THE OXFORD

New Desk
Dictionary and Thesaurus

THIRD EDITION

BERKLEY BOOKS, NEW YORK

THE BERKLEY PUBLISHING GROUP
Published by the Penguin Group
Penguin Group (USA) Inc.
375 Hudson Street, New York, New York 10014, USA
Penguin Group (Canada), 90 Eglinton Avenue East, Suite 700, Toronto, Ontario M4P 2Y3, Canada
(a division of Pearson Penguin Canada Inc.)
Penguin Books Ltd., 80 Strand, London WC2R 0RL, England
Penguin Group Ireland, 25 St. Stephen's Green, Dublin 2, Ireland (a division of Penguin Books Ltd.)
Penguin Group (Australia), 250 Camberwell Road, Camberwell, Victoria 3124, Australia
(a division of Pearson Australia Group Pty. Ltd.)
Penguin Books India Pvt. Ltd., 11 Community Centre, Panchsheel Park, New Delhi—110 017, India
Penguin Group (NZ), 67 Apollo Drive, Rosedale, North Shore 0632, New Zealand
(a division of Pearson New Zealand Ltd.)
Penguin Books (South Africa) (Pty.) Ltd., 24 Sturdee Avenue, Rosebank, Johannesburg 2196, South Africa

Penguin Books Ltd., Registered Offices: 80 Strand, London WC2R 0RL, England

The publisher does not have any control over and does not assume any responsibility for author or
third-party websites or their content.

THE OXFORD NEW DESK DICTIONARY AND THESAURUS

A Berkley Book / published by arrangement with Oxford University Press, Inc.

PRINTING HISTORY
Oxford University Press edition / July 1997
Berkley mass-market first edition / August 1997
Berkley mass-marked second edition / July 2001
Berkley mass-marked third edition / July 2009

Copyright © 1997, 2001, 2009 by Oxford University Press
Published in 1997 as *The Oxford Desk Dictionary and Thesaurus: American Edition.*
Published in 2001 as *The Oxford American Desk Dictionary and Thesaurus, Second Edition.*
All rights reserved.
No part of this book may be reproduced, scanned, or distributed in any printed or electronic form
without permission. Please do not participate in or encourage piracy of copyrighted materials in
violation of the author's rights.
Purchase only authorized editions.
For information, address: Oxford University Press, Inc.,
198 Madison Avenue, New York, New York, 10016

ISBN: 978-0-425-22862-3

BERKLEY®
Berkley Books are published by The Berkley Publishing Group,
a division of Penguin Group (USA) Inc.,
375 Hudson Street, New York, New York 10014.
BERKLEY is a registered trademark of Penguin Group (USA) Inc.
The "B" design is a trademark belonging to Penguin Group (USA) Inc.

PRINTED IN THE UNITED STATES OF AMERICA

20   19

Contents

Preface

The Oxford New Desk Dictionary and Thesaurus combines the information you would expect to find in a conventional dictionary and a thesaurus in a single handy volume. Within an individual entry it offers a guide to the spelling, syllabification, pronunciation, and meaning of a word, together with lists of synonyms where appropriate. The second edition of this popular reference book also features synonym studies and detailed explorations of the fine nuances in the meanings of closely related words.

Based on *The Oxford Dictionary and Thesaurus*, the first American reference work to offer integrated dictionary and thesaurus entries, *The Oxford New Desk Dictionary and Thesaurus* offers a valuable and portable tool for students, writers, businesspeople, and all those who need to use English with accuracy and flexibility.

How to Use *The Oxford New Desk Dictionary and Thesaurus*

The "entry map" below explains the different parts of an entry.

Pronunciation set off with slashes / /

Parts of speech in *italic*

Bold face main entry

Inflected forms in **bold face**

Sense numbers and letters in **bold face**

a•cute /əkyo͞ot/ • *adj.* (**a•cut•er, a•cut•est**) **1 a** (of senses, etc.) keen; penetrating. **b** (of pain) intense; severe. **2** (of a disease) coming sharply to a crisis; not chronic. **3 a** (of an angle) less than 90°. **b** sharp; pointed. See synonym studies at KEEN, CRUCIAL. • *n.* = *acute accent.* □ **acute accent** mark (´) placed over letters in some languages to show vowel length, pronunciation (e.g., *maté*), etc. □□ **a•cute′ly** *adv.* **a•cute′ness** *n.*
■ *adj.* **1 a** sharp, sensitive, discriminating. **b** cutting, keen, piercing. **2** intense, critical, dangerous, grave. **3 b** narrow. □□ **acutely** see *severely* (SEVERE), VERY *adv.* **acuteness** see GRAVITY 3a, *penetration* (PENETRATE).

New part of speech signaled by •

Idioms and phrases signaled by □

Derivatives signaled by □□

Synonym section introduced by ■

Sense numbers refer to definition section

Main entries and other boldface forms

Main entries appear in boldface type, as do inflected forms, idioms and phrases, and derivatives. Main entries, inflected forms, and derivatives of two or more syllables show syllabication with centered dots. Stressed syllable(s) are shown on derivatives by an accent mark following the stressed syllable.

Cross references

Cross references to main entries appear in small capitals, and cross references to derivatives, idioms, and phrases are given in italic type. For example, in the synonym section of the entry **acute** seen above, cross references are given in small capitals to the entries for VERY and GRAVITY. A cross reference is also given to *severely* (SEVERE); the italic type indicates that the derivative (*severely*) can be found under its main entry (SEVERE).

Arrangement of synonym sections

Synonyms are offered for many of the words defined in *The Oxford New Desk Dictionary and Thesaurus.* The sense numbering in the synonym sections refers to that of the defining sections, so that users can easily see which synonyms are appropriate to which meaning of the entry. Synonyms are not always offered for every dictionary sense, and in some cases a single list of synonyms is offered for several senses. The sense numbering may then take the form of a list, as, for example, **1, 3, 4,** indicating that the words following are synonyms for dictionary definitions numbered 1, 3, and 4. Wherever a single synonym list covers all the meanings explained in the defining section, sense numbers are dispensed with and the synonym list is simply introduced by the symbol ■.

A list of synonyms may be divided by a semicolon to indicate a different "branch" of meaning.

> **bound**[1] /bownd/ • *v.intr.* **1 a** spring; leap. **b** walk or run with leaping strides. **2** (of a ball, etc.) bounce. • *n.* **1** springy leap. **2** bounce.
> ■ *v.* **1** jump, hop, vault; gambol, caper, romp. **2** see BOUNCE *v.* 1. *n.* **1** jump, vault, spring, hop.

Semicolon indicates new "branch" of meaning

Occasionally, the synonyms offered are for a form other than the exact form of the main entry. In these cases, this altered form is given in parentheses at the beginning of the synonym list.

> **com•pli•ment** • *n.* /kómplimənt/ **1 a** polite expression of praise. **b** act implying praise. **2** [in *pl.*] formal greetings or praise. • *v.tr.* /kómpliment/ congratulate; praise.
> ■ *n.* **1** commendation, bouquet, tribute, honor. **2** (*compliments*) respects, regards, good *or* best wishes, felicitations, salutations. *v.* pay homage *or* tribute to, commend, laud, honor; flatter.

Synonyms offered for a plural form of the headword

List Words

Words beginning with common prefixes (*in-, non-, over-, re-, self-, sub-,* and *un-*) are given in lists where the sense of the word (e.g., *inexpensive*) is clear from an understanding of the meaning of the prefix (*in-* = 'not,' 'without') and the root of the word (*expensive* = 'costing or charging too much').

Synonym Studies

Special synonym studies compare the nuances of meanings among a group of closely related words. At the entry for **absolve,** the synonym study compares *absolve* with *acquit, exempt, exonerate, forgive, pardon,* and *vindicate.* Cross-references at related entries make the synonym studies easy to find.

Special Reference Sections

Refer to the table of contents or the pages at the back of this volume for a number of handy special reference sections covering weights and measures, signs and symbols, countries of the world, and other useful information.

Key to the Pronunciations

This dictionary uses a simple respelling system to show how entries are pronounced, using the following symbols:

a, á	*as in*	**pat** /pat/, **fasten** /fásən/
aa, áa	*as in*	**father** /faáthər/, **barnyard** /baárnyaard/
air, áir	*as in*	**fair** /fair/, **share** /shair/, **heir** /air/
aw, áw	*as in*	**law** /law/, **caught** /kawt/, **thought** /thawt/
ay, áy	*as in*	**day** /day/, **raid** /rayd/, **made** /mayd/, **prey** /pray/
ch	*as in*	**church** /chərch/, **picture** /píkchər/
e, é	*as in*	**men** /men/, **said** /sed/
ee, eé	*as in*	**feet** /feet/, **receive** /riseév/
ə	*as in*	**along** /əlóng/, **soda** /sódə/, **civil** /sívəl/
ər, ór	*as in*	**parade** /pəráyd/, **bitter** /bítər/, **person** /pórsən/
g	*as in*	**get** /get/, **exhaust** /igzáwst/, **egg** /eg/
i, í	*as in*	**pin** /pin/, **guild** /gild/, **women** /wímin/
ī, í	*as in*	**time** /tīm/, **fight** /fīt/, **guide** /gīd/
īr, ír	*as in*	**fire** /fīr/, **desire** /dizír/
j	*as in*	**judge** /juj/, **carriage** /kárij/
kh	*as in*	**loch** /lokh/, **Bach** /baakh/
N	*as in*	**en route** /oN root/ (preceding vowel is nasalized)
ng	*as in*	**sing** /sing/, **anger** /ánggər/
o, ó	*as in*	**rob** /rob/, **pocket** /pókit/
ō, ő	*as in*	**go** /gō/, **promote** /prəmót/
ö, ő	*as in*	**jeu** /zhő/, **schön** /shön/
ŏo, ŏ́o	*as in*	**wood** /wŏod/, **football** /fŏotbawl/
ōo, óo	*as in*	**food** /food/, **music** /myóosik/
ow, ów	*as in*	**mouse** /mows/, **coward** /kówərd/
oy, óy	*as in*	**boy** /boy/, **noisy** /nóyzee/
r	*as in*	**run** /run/, **fur** /fər/, **spirit** /spírit/
sh	*as in*	**shut** /shut/, **social** /sóshəl/, **action** /ákshən/
th	*as in*	**thin** /thin/, **truth** /trooth/
th	*as in*	**then** /then/, **mother** /múthər/
u, ú	*as in*	**cut** /kut/, **blood** /blud/, **enough** /inúf/
y	*as in*	**yet** /yet/, **accuse** /əkyóoz/
Y	*as in*	**aperçu** /aapersY/
zh	*as in*	**measure** /mézhər/, **vision** /vizhən/

More than one acceptable pronunciation may be given, with commas between the variants; for example:

news /nŏŏz, nyŏŏz/

If the pronunciations of a word differ only in part, then the syllable or syllables affected are shown as follows:

bedroom /bédrŏŏm, –rŏŏm/, **forest** /fáwrist, fór–/

The same principle applies to derivative forms that are given within the main entry; for example:

complete /kəmpleét/, **completion** /–pleéshən/

STRESS

The mark that appears over the vowel symbol in words of more than one syllable indicates the part of the word that carries the stress. Where a word has two or more stress markers then the main stress may vary according to the context in which a word is used; for example:

afternoon /áftərnŏón/

In the phrase "afternoon tea" the main stress falls on the first syllable /áftər–/, but in the phrase "all afternoon" the main stress falls on the last syllable /–nŏón/.

Abbreviations

Abbreviations in general use (such as etc. and i.e.) are explained in the dictionary text itself.

abbr.	abbreviation	cogn.	cognate
ablat.	ablative	collect.	collective(ly)
absol.	absolute(ly)	colloq.	colloquial(ly)
acc.	according	comb.	combination, combining
accus.	accusative		
adj.	adjective	compar.	comparative
adv.	adverb	compl.	complement
Aeron.	Aeronautics	conj.	conjunction
alt.	alteration	conn.	connected
Amer.	America, American	constr.	construction
Anat.	Anatomy	contr.	contraction
anc.	ancient	corresp.	corresponding
Anthropol.	Anthropology	corrupt.	corruption
Antiq.	Antiquities, Antiquity	Criminol.	Criminology
app.	apparently	def.	definite
arbitr.	arbitrary, arbitrarily	Demog.	Demography
Archaeol.	Archaeology	demons.	demonstrative
Archit.	Architecture	demons.adj.	demonstrative adjective
Arith.	Arithmetic	demons.pron.	demonstrative pronoun
assim.	assimilated	deriv.	derivative
assoc.	associated, association	derog.	derogatory
Astrol.	Astrology	dial.	dialect
Astron.	Astronomy	dimin.	diminutive
Astronaut.	Astronautics	disp.	disputed (use or pronunciation)
attrib.	attributive(ly)		
attrib.adj.	attributive adjective	dissim.	dissimilated
Austral.	Australia, Australian	distrib.	distributive
aux.	auxiliary		
		Eccl.	Ecclesiastical
Bibl.	Biblical	Ecol.	Ecology
Biochem.	Biochemistry	Econ.	Economics
Biol.	Biology	Electr.	Electricity
Bot.	Botany	elem.	elementary
Brit.	British	ellipt.	elliptical(ly)
		emphat.	emphatic(ally)
c.	century	Engin.	Engineering
c.	*circa*	Engl.	England, English
Ch.	Church	Entomol.	Entomology
Chem.	Chemistry	erron.	erroneous(ly)
Cinematog.	Cinematography	esp.	especial(ly)
class.	classical	euphem.	euphemism
coarse sl.	coarse slang	ex.	example

exc.	except	masc.	masculine
exclam.	exclamation	Math.	Mathematics
		Mech.	Mechanics
f.	from	Med.	Medicine
fam.	familiar	metaph.	metaphorical
fem.	feminine	Meteorol.	Meteorology
fig.	figurative(ly)	Mil.	Military
fl.	flourished	Mineral.	Mineralogy
foll.	followed, following	mod.	modern
form.	formation	Mus.	Music
frequent.	frequentative(ly)	Mythol.	Mythology
gen.	general	n.	noun
genit.	genitive	N.Amer.	North America, North American
Geog.	Geography		
Geol.	Geology	Nat.	National
Geom.	Geometry	Naut.	Nautical
Grk Hist.	Greek History	neg.	negative(ly)
Gram.	Grammar	neut.	neuter
		N.Engl.	New England
Hist.	History	No. of Engl.	North of England
hist.	with historical reference	north.	northern
Horol.	Horology	n.pl.	noun plural
Hort.	Horticulture	num.	numeral
illit.	illiterative	obj.	object, objective
imit.	imitative	obs.	obsolete
immed.	immediate(ly)	Obstet.	Obstetrics
imper.	imperative	occas.	occasional(ly)
impers.	impersonal	offens.	offensive
incept.	inceptive	opp.	(as) opposed (to), opposite (of)
incl.	including, inclusive		
ind.	indirect	orig.	origin, original(ly)
indecl.	indeclinable	Ornithol.	Ornithology
indef.	indefinite		
infin.	infinitive	Paleog.	Paleography
infl.	influence(d)	Parl.	Parliament, Parliamentary
instr.	instrumental (case)		
int.	interjection	part.	participle
interrog.	interrogative(ly)	past part.	past participle
interrog.adj.	interrogative adjective	Pathol.	Pathology
interrog.pron.	interrogative pronoun	pejor.	pejorative
intr.	intransitive	perf.	perfect (tense)
iron.	ironical(ly)	perh.	perhaps
irreg.	irregular(ly)	pers.	person(ai)
		Pharm.	Pharmacy, Pharmacology
joc.	jocular(ly)		
		Philol.	Philology
lang.	language	Philos.	Philosophy
lit.	literal(ly)	Phonet.	Phonetics

Photog.	Photography	Sociol.	Sociology
phr.	phrase	spec.	special(ly)
Phrenol.	Phrenology	Stock Exch.	Stock Exchange
Physiol.	Physiology	subj.	subject, subjunctive
pl.	plural	superl.	superlative
poet.	poetical	syll.	syllable
Polit.	Politics	symb.	symbol
pop.	popular, not technical	syn.	synonym
poss.	possessive		
prec.	preceded, preceding	techn.	technical(ly)
predic.	predicate, predicative(ly)	Telev.	Television
		Theatr.	Theater, Theatrical
prep.	preposition	Theol.	Theology
pres.part.	present participle	tr.	transitive
prob.	probable, probably	transf.	in transferred sense
pron.	pronoun	transl.	translation
pronunc.	pronunciation	Typog.	Typography
propr.	proprietary term		
Psychol.	Psychology	ult.	ultimate(ly)
		univ.	university
RC Ch.	Roman Catholic Church	unkn.	unknown
		US	American, in American use, in the United States
ref.	reference		
refl.	reflexive(ly)		
rel.	related, relative	usu.	usual(ly)
rel.adj.	relative adjective		
Relig.	Religion	v.	verb
rel.pron.	relative pronoun	var.	variant(s)
repr.	representing	v.aux.	auxiliary verb
Rhet.	Rhetoric	Vet.	Veterinary
rhet.	rhetorical(ly)	v.intr.	intransitive verb
Rom.Hist.	Roman History	voc.	vocative
		v.refl.	reflexive verb
Sci.	Science	v.tr.	transitive verb
sing.	singular		
sl.	slang	Zool.	Zoology

Note on proprietary status

This book includes some words that are, or are asserted to be, proprietary names or trademarks. Their inclusion does not imply that they have acquired for legal purposes a non-proprietary or general significance, nor is any other judgment implied concerning their legal status. In cases where the editor has some evidence that a word is used as a proprietary name or trademark, this is indicated by the designation *propr.*, but no judgment concerning the legal status of such words is made or implied thereby.

Aa

A[1] /ay/ *n.* (also **a**) (*pl.* **As** or **A's**; **a's**) **1** first letter of the alphabet. **2** *Mus.* sixth note of the diatonic scale of C major. **3** first hypothetical person or example. **4** highest class or category (of academic grades, etc.). **5** human blood type.

A[2] /ay/ *abbr.* (also **A.**) **1** ampere(s). **2** answer. **3** Associate of. **4** atomic (energy, etc.).

a[1] /ə, ay/ *adj.* (also **an** before a vowel) **1** one; some; any. **2** one like (*a Judas*). **3** one single (*not a thing in sight*). **4** the same. **5** in, to, or for each (*twice a year*).

a[2] /ə/ *prep.* [usu. as *prefix*] **1** to; toward (*ashore*). **2** in the process of; in a specified state (*a-wandering, abuzz*). **3** on (*afire*).

Å *abbr.* ångström(s).

a- /ay, ə/ *prefix* not; without (*amoral*).

AA *abbr.* **1** Alcoholics Anonymous. **2** *Mil.* antiaircraft.

aard•vark /áardvaark/ *n.* anteating nocturnal mammal of southern Africa.

aargh /aar, aarg/ • *int.* expressing anguish, horror, rage, or other strong emotion, often with humorous intent.

AB /áybeé/ *n.* human blood type.

ab- /əb, ab/ *prefix* off; away; from (*abduct, abnormal, abuse*).

a•back /əbák/ *adv. archaic* backward; behind.
□ **take aback** surprise; disconcert (*your request took me aback*).
■ □ **take aback** astound, astonish, shock, stun.

ab•a•cus /ábəkəs, əbákəs/ *n.* (*pl.* **ab•a•cus•es**) oblong frame with wires along which beads are slid, used for calculating.

a•baft /əbáft/ *Naut.* • *adv.* in the stern half of a ship. • *prep.* nearer the stern than; aft of.

ab•a•lo•ne /ábəlóne/ *n.* salt-water mollusk with a shallow ear-shaped shell.

a•ban•don /əbándən/ • *v.tr.* **1** give up completely or before completion. **2** forsake, desert, or leave. See synonym study at RELINQUISH. • *n.* lack of inhibition or restraint. □□ **a•ban′do•ner** *n.* **a•ban′don•ment** *n.*
■ *v.* **1** relinquish, renounce, leave; withdraw from, pull out of. **2** abdicate; jilt, walk *or* run out on, cast off *or* aside; jettison, evacuate.

a•ban•doned /əbándənd/ *adj.* **1** deserted; forsaken. **2** unrestrained; profligate.
■ **1** neglected, rejected, shunned, castaway, jilted, forlorn; *predic.* left alone, cast-off, cast aside. **2** uninhibited, licentious, unprincipled, disreputable, loose.

a•base /əbáys/ *v.tr.* humiliate or degrade. See synonym study at HUMBLE. □□ **a•base′ment** *n.*

a•bash /əbásh/ *v.tr.* (usu. as **abashed** *adj.*) embarrass; disconcert. □□ **a•bash′ment** *n.*

a•bate /əbáyt/ *v.* make or become less strong, severe, intense, etc. See synonym study at ALLEVIATE. □□ **a•bate′ment** *n.*

ab•at•toir /ábətwaar/ *n.* slaughterhouse.

ab•bess /ábis/ *n.* head of a community of nuns.

ab•bey /ábee/ *n.* (*pl.* **–beys**) **1** building(s) occupied by a community of monks or nuns. **2** the community itself.

ab•bot /ábət/ *n.* head of a community of monks.

abbr. *abbr.* (also **abbrev.**) abbreviation.

ab•bre•vi•ate /əbréevee-ayt/ *v.tr.* shorten, esp. represent (a word, etc.) by a part of it. □□ **ab•bre•vi•a′tion** /–áyshən/ *n.*
■ compress, telescope, contract, truncate, trim. □□ **abbreviation** initialism, acronym; abridgment, contraction.

ABC /áybeesée/ *n.* **1** the alphabet. **2** [usu. *pl.*] rudiments of any subject.

ab•di•cate /ábdikayt/ *v.tr.* **1** give up or renounce (esp. a throne). **2** renounce (a responsibility, duty, etc.). □□ **ab•di•ca′tion** /–káyshən/ *n.* **ab′di•ca•tor** *n.*
■ surrender, yield, disclaim, relinquish, vacate, resign (from); quit, waive, disown; (*absol.*) step down.

ab•do•men /ábdəmən, abdó–/ *n.* **1** part of the body containing digestive and reproductive organs. **2** *Zool.* hind part of an insect, crustacean, etc. □□ **ab•dom•i•nal** /abdóminəl/ *adj.* **ab•dom′i•nal•ly** /abdóminəlee/ *adv.*

ab•duct /əbdúkt/ *v.tr.* carry off or kidnap (a person) illegally. □□ **ab•duc′tion** /–dúkshən/ *n.* **ab•duc′tor** *n.*
■ make off with, seize, snatch, grab.

A•be•na•ki /aabənáakee/ • *n.* (also **Ab•na′ki** /aabnáakee/) **1a** N. American people native to northern New England and adjoining parts of Quebec. **b** member of this people. **2** either of the two languages of this people.

ab•er•ra•tion /ábəráyshən/ *n.* **1** departure from what is normal or regarded as right. **2** moral or mental lapse. □□ **ab•er′rant** *adj.* **ab•er•ra′tion•al** *adj.*

a•bet /əbét/ *v.tr.* (**a•bet•ted, a•bet•ting**) (usu. in **aid and a•bet**) encourage or assist (an offender or offense). □□ **a•bet′ment** *n.*
■ urge, instigate, prompt; aid, help.

a•bey•ance /əbáyəns/ *n.* [usu. prec. by *in, into*] state of temporary disuse or suspension. □□ **a•bey′ant** /–ənt/ *adj.* See synonym study at LATENT.
■ see PAUSE *n.*; (*in abeyance*) pending, reserved, shelved, pushed aside, postponed.

abhor /əbháwr/ *v.tr.* (**ab•horred, ab•hor•ring**) detest; regard with disgust and hatred. □□ **ab•hor′rence** *n.* **ab•hor′rer** *n.*
■ hate, loathe, abominate, execrate; despise, shudder at, recoil *or* shrink from.

ab•hor•rent /əbháwrənt, –hór–/ *adj.* disgusting; repugnant; hateful; detestable. See synonym study at OFFENSIVE.

■ abominable, contemptible, loathsome; vile; repulsive, repellent.

a·bide /əbíd/ v. (past **a·bode** /əbṓd/ or **a·bid·ed**) **1** tr. tolerate; endure. **2** intr. **a** act in accordance with. **b** remain faithful to (a promise). □□ **a·bid'ance** n.

■ **1** stand, suffer, support, bear, put up with.

a·bid·ing /əbídiŋ/ adj. enduring; permanent (an abiding sense of loss). □□ **a·bid'ing·ly** adv.

■ lasting, constant, steadfast, everlasting; unchanging, (hard and) fast, fixed, firm, immutable.

a·bil·i·ty /əbílitee/ n. (pl. **–ties**) **1** capacity or power. **2** cleverness; talent; mental power.

■ **1** adeptness, aptitude, facility, knack. **2** skill(s), gift(s), faculties; genius, knowhow.

-ability /əbílitee/ suffix forming nouns of quality from, or corresponding to, adjectives in –able (capability, vulnerability).

ab·ject /ábjekt, abjékt/ adj. **1** miserable; wretched. **2** degraded; self-abasing; humble. **3** despicable. □□ **ab·jec'tion** n. **ab·ject'ly** adv. **ab·ject'ness** n.

■ **1** see MISERABLE 1, 2. **2** see SERVILE 2.

ab·jure /əbjóor/ v.tr. renounce under oath. □□ **ab·ju·ra'tion** /–ráyshən/ n.

ab·la·tive /áblətiv/ Gram. • n. case (esp. in Latin) of nouns and pronouns indicating an agent, instrument, or location. • adj. of or in the ablative.

a·blaze /əbláyz/ adj. & adv. **1** on fire. **2** glittering; glowing; radiant. **3** greatly excited.

■ adj. **1** aflame, afire, burning. **2** brilliantly or brightly lit, sparkling, gleaming, brilliant, luminous. **3** see FERVENT 1.

a·ble /áybəl/ adj. (**a·bler, a·blest**) **1** [often foll. by to] having the capacity or power (able to come). **2** having great ability; clever. □ **able-bodied** fit; healthy.

■ **1** (able to) capable of, qualified to, competent to. **2** talented, quick, skilled, adept. □ **able-bodied** see FIT¹ adj. 2.

-able /əbəl/ suffix forming adjectives meaning: **1** that may or must be (eatable). **2** that can be made the subject of (dutiable, objectionable). **3** relevant to or in accordance with (fashionable).

ab·lu·tion /əblóoshən/ n. [usu. in pl.] **1** ceremonial washing of hands, sacred vessels, etc. **2** colloq. ordinary washing of the body. □□ **ab·lu'tion·ar·y** adj.

-ably /əblee/ suffix forming adverbs corresponding to adjectives in –able.

ABM abbr. antiballistic missile.

ab·ne·gate /ábnigayt/ v.tr. **1** give up or deny oneself (a pleasure, etc.). **2** renounce or reject (a right or belief). □□ **ab·ne·ga'tion** /–gáyshən/ n. **ab'ne·ga·tor** n. See synonym study at ABSTINENCE

ab·nor·mal /ábnáwrməl/ adj. deviating from the norm; exceptional. □□ **ab·nor·mal'i·ty** n. **ab·nor'mal·ly** adv.

■ peculiar, strange, curious, unconventional, unnatural, extraordinary, singular, weird.

a·board /əbáwrd/ adv. & prep. **1** on or into (a ship, aircraft, etc.). **2** alongside.

a·bode¹ /əbṓd/ n. dwelling; one's home.

■ residence, house, domicile, habitat.

a·bode² past of ABIDE.

a·bol·ish /əbólish/ v.tr. put an end to (esp. a custom or institution). □□ **a·bol'ish·a·ble** adj. **a·bol'ish·er** n. **a·bol'ish·ment** n.

■ eliminate, terminate, stop; destroy, annihilate, nullify, repeal, cancel.

ab·o·li·tion /ábəlishən/ n. **1** abolishing or being abolished. **2** the ending of a practice or institution, esp. (in US hist.) slavery. □□ **ab·o·li'tion·ist** n.

■ **1** elimination, end, ending, termination; eradication.

A-bomb /áybom/ n. = atom bomb:

a·bom·i·na·ble /əbómənəbəl/ adj. **1** detestable; loathsome; morally reprehensible. **2** colloq. very unpleasant. See synonym study at OFFENSIVE. □□ **a·bom'i·na·bly** adv.

■ **1** offensive, repugnant, repulsive, vile, monstrous, outrageous; see also EVIL adj. 1. **2** atrocious, distasteful, unpleasant, disagreeable.

a·bom·i·nate /əbóminayt/ v.tr. detest; loathe. □□ **a·bom·i·na'tion** /–náyshən/ n. **a·bom'i·na·tor** n.

ab·o·rig·i·nal /ábərijinəl/ adj. **1** inhabiting or existing in a land from the earliest times or from before the arrival of colonists. **2** (usu. **Aboriginal**) of the Australian Aborigines. See synonym study at NATIVE.

ab·o·rig·i·ne /ábərijinee/ n. [usu. in pl.] **1** aboriginal inhabitant. **2** (usu. **Aborigine**) aboriginal inhabitant of Australia. **3** aboriginal plant or animal.

a·bort /əbáwrt/ • v. **1** intr. miscarry. **2** tr. effect abortion. **3 a** tr. cause to end fruitlessly or prematurely. **b** intr. end unsuccessfully or prematurely. • n. **1** prematurely terminated space flight or other undertaking. **2** termination of such an undertaking.

■ v. **1** see MISCARRY. **3a** see PREVENT, TERMINATE 1. **3b** see FAIL 1, 2a, MISCARRY.

a·bor·tion /əbáwrshən/ n. expulsion of a fetus (naturally or esp. by medical induction) from the womb before it is able to survive independently. □□ **a·bor'tion·ist** n.

■ miscarriage, termination.

a·bor·tive /əbáwrtiv/ adj. fruitless; unsuccessful; unfinished. □□ **a·bor'tive·ly** adv.

ABO system /áybee-ṓ/ n. system of four types (A, AB, B, and O) by which human blood may be classified.

a·bound /əbównd/ v.intr. **1** be plentiful. **2** [foll. by in, with] be rich; teem or be infested.

■ **1** prevail, thrive, flourish, be prolific. **2** (abound in, abound with) be well supplied or furnished with, be crowded with, be abundant in.

a·bout /əbówt/ • prep. **1 a** on the subject of. **b** relating to. **c** in relation to (symmetry about a plane). **d** so as to affect (can do nothing about it). **2** at a time near to. **3** in; around. • adv. **1 a** approximately. **b** colloq. used to indicate understatement (just about had enough). **2** at points nearby (a lot of flu about). **3** in every direction.

■ *prep.* **1 a,b,d** concerning, concerned with, on, involving. **2** around, close to. **3** encircling, encompassing. ● *adv.* **1 a** around, nearly, roughly, more or less. **b** really, honestly. **2** around, close by; in the area; in the air. **3** around, all over, on every side.

a•bout-face /əbówtfáys/ ● *n.* **1** turn made to face the opposite direction. **2** change of opinion or policy, etc. ● *v.intr.* make an about-face. ● *int. Mil.* a command to make an about-face.

■ *n.* **1, 2** volte-face, reversal, U-turn. **2** change of heart.

a•bove /əbúv/ ● *prep.* **1** over; on the top of; higher than. **2** more than (*above average*). **3** higher in rank, importance, etc., than. ● *adv.* **1** at or to a higher point; overhead. **2** upstairs. **3** (of a text reference) further back on a page or in a book (*as noted above*). ● *adj.* preceding. ● *n.* [prec. by *the*] what is mentioned above. □ **above all** more than anything else.

■ *prep.* **1** on, upon, atop. **2** over, exceeding, greater than. ● *adv.* **1** on high, aloft, in the sky. **3** earlier, before, previously. ● *adj.* former, previous, prior. ● *adj. & n.* abovementioned, aforementioned, above-stated. □ **above all** first *or* most of all, chiefly.

a•bove-board /əbúvbawrd/ *adj. & adv.* without concealment; fair or fairly; open or openly.

■ candid, frank, straight, direct, honorable.

ab•ra•ca•da•bra /ábrəkədábrə/ *int.* word used in performing a magic trick.

a•brade /əbráyd/ *v.tr.* scrape or wear away (skin, rock, etc.) by rubbing. □□ **a•brad′er** *n.*

ab•ra•sion /əbráyzhən/ *n.* **1** result of abrading. **2** damaged area resulting from this.

■ **1** see EROSION. **2** see SCRAPE *n.* 2.

ab•ra•sive /əbráysiv/ ● *adj.* **1 a** tending to rub or abrade. **b** capable of polishing by rubbing or grinding. **2** harsh or hurtful in manner. ● *n.* abrasive substance.

■ see *gritty* (GRIT). **2** see ABRUPT 2.

a•breast /əbrést/ *adv.* **1** side by side and facing the same way. **2 a** up to date. **b** well-informed.

a•bridge /əbríj/ *v.tr.* **1** shorten (a book, movie, etc.). **2** curtail. □□ **a•bridg′a•ble** *or* **a•bridge′a•ble** *adj.* **a•bridg′er** *n.* **a•bridg′ment** *or* **a•bridge′ment** *n.*

■ **1** reduce, condense, abbreviate, trim, clip, curtail, digest, summarize, abstract, précis, synopsize. □□ **abridgment** digest, condensation; synopsis, summary.

a•broad /əbráwd/ *adv.* **1** in or to a foreign country or countries. **2** over a wide area. **3** in circulation.

■ **1** overseas, out of the country. **2** about, around, all over, broadly. **3** at large, in the air.

ab•ro•gate /ábrəgayt/ *v.tr.* repeal, annul, or abolish (a law or custom). □□ **ab•ro•ga′tion** /-gáyshən/ *n.* **ab′ro•ga•tor** *n.*

ab•rupt /əbrúpt/ *adj.* **1** sudden; hasty. **2** (of speech, manner, etc.) curt. **3** steep. □□ **ab•rupt′ly** *adv.* **ab•rupt′ness** *n.*

■ **1** quick, precipitate, immediate. **2** broken, jerky; short, brusque. **3** precipitous,

sheer, sharp. □□ **abruptly** see *suddenly* (SUDDEN). **abruptness** see SPEED *n.* 1.

ABS *abbr.* antilock brake (or braking) system.

abs /abs/ ● *n. sl.* abdominal muscles (*toned abs through lots of exercise*).

ab•scess /ábses/ *n.* swelling containing pus. □□ **ab′scessed** *adj.*

ab•scis•sa /əbsísə/ *n.* (*pl.* **ab•scis•sae** /–ee/ *or* **ab•scis•sas**) *Math.* (in a system of coordinates) shortest distance from a point to the vertical or *y*–axis (cf. ORDINATE).

ab•scond /əbskónd/ *v.intr.* depart hurriedly and furtively, esp. unlawfully or to avoid arrest. □□ **ab•scond′er** *n.*

ab•sence /ábsəns/ *n.* **1** state of being away. **2** time of this. **3** lack. See synonym study at LACK.

■ **1, 2** nonattendance, nonappearance, truancy; leave. **3** want, deficiency, insufficiency, scantiness.

ab•sent ● *adj.* /ábsənt/ **1** not present. **2** not existing. **3** inattentive. ● *v.refl.* /absént/ **1** stay away. **2** withdraw. □□ **ab′sent•ly** *adv.* (in sense 3 of *adj.*).

■ *adj.* **1** out, off, elsewhere, not here, away. **2** missing, lacking, nonexistent. **3** see AB-SENTMINDED. ● *v.* (*absent oneself*) **1** keep away. **2** retire, take one's leave.

ab•sen•tee /ábsəntée/ *n.* person not present.

ab•sen•tee•ism /ábsəntéeizəm/ *n.* habitual absence from work, school, etc.

■ truancy, malingering, playing hooky.

ab•sent•mind•ed /ábsəntmíndid/ *adj.* forgetful or inattentive. □□ **ab′sent•mind′ed•ly** *adv.* **ab′sent•mind′ed•ness** *n.*

■ preoccupied, absorbed, unmindful, withdrawn. □□ **absentmindedly** absently, vaguely, inattentively. **absentmindedness** forgetfulness, obliviousness, carelessness, heedlessness.

ab•sinthe /ábsinth/ *n.* (also **ab′sinth**) aniseed-flavored potent liqueur based on wormwood.

ab•so•lute /ábsəloot/ *adj.* **1** complete; utter. **2** unconditional. **3** despotic. **4** (of a standard or other concept) not relative or comparative. **5** (of a legal decree, etc.) final. □ **absolute majority 1** majority over all others combined. **2** more than half. **absolute pitch** *Mus.* ability to recognize or sound any given note. **absolute zero** theoretical lowest possible temperature, calculated as –273.15° C (or 0° K). □□ **ab•so•lute′ness** *n.*

■ **1** perfect, unmitigated, categorical, unqualified. **2** unlimited, limitless, untrammeled; total. **3** unrestrained, dictatorial, totalitarian, supreme. **4** certain, sure, unambiguous, definite.

ab•so•lute•ly /ábsəlootlee/ *adv.* **1** completely; utterly. **2** in an absolute sense. **3** *colloq.* in actual fact; positively. **4** *colloq.* (used in reply) quite so; yes.

■ **1** totally, perfectly, entirely, wholly; unqualifiedly. **4** certainly, assuredly, definitely.

ab•so•lu•tion /ábsəlooshən/ *n. formal* release or forgiveness from guilt, sin, obligation, or punishment.

ab•so•lut•ism /ábsəlootizəm/ *n.* acceptance

of or belief in absolute principles in politics, theology, etc. □□ **ab'so•lut•ist** *n. & adj.*

ab•solve /əbzólv, –sólv/ *v.tr.* **1 a** free from blame or obligation, etc. **b** acquit; pronounce not guilty. **2** pardon or give absolution for (a sin, etc.). □□ **ab•solv'er** *n.*

■ *see* FORGIVE, PARDON *v.*

SYNONYM STUDY: **absolve**

ACQUIT, EXEMPT, EXONERATE, FORGIVE, PARDON, VINDICATE. To varying degrees, all of these words mean to free from guilt or blame, and some are most frequently heard in a legal or political context. **Absolve** is the most general term, meaning to set free or release—not only from guilt or blame, but from a duty or obligation (*absolved from her promise to serve on the committee*) or, in a religious context, from having committed a sin. **Pardon** is usually associated with the actions of a government or military official (*President Gerald Ford pardoned Richard Nixon following his resignation in the wake of the Watergate scandal*) and specifically refers to a release from prosecution or punishment. It is usually a legal official who decides to **acquit**, or release someone from a specific and formal accusation of wrongdoing (*the court acquitted the accused due to lack of evidence*). **Exonerate** suggests relief (its origin suggests the lifting of a burden), often in a moral sense, from a definite charge so that not even the suspicion of wrongdoing remains (*completely exonerated from the accusation of cheating*). A person who is **vindicated** is also off the hook, usually due to the examination of evidence (*she vindicated herself by producing the missing documents*). **Exempt** has less to do with guilt and punishment and more to do with duty and obligation (*exempt from paying taxes*). To **forgive**, however, is the most magnanimous act of all: It implies not only giving up on the idea that an offense should be punished, but also relinquishing any feelings of resentment or vengefulness (*"To err is human; to forgive divine"*).

---

ab•sorb /əbsáwrb, –záwrb/ *v.tr.* **1** incorporate as part of itself or oneself. **2** take in; suck up. **3** reduce the effect or intensity of. **4** consume. **5** engross the attention of. □□ **ab•sorb'a•ble** *adj.* **ab•sorb•a•bil'i•ty** *n.* **ab•sorb'er** *n.*

■ **1** *see* INCLUDE 1. **2** *see* SOAK *v.* 3. **5** *see* OCCUPY 5.

ab•sorbed /əbsáwrbd, –záwrbd/ *adj.* intensely engaged or interested. □□ **ab•sorb•ed•ly** /–bidlee/ *adv.*

■ engrossed, involved, lost, wrapped up, immersed.

ab•sor•bent /əbsáwrbənt, –záwr–/ • *adj.* tending to absorb. • *n.* absorbent substance. □□ **ab•sor•ben•cy** /–bənsee/ *n.*

ab•sorb•ing /əbsáwrbing, –záwr–/ *adj.* engrossing; intensely interesting. □□ **ab•sorb'ing•ly** *adv.*

■ engaging, riveting, captivating, fascinating, spellbinding, gripping.

ab•sorp•tion /əbsáwrpshən, –záwrp–/ *n.* **1** absorbing or being absorbed. **2** mental engrossment. □□ **a•bsorp'tive** *adj.*

ab•stain /əbstáyn/ *v.intr.* **1** refrain from. **2** formally decline to use one's vote. □□ **ab•stain'er** *n.* **ab•sten•tion** /əbsténshən/ *n.*

ab•ste•mi•ous /əbsteémeeəs/ *adj.* moderate, esp. in eating and drinking. See synonym study at ABSTINENCE. □□ **ab•ste'mi•ous•ly** *adv.* **ab•ste'mi•ous•ness** *n.*

ab•sti•nence /ábstinəns/ *n.* abstaining, esp. from food, alcohol, or sexual relations. □□ **ab'sti•nent** *adj.*

■ *see* SELF-DENIAL, TEMPERANCE 2.

SYNONYM STUDY: **abstinence**

ABNEGATION, ABSTEMIOUSNESS, CONTINENCE, FORBEARANCE, MODERATION, TEMPERANCE. **Abstinence** implies voluntary self-denial and is usually associated with the non-indulgence of an appetite (*total abstinence from cigarettes and alcohol*). **Abstemiousness** is the quality or habit of being abstinent; an abstemious person would be one who is moderate when it comes to eating and drinking. **Continence, temperance, and moderation** all imply various forms of self-restraint or self-denial: *moderation* is the avoidance of extremes or excesses (*he drank in moderation*); *temperance* is habitual moderation, or even total abstinence, particularly with regard to alcohol (*the 19th-century temperance movement*); and *continence* (in this regard) refers to self-restraint with regard to sexual activity. **Forbearance** is self-control, the patient endurance that characterizes deliberately holding back from action or response. **Abnegation** is the rejection or renunciation of something that is generally held in high esteem (*abnegation of the Christian Church*), although it can also mean to refuse or deny oneself a particular right, claim, or convenience (*abnegation of worldly goods*).

---

ab•stract • *adj.* /ábstrakt/ **1 a** of or existing in thought or theory rather than matter or practice; not concrete. **b** (of a word, esp. a noun) denoting a quality, condition, etc., not a concrete object. **2** (of art) achieving its effect by shapes and colors rather than by realism. • *v.tr.* /əbstrákt/ **1** extract; remove. **2** summarize. • *n.* /ábstrakt/ **1** summary. **2** abstract work of art. □□ **ab•stract'ly** *adv.* **ab•stract'or** *n.* (in sense 2 of *v.*).

■ *adj.* **1 a** theoretical, unapplied, pure, notional; intangible. **2** nonrepresentational. • *v.* **1** take away, draw out. **2** epitomize, abbreviate, digest. • *n.* **1** epitome, synopsis, essence; outline, précis.

ab•strac•tion /əbstrákshən/ *n.* **1** removal or taking away. **2** abstract or visionary idea. **3 a** abstract qualities (esp. in art). **b** abstract work of art. **4** absentmindedness.

ab•struse /əbstroos/ *adj.* hard to understand; obscure; profound. □□ **ab•struse'ly** *adv.* **ab•struse'ness** *n.*

ab•surd /əbsórd/ *adj.* wildly illogical or inappropriate. □□ **ab•surd'i•ty** *n.* **ab•surd'ly** *adv.*

■ ridiculous, silly, nonsensical, senseless, outlandish; preposterous; laughable, ludicrous. □□ **absurdity** folly, silliness, ridiculousness.

SYNONYM STUDY: **absurd**

FOOLISH, LUDICROUS, PREPOSTEROUS, RIDICULOUS, UNREASONABLE. We call something **absurd** when it is utterly inconsistent with what common sense or experience tells us (*she found herself in the absurd position of having to defend the intelligence of a cockroach*). **Ludicrous** applies to whatever is so incongruous that it provokes laughter or scorn (*a ludicrous suggestion that he might escape unnoticed if he dressed up as a woman*), and **ridiculous** implies that ridicule or mockery is the only appropriate response (*she tried to look younger, but succeeded only in making herself look ridiculous*). **Foolish** behavior shows a lack of intelligence or good judgment (*it was foolish to keep that much money under a mattress*), while **unreasonable** behavior implies that the person has acted contrary to good sense (*his response was totally unreasonable in view of the fact that he'd asked for their honest opinion*). **Preposterous** should be reserved for those acts or situations that are glaringly absurd or ludicrous. For example, it might be *unreasonable* to judge an entire nation on the basis of one tourist's experience and *foolish* to turn down an opportunity to visit that country on those grounds alone, but it would be *preposterous* to suggest that everyone who comes to the United States will be robbed at gunpoint.

a·bun·dance /əbúndəns/ *n.* very great quantity; more than enough. □□ **a·bun′dant** *adj.* **a·bun′dant·ly** *adv.* See synonym study at PREVALENT

■ overflow, superfluity, excess; plethora, wealth, copiousness, profusion; *colloq.* pile. □□ **abundant** ample, generous, copious; rich in, teeming with.

a·buse • *v.tr.* /əbyōōz/ **1 a** use improperly; misuse. **b** take (a drug) for a purpose other than a therapeutic one; be addicted to (a substance). **2** insult verbally. **3** maltreat; assault (esp. sexually). • *n.* /əbyōōs/ **1** improper use. **2** insulting language. **3** unjust or corrupt practice. **4** maltreatment. □□ **a·bused** /əbyōōzd/ *adj.* **a·bus·er** /əbyōōzər/ *n.* **a·bu·sive** /əbyōōsiv/ *adj.* **a·bu′sive·ly** *adv.* **a·bu′sive·ness** *n.*

■ *v.* **1 a** take advantage of, pervert. **b** use, be dependent on. **2** malign, call a person names, revile. **3** ill-use, injure, wrong, hurt; rape, violate. • *n.* **1** misuse, misusage, perversion; misappropriation; addiction. **2** revilement, mudslinging, vituperation, namecalling. **3** injustice, wrong, corruption. **4** ill-treatment, molestation; beating; rape, violation. □□ **abusive** insulting, scurrilous, vituperative; brutal, cruel, injurious.

a·but /əbút/ *v.* (**a·but·ted, a·but·ting**) **1** *intr.* (of land, etc.) adjoin (another). **2** *tr.* border on.

a·but·ment /əbútmənt/ *n.* **1** lateral supporting structure of a bridge, arch, etc. **2** point of junction between such a support and the thing supported.

a·bys·mal /əbízməl/ *adj.* **1** *colloq.* extremely

---

bad. **2** profound; utter. □□ **a·bys′mal·ly** *adv.*

■ **1** awful, appalling, dreadful, terrible, abominable. **2** abyssal, bottomless, unfathomable; complete. □□ **abysmally** see BADLY 1.

a·byss /əbís/ *n.* **1** deep chasm. **2** immeasurable depth. **3** primal chaos; hell.

■ **1** deep, gulf, (gaping) void. **2** see DEPTH 4a. **3** see HELL 1.

AC *abbr.* **1** (also **ac**) alternating current. **2** air conditioning.

Ac *symb. Chem.* actinium.

ac- /ək/ *prefix* assim. form of AD- before *c, k, q*.

-ac /ak/ *suffix* forming adjectives often (or only) used as nouns (*cardiac, maniac*).

a·ca·cia /əkáyshə/ *n.* tree with yellow or white flowers, esp. one yielding gum arabic.

ac·a·de·mi·a /ákədéemeeə/ *n.* (also **ac·a·deme** /ákədeem/) academic world; scholastic life. □□ **ac·a·de·mi·cian** /ákədəmíshən/ *n.*

ac·a·dem·ic /ákədémik/ • *adj.* **1 a** scholarly; of learning. **b** of or relating to a scholarly institution (*academic dress*). **2** theoretical; not of practical relevance. • *n.* teacher or scholar in a university, etc. □□ **ac·a·dem′i·cal·ly** *adv.*

■ *adj.* **1 a** learned, lettered, erudite. **b** scholastic, collegiate. **2** hypothetical; ivory-tower, idealistic; impractical. • *n.* lecturer, tutor, professor, fellow, doctor, instructor; intellectual.

a·cad·e·my /əkádəmee/ *n.* (*pl.* **–mies**) **1 a** place of specialized training. **b** *hist.* place of study. **2** (usu. **Academy**) society or institution of distinguished scholars, artists, scientists, etc.

a·can·thus /əkánthəs/ *n.* herbaceous plant with spiny leaves.

a cap·pel·la /aa kəpélə/ *adj. & adv. Mus.* (of choral singing) unaccompanied.

ac·cede /akséed/ *v.intr.* **1** assent or agree. **2** take office.

■ **1** see AGREE 2.

ac·cel·er·ate /aksélərayt/ *v.* **1** *intr.* **a** move or begin to move more quickly; increase speed. **b** happen or reach completion more quickly. **2** *tr.* **a** cause to increase speed. **b** cause to happen more quickly. □□ **ac·cel·er·a·tion** /–ráyshən/ *n.*

ac·cel·er·a·tor /akséləraytər/ *n.* **1** device for increasing speed, esp. the pedal that controls the speed of a vehicle's engine. **2** *Physics* apparatus for imparting high speeds to charged particles.

ac·cent • *n.* /áksent/ **1** particular mode of pronunciation, esp. local or national. **2** prominence given to a syllable by stress or pitch. **3** mark on a letter or word to indicate pitch, stress, or vowel quality. **4** distinctive feature or emphasis. • *v.tr.* (also /aksént/) **1** emphasize (a word or syllable). **2** write or print accents on (words, etc.). **3** accentuate. □□ **ac·cen·tu·al** /aksénchŏŏəl/ *adj.*

■ *n.* **1** intonation, speech pattern, inflection. **2, 4** force, prominence, weight; inflection; cadence, beat. **3** diacritic, (diacritical)

mark, accent mark. • v. **1, 3** stress, give prominence or weight to, mark, underline.
ac•cen•tu•ate /aksénchŏoayt/ v.tr. emphasize; make prominent. □□ **ac•cen•tu•a•tion** /-áyshən/ n.
ac•cept /aksépt/ v.tr. **1** willingly receive. **2** answer affirmatively. **3** regard favorably; treat as welcome. **4** a believe. **b** be prepared to subscribe to (a belief, philosophy, etc.).
■ **1** take, be the recipient of. **2** agree or say yes to, acknowledge; assent, accede. **3** favor, warm to; receive, welcome.
ac•cept•a•ble /akséptəbəl/ adj. **1** a worth accepting. **b** welcome. **2** adequate. **3** tolerable. □□ **ac•cept•a•bil•i•ty** /-bílitee/ n. **ac•cept'a•ble•ness** n. **ac•cept'a•bly** adv.
■ **1** a deserving, suitable, appropriate, apt. **b** agreeable, pleasing, satisfying. **2** satisfactory, all right, fair, sufficient, colloq. OK, okay. **3** reasonable, understandable, allowable.
ac•cept•ance /akséptəns/ n. **1** willingness to receive. **2** affirmative answer to an invitation.
ac•cess /ákses/ • n. **1** way of approach or entry. **2** a right or opportunity to reach or use or visit; admittance. **b** accessibility. • v.tr. Computing gain access to (data, a file, etc.).
■ n. **2** a see ADMISSION 2a.
ac•ces•si•ble /aksésibəl/ adj. **1** readily reached, entered, or used. **2** readily available. **3** easy to understand. □□ **ac•ces•si•bil•i•ty** /-bílitee/ n. **ac•ces'si•bly** adv.
■ **1** open, available, attainable, obtainable, reachable. **2** approachable, accommodating. **3** simple, comprehensible.
ac•ces•sion /akséshən/ • n. **1** taking office (esp. the throne). **2** thing added (e.g., book to a library); increase. • v.tr. record the addition of (a new item) to a library, etc.
ac•ces•so•ry /aksésəree/ • n. (pl. –ries) **1** additional or extra thing. **2** [usu. in pl.] a small attachment or fitting. **b** small item of (esp. a woman's) dress (e.g., shoes, gloves, etc.). **3** person who helps in or knows the details of an (esp. illegal) act. • adj. additional; contributing or aiding in a minor way; dispensable. □□ **ac•ces•so•ri•al** /áksesáwreeəl/ adj.
■ n. **1** adjunct, attachment, add-on. **2** (accessories) extras, trappings, frills, trimmings. **3** accomplice, confederate, colleague, collaborator. • adj. extra, subordinate, auxiliary; see also DISPENSABLE.
ac•ci•dent /áksidənt/ n. **1** event that is without apparent cause or that is unexpected. **2** unfortunate event, esp. one causing physical harm or damage. **3** occurrence of things by chance. □ **accident-prone** (of a person) subject to frequent accidents.
■ **1, 3** chance, coincidence, fluke; serendipity. **2** mishap, misfortune, mistake; casualty, disaster.
ac•ci•den•tal /áksidént'l/ • adj. happening by chance or unexpectedly. • n. **1** Mus. sign indicating a momentary departure from the key signature. **2** something not essential. □□ **ac•ci•den'tal•ly** adv.

■ adj. fortuitous, serendipitous, incidental; undesigned, unpremeditated; uncalculated, unintended; unplanned. • n. **2** incidental, inessential, extra, addition.

SYNONYM STUDY: accidental
ADVENTITIOUS, CASUAL, CONTINGENT, FORTUITOUS, INCIDENTAL. Things don't always go as planned, but there are many ways to describe the role that chance plays. **Accidental** applies to events that occur entirely by chance (an accidental encounter with the candidate outside the men's room); but it is so strongly influenced by the noun "accident" that it carries connotations of undesirable or possibly disastrous results (an accidental miscalculation of the distance he had to jump). A **casual** act or event is one that is random or unpremeditated (a casual conversation with her son's teacher in the grocery store), in which the role that chance plays is not always clear. Something that is **incidental** may or may not involve chance; it typically refers to what is secondary or nonessential (incidental expenses in the budget) or what occurs without design or regularity (incidental lighting throughout the garden). **Adventitious** also implies the lack of an essential relationship, referring to something that is a mere random occurrence (adventitious circumstances that led to victory). In contrast, **contingent** points to something that is entirely dependent on an uncertain event for its existence or occurrence (travel plans that are contingent upon the weather). **Fortuitous** refers to chance events of a fortunate nature; it is about as far as one can get from accidental (a fortuitous meeting with the candidate outside the men's room just before the press conference).

ac•claim /əkláym/ • v.tr. welcome or applaud enthusiastically; praise publicly. See synonym study at PRAISE. • n. applause; welcome; public praise. □□ **ac•claim'er** n.
■ v. see PRAISE v. **1**. ■ n. see PRAISE n.
ac•cla•ma•tion /ákləmáyshən/ n. **1** loud and eager assent. **2** act or process of acclaiming.
ac•cli•mate /áklimayt, əklímit/ v.tr. acclimatize.
ac•cli•ma•tize /əklímətīz/ v. **1** tr. accustom to a new climate or conditions. **2** intr. become acclimatized. □□ **ac•cli•ma•tiz•a'tion** n.
ac•co•lade /ákəláyd/ n. awarding of praise; acknowledgment of merit.
■ see HONOR n. **1**, PRAISE n.
ac•com•mo•date /əkómədayt/ v.tr. **1** provide lodging or room for. **2** adapt; harmonize; reconcile. **3** do a favor for.
■ **1** put up, house, lodge, shelter, quarter, Mil. billet. **2** (accommodate a thing to) make consistent with, adapt to; (accommodate oneself to) become accustomed or acclimatized to, get used to. **3** oblige, favor; aid, assist.
ac•com•mo•dat•ing /əkómədayting/ adj. obliging; compliant. □□ **ac•com'mo•dat•ingly** adv.
■ cooperative, helpful, considerate, easy to deal with.
ac•com•mo•da•tion /əkómədáyshən/ n. **1** [in pl.] a lodgings; place to live. **b** room

and board. **2 a** adjustment or adaptation. **b** settlement or compromise. **3** act or process of accommodating or being accommodated. **4** [in *pl.*] seat or other facilities for a passenger of a public vehicle.

■ **1 a** room(s), quarters, shelter, housing. **2 a** modification, change, alteration, conformation. **b** treaty, arrangement, terms, contract, deal. **3** conformity, orientation.

ac•com•pa•ni•ment /əkúmpəniment/ *n.* **1** *Mus.* instrumental or orchestral support for a solo instrument, voice, or group. **2** accompanying thing. □□ **ac•com′pa•nist** *n.*

ac•com•pa•ny /əkúmpənee/ *v.tr.* (**-nies, -nied**) **1** go with; escort. **2 a** supplement. **b** have as a result (*pills accompanied by side effects*). **3** *Mus.* support or partner with accompaniment.

■ **1** chaperon, go (along) with, guide, conduct. **2** go (along) with, come with, occur with, be associated with.

ac•com•plice /əkómplis, əkúm-/ *n.* partner in a crime.

■ accessory, confederate; henchman, collaborator; ally.

ac•com•plish /əkómplish/ *v.tr.* perform; complete; succeed in doing. □□ **ac•com′plish•a•ble** *adj.*

■ fulfill, achieve, carry out; attain, reach.

ac•com•plished /əkómplisht/ *adj.* clever; skilled.

■ consummate, expert, masterful, adept.

ac•com•plish•ment /əkómplishmənt/ *n.* **1** completion (of a task, etc.). **2** acquired (esp. social) skill. **3** thing achieved.

■ **1** consummation, realization, attainment. **2** talent, gift, ability. **3** achievement, attainment, acquirement.

ac•cord /əkáwrd/ • *v.* **1** *intr.* be in harmony; be consistent. **2** *tr.* grant (permission, a request, etc.). • *n.* **1** agreement; consent. **2** harmony. **3** *formal* treaty or agreement. □ **of one's own accord** voluntarily.

■ *v.* **1** agree, harmonize, concur, be at one, correspond. **2** see GIVE *v.* 4. ■ *n.* **1** unanimity, concord, harmony. **2** agreement, sympathy, concord. **3** pact, compact, contract. □ **of one's own accord** see *voluntarily* (VOLUNTARY).

ac•cord•ance /əkáwrd'ns/ *n.* harmony; agreement.

ac•cord•ing /əkáwrding/ *adv.* **1** [foll. by *to*] as stated by (*according to my sister*). **2** in proportion to.

■ **1** (*according to*) on the authority of, in conformity *or* agreement with, as said by. **2** by, in keeping with.

ac•cord•ing•ly /əkáwrdinglee/ *adv.* **1** as suggested or required by the (stated) circumstances. **2** consequently.

■ **1** correspondingly, in accordance, in conformity. **2** hence, therefore.

ac•cor•di•on /əkáwrdeeən/ *n.* musical reed instrument with bellows, keys, and buttons. □□ **ac•cor′di•on•ist** *n.*

ac•cost /əkáwst, əkóst/ *v.tr.* **1** approach and address (a person), esp. boldly. **2** (of a prostitute) solicit.

■ **1** see HAIL² *v.* 2. **2** see PROPOSITION *v.*

ac•count /əkównt/ • *n.* **1** narration or de-

scription. **2** arrangement at a bank, etc., for commercial or financial transactions, esp. for depositing and withdrawing money. **3** [often in *pl.*] record or statement of financial transactions. • *v.tr.* [foll. by *to be* or compl.] consider; regard as (*account it a misfortune*). ¶Use with *as* (*we accounted him as wise*) is considered incorrect. □ **account for 1** serve as or provide an explanation for. **2 a** give a reckoning of (money, etc., entrusted). **b** answer for (one's conduct). **on no account** under no circumstances. **take account of** (or **take into account**) consider along with other factors (*took their age into account*).

■ *n.* **1** explanation, narrative, statement; history, chronicle. **3** books, (financial) statement; invoice. • *v.* count (as), view as, look upon as. □ **on no account** see *by no means* (MEANS). □ **take account of** (or **take into account**) notice, take note of, allow for.

ac•count•a•ble /əkówntəbəl/ *adj.* **1** responsible; required to account for (one's conduct). **2** understandable. □□ **ac•count•a•bil•i•ty** /-bílitee/ *n.* **ac•count′a•ble•ness** *n.* **ac•count′a•bly** *adv.*

■ **1** answerable, liable, chargeable. **2** explicable; explainable. □□ **accountability**, accountableness answerability, responsibility, liability. **accountably** understandably, discernibly.

ac•count•ant /əkównt'nt/ *n.* professional keeper or inspector of accounts. □□ **ac•count′an•cy** *n.*

ac•count•ing /əkównting/ *n.* **1** process or practice of keeping and verifying accounts. **2** in sense of ACCOUNT *v.*

ac•cou•ter•ment /əkóõtərmənt, -trəmənt/ *n.* (also **ac•cou′tre•ment**) [usu. in *pl.*] **1** equipment. **2** *Mil.* soldier's equipment.

ac•cred•it /əkrédit/ *v.tr.* **1** attribute. **2** send (an ambassador, etc.) with credentials. **3** make credible (an adviser, a statement, etc.). **4** certify (esp. an educational institution) as maintaining professional standards. □□ **ac•cred•i•ta′tion** *n.* **ac•cred′it•ed** *adj.*

■ **1** see ATTRIBUTE *v.* **2** see DELEGATE *v.* 2. **3** see CONFIRM 2. □□ **accredited** see OFFICIAL *adj.* 3.

ac•cre•tion /əkreeshən/ *n.* **1** growth by organic enlargement. **2 a** growing of separate things into one. **b** product of such growing. **3 a** extraneous matter added to anything. **b** the adhesion of this. □□ **ac•cre′tive** *adj.*

ac•crue /əkróõ/ *v.intr.* (**ac•crued, ac•cru•ing**) come as a natural increase or advantage, esp. financial. □□ **ac•cru′al** *n.* **ac•crued′** *adj.* **ac•crue′ment** *n.*

acct. *abbr.* **1** account. **2** accountant.

ac•cu•mu•late /əkyóõmyəlayt/ *v.tr.* **1** acquire an increasing number or quantity of. **2** produce or acquire (a resulting whole) in this way. □□ **ac•cu•mu•la′tion** /-láyshən/ *n.* **ac•cu•mu•la•tive** /-laytiv, -lətiv/ *adj.* **ac•cu′mu•la•tor** *n.*

■ collect, gather, amass, pile up, hoard. □□ **accumulation** collecting, amassing, gathering.

ac•cu•ra•cy /ákyərəsee/ *n.* exactness or careful precision.

■ correctness, accurateness, exactitude, preciseness.

ac•cu•rate /ákyərət/ *adj.* **1** careful; precise; lacking errors. **2** conforming exactly with a qualitative standard, physical or quantitative target, etc. □□ **ac'cu•rate•ly** *adv.* **ac'cu•rate•ness** *n.*

■ meticulous, with an eye for detail, scrupulous; exact, correct. □□ **accurately** see EXACTLY 1, TRULY 4.

ac•curs•ed /ákórsid, əkórst/ *adj.* **1** under a curse. **2** *colloq.* detestable; annoying.

ac•cu•sa•tion /ákyəzáyshən/ *n.* **1** accusing or being accused. **2** statement charging a person with an offense or crime. □□ **ac'cu•sa•to•ry** /əkyóőzətawree/

■ accusal, charge, allegation; incrimination, denunciation.

ac•cu•sa•tive /əkyóőzótiv/ *Gram.* • *n.* case of nouns, pronouns, and adjectives expressing the object of an action. • *adj.* of or in this case. □□ **ac•cu•sa•ti•val** /–tívəl/ *adj.* **ac•cu' sa•tive•ly** *adv.*

ac•cuse /əkyóőz/ *v.tr.* **1** [foll. by *of*] charge with a fault or crime; indict. **2** blame. □□ **ac•cus'er** *n.* **ac•cus'ing•ly** *adv.*

■ **1** (*accuse of*) impeach, arraign for, incriminate in. **2** censure, hold responsible *or* accountable, charge. □□ **ac•cus'er** prosecutor, indicter, informer. **ac•cus'ing•ly** censoriously.

ac•cus•tom /əkústəm/ *v.tr.* [foll. by *to*] make (a person or thing) used to (*the army accustomed him to discipline*).

■ (*accustom to*) familiarize with, acquaint with; adapt to.

ac•cus•tomed /əkústəmd/ *adj.* **1** [usu. foll. by *to*] used to. **2** customary; usual.

■ **1** (*accustomed to*) inured *or* acclimatized to. **2** habitual, traditional.

ace /ays/ • *n.* **1** playing card with a single spot and generally having the highest value. **2 a** person who excels in some activity. **b** *Mil.* pilot who has shot down many enemy aircraft. **3** *Tennis* a unreturnable serve. **b** point scored in this way. **4** *Golf* hole in one. • *adj. sl.* excellent.

■ *n.* **2 a** see EXPERT *n.* • *adj.* see SUPERLATIVE *adj.*

Ace band•age /ays/ • *n. propr.* elasticized bandage designed to support an injury such as a sprained ankle, pulled muscle, etc.

-aceous /áyshəs/ *suffix* forming adjectives, esp. from nouns in -acea, -aceae (*herbaceous, rosaceous*).

a•cer•bic /əsérbik/ *adj.* **1** astringently sour; harsh-tasting. **2** bitter in speech, manner, or temper. □□ **a•cer'bi•cal•ly** *adv.* **a•cer'bi•ty** *n.* (*pl.* **-ties**.)

■ **1** see TART³ 1. **2** see TART³ 2.

a•ce•ta•min•o•phen /əseetəmínəfən/ *n.* common drug used medically to reduce fever and pain.

ac•e•tate /ásitayt/ *n.* **1** salt or ester of acetic acid. **2** fabric made from this.

a•ce•tic /əseétik/ *adj.* of or like vinegar.

□ **acetic acid** clear liquid acid that gives vinegar its characteristic taste.

ac•e•tone /ásitōn/ *n.* colorless, volatile liquid that dissolves organic compounds, esp. paints, varnishes, etc.

a•cet•y•lene /əsétileen/ *n.* colorless hydrocarbon gas, burning with a bright flame, used esp. in welding.

ache /ayk/ • *n.* **1** continuous dull pain. **2** mental distress. • *v.intr.* **1** suffer an ache. **2** desire greatly. □□ **ach'ing•ly** *adv.* **ach'y** *adj.* (**ach•i•er, ach•i•est**.)

■ *n.* **1** pang, throbbing, pounding, soreness; discomfort. **2** pang; sorrow, grief. • *v.* **1** hurt, smart, throb. **2** yearn, long, hunger; crave.

a•chieve /əcheév/ *v.tr.* **1 a** attain by effort. **b** acquire; gain; earn. **2** accomplish. **3** *absol.* be successful. □□ **a•chiev'a•ble** *adj.* **a• chiev'er** *n.*

■ **1** reach, get, manage, win. **2** carry out, execute, succeed in; realize. **3** succeed, triumph, flourish. □□ **achievable** see POSSIBLE *adj.* 2. **achiever** high-flyer, success story, *colloq.* golden boy.

a•chieve•ment /əcheévmənt/ *n.* **1** something achieved. **2** act of achieving.

■ **1** see ACCOMPLISHMENT 3, ACT *n.* 1.

A•chil•les heel /əkileez/ *n.* person's weak or vulnerable point.

A•chil•les ten•don /əkileez/ *n.* tendon connecting the heel with the calf muscles.

ach•ro•mat•ic /ákrōmátik/ *adj. Optics* transmitting light without separating it into constituent colors. □□ **ach•ro•ma'tic•al•ly** *adv.* **ach•ro•ma•tic•i•ty** /əkrōmətísitee/ *n.* **a• chro•ma•tism** /əkrōmətizəm/ *n.*

ac•id /ásid/ • *n.* **1** *Chem.* **a** any of a class of substances that liberate hydrogen ions in water, are usu. sour and corrosive, and have a pH of less than 7. **b** any compound or atom donating protons. **2** any sour substance. **3** *sl.* the drug LSD. • *adj.* **1** sour. **2** biting; sharp. **3** *Chem.* having the properties of an acid. □ **acid rain** overly acidic rainwater, as from pollution. **acid test** severe or conclusive test. □□ **a•cid•ic** /əsídik/ *adj.* **a•cid•i•fy** /əsidifī/ *v.* **a•cid'i•ty** *n.* **ac'id•ly** *adv.* **ac'id• ness** *n.*

a•cid•u•lous /əsídyoolɘs/ *adj.* somewhat acid.

-acity /ásitee/ *suffix* forming nouns of quality or state corresponding to adjectives in -*acious*.

ac•knowl•edge /əknólij/ *v.tr.* **1** recognize; accept as truth. **2** confirm the receipt of (*acknowledged her letter*). **3 a** show that one has noticed. **b** express appreciation for. **4** recognize the validity of. □□ **ac•knowl'edge•a• ble** *adj.* **ac•knowl'edg•ment** *or* **ac•knowl' edge•ment** *n.*

■ **1** admit, own up to, concede. **2** answer, reply to, respond to. **3 a** greet, mark, note. **b** thank a person for, honor, reward. **4** grant, accept. □□ **acknowledgeable** admittable, confessable; answerable; rewardable. **acknowledgment** admission, confession, avowal; tribute, (show of) appreciation.

ACLU *abbr.* American Civil Liberties Union.

ac•me /ákmee/ *n.* highest point.
■ climax, culmination; apex, top, summit.

ac•ne /áknee/ *n.* skin condition characterized by pimples. □□ **ac′ned** *adj.*

ac•o•lyte /ákəlīt/ *n.* **1** person assisting a priest; altar boy or girl. **2** assistant; beginner.

ac•o•nite /ákənīt/ *n.* **1** any of various poisonous plants, esp. monkshood or wolfsbane. **2** drug obtained from this. □□ **ac•o•nit•ic** /–nítik/ *adj.*

a•corn /áykorn/ *n.* fruit of the oak, with a smooth nut in a rough cuplike base.

a•cous•tic /əkṓóstik/ • *adj.* **1** relating to sound or the sense of hearing. **2** (of a musical instrument) not having electrical amplification. **3** (of building materials) used for soundproofing. • *n.* **1** [usu. in *pl.*] properties or qualities (esp. of a room, etc.) in transmitting sound. **2** [in *pl.*; usu. treated as *sing.*] science of sound. □□ **a•cous′ti•cal** *adj.* **a•cous′ti•cal•ly** *adv.* **ac•ous•ti•cian** /ákoostíshən/ *n.*

ac•quaint /əkwáynt/ *v.tr.* [usu. foll. by *with*] make aware of or familiar with.
■ (*acquaint with*) familiarize with, inform about, advise of.

ac•quaint•ance /əkwáyntəns/ *n.* **1** slight knowledge (of a person or thing). **2** being acquainted. **3** person one knows slightly. □□ **ac•quaint′ance•ship** *n.*
■ **1** familiarity, acquaintanceship; experience. **2** association, friendship, relationship. **3** associate, fellow, colleague.

ac•qui•esce /ákwee-és/ *v.intr.* **1** agree, esp. tacitly. **2** raise no objection. **3** accept (an arrangement, etc.). □□ **ac•qui•es′cence** *n.* **ac′qui•es′cent** *adj.*
■ **1** see AGREE 1. **2** see AGREE 2. □□ **acquiescent** see YIELDING 1.

ac•quire /əkwīr/ *v.tr.* **1** gain by and for oneself. **2** come into possession of. See synonym study at GET. □ **acquired immune deficiency syndrome** *Med.* see AIDS. □□ **ac•quir′a•ble** *adj.* **ac•quire′ment** *n.*
■ **1** get, obtain, win, earn. **2** receive, amass, pick up; inherit. □□ **acquirable** obtainable, gettable, procurable. **acquirement** see ACCOMPLISHMENT 3, ACQUISITION 2.

ac•qui•si•tion /ákwizíshən/ *n.* **1** something acquired. **2** act of acquiring.
■ **1** possession(s), belongings, purchase; object. **2** gain, procurement, inheritance.

ac•quis•i•tive /əkwízitiv/ *adj.* eager to acquire things. See synonym study at GREEDY. □□ **ac•quis′i•tive•ly** *adv.* **ac•quis′i•tive•ness** *n.*
■ see *avaricious* (AVARICE).

ac•quit /əkwít/ *v.* (**ac•quit•ted, ac•quit•ting**) **1** *tr.* declare not guilty. **2** *refl.* **a** conduct oneself or perform in a specified way. **b** discharge (a duty or responsibility). See synonym study at ABSOLVE. □□ **ac•quit′tal** /əkwít′l/ *n.*
■ **1** see FORGIVE. **2** see CONDUCT *v.* 4.

a•cre /áykər/ *n.* measure of land, 4,840 sq. yds. □□ **a′cred** *adj.* [also in *comb.*]

a•cre•age /áykərij, áykrij/ *n.* unspecified number of acres.

ac•rid /ákrid/ *adj.* (**ac•rid•er, ac•rid•est**) bit-

terly pungent. □□ **a•crid′i•ty** *n.* **ac′rid•ly** *adv.*
■ **1** see BITTER[3] *adj.* 1, TART 1.

ac•ri•mo•ni•ous /ákrimṓneeəs/ *adj.* bitter in manner or temper. □□ **ac•ri•mo′ni•ous•ly** *adv.* **ac•ri•mo′ny** /ákrimṓnee/ *n.*
■ see TART[3] 2. □□ **acrimony** see ANIMOSITY.

ac•ro•bat /ákrəbat/ *n.* performer of gymnastic feats. □□ **ac•ro•bat′ic** *adj.* **ac•ro•bat′i•cal•ly** *adv.*

ac•ro•bat•ics /ákrəbátiks/ *n.pl.* **1** acrobatic feats. **2** [as *sing.*] art of performing these. **3** skill requiring ingenuity (*mental acrobatics*).

ac•ro•nym /ákrənim/ *n.* usu. pronounceable word formed from the initial letters of other words (e.g., *laser, NATO*).

ac•ro•pho•bi•a /ákrəfṓbeeə/ *n. Psychol.* abnormal dread of heights. □□ **ac•ro•pho•bic** /–fṓbik/ *adj.*

a•crop•o•lis /əkrópəlis/ *n.* **1** elevated, fortified part of esp. an ancient Greek city. **2** (**Acropolis**) ancient citadel at Athens.

a•cross /əkráws, əkrós/ • *prep.* **1** to or on the other side of. **2** from one side to another side of. **3** at or forming an angle (esp. a right angle) with. • *adv.* **1** to or on the other side. **2** from one side to another. □ **across the board** generally; applying to all.
■ *prep.* **1, 2** see OVER *prep.* 4. • *adv.* **1, 2** see OVER *adv.* 4.

a•cryl•ic /əkrílik/ • *adj.* **1** of synthetic material made from acrylic acid. **2** *Chem.* of or derived from acrylic acid. • *n.* acrylic fiber.

act /akt/ • *n.* **1** something done; deed. **2** process of doing. **3 a** piece of entertainment. **b** performer(s) of this. **4** pretense. **5** main division of a play or opera. **6** statute law. • *v.intr.* **1** behave. **2** perform actions or functions; take action. **3** [also foll. by *on*] exert energy or influence. **4 a** perform a part in a play, movie, etc. **b** pretend. □ **act up** *colloq.* misbehave; give trouble. **get one's act together** *sl.* become properly organized.
■ *n.* **1** undertaking, move; exploit; accomplishment. **2** see PERFORMANCE 1. **3 a** performance, show, skit. **b** see CAST *n.* 3. **4** posture, pose, stance, front. **5** bill, decree, edict, statute. • *v.* **1** carry on, conduct oneself. **3** take effect, work. **4 a** appear. **b** feign, fake, dissemble, make believe. □ **act up** see MISBEHAVE. **get one's act together** pull oneself together, rally oneself; hurry up, *colloq.* get moving.

act•ing /ákting/ • *n.* art or occupation of an actor. • *attrib.adj.* serving temporarily.
■ *attrib. adj.* see TEMPORARY *adj.*

ac•tin•i•um /aktíneeəm/ *n. Chem.* radioactive metallic element. ¶Symb.: **Ac**

ac•tion /ákshən/ • *n.* **1** process of doing or acting. **2** forcefulness or energy. **3** exertion of energy or influence. **4** deed or act. **5** a series of events in a story, play, etc. **b** *sl.* exciting activity. **6 a** armed conflict; fighting (*killed in action*). **b** minor military engagement. **7 a** way in which a machine, instrument, etc., works. **b** mechanism of an instrument, etc. **8** lawsuit. • *v.tr.* bring a legal action against.

■ *n.* **1** activity, performance, movement. **2** liveliness, vim, vigor, spirit. **3** effect, power, force, strength. **4** undertaking, operation, feat; (*actions*) behavior, conduct. **5 b** excitement, interest, adventure, thrills. **6 a** combat, battle, war. **b** fight, battle, skirmish. **7 a, b** see MOVEMENT 2, MECHANISM 2, 3. **8** litigation, proceeding, case; remedy. ● *v.* proceed against, institute proceedings against.

ac•tion•a•ble /ákshənəbəl/ *adj.* giving cause for legal action. □□ **ac′tion•a•bly** *adv.*

ac•ti•vate /áktivayt/ *v.tr.* **1** make active. **2** *Chem.* cause reaction in. **3** *Physics* make radioactive. □□ **ac•ti•va•tion** /–váyshən/ *n.* **ac′ti•va•tor** *n.*

■ **1** move, actuate, set in motion, get started, energize. □□ **activation** operation, movement. **activator** initiator, starter.

ac•tive /áktiv/ ● *adj.* **1 a** marked by action; energetic. **b** able to move about or accomplish practical tasks. **2** working; operative (*active volcano*). **3** originating action (*active support*). **4** *Gram.* designating the voice that attributes the action of a verb to the person or thing from which it logically proceeds (e.g., of the verb in *guns kill*). ● *n. Gram.* active form or voice of a verb. □□ **ac′tive•ly** *adv.* **ac′tive•ness** *n.*

■ *adj.* **1 a** strenuous, vigorous, full, dynamic; tireless, industrious. **b** agile, spry. **2, 3** effective, effectual, functioning, potent.

ac•tiv•ism /áktivizəm/ *n.* policy of vigorous action in a cause, esp. in politics. □□ **ac′tiv•ist** *n.*

ac•tiv•i•ty /aktívitee/ *n.* (*pl.* –**ties**) **1 a** condition of being active or moving about. **b** exertion of energy; vigorous action. **2** [often in *pl.*] particular occupation or pursuit.

■ **1** action, movement; liveliness; exertion, vigor. **2** work, employment, function; interest, avocation, pastime.

ac•tor /áktər/ *n.* performer in a play, movie, etc.

■ see PLAYER 3.

ac•tress /áktris/ *n.* female actor.

ac•tu•al /ákchōōəl/ *adj.* [usu. *attrib.*] **1** existing in fact; real. **2** current. See synonym study at GENUINE. □□ **ac′tu•al•ize** *v.* **ac•tu•al•i•za′tion** *n.*

■ **1** genuine, factual, authentic. **2** existent, present, extant. □□ **actualize** see REALIZE 4. **actualization** see *realization* (REALIZE).

ac•tu•al•i•ty /ákchōō-álitee/ *n.* (*pl.* –**ties**) **1** reality. **2** [in *pl.*] existing conditions.

■ **1** see CASE¹ 2, REALITY 1.

ac•tu•al•ly /ákchōōəlee/ *adv.* **1** as a fact; really. **2** in truth; strange as it may seem. **3** at present.

■ **1** in reality, in actuality, in point of fact. **2** even, as a matter of fact. **3** for the time being, currently, (just) now.

ac•tu•ar•y /ákchōōeree/ *n.* (*pl.* –**ies**) statistician, esp. one who calculates insurance risks and premiums. □□ **ac•tu•ar•i•al** /–chōōáir-eeəl/ *adj.* **ac•tu•ar′i•al•ly** *adv.*

ac•tu•ate /ákchōō-ayt/ *v.tr.* **1** cause the operation of (an electrical device, etc.). **2** cause

to act. □□ **ac•tu•a•tion** /–áyshən/ *n.* **ac′tu•a•tor** *n.*

■ see ACTIVATE.

a•cu•i•ty /əkyóōitee/ *n.* sharpness; acuteness.

a•cu•men /ákyəmən, əkyóō–/ *n.* keen insight or discernment.

ac•u•pres•sure /ákyəpreshər/ *n.* method of treating various conditions by applying pressure with the fingers to specific points on the body.

ac•u•punc•ture /ákyəpungkchər/ *n.* method (orig. Chinese) of treating various conditions by pricking the skin with needles. □□ **ac•u•punc′tur•ist** *n.*

a•cute /əkyōōt/ ● *adj.* (**a•cut•er, a•cut•est**) **1 a** (of senses, etc.) keen; penetrating. **b** (of pain) intense; severe. **2** (of a disease) coming sharply to a crisis; not chronic. **3 a** (of an angle) less than 90°. **b** sharp; pointed. See synonym studies at KEEN, CRUCIAL. ● *n.* = *acute accent.* □ **acute accent** mark (′) placed over letters in some languages to show vowel length, pronunciation (e.g., *maté*), etc. □□ **a•cute′ly** *adv.* **a•cute′ness** *n.*

■ *adj.* **1 a** sharp, sensitive, discriminating. **b** cutting, keen, piercing. **2** intense, critical, dangerous, grave. **3 b** narrow. □□ **acutely** see *severely* (SEVERE), VERY *adv.* **acuteness** see GRAVITY 3a, *penetration* (PENETRATE).

-acy /əsee/ *suffix* forming nouns of state or quality (*accuracy, piracy, supremacy*), or an instance of it (*conspiracy, fallacy*).

A.D. *abbr.* (of a date) of the Christian era (Latin *Anno Domini*, 'in the year of the Lord').

ad /ad/ *n. colloq.* advertisement.

ad- /əd, ad/ *prefix* (also **a-** before *sc, sp, st,* **ac-** before *c, k, q,* **af-** before *f,* **ag-** before *g,* **al-** before *l,* **an-** before *n,* **ap-** before *p,* **ar-** before *r,* **as-** before *s,* **at-** before *t*) with the sense of motion or direction to; reduction or change into; addition, adherence, increase, or intensification.

ad•age /ádij/ *n.* traditional maxim; proverb. See synonym study at SAYING.

■ see MAXIM.

a•da•gio /ədáazheeō/ *Mus.* ● *adv. & adj.* in slow time. ● *n.* (*pl.* –**gios**) adagio movement or passage.

Ad•am /ádəm/ *n.* Biblical first man. □ **Adam's apple** projection of cartilage of the larynx, esp. as prominent in men.

ad•a•mant /ádəmənt/ *adj.* stubbornly resolute; resistant to persuasion. □□ **ad′a•mant•ly** *adv.*

■ see RESOLUTE.

a•dapt /ədápt/ *v.* **1** *tr.* [foll. by *to*] fit; adjust (one thing to another). **2** *intr. & refl.* [usu. foll. by *to*] become adjusted to new conditions. □□ **a•dapt′a•ble** *adj.* **ad•ap•ta′tion** *n.* **a•dapt′er** or **a•dap′tor** *n.* **a•dap′tive** *adj.* **a•dap′tive•ly** *adv.*

■ **1** (*adapt to*) align to, coordinate with, attune to. **2** (*adapt oneself to*) accustom or acclimatize oneself to, get used to. □□ **adaptable** flexible, versatile; compliant. **adaptation** modification, change, adjustment.

add /ad/ *v.tr.* **1** join (one thing to another) as an increase or supplement. **2** put to-

gether (numbers) to find their total value.
3 say further. □ **add up 1** find the total
of. **2** [foll. by *to*] amount to (*adds up to a
disaster*). **3** *colloq.* make sense. □□ **add′ed**
adj.
■ **1** unite, aggregate, combine, annex.
2 add up, total, sum (up). **3** continue, go on.
□ **add up 1** see ADD 2 above. **2** constitute,
signify, mean. **3** hang together, be understandable. □□ **added** see EXTRA *adj.*

ad·den·dum /ədéndəm/ *n.* (*pl.* **ad·den·da**
/–də/) **1** thing to be added, esp. [in *pl.*] as additional matter at the end of a book. **2** appendix; addition.
■ see ADDITION 2.

ad·der /ádər/ *n.* any of various small venomous snakes, esp. the common viper.

ad·dict • *v.tr. & refl.* /ədíkt/ [usu. foll. by *to*]
devote or apply habitually or compulsively;
make addicted. • *n.* /ádikt/ **1** person addicted to a habit, esp. to a drug. **2** *colloq.* devotee. □□ **ad·dic·tion** /–díkshən/ *n.* **ad·dic′**
tive *adj.*
■ *v.* (be(come) *addicted*) be(come) dependent, *sl.* be(come) hooked. • *n.* **1** (habitual)
user, drug abuser. **2** aficionado, fan, admirer, supporter, enthusiast. □□ **addiction**
see HABIT 2, 4. **addictive** habit-forming,
compulsive, obsessive.

ad·di·tion /ədíshən/ *n.* **1** adding or being
added. **2** person or thing added. □ **in addition** moreover; furthermore. **in addition to**
as well as; as something added to.
■ **1** increase, augmentation, attachment;
calculation. **2** supplement, increment; extra;
annex. □ **in addition** additionally, to boot,
too. **in addition to** besides, beyond, over
and above.

ad·di·tion·al /ədíshənəl/ *adj.* added; extra;
supplementary. □□ **ad·di′tion·al·ly** *adv.*
■ see EXTRA *adj.*

ad·di·tive /áditiv/ • *n.* substance added to
another so as to give it specific qualities.
• *adj.* characterized by addition (*additive
process*).

ad·dle /ád′l/ • *v.* **1** *tr.* muddle; confuse.
2 *intr.* (of an egg) become rotten. • *adj.*
1 muddled; unsound (*addlebrained*).
2 empty; vain.

ad·dress /ədrés/ • *n.* **1** (also /ádres/) **a** place
where a person lives or an organization is situated. **b** particulars of this, esp. for postal
purposes. **c** *Computing* location of an item of
stored information. **2** discourse delivered to
an audience. • *v.tr.* **1** write postal directions
on (an envelope, package, etc.). **2** speak or
write to, esp. formally (*addressed the audience*). **3** direct one's attention to. □□ **ad·
dress′er** *n.*
■ *n.* **1 a** location, whereabouts, position,
site, situation. **2** speech, talk, lecture; sermon. • *v.* **2** talk to, deliver *or* give a speech
to, present a paper to, lecture. **3** focus on,
aim at, turn to, concentrate on.

ad·dress·ee /ádresée/ *n.* person to whom
something (esp. a letter) is addressed.

ad·duce /ədóos, ədyóos/ *v.tr.* cite as an instance or as proof or evidence. □□ **ad·duc′i·**
ble *adj.*

ad·duc·tor /ədúktər/ *n.* muscle that moves

one part of the body toward another or toward the midline of the body.

-ade¹ /ayd/ *suffix* forming nouns: **1** an action
done (*blockade, tirade*). **2** the body concerned in an action or process (*cavalcade*).
3 the product or result of a material or action
(*arcade, lemonade, masquerade*).

-ade² /ayd/ *suffix* forming nouns: (*decade*).

-ade³ /ayd/ *suffix* forming nouns: **1** = -ADE¹
(*brocade*). **2** a person concerned (*renegade*).

ad·e·noids /ád′noydz/ *n.pl. Med.* mass of
lymphatic tissue between the back of the
nose and the throat. □□ **ad·e·noi·dal** /–nóy-
d′l/ *adj.*

a·dept • *adj.* /ədépt/ thoroughly proficient.
• *n.* /ádept/ skilled performer; expert. □□ **a·
dept′ly** *adv.* **a·dept′ness** *n.*
■ *adj.* versed, skilled, expert, accomplished.
• *n.* master, specialist, authority. □□ **adeptly**
see WELL¹ *adv.* 3. **adeptness** see *proficiency*
(PROFICIENT).

ad·e·quate /ádikwət/ *adj.* sufficient; satisfactory. □□ **ad′e·qua·cy** *n.* **ad′e·quate·ly**
adv.
■ enough; fitting, good enough; passable,
fair. □□ **adequacy** see *fitness* (FIT¹). **adequately** see FAIRLY 2.

ad·here /ədhéer/ *v.intr.* **1** (of a substance)
stick fast to a surface, etc. **2** [foll. by *to*] behave according to. **3** [foll. by *to*] give support
or allegiance.
■ **1** see STICK² 4. **2** (adhere to) see FOLLOW 5.

ad·her·ent /ədhéerənt, –hér–/ • *n.* **1** supporter. **2** devotee. • *adj.* **1** faithfully observing a rule, etc. **2** (of a substance) sticking
fast. □□ **ad·her·ence** /–rəns/ *n.*
■ **2** see FOLLOWER. □□ **adherence** see DEDI-
CATION 1.

ad·he·sion /ədhéezhən/ *n.* **1** adhering.
2 *Med.* unnatural union of body tissues.

ad·he·sive /ədhéesiv, –ziv/ • *adj.* sticky;
causing adhesion. • *n.* adhesive substance.
□□ **ad·he′sive·ly** *adv.* **ad·he′sive·ness** *n.*
■ *adj.* see STICKY *adj.* 1. • *n.* see GLUE *n.*

ad hoc /ád hók/ *adv. & adj.* for one particular
(usu. exclusive) purpose (*an ad hoc appointment*).

a·dieu /ədyóo, ədóo/ • *int.* good-bye. • *n.* (*pl.*
a·dieus or **a·dieux** /ədyóoz, ədóoz/) a good-
bye.

ad in·fi·ni·tum /ád ínfinítəm/ *adv.* without
limit; for ever.

ad·i·os /áadee-ós, ádee–/ *int.* good-bye.

ad·i·pose /ádipōs/ *adj.* fat; fatty. □□ **ad·i·
pos′i·ty** /–pósitee/ *n.*

Ad·i·ron·dack chair /ádəróndak/ • *n.* chair
with a sloping back and wide arms, usu.
made of wood and used outdoors.

ad·ja·cent /əjáysənt/ *adj.* [often foll. by *to*] lying near or adjoining. □□ **ad·ja·cen·cy**
/–sənsee/ *n.*
■ see *adjoining* (ADJOIN).

ad·jec·tive /ájiktiv/ *n.* word used to modify or
describe a noun or pronoun. □□ **ad·jec·ti·
val** /ájiktívəl/ *adj.* **ad·jec·ti′val·ly** *adv.*

ad·join /əjóyn/ *v.tr.* (often as **adjoining** *adj.*)
be next to and joined with.
■ see BORDER *v.* 3a; (**adjoining**) neighbor-

ing, contiguous, adjacent, abutting, bordering, next.

ad•journ /əjórn/ v. **1** tr. **a** put off; postpone. **b** break off (a meeting, etc.) temporarily. **2** intr. of persons at a meeting: **a** break off proceedings and disperse. **b** [foll. by to] transfer the meeting to another place. See synonym study at POSTPONE. □□ **ad•journ´ment** n.

■ **1 b** see DISSOLVE v. 3a.

ad•judge /əjúj/ v.tr. **1** adjudicate (a matter). **2** pronounce or award judicially.

ad•ju•di•cate /əjōōdikayt/ v. **1** intr. act as judge in a competition, court, etc. **2** tr. a decide judicially regarding (a claim, etc.). **b** [foll. by to be + compl.] pronounce (was adjudicated to be bankrupt). □□ **ad•jud•i•ca´tion** /–dikáyshən/ n. **ad•ju´di•ca•tive** adj. **ad•ju´di•ca•tor** n.

■ **1** see JUDGE v. 3. **2 a** see JUDGE v. 1a.

ad•junct /ájungkt/ n. **1** [foll. by to, of] subordinate or incidental thing. **2** subordinate person, esp. one with temporary appointment only. □□ **ad•junc•tive** /əjúngktiv/ adj. **ad•junc´tive•ly** adv.

■ **1** see ACCESSORY n. 1, EXTENSION 3. **2** see ASSISTANT 2.

ad•jure /əjōōr/ v.tr. [usu. foll. by to + infin.] charge or request (a person) solemnly or earnestly, esp. under oath. □□ **ad•ju•ra´tion** n. **ad•jur´a•to•ry** adj.

ad•just /əjúst/ v. **1** tr. **a** put in the correct order or position. **b** regulate. **2** tr. make suitable. **3** tr. assess (loss or damages). **4** intr. [usu. foll. by to] adapt oneself. □□ **ad•just´a•ble** adj. **ad•just•a•bil´i•ty** n. **ad•just´er** n. **ad•just´ment** n.

■ **1** set to rights, (fine–)tune, fix, rearrange. **2** see ADAPT 1b. **3** see EVALUATE 1. **4** (adjust to) accommodate oneself to, accustom oneself to; get used to. □□ **adjustability** see flexibility (FLEXIBLE). **adjustment** alteration, setting, regulation.

ad•ju•tant /ájət'nt/ n. **1** Mil. officer who assists superior officers. **2** assistant. □□ **ad•ju•tan•cy** /–t'nsee/ n.

ad lib /ád líb/ • v.intr. (**ad libbed, ad lib•bing**) improvise. • adj. improvised. • adv. as one pleases. • n. something spoken or played extempore.

■ v. see IMPROVISE 1. • adj. see EXTEMPORANEOUS.

ad loc abbr. to or at that place.

ad•man /ádman/ n. (pl. **ad•men**) colloq. person who produces advertisements commercially.

ad•min•is•ter /ədmínistər/ v. **1** tr. manage. **2** tr. **a** be responsible for the implementation of (the law, justice, punishment, etc.). **b** Eccl. perform the rites of (a sacrament). **3** tr. **a** provide; apply (a remedy). **b** give; deliver (a rebuke). **4** intr. act as administrator. □□ **ad•min´is•tra•ble** adj.

■ **1** administrate, control, direct, conduct. **2 a** execute, carry out, dispense; implement. **3 a** dispense, supply, furnish. **b** see DELIVER 4b. □□ **administrable** manageable; executable.

ad•min•is•trate /ədmínistrayt/ v. administer (esp. business affairs); act as an administrator. □□ **ad•min´is•tra•tive** adj. **ad•min´is•tra•tive•ly** adv.

ad•min•is•tra•tion /ədminístráyshən/ n. **1** management; government. **2** the government in power. **3** president's period of office. **4** [foll. by of] **a** administering of justice, an oath, etc. **b** application of remedies.

■ **1** direction, conduct, supervision. **2** authority, ministry, leadership. **3** presidency, term, office. **4** dispensation, provision, delivery.

ad•min•is•tra•tor /ədmínistraytər/ n. **1** manager. **2** Law person appointed to manage the estate of one who has died intestate.

ad•mi•ra•ble /ádmərəbəl/ adj. **1** deserving admiration. **2** excellent. □□ **ad´mi•ra•bly** adv.

■ **1** see PRAISEWORTHY. **2** wonderful, awe-inspiring, estimable, splendid, superb; see also GREAT adj. 4a. □□ **admirably** marvelously, wonderfully, superbly.

ad•mi•ral /ádmərəl/ n. **1** commander in chief of a fleet. **2** naval officer of high rank. □□ **ad´mi•ral•ship** n.

ad•mi•ra•tion /ádmiráyshən/ n. **1** pleased contemplation. **2** respect; warm approval. **3** object of this.

■ **1** wonder, awe, delight. **2** esteem, (high) regard, appreciation. **3** center of attention, sensation, cynosure.

ad•mire /ədmír/ v.tr. **1** regard with approval, respect, or satisfaction. **2** express one's admiration of. See synonym study at ESTEEM. □□ **ad•mir´er** n. **ad•mir´ing** adj. **ad•mir´ing•ly** adv.

■ **1** respect, approve of, esteem. **2** wonder at, delight in. □□ **admirer** suitor; lover; devotee.

ad•mis•si•ble /ədmísibəl/ adj. **1** (of an idea or plan) worth accepting or considering. **2** Law allowable as evidence. □□ **ad•mis•si•bil•i•ty** /–bílitee/ n.

ad•mis•sion /ədmíshən/ n. **1** acknowledgment. **2 a** process or right of entering. **b** charge for this.

■ **1** confession, concession, avowal, disclosure. **2 a** access, admittance, reception, acceptance. **b** ticket, (entry or entrance) fee.

ad•mit /ədmít/ v. (**ad•mit•ted, ad•mit•ting**) **1** tr. acknowledge; recognize as true. **2** intr. **a** [foll. by to] confess. **b** [foll. by of] allow for something to exist, have influence, etc. **3** tr. allow (a person) entrance or access. **4** tr. (of an enclosed space) accommodate. □□ **ad•mit´ta•ble** adj. **ad•mit´tance** n.

■ **1** accept, concede, allow, grant. **2 a** (admit to) own (up to); concede, divulge. **b** (admit of) permit, grant, tolerate. **3** let in, give access to, take in; accept, receive. **4** hold, receive, embrace.

ad•mit•ted•ly /ədmítidlee/ adv. as an acknowledged fact.

ad•mix•ture /admíkschər/ n. **1** thing added, esp. a minor ingredient. **2** act of adding this.

ad•mon•ish /ədmónish/ v.tr. **1** reprove. **2** urge. **3** give earnest advice to. **4** warn. See synonym study at REBUKE. □□ **ad•mon´ish•**

ment n. **ad·mo·ni·tion** /ádməníshən/ n. **ad·mon'i·to·ry** adj.

■ **1** see REPRIMAND v. **2** see URGE v. 2. **3** see ADVISE 1, 2. **4** see WARN.

ad nau·se·am /ad náwzeeəm/ adv. to an excessive or disgusting degree.

a·do /ədóō/ n. (pl. **a·dos**) fuss; busy activity; trouble; difficulty. □ **without further** (or **more**) **ado** immediately.

a·do·be /ədóbee/ n. **1** sun-dried brick of clay and straw. **2** clay used for making this. **3** structure of such bricks.

ad·o·les·cent /ádəlésənt/ • adj. between childhood and adulthood. See synonym study at YOUTHFUL. • n. adolescent person. □□ **ad·o·les'cence** /-səns/ n.

■ adj. teenage(d), maturing, pubescent; immature, callow. • n. teenager, juvenile, minor; see also YOUTH 4. □□ **adolescence** puberty, teenage years.

A·don·is /ədónis, ədó-/ n. handsome young man.

a·dopt /ədópt/ v.tr. **1** legally take another's child as one's own. **2** choose to follow (a course of action, etc.). **3** take over (a name, idea, etc.). □□ **a·dop·tion** /-dópshən/ n. **a·dop'tive** adj.

■ **1** take (in), accept, take or accept as one's own. **2** select, take on, assume. **3** take (up or on or over); espouse; arrogate, appropriate.

a·dor·a·ble /ədáwrəbəl/ adj. **1** deserving adoration. **2** colloq. delightful; charming. □□ **a·dor'a·bly** adv.

■ **1** lovable, wonderful, estimable, honorable, praiseworthy; beloved, loved, cherished, prized. **2** appealing, attractive, lovely, enchanting, gorgeous, captivating, fetching; darling, sweet, dear, cunning, colloq. cute.

a·dore /ədáwr/ v.tr. **1** regard with honor and deep affection. **2** worship as divine. **3** colloq. like very much. □□ **ad·o·ra·tion** /ádəráyshən/ n. **a·dor'er** n. **a·dor'ing** adj. **a·dor'ing·ly** adv.

■ **1** esteem, respect, admire; love, idolize. **2** venerate, reverence, revere, exalt; hallow. **3** cherish, fancy; carry a torch for; be mad about. □□ **adoration** see LOVE n. 1, reverence (REVERE).

a·dorn /ədáwrn/ v.tr. add beauty to; decorate. □□ **a·dorn'ment** n.

■ see EMBELLISH 1.

ADP abbr. **1** adenosine diphosphate, a nucleic acid essential to living cells. **2** automatic data processing.

a·dre·nal /ədréenəl/ • adj. **1** at or near the kidneys. **2** of the adrenal glands. • n. (in full **adre'nal gland**) either of two ductless glands above the kidneys, secreting adrenaline.

a·dren·a·line /ədrénəlin/ = EPINEPHRINE.

a·drift /ədríft/ adv. & predic. adj. **1** drifting. **2** powerless; aimless.

a·droit /ədróyt/ adj. dexterous; skillful. □□ **a·droit'ly** adv. **a·droit'ness** n.

■ see SKILLFUL.

ad·sorb /adsáwrb, -záwrb/ v.tr. (usu. of a solid) hold (molecules of a gas or liquid, etc.) to its surface, as a thin film. □□ **ad·sorb'a·ble** adj. **ad·sorb'ent** adj. & n. **ad·**

sorp·tion /-sáwrp-, -záwrp-/ n. (also **ad·sorb'tion**).

ad·u·late /ájəlayt/ v.tr. flatter obsequiously. □□ **ad·u·la·tion** /-láyshən/ n. **ad'u·la·tor** n. **ad·u·la·to·ry** /-lətáwree/ adj.

a·dult /ədúlt, ádult/ • adj. **1** mature; grown-up. **2 a** of or for adults. **b** euphem. sexually explicit; indecent (adult films). • n. adult person. □□ **a·dult'hood** n. **a·dult'ly** adv.

■ adj. **1** full-grown, matured, of age. **2 b** see INDECENT. • n. **1** grown-up. □□ **adulthood** see maturity (MATURE). **adult·ly** maturely, sensibly.

a·dul·ter·ate • v.intr. /ədúltərayt/ debase (esp. foods) by adding other or inferior substances. See synonym study at POLLUTE. • adj. /ədúltərət/ spurious; debased; counterfeit. □□ **a·dul'ter·ant** /ədúltərənt/ adj. & n. **a·dul·ter·a·tion** /-ráyshən/ n. **a·dul'ter·a·tor** n.

■ v. falsify, corrupt, alloy, spoil, water (down), weaken, dilute, bastardize, contaminate, pollute, taint, doctor, cut. • adj. see SPURIOUS. □□ **adulteration** see pollution (POLLUTE).

a·dul·ter·y /ədúltəree/ n. voluntary sexual intercourse between a married person and a person (married or not) other than his or her spouse. □□ **a·dul'ter·er** n. **a·dul'ter·ous** adj. **a·dul'ter·ous·ly** adv.

ad·vance /ədváns/ • v. **1** tr. & intr. move or put forward. **2** intr. make progress. **3** tr. **a** pay (money) before it is due. **b** lend (money). **4** tr. promote (a person, cause, or plan). **5** tr. put forward (a suggestion, etc.). **6** tr. (as **advanced** adj.) a far on in progress. **b** ahead of the times. • n. **1** progress. **2** prepayment. **3** loan. **4** [esp. pl.] amorous approach. **5** rise in price. • adj. beforehand (advance warning). □ **in advance** ahead in place or time. □□ **ad·vance'ment** n. **ad·vanc'er** n.

■ v. **1, 2** send on(ward); go or push or press on, proceed. **3** prepay; lend. **4** support, further, assist; benefit, improve; contribute to. **6** (**advanced**) a well-ahead; nearing completion. **b** see PROGRESSIVE adj. 1. • n. **1** progression; headway; improvement. **2** deposit. **4** see APPROACH n. 3. **5** increase, appreciation. □ **in advance** beforehand, before, previously; in front. □□ **advancement** see promotion (PROMOTE).

ad·van·tage /ədvántij/ • n. **1** beneficial feature. **2** benefit; profit. **3** superiority. **4** (in tennis) the next point won after deuce. • v.tr. **1** be beneficial or favorable to. **2** further; promote. □ **take advantage of 1** make good use of. **2** exploit, esp. unfairly. **3** euphem. seduce. □□ **ad·van·ta·geous** /ádvəntáyjəs/ adj. **ad·van·ta'geous·ly** adv.

■ n. **1, 3** strength, feature, attraction; upper hand, dominance, edge. **2** gain, interest, betterment, advancement; use. • v. **1, 2** see BENEFIT v. 1. □ **take advantage of 1** see PROFIT v. 2. **2** see EXPLOIT v. **3** see SEDUCE 1. □□ **advantageous** profitable, worthwhile, beneficial. **advantageously** see favorably (FAVORABLE).

Ad•vent /ádvent/ *n.* **1** season before Christmas. **2** coming of Christ. **3** (**advent**) important arrival.

adven•ti•tious /ádventíshəs/ *adj.* accidental; casual. See synonym study at ACCIDENTAL. □□ **adven•ti′tious•ly** *adv.*

ad•ven•ture /ədvénchər/ • *n.* **1** unusual and exciting experience. **2** daring enterprise. • *v.intr.* **1** (often foll. by *into, upon*) dare to go or come. **2** dare to undertake. **3** incur risk. □□ **ad•ven′ture•some** *adj.* **ad•ven′tur•ous** *adj.*

■ *n.* **1** incident, event, occurrence. **2** exploit, escapade, affair; danger, peril, risk. *v.* **1** (*adventure into* or *upon*) venture upon, brave. **2, 3** try one's luck, take a risk (on). □□ **adventuresome** see *adventurous* (ADVENTURE). **adventurous** daring, bold; rash, reckless.

ad•ven•tur•er /ədvénchərər/ *n.* (*fem.* **ad•ven•tur•ess** /-chəris/) **1** person who seeks adventure. **2** financial speculator.

■ **1** soldier of fortune, swashbuckler, hero, heroine, daredevil. **2** opportunist.

ad•verb /ádvərb/ *n.* word or phrase that modifies or qualifies an adjective, verb, or other adverb (e.g., *gently, quite, then, there*). □□ **ad•ver•bi•al** /ədvə́rbeeəl/ *adj.*

ad•ver•sar•y /ádvərseree/ • *n.* (*pl.* **–ies**) **1** enemy. **2** opponent. • *adj.* opposed; antagonistic. □□ **ad•ver•sar•i•al** /ádvərsáireeəl/ *adj.*

■ *n.* **1** opponent, antagonist, opposition, other side, *esp. poet. or formal* foe. **2** antagonist, competitor, rival. • *adj.* hostile, competitive, adversarial.

ad•verse /ádvə́rs, ád-/ *adj.* **1** contrary; hostile. **2** harmful; injurious. See synonym study at ADVERSE. □□ **ad•verse′ly** *adv.*

■ **1** see HOSTILE 2. **2** see INJURIOUS 1.

ad•ver•si•ty /ədvə́rsitee/ *n.* (*pl.* **–ties**) **1** adverse fortune. **2** misfortune.

■ see MISFORTUNE.

ad•ver•tise /ádvərtiz/ *v.* **1** *tr.* promote (goods or services) publicly to increase sales. **2** *tr.* make generally known. **3** *intr.* [foll. by *for*] place an advertisement. **4** *tr.* [usu. foll. by *that* + clause] notify. □□ **ad′ver•tis•er** *n.*

■ **1, 2** see PUBLICIZE. **3** see NOTIFY 2.

ad•ver•tise•ment /ádvərtízmənt, ədvə́rtis–, –tiz–/ *n.* public notice or announcement.

■ handbill, circular, junk mail, classified advertisement.

ad•vice /ədvís/ *n.* **1** recommendation about future action or behavior. **2** information given; news.

■ **1** counsel, guidance, suggestion. **2** intelligence, notice, notification; communication.

ad•vis•a•ble /ədvízəbəl/ *adj.* **1** to be recommended. **2** expedient. □□ **ad•vis•a•bil′i•ty** *n.* **ad•vis′a•bly** *adv.*

■ recommendable, prudent, practical, sensible. □□ **advisability** see *prudence* (PRUDENT).

ad•vise /ədvíz/ *v.tr.* **1** [also *absol.*] give advice to. **2** recommend. **3** inform. □□ **ad•vis′er** or **ad•vi′sor** *n.*

■ **1, 2** counsel, guide, steer; caution, ad-

monish, warn; suggest. **3** tell, notify, announce to. □□ **adviser** counselor, mentor, guide.

ad•vis•ee /ədvízée/ • *n.* person, esp. a student, who receives advice from another.

ad•vi•so•ry /ədvízəree/ • *adj.* giving advice. • *n.* (*pl.* **–ries**) information, esp. warning about bad weather, etc.

■ *adj.* consultative, counseling, admonitory. • *n.* bulletin, notice.

ad•vo•cate • *n.* /ádvəkət/ **1** person who supports or speaks in favor. **2** person who pleads for another. **3** professional pleader in a court of justice. • *v.tr.* /ádvəkayt/ **1** recommend by argument (a cause, etc.). **2** plead for; defend. □□ **ad′vo•ca•cy** *n.* **ad•vo•cate′ship** *n.* **ad•voc•a•to•ry** /advókətáwree, ádvəkə–, ádvəkaytəree/ *adj.*

■ *n.* **1** supporter, champion, backer, upholder, proponent. **2, 3** lawyer, counselor; intercessor; attorney. • *v.* support, champion, back, endorse; urge; preach, teach.

adze /adz/ (also **adz**) *n.* axelike tool for cutting away the surface of wood.

ae•gis /éejis/ *n.* protection; impregnable defense.

ae•on var. of EON.

aer•ate /áirayt/ *v.tr.* **1** charge a liquid with carbon dioxide. **2** expose to air. □□ **aer•a•tion** /-ráyshən/ *n.* **aer′a•tor** *n.*

aer•i•al /áireeəl/ • *n.* radio or TV antenna. • *adj.* **1** by, in, or from the air. **2** existing, moving, or happening in the air. **3** thin as air; ethereal. □□ **aer′i•al•ly** *adv.*

aer•i•al•ist /áireeəlist/ *n.* high-wire or trapeze artist.

aer•ie /áiree, áree/ *n.* (also **ey′rie**) **1** lofty nest of a bird of prey. **2** house, etc., perched high up.

aer•o•bat•ics /áirəbátiks/ *n.pl.* feats of expert and usu. spectacular flying of aircraft.

aer•o•bic /airóbik/ *adj.* **1** existing or active only in the presence of oxygen. **2** of or relating to aerobics.

aer•o•bics /airóbiks/ *n.pl.* vigorous exercises designed to increase the body's heart rate and oxygen intake.

aer•o•dy•nam•ics /áirōdīnámiks/ *n.pl.* [usu. treated as *sing.*] study of solid bodies moving through air. □□ **aer•o•dy•nam′ic** *adj.* **aer•o•dy•nam′i•cal•ly** *adv.* **aer•o•dy•nam•i•cist** /-misist/ *n.*

aer•o•nau•tics /áirənáwtiks/ *n.pl.* [usu. treated as *sing.*] science or practice of motion in the air. □□ **aer•o•nau′tic** *adj.* **aer•o•nau′ti•cal** *adj.*

aer•o•sol /áirəsawl, –sol/ *n.* **1** pressurized container for releasing a substance as a fine spray. **2** system of colloidal particles dispersed in a gas (e.g., fog or smoke).

aer•o•space /áirōspays/ *n.* **1** earth's atmosphere and outer space. **2** technology of aviation in this region.

aes•thete /és-theet/ *n.* (also **es′thete**) person who has or professes a special appreciation of beauty.

■ connoisseur, art lover, lover of beauty.

aes•thet•ic /es-thétik/ (also **es•thet′ic**) • *adj.* **1** concerned with beauty or the appreciation of beauty. **2** sensitive to beauty. • *n.* **1** [in *pl.*] philosophy of the beautiful, esp. in art. **2** set of principles of good taste and the appreciation of beauty. □□ **aes•thet'i•cal•ly** *adv.* **aes•thet•i•cism** /–tisizəm/ *n.*

■ *adj.* **1** artistic. **2** refined, discriminating, cultivated, cultured. □□ **aesthetically** artistically; sensitively, tastefully. **aestheticism** beauty; tastefulness, elegance.

a•far /əfáar/ *adv.* at or to a distance.

AFB *abbr.* Air Force Base.

af•fa•ble /áfəbəl/ *adj.* **1** friendly. **2** kind and courteous. □□ **af•fa•bil'i•ty** *n.* **af'fa•bly** *adv.*

■ see FRIENDLY *adj.* 1.

af•fair /əfáir/ *n.* **1** concern, business, or matter to be attended to. **2 a** celebrated or notorious happening. **b** *colloq.* noteworthy thing or event. **3** amorous relationship. **4** [in *pl.*] **a** ordinary pursuits of life. **b** business dealings. **c** public matters (*current affairs*).

■ **1** interest, area. **2 b** occasion, episode, happening. **3** romance, fling, relationship. **4** (*affairs*) **a**, **b** concerns, undertakings, transactions. **c** topics, issues.

af•fect¹ /əfékt/ *v.tr.* **1 a** produce an effect on. **b** (of a disease, etc.) attack (*his liver is affected*). **2** touch the feelings of. □□ **af•fect'ing** *adj.* **af•fect'ing•ly** *adv.*

■ **1 a** influence; sway, change. **b** act upon, damage. **2** stir, impress, strike; perturb, upset.

af•fect² /əfékt/ *v.tr.* **1** pretend. **2** pose as.

■ **1** assume, adopt, put on, feign, sham, fake, counterfeit. **2** see POSE *v.* 2.

af•fect³ /áfekt/ *n. Psychol.* feeling or emotion.

af•fec•ta•tion /áfektáyshən/ *n.* **1** assumed or contrived manner of behavior. **2** pretense.

■ **1** affectedness, pretension, airs, posturing. **2** pose, false display, act.

af•fect•ed /əféktid/ *adj.* **1** in senses of AFFECT¹, AFFECT². **2** artificial; pretended. **3** disposed, inclined. □□ **af•fect'ed•ly** *adv.* **af•fect'ed•ness** *n.*

■ **1** (AFFECT¹) attacked, seized, afflicted; moved, touched. **2** unnatural, specious, studied; hollow, feigned, fake. **3** see *inclined* (INCLINE *v.*).

af•fec•tion /əfékshən/ *n.* **1** goodwill; fond feeling. **2** disease; diseased condition.

■ **1** (high) regard, liking, fondness, warmth, love. **2** see ILLNESS.

af•fec•tion•ate /əfékshənət/ *adj.* loving, tender; showing love or tenderness. □□ **af•fec'tion•ate•ly** *adv.*

■ fond, caring, devoted, doting, warm. □□ **affectionately** see *fondly* (FOND).

af•fi•da•vit /áfidáyvit/ *n.* written statement confirmed under oath, for use as evidence in court.

af•fil•i•ate ■ *n.* /əfíleeayt/ *v.tr.* **1** attach or connect (a person or society) with a larger organization. **2** *tr.* (of an institution) adopt (persons as members, societies as branches, etc.). **3** *intr.* associate oneself with a society. ● *n.* /əfíleeət, -eeayt/ affiliated person or organization. □□ **af•fil'i•a•tion** /–áyshən/ *n.*

■ *v.* **1, 2** associate; combine, unite, join. □□ **affiliation** see ASSOCIATION 2–4.

af•fin•i•ty /əfínitee/ *n.* (*pl.* **–ties**) **1** liking for or attraction to a person or thing. **2** relationship, esp. by marriage. **3** similarity of character suggesting a relationship. See synonym study at LIKENESS.

■ **1** friendliness, fondness, partiality, rapport. **2, 3** kinship, closeness, alliance; similitude, resemblance.

af•firm /əfórm/ *v.* **1** *tr.* assert strongly; state as a fact. **2** *intr.* **a** *Law* make an affirmation. **b** make a formal declaration. □□ **af•fir•ma'tion** *n.* **af•firm'a•to•ry** *adj.* **af•firm'er** *n.*

■ **1** see DECLARE 3. **2 b** see DECLARE 1, 2. □□ **affirmation** see DECLARATION 1, 2a.

af•fir•ma•tive /əfórmətiv/ ● *adj.* **1** affirming; asserting that a thing is so. **2** (of a vote) expressing approval. ● *n.* **1** affirmative statement, reply, or word. **2** [prec. by *the*] positive or affirming position. □ **affirmative action** action favoring minorities, etc., who have been discriminated against. □□ **af•firm'a•tive•ly** *adv.*

■ *adj.* **2** see FAVORABLE 1.

af•fix ● *v.tr.* /əfíks/ **1** attach; fasten. **2** add in writing. **3** impress (a seal or stamp). ● *n.* /áfiks/ **1** addition. **2** *Gram.* prefix or suffix.

af•flict /əflíkt/ *v.tr.* inflict bodily or mental suffering on. □□ **af•flic•tion** /əflíkshən/ *n.* **af•flic'tive** *adj.*

■ affect, bother, distress; weaken, enfeeble, debilitate. □□ **affliction** hardship, misery, misfortune.

af•flu•ent /áflooənt/ *adj.* **1** wealthy; rich. **2** abundant. See synonym study at WEALTHY. □□ **af'flu•ence** *n.* **af'flu•ent•ly** *adv.*

■ **1** see WEALTHY. **2** see *abundant* (ABUNDANCE). □□ **affluence** see WEALTH 1, 2.

af•ford /əfáwrd/ *v.tr.* **1 a** have enough money, means, time, etc., for; be able to spare (*can afford $50*). **b** be in a position to do something **2** yield a supply of. **3** provide. See synonym study at GIVE. □□ **af•ford'a•ble** *adj.* **af•ford•a•bil'i•ty** *n.*

■ **1 a** have sufficient means, be rich enough, manage, *colloq.* have the wherewithal. **2** give, produce; give forth. **3** see PROVIDE 1. □□ **af•fordable** reasonably priced, inexpensive; reasonable.

af•fray /əfráy/ *n.* loud public brawl.

af•front /əfrúnt/ ● *n.* open insult. ● *v.tr.* **1** insult openly. **2** offend the modesty or self respect of.

■ *n.* see INSULT *n.* ● *v.* **1** see INSULT *v.* 1. **2** see INSULT *v.* 2.

Af•ghan /áfgan/ ● *n.* **1 a** a native or inhabitant of Afghanistan. **b** person of Afghan descent. **2** official language of Afghanistan (also called PASHTO). **3** (**afghan**) knitted or crocheted shawl or throw. ● *adj.* of or relating to Afghanistan or its people or language. □ **Af•ghan hound** tall hunting dog with long silky hair.

a•fi•cio•na•do /əfisheeənaádo, əfisee-/ *n.* (*pl.* **–dos**) devotee of a sport or pastime (orig. of bullfighting).

a•field /əfeeld/ *adv.* **1** away from home. **2** to or on a field. **3** astray.

a•flame /əfláym/ *adv. & adj.* in flames.

a•float /əflót/ *adv. & adj.* **1** floating in water or on air. **2** at sea; on board ship.

a•foot /əfŏŏt/ *adv. & adj.* **1** in operation; progressing. **2** astir; on the move.

afore- /əfáwr/ *comb. form* before; previously (*aforesaid*).

a•fore•thought /əfáwrthawt/ *adj.* premeditated.

a•foul /əfówl/ *adv.* foul. □ **run afoul of** come into conflict with.

■ □ **run afoul of** become entangled with, be at odds with.

a•fraid /əfráyd/ *adj.* alarmed; frightened. □ **be afraid** *colloq.* politely regret (*I'm afraid there's none left*).

■ fearful, scared, intimidated, apprehensive; cowardly. □ **be afraid** be sorry *or* apologetic *or* rueful.

a•fresh /əfrésh/ *adv.* anew; with a fresh beginning.

Af•ri•can /áfrikən/ • *n.* **1** native of Africa (esp. a black person). **2** person of African descent. • *adj.* of or relating to Africa. □ **African-American** *n.* American citizen of black African origin or descent. • *adj.* of or relating to American blacks or their culture. **African violet** houseplant with heart-shaped velvety leaves and blue, purple, or pink flowers.

Af•ri•kaans /áfrikáans/ *n.* language derived from Dutch, spoken in S. Africa.

Af•ri•ka•ner /áfrikáánər/ *n.* Afrikaans-speaking white person in S. Africa.

Afro- /áfrō/ *comb. form* African (*Afro-Asian*).

Af•ro-A•mer•i•can /áfrōōmérikən/ *adj. & n.* = *African-American*.

Af•ro-Car•ib•be•an /áfrōkáribéeən, –kárí-beeən/ • *n.* person of African descent in or from the Caribbean. • *adj.* of or relating to the Afro-Caribbeans or their culture.

aft /aft/ *adv. Naut. & Aeron.* at or toward the stern or tail.

af•ter /áftər/ • *prep.* **1 a** following in time; later than (*after six months*). **b** in specifying time (*quarter after eight*). **2** in view of (*after your behavior tonight what do you expect?*). **3** in spite of (*after all my efforts I'm no better off*). **4** behind (*shut the door after you*). **5** in pursuit or quest of. **6** about; concerning. **7** in allusion to (*named after his uncle*). **8** in imitation of. **9** next in importance to. **10** according to (*after a fashion*). • *conj.* later than. • *adv.* **1** later in time (*soon after*). **2** behind. • *adj.* **1** later; following. **2** *Naut.* nearer the stern.

af•ter•birth /áftərbərth/ *n. Med.* placenta and fetal membranes discharged from the womb after childbirth.

af•ter•burn•er /áftərbərnər/ *n.* auxiliary burner in a jet engine to increase thrust.

af•ter•care /áftərkair, –ker/ *n.* care of a patient after a stay in the hospital or of a person on release from prison.

af•ter•ef•fect /áftərəfékt/ *n.* delayed effect following an accident, trauma, etc.

af•ter•life /áftərlif/ *n.* **1** life after death. **2** life at a later time.

af•ter•math /áftərmath/ *n.* consequences; aftereffects.

■ see OUTCOME.

af•ter•noon /áftərnŏŏn/ *n.* time from noon to evening.

af•ter•thought /áftərthawt/ *n.* thing thought of or added later.

af•ter•ward /áftərwórd/ *adv.* (also **af•ter•wards**) later; subsequently.

■ see *subsequently* (SUBSEQUENT).

Ag *symb. Chem.* silver.

a•gain /əgén/ *adv.* **1** another time; once more. **2** as previously (*back again*). **3** in addition. **4** further; besides. **5** on the other hand. □ **again and again** repeatedly.

a•gainst /əgénst/ *prep.* **1** in opposition to (*arson is against the law*). **2** into collision or in contact with. **3** to the disadvantage of. **4** in contrast to. **5** in anticipation of.

■ **1, 4** opposed to, anti, averse to, resistant toward.

a•gape /əgáyp/ *adv. & adj.* gaping, open-mouthed.

a•gar /áygaar/ *n.* (also **a'gar-a'gar**) gelatinous substance from seaweed, used in food, microbiological media, etc.

ag•ate /ágət/ *n.* **1** any of several varieties of hard usu. streaked chalcedony. **2** colored toy marble resembling this.

a•ga•ve /əgáavee, əgáy–/ *n.* plant with rosettes of narrow spiny leaves and tall inflorescences, e.g., the aloe.

age /ayj/ *n.* **1 a** length of time that a person or thing has existed. **b** particular point in or part of one's life (*old age*). **2 a** *colloq.* [often in *pl.*] a long time. **b** distinct historical or geological period. **3** old age. • *v.intr.* (*pres, part.* **ag•ing,** **age•ing**) **1** show signs of advancing age. **2** grow old. **3** mature. See synonym study at MATURE. □ **of age** adult.

■ *n.* **1 a** lifetime, duration; lifespan. **b** period, time, point; see also STAGE *n.* 1. **2 a** eon; years, *colloq.* for ever. **b** era, epoch, period. **3** declining years, senescence; senility, dotage. • *v.* **1, 2** grow old(er), get on (in years); decline. **3** ripen, mellow.

-age /ij/ *suffix* forming nouns denoting: **1** action (*breakage*). **2** condition (*bondage*). **3** aggregate or number of (*acreage*). **4** cost (*postage*). **5** product of an action (*wreckage*). **6** place; abode (*anchorage, orphanage*).

a•ged *adj.* **1** /ayjid/ **a** of the age of (*aged ten*). **b** allowed to reach maturity or ripeness in storage (*aged cheese*). **2** /áyjid/ old. See synonym study at OLD.

■ **1 b** mature(d), ripe(ned), mellow(ed). **2** elderly, ancient, gray, antediluvian.

age•ism /áyjizəm/ *n.* (also **ag'ism**) prejudice or discrimination on the grounds of age. □□ **age'ist** *adj. & n.*

age•less /áyjlis/ *adj.* **1** never growing or appearing old or outmoded. **2** eternal; timeless.

■ **2** see TIMELESS.

a•gen•cy /áyjənsee/ *n.* (*pl.* **–cies**) **1** business or establishment of an agent. **2 a** action. **b** intervention. **3** governmental department.

■ **1 a** see BUSINESS 5. **2 a** activity, working(s), operation. **b** means, medium; intercession; operation.

a•gen•da /əjéndə/ *n.* **1** (*pl.* **agen•das**) list of items of business to be considered at a meet-

a•gent /áyjənt/ *n.* **1 a** a person who acts for another in business, etc. **b** a spy. **2 a** a person or thing that exerts power or produces an effect. **b** cause of a natural force or effect on matter (*oxidizing agent*). □□ **a•gen•tial** /əjénshəl/ *adj.*

  ■ **1 a** representative, intermediary, mediator, go-between. **b** secret *or* undercover *or* double agent, informer. **2 a** see INFLUENCE *n.* **b** factor, agency, means, medium.

ag•glom•er•ate • *v.* /əglómərayt/ **1** collect into a mass. **2** accumulate in a disorderly way. • *n.* /əglómərət/ **1** mass or collection of things. **2** *Geol.* mass of large volcanic fragments bonded under heat (cf. CONGLOMERATE). • *adj.* /əglómərət/ collected into a mass.

ag•glu•ti•nate /əglꝏ́t'nayt/ *v.tr.* unite as with glue. □□ **ag•glu•ti•na•tion** /–náyshən/ *n.* **ag•glu•ti•na•tive** /əglꝏ́t'nətiv, –aytiv/ *adj.*

ag•gran•dize /əgrándiz/ *v.tr.* **1** increase the power, rank, or wealth of (a person or nation). **2** cause to appear greater than is the case. ·□□ **ag•gran•dize•ment** /–dizmənt/ *n.* **ag•gran'diz•er** *n.*

ag•gra•vate /ágrəvayt/ *v.tr.* **1** increase the seriousness of (an illness, offense, etc.). **2** *disp.* annoy; exasperate (a person). □□ **ag•gra•va•tion** /–váyshən/ *n.*

  ■ **1** worsen, intensify, exacerbate, heighten, magnify. **2** frustrate, infuriate, irritate; harass; anger.

ag•gre•gate • *n.* /ágrigət/ **1** total amount assembled. **2** crushed stone, gravel, etc., used in making concrete. **3** *Geol.* mass of minerals formed into solid rock. • *adj.* /ágrigət/ **1** (of disparate elements) collected into one mass. **2** constituted by the collection of many units into one body. • *v.* /ágrigayt/ **1** *tr. & intr.* combine into one mass. **2** *tr. colloq.* amount to. □□ **ag•gre•ga•tion** /–gáyshən/ *n.* **ag•gre•ga'tive** *adj.*

  ■ *n.* **1** see TOTAL¹ *n.* **1, 2.** • *v.* **1** see AMASS.

ag•gres•sion /əgréshən/ *n.* **1** unprovoked attack. **2** self-assertiveness; forcefulness. **3** *Psychol.* hostile or destructive behavior. □□ **ag•gres•sor** /əgrésər/ *n.*

  ■ **1** assault, onslaught, invasion. **2** (self-) assertion, boldness. □□ **aggressor** assailant, attacker, belligerent, provoker.

ag•gres•sive /əgrésiv/ *adj.* **1** of a person: **a** given to aggression; hostile. **b** forceful; self-assertive. **2** (of an act) offensive; hostile. **3** of aggression. See synonym study at BOLD. □□ **ag•gres'sive•ly** *adv.* **ag•gres'sive•ness** *n.*

  ■ **1 a** combative, antagonistic, warlike, belligerent. **b** forward, bold, brash. **2** unfriendly, threatening, provocative. □□ **aggressively** forcefully, assertively, belligerently; pugnaciously, truculently, angrily. **aggressiveness** see AGGRESSION 1.

ag•grieved /əgrévd/ *adj.* having a grievance. □□ **ag•griev'ed•ly** *adv.*

a•ghast /əgást/ *adj.* filled with dismay or consternation.

ag•ile /ájəl, ájil/ *adj.* quick-moving; nimble; active. □□ **ag'ile•ly** *adv.* **a•gil•i•ty** /əjílitee/ *n.*

  ■ quick, brisk, swift, lively; dexterous. □□ **agility** see DEXTERITY 2.

ag•i•tate /ájitayt/ *v.* **1** *tr.* (often as **agitated** *adj.*) disturb or excite (a person or feelings). **2** *intr.* stir up concern, esp. publicly (*agitated for tax reform*). **3** *tr.* shake or move, esp. briskly. □□ **ag'i•tat•ed•ly** *adv.* **ag•i•ta•tion** /–táyshən/ *n.* **ag'i•ta•tive** *adj.* **ag'i•ta•tor** *n.*

  ■ **1** arouse, move, perturb, stir up; (**agitated**) nervous, jittery, fidgety. **2** push, press, campaign; (*agitate for*) promote. **3** stir (up), churn, disturb. □□ **agitator** activist, rabble-rouser, troublemaker, demagogue.

a•glow /əgló/ • *adv.* glowingly. • *adj.* glowing.

ag•nos•tic /agnóstik/ • *n.* person who believes that the existence or nature of God cannot be proven. • *adj.* of agnosticism. □□ **ag•nos'ti•cism** *n.*

a•go /əgó/ *adv.* earlier; before the present.

a•gog /əgóg/ • *adv.* eagerly; expectantly. • *adj.* eager; expectant.

ag•o•nize /ágoniz/ *v.* **1** *intr.* suffer agony. **2** *tr.* (often as **agonizing** *adj.*) cause agony to. □□ **ag'o•niz•ing•ly** *adv.*

  ■ **1** see WORRY *v.* 1. **2** see TORMENT *v.* 1; (**agonizing**) painful, distressful, distressing, harrowing, torturous.

ag•o•ny /ágənee/ *n.* (*pl.* **–nies**) **1** extreme mental or physical suffering. **2** severe struggle.

  ■ **1** anguish, trouble, pain, misery, torment. **2** see STRUGGLE *n.* 1, 3.

ag•o•ra•pho•bi•a /ágərəfóbeeə/ *n. Psychol.* abnormal fear of open spaces or public places. □□ **ag•o•ra•pho'bic** *adj. & n.*

a•grar•i•an /əgráreeən/ *adj.* **1** of the land or its cultivation. **2** relating to the ownership of land.

a•gree /əgrée/ *v.* (**a•grees, a•greed, a•gree•ing**) **1** hold a similar opinion. **2** consent. **3 a** become or be in harmony. **b** be good for; suit. **c** *Gram.* have the same number, gender, case, or person as.

  ■ **1** concur, see eye to eye, be at one; concede, grant. **2** acquiesce, approve, accede, assent. **3 a** concur, conform, correspond, harmonize, *colloq.* jibe.

a•gree•a•ble /əgréeəbəl/ *adj.* **1** pleasing. **2** willing to agree. □□ **a•gree•a•bil•i•ty** /–bilitee/ *n.* **a•gree'a•ble•ness** *n.* **a•gree'a•bly** *adv.*

  ■ **1** pleasant, enjoyable, pleasurable, favorable, delightful. **2** in favor, consenting, acquiescent, compliant. □□ **agreeably** see *willingly* (WILLING), *favorably* (FAVORABLE).

a•gree•ment /əgréemənt/ *n.* **1** act of agreeing. **2** mutual understanding. **3** arrangement or contract.

  ■ **1, 2** concord, concurrence, consensus, harmony. **3** understanding, covenant, treaty, pact, accord.

ag•ri•busi•ness /ágribiznis/ *n.* large-scale farming and related commerce, as food processing, etc.

ag•ri•cul•ture /ágrikulchər/ *n.* cultivating the

soil and rearing animals. □□ **ag•ri•cul•tur•al** /-kúlchərəl/ adj. **ag•ri•cul'tur•al•ist** n. **ag•ri•cul'tur•al•ly** adv. **ag•ri•cul'tur•ist** n.

a•gron•o•my /əgrónəmee/ n. science of soil management and crop production. □□ **ag•ro•nom•ic** /ágrənómik/ adj. **a•gron•o•mist** /-grón-/ n.

a•ground /əgrównd/ adj. & adv. (of a ship) on or on to the bottom of shallow water (run aground).

a•gue /áygyōō/ n. **1** hist. malarial fever. **2** shivering fit. □□ **a'gued** adj. **a'gu•ish** adj.

ah /aa/ int. expressing surprise, pleasure, realization, etc.

a•ha /aaháa, əháa/ int. expressing surprise, triumph, mockery, irony, etc.

a•head /əhéd/ adv. **1** further forward in space or time. **2** in the lead.
■ **1** at the front, in front, in advance, in the lead. **2** winning, in front.

a•hem /əhém/ int. used to attract attention, gain time, or express disapproval.

-aholic /əhólik/ suffix (also **-oholic**) denoting one addicted to or compulsively in need of what is specified in the initial element (workaholic, chocoholic).

a•hoy /əhóy/ int. Naut. call used in hailing.

AI abbr. **1** artificial intelligence. **2** artificial insemination.

aid /ayd/ • n. **1** help. **2** financial or material help. **3** person or thing that helps. • v.tr. **1** help. **2** promote or encourage.
■ n. **1** support, assistance, backing, relief, service. **2** funding, subsidy, grant. **3** see AIDE, AUXILIARY n. • v. **1** support, assist, facilitate; succor, relieve, subsidize. **2** see PROMOTE 2.

aide /ayd/ n. **1** aide-de-camp. **2** assistant.
■ aid, helper; right hand; colleague, partner.

aide-de-camp /áyd-dəkámp/ n. (pl. **aides-de-camp** pronunc. same) officer acting as a confidential assistant to a senior officer.

AIDS /aydz/ n. acquired immune deficiency syndrome, a viral disorder marked by severe loss of resistance to infection. □ **AIDS-related complex** symptoms of a person affected with the AIDS virus who has not developed the disease.

ail /ayl/ v. **1** tr. trouble or afflict (what ails him?). **2** intr. (usu. **be ailing**) be ill.
■ **1** affect, bother, distress, upset, worry. **2** suffer, be sick, decline.

ai•le•ron /áyləron/ n. hinged surface in the trailing edge of an airplane wing, used to control lateral balance, etc.

ail•ment /áylmənt/ n. minor or chronic illness.
■ sickness, affliction, disorder, indisposition.

aim /aym/ • v. **1** intr. [foll. by at, to] intend or try. **2** tr. direct or point (a weapon, remark, etc.). **3** intr. take aim. **4** intr. [foll. by at, for] seek to attain or achieve. See synonym study at INTEND. • n. **1** purpose or object. **2** directing of a weapon, etc., at an object. □ **take aim** direct a weapon, etc., at an object.
■ v. **1, 4** (aim at, aim for) focus on, strive for, plan on; (aim to) seek to, intend to, plan

to. **2** focus, train, level. • n. **1** goal, design, ambition, objective. □ **take aim** aim; (take aim at) draw a bead on, zero in on.

aim•less /áymlis/ adj. without aim or purpose. □□ **aim'less•ly** adv. **aim'less•ness** n.
■ purposeless, pointless, undirected, erratic, haphazard. □□ **aimlessly** pointlessly, unsystematically, randomly.

ain't /aynt/ contr. colloq. **1** am not; are not; is not. **2** has not; have not. ¶Often regarded as an uneducated use but used informally and jocularly

air /air/ • n. **1** gaseous mixture, mainly of oxygen and nitrogen, surrounding the earth. **2** earth's atmosphere. **3 a** distinctive impression. **b** one's manner or bearing, esp. a confident one. **c** [esp. in pl.] pretentiousness. **4** Mus. tune. • v.tr. **1** expose (a room, etc.) to the open air; ventilate. **2** express publicly. **3** broadcast. □ **air bag** safety device that fills with nitrogen on impact to protect the occupants of a vehicle in a collision. **air base** base for the operation of military aircraft. **air-conditioned** (of a room, building, etc.) equipped with air-conditioning. **air conditioner** air-conditioning apparatus. **air-conditioning** system for regulating the humidity, ventilation, and temperature in a building. **air force** branch of the armed forces concerned with fighting or defense in the air. **air raid** attack by aircraft. **in the air** prevalent. **up in the air** uncertain. □□ **air'less** adj. **air'less•ness** n.
■ n. **3 a** atmosphere, ambience, climate, feeling. **b** style, appearance, attitude. **c** (airs) pretension(s), show, affectedness; haughtiness, arrogance. **4** melody, song, music. • v. **1** freshen. **2** publish, broadcast, circulate, publicize. □ **by air** colloq. by plane; by airmail. **up in the air** see UNCERTAIN 1.

air•borne /áirbawrn/ adj. **1** transported by air. **2** (of aircraft) in the air after taking off.

air•craft /áirkraft/ n. (pl. same) machine capable of flight, esp. an airplane or helicopter. □ **aircraft carrier** warship that carries and serves as a base for airplanes.

Aire•dale /áirdayl/ n. **1** large terrier of a rough-coated breed. **2** this breed.

air•fare /áirfair/ • n. the price of a passenger ticket for travel by aircraft.

air•field /áirfeeld/ n. area with runways for aircraft.

Air Force One • n. the official aircraft of the president of the United States.

air•head /áirhed/ n. sl. silly or stupid person.

air•lift /áirlift/ • n. emergency transport of supplies by air. • v.tr. transport in this way.

air•line /áirlīn/ n. organization providing a regular public service of air transport on one or more routes.

air•lin•er /áirlīnər/ n. passenger aircraft, esp. a large one.

air•lock /áirlok/ n. **1** stoppage of the flow in a pump or pipe, caused by an air bubble. **2** airtight compartment between areas of different pressures.

air•mail /áirmayl/ • n. **1** system of transporting mail by air. **2** mail carried by air. • v.tr. send by airmail.

air•man /áirmən/ n. (pl. **–men**) **1** pilot or

member of the crew of an aircraft. **2** member of the USAF below commissioned rank.

air•plane /áirplayn/ n. powered heavier-than-air flying vehicle with fixed wings.

air•port /áirpawrt/ n. complex of runways and buildings for the takeoff, landing, and maintenance of civil aircraft, with facilities for passengers.

air•ship /áirship/ n. power-driven aircraft lighter than air.

air•sick /áirsik/ adj. nauseated from air travel. □□ **air′sick•ness** n.

air•space /áirspays/ n. air above a country and subject to its jurisdiction.

air•speed /áirspeed/ n. speed of an aircraft relative to the air.

air•strip /áirstrip/ n. strip of ground suitable for the takeoff and landing of aircraft but usu. without other facilities.

air•tight /áirtīt/ adj. **1** not allowing air to pass through. **2** having no visible or apparent weaknesses (an airtight alibi).

air•time /áirtīm/ n. **1a** time allotted for a broadcast. **b** time at which a broadcast is scheduled. **2** time allotted or spent on a wireless telephone call.

air•waves /áirwayvz/ n.pl. colloq. radio waves used in broadcasting.

air•way /áirway/ n. **1 a** recognized route followed by aircraft. **b** [often in pl.] = AIRLINE. **2** Med. [often in pl.] breathing passage(s).

air•wom•an /áirwoomən/ n. (pl. **-wom•en**) **1** woman pilot or member of the crew of an aircraft. **2** woman member of the USAF below commissioned rank.

air•wor•thy /áirwərthee/ adj. (of an aircraft) fit to fly.

air•y /áiree/ adj. (**air•i•er, air•i•est**) **1** well ventilated; breezy. **2** flippant; superficial. **3 a** light as air. **b** graceful; delicate. **4** insubstantial; ethereal. □□ **air′i•ly** adv. **air′i•ness** n.

■ **1** see BREEZY 1. **3 b** see DELICATE 1a. **4** see IMMATERIAL 2.

aisle /īl/ n. **1** passage between rows of pews, seats, etc. **2** passageway in a supermarket, department store, etc. □□ **aisled** adj.

aitch /aych/ n. name of the letter H.

a•jar /əjáar/ adv. & adj. (of a door) slightly open.

AK abbr. Alaska (in official postal use).

a.k.a. abbr. also known as.

AK-47 ● n. a Soviet-designed assault rifle.

a•kim•bo /əkímbō/ adj. & adv. (of the arms) with hands on the hips and elbows turned outwards.

a•kin /əkín/ adj. **1** related by blood. **2** [often foll. by to] of similar or kindred character.

■ **1** see KIN adj. **2** kindred; see also ALIKE adj.; (akin to) related to, germane to, like.

AL abbr. Alabama (in official postal use).

Al symb. Chem. aluminum.

-al /əl/ suffix **1** forming adjectives meaning 'relating to; of the kind of': **a** from Latin or Greek words (central, tropical) (cf. –IAL, – ICAL). **b** from English nouns (tidal). **2** forming nouns, esp. of verbal action (arrival, trial).

Ala. abbr. Alabama.

à la /aa laa/ prep. after the manner of (à ʳ russe).

al•a•bas•ter /áləbastər/ ● n. translucent usu. white form of gypsum, often carved. ● adj. **1** of alabaster. **2** white or smooth. □□ **al•a•bas•trine** /–bástrin/ adj.

à la carte /aa laa kaart/ adv. & adj. ordered as separately priced item(s) from a menu, not as part of a set meal.

a•lac•ri•ty /əlákritee/ n. briskness or cheerful readiness.

à la mode /aa laa mṓd/ adv. & adj. **1** in fashion; fashionable. **2** served with ice cream, esp. pie or cake.

a•larm /əláarm/ ● n. **1** warning of danger, etc. **2 a** warning sound or device. **b** = alarm clock. **3** apprehension. ● v.tr. **1** frighten or disturb. **2** warn. □ **alarm clock** clock that rings at a set time. □□ **a•larm′ing** adj. **a•larm′ing•ly** adv.

■ n. **1** alert, danger signal, distress signal. **2 a** tocsin, bell, gong, siren. **3** fear, fright, dismay, trepidation, terror. ● v. **1** scare, startle, terrify; unnerve, dismay. **2** alert, rouse. □□ **alarming** see frightening (FRIGHTEN).

a•larm•ist /əláarmist/ ● n. person spreading needless alarm. ● adj. creating needless alarm. □□ **a•larm′ism** n.

Alas. abbr. Alaska.

a•las /əlás/ int. expression of grief, pity, or concern.

alb /alb/ n. long white vestment worn by Christian priests.

al•ba•core /álbəkawr/ n. **1** long-finned tuna. **2** any of various other related fish.

Al•ba•ni•an /albáyneeən, awl–/ ● n. **1 a** native or inhabitant of Albania in SE Europe. **b** person of Albanian descent. **2** language of Albania. ● adj. of or relating to Albania or its people or language.

al•ba•tross /álbətraws, –tros/ n. **1** long-winged, web-footed, stout-bodied sea bird. **2** encumbrance.

al•be•it /awlbéeit/ conj. formal though.

al•bi•no /albī́nō/ n. (pl. **-nos**) **1** person or animal lacking pigment in the skin and hair (which are white), and the eyes (usu. pink). **2** plant lacking normal coloring. □□ **al•bi•nism** /álbinizəm/ n. **al•bi•not•ic** /álbinṓtik/ adj.

al•bum /álbəm/ n. **1** blank book for photographs, stamps, etc. **2 a** long-playing phonograph, audio cassette, or compact disc recording. **b** set of these.

al•bu•men /álbyoomən/ n. **1** egg white. **2** Bot. substance found between the skin and embryo of many seeds, usu. the edible part.

al•bu•min /albyoomin/ n. water-soluble proteins found in egg white, milk, blood, etc. □□ **al•bu′min•ous** adj.

al•che•my /álkəmee/ n. (pl. **-mies**) medieval chemistry, esp. seeking to turn base metals into gold. □□ **al•chem•ic** /alkémik/ adj. **al•chem′i•cal** adj. **al′che•mist** n. **al′che•mize** v.tr.

al•co•hol /álkəhawl, –hol/ n. **1** colorless volatile flammable liquid forming the intoxicating element in wine, beer, liquor, etc., and

also used as a solvent, as fuel, etc. **2** any liquor containing this. **3** *Chem.* any of a large class of organic compounds that contain one or more hydroxyl groups attached to carbon atoms.
■ **2** spirits, liquor, (strong) drink, *colloq.* booze.

al•co•hol•ic /álkəháwlik, –hól–/ • *adj.* of, relating to, containing, or caused by alcohol.
• *n.* person suffering from alcoholism.
■ *adj.* intoxicating, intoxicant, inebriating.
• *n.* drunk, dipsomaniac, sot, boozer.

al•co•hol•ism /álkəhawlízəm, –ho–/ *n.* addiction to the consumption of alcoholic liquor; condition resulting from this.

al•cove /álkōv/ *n.* recess, esp. in the wall of a room.

al den•te /aal déntay, al déntee/ *adj.* (of pasta, etc.) cooked so as to be still firm when bitten.

al•der /áwldər/ *n.* tree related to the birch.

al•der•man /áwldərmən/ *n.* (*pl.* **-men**; *fem.* **al•der•wom•an**, *pl.* **-wom•en**) elected municipal official serving on the governing council of a city. □□ **al•der•man•ic** /–mánik/ *adj.* **al•der•man•ship** *n.*

ale /ayl/ *n.* beverage like beer, but stronger.

a•le•a•to•ry /áyleeətawree/ *adj.* depending on chance.

a•lert /əlórt/ • *adj.* **1** watchful or vigilant. **2** quick (esp. of mental faculties); attentive. See synonym study at VIGILANT. • *n.* **1** alarm. • *v.tr.* warn. □ **on the alert** vigilant. • *v.tr.* state or period of special vigilance. • *v.tr.* warn. □ **on the alert** vigilant. □□ **a•lert'ly** *adv.* **a•lert'ness** *n.*
■ *adj.* **1** awake, attentive, wary, cautious. **2** active, nimble, lively, agile, spry, sprightly.
• *n.* **1** warning, signal, call, siren. • *v.* caution, alarm; (*alert to*) advise of. □ **on the alert** on the qui vive, on guard, watchful. □□ **alertness** see VIGILANCE, INTELLIGENCE 1b.

Al•eut /əlóōt/ *n.* **1 a** N. American people native to the Aleutian Islands and western Alaska. **b** member of this people. **2** language of this people. □□ **A•leu'tian** /–shən/ *adj.*

al•fal•fa /alfálfə/ *n.* cloverlike plant used for fodder.

al•fres•co /alfréskō/ *adv. & adj.* in the open air.

al•ga /álgə/ *n.* (*pl.* **al•gae** /áljee/ also **al•gas**) [usu. in *pl.*] nonflowering stemless water plant, esp. seaweed and phytoplankton. □□ **al'gal** *adj.* **al'goid** *adj.*

al•ge•bra /áljibrə/ *n.* branch of mathematics that uses letters, etc., to represent numbers and quantities. □□ **al•ge•bra'ic** /áljibráyik/ *adj.* **al•ge•bra'i•cal** *adj.* **al•ge•bra'i•cal•ly** *adv.*

Al•gon•qui•an /algóngkweeən/ *n.* any of the languages or dialects used by the Algonquin peoples, native to eastern N. America.

al•go•rithm /álgərithəm/ *n. Math.* process or set of rules used for calculation or problem-solving, esp. with a computer. □□ **al•go• rith'mic** /álgərithmik/ *adj.*

a•li•as /áyleeəs/ *adv.* also named or known as. • *n.* false or assumed name.
■ *n.* see PSEUDONYM.

a•li•bi /álibī/ (*pl.* **al•i•bis**) • *n.* **1** claim or proof that when an alleged act took place one was elsewhere. **2** excuse. • *v.* (**al•i•bis, al•i•bied, al•i•bi•ing**) *colloq.* **1** *tr.* provide an alibi or offer an excuse for (a person). **2** *intr.* provide an alibi.
■ *n.* explanation; justification; reason. • *v.* explain, justify; give an explanation or excuse.

al•ien /áyleeən/ • *adj.* **1 a** unfamiliar; unacceptable or repugnant. **b** different or separated. **2** foreign. **3** of or relating to beings supposedly from other worlds. • *n.* **1** foreigner, esp. one who is not a citizen of the country where he or she is living. **2** being supposedly from another world. □□ **al'ien• ness** *n.*
■ *adj.* **1 a** foreign, strange, odd; exotic, remote, outlandish; see also HOSTILE 2. **b** unalike, dissimilar, differing. **2** see FOREIGN 1. **3** extraterrestrial, unearthly. • *n.* **1** stranger, outsider, immigrant, newcomer. **2** extraterrestrial, E.T.; martian.

al•ien•ate /áyleeənayt/ *v.tr.* **1 a** cause (a person) to become unfriendly or hostile. **b** [often foll. by *from*] cause (a person) to feel isolated or estranged from (friends, society, etc.). **2** transfer ownership of. □□ **al•ien•a' tion** /–ayshən/ *n.* **al'ien•a•tor** *n.*
■ **1** estrange, detach, distance, put at a distance; antagonize; (*alienate from*) turn away from.

a•light¹ /əlít/ *v.intr.* **1 a** descend from a vehicle. **b** dismount from a horse. **2** settle; come to earth from the air.

a•light² /əlít/ *adj.* **1** on fire. **2** lit up; excited.

a•lign /əlín/ *v.tr.* (also **a•line'**) **1** put or bring into line. **2** bring (oneself, etc.) into agreement or alliance with (a cause, party, etc.). □□ **a•lign'ment** *n.*

a•like /əlík/ • *adj.* similar; like. • *adv.* in a similar way.
■ *adj.* akin, resembling one another; allied, related; indistinguishable. • *adv.* in like manner, similarly, equally.

al•i•men•ta•ry /áliméntəree/ *adj.* of or providing nourishment or sustenance. □ **alimentary canal** *Anat.* passage along which food is passed during digestion. □□ **al•i• men•ta'tion** *n.*

al•i•mo•ny /álimōnee/ *n.* money payable to a spouse after divorce or legal separation.
■ maintenance.

a•live /əlív/ *adj.* **1** living; not dead. **2 a** (of a thing) existing; continuing (*kept his interest alive*). **b** under discussion (*topic is very much alive*). **3** lively; active. **4** [foll. by *to*] aware of; alert. **5** [foll. by *with*] swarming or teeming with. □□ **a•live'ness** *n.*
■ **1** live, breathing. **2** in operation or action; in existence; on the agenda. **3** alert, vivacious, vibrant, quick, spirited. **4** (*alive to*) sensitive or responsive to, conscious of. **5** astir, thronging, crowded, packed.

al•ka•li /álkəlī/ *n.* (*pl.* **al•ka•lis**) **1** any of a class of substances that liberate hydroxide ions in water, usu. form caustic or corrosive solutions, and have a pH of more than 7. **2** *Chem.* any substance that reacts with or neutralizes acids. □□ **al'ka•line** /–līn/ *adj.* **al• ka•lin'i•ty** /–línitee/ *n.*

al•ka•loid /álkəloyd/ *n.* nitrogenous organic

compounds of plant origin, e.g., morphine, quinine.

al•kyd /álkid/ *n.* synthetic resin derived from various alcohols and acids.

all /awl/ • *adj.* **1 a** whole amount, quantity, or extent of. **b** [with *pl.*] entire number of (*all the others left*). **2** any whatever (*beyond all doubt*). **3** greatest possible (*with all speed*). • *n.* **1 a** all concerned (*all were present*). **b** everything. **2** [foll. by *of*] **a** the whole of. **b** every one of. **3** (in games) each (*score was two all*). • *adv.* **1 a** entirely; quite (*dressed all in black*). **b** as an intensifier (*a book all about ships*). **2** to that extent (*if they go, all the better*). □ **all-America(n) 1** representing the whole of (or only) America or the US. **2** truly American (*all-American boy*). **3** *Sports* recognized as one of the best in a particular sport. **all-around** (of a person) versatile. **all but** very nearly (*it was all but impossible*). **all in all** everything considered. **all right** [*predic.*] **1** satisfactory; in good condition. **2** satisfactorily; as desired. **at all** in any way; to any extent.

■ *n.* **1 a** see EVERYONE[1], EVERYTHING 1. **b** see EVERYTHING 1. **2 a** see WHOLE *n.* 2. □ **all in all** see *on the whole* (WHOLE). **all right 2** see OK *adv.* **at all** see SCARCELY 1.

Al•lah /álə, áálaa/ *n.* name of God in Islam.

al•lay /əláy/ *v.tr.* **1** diminish (fear, suspicion, etc.). **2** relieve or alleviate (pain, hunger, etc.). See synonym study at ALLEVIATE.

■ **2** see RELIEVE 2.

al•le•ga•tion /áligáyshən/ *n.* **1** assertion, esp. unproved. **2** alleging.

■ avowal, claim, declaration; charge, accusation.

al•lege /əléj/ *v.tr.* **1** declare, esp. without proof. **2** advance as an argument or excuse. □□ **al•leged** *adj.* **al•leg•ed•ly** *adv.*

■ claim, profess, state; maintain, contend. □□ **alleged** claimed, avowed, stated; purported, so-called.

al•le•giance /əléejəns/ *n.* **1** loyalty (to a person or cause, etc.). **2** the duty of a subject to his or her government.

■ see *loyalty* (LOYAL).

al•le•go•ry /áligawree/ *n.* (*pl.* **–ries**) story, etc., whose characters are represented symbolically. □□ **al'le•go•rist** *n.*

al•le•gret•to /áligrétō/ *Mus.* • *adv. & adj.* in a fairly brisk tempo. • *n.* (*pl.* **–tos**) such a passage or movement.

al•le•gro /əléggrō, əláy–/ *Mus.* • *adv. & adj.* in a brisk tempo. • *n.* (*pl.* **–gros**) such a passage or movement.

al•le•lu•ia /álilṓyə/ (also **al•le•lu'ya, hal•le•lu•jah** /hál–/) • *int.* God be praised. • *n.* praise to God.

Al•len wrench /álən/ *n.* hexagonal wrench designed to fit into and turn a screw with a hexagonal head.

al•ler•gen /álərjən/ *n.* any substance that causes an allergic reaction. □□ **al•ler•gen'ic** /–jénik/ *adj.*

al•ler•gic /əlórjik/ *adj.* **1** [foll. by *to*] **a** having an allergy to. **b** *colloq.* having a strong dislike for. **2** caused by an allergy.

al•ler•gy /álərjee/ *n.* (*pl.* **–gies**) **1** *Med.* adverse reaction to certain substances, as par-

---

ticular foods, pollen, fur, or dust. **2** ᴄ dislike. □□ **al'ler•gist** *n.*

al•le•vi•ate /əléeveeayt/ *v.tr.* lessen or ma less severe (pain, suffering, etc.). □□ **al•le vi•a•tion** /–áyshən/ *n.* **al•le'vi•a•tive** *adj.* **al le'vi•a•tor** *n.* **al•le•vi•a•to•ry** /–veeətáwree/ *adj.*

■ see EASE *v.* 1a, 2a.

al•ley /álee/ *n.* (*pl.* **–leys**) **1** (also **al•ley•way**) narrow streetlike passageway, esp. between or behind buildings. **2** place for bowling, etc.

al•li•ance /əlíəns/ *n.* **1** union or agreement to cooperate, esp. of nations by treaty or families by marriage. **2** the parties involved.

■ **1** confederation, federation, league; axis, pact.

al•lied /əlíd, álíd/ *adj.* **1 a** associated in an alliance. **b** (**Allied**) of or relating to the US and its allies in World War I and World War II. **2** connected or related.

al•li•ga•tor /áligaytər/ *n.* large reptile of the crocodile family native to the Americas and China, with a head broader and shorter than that of the crocodile. □ **alligator pear** avocado.

al•lit•er•a•tion /əlítəráyshən/ *n.* occurrence of the same letter or sound at the beginning of adjacent or closely connected words (e.g., *calm, cool, and collected*). □□ **al•lit•er•ate** /əlítərayt/ *v.* **al•lit'er•a•tive** /əlítəraytiv, –rətiv/ *adj.*

all-night•er /awl–nítər/ • *n.* a night during which one remains awake, usu. in order to study or work.

al•lo•cate /áləkayt/ *v.tr.* assign, apportion, or devote to (a purpose, person, or place). □□ **al•lo•ca•ble** /–kəbəl/ *adj.* **al•lo•ca•tion** /–káyshən/ *n.* **al'lo•ca•tor** *n.*

■ see ALLOT, ALLOW 2, ASSIGN 1a.

al•lot /əlót/ *v.tr.* (**al•lot•ted, al•lot•ting**)

...portion or distribute to (a person) as a share or task. □□ **al•lot′ment** n.

■ allocate, allow, assign; (allot to) divide among(st), share (out) among(st), distribute to.

al•low /əlów/ v. **1** tr. permit (a thing to happen, etc.). **2** tr. permit (a person) to have (a limited quantity or sum) (we were allowed $500 a year). **3** tr. provide or set aside for a purpose. **4** tr. **a** admit; concede. **b** assert. **5** refl. indulge oneself in (conduct). **6** intr. take into consideration or account. □□ **al•low′a•ble** adj. **al•low′a•bly** adv.

■ **1** agree to, give permission for, authorize; tolerate, put up with; (allow to) let. **2** give, let have, grant, allot, allocate. **3** make allowance(s) for, put aside, take into account or consideration; add (in), include; deduct, take away, exclude. **4 a** agree, acknowledge, confess. **5** permit oneself, grant oneself; (allow oneself to) let oneself. **6** see CONSIDER 4. □□ **allowable** see PERMISSIBLE. **allowably** see acceptably (ACCEPTABLE).

al•low•ance /əlówəns/ • n. **1** amount or sum allowed. **2** deduction or discount. **3** tolerance of. • v.tr. make an allowance to (a person). □ **make allowances 1** take into consideration (mitigating circumstances). **2** look with tolerance upon.

■ n. **1** stipend, grant, dole, pin or pocket money; remuneration; pension, annuity, per diem. **2** reduction, rebate, payment, recompense. **3** toleration, sufferance, concession. □ **make allowances**(make allowances for) **1** take into account, consider, bear in mind. **2** be patient with, excuse.

al•loy /áloy, əlóy/ • n. **1** mixture of two or more metals. **2** inferior metal mixed esp. with gold or silver. • v.tr. **1** mix (metals). **2** debase (a pure substance) by admixture. **3** moderate.

■ n. **1** mix, combination, compound, composite, blend, amalgam. **2** admixture. • v. **1** see MIX v. 1, 3a. **2** contaminate, pollute, adulterate. **3** change, modify, temper.

all•spice /áwlspis/ n. **1** aromatic spice obtained from the ground berry of the pimento tree. **2** berry of this.

all-ter•rain ve•hi•cle /awl-teráyn/ • n. a small open motor vehicle with one seat and three or more wheels fitted with large tires, designed for use on rough ground ¶Abbr.: **ATV.**

al•lude /əlō̄d/ v.intr. **1** refer, esp. indirectly, covertly, or briefly to. **2** mention.

■ **1** see REFER 4.

al•lure /əlōōr/ • v.tr. attract, charm, or fascinate. • n. attractiveness; personal charm; fascination. □□ **al•lure′ment** n. **al•lur′ing** adj. **al•lur′ing•ly** adv.

■ v. see ATTRACT 2, CAPTIVATE. • n. see CHARM n. 1a, b.

al•lu•sion /əlō̄ozhən/ n. reference, esp. a covert, passing, or indirect one. □□ **al•lu•sive** /əlō̄osiv/ adj.

■ see REFERENCE n. 2a.

al•lu•vi•um /əlō̄oveeəm/ n. (pl. **al•lu•vi•ums** or **al•lu•vi•a** /-ə/) deposit of usu. fine fertile

soil left behind by a flood. □□ **al•lu′vi•al** adj.

al•ly /álī/ • n. (pl. **–lies**) **1** government formally cooperating or united with another, esp. by a treaty. **2** person or organization that cooperates with or helps another. • v.tr. (also /əlī/) (**–lies, –lied**) combine or unite in alliance.

-ally /əlee/ suffix forming adverbs from adjectives in -al (cf. -AL², -LY, -ICALLY).

al•ma ma•ter /áalmə maátər, álmə máytər/ n. (also **Al•ma Ma•ter**) **1** university, school, or college one attends or attended. **2** official school anthem or song.

al•ma•nac /áwlmənak, ál-/ n. calendar, usu. with astronomical data and other reference information.

al•might•y /áwlmítee/ • adj. **1** having complete power; omnipotent. **2** (**the Al•might•y**) God. **3** sl. very great (an almighty crash). • adv. sl. extremely; very much.

al•mond /áamənd, ám-/ n. **1** nutlike seed (kernel) of a fruit related to the peach and plum. **2** tree itself.

al•most /áwlmohst/ adv. all but; very nearly.

■ nearly, (just) about, practically, virtually, on the brink of.

alms /aamz/ n.pl. hist. charitable donation of money or food to the poor.

alms•house /áamz-hows/ n. esp. Brit. hist. a house founded by charity for the poor.

al•oe /áló/ n. plant of the lily family, usu. having toothed fleshy leaves.

a•loft /əláwft, əlóft/ predic.adj. & adv. **1** high up; overhead. **2** upwards.

a•lo•ha /əlóhaa, aa-/ int. Hawaiian salutation at meeting or parting.

a•lone /əlón/ predic. adj. & adv. **1** without others. **2** lonely. **3** only; exclusively. □□ **a•lone′ness** n.

■ **1** unaccompanied, unescorted, solitar(il)y, by oneself or itself, isolated; unassisted, unaided, single-handed. **2** wretched, friendless, abandoned, forsaken.

a•long /əláwng, əlóng/ • prep. **1** from one end to the other end of. **2** on, beside, or through any part of the length of. • adv. **1** onward. **2** arriving. **3** with oneself or others.

a•long•side /əláwngsíd, əlóng-/ • adv. at or to the side. • prep. close to the side of.

a•loof /əlóof/ • adj. distant; unsympathetic. • adv. away; apart. □□ **a•loof′ness** n.

■ adj. remote, cold, undemonstrative; unsympathetic. □□ **aloofness** see DISTANCE n. 4.

a•loud /əlówd/ adv. audibly; not silently or in a whisper.

alp /alp/ n. **1** high mountain. **2** (**the Alps**) high range of mountains in Switzerland and adjoining countries.

al•pac•a /alpákə/ n. **1** S. American mammal related to the llama, with long shaggy hair. **2** wool from the animal. **3** fabric made from the wool.

al•pha /álfə/ n. **1** first letter of the Greek alphabet (A, α). **2** beginning. □ **alpha and omega** beginning and end. **alpha particle** helium nucleus emitted by a radioactive substance.

al•pha•bet /álfəbet/ n. set of letters used in writing a language. □□ **al•pha•bet'i•cal** adj. **al•pha•bet'i•cal•ly** adv.

al•pha•bet•ize /álfəbətíz/ v.tr. arrange (words, names, etc.) in alphabetical order. □□ **al•pha•bet•i•za•tion** /-izáyshən/ n.

al•pha•nu•mer•ic /álfənōōmérik, –nyōō–/ adj. (also **al•pha•nu•mer'i•cal**) containing both alphabetical and numerical symbols.

al•pine /álpɪn/ adj. 1 of, relating to, or found in high mountains. 2 (**Alpine**) of or relating to the Alps.

al•read•y /áwlrédee/ adv. 1 before the time in question. 2 as early or as soon as this.

al•right /áwlrít/ adj., adv., & int. disp. = all right.

ALS abbr. AMYOTROPHIC LATERAL SCLEROSIS.

al•so /áwlsō/ adv. in addition; likewise; besides. □ **also-ran** 1 one who does not win a competition. 2 undistinguished person.

alt. abbr. 1 alternate. 2 altimeter. 3 altitude.

al•tar /áwltər/ n. 1 table or flat block for sacrifice or offering to a deity. 2 raised surface or table used in a Christian service.

al•tar•piece /áwltərpees/ n. piece of art, esp. a painting, set above or behind an altar.

al•ter /áwltər/ v. 1 tr. & intr. make or become different; change. 2 tr. castrate or spay. □□ **al'ter•a•ble** adj. **al•ter•a'tion** n.

■ 1 revise, modify, transform; adjust. 2 neuter, desex, doctor, fix, geld. □□ **alterable** see CHANGEABLE 2. **alteration** change, modification, shift; adjustment, adaptation, conversion.

al•ter•cate /áwltərkayt/ v.intr. dispute hotly; wrangle. □□ **al•ter•ca'tion** /-káyshən/ n. See synonym study at QUARREL.

al•ter e•go /áwltər éegō, égō/ n. 1 intimate and trusted friend. 2 person's secondary or alternative personality.

al•ter•nate • v.intr. /áwltərnayt, ál–/ 1 (of two things) succeed each other in turn. 2 change repeatedly (between two conditions). • adj. /áwltərnət, ál–/ 1 every other. 2 (of things of two kinds) each following and succeeded by one of the other kind. • n. /áwltərnət, ál–/ alternative; deputy or substitute. □ **alternating current** electric current that reverses its direction at regular intervals. □□ **al'ter•nate•ly** adv. **al•ter•na•tion** /-náyshən, ál–/ n.

■ v. 2 see OSCILLATE. • adj. 1 every second. 2 successive, alternating, rotating, in rotation. • n. delegate, proxy, representative. □□ **alternately** by turns, reciprocally, in rotation.

al•ter•na•tive /awltórnətiv, ál–/ • adj. 1 available or usable instead of another. 2 (of two things) mutually exclusive. 3 unconventional. • n. 1 any of two or more possibilities. 2 choice. □□ **al'ter•na•tive•ly** adv.

• adj. 1 second, additional, substitute. 3 see DIFFERENT 3. • n. 1 see ALTERNATE 1. 2 see CHOICE 2, OPTION 1, 2.

al•ter•na•tor /áwltərnaytər, ál–/ n. generator that produces an alternating current.

al•though /awlthó/ conj. = THOUGH conj. 1–3.

al•tim•e•ter /áltímitər, áltimeetər/ n. instrument for showing height above sea or ground level.

al•ti•tude /áltitōōd, –tyōōd/ n. height of a object in relation to a given point, esp. sea level or the horizon.

■ elevation, level.

al•to /áltō/ n. (pl. **-tos**) 1 = CONTRALTO. 2 = COUNTERTENOR. 3 instrument pitched next below a soprano of its type.

al•to•geth•er /áwltəgéthər/ adv. 1 totally; completely. 2 on the whole. 3 in total. □ **in the altogether** colloq. naked.

■ 1 entirely, utterly, wholly, totally. 2 by and large, in the main, generally. 3 in all, all included. □ **in the altogether** see NAKED 1.

al•tru•ism /áltrōōizəm/ n. unselfishness as a principle of action. □□ **al•tru•ist** /–trooist/ n. **al•tru•is'tic** /–ístik/ adj. **al•tru•is'ti•cal•ly** adv.

■ selflessness, self-sacrifice, philanthropy. □□ **altruist** see philanthropist (PHILAN-THROPY). **altruistic** see SELFLESS.

al•um /áləm/ n. sulfate of aluminum and potassium.

a•lu•mi•na /əlōōminə/ n. aluminum oxide occurring naturally as corundum and emery.

a•lu•mi•num /əlōōminəm/ n. silvery light and malleable metallic element. ¶Symb.: Al

a•lum•nus /əlúmnəs/ n. (pl. **a•lum•ni** /–ni/; fem. **a•lum•na**, pl. **a•lum•nae** /–nee, nī/) former pupil or student of a particular school, college, or university.

al•ways /áwlwayz/ adv. 1 at all times; on all occasions. 2 whatever the circumstances. 3 repeatedly; often.

■ 1 again and again, every or each time, each and every time, without exception. 2 in any case or event, as a last resort, if necessary. 3 usually; see also OFTEN.

Alz•hei•mer's dis•ease /áalts-hímərz, álts–, áwlts–, áwlz–/ n. brain disorder causing premature senility.

AM abbr. 1 amplitude modulation. 2 Master of Arts.

Am symb. Chem. americium.

am 1st person sing. present of BE.

a.m. abbr. (also **A.M.** or **AM**) between midnight and noon.

a•mal•gam /əmálgəm/ n. 1 mixture or blend. 2 alloy of mercury with one or more other metals.

■ 1 combination, mix, composite, compound.

a•mal•ga•mate /əmálgəmayt/ v. combine or unite. □□ **a•mal•ga•ma'tion** /–máyshən/ n.

■ blend, mix, join, merge, fuse; consolidate, integrate. □□ **amalgamation** blend, fusion, alloy, combination, mix(ture), amalgam, composite, compound, union.

a•man•u•en•sis /əmányōō–énsis/ n. (pl. **a•man•u•en'ses** /–seez/) person who writes from dictation or copies manuscripts.

am•a•ranth /áməranth/ n. 1 plant with small green, red, or purple tinted flowers. 2 imaginary flower that never fades. □□ **am•a•ran'thine** /–əránthin, –thin/ adj.

am•a•ryl•lis /ámərílis/ n. bulbous lilylike plant with white, pink, or red flowers.

a•mass /əmás/ v.tr. 1 gather or heap

together. **2** accumulate (esp. riches). □□ **a‧mass′er** n. **a‧mass′ment** n.

■ pile or heap up, collect, assemble, stockpile, hoard.

am‧a‧teur /ámǝchoŏr, –chǝr, –tǝr, –tór/ • n. **1** person who engages in a pursuit as a pastime rather than a profession. **2** derog. person who does something unskillfully. • adj. for or done by amateurs; amateurish; unskillful. □□ **am′a‧teur‧ish** adj. **am‧a‧teur′ish‧ly** adv.

■ n. **1** layman, nonprofessional, nonspecialist; tyro; dabbler, dilettante. • adj. lay, nonprofessional, untrained; dilettante, inept, incompetent. □□ **amateurism** unprofessionalism, dilettantism, ineptitude, incompetence.

am‧a‧to‧ry /ámǝtawree/ adj. sexual love or desire.

a‧maze /ǝmáyz/ v.tr. surprise greatly; overwhelm with wonder. □□ **a‧maze′ment** n. **a‧maz‧ing** adj. **a‧maz′ing‧ly** adv.

■ astound, astonish, awe, stun, stagger; (be amazed) be thunderstruck or dumbstruck. □□ **amazement** astonishment, surprise, awe, wonder. **amazing** astonishing, astounding, awe-inspiring. **amazingly** astonishingly, astoundingly, remarkably, extraordinarily.

Am‧a‧zon /ámǝzon, –zǝn/ n. **1** female warrior of a mythical race. **2** (**amazon**) tall, strong, or athletic woman. □□ **Am‧a‧zo′ni‧an** /–zōneeǝn/ adj.

am‧bas‧sa‧dor /ámbásǝdǝr, –dawr/ n. **1** accredited diplomat sent by a nation as its representative in a foreign country. **2** representative or promoter. □□ **am‧bas‧sa‧do′ri‧al** /–dáwreeǝl/ adj. **am‧bas′sa‧dor‧ship** n.

■ envoy, delegate, emissary, minister; agent.

am‧ber /ámbǝr/ n. **1** yellowish translucent fossilized resin deriving from extinct (esp. coniferous) trees and used in jewelry. **2** color of this.

am‧ber‧gris /ámbǝrgris, –grees/ n. waxlike secretion of the sperm whale, used in perfumes.

am‧bi‧dex‧trous /ámbidékstrǝs/ adj. **1** able to use either hand equally well. **2** versatile; skillful. □□ **am‧bi‧dex‧ter′i‧ty** /–stéritee/ n. **am‧bi‧dex′trous‧ly** adv. **am‧bi‧dex′trous‧ness** n.

am‧bi‧ence /ámbeeǝns, aanbeeáans/ n. (also **am′bi‧ance**) surroundings or atmosphere of a place.

■ see ATMOSPHERE 2a.

am‧bi‧ent /ámbeeǝnt/ adj. surrounding.

am‧big‧u‧ous /ambígyŏŏǝs/ adj. **1** having an obscure or double meaning. **2** difficult to classify. See synonym study at DOUBTFUL. □□ **am‧bi‧gu‧i‧ty** /ámbigyŏŏitee/ n. **am‧big′u‧ous‧ly** adv.

■ equivocal, indistinct, inconclusive, vague, unclear; unreliable, undependable. **ambiguity** equivocalness, vagueness, indistinctness, double-talk, doublespeak. **ambiguously** equivocally; see also vaguely (VAGUE).

am‧bi‧tion /ambíshǝn/ n. **1** determination to succeed. **2** object of this.

■ **1** drive, enterprise, energy, initiative, push, vigor. **2** goal, aim, end, aspiration.

am‧bi‧tious /ambíshǝs/ adj. **1 a** full of ambition. **b** showing ambition. **2** strongly determined. □□ **am‧bi′tious‧ly** adv.

■ **1 a** energetic, enterprising, vigorous, zealous, keen; greedy, avaricious, overzealous. **b** enterprising, grandiose. **2** see DETERMINED 1.

am‧biv‧a‧lence /ambívǝlǝns/ n. (also **am‧biv′a‧len‧cy**) simultaneous conflicting feelings. □□ **am‧biv′a‧lent** adj. **am‧biv′a‧lent‧ly** adv.

am‧ble /ámbǝl/ • v.intr. move at an easy pace. • n. such a pace.

am‧bro‧sia /ambrṓzhǝ/ n. **1** (in Greek and Roman mythology) food of the gods. **2** anything very pleasing to taste or smell. □□ **am‧bro′sial** adj. **am‧bro′sian** adj.

am‧bu‧lance /ámbyǝlǝns/ n. vehicle equipped for conveying the sick or injured to and from a hospital.

am‧bu‧la‧to‧ry /ámbyǝlǝtawree/ adj. **1** (of a patient) able to walk about. **2** of or for walking.

am‧bus‧cade /ámbǝskáyd/ n. & v. = AMBUSH.

am‧bush /ámbŏŏsh/ • n. **1** surprise attack from a concealed position. **2 a** concealment of troops, etc., to make such an attack. **b** place where they are concealed. • v.tr. **1** attack by ambush. **2** lie in wait for.

■ n. **1** trap, ambuscade. • v. **1** trap, waylay, ambuscade, jump. **2** bushwhack.

a‧me‧ba var. of AMOEBA.

a‧me‧lio‧rate /ǝméelyǝrayt/ v. make or become better; improve. □□ **a‧mel‧io‧ra′tion** /–ráyshǝn/ n. **am‧el′io‧ra‧tive** adj. **a‧mel′io‧ra‧tor** n.

a‧men /áamén, áy–/ int. word uttered at the end of a prayer, etc., meaning 'so be it.'.

a‧me‧na‧ble /ǝméenǝbǝl, ǝmén–/ adj. **1** responsive. **2** (of a person) responsible to law. □□ **a‧me‧na‧bil′i‧ty** n. **a‧me′na‧bly** adv.

a‧mend /ǝménd/ v.tr. **1** make minor improvements in (a text, etc.). **2** correct an error in (a document). **3** improve. **4** modify formally, as a legal document. □□ **a‧mend′a‧ble** adj. **a‧mend′er** n.

■ **1** enhance, revise, edit, refine, polish (up), improve. **2** emend, rectify, set to rights, right, fix. **3** reform, mend, change for the better. □□ **amendable** correctable, emendable, rectifiable.

a‧mend‧ment /ǝméndmǝnt/ n. **1** minor change in a document (esp. a legal or statutory one). **2** article added to the US Constitution.

■ **1** correction, emendation, change, alteration.

a‧mends /ǝméndz/ n. □ **make amends** compensate or make up (for).

■ □ **make amends** (make amends for) make reparation or restitution for, atone for; (make amends to) make it up to, pay, repay, recompense.

a‧men‧i‧ty /ǝménitee, ǝmée–/ n. (pl. **–ties**) **1** [usu. in pl.] pleasant or useful feature. **2** pleasantness (of a place, etc.).

Am•er•a•sian /aməráyzhən/ n. person of American and Asian descent.

a•merce /əmérs/ v.tr. **1** Law punish by fine. **2** punish arbitrarily. □□ **a•merce′ment** n.

A•mer•i•can /əmérikən/ • adj. **1** of, relating to, or characteristic of the United States or its inhabitants. **2** [usu. in comb.] of or relating to the continents of America (Latin-American). • n. **1** native or citizen of the United States. **2** native or inhabitant of the continents of America. **3** (also **Amer′ican Eng′lish**) the English language as it is used in the United States. □ **American Indian** member of the aboriginal peoples of America or their descendants. □□ **A•mer′i•can•i•za′tion** n. **A•mer′i•can•ize** v.

A•mer•i•ca•na /əmérikánə, –káanə, –káynə/ n.pl. things connected with America, esp. with the United States.

A•mer•i•can•ism /əmérikənizəm/ n. **1 a** word, sense, or phrase peculiar to or originating from the United States. **b** thing or feature characteristic of the United States. **2** attachment to or sympathy for the United States.

am•er•i•ci•um /əmərísheeəm/ n. Chem. artificial radioactive metallic element. ¶Symb.: **Am**

Am•er•in•di•an /ámərindeeən/ adj. & n. (also **Am•er•ind** /ámərínd/) = American Indian. □□ **Am•er•in′dic** /–rindik/ adj.

am•e•thyst /ámithist/ n. semiprecious stone of a violet or purple variety of quartz. □□ **am•e•thys•tine** /–thisteen/ adj.

a•mi•a•ble /áymeeəbəl/ adj. friendly and pleasant, likable. □□ **a•mi•a•bil′i•ty** n. **a′mi•a•ble•ness** n. **a′mi•a•bly** adv.
  ■ amicable, agreeable, cordial, congenial; warm, kindly.

am•i•ca•ble /ámikəbəl/ adj. showing or done in a friendly spirit. □□ **am•i•ca•bil′i•ty** n. **am′i•ca•bly** adv.
  ■ amiable, congenial, harmonious; warm, courteous, cordial, polite, civil.

a•mid /əmíd/ prep. (also **a•midst** /əmídst/) **1** in the middle of. **2** in the course of.
  ■ **1** in the midst or thick of, among; surrounded by. **2** in the middle of, during.

am•ide /áymīd, ám–/ n. Chem. compound formed from ammonia.

a•mid•ships /əmídships/ adv. (also **a•mid′ship**) in or into the middle of a ship.

a•mi•go /əmeégō/ n. (pl. **–gos**) friend or comrade.

a•mine /əmeén, ámeen/ n. Chem. compound formed from ammonia.

a•mi•no ac•id /əmeénō/ n. Biochem. any of a group of nitrogenous organic acids forming the basic constituents of proteins.

a•miss /əmís/ • adj. wrong; out of order. • adv. wrong; wrongly; inappropriately.
  ■ adj. at fault, awry, out of kilter, faulty, defective. • adv. awry, badly, poorly; unfavorably; out of place.

am•i•ty /ámitee/ n. friendship; friendly relations.

am•me•ter /ám-meetər/ n. instrument for measuring electric current in amperes.

am•mo /ámō/ n. colloq. ammunition.

am•mo•ni•a /əmṓnyə/ n. **1** pungent, strongly

alkaline gas. ¶Chem. formula: NH_3. **2** solution of ammonia gas in water.

am•mu•ni•tion /ámyənishən/ n. **1** supply of bullets, shells, grenades, etc. **2** points usable to advantage in an argument.

am•ne•sia /amneézhə/ n. partial or total loss of memory. □□ **am•ne′si•ac** /–zeeak/, –zheeak/ n. **am•ne′sic** adj. & n.

am•nes•ty /ámnistee/ • n. (pl. **–ties**) general pardon, esp. for political offenses. • v.tr. (**–ties, –tied**) grant an amnesty to.
  ■ n. see PARDON n. • v. see PARDON v.

am•ni•o•cen•te•sis /ámneeōsenteésis/ n. (pl. **am•ni•o•cen•te•ses** /–seez/) Med. sampling of amniotic fluid to determine health of a fetus.

am•ni•on /ámneeən/ n. (pl. **am•ni•a**) Zool. & Physiol. innermost membrane that encloses an embryo. □□ **am•ni•ot•ic** /ámneeótik/ adj.

a•moe•ba /əmeébə/ n. (also **a•me′ba**) (pl. **a•moe•bas** or **a•moe•bae** /–bee/) any usu. aquatic protozoan capable of changing shape. □□ **a•moe′bic** adj. **a•moe′boid** adj.

a•mok /əmúk, əmók/ adv. (also **a•muck** /əmúk/) □ **run amok** run about wildly in an uncontrollable violent rage.

a•mong /əmúng/ prep. (also **a•mongst** /əmúngst/) **1** surrounded by; in the company of. **2** included in. **3** in the class or category of (is among the richest men alive). **4 a** shared by (had $5 among us). **b** from the joint resources of. **5** with one another. **6** as distinguished from (she is one among many).
  ■ **1** amid, amidst, in the midst or middle or center of. **3** one of, an example of. **4 a** to each or all (of), between. **6** out of, from.

a•mor•al /áymáwrəl, –mór–/ adj. **1** not concerned with or outside the scope of morality (cf. IMMORAL). **2** having no moral principles. □□ **a•mor′al•ism** n. **a•mo•ral′i•ty** /–rálitee/ n.

am•o•rous /ámərəs/ adj. **1** showing, feeling, or inclined to sexual love. **2** of or relating to sexual love. □□ **am′o•rous•ly** adv. **am′o•rous•ness** n.
  ■ see PASSIONATE.

a•mor•phous /əmáwrfəs/ adj. **1** shapeless. **2** ill-organized; unclassifiable. **3** Mineral. & Chem. noncrystalline. □□ **a•mor′phous•ly** adv. **a•mor′phous•ness** n.
  ■ **2** see VAGUE 1.

am•or•tize /ámərtīz, əmáwr–/ v.tr. Commerce gradually extinguish (a debt) by regular payments.

a•mount /əmównt/ • n. **1** quantity, esp. the total in number, size, value, extent, etc. **2** full effect. • v.intr. [foll. by to] **1** be equivalent to in number, significance, etc. **2** (of a person) develop into; become.
  ■ n. **1** volume, mass, expanse, area, bulk. **2** see significance (SIGNIFICANT). • v. (amount to) **1** add up to, total, come (up) to; be equal to. **2** be capable of.

a•mour /əmoͤor/ n. love affair, esp. a secret one.

a•mour pro•pre /áamoͤorr práwprə/ n. self-respect.

a•mox•i•cil•lin /əmoksəsilən/ • n. a synthetic

...penicillin used in treating bacterial infections.

amp /amp/ *n.* **1** ampere. **2** amperage. **3** amplifier.

amp•er•age /ámpərij/ *n. Electr.* strength of an electric current in amperes.

am•pere /ámpeer/ *n. Electr.* base unit of electric current. ¶Symb.: **A.**

am•per•sand /ámpərsand/ *n.* character representing the word *and*: &.

am•phet•a•mine /amfétəmeen, –min/ *n.* synthetic drug used esp. as a stimulant.

am•phib•i•an /amfíbeeən/ • *adj.* **1** of a class of vertebrates living both on land and in water. **2** (of a vehicle) able to operate on land and water. • *n.* **1** *Zool.* class of vertebrates including frogs, toads, newts, and salamanders. **2** (in general use) creature living both on land and in water. **3** amphibian vehicle. □□ **am•phib'i•ous** *adj.* **am•phib'i•ous•ly** *adv.*

am•phi•the•a•ter /ámfitheeətər/ *n.* round, usu. unroofed building with tiers of seats surrounding a central space.

am•pho•ra /ámfərə/ *n.* (*pl.* **am•pho•rae** /–ree/ or **am•pho•ras**) Greek or Roman vessel with two handles and a narrow neck.

am•ple /ámpəl/ *adj.* (**am•pler**, **am•plest**) **1 a** plentiful; abundant; extensive. **b** *euphem.* (esp. of a person) large; stout. **2** enough or more than enough. □□ **am'ple•ness** *n.* **am'ply** *adv.*

■ **1 a** full, complete, copious; wide-ranging, broad; liberal, unsparing. □□ **ampleness** see ABUNDANCE. **amply** to a great extent, largely; unstintingly, generously; sufficiently, adequately, satisfactorily.

am•pli•fi•er /ámplifīər/ *n.* electronic device for increasing the strength of electrical signals, esp. for conversion into sound.

am•pli•fy /ámplifī/ *v.* (**–fies, –fied**) **1** *tr.* increase the strength of (sound, electrical signals, etc.). **2** *tr.* enlarge upon or add detail to (a story, etc.). **3** *intr.* expand what is said or written. □□ **am•pli•fi•ca'tion** *n.*

■ **1** magnify, add to, augment, make larger *or* greater *or* louder *or* bigger. **2** elaborate (on), expand (on), develop. **3** elaborate, go into detail. □□ **amplification** see *elaboration* (ELABORATE), INCREASE *n.* 1, 2.

am•pli•tude /ámplitōōd, –tyōōd/ *n.* **1 a** *Physics* maximum extent of a vibration or oscillation from the position of equilibrium. **b** *Electr.* maximum departure of the value of an alternating current or wave from the average value. **2 a** spaciousness; breadth; wide range. **b** abundance. □ **amplitude modulation** *Electr.* **1** modulation of a wave by variation of its amplitude. **2** system using such modulation.

■ **2 a** see BREADTH 2. **b** see ABUNDANCE.

am•poule /ámpyōōl, –pōōl/ *n.* (also **am'pule** or **am'pul**) sealed capsule holding a solution for injection.

am•pu•tate /ámpyətayt/ *v.tr.* cut off by surgical operation (a limb, etc.). □□ **am•pu•ta'tion** /–táyshən/ *n.* **am'pu•ta•tor** *n.*

am•pu•tee /ámpyətée/ *n.* person who has lost a limb, etc., by amputation.

a•muck var. of AMOK.

am•u•let /ámyəlit/ *n.* charm worn against evil. ■ talisman, good-luck piece.

a•muse /əmyōōz/ *v.* **1** *tr.* cause to laugh or smile. **2** *tr.* & *refl.* interest or occupy; keep entertained. □□ **a•mus'ing** *adj.* **a•mus'ing•ly** *adv.*

■ **1** delight, tickle, cheer, *colloq.* get. **2** divert, entertain, please, beguile, distract. □□ **amusing** see *entertaining* (ENTERTAIN).

a•muse•ment /əmyōōzmənt/ *n.* **1** something that amuses. **2 a** state of being amused. **b** act of amusing. □ **amusement park** park with rides such as a roller coaster, etc., and other entertainment.

■ **1** entertainment, diversion, divertissement, recreation, distraction, pastime. **2** entertainment, diversion, recreation, pleasure.

a•my•o•troph•i•clat•er•al scle•ro•sis /aymīətrōfik, –trō–/ *n.* incurable degenerative disease of the nervous system leading to paralysis. (Also called **Lou Gehrig's disease.**) ¶Abbr.: **ALS.**

an /an, ən/ *adj.* form of the indefinite article see A.

an– /ən, an/ *prefix* **1** not; without (*anarchy*) (cf. A-). **2** assim. form of AD- before *n.*

-an /ən/ *suffix* (also **–ean, –ian**) forming adjectives and nouns, esp. from names of places, systems, classes or orders, and founders (*Mexican, Anglican, crustacean, Lutheran*).

an•a•bol•ic /ánəbólik/ *adj. Biochem.* of or relating to anabolism. □ **anabolic steroid** synthetic steroid hormones used to increase muscle size.

a•nab•o•lism /ənábəlizəm/ *n. Biochem.* synthesis of complex molecules in living organisms from simpler ones.

a•nach•ro•nism /ənákrənizəm/ *n.* **1 a** attribution of a custom, event, etc., to the wrong period. **b** thing attributed in this way. **2** out-of-date person or thing. □□ **a•nach•ro•nis•tic** /–nístik/ *adj.* **a•nach•ro•nis'ti•cal•ly** *adv.*

■ **1** misdating. **2** (old) fogy, conservative, *colloq.* stick-in-the-mud. □□ **anachronistic** see *old-fashioned.*

an•a•con•da /ánəkóndə/ *n.* large nonpoisonous snake that kills its prey by constriction.

an•a•dam•a bread /anədámə/ • *n.* a yeast bread made with flour, cornmeal, and molasses.

an•aer•obe /ánərōb, anáirōb/ *n.* organism able to live without air or water. □□ **an•aer•o'bic** *adj.*

an•a•gram /ánəgram/ *n.* word or phrase formed by transposing the letters of another word or phrase. □□ **an•a•gram•ma•tic** /–mátik/ *adj.* **an•a•gram•mat'i•cal** *adj.* **an•a•gram•ma•tize** /–grámətīz/ *v.tr.*

a•nal /áynəl/ *adj.* **1** of or near the anus. **2** = *anal retentive.* □ **anal retentive** (of a person) excessively orderly and fussy. □□ **a'nal•ly** *adv.*

an•al•ge•si•a /ánəljeézeeə, –seeə/ *n.* absence or relief of pain.

an•al•ge•sic /ánəljeézik, –sik/ • *adj.* relieving pain. • *n.* analgesic drug.

an·a·log /ánəlog/ *n.* **1** analogous thing. **2** [*attrib.*] (of a computer or electronic process) using physical variables, e.g., voltage weight, etc., to represent numbers (cf. DIGITAL).

■ **1** see METAPHOR, PARALLEL *n.* 1.

a·nal·o·gize /ənáləjīz/ *v.* **1** *tr.* represent or explain by analogy. **2** *intr.* use analogy.

a·nal·o·gous /ənáləgəs/ *adj.* [usu. foll. by to] partially similar or parallel; showing analogy. □□ **a·nal'o·gous·ly** *adv.*

a·nal·o·gy /ənáləjee/ *n.* (*pl.* **–gies**) **1** correspondence or partial similarity. **2** *Logic* arguing from parallel cases. **3** = ANALOG 1. See synonym study at LIKENESS. □□ **an·a·log·i·cal** /ánəlójikəl/ *adj.* **an·a·log'i·cal·ly** *adv.*

■ **1** see METAPHOR. **3** see METAPHOR, PARALLEL *n.*

a·nal·y·sis /ənálisis/ *n.* (*pl.* **a·nal·y·ses** /–seez/) **1 a** detailed examination of elements or structure. **b** statement of the result of this. **2** *Chem.* determination of the constituent parts of a mixture or compound. **3** psychoanalysis. □□ **an·a·lyt·ic** /ánəlítik/ *adj.* **an·a·lyt'i·cal** *adj.* **an·a·lyt'i·cal·ly** *adv.*

■ **1** investigation, study, scrutiny, inquiry; interpretation; review. **2** assay, breakdown, division. **3** see THERAPY.

an·a·lyst /ánəlist/ *n.* **1** person skilled in analysis. **2** psychoanalyst.

an·a·lyze /ánəlīz/ *v.tr.* **1** examine in detail. **2 a** *Chem.* ascertain the constituents of. **b** break (something) down into its constituent parts. **3** psychoanalyze. □□ **an'a·lyz·a·ble** *adj.* **an'a·lyz·er** *n.*

■ **1** investigate, study, scrutinize. **2 b** separate, dissect. **3** give therapy to, put in therapy.

an·a·pest /ánəpest/ *n.* *Prosody* metrical foot consisting of two short or unstressed syllables followed by one long or stressed syllable. □□ **an·a·pes'tic** *adj.*

an·a·phy·lax·is /ánəfiláksis/ *n.* (*pl.* **an·a·phy·lax·es** /–seez/) *Med.* hypersensitivity of tissues to a dose of antigen, as a reaction against a previous dose. □□ **an·a·phy·lac·tic** /–láktik/ *adj.*

an·ar·chism /ánərkizəm/ *n.* doctrine that all government and laws should be abolished. □□ **an'ar·chist** *n.* **an·ar·chis'tic** *adj.*

an·ar·chy /ánərkee/ *n.* **1** disorder, esp. political or social. **2** lack of government in a society. □□ **an·ar'chic** *adj.* **an·ar'chi·cal** *adj.* **an·ar'chi·cal·ly** *adv.*

A·na·sa·zi /onəsáazee/ *n.* **1 a** prehistoric N. American people native to the southwestern US. **b** member of this people. **2** language of this people.

anat. *abbr.* **1** anatomical. **2** anatomy.

a·nath·e·ma /ənáthəmə/ *n.* (*pl.* **a·nath·e·mas**) **1** detested thing or person. **2** ecclesiastical rejection of a person or doctrine.

a·nath·e·ma·tize /ənáthəmətīz/ *v.* curse.

a·nat·o·mize /ənátəmīz/ *v.tr.* **1** examine in detail. **2** dissect.

a·nat·o·my /ənátəmee/ *n.* (*pl.* **–mies**) **1** science of the bodily structure of animals and plants. **2** this structure. **3** *colloq.* human body. **4** analysis. □□ **an·a·tom·i·cal** /ánətómikəl/ *adj.* **a·nat·o·mist** /ənátəmist/ *n.*

■ **2** see FORM *n.* 1. **3** see BODY *n.* 1.

ANC *abbr.* African National Congress.

-ance /əns/ *suffix* forming nouns expressing: **1** quality or state or an instance of (*appearance, resemblance*). **2** action (*assistance*).

an·ces·tor /ánsestər/ *n.* (*fem.* **an·ces·tress** /–stris/) **1** any (esp. remote) person from whom one is descended. **2** early type of animal or plant from which others have evolved. **3** prototype or forerunner. □□ **an·ces·tral** /anséstrəl/ *adj.*

■ **1** forebear, forefather, progenitor, predecessor. **3** precursor, antecedent; archetype; harbinger

an·ces·try /ánsestree/ *n.* (*pl.* **–tries**) **1** family descent. **2** one's ancestors collectively.

an·chor /ángkər/ *n.* **1** heavy metal weight used to moor a ship or a balloon. **2** thing affording stability. **3** source of confidence. **4** (in full **anchor·man**, **an'chor·per·son**, **an'chor·wom·an**) a person who plays a vital part, as the last member of a relay team, etc, **b** news broadcaster who introduces segments and reads news. • *v.* **1** *tr.* secure by means of an anchor. **2** *tr.* fix firmly. **3** *intr.* cast anchor. **4** *intr.* be moored by means of an anchor.

■ *n.* **1** sheet anchor. **2** mainstay, support, stabilizer; hold, grasp, grip. **4 b** presenter, announcer, newsreader. • *v.* **1, 2** attach, affix, moor. **3, 4** drop anchor, harbor, moor, be moored, be at anchor.

an·chor·age /ángkərij/ *n.* **1** place where a ship may be anchored. **2** anchoring or lying at anchor.

an·cho·rite /ángkərīt/ *n.* hermit; religious recluse.

an·cho·vy /ánchōvee/ *n.* (*pl.* **–vies**) small strong-flavored fish of the herring family.

an·cient /áynshənt/ • *adj.* **1** of long ago. **2** having lived or existed long. See synonym study at OLD. • *n.* very old person. □□ **an'cient·ness** *n.*

■ *adj.* **1** old, archaic, antique, bygone, past, antediluvian, primitive, prehistoric, primeval. **2** old, timeworn, aged, aging, age-old, obsolescent, hoary. • *n.* Methuselah.

an·cil·lar·y /ánsəleree/ • *adj.* **1** providing essential support to a central service or industry, esp. the medical service. **2** subordinate; subservient. • *n.* (*pl.* **–ies**) ancillary worker. **2** accessory.

■ *adj.* see AUXILIARY *adj.* • *n.* see AUXILIARY *n.*

-ancy /ənsee/ *suffix* forming nouns denoting a quality (*constancy*) or state (*infancy*) (cf. –ANCE).

and /and, ənd/ *conj.* **1** connecting words, clauses, or sentences to be taken jointly (*buy and sell*). **2** implying: **a** progression (*better and better*). **b** causation (*do that and I'll hit you*). **c** great duration (*he cried and cried*). **d** great number (*miles and miles*). **e** addition (*two and two*). **3** *colloq.* to (*try and open it*). □ **and/or** either or both of two stated possibilities.

an·dan·te /aandáantay, andántee/ *Mus.* • *adv. & adj.* in a moderately slow tempo. • *n.* andante passage or movement.

and•i•ron /ándīrn/ n. one of a pair of supports for logs in a fireplace.

an•dro•gen /ándrəjən/ n. male sex hormone or other substance that reinforces certain male sexual characteristics. □□ **an•dro•gen•ic** /–jénik/ adj.

an•drog•y•nous /andrójinəs/ adj. 1 hermaphroditic. 2 exhibiting the appearance or attributes of both sexes. 3 Bot. with stamens and pistils in the same flower. □□ **an•drog′y•ny** /andrójinee/ n.

an•droid /ándroyd/ n. robot with a human appearance.

-ane¹ /ayn/ suffix var. of -AN; usu. with distinction of sense (germane, humane, urbane) but sometimes with no corresponding form in -an (mundane).

-ane² /ayn/ suffix Chem. forming names of saturated hydrocarbons (methane, propane).

an•ec•dote /ánikdōt/ n. short account of an entertaining or interesting incident. □□ **an•ec•do′tal** /–dōt′l/ adj. **an•ec•do′tal•ist** n. **an•ec•dot•ic** /–dótik/ adj. **an•ec•dot•ist** /–dōt–/ n.

■ see STORY¹ 1.

a•ne•mi•a /əneémeeə/ n. deficiency of red cells or their hemoglobin.

a•ne•mic /əneémik/ adj. 1 relating to or suffering from anemia. 2 pale; lacking in vitality.

■ 2 see PALE¹ adj. 1, WEAK 1.

an•e•mom•e•ter /ánimómitər/ n. instrument for measuring the force of the wind.

a•nem•o•ne /ənémənee/ n. plant akin to the buttercup, with flowers of various vivid colors.

-aneous /áyneeəs/ suffix forming adjectives (cutaneous, miscellaneous).

an•es•the•sia /ánis-theézhə/ n. absence of sensation, esp. artificially induced before surgery. □□ **an•es•the•si•ol•o•gy** /–zeeóləjee/ n.

an•es•thet•ic /ánis-thétik/ • n. substance that produces insensibility to pain, etc. • adj. producing partial or complete insensibility to pain, etc. □□ **an•es•the•tize** /ənés-thətiz/ v.

■ n. see PAINKILLER. • adj. see NARCOTIC adj.

an•es•the•tist /ənés-thətist/ n. specialist in the administration of anesthetics.

an•eu•rysm /ányərizəm/ n. (also **an′eu•rism**) excessive localized enlargement of an artery. □□ **an•eu•rys′mal** /–rízməl/ adj. (-also **an•eu•ris′mal**).

a•new /ənoó, ənyoó/ adv. 1 again. 2 in a different way.

an•gel /áynjəl/ n. 1 a attendant or messenger of God. b conventional representation of this in human form with wings. 2 a very virtuous person. b obliging person (be an angel and answer the door). 3 sl. financial backer of an enterprise, esp. in the theater. □□ **an•gel•ic** /–jél–/ adj. **an•gel′i•cal** adj. **an•gel′i•cal•ly** adv.

an•ger /ánggər/ • n. extreme or passionate displeasure. • v.tr. make angry; enrage.

■ n. rage, fury, pique; antagonism, irritation, vexation, outrage. • v. infuriate, madden, incense; vex, nettle, displease.

an•gin•a /anjínə, ánjənə/ n. 1 attack of intense constricting pain often causing suffocation. 2 (in full **an•gi•na pec•tor•is** /péktəris/) pain in the chest brought on by exertion, owing to an inadequate blood supply to the heart.

an•gi•o•sperm /ánjeeəspərm/ n. plant propagating by seeds in pods opp. GYMNOSPERM. □□ **an•gi•o•sper′mous** adj.

an•gle¹ /ánggəl/ • n. 1 a space between two meeting lines or surfaces. b inclination of two lines or surfaces to each other. 2 corner. 3 a point of view. b approach, technique, etc. • v. 1 tr. & intr. move or place obliquely. 2 tr. present (information) in a biased way. □□ **an•gled** adj.

■ n. 1 b slant. 2 bend, intersection, cusp; sharp end, projection. 3 direction, slant, aspect, perspective, bias. v. 1 slant, bend, point. 2 see SLANT v. 3.

an•gle² /ánggəl/ v.intr. 1 fish with hook and line. 2 [foll. by for] seek an objective by devious means (angled for a pay raise).

■ 2 (angle for) fish (for); look or hope for, seek, go after.

An•gli•can /ángglikən/ • adj. of or relating to the Church of England or any church in communion with it. • n. member of an Anglican Church. □□ **An′gli•can•ism** n.

An•gli•cism /ánggəlisizəm/ n. peculiarly English word or custom.

An•gli•cize /ángglisiz/ v.tr. make English in form or character.

An•glo /ánggló/ n. (pl. –glos) 1 person of British or northern European origin. 2 non-Hispanic white person.

Anglo- /ángglo/ comb. form 1 Anglican (Anglo-Catholic). 2 of English origin (an Anglo-American). 3 English or British and (Anglo-American agreement).

Anglo-French /ángglofrénch/ • adj. English (or British) and French. • n. French language as developed in England after the Norman Conquest.

An•glo•phile /ángglafil/ • n. person who greatly admires England or the English. • adj. being or characteristic of an Anglophile.

An•glo-Sa•xon /ángglosáksən/ • adj. 1 of the English Saxons (as distinct from the Old Saxons of the European continent, and from the Angles) before the Norman Conquest. 2 of English descent. • n. 1 Anglo-Saxon person. 2 Old English. 3 colloq. plain (esp. crude) English.

an•go•ra /anggáwrə/ n. 1 fabric or wool made from the hair of the angora goat or rabbit. 2 long-haired variety of cat, goat, or rabbit.

an•gry /ánggree/ adj. (**an•gri•er, an•gri•est**) 1 feeling or showing anger. 2 (of a wound, sore, etc.) inflamed; painful. 3 stormy (an angry sky). □□ **an′gri•ly** adv.

■ 1 enraged, furious, irate, incensed; irritated, annoyed, vexed, cross. 2 irritated, sore, smarting, stinging. 3 black, lowering, dark, savage, glowering. □□ **angrily** furiously, irately, crossly; blackly, darkly, savagely.

angst /aangkst/ n. 1 anxiety. 2 feeling of guilt or remorse.

ang•strom /ángstrəm/ *n.* (also **ång•ström** /áwngström/) unit of length equal to 10^{-10} meter. ¶Symb.: Å.

an•guish /ánggwish/ • *n.* severe mental suffering. • *v.tr.* (often as **anguished** *adj.*) cause to suffer physical or mental pain.

■ *n.* pain, angst, distress, agony, torment. • *v.* disturb, upset, distress; torment, torture; (**anguished**). see *worried* (WORRY *v.* 4).

an•gu•lar /ánggyələr/ *adj.* **1 a** having angles or sharp corners. **b** (of a person) having sharp features. **2** forming an angle. **3** measured by angle. □□ **an•gu•lar•i•ty** /–láritee/ *n.* **an'gu•lar•ly** *adv.*

an•i•line /ánillin, –līn/ *n.* colorless oily liquid used in the manufacture of dyes, drugs, and plastics.

an•i•mad•vert /ánimadvórt/ *v.intr.* criticize; censure. □□ **an•i•mad•ver•sion** /–vórzhən/ *n.*

an•i•mal /ánimal/ • *n.* **1** living organism that feeds on organic matter, usu. one with specialized sense organs and a nervous system, and able to respond rapidly to stimuli. **2** such an organism other than a human being. **3** brutish or uncivilized person. • *adj.* characteristic of animals.

■ *n.* **1** creature, (sentient) being, living thing. **3** beast, barbarian, savage, monster. • *adj.* zoological, biological.

an•i•mal•ism /ániməlizəm/ *n.* **1** nature and activity of animals. **2** belief that humans are mere animals. **3** sensuality.

an•i•mate • *adj.* /ánimət/ **1** having life **2** lively. • *v.tr.* /ánimayt/ **1** enliven. **2** give life to. **3** inspire. **4** encourage. See synonym study at QUICKEN.

■ *adj.* **1** alive, living, animated, moving, breathing. **2** spirited, vivacious, vigorous. *v.* **1, 2** activate, invigorate, stimulate. **3, 4** inspirit, stimulate, actuate, move, motivate.

an•i•mat•ed /ánimaytid/ *adj.* **1** lively, vigorous. **2** having life. **3** (of a movie, etc.) using techniques of animation. □□ **an•i•mat•ed•ly** *adv.* **an'i•ma•tor** *n.* (in sense 3)

■ **1** alive, quick, spirited, active, energetic. **2** see ANIMATE *adj.* 1. □□ **animatedly** see *vigorously* (VIGOR). **animator** cartoonist.

an•i•ma•tion /ánimáyshən/ *n.* **1** vivacity; ardor. **2** state of being alive. **3** *Cinematog.* technique of filming successive drawings, positions of puppets, etc., to create an illusion of movement.

■ **1** vivaciousness, spirit, vitality, dash, élan, zest; fire, fervor.

an•i•mism /ánimizəm/ *n.* attribution of a living soul to plants, inanimate objects, and natural phenomena. □□ **an'i•mist** *n.* **an•i•mis'tic** /–místik/ *adj.*

an•i•mos•i•ty /ánimósitee/ *n.* (*pl.* **–ties**) spirit or feeling of strong hostility.

■ antagonism, antipathy, ill will, malevolence; bitterness, acrimony, resentment, rancor.

an•i•mus /ániməs/ *n.* **1** animosity. **2** ill feeling.

an•i•on /ánīən/ *n.* negatively charged ion opp. CATION. □□ **an•i•on•ic** /ánīónik/ *adj.*

an•ise /ánis/ *n.* umbelliferous plant having aromatic seeds, used to flavor liqueurs and candy.

ankh /angk/ *n.* cross with a loop at the top.

an•kle /ángkəl/ *n.* **1** joint connecting the foot with the leg. **2** this part of the leg.

ank•let /ángklit/ *n.* **1** ornament worn around the ankle. **2** short sock.

an•ky•lo•sis /ángkilósis/ *n.* **1** abnormal stiffening of a joint by fusion of the bones. **2** such fusion. □□ **an•ky•lot•ic** /–lótik/ *adj.*

an•nals /ánəlz/ *n.pl.* **1** narrative of events year by year. **2** historical records. □□ **an'nal•ist** *n.* **an•nal•is'tic** *adj.* **an•nal•is'ti•cal•ly** *adv.*

an•neal /ənéél/ *v.tr.* **1** heat (metal or glass) and cool slowly, esp. to toughen it. **2** toughen. □□ **an•neal'er** *n.*

an•ne•lid /án'lid/ *n.* segmented worm, e.g., earthworms, etc.

an•nex /anéks, áneks/ • *v.tr.* **1** add as a subordinate part. **2** incorporate (territory of another) into one's own. • *n.* **1** separate or added building, esp. for extra accommodation. **2** addition to a document. □□ **an•nex•a'tion** *n.*

■ **1** see ADD 1. **2** see CONQUER 1a. • *n.* **1** extension, addition; wing. **2** see ADDITION 2.

an•ni•hi•late /ənílayt/ *v.tr.* **1** completely destroy. **2** defeat utterly; make powerless. See synonym study at DESTROY. □□ **an•ni•hi•la•tion** /–láyshən/ *n.* **an•ni'hi•la•tor** *n.*

■ **1** see DESTROY 1, 2. **2** see DEFEAT *v.* 1.

an•ni•ver•sa•ry /ánivərsáree/ *n.* (*pl.* **–ries**) **1** date on which an event took place in a previous year. **2** celebration of this.

an•no•tate /ánōtayt/ *v.tr.* add explanatory notes to (a book, document, etc.). □□ **an•no•ta•tion** /–táyshən/ *n.* **an'no•ta•tive** *adj.* **an'no•ta•tor** *n.*

■ see GLOSS² *v.* 1.

an•nounce /ənówns/ *v.* **1** *tr.* make publicly known. **2** *tr.* make known the arrival or imminence of (a guest, etc.). **3** *intr.* declare one's candidacy for office. **4** *tr.* be a sign of. □□ **an•nounce'ment** *n.*

■ **1** proclaim, put out, publish, advertise; circulate; reveal, disclose. **2** introduce, present. **4** intimate, suggest, hint at; foretell, augur. □□ **announcement** declaration, notice, report, bulletin.

SYNONYM STUDY: **announce**
BLAZON, PUBLISH, PROCLAIM, DECLARE, PROMULGATE. When you **announce** something, you communicate it in a formal and public manner, often for the first time (*to announce the arrival of the guest of honor*). But just how you go about announcing something depends on what you're trying to convey. If you want to make sure no one misses your message, use **blazon** (*signs along the highway blazoned the local farmers' complaints*). If you plan to make your views known to the general public through the medium of writing, use **publish** (*to publish a story on drunk driving in the local newspaper*). Use **proclaim** if you have something of great importance that you want to announce very formally and official-

ly (*proclaim a national day of mourning*). Although **declare** also implies a very formal announcement (*declare war*), it can refer to any clear and explicit statement (*declare one's love*). **Promulgate** is usually associated with the communication of a creed, doctrine, or law (*promulgate the views of the Democratic Party*).

---

an•nounc•er /ənównsər/ *n.* person who announces, esp. in broadcasting.
  ■ presenter, anchor, newscaster, reporter, broadcaster.

an•noy /ənóy/ *v.tr.* **1** cause slight anger or mental distress to. **2** [in *passive*] be somewhat angry. **3** molest; harass repeatedly. □□ **an•noy′ance** *n.* **an•noy′er** *n.* **an•noy′ ing** *adj.*
  ■ **1** irritate, bother, irk, vex, get on a person's nerves. **3** pester, harry, badger, nag. □□ **annoying** irritating, maddening, infuriating, irksome, exasperating.

an•nu•al /ányōoəl/ • *adj.* **1** reckoned by the year. **2** occurring every year. **3** living or lasting for one year. • *n.* **1** book, etc., published once a year; yearbook. **2** plant that lives only for a year or less. □□ **an′nu•al•ly** *adv.*
  ■ *adj.* **2** yearly, once a year, regular.

an•nu•i•ty /ənóoitee, ənyóo–/ *n.* (*pl.* **–ties**) **1** yearly grant or allowance. **2** investment yielding a fixed annual sum. **3** sum paid.

an•nul /ənúl/ *v.tr.* (**an•nulled, an•nul•ling**) **1** declare (a marriage, etc.) invalid. **2** cancel; abolish. □□ **an•nul′ment** *n.*
  ■ **2** see CANCEL *v.* 2.

an•nu•lar /ányələr/ *adj.* ring-shaped; forming a ring. See synonym study at ROUND. □ **annular eclipse** eclipse of the sun in which the moon leaves a ring of sunlight visible around it. □□ **an′nu•lar•ly** *adv.*

an•nun•ci•a•tion /ənúnseeáyshən/ *n.* **1** (**Annunciation**) **a** announcing of the Incarnation, made by the angel Gabriel to Mary, related in Luke 1:26–38. **b** festival commemorating this. **2 a** act or process of announcing. **b** announcement.

an•ode /ánōd/ *n.* *Electr.* positive electrode in an electrolytic cell. □□ **an•od•ic** /ənódik/ *adj.*

an•o•dize /ánədīz/ *v.tr.* coat (a metal, esp. aluminum) with a protective oxide layer by electrolysis. □□ **an′o•diz•er** *n.*

an•o•dyne /ánədīn/ • *adj.* **1** able to relieve pain. **2** mentally soothing. • *n.* anodyne drug or medicine.

a•noint /ənóynt/ *v.tr.* **1** apply oil or ointment to, esp. as a religious ceremony (e.g., at baptism, etc.). **2** smear; rub. □□ **a•noint′er** *n.*

a•nom•a•lous /ənómələs/ *adj.* irregular; deviant; abnormal. □□ **a•nom′a•lous•ly** *adv.* **a•nom′a•lous•ness** *n.*
  ■ see ABNORMAL.

a•nom•a•ly /ənóməlee/ *n.* (*pl.* **–lies**) **1** anomalous thing; irregularity. **2** irregularity of motion, behavior, etc.
  ■ **1** see ODDITY 1. **2** see ODDITY 3.

a•non /ənón/ *adv.* archaic or *literary* soon; shortly.

anon. /ənón/ *abbr.* anonymous; anonymous author.

a•non•y•mous /ənóniməs/ *adj.* **1** of unknown name. **2** of unknown or undeclared authorship. **3** without character; featureless. □□ **an•o•nym•i•ty** /ánənímitee/ *n.* **a•non′y•mous•ly** *adv.*
  ■ **1** see NAMELESS 1, 3.

a•noph•e•les /ənófileez/ *n.* any of various mosquitoes that transmit malaria to humans.

an•o•rak /ánərak/ *n.* warm jacket, usu. with a hood; parka.

an•o•rex•i•a /ánərékseeə/ *n.* **1** lack of appetite for food. **2** (in full **an•o•rex′ia ner•vo•sa**) /nərvósə/) psychological illness, esp. in young women, characterized by an obsessive desire to lose weight by refusing to eat. □□ **an•o•rex′ic** *adj.*

an•oth•er /ənúthər/ • *adj.* **1** additional (*have another piece of cake*). **2** person like (*another Lincoln*). **3** a different (*quite another matter*). **4** some or any other (*will not do another person's work*). • *pron.* **1** additional one. **2** different one. **3** some or any other one (*I love another*).

an•swer /ánsər/ • *n.* **1** something said or done in reaction to a question, statement, or circumstance. **2** solution to a problem. • *v.* **1** *tr. & intr.* make an answer to (*answer me*). **2** *tr.* respond to the summons or signal of (*answer the door*). **3** *tr.* be satisfactory for (a purpose or need). **4** *intr.* **a** [foll. by *for, to*] be responsible. **b** vouch (for a person, etc.). **5** *intr.* correspond, esp. to a description. □ **answer back** answer impudently. **answering machine** device that supplies a recorded answer to a telephone call and usu. records incoming messages. □□ **an′swer•a•ble** *adj.*
  ■ *n.* **1** reply, response, rejoinder, retort; *Law* defense, plea. **2** explanation, explication; key. • *v.* **1** reply to, respond to. **3** satisfy, fulfill, meet, suit. **4** be accountable *or* answerable; (*answer for*) take *or* accept the blame for; take *or* undertake responsibility for. **5** see CORRESPOND 1. □ **answer back** talk back. □□ **answerable** see RESPONSIBLE 1, 2.

ant /ant/ *n.* small insect living in complex social colonies, usu. wingless, and proverbial for industry.

-ant /ənt/ *suffix* **1** forming adjectives denoting attribution of an action (*repentant*) or state (*arrogant*). **2** forming nouns denoting an agent (*assistant*).

ant•ac•id /ántásid/ *n.* substance that prevents or corrects acidity.

an•tag•o•nism /antágənizəm/ *n.* active opposition or hostility.
  ■ animosity, enmity, rancor, antipathy; conflict, rivalry.

an•tag•o•nist /antágənist/ *n.* opponent or adversary. □□ **an•tag•o•nis′tic** *adj.* **an•tag•o•nis′ti•cal•ly** *adv.*
  ■ enemy, contender, competitor. □□ **antagonistic** see HOSTILE 2.

an•tag•o•nize /antágənīz/ *v.tr.* evoke hostility or opposition or enmity in. □□ **an•tag•o•ni•za′tion** *n.*
  ■ see ALIENATE 1.

Ant•arc•tic /antaárktik/ • adj. of the south polar regions. • n. this region. □ **Antarctic Circle** parallel of latitude 66° 32- S., delimiting this region.

an•te /ántee/ • n. **1** stake put up by a player in poker, etc., before receiving cards. **2** amount to be paid in advance. • v.tr. (**an•tes, an•ted**) **1** put up as an ante. **2 a** bet; stake. **b** (foll. by up) pay.

ante- /ántee/ prefix forming nouns and adjectives meaning 'before; preceding' (anteroom).

ant•eat•er /ánteetər/ n. any of various mammals feeding on ants and termites.

an•te•bel•lum /ánteebéləm/ adj. before the US Civil War.

an•te•ced•ent /ántiseéd'nt/ • n. **1** preceding thing or circumstance. **2** Gram. word, phrase, etc., to which another word (esp. a relative pronoun) refers. **3** [in pl.] past history, esp. of a person, • adj. previous. □□ **an•te•ce'dence** n. **an•te•ced'ent•ly** adv.

an•te•cham•ber /ánteechaymbər/ n. = ANTEROOM.

an•te•date /ántidáyt/ • v.tr. **1** precede in time. **2** assign an earlier date to. • n. date earlier than the actual one.
■ v. 1 see PRECEDE.

an•te•di•lu•vi•an /ánteediloóveeən/ adj. **1** of the time before the Biblical flood. **2** colloq. very old or out of date. See synonym study at OLD.

an•te•lope /ántilōp/ n. (pl. same or **an•te•lopes**) **1** swift-moving deerlike ruminant, e.g., gazelle and impala. **2** leather made from the skin of any of these.

an•ten•na /ántenə/ n. (pl. **an•ten•nae** /-nee/) **1** Zool. one of a pair of feelers on the heads of insects, crustaceans, etc. **2** (pl. **an•ten•nas**) metal rod, wire, or other structure by which broadcast signals are transmitted or received.

an•te•ri•or /ánteereeər/ adj. **1** nearer the front. **2** earlier; prior. □□ **an•te•ri•or•i•ty** /-reeáwritee/ n. **an•te'ri•or•ly** adv.
■ **1** see FRONT adj. 1. **2** see FOREGOING.

an•te•room /ánteeroóm, -roóm/ n. small room leading to a main one.

an•them /ánthəm/ n. **1** elaborate choral composition usu. based on a passage of scripture. **2** solemn hymn of praise, etc., esp. = national anthem.

an•ther /ánthər/ n. Bot. apical portion of a stamen containing pollen. □□ **an'the•ral** adj.

ant•hill /ánt-hil/ n. moundlike nest built by ants or termites.

an•thol•o•gy /anthóləjee/ n. (pl. **-gies**) published collection of passages from literature, songs, reproductions of paintings, etc. □□ **an•thol'o•gist** n. **an•thol'o•gize** v.

an•thra•cite /ánthrəsīt/ n. coal of a hard variety burning with little flame and smoke. □□ **an•thra•cit•ic** /-sítik/ adj.

an•thrax /ánthraks/ n. disease of sheep and cattle transmissible to humans.

an•thro•po•cen•tric /ánthrəpōséntrik/ adj. regarding humankind as the center of existence. □□ **an•thro•po•cen'tri•cal•ly** adv. **an•thro•po•cen'trism** n.

an•thro•poid /ánthrəpoyd/ • adj. **1** human in form. **2** colloq. (of a person) apelike. • n. anthropoid ape.

an•thro•pol•o•gy /ánthrəpóləjee/ n. study of humankind, esp. its societies and customs. □□ **an•thro•pol•og•i•cal** /-pəlójikəl/ adj. **an•thro•pol'og•ist** n.

an•thro•po•mor•phism /ánthrəpəmáwrfizəm/ n. attribution of human characteristics to a god, animal, or thing. □□ **an•thro•po•mor'phic** adj. **an•thro•po•mor'phi•cal•ly** adv. **an•thro•po•mor'phize** v.tr.

an•thro•po•mor•phous /ánthrəpəmáwrfəs/ adj. human in form.

an•ti /ántee, -tī/ • prep. opposed to (is anti everything). • n. (pl. **an•tis**) person opposed to a particular policy, etc.

anti- /ántee/ prefix (also **ant-** before a vowel or h) forming nouns and adjectives meaning: **1** opposed to; against (antivivisectionism). **2** preventing (antiscorbutic). **3** opposite of (anticlimax). **4** rival (antipope). **5** unlike the conventional form (antihero).

an•ti•air•craft /ánteeáirkraft, ántī-/ adj. (of a gun, missile, etc.) used to attack enemy aircraft.

an•ti•bal•lis•tic mis•sile /ánteebəlistik, ántī-/ n. a missile designed for intercepting and destroying a ballistic missile while in flight.

an•ti•bi•ot•ic /ántibīótik, ántī-/ Pharm. • n. substance (e.g., penicillin) that can inhibit or destroy susceptible microorganisms. • adj. functioning as an antibiotic.

an•ti•bod•y /ántibodee, ántī-/ n. (pl. **-ies**) blood protein produced in response to and then counteracting antigens.

an•tic /ántik/ n. [usu. in pl.] absurd or foolish behavior or action; prank.
■ see CAPER[1] n. 2a.

An•ti•christ /ántikrīst, ántī-/ n. archenemy of Christ.

an•tic•i•pate /antisipayt/ v.tr. **1** deal with or use before the proper time. **2** expect; foresee. **3** forestall (a person or thing). **4** look forward to. □□ **an•tic•i•pa•tion** /-páyshən/ n. **an•tic'i•pat•or** n. **an•tic'i•pa•tor•y** /-pətawree/ adj.
■ **2** foretell, forecast, predict; bank or count on. **3** preempt, intercept, head off. **4** prepare for, wait for, await. □□ **anticipation** expectation, hope.

an•ti•cli•max /ántiklímaks, ántī-/ n. disappointingly trivial conclusion to something significant. □□ **an•ti•cli•mac•tic** /-máktik/ adj. **an•ti•cli•mac'ti•cal•ly** adv.

an•ti•de•pres•sant /ánteediprésənt, ántī-/ • n. drug that alleviates depression. • adj. alleviating depression.

an•ti•dote /ántidōt/ n. **1** medicine, etc., used to counteract poison. **2** anything that counteracts something unpleasant. □□ **an•ti•dot'al** adj.
■ **1** antitoxin, antiserum; cure, remedy. **2** countermeasure, corrective, remedy.

an•ti•freeze /ántifreez, ántee-/ n. substance added to water to lower its freezing point, esp. in the radiator of a motor vehicle.

an•ti•gen /ántijən/ *n.* foreign substance (e.g., toxin) that causes the body to produce antibodies. □□ **an•ti•gen•ic** /–jénik/ *adj.*

an•ti•he•ro /ánteeheerŏ, ántī–/ *n.* (*pl.* **–roes**) (in a story) central character lacking conventional heroic attributes.

an•ti•his•ta•mine /ánteehístəmin, –meen, ántī–/ *n.* substance used esp. in the treatment of allergies.

an•ti•lock /ánteelók, ántī–/ *adj.* (of brakes) designed so as to prevent locking and skidding when applied suddenly.

an•ti•mat•ter /ánteemátər, ántī–/ *n. Physics* matter composed solely of antiparticles.

an•ti•mo•ny /ántimŏnee/ *n. Chem.* brittle silvery metallic element used esp. in alloys. ¶Symb.: **Sb**.

an•ti•par•ti•cle /ánteepaartikəl, ántī–/ *n. Physics* elementary particle having the same mass as a given particle but opposite electric or magnetic properties.

an•ti•pas•to /ánteepaástŏ/ *n.* (*pl.* **–tos** or **an•ti•pas•ti** /–tee/) assorted appetizers, esp. of marinated vegetables.

an•tip•a•thy /antípəthee/ *n.* (*pl.* **–thies**) strong or deep-seated aversion or dislike.
■ see AVERSION 1.

an•ti•per•spi•rant /ánteepórspirənt, ántī–/ *n.* substance applied to the skin to prevent or reduce perspiration.

an•ti•phon /ántifon/ *n.* **1** hymn sung or recited alternately by two groups. **2** phrase from this. □□ **an•tiph•o•nal** /antífənəl/ *adj. & n.* **an•tiph′o•nal•ly** *adv.*

an•tip•o•des /antípədeez/ *n.pl.* (also **Antipodes**) places diametrically opposite to one another, esp. Australasia in relation to N. America or Europe. □□ **an•tip′o•dal** *adj.* **an•tip•o•de•an** /–déeən/ *adj. & n.*

an•ti•quar•i•an /ántikwáireeən/ • *adj.* of or dealing in antiques or rare books. • *n.* antiquary. □□ **an•ti•quar′i•an•ism** *n.*

an•ti•quar•y /ántikweree/ *n.* (*pl.* **–ies**) student or collector of antiques or antiquities.

an•ti•quat•ed /ántikwaytid/ *adj.* old-fashioned; out of date. See synonym study at OLD.
■ old, outmoded, passé, dated, archaic.

an•tique /antéek/ • *n.* old object, item of furniture, etc., esp. one valued for its beauty or quality. • *adj.* **1** of or existing from an early date. **2** old-fashioned. • *v.tr.* (**an•tiques**, **an•tiqued**, **an•ti•quing**) give an antique appearance to (furniture, etc.) by artificial means.
■ *n.* collectible, bibelot, objet d'art, heirloom, curio, rarity, treasure. • *adj.* **1** old, age-old, ancient, historic(al), timeworn. **2** archaic, antiquated, outmoded.

an•tiq•ui•ty /antíkwitee/ *n.* (*pl.* **–ties**) **1** ancient times, esp. before the Middle Ages. **2** great age. **3** [usu. in *pl.*] relics from ancient times, esp. buildings and works of art.

an•ti-Sem•ite /ánteesémīt, ántī–/ *n.* person prejudiced against Jews. □□ **an•ti-Se•mit•ic** /–simítik/ *adj.* **an•ti-Sem•i•tism** /–sémi-tizəm/ *n.*

an•ti•sep•tic /ántiséptik/ • *adj.* **1** counter-

acting sepsis, esp. by preventing the growth of disease-causing microorganisms. **2** sterile or free from contamination. **3** lacking character. See synonym study at SANITARY. • *n.* antiseptic agent. □□ **an•ti•sep′ti•cal•ly** *adv.*
■ *adj.* **2** see STERILE 3. • *n.* see *disinfectant* (DISINFECT).

an•ti•se•rum /ántiseérəm/ *n.* (*pl.* **an•ti•se•ra** /–rə/) blood serum with a high antibody count.

an•ti•so•cial /ánteesóshəl, ántī–/ *adj.* **1** harmful to the existing social order. **2** not sociable.

an•tith•e•sis /antíthisis/ *n.* (*pl.* **an•tith•e•ses** /–seez/) **1** direct opposite. **2** contrast or opposition between two things. □□ **an•ti•thet•i•cal** /–thót–/ *adj.* **an•ti•thet′i•cal•ly** *adv.* See synonym study at OPPOSITE.

an•ti•tox•in /ánteetóksin/ *n.* antibody that counteracts a toxin. □□ **an•ti•tox′ic** *adj.*

an•ti•trust /ánteetrúst, ántī–/ *adj.* (of a law, etc.) opposed to or controlling trusts or other monopolies.

an•ti•vi•ral /ánteevírəl, ántī–/ *adj.* effective against viruses.

ant•ler /ántlər/ *n.* each of the branched horns of a stag or other (usu. male) deer. □□ **ant•lered** *adj.*

an•to•nym /ántənim/ *n.* word opposite in meaning to another opp. SYNONYM. □□ **an•ton•y•mous** /antóniməs/ *adj.*

a•nus /áynəs/ *n. Anat.* excretory opening at the end of the alimentary canal.

an•vil /ánvil/ *n.* block (usu. of iron) on which metals are shaped.

anx•i•e•ty /angzíətee/ *n.* (*pl.* **–ties**) **1** being anxious. **2** worry or concern. **3** anxious desire.
■ **1, 2** solicitude, uneasiness, nervousness; depression; see also STRESS *n.* 2. **3** longing, yearning, ache; appetite, hunger, thirst.

anx•ious /ángkshəs/ *adj.* **1** mentally troubled. **2** causing or marked by anxiety. **3** earnestly or uneasily wanting or trying. □□ **anx′ious•ly** *adv.* **anx′ious•ness** *n.*
■ **1** uneasy, disquieted, uncertain; solicitous, concerned, worried. **3** desirous, eager, keen, enthusiastic. □□ **anxiousness** see ANXIETY 1, 2.

an•y /énee/ • *adj.* **1** [with *interrog.*, *neg.*, or conditional expressed or implied] **a** one, no matter which, of several. **b** some, no matter how much or many or of what sort. **2** whichever (*any fool knows that*). **3** appreciable or significant. • *pron.* **1** any one. **2** any number or amount. • *adv.* [usu. with *neg.* or *interrog.*] at all; in some degree.

an•y•bod•y /éneebudee, –bodee/ *n. & pron.* **1** person of any kind. **2** person of importance.

an•y•how /éneehow/ *adv.* **1** anyway. **2** in a disorderly manner or state (*does his work anyhow*).

an•y•one /éneewun/ *pron.* anybody.

an•y•thing /éneething/ *pron.* **1** a thing, no matter which. **2** thing of any kind. □ **anything but** not at all.

an•y•way /éneeway/ *adv.* (also *dial.* **an•y•ways** /éneewayz/) **1** in any way or manner.

2 at any rate. 3 in any case. 4 to resume (*anyway, as I was saying*).

■ 2, 3 see *at any rate* (RATE[1]).

an•y•where /éneehwair, –wair/ • *adv.* in or to any place. • *pron.* any place (*anywhere will do*).

A-OK *abbr. colloq.* excellent; in good order.

a•or•ta /ayáwrtə/ *n.* (*pl.* **a•or•tas**) main artery through which oxygenated blood is supplied to the body from the heart. □□ **a•or′tic** *adj.*

a•pace /əpáys/ *adv. literary* swiftly; quickly.

A•pach•e /əpáchee/ *n.* member of a N. American Indian tribe of the southwestern US.

a•part /əpaart/ *adv.* **1** separately; not together. **2** into pieces. **3** to or on one side. **4** to or at a distance. □ **apart from 1** excepting; not considering. **2** in addition to (*apart from roses we grow irises*).

■ **1** individually, singly, alone, independently. **2** to bits, in two. **3** aside, by oneself or itself, at a distance. □ **apart from 1** except (for), separately from, besides.

a•part•heid /əpaart-hayt, –hīt/ *n.* (in S. Africa) racial segregation or discrimination.

a•part•ment /əpaartmənt/ *n.* room or suite of rooms, usu. on one floor, used as a residence. □ **apartment building** (or **house**) building containing a number of separate apartments.

ap•a•thy /ápəthee/ *n.* lack of interest or feeling; indifference. □□ **ap•a•thet•ic** /úpəthétik/ *adj.* **ap•a•thet′i•cal•ly** *adv.*

■ see *indifference* (INDIFFERENT). □□ **apathetic** see UNMOVED 3.

ap•a•to•sau•rus /ápátəsáwrəs/ *n.* = BRONTOSAURUS.

ape /ayp/ • *n.* **1** monkeylike primate characterized by the absence of a tail, e.g., the gorilla, chimpanzee, etc. **2** (in general use) any monkey. **3 a** imitator. **b** apelike person. • *v. tr* imitate; mimic. See synonym study at APE.

■ *n.* **1, 2** monkey, simian, primate. • *v.* see IMITATE 2.

a•pe•ri•tif /əpéritéef/ *n.* alcoholic drink taken before a meal to stimulate the appetite.

ap•er•ture /ápərchər/ *n.* opening; gap.

■ space, cleft, chink, crevice, crack.

a•pex /áypeks/ *n.* (*pl.* **a•pex•es** or **a•pi•ces** /áypiseéz/) **1** highest point. **2** climax. **3** tip or pointed end.

■ **1, 3** see VERTEX[1], TIP n. **1. 2** see ACME.

a•pha•sia /əfáyzhə/ *n. Med* loss of ability to understand or express speech. □□ **a•pha•sic** /–zik/ *adj. & n.*

aph•e•li•on /əféeleeən, ap-héeleeən/ *n.* (*pl.* **a•phe•li•a** /–leeə/) point in an orbit furthest from the sun opp. PERIHELION. ¶Symb.: Q.

a•phid /áyfid, áfid/ *n.* small insect that feeds by sucking sap from leaves, stems, or roots of plants.

aph•o•rism /áfərizəm/ *n.* short pithy maxim. See synonym study at SAYING. □□ **aph′o•rist** *n.* **aph•o•ris′tic** *adj.* **aph•o•ris′ti•cal•ly** *adv. aph•o•rize v.intr.*

■ see MAXIM.

aph•ro•di•si•ac /áfrədeézeeak, –díz–/ *adj.* that arouses sexual desire. • *n.* aphrodisiac drug.

■ *adj.* see EROTIC.

---

a•pi•ar•y /áypee-eree/ *n.* (*pl.* **–ies**) place where bees are kept. □□ **a′pi•a•rist** *n.*

ap•i•cal /áypikəl, áp–/ *adj.* of, at, or forming an apex. □□ **a′pi•cal•ly** *adv.*

a•piece /əpées/ *adv.* for each one; severally; individually.

a•plomb /əplóm, əplúm/ *n.* assurance; self-confidence.

■ see ASSURANCE 4a.

APO *abbr.* Army post office.

a•poc•a•lypse /əpókəlips/ *n.* **1** (**the Apocalypse**) Revelation, the last book of the New Testament. **2** grand or violent event resembling those described in the Apocalypse. □□ **a•poc•a•lyp•tic** /–líptik/ *adj.* **a•poc•a•lyp′ti•cal•ly** *adv.*

A•poc•ry•pha /əpókrifə/ *n.pl.* **1** books included in the Septuagint and Vulgate versions of the Old Testament but not in the Hebrew Bible. **2** (**apocrypha**) writings or reports not considered genuine.

a•poc•ry•phal /əpókrifəl/ *adj.* of doubtful authenticity. See synonym study at SPURIOUS.

ap•o•gee /ápəjee/ *n.* **1** point in an orbit farthest from the earth opp. PERIGEE. **2** point in a celestial body's orbit where it is farthest from the body being orbited. □□ **ap•o•ge′an** *adj.*

a•po•lit•i•cal /áypəlítikəl/ *adj.* not interested in or concerned with politics.

ap•o•lo•get•ic /əpóləjétik/ • *adj.* **1** regretfully acknowledging or excusing an offense or failure. **2** diffident. • *n.* (usu. in *pl.*) reasoned defense, esp. of Christianity. □□ **a•pol•o•get′i•cal•ly** *adv.*

■ *adj.* **1** sorry, contrite, remorseful, penitent. **2** retiring, meek, self-effacing, modest. □□ **apologetically** contritely, remorsefully, penitently; meekly, shyly.

a•pol•o•gist /əpóləjist/ *n.* person who defends something by argument.

a•pol•o•gize /əpólajīz/ *v.intr.* make an apology for an offense or failure; express regret.

■ beg *or* ask pardon.

a•pol•o•gy /əpólajee/ *n.* (*pl.* **–gies**) **1** regretful acknowledgment of an offense or failure. **2** assurance that no offense was intended. **3** explanation or defense. **4** [foll. by *for*] poor or scanty specimen of (*this apology for a letter*).

■ **1** see EXCUSE n. 2. **3** see EXCUSE n. 1, DEFENSE 3. **4** excuse, farce, mockery, travesty.

ap•o•plex•y /ápəpleksee/ *n.* sudden loss of consciousness, voluntary movement, and sensation caused by blockage or rupture of a brain artery; stroke.

a•pos•ta•sy /əpóstəsee/ *n.* (*pl.* **–sies**) **1** renunciation of a belief or faith, esp. religious. **2** abandonment of principles or of a party. **3** instance of apostasy.

a•pos•tate /əpóstayt/ • *n.* person who renounces a former belief, adherence, etc. • *adj.* engaged in apostasy. □□ **ap•o•stat•i•cal** /ápəstátikəl/ *adj.* **a•pos•ta•tize** /–tətīz/ *v.*

a pos•te•ri•o•ri /áy postéeree-áwree, –áwrī/ • *adj.* (of reasoning) inductive; empirical; proceeding from effects to causes. • *adv.* inductively opp. A PRIORI.

a•pos•tle /əpósəl/ *n.* **1 (Apostle) a** any of the twelve men first sent out by Christ to preach the gospel. **b** first successful Christian missionary in a country or to a people. **2** leader or outstanding figure, esp. of a reform movement. □□ **a•pos´tle•ship** *n.*
■ 2 see ADVOCATE *n.* 1.

ap•os•tol•ic /ápəstólik/ *adj.* **1** of or relating to the Apostles. **2** of the pope regarded as the successor of St. Peter.

a•pos•tro•phe /əpóstrəfee/ *n.* punctuation mark used to indicate: **1** omission of letters or numbers (e.g., *can't; Class of '92*). **2** possessive case (e.g., *Harry's book*).

a•poth•e•car•y /əpóthəkeree/ *n.* (*pl.* **–ies**) *archaic* pharmacist.

ap•o•thegm /ápəthem/ = APHORISM. See synonym study at SAYING. □□ **ap•o•theg•mat•ic** /–thegmátik/ *adj.*

a•po•the•o•sis /əpóthee-ōsis/ *n.* (*pl.* **a•poth•e•o•ses** /–seez/) **1** elevation to divine status; deification. **2** glorification of a thing; sublime example.

ap•pall /əpáwl/ *v.tr.* (also **ap•pal**) (**ap•palled, ap•pal•ling**) **1** greatly dismay or horrify. **2** (as **appalling** *adj.*) *colloq.* shocking; unpleasant; bad. □□ **ap•pal´ling•ly** *adv.*
■ 1 shock, outrage; revolt, disgust, sicken, offend. 2 (**appalling**) see ATROCIOUS 1. □□ **appallingly** horrifically, shockingly, outrageously; awfully, horrendously.

ap•pa•rat•us /ápərátəs, –ráytəs/ *n.* **1** equipment for a particular function, esp. scientific or technical. **2** political or other complex organization. See synonym study at TOOL.
■ 1 gear, paraphernalia, machinery; requisites, tools, instruments, utensils, implements; machine, appliance.

ap•par•el /əpárəl/ *n.* clothing; dress. • *v.tr.* (**ap•par•eled, ap•par•el•ing; ap•par´elled, ap•par•el•ling**) clothe.
■ *n.* clothes, garments, outfit. • *v.* see CLOTHE 1.

ap•par•ent /əpárənt/ *adj.* **1** readily visible or perceivable. **2** seeming. See synonym study at OSTENSIBLE. □□ **ap•par´ent•ly** *adv.*
■ 1 evident, plain, clear, obvious; conspicuous, marked. 2 ostensible, outward; see also PROFESSED 2. □□ **apparently** evidently, plainly, clearly, obviously, patently; seemingly, ostensibly, superficially, outwardly; purportedly, allegedly.

ap•pa•ri•tion /ápərishən/ *n.* sudden or dramatic appearance, esp. of a ghost or phantom; visible ghost.
■ see PHANTOM *n.* 1.

ap•peal /əpeél/ • *v.intr.* **1** make an earnest or formal request; plead. **2** be attractive or of interest; be pleasing. **3** [foll. by *to*] resort to for support. **4** *Law* apply (to a higher court) for a reconsideration of a decision. • *n.* **1** act or instance of appealing. **2** formal or urgent request for public support, esp. financial. **3** *Law* referral of a case to a higher court. **4** attractiveness. □□ **ap•peal´er** *n.*
■ *v.* 1 supplicate, solicit, beg, cry; (*appeal to*) entreat, beseech, implore. 2 (*appeal to*) attract, allure, please, charm. 3 see RESORT *v.*

• *n.* **1** entreaty, supplication, solicitation, petition, plea. **4** attraction, allure, (personal) charm, charisma.

ap•peal•ing /əpeéling/ *adj.* attractive; likable. □□ **ap•peal´ing•ly** *adv.*
■ see ATTRACTIVE 1.

ap•pear /əpeér/ *v.intr.* **1** become or be visible. **2** be evident (*a new problem appeared*). **3** seem. **4** present oneself publicly or formally. **5** be published.
■ 1 come forth, put in an appearance, arrive. 2 materialize, surface, emerge, rise, come up. 3 see SEEM. 4 (*appear as*) play, perform *or* act *or* take the part *or* role of. 5 come out; become available.

ap•pear•ance /əpeérəns/ *n.* **1** act or instance of appearing. **2** outward form as perceived (*gives the appearance of trying hard*). **3** semblance. □ **keep up appearances** maintain an impression or pretense. **make** (or **put in**) **an appearance** be present, esp. briefly.
■ 1 arrival, advent, coming, emergence, debut; presence; publication; compare APPEAR. 2 aspect, look(s); air, demeanor; bearing. 3 show, hint, suggestion; illusion; pretense.

ap•pease /əpeéz/ *v.tr.* **1** make calm or quiet, esp. conciliate (a potential aggressor) by making concessions. **2** satisfy (an appetite, scruples). See synonym study at PACIFY. □□ **ap•pease´ment** *n.* **ap•peas´er** *n.*
■ 1 see CALM *v.* 2 meet, comply with, answer, serve; see also FULFILL 2.

ap•pel•lant /əpélənt/ *n.* *Law* person who appeals to a higher court.

ap•pel•late /əpélət/ *adj.* *Law* (esp. of a court) concerned with or dealing with appeals.

ap•pel•la•tion /ápəláyshən/ *n.* *formal* name or title; nomenclature.

ap•pend /əpénd/ *v.tr.* [usu. foll. by *to*] attach, affix, add, esp. to a written document, etc.
■ see TACK¹ *v.* 3.

ap•pend•age /əpéndij/ *n.* something attached; addition.

ap•pen•dec•to•my /ápəndéktəmee/ *n.* (*pl.* **–mies**) surgical removal of the appendix.

ap•pen•di•ci•tis /əpéndisítis/ *n.* inflammation of the appendix.

ap•pen•dix /əpéndiks/ *n.* (*pl.* **ap•pen•di•ces** /–diseez/; **ap•pen•dix•es**) **1** (in full **verm•i•form ap•pen•dix**) *Anat.* small outgrowth of tissue attached to the large intestine. **2** subsidiary matter at the end of a book or document.
■ 2 see ADDITION 2.

ap•per•tain /ápərtáyn/ *v.intr.* [foll. by *to*] **1** relate. **2** belong as a possession or right. **3** be appropriate.

ap•pe•tite /ápitīt/ *n.* **1** natural desire to satisfy bodily needs, esp. for food or sexual activity. **2** inclination or desire. □□ **ap•pe•ti´tive** *adj.*
■ 1 see HUNGER *n.* 2. 2 proclivity, tendency, disposition, bent, preference; craving, hunger, yearning.

ap•pe•tiz•er /ápitīzər/ *n.* small amount, esp. of food served before a meal, to stimulate an appetite.
■ see HORS D'OEUVRE.

ap•pe•tiz•ing /ápitīzing/ *adj.* stimulating an appetite, esp. for food. □□ **ap´pe•tiz•ing•ly** *adv.*

■ see TEMPTING.

ap•plaud /əpláwd/ v. express approval or praise, esp. by clapping.

■ approve, clap, cheer; praise, acclaim, congratulate; commend, laud.

ap•plause /əpláwz/ n. 1 approbation, esp. from an audience, etc., by clapping. 2 emphatic approval.

■ 1 (standing) ovation, plaudit; cheering. 2 acclamation, acclaim, congratulation, commendation.

ap•ple /ápəl/ n. 1 rounded firm edible fruit with a crisp flesh. 2 tree bearing this. □ **apple-pie order** extreme neatness.

ap•ple•jack /ápəljak/ n. brandy distilled from fermented apple cider.

ap•ple•sauce /ápəlsaws/ • n. apples stewed and sometimes blended until pulp remains.

ap•pli•ance /əplíəns/ n. device for a specific task, esp. a household device for washing, drying, cooking, etc. See synonym study at TOOL.

ap•pli•ca•ble /áplikəbəl, əplíka–/ adj. 1 that may be applied. 2 having reference; appropriate. □□ **ap•pli•ca•bil•i•ty** n. **ap'pli•ca•bly** adv.

■ 2 fit, fitting, suitable, proper, relevant. □□ **applicability** see relevance (RELEVANT).

ap•pli•cant /áplikənt/ n. person who applies for something, esp. a job.

■ candidate, job seeker, job-hunter; applier, auditioner.

ap•pli•ca•tion /áplikáyshən/ n. 1 act or instance of applying. 2 formal request, usu. in writing. 3 a relevance. b use. 4 diligence.

■ 1 utilization; administration, rubbing in, putting on. 2 solicitation; appeal, petition. 3 a relevancy, reference, pertinence; bearing. b purpose, function. 4 attention, industriousness, perseverance.

ap•pli•ca•tor /áplikaytər/ n. device for applying a substance to a surface.

ap•plied /əplíd/ adj. (of a subject of study) put to practical use as opposed to being theoretical (cf. PURE adj. 5).

■ see PRACTICAL 1.

ap•pli•qué /áplikáy/ • n. attachment of cut-out fabric patterns to the surface of another fabric to form pictures or patterns. • adj. executed in appliqué. • v.tr. (**ap•pli•qués, ap•pli•quéd, ap•pli•qué•ing**) decorate with appliqué.

ap•ply /əplí/ v. (**–plies, –plied**) 1 intr. formally request. 2 intr. have relevance. 3 tr. a make use of; employ. b operate (apply the hand brake). 4 tr. put or spread on. 5 refl. devote oneself. □□ **ap•pli'er** n.

■ 1 make application, register; audition; (apply for) seek, go after; (apply to) petition, solicit. 2 have bearing, pertain; (apply to) involve, include, suit; bear on, refer to. 3 a use, put to use. b engage, put or turn on, activate. 4 administer, rub in or on; put. 5 dedicate, commit; (apply oneself) focus, concentrate, pay attention; (apply oneself to) work at, do.

ap•point /əpóynt/ v.tr. 1 assign a job or office to (appoint him governor). 2 fix (a time, place, etc.). 3 (as **appointed** adj.) equipped; furnished. □□ **ap•point•ee** /–tée/ n. **ap•point'er** n. **ap•poin'tive** adj.

35 applaud ~ apprehension

■ 1 name, designate; assign, delegate; select, choose. 2 set, settle, determine. 3 (**appointed**) decorated, presented. □□ **appointee** see APPOINTMENT 2b.

ap•point•ment /əpóyntmənt/ n. 1 arrangement to meet at a specific time and place. 2 a job or office, esp. one available for applicants. b person appointed. c act or instance of appointing. 3 [usu. in pl.] a furniture; fittings. b equipment.

■ 1 meeting, rendezvous, engagement; time; assignation, colloq. date. 2 a position, post, situation b appointee. c nomination, election; assignment; choice. 3 (appointments) see FITTING n. 2.

ap•por•tion /əpáwrshən/ v.tr. share out; assign as a share. □□ **ap•por'tion•a•ble** adj.

ap•por'tion•ment n.

ap•po•site /ápəzit/ adj. 1 apt; well chosen 2 well expressed. □□ **ap•pos'ite•ly** adv. **ap'po•site•ness** n.

■ see APPLICABLE 2.

ap•po•si•tion /ápəzíshən/ n. Gram. placing of a word next to another to qualify or explain the first (e.g., William the Conqueror; my friend Sue). □□ **ap•po•si'tion•al** adj.

ap•praise /əpráyz/ v.tr. 1 estimate the value or quality of. 2 (esp. officially) set a price on. □□ **ap•prais'a•ble** adj. **ap•prais'al** n. **ap•prais'er** n.

■ 1 evaluate, assess, value.

ap•pre•cia•ble /əpréeshəbəl/ adj. significant; considerable. See synonym study at TANGIBLE □□ **ap•pre'cia•bly** adv.

■ see CONSIDERABLE 2.

ap•pre•ci•ate /əpréeshee áyt/ v. 1 tr. a esteem highly; value. b be grateful for. 2 tr. understand; recognize. 3 a intr. (of property, etc.) rise in value. b tr. raise in value. See synonym study at ESTEEM. □□ **ap•pre'cia•tive** /–shətiv, –shee-áytiv/ adj. **ap•pre'cia•tive•ly** adv. **ap•pre'cia•tive•ness** n. **ap•pre'ci•a•tor** n. **ap•pre'ci•a•to•ry** /–shee-ətáwree/ adj.

■ 1 a find worthwhile or valuable, cherish, prize, treasure, respect. b be thankful for. 2 comprehend, realize. 3 a increase or gain in value or worth. □□ **appreciative**, **appreciatory** understanding, aware, cognizant; see also THANKFUL. **appreciatively** in recognition or admiration, respectfully, thankfully. see APPRECIATION 1.

ap•pre•ci•a•tion /əpréeshee-áyshən/ n. 1 favorable or grateful recognition. 2 sensitive understanding or judgment. 3 increase in value.

■ 1 gratitude, thankfulness, gratefulness, thanks; acknowledgment. 2 evaluation, assessment, appraisal, comprehension. 3 rise, advance, growth.

ap•pre•hend /áprihénd/ v.tr. 1 seize; arrest. 2 understand; perceive. 3 anticipate with uneasiness or fear.

■ 1 see ARREST v. 1. 2 see PERCEIVE 1, 2. 3 see DREAD v.

ap•pre•hen•sion /áprihénshən/ n. 1 uneasiness; dread. 2 understanding; perception. 3 arrest; capture.

■ **1** see DREAD *n.* **2** see UNDERSTANDING 1, 2.
3 see ARREST *n.* 1.

ap•pre•hen•sive /áprihénsiv/ *adj.* uneasily fearful; dreading. □□ **ap•pre•hen′sive•ly** *adv.* **ap•pre•hen′sive•ness** *n.*

■ see FEARFUL 1.

ap•pren•tice /əpréntis/ • *n.* **1** person learning a trade by being employed in it usu. at low wages. **2** novice. • *v.tr.* engage or bind as an apprentice. □□ **ap•pren′tice•ship** *n.*

■ *n.* trainee, probationer, tyro, learner, beginner. • *v.* article, contract, *hist.* indenture; (*be apprenticed to*) be enrolled *or* employed *or* taken on by. □□ **apprenticeship** training, probation.

ap•prise /əpríz/ *v.tr.* inform. □ **be apprised of** be aware of.

■ see INFORM 1. □ **be apprised of** be conscious *or* cognizant *or* sensible of.

ap•proach /əpróch/ • *v.* **1** *tr.* come near or nearer to (a place or time). **2** *intr.* come near or nearer in space or time (*the hour approaches*). **3** *tr.* make a tentative proposal or suggestion to. **4** *tr.* **a** be similar to. **b** approximate to. **5** *tr.* set about. • *n.* **1** act or means of approaching. **2** approximation. **3** way of dealing with a person or thing.

■ *v.* **1, 2** draw near. **2** advance, creep up on, loom. **3** make advances *or* overtures to, proposition, sound out. **4 a** see COMPARE *v.* 3, 4. **b** near, come close to. **5** see TACKLE *v.* 1. • *n.* **1** access, entrance, passage; entry, advance. **3** method, procedure, technique; attitude, angle.

ap•proach•a•ble /əpróchəbəl/ *adj.* **1** friendly; easy to talk to. **2** able to be approached. □□ **ap•proach•a•bil′i•ty** *n.*

■ **1** see FRIENDLY *adj.* 1. **2** see ACCESSIBLE 2.

ap•pro•ba•tion /áprəbáyshən/ *n.* approval; consent. □□ **ap•pro•ba′tive** *adj.* **ap•pro•ba•to•ry** /əpróbətawree/ *adj.*

ap•pro•pri•ate • *adj.* /əprópreeət/ suitable or proper. • *v.tr.* /əprópreeayt/ **1** take possession of, esp. without authority. **2** devote (money, etc.) to special purposes. □□ **ap•pro′pri•ate•ly** *adv.* **ap•pro′pri•ate•ness** *n.* **ap•pro•pri•a•tion** /–áyshən/ *n.* **ap•pro′pri•a′tor** *n.*

■ *adj.* apt, fitting, fit, right, deserved, becoming. • *v.* **1** take (over), seize, expropriate, usurp; steal, pilfer, filch. **2** set aside *or* apart, assign, earmark. □□ **appropriately** fittingly, aptly, suitably, properly, correctly. **appropriateness** see *fitness* (FIT¹), *relevance* (RELEVANT).

ap•prov•al /əpróōvəl/ *n.* **1** approving. **2** consent; favorable opinion. □ **on approval** (of goods supplied) to be returned if not satisfactory.

■ sanction, approbation, blessing; endorsement, acceptance; license, permission.

ap•prove /əpróōv/ *v.* **1** *tr.* confirm; sanction. **2** *intr.* give or have a favorable opinion. **3** *tr.* commend. □□ **ap•prov′er** *n.* **ap•prov′ing•ly** *adv.*

■ **1, 3** affirm, support, ratify, uphold; allow, countenance, condone, permit, sanction.

SYNONYM STUDY: approve
CERTIFY, COMMEND, ENDORSE, RATIFY, SANCTION. There are a number of ways to show your support for something. The most general way is to **approve** it, a term that covers everything from simple, technical agreement (*to approve the plan*) to enthusiastic support (*she was quick to approve her son's decision to marry*). **Endorse** implies a more public and official expression of support and is used primarily in reference to things that require promotion or publicity (*endorse a political candidate*), while **commend** is to make a formal and usually public statement of approval or congratulation (*he was commended for his heroism*). **Sanction, certify,** and **ratify** imply that approval is not only official but that it makes something legal. To *sanction* is not only to *approve* but to authorize (*school authorities would not sanction the wearing of hats in class*), while *certify* implies conformity with certain standards (*certified to teach in the State of New York*). *Ratify* is usually confined to only the most official and authoritative settings. For example, an employer might *sanction* the idea of hiring a woman to perform a job that only men have performed in the past, and the woman in question might have to *certify* that she possesses the necessary training and qualifications. But to *ratify* a constitutional amendment granting equal rights to women requires a lengthy set of legislative procedures. However, note that **sanction** has another, nearly opposite meaning: it means to threaten a penalty for disobeying a rule or law.

---

approx. *abbr.* **1** approximate. **2** approximately.

ap•prox•i•mate • *adj.* /əpróksimət/ fairly correct; near to the actual. • *v.* /əpróksimayt/ bring or come near (esp. in quality, number, etc.). □□ **ap•prox′i•mate•ly** /–mətlee/ *adv.* **ap•prox•i•ma•tion** /–máyshən/ *n.*

■ *adj.* rough, inexact, loose, imprecise, estimated. • *v.* approach, come close to; resemble; simulate. □□ **approximately** approaching; nearly, almost. **approximation** guess, (rough) estimate.

ap•pur•te•nance /əpórt′nəns/ *n.* [usu. *pl.*] belonging; appendage; accessory.

APR *abbr.* annual or annualized percentage rate.

Apr. *abbr.* April.

ap•ri•cot /áprikot, áypri–/ • *n.* **1 a** small, juicy, soft fruit, of an orange-yellow color. **b** tree bearing it. **2** its color. • *adj.* orange-yellow.

A•pril /áypril/ *n.* fourth month of the year. □ **April Fool's (or Fools') Day** April 1.

a pri•o•ri /áa pree-áwree, áy prī–áwrī/ • *adj.* **1** (of reasoning) deductive; proceeding from causes to effects opp. A POSTERIORI. **2** (of concepts, etc.) logically independent of experience opp. EMPIRICAL. **3** not submitted to critical investigation. • *adv.* **1** deductively. **2** as far as one knows. □□ **a•pri•o•rism** /aypríərizəm/ *n.*

a•pron /áyprən/ *n.* **1** garment covering and protecting the front of a person's clothes.

2 *Theatr.* part of a stage in front of the curtain. **3** paved area of an airfield for maneuvering or loading aircraft. □□ a′**proned** *adj.*

a′**pron•ful** *n.* (*pl.* **-fuls**)

ap•ro•pos /áprəpó/ • *adj.* to the point; appropriate. • *adv.* appropriately. • *prep.* in respect to.

■ *adj.* see APPROPRIATE *adj.* • *prep.* see CONCERNING.

apse /aps/ *n.* large semicircular or polygonal recess, arched or with a domed roof, at the eastern end of a church.

apt /apt/ *adj.* **1** appropriate; suitable. **2** having a tendency. **3** clever; quick to learn. □□ **apt′ly** *adv.* **apt′ness** *n.*

■ **1** see APPROPRIATE *adj.* **2** see PRONE 2. **3** see QUICK *adj.* 4. □□ **aptness** see APTITUDE 2.

apt. *abbr.* **1** apartment. **2** aptitude.

ap•ti•tude /áptitóod, -tyóod/ *n.* **1** natural talent. **2** ability or suitability.

■ **1** gift, ability, facility, flair; tendency, bent, proclivity. **2** fitness, appropriateness, relevance; quick-wittedness, intelligence.

aq•ua /ákwə, aákwə/ *n.* the color aquamarine.

aq•ua•ma•rine /ákwəməréen, aákwə-/ *n.* **1** light bluish green beryl. **2** its color.

aq•ua•plane /ákwəplayn, aákwə-/ • *n.* board for riding on the water, pulled by a speedboat. • *v.intr.* ride on this.

a•quar•i•um /əkwáireeəm/ *n.* (*pl.* **a•quar•i•ums** or **a•quar•i•a** /-reeə/) **1** tank of water with transparent sides for keeping live aquatic plants and animals. **2** building where aquatic plants and animals are kept for study and exhibition.

A•quar•i•us /əkwáireeəs/ *n.* **1** constellation and eleventh sign of the zodiac (the Water Carrier). **2** person born under this sign. □□ **A•quar′i•an** *adj. & n.*

a•quat•ic /əkwátik, əkwótik/ • *adj.* **1** growing or living in water. **2** (of a sport) played in or on water. • *n.* **1** aquatic plant or animal. **2** [in *pl.*] aquatic sports.

aq•ua vi•tae /aákwə víttee, vee-/ *n.* strong alcoholic liquor.

aq•ue•duct /ákwidukt/ *n.* artificial channel for conveying water, esp. in the form of a bridge supported by tall columns across a valley.

a•que•ous /áykweeəs, ák-/ *adj.* of, containing, or like water.

aq•ui•fer /ákwifər/ *n.* Geol. layer of rock or soil able to hold or transmit much water.

aq•ui•line /ákwilīn/ *adj.* **1** of or like an eagle. **2** (of a nose) curved like an eagle's beak.

AR *abbr.* Arkansas (in official postal use).

Ar *symb. Chem.* argon.

-ar[1] /ər/ *suffix* **1** forming adjectives (*angular, linear, nuclear, titular*). **2** forming nouns (*scholar*).

-ar[2] /ər/ *suffix* forming nouns (*pillar*).

-ar[3] /ər/ *suffix* forming nouns (*bursar, exemplar, mortar, vicar*).

-ar[4] /ər/ *suffix* assim. form of -ER[1], -OR[1] (*liar, beggar*).

Ar•ab /árəb/ • *n.* member of a Semitic people inhabiting Saudi Arabia and the Middle East generally. • *adj.* of Arabia or the Arabs (esp. with ethnic reference).

ar•a•besque /árəbésk/ *n.* **1** *Ballet* posture with one leg extended horizontally backward, torso extended forward, and arms outstretched. **2** design of intertwined leaves, scrolls, etc.

A•ra•bi•an /əráybeeən/ • *adj.* of or relating to Arabia (esp. with geographical reference). • *n.* **1** native of Arabia. **2** (in full **Ara′bian horse′**) horse of a breed orig. native to Arabia.

Ar•a•bic /árəbik/ • *n.* Semitic language of the Arabs. • *adj.* of or relating to Arabia (esp. with reference to language or literature). □ **Arabic numeral** any of the numerals 0, 1, 2, 3, 4, 5, 6, 7, 8, and 9 (cf. *Roman numeral*).

ar•a•ble /árəbəl/ *adj.* (of land) suitable for crop production.

a•rach•nid /əráknid/ *n.* any arthropod of a class comprising scorpions, spiders, etc. • *adj.* of or pertaining to the arachnids. □□ a•**rach′ni•dan** *adj. & n.*

Ar•a•ma•ic /árəmáyik/ • *n.* branch of the Semitic languages, esp. the language of Syria, used as a lingua franca in the Near East. • *adj.* of or in Aramaic.

A•rap•a•ho /ərápəhó/ *n.* **1 a** N. American people native to the central plains of Canada and the US. **b** member of this people. **2** the language of this people.

ar•bi•ter /aárbitər/ *n.* arbitrator; judge.

■ see JUDGE *n.* 2, *negotiator* (NEGOTIATE); JUDGE *n.* 3b, AUTHORITY 3c.

ar•bi•trar•y /aárbitreree/ *adj.* **1** random; capricious. **2** despotic. □□ **ar•bi•trar′i•ly** *adv.* **ar•bi•trar′i•ness** *n.*

■ **1** erratic, uncertain, inconsistent, unpredictable, whimsical. **2** absolute, tyrannical, authoritarian, imperious, dictatorial. □□ **arbitrarily** inconsistently, despotically, tyrannically, autocratically; see also *at random* (RANDOM), **arbitrariness** irrationality, randomness; see also TYRANNY.

ar•bi•trate /aárbitrayt/ *v.* decide by or as an arbitrator. □□ **ar•bi•tra•tion** /-tráyshən/ *n.*

■ see DECIDE 2, JUDGE *v.* 3.

ar•bi•tra•tor /aárbitraytər/ *n.* person appointed to settle a dispute; arbiter.

ar•bor /aárbər/ *n.* shady garden alcove enclosed by trees or climbing plants; bower. □□ **ar•bored** *adj.*

ar•bo•re•al /aarbáwreeəl/ *adj.* of or living in trees.

ar•bo•re•tum /aárbəreetəm/ *n.* (*pl.* **ar•bo•re•tums** or **ar•bo•re•ta** /-tə/) botanical garden devoted to trees, shrubs, etc.

ar•bor vi•tae /aárbər vítee/ *n.* any of various evergreen conifers, usu. of pyramidal shape with flattened shoots bearing scalelike leaves.

ar•bu•tus /aarbyóotəs/ *n.* evergreen tree or shrub having white or pink clusters of flowers and strawberrylike berries. ■ **trailing arbutus** mayflower, a creeping plant of the heath family with pink or white flowers.

arc /aark/ • *n.* **1** part of the circumference of a circle or any other curve. **2** *Electr.* luminous discharge between two electrodes. • *v.intr.* (**arced** /aarkt/, **arc•ing** /aárking/) form an arc or move in a curve.

ar•cade /aarkáyd/ *n.* **1** passage with an arched roof. **2** covered walk, esp. lined with shops. **3** *Archit.* series of arches supporting or set along a wall. **4** entertainment establishment with coin-operated games, etc. □□ **ar•cad′ed** *adj.*

ar•cane /aarkáyn/ *adj.* mysterious; secret. □□ **ar•cane′ly** *adv.*

arch[1] /aarch/ • *n.* **1 a** curved structure as an opening or a support for a bridge, roof, floor, etc. **b** arch used in building as an ornament. **2** any arch-shaped curve. • *v.tr.* **1** form an arch. **2** span like an arch.

arch[2] /aarch/ *adj.* self-consciously or affectedly playful or teasing. □□ **arch′ly** *adv.* **arch′ness** *n.*

arch- /aarch/ *comb. form* chief; principal (*archbishop*, *archenemy*).

ar•chae•ol•o•gy /aarkee-ólajee/ *n.* (also **ar•che•ol′o•gy**) study of ancient cultures, esp. through the excavation and analysis of physical remains. □□ **ar•chae•o•log•ic** /-keeəlój-ik/ *adj.* **ar•chae•o•log′i•cal** *adj.* **ar•chae•ol′o•gist** *n.*

ar•cha•ic /aarkáyik/ *adj.* **1 a** antiquated. **b** (of a word, etc.) no longer in ordinary use. **2** primitive. **3** of an early period of culture. See synonym study at OLD. □□ **ar•cha′i•cal•ly** *adv.*

 ■ **1** see ANTIQUATED, OBSOLETE. **2, 3** see ANCIENT *adj.* 1.

ar•cha•ism /aarkeeizəm, -kay-/ *n.* **1** retention or imitation of the old or obsolete, esp. in language or art. **2** *archaic* word or expression. □□ **ar′cha•ist** *n.* **ar•cha•is′tic** *adj.*

arch•an•gel /aarkaynjəl/ *n.* angel of the highest rank.

arch•bish•op /aarchbíshəp/ *n.* bishop of highest rank. □□ **arch•bish′op•ric** *n.*

arch•dea•con /aarchdeékən/ *n.* cleric in various churches ranking below a bishop. □□ **arch•dea′con•ry** *n.* (*pl.* **-ries**) **arch•dea′con•ship** *n.*

arch•di•o•cese /aarchdíəsis, -sees, -seez/ *n.* diocese of an archbishop. □□ **arch•di•oc′e•san** /aarchdíósisən/ *adj.*

arch•duke /aarchdóōk, -dyóōk/ *n.* (*fem.* **arch•duch•ess** /-dúchis/) *hist.* chief duke (esp. as the title of a son of the Emperor of Austria). □□ **arch•du′cal** *adj.* **arch•duch•y** /-dúchee/ *n.* (*pl.* **-ies**)

arch•en•e•my /aarchénəmee/ *n.* (*pl.* **-mies**) **1** chief enemy. **2** the Devil.

ar•che•ol•o•gy var. of ARCHAEOLOGY.

arch•er /aarchər/ *n.* **1** person who shoots with a bow and arrows. **2 (the Archer)** the zodiacal sign or constellation Sagittarius.

arch•er•y /aarchəree/ *n.* shooting with a bow and arrows, esp. as a sport.

ar•che•type /aarkitīp/ *n.* **1** original model; prototype. **2** typical specimen. See synonym study at ARCHETYPE. □□ **ar′che•typ•al** *adj.* **ar•che•typ•i•cal** /-típikəl/ *adj.*

ar•chi•pel•a•go /aarkipéləgō/ *n.* (*pl.* **-gos** or **-goes**) **1** group of islands. **2** sea with many islands.

ar•chi•tect /aarkitekt/ *n.* **1** designer of buildings, ships, etc., supervising their construc-

tion. **2** person who brings about a specified thing (*the architect of the tax reform bill*).

ar•chi•tec•ton•ic /aarkitektónik/ • *adj.* **1** of or relating to architecture or architects. **2** of or relating to the systematization of knowledge. • *n.* [in *pl.*; usu. treated as *sing.*] **1** scientific study of architecture. **2** study of the systematization of knowledge.

ar•chi•tec•ture /aarkitekchər/ *n.* **1** design and construction of buildings. **2** style of a building. **3** buildings collectively. □□ **ar•chi•tec′tur•al** *adj.* **ar•chi•tec′tur•al•ly** *adv.*

ar•chi•trave /aarkitrayv/ *n.* **1** (in classical architecture) main beam resting across the tops of columns. **2** molded frame around a doorway or window. **3** molding around the exterior of an arch.

ar•chive /aarkīv/ • *n.* [usu. in *pl.*] **1** collection of esp. public or corporate documents or records. **2** place where these are kept. • *v.tr.* **1** place or store in an archive. **2** *Computing* transfer (data) to a less frequently used file or less easily accessible medium, e.g., from disk to tape. □□ **ar•chi′val** *adj.* **ar•chi•vist** /aarkivist, aarki-/ *n.*

 ■ *n.* **1** see CHRONICLE *n.* • *v.* **1** see CHRONICLE *v.*

arch•way /aarchway/ *n.* **1** vaulted passage. **2** arched entrance.

Arc•tic /aarktik, aartik/ • *adj.* **1** of the north polar regions. **2** (**arctic**) *colloq.* very cold. • *n.* Arctic regions. □ **Arctic Circle** parallel of latitude 66° 30′ N, forming an imaginary line around this region.

-ard /ərd/ *suffix* **1** forming nouns in depreciatory senses (*drunkard*, *sluggard*). **2** forming nouns in other senses (*Spaniard*, *wizard*).

ar•dent /aard′nt/ *adj.* **1** eager; zealous; fervent; passionate. **2** burning. See synonym study at EAGER. □□ **ar•den•cy** /-d′nsee/ *n.* **ar′dent•ly** *adv.*

 ■ **1** intense, keen, enthusiastic, avid, fierce; earnest, sincere.

ar•dor /aardər/ *n.* zeal; burning enthusiasm; passion.

 ■ desire, fervency, ardency, burning desire; enthusiasm.

ar•du•ous /aarjōōəs/ *adj.* **1** hard to achieve or overcome; difficult; laborious. **2** strenuous. □□ **ar′du•ous•ly** *adv.* **ar′du•ous•ness** *n.*

 ■ hard, tough, energetic, onerous, backbreaking; exhausting.

are *2nd sing. present* & *1st, 2nd, 3rd pl. present* of BE.

a•re•a /áireeə/ *n.* **1** extent or measure of a surface (*3 acres in area*). **2** region. **3** space for a specific purpose. **4** scope or range. □ **area code** three-digit number that identifies telephone service region. □□ **ar′e•al** *adj.*

 ■ **1** limit, compass, size, space. **2** tract, territory, district; section, quarter, precinct. **3** room, ground, zone. **4** margin, sphere; section; subject.

a•re•na /əreénə/ *n.* **1** central part of an amphitheater, etc. **2** scene of conflict; sphere of action or discussion.

aren't /aarnt, aarənt/ *contr.* **1** are not. **2** [in *interrog.*] am not (*aren't I coming too?*).

Ar•gen•tine /aarjənteen, -tīn/ (also **Ar•gen•tin•i•an** /-tineeən/) • *adj.* of or relating to

Argentina in S. America. • *n.* **1** native or citizen of Argentina. **2** person of Argentine descent.

ar•gon /áargon/ *n. Chem.* inert gaseous element. ¶Symb.: **Ar.**

ar•go•sy /áargosee/ *n.* (*pl.* **-sies**) *poet.* large merchant ship.

ar•got /áargō, -gət/ *n.* jargon of a group or class. See synonym study at DIALECT.

ar•gue /áargyōō/ *v.* (**ar•gues, ar•gued, ar•gu•ing**) **1** *intr.* exchange views or opinions heatedly or contentiously. **2** *tr. & intr.* indicate; maintain by reasoning. **3** *tr.* persuade. □□ **ar′gu•a•ble** *adj.* **ar′gu•a•bly** *adv.* **ar′gu•er** *n.*
 ■ **1** bicker, wrangle, quarrel, squabble, altercate. **2** reason, assert, maintain; suggest, show. **3** prevail (up)on, convince; dissuade; see also COAX.

ar•gu•ment /áargyəmənt/ *n.* **1** exchange of views, esp. a contentious or prolonged one. **2** reason advanced; reasoning process.
 ■ **1** debate, dispute, disagreement, quarrel; conflict, fight. **2** (line of) reasoning, case, assertion, contention; defense; explanation, excuse.

ar•gu•men•ta•tion /áargyəməntáyshən/ *n.* **1** methodical reasoning. **2** debate or argument.

ar•gu•men•ta•tive /áargyəméntətiv/ *adj.* fond of arguing. □□ **ar•gu•men′ta•tive•ly** *adv.* **ar•gu•men′ta•tive•ness** *n.*
 ■ quarrelsome, cantankerous, contentious.

a•ri•a /áareeə/ *n. Mus.* solo in an opera, etc.

-arian /áireeən/ *suffix* forming adjectives and nouns meaning '(one) concerned with or believing in' (*agrarian, antiquarian, humanitarian, vegetarian*).

ar•id /árid/ *adj.* **1 a** dry; parched. **b** barren. **2** uninteresting. See synonym study at DRY. □□ **a•rid•i•ty** /əríditee/ *n.* **ar′id•ly** *adv.* **ar′id•ness** *n.*
 ■ **1 a** see DRY *adj.* 1c. **2** see DRY *adj.* 3b.

Ar•ies /áireez/ *n.* **1** constellation and the first sign of the zodiac (the Ram). **2** person born under this sign. □□ **Ar•i•an** /-reeən/ *adj. & n.*

a•right /ərít/ *adv.* rightly.

a•rise /əríz/ *v.intr.* (*past* **a•rose** /əróz/; *past part.* **a•risen** /ərízən/) **1** originate. **2** result. **3** emerge. **4** rise.
 ■ **1** spring up, begin, start (up or off). **2** see DERIVE 2. **3** come up, be brought up, be mentioned, surface. **4** stand up, get to one's feet; wake up, get out of bed, be resurrected, be raised.

ar•is•to•cra•cy /áristókrəsee/ *n.* (*pl.* **-cies**) **1 a** highest class in society; the nobility. **b** the nobility as a ruling class. **2 a** government by a privileged group. **b** nation so governed.

a•ris•to•crat /ərístəkrat, áris-/ *n.* member of the aristocracy. □□ **a•ris•to•crat′ic** *adj.* **a•ris•to•crat′i•cal•ly** *adv.*
 ■ see NOBLE *n.* □□ **aristocratic** see NOBLE *adj.* 1.

ar•ith•me•tic • *n.* /əríthmətik/ **1** science of numbers. **2** use of numbers; computation. • *adj.* /árithmétik/ (also **ar•ith•met′i•cal**

/-métikəl/) of arithmetic. □□ **a•rith•me•ti•cian** /ərìthmətíshən/ *n.*

Ariz. *abbr.* Arizona.

Ark. *abbr.* Arkansas.

ark /aark/ *n.* **1** (usu. **Noah's Ark**) ship used by Noah to save his family and the animals from the biblical flood. **2** *archaic* chest; box.

arm¹ /aarm/ *n.* **1** each of the upper limbs of the human body from shoulder to hand. **2** forelimb or tentacle of an animal. **3 a** sleeve of a garment. **b** arm support of a chair. **c** thing resembling an arm in branching from a main stem (*an arm of the sea*). □ **at arm's length** at a distance. **with open arms** cordially. □□ **arm′ful** *n.* (*pl.* **-fuls**) **arm′less** *adj.*

arm² /aarm/ • *n.* **1** [usu. *pl.*] a weapon. **b** = FIREARM. **2** [*pl.*] military profession. **3** branch of the military. • *v.tr. & refl.* **1** supply with weapons. **2** make (a bomb, etc.) able to explode. □ **take up arms** begin fighting.
 ■ *n.* **1** see HARDWARE 2.

ar•ma•da /aarmaadə/ *n.* fleet of warships, esp. that sent by Spain against England in 1588.

ar•ma•dil•lo /aarmədíllo/ *n.* (*pl.* **-los**) tropical American mammal with a body covered in bony plates.

Ar•ma•ged•don /aarməgéd'n/ *n.* **1** (in the New Testament) last battle between good and evil before the Day of Judgment. **2** any huge bloody battle or struggle.

ar•ma•ment /aarməmənt/ *n.* **1** [often *pl.*] military weapons and equipment. **2** equipping for war. **3** force equipped for war.

ar•ma•ture /aarməchŏŏr/ *n.* **1 a** rotating part of a generator or electric motor. **b** any moving part of an electrical machine in which a voltage is induced by a magnetic field. **2** iron bar placed in contact with the poles of a horseshoe magnet to preserve its power. **3** metal framework on which a clay, etc., sculpture is molded.

arm•chair /aarmchair/ *n.* **1** chair with arm supports. **2** [*attrib.*] theoretical rather than active (*armchair critic*).

Ar•me•ni•an /aarmeeneeən/ • *n.* **1 a** native of Armenia. **b** person of Armenian descent. **2** language of Armenia. • *adj.* of or relating to Armenia, its language, or the Christian Church established there *c.*300.

arm•hole /aarmhōl/ *n.* each of two holes for arms in a garment.

ar•mi•stice /aarmistis/ *n.* truce, esp. permanent. □ **Armistice Day** former name of Veteran's Day.
 ■ see TRUCE.

arm•load /aarmlōd/ • *n.* amount that can be or is carried in one's arms.

ar•moire /aarmwaar/ *n.* tall, upright cupboard or closet.

ar•mor /aarmər/ • *n.* **1** defensive covering, usu. of metal. **2** armored vehicles collectively. • *v.tr.* (usu. as **armored** *adj.*) provide with armor and often with guns.

ar•mor•y /aarmoree/ *n.* (*pl.* **-ies**) **1** arsenal. **2** arms factory.

arm•pit /áarmpit/ *n.* hollow under the arm at the shoulder.

arm•rest /áarmrest/ *n.* = ARM[1] 3b.

ar•my /áarmee/ *n.* (*pl.* **–mies**) **1** organized armed land force. **2** very large number.
- **1** troops, soldiers, armed forces. **2** see HOST[1].

a•ro•ma /ərómə/ *n.* fragrance; distinctive and esp. pleasing smell. See synonym study at SMELL.
- odor, scent, perfume, bouquet.

ar•o•mat•ic /árəmátik/ • *adj.* fragrant; pleasantly pungent. • *n.* aromatic substance. □□ **ar•o•mat′i•cal•ly** *adv.*
- *adj.* spicy, perfumed, sweet-smelling, balmy.

a•rose *past of* ARISE.

a•round /ərównd/ • *adv.* **1** on every side; on all sides. **2** in various places; here and there (*shop around*). **3** *colloq.* **a** in existence; available. **b** near at hand. **4** approximately. **5** in circumference. • *prep.* **1** on or along the circuit of. **2** on every side of. **3** here and there; in or near. **4** about; at a time near to.
- *adv.* **1** all around *or* about, everywhere, in every direction. **2** all about, everywhere, all over, back and forth, up and down, to and fro. **3** see ABOUT *adv.* 2, AVAILABLE 1.
- *prep.* **2** surrounding, encompassing, enveloping, encircling. **4** (at) approximately, (at) roughly, (at) nearly, circa; sometime in *or* during.

a•rouse /ərówz/ *v.tr.* **1** induce (esp. a feeling, etc.). **2** awake from sleep. **3** stir into activity. **4** stimulate sexually. See synonym study at INCITE. □□ **a•rous′a•ble** *adj.* **a•rous′al** *n.* **a•rous′er** *n.*
- **1** initiate, excite, stir up, stimulate, kindle. **2** awaken, raise (up), wake up, rouse. **3** rouse, activate, stir up, animate, enliven. **4** excite, *colloq.* turn on. □□ **arousal** excitement, stimulation, incitement; activation. **arouser** stimulator, inciter, encourager; inspiration.

ar•peg•gio /aarpéjeeō/ *n.* (*pl.* **–gios**) *Mus.* notes of a chord played in succession.

ar•raign /əráyn/ *v.tr.* indict; formally accuse. □□ **ar•raign′ment** *n.*

ar•range /əráynj/ *v.* **1** *tr.* put into order; classify. **2** *tr.* plan or provide for. **3** *tr.* agree about. **4** *intr.* make plans. **5** *tr. Mus.* adapt (a composition) for performance with instruments or voices. □□ **ar•range′a•ble** *adj.* **ar•rang′er** *n.* (esp. in sense 5).
- **1** dispose, array, organize, sort (out). **2, 3** settle, convene, set (up), organize. **5** orchestrate, score, adapt, transcribe. □□ **arranger** organizer, planner; transcriber, adapter.

ar•range•ment /əráynjmənt/ *n.* **1** arranging or being arranged. **2** manner in which a thing is arranged. **3** something arranged. **4** [*pl.*] plans; preparations. **5** *Mus.* composition arranged for performance by different instruments or voices.
- **1–3** classification, ordering, organization, grouping; configuration; order, array. **4** (*arrangements*) measures, program, schedule, itinerary. **5** orchestration, instrumentation, adaptation; version.

ar•rant /árənt/ *attrib.adj.* downright; utter. □□ **ar′rant•ly** *adv.*

ar•ras /árəs/ *n. hist.* rich tapestry or hanging.

ar•ray /əráy/ • *n.* **1** imposing or well-ordered series or display. **2** ordered arrangement, esp. of troops. • *v.tr.* **1** deck; adorn. **2** set in order; marshal (forces).
- *n.* **1** see DISPLAY *n.* 2. **2** see ARRANGEMENT 1–3. • *v.* **1** see DRESS *v.* 1a, 3. **2** see ARRANGE 1.

ar•rears /əréerz/ *n.pl.* amount (esp. of work or debt) still outstanding or uncompleted. □□ **ar•rear′age** *n.*

ar•rest /ərést/ • *v.tr.* **1** lawfully seize (a person, ship, etc.). **2** stop or check (esp. a process or moving thing). **3** attract (a person's attention). • *n.* **1** arresting or being arrested. **2** stoppage. □ **under arrest** in custody. □□ **ar•rest′ing** *adj.* **ar•rest′ing•ly** *adv.*
- *v.* **1** catch, capture, apprehend, detain. **2** halt, stall, retard, slow. **3** draw, catch, get hold of, secure. • *n.* **1** seizure, capture, apprehension, detention. **2** stop, check; slowness; blockage, obstruction; abortion. □ **under arrest** under legal restraint, imprisoned. □□ **arresting** striking, shocking, remarkable, impressive, electrifying.

ar•riv•al /əríval/ *n.* **1 a** arriving. **b** appearance on the scene. **2** person or thing that has arrived.
- **1** coming, advent, entry, entrance. **2** newcomer; immigrant; traveler; tourist.

ar•rive /ərív/ *v.intr.* [often foll. by *at, in*] **1** reach a destination. **2** [foll. by *at*] reach (a conclusion, etc.). **3** *colloq.* become successful. **4** (of a thing) be brought. **5** come.
- **1** come, appear, show, turn up (*arrive at*) make, hit, reach. **2** (*arrive at*) come *or* get to, attain (to). **3** succeed, prosper.

ar•ri•viste /áreevéest/ *n.* **1** ambitious or ruthless person. **2** person who is newly arrived in social status, wealth, etc.

ar•ro•gant /árəgənt/ *adj.* aggressively assertive or presumptuous. □□ **ar′ro•gance** *n.* **ar′ro•gant•ly** *adv.* See synonym study at PRIDE.
- assuming, conceited, egotistical, pompous; haughty, overbearing. □□ **arrogance** self-assertion, impertinence, insolence, presumption, nerve, effrontery.

ar•ro•gate /árəgayt/ *v.tr.* claim (power, responsibility, etc.) without justification. □□ **ar•ro•ga′tion** /–gáyshən/ *n.*

ar•row /árō/ *n.* **1** sharp pointed wooden or metal missile shot from a bow. **2** representation of an arrow indicating a direction.
- **1** see BOLT *n.* 5. **2** see POINTER 1.

ar•row•head /árōhed/ *n.* pointed end of an arrow.

ar•row•root /árōrōōt, –rŏŏt/ *n.* **1** type of nutritious starch. **2** plant yielding this.

ar•se•nal /áarsənəl/ *n.* **1** store of weapons. **2** government establishment for the storage and manufacture of weapons and ammunition. **3** resources regarded collectively.

ar•se•nic • *n.* /áarsənik/ **1** nonscientific name for arsenic trioxide, a poisonous white powder used in weed killers, rat poison, etc. **2** *Chem.* brittle semimetallic element.

¶Symb.: **As.** • adj. /aarsénik/ of or containing arsenic. □□ **ar•sen'i•cal** adj. & n.

41

arson ~ -ary

ar•son /aarsən/ n. act of maliciously setting fire to property. □□ **ar'son•ist** n.

art¹ /aart/ n. **1 a** human creative skill or its application. **b** work exhibiting this. **2 a** [pl.; prec. by *the*] various branches of creative activity concerned with the production of imaginative designs, sounds, or ideas, e.g., painting, music, writing, etc. **b** any one of these branches. **3** creative activity, esp. painting and drawing, resulting in visual representation. **4** human skill as opposed to nature. **5** skill, aptitude, or knack. **6** [pl.; usu. prec. by *the*] = liberal arts.

■ **1** creativity, artistry, inventiveness, imagination; creation. **2, 3** visual art(s). **4** ingenuity, talent, artistry; expertise; craft, technique. **5** talent, craft, faculty.

art² /aart/ archaic or dial. 2nd sing. present of BE.

ar•te•ri•al /aarteereeəl/ adj. **1** of or relating to an artery. **2** (esp. of a road) main, important.

ar•te•rio•scle•ro•sis /aartéereeósklərósis/ n. loss of elasticity and thickening of the walls of the arteries, esp. in old age; hardening of the arteries. □□ **ar•te•ri•o•scle•rot•ic** /-rótik/ adj.

ar•ter•y /aartəree/ n. (pl. **-ies**) **1** any of the blood vessels carrying oxygen-enriched blood from the heart (cf. VEIN). **2** main road or railroad line.

ar•te•sian well /aartéezhən/ n. well in which natural pressure produces a constant supply of water.

art•ful /aartfool/ adj. **1** crafty; deceitful. **2** skillful; clever. □□ **art'ful•ly** adv. **art'ful•ness** n.

■ **1** scheming, wily, sly, cunning, foxy. **2** ingenious, astute, shrewd. □□ **artfully** see astutely (ASTUTE¹). **artfulness** see ART 7, ARTIFICE 2.

ar•thri•tis /aarthrítis/ n. inflammation of a joint or joints. □□ **ar•thrit•ic** /-thrítik/ adj & n.

ar•thro•pod /aarthrəpod/ n. Zool. invertebrate with a segmented body, jointed limbs, and an external skeleton, e.g., spider, crustacean, etc.

ar•ti•choke /aartichōk/ n. **1** plant allied to the thistle. **2** flower head of the artichoke, the bracts of which have edible bases.

ar•ti•cle /aartikəl/ • n. **1** [often in pl.] item or commodity. **2** nonfictional journalistic essay. **3** separate clause or portion of any document. **4** Gram. word (e.g., (a, an, the) preceding a noun and signifying a specific instance (the) or any of several instances (a, an). • v.tr. bind by articles of apprenticeship.

■ n. **1** see THING 2, 3, ITEM 1, 2. **2** see ESSAY n. **1.** • v. see APPRENTICE v.

ar•ti•cu•lar /aartíkyələr/ adj. of or relating to the joints.

ar•tic•u•late • adj. /aartíkyələt/ **1** able to speak fluently and coherently. **2** (of sound or speech) having clearly distinguishable parts. **3** having joints. • v. /aartíkyəlayt/ **1** pronounce clearly and distinctly. **2** express (an idea, etc.) coherently (was quite unable to arti-

culate). **3** connect by joints. □□ **ar•tic'u•late•ly** adv. **ar•tic'u•late•ness** n. **ar•tic•u•la•tion** /-láyshən/ n.

■ adj. **1** see FLUENT¹, COHERENT. **3** articulated, jointed, hinged. • v. **1** see ENUNCIATE 1, PRONOUNCE 1, see EXPRESS 1, 2.

ar•ti•fact /aartifakt/ n. man-made object.

■ product, commodity, item, article, object.

ar•ti•fice /aartifis/ n. **1** clever device; contrivance. **2** cunning. **3** skill; dexterity.

■ **1** stratagem, maneuver, trick, wile, ruse. **2** trickery, craftiness, artfulness, guile, duplicity. **3** see DEXTERITY 1.

ar•ti•fi•cer /aartífisər/ n. **1** inventor. **2** craftsman.

ar•ti•fi•cial /aartifíshəl/ adj. **1** produced by human art or effort; not natural. **2** imitation; fake. **3** affected; insincere. See synonym study at SPURIOUS. □ **artificial insemination** injection of semen into the uterus other than by sexual intercourse. **artificial intelligence** application of computers to areas normally regarded as requiring human intelligence. **artificial respiration** restoration or initiation of breathing by manual or mechanical methods. □□ **ar•ti•fi•ci•al•i•ty** /-sheeálitee/ n. **ar•ti•fi'cial•ly** adv.

■ **1, 2** synthetic, man-made, fabricated; simulated, plastic; made-up, concocted. **3** unnatural, forced, pretended; sham, false, meretricious

ar•til•ler•y /aartíləree/ n. (pl. **-ies**) **1** large-caliber guns used in warfare on land. **2** branch of the armed forces that uses these. □□ **ar•til'ler•y•man** n.

ar•ti•san /aartizən, -sən/ n. skilled manual worker or craftsman.

art•ist /aartist/ n. **1** painter. **2** person who practices any of the arts. **3** professional performer, esp. a singer or dancer. **4** habitual or skillful practitioner of a specified activity. □□ **art'ist•ry** n.

■ **3** see performer (PERFORM). **4** see SPECIALIST. □□ **artistry** see SKILL.

ar•tis•tic /aartístik/ adj. **1** having natural skill in art. **2** made or done with art. **3** of art or artists. □□ **ar•tis'ti•cal•ly** adv.

■ **1** see CREATIVE.

art•less /aartlis/ adj. **1** guileless; ingenuous. **2** not resulting from or displaying art. **3** clumsy. □□ **art'less•ly** adv. **art'less•ness** n.

■ **1** innocent, sincere, true, natural; unassuming, unaffected, naive. **2** unartistic, unimaginative, uncreative, talentless. **3** inept, unskilled, untalented, unskillful, awkward, bungling.

art•work /aartwərk/ n. **1** artistic work, esp. in the visual arts. **2** illustrations in a printed work.

art•y /aartee/ adj. (**art•i•er, art•i•est**) colloq. pretentiously or affectedly artistic. □□ **art'i•ness** n.

a•rum /áirəm/ n. usu. stemless plant with arrow-shaped leaves.

-ary¹ /eree/ suffix **1** forming adjectives (budgetary, contrary, primary). **2** forming nouns (dictionary, fritillary, granary).

-ary² /eree/ *suffix* **1** forming adjectives (*military*).

Ar•y•an /áireeən/ • *n.* **1** member of the peoples speaking any of the Indo-European languages. **2** parent language of this family. **3** *improperly* (in Nazi ideology) a Caucasian not of Jewish descent. • *adj.* of or relating to Aryan or the Aryans.

As *symb. Chem.* arsenic.

as /az, *unstressed* əz/ • *adv. & conj.* [*adv.* as antecedent in main sentence; *conj.* in relative clause expressed or implied] ... to the extent to which ... is or does, etc. (*I am as tall as he, it is not as easy as you think*). • *conj.* [with relative clause expressed or implied] **1** [with antecedent *so*] expressing result or purpose (*came early so as to meet us*). **2** although (*good as it is* = although it is good). **3** [without antecedent adverb] **a** in the manner in which (*do as you like*). **b** in the capacity or form of (*Olivier as Hamlet*). **c** during or at the time that (*fell just as I reached the door*). **d** since (*as you are here, we can talk*). **e** for instance (*composers, as Monteverdi*). • *pron.* [with verb of relative clause expressed or implied] **1** that; who; which (*I had the same trouble as you*). **2** [with sentence as antecedent] a fact that (*he lost, as you know*). □ **as for** with regard to. **as if** (or **though**) as would be the case if (*acts as if she were in charge*). **as it is** (or **as is**) in the existing circumstances or state. **as it were** in a way; to a certain extent. **as well** see WELL¹.

a.s.a.p. *abbr.* (also **ASAP**) as soon as possible.

as•bes•tos /asbéstəs, az–/ *n.* fibrous silicate mineral, esp. used as a heat-resistant or insulating material.

as•cend /əsénd/ *v.* **1** *intr.* move upwards; rise. **2** *intr.* **a** slope upwards. **b** lie along an ascending slope. **3** *tr.* climb; go up. □ **ascend the throne** become king or queen.
■ **2 a** see RISE *v.* 2. **3** see CLIMB *v.* 1.

as•cen•dan•cy /əséndənsee/ *n.* (also **as•cen'den•cy**) superior or dominant condition or position.
■ see SUPREMACY.

as•cen•dant /əséndənt/ *adj.* **1** rising. **2** *Astron.* rising toward the zenith. **3** predominant. □ **in the ascendant** rising; gaining power or authority.
■ *adj.* **3** see PREDOMINANT 1.

as•cen•sion /əsénshən/ *n.* **1** ascent. **2** (**Ascension**) ascent of Christ into heaven. □□ **as•cen'sion•al** *adj.*

as•cent /əsént/ *n.* **1** ascending; rising; progressing. **2** upward slope.

as•cer•tain /ásərtáyn/ *v.tr.* find out as a definite fact. □□ **as•cer•tain'a•ble** *adj.* **as•cer•tain'ment** *n.*
■ see DETERMINE 1.

as•cet•ic /əsétik/ • *n.* person who practices severe self-discipline and abstains from all forms of pleasure, esp. for religious or spiritual reasons. See synonym study at SEVERE. • *adj.* relating to or characteristic of ascetics or asceticism; abstaining from pleasure. □□ **as•cet'i•cal•ly** *adv.* **as•cet•i•cism** /–ti-sizəm/ *n.*

■ *adj.* see SPARTAN *adj.*

ASCII /áskee/ *abbr. Computing* American Standard Code for Information Interchange.

a•scor•bic ac•id /əskáwrbik/ *n.* vitamin C.

as•cot /áskot, –kət/ *n.* scarflike item of neckwear with broad ends worn looped to lie flat one over the other against the chest.

as•cribe /əskríb/ *v.tr.* [usu. foll. by *to*] **1** attribute or impute. **2** regard as belonging. □□ **a•scrib'a•ble** *adj.* **as•crip•tion** /–kríp–/ *n.*
■ see ATTRIBUTE *v.*

a•sep•sis /aysépsis/ *n.* **1** absence of harmful microorganisms. **2** method of achieving asepsis in surgery. □□ **a•sep'tic** *adj.*

a•sex•u•al /aysékshōoəl/ *adj. Biol.* **1** without sex or sexual organs. **2** (of reproduction) not involving the fusion of gametes. □□ **a•sex•u•al•i•ty** /–shōoálitee/ *n.* **a•sex'u•al•ly** *adv.*

ash¹ /ash/ *n.* **1** [often in *pl.*] powdery residue left after burning. **2** [*pl.*] remains of the human body after cremation. **3** grayish color. □ **Ash Wednesday** first day of Lent.

ash² /ash/ *n.* **1** tree with silvery-gray bark. **2** its hard, pale wood.

a•shamed /əsháymd/ *adj.* **1** embarrassed by shame. **2** hesitant; reluctant (but usu. not actually refusing or declining) (*ashamed to admit I was wrong*). □□ **a•sham•ed•ly** /–midlee/ *adv.*
■ **1** conscience-stricken, remorseful, abashed, disconcerted, humiliated, mortified. **2** afraid, sorry.

ash•en /áshən/ *adj.* like ashes; esp. gray or pale. See synonym study at PALE.

a•shore /əsháwr/ *adv.* toward or on the shore or land.

ash•ram /áashrəm/ *n. Ind.* place of religious retreat for Hindus; a hermitage.

ash•tray /áshtray/ *n.* small receptacle for cigarette ashes, butts, etc.

ash•y /áshee/ *adj.* (**ash•i•er, ash•i•est**) **1** = ASHEN. **2** covered with ashes.

A•sian /áyzhən, –shən/ • *n.* **1** native of Asia. **2** person of Asian descent. • *adj.* of or relating to Asia or its people, customs, or languages.

A•si•at•ic /áyzheeátik, –shee–, –zee–/ • *n.* offens. an Asian. • *adj.* Asian.

a•side /əsíd/ • *adv.* **1** to or on one side; away. **2** out of consideration [placed after noun]: (*joking aside*). • *n.* **1** words spoken in a play for the audience to hear, but supposed not to be heard by the other characters. **2** incidental remark.
■ *adv.* see APART 3.

as•i•nine /ásinin/ *adj.* like an ass, esp. stubborn or stupid. □□ **as•i•nin•i•ty** /–nínitee/ *n.*
■ see STUPID *adj.* 1, 2.

ask /ask/ *v.* **1** *tr.* call for an answer to or about. **2** *tr.* seek to obtain from another person. **3** *tr.* invite; request the company of. **4** *intr.* **a** seek to obtain, meet, or be directed to (*ask for a donation, asking for you*). **b** bring upon oneself (*they were asking for trouble*). □ **ask after** inquire about (esp. a person). □□ **ask'er** *n.*
■ **1** question, interrogate, quiz; inquire of. **2** request, seek, demand, plead for; entreat, implore. **3** summon. **4** (*ask for*) a request,

demand, seek, beg. **b** invite, attract, provoke.

a•skance /əskáns/ *adv.* (also **a•skant** /–skánt/) sideways or squinting. □ **look askance** at regard with suspicion.

a•skew /əskyoō/ • *adv.* obliquely; awry. • *adj.* oblique; awry.
  ■ *adv.* aslant, crookedly. • *adj.* bent, crooked, lopsided.

ASL • *abbr.* American Sign Language.

a•slant /əslánt/ • *adv.* obliquely or at a slant. • *prep.* obliquely across (*lay aslant the path*).

a•sleep /əsleép/ *adj. & adv.* **1 a** in or into a state of sleep. **b** inactive; inattentive. **2** (of a limb, etc.) numb. **3** *euphem.* dead.
  ■ **2** see NUMB *adj*

asp /asp/ *n.* small venomous snake of North Africa and southern Europe.

as•par•a•gus /əspárəgəs/ *n.* **1** plant of the lily family. **2** edible young shoots of this.

as•par•tame /əspáartaym, áspər–/ • *n.* a very sweet, low-calorie substance used as a sweetener instead of sugar or saccharin.

ASPCA • *abbr.* American Society for the Prevention of Cruelty to Animals.

as•pect /áspekt/ *n.* **1 a** particular component or feature of a matter (*one aspect of the problem*). **b** particular way in which a matter may be considered. **2** appearance.
  ■ **1 a** part, constituent, ingredient, attribute, characteristic. **b** viewpoint, position, approach; interpretation. **2** look; complexion, face; bearing.

as•pen /áspən/ *n.* poplar tree with especially tremulous leaves.

as•per•i•ty /əspéritee/ *n.* (*pl.* **–ies**) **1** harshness or sharpness of temper or tone. **2** roughness. **3** rough excrescence.
  ■ **1** see *bitterness* (BITTER).

as•per•sion /əspérzhən/ *n.* slander; false insinuation.
  ■ libel, calumny, defamation.

as•phalt /ásfalt/ • *n.* **1** dark bituminous pitch occurring naturally or made from petroleum. **2** mixture of this with sand, gravel, etc., for surfacing roads, etc. • *v.tr.* surface with asphalt. □□ **as•phalt•er** *n.* **as•phal•tic** /–fáltik/ *adj.*

as•pho•del /ásfədel/ *n.* plant of the lily family.

as•phyx•i•ate /əsfikseeayt/ *v.tr.* suffocate. □□ **as•phyx•i•a•tion** /–áyshən/ *n.* **as•phyx•i•a•tor** *n.*
  ■ see SMOTHER *v.* 1.

as•pic /áspik/ *n.* savory meat jelly used as a garnish or to contain meat, eggs, etc.

as•pir•ant /áspirənt, əspíerənt/ • *adj.* aspiring. • *n.* person who aspires.

as•pir•ate /áspirət/ • *adj.* pronounced with an exhalation of breath with the sound of *h*. • *n.* **1** consonant pronounced in this way. **2** sound of *h*. • *v.* (also /áspiráyt/) **1 a** *tr.* pronounce with a breath. **b** *intr.* make the sound of *h*. **2** *tr.* draw (fluid) by suction from a vessel or cavity. **3** *tr.* draw (air, fluid, etc.) into the lungs, as by breathing.

as•pi•ra•tion /áspiráyshən/ *n.* **1** strong desire; ambition. **2** drawing breath. **3** aspirating.
  ■ **1** aim, goal, objective, end, purpose; longing.

as•pi•ra•tor /áspiraytər/ *n.* apparatus for aspirating fluid.

as•pire /əspír/ *v.intr.* have ambition or strong desire.
  ■ hope, long, wish; (*aspire to*) dream of, go after.

as•pi•rin /ásprin/ *n.* (*pl.* same or **as•pir•ins**) **1** white powder, acetylsalicylic acid, used to relieve pain and reduce fever. **2** tablet of this.

ass /as/ *n.* **1 a** four-legged long-eared mammal related to the horse. **b** donkey. **2** stupid person.
  ■ **2** see DOLT.

as•sail /əsáyl/ *v.tr.* attack physically or verbally. See synonym study at ATTACK. □□ **as•sail•a•ble** *adj.* **as•sail•ant** *n.*
  ■ see ATTACK *v.* 1, 4. □□ **assailant** assaulter, mugger.

as•sas•sin /əsásin/ *n.* killer, esp. of a political or religious leader.
  ■ see KILLER 1.

as•sas•si•nate /əsásinayt/ *v.tr.* kill for political or religious motives. See synonym study at KILL. □□ **as•sas•si•na•tion** /–náyshən/ *n.* **as•sas•si•na•tor** *n.*
  ■ see KILL *v.* 1.

as•sault /əsáwlt/ • *n.* **1** violent physical or verbal attack. **2 a** *Law* act that threatens physical harm. **b** *euphem.* rape. • *v.tr.* **1** make an assault on. **2** *euphem.* rape. See synonym study at ATTACK. □□ **as•sault•er** *n.*
  ■ *n.* **1** beating, mugging; onslaught, charge, offensive, blitzkrieg. **2 b** sexual assault, violation, molestation. • *v.* **1** attack, assail, storm, come at, charge; beat (up), batter, harm. **2** violate, molest.

as•say /əsáy, ásay/ • *n.* testing of a metal or ore to determine its ingredients and quality. • *v.* make an assay of (a metal or ore). □□ **as•say•er** *n.*

as•sem•blage /əsémblij/ *n.* **1** bringing or coming together. **2** assembled group. **3** work of art made by grouping found or unrelated objects.

as•sem•ble /əsémbəl/ *v.* **1** *tr. & intr.* gather together; collect. **2** *tr.* arrange in order. **3** *tr.* esp. *Mech.* fit together the parts of. See synonym study at GATHER. □□ **as•sem•bler** *n.*
  ■ **1** convene, meet, muster, marshal; congregate; accumulate, amass. **2** see ARRANGE 1. **3** construct, put together, set up.

as•sem•bly /əsémblee/ *n.* (*pl.* **–blies**) **1** assembling. **2 a** group of persons gathered together, esp. as a deliberative body. **b** gathering of the entire membership of a school. **3** assembling of a machine or structure or its parts.
  ■ **1, 2a** gathering, group, meeting; convocation, council, convention. **3** construction, fitting or joining or piecing together.

as•sent /əsént/ • *v.intr.* [usu. foll. by *to*] express agreement. **2** consent. • *n.* **1** mental or inward acceptance or agreement. **2** consent or sanction, esp. official. □□ **as•sen•tor** *n.* (also **as•sent•er**).
  ■ *v.* **1** see AGREE 1. **2** see AGREE 2. • *n.* **1** see CONSENT *n.* **2** see CONSENT *n.*, SANCTION *n.* 1.

as•sert /əsɔ́rt/ *v.* **1** *tr.* declare; state clearly. **2** *refl.* insist on one's rights. **3** *tr.* vindicate a claim to. □□ **as•ser′tor** *n.*
  ■ **1** see DECLARE 3.

as•ser•tion /əsɔ́rshən/ *n.* **1** declaration; forthright statement. **2** act or instance of asserting.
  ■ claim, affirmation, contention.

as•ser•tive /əsɔ́rtiv/ *adj.* tending to assert oneself; forthright. □□ **as•ser′tive•ly** *adv.* **as•ser′tive•ness** *n.*
  ■ declaratory, affirmative; definite, confident, firm; aggressive, insistent, forceful. □□ **assertively** forcefully, boldly, firmly, emphatically; dogmatically, domineeringly; see also *aggressively* (AGGRESSIVE). **assertiveness** forcefulness, boldness, firmness.

as•sess /əsés/ *v.tr.* **1** estimate the size or quality of. **2** estimate the value of (a property) for taxation. □□ **as•sess′a•ble** *adj.* **as•sess′ment** *n.* **as•ses′sor** *n.*
  ■ **1** see ESTIMATE *v.* 1, 2. □□ **assessment** see MEASUREMENT 1, REVIEW *n.* 1.

as•set /áset/ *n.* **1 a** useful or valuable quality. **b** person or thing possessing such a quality. **2** property and possessions.
  ■ **1 a** talent, strength, advantage, resource, benefit; see also PLUS *n.* 3. **2** (*assets*) resources, holdings.

as•sev•er•ate /əsévərayt/ *v.tr.* declare solemnly. □□ **as•sev•er•a•tion** /-ráyshən/ *n.* **as•sev•er•a•tive** /-rətiv/ *adj.*
  ■ see ATTEST 1, 2.

as•sid•u•ous /əsíjŏŏəs/ *adj.* **1** persevering; hardworking. **2** attending closely. See synonym study at BUSY. □□ **as•sid′u•ous•ly** *adv.* **as•sid′u•ous•ness** *n.*
  ■ see DILIGENT. □□ **assiduousness** see APPLICATION 4.

as•sign /əsín/ • *v.tr.* **1 a** allot as a share or responsibility. **b** appoint to a position, task, etc. **2** fix (a time, place, etc.) for a specific purpose. **3** ascribe or refer to. • *n.* person to whom property or rights are legally transferred. □□ **as•sign′a•ble** *adj.* **as•sign′er** *n.*
  ■ *v.* **1 a** allocate, apportion, consign, distribute. **b** designate, order; name. **2** fix (on), set apart or aside; choose, select. **3** attribute, accredit.

as•sig•na•tion /ásignáyshən/ *n.* appointment to meet, esp. in secret.

as•sign•ee /ásineé/ *n. Law* person assigned a property, duty, etc.

as•sign•ment /əsínmənt/ *n.* **1** task or mission. **2** assigning or being assigned.
  ■ **1** obligation, responsibility, chore; lesson, homework. **2** allotment, allocation; appointment, designation.

as•sim•i•late /əsímilayt/ *v.* **1** *tr.* **a** absorb and digest (food, etc.) into the body. **b** absorb (information, etc.) into the mind. **2** *tr.* make like; cause to resemble. **3** *intr.* be absorbed into the body, mind, or a larger group. □□ **as•sim•i•la•tion** /-láyshən/ *n.* **as•sim′i•la•tive** *adj.* **as•sim′i•la•tor** *n.*
  ■ **1 b** see DIGEST *v.* 2.

as•sist /əsíst/ • *v.tr.* help. • *n.* act of helping. □□ **as•sis′tance** *n.* **as•sist′er** *n.*

■ *v.* aid, support, succor; further, promote, abet. □□ **assistance** help, aid, support, backing.

as•sis•tant /əsístənt/ *n.* **1** helper. **2** person who assists, esp. as a subordinate.
  ■ **1** mate, aide, right-hand man *or* woman; see also ACCOMPLICE. **2** deputy, auxiliary.

as•sist•ed liv•ing • *n.* housing arrangement, usu. for the elderly, offering private apartments and services such as meals, social activities, and nursing assistance.

assn. *abbr.* association.

Assoc. *abbr.* (as part of a title) Association.

as•so•ci•ate • *v.* /əsŏsheeayt, -seet/ **1** *tr.* connect in the mind. **2** *tr.* join or combine. **3** *refl.* declare oneself in agreement (*want to associate ourselves with the plan*). **4** *intr.* combine for a common purpose. **5** *intr.* meet frequently or have dealings. • *n.* /əsŏsheeət, -seet/ **1** business partner or colleague. **2** friend or companion. **3** subordinate member of a body, institute, etc. • *adj.* /əsŏshiət, əsŏsee-/ **1** joined or allied. **2** of less than full status. □□ **as•so′ci•ate•ship** *n.* **as•so•ci•a•tive** /əsŏsheeətiv, -seet-/ *adj.*
  ■ *v.* **1** link; affiliate, relate. **2** ally, unite. **3** (*associate oneself*) ally, align, affiliate. **4** unite, join (up *or* together), join ranks *or* forces. **5** (*associate with*) see, be seen with, socialize *or* fraternize with. • *n.* **1** fellow worker, workmate, coworker; see also ACCOMPLICE. **2** comrade, mate. **3** junior member. • *adj.* **1** affiliated, associated; related, connected. **2** subsidiary, secondary; deputy, auxiliary.

as•so•ci•a•tion /əsŏseeáyshən/ *n.* **1** group organized for a joint purpose; society. **2** associating. **3** fellowship. **4** mental connection between ideas.
  ■ **1** organization, confederation, union. **2** combination, alliance, marriage, union. **3** companionship, intimacy, friendship; affiliation, cooperation. **4** interconnection, link.

as•so•nance /ásənəns/ *n.* resemblance of sound (often of vowels) between two syllables in nearby words, e.g., *saw, caught; cold, culled.* □□ **as′so•nant** *adj.* **as•so•nate** /-nayt/ *v.intr.*

as•sort /əsɔ́wrt/ *v.* **1** *tr.* classify or arrange in groups. **2** *intr.* suit; harmonize with.

as•sort•ed /əsɔ́wrtid/ *adj.* **1** of various kinds put together. **2** sorted into groups. **3** matched.
  ■ **1** see MISCELLANEOUS.

as•sort•ment /əsɔ́wrtmənt/ *n.* diverse group or mixture.
  ■ collection, miscellany, jumble, medley.

Asst. *abbr.* Assistant.

as•suage /əswáyj/ *v.tr.* **1** calm or soothe. **2** appease (an appetite). See synonym study at ALLEVIATE. □□ **as•suage′ment** *n.* **as•suag′er** *n.*
  ■ **1** see STILL[1] *v.* **2** see SLAKE.

as•sume /əsŏŏm/ *v.tr.* **1** take or accept as being true. **2** simulate or pretend (ignorance, etc.). **3** undertake (an office or duty). **4** take or put on (an aspect, attribute, etc.). □□ **as•sum′a•ble** *adj.* **as•sum′ed•ly** *adv.*
  ■ **1** presume, suppose, accept; surmise, guess. **2** feign, affect, fake; profess. **3** take

control of, accept; arrogate, claim. **4** don, adopt, acquire.

as•sumed /əsōōmd/ *adj.* **1** false; adopted. **2** supposed; accepted.

■ **1** sham, feigned, affected, counterfeit, spurious, bogus, fake; made-up. **2** presumed, expected, presupposed; hypothetical, theoretical.

as•sum•ing /əsōōming/ *adj.* arrogant; presumptuous.

as•sump•tion /əsúmpshən/ *n.* **1** assuming. **2** accepting without proof. **3** arrogance. **4** (**Assumption**) reception of the Virgin Mary bodily into heaven.

■ **1, 2** see PRESUMPTION 2. **3** see PRESUMPTION 1.

as•sur•ance /əshŏŏrəns/ *n.* **1** positive declaration. **2** solemn promise or guarantee. **3** certainty. **a** self-confidence. **b** impudence.

■ **1** see DECLARATION 2. **2** pledge, word (of honor), oath. **3** sureness, positiveness, certitude, conviction. **4 a** self-reliance, confidence; conviction. **b** audacity, presumption, boldness.

as•sure /əshŏŏr/ *v.tr.* **1 a** convince. **b** confirm confidently. **2 a** make certain of. **b** make safe (against overthrow, etc.). **3** (as **assured** *adj.*) **a** guaranteed. **b** self-confident. □□ **as•sur'a•ble** *adj.* **as•sur'er** *n.*

■ **1 a** persuade, reassure. **b** promise, reassure; assert. **2** ensure, confirm, secure; see also PROTECT. **3** (**assured**) **a** warranted, certain, sure. **b** see CONFIDENT *adj.* □□ **as•surable** insurable, warrantable. **assurer** in sures, guarantor.

as•ta•tine /ástəteen, -tin/ *n. Chem.* radioactive element. ¶Symb.: **At**.

as•ter /ástər/ *n.* plant with bright daisylike flowers.

as•ter•isk /ástərisk/ • *n.* symbol (*) used in printing and writing to mark words, etc., for reference, to stand for omitted matter, etc. • *v.tr.* mark with an asterisk.

a•stern /əstórn/ *adv. Naut. & Aeron.* **1** aft; away to the rear. **2** backward.

as•ter•oid /ástəroyd/ *n.* any of the small celestial bodies revolving around the sun, mainly between the orbits of Mars and Jupiter. □□ **as•ter•oi'dal** /ástəróyd'l/ *adj.*

asth•ma /ázmə, ás-/ *n.* usu. allergic respiratory disorder, often with paroxysms of difficult breathing. □□ **asth•mat•ic** /azmátik, as-/ *adj. & n.*

a•stig•ma•tism /əstigmətizəm/ *n.* defect in the eye or lens resulting in distorted images. □□ **as•tig•mat•ic** /ástigmátik/ *adj.*

a•stir /əstór/ *predic.adj. & adv.* **1** in motion. **2** out of bed.

as•ton•ish /əstónish/ *v.tr.* amaze; surprise greatly. □□ **as•ton'ish•ing** *adj.* **ast•on'ish•ing•ly** *adv.* **as•ton'ish•ment** *n.*

■ shock, astound, stun, stagger. □□ **astonishing** see *amazing* (AMAZE). **astonishingly** see *amazingly* (AMAZE). **astonishment** amazement, surprise, shock, awe.

as•tound /əstównd/ *v.tr.* shock with alarm or surprise; amaze. □□ **as•tound'ing** *adj.* **as•tound'ing•ly** *adv.*

■ astonish, stun, stagger, take aback.

□□ **astounding** see *amazing* (AMAZE). **astoundingly** see *amazingly* (AMAZE).

a•strad•dle /əstrád'l/ *adv. & predic.adj.* in a straddling position.

as•tra•khan /ástrəkán/ *n.* dark curly fleece of young lambs from Astrakhan.

as•tral /ástrəl/ *adj.* **1** of the stars. **2** starry.

a•stray /əstráy/ *adv. & predic.adj.* **1** in or into error or sin (esp. *lead astray*). **2** out of the right way.

■ **1** (*lead astray*) lead on, mislead, misguide; fool, decoy, hoodwink.

a•stride /əstríd/ • *adv.* **1** with a leg on each side. **2** with legs apart. • *prep.* with a leg on each side of; extending across.

as•trin•gent /əstrínjənt/ • *adj.* **1** causing the contraction of body tissues. **2** checking bleeding. **3** severe; austere. • *n.* astringent substance or drug. □□ **as•trin•gen•cy** /-jənsee/ *n.* **as•trin'gent•ly** *adv.*

■ *adj.* **3** styptic.

astro- /ástrō/ *comb. form* **1** relating to the stars or celestial bodies. **2** relating to outer space.

as•tro•labe /ástrəlayb/ *n.* instrument formerly used to measure the altitudes of celestial bodies.

as•trol•o•gy /əstróləjee/ *n.* study of the movements and relative positions of celestial bodies interpreted as an influence on human affairs. □□ **as•trol'o•ger** *n.* **as•tro•log•i•cal** /ástrəlójikəl/ *adj.* **as•trol'o•gist** *n.*

as•tro•naut /ástrənawt/ *n.* person trained to travel in a spacecraft. □□ **as•tro•nau'ti•cal** *adj.* **as•tro•nau'tics** *n.*

as•tro•nom•i•cal /ástrənómikəl/ *adj.* (also **as•tro•nom'ic**) **1** of astronomy. **2** extremely large. □ **astronomical unit** unit of measurement equal to the mean distance from the center of the earth to the center of the sun, 1.496×10^{11} meters or 92.9 million miles. □□ **as•tro•nom'i•cal•ly** *adv.*

■ **2** see INFINITE *adj.* 1, 2.

as•tron•o•my /əstrónəmee/ *n.* scientific study of celestial bodies. □□ **as•tron'o•mer** *n.*

as•tro•phys•ics /ástrōfiziks/ *n.* branch of astronomy concerned with the physics and chemistry of celestial bodies. □□ **as•tro•phys'i•cal** *adj.* **as•tro•phys'i•cist** /-zisist/ *n.*

as•tute /əstōōt, əstyōōt/ *adj.* **1** shrewd; sagacious. **2** crafty. See synonym study at KEEN. □□ **as•tute'ly** *adv.* **as•tute'ness** *n.*

■ **1** sharp, keen, perceptive, observant. **2** shrewd, subtle, clever, ingenious, adroit, wily. □□ **astutely** perceptively, insightfully; shrewdly; artfully; craftily. **astuteness** shrewdness, subtleness, artfulness.

a•sun•der /əsúndər/ *adv. literary* apart.

a•sy•lum /əsîləm/ *n.* **1** sanctuary; protection, esp. for those pursued by the law. **2** *hist.* institution for the mentally ill or destitute.

■ **1** see SANCTUARY 3a.

a•sym•me•try /aysímitree/ *n.* lack of symmetry. □□ **a•sym•met•ric** /–métrik/ *adj.* **a•sym•met'ri•cal** *adj.* **a•sym•met'ri•cal•ly** *adv.*

■ see DISPROPORTION.

At *symb. Chem.* astatine.

at /at, *unstressed* ət/ *prep.* **1** expressing position (*at the corner*). **2** expressing a time (*at dawn*). **3** expressing a point in a scale (*at his best*). **4** expressing engagement in a state or activity (*at war*). **5** expressing a value or rate (*sell at $10 each*). **6 a** with or with reference to (*at a disadvantage, annoyed at losing*). **b** by means of (*starts at a touch*). **7** expressing: **a** motion toward (*arrived at the station*). **b** aim toward or pursuit of (*aim at the target, work at a solution*).

at•ax•i•a /ətákseeə/ *n.* (also **a•tax•y** /–see/) *Med.* loss of full control of bodily movements. □□ **a•tax′ic** *adj.*

ate *past of* EAT.

-ate[1] /ət, ayt/ *suffix* **1** forming nouns denoting status or office (*doctorate, episcopate*). **2** forming nouns denoting state or function (*curate, mandate*).

-ate[2] /ayt/ *suffix* forming verbs (*associate, duplicate, hyphenate*).

a•te•lier /átəlyáy/ *n.* workshop or artist's studio.

a•the•ism /áytheeizəm/ *n.* belief that God does not exist. □□ **a′the•ist** *n.* **a•the•is′tic** *adj.* **a•the•is′ti•cal** *adj.*

ath•er•o•scle•ro•sis /áthərösklərósis/ *n.* degeneration of the arteries because of a buildup of fatty deposits. □□ **ath•er•o•scle•rot•ic** /–rótik/ *adj.*

ath•lete /áthleet/ *n.* skilled performer in sports and physical activities. □ **athlete's foot** fungal foot condition.

ath•let•ic /athlétik/ *adj.* **1** of athletes or athletics. **2** muscular or physically powerful. □□ **ath•let′i•cal•ly** *adv.* **ath•let•i•cism** /–tisizəm/ *n.*

ath•let•ics /athlétiks/ *n.pl.* [usu. treated as *sing.*] **1** physical exercises, games, sports, etc. **2** practice of these.

-atic /átik/ *suffix* forming adjectives and nouns (*aquatic, fanatic, idiomatic*).

-ation /áyshən/ *suffix* **1** forming nouns denoting an action or an instance of it (*alteration*). **2** forming nouns denoting a result or product of action (*plantation, starvation*) (see also see also –FICATION).

-ative /ətiv, aytiv/ *suffix* forming adjectives denoting a characteristic or propensity (*authoritative, imitative, talkative*).

At•lan•tic /ətlántik/ • *n.* ocean separating the Americas from Europe and Africa. • *adj.* of or adjoining the Atlantic.

at•las /átləs/ *n.* book of maps or charts.

ATM *abbr.* automatic teller machine.

at•mo•sphere /átməsfeer/ *n.* **1 a** gases surrounding the earth, any other planet, or any substance. **b** air in any particular place. **2 a** pervading tone or mood of a place or situation. **b** feelings or emotions evoked by a work of art, a piece of music, etc. **3** *Physics* unit of pressure equal to mean atmospheric pressure at sea level, 101,325 pascals or 14.7 pounds per square inch. ¶Abbr.: **atm.** □□ **at•mos•pher•ic** /–férik, –feer–/ *adj.* **at•mos′pher′i•cal** *adj.* **at•mos•pher′i•cal•ly** *adv.* ■ **1** heaven(s), sky, ether. **2 a** air, ambience, environment, climate, mood, feeling.

at•mos•phe•rics /átməsfériks, –feer–/ *n.pl.*

1 electrical disturbance in the atmosphere, esp. caused by lightning. **2** interference with telecommunications caused by this.

at•oll /átawl, átol, áy–/ *n.* ring-shaped coral reef enclosing a lagoon.

at•om /átəm/ *n.* **1** smallest particle of a chemical element that can take part in a chemical reaction. **2** this as a source of nuclear energy. □ **atom bomb** bomb involving the release of energy by nuclear fission. ■ **1** particle, molecule.

a•tom•ic /ətómik/ *adj.* **1** concerned with or using atomic energy or atomic bombs. **2** of atoms. □ **atomic bomb** = *atom bomb.* **atomic energy** nuclear energy. **atomic number** number of protons in the nucleus of an atom. **atomic weight** ratio of the average mass of one atom of an element to one twelfth of the mass of an atom of carbon-12. □□ **a•tom′i•cal•ly** *adv.* ■ **1** see NUCLEAR.

at•om•ize /átəmíz/ *v.tr.* reduce to atoms or fine particles. □□ **at•om•i•za′tion** *n.* ■ break apart, fragment; separate, disperse, scatter.

at•om•iz•er /átəmízər/ *n.* instrument for emitting liquids as a fine spray.

a•ton•al /áytón′l/ *adj. Mus.* not written in any key or mode. □□ **a•to•nal•i•ty** /–nálitee/ *n.*

a•tone /ətón/ *v.intr.* make amends. ■ pay, repay, compensate; (*atone for*) expiate, make up for.

a•tone•ment /ətónmənt/ *n.* **1** expiation; reparation for a wrong. ■ **1** repayment, compensation, satisfaction, restitution, recompense.

-ator /áytər/ *suffix* forming agent nouns, usu. from Latin words (sometimes via French) (*agitator, creator, escalator*). See also –OR[1].

-atory /ətáwree/ *suffix* forming adjectives meaning 'relating to or involving (a verbal action)' (*amatory, explanatory, predatory*). See also –ORY[2].

a•tri•um /áytreeəm/ *n.* (*pl.* **a•tri•ums** or **a•tri•a** /–treeə/) **1 a** central court of an ancient Roman house. **b** usu. skylit central court rising through several stories. **c** (in a modern house) central hall or courtyard with rooms opening off it. **2** *Anat.* one of the two upper cavities of the heart. □□ **a′tri•al** *adj.*

a•tro•cious /ətróshəs/ *adj.* **1** very bad or unpleasant. **2** extremely savage or wicked. □□ **a•tro′cious•ly** *adv.* ■ **1** disagreeable, horrible, objectionable, woeful, horrendous. **2** cruel, iniquitous, villainous, fiendish, monstrous, inhuman.

a•troc•i•ty /ətrósitee/ *n.* (*pl.* **–ties**) **1** extremely evil or cruel act. **2** extreme wickedness. ■ **1** outrage, crime, villainy, offense, violation, evil. **2** enormity, iniquity, infamy, cruelty, heinousness.

at•ro•phy /átrəfee/ • *v.* (**–phies, –phied**) **1** *intr.* waste away through lack of use; become emaciated. **2** *tr.* cause to atrophy. • *n.* process of atrophying; emaciation.

at•ro•pine /átrəpeen, –pin/ *n.* poisonous alkaloid in deadly nightshade.

at•tach /ətách/ *v.* **1** *tr.* fasten; affix; join. **2** *tr.* [in *passive*; foll. by *to*] be very fond of or devoted to. **3** *tr.* attribute; assign. **4 a** *tr.* include. **b** *intr.* [foll. by *to*] be an attribute or characteristic. **5** *refl.* [usu. foll. by *to*] (of a thing) adhere; (of a person) join. **6** *tr. Law* seize by legal authority. □□ **at•tach′a•ble** *adj.* **at•tach′er** *n.*

■ **1** connect, secure, fix, unite. **2** (*be attached to*) love, adore, dote on, have a fondness for; like. **3** ascribe, apply; affix, pin, put, place. **4 a** see INCLUDE 1. **5** stick; see also JOIN *v.* 1, 3. **6** lay hold of, take into custody, confiscate. □□ **attachable** joinable, connectable, securable; attributable, assignable.

at•ta•ché /atasháy/ *n.* person appointed to an ambassador's staff, usu. with a special sphere of activity. □ **attaché case** small flat rectangular case for carrying documents, etc.

at•tach•ment /ətáchmənt/ *n.* **1** thing attached, esp. for a special function. **2** affection; devotion. **3** means of attaching. **4** attaching or being attached. **5** legal seizure.

■ **1** fixture; adjunct, addition, accessory. **2** liking, fondness, warmth. **3** see FASTENING, BOND *n.* 2a. **4** linkage, connection.

at•tack /əták/ • *v.tr.* **1** act against with (esp. armed) force. **2** seek to hurt or defeat. **3** criticize adversely. **4** act harmfully upon. **5** vigorously apply oneself to. • *n.* **1** act of attacking. **2 a** offensive operation **b** severe criticism. **3** sudden occurrence of an illness. □□ **at•tack′er** *n.*

■ *v.* **1** assail, assault, lay into; charge, rush; fight. **3** censure, berate, revile. **4** affect, afflict, damage; waste, erode. **5** launch into, embark on; approach, undertake. • *n.* **1** assault, bombardment, onset, offensive. **2 b** censure, abuse, denunciation, condemnation, disparagement. **3** seizure, spell; fit, bout, outbreak. □□ **attacker** see *aggressor* (AGGRESSION).

SYNONYM STUDY: **attack**

ASSAIL, ASSAULT, BESET, BESIEGE, BOMBARD, CHARGE, MOLEST, STORM. There is no shortage of "fighting words." **Attack** is the most general verb, meaning to set upon someone or something in a violent, forceful, or aggressive way (*the rebels attacked at dawn*); but it can also be used figuratively (*attack the government's policy*). **Assault** implies a greater degree of violence or viciousness and the infliction of more damage. As part of the legal term "assault and battery," it suggests an attempt or threat to injure someone physically. **Molest** is another word meaning to *attack* and is used today almost exclusively of sexual molestation (*she had been molested as a child*). **Charge** and **storm** are primarily military words, both suggesting a forceful assault on a fixed position. To *charge* is to make a violent onslaught (*the infantry charged the enemy camp*) and is often used as a command (*"Charge!" the general cried*). To *storm* means to take by force, with all the momentum and fury of a storm (*after days of planning, the soldiers stormed the castle*), but there is often the suggestion of a last-ditch, all-out effort to end a long siege or avoid defeat. To **assail** is to attack with repeated thrusts or blows, implying that victory depends not so much on force as on persistence. To **bombard** is to assail continuously with bombs or shells (*they bombarded the city without mercy for days*). **Besiege** means to surround with an armed force (*to besiege the capital city*). When used figuratively, its meaning comes close to that of *assail*, but with an emphasis on being hemmed in and enclosed rather than punished repeatedly (*besieged with fears*). **Beset** also means to attack on all sides (*beset by enemies*), but it is also used in other contexts to mean set or placed upon (*a bracelet beset with diamonds*).

---

at•tain /ətáyn/ *v.* **1** *tr.* reach (a goal, etc.). **2** *tr.* gain; accomplish. **3** *intr.* arrive at. See synonym study at GET. □□ **at•tain′a•ble** *adj.* **at•tain•a•bil′i•ty** *n.* **at•tain′ment** *n.*

■ **1** see REACH *v.* 4. **2** see GAIN *v.* 1.

at•tar /átaar/ *n.* (also **ot•to** /ótō/) fragrant essential oil, esp. from rose petals.

at•tempt /ətémpt/ • *v.tr.* seek to achieve, complete, or master. • *n.* attempting; endeavor. □□ **at•tempt′a•ble** *adj.*

■ *v.* try, undertake, take on; (*attempt to*) endeavor or strive or struggle or make an effort to. • *n.* try, effort, undertaking.

at•tend /əténd/ *v.* **1** *tr.* **a** be present at. **b** go regularly to. **2** *intr.* **a** be present. **b** wait on. **3** *tr.* escort. **4** *intr.* **a** turn or apply one's mind. **b** deal with. □□ **at•tend′er** *n.*

■ **1a**, **2a** go (to), appear (at); be there. **1 b** be at, take, be enrolled or registered at. **2 b** see WAIT *v.* 6b. **3** accompany, serve. **4** (*attend to*) **a** pay attention to, heed, listen to. **b** take care of, handle, look after; tend, watch over.

at•tend•ance /əténdəns/ *n.* **1** attending or being present. **2** number present.

■ **1** presence, appearance, being. **2** turnout, gate, audience; gathering.

at•tend•ant /əténdənt/ • *n.* person employed to wait on others or provide a service. • *adj.* **1** accompanying. **2** waiting on; serving.

■ *n.* escort, servant, helper, valet, usher; aide, subordinate. • *adj.* **1** following; resultant, related. **2** ministering to.

at•tend•ee /átendée/ *n.* person who attends.

at•ten•tion /əténshən/ *n.* **1** act or faculty of applying one's mind. **2 a** consideration. **b** care. **3** [in *pl.*] **a** ceremonious politeness. **b** wooing; courting. **4** *Mil.* erect stance.

■ *n.* **1** awareness, consciousness, attentiveness. **2 a** heed, regard, notice, concentration. **b** see CARE *n.* 3. **3** (*attentions*) **a** see RESPECT *n.* 1. **b** suit, courtship.

at•ten•tive /əténtiv/ *adj.* **1** concentrating; paying attention. **2** assiduously polite. □□ **at•ten′tive•ly** *adv.* **at•ten′tive•ness** *n.*

■ **1** observant, awake, alert, on the qui vive, aware. **2** courteous, courtly, gallant. □□ **attentively** intently, closely, carefully; politely, courteously. **attentiveness** attention; see also RESPECT *n.* 1.

at•ten•u•ate • *v.tr.* /ətényŏoayt/ **1** make thin. **2** reduce in force, value, etc. • *adj.* /ətényŏoət/ **1** slender. **2** tapering gradually.

□□ **at•ten′u•at•ed** adj. **at•ten•u•a′tion** /-áyshən/ n. **at•ten′u•a•tor** n.

at•test /ətést/ v. **1** tr. certify the validity of. **2** intr. [foll. by to] bear witness to. □□ **at•test′a•ble** adj. **at•tes•ta′tion** n. **at•tes′tor** n.
■ confirm, verify, substantiate, vouch for; (attest to) swear to.

At•tic /átik/ • adj. of ancient Athens or Attica, or the form of Greek spoken there. • n. form of Greek used by the ancient Athenians.

at•tic /átik/ n. uppermost story in a house, usu. under the roof.

at•tire /ətír/ formal • v.tr. dress. • n. clothes.
■ v. see DRESS v. 1a. ■ n. see CLOTHES.

at•ti•tude /átitōōd, -tyōōd/ n. **1 a** opinion or way of thinking. **b** behavior reflecting this. **2 a** bodily posture. **b** pose. **3** position of an aircraft, spacecraft, etc., in relation to specified directions. □□ **at•ti•tu′di•nal** /-tōō-d′nəl, -tyōōd-/ adj.
■ **1** position, feeling, view; disposition, demeanor. **2** position, stance; form, shape. □□ **attitudinal** postural, positional, aspectual.

at•ti•tu•di•nize /átitōōd′nīz, -tyōōd-/ v.intr. adopt esp. affected attitudes.

at•tor•ney /ətə́rnee/ n. (pl. **-neys**) **1** person, esp. a lawyer, appointed to act for another in business or legal matters. **2** lawyer. □ **attorney general** chief legal officer in the US and some other countries.
■ see LAWYER.

at•tract /ətrákt/ v.tr. **1** draw or bring to oneself or itself. **2** be attractive to; fascinate. □□ **at•tract′a•ble** adj. **at•trac′tor** n.
■ **1** catch, capture. **2** entice, lure, allure, appeal to, charm.

at•trac•tion /ətrákshən/ n. **1 a** attracting or being attracted. **b** person or thing that attracts. **2** Physics the force by which bodies attract or approach each other (opp. REPULSION).
■ **1 a** draw, appeal, lure, magnetism. **b** draw, lure, enticement; show, entertainment. **2** magnetism, polarity; gravitation.

at•trac•tive /ətráktiv/ adj. **1** attracting. **2** aesthetically pleasing. □□ **at•trac′tive•ly** adv. **at•trac′tive•ness** n.
■ **1** captivating, appealing, luring, inviting. **2** good-looking, pretty, handsome. □□ **attractiveness** see ATTRACTION 1a, BEAUTY 1.

at•trib•ute • v.tr. /ətríbyōōt/ **1** regard as belonging or appropriate. **2** ascribe to a cause. • n. /átribyōōt/ **1** characteristic quality ascribed to a person or thing. **2** material object recognized as appropriate to a person, office, or status. See synonym study at EMBLEM. □□ **at•trib′ut•a•ble** adj. **at•tri•bu′tion** n.
■ v. ascribe, impute, assign. ■ n. **1** character, property, feature. □□ **attributable** assignable, imputable; chargeable; connectable. **attribution** assignment, ascription; connection, association, linkage.

at•trib•u•tive /ətríbyətiv/ adj. Gram. (of an adjective or noun) preceding the word described, as (old) in (the old dog) opp. PREDICATIVE. □□ **at•trib′u•tive•ly** adv.

at•tri•tion /ətríshən/ n. **1 a** gradual wearing out, esp. by friction. **b** abrasion. **2** gradual reduction, as by retirement, etc., in a work force. □□ **at•tri′tion•al** adj.
■ **1** see EROSION.

at•tune /ətōōn, ətyōōn/ v.tr. **1** adjust to a situation. **2** bring (an orchestra, instrument, etc.) into musical accord.
■ **1** (attune to) see ADAPT 2. **2** see TUNE v. 1.

atty. abbr. attorney.

ATV abbr. all-terrain vehicle.

a•typ•i•cal /áytípikəl/ adj. not typical. □□ **a•typ′i•cal•ly** adv.

Au symb. Chem. gold.

au•burn /áwbərn/ adj. reddish brown (usu. of a person's hair).

auc•tion /áwkshən/ • n. sale in which articles are sold to the highest bidder. • v.tr. sell at auction.

auc•tion•eer /áwkshəneér/ n. person who conducts auctions professionally. □□ **auc′tion•eer′ing** n.

au•da•cious /awdáyshəs/ adj. **1** daring; bold. **2** impudent. See synonym study at BOLD. □□ **au•da′cious•ly** adv. **au•da′cious•ness** n. **au•dac•i•ty** /awdásitee/ n. See synonym study at TEMERITY
■ **1** confident, intrepid, brave, adventurous; reckless, rash, foolhardy, daredevil. **2** presumptuous, shameless, bold, defiant. □□ **audaciousness, audacity** see GUT[1] n. 3, GALL 1.

au•di•ble /áwdibəl/ adj. capable of being heard. □□ **au•di•bil′i•ty** n. **au′di•ble•ness** n. **au′di•bly** adv.

au•di•ence /áwdeeəns/ n. **1 a** assembled listeners or spectators at an event, esp. a stage performance, concert, etc. **b** people addressed by a movie, book, play, etc. **2** formal interview with a person in authority.
■ **1 a** see ATTENDANCE 2. **2** see INTERVIEW n. 3.

au•di•o /áwdeeō/ n. sound or its reproduction. □ **audio frequency** frequency perceivable by the human ear.

au•di•o•phile /áwdeeōfīl/ n. high-fidelity sound enthusiast.

au•di•o•vis•u•al /áwdeeōvízhyōōəl/ adj. (esp. of teaching methods) using both sight and sound.

au•dit /áwdit/ • n. official examination of accounts. • v.tr. **1** conduct an audit of. **2** attend (a college-level class) for no credit.
■ v. **1** see MONITOR v. **2** see ATTEND 1b.

au•di•tion /awdíshən/ • n. test for a performer's ability or suitability. • v. assess or be assessed at an audition.

au•di•tor /áwditər/ n. **1** person who audits accounts. **2** person who audits a class.

au•di•to•ri•um /áwditáwreeəm/ n. (pl. **au•di•to•ri•ums** or **au•di•to•ri•a** /-reeə/) **1** large room or building for meetings, etc. **2** part of a theater, etc., in which the audience sits.

au•di•to•ry /áwditawree/ adj. concerned with hearing.

au fait /ō fáy/ adj. conversant.

Aug. abbr. August.

au•ger /áwgər/ n. tool resembling a large corkscrew, for boring holes in wood, the ground, etc.

aught[1] /awt/ *n.* (also **ought**) *archaic* anything.

aught[2] /awt/ *n.* (also **ought**) *colloq.* zero.

aug•ment /awgmént/ *v.* **1** make or become greater; increase. **2** add to; supplement. □□ **aug•men•ta'tion** *n.* **aug•men'ta•tive** *adj.* **aug•ment'er** *n.*
   ■ *v.* see INCREASE *v.* 1.

au gra•tin /ó gratán/ *adj. Cookery* cooked with a crisp brown crust, usu. of bread crumbs or melted cheese.

au•gur /áwgər/ • *v.intr.* **1** (of an event, circumstance, etc.) suggest a specified outcome (usu. (*augur well*) or (*ill*). **2** portend; bode. See synonym study at PREDICT. • *n.* ancient Roman religious soothsayer.

au•gu•ry /áwgyəree/ *n.* (*pl.* **–ries**) **1** omen; portent. **2** interpretation of omens; prophecy. See synonym study at OMEN. □□ **au'gu•ral** *adj.*

Au•gust /áwgəst/ *n.* eighth month of the year.

au•gust /awgúst/ *adj.* inspiring reverence and admiration; venerable; impressive. □□ **au•gust'ly** *adv.* **au•gust'ness** *n.*
   ■ see VENERABLE.

Au•gus•tan /awgústən/ *adj.* of the reign of the Roman emperor Augustus, esp. as an outstanding period of Latin literature.

au jus /ó zhoo, ó zhoos/ • *adj.* with juice, usu. describing roast beef, veal, or other meat served with its juices.

auk /awk/ *n.* black and white diving bird, e.g., the puffin and razorbill.

auld lang syne /áwld lang zín, sín/ *n.* times long past.

aunt /ant, aant/ *n.* **1** sister of one's father or mother. **2** uncle's wife. **3** *colloq.* unrelated woman friend of a child or children.

au pair /ó páir/ *n.* young foreign person who helps with child care, housework, etc., in exchange for room and board.

au•ra /áwrə/ *n.* (*pl.* **au•rae** /–ree/ or **au•ras**) **1** distinctive atmosphere. **2** subtle emanation or aroma.
   ■ **1** air, feeling, ambience, sense, mood. **2** odor, fragrance; see also HINT *n.* 3.

au•ral /áwrəl/ *adj.* of the ear, or hearing. □□ **au'ral•ly** *adv.*
   ■ auditive, auditory, auricular.

au•re•ole /áwreeōl/ *n.* (also **au•re•o•la** /awreeólə/) **1** halo, esp. around the head in a religious painting. **2** corona around the sun or moon.

au re•voir /ó rəvwaár/ *int. & n.* good-bye (until we meet again).

au•ri•cle /áwrikəl/ *n. Anat.* **1 a** small muscular pouch on the surface of each atrium of the heart. **b** the atrium itself. **2** external ear of animals. (Also called **pinna**).

au•ro•ra /awráwrə/ *n.* (*pl.* **au•ro•ras** or **au•ro•rae** /–ree/) luminous phenomenon, usu. of streamers of light in the night sky above the northern or southern magnetic pole. □ **aurora australis** /awstráylis/ southern occurrence of aurora. **aurora borealis** /báwree-ális/ northern occurrence of aurora.

aus•cul•ta•tion /áwskəltáyshən/ *n.* listening, esp. to sounds from the heart, lungs, etc., as a part of medical diagnosis.

aus•pice /áwspis/ *n.* **1** [in *pl.*] patronage. **2** forecast.
   ■ **1** (*auspices*) aegis, sponsorship, authority, protection, support, backing. **2** see FORECAST *n.*

aus•pi•cious /awspíshəs/ *adj.* of good omen; favorable. □□ **aus•pi'cious•ly** *adv.* **aus•pi'cious•ness** *n.*
   ■ see PROPITIOUS 1.

Aus•sie /áwsee, –zee/ (also **Os•sie, Oz•zie**) *colloq.* • *n.* **1** an Australian. **2** Australia. • *adj.* Australian.

aus•tere /awstéer/ *adj.* (**aus•ter•er, aus•ter•est**) **1** severely simple. **2** morally strict. **3** harsh; stern. See synonym study at SEVERE. □□ **aus•tere'ly** *adv.*
   ■ **1** see SIMPLE[1] *adj.* 2. **2** see STRICT 2. **3** see STERN.

aus•ter•i•ty /awstéritee/ *n.* (*pl.* **–ties**) **1** sternness; moral severity. **2** severe simplicity, e.g., of economics. **3** [esp. in *pl.*] austere practice (*the austerities of a monk's life*).
   ■ **1** see *severity* (SEVERE). **3** rigors, asceticism; see also HARDSHIP.

Aus•tral•ian /awstráylyən/ • *n.* **1** native or inhabitant of Australia. **2** person of Australian descent. **3** any of the aboriginal languages of Australia. • *adj.* of or relating to Australia. □□ **Aus•tral'ian•ism** *n.*

auth. *abbr.* **1** authentic. **2** author. **3** authority. **4** authorized.

au•then•tic /awthéntik/ *adj.* **1** of undisputed origin; genuine. **2** reliable or trustworthy. See synonym study at GENUINE. □□ **au•then'ti•cal•ly** *adv.* **au•then•tic•i•ty** /–tísitee/ *n.*
   ■ **1** real, actual, bona fide; authoritative, reliable, incontrovertible. □□ **authentically** genuinely, bona fide; reliably. **authenticity** reality, realness, fact, truth, genuineness.

au•then•ti•cate /awthéntikayt/ *v.tr.* **1** establish the truth or genuineness of. **2** validate. □□ **au•then•ti•ca•tion** /–káyshən/ *n.* **au•then'ti•ca•tor** *n.*
   ■ verify, certify, endorse; seal; corroborate. □□ **authentication** verification, validation; corroboration; see also PROOF *n.* 2.

au•thor /áwthər/ • *n.* (*fem.* **au•thor•ess** /áwthris, áwthərés/) **1** writer, esp. of books. **2** originator of an event, condition, etc. • *v.tr.* be the author of (a book, the universe, a child, etc.). □□ **au•tho•ri•al** /awtháwriəl/ *adj.* **au'thor•ship** *n.*
   ■ *n.* **1** man or woman of letters; novelist, playwright, dramatist, essayist, poet; journalist, columnist. **2** creator, inventor, father, founder. • *v.* see CREATE 1, WRITE 5.

au•thor•i•tar•i•an /əthawritáireeən, əthór-/ • *adj.* **1** favoring or enforcing strict obedience to authority. **2** tyrannical or domineering. • *n.* person favoring absolute obedience to a constituted authority. □□ **au•thor•i•tar'i•an•ism** *n.*
   ■ *adj.* dictatorial, imperious, totalitarian, autocratic, tyrannical. • *n.* disciplinarian, absolutist. □□ **authoritarianism** strictness, inflexibility, rigidity, severity; see also TYRANNY.

au•thor•i•ta•tive /ətháwritáytiv, əthór-/ *adj.*

1 recognized as true or dependable. **2** (of a person, behavior, etc.) commanding or self-confident. **3** official. □□ **au·thor'i·ta·tive·ly** adv. **au·thor'i·ta·tive·ness** n.
■ **1** reliable, trustworthy, authentic. **2** see DOMINANT adj. **3** approved, valid, authentic, certified. □□ **authoritatively** officially, knowledgeably; reliably, truthfully; confidently. **authoritativeness** authority, scholarliness; reliability, dependability, legitimacy; see also CONFIDENCE 2b.

au·thor·i·ty /əthávwritee, əthór-/ n. (pl. **-ties**) **1 a** power or right to enforce obedience. **b** delegated power. **2** [esp. pl.] person or body having authority. **3 a** influence based on recognized knowledge or expertise. **b** such an influence expressed in a book, etc. **c** expert. See synonym study at JURISDICTION.
■ **1 a** jurisdiction, dominion, right, control. **b** authorization; see also PERMISSION. **2** (authorities) government, establishment, officials. **3 a** see INFLUENCE n. **c** specialist, scholar, sage, judge.

au·thor·ize /áwthərīz/ v.tr. **1** sanction. **2 a** give authority. **b** commission (a person or body) (authorized to trade). □□ **au·thor·i·za'tion** n.
■ **1** approve, consent to, permit; legalize. **2 a** permit, allow, license, entitle, empower. **b** license. □□ **authorization** see LICENSE, PERMISSION.

au·tism /áwtizəm/ n. Psychol. mental condition, usu. present from childhood, characterized by complete self-absorption and social withdrawal. □□ **au·tis·tic** /awtístik/ adj.

au·to /áwtō/ n. (pl. **-tos**) colloq. automobile.

auto- /áwtō/ comb. form (usu. **aut-** before a vowel) **1** self (autism). **2** one's own (autobiography). **3** by oneself or spontaneous (autosuggestion). **4** by itself or automatic (automobile).

au·to·bi·og·ra·phy /áwtōbīógrəfee/ n. (pl. **-phies**) **1** written account of one's own life. **2** this as a literary form. □□ **au·to·bi·og'ra·pher** n. **au·to·bi·o·graph·ic** /-bíəgráfik/ adj. **au·to·bi·o·graph'i·cal** adj.

au·to·clave /áwtōklayv/ n. sterilizer using steam.

au·toc·ra·cy /awtókrəsee/ n. (pl. **-cies**) **1** absolute government by one person; tyranny. **2** dictatorship. □□ **au·to·crat** /áwtəkrat/ n. **au·to·crat'ic** adj. **au·to·crat'i·cal·ly** adv.

au·to-da-fé /áwtōdaafáy/ n. (pl. **au·tos-da-fé** /áwtōz-/) **1** judgment of heretics by the Spanish Inquisition. **2** public burning of a heretic.

au·to·graph /áwtəgraf/ • n. **1** signature, esp. that of a celebrity. **2** manuscript in an author's own handwriting. • v.tr. sign (a photograph, autograph album, etc.).
■ n. **2** holograph. • v. see SIGN v. 1.

au·to·im·mune /áwtōimyóōn/ adj. Med. (of a disease) caused by antibodies produced against substances naturally present in the body. □□ **au·to·im·mu'ni·ty** n.

au·to·mate /áwtəmayt/ v.tr. convert to or opcrate by automation. □ **automated teller**

machine electronic machine that allows customers to deposit or withdraw funds, etc. ¶Abbr.: ATM.

au·to·mat·ic /áwtəmátik/ • adj. **1** (of a machine, etc.) working by itself, without direct human intervention. **2 a** done spontaneously. **b** necessary and inevitable. **3** Psychol. performed unconsciously or subconsciously. **4** (of a firearm) able to be loaded and fired continuously. **5** (of a motor vehicle or its transmission) using gears that change automatically. • n. **1** automatic device, esp. a gun or transmission. **2** colloq. vehicle with automatic transmission. □ **automatic pilot** device for keeping an aircraft on a set course. □□ **au·to·mat'i·cal·ly** adv. **au·to·ma·tic·i·ty** /áwtəmətísitee/ n.
■ adj. **1** mechanical, robotic, automated. **2 a** involuntary, instinctive, instinctual. **b** unavoidable, inevitable; mandatory; definite. **3** see sense 2a above. □□ **automatically** mechanically, by itself or oneself; involuntarily, instinctively, intuitively.

au·to·ma·tion /áwtəmáyshən/ n. use of automatic manufacturing equipment.

au·tom·a·tism /awtómətizəm/ n. involuntary, unthinking action.

au·tom·a·ton /awtómətən, -ton/ n. (pl. **au·tom·a·ta** /-tə/ or **au·tom·a·tons**) **1** mechanism with concealed motive power. **2** person who behaves like a robot.

au·to·mo·bile /áwtəməbeel/ n. motor vehicle for road use with an enclosed passenger compartment; car.

au·to·mo·tive /áwtəmōtiv/ adj. concerned with motor vehicles.

au·to·nom·ic /áwtənómik/ adj. esp. Physiol. functioning involuntarily. □ **autonomic nervous system** nervous system controlling involuntary bodily functions, e.g., heartbeat.

au·ton·o·mous /awtónəməs/ adj. **1** having self-government. **2** acting independently or having the freedom to do so. □□ **au·ton'o·mous·ly** adv.
■ **1** see INDEPENDENT adj. 1b.

au·ton·o·my /awtónəmee/ n. (pl. **-mies**) **1** self-government. **2** personal freedom. □□ **au·ton'o·mist** n.
■ **2** see FREEDOM 1, 2.

au·to·pi·lot /áwtōpīlət/ n. = automatic pilot.

au·top·sy /áwtopsee/ n. (pl. **-sies**) postmortem examination to determine cause of death, etc.

au·tumn /áwtəm/ n. **1** season between summer and winter. (Also called **fall**). **2** time of maturity or incipient decay. □□ **au·tum·nal** /awtúmnəl/ adj. (see also EQUINOX).

aux·il·ia·ry /awgzílyaree/ • adj. **1** (of a person or thing) that gives help. **2** (of services or equipment) subsidiary; additional. • n. (pl. **-ries**) **1** auxiliary person or thing. **2** Gram. = auxiliary verb. □ **auxiliary verb** Gram. one used in forming tenses or moods of other verbs, e.g., (have) in (I have seen).
■ adj. supportive, support; additional, supplemental. • n. **1** help, assistance, aid; assistant, supporter; subordinate, deputy.

AV abbr. audiovisual (teaching aids, etc.).

a·vail /əváyl/ • v. **1** tr. help; benefit. **2** refl.

[foll. by *of*] profit by; take advantage of. **3** *intr.* **a** provide help. **b** be of use, value, or profit. • *n.* use; profit (*to no avail*).

a•vail•a•ble /əváyləbəl/ *adj.* **1** capable of being used; at one's disposal. **2** within one's reach. **3** (of a person) **a** free. **b** able to be contacted. □□ **a•vail•a•bil•i•ty** *n.* **a•vail'a•bly** *adv.*

■ **1** free, unoccupied, not busy; on sale. **2** at *or* to hand, close at hand, accessible. **3** unoccupied, at liberty, not busy; accessible.

av•a•lanche /ávəlanch/ *n.* **1** mass of snow and ice tumbling rapidly down a mountain. **2** sudden appearance or arrival of anything in large quantities.

a•vant-garde /avón-gaard/ • *n.* pioneers or innovators, esp. in art and literature. • *adj.* (of ideas, etc.) new; progressive. □□ **a•vant' -gard'ism** *n.* **a•vant'-gard'ist** *n*

■ *n.* vanguard, trendsetters. • *adj.* innovative, advanced, experimental; unconventional, eccentric, revolutionary, extreme.

av•a•rice /ávəris/ *n.* extreme greed for money or gain; cupidity. □□ **av•a•ri•cious** /ríshəs/ *adj.* **av•a•ri'cious•ly** *adv.* **av•a•ri'cious•ness** *n.* See synonym study at GREEDY.

■ greed, greediness, acquisitiveness, cupidity, rapacity, selfishness. □□ **avaricious** greedy, acquisitive, grasping. **avariciously** greedily, covetously. **avariciousness** see AVARICE above.

a•vast /əvást/ *int.* *Naut.* stop; cease.

av•a•tar /ávətaar/ *n.* (in Hindu mythology) descent of a deity, etc., to earth in bodily form.

Ave. *abbr.* Avenue.

a•venge /əvénj/ *v.tr.* **1** inflict retribution on behalf of. **2** take vengeance for (an injury). □□ **a•veng'er** *n.*

■ **2** see REVENGE *v.* 2.

av•e•nue /ávənoo, -nyoo/ *n.* **1** broad, often tree-lined road or street. **2** approach.

■ **1** see ROAD 1. **2** see ROUTE *n.*

a•ver /əvér/ *v.tr.* (**averred, a•ver•ring**) *formal* assert; affirm; declare.

av•er•age /ávərij, ávrij/ • *n.* **1 a** usual amount, extent, or rate. **b** ordinary standard. **2** amount obtained by dividing the total of given amounts by the number of amounts in the set. • *adj.* **1 a** usual; typical. **b** mediocre. **2** estimated by average. See synonym study at NORMAL. • *v.tr.* **1** amount on average to (*sales averaged $1000 a day*). **2** do on average. **3** estimate average of. □ **average out** result in an average of. **on** (*or* **on an**) **average** as an average rate or estimate.

■ *n.* **1** standard, mean, norm. • *adj.* **1 a** normal, common, customary. **b** middling, run-of-the-mill, commonplace. **2** mean. □ **on average** in the main, generally, normally, usually.

a•verse /əvórs/ *predic.adj.* opposed; disinclined.

■ unwilling, reluctant, resistant, loath.

a•ver•sion /əvórzhən, -shən/ *n.* **1** dislike or unwillingness. **2** object of dislike.

■ **1** abhorrence, repugnance, antipathy; disinclination, resistance. **2** bugbear, bête noire.

a•vert /əvórt/ *v.tr.* **1** turn away (one's eyes or

thoughts). **2** prevent or ward off (an undesirable occurrence).

avg. *abbr.* average.

a•vi•an /áyveeən/ *adj.* of or relating to birds.

■ ornithological.

a•vi•ar•y /áyvee-eree/ *n.* (*pl.* **-ies**) large enclosure or building for keeping birds.

a•vi•a•tion /áyveeáyshən/ *n.* **1** skill or practice of operating aircraft. **2** aircraft manufacture.

a•vi•a•tor /áyveeaytər/ *n.* (*fem.* **a•vi•a•trix** /áyveeáytriks/) person who pilots an aircraft.

av•id /ávid/ *adj.* eager; greedy. See synonym study at EAGER. □□ **a•vid•i•ty** /əvíditee/ *n.* **a'vid•ly** *adv.*

■ see EAGER.

a•vi•on•ics /áyveeóniks/ *n.pl.* [treated as *sing.*] electronics as applied to aviation.

av•o•ca•do /ávəkaadō, aávə-/ *n.* (*pl.* **-dos**) **1** pear-shaped fruit with rough leathery skin, smooth flesh, and a large stone. **2** tropical tree bearing this fruit. (Also called **alligator pear**).

av•o•ca•tion /ávōkáyshən/ *n.* hobby.

■ calling; see also INTEREST *n.* 2.

a•void /əvóyd/ *v.tr.* **1** refrain or keep away from. **2** escape; evade. **3** quash. □□ **a•void'a•ble** *adj.* **a•void'a•bly** *adv.* **a•void'ance** *n.* **a•void'er** *n.*

■ **1** shun, leave alone, steer clear of, keep at arm's length. **2** get away from, miss; dodge, circumvent. □□ **avoidable** escapable, evadable. **avoidance** see EVASION 1.

av•oir•du•pois /ávərdəpóyz/ *n.* (in full **av' oir•du•pois' weight'**) system of weights based on a pound of 16 ounces or 7,000 grains.

a•vow /əvów/ *v.tr.* admit; confess. □□ **a•vow'• al** *n.* **a•vow'ed•ly** *adv.*

a•vun•cu•lar /əvúngkyələr/ *adj.* like or of an uncle; kind and friendly, esp. toward a younger person.

a•wait /əwáyt/ *v.tr.* **1** wait for. **2** be in store for.

a•wake /əwáyk/ • *v.* (*past* **a•woke** /əwók/; *past part.* **a•wok•en** /əwókən/) **1** *intr.* **a** cease to sleep. **b** become active. **2** *intr.* [foll. by *to*] become aware of. **3** *tr.* rouse, esp. from sleep. • *predic.adj.* **1 a** not asleep. **b** vigilant. **2** [foll. by *to*] aware of

■ *v.* **1 a** wake (up), awaken, get up, rouse oneself. **b** see STIR[1] *v.* 2b. **2** (*awake to*) awaken to, wake up to, realize, understand. **3** awaken, animate, arouse; stir up, kindle. *predic.adj.* **1 a** up (and about), aroused, roused, astir. **b** alert, on the alert, watchful. **2** see AWARE 1.

a•wak•en /əwáykən/ *v.* = AWAKE *v.*

a•ward /əwáwrd/ • *v.tr.* **1** give or order to be given as a payment or prize. **2** grant; assign. See synonym study at GIVE. • *n.* **1 a** payment, compensation, or prize awarded. **b** the act or process of awarding. **2** judicial decision. □□ **a•ward'er** *n.*

■ *v.* donate; confer on; apportion. • *n.* **1 a** trophy, reward, honor(s); subsidy, grant. **b** grant, bestowal, presentation. **2** see DECISION 2, 3.

a•ware /əwáir/ *predic.adj.* **1** conscious; having knowledge. **2** well-informed. □□ **a•ware′ ness** *n.*

■ **1** awake, alert; (*aware of*) conscious or cognizant of, informed. **2** knowledgeable, knowing, enlightened. □□ **awareness** see *sensitivity* (SENSITIVE), UNDERSTANDING *n.*

a•wash /əwósh, əwáwsh/ *predic.adj.* **1** level with the surface of water, so that it just washes over. **2** overflowing, abounding.

a•way /əwáy/ • *adv.* **1** to or at a distance from. **2** toward or into nonexistence. **3** constantly; persistently. **4** without delay. • *adj.* **1** *Sports* played at an opponent's field, etc. **2** absent or distant. **3** *Baseball* out. • *n. Sports* away game or win. □ **away with** [as *imper.*] take away.

awe /aw/ • *n.* reverential fear or wonder. • *v.tr.* inspire with awe. □ **awe-inspiring** causing awe; magnificent.

■ *n.* see WONDER *n.* 1. □□ **awe-inspiring** see AWESOME 1.

a•weigh /əwáy/ *predic.adj. Naut.* (of an anchor) clear of the sea or river bed; hanging.

awe•some /áwsəm/ *adj.* **1** inspiring awe. **2** *colloq.* excellent; superb. □□ **awe′some•ly** *adv.* **awe′some•ness** *n.*

■ **1** awe-inspiring, imposing, overwhelming, formidable; breathtaking, amazing; incredible; alarming. **2** (**the A•x•is**) *colloq.* excellent; superb.

aw•ful /áwfool/ *adj.* **1** *colloq.* **a** unpleasant or horrible. **b** poor in quality. **c** excessive. **2** *poet.* inspiring awe. □□ **aw′ful•ness** *n.*

■ **1 a, b** atrocious, horrendous, disagreeable, nasty; bad, inferior. **c** see *excessive* (EXCESS), LARGE *adj.* 1, 2. **2** see AWESOME 1.

aw•ful•ly /áwfəlee, –flee/ *adv.* **1** *colloq.* unpleasantly, badly. **2** *colloq.* very.

■ **1** terribly, woefully, atrociously; see also BADLY 1. **2** extremely, really, greatly.

a•while /əhwíl, əwíl/ *adv.* for a short time.

awk•ward /áwkwərd/ *adj.* **1** difficult to use. **2** clumsy or bungling. **3 a** embarrassed. **b** embarrassing. □□ **awk′ward•ly** *adv.* **awk′ ward•ness** *n.*

■ **1** unwieldy, cumbersome; ill-adapted; tricky. **2** ungainly, heavy-handed. **3 a** shamefaced, uncomfortable, ill at ease. **b** uncomfortable, humiliating.

awl /awl/ *n.* small pointed tool used for piercing holes.

awn•ing /áwning/ *n.* sheet of canvas or similar material stretched on a frame and used as a shelter from the sun or rain.

■ see SHADE *n.* 5.

a•woke *past* of AWAKE.

a•wok•en *past part.* of AWAKE.

AWOL /áywawl/ *abbr.* absent without leave.

a•wry /ərí/ • *adv.* **1** crookedly or askew. **2** improperly or amiss. • *predic. adj.* crooked; unsound.

■ *adv.* **1** see ASKEW *adv.* **2** see AMISS *adv.* • *adj.* see CROOKED 1, WRONG *adj.* 4.

ax /aks/ (also **axe**) • *n.* **1** chopping tool, usu. of iron with a steel edge at a right angle to a wooden handle. **2** drastic cutting or elimination of expenditure, staff, etc. • *v.tr.* (**ax•ing**) **1** use an ax. **2** cut (esp. costs or services) drastically. **3** remove or dismiss. □ **an ax to grind** private or selfish purpose to serve.

ax•i•al /ákseeəl/ *adj.* of, forming, or placed around an axis. □□ **ax′i•al•ly** *adv.*

ax•i•om /ákseeəm/ *n.* **1** established or widely accepted principle. **2** esp. *Geom.* self-evident truth. □□ **ax•i•o•mat′ic** *adj.* **ax•i•o•mat′i•cal•ly** *adv.*

■ **1** see PRINCIPLE 1.

ax•is /áksis/ *n.* (*pl.* **ax•es** /–seez/) **1 a** imaginary line about which a body rotates. **b** line that divides a regular figure symmetrically. **2** *Math.* fixed reference line for the measurement of coordinates, etc. **3** (**the Ax•is**) alliance of Germany and Italy during World War II, later also Japan.

ax•le /áksəl/ *n.* spindle on which a wheel is fixed.

ax•o•lotl /áksəlot'l/ *n.* aquatic newtlike salamander from Mexico.

ax•on /ákson/ *n.* *Anat. & Zool.* long threadlike part of a nerve cell, conducting impulses from the body.

a•ya•tol•lah /íətólə/ *n.* Shiite religious leader in Iran.

aye /ī/ (also **ay**) • *adv. archaic* or *dial.* yes. • *n.* affirmative answer or assent, esp. in voting.

■ yes, *archaic* yea.

AZ *abbr.* Arizona (in official postal use).

a•za•lea /əzáylyə/ *n.* kind of rhododendron.

az•i•muth /áziməth/ *n.* angular distance from a north or south point of the horizon to the intersection with the horizon of a vertical circle passing through a given celestial body. □□ **az•i•muth•al** /–múthəl/ *adj.*

AZT *n.* drug used against the AIDS virus.

Az•tec /áztek/ • *n.* **1** member of the native people dominant in Mexico before the Spanish conquest of the 16th century. **2** language of the Aztecs. • *adj.* of the Aztecs or their language (see also NAHUATL).

az•ure /ázhər/ • *n.* **1** deep sky-blue color. **2** *poet.* clear sky. • *adj.* of the color azure.

Bb

B[1] /bee/ *n.* (also **b**) (*pl.* **Bs** or **B's; b's**) **1** second letter of the alphabet. **2** second class or category (of sizes, academic marks, etc.). **3** *Algebra* (usu. **b**) second known quantity. **4** human blood type. □ **B movie** low-budget movie.

B[2] *symb.* **1** *Chem.* boron. **2** *Physics* magnetic flux density.

B[3] *abbr.* (also **B.**) **1** bachelor. **2** bishop. **3** black (pencil lead). **4** *Baseball* base; baseman.

b *abbr.* (also **b.**) *Physics* barn.

b. *abbr.* **1** born. **2** billion.

BA *abbr.* **1** Bachelor of Arts. **2** *Baseball* batting average.

Ba *symb. Chem.* barium.

baa /baa/ • *v.intr.* (**baas, baaed** or **baa'd**) (esp. of a sheep) bleat. • *n.* (*pl.* **baas**) cry of a sheep or lamb.

bab•ble /bábəl/ • *v.* **1** *intr.* **a** talk inarticulately or incoherently. **b** chatter excessively or irrelevantly. **c** (of a stream, etc.) murmur. **2** *tr.* repeat foolishly; divulge through chatter. • *n.* **1 a** incoherent speech. **b** foolish talk. **2** murmur of voices, water, etc. □□ **bab'bler** *n.*

■ *v.* **1 a, b** gabble, jabber, blab, blabber; prattle, prate, blather, gossip, *colloq.* gab, natter, *colloq. or dial.* yammer, *sl.* yak. **c** gurgle, purl. **2** disclose, broadcast, blurt (out), give away, blab, let out, *colloq.* let on. • *n.* **1 a** gibberish. **b** twaddle, prattle, gossip, *colloq.* chitchat. **2** gurgle, buzz.

babe /bayb/ *n.* **1** esp. *literary* baby. **2** innocent or helpless person. **3** sometimes *derog. sl.* young woman.

ba•bel /báybəl, báb-/ *n.* **1** confused noise, esp. of voices. **2** noisy assembly. **3** scene of confusion.

■ **2** see DIN *n.*

ba•boon /babóŏn/ *n.* **1** monkey having a long doglike snout, large teeth, and a short tail. **2** ugly or uncouth person.

ba•by /báybee/ • *n.* (*pl.* **–bies**) **1** very young child or infant. **2** childish person (*is a baby about injections*). **3** youngest member of a family, team, etc. **4** young or newly born animal. **5** *sl.* young woman; sweetheart (often as a form of address). **6** *sl.* person or thing regarded with affection or familiarity. • *v.tr.* (**–bies, –bied**) **1** treat like a baby. **2** pamper. □ **baby boom** *colloq.* temporary marked increase in the birthrate. **baby boomer** person born during a baby boom, esp. that following World War II. **baby carriage** four-wheeled carriage for pushing a baby. **baby grand** smallest grand piano. **baby-sit** see **baby-sitter** person who baby-sits. **baby talk** childish talk used by or to young children. **throw out the baby with the bath water** reject the essential with the inessential. □□ **ba'by•hood** *n.* **ba'by•ish** *adj.*

■ *n.* **1** neonate, toddler, tot, *colloq.* new arrival, *literary* babe (in arms). **3** smallest, littlest. **5** see DARLING *n.* **1**. • *v.* cosset, coddle, mollycoddle, indulge, spoil. □ **baby-sit** see MIND *v.* **3**. **baby talk** see BABBLE *n.* **1**b.

bac•ca•lau•re•ate /bákəláwreeət/ *n.* **1** college or university bachelor's degree. **2** examination intended to qualify successful candidates for higher education.

bac•cha•nal /bákənál, bákənəl/ • *n.* **1** (also **bac•cha•na•li•a** /bákənáyleeə/) wild and drunken revelry. **2** reveler. **3** priest, worshiper, or follower of Bacchus. • *adj.* **1** of or like Bacchus, the Greek or Roman god of wine, or his rites. **2** riotous.

bach•e•lor /báchələr, báchlər/ *n.* **1** unmarried man. **2** man or woman who has taken the degree of Bachelor of Arts or Science, etc. □□ **bach'e•lor•hood** *n.*

■ **2** graduate.

ba•cil•lus /bəsíləs/ *n.* (*pl.* **ba•cil•li** /–lī/) **1** any rod-shaped bacterium. **2** [usu. in *pl.*] any pathogenic bacterium.

back /bak/ • *n.* **1 a** rear surface of the human body from shoulders to hips. **b** upper surface of an animal's body. **c** spine. **2 a** any backlike surface, e.g., of the head, a chair, etc. **b** part of a garment that covers the back. **3 a** less active or visible or important part (*write it on the back*). **b** distant part. **4** player or position in some games. • *adv.* **1** to the rear. **2 a** in or into an earlier or normal position or condition (*went back home*). **b** in return (*pay back*). **3** in or into the past (*back in June*). **4** at a distance (*stand back from the road*). **5** in check (*hold him back*). **6** [foll. by *of*] behind. • *v.* **1** *tr.* **a** help with moral or financial support. **b** bet on. **2** *tr.* & *intr.* move, or cause (a vehicle, etc.) to move, backward. **3** *tr.* **a** put or serve as a back or support to. **b** *Mus.* accompany. **4** *tr.* lie at the back of (*a beach backed by steep cliffs*). • *adj.* **1** situated behind, esp. as remote or subsidiary (*back entrance*). **2** past; not current (*back pay*). **3** reversed (*back flow*). □ **back and forth** to and fro. **back down** withdraw one's claim; concede defeat in an argument. **back off 1** draw back; retreat. **2** abandon one's intention, stand, etc. **back out** withdraw from a commitment. **back talk** *colloq.* rude or impudent response. **back up 1** give (esp. moral) support to. **2** *Computing* copy (a file, disk, etc.). **3** (of running water, etc.) accumulate behind an obstruction. **4** move (a vehicle) backward. **get** (or **put**) **a person's back up** annoy or anger a person. **get off a person's back** stop troubling a person. **go back on** fail to honor (a promise or commitment). **turn one's back on 1** abandon. **2** disregard; ignore. □□ **back'er** *n.* (in sense 1 of *v.*). **back'less** *adj.*

■ *n.* **3 a** other side, wrong side, *colloq.* flip

side. **b** far side *or* corner. **4** fullback, half-back. • *adv.* **1** rearward(s), backward(s). **2 a** again, re–. **b** repayment, retaliation. **3** ago, before. **4** away, at arm's length; to one side. **5** under control. **6** (*back of*) on the other side of. • *v.* **1 a** stand behind, encourage; uphold, endorse; *colloq.* bankroll, stake. **b** invest in, wager on. **2** reverse. • *adj.* **1** rear, side; service, servants'. **2** in arrears, overdue, late; old, out-of-date. **3** backward. □ **back and forth** see AROUND *adv.* 2. **back down** see *give in*, WITHDRAW 2. **back off** 1 see RETREAT *v.* 1. **2** see *give in*. **back out** see RENEGE 1. **back talk** see *impudence* (IMPUDENT). **back up** 1 see BACK *v.* 1a above. **get a person's back up** get on a person's nerves; see also ANNOY 1. **go back on** renege on, default on, repudiate; *colloq.* chicken out of. **turn one's back on** 1 forsake, reject. **2** overlook; see also IGNORE 2. □□ **backer** investor, benefactor, underwriter, patron, *sl.* angel; bettor.

back•ache /bákayk/ *n.* (usu. prolonged) pain in one's back.

back•bite /bákbīt/ *v.tr.* speak badly of. □□ **back'bit•er** *n.*

back•bone /bákbōn/ *n.* **1** spine. **2** main support. **3** firmness of character.
■ **1** vertebrae. **2** mainstay, pillar. **3** resoluteness, sturdiness, perseverance, tenacity, courage, *colloq.* guts, grit.

back•break•ing /bákbrayking/ *adj.* extremely hard.
■ see *exhausting* (EXHAUST).

back•date /bákdáyt/ *v.tr.* put an earlier date on (an agreement, etc.) than the actual one.

back•door /bákdáwr/ *adj.* (of an activity) clandestine; underhand (*backdoor deal*).
■ covert, secret, hidden; furtive, shady.

back•drop /bákdrop/ *n. Theatr.* painted cloth at the back of the stage as a main part of the scenery.

back•fire /bákfīr/ • *v.intr.* **1** undergo a mistimed explosion in the cylinder or exhaust of an internal combustion engine. **2** (of a plan, etc.) fail adversely. • *n.* instance of backfiring.
■ *v.* **2** see BOOMERANG *v.* • *n.* see REPORT *n.* 6.

back•gam•mon /bákgámən/ *n.* board game for two with pieces moved according to throws of the dice.

back•ground /bákgrownd/ *n.* **1** part of a scene or picture farthest from the observer. **2** inconspicuous or obscure position (esp. as *in the background*). **3** person's education, knowledge, or social circumstances. **4** explanatory or contributory information or circumstances.
■ **1** surroundings; field, distance. **2** (*in the background*) unnoticed, unobtrusive; see also *hidden* (HIDE¹). **3** history, experience, qualifications, upbringing, family; curriculum vitae, c.v.

back•hand /bák-hand/ *n. Tennis,* etc. **1** stroke played with the back of the hand turned toward the opponent. **2** [*attrib.*] of or made with a backhand (*backhand volley*).

back•hand•ed /bák-hándid/ *adj.* **1** (of a

blow, etc.) delivered with the back of the hand. **2** indirect. **3** = BACKHAND *attrib.*

back•ing /báking/ *n.* **1 a** support. **b** body of supporters. **c** material used to form a back or support. **2** musical accompaniment, esp. to a singer; backup.
■ **1 a** help, aid, assistance; approval, endorsement, sponsorship, funding. **b** backers, campaigners, patrons. **c** lining, interlining, reinforcement.

back•lash /báklash/ *n.* **1** excessive or marked adverse reaction. **2** sudden recoil in a mechanism.
■ **1** retaliation, repercussion, *sl.* comeback. **2** counteraction, rebound.

back•log /báklawg, –log/ *n.* **1** accumulation of uncompleted work, etc. **2** reserve; reserves (*backlog of goodwill*).

back•pack /bákpak/ • *n.* bag with shoulder straps for carrying on the back. • *v.intr.* travel or hike with this. □□ **back'pack•er** *n.*

back•ped•al /bákped'l/ *v.* (**-ped•aled, –ped•al•ing**) **1** pedal backward. **2** reverse one's previous action or opinion.
■ back up, backtrack.

back•rest /bákrest/ *n.* support for the back.

back•seat /bákseet/ *n.* **1** seat in the rear. **2** inferior position or status. □ **backseat driver** person eager to advise without taking or having responsibility.

back•side /báksīd/ *n. colloq.* buttocks.

back•slash /bákslash/ *n.* backward-sloping diagonal line.

back•slide /bákslīd/ *v.intr.* (*past* **–slid** /–slid/; *past part.* **–slid** *or* **–slid•den** /–slid'n/) relapse into bad ways or error. □□ **back'slid•er** *n.*

back•space /bákspays/ *v.intr.* move a computer cursor, etc., back one or more spaces.

back•spin /bákspin/ *n.* backward spin imparted to a ball.

back•stage /bákstáyj/ • *adv. Theatr.* out of view of the audience. • *adj.* concealed.
■ *adv.* see BACKGROUND 2. • *adj.* see BACKDOOR.

back•stairs /bákstairz/ *adj.* (also **back'stair**) underhand; clandestine.
■ see STEALTHY.

back•stop /bákstop/ *n. Baseball* fence or screen positioned behind home plate.

back•stroke /bákstrōk/ *n.* swimming stroke performed on the back.

back•track /báktrak/ *v.intr.* **1** retrace one's steps. **2** reverse one's previous action or opinion.

back•up /bákup/ *n.* **1** moral or technical support. **2** reserve. **3** *Computing* security copies of data.
■ **1** see SUPPORT *n.* 1. **2** see RESERVE 4.

back•ward /bákwərd/ • *adv.* (also **back'wards**) **1** away from one's front. **2 a** with the back foremost. **b** in reverse of the usual way. **3 a** into a worse state. **b** into the past. **c** back toward the starting point. • *adj.* **1** directed to the rear or starting point. **2** reversed. **3 a** mentally retarded or slow. **b** slow to progress. **4** reluctant; shy. □ **bend** (*or* **fall** *or* **lean**) **over backward** *colloq.* make every effort, esp. to be fair or helpful. □□ **back'ward•ness** *n.*

■ *adv.* **1** see BACK *adv.* 1. **2** rearward(s), regressively; counterclockwise. **3 a** see DETERIORATE. • *adj.* **1** rearward, behind. **2** in the opposite direction; retrograde, retrogressive, regressive. **3 a** dull, slow-witted, *colloq.* dim. **b** late, behindhand. **4** bashful, reticent. □ **bend over backward** do one's best.

back•wash /bákwosh, –wawsh/ *n.* **1** receding waves created by the motion of a ship, etc. **2** repercussions.

■ **1** see WAKE² 1. **2** see UPSHOT.

back•wa•ter /bákwawtər, –wotər/ *n.* **1** place remote from the center of activity. **2** stagnant water.

back•woods /bákwóodz/ *n.pl.* **1** remote uncleared forest land. **2** any remote or sparsely inhabited region. □□ **back'woods•man** *n.* (*pl.* **-men**)

back•yard /bakyaárd/ *n.* yard at the back of a house, etc. □ **in one's own backyard** *colloq.* near at hand.

ba•con /báykən/ *n.* cured meat from the back or sides of a pig.

bac•te•ri•a *pl.* of BACTERIUM.

bac•te•ri•cide /bakteérisīd/ *n.* substance capable of destroying bacteria. □□ **bac•te•ri•ci'dal** *adj.*

bac•te•ri•ol•o•gy /bákteereeóləjee/ *n.* the study of bacteria. □□ **bac•te•ri•o•log'i•cal** /–reeəlójikəl/ *adj.* **bac•te•ri•o•log'i•cal•ly** *adv.* **bac•te•ri•ol•o•gist** / óləjist/ *n.*

bac•te•ri•um /bakteéreeəm/ *n.* (*pl.* **bac•te•ri•a** /–reeə/) unicellular microorganism lacking an organized nucleus, esp. that can cause disease. □□ **bac•te'ri•al** *adj.*

bad /bad/ • *adj.* (**worse** /wərs/; **worst** /wərst/) **1** inferior; inadequate; defective. **2 a** unpleasant; unwelcome. **b** unsatisfactory; unfortunate. **c** harmful. **4 a** (of food) decayed; putrid. **b** polluted. **5** ill; injured. **6** *colloq.* regretful; guilty. **7** serious; severe. **8 a** morally unacceptable. **b** disobedient. **9** not valid. **10** (**bad'der, bad'dest**) *sl.* good; excellent. • *n.* **1** ill fortune. **2** ruin. • *adv. colloq.* badly. □ **bad blood** ill feeling. **bad debt** debt that is not recoverable. **bad faith** see FAITH. **bad-mouth** *v.tr.* subject to malicious gossip or criticism. **bad news** *colloq.* unpleasant or troublesome person or thing. **not** (**or not so**) **bad** *colloq.* fairly good. **too bad** *colloq.* regrettable. □□ **bad'ness** *n.*

■ *adj.* **1** poor, worthless, substandard, low-quality, wretched, *colloq.* lousy, crummy, *sl.* rotten; see also AWFUL² 1a, b. **2 a** offensive, disagreeable, inclement, adverse. **b** unfavorable, unlucky, inopportune; lamentable. **3** injurious, dangerous, hurtful; unhealthful, unhealthy, noxious. **4 a** spoiled, moldy. **5** wounded, diseased, lame; see also ILL *adj.* 1. **6** sorry, apologetic, ashamed. **7** distressing, grave, critical, terrible, dreadful. **8 a** evil, immoral, wicked, vicious, vile, sinful; see also OFFENSIVE *adj.* 1. **b** naughty, ill-behaved, unruly. **9** see INVALID. **10** see EXCELLENT. • *adv.* see BADLY. □ **bad blood** see *ill will*. **bad-mouth** attack, *colloq.* pan, trash. **too bad** see *regrettable* (REGRET). □□ **badness** see EVIL *n.* 2, *misbehavior* (MISBEHAVE).

bade see BID.

badge /baj/ *n.* **1** distinctive emblem worn as

a mark of office, membership, achievement, etc. **2** thing that reveals a condition or quality.

■ **1** see EMBLEM 1.

bad•ger /bájər/ • *n.* omnivorous gray-coated nocturnal mammal with a black and white striped head. • *v.tr.* pester; harass; tease.

■ *v.* see HARASS 1.

bad•i•nage /bád'naazh/ *n.* humorous or playful ridicule.

bad•lands /bádlandz/ *n.* extensive barren eroded tracts in arid areas.

bad•ly /bádlee/ *adv.* (**worse** /wərs/; **worst** /wərst/) **1** in a bad manner. **2** *colloq.* very much (*wants it badly*). **3** severely.

■ **1** poorly, defectively, incorrectly, shoddily; inaccurately, erroneously, unsatisfactorily, ineptly; unkindly, cruelly, wickedly, harshly, severely; atrociously, horribly. **2** greatly, seriously, *colloq.* bad. **3** gravely, critically, grievously.

bad•min•ton /bádmint'n/ *n.* game with rackets in which a shuttlecock is volleyed back and forth across a net.

bad-tem•pered /bádtémpərd/ *adj.* having a bad temper.

■ see IRRITABLE 1.

baf•fle /báfəl/ • *v.tr.* **1** confuse. **2** frustrate, hinder. See synonym study at THWART. • *n.* device that checks the flow of fluid, gas, sound, etc. □□ **baf'fle•ment** *n.* **baf'fling** *adj.* **baf'fling•ly** *adv.*

■ *v.* **1** see PERPLEX 1. **2** see FRUSTRATE *v.* 2.

bag /bag/ • *n.* **1** receptacle of flexible material with an opening at the top. **2 a** piece of luggage. **b** handbag. **3** [in *pl.*] *colloq.* large amount. **4** amount of game shot or allowed. **5** [usu. in *pl.*] baggy skin under the eyes. **6** *sl.* particular interest. • *v.* (**bagged, bagging**) **1** *tr.* put in a bag. **2** *colloq. tr.* **a** secure. **b** *colloq.* steal. **c** shoot (game). **3** *tr.* hang loosely; bulge. **b** *tr.* cause to do this. □ **bag lady** homeless woman who carries her possessions in shopping bags. **in the bag** achieved; secured. □□ **bag'ful** *n.* (*pl.* **-fuls**)

■ *n.* **1** sack, shopping bag. **2 a** valise, satchel, grip, suitcase. **b** pocketbook, purse. **3** (*bags*) see LOT *n.* 1. **6** occupation, hobby, avocation. • *v.* **2 a** see SECURE *v.* 3. **b** see STEAL *v.* 1. **c** kill; trap, snare. **3** see SWELL *v.* 3.

bag•a•telle /bágətél/ *n.* mere trifle.

ba•gel /báygəl/ *n.* hard bread roll in the shape of a ring.

bag•gage /bágij/ *n.* luggage.

■ see LUGGAGE.

bag•gy /bágee/ *adj.* (**bag•gi•er, bag•gi•est**) **1** hanging in loose folds. **2** puffed out. □□ **bag'gi•ly** *adv.* **bag'gi•ness** *n.*

■ **1** see LOOSE *adj.* 2–3.

bag•pipe /bágpīp/ *n.* [usu. in *pl.*] musical instrument consisting of a windbag connected to reeded pipes. □□ **bag'pip•er** *n.*

ba•guette /bagét/ *n.* long narrow French loaf.

bah /baa/ *int.* expression of contempt or disbelief.

bail¹ /bayl/ • *n.* **1** money, etc., required as

security for the temporary release of a person in custody pending trial. **2** person(s) giving such security. • *v.tr.* **1** release or secure the release of (a prisoner) on payment of bail. **2** release from a difficulty; rescue. □ **forfeit** (*colloq.* **jump**) **bail** fail to appear for trial after being released on bail. □□ **bail′a•ble** *adj.*

■ *n.* **1** see PAWN[2] *n.* • *v.* (*bail out*) see SAVE[1] *v.* **1**.

bail[2] /bayl/ *n.* **1** bar on a typewriter holding the paper against the platen. **2** arched usu. wire handle, as of a pail.

bail[3] /bayl/ *v.tr.* scoop water out of (a boat, etc.). □ **bail out 1** parachute from an aircraft. **2** leave or desert a problematic situation. □□ **bail′er** *n.*

bai•liff /báylif/ *n.* official in a court of law who keeps order, looks after prisoners, etc.

bai•li•wick /báyliwik/ *n.* **1** *Law* district or jurisdiction of a bailiff. **2** *joc.* person's sphere of operations or particular area of interest.

■ **1** see JURISDICTION 2. **2** see AREA 4.

bail•out /báylowt/ *n.* a rescue from a dire situation (*a financial bailout for an ailing company*).

bait /bayt/ • *n.* **1** food used to entice a prey, esp. a fish or an animal. **2** allurement. • *v.* **1** *tr.* **a** harass or annoy (a person). **b** torment (a chained animal). **2** *tr.* put bait on (a hook, trap, etc.).

■ *n.* see *enticement* (ENTICE). • *v.* **1 a** see HARASS 1. **b** see TANTALIZE.

baize /bayz/ *n.* coarse, usu. green woolen material resembling felt used as a covering or lining, esp. on the tops of billiard and card tables.

bake /bayk/ • *v.* **1** *tr.* cook or process (food, etc.) by dry heat in an oven or on a hot surface, without direct exposure to a flame. **2** *intr.* undergo the process of being baked. • *n.* act or an instance of baking. □ **baked Alaska** sponge cake and ice cream with a meringue covering browned in an oven. **baking powder** mixture of sodium bicarbonate, cream of tartar, etc., used as a leavening agent. **baking soda** sodium bicarbonate. □□ **bak′er** *n.*

bak•er•y /báykəree/ *n.* (*pl.* **–ies**) place where bread and cakes are made or sold.

bak•la•va /baáklɔvaà/ *n.* rich dessert of flaky pastry, honey, and nuts.

bak•sheesh /báksheesh/ *n.* gratuity.

bal•a•cla•va /bálɔklaàvɔ/ *n.* tight covering for the whole head and neck except for the eyes, nostrils, and mouth.

bal•a•lai•ka /bálɔlíkɔ/ *n.* guitarlike stringed instrument with a triangular body.

bal•ance /bálɔns/ • *n.* **1** apparatus for weighing, esp. one with a central pivot, beam, and two scales. **2 a** counteracting weight or force. **b** (in full **bal′ance wheel**) regulating device in a clock, etc. **3 a** even distribution of weight or amount. **b** stability of body or mind. **4** decisive weight or amount. **5 a** agreement between or the difference between credits and debits in an account. **b** amount outstanding. **6 a** *Art* harmony and proportion. **b** *Mus.* relative volume of

sources of sound. **7** (**the Balance**) zodiacal sign or constellation Libra. • *v.* **1** *tr.* offset or compare (one thing) with another. **2** *tr.* counteract, equal, or neutralize the weight or importance of. **3 a** *tr.* bring into or keep in equilibrium. **b** *intr.* be in equilibrium (*balanced on one leg*). **4** *tr.* make well-proportioned and harmonious. **5 a** *tr.* compare and esp. equalize debits and credits of (an account). **b** *intr.* (of an account) have credits and debits equal. □ **balance of payments** difference in value between payments into and out of a country. **balance of power** situation in which the chief nations of the world have roughly equal power. **balance of trade** difference in value between imports and exports. **balance sheet** statement giving the balance of an account. □□ **bal′anc•er** *n.*

■ *n.* **1** scales. **3 a** evenness, symmetry. **b** steadiness; poise, control. **4** preponderance; control, command. **5 b** difference, remainder; surplus. **6** see PROPORTION *n.* 2. • *v.* **1** weigh, estimate, measure; make up. **2** cancel (out); counterbalance, compensate (for). **3** steady. **b** stabilize, level (up *or* out). **4** equilibrate. □□ **balancer** harmonizer, steadier.

bal•co•ny /bálkɔnee/ *n.* (*pl.* **–nies**) **1 a** usu. balustraded platform on the outside of a building, with access from an upper floor window or door. **b** such a balustraded platform inside a building; gallery. **2** upper tier of seats in a theater, etc. □□ **bal′co•nied** *adj.*

bald /bawld/ *adj.* **1** with the scalp wholly or partly lacking hair. **2** lacking the usual hair, feathers, leaves, etc. **3** *colloq.* with the surface worn away (*a bald tire*). **4** blunt; unelaborated (*a bald statement*). **5** marked with white, esp. on the face (*a bald horse*). See synonym study at NAKED. □ **bald eagle** white-headed eagle used as the emblem of the United States. □□ **bald′ing** *adj.* (in senses 1–3). **bald′ish** *adj.* **bald′ly** *adv.* (in sense 4). **bald′ness** *n.*

■ **1, 2** see *hairless* (HAIR).

bal•der•dash /báwldɔrdash/ *n.* nonsense.

bale /bayl/ • *n.* tightly bound bundle of merchandise or hay. • *v.tr.* make up into bales.

ba•leen /bɔleén/ *n.* whalebone.

bale•ful /báylfʊʊl/ *adj.* **1** (esp. of a manner, look, etc.) gloomy; menacing. **2** harmful; malignant; destructive. □□ **bale′ful•ly** *adv.* **bale′ful•ness** *n.*

balk /bawk/ • *v.intr.* **1** refuse to go on. **2** (often foll. by *at*) hesitate. See synonym study at THWART. • *n.* **1** hindrance; stumbling block. **2** heavy timber. **3** *Baseball* illegal action made by a pitcher. □□ **balk′er** *n.*

■ *v.* see RECOIL *v.* 1, 2. • *n.* **1** see *prevention* (PREVENT).

ball[1] /bawl/ • *n.* **1 a** sphere, esp. for use in a game. **b** game played with such a sphere. **2 a** ball-shaped object; material forming the shape of a ball (*ball of snow*). **b** rounded part of the body (*ball of the foot*). **3** solid nonexplosive missile for a cannon, etc. **4** *Baseball* pitched ball that is not swung at by the batter and that does not pass through the strike zone. • *v.* form into a ball. □ **ball-and-socket joint** *Anat.* joint in which a rounded end pivots in a concave socket. **ball bearing 1** bearing in which friction is relieved by a ring of metal balls. **2** one of these balls. **ball cock** floating ball on a hinged arm that controls the water level in a cistern, etc. **ball game 1** game played with a ball, esp. a game of baseball. **2** colloq. affair or concern (a whole new ball game). **on the ball** colloq. alert. **play ball 1** start or continue a ball game. **2** colloq. cooperate. **start (or get) the ball rolling** set an activity in motion; make a start.

  ■ n. **1a, 2a** see ORB[1] n. **3** see SHOT 3. □ **on the ball** see ALERT adj. 1. **play ball 2** agree, work together.

ball[2] /bawl/ n. **1** formal social gathering for dancing. **2** sl. enjoyable time (esp. have a ball).

bal•lad /bálǝd/ n. **1** poem or song narrating a popular story. **2** slow sentimental song. □□ **bal•lad•eer** n. **bal•lad•ry** n.

bal•last /bálǝst/ • n. **1** any heavy material placed in a ship's hold, etc., for stability. **2** coarse stone, etc., used to form the bed of a railroad track or road. • v.tr. provide with ballast.

ball•boy /báwlboy/ n. (fem. **ball•girl** /–gǝrl/) boy or girl who retrieves balls that go out of play during a game.

bal•le•ri•na /bálǝreénǝ/ n. female ballet dancer.

bal•let /haláy, hálay/ n. **1** dramatic or representational style of dancing to music. **2** particular piece or performance of ballet. □□ **bal•let•ic** /balétik/ adj.

bal•lis•tic /balístik/ adj. **1** of or relating to projectiles. **2** moving under the force of gravity only. □ **ballistic missile** missile that is initially powered and guided but falls under gravity on its target. □□ **bal•lis•ti•cal•ly** adv.

bal•lis•tics /balístiks/ n.pl. [usu. treated as sing.] science of projectiles and firearms.

bal•loon /balóon/ • n. **1** small inflatable rubber pouch with a neck, used as a toy or decoration. **2** large bag inflatable with hot air or gas to make it rise in the air, often carrying a basket for passengers. **3** balloon shape enclosing dialogue in a comic strip or cartoon. • v. **1** intr. & tr. swell out or cause to swell out like a balloon. **2** intr. travel by balloon. □□ **bal•loon'ist** n.

  ■ v. **1** see SWELL v. 3.

bal•lot /bálǝt/ • n. **1** process of recorded voting, usu. secret. **2** total of votes recorded in a ballot. **3** paper or ticket, etc., used in voting. • v. (**bal•lot•ed, bal•lot•ing**) **1** intr. give a vote. **2** tr. take a ballot of (the union balloted its members). □ **ballot box** sealed box into which voters put completed ballot papers.

  ■ n. **1** see VOTE n. 1. • v. **1** see VOTE v. 1.

ball•park /báwlpaark/ n. **1** baseball field. **2** [attrib.] colloq. approximate. □ **in the (right) ballpark** colloq. approximately correct.

ball•point /báwlpoint/ n. (in full **ball'point pen'**) pen with a tiny ball as its writing point.

ball•room /báwlrōōm, –rŏŏm/ n. large room for dancing.

bal•ly•hoo /báleehōō/ n. **1** loud noise or fuss; confused state or commotion. **2** extravagant or sensational publicity.

  ■ **1** see NOISE n. **2** see FANFARE 2.

balm /baam/ n. aromatic soothing ointment or oil.

  ■ see OINTMENT.

balm•y /báamee/ adj. (**balm•i•er, balm•i•est**) **1** mild; soothing. **2** fragrant. □□ **balm'i•ly** adv. **balm'i•ness** n.

  ■ **1** see MILD 2.

ba•lo•ney /bǝlónee/ n. (pl. **–neys**) sl. **1** nonsense. **2** = BOLOGNA.

  ■ **1** see NONSENSE.

bal•sa /báwlsǝ/ n. **1** (in full **bal'sa wood**) tough lightweight wood used for making models, etc. **2** tropical American tree from which it comes.

bal•sam /báwlsǝm/ n. **1** resin exuded from various trees and shrubs. **2** ointment, esp. containing oil or turpentine. **3** any of various trees or shrubs that yield balsam. □□ **bal•sam•ic** /–sámik/ adj.

  ■ □□ **balsamic** see soothing (SOOTHE).

bal•us•ter /bálǝstǝr/ n. short post or pillar supporting a rail.

bal•us•trade /bálǝstráyd/ n. railing supported by balusters.

bam•boo /bambōō/ n. **1** tropical giant woody grass with hollow jointed stem. **2** its stem used for canes, furniture, etc.

bam•boo•zle /bambōōzǝl/ v.tr. colloq. cheat; hoax; mystify. □□ **bam•boo'zle•ment** n. **bam•boo'zler** n.

  ■ see CHEAT v. 1.

ban /ban/ • v.tr. (**banned, ban•ning**) forbid; prohibit, esp. formally. See synonym study at PROHIBIT. • n. formal or authoritative prohibition.

  ■ v. outlaw, interdict, stop, bar, proscribe. • n. taboo, proscription, interdiction.

ba•nal /bǝnál, báynǝl, bánǝl/ adj. trite; feeble; commonplace. □□ **ba•nal•i•ty** /–nálitee/ n. (pl. **–ties**). **ba•nal•ly** adv.

  ■ hackneyed, stereotyped, clichéd, stereotypical, pedestrian, humdrum, tired, well-worn, feeble, unoriginal, unimaginative, uninspired, bourgeois; colloq. corny, old hat.

ba•nan•a /bǝnánǝ/ n. **1** long curved fruit with soft pulpy flesh and yellow skin. **2** treelike plant bearing this. □ **banana republic** derog. small nation, esp. in Central America, dependent on one export crop. **go bananas** sl. go crazy.

band[1] /band/ • n. **1** flat, thin strip or loop of material (e.g., paper, metal, or cloth) put around something esp. to hold or decorate it. **2 a** strip of material forming part of a garment. **b** stripe. **3 a** range of frequencies or wavelengths in a spectrum (esp. of radio frequencies). **b** range of values within a series. • v.tr. **1** put a band on. □ **band saw** mechanical saw with a blade formed by an endless toothed band.

  ■ n. **1** ribbon, headband, belt. **2 b** strip, line, streak, bar, border, edging. • v. **1** tie (up), bind; encircle.

band[2] /band/ • n. organized group, esp. of

nonclassical musicians. • *v.tr* unite (esp. as *band together*).

■ *n.* company, troop, platoon, corps, body, gang, horde, party, pack, *colloq.* bunch, crew, mob; ensemble, combination, orchestra, *sl.* combo. • *v.* (*band together*) confederate, ally, team *or* join up.

band•age /bándij/ • *n.* strip of material for binding up a wound, etc. • *v.tr.* bind with a bandage.

■ *v.* see BIND *v.* 9.

Band-Aid /bándayd/ *n.* **1** *propr.* adhesive strip with a gauze pad for covering minor wounds. **2** (**band-aid**) stopgap solution to a problem.

ban•dan•na /bandánə/ *n.* (also **ban•dan'a**) a large patterned handkerchief.

b. & b. *abbr.* (also **B & B**) bed and breakfast.

ban•deau /bándō/ *n.* (*pl.* **ban•deaux** /–dōz/) narrow ribbon.

ban•dit /bándit/ *n.* robber; outlaw. □□ **ban'dit•ry** *n.*

■ see OUTLAW *n.*

ban•do•lier /bándəleˈer/ *n.* (also **ban•do• leer'**) shoulder belt with loops or pockets for cartridges.

band•stand /bándstand/ *n.* covered outdoor platform for a band to play on, usu. in a park.

band•wag•on /bándwagən/ *n.* wagon used for carrying a band in a parade, etc. □ **climb** (or **jump**) **on the bandwagon** join a popular or successful cause, etc.

ban•dy[1] /bándee/ *adj.* (**ban•di•er, ban•di• est**) **1** (of the legs) curved so as to be wide apart at the knees. **2** (also **ban'dy-leg•ged** /–légəd, –legd/) (of a person) having bandy legs.

ban•dy[2] /bándee/ *v.tr.* (**–dies, –died**) **1** pass (a story, rumor, etc.) back and forth. **2** discuss disparagingly. **3** exchange (blows, insults, etc.).

bane /bayn/ *n.* **1** cause of ruin or trouble. **2** ruin; woe. □□ **bane'ful** *adj.* **bane'ful•ly** *adv.*

■ **1** see CURSE *n.* 4. **2** see RUIN *n.* 2.

bang /bang/ • *n.* **1** loud short sound. **2** sharp blow. **3** [esp. in *pl.*] fringe of hair cut straight across the forehead. • *v.* **1** strike or shut noisily. **2** make or cause to make a bang. • *adv.* with a bang.

■ *n.* **1** see EXPLOSION[1] 2. **2** see HIT *n.* 1a. • *v.* **1** see HIT *v.* 1a, BEAT *v.* 1. **2** see BOOM *v.*

ban•gle /bánggəl/ *n.* rigid bracelet or anklet.

ban•ish /bánish/ *v.tr.* **1** condemn to exile. **2** dismiss from one's presence or mind. □□ **ban'ish•ment** *n.*

■ **1** expatriate, deport. **2** drive out *or* away, expel, cast out. □□ **banishment** see EXILE *n.* 1.

ban•is•ter /bánistər/ *n.* (also **ban'nis•ter**) uprights and handrail at the side of a staircase.

ban•jo /bánjō/ *n.* (*pl.* **–jos** *or* **–joes**) guitarlike stringed instrument with a circular body. □□ **ban'jo•ist** *n.*

bank[1] /bangk/ • *n.* **1** area of sloping land alongside a river. **2** raised shelf of ground; slope. **3** mass of cloud, fog, snow, etc. • *v.* **1** *tr. & intr.* heap or rise into banks. **2** *tr.* heap

up (a fire) tightly so that it burns slowly. **3 a** *intr.* (of a vehicle or aircraft or its occupant) travel with one side higher than the other in rounding a curve. **b** *tr.* cause to do this.

■ *n.* **1, 2** see SLOPE *n.* 1–3.

bank[2] /bangk/ • *n.* **1 a** establishment for depositing, withdrawing, and borrowing money. **b** building in which this business takes place. **2** kitty in some gambling games. **3** storage place. • *v.tr.* deposit (money or valuables) in a bank. □ **bank on** rely on. □□ **bank'a•ble** *adj.*

■ *n.* **3** see STOREHOUSE. • *v.* see DEPOSIT *v.* 2. □ **bank on** see RELY.

bank[3] /bangk/ *n.* row of similar objects, e.g., lights, switches, oars.

bank•book /bángkbʊk/ *n.* = PASSBOOK.

bank•card /bángk-kard/ *n.* bank-issued credit card or automatic teller machine card.

bank•er /bángkər/ *n.* **1** person who manages or owns a bank. **2** keeper of the bank in some gambling games.

bank•ing /bángking/ *n.* business transactions of a bank.

bank•note /bángknōt/ *n.* banker's promissory note, payable on demand.

bank•rupt /bángkrupt/ • *adj.* **1** insolvent; declared in law unable to pay debts. **2** exhausted or drained (of some quality, etc.); deficient; lacking. • *n.* insolvent person. • *v.tr.* make bankrupt. □□ **bank•rupt•cy** /–rupt-see/ *n.* (*pl.* **–cies**).

■ *adj.* **1** see INSOLVENT *adj.* • *n.* see PAUPER. • *v.* see RUIN *v.* 1.

ban•ner /bánər/ *n.* **1** large sign bearing a slogan or design used esp. in a demonstration or procession. **2** flag. □□ **ban'nered** *adj.*

■ standard, pennant, ensign, burgee, pennon.

ban'nis•ter var. of BANISTER.

banns /banz/ *n.pl.* notice in a parish church announcing an intended marriage.

ban•quet /bángkwit/ • *n.* elaborate usu. extensive feast. • *v.* **1** *intr.* hold a banquet; feast. **2** *tr.* entertain with a banquet. □□ **ban'quet•er** *n.*

■ *n.* sumptuous meal, ceremonial dinner.

ban•quette /bangkét/ *n.* upholstered bench along a wall, esp. in a restaurant or bar.

ban•shee /bánshee, –sheé/ *n.* female spirit whose wailing warns of a death in a house.

ban•tam /bántəm/ *n.* **1** any of several small breeds of domestic fowl. **2** small but aggressive person.

ban•tam•weight /bántəmwayt/ *n.* **1** weight in certain sports between flyweight and featherweight. **2** athlete of this weight.

ban•ter /bántər/ • *n.* good-humored teasing. • *v.* **1** *tr.* ridicule in a good-humored way. **2** *intr.* talk humorously or teasingly. □□ **ban'ter•er** *n.*

■ *n.* raillery, badinage, persiflage, jesting. • *v.* **1** tease, kid, poke fun at, *colloq.* rib. **2** joke (around).

Ban•tu /bántōō/ • *n.* (*pl.* same or **Ban•tus**) **1** often *offens.* large group of Negroid peoples of central and southern Africa. **2** group of languages spoken by them. • *adj.* of these peoples or languages.

ban•yan /bányən/ n. Indian fig tree with self-rooting branches.

ba•o•bab /báyōbab, báa–/ n. African tree with a massive trunk and large edible fruit.

bap•tism /báptizəm/ n. **1** religious rite symbolizing admission to the Christian Church, with water and usu. name given. **2** any initiation. □□ **bap•tis•mal** /–tizməl/ adj.

Bap•tist /báptist/ n. Christian advocating baptism by total immersion.

bap•tis•ter•y /báptistree/ n. (also **bap′tis•try**) (pl. **–tries**) **1** part of a church used for baptism. **2** (in a Baptist chapel) sunken receptacle used for total immersion.

bap•tize /báptīz/ v.tr. **1** administer baptism to. **2** give a name or nickname to.
■ **1** christen. **2** see CALL v. 6.

bar¹ /baar/ • n. **1** long piece of rigid material used to confine or obstruct. **2** something resembling this in being straight, rigid, narrow, etc. **3** barrier or restriction. **4 a** counter in a restaurant, etc., for serving alcohol or refreshments. **b** room in which alcohol is served and customers may sit and drink. **c** establishment selling alcoholic drinks to be consumed on the premises. **d** small store or stall serving refreshments. **5** enclosure in which a defendant stands in a court of law. **6** Mus. any of the sections of usu. equal time value into which a musical composition is divided by vertical lines. **7** (**the Bar**) Law **a** lawyers collectively. **b** the profession of lawyers. • v.tr. (**barred**, **barring**) **1 a** fasten (a door, window, etc.) with a bar or bars. **b** [usu. foll. by in, out] shut or keep in or out. **2** obstruct; prevent. • prep. except (all were there bar a few). □ **bar code** machine-readable striped code on packaging. **behind bars** in prison.
■ n. **1** rod, shaft, pole, stick. **2** see BLOCK n. 1. **3** obstacle, obstruction, barricade, hindrance, deterrent, impediment, control, check, restraint, constraint. **4 b, c** barroom, saloon, café, cocktail lounge. **d** kiosk. • v. **1 a** close up, secure, make fast. **b** (bar out) see shut out 1. **2** stop, hinder. • prep. excepting, excluding, barring. □ **behind bars** colloq. doing time, sl. inside.

bar² /baar/ n. esp. Meteorol. unit of pressure, 10⁵ newtons per square meter, approx. one atmosphere.

barb /baarb/ • n. **1** secondary, backward facing projection from an arrow, fishhook, etc. **2** hurtful remark. • v.tr. **1** provide (an arrow, fishhook, etc.) with a barb or barbs. **2** (as **barbed** adj.) (of a remark, etc.) deliberately hurtful.
■ n. **1** see SPINE³ 2. **2** see WISECRACK n. • v. **2** (barbed) see TART 2.

bar•bar•i•an /baarbáireeən/ • n. **1** uncultured or brutish person. **2** member of a primitive community or tribe. • adj. **1** rough and uncultured. **2** uncivilized.
■ n. **1** boor, lowbrow; tough, hoodlum, skinhead. **2** savage, brute, native. • adj. uncultivated, philistine, savage.

bar•bar•ic /baarbárik/ adj. **1** brutal; cruel. **2** rough and uncultured. **3** primitive. □□ **bar•bar′i•cal•ly** adv.
■ **1** see BRUTAL. **2, 3** see SAVAGE adj. 2.

bar•ba•rism /báarbərizəm/ n. **1** absence of culture and civilized standards; rudeness. **2** nonstandard word or expression.

bar•bar•i•ty /baarbáritee/ n. (pl. **–ties**) **1** savage cruelty. **2** example of this.
■ **1** inhumanity, ruthlessness, savagery. **2** atrocity, outrage.

bar•ba•rous /báarbərəs/ adj. = BARBARIC. □□ **bar′ba•rous•ly** adv. **bar′ba•rous•ness** n.

bar•be•cue /báarbikyōō/ • n. **1 a** meal cooked over an open fire, often out of doors. **b** party at which such a meal is cooked and eaten. **c** marinated or seasoned meat prepared for cooking this way. **2 a** grill used for this. **b** fireplace containing such a grill. • v.tr. (**bar•be•cues**, **bar•be•cued**, **bar•be•cuing**) cook on a barbecue.

bar•bel /báarbəl/ n. fleshy filament growing from the mouth of some fishes.

bar•bell /báarbel/ n. iron bar with removable weights at each end, used for weightlifting.

bar•ber /báarbər/ • n. person who cuts men's hair as an occupation. • v.tr. cut the hair of; shave or trim the beard of. □□ **bar′ber•shop** n.

bar•ber•ry /báarberee/ n. (pl. **–ries**) **1** shrub with yellow flowers and red berries. **2** its berry.

bar•bi•tu•rate /baarbítchərət, –rayt/ n. sedative or sleep-inducing drug derived from an organic, white crystalline acid.

bar•ca•role /báarkərōl/ n. (also **bar′ca•rolle**) **1** song sung by Venetian gondoliers. **2** music in imitation of this.

bard /baard/ n. **1** poet. **2** hist. Celtic minstrel. □□ **bard′ic** adj.
■ **2** see MINSTREL.

bare /bair/ • adj. **1** unclothed or uncovered. **2** leafless, unfurnished; empty. **3** unadorned. **4** scanty; mere. See synonym study at NAKED. • v.tr. uncover; reveal. □□ **bare′ness** n.
■ adj. **1** naked, nude, exposed. **2** stripped, defoliated, shorn; vacant. **3** plain, simple; undisguised, open. **4** minimal; meager, scant. • v. expose, lay bare, unsheathe; disclose, divulge. □□ **bareness** nakedness, nudity; see also emptiness (EMPTY), SIMPLICITY.

bare•back /báirbak/ adj. & adv. without a saddle.

bare•faced /báirfayst/ adj. undisguised; impudent (barefaced lie).
■ unconcealed, open, blatant; audacious, shameless, insolent.

bare•foot /báirfoŏt/ adj. & adv. (also **bare•foot•ed** /–foŏtid/) with nothing on the feet.

bare•head•ed /báirhédid/ adj. & adv. without a covering for the head.

bare•ly /báirlee/ adv. **1** only just; scarcely. **2** scantily.
■ **1** not quite, hardly, no more than. **2** sparsely, sparely, austerely, simply, plainly.

bar•gain /báargin/ • n. **1 a** agreement on the terms of a transaction or sale. **b** this from the buyer's viewpoint. **2** something acquired or offered cheaply. • v.intr. discuss the terms of a transaction. □ **bargain for** (or colloq.

on) [usu. with *neg.* actual or implied] be prepared for; expect. **in** (also **into**) **the bargain** moreover; in addition to what was expected. □□ **bar′gain•er** *n.*

■ *n.* 1 contract, understanding, arrangement. 2 good deal, best buy, square deal. ● *v.* negotiate, trade, haggle, barter. □ **bargain for** count on, envision, foresee. **in the bargain** see MOREOVER.

barge /baarj/ ● *n.* 1 long flat-bottomed cargo boat on canals, rivers, etc. 2 long ornamental pleasure boat. ● *v.intr.* 1 intrude or interrupt rudely or awkwardly. 2 collide with.

■ *v.* 1 see INTRUDE 1.

bar•i•tone /báritōn/ *n.* 1 a second-lowest adult male singing voice. **b** singer with this voice. 2 instrument pitched second-lowest in its family.

bar•i•um /báireeəm, bár-/ *n. Chem.* white, reactive, soft metallic element of the alkaline earth group. ¶Symb.: **Ba.**

bark[1] /baark/ ● *n.* 1 sharp explosive cry of a dog, fox, etc. 2 sound resembling this. ● *v.* 1 *intr.* (of a dog, fox, etc.) give a bark. 2 *tr. & intr.* speak or utter sharply or brusquely. □ **bark up the wrong tree** make an effort in the wrong direction.

bark[2] /baark/ ● *n.* 1 tough protective outer sheath of tree trunks, branches, etc. ● *v.tr.* graze or scrape (one's shin, etc.).

bar•keep•er /báarkeepər/ *n.* (also **bar′keep**) person who owns or serves drinks in a bar.

bark•er /báarkər/ *n.* person at an auction, sideshow, etc., who calls out to passersby as advertising.

bar•ley /báarlee/ *n.* cereal widely used as food and in malt liquors and spirits.

bar•maid /báarmayd/ *n.* female bartender.

bar•man /báarmən/ *n.* (*pl.* **–men**) male bartender.

bar mitz•vah /baar mítsvə/ *n.* 1 religious initiation ceremony of a Jewish boy who has reached the age of 13. 2 boy undergoing this ceremony.

barn /baarn/ *n.* large farm building for storing grain, housing livestock, etc.

bar•na•cle /báarnəkəl/ *n.* 1 any of various species of small marine crustaceans that cling to rocks, ships' hulls, etc. 2 tenacious attendant or follower. □□ **bar′na•cled** *adj.*

barn•storm /báarnstawrm/ *v.intr.* 1 tour rural districts as an entertainer or political campaigner. 2 *Aeron.* give informal flying exhibitions; do stunt flying. □□ **barn′storm•er** *n.*

barn•yard /báarnyaard/ *n.* area around a barn.

ba•rom•e•ter /bərómitər/ *n.* 1 instrument measuring atmospheric pressure, esp. in forecasting the weather. 2 anything that reflects change. □□ **bar•o•met•ric** /bárəmétrik/ *adj.* **bar•o•met′ri•cal** *adj.* **ba•rom′e•try** *n.*

bar•on /báran/ *n.* 1 member of the lowest order of the British nobility. 2 important businessman or other powerful or influential person (*newspaper baron*).

bar•on•ess /báranis/ *n.* 1 woman holding

the rank of baron. 2 wife or widow of a baron.

bar•on•et /báranit, –nét/ *n.* member of the lowest hereditary titled British order.

bar•o•ny /báranee/ *n.* (*pl.* **–nies**) domain or rank of a baron.

ba•roque /bərók/ ● *adj.* 1 highly ornate and extravagant in style, esp. of European art, architecture, and music of the 17th and 18th c. 2 of or relating to this period. ● *n.* baroque style or art.

■ *adj.* 1 see ORNATE.

bar•rack /bárək/ ● *n.* [usu. in *pl.*, often treated as *sing.*] 1 housing for soldiers. 2 large bleak building. ● *v.tr.* place (soldiers, etc.) in barracks.

bar•ra•cu•da /bárəkŏŏdə/ *n.* (*pl.* same or **–das**) large voracious tropical marine fish.

bar•rage /bəráazh/ *n.* 1 concentrated artillery bombardment. 2 rapid succession of questions or criticisms.

■ 1 see VOLLEY *n.* 1. 2 see STREAM *n.* 2.

barre /baar/ *n.* horizontal bar at waist level used in dance exercises.

bar•rel /bárəl/ ● *n.* 1 cylindrical container usu. bulging out in the middle. 2 its contents. 3 measure of capacity, usu. varying from 30 to 40 gallons. 4 cylindrical tube forming part of an object such as a gun or pen. ● *v.* (**bar•reled, bar•rel•ing; bar•relled, bar•rel•ling**) 1 *tr.* put into a barrel or barrels. 2 *intr. sl.* drive or move fast. □ **barrel organ** mechanical musical instrument in which a rotating pin-studded cylinder acts on a series of pipe valves, strings, or metal tongues.

■ *n.* 1, 2 see KEG.

bar•ren /báran/ *adj.* 1 a unable to bear young. **b** unable to produce fruit or vegetation. 2 unprofitable. 3 dull. See synonym study at NAKED. □□ **bar′ren•ly** *adv.* **bar′ren•ness** *n.*

■ 1 a sterile, childless, infertile. **b** unproductive, fruitless, unfruitful. 2 unrewarding, poor, meager. 3 see DREARY. □□ **barrenness** sterility; desolation; tedium, dreariness.

bar•rette /bərét/ *n.* hair clip.

bar•ri•cade /bárikáyd/ ● *n.* barrier, esp. improvised. ● *v.tr.* block or defend with a barricade.

■ *n.* see BAR[1] *n.* 3. ● *v.* see BAR[1] *v.* 1a.

bar•ri•er /báreeər/ *n.* 1 fence, etc., that bars advance or access. 2 obstacle (*language barrier*).

■ 1 bar, railing, wall. 2 obstruction, block, impediment.

bar•ring /báaring/ *prep.* except; not including.

■ excluding, exclusive of, bar, omitting.

bar•ri•o /báareeō, bár–/ *n.* (*pl.* **–os**) Spanish-speaking quarter or neighborhood of a town or city.

bar•room /báarōōm, –rŏŏm/ *n.* establishment specializing in serving alcoholic drinks.

bar•row[1] /báarō/ *n.* 1 two-wheeled handcart. 2 = WHEELBARROW.

bar•row[2] /báarō/ *n. Archaeol.* ancient grave mound.

bar•tend•er /báartendər/ *n.* person serving behind the bar of a tavern, bar, etc.

bar•ter /báartər/ ● *v.* 1 *tr.* exchange (goods or

services) without using money. **2** *intr.* make such an exchange. • *n.* trade by exchange of goods. □□ **bar'ter•er** *n.*

■ *v.* see EXCHANGE *v.* • *n.* see EXCHANGE *n.* 1.

bar•y•on /báreeon/ *n.* x*Physics* heavy elementary particle (i.e., a nucleon or hyperon). □□ **bar•y•on'ic** *adj.*

ba•sal /báysəl, –zəl/ *adj.* of, at, or forming a base. □ **ba'sal me•tab'o•lism** amount of energy consumed by an organism at complete rest.

ba•salt /bəsáwlt, báysawlt/ *n.* dark volcanic rock. □□ **ba•sal'tic** /–sáwltik/ *adj.*

base¹ /bays/ • *n.* **1 a** part supporting from beneath or serving as a foundation. **b** notional structure or entity (*power base*). **2** principle or starting point. **3** headquarters. **4** main or important ingredient. **5** *Chem.* substance capable of combining with an acid to form a salt. **6** *Math.* number in terms of which other numbers or logarithms are expressed. **7** *Baseball*, etc., one of the four stations that must be reached in turn to score a run. • *v.tr.* **1** found or establish. **2** station (*troops were based in Malta*).

■ *n.* **1 a** bottom, foot, stand. **b** center, hub, focus. **2** basis, point of departure. **3** home, station, camp. • *v.* **1** secure, build, ground. **2** post, position.

base² /bays/ *adj.* **1** cowardly; despicable. **2** menial. **3** not pure; alloyed. **4** (of a metal) low in value. □□ **base'ly** *adv.* **base'ness** *n.*

■ **1** low, undignified, mean, contemptible, dastardly, vile, sordid, ignoble. **2** degrading, inferior. **3** see IMPURE 1.

base•ball /báysbawl/ *n.* **1** game played with a bat and ball, and a circuit of four bases that must be completed to score. **2** ball used in this game.

base•board /báysbawrd/ *n.* narrow board, etc., along the bottom of the wall of a room.

base•less /báyslis/ *adj.* unfounded; groundless. □□ **base'less•ly** *adv.* **base'less•ness** *n.*

■ see UNFOUNDED.

base•line /báyslīn/ *n.* **1** line used as a base or starting point. **2** (in tennis, basketball, etc.) line marking each end of a court. **3** *Baseball* either of the lines leading from home plate and determining the boundaries of fair territory.

base•ment /báysmənt/ *n.* lowest floor of a building, usu. at least partly below ground level.

■ see CELLAR *n.*

bash /bash/ • *v.tr.* strike bluntly or heavily. • *n.* **1** heavy blow. **2** *sl.* party. □□ **bash'er** *n.*

■ *v.* see STRIKE *v.* 1. • *n.* **2** see PARTY *n.* 1.

bash•ful /báshfŏŏl/ *adj.* **1** shy; diffident; self-conscious. **2** sheepish. □□ **bash'ful•ly** *adv.* **bash'ful•ness** *n.*

■ retiring, embarrassed, meek, abashed, shamefaced.

BASIC /báysik/ *n.* computer programming language using familiar English words and designed for beginners.

bas•ic /báysik/ • *adj.* **1** serving as a base. **2** fundamental. • *n.* [usu. in *pl.*] fundamental facts or principles. □□ **ba'si•cal•ly** *adv.*

■ *adj.* **2** essential, key, underlying. • *n.* (ba-

sics) see ELEMENT 6. □□ **basically** see *in essence* (ESSENCE).

ba•sil /bázəl, báyzəl/ *n.* aromatic herb used as a flavoring.

ba•sil•i•ca /bəsílikə/ *n.* **1** ancient Roman public hall used as a court of law, etc. **2** similar building used as a Christian church.

ba•sin /báysən/ *n.* **1** shallow, open container for holding water; sink. **2** hollow depression. **3** any sheltered mooring area. **4** area drained by rivers and tributaries. □□ **ba'sin•ful** *n.* (*pl.* **–fuls**).

■ **2** see HOLLOW *n.* 1.

ba•sis /báysis/ *n.* (*pl.* **ba•ses** /–seez/) **1** foundation or support. **2** main or determining principle or ingredient. **3** starting point for a discussion, etc.

■ **1, 2** base, footing, grounding; essence, bottom, heart. **3** point of departure.

bask /bask/ *v.intr.* **1** relax in warmth and light. **2** [foll. by *in*] derive great pleasure (from).

■ **2** see REVEL *v.* 2.

bas•ket /báskit/ *n.* **1** container made of interwoven cane, etc. **2** amount held by this. **3** goal in basketball, or a goal scored. □ **basket case** person who cannot function because of tension, etc. □□ **bas'ket•ful** *n.* (*pl.* **–fuls**).

bas•ket•ball /báskitbawl/ *n.* **1** game between two teams in which points are scored by making the ball drop through hooped nets fixed at each end of the court. **2** ball used in this game.

bas•ket•ry /báskitree/ *n.* **1** art of making baskets. **2** baskets collectively.

bas•ket•work /báskitwərk/ *n.* = BASKETRY.

bas mitz•vah /bas mítsvə/ *n.* (also **bat mitz'vah**) **1** initiation ceremony for a Jewish girl who has reached the age of 12 or 13. **2** girl undergoing this ceremony.

Basque /bask/ • *n.* **1** member of a people of the Western Pyrenees. **2** their language. • *adj.* the Basques or their language.

bas-re•lief /báa-rileéf, bás–/ *n.* sculpture or carving in which the figures project slightly from the background.

bass¹ /bays/ • *n.* **1 a** lowest adult male singing voice. **b** singer with this voice. **2** instrument pitched lowest in its family. **3** *colloq.* bass guitar or double bass. **4** low-frequency output of a radio, CD player, etc. • *adj.* **1** lowest in musical pitch. **2** deep sounding. □□ **bass'ist** *n.* (in sense 3).

bass² /bas/ *n.* (*pl.* same or **bass•es**) any of various edible fishes including the common perch.

bas•set /básit/ *n.* (in full **bas'set hound**) sturdy hunting dog with a long body, short legs, and big ears.

bas•si•net /básinét/ *n.* baby's wicker cradle, usu. hooded.

bas•so /básō, báa–/ *n.* (*pl.* **–sos** or **bas•si** /–see/) singer with a bass voice.

bas•soon /bəsōōn/ *n.* bass instrument of the oboe family.

bast /bast/ *n.* fiber from the inner bark of a tree used for ropes, etc.

bas•tard /bástərd/ usu. *offens.* • *n.* **1** person born of parents not married to each other. **2** *sl.* unpleasant or despicable person. **3** *sl.* difficult or awkward thing, undertaking, etc. • *adj.* **1** illegitimate by birth. **2** (of things) unauthorized; counterfeit; hybrid. □□ **bas′tard•y** *n.* (in sense 1 of *n.*).

■ *n.* **2** son of a bitch, *sl.* bummer. • *adj.* **1** see ILLEGITIMATE *adj.* 1.

bas•tard•ize /bástərdīz/ *v.tr.* **1** declare (a person) illegitimate. **2** corrupt; debase. □□ **bas•tard•i•za′tion** *n.*

■ **2** see ADULTERATE *v.*

baste[1] /bayst/ *v.tr.* moisten (meat) with gravy or melted fat during cooking.

baste[2] /bayst/ *v.tr.* stitch loosely together in preparation for sewing; tack.

bas•tion /báschən, -teeən/ *n.* **1** projecting part of a fortification. **2** thing regarded as protecting (*bastion of freedom*).

■ see STRONGHOLD 1, 3.

bat[1] /bat/ • *n.* **1** implement with a handle, used for hitting balls in games. **2** player's turn with this. • *v.* (**bat•ted, bat•ting**) **1** *tr.* hit with or as with a bat. **2** *intr.* take a turn at batting.

■ *v.* **1** see HIT *v.* 1a.

bat[2] /bat/ *n.* mouselike nocturnal flying mammal.

bat[3] /bat/ *v.tr.* (**bat•ted, bat•ting**) blink.

batch /bach/ • *n.* **1** group of things or persons dealt with together. **2** loaves, panfuls, etc., produced at one baking. **3** *Computing* group of records processed as a single unit. • *v.tr.* arrange or deal with in batches.

■ *n.* **1** set, number, quantity, assortment, lot. • *v.* sort, bunch.

bat•ed /báytid/ *adj.* □ **with bated breath** very anxiously.

bath /bath/ *n.* (*pl.* **baths** /bathz, baths/) **1** = BATHTUB. **2** act of washing the body in a tub. **3** liquid in which something is immersed, treated, etc.

■ **2** see WASH *n.* 1.

bathe /bayth/ *v.* **1** *intr.* immerse oneself in water, esp. to wash. **2** *tr.* soak. **3** *tr.* (of sunlight, etc.) envelop. □ **bathing suit** garment worn for swimming.

■ **3** see SUFFUSE.

bath•house /báth-hows/ *n.* **1** building with baths for public use. **2** building with changing rooms, as at the beach.

ba•thos /báythaws, -thos/ *n.* lapse in mood from the sublime to the absurd or trivial; anticlimax. □□ **ba•thet•ic** /bəthétik/ *adj.*

bath•robe /báthrōb/ *n.* loose robe, often of toweling, worn before and after taking a bath.

bath•room /báthrōom, -rōōm/ *n.* room with a toilet and sink and often a bathtub or shower.

■ see LAVATORY.

bath•tub /báthtəb/ *n.* container for liquid, usu. water, used for bathing the body.

bath•y•scaphe /báthiskaf/ *n.* manned vessel controlled by ballast for deep-sea diving.

bath•y•sphere /báthisfeer/ *n.* spherical vessel connected to a surface vessel by cables, used for deep-sea observation.

ba•tik /bətéek, bátik/ *n.* method of producing colored designs on textiles by applying wax to the parts to be left uncolored; piece of cloth treated in this way.

bat mitz•vah /bat mítsvə/ var. of BAS MITZVAH.

ba•ton /bətón, ba–, bát′n/ *n.* **1** thin stick used by a conductor to direct an orchestra. **2** *Sports* short stick carried and passed on in a relay race. **3** stick carried by a drum major. **4** staff of office.

■ see STAFF *n.* 1a, b.

bat•tal•ion /bətályən/ *n.* army unit, part of a division.

bat•ten[1] /bát′n/ • *n.* **1** narrow flat strip of wood used as a stiffener, etc. **2** strip of wood used for clamping the boards of a door, etc. **3** *Naut.* strip for securing tarpaulin over a ship's hatchway. • *v.tr.* strengthen or fasten with battens. □ **batten down the hatches 1** *Naut.* secure a ship's tarpaulins. **2** prepare for a difficulty or crisis.

bat•ten[2] /bát′n/ *v.intr.* [foll. by *on*] thrive or prosper at another's expense.

bat•ter[1] /bátər/ *v.* **1 a** *tr.* strike repeatedly with hard blows. **b** *intr.* pound heavily and insistently (*batter at the door*). **2** *tr.* handle roughly, esp. over a long period. □□ **bat′ter•er** *n.* **bat′ter•ing** *n.*

■ **1 a** beat, beat up, knock about. **b** bang, thrash. **2** maltreat, mistreat, abuse.

bat•ter[2] /bátər/ *n.* mixture of flour, egg, and liquid used in cooking, esp. for cakes, etc.

bat•ter[3] /bátər/ *n.* *Sports* player batting, esp. in baseball.

bat•ter•y /bátəree/ *n.* (*pl.* **-ies**) **1** cell or cells carrying an electric charge, as a source of current. **2** set of similar units of equipment, esp. connected. **3** series of tests. **4** fortified emplacement for heavy guns. **5** *Law* unlawful personal violence on another (see ASSAULT).

bat•tle /bát′l/ • *n.* **1** prolonged fight between armed forces. **2** contest; difficult struggle. • *v.* **1** *intr.* struggle; fight. **2** *tr.* engage in battle with. □ **battle-ax 1** large ax used in ancient warfare. **2** *colloq.* formidable older woman. **battle cruiser** warship faster and more lightly armored than a battleship. **battle cry** cry or slogan used in a battle. **battle fatigue** = *combat fatigue.* **battle royal 1** battle of many combatants; free fight. **2** heated argument. □□ **bat′tler** *n.*

■ *n.* **1** conflict, combat, war. **2** competition, match, tournament, game. • *v.* **1** combat, wage war; (*battle with* or *against*) oppose. **2** see FIGHT[3] *v.* 1a. □ **battle cry** see SLOGAN. **battle royal 1** see BRAWL *n.* **2** see ROW *n.* □□ **battler** fighter, soldier, pugilist.

bat•tle•field /bát′lfeeld/ *n.* (also **bat•tle•ground** /–grownd/) piece of ground on which a battle is or was fought.

bat•tle•ment /bát′lmənt/ *n.* [usu. in *pl.*] recessed parapet along the top of a fortification.

bat•tle•ship /bát′lship/ *n.* heaviest armored warship.

bat•ty /bátee/ *adj.* (**bat•ti•er, bat•ti•est**) *sl.* crazy.

■ see CRAZY 1.

bau•ble /báwbəl/ *n.* showy trinket or toy of little value.
  ■ gewgaw, bijou, ornament, trifle, gimcrack.

baud /bawd/ *n.* (*pl.* same or **bauds**) *Computing,* etc., unit to express the speed of electronic code signals, corresponding to one information unit or one bit per second.

baux•ite /báwksīt/ *n.* claylike ore, the source of aluminum.

bawd /bawd/ *n.* woman who runs a brothel.

bawd•y /báwdee/ • *adj.* (**bawd•i•er, bawd•i•est**) (esp. humorously) indecent; raunchy.
  • *n.* bawdy talk or writing. □ **bawdy house** brothel. □□ **bawd'i•ly** *adv.* **bawd'i•ness** *n.*
  ■ *adj.* lewd, obscene, taboo, ribald, risqué.
  • *n.* scatology, ribaldry. □ **bawdy house** see BROTHEL.

bawl /bawl/ *v.* **1** *tr.* speak or call out noisily. **2** *intr.* weep loudly. □ **bawl out** *colloq.* reprimand angrily. □□ **bawl'er** *n.*
  ■ **1** shout, bellow, vociferate, roar. **2** cry, wail, howl. □ **bawl out** see REPRIMAND *v.*
  □□ **bawler** crybaby.

bay[1] /bay/ *n.* broad inlet of the sea where the land curves inward.
  ■ see GULF *n.* 1.

bay[2] /bay/ *n.* **1** laurel having deep green leaves and purple berries. **2** [in *pl.*] bay wreath for a victor or poet. □ **bay leaf** aromatic (usu. dried) leaf of the bay tree, used in cooking.

bay[3] /bay/ *n.* **1** space created by a window line projecting outward from a wall. **2** recess; alcove. **3** compartment (*bomb bay*). **4** area specially allocated (*loading bay*).
  ■ **1, 2** see RECESS *n.* 1.

bay[4] /bay/ • *adj.* (esp. of a horse) dark reddish brown. • *n.* bay horse with a black mane and tail.

bay[5] /bay/ • *v.* **1** *intr.* bark or howl loudly and plaintively. **2** *tr.* bay at. • *n.* sound of baying, esp. in chorus from hounds in close pursuit. □ **at bay** cornered, unable to escape. **hold** (or **keep**) **at bay** hold off (a pursuer).

bay•ber•ry /báyberee/ *n.* (*pl.* **-ries**) N. American plants bearing waxy berries.

bay•o•net /báyənét/ • *n.* **1** stabbing blade attachable to the muzzle of a rifle. **2** electrical or other fitting engaged by being pushed into a socket and twisted. • *v.tr.* stab with a bayonet.

bay•ou /bí ōō/ *n.* marshy offshoot of a river, etc.

ba•zaar /bəzaàr/ *n.* **1** market in an Eastern or Middle Eastern country. **2** fund-raising sale, esp. for charity.
  ■ **2** see FAIR[2] 2.

ba•zoo•ka /bəzōōkə/ *n.* **1** anti-tank rocket launcher. **2** crude trombone-like musical instrument.

BB *abbr.* pellet about .18 inch in diameter, for use in a BB gun or air gun.

bbl. *abbr.* barrels (esp. of oil).

BC *abbr.* **1** (of a date) before Christ. **2** British Columbia.

bdrm. *abbr.* bedroom.

Be *symb. Chem.* beryllium.

be /bee/ (*sing. present* **am** /am, əm/, **is** /iz/; *pl. present* **are** /wuz,

woz, wəz/; *2nd sing. past and pl. past* **were** /wər/; *present subj.* **be**; *past subj.* **were**; *pres. part.* **be•ing**; *past part.* **been** /bin/ • *v.intr.*
1 exist; live (*I think, therefore I am*). **2 a** occur; take place. **b** occupy a position. **3** remain; continue. **4** linking subject and predicate, expressing: **a** identity (*she is the person*). **b** condition (*he is ill*). **c** state or quality (*he is kind*). **d** opinion (*I am against hanging*). **e** total (*two and two are four*). **f** cost or significance (*it is nothing to me*). • *v.aux.* **1** with a past participle to form the passive mood (*it was done*). **2** with a present participle to form continuous tenses (*we are coming*). **3** with an infinitive to express duty or commitment, intention, possibility, destiny, or hypothesis (*we are to wait here*).
  ■ *v.intr.* **1** see EXIST 1.

be- /bee/ *prefix forming verbs:* **1** (from transitive verbs) **a** all over; all around (*beset*). **b** thoroughly; excessively (*begrudge, belabor*). **2** (from intransitive verbs) expressing transitive action (*bemoan*). **3** (from adjectives and nouns) expressing transitive action (*befoul*). **4** (from nouns) **a** affect with (*befog*). **b** treat as (*befriend*). **c** [forming adjectives, ending in −ed] having (*bejeweled*).

beach /beech/ • *n.* pebbly or sandy shore. • *v.tr.* run or haul up (a boat, etc.) onto a beach.
  ■ *n.* lakeshore, bank, seashore. • *v.* ground; land.

beach•head /beech-hed/ *n.* Mil. fortified position established on a beach by landing forces.

bea•con /beekən/ *n.* **1** visible warning or guiding device (e.g., lighthouse, navigation buoy, etc.). **2** radio transmitter whose signal helps fix the position of a ship or aircraft.
  ■ **1** fire, light; signal, guide.

bead /beed/ • *n.* **1 a** small usu. rounded and perforated piece of glass, stone, etc., for threading with others or sewing on to fabric, etc. **b** [in *pl.*] string of beads; rosary. **2** drop of liquid. **3** small knob in the foresight of a gun. **4** inner edge of a pneumatic tire that grips the rim of the wheel. • *v. tr.* decorate with beads. □ **draw a bead on** take aim at. □□ **bead'ed** *adj.*
  ■ *n.* **1a** see ROUND *n.* 2. **2** see DROP *n.* 1a.

bead•ing /beeding/ *n.* **1** decoration of or resembling beads. **2** *Archit.* molding like a series of beads. **3** bead of a tire.

bead•y /beedee/ *adj.* (**bead•i•er, bead•i•est**) **1** (of the eyes) small, round, and bright. **2** covered with beads or drops. □ **beady-eyed** with beady eyes. □□ **bead'i•ly** *adv.* **bead'i•ness** *n.*

bea•gle /beegəl/ *n.* small short-haired hound.

beak /beek/ *n.* **1** bird's horny projecting jaws; bill. **2** similar jaw of a turtle, etc. □□ **beaked** *adj.* **beak'y** *adj.*

beak•er /beekər/ *n.* **1** tall drinking vessel. **2** lipped cylindrical vessel for scientific experiments.
  ■ **1** see GLASS *n.* 2.

beam /beem/ • *n.* **1** long sturdy piece of timber or metal spanning an opening or room, usu. to support the structure above. **2** ray or shaft of light. **3** series of radio or radar signals as a guide to a ship or aircraft. **4** crossbar of a balance. **5** ship's breadth at its widest point. • *v.* **1** *tr.* emit or direct (light, radio waves, etc.). **2** *intr.* **a** shine. **b** look or smile radiantly. □ **off** (*or* **off the**) **beam** *colloq.* mistaken. **on the beam** *colloq.* on the right track.

  ■ *n.* **1** pile, purlin, collar beam, tie beam. **2** gleam. • *v.* **1** radiate, shed, give off *or* out. **2 a** pour out *or* forth. **b** grin. □ **off** (*or* **off the**) **beam** see WRONG *adj.* 1. **on the beam** along the right lines, close, *colloq.* warm.

bean /been/ • *n.* **1** a plant with edible seeds in long pods. **b** one of these seeds. **2** similar seed of coffee, etc. **3** *sl.* the head, esp. as a source of common sense. • *v.tr. sl.* hit on the head. □ **bean counter** *colloq.* accountant.

bean•bag /beénbag/ *n.* **1** small bag filled with dried beans and used esp. in children's games. **2** (in full **bean′bag chair**) large cushion filled usu. with polystyrene beads and used as a seat.

bean•pole /beénpōl/ *n.* **1** stick for supporting bean plants. **2** *colloq.* tall thin person.

bear[1] /bair/ *v.* (*past* **bore** /bor/; *past part.* **borne, born** /bawrn/) ¶In the passive *born* is used with reference to birth (e.g., *was born in July*), except for *borne by* foll. by the name of the mother (e.g., *was borne by Sarah*). **1** *tr.* carry, bring, or take. **2** *tr.* show; have as an attribute or characteristic (*bear marks of violence*). **3** *tr.* **a** produce; yield (fruit, etc.). **b** give birth to. **4** *tr.* **a** sustain (a weight, responsibility, cost, etc.). **b** endure (an ordeal, difficulty, etc.). **5** *tr.* **a** tolerate. **b** admit of. **6** *intr.* veer in a given direction (*bear left*). □ **bear down** exert downward pressure. **bear down on** approach rapidly or purposefully. **bear on** (*or* **upon**) be relevant to. **bear out** support or confirm (an account or the person giving it). **bear with** tolerate. **bear witness** testify. □□ **bear′a•ble** *adj.* **bear′a•bly** *adv.* **bear′er** *n.*

  ■ **1** transport, convey, move. **2** have, exhibit, be marked by. **3** develop, breed, generate; spawn, bring forth, have; (*be born*) come into the world. **4** support; withstand. **5 a** stand, put up with, abide. **b** merit, be worthy of. **6** turn, swing. □ **bear down on** travel headlong toward, head toward. **bear on** (*or* **upon**) relate to. **bear out** corroborate, substantiate, uphold. **bear with** put up with, be patient *or* tolerant with. **bear witness** see TESTIFY 1.

bear[2] /bair/ *n.* **1** large heavy mammal having thick fur and walking on its soles. **2** rough or uncouth person. **3** *Stock Exch.* person who sells shares hoping to buy them back later at a lower price. □□ **bear•ish** *adj.*

beard /beerd/ • *n.* **1** facial hair growing on the chin, etc. **2** similar tuft on an animal. • *v.tr.* oppose openly; defy. □□ **beard′ed** *adj.* **beard′less** *adj.*

bear•ing /báiring/ *n.* **1** person's bodily attitude or outward behavior. **2** relevance (*has*

no bearing on the subject). **3** part of a machine that supports a rotating or other moving part. **4** direction or position relative to a fixed point. **5** [in *pl.*] sense of one's orientation (*get my bearings*).

  ■ **1** carriage, deportment, manner, conduct. **2** relation, reference, relationship, correlation. **5** (*bearings*) (sense of) direction, (relative) position.

Bé•ar•naise sauce /báirnáyz/ *n.* rich, savory sauce thickened with egg yolks.

bear•skin /báirskin/ *n.* **1** skin of a bear. **2** wrap, etc., made of this.

beast /beest/ *n.* **1** animal, esp. a wild quadruped. **2** brutal; objectionable person.

  ■ **1** creature, living thing; being. **2** brute, savage, animal, monster, fiend.

beast•ly /beéstlee/ *adj.* (**beast•li•er, beast•li•est**) **1** *colloq.* objectionable; unpleasant. **2** like a beast; brutal. □□ **beast′li•ness** *n.*

  ■ *adj.* **1** horrible, awful, unpleasant, atrocious, disagreeable, intolerable. **2** uncivilized, uncultivated, uncivil; cruel, inhuman, savage, barbaric. □□ **beastliness** see *brutality* (BRUTAL).

beat /beet/ • *v.* (*past* **beat**; *past part.* **beat•en** /beét′n/) **1 a** strike persistently or repeatedly, esp. to harm or punish. **b** strike (a thing) repeatedly, e.g., to remove dust from (a carpet, etc.), or to sound (a drum, etc.). **2** *tr.* **a** overcome; surpass. **b** complete an activity before (another person, etc.). **c** be too hard for; perplex. **3** *tr.* stir (eggs, etc.) vigorously. **4** *tr.* shape (metal, etc.) by blows. **5** *intr.* (of the heart, etc.) pulsate rhythmically. **6** *tr.* **a** indicate (a tempo or rhythm) by tapping, etc. **b** sound (a signal, etc.) by striking a drum. **7** move or cause (wings) to move up and down. **8** *tr.* make (a path, etc.) by trampling. • *n.* **1 a** main stress accent in music or verse. **b** indication of rhythm by a conductor. **2** stroke, blow, or measured sequence of strokes. **3** route or area allocated to a police officer, etc. • *adj. sl.* exhausted; tired out. □ **beat generation** members of a movement of young people, esp. in the 1950s, who rejected conventional society in their dress, habits, and beliefs. **beat it** *sl.* go away. **beat off** drive back (an attack, etc.). **beat up** give a beating to, esp. with punches and kicks. **beat-up** *adj. colloq.* dilapidated; in a state of disrepair. □□ **beat′a•ble** *adj.*

  ■ *v.* **1** pound, bash, batter, baste, pummel, belabor, pelt, clout, thrash, trounce. **2 a** defeat, worst, win (out) over, trounce, rout, break, outdo. **b** preempt. **c** see PERPLEX 1. **3** mix, whip (up). **4** hammer (out), forge, form. **5** throb, pulse, palpitate. **7** flap, flutter. **8** tread, wear. • *n.* **1 a** pulsation. **2** rap. **3** course, round, tour; zone, territory. • *adj.* spent, drained, worn out. □ **beat it** depart, leave, abscond. **beat off** drive off *or* away, repel. **beat-up** see DILAPIDATED.

beat•en /beét′n/ *adj.* **1** outwitted; defeated. **2** exhausted; dejected. **3** (of metal) shaped by a hammer. **4** (of a path, etc.) much used.

beat•er /beétər/ *n.* implement used for beating (esp. a carpet or eggs).

be•a•tif•ic /beéətifik/ *adj.* **1** *colloq.* blissful

(*beatific smile*). **2 a** of or relating to blessedness. **b** making blessed. □□ **be·a·tif'i·ca·lly** *adv*.

■ **2** see *saintly* (SAINT).

be·at·i·fy /beeátifí/ *v.tr.* (**–fies, –fied**) **1** *RC Ch.* declare a dead person "blessed"; often a step toward canonization. **2** make happy. □□ **be·at·i·fi·ca'tion** *n*.

■ **1** see SANCTIFY 1.

beat·ing /beeting/ *n.* **1** physical punishment or assault. **2** defeat. □ **take a beating** suffer a defeat or setback.

be·at·i·tude /beeátitōod, –tyōod/ *n.* **1** blessedness. **2** [in *pl.*] declarations of blessedness in Matt. 5:3–11.

beat·nik /beétnik/ *n.* member of the beat generation (see BEAT).

beau /bō/ *n.* (*pl.* **beaux** or **beaus** /bōz/) boyfriend.

Beau·fort scale /bṓtərt/ *n.* scale of wind speed ranging from 0 (calm) to 12 (hurricane).

beau·te·ous /byóōteəs/ *adj. poet.* beautiful.

beau·ti·cian /byōōtíshən/ *n.* specialist in beauty treatment.

beau·ti·ful /byóōtifool/ *adj.* **1** delighting the aesthetic senses. **2** pleasant; enjoyable (*had a beautiful time*). **3** excellent (*beautiful specimen*). □□ **beau'ti·ful·ly** *adv*.

■ **1** attractive, charming, comely, lovely; scenic, picturesque. **2** see PLEASANT. **3** first-rate, unequaled, fine, skillful, admirable. □□ **beautifully** exquisitely, gorgeously, prettily, alluringly.

beau·ti·fy /byóōtifí/ *v.tr.* (**–fies, –fied**) make beautiful; adorn. □□ **beau·ti·fi·ca·tion** *n*. **beau'ti·fi·er** *n*.

■ adorn, embellish, decorate, ornament, elaborate. □□ **beautification** see *embellishment* (EMBELLISH). **beautifier** decorator.

beau·ty /byóōtee/ *n.* (*pl.* **–ties**) **1** combination of shape, color, etc., that pleases the senses. **2** *colloq.* **a** excellent specimen. **b** attractive feature; advantage. **3 beauty parlor** (or **salon** or **shop**) establishment for manicure, hairdressing, makeup, etc.

■ **1** loveliness, attractiveness, handsomeness; picturesqueness, aestheticism, elegance. **2 a** jewel, pearl, gem, dream. **b** attraction, appeal, charm; asset, benefit, boon, selling point.

bea·ver /beevər/ • *n.* (*pl.* same or **bea·vers**) **1 a** amphibious broad-tailed rodent native to N. America, Europe, and Asia able to cut down trees and build dams. **b** its fur. **c** hat of this. • *v.intr. colloq.* work hard. □ **eager beaver** *colloq.* over-zealous person.

■ □ **eager beaver** fanatic, zealot, workaholic, *colloq.* buff.

be·bop /beebop/ *n.* type of jazz characterized by complex harmony and rhythms. □□ **be'bop·per** *n*.

be·calm /bikaám/ *v.tr.* deprive (a ship) of wind.

be·came *past of* BECOME.

be·cause /bikáwz, –kúz/ *conj.* for the reason that; since. □ **because of** on account of; by reason of.

bé·cha·mel /béshəmel/ *n.* kind of thick white sauce.

beck /bek/ □ **at a person's beck and call** having constantly to obey a person's orders.

beck·on /békən/ *v.* **1** *tr.* summon by gesture. **2** *intr.* make a signal to attract a person's attention.

■ **1** call, *archaic or literary* bid. **2** motion, sign.

be·come /bikúm/ *v.* (*past* **be·came** /bikáym/; *past part.* **be·come**) **1** *intr.* begin to be; come to be; turn into (*tadpoles become frogs*). **2** *tr.* **a** look well on; suit. **b** befit (*it ill becomes you to complain*). **3** *intr.* (as **becoming** *adj.*) **a** flattering the appearance. **b** suitable; decorous. □ **become of** happen to (*what will become of me?*). □□ **be·com'ing·ly** *adv*.

■ **1** change or transform or metamorphose into, grow or develop or evolve into. **2** fit. **3** (**becoming**) **a** seemly; attractive, flattering, chic. **b** appropriate, apt, fitting; see also DECOROUS. □ **become of** come of, *poet.* befall. □□ **becomingly** stylishly, tastefully.

bed /bed/ • *n.* **1** piece of furniture or padding, etc., for sleeping on. **2** garden plot, esp. for flowers. **3 a** bottom of the sea or a river. **b** foundations of a road or railroad. **4** stratum; layer. • *v.* (**bed·ded, bed·ding**) **1** *tr. & intr.* put or go to bed. **2** *tr.* plant in a garden bed. **3 a** *tr.* arrange as a layer. **b** *intr.* be or form a layer. □ **bed and board** lodging and food. **bed and breakfast 1** one night's lodging and breakfast in a hotel, etc. **2** establishment that provides this. **get out of bed on the wrong side** be bad-tempered all day long. **make one's bed and lie in it** accept the consequences of one's acts.

■ *n.* **4** see SEAM *n.* 4. • *v.* **2** see PLANT *v.* 1.

be·daz·zle /bidázəl/ *v.tr.* **1** dazzle. **2** confuse (a person). □□ **be·daz'zle·ment** *n*.

■ see DAZE *v.*

bed·bug /bédbug/ *n.* biting parasites infesting beds, etc.

bed·clothes /bédklōthz, –klōz/ *n.pl.* coverings for a bed, such as sheets, blankets, etc.

bed·ding /béding/ *n.* **1** mattress and bedclothes. **2** geological strata.

■ **1** see COVER *n.* 1d.

be·deck /bidék/ *v.tr.* adorn.

be·dev·il /bidévəl/ *v.tr.* (**–iled, –il·ing**) **1** plague; afflict. **2** confound; confuse. **3** bewitch. **4** torment or abuse. □□ **be·dev'il·ment** *n*.

■ **1** see PESTER. **3** see OBSESS.

bed·fel·low /bédfelō/ *n.* **1** person who shares a bed. **2** associate.

bed·lam /bédləm/ *n.* scene of uproar and confusion.

■ pandemonium, chaos, hubbub, commotion, tumult, turmoil, furor, *colloq.* madhouse.

Bed·ou·in /bédōōin/ (also **Bed'u·in**) (*pl.* same) *n.* **1** nomadic Arab of the desert. **2** wanderer; nomad.

bed·pan /bédpan/ *n.* toilet for a bedridden patient.

be·drag·gle /bidrágəl/ *v.tr.* **1** (often as **bedraggled** *adj.*) wet (a dress, etc.) by trailing it, or so that it hangs limp. **2** (as **bedraggled** *adj.*) untidy; disheveled.

■ (**bedraggled**) **1** sloppy, soaking (wet), sopping (wet). **2** scruffy, messy, unkempt.

bed•rid•den /bédrid'n/ *adj.* confined to bed by infirmity.

bed•rock /bédrok/ *n.* **1** solid underlying rock. **2** underlying principles or facts.

bed•room /bédroom, –room/ *n.* room for sleeping in.

bed•side /bédsīd/ *n.* space beside esp. a patient's bed. □ **bedside manner** (of a doctor) way with a patient.

bed•sore /bédsawr/ *n.* sore developed by lying in bed.

bed•spread /bédspred/ *n.* decorative cover for a bed.

bed•stead /bédsted/ *n.* framework of a bed.

bed•wet•ting /bédweting/ *n.* involuntary urination during the night.

bee /bee/ *n.* **1** any four-winged social insect that collects nectar and pollen and produces wax and honey. **2** meeting for communal work or amusement. □ **bee in one's bonnet** obsession.

beech /beech/ *n.* **1** large tree with smooth gray bark and glossy leaves. **2** its wood.

beef /beef/ • *n.* **1** flesh of the ox, bull, or cow for eating. **2** *colloq.* well-developed male muscle. **3** (*pl.* **beeves** /beevz/ or **beefs**) cow, bull, or ox fattened for beef. **4** (*pl.* **beefs**) *sl.* complaint. • *v.intr. sl.* complain. □ **beef up** *sl.* strengthen; reinforce.
   ■ *n.* **4** see PROTEST *n.* • *v.* see COMPLAIN 1.

beef•cake /béefkayk/ *n. sl.* well-developed male muscles, esp. when photographed and displayed for admiration.

beef•steak /béefstáyk/ *n.* thick slice of beef, usu. for grilling or frying.

beef•y /béefee/ *adj.* (**beef•i•er**, **beef•i•est**) **1** like beef. **2** solid; muscular. □□ **beef′i•ly** *adv.* **beef′i•ness** *n.*
   ■ **2** see *brawny* (BRAWN).

bee•hive /béehīv/ *n.* **1** artificial habitation for bees. **2** busy place.

bee•keep•er /béekəpər/ *n.* keeper of bees. □□ **bee′keep•ing** *n.*

bee•line /béelīn/ *n.* straight line between two places.

Be•el•ze•bub /bee-élzibub/ *n.* the Devil.

been *past part.* of BE.

beep /beep/ • *n.* **1** sound of an automobile horn. **2** any similar high-pitched noise. • *v.intr.* emit a beep.

beep•er /bépər/ *n.* portable electronic device that receives signals and emits a beep to page the person carrying it.

beer /beer/ *n.* **1** alcoholic drink made from yeast-fermented malt, etc., flavored with hops. **2** fermented nonalcoholic drinks, e.g., ginger beer, root beer.

beet /beet/ *n.* plant with an edible root (see *sugar beet*).

bee•tle[1] /béet'l/ *n.* insect with modified front wings forming hard protective cases closing over the back wings.

bee•tle[2] /béet'l/ *n.* tool with a heavy head and handle, used for ramming, crushing, driving wedges, etc.

bee•tle[3] /béet'l/ • *adj.* (esp. of the eyebrows) projecting; shaggy; scowling. • *v.intr.* (usu. as **beetling** *adj.*) (of brows, cliffs, etc.) projecting; overhanging threateningly. □ **beetle-browed** with shaggy or projecting eyebrows.

beeves *pl.* of BEEF.

be•fall /bifáwl/ *v.* (*past* **be•fell** /bifél/; *past part.* **be•fall•en** /bifáwlən/) *poet.* **1** *intr.* happen (*so it befell*). **2** *tr.* happen to. See synonym study at HAPPEN.
   ■ **1** see HAPPEN *v.* 1. **2** see HAPPEN *v.* 3.

be•fit /bifít/ *v.tr.* (**be•fit•ted**, **be•fit•ting**) be appropriate for; suit. □□ **be•fit′ting** *adj.* **be•fit′ting•ly** *adv.*
   ■ be fitting *or* apt for; be required of, be incumbent on, be proper to *or* for. □□ **befitting** fitting, becoming, due, suitable. **befittingly** see *appropriately* (APPROPRIATE).

be•fog /bifawg, –fóg/ *v.tr.* (**be•fogged**, **be•fog•ging**) **1** confuse; obscure. **2** envelop in fog.

be•fore /bifáwr/ • *conj.* **1** earlier than the time when. **2** rather than that. • *prep.* **1** in front of; ahead of. **2** earlier than; preceding. **3** rather than. **4 a** in the presence of. **b** for the attention of. • *adv.* **1 a** earlier than the time in question; already. **b** in the past (*happened long before*). **2** ahead.
   ■ *prep.* **1** in advance of. **2** previous to; on the eve of; ante–, pre–. **3** in preference to; instead of, in place of, in lieu of. • *adv.* **1 a** previously. **b** formerly; once.

be•fore•hand /bifáwrhand/ *adv.* in advance; in readiness.
   ■ see *in advance* (ADVANCE).

be•fud•dle /bifúd'l/ *v.tr.* **1** make drunk. **2** confuse. □□ **be•fud′dle•ment** *n.*
   ■ **1** see INTOXICATE 1. **2** see CONFUSE 1.

beg /beg/ *v.* (**begged**, **beg•ging**) **1 a** *tr. & intr.* ask for (esp. food, money, etc.). **b** *intr.* live by begging. **2** *tr.* ask earnestly or humbly. **3** *tr.* ask formally for. **4** *intr.* (of a dog, etc.) sit up with the front paws raised expectantly. **5** *tr.* take or ask leave (to do something). □ **beg off 1** decline to take part in or attend. **2** get (a person) excused from a penalty, etc.
   ■ **1 a** (*beg for*) see ASK 4a. **b** beg one's bread, solicit, sponge, cadge, *colloq.* scrounge. **2** entreat, beseech, plead (with), ask for. □ **beg off 1** abstain from, take a rain check on.

SYNONYM STUDY: beg
BESEECH, ENTREAT, IMPLORE, IMPORTUNE, PETITION, PLEAD, SOLICIT. How badly do you want something? You can **beg** for it, which implies a humble and earnest approach. If you **entreat**, you're trying to get what you want by ingratiating yourself (*she entreated her mother to help her prepare for the exam*). To **plead** involves more urgency (*he pleaded with the judge to spare his life*) and is usually associated with the legal system (*she was advised to plead guilty*). **Beseech** also suggests urgency, as well as an emotional appeal (*he beseeched her to tell the truth*). **Implore** is still stronger, suggesting desperation or great distress (*the look in his mother's eyes implored him to have mercy*). If you really want to get your way,

you can **importune**, which means to *beg* not only urgently but persistently and to risk making a pest of yourself (*he importuned her daily to accept his invitation*). **Petition** suggests an appeal to authority (*to petition the government to repeal an unjust law*), while **solicit** suggests petitioning in a courteous, formal way (*soliciting financial support for the school carnival*).

---

be•get /bigét/ *v.tr.* (**be•get•ting**; *past* **be•got** /bigót/; *archaic* **be•gat** /bigát/; *past part.* **be•got•ten** /bigót'n/) *literary* **1** father; procreate. **2** cause. □□ **be•get′ter** *n.*

beg•gar /bégər/ • *n.* **1** person who lives by begging. **2** poor person. • *v.tr.* **1** reduce to poverty. **2** cause one's ability for (description, etc.) to be inadequate. □□ **beg•gar•ly** *adj.* **beg•gar•y** *n.*

■ *n.* **1, 2** mendicant, sponger, tramp, vagrant, pauper. • *v.* **2** see EXCEED.

be•gin /bigín/ *v.* (**be•gin•ning**; *past* **be•gan** /bigán/; *past part.* **be•gun** /bigún/) **1** *tr.* perform the first part of, start. **2** *intr.* come into being. **3** *tr.* start at a certain time. **4** *intr.* be begun.

■ **1** start (out *or* off *or* in *or* on), initiate, enter on *or* upon, set out *or* about. **2, 4** originate, emerge, open, get under way.

be•gin•ner /bigínər/ *n.* person just beginning to learn.

be•gin•ning /bigíning/ *n.* **1** time or place at which anything begins. **2** source or origin **3** first part.

■ **1, 2** start, outset, onset, inception, dawn, dawning. **3** opening.

be•gone /bigáwn, -gón/ *int. poet.* go away at once!.

be•go•nia /bigónyə/ *n.* plant with brightly colored sepals and no petals, and often having brilliant glossy foliage.

be•got *past of* BEGET.

be•got•ten *past part.* of BEGET.

be•grudge /bigrúj/ *v.tr.* **1** resent; be dissatisfied at. **2** envy (a person) the possession of. □□ **be•grudg′ing•ly** *adv.*

■ feel jealous about, feel embittered *or* bitter about, have hard feelings about. □□ **begrudgingly** unwillingly, grudgingly, under protest.

be•guile /bigíl/ *v.tr.* **1** charm; amuse. **2** divert attention pleasantly from (work, etc.). **3** delude; cheat. □□ **be•guile′ment** *n.* **be•guil′er** *n.* **be•guil′ing** *adj.* **be•guil′ing•ly** *adv.*

■ **1** divert, distract, fascinate; captivate, enchant, enthrall. **3** deceive, swindle, dupe, gull, fool. □□ **beguilement** see AMUSEMENT 2, TRICKERY. **beguiler** see *charmer* (CHARM), *swindler* (SWINDLE). **beguiling** see *enchanting* (ENCHANT). **beguilingly** seductively.

be•gine /bigéen/ *n.* popular dance of W. Indian origin.

be•gun *past part.* of BEGIN.

be•half /bihàf/ *n.* □ **on** (also **in**) **behalf of** (or **on a person's behalf**) **1** in the interests of (a person, principle, etc.). **2** as representative of (*acting on behalf of my client*).

■ for the benefit *or* advantage of, for, in place of.

be•have /biháyv/ *v.intr.* **1** act or react (in a specified way). **2** (esp. to or of a child) conduct oneself properly. **3** (of a machine, etc.) work well (or in a specified way).

■ **1, 3** function, operate, perform. **2** act obediently, act properly, be good, *sl.* keep one's nose clean.

be•hav•ior /biháyvyər/ *n.* **1 a** way one conducts oneself; manners. **b** treatment of others. **2** way in which a ship, machine, etc., acts or works. **3** *Psychol.* response (of a person, animal, etc.) to a stimulus. □□ **be•hav′ior•al** *adj.*

■ **1 a** demeanor, deportment, bearing. **2** operation, action, performance.

be•head /bihéd/ *v.tr.* cut off the head

■ decapitate, guillotine, *formal* decollate.

be•held *past* and *past part.* of BEHOLD.

be•he•moth /biheemoth, beeə-/ *n.* huge creature or thing.

be•hest /bihést/ *n. literary* command; entreaty.

be•hind /bihínd/ • *prep.* **1 a** in, toward, or to the rear of. **b** on the farther side of. **c** hidden by. **2 a** in the past in relation to. **b** late in relation to. **3** inferior to; weaker than. **4 a** in support of. **b** responsible for. • *adv.* **1 a** in or to the rear; farther back. **b** on the farther side (*a high wall with a field behind*). **2** remaining. **3 a** in arrears. **b** late in accomplishing a task, etc. **4** in a weak position; backward (*behind in Latin*). • *n.* *colloq.* buttocks. □ **behind the times** old-fashioned, antiquated.

■ *prep.* **1 a, b** around the back of, on or to the other side of. **c** concealed by. **3** below, worse or lower than. **4 a** at a person's back, for, pro, in favor of. **b** explaining. • *adv.* **3** late, overdue, behindhand. • *n.* see BUTTOCK. □ **behind the times** outdated, out-of-date, outmoded, passé.

be•hold /bihóld/ *v.tr.* (*past & past part.* **beheld** /bihéld/) *literary* [esp. in *imper.*] see; observe. □□ **be•hold′er** *n.*

■ look at *or* upon, regard, set *or* lay eyes on.

be•hold•en /bihóldən/ *adj.* under obligation.

■ obliged, obligated, indebted, bound, grateful, in debt.

be•hoove /bihóov/ *v.tr.* **1** be incumbent on. **2** befit.

■ be required of, be proper to *or* for; be appropriate *or* suitable; be advisable for, be worthwhile for.

beige /bayzh/ • *n.* pale sandy color. • *adj.* of this color.

be•ing /béeing/ *n.* **1** existence. **2** nature or essence. **3** human being. **4** anything that exists or is imagined.

■ **1** see EXISTENCE 1. **2** see ESSENCE 1. **3** see PERSON. **4** see ENTITY 1.

be•la•bor /biláybər/ *v.tr.* **1** thrash; beat. **2** argue or elaborate (a subject) in excessive detail.

■ **1** see BEAT *v.* 1. **2** dissect, scrutinize, go over *or* through again, look at again.

be•lat•ed /biláytid/ *adj.* late or too late. □□ **be•lat′ed•ly** *adv.* **be•lat′ed•ness** *n.*

■ behind time, behindhand, out of date, overdue. □□ **belatedness** tardiness.

be•lay /biláy/ v. **1** tr. fix (a running rope) around a cleat, etc., to secure it. **2** tr. & intr. [usu. in imper.] Naut. sl. stop; enough!.

bel can•to /bel kántō, kaàn–/ n. lyrical style of operatic singing using a full rich broad tone and smooth phrasing.

belch /belch/ • v. **1** intr. emit wind noisily from the stomach through the mouth. **2** tr. (of a chimney, gun, etc.) send (smoke, etc.) out or up. • n. act of belching.

be•lea•guer /bileégər/ v.tr. **1** besiege. **2** vex; harass.

■ **2** see MOLEST 1.

bel•fry /bélfree/ n. (pl. **–fries**) **1** bell tower. **2** space for bells in a church tower. □ **have bats in the belfry** be eccentric or crazy.

be•lie /bilī/ v.tr. (**be•lied**, **be•ly•ing**) **1** give a false notion of. **2** fail to fulfill or justify.

■ **1** see MISREPRESENT.

be•lief /bileéf/ n. **1 a** a religious conviction. **b** firm opinion. **c** acceptance. **2** trust or confidence.

■ **1** religion, faith, creed, judgment. **2** certitude.

be•lieve /bileév/ v. **1** tr. accept as true or as conveying the truth. **2** tr. think; suppose. **3** intr. [foll. by in] **a** have faith in the existence of. **b** have confidence in. **c** have trust in the advisability of. **4** intr. have (esp. religious) faith. □ **make believe** pretend. □□ **be•liev•a•ble** adj. **be•liev•a•bil•i•ty** n. **be•liev•er** n.

■ **1** put faith or credence in or into, find credible or believable. **2** assume, hold, maintain. **3** (believe in) trust to or in, rely upon or on, have faith or confidence in. **4** have seen the light. □ **make believe** suppose, imagine, fancy. □□ **believable** see PLAUSIBLE 1. **believability** credibility, feasibility, likelihood.

be•lit•tle /bilít'l/ v.tr. **1** disparage. **2** make small; dwarf. □□ **be•lit'tle•ment** n. **be•lit'tler** n. **be•lit'tling•ly** adv.

■ decry, cry down, detract from, depreciate, trivialize, deprecate, degrade, denigrate. □□ **belittlement** disparagement, deprecation, depreciation.

bell /bel/ • n. **1** hollow usu. metal object in the shape of a cup usu. widening at the lip, made to sound a clear musical note when struck. **2** sound or stroke of a bell, esp. as a signal. **3** anything that sounds like or functions as a bell. • v.tr. provide with a bell or bells. □ **bell-bottom** marked flare below the knee (of a pants leg). **bell jar** bell-shaped glass cover or container. **bells and whistles** colloq. attractive but unnecessary additional features. **saved by the bell 1** Boxing spared a knockout by the bell signaling the end of a round. **2** spared an unwanted task, etc., by another claim on one's attention.

bel•la•don•na /bélədónə/ n. **1** Bot. poisonous plant with purple flowers and purple-black berries. (Also called **deadly nightshade**.) **2** Med. drug from this.

bell•boy /bélboy/ n. = BELLHOP.

belle /bel/ n. beautiful woman.

bel•les let•tres /bel-létrə/ n.pl. [also treated as sing.] writings or studies of a literary nature, esp. essays and criticisms. □□ **bel•le•trism** /bel-létrizəm/ n. **bel•let•rist** /bel-létrist/ n. **bel•let•ris•tic** /bèl-letrístik/ adj.

bell•hop /bélhop/ n. person who carries luggage, runs errands, etc., in a hotel or club.

bel•li•cose /bélikōs/ adj. eager to fight; warlike. See synonym study at HOSTILE. □□ **bel•li•cos•i•ty** /–kósitee/ n.

■ see WARLIKE 1.

bel•lig•er•ent /bilíjərənt/ • adj. **1** engaged in war or conflict. **2** given to constant fighting; pugnacious. See synonym study at HOSTILE. • n. nation or person engaged in war or conflict. □□ **bel•lig'er•ence** n. **bel•lig'er•ent•ly** adv.

■ adj. **1** warring, militant, warmongering, hawkish. **2** quarrelsome, contentious, disputatious. • n. warring party, fighter, antagonist, adversary.

bel•low /bélō/ • v. **1** intr. emit a deep loud roar. **2** tr. utter loudly. • n. bellowing sound.

■ v. yell, shout, cry. • n. call, howl.

bel•lows /bélōz/ n.pl. [also treated as sing.] **1** device that emits a stream of air when squeezed, esp. (in full **pair of bel•lows**) kind with two handles used for blowing air onto a fire. **2** expandable component, e.g., of a camera.

bel•ly /bélee/ • n. (pl. **–lies**) **1** part of the human body below the chest, containing the stomach and bowels. **2** stomach. **3** front of the body from the waist to the groin. **4** underside of a four-legged animal. **5** cavity or bulging part. • v. (**–lies**, **–lied**) swell or cause to swell; bulge. □ **belly button** colloq. navel. **belly dance** Middle Eastern dance performed by a woman, involving voluptuous movements. **belly laugh** loud unrestrained laugh.

■ n. **1–3** see STOMACH n. 2. • v. see SWELL v. 3. □ **belly button** see NAVEL.

bel•ly•ache /béleeayk/ • n. colloq. stomach pain. • v.intr. sl. complain noisily or persistently. □□ **bel'ly•ach•er** n.

bel•ly•flop /béleeflop/ colloq. n. dive with the belly landing flat on the water.

bel•ly•ful /béleefŏol/ n. (pl. **–fuls**) **1** enough to eat. **2** colloq. more than enough of anything (esp. unwelcome).

be•long /bilawng, –lóng/ v.intr. **1** [foll. by to] **a** be the property of. **b** be rightly assigned to. **c** be a member of. **2** fit socially.

■ **1** (belong to) **a** be owned by. **b** be allocated to. **c** be affiliated or associated or connected with. **2** be suited, have a (proper) place, be suitable.

be•long•ing /bilawnging, –lóng–/ n. **1** [in pl.] movable possessions or luggage. **2** membership; relationship.

■ **1** (belongings) (personal) property, effects, goods; baggage. **2** association, connection, alliance.

be•lov•ed /bilúvid, –lúvd/ • adj. much loved. • n. much loved person.

■ adj. cherished, adored, dear, dearest, darling. • n. sweetheart, darling, dearest, love.

be•low /bilō/ • prep. **1 a** lower in position

than. **b** south of. **2** beneath the surface of. **3** unworthy of. • *adv.* **1** at or to a lower point or level. **2 a** downstairs. **b** downstream. **3** (of a text reference) further forward on a page or in a book (*as noted below*). ■ *prep.* **1, 2** under, underneath. **3** beneath, unbefitting (of). • *adv.* **1** lower down, further *or* farther down. **2 a** beneath, underneath. **3** further on *or* down, infra.

belt /belt/ • *n.* **1** strip of leather, etc., esp. worn around the waist. **2 a** circular band of material used as a driving medium in machinery. **b** conveyor belt. **3** distinct region or extent. **4** *sl.* heavy blow. • *v.* **1** *tr.* put a belt around. **2** *tr.* fasten with a belt. **3** *tr. sl.* hit hard. □ **below the belt** unfair or unfairly. **belt out** *sl.* sing loudly. **tighten one's belt** live more frugally. **under one's belt** securely acquired. □□ **belt'er** *n.* (esp. in sense of *belt out*).
■ *n.* **1** sash, girdle, cord. **3** zone, sector. **4** see BLOW² 1. • *v.* **3** see BEAT *v.* 1.

belt•way /béltway/ *n.* highway skirting a metropolitan region.

be•moan /bimṓn/ • *v.tr.* express regret or sorrow over; lament.

be•muse /bimyṓoz/ *v.tr.* stupefy or bewilder (a person). □□ **be•mus•ed•ly** /-zidlee/ *adv.* **be•muse'ment** *n.*
■ confuse, mystify, perplex, puzzle, baffle.

bench /bench/ • *n.* **1** long seat of wood, stone, etc. **2** strong worktable. **3** [prec. by *the*] **a** office of judge or magistrate. **b** judge's seat in a court of law. **c** court of law. **d** judges and magistrates collectively. **4** *Sports* **a** seating to the side of a field for coaches and players not taking part. **b** those players not taking part in a game. • *v.tr.* **1** *Sports* **a** keep (a player) on the bench. **b** withdraw (a player) from a game.

bench•mark /bénchmaark/ *n.* **1** surveyor's mark used as a reference point. **2** standard or point of reference.
■ **2** see STANDARD *n.* 1, 2.

bend¹ /bend/ • *v.* (*past* **bent**; *past part.* **bent** *exc.* in *bended knee*) **1 a** *tr.* force or adapt (something straight) into a curve or angle. **b** *intr.* (of an object) be so altered. **2** *intr.* move or stretch in a curved course. **3** *intr. & tr.* [often foll. by *down, over,* etc.] incline or cause to incline from the vertical. **4** *tr.* interpret or modify (a rule) to suit oneself. **5** *tr. & refl.* [foll. by *to, on*] direct or devote (oneself or one's attention, energies, etc.). **6** *tr.* turn (one's steps or eyes) in a new direction. **7 a** *intr.* stoop or submit. **b** *tr.* force to submit. • *n.* **1** curve. **2** departure from a straight course. **3** bent part. **4** [in *pl.*; prec. by *the*] *colloq.* decompression sickness. □□ **bend'a•ble** *adj.*
■ *v.* **1** arch, bow, crook. **2** turn, wind. **3** see STOOP¹ *v.* 1. **4** change, adapt, revise; see also TWIST *v.* 5. **5, 6** incline, channel, focus. **7 a** bow, curtsy; kowtow. • *n.* **1, 3** turn, turning; angle, crook. □□ **bendable** see PLASTIC *adj.*

bend² /bend/ *n. Naut.* any of various rope knots.

bend•er /béndər/ *n. sl.* wild drinking spree.
■ drinking bout, revel, carousal.

be•neath /binéeth/ • *prep.* **1** not worthy of. **2** below; under. • *adv.* below; underneath. ■ *prep.* **1** unbefitting of, undeserving of. **2** behind. • *adv.* low *or* lower down; underground.

ben•e•dic•tion /bénidíkshən/ *n.* **1** blessing, esp. as part of a religious service. **2** state of being blessed.

ben•e•fac•tion /bénifákshən/ *n.* **1** donation or gift. **2** giving or doing good.

ben•e•fac•tor /bénifaktər/ *n.* (*fem.* **ben•e•fac•tress** /-tris/) person who gives support (esp. financial) to a person or cause.
■ patron, philanthropist; backer, *sl.* angel.

ben•e•fice /bénifis/ *n.* income from a church office.

be•nef•i•cent /binéfisənt/ *adj.* doing good; generous, actively kind. □□ **be•nef'i•cence** *n.* **be•nef'i•cent•ly** *adv.*
■ see GENEROUS 2. □□ **beneficence** see KINDNESS 1.

ben•e•fi•cial /bénifíshəl/ *adj.* advantageous; having benefits. □□ **ben•e•fi'cial•ly** *adv.*
■ serviceable, useful, profitable; healthful.

ben•e•fi•ci•ar•y /bénifíshee-e-ree, -físhəree/ *n.* (*pl.* **-ies**) person who benefits, esp. from a will.
■ see HEIR.

ben•e•fit /bénifit/ • *n.* **1** favorable or helpful factor or circumstance. **2** [often in *pl.*] insurance, social security, welfare, etc., payment. **3** public performance or game in aid of a charitable cause. • *v.* (**ben•e•fit•ed**, **ben•e•fit•ing**; **ben•e•fit•ted**, **ben•e•fit•ting**) **1** *tr.* do good to; bring advantage to. **2** *intr.* receive an advantage. □ **the benefit of the doubt** concession that a person is innocent, etc., although doubt exists.
■ *n.* **1** advantage, profit, good, gain, aid, help, service. **2** payout; sick pay; (*benefits*) perquisites. **3** charity event. • *v.* **1** improve, aid, help, better; promote. **2** profit, gain.

be•nev•o•lent /binévələnt/ *adj.* wishing to do good; actively friendly and helpful. **2** charitable. □□ **be•nev'o•lence** *n.* **be•nev'o•lent•ly** *adv.* See synonym study at MERCY.
■ **1** well-disposed, gracious, good, kind; magnanimous. **2** good, philanthropic. □□ **benevolence** charity, kindness, kindliness, kindheartedness, warmheartedness.

be•night•ed /binítid/ *adj.* intellectually or morally ignorant. □□ **be•night'ed•ness** *n.*
■ unenlightened, naive, uninformed, in the dark.

be•nign /binín/ *adj.* **1** gentle; mild; kind. **2** fortunate; salutary. **3** *Med.* (of a tumor, etc.) not malignant. □□ **be•nign'ly** *adv.*
■ **1** kindly, gracious, good, kindhearted. **2** congenial, propitious, beneficial; advantageous, favorable. **3** nonfatal, nonvirulent, curable.

be•nig•nant /bínignənt/ *adj.* **1** kindly, esp. to inferiors. **2** salutary; beneficial. □□ **be•nig•nan•cy** /-nənsee/ *n.* **be•nig'nant•ly** *adv.*
■ **1** see BENEVOLENT 1, BENIGN 1. **2** see BENIGN 2.

bent¹ /bent/ *past* and *past part.* of BEND¹ *v.* • *adj.* **1** curved; having an angle. **2** [foll. by *on*] determined to do or have. • *n.* 1 inclination or bias. 2 talent for something specified (*bent for mimicry*).

■ *adj.* 1 deflected, bowed, crooked, distorted. 2 (*bent on*) intent on, set on, resolved about *or* to. • *n.* 1 direction, disposition, predisposition, tendency.

bent[2] /bent/ *n.* 1 any of various grasslike reeds, rushes, *or* sedges. 2 stiff stalk of a grass usu. with a flexible base.

bent•wood /béntwŏŏd/ *n.* wood that is artificially shaped for use in making furniture.

be•numb /binúm/ *v.tr.* 1 make numb; deaden. 2 paralyze (the mind or feelings).

■ see DEADEN 2.

ben•zene /bénzeen/ *n.* colorless carcinogenic volatile liquid found in coal tar, petroleum, etc., and used as a solvent and in the manufacture of plastics, etc.

be•queath /bikwéeth, –kwéeth/ *v.tr.* 1 leave (a personal estate) to a person by a will. 2 hand down to posterity. □□ **be•queath'al** *n.* **be•queath'er** *n.*

■ make over, will, pass on, hand down *or* on.

be•quest /bikwést/ *n.* 1 bequeathing. 2 thing bequeathed.

■ 2 legacy, inheritance, heritage, patrimony.

be•rate /biráyt/ *v.tr.* scold; rebuke. See synonym study at SCOLD.

■ reprimand, rate, upbraid, chastise, reprove.

Ber•ber /bárbər/ • *n.* 1 member of the indigenous mainly Muslim peoples of N. Africa. 2 language of these peoples. • *adj.* of the Berbers or their language.

be•reave /biréev/ *v.tr.* (esp. as **bereaved** *adj.*) deprive of a relation, friend, etc., esp. by death. □□ **be•reave'ment** *n.*

■ strip, rob, dispossess; widow. □□ **bereavement** see LOSS 1, MOURNING 1.

be•reft /biréft/ *adj.* deprived (esp. of a nonmaterial asset).

be•ret /bəráy/ *n.* round, flattish, visorless cap of felt or cloth.

berg /bərg/ *n.* = ICEBERG.

beri•beri /béreebéree/ *n.* nerve disease caused by a deficiency of vitamin B[1].

ber•ke•li•um /bárkeélee̊əm, bórkleeăm/ *n.* *Chem.* transuranic radioactive metallic element. ¶Symb.: **Bk**.

ber•ry /béree/ *n.* (*pl.* **–ries**) 1 any small roundish juicy fruit without a stone. 2 *Bot.* fruit with its seeds contained in a pulp (e.g., banana, tomato). □□ **ber'ried** *adj.* [also in *comb.*].

ber•serk /bərsórk, –zórk/ *adj.* (esp. in **go berserk**) wild; frenzied; in a violent rage.

■ mad, crazy, deranged, crazed.

berth /bərth/ *n.* 1 fixed bunk on a ship, train, etc. 2 ship's place at a wharf. • *v.* 1 *tr.* moor (a ship) in its berth. 2 *tr.* provide a sleeping place for. □ **give a wide berth to** stay away from.

■ *n.* 1 compartment, cabin, room. • *v.* 1 see MOOR[2].

ber•yl /béril/ *n.* transparent precious stone, esp. emerald and aquamarine.

be•ryl•li•um /bəríleeəm/ *n.* *Chem.* hard white metallic element. ¶Symb.: **Be**.

be•seech /biséech/ *v.tr.* (*past* and *past part.* **be•sought** /–sáwt/ *or* **be•seeched**) ask earnestly. See synonym study at BEG. □□ **be•seech•ing** *adj.*

■ supplicate, entreat, implore, plead (with), beg.

be•set /bisét/ *v.tr.* (**be•set•ting**; *past* and *past part.* **be•set**) 1 attack or harass persistently. 2 surround or hem in. See synonym study at ATTACK. □□ **be•set' ment** *n.*

■ 1 assail, beleaguer, bedevil, harry, hector. 2 encompass, besiege, encircle.

be•side /bisíd/ *prep.* 1 at the side of; near. 2 compared with. 3 irrelevant to. □ **beside oneself** overcome with worry, anger, etc.

■ 1 alongside, next to, close to. 3 away from, wide of, apart from. □ **beside oneself** out of one's mind *or* wits, at the end of one's tether; excited, worked up.

be•sides /bisídz/ • *prep.* in addition to; apart from. • *adv.* also; as well; moreover.

■ *prep.* over and above, above and beyond; barring, excepting. • *adv.* in addition, additionally; further, furthermore.

be•siege /biséej/ *v.tr.* 1 lay siege to. 2 crowd around oppressively. 3 harass with requests. See synonym study at ATTACK. □□ **be•sieg'er** *n.*

■ 1 beleaguer, invest. 2 blockade, block (off *or* up), hem in. 3 bedevil, beset.

be•smirch /bismárch/ *v.tr.* 1 soil. 2 dishonor.

be•sot•ted /bisótid/ *adj.* 1 intoxicated; stupefied. 2 infatuated.

be•sought *past* and *past part.* of BESEECH.

be•spat•ter /bispátər/ *v.tr.* 1 spatter (an object) all over. 2 overwhelm with abuse, slander, etc.

be•speak /bispéek/ *v.tr.* (*past* **be•spoke** /–spók/; *past part.* **be•spo•ken** /–spókən/ *or* as *adj.* **be•spoke**) 1 engage in advance. 2 suggest; be evidence of.

best /best/ • *adj.* (*superl.* of GOOD[1]) of the most excellent or desirable kind. • *adv.* (*superl.* of WELL). 1 in the best manner. 2 to the greatest degree. 3 most usefully. • *n.* 1 that which is best. 2 chief merit or advantage. 3 [foll. by *of*] winning majority of (games, etc., played). 4 = *Sunday best.* • *v.tr. colloq.* defeat, outwit, outbid, etc. □ **at best** on the most optimistic view. **get the best of** defeat; outwit. **had best** would find it wisest to. **make the best of** derive what limited advantage one can from (something unsatisfactory or unwelcome).

■ *adj.* top, superlative, unexcelled. • *adv.* 2 most. 3 better. • *n.* 1, 2 finest, first, prime. 4 finery, best clothes. • *v.* win (out) over, conquer, beat; see also BEAT[1] *v.* 2a. □ **get the best of** see BEAT *v.* 2a. **had best** had better, ought to, must. **make the best of** see *put up with* (PUT).

best boy *n.* the assistant to the chief electrician of a movie crew.

bes•tial /béschəl, bées–/ *adj.* 1 brutish; cruel; savage. 2 of or like a beast. □□ **bes'tial•ize** *v.tr.* **bes'tial•ly** *adv.*

■ 1 see SAVAGE *adj.* 1, 2.

bes•ti•al•i•ty /béscheeálitee, bées–/ n. (pl. –ties) 1 bestial behavior. 2 sexual intercourse between a person and an animal.

bes•ti•ar•y /béschee-eree, bées–/ n. (pl. –ies) moralizing medieval treatise on real and imaginary beasts.

be•stir /bistér/ v.refl. (**be•stirred, be•stir•ring**) exert or rouse (oneself).

be•stow /bistó/ v.tr. confer (a gift, right, etc.). See synonym study at GIVE. □□ **be•stow'al** n. ■ give, award. □□ **bestowal** see AWARD n. 1b.

be•strew /bistróō/ v.tr. (past part. **be•strewed** or **be•strewn** /–stróōn/) 1 [foll. by with] cover or partly cover (a surface). 2 scatter (things) about. 3 lie scattered over.

bet /bet/ • v. (**bet•ting**; past and past part. **bet** or **bet•ted**) 1 intr. risk money, etc., on the outcome of an event (esp. a race, game, etc.). 2 tr. risk (an amount) on such an outcome. 3 tr. colloq. feel sure. • n. 1 act of betting. 2 money, etc., staked. 3 colloq. choice or course of action. □ **you bet** colloq. you may be sure. □□ **bet•tor** or **bet•ter** n.
■ v. 1, 2 wager, stake, gamble. • n. 1, 2 wager, risk. 3 see OPTION 1.

bet. abbr. between.

be•ta /báyta, bee–/ n. second letter of the Greek alphabet (Β, β). □ **beta-blocker** Pharm. drug that prevents the stimulation of increased cardiac action, used to treat angina and reduce high blood pressure. **beta parti-cle** (or **ray**) fast-moving electron emitted by radioactive decay.

be•ta•tron /báytatron, bée–/ n. Physics apparatus for accelerating electrons in a circular path by magnetic induction.

bête noire /bet nwáar/ n. (pl. **bêtes noires** pronunc. same) person or thing one particularly dislikes or fears.

be•think /bithíngk/ v.refl. (past and past part. **be•thought** /–tháwt/) [foll. by of, how, or that + clause] formal 1 reflect; stop to think. 2 be reminded by reflection.

be•tray /bitráy/ v.tr. 1 be disloyal or treacherous to (another person, etc.). 2 reveal involuntarily or treacherously; be evidence of. □□ **be•tray'al** n. **be•tray'er** n.
■ 1 be or prove false to, sell out, break faith with. 2 disclose, divulge, display, show. □□ **betrayal** treachery, treason, disloyalty, perfidy.

be•troth /bitróth, –tráwth/ v.tr. (usu. as **be•trothed** adj.) bind with a promise to marry. □□ **be•troth'al** n.
■ (**betrothed**) see ENGAGED¹ 1. □□ **be•trothal** see MATCH n. 3.

bet•ter /bétər/ • adj. (compar. of GOOD¹). 1 of a more excellent or desirable kind. 2 partly or fully recovered from illness. • adv. (compar. of WELL). 1 in a better manner. 2 to a greater degree. 3 more usefully or advantageously. • n. 1 that which is better. 2 [usu. in pl.; prec. by my, etc.] one's superiors. • v.tr. 1 surpass. 2 improve. □ **better off** in a better (esp. financial) position. **get the better of** defeat; outwit. **had better** would find it wiser to.
■ adj. 1 superior; preferable. 2 healthier; cured. • adv. 3 best. • n. 1 advantage, mastery. 2 (betters) masters, elders. • v. 1 excel, outdo. 2 advance, raise, upgrade. □ **better off** improved; wealthier. **get the better of** see DEFEAT v. 1. **had better** had best, ought to.

bet•ter•ment /bétərmənt/ n. improvement.

be•tween /bitwéen/ • prep. 1 a at or to a point in the area or interval bounded by two points in space, time, etc. (broke down between Boston and Providence). b along the extent of such an area. 2 separating. 3 a shared by. b by joint action. ¶Use in sense 3 with reference to more than two people or things is established and acceptable (e.g., relations between the United States, Canada, and Mexico). 4 to and from. 5 taking one and rejecting the other of. • adv. (also in **between**) at a point or in the area bounded by two or more other points in space, time, sequence, etc. (not fat or thin but in between). □ **between ourselves** (or **you and me**) in confidence.

be•twixt /bitwíkst/ prep. & adv. between. □ **betwixt and between** colloq. neither one thing nor the other.

bev•el /bévəl/ • n. 1 slope from the horizontal or vertical; sloping surface or edge. 2 (in full **bevel square**) tool for marking angles. • v. (**beveled, bev•el•ing; bev•elled, bev•el•ling**) 1 tr. reduce (a square edge) to a sloping edge. 2 intr. slope at an angle. □ **bevel gear** gear working another gear at an angle.
■ n. 1 see SLOPE 1–3. • v. see SLANT 1, 2.

bev•er•age /bévərij, bévrij/ n. drink.

bev•y /bévee/ n. (pl. –ies) 1 flock of quails or larks. 2 company or group (orig. of women).
■ 2 see GROUP n. 1.

be•wail /biwáyl/ v.tr. 1 lament. 2 wail over. □□ **be•wail'er** n.
■ regret, mourn (for or over), bemoan.

be•ware /biwáir/ v. [only in imper. or infin.] 1 intr. take heed. 2 tr. be cautious of.
■ be careful, be wary, be on one's guard.

be•wil•der /biwíldər/ v.tr. utterly perplex or confuse. □□ **be•wil'der•ed•ly** adv. **be•wil'der•ing** adj. **be•wil'der•ing•ly** adv. **be•wil'der•ment** n.
■ confound, puzzle, mystify, befuddle, baffle. □□ **bewildering** see perplexing (PERPLEX).

be•witch /biwích/ v.tr. 1 enchant; greatly delight. 2 cast a spell on. □□ **be•witch'ing** adj. **be•witch'ing•ly** adv.
■ 1 entrance, spellbind, charm, fascinate, beguile. 2 bedevil, voodoo.

be•yond /biyónd/ • prep. 1 at or to the farther side of. 2 outside the scope or understanding of. 3 more than. • adv. 1 at or to the farther side. 2 farther on. • n. [prec. by the] the unknown after death.

bez•el /bézəl/ n. 1 sloped edge of a chisel. 2 oblique faces of a cut gem. 3 groove holding a watch crystal or gem.

Bi symb. Chem. bismuth.

bi- /bī/ comb. form (often **bin-** before a vowel) forming nouns and adjectives meaning: 1 having two; thing having two (bilateral).

2 a occurring twice in every one or once in every two (*biweekly*). **b** lasting for two (*biennial*).

bi•an•nu•al /bī-ányōōəl/ • *adj.* occurring, appearing, etc., twice a year (cf. BIENNIAL). □□ **bi•an′nu•al•ly** *adv.*

bi•as /bīəs/ • *n.* **1** predisposition or prejudice. **2** edge cut obliquely across the weave of a fabric. • *v.tr.* (**bi•ased, bi•as•ing**) (esp. as **biased** *adj.*) influence (usu. unfairly); prejudice. □ **on the bias** obliquely; diagonally.

■ *n.* **1** partiality, inclination, leaning, bent. **2** angle, slant. • *v.* affect unduly, color, taint.

bi•ath•lon /bī-áthlon, -lən/ *n. Sports* athletic contest in skiing and shooting. □□ **bi•ath′lete** *n.*

bib /bib/ *n.* **1** piece of cloth fastened around a child's neck while eating. **2** top front part of an apron, overalls, etc.

bibl. *abbr.* (also **Bibl.**) biblical.

Bi•ble /bībəl/ *n.* **1 a** Christian scriptures consisting of the Old and New Testaments. **b** Jewish scriptures. **2** (**bible**) *colloq.* any authoritative book (*the woodworker's bible*).

□ **Bible belt** area of the southern and central US where fundamentalist Protestant beliefs prevail. □□ **bib•li•cal** /bíblikəl/ *adj.* **bib′li•cal•ly** *adv.*

bibliog. *abbr.* bibliography.

bib•li•og•ra•phy /bíbleeógrəfee/ *n.* (*pl.* **-phies**) **1 a** list of books referred to in a scholarly work, usu. as an appendix. **b** list of books by a specific author or publisher, or on a specific subject, etc. **2** history or description of books, including authors, editions, etc. □□ **bib•li•og′ra•pher** *n.* **bib•li•o•graph•ic** /-leeəgráfik/ *adj.* **bib•li•o•graph′i•cal** *adj.* **bib•li•o•graph′i•cal•ly** *adv.*

bib•li•o•phile /bíbleeōfīl/ *n.* collector or lover of books. □□ **bib•li•o•phil•ic** /-fílik/ *adj.* **bib•li•oph•i•ly** /-leeófilee/ *n.*

bib•u•lous /bíbyələs/ *adj.* given to drinking alcoholic beverages. □□ **bib′u•lous•ly** *adv.* **bib′u•lous•ness** *n.*

■ □□ **bibulousness** see *drunkenness* (DRUNKEN).

bi•cam•er•al /bíkámərəl/ *adj.* (of a legislative body) having two chambers. □□ **bi•cam′er•al•ism** *n.*

bi•carb /bíkaárb/ *n. colloq.* = BICARBONATE.

bi•car•bon•ate /bíkaárbənit/ *n.* (in full **bi•car′bo•nate of so′da**) sodium bicarbonate used as an antacid or in baking powder.

bi•cen•ten•ni•al /bísenténeeəl/ • *n.* two-hundredth anniversary. • *adj.* lasting two hundred years or occurring every two hundred years.

bi•ceps /bíseps/ *n.* muscle having two heads or attachments, esp. the one that bends the elbow.

bick•er /bíkər/ *v.intr.* quarrel pettily; wrangle.

■ squabble, dispute, argue, disagree.

bi•con•cave /bíkónkayv, bíkonkáyv/ *adj.* (esp. of a lens) concave on both sides.

bi•con•vex /bíkónveks, bíkonvéks/ *adj.* (esp. of a lens) convex on both sides.

bi•cus•pid /bíkúspid/ • *adj.* having two cusps. • *n.* the premolar in humans. □□ **bi•cus′pi•date** *adj.*

bi•cy•cle /bísikəl, –sīkəl/ • *n.* two-wheeled vehicle propelled by pedals and steered with handlebars attached to the front wheel. • *v.intr.* ride a bicycle.

■ *n.* cycle, bike.

bid /bid/ • *v.* (**bid•ding**; *past* **bid, bade** /bayd, bad/; *past part.* **bid**) **1** *tr. & intr.* (*past* and *past part.* **bid**) [often foll. by *for, against*] **a** (esp. at an auction) offer (a certain price) (*bid $20*). **b** offer to do work, etc., for a stated price. **2** *tr.* command; invite. **3** *tr. archaic* or *literary* utter (greeting or farewell) (to. **4** *tr. & intr.* (*past* and *past part.* **bid**) *Cards* state before play how many tricks one intends to make. • *n.* **1 a** offer (of a price). **b** offer (to do work, etc.) at a stated price. **2** attempt; effort. □□ **bid′da•ble** *adj.* **bid′der** *n.*

■ *v.* **1** (*tr.*) tender, proffer. **2** order *or* direct to; summon *or* ask to. • *n.* **1** tender. **2** see ATTEMPT *n.*

bid•ding /bíding/ *n.* **1** bids at an auction or card game. **2** command; request; invitation.

■ **2** summons, call; order.

bid•dy /bídee/ *n.* (*pl.* **–dies**) *sl. derog.* woman (esp. *old biddy*).

bide /bīd/ □ **bide one's time** await one's best opportunity.

bi•det /beedáy/ *n.* low, oval, basinlike bathroom fixture used esp. for washing the genital area.

bi•en•ni•al /bí-éneeəl/ • *adj.* **1** lasting two years. **2** recurring every two years (cf. BIANNUAL). • *n.* **1** *Bot.* plant that takes two years to grow from seed to fruition and die. **2** event celebrated or taking place every two years. □□ **bi•en′ni•al•ly** *adv.*

bier /beer/ *n.* movable frame for a coffin.

bi•fo•cal /bífōkəl/ • *adj.* having two focuses, esp. of a lens with a part for distant vision and a part for near vision. • *n.* [in *pl.*] bifocal eyeglasses.

bi•fur•cate /bífərkayt/ • *v.* divide into two branches; fork. • *adj.* forked; branched. □□ **bi•fur•ca′tion** /-káyshən/ *n.*

big /big/ • *adj.* (**big•ger, big•gest**) **1 a** of considerable size, amount, intensity, etc. **b** of a large or the largest size. **2** important; significant; outstanding. **3 a** grown up. **b** elder. **4** *colloq.* **a** boastful. **b** often *iron.* generous. **c** ambitious. **d** popular. **5** advanced in pregnancy. • *adv. colloq.* in a big manner, esp.: **1** effectively (*went over big*). **2** boastfully. **3** ambitiously. □ **Big Apple** *sl.* New York City. **big bang theory** theory that the universe began with the explosion of dense matter. **Big Dipper** constellation of seven bright stars in Ursa Major in the shape of a dipper. **big top** main tent in a circus. □□ **big′gish** *adj.* **big′ness** *n.*

■ *adj.* **1 a** great, grand. **2** weighty, consequential, major. **3 a** mature. **b** older. **4 b** magnanimous, charitable. **c** grandiose, showy. • *adv.* **1** successfully, well. **2** pompously, conceitedly. **3** determinedly, enterprisingly.

big•a•my /bígəmee/ *n.* (*pl.* **–mies**) crime of

marrying when one is lawfully married to another person. □□ **big'a•mist** *n.* **big'a•mous** *adj.*

big•heart•ed /bíghártid/ *adj.* generous.
■ see GENEROUS 1.

big•horn /bíghawrn/ *n.* American wild sheep, esp. native to the Rocky Mountains.

bight /bīt/ *n.* **1** curve or recess in a coastline, river, etc. **2** loop of rope.

big•ot /bígət/ *n.* obstinate and intolerant believer in a religion, etc. See synonym study at ZEALOT. □□ **big'ot•ed** *adj.* **big'ot•ry** *n.*
■ dogmatist, partisan, sectionalist, intransigent. □□ **bigoted** uncompromising, inflexible, prejudiced, biased. **bigotry** prejudice, intolerance, narrow-mindedness.

big•wig /bígwig/ *n. colloq.* important person.
■ VIP, *colloq.* big shot, brass.

bike /bīk/ *n. colloq.* bicycle or motorcycle.
• *v.intr.* ride a bicycle or motorcycle. □□ **bik'er** *n.*
■ *n.* bicycle, tricycle, cycle.

bi•ki•ni /bikeénee/ *n.* brief two-piece swimsuit for women.

bi•lat•er•al /bílátərəl/ *adj.* **1** of, on, or with two sides. **2** affecting or between two parties, countries, etc. (*bilateral negotiations*). □ **bilateral symmetry** symmetry about a plane. □□ **bi•lat'er•al•ly** *adv.*

bile /bīl/ *n.* **1** bitter fluid that aids digestion and is secreted by the liver. **2** bad temper; peevish anger.

bilge /bilj/ *n.* **1 a** almost flat part of a ship's bottom, inside or out. **b** (in full **bilge wa•ter**) filthy water that collects there. **2** *sl.* nonsense; worthless ideas.
■ **1 b** see MUCK *n.* 2. **2** see NONSENSE.

bi•lin•gual /bílínggwəl/ • *adj.* **1** able to speak two languages. **2** spoken or written in two languages. • *n.* bilingual person. □□ **bi•lin'gual•ism** *n.*

bil•ious /bílyəs/ *adj.* **1** affected by a disorder of the bile. **2** bad-tempered. □□ **bil'ious•ly** *adv.* **bil'ious•ness** *n.*
■ ill-tempered, peevish, irritable.

bilk /bilk/ *v.tr. sl.* **1** cheat. **2** give the slip to. **3** avoid paying (a creditor or debt). □□ **bilk'er** *n.*
■ **1** see CHEAT *v.* 1.

bill¹ /bil/ • *n.* **1 a** statement of charges for goods or services rendered. **b** amount owed (*ran up a bill of $300*). **2** draft of a proposed law. **3 a** poster; placard. **b** = HANDBILL. **4** a printed list, esp. a theater program. **b** the entertainment itself (*top of the bill*). **5** piece of paper money. • *v.tr.* **1** put in the program; announce. **2** send a note of charges to. □ **bill of exchange** *Econ.* written order to pay a sum of money on a given date to the drawer or to a named payee. **bill of fare** menu. **bill of goods** shipment of merchandise, often for resale. **2** *colloq.* item that is misrepresented, fraudulent, etc. **bill of lading** *Naut.* detailed list of cargo. **Bill of Rights** original ten amendments to the U.S. Constitution, affirming civil rights. **bill of sale** *Econ.* certificate of transfer of personal property. □□ **bill'a•ble** *adj.*
■ *n.* **1** invoice, account. **3 a** notice, sign, poster. **b** flyer. **4 a** playbill. **5** banknote;

greenback. • *v.* **1** see ANNOUNCE 1. **2** invoice, charge, debit.

bill² /bil/ • *n.* bird's beak. • *v.intr.* (of doves, etc.) stroke a bill with a bill. □□ **billed** *adj.* [usu. in *comb.*].

bill•board /bílbawrd/ *n.* large outdoor advertising sign.

bil•let /bílit/ • *n.* **1** place where troops, etc., are lodged. **2** *colloq.* job. • *v.tr.* [usu. foll. by *on, in, at*] quarter (soldiers, etc.). □□ **bil'let•er** *n.*
■ *n.* **1** see QUARTER *n.* 6b. • *v.* see QUARTER *v.* 2.

bil•let-doux /bílaydóō/ *n.* (*pl.* **bil•lets-doux** /-dóōz/) often *joc.* love letter.

bill•fold /bílfold/ *n.* wallet for keeping paper money.

bil•liards /bílyərdz/ *n.* any of several games played on an oblong cloth-covered table, esp. one with three balls struck with cues into pockets around the edge of the table.

bil•lion /bílyən/ *n.* (*pl.* same or (in sense 2) **bil•lions**) [in *sing.* prec. by *a* or *one*] **1 a** thousand million (1,000,000,000 or 10⁹). **2** *colloq.* very large number (*billions of years*). □□ **bil'lionth** *adj.* & *n.*

bil•lion•aire /bílyənáir/ *n.* person possessing over a billion dollars, pounds, etc.

bil•low /bílō/ *n.* **1** wave. **2** any large soft mass. □□ **bil'low•y** *adj.*

bil•ly /bílee/ *n.* (*pl.* **-lies**) (in full **bil'ly club**) bludgeon.

bil•ly goat /bíligōt/ *n.* male goat.

bim•bo /bímbō/ *n.* (*pl.* **-bos** or **-boes**) *sl.* usu. *derog.* **1** foolish person. **2 a** physically attractive but simple-minded woman. **b** disreputable woman.

bi•me•tal•lic /bímitalik/ *adj.* made of two metals.

bi•month•ly /bímúnthlee/ • *adj.* occurring twice a month or every two months. • *adv.* twice a month or every two months. • *n.* (*pl.* **-lies**) periodical produced bimonthly.

bin /bin/ *n.* large receptacle for storage or garbage.

bi•na•ry /bínəree/ • *adj.* **1 a** dual. **b** of or involving pairs. **2** of the arithmetical system using 2 as a base. • *n.* (*pl.* **-ries**) **1** something having two parts. **2** binary number. □ **binary code** *Computing* coding system using the binary digits 0 and 1 to represent a letter, digit, or other character. **binary star** system of two stars orbiting each other.

bind /bīnd/ • *v.* (*past* and *past part.* **bound** /bownd/) **1** tie or fasten tightly. **2** *tr.* **a** restrain. **b** (as **-bound** *adj.*) constricted; obstructed (*snowbound*). **3** *tr.* cause to cohere. **4** *tr.* fasten or hold together as a single mass. **5** *tr.* compel; impose. **6** *tr.* **a** edge (fabric, etc.) with braid, etc. **b** fasten (the pages of a book) in a cover. **7** *tr.* ratify (a bargain, agreement, etc.). **8** *tr.* [in *passive*] be required by an obligation or duty (*am bound to answer*). **9** *tr.* [often foll. by *up*] bandage. • *n.* *colloq.* **1** nuisance; restriction. **2** tight or difficult situation.
■ *v.* **1** make fast, secure; cement, fuse. **2 a** see TIE *v.* 1a, 3. **3** mix, blend, combine.

5 constrain, restrain; oblige, obligate. **6 a** border, band. **8** see sense 5 above. **9** bind up, swathe, cover. • *n.* **1** annoyance, irritant, bother, bore, pest. **2** predicament, tight corner *or* spot, *colloq.* pickle, fix.

bind•er /bíndər/ *n.* **1** cover for sheets of paper, etc. **2** substance that acts cohesively. **3** reaping machine that binds grain into sheaves. **4** bookbinder.

bind•er•y /bíndəree/ *n.* (*pl.* **–ies**) bookbinder's workshop.

bind•ing /bínding/ • *n.* something that binds, esp. the covers, glue, etc., of a book. • *adj.* obligatory.

■ *n.* see COVER *n.* 1b. • *adj.* see INCUMBENT *adj.* 1.

binge /binj/ *sl.* • *n.* spree; period of uncontrolled eating, drinking, etc. • *v.intr.* indulge in a binge.

■ *n.* see SPREE *n.* 2. • *v.* see DRINK *v.* 2.

bin•go /bínggō/ *n.* game in which each player has a card of squares with numbers that are marked off as they are randomly drawn and called.

bin•oc•u•lar /bínókyələr/ *adj.* adapted for or using both eyes.

bin•oc•u•lars /binókyələrz/ *n.pl.* optical instrument with a lens for each eye, for viewing distant objects.

bi•no•mi•al /bīnōmeeəl/ • *n.* algebraic expression of the sum or the difference of two terms. • *adj.* consisting of two terms. □□ **bi•no′mi•al•ly** *adv.*

bi•o / bī-ō/ • *n.* **1** biography. **2** (*pl.* **bi•os**) biography. • *adj.* biological.

bio- /bī-ō/ *comb. form* **1** life (*biography*). **2** biological (*biomathematics*). **3** of living beings (*biophysics*).

bi•o•chem•is•try /bī-ōkémistree/ *n.* study of the chemical and physicochemical processes of living organisms. □□ **bi•o•chem′i•cal** *adj.* **bi•o•chem′ist** *n.*

bi•o•de•grad•a•ble /bī-ōdigráydəbəl/ *adj.* capable of being decomposed by bacteria or other living organisms. □□ **bi•o•de•grad•a•bil′i•ty** *n.* **bi•o•deg•ra•da′tion** /bī-ōdégrədáyshən/ *n.*

bi•o•feed•back /bī-ōfeédbak/ *n.* technique of using the feedback of a normally automatic bodily response to a stimulus in order to acquire voluntary control of that response.

biog. *abbr.* **1** biographer. **2** biographical. **3** biography.

bi•o•gen•e•sis /bī-ōjénisis/ *n.* **1** synthesis of substances by living organisms. **2** hypothesis that a living organism arises only from another similar living organism. □□ **bi•o•ge•net′ic** /–jinétik/ *adj.*

bi•og•ra•phy /bīógrəfee/ *n.* (*pl.* **–phies**) **1** written account of a person's life, usu. by another. **2** such writing as a branch of literature. □□ **bi•og′ra•pher** *n.* **bi•o•graph•ic** /bíəgráfik/ *adj.* **bi•o•graph′i•cal** *adj.*

■ **1** see LIFE 8.

biol. *abbr.* **1** biologic. **2** biological. **3** biologist. **4** biology.

bi•o•log•i•cal /bíəlójikəl/ *adj.* **1** of or relating to biology or living organisms. **2** related genetically, not by marriage, adoption, etc. □ **biological clock** innate mechanism controlling the rhythmic physiological activities of an organism. **biological warfare** warfare involving the use of toxins or microorganisms. □□ **bi•o•log′i•cal•ly** *adv.*

bi•ol•o•gy /bīóləjee/ *n.* the study of living organisms. □□ **bi•ol′o•gist** *n.*

bi•o•mass /bí-ōmas/ *n.* total quantity or weight of organisms in a given area or volume.

bi•on•ic /bīónik/ *adj.* having electronically or mechanically operated body parts. □□ **bi•on′i•cal•ly** *adv.*

bi•on•ics /bīóniks/ *n.pl.* [treated as *sing.*] the study of mechanical systems that function like living organisms.

bi•o•phys•ics /bí-ōfiziks/ *n.pl.* [treated as *sing.*] science of the application of the laws of physics to biological phenomena. □□ **bi•o•phys′i•cal** *adj.* **bi•o•phys′i•cist** *n.*

bi•op•sy /bíopsee/ *n.* (*pl.* **–sies**) examination of tissue removed for diagnosis.

bi•o•rhythm /bí-ōrithəm/ *n.* any recurring biological cycle thought to affect a person's emotional, intellectual, and physical activity. □□ **bi•o•rhyth•mic** /–ərithmik/ *adj.* **bi•o•rhyth′mi•cal•ly** *adv.*

bi•o•sphere /bí-ōsfeer/ *n.* regions of the earth's crust and atmosphere occupied by living organisms.

bi•o•syn•the•sis /bí-ōsínthisis/ *n.* production of organic molecules by living organisms. □□ **bi•o•syn•thet•ic** /–thétik/ *adj.*

bi•o•tech•nol•o•gy /bí-ōteknóləjee/ *n.* exploitation of biological processes in industry, medicine, etc.

bi•o•tin /bíətin/ *n.* vitamin of the B complex.

bi•par•ti•san /bīpáartizan, –sən/ *adj.* of or involving two (esp. political) parties. □□ **bi•par′ti•san•ship** *n.*

bi•par•tite /bípaártit/ *adj.* **1** consisting of two parts. **2** shared by or involving two parties.

bi•ped /bíped/ • *n.* two-footed animal. • *adj.* two-footed. □□ **bi•ped′al** *adj.*

bi•plane /bíplayn/ *n.* type of airplane having two sets of wings, one above the other.

birch /bərch/ • *n.* **1** hardwood tree with thin peeling bark. **2** its wood. **3** (in full **birch rod**) bundle of birch twigs used for flogging. • *v.tr.* beat with a birch (in sense 3).

bird /bərd/ *n.* egg-laying feathered vertebrate with a beak, two wings, and two feet, and usu. able to fly. □ **bird in the hand** something secured or certain. **the birds and the bees** *euphem.* sexual activity and reproduction. **bird's-eye view** general view from above. **birds of a feather** people of like character. **for** (or **strictly for**) **the birds** *colloq.* trivial; uninteresting.

bird•bath /bɔ́rdbath/ *n.* basin in a garden, etc., with water for birds to bathe in.

bird•brain /bɔ́rdbrayn/ *n. colloq.* stupid or flighty person. □□ **bird′brained** *adj.*

■ see HALFWIT. □□ **birdbrained** see FRIVOLOUS 2.

bird•ie /bɔ́rdee/ *Golf* • *n.* score of one stroke less than par at any hole. • *v.tr.* (**–ies, –ied, –ie•ing**) play (a hole) in one stroke less than par.

bi•ret•ta /birétə/ n. square, usu. black cap worn by (esp. Roman Catholic) clergymen.

birth /bərth/ • n. 1 emergence of an infant or other young from the body of its mother. 2 rhet. beginning (*birth of socialism*). 3 origin; descent; ancestry (*of noble birth*). • v.tr. colloq. give birth to. □ **birth control** contraception.

■ n. 1 childbirth, delivery. 2 origin, creation. 3 extraction, parentage, lineage. • v. have, deliver, bear.

birth•day /bərthday/ n. 1 day on which one was born. 2 anniversary of this. □ **in one's birthday suit** joc. naked.

birth de•fect • n. physical, mental, or biochemical abnormality present at birth.

birth•mark /bərthmaark/ n. brown or red mark on one's body at or from birth.

birth par•ent • n. a biological as opposed to an adoptive parent.

birth•place /bərthplays/ n. place where one was born.

birth•right /bərthrit/ n. right of possession or privilege one has from birth.

■ see INHERITANCE 1.

birth•stone /bərthstōn/ n. gemstone popularly associated with the month of one's birth.

bis•cuit /bískit/ n. small leavened bread or cake.

bi•sect /bīsékt/ v.tr. divide into two (equal) parts. □□ **bi•sec•tion** /-sékshən/ n. **bi•sec′tor** n.

■ see CLEAVE[1] 1.

bi•sex•u•al /bīsékshōōəl/ • adj. 1 sexually attracted to persons of both sexes. 2 Biol. having characteristics of both sexes. 3 of or concerning both sexes. • n. bisexual person. □□ **bi•sex•u•al•i•ty** /-sékshoo-álitee, -séksy-oo-álitee/ n.

■ adj. 2 hermaphroditic, androgynous. • n. hermaphrodite, androgyne.

bish•op /bíshəp/ n. 1 senior member of the Christian clergy usu. in charge of a diocese. 2 chess piece that is moved diagonally.

bish•op•ric /bíshəprik/ n. office or diocese of a bishop.

bis•muth /bízməth/ n. Chem. metallic element used in alloys. ¶Symb.: **Bi**.

bi•son /bísən/ n. (pl. same) humpbacked shaggy-haired oxen of N. America or Europe.

bisque /bisk/ n. rich shellfish soup, made esp. from lobster.

bis•tro /béestrō, bís-/ n. (pl. -tros) small restaurant.

■ see CAFÉ 1.

bit[1] /bit/ n. 1 small piece or quantity. 2 [prec. by a] a fair amount. b colloq. somewhat (*am a bit tired*). 3 short time or distance. □ **bit by bit** gradually. **do one's bit** colloq. make a useful contribution. **two bits** 25 cents.

■ 1 segment, share; morsel, scrap. 2 b see RATHER 4. 3 moment, minute, second, little while. □ **bit by bit** see *gradually* (GRADUAL). **two bits** quarter.

bit[2] /bit/ n. 1 metal mouthpiece on a bridle. 2 (usu. metal) tool or piece for boring or

drilling. 3 cutting or gripping part of a plane, pliers, etc.

bit[3] /bit/ n. Computing unit of information; 0 or 1 in binary notation.

bitch /bich/ • n. 1 female dog or other canine animal. 2 sl. offens. spiteful woman. 3 sl. very unpleasant or difficult thing. • v. colloq. 1 intr. [often foll. by *about*] speak scathingly. 2 complain.

■ n. 2 shrew, hag, termagant. 3 colloq. beast, pain. • v. 1 (*bitch about*) criticize, censure, find fault with. 2 object, protest, grumble.

bitch•y /bíchee/ adj. (**bitch•i•er**, **bitch•i•est**) sl. spiteful; bad-tempered. □□ **bitch′i•ly** adv. **bitch′i•ness** n.

■ see VICIOUS 1. □□ **bitchiness** see SPITE n.

bite /bīt/ • v. (past **bit** /bit/; past part. **bit•ten** /bít'n/) 1 tr. cut or puncture using the teeth. 2 tr. [often foll. by *off*, etc.] detach with the teeth. 3 tr. (of an insect, etc.) sting. 4 intr. (of a wheel, screw, etc.) grip; penetrate. 5 intr. accept bait or an inducement. 6 tr. (as **bitten** adj.) cause smarting pain. • n. 1 act of biting. 2 wound made by biting. 3 a mouthful of food. b snack. 4 taking of bait by a fish. 5 pungency (esp. of flavor). 6 incisiveness; sharpness. □ **bite the bullet** sl. behave bravely or stoically. □ **bite the dust** sl. 1 die. 2 fail; break down. **bite a person's head off** colloq. respond angrily. **bite one's lip** see LIP.

■ v. 1, 2 nip, chew, gnaw. • n. 1 nibble. 2 sting. 3 a taste; morsel. b meal, lunch. 5 see SPICE[1] n. 1. 6 see EDGE n. 7a. □ **bite the bullet** bear up, steel oneself, face up to it, grit one's teeth. **bite the dust** 1 see DIE 1. 2 stop, stall, colloq. conk (out).

bit•ing /bíting/ adj. 1 stinging; intensely cold. 2 sharp; effective. □□ **bit′ing•ly** adv.

■ 1 wintry, freezing, raw. 2 cutting, piercing, keen.

bit•ter /bítər/ • adj. 1 having a sharp pungent taste; not sweet. 2 caused by, feeling, or showing mental pain or resentment. 3 a harsh; virulent. b piercingly cold. • n. [in pl.] liquor with a bitter flavor used as an additive in cocktails. □□ **bit′ter•ly** adv. **bit′ter•ness** n.

■ adj. 1 acerbic. 2 disturbing, dispiriting; aggrieved, pained; painful, unwelcome, unpalatable. 3 a stinging, cutting. b see BITING 1. □□ **bitterness** harshness, acerbity, spleen.

bit•tern /bítərn/ n. wading bird of the heron family.

bit•ter•sweet /bítərswēt/ • adj. sweet with a bitter aftertaste. • n. 1 such sweetness. 2 scarlet-berried climbing nightshade of N. America.

bi•tu•men /bitōōmin, -tyōō-, bi-/ n. any of various tarlike mixtures of hydrocarbons derived from petroleum.

bi•tu•mi•nous /bitōōminəs, -tyōō-, bi-/ adj. of, relating to, or containing bitumen. □ **bi•tuminous coal** soft coal burning with a smoky flame.

bi•valve /bívalv/ n. any of a group of aquatic

mollusks with two hinged shells, e.g., oysters.

biv•ou•ac /bívōō-ak, bívwak/ • *n.* temporary open encampment without tents. • *v.intr.* (**biv•ou•acked, biv•ou•ack•ing**) camp in a bivouac.

■ *n.* see CAMP[1] *n.* 2. • *v.* see CAMP[1] *v.*

biz /biz/ *n. colloq.* business.

bi•zarre /bizaár/ *adj.* strange; eccentric; grotesque. □□ **bi•zarre′ly** *adv.* **bi•zarre′ness** *n.*

■ unusual, weird, odd, peculiar.

Bk *symb. Chem.* berkelium.

bk. *abbr.* book.

blab /blab/ • *v.* (**blabbed, blab•bing**) **1** talk foolishly or indiscreetly. **2** reveal secrets. • *n.* person who blabs.

■ *v.* **1** gossip, prattle, chatter; see also BABBLE *v.* 1a, b. **2** broadcast, betray; see also BABBLE *v.* 2. • *n.* telltale, gossip.

black /blak/ • *adj.* **1** having no color from the absorption of all or nearly all incident light (like coal or soot). **2** completely dark. **3 a** of the human group having dark-colored skin, esp. of African descent. **b** of or relating to black people. **4** (of the sky, etc.) dusky; heavily overcast. **5** angry; threatening. **6** wicked; sinister; deadly. **7** gloomy; depressed; sullen (*a black mood*). **8** with sinister or macabre, as well as comic, import (*black comedy*). **9** (of coffee or tea) without milk. • *n.* **1** black color or pigment. **2** black clothes (*wears nothing but black*). **3** credit side of an account (*in the black*). **4** member of a dark-skinned race, esp. one of African descent. • *v.tr.* make black (*blacked his eyebrows*). □ **black and blue** discolored by bruises. **black belt 1** black belt worn by an expert in judo, etc. **2** person qualified to wear this. **black box** flight recorder in an aircraft. **black eye** bruised skin around the eye resulting from a blow. **black-eyed Susan** daisylike flower with yellow petals and a dark center. **black hole** region of space possessing a strong gravitational field from which matter and radiation cannot escape. **black ice** thin, hard transparent ice, esp. on a road surface. **black light** *Physics* invisible ultraviolet or infrared radiations of the electromagnetic spectrum. **black magic** magic involving supposed invocation of evil spirits. **black mark** mark of discredit. **black market** illicit traffic in officially controlled or scarce commodities. **black marketeer** person who engages in a black market. **Black Mass** ceremony in worship of Satan. **Black Power** movement, esp. in the 1960s in support of black rights and political power. **black sheep** *colloq.* unsatisfactory or disreputable member of a family, group, etc. **black tie 1** black bow tie worn with a dinner jacket. **2** *colloq.* man's formal evening dress. **black widow** venomous spider, of which the female has an hourglass-shaped red mark on her abdomen. □□ **black′ish** *adj.* **black′ly** *adv.* **black′ness** *n.*

■ *adj.* **1** jet-black, coal-black, inky, sooty, swarthy. **2** pitch-black; starless, moonless.

3 nonwhite, colored, dark-skinned, negroid. **4** dark, somber. **5** furious, frowning, bad-tempered, sulky. **6** bad, foul, iniquitous, evil. **7** see GLOOMY 2. • *v.* blacken. □ **black and blue** contused. **black eye** *colloq.* shiner, *sl.* mouse. **black magic** see MAGIC *n.* 1. **black sheep** scoundrel, wastrel, good-for-nothing.

black•ball /blákbawl/ *v.tr.* **1** reject (a candidate) in a ballot (orig. by voting with a black ball). **2** exclude; ostracize.

black•ber•ry /blákberee/ *n.* (*pl.* **–ries**) **1** thorny rosaceous shrub. (Also called **bramble**). **2** black fleshy edible fruit of this plant.

black•bird /blákbərd/ *n.* **1** common thrush of which the male is black with an orange beak. **2** any of various birds, esp. a grackle, with black plumage.

black•board /blákbawrd/ *n.* board with a smooth, usu. dark surface for writing on with chalk.

black•en /blákən/ *v.* **1** *tr. & intr.* make or become black or dark. **2** *tr.* speak evil of; defame.

■ **1** smudge, begrime. **2** slander, libel, smear.

black•guard /blágaard, –ərd/ *n.* villain; scoundrel. □□ **black′guard•ly** *adj.*

black•head /blák-hed/ *n.* black-topped pimple on the skin.

■ see PIMPLE.

black•jack /blákjak/ *n.* **1** card game in which players try to acquire cards with a face value totaling 21 and no more. **2** flexible leaded bludgeon. .

black•list /bláklist/ • *n.* list of people in disfavor, etc. • *v.tr.* put on a blacklist.

■ *n.* see BOYCOTT *n.* • *v.* see BOYCOTT *v.*

black•mail /blákmayl/ • *n.* **1** extortion of payment in return for not disclosing a secret, etc. **2** any payment extorted in this way. • *v.tr.* extort money, etc., by blackmail. □□ **black′mail•er** *n.*

■ *n.* **1** bribe, protection money, hush money. • *v.* see *shake down* 3.

black•out /blákowt/ *n.* **1** temporary loss of consciousness or memory. **2** temporary loss of power, etc. **3** compulsory darkness as a precaution against air raids. **4** suppression of news. **5** sudden darkening of a theater stage.

■ **1** see FAINT *n.*

black•smith /blásmith/ *n.* smith who works in iron.

black•thorn /blákthawrn/ *n.* thorny rosaceous shrub bearing white flowers and small blue-black fruits.

black•top /bláktop/ *n.* type of surfacing material for roads, playgrounds, etc.

blad•der /bládər/ *n.* **1 a** membranous sac in some animals, esp. that which stores urine. **b** this or a similar object prepared for various uses. **2** inflated vesicle in various plants.

blade /blayd/ *n.* **1 a** cutting edge of a knife, etc. **b** flat piece of metal with a sharp edge or edges used in a razor. **2** flattened part of an oar, propeller, etc. **3 a** flat, narrow leaf of grass and cereals. **b** *Bot.* broad thin part of a leaf. **4** *poet.* sword. □□ **blad•ed** *adj.* [also in *comb.*].

■ **3** leaflet, frond. **4** rapier, saber, dagger, stiletto, cutlass.

blame /blaym/ • *v.tr.* **1** assign fault or responsibility to. **2** [foll. by *on*] assign the responsibility for (an error or wrong) to a person, etc. • *n.* **1** responsibility for a bad result. **2** blaming or attributing responsibility. □ **be to blame** [often foll. by *for*] be responsible; deserve censure. □□ **blam′a•ble** or **blame′a•ble** *adj.* **blame′ful** *adj.*

■ *v.* **1** censure, criticize; accuse. • *n.* **1** culpability; guilt. **2** criticism, reproof.

blame•less /bláymlis/ *adj.* innocent; free from blame. □□ **blame′less•ly** *adv.* **blame′less•ness** *n.*

■ faultless, guiltless, irreproachable.

blanch /blanch/ • *v.* **1** make or become white or pale. **2** *tr. Cookery* prepare by briefly immersing in boiling water.

bland /bland/ *adj.* **1 a** mild; not irritating. **b** tasteless; insipid. **2** gentle in manner; smooth. □□ **bland′ly** *adv.* **bland′ness** *n.*

■ **1 a** soothing. **b** boring, dull; flavorless. **2** suave, urbane, cool, unruffled, calm, composed.

blan•dish /blándish/ *v.tr.* flatter; coax; cajole. □□ **blan′dish•ment** *n.*

■ see ENTICE.

blank /blangk/ • *adj.* **1 a** (of paper) not written or printed on. **b** (of a document) with spaces left for a signature or details. **2 a** empty. **b** undecorated. **3 a** puzzled; nonplussed. **b** having (temporarily) no knowledge. • *n.* **1 a** unfilled space in a document. **b** document having blank spaces to be filled. **2** (in full **blank cartridge**) cartridge containing gunpowder but no bullet. • *v.tr.* [usu. foll. by *off*, *out*] screen; obscure. □ **blank check 1** check with the amount left for the payee to fill in. **2** *colloq.* freedom of action. **blank verse** unrhymed verse, esp. iambic pentameters. □□ **blank′ly** *adv.* **blank′ness** *n.*

■ *adj.* **1 a** unused, plain. **2 a** bare, vacant. **b** unornamented, unadorned. **3 a** disconcerted, discomfited, confused. • *n.* **1 a** line, box. □ **blank check** carte blanche.

blan•ket /blángkit/ • *n.* **1** large piece of woolen or other material used for warmth, esp. as a bed covering. **2** [usu. foll. by *of*] thick covering mass or layer. • *adj.* covering all cases or classes; inclusive • *v.tr.* **1** cover. **2** stifle; keep quiet.

■ *n.* **1** see COVER *n.* **1d. 2** see MANTLE *n.* **2.** • *adj.* see INCLUSIVE 3. • *v.* **1** see COVER *v.* **1. 2** see SMOTHER *v.* **1.**

blare /blair/ • *v.* **1** *tr. & intr.* sound or utter loudly. **2** *intr.* make the sound of a trumpet. • *n.* loud sound.

■ *v.* blast, bellow; reverberate. • *n.* ring, roar, boom.

blar•ney /bláarnee/ • *n.* cajoling talk; flattery. • *v.* (**-neys, -neyed**) *tr.* flatter; cajole.

blasé /blaazáy/ *adj.* bored; indifferent.

■ cool, supercilious, sophisticated; jaded, weary.

blas•pheme /blasfeém, blásfeem/ *v.* **1** *intr.* talk profanely, making use of religious names, etc. **2** *tr.* talk profanely about; revile. □□ **blas•phem′er** *n.*

■ **1** curse, swear, damn. **2** abuse, malign.

blas•phe•my /blásfəmee/ *n.* (*pl.* **-mies**) **1** profane talk. **2** instance of this. □□ **blas′phe•mous** *adj.* **blas′phe•mous•ly** *adv.*

■ see PROFANITY 2. □□ **blasphemous** profane, impious.

blast /blast/ • *n.* **1** strong gust of wind, heat, etc. **2 a** explosion. **b** destructive wave of air from this. **3** loud note of a wind instrument, car horn, etc. **4** *colloq.* severe reprimand. • *v.* **1** *tr.* blow up with explosives. **2** *tr.* wither; shrivel. **3** *intr. & tr.* make or cause to make a loud noise. **4** *colloq.* reprimand severely. □ **at full blast** *colloq.* working at maximum speed, etc. **blast off** (of a rocket, etc.) take off from a launching site.

■ *n.* **1** blow, gale. **2** burst; detonation. **3** blare, racket; boom, report. • *v.* **1** explode, dynamite, demolish. **4** defame, discredit, denounce. □ **at full blast** fully, at full tilt.

bla•tant /blát′nt/ *adj.* **1** flagrant; unashamed. **2** offensively obtrusive. See synonym study at VOCIFEROUS. □□ **bla•tan•cy** /-t′nsee/ *n.* **bla′tant•ly** *adv.*

■ **1** obvious, palpable. **2** noisy, clamorous, loud.

blaze¹ /blayz/ • *n.* **1** bright flame or fire. **2** bright glaring light. **3** violent outburst (of passion, etc.). • *v.intr.* **1** burn with a bright flame. **2** be brilliantly lit. **3** be consumed with anger, excitement, etc. □ **blaze away** [often foll. by *at*] shoot continuously. □□ **blaz′ing** *adj.* **blaz′ing•ly** *adv.*

■ *n.* **1** holocaust, inferno. **2** brightness, brilliance. **3** eruption, flare-up. • *v.* **1** flare (up). **2** glow, glare, dazzle; see also FLASH *v.* 1, 2. □ **blaze away** fire; (*blaze away at*) bombard, pelt, shell.

blaze² /blayz/ • *n.* **1** white mark on an animal's face. **2** mark cut on a tree, esp. to mark a route. • *v.tr.* mark (a tree or path) with blazes.

blaz•er /bláyzər/ *n.* solid-color jacket not worn with matching trousers.

bla•zon /bláyzən/ • *v.tr.* proclaim. See synonym study at ANNOUNCE. • *n. Heraldry* coat of arms.

bldg. *abbr.* building.

bleach /bleech/ • *v.* whiten by sunlight or chemical process. • *n.* bleaching substance.

■ *n.* fade, blanch. • *n.* whitener, chlorine.

bleach•er /bleéchər/ *n.* [usu. in *pl.*] usu. uncovered, inexpensive bench seat at a sports field or arena.

bleak /bleek/ *adj.* **1** exposed; windswept. **2** dreary. □□ **bleak′ly** *adv.* **bleak′ness** *n.*

■ **1** austere, inhospitable, desolate. **2** cheerless, unpromising, disheartening.

blear•y /bleéree/ *adj.* (**blear•i•er, blear•i•est**) **1** (of the eyes or mind) dim; blurred. **2** indistinct. □ **bleary-eyed** having dim sight or wits. □□ **blear′i•ly** *adv.* **blear′i•ness** *n.*

■ **1** see FILMY 2.

bleat /bleet/ • *v.* **1** *intr.* (of a sheep, goat, or calf) make a wavering cry. **2** *intr. & tr.* [often foll. by *out*] speak feebly, foolishly, or plaintively. • *n.* **1** sound made by a sheep, goat, etc. **2** weak cry. □□ **bleat′er** n. **bleat′ing•ly** adv.

bleed /bleed/ v. (past and past part. **bled** /bled/) **1** intr. emit blood. **2** tr. draw blood from surgically. **3** tr. extort money from. **4** tr. allow (fluid or gas) to escape from a closed system through a valve, etc.

bleed•er /bleédər/ n. colloq. hemophiliac.

bleep /bleep/ • n. intermittent high-pitched sound made electronically. • v. **1** intr. & tr. make such a sound, esp. as a signal. **2** tr. obliterate obscenities with a bleep, as on a broadcast.

blem•ish /blémish/ • n. defect; stain; flaw. See synonym study at FAULT. • v.tr. spoil; stain.

■ n. disfigurement; scar; blot; error, fault. ● v. deface, mar, scar, impair, disfigure, tarnish.

blench /blench/ v.intr. flinch; quail.

blend /blend/ • v. **1** tr. **a** mix together. **b** produce by this method. **2** intr. harmonize; become one. **3** intr. (esp. of colors): **a** merge imperceptibly. **b** go well together; harmonize. • n. mixture.

■ v. **1 a** mingle, combine, meld. **2** join, amalgamate. **3 a** shade, grade. • n. amalgamation, fusion.

blend•er /bléndər/ n. kitchen appliance for liquefying, chopping, or puréeing food.

bless /bles/ v.tr. (past and past part. **blessed**, poet. **blest** /blest/) **1** (of a priest, etc.) pronounce words, esp. in a religious rite, asking for divine favor. **2 a** consecrate (esp. bread and wine). **b** sanctify by the sign of the cross. **3** glorify (God). **4** thank. **5** [usu. in passive; often foll. by with] make happy or successful. □ **(God) bless you!** exclamation of endearment, gratitude, etc., or to a person who has just sneezed.

■ **2** hallow, dedicate. **3** extol, praise, adore. **4** pay homage to. **5** make fortunate, endow, favor.

bless•ed /blésid, blest/ adj. (also poet. **blest**) **1** consecrated. **2** /blest/ [usu. foll. by with] often iron. fortunate (in the possession of). **3** euphem. cursed. **4** RC Ch. beatified. □□ **bless′ed•ly** adv. **bless′ed•ness** n.

■ **2** see FORTUNATE 1.

bless•ing /blésing/ n. **1** invoking (esp. divine) favor. **2** grace said before or after a meal. **3** gift of God, nature, etc.

■ **1** benediction, prayer; see also APPROVAL. **3** boon, favor, advantage, good fortune.

blew past of BLOW[1].

blight /blīt/ • n. **1** plant disease caused by mildew, insects, etc. **2** such an insect. **3** harmful or destructive force. **4** unsightly or neglected urban area. • v.tr. **1** affect with blight. **2** harm; destroy. **3** spoil.

■ n. **1** plague, infestation. **3** affliction, disease, plague. **4** eyesore, wasteland. • v. **1** afflict, infect. **2** wither, blast. **3** mar, taint, deface.

blimp /blimp/ n. small nonrigid airship.

blind /blīnd/ • adj. **1** lacking the power of sight. **2 a** without discernment. **b** [often foll. by to] unwilling or unable to appreciate (a circumstance, etc.). **3** not governed by purpose

or reason. **4 a** concealed. **b** closed at one end. **5** Aeron. (of flying) using instruments only. • v.tr. **1** deprive of sight. **2** [often foll. by to] rob of judgment. • n. **1** shade for a window. **2** pretext. **3** obstruction to sight or light. **4** camouflaged shelter used for observing wildlife or hunting animals. □ **blind date 1** social engagement between two people who have not previously met. **2** either of such people. **blind spot 1** Anat. point on the retina insensitive to light. **2** area in which a person lacks understanding or impartiality. **turn a (or one's) blind eye to** pretend not to notice. □□ **blind′ly** adv. **blind′ness** n.

■ adj. **1** sightless, eyeless, visionless, unseeing. **2 a** imperceptive, slow, myopic. **b** (blind to) unaware of, impervious or insensible to. **3** indiscriminate, unreasoning, mindless. • v. **2** deceive; hoodwink. • n. **1** curtain, screen, shutter(s). **2** pretense, front, smokescreen. □ **turn a blind eye to** see IGNORE 2. □□ **blindly** recklessly, heedlessly, deludedly, indiscriminately, rashly, impetuously.

blind•er /blíndər/ n. colloq. [in pl.] either of a pair of flaps attached to a horse's bridle to prevent it from seeing sideways.

blind•fold /blíndfōld/ • v.tr. **1** cover the eyes with a cloth, etc. **2** deprive of understanding; hoodwink. • n. cloth used to blindfold. • adj. & adv. with eyes bandaged.

■ adj. & adv. with eyes bandaged.

blind•side /blíndsīd/ v.tr. strike or attack unexpectedly.

blink /blingk/ • v. **1** intr. shut and open the eyes quickly. **2** intr. look with eyes opening and shutting. **3** tr. [often foll. by back] prevent (tears) by blinking. **4** tr. & [foll. by at] intr. ignore; condone. • n. **1** act of blinking. **2** momentary gleam or glimpse. □ **on the blink** sl. out of order.

■ v. **1** wink, flicker, flutter. **3** squint; be shocked, be surprised. **4** (blink at) wink at, overlook; turn a blind eye to. • n. **1** wink, flicker. **2** flash, sparkle, twinkle. □ **on the blink** broken, in disrepair, down.

blink•er /blíngkər/ • n. **1** device that blinks, esp. a vehicle's turn indicator. **2** = BLINDER. • v.tr. obscure with blinders.

blip /blip/ • n. **1** small image of an object on a radar screen. **2** minor deviation or error. • v. (**blipped, blip•ping**) intr. make a blip.

■ n. **2** see MISTAKE n.

bliss /blis/ n. **1** perfect joy; gladness. **2** being in heaven. See synonym study at RAPTURE. □□ **bliss′ful** adj. **bliss′ful•ly** adv. **bliss′ful•ness** n.

■ **1** happiness, blessedness, delight, felicity. **2** paradise; see also HEAVEN 2. □□ **blissful** see elated (ELATE).

blis•ter /blístər/ • n. **1** small bubble on the skin filled with fluid and caused by friction, etc. **2** similar swelling on any surface. • v. **1** tr. raise a blister on. **2** intr. come up in blisters. **3** tr. attack sharply. **4** (as **blistering** adj.) causing blisters. □□ **blis′ter•y** adj.

■ n. **1, 2** see LUMP[1] n. 2.

blithe /blīth/ adj. poet. **1** joyous. **2** careless; casual. □□ **blithe′ly** adv. **blithe′ness** n. **blithe′some** /blíthsəm/ adj.

■ **1** blissful, happy, cheerful, joyous. **2** happy-go-lucky, insouciant, heedless.

blitz /blits/ *colloq.* • *n.* **1** intensive or sudden (esp. aerial) attack. **2** (**the Blitz**) German air raids on London in 1940 during World War II. • *v.tr.* attack, damage, or destroy by a blitz.
■ *n.* **1** see RAID *n.* 1. • *v.* see SHELL *v.* 2.

bliz•zard /blízərd/ *n.* severe snowstorm with high winds.

bloat /blōt/ *v.* **1** *tr. & intr.* inflate; swell. **2** *tr.* (as **bloated** *adj.*) **a** swollen; puffed. **b** puffed up with pride or excessive wealth (*bloated plutocrat*).
■ **1** see SWELL *v.* 3. **2** (**bloated**) **a** distended, full, bulging. **b** inflated, pompous, conceited.

blob /blob/ *n.* **1** small drop of matter. **2** drop; spot.
■ **1** gobbet, globule, bit. **2** droplet, bead, drip.

bloc /blok/ *n.* combination of parties, governments, etc., sharing a common purpose.
□ **bloc vote** vote proportional in power to the number of people a delegate represents.

block /blok/ • *n.* **1** solid piece of hard material, esp. of stone or wood. **2** this as a base for chopping, etc. **3** compact mass of buildings bounded by (usu. four) streets. **4** obstruction. **5** pulley or system of pulleys mounted in a case. **6** [in *pl.*] any of a set of solid cubes, etc., used as a child's toy. **7** *Printing* piece of wood or metal engraved for printing. • *v.tr.* obstruct. □ **block and tackle** system of pulleys and ropes, esp. for lifting. □□ **block'er** *n.*
■ *n.* **1** chunk, hunk; lump, slab. **2** plinth. **4** bar, obstacle, hindrance. • *v.* clog, close off, barricade; bar, shut off.

block•ade /blokáyd/ • *n.* blocking of a place, esp. a port, by an enemy to prevent entry and exit. • *v.tr.* subject to a blockade.

block•bust•er /blókbustər/ *n. sl.* **1** thing of great power, esp. an extremely popular movie or book. **2** highly destructive bomb.

block•head /blókhed/ *n.* stupid person. □□ **block'head•ed** *adj.*
■ see CLOD 2. □□ **blockheaded** see FOOLISH.

block•house /blókhows/ *n.* **1** reinforced concrete shelter. **2** *hist.* small timber fort.

blond /blond/ • *adj.* (also *fem.* **blonde**) **1** (of hair) light-colored; fair. **2** (of the complexion, esp. as an indication of hair color) light-colored. • *n.* person with fair hair and skin. □□ **blond'ish** *adj.* **blond'ness** *n.*
■ *adj.* see FAIR¹ *adj.* 2.

blood /blud/ • *n.* **1** usu. red fluid circulating in the arteries and veins of vertebrates. **2** corresponding fluid in invertebrates. **3** bloodshed. **4** passion; temperament. **5** race; descent; parentage. **6** relationship; relations. • *v.tr.* **1** give (a hound) a first taste of blood. **2** initiate (a person) by experience. □ **blood bank** store of blood or plasma for transfusion. **blood bath** massacre. **blood count** number of corpuscles in a specific amount of blood. **blood group** any of the types of human blood. **blood relation** or **relative** relative by birth. **blood vessel** vein, artery, or capillary carrying blood.
■ *n.* **3** see GORE¹ 1. **5** see RACE² 1. **6** see *one's*

own flesh and blood (FLESH). □ **blood bath** see MASSACRE *n.* 1.

blood•cur•dling /blúdkərdling/ *adj.* horrifying.

blood•hound /blúdhownd/ *n.* **1** large hound used in tracking, having a keen sense of smell. **2** this breed.

blood•less /blúdlis/ *adj.* **1** without blood. **2** unemotional; cold. **3** pale. **4** without bloodshed. **5** feeble; lifeless. □□ **blood'less•ly** *adv.* **blood'less•ness** *n.*
■ **3** see PALE¹ *adj.* 1.

blood•mo•bile /blúdmōbeel/ *n.* van, truck, or bus equipped and staffed to take blood from donors.

blood•shed /blúdshed/ *n.* **1** spilling of blood. **2** slaughter.
■ **2** carnage, butchery, killing, murder.

blood•shot /blúdshot/ *adj.* (of an eyeball) inflamed.

blood•stain /blúdstayn/ *n.* discoloration caused by blood. □□ **blood'stained** *adj.*

blood•stream /blúdstreem/ *n.* blood in circulation.

blood•suck•er /blúdsukər/ *n.* **1** animal or insect that sucks blood, esp. a leech. **2** extortionist. **3** person who lives off others. □□ **blood'suck•ing** *adj.*
■ **2** blackmailer. **3** leech, parasite.

blood•thirst•y /blúdthərstee/ *adj.* (**blood•thirst•i•er**, **blood•thirst•i•est**) eager for bloodshed. □□ **blood'thirst•i•ly** *adv.* **blood'thirst•i•ness** *n.*
■ murderous, slaughterous, homicidal, savage, feral.

blood•y /blúdee/ • *adj.* (**blood•i•er**, **blood•i•est**) **1 a** of or like blood. **b** running or smeared with blood. **2 a** involving bloodshed. **b** sanguinary; cruel. **3** red. • *v.tr.* (**-ies**, **-ied**) stain with blood. □ **Bloody Mary** mixed drink of vodka and tomato juice. □□ **blood'i•ly** *adv.* **blood'i•ness** *n.*
■ *adj.* **2 a** see GORY. **b** see MURDEROUS 1.

bloom /bloom/ • *n.* **1 a** flower, esp. cultivated. **b** state of flowering. **2** one's prime. **3 a** (of the complexion) glow. **b** delicate powder on fruits, leaves, etc. • *v.* **1** *intr.* bear flowers; be in flower. **2** *intr.* **a** come into, or remain in, full beauty. **b** flourish.
■ *n.* **1 a** see FLOWER¹ *n.* **3 a** see FLUSH *n.* 1. • *v.* **1** see FLOWER *v.* 1. **2 b** see THRIVE 3.

bloom•ers /bloomərz/ *n.pl.* women's loose, almost knee-length underpants or knee-length trousers.

bloom•ing /blooming/ *adj.* flourishing; healthy.
■ *adj.* see SOUND² *adj.* 1.

bloop•er /bloopər/ *n. colloq.* **1** an embarrassing error. **2** a brief television or radio segment containing a humorous error, collected with others for broadcast as a group. **3** *Baseball* a weakly hit fly ball landing just beyond the reach of the infielders.

blos•som /blósəm/ • *n.* **1** flower or mass of flowers, esp. of a fruit tree. **2** promising stage. • *v.intr.* **1** open into flower. **2** mature; thrive. □□ **blos'som•y** *adj.*
■ *n.* **1** see FLOWER *n.* • *v.* **1** see FLOWER *v.* 1.

blot /blot/ • *n.* **1** spot or stain esp. of ink, etc. **2** disgraceful act or quality. **3** any blemish. • *v.* (**blot•ted, blot•ting**) **1 a** *tr.* spot or stain, esp. with ink. **b** *intr.* (of a pen, ink, etc.) make blots. **2** *tr.* **a** use blotting paper to absorb excess liquid, esp. ink. **b** (of blotting paper, etc.) soak up (esp. ink). □ **blot out 1** obliterate (writing). **2** obscure (a view, sound, etc.). **blotting paper** absorbent paper for drying excess ink.

■ *n.* **1** mark, smudge, blotch, discoloration. **2, 3** smear, smirch, scar, taint. • *v.* **1 a** spatter, smudge. □ **blot out** conceal, cover (up), hide; erase, efface, delete.

blotch /bloch/ • *n.* **1** discolored or inflamed patch on the skin. **2** irregular patch of color. • *v.tr.* cover with blotches. □□ **blotch•y** *adj.* (**blotch•i•er, blotch•i•est**).

■ *n.* see SPOT *n.* 1a, b. • *v.* see STAIN *v.* 1.

blot•ter /blótər/ *n.* **1** sheet of blotting paper. **2** logbook, esp. a police charge sheet.

blouse /blows, blowz/ • *n.* **1** woman's loose upper garment, usu. buttoned and collared. **2** upper part of a military uniform. • *v.tr.* make (a shirt, etc.) full like a blouse.

blow¹ /blō/ • *v.* (*past* **blew** /blōō/; *past part.* **blown** /blōn/) **1 a** *intr.* (of the wind or air) move rapidly. **b** *intr.* be driven by an air current. **c** *tr.* drive with an air current. **2 a** *tr.* send out (esp. air) by breathing. **b** *intr.* send a directed air current from the mouth. **3** *tr. & intr.* sound or be sounded by blowing. **4** *tr.* clear (the nose) by blowing. **5 a** *intr.* puff; pant. **b** *tr.* [esp. in *passive*] exhaust of breath. **6** *sl.* **a** *tr.* depart suddenly from (*blew town yesterday*). **b** *intr.* depart suddenly. **7** *tr.* shatter by an explosion. **8** *tr.* make or shape (glass or a bubble) by blowing. **9** *tr. & intr.* melt or cause to melt from overloading (*the fuse has blown*). **10** *tr.* break into (a safe, etc.) with explosives. **11** *tr.* *sl.* **a** squander; spend recklessly (*blew $20 on a meal*). **b** spoil; bungle (an opportunity, etc.). **c** reveal (a secret, etc.). • *n.* **1** act of blowing (e.g., one's nose, a wind instrument). **2 a** gust of wind or air. **b** exposure to fresh air. □ **blow-dry** arrange (the hair) while drying it with a hand-held dryer. **blow hot and cold** *colloq.* vacillate. **blow in** *colloq.* arrive unexpectedly. **blow a person's mind** *sl.* **1** cause to have drug-induced hallucinations, etc. **2** amaze. **blow out 1** extinguish by blowing. **2** (of a tire) burst. **blow over** (of trouble, etc.) fade away. **blow one's top** (or **stack**) *colloq.* explode in rage. **blow up 1 a** shatter or destroy by an explosion. **b** explode; erupt. **2** *colloq.* rebuke strongly. **3** inflate (a tire, etc.). **4** *colloq.* **a** enlarge (a photograph). **b** exaggerate. **5** *colloq.* lose one's temper. **blow-up** *n.* **1** *colloq.* enlargement (of a photograph, etc.). **2** explosion.

■ *v.* **1 a, b** waft, whistle. **2** exhale; expel. **5a** see PUFF *v.* 1. **6 b** see ESCAPE *v.* 1. **7** blast. **9** short-circuit, burn out. **11 a** lavish, waste, throw away. **b** botch, mess up, make a mess of. **c** see REVEAL 2. • *n.* **1** exhalation, breath, expiration. **2 a** breeze. □ **blow hot and cold** be inconsistent, be fickle, shilly-shally.

blow out 1 snuff (out), smother. **blow one's top** (**stack**) become angry. **blow up 1 a** puncture, rupture. **b** fly apart, go off. **3** dilate, pump up. **4 a** magnify. **b** amplify, expand, overstate. **5** flare up.

blow² /blō/ *n.* **1** hard stroke with a hand or weapon. **2** sudden shock or misfortune. □ **blow-by-blow** (of a description, etc.) giving all the details in sequence.

■ **1** cuff, rap, smack, punch, clout, hit, knock. **2** surprise, bombshell, jolt, bolt from the blue.

blow•fly /blófli/ *n.* (*pl.* **–flies**) fly that lays eggs on meat or flesh.

blow•gun /blógun/ *n.* tube for propelling arrows or darts by blowing.

blow•hole /blóhōl/ *n.* **1** nostril of a whale or other cetacean, on the top of its head. **2** vent for air, smoke, etc.

blown *past part.* of BLOW¹.

blow•out /blō-owt/ *n. colloq.* **1** burst tire. **2** melted fuse. **3** large party. **4** victory by a wide margin.

blow•pipe /blópīp/ *n.* **1** = BLOWGUN. **2** tube used to intensify the heat of a flame by blowing air or other gas through it.

blow•torch /blótawrch/ *n.* portable device with a very hot flame used for burning off paint, soldering, etc.

blow•zy /blówzee/ *adj.* (**blow•zi•er, blow•zi•est**) slovenly. □□ **blow'zi•ly** *adv.* **blow'zi•ness** *n.*

■ see UNKEMPT.

BLT *abbr.* bacon, lettuce, and tomato sandwich.

blub•ber /blúbər/ • *n.* **1 a** whale fat. **b** thick or excessive fat. **2** spell of weeping. • *v.* **1** *intr.* sob loudly. **2** *tr.* sob out (words). □□ **blub'ber•er** *n.* **blub'ber•ing•ly** *adv.* **blub'ber•y** *adj.*

■ *v.* see SOB *v.*

blud•geon /blújən/ • *n.* heavy club. • *v.tr.* **1** beat with a bludgeon. **2** coerce.

■ *n.* see CLUB *n.* 1. • *v.* **1** see BEAT *v.* 1.

blue /blōō/ • *adj.* **1** having the color of a clear sky. **2** sad; depressed. **3** pornographic. • *n.* **1** blue color or pigment. **2** blue clothes or material (*looks good in blue*). □ **blue baby** baby with a blue complexion due to a congenital heart defect. **blue blood** aristocrat. **blue cheese** cheese with veins of blue mold. **blue-chip 1** (of stock) sound and usu. paying a dividend. **2** high quality. **blue-collar** manual; industrial. **blue jay** common crested bird with a blue back and head. **blue jeans** pants made of blue denim. **blue-pencil** (**–pen•ciled, –pen•cil•ing**) edit (a manuscript, movie, etc.).

■ *adj.* **1** azure, sapphire, aquamarine, turquoise, ultramarine, lapis lazuli, navy, indigo, cyan, hyacinth, cobalt, teal, Wedgwood. **2** low-spirited, dispirited, dismal, gloomy. **3** obscene, vulgar, indecent, risqué; indelicate.

blue•bell /blóobel/ *n.* any of various woodland plants with bell-shaped blue flowers.

blue•ber•ry /blóoberee/ *n.* (*pl.* **–ries**) small, blue-black edible fruit of various plants.

blue•bird /blóobərd/ *n.* any of various blue songbirds.

blue•bot•tle /bloobot'l/ *n.* large buzzing blowfly with a metallic blue body.

blue•grass /bloogras/ *n.* **1** any of several bluish green grasses, esp. Kentucky bluegrass. **2** variety of country music.

blue moon • *n. colloq.* second full moon during a calendar month. □ **once in a blue moon** infrequently; rarely.

blue•print /blooprint/ • *n.* **1** photographic print of plans in white on a blue background. **2** detailed plan. • *v.tr.* work out (a program, plan, etc.).

■ *n.* see PLAN *n.* 2.

blues /blooz/ *n.pl.* **1** [prec. by *the*] bout of depression. **2** [prec. by *the*; often treated as *sing.*] melancholic music of African-American folk origin. □□ **blues'y** *adj.* (in sense 2).

bluff[1] /bluf/ • *v.* **1** *intr.* feign strength, confidence, etc. **2** *tr.* mislead by bluffing. • *n.* act of bluffing. □ **call a person's bluff** challenge a person to prove a claim. □□ **bluff'er** *n.*

■ *v.* **1** pretend, fake, boast. **2** deceive, hoodwink, dupe. • *n.* bombast, bravado; *sl.* hot air.

bluff[2] /bluf/ • *adj.* **1** (of a cliff, or a ship's bows) having a steep broad front. **2** (of a person or manner) blunt; frank. See synonym study at BRUSQUE. • *n.* steep cliff or headland. □□ **bluff'ly** *adv.* (in sense 2 of *adj.*). **bluff'ness** *n.* (in sense 2 of *adj.*).

■ *adj.* **1** abrupt, sheer, perpendicular, precipitous. **2** blustering, gruff, rough; hearty, straightforward. • *n.* precipice, scarp; promontory, palisades.

blun•der /blundar/ • *n.* serious or foolish mistake. • *v.* **1** *intr.* make a blunder; act clumsily or ineptly. **2** *tr.* deal incompetently with. **3** *intr.* stumble. □□ **blun'der•er** *n.* **blun'der•ing•ly** *adv.*

■ *n.* error, gaffe, faux pas, impropriety. • *v.* **1** make a mess or mistake. **2** botch, bungle, mismanage. **3** flounder, grope about, stagger.

blun•der•buss /blundarbus/ *n. hist.* short, large-bored gun.

blunt /blunt/ • *adj.* **1** (of a knife, pencil, etc.) not sharp or pointed. **2** (of a person or manner) direct; outspoken. See synonym study at BRUSQUE. • *v.tr.* make less sharp. □□ **blunt'ly** *adv.* (in sense 2 of *adj.*). **blunt'ness** *n.*

■ *adj.* **1** dull, blunted, obtuse, unpointed, worn (down). **2** abrupt, curt, rough-spoken, plainspoken, short. • *v.* dull, take the edge off, soften.

blur /blər/ • *v.* (**blurred, blur•ring**) **1** *tr.* & *intr.* make or become unclear or less distinct. **2** *tr.* smear. • *n.* something that appears or sounds indistinct or unclear. □□ **blur'ry** *adj.* (**blur•ri•er, blur•ri•est**).

■ *v.* **1** obscure, hide, conceal; confuse. **2** smudge. • *n.* dimness, haziness; cloudiness, fogginess; haze.

blurb /blərb/ *n.* promotional description of a book.

blurt /blərt/ *v.tr.* [usu. foll. by *out*] utter abruptly, thoughtlessly, or tactlessly.

■ (*blurt out*) burst out with, utter, tattle; reveal, disclose.

blush /blush/ • *v.intr.* **1 a** become pink in the face from embarrassment. **b** (of the face) redden thus. **2** feel embarrassed or ashamed. **3** become red or pink. • *n.* **1** act of blushing. **2** pink tinge. □ **at first blush** on the first glimpse.

■ *v.* **1, 3** flush, color. **2** be or feel shamefaced, be red-faced or mortified.

blush•er /blushər/ *n.* rouge.

blus•ter /blustər/ • *v.intr.* **1** behave pompously and boisterously. **2** (of the wind, etc.) blow fiercely. • *n.* **1** noisily self-assertive talk. **2** empty threats. □□ **blus'ter•er** *n.* **blus'ter•y** *adj.*

■ *v.* **1** swagger, strut, boast, brag. **2** storm, rage. • *n.* **1** swagger, rhetoric, bombast, puffery, bravado.

blvd. *abbr.* boulevard.

BM *abbr.* **1** Bachelor of Medicine. **2** Bachelor of Music. **3** British Museum. **4** basal metabolism. **5** bowel movement.

BMOC • *n. abbr.* a popular, well known, or influential person (from *b*ig *m*an *o*n *c*ampus).

BO *abbr. colloq.* body odor.

bo•a /boə/ *n.* **1** large snake that kills its prey by crushing and suffocating. **2** long scarf of feathers or fur.

■ **2** see STOLE[1].

boar /bawr/ *n.* **1** tusked wild pig. **2** uncastrated male pig.

board /bawrd/ • *n.* **1** long, flat, thin piece of sawn lumber. **2** provision of regular meals for payment. **3** directors of a company; committee or group of councillors, etc. **4** [in *pl.*] stage of a theater. **5** *Naut.* side of a ship. • *v.* **1** *tr.* go on board (a ship, train, etc.). **2** *intr.* **a** receive regular meals for payment. **b** *tr.* provide with regular meals. **3** *tr.* cover with boards. □ **go by the board** be neglected or discarded. **on board** on or onto a ship, aircraft, etc. on **board'er** *n.*

■ *n.* **1** plank. **2** food. **3** council, directorship, management. • *v.* **1** enter. **2 a** eat. **3** see SEAL[1] *v.* 1. □ **go by the board** see STOP *v.* 2. **on board** aboard.

board cer•ti•fied • *adj.* (usu. of a physician) officially recognized by a professional organization as possessing certain qualifications or meeting certain standards.

board•ing•house /bawrdinghows/ *n.* establishment providing board and lodging.

board•walk /bawrdwawk/ *n.* promenade, esp. of wood, along a beach.

boast /bōst/ • *v.* **1** *intr.* talk about oneself with indulgent pride. **2** *tr.* own or have with pride. • *n.* **1** act of boasting. **2** thing one is proud of. □□ **boast'er** *n.* **boast'ful** *adj.* **boast'ful•ly** *adv.* **boast'ful•ness** *n.* **boast'ing•ly** *adv.*

■ *v.* **1** brag, blow one's (own) trumpet, crow. □□ **boaster** see BRAGGART *n.*

boat /bōt/ • *n.* **1** small vessel propelled on water by an engine, oars, or sails. **2** (in general use) any ship. **3** elongated boat-shaped container used for sauce, gravy, etc. • *v.intr.* go in a boat for pleasure. □ **boat peo•ple** refugees who have left a country by sea. **in the same boat** sharing the same problems. □□ **boat'ful** *n.* (*pl.* **–fuls**).

■ *n.* **1** craft, skiff, motorboat, speedboat, launch. • *v.* sail, cruise.

boat•er /bótər/ *n.* **1** person who boats. **2** flat-topped straw hat with a stiff brim.

boat•house /bót-hows/ *n.* waterside shelter for housing boats.

boat•ing /bóting/ *n.* rowing or sailing as recreation.

boat•swain /bós'n/ *n.* (also **bo'sun**, **bo'sun**, **bo's'n**) ship's officer in charge of equipment and the crew. □ **boatswain's chair** seat suspended from ropes for work on the side of a ship or building.

bob /bob/ • *v.intr.* (**bobbed**, **bob•bing**) **1** move quickly up and down. **2** emerge suddenly; become active or conspicuous again after a defeat, etc. • *n.* jerking or bouncing movement, esp. upward.

■ *v.* **1** see WAG¹ *v.*

bob•bin /bóbin/ *n.* cylinder for thread.

bob•ble /bóbəl/ *n.* fumble, esp. of a baseball or football.

bob•by pin /bóbeepin/ *n.* flat, closed hairpin.

bob•by socks *n.pl.* (also **bob'by sox**) short socks reaching just above the ankle.

bob•cat /bóbkat/ *n.* small N. American lynx with a spotted reddish-brown coat and a short tail.

bob•sled /bóbsled/ • *n.* mechanically steered and braked sled used for racing down a steep ice-covered run. • *v.intr.* race in a bobsled.

bob•white /bóbhwít, bóbwít/ *n.* American quail.

bode /bód/ *v. tr.* portend; foreshow. □ **bode well** (or **ill**) be a good (or bad) sign. □□ **bod'ing** *n.*

■ promise, augur, betoken, omen, presage.

bod•ice /bódis/ *n.* part of a woman's dress above the waist.

bod•i•ly /bód'lee/ • *adj.* of the body. • *adv.* **1** as a whole (*threw them bodily*). **2** in the body; as a person.

■ *adj.* physical, corporal.

bod•kin /bódkin/ *n.* **1** blunt thick needle for drawing tape, etc., through a hem. **2** small pointed instrument for piercing cloth, etc.

bod•y /bódee/ *n.* (*pl.* **-ies**) **1** physical structure, including the bones, flesh, and organs, of a person or animal. **2** = TRUNK 2. **3 a** main or central part. **b** bulk or majority. **4 a** group regarded collectively. **b** collection. **5** quantity. **6** piece of matter. **7** full or substantial quality of flavor, tone, etc. □ **body language** communicating through gestures and poses. **body politic** nation or government as a corporate body. **body shop** workshop where bodies of vehicles are repaired.

■ *n.* **1** (*dead body*) corpse, remains, *esp. Med.* cadaver. **2** torso. **3 a** hull, chassis; substance, essentials. **b** aggregate. **4 a** association, league, band, organization, corps, union. **b** see COLLECTION 1, 2. **5** see AMOUNT *n.* 1. **7** richness, substance, firmness.

bod•y•build•ing /bódeebilding/ *n.* strengthening and enlarging the muscles by exercise.

bod•y•guard /bódeegaard/ *n.* person or group of persons escorting and protecting another person (esp. a dignitary).

■ see ESCORT *n.* 1.

bod•y•suit /bódeesōōt/ *n.* close-fitting, one-piece stretch garment, used mainly for sport.

Boer /bōr, bawr/ • *n.* South African of Dutch descent. • *adj.* of or relating to the Boers.

bog /bog, bawg/ • *n.* wet, spongy ground. • *v.tr.* (**bogged**, **bog•ging**) [foll. by *down*] impede. □□ **bog'gy** *adj.* (**bog•gi•er**, **bog•gi•est**). **bog'gi•ness** *n.*

■ *n.* swamp, fen, marsh, quagmire. • *v.* (*bog down*) slow (down), hamper.

bo•gey¹ /bógee/ *Golf* • *n.* (*pl.* **-geys**) score of one stroke more than par at any hole. • *v.tr.* (**-geys**, **-geyed**) play (a hole) in one stroke more than par.

bo•gey² /bógee/ *n.* (also **bo•gy**) (*pl.* **-geys** or **-gies**) evil or mischievous spirit; devil.

■ see DEVIL *n.* 1, 2.

bo•gey•man /bōogeeman, bógee-, bōogee-/ *n.* (also **bo'gy•man**, **boog'ey•man**, **boog'ie•man**) (*pl.* **-men**) person (real or imaginary) causing fear or difficulty.

■ see MONSTER 1.

bog•gle /bógəl/ *v.intr. colloq.* **1** be startled or baffled (esp.*the mind boggles*). **2** [usu. foll. by *about*, *at*] hesitate; demur.

bo•gus /bógəs/ *adj.* sham; fictitious; spurious. □□ **bo'gus•ly** *adv.* **bo'gus•ness** *n.*

■ counterfeit, fake, false, fraudulent.

Bo•he•mi•an /bōheemeeən/ • *n.* **1** native of Bohemia; Czech. **2** (also **bohemian**) socially unconventional person, esp. an artist or writer. • *adj.* **1** of Bohemia or its people. **2** socially unconventional. □□ **bo•he'mi•an•ism** *n.* (in sense 2).

■ *n.* **2** eccentric, nonconformist; *colloq.* hippie. • *adj.* **2** alternative, radical, experimental, avant-garde.

boil¹ /boyl/ • *v.* **1** *intr.* **a** (of a liquid) start to bubble up and turn into vapor; reach a temperature at which this happens. **b** (of a vessel) contain boiling liquid. **2 a** *tr.* cause to boil. **b** *tr.* cook by boiling. **c** *intr.* (of food) be cooked by boiling. **3** *intr.* be very angry. • *n.* act or process of boiling; boiling point. □ **boil down 1** reduce volume by boiling. **2** reduce to essentials. **3** [foll. by *to*] amount to. **boil over** lose one's temper.

■ *v.* **2 b, c** simmer, stew. **3** seethe, fume, foam at the mouth. □ **boil down** see TELESCOPE *v.* 3. **3** (*boil down to*) come down to, signify. **boil over** see EXPLODE 2.

boil² /boyl/ *n.* inflamed pus-filled swelling caused by infection of a hair follicle, etc.

■ abscess, carbuncle, pustule.

boil•er /bóylər/ *n.* **1** apparatus for heating a hot water supply. **2** tank for turning water to steam.

boil•ing point /bóyling poynt/ *n.* **1** temperature at which a liquid starts to boil. **2** high excitement.

bois•ter•ous /bóystərəs/ *adj.* **1** (of a person) rough; noisily exuberant. **2** (of the sea, etc.) stormy. See syonym study at VOCIFEROUS. □□ **bois'ter•ous•ly** *adv.* **bois'ter•ous•ness** *n.*

■ **1** rowdy, clangorous, uproarious, rip-roaring. **2** rough, tempestuous, turbulent.

bold /bōld/ *adj.* **1** confidently assertive; adventurous; courageous. **2** impudent. **3** vivid. □□ **bold'ly** *adv.* **bold'ness** *n.*

■ **1** brave, gallant, plucky, spirited. **2** audacious, forthright, self-assertive, outspoken. **3** pronounced, prominent, well-marked, strong. □□ **boldly** see *assertively* (ASSERTIVE).

SYNONYM STUDY: **bold**
AGGRESSIVE, AUDACIOUS, BUMPTIOUS, BRAZEN, INTREPID, PRESUMPTUOUS. Is walking up to an attractive stranger and asking him or her to have dinner with you tonight a **bold** move or merely an **aggressive** one? Both words suggest assertive, confident behavior that is a little on the shameless side, but *bold* has a wider range of application. It can suggest self-confidence that borders on impudence (*to be so bold as to call the president by his first name*), but it can also be used to describe a daring temperament that is either courageous or defiant (*he began to be known in military circles as a bold, cool, and remarkably clear-sighted man*). *Aggressive* behavior, on the other hand, usually falls within a narrower range, somewhere between menacing (*aggressive attacks on innocent villagers*) and just plain pushy (*an aggressive salesperson*). *Brazen* implies a defiant lack of modesty (*a brazen stare*), and **presumptuous** goes even further, suggesting a failure to observe appropriate limits to the point of causing offense (*a presumptuous request for money*). *Bumptious* behavior can also be offensive, but it is usually associated with the kind of pride or cockiness that can't be helped (*a bumptious young upstart*). An **audacious** individual is bold to the point of recklessness (*an audacious explorer*), which brings it very close in meaning to **intrepid**, suggesting fearlessness in the face of danger or the unknown (*an intrepid mountaineer may still have a safety rope*).

bole /bōl/ *n.* stem or trunk of a tree.

bo•le•ro /bōláirō, bə/ *n.* (*pl.* -**ros**) **1 a** Spanish dance in simple triple time. **b** music for it. **2** woman's short open jacket.

boll /bōl/ *n.* rounded seedpod of flax or cotton.

bo•lo•gna /bəlōnee, -nyə/ *n.* large meat sausage sold ready for eating.

Bol•she•vik /bṓlshəvik, bōl-/ • *n.* **1** *hist.* member of the radical faction of the Russian Social Democratic party, which became the Communist party in 1918. **2** Russian communist. **3** any revolutionary socialist. • *adj.* **1** of the Bolsheviks. **2** communist. □□ **Bol'she•vism** *n.* **Bol'she•vist** *n.*

bol•ster /bṓlstər/ • *n.* long, thick pillow. • *v.tr.* [usu. foll. by *up*] encourage; reinforce. □□ **bol'ster•er** *n.*

■ *v.* support, uphold, reinforce; help.

bolt /bōlt/ • *n.* **1** sliding bar and socket used to fasten a door, etc. **2** threaded pin, usu. metal, used with a nut to hold things together. **3** discharge of lightning. **4** act of bolting (cf. sense 3 of *v.*). **5** *hist.* arrow for shooting from a crossbow. **6** roll of fabric, wallpaper, etc. • *v.* **1** *tr.* fasten with a bolt. **2** *tr.* fasten together with bolts. **3** *intr.*

a dash suddenly away. **b** (of a horse) suddenly gallop out of control. **4** *tr.* gulp down (food) unchewed. • *adv.* rigidly; stiffly (esp. as *bolt upright*). □ **bolt from the blue** complete surprise. □□ **bolt'er** *n.* (in sense 3 of *v.*).

■ *n.* **1** pin, rod, latch. **3** thunderbolt. **4** see DASH *n.* 1. **5** arrow, *hist.* quarrel. • *v.* **1** lock, latch, secure. **2** fix, attach, connect. **3 a** dart off, race off, shoot off. **b** break away. **4** swallow whole; wolf down. • *adv.* (*bolt upright*) erect; woodenly, fixedly. □ **bolt from the blue** shock, bombshell.

bomb /bom/ • *n.* **1** container with explosive, incendiary material, etc., designed to explode and cause damage. **2** small pressurized container that sprays liquid, foam, or gas. **3** *colloq.* failure (esp. a theatrical one). • *v.* **1** *tr.* attack with bombs. **2** *intr.* throw or drop bombs. **3** *intr. sl.* fail badly.

■ *n.* **1** bombshell, shell, torpedo. **3** see FLOP *n.* **•** *v.* **1** bombard, shell, blow up. **3** see FAIL *v.* 1, 2a.

bom•bard /bombáärd/ *v.tr.* **1** attack with heavy guns or bombs. **2** subject to persistent questioning. **3** *Physics* direct a stream of high-speed particles at (a substance). See synonym study at ATTACK. □□ **bom•bard'ment** *n.*

■ **1, 2** bomb, shell; assail; see also BESIEGE 3. □□ **bombardment** see ATTACK *n.* 1.

bom•bar•dier /bómbərdéer/ *n.* member of a bomber crew responsible for aiming and releasing bombs.

bom•bast /bómbast/ *n.* pompous, pretentious, or extravagant language. □□ **bom•bas'tic** *adj.* **bom•bas'ti•cal•ly** *adv.*

■ bluster, grandiloquence. □□ **bombastic** high-flown, rhetorical.

bomb•er /bómər/ *n.* **1** aircraft equipped to drop bombs. **2** person using bombs.

bomb•shell /bómshel/ *n.* **1** overwhelming surprise. **2** artillery bomb. **3** *sl.* very attractive woman.

■ **1** shock, blow. **3** see BEAUTY 2a.

bo•na fide /bónə fíd, fídee, bóna/ • *adj.* genuine; sincere. See synonym study at GENUINE. • *adv.* genuinely; sincerely.

■ *adj.* authentic, attested; reliable. • *adv.* see *authentically* (AUTHENTIC).

bo•nan•za /bənánzə/ *n.* **1** source of wealth. **2** rich lode. **3** prosperity.

■ **3** see WINDFALL.

bon•bon /bónbon/ *n.* piece of candy.

bond /bond/ • *n.* **1 a** thing that fastens another down or together. **b** [usu. in *pl.*] thing restraining bodily freedom. **2** [often in *pl.*] **a** uniting force. **b** restraint; responsibility. **3** binding agreement. **4** *Commerce* certificate issued by a government or a company promising to repay borrowed money at a fixed rate of interest. **5** (also **bail bond**) money deposited to guarantee appearance in court. • *v.* **1** *intr.* adhere; hold together. **2** *tr.* connect with a bond. **3** *tr.* place (goods) in bond. □ **bond paper** high-quality writing paper.

■ *n.* **1 a** cement, adhesive, glue. **b** (*bonds*)

tie(s), shackles, chains, fetters. **2 a** connection, tie, attachment. **b** charge, duty, obligation; see also sense 1b above. **3** covenant, pact, contract. • *v.* **2, 3** cement, bind, glue, weld.

bond•age /bóndij/ *n.* **1** slavery. **2** subjection to constraint, influence, etc.

■ **1** servitude, serfdom, subjection, enslavement. **2** subjugation, oppression; restraint; imprisonment.

bonds•man /bóndzmən/ *n.* (*pl.* **–men**) **1** slave. **2** person who provides bond (sense 5).

bone /bón/ • *n.* **1** any piece of hard tissue making up the skeleton in vertebrates. **2** [in *pl.*] **a** skeleton, esp. as remains after death. **b** the body, esp. as a seat of intuitive feeling (*felt it in my bones*). **3 a** material of which bones consist. **b** similar substance such as ivory, dentine, or whalebone. • *v. tr.* take out bones from (meat or fish). □ **bone china** fine china made of clay mixed with bone ash. **bone-dry** quite dry. **bone of contention** source of dispute. **bone up** [often foll. by *on*] *colloq.* study (a subject) intensively. □□ **bone′less** *adj.*

bone•meal /bónmeel/ *n.* crushed or ground bones used esp. as a fertilizer.

bon•fire /bónfīr/ *n.* large open-air fire.

bon•go /bónggō/ *n.* (*pl.* **–gos** or **–goes**) either of a pair of small connected drums usu. held between the knees and played with the fingers.

bo•ni•to /bənéetō/ *n.* (*pl.* same or **–tos**) any of several fish similar to the tuna and striped like mackerel.

bonk /bongk/ • *v.* **1** *tr.* hit resoundingly. **2** *intr.* bang; bump. • *n.* instance of bonking (*a bonk on the head*). □□ **bonk′er** *n.*

bonk•ers /bóngkərz/ *adj. sl.* crazy.

bon mot /bawn mó/ *n.* (*pl.* **bons mots** *pronunc.* same or /–móz/) witty saying.

■ see WITTICISM.

bon•net /bónit/ *n.* woman's or child's hat tied under the chin.

bon•sai /bónsī, –zī/ *n.* (*pl.* same) **1** art of cultivating ornamental, artificially dwarfed trees and shrubs. **2** such a tree or shrub.

bo•nus /bónəs/ *n.* **1** extra benefit. **2** usu. seasonal gratuity to employees beyond their normal pay.

■ **1** see BENEFIT *n.* 1. **2** reward, perquisite.

bon voyage /báwn vwaayaázh/ expression of good wishes to a departing traveler.

bon•y /bónee/ *adj.* (**bon•i•er**, **bon•i•est**) **1** thin with prominent bones. **2** having many bones. **3** of or like bone. □□ **bon′i•ness** *n.*

■ **1** see THIN *adj.* 4.

boo /boo/ • *int.* **1** expression of disapproval or contempt. **2** sound intended to surprise. • *n.* utterance of *boo*, esp. made to a performer, etc. • *v.* (**boos, booed**) **1** *intr.* utter boos. **2** *tr.* jeer at by booing.

■ *v.* see JEER *v.* 1.

boob /boob/ *sl.* • *n.* simpleton. □ **boob tube** *sl.* television set.

■ see FOOL *n.* 1. □ **boob tube** the tube, TV, idiot box.

boo•boo /bóoboo/ *n. sl.* **1** mistake. **2** (esp. by or to a child) minor injury.

boo•by /bóobee/ *n.* (*pl.* **–bies**) **1** stupid or childish person. **2** gannet with a bright bill and bright feet. □ **booby prize** prize given to the least successful competitor in any contest. **booby trap** *Mil.* apparently harmless explosive device intended to kill or injure anyone touching it. **booby-trap** *v.tr.* place a booby trap or traps in or on.

■ **1** see SILLY *n.* □ **booby hatch** see BEDLAM 2. **booby trap** see TRAP *n.* 3.

boo•dle /bóod'l/ *n. sl.* money, esp. gained or used dishonestly.

boog•er /bóogar/ • *n.* **1** (also **booger man**) = BOGEYMAN. **2** piece of dried nasal mucus.

boog•ey•man var. of BOGEYMAN.

boo•gie /bóogee/ • *v.intr.* (**–gies, –gied, –gy•ing**) *sl.* **1** dance enthusiastically to pop music. **2** leave, esp. quickly. • *n.* **1** = BOOGIE-WOOGIE. **2** *sl.* dance to jazz music.

boog•ie•man var. of BOGEYMAN.

boog•ie-woog•ie /bóogeewóogee, bóogeewóogee/ *n.* style of playing blues or jazz, esp. on the piano.

book /book/ • *n.* **1 a** written or printed work consisting of pages glued or sewn together along one side and bound in covers. **b** literary composition intended for publication (*working on her book*). **2** bound set of tickets, stamps, matches, etc. **3** [in *pl.*] set of records or accounts. **4** main division of a literary work, or of the Bible. **5** libretto, script of a play, etc. **6** telephone directory. **7** record of bets. • *v.* **1** *tr.* **a** reserve (a seat, etc.) in advance. **b** engage (a guest, musical act, etc.) for some occasion. **2** *tr.* record the personal details of (esp. a criminal offender). □ **go by the book** proceed according to the rules. **the Good Book** the Bible. **make book** take bets and pay out winnings on a race, etc. **throw the book at** see ACCUSE 2, PUNISH 1.

■ *n.* **1** volume, tome, work, publication; paperback, hardback. **5** words, lyrics; continuity. • *v.* **1** earmark, save; order. □ **go by the book** follow *or* stick to the rules. **throw the book at** see ACCUSE 2, PUNISH 1.

book•bind•er /bóokbindər/ *n.* person who binds books professionally. □□ **book′bind•ing** *n.*

book•case /bóok-kays/ *n.* set of shelves for books in the form of a cabinet.

book•end /bóokend/ *n.* usu. ornamental prop used to keep a row of books upright.

book•ie /bóokee/ *n. colloq.* = BOOKMAKER.

book•ing /bóoking/ *n.* reservation or engagement (see BOOK *v.* 1).

■ order, arrangement.

book•ish /bóokish/ *adj.* **1** studious; fond of reading. **2** acquiring knowledge mainly from books. □□ **book′ish•ly** *adv.* **book′ish•ness** *n.*

■ **1** see STUDIOUS 1.

book•keep•er /bóok-keepər/ *n.* person who keeps accounts for a business, etc. □□ **book′keep•ing** *n.*

book•let /bóoklit/ *n.* small book, usu. with paper covers.

book•mak•er /boŏokmaykər/ n. professional taker of bets. □□ **book′mak•ing** n.

book•mark /boŏokmaark/ • n. **1** strip of leather, cardboard, etc., used to mark one's place in a book. **2** Computing record of the address of a web page, etc., for quick access by the user. • v. Computing make a record of the address of a web page, etc., for quick access.

book•mo•bile /boŏokmōbeēl/ n. mobile library.

book•plate /boŏokplayt/ n. decorative personalized label stuck in the front of a book.

book•sell•er /boŏokselər/ n. dealer in books.

book•store /boŏokstawr/ n. store where books are sold.

boom[1] /boŏom/ • n. deep resonant sound. • v.intr. make or speak with a boom. □ **boom box** sl. stereo with powerful speakers. • n. rumble, roar, blare. • v. resound, thunder, roar, bellow.

boom[2] /boŏom/ • n. period of economic prosperity or activity. • v.intr. be suddenly prosperous. • n. growth, increase, development; profitability. • v. thrive, flourish, succeed, progress.

boom[3] /boŏom/ n. **1** Naut. pivoted spar to which a sail is attached. **2** long pole over a movie or television stage set, carrying microphones and other equipment. **3** floating barrier across the mouth of a harbor or river, or enclosing an oil spill.

boo•mer•ang /boŏomərang/ • n. **1** curved flat missile able to return to the thrower. **2** plan that recoils on its originator. • v.intr. (of a plan, etc.) backfire. • v. rebound, recoil, redound; miscarry, fail.

boon[1] /boŏon/ n. **1** advantage; blessing. **2 a** thing asked for. **b** gift. • n. **1** godsend, stroke of good fortune, piece of luck. **2 a** see REQUEST n. 1, 2. **b** award, reward, gratuity, present.

boon[2] /boŏon/ adj. intimate; favorite (esp. as boon companions).

boon•docks /boŏondoks/ (also **boon•ies** n. sl. rough, remote, or isolated country.

boon•dog•gle /boŏondogəl, –daw–/ n. **1** trivial work done to appear busy. **2** questionable public project that typically involves political patronage and graft. • v.intr. participate in a boondoggle.

boor /boŏor/ n. rude, unmannerly person. □□ **boor′ish** adj. **boor′ish•ly** adv. **boor′ish•ness** n. • n. barbarian, yahoo, brute, hoodlum, colloq. slob, pig.

boost /boŏost/ colloq. • v.tr. **1 a** promote by praise or advertising; push; increase. **b** push from below. **2** increase or amplify (voltage, a radio signal, etc.). • n. act or result of boosting. • v. **1 a** encourage, help, kick-start, aid, support. **b** lift or shove (up); raise. **2** see AMPLIFY 1. • n. leg up.

boost•er /boŏostər/ n. **1** device for increasing power or voltage. **2** auxiliary engine or rocket for initial acceleration. **3** (also **boost•er shot**) Med. dose of an immunizing agent to reinforce an earlier one. **4** colloq. person who boosts by helping or encouraging.

■ **4** see FAN[2].

boot[1] /boŏot/ • n. outer foot covering reaching above the ankle. • v.tr. **1** kick. **2** [often foll. by out] dismiss (a person) forcefully. **3** put (a computer) in a state of readiness. □ **you bet your boots** sl. it is quite certain. □□ **boot′ed** adj. • v. **1** see KICK v. 1. **2** (boot out) eject, expel, throw out; see also DISMISS 2.

boot[2] /boŏot/ n. □ **to boot** as well; to the good; in addition. ■ □ **to boot** into the bargain, besides, moreover, also, too, additionally.

booth /boŏoth/ n. (pl. **booths** /boŏothz, boŏoths/) **1** small temporary structure used esp. for sale or display of goods at a market, etc. **2** enclosure for telephoning, voting, etc. **3** set of a table and benches in a restaurant or bar. ■ **1** stall, stand, table. **2** compartment, cubicle, box.

boot•leg /boŏotleg/ • adj. (esp. of liquor) smuggled; illicitly sold. • v.tr. (–legged, –leg•ging) make, distribute, or smuggle (illicit goods). □□ **boot′leg•ger** n.

boot•less /boŏotlis/ adj. unavailing; useless. ■ pointless, vain, purposeless, hopeless, futile.

boot•strap /boŏotstrap/ n. loop at the back of a boot used to pull it on. □ **pull oneself up by one's bootstraps** better oneself by one's own efforts.

boo•ty /boŏotee/ n. **1** plunder gained esp. in war or by piracy. **2** colloq. something gained or won. ■ **1** spoil(s), contraband, takings, loot. **2** pickings, takings; prize, haul.

booze /boŏoz/ colloq. • n. alcohol, esp. hard liquor. • v.intr. drink alcohol esp. excessively or habitually. □□ **booz′er** n. ■ n. drink, spirit(s), colloq. firewater. • v. tipple, imbibe, sl. hit the bottle. □□ **boozer** see DRUNK n. 1.

bop[1] /bop/ • n. colloq. = BEBOP. • v.intr. sl. proceed; go (let's bop on over to the library). □□ **bop′per** n.

bop[2] /bop/ colloq. • v.tr. (**bopped, bopping**) hit; punch lightly. • n. light blow or hit.

bor. abbr. borough.

bo•rax /báwraks/ n. mineral salt, sodium borate, used in making glass and china, and as an antiseptic.

bor•der /báwrdər/ • n. **1** edge or boundary, or the part near it. **2 a** line separating two countries. **b** district on each side of this. **3** edging around anything. • v. **1** tr. be on or along a border. **2** tr. provide with a border. **3** intr. [usu. foll. by on, upon] **a** adjoin; come close to being. **b** approximate; resemble. ■ n. **1** verge, rim; periphery, outskirts. **2 a** frontier, borderline. **b** hinterland(s). **3** margin, hem, band; frame, frieze. • v. **1**, **2** edge, trim, bind; ring. **3 a** (border on) lie alongside, abut. **b** (border on) seem or be similar to, be like.

SYNONYM STUDY: border

BRIM, BRINK, EDGE, MARGIN, RIM, VERGE. A **border** is the part of a surface that is nearest to its boundary (*a rug with a flowered border*)—although it may also refer to the boundary line itself (*the border between Vermont and New Hampshire*). A **margin** is a *border* of a definite width that is usually distinct in appearance from what it encloses; but unlike *border*, it usually refers to the blankness or emptiness that surrounds something (*the margin on a printed page*). While *border* and *margin* usually refer to something that is circumscribed, **edge** may refer to only a part of the perimeter (*the edge of the lawn*) or the line where two planes or surfaces converge (*the edge of the table*). *Edge* can also connote sharpness (*the edge of a knife*) and can be used metaphorically to suggest tension, harshness, or keenness (*there was an edge in her voice; take the edge off their nervousness*). **Verge** may also be used metaphorically to describe the extreme limit of something (*on the verge of a nervous breakdown*), but in a more literal sense, it sometimes is used of the line or narrow space that marks the limit or termination of something (*the verge of a desert or forest*). **Brink** denotes the edge of something very steep or an abrupt division between land and water (*the brink of the river*), or metaphorically the very final limit before an abrupt change (*on the brink of disaster*). **Rim** and **brim** apply only to things that are circular or curving. But while *rim* describes the edge or lip of a rounded or cylindrical shape (*the rim of a glass*), *brim* refers to the inner side of the rim when the container is completely full (*a cup filled to the brim with steaming coffee*). However, when one speaks of the *brim* of a hat, it comes closer to the meaning of *margin* or *border*.

---

bor•der•line /báwrdərlīn/ • *n.* **1** line dividing two conditions. **2** line marking a boundary. • *adj.* **1** on the borderline. **2** barely acceptable.
  ■ *n.* see LINE[1] *n.* 4. • *adj.* **2** see *marginal* (MARGIN).

bore[1] /bawr/ • *v.tr.* **1** make a hole, esp. with a revolving tool. **2** hollow out (a tube, etc.).
• *n.* **1** hollow of a firearm barrel or of a cylinder in an internal combustion engine. **2** diameter of this; caliber.
  ■ *v.* pierce, drill, perforate, penetrate; tunnel, excavate, sink; scoop out. • *n.* **2** see CALIBER 1a.

bore[2] /bawr/ • *n.* tiresome or dull person or thing. • *v.tr.* weary by tedious talk or dullness. □□ **bor'ing** *adj.*
  ■ *n.* see NUISANCE. • *v.* wear out, tire, exhaust, jade. • *adj.* monotonous, humdrum, routine, mundane.

bore[3] /bawr/ *n.* high tidal wave rushing up a narrow estuary.

bore[4] *past* of BEAR[1].

bore•dom /báwrdəm/ *n.* state of being bored; ennui.

■ dullness, dreariness, tedium, monotony.

bor•ic /báwrik/ □ **boric acid** acid derived from borax, used as a mild antiseptic.

born /bawrn/ *adj.* **1** existing as a result of birth. **2 a** of natural ability or quality. **b** destiny. **3** [in *comb.*] of a certain born by birth (*French-born, well-born*). □ **born-again** [*attrib.*] converted (esp. to fundamentalist Christianity).

borne /bawrn/ **1** *past part.* of BEAR[1]. **2** [in *comb.*] carried by.

bo•ron /báwron/ *n. Chem.* nonmetallic crystalline element. ¶Symb.: **B**.

bor•ough /bárō, búrō/ *n.* **1** (in some states) incorporated municipality. **2** each of five political divisions of New York City. **3** (in Alaska) a county equivalent.

bor•row /bórō, báwrō/ *v.* **1 a** *tr.* acquire temporarily with the promise or intention of returning. **b** *intr.* obtain money in this way. **2** *tr.* use (an idea, etc.) originated by another; plagiarize. □□ **bor'row•er** *n.* **bor'row•ing** *n.*
  ■ **1** be lent *or* loaned; cadge, sponge. **2** see TAKE *v.* 11a.

borscht /bawrsht/ *n.* (also **borsch** /bawrsh, bawrshch/) Russian soup made primarily with beets.

bor•zoi /báwrzoy/ *n.* **1** large Russian wolfhound of a breed with a narrow head and silky, usu. white, coat. **2** this breed.

bosh /bosh/ *n. & int. sl.* nonsense; foolish talk.

bo's'n var. of BOATSWAIN.

bo•som /bòozəm/ • *n.* **1 a** person's breast. **b** *colloq.* each of a woman's breasts. **c** enclosure formed by the breast and arms. **2** emotional center. • *adj.* (esp. in **bos•om friend**) close; intimate. □□ **bos'om•y** *adj.*
  ■ *n.* **1** chest, bust. **2** soul, heart; core, center. • *adj.* dear, beloved, cherished; (**bosom friend**) best friend, intimate; see also FRIEND *n.* 1. □□ **bosomy** busty, buxom.

boss[1] /baws, bos/ • *n.* **1** employer; manager; overseer. **2** one who controls a political organization. • *v.tr.* **1** treat domineeringly. **2** be the master or manager of.
  ■ *n.* **1** chief, supervisor, head, administrator, foreman, superintendent. • *v.* **1** push or shove around, dominate, lord it over. **2** supervise, head, run, oversee.

boss[2] /baws, bos/ *n.* round knob, stud, or other protuberance, esp. in the center of a shield or in ornamental work.

bos•sa no•va /bòsə nòvə, báwsə/ *n.* **1** Brazilian dance like the samba. **2** music for this.

boss•y /báwsee, bós-/ *adj.* (**boss•i•er, boss•i•est**) *colloq.* domineering; tending to boss. □□ **boss'i•ly** *adv.* **boss'i•ness** *n.*
  ■ overbearing, high-handed, dictatorial, authoritarian.

bo•sun (also **bo'sun**) var. of BOATSWAIN.

bot. *abbr.* **1** bottle. **2** botanic; botanical; botany.

bot•a•ny /bót'nee/ *n.* the study of plants. □□ **bo•tan•ic** /bətánik/ *adj.* **bo•tan'i•cal** *adj.* **bo•tan'i•cal•ly** *adv.* **bot•a•nist** /bót'nist/ *n.*

botch /boch/ • *v.tr.* **1** bungle; do badly. **2** repair clumsily. • *n.* bungled or spoiled work. □□ **botch'er** *n.*

■ *v.* **1** mismanage, spoil, mess up. **2** patch up. ■ *n.* mess, hash.

both /bŏth/ • *adj. & pron.* the two; not only one (*both boys, both the boys, both of the boys, the boys are both here*). • *adv.* with equal truth in two cases (*both angry and sad*).

both•er /bŏthər/ • *v.* **1** *tr.* **a** give trouble to; worry; disturb. **b** *refl.* be anxious or concerned. **2** *intr.* **a** worry oneself. **b** [foll. by *with*] be concerned. • *n.* **1** person or thing that bothers; nuisance. **2** trouble; worry; fuss. □□ **both'er•some** *adj.*

■ *v.* **1 a** annoy, pester, keep on at, irritate. **1b, 2** trouble (oneself), fret; fuss. • *n.* **1** pest, annoyance, inconvenience, vexation, irritation. **2** inconvenience, discomfort.

bot•tle /bŏt'l/ • *n.* **1** container, usu. of glass or plastic, for storing liquid. **2** amount filling it. • *v.tr.* **1** put into bottles or jars. **2** [foll. by *up*] **a** conceal or restrain (esp. a feeling). **b** keep (an enemy force, etc.) contained or entrapped. □ **hit the bottle** *sl.* drink heavily. □□ **bot'tle•ful** *n.* (*pl.* **-fuls**). **bot•tler** /bŏtlər/ *n.*

■ *n.* **1** flask, decanter. • *v.* **2** (*bottle up*) **a** contain, hold back, control, suppress. **b** trap, confine, hem in; surround.

bot•tle law • *n.* any of several laws relating to the bottles in which beverages are sold, including a law requiring consumers to pay a deposit on beverage bottles so as to encourage recycling of the bottles, or a law requiring that such bottles be recycled.

bot•tle•neck /bŏt'lnĕk/ *n.* **1** point at which the flow of traffic, production, etc., is constricted. **2** any impedance to progress.

bot•tom /bŏtəm/ • *n.* **1 a** lowest point or part. **b** base. **c** underneath part. **2** *colloq.* **a** buttocks. **b** seat of a chair, etc. **3** ground under the water of a lake, etc. **4** basis; origin. • *adj.* **1** lowest. **2** last. □ **at bottom** basically; essentially. **bottom line** *colloq.* underlying truth; ultimate, esp. financial, criterion. □□ **bot'tom•most** *adj.*

■ *n.* **1 a, b** foot, foundation. **c** underside. **2 a** rump. **4** root, source. □ **at bottom** fundamentally, in the final *or* last analysis, in reality.

bot•tom•less /bŏtəmlĭs/ *adj.* **1** without a bottom. **2** (of a supply, etc.) inexhaustible.

■ **2** unlimited, boundless, limitless; interminable, never-ending, endless, unending, immeasurable, infinite.

bot•u•lism /bŏchəlĭzəm/ *n.* poisoning caused by a bacillus growing in spoiled food.

bou•doir /boodwaar/ *n.* woman's private room or bedroom.

bouf•fant /boofaänt/ *adj.* (of a dress, hair, etc.) puffed out.

bou•gain•vil•le•a /boogənvĭlyə, -vēə/ *n.* tropical plant with large colored bracts.

bough /bow/ *n.* branch of a tree, esp. a main one.

■ see BRANCH *n.* 1.

bought *past* and *past part.* of BUY.

bouil•la•baisse /booyəbĕs, boolyəbáys/ *n.* Cookery rich, spicy fish stew.

bouil•lon /boolyən, -yon, booyóN/ *n.* clear soup; broth.

boul•der /bóldər/ *n.* large rock.

■ see ROCK[1] 3.

bou•le•vard /booləvaard/ *n.* **1** broad, tree-lined avenue. **2** broad main road.

■ see STREET 1.

bounce /bowns/ • *v.* **1 a** *intr.* (of a ball, etc.) rebound. **b** *tr.* cause to rebound. **2** *intr. sl.* (of a check) be returned by a bank when there are insufficient funds to meet it. **3** *intr.* jump, spring, or rush noisily, enthusiastically, etc. • *n.* **1 a** rebound. **b** power of rebounding. **2** *colloq.* **a** liveliness. **b** resilience. **3** *sl.* [often prec. by *the*] dismissal or ejection. □□ **bounc'i•ness** *n.* **bounc'y** *adj.* (**bounc•i•er, bounc•i•est**).

■ *v.* **1** bound, ricochet; (*bounce back*) recoil, spring *or* jump back. **3** see SPRING *v.* 1. • *n.* **1** bound, leap, hop; recoil, ricochet. **2 a** vitality, energy, verve, zest. **3** see EXPULSION.

bounc•er /bównsər/ *n. sl.* person employed to eject troublemakers from a bar, club, etc.

bounc•ing /bównsing/ *adj.* (esp. of a baby) big and healthy.

bound[1] /bownd/ • *v.intr.* **1 a** spring; leap. **b** walk or run with leaping strides. **2** (of a ball, etc.) bounce. • *n.* **1** springy leap. **2** bounce.

■ *v.* **1** jump, hop, vault; gambol, caper, romp. **2** see BOUNCE *v.* 1. • *n.* **1** jump, vault, spring, hop.

bound[2] /bownd/ • *n.* [usu. in *pl.*] **1** limitation; restriction. **2** border; boundary. ■ *v.tr.* **1** [esp. in *passive*; foll. by *by*] set bounds to; limit. **2 b** be the boundary of. □ **out of bounds 1** outside a permitted area. **2** beyond what is acceptable.

■ *n.* **1** (*bounds*) limit(s), extent, confines, margin(s). **2** (*bounds*) circuit. • *v.* restrict, confine, enclose, surround, delimit, define. □ **out of bounds 1** off limits. **2** forbidden, prohibited, proscribed; inadmissible, unacceptable.

bound[3] /bownd/ *adj.* **1** on one's way. **2** [in *comb.*] moving in a specified direction (*north-bound*).

■ **1** destined, headed, directed, en route.

bound[4] /bownd/ *past* and *past part.* of BIND. □ **bound to** be certain to (*he's bound to come*).

bound•a•ry /bówndəree, -dree/ *n.* (*pl.* **-ries**) real or notional line marking the limits of an area, territory, etc.

■ border, frontier, boundary line; parameter, limit; confines, perimeter.

bound•en /bówndən/ *adj. archaic* □ **bounden duty** solemn responsibility.

bound•less /bówndlis/ *adj.* unlimited; immense (*boundless enthusiasm*). □□ **bound'less•ly** *adv.* **bound'less•ness** *n.*

■ limitless, unbounded, endless, unending, never-ending, infinite, immeasurable, incalculable, untold, inexhaustible.

boun•te•ous /bównteeəs/ *adj. poet.* generous; liberal. □□ **boun'te•ous•ly** *adv.* **boun'te•ous•ness** *n.*

■ beneficent, munificent, liberal, ungrudging; free, unsparing, unstinting.

boun•ti•ful /bówntifool/ *adj.* **1** = BOUNTEOUS. **2** ample. □□ **boun'ti•ful•ly** *adv.*

■ **2** abundant, plentiful, copious, generous, lavish.

boun•ty /bówntee/ n. (pl. **–ties**) **1** generosity. **2** reward; premium.

■ **1** generosity, munificence, prodigality, charitableness. **2** present, gratuity, prize, tribute, honor, award.

bou•quet /bōōkáy,bō–/ n. **1** bunch of flowers. **2** scent of wine, etc. **3** compliment. See synonym study at SMELL.

■ **1** nosegay, posy, bunch. **2** aroma, odor, fragrance, perfume. **3** honor, tribute, homage, commendation.

bour•bon /bárbən/ n. whiskey distilled from corn mash.

bour•geois /bŏŏrzhwaá/ often derog. • adj. **1 a** conventional. **b** humdrum. **c** selfishly materialistic. **2** capitalistic; noncommunist. • n. bourgeois person.

■ adj. **1 a** middle-class, conservative, conformist; see also NARROW-MINDED, PHILISTINE adj. **b** see BANAL. **c** greedy, acquisitive. • n. capitalist, materialist, professional.

bour•geoi•sie /bŏŏrzhwaazée/ n. **1** capitalist class. **2** middle class.

bout /bowt/ n. **1** limited period. **2 a** wrestling or boxing match. **b** trial of strength.

■ **1** spell, session; round; attack, fit, outburst. **2 a** fight, contest, prizefight.

bou•tique /bŏŏteék/ n. small shop, esp. one selling fashionable goods.

bou•ton•niere /bŏŏtənéer, –tənyáir/ n. (also **bou•ton•nière'**) flower worn in a buttonhole.

■ buttonhole, corsage.

bo•vine /bóvin, –veen/ adj. **1** of or relating to cattle. **2** stupid; dull. □□ **bo'vine•ly** adv.

■ **2** see DULL adj. 1.

bow¹ /bō/ • n. **1 a** slipknot with a double loop. **b** ribbon, shoelace, etc., tied with this. **2** device for shooting arrows with a taut string joining the ends of a curved piece of wood, etc. **3** rod with horsehair stretched along its length, used for playing the violin, cello, etc. **4** shallow curve or bend. • v.tr. use a bow on (a violin, etc.). □ **bow tie** necktie in the form of a bow (sense 1).

bow² /bow/ • v. **1** intr. incline the head or trunk, esp. in greeting or acknowledgment. **2** intr. submit. **3** tr. cause to incline or submit. • n. act of bowing. □ **take a bow** acknowledge applause.

■ v. **1** nod; curtsy, salaam. **2** defer, yield, give in, give way, bow down; (bow to) see OBEY. **3** bend; make surrender or yield. • n. nod; salaam, obeisance.

bow³ /bow/ n. Naut. forward end of a boat or ship.

bowd•ler•ize /bówdlərìz/ v.tr. delete offensive words from (a book, etc.). □□ **bowd'ler•ism** n. **bowd•ler•i•za'tion** n.

bow•el /bówəl/ n. **1** intestine. **2** [in pl.] depths; innermost parts. □ **bowel movement** defecation.

■ **1** gut, guts; (bowels) viscera, vitals. **2** (bowels) interior, inside(s), center, core.

bow•er /bówər/ n. secluded place enclosed by foliage; arbor. □□ **bow'er•y** adj.

bowl¹ /bōl/ n. **1 a** usu. round deep basin for food or liquid. **b** contents of a bowl. **2 a** any deep-sided container shaped like a bowl. **b** bowl-shaped part of a tobacco pipe, spoon, balance, etc. □□ **bowl'ful** n. (pl. **–fuls**).

■ **1** dish, plate; pan.

bowl² /bōl/ • n. **a** wooden or hard rubber ball used in the game of bowls. • v. **1 a** tr. roll (a hoop, etc.) along the ground. **b** intr. play bowling or skittles. **2** intr. [often foll. by along] go along rapidly. □ **bowl over 1** knock down. **2** colloq. **a** impress greatly. **b** overwhelm.

■ v. **2** move, trundle, wheel, roll, spin, whirl; hurtle. □ **bowl over 1** bring down, fell, floor.

bow•legs /bólegz/ n. legs that curve outward at the knee. □□ **bow•leg•ged** /bólegid/ adj.

bowl•er¹ /bólər/ n. player at bowls or bowling.

bowl•er² /bólər/ n. (in full **bowl'er hat**) man's hard felt hat.

bowl•ing /bóling/ n. games of tenpins, skittles, or bowls as a sport or recreation.

bow•man /bómən/ n. (pl. **–men**) archer.

bow•sprit /bówsprit/ n. Naut. spar running out from a ship's bow to which the forestays are fastened.

bow•string /bóstring/ n. string of an archer's bow.

box¹ /boks/ • n. **1** container, usu. flat sided and firm. **2** amount that will fill a box. **3** separate seating area in a theater, etc. **4** facility at a post office, etc., for receiving mail or messages. **5** enclosed area for a jury or witnesses in a courtroom. **6** space or area of print on a page, enclosed by a border. • v.tr. **1** put in or provide with a box. **2** confine. □ **box office 1** ticket office at a theater, etc. **2** the commercial aspect of a performance. □□ **box'ful** n. (pl. **–fuls**). **box'like** adj.

■ n. **1, 2** case, crate, carton, container, chest. **3** compartment, booth, cubicle, enclosure. • v. **1** crate, encase, package, pack. **2** (box in or up) trap, hem or block in, shut up or in, coop up.

box² /boks/ • v. **1 a** tr. fight (an opponent) at boxing. **b** intr. practice boxing. **2** slap (esp. a person's ears). • n. slap with the hand, esp. on the ears.

■ v. **1 a** come to blows with, spar with, sl. mill. **b** fight, spar, battle. **2** strike, smack, rap, punch, hit. • n. blow, smack, rap, hit, strike, cuff.

box³ /boks/ n. **1** small evergreen tree with glossy dark green leaves. **2** its wood.

box•car /bókskaar/ n. enclosed railroad freight car.

box•er /bóksər/ n. **1** person who boxes, esp. for sport. **2** medium-sized dog with a smooth brown coat and puglike face. □ **boxer shorts** (also **box•ers**) underpants similar to shorts worn in boxing, with an elastic waist.

■ **1** see PUGILIST.

box•ing /bóksing/ n. fighting with the fists, esp. as a sport.

■ see pugilism (PUGILIST).

boy /boy/ • n. **1** male child or youth. **2** young man. **3** (**the boys**) colloq. group of men mixing socially. • *int.* expressing pleasure, surprise, etc. □ **boy scout** (also **Boy Scout**) member of an organization of boys, esp. the Boy Scouts of America, that promotes character, outdoor activities, community service, etc. □□ **boy'hood** *n.* **boy'ish** *adj.* **boy'ish•ly** *adv.* **boy'ish•ness** *n.*

■ *n.* **1, 2** lad, young man, stripling, youngster, schoolboy, juvenile, minor. *int.* wow, (my) god, Lord, whew. □□ **boyish** young, youthful, adolescent, childlike; childish, puerile, juvenile.

boy•cott /bóykot/ • *v.tr.* refuse social or commercial relations with (a person, country, etc.). • *n.* such a refusal.

■ *v.* blacklist, embargo, ostracize; avoid, refuse, shun. • *n.* embargo, ban; interdiction, prohibition.

boy•friend /bóyfrend/ *n.* person's regular male companion or lover.

■ see SWEETHEART 1.

bps *abbr.* (also **BPS**) *Computing* bits per second.

Br *symb. Chem.* bromine.

bra /braa/ *n. colloq.* = BRASSIERE.

brace /brays/ • *n.* **1 a** device that clamps or fastens tightly. **b** strengthening piece of metal, wood, etc., in building. **2** [in *pl.*] wire device for straightening the teeth. **3** (*pl.* same) pair (esp. of game). **4** connecting mark { or } in printing. • *v.tr.* **1** give strength to. **2** make steady by supporting. **3** (esp. as **bracing** *adj.*) invigorate; refresh. **4** [often *refl.*] prepare for a difficulty, shock, etc. □ **brace and bit** revolving tool with a D-shaped central handle for boring. □□ **brac'ing•ly** *adv.* **brac'ing•ness** *n.*

■ *n.* **1 a** clasp, vice, fastener. **b** bracket, reinforcement, support, buttress. **3** couple, set. • *v.* **1** see SECURE *v.* 2. **2** stabilize, reinforce, secure. **3** (**bracing**) tonic, stimulating, exhilarating. **4** (*brace oneself*) steady oneself; get or make ready, hold on.

brace•let /bráyslit/ *n.* **1** ornamental band or chain worn on the wrist or arm. **2** *sl.* handcuff.

brack•en /brákən/ *n.* **1** large coarse fern. **2** mass of such ferns.

brack•et /brákit/ • *n.* **1** support projecting from a vertical surface. **2 a** each of a pair of marks [ ] (**square brack•ets**) or < > (**angle brack•ets**) used to enclose words or figures. **b** = PARENTHESIS 1b. **c** = BRACE 4. **3** group or classification. • *v.tr.* **1 a** combine within brackets. **b** imply a connection or equality between. **2** enclose in brackets.

■ *n.* **1** console, cantilever, gusset, *Archit.* corbel. **3** category, class, set; range; grade. • *v.* **1** couple, join, link, connect.

brack•ish /brákish/ *adj.* (of water, etc.) slightly salty. □□ **brack'ish•ness** *n.*

bract /brakt/ *n.* often brightly colored leaflike part of a plant growing below a flower. □□ **brac'te•al** *adj.* **brac•te•ate** /–tee-it, –ayt/ *adj.*

brad /brad/ *n.* thin flat nail with a small head.

brag /brag/ • *v.* (**bragged, brag•ging**) **1** *intr.* talk boastfully. **2** *tr.* boast about. • *n.* boastful statement or talk. □□ **brag'ger** *n.* **brag' ging•ly** *adv.*

89

boycott ~ brake

■ *v.* **1** crow, swagger, rodomontade, blow one's (own) trumpet. **2** trumpet. • *n.* **2** see BOAST *n.* □□ **bragger** see BRAGGART *n.*

brag•gart /brágərt/ • *n.* person given to bragging. • *adj.* boastful.

■ *n.* boaster, *colloq.* show-off, bigmouth, loudmouth.

Brah•ma /braamə/ *n.* supreme Hindu divinity.

Brah•man /braamən/ *n.* (also **brah'man**) (*pl.* **–mans**) **1** member of the highest or priestly Hindu caste. **2** = BRAHMA. □□ **Brah•man•ic** /–mánik/ *adj.* **Brah•man' i•cal** *adj.* **Brah'man•ism** *n.*

Brah•min /braamin/ *n.* **1** = BRAHMAN. **2** (esp. in New England) socially or culturally superior person.

braid /brayd/ • *n.* **1** woven band as edging or trimming. **2** length of hair, straw, etc., in three or more interlaced strands. • *v.tr.* intertwine. □□ **braid'er** *n.* **braid'ing** *n.*

■ *n.* **1** trim, fillet, ribbon, twine, soutache. **2** plait. • *v.* interlace, weave, plait.

Braille /brayl/ *n.* system of writing and printing for the blind with patterns of raised dots.

brain /brayn/ • *n.* **1** organ of soft nervous tissue contained in the skull of vertebrates, the center of sensation and of intellectual and nervous activity. **2** [in *pl.*] the substance of the brain, esp. as food. **3 a** person's intellectual capacity. **b** [often in *pl.*] intelligence. **4** *colloq.* intelligent person. • *v.tr. colloq.* strike very hard on the head. □ **brain drain** *colloq.* loss of skilled personnel by emigration. **brain wave 1** [usu. in *pl.*] electrical impulse in the brain. **2** *colloq.* sudden bright idea.

■ *n.* **3** intellect, brainpower, understanding, cleverness, brightness, smartness, sense. **4** genius, mastermind, intellectual. • *v.* clout, cuff. □ **brain wave 2** see INSPIRATION 2.

brain•child /bráynchīld/ *n.* (*pl.* **–chil•dren**) *colloq.* clever idea or invention.

brain•less /bráynlis/ *adj.* stupid; foolish.

■ see STUPID *adj.* 1.

brain•storm /bráynstawrm/ • *n.* spontaneous ingenious idea or invention. • *v.* **1** *intr.* discuss ideas spontaneously and openly. **2** *tr.* discuss (an issue) in this way. □□ **brain• storm•ing** *n.*

brain•wash /bráynwosh, –wawsh/ *v.tr.* subject (a person) to a process by which ideas are implanted in the mind. □□ **brain•wash• ing** *n.*

■ see INDOCTRINATE.

brain•y /bráynee/ *adj.* (**brain•i•er, brain•i• est**) intellectually clever or active. □□ **brain' i•ly** *adv.* **brain'i•ness** *n.*

■ see INTELLECTUAL *adj.* 2.

braise /brayz/ *v.tr.* sauté lightly and then stew slowly with a little liquid in a closed container.

brake /brayk/ • *n.* [often *pl.*] device for stopping or slowing a wheel, vehicle, etc. • *v.* **1** *intr.* apply a brake. **2** *tr.* retard or stop with a brake. □□ **brake'less** *adj.*

■ *n.* curb, check, restraint, restriction,

constraint. • v. 1 put on the brakes. 2 slow, slow up or down, pull up, reduce the speed of.

brake•man /bráykmən/ n. (pl. –men) railroad worker responsible for maintenance on a journey.

bram•ble /brámbəl/ n. any of various thorny shrubs bearing fleshy red or black berries. □□ **bram′bly** adj.

bran /bran/ n. grain husks separated from the flour.

branch /branch/ • n. 1 limb of a tree. 2 lateral extension or subdivision, esp. of a river or railroad. 3 conceptual extension or subdivision, as of a family, knowledge, etc. 4 local office, etc., of a large business. • v.intr. [often foll. by off] 1 diverge. 2 divide into branches. □ **branch out** extend one's field of interest. □□ **branched** adj. **branch′let** n. **branch′like** adj.

■ n. 1 offshoot, arm; bough. 2, 3 offshoot; wing; department, section. 4 bureau; affiliate, subsidiary. • v. 1 (branch off) deviate, turn off or away, separate. 2 subdivide, fork, split. ■ **branch out** diversify, spread or stretch one's wings.

brand /brand/ • n. 1 a particular make of goods. b identifying trademark, label, etc. 2 characteristic kind. 3 identifying mark burned on livestock, etc. 4 iron used for this. 5 piece of burning, smoldering, or charred wood. 6 stigma; mark of disgrace. • v.tr. 1 mark with a hot iron. 2 stigmatize (was branded for life). 3 impress unforgettably on one's mind. □ **brand-new** completely new. □□ **brand′er** n.

■ n. 1 a kind, type, sort. b brand name, trade name. 2 see TYPE n. 1. 6 see STIGMA 1. • v. 2 discredit, disgrace, dishonor, besmirch, smear. 3 see IMPRESS v. 3, 4. □ – **brand-new** unused, fresh, firsthand, mint, virgin; latest; today's.

bran•dish /brándish/ v.tr. wave or flourish as a threat or in display. □□ **bran′dish•er** n.

■ see FLOURISH v. 2.

bran•dy /brándee/ n. (pl. –dies) strong alcoholic spirit distilled from wine or fermented fruit juice.

brash /brash/ adj. 1 vulgarly self-assertive. 2 hasty; rash. 3 impudent. □□ **brash′ly** adv. **brash′ness** n.

■ 1 see BOLD 2. 2 abrupt, impetuous, precipitate, impulsive. 3 rude, impertinent, disrespectful, insolent.

brass /bras/ • n. 1 yellow alloy of copper and zinc. 2 brass objects collectively. 3 Mus. brass wind instruments. 4 (in full **top brass**) colloq. persons of high (esp. military) rank. 5 colloq. effrontery. • adj. made of brass. □ **brass tacks** sl. actual details.

■ n. 4 see MANAGEMENT 2b. 5 nerve, cheek, audacity, presumption, brazenness.

bras•siere /brəzeér/ n. undergarment worn by women to support the breasts.

brass•y /brásee/ adj. (**brass•i•er**, **brass•i•est**) 1 impudent. 2 pretentious; showy. 3 loud and blaring. 4 of or like brass. □□ **brass′i•ly** adv. **brass′i•ness** n.

■ 1 forward, insolent, saucy, brash, rude, brazen, colloq. fresh. 2 ostentatious, flashy, flamboyant. 3 harsh, strident.

brat /brat/ n. usu. derog. child, esp. a badly behaved one. □□ **brat′ty** adj.

■ see IMP n. 1.

bra•va•do /brəvaádō/ n. show of boldness.

■ bluster, boasting, bluff, braggadocio, swagger.

brave /brayv/ • adj. 1 able or ready to face and endure danger or pain. 2 splendid; spectacular. • n. Native American warrior. • v.tr. defy; encounter bravely. □□ **brave′ly** adv. **brave′ness** n. **brav′er•y** n.

■ adj. 1 fearless, intrepid, bold, courageous, daring. 2 fine, handsome, grand, dramatic. • v. brazen out, weather, face (up to), confront. □□ **bravery** daring, courage, valor, heroism, gallantry.

bra•vo /braávō/ • int. expressing approval. • n. (pl. –vos) cry of bravo.

bra•vu•ra /brəvóŏrə, –vyóŏrə/ n. 1 brilliant action or display. 2 passage of (esp. vocal) music requiring exceptional ability.

■ 1 see VIRTUOSO 1.

brawl /brawl/ • n. noisy quarrel or fight. • v.intr. quarrel noisily or roughly. □□ **brawl′er** n.

■ n. fistfight, mêlée, scrimmage, scuffle, battle, battle royal, donnybrook. • v. fight, scuffle, wrangle, clash.

brawn /brawn/ n. 1 muscular strength. 2 muscle; lean flesh. □□ **brawn•y** adj. (**brawn•i•er**, **brawn•i•est**). **brawn′i•ness** n.

■ 1 muscle(s), robustness, brawniness, might. 2 sinew. □□ **brawny** muscular, strong, tough, robust, mighty.

bray /bray/ • n. cry of a donkey. • v.intr. make such a sound.

bra•zen /bráyzən/ • adj. 1 (also **bra′zen-faced**) shameless; insolent. 2 made of brass. 3 of or like brass. See synonym study at BOLD. • v.tr. [foll. by out] face or undergo defiantly. □□ **bra′zen•ly** adv. **bra′zen•ness** n.

■ adj. 1 brassy, barefaced, unashamed, unabashed. □□ **brazenness** see BRASS n. 5.

bra•zier /bráyzhər/ n. metal pan or stand for holding lighted coals.

breach /breech/ • n. 1 breaking of or failure to observe a law, contract, etc. 2 a breaking of relations. b quarrel. 3 gap; opening. • v.tr. 1 break through; make a gap in. 2 break (a law, contract, etc.).

■ n. 1 violation, nonobservance, infringement, contravention, Law infraction. 2 a rift, gulf, split, breakup, separation. b see QUARREL n. 1. 3 fissure, crack, hole. • v. 1 rupture, burst, break through. 2 see BREAK v. 4a, b.

bread /bred/ • n. 1 baked dough of flour and liquid usu. leavened with yeast. 2 a necessary food. b (also **dai•ly bread**) one's livelihood. 3 sl. money. • v.tr. coat with breadcrumbs for cooking. □ **bread basket** 1 sl. the stomach. 2 farming area producing staple crops.

bread•box /brédboks/ • n. container for keeping bread and other baked goods in.

breadth /bredth/ n. 1 distance or measurement from side to side of a thing. **2** extent; distance; room. □□ **breadth'ways** *adv.* **breadth'wise** *adv.*

■ **1** width, wideness, broadness, span, spread, thickness. **2** magnitude, degree, amount; stretch, measurement.

bread•win•ner /brédwinər/ *n.* person who earns the money to support a family.

break /brayk/ • *v.* (*past* **broke** /brōk/; *past part.* **bro•ken** /brōkən/) **1** *tr. & intr.* a separate into pieces, as from a blow; shatter. **b** make or become inoperative. **2 a** *tr.* cause or effect an interruption in. **b** *intr.* have an interval between periods of work. **3** *tr.* fail to keep (a law, promise, etc.). **4 a** *tr. & intr.* make or become subdued or weakened; yield or cause to yield. **b** *tr.* weaken the effect of (a fall, etc.). **c** *tr.* tame or discipline (an animal); accustom (a horse) to saddle and bridle, etc. **d** *tr.* defeat; destroy. **e** *tr.* defeat the object of (a strike, e.g., by hiring other personnel). **5** *tr.* surpass (a record, etc.). **6** *intr.* [foll. by *with*] quarrel or cease association with (another person, etc.). **7** *tr.* a be no longer subject to (a habit). **b** free (a person) of a habit. **8** *tr. & intr.* reveal or be revealed. **9** *intr.* **a** (of the weather) change suddenly. **b** (of waves) curl over and foam. **c** (of the day) dawn. **d** (of clouds) move apart. **e** (of a storm) begin violently. **10** *tr. Electr.* disconnect (a circuit). **11** *intr.* **a** (of the voice) change with emotion. **b** (of a boy's voice) change at puberty. **12** *tr.* **a** divide (a set, etc.) into parts. **b** change (a bill, etc.) for coins or smaller denominations. **13** *tr.* ruin financially (*see also* BROKE *adj.*). **14** *tr.* penetrate (e.g., a safe) by force. **15** *tr.* decipher (a code). **16** *tr.* make (a path, etc.) by separating obstacles. **17** *intr.* burst forth. **18** *tr.* escape from constraint by a sudden effort. **b** *tr.* escape or emerge from (prison, cover, etc.). • *n.* **1** a act or instance of breaking. **b** gap; split. **2** interval; interruption; pause. **3** sudden dash (esp. in Rugby). **4** *colloq.* piece of good luck. □ **bad break** *colloq.* **1** piece of bad luck. **2** mistake or blunder. **break down 1 a** fail; cease to function. **b** (of human relationships, etc.) collapse. **c** be overcome by emotion. **2 a** demolish. **b** suppress (resistance). **c** force (a person) to yield under pressure. **3** analyze into components (*see also* BREAKDOWN). **break even** make neither profit nor loss. **break in 1** enter by force. **2** interrupt. **3 a** accustom to a habit, etc. **b** wear, etc., until comfortable. **c** = BREAK 4c. **break-in** *n.* illegal forced entry into premises, esp. with criminal intent. **break into 1** enter forcibly. **2 a** burst forth with. **b** suddenly change one's pace for (a faster one). **3** interrupt. **break off 1** detach by breaking. **2** bring to an end. **break out 1** escape by force, esp. from prison. **2** begin suddenly; burst forth. **3** become covered in (a rash, etc.). **break up 1** disperse; disband. **2** terminate a relationship. **3** convulse or be convulsed (*see also* BREAKUP). □□ **break'a•ble** *adj.*

■ *v.* **1 a** break apart *or* up, fracture, rupture. **b** (*tr.*) stop, *colloq.* bust; (*intr.*) break down, stop working *or* functioning, go

wrong, give out. **2 a** break off, discontinue, suspend. **b** have *or* take a break, stop, pause. **3** violate, transgress, disobey. **4 a** weary, exhaust, sap, drain. **b** lessen, soften, mitigate. **c** train, condition, domesticate. **d** demolish, smash, crush, ruin. **5** *see* EXCEED[1]. **6** (*break with*) *see* LEAVE *v.* 1b, 3, QUARREL *v.* 2. **7 a** give up, put an end to. **8** announce, disclose, divulge. **9 a** fail; shift, vary. **c** begin, start. **d** break up, divide, disperse. **e** burst forth, erupt. **11 a** *see* QUAVER *v.* **13** bankrupt, put out of business. **14** break *or* force open. **15** decode, decrypt. **17** emerge, come out, appear. **18 a** *see* ESCAPE *v.* 1. • *n.* **1 a** fracture, split, separation, rupture, opening, hole, space. **2** discontinuation, disruption, hesitation; stop, cease; rest, respite, rest period, time off. **3** *see* DASH *n.* 1, ESCAPE *n.* 1. **4** chance, opportunity, opening. □ **bad break 1** *see* MISFORTUNE 2. **2** *see* BLUNDER *n.* **break down 1 a** *see* BREAK *v.* 1b above. **b** *see* FAIL 7a. **c** burst *or* dissolve into tears. **2 a** *see* DESTROY 1. **b** *see* SUPPRESS 1. **3** separate, dissect; classify. **break in 1** force one's way in, intrude. **2** *see* INTERRUPT 1. **3 a** train, educate; condition, habituate. **break into 1** force one's way into, burst into. **2 a** erupt *or* explode into. **3** *see* INTERRUPT 1. **break off 1** *see* SNAP *v.* 1. **2** *see* STOP *v.* 1a, b. **break out 1** *see* ESCAPE *v.* 1. **3** come out in. **break up 1** *see* DISPERSE 2. **2** *see* SPLIT *v.* 3a. □□ **breakable** *see* FRAGILE 1.

break•age /bráykij/ *n.* **1 a** broken thing. **b** damage or loss caused by breaking. **2** act or instance of breaking.

■ **2** *see* FRACTURE *n.* 1.

break•down /bráykdown/ *n.* **1 a** mechanical failure. **b** loss of (esp. mental) health. **2** collapse. **3** detailed analysis.

■ **1** a collapse, *Computing* crash. **b** (mental) collapse, nervous breakdown. **2** disintegration, failure, downfall. **3** review, rundown; itemization, classification, listing.

break•er /bráykər/ *n.* heavy breaking wave.

■ *see* WAVE *n.* 1, 2.

break•fast /brékfəst/ • *n.* first meal of the day. • *v.intr.* have breakfast. □□ **break'fas•ter** *n.*

break•neck /bráyknek/ *adj.* (of speed) dangerously fast.

■ reckless, daredevil, careless; excessive; (*at breakneck speed*) at full speed *or* gallop, headlong.

break•through /bráykthro͞o/ *n.* **1** major advance or discovery. **2** act of breaking through an obstacle, etc.

break•up /bráykup/ *n.* **1** disintegration; collapse. **2** dispersal.

■ **1** *see* DISSOLUTION 1. **2** *see* DISSOLUTION 3.

break•wa•ter /bráykwawtər, –wotər/ *n.* barrier built out into the sea to break the force of waves.

breast /brest/ • *n.* **1 a** either of two milk-secreting organs on a woman's chest. **b** corresponding part of a man's body. **2 a** chest. **b** corresponding part of an animal. **3** part of a garment that covers the breast. • *v.tr.*

1 face; meet in full opposition. **2** contend with. □□ **breast′ed** *adj.* [also in *comb.*]. **breast′less** *adj.*

■ *n.* **1 a** teat, mammary gland. **2** bust, front. • *v.* **1, 2** see FACE *v.* 3.

breast•bone /bréstbōn/ *n.* thin, flat vertical bone and cartilage in the chest connecting the ribs.

breast•stroke /bréststrōk/ *n.* stroke made while swimming face down by extending arms forward and sweeping them back in unison.

breath /breth/ *n.* **1 a** air taken into or expelled from the lungs. **b** respiration. **2 a** breeze. **b** whiff of perfume, etc. **3** whisper. **4** spirit; vitality. □ **below** (or **under**) **one's breath** in a whisper. **catch one's breath 1** cease breathing momentarily in surprise, suspense, etc. **2** rest to restore normal breathing. **hold one's breath 1** cease breathing temporarily. **2** *colloq.* wait in eager anticipation. **take a person's breath away** awe; delight.

■ **1** see *exhalation* (EXHALE). **2 a** gust, puff, stirring, stir. **b** smell, aroma, sniff, scent. **3** murmur, suggestion, hint, suspicion. **4** life. □ **take a person's breath away** astound, astonish, surprise, dazzle, startle.

breathe /breeth/ *v.* **1** *intr.* take air into and expel it from the lungs. **2** *intr.* be or seem alive. **3** *tr.* **a** utter. **b** express; display.

■ **1** inhale and exhale, respire. **2** live, exist. **3 a** whisper, murmur; tell, speak, say.

breath•er /bréethər/ *n.* *colloq.* brief pause for rest.

■ see BREAK *n.* 2.

breath•ing /bréething/ *n.* process of taking air into and expelling it from the lungs.

breath•less /bréthlis/ *adj.* **1** panting; out of breath. **2** (as if) holding the breath because of excitement, etc. **3** windless; still. □□ **breath′less•ly** *adv.* **breath′less•ness** *n.*

■ **1** winded, short-winded, gasping. **2** eager, agog, feverish, excited. **3** see STILL[1] *adj.* 1.

breath•tak•ing /bréthtayking/ *adj.* astounding; awe-inspiring. □□ **breath′tak•ing•ly** *adv.*

■ see TERRIFIC 1b.

breath•y /bréthee/ *adj.* (**breath•i•er, breath•i•est**) (of a voice, etc.) containing the sound of breathing. □□ **breath′i•ly** *adv.* **breath′i•ness** *n.*

bred /bred/ *past* and *past part.* of BREED.

breech /breech/ *n.* back part of a rifle or gun barrel. □ **breech birth** (or **delivery**) delivery of a baby with the buttocks or feet foremost.

breech•es /bríchiz/ *n.pl.* (also **pair of breeches** *sing.*) short trousers, esp. fastened below the knee, now used esp. for riding. □ **breeches buoy** lifebuoy suspended from a rope with canvas breeches for the user's legs.

breed /breed/ • *v.* (*past* and *past part.* **bred** /bred/) **1** *tr. & intr.* generate (offspring); reproduce. **2** *tr. & intr.* propagate or cause to propagate. **3** *tr.* **a** produce; result in. **b** spread (*discontent bred by rumor*). **4** *intr.* arise; spread. **5** *tr.* bring up; train. • *n.* **1** stock of genetically similar animals or plants. **2** race; lineage. **3** sort; kind. □ **breeder reactor** nuclear reactor creating surplus fissile material. □□ **breed′er** *n.*

■ *v.* **1** produce, bring forth, give birth to; see also REPRODUCE 3. **2** raise, rear, cultivate; mate. **3 a** yield, make, generate. **b** see SPREAD *v.* 3. **4** originate, appear; develop, grow. **5** see *bring up* 1, TRAIN *v.* 1a. • *n.* **1** strain. **2** stock, family, tribe. **3** type, form, variety, species.

breed•ing /bréeding/ *n.* **1** developing or propagating (animals, plants, etc.). **2** generation; childbearing. **3** good manners (*has no breeding*).

■ **1** rearing, bringing up, raising. **2** (re)production, creation, making, bearing. **3** (good) upbringing, civility, politeness.

breeze /breez/ • *n.* **1** gentle wind. **2** *colloq.* easy task. • *v.intr.* [foll. by *in, out, along*, etc.] *colloq.* come or go casually.

■ *n.* **1** breath, puff, stir. **2** easy *or* simple job, child's play, nothing. • *v.* drift, float; saunter, cruise.

breez•y /bréezee/ *adj.* (**breez•i•er, breez•i•est**) **1** pleasantly windy. **2** *colloq.* lively; jovial. **3** *colloq.* careless. □□ **breez′i•ly** *adv.* **breez′i•ness** *n.*

■ **1** airy, fresh, blowy; windswept. **2** carefree, lighthearted, free and easy. **3** careless, heedless.

breth•ren see BROTHER 3.

breve /brev, breev/ *n.* **1** *Mus.* note having the time value of two whole notes. **2** written or printed mark (˘) indicating a short or unstressed vowel.

brev•i•ty /brévitee/ *n.* **1** conciseness. **2** shortness (of time, etc.).

■ concision, terseness, succinctness, pithiness.

brew /brōō/ • *v.* **1** *tr.* **a** make (beer, etc.) by infusion, boiling, and fermentation. **b** make (tea, etc.) by infusion. **2** *intr.* undergo these processes. **3** *intr.* gather force; threaten. **4** *tr.* bring about; concoct. • *n.* **1 a** amount brewed. **b** serving (of beer, etc.). □□ **brew′er** *n.*

■ *v.* **1, 2** ferment, boil; infuse. **3** impend, approach, be imminent. **4** brew up, devise, plan, plot, contrive.

brew•er•y /brōōəree, brōōree/ *n.* (*pl.* **–ies**) place where beer, etc., is brewed commercially.

brew•pub /brōōpub/ • *n.* establishment selling beer brewed on the premises and often including a restaurant.

bri•ar[1] var. of BRIER[1].

bri•ar[2] var. of BRIER[2].

bribe /brīb/ • *v.tr.* persuade to act improperly by a gift of money, etc. • *n.* money or services offered in bribing. □□ **brib′a•ble** *adj.* **brib′er** *n.* **brib′er•y** *n.*

■ *v.* pay *or* buy off, oil a person's palm; corrupt, suborn. • *n.* inducement, payoff, *colloq.* kickback, graft. □□ **bribery** extortion, blackmail, subornation.

bric-à-brac /bríkəbrak/ *n.* (also **bric′-a-brac, bric′a•brac**) miscellaneous, cheap ornaments.

■ curiosities, knickknacks, collectibles, gew-gaws.

brick /brik/ • n. **1 a** block of fired or sun-dried clay, used in building. **b** similar block of concrete, etc. **2** brick-shaped solid object. • v.tr. close, pave, or block with bricks. • adj. built of brick.

■ n. **2** block, cube, chunk. • v. see WALL v.

brick•lay•er /bríklayər/ n. worker who builds with bricks. □□ **brick'lay•ing** n.

brid•al /bríd'l/ adj. of a bride or wedding.

■ nuptial, wedding, marriage.

bride /brīd/ n. woman on her wedding day and for some time before and after it.

■ see WIFE.

bride•groom /brīdgrōōm, –grŏŏm/ n. man on his wedding day and for some time before and after it.

■ see HUSBAND.

brides•maid /brīdzmayd/ n. girl or woman attending a bride on her wedding day.

bridge[1] /brij/ • n. **1 a** structure providing a way across a river, ravine, road, etc. **b** thing joining or connecting. **2** operational super-structure on a ship. **3** upper bony part of the nose. **4** Mus. upright piece of wood on a vi-olin, etc., over which the strings are stretched. **5** = BRIDGEWORK. • v.tr. **1 a** be a bridge over. **b** make a bridge over. **2** span as if with a bridge. □□ **bridge'a•ble** adj.

■ n. **1** a viaduct. **b** link, tie, bond. • v. **1** span, cross (over), traverse. **2** overcome, reconcile.

bridge[2] /brij/ n. card game derived from whist.

bridge•head /bríjhed/ n. Mil. fortified posi-tion held on the enemy's side of a river or other obstacle.

bridge•work /bríjwərk/ n. Dentistry dental structure used to cover a gap.

bri•dle /bríd'l/ • n. **1** headgear to control a horse, including reins and bit. **2** restraining thing. • v. **1** tr. put a bridle on. **2** tr. bring under control; curb. **3** intr. [often foll. by at or up or] express offense, etc., esp. by throw-ing up the head. □□ **bridle path** rough path or road suitable for horseback riding.

■ n. **2** restraint, curb, check. • v. **2** check, restrain, hold in (check). **3** (bridle (up) at) bristle at, draw oneself up at.

brief /breef/ • adj. **1** of short duration. **2** concise. **3** abrupt; brusque. • n. **1** [in pl.] brief underpants. **2** Law summary of a case. • v.tr. instruct in preparation for a task; inform in advance. □□ **brief'ly** adv. **brief'ness** n.

■ adj. **1** momentary, short-lived; flying, brisk. **2** short, thumbnail, succinct. **3** curt, terse, short. **4** see SCANTY. • n. **1** (briefs) bi-kini briefs, G-string. • v. coach, train, drill; advise. □□ **briefly** momentarily, fleetingly, hurriedly.

brief•case /bréefkays/ n. flat, rectangular document case.

■ see BAG n. 2a.

bri•er[1] /bríər/ n. (also **bri'ar**) any prickly bush, esp. of a wild rose. □□ **bri'er•y** adj.

bri•er[2] /bríər/ n. (also **bri'ar**) **1** white heath native to S. Europe. **2** tobacco pipe made from its root.

brig /brig/ n. **1** two-masted square-rigged ship. **2** prison, esp. in the navy.

■ **2** see PRISON n. 1.

bri•gade /brigáyd/ n. **1** Mil. subdivision of an army consisting usu. of three battalions and forming part of a division. **2** organized or uniformed band of workers (fire brigade).

brig•a•dier /brígədéer/ n. Mil. (in full **brig'a•dier gen'er•al**) officer ranking between col-onel and major general.

brig•and /brígənd/ n. member of a robber band. □□ **brig'and•age** n.

■ see robber (ROB).

brig•an•tine /brígənteen/ n. type of two-masted ship.

bright /brīt/ adj. **1** emitting or reflecting much light; shining. **2** intense; vivid. **3** tal-ented. **4 a** (of a person) cheerful; vivacious. **b** (of prospects, etc.) promising; hopeful. □□ **bright'ish** adj. **bright'ly** adv. **bright'ness** n.

■ adj. **1** gleaming, radiant, brilliant, lumi-nous. **2** brilliant, bold. **3** intelligent, clever, brilliant, keen. **4 a** gay, happy, cheery, exu-berant, bubbly. **b** optimistic, favorable, pro-pitious, auspicious. □□ **brightly** see BRIGHT adv. above.

bright•en /brít'n/ v. **1** make or become brighter. **2** make or become more cheerful or hopeful.

■ **1** see LIGHTEN[2]. **2** enliven, lighten, liven up, hearten.

bril•liant /brílyənt/ • adj. **1** very bright; sparkling. **2** outstandingly talented. **3** showy. • n. diamond of the finest cut with many facets. □□ **bril'liance** n. **bril'liant•ly** adv.

■ adj. **1** shining, lustrous, radiant; incan-descent, glittering. **2** intelligent, clever, gift-ed; exceptional. **3** glittering, dazzling, sparkling, scintillating.

brim /brim/ • n. **1** edge or lip of a vessel. **2** projecting edge of a hat. See synonym study at BORDER. • v. (**brimmed, brim•ming**) fill or be full to the brim. □□ **brim'less** adj. **brimmed** adj. [usu. in comb].

■ n. **1** margin, rim, side; brink. • v. be full or filled.

brim•stone /brímstōn/ n. sulfur.

brin•dled /bríndld/ adj. (also **brin'dle**) brownish or tawny with streaks of other color(s) (esp. of domestic animals).

brine /brīn/ n. **1** water saturated or strongly impregnated with salt. **2** sea water. □□ **brin'y** adj. (**brin•i•er, brin•i•est**). **brin'i•ness** n.

bring /bring/ v.tr. (past and past part. **brought** /brawt/) **1 a** come carrying or lead-ing. **b** come with. **2** cause to come or be present. **3** cause or result in (war brings mis-ery). **4** be sold for; produce as income. □ **bring about** cause to happen. **bring forth** give birth to. **bring off** achieve suc-cessfully. **bring in 1** earn; make evi-dent. **2** publish and broadcast. **bring up 1** rear (a child). **2** vomit. **3** call attention to. □□ **bring'er** n.

■ **1 a** bring along, bear, transport. **b** escort, invite; usher, show. **2** lead, draw, direct, at-tract. **3** lead to, bring on, bring about.

□ **bring about** occasion, give rise to. **bring forth** bear, bring into the world, spawn, pro-create. **bring off** succeed (in), accomplish, do. **bring out 1** focus on, make noticeable or conspicuous. **2** issue, release, put or turn out. **bring up 1** raise, care for, look after; educate, teach. **2** throw up, regurgitate. **3** introduce, broach, bring in, raise.

brink /bringk/ n. **1** extreme edge. **2** furthest point before something dangerous or exciting is discovered. See synonym study at BORDER. □ **on the brink of** about to experience or suffer.

■ **1** brim, rim, margin, lip, border. □ **on the brink of** on the threshold of, within an ace of; about to.

brink•man•ship /bringkmənship/ n. pursuing a dangerous course to the brink of catastrophe.

bri•quette /brikét/ n. (also **bri•quet**) block of compressed coal dust or charcoal used as fuel.

brisk /brisk/ • adj. **1** quick; lively. **2** enlivening. **3** curt; peremptory. • v. make or grow brisk. □□ **brisk′ly** adv. **brisk′ness** n.

■ adj. **1** active, busy; fast, prompt; animated, sprightly. **2** breezy, strong, steady, fresh; crisp, biting. □□ **briskly** see FAST[1] adv. 1.

bris•ket /brískit/ n. animal's breast, esp. as a cut of meat.

bris•tle /brísəl/ • n. **1** short stiff hair, esp. one of those on an animal's back. **2** this, or an artificial substitute, used in brushes. • v. **1** a intr. (of the hair) stand upright. **b** tr. make (the hair) do this. **2** intr. show irritation. **3** intr. be covered or abundant (in).

■ n. **1** whisker(s); Bot. & Zool. seta. • v. **1** rise, stand up. **2** draw oneself up; seethe, be angry or infuriated. **3** teem, crawl, swarm, throng.

Brit /brit/ n. colloq. British person.

Brit. abbr. **1** British. **2** Britain.

Bri•tan•nia /britányə/ n. personification of Britain, esp. as a helmeted woman with shield and trident.

Brit•i•cism /brítisizəm/ n. (also **Brit•ish•ism** /-tishizəm/) term used or originating in Britain.

Brit•ish /brítish/ • adj. **1** of Great Britain or the United Kingdom, or to its people or language. **2** of the British Commonwealth. • n. **1** [prec. by the; treated as pl.] the British people. **2** = British English. □ **British English** English as used in Great Britain. **British thermal unit** see THERMAL. □□ **Brit′ish•ness** n.

Brit•on /brítən/ n. **1** one of the people of S. Britain before the Roman conquest. **2** native or inhabitant of Great Britain.

brit•tle /brít′l/ • adj. **1** hard and fragile; apt to break. **2** frail; weak; unstable. • n. brittle confection made from nuts and hardened melted sugar. □□ **brit′tle•ly** adv. **brit′tle•ness** n.

■ adj. **1** frangible, delicate; friable. **2** delicate, sensitive, insecure.

broach /brōch/ • v.tr. **1** raise for discussion.

2 pierce (a cask) to draw liquor, etc. • n. bit for boring.

■ v. **1** introduce, venture, put or bring forward.

broad /brawd/ • adj. **1** large in extent from one side to the other; wide. **2** spacious or extensive (broad plain). **3** full and clear (broad daylight). **4** explicit. **5** not taking account of detail. • n. **1** broad part of something. **2** sl. woman. □ **broad-minded** tolerant; liberal. **broad spectrum** (of a drug) effective against many microorganisms. □□ **broad′ly** adv. **broad′-mind•ed•ly** adv. **broad′-mind′ed•ness** n. **broad′ness** n. **broad′ways** adv. **broad′wise** adv.

■ adj. **2** wide, expansive, sweeping. **3** bright, plain, open. **4** plain, clear, obvious, unmistakable. • n. **2** girl, sl. chick, dame. □ **broad-minded** see LIBERAL adj. 3.

broad•cast /bráwdkast/ • v. (past **broad•cast** or **broad•cast•ed**; past part. **broad•cast**) **1** tr. a transmit by radio or television. **b** disseminate widely. **2** intr. undertake or take part in a radio or television transmission. **3** tr. scatter (seed, etc.) widely. See synonym study at SCATTER. • n. radio or television program or transmission. • adj. **1** transmitted by radio or television. **2 a** scattered widely. **b** widely disseminated. • adv. over a large area. □□ **broad′cast•er** n. **broad′cast•ing** n.

■ v. **1** a air, relay. **b** announce, advertise, circulate. **3** sow, strew. • n. show; telecast. □□ **broadcaster** see ANNOUNCER.

broad•cloth /bráwdklawth, -kloth/ n. fine cloth of wool, cotton, or silk.

broad•en /bráwdən/ v. make or become broader.

■ see WIDEN.

broad•loom /bráwdlōōm/ adj. (esp. of carpet) woven in broad widths.

broad•side /bráwdsīd/ n. **1** firing of all guns from one side of a ship. **2** vigorous verbal onslaught. **3** side of a ship above the water.

broad•sword /bráwdsawrd/ n. sword with a broad blade, for cutting rather than thrusting.

bro•cade /brōkáyd/ • n. rich fabric woven with a raised pattern. • v.tr. weave with this design.

broc•co•li /brókəlee/ n. green vegetable with edible flower heads.

bro•chure /brōshŏŏr/ n. pamphlet or leaflet.

■ booklet, insert, catalog, folder.

brogue[1] /brōg/ n. **1** strong outdoor shoe with ornamental perforated bands. **2** rough shoe of untanned leather.

brogue[2] /brōg/ n. marked dialect or accent, esp. Irish.

broil /broyl/ v. **1** tr. cook (meat) on a rack or a grill. **2** tr. & intr. make or become very hot.

■ **1** grill, barbecue, griddle, frizzle. **2** swelter, roast.

broil•er /bróylər/ n. **1** young chicken for broiling. **2** device or oven setting on a stove for radiating heat downward. **3** colloq. a very hot day.

broke /brōk/ past of BREAK predic.adj. colloq. having no money; financially ruined. □ **go**

for broke *sl.* risk everything in a strenuous effort.

■ penniless, indigent, down and out, poverty-stricken, penurious, impoverished, insolvent, destitute, poor, needy. □ **go for broke** throw caution to the wind, give one's all.

bro·ken /brṓkən/ *past part.* of BREAK. *adj.* **1** that has been broken. **2** reduced to despair. **3** (of language) badly spoken, as by a foreigner. **4** interrupted. **5** uneven (*broken ground*). **6** tamed. □ **broken-down 1** worn out by age, use, etc. **2** out of order. **broken home** family in which the parents are divorced or separated. □□ **bro′ken·ly** *adv.* **bro′ken·ness** *n.*

■ **1** fragmented, shattered, cracked, fractured, split, smashed; broken-down, out of order *or* commission, not working *or* functioning, in (a state of) disrepair, in pieces, inoperative. **2** defeated, beaten, ruined; dispirited. **3** faltering, hesitant, halting. **4** disturbed, discontinuous, disjointed. **5** see *bumpy* (BUMP). **6** trained, disciplined, docile. □ **broken-down 1** worn, decrepit; dilapidated; see also BEAT *adj.*, BROKEN 2 above. **2** see BROKEN 1 above.

bro·ken·heart·ed /brṓkənhaártid/ *adj.* overwhelmed with sorrow or grief. □□ **bro′ken·heart′ed·ness** *n.*

■ heartbroken, depressed, downhearted, dejected, devastated, crushed, desolate, overwhelmed, heartsick, downcast, sorrowful, disconsolate, inconsolable, grief-stricken, heavyhearted, sad, doleful. □□ **broken-heartedness** see GRIEF 1.

bro·ker /brṓkər/ *n.* **1** agent who buys and sells for others; intermediary. **2** member of the stock exchange dealing in stocks and bonds. □□ **bro′ker·age** *n.* **bro′ker·ing** *n.*

■ **1** dealer, merchant, trader. **2** brokerdealer, stockbroker.

bro·mide /brṓmīd/ *n.* **1** *Chem.* any binary compound of bromine. **2** *Pharm.* preparation of (esp. potassium) bromide, used as a sedative. **3** trite remark.

bro·mine /brṓmeen/ *n. Chem.* poisonous liquid element with a choking irritating smell ¶Symb.: **Br**.

bron·chi·al /bróngkeeəl/ *adj.* of or relating to the bronchi or bronchioles.

bron·chi·tis /brongkítis/ *n.* inflammation of the mucous membrane in the bronchial tubes. □□ **bron·chit·ic** /-kítik/ *adj. & n.*

bron·chus /bróngkəs/ *n.* (*pl.* **bron·chi** /-kī/) either of the two main divisions of the windpipe.

bron·co /bróngkō/ *n.* (*pl.* **-cos**) wild or halftamed horse of western N. America.

bron·to·sau·rus /bróntəsáwrəs/ *n.* (also **bron·to·saur** /bróntəsawr/) large planteating dinosaur with a long whiplike tail and trunk-like legs. (Now more correctly **apatosaurus**).

bronze /bronz/ • *n.* **1** alloy of copper and tin. **2** its brownish color. **3** thing of bronze, esp. a sculpture. • *adj.* made of or colored like bronze. • *v.* **1** *tr.* give a bronzelike surface to. **2** *tr. & intr.* make or become brown; tan. □□ **bronz′y** *adj.*

■ *n.* **3** see SCULPTURE. • *v.* **2** see SUN *v.*

brooch /brōch, brōōch/ *n.* ornamental pin.

■ clasp, badge; fastening, clip.

brood /brōōd/ • *n.* **1** young of an animal (esp. a bird) produced at one time. **2** *colloq.* children in a family. • *v.* **1** *intr.* [often foll. by *on*, *over*, etc.] worry or ponder (esp. resentfully). **2** *tr.* sit as a hen on eggs to hatch them. **3** *intr.* [usu. foll. by *over*] (of silence, a storm, etc.) hang or hover closely. □□ **brood′ing·ly** *adv.*

■ *n.* **1** offspring, litter, progeny, issue. **2** family, *colloq.* kids. • *v.* **1** deliberate, reflect; mope, sulk; (*brood over*) mull over. **2** incubate, hatch. **3** see LOOM[2] *v.* 2.

brook[1] /brōōk/ *n.* small stream. □□ **brook·let** /-lət/ *n.*

■ rivulet, streamlet, creek.

brook[2] /brōōk/ *v.tr.* [usu. with *neg.*] *formal* tolerate; allow.

■ endure, stand, abide; see also ALLOW 1.

broom /brōōm, brŏŏm/ *n.* **1** long-handled brush for sweeping. **2** any of various shrubs bearing bright yellow flowers.

broom·stick /brṓōmstik, brŏŏm-/ *n.* handle of a broom.

Bros. *abbr.* Brothers (esp. in the name of a business).

broth /brawth, broth/ *n. Cookery* thin soup of meat or fish stock.

■ stock, consommé; bouillon.

broth·el /bróthəl/ *n.* house for prostitutes.

■ whorehouse, bawdy house, bagnio, bordello.

broth·er /brúthər/ *n.* **1** male sibling. **2** close male friend or associate. **3** (*pl.* also **breth·ren** /bréthrin/) **a** a member of a male religious order, esp. a monk. **b** fellow member of a congregation, religion, or (formerly) guild, etc. □ **brother-in-law** (*pl.* **brothers-in-law**) **1** brother of one's wife or husband. **2** husband of one's sister or sister-in-law. □□ **broth′er·less** *adj.* **broth′er·ly** *adj. & adv.* **broth′er·li·ness** *n.*

■ **1** cousin, relation, relative. **2** fellow; associate, colleague, comrade. **3 a** see MONK. □□ **brotherly** fraternal, neighborly, comradely.

broth·er·hood /brúthərhŏŏd/ *n.* **1 a** relationship between brothers. **b** brotherly friendliness **2 a** association of people linked by a common interest. **b** its members collectively. **3** labor union.

■ **1 b** brotherliness, fellowship, companionship, alliance. **2** fraternity, confraternity, guild, society.

brought *past* and *past part.* of BRING.

brou·ha·ha /brṓōhaahaa/ *n.* commotion; sensation.

■ see UPROAR.

brow /brow/ *n.* **1** forehead. **2** [usu. in *pl.*] eyebrow. **3** summit of a hill or pass. **4** edge of a cliff, etc. □□ **browed** *adj.*

brow·beat /brówbeet/ *v.tr.* (*past* **-beat**; *past part.* **-beat·en**) intimidate with stern looks and words. □□ **brow′beat·er** *n.*

■ bully, persecute, torment, threaten, badger.

brown /brown/ • *adj.* **1** having the color as of dark wood or rich soil. **2** dark-skinned or suntanned. **3** (of bread) made from a dark flour such as whole wheat. • *n.* **1** brown color or pigment. **2** brown clothes or material. • *v.* make or become brown by cooking, sunburn, etc. □ **brown-bag** take one's lunch to work, etc., in a brown paper bag. **brown rice** unpolished rice. □□ **brown'ish** *adj.* **brown'ness** *n.* **brown'y** *adj.*
■ *adj.* **2** see DARK *adj.* 3. • *v.* see SUN *v.*

brown•ie /brównee/ *n.* **1** (**Brownie**) junior Girl Scout. **2** *Cookery* small square of rich, usu. chocolate, cake with nuts. **3** benevolent elf. □ **Brownie point** *colloq.* notional credit for something done to please.

brown•out /brównowt/ *n.* period during which electrical voltage is reduced to avoid a blackout.

brown•stone /brównstōn/ *n.* **1** kind of reddish brown sandstone used for building. **2** building faced with this.

browse /browz/ • *v.* **1** *intr. & tr.* read or survey desultorily. **2** *intr.* feed (on leaves, twigs, etc.). • *n.* **1** twigs, young shoots, etc., as fodder. **2** act of browsing. □□ **brows'er** *n.*
■ *v.* **1** (*tr.*) look over or through, skim (through), scan. **2** graze, pasture. • *n.* **2** look, scan, skim.

bruise /brooz/ • *n.* **1** injury appearing as a discoloration of the skin. **2** similar damage on a fruit, etc. • *v.* **1** *tr.* **a** inflict a bruise on. **b** hurt mentally. **2** *intr.* be susceptible to bruising.
■ *n.* hurt, contusion; blotch, blemish. • *v.* **1** contuse, harm; see also INJURE 1, 2.

bruis•er /broozar/ *n. colloq.* large tough-looking person.
■ tough, ruffian, thug, hoodlum, bouncer.

bruit /broot/ *v.tr.* [often foll. by *about*] spread (a report or rumor).
■ *v.* see RUMOR *v.*

brunch /brunch/ • *n.* late-morning meal eaten as the first meal of the day. • *v.intr.* eat brunch.

bru•nette /broonét/ (also *masc.* **bru•net'**) • *n.* person with dark hair. • *adj.* having dark hair.

brunt /brunt/ *n.* chief impact of an attack, task, etc. (esp. *bear the brunt of*).
■ (full) force, burden, onus; effect, repercussion(s).

brush /brush/ • *n.* **1** implement with bristles, hair, wire, etc., set into a handle, for arranging the hair, painting, etc. **2** application of a brush; brushing. **3 a** short, esp. unpleasant encounter. **b** skirmish. **4** bushy tail of a fox. **5** *Electr.* piece of carbon or metal serving as an electrical contact, esp. with a moving part. **6** undergrowth. • *v.* **1** *tr.* **a** sweep, scrub, or put in order with a brush. **b** treat (a surface) with a brush so as to change its nature or appearance. **2** *tr.* remove or apply with a brush. **3** *tr. & intr.* graze in passing. **4** *intr.* perform a brushing action or motion. □ **brush aside** dismiss curtly. **brush-off** *n.* abrupt dismissal. **brush**

up [often foll. by *on*] revive one's former knowledge of (a subject). □□ **brush'like** *adj.* **brush'y** *adj.*
■ *n.* **1** hairbrush; broom, besom. **2** groom; sweep. **3** altercation, exchange, incident; see also SKIRMISH *n.* **6** brushwood, shrubs; underbrush. • *v.* **1, 4** dust, clean, wipe; groom. **3** touch, rub *or* press against. □ **brush aside** disregard, discount, discard, shrug off. **brush-off** see REBUFF *n.*

brush•wood /brúshwood/ *n.* **1** cut or broken twigs, etc. **2** undergrowth; a thicket.

brush•work /brúshwark/ *n.* **1** manipulation of the brush in painting. **2** painter's style in this.

brusque /brusk/ *adj.* abrupt or offhand. □□ **brusque'ly** *adv.* **brusque'ness** *n.*
■ blunt, gruff, short, curt.

BLUNT, BLUFF, CURT, GRUFF, SURLY. **Brusque**, which comes from an Italian word meaning rude, describes an abruptness of speech or manner that is not necessarily meant to be rude (*a brusque handshake; a brusque reply*). **Curt** is more deliberately unfriendly, suggesting brevity and coldness of manner (*a curt dismissal*). There's nothing wrong with being **blunt**, although it implies an honesty and directness that can border on tactlessness (*a blunt reply to his question about where the money went*). Someone who is **bluff** is usually more likable, possessing a frank, hearty manner that may be a little too outspoken but is seldom offensive (*a bluff man who rarely minced words*). Exhibiting **gruff** or **surly** behavior will not win friends, since both words suggest bad temper if not rudeness. But **gruff** is used to describe a rough or grouchy disposition and, like *bluff*, is applied more often to a man. Anyone who has had to deal with an overworked store clerk while shopping during the holidays knows the meaning of *surly*, which is worse than *gruff*. It describes not only a sour disposition but an outright hostility toward people, and it can apply to someone of either sex (*that surly woman at the customer service desk*).

Brus•sels sprout /brúsalz/ *n.* **1** vegetable with small, compact cabbage-like buds. **2** any of these buds.

bru•tal /broot'l/ *adj.* **1** savagely or viciously cruel. **2** harsh; merciless. □□ **bru•tal•i•ty** /-tálitee/ *n.* (*pl.* **–ties**). **bru'tal•ly** *adv.*
■ inhuman, pitiless, merciless; inhumane, heartless. □□ **brutality** bestiality, cruelty, savagery, barbarousness, barbarity, inhumanity.

bru•tal•ize /broot'līz/ *v.tr.* **1** make brutal. **2** treat brutally. □□ **bru•tal•i•za'tion** *n.*
■ **2** see MISTREAT.

brute /broot/ *n.* **1** brutal or violent person or animal. **2** animal as opposed to a human being. • *adj.* **1** not possessing the capacity to reason. **2 a** cruel. **b** stupid. **3** unthinking; merely physical. □□ **brut'ish** *adj.* **brut'ish•ly** *adv.* **brut'ish•ness** *n.*
■ *n.* **1** see BEAST 2. **2** creature, beast. • *adj.* **2 a** see CRUEL *adj.* **b** see CARNAL 1, SIMPLE 5. **3** brutish, unfeeling.

BS *abbr.* **1** Bachelor of Science. **2** Bachelor of Surgery. **3** Blessed Sacrament.

B.Sc. *abbr.* Bachelor of Science.

BTU *abbr.* (also **B.t.u.**) British thermal unit(s).

B-school • *n. abbr.* business school (*most B-school graduates have several years of work experience*).

bub•ble /búbəl/ • *n.* **1 a** a thin sphere of liquid enclosing air, etc. **b** air-filled cavity in a liquid or a solidified liquid such as glass or amber. **c** [in *pl.*] froth; foam. **2** sound or appearance of boiling. **3** semicylindrical or domed structure. **4** visionary or unrealistic project. • *v.intr.* **1** rise in or send up bubbles. **2** make the sound of boiling. □ **bubble gum** chewing gum that can be blown into bubbles. **bubble memory** *Computing* type of memory that stores data as a pattern of magnetized regions in a thin layer of magnetic material. **bubble wrap** clear plastic wrap with air bubbles in it.

■ *n.* **1 a, b** blister, air pocket, globule, droplet. **c** (*bubbles*) suds, lather, spume; effervescence. **4** pipe dream, fantasy, illusion, daydream. • *v.* foam, froth, boil.

bub•bly /búblee/ • *adj.* **1** having bubbles. **2** (**bub•bli•er, bub•bli•est**) exuberant. • *n. colloq.* champagne.

■ *adj.* **1** effervescent, sudsy, fizzy, sparkling, sparkly. **2** effervescent, merry, ebullient, bouncy, animated, vivacious, dynamic, vibrant.

bu•bo /byóōbō, bóō–/ *n.* (*pl.* **–boes**) swollen inflamed lymph node, esp. in the armpit or groin

bu•bon•ic plague /byoōbónik, boō–/ *n.* contagious bacterial disease characterized by fever, delirium, and buboes.

buc•ca•neer /búkəneer/ • *n.* **1** pirate. **2** unscrupulous adventurer. • *v.intr.* be a buccaneer. □□ **buc•ca•neer'ing** *n. & adj.* **buc•ca•neer'ish** *adj.*

■ *n.* **1** see PIRATE *n.* 1a.

buck¹ /buk/ • *n.* male deer, hare, rabbit, etc. • *v.* **1** *intr.* (of a horse) jump upward with back arched and feet drawn together. **2** *tr.* **a** throw (a rider) in this way. **b** oppose; resist. **3** *tr. & intr.* [usu. foll. by *up*] *colloq.* make or become more cheerful. □□ **buck'er** *n.*

■ *v.* **3 a** see CHEER *v.* 3.

buck² /buk/ *n. sl.* dollar. □ **a fast buck** easy money.

buck³ /buk/ *n. sl.* article placed as a reminder before a player whose turn it is to deal at poker. □ **pass the buck** *colloq.* shift responsibility (to another).

buck•board /búkbawrd/ *n.* horse-drawn vehicle with the body formed by a plank fixed to the axles.

buck•et /búkit/ • *n.* **1 a** roughly cylindrical open container with a handle, for carrying, catching, or holding water, etc. **b** amount contained in this. **2** [in *pl.*] large quantities, esp. rain or tears. **3** compartment on the outer edge of a waterwheel. **4** scoop of a dredger or a grain elevator. • *v.intr.* (esp. of rain) pour heavily. □ **bucket seat** seat with a rounded back to fit one person, esp. in a car. □□ **buck'et•ful** *n.* (*pl.* **–fuls**).

■ *n.* **1** pail, scuttle. • *v.* see POUR 3.

buck•le /búkəl/ • *n.* **1** clasp with a hinged pin, used for securing a belt, strap, etc. **2** similarly shaped ornament, esp. on a shoe. • *v.* **1** *tr.* [often foll. by *up, on*, etc.] fasten with a buckle. **2** *tr. & intr.* give way or cause to give way under longitudinal pressure; crumple. □ **buckle down** make a determined effort.

■ *n.* **1** fastener, clip, hook, catch. **2** brooch, pin. • *v.* **1** clasp, bracket, strap. **2** collapse, cave in, give way.

buck•ram /búkrəm/ *n.* coarse linen or other cloth stiffened with gum or paste.

buck•saw /búksaw/ *n.* two-handed saw set in an H-shaped frame and used for sawing wood.

buck•shot /búkshot/ *n.* large-sized lead shot.

buck•skin /búkskin/ *n.* **1** leather made from a buck's skin. **2** thick, smooth cotton or wool cloth.

buck•tooth /búktooth/ *n.* upper tooth that projects.

buck•wheat /búkhweet, –weet/ *n.* any cereal plant with seeds used for fodder and flour.

bu•col•ic /byoōkólik/ • *adj.* of or concerning shepherds, etc.; rural. • *n.* **1** [usu. in *pl.*] pastoral poem or poetry. **2** peasant. □□ **bu•col'i•cal•ly** *adv.*

bud /bud/ • *n.* **1 a** shoot from which a stem, leaf, or flower develops. **b** flower or leaf not fully open. **2** anything still undeveloped. • *v.intr.* (**bud•ded, bud•ding**) **1** *Bot. & Zool.* form a bud. **2** begin to grow or develop.

■ *n.* **1** see SHOOT. *v.* **2** see SPROUT *v.* 2.

Bud•dha /bōōdə, bóōdə/ *n.* title given to successive teachers of Buddhism, esp. to its founder, Gautama.

Bud•dhism /bōōdizəm, bóōd–/ *n.* widespread Asian religion or philosophy, founded by Gautama Buddha in India in the 5th c. BC. □□ **Bud'dhist** *n. & adj.*

bud•dy /búdee/ *colloq.* • *n.* (*pl.* **–dies**) close friend or companion. • *v.intr.* (**–dies, –died**) become friendly.

■ *n.* see MATE¹ *n.* 1.

budge /buj/ *v.* [usu. with *neg.*] **1** *intr.* **a** make the slightest movement. **b** change one's opinion. **2** *tr.* cause or compel to budge.

■ **1 a, 2** see SHIFT *v.* 1.

bud•ger•i•gar /bújəreegaar/ *n.* small parrot kept as a pet.

bud•get /bújit/ • *n.* **1** amount of money needed or available. **2** estimate or plan of revenue and expenditure. **3** quantity or arrange for in a budget. □□ **budg'et•ar•y** *adj.*

■ *v.* ration, restrict. □□ **budgetary** see ECONOMIC 1.

buff /buf/ • *adj.* of a yellowish beige color. • *n.* **1** this color. **2** *colloq.* enthusiast. **3** *colloq.* human skin unclothed. **4** velvety dull yellow ox leather. • *v.tr.* **1** polish (metal, etc.). **2** make (leather) velvety. □ **in the buff** *colloq.* naked.

■ *n.* **2** see *enthusiast* (ENTHUSIASM). • *v.* **1** see POLISH *v.* 1.

buf•fa•lo /búfəlō/ • *n.* (*pl.* same or **–loes**)

buffer ~ bull

1 N. American bison. **2** wild ox of Africa or Asia. • *v.tr.* (**–loes, –loed**) *sl.* outwit.

buf•fer /búfər/ • *n.* **1 a** device that deadens an impact, etc. **b** such a device on the front and rear of a railroad vehicle or at the end of a track. **2** *Biochem.* substance that maintains the hydrogen ion concentration of a solution when an acid or alkali is added. **3** *Computing* temporary memory area for data. • *v.tr.* **1** act as a buffer to. **2** *Biochem.* treat with a buffer. □ **buffer state** small nation situated between two larger ones regarded as reducing friction. **buffer zone** any area separating those in conflict.

■ *n.* **1** see PROTECTION 1b. • *v.* **1** see CUSHION *v.* 2.

buf•fet¹ /bŏōfáy, bə–/ *n.* **1** meal consisting of several dishes set out on a table from which guests serve themselves. **2** restaurant or counter where light meals or snacks may be bought. **3** sideboard. □ **buffet car** railroad car serving refreshments.

buf•fet² /búfit/ • *v. tr.* strike repeatedly. • *n.* **1** blow, esp. of the hand or fist. **2** shock.

■ *v.* see STRIKE *v.* 1. • *n.* **1** see BUMP *n.* 1.

buf•foon /bəfŏōn/ *n.* **1** jester; mocker. **2** stupid person. □□ **buf•foon′er•y** *n.* **buf•foon′ ish** *adj.*

■ **1** see FOOL *n.* **2** see FOOL *n.* 1.

bug /bug/ • *n.* **1 a** any of various insects with mouthparts modified for piercing and sucking. **b** *colloq.* any insect. **2** *sl.* virus; infection. **3** concealed microphone. **4** error in a computer program or system, etc. **5** *sl.* **a** obsession, enthusiasm, etc. **b** enthusiast. • *v.* (**bugged, bug•ging**) **1** *tr.* conceal a microphone in. **2** *tr. sl.* annoy. **3** *intr. sl.* leave quickly. □ **bug-eyed** with bulging eyes.

■ *n.* **1** beetle, fly, midge, no-see-um. **2** microbe, microorganism, germ; disease, illness. **3** transmitter. **4** fault, mistake, failing. **5 a** craze, fad, mania. **b** faddist, fan, fanatic. • *v.* **1** tap, wiretap. **2** see ANNOY 1, BOTHER *v.* 1a.

bug•gy /búgee/ *n.* (*pl.* **–gies**) **1** small light, horse-drawn vehicle. **2** small, sturdy, esp. open, motor vehicle (*beach buggy*). **3** baby carriage.

bu•gle /byŏōgəl/ • *n.* (also **bu′gle horn**) brass military instrument like a small trumpet. • *v.* **1** *intr.* sound a bugle. **2** *tr.* sound (a note, a call, etc.) on a bugle. □□ **bu′gler** /byŏōglər/ *n.* **bu′glet** /byŏōglit/ *n.*

build /bild/ • *v.tr.* (*past & past. part.* **built** /bilt/) **1 a** construct. **b** commission, finance, and oversee the building of. **2 a** establish, develop, make, or accumulate. **b** [often foll. by *on*] base (hopes, theories, etc.). **3** (as **built** *adj.*) having a specified build. • *n.* **1** physical proportions. **2** style of construction. □ **build in** incorporate. **build on** add (an extension, etc.). **build up 1** increase in size or strength. **2** praise; boost. **3** gradually become established. **built-in** integral. **built-up 1** (of a locality) densely developed. **2** increased in height, etc., by the addition of parts. □□ **build′er** *n.*

■ *v.* **1** erect, raise, set up, assemble, put to-

gether. **2** build up, expand; base, found. **3** (**built**) made, constructed. • *n.* **1** physique, figure, body, shape. **2** see MOLD¹ *n.* 2. □ **build on** annex, append, attach. **build up 1** see BUILD *v.* 2 above. **2** see BOOST *v.* 1a.

built-in see INHERENT. **built-up 1** populous, (heavily) populated.

build•ing /bílding/ *n.* **1** permanent fixed structure. **2** constructing of such structures. ■ edifice; construction, erection, fabrication.

build•up /bíldəp/ *n.* **1** favorable advance publicity. **2** gradual approach to a climax. ■ **2** see INCREASE *n.* 1, 2.

built *past and past part.* of BUILD.

bulb /bulb/ *n.* **1 a** underground fleshy-leaved storage organ of some plants (e.g., lily, onion) sending roots downward and leaves upward. **b** plant grown from this. **2** = LIGHTBULB. **3** any object or part shaped like a bulb.

bul•bous /búlbəs/ *adj.* shaped like a bulb; fat or bulging.

bulge /bulj/ • *n.* **1** irregular swelling; lump. **2** *colloq.* temporary increase in quantity or number. • *v.* **1** *intr.* swell. **2** *intr.* be full or replete. **3** *tr.* swell (a bag, etc.). □□ **bulg′ ing•ly** *adv.* **bulg′y** *adj.*

■ *n.* **1** hump, protuberance, bump, protrusion. **2** see BOOM² *n.* • *v.* **1** protrude, stick out; belly out. **2** (*bulging*) see REPLETE 1. **3** see SWELL *v.* 3.

bu•lim•a•rex•i•a /bŏōlímərékseeə, –leemə–, byŏō–/ *n.* = BULIMIA 2. □□ **bu•lim•a•rex′ic** *adj. & n.*

bu•lim•i•a /bŏōleémeeə, –li–, byŏō–/ *n. Med.* **1** insatiable overeating. **2** (in full **bu•lim′ia ner•vo′sa**) emotional disorder in which bouts of overeating are followed by self-induced vomiting, etc. □□ **bu•lim′ic** *adj. & n.*

bulk /bulk/ • *n.* **1 a** magnitude (esp. large). **b** large mass. **c** large quantity. **2** large shape, body, or person. **3** [treated as *pl.*] the greater part or number. **4** roughage. • *v.* **1** *intr.* seem in respect to size or importance; loom. **2** *tr.* make (a book, etc.) seem thicker (*bulked it with irrelevant stories*). □ **in bulk** in large quantities.

■ *n.* **1 a** volume, size, weight; immensity; obesity. **3** see MAJORITY¹ 1. **4** fiber. • *v.* **2** see PAD *v.* 2. □ **in bulk** wholesale, *en bloc*, by the gross.

bulk•head /búlk-hed/ *n.* **1** upright partition separating compartments in a ship, aircraft, etc. **2** embankment, esp. along a waterfront. ■ see WALL *n.* 2.

bulk•y /búlkee/ *adj.* (**bulk•i•er, bulk•i•est**) awkwardly large; unwieldy. □□ **bulk′i•ly** *adv.* **bulk′i•ness** *n.*

■ voluminous, ungainly; chunky, hefty, brawny.

bull¹ /bŏōl/ • *n.* **1 a** uncastrated male bovine animal. **b** male of the whale, elephant, etc. **2** (**the Bull**) zodiacal sign or constellation Taurus. **3** *Stock Exch.* person who buys shares hoping to sell them at a higher price (cf. BEAR²). • *adj.* like that of a bull. • *v.* **1** *tr. & intr.* act or treat violently. **2** *Stock Exch.* **a** *intr.* speculate for a rise in stock prices. **b** *tr.* raise price of (stocks, etc.). □ **bull pen** (also **bull′pen**) **1** *Baseball* **a** area where relief pitchers warm up. **b** relief pitchers on a team. **2** large temporary holding cell for prisoners. **bull's-eye** center of a target; direct hit. **take the bull by the horns** face danger or challenge boldly. □□ **bull′ish** adj.

bull² /bool/ n. a papal edict.

bull³ /bool/ • n. **1** (also **Irish bull**) expression containing a contradiction in terms. **2** sl. **a** unnecessary routine tasks or discipline. **b** nonsense. **c** trivial or insincere talk or writing.

bull•dog /booldawg, -dog/ n. **1 a** dog of a sturdy powerful breed with a large head and smooth hair. **b** this breed. **2** tenacious and courageous person.

bull•doze /booldoz/ v.tr. **1** clear with a bulldozer. **2** colloq. **a** intimidate. **b** make (one's way) forcibly.

  ■ **1** see LEVEL v. 2. **2** see FORCE v. 2.

bull•doz•er /booldozar/ n. powerful tractor with a broad curved vertical blade at the front for clearing ground.

bul•let /boolit/ n. small missile fired from a rifle, revolver, etc.

  ■ see PROJECTILE n.

bul•le•tin /boolitin/ n. **1** short official statement of news. **2** regular periodical issued by an organization. □ **bulletin board 1** board for posting notices, information, etc. **2** Computing public computer file serving the function of a bulletin board.

  ■ **1** report, account, flash, update, announcement; see also WORD n. 7. **2** newsletter, pamphlet.

bul•let•proof /boolitproof/ • adj. (of a material) designed to protect from bullets. • v.tr. make bulletproof.

bull•fight /boolfit/ n. sport of baiting and (usu.) killing bulls. □□ **bull′fight•er** n. **bull′fight•ing** n.

bull•frog /boolfrawg, -frog/ n. large frog native to eastern N. America, with a deep croak.

bull•head•ed /boolhédid/ adj. obstinate; impetuous; blundering. □□ **bull′head•ed•ly** adv. **bull′head•ed•ness** n.

  ■ see STUBBORN.

bull•horn /boolhawrn/ n. portable voice amplifier.

bul•lion /boolyan/ n. gold or silver in bulk before coining, or valued by weight.

bull•ish /boolish/ adj. **1** like a bull, esp. in size or temper. **2 a** associated with rising stock prices. **b** optimistic.

bul•lock /boolak/ n. castrated bull; steer.

bull•ring /boolring/ n. arena for bullfights.

bul•ly /boolee/ • n. (pl. **-lies**) person intimidating others. • v.tr. (**-lies, -lied**) **1** persecute. **2** pressure (a person) to do something (bullied him into agreeing).

  ■ n. hooligan, rowdy, thug; persecutor, oppressor. • v. victimize, intimidate, tyrannize. **2** see RAILROAD v.

bul•rush /boolrush/ n. **1** rushlike water plant. **2** Bibl. papyrus.

bul•wark /boolwark/ • n. **1** defensive wall, esp. of earth; a rampart. **2** person, principle, etc., that acts as a defense. **3** [usu. in pl.] ship's side above deck. • v.tr. serve as a bulwark to; protect.

  ■ n. **1** see RAMPART n. 1. **2** defense, safe-

guard, protection, shield. • v. defend, protect, shelter.

bum /bum/ sl. • n. habitual loafer or tramp; lazy dissolute person. • v. (**bummed, bumming**) **1** intr. loaf or wander around. **2** tr. cadge. • attrib.adj. **1** of poor quality. **2** false; fabricated. **3** not entirely functional (bum ankle).

  ■ n. beggar, down-and-out, vagrant, drifter. • v. **1** see LOAF² v. **2** borrow, beg, sponge; freeload. • attrib. adj. **1** see BAD adj. 1. **2** improper, unjustified, trumped up.

bum•ble /bumbal/ v.intr. **1** speak in a rambling way. **2** (often as **bumbling** adj.) blunder. □□ **bum′bler** n.

  ■ **2** (**bumbling**) see INEPT 1.

bum•ble•bee /bumbalbee/ n. any large loud humming bee.

bump /bump/ • n. **1** dull-sounding blow or collision. **2** swelling or dent so caused. **3** uneven patch on a road, etc. • v. **1 a** tr. hit or come against with a bump. **b** intr. (of two objects) collide. **2** intr. hit with a bump; collide with. **3** tr. hurt or damage by striking. **4** intr. [usu. foll. by along] move with much jolting. • adv. with a bump. □ **bump into** colloq. meet by chance. **bump off** sl. murder. □□ **bump′i•ly** adv. **bump′i•ness** n. **bump′y** adj. (**bump•i•er, bump•i•est**).

  ■ n. **1** thud, thump, hit, knock, buffer. **2** lump, protuberance, welt; indentation. • v. **1, 2** knock (against), strike, bang, bash. **3** injure, bruise; scrape. **4** lurch, jerk, bounce. • adv. crash; suddenly; violently. □ **bump into** encounter, run into or across, chance upon. **bump off** see MURDER v. 1. □□ **bumpy** lumpy, rough, potholed, rutted, bouncy, jarring.

bump•er /bumpar/ n. **1** horizontal bar across the front or back of a vehicle, at the end of a track, etc., to reduce damage in a collision. **2** unusually large or fine (a bumper crop).

  ■ **2** (attrib.) see PLENTIFUL.

bump•kin /bumpkin/ n. rustic or socially inept person.

bump•tious /bumpshas/ adj. offensively self-assertive or conceited. See synonym study at BOLD. □□ **bump′tious•ly** adv. **bump′tious•ness** n.

  ■ see PUSHY.

bun /bun/ n. **1** small bread, roll, or cake. **2** hair worn in the shape of a bun.

  ■ **1** bread roll, brioche.

bunch /bunch/ • n. **1** things growing or fastened together (bunch of grapes). **2** collection. **3** colloq. group; gang. • v. **1** tr. gather into close folds. **2** intr. form into a group or crowd. □□ **bunch′y** adj.

  ■ n. **1** bundle, cluster, batch, clump; bouquet. **2** group, lot, set. **3** body, band, gathering; party. • v. sort, class, classify; collect.

bun•co /bungko/ n. (also **bun′ko**) sl. (pl. **-cos**) swindle, esp. by card sharping or a confidence trick.

bun•dle /bundal/ • n. **1** things tied or fastened together. **2** set of nerve fibers, etc. **3** sl. large amount of money. • v.tr. **1** tie or make into a bundle. **2** [usu. foll. by into] throw or push, esp. quickly or confusedly. **3** send away hurriedly.

■ *n.* **1** bunch, collection, assemblage, cluster, group. **3** (*make a bundle*) make a killing *or* a fortune. ● *v.* **1** tie up; collect, gather (together), package. **2** thrust, stuff, cram. **3** (*bundle off*) dispatch, pack off.

bung /bung/ ● *n.* stopper for a cask. ● *v.tr.* stop with a bung.

bun•ga•low /búnggəlō/ *n.* one-storied house.

■ see CABIN *n.* 1.

bun•gee /búnjee/ *n.* (in full **bun'gee cord**) elasticized cord used for securing baggage, etc. □ **bungee jumping** sport of jumping from a height while secured by a bungee from the ankles or a harness.

bun•gle /búnggəl/ ● *v.* **1** *tr.* mismanage or fail at (a task). **2** *intr.* work badly or clumsily. ● *n.* bungled attempt or work. □□ **bun'gler** *n.*

■ *v.* **1** see BOTCH *v.* 1. **2** bumble, fumble, make a blunder, flub. ■ *n.* see MISTAKE *n.*

bun•ion /búnyən/ *n.* swelling on the foot, esp. at the base of the big toe.

bunk[1] /bungk/ ● *n.* shelflike bed against a wall, e.g., in a ship. ● *v.intr.* sleep in a bunk. □ **bunk bed** each of two or more beds one above the other, forming a unit.

bunk[2] /bungk/ *n. sl.* nonsense; humbug.

bunk•er /búngkər/ ● *n.* **1** large container or compartment for storing fuel. **2** reinforced underground shelter. **3** sand-filled hollow as an obstacle in a golf course. ● *v.tr.* fill the fuel bunkers of (a ship, etc.).

bun•kum /búngkəm/ *n.* nonsense; humbug.

■ see NONSENSE.

bun•ny /búnee/ *n.* (*pl.* **–nies**) child's word for a rabbit.

Bun•sen burn•er /búnsən/ *n.* small adjustable gas burner used in scientific work as a source of intense heat.

bunt /bunt/ ● *v.* **1** *tr. & intr.* push with the head or horns; butt. **2** *tr. Baseball* tap or push (a ball) with the bat without swinging. ● *n.* act of bunting.

bunt•ing[1] /búnting/ *n.* any of numerous seedeating birds related to the finches and sparrows.

bunt•ing[2] /búnting/ *n.* **1** flags and other decorations. **2** loosely woven fabric used for these.

buoy /bōó-ee, boy/ ● *n.* **1** anchored float as a navigation mark, etc. **2** lifebuoy. ● *v.tr.* **1** [usu. foll. by *up*] **a** keep afloat. **b** uplift; encourage. **2** mark with a buoy.

■ *n.* **1** (navigational *or* channel) marker, beacon. **2** lifebelt. ● *v.* **1** keep a person's head above water; uplift, support.

buoy•ant /bóyənt/ *adj.* **1 a** able or apt to keep afloat. **b** (of a liquid or gas) able to keep something afloat. **2** lighthearted; resilient. □□ **buoy•an•cy** /bóyənsee/ *n.* **buoy'ant•ly** *adv.*

■ **1 a** floating, floatable. **2** light, lively, vivacious, bubbly.

bur /bər/ *n.* var. of BURR.

bur. *abbr.* bureau.

bur•den /bɔ́rdən/ ● *n.* **1** load, esp. a heavy one. **2** oppressive duty, expense, emotion, etc. **3** ship's carrying capacity; tonnage.

● *v.tr.* load with a burden; oppress. □□ **bur'den•some** *adj.* **bur'den•some•ness** *n.* See synonym study at HEAVY

■ *n.* **1, 2** weight, onus; strain, stress, pressure; see also BOTHER *n.* 1. ● *v.* weigh down, saddle, encumber; tax, trouble. □□ **burden-some** onerous, cumbersome, oppressive.

bur•dock /bɔ́rdok/ *n.* plant with prickly flowers and leaves.

bu•reau /byŏŏrō/ *n.* (*pl.* **bu•reaus** or **bu•reaux** /–rōz/) **1** chest of drawers. **2 a** office or department for specific business. **b** government department.

■ **1** commode, dresser, highboy. **2** agency, division, section; ministry.

bu•reau•cra•cy /byŏŏrókrəsee/ *n.* (*pl.* **–cies**) **1 a** government by central administration. **b** nation so governed. **2** officials of such a government, esp. regarded as oppressive and inflexible. **3** conduct typical of these. □□ **bu•reau•crat** /byŏŏrəkrat/ *n.* **bu•reau•crat'ic** *adj.* **bu•reau•crat'i•cal•ly** *adv.*

■ **2, 3** officialdom, officialism, red tape, rigmarole.

bur•geon /bɔ́rjən/ *literary* ● *v.intr.* grow rapidly; flourish. ● *n.* bud; sprout.

■ *v.* see FLOURISH *v.* 1a, b.

burg•er /bɔ́rgər/ *n. colloq.* hamburger.

bur•gher /bɔ́rgər/ *n.* citizen of a town.

bur•glar /bɔ́rglər/ *n.* person who commits burglary.

■ housebreaker, thief, robber.

bur•glar•ize /bɔ́rglərīz/ *v.* **1** *tr.* commit burglary against (a building or person). **2** *intr.* commit burglary.

■ see ROB 1.

bur•gla•ry /bɔ́rgləree/ *n.* (*pl.* **–ries**) **1** entry into a building illegally with intent to commit a felony. **2** instance of this.

bur•gle /bɔ́rgəl/ *v.* = BURGLARIZE.

bur•gun•dy /bɔ́rgəndee/ *n.* (*pl.* **–dies**) **1 a** wine of Burgundy in E. France. **b** similar wine from another place. **2** dark red color of Burgundy wine.

bur•i•al /béreeəl/ *n.* **1** burying of a dead body. **2** *Archaeol.* grave or its remains.

■ **1** interment, entombment; funeral, obsequies. **2** tomb, burial vault or chamber *or* mound.

bur•ka /bɔ́rkə/ *n.* (also **burkha**) a full, loose garment worn in public by Muslim women, covering the entire body except for the hands and feet, with a screenlike grid for the eyes.

bur•lesque /bərlésk/ ● *n.* **1 a** comic imitation; parody. **b** performance or work of this kind. **2** variety show, often including striptease. See synonym study at CARICATURE. ● *adj.* of or in the nature of burlesque. ● *v.tr.* (**bur•lesques**, **bur•lesqued**, **bur•lesqu•ing**) parody. □□ **bur•lesqu'er** *n.*

■ *n.* **1** caricature, satirization; lampoon. **2** vaudeville. ● *adj.* satirical, derisive, mocking, sardonic. ● *v.* satirize, lampoon, caricature.

bur•ly /bɔ́rlee/ *adj.* (**bur•li•er**, **bur•li•est**) of stout sturdy build; big and strong. □□ **bur'li•ness** *n.*

■ corpulent, large, hefty, stocky, thickset.

burn /bərn/ ● *v.* (*past* and *past part.* **burned** or **burnt**) **1** *tr. & intr.* be or cause to be consumed or destroyed by fire. **2** *intr.* blaze or glow with fire. **3** *tr. & intr.* be or cause to be injured or damaged by fire, heat, or radiation. **4** *tr. & intr.* use or be used as fuel. **5** *tr. & intr.* char in cooking. **6** *tr.* produce (a hole, a mark, etc.) by fire or heat. **7** *tr. & intr.* put or be put to death by fire or electrocution. **8** *tr.* cauterize; brand. **9** *tr. & intr.* make, be, or feel hot, esp. painfully. **10 a** *tr. & intr.* make or be passionate; feel or cause to feel great emotion. **b** *intr.* [usu. foll. by *to* + infin.] desire passionately; long. • *n.* mark or injury caused by burning. □ **burn down** destroy or be destroyed by fire. **burn out 1** be reduced to nothing by burning. **2** fail or cause to fail by burning. **3** [usu. *refl.*] suffer exhaustion. **burn up 1** get rid of by fire. **2** *sl.* be or make furious.

■ *v.* **1** ignite, set on fire, set alight, set fire to; burn up. **2** flame, flare (up), smolder. **5** overcook, blacken. **9** see BROIL 2. **10 b** yearn, wish. □ **burn out 3** see EXHAUST *v.* 2. **burn up 2** see MADDEN.

burn•er /bórnər/ *n.* part of a gas stove, lamp, etc., that emits and shapes the flame.
burn•ing /bórning/ *adj.* **1** ardent; intense. **2** hotly discussed; exciting. **3** flagrant (*burning shame*). **4** that burns; on fire; very hot. □□ **burn'ing•ly** *adv.*

■ **1** vehement, excited, passionate. **2** see *thrilling* (THRILL). **3** see FLAGRANT. **4** flaming, blazing; ablaze; see also HOT *adj.* 1.
burn•ish /bórnish/ *v.tr.* polish by rubbing. □□ **bur'nish•er** *n.*

■ see POLISH *v.* 1.

bur•noose /bərnóos/ *n.* Arab or Moorish hooded cloak.
burn•out /bórnowt/ *n.* **1** physical or emotional exhaustion. **2** extinguishing of a rocket motor when fuel is exhausted.

■ **1** see EXHAUSTION 2.

burnt see BURN.
burp /bərp/ *colloq.* • *v.* **1** *intr.* belch. **2** *tr.* make (a baby) belch. • *n.* belch.
burr /bər/ • *n.* **1 a** whirring sound. **b** rough sounding of the letter *r*. **2 a** rough edge on cut metal or paper. **b** surgeon's or dentist's small drill. **3 a** prickly clinging seedcase or flowerhead. **b** any plant producing these. • *v.* **1** *tr.* pronounce with a burr. **2** *intr.* speak indistinctly. **3** *intr.* make a whirring sound.
bur•ri•to /bəréetō/ *n.* (*pl.* **-tos**) tortilla rolled around a usu. meat or bean filling.
bur•ro /bóro, bóoro, búro/ *n.* (*pl.* **-ros**) small donkey.
bur•row /bóro, búro/ • *n.* hole or tunnel dug by a small animal as a dwelling. • *v.* **1** *intr.* make a burrow. **2** *tr.* make (a hole, etc.) by digging. **3** *intr.* hide oneself. **4** *intr.* [foll. by *into*] investigate; search. □□ **bur'row•er** *n.*

■ *n.* excavation, warren; den, lair. • *v.* **1, 2** tunnel, bore; excavate. **3** see HIDE[1] *v.* 2. **4** (*burrow into*) see INVESTIGATE.

bur•sa /bórsə/ *n.* (*pl.* **bur•sae** /-see/ or **bur•sas**) *Anat.* fluid-filled sac or cavity that eases friction. □□ **bur'sal** *adj.*
bur•sar /bórsər/ *n.* treasurer, esp. of a college.
bur•si•tis /bərsítis/ *n.* inflammation of a bursa.
burst /bərst/ • *v.* (*past* and *past part.* **burst**) **1 a** *intr.* break suddenly apart from within. **b** *tr.* cause to do this. **2 a** *tr.* open forcibly. **b** *intr.* come open or be opened forcibly. **3 a** *intr.* make one's way suddenly, dramatically, or by force. **b** *tr.* break away from or through. **4** *tr. & intr.* fill or be full to overflowing. **5** *intr.* appear or come suddenly (*burst into flame*). **6** *intr.* suddenly begin to shed or utter (*burst into tears* or *laughter* or *song*). **7** *intr.* be as if about to burst because of effort, excitement, etc. • *n.* **1** act of bursting; split. **2** sudden issuing forth. **3** sudden outbreak. **4** sudden effort; spurt. **5** explosion.

■ *v.* **1** rupture, split, shatter; puncture. **2** break open. **3 a** force or break or push one's way. **5** break (out or forth), erupt; (*burst out*) emerge, appear. **6** (*burst into*) burst out in, break into, burst forth with. **7** (*bursting*) see TENSE[1] *adj.* 1. • *n.* **1** see SPLIT *n.* 2. **3** see OUTBURST. **4** see SPURT *n.* 2. **5** blast, detonation.

bur•y /béree/ *v.tr.* (**-ies, -ied**) **1** place (a dead body) in the earth, a tomb, or the sea. **2** lose by death. **3 a** put under ground (*bury alive*). **b** hide (treasure, a bone, etc.) in the earth. **c** cover up; submerge. **4** involve deeply.

■ **1** inter, lay to rest. **3 b, c** conceal, secrete; obscure, cloak, veil. **4** see IMMERSE 2.
bus /bus/ • *n.* (*pl.* **bus•es** or **bus•ses**) **1** large passenger vehicle, usu. on a fixed route. **2** *Computing* defined set of conductors carrying data and control signals within a com-

puter. • v. (bus•es, bused, bus•ing; bus•ses, bussed, bus•sing) 1 intr. go by bus. 2 tr. transport by bus.

bus. abbr. business.

bus•boy /búsboy/ n. assistant to a restaurant waiter who fills water glasses, removes dirty dishes, etc.

bush /boŏsh/ n. 1 shrub or clump of shrubs. 2 thing resembling this, esp. a clump of hair or fur. □□ **bush'i•ly** adv. **bush'i•ness** n. **bush'y** adj. (bush•i•er, bush•i•est)

bushed /boŏsht/ adj. colloq. tired out.

■ see TIRED 1.

bush•el /boŏshəl/ n. measure of capacity equivalent to 64 pints. □□ **bush'el•ful** n. (pl. –fuls)

bush•ing /boŏshing/ n. metal lining for a hole enclosing a revolving shaft, etc.

bush•man /boŏshmən/ n. (pl. –men) 1 person who lives or travels in the Australian bush. 2 (**Bushman**) member or language of an aboriginal people in S. Africa.

bush•mas•ter /boŏshmastər/ n. venomous viper of Central and S. America.

bush•whack /boŏsh–hwak, –wak/ v. 1 intr. a clear woods and bush country. b live or travel in bush country. 2 tr. ambush.

■ 2 see AMBUSH v.

busi•ness /bíznis/ n. 1 one's regular occupation, profession, or trade. 2 one's own concern. 3 a task or duty. b reason for coming. 4 derog. affair; matter. 5 commercial firm. □ **business card** card printed with one's name and professional details. **the business end** colloq. functional part of a tool or device. **business reply mail** system of sending business mail in envelopes prepaid by the addressee. **business suit** 1 man's suit consisting of a jacket, trousers, and sometimes a vest. 2 woman's suit, consisting of a jacket and usu. a skirt. **has no business to** has no right to. **in business** 1 trading or dealing. 2 able to begin operations. **in the business of** 1 engaged in. 2 intending to (we are not in the business of surrendering). **mind one's own business** not meddle.

■ 1 calling, vocation, career. 2 affair, interest, responsibility. 3 function, job, responsibility. 4 topic, subject, problem; see also PALAVER. 5 concern, establishment, operation; corporation, partnership. □ **mind one's own business** stop butting in or prying or interfering, stick to one's last, keep off or out, colloq. keep one's paws off, stop poking or sticking one's nose in.

busi•ness•like /bíznislik/ adj. efficient; systematic; practical.

■ see SYSTEMATIC 1.

busi•ness•man /bíznismən/ n. (pl. –men; fem. **busi•ness•wom•an**, pl. –wom•en) person engaged in commerce.

■ dealer, merchant, broker, distributor, seller, salesperson.

bus•man /búsmən/ n. (pl. –men) driver of a bus. □ **busman's holiday** leisure time spent in an activity similar to one's regular work.

buss /bus/ colloq. • n. kiss. • v.tr. kiss.

bust¹ /bust/ n. 1 human chest, esp. that of a woman; bosom. 2 sculpture of a person's head, shoulders, and chest.

■ 1 bosom, chest. 2 see STATUE.

bust² /bust/ colloq. • v. (past and past part. **bust•ed** or **bust**) 1 tr. & intr. burst; break. 2 tr. reduce (a soldier, etc.) to a lower rank. 3 tr. a raid; search. b arrest. • n. 1 sudden failure. 2 a police raid. b arrest. • adj. (also **bust•ed**) 1 broken; burst. 2 bankrupt. 3 arrested. □ **bust up** (of esp. a married couple) separate.

■ v. 1 see BREAK v. 1. 2 see DOWNGRADE v. 1. 3 a see RAID v. b see ARREST v. 1. • n. 2 search; see also ARREST n. 1. • adj. 2 see INSOLVENT adj.

bus•tle /búsəl/ • v. 1 intr. a work, etc., showily and energetically. b hasten. 2 tr. make (a person) hurry or work hard. 3 intr. (as **bustling** adj.) colloq. full of activity. • n. excited activity; fuss. □□ **bus'tler** n.

■ v. 1 see RUSH¹ v. 1. 3 (bustling) see ACTIVE adj. 1a. • n. rush, hustle (and bustle), hurry; haste.

bus•y /bízee/ • adj. (bus•i•er, bus•i•est) 1 occupied or engaged. 2 full of activity; fussy. 3 (of a telephone line) in use. • v.tr. (–ies, –ied) [often refl.] keep busy; occupy. □ **busy signal** intermittent buzzing sound indicating that a telephone line is in use. □□ **bus'i•ly** /bízilee/ adv. **bus'y•ness** /bízeenis/ n. (cf. BUSINESS).

■ adj. 1 tied up, wrapped up. 2 hectic, frantic; fancy, ornate, (over)decorated. • v. involve, employ, divert.

SYNONYM STUDY: busy

ASSIDUOUS, DILIGENT, ENGAGED, INDUSTRIOUS, SEDULOUS. There are varying degrees of busyness. **Busy** implies actively and attentively involved in work or a pastime (too busy to come to the phone). It can also be used to describe intensive activity of any kind (a busy intersection; a busy day). Someone who is **engaged** is also busy, but in a more focused way (engaged in compiling a dictionary). **Diligent** is used to describe earnest and constant effort, and it often connotes enjoyment of or dedication to what one is doing (diligent efforts to rescue injured animals). To be **industrious** is to be more focused still, often with a definite goal in mind (an industrious employee working for a promotion). **Sedulous** also applies to goal-oriented activity, but it suggests more close care and perseverance than industrious does (a sedulous investigation of the accident). The award for concentrated effort goes to the person who is **assiduous**, which suggests painstaking preoccupation with a specific task (an assiduous student is the one most likely to win his or her teacher's favor).

---

bus•y•bod•y /bízeebodee, –budee/ n. (pl. –ies) 1 meddlesome person. 2 mischief maker.

■ 1 snoop(er), gossip, Nosy Parker. 2 see TROUBLEMAKER.

but /but, bət/ • conj. 1 a nevertheless; however. b on the other hand; on the contrary. 2 except; other than; otherwise than (what could we do but run?). 3 without the result that (it never rains but it pours). • prep. except;

apart from; other than (*everyone went but me*). • *adv.* **1** only; no more than; only just (*we can but try, did it but once*). **2** introducing emphatic repetition; definitely (*wanted to see nobody, but nobody*). • *rel.pron.* who not; that not (*there is not a man but feels pity*). • *n.* objection (*ifs and buts*). □ in phr. **but me no buts** do not raise objections. □ **but for** without the help or hindrance, etc., of (*but for you I'd be rich by now*).

bu•tane /byŏtayn/ *n. Chem.* gaseous hydrocarbon used as fuel.

butch /bŏŏch/ *sl.* • *adj.* masculine; tough-looking. • *n.* **1** mannish woman. **2** mannish lesbian.

butch•er /bŏŏchər/ • *n.* **1 a** person who deals in meat. **b** person who slaughters animals for food. **2** person who kills indiscriminately or brutally. • *v.tr.* **1** slaughter or cut up (an animal) for food. **2** kill (people) wantonly or cruelly. **3** ruin through incompetence.

■ *n.* **2** murderer, slaughterer, killer. • *v.* **2** slaughter, massacre, murder; cut *or* hack to pieces, mutilate. **3** see RUIN *v.* 1.

butch•er•y /bŏŏchəree/ *n.* (*pl.* **–ies**) **1** needless or cruel slaughter (of people). **2** butcher's trade.

■ **1** see SLAUGHTER *n.* 2.

but•ler /bŭtlər/ *n.* principal manservant of a household.

butt¹ /but/ • *v.* **1** *tr. & intr.* push with the head or horns. **2** *intr.* meet end to end with; abut. • *n.* **1** a push with the head. **2** joining of two edges. □ **butt in** interrupt; meddle.

■ *v.* **1** ram, prod, poke. **2** (*butt on to*) join. • *n.* **1** poke, jab, prod, nudge. □ **butt in** interfere, intrude, intervene.

butt² /but/ *n.* **1** object (of ridicule, etc.). **2** a mound behind a target. **b** [in *pl.*] shooting range.

■ **1** target; prey, victim.

butt³ /but/ *n.* **1** (also **butt end**) thicker end, esp. of a tool or a weapon. **2** stub of a cigar or a cigarette. **3** *sl.* buttocks.

butt⁴ /but/ *n.* cask, esp. as a measure of wine or ale.

but•ter /bŭtər/ • *n.* **1 a** solidified churned cream used as a spread and in cooking. **b** substance of a similar consistency. • *v.tr.* spread, cook, or serve with butter. □ **butter bean 1** dried lima bean. **2** wax bean. **butter cream** (or **icing**) mixture of butter, confectioner's sugar, etc., used as a filling or topping for a cake. **butter up** *colloq.* flatter excessively.

but•ter•fat /bŭtərfat/ *n.* essential fats of pure butter.

but•ter•fly /bŭtərflī/ *n.* (*pl.* **–flies**) **1** insect with four usu. brightly colored wings erect when at rest. **2** [in *pl.*] *colloq.* nervous sensation felt in the stomach. □ **butterfly stroke** stroke in swimming, with both arms raised out of the water and lifted forward together.

but•ter•milk /bŭtərmilk/ *n.* slightly acid liquid left after churning butter.

but•ter•scotch /bŭtərskoch/ *n.* **1** brittle candy made from butter, brown sugar, etc. **2** this flavor in desserts, etc.

but•ter•y¹ /bŭtəree/ *n.* (*pl.* **–ies**) pantry.

but•ter•y² /bŭtəree/ *adj.* like, containing, or spread with butter. □□ **but'ter•i•ness** *n.*

but•tock /bŭtək/ *n.* [usu. in *pl.*] **1** each of two fleshy protuberances on the lower rear part of the human trunk. **2** the corresponding part of an animal.

■ (*buttocks*) seat, posterior, rump, hindquarters, hams.

but•ton /bŭt'n/ • *n.* **1** small disk or knob sewn to a garment as a fastener or as an ornament. **2** knob on electronic equipment that is pressed to operate it. • *v.* **1** *tr. & intr.* – *button up* fasten with buttons. □ **button up 1** fasten with buttons. **2** *colloq.* complete (a task, etc.) satisfactorily. **3** *colloq.* become silent. □□ **but'toned** *adj.* **but'ton•less** *adj.*

but•ton•hole /bŭt'nhōl/ • *n.* **1** slit in a garment for a button. **2** flower worn in a lapel buttonhole; boutonniere. • *v.tr. colloq.* accost and detain (a reluctant listener).

■ *v.* corner, hold up, importune, waylay.

but•tress /bŭtris/ • *n.* **1** projecting support of stone or brick, etc., built against a wall. **2** source of help or encouragement. • *v.tr.* **1** support with a buttress. **2** support by argument, etc.

■ *n.* **1** prop, stay, reinforcement. • *v.* sustain, bolster, strengthen, reinforce.

bux•om /bŭksəm/ *adj.* (esp. of a woman) plump and healthy looking; large bosomed. □□ **bux'om•ly** *adv.* **bux'om•ness** *n.*

■ hearty, vigorous, solid, sizable, large.

buy /bī/ • *v.* (**buys**, **buy•ing**; *past* and *past part.* **bought** /bawt/) **1** *tr.* **a** obtain in exchange for money. **b** [usu. in *neg.*] serve to obtain (*money can't buy happiness*). **2** *tr.* bribe. **3** *tr.* get by sacrifice, great effort, etc. **4** *tr. sl.* accept; believe in; approve of. **5** *absol.* be a buyer for a store, etc. • *n. colloq.* purchase. □ **buy off** get rid of by payment. **buy out** pay (a person) to give up an ownership, interest, etc. **buy up** buy as much as possible of.

■ *v.* **1** purchase; acquire. **2** pay off, buy off, suborn, corrupt. **4** allow, take, find credible *or* believable. **5** trade. • *n.* acquisition, deal.

buy•er /bīər/ *n.* **1** person employed to purchase stock for a large store, etc. **2** customer. □ **buyer's** (or **buyers'**) **market** trading conditions favorable to buyers.

■ **2** consumer, purchaser; (*buyers*) see CLIENTELE.

buy•out /bīowt/ *n.* purchase of a controlling share in a company, etc.

buzz /buz/ • *n.* **1** hum of a bee, etc. **2** sound of a buzzer. **3 a** murmur, as of conversation. **b** stir; hurried activity. **c** *colloq.* rumor. **4** *sl.* telephone call. **5** *sl.* thrill; euphoric sensation. • *v.* **1** *intr.* make a humming sound. **2 a** *tr. & intr.* signal or signal to with a buzzer. **b** *tr. sl.* telephone. **3** *intr.* **a** [often foll. by *about*] move busily. **b** (of a place) have an air of excitement or purposeful activity. **4** *tr. Aeron. colloq.* fly fast and very close to (another aircraft, the ground, etc.). □ **buzz off** *sl.* go or hurry away. **buzz saw** circular saw.

■ *n.* **1** drone. **3 a** undercurrent, undertone, background noise. **b** see STIR[1] *n.* 2. **c** piece of gossip *or* hearsay; *colloq.* lowdown, info, *sl.* dope, poop. **4** phone call, call. **5** feeling of excitement, sensation, stimulation. ● *v.* **1** hum, murmur, drone. **2 a** summon, ring for. **b** call (up). **3 a** bustle, fuss (about); flutter, hover. **b** be alive, bristle, swarm, hum. **4** fly down on, zoom on to. □ **buzz off** see *beat it.*

buz•zard /búzərd/ *n.* turkey vulture.

buzz•er /búzər/ *n.* **1** electrical device that makes a buzzing noise. **2** whistle or siren.

buzz•word /búzwərd/ *n.* sl. **1** fashionable technical or computer jargon. **2** catchword; slogan.

■ **2** see SLOGAN.

BVM *abbr.* Blessed Virgin Mary.

by /bī/ ● *prep.* **1** near; beside. **2** through the agency or means of. **3** not later than. **4 a** past; beyond. **b** passing through; via. **5** in the circumstances of (*by day*). **6** to the extent of. **7** according to. **8** with the succession of. **9** concerning; in respect of. **10** placed between specified lengths in two directions (*three feet by two*). **11** inclining to (*north by northwest*). ● *adv.* **1** near. **2** aside; in reserve (*put $5 by*). **3** past (*marched by*). ● *n.* = BYE[2]. □ **by and by** before long; eventually. **by and large** on the whole. **by the by** (or **bye**) incidentally.

■ *prep.* **1** next to, close to, alongside. **2** by means of, through. **3** before, as soon as. **4 b** by way of, through. **5** during, at. **7** see ACCORDING 1. **9** see CONCERNING. ● *adv.* **1** nearby, at hand, close. **2** away, on one side. □ **by and by** see PRESENTLY 1. **by and large** see *on the whole* (WHOLE). **by the by** see INCIDENTALLY 1.

by- /bī/ *prefix* (also **bye-**) subordinate; incidental (*byroad*).

bye[1] /bī/ *n.* status of an unpaired competitor in a sport, who proceeds to the next round as if having won.

bye[2] /bī/ *int. colloq.* = GOOD-BYE.

by•gone /bígawn, –gon/ ● *adj.* past; antiquated. ● *n.* [in *pl.*] past offenses (*let bygones be bygones*).

■ *adj.* former, ancient; of old. ● *n.* (bygones) past indiscretions; (*let bygones be bygones*) let sleeping dogs lie, call a truce.

by•law /bílaw/ *n.* (also **bye'law**) regulation made by a society or corporation.

by•line /bílīn/ *n.* **1** line in a newspaper, etc., naming the writer of an article. **2** secondary line of work.

by•pass /bípas/ ● *n.* **1** road passing around a town or its center. **2 a** secondary channel or pipe, etc., used in emergencies. **b** alternative passage for the circulation of blood to the heart. ● *v.tr.* avoid; go around.

■ *n.* **1** detour, alternative way *or* route, diversion. ● *v.* evade, circumvent, sidestep, skirt.

by-prod•uct /bíprodəkt/ *n.* **1** incidental product of the manufacture of something else. **2** secondary result.

■ see DERIVATIVE *n.*

by•road /bíröd/ *n.* minor road.

by•stand•er /bístandər/ *n.* person who stands by but does not take part; mere spectator.

■ onlooker, looker-on, observer, witness.

byte /bīt/ *n.* Computing group of eight binary digits, often used to represent one character.

by•way /bíway/ *n.* small seldom-traveled road.

■ byroad, bypath, minor road, lane, track.

by•word /bíwərd/ *n.* **1** person or thing as a notable example. **2** familiar saying; proverb.

■ **2** proverbial saying, maxim, adage, motto, slogan.

Byz•an•tine /bízənteen, –tīn, bizántin/ ● *adj.* **1** of Byzantium or the E. Roman Empire. **2** (of a political situation, etc.): **a** extremely complicated. **b** inflexible. **c** underhand. **3** *Archit.* & *Painting* of Byzantium's highly decorated style. ● *n.* citizen of Byzantium or the E. Roman Empire. □□ **By'zan•tin•ism** *n.* **Byz'an•tin•ist** *n.*

Cc

C[1] /see/ *n.* (also **c**) (*pl.* **Cs** or **C's**; **c's**) **1** third letter of the alphabet. **2** *Mus.* first note of the diatonic scale of C major. **3** third hypothetical person or example. **4** third highest class or category. **5** (as a Roman numeral) 100. **6** (also ©) copyright.

C[2] *symb. Chem.* carbon.

C[3] *abbr.* (also **C.**) Celsius; centigrade.

c. *abbr.* **1** century; centuries. **2** chapter. **3** cent(s). **4** cubic. **5** *Baseball* catcher. **6** circa; about.

CA *abbr.* California (in official postal use).

Ca *symb. Chem.* calcium.

cab /kab/ *n.* **1** taxi. **2** driver's compartment in a truck, train, crane, etc.

ca•bal /kəbál/ *n.* **1** secret intrigue. **2** political clique see synonym study at PLOT.

■ **1** plot, conspiracy, scheme, machination. **2** junta, faction, set, sect, coterie, body, band.

cab•a•ret /kabəráy/ *n.* **1** entertainment in a nightclub or restaurant. **2** such a nightclub, etc.

■ **1** floor show, show, performance, amusement.

cab•bage /kábij/ *n.* vegetable with thick green or purple leaves forming a round heart or head.

cab•by /kábee/ *n.* (also **cab'bie**) (*pl.* **–bies**) *colloq.* cab driver.

cab•in /kábin/ *n.* **1** small shelter or house, esp. of wood. **2** room or compartment in an aircraft or ship. □ **cabin fever** state of restlessness and irritability from having been confined for an extended period.
  ■ **1** hut, shack, cottage, shanty, shelter. **2** berth.

cab•i•net /kábinit/ *n.* **1 a** cupboard or case for storing or displaying articles. **b** piece of furniture housing a radio or television, etc. **2** (**Cabinet**) committee of senior government advisers.
  ■ **1 a** bureau, commode, chiffonier, chest (of drawers), tallboy, highboy, lowboy. **2** council, ministry.

cab•i•net•mak•er /kábinitmáykər/ *n.* skilled furniture maker.

cab•i•net•ry /kábinitree/ *n.* finished woodwork, esp. of professional quality.

ca•ble /káybəl/ • *n.* **1** thick rope of wire or hemp. **2** encased group of insulated wires for transmitting electricity or electrical signals. **3** cablegram. • *v.tr.* **1** transmit (a message) by cablegram. **2** inform (a person) by cablegram. □ **cable-ready** (of a TV, VCR, etc.) designed for direct connection to a coaxial cable TV system. **cable television** broadcasting system with signals transmitted by cable to subscribers' sets.
  ■ *n.* **1** wire, line, lead, chain, strand, twine, guy. **2** lead, cord. • *v.* **1, 2** telegraph, radio, *colloq.* wire; see also TRANSMIT 1a.

ca•ble•gram /káybəlgram/ *n.* telegraph message sent by undersea cable, etc.

ca•boose /kəbóos/ *n.* crew car at the rear of a freight train.

ca•ca•o /kəkaa-ō, -káyō/ *n.* (*pl.* **-os**) **1** seed pod from which cocoa and chocolate are made. **2** small, widely cultivated evergreen tree bearing these.

cache /kash/ • *n.* **1** hiding place for treasure, provisions, ammunition, etc. **2** what is hidden in a cache. • *v.tr.* put in a cache.
  ■ *n.* **1** hole, vault, repository, stash. **2** store, hoard, supply, reserve, stock, fund. • *v.* hide, store, conceal, hoard, put *or* stash away.

ca•chet /kasháy/ *n.* **1** distinguishing mark or seal. **2** prestige.
  ■ **1** stamp, sign, hallmark, tag. **2** distinction, importance, status, stature, reputation, renown, prominence, preeminence, superiority, merit, value.

cack•le /kákəl/ • *n.* **1** clucking sound as of a hen or a goose. **2** loud, silly laugh. **3** noisy, inconsequential talk. • *v.* **1** *intr.* emit a cackle. **2** *intr.* talk noisily and inconsequentially. **3** *tr.* utter or express with a cackle.
  ■ *n.* **3** see PRATTLE *n.* • *v.* **1, 3** see SQUAWK *v.* **2** see JABBER *v.* 1.

ca•coph•o•ny /kəkófonee/ *n.* (*pl.* **-nies**) **1** harsh discordant mixture of sound. **2** dissonance; discord. □□ **ca•coph'o•nous** *adj.*

cac•tus /káktəs/ *n.* (*pl.* **cac•ti** /-tī/ or **cac•tus•es**) succulent plant with a thick fleshy stem and usu. spines but no leaves.

CAD /kad/ *abbr.* computer-aided design.

cad /kad/ *n.* person (esp. a man) who behaves dishonorably. □□ **cad'dish** *adj.* **cad'dish•ly** *adv.* **cad'dish•ness** *n.*
  ■ see ROGUE *n.* 1.

ca•dav•er /kədávər/ *n.* esp. *Med.* corpse.
  ■ (dead) body, remains, *sl.* stiff.

ca•dav•er•ous /kədávərəs/ *adj.* **1** corpselike. **2** deathly pale.

cad•die /kádee/ (also **cad'dy**) • *n.* (*pl.* **-dies**) person who assists a golfer during a match, by carrying clubs, etc. • *v.intr.* (**cad•dies, cad•died, cad•dy•ing**) act as caddie.

cad•dy¹ /kádee/ *n.* (*pl.* **-dies**) small container, esp. a box for holding tea.

cad•dy² var. of CADDIE.

ca•dence /káyd'ns/ *n.* **1** fall in pitch of the voice, esp. at the end of a phrase or sentence. **2** intonation; tonal inflection. **3** *Mus.* close of a musical phrase. **4** rhythm; measure or beat of sound or movement. □□ **ca'denced** *adj.*
  ■ **2** see INTONATION 1. **4** tempo, accent, pulse, meter.

ca•den•za /kədénzə/ *n. Mus.* virtuosic passage for a solo instrument or voice, sometimes improvised.

ca•det /kədét/ *n.* young trainee, as in the armed services or police force.

cadge /kaj/ *v.* **1** *tr.* get or seek by begging. **2** *intr.* beg. □□ **cadg'er** *n.*

cad•mi•um /kádmeeəm/ *n.* soft, bluish-white metallic element. ¶Symb.: **Cd.** □ **cadmium yellow** an intense yellow pigment.

cad•re /kádree, kaádray/ *n.* basic unit, esp. of servicemen.
  ■ see CORPS.

ca•du•ce•us /kədóoseeəs, -shəs, -dyóo/ *n.* (*pl.* **ca•du•ce•i** /-see-ī/) winged staff of Mercury; symbol of the medical profession.

Cae•sar /séezər/ *n.* **1** title of the Roman emperors, esp. from Augustus to Hadrian. **2** autocrat.

cae•su•ra /sizhóorə, -zóorə/ *n.* (*pl.* **cae•su•ras** or **cae•su•rae** /-zhóoree, -zóoree/) *Prosody* pause near the middle of a line. □□ **cae•su'ral** *adj.*

ca•fé /kafáy/ *n.* (also **ca•fe**) **1** small coffeehouse; simple restaurant. **2** bar. □ **café au lait** /ō láy/ **1** coffee with milk. **2** color of this. **café noir** /nwaar/ black coffee.
  ■ **1** coffee bar, coffee shop, bistro, snack bar, brasserie; tearoom, lunchroom, canteen, diner, cafeteria.

ca•fé con le•che /kafáy kon léchay/ *n.* coffee, esp. strong coffee, with milk.

caf•e•te•ri•a /káfitéereeə/ *n.* restaurant in which customers collect their meals on trays at a counter.

caf•feine /káfeen, kaféen/ *n.* alkaloid drug with stimulant action found in tea leaves and coffee beans.

caf•tan /káftan/ *n.* (also **kaf'tan**) **1** long tunic worn in the Near East. **2 a** long, loose dress. **b** loose shirt or top.

cage /kayj/ • *n.* **1** structure of bars or wires, esp. for confining animals or birds. **2** any similar open framework, as in a freight elevator, etc. • *v.tr.* place or keep in a cage.
  ■ *n.* **1** crate, enclosure, pen, pound, coop, hutch. • *v.* confine, enclose, pen, impound, imprison.

ca•gey /káyjee/ *adj.* (also **cag'y**) (**cag•i•er,**

cag·i·est) *colloq.* cautious and uncommunicative; wary. □□ **cag'i·ly** *adv.* **cag'i·ness** *n.*
■ see WARY.

ca·hoots /kəhŏŏts/ *n.pl.* □ **in cahoots** *sl.* in collusion.

CAI *abbr.* computer-assisted (or –aided) instruction.

cairn /kairn/ *n.* mound of rough stones as a monument or landmark.

cais·son /káyson, –sən/ *n.* watertight chamber in which underwater construction work can be done.

ca·jole /kəjṓl/ *v.tr.* persuade by flattery, deceit, etc. □□ **ca·jole'ment** *n.* **ca·jol'er** *n.* **ca·jol'er·y** *n.*
■ wheedle, coax, beguile, seduce, inveigle, entice, *colloq.* soft-soap, butter (up), sweet-talk, smooth-talk. □□ **cajolery** wheedling, coaxing, blandishment, beguilement, persuasion, blarney, *colloq.* soft soap, buttering up, sweet talk.

cake /kayk/ • *n.* **1** baked mixture of flour, butter, eggs, sugar, etc., often iced. **2** other food in a flat round shape. **3** flattish compact mass. • *v.* **1** *tr. & intr.* form into a compact mass. **2** *tr.* cover (with a hard or sticky mass). □ **piece of cake** *colloq.* something easily achieved.
■ *n.* **1** pastry, bun, gateau. **2** burger, patty, pat. **3** piece, chunk, bar, block, cube, lump, loaf, slab, hunk. • *v.* **1** harden, solidify, thicken, congeal, dry, coagulate, set. **2** encrust, coat, layer. □ **piece of cake** see BREEZE *n.* 2.

Cal *abbr.* large calorie(s).

cal *abbr.* small calorie(s).

cal·a·bash /kálabash/ *n.* **1 a** gourd-bearing evergreen tree native to tropical America. **b** gourd from this tree. **2** shell of this or a similar gourd used as a vessel for water, etc.

cal·a·boose /káləbōōs/ *n. sl.* prison.

cal·a·mine /káləmīn/ *n.* pink powder consisting of zinc carbonate and ferric oxide, used in lotion or ointment.

ca·lam·i·ty /kəlámitee/ *n.* (*pl.* **–ties**) **1** disaster; great misfortune. **2 a** adversity. **b** deep distress. □□ **ca·lam'i·tous** *adj.* **ca·lam'i·tous·ly** *adv.*
■ **1** catastrophe, cataclysm, devastation, tragedy, blight, crisis. **2** affliction, trouble, tragedy, misfortune, hardship. □□ **calamitous** dire, troublesome, woeful, sad, grievous, destructive, ruinous, dreadful, terrible, devastating, desperate, pernicious.

cal·cif·er·ous /kalsífərəs/ *adj.* yielding calcium salts, esp. calcium carbonate.

cal·ci·fy /kálsifī/ *v.* (**–fies, –fied**) **1** harden or become hardened by deposition of calcium salts; petrify. **2** convert or be converted to calcium carbonate. □□ **cal·cif'ic** /–sifik/ *adj.* **cal·ci·fi·ca'tion** *n.*

cal·cine /kálsīn, –sin/ *v.* **1** *tr.* **a** reduce, oxidize, or desiccate by strong heat. **b** burn to ashes. **2** *tr.* consume or purify as if by fire. **3** *intr.* undergo any of these. □□ **cal·ci·na'tion** /–sináyshən/ *n.*

cal·cite /kálsīt/ *n.* natural crystalline calcium carbonate.

cal·ci·um /kálseeəm/ *n.* soft, gray metallic element of the alkaline earth group occurring naturally in limestone, marble, chalk, etc. ¶Symb.: **Ca.** □ **calcium carbonate** white, insoluble solid occurring naturally as chalk, limestone, marble, and calcite.

cal·cu·late /kálkyəlayt/ *v.tr.* **1** ascertain or determine beforehand, esp. by arithmetic. **2** plan deliberately. □□ **cal·cu·la·ble** /–ləbəl/ *adj.* **cal·cu·la·tive** /–lətiv/ *adj.*
■ **1** compute, work out, assess, evaluate, gauge.

cal·cu·lat·ed /kálkyəlaytid/ *adj.* **1** (of an action) done with awareness of the likely consequences. **2** [foll. by *to* + infin.] designed or suitable; intended. □□ **cal'cu·lat·ed·ly** *adv.*
■ **2** arranged, planned, fit, fitted, suited; deliberate, purposeful, purposive, intentional.

cal·cu·lat·ing /kálkyəlayting/ *adj.* shrewd; scheming.
■ conniving, crafty, sly, wily, designing.

cal·cu·la·tion /kálkyəláyshən/ *n.* **1** act or process of calculating. **2** result from calculating. **3** reckoning or forecast.
■ **1** computation, reckoning, estimation, determining. **2** answer, product, figure. **3** projection, expectation.

cal·cu·la·tor /kálkyəlaytər/ *n.* device (esp. a small electronic one) used for making mathematical calculations.

cal·cu·lus /kálkyələs/ *n.* (*pl.* **cal·cu·li** /–lī/ or **cal·cu·lus·es**) **1** *Math.* particular method of calculation or reasoning (*calculus of probabilities*). **2** *Med.* stone or concretion of minerals formed within the body.

cal·dron var. of CAULDRON.

cal·en·dar /kálindər/ *n.* **1** system by which the beginning, length, and subdivisions of the year are fixed. **2** chart or series of pages showing the days, weeks, and months of a particular year. **3** timetable of appointments, special events, etc.
■ **2** almanac, chronicle; journal, diary. **3** schedule, register, diary, listing.

cal·en·der /kálindər/ • *n.* machine in which cloth, paper, etc., is rolled to glaze or smooth it. • *v.tr.* press in a calender.

calf[1] /kaf/ *n.* (*pl.* **calves** /kavz/) **1** young bovine animal. **2** young of other animals, e.g., elephant, deer, and whale. □□ **calf'hood** *n.* **calf'ish** *adj.* **calf'like** *adj.*

calf[2] /kaf/ *n.* (*pl.* **calves** /kavz/) fleshy hind part of the human leg below the knee.

calf·skin /káfskin/ *n.* calf leather.

cal·i·ber /kálibər/ *n.* **1 a** internal diameter of a gun or tube. **b** diameter of a bullet or shell. **2** strength or quality of character; importance. □□ **cal'i·bered** *adj.* [also in *comb.*]
■ **1** size, bore, gauge, width, breadth. **2** merit, capability, competence, proficiency, capacity, stature.

cal·i·brate /kálibrayt/ *v.tr.* **1** mark (a gauge) with a scale of readings. **2** correlate the readings of (an instrument) with a standard. □□ **cal·i·bra·tion** /–bráyshən/ *n.* **cal'i·bra·tor** *n.*
■ adjust, tune (up), regulate, attune, align, set; graduate, scale, grade; standardize.

cal·i·co /káliko/ • *n.* (*pl.* **–coes** or **–cos**)

printed cotton fabric. • *adj.* **1** made of calico. **2** multicolored; piebald.

Calif. *abbr.* California.

cal•i•for•ni•um /kálifáwrneeəm/ *n. Chem.* transuranic radioactive metallic element produced artificially. ¶Symb.: **Cf.**

cal•i•per /kálipər/ *n.* [in *pl.*] compasses for measuring diameters or internal dimensions.

ca•liph /káylif, kál–/ *n.* esp. *hist.* chief Muslim civil and religious ruler. □□ **ca'liph•ate** *n.*

cal•is•then•ics /kálisthéniks/ *n.pl.* fitness exercises. □□ **cal•is•then'ic** *adj.*

calk var. of CAULK.

call /kawl/ • *v.* **1** *intr.* **a** cry; shout; speak loudly. **b** (of a bird or animal) emit its characteristic note or cry. **2** *tr.* communicate with by telephone or radio. **3** *tr.* summon. **4** *intr.* pay a brief visit (*called at the house*). **5** *tr.* announce or order to take place. **6** *tr.* name; describe as. **7** *intr.* guess the outcome of tossing a coin, etc. **8** *intr.* [foll. by *for*] order; demand (*called for silence*). **9** *intr.* [foll. by *on, upon*] appeal to; request (*called on us to be quiet*). • *n.* **1** shout or cry. **2 a** characteristic cry of a bird or animal. **b** imitation of this. **c** instrument for imitating it. **3** brief visit (*paid them a call*). **4** act of telephoning. **5** invitation; appeal. **6** duty, need, or occasion (*no call to be rude*). **7** signal on a bugle, etc. **8** *Stock Exch.* option of buying stock at a fixed price at a given date. □ **call girl** female prostitute who accepts appointments by telephone. **calling card 1** card with a person's name, etc., sent or left in lieu of a personal visit. **2** identifying mark, etc., left behind (by someone). **3** card used to pay for a telephone call. **call off 1** cancel (an arrangement, etc.). **2** order (an attacker or pursuer) to desist. **call of nature** a need to urinate or defecate. **call out 1** summon (troops, etc.) to action. **2** order (workers) to strike. **call the shots** (or **tune**) be in control; take the initiative. **call to order 1** request to be orderly. **2** declare (a meeting) open. **call up 1** reach by telephone. **2** imagine; recollect. **3** summon, esp. to military duty. **on call** (of a doctor, etc.) available if required.

■ *v.* **1 a** hail, yell, roar, bellow, bawl, howl, *colloq.* holler. **2** call up, telephone, dial, *colloq.* buzz, phone, give a person a ring, radio. **3** collect, muster, rally, assemble, convene, *formal* convoke; page, send for. **4** call at or on, visit, attend, look in, stop in or by, pop in or by, come by, *colloq.* drop in or by. **5** see AR RANGE 2, see ORDER *v.* 1, 2. **6** designate, denominate, term, style, nickname, label, title, tag, identify, dub, christen. **8** (*call for*) see DEMAND *v.* 1. **9** (*call on*) invoke, entreat, ask. • *n.* **1** yell, hail, whoop, *colloq.* holler. **2 a** song. **4** telephone call, phone call, *colloq.* ring, *sl.* buzz. **5** summons, bidding, notice, notification, order, demand, command, dictate, instruction, requisition; request, entreaty, plea, petition; vocation, calling. **6** reason, justification, case, pretext, ground(s), cause, motive, right, excuse; requirement; responsibility. □ **call off 1** see POSTPONE. **call the shots** (or **tune**) be in charge or command, rule the roost, be in the driver's seat, be in the saddle, be at the wheel, pull the

strings, *colloq.* run the show. **call up 1** see CALL *v.* 2 above. **2** see IMAGINE 1. **3** enlist, recruit, conscript, draft. **on call** ready, on duty, standing by, on standby, awaiting orders.

call•er /káwlər/ *n.* person who calls, esp. one who pays a visit or makes a telephone call.

■ see *visitor* (VISIT).

cal•lig•ra•phy /kəlígrəfee/ *n.* art of fine handwriting. □□ **cal•lig'ra•pher** *n.* **cal•li•graph•ic** /káligráfik/ *adj.* **cal•lig'ra•phist** *n.*

call•ing /káwling/ *n.* profession or occupation.

■ business, trade, employment, work, line, job, métier, pursuit, career, craft, area, province.

cal•li•o•pe /kəlíəpee/ *n.* keyboard instrument resembling an organ, with a set of steam whistles producing musical notes.

cal•lous /kálos/ *adj.* **1** unfeeling; insensitive. **2** (of skin) hardened. □□ **cal'lous•ly** *adv.* (in sense 1). **cal'lous•ness** *n.*

■ **1** thick-skinned, uncaring, hard-hearted, cold-hearted, heartless, cruel, ruthless. **2** tough, leathery.

cal•low /kálō/ *adj.* inexperienced; immature. See synonym study at GULLIBLE. See synonym study at RUDE. See synonym study at YOUTHFUL.

■ young, naive, green, guileless, unsophisticated, innocent.

cal•lus /káləs/ *n.* hard thick area of skin or tissue.

calm /kaam/ • *adj.* **1** tranquil; quiet; windless. **2** settled; not agitated. • *n.* **1** state of being calm; stillness; serenity. **2** period without wind or storm. • *v.* make or become calm. □□ **calm'ly** *adv.* **calm'ness** *n.*

■ *adj.* **1** still, serene, peaceful, balmy, halcyon, undisturbed, windless. **2** composed, cool, controlled, self-controlled, impassive, dispassionate, unexcitable, unruffled, equable, collected, sedate, stoical, *colloq.* laidback, together. • *n.* **1** tranquillity, composure, placidity, placidness, sangfroid, coolness, self-control, equanimity, self-possession; motionlessness. **2** hush, peace; see also LULL *n.*

SYNONYM STUDY: calm

HALCYON, PEACEFUL, PLACID, SERENE, TRANQUIL. We usually speak of the weather or the sea as **calm**, meaning free from disturbance or storm. When applied to people and their feelings or moods, **calm** implies an unruffled state, often under disturbing conditions (*to remain calm in the face of disaster*). **Halcyon** is another adjective associated with the weather (*the halcyon days of summer*); it comes from the name of a mythical bird, usually identified with the kingfisher, that builds its nest on the sea and possesses a magical power to calm the winds and waves. **Peaceful** also suggests a lack of turbulence or disorder, although it is usually applied to situations, scenes, and activities rather than to people (*a peaceful gathering of protesters; a peaceful resolution to their problems*). Often, however,

peaceful is used of a corpse (*Aunt Helen looks so peaceful now*). **Serene, tranquil,** and **placid** are more often used to describe human states of being. *Serene* suggests a lofty and undisturbed calmness (*the monastery is severe, spacious, and very serene*), while *tranquil* implies an intrinsic calmness (*they led a tranquil life in the country*). **Placid** usually refers to a prevailing tendency and is sometimes used disparagingly to suggest a lack of responsiveness or a dull complacency (*with her placid disposition, she seldom got involved in family arguments*).

---

ca•lor•ic /kəláwrik, –lór–/ *adj.* of heat or calories.

cal•o•rie /kálэree/ *n.* unit of quantity of heat: **1** (in full **small calorie**) amount needed to raise the temperature of 1 gram of water through 1°C. ¶Abbr.: **cal. 2** (in full **large calorie**) amount needed to raise the temperature of 1 kilogram of water through 1°C, often used to measure the energy value of foods. ¶Abbr.: **Cal.**

cal•o•rif•ic /kálərífik/ *adj.* producing heat.

cal•u•met /kályəmét/ *n.* Native American ceremonial peace pipe.

ca•lum•ni•ate /kəlúmneeayt/ *v.tr.* slander. See synonym study at MALIGN. □□ **ca•lum•ni•a•tion** /–neeáyshən/ *n.* **ca•lum′ni•a•tor** *n.*

cal•um•ny /kálэmnee/ *n.* (*pl.* **–nies**) slander. □□ **ca•lum•ni•ous** /–lúmneeəs/ *adj.*

cal•va•dos /kálvədōs/ *n.* (also **Cal•va•dos**) apple brandy.

calve /kav/ *v.intr.* give birth to a calf.

calves *pl.* of CALF[1], CALF[2].

Cal•vin•ism /kálvinizəm/ *n.* theology of J. Calvin (d. 1564) or his followers, in which predestination and justification by faith are important elements. □□ **Cal′vin•ist** *n.* **Cal•vin•is′tic** *adj.*

ca•lyp•so /kəlípsō/ *n.* (*pl.* **–sos**) W. Indian musical style with syncopated rhythm.

ca•lyx /káyliks, kál–/ *n.* (*pl.* **ca•lyx•es** or **ca•ly•ces** /–liseez/) **1** *Bot.* sepals collectively, forming the protective layer of a flower in bud. **2** *Biol.* any cuplike cavity or structure.

cam /kam/ *n.* projection on a rotating part in machinery, shaped to impart a particular motion.

ca•ma•ra•de•rie /kaàmərəàdəree/ *n.* mutual trust and sociability among friends.

cam•ber /kámbər/ • *n.* slightly convex or arched shape of the surface of a ship's deck, aircraft wing, etc. • *v.* **1** *intr.* (of a surface) have a camber. **2** *tr.* build with a camber.

Cam•bo•di•an /kambódeeən/ • *n.* **1 a** native or national of Cambodia (Kampuchea) in SE Asia. **b** person of Cambodian descent. **2** language of Cambodia. • *adj.* of or relating to Cambodia or its people or language.

Cam•bri•an /kámbreeən/ • *adj.* **1** Welsh. **2** *Geol.* of the first period in the Paleozoic era. • *n.* this period.

cam•bric /kámbrik/ *n.* a fine white linen or cotton fabric.

cam•cor•der /kámkawrdər/ *n.* combined video camera and sound recorder.

came *past* of COME.

cam•el /káməl/ *n.* large, cud-chewing mammal having slender legs and one hump (**Arabian camel**) or two humps (**Bactrian camel**).

ca•mel•li•a /kəméelyə/ *n.* evergreen shrub native to E. Asia, with shiny leaves and showy flowers.

Cam•em•bert /káməmbair/ *n.* a soft, creamy cheese, usu. with a strong flavor.

cam•e•o /kámeeō/ *n.* (*pl.* **–os**) **1** relief carving with a background of a different color. **2** small character part in a play or film played by a distinguished actor.

cam•er•a /kámrə, kámərə/ *n.* **1** apparatus for taking still or motion pictures. **2** *Telev.* equipment that converts images into electrical impulses for transmission or storage. □ **in camera** *Law* in a judge's private room.

cam•i•sole /kámisōl/ *n.* an upper-body undergarment.

cam•o•mile var. of CHAMOMILE.

cam•ou•flage /káməflaazh/ • *n.* **1** disguising of soldiers, vehicles, aircraft, etc., so that they blend with their surroundings. **2** such a disguise. **3** misleading or evasive precaution or expedient. • *v.tr.* hide by camouflage.

■ *n.* **1** concealment. **3** smokescreen, coverup, cover, cloak, mask, screen, blind. • *v.* disguise, cloak, mask, cover (up), obscure, conceal, screen, veil, shroud, dress up.

camp[1] /kamp/ • *n.* **1** place where troops are lodged or trained. **2** temporary accommodations, as huts or tents. **3** adherents of a particular party or doctrine regarded collectively. • *v.intr.* set up or spend time in a camp. □□ **camp′ing** *n.*

■ *n.* **1** base, station, barrack(s), cantonment, encampment. **3** faction, wing, front, set, coterie, clique, side, group, lobby. • *v.* encamp, tent, lodge, bivouac.

camp[2] /kamp/ *colloq.* • *adj.* done in an exaggerated way for effect. • *v.* behave or do in a camp way. □□ **camp′y** *adj.* (**camp•i•er, camp•i•est**). **camp′i•ly** *adv.* **camp′i•ness** *n.*

■ *adj.* outré, outrageous, outlandish, affected, extravagant. • *v.* overact, go too far, overdo it.

cam•paign /kampáyn/ • *n.* **1** organized course of action. **2** series of military operations. • *v.intr.* conduct or take part in a campaign. □□ **cam•paign′er** *n.*

■ *n.* **1** drive, offensive, push, effort, crusade; strategy, plan. **2** maneuver(s), movement, crusade, action, offensive. • *v.* run, compete, vie, contend, stump; (*campaign for*) promote, support, back, advocate, champion.

cam•pa•ni•le /kámpəneélee, –neél/ *n.* bell tower (usu. freestanding), esp. in Italy.

camp•er /kámpər/ *n.* **1** person who camps. **2** large motor vehicle with beds, etc.

cam•phor /kámfər/ *n.* white, crystalline volatile substance with aromatic smell used to make celluloid and in medicine.

camp•site /kámpsit/ *n.* place suitable for camping.

cam•pus /kámpəs/ *n.* (*pl.* **cam•pus•es**)

cam•shaft /kámshaft/ n. shaft with one or more cams.

can[1] /kan, kən/ v.aux. (past **could** /kŏŏd/) **1 a** be able to; know how to (I can run fast, can you speak German?). **b** be potentially capable of (you can do it if you try). **2** be permitted to (can we go to the party?).

can[2] /kan/ n. **1** metal vessel for liquid. **2** metal container in which food or drink is sealed. **3** [prec. by the] sl. **a** prison. **b** toilet. • v.tr. (**canned, can•ning**) put or preserve in a can. □ **can of worms** colloq. complicated problem. **in the can** colloq. completed; ready. □□ **can'ner** n.
■ n. **1, 2** see RECEPTACLE. **3 a** see PRISON 1. **b** see TOILET. • v. see PRESERVE v. 3.

Can•a•da goose /kánədə/ n. wild goose of N. America, with a brownish-gray body and white cheeks and breast.

ca•nal /kənál/ n. **1** artificial waterway for inland navigation or irrigation. **2** tubular duct in a plant or animal.
■ **1** see CHANNEL n. 5.

ca•na•pé /kánəpay, –pee/ n. small piece of bread or pastry with a savory food on top, often served as an hors d'oeuvre.

ca•nard /kənaárd/ n. unfounded rumor or story.

ca•nar•y /kənáiree/ n. (pl. **–ies**) songbird native to the Canary Islands, with mainly yellow plumage.

ca•nas•ta /kənástə/ n. **1** card game using two decks and resembling rummy. **2** set of seven cards in this game.

can•can /kánkan/ n. lively stage dance with high kicking.

can•cel /kánsəl/ v. (**can•celed, can•cel•ing; can•celled, can•cel•ling**) **1** tr. withdraw, revoke, or discontinue (an arrangement). **2** tr. obliterate; delete; invalidate. **3** intr. & tr. neutralize; counterbalance. **4** tr. Math. strike out (an equal factor) on each side of an equation, etc. □□ **can•cel•la'tion** n.
■ **1** call off, retract, rescind, colloq. scrub, sl. nix, see also STOP v. 1c. **2** cross or strike or blot or scratch out, rub out, erase, Printing dele; expunge, efface, eradicate, void **3** nullify, countervail, counter, compensate (for), make up for, offset, counteract. □□ **cancellation** annulment, nullification, abrogation, invalidation, withdrawal, revocation; deletion, elimination; discontinuance, termination, stoppage.

can•cer /kánsər/ n. **1** malignant growth or tumor of body cells. **2** evil influence or corruption spreading uncontrollably. **3** (**Cancer**) **a** constellation and fourth sign of the zodiac (the Crab). **b** person born under this sign. □□ **Can•cer•i•an** /–sérecən/ n. & adj. (in sense 3). □□ **can'cer•ous** adj.
■ n. **2** see ULCER 1. **3** see POISON n. 2.

can•de•la•brum /kánd'laábrəm/ n. (also **can•de•la•bra** /–brə/) (pl. **can•de•la•bra, can•de•la•brums, can•de•la•bras**) large branched candlestick or lamp holder.

can•did /kándid/ adj. **1** frank. **2** (of a photograph) taken informally. □□ **can'did•ly** adv. **can'did•ness** n.
■ **1** open, plain, sincere, ingenuous,

straight, straightforward, truthful, honest, colloq. upfront, on the level. **2** unposed, impromptu.

can•di•date /kándidət, –dayt/ n. nominee, office seeker, or entrant. □□ **can•di•da•cy** /–dəsee/ n.
■ runner; interviewee; prospect.

can•dle /kánd'l/ n. cylinder or block of wax or tallow with a central wick, for giving light when burning. □ **cannot hold a candle to** cannot be compared with; is much inferior to. □□ **can'dler** n.
■ light, taper, votive.

can•dle•light /kánd'l-līt/ n. light provided by candles. □□ **can'dle•lit** adj.

can•dle•power /kánd'lpowr/ n. unit of luminous intensity.

can•dle•stick /kánd'lstik/ n. holder for one or more candles.

can•dor /kándər/ n. candid behavior or action.
■ openness, frankness, straightness, straightforwardness, ingenuousness, simplicity, naïveté.

can•dy /kándee/ n. (pl. **–dies**) sweet confection, usu. containing sugar, chocolate, etc. • v.tr. (**–dies, –died**) (usu. as **candied** adj.) preserve by coating and impregnating with a sugar syrup (candied fruit). □ **candy stripe** pattern consisting of alternate stripes of white and a color (usu. pink). **candy striper** hospital volunteer, esp. a teenager
■ n. sweet(s), bonbon(s), sweetmeat(s), confectionery. • v. (**candied**) sugar-coated, preserved, crystallized.

cane /kayn/ • n. **1 a** hollow jointed stem of giant reeds or grasses. **b** solid stem of slender palms. **2** = sugar cane. **3** material of cane used for wickerwork, etc. **4** cane used as a walking stick or an instrument of punishment. • v.tr. **1** beat with a cane. **2** weave cane into (a chair, etc.). □ **cane sugar** sugar obtained from sugar cane. □□ **can•er** n. (in sense 2 of v.). **can•ing** n.
■ n. **1** see STEM[1] 1, 2. **4** see STICK[1] 1b. • v. **1** see BEAT v. 1.

ca•nine /káynīn/ • adj. of a dog or dogs. • n. **1** dog. **2** (in full **canine tooth**) pointed tooth between incisors and premolars

can•is•ter /kánistər/ n. **1** rigid container for storage. **2** cylinder of shot, tear gas, etc.

can•ker /kángkər/ • n. **1** destructive fungus disease of trees and plants. **2** Zool. ulcerous ear disease of animals, esp. cats and dogs. **3** corrupting influence. • v.tr. **1** consume with canker. **2** corrupt. □□ **can'ker•ous** adj.
■ n. see ULCER 1. **3** see POISON n. 2.

can•na•bis /kánəbis/ n. **1** hemp plant. **2** parts of this used as an intoxicant or hallucinogen.

canned /kand/ adj. **1** prerecorded. **2** supplied in a can.

can•nel•lo•ni /kánəlṓnee/ n.pl. tubes or rolls of pasta stuffed with meat or a vegetable mixture.

can•ner•y /kánəree/ n. (pl. **–ies**) canning factory.

can•ni•bal /kánibəl/ n. **1** person who eats human flesh. **2** animal that feeds on flesh of its own species. □□ **can'ni•bal•ism** n. **can'ni•bal•is'tic** adj.

can•ni•bal•ize /kánibəliz/ v.tr. use (a machine, etc.) as a source of spare parts for others. □□ **can•ni•bal•i•za'tion** n.

can•non /kánən/ n. hist. (pl. same) heavy gun installed on a carriage or mounting.

can•non•ade /kánənáyd/ • n. period of continuous heavy gunfire. • v.tr. bombard with a cannonade.

can•non•ball /kánənbawl/ n. large, usu. metal ball fired by a cannon.

can•not /kánot, kanót/ v.aux. can not.

can•ny /kánee/ adj. (**can•ni•er, can•ni•est**) shrewd; worldly-wise. □□ **can'ni•ly** adv. **can'ni•ness** n.

■ see SHREWD.

ca•noe /kənóó/ • n. narrow boat with pointed ends usu. propelled by paddling. • v.intr. (**ca•noes, ca•noed, ca•noe•ing**) travel in a canoe. □□ **ca•noe'ist** n.

can•o•la oil' /kənólə/ n. type of cooking oil derived from the seed of a variety of the rape plant.

can•on /kánən/ n. **1 a** general law, rule, principle, or criterion. **b** church decree or law. **2** (fem. **can•on•ess**) member of a cathedral chapter. **3** collection or list of books, etc., accepted as genuine. **4** Mus. piece with different parts taking up the same theme successively. □ **canon law** ecclesiastical law.

ca•non•i•cal /kənónikəl/ adj. (also **ca•non•ic** /kənónik/) **1 a** according to or ordered by canon law. **b** included in the canon of Scripture. **2** authoritative; standard; accepted. □□ **ca•non'i•cal•ly** adv.

can•on•ize /kánəniz/ v.tr. declare officially to be or regard as a saint. □□ **can•on•i•za'tion** n.

can•o•py /kánəpee/ n. (pl. **–pies**) **1** covering hung or held up over a throne, bed, person, etc. **2** overhanging shelter.

canst /kanst/ archaic 2nd person sing. present of CAN[1].

cant[1] /kant/ n. **1** insincere pious or moral talk. **2** language peculiar to a class, profession, sect, etc.; jargon. See synonym study at DIALECT.

■ **1** hypocrisy, insincerity, sham, pretense, humbug, sanctimony, sanctimoniousness. **2** argot, vernacular, idiom, slang, colloq. lingo.

cant[2] /kant/ • n. **1** slanting surface; bevel. **2** oblique push or movement. **3** tilted or sloping position. • v.tr. push or pitch out of level; tilt.

can't /kant/ contr. can not.

can•ta•loupe /kánt'lōp/ n. variety of melon with orange flesh.

can•tan•ker•ous /kantángkərəs/ adj. bad-tempered; quarrelsome. □□ **can•tan'ker•ous•ly** adv. **can•tan'ker•ous•ness** n.

■ ill-natured, cross, grumpy, choleric, cross-grained, crabby, curmudgeonly, crusty, surly, irascible, contrary, cranky, colloq. grouchy, literary atrabilious.

can•ta•ta /kəntaátə/ n. Mus. short composition with vocal solos and usu. chorus and orchestral accompaniment.

can•teen /kanteén/ n. **1 a** restaurant for employees in an office or factory, etc. **b** store selling provisions or liquor in a barracks or camp. **2** water flask.

■ **1** see CAFÉ 1.

cant•er /kántər/ • n. gentle gallop. • v.intr. (of a horse or its rider) go at a canter.

can•ti•cle /kántikəl/ n. **1** song or chant with a Biblical text. **2** (also **Can'ticle of Can'ticles**) the Song of Solomon.

can•ti•le•ver /kánt'leevər, –evər/ **1** long bracket or beam, etc., projecting from a wall to support a balcony, etc. **2** beam or girder fixed at only one end. □ **cantilever bridge** bridge made of cantilevers projecting from the piers and connected by girders.

can•to /kántō/ n. (pl. **–tos**) division of a long poem.

can•ton /kánton/ n. **1** subdivision of a country. **2** state of the Swiss confederation. □□ **can•ton•al** /kánt'nəl, kantónəl/ adj.

can•tor /kántər/ n. liturgical leader in a synagogue or church.

can•vas /kánvəs/ n. **1 a** strong coarse kind of cloth used for sails and tents, etc., and as a surface for oil painting. **b** piece of this. **2** painting on canvas, esp. in oils. • v.tr. (**can•vased, can•vas•ing; can•vassed, can•vass•ing**) cover with canvas. □ **under canvas 1** in a tent or tents. **2** with sails spread.

can•vass /kánvəs/ • v. **1** intr. solicit votes. **2** tr. ascertain opinions of. • n. canvassing, esp. of electors. □□ **can'vass•er** n.

• v. **2** survey, poll, study, examine. • n. solicitation, campaign; survey, study, investigation, poll.

can•yon /kányən/ n. deep gorge, often with a stream or river.

■ ravine, gully, pass, defile, coulée, gulch.

cap /kap/ • n. **1** covering for the head, often soft and with a visor. **2** device to seal a bottle or protect the point of a pen, lens of a camera, etc. **3** = CROWN n. 9b. • v.tr. (**capped, cap•ping**) **1 a** put a cap on. **b** cover the top or end of. **c** set a limit to (rate-capping). **2 a** lie on top of; form the cap of. **b** surpass; excel. □□ **cap'ful** n. (pl. **–fuls**). **cap'ping** n.

■ n. **1** hat, head covering; mortarboard. **2** lid, top, cover, covering. • v. **1 a, b** protect, shelter, shield, screen, sheathe. **c** curb, check, restrain. **2 a** see COVER v. 2a. **b** exceed, break, top, improve on, outdo, outmatch.

cap. abbr. **1** capital. **2** capital letter. **3** chapter.

ca•pa•bil•i•ty /káypəbilitee/ n. (pl. **–ties**) **1** ability; power; condition of being capable. **2** undeveloped or unused faculty.

■ capacity, means, faculty, talent, gift, touch, proficiency, aptitude, facility, adeptness; potential, promise.

ca•pa•ble /káypəbəl/ adj. **1** competent; able. **2 a** having the ability or fitness, etc., for. **b** susceptible or admitting of (explanation or improvement, etc.). □□ **ca'pa•bly** adv.

1 efficient, proficient, qualified, experienced, effectual. **2 a** (*capable of*) disposed to, inclined to, predisposed to; up to.

ca•pa•cious /kəpáyshəs/ *adj.* roomy; able to hold much. □□ **ca•pa′cious•ly** *adv.* **ca•pa′cious•ness** *n.*

ca•pac•i•tance /kəpásit'ns/ *n.* *Electr.* **1** ability of a system to store an electric charge. **2** ratio of the change in an electric charge in a system to the corresponding change in its electric potential. ¶Symb.: **C.**

ca•pac•i•tor /kəpásitər/ *n.* *Electr.* device used to store an electric charge.

ca•pac•i•ty /kəpásitee/ *n.* (*pl.* **–ties**) **1 a** power of containing, receiving, experiencing, or producing (*capacity for heat, pain,* etc.). **b** maximum amount that can be contained or produced, etc. **2** mental power. **3** position or function (*in a civil capacity*). **4** legal competence. □□ **ca•pac•i•ta•tive** /-táytiv/ *adj.*

■ **1 a** see POTENTIAL *n.* 1. **b** volume, content, size; range, scope, extent, reach, limit; room, space. **2** potential, ability, capability, competence, intelligence, brainpower, cleverness, brightness, wit. **3** condition, character, place, post, role, job, office, duty, responsibility. **4** *Law* competency, qualification.

ca•par•i•son /kəpárisən/ • *n.* **1** [usu. in *pl.*] horse's trappings. **2** equipment; finery. • *v.tr.* put caparisons on; adorn.

cape¹ /kayp/ *n.* sleeveless cloak.

■ mantle, shawl, stole, wrap.

cape² /kayp/ *n.* **1** headland or promontory. **2** (**the Cape**) **a** Cape of Good Hope. **b** Cape Cod, Massachusetts.

■ **1** neck, point, tip, ness, bluff, foreland, point, tongue.

ca•per¹ /káypər/ • *v.intr.* jump or run playfully. • *n.* **1** playful jump or leap. **2 a** prank. **b** *sl.* any activity or occupation. □ **cut a caper** (or **capers**) act friskily. □□ **ca′per•er** *n.*

■ *v.* skip, hop, frolic, leap, frisk, romp, bound. • *n.* **1** skip, spring, frolic, hop, gambol, frisk, bound. **2 a** escapade, stunt, trick, *colloq.* shenanigans. **b** affair, matter, thing.

ca•per² /káypər/ *n.* **1** bramblelike shrub. **2** [in *pl.*] its buds pickled for use as flavoring.

cap•il•lar•y /kápəleree/ • *adj.* **1** of or like a hair. **2** (of a tube) of hairlike internal diameter. **3** of one of the delicate ramified blood vessels intervening between arteries and veins. • *n.* (*pl.* **–ies**) **1** capillary tube. **2** capillary blood vessel. □ **capillary action** rise or depression of a liquid in contact with a solid, owing to surface tension, etc.

cap•i•tal¹ /kápit'l/ • *n.* **1** most important town or city of a country, state, or region. **2 a** money or other assets with which a company starts in business. **b** accumulated wealth. **3** capital letter. • *adj.* **1** principal; most important. **2** involving or punishable by death. **3** (of letters of the alphabet) large in size and of the form used to begin sentences and names, etc. □ **capital gain** profit from the sale of investments or property. □□ **cap′i•tal•ly** *adv.*

■ *n.* **2** funds, stocks, finance(s), cash; means, property, resources. **3** upper case let-

111   **capacious ~ captain**

ter. • *adj.* **1** chief, main, major, cardinal. **3** upper case, initial, large, big.

cap•i•tal² /kápit'l/ *n. Archit.* head of a pillar or column.

■ top, crown, cap, cornice.

cap•i•tal•ism /kápit'lizəm/ *n.* economic system in which the production and distribution of goods depend on invested private capital and profit making.

cap•i•tal•ist /kápit'list/ • *n.* **1** person using or possessing capital. **2** advocate of capitalism. • *adj.* of or favoring capitalism. □□ **cap′i•tal•is′tic** *adj.* **cap•i•tal•is′ti•cal•ly** *adv.*

cap•i•tal•ize /kápit'līz/ *v.* **1** *tr.* convert into or provide with capital. **2** *tr.* **a** write (a letter of the alphabet) as a capital. **b** begin (a word) with a capital letter. **3** *intr.* [foll. by *on*] use to one's advantage; profit from. □□ **cap•i•tal•i•za′tion** *n.*

ca•pit•u•late /kəpíchəlayt/ *v.intr.* surrender, esp. on stated conditions. □□ **ca•pit′u•la•tor** *n.* **ca•pit•u•la•to•ry** /-lətáwree/ *adj.*

■ yield, give up *or* in *or* way, submit, succumb.

ca•pon /káypon, -pən/ *n.* domestic cock castrated and fattened for eating.

cap•puc•ci•no /kápoocheenō/ *n.* (*pl.* **–nos**) espresso coffee with milk made frothy with pressurized steam.

ca•price /kəprées/ *n.* **1 a** unaccountable or whimsical change of mind or conduct. **b** tendency to this. **2** work of lively fancy in painting, drawing, or music.

■ **1** see FANCY *n.* 2.

ca•pri•cious /kəpríshəs, -prée-/ *adj.* subject to caprice; unpredictable. □□ **ca•pri′cious•ly** *adv.* **ca•pri′cious•ness** *n.*

■ erratic, unsteady, variable, fitful, unstable, wayward, undependable; giddy, mercurial, volatile, temperamental, wanton, fickle, impulsive.

Cap•ri•corn /kápilkawrn/ *n.* **1** constellation and tenth sign of the zodiac (the Goat). **2** person born under this sign.

cap•size /kápsīz, -síz/ *v.* **1** *tr.* upset or overturn (a boat). **2** *intr.* be capsized. □□ **cap′siz•al** /-sízəl/ *n.*

■ keel, turn upside down, invert, tip over; upset.

cap•stan /kápstən/ *n.* revolving cylinder with a vertical axis, for winding cable, tape, etc.

cap•sule /kápsəl, -sōōl/ *n.* **1** small gelatinous case enclosing a dose of medicine and swallowed with it. **2** detachable compartment of a spacecraft or nose cone of a rocket. **3** enclosing membrane in the body. **4** dry fruit that releases its seeds when ripe. **5** [*attrib.*] concise; highly condensed (*a capsule history*). □□ **cap′su•lar** *adj.* **cap′su•late** *adj.*

■ **1** see PILL 1a.

cap•sul•ize /kápsəlīz, -syōō-/ *v.tr.* put (information, etc.) in compact form.

Capt. *abbr.* Captain.

cap•tain /káptin/ • *n.* **1** chief, leader, or commander. **2 a** army or air force officer next above lieutenant. **b** navy officer in command of a warship; one ranking below commodore or rear admiral and above commander. • *v.tr.* be captain of; lead. □□ cap′tain•cy *n.* (*pl.* –cies). cap′tain•ship *n.*

■ *n.* **1** see CHIEF¹ *n.* • *v.* see LEAD *v.* 6, 7a.

cap•tion /kápshən/ • *n.* **1** title or brief explanation appended to an illustration, cartoon, etc. **2** heading of a chapter or article, etc. • *v.tr.* provide with a caption.

■ *n.* see TITLE *n.* 2.

cap•tious /kápshəs/ *adj.* given to finding fault or raising petty objections. □□ cap′tious•ly *adv.* cap′tious•ness *n.*

cap•ti•vate /káptivayt/ *v.tr.* charm; fascinate. □□ cap′ti•vat•ing *adj.* cap′ti•vat•ing•ly *adv.* cap•ti•va•tion /–váyshən/ *n.*

■ beguile, delight, enamor, enchant, bewitch, enrapture, dazzle, infatuate; intrigue, enthrall, hypnotize.

cap•tive /káptiv/ • *n.* person or animal that has been taken prisoner or confined. • *adj.* **1** taken prisoner. **2** kept in confinement or under restraint. □□ cap•tiv′i•ty *n.*

■ *n.* hostage, detainee, internee; slave, bondsman. • *adj.* imprisoned, incarcerated, confined, caged, locked up. □□ captivity confinement, imprisonment, internment, detention, custody, incarceration.

cap•tor /káptər, –tawr/ *n.* person who captures.

cap•ture /kápchər/ • *v.tr.* **1** take prisoner; seize. **2** portray in permanent form. **3** cause (data) to be stored in a computer. • *n.* act of capturing. □□ cap′tur•er *n.*

■ *v.* **1** catch, lay *or* take hold of, grab, ensnare, entrap, snare, hook; snatch, take possession of, take over, get, net, conquer. **2** see CHARACTERIZE 1, 2. • *n.* seizure, taking, arrest, apprehension.

cap•y•ba•ra /kápəbaárə/ *n.* very large semiaquatic rodent native to S. America.

car /kaar/ *n.* **1** automobile. **2** vehicle that runs on rails, esp. a railroad car or a streetcar. **3** passenger compartment of an elevator, cable railway, balloon, etc. □ **car bomb** terrorist bomb concealed in or under a parked car. □□ car′ful *n.* (*pl.* –fuls).

■ **1** *colloq.* auto, wagon, *sl.* wheels. **2** streetcar, coach, caboose.

ca•rafe /kəráf/ *n.* glass container for water or wine.

car•a•mel /kárəmel, –məl, kaárməl/ *n.* **1 a** sugar or syrup heated until it turns brown, then used as a flavoring or coloring. **b** kind of soft toffee made with sugar, butter, etc., melted and further heated. **2** lightbrown color. □□ car•a•mel•i•za′tion *n.* car′a•mel•ize *v.*

car•a•pace /kárəpays/ *n.* hard upper shell of a turtle or a crustacean.

car•at /kárət/ *n.* unit of weight for precious stones, now equivalent to 200 milligrams.

car•a•van /kárəvan/ *n.* company of merchants or pilgrims, etc., traveling together, esp. across a desert. □□ car′a•van•ner *n.*

car•a•van•sa•ry /kárəvánsəree, –rī/ *n.* (also **car•a•van•se•rai**) Near Eastern inn with a central court.

car•a•way /kárəway/ *n.* umbelliferous plant,

bearing clusters of tiny white flowers. □ **caraway seed** its fruit used as flavoring and as a source of oil.

car•bide /kaárbīd/ *n.* Chem. binary compound of carbon.

car•bine /kaárbeen, –bīn/ *n.* lightweight firearm, usu. a rifle, orig. for cavalry use.

car•bo•hy•drate /kaárbəhídrayt, –bō–/ *n.* Biochem. energy-producing organic compound containing carbon, hydrogen, and oxygen, e.g., starch, glucose, and other sugars.

car•bol•ic /kaarbólik/ *n.* (in full **car•bol′ic ac′id**) phenol.

car•bon /kaárbən/ *n.* **1** nonmetallic element occurring naturally as diamond, graphite, and charcoal, and in all organic compounds. ¶Symb.: **C**. **2 a** = *carbon copy*. **b** = *carbon paper*. □ **carbon copy 1** copy made with carbon paper. **2** person or thing identical or similar to another (*is a carbon copy of his father*). **carbon paper** thin carbon-coated paper used between two sheets of paper when writing to make a copy onto the bottom sheet.

car•bon•ate /kaárbənayt/ • *n.* Chem. salt of carbonic acid. • *v.tr.* **1** impregnate with carbon dioxide; aerate. **2** convert into a carbonate. □□ car•bon•a′tion /–náyshən/ *n.*

car•bon•ic /kaarbónik/ *adj.* Chem. containing carbon. □ **carbonic acid** very weak acid formed from carbon dioxide dissolved in water.

car•bon•if•er•ous /kaárbənífərəs/ *adj.* producing coal.

car•bo•run•dum /kaábərúndəm/ *n.* compound of carbon and silicon used esp. as an abrasive.

car•boy /kaárboy/ *n.* large bottle often held in a frame, used for containing liquids.

car•bun•cle /kaárbungkəl/ *n.* **1** severe abscess in the skin. **2** bright red gem. □□ car•bun•cu•lar /–búngkyələr/ *adj.*

car•bu•re•tor /kaárbəráyttər, –byə–/ *n.* (also **car′bu•rat•or**) apparatus for mixing fuel and air in an internal combustion engine to make an explosive mixture.

car•cass /kaárkəs/ *n.* **1** dead body of an animal. **2** framework of a building, ship, etc.

■ **1** see BODY *n.* 1.

car•cin•o•gen /kaarsínəjən, kaársinəjen/ *n.* any substance that produces cancer. □□ car•ci•no•gen•ic /kaársinəjénik/ *adj.*

car•ci•no•ma /kaársinómə/ *n.* (*pl.* **car•ci•no•mas** or **car•ci•no•ma•ta** /–mətə/) cancer, esp. one arising in epithelial tissue. □□ car•ci•no′ma•tous *adj.*

■ see TUMOR.

card /kaard/ *n.* **1** thick, stiff paper or thin pasteboard. **2** flat piece of this, esp. for writing or printing on. **3** rectangular piece of paper or plastic for identity, etc. **4 a** = PLAYING CARD. **b** [in *pl.*] card playing; a card game. **5** program of events. **6** *colloq.* person, esp. an odd or amusing one (*what a card!*). □ **card-carrying** being a registered member of an organization, esp. a political party or labor union. **in the cards** possible or likely. **put** (or **lay**) **one's cards on the table** reveal one's resources, intentions, etc.

■ *n.* **6** character, eccentric, original; joker, prankster, practical joker. □ **in the cards** probable, expected, in the offing, on the horizon.

card•board /káardbawrd/ *n.* pasteboard or stiff paper, esp. for making cards or boxes.

car•di•ac /káardeeak/ *adj.* of or relating to the heart.

car•di•gan /káardigən/ *n.* sweater fastening down the front.

car•di•nal /káard'nəl/ • *n.* **1** (as a title **Cardinal**) leading dignitary of the RC Church, one of the college electing the pope. **2** small scarlet American songbird. • *adj.* **1** chief; fundamental; on which something hinges. **2** of deep scarlet. □ **cardinal numbers** those denoting quantity (one, two, three, etc.), as opposed to ordinal numbers (first, second, third, etc.). **cardinal points** four main points of the compass (N., S., E., W.). **cardinal virtues** chief moral attributes: justice, prudence, temperance, and fortitude. □□ **car•di•nal•ate** /-nəlayt/ *n.* (in sense 1 of *n.*), **car'di•nal•ly** *adv.* **car'din•al•ship** *n.* (in sense 1 of *n.*).

■ *adj.* **1** important, major, key, special, main, central, principal; first, foremost, leading. **2** cinnabar, vermilion.

car•di•o•gram /káardeeəgram/ *n.* record of muscle activity within the heart, made by a cardiograph.

car•di•o•graph /káardeeəgraf/ *n.* instrument for recording heart muscle activity. □□ **car•di•og'ra•pher** /-deeógrəfər/ *n.* **car•di•og'ra•phy** *n.*

car•di•ol•o•gy /káardeeóləjee/ *n.* branch of medicine concerned with the heart. □□ **car•di•ol'o•gist** *n.*

car•di•o•pul•mo•nar•y re•sus•ci•ta'tion /kardeeópoolmənéree/ *n.* emergency medical procedures for restoring normal heartbeat and breathing to victims of heart failure, drowning, etc. ¶Abbr.: **CPR.**

car•di•o•vas•cu•lar /káardeeóváskyələr/ *adj.* of or relating to the heart and blood vessels.

card•sharp /káardshaarp/ *n.* (also **card' sharp•er**) swindler at card games.

care /kair/ • *n.* **1** worry; anxiety. **2** occasion for this. **3** serious attention; heed; caution; pains (*assembled with care*). **4** protection; charge. • *v.intr.* **1** feel concern or interest. **2** wish or be willing to (*do not care to be seen with him*). □ **care for** provide for, look after. **care of** at the address of (*sent it care of his sister*). **have a care** take care; be careful. **2** have worries or responsibilities (*don't have a care in the world*). **take care** be careful. **take care of** look after.

■ *n.* **1, 2** trouble, anguish, uneasiness, disquiet, distress, grief, sorrow, sadness, suffering, misery, tribulation, see also BURDEN *n.* 1, 2. **3** thought, consideration, deliberation, awareness, pains; vigilance, mindfulness. **4** responsibility, guardianship, custody, safekeeping, trust; control, direction, supervision. • *v.* **1** worry, fret, trouble, mind.

ca•reen /kəréen/ *v.* **1** *tr.* turn (a ship) on one side for cleaning, caulking, or repair.

2 a *intr.* tilt; lean over. **b** *tr.* cause to do this. **3** *intr.* swerve about. □□ **ca•reen'age** *n.*

■ **2** see TILT *v.* 1. **3** career, sway, veer, swerve, lurch, reel.

ca•reer /kəréer/ • *n.* **1** one's advancement through life, esp. in a profession. **2** profession; occupation. • *v.intr.* **1** move or swerve about wildly. **2** go swiftly.

■ *n.* **1** life's work *or* journey. **2** job, trade, craft, métier. • *v.* **1** see SWERVE *v.* **2** speed, race, rush, dash.

care•free /káirfree/ *adj.* free from anxiety or responsibility; lighthearted.

■ nonchalant, easy, easygoing, insouciant, blithe.

care•ful /káirfool/ *adj.* **1** painstaking; thorough. **2** cautious. **3** taking care; not neglecting. See synonym study at VIGILANT. □□ **care'ful•ly** *adv.* **care'ful•ness** *n.*

■ **1** meticulous, attentive, punctilious, accurate, assiduous, diligent, particular, finicky. **2** wary, circumspect, guarded, chary, prudent.

care•giv•er /káirgivər/ *n.* person who provides care for children, the sick, the elderly, etc.

care•less /káirlis/ *adj.* **1** not taking care nor paying attention. **2** unthinking; insensitive. **3** lighthearted. □□ **care'less•ly** *adv.* **care'less•ness** *n.*

■ **1** negligent, thoughtless, foolhardy, absentminded, unobservant, unthinking, unmindful. **2** unconcerned, thoughtless, casual, blithe. **3** see CAREFREE.

ca•ress /kərés/ • *v.tr.* touch or stroke gently or lovingly. • *n.* loving or gentle touch.

■ *v.* pet, fondle, pat, cuddle. • *n.* stroke, embrace, hug.

car•et /kárət/ *n.* mark (^) indicating a proposed insertion in printing or writing.

care•tak•er /káirtaykər/ *n.* person employed to look after something, esp. a house in the owner's absence.

care•worn /káirwawrn/ *adj.* showing the effects of prolonged worry.

car•go /káargō/ *n.* (*pl.* **goes** or **-gos**) goods carried on a ship or aircraft.

■ freight, merchandise, freightage, *Naut.* bulk.

car•go pants • *n.* pants featuring large pockets (usu. on the thighs and with flaps or zippers).

Car•ib /kárib/ *n.* **1** aboriginal inhabitant of the southern W. Indies or the adjacent coasts. **2** language of this people.

Car•ib•be•an /káribeeən, kəríbeeən/ *n.* part of the Atlantic between the southern W. Indies and Central America.

car•i•bou /káriboo/ *n.* (*pl.* same) N. American reindeer.

car•i•ca•ture /kárikəchər, -choor/ • *n.* **1** usu. comic representation of a person by exaggeration of characteristic traits. **2** ridiculously poor imitation or version. • *v.tr.* make a caricature of. □□ **car•i•ca•tur•al** /-chóorəl/ *adj.* **car'i•ca•tur•ist** *n.*

■ *n.* **1** cartoon, parody, satire. **2** see JOKE *n.* 2. • *v.* lampoon, burlesque; ridicule, mock.

SYNONYM STUDY: caricature

BURLESQUE, LAMPOON, MIMICRY, PARODY, TRAV-
ESTY. Skilled writers and artists who want to
poke fun at someone or something have a
number of weapons at their disposal. An
artist might come up with a **caricature**,
which is a drawing or written piece that ex-
aggerates its subject's distinguishing features
or peculiarities (*the cartoonist's caricature of
the presidential candidate*). A **parody** is similar to a caricature in purpose, but is used of
written work, or performances that ridicule
an author or performer's work by imitating
its language and style for comic effect (*a parody of the scene between Romeo and Juliet*).
While a *parody* concentrates on distorting
the content of the original work, a **travesty**
retains the subject matter but imitates the
style in a grotesque or absurd way (*their version of the Greek tragedy was a travesty*). A
lampoon is a strongly satirical piece of writing that attacks or ridicules an individual or
an institution; it is more commonly used as a
verb (*to lampoon the government in a local
newspaper*). While a *caricature*, a *parody*, and a
travesty must have an original to imitate, a
burlesque can be an independent comic or
satiric creation or composition; it can also be
an imitation, often a theatrical one, that
treats a serious subject lightly or a trivial subject with mock seriousness (*the play was a
burlesque of Homer's great epic*). **Mimicry** is
something you don't have to be an artist, a
writer, or an actor to be good at. Anyone who
successfully imitates another person's speech
or gestures is a good mimic, whether the intent is playful or mocking (*he showed an early
talent for mimicry*).

car•ies /káireez/ *n.* (*pl.* same) decay of a tooth
or bone. □□ **car•i•ous** /káireeəs/ *adj.*

car•il•lon /kárilon, –lən/ *n.* set of bells.

car•ing /káiring/ *adj.* compassionate.
■ see SYMPATHETIC *adj.* 1.

car•jack•ing /kárjaking/ *n.* theft of an automobile whose driver is forced to leave the vehicle, kept captive while the thief drives, or
forced to drive while at gunpoint, etc.
□□ **car'jack•er** *n.*

car•mine /káarmin, –mīn/ • *adj.* of a vivid
crimson color. • *n.* this color.

car•nage /káarnij/ *n.* great slaughter, esp. in
battle.
■ bloodshed, butchery, massacre, killing,
blood bath.

car•nal /káarnəl/ *adj.* 1 of the body or flesh;
worldly. 2 sensual; sexual. □ **carnal knowledge** *Law* sexual intercourse. □□ **car•nal•i-
ty** /–áalitee/ *n.* **car'nal•ize** *v.tr.* **car'nal•ly**
adv.
■ 1 physical, corporeal, animal, brute;
earthly, material. 2 fleshly, erotic, volupt-
ous, libidinous.

car•na•tion¹ /kaarnáyshən/ *n.* variously colored clove-scented flower.

car•na•tion² /kaarnáyshən/ *n.* rosy pink
color.

car•ne•lian /kaarneélyən/ *n.* (also **cor•ne•**

lian /kawr–/) 1 dull red or reddish-white variety of chalcedony. 2 this color.

car•ni•val /káarnivəl/ *n.* 1 a festivities usual
during the period before Lent in Roman
Catholic countries. b any festivities. 2 merrymaking; revelry. 3 traveling fair or circus.

car•ni•vore /káarnivawr/ *n.* any flesh-eating
mammal or plant.

car•niv•o•rous /kaarnívərəs/ *adj.* feeding on
flesh. □□ **car•niv'or•ous•ly** *adv.* **car•niv'
or•ous•ness** *n.*

car•ob /kárəb/ *n.* 1 evergreen tree native to
the Mediterranean, bearing edible pods.
2 its bean-shaped edible seed pod sometimes
used as a substitute for chocolate.

car•ol /kárəl/ • *n.* joyous song, esp. a Christmas hymn. • *v.intr.* sing carols. □□ **car'ol•er**
n.
■ *n.* see SONG. • *v.* see SING *v.* 1, 2.

car•o•tene /kárəteen/ *n.* orange-colored
plant pigment found in carrots, tomatoes,
etc., acting as a source of vitamin A.

ca•rot•id /kərótid/ • *n.* each of the two main
arteries carrying blood to the head and
neck. • *adj.* of or relating to either of these
arteries.

ca•rouse /kərówz/ • *v.intr.* 1 have a noisy or
lively drinking party. 2 drink heavily. • *n.*
noisy or lively drinking party. □□ **ca•rous'al**
n. **ca•rous'er** *n.*
■ *v.* 1 revel, *colloq.* go on a spree. 2 see
BOOZE *v.* • *n. sl.* jag, bender, binge.

car•ou•sel /kárəsél, –zél/ *n.* 1 merry-go-
round. 2 rotating delivery or conveyor system, esp. for passengers' luggage at an airport.

carp¹ /kaarp/ *n.* (*pl.* same) freshwater food
fish.

carp² /kaarp/ *v.intr.* [usu. foll. by *at*] find
fault; complain pettily. □□ **carp'er** *n.*
■ cavil, grumble, niggle, *colloq.* gripe.

car•pal /káarpəl/ • *adj.* of or relating to the
bones in the wrist. • *n.* any of the bones
forming the wrist.

car•pel /káarpəl/ *n. Bot.* female reproductive
organ of a flower. □□ **car'pel•lar•y** *adj.*

car•pen•ter /káarpintər/ • *n.* person skilled in
woodwork, esp. of a structural kind. □□ **car'
pen•try** *n.*

car•pet /káarpit/ • *n.* 1 a thick fabric for covering a floor or stairs. b piece of this fabric.
2 expanse or layer resembling a carpet in being smooth, soft, bright, or thick (*carpet of
snow*). • *v.tr.* cover with or as with a carpet.
□ **on the carpet** *colloq.* being reprimanded.
sweep under the carpet conceal (a problem or difficulty).

car•pet•bag•ger /káarpitbagər/ *n.* 1 political
candidate who has no local connections.
2 unscrupulous opportunist (orig. a North-
erner in the South after the Civil War).

car•pet•ing /káarpiting/ *n.* 1 material for carpets. 2 carpets collectively.

car•pool /kárpōōl/ • *n.* (also **car' pool**) 1 arrangement by which a group of commuters
travel to and from their destination in a single vehicle. 2 commuters taking part in such
an arrangement (*there are four people in our
carpool*). • *v.intr.* (also **car'-pool**) participate in or organize a carpool.

car•port /káarpawrt/ n. shelter with a roof and open sides for a car, usu. beside a house.

car•pus /káarpəs/ n. (pl. car•pi /-pī/) small bones between the forelimb and metacarpus in terrestrial vertebrates, forming the wrist in humans.

car•rel /kárəl/ n. small cubicle for a reader in a library.

car•riage /kárij/ n. 1 wheeled vehicle, esp. one pulled by horses. 2 carrying part of a machine (e.g., a typewriter). 3 gun carriage. 4 bearing; deportment.
   ■ 4 air, demeanor, attitude, posture.

car•ri•er /káreeər/ n. 1 person or thing that carries. 2 transport or freight company. 3 person or animal that may transmit a disease or a hereditary characteristic. 4 = *aircraft carrier*. □ **carrier pigeon** pigeon trained to carry messages.
   ■ 1, 2 bearer, porter, conveyor, carter, shipper. 3 transmitter, *Immunology* vector.

car•ri•on /káree-ən/ n. dead putrefying flesh.

car•rot /kárət/ n. 1 umbelliferous plant, with a tapering, edible orange-colored root. 2 means of enticement or persuasion. □□ **car'rot•y** adj.

car•ry /káree/ • v. (–ries, –ried) 1 tr. support or hold up, esp. while moving. 2 tr. convey with one or have on one's person. 3 tr. conduct or transmit (*pipe carries water*). 4 tr. take (a process, etc.) to a specified point; continue (*carry into effect, carry a joke too far*). 5 tr. involve; imply; entail as a feature or consequence (*principles carry consequences*). 6 tr. (in reckoning) transfer (a figure) to a column of higher value. 7 tr. hold in a specified way (*carry oneself erect*). 8 tr. publish or broadcast esp. regularly. 9 tr. keep a regular stock of. 10 intr. be audible at a distance. 11 tr. **a** win victory or acceptance for (a proposal, etc.). **b** gain (a state or district) in an election. **c** *Golf* cause the ball to pass beyond (a bunker, etc.). 12 tr. endure the weight of; support. 13 tr. be pregnant with. • n. (pl. **ries**) 1 act of carrying. 2 *Golf* distance a ball travels in the air. □ **carry away 1** remove. 2 inspire; affect emotionally or spiritually. 3 deprive of self-control (*got carried away*). **carry the day** be victorious or successful. **carry off 1** take away, esp. by force. 2 win (a prize). 3 (esp. of a disease) kill. 4 render acceptable or passable. **carry on 1** continue. 2 engage in (a conversation or a business). 3 *colloq.* behave strangely or excitedly. 4 advance (a process) by a stage. **carry out** put (ideas, instructions, etc.) into practice. **carry weight** be influential or important.
   ■ v. 1, 2 transport, bear, deliver, bring, haul, lug, cart, ship, move, *colloq.* schlep, tote; drive, take; hold. 3 convey, take, transport, transfer, bear. 7 bear, deport, hold up, maintain, keep. 8 put out; air, screen; disseminate, communicate, present, announce, offer, give, release. 9 stock, keep, have in stock, sell, offer, trade in, deal in, have. 11 b win, take, sweep, capture, pick up. 12 see SUPPORT v. 1, 2. □ **carry away 1** see REMOVE v. 2. 2 see INSPIRE 1, 2. **carry the day** see TRIUMPH v. 1. **carry off 1** abscond

with, make away *or* off with, run off with, spirit off *or* away, whisk away *or* off, cart off, drag away, kidnap, abduct. 2 gain, capture, pick up, take, *colloq.* walk away *or* off with. 3 be *or* cause the death of, cause to die, *colloq.* finish off. 4 accomplish, achieve, perform, effect, effectuate, do, execute, succeed in *or* with, handle, manage, work, bring off, carry out *or* through, pull off. **carry on 1** go on, keep on; keep (on) going, last, remain; persist, persevere, push *or* press on. 2 be involved *or* busy, occupy oneself with; follow, pursue, prosecute; manage, conduct, operate, run, administer. **carry out** perform, continue, implement, administer, transact, see through, execute, discharge, prosecute; effect, complete, accomplish, conclude.

car•sick /káarsik/ adj. affected with nausea caused by the motion of a car. □□ **car'sick•ness** n.

cart /kaart/ • n. 1 strong vehicle with two or four wheels for carrying loads, usu. drawn by a horse. 2 light vehicle for pulling by hand. • v.tr. convey in or as in a cart. □ **cart off** remove, esp. by force. **put the cart before the horse 1** reverse the proper order or procedure. 2 take an effect for a cause. □□ **cart'er** n. **cart'ful** n. (pl. **-fuls**).
   ■ n. 1 dray, trailer, wagon. 2 handcart, pushcart.

carte blanche /káart blónsh, blánch/ n. full discretionary power given to a person.
   ■ license, free rein, permission, sanction, warrant.

car•tel /kaartél/ n. informal association of manufacturers or suppliers to maintain prices at a high level. □□ **car•tel•ize** /káartəliz/ v.
   ■ see SYNDICATE n.

car•ti•lage /káart'lij/ n. gristle; firm flexible connective tissue. □□ **car•ti•lag•i•noid** /-lájinoyd/ adj. **car•ti•lag'i•nous** adj.

car•tog•ra•phy /kaartógrəfee/ n. science or practice of map drawing. □□ **car•tog'ra•pher** n. **car•to•graph•ic** /-təgráfik/ adj.

car•ton /káart'n/ n. light box or container, esp. one made of cardboard.
   ■ see BOX[1] n. 1, 2.

car•toon /kaartoon/ n. 1 humorous drawing in a newspaper, magazine, etc., esp. as a topical comment. 2 sequence of drawings telling a story. 3 animated sequence of these. □□ **car•toon'ist** n.

car•tridge /káartrij/ n. 1 case containing a charge of propelling explosive for firearms or blasting; with a bullet or shot if for small arms. 2 spool of film, magnetic tape, etc., in a sealed container ready for insertion. 3 ink container for insertion in a pen. □ **cartridge belt** belt with pockets or loops for cartridges (in sense 1).
   ■ 1 see SHELL n. 2.

cart•wheel /káart-hweel, -weel/ n. 1 wheel of a cart. 2 circular sideways handspring.

carve /kaarv/ v.tr. 1 produce or shape (a statue, representation in relief, etc.) by cutting into a hard material (*carved a figure out of rock*). 2 cut patterns, designs, letters, etc., in

(hard material). **3** [*absol.*] cut (meat, etc.) into slices for eating. □ **carve out 1** take from a larger whole. **2** establish (a career, etc.) purposefully (*carved out a name for themselves*). □□ **carv′er** *n.*
■ **1, 2** hew, sculpt, sculpture, chisel, model; engrave, incise, inscribe. □ **carve out 2** see ESTABLISH[1] 1, FORGE 2.

carv•ing /káarving/ *n.* carved object, esp. as a work of art.

Cas•a•no•va /kásənōvə/ *n.* man notorious for seducing women.

cas•cade /kaskáyd/ • *n.* **1** small waterfall, esp. one in a series. **2** material, etc., draped in descending folds. • *v.intr.* fall in or like a cascade.
■ *n.* **1** see WATERFALL. • *v.* see STREAM *v.* 1.

case[1] /kays/ *n.* **1** instance of something occurring. **2** state of affairs, hypothetical or actual. **3 a** instance of a person receiving professional guidance, e.g., from a doctor or social worker. **b** such a person. **4** matter under official investigation, esp. by the police. **5** *Law* cause or suit for trial. **6 a** sum of the arguments on one side, esp. in a lawsuit. **b** set of arguments, esp. in relation to persuasiveness (*have a good case*). **c** valid set of arguments (*have no case*). **7** *Gram.* **a** relation of a word to other words in a sentence. **b** form of a noun, adjective, or pronoun expressing this. □ **in any case** whatever the truth is; whatever may happen. **in case** in the event that; if.
■ **1** example, specimen, illustration. **2** happening, occasion, event, occurrence. **3 b** patient, client; subject. **5** action, lawsuit. **6 a, b** see ARGUMENT 2. □ **in any case** in any event, come what regardless, just the same, for all that; always.

case[2] /kays/ • *n.* **1** container or covering serving to enclose or contain. **2** container with its contents. • *v.tr.* **1** enclose in a case. **2** *sl.* reconnoiter (a house, etc.), esp. with a view to robbery.
■ *n.* **1** box, carton, crate, chest, holder, receptacle. • *v.* **1** encase, box, crate, wrap, envelop. **2** see RECONNOITER *v.*

case•ment /káysmənt/ *n.* window or part of a window hinged to open on its outer frame.

case•work /káyswərk/ *n.* social work concerned with family and background. □□ **case′work•er** *n.*

cash /kash/ • *n.* **1** money in coins or bills. **2** (also **cash down**) full payment at the time of purchase, as distinct from credit. • *v.tr.* give or obtain cash for (a note, check, etc.). □ **cash cow** business, product, etc., generating steady profits. **cash flow** movement of money into and out of a business. **cash in 1** obtain cash for. **2** *colloq.* profit (from); take advantage (of). **3** (in full **cash in one's chips**) *colloq.* die. **cash machine** = *automated teller machine.* □□ **cash′a•ble** *adj.* **cash′less** *adj.*
■ *n.* **1** currency, funds, change, hard cash, *sl.* moolah, dough, bread, loot. • *v.* cash in, redeem. □ **cash in 1** redeem. **2** see PROFIT[1] *v.* 2. **3** see DIE 1.

ca•shew /káshōō, kashōō/ *n.* **1** bushy evergreen tree native to Central and S. America, bearing kidney-shaped nuts. **2** (in full **cashew nut**) edible nut of this tree.

cash•ier[1] /kasheér/ *n.* person dealing with cash transactions in a store, bank, etc. □ **cashier's check** check drawn by a bank on its own funds and signed by a cashier of the bank.

cash•mere /kázhmeer, kásh–/ *n.* **1** fine soft wool, esp. that of a Kashmir goat. **2** material made from this.

cas•ing /káysing/ *n.* **1** protective or enclosing cover or shell. **2** material for this.

ca•si•no /kəseénō/ *n.* (*pl.* **–nos**) place for gambling.

cask /kask/ *n.* **1** large barrellike container made of wood, metal, or plastic, esp. one for alcoholic liquor. **2** its contents.
■ see KEG.

cas•ket /káskit/ *n.* **1** coffin. **2** small, often ornamental box or chest for jewels, letters, etc.

cas•sa•va /kəsáavə/ *n.* **1** plant with starchy tuberous roots. **2** starch or flour obtained from these roots. (Also called **tapioca** or **manioc**).

cas•se•role /kásərōl/ *n.* **1** covered dish for baking. **2** food cooked in a casserole.

cas•sette /kəsét, ka–/ *n.* sealed case containing a length of tape, film, etc., ready for insertion in tape recorder, camera, etc.

cas•si•a /kásha/ *n.* **1** tree bearing leaves from which senna is extracted. **2** cinnamonlike bark of this used as a spice.

cas•sock /kásək/ *n.* long garment worn by clergy, members of choirs, etc. □□ **cas′socked** *adj.*

cas•so•war•y /kásəwairee/ *n.* (*pl.* **–ies**) large flightless Australasian bird.

cast /kast/ • *v.tr.* (*past* and *past part.* **cast**) **1** throw, esp. deliberately or forcefully. **2 a** direct or cause to fall (one's eyes, a glance, light, a shadow, a spell, etc.). **b** express (doubts, aspersions, etc.). **3** throw out (a fishing line) into the water. **4** let down (an anchor, etc.). **5** record, register, or give (a vote). **6 a** shape (molten metal or plastic material) in a mold. **b** make (a product) in this way. **7 a** assign (an actor) to play a particular character. **b** allocate roles in (a play, motion picture, etc.). • *n.* **1** the throwing of a missile, dice, line, etc. **2 a** object of metal, clay, etc., made in a mold. **b** rigid case to support an injured limb. **3** the actors in a play, motion picture, etc. □ **cast aside** give up using; abandon. **cast iron** hard alloy of iron, carbon, and silicon cast in a mold. **cast-iron** *adj.* **1** made of cast iron. **2** hard; unchangeable. **cast off 1** abandon. **2** loosen and throw off (rope, etc.). **cast-off** abandoned; discarded. **cast out** expel.
■ *v.* **1** toss, pitch, fling, let fly, sling, hurl, bowl, launch, discharge, dash, send, shoot, shy, *colloq.* chuck. **2 a** see DIRECT[2] *v.* 4, SHED 4. **6** mold, form, fashion. **7 a** give the part; appoint, designate, name, nominate, choose, pick, select. • *n.* **1** throw, toss, pitch, lob, hurl. **2 a** model, casting, mold. **3** players, performers, troupe, company, act. □ **cast aside** reject, discard, cast *or* throw away, cast

or throw out, dispense with, get rid of, dispose of; see also REJECT *v.* 1. **cast-iron** 2 see SOLID *adj.* 4, 6. **cast off** 1 see ABANDON *v.* 2. **cast-off** (*adj.*) see ABANDONED 1; (*n.*) see REJECT *n.* **cast out** evict, eject, oust, exile, banish, remove, *colloq.* chuck out, *sl.* bounce.

cas•ta•net /kástənét/ *n.* [usu. in *pl.*] hand-held, concave piece of hardwood, ivory, etc., in pairs, clicked together, esp. by Spanish dancers.

cast•a•way /kástəway/ • *n.* shipwrecked person. • *adj.* 1 shipwrecked. 2 cast aside; rejected.
  ■ *adj.* 1 marooned, stranded. 2 see ABANDONED 1.

caste /kast/ *n.* 1 Hindu hereditary class. 2 more or less exclusive social class. 3 system of such classes.
  ■ 1, 2 order, level, stratum, rank, station.

cas•tel•lat•ed /kástəlaytid/ *adj.* 1 having battlements. 2 castlelike. □□ **cas•tel•la•tion** /-láyshən/ *n.*

cast•er /kástər/ *n.* 1 small swiveled wheel as on furniture. 2 small container with holes in the top for sprinkling the contents. □ **caster action** swiveling of vehicle wheels to ensure stability.

cas•ti•gate /kástigayt/ *v.tr.* rebuke or punish severely. □□ **cas•ti•ga•tion** /-gáyshən/ *n.* **cas•ti•ga•tor** *n.* **cas•ti•ga•to•ry** /-gətáwree/ *adj.*
  ■ chastise, scold, reprimand, berate, upbraid, *colloq.* tell off, dress down, bawl out, blast, discipline, chasten, correct, penalize.

cast•ing /kásting/ *n.* object made by casting, esp. of molten metal.

cas•tle /kásəl/ *n.* 1 large fortified building or group of buildings; stronghold. 2 *Chess* = ROOK³. □ **castles in the air** visionary unattainable scheme; daydream. □□ **cas'tled** *adj.*
  ■ *n.* 1 fortress, citadel, fastness, tower.

cast-off /kástawf/ *n.* cast-off thing, esp. a garment.

castor oil /kástər/ *n.* oil from the seeds of a plant, used as a purgative and lubricant.

cas•trate /kástrayt/ *v.tr.* 1 remove the testicles of; geld. 2 deprive of vigor. □□ **cas•tra•tion** /-tráyshən/ *n.* **cas'tra•tor** *n.*
  ■ 1 see NEUTER *v.*

ca•su•al /kázhōōəl/ *adj.* 1 accidental; due to chance. 2 not regular nor permanent (*casual work*). 3a unconcerned (*was very casual about it*). b careless. 4 (of clothes) informal. See synonym study at ACCIDENTAL. □□ **cas'u•al•ly** *adv.* **cas'u•al•ness** *n.*
  ■ 1 coincidental, adventitious, random, incidental, spontaneous, fortuitous. 2 occasional, temporary, part-time; superficial, passing, transient, fleeting. 3a indifferent, nonchalant, offhand, lax, insouciant, apathetic. b unthinking, offhand, extempore; haphazard, sporadic, erratic. 4 see INFORMAL.

ca•su•al•ty /kázhōōəltee/ *n.* (*pl.* **–ties**) 1 person killed or injured in a war or accident. 2 thing lost or destroyed.
  ■ 1 victim, fatality, death; (*casualties*) wounded, injured, dead, *Mil.* missing in action, losses.

117 castanet ~ cataract

ca•su•ist /kázhōōist/ *n.* person who resolves problems of conscience, duty, etc., with clever but false reasoning. □□ **cas•u•is'tic** *adj.* **cas•u•is'ti•cal** *adj.* **cas•u•is'ti•cal•ly** *adv.* **cas•u•ist•ry** /kázhōōəstree/ *n.*

CAT /kat/ *abbr. Med.* computerized axial tomography.

cat /kat/ *n.* 1 small, soft-furred, four-legged domesticated animal. 2 any wild animal of the same family, e.g., a lion, tiger, or leopard. □ **cat burglar** burglar who enters by climbing to an upper story. **cat-o'-nine-tails** *hist.* rope whip with nine knotted lashes. **cat's cradle** child's game in which a loop of string is held between the fingers and patterns are formed. **cat's-paw** person used as a tool by another. **let the cat out of the bag** reveal a secret, esp. involuntarily. **rain cats and dogs** *colloq.* rain very hard.

cata- /kátə/ *prefix* 1 down; downward. 2 wrongly; badly.

cat•a•clysm /kátəklizəm/ *n.* 1 violent, esp. social or political, upheaval or disaster. 2 a great change. □□ **cat•a•clys•mal** /-klízməl/ *adj.* **cat•a•clys•mic** *adj.* **cat•a•clys•mi•cal•ly** *adv.*
  ■ 1 see DISASTER 1.

cat•a•comb /kátəkōm/ *n.* [often in *pl.*] underground cemetery, esp. in Rome.

cat•a•falque /kátəfawk, –fawlk/ *n.* framework for supporting the coffin during a funeral.

Cat•a•lan /kát'lan/ • *n.* 1 native of Catalonia in Spain. 2 language of Catalonia. • *adj.* of or relating to Catalonia or its people or language.

cat•a•lep•sy /kát'lepsee/ *n.* trance or seizure with loss of sensation and consciousness. □□ **cat•a•lep'tic** /-léptik/ *adj. & n.*

cat•a•log /kát'lawg, –log/ (also **cat•a•logue**) • *n.* ordered list of items often with a description of each. • *v.tr.* (**cat•a•logs, cat•a•loged, cat•a•log•ing; cat•a•logues, cat•a•logued, cat•a•logu•ing**) 1 make a catalog of. 2 enter in a catalog. □□ **cat'a•log•er** *n.* (also **cat'a•logu•er**).
  ■ *n.* see LIST¹ *n.* ■ *v.* see LIST¹ *v.*

ca•tal•y•sis /kətálisis/ *n.* (*pl.* **ca•tal•y•ses** /-seez/) acceleration of a chemical or biochemical reaction by a catalyst.

cat•a•lyst /kát'list/ *n.* 1 *Chem.* substance that increases the rate of a reaction. 2 person or thing that precipitates a change.

cat•a•lyt•ic /kát'lítik/ *adj. Chem.* relating to or involving catalysis. □ **catalytic converter** device in a motor vehicle for converting pollutant gases into harmless products.

cat•a•ma•ran /kátəmərán/ *n.* 1 boat with twin hulls in parallel. 2 raft of yoked logs or boats.

cat•a•pult /kátəpult, –pŏolt/ • *n.* 1 mechanical device for launching a glider, an aircraft from the deck of a ship, etc. 2 *hist.* military machine for hurling large stones, etc. • *v.* 1 *tr.* a hurl from or launch with a catapult. b fling forcibly. 2 *intr.* leap or be hurled forcibly.

cat•a•ract /kátərakt/ *n.* 1 a large waterfall or cascade. b downpour; rush of water. 2 *Med.*

condition in which the lens of the eye becomes progressively opaque.

ca•tas•tro•phe /kətástrəfee/ *n.* **1** great and usu. sudden disaster. **2** disastrous end; ruin. □□ **cat•a•stroph•ic** /kátəstrófik/ *adj.* **cat•a•stroph'i•cal•ly** *adv.*
■ **1** calamity, cataclysm, casualty, misfortune, tragedy. **2** destruction, devastation, downfall.

cat•a•to•ni•a /kátətóneeə/ *n.* **1** schizophrenia with intervals of catalepsy and sometimes violence. **2** catalepsy. □□ **cat•a•ton•ic** /-tónik/ *adj. & n.*

cat•call /kátkawl/ *n.* shrill whistle of disapproval.
■ see JEER *n.*

catch /kach/ • *v.* (*past* and *past part.* **caught** /kawt/) **1** *tr.* lay hold of so as to restrain; capture in a trap, in one's hands, etc. **2** *tr.* detect or surprise (esp. a guilty person). **3** *tr.* intercept and hold (a moving thing) in the hands, etc. **4** *tr.* **a** contract (a disease) by infection or contagion. **b** acquire (a quality or feeling). **5** *tr.* **a** reach in time and board (a train, bus, etc.). **b** be in time to see, etc. (a person or thing about to leave or finish). **6** *tr.* apprehend with the mind (esp. a thing occurring quickly or briefly). **7** *a* *intr.* become fixed or entangled. **b** *tr.* cause to do this (*caught her tights on a nail*). **8** *tr.* draw the attention of; captivate. **9** *intr.* begin to burn. • *n.* **1** act of catching. **2 a** amount of a thing caught, esp. of fish. **b** thing or person caught or worth catching. **3 a** question, trick, etc., intended to deceive, incriminate, etc. **b** unexpected or hidden difficulty or disadvantage. **4** device for fastening a door or window, etc. □ **catch on** *colloq.* **1** (of a practice, fashion, etc.) become popular. **2** (of a person) understand what is meant. **catch up 1 a** reach a person, etc., ahead. **b** make up arrears (of work, etc.). **2** pick up hurriedly. **3** involve; entangle. □□ **catch'a•ble** *adj.*
■ *v.* **1** seize, apprehend, take *or* get (hold of), grab, take captive, arrest, take prisoner, collar, *sl.* nab, pinch; trap, ensnare, entrap, snare, net, bag, hook, land. **2** discover, find, uncover, take unawares. **3** field, stop; grab, seize, snatch, take possession of. **4 a** get, develop, come down with, pick up, acquire, be afflicted by *or* with, suffer from. **5 a** make; take, get, get on (to), *colloq.* hop. **6** understand, comprehend, ascertain, grasp, follow, take in, hear, gather, perceive, *colloq.* get, catch on to, get the drift of. **7 a** tangle, be enmeshed, stick, lodge, become stuck *or* trapped *or* hooked *or* wedged. **b** snag, wedge, fix, entangle, hook; tear, rip. **8** attract, capture; appeal to, engage, bewitch. **9** ignite, light, flare up. • *n.* **2 a** take, bag, haul, yield, harvest. **b** find; conquest. **3 a** trap, wile, dodge, *colloq.* ploy, *sl.* con. **b** hitch, snag, problem, drawback, twist, rub, fly in the ointment, complication, small print. **4** clasp, bolt, hook, pin, clip, fastener.

catch•all /káchawl/ *n.* [often *attrib.*] **1** something designed to be all-inclusive. **2** container for odds and ends.

catch•ing /káching/ *adj.* infectious; likely to be imitated.
■ contagious, transmissible, transmittable, communicable; attractive, captivating, fascinating.

catch•phrase /káchfrayz/ *n.* phrase in frequent use.

catch-22 /káchtwenteetóō/ *n.* [often *attrib.*] *colloq.* circumstance that presents a dilemma because of mutually conflicting or dependent conditions.

catch•word /káchwərd/ *n.* word or phrase in common (often temporary) use; topical slogan.

catch•y /káchee/ *adj.* (**catch•i•er, catch•i•est**) (of a tune) easy to remember; attractive. □□ **catch'i•ly** *adv.* **catch'i•ness** *n.*
■ see MEMORABLE.

cat•e•chism /kátikizəm/ *n.* **1 a** principles of a religion in the form of questions and answers. **b** book containing this. **2** series of questions put to anyone. □□ **cat•e•chis•mal** /-kízməl/ *adj.*

cat•e•chize /kátikīz/ *v.tr.* **1** instruct by means of a catechism. **2** put questions to; examine. □□ **cat'e•chiz•er** *n.*

cat•e•gor•i•cal /kátigáwrikəl, -gór-/ *adj.* (also **cat•e•gor'ic**) unconditional; absolute; explicit. □□ **cat•e•gor'i•cal•ly** *adv.*
■ direct, express, firm, positive, unmitigated, unqualified, definitive, unequivocal, unambiguous.

cat•e•go•rize /kátigərīz/ *v.tr.* place in a category or categories. □□ **cat•e•go•ri•za'tion** *n.*
■ compartmentalize, classify, class, sort, organize, group.

cat•e•go•ry /kátigawree, -goree/ *n.* (*pl.* **-ries**) class or division. □□ **cat•e•go•ri•al** /-gáwreeəl/ *adj.*
■ **1** type, sort, kind, variety, species, form, order; section, sector, league, bracket, genre; set, group.

ca•ter /káytər/ *v.* **1 a** *intr.* provide food. **b** *tr.* provide food and service (*cater a party*). **2** *intr.* provide what is desired or needed by. **3** *intr.* pander to (esp. low tastes).
■ **1 a** provision, victual. **2** accommodate, host, entertain; care for, look after, minister to. **3** indulge, minister to, humor, serve.

ca•ter•cor•nered /kátərkáwrnərd/ (also **cat'er•cor'ner, cat•ty-cor'nered** /kátee-/, **kit•ty-cor'ner** /kítee-/) • *adj.* placed or situated diagonally. • *adv.* diagonally.

ca•ter•er /káytərər/ *n.* person who supplies food for social events, esp. professionally.

cat•er•pil•lar /kátərpilər/ *n.* larva of a butterfly or moth.

cat•er•waul /kátərwawl/ • *v.intr.* make the shrill howl of a cat. • *n.* caterwauling noise.

cat•fish /kátfish/ *n.* any of various esp. freshwater fish, usu. having whiskerlike barbels around the mouth.

cat•gut /kátgut/ *n.* material used for surgical sutures, etc., made of animal intestine (but not of the cat).

ca•thar•sis /kətháarsis/ *n.* (*pl.* **ca•thar•ses** /-seez/) **1** emotional release in drama or art. **2** *Psychol.* process of freeing and eliminating repressed emotion.

ca•thar•tic /kəthaártik/ • *adj.* **1** effecting catharsis. **2** purgative. • *n.* cathartic drug. □□ **ca•thar'ti•cal•ly** *adv.*

ca•the•dral /kətheédrəl/ *n.* principal church of a diocese.

cath•e•ter /káthitər/ *n. Med.* tube inserted into a body cavity for introducing or removing fluid. □□ **cath'e•ter•ize** *v.*

cath•ode /káthōd/ *n. Electr.* **1** negative electrode in an electrolytic cell or electronic valve or tube. **2** positive terminal of a primary cell such as a battery (opp. ANODE). □ **cathode ray** beam of electrons emitted from the cathode of a high-vacuum tube. □□ **cath'o•dal** *adj.* **ca•thod•ic** /kəthódik/ *adj.*

cath•o•lic /káthəlik, káthlik/ • *adj.* **1** of interest or use to all; universal. **2** all-embracing, of wide sympathies or interests (*has catholic tastes*). See synonym study at UNIVERSAL. • *n.* **(Catholic)** Roman Catholic. □□ **ca•thol•i•cal•ly** /kəthóliklee/ *adv.* **Ca•thol•i•cism** /kəthólisizəm/ *n.* **cath•o•lic•i•ty** /káthəlísitee/ *n.*

■ *adj.* **1** general, widespread. **2** inclusive, all-inclusive, broad, eclectic, liberal.

cat•i•on /kátīən/ *n.* positively charged ion; ion that is attracted to the cathode in electrolysis (opp. ANION). □□ **cat•i•on•ic** /-ónik/ *adj.*

cat•kin /kátkin/ *n.* spike of usu. downy or silky flowers hanging from a willow, hazel, etc.

cat•nap /kátnap/ • *n.* short sleep. • *v.intr.* (**-napped, -nap•ping**) have a catnap.

cat•nip /kátnip/ *n.* white-flowered plant that attracts cats.

CAT scan /kat/ *n.* X-ray image made using computerized axial tomography. □□ **CAT scan'ner** *n.*

cat•sup /kátsəp, kéchəp, kách-/ var. of KETCHUP.

cat•tle /kát'l/ *n.pl.* domesticated bovine animals bred for meat and milk.

■ cows, bulls, bullocks, steers, oxen; stock, livestock.

cat•ty /kátee/ *adj.* (**cat•ti•er, cat•ti•est**) sly; spiteful; deliberately hurtful in speech. □□ **cat'ti•ly** *adv.* **cat'ti•ness** *n.*

CATV *abbr.* community antenna television.

cat•walk /kátwawk/ *n.* narrow footway or platform.

Cau•ca•sian /kawkáyzhən/ • *adj.* **1** of or relating to the white or light-skinned division of mankind. **2** of or relating to the Caucasus. • *n.* Caucasian person. □□ **Cau•ca•soid** /káwkəsoyd/ *adj.*

■ *adj.* **1** see WHITE *adj.* 3.

cau•cus /káwkəs/ *n.* meeting of a political party, esp. in a legislature or convention, to decide policy.

■ see MEETING 2.

cau•dal /káwd'l/ *adj.* of or like a tail. □□ **cau'dal•ly** *adv.*

caught *past* and *past part.* of CATCH.

caul•dron /káwldrən/ *n.* (also **cal'dron**) large, deep, bowl-shaped vessel for boiling over an open fire.

■ see POT¹ *n.* 1.

cau•li•flow•er /káwliflowr, kól-/ *n.* cabbage with a large flower head of small usu.

creamy-white buds. □ **cauliflower ear** ear deformed by injury, as in boxing.

caulk /kawk/ *v.tr.* (also **calk**) stop up (the seams of a boat, etc.) with a pliable sealant. □□ **caulk'er** *n.*

caus•al /káwzəl/ *adj.* **1** of, forming, or expressing a cause or causes. **2** relating to, or of the nature of, cause and effect. □□ **caus'al•ly** *adv.*

cau•sal•i•ty /kawzálitee/ *n.* the relation of cause and effect.

cau•sa•tion /kawzáyshən/ *n.* **1** act of causing or producing an effect. **2** = CAUSALITY.

caus•a•tive /káwzətiv/ *adj.* **1** acting as cause. **2** [foll. by *of*] producing; having as effect. □□ **caus'a•tive•ly** *adv.*

cause /kawz/ • *n.* **1** person or thing that produces an effect. **2** reason or motive; ground that may be held to justify something (*no cause for complaint*). **3** principle, belief, or purpose (*faithful to the cause*). **4** matter to be settled at law. • *v.tr.* be the cause of; produce; make happen (*caused a commotion*). □□ **caus'a•ble** *adj.* **cause'less** *adj.* **caus'er** *n.*

■ *n.* **1** agent, reason, occasion; source, originator, creator, producer, initiator, instigator. **2** ground(s), justification, basis. **3** see PRINCIPLE¹ 1. **4** see CASE 5. • *v.* **1** effect, create, precipitate, occasion, lead to, spark (off).

cause cé•lè•bre /káwz selébrə/ *n.* (*pl.* **causes cé•lè•bres** *pronunc.* same) trial or case that attracts much attention.

cause•way /káwzway/ *n.* raised road or track across low or wet ground or a stretch of water.

caus•tic /káwstik/ • *adj.* **1** corrosive; burning. **2** sarcastic; biting. • *n.* caustic substance. □□ **caus'ti•cal•ly** *adv.* **caus•tic•i•ty** /-tísitee/ *n.*

■ *adj.* **1** destructive, mordant, **2** acrimonious, sharp, bitter, sardonic, cutting, trenchant.

cau•ter•ize /káwtərīz/ *v.tr. Med.* burn or coagulate (tissue); esp. to stop bleeding. See synonym study at BURN. □□ **cau•ter•i•za'tion** *n.*

cau•tion /káwshən/ • *n.* **1** attention to safety; prudence; carefulness. **2** warning. • *v.tr.* warn or admonish.

■ *n.* **1** wariness, care, vigilance, forethought, heed, heedfulness, watchfulness. • *v.* **1** see WARN.

cau•tion•ar•y /káwshəneree/ *adj.* giving or serving as a warning.

cau•tious /káwshəs/ *adj.* careful; prudent; attentive to safety. See synonym study at VIGILANT. □□ **cau'tious•ly** *adv.* **cau'tious•ness** *n.*

■ wary, heedful, circumspect, watchful, vigilant.

cav•al•cade /kávəlkáyd/ *n.* procession or formal company of riders, motor vehicles, etc.

■ see PROCESSION 1.

cav•a•lier /kávəleèr/ • *n.* courtly gentleman. • *adj.* offhand; supercilious. □□ **cav•a•lier'ly** *adv.*

■ *adj.* see OFFHAND *adj.*

cav•al•ry /kávəlree/ n. (pl. **–ries**) [usu. treated as pl.] soldiers on horseback or in armored vehicles.

cave /kayv/ • n. large hollow in the side of a cliff, hill, etc., or underground. • v.intr. explore caves. □ **cave in 1 a** (of a wall, earth over a hollow, etc.) subside; collapse. **b** cause (a wall, earth, etc.) to do this. **2** yield; give up. □□ **cave′like** adj. **cav′er** n.
■ n. **1** cavern, grotto; den, lair. □ **cave in 1 a** buckle, fall in. **b** knock or break down. **2** submit, surrender.

ca•ve•at /kávee-aat, kaá–, –at/ n. warning or proviso.

cave•man /káyvman/ n. (pl. **–men**) prehistoric human living in a cave.

cav•ern /kávərn/ n. cave, esp. a large or dark one. □□ **cav′ern•ous** adj. **cav′ern•ous•ly** adv.

cav•i•ar /kávee-aár/ n. (also **cav′i•are**) pickled roe of sturgeon or other large fish, eaten as a delicacy.

cav•il /kávil/ • v.intr. make petty objections; carp. • n. trivial objection. □□ **cav′il•er** n.
■ v. quibble, split hairs, complain, find fault. • n. quibble, complaint, criticism, niggle, colloq. gripe.

cav•ing /káyving/ n. exploring caves as a sport or pastime.
■ speleology, spelunking.

cav•i•ty /kávitee/ n. (pl. **–ties**) **1** hollow within a solid body. **2** decayed part of a tooth.
■ **1** pit, hole, gap, space, opening, crater, pan.

ca•vort /kəváwrt/ v.intr. sl. caper excitedly; gambol; prance.
■ frisk, bound, frolic, romp, skip, leap, jump.

caw /kaw/ • n. harsh cry of a crow, etc. • v.intr. utter this cry.

cay•enne /kī–én, kay–/ n. (in full **cay•enne′ pep′per**) powdered red pepper.

CB abbr. citizens' band.

CCTV abbr. closed-circuit television.

CCU abbr. **1** cardiac care unit. **2** coronary care unit. **3** critical care unit.

CD abbr. **1** compact disc. **2** certificate of deposit.

Cd symb. Chem. cadmium.

CDC abbr. Centers for Disease Control (and Prevention).

CD-ROM /seédeeróm/ abbr. Computing compact disc read-only memory, a medium for data storage and distribution.

CDT abbr. central daylight time.

Ce symb. Chem. cerium.

cease /sees/ v. stop; bring or come to an end (ceased breathing). □ **cease-fire** n. **1** order to stop firing. **2** period of truce; suspension of hostilities.
■ end, finish, terminate, halt, discontinue; abandon, cut off, suspend, drop, sever. □ **cease-fire 2** see TRUCE.

cease•less /seéslis/ adj. without end. □□ **cease′less•ly** adv.

ce•cum /seékəm/ n. (pl. **ce•ca** /–kə/) blind-ended pouch at the junction of the small and large intestines. □□ **ce′cal** adj.

ce•dar /seédər/ n. **1** spreading evergreen conifer. **2** (in full **cedar wood**) fragrant durable wood of any cedar tree. □□ **ce′darn** adj. poet.

cede /seed/ v.tr. give up one's rights to or possession of. See synonym study at RELINQUISH.
■ yield, grant, surrender, deliver up; relinquish, forgo, abandon, renounce, abdicate, forfeit, resign.

ce•dil•la /sidílə/ n. mark written under the letter c, esp. in French, to show that it is sibilant (as in façade).

ceil•ing /seéling/ n. **1** upper interior surface of a room or other similar compartment. **2** upper limit. **3** Aeron. maximum altitude a given aircraft can reach.

cel•e•brant /sélibrənt/ n. person who performs a rite, esp. a priest at the Eucharist.
■ officiant, officiator, celebrator.

cel•e•brate /sélibrayt/ v. **1** tr. mark with festivities. **2** tr. perform publicly and duly (a religious ceremony, etc.). **3** intr. engage in festivities. **4** tr. (as **celebrated** adj.) honor publicly. □□ **cel•e•bra•tion** /–bráyshən/ n. **cel′e•bra•tor** n. **cel•e•bra•to•ry** /–brətáwree, sələbrətáwree/ adj.
■ **1** memorialize, commemorate, hold, keep, observe. **2** solemnize; sanctify. **3** revel, rejoice, colloq. party. **4** extol, praise, eulogize; publicize; (**celebrated**) acclaimed; famous, renowned, famed, legendary. □□ **celebration** commemoration, memorialization, observance; performance, officiation; festival, fete, gala, revel.

ce•leb•ri•ty /silébritee/ n. (pl. **–ties**) **1** well-known person. **2** fame.
■ **1** notable, dignitary, star, luminary, personage. **2** renown, repute, reputation, prominence; notoriety.

cel•er•y /sélaree/ n. umbelliferous plant, with closely packed succulent leafstalks used as a vegetable.

ce•les•tial /siléschəl/ adj. **1** divinely good; sublime. **2** of the sky or heavenly bodies. □□ **ce•les′tial•ly** adv.
■ **1** spiritual, godly, godlike, holy, paradisiacal; perfect, ideal, exquisite. **2** astronomical; astral.

cel•i•bate /sélibət/ • adj. **1** committed to abstention from sexual relations and from marriage. **2** abstaining from sexual relations. • n. celibate person. □□ **cel•i•ba•cy** /–bəsee/ n.
■ adj. **1** abstinent, abstemious, continent, ascetic. **2** virgin, virginal, pure, chaste, unsullied. □□ **celibacy** abstemiousness, self-denial, continence.

cell /sel/ n. **1** small room, esp. in a prison or monastery. **2** small compartment, e.g., in a honeycomb. **3** Biol. the structural and functional, usu. microscopic unit of an organism, consisting of cytoplasm and a nucleus enclosed in a membrane. **4** Electr. vessel for containing electrodes within an electrolyte for current generation or electrolysis. □□ **celled** adj. [also in comb.].
■ **1** closet, cubby(hole), den, cubicle, stall, apartment. **2** division, section, chamber.

cel•lar /sélər/ n. storage room below ground level.

■ *n.* basement, vault.

cel•lo /chélō/ *n.* (*pl.* **–los**) bass instrument of the violin family, held between the legs of the seated player. □□ **cel′list** *n.*

cel•lo•phane /séləfayn/ *n. formerly propr.* thin transparent wrapping material made from viscose.

cell•phone /sélfōn/ *n.* portable radiotelephone having access to a cellular telephone system.

cel•lu•lar /sélyələr/ *adj.* consisting of cells; of open texture; porous. □ **cellular telephone** (or **phone**) system of mobile radiotelephone transmission with an area divided into "cells," each served by its own small transmitter. □□ **cel•lu•lar•i•ty** /–láritee/ *n.* **cel′lu•late** *adj.* **cel•lu•la•tion** /–láyshən/ *n.*

cel•lu•lite /sélyəlīt/ *n.* lumpy fat, esp. on the hips and thighs.

cel•lu•loid /sélyəloyd/ *n.* **1** transparent plastic made from camphor and cellulose nitrate. **2** motion-picture film.

cel•lu•lose /sélyəlōs, –lōz/ *n.* **1** carbohydrate forming the main constituent of plant cell walls, used in textile fibers. **2** paint or lacquer containing cellulose acetate or nitrate.

Cel•si•us /sélseeəs/ *adj.* of a scale of temperature on which water freezes at 0° and boils at 100°.

Celt /kelt, selt/ *n.* (also **Kelt**) member of a group of W. European peoples, including inhabitants of Ireland, Wales, Scotland, Cornwall, Brittany, and the Isle of Man.

Celt•ic /kéltik, séltik/ (also **Kelt′ic**) • *adj.* of or relating to the Celts. • *n.* group of languages spoken by Celtic peoples, including Gaelic, Welsh, Cornish, and Breton.

ce•ment /simént/ • *n.* **1** powdery substance made by calcining lime and clay, mixed with water to form mortar or used in concrete. **2** similar substance that hardens and fastens on setting. **3** uniting factor or principle. **4** substance for filling cavities in teeth. • *v. tr.* **1 a** unite with or as with cement. **b** establish or strengthen (a friendship, etc.). **2** apply cement to. □□ **ce•ment′er** *n.*

■ *n.* **2** glue, gum, paste, solder. • *v.* **1 a** stick, solder, weld; join, bind, fuse. **b** see REINFORCE.

cem•e•ter•y /sémiteree/ *n.* (*pl.* **–ies**) burial ground.

■ see GRAVEYARD.

cen•o•taph /sénətaf/ *n.* tomblike monument, esp. a war memorial, to a person whose body is elsewhere.

Ce•no•zo•ic /séenəzṓik, sén–/ (also **Cai•no•zo•ic** /kínə–/, **Cae•no•zo•ic** /séenə–/) *Geol.* • *adj.* of or relating to the most recent era of geological time, marked by the evolution and development of mammals, birds, and flowers. • *n.* this era.

cen•ser /sénsər/ *n.* vessel in which incense is burned.

cen•sor /sénsər/ • *n.* person who examines printed matter, movies, news, etc., to suppress any parts on the grounds of obscenity, security, etc. • *v. tr.* **1** act as a censor of. **2** make deletions or changes in. □□ **cen•so′ri•al** /–sáwreeəl/ *adj.* **cen•so•ri•ous** /–sáwreeəs/ *adj.* **cen′sor•ship** *n.*

■ *v.* bowdlerize, expurgate, blue-pencil, edit, delete.

cen•sure /sénshər/ • *v. tr.* criticize harshly; reprove. See synonym study at REBUKE. • *n.* harsh criticism; expression of disapproval. □□ **cen′sur•a•ble** *adj.*

cen•sus /sénsəs/ *n.* (*pl.* **cen•sus•es**) official count of a population or of a class of things.

■ poll, canvas.

cent /sent/ *n.* **1** monetary unit valued at one-hundredth of a dollar. **2** coin of this value.

cen•taur /séntawr/ *n. Gk mythol.* creature with the head, arms, and torso of a man and the body and legs of a horse.

cen•te•nar•i•an /séntináreeən/ • *n.* person a hundred or more years old. • *adj.* a hundred or more years old.

cen•te•nar•y /sénténəree, séntəneree/ *n.* (*pl.* **–ries**) = CENTENNIAL • *adj.* **1** of or relating to a centenary. **2** occurring every hundred years.

cen•ten•ni•al /senténeeəl/ • *adj.* **1** lasting for a hundred years. **2** occurring every hundred years. • *n.* **1** hundredth anniversary. **2** celebration of this.

cen•ter /séntər/ • *n.* **1** middle point. **2** pivot or axis of rotation. **3** place or group of buildings forming a central point or a main area for an activity. **4** point of concentration or dispersion; nucleus or source. **5** political party or group holding moderate opinions. • *v.* **1** *intr.* have as its main center. **2** *tr.* place in the center. **3** *tr.* concentrate. □ **center of gravity** (or **mass**) point at which the weight of a body may be considered to act. □□ **cen′tered** *adj.* [often in *comb.*]. **cen′ter•most** *adj.* **cen′tric** *adj.*

■ *n.* **1** midpoint; bull's-eye. **2** fulcrum, hub. **3** focal point, hub. **4** nub, core, heart, kernel. • *v.* **3** focus, direct, train, turn.

cen•ter•board /séntərbawrd/ *n.* retractable keel.

cen•ter•fold /séntərfōld/ *n.* printed and usu. illustrated sheet folded to form the center spread of a magazine, etc.

cen•ter•piece /séntərpees/ *n.* **1** ornament for the middle of a table. **2** principal item.

centi- /séntee/ *comb. form* **1** one-hundredth, esp. of a unit in the metric system (*centigram*). **2** hundred. ¶Abbr.: **c**.

cen•ti•grade /séntigrayd/ *adj.* = CELSIUS.

cen•ti•me•ter /séntimeetər/ *n.* one-hundredth of a meter.

cen•ti•pede /séntipeed/ *n.* arthropod with a wormlike body of many segments each with a pair of legs.

cen•tral /séntrəl/ *adj.* **1** of, at, or forming the center. **2** from the center. **3** chief; essential; most important. □ **Central America** isthmus joining N. and S. America. **central nervous system** *Anat.* brain and spinal cord. **central processor** (or **processing unit**) principal operating part of a computer. □□ **cen•tral•i•ty** /–trálitee/ *n.* **cen′tral•ly** *adv.*

■ **1** middle, medial, median. **3** main, principal, major, key, leading, dominant; vital, crucial, critical.

cen•tral•ize /séntrəliz/ v. **1** tr. & intr. bring or come to a center. **2** tr. **a** concentrate (administration) at a single center. **b** subject (a government) to this system. □□ **cen•tral•i•za′tion** n.
  ■ **1** see CONCENTRATE v. 2, CONVERGE.

cen•trif•u•gal /sentrífyəgəl, –trifə–/ adj. moving or tending to move from a center (cf. CENTRIPETAL). □ **centrifugal force** apparent force that acts outward on a body moving about a center. □□ **cen•trif′u•gal•ly** adv.

cen•tri•fuge /séntrifyŏŏj/ n. machine with a rapidly rotating device designed to separate liquids from solids or other liquids (e.g., cream from milk).

cen•trip•e•tal /sentrípit′l/ adj. moving or tending to move toward a center (cf. CENTRIFUGAL). □ **centripetal force** force acting on a body causing it to move about a center. □□ **cen•trip′e•tal•ly** adv.

cen•trist /séntrist/ n. Polit. person who holds moderate views. □□ **cen′trism** n.

cen•tu•ri•on /sentyŏŏreeən, –tyŏŏr–/ n. commander of a century in the ancient Roman army.

cen•tu•ry /sénchəree/ n. (pl. **–ries**) **1 a** period of one hundred years. **b** any of the centuries calculated from the birth of Christ (twentieth century = 1901–2000). ¶In modern use often calculated as, e.g., 1900–1999. **2** company in the ancient Roman army, orig. of 100 men.

CEO abbr. chief executive officer.

ce•phal•ic /sifálik/ adj. of or in the head.

ceph•a•lo•pod /séfələpod/ n. mollusk having a distinct tentacled head, e.g., octopus, squid, and cuttlefish.

ce•ram•ic /sirámik/ • adj. **1** made of (esp.) clay and permanently hardened by heat (ceramic bowl). **2** of or relating to ceramics (ceramic arts). • n. ceramic article or product.

ce•ram•ics /sirámiks/ n.pl. **1** ceramic products collectively. **2** [usu. treated as sing.] art of making ceramic articles.
  ■ **1** see POTTERY.

ce•re•al /séereeəl/ • n. **1 a** grain used for food. **b** any grass producing this, e.g., wheat, corn, rye, etc. **2** breakfast food made from a cereal. • adj. of edible grain or products of it.

cer•e•bel•lum /séribéləm/ n. (pl. **cer•e•bel•lums** or **cer•e•bel•la** /–lə/) part of the brain at the back of the skull.

ce•re•bral /séribrəl, sərée–/ adj. **1** of the brain. **2** intellectual rather than emotional. □ **cerebral palsy** Med. spastic paralysis from brain damage before or at birth, with jerky or uncontrolled movements. □□ **ce•re′bral•ly** adv.
  ■ **2** see INTELLECTUAL adj. 1.

ce•re•brum /séribrəm, sərée–/ n. (pl. **cer•e•brums** or **cer•e•bra** /–brə/) principal part of the brain in vertebrates, located in the front area of the skull.

cer•e•mo•ni•al /sérimōneeəl/ • adj. **1** with or concerning ritual or ceremony. **2** formal (a ceremonial bow). See synonym study at FORMAL. • n. system of rites, etc., to be used esp. at a formal or religious occasion. □□ **cer•e•mo′ni•al•ism** n. **cer•e•mo′ni•al•ist** n. **cer•e•mo′ni•al•ly** adv.
  ■ adj. **1** celebratory, commemorative, state. **2** solemn, stately, official, dignified, ritual.

cer•e•mo•ni•ous /sérimōneeəs/ adj. **1** excessively polite. **2** having or showing a fondness for ritualistic observance or formality. See synonym study at FORMAL. □□ **cer•e•mo′ni•ous•ly** adv.
  ■ **1** punctilious, nice, courtly, overnice, exact, precise. **2** ceremonial, formal, dignified, solemn, ritual.

cer•e•mo•ny /sérimōnee/ n. (pl. **–nies**) **1** formal religious or public occasion, esp. celebrating a particular event or anniversary. **2** formalities, esp. of an empty or ritualistic kind. **3** excessively polite behavior. □ **master of ceremonies** (also **MC** or **emcee**) person in charge of a ceremonial or social occasion. **stand on ceremony** insist on the observance of formalities.
  ■ **1** rite(s), solemnity, service; function, celebration. **2** pomp, convention(s), niceties, proprieties. **3** punctiliousness, courtesy, etiquette, decorum.

ce•rise /sərées, –réez/ • adj. of a light, clear red. • n. this color.

ce•ri•um /séereeəm/ n. Chem. silvery metallic element. ¶Symb.: **Ce**.

cer•tain /sárt′n/ • adj. **1 a** confident; convinced. **b** indisputable. **2 a** that may be relied on to happen (it is certain to rain). **b** destined (certain to become a star). **3** unfailing; reliable. **4** that might be specified, but is not (a certain lady). **5** some though not much (a certain reluctance). • pron. [as pl.] some but not all (certain of them were wounded). □ **for certain** without doubt.
  ■ adj. **1 a** sure, positive, satisfied. **b** definite, indubitable, undoubted, clear, unequivocal. **2 a** bound, sure. **b** fated. **3** definite, firm, sure, decided; unerring, dependable, unfailing. **4** unnamed; particular. pron. a number. □ **for certain** assuredly, definitely, surely, positively; undoubtedly, absolutely, colloq. for sure.

cer•tain•ly /sárt′nlee/ adv. **1** undoubtedly; definitely. **2** (in answer) yes; by all means.
  ■ **1** see undoubtedly (UNDOUBTED). **2** see ABSOLUTELY 4.

cer•tain•ty /sárt′ntee/ n. (pl. **–ties**) **1** undoubted fact or prospect. **2** absolute conviction. **3** thing or person that may be relied on.
  ■ **1** actuality, reality, truth, sure thing, colloq. cinch. **2** assurance, definiteness, confidence, certitude, sureness, fixedness.

cer•ti•fi•a•ble /sórtifiəbəl/ adj. **1** able or needing to be certified. **2** colloq. insane.
  ■ see DOCUMENT n.

cer•tif•i•cate /sərtifikət/ n. formal document attesting a fact, esp. birth, marriage, death, a medical condition, a level of achievement, etc. □□ **cer•ti•fi•ca•tion** /sórtifikáyshən/ n.
  ■ n. see DOCUMENT n.

cer•ti•fy /sórtifi/ v.tr. (**–fies, –fied**) **1** make a formal statement of; attest; attest to. **2** declare by certificate (that a person is qualified or competent) (certified as a trained bookkeeper). **3** officially declare insane. See synonym study at APPROVE.

■ **1** confirm, verify, vouch for, testify (to), bear witness to, affirm, declare, asseverate, corroborate; swear.

cer•ti•tude /sɔ́rtitōod, –tyōod/ n. feeling of absolute certainty.

■ see CONVICTION 2a.

ce•ru•le•an /sɔrōōleeən/ literary • adj. deep blue like a clear sky. • n. this color.

cer•vi•cal /sɔ́rvikəl/ adj. Anat. **1** of or relating to the neck (cervical vertebrae). **2** of or relating to the cervix.

cer•vix /sɔ́rviks/ n. (pl. cer•vic•es /–viseez/ or cer•vix•es) Anat. any necklike structure, esp. the neck of the womb.

Ce•sar•e•an /sizáireeən/ (also Ce•sar'i•an, Cae•sar'e•an, Cae•sar'i•an) • adj. (ot a birth) effected by cesarean section. • n. cesarean section. □ cesarean section (also C–section) operation for delivering a child by cutting through the wall of the abdomen.

ce•si•um /séezeeəm/ n. soft, silver-white element. ¶Symb.: Cs. □ cesium clock atomic clock that uses cesium.

ces•sa•tion /sesáyshən/ n. **1** ceasing. **2** pause.

■ **1** see END[1] n. 3a, b. **2** see REST n. 3.

ces•sion /séshən/ n. **1** ceding (of rights, property, and esp. of territory by a nation). **2** the territory, etc., so ceded.

cess•pool /séspōol/ n. pit for waste or sewage.

ce•ta•cean /sitáyshən/ • n. any marine mammal with dorsal blowhole for breathing, including whales, dolphins, and porpoises. • adj. of cetaceans. □□ ce•ta•ceous /–táy-shəs/ adj.

Cf symb. Chem. californium.

cf. abbr. compare.

CFA abbr. chartered financial analyst.

CFC abbr. Chem. chlorofluorocarbon, a compound of carbon, hydrogen, chlorine, and fluorine, used in refrigerants, etc., and thought to be harmful to the ozone layer.

cfm abbr. cubic feet per minute.

cfs abbr. cubic feet per second.

cg abbr. centigram(s).

c.h. abbr. (also C.H.) **1** clearinghouse. **2** courthouse.

Cha•blis /shableé, shāblee/ n. (pl. same /–leez/) type of dry white wine.

cha-cha /chaáchaa/ (also cha-cha-cha /cháachaachaá/) n. **1** ballroom dance with a Latin-American rhythm **2** music for or in the rhythm of a cha-cha.

chafe /chayf/ v. **1** make or become sore or damaged by rubbing. **2** make or become annoyed; fret (was chafed by the delay).

■ **1** abrade, fret, gall, irritate. **2** fume, rage, seethe; see also IRRITATE 1.

chaff /chaf/ • n. **1** husks of grain or other seed. **2** chopped hay and straw used as fodder. **3** lighthearted joking. **4** worthless things. • v.tr. tease; banter. □ separate the wheat from the chaff distinguish good from bad. □□ chaff'y adj.

■ n. **3** banter, raillery, colloq. ribbing. **4** see RUBBISH n. 1, 2. • v. **1** poke fun (at); kid, pull a person's leg.

chaf•ing dish /cháyfing/ n. **1** cooking pot with an outer pan of hot water, used for keeping food warm. **2** dish with an alcohol lamp, etc., for cooking at table.

cha•grin /shəgrín/ • n. acute vexation or mortification. • v.tr. affect with chagrin.

chain /chayn/ • n. **1 a** connected flexible series of esp. metal links. **b** something resembling this (formed a human chain). **2** [in pl.] fetters, restraining force. **3** sequence, series, or set (chain of events, mountain chain). **4** group of associated restaurants, newspapers, etc. • v.tr. secure or confine with a chain. □ chain gang team of convicts chained together and forced to work in the open air. chain reaction **1** Physics self-sustaining nuclear reaction. **2** Chem. self-sustaining molecular reaction. **3** series of events, each caused by the previous one. chain saw motor-driven saw with teeth on an endless chain.

■ n. **2** (chains) see BOND n. 1b; restriction(s), constraint(s). **3** string, stream; train, course • n. **1** shackle, fasten, bind (up), fetter.

chair /chair/ • n. **1** separate seat for one person, of various forms, usu. having a back and four legs. **2** professorship. **3 a** chairperson. **b** seat or office of a chairperson (I'm in the chair). • v.tr. act as chairperson of or preside over (a meeting).

■ n. **3 a** chairman, chairwoman, presiding officer. • v. head (up), lead, moderate, run, direct.

chair•lift /cháirlift/ n. series of chairs on an endless cable for carrying passengers up and down a mountain, etc.

chair•man /cháirmən/ n. (pl. –men; fem. chair•wom•an, pl. –wom•en) **1** person chosen to preside over a meeting. **2** permanent president of a committee, board of directors, etc. □□ chair'man•ship n.

chair•per•son /cháirpərsən/ n. chairman or chairwoman.

chaise longue /sháyz lóng, shéz/ n. reclining chair with a lengthened seat forming a leg rest.

cha•let /shalay, shálay/ n. **1** small house, bungalow, or hut, esp. with an overhanging roof. **2** Swiss cowherd's hut, or wooden cottage, with overhanging eaves.

chal•ice /chális/ n. **1** wine cup used in the Communion service. **2** literary goblet.

chalk /chawk/ • n. **1** white, soft, earthy limestone. **2** similar substance (calcium sulfate), sometimes colored, used for writing or drawing. • v.tr. **1** rub, mark, draw, or write with chalk. **2** [foll. by up] **a** write or record with chalk. **b** register (a success, etc.). □□ chalk•y /cháwkee/ adj. (chalk•i•er, chalk•i•est) chalk'i•ness n.

chal•lenge /chálinj/ • n. **1 a** summons to take part in a contest or a trial of strength, etc. **b** summons to prove or justify something. **2** demanding or difficult task. **3** Law objection made to a jury member. • v.tr. **1 a** invite to take part in a contest, game, debate, duel, etc. **b** invite to prove or justify something. **2** dispute; deny. **3 a** stretch; stimulate (challenges him to produce his best). **b** (as challenging adj.) demanding; stimulatingly difficult. **4** *Law* object to (a jury member, evidence, etc.). **5** (as **challenged** *adj.*) disabled. □□ **chal'lenge•a•ble** *adj.* **chal'leng•er** *n.*

■ *n.* **1** defiance, gage, dare; ultimatum. **2** needs; test, trial. • *v.* **1 a** dare, summon, call out, provoke; take on. **b** defy. **2** question, object to, take exception to; disagree with; oppose. **3 a** test; drive. **b** (**challenging**) formidable, exacting.

cha•lu•pa /chaalōōpaa/ *Cookery* **1** Mexican-American dish consisting of a fried tortilla holding refried beans or ground meat and shredded cheese, lettuce, tomato, and hot sauce. **2** Mexican-American stew made from pork, beans, chili peppers, and spices.

cham•ber /cháymbər/ *n.* **1 a** hall used by a legislative or judicial body. **b** body that meets in it. **2** [in *pl.*] judge's room. **3** enclosed space in machinery, etc. (esp. the part of a gun bore that contains the charge). **4 a** cavity in a plant or in the body of an animal. **b** compartment in a structure. **5** *poet.* or *archaic* room, esp. a bedroom. □ **chamber of commerce** association to promote local commercial interests.

■ **1 b** assembly, legislature, judicature, judiciary, house, congress, senate. **3** enclosure, magazine, *Mech.* manifold. **4 a** *Anat.* antrum, vestibule. **b** cell, cavity, space.

cham•ber•lain /cháymbərlin/ *n.* officer managing a royal or noble household.

cham•ber•maid /cháymbərmayd/ *n.* housemaid who cleans bedrooms, esp. in a hotel, etc.

cha•me•le•on /kəmeélyən/ *n.* small lizard having the power of changing color. □□ **cha•me•le•on•ic** /–leeónik/ *adj.*

cham•ois /shámee/ *n.* (*pl.* same /–eez/) **1** agile goat antelope native to Europe and Asia. **2 a** soft leather from sheep, goats, deer, etc. **b** a piece of this or similar soft material used for polishing, etc.

cham•o•mile /kámɔmil, –meel/ *n.* (also **cam'o•mile**) aromatic plant with daisylike flowers. □ **chámomile tea** infusion of its dried flowers used as a tonic.

champ[1] /champ/ *v.* **1** *tr. & intr.* munch or chew noisily. **2** *tr.* (of a horse, etc.) work (the bit) noisily between the teeth.

champ[2] /champ/ *n. sl.* champion.

cham•pagne /shampáyn/ *n.* **1** white sparkling wine, originally from Champagne in France. **2** pale cream or straw color.

cham•pi•on /chámpeeən/ • *n.* **1** person, animal, plant, etc., that has defeated or surpassed all rivals in a competition, etc. **2** person who fights or argues for a cause or on behalf of another person. • *v.tr.* support the cause of; defend; argue in favor of.

■ *n.* **1** victor, winner, conqueror, titleholder. **2** defender, guardian, protector, advocate, proponent. • *v.* protect, guard; back, stand up for; espouse, forward, promote, advocate, urge.

cham•pi•on•ship /chámpeeənship/ *n.* **1** [often in *pl.*] contest for the position of champion. **2** position of champion.

■ **1** see CONTEST *n.* **1**. **2** title, crown.

chance /chans/ • *n.* **1 a** possibility. **b** [often in *pl.*] probability (*the chances are against it*). **2** opportunity (*didn't have a chance to speak*). **3** the way things happen; fortune; luck (*we'll just leave it to chance*). • *adj.* fortuitous; accidental (*a chance meeting*). • *v.* **1** *tr. colloq.* risk (*we'll chance it and go*). **2** *intr.* happen without intention (*I chanced to find it*). See synonym study at HAPPEN. □ **by any chance** as it happens; perhaps. **by chance** without design; unintentionally. **chance on** (or **upon**) happen to find, meet, etc. **stand a chance** have a prospect of success, etc.

■ *n.* **1** conceivably; (*chances*) likelihood, odds. **2** occasion; window, opening; see also SHOT[1] 5b. **3** fate, destiny, fortuity. • *adj.* casual, coincidental, adventitious; unintentional, inadvertent, unplanned. • *v.* **1** hazard, venture. □ **by any chance** see POSSIBLY 2. **by chance** accidentally, coincidentally, fortuitously.

chan•cel /chánsəl/ *n.* part of a church near the altar.

chan•cel•ler•y /chánsələree, chánslə–/ *n.* (*pl.* –**ies**) **1 a** position, office, staff, department, etc., of a chancellor. **b** official residence of a chancellor. **2** office attached to an embassy or consulate.

chan•cel•lor /chánsələr, chánslər/ *n.* **1** government official of various kinds; head of the government in some European countries, e.g., Germany. **2** chief administrator at certain universities. □□ **chan'cel•lor•ship** *n.*

■ **1** see PREMIER *n.*

chan•cer•y /chánsəree/ *n.* (*pl.* –**ies**) **1** (in full **court of chancery**) court of equity. **2** administrative office for a diocese. **3** office attached to an embassy or consulate.

chanc•y /chánsee/ *adj.* (**chanc•i•er, chanc•i•est**) subject to chance; uncertain; risky. □□ **chanc'i•ly** *adv.* **chanc'i•ness** *n.*

■ see *risky* (RISK).

chan•de•lier /shándəleer/ *n.* ornamental branched hanging support for several candles or electric lightbulbs.

change /chaynj/ • *n.* **1 a** making or becoming different. **b** alteration or modification. **2 a** money given in exchange for money in larger units or a different currency. **b** money returned as the balance of that given in payment. **3** new experience; variety (*for a change*). **4** substitution of one thing for another (*change of scene*). • *v.* **1** *tr. & intr.* undergo, show, or subject to change; make or become different. **2** *tr.* **a** take or use another instead of (*changed trains*). **b** give up or get rid of in exchange (*changed the car for a van*). **3** *tr.* **a** give or get change in smaller denominations for (*can you change a ten-dollar bill?*). **b** exchange (a sum of money) for (*changed his dollars for pounds*). **4** *tr. & intr.* put fresh clothes or coverings on (*changed into something loose*). **5** *tr.* give and receive; exchange (*we changed places*). □ **change hands 1** pass to a different owner. **2** substitute one hand for another. **change one's tune 1** voice a different opinion from that expressed previously. **2** change one's style of language or manner. □□ **change'ful** *adj.* **chang'er** *n.*

■ *n.* **1** transformation, mutation, shift; adjustment, transition, flux. **2 c** coin(s), silver. **3** variation, novelty. **4** switch, exchange, trade. • *v.* **1** modify, alter, modulate, convert; mutate; fluctuate, shift, distort, warp. **2, 5** interchange, switch; replace, substitute.

change•a•ble /cháynjəbəl/ *adj.* **1** irregular; inconstant. **2** that can change or be changed. □□ **change•a•bil•i•ty** *n.* **change′a•ble•ness** *n.* **change′a•bly** *adv.*

■ **1** variable, protean, unstable, unsettled, shifting; capricious, erratic, fickle. **2** alterable, modifiable, transformable, convertible.

change•less /cháynjlis/ *adj.* unchanging.

■ unvaried, constant, steadfast; see also ABIDING.

change•ling /cháynjling/ *n.* child believed to be substituted for another by stealth, esp. in folklore.

change•o•ver /cháynjōvər/ *n.* change from one system or situation to another.

■ conversion, switch, shift, revolution; transition, move.

chan•nel /chánəl/ • *n.* **1 a** length of water wider than a strait, joining two larger areas, esp. seas. **b (the Channel)** the English Channel between Britain and France. **2** medium of communication; agency. **3** *Broadcasting* band of frequencies used in radio and television transmission, esp. as used by a particular station. **4** course in which anything moves; direction. **5 a** natural or artificial hollow bed of water. **b** navigable part of a waterway. • *v.tr.* guide; direct.

■ *n.* **2** avenue, path, course; vehicle, method. **5a** watercourse, canal, waterway, stream, ditch. • *v.* **1** convey, pass, lead, conduct, focus, train.

chant /chant/ • *n.* **1** spoken singsong phrase. **2** *Mus.* a short musical passage in two or more phrases used for singing unmetrical words, e.g., psalms, canticles. **b** song, esp. monotonous or repetitive. • *v.* sing or intone (a psalm, etc.).

■ *n.* **2 b** psalm, canticle, plainsong, mantra.

chan•teuse /shaantöz/ *n.* female singer of popular songs.

Cha•nu•kkah var. of HANUKKAH.

cha•os /káyos/ *n.* utter confusion. □ **chaos theory** *Math.* the study of the apparently random behavior of deterministic systems. □□ **cha•ot•ic** /kayótik/ *adj.* **cha•ot′i•cal•ly** *adv.*

■ pandemonium, bedlam, havoc, mayhem, babel, turmoil, disarray; disorder, disorganization. □□ **chaotic** formless, shapeless, incoherent, disordered, at sixes and sevens, jumbled, turbulent, tumultuous.

chap[1] /chap/ • *v.* **(chapped, chap•ping) 1** *intr.* (esp. of the skin; also of dry ground, etc.) crack in fissures, esp. because of exposure and dryness. **2** *tr.* (of the wind, cold, etc.) cause to chap. • *n.* [usu. in *pl.*] crack in the skin.

chap[2] /chap/ *n.* man; boy; fellow.

■ lad, *colloq.* guy.

chap. *abbr.* chapter.

chap•ar•ral /shápərál, cháp–/ *n.* dense, tangled brushwood.

chap•el /chápəl/ *n.* **1** place for private Chris-

---

tian worship in a large church or esp. a cathedral, with its own altar and dedication. **2** place of worship attached to a private house or institution.

■ see SANCTUARY 1.

chap•er•on /shápərōn/ (also **chap′er•one**) • *n.* **1** person, esp. an older woman, who ensures propriety by accompanying a young unmarried woman on social occasions. **2** person who takes charge of esp. young people in public. • *v.tr.* act as a chaperon to. □□ **chap•er•on•age** /shápərōnij/ *n.*

■ *n.* see ESCORT *n.* 1. • *v.* see ACCOMPANY 1.

chap•lain /cháplin/ *n.* member of the clergy attached to a private chapel, institution, ship, regiment, etc. □□ **chap′lain•cy** *n.* (*pl.* –cies)

chap•let /cháplit/ *n.* **1** garland or circlet for the head. **2** string of 55 beads (one-third of the rosary number) for counting prayers, or as a necklace. □□ **chap′let•ed** *adj.*

■ **1** see GARLAND *n.*

chap•ter /cháptər/ *n.* **1** main division of a book. **2** period of time (in a person's life, a nation's history, etc.). **3** local branch of a society.

■ **1** see EPISODE 2. **2** see ERA. **3** see LODGE *n.* 4.

char[1] /chaar/ *v.* **(charred, char•ring) 1** make or become black by burning; scorch. **2** burn to charcoal. See synonym study at BURN.

char•ac•ter /káriktər/ *n.* **1** collective qualities or characteristics, esp. mental and moral, that distinguish a person or thing. **2 a** moral strength (*has a weak character*). **b** reputation, esp. good reputation. **3** a person in a novel, play, etc. **b** part played by an actor; role. **4** *colloq.* person, esp. an eccentric or outstanding individual (*he's a real character*). **5** printed or written letter, symbol, or distinctive mark (*Chinese characters*). □□ **char′ac•ter•less** *adj.*

■ **1** personality, nature, temperament, disposition, features, properties. **2 a** morality, honesty, integrity, uprightness. **b** see REPUTATION. **3** (*characters*) dramatis personae. **4** original, *colloq.* card. **5** monogram, sign; number, figure.

char•ac•ter•is•tic /káriktərístik/ • *adj.* typical; distinctive (*with characteristic expertise*). • *n.* distinguishing feature or quality. □□ **char•ac•ter•is′ti•cal•ly** *adv.*

■ *adj.* representative; emblematic, symbolic. • *n.* mark, trait, attribute, property, hallmark, indication.

char•ac•ter•ize /káriktəriz/ *v.tr.* **1 a** describe the character of. **b** describe as. **2** be characteristic of. **3** impart character to. □□ **char•ac•ter•i•za′tion** *n.*

■ **1, 2** define; delineate, portray. **3** see TYPIFY.

cha•rade /shəráyd/ *n.* **1** [usu. in *pl.*, treated as *sing.*] game of guessing a word from a written or acted clue given for each syllable and for the whole. **2** absurd pretense.

■ **2** travesty, absurdity, mockery, farce, parody, nonsense.

char•coal /cháarkōl/ *n.* **1 a** amorphous form

of carbon consisting of a porous black residue from partially burned wood, bones, etc. **b** piece of this used for drawing. **2** drawing in charcoal. **3** (in full **charcoal gray**) dark gray color.

charge /chaarj/ • v. **1** tr. **a** ask (an amount) as a price. **b** ask (a person) for an amount as a price. **2** tr. **a** debit the cost of to (a person or account). **b** debit (a person or an account). **3** tr. **a** accuse (of an offense) (charged him with theft). **b** make an accusation that. **4** tr. instruct or urge. **5** tr. entrust with. **6 a** intr. make a rushing attack. **b** tr. make a rushing attack on. **7** tr. **a** give an electric charge to (a body). **b** store energy in (a battery). **8** tr. load or fill, as with fuel, emotion, etc. See synonym study at ATTACK. • n. **1 a** price asked for goods or services. **b** financial liability or commitment. **2** accusation, esp. against a defendant. **3 a** task, duty, or commission. **b** care, custody, responsible possession. **c** person or thing entrusted; minister's congregation. **4 a** impetuous rush or attack, esp. in a battle. **b** signal for this. **5** appropriate amount of material to be put into a receptacle, mechanism, etc. **6 a** property of matter causing electrical phenomena. **b** quantity of this carried by a body. **7** exhortation; directions; orders. □ **charge account** credit account at a store, etc. **charge card** credit card for which the account must be paid in full when a statement is issued. **in charge** having command. **take charge** assume control or direction. □□ **charge′a•ble** adj.

• v. **1 a** demand, claim, require, expect. **b** bill, invoice. **2 a** (charge to) put on a person's account, chalk up to. **3** indict, impeach, arraign, incriminate, inculpate; allege; assert, claim, hold, asseverate, maintain, contend. **4** command, order, direct, tell, enjoin, exhort, beg, call on, archaic or literary bid. **5** trust. **6 a** assault, charge, storm, rush. **b** rush at, assault, storm, assail, set upon, come at, descend upon. • n. **1 a** fee, cost, payment, rate, tariff, fare, toll, sl. damages. **b** debt, debit, expense, assessment. **2** imputation, indictment, allegation, complaint. **3 a** see OBLIGATION 2. **b** protection, safekeeping, keeping, trust, guardianship, wardship, custodianship; supervision, jurisdiction, control, guidance, leadership. **c** concern, responsibility; protégé. **4 a** onset, assault, sally, sortie, going forth, raid, foray. **7** mandate, injunction, precept, command, dictate, instruction, demand. □ **in charge** see call the shots. **take charge** see HEAD v. 2.

char•ger /chaarjər/ n. **1** cavalry horse. **2** apparatus for charging a battery. **3** person or thing that charges.

char•i•ot /chareeot/ n. hist. two-wheeled vehicle drawn by horses, used in ancient warfare and racing. □□ **char•i•o•teer′** n.

cha•ris•ma /kərízmə/ n. (pl. **cha•ris•ma•ta** /-mətə/) **1** ability to inspire followers with devotion and enthusiasm. **2** attractive aura; great charm. □□ **char•is•mat•ic** /kárizmátik/ adj. **char•is•mat′i•cal•ly** adv.

■ **2** see APPEAL n. 4. □□ **charismatic** see MAGNETIC.

char•i•ta•ble /cháritəbəl/ adj. **1** generous in giving to those in need. **2** of, relating to, or connected with a charity or charities. **3** apt to judge favorably of persons, acts, and motives. □□ **char′i•ta•ble•ness** n. **char′i•ta•bly** adv.

■ **1** liberal, bountiful, munificent, free, unsparing, unstinting. **2** sympathetic, magnanimous, understanding, compassionate.

char•i•ty /cháritee/ n. (pl. **–ties**) **1** giving voluntarily to those in need. **2** institution or organization for helping those in need. **3 a** kindness; benevolence. **b** tolerance. See synonym study at MERCY.

■ **1** help, aid, support; relief, benefit. **3 a** generosity, philanthropy, unselfishness, altruism. **b** leniency, bigheartedness, magnanimity, indulgence.

char•la•tan /shaarlətən/ n. person falsely claiming a special knowledge or skill. □□ **char′la•tan•ism** n. **char′la•tan•ry** n.

■ see FRAUD 3.

char•ley horse /chaarlee/ n. sl. stiffness or cramp in a thigh.

charm /chaarm/ • n. **1 a** power or quality of giving delight or arousing admiration. **b** fascination; attractiveness. **c** [usu. in pl.] attractive or enticing quality. **2** trinket on a bracelet, etc. **3 a** object, act, or word(s) supposedly having occult or magic power; spell. **b** thing worn to avert evil, etc.; amulet. • v.tr. **1** delight; captivate. **2** influence or protect as if by magic (leads a charmed life). **3** gain or influence by charm. □ **like a charm** perfectly; wonderfully. □□ **charm′er** n.

■ n. **1 a, b** appeal, attraction, allure, magnetism, draw. **3 a** spell, incantation, conjuration. **b** talisman, good-luck piece, juju. • v. **1** see CAPTIVATE, DELIGHT v. 1. **3** seduce, coax, see also BEGUILE 1. □ **like a charm** successfully, marvelously, like a dream, like clockwork. □□ **charmer** enchanter, enchantress, sorcerer, sorceress, magician; vamp, siren, temptress, seductress; seducer, Romeo, Don Juan.

charm•ing /chaarming/ adj. **1** delightful; attractive; pleasing. **2** [often as int.] iron. expressing displeasure or disapproval. □□ **charm′ing•ly** adv.

■ **1** see DELIGHTFUL.

chart /chaart/ • n. **1** geographical map or plan, esp. for navigation by sea or air. **2** sheet of information in the form of a table, graph, or diagram. **3** [usu. in pl.] colloq. listing of the currently most popular music recordings. • v.tr. make a chart of; map.

■ n. **2** tabulation. • v. plot, draw, mark (out); delineate, sketch (out), trace, rough out, outline.

charter /chaartər/ • n. **1** written grant of rights, by a sovereign or legislature, esp. the creation of a city, company, university, etc. **2** written constitution or description of an organization's functions, etc. • v.tr. **1** grant a charter to. **2** hire (an aircraft, ship, etc.). □ **charter member** original member of a society, corporation, etc. □□ **char′ter•er** n.

■ *n.* **1** contract, compact, agreement; permit, license. • *v.* **1** license, authorize, commission, franchise. **2** let, lease, rent, engage.

char•treuse /shaartrōōz, –trōōs/ *n.* **1** pale green or yellow liqueur made from brandy. **2** pale yellow or pale green color of this.

char•y /cháiree/ *adj.* (**char•i•er, char•i•est**) **1** cautious; wary. **2** sparing; ungenerous. □□ **char′i•ly** *adv.* **char′i•ness** *n.*
■ **1** see WARY.

chase[1] /chays/ • *v.tr.* **1** pursue in order to catch. **2** drive. **3** *colloq.* **a** try to attain. **b** court persistently and openly. • *n.* **1** pursuit. **2** [*prec. by the*] hunting, esp. as a sport.
■ *v.* **1** follow, track, hunt. **2** hound. **3 a** see PURSUE 5. **b** see COURT *v.* 1b. • *n.* **1** search, hunt, tracking, stalking; pursuance.

chase[2] /chays/ *v.tr.* emboss or engrave (metal)

chas•er /cháysər/ *n. colloq.* drink taken after another of a different kind, e.g., beer after liquor.

chasm /kázəm/ *n.* **1** deep fissure or opening in the earth, rock, etc. **2** wide difference of; a gulf. □□ **chas′mic** *adj.*
■ **1** see GORGE *n.* 1.

chas•sis /shásee, chás–/ *n.* (*pl.* same /–siz/) **1** base frame of a motor vehicle, carriage, etc. **2** frame to carry radio, etc., components.

chaste /chayst/ *adj.* **1** abstaining from extramarital, or from all, sexual intercourse. **2** (of behavior, speech, etc.) pure, virtuous, decent. **3** (of artistic, etc., style) simple; unadorned. □□ **chaste′ly** *adv.* **chaste′ness** *n.*
■ **1** pure, virginal, virgin, celibate, abstinent, continent, virtuous. **2** innocent, platonic, uncorrupted, sinless, blameless, immaculate, spotless, unblemished. **3** undecorated, unembellished, subdued, restrained.

chast•en /cháysən/ *v.tr.* **1** (esp. as **chastening, chastened** *adjs.*) subdue; restrain. **2** discipline; punish. □□ **chas′ten•er** *n.*
■ **1** humble, shame; curb, control, check, correct, chastise; see also CASTIGATE.

chas•tise /chastīz, chástīz/ *v.tr.* **1** rebuke or reprimand severely. **2** punish, esp. by beating. □□ **chas•tise′ment** *n.* **chas•tis′er** *n.*
■ **1** see REDUCE *v.* **2** thrash, belabor, spank, whip, flog; discipline, chasten, castigate.

chas•ti•ty /chástitee/ *n.* being chaste.
■ purity, continence, virginity, abstention, restraint.

cha•su•ble /cházəbəl, cházyə–, chás–/ *n.* loose, sleeveless, often ornate outer vestment worn by a priest.

chat /chat/ • *v.intr.* (**chat•ted, chat•ting**) talk in a light familiar way. • *n.* informal conversation or talk. See synonym study at CONVERSATION. □□ **chat′ty** *adj.* (**chat•ti•er, chat•ti•est**). **chat′ti•ly** *adv.* **chat′ti•ness** *n.*
■ *v.* converse, gossip, chatter, *colloq.* chitchat, *sl.* rap. • *n.* **1** gossip, *colloq.* gab.

châ•teau /shatṓ/ *n.* (*pl.* **châ•teaus** or **châ•teaux** /–tṓz/) large French country house or castle.
■ mansion, palace, manor house, hall.

chat•e•laine /shát′layn/ *n.* mistress of a large house.

chat•tel /chát′l/ *n.* [usu. in *pl.*] moveable pos-

session; any possession or piece of property other than real estate or a freehold.

chat•ter /chátər/ • *v.intr.* **1** talk quickly, incessantly, trivially, or indiscreetly. **2** (of a bird) emit short, quick notes. **3** (of the teeth) click repeatedly together (usu. from cold). • *n.* chattering talk or sounds. □□ **chat′ter•er** *n.* **chat′ter•y** *adj.*
■ *v.* **1** prattle, gabble, jabber, prate, *colloq.* gab, jaw, natter. **3** clatter, rattle, shake, shiver. • *n.* prattle, babble, twaddle, blather, *colloq.* chitchat, gab.

chat•ter•box /chátərboks/ *n.* talkative person.
■ blabber(mouth), gossip, *colloq.* blab, bigmouth.

chauf•feur /shṓfər, –fȯ́r/ • *n.* person employed to drive a private or rented automobile or limousine. • *v.tr.* drive (a car or a person) as a chauffeur.

chau•vin•ism /shṓvinizm/ *n.* **1** exaggerated or aggressive patriotism. **2** excessive or prejudiced support or loyalty.

chau•vin•ist /shṓvinist/ *n.* **1** person exhibiting chauvinism. **2** (in full **male chauvinist**) man showing excessive loyalty to men and prejudice against women. □□ **chau•vin•is′tic** *adj.* **chau•vin•is′ti•cal•ly** *adv.*

cheap /cheep/ • *adj.* **1** low in price; worth more than its cost (*cheap labor*). **2** charging low prices; offering good value (*a cheap restaurant*). **3** of poor quality; inferior. **4** costing little effort and hence of little worth (*a cheap joke*). • *adv.* cheaply (*got it cheap*). □ **dirt cheap** very cheap. **feel cheap** feel ashamed or contemptible. □□ **cheap′ish** *adj.* **cheap′ly** *adv.* **cheap′ness** *n.*
■ *adj.* **1, 2** inexpensive, reasonable, budget, *sl.* cheapo. **3** shoddy, shabby, tawdry; inferior, trashy, worthless, chintzy. • *adv.* inexpensively, on the cheap.

cheap•en /cheepan/ *v.* make or become cheap or cheaper; depreciate; degrade.
■ see DEPRECIATE 1.

cheap•skate /cheepskayt/ *n. colloq.* stingy person.

cheat /cheet/ • *n.* **1** *tr.* deceive; trick. **2** *intr.* gain unfair advantage by deception or breaking rules. • *n.* **1** person who cheats. **2** trick, fraud, or deception. □ **cheat on** *colloq.* be sexually unfaithful to. □□ **cheat′er** *n.* **cheat′ing•ly** *adv.*
■ *v.* **1** swindle, fleece, defraud, *colloq.* rip off, *sl.* con. • *n.* **1** cheater, swindler, deceiver, impostor, faker, trickster, confidence man, charlatan. **2** see TRICK *n.* 1.

check /chek/ • *v.* **1** *tr.* **a** examine the accuracy, quality, or condition of. **b** make sure; verify. **2** *tr.* **a** stop or slow the motion of; curb. **b** *colloq.* find fault with; rebuke. **3** *tr. Chess* directly threaten (the opposing king). **4** *intr.* agree or correspond when compared. **5** *tr.* mark with a check mark, etc. **6** *tr.* deposit (luggage, etc.) for storage or dispatch. • *n.* **1** means or act of testing or ensuring accuracy, quality, etc. **2 a** stopping or slowing of motion. **b** rebuff or rebuke. **c** person or thing that restrains. **3** *Chess* exposure of a king to direct attack. **4** bill in a restaurant. **5** written order to a bank to pay the stated sum from one's account. **6** token of identification for left luggage, etc. **7** crack or flaw in lumber. **8 a** pattern of small squares. **b** fabric having this pattern. • *int.* expressing assent or agreement. □ **check in 1** arrive or register at a hotel, airport, etc. **2** record the arrival of. **check into** register one's arrival at (a hotel, etc.). **check mark** a mark (√) to denote correctness, check items in a list, etc. **check off** mark on a list, etc., as having been examined or dealt with. **check on** examine carefully; keep a watch on (a person, work done, etc.). **check out 1** leave a hotel, etc., after paying. **2** *colloq.* investigate; examine for authenticity or suitability. **in check** under control; restrained. □□ **check′a•ble** *adj.*

■ *v.* **1** authenticate, substantiate, validate, corroborate, look into, test out, investigate, inspect, scrutinize, look at *or* over, keep an eye on, monitor. **2 a** arrest, halt, hold up, stall; limit, stunt; retard, brake, stanch, stem; obstruct, block, hinder, hamper, impede; restrain, contain, restrict. **b** see REBUKE *v.* **4** coincide, tally, accord, concur, match, *colloq.* jibe. • *n.* **1** control, test, verification, substantiation, authentication, confirmation, validation. **2 a** stop, arrest, halt, cessation; break, pause, hesitation, interruption, suspension, delay. **b** see REBUKE *n.* **c** restraint, curb, restriction, control, constraint, hindrance, brake, deterrent, obstruction, impediment, damper, limitation. **4** *colloq.* tab. **5** receipt, stub; voucher, chit. □ **check in 1** sign in. **check on** see CHECK *v.* 1 above. **check out 1** depart, go. **2** research, explore, inquire into, look into *or* at *or* over, inspect, probe.

check•er /chékər/ • *n.* **1** person or thing that examines, esp. in a factory, etc. **2** cashier in a supermarket, etc. **3** [often in *pl.*] pattern of squares often alternately colored. **4 a** [in *pl.*] game for two played with 12 pieces each on a checkerboard. **b** pieces used in a game of checkers. • *v.tr.* **1** mark with checkers. **2** (as **checkered** *adj.*) with varied fortunes (*a checkered career*).

■ *v.* **2** (**checkered**) variable, mixed, unsettled.

check•er•board /chékərbawrd/ *n.* checkered board, identical to a chessboard, used in the game of checkers.

check•ing ac•count /chéking/ *n.* account at a bank against which checks can be drawn by the account depositor.

check•mate /chékmayt/ • *n. Chess* check from which a king cannot escape. • *v.tr.* **1** *Chess* put into checkmate. **2** defeat; frustrate.

check•out /chékowt/ *n.* **1** act of checking out. **2** point at which goods are paid for in a supermarket, etc.

check•point /chékpoynt/ *n.* barrier or gate for inspection.

check•up /chékup/ *n.* thorough (esp. medical) examination.

■ *colloq.* going-over.

ched•dar /chédər/ *n.* (in full **ched•dar cheese**) kind of firm smooth cheese orig. made in Cheddar in S. England.

cheek /cheek/ *n.* **1 a** side of the face below the eye. **b** sidewall of the mouth. **2** impertinence; cool confidence. **3** *sl.* either buttock. □ **cheek by jowl** close together; intimate.

cheek•bone /cheekbōn/ *n.* bone below the eye.

cheek•y /cheékee/ *adj.* (**cheek•i•er, cheek•i•est**) impertinent; impudent. □□ **cheek′i•ly** *adv.* **cheek′i•ness** *n.*

■ insolent, audacious, disrespectful, rude.

cheep /cheep/ • *n.* weak shrill cry of a young bird. • *v.intr.* make such a cry.

cheer /cheer/ • *n.* **1** shout of encouragement or applause. **2** mood; disposition (*full of good cheer*). **3** [in *pl.*; as *int.*] *colloq.* expressing good wishes on parting or before drinking. • *v.* **1** *tr.* **a** applaud with shouts. **b** urge or encourage with shouts. **2** *intr.* shout for joy. **3** *tr.* gladden; comfort.

■ *n.* **1** cry, whoop, hurrah. **2** temper, spirit(s). **3** (*cheers!*) see GOOD-BYE *int.* • *v.* **1 a** clap, *colloq.* give a person a (big) hand. **b** (*cheer on*) egg on, spur on. **2** hurrah; see also APPLAUD. **3** enliven, hearten, console, *colloq.* buck up.

cheer•ful /cheerfool/ *adj.* **1** in good spirits; noticeably happy. **2** bright; pleasant. □□ **cheer′ful•ly** *adv.* **cheer′ful•ness** *n.*

■ **1** cheery, jolly, merry, gay, lighthearted, breezy, sunny. **2** cheering, enlivening, gay; pleasant, charming.

cheer•lead•er /cheerleedər/ *n.* person who leads cheers of applause, etc., esp. at a sports event.

cheer•less /cheerlis/ *adj.* gloomy; dreary; miserable. □□ **cheer′less•ly** *adv.* **cheer′less•ness** *n.*

■ see GLOOMY 2.

cheer•y /cheeree/ *adj.* (**cheer•i•er, cheer•i•est**) lively; in good spirits; genial; cheering. □□ **cheer′i•ly** *adv.* **cheer′i•ness** *n.*

■ see GENIAL 1.

cheese /cheez/ *n.* **1** a food made from the pressed curds of milk. **2** complete cake of this with rind.

cheese•burg•er /cheezbərgər/ *n.* hamburger with cheese on it.

cheese•cake /cheezkayk/ *n.* **1** rich dessert cake made with cream cheese, etc. **2** *sl.* portrayal of women in a sexually attractive manner.

cheese•cloth /cheezklawth, –kloth/ *n.* thin loosely woven cloth, used orig. for wrapping cheese.

chees•y /cheezee/ *adj.* (**chees•i•er, chees•i•est**) **1** like cheese in taste, smell, appearance, etc. **2** *sl.* inferior; cheap and nasty. □□ **chees′i•ness** *n.*

■ **2** see INFERIOR *adj.* 2.

chee•tah /cheetə/ *n.* swift, spotted leopard-like feline.

chef /shef/ *n.* cook, esp. the chief cook in a restaurant, etc.

chem. *abbr.* **1** chemical. **2** chemist. **3** chemistry.

chem•i•cal /kémikəl/ • *adj.* of, made by, or

employing chemistry or chemicals. • *n.* substance obtained or used in chemistry. □ **chemical engineering** design, manufacture, and operation of industrial chemical plants. **chemical warfare** warfare using poison gas and other chemicals. □□ **chem′i·cal·ly** *adv.*

che·mise /shəmeéz/ *n. hist.* woman's loose-fitting undergarment or dress hanging straight from the shoulders.

chem·ist /kémist/ *n.* person practicing or trained in chemistry.

chem·is·try /kémistree/ *n.* (*pl.* **–tries**) **1** the study of the elements and the compounds they form and the reactions they undergo. **2** any complex (esp. emotional) change or process. **3** *colloq.* person's personality or temperament.

che·mo·ther·a·py /keémōthérəpee/ *n.* treatment of disease, esp. cancer, by chemical substances. □□ **che·mo·ther′a·pist** *n.*

che·nille /shəneél/ *n.* **1** tufty, velvety cord or yarn, used in trimming furniture, etc. **2** fabric made from this.

cher·ish /chérish/ *v.tr.* **1** protect or tend (a child, plant, etc.) lovingly. **2** hold dear; cling to (hopes, feelings, etc.).

 ■ **1** foster, cultivate, nurture. **2** treasure, prize.

Cher·o·kee /chérəkee/ *n.* **1 a** N. American people formerly inhabiting much of the southern US. **b** member of this people. **2** language of this people.

che·root /shəroót/ *n.* cigar with both ends open.

cher·ry /chéree/ • *n.* (*pl.* **–ries**) **1** small, soft, round stone fruit. **2** tree bearing this, also grown for its wood and its ornamental flowers. • *adj.* of a light red color. □ **cherry picker** *colloq.* crane for raising and lowering people. **cherry tomato** miniature tomato.

cher·ub /chérəb/ *n.* **1** (*pl.* **cher·u·bim** /-bim/) angelic being, usu. depicted as a winged child or the head of a winged child. **2** beautiful or innocent child. □□ **che·ru·bic** /chiroóbik/ *adj.* **che·ru′bi·cal·ly** *adv.*

cher·vil /chérvil/ *n.* umbelliferous plant, with small white flowers, used as an herb.

chess /ches/ *n.* game for two with 16 pieces each, played on a chessboard.

chess·board /chésbawrd/ *n.* checkered board of 64 squares on which chess and checkers are played.

chess·man /chésman, -mən/ *n.* (*pl.* **–men**) any of the 32 pieces with which chess is played.

chest /chest/ *n.* **1** large strong box. **2 a** part of a human or animal body enclosed by the ribs. **b** front surface of the body from neck to waist. **3** small cabinet for medicines, etc. □ **get a thing off one's chest** *colloq.* disclose a fact, secret, etc., to relieve one's anxiety about it.

 ■ **1** coffer, trunk, crate. **2** breast; *Anat. & Zool.* thorax.

chest·nut /chésnut/ *n.* **1 a** glossy, hard, brown edible nut. **b** tree bearing it. **2** = *horse chestnut.* **3** (in full **chestnut wood**) the heavy wood of any chestnut tree. **4** horse of a reddish-brown or yellowish-brown color.

5 *colloq.* stale joke or anecdote. **6** reddish-brown color.

chev·ron /shévrən/ *n.* **1** V-shaped line or stripe. **2** badge, etc., of such lines or stripes.

chew /choo/ • *v.tr.* [also *absol.*] work (food, etc.) between the teeth. • *n.* **1** act of chewing. **2** something for chewing, esp. a chewy candy. □ **chew the cud** reflect; ruminate. **chew the fat** (or **rag**) *sl.* chat. **chewing gum** flavored gum, for chewing. **chew out** *colloq.* reprimand. □□ **chew′a·ble** *adj.* **chew′er** *n.*

 ■ *v.* **1** masticate, munch, grind; bite, gnaw. □ **chew the cud** see MEDITATE 1. **chew the fat** (or **rag**) see CHAT *v.* **chew out** see REPRIMAND *v.*

chew·y /chóoee/ *adj.* (**chew·i·er**, **chew·i·est**) **1** needing much chewing. **2** suitable for chewing. □□ **chew′i·ness** *n.*

 ■ **1** see TOUGH *adj.* 1.

Chey·enne /shīán, -én/ *n.* **1 a** N. American people formerly living between the Missouri and Arkansas rivers. **b** member of this people. **2** language of this people.

chi /kī/ *n.* twenty-second letter of the Greek alphabet (Ψ, ψ).

Chi·an·ti /keeáantee, keeán-/ *n.* (*pl.* **Chi·an·tis**) dry, red Italian-style wine.

chi·a·ro·scu·ro /keeáarəskoóró/ *n.* treatment of light and shade in drawing and painting.

chic /sheek/ • *adj.* (**chic·er**, **chic·est**) stylish; elegant. • *n.* stylishness; elegance. □□ **chic′ly** *adv.*

 ■ *adj.* fashionable, modish, smart, snappy. • *n.* good taste, style, fashion, modishness. □□ **chicly** see *beautifully* (BEAUTIFUL).

chi·can·er·y /shikáynəree/ *n.* (*pl.* **–ies**) **1** clever but misleading talk; false argument. **2** trickery; deception.

 ■ **1** sophistry, equivocation, humbug. **2** deceit, sharp practice, cheating, deviousness, duplicity.

Chi·ca·no /chikáanō/ *n.* (*pl.* **–nos**; *fem.* **Chi·ca·na**, *pl.* **–nas**) American of Mexican origin.

chick /chik/ *n.* **1** young bird. **2** *derog. sl.* young woman.

Chick·a·saw /chíkəsaw/ *n.* **1 a** N. American people native to Mississippi and Alabama. **b** member of this people. **2** language of this people.

chick·en /chíkin/ • *n.* (*pl.* same or **chick·ens**) **1** common breed of domestic fowl. **2 a** domestic fowl prepared as food. **b** its flesh. • *adj. colloq.* cowardly. • *v.intr.* [foll. by *out*] *colloq.* withdraw through fear or lack of nerve. □ **chicken feed 1** food for poultry. **2** *colloq.* unimportant amount, esp. of money. **chicken pox** infectious disease, esp. of children, with a rash of small blisters. **chicken wire** light wire netting with a hexagonal mesh.

chick·pea /chíkpee/ *n.* **1** leguminous plant with pods containing yellow, beaked seeds. **2** this seed used as a vegetable. □□ **gar·ban′zo (bean)**

chick·weed /chíkweed/ *n.* small weed with tiny white flowers.

chic•le /chíkəl/ n. milky juice of the sapodilla tree, used in the manufacture of chewing gum.

chic•o•ry /chíkəree/ n. (pl. **–ries**) 1 blue-flowered plant cultivated for its salad leaves and its root. 2 its root, roasted and ground for use with or instead of coffee.

chide /chīd/ v. (past **chid•ed** or **chid** /chid/; past part. **chid•ed** or **chid** or **chid•den** /chíd'n/) literary scold; rebuke. See synonym study at REBUKE. See synonym study at SCOLD. □□ **chid'er** n. **chid'ing•ly** adv.

■ see SCOLD v.

chief /cheef/ • n. 1 a leader or ruler. b head of a tribe, clan, etc. 2 head of a department; highest official. • adj. [usu. attrib.] 1 first in position, importance, influence, etc. 2 prominent; leading. □ **chief executive officer** highest ranking executive in a corporation, organization, etc. ¶Abbr.: CEO.

■ n. 1, 2 principal, employer, manager, superior, director, supervisor, king, colloq. boss, sl. big cheese. • adj. 1 premier, greatest, leading, ranking. 2 principal, key, prime, main, major.

chief•ly /chéeflee/ adv. above all; mainly but not exclusively.

■ especially, primarily, particularly, preeminently, principally, primarily, mostly, largely.

chief•tain /chéeftən/ n. (fem. **chief•tain•ess** /–tənis/) leader of a tribe, clan, etc. □□ **chief' tain•cy** n. (pl. **–cies**). **chief'tain•ship** n.

■ see LEADER 1.

chif•fon /shifón, shífon/ • n. light, diaphanous fabric of silk, nylon, etc. • adj. 1 made of chiffon. 2 light-textured.

chig•ger /chígər/ n. harvest mite with parasitic larvae.

chi•gnon /shéenyon, sheenyón/ n. coil or knot of hair worn at the back of the head.

chi•hua•hua /chiwaáwə/ n. 1 very small dog of a smooth-haired, large-eyed breed originating in Mexico. 2 this breed.

chil•blain /chílblayn/ n. painful, itchy swelling of the skin, usu. on a hand, foot, etc., caused by exposure to cold. □□ **chil' blained** adj.

child /chīld/ n. (pl. **chil•dren** /chíldrən/) 1 a young human being below the age of puberty. b unborn or newborn human being. 2 one's son or daughter. 3 descendant, follower, or product (of) (child of God). 4 childish person. □ **child care** care of children, esp. by someone other than a parent. **child's play** easy task. □□ **child'less** adj. **child' less•ness** n.

■ 1 a toddler, youngster, little one, juvenile, minor; colloq. kid, boy, lad, youth; girl. b neonate, infant, baby. 2 descendant; (children) offspring, family, progeny. 3 adherent, disciple; result. □ **child's play** see BREEZE n. 2.

child•bear•ing /chíldbairing/ n. act of giving birth to a child or children.

child•birth /chíldbərth/ n. act of giving birth to a child.

child•hood /chíldhŏŏd/ n. state or period of being a child.

child•ish /chíldish/ adj. 1 of, like, or proper to a child. 2 immature, silly. □□ **child'ish• ly** adv. **child'ish•ness** n.

■ 1 childlike, boyish, girlish. 2 juvenile, puerile, adolescent, infantile; immature, silly.

child•like /chíldlīk/ adj. having the good qualities of a child; as innocence, frankness, etc.

■ youthful, young, innocent, trustful, ingenuous.

Chil•e•an /chíleeən, chiláyən/ • n. 1 native or national of Chile in S. America. 2 person of Chilean descent. • adj. of or relating to Chile.

chil•i /chílee/ n. (pl. **–ies**) small, hot-tasting dried pod of a certain red pepper, used as a spice. □ **chili con carne** /kon kaárnee/ stew of chili-flavored ground meat and usu. beans.

chill /chil/ • n. 1 a unpleasant cold sensation; lowered body temperature. b feverish cold. 2 unpleasant coldness (of air, water, etc.). 3 depressing influence (cast a chill over). 4 coldness of manner. • v. 1 tr. & intr. make or become cold. 2 tr. depress; dispirit. 3 tr. cool (food or drink); preserve by cooling. • adj. = CHILLY. □ **chill out** become calm or less agitated. □□ **chill'er** n. **chill'ing•ly** adv.

■ n. 1 b sniffle(s), influenza, colloq. flu. 2 nip, chilliness; rawness. 3 pall, black or dark cloud, dampener. 4 iciness, frigidity, aloofness. • v. 2 see DEPRESS 2. 3 refrigerate, freeze, ice. • adj. see CHILLY.

chill•y /chílee/ adj. (**chill•i•er**, **chill•i•est**) 1 somewhat cold. 2 unfriendly; unemotional. □□ **chill'i•ness** n.

■ 1 cool, frosty, crisp, colloq. nippy. 2 unfeeling, lukewarm, unresponsive, stiff, cool, cold.

chime /chīm/ • n. 1 a set of attuned bells. b series of sounds given by this. • v. 1 intr. (of bells) ring. 2 tr. show (the hour) by chiming. □ **chime in** interject a remark. □□ **chim'er** n.

■ n. 1 a carillon, peal. b ringing, peal, tolling, jingle. • v. 1 toll, sound; see also PEAL v. 2 sound, mark. □ **chime in 1** interrupt, break in, butt in.

chi•me•ra /kīméerə, kee–/ (also **chi•mae'ra**) n. 1 Gk. mythol. fire-breathing female monster with a lion's head, a goat's body, and a serpent's tail. 2 fantastic or grotesque product of the imagination. □□ **chi•mer•ic** /–mérik/ adj. **chi•mer'i•cal** adj. **chi•mer'i• cal•ly** adv.

■ 2 see PHANTOM n. 2. □□ **chimerical** see IMAGINARY.

chim•ney /chímnee/ n. (pl. **–neys**) 1 vertical channel conducting smoke or combustion gases, etc., up and away from a fire, furnace, etc. 2 part of this that projects above a roof. 3 glass tube protecting the flame of a lamp. 4 narrow vertical crack in a rock face.

■ 1 stack, funnel.

chim•pan•zee /chímpanzeé, chimpánzee/ n. (also colloq. **chimp**) small African anthropoid ape.

chin /chin/ n. front of the lower jaw. □ **chin-up** exercise in which the chin is raised up to the level of an overhead bar that one grasps.

keep one's chin up *colloq.* remain cheerful, esp. in adversity.

chi•na /chína/ • *n.* **1** fine white or translucent ceramic ware, porcelain, etc. **2** things made from ceramic, esp. household tableware. • *adj.* made of china.
 ■ **1, 2** see POTTERY.

chin•chil•la /chinchílə/ *n.* **1** S. American small rodent having soft, silver-gray fur. **2** its highly valued fur.

chine /chin/ *n.* **1** backbone, esp. of an animal. **2** joint of meat containing all or part of this.

Chi•nese /chíneéz/ • *adj.* **1** of or relating to China. **2** of Chinese descent. • *n.* **1** the Chinese language. **2** (*pl.* same) **a** native or national of China. **b** person of Chinese descent. □ **Chinese lantern** collapsible paper lantern. **Chinese puzzle** very intricate puzzle or problem.

chink[1] /chingk/ *n.* narrow opening; slit.
 ■ aperture, gap.

chink[2] /chingk/ • *v.* **1** *intr.* make a slight ringing sound, as of glasses or coins striking together. **2** *tr.* cause to make this sound. • *n.* this sound.

chi•no /cheénó/ *n.* (*pl.* **–nos**) **1** cotton twill fabric, usu. khaki-colored. **2** [in *pl.*] garment, esp. trousers, made from this.

Chi•nook /shənóók, chə–/ *n.* **1 a** N. American people native to the northwestern coast of the US. **b** member of this people. **2** language of this people.

chintz /chints/ *n.* printed, multicolored cotton fabric with a glazed finish.

chintz•y /chíntsee/ *adj.* (**chintz•i•er, chintz•i•est**) **1** like chintz. **2** gaudy; cheap. □□ **chintz′i•ly** *adv.* **chintz′i•ness** *n.*
 ■ **2** see GAUDY.

chip /chip/ • *n.* **1** small piece removed by or in the course of chopping, cutting, or breaking. **2** place where such a chip has been made. **3 a** = *potato chip.* **b** [usu. in *pl.*] = *French fries (fish and chips).* **4** counter used in some gambling games to represent money. **5** *Electronics* = MICROCHIP. • *v.* (**chipped, chip•ping**) **1** *tr.* cut or break (a piece) from a hard material. **2** *intr.* cut pieces off. **3** *tr.* (of stone, china, etc.) be apt to break at the edge (*will chip easily*). □ **chip in** *colloq.* **1** interrupt or contribute abruptly to a conversation. **2** contribute (money or resources). **chip off the old block** child who resembles a parent, esp. in character. **chip on one's shoulder** *colloq.* inclination to feel resentful or aggrieved. **when the chips are down** *colloq.* in times of discouragement or disappointment.
 ■ *n.* **1** fragment, shard, flake. **2** nick. **3 b** (*chips*) fries. **4** marker, token. • *v.* **1** snap. **2** chisel, whittle. □ **chip in 1** break in, interpose, cut in. **2** help out, *colloq.* shell out.

chip•munk /chípmungk/ *n.* small ground squirrel having alternate light and dark stripes.

chip•per /chípər/ *adj. colloq.* **1** cheerful. **2** smartly dressed.
 ■ **1** see SPRIGHTLY.

Chip•pe•wa /chípəwaw, –wə, –waa, –way/ *n.* = OJIBWA.

chiro- /kírō/ *comb. form* of the hand.

chi•ro•man•cy /kírəmansee/ *n.* palmistry.

chi•rop•o•dy /kirópədee/ = PODIATRY. □□ **chi•rop′o•dist** *n.*

chi•ro•prac•tic /kírəpráktik/ *n.* manipulative treatment of mechanical disorders of the joints, esp. of the spinal column. □□ **chi′ro•prac•tor** *n.*

chirp /chərp/ • *v.* **1** *intr.* (usu. of small birds, grasshoppers, etc.) utter a short, sharp note. **2** *tr. & intr.* speak or utter merrily. • *n.* chirping sound. □□ **chirp′er** *n.*
 ■ *v.* **1** tweet, sing, twitter, chirrup. • *n.* peep, warble.

chir•rup /chírəp/ • *v.intr.* (**chir•ruped, chir•rup•ing**) chirp, esp. repeatedly. • *n.* chirruping sound. □□ **chir′rup•y** *adj.*

chis•el /chízəl/ • *n.* hand tool with a squared, beveled blade. • *v.* **1** *tr.* cut or shape with a chisel. **2** *tr. & intr. sl.* cheat; swindle. □□ **chis′el•er** *n.*
 ■ *v.* **1** carve, sculpt; incise; gouge, groove. **2** see CHEAT *v.* 1.

chit[1] /chit/ *n.* note of a sum owed, esp. for food or drink.

chit•chat /chítchat/ *colloq.* • *n.* light conversation; gossip. • *v.intr.* (**–chat•ted, –chat•ting**) talk informally.
 ■ *n.* see GOSSIP *n.* 1. • *v.* see CHAT *v.*

chi•tin /kít′n/ *n. Chem.* polysaccharide forming the major constituent in the exoskeleton of insects, etc. □□ **chi′tin•ous** *adj.*

chit•ter•lings /chítlinz/ *n.* (also **chit′lings, chit′lins**) small intestines of pigs, etc., esp. as cooked for food.

chiv•al•rous /shívəlrəs/ *adj.* **1** gallant; honorable; courteous. **2** involving or showing chivalry. □□ **chiv′al•rous•ly** *adv.*
 ■ courtly, gracious, heroic, noble, well-bred.

chiv•al•ry /shívəlree/ *n.* **1** medieval knightly system with its religious, moral, and social code. **2** selfless gallantry. □□ **chi′val•ric** *adj.*
 ■ **2** honor, courtliness, nobility, knightliness, virtuousness; bravery, courage; see COURTESY.

chive /chiv/ *n.* plant with onion-flavored tubular leaves.

chla•myd•i•a /kləmídeeə/ *n.* venereal disease caused by a parasitic microorganism.

chlo•ride /kláwrīd/ *n. Chem.* **1** any compound of chlorine with another element or group. **2** any bleaching agent containing chloride.

chlo•ri•nate /kláwrinayt/ *v.tr.* impregnate or treat with chlorine. □□ **chlo•ri•na•tion** /–áyshən/ *n.* **chlo′ri•na•tor** *n.*

chlo•rine /kláwreen/ *n. Chem.* poisonous gaseous element used for purifying water, bleaching, etc. ¶*Symb.:* **Cl**.

chlo•ro•fluor•o•car•bon /kláwrōflóórōkaárbən, –flawr–/ see CFC.

chlo•ro•form /kláwrəfawrm/ • *n.* colorless, volatile, sweet-smelling liquid used as a solvent and formerly used as a general anesthetic. ¶*Chem.* formula: $CHCl_3$. • *v.tr.* render (a person) unconscious with this.

chlo•ro•phyll /kláwrəfil/ *n.* green pigment

found in most plants. ▫▫ **chlo•ro•phyl•lous** /-fílǝs/ *adj.*

chock /chok/ • *n.* block or wedge of wood to check motion, esp. of a cask or a wheel. • *v.tr.* fit or make fast with chocks. ▫ **chock-full** = CHOCKABLOCK.

chock•a•block /chókǝblók/ *adj. & adv.* crammed full.

choc•o•late /cháwkǝlǝt, cháwklǝt, chók-/ • *n.* **1 a** food preparation made from roasted and ground cacao seeds, usually sweetened. **b** candy made with this. **c** drink made with chocolate. **2** deep brown color. • *adj.* made from or of chocolate. ▫▫ **choc'o•lat•y** *adj.* (also **choc'o•late•y**).

Choc•taw /chóktaw/ *n.* (*pl.* same or **–taws**) **1 a** N. American people originally from Alabama. **b** member of this people. **2** language of this people.

choice /choys/ • *n.* **1 a** act or instance of choosing. **b** thing or person chosen (*not a good choice*). **2** range from which to choose. **3** power or opportunity to choose (*what choice have I?*). • *adj.* of superior quality; carefully chosen. ▫▫ **choice'ly** *adv.*
■ *n.* **1** selection, election, preference, pick. **3** option, alternative. • *adj.* prime, outstanding, best, prize; select, handpicked.

choir /kwīr/ *n.* **1** group of singers, esp. taking part in church services. **2** part of a cathedral or large church used by the choir and clergy.

choke /chōk/ • *v.* **1** *tr.* hinder or impede the breathing of (a person or animal), esp. by constricting the windpipe or (of gas, smoke, etc.) by being unbreathable. **2** *intr.* suffer a hindrance or stoppage of breath. **3** *tr. & intr.* make or become speechless from emotion. **4** *tr.* retard the growth of or kill (esp. plants). **5** *tr.* suppress (feelings) with difficulty. • *n.* valve of an internal combustion engine that controls the intake of air. ▫ **choke up** become overly anxious or emotionally affected.
■ *v.* **1** suffocate, asphyxiate, smother. **2** gag, retch. **5** (*choke back*) repress, stifle, restrain.

chok•er /chókǝr/ *n.* close-fitting necklace.

chol•er /kólǝr/ *n. poet.* anger; irascibility.

chol•er•a /kólǝrǝ/ *n. Med.* infectious and often fatal bacterial disease of the small intestine. ▫▫ **chol•e•ra•ic** /-ráyik/ *adj.*

chol•er•ic /kólǝrik, kǝlérik/ *adj.* irascible; angry. ▫▫ **chol'er•i•cal•ly** *adv.*

cho•les•ter•ol /kǝléstǝrawl, –rōl/ *n. Biochem.* sterol found in most body tissues, including the blood, where high concentrations promote arteriosclerosis.

chomp /chomp/ *v.tr.* = CHAMP[1].

choose /chōoz/ *v.* (*past* **chose** /chōz/; *past part.* **chos•en** /chōzǝn/) **1** *tr.* select out of a greater number. **2** *intr.* take or select one or another. **3** *tr.* decide; be determined (*chose to stay behind*). **4** *tr.* select as (*was chosen king*). ▫▫ **choos'er** *n.*
■ **1** elect, pick (out), opt for, go for. **3** determine, opt, elect, resolve, see also DECIDE 1.

choos•y /chōozee/ *adj.* (**choos•i•er, choos•i•est**) *colloq.* fastidious. ▫▫ **choos'i•ly** *adv.* **choos'i•ness** *n.*

■ discriminating, discerning, finicky, particular, fussy, demanding, exacting, *colloq.* picky.

chop[1] /chop/ • *v.tr.* (**chopped, chop•ping**) **1** cut or fell by a blow, usu. with an ax. **2** cut into small pieces. • *n.* **1** cutting blow. **2** thick slice of meat (esp. pork or lamb) usu. including a rib. ▫ **chop shop** *colloq.* garage in which stolen cars are dismantled so that the parts can be sold separately.
■ *v.* **1** hack, hew, lop. **2** (*chop up*) cut up, mince, dice. • *n.* **1** cut, stroke; swing.

chop[2] /chop/ *n.* [usu. in *pl.*] jaw of an animal, etc.

chop•per /chópǝr/ *n.* **1** person or thing that chops. **2** *colloq.* helicopter.

chop•py /chópee/ *adj.* (**chop•pi•er, chop•pi•est**) (of the sea, etc.) fairly rough. ▫▫ **chop'pi•ly** *adv.* **chop'pi•ness** *n.*
■ agitated, turbulent, stormy.

chop•stick /chópstik/ *n.* each of a pair of small thin sticks, used as eating utensils.

chop su•ey /chopsǒo-ee/ *n.* (*pl.* **–eys**) Chinese-style dish of meat, bean sprouts, bamboo shoots, etc.

cho•ral /káwrǝl/ *adj.* of, for, or sung by a choir or chorus. ▫▫ **cho'ral•ly** *adv.*

cho•rale /kǝrál, –rául/ *n.* (also **cho•ral**) **1** stately and simple hymn tune; harmonized version of this. **2** choir.

chord[1] /kawrd/ *n. Mus.* group of (usu. three or more) notes sounded together, as a basis of harmony. ▫▫ **chord'al** *adj.*

chord[2] /kawrd/ *n.* **1** *Math. & Aeron.*, etc., straight line joining the ends of an arc, the wings of an airplane, etc. ▫ **strike a chord 1** recall something to a person's memory. **2** elicit sympathy. ▫▫ **chord'al** *adj.*

chor•date /káwrdayt/ *n.* animal possessing a notochord at some stage during its development. • *adj.* of chordates.

chore /chawr/ *n.* tedious or routine task, esp. domestic.
■ see TASK *n.*

cho•re•o•graph /káwreeǝgraf/ *v.tr.* compose the choreography for (a ballet, etc.). ▫▫ **cho•re•og•ra•pher** /-reeógrǝfǝr/ *n.*

cho•re•og•ra•phy /káwreeógrǝfee/ *n.* design or arrangement of a ballet or other staged dance. ▫▫ **cho•re•o•graph•ic** /-reeǝgráfik/ *adj.* **cho•re•o•graph'i•cal•ly** *adv.*

cho•ris•ter /káwristǝr, kór-/ *n.* a member of a choir.

chor•tle /cháwrt'l/ • *v.intr. colloq.* chuckle gleefully. • *n.* gleeful chuckle.
■ *v.* see CHUCKLE *v.* • *n.* see CHUCKLE *n.*

cho•rus /káwrǝs/ • *n.* (*pl.* **cho•rus•es**) **1** group (esp. a large one) of singers; choir. **2** piece of music composed for a choir. **3** refrain or main part of a popular song. **4** group of singers and dancers performing in concert in a musical comedy, opera, etc. **5** *Gk Antiq.* **a** in Greek tragedy, a group of performers who comment on the main action. **b** utterance of the chorus. • *v.* (of a group) speak or utter simultaneously.
■ *n.* **1** see ENSEMBLE[2] 3. **3** see REFRAIN.

chose *past* of CHOOSE.

cho•sen *past part.* of CHOOSE.

chow /chow/ *n.* **1** *sl.* food. **2** (in full **chow**

chow) dog of a Chinese breed with long hair and bluish-black tongue.
■ **1** see FOOD 1.

chow•der /chówdər/ *n.* rich soup or stew usu. containing fish, clams, or corn with potatoes, onions, etc.

chow mein /chów máyn/ *n.* Chinese-style dish of fried noodles with shredded meat or shrimp, etc., and vegetables.

Christ /kríst/ *n. Relig.* **1** title, also now treated as a name, given to Jesus of Nazareth. **2** Messiah as prophesied in the Old Testament. □□ **Christ′hood** *n.* **Christ′like** *adj.*

chris•ten /krísən/ *v.tr.* **1** baptize. **2** give a name to. **3** *colloq.* use for the first time. □□ **chris′ten•er** *n.* **chris′ten•ing** *n.*
■ **1** baptize. **2** see CALL *v.* 6.

Chris•ten•dom /krísəndəm/ *n.* Christians worldwide.

Chris•tian /kríschən/ • *adj.* **1** of Christ's teachings or religion. **2** believing in or following the religion based on the teachings of Jesus Christ. **3** showing the qualities associated with Christ's teachings. **4** *colloq.* (of a person) kind; fair; decent. • *n.* adherent of Christianity. □ **Christian name** forename, esp. as given at baptism. □□ **Chris′tian•ize** *v.* **Chris′tian•i•za′tion** *n.*

Chris•ti•an•i•ty /krischeeánitee/ *n.* **1** Christian religion. **2** being a Christian. **3** = CHRISTENDOM.

Christ•mas /krísməs/ *n.* (*pl.* **Christ•mas•es**) **1** (also **Christmas Day**) annual festival of Christ's birth, celebrated on Dec. 25. **2** season in which this occurs. □□ **Christ′mas•sy** *adj.*

chro•mat•ic /krōmátik/ *adj.* **1** of or produced by color; in (esp. bright) colors. **2** *Mus.* (of a scale) ascending or descending by semitones. □□ **chro•mat′i•cal•ly** *adv.* **chro•mat•i•cism** /-tisizəm/ *n.*

chro•ma•tin /krómətin/ *n.* material in a cell nucleus that stains with basic dyes and consists of protein, RNA, and DNA.

chrome /krōm/ *n.* **1** chromium, esp. as plating. **2** (in full **chrome yellow**) yellow pigment obtained from lead chromate. □ **chrome steel** hard, fine-grained steel containing much chromium and used for tools, etc.

chro•mi•um /krómeeəm/ *n. Chem.* hard, white metallic element used as a shiny electroplated coating. ¶Symb.: **Cr**. □ **chromium steel** = *chrome steel.*

chro•mo•some /króməsōm/ *n. Biochem.* threadlike cellular structures that carry the genetic information in the form of genes. □□ **chro•mo•so′mal** *adj.*

chron•ic /krónik/ *adj.* **1** persisting for a long time (usu. of an illness or a personal or social problem). **2** having a chronic complaint. **3** *colloq. disp.* habitual; inveterate (*a chronic liar*). □□ **chron′i•cal•ly** *adv.* **chro•nic•i•ty** /-nísitee/ *n.*
■ **1** lingering, inveterate, persistent, lasting. **3** persistent, confirmed, incorrigible.

chron•i•cle /krónikəl/ • *n.* register of events in order of their occurrence. • *v.tr.* record (events) in the order of their occurrence. □□ **chron′i•cler** *n.*

■ *n.* **1** record, history, account, narrative. • *v.* register, list, document; recount.

chro•nol•o•gy /krənóləjee/ *n.* (*pl.* **–gies**) **1** study of historical records to establish the dates of past events. **2 a** arrangement of events, dates, etc., in the order of their occurrence. **b** table or document displaying this. □□ **chron•o•log•i•cal** /krónəlójikəl/ *adj.* **chro•nol′o•gist** *n.* **chron•o•log′i•cal•ly** *adv.* **chro•nol′o•gize** *v.tr.*
■ **2 a** see SEQUENCE *n.* **b** calendar, journal, log.

chro•nom•e•ter /krənómitər/ *n.* time-measuring instrument, esp. one keeping accurate time at all temperatures. □□ **chro•nom•e•try** /krənómitree/ *n.* **chron•o•met•ric** /krónəmétrik/ *adj.* **chron•o•met′ri•cal** *adj.* **chron•o•met′ri•cal•ly** *adv.*

chrys•a•lis /krísəlis/ *n.* (also **chrys′a•lid**) (*pl.* **chrys•a•lis•es** or **chry•sal•i•des** /krisálideez/) **1** quiescent pupa of a butterfly or moth. **2** hard outer case enclosing it.

chry•san•the•mum /krisánthəməm/ *n.* garden plant of the daisy family having brightly colored flowers.

chub•by /chúbee/ *adj.* (**chub•bi•er**, **chub•bi•est**) plump and rounded. □□ **chub′bi•ly** *adv.* **chub′bi•ness** *n.*
■ tubby, dumpy, rotund, *colloq.* pudgy.

chuck¹ /chuk/ • *v.tr.* **1** *colloq.* fling or throw carelessly or with indifference. **2** *colloq.* give up; reject; abandon; jilt (*chucked my job*). **3** touch playfully, esp. under the chin. • *n.* playful touch under the chin.
■ *v.* **1** see THROW *v.* 1, 2. **2** see DROP *v.* 4.

chuck² /chuk/ • *n.* **1** cut of beef between the neck and the ribs. **2** device for holding a workpiece in a lathe or a tool in a drill. • *v.tr.* fix (wood, a tool, etc.) to a chuck.

chuck•le /chúkəl/ • *v.intr.* laugh quietly or inwardly • *n.* quiet or suppressed laugh. □□ **chuck′ler** *n.*
■ *v.* chortle, giggle, titter, tehee, snigger, snicker.

chug /chug/ • *v.intr.* (**chugged**, **chug•ging**) **1** emit a regular muffled explosive sound, as of an engine running slowly. **2** move with this sound. • *n.* chugging sound.

chum /chum/ *n. colloq.* close friend. □□ **chum′my** *adj.* (**chum•mi•er**, **chum•mi•est**). **chum′mi•ly** *adv.* **chum′mi•ness** *n.*
■ comrade, companion, *colloq.* pal, buddy. □□ **chummy** friendly, intimate, close, *colloq.* pally, thick.

chump /chump/ *n. colloq.* foolish person.

chunk /chungk/ *n.* **1** thick, solid slice or piece of something firm or hard. **2** substantial amount or piece.
■ see PIECE *n.* 1a.

chunk•y /chúngkee/ *adj.* (**chunk•i•er**, **chunk•i•est**) **1** containing or consisting of chunks. **2** short and thick; small and sturdy. **3** (of clothes) made of a thick material. □□ **chunk′i•ness** *n.*
■ **1** see *lumpy* (LUMP¹). **2** see STOCKY. **3** see BULKY.

church /chərch/ *n.* **1** building for public

(usu. Christian) worship. **2** meeting for public worship in such a building (*go to church*). **3** (**Church**) body of all Christians. **4** (**Church**) clergy or clerical profession. **5** institutionalized religion as a political or social force (*church and state*). ■ *n.* **1** see TEMPLE¹. **4** see MINISTRY 2, 3.

church•go•er /chə́rchgōər/ *n.* person who goes to church, esp. regularly. □□ **church' go•ing** *n. & adj.*

churl /chərl/ *n.* ill-bred person.

churl•ish /chə́rlish/ *adj.* surly; mean. □□ **churl'ish•ly** *adv.* **churl'ish•ness** *n.*

churn /chərn/ • *n.* machine for making butter. • *v.* **1** *tr.* agitate (milk or cream) in a churn. **2** *tr.* produce (butter) in this way. **3** *tr.* upset; agitate. **4** *intr.* (of a liquid) seethe; foam violently (*the churning sea*). □ **churn out** produce routinely or mechanically, esp. in large quantities. ■ *v.* **1** see STIR¹ *v.* **1**. **3** see DISTURB. **4** see SWIRL *v.* □ **churn out** see *run off* 2.

chute¹ /shōōt/ *n.* sloping channel or slide, for conveying things to a lower level. ■ shaft, ramp, runway, trough, conduit, race.

chute² /shōōt/ *n. colloq.* parachute. □□ **chut' ist** *n.*

chut•ney /chútnee/ *n.* (*pl.* **–neys**) pungent condiment made of fruits or vegetables, vinegar, spices, sugar, etc.

chutz•pah /khŏ́ŏtspə/ *n.* (also **chutz'pa**) *sl.* shameless audacity; gall. ■ see NERVE *n.* 2b.

chyme /kīm/ *n.* acidic, semisolid, and partly digested food produced by the action of gastric secretion. □□ **chy'mous** *adj.*

CIA *abbr.* Central Intelligence Agency.

ciao /chow/ *int. colloq.* **1** good-bye. **2** hello.

ci•ca•da /sikáydə, -kaádə/ *n.* (*pl.* **ci•ca•das** or **ci•ca•dae** /–dee/) transparent-winged large insect that makes a loud, rhythmic, chirping sound.

cic•a•trix /sikətriks, sikáy–/ *n.* (also **cic•a• trice** /síkətris/) (*pl.* **cic•a•tri•ces** /–tríseez/) scar. □□ **cic•a•tri•cial** /–tríshəl/ *adj.*

-cide /sīd/ *suffix* forming nouns meaning: **1** person or substance that kills (*regicide*). **2** killing of (*suicide*).

ci•der /sídər/ *n.* usu. unfermented drink made from crushed apples.

ci•gar /sigaár/ *n.* tight roll of tobacco leaves for smoking.

cig•a•rette /sigərét/ *n.* (also **cig•a•ret'**) thin cylinder of finely cut tobacco rolled in paper for smoking. □ **cigarette butt** unsmoked remainder of a cigarette.

cil•i•um /síleeəm/ *n.* (*pl.* **cil•i•a** /–leeə/) **1** minute hairlike cellular structure. **2** eyelash. □□ **cil'i•ar•y** *adj.* **cil•i•ate** /–ayt, –ət/ *adj.* **cil•i•at•ed** *adj.* **cil•i•a'tion** *n.*

cinch /sinch/ • *n.* **1** *colloq.* a sure thing; certainty. **b** easy task. **2** firm hold. **3** girth for a saddle or pack. • *v.tr.* **1 a** tighten. **b** secure a grip on. **2** *sl.* make certain of. ■ *n.* **1 a** see CERTAINTY 1b. **b** see PUSHOVER 1. **3** see GIRTH *n.* 2.

cin•cho•na /singkṓnə/ *n.* **a** S. American ev-

ergreen tree or shrub. **b** bark of this tree, containing quinine. □□ **cin•chon•ic** /–kónik/ *adj.* **cin•cho•nine** /síngkəneen/ *n.*

cinc•ture /síngkchər/ *n. literary* girdle; belt.

cin•der /síndər/ *n.* **1** residue of coal or wood, etc., after burning. **2** slag. **3** [in *pl.*] ashes. □ **cinder block** concrete building block. □□ **cin'der•y** *adj.*

Cin•der•el•la /síndərélə/ *n.* person or thing of unrecognized or disregarded merit or beauty.

cin•e•ma /sínəmə/ *n.* **1** films collectively. **2** production of films as an art or industry; cinematography. □□ **cin•e•mat•ic** /sínəmátik/ *adj.* **cin•e•mat'i•cal•ly** *adv.* ■ **1** see PICTURE *n.* 3.

cin•e•ma•tog•ra•phy /sínəmətógrəfee/ *n.* art of making motion pictures. □□ **cin•e• ma•tog'ra•pher** *n.* **cin•e•mat•o•graph•ic** /–mátəgráfik/ *adj.* **cin•e•mat•o•graph'i•cal• ly** *adv.*

cin•na•bar /sínəbaar/ *n.* **1** bright red mineral form of mercuric sulfide from which mercury is obtained. **2** vermilion.

cin•na•mon /sínəmən/ *n.* **1** aromatic spice from the peeled, dried, and rolled bark of a SE Asian tree. **2** this tree.

ci•pher /sífər/ *n.* **1 a** secret or disguised way of writing. **b** thing written in this way. **c** key to it. **2** arithmetical symbol (0; zero). **3** person or thing of no importance. ■ **1 a** see CODE *n.* 1. **2** see ZERO *n.* 1. **3** see NOBODY *n.*

cir. *abbr.* (also **circ.**) **1** circle. **2** circuit. **3** circular. **4** circulation. **5** circumference.

cir•ca /sárkə/ *prep.* (preceding a date) about.

cir•ca•di•an /sərkáydeeən/ *adj. Physiol.* occurring or recurring about once per day.

cir•cle /sárkəl/ • *n.* **1 a** round plane figure whose circumference is everywhere equidistant from its center. **b** line enclosing a circle. **2** roundish enclosure or structure. **3** persons grouped around a center of interest. **4** set or class or restricted group (*literary circles*). • *v.* **1** *intr.* move in a circle. **2** *tr.* **a** revolve around. **b** form a circle around. □□ **cir'cler** *n.*

■ *n.* **1** disk, round. **4** coterie, clique, camp, faction; society, company. • *v.* **1** see REVOLVE 1, 2. **2** go around, tour; encircle, surround, enclose, ring, hoop.

cir•clet /sárklit/ *n.* **1** small circle. **2** circular band, esp. of gold or jeweled, etc., as an ornament.

cir•cuit /sárkit/ *n.* **1** line or course enclosing an area; circumference. **2** *Electr.* **a** path of a current. **b** apparatus through which a current passes. **3** journey of a judge or preacher for work in a particular district. □ **circuit breaker** automatic device for stopping the flow of current in an electrical circuit.

■ *n.* **1** round, tour, circle, orbit; compass, perimeter, border, boundary, edge. **3** see ROUND *n.* 2.

cir•cu•i•tous /sərkyōō-itəs/ *adj.* **1** indirect. **2** going a long way around. □□ **cir'cu•i• tous•ly** *adv.* **cir•cu'i•tous•ness** *n.* ■ see INDIRECT 1, 2.

cir•cuit•ry /sárkitree/ *n.* (*pl.* **–ries**) **1** system of electric circuits. **2** equipment forming this.

cir•cu•lar /sórkyələr/ • *adj.* **1 a** having the form of a circle. **b** moving or taking place along a circle; indirect; circuitous (*circular route*). **2** *Logic* (of reasoning) depending on a vicious circle. See synonym study at ROUND. • *n.* letter, leaflet, etc., distributed to a large number of people. □□ **cir•cu•lar•i•ty** /-lári-tee/ *n.* **cir•cu•lar•ly** *adv.*
■ *adj.* **1 a** round, disk-shaped. **b** roundabout, tortuous; periphrastic. **2** illogical, fallacious.

cir•cu•late /sórkyəlayt/ *v.* **1** *intr.* be in circulation. **2** *tr.* cause to go around; put into circulation. **3** *intr.* be actively sociable at a party, gathering, etc. □□ **cir•cu•la•tive** *adj.* **cir•cu•la•tor** *n.*
■ **1** move *or* go about *or* around, flow. **2** spread, distribute, publish, air, report, broadcast, advertise. **3** mix, mingle, socialize.

cir•cu•la•tion /sórkyəláyshən/ *n.* **1** movement within or around, esp. of blood from and to the heart. **2 a** transmission or distribution (of news; etc.). **b** number of copies sold, esp. of journals and newspapers. □ **in** (*or* **out of**) **circulation** participating (or not participating) in activities, etc.
■ **1** circuit, course, flow. **2 a** spreading, dissemination, diffusion, publication, issuance, proclamation.

cir•cu•la•to•ry /sórkyələtawree/ *adj.* of or relating to the circulation of blood or sap.

circum- /sórkəm/ *comb. form* round; about; around.

circum. *abbr.* circumference.

cir•cum•cise /sórkəmsīz/ *v.tr.* cut off the foreskin or clitoris. □□ **cir•cum•ci•sion** /sórkəmsízhən/ *n.*

cir•cum•fer•ence /sərkúmfərəns/ *n.* **1** enclosing boundary, esp. of a circle. **2** distance around. □□ **cir•cum•fer•en•tial** /-fərénshəl/ *adj.* **cir•cum•fer•en'tial•ly** *adv.*
■ **1** see PERIMETER.

cir•cum•flex /sórkəmfleks/ *n.* mark (^) placed over a vowel in some languages to indicate a contraction or a special quality.

cir•cum•lo•cu•tion /sórkəmlōkyóoshən/ *n.* roundabout expression; evasive talk. □□ **cir•cum•lo•cu'tion•al** *adj.* **cir•cum•lo•cu'tion•ar•y** *adj.* **cir•cum•lo•cu'tion•ist** *n.* **cir•cum•loc•u•to•ry** /-lókyətáwree/ *adj.*
■ periphrasis; see also EVASION 2.

cir•cum•nav•i•gate /sórkəmnávigayt/ *v.tr.* sail around (esp. the world). □□ **cir•cum•nav•i•ga•tion** /-gáyshən/ *n.* **cir•cum•nav'i•ga•tor** *n.*
■ see CIRCLE *v.* 2.

cir•cum•scribe /sórkəmskrīb/ *v.tr.* **1** enclose or outline. **2** lay down the limits of; confine. □□ **cir•cum•scrib'a•ble** *adj.* **cir•cum•scrib•er** *n.* **cir•cum•scrip•tion** /-skrípshən/ *n.*
■ **1** see DEFINE 3. **2** see RESTRICT.

SYNONYM STUDY: circumscribe

ENCIRCLE, ENCLOSE, ENCOMPASS, ENVELOP, SURROUND. Strictly speaking, to **circumscribe** is to draw a line around something to mark

its limits or boundary (*a square circumscribed by a circle*). Beyond the realm of geometry, however, it suggests something that is hemmed in on all sides (*a lake circumscribed by mountains*); when used of people, it describes a limitation on their actions (*her movements were circumscribed by the long, narrow skirt she wore; the journalists were circumscribed by political considerations*). **Encompass** is used when something is set within a circle or within limits (*a road that encompassed the grounds of the estate; a view that encompassed the harbor*). **Surround** is a less formal word for *circumscribe*, but it can also refer to an undesirable, threatening, or dangerous situation (*surrounded by angry demonstrators; surrounded by skyscrapers*). **Encircle** is similar to *surround* in meaning, but it suggests a tight or quite circular clustering around a central object (*a bowl of fruit encircled by flowers*) or a deliberate attempt to surround someone or something for a definite reason (*to encircle the enemy camp*). **Envelop** is the right word if something is surrounded to the point where it can barely be seen (*a lonely figure enveloped in fog*) or if it is surrounded by layers or folds of an amorphous material (*enveloped in soft cotton to prevent breakage*). **Enclose** is very similar to *envelop*, but it suggests that something has been especially designed to fit around something else for protection or containment (*a ship model enclosed in a glass case*).

cir•cum•spect /sórkəmspekt/ *adj.* wary; cautious. See synonym study at VIGILANT. □□ **cir•cum•spec•tion** /-spékshən/ *n.* **cir•cum•spect'ly** *adv.*
■ see CAUTIOUS.

cir•cum•stance /sórkəmstans/ *n.* **1 a** fact, occurrence, or condition, esp. [in *pl.*] the time, place, occasion, etc., or surroundings of an act or event. **b** [in *pl.*] external conditions. **2** [in *pl.*] one's state of financial or material welfare. **3** ceremony; fuss (*pomp and circumstance*). □ **in** (*or* **under**) **the** (*or* **these**) **circumstances** the state of affairs being what it is. **in** (*or* **under**) **no circumstances** not at all; never. □□ **cir•cum•stanced** *adj.*
■ **1** situation, state (of affairs); incident, episode. **2** (*circumstances*) status, station, resources. **3** see CEREMONY 2, 3. □ **in** (*or* **under**) **no circumstances** see NEVER.

cir•cum•stan•tial /sórkəmstánshəl/ *adj.* **1** given in full detail. **2 a** depending on circumstances. **b** adventitious. □□ **cir•cum•stan•ti•al•i•ty** /-sheeálitee/ *n.* **cir•cum•stan'tial•ly** *adv.*
■ **1** detailed, particular, precise. **2 b** accidental, incidental, indirect, unimportant, provisional.

cir•cum•vent /sórkəmvént/ *v.tr.* evade (a difficulty); find a way around. □□ **cir•cum•ven•tion** /-vénshən/ *n.*
■ see EVADE.

cir•cus /sórkəs/ *n.* (*pl.* **cir•cus•es**) **1** traveling show of performing animals, acrobats, clowns, etc. **2** *colloq.* scene of lively action; a disturbance.

cir•rho•sis /sirṓsis/ *n.* chronic disease of the liver, a result of alcoholism, hepatitis, etc. □□ **cir•rhot•ic** /sirótik/ *adj.*

cir•rus /síros/ *n.* (*pl.* **cir•ri** /–rī/) *Meteorol.* white wispy cloud, esp. at high altitude. □□ **cir′rose** *adj.* **cir′rous** *adj.*

cis•tern /sístərn/ *n.* **1** tank or container for storing water, etc. **2** underground reservoir for rainwater.

cit. *abbr.* **1** citation. **2** cited. **3** citizen.

cit•a•del /sítəd′l, –del/ *n.* fortress, usu. on high ground protecting or dominating a city.
■ see STRONGHOLD 1.

ci•ta•tion /sītáyshən/ *n.* **1** citing of a book or other source; passage cited. **2** mention in an official dispatch. **3** note accompanying an award, describing the reasons for it.
■ **1** see QUOTATION 2. **2** see MENTION *n.* 1.

cite /sīt/ *v.tr.* **1** adduce as an instance. **2** quote (a passage, etc.) in support. **3** mention in an official dispatch. **4** summon to appear in a court of law. □□ **cit′a•ble** *adj.*
■ **1, 2** see QUOTE *v.* 1. **3** see MENTION *v.* 1, 2. **4** subpoena.

cit•i•zen /sítizən/ *n.* member of a country, state, city, etc. □ **citizen's arrest** arrest by an ordinary person without a warrant. □□ **cit′i•zen•ry** *n.* **cit′i•zen•ship** *n.*
■ voter; native, resident, inhabitant, dweller.

cit•ric /sítrik/ *adj.* derived from citrus fruit. □ **citric acid** sharp-tasting acid found in citrus. □□ **cit′rate** *n.*

cit•ron /sítrən/ *n.* **1** shrubby tree bearing large lemonlike fruits with thick fragrant peel. **2** this fruit.

cit•ro•nel•la /sítrənélə/ *n.* scented oil used in insect repellent, perfume, and soap manufacture.

cit•rus /sítrəs/ *n.* **1** tree of a group including citron, lemon, lime, orange, and grapefruit. **2** (in full **citrus fruit**) fruit from such a tree. □□ **cit′rous** *adj.*

cit•y /sítee/ *n.* (*pl.* **–ies**) **1** large town. **2** *US* state-chartered municipal corporation occupying a definite area. □ **city hall** municipal offices or officers. **city slicker** usu. *derog.* **1** smart and sophisticated city dweller. **2** plausible rogue as found in cities. □□ **cit′y•ward** *adj. & adv.* **cit′y•wards** *adv.*
■ **1** metropolis, municipality, borough, conurbation. **2** see CITY SLICKER *colloq.* slicker.

cit•y•scape /síteeskayp/ *n.* **1** view of a city (actual or depicted). **2** city scenery.
■ see VIEW *n.* 2a, b.

civ•et /sívit/ *n.* **1** (in full **civet cat**) catlike animal of Central Africa. **2** strong musky perfume obtained from it.

civ•ic /sívik/ *adj.* **1** of a city; municipal. **2** of or proper to citizens (*civic virtues*). □□ **civ′i•cal•ly** *adv.*
■ **1** see MUNICIPAL. **2** see PUBLIC *adj.* 1.

civ•ics /síviks/ *n.pl.* [usu. treated as *sing.*] the study of the rights and duties of citizenship.

civ•il /sívəl/ *adj.* **1** of or belonging to citizens. **2** of ordinary citizens and their concerns, as distinct from military or ecclesiastical matters. **3** polite; obliging; not rude. **4** *Law* concerning private rights and not criminal offenses. □ **civil disobedience** refusal to comply with certain laws or to pay taxes, etc., as a peaceful form of political protest. **civil engineer** engineer who designs or maintains roads, bridges, dams, etc. **civil liberty** freedom of action and speech subject to the law. **civil rights** rights of citizens to political and social freedom and equality. **civil servant** member of the civil service. **civil service** nonelected civilian branches of governmental administration. **civil war** war between citizens of the same country. □□ **civ′il•ly** *adv.*
■ **2** civilian, nonmilitary; lay, secular. **3** courteous, respectful, well-mannered, cordial, genial. □ **civil servant** public servant, government worker.

ci•vil•ian /sivílyən/ • *n.* person not in the armed services or the police force. • *adj.* of or for civilians.

ci•vil•i•ty /sivílitee/ *n.* (*pl.* **–ties**) **1** politeness. **2** act of politeness.
■ **1** courtesy, respect, amiability.

civ•i•li•za•tion /síviləzáyshən/ *n.* **1** advanced stage or system of social development. **2** those peoples of the world regarded as having this. **3** a people or nation (esp. of the past) regarded as an element of social evolution.
■ **1** culture, refinement. **3** see PEOPLE *n.* 1a, NATION.

civ•i•lize /síviliz/ *v.tr.* **1** bring out of a less developed stage of society. **2** refine and educate. □□ **civ′i•liz•a•ble** *adj.* **civ′i•liz•er** *n.*
■ **2** polish, edify, acculturate, broaden, elevate.

civ•vies /síveez/ *n.pl. sl.* civilian clothes.

Cl *symb. Chem.* chlorine.

cl *abbr.* **1** centiliter(s). **2** class.

clack /klak/ • *v.intr.* make a sharp sound as of boards struck together. • *n.* clacking sound or talk. □□ **clack′er** *n.*

clad /klad/ *adj.* **1** clothed. **2** provided with cladding.

clad•ding /kláding/ *n.* covering or coating.

claim /klaym/ • *v.tr.* **1** demand as one's due or property. **2 a** represent oneself as having or achieving (*claim victory*). **b** assert; contend (*claim that one knows*). **3** have as an achievement or a consequence (*the fire claimed many victims*). **4** (of a thing) deserve (one's attention, etc.). • *n.* **1** demand or request for something considered one's due (*lay claim to*). **2** right or title. **3** contention or assertion. **4** thing claimed. □□ **claim′a•ble** *adj.* **claim′ant** *n.* **claim′er** *n.*
■ *v.* **1** seek, call (for). **2** profess, declare, assert. **4** see DESERVE 1. • *n.* **1** petition, application. **3** see ASSERTION 1, 2.

clair•voy•ance /klairvóyəns/ *n.* supposed faculty of perceiving things or events in the future or beyond normal sensory contact. □□ **clair•voy′ant** *n. & adj.* **clair•voy′ant•ly** *adv.*

clam /klam/ • *n.* edible bivalve mollusk. • *v.intr.* (**clammed, clam•ming**) **1** dig for clams. **•2** [foll. by *up*] *colloq.* refuse to talk.

clam•bake /klámbayk/ *n.* picnic at the seashore typically featuring steamed clams, lobsters, and ears of corn.

clam•ber /klámbər/ • *v.intr.* climb with hands and feet, esp. with difficulty or laboriously. • *n.* difficult climb.

■ *v.* see SCRAMBLE *v.* 1.

clam•my /klámee/ *adj.* (**clam•mi•er, clam•mi•est**) unpleasantly damp and sticky. □□ **clam'mi•ly** *adv.* **clam'mi•ness** *n.*

clam•or /klámər/ • *n.* **1** loud or vehement shouting or noise. **2** protest; demand. • *v. intr.* make a clamor. □□ **clam'or•ous** *adj.* **clam'or•ous•ly** *adv.* **clam'or•ous•ness** *n.* See synonym study at VOCIFEROUS

■ *n.* **1** see NOISE *n.* 1. **2** see OUTCRY.

clamp /klamp/ • *n.* device, esp. a brace or band of iron, etc., for strengthening other materials or holding things together. • *v.tr.* **1** strengthen or fasten with a clamp. **2** place or hold firmly. □ **clamp down 1** be rigid in enforcing a rule, etc. **2** [foll. by *on*] suppress.

■ *n.* clasp, vice. • *v.* **1** clip (together), bracket. **2** grip, grasp. □ **clamp down 2** see SUPPRESS 1.

clan /klan/ *n.* **1** group of people with a common ancestor. **2** group with a strong common interest. □□ **clan'nish** *adj.* **clan'nish•ly** *adv.* **clan'nish•ness** *n.*

■ **1** tribe, family, dynasty. **2** fraternity, brotherhood; gang. □□ **clannish** see EXCLUSIVE *adj.* 3.

clan•des•tine /klandéstin/ *adj.* surreptitious; secret. □□ **clan•des'tine•ly** *adv.*

■ see SECRET *adj.* 2.

clang /klang/ • *n.* loud, resonant, metallic sound. • *v.* **1** *intr.* make a clang. **2** *tr.* cause to clang.

■ *n.* see CLASH *n.* 1. • *v.* see CLASH *v.* 1.

clan•gor /klánggər/ *n.* **1** prolonged or repeated clanging noise. **2** uproar or commotion □□ **clan'gor•ous** *adj.* **clan'gor•ous•ly** *adv.*

clank /klangk/ • *n.* sound as of heavy pieces of metal meeting or a chain rattling. • *v.* **1** *intr.* make a clanking sound. **2** *tr.* cause to clank. □□ **clank'ing•ly** *adv.*

■ *n.* see JANGLE *n.* • *v.* see JANGLE *v.* 1.

clap /klap/ • *v.* (**clapped, clap•ping**) **1** *intr.* strike the palms of one's hands together as a signal or repeatedly as applause. **2** *tr.* strike (the hands) together in this way. • *n.* **1** act of clapping, esp. as applause. **2** explosive sound, esp. of thunder. **3** slap; pat.

■ *v.* **1** applaud, cheer. • *n.* **2** crack, slap, report, crash, bang. **3** see SLAP[1] *n.*, PAT *n.* 1, 2.

clap•per /klápər/ *n.* tongue or striker of a bell.

clap•trap /kláptrap/ *n.* insincere or pretentious talk.

■ see NONSENSE.

claque /klak/ *n.* hired applauders.

clar•et /klárət/ *n.* **1** red wine, esp. from Bordeaux. **2** deep purplish-red.

clar•i•fy /klárifī/ *v.* (**-fies, -fied**) make or become clearer. □□ **clar•i•fi•ca'tion** *n.* **clar'i•fi•er** *n.*

■ elucidate, simplify, make plain, clear up, explain.

SYNONYM STUDY: clarify

CONSTRUE, ELUCIDATE, EXPLAIN, EXPLICATE, INTERPRET. When a biology teacher gets up in front of a class and tries to **explain** how two brown-eyed parents can produce a blue-eyed child, the purpose is to make an entire process or sequence of events understandable. In a less formal sense, to *explain* is to make a verbal attempt to justify certain actions or to make them understood (*she tried to explain why she was so late*). That same teacher might **clarify** a particular exam question—a word that means to make an earlier event, situation, or statement clear. **Elucidate** is a more formal word meaning to *clarify*, but where the root of the latter refers to clearness, the root of the former refers to light; to *elucidate* is to shed light on something through explanation, illustration, etc. (*the principal's comments were an attempt to elucidate the school's policy on cheating*). A teacher who **explicates** something discusses a complex subject in a point-by-point manner (*to explicate a poem*). If a personal judgment is inserted in making such an explication, the correct word is **interpret** (*to interpret a poem's symbolic meanings*). To **construe** is to make a careful interpretation of something, especially where the meaning is ambiguous. For example, when a class misbehaves in front of a visitor, the teacher is likely to *construe* that behavior as an attempt to cause embarrassment or ridicule.

---

clar•i•net /klárinét/ *n.* woodwind instrument with a single-reed mouthpiece. □□ **clar•i•net'ist** *n.* (also **clar•i•net'tist**).

clar•i•on /kláreeən/ *n.* clear, rousing sound.

clar•i•ty /kláritee/ *n.* state or quality of being clear, esp. of sound or expression.

■ clearness, lucidity, limpidity; comprehensibility.

clash /klash/ • *n.* **1** loud, jarring sound as of metal objects being struck together. **2 a** conflict. **b** discord of colors, etc. • *v.* **1 a** *intr.* make a clashing sound. **b** *tr.* cause to clash. **2** *intr.* collide; coincide awkwardly. **3** *intr.* come into conflict or be discordant. □□ **clash'er** *n.*

■ *n.* **1** crash, clang, clank, clangor. **2 a** fight, battle, disagreement, difference. • *v.* **1** smash, bang, boom. **3** disagree, differ, argue; disharmonize, jar.

clasp /klasp/ • *n.* **1** device with interlocking parts for fastening. **2 a** embrace. **b** grasp or handshake. • *v.tr.* **1** fasten with or as with a clasp. **2 a** grasp; hold closely. **b** embrace. □□ **clasp'er** *n.*

■ *n.* **1** hook, catch, clip, pin. **2** hug, hold, grip. • *v.* **1** secure, close, clip, pin. **2** hug, enclose; grab, seize.

class /klas/ • *n.* **1** any set of persons or things grouped together, or graded or differentiated from others. **2** division or order of society. **3** *colloq.* distinction; high quality. **4 a** group of students taught together. **b** occasion when they meet. **c** their course of instruction. **5** *Biol.* grouping of organisms, below a division or phylum. • *v.tr.* assign to a class or category. □ **class-conscious** aware of one's place in a system of social class. **class-consciousness** this awareness.

■ *n.* **1** category, division, classification. **2** rank, grade, level; caste, lineage. **3** excellence, refinement, stylishness. • *v.* classify, group, arrange, rank, grade.

clas•sic /klásik/ • *adj.* **1 a** of the first class; of acknowledged excellence. **b** remarkably typical; outstandingly important (*a classic case*). **c** having enduring worth; timeless. **2 a** of ancient Greek and Latin literature, or culture. **b** (of style in art, music, etc.) simple, harmonious, well-proportioned. • *n.* **1** classic writer, artist, work, or example. **2 a** ancient Greek or Latin writer. **b** [in *pl.*] the study of ancient Greek and Latin literature and history. **3** follower of classic models.

■ *adj.* **1 a** outstanding, first-rate, superior. **b** standard, leading, definitive; see also IMPORTANT 1, 2. **c** legendary, immortal, ageless. **2b** see SIMPLE *adj.* 2. • *n.* **1** paragon, epitome; masterpiece, masterwork.

clas•si•cal /klásikəl/ *adj.* **1 a** of ancient Greek or Latin literature or art. **b** (of language) having the form used by the ancient standard authors. **2** (of music) serious or conventional; following traditional principles. **3** restrained in style. □□ **clas'si•cal•ism** *n.* **clas'si•cal•ist** *n.* **clas'si•cal•ly** *adv.*

■ **1 a** Greek, Latin, Roman. **3** standard, traditional, established, authoritative, serious.

clas•si•cism /klásisizəm/ *n.* **1** the following of a classic style. **2** classical scholarship. □□ **clas'si•cist** *n.*

clas•si•fy /klásifī/ *v.tr.* (**–fies, –fied**) **1 a** arrange in classes or categories. **b** assign (a thing) to a class or category. **2** designate as officially secret. □□ **clas•si•fi'a•ble** *adj.* **clas•si•fi•ca'tion** *n.* **clas•si•fi•ca•to•ry** /klásifikətawree, kləsifi–, klásifikáytəree/ *adj.* **clas'si•fied** *adj.* **clas'si•fi•er** *n.*

■ **1** see ORGANIZE 1. □□ **classified** see CONFIDENTIAL 1.

class•less /kláslis/ *adj.* making or showing no distinction of classes (*classless society*). □□ **class'less•ness** *n.*

class•mate /klásmayt/ *n.* person in the same class at school.

class•room /klásrōōm, –rŏŏm/ *n.* room in which a class of students is taught.

class•y /klásee/ *adj.* (**class•i•er, class•i•est**) *colloq.* superior; stylish. □□ **class'i•ly** *adv.* **class'i•ness** *n.*

■ see STYLISH 1.

clat•ter /klátər/ *n.* **1** rattling sound as of many hard objects struck together.

■ *n.* **1** see RATTLE *n.* 1.

clause /klawz/ *n.* **1** *Gram.* distinct part of a sentence, including a subject and predicate. **2** single statement in a treaty, law, bill, or contract. □□ **claus'al** *adj.*

■ **1** see PHRASE *n.* 1. **2** see *stipulation* (STIPULATE).

claus•tro•pho•bi•a /kláwstrəfōbeeə/ *n.* abnormal fear of confined places. □□ **claus•tro•phobe** /–rəfōb/ *n.* **claus•tro•pho'bic** *adj.*

clav•i•chord /klávikawrd/ *n.* small keyboard instrument with a very soft tone.

clav•i•cle /klávikəl/ *n.* collarbone. □□ **cla•vic•u•lar** /kləvíkyələr/ *adj.*

claw /klaw/ • *n.* **1 a** pointed horny nail on an animal's foot. **b** foot armed with claws. **2** pincers of a shellfish. • *v.* scratch, maul, or pull with claws or fingernails. □□ **clawed** *adj.* [also in *comb.*]. **claw'er** *n.* **claw'less** *adj.*

■ *n.* **1** talon, nail. • *v.* tear, scrape, rake.

clay /klay/ *n.* **1** stiff, sticky earth, used for making bricks, pottery, ceramics, etc. **2** *poet.* substance of the human body. □□ **clay'ey** *adj.* **clay'ish** *adj.* **clay'like** *adj.*

■ **1** see EARTH *n.* 2b.

clean /kleen/ • *adj.* **1** free from dirt or contaminating matter; unsoiled. **2** clear; unused or unpolluted; pristine. **3** free from obscenity or indecency. **4** attentive to personal hygiene. **5** complete; clear-cut. **6** streamlined; well-formed. **7** free from any record of a crime, offense, etc. • *adv.* **1** completely; outright; simply (*clean forgot*). **2** in a clean manner. • *v.* make or become clean. □ **clean-cut 1** sharply outlined. **2** neatly groomed. **clean out 1** clean or clear thoroughly. **2** *sl.* empty or deprive (esp. of money). **clean up 1 a** clear (a mess) away. **b** make (things) neat. **c** make (oneself) clean. **2** restore order or morality to. **3** *sl.* acquire as or make a profit. **come clean** *colloq.* confess everything. □□ **clean'a•ble** *adj.* **clean'ish** *adj.* **clean'ness** *n.*

■ *adj.* **1** pure, unpolluted, unsoiled, sanitary, antiseptic, sterile; washed, scrubbed; spotless. **2, 3** see PURE 3, 4. **4** hygienic, cleanly. **5** clean-cut, neat, trim, tidy. **6** see STREAMLINE *v.* 3a, SLENDER 1, SHAPELY. **7** innocent; see also BLAMELESS. • *adv.* **1** entirely, thoroughly, fully, totally. • *v.* wash, sponge, mop, scrub, scour, sweep, launder, tidy, neaten. □ **clean-cut 1** see CLEAR *adj.* 4. **clean out 2** see DEFRAUD. **clean up 1** wash, (have *or* take a) shower, have *or* take a bath. **come clean** acknowledge *or* admit guilt, own up.

clean•er /kleenər/ *n.* **1** person employed to clean the interior of a building. **2** [usu. in *pl.*] commercial establishment for cleaning clothes. **3** device or substance for cleaning. □ **take to the cleaners** *sl.* defraud or rob.

clean•ly¹ /kleenlee/ *adv.* **1** in a clean way. **2** efficiently; without difficulty.

■ **1** clean. **2** see EASILY 1.

clean•ly² /klénlee/ *adj.* (**clean•li•er, clean•li•est**) habitually clean; with clean habits. □□ **clean'li•ness** *n.*

■ □□ **cleanliness** see PURITY 1.

cleanse /klenz/ *v.tr.* make clean or pure. □□ **cleans'er** /klénzər/ *n.*

■ wash, scour; see also CLEAN *v.*

clear /kleer/ • *adj.* **1** free from dirt or contamination. **2** (of weather, the sky, etc.) not dull or cloudy. **3** transparent. **4 a** distinct; easily perceived by the senses. **b** easily understood (*make oneself clear*). **5** that discerns or is able to discern readily and accurately (*clear-sighted*). **6** confident; convinced. **7** free from guilt. **8** without deduction (*a* *clear $1,000*). **9** free; unhampered. • *adv.* **1** clearly. **2** completely (*he got clear away*). **3** apart; out of contact (*keep clear*). • *v.* **1** *tr. & intr.* make or become clear. **2** *tr.* free from prohibition or obstruction. **3** *tr.* show or declare (a person) to be innocent. **4** *tr.* approve (a person) for access to information, etc. **5** *tr.* pass over or by safely or without touching. **6** *tr.* make (an amount of money) as a net gain. **7** *tr.* pass through (a customs office, etc.). □ **clear the air** disperse suspicion, tension, etc. **clear-cut 1** sharply defined. **2** obvious. **clear out 1** empty. **2** remove. **3** *colloq.* go away. **in the clear** free from suspicion or difficulty. □□ **clear′a•ble** *adj.* **clear′er** *n.* **clear′ly** *adv.* **clear′ness** *n.*

■ *adj.* **1** see CLEAN *adj.* 1. **2** sunny, fair, fine. **3** limpid, translucent, pellucid. **4** *a* sharp, well defined, legible. *b* intelligible, lucid, comprehensible, plain, obvious, patent. **5** acute, sensitive, perspicacious; see also PERCEPTIVE. **6** certain, sure, positive. **7** pure, blameless; see also INNOCENT *adj.* 2. **8** net, unencumbered, free. • *adv.* **1** distinctly, audibly. **2** utterly, entirely, totally. **3** see APART 3. • *v.* **1** (*tr.*) clarify, clean, purify. **3** exonerate, absolve, acquit; excuse, forgive. **5** vault, hurdle. □ **clear-cut** manifest, distinct, explicit, plain. **clear out 1** see EMPTY *v.* 1. **2** see REMOVE *v.* 2. **in the clear** innocent, not guilty; exonerated, forgiven, absolved; unburdened. □□ **clearly** distinctly, audibly, understandably; evidently, plainly, apparently, manifestly, obviously, certainly.

clear•ance /kleerəns/ *n.* **1** removal of obstructions, etc. **2** clear space allowed for the passing of two objects or two parts in machinery, etc. **3** special authorization or permission. □ **clearance sale** sale to get rid of superfluous stock.

■ **2** margin, leeway, room, allowance. **3** approval, endorsement, license, consent.

clear•ing /kleering/ *n.* area in a forest cleared for cultivation.

■ see FIELD *n.* 1.

clear•ing•house /kleeringhows/ *n.* **1** bankers' establishment where checks and bills are exchanged and resolved. **2** agency for collecting and distributing information, etc.

cleat /kleet/ *n.* **1** fixed piece of metal, wood, etc., for fastening ropes to, or to strengthen woodwork, etc. **2** projecting piece to give footing or prevent slipping.

cleav•age /kleevij/ *n.* **1** hollow between a woman's breasts. **2** division; splitting.

cleave[1] /kleev/ *v.* (*past* **cleaved** or **cleft** /kleft/ or **clove** /klōv/; *past part.* **cleaved** or **cleft** or **clo•ven** /klōvən/) *literary* **1** *tr.* chop or break apart; split, esp. along the grain. **2** *intr.* come apart in this way. □□ **cleav′a•ble** *adj.*

■ **1** divide, cut, bisect, halve, slit.

cleave[2] /kleev/ *v.intr.* (*past* **cleaved** or **clove** /klōv/ or **clave** /klayv/) [foll. by *to*] *literary* stick fast; adhere.

cleav•er /kleevər/ *n.* heavy tool for cutting or chopping.

clef /klef/ *n.* *Mus.* symbol placed at the beginning of a staff, indicating the pitch of the notes written on it.

cleft[1] /kleft/ *adj.* split; partly divided. □ **cleft lip** (or **palate**) congenital split in the lip or the roof of the mouth.

■ see SPLIT *n.* 2.

cleft[2] /kleft/ *n.* split; fissure.

cle•ma•tis /klémətis, kləmátis/ *n.* erect or climbing plant bearing white, pink, or purple flowers and feathery seeds.

clem•ent /klémənt/ *adj.* **1** mild (*clement weather*). **2** merciful. □□ **clem•en•cy** /-mən-see/ *n.* See synonym study at MERCY

clem•en•tine /kléməntīn, –teen/ *n.* small citrus fruit, similar to a tangerine.

clench /klench/ • *v.tr.* **1** close (teeth or fingers) tightly. **2** grasp firmly. • *n.* **1** clenching action. **2** clenched state.

clere•sto•ry /kleerstawree/ *n.* (also **clear′sto•ry**) (*pl.* **–ries**) upper row of windows in a cathedral or large church.

cler•gy /klárjee/ *n.* (*pl.* **–gies**) [usu. treated as *pl.*] [usu. prec. by *the*] the body of all persons ordained for religious duties.

■ see MINISTRY 2.

cler•gy•man /klárjeemən/ *n.* (*pl.* **–men**; *fem.* **cler•gy•wom•an**, *pl.* **–wom•en**) member of the clergy.

■ ecclesiastic, churchman, cleric, divine, priest, minister, chaplain, father, pastor, parson.

cler•ic /klérik/ *n.* member of the clergy.

cler•i•cal /klérikəl/ *adj.* **1** of the clergy or clergymen. **2** of or done by a clerk or clerks. □□ **cler′i•cal•ism** *n.* **cler′i•cal•ist** *n.* **cler′i•cal•ly** *adv.*

■ **1** ecclesiastical, churchly, pastoral, priestly. **2** white-collar, office, secretarial, stenographic.

clerk /klərk/ • *n.* **1** person employed to keep records, accounts, etc. **2** secretary, agent, or record keeper of a municipality, court, etc. • *v.intr.* work as a clerk □□ **clerk′ish** *adj.* **clerk′ly** *adj.* **clerk′ship** *n.*

■ *n.* **1** see BOOKKEEPER. **2** see SCRIBE *n.* 1.

clev•er /klévər/ *adj.* (**clev•er•er**, **clev•er•est**) skillful; talented; quick; adroit; ingenious; cunning. □□ **clev′er•ly** *adv.* **clev′er•ness** *n.*

■ skilled, gifted, intelligent, brainy, sharp, adept, wise, sage, deft, handy; resourceful, inventive, creative, imaginative; shrewd; see also DEXTEROUS.

cli•ché /kleesháy/ *n.* (also **cli•che**) hackneyed phrase or opinion. □□ **cli•ché′d** *adj.*

■ stereotype, bromide, truism, platitude.

click /klik/ • *n.* slight, sharp sound. • *v.* **1** *intr.* make a click. **2** *tr.* cause (one's tongue, heels, etc.) to click. □□ **click′er** *n.*

■ *n.* see SNAP *n.* 1. • *v.* **1** see SNAP *v.* 2.

cli•ent /klīənt/ *n.* **1** person using the services of a lawyer, architect, social worker, or other professional person. **2** customer.

■ **1** patron; patient. **2** shopper; patron.

cli•en•tele /klīəntél, kleeon–/ *n.* **1** clients collectively. **2** customers. **3** patrons of a theater, etc.

■ **1** patrons, customers. **2** custom, business, trade, patronage. **3** public, audience.

cliff /klif/ *n.* steep rock face, as at the edge of

the sea. □ **cliff-hanger** very suspenseful story, ending, etc. □□ **cliff'like** adj.

■ precipice, bluff, escarpment, scarp.

cli•mac•ter•ic /klīmáktərik, klīmaktérik/ n. supposed critical period in life, as menopause.

cli•mate /klímit/ n. **1** prevailing weather conditions. **2** region with particular weather conditions. **3** prevailing opinion or public feeling. □□ **cli•mat•ic** /-mátik/ adj. **cli•mat' i•cal** adj. **cli•mat'i•cal•ly** adv.

■ **3** consensus; atmosphere; feeling, mood, milieu.

cli•max /klímaks/ n. **1** event or point of greatest intensity or interest; culmination or apex. **2** sexual orgasm. □□ **cli•mac•tic** /-máktik/ adj.

■ **1** height, acme, summit, zenith, apogee, peak.

climb /klīm/ • v. **1** tr. & intr. ascend, mount, go or come up. **2** intr. (of a plant) grow up a wall, tree, trellis, etc., by clinging or twining. **3** intr. make progress from one's own efforts. • n. **1** ascent by climbing. **2** place, esp. a hill, climbed or to be climbed. □□ **climb'a•ble** adj. **climb'er** n.

■ v. **1** scale, shin (up), clamber up. **2** creep, trail, twine. **3** see PROGRESS v. 1.

clime /klīm/ n. literary **1** region. **2** climate.

clinch /klinch/ • v. **1** tr. confirm or settle (an argument, bargain, etc.) conclusively. **2** intr. embrace. **3** tr. secure (a nail or rivet) by driving the point sideways when through. • n. **1** clinching action or state. **2** colloq. embrace.

■ v. **1** secure, determine, conclude, wind up. **2** see EMBRACE v. 1. • n. **2** hug, clasp, squeeze.

clinch•er /klínchər/ n. colloq. remark or argument that settles a matter conclusively.

■ punch line, coup de grâce, sl. pay off.

cling /kling/ v.intr. (past and past part. **clung** /klung/) **1** adhere, stick, or hold on. **2** remain persistently or stubbornly faithful (to a friend, habit, idea, etc.). **3** maintain one's grasp; keep hold; resist separation. □□ **cling' er** n. **cling'y** adj. (**cling•i•er, cling•i•est**). **cling'ing•ly** adv. **cling'i•ness** n.

■ v. **1** see STICK² 4. **2** (cling to) embrace, hang on to, retain, keep, cherish.

clin•ic /klínik/ n. **1** private or specialized hospital. **2** place or occasion for giving specialist medical treatment or advice. **3** instructional session. □□ **cli•ni•cian** /kliníshən/ n.

■ **1** see INFIRMARY 1.

clin•i•cal /klínikəl/ adj. **1** Med. of or for the treatment of patients. **2** dispassionate; detached. □□ **clin'i•cal•ly** adv.

■ **2** see COLD adj. 4.

clink¹ /klingk/ • n. sharp ringing sound. • v. **1** intr. make a clink. **2** tr. cause (glasses, etc.) to clink.

■ n. see JINGLE n. 1. • v. see JINGLE v.

clink² /klingk/ n. sl. prison (in the clink).

clink•er¹ /klíngkər/ n. **1** mass of slag or lava. **2** stony residue from burned coal.

clink•er² /klíngkər/ n. sl. mistake or blunder.

clip¹ /klip/ • n. **1** device for holding things together or for attachment. **2** piece of jewelry fastened by a clip. **3** set of attached cartridges for a firearm. • v.tr. (**clipped, clip' ping**) fix with a clip.

■ n. **1** clasp, fastener. • v. attach, hold; staple.

clip² /klip/ • v.tr. (**clipped, clip•ping**) **1** cut with shears or scissors, esp. cut short or trim (hair, wool, etc.). **2** trim or remove the hair or wool of. **3** colloq. hit smartly. **4** cut short or omit. **5** cut (an extract) from a newspaper, etc. **6** sl. swindle; rob. • n. **1** act of clipping. **2** colloq. smart blow. **3** short sequence from a motion picture. **4** colloq. speed, esp. rapid. □ **clip joint** sl. club, etc., charging exorbitant prices. □□ **clip'pa•ble** adj.

■ v. **1** lop (off), crop, snip. **2** shear, fleece. **3** strike, punch, smack. **4** abbreviate, diminish, curtail. **6** cheat, sl. rook; see also SWINDLE v. • n. **1** cut, trim. **2** cuff, punch, hit, strike, smack, box. **3** segment, section, part, excerpt. **4** pace, rate.

clip•board /klípbawrd/ n. small board with a spring clip for holding papers, etc.

clip•per /klípər/ n. **1** instrument for clipping hair, hedges, etc. **2** fast sailing ship.

clip•ping /klíping/ n. piece clipped or cut from something, esp. from a newspaper.

clique /kleek/ n. small exclusive group of people. □□ **cli'quey** adj. (**cliqu•i•er, cliqu•i• est**). **cli'quish** adj. **cli'quish•ness** n. **cli' quism** n.

■ set, coterie, crowd, circle, group.

cli•to•ris /klítəris, klī-/ n. small erectile part of the female genitals at the upper end of the vulva. □□ **cli'to•ral** adj.

cloak /klōk/ • n. **1** outdoor overgarment, usu. sleeveless. **2** covering (cloak of snow). • v.tr. **1** cover with a cloak. **2** conceal; disguise.

■ n. **1** mantle, cape, robe. **2** mantle, screen, shroud, veil. • v. **1** see DRESS v. 1. **2** hide, mask; disguise.

clob•ber /klóbər/ v.tr. sl. **1** hit; beat up. **2** defeat.

■ **1** see HIT v. 1a.

cloche /klōsh/ n. (in full **cloche hat**) woman's close-fitting, bell-shaped hat.

clock /klok/ • n. **1** instrument for measuring and showing time. **2** any measuring device resembling a clock. • v.tr. **1** colloq. attain or register (a stated time, distance, or speed, esp. in a race). **2** time (a race) with a stopwatch.

■ n. **1** see WATCH n. 1.

clock•wise /klókwīz/ adj. & adv. in a curve corresponding in direction to the movement of the hands of a clock.

clock•work /klókwərk/ n. mechanism of or like that of a clock. □ **like clockwork** smoothly; regularly; automatically.

clod /klod/ n. **1** lump of earth, clay, etc. **2** sl. silly or foolish person.

■ **1** mass, wad, hunk, chunk, piece. **2** idiot, fool, dolt, blockhead, colloq. imbecile, sl. jerk, dope.

clod•hop•per /klódhopər/ n. [usu. pl.] colloq. large heavy shoe.

clog /klawg, klog/ • *n.* shoe with a thick wooden sole. • *v.* (**clogged, clog•ging**) **1** *tr.* obstruct; choke. **2** *intr.* become obstructed; choke.

▪ *v.* **1** block, congest, jam.

clois•ter /klóystər/ • *n.* **1** covered walk, often open to a courtyard on one side. **2** monastic life or seclusion. **3** convent or monastery. • *v.tr.* seclude. □□ **clois´tered** *adj.* **clois´tral** *adj.*

▪ *n.* **3** see MONASTERY. • *v.* see ISOLATE 1. □□ **cloistered 1** see SECLUDE 2.

clomp var. of CLUMP *v.* 2.

clone /klōn/ • *n.* **1 a** group of organisms produced asexually from one stock or ancestor. **b** one such organism. **2** person or thing regarded as identical with another. • *v.tr.* propagate as a clone. □□ **clon´al** *adj.*

▪ *n.* **1b, 2** see DUPLICATE *n.* 1. • *v.* see IMITATE 3.

clonk /klongk, klawngk/ • *n.* abrupt heavy sound of impact. • *v.* **1** *intr.* make such a sound. **2** *tr.* *colloq.* hit.

▪ *n.* see THUD *n.* • *v.* **1** see THUD *v.* **2** see HIT *v.* 1a.

close¹ /klōs/ • *adj.* **1** situated at only a short distance or interval. **2 a** having a strong or immediate relation or connection (*close friend*). **b** in intimate association (*were very close*). **c** corresponding almost exactly (*close resemblance*). **3** in or almost in contact (*close combat*). **4** dense; compact. **5** in which competitors are almost equal (*close contest*). **6** rigorous (*close reasoning*). **7** concentrated; searching (*close attention*). **8** (of air, etc.) stuffy or humid. • *adv.* at only a short distance or interval (*they live close to us*). □ **close-knit** tightly bound or interlocked; closely united in friendship. **close shave** *colloq.* narrow escape. **close-up 1** photograph, etc., taken at close range. **2** intimate description. □□ **close´ly** *adv.* **close´ness** *n.*

▪ *adj.* **1** adjacent, near. **2 a, b** devoted, familiar, inseparable, close-knit; attached, friendly. **4** tight, cramped, compressed. **5** neck and neck, tight. **6** see METICULOUS. **7** careful, assiduous, precise, detailed, intense, thorough. **8** oppressive, airless, stifling, suffocating. • *adv.* near, in the neighborhood (of), not far (from *or* off), adjacent (to); nearby, close by; (*close to* or *on*) nearly, almost, practically. □ **close-knit** see CLOSE *adj.* 2a, b above.

close² /klōz/ • *v.* **1 a** *tr.* shut. **b** *intr.* become shut. **c** *tr.* block up. **2** *tr. & intr.* bring or come to an end. **3** *intr.* end the day's business. **4** *tr. & intr.* bring or come closer or into contact. • *n.* conclusion; end. □ **close down** discontinue business. **close in 1** enclose. **2** come nearer. **close up 1** move closer. **2** shut, esp. temporarily. **3** block up. **4** (of an aperture) grow smaller. □□ **clos´able** *adj.* **clos´er** *n.*

▪ *v.* **1 a** close up, seal; lock, secure, fasten. **2** conclude, end, finish; complete, wind up; conclude, terminate. **3** shut. • *n.* **1** termination, finish, completion; culmination. □ **close down** shut down, go out of business, shut up shop. **close in 1** see ENCLOSE 1, 6.

2 see APPROACH *v.* 1, 2. **close up 1** see APPROACH *v.* 1, 2. **2** close, lock up. **3** see CLOG *v.*

closed-cap•tioned • *adj.* (of a television program) broadcast with captions visible to viewers who have selected a decoding option on their television set.

closed /klōzd/ *adj.* **1** not giving access; shut. **2** (of a store, etc.) having ceased business. **3** not communicating with others. □ **closed-circuit** (of television) transmitted to a restricted set of receivers.

▪ **3** withdrawn, uncommunicative, aloof, distant.

clos•et /klózit/ • *n.* **1** small room. **2** storage area. • *adj.* secret; covert (*closet drinker*). • *v.tr.* (**clos•et•ed, clos•et•ing**) shut away.

▪ *n.* **1** see CABINET 1. **2** see WARDROBE 1. • *adj.* see STEALTHY.

clo•sure /klózhər/ *n.* **1** act or process of closing. **2** closed condition.

clot /klot/ • *n.* thick mass of coagulated liquid, esp. of blood. • *v.* (**clot•ted, clot•ting**) form into clots.

▪ *n.* see LUMP¹ *n.* 1, 2. • *v.* see COAGULATE.

cloth /klawth, kloth/ *n.* (*pl.* **cloths** /kloths, klothz/) **1** woven or felted material. **2** piece of this. **3** piece of this for a particular purpose. **4** [prec. by *the*] the clergy.

▪ **1** fabric, textile.

clothe /klōth/ *v.tr.* (*past and past part.* **clothed** or *formal* **clad**) **1** provide with clothes. **2** cover as with clothes.

▪ **1** dress, garb, outfit, *formal* attire. **2** garb, robe, sheathe, *formal* attire.

clothes /klōz, klōthz/ *n.pl.* garments worn to cover the body and limbs.

▪ clothing, wear, dress, wardrobe, *colloq.* togs, gear, *formal* attire, apparel, *sl.* threads, duds.

cloth•ier /klóthēeər/ *n.* seller of clothes.

cloth•ing /klóthing/ *n.* clothes collectively.

clo•ture /klóchər/ • *n.* legislative procedure for ending debate and taking a vote. • *v.tr.* apply cloture.

cloud /klowd/ • *n.* **1** visible mass of condensed watery vapor floating above the ground. **2** mass of smoke or dust. **3** great number of insects, birds, etc. **4** state of gloom, trouble, or suspicion. • *v.* **1** *tr.* cover or darken with clouds or gloom or trouble. **2** *intr.* become overcast or gloomy. □ **on cloud nine** *colloq.* extremely happy. **under a cloud** out of favor, under suspicion. **with one's head in the clouds** daydreaming; unrealistic. □□ **cloud´less** *adj.* **cloud´less•ly** *adv.* **cloud´let** *n.*

▪ *n.* **1, 2** see VAPOR *n.* 1. **3** see SWARM *n.* 1–3. • *v.* **1** see SHADE *v.* 1, 2. **2** see FOG *v.* 2. □ **on cloud nine** see HAPPY 1. □□ **cloudless** clear, sunny, fair.

cloud•burst /klówdbərst/ *n.* sudden violent rainstorm.

cloud•y /klówdee/ *adj.* (**cloud•i•er, cloud•i•est**) **1** (of the sky or weather) covered with clouds; overcast. **2** not transparent; unclear. □□ **cloud´i•ly** *adv.* **cloud´i•ness** *n.*

▪ **1** see DULL *adj.* 3. **2** see OPAQUE *adj.* 1, 2.

clout /klowt/ • *n.* **1** heavy blow. **2** *colloq.* influence; power. • *v.tr.* hit hard.
■ *n.* **1** see BLOW² 1. **2** see INFLUENCE *n.* • *v.* see HIT *v.* 1a.

clove¹ /klōv/ *n.* dried flower bud of a tropical plant used as a pungent aromatic spice.

clove² /klōv/ *n.* any of the small bulbs making up a compound bulb of garlic, shallot, etc.

clove³ *past of* CLEAVE¹.

clo•ven /klō'v'n/ *adj.* split; partly divided. □□ **clo•ven-foot•ed** /–foŏtid/ *adj.* **clo•ven-hoofed** /–hoŏft/ *adj.*

clo•ver /klō'vər/ *n.* fodder plant. □ **in clover** in ease and luxury.
■ □ **in clover** see OPULENT 1.

clown /klown/ • *n.* **1** comic entertainer, esp. in a pantomime or circus. **2** silly, foolish, or playful person. • *v. intr.* behave like a clown. □□ **clown'er•y** *n.* **clown'ish** *adj.* **clown'ish•ly** *adv.* **clown'ish•ness** *n.*
■ *n.* **1** jester, fool, zany, comic, comedian, comedienne. **2** buffoon, clod, fool. • *v.* (*clown around*) fool (around), play *or* act the fool, horse around.

cloy /kloy/ *v.tr.* [usu. foll. by *with*] satiate or sicken with an excess of sweetness, richness, etc. □□ **cloy'ing•ly** *adv.*

club /klub/ • *n.* **1** heavy stick with a thick end, used as a weapon, etc. **2** headed stick used in golf. **3 a** playing card of a suit denoted by a black trefoil. **b** [in *pl.*] this suit. **4** association of persons meeting periodically. **5** members' organization or premises. **6** organization offering subscribers certain benefits (*book club*). • *v.tr.* (**clubbed, club•bing**) beat with or as with a club. □ **club sandwich** sandwich with two layers of filling between three slices of toast or bread. **club soda** = SODA *n.* 2. □□ **club'ber** *n.*
■ *n.* **1** cudgel, bat, blackjack, bludgeon, billy. **4** society, organization, fraternity, sorority, union, guild, lodge. • *v.* cudgel, bludgeon, bat, belabor, baste, thrash, trounce, *colloq.* lambaste.

club•foot /klub'foŏt/ *n.* congenitally deformed foot. □□ **club'foot•ed** *adj.*

club•house /klub'hows/ *n.* premises used by a club.

cluck /kluk/ • *n.* guttural cry like that of a hen. • *v.intr.* emit a cluck or clucks.

clue /kloō/ • *n.* **1** fact or idea that serves as a guide, or suggests a line of inquiry, in a problem or investigation. **2** piece of evidence. **3** verbal hint in a crossword. • *v.tr.* (**clues, clued, clue•ing** or **clu•ing**) provide a clue to.
■ *n.* **1, 2** hint, indication, pointer, lead, suggestion; inkling; key, answer, indicator.

clue•less /kloō'lis/ *adj. colloq.* ignorant; stupid. □□ **clue'less•ly** *adv.* **clue'less•ness** *n.*

clump /klump/ • *n.* cluster or mass. • *v.* **1 a** *intr.* form a clump. **b** *tr.* heap or plant together. **2** *intr.* (also **clomp** /klomp/) walk with heavy tread. □□ **clump'y** *adj.* (**clump•i•er, clump•i•est**).
■ *n.* **1** bunch; lump, clot, clod, glob, *sl.* gob. • *v.* **1 b** mass, collect, gather, bunch, pile.

clum•sy /klúmzee/ *adj.* (**clum•si•er, clum•si•est**) **1** awkward in movement or shape; ungainly. **2** difficult to handle or use. **3** tactless. □□ **clum'si•ly** *adv.* **clum'si•ness** *n.*
■ **1** ungraceful, gawky, maladroit, inept, bungling, bumbling. **2** see UNWIELDY. **3** see TACTLESS.

clung *past* and *past part.* of CLING.

clunk /klungk/ • *n.* dull sound as of thick pieces of metal meeting. • *v.intr.* make such a sound.
■ *n.* see THUD *n.* • *v.* see THUD *v.*

clus•ter /klústər/ • *n.* aggregated or close group or bunch. • *v.* **1** *tr.* bring into a cluster or clusters. **2** *intr.* be or come into a cluster or clusters.
■ *n.* collection, clutch, tuft, bundle; swarm, body, band. • *v.* **2** collect, gather, bunch, group; throng.

clutch¹ /kluch/ • *v.* **1** *tr.* seize eagerly; grasp tightly. **2** *intr.* snatch suddenly. • *n.* **1 a** tight grasp. **b** grasping. **2** [in *pl.*] cruel or relentless grasp or control. **3 a** (in a vehicle) device for connecting and disconnecting the engine to the transmission. **b** control operating this.
■ *v.* **1** snatch, grab; hold, grip. **2** grab, grasp, pluck. • *n.* **1 a** hold, grip, lock. **2** (*clutches*) hold; embrace; domination, influence, power.

clutch² /kluch/ *n.* **1** set of eggs for hatching. **2** brood of chickens.

clut•ter /klútər/ • *n.* **1** crowded and untidy collection of things. **2** untidy state. • *v.tr.* crowd untidily.
■ *n.* **1** mess, litter, jumble, hodgepodge. **2** confusion, tangle; see also CHAOS. • *v.* mess up, litter, strew.

Cm *symb. Chem.* curium.

cm *abbr.* centimeter(s).

Cmdr. *abbr.* commander.

CNS *abbr.* central nervous system.

CO *abbr.* **1** Colorado (in official postal use). **2** commanding officer. **3** conscientious objector. **4** carbon monoxide.

Co *symb. Chem.* cobalt.

Co. *abbr.* **1** company. **2** county.

c/o *abbr.* care of.

co- /kō/ *prefix* added to: **1** nouns, with the sense 'joint, mutual, common' (*coauthor*). **2** adjectives and adverbs, with the sense 'jointly, mutually' (*coequal, coequally*). **3** verbs, with the sense 'together with another or others' (*coauthor*).

coach /kōch/ • *n.* **1** bus, usu. comfortably equipped for longer journeys. **2** railroad car. **3** horse-drawn carriage, usu. closed. **4** instructor or trainer in a sport, etc. • *v. tr.* train or teach as a coach.
■ *n.* **4** tutor; see also TEACHER. • *v.* tutor, instruct, guide, direct, drill, prepare, prompt, *colloq.* cram.

co•ag•u•late /kō-ágyəlayt/ *v.* **1** change from a fluid to a solid or semisolid state. **2** clot; curdle. **3** set; solidify. □□ **co•ag'u•la•ble** *adj.* **co•ag'u•lant** *n.* **co•ag•u•la•tion** /–láyshən/ *n.* **co•ag'u•la•tive** /–láytiv, –lətiv/ *adj.* **co•ag'u•la•tor** *n.*
■ congeal, gel, *colloq.* jell.

coal /kōl/ *n.* **1** hard black mineral used as

fuel. **2** red-hot piece of coal, wood, etc., in a fire.

co•a•lesce /kốəlés/ v.intr. come together and form one whole. □□ **co•a•les′cence** n. **co•a•les′cent** adj.

■ see MERGE.

co•a•li•tion /kốəlíshən/ n. Polit. temporary alliance for combined action, esp. of political parties. □□ **co•a•li′tion•ist** n.

■ see ALLIANCE 1.

coarse /kawrs/ adj. **1** rough or loose in texture or grain; made of large particles. **2** lacking refinement; crude; obscene. □□ **coarse′ly** adv. **coarse′ness** n.

■ **1** uneven, scratchy, prickly; crude, roughhewn. **2** boorish, unpolished, unrefined; rude, indecent, lewd, vulgar, gross, smutty, foul.

coars•en /káwrsən/ v. make or become coarse.

coast /kōst/ • n. border of the land near the sea; seashore. • v.intr. **1** ride or move, usu. downhill, without use of power. **2** make progress without much effort. □ **the coast is clear** there is no danger of being observed or caught. □□ **coast′al** adj.

■ n. seaside, shore, beach, littoral. • v. **1** glide, skim, slide, sail. **2** freewheel.

coast•er /kốstər/ n. small tray or mat for a bottle or glass.

coast•line /kốstlin/ n. line of the seashore.

coat /kōt/ • n. **1** outer garment with sleeves and often extending below the hips. **2** animal's fur, hair, etc. **3** single covering of paint, etc. • v.tr. **1 a** provide with a layer or covering. **b** (as **coated** adj.) covered with. **2** (of paint, etc.) form a covering to. □ **coat of arms** heraldic bearings or shield of a person, family, or corporation. □□ **coat′ed** adj. [also in comb.]

■ n. **1** overcoat, topcoat; jacket, anorak, parka. **3** coating, layer, film. • v. **1 a** cover, paint, spread. **b** (**coated**) see SPREAD v. 1b.

coat•ing /kốting/ n. thin layer or covering of paint, etc.

coat•tail /kốttayl/ n. back flap of a jacket or coat.

coax /kōks/ v.tr. **1** persuade (a person) gradually or by flattery. **2** obtain by coaxing. **3** manipulate (a thing) carefully or slowly. □□ **coax′er** n. **coax′ing•ly** adv.

■ **1, 2** wheedle, cajole, beguile, charm, inveigle.

co•ax•i•al /kō-ákseeəl/ adj. **1** having a common axis. **2** Electr. (of a cable or line) transmitting by means of two concentric conductors separated by an insulator. □□ **co•ax′i•al•ly** adv.

cob /kob/ n. **1** = CORN COB. **2** sturdy riding or driving horse with short legs. **3** male swan.

co•balt /kốbawlt/ n. Chem. silvery-white, magnetic metallic element. ¶Symb.: **Co**. □ **cobalt blue 1** pigment containing a cobalt salt. **2** deep-blue color of this.

cob•ble¹ /kóbəl/ n. (in full **cob′ble•stone**) small rounded stone of a size used for paving. • v.tr. pave with cobbles.

cob•ble² /kóbəl/ v.tr. **1** mend or patch up (esp. shoes). **2** [often foll. by together] join or assemble roughly.

cob•bler /kóblər/ n. **1** person who mends shoes, esp. professionally. **2** deep-dish fruit pie.

co•bra /kốbrə/ n. venomous snake of Africa and Asia.

cob•web /kóbweb/ n. **1** fine network of threads spun by a spider from a liquid secreted by it. **2** thread of this. □□ **cob′webbed** adj.

co•ca /kốkə/ n. **1** S. American shrub. **2** its dried leaves, chewed as a stimulant.

co•caine /kōkáyn/ n. drug derived from coca or prepared synthetically, used as a local anesthetic and as a stimulant.

coc•cyx /kóksiks/ n. (pl. **coc•cy•ges** /–sijeez/) small triangular bone at the base of the spinal column in humans and some apes. □□ **coc•cyg•e•al** /koksíjeeəl/ adj.

cock /kok/ • n. **1** male bird, esp. of a domestic fowl. **2 a** firing lever in a gun. **b** cocked position of this (at full cock). **3** tap or valve controlling flow. • v.tr. **1** turn or move (the eye or ear) attentively or knowingly. **2** set aslant, or turn up the brim of (a hat). **3** raise the cock of (a gun). □ **cock-and-bull story** absurd or incredible account.

■ n. **3** see TAP¹ n. 1.

cock•a•too /kókətŏo/ n. crested parrots.

cock•er /kókər/ n. (in full **cock′er span′iel**) **1** small spaniel of a breed with a silky coat. **2** this breed.

cock•er•el /kókrəl/ n. young cock.

cock•eyed /kókīd/ adj. colloq. **1** crooked; askew; not level. **2** (of a scheme, etc.) absurd; not practical.

■ **1** see LOPSIDED. **2** see STUPID adj. 2.

cock•fight /kókfīt/ n. fight between cocks as sport. □□ **cock′fight•ing** n.

cock•le /kókəl/ n. **1** bivalve edible mollusk. **2** (in full **cock′le•shell**) its shell. □ **warm the cockles of one's heart** make one contented; be satisfying.

cock•ney /kóknee/ n. (pl. **–neys**) **1** native of London, esp. of the East End. **2** dialect or accent typical of this area. □□ **cock′ney•ism** n.

cock•pit /kókpit/ n. **1** compartment for the pilot (or the pilot and crew) of an airplane or other craft. **2** place where cockfights are held.

cock•roach /kókrōch/ n. flat brown verminous insect.

cock•sure /kókshŏor/ adj. presumptuously or arrogantly confident. □□ **cock′sure′ly** adv. **cock′sure′ness** n.

■ see CONFIDENT.

cock•tail /kóktayl/ n. **1** usu. alcoholic drink made by mixing various spirits, fruit juices, etc. **2** dish of mixed ingredients (fruit cocktail). **3** any hybrid mixture.

cock•y /kókee/ adj. (**cock•i•er**, **cock•i•est**) **1** conceited; arrogant. **2** saucy; impudent. □□ **cock′i•ly** adv. **cock′i•ness** n.

■ **1** overconfident, haughty, self-important, egotistical, proud. **2** saucy; see also IMPUDENT.

co•co /kốkō/ n. (pl. **co•cos**) coconut palm.

co•coa /kốkō/ n. **1** powder made from

crushed cacao seeds, often with other ingredients. **2** hot drink made from this. □ **cocoa butter** fatty substance obtained from cocoa beans.

co•co•nut /kókənut/ n. (also **co'coa•nut**) large ovate brown seed of the coco, with a hard shell and edible white fleshy lining enclosing a milky juice.

co•coon /kəkōōn/ n. **1** silky case spun by many insect larvae for protection as pupae. **2** protective covering.

COD abbr. **1** cash on delivery. **2** collect on delivery.

cod /kod/ n. (pl. same) large marine fish used as food. □ **cod-liver oil** oil pressed from the fresh liver of cod, which is rich in vitamins D and A.

co•da /kódə/ n. **1** Mus. concluding passage of a piece or movement. **2** concluding event or series of events.

cod•dle /kód'l/ v.tr. **1** treat as an invalid; protect attentively. **2** cook (an egg) in water below boiling point. □□ **cod'dler** n.
■ **1** pamper, baby, cosset, mollycoddle, indulge.

code /kōd/ • n. **1** system of words, letters, figures, or symbols, used to represent others for secrecy or brevity. **2** system of laws, etc. **3** standard of moral behavior. • v.tr. put into code.
■ n. **1** cipher. **2** rule(s), constitution. **3** practice(s), convention(s), criteria, principle(s). • v. encode, encipher, encrypt.

co•deine /kódeen/ n. analgesic alkaloid from morphine.

co•dex /kódeks/ n. (pl. **co•di•ces** /kódiseez, kód–/) ancient manuscript text in book form.

cod•fish /kódfish/ n. = COD.

cod•ger /kójər/ n. (usu. in **old codger**) colloq. person, esp. an old or strange one.

cod•i•cil /kódisil/ n. addition explaining, modifying, or revoking a will or part of one. □□ **cod•i•cil•la•ry** /kódisíləree/ adj.

cod•i•fy /kódifī, kód–/ v.tr. (**-fies, -fied**) arrange (laws, etc.) systematically. □□ **cod•i•fi•ca'tion** n. **cod'i•fi•er** n.

cod•piece /kódpees/ n. hist. appendage like a small bag or flap at the front of a man's breeches.

co•ed /kó-ed, –éd/ colloq. • n. female student at a coeducational institution. • adj. coeducational.

co•ed•u•ca•tion /kóejōōkáyshən/ n. education of pupils of both sexes together. □□ **co•ed•u•ca'tion•al** adj.

co•ef•fi•cient /kóifíshənt/ n. **1** Math. quantity placed before and multiplying an algebraic expression (e.g., 4 in $4x$). **2** Physics multiplier or factor that measures some property (coefficient of expansion).

coe•len•ter•ate /seeléntərayt, –tərit/ n. marine animal with a simple tube-shaped or cup-shaped body, e.g., jellyfish.

co•erce /kó-órs/ v.tr. persuade or restrain by force (coerced you into signing). See synonym study at COMPEL. □□ **co•er'ci•ble** adj. **co•er•cion** /kō-órzhən, –shən/ n. **co•er'cive** adj.

■ see FORCE v. 1. □□ **coercion** see FORCE n. 2.

co•e•val /kō-eévəl/ • adj. **1** having the same age or date of origin. **2** existing at the same epoch. • n. coeval person; contemporary. □□ **co•e•val•i•ty** /–válitee/ n. **co•e'val•ly** adv.

co•ex•ist /kóigzíst/ v.intr. **1** exist together (in time or place). **2** (esp. of nations) exist in mutual tolerance. □□ **co•ex•ist'ence** n. **co•ex•is'tent** adj.

co•ex•ten•sive /kóiksténsiv/ adj. extending over the same space or time.

cof•fee /káwfee, kófee/ n. **1 a** drink made from the roasted and ground beanlike seeds of a tropical shrub. **b** cup of this. **2 a** the shrub. **b** its seeds. **3** pale brown color. □ **coffee break** short rest from work. **coffee cake** type of cake or sweetened bread, often served with coffee. **coffee shop** small informal restaurant. **coffee table** small low table.

cof•fee•house /káwfeehows, kóf–/ n. place serving coffee and other refreshments, often with informal entertainment.

cof•fer /káwfər, kóf–/ n. **1** large strongbox for valuables. **2** [in pl.] treasury or store of funds. □□ **cof'fered** adj.
■ **1** see SAFE n. **2** (coffers) see TREASURY 1.

cof•fer•dam /káwfərdam, kóf–/ n. watertight enclosure pumped dry to permit work below the waterline.

cof•fin /káwfin, kóf–/ n. long, narrow, usu. wooden box in which a corpse is buried or cremated.
■ casket; sarcophagus.

cog /kawg, kog/ n. **1** each of a series of projections on the edge of a wheel or bar transferring motion by engaging with another series. **2** unimportant worker. □□ **cogged** adj.
■ **1** tooth, sprocket. **2** underling, pawn, nonentity.

co•gent /kójənt/ adj. (of arguments, reasons, etc.) convincing; compelling. □□ **co•gen•cy** /–jənsee/ n. **co'gent•ly** adv.
■ see PERSUASIVE. □□ **cogency** see FORCE n. 4.

cog•i•tate /kójitayt/ v. ponder; meditate. □□ **cog•i•ta•tion** /–táyshən/ n. **cog'i•ta•tive** adj. **cog'i•ta•tor** n.
■ see PONDER. □□ **cogitative** see THOUGHTFUL 1.

cog•nac /káwnyak, kón–/ n. high-quality brandy, properly that distilled in Cognac in W. France.

cog•nate /kógnayt/ • adj. **1** related to or descended from a common ancestor. **2** Philol. (of a word) having the same derivation. • n. cognate word. □□ **cog'nate•ly** adv.
■ adj. **1** see LIKE[1] adj. 1.

cog•ni•tion /kognishən/ n. **1** Philos. knowing, perceiving, or conceiving as an act or faculty. **2** a result of this. □□ **cog•ni'tion•al** adj. **cog•ni•tive** /kógnitiv/ adj.
■ **1** see KNOWLEDGE 1.

cog•ni•zance /kógnizəns/ n. knowledge or awareness; perception; sphere of one's observation or concern.
■ notice, consciousness, mindfulness; scope, province, domain.

cog·ni·zant /kógnizənt/ adj. [foll. by of] having knowledge or being aware of.

cog·no·men /kognṓmen/ n. nickname.

cog·wheel /kóghweel, –weel/ n. wheel with cogs.

co·hab·it /kōhábit/ v.intr. (–it·ed, –it·ing) live together, esp. as an unmarried couple. □□ **co·hab'it·ant** n. **co·hab·i·ta'tion** n.

co·here /kōheér/ v.intr. 1 (of parts or a whole) stick together; remain united. 2 (of reasoning, etc.) be logical or consistent.
■ 1 see STICK² v. 4. 2 hold, hang together.

co·her·ent /kōheérent, –hér–/ adj. 1 intelligible and articulate. 2 (of an argument, etc.) consistent. 3 Physics (of waves) having a fixed phase relationship. □□ **co·her'ence** /–rəns/ n. **co·her'en·cy** n. **co·her'ent·ly** adv.
■ 1, 2 orderly, logical, rational, reasonable, sensible, well-ordered; lucid, clear. □□ **co·herence** see UNITY 1.

co·he·sion /kōheézhən/ n. tendency to cohere. □□ **co·he·sive** /–heésiv/ adj. **co·he·sive·ly** /–heésivlee/ adv. **co·he·sive·ness** /–heésivnis/ n.

co·hort /kóhawrt/ n. 1 band of warriors. 2 persons banded or grouped together, esp. in a common cause.
■ 1 troop, squad, squadron, platoon, brigade, unit. 2 company, band, group, faction, set, body, corps.

coif·fure /kwaafyŏōr/ • n. hairstyle. • v. (also **coif**) provide a coiffure.

coil /koyl/ • n. 1 anything arranged in a joined sequence of concentric circles; rope, etc. 2 Electr. device consisting of a coiled wire for converting low voltage to high voltage. 3 piece of wire, piping, etc., wound in circles or spirals. • v. 1 tr. arrange in a series of concentric loops or rings. 2 tr. & intr. twist or be twisted into a circular or spiral shape. 3 intr. move sinuously.
■ n. 1 circle, loop, twist; whorl, spiral, helix. • v. 1, 2 wind, snake, wrap, spiral. 3 see WIND² v. 1.

coin /koyn/ • n. 1 piece of flat, usu. round metal stamped and issued by authority as money. 2 [collect.] metal money. • v.tr. 1 make (coins) by stamping. 2 invent or devise (esp. a new word or phrase). □□ **coin'age** n.
■ n. 2 specie; change, cash, silver. • v. 1 mint, stamp. 2 make up, create, conceive, originate, fabricate. □□ **coinage** 3 see NEOLOGISM.

co·in·cide /kṓinsíd/ v.intr. 1 occur in or during the same time. 2 occupy the same portion of space. 3 be in agreement.
■ 1, 2 fall or come or go together, co-occur, synchronize. 3 agree, (be in) accord, colloq. jibe; correspond, match.

co·in·ci·dence /kō-insidəns/ n. 1 a occurring or being together. b instance of this. 2 remarkable concurrence of events or circumstances, apparently by chance.
■ 1 simultaneity, correspondence, concurrence, contemporaneity. 2 chance, fluke, accident, luck.

co·in·ci·den·tal /kō-insidént'l/ adj. in the nature of or resulting from a coincidence. □□ **co·in·ci·den'tal·ly** adv.

■ chance, fortuitous, accidental, unexpected.

co·i·tus /kṓ-itəs, kō-eé–/ n. Med. sexual intercourse. □□ **co'i·tal** adj.

coke¹ /kōk/ n. solid substance left after the gases have been extracted from coal.

coke² /kōk/ n. sl. cocaine.

Col. abbr. 1 colonel. 2 Colossians (New Testament).

col– /kol/ prefix assim. form of COM–before l.

COLA /kṓlə/ abbr. cost-of-living adjustment or allowance.

co·la /kṓlə/ n. (also **ko'la**) 1 small tree, native to W. Africa, bearing seeds containing caffeine. 2 carbonated drink usu. flavored with these seeds.

col·an·der /kúləndər, kól–/ n. perforated vessel used to strain off liquid in cookery.

cold /kōld/ • adj. 1 of or at a low or relatively low temperature. 2 not heated. 3 feeling cold. 4 lacking ardor, friendliness, or affection. 5 depressing; uninteresting. 6 a dead. b colloq. unconscious. 7 (in games) far from finding what is sought. • n. 1 a prevalence of a low temperature, esp. in the atmosphere. b cold weather or environment. 2 infection of the nose or throat, causing sneezing, sore throat, etc. • adv. completely; entirely (stopped cold). □ **cold cream** ointment for cleansing and softening the skin. **cold cuts** slices of cold cooked meats. **cold feet** colloq. loss of nerve. **cold shoulder** intentional unfriendliness. **cold sore** viral inflammation and blisters in and around the mouth. **cold turkey** sl. abrupt withdrawal from addictive drugs. **cold war** state of hostility between nations without actual fighting. **in cold blood** without feeling or passion; deliberately. **out in the cold** ignored; neglected. □□ **cold'ish** adj. **cold'ly** adv. **cold'ness** n.
■ adj. 1 chilly, frosty, icy, freezing, frigid, ice-cold, stone-cold, bitter, raw, keen, biting, gelid, wintry, glacial. 3 freezing, frozen, stone-cold. 4 indifferent, apathetic, chilly, cool, icy, dispassionate, unsympathetic, aloof, unresponsive, clinical, spiritless, frigid, unfriendly; cold-blooded, insensitive, uncaring, unemotional, undemonstrative, reserved. 5 cheerless, gloomy, dispiriting, deadening. 6 a see DEAD adj. 1. b see DEAD adj. 4. 7 off the track, far away, distant. • n. 1 coldness, frigidity, iciness. 2 common cold, sniffle(s), Med. coryza,. sl. bug. • adv. thoroughly, absolutely, unhesitatingly, promptly, immediately.

cold-blood·ed /kṓldblúdid/ adj. 1 having a body temperature varying with that of the environment. 2 callous; deliberately cruel. □□ **cold'-blood'ed·ly** adv. **cold'-blood'ed·ness** n.
■ 2 brutal, savage, inhuman, barbarous; thick-skinned, insensitive, heartless, uncaring.

cold-heart·ed /kṓldhaártid/ adj. lacking affection or warmth; unfriendly. □□ **cold'-heart'ed·ly** adv. **cold'-heart'ed·ness** n.
■ unsympathetic, indifferent, unfeeling, uncaring, callous, thick-skinned, heartless.

cole•slaw /kőlslaw/ *n.* dressed salad of sliced raw cabbage.

co•le•us /kőleeəs/ *n.* decorative plant with variegated leaves.

col•ic /kólik/ *n.* severe spasmodic abdominal pain. □□ **col'ick•y** *adj.*

col•i•se•um /kóliseéəm/ *n.* large stadium.

co•li•tis /kəlítis/ *n.* inflammation of the lining of the colon.

col•lab•o•rate /kəlábərayt/ *v.intr.* 1 work jointly. 2 cooperate traitorously with an enemy. □□ **col·lab·o·ra'tion** /-ráyshən/ *n.* **col·lab·o·ra'tion·ist** *n. & adj.* **col·lab·o·ra'tive** /-ráytiv –rətiv/ *adj.* **col·lab'o·ra·tor** *n.*

■ 1 cooperate, join (forces), work together, team up.

col•lage /kəlaázh/ *n.* work of art in which various materials are arranged and glued to a backing. □□ **col•lag'ist** *n.*

col•lapse /kəláps/ • *n.* 1 tumbling down or falling in of a structure. 2 sudden failure. 3 physical or mental breakdown. • *v.* 1 a *intr.* undergo or experience a collapse. b *tr.* cause to collapse. 2 *intr. colloq.* lie or sit down and relax. 3 *tr. & intr.* fold. □□ **col•lap'si•ble** *adj.* **col•lap•si•bil'i•ty** *n.*

■ *n.* 1 cave-in, breakdown; see also RUIN *n.* 3. 2 downfall, ruin; bankruptcy. 3 (mental or nervous) breakdown. • *v.* 1 a crumple, cave in, deflate; fail, (come to an) end, go bankrupt, go under; pass out, faint, drop.

col•lar /kólər/ • *n.* 1 part of a garment, that goes around the neck. 2 band of leather or other material put around an animal's neck. 3 encircling part, device, etc. • *v.tr.* 1 seize (a person) by the collar or neck. 2 capture; apprehend. □□ **col'lared** *adj.* [also in *comb.*]. **col'lar•less** *adj.*

col•lar•bone /kólərbōn/ *n.* either of two bones joining the breastbone and the shoulder blades; the clavicle.

col•late /kəláyt, kólayt, kő–/ *v.tr.* 1 compare (texts, statements, etc.). 2 arrange in proper sequence. □□ **col'la•tor** *n.*

■ 1 see SEPARATE *v.* 4.

col•lat•er•al /kəlátərəl/ • *n.* 1 security pledged as a guarantee for repayment of a loan. 2 person having the same descent as another but by a different line. • *adj.* 1 descended from the same stock but by a different line. 2 side by side; parallel. 3 a additional but subordinate. b contributory. □□ **col•lat'er•al•ly** *adv.*

■ *n.* 1 see SECURITY 3. • *adj.* 3 see EXTRA *adj.*

col•la•tion /kəláyshən, ko–/ *n.* 1 collating. 2 light meal.

col•league /kóleeg/ *n.* fellow official or worker.

■ teammate, coworker, associate, comrade.

col•lect /kəlékt/ • *v.* 1 *tr. & intr.* bring or come together; assemble; accumulate. 2 *tr.* systematically seek and acquire, esp. as a hobby. 3 *tr.* obtain (taxes, contributions, etc.). 4 a *refl.* regain control of oneself. b *tr.* concentrate (one's thoughts, etc.). c *tr.* (as **collected** *adj.*) not perturbed nor distracted. See synonym study at GATHER. • *adj. & adv.*

to be paid for by the receiver (of a telephone call, parcel, etc.). □□ **col·lect'a·ble** *adj.* **col·lect'ed·ly** *adv.*

■ *v.* 1 gather, amass, compile; convene, meet. 4 a see COMPOSE 4a. b summon (up), muster, gather (up). c (**collected**) calm, serene, controlled, cool; confident.

col•lect•i•ble /kəléktibəl/ • *adj.* worth collecting. • *n.* item sought by collectors.

col•lec•tion /kəlékshən/ *n.* 1 collecting or being collected. 2 things collected. 3 money collected, esp. in church or for a charitable cause.

■ 1 accumulation, amassment, aggregation. 2 hoard, store; anthology. 3 contribution(s), alms.

col•lec•tive /kəléktiv/ • *adj.* 1 taken as a whole; aggregate. 2 of or from several or many individuals; common. • *n.* 1 cooperative enterprise. 2 = *collective noun.* □□ **collective bargaining** negotiation of wages, etc., by an organized body of employees. **collective noun** *Gram.* noun that denotes a collection or number of individuals (e.g., *assembly*, *family*, *troop*). □□ **col•lec'tive•ly** *adv.* **col•lec'tive•ness** *n.*

■ *adj.* 1 see JOINT *adj.* 2 see COMMON *adj.* 2.

col•lec•tiv•ism /kəléktivizəm/ *n.* theory and practice of the collective ownership of land and the means of production. □□ **col•lec'tiv•ist** *n.* **col•lec•tiv•is'tic** *adj.*

col•lec•tor /kəléktər/ *n.* 1 person who collects things of interest as a hobby. 2 person who collects money, etc., due.

■ 1 gatherer, accumulator, hoarder.

col•lege /kólij/ *n.* 1 establishment for further or higher education, sometimes part of a university. 2 establishment for specialized professional education (*naval college*). 3 organized body of persons with shared functions and privileges (*college of cardinals*). □□ **col•le•gi•al** /kəleéjəl/ *adj.*

col•le•giate /kəleéjət/ *adj.* constituted as or belonging to a college; corporate. □□ **col•le'giate•ly** *adv.*

col•lide /kəlíd/ *v.intr.* come into collision or conflict.

■ (**collide with**) crash into, smash into; run into, bump into, smack into; see CONFLICT *v.*

col•lie /kólee/ *n.* longhaired dog orig. of a Scottish breed.

col•lier•y /kólyəree/ *n.* (*pl.* **–ies**) coal mine and its buildings.

col•li•sion /kəlízhən/ *n.* 1 violent impact of a moving body with another or with a fixed object. 2 clashing of opposed interests or considerations.

■ 1 smash, crash. 2 clash, conflict; see also STRUGGLE *n.* 2.

col•loid /kóloyd/ *n. Chem.* substance consisting of ultramicroscopic particles suspended in a liquid or other medium. □□ **col•loi•dal** /kəlóyd'l/ *adj.*

col•lo•qui•al /kəlőkweeəl/ *adj.* of ordinary or familiar conversation. □□ **col•lo'qui•al•ism** *n.* **col•lo'qui•al•ly** *adv.*

■ see VERNACULAR *n.*

col•lo•qui•um /kəlőkweeəm/ *n.* (*pl.* **col•lo•qui•ums** or **col•lo•qui•a** /–kweeə/) academic conference or seminar.

col•lo•quy /kólǝkwee/ n. (pl. **–quies**) conversation; talk. See synonym study at CONVERSATION.

col•lude /kǝlōōd/ v.intr. come to an understanding or conspire together. □□ **col•lud'er** n. **col•lu•sion** /kǝlōōzhǝn/ n. **col•lu•sive** /-lōōsiv/ adj. **col•lu'sive•ly** adv.

■ see PLOT v. 2. □□ **collusion** see INTRIGUE n. 1.

Colo. abbr. Colorado.

co•logne /kǝlōn/ n. perfumed water for the face, etc.

co•lon[1] /kólǝn/ n. punctuation mark (:), used esp. to set off something to follow.

co•lon[2] /kólǝn/ n. Anat. lower and greater part of the large intestine. □□ **co•lon•ic** /kǝlónik/ adj.

col•o•nel /kǝrnǝl/ n. military officer, just below a brigadier general in rank. □□ **colo'nel•cy** n. (pl. **–cies**)

co•lo•ni•al /kǝlṓneeǝl/ • adj. 1 pertaining to a colony or colonies. 2 (esp. of architecture or furniture) built or in the style of the period in America before independence. • n. native or inhabitant of a colony. □□ **co•lo'ni•al•ly** adv.

co•lo•ni•al•ism /kǝlṓneeǝlizǝm/ n. policy of acquiring or maintaining colonies, esp. for economic advantage. □□ **co•lo'ni•al•ist** n. ■ neocolonialism, usu. derog. imperialism.

col•o•nize /kólǝnīz/ v.tr. establish a colony or colonies in (a country or area). □□ **col•o•ni•za'tion** n. **col'o•niz•er** n.

■ see SETTLE 10.

col•on•nade /kólǝnáyd/ n. row of columns, esp. supporting an entablature or roof. □□ **col•on•nad'ed** adj.

■ see PORTICO.

col•o•ny /kólǝnee/ n. (pl. **–nies**) 1 group of settlers or settlement in a new country fully or partly subject to the mother country. 2 people of one nationality, race, occupation, etc., forming a community. 3 Biol. collection of animals, plants, etc., connected, in contact, or living close together. □□ **col'o•nist** n.

■ 1 see SETTLEMENT 3. □□ **colonist** see settler (at SETTLE).

col•o•phon /kólǝfon, –fǝn/ n. publisher's identifying device or imprint, as on a title page, etc.

col•or /kúlǝr/ • n. 1 sensation produced by visible wavelengths of light. 2 one, or any mixture, of the constituents into which light can be separated as in a spectrum or rainbow. 3 coloring substance, esp. paint. 4 use of colors, as in photography and television. 5 pigmentation of the skin, esp. when dark. 6 ruddiness. 7 [pl.] appearance or aspect (see things in their true colors). 8 [pl.] flag, insignia, etc. 9 quality or mood in art, speech, etc. • v. 1 tr. apply color to. 2 tr. influence. 3 tr. misrepresent; exaggerate. 4 intr. take on color; blush. □ **color-blind** 1 unable to distinguish certain colors. 2 ignoring racial prejudice. **color-blindness** condition of being color-blind. **show one's true colors** reveal one's true character or intentions. □□ **col•or•a'tion** n.

■ n. 2 hue, tint, shade, tone, tinge, tincture.

---

3 pigmentation, pigment, dye. 5 coloration, coloring. 6 bloom, flush, blush. 7 (colors) identity, light. 8 (colors) ensign, standard, pennant. 9 see CHARACTER n. 1. • v. 1 tint, dye, stain, paint; pigment. 2 affect, bias; see also INFLUENCE v. 3 distort, falsify, taint, warp, twist. 4 redden, flush, become red-faced.

col•or•a•tu•ra /kúlǝrǝtṓorǝ, –tyŏor–/ n. 1 elaborate ornamentation of a vocal melody. 2 soprano skilled in this.

col•ored /kúlǝrd/ adj. 1 having color(s). 2 often offens. wholly or partly of nonwhite descent.

col•or•fast /kúlǝrfast/ adj. dyed in colors that will not fade nor be washed out. □□ **col'or•fast•ness** n.

col•or•ful /kúlǝrfool/ adj. 1 having much or varied color; bright. 2 vivid; lively. □□ **col'or•ful•ly** adv. **col'or•ful•ness** n.

■ 1 see VIVID 1. 2 see dramatic (DRAMA).

col•or•ing /kúlǝring/ n. 1 process of or skill in using color(s). 2 appearance as regards color, esp. complexion.

col•or•ize /kúlǝrīz/ v.tr. add color to (orig. black-and-white film) with computer technology.

col•or•less /kúlǝrlis/ adj. 1 without color. 2 lacking character or interest. 3 dull or pale in hue. □□ **col'or•less•ly** adv.

■ 1, 3 pallid, white; wan, washed out, ashen. 2 dull, drab, lifeless, boring, tedious, bland, lackluster, uninspired.

co•los•sal /kǝlósǝl/ adj. 1 huge; gigantic. 2 colloq. remarkable; splendid. 3 Archit. (of an order) having more than one story of columns.

■ 1 vast, enormous, giant, mammoth, massive, gargantuan, immense. 2 spectacular, stupendous, wonderful, awe-inspiring, extraordinary, incredible, overwhelming, unbelievable, fantastic.

co•los•sus /kǝlósǝs/ n. (pl. **co•los•si** /-sī/ or **co•los•sus•es**) 1 gigantic statue. 2 gigantic or important person or thing.

co•los•to•my /kǝlóstǝmee/ n. (pl. **–mies**) Surgery operation on the colon to make an artificial anus in the abdominal wall.

colt /kōlt/ n. young, uncastrated male horse.

col•um•bine /kólǝmbīn/ n. garden plant having drooping belled flowers.

col•umn /kólǝm/ n. 1 Archit. upright, usu. cylindrical pillar. 2 column-shaped structure or part. 3 vertical cylindrical mass of liquid or vapor. 4 vertical division of a page, etc., containing a sequence of figures or words. 5 regular newspaper feature devoted to a particular subject. 6 arrangement of troops or ships in successive lines, with a narrow front. □□ **co•lum•nar** /kǝlúmnǝr/ adj. **col'umned** adj.

■ 1–3 see PILLAR 1. 5 see EDITORIAL.

col•um•nist /kólǝmnist, –mist/ n. journalist contributing regularly to a newspaper.

com /kom/ • abbr. used by commercial organizations in Internet addresses.

com- /kom, kǝm, kum/ prefix (also **co-, col-, con-, cor-**) with; together; jointly.

co•ma /kṓmə/ *n.* prolonged deep unconsciousness.

■ see STUPOR.

Co•man•che /kəmánchee/ *n.* **1 a** a N. American people native to the western plains.
b member of this people. **2** language of this
people.

co•ma•tose /kṓmətōs, kóm–/ *adj.* **1** in a
coma. **2** lethargic.

■ **1** see UNCONSCIOUS *adj.* **2** see *lethargic*
(LETHARGY).

comb /kōm/ • *n.* **1** toothed strip of rigid material for grooming hair. **2** tool having a similar design. **3** red, fleshy crest of esp. male
fowl. • *v.tr.* **1** groom (hair) with a comb.
2 dress (wool or flax) with a comb. **3** search
(a place) thoroughly.

■ *v.* **3** see SEARCH *v.* 1, 3.

com•bat • *n.* /kómbat, kúm–/ **1** armed conflict; battle. **2** struggle; contest. • *v.*
/kəmbát, kómbat/ **1** *intr.* engage in combat.
2 *tr.* engage in combat with. **3** *tr.* oppose.
□ **combat fatigue** mental disorder caused
by stress in wartime combat.

■ *n.* **1** fight, engagement, fighting, skirmish. **2** strife, controversy, dispute, quarrel,
disagreement, confrontation. • *v.* **1** fight,
(do) battle, war, clash, contend, duel, wrestle, spar, grapple. **3** fight, struggle *or* strive
against, defy. □ **combat fatigue** shell shock.

com•bat•ant /kəmbát′nt, kómbət′nt/ • *n.*
person engaged in fighting. • *adj.* **1** fighting.
2 for fighting.

com•bat•ive /kəmbátiv/ *adj.* ready or eager to
fight.

■ see PUGNACIOUS.

com•bi•na•tion /kómbináyshən/ *n.* **1 a** combining; process of being combined. **2** combined state (*in combination with*). **3** combined set of things or people. **4** sequence of
numbers used to open a combination lock.
□ **combination lock** lock that opens only by
a specific sequence of movements.

■ **1** union, conjunction, mixture, mix,
grouping, amalgamation, compound; blend.
2 conjunction, tandem; see also ASSOCIATION
2. **3** array; association, alliance, coalition,
union, federation, confederation.

com•bine • *v.* /kəmbín/ **1** *tr.* & *intr.* join together; unite. **2** *tr.* possess (qualities usually
distinct) together. **3** *intr.* form or cause to
form a chemical compound. • *n.* /kómbīn/
combination of esp. commercial interests.
□ **combine harvester** /kómbīn/ machine
that reaps and threshes. **combining form**
Gram. linguistic element used with another
element to form a word (e.g., *bio–* = life,
–graphy = writing).

■ *v.* **1** unify, connect, relate, link, integrate,
merge, pool; join forces. **2** see FUSE[1] *v.*
3 blend, synthesize, bind, bond, mingle,
amalgamate, mix.

com•bo /kómbō/ *n.* (*pl.* **–bos**) *sl.* small jazz or
dance band.

com•bus•ti•ble /kəmbústibəl/ • *adj.* capable
of or used for burning. • *n.* combustible substance. □□ **com•bus•ti•bil′i•ty** *n.*

■ *adj.* see FLAMMABLE.

com•bus•tion /kəmbúschən/ *n.* **1** burning;
consumption by fire. **2** *Chem.* development
of light and heat from the chemical combination of a substance with oxygen. □□ **com•
bus•tive** /–bústiv/ *adj.*

Comdr. *abbr.* commander.

come /kum/ *v.intr.* (*past* **came** /kaym/; *past
part.* **come**) **1** move, be brought toward, or
reach a place. **2** reach or be brought to a
specified situation or result (*you'll come to no
harm, came into prominence*). **3** reach or extend to a specified point. **4** traverse or accomplish (*have come a long way*). **5** occur;
happen (*how did you come to break your leg?*).
6 take or occupy a specified position in space
or time (*it comes on the third page*). **7** become
perceptible or known (*the news comes as a surprise*). **8** be available (*comes in three sizes*).
9 become (*the handle has come loose*). **10** [foll.
by *from, of*] **a** be descended from (*comes from
a rich family*). **b** be the result of (*that comes of
complaining*). **11** [in *subj.*] *colloq.* when a
specified time is reached (*come next month*).
□ **come about** happen; take place. **come
across 1 a** be effective or understood. **b** appear or sound in a specified way (*the ideas
came across clearly*). **2** meet or find by chance
(*came across an old jacket*). **come along
1** make progress. **2** [as *imper.*] hurry up.
come around 1 pay an informal visit. **2** recover consciousness. **3** be converted to another opinion. **come away** become detached
or broken off. **come back 1** return. **2** recur
to one's memory. **3** become fashionable or
popular again. **4** reply; retort. **come between 1** interfere with the relationship of.
2 separate; prevent contact between. **come
by 1** pass; go past. **2** call on; visit. **3** acquire;
obtain. **come down 1** lose position or
wealth. **2** reach a decision or recommendation (*the report came down against change*).
3 [foll. by *to*] signify; be dependent on (a factor) (*it comes down to who is willing to go*).
4 [foll. by *on*] criticize harshly. **5** [foll. by
with] begin to suffer from (a disease). **come
in 1** take a specified position in a race, etc.
(*came in third*). **2 a** have a useful role or function. **b** prove to be (*came in very handy*).
3 begin speaking, esp. in radio transmission.
come into receive, esp. as heir. **come off
1** *colloq.* (of an action) succeed; be accomplished. **2** fare; turn out (*came off badly, came
off the winner*). **3** be detached or detachable
(from). **come off it** [as *imper.*] *colloq.* expression of disbelief or refusal to accept another's
opinion, behavior, etc. **come on 1 a** advance, esp. to attack. **b** [foll. by *to*] make sexual advances. **2** be heard or seen on television, on the telephone, etc. **3** [as *imper.*]
expressing encouragement. **come-on** *n. sl.*
lure or enticement. **come out 1 a** emerge;
become known. **b** end; turn out. **2** appear or
be published. **3 a** declare oneself; make a decision (*came out in favor of joining*). **b** openly
declare that one is a homosexual. **4** turn out
in a specified way (esp. the subject of a photograph). **5** (of a stain, etc.) be removed.
come over 1 (of a feeling, etc.) overtake or
affect (a person). **2** affect or influence (*I
don't know what came over me*). **come**

through 1 be successful; survive. **2** survive or overcome (a difficulty). **come to 1** recover consciousness. **2** *Naut.* bring a vessel to a stop. **3** reach in total; amount to. **4** have as a destiny; reach (*what is the world coming to?*). **5** be a question of (*when it comes to wine, he is an expert*). **come to pass** happen; occur. **come to rest** cease moving. **come up 1** (of an issue, problem, etc.) arise; present itself. **2** [foll. by *with*] produce (an idea, etc.). **come up against** be faced with or opposed by. **come upon 1** meet or find by chance. **2** attack by surprise. **come what may** no matter what happens.

■ **1** approach, advance, (draw) near, move closer, *archaic or dial.* draw nigh; arrive, appear, make *or* put in an appearance, turn *or* show up, *colloq.* blow in. **3** stretch *or* spread (out), range, go. **5** see CHANCE *v.* 2. **9** see BECOME 1. **10** a see SPRING *v.* 3. **b** see SPRING *v.* 4. □ **come about** occur, *disp.* transpire, *poet.* befall. **come across 1** be communicated *or* understandable, penetrate, sink in; go over, be received. **2** discover, encounter, run across *or* into, happen *or* chance upon, hit *or* light upon, stumble (up)on. **come along 1** do, progress, move along, *literary* fare; see also get on 1. **2** see HURRY *v.* 1. **come around 1** see VISIT *v.* 1. **2** see *come to* 1 below. **come away** see DETACH 1. **come back 1** see RETURN *v.* 1. **4** answer, respond, rejoin, return. **come between 1** see INTERFERE 3. **2** see SEPARATE *v.* 1. **come by 1** move *or* proceed past. **2** see CALL *v.* 4. **3** get, procure; secure, find, take *or* get possession of, get *or* lay hold of, get *or* lay *or* put (one's) hands on; win, earn, attain. **come down 3** see DEPEND 1. **4** (*come down on*) punish, pounce on *or* upon, rebuke, revile, reprimand, bear down on. **5** (*come down with*) succumb to, contract, catch; be afflicted with, get, *archaic* be stricken with. **come in 1** finish, end up, arrive. **2 b** be, turn out (to be) elected; see RECEIVE 1, 2. **come off 1** occur, happen, come to pass, take place. **2** emerge, result as, end up; see also FARE *v.* 3. see DETACH 1. **come on 2** appear. **come-on** attraction, inducement, temptation, bait. **come out 1 a** be revealed, become public *or* common knowledge, get about *or* around, get *or* leak out. **b** conclude, terminate, finish. **2** be issued *or* produced *or* distributed, be shown, be in print, première. **3 a** see DECIDE 1. **b** come out of the closet. **5** go, vanish, disappear. **come over 1** see OVERTAKE 2, AFFECT 1a. **come through 1** succeed, not fail *or* disappoint; get well *or* better. **2** recover from, recuperate from. **come to 1** regain consciousness, awake(n), revive, wake up, come around. **3** add up to, total, aggregate, (be) equal (to), mount up to, tot up to, make. **5** regard, concern, relate to, involve, be relevant to, be involved. **come to pass** see HAPPEN *v.* 1. **come to rest** see STOP *v.* 3. **come up 1** surface, be brought up, be broached, crop up. **2** see *think v.* **come up against** face, experience, meet (with), contend with, come into contact with, wrestle with. **come upon 1** see STUMBLE *v.* 4.

come•back /kúmbak/ *n.* **1** return to a previ-

ous (esp. successful) state. **2** *sl.* retaliation or retort.

■ **1** see REVIVAL¹ 1, 3. **2** see RETORT *n.*

co•me•di•an /kəmeédeeən/ *n.* humorous entertainer.

■ comic, humorist, wit, wag, funny man *or* woman.

co•me•di•enne /kəmeédee-én/ *n.* female comedian.

come•down /kúmdown/ *n.* **1** loss of status; decline or degradation. **2** disappointment.

com•e•dy /kómidee/ *n.* (*pl.* **–dies**) **1 a** amusing *or* satirical play, film, etc. **b** dramatic genre of such works. **2** humor, esp. in a work of art, etc. □□ **co•me•dic** /kəmeédik/ *adj.*

■ **2** see HUMOR *n.* 1.

come•ly /kúmlee/ *adj.* (**come•li•er, come•li•est**) pleasant to look at; lovely. □□ **come'li•ness** *n.*

co•mes•ti•ble /kəméstibəl/ *n.* [usu. in *pl.*] *formal or joc.* food.

com•et /kómit/ *n.* celestial tailed object of ice, dust, and gas, orbiting the sun.

■ see STAR *n.* 1.

come•up•pance /kúmúpəns/ *n. colloq.* one's deserved fate.

■ see DESERT³ 2.

com•fort /kúmfərt/ ● *n.* **1** consolation, relief in affliction. **2 a** state of physical well-being. **b** [usu. in *pl.*] things that make life easy *or* pleasant. **3** cause or provider of satisfaction. ● *v.tr.* **1** console. **2** make comfortable.

■ *n.* **1** solace, cheer. **2 a** ease, luxury, security. **3** pleasure, delight, joy, blessing. ● *v.* **1** soothe, assuage, reassure, relieve, cheer, gladden.

com•fort•a•ble /kúmftəbəl, –fərtəbəl/ *adj.* **1 a** such as to avoid hardship and give comfort. **b** (of a person) relaxing to be with; congenial. **2** free from discomfort. **3** *colloq.* free from (esp. financial) worry **4** having an easy conscience (*did not feel comfortable about refusing him*).

■ **1** amiable, pleasant, agreeable, relaxing; see also SNUG¹ *adj.* 1, 2 at ease, relaxed, untroubled, undisturbed. **3** easy, secure; see also *well off* 1 (WELL). **4** see RIGHT *adj.* 1.

com•fort•er /kúmfərtər/ *n.* **1** person who comforts. **2** quilt.

com•fy /kúmfee/ *adj.* (**com•fi•er, com•fi•est**) *colloq.* comfortable. □□ **com'fi•ly** *adv.* **com'fi•ness** *n.*

com•ic /kómik/ ● *adj.* **1** of, or in the style of, comedy. **2** funny. ● *n.* **1** comedian. **2** (*pl.*) comic-strip section of a newspaper. □ **comic book** magazine of comic strips. **comic strip** sequence of drawings in a newspaper, etc., telling a story. □□ **com'i•cal** *adj.* **com'i•cal•ly** *adv.*

■ *adj.* **2** amusing, droll, comedic, humorous, hilarious, sidesplitting, jocular, witty. ● *n.* **1** see COMEDIAN.

com•ing /kúming/ ● *attrib.adj.* approaching; next (*this coming Sunday*). ● *n.* arrival; approach.

comm. *abbr.* **1** commerce. **2** commercial. **3** commissioner. **4** commission. **5** committee. **6** common.

com•ma /kómə/ n. **1** punctuation mark (,) indicating pause or division. **2** Mus. definite minute interval or difference of pitch.

com•mand /kəmánd/ • v.tr. **1** give formal order to. **2** have authority or control over. **3 a** restrain; master. **b** gain or have the use of (skill, resources, etc.). **4** deserve and get (respect, etc.). **5** Mil. dominate (a strategic position) from a superior height. • n. **1** authoritative order. **2** mastery; possession (a good command of languages). **3** exercise of authority, esp. naval or military (has command of this ship). **4** Mil. **a** body of troops, etc. **b** district under a commander. **5** Computing **a** instruction causing a computer to perform a function. **b** signal initiating such an operation. See synonym study at JURISDICTION. □ **command performance** performance given at the request of a head of state or sovereign.

■ v. **1** direct, enjoin, charge, request, require, demand, instruct, decree. **2, 5** lead, rule, govern. **3 b** enjoy, possess; summon. **4** attract, earn; exact, compel. • n. **1** direction, instruction, mandate, charge. **2** (thorough) grasp or knowledge. **3** power, sovereignty, dominion, regulation, direction, management, government, supervision, leadership, jurisdiction.

com•man•dant /kómandánt, –daant/ n. commanding officer.

■ see LEADER 1.

com•man•deer /kómandéer/ v.tr. **1** seize for military purposes. **2** take possession of without authority.

■ see SEIZE 2.

com•mand•er /kəmándər/ n. person who commands, esp. a naval officer next in rank below captain. □ **commander in chief** supreme commander, esp. of a nation's forces.

■ see MASTER n. 1.

com•mand•ing /kəmánding/ adj. **1** exalted; impressive. **2** (of a hill, etc.) giving a wide view. **3** substantial (has a commanding lead).

■ **1** see MAGNIFICENT 1. **2** see panoramic (PANORAMA). **3** see DOMINANT adj.

com•mand•ment /kəmándmənt/ n. divine command. □ **Ten Commandments** divine rules of conduct given by God to Moses (Exod. 20:1–17).

■ see ORDER n. 2.

com•man•do /kəmándō/ n. (pl. **–dos**) Mil. member of a unit trained for raids.

com•mem•o•rate /kəmémərayt/ v.tr. **1** preserve in memory by ceremony or celebration. **2** be a memorial of. □□ **com•mem•o•ra•tive** /–ráytiv, –rotiv/ adj. **com•mem•o•ra•tion** /–ráyshən/ n.

■ **1** memorialize, remember, observe; revere, honor, venerate, pay tribute or homage to.

com•mence /kəméns/ v. formal begin.

■ start, open, initiate, launch, inaugurate.

com•mence•ment /kəménsmənt/ n. formal **1** a beginning. **2** ceremony of degree conferment.

com•mend /kəménd/ v.tr. **1** entrust. **2** praise. **3** recommend. See synonym study at APPROVE. See synonym study at PRAISE.

■ **1** see TRUST v. 4. **2** see PRAISE v. 1. **3** see RECOMMEND 1, SUGGEST 1.

com•mend•a•ble /kəméndəbəl/ adj. praiseworthy.

com•men•da•tion /kómendáyshən/ n. **1** act of commending or recommending. **2** praise.

com•men•su•rate /kəménsərət, –shərət/ adj. **1** having the same size, duration, etc. **2** proportionate.

■ **1** see EQUAL adj. 1, 3. **2** see PROPORTIONAL adj.

com•ment /kóment/ • n. **1 a** remark, esp. critical. **b** criticism. **2 a** explanatory note (e.g., on a written text). **b** written criticism. **3** (of a play, poem, etc.) critical illustration (his art is a comment on society). • v.intr. **1** make (esp. critical) remarks. **2** write explanatory notes.

■ n. **1** opinion, view, observation. **2 a** reference, annotation, elucidation, clarification, footnote. **3** see CRITICISM 2. • v. **1** observe, opine. **2** annotate.

com•men•tar•y /kómanteree/ n. (pl. **–ies**) **1** set of critical notes on a text, etc. **2** descriptive spoken account of an event or a performance as it happens.

■ **1** see EXPLANATION 1.

com•men•ta•tor /kómantaytər/ n. person who provides commentary. □□ **com′men•tate** v.

■ see journalist (JOURNALISM).

com•merce /kómərs/ n. **1** large-scale business transactions. **2** social intercourse.

■ **1** marketing; see also TRADE n. 1a, b. **2** see INTERCOURSE.

com•mer•cial /kəmórshəl/ • adj. **1** engaged in, or concerned with, commerce. **2** having profit as a primary aim. • n. broadcast advertisement. □□ **com′mer′cial•ism** n. **com•mer′cial•i•za′tion** n. **com•mer′cial•ize** v.

com•min•gle /kəmínggəl/ v. literary mingle together.

com•mis•er•ate /kəmízərayt/ v.intr. express or feel pity. □□ **com•mis•er•a•tion** /–ráyshən/ n. **com•mis•er•a′tive** adj. **com•mis′er•a•tor** n.

■ see SYMPATHIZE 1.

com•mis•sar•y /kómiseree/ n. (pl. **–ies**) **1** Mil. **a** store for the supply of food, etc., to soldiers. **b** officer responsible for this. **2 a** restaurant in a movie studio, etc. **b** food supplied. **3** deputy or delegate.

com•mis•sion /kəmíshən/ • n. **1 a** authority to perform a task or certain duties. **b** person or group entrusted with such authority. **c** instruction or duty given. **2** order for something, esp. a work of art, to be produced. **3** Mil. **a** warrant conferring the rank of officer. **b** rank so conferred. **4 a** authority to act as agent for a company, etc., in trade. **b** percentage paid to the agent from profits obtained. **5** act of committing (a crime, sin, etc.). **6** office or department of a commissioner. • v.tr. **1** authorize by a commission. **2 a** give (an artist, etc.) a commission for a piece of work. **b** order (a work) to be created. **3** Naut. **a** give (an officer) command of a ship. **b** prepare (a ship) for active service. □ **out of commission** not in service.

■ *n.* **1 b** see COMMITTEE. **4 b** see CUT *n.* 8. **6** see OFFICE 2. • *v.* **1** see AUTHORIZE 2. **2** see ORDER *v.* 3. □ **out of commission** see *out of order* 1 (ORDER).

com•mis•sion•er /kəmíshənər/ *n.* leader appointed by a commission.

com•mit /kəmít/ *v.tr.* (**com•mit•ted, com•mit•ting**) **1** entrust or consign for safekeeping, treatment, etc. **2** perpetrate, do (esp. a crime or blunder). **3** pledge or bind (esp. oneself) to a certain course. **4** (as **committed** *adj.*) **a** morally dedicated; politically aligned. **b** obliged (to take certain action). ■ **1** transfer, assign, delegate, hand over, deliver; sentence, confine, imprison, incarcerate. **2** see PERPETRATE. **3** promise, agree, assure, swear, give one's word, vow, undertake, guarantee. **4 a** (**committed**) see DEVOTED.

com•mit•ment /kəmítmənt/ *n.* **1** obligation that restricts freedom of action. **2** process or instance of committing oneself. **3** dedication. ■ **1** see BOND *n.* 2b. **2** see UNDERTAKING 2. **3** see APPLICATION 4.

com•mit•tal /kəmít'l/ *n.* **1** act of committing a person to an institution, esp. prison or a mental hospital. **2** burial.

com•mit•tee *n.* **1** /kəmítee/ body of persons appointed for a specific function by, and usu. out of, a larger body. **2** /kómitee/ *Law* person entrusted with the charge of another person or another person's property. ■ **1** council, board, cabinet, panel, commission.

com•mode /kəmód/ *n.* **1** chest of drawers. **2** = TOILET 1.

com•mo•di•ous /kəmódeeəs/ *adj.* roomy and comfortable.

com•mod•i•ty /kəmóditee/ *n.* (*pl.* **–ties**) **1** *Commerce* article or raw material that can be bought and sold. **2** useful thing. ■ **1** see PRODUCT 1. **2** see THING 2, 3.

com•mo•dore /kómədawr/ *n.* **1** naval officer just above captain. **2** commander of a fleet division. **3** president of a yacht club.

com•mon /kómən/ • *adj.* **1 a** occurring often. **b** overused; trite. **c** ordinary; without special rank. **2** shared by or coming from more than one (*common knowledge*). **3** *derog.* low-class; inferior. **4** familiar. **5** *Math.* belonging to two or more quantities (*common denominator*). See synonym study at MUTUAL. See synonym study at PREVALENT. See synonym study at UNIVERSAL. • *n.* piece of open public land. □ **common fraction** fraction expressed by numerator and denominator. **common ground** argument accepted by both sides in a dispute. **common law** law derived from custom and judicial precedent rather than statutes. **common sense** sound practical sense.

■ *adj.* **1 a** frequent, usual, customary, prevalent. **b** stale, hackneyed, worn-out, banal. **c** everyday, commonplace, prosaic, run-of-the-mill, general, normal, standard, conventional, regular, routine, stock, average, mediocre, undistinguished, unexceptional. **2** public, general, community, communal, collective, nonprivate; well-known;

universal, joint, shared, mutual. **3** low-grade, mean, cheap, vulgar, base, ordinary, plain, simple, plebeian, bourgeois, proletarian, unrefined. **4** see FAMILIAR 1.

com•mon•al•i•ty /kómənálitee/ *n.* (*pl.* **–ties**) **1** sharing of an attribute. **2** common occurrence.

com•mon•er /kómənər/ *n.* one of the common people, as opposed to the aristocracy. ■ see PLEBEIAN *n.*

com•mon•place /kómənplays/ • *adj.* lacking originality; trite. • *n.* **1 a** everyday saying; platitude. **b** ordinary topic of conversation. **2** anything usual or trite. ■ *adj.* see BANAL. • *n.* **1 a** see TRUISM.

com•mons /kómənz/ *n.pl.* **1** dining hall at a university, etc. **2** *New Eng.* central public park or ground.

com•mon•wealth /kómənwelth/ *n.* **1 a** independent state or community, esp. a democratic republic. **b** designation of four US states (Ky., Mass., Penn., Va.). **2** (**the Commonwealth**) association of the UK with nations previously part of the British Empire. **3** federation of states.

com•mo•tion /kəmóshən/ *n.* **1** confused and noisy disturbance. **2** civil insurrection. ■ **1** see NOISE 1, 2. **2** see DISORDER *n.* 2.

com•mu•nal /kəmyóōnəl, kómyə–/ *adj.* relating to or benefiting a community; for common use. □□ **com•mu′nal•ize** *v.* **com•mu′ral•ly** *adv.* ■ see COMMON *adj.* 2.

com•mune[1] /kómyōōn/ *n.* **1 a** group of people sharing living accommodation, goods, etc. **b** communal settlement. **2 a** smallest French territorial division for administrative purposes. **b** similar division elsewhere.

com•mune[2] /kəmyōōn/ *v.intr.* **1** speak confidentially and intimately. **2** feel in close touch (with nature, etc.).

com•mu•ni•ca•ble /kəmyóōnikəbəl/ *adj.* (esp. of disease) able to be passed on. □□ **com•mu•ni•ca•bil′i•ty** *n.* **com•mu′ni•ca•bly** *adv.* ■ see INFECTIOUS 2.

com•mu•ni•cant /kəmyóōnikənt/ *n.* person who receives Holy Communion.

com•mu•ni•cate /kəmyóōnikayt/ *v.* **1** *tr.* **a** transmit by speaking or writing. **b** transmit (heat, motion, etc.). **c** pass on (an infectious illness). **d** impart (feelings, etc.) nonverbally. **2** *intr.* convey information. **3** *intr.* share a feeling or understanding. □□ **com•mu′ni•ca•tor** *n.*

■ **1 a** make known, impart, confer, transfer, hand on *or* down, share, pass on *or* along, get *or* put across. **2** converse, talk, correspond. **3** be of one mind, *colloq.* be on the same wavelength.

com•mu•ni•ca•tion /kəmyóōnikáyshən/ *n.* **1 a** act of imparting, esp. news. **b** information, etc., communicated. **2** social intercourse. **3** [in *pl.*] science and practice of transmitting information. ■ **1** see INFORMATION 1b. **3** (*communications*) see TRANSMISSION 2.

com•mu•ni•ca•tive /kəmyóōnikáytiv, –kətiv/

adj. open; talkative; ready to inform. □□ com•mu′ni•ca•tive•ly *adv.*

■ see TALKATIVE, RESPONSIVE.

com•mu•nion /kəmyo͞onyən/ *n.* **1** sharing, esp. of thoughts, etc.; fellowship. **2** sharing in common (*communion of interests*). **3** (**Communion, Holy Communion**) the Eucharist. **4** Christian denomination (*the Methodist communion*). See synonym study at CONVERSATION.

com•mu•ni•qué /kəmyo͞onikáy/ *n.* official communication.

com•mu•nism /kómyənizəm/ *n.* **1** political theory advocating public ownership of property. **2** (usu. **Communism**) communistic form of society, as established in the former USSR.

com•mu•nist /kómyənist/ • *n. & adj.* **1** person advocating communism. **2** (**Communist**) member of a Communist party. • *adj.* relating to communism. □□ com•mu•nis′tic *adj.*

com•mu•ni•ty /kəmyo͞onitee/ *n.* (*pl.* **–ties**) **1 a** body of people living in one locale. **b** locality, including its inhabitants. **2** body of people having religion, profession, etc., in common. **3** [prec. by *the*] the public. □ **community college** nonresidential junior college offering college courses to a local community or region. **community service** unpaid work performed in service to the community, esp. as part of a criminal sentence.

■ **1 b** see DISTRICT *n.* **2** see BROTHERHOOD 2. **3** see PUBLIC *n.* 1.

com•mu•ta•tive /kəmyo͞otətiv/ *adj.* **1** relating to or involving substitution. **2** *Math.* unchanged in result by the interchange of the order of quantities.

com•mute /kəmyo͞ot/ • *v.* **1** *intr.* travel to and from one's daily work. **2** *tr. Law* change (a judicial sentence, etc.) to another less severe. **3** *tr.* change (one kind of payment) for another. **4** *tr.* **a** exchange; interchange (two things). **b** change (to another thing). • *n.* trip made by one who commutes.

■ *v.* **1** see TRAVEL *v.* 1. **2** see REPRIEVE *v.* **3, 4** see TRANSPOSE.

com•mut•er /kəmyo͞otər/ *n.* person who travels some distance to work.

comp. *abbr.* **1** companion. **2** comparative. **3** compensation. **4** compilation. **5** compiled. **6** compiler. **7** complete. **8** composite. **9** composition. **10** compositor. **11** comprehensive.

com•pact¹ • *adj.* /kəmpákt, kóm-/ **1** closely or neatly packed together. **2** (of a piece of equipment, a room, etc.) well-fitted and practical though small. **3** (of style, etc.) condensed; brief. **4** (esp. of the human body) small but well-proportioned. • *v.tr.* /kəmpákt/ **1** join or press firmly together. **2** condense. • *n.* /kómpakt/ **1** small, flat case for face powder, a mirror, etc. **2** medium-sized automobile. □ **compact disc** /kómpakt/ disc on which information or sound is recorded digitally and reproduced by laser reflection. □□ com•pact′ly *adv.* com•pact′ness *n.*

■ *adj.* **1** closely knit, consolidated, compressed; dense, solid, firm, tight, thick. **3** terse, laconic, close, pithy, succinct, concise. • *v.* compress.

com•pact² /kómpakt/ *n.* agreement; contract.

com•pan•ion /kəmpányən/ *n.* **1 a** person who accompanies or associates with another. **b** person employed to live with and assist another. **2** handbook on a particular subject. **3** thing that matches another.

■ **1 a** fellow, comrade, colleague, *colloq.* pal, chum, buddy. **2** manual, guide. **3** complement, counterpart.

com•pan•ion•a•ble /kəmpányənəbəl/ *adj.* friendly; sociable. □□ com•pan′ion•a•bly *adv.*

■ see SOCIABLE *adj.*

com•pan•ion•ship /kəmpányənship/ *n.* fellowship; friendship.

■ camaraderie, comradeship, company, amity, fraternity.

com•pan•ion•way /kəmpányənway/ *n.* ship's stairway.

com•pa•ny /kúmpənee/ *n.* (*pl.* **–nies**) **1 a** number of people assembled; crowd. **b** guest(s). **2** state of being a companion or fellow; companionship, esp. of a specific kind (*do not care for his company*). **3** commercial business. **4** troupe of entertainers. **5** *Mil.* subdivision of a battalion. □ **be in good company** discover that one's companions, or better people, have done the same as oneself.

■ **1 a** assemblage, party, band, group, circle, assembly, gathering, convention, throng; troop, followers, following, retinue, entourage. **b** visitor(s), caller(s). **2** fellowship; attendance, presence. **3** firm, house, concern, institution, establishment, enterprise; partnership, corporation. **4** cast, ensemble, players, actors and actresses, performers.

com•pa•ra•ble /kómpərəbəl/ *adj.* able or fit to be compared. □□ com•pa•ra•bil′i•ty *n.* com′pa•ra•bly *adv.*

com•par•a•tive /kəmpárətiv/ • *adj.* **1** perceptible by comparison; relative. **2** of or involving comparison. **3** *Gram.* (of an adjective or adverb) expressing a higher degree (e.g., *braver, more fiercely*). • *n. Gram.* comparative expression or word. □□ com•par′a•tive•ly *adv.*

com•pare /kəmpáir/ • *v.* **1** *tr.* express similarities in; liken. **2** *tr.* estimate the similarity of. **3** *intr.* bear comparison. **4** *intr.* be equivalent to. **5** *tr. Gram.* form comparative and superlative degrees of (an adjective or adverb). • *n.* comparison (*beyond compare*). □ **compare notes** exchange ideas or opinions.

■ *v.* **1** associate, analogize. **2** contrast, weigh up, juxtapose, relate, correlate. **3, 4** (*compare with*) resemble, be on a par with, be in the same class with, correspond, match, parallel, approach; rival, be a match for. • *n.* see COMPARISON 3.

com•par•i•son /kəmpárisən/ *n.* **1** comparing. **2** simile or semantic illustration. **3** similarity (*there's no comparison*). **4** (in full **degrees of comparison**) *Gram.* positive, comparative, and superlative forms of adjectives and adverbs. □ **beyond comparison** **1** totally different in quality. **2** greatly superior.

■ **1** contrast, juxtaposition, balance, weighing, likening. **3** match, resemblance, likeness, comparability, relation, relationship, commensurability, kinship.

com•part•ment /kəmpaártmənt/ *n.* **1** partitioned space within a larger space. **2** watertight division of a ship.

■ **1** division, section, chamber, bay, alcove, cell, pigeonhole, locker, cubbyhole, niche, cubicle, slot.

com•part•men•tal /kómpaartmént'l/ *adj.* of or divided into compartments. □□ **com•part•men•tal•ly** *adv.*

com•part•men•tal•ize /kómpaartmént'līz, kómpaart-/ *v.tr.* divide into compartments or categories. □□ **com•part•men•tal•i•za'tion** *n.*

com•pass /kúmpəs, kóm-/ *n.* **1** instrument showing the direction of magnetic north and bearings from it. **2** [*often pl.*] instrument within two hinged legs for taking measurements and describing circles. **3** circumference or boundary. See synonym study at RANGE.

com•pas•sion /kəmpáshən/ *n.* pity inclining one to be merciful. See synonym study at MERCY.

■ see PITY *n.* 1.

com•pas•sion•ate /kəmpáshənət/ *adj.* sympathetic; pitying. □□ **com•pas'sion•ate•ly** *adv.*

■ see SYMPATHETIC *adj.* 1.

com•pat•i•ble /kəmpátəbəl/ *adj.* **1 a** able to coexist; mutually tolerant. **b** consistent. **2** (of equipment, etc.) able to be used in combination. □□ **com•pat•i•bil'i•ty** *n.* **com•pat'i•bly** *adv.*

■ **1 a** well-matched, well-suited. **b** see CONSISTENT 1.

com•pa•tri•ot /kəmpáytreeət, -ot/ *n.* fellow countryman.

com•pel /kəmpél/ *v.tr.* (**com•pel•led, com•pel•ling**) **1** force; constrain (*compelled them to admit it*). **2** (as **compelling** *adj.*) rousing strong interest. □□ **com•pel'ling•ly** *adv.*

■ **1** see FORCE *v.* 1. **2** (**compelling**) see INTERESTING.

SYNONYM STUDY: compel

COERCE, CONSTRAIN, FORCE, NECESSITATE, OBLIGE. A parent faced with a rebellious teenager may try to **compel** him to do his homework by threatening to take away his allowance. *Compel* commonly implies the exercise of authority or force (*compelled to pull over by the insistent siren behind us*), but often the source of the compulsion is internal (*felt compelled to explain his angry reaction*). It typically requires a personal object, although it is possible to *compel* a reaction or response (*she compels admiration*). **Force**, even more than *compel*, suggests the exertion of power, energy, physical strength, or inward drives to accomplish something or to subdue resistance (*his mother forced him to confess that he'd broken the basement window*). **Coerce** can

imply the use of force or merely the threat of force or some other unpleasantness (*coerced by thugs into repaying the loan sharks; he coerced his friends into seeing the avant-garde film*). **Constrain** means *compel*, but by means of restriction, confinement, or limitation (*art forms constrained by classical rules; constrained by his acute shyness from speaking*). **Necessitate** and **oblige** make an action necessary by imposing certain conditions that demand a response (*her mother's illness obliged her to be more cooperative; it also necessitated giving up her social life*).

---

com•pen•di•ous /kəmpéndeeəs/ *adj.* comprehensive but brief.

com•pen•di•um /kəmpéndeeəm/ *n.* (*pl.* **com•pen•di•ums** or **com•pen•di•a** /-deeə/) concise summary or abridgment.

com•pen•sate /kómpənsayt/ *v.* **1** *tr.* pay. **2** *intr.* make amends. **3** *tr.* counterbalance. **4** *intr.* offset a disability, etc., by development in another direction. □□ **com•pen•sa•to•ry** /-pénsətáwree/ *adj.*

■ **1** recompense, make restitution *or* reparation to, reimburse, requite. **2** atone; expiate; offset, make up for, redress. **3** balance, counterpoise, equalize, neutralize, even (up).

com•pen•sa•tion /kómpənsáyshən/ *n.* **1 a** compensating. **b** being compensated. **2** something given as recompense. □□ **com•pen•sa'tion•al** *adj.*

■ see RESTITUTION 1.

com•pete /kəmpeet/ *v.intr.* **1** contend; vie. **2** take part in a contest.

■ **1** struggle.

com•pe•tence /kómpit'ns/ *n.* (also **com•pe•ten•cy** /-tənsee/) **1** ability; being competent. **2** *Law* legal capacity to deal with a matter.

■ **1** see *proficiency* (PROFICIENT).

com•pe•tent /kómpit'nt/ *adj.* adequately qualified or skilled. □□ **com'pe•tent•ly** *adv.*

■ fit, capable; suitable, sufficient, satisfactory, acceptable.

com•pe•ti•tion /kómpətíshən/ *n.* **1** competing. **2** event in which people compete. **3** the others competing; opposition.

■ **1** contention, striving; see also *rivalry* (RIVAL). **2** contest, match, meet, game, tournament. **3** see COMPETITOR.

com•pet•i•tive /kəmpétitiv/ *adj.* **1** of or involving competition. **2** (of prices, etc.) comparing favorably. **3** driven to win. □□ **com•pet'i•tive•ly** *adv.* **com•pet'i•tive•ness** *n.*

com•pet•i•tor /kəmpétitər/ *n.* person who competes; rival, esp. in business.

■ opponent, adversary, antagonist; contestant, contender; (*competitors*) competition, opposition.

com•pile /kəmpíl/ *v.tr.* **1** collect (material) into a list, volume, etc. **2** produce (a volume, etc.) from such material. **3** accumulate (a large number of). □□ **com•pi•la•tion** /kómpiláyshən/ *n.* **com•pil'er** *n.*

■ **1, 2** assemble, collate, organize, order, systematize; anthologize, compose. **3** see AMASS.

com•pla•cent /kəmpláysənt/ *adj.* smugly

self-satisfied; content. □□ **com•pla'cence** *n.*
com•pla'cen•cy *n.* **com•pla'cent•ly** *adv.*
■ see SMUG.

com•plain /kəmpláyn/ *v.intr.* **1** express dissatisfaction. **2 a** say that one is suffering from (an ailment). **b** state a grievance. □□ **com•plain'er** *n.* **com•plain'ing•ly** *adv.*
■ **1, 2b** grumble, moan, groan, wail, carp, squawk, kick, *colloq.* gripe, grouch, grouse, bitch, crab, bellyache.

com•plain•ant /kəmpláynənt/ *n. Law* plaintiff.

com•plaint /kəmpláynt/ *n.* **1** complaining. **2** grievance. **3** ailment.
■ **2** grumble, squawk, *colloq.* gripe, grouse, beef. **3** see AILMENT.

com•plai•sant /kəmpláysənt/ *adj.* willing to please; acquiescent. □□ **com•plai'sance** *n.*
■ see PASSIVE 2, ACCOMMODATING.

com•ple•ment • *n.* /kómplimənt/ **1** thing that completes; counterpart. **2** full number needed. • *v.tr.* /kómpliment/ **1** complete. **2** form a complement to. □□ **com•ple•men'tal** /-mént'l/ *adj.*
■ *n.* **1** finishing touch, consummation; companion, twin, fellow. **2** crew, team, company, band, outfit; quota, allowance, quorum. • *v.* **1** perfect, round out. **2** supplement, add to; see also ENHANCE.

com•ple•men•ta•ry /kómpliméntəree/ *adj.* **1** forming a complement. **2** (of two or more things) complementing each other. □ **complementary angle** either of two angles making up 90°.
■ **2** see HARMONIOUS 2.

com•plete /kəmpléet/ • *adj.* **1** having all its parts; entire. **2** finished. **3** of the maximum extent (*a complete surprise*). • *v.tr.* **1** finish. **2** make whole. **3** fill in (a form, etc.). □□ **com•plete'ly** *adv.* **com•plete'ness** *n.* **com•ple'tion** /-pléeshən/ *n.*
■ *adj.* **1** intact, uncut, unbroken, undivided, unabridged, full. **2** ended, concluded, over, done, accomplished, terminated; settled, executed, performed. **3** entire, total, thorough, absolute, utter, unqualified, pure, unmitigated. • *v.* **1** conclude, end, bring to an end, wrap up; accomplish, achieve, do; finalize. **2** round out, perfect; crown, culminate; see also *make up* 2. □□ **completely** altogether, *in toto*; lock, stock, and barrel; hook, line, and sinker; expressly, explicitly, unequivocally, truly, categorically, flatly.

com•plex • *n.* /kómpleks/ **1** building, series of rooms, etc., of related parts. **2** *Psychol.* group of usu. repressed feelings or thoughts that influence behavior. **3** preoccupation. • *adj.* /kəmpléks, kómpleks/ complicated. □ **complex sentence** sentence containing a subordinate clause or clauses. □□ **com•plex•i•ty** /-pléksitee/ *n.* (*pl.* **-ties**)
■ *n.* **3** see OBSESSION. • *adj.* see COMPLICATE 2. □□ **complexity** convolution; intricacy, involvement.

com•plex•ion /kəmplékshən/ *n.* **1** natural appearance of skin, esp. of the face. **2** aspect; interpretation.

com•pli•ance /kəmplíəns/ *n.* **1** obedience to

a request, command, etc. **2** *Mech.* capacity to yield.

com•pli•ant /kəmplíənt/ *adj.* yielding. □□ **com•pli'ant•ly** *adv.*
■ see OBEDIENT.

com•pli•cate /kómplikayt/ *v.* **1** make difficult or complex. **2** (as **complicated** *adj.*) complex.
■ **1** entangle, mix up, confuse, confound, muddle. **2** (**complicated**) involved, intricate.

com•pli•ca•tion /kómplikáyshən/ *n.* **1** involved or confused condition; difficulty. **2** *Med.* condition aggravating a previous one.
■ **1** complexity, intricacy, convolution; problem, predicament, obstacle, obstruction, snag; see also *subtlety* (SUBTLE).

com•plic•i•ty /kəmplísitee/ *n.* partnership in wrongdoing.

com•pli•ment • *n.* /kómplimənt/ **1 a** polite expression of praise. **b** act implying praise. **2** [in *pl.*] formal greetings or praise. • *v.tr.* /kómpliment/ congratulate; praise.
■ *n.* **1** commendation, bouquet, tribute, honor. **2** (**compliments**) respects, regards, good *or* best wishes, felicitations, salutations. • *v.* pay homage *or* tribute to, commend, laud, honor; flatter.

com•pli•men•ta•ry /kómpliméntəree/ *adj.* **1** expressing a compliment. **2** given free.
■ **1** laudatory, laudative, congratulatory, commendatory, flattering. **2** gratis, on the house; see also FREE *adj.* 6a.

com•ply /kəmplí/ *v.intr.* (**-plies, -plied**) act in accordance (with a wish, command, etc.).
■ agree, obey, conform, consent, acquiesce, concur, submit, yield, accede.

com•po•nent /kəmpónənt/ • *n.* part of a larger whole. • *adj.* being part of a larger whole. □□ **com•po•nen•tial** /kómpənén-shəl/ *adj.*
■ *n.* see PART *n.* 1.

com•port /kəmpáwrt/ *v.refl.* conduct oneself; behave. □ **comport with** suit; befit. □□ **com•port'ment** *n.*
■ see BEHAVE 1. □□ **comportment** see BEHAVIOR 1a.

com•pose /kəmpóz/ *v.tr.* **1** create in music or writing. **2** constitute; make up. **3** arrange artistically. **4 a** [often *refl.*] calm. **b** (as **composed** *adj.*) calm; settled. **5** *Printing* a set (type). **b** set (manuscript, etc.) in type. □□ **com•pos'er** *n.*
■ **1** write, imagine, think up, originate, frame, formulate, make (up), devise, construct, *disp.* author; set to music, arrange. **2** form. **4 a** settle; quiet, pacify, control oneself. **b** (**composed**) see *collected* (COLLECT *v.* 4).

com•pos•ite /kəmpózit/ • *adj.* **1** made up of various parts. **2** (of a plant) having a bloom head of many flowers. • *n.* composite thing or plant.
■ *adj.* **1** compound, multiform, multifaceted.

com•po•si•tion /kómpəzíshən/ *n.* **1 a** putting together; composing. **b** thing so composed, esp. music. **2** constitution of a substance. **3** school essay. **4** artistic arrangement. **5** compound artificial substance. □□ **com•po•si′tion•al** *adj.* **com•po•si′tion•al•ly** *adv.*

■ **1**, **4** formation, construction, combination, makeup, structure, form, assembly, setup, organization, layout, arrangement, configuration, shaping; balance, harmony, proportion, placement, placing. **2** combination, aggregate, mixture, compound, mix, formulation, composite, amalgam, alloy, mélange, medley; creation, production, making, generation; writing; see also FORMATION 2. **3** article, paper, story.

com•pos•i•tor /kəmpózitər/ *n.* person who sets type for printing; typesetter.

com•post /kómpōst/ • *n.* organic fertilizing mixture. • *v.tr.* **1** treat with compost. **2** make into compost.

■ *v.* **1** see FERTILIZE 1.

com•po•sure /kəmpṓzhər/ *n.* tranquil manner; calmness.

■ see CALM *n.* 1.

com•pote /kómpōt/ *n.* fruit preserved or cooked in syrup.

com•pound¹ • *n.* /kómpownd/ **1** mixture of two or more things. **2** word made up of two or more existing words. **3** substance chemically formed from two or more elements. • *adj.* /kómpownd/ **1** made up of several ingredients. **2** combined; collective. • *v.tr.* /kəmpównd/ **1** mix or combine (ingredients, elements, etc.). **2** increase or complicate (difficulties, etc.). **3** make up (a composite whole).

■ *n.* **1** composite, blend, synthesis, combination, consolidation, amalgam, alloy. • *adj.* **1** composite, multiform, multifaceted. **2** see JOINT *adj.* • *v.* **1** put together, blend, merge, unite, fuse; see also COMBINE *v.* 3. **2** aggravate, intensify, exacerbate, heighten, augment, add to, worsen, enhance, multiply. **3** concoct, compose, formulate; see also MAKE *v.* 1.

com•pound² /kómpownd/ *n.* enclosure or fenced-in space.

com•pre•hend /kómprihénd/ *v.tr.* **1** grasp mentally; understand. **2** include. □□ **com•pre•hen•si•bil•i•ty** /-síbilítee/ *n.* **com•pre•hen′si•ble** *adj.* **com•pre•hen′si•bly** *adv.* **com•pre•hen′sion** *n.*

■ **1** see, conceive, take in, apprehend, realize, fathom, perceive, discern, appreciate; see also DIGEST *v.* 2. **2** take in, comprise, assimilate, absorb.

com•pre•hen•sive /kómprihénsiv/ *adj.* **1** including all or nearly all. **2** (of insurance) providing complete protection. □□ **com•pre•hen′sive•ly** *adv.* **com•pre•hen′sive•ness** *n.*

■ **1** (all-)inclusive, (all-)encompassing, thorough, extensive, full, exhaustive, complete, sweeping, all-embracing, wide, broad.

com•press • *v.tr.* /kəmprés/ **1** squeeze together. **2** bring into a smaller space or shorter extent. • *n.* /kómpres/ pad applied to a wound. □□ **com•press•i•ble** /kəmprésəbəl/ *adj.* **com•press′i•bil′i•ty** *n.*

■ *v.* **1** see SQUEEZE *v.* 1. **2** see CONTRACT *v.* 1.

com•pres•sion /kəmpréshən/ *n.* compressing.

■ see PRESSURE *n.* 1a, b.

com•pres•sor /kəmprésər/ *n.* instrument or device for compressing esp. air or other gases.

com•prise /kəmpríz/ *v.tr.* **1** include. **2** consist of. **3** make up, compose.

■ **1** see INCLUDE 1.

com•pro•mise /kómprəmīz/ • *n.* **1** mutual settlement of a dispute. **2** intermediate state between conflicting opinions, actions, etc. • *v.* **1 a** *intr.* mutually settle a dispute. **b** *tr.* modify one's opinions, demands, etc. **2** *tr.* bring into disrepute or danger esp. by indiscretion. □□ **com′pro•mis•er** *n.* **com′pro•mis•ing•ly** *adv.*

■ *n.* see ACCOMMODATION 2b. • *v.* **1** see *come to terms with* (TERM).

comp•trol•ler /kəntrṓlər/ *n.* financial officer.

com•pul•sion /kəmpúlshən/ *n.* **1** constraint; obligation. **2** irresistible urge.

■ **1** see OBLIGATION 1, 3. **2** see URGE *n.* 1.

com•pul•sive /kəmpúlsiv/ *adj.* **1** resulting or acting (as if) from compulsion. **2** irresistible. □□ **com•pul′sive•ly** *adv.* **com•pul′sive•ness** *n.*

■ **1** obsessive, unshakable; see also INCORRIGIBLE 2. **2** compelling, gripping; see also FORCEFUL 2.

com•pul•so•ry /kəmpúlsəree/ *adj.* **1** required by law or a rule. **2** essential. □□ **com•pul′so•ri•ly** *adv.*

■ **1** see MANDATORY *adj.* **2** see NECESSARY *adj.* 1.

com•punc•tion /kəmpúngkshən/ *n.* **1** pricking of the conscience. **2** slight regret; scruple. See synonym study at QUALM. □□ **com•punc′tious** /-shəs/ *adj.*

■ **1** remorse, contrition, uneasiness of mind. **2** second thought(s), misgiving, qualm; see also SCRUPLE *n.*

com•pute /kəmpyṓt/ *v.* **1** *tr.* reckon or calculate. **2** *intr.* use a computer. □□ **com•put•a•bil′i•ty** *n.* **com•put′a•ble** *adj.* **com•pu•ta′tion** /-táyshən/ *n.* **com•pu•ta′tion•al** *adj.*

■ **1** figure (out), work out, determine, ascertain, estimate. □□ **com•pu•ta•tion** see CALCULATION 1.

com•put•er /kəmpyṓtər/ *n.* electronic device for storing and processing data. □ **computer virus** hidden code within a computer program intended to corrupt a system.

com•put•er•ize /kəmpyṓtərīz/ *v.tr.* **1** equip with a computer. **2** store or produce by computer. □□ **com•put•er•i•za′tion** *n.*

com•rade /kómrad, –rid/ *n.* **1** associate or companion. **2** fellow socialist or communist. □□ **com′rade•ly** *adj.* **com′rade•ship** *n.*

■ **1** colleague, friend, crony.

con¹ /kon/ *sl.* • *n.* **1** confidence trick. • *v.tr.* (**conned, con′ning**) swindle; deceive.

■ *n.* see CON *n.* • *v.* see SWINDLE *v.*

con² /kon/ • *n.* [usu. in *pl.*] reason against. • *prep. & adv.* against.

con³ /kon/ *sl.* convict.

con- /kon, kən/ *prefix* assim. form of COM-.

con•cat•e•nate /konkát′nayt/ • *v.tr.* link

together (events, things, etc.). • *adj.* joined; linked. □□ **con•cat•e•na•tion** /-náyshən/ *n.*

■ *v.* see LINK *v.* 1. □□ **concatenation** see CHAIN *n.* 3.

con•cave /kónkáyv/ *adj.* curved like the interior of a circle or sphere. □□ **con•cav•i•ty** /-kávitee/ *n.*

■ see HOLLOW *adj.* 1b.

con•ceal /kənseél/ *v.tr.* 1 keep secret. 2 hide. □□ **con•ceal'er** *n.* **con•ceal'ment** *n.*

■ 1 keep quiet about, disguise; see also HIDE[1] *v.* 3. 2 secrete, bury, squirrel away, cover (up), camouflage.

con•cede /kənseéd/ *v.tr.* 1 a admit to be true. b admit defeat in. 2 grant (a right, privilege, etc.).

■ 1 a allow, acknowledge, confess, own (up to), accept. b see *give up* 1. 2 yield, surrender, cede, give up, submit, resign, relinquish, abandon, waive.

con•ceit /kənseét/ *n.* 1 personal vanity; pride. 2 *literary* a elaborate metaphoric comparison. b fanciful notion. See synonym study at PRIDE.

■ 1 egotism, self-admiration, self-love, narcissism, arrogance, vainglory. 2 a trope, affectation.

con•ceit•ed /kənseétid/ *adj.* vain; proud. □□ **con•ceit'ed•ly** *adv.*

■ egotistical, self-centered, egocentric, self-admiring, narcissistic, prideful, arrogant, self-important, self-satisfied, smug, complacent, snobbish.

con•ceiv•a•ble /kənseévəbəl/ *adj.* capable of being grasped or imagined. □□ **con•ceiv'a•bly** *adv.*

■ see PLAUSIBLE 1.

con•ceive /kənseév/ *v.* 1 *intr.* become pregnant. 2 *tr.* become pregnant with (a child). 3 *tr.* imagine; formulate.

■ 3 think (up), fancy, speculate (on), perceive, understand, realize, comprehend, envision, conjure up, dream up, hypothesize, postulate, posit, suggest, suppose.

con•cen•trate /kónsəntrayt/ *v.* 1 *intr.* focus one's attention. 2 *tr.* bring together to one point. 3 *tr.* make less dilute. • *n.* concentrated substance. □□ **con'cen•tra•tor** *n.*

■ *v.* 1 think. 2 direct, center, centralize, consolidate; gather, collect, congregate. 3 condense, reduce, distill, intensify. • *n.* see ESSENCE 2a.

con•cen•tra•tion /kónsəntráyshən/ *n.* 1 act or instance of concentrating, esp. of mental attention. 2 something concentrated. □ **concentration camp** camp holding political prisoners.

■ 1 see THOUGHT[1] 3. 2 see POCKET *n.* 3.

con•cen•tric /kənséntrik/ *adj.* (esp. of circles) having a common center. □□ **con•cen'tri•cal•ly** *adv.* **con•cen•tric•i•ty** /kónsentrísi-tee/ *n.*

con•cept /kónsept/ *n.* general notion; abstract idea. See synonym study at IDEA.

■ see IDEA 1, 2a, b.

con•cep•tion /kənsépshən/ *n.* 1 act or instance of conceiving. 2 idea; plan. See synonym study at IDEA. □□ **con•cep'tion•al** *adj.*

■ 1 birth, beginning, genesis, inception, emergence, start, inauguration, initiation, launch, origin, origination, formation, formulation, *formal* commencement; impregnation, fertilization, insemination. 2 understanding, apprehension, knowledge, comprehension. 2 design, scheme; see also IDEA 1, 2a, b, PLAN *n.* 1.

con•cep•tu•al /kənsépchōōəl/ *adj.* of mental conceptions or concepts. □□ **con•cep'tu•al•ly** *adv.*

■ see ABSTRACT *adj.* 1a.

con•cep•tu•al•ize /kənsépchōōəliz/ *v.tr.* form a concept or idea of. □□ **con•cep•tu•al•i•za'tion** *n.*

■ see IMAGINE 1.

con•cern /kənsórn/ • *v.tr.* 1 a be relevant or important to. b relate to; be about. 2 interest or involve oneself. 3 worry; affect. • *n.* 1 anxiety; worry. 2 matter of interest or importance. 3 business; firm.

■ *v.* 1 a affect, have (a) bearing *or* (an) influence on, involve, touch; interest, be of importance *or* interest to. b refer to, have relation *or* reference to, pertain to, be pertinent *or* relevant to, regard, apply to, be connected *or* involved with, bear on, be germane to, involve, touch (on). 2 see BOTHER *v.* 2. 3 trouble, disturb, bother, perturb, unsettle, upset, distress. • *n.* 1 solicitude, apprehension, distress, apprehensiveness, uneasiness, disquiet, disquietude; interest, regard, consideration, care, thought, awareness, attention. 2 affair, problem, issue. 3 company, house, establishment, enterprise, organization.

con•cerned /kənsórnd/ *adj.* 1 involved; interested. 2 troubled; anxious. □□ **con•cern'ed•ly** *adv.*

■ 1 responsible. 2 vexed, worried, distressed, uneasy, perturbed, bothered, upset, disturbed.

con•cern•ing /kənsórning/ *prep.* about; regarding.

■ relative *or* relating to, referring to, with *or* in reference to, as regards, in *or* with regard to, with an eye to, with respect to, respecting, apropos (of), as to *or* for, in the matter of, on the subject of.

con•cert /kónsərt/ *n.* 1 a musical performance. b comedy, etc., stage performance. 2 agreement. 3 combination of voices or sounds.

■ 1 see PERFORMANCE 2. 2 see ACCORD *n.* 1.

con•cert•ed /kənsórtid/ *adj.* jointly arranged or planned.

con•cer•ti•na /kónsərteénə/ *n.* small accordionlike musical instrument.

con•cer•to /kəncháirtō/ *n.* (*pl.* **con•cer•ti** /-tee/ *or* **–tos**) *Mus.* composition for solo instrument(s) and orchestra.

con•ces•sion /kənséshən/ *n.* 1 a conceding. b thing conceded. 2 right to sell goods in a particular territory. □□ **con•ces'sion•ar•y** *adj.* (also **con•ces'sion•al**).

■ 1 see ADMISSION 1. 2 see PRIVILEGE *n.* 1.

conch /kongk, konch/ *n.* (*pl.* **conchs** /kongks/ *or* **conches** /kónchiz/) 1 spiral shell of various marine gastropod mollusks. 2 any such gastropod.

con•ci•erge /konseeáirzh, káwNsyáirzh/ *n.*

1 hotel worker who arranges special services for guests. **2** porter for an apartment building, etc.

con•cil•i•ate /kənsíleeayt/ v.tr. **1** make calm and amenable; pacify. **2** gain (esteem or goodwill). **3** reconcile. See synonym study at PACIFY. □□ **con•cil•i•a•tive** /–síleeətiv, –áytiv/ adj. **con•cil•i•a•tor** n. **con•cil•i•a•tory** /–síleeətáwree/ adj.

■ **1** see DISARM 5. □□ **conciliator** see *mediator* (MEDIATE).

con•cise /kənsís/ adj. brief but comprehensive. See synonym study at TERSE. □□ **con•cise'ly** adv. **con•cise'ness** n.

■ terse, laconic, compact, direct, succinct, cogent, pithy, compendious, summary, condensed, short; shortened, abridged, abbreviated.

con•clave /kónklayv, kóng–/ n. **1** private meeting. **2** RC Ch. assembly of cardinals for the election of a pope.

con•clude /kənklốod/ v. **1** tr. & intr. bring or come to an end. **2** tr. infer. **3** tr. settle (a treaty, etc.).

■ **1** see END v. 1. **2** see INFER 1. **3** see SETTLE 5–7.

con•clu•sion /kənklốozhən/ n. **1** final result; end. **2** judgment reached by reasoning. **3** summing-up. **4** settling (of peace, etc.).

■ **1** see RESULT n. 1. **2** see THINKING n.

con•clu•sive /kənklốosiv/ adj. decisive; convincing. □□ **con•clu'sive•ly** adv. **con•clu'sive•ness** n.

■ see UNQUESTIONABLE.

con•coct /kənkókt/ v.tr. **1** make by mixing ingredients. **2** invent. □□ **con•coc'tion** /–kókshən/ n.

■ **2** see INVENT 1.

con•com•i•tant /kənkómit'nt/ • adj. going together; associated. • n. accompanying thing. □□ **con•com'i•tance** n. **con•com'i•tant•ly** adv.

con•cord /kónkawrd, kóng–/ n. agreement; harmony.

■ see AGREEMENT 1, 2, PACT.

con•cor•dance /kənkáwrd'ns/ n. **1** agreement. **2** book or book part containing an index of important words used in a book or by an author.

■ **1** see AGREEMENT 1, 2. **2** see INDEX n. 1.

con•course /kónkawrs/ n. **1** crowd; gathering. **2** large open area in a building for public use.

con•crete /kónkreet, kóng–, konkrèet, kong–/ • adj. **1 a** existing in a material form. **b** specific; definite. **2** Gram. (of a noun) denoting a material object as opposed to a quality, state, action, etc. • n. mixture of gravel, sand, cement, and water, used for building. □□ **con•crete'ly** adv. **con•crete'ness** n.

■ adj. **1** real, actual, literal, realistic, authentic, valid, genuine, bona fide, reliable; particular, definitive, clear-cut, physical, tangible, substantial.

con•cre•tion /kənkréeshən/ n. **1** hard, solid mass. **2** forming of this.

con•cu•bine /kóngkyəbīn/ n. **1** mistress. **2** (in some societies) secondary wife.

con•cu•pis•cence /konkyốopisəns/ n. lust. □□ **con•cu'pis•cent** adj.

con•cur /kənkɔ́r/ v.intr. (**con•curred, con•cur•ring**) **1** coincide. **2** agree (with).

■ **1** see AGREE 3a. **2** see AGREE 1.

con•cur•rent /kənkɔ́rənt, –kúr–/ adj. existing or in operation at the same time or together. □□ **con•cur'rent•ly** adv.

■ see SIMULTANEOUS.

con•cus•sion /kənkúshən/ n. **1** Med. temporary incapacity due to head injury. **2** violent shaking; shock.

con•demn /kəndém/ v.tr. **1** express utter disapproval of. **2 a** find guilty, convict. **b** sentence (to). **3** pronounce (a building, etc.) unfit for use. **4** doom or assign (to something unpleasant). □□ **con•dem•na•ble** /–démnəb'l/ adj. **con•dem•na•tion** /kóndemnáyshən/ n. **con•dem•na•to•ry** /–démnətáwree/ adj.

■ **1** censure, blame, criticize, denounce, disparage, reproach, rebuke, reprove, scold, reprimand, upbraid. **4** damn, decree, ordain.

con•den•sa•tion /kóndensáyshən/ n. **1** condensing. **2** condensed liquid. **3** abridgment.

■ **3** see *abridgment* (ABRIDGE).

con•dense /kəndéns/ v. **1** tr. make denser or more concentrated. **2** tr. express in fewer words. **3** tr. & intr. reduce or be reduced to a liquid.

■ **1, 3** see CONCENTRATE v. 3. **2** see ABRIDGE 1.

con•dens•er /kəndénsər/ n. **1** apparatus or vessel for condensing vapor. **2** Electr. = CAPACITOR.

con•de•scend /kóndisénd/ v.intr. **1** be gracious enough (to do a thing unworthy of one). **2** behave as if one is on equal terms with (an inferior). **3** (as **condescending** adj.) patronizing. □□ **con•de•scend'ing•ly** adv. **con•de•scen'sion** n.

■ **1** stoop, deign, lower or humble or demean oneself. **3** (**condescending**) belittling, disdainful, contemptuous, pompous, overbearing, high-handed, imperious, snobbish, haughty, supercilious.

con•dign /kəndín/ adj. (of punishment, etc.) severe and well-deserved. □□ **con•dign'ly** adv.

con•di•ment /kóndimənt/ n. seasoning or relish for food.

con•di•tion /kəndíshən/ • n. **1** stipulation; term(s). **2 a** state of fitness. **b** ailment; abnormality. **3** [in pl.] circumstances. • v.tr. **1 a** bring into a good or desired state. **b** make fit. **2** teach or accustom.

■ n. **1** proviso, demand, requirement, qualification, contingency, requisite, prerequisite. **2 a** shape; working order; form, fettle, health. **3** (**conditions**) environment, surroundings. • v. **1 a** ready, prepare, equip, outfit, adapt, modify. **2** train, educate; brainwash; influence, mold; inure, acclimate.

con•di•tion•al /kəndíshənəl/ adj. **1** dependent; not absolute. **2** Gram. (of a clause, mood, etc.) expressing a condition. □□ **con•di'tion•al•ly** adv.

■ **1** see PROVISIONAL adj.

con•di•tion•er /kəndíshənər/ n. agent that conditions, as for the hair.

con·do /kóndō/ *n.* (*pl.* **-dos**) *colloq.* condominium.

con·do·lence /kəndṓləns/ *n.* [often *pl.*] expression of sympathy (*sent my condolences*).
■ see PITY *n.* 1.

con·dom /kóndom/ *n.* prophylactic or contraceptive sheath worn on the penis.

con·do·min·i·um /kóndəmíneeəm/ *n.* 1 building or complex containing individually owned apartments. 2 joint sovereignty.

con·done /kəndṓn/ *v.tr.* forgive or overlook.

con·dor /kóndawr/ *n.* 1 large S. American vulture. 2 smaller vulture of California.

con·du·cive /kəndōōsiv, –dyṓō–/ *adj.* contributing or helping (toward something).
■ see INSTRUMENTAL *adj.*

con·duct • *n.* /kóndukt/ 1 behavior. 2 action or manner of directing or managing. • *v.* /kəndúkt/ 1 *tr.* direct or manage (business, etc.). 2 *tr.* be the conductor of (an orchestra, etc.). 3 *tr.* transmit (heat, electricity, etc.). 4 *refl.* behave. □□ **con·duct·i·ble** /kəndúktibəl/ *adj.* **con·duct·i·bil'i·ty** *n.*
■ *n.* 1 actions, demeanor, manners, deportment, attitude, comportment. 2 guidance, supervision, leadership, administration, government, running, handling, control, command, regulation, operation. • *v.* 1 supervise, run, control, administer, regulate, operate. 3 channel, carry, convey. 4 see BEHAVE 2.

con·duc·tance /kəndúktəns/ *n.* ability to conduct electricity.

con·duc·tion /kəndúkshən/ *n.* transmission of heat, electricity, etc., through a substance. □□ **con·duc·tive** /–tiv/ *adj.* **con·duc·tiv'i·ty** *n.*

con·duc·tor /kəndúktər/ *n.* 1 person who directs an orchestra, choir, etc. 2 official in charge of passengers on a train, etc. 3 thing that conducts heat or electricity.
■ 1 maestro, leader.

con·duit /kóndōōit, –dyōōit, –dit/ *n.* 1 channel or pipe conveying liquids. 2 tube protecting electric wires.

cone /kōn/ *n.* 1 solid figure with a circular (or other curved) plane base, tapering to a point. 2 thing or holder of similar shape. 3 dry fruit of a conifer.

con·fec·tion /kənfékshən/ *n.* sweet dish; candy.
■ see CANDY *n.*

con·fec·tion·er /kənfékshənər/ *n.* maker or retailer of confections. □ **confectioners' sugar** fine powdered sugar.

con·fed·er·a·cy /kənfédərəsee/ *n.* (*pl.* **-cies**) 1 league or alliance. 2 (**the Confederacy**) the 11 Southern states that seceded from the US in 1860–61.
■ 1 see LEAGUE[1] *n.* 1. 2 Confederate States of America.

con·fed·er·ate • *adj.* /kənfédərət/ allied. • *n.* /kənfédərət/ 1 ally; accomplice. 2 (**Confederate**) supporter of the Confederacy. • *v.* /kənfédərayt/ 1 *tr.* bring into alliance. 2 *intr.* come into alliance.
■ *n.* 1 see ACCOMPLICE. • *v.* see ASSOCIATE *v.* 2.

con·fed·er·a·tion /kənfédəráyshən/ *n.*

1 union or alliance. 2 confederating; being confederated.
■ 1 see ALLIANCE 1.

con·fer /kənfər/ *v.* (**con·ferred, con·fer·ring**) 1 *tr.* grant or bestow. 2 *intr.* converse; consult. See synonym study at GIVE. □□ **con·fer'ment** *n.* **con·fer'ra·ble** *adj.*
■ 1 give, present, award. 2 talk, take counsel, communicate, parley, negotiate.

con·fer·ence /kónfərəns, –frəns/ *n.* 1 consultation. 2 meeting. □ **conference call** telephone call in which several people are connected.
■ 1 talk, colloquy; see also *discussion* (DISCUSS). 2 convention, symposium, congress, seminar, forum, colloquium.

con·fer·ral /kənfôrəl/ *n.* conferring of a degree, honor, etc.

con·fess /kənfés/ *v.* 1 a *tr.* acknowledge or admit. b *intr.* admit (to). 2 *tr.* admit reluctantly. 3 a *tr.* declare (one's sins) to a priest. b *tr.* (of a priest) hear the confession of. ·
■ 1 a own (up to), declare, confirm, concede, affirm, testify, avow, reveal, divulge. b see *come clean* (CLEAN).

con·fes·sion /kənféshən/ *n.* 1 a confessing. b thing confessed. 2 declaration of one's beliefs. □□ **con·fes'sion·ar·y** *adj.*
■ 1 see ADMISSION 1. 2 see PROFESSION 3.

con·fes·sion·al /kənféshənəl/ • *n.* enclosed stall in a church in which a priest hears confessions. • *adj.* of confession.

con·fes·sor /kənfésər/ *n.* priest who hears confessions.

con·fet·ti /kənfétee/ *n.* bits of colored paper thrown during celebrations, etc.

con·fi·dant /kónfidánt, –dáant/ *n.* (*fem.* **con·fi·dante**) person trusted with knowledge of one's private affairs.
■ see INTIMATE[1] *n.*

con·fide /kənfíd/ *v.* 1 *tr.* tell in confidence. 2 *tr.* entrust (an object, a task, etc.) to. 3 *intr.* [foll. by *in*] talk confidentially to.
■ 1 see IMPART 1. 3 see TRUST *v.* 1.

con·fi·dence /kónfidəns/ *n.* 1 firm trust. 2 a feeling of reliance or certainty. b sense of self-reliance; boldness. 3 something told confidentially. □ **confidence game** swindle in which the victim is persuaded to trust the swindler. **confidence man** swindler in a confidence game.
■ 1 faith, belief. 2 a conviction; see also CERTAINTY 2. b assurance, self-confidence, courage, nerve, self-assurance, poise, aplomb, coolness. 3 secret, private matter *or* affair.

con·fi·dent /kónfid'nt/ *adj.* feeling or showing confidence. □□ **con'fi·dent·ly** *adv.*
■ self-assured, self-reliant, dauntless, bold, fearless, courageous; secure, sure, certain, assured, positive, convinced, trusting, satisfied.

con·fi·den·tial /kónfidénshəl/ *adj.* spoken or written in confidence. □□ **con·fi·den·ti·al·i·ty** /–sheeálitee/ *n.* **con·fi·den'tial·ly** *adv.*
■ private, secret, classified, top secret, *colloq.* hush-hush.

con·fig·u·ra·tion /kənfigyəráyshən/ *n.* arrangement in a particular form.
■ see FORM *n.* 1.

con•fine • *v.tr.* /kənfín/ **1** keep or restrict (within certain limits, etc.). **2** imprison. • *n.* /kónfīn/ [usu. *pl.*] limit; boundary.

■ *v.* **1** see RESTRICT². **2** see IMPRISON. • *n.* see BOUND *n.* 1.

con•fine•ment /kənfínmənt/ *n.* **1** confining; being confined. **2** time of childbirth.

■ **1** see *captivity* (CAPTIVE). **2** see LABOR *n.* 3.

con•firm /kənfárm/ *v.tr.* **1** settle the truth or correctness of. **2** make formally valid. **3** encourage (a person) in (an opinion, etc.). **4** administer the religious rite of confirmation to. □□ **con•firm′a•tive** *adj.* **con•firm′a•to•ry** *adj.*

■ **1, 2** strengthen, reinforce, uphold, back up, corroborate, substantiate, prove; ratify, sanction, authorize, endorse, sustain, approve, verify, recognize; authenticate. **3** see SUPPORT *v.* 4, 6.

con•fir•ma•tion /kónfərmáyshən/ *n.* **1** confirming; being confirmed. **2** rite confirming a baptized person as a church member.

con•firmed /kənfármd/ *adj.* firmly settled in some habit or condition (*a confirmed bachelor*).

■ see HABITUAL 3.

con•fis•cate /kónfiskayt/ *v.tr.* take or seize by authority. □□ **con•fis•ca•tion** /-káyshən/ *n.* **con′fis•ca•tor** *n.*

■ appropriate, impound, expropriate, commandeer.

con•fla•gra•tion /kónfləgráyshən/ *n.* great and destructive fire.

■ holocaust, inferno.

con•flate /kənfláyt/ *v.tr.* blend or fuse together (esp. two variant texts into one). □□ **con•fla•tion** /-fláyshən/ *n.*

con•flict • *n.* /kónflikt/ **1** state of opposition. **2** fight; struggle. • *v.intr.* /kənflíkt/ clash; be incompatible.

■ *n.* **1** battle, combat, war, dispute, controversy, contention. **2** engagement, fray, fracas, donnybrook; argument, altercation, feud, quarrel. • *v.* disagree, differ, be at odds.

con•flu•ence /kónflØəns/ *n.* **1** place where two rivers meet. **2** coming together.

con•form /kənfáwrm/ *v.* **1** *intr.* comply with rules or general custom. **2** *tr.* make similar. **3** *intr.* comply with; be in accordance with.

■ **1** fit (in), harmonize. **3** follow, observe, obey, respect, abide by, adapt *or* adjust to.

con•form•a•ble /kənfáwrməbəl/ *adj.* **1** similar. **2** consistent. **3** adaptable. □□ **con•form•a•bil′i•ty** *n.* **con•form′a•bly** *adv.*

con•for•ma•tion /kónfawrmáyshən/ *n.* way a thing is formed; shape.

■ see FORM *n.* 1.

con•form•ist /kənfáwrmist/ • *n.* person who conforms to established practice. • *adj.* conforming; conventional. □□ **con•form′ism** *n.*

■ *n.* see SQUARE *n.* 5. • *adj.* see CONSERVATIVE *adj.* 1a.

con•form•i•ty /kənfáwrmitee/ *n.* **1** accordance with established practice. **2** agreement; suitability.

■ **2** see ACCORD *n.* 1.

con•found /kənfównd/ *v.tr.* **1** perplex. **2** confuse (in one's mind).

■ **1** see PERPLEX 1. **2** see CONFUSE 2.

con•front /kənfrúnt/ *v.tr.* **1 a** face in hostility or defiance. **b** face up to and deal with. **2** present itself to. **3** bring (a person) face to face with. **4** meet or stand facing. □□ **con•fron•ta•tion** /kónfruntáyshən/ *n.* **con•fron•ta′tion•al** *adj.*

■ **1** see FACE *v.* 3.

Con•fu•cian /kənfyōōshən/ *adj.* of or relating to Confucius, Chinese philosopher d. 479 BC, or his philosophy. □□ **Con•fu′cian•ism** *n.* **Con•fu′cian•ist** *n.*

con•fuse /kənfyōōz/ *v.tr.* **1** perplex; bewilder. **2** mix up in the mind; mistake (one for another). **3** make indistinct (*that point confuses the issue*). □□ **con•fus′ed•ly** *adv.* **con•fus′ing** *adj.* **con•fus′ing•ly** *adv.*

■ **1** disconcert, puzzle, mystify, baffle, bemuse, befuddle, discomfit, confound, fluster, upset, disorient. **3** disorder, muddle, entangle; blur.

con•fu•sion /kənfyōōzhən/ *n.* confusing or being confused. See synonym study at JUMBLE.

■ misconception, mix-up; disorder, disarray, chaos, tumult, commotion, turmoil, pandemonium, bedlam; mess, jumble, muddle.

con•fute /kənfyōōt/ *v.tr.* prove to be in error. □□ **con•fu•ta•tion** /kónfyootáyshən/ *n.*

Cong. *abbr.* **1** Congress. **2** Congressional. **3** Congregational.

con•ga /kónggə/ *n.* **1** Latin American line dance. **2** tall, narrow drum beaten with the hands.

con•geal /kənjéel/ *v.* **1** make or become semisolid by cooling. **2** coagulate.

■ see COAGULATE.

con•gen•ial /kənjéenyəl/ *adj.* **1** pleasantly sociable. **2** suited or agreeable. □□ **con•gen•i•al•i•ty** /-jeeneeálitee/ *n.* **con•gen′ial•ly** *adv.*

■ **1** see LIKABLE.

con•gen•i•tal /kənjénitəl/ *adj.* (esp. of a disease, defect, etc.) existing from birth. See synonym study at INHERENT. □□ **con•gen′i•tal•ly** *adv.*

■ see INBORN, INHERENT 1.

con•ger /kónggər/ *n.* large marine eel.

con•ge•ries /kónjəreez, kónjə-/ *n.* (*pl.* same) disorderly collection; mass or heap.

con•gest /kənjést/ *v.tr.* (esp. as **congested** *adj.*) affect with congestion. □□ **con•ges′tive** *adj.*

■ see BLOCK *v.*; (**congested**) snarled up, obstructed, (over)crowded; blocked (up), stuffed (up).

con•ges•tion /kənjés-chən/ *n.* abnormal accumulation or obstruction.

con•glom•er•ate • *adj.* /kənglómərət/ gathered into a rounded mass. • *n.* /kənglómərət/ **1** heterogeneous mass. **2** group or corporation. • *v.* /kənglómərayt/ collect into a coherent mass. □□ **con•glom•er•a•tion** /-ráyshən/ *n.* See synonym study at JUMBLE.

■ *n.* **2** see ORGANIZATION 2.

con•grat•u•late /kəngráchəlayt, -gráj-, kəng-/ *v.tr.* express pleasure at the good fortune or excellence of (a person). □□ **con•grat•u•la•to•ry** /-lətáwree/ *adj.*

■ see COMPLIMENT *v.*

con•grat•u•la•tion /kəngráchəláyshən, –gráj–, kəng–/ n. 1 congratulating. 2 [usu. pl.] expression of this.

■ 2 (*congratulations*) felicitations, well done, good for you, nice going; many happy returns.

con•gre•gate /kónggrigayt/ v. collect or gather into a crowd or mass. See synonym study at GATHER.

■ see GATHER v. 1.

con•gre•ga•tion /kónggrigáyshən/ n. 1 gathering of people, esp. for religious worship. 2 body of persons regularly attending a particular church, etc.

con•gre•ga•tion•al /kónggrigáyshənəl/ adj. 1 of a congregation. 2 (**Congregational**) of or adhering to Congregationalism, a Christian denomination of churches that are largely self-governing. □□ **Con•gre•ga′tion•al•ist** n.

con•gress /kónggris/ n. 1 formal meeting of delegates for discussion. 2 (**Congress**) national legislative body of the US. □□ **con•gres•sion•al** /kəngréshən'l/ adj.

■ 1 see CONFERENCE 2. 2 see PARLIAMENT.

con•gress•man /kónggrismən/ n. (pl. –men; fem. **con•gress•wom•an**, pl. –wom•en) member of the US Congress.

■ see REPRESENTATIVE n. 3.

con•gru•ent /kónggrō̄ənt, kəngrōō–/ adj. 1 suitable; agreeing. 2 Geom. coinciding when superimposed. □□ **con′gru•ence** n.

con•gru•ous /kónggrōōəs/ adj. suitable; fitting. □□ **con•gru′i•ty** n. **con′gru•ous•ly** adv.

con•ic /kónik/ adj. of a cone. □□ **con′i•cal** adj. **con′i•cal•ly** adv.

co•ni•fer /kónifər, kō–/ n. any cone-bearing tree or shrub, usu. evergreen. □□ **co•nif′er•ous** /kənifərəs/ adj.

conj. abbr. conjunction.

con•jec•ture /kənjékchər/ • n. formation of an opinion on incomplete information. • v. guess. □□ **con•jec′tur•al** adj.

■ n. see GUESS n. • v. see GUESS v. 2.

con•join /kənjóyn/ v. join; combine.

■ see COMBINE v. 1.

con•joint /kənjóynt/ adj. associated; conjoined. □□ **con•joint′ly** adv.

con•ju•gal /kónjəgəl/ adj. pertaining to marriage. □□ **con•ju•gal•i•ty** /–gálitee/ n. **con′ju•gal•ly** adv.

■ see matrimonial (MATRIMONY).

con•ju•gate • v. /kónjəgayt/ 1 tr. Gram. give the different forms of (a verb). 2 intr. a unite. b become fused. • adj. /kónjəgət, –gayt/ joined together; fused.

con•ju•ga•tion /kónjəgáyshən/ n. Gram. system of verbal inflection. □□ **con•ju•ga′tion•al** adj.

con•junct /kənjúngkt/ adj. joined together; associated.

con•junc•tion /kənjúngkshən/ n. 1 joining; connection. 2 Gram. connective word (e.g., and, but, if). 3 combination (of events or circumstances).

■ 1 see JUNCTION 3.

con•junc•ti•va /kónjungktívə, kənjúngktívə/

n. (pl. **con•junc•ti•vas** or **con•junc•ti•vae** /–vee/) Anat. mucous membrane of the eye. □□ **con•junc•ti′val** adj.

con•junc•tive /kənjúngktiv/ adj. 1 serving to join; connective. 2 Gram. of the nature of a conjunction.

con•junc•ti•vi•tis /kənjúngktivítis/ n. inflammation of the conjunctiva.

con•jure /kónjər/ v. 1 tr. call upon (a spirit) to appear. 2 tr. evoke. 3 intr. perform seemingly magical tricks. □ **conjure up** produce as if by magic.

■ □ conjure up see EVOKE 2.

conk /kongk/ v.tr. sl. hit on the head, etc. □ **conk out** 1 (of a machine, etc.) break down. 2 (of a person) be exhausted and give up; faint.

■ see HIT v. 1a. □ **conk out** 1 see BREAK v. 1b.

Conn. abbr. Connecticut.

con•nect /kənékt/ v. 1 a tr. join (one thing with another). b intr. be joined or joinable. 2 tr. associate mentally or practically. 3 intr. (of a train, etc.) be timed such that passengers can transfer (to another train, etc.). 4 tr. put into communication. 5 intr. colloq. hit or strike effectively. □□ **con•nec′tor** n.

■ 1 link or tie (together); fasten, bind, attach, couple, secure, affix; pin, hook, staple, tack, glue, cement, fuse, seal, strap, bolt, lash. 2 affiliate, relate, tie (in).

con•nec•tion /kənékshən/ n. 1 connecting; being connected. 2 meeting point. 3 link, esp. by telephone. 4 connecting train, flight, etc. 5 [often in pl.] relevant or helpful acquaintance. 6 relation of ideas.

■ 1 linking, linkage, union, bond, link; tie, relationship, association, relevance, appropriateness. 2 see JOINT n. 1. 3 see LINK n. 2a, b. 5 (connections) contacts, friends; influence, pull, clout. 6 see CONTEXT.

con•nec•tive /kənéktiv/ adj. serving or tending to connect, esp. of body tissue.

conn•ing tow•er /kóning/ n. 1 superstructure of a submarine containing the periscope. 2 pilothouse of a warship.

con•nive /kənív/ v.intr. 1 [foll. by at] disregard or tacitly consent to (a wrongdoing). 2 conspire.

■ 1 see ABET. 2 see SCHEME v.

con•nois•seur /kónəsőr/ n. expert judge in matters of taste.

■ see EXPERT n.

con•note /kənṓt/ v.tr. imply in addition to the literal or primary meaning. □□ **con•no•ta′tion** n. **con•no•ta•tive** /kónətaytiv, kənṓtətiv/ adj.

■ see IMPLY 3.

con•nu•bi•al /kənṓbeeəl, kənyṓ–/ adj. of or relating to marriage. □□ **con•nu′bi•al•ly** adv.

■ see matrimonial (MATRIMONY).

con•quer /kóngkər/ v.tr. 1 a overcome militarily. b be victorious. 2 overcome (a habit, challenge, etc.) by effort. □□ **con′quer•a•ble** adj. **con′quer•or** n.

■ 1 a beat, defeat, subdue, crush, subjugate, vanquish; capture, seize, win, gain, acquire, obtain; occupy, annex. 2 triumph or prevail over, surmount, master.

con•quest /kóngkwest/ *n.* **1** conquering; being conquered. **2** something won. **3** person whose affection has been won.

■ **1** subjugation, domination, subjection; (*conquest of*) mastery *or* control of, triumph over; see also DEFEAT *n.* **2** see TROPHY *n.*

con•quis•ta•dor /konkwístədawr, kongkeéstə‑/ *n.* (*pl.* **con•quis•ta•dor•es** /‑dáwrez/ *or* **con•quis•ta•dors**) conqueror, esp. a 16th‑c. Spanish conqueror of Mexico and Peru.

con•san•guin•e•ous /kónsanggwineeəs/ *adj.* descended from the same ancestor; akin. □□ **con•san•guin′i•ty** *n.*

con•science /kónshəns/ *n.* moral sense of right and wrong. □ **in all conscience** by any reasonable standard.

■ morality, judgment, fairness, ethics, honor, standards, principles, scruples. □ **in all conscience** in all fairness, reasonably.

con•sci•en•tious /kónshee‑énshəs/ *adj.* diligent and scrupulous. □ **conscientious objector** person who refrains from military service on moral grounds. □□ **con•sci•en′tious•ly** *adv.* **con•sci•en′tious•ness** *n.*

■ principled, fair, moral, ethical, righteous, upstanding, upright, honorable, just, responsible, incorruptible; careful, meticulous, punctilious, painstaking, particular, rigorous, thorough; prudent, sensible, attentive, serious.

con•scious /kónshəs/ *adj.* **1** awake and aware of one's surroundings and identity. **2 a** aware; knowing. **b** intentional. **3** [*in comb.*] aware of; concerned with (*appearance‑conscious*). ● *n.* [prec. by *the*] the conscious mind. □□ **con′scious•ly** *adv.* **con′scious•ness** *n.*

■ *adj.* **1** see AWAKE *adj.* 1. **2 a** see AWARE 1. **b** deliberate, willful, studied.

con•script ● *v.tr.* /kənskrípt/ summon for compulsory (esp. military) service. ● *n.* /kónskript/ conscripted person. □□ **con•scrip′tion** *n.*

■ *v.* see ENLIST 1. ● *n.* see RECRUIT *n.* 1, 2.

con•se•cra•te /kónsikrayt/ *v.tr.* **1** make or declare sacred. **2** [foll. by *to*] devote to (a purpose). □□ **con•se•cra′tion** /‑kráyshən/ *n.* **con′se•cra′tor** *n.*

■ **1** see SANCTIFY 1. **2** see DEVOTE.

con•sec•u•tive /kənsékyətiv/ *adj.* following continuously, in unbroken or logical order. □□ **con•sec′u•tive•ly** *adv.* **con•sec′u•tive•ness** *n.*

■ see SUCCESSIVE.

con•sen•sus /kənsénsəs/ *n.* general agreement or opinion.

■ see AGREEMENT 1, 2.

con•sent /kənsént/ ● *v.intr.* express willingness; agree. ● *n.* voluntary agreement; permission.

■ *v.* comply, concur, accede, acquiesce, concede, yield, submit, cede, conform, give in; (*consent to*) permit, allow, approve, authorize. ● *n.* approval, assent, sanction, authorization.

con•se•quence /kónsikwens, ‑kwəns/ *n.* **1** result or effect of an action or condition. **2** importance.

■ **1** see RESULT *n.* 1. **2** see *importance* (IMPORTANT).

con•se•quent /kónsikwənt/ *adj.* following as a result or consequence.

■ see ATTENDANT *adj.* 1.

con•se•quen•tial /kónsikwénshəl/ *adj.* **1** following as a consequence. **2** resulting indirectly. **3** significant. □□ **con•se•quen′tial•ly** *adv.*

con•se•quent•ly /kónsikwentlee/ *adv. & conj.* as a result; therefore.

■ so, accordingly, ergo, hence, thus.

con•ser•van•cy /kənsárvənsee/ *n.* (*pl.* **–cies**) **1** body concerned with the preservation of natural resources. **2** official preservation (of forests, etc.).

con•ser•va•tion /kónsərváyshən/ *n.* preservation, esp. of the natural environment. □ **conservation of energy** *Physics* principle that the total quantity of energy of any system not subject to external action remains constant. □□ **con•ser•va′tion•al** *adj.* **con•ser•va′tion•ist** *n.*

■ protection, safekeeping, maintenance, upkeep, management, safeguarding; environmentalism. □□ **conservationist** environmentalist, ecologist, preservationist; see also NATURALIST.

con•ser•va•tive /kənsárvətiv/ ● *adj.* **1 a** averse to rapid change. **b** moderate; avoiding extremes. **2** (of an estimate, etc.) purposely low. **3** tending to conserve. ● *n.* conservative person. □□ **con•ser′va•tism** *n.* **con•ser′va•tive•ly** *adv.* **con•ser′va•tive•ness** *n.*

■ *adj.* **1 a** unprogressive, orthodox, traditional, conformist, conventional, fundamentalist. **b** cautious, careful, prudent, temperate. ● *n.* reactionary, fundamentalist; moderate, middle‑of‑the‑roader.

con•ser•va•to•ry /kənsárvətawree/ *n.* (*pl.* **–ries**) **1** greenhouse. **2** music school.

con•serve /kənsárv/ ● *v.tr.* **1** keep from harm or damage, esp. for later use. **2** *Physics* maintain a quantity of (heat, etc.). **3** preserve (food, esp. fruit), usu. with sugar. ● *n.* (also /kónsərv/) fresh fruit jam.

■ *v.* **1** preserve, store up, save, spare, reserve; maintain, keep up, take care of, **3** see PRESERVE *v.* 3. ● *n.* see PRESERVE *n.* 1.

con•sid•er /kənsídər/ *v.tr.* **1** contemplate; weigh and evaluate. **2** examine the merits of. **3** give attention to. **4** take into account. **5** regard as. **6** (as **considered** *adj.*) deliberated. □ **all things considered** taking everything into account.

■ **1** think about *or* over, ponder, mull over, meditate (on *or* upon *or* over *or* about), reflect (on *or* upon *or* about), ruminate (on *or* over *or* about). **2** see DELIBERATE *v.* 2. **3** see HEED *v.* **4** reckon with, bear in mind, observe, make allowance for; respect, have regard for. **5** look upon; judge, take to be, believe, gauge, rate, estimate, deem.

con•sid•er•a•ble /kənsídərəbəl/ *adj.* **1** much; a lot of. **2** notable; important. □□ **con•sid′er•a•bly** *adv.*

■ **1** sizable, substantial, great, no little,

appreciable, respectable, noticeable, decent, fair. **2** worthy, of consequence, of distinction, distinguished, illustrious, noteworthy, remarkable, estimable.

con•sid•er•ate /kənsídərət/ *adj.* thoughtful toward others. □□ **con•sid′er•ate•ly** *adv.*

■ kind, helpful, friendly, gracious, obliging, accommodating, charitable, generous, unselfish; sympathetic, compassionate, sensitive, attentive.

con•sid•er•a•tion /kənsídəráyshən/ *n.* **1** careful thought. **2** thoughtfulness. **3** fact or thing taken into account. **4** compensation; payment or reward.

■ **1** deliberation, reflection, contemplation; study, examination. **2** regard, concern, attentiveness, solicitude, compassion, kindness, respect, care. **3** see POINT *n.* 11. **4** remuneration, recompense.

con•sid•er•ing /kənsídəring/ • *prep.* in view of; because of. • *adv. colloq.* all in all *(not so bad, considering)*.

■ *prep.* in light of, bearing in mind, taking into account, looking at, inasmuch as, insomuch as. • *adv.* all things or everything considered; see also *on the whole* (WHOLE).

con•sign /kənsín/ *v.tr.* **1** hand over; deliver. **2** assign; commit. **3** transmit or send (goods). □□ **con•sign•ee** /kónsīneé/ *n.* **con•sign′or** *n.*

■ **1** see ENTRUST. **2** dispatch, dismiss, relegate; see also DOWNGRADE *v.* 1. **3** see SEND 1a.

con•sign•ment /kənsínmənt/ *n.* **1** consigning; being consigned. **2** goods consigned. **3** agreement to pay a supplier of goods after the goods are sold.

■ **2** see CARGO 1b, 2b.

con•sist /kənsíst/ *v.intr.* be composed; have as ingredients or essential features.

■ *(consist of)* contain, comprise, include, have in it.

con•sis•ten•cy /kənsístənsee/ *n.* (*pl.* –**cies**) **1** degree of density, viscosity, etc., esp. of liquids. **2** being consistent.

■ **1** texture, firmness, compactness. **2** see *uniformity* (UNIFORM).

con•sis•tent /kənsístənt/ *adj.* **1** compatible or in harmony. **2** (of a person) constant. □□ **con•sist′ent•ly** *adv.*

■ **1** in agreement, in keeping, harmonious, accordant, in accordance, consonant, consequent. **2** dependable, regular, predictable, undeviating, steady, steadfast, unchanging, unswerving. □□ **consistently** steadily, often, frequently; reliably, devotedly, firmly, resolutely, faithfully, unfailingly.

con•so•la•tion /kónsəláyshən/ *n.* **1** consoling; being consoled. **2** consoling thing, person, or circumstance.

■ see COMFORT *n.* 1.

con•sole[1] /kənsól/ *v.tr.* comfort, esp. in grief or disappointment. □□ **con•sol′a•ble** *adj.* **con•sol′er** *n.* **con•sol′ing•ly** *adv.*

■ soothe, calm, assuage, solace, cheer (up), reassure, relieve, hearten, cheer, gladden.

con•sole[2] /kónsól/ *n.* **1** panel for switches, controls, etc. **2** appliance cabinet. **3** cabinet for an organ's keyboards, etc.

con•sol•i•date /kənsólidayt/ *v.* **1** *tr. & intr.* make or become strong or solid. **2** *tr.* combine into one whole. □□ **con•sol•i•da′tion** /–dáyshən/ *n.* **con•sol′i•da•tor** *n.*

■ **1** see STRENGTHEN. **2** see AMALGAMATE.

con•som•mé /kónsəmáy/ *n.* clear soup from meat stock.

con•so•nant /kónsənənt/ • *n.* **1** speech sound in which the breath is at least partly obstructed. **2** letter(s) representing this. • *adj.* consistent; in agreement or harmony.

■ *adj.* see CONSISTENT 1.

con•sort[1] • *n.* /kónsawrt/ spouse, esp. of royalty. • *v.intr.* /kənsórt/ keep company; associate.

con•sort[2] /kónsawrt/ *n. Mus.* group of players, singers, etc.

con•sor•tium /kənsáwrsheeəm, –teeəm/ *n.* (*pl.* –**ti•a** /–sheeə, –teeə/ or –**ti•ums**) association, esp. of several firms.

con•spic•u•ous /kənspíkyŏŏəs/ *adj.* **1** clearly visible; attracting notice. **2** remarkable of its kind. See synonym study at NOTICEABLE. □□ **con•spic′u•ous•ly** *adv.* **con•spic′u•ous•ness** *n.*

■ **1** obvious, unmistakable, prominent, outstanding, impressive, vivid, obtrusive; striking, loud, blatant; evident, apparent. **2** notable, noteworthy, exceptional, eminent, unusual, marked, extraordinary.

con•spir•a•cy /kənspírəsee/ *n.* (*pl.* –**cies**) **1** secret plan to commit a crime; a plot. **2** conspiring. See synonym study at PLOT.

■ **1** scheme, stratagem, cabal, intrigue, machination. **2** collusion, connivance, foul play.

con•spir•a•tor /kənspírətər/ *n.* person who takes part in a conspiracy. □□ **con•spir•a•to′ri•al** /–táwreeəl/ *adj.*

■ see ACCOMPLICE.

con•spire /kənspír/ *v.intr.* **1** collude for an unlawful or harmful act. **2** (of events) seem to be working together.

■ **1** see PLOT *v.* 2.

con•sta•ble /kónstəbəl, kún–/ *n.* peace officer, esp. in a small town.

con•stab•u•lar•y /kənstábyələree/ *n.* (*pl.* –**ies**) constables, collectively.

■ see POLICE *n.*

con•stan•cy /kónstənsee/ *n.* dependability; faithfulness.

■ see *loyalty* (LOYAL), DETERMINATION 1.

con•stant /kónstənt/ • *adj.* **1** continuous. **2** occurring frequently. **3** faithful; dependable. See synonym study at RESOLUTE. • *n.* anything that does not vary. □□ **con′stant•ly** *adv.*

■ *adj.* **1** continual; incessant, unceasing, ceaseless, perpetual, persistent, uninterrupted, steady, invariable, unremitting, unvarying, relentless, unrelenting, unending, endless, never-ending, nonstop. **3** unchanging, invariable, unvarying, immutable; resolute, immovable, steadfast, firm, unshakable, unswerving, undeviating, persevering, unwearying, tireless, unflagging, unwavering, unfaltering; loyal, true, devoted.

con•stel•la•tion /kónstəláyshən/ *n.* **1** group of associated stars. **2** assemblage of persons, ideas, etc.

con•ster•na•tion /kónstərnáyshən/ *n.* anxiety; dismay.
 ■ see DISMAY *n.* 1.

con•sti•pate /kónstipayt/ *v.tr.* affect with constipation.

con•sti•pa•tion /kónstipáyshən/ *n.* difficulty in emptying the bowels.

con•stit•u•en•cy /kənstíchŏŏənsee/ *n.* (*pl.* –cies) **1** body of voters who elect a representative. **2** area so represented.

con•stit•u•ent /kənstíchŏŏənt/ • *adj.* **1** composing; constituting. **2** able to make or change a constitution. **3** electing. • *n.* **1** member of a constituency. **2** component.
 ■ *n.* **2** see INGREDIENT.

con•sti•tute /kónstitŏŏt, tyŏŏt/ *v.tr.* **1** be the components or essence of; make up. **2** amount to. **3** give legal or constitutional form to. □□ **con'sti•tu•tor** *n.*
 ■ **1** see FORM *v.* 3. **2** see MAKE *v.* 5.

con•sti•tu•tion /kónstitŏŏshən, –tyŏŏ–/ *n.* **1** act or method of constituting; composition. **2** body of fundamental governing principles. **3** person's health, strength, etc.
 ■ **1** see STRUCTURE *n.* 2. **2** see LAW 1. **3** see HEALTH 2.

con•sti•tu•tion•al /kónstitŏŏshənəl, –tyŏŏ–/ • *adj.* **1** pertaining to a constitution. **2** inherent. • *n.* walk taken regularly for health. □□ **con•sti•tu•tion•al•i•ty** /–álitee/ *n.* **con•sti•tu'tion•al•ly** *adv.*
 ■ *adj.* **1** see LEGITIMATE *adj.* 2. **2** see INHERENT 1. • *n.* see WALK *n.* 2*b*.

con•strain /kənstráyn/ *v.tr.* **1** compel. **2 a** confine forcibly. **b** restrict severely. **3** (as **constrained** *adj.*) forced; embarrassed. See synonym study at COMPEL.
 ■ **1** see FORCE[2] *v.* 1. **2** see BOUND *v.* 1.

con•straint /kənstráynt/ *n.* **1** constraining; being constrained. **2** restriction. **3** self-control.

con•strict /kənstríkt/ *v.tr.* make narrow or tight; compress. □□ **con•stric•tion** /–stríkshən/ *n.* **con•stric'tive** *adj.*
 ■ see CONTRACT *v.* 1.

con•stric•tor /kənstríktər/ *n.* **1** snake that kills by compressing. **2** muscle that compresses a part of the body.

con•struct • *v.tr.* /kənstrúkt/ make by fitting together; build. • *n.* /kónstrukt/ thing constructed, esp. by the mind. □□ **con•struc'tor** *n.*
 ■ *v.* erect, put together, frame, set up, put up, assemble; fabricate, devise, create, forge, invent, formulate, compose, form, shape, fashion. • *n.* see INVENTION 1.

con•struc•tion /kənstrúkshən/ *n.* **1** constructing. **2** thing constructed. **3** interpretation or explanation. **4** particular arrangement of words. □□ **con•struc'tion•al** *adj.*
 ■ **1, 2** see STRUCTURE *n.* 1, 2. **3** see RENDITION.

con•struc•tive /kənstrúktiv/ *adj.* **1** tending to form a basis for ideas. **2** helpful; positive. □□ **con•struc'tive•ly** *adv.*
 ■ **2** useful, practical, productive, beneficial.

con•strue /kənstrŏŏ/ *v.tr.* **1** interpret. **2** analyze the syntax of (a sentence). **3** translate word for word. See synonym study at CLARIFY.
 ■ **1** see INTERPRET 4.

con•sul /kónsəl/ *n.* **1** official appointed by a government to protect its citizens and interests in a foreign city. **2** *hist.* either of two chief magistrates in ancient Rome. □□ **con'sul•ar** *adj.* **con'sul•ship** *n.*

con•sul•ate /kónsələt/ *n.* **1** building officially used by a consul. **2** position of consul.

con•sult /kənsúlt/ *v.* **1** *tr.* seek information or advice from. **2** *intr.* solicit counsel. **3** *intr.* give counsel. **4** *tr.* take into account (feelings, interests, etc.). □□ **con•sul•ta•tive** /–súltətiv/ *adj.*
 ■ **1, 2** refer to, look in or at; confer (with). **4** see CONSIDER 4.

con•sult•ant /kənsúlt'nt/ *n.* person providing professional advice, etc.
 ■ expert, counselor.

con•sul•ta•tion /kónsəltáyshən/ *n.* **1** meeting arranged to consult. **2** act or instance of consulting.
 ■ see TALK *n.* 1

con•sume /kənsŏŏm/ *v.tr.* **1** eat or drink. **2** destroy. **3** possess (*consumed with rage*). **4** use up. □□ **con•sum'a•ble** *adj. & n.*
 ■ **1** devour, swallow, put away. **2** ruin, (lay) waste, demolish, devastate. **3** overcome, overwhelm; preoccupy, obsess. **4** exhaust, deplete, drain, expend.

con•sum•er /kənsŏŏmər/ *n.* person who consumes, esp. one who uses a product or service.
 ■ see BUYER.

con•sum•er•ism /kənsŏŏmərizəm/ *n.* protection or promotion of consumers' interests. □□ **con•sum'er•ist** *adj. & n.*

con•sum•mate • *v.tr.* /kónsəmayt/ **1** complete; make perfect. **2** complete (a marriage) by sexual intercourse. • *adj.* /kənsúmit, kónsəmit/ complete; perfect. □□ **con•sum'mate•ly** *adv.* **con•sum•ma•tion** /–máyshən/ *n.* **con•sum•ma'tive** *adj.* **con'sum•ma•tor** *n.*
 ■ *v.* **1** see FINISH *v.* 1*a*. • *adj.* see COMPLETE *adj.* 1.

con•sump•tion /kənsúmpshən/ *n.* **1** consuming; being consumed. **2** purchase and use of goods, etc. **3** amount consumed. **4** *obs.* tuberculosis.
 ■ **1, 2** see USE *n.* 1.

cont. *abbr.* **1** contents. **2** continued.

con•tact • *n.* /kóntakt/ **1** state or condition of touching, meeting, or communicating. **2** person useful to deal with. **3** connection for electric current. **4** *colloq.* contact lens. • *v.tr.* /kóntakt, kəntákt/ get in touch with. □ **contact lens** small lens placed directly on eyeball to correct vision.
 ■ *n.* **1** conjunction, connection, association. **2** see CONNECTION 5.

con•ta•gion /kəntáyjən/ *n.* **1 a** communication of disease by bodily contact. **b** contagious disease. **2** moral corruption.
 ■ **1 b** see DISEASE 3. **2** see POISON *n.* 2.

con•ta•gious /kəntáyjəs/ *adj.* **1 a** (of a person) likely to transmit disease by contact. **b** (of a disease) transmitted in this way. **2** (of emotions, etc.) likely to spread.
 ■ **1b, 2** see INFECTIOUS 2, 3.

con•tain /kəntáyn/ v.tr. **1** hold or be capable of holding within itself. **2** (of measures) be equal to. **3** prevent from moving or extending. **4** control or restrain (feelings, etc.).

■ **1** comprise, lodge; bear, carry; see also INCLUDE 1. **2** consist of. **3, 4** restrict, confine, repress, hold back or in, curb, bridle, keep under control, suppress, check, stifle.

con•tain•er /kəntáynər/ n. jar, box, etc., for holding things.

■ see RECEPTACLE.

con•tain•er•ize /kəntáynərīz/ v.tr. pack in or transport by container. □□ **con•tain•er•i•za′tion** n.

con•tain•ment /kəntáynmənt/ n. prevention of hostile incursion.

con•tam•i•nate /kəntámináyt/ v.tr. **1** pollute. **2** infect. See synonym study at POLLUTE. □□ **con•tam•i•nant** /-minənt/ n. **con•tam•i•na•tion** /-náyshən/ n. **con•tam′i•na•tor** n.

■ **1** defile, poison, spoil, sully; debase, adulterate. **2** stain, corrupt, soil, taint.

con•tem•plate /kóntəmplayt/ v. **1** tr. survey visually or mentally. **2** tr. regard (an event) as possible. **3** tr. intend. **4** intr. meditate. □□ **con•tem•pla•tion** /-pláyshən/ n. **con•tem′pla•tive** adj.

■ **1** look at or (up)on, observe, regard, ruminate on or over, ponder on or over, deliberate over, reflect on, think about or over, mull over. **2** see ENVISAGE 2. **3** see INTEND 1, 2. **4** see MEDITATE 1.

con•tem•po•ra•ne•ous /kəntémpəráyneeəs/ adj. existing or occurring at the same time. □□ **con•tem•po•ra′ne•ous•ly** adv.

■ see SIMULTANEOUS.

con•tem•po•rar•y /kəntémpəreree/ • adj. **1** living or occurring at the same time. **2** about the same age. **3** modern in style. • n. (pl. **-ies**) contemporary person or thing.

■ adj. **1** coexistent, concurrent, synchronous, synchronic. **3** current, present-day, new, up-to-date, stylish, fashionable. • n. peer, coeval.

con•tempt /kəntémpt/ n. **1** feeling of scorn or extreme reproach. **2** being so regarded. **3** disrespect shown to a court, etc. □ **beneath contempt** utterly despicable. **hold in contempt** despise.

■ **1** disdain, disgust; loathing, abhorrence, hatred. **2** contumely.

con•tempt•i•ble /kəntémptibəl/ adj. deserving contempt. □□ **con•tempt′i•bly** adv.

■ despicable, unworthy, shabby, shameful, low, mean, base, measly, miserable, wretched, petty, pitiable, pitiful, nasty, pathetic, loathsome, detestable.

con•temp•tu•ous /kəntémpchōōəs/ adj. showing contempt. □□ **con•temp′tu•ous•ly** adv.

■ scornful, disdainful, sneering, derisive, insulting, insolent.

con•tend /kənténd/ v. **1** intr. strive; fight. **2** intr. compete. **3** tr. assert; maintain. □□ **con•tend′er** n.

■ **1, 2** see STRIVE 2. **3** see MAINTAIN 3.

con•tent¹ /kəntént/ • adj. **1** satisfied; adequately happy. **2** willing. • v.tr. satisfy. • n. contented state.

■ adj. **1** pleased, delighted, gratified, glad, cheerful; comfortable, fulfilled. **2** see WILLING adj. • v. please, gratify, soothe, cheer, gladden. • n. pleasure, satisfaction, gratification, happiness, contentment.

con•tent² /kóntent/ n. **1** [usu. in pl.] what is contained, as in a vessel, book, or house. **2** amount contained. **3** substance (of a speech, etc.) as distinct from form. **4** capacity or volume.

■ **1** (contents) components, constituents; load. **3** subject matter, theme, thesis, text.

con•tent•ed /kəntQuéntid/ adj. happy; satisfied. □□ **con•tent′ed•ly** adv. **con•tent′ed•ness** n.

con•ten•tion /kənténshən/ n. **1** dispute or argument; rivalry. **2** point contended.

■ **1** see rivalry (RIVAL). **2** see ARGUMENT 2.

con•ten•tious /kənténshəs/ adj. **1** quarrelsome. **2** likely to cause an argument. □□ **con•ten′tious•ly** adv. **con•ten′tious•ness** n.

■ **1** see ARGUMENTATIVE. **2** see CONTROVERSIAL 1.

con•tent•ment /kəntQuéntmənt/ n. satisfied state; tranquil happiness.

■ ease, comfort, serenity, peace, peacefulness.

con•test • n. /kóntest/ **1** contending; competition. **2** dispute. • v.tr. /kəntést, kóntest/ **1** dispute. **2** contend or compete for. □□ **con•test•a•ble** /kəntéstəbəl/ adj.

■ n. **1** match, tournament, championship, meet, game. **2** controversy, debate, altercation, argument. • v. **1** argue against, challenge, oppose.

con•test•ant /kəntéstənt/ n. person taking part in a contest.

■ contender, competitor, entrant, player, participant.

con•text /kóntekst/ n. **1** parts that surround and clarify a word or passage. **2** relevant circumstances. □□ **con•tex•tu•al** /kəntékschōōəl/ adj. **con•tex′tu•al•ize** v.tr. **con•tex•tu•al•i•za′tion** n. **con•tex′tu•al•ly** adv.

■ structure, circumstance(s); frame (of reference).

con•tig•u•ous /kəntigyōōəs/ adj. touching; in contact. □□ **con•tig′u•ous•ly** adv.

con•ti•nent¹ /kóntinənt/ n. any of earth's main land masses.

con•ti•nent² /kóntinənt/ adj. **1** able to control one's bowels and bladder. **2** exercising self-restraint. □□ **con′ti•nence** n. See synonym study at ABSTINENCE.

■ **2** see TEMPERATE 4.

con•ti•nen•tal /kóntinént'l/ adj. of a continent. □ **continental breakfast** light breakfast of coffee, rolls, etc.

con•tin•gen•cy /kəntínjənsee/ n. (pl. **-cies**) **1** event that may or may not occur. **2** uncertainty; chance.

■ **1** see EVENTUALITY.

con•tin•gent /kəntínjənt/ • adj. **1** conditional; dependent (on an uncertain circumstance). **2** that may or may not occur. See synonym study at ACCIDENTAL. • n. body (of troops, ships, etc.) forming part of a larger group.

■ *adj.* **1** see PROVISIONAL. • *n.* see COHORT 2.

con•tin•u•al /kəntínyōōəl/ *adj.* constantly or frequently recurring. □□ **con•tin'u•al•ly** *adv.*

■ incessant, perpetual, nonstop, uninterrupted, unceasing, unremitting, endless, unending, continuous.

con•tin•u•ance /kəntínyōōəns/ *n.* **1** continuing in existence or operation. **2** duration. **3** *Law* postponement.

con•tin•u•a•tion /kəntínyōō-áyshən/ *n.* **1** continuing; being continued. **2** part that continues something else.

■ **1** see MAINTENANCE 1. **2** see SUPPLEMENT *n.* 1.

con•tin•ue /kəntínyōō/ *v.* **1** *tr.* maintain; not stop. **2** *tr.* resume or prolong (a narrative, journey, etc.). **3** *tr.* be a sequel to. **4** *intr.* remain.

■ **1** proceed with, pursue, sustain. **3** pick up, take up, carry on (with). **4** endure, persist.

con•ti•nu•i•ty /kóntinōōitee, -nyōō-/ *n.* (*pl.* **-ties**) **1** state of being continuous. **2** logical sequence.

■ see UNITY 2.

con•tin•u•ous /kəntínyōōəs/ *adj.* unbroken; uninterrupted. □□ **con•tin'u•ous•ly** *adv.*

■ incessant, persistent, perpetual, nonstop, unceasing, ceaseless, constant, unremitting, interminable, endless.

con•tin•u•um /kəntínyōōəm/ *n.* (*pl.* **con•tin•ua** /-yōōə/ or **con•tin•u•ums**) thing having a continuous structure.

con•tort /kəntáwrt/ *v.tr.* twist or force out of normal shape. □□ **con•tor'tion** /kəntáwrshən/ *n.*

con•tor•tion•ist /kəntáwrshənist/ *n.* entertainer who adopts contorted postures.

con•tour /kóntōōr/ • *n.* outline. • *v.tr.* mark with contour lines.

■ *n.* see OUTLINE[1] *n.* 4. • *v.* see LINE[1] *v.* 1.

contra- /kóntrə/ *comb. form* against; opposite.

con•tra•band /kóntrəband/ • *n.* smuggled goods. • *adj.* forbidden from import or export.

con•tra•cep•tion /kóntrəsépshən/ *n.* prevention of pregnancy esp. by artificial means. □□ **con•tra•cep'tive** *adj. & n.*

■ birth control.

con•tract • *n.* /kóntrakt/ **1** written or spoken agreement, esp. one enforceable by law. **2** document recording this. • *v.* /kəntrákt, kóntrakt/ **1** *tr. & intr.* make or become smaller. **2 a** *intr.* make a contract. **b** *tr.* arrange (work) to be done by contract. **3** *tr.* catch or develop (a disease).

■ *n.* **1** understanding, deal, arrangement, pact, compact. **2** agreement, memorandum. • *v.* **1** diminish, reduce, shrink, condense. **3** come down with, develop.

con•trac•tile /kəntrákt'l, -tīl/ *adj.* capable of or producing contraction. □□ **con•trac•til•i•ty** /kóntraktílitee/ *n.*

■ see ELASTIC *adj.* 1, 2.

con•trac•tion /kəntrákshən/ *n.* **1** contracting. **2** *Med.* shortening of the uterine muscles during childbirth. **3** shortened word form (e.g., *it's* for *it is*).

■ **2** see LABOR *n.* 3.

con•trac•tor /kóntraktər; kəntráktər/ *n.* person who makes a contract, as to provide services.

con•trac•tu•al /kəntrákchōōəl/ *adj.* of or in the nature of a contract. □□ **con•trac'tu•al•ly** *adv.*

con•tra•dict /kóntrədíkt/ *v.tr.* **1** deny (a statement). **2** deny a statement made by (a person). **3** be in opposition to or in conflict with. □□ **con•tra•dic•tion** /-díkshən/ *n.* **con•tra•dic•to•ry** /-tawree/ *adj.* See synonym study at OPPOSITE

■ **1, 2** counter, dispute, rebut, reject, refute.

con•tra•dis•tinc•tion /kóntrədistíngkshən/ *n.* distinction made by contrast.

con•trail /kóntrayl/ *n.* condensation trail, esp. from a jet.

con•tral•to /kəntráltō/ *n.* (*pl.* **-tos**) **1** lowest female singing voice. **2** singer with this voice.

con•trap•tion /kəntrápshən/ *n.* machine or device, esp. a strange one.

■ contrivance, gadget, doodad, *sl.* gizmo.

con•tra•pun•tal /kóntrəpúnt'l/ *adj. Mus.* of or in counterpoint. □□ **con•tra•pun'tal•ly** *adv.* **con•tra•pun'tist** *n.*

con•tra•ri•wise /kəntráireewiz/ *adv.* **1** on the other hand. **2** in the opposite way.

■ **2** see VICE VERSA.

con•tra•ry /kóntreree/ • *adj.* **1** opposed in nature or tendency. **2** /kəntráirec/ self-willed. **3** (of a wind) unfavorable. **4** opposite in position or direction. See synonym study at OPPOSITE. • *n.* (*pl.* **-ies**) [prec. by *the*] the opposite. • *adv.* [foll. by *to*] in utter contrast. □□ **con•trar'i•ly** *adv.* **con•trar'i•ness** *n.*

■ *adj.* **1** contradictory, conflicting, antagonistic. **2** perverse, hostile, unfriendly, refractory, argumentative. **3** adverse. • *n.* reverse, converse, antithesis.

con•trast • *n.* /kóntrast/ **1 a** juxtaposition or comparison showing differences. **b** difference so revealed. **2** thing or person having different qualities. **3** range of color or tone in a picture. • *v.tr.* /kəntrást, kóntrast/ set together so as to reveal a contrast.

■ *n.* **1** distinction, disparity, dissimilarity. • *v.* juxtapose, oppose, compare, distinguish, differentiate.

con•tra•vene /kóntrəveen/ *v.tr.* **1** infringe (a law, etc.). **2** (of things) conflict with. □□ **con•tra•ven'tion** /-vénshən/ *n.*

■ **1** see INFRINGE 1.

con•tre•temps /kóntrətoN/ *n.* awkward or unfortunate occurrence.

con•trib•ute /kəntríbyōōt/ *v.tr.* **1** give (money, help, etc.) toward a common purpose. **2** supply (an article, etc.) for publication. □□ **con•trib'u•tor** *n.*

■ **1** donate, bestow, grant; promote, have a hand in.

con•tri•bu•tion /kóntribyōōshən/ *n.* **1** act of contributing. **2** thing contributed.

■ **1** see DONATION 1. **2** see DONATION 2.

con•trite /kəntrít, kóntrīt/ *adj.* penitent; feeling remorse. □□ **con•trite'ly** *adv.* **con•trite'ness** *n.* **con•tri'tion** *n.*

■ see *remorseful* (REMORSE).

con•triv•ance /kəntrívəns/ n. **1** something contrived, esp. a mechanical device or a plan. **2** act of contriving.
  ■ **1** see DEVICE 1. **2** see SUBTERFUGE 1.

con•trive /kəntrív/ v.tr. devise; plan or make resourcefully.
  ■ see DEVISE v. 1.

con•trived /kəntrívd/ adj. artificial; forced.
  ■ see ARTIFICIAL 3.

con•trol /kəntról/ • n. **1** power of directing. **2** power of restraining, esp. self-restraint. **3** means of restraint. **4** [usu. in pl.] means of regulating. **5** [usu. in pl.] switches, etc., by which a machine is controlled. **6** place where something is overseen. **7** standard of comparison in an experiment. • v.tr. (**con•trolled**, **con•trol•ling**) **1** have control of; regulate. **2** hold in check. □□ **con•trol′la•ble** adj. **con•trol•la•bil′i•ty** n. **con•trol′la•bly** adv.
  ■ n. **1** command, authority, leadership, management, guidance, supervision. **2** mastery, dominance, domination. **3** check, curb. • v. **1** direct, steer, pilot, manage, conduct. **2** restrain, curb, repress, contain.

con•trol•ler /kəntrólər/ n. **1** person or thing that controls. **2** person in charge of expenditures.

con•tro•ver•sial /kóntrəvórshəl/ adj. causing or subject to controversy. □□ **con•tro•ver′sial•ly** adv.
  ■ debatable, contentious, disputable, questionable, litigious, polemic(al), provocative.

con•tro•ver•sy /kóntrəvərsē/ n. (pl. **–sies**) prolonged argument or dispute.
  ■ debate, contention, disagreement, argument.

con•tro•vert /kóntrəvórt/ v.tr. dispute; deny. □□ **con•tro•vert′i•ble** adj.

con•tu•ma•cious /kóntōōmáyshəs, –tyōō–/ adj. stubbornly or willfully disobedient.

con•tu•me•ly /kóntōōməlee, –tōōmlee, –tōō–, –tyōō–/ n. **1** insolent language or treatment. **2** disgrace.
  ■ **1** see DERISION. **2** see DISGRACE n.

con•tuse /kəntōōz, –tyōōz/ v.tr. bruise. □□ **con•tu•sion** /–zhən/ n.
  ■ see BRUISE v. 1. □□ **contusion** see BRUISE n.

co•nun•drum /kənúndrəm/ n. **1** riddle, esp. one with a pun in its answer. **2** puzzling question. See synonym study at RIDDLE.
  ■ **1** see RIDDLE[1] n.

con•ur•ba•tion /kónərbáyshən/ n. extended urban area.

con•va•lesce /kónvəlés/ v.intr. recover health after illness. □□ **con•va•les′cence** n. **con•va•les′cent** adj.
  ■ improve, get better, recuperate.

con•vec•tion /kənvékshən/ n. heat transfer by upward movement of a heated and less dense medium.

con•vene /kənveen/ v. **1** tr. summon or arrange (a meeting, etc.). **2** intr. assemble. See synonym study at GATHER.
  ■ **1** see SUMMON 3. **2** see ASSEMBLE 1.

con•ven•ience /kənveenyəns/ n. **1** state of being convenient; suitability. **2** useful thing.

□ **at one's convenience** at a time or place that suits one. **convenience store** store with basic groceries, etc., usu. having extended hours.

con•ven•ient /kənveenyənt/ adj. serving one's comfort or interests; suitable. □□ **con•ven′ient•ly** adv.
  ■ useful, helpful, handy, advantageous, opportune, accessible, available.

con•vent /kónvent, –vənt/ n. **1** religious community, esp. of nuns. **2** premises for this.

con•ven•tion /kənvénshən/ n. **1** general custom or customary practice. **2** assembly for a common purpose. **3** formal agreement, esp. between nations.
  ■ **1** tradition, usage, formality, rule. **2** gathering, congregation, congress, conference, symposium, seminar.

con•ven•tion•al /kənvénshənəl/ adj. **1** depending on or according to convention. **2** (of a person) attentive to social conventions. **3** usual; commonplace. **4** (of weapons, etc.) nonnuclear. □□ **con•ven′tion•al•ism** n. **con•ven′tion•al•ist** n. **con•ven•tion•al•i•ty** /–shənálitee/ n. **con•ven′tion•al•ly** adv.
  ■ **1** traditional, orthodox, established. **2** formal, conservative, conformist. **3** normal, standard, customary, ordinary.

con•verge /kənvórj/ v.intr. **1** come together or toward the same point. **2** approach from different directions. □□ **con•ver′gence** n. **con•ver′gent** adj.
  ■ **1** meet, join, unite, merge, coincide.

con•ver•sant /kənvórsənt, kónvərs–/ adj. well acquainted (with).
  ■ see FAMILIAR adj. 2.

con•ver•sa•tion /kónvərsáyshən/ n. **1** informal spoken communication. **2** instance of this. □□ **con•ver•sa′tion•al** adj. **con•ver•sa′tion•al•ist** n.
  ■ discussion, colloq. chitchat, talk, dialogue.

SYNONYM STUDY: conversation
CHAT, COLLOQUY, COMMUNION, DIALOGUE, PARLEY, TÊTE-À-TÊTE. It is nearly impossible for most people to get through a day without having a **conversation** with someone, even if it's only a **chat** with a neighbor. Although *conversation* can and does take place in all sorts of contexts, both formal and informal, the word usually implies a relaxed, casual exchange. A *chat* is the least formal of all conversations, whether it's a father talking to his son about girls or two women having a **tête-à-tête** (French for "head to head," meaning a confidential conversation) about their exasperating husbands. Men, of course, often complain that women don't understand the meaning of **dialogue**, which is a two-way conversation that may involve opposing points of view. Argument is even more likely to play a role in a **parley**, which formally is a discussion between enemies regarding the terms of a truce. A **colloquy** is the most formal of all conversations (*a colloquy on nuclear disarmament*); it can also be used jocularly to describe a guarded exchange (*a brief colloquy with the arresting officer*). **Communion** is a

form of conversation as well—one that may take place on such a profound level that no words are necessary (*communion with Nature*).

　■ **2** see *complexity* (COMPLEX).

con•voy /kónvoy/ *n.* group of ships, vehicles, etc., traveling together or under escort.
　■ see FLEET[1].

con•verse[1] /kənvɔ́rs/ *v.intr.* talk.
　■ discuss, speak, chat, parley, discourse.

con•verse[2] • *adj.* /kənvɔ́rs, kónvərs/ opposite; contrary; reversed. • *n.* /kónvərs/ something opposite or contrary. □□ **con•verse′ly** *adv.*

con•ver•sion /kənvɔ́rzhən, –shən/ *n.* converting; being converted.

con•vert • *v.* /kənvɔ́rt/ **1 a** *tr.* change in form or function. **b** *intr.* be converted. **2** *tr.* cause (a person) to change beliefs, etc. **3** *tr.* change (money, etc.). **4** *tr.* modify structurally. **5** *tr.* (in certain sports) score an extra point or points. • *n.* /kónvərt/ person converted to a different belief, etc. □□ **con•vert′er** *n.*
　■ *v.* **1 a**, **4** alter, transform, transmute, transfigure, remodel, remake. **2** proselytize. • *n.* proselyte, neophyte.

con•vert•i•ble /kənvɔ́rtibəl/ • *adj.* that may be converted. • *n.* car with a folding roof. □□ **con•vert•i•bil′i•ty** *n.* **con•vert′i•bly** *adv.*
　■ *adj.* see CHANGEABLE 2, LIQUID *adj.* 3.

con•vex /kónveks, kənvéks/ *adj.* curved like the exterior of a circle or sphere (cf. CONCAVE). □□ **con•vex′i•ty** *n.* **con•vex′ly** *adv.*

con•vey /kənváy/ *v.tr.* **1** transport or carry. **2** communicate or transmit (an idea, meaning, etc.). □□ **con•vey′a•ble** *adj.* **con•vey′or** *n.*
　■ **1** see TRANSPORT *v.* 1. **2** see COMMUNICATE 1a, TRANSMIT 1a.

con•vey•ance /kənváyəns/ *n.* **1** conveying; being conveyed. **2** means of transport.
　■ **1** see TRANSMISSION 1. **2** vehicle.

con•vict • *v.tr.* /kənvíkt/ **1** prove to be guilty. **2** declare guilty by legal process. • *n.* /kónvikt/ prison inmate.
　■ *n.* prisoner, *sl.* jailbird, con, yardbird.

con•vic•tion /kənvíkshən/ *n.* **1** convicting; being convicted. **2 a** being convinced. **b** firm belief.
　■ **2 a** certainty, sureness, confidence, assurance, certitude. **b** opinion, view, persuasion, position.

con•vince /kənvíns/ *v.tr.* firmly persuade. □□ **con•vinc′ing** *adj.* **con•vinc′ing•ly** *adv.*
　■ win over, bring around, sway.

con•viv•i•al /kənvíveeəl/ *adj.* fond of good company; sociable; lively. □□ **con•viv•i•al′i•ty** /–veeálitee/ *n.* **con•viv′i•al•ly** *adv.*
　■ see SOCIABLE.

con•vo•ca•tion /kónvəkáyshən/ *n.* **1** act of calling together. **2** large formal gathering, as for giving awards, etc. □□ **con•vo•ca′tion•al** *adj.*
　■ **2** see ASSEMBLY 1, 2a.

con•voke /kənvók/ *v.tr. formal* call together.
　■ see SUMMON 3.

con•vo•lut•ed /kónvəlootid/ *adj.* **1** coiled; twisted. **2** complex. □□ **con′vo•lut•ed•ly** *adv.*
　■ **1** see TORTUOUS 1. **2** see INTRICATE.

con•vo•lu•tion /kónvəlooshən/ *n.* **1** coiling; twisting. **2** complexity.

con•vulse /kənvúls/ *v.tr.* **1** [usu. *passive*] affect with convulsions. **2** cause to laugh uncontrollably.

con•vul•sion /kənvúlshən/ *n.* **1** [usu. *pl.*] violent body spasm. **2** violent disturbance. **3** [in *pl.*] uncontrollable laughter. □□ **con•vul′sive** /kənvúlsiv/ *adj.* **con•vul′sive•ly** *adv.*
　■ **1** see FIT[2] 1.

coo /koo/ • *n.* soft murmuring sound as of a dove. • *v.* **1** *intr.* emit a coo. **2** *intr. & tr.* talk or say in a soft voice.

cook /kook/ • *v.* **1** *tr.* prepare (food) by heating it. **2** *intr.* (of food) undergo cooking. **3** *tr. colloq.* falsify (accounts, etc.). • *n.* person who cooks. □ **cook one's goose** ruin one's chances. **cook up** *colloq.* concoct (a story, excuse, etc.). □□ **cook′ing** *n.*
　■ **1** see PREPARE 2. **3** see FALSIFY 1. □ **cook up** see INVENT 2.

cook•book /kookbook/ *n.* book of recipes, etc.

cook•er•y /kookəree/ *n.* art or practice of cooking.

cook•ie /kookee/ *n.* (also **cook′y**) (*pl.* **cook•ies**) small sweet cake. □ **that's the way the cookie crumbles** *colloq.* that is how things turn out.

cook•out /kookowt/ *n.* gathering with an open-air cooked meal.

cook•ware /kookwair/ *n.* utensils for cooking, esp. pots, etc.

cool /kool/ • *adj.* **1** of or at a fairly low temperature. **2** calm; unexcited. **3** lacking enthusiasm. **4** unfriendly. **5** calmly audacious. **6** *sl.* excellent. • *n.* **1** coolness. **2** *sl.* calmness; composure. • *v.* make or become cool. □ **cool it** *sl.* relax; calm down. □□ **cool′ly** *adv.* **cool′ness** *n.*
　■ *adj.* **1** chilly, cold; chilled; unheated. **2** serene, unemotional, undisturbed, unexcitable, unruffled, relaxed, self-controlled, unperturbed, composed; dispassionate. **3** uninterested, apathetic. **4** lukewarm, uncordial, unsociable, unapproachable, standoffish, unwelcoming, aloof. **5** bold, brazen, presumptuous. **6** see SUPERB, WORLDLY 2. • *n.* **1** chill, chilliness. **2** self-control, aplomb, poise, sedateness. • *v.* (*tr.*) chill, refrigerate, ice. (*intr.*) diminish, lessen, moderate. □ **cool it** see RELAX 1.

cool•ant /koolənt/ *n.* cooling agent, esp. fluid.

cool•er /koolər/ *n.* **1** vessel in which a thing is cooled or kept cool. **2** cold drink. **3** *sl.* prison cell.

coo•lie /koolee/ *n. offens.* unskilled native laborer in Asian countries.

coon /koon/ *n.* raccoon.

coop /koop/ • *n.* cage for keeping poultry. • *v.tr.* confine (a person, etc.).
　■ *n.* see CAGE *n.* • *v.* see *shut up* 2.

co-op /kó-op/ *n. colloq.* cooperative business, apartment building, etc.

co•op•er•ate /kō-ópərayt/ *v.intr.* **1** work or

act together; assist. **2** (of things) concur in producing an effect. □□ **co•op•er•a•tion** /–áyshən/ n.

■ **1** collaborate, interact, team up, join forces; participate, contribute, lend a hand.

co•op•er•a•tive /kō-ópərətiv, –óprə–/ • adj. **1** of or affording cooperation. **2** willing to cooperate. **3** (of a business) owned and run jointly by its members, with profits shared. **4** (of an apartment building) with individual units owned by tenants. • n. cooperative farm, society, or business. □□ **co•op′er•a•tive•ly** adv.

co-opt /kō-ópt, kó-opt/ v.tr. appoint to membership of a body by invitation. □□ **co-op′tion** /–ópshən/ n. **co-op′tive** adj.

co•or•di•nate • v. /kō-áwrd′nayt/ **1** tr. cause to function together effectively. **2** intr. work or act together effectively. • adj. /kō-áwrd′nət/ equal in rank or importance. • n. /kō-áwrd′nət/ Math. value used to fix the position of a point, line, or plane. □□ **co•or′di•na•tion** /–náyshən/ n. **co•or′di•na•tor** n.

■ v. **1** harmonize, correlate, synchronize, integrate; see also UNIFY. **2** pull together; see also COOPERATE. • adj. equivalent, parallel, corresponding, complementary **1**. □□ **coordination** see ORGANIZATION **1**.

coot /kōōt/ n. **1** black aquatic bird with upper mandible extended on the forehead. **2** colloq. crotchety person.

coot•ie /kōōtee/ • n. sl. (usu. pl. **cooties**) a body louse.

cop /kop/ • n. police officer. • v.tr. (**copped, cop•ping**) **1** catch or arrest (an offender). **2** take; seize. □ **cop out** withdraw; renege. **cop a plea** sl. = plea-bargain.

■ n. see police officer. • v. **1** see ARREST v. **1**.

co•pa•cet•ic /kōpəsétik/ adj. sl. excellent; in good order.

cope¹ /kōp/ v.intr. deal effectively or contend with; manage.

■ (cope with) withstand, handle; see also DEAL v. **1**a.

cope² /kōp/ n. priest's cloaklike vestment.

cop•i•er /kópeeər/ n. machine that copies (esp. documents).

co•pi•lot /kópīlət/ n. second pilot in an aircraft.

cop•ing /kóping/ n. top (usu. sloping) course of wall masonry.

co•pi•ous /kópeeəs/ adj. **1** abundant. **2** productive. See synonym study at PREVALENT. □□ **co′pi•ous•ly** adv. **co′pi•ous•ness** n.

■ **1** see abundant (ABUNDANCE). **2** see PROFUSE **2**.

cop•per /kópər/ • n. **1** malleable, red-brown metallic element. ¶Symb.: **Cu**. **2** bronze coin. • adj. made of or colored like copper.

cop•per•head /kópərhed/ n. venomous N. American or Australian snake.

co•pra /kóprə/ n. dried kernels of the coconut.

copse /kops/ n. small dense forest.

cop•ter /kóptər/ n. helicopter.

cop•u•la /kópyələ/ n. (pl. **cop•u•las** or **cop•u•lae** /–lee/) Gram. connecting word, esp. a part of the verb be connecting subject and predicate. □□ **cop′u•lar** adj.

cop•u•late /kópyəlayt/ v.intr. have sexual intercourse. □□ **cop•u•la′tion** /–láyshən/ n.

■ see MATE¹ v. **2**.

cop•u•la•tive /kópyəlaytiv, –lətiv/ adj. **1** serving to connect. **2** Gram. **a** (of a word) that connects words or clauses linked in sense. **b** connecting a subject and predicate. **3** relating to sexual union. □□ **cop′u•la•tive•ly** adv.

cop•y /kópee/ • n. (pl. **–ies**) **1** thing made to imitate another. **2** issue of a publication. **3** matter to be printed (scandals make good copy). • v.tr. (**–ies, –ied**) **1** make a copy of. **2** do the same as; imitate. See synonym study at IMITATE.

■ n. **1** reproduction, replica, facsimile, likeness, duplication, duplicate, transcript, replication. **3** text, writing, material. • v. **1** reproduce, duplicate, replicate, transcribe; see also IMITATE **3**. **2** mimic, impersonate, emulate, ape, echo; see also IMITATE **1**, **2**.

cop•y•cat /kópeekat/ n. colloq. imitator.

■ see MIMIC n.

cop•y•right /kópeerīt/ • n. exclusive legal right to print, publish, perform, film, or record material. • adj. (of such material) protected by copyright. • v.tr. secure copyright for (material).

cop•y•writ•er /kópeerītər/ n. person who writes or edits (esp. advertising) copy for publication. □□ **cop′y•writ•ing** n.

co•quette /kōkét/ n. woman who flirts. □□ **co•quet′tish** adj. **co•quet′tish•ly** adv. **co•quet′tish•ness** n.

■ see FLIRT n. **1**.

cor- /kər/ prefix assim. form of COM-before r.

cor•al /káwrəl, kór–/ • n. **1** hard red, pink, or white calcareous substance secreted by marine polyps. **2** any of these usu. colonial organisms. • adj. **1** like coral, esp. in color. **2** made of coral. □ **coral snake** brightly colored poisonous snake of the southeastern US.

cor•bel /káwrbəl, –bel/ • n. jutting support of stone, timber, etc. • v. [foll. by out, off] support or project on corbels.

cord /kawrd/ n. **1 a** long, thin, flexible material made from several twisted strands. **b** piece of this. **2** body structure resembling a cord (spinal cord). **3 a** ribbed fabric, esp. corduroy. **b** [in pl.] corduroy trousers. **4** unit of cut firewood (usu. 128 cu.ft.).

■ **1** line, twine, rope; see also STRING n. **1**, **2**.

cor•dial /káwrjəl/ • adj. heartfelt; warm, friendly. • n. a liqueur. □□ **cor•di•al•i•ty** /–jeeálitee/ n. **cor′dial•ly** adv.

■ adj. affable, amiable, kindly, genial, gracious, welcoming, pleasant, courteous, polite.

cord•ite /káwrdīt/ n. smokeless explosive.

cord•less /káwrdlis/ adj. (of an electrical appliance, etc.) not connected by wire to an external source of energy, data, etc.

cor•don /káwrd′n/ n. **1** protective line or circle of police, soldiers, guards, etc. **2** ornamental cord or braid. • v.tr. enclose or separate with a cordon of police, etc.

■ n. **2** see BRAID n. **1**.

cor•du•roy /káwrdəroy/ n. 1 thick cotton fabric with velvety ribs. 2 [in pl.] corduroy trousers.

core /kawr/ • n. 1 central part of various fruits, containing the seeds. 2 central or most important part of anything. 3 central region of the earth. • v.tr. remove the core from.
■ n. 1 kernel, pith, stone, pip(s). 2 essence, marrow, heart, pith, quintessence, substance, crux.

co•re•spon•dent /kó-rispóndənt/ n. person cited in a divorce case as having committed adultery with the respondent.

cor•gi /káwrgee/ n. (pl. **cor•gis**) (in full **Welsh corgi**) short-legged dog with a foxlike head.

co•ri•an•der /káwreeándər/ n. 1 aromatic herb of the carrot family. 2 its seeds used for flavoring.

Co•rin•thi•an /kərintheeən/ adj. Archit. of an ornate order characterized by flared capitals with rows of acanthus leaves.

cork /kawrk/ • n. 1 buoyant light-brown bark of a S. European oak. 2 bottle stopper, esp. of cork. • adj. made of cork. • v.tr. stop up, as with a cork.
■ n. 2 see STOPPER n. • v. see PLUG v. 1.

cork•screw /káwrkskrōō/ • n. 1 spiral device for extracting corks from bottles. 2 thing with a spiral shape. • v. move spirally; twist.

corm /kawrm/ n. Bot. underground swollen stem base of some plants, e.g., crocus.

cor•mo•rant /káwrmərənt, -mərant/ n. diving black sea bird.

corn[1] /kawrn/ • n. 1 a cereal plant bearing kernels on a long ear (cob). b cobs or kernels of this plant. 2 colloq. something corny or trite. • v.tr. (as **corned** adj.) preserved with salt or brine (corned beef).
■ n. 2 see sentimentality (SENTIMENTAL). • v. (corned) see SALT adj.

corn[2] /kawrn/ n. tender area of horny skin, esp. on the toe.

corn•ball /kórnbawl/ • n. mawkishly sentimental person. • adj. = CORNY 1.

corn•cob /káwrnkaab/ n. cylindrical center of a corn ear.

cor•ne•a /káwrneeə/ n. transparent covering of the front of the eyeball. □□ **cor′ne•al** adj.

cor•ner /káwrnər/ • n. 1 place where sides or edges meet. 2 projecting angle, esp. where two streets meet. 3 internal space or recess formed by the meeting of two sides, esp. of a room. 4 difficult position. 5 secluded or remote place. 6 monopoly on a stock or commodity. • v. 1 tr. force into a difficult or inescapable position. 2 tr. establish a monopoly in. 3 intr. (esp. of or in a vehicle) go around a corner.
■ n. 1, 2 see ANGLE[1] n. 2. 3 see NOOK. 4 see HOLE n. 5. • v. 1 see TRAP v. 1, 2. 2 see MONOPOLIZE. 3 see TURN v. 3b.

cor•ner•stone /káwrnərstōn/ n. 1 foundation stone at the corner of a building. 2 indispensable part or basis.
■ 2 see KEYSTONE.

cor•net /kawrnét/ n. brass instrument resembling a trumpet but shorter and wider. □□ **cor•net′ist** or **cor•net′tist** n.

corn•flow•er /káwrnflowər/ n. plant with deep-blue flowers.

cor•nice /káwrnis/ n. ornamental molding just below the ceiling.

corn•meal /káwrnmeel/ n. coarsely ground corn.

corn•row /kórnrō/ n. any of usu. several narrow plaits of hair braided close to the scalp.

corn•starch /káwrnstaarch/ n. fine-ground flour from corn.

cor•nu•co•pi•a /káwrnəkópeeə, -nyə-/ n. 1 symbol of plenty consisting of a goat's horn overflowing with flowers, fruit, etc. 2 abundant supply. □□ **cor•nu•co′pi•an** adj.
■ 2 see ABUNDANCE.

corn•y /káwrnee/ adj. (**corn•i•er**, **corn•i•est**) colloq. 1 feebly humorous. 2 tritely sentimental. □□ **corn′i•ly** adv. **corn′i•ness** n.
■ 1 see BANAL. 2 see SENTIMENTAL.

co•rol•la /kərólə, -rṓ-/ n. petals forming a flower.

cor•ol•lar•y /káwrəleree, kór-/ n. (pl. **-ies**) 1 proposition that follows from one already proved. 2 natural consequence.

co•ro•na /kərṓnə/ n. (pl. **co•ro•nas** or **co•ro•nae** /-nee/) 1 halo around the sun or moon. 2 rarefied gaseous envelope of the sun, seen during a total solar eclipse.
■ see HALO n. 2.

cor•o•nar•y /káwrəneree, kór-/ • adj. Anat. resembling or encircling like a crown • n. (pl. **-ies**) 1 = coronary thrombosis. 2 heart attack. □ **coronary artery** artery supplying blood to the heart. **coronary thrombosis** blockage caused by a blood clot in a coronary artery.

cor•o•na•tion /káwrənáyshən, kór-/ n. ceremony of crowning.

cor•o•ner /káwrənər, kór-/ n. officer holding inquests on deaths thought to be violent or accidental.

cor•o•net /káwranit, -nét, kór-/ n. small crown or band worn on the head. □□ **cor′o•net•ed** adj.
■ see CROWN n. 1.

Corp. abbr. 1 corporal. 2 corporation.

cor•po•ra pl. of CORPUS.

cor•po•ral[1] /káwrpərəl, -prəl/ n. noncommissioned officer ranking next below sergeant.

cor•po•ral[2] /káwrpərəl, -prəl/ adj. of the human body. □ **corporal punishment** physical punishment. □□ **cor′po•ral•ly** adv.
■ bodily, physical.

cor•po•rate /káwrpərət, -prit/ adj. 1 forming a corporation. 2 forming one body of many individuals.

cor•po•ra•tion /káwrpəráyshən/ n. group of people authorized to act as an individual, esp. in business.
■ see COMPANY n. 3.

cor•po•re•al /kawrpáwreeəl/ adj. bodily; physical; material. See synonym study at TANGIBLE. ■ □□ **cor•po•re•al•i•ty** /-reeálitee/ n. **cor•po′re•al•ly** adv.
■ see PHYSICAL 1.

corps /kawr/ n. (pl. **corps** /kawrz/) 1 military body or subdivision with special duties. 2 body of people engaged in a special activity.

■ **1** troop(s), cadre, unit, detachment, cohort, battalion, brigade, platoon, squad, squadron.

corpse /kawrps/ n. dead body.

■ remains, cadaver, carcass.

cor•pu•lent /káwrpyələnt/ adj. bulky in body; fat. □□ **cor′pu•lence** n.

■ see FAT adj. 1.

cor•pus /káwrpəs/ n. (pl. **cor•po•ra** /káwr-pərə/ or **corpuses**) body or collection of writings, texts, etc.

cor•pus•cle /káwrpusəl/ n. minute body in an organism, esp. a red or white cell in the blood of vertebrates. □□ **cor•pus•cu•lar** /kawrpúskyələr/ adj.

corr. abbr. **1** correction. **2** correspondence.

cor•ral /kərál/ • n. pen for cattle, horses, etc. • v.tr. (**cor•ralled**, **cor•ral•ling**) **1** put or keep in a corral. **2** colloq. gather in; acquire.

■ n. see PEN² n. • v. **1** see PEN² v.

cor•rect /kərékt/ • adj. **1** true; right; accurate. **2** proper; in accordance with good standards of taste, etc. • v.tr. **1** set right; amend. **2** mark errors in. **3 a** admonish (a person). **b** punish (a person or fault). **4** counteract (a harmful quality). □□ **cor•rect′ly** adv. **cor•rect′ness** n.

■ adj. **1** precise, exact, factual, valid. **2** decorous, decent, appropriate, (socially) acceptable, suitable, fitting, befitting. • v. **1** redress, rectify, remedy, repair, fix, cure. **2** revise, edit. **3 a** scold, rebuke, reprimand, berate, reprove, castigate, chastise. **b** chasten, discipline; see also PUNISH 1. **4** reverse, offset, counterbalance, neutralize, nullify, make up for, annul.

cor•rec•tion /kərékshən/ n. **1 a** correcting. **b** instance of this. **2** thing substituted for what is wrong. **3** program of punishment, esp. of convicted offenders. □□ **cor•rec′tion•al** adj.

■ **1** emendation, rectification, redress, reparation, amendment; improvement.

cor•rec•tive /kəréktiv/ • adj. serving to correct or counteract something undesired or harmful. • n. corrective measure or thing. □□ **cor•rec′tive•ly** adv.

■ adj. see THERAPEUTIC 1. • n. see ANTIDOTE 2.

cor•re•late /káwrəlayt, kór-/ • v. **1** intr. have a mutual relation. **2** tr. bring into a mutual relation. • n. each of two complements. □□ **cor•re•la′tion** n. **cor•re•la′tion•al** adj.

■ v. see RELATE 3.

cor•rel•a•tive /kərélətiv/ • adj. **1** having a mutual relation. **2** Gram. used together (as neither and nor). • n. correlative word or thing. □□ **cor•rel′a•tive•ly** adv. **cor•rel•a•tiv′i•ty** n.

■ adj. **1** see RECIPROCAL adj. 2.

cor•re•spond /káwrispónd, kór-/ v.intr. **1 a** be analogous or similar (to). **b** be in agreement with. **2** exchange letters with. □□ **cor•re•spond′ing•ly** adv.

■ **1** be alike; conform, tally, comply, accord, harmonize, be congruous, coincide; (correspond to) match. **2** write (letters), communicate.

cor•re•spon•dence /káwrispóndəns, kór-/

n. **1** agreement, similarity, or harmony. **2 a** communication by letters. **b** letters.

■ **1** see ACCORD n. 1. **2** see LETTER n. 2.

cor•re•spond•ent /káwrispóndənt, kór-/ n. **1** person who writes letters. **2** reporter or news source. □□ **cor•re•spond′ent•ly** adv.

■ **2** journalist, newsperson, colloq. stringer.

cor•ri•dor /káwridər, –dor, kór-/ n. **1** passage giving access into rooms, compartments, etc. **2** strip of the territory of one nation passing through that of another.

■ **1** hallway, passageway, hall.

cor•rob•o•rate /kərábərayt/ v.tr. confirm or give support to (a statement or belief, etc.). □□ **cor•rob•o•ra′tion** /–ráyshən/ n. **cor•rob•o•ra•tive** /–rətiv, –ráytiv/ adj. **cor•rob′o•ra•tor** n.

■ see SUBSTANTIATE.

cor•rode /kəród/ v. **1 a** tr. wear away, esp. by chemical action. **b** intr. be worn away. **2** tr. destroy gradually. □□ **cor•rod′i•ble** adj.

■ **1** see WEAR v. 5.

cor•ro•sion /kərózhən/ n. **1** corroding. **2** damage caused by corroding. □□ **cor•ro•sive** /–siv/ adj. **cor•ro′sive•ly** adv. **cor•ro′sive•ness** n.

cor•ru•gate /káwrəgayt, kór-/ v.tr. (esp. as **corrugated** adj.) form into ridges and grooves. □□ **cor•ru•ga′tion** /–gáyshən/ n.

cor•rupt /kərúpt/ • adj. **1** morally depraved; wicked. **2** influenced by or using bribery or fraudulent activity. **3** (of a text, etc.) harmed by errors or alterations. See synonym study at DEPRAVED. • v. make or become corrupt. □□ **cor•rup′ter** n. **cor•rupt′i•ble** adj. **cor•rupt•i•bil′i•ty** n. **cor•rup′tive** adj. **cor•rupt′ly** adv. **cor•rupt′ness** n.

■ adj. **1** debased, perverted, evil; see also DEGENERATE adj. **2** dishonest, untrustworthy, dishonorable, underhand(ed), venal, colloq. crooked. • v. subvert, degrade, deprave, warp; bribe; infect, contaminate, pollute, taint, defile, spoil, poison, adulterate.

cor•rup•tion /kərúpshən/ n. **1** moral deterioration. **2** use of corrupt practices, esp. bribery or fraud. **3** irregular alteration (of a text, language, etc.) from its original state. **4** rot; decay.

■ **1** see SIN¹ n. 1. **2** see GRAFT². **3** see MISUSE n. **4** see ROT n. 1.

cor•sage /kawrsáazh/ n. small bouquet worn by a woman.

cor•sair /káwrsair/ n. **1** pirate ship. **2** pirate.

cor•set /káwrsit/ n. closely fitting undergarment worn for support. □□ **cor′set•ed** adj.

cor•tex /káwrteks/ n. (pl. **cor•ti•ces** /–tiseez/ or **cor•tex•es**) outer part of an organ, esp. of the brain (**cerebral cortex**) or kidneys (**renal cortex**). □□ **cor•ti•cal** /káwrtikəl/ adj.

cor•ti•sone /káwrtisōn, –zōn/ n. hormone used esp. against inflammation and allergy.

co•run•dum /kərúndəm/ n. extremely hard crystallized alumina, used esp. as an abrasive or as a gemstone.

cor•us•cate /káwrəskayt, kór-/ v.intr. sparkle. □□ **cor•us•ca′tion** /–káyshən/ n.

cor•vette /kawrvét/ n. small naval escort vessel.

cos¹ /kaws, kos/ n. long-headed variety of lettuce; romaine.

cos² /kos, koz/ *abbr.* cosine.

co•sec /kósek/ *abbr.* cosecant.

co•se•cant /kōséekant, –kənt/ *n.* Math. ratio of the hypotenuse (in a right triangle) to the side opposite an acute angle.

co•sign /kósīn/ *v.tr.* sign (a promissory note) jointly with another person. □□ **co′sign•er** *n.*

co•sig•na•to•ry /kōsígnətáwree/ *n.* (*pl.* **–ries**) party signing (a treaty, etc.) jointly.

co•sine /kósīn/ *n.* Math. ratio of the side adjacent to an acute angle (in a right triangle) to the hypotenuse.

cos•met•ic /kozmétik/ • *adj.* **1** enhancing; beautifying. **2** only superficially improving. **3** (of surgery or a prosthesis) imitating, restoring, or enhancing normal appearance. • *n.* cosmetic preparation, esp. for the face. □□ **cos•met′i•cal•ly** *adv.*
■ *adj.* **2** see SUPERFICIAL 4.

cos•me•tol•o•gy /kozmətóləjee/ *n.* the art and technique of using cosmetics. □□ **cos•me′tol•o•gist** *n.*

cos•mic /kózmik/ *adj.* of the universe or cosmos, esp. as distinct from the earth. See synonym study at UNIVERSAL. □□ **cos′mi•cal** *adj.* **cos′mi•cal•ly** *adv.*
■ see UNIVERSAL *adj.*

cos•mog•o•ny /kozmógənee/ *n.* (*pl.* **–nies**) **1** origin of the universe. **2** theory about this. □□ **cos•mo•gon•ic** /–məgónik/ *adj.* **cos•mo•gon′i•cal** *adj.* **cos•mog•o•nist** /–móg–/ *n.*

cos•mol•o•gy /kozmóləjee/ *n.* science of the origin of the universe. □□ **cos•mo•log•i•cal** /–mələójikəl/ *adj.* **cos•mol•o•gist** /–mól–/ *n.*

cos•mo•naut /kózmənawt/ *n.* Russian or Soviet astronaut.

cos•mo•pol•i•tan /kózməpólit'n/ • *adj.* of, from, or knowing many parts of the world. See synonym study at COSMOPOLITAN. • *n.* cosmopolitan person. □□ **cos•mo•pol′i•tan•ism** *n.*

cos•mos /kózmos, –məs, –mos/ *n.* the universe, esp. as a well-ordered whole.
■ see UNIVERSE 1a.

Cos•sack /kósak/ *n.* hist. **1** member of a people of southern Russia. **2** member of a Cossack military unit.

cost /kawst/ • *v.tr.* (*past and past part.* **cost**) **1** be obtainable for (a sum); have as a price. **2** involve as a loss or sacrifice (*it cost me my job*). • *n.* **1** what a thing costs; price. **2** loss or sacrifice. □ **at all costs** (or **at any cost**) no matter what. **cost-benefit** assessing the cost of an operation and the value of the resulting benefits. **cost-effective** effective or productive in relation to its cost. **cost of living** level of prices, esp. of the basic necessities of life.
■ *v.* **1** sell for, get, fetch, bring in. • *n.* **1** payment, charge, cost, expenditure; outlay. **2** see LOSS 1.

cost•ly /káwstlee/ *adj.* (**cost•li•er, cost•li•est**) **1** costing much; expensive. **2** of great value. □□ **cost′li•ness** *n.*
■ **1** see EXPENSIVE. **2** see PRECIOUS *adj.* 1.

cos•tume /kóstoōm, –tyoōm/ • *n.* **1** style of dress, esp. of a particular place, time, or class. **2** set of clothes. **3** clothing for a particular activity or role. • *v.tr.* provide with a

costume. □ **costume jewelry** jewelry made of artificial or inexpensive materials.
■ *n.* **1, 2** garb, garments, outfit, vestment; raiment, attire, apparel. • *v.* see DRESS *v.* 1a.

cot¹ /kot/ *n.* small folding or portable bed.

cot² /kot/ *abbr.* Math. cotangent.

co•tan•gent /kōtánjənt/ *n.* Math. ratio of the side adjacent to an acute angle (in a right triangle) to the opposite side.

cote /kōt/ *n.* shelter, esp. for animals or birds.

co•te•rie /kótəree/ *n.* exclusive clique or circle.

co•ter•mi•nous /kōtórminəs/ *adj.* having the same boundaries or extent (in space, time, or meaning).
■ coextensive

co•til•lion /kətílyən/ *n.* **1** formal ball. **2** ballroom dance resembling a quadrille.

cot•tage /kótij/ *n.* small, simple house, esp. in the country. □ **cottage cheese** soft white cheese made from milk curds. **cottage industry** business activity carried on at home.
■ hut, cabin, bungalow, lodge, chalet, shanty.

cot•ter /kótər/ *n.* **1** securing bolt or wedge. **2** (in full **cotter pin**) split pin that opens after passing through a hole.

cot•ton /kót'n/ • *n.* **1** soft, white fibrous substance covering the seeds of certain plants. **2** such a plant, esp. one cultivated for its fiber or seeds. **3** [*attrib.*] made of cotton. • *v.intr.* [foll. by *to*] be attracted by. □ **cotton candy** fluffy mass of spun sugar. **cotton gin** machine for separating cotton from its seeds. **cotton-picking** sl. unpleasant; wretched. □□ **cot′ton•y** *adj.*

cot•ton•mouth /kót'nmowth/ *n.* venomous pit viper of the southeastern US.

cot•ton•tail /kót'ntayl/ *n.* fluffy-tailed N. American rabbit.

cot•ton•wood /kót'nwood/ *n.* N. American poplar, having seeds covered in cottony hairs.

cot•y•le•don /kót'leéd'n/ *n.* embryonic leaf in seed-bearing plants.

couch /kowch/ • *n.* upholstered piece of furniture for several people; sofa. • *v.tr.* [foll. by *in*] express in words of a specified kind (*couched in simple language*). □ **couch potato** sl. person who likes lazing, esp. watching television.
■ *n.* settee, divan, love-seat, davenport. • *v.* phrase, formulate; see also EXPRESS¹ 1, 2.

cou•gar /koógər/ *n.* puma.

cough /kawf, kof/ • *v.intr.* **1** expel air from the lungs with a sudden, sharp sound. **2** (of an engine, etc.) make a similar sound. • *n.* **1** act of coughing. **2** condition of the respiratory organs causing coughing. □ **cough drop** medicated lozenge to relieve a cough. **cough up** sl. bring out or give (money or information) reluctantly.

could *past* of CAN¹.

couldn't /kood'nt/ *contr.* could not.

cou•lomb /koólom/ *n.* Electr. unit of electric charge, equal to the quantity of electricity conveyed in one second by a current of one ampere. ¶Symb.: **C**.

coun•cil /kównsəl/ *n.* advisory, deliberative, or administrative body.

■ board, ministry, directors, cabinet, panel, committee, directorate; assembly, conclave, congress.

coun•cil•man /kównsəlmən/ *n.* (*pl.* –men; *fem.* **coun•cil•wom•an**, *pl.* **–wom•en**) member of a council.

coun•sel /kównsəl/ • *n.* 1 advice, esp. formally given. 2 (*pl.* same) legal adviser. • *v.tr.* 1 advise (a person). 2 give advice on personal problems, esp. professionally. 3 recommend (a course of action). □□ **coun′sel•ing** *n.*

■ *n.* 1 direction, opinion, guidance, instruction, recommendation. 2 counselor; lawyer, attorney. • *v.* 1 direct, instruct; see also ADVISE 1. 3 urge, exhort, advocate; see also SUGGEST 1.

coun•sel•or /kównsələr, –slər/ *n.* 1 adviser; professional guide. 2 lawyer.

■ 2 counsel, attorney.

count¹ /kównt/ • *v.* 1 *tr.* determine, esp. one by one, the total number of. 2 *intr.* repeat numbers in order. 3 **a** *tr.* include. **b** *intr.* be included. 4 *tr.* consider (a thing or a person) to be (lucky, etc.). 5 *intr.* have value; matter (*his opinion counts for a great deal*). • *n.* 1 **a** counting; reckoning. **b** total of a reckoning (*pollen count*). 2 *Law* each charge in an indictment. □ **count one's blessings** be grateful for what one has. **count one's chickens** be hasty in anticipating good fortune. **count down** recite numbers backward to zero. **count on** (or **upon**) depend on. **count out** *colloq.* exclude from. **down for the count** 1 *Boxing* defeated by being unable to rise within ten seconds. 2 **a** defeated or demoralized. **b** asleep.

■ *v.* 1 enumerate, calculate, add up, total, reckon, compute, tally, figure (out). 3 **a** consider. 4 see CONSIDER 6. 5 see MATTER *v.* □ **count on** (or **upon**) rely on *or* upon, be sure of, trust, bank on. **count out** see EXCLUDE 2 **b** sleeping like a baby; see also *dead to the world*.

count² /kównt/ *n.* noble corresponding to a British earl.

count•a•ble /kówntəbəl/ *adj.* that can be counted.

count•down /kówntdown/ *n.* 1 act of counting down. 2 final moments before any significant event.

coun•te•nance /kówntinəns/ • *n.* 1 **a** the face. **b** facial expression. 2 composure. • *v.tr.* give approval to (an act, etc.).

■ *n.* 1 **a** see FACE *n.* 1. **b** see EXPRESSION 4. • *v.* see APPROVE.

counter¹ /kówntər/ *n.* 1 **a** long, flat-topped fixture in a store, etc., across which business is conducted. **b** similar structure used for serving food, etc. 2 **a** small disk used in board games. **b** token representing a coin. 3 apparatus used for counting. □ **over the counter** 1 (of stock) sold through a broker directly. 2 by ordinary retail purchase. **under the counter** surreptitiously, esp. sold illegally.

■ 1 table, bar; desk. 2 **a, b** chip, piece, marker. □ **under the counter** see *on the sly* (SLY), *illegally* (ILLEGAL).

counter² /kówntər/ • *v.* 1 *tr.* **a** oppose; contradict. **b** meet by countermove. 2 *intr.* **a** make a countermove. **b** make an opposing statement. 3 *intr. Boxing* give a return blow. • *adv.* in the opposite direction or manner. • *adj.* 1 opposite. 2 duplicate; serving as a check. • *n.* 1 countermove. 2 something opposite. □ **run counter to** act contrary to.

counter- /kówntər/ *comb. form* denoting: 1 retaliation, opposition, or rivalry (*counterthreat*). 2 opposite direction (*counterclockwise*). 3 correspondence (*counterpart*).

coun•ter•act /kówntərákt/ *v.tr.* hinder or neutralize by contrary action. □□ **coun•ter•ac•tion** /-ákshən/ *n.* **coun•ter•ac′tive** *adj.*

■ counterbalance, annul, nullify, cancel, mitigate; see also HINDER, OPPOSE 1.

coun•ter•at•tack • *n.* /kówntərətak/ attack in reply to an attack. • *v.* /kówntərəták/ attack in reply.

■ *v.* see OPPOSE 1.

coun•ter•bal•ance • *n.* /kówntərbaləns/ weight or influence balancing another. • *v.tr.* /kówntərbáləns/ act as a counterbalance to.

■ *n.* see OFFSET *n.* • *v.* see BALANCE *v.* 2.

coun•ter•clock•wise /kówntərklókwiz/ *adv. & adj.* circling in a direction opposite to the movement of the hands of a clock.

coun•ter•cul•ture /kówntərkulchər/ *n.* way of life, etc., opposed to that usually considered normal.

coun•ter•es•pi•o•nage /kówntəréspeeənaazh, –nij/ *n.* action taken to frustrate enemy spying.

coun•ter•feit /kówntərfit/ • *adj.* made in imitation; not genuine; forged. See synonym study at SPURIOUS. • *n.* forgery; imitation. • *v.tr.* imitate fraudulently; forge. □□ **coun′ter•feit•er** *n.*

■ *adj.* fake, fraudulent, bogus, spurious, sham, *colloq.* phony; make-believe, feigned, insincere, artificial. • *n.* fake, reproduction. • *v.* falsify; reproduce; simulate.

coun•ter•in•tel•li•gence /kówntərintélijəns/ *n.* = COUNTERESPIONAGE.

coun•ter•mand • *v.tr.* /kówntərmánd/ revoke (an order or command). • *n.* /kówntərmand/ order revoking a previous one.

■ *v.* see CANCEL *v.* 1.

coun•ter•meas•ure /kówntərmezhər/ *n.* action taken to counteract a danger, threat, etc.

coun•ter•pane /kówntərpayn/ *n.* bedspread.

coun•ter•part /kówntərpaart/ *n.* 1 complement or equivalent to another. 2 duplicate, esp. of a document.

■ 1 see MATCH¹ *n.* 2b.

coun•ter•point • *n.* /kówntərpoynt/ 1 *Mus.* **a** art or technique of combining melodies according to fixed rules. **b** melody played in conjunction with another. 2 contrasting argument, theme, etc., used to set off the main element. • *v.tr.* 1 *Mus.* add counterpoint to. 2 set (an argument, etc.) in contrast to (a main element).

coun•ter•poise • *n.* /kówntərpoyz/ 1 counterbalance. 2 state of equilibrium. • *v.tr.*

/kównt∂rpóyz/ **1** counterbalance. **2** compensate.

coun•ter•pro•duc•tive /kównt∂rpr∂dúktiv/ adj. having the opposite of the desired effect.

coun•ter•rev•o•lu•tion /kównt∂rrèv∂lóōshən/ n. revolution opposing a former one or reversing its results. □□ **coun´ter•rev•o•lu´ tion•ar•y** adj. & n. (pl. **–ies**).

coun•ter•sign /kównt∂rsīn/ • v.tr. add a ratifying signature to (a document). • n. watchword or password. □□ **coun•ter•sig•na´ ture** /–sígn∂chər/ n.

■ v. see SIGN v. 1, ENDORSE 2. • n. see PASSWORD.

coun•ter•sink /kównt∂rsíngk/ v.tr. (past and past part. **–sunk**) **1** enlarge and bevel (the rim of a hole) so that a screw or bolt can be inserted flush with the surface. **2** sink (a screw, etc.) in such a hole.

coun•ter•ten•or /kównt∂rtenər/ n. **1** highest adult male singing voice. **2** singer with this voice.

coun•ter•top /kównt∂rtop/ n. horizontal, flat work surface, as in a kitchen.

coun•ter•vail /kównt∂rváyl/ v. **1** tr. counterbalance. **2** tr. & intr. oppose forcefully and usu. successfully.

coun•ter•weight /kównt∂rwayt/ n. counterbalancing weight.

count•ess /kówntis/ n. **1** wife or widow of a count or an earl. **2** woman holding the rank of count or earl.

count•less /kówntlis/ adj. too many to be counted.

coun•tri•fied /kúntrifīd/ adj. rustic, esp. of manners, appearance, etc.

■ see RUSTIC adj. 2.

coun•try /kúntree/ n. (pl. **–tries**) **1** nation or its territory. **2** [often attrib.] rural area. **3** land of a person's birth or citizenship. **4** region associated with a particular person, feature, etc. (Elvis country; mountain country). **5** national population, esp. as voters. □ **country and western** popular music originating in the southern US. **country club** golfing and social club. **country cousin** often derog. countrified person.

■ **1** state, power. **2** countryside. **3** (native) land, homeland, fatherland, motherland, mother country. **4** see TERRITORY 1, SPHERE n. 3. **5** see POPULATION 1.

coun•try•man /kúntreemən/ n. (pl. **–men**) fem. **coun•try•wom•an**, pl. **–wom•en**) person of one's own country.

coun•try•side /kúntreesīd/ n. **1** rural area. **2** rural areas in general.

coun•try•wide /kúntreewīd/ adj. extending throughout a nation.

coun•ty /kówntee/ n. (pl. **–ties**) **1** political and administrative division of a state, as in the US. **2** administrative divisions of some countries. □ **county seat** administrative capital of a county.

coup /kōō/ n. (pl. **coups** /kōōz/) **1** successful stroke or move. **2** = COUP D'ÉTAT.

■ **1** see TRIUMPH n. 1b.

coup de grâce /kōō də gráas/ n. finishing stroke, esp. to kill a wounded animal or person.

■ see KILL n. 1.

coup d'é•tat /kōō daytaá/ n. violent or illegal seizure of power.

■ see REVOLT n.

coupe /kōōp/ n. two-door car with a hard top.

cou•ple /kúpəl/ • n. **1 a** two. **b** about two (a couple of hours). **2 a** married or engaged pair. **b** pair of partners in a dance, etc. • v. **1** tr. link together. **2** tr. associate in thought or speech. **3** intr. copulate.

■ n. **1 a** pair, brace, yoke. **b** (a couple of) a few, a handful (of), one or three. **2** duo, twosome. • v. **1** join, connect, fasten, yoke, lock, combine, unite. **2** see ASSOCIATE v. 1. **3** see make love (LOVE).

cou•plet /kúplit/ n. two successive lines of verse, usu. rhyming and of the same length.

cou•pling /kúpling/ n. link connecting machinery parts, railroad cars, etc.

■ see JUNCTION 3.

cou•pon /kōōpon, kyōō–/ n. **1** discount voucher presented at purchase. **2** detachable ticket or form entitling holder to payment, goods, a discount, services, etc.

cour•age /kórij, kúr–/ n. ability to disregard fear; bravery.

■ valor, boldness, gallantry, dauntlessness, daring, fearlessness, heroism, nerve, pluck, colloq. grit, guts, spunk, sl. moxie.

cou•ra•geous /kəráyjəs/ adj. brave; fearless. □□ **cou•ra´geous•ly** adv.

■ valiant, valorous, bold, intrepid, unafraid, gallant, dauntless, undaunted, daring, heroic, plucky, audacious, stalwart, colloq. spunky, gutsy.

cou•ri•er /kóōreeər, kór–, kúr–/ n. special messenger.

■ see MESSENGER.

course /kawrs/ • n. **1** onward movement or progression. **2** direction taken. **3 a** ground on which a race, etc., takes place. **b** series of hurdles, etc., to be crossed in a race, etc. **4** series of lessons, etc., in a particular subject. **5** each successive part of a meal. **6** stretch of land or water. **7** line of conduct. **8** horizontal layer of brick, stone, etc. **9** water channel. • v.intr. (esp. of liquid) run, esp. fast. □ **in the course of** during. **matter of course** natural or expected thing. **of course** naturally; as is or was to be expected. **run its course** (esp. of an illness) complete its natural development.

■ n. **2** path, way, orbit, route, run, track, circuit. **4** class, seminar. **9** see CHANNEL n. 5a. • v. see RUN v. 11. □ **of course** certainly, positively, obviously, definitely, assuredly, by all means; undoubtedly, indubitably, without (a) doubt, absolutely, that goes without saying, needless to say.

court /kawrt/ • n. **1** (in full **court of law**) **a** judicial body hearing legal cases. **b** = COURTROOM. **2** quadrangular area for games. **3** = COURTYARD. **4** milieu or attendants of a sovereign. **5** attention paid to a person for favor. • v.tr. **1** try to win affection or favor of. **2** seek to win (applause, fame, etc.). **3** invite (misfortune) by one's actions (courting disaster).

■ n. **1 a** see TRIBUNAL 2. **4** see TRAIN n. 3. •

v. **1** woo, seek the hand of, set one's cap at, go after, pursue; see also CULTIVATE 3b.

cour•te•ous /kárteeəs/ *adj.* polite; considerate. □□ **cour′te•ous•ly** *adv.* **cour′te•ous•ness** *n.*

■ well-mannered, well-behaved, urbane, civilized, respectful, civil.

cour•te•san /káwrtizán/ *n. literary* **1** prostitute, esp. for wealthy clients. **2** mistress of a wealthy man.

cour•te•sy /kártisee/ *n.* (*pl.* **-sies**) courteous behavior or act.

■ politeness, courteousness, respect, respectfulness, good manners, civility.

court•house /káwrthows/ *n.* **1** judicial building. **2** county administrative building.

cour•ti•er /káwrteeər/ *n.* person who attends or frequents a sovereign's court.

court•ly /káwrtlee/ *adj.* (**court•li•er, court•li•est**) polished or refined in manners. □□ **court′li•ness** *n.*

■ see *polished* (POLISH *v.* 2).

court-mar•tial /káwrt máarshəl/ • *n.* (*pl.* **courts-mar•tial**) military judicial court. • *v.tr.* try by court-martial.

court•room /káwrtrōom, -rŏŏm/ *n.* room in which a court of law meets.

court•ship /káwrtship/ *n.* **1** process or period of courting with a view to marriage. **2** courting behavior of animals, birds, etc.

court•yard /káwrtyaard/ *n.* area enclosed by walls or buildings.

■ see AREA 2.

cous•cous /kŏŏskŏŏs/ *n.* N. African dish of semolina steamed over broth, often with meat or fruit added.

cous•in /kúzan/ *n.* **1** (also **first cousin**) child of one's uncle or aunt. **2** person of kindred race or nation. □ **second cousin** child of one's parent's first cousin.

cou•ture /kŏŏtŏŏr, -tүr/ *n.* design and manufacture of fashionable clothes.

cou•tu•ri•er /kŏŏtŏŏree-ay, -eeər/ *n.* (*fem.* **cou•tu•ri•ère** /-reeáir/) fashion designer.

co•va•len•cy /kóváylənsee/ *n. Chem.* **1** linking of atoms by a bond of shared electrons. **2** number of pairs of electrons an atom can share with another. □□ **co•va′lent** *adj.*

cove /kōv/ *n.* **1** small, esp. sheltered, bay or creek. **2** sheltered recess.

co•ven /kúvən/ *n.* assembly of witches.

cov•e•nant /kúvənənt/ • *n.* **1** agreement; contract. **2** *Law* sealed contract, esp. a deed of covenant. **3** (**Covenant**) *Bibl.* agreement between God and the Israelites. • *v.* agree, esp. by legal covenant. □□ **cov•e•nan•tal** /-nánt′l/ *adj.* **cov′e•nan•tor** *n.*

■ *n.* **1, 2** see AGREEMENT 3. • *v.* see UNDERTAKE 2.

cov•er /kúvər/ *v.tr.* **1** protect or conceal with a cloth, lid, etc. **2 a** extend over the surface of. **b** strew thickly or thoroughly. **c** lie over. **3** protect; clothe. **4** include; comprise; deal with. **5** travel (a specified distance). **6** *Journalism* investigate or describe as a reporter. **7** be enough to defray (expenses, etc.). **8 a** *refl.* protect oneself. **b** [*absol.*; foll. by *for*] stand in for (*will you cover for me?*). **9 a** aim a

gun, etc., at. **b** (of a fortress, etc.) command (a territory). **c** protect (an exposed person, etc.) with a gun, etc. • *n.* **1** something that covers, esp.: **a** a lid. **b** binding of a book. **c** envelope or wrapping (*under separate cover*). **d** [in *pl.*] bedclothes. **2** shelter. **3 a** pretense; screen. **b** pretended identity. **c** *Mil.* force protecting an advance party from attack. □ **cover charge** charge levied per head in a restaurant, nightclub, etc. **cover crop** crop grown for protection and enrichment of the soil. **cover girl** female model appearing on magazine covers, etc. **cover letter** explanatory letter sent with an enclosure. **cover story** news story in a magazine, as illustrated on the front cover. **cover up** conceal (circumstances, etc., esp. illicitly). **cover-up** *n.* act of concealing circumstances, esp. illicitly. **take cover** find shelter, esp. against an attack.

■ *v.* **1** bury, mask, shroud, obscure; enclose, envelop, wrap, swaddle; see also HIDE[1] *v.* 4. **2 a** overlie, overspread, lie on, coat, blanket. **b** see STREW[1]. **3** shelter, shield, screen; sheathe. **4** comprehend, take in, contain, embody, incorporate, account for, take into account. **5** traverse, complete, pass over, cross. **7** pay *or* compensate for; offset, make up for. **8 b** deputize, take over responsibility, sit in, substitute, run things, hold the fort. **9 b** guard, defend. • *n.* **1 a** top, cap, covering. **b** dust jacket, jacket. **d** (*covers*) blankets, bedding, (bed) linen, quilt, comforter. **2** hiding place, hideout, retreat, refuge. **3 a** cloak, disguise, front, camouflage, smokescreen. □ **cover up** see CONCEAL 2, HIDE *v.* 3. **cover-up** see PRETENSE 2.

cov•er•age /kúvərij/ *n.* **1** area or amount covered. **2** amount of publicity received by a particular story, person, event, etc.

cov•er•all /kúvərawl/ *n.* [usu. in *pl.*] full-length protective garment.

cov•er•let /kúvərlit/ *n.* bedspread.

co•vert /kóvərt, kú-/ • *adj.* secret or disguised (*covert glance*). • *n.* shelter, esp. a thicket hiding game. □□ **co′vert•ly** *adv.* **co′vert•ness** *n.*

■ *adj.* see SECRET *adj.* 2. • *n.* see THICKET.

cov•et /kúvit/ *v.tr.* desire greatly (another's possession, attribute, etc.). □□ **cov′et•a•ble** *adj.*

■ see DESIRE *v.* 1.

cov•et•ous /kúvitəs/ *adj.* coveting; grasping. See synonym study at GREEDY. See synonym study at JEALOUS. □□ **cov′et•ous•ly** *adv.* **cov′et•ous•ness** *n.*

■ see *hungry* (HUNGER), *avaricious* (AVARICE).

cov•ey /kúvee/ *n.* (*pl.* **-eys**) **1** brood of partridges. **2** small group of people, etc.

■ **2** see GROUP *n.*

cow[1] /kow/ *n.* **1** grown female of any bovine animal, used esp. as a source of milk and beef. **2** female of other large animals, esp. the elephant, whale, and seal. □ **till the cows come home** *colloq.* an indefinitely long time.

cow[2] /kow/ *v.tr.* intimidate; dispirit.

■ see INTIMIDATE.

cow•ard /kówərd/ *n.* person easily frightened or intimidated.

■ *n.* poltroon, mouse, milksop, *colloq.* sissy.

cow•ard•ice /ˈkówərdis/ *n.* lack of bravery.

■ faintheartedness, timidity, pusillanimity.

cow•ard•ly /ˈkówərdlee/ *adj.* **1** lacking courage. **2** (of an action) done against one who cannot retaliate. □□ **cow′ard•li•ness** *n.*

■ **1** timid, fainthearted, timorous, chicken-hearted, chicken-livered, lily-livered, craven, pusillanimous, *colloq.* yellow, yellow-bellied, chicken.

cow•boy /ˈkówboy/ *n.* **1** (*fem.* **cow•girl**) person who tends cattle. **2** *colloq.* unscrupulous or reckless person in business.

cow•catch•er /ˈkówkachər/ *n.* peaked metal frame at the front of a locomotive for pushing aside obstacles.

cow•er /ˈkowər/ *v.intr.* crouch or shrink in fear. See synonym study at WINCE.

■ see CRINGE *v.* 1.

cow•hand /ˈkówhand/ *n.* = COWBOY 1.

cow•hide /ˈkówhīd/ *n.* **1** cow's hide; leather. **2** whip made from this.

cowl /kowl/ *n.* **1** monk's hooded habit. **2** a loose hood of a monk's cowl. **b** any such hood. □□ **cowled** *adj.* (in sense 1).

cow•lick /ˈkówlik/ *n.* projecting lock of hair.

cowl•ing /ˈkówling/ *n.* removable cover of a vehicle or aircraft engine.

co•work•er /kōˈwórkər/ *n.* person who works with another.

■ see COLLEAGUE.

cow•poke /ˈkówpōk/ *n.* = COWBOY 1.

cow•pox /ˈkówpoks/ *n.* disease of cows, whose virus was formerly used in smallpox vaccination.

cox•comb /ˈkókskōm/ *n.* ostentatiously conceited person.

cox•swain /ˈkóksən, -swayn/ *n.* person who steers and directs the crew, esp. in a rowing boat.

coy /koy/ *adj.* (**coy•er, coy•est**) **1** modestly or affectedly shy. **2** irritatingly reticent. □□ **coy′ly** *adv.* **coy′ness** *n.*

■ **1** diffident, demure. **2** reluctant, evasive.

coy•o•te /īəˈyōtee, kīˈyōt/ *n.* (*pl.* same or **coy•otes**) N. American wolflike wild dog.

coz•en /ˈkúzən/ *v. literary* **1** *tr.* cheat; defraud. **2** *tr.* beguile; persuade. **3** *intr.* act deceitfully. □□ **coz′en•age** *n.*

co•zy /ˈkōzee/ • *adj.* (**co•zi•er, co•zi•est**) comfortable and warm; snug. • *n.* (*pl.* **-zies**) cover to keep something hot, esp. a teapot. □ **cozy up to** *colloq.* **1** ingratiate oneself with. **2** snuggle up to. □□ **co′zi•ly** *adv.* **co′zi•ness** *n.*

■ *adj.* secure, relaxing, *colloq.* comfy. □ **cozy up to 1** see INGRATIATE.

cp. *abbr.* compare.

CPA *abbr.* certified public accountant.

cpd. *abbr.* compound.

CPI *abbr.* consumer price index.

Cpl. *abbr.* corporal.

CPR *abbr.* cardiopulmonary resuscitation.

cps *abbr.* (also **c.p.s.**) **1** *Computing* characters per second. **2** cycles per second.

CPU *abbr. Computing* central processing unit.

Cr *symb. Chem.* chromium.

crab[1] /krab/ • *n.* **1** crustacean with four pairs of legs and two pincers. **2** (**the Crab**) zodiacal sign or constellation Cancer. **3** (in full

crab louse) [often in *pl.*] parasitic louse, infesting hairy parts of the body. **4** irritable person. • *v.* (**crabbed, crabbing**) criticize adversely; grumble. □□ **crab′like** *adj.*

crab[2] /krab/ *n.* (in full **crab apple**) **1** small sour, applelike fruit. **2** tree bearing this fruit.

crab•bed /ˈkrábid/ *adj.* **1** irritable. **2** (of handwriting) hard to decipher. □□ **crab′bed•ly** *adv.* **crab′bed•ness** *n.*

■ **1** see IRRITABLE 1.

crab•by /ˈkrábee/ *adj.* (**crab•bi•er, crab•bi•est**) = CRABBED 1. □□ **crab′bi•ly** *adv.* **crab′bi•ness** *n.*

crab•grass /ˈkrábgras/ *n.* creeping grass infesting lawns.

crack /krak/ • *n.* **1 a** sharp, explosive noise. **b** (in a voice) sudden change in pitch. **2** sharp blow. **3** narrow opening; break; partial fracture. **4** *colloq.* mischievous or malicious remark. **5** *colloq.* attempt (*I'll have a crack at it*). **6** exact moment (*the crack of dawn*). **7** *sl.* potent crystalline form of cocaine. • *v.* **1** *tr. & intr.* break without separating the parts. **2** *tr. & intr.* make or cause to make a sharp, explosive sound. **3** *tr. & intr.* break or cause to break with a sharp sound. **4** *tr. & intr.* give way or cause to give way (under torture, etc.); break. **5** *intr.* (of the voice) become dissonant; break. **6** *tr. colloq.* find a solution to. **7** *tr.* say (a joke, etc.) in a jocular way. **8** *tr. colloq.* hit sharply. **9** *tr.* break (grain) into coarse pieces. • *attrib.adj. colloq.* excellent; first-rate. □ **crack down on** *colloq.* take severe measures against. **crack up** *colloq.* **1** collapse under strain. **2** laugh. **3** repute (*not all it's cracked up to be*). **get cracking** *colloq.* begin promptly and vigorously.

■ *n.* **1 a** snap, report, bang, clap, shot, slap. **2** see KNOCK *n.* 3. **3** crevice, rift, rupture, breach, slit, gap, cleft, check; split, fissure, flaw; chink. **4** see JOKE *n.* **5** see ATTEMPT *n.* **6** instant, time, second. • *v.* **1** fracture, rupture. **2** snap. **4** see *give way* 1 (WAY). **6** see SOLVE. **8** see HIT *v.* 1a. □ **crack up 1** see COLLAPSE *v.* **2** see LAUGH *v.* 1. **3** (*cracked up*) supposed, suggested, rumored, reported. **get cracking** see *get a move on* 2 (MOVE).

crack•down /ˈkrákdown/ *n. colloq.* severe measures (esp. against lawbreakers, etc.).

■ see *suppression* (SUPPRESS).

crack•er /ˈkrákər/ *n.* **1** thin, dry biscuit. **2** firework exploding with a sharp noise.

crack•er•jack /ˈkrákərjak/ *sl.* • *adj.* exceptionally fine or expert. • *n.* exceptionally fine thing or person.

■ *adj.* see EXPERT *adj.* 1. • *n.* see MASTER *n.* 4.

crack•ers /ˈkrákərz/ *predic.adj. sl.* crazy.

crack•le /ˈkrákəl/ • *v.intr.* make repeated slight cracking sound. • *n.* **1** such a sound. **2** paintwork, china, or glass decorated with a pattern of minute surface cracks. □□ **crack′ly** *adj.*

■ *n.* **1** see RATTLE *n.* 1.

crack•pot /ˈkrákpot/ *sl.* • *n.* eccentric person. • *adj.* mad; unworkable (*crackpot scheme*).

■ *n.* see WEIRDO. • *adj.* see IMPRACTICAL 1.

cra•dle /ˈkráydᵊl/ • *n.* **1 a** baby's bed, esp. on

rockers. **b** place in which a thing begins or is nurtured in its infancy (*cradle of democracy*). **2** supporting structure or framework. • *v.tr.* contain or shelter as if in a cradle. □ **cradle-robber** (or **-snatcher**) *sl.* person amorously attached to a much younger person.

■ *n.* **1 a** crib, cot. **b** see ORIGIN[1] 1. • *v.* see HOLD *v.* 1a, c.

craft /kraft/ • *n.* **1** skill, esp. in practical arts. **2** [esp. in *comb.*] trade or art. **3** (*pl.* **craft**) **a** boat or vessel. **b** aircraft or spacecraft. **4** cunning; deceit. • *v.tr.* make in a skillful way.

■ *n.* **1** ability, artisanship, craftsmanship, workmanship, ingenuity, talent, dexterity, cleverness, mastery, expertness, expertise, flair, genius, technique, know-how. **2** occupation, calling, vocation, profession. **3** ship; airplane; spaceship, rocket. **4** guile, art, fraud, trickery, wiliness, foxiness, artfulness, craftiness, duplicity. • *v.* fashion, fabricate.

crafts•man /kráftsmən/ *n.* (*pl.* **-men**; *fem.* **crafts•wom•an,** *pl.* **-wom•en**) skilled worker; artisan. □□ **crafts'man•ship** *n.*

■ see TRADESMAN. □□ **craftsmanship** see WORKMANSHIP.

craft•y /kráftee/ *adj.* (**craft•i•er, craft•i•est**) cunning; artful; wily. □□ **craft'i•ly** *adv.* **craft'i•ness** *n.*

■ clever, shrewd, foxy, canny, sly, scheming, calculating, designing, plotting, tricky, sneaky, deceitful, insidious, double-dealing, two-faced, duplicitous, treacherous, *colloq.* shifty.

crag /krag/ *n.* steep or rugged rock.

■ cliff, bluff, tor, scarp, precipice, *Geol.* escarpment; (*crags*) palisades.

crag•gy /krágee/ *adj.* (**crag•gi•er, crag•gi•est**) (of facial features, landscapes, etc.) rugged. □□ **crag'gi•ly** *adv.* **crag'gi•ness** *n.*

cram /kram/ *v.* (**crammed, cram•ming**) **1** *tr.* **a** fill to bursting; stuff. **b** force (a thing) into. **2** *tr. & intr.* prepare for an exam by intensive study.

■ **1** pack, overstuff, overcrowd, jam. **2** burn the midnight oil.

cramp /kramp/ • *n.* painful involuntary muscle contraction. • *v.tr.* **1** affect with cramp. **2** confine narrowly. **3** restrict (energies, etc.). **4** (as **cramped** *adj.*) **a** (of handwriting) small and difficult to read. **b** (of a room, etc.) uncomfortably crowded.

■ *n.* stomachache. • *v.* **2** see BOX[1] *v.* 2. **3** see INHIBIT 1. **4 b** (**cramped**) tight, incommodious, uncomfortable, close.

cram•pon /krámpon/ *n.* [usu. in *pl.*] spiked plate fixed to a boot for walking on ice, climbing, etc.

cran•ber•ry /kránberee/ *n.* (*pl.* **-ries**) **1** N. American evergreen shrub yielding edible small, red, acid berries. **2** berry from this.

crane /krayn/ • *n.* **1** machine with long hoisting arm. **2** tall wading bird with long legs, long neck, and straight bill. • *v.tr.* [also *absol.*] stretch out (one's neck) to see.

■ *n.* **1** see HOIST[1] *n.* • *v.* see STRAIN *v.* 1.

cra•ni•um /kráyneeəm/ *n.* (*pl.* **cra•ni•ums** or

cra•ni•a /-neeə/) skull, esp. the part enclosing the brain. □□ **cra'ni•al** *adj.*

■ see HEAD *n.* 1.

crank /krangk/ • *n.* **1** part of an axle or shaft bent at right angles for interconverting reciprocal and circular motion. **2 a** eccentric person. **b** bad-tempered person. • *v.tr.* cause to move by means of a crank. □ **crank up** *sl.* increase (speed, etc.) by intensive effort.

■ **2 a** character, oddity, *sl.* nut, nutcase.

crank•case /krángk-kays/ *n.* case enclosing a crankshaft.

crank•shaft /krángkshaft/ *n.* shaft driven by a crank (see CRANK *n.* 1).

crank•y /krángkee/ *adj.* (**crank•i•er, crank•i•est**) ill-tempered; crotchety. □□ **crank'i•ly** *adv.* **crank'i•ness** *n.*

■ testy, grouchy, crabby, short-tempered, surly, irascible, waspish, churlish, gruff, curmudgeonly, cantankerous, choleric, bilious, snappish, petulant, peevish, contentious, querulous, irritable, splenetic. □□ **crankiness** see ECCENTRICITY (ECCENTRIC), *ill humor*.

cran•ny /kránee/ *n.* (*pl.* **-nies**) chink; crevice; crack. □□ **cran'nied** /-need/ *adj.*

■ fissure, fracture, break, furrow, split, cleft.

crap /krap/ *coarse sl.* • *n.* **1** nonsense; rubbish. **2** feces. • *v.intr.* (**crapped, crap•ping**) defecate. □ **crap out** be unsuccessful. □□ **crap'py** *adj.*

■ *n.* see NONSENSE.

craps /kraps/ *n.pl.* gambling game played with dice.

crap•shoot /krápshoot/ *n. sl.* venture marked by uncertainty.

crap•u•lent /krápyələnt/ *adj.* suffering the effects of drunkenness. □□ **crap'u•lence** *n.* **crap'u•lous** *adj.*

crash /krash/ • *v.* **1** *tr. & intr.* make or cause to make a loud smashing noise. **2** *tr. & intr.* throw, drive, move, or fall with a loud smashing noise. **3** *tr. & intr.* **a** collide or cause (a vehicle, etc.) to collide violently. **b** fall or cause (an aircraft) to fall and land violently. **4** *intr.* undergo financial ruin. **5** *tr. colloq.* enter without permission (*crashed the party*). **6** *intr. Computing* (of a system) fail suddenly. **7** *intr. sl.* sleep, esp. in an improvised setting. • *n.* **1** loud and sudden smashing noise. **2 a** violent collision, esp. of a vehicle. **b** violent fall and landing of an aircraft. **3** ruin, esp. financial. **4** *Computing* sudden failure (of a system). **5** [*attrib.*] done rapidly or urgently (*crash course in first aid*). • *adv.* with a crash (*the window went crash*). □ **crash-dive 1** *intr.* (of an aircraft or pilot, etc.) dive and crash. **2** *tr.* cause to crash-dive. **crash helmet** helmet worn esp. by a motorcyclist to protect the head. **crash-land 1** *intr.* (of an aircraft or airman) land hurriedly with a crash. **2** *tr.* cause (an aircraft) to crash-land.

■ *v.* **1** bang, boom, clash, clang, clank. **3 a** smash (into); (*crash into*) drive or run into. **5** gatecrash, invade, intrude. • *n.* **1** bang, smash, clash, explosion, blast, clangor; see also BOOM[1] *n.* **2 a** see COLLISION 1. **3** disaster, collapse, failure.

crass /kras/ *adj.* gross; grossly stupid. □□ **crass'ly** *adv.* **crass'ness** *n.*

■ see GROSS *adj.* 2.

-crat /krat/ *comb. form* member or supporter of a particular form of government or rule (*autocrat, democrat*). □□ **-cratic** /krátik/ (also **-cratical**) *comb. form (adj.)* **-cratically** *comb. form (adv.)*

crate /krayt/ • *n.* **1 a** slatted wooden case for transporting goods. **b** any similar case. **2** *sl.* old airplane or other vehicle. • *v.tr.* pack in a crate. □□ **crate'ful** *n.* (*pl.* **-fuls**).
■ *n.* **1** see BOX¹ *n.* 1, 2. • *v.* see BOX¹ *v.* 1.

cra·ter /kráytər/ • *n.* **1** mouth of a volcano. **2** bowl-shaped cavity, esp. from a shell or bomb. **3** hollow on the surface of a planet or moon. • *v.tr.* form a crater in. □□ **cra·ter·ous** *adj.*
■ *n.* see HOLLOW *n.* 1.

cra·vat /krəvát/ *n.* **1** scarf worn inside an open-necked shirt. **2** *hist.* necktie. □□ **cra·vat·ted** *adj.*

crave /krayv/ *v.* long or beg for.
■ see LONG², BEG 2.

cra·ven /kráyvən/ *adj.* cowardly. □□ **cra·ven·ly** *adv.* **cra'ven·ness** *n.*
■ see COWARDLY *adj.*

crav·ing /kráyving/ *n.* strong desire or longing.
■ see LONGING *n.*

craw /kraw/ *n. Zool.* crop of a bird or insect. □ **stick in one's craw** be unacceptable.

craw·fish /kráwfish/ *n.* = CRAYFISH.

crawl /krawl/ • *v.intr.* **1** move slowly, esp.: a person on hands and knees;. **b** insect, snake, etc., with the body close to the ground. **2** walk or move slowly (*the train crawled into the station*) **3** *colloq.* behave obsequiously. **4** be covered or filled with crawling or moving things, people, etc. • *n.* **1** crawling. **2** slow rate of movement. **3** high-speed overarm swimming stroke. □□ **crawl'ing·ly** *adv.* **crawl'y** *adj.* (in sense 4 of *v.*).
■ *v.* **1 a** creep. **b** worm, wriggle, squirm, slither. **2** inch; see also EDGE *v.* 1. **3** grovel, fawn, cower, *colloq.* suck up; lackey; see also CRINGE *v.* 4 (*crawl with*) see TEEM 2.

cray·fish /kráyfish/ *n.* (*pl.* same) small, lobsterlike freshwater crustacean.

cray·on /kráyon/ *n.* stick or pencil of colored wax, chalk, etc. • *v.tr.* draw with crayons.

craze /krayz/ • *v.* **1** *tr.* (usu. as **crazed** *adj.*) make insane. **2 a** *tr.* produce fine surface cracks on (pottery glaze, etc.). **b** *intr.* develop such cracks. • *n.* fad; rage.
■ *v.* **1** (**crazed**) see MAD *adj.* 1. • *n.* fashion, trend, craze, mania, obsession.

cra·zy /kráyzee/ *adj.* (**cra·zi·er, cra·zi·est**) **1** *colloq.* insane; mad; foolish. **2** *colloq.* extremely enthusiastic. □□ **cra'zi·ly** *adv.* **cra'zi·ness** *n.*
■ **1** demented, deranged, unbalanced, unhinged, lunatic, touched, out of one's mind *or* head, *sl.* bananas, nuts, batty, loony, screwy, flaky; inane, ridiculous, preposterous, laughable, ludicrous; (*be crazy*) have a screw loose. **2** avid, zealous, keen, excited; infatuated, obsessed, wild. □□ **crazily** see MADLY 1.

creak /kreek/ • *n.* harsh scraping or squeaking sound. • *v.intr.* **1** make a creak.

2 a move with a creaking noise. **b** move stiffly. **c** show weakness or frailty under strain. □□ **creak'ing·ly** *adv.* **creak'y** *adj.*
■ □□ **creaky** see DECREPIT 2.

cream /kreem/ • *n.* **1** fatty content of milk. **2** [usu. prec. by *the*] best part of something. **3** creamlike cosmetic, etc. **4** pale yellow or off-white color. • *v.* **1** *tr.* work (butter, etc.) to a creamy consistency. **2** *intr.* form a cream or scum. **3** *tr. colloq.* defeat soundly (esp. in a sporting contest). • *adj.* pale yellow; off-white. □ **cream of tartar** crystalline potassium hydrogen tartrate, used in medicine, baking powder, etc.
■ *n.* **2** see BEST¹ *n.* 1, 2. **3** see LOTION. • *v.* **1** see PUREE *v.* 2b. **3** see DEFEAT *v.* 1b.

cream·er /kréemər/ *n.* small pitcher for cream.

cream·er·y /kréeməree/ *n.* (*pl.* **-ies**) factory or store for dairy products.

cream·y /kréemee/ *adj.* (**cream·i·er, cream·i·est**) **1** like cream. **2** rich in cream. □□ **cream'i·ness** *n.*
■ **1** see WHITE *adj.* 1. **2** see RICH 6.

crease /krees/ • *n.* line caused by folding; wrinkle. • *v.* **1** *tr.* make creases in. **2** *intr.* become creased.
■ *n.* see FOLD¹ *n.* 2. • *v.* **1** see FOLD¹ *v.* 1.

cre·ate /kree-áyt/ *v.tr.* **1** bring into existence; cause. **2** originate.
■ **1** make, produce, form, bring into being, conceive, generate, invent, imagine, think up, frame, forge, fashion, fabricate, manufacture, develop, design, contrive, devise.

cre·a·tion /kree-áyshən/ *n.* **1** creating; being created. **2 a** (usu. **the Creation**) God's creating of the universe. **b** (usu. **Creation**) everything so created; the universe. **3** product of imagination, art, etc.
■ **1** generation, making; beginning, origin, start, inception, genesis; see also FORMATION 1, 2. **2 b** the world, the cosmos. **3** see INVENTION 2.

cre·a·tion·ism /kree-áyshənizəm/ *n. Theol.* theory of the origin of life in accordance with the Bible. □□ **cre·a'tion·ist** *n.*

cre·a·tive /kree-áytiv/ *adj.* **1** inventive; imaginative. **2** able to create. □□ **cre·a'tive·ly** *adv.* **cre·a'tive·ness** *n.* **cre·a·tiv·i·ty** /-ay-tívitee, éti-/ *n.*
■ **1** originative, artistic, original, ingenious, resourceful. **2** see PRODUCTIVE 2.

SYNONYM STUDY: creative

INVENTIVE, ORIGINAL, RESOURCEFUL, IMAGINATIVE, INGENIOUS. Everyone likes to think that he or she is *creative*, a term used to describe the active, exploratory minds possessed by artists, writers, and inventors (*a creative approach to problem-solving*). Today, however, *creative* has become an advertising buzzword (*creative cooking, creative hair-styling*) that simply means new or different. **Original** is more specific and limited in scope. Someone who is *original* comes up with things that no one else has thought of (*an original approach to constructing a dog-house*), or thinks in an independent and

creative way (*a highly original filmmaker*).
Imaginative implies having an active and
creative imagination, which often means
that the person visualizes things quite differently than the way they appear in the real
world (*imaginative illustrations for a children's
book*). The practical side of *imaginative* is in-
ventive; the *inventive* person figures out
how to make things work better (*an inventive
solution to the problem of getting a wheelchair
into a van*). But where an *inventive* mind
tends to comes up with solutions to problems it has posed for itself, a **resourceful**
mind deals successfully with externally imposed problems or limitations using the materials available (*a resourceful child can amuse
herself with simple wooden blocks*). Someone
who is **ingenious** is both *inventive* and *resourceful*, with a dose of cleverness thrown in
(*the ingenious idea of using recycled plastic to
create a warm, fleecelike fabric*).

cre•a•tor /kree-áytər/ n. **1** person who cre-
ates. **2 (the Creator)** God.
  ■ **1** originator, author, architect, designer,
framer, maker.

crea•ture /kréechər/ n. **1** any living being.
2 person of a specified kind (*poor creature*).
□ **creature comforts** material comforts.
creature of habit person set in an unvarying routine.
  ■ **1** animal, beast; organism, entity, living
thing. **2** see PERSON.

crèche /kresh/ n. representation of a Nativity
scene.

cre•dence /kréed'ns/ n. belief. □ **give credence to** believe.
  ■ see BELIEF 1.

cre•den•tial /kridénshəl/ n. [usu. in *pl.*] evidence of a person's qualifications, etc., usu.
in the form of certificates, references, etc.
  ■ see WARRANT n. 2.

cre•den•za /kridénzə/ n. sideboard or cupboard.

cred•i•bil•i•ty /krédibílitee/ n. **1** being credible; believable. **2** reputation; status.

cred•i•ble /krédibəl/ adj. believable; worthy
of belief. □□ **cred′i•bly** adv.
  ■ see PLAUSIBLE 1.

cred•it /krédit/ • n. **1** source of honor, pride,
etc. **2** acknowledgment of merit. **3** good
reputation. **4 a** person's financial standing.
b power to obtain goods, etc., before payment. **5** [usu. in *pl.*] acknowledgment of a
contribution. **6** reputation for solvency and
honesty in business. **7 a** entry in an account
of a sum paid into it. **b** sum entered. • v.tr.
1 believe (*cannot credit it*). **2 a** enter on the
credit side of an account. **b** ascribe a good
quality or achievement to. □ **do credit to**
enhance the reputation of. **on credit** with an
arrangement to pay later. **to one's credit** in
one's praise, commendation, or defense.
  ■ n. **2** praise, commendation, tribute, recognition. **3** honor, esteem, standing, stature,
repute. • v. **1** trust, accept, have faith *or* confidence in, rely on, depend on *or* upon.
2 b accredit, attribute, assign.

cred•it•a•ble /kréditəbəl/ adj. bringing credit
or honor. □□ **cred•it•a•bil′i•ty** n. **cred′it•a•
bly** adv.
  ■ see MERITORIOUS.

cred•i•tor /kréditər/ n. person to whom a
debt is owed.

cre•do /kréedō, kráy-/ n. (*pl.* **-dos**) creed.
  ■ see CREED.

cred•u•lous /kré jələs/ adj. too ready to believe; gullible. See synonym study at GULLI-
BLE. □□ **cre•du•li•ty** /kridōolitee, -dyōō-/ n.
cred′u•lous•ly adv. **cred′u•lous•ness** n.

Cree /kree/ n. (*pl.* same *or* **Crees**) **1 a** N.
American people of eastern and central
Canada. **b** member of this people. **2** lan-
guage of this people.

creed /kreed/ n. **1** set of principles or beliefs.
2 a (the Creed *or* **Apostles' Creed)** early
statement of the Christian creed, ascribed to
the Apostles. **b** formal summary of Christian doctrine (*Nicene Creed*). □□ **creed′al** *or*
cred′al adj.
  ■ **1** dogma, doctrine, credo, teaching, philosophy, maxim.

Creek /kreek/ n. **1 a** confederacy of N. American peoples formerly of Alabama and Georgia. **b** member of these peoples. **2** language
of these peoples.

creek /kreek, krik/ n. stream. □ **up the creek**
sl. in difficulties.
  ■ brook, rivulet, rill.

creel /kreel/ n. fisherman's large wicker basket.

creep /kreep/ • v.intr. (*past* and *past part.*
crept /krept/) **1** move with the body prone
and close to the ground. **2** move stealthily
or timidly. **3** enter or overcome slowly.
4 colloq. act obsequiously. **5** (of a plant)
grow along the ground or up a wall, etc.
6 (of flesh) shiver; shudder. • n. **1** act or instance of creeping. **2** [in *pl.*; prec. by *the*]
colloq. feeling of revulsion or fear. **3** sl. unpleasant person.
  ■ v. **1** crawl, slither, inch, squirm, wriggle,
2 steal, sneak; slink, skulk, tiptoe, pussyfoot,
sidle. **3** make its way. **4** see CRAWL v. 3. • n.
2 (*the creeps*) see JITTER n. **3** see WRETCH 2.

creep•y /kréepee/ adj. (**creep•i•er, creep•i•
est**) colloq. producing a feeling of horror or
revulsion. □□ **creep′i•ly** adv. **creep′i•ness**
n.
  ■ see SCARY.

cre•mate /kréemayt, krimáyt/ v.tr. consume
(a corpse, etc.) by fire. □□ **cre•ma′tion**
/krimáyshən/ n. **cre′ma•tor** n. **cre′ma•to•
ry** adj.

cre•ma•to•ri•um /kréemətáwreeəm/ n. (*pl.*
cre•ma•to•ri•ums *or* **cre•ma•to•ri•a**
/-reeə/) place for cremating corpses.

crème de la crème /krém də laa krém/ n.
best part; elite.
  ■ see BEST n. 1, 2.

cren•el•late /krénəlayt/ v.tr. provide (a tower,
etc.) with battlements. □□ **cren•el•la′tion**
/-láyshən/ n.

Cre•ole /kree-ōl/ • n. **1 a** descendant of European (esp. Spanish) settlers in the W. Indies or Central or S. America. **b** white descendant of French settlers, esp. in
Louisiana. **c** person of mixed European and

black descent. **2** language formed from a European language (esp. English, French, or Portuguese) and another (esp. African) language. • *adj.* **1** of Creoles. **2** (usu. **creole**) of Creole origin (*creole cooking*).

cre•o•sote /krēəsōt/ *n.* distillate of wood or coal tar, used as wood preservative, antiseptic, etc.

crepe /krayp/ *n.* (also **crêpe**) **1** fine, gauzelike wrinkled fabric. **2** thin pancake, usu. with a filling. **3** hard-wearing wrinkled rubber used for the soles of shoes, etc. □ **crêpe paper** thin crinkled paper. □□ **crep′ey** *adj.* (also **crep′y**).

crept *past and past part.* of CREEP.

cre•scen•do /krishéndō/ • *n.* (*pl.* **–dos**) **1** *Mus.* gradual increase in loudness. **2 a** progress toward a climax. **b** *disp.* climax. • *adv. & adj.* increasing in loudness. • *v.intr.* (**–does, –doed**) increase gradually in loudness or intensity.
 ■ *n.* **2** see HEAD *n.* 14.

cres•cent /krésənt/ *n.* **1** curved sickle shape, as of the waxing or waning moon. **2** anything of this shape.
 ■ **2** arc, lunette.

cress /kres/ *n.* cruciferous plant with edible leaves.

crest /krest/ • *n.* **1 a** comb, tuft, etc., on a bird's or animal's head. **b** plume, etc., on a helmet, etc. **2** top of a mountain, wave, roof, etc. **3** heraldic device, as on seals, etc. • *v.* **1** *tr.* reach the crest of. **2** *intr.* (of a wave, etc.) form into a crest. □□ **crest′ed** *adj.* [also in *comb.*].
 ■ *n.* **2** summit, pinnacle, peak, head, ridge. **3** badge, emblem, insignia, symbol. • *v.* **2** level out *or* off.

crest•fall•en /créstfawlən/ *adj.* dejected; dispirited.
 ■ see *dejected* (DEJECT).

cre•ta•ceous /kritáyshəs/ • *adj.* **1** of or like chalk. **2** (**Cretaceous**) *Geol.* of or relating to the last period of the Mesozoic era, with evidence of extensive chalk deposits. • *n.* (**Cretaceous**) *Geol.* this era or system.

cre•tin /krḗtin/ *n.* **1** deformed and mentally deficient person. **2** *colloq.* stupid person. □□ **cre′tin•ism** *n.* **cre′tin•ize** *v.tr.* **cre′tin•ous** *adj.*

cre•vasse /krəvás/ *n.* deep open crack, esp. in a glacier.
 ■ gorge, chasm, abyss, ravine, fissure, furrow.

crev•ice /krévis/ *n.* narrow opening or fissure, esp. in a rock.
 ■ crack, chink, cleft, cranny, groove, furrow, split, rift.

crew /krōō/ • *n.* [often treated as *pl.*] **1 a** people manning a ship, aircraft, train, etc. **b** these as distinct from the captain or officers. **c** people working together; team. **2** *colloq.* company of people; gang (*a motley crew*). • *v.* **1** *tr.* supply or act as a crew or crew member for. **2** *intr.* act as a crew or crew member. □ **crew cut** very short haircut. **crew neck** close-fitting round neckline.
 ■ *n.* group, band, troupe, party, corps.

crew•el /krōōəl/ *n.* thin worsted yarn for tapestry and embroidery.

crew•el•work /krōōəlwərk/ *n.* design in crewel.

crib /krib/ • *n.* **1** baby's bed with high sides. **2** rack for animal fodder. **3** *colloq.* furtively used study notes. • *v.tr.* [also *absol.*] (**cribbed, crib•bing**) **1** *colloq.* copy without acknowledgment. **2** confine in a small space. □ **crib death** = *sudden infant death syndrome.*
 ■ *n.* **1** cradle, cot. • *v.* **1** plagiarize. **2** see RESTRICT.

crib•bage /kríbij/ *n.* card game for up to four players. □ **cribbage board** board with pegs for scoring at cribbage.

crick /krik/ *n.* sudden painful stiffness.

crick•et[1] /kríkit/ *n.* team game played with ball, bats, and wickets. □ **not cricket** esp. *Brit. colloq.* underhand behavior.

crick•et[2] /kríkit/ *n.* grasshopperlike chirping insect.

cried *past and past part.* of CRY.

cri•er /krīər/ *n.* (also **cry′er**) **1** person who cries. **2** official making public announcements, as in a court of law.

crime /krīm/ *n.* **1 a** offense punishable by law. **b** illegal acts. **2** evil or shameful act. See synonym study at SIN.
 ■ *n.* **1 a** violation, misdeed, wrong, misdemeanor; felony. **b** lawlessness. **2** see EVIL *n.* 1.

crim•i•nal /kríminəl/ • *n.* person guilty of a crime. • *adj.* **1** of, involving, or concerning crime. **2** guilty of crime. **3** *Law* relating to or expert in criminal law. **4** *colloq.* scandalous; deplorable. □□ **crim•i•nal•i•ty** /–nálitee/ *n.* **crim′i•nal•ly** *adv.*
 ■ *n.* felon, lawbreaker, outlaw, culprit, offender, malefactor, wrongdoer, *colloq.* crook. • *adj.* **2** illegal, unlawful, illicit, lawless, dishonest, *colloq.* crooked. **4** reprehensible; wicked, corrupt, immoral, amoral, sinful.

crim•i•nol•o•gy /kríminóləjee/ *n.* study of crime. □□ **crim•i•no•log•i•cal** /–nəlójikəl/ *adj.* **crim•i•nol′o•gist** *n.*

crimp /krimp/ • *v.tr.* **1** compress into small folds. **2** corrugate. **3** make waves in (hair). • *n.* crimped thing or form. □ **put a crimp in** *sl.* thwart. □□ **crimp′er** *n.* **crimp′y** *adj.* **crimp′i•ness** *n.*
 ■ *v.* **1, 2** see WRINKLE[1] *v.* 1. • *n.* see FOLD *n.* 2.

crim•son /krímzən/ • *adj.* of a rich, deep red. • *n.* this color.
 ■ *adj.* see RED *adj.* 1.

cringe /krinj/ • *v.intr.* shrink in fear; cower. See synonym study at WINCE. See synonym study at WINCE. • *n.* act or instance of cringing. □□ **cring′er** *n.*
 ■ *v.* wince, flinch, quail, recoil, blench, tremble, quiver, *colloq.* quake *or* shake in one's boots *or* shoes. • *n.* embarrassment.

crin•kle /kríngkəl/ • *n.* wrinkle; crease. • *v.* **1** *intr.* form crinkles. **2** *tr.* form crinkles in. □ **crinkle-cut** (of vegetables) cut with wavy edges. □□ **crin′kly** *adj.*
 ■ *n.* see WRINKLE *n.* 1, 2. • *v.* see WRINKLE *v.* 2.

crin•o•line /krínəlin/ *n.* **1** stiffened or hooped petticoat. **2** stiff fabric of horsehair, etc., used for linings, hats, etc.

crip•ple /krípəl/ • *n.* usu. *offens.* lame person or animal. • *v.tr.* **1** make a cripple of. **2** disable; impair.

■ *n.* invalid, paralytic, paraplegic. • *v.* incapacitate, handicap, maim; damage, weaken, debilitate.

cri•sis /krísis/ *n.* (*pl.* **cri•ses** /–seez/) **1 a** decisive moment. **b** time of danger or great difficulty. **2** turning point.

■ **1 b** disaster, emergency, calamity, catastrophe.

crisp /krisp/ • *adj.* **1** hard but brittle. **2 a** (of air) bracing. **b** (of a style or manner) lively; brisk and decisive. **c** (of paper) stiff and crackling. • *v.* make or become crisp. □□ **crisp′ly** *adv.* **crisp′ness** *n.*

■ *adj.* **1** crunchy, friable, breakable, crumbly. **2 a** see *bracing* (BRACE *v.* 3). **b** see LIVE-LY 1, 2, EMPHATIC.

crisp•er /kríspər/ *n.* refrigerator compartment for produce.

crisp•y /kríspee/ *adj.* (**crisp•i•er, crisp•i•est**) crisp; brittle. □□ **crisp′i•ness** *n.*

criss•cross /krískráws, –krós/ • *n.* pattern of crossing lines. • *adj.* crossing; in cross lines. • *adv.* crosswise; at cross purposes. • *v.* **1** *intr.* **a** intersect repeatedly. **b** move crosswise. **2** *tr.* mark or make with a crisscross pattern.

■ *n.* see NETWORK *n.* 2. • *v.* **1** see TRAVERSE *v.*

cri•te•ri•on /kríteéreeən/ *n.* (*pl.* **cri•te•ri•a** /–reeə/ or **cri•te•ri•ons**) principle or standard that a thing is judged by.

■ see STANDARD *n.* 1.

crit•ic /krítik/ *n.* **1** person who censures or criticizes. **2** person who reviews literary, artistic, etc. works.

■ **2** see JUDGE *n.* 3b.

crit•i•cal /krítikəl/ *adj.* **1** involving adverse comments; faultfinding. **2** providing textual criticism. **3 a** of or at a crisis. **b** decisive; crucial (*of critical importance*). **4** (of a nuclear reactor) maintaining a self-sustaining chain reaction. See synonym study at CRUCIAL. □ **critical list** list of critically ill patients. □□ **crit′i•cal•ly** *adv.* **crit′i•cal•ness** *n.*

■ **1** disparaging, deprecatory, deprecating, judgmental; adverse. **3 a** risky, uncertain, perilous, dangerous, touch and go. **b** important, essential, pivotal, vital.

crit•i•cism /krítisizəm/ *n.* **1 a** finding fault; censure. **b** critical remark, etc. **2 a** work of a critic. **b** judgmental analysis.

■ **1 a** faultfinding, disapproval, condemnation, disparagement. **2** evaluation, appraisal, assessment, estimation, valuation; critique, review, commentary.

crit•i•cize /krítisīz/ *v.tr.* [also *absol.*] **1** find fault with; censure. **2** discuss critically. □□ **crit′i•ciz•able** *adj.* **crit′i•ciz•er** *n.*

■ **1** carp (at); condemn, attack, cut up, denounce, impugn, *colloq.* pan, lambaste, put down, *sl.* knock. **2** judge, evaluate, assess, appraise; analyze, critique.

cri•tique /kriteék/ • *n.* expression of critical analysis. • *v.tr.* (**cri•tiques, cri•tiqued, cri•ti•quing**) discuss critically.

■ *n.* see ANALYSIS 1. • *v.* interpret, evaluate, review.

crit•ter /krítər/ *n. dial.* or joc. creature.

croak /krōk/ • *n.* deep, hoarse sound, as of a frog. • *v.* **1 a** *intr.* utter a croak. **b** *tr.* utter with a croak or in a dismal manner. **2** *sl.* **a** *intr.* die. **b** *tr.* kill.

■ *v.* **1** see RASP[1] *v.* 2. **2 a** see DIE 1.

Croat /krō-at/ • *n.* (also **Cro•a•tian** /krōáyshən/) **1** a native of Croatia. **b** person of Croatian descent. **2** Slavic dialect of the Croats. • *adj.* of the Croats or their dialect.

cro•chet /krōsháy/ • *n.* handicraft in which yarn is hooked into a patterned fabric. • *v.* create crochet. □□ **cro•chet′er** *n.*

crock[1] /krok/ *n.* **1** earthenware pot or jar. **2** broken piece of earthenware.

■ **1** see JAR[1] 1.

crock[2] /krok/ *n. colloq.* nonsense; exaggeration.

crock•er•y /krókəree/ *n.* earthenware; china dishes, etc.

croc•o•dile /krókədīl/ *n.* **1** large, long-jawed tropical amphibious reptile. **2** leather from its skin. □ **crocodile tears** insincere grief. □□ **croc•o•dil•i•an** /–dileeən/ *adj.*

cro•cus /krōkəs/ *n.* (*pl.* **cro•cus•es**) early spring plant growing from a corm and having white, yellow, or purple flowers.

Croe•sus /kreésəs/ *n.* person of great wealth.

crois•sant /krwaasaán, krəsánt/ *n.* crescent-shaped pastry.

Cro-Mag•non /krōmágnən, –mányən/ *adj. Anthropol.* of a tall, broad-faced European race of late Paleolithic times.

crone /krōn/ *n.* withered old woman.

■ see HAG 1.

cro•ny /krōnee/ *n.* (*pl.* **–nies**) close friend or companion.

■ see FRIEND *n.* 1.

crook /krook/ • *n.* **1** hooked staff of a shepherd or bishop. **2 a** bend; curve; hook. **b** anything hooked or curved. **3** *colloq.* swindler; criminal. • *v.* bend; curve.

■ *n.* **1** see STAFF[1] *n.* 1a, b. **2** see BEND *n.* 3 see CRIMINAL[1] *n.* • *v.* see BEND *v.* 1.

crook•ed /krookid/ *adj.* **1 a** not straight or level; bent. **b** deformed. **2** *colloq.* not straightforward; dishonest. □□ **crook′ed•ly** *adv.* **crook′ed•ness** *n.*

■ **1** bowed, curved, askew, awry, distorted, contorted, lopsided, twisted, misshapen, disfigured, warped, gnarled. **2** criminal; illegal, unlawful, illicit, perverse.

croon /kroon/ *v.* hum or sing in a low sentimental voice. □□ **croon′er** *n.*

crop /krop/ • *n.* **1 a** produce of cultivated plants. **b** season's yield of this. **2** group or amount produced or appearing at one time. **3** handle of a whip. **4** predigestive pouch in a bird's gullet. • *v.tr.* (**cropped, crop•ping**) **1 a** cut off. **b** bite off. **2** cut (hair, etc.) short. □ **crop circle** circular depression in a standing crop. **crop-dusting** sprinkling of insecticide or fertilizer, esp. from the air. **crop out** *Geol.* appear at the surface. **crop up** occur unexpectedly.

■ *n.* **1** see HARVEST *n.* 2. **3** see WHIP *n.* • *v.* see CUT *v.* 3. □ **crop up** see ARISE 3.

crop•per /krópər/ *n.* crop-producing plant of

specified quality (*a good cropper*). □ **come a cropper** *sl.* fail badly.

cro·quet /krōkáy/ *n.* lawn game with hoops, mallets, and wooden balls.

cro·quette /krōkét/ *n.* fried, breaded ball of mashed potato or ground meat, etc.

cro·sier /krṓzhər/ *n.* (also **cro'zier**) bishop's hooked staff.

cross /kraws, kros/ • *n.* **1** upright post with a transverse bar, as used for crucifixion. **2 a** (**the Cross**) cross on which Christ was crucified. **b** representation of this. **3** thing or mark like a cross. **4** cross-shaped decoration indicating rank, etc. **5** hybrid. **6** (foll. by *between*) mixture or compromise of two things. **7** trial; affliction. • *v.* **1** *tr.* go across. **2 a** *intr.* intersect; be across. **b** *tr.* cause to do this. **3** *tr.* draw a line or lines across, esp. to delete. **4** *tr.* [often *refl.*] make the sign of the cross on or over. **5** *intr.* **a** pass in opposite or different directions. **b** (of letters, etc.) be sent before receipt of the other. **6** *tr.* a cause to interbreed. **b** cross-fertilize (plants). **7** *tr. sl.* cheat. • *adj.* **1** peevish; angry; contrary. **2** transverse; reaching from side to side. **3** intersecting. □ **at cross purposes** misunderstanding; conflicting. **cross-dress** wear clothing typically worn by the opposite sex. **cross one's fingers** (or **keep one's fingers crossed**) **1** put one finger across another as a sign of hoping for good luck. **2** trust in good luck. **cross one's heart** make a solemn pledge. **cross one's mind** (of a thought, etc.) occur to one. **cross a person's palm** bribe. **cross swords** encounter in opposition. **cross wires** (or **get one's wires crossed**) **1** become wrongly connected by telephone. **2** have a misunderstanding. □□ **cross'ly** *adv.* **cross'ness** *n.*

■ *n.* **1, 2b** crucifix, rood. **5** crossbreed, mongrel. **6** blend, combination. **7** see TRIAL 3. • *v.* **1** span, traverse. **2 a** meet, join. **3** (*cross off* or *out*) obliterate, strike out, cancel. **6** crossbreed. • *adj.* **1** irritated, annoyed, piqued, irritable, testy, irascible, grouchy, grumpy, fractious, petulant, cantankerous, short-tempered, cranky. □ **cross one's fingers 2** hope *or* pray for the best. **cross one's heart** see SWEAR *v.* 1a, 2. **cross one's mind** see OCCUR 3. **cross swords** see CLASH *v.* 3.

cross·bar /kráwsbaar, krós-/ *n.* horizontal bar, esp. on a bicycle.

cross·bow /kráwsbō, krós-/ *n.* bow fixed on a wooden stock, with a groove for an arrow. □□ **cross'bow'man** *n.* (pl. **-men**).

cross·breed • *n.* /kráwsbreed, krós-/ **1** hybrid breed of animals or plants. **2** individual hybrid. • *v.tr.* /kráwsbréed, krós-/ (*past* and *past part.* **-bred**) produce by crossing.

■ *n.* see HYBRID *n.* 1.

cross-check • *v.tr.* /kraws-chék, krós-/ check by alternative methods. • *n.* /kráws-chek, krós-/ cross-checking.

cross-coun·try /kráwskúntree, krós-/ *adj. & adv.* **1** across open country. **2** not keeping to main roads.

cross·cut • *adj.* /kráwskút, krós-/ cut across the main grain or axis. • *n.* /kráwskut, krós-/ diagonal cut, path, etc.

cross-ex·am·ine /kráwsigzámin, krós-/ *v.tr.*

examine (esp. a witness in a court of law) to check or extend testimony already given. □□ **cross-ex·am·in·a'tion** *n.* **cross'-ex·am'in·er** *n.*

cross-eyed /kráwsíd, krós-/ *adj.* having one or both eyes turned inward.

cross-fer·til·ize /kráwsfért'líz, krós-/ *v.tr.* **1** fertilize (an animal or plant) from one of a different species. **2** interchange ideas, etc. □□ **cross'-fer·ti·li·za'tion** *n.*

cross·fire /kráwsfir, krós-/ *n.* (also **cross'fire**) **1** firing in two crossing directions. **2 a** attack or criticism from several sources. **b** combative exchange of views, etc.

cross·ing /kráwsing, krós-/ *n.* **1** place where things (esp. roads) cross. **2** place for crossing a street, etc. **3** journey across water, mountains, etc.

■ **1** see JUNCTION 2. **3** see PASSAGE 1, 4.

cross·o·ver /kráwsōvər, krós-/ • *n.* point or place of crossing. • *adj.* having a crossover.

cross·piece /kráwspees, krós-/ *n.* transverse beam or other component of a structure, etc.

cross-ref·er·ence /kráwsréfərəns, krós-/ • *n.* reference from one part of a book, etc., to another. • *v.tr.* provide with cross-references.

cross·road /kráwsrōd, krós-/ *n.* [usu. in pl.] intersection of two or more roads. □ **at the crossroads** at a critical point.

cross sec·tion /kráws-sékshən, krós-/ *n.* **1 a** cutting across a solid. **b** plane surface produced in this way. **c** representation of this. **2** representative sample. □□ **cross'-sec'tion·al** *adj.*

■ **2** see SAMPLE *n.* 1.

cross·walk /kráwswawk, krós-/ *n.* pedestrian crossing.

cross·wind /kráwswind, krós-/ *n.* wind blowing across one's direction of travel.

cross·wise /kráwswiz, krós-/ *adj. & adv.* **1** in the form of a cross; intersecting. **2** transverse or transversely.

cross·word /kráwswərd, krós-/ *n.* (also **cross'word puz'zle**) grid of squares and blanks for words crossing vertically and horizontally to be filled in from clues.

crotch /kroch/ *n.* place where something forks, esp. the legs of the human body or a garment.

crotch·et·y /króchitee/ *adj.* peevish. □□ **crotch'et·i·ness** *n.*

crouch /krowch/ • *v.intr.* lower the body with limbs close to the chest; be in this position. • *n.* crouching; crouching position.

■ *v.* bend (down), squat (down); scrunch down, stoop. • *n.* see STOOP[1] *n.* 1.

croup /kroop/ *n.* inflammation of the larynx and trachea in children, with a hard cough. □□ **croup'y** *adj.*

crou·pi·er /króopeeər, -eeay/ *n.* person in charge of a gaming table.

crou·ton /króoton/ *n.* cube of toasted bread served with soup, etc.

Crow /krō/ *n.* **1 a** N. American people native to eastern Montana. **b** member of this people. **2** language of this people.

crow[1] /krō/ *n.* large black bird having a

powerful black beak. □ **as the crow flies** in a straight line. **crow's-foot** (*pl.* **-feet**) [usu. in *pl.*] wrinkle at the outer corner of the eye. **crow's nest** lookout platform at the masthead of a sailing vessel. **eat crow** submit to humiliation.

crow[2] /krō/ • *v.intr.* **1** (of a cock) utter a loud cry. **2** express glee. • *n.* cry of a cock.
  ■ *v.* **2** see GLOAT *v.*

crow•bar /krṓbaar/ *n.* iron bar with a flattened end, used as a lever.

crowd /krowd/ • *n.* **1** large gathering of people. **2** spectators; audience. **3** *colloq.* particular set of people. • *v.* **1 a** *intr.* come together in a crowd. **b** *tr.* cause to do this. **c** *intr.* force one's way. **2** *tr.* **a** [foll. by *into*] force or compress into a confined space. **b** fill or make abundant with. **3** *tr.* come aggressively close to. □ **crowd out** exclude by crowding. □□ **crowd′ed•ness** *n.*
  ■ *n.* **1** throng, multitude, horde, host, swarm, mass, press, flood, mob, flock, pack. **3** company, circle, gang, bunch, coterie, clique. • *v.* **1 a** herd, pour, gather, get together, assemble, congregate. **2 a** squeeze, pack, jam, stuff, cram, push, press, drive, shove, thrust, force, load.

crown /krown/ • *n.* **1** monarch's jeweled headdress. **2** (**the Crown**) **a** monarch, esp. as head of state. **b** power or authority of the monarchy. **3 a** wreath worn on the head, esp. as an emblem of victory. **b** award or distinction, esp. in sport. **4** crown-shaped device or ornament. **5** top part of a thing, esp. of the head or a hat. **6** highest part. **7 a** part of a tooth projecting from the gum. **b** artificial replacement for this. • *v.tr.* **1** put a crown on. **2** invest with royal authority. **3** be a crown to; rest on top of. **4** (as **crowning** *adj.*) be or cause to be the reward or finishing touch to (*the crowning glory*). **5** promote (a piece in checkers) to king. **6** *sl.* hit on the head. □ **crown prince** male heir to a sovereign throne. **crown princess 1** wife of a crown prince. **2** female heir to a sovereign throne.
  ■ *n.* **1** coronet, diadem, circlet, tiara. **2 a** ruler, sovereign, potentate; king, queen. **b** government, realm. • *v.* **2** enthrone. **3** see TOP[1] *v.* 1. **4** cap, top, surmount, culminate, climax, consummate. **6** see BRAIN *v.*

cro•zier var. of CROSIER.

CRT *abbr.* cathode-ray tube.

cru•ces *pl.* of CRUX.

cru•cial /krṓshəl/ *adj.* **1** decisive; critical. **2** very important. □□ **cru•ci•al•i•ty** /-sheeálitee/ *n.* (*pl.* **-ties**). **cru′cial•ly** *adv.*
  ■ **1** pivotal, vital, momentous, essential, major; key.

SYNONYM STUDY: crucial

ACUTE, CRITICAL, DECIDING, PRESSING, URGENT. In any emergency or crisis situation, there is usually a turning point. Such an event is called **critical** if it determines the outcome of a situation (*a critical point in the nuclear disarmament negotiations; a critical election for the Democratic Party*). **Crucial** can also refer to a

---

turning point, but it emphasizes the necessity of something happening before a result can be achieved (*the battle was crucial to their victory*), while **critical** suggests more of a balance between positive and negative outcomes (*a critical debate on foreign policy*). **Acute** describes the intensification of a situation that is rapidly approaching a climax (*an acute shortage of O-negative blood*), while **deciding** refers to something that forces a certain outcome (*a deciding factor in his recovery*). **Pressing** and **urgent** are milder words. A situation that is *pressing* may be chronic rather than *acute* (*a pressing need for changes in the political system*), while an *urgent* situation may be approaching a crisis without reference to a specific turning point (*an urgent meeting between the two presidents*). While *urgent* expresses more intensity than *pressing*, neither adjective conveys the same sense of intensity as *crucial*, *critical*, or *acute*.

cru•ci•ble /krṓsibəl/ *n.* **1** melting pot for metals, etc. **2** severe test or trial.

cru•cif•er•ous /krṓsíferəs/ *adj.* of a botanical family having flowers with four petals arranged in a cross.

cru•ci•fix /krṓsifiks/ *n.* image of a cross with a figure of Christ on it.

cru•ci•fix•ion /krṓsifikshən/ *n.* **1** crucifying; being crucified. **2** (**Crucifixion**) crucifixion of Christ.

cru•ci•form /krṓsifawrm/ *adj.* cross-shaped.

cru•ci•fy /krṓsifī/ *v.tr.* (**-fies, -fied**) **1** put to death by fastening to a cross. **2** persecute; torment. **3** *sl.* defeat thoroughly. □□ **cru′ci•fi•er** *n.*
  ■ **2** see TORMENT *v.* 1. **3** humiliate.

crud /krud/ *n.* *sl.* **1** deposit of dirt, grease, etc. **2** unpleasant person. **3** nonsense. □□ **crud′dy** *adj.* (**crud•di•er, crud•di•est**).
  ■ **1** see FILTH 1. □□ **cruddy** see *filthy* (FILTH).

crude /krōōd/ • *adj.* **1 a** in the natural state; not refined. **b** unpolished; lacking finish. **2 a** rude; blunt. **b** offensive; indecent. **3** inexact; rough (*a crude estimate*). See synonym study at RUDE. • *n.* natural mineral oil. □□ **crude′ly** *adv.* **crude′ness** *n.* **cru′di•ty** *n.*
  ■ *adj.* **1 a** raw, unprocessed. **b** rough, rudimentary, undeveloped, primitive. **2 a** coarse, unsophisticated, indelicate, unrefined, uncouth, crass, gross, uncivil, impolite. **b** obscene, vulgar, tasteless. **3** see ROUGH *adj.* 7.

cru•di•tés /krōōditáy/ *n.pl.* hors-d'oeuvre of mixed raw vegetables.

cru•el /krṓəl/ *adj.* **1** harsh; severe. **2** causing pain or suffering, esp. deliberately. □□ **cru′el•ly** *adv.* **cru′el•ness** *n.* **cru′el•ty** *n.* (*pl.* **-ties**).
  ■ merciless, pitiless, hard-hearted, heartless, unsparing, callous, sadistic, beastly, cold-blooded, ruthless, vicious, unkind; ferocious, inhuman, barbaric, barbarous, brutal, brute, savage, fiendish.

cru•et /krṓit/ *n.* small container (esp. for oil or vinegar) for use at the table.

cruise /krōōz/ • *v.* **1** *intr.* make a journey by

sea, esp. for pleasure. **2** *intr.* travel at a moderate or steady speed. **3** *intr.* achieve an objective, win a race, etc., with ease. **4** *intr. & tr. sl.* search for a sexual partner, esp. on streets, in bars, etc. • *n.* cruising voyage. □ **cruise control** device for automatically maintaining the speed of an automobile, etc. **cruise missile** low-flying, self-guiding missile.

■ *v.* **1** sail, coast, travel, journey. • *n.* boat trip.

cruis•er /krōōzər/ *n.* **1** high-speed warship. **2** police patrol car.

cruis•er•weight /krōōzərwayt/ *n.* weight class in professional boxing between light heavyweight and heavyweight.

crul•ler /krúlər/ *n.* small fried cake made of twisted dough.

crumb /krum/ *n.* **1 a** small fragment, esp. of bread. **b** small particle. **2** *sl.* objectionable person.

■ **1** morsel, bite, scrap, shred, snippet, sliver, bit, speck, *colloq.* atom. **2** see WRETCH 2.

crum•ble /krúmbəl/ *v.* **1** *tr. & intr.* break or fall into fragments. **2** *intr.* (of power, reputation, etc.) gradually disintegrate. □□ **crum′bli•ness** /-blee-/ *n.* **crum′bly** *adj.* (**crum•bli•er, crum•bli•est**).

■ *v.* **1** come to pieces. **2** see COLLAPSE *v.*

crumb•y /krúmee/ *adj.* (**crumb•i•er, crumb•i•est**) **1** like or covered in crumbs. **2** = CRUMMY.

crum•my /krúmee/ *adj.* (**crum•mi•er, crum•mi•est**) *colloq.* squalid; worthless □□ **crum′mi•ly** *adv.* **crum′mi•ness** *n.*

■ see INFERIOR *adj.* 2.

crum•ple /krúmpəl/ • *v.* **1** *tr. & intr.* **a** crush or become crushed into creases. **b** ruffle; wrinkle. **2** *intr.* collapse; give way. • *n.* crease or wrinkle. □□ **crum′ply** *adj.*

■ *v.* **1** rumple, crinkle, mangle. **2** see COLLAPSE *v.* • *n.* see WRINKLE *n.* 1, 2.

crunch /krunch/ • *v.tr.* **1** crush noisily with the teeth. **2** grind under foot, wheels, etc. • *n.* **1** crunching; crunching sound. **2** *colloq.* decisive event; moment of pressure. □□ **crunch′i•ly** *adv.* **crunch′i•ness** *n.* **crunch′y** *adj.* (**crunch•i•er, crunch•i•est**).

■ *v.* chew, bite, munch, champ, chomp, scrunch. • *n.* **2** crisis, critical moment; crux, juncture. □□ **crunchy** see CRISP *adj.* 1.

cru•sade /krōōsáyd/ • *n.* **1** any of several medieval military expeditions made by Europeans to recover the Holy Land from the Muslims. **2** vigorous campaign in favor of a cause. • *v.intr.* engage in a crusade. □□ **cru•sad′er** *n.*

■ *n.* **1** holy war. **2** see CAMPAIGN *n.* 2. • *v.* campaign, war, battle; lobby.

crush /krush/ • *v.tr.* **1** compress with force or violence, so as to break, bruise, etc. **2** reduce to powder by pressure. **3** crumple. **4** defeat or subdue completely. • *n.* **1** act of crushing. **2** crowded mass of people. **3** drink made from crushed fruit. **4** *colloq.* infatuation.

■ *v.* **1** smash, crunch; squash, mash, mangle, squeeze. **2** pulverize; see also GRIND *v.* 1a. **3** wrinkle, crease, crinkle, rumple. **4** overcome, conquer, beat, thrash, quash,

quell, overwhelm, squelch, suppress, repress. • *n.* **2** crowd, jam, throng.

crust /krust/ • *n.* **1 a** hard outer part of bread. **b** dry scrap of bread. **2** pastry covering of a pie. **3** hard casing of a softer thing. **4** outer portion of the earth. **5** hard residue or deposit. **6** *sl.* impudence. • *v.* **1** cover or become covered with a crust. **2** form into a crust. □□ **crus′tal** *adj.* (in sense 4 of *n.*).

■ *n.* **1** see HEEL¹ *n.* 4. **3–5** see SKIN¹ *n.* 3. **6** see GALL 1.

crus•ta•cean /krustáyshən/ • *n.* hardshelled, esp. aquatic arthropod, e.g., crab, lobster, shrimp. • *adj.* of crustaceans.

crust•y /krústee/ *adj.* (**crust•i•er, crust•i•est**) **1** having a crisp crust. **2** irritable; curt. □□ **crust′i•ly** *adv.* **crust′i•ness** *n.*

■ **2** see IRRITABLE 1.

crutch /kruch/ *n.* **1** support for walking used by a lame person, usu. with a crosspiece fitting under the armpit. **2** support or object of dependency.

crux /kruks/ *n.* (*pl.* **crux•es** or **cru•ces** /krōōseez/) decisive point at issue.

■ see NUB 1.

cry /krī/ • *n.* (**cries, cried**) **1** *intr.* make a loud or shrill sound, esp. to express pain, appeal for help, etc. **2 a** *intr.* shed tears; weep. **b** *v.* shed (tears). **3** *tr.* say or exclaim loudly or excitedly. **4** *intr.* (of an animal, esp. a bird) make a loud call. • *n.* (*pl.* **cries**) **1** loud shout of grief, pain, joy, etc. **2** loud excited utterance. **3** urgent appeal. **4** spell of weeping. **5 a** public demand. **b** rallying call. **6** call of an animal. □ **cry out for** demand as a self-evident requirement or solution. **far cry 1** long way. **2** very different thing. **for crying out loud** *colloq.* exclamation of surprise or annoyance.

■ *v.* **1** see SHOUT *v.* **2 a** sob, wail, bawl, whimper, snivel. • *n.* **1, 2** scream, shriek, wail, howl, yowl, screech, yelp, whoop, yell. **3** see APPEAL *n.* 1. **5 b** battle cry; slogan, watchword. **6** sound, note. □ **cry out for** call for. **far cry 1** remote, distant, faraway, faroff. **2** (*far cry from*) not (at all), anything but.

cry•ba•by /krībaybee/ *n.* person who sheds tears or complains frequently.

cry•er var. of CRIER.

cry•ing /krī-ing/ *attrib.adj.* flagrant (*a crying shame*).

cry•o•gen•ics /krīəjéniks/ *n.* branch of physics dealing with very low temperatures. □□ **cry•o•gen′ic** *adj.*

crypt /kript/ *n.* underground vault, used usu. for burial.

■ tomb, mausoleum, sepulcher, grave, catacomb.

cryp•tic /kríptik/ *adj.* obscure in meaning; secret; mysterious. □□ **cryp′ti•cal•ly** *adv.*

■ unclear, nebulous, vague, inscrutable, recondite, puzzling; mystical, esoteric, enigmatic.

crypto- /kríptō/ *comb. form* concealed; secret (*crypto-Nazi*).

cryp•to•gram /kríptəgram/ *n.* text written in code.

cryp•tog•ra•phy /kríptógrəfee/ *n.* art of

writing or solving ciphers. □□ **cryp•to'gra• pher** *n.* **cryp•to•graph•ic** /–təgráfik/ *adj.* **cryp•to•graph'i•cal•ly** *adv.*

crys•tal /krístˈl/ • *n.* **1 a** clear transparent mineral. **b** piece of this. **2 a** highly transparent glass. **b** articles of this. **3** glass over a watch face. **4** crystalline piece of semiconductor. **5** substance with a definite internal structure and a solid form enclosed by symmetrical plane faces. • *adj.* made of, like, or clear as crystal.

■ *n.* **1 b** see GRAIN *n.* 3.

crys•tal•line /krístˈlin, –lin/ *adj.* **1** of, like, or clear as crystal. **2** having the structure and form of a crystal. □□ **crys•tal•lin•i•ty** /–líni-tee/ *n.*

■ **1** see CLEAR *adj.* 3.

crys•tal•lize /krístˈliz/ *v.* **1** *tr. & intr.* form or cause to form crystals. **2** (of ideas or plans) **a** *intr.* become definite. **b** *tr.* make definite. □□ **crys•tal•li•za'tion** *n.*

Cs *symb. Chem.* cesium.

CST *abbr.* central standard time.

CT *abbr.* Connecticut (in official postal use).

ct. *abbr.* **1** carat. **2** cent.

ctn. *abbr.* **1** carton. **2** cotangent.

Cu *symb. Chem.* copper.

cu. *abbr.* cubic.

cub /kub/ *n.* **1** young of a fox, bear, lion, etc. **2** (in full **cub reporter**) young newspaper reporter.

cub•by /kúbee/ *n.* (*pl.* **–bies**) (in full **cub•by• hole**) small enclosed space, esp. for storage, etc.

■ see COMPARTMENT *n.* 1.

cube /kyoob/ • *n.* **1** solid of six equal square sides. **2** *Math.* product of a number multiplied by its square. • *v.tr.* **1** find the cube of (a number). **2** cut (food, etc.) into small cubes. □ **cube root** number for which a given number is the cube.

■ *n.* **1** see BLOCK *n.* 1.

cu•bic /kyoobik/ *adj.* **1** cube-shaped. **2** of three dimensions. **3** involving the cube (and no higher power) of a number.

cu•bi•cal /kyoobikəl/ *adj.* cube-shaped. □□ **cu'bi•cal•ly** *adv.*

cu•bi•cle /kyoobikəl/ *n.* small partitioned space; compartment.

■ see BOOTH 2.

cub•ism /kyoobizəm/ *n.* geometric style in art, esp. painting. □□ **cub'ist** *n. & adj.*

cu•bit /kyoobit/ *n.* ancient measure about the length of a forearm.

cuck•old /kúkōld/ • *n.* husband of an adulteress. • *v.tr.* make a cuckold of. □□ **cuck' old•ry** *n.*

cuck•oo /kookoo/ • *n.* bird with a characteristic cry, known to lay its eggs in the nests of other birds. • *predic.adj. sl.* crazy; foolish. □ **cuckoo in the nest** unwelcome intruder.

■ *adj.* see CRAZY 1.

cu•cum•ber /kyookumbər/ *n.* long, green, fleshy fruit, used in salads and for pickles.

cud /kud/ *n.* half-digested food returned from the first stomach of ruminants to the mouth for further chewing.

cud•dle /kúd'l/ • *v.* **1** *tr.* hug; fondle. **2** *intr.*

nestle together; lie close and snug. • *n.* prolonged hug. □□ **cud'dle•some** *adj.* **cud'dly** *adj.* (**cud•dli•er, cud•dli•est**).

■ *v.* **1** see CARESS *v.* **2** embrace, snuggle up. • *n.* see CARESS *n.*

cud•gel /kújəl/ • *n.* short, thick stick used as a weapon. • *v.tr.* beat with a cudgel.

■ *n.* see CLUB *n.* 1. • *v.* see CLUB *v.* 1.

cue[1] /kyoo/ • *n.* **1 a** last words of an actor's line as a signal to another to enter or speak. **b** similar signal to a musician, etc. **2 a** stimulus to perception, etc. **b** signal for action. **c** hint on how to behave. • *v.tr.* (**cues, cued, cu•ing** or **cue•ing**) **1** give a cue to. **2** put (audio equipment) in readiness.

■ *n.* **1, 2** prompt, reminder, sign. • *v.* -**1** signal, prompt.

cue[2] /kyoo/ *n. Billiards* long rod for striking the ball. □□ **cue'ist** *n.*

cuff[1] /kuf/ *n.* **1** end part of a sleeve. **2** turned-up hem on pants. **3** [in *pl.*] *colloq.* handcuffs. □ **off-the-cuff** *colloq.* impromptu. □□ **cuffed** *adj.* [also in *comb.*].

■ □ **off-the-cuff** see EXTEMPORANEOUS.

cuff[2] /kuf/ • *v.tr.* strike with an open hand. • *n.* such a blow.

■ *v.* see HIT[2] *v.* 1a. • *n.* see BLOW 1.

cui•sine /kwizeén/ *n.* style or method of cooking.

cul-de-sac /kúldəsak, kool–/ *n.* (*pl.* **culs-de-sac** *pronunc.* same) **1** dead-end street. **2** futile course.

cu•li•nar•y /kyóoləneree, kúl–/ *adj.* pertaining to cooking.

cull /kul/ *v.tr.* **1** gather; derive. **2** pick selectively.

■ see PICK[1] *v.* 1, 2.

cul•mi•nate /kúlminayt/ *v.* **1** *intr.* reach its highest or final point. **2** *tr.* bring to its highest or final point. □□ **cul•mi•na•tion** /–náy-shən/ *n.*

■ see FINISH *v.* 2a.

cu•lottes /kóolóts, kyoo–/ *n.pl.* skirtlike trousers.

cul•pa•ble /kúlpəbəl/ *adj.* deserving blame. □□ **cul•pa•bil'i•ty** *n.*

■ see GUILTY 1, 4.

cul•prit /kúlprit/ *n.* guilty person.

■ offender, criminal, malefactor, wrongdoer.

cult /kult/ *n.* **1** ritualistic religious system. **2 a** devotion to a person or thing (*cult of aestheticism*). **b** popular fashion. **3** [*attrib.*] denoting a fashionable person or thing (*cult film*). □□ **cult'ism** *n.* **cult'ist** *n.*

cul•ti•vate /kúltivayt/ *v.tr.* **1** prepare and use (soil, etc.) for crops or gardening. **2 a** raise (crops). **b** culture (bacteria, etc.). **3 a** (often as **cultivated** *adj.*) improve or develop (the mind, manners, etc.). **b** nurture (a person, friendship, etc.). □□ **cul•ti•va'tion** *n.*

■ **1** till, plow, farm, work. **2 a** grow, tend, produce. **3 a** (**cultivated**) sophisticated, cultured, refined, civilized, polished, aristocratic, urbane, suave, cosmopolitan. **b** work on, promote, further, encourage, foster, advance. □□ **cultivation** see CULTURE *n.* 1b.

cul•tur•al /kúlchərəl/ *adj.* relating to artistic or intellectual matters or to a specific culture. □□ **cul'tur•al•ly** *adv.*

cul•ture /kúlchər/ • n. **1 a** artistic and intellectual achievement. **b** refined appreciation of this. **2** customs, achievements, etc., of a particular civilization. **3 a** cultivation of plants; rearing of bees, silkworms, etc. **b** cultivation of the soil. **4** quantity of microorganisms and the nutrient material supporting their growth. • v.tr. maintain (bacteria, etc.) in suitable growth conditions. □ **culture shock** disorientation experienced by a person suddenly subjected to an unfamiliar culture. □□ **cul′tured** adj.

■ n. **1 b** sophistication, urbanity, taste. **2** mores. **3** see BREEDING 1.

cul•vert /kúlvərt/ n. channel carrying water under a road, etc.

■ see DRAIN n. 1a.

cum /kum/ prep. [usu. in comb.] with; combined with; also used as (a bedroom-cum-study).

cum. abbr. cumulative.

cum•ber•some /kúmbərsəm/ adj. inconvenient in size, weight, or shape; unwieldy. See synonym study at HEAVY.

■ see UNWIELDY.

cum•in /kúmin, kŏŏ-, kyŏŏ-/ n. **1** plant with aromatic seeds. **2** these seeds used as flavoring.

cum•mer•bund /kúmərbund/ n. waist sash.

cu•mu•la•tive /kyŏŏmyələtiv, -lətiv/ adj. **1** increasing progressively in amount, force, etc. **2** formed by successive additions. □□ **cu′mu•la•tive•ly** adv. **cu′mu•la•tive•ness** n.

cu•mu•lus /kyŏŏmyələs/ n. (pl. **cu•mu•li** /-lī/) cloud formation of heaped, rounded masses. □□ **cu′mu•lous** adj.

cu•ne•i•form /kyŏŏnéeəfawrm, kyŏŏnéeə-, kyŏŏni-/ • adj. **1** wedge-shaped. **2** of or using wedge-shaped writing, as in ancient Babylonian, etc., inscriptions. • n. cuneiform writing.

cun•ning /kúning/ • adj. **1** deceitful; clever; crafty. **2** ingenious. **3** attractive; quaint. • n. **1** craftiness; skill in deceit. **2** skill; ingenuity. □□ **cun′ning•ly** adv.

■ adj. **1** see CRAFTY. **2** see INGENIOUS. • n. **1** see CRAFT n. 4. **2** see INGENUITY.

cup /kup/ • n. **1** small bowl-shaped container for drinking from. **2 a** its contents. **b** = CUPFUL. **3** cup-shaped thing. **4** cup-shaped trophy. • v.tr. (**cupped, cup•ping**) **1** form (esp. one's hands) into the shape of a cup. **2** take or hold as in a cup. □ **one's cup of tea** colloq. what interests or suits one.

■ n. **1** see MUG n. 1a. **4** see TROPHY 1.

cup•board /kúbərd/ n. recess or piece of furniture with a door and (usu.) shelves.

■ see CABINET 1a.

cup•cake /kúpkayk/ n. small cup-shaped cake.

cup•ful /kúpfŏŏl/ n. (pl. **-fuls**) amount held by a cup, esp. a half-pint (8-ounce) measure.

Cu•pid /kyŏŏpid/ n. **1** Roman god of love, represented as a naked winged archer. **2** (also **cupid**) representation of Cupid.

cu•pid•i•ty /kyŏŏpíditee/ n. greed for gain; avarice.

cu•po•la /kyŏŏpələ/ n. dome forming or adorning a roof.

cu•pric /kŏŏprik, kyŏŏ-/ adj. of copper.

cu•prous /kŏŏprəs, kyŏŏ-/ adj. of copper.

cur /kər/ n. **1** mongrel. **2** colloq. contemptible person.

■ **1** see MONGREL n. **2** see WRETCH 2.

cur. abbr. **1** currency. **2** current.

cur•a•ble /kyŏŏrəbəl/ adj. that can be cured. □□ **cur•a•bil′i•ty** n.

■ see BENIGN 3.

cu•ra•cao /kyŏŏrəsố, -sốw/ n. orange-flavored liqueur.

cu•ra•re /kyŏŏraáree, kŏŏ-/ n. bitter, poisonous extract of various S. American plants.

cu•rate /kyŏŏrət/ n. assistant to a parish priest.

cu•ra•tive /kyŏŏrətiv/ • adj. tending or able to cure. • n. curative agent.

■ adj. see THERAPEUTIC 1.

cu•ra•tor /kyŏŏráytər, kyŏŏrə-/ n. keeper or custodian of a museum, etc. □□ **cu•ra•to•ri•al** /kyŏŏrətáwreeəl/ adj. **cu•ra′tor•ship** n.

curb /kərb/ • n. **1** check; restraint. **2** street edge or sidewalk border. **3** strap, etc., to restrain a horse. **4** enclosing border. • v.tr. restrain.

■ n. **1** control; see also CHECK n. 2c. • v. check, bridle, control, contain, repress, subdue, suppress; see also RESTRAIN 1.

curd /kərd/ n. [often pl.] coagulated milk product, often made into cheese.

cur•dle /kərd′l/ v. make into or become curds; (of milk) turn sour; congeal. □ **make one's blood curdle** fill one with horror. □□ **cur′dler** n.

■ see TURN v. 10, COAGULATE.

cure /kyŏŏr/ • v.tr. **1** restore to health. **2** eliminate (disease, evil, etc.). **3** preserve (meat, fruit, etc.) by salting, drying, etc. • n. **1** restoration to health. **2** thing that effects a cure. **3** course of treatment. □ **cure-all** panacea.

■ v. **1** heal, make better. **2** see ELIMINATE 1a. **3** smoke, pickle, corn, marinate. • n. **1** healing. **2, 3** therapy, remedy, medication.

cu•rette /kyŏŏrét/ n. surgeon's scraping instrument.

cur•few /kárfyŏŏ/ n. regulation requiring people to remain indoors between specified hours, usu. at night.

cu•ri•a /kyŏŏreeə/ n. (also **Curia**) (pl. **cu•ri•ae** /-ree-ee/) the papal court; government departments of the Vatican. □□ **Cu′ri•al** adj.

cu•rie /kyŏŏree/ n. unit of radioactivity.

cu•ri•o /kyŏŏreeố/ n. (pl. **-os**) rare or unusual object.

■ see RARITY 2.

cu•ri•os•i•ty /kyŏŏreeósitee/ n. (pl. **-ties**) **1** eager desire to know; inquisitiveness. **2** strange, rare, or interesting thing.

■ **1** interest, colloq. nosiness. **2** strangeness, peculiarity; oddity, rarity.

cu•ri•ous /kyŏŏreeəs/ adj. **1** eager to learn; inquisitive. **2** strange; surprising; odd. □□ **cu′ri•ous•ly** adv. **cu′ri•ous•ness** n.

■ **1** interested, inquiring, prying, investigative, colloq. nosy, snoopy. **2** peculiar, eccentric, queer, unusual, outrageous, offbeat, weird, bizarre, unconventional, irregular.

cu·ri·um /kyŏoreeəm/ n. artificial radioactive metallic element. ¶Symb.: **Cm**.

curl /kərl/ • v. **1** tr. & intr. bend or coil into a spiral; form or cause to form curls. **2** intr. move in a spiral form. • n. **1** lock of curled hair. **2** anything spiral or curved inward. **3 a** curling movement. **b** being curled. □ **make a person's hair curl** colloq. shock or horrify a person.
■ v. **1, 2** see WIND² v. 4. • n. **1** see LOCK² 1. **2** see SPIRAL n.

curl·er /kərlər/ n. pin or roller, etc., for curling the hair.

cur·lew /kərlŏo, –lyŏo/ n. wading bird, usu. with long, slender, bill.

cur·li·cue /kərlikyŏo/ n. decorative curl or twist.

curl·ing /kərling/ n. game played on ice in which round, flat stones are slid across the surface toward a mark. □□ **curl'i·ness** n.

curl·y /kərlee/ adj. (**curl·i·er**, **curl·i·est**) **1** having or arranged in curls. **2** moving in curves. □□ **curl'i·ness** n.
■ **1** see KINKY 3.

cur·mud·geon /kərmújən/ n. bad-tempered person. □□ **cur·mud'geon·ly** adj.
■ □□ **curmudgeonly** see IRRITABLE 1.

cur·rant /kərənt, kúr–/ n. **1** small seedless dried grape. **2 a** any of various shrubs producing red, white, or black berries. **b** such a berry.

cur·ren·cy /kərənsee, kúr–/ n. (pl. **–cies**) **1 a** money in use in a country. **b** other commodity used as money. **2** being current; prevalence.
■ **1** see MONEY 1.

cur·rent /kərənt, kúr–/ • adj. belonging to the present time; happening now. • n. **1** narrow body of water, air, etc., moving in a definite direction. **2 a** ordered movement of electrically charged particles. **b** quantity representing the intensity of this.
■ adj. contemporary, ongoing, contemporaneous, latest, up-to-date. • n. **1** stream, flow, undercurrent, tide.

cur·rent·ly /kərəntlee, kúr–/ adv. at the present time; now.

cur·ric·u·lum /kərikyələm/ n. (pl. **cur·ric·u·la** /–lə/ or **cur·ric·u·lums**) subjects in a course of study. □□ **cur·ric'u·lar** adj.
■ see PROGRAM n. 4.

cur·ric·u·lum vi·tae /kərikyələm vítee, veéti/ n. (pl. **cur·ric·u·la vi·tae** /kərikyələm vítee, veéti/) brief account of one's education, qualifications, etc.
■ see RÉSUMÉ.

cur·ry¹ /kóree, kúree/ • n. (pl. **–ries**) dish prepared with curry powder. • v.tr. (**–ries**, **–ried**) flavor with curry powder. □ **curry powder** usu. hot-tasting preparation of various spices.

cur·ry² /kóree, kúree/ v.tr. (**–ries**, **–ried**) **1** groom (a horse) with a currycomb. **2** treat (tanned leather) to improve it. **3** thrash. □ **curry favor** ingratiate oneself.
■ **1** see GROOM v. 1. □ **curry favor** see INGRATIATE.

cur·ry·comb /kóreekōm, kúree–/ n. metal serrated device for grooming horses.

curse /kərs/ • n. **1** solemn invocation of supernatural wrath. **2** evil supposedly resulting from a curse. **3** violent exclamation of anger; profane oath. **4** thing that causes evil or harm. • v. **1** tr. **a** utter a curse against. **b** [in imper.] may God curse. **2** tr. afflict (with). **3** intr. utter expletive curses.
■ n. **1** malediction, imprecation, denunciation, execration, anathema. **3** profanity, expletive, blasphemy, obscenity. **4** bane, misfortune, affliction, torment, scourge, blight, cross to bear. • v. **1 a** damn, execrate, denounce. **b** damn, confound, colloq. drat. **2** burden, saddle, handicap. **3** swear.

cursed /kərsid, kərst/ adj. damnable; abominable. □□ **curs'ed·ly** adv. **curs'ed·ness** n.
■ see DAMNABLE.

cur·sive /kərsiv/ • adj. (of writing) done with joined characters. • n. cursive writing. □□ **cur'sive·ly** adv.

cur·sor /kərsər/ n. Computing positional indicator on a screen.

cur·so·ry /kərsəree/ adj. hasty; hurried (cursory glance). See synonym study at SUPERFICIAL. □□ **cur'so·ri·ly** adv. **cur'so·ri·ness** n.
■ superficial, passing, quick, slapdash, perfunctory.

curt /kərt/ adj. rudely brief. See synonym study at BRUSQUE. □□ **curt'ly** adv. **curt'ness** n.
■ abrupt, short, terse, laconic; blunt, gruff, brusque.

cur·tail /kərtáyl/ v.tr. cut short; reduce. □□ **cur·tail'ment** n.
■ shorten, abbreviate, abridge; diminish, cut back or down; terminate.

cur·tain /kərtən/ • n. **1** piece of cloth, etc., hung as a screen, esp. at a window. **2 a** rise or fall of a stage curtain. **b** = curtain call. **3** partition or cover. **4** [in pl.] sl. the end. • v.tr. [foll. by off] shut off with curtains. □ **curtain call** audience's summons to actor(s) to take a bow.

curt·sy /kərtsee/ (also **curt'sey**) • n. (pl. **–sies** or **–seys**) woman's or girl's formal greeting or salutation made by bending the knees and lowering the body. • v.intr. (**–sies**, **–sied** or **–seys**, **–seyed**) make a curtsy.

cur·va·ceous /kərváyshəs/ adj. colloq. (esp. of a woman) having a shapely figure.
■ see SHAPELY.

cur·va·ture /kərvəchər/ n. curving or degree of curve.
■ see BEND¹ n.

curve /kərv/ • n. **1** line or surface of which no part is straight or flat. **2** curved form or thing. • v. bend or shape to form a curve. □□ **curved** adj. **cur'vi·ness** n. **curv'y** adj. (**curv·i·er**, **curv·i·est**).
■ n. see BEND¹ n. • v. see BEND¹ v. 1. □□ **curvy** see SERPENTINE adj.

cush·ion /kŏoshən/ • n. **1** bag stuffed with soft material, for sitting or leaning on, etc. **2** protection against shock. • v.tr. **1** provide or protect with a cushion or cushions. **2** mitigate the adverse effects of. □□ **cush'ion·y** adj.
■ n. **1** pillow, bolster, pad. **2** see DEFENSE 2. • v. **2** soften, absorb, buffer, dampen, lessen.

cush·y /kŏoshee/ adj. (**cush·i·er**, **cush·i·est**) colloq. easy and pleasant. □□ **cush'i·ness** n.

cusp /kusp/ *n.* **1** point or pointed end. **2** point at which two arcs meet.

cus•tard /kústərd/ *n.* pudding or sweet sauce made with milk, eggs, and flavored cornstarch.

cus•to•di•an /kustṓdeeən/ *n.* caretaker, esp. of a public building, etc. □□ **cus•to′di•an•ship** *n.*

■ see GUARD *n.* 2. □□ **custodianship** see CARE *n.* 4.

cus•to•dy /kústədee/ *n.* **1** guardianship; protective care. **2** imprisonment. □ **take into custody** arrest. □□ **cus•to•di•al** /kustṓdeeəl/ *adj.*

■ **1** custodianship, safekeeping, protection, charge, keeping. **2** detention, incarceration, confinement.

cus•tom /kústəm/ *n.* **1 a** usual behavior. **b** particular established way of behaving. **2** *Law* established usage having the force of law. **3** [in *pl.*; also treated as *sing.*] **a** duty on imports and exports. **b** officials or area administering this.

■ **1 a** practice, habit, usage, fashion, tradition, routine. **b** (*customs*) traditions, conventions, mores. **3** (*customs*) **a** impost, tax, excise, levy, dues, tariff.

cus•tom•ar•y /kústəmeree/ *adj.* usual; in accordance with custom. □□ **cus•tom•ar′i•ly** *adv.*

■ normal, conventional, routine, commonplace, ordinary, traditional.

cus•tom•er /kústəmər/ *n.* **1** person who buys goods or services. **2** person one has to deal with (*tough customer*).

■ **1** client, patron, purchaser; consumer. **2** character.

cus•tom•ize /kústəmīz/ *v.tr.* make or modify according to individual requirements.

cut /kut/ • *v.* (**cut•ting**; *past* and *past part.* **cut**) **1** *tr.* penetrate or wound with a sharp-edged instrument. **2** *tr. & intr.* divide or be divided with a knife, etc. **3** *tr.* reduce the length of or detach by cutting. **4** *tr.* reduce (wages, prices, time, etc.) or cease (services, etc.). **5** *tr.* **a** make (a coat, gem, key, record, etc.) by cutting. **b** make (a path, tunnel, etc.) by removing material. **6** *tr.* perform; make (*cut a deal*). **7** *tr.* cross; intersect. **8** *intr.* traverse, esp. as a shorter way. **9** *tr.* refuse to recognize (a person). **10** *tr.* deliberately miss (a class, etc.). **11** *Cards* divide (a deck) into two parts. **12** *tr.* switch off (an engine, etc.). **13** *tr.* dilute. • *n.* **1** cutting. **2** division or wound made by cutting. **3** stroke with a knife, etc. **4** reduction or excision. **5** wounding remark or act. **6** style in which a garment, the hair, etc., is cut. **7** piece of butchered meat. **8** *colloq.* commission; share of profits. □ **a cut above** *colloq.* noticeably superior to. **be cut out be** suited (*was not cut out to be a teacher*). **cut-and-dried** completely decided; inflexible. **cut corners** do a task, etc., perfunctorily, esp. to save time. **cut a person down to size** *colloq.* deflate a person's pretensions. **cut in 1** interrupt. **2** pull in closely in front of another vehicle. **3** give a share of profits, etc., to. **4** interrupt a dancing couple to take over from one partner. **cut into** interfere with and reduce (*cuts into my free time*). **cut it out** [usu. in *imper.*] *sl.* stop doing that. **cut loose** begin to act freely. **cut the mustard** *sl.* reach the required standard. **cut short** terminate prematurely (*cut short his visit*). **cut one's teeth on** acquire initial practice or experience from (something). **cut a tooth** have it appear through the gum. **cut up 1** criticize severely. **2** behave in a comical or unruly manner.

■ *v.* **1** gash, slash; see also SLIT¹ *v.* **2** slice, carve. **3** trim, snip, lop, clip, crop, shorten, shear, chop off; mow; dock; abbreviate, condense, abridge, edit. **4** slash, diminish, decrease, curtail; discount, mark down; lower. **5 a** see SHAPE *v.* 1. **b** dig, burrow, hollow out. **6** present, exhibit, display; execute, do; conclude, settle. **7** meet. **8** pass; take a short cut. **9** see IGNORE 1. **10** avoid, fail to attend, *colloq.* skip; eschew. **12** turn off. **13** thin, water (down), weaken; degrade, adulterate. • *n.* **2** gash, slash, incision, nick, wound. **3** *colloq.* swipe. **4** cutback, curtailment, decrease; deletion, omission. **5** affront, insult, offense, slight, snub, dig, slap in the face, *colloq.* jibe. **6** see STYLE *n.* 1, 4. **8** portion, percentage, dividend. □ **a cut above** better than. **cut and dried** clear-cut, settled, arranged; predetermined. **cut in 1** interrupt, butt in. **cut it out** see *pack it in* (PACK). **cut the mustard** see *make it* 2. **cut short** interrupt; abbreviate, condense, abridge, edit. **cut up 1** see CRITICIZE 1. **2** misbehave.

cu•ta•ne•ous /kyoōtáyneeəs/ *adj.* of the skin.

cut•a•way /kútəway/ *adj.* **1** (of a diagram, etc.) with parts of the interior exposed. **2** (of a coat) with the front below the waist cut away.

cut•back /kútbak/ *n.* cutting back, esp. a reduction in expenditure.

■ see DECREASE *n.*

cute /kyoōt/ *adj. colloq.* **1 a** attractive; quaint. **b** affectedly attractive. **2** clever; ingenious. □□ **cute′ly** *adv.* **cute′ness** *n.*

■ **1 a** pretty, adorable, dainty, lovely, beautiful; cunning. **2** shrewd, adroit, crafty, cunning.

cu•ti•cle /kyoōtikəl/ *n.* dead skin at the base of a fingernail or toenail.

cut•lass /kútləs/ *n.* short sword with a slightly curved blade.

cut•ler•y /kútləree/ *n.* **1** knives, etc., for kitchen use. **2** knives, forks, and spoons for use at table.

■ **2** flatware.

cut•let /kútlit/ *n.* **1** small piece of veal, etc., for frying. **2** flat cake of ground meat, etc.

cut•off /kútawf/ *n.* **1** point at which something is cut off. **2** device for stopping a flow. **3** shortcut. **4** (*pl.*) shorts made from jeans, etc.

cut•throat /kútthrōt/ • *n.* murderer. • *adj.* ruthless and intense.

■ *n.* pirate, killer, assassin. • *adj.* merciless, unmerciful, brutal, cold-blooded, cold-hearted; murderous, barbaric, cruel, savage, inhuman, brutal, vicious.

cut•ting /kúting/ • *n.* piece cut from a plant for propagation. • *adj.* hostile; wounding. □ **cutting edge** forefront; vanguard. □□ **cut′ting•ly** *adv.*
■ *n.* scion, slip; clipping. • *adj.* sarcastic, sardonic, scornful, sneering, harsh, caustic, contemptuous; malicious, vicious, venomous; severe, biting.

cut•tle•fish /kút'lfish/ *n.* mollusk with ten arms that ejects a black fluid when threatened.

cut•worm /kútwərm/ *n.* caterpillar that eats through stems at ground level.

c.v. *abbr.* curriculum vitae.

cwt. *abbr.* hundredweight.

cy•an /sían/ • *adj.* of a greenish-blue. • *n.* greenish-blue color.

cy•a•nide /síənīd/ *n.* highly poisonous substance used in mineral extraction.

cy•a•no•sis /síənósis/ *n.* bluish discoloration of the skin due to oxygen-deficient blood. □□ **cy•a•not•ic** /–nótik/ *adj.*

cy•ber•ca•fe /síbərkafáy/ • *n.* cafe with computers from which patrons may access the Internet.

cy•ber•net•ics /síbərnétiks/ *n.pl.* [usu. treated as *sing.*] science of communications and control systems in machines and living things. □□ **cy•ber•net′ic** *adj.* **cy•ber•net•i•cist** /–tisist/ *n.*

cy•borg /síbawrg/ *n.* (in science fiction) human being whose biological functions are bionically enhanced.

cy•cla•men /síkləmən, sík–/ *n.* plant with pink, red, or white flowers.

cy•cle /síkəl/ • *n.* **1 a** a recurrent round or period (of events, phenomena, etc.). **b** time needed for this. **2** *Electr.* = HERTZ. **3** series of related songs, poems, etc. **4** bicycle, tricycle, etc. • *v.intr.* **1** ride a bicycle, etc. **2** move in cycles.
■ *n.* **1 a** rotation, circle, course; run, succession, pattern. **4** *colloq.* bike. • *v.* **2** recur, rotate, circle.

cy•clic /síklik, sík–/ *adj.* (also **cy•cli•cal**) /síklikəl, sík–/ **1 a** recurring in cycles. **b** belonging to a chronological cycle. **2** *Chem.* with constituent atoms forming a ring. □□ **cy′cli•cal•ly** *adv.*
■ **1** see PERIODIC.

cy•clist /síklist/ *n.* rider of a bicycle, etc.

cy•clo- /síklō/ *comb. form* circle, cycle, or cyclic.

cy•clone /síklōn/ *n.* violent, low-pressure hurricane of limited diameter. □□ **cy•clon•ic** /–klónik/ *adj.* **cy•clon′i•cal•ly** *adv.*
■ see HURRICANE 1, 2.

cy•clo•tron /síklətron/ *n.* apparatus for acceleration of charged atomic and subatomic particles revolving in a magnetic field.

cyg•net /signit/ *n.* young swan.

cyl•in•der /sílindər/ *n.* **1** uniform solid or hollow body with straight sides and a circular cross section. **2** thing of this shape. □□ **cy•lin•dri•cal** /silíndrikəl/ *adj.* **cy•lin′dri•cal•ly** *adv.*
■ **1** see ROLL *n.* 5.

cym•bal /símbəl/ *n.* brass or bronze plate struck to make a ringing sound. □□ **cym′bal•ist** *n.*

cyn•ic /sínik/ *n.* person with little faith in human nature. □□ **cyn′i•cal** *adj.* **cyn′i•cism** /–nisizəm/ *n.*
■ see SKEPTIC *n.* □□ **cynical** skeptical; see also SARDONIC 1.

cy•no•sure /sínəshŏŏr, sín–/ *n.* **1** center of attraction or admiration. **2** guiding star.

cy•press /síprəs/ *n.* conifer with hard wood and dark foliage.

Cy•ril•lic /sirílik/ • *adj.* of the alphabet used by the Slavic peoples of the Orthodox Church; now used esp. for Russian and Bulgarian. • *n.* this alphabet.

cyst /sist/ *n.* sac formed in the body, containing liquid or semiliquid.

cys•tic /sístik/ *adj.* **1** of the bladder. **2** like a cyst.

cyto- /sítō/ *comb. form* *Biol.* cells or a cell.

cy•tol•o•gy /sítóləjee/ *n.* study of cells. □□ **cy•to•log•i•cal** /sítəlójikəl/ *adj.* **cy•to•log′i•cal•ly** *adv.* **cy•tol′o•gist** *n.*

cy•to•plasm /sítəplazəm/ *n.* protoplasmic content of a cell apart from its nucleus. □□ **cy•to•plas•mic** /–plázmik/ *adj.*

czar /zaar/ *n.* (also **tsar**; *fem.* **cza•ri′na, tsa•ri′na**) **1** *hist.* title of the former emperor of Russia. **2** person with great authority. □□ **czar′dom** *n.* **czar′ism** *n.* **czar′ist** *n.*

Czech /chek/ • *n.* **1** native or national of the Czech Republic. **2** language of the Czech people. • *adj.* of the Czechs or their language.

Czech•o•slo•vak /chékəslóvak, –vaak/ (also **Czech•o•slo•va•ki•an** /–sləvaákeeən/) • *n.* native or national of Czechoslovakia, a former nation in central Europe. • *adj.* of or relating to Czechoslovaks or Czechoslovakia.

Dd

D¹ /dee/ *n.* (also **d**) (*pl.* **Ds** or **D's**; **d's**) **1** fourth letter of the alphabet. **2** *Mus.* second note of the diatonic scale of C major. **3** (as a Roman numeral) 500.
D² *symb. Chem.* deuterium.
D³ *abbr.* **1** (also **D.**) Democrat. **2** dimension (3-*D*).

d. *abbr.* **1** died. **2** departs. **3** delete. **4** daughter. **5** depth.
'd *v.* colloq. (usu. after pronouns) had; would (*I'd, he'd*).
DA *abbr.* district attorney.
dab /dab/ • *v.* (**dabbed, dab•bing**) **1** *tr.* press (a surface) briefly with a cloth, etc.,

without rubbing. **2** *tr.* [foll. by *on*] apply (a substance). • *n.* **1** brief application of a cloth, etc., to a surface. **2** small amount applied in this way. □□ **dab′ber** *n.*

■ *v.* **2** daub, touch; see also APPLY 4. • *n.* **1** touch. **2** drop, trace, bit, hint, suggestion, pinch, dash, *colloq.* smidgen.

dab•ble /dábəl/ *v.intr.* **1** take a casual interest (in an activity, etc.). **2** move the feet, hands, etc., in liquid. □□ **dab′bler** *n.*

■ **1** tinker, trifle, dally; experiment. □□ **dabbler** see DILETTANTE *n.*

da•cha /daachə/ *n.* country house or cottage in Russia.

dachs•hund /daaks-hoont, daaksənt/ *n.* dog of a short-legged, long-bodied breed.

Dacron /dáykron/ *n. propr.* synthetic polyester fiber used in textiles.

dac•tyl /dáktil/ *n.* metrical foot (⌣⌣) consisting of one long (or stressed) syllable followed by two short (or unstressed). □□ **dac•tyl′ic** *adj.*

dad /dad/ *n. colloq.* father.

■ see FATHER *n.* 1.

dad•dy /dádee/ *n.* (*pl.* **-dies**) *colloq.* father.

□ **daddy longlegs** harvestman arachnid.

da•do /dáydō/ *n.* (*pl.* **-dos**) **1** lower part of the wall of a room, visually distinct from the upper part. **2** plinth of a column.

daf•fo•dil /dáfədil/ *n.* **1** bulbous plant with a yellow trumpet-shaped flower. **2** pale-yellow color.

daf•fy /dáfee/ *adj.* (**daf•fi•er, daf•fi•est**) *sl.* = DAFT. □□ **daf′fi•ness** *n.*

daft /daft/ *adj. colloq.* silly; foolish; crazy. □□ **daft′ly** *adv.* **daft′ness** *n.*

■ giddy, senseless, ridiculous, nonsensical, imbecilic, dim-witted, witless, simpleminded, brainless, featherbrained, harebrained, slow-witted, addlebrained, *colloq.* dumb, dopey, moronic, *sl.* daffy; see also CRAZY 1.

dag•ger /dágər/ *n.* **1** short pointed knife for stabbing. **2** *Printing* = OBELUS.

■ **1** short sword, stiletto, dirk, *literary* poniard, *poet.* blade.

da•go /dáygō/ *n.* (*pl.* **-gos** or **-goes**) *sl. offens.* person of Italian, Spanish, or Portuguese ancestry.

da•guerre•o•type /dəgérətīp/ *n.* photograph taken by an early process using a silvered plate and mercury vapor.

dahl•ia /dályə, daal-, dáyl-/ *n.* composite garden plant of Mexican origin, cultivated for its many-colored flowers.

dai•ly /dáylee/ • *adj.* done or occurring every day. • *adv.* every day. • *n.* (*pl.* **-lies**) *colloq.* daily newspaper. □ **daily bread** necessary food. **daily dozen** *colloq.* regular exercises.

■ *adj.* constant, continual, everyday, routine, common. • *adv.* day after day, always, habitually, routinely, continuously. □ **daily bread** see SUSTENANCE 1a.

dain•ty /dáyntee/ • *adj.* (**dain•ti•er, dain•ti•est**) **1** delicately pretty. **2** delicate. **3** (of food) choice. **4** fastidious. • *n.* (*pl.* **-ties**) choice morsel; delicacy. □□ **dain′ti•ly** *adv.* **dain′ti•ness** *n.*

■ *adj.* **1, 2** graceful, elegant, exquisite. **3** delicious, tasty, appetizing; see also CHOICE *adj.* **4** sensitive, finicky. • *n.* treat, tidbit.

dai•qui•ri /dákəree, dī-/ *n.* cocktail of rum, lime juice, etc.

dair•y /dáiree/ • *n.* (*pl.* **-ies**) **1** place for the storage, processing, and distribution of milk and its products. **2** store where milk and milk products are sold. • *adj.* pertaining to milk and its products (and sometimes eggs).

da•is /dáyis, dí-/ *n.* low platform, usu. at the front of a hall, used to support a table, lectern, etc.

dai•sy /dáyzee/ *n.* (*pl.* **-sies**) small composite plant bearing white-petaled flowers ■ **daisy wheel** disk of spokes extending radially from a hub, each ending in a character, used as a printer in word processors and typewriters, **pushing up daisies** *sl.* dead and buried.

Da•ko•ta /dəkōtə/ *n.* **1** N. American people native to the northern Mississippi valley. **2** language of this people (Also called Lakota or Sioux). □□ **Da•ko′tan** *adj.*

Da•lai La•ma /daalī laamə/ *n.* spiritual head of Tibetan Buddhism, formerly also the chief ruler of Tibet (see LAMA).

dale /dayl/ *n.* valley.

dal•li•ance /dáleeəns, -yəns/ *n.* **1** leisurely or frivolous passing of time. **2** act or instance of lighthearted flirting.

■ **1** see SPORT *n.* 2.

dal•ly /dálee/ *v.intr.* (**-lies, -lied**) **1** delay; waste time. **2** flirt; treat frivolously. See synonym study at LOITER.

■ **1** see DELAY *v.* 3, **2** see FLIRT *v.* 1.

Dal•ma•tian /dalmáyshən/ *n.* dog of a large, white, short-haired breed with dark spots.

dam¹ /dam/ • *n.* barrier constructed to hold back water, forming a reservoir or preventing flooding. • *v.tr.* (**dammed, dam•ming**) **1** furnish or confine with a dam. **2** block up; obstruct.

■ *v.* **2** see PLUG *v.* 1.

dam² /dam/ *n.* mother, esp. of a four-footed animal.

dam•age /dámij/ • *n.* **1** harm or injury. **2** [in *pl.*] *Law* financial compensation for a loss or injury. **3** [prec. by *the*] *sl.* cost. • *v.tr.* inflict damage on. □□ **dam′ag•ing•ly** *adv.*

■ *n.* **1** hurt, impairment, mutilation, destruction, devastation. **2** (*damages*) reparation, indemnity. **3** expense, price. • *v.* harm, hurt, injure, impair, mar, deface.

dam•ask /dáməsk/ • *n.* **1 a** woven fabric (esp. silk or linen) with a pattern visible on both sides. **b** twilled table linen. **2** tablecloth made of this material. • *adj.* **1** made of or resembling damask. **2** colored like a damask rose, velvety pink or vivid red. • *v.tr.* weave with figured designs. □ **damask rose** sweet-scented variety of rose with very soft petals.

dame /daym/ *n.* **1** (**Dame**) (in the UK) honorific title given to a woman. **2** *sl.* a woman.

dam•mit /dámit/ *int.* damn it.

damn /dam/ • *v.tr.* **1** curse (a person or thing). **2** doom to hell. **3** condemn; censure. **4** (often as **damning** *adj.*) (of evidence, etc.) show or prove to be guilty. • *n.* **1** uttered curse. **2** *sl.* negligible amount (*not worth a damn*). • *adj. & adv. colloq.* = DAMNED.

□ **damn with faint praise** commend so unenthusiastically as to imply disapproval. □□ **damn'ing•ly** adv.

■ v. **1** see CURSE v. 1. **2** condemn, sentence. **3** criticize, berate, reprimand, denounce. ● n. **1** see CURSE n. 1. **2** sl. hoot, two hoots (in hell).

dam•na•ble /dámnəbəl/ adj. hateful; annoying. □□ **dam'na•bly** adv.

■ terrible, horrible, atrocious, abominable, dreadful, cursed, wicked, colloq. awful, damned; see also IRKSOME.

dam•na•tion /damnáyshən/ n. eternal punishment in hell.

■ see PERDITION.

damned /damd/ colloq. ● adj. damnable. ● adv. extremely (damned lovely). □ **do one's damnedest** do one's utmost.

■ adj. see INFERNAL 1.

damp /damp/ ● adj. slightly wet. ● n. moisture, esp. inconvenient or dangerous. ● v.tr. **1** make damp; moisten. **2 a** take the force or vigor out of. **b** make (a fire) burn less strongly by reducing the flow of air. □□ **damp'ly** adv. **damp'ness** n.

■ adj. moist; humid, steamy, clammy, muggy. ● n. dampness, humidity. ● v. **1** see DAMPEN 1. **2 a** see DAMPEN 2. □□ **dampness** see DAMP n. above.

damp•en /dámpən/ v. **1** tr. & intr. make or become damp. **2** tr. make less forceful or vigorous; choke. □□ **damp'en•er** n.

■ **1** moisten, see also WET v. **2** stifle, deaden, check, cool, restrain, lessen, diminish, reduce, suppress, temper.

damp•er /dámpər/ n. **1** person or thing that discourages. **2** metal plate in a flue to control the draft, and so the rate of combustion. □ **put a damper on** take the enjoyment out of.

dam•sel /dámzəl/ n. literary young unmarried woman.

■ see MAID 2.

dam•sel•fly /dámzəlfli/ n. (pl. **–flies**) any of various insects like a dragonfly but with its wings folded when resting.

dance /dans/ ● v. **1** intr. move about rhythmically, usu. to music, for pleasure or as an entertainment. **2** intr. move in a lively way; skip or jump about. **3** tr. **a** perform (a specified dance). **b** perform (a specified role) in a ballet, etc. **4** intr. move up and down. ● n. **1** piece of dancing; sequence of steps in dancing. **2** social gathering for dancing. **3** piece of music for dancing. **4** lively motion. □□ **dance'a•ble** adj. **danc'er** n.

■ v. **1** colloq. bop, sl. boogie, hoof it. **2** gambol, caper, frolic. **4** see WAG¹ v. ● n. **2** ball, social, colloq. hop, prom.

dan•de•lion /dánd'lfən/ n. composite plant with jagged leaves and a yellow flower, then a head of seeds with downy tufts.

dan•der² /dándər/ ● n. skin flakes in an animal's fur or hair.

dan•der¹ /dándər/ n. colloq. temper; anger; indignation.

dan•dle /dánd'l/ v.tr. dance (a child) on one's knees.

dan•druff /dándruf/ n. dead skin in small scales among the hair.

dan•dy /dándee/ ● n. (pl. **–dies**) **1** man unduly devoted to style and fashion. **2** colloq. excellent thing. ● adj. (**dan•di•er**, **dan•di•est**) colloq. splendid; first-rate. □□ **dan'dy•ish** adj. **dan'dy•ism** n.

■ n. **1** fop, coxcomb, beau, colloq. swell, clotheshorse, sl. dude. ● adj. see SPLENDID 3.

Dane /dayn/ n. native or national of Denmark. □ **Great Dane** dog of a very large, short-haired breed.

dan•ger /dáynjər/ n. **1** liability or exposure to harm. **2** thing that causes or may cause harm. □ **in danger of** likely to incur or to suffer from.

■ peril, risk, threat, jeopardy, hazard; (in danger) in jeopardy, at risk, under threat. □ **in danger of** likely to.

dan•ger•ous /dáynjərəs/ adj. involving or causing danger. □□ **dan'ger•ous•ly** adv. **dan'ger•ous•ness** n.

■ risky, perilous, treacherous, hazardous, unsafe, precarious, chancy; threatening, menacing, harmful. □□ **dangerously** recklessly; ominously, alarmingly.

dan•gle /dánggəl/ v. **1** intr. be loosely suspended, so as to be able to sway. **2** tr. hold or carry loosely suspended. **3** tr. hold out (hope, temptation, etc.) enticingly. □□ **dan'gler** n.

■ **1** hang down, droop, swing. **3** flaunt, brandish, wave, flourish.

Dan•ish /dáynish/ ● adj. of or relating to Denmark or the Danes. ● n. **1** Danish language. **2** [prec. by the; treated as pl.] the Danish people. □ **Danish blue** soft, salty white cheese with blue veins. **Danish pastry** sweetened yeast pastry topped with icing, fruit, nuts, etc.

dank /dangk/ adj. disagreeably damp and cold. □□ **dank'ly** adv. **dank'ness** n.

■ see DAMP adj.

dap•per /dápər/ adj. **1** neat and precise, esp. in dress or movement. **2** sprightly. □□ **dap'per•ly** adv. **dap'per•ness** n.

■ **1** smart, trim, swanky, colloq. nifty, swell, classy, sharp, ritzy, swank, sl. snazzy, spiffy. **2** see SPRIGHTLY.

dap•ple /dápəl/ ● v. **1** tr. mark with spots. **2** intr. be marked in this way. ● n. **1** dappled effect. **2** dappled horse.

■ v. **1** spot, mottle, stipple. ● n. **2** piebald, pinto.

dare /dair/ ● v.tr. **1** have the courage or impudence (to) (I dare not speak, I do not dare to jump). **2** defy or challenge (a person). ● n. **1** act of daring. **2** challenge, esp. to prove courage. □ **I daresay** it is probable.

■ v. **1** venture, risk, hazard. ● n. **2** provocation, taunt.

dare•dev•il /dáirdevəl/ ● n. recklessly daring person. ● adj. recklessly daring. □□ **dare'dev•il•ry** n.

■ n. adventurer, hero, heroine. ● adj. rash, impulsive, wild, foolhardy, madcap; audacious, bold, fearless, intrepid.

dar•ing /dáiring/ ● n. adventurous courage. ● adj. adventurous; bold; prepared to take risks. □□ **dar'ing•ly** adv.

■ *n.* bravery, valor, pluck, spirit, mettle, nerve, *colloq.* guts, grit, spunk. ● *adj.* audacious, intrepid, *colloq.* nervy; rash, reckless.

dark /daark/ ● *adj.* **1** with little or no light. **2** of deep or somber color. **3** (of a person) with dark coloring. **4** gloomy; depressing; dismal. **5** evil; sinister. **6** sullen; angry. **7** secret; mysterious. ● *n.* **1** absence of light. **2** nightfall. □ **dark chocolate** chocolate without milk. **the Dark Continent** Africa, esp. when little known to Europeans. **dark horse** little-known person who is unexpectedly prominent. **in the dark** lacking information. □□ **dark'ly** *adv.* **dark'ness** *n.*

■ *adj.* **1** unlit, unlighted, poorly-lit; dim, murky, shady; black. **2** inky, sooty; dreary. **3** brunette; black, swarthy; (sun)tanned. **4** bleak, cheerless, somber, grim. **5** wicked, vile, foul, nefarious. **6** see SULLEN *adj.* 1. **7** remote, hidden, puzzling. ● *n.* **1** gloominess, murkiness; see GLOOM *n.* 1. **2** night, nighttime, dusk, twilight. ■ **in the dark** *ignorant* (IGNORANCE). □□ **darkness** see DARK *n.* 1 above.

dark•en /daárkən/ *v.* **1** *tr.* make dark or darker. **2** *intr.* become dark or darker.

■ **1** see SHADE *v.* 3. **2** see DIM *v.*

dark•room /daárkrŏŏm, –rŏŏm/ *n.* room for photographic work, with normal light excluded.

dar•ling /daárling/ ● *n.* **1** beloved or lovable person or thing. **2** favorite ● *adj.* **1** beloved; lovable. **2** favorite. **3** *colloq.* charming or pretty.

■ *n.* **1** sweetheart, love, dear. **2** pet, *colloq.* golden boy *or* girl. ● *adj.* **1** cherished, adored, dear. **2** see FAVORITE *adj.* **3** pleasing, adorable, enchanting.

darn[1] /daarn/ ● *v.tr.* mend (esp. knitted material) by filling a hole with stitching. ● *n.* darned area in material. □ **darning needle 1** long needle with a large eye. **2** dragonfly.

■ *v.* see PATCH *v.* 1, 2.

darn[2] /daarn/ *v.tr., int., adj., & adv. colloq.* = DAMN (in *imprecatory senses*)

dart /daart/ ● *n.* **1** small pointed missile used as a weapon or in a game. **2** [in *pl.*; usu. treated as *sing.*] indoor game of throwing these at a target to score points. **3** sudden rapid movement. **4** tapering tuck stitched in a garment. ● *v.* **1** *intr.* move or go suddenly or rapidly. **2** *tr.* direct suddenly (a glance, etc.).

■ *n.* **1** see BOLT *n.* 5. **3** see DASH *n.* 1. ● *v.* **1** see DASH *v.* 1.

dart•board /daártbawrd/ *n.* circular target in darts.

dash /dash/ ● *v.* **1** *intr.* rush. **2** *tr.* strike or fling with force, esp. to shatter. **3** *tr.* frustrate; daunt; dispirit. **4** *tr.* *colloq.* (esp. **dash it all**) = DAMN *v.* ● *n.* **1** rush; sudden advance. **2** horizontal stroke in writing or printing to mark a pause, break in sense, etc. **3** impetuous vigor. **4** showy appearance or behavior. **5** sprinting race. **6** slight admixture. **7** = DASHBOARD. **8** longer signal of the two in Morse code (cf. DOT *n.* 2). □ **dash off** depart or write hurriedly.

● *v.* **1** run, race; hasten, fly. **2** hurl, toss, *colloq.* chuck. **3** destroy, ruin, spoil. ● *n.*

---

1 bolt; run; sprint. **3** energy, vivacity, zest. **4** see OSTENTATION. **6** pinch, soupçon, *colloq.* smidgen, tad. □ **dash off** scribble, rush off.

dash•board /dáshbawrd/ *n.* instrument panel of a vehicle.

dash•ing /dáshing/ *adj.* **1** spirited; lively. **2** stylish. □□ **dash'ing•ly** *adv.*

■ **1** energetic, vigorous, *colloq.* peppy; see also LIVELY 1. **2** fashionable, chic.

das•tard•ly /dástərdlee/ *adj.* cowardly; despicable. □□ **das'tard•li•ness** *n.*

DAT *abbr.* digital audiotape.

da•ta /dáytə, dátə, dáa–/ *n.pl.* [also treated as *sing.*, although the singular form is strictly *datum*] **1** known facts used as a basis for conclusions. **2** quantities or characters operated on by a computer, etc. □ **data capture** entering data into a computer. **data processing** series of operations on data, esp. by a computer. **data processor** machine, esp. a computer, that carries out data processing.

■ **1** information, statistics, figures, details, observations.

da•ta•base /dáytəbays, dátə–/ *n.* structured set of data held in a computer.

date[1] /dayt/ ● *n.* **1** day of the month, esp. as a number. **2** particular day or year. **3** statement in a document, etc., of the time of composition or publication. **4** period to which a work of art, etc., belongs. **5** *colloq.* **a** appointment, esp. social. **b** person with whom one has a social engagement. ● *v.* **1** *tr.* mark with a date. **2** *tr.* assign a date to (an object, etc.). **3** *intr.* have its origins at a particular time. **4** *intr.* be recognizable as from the past. **5** *tr.* indicate as out of date. **6** *colloq.* **a** *tr.* arrange with (a person) to meet socially. **b** *intr.* meet socially by agreement. □ **date rape** sexual assault involving two people who have met socially. **out of date** (*attrib.* **out-of-date**) old-fashioned; obsolete. **to date** until now. **up to date** (*attrib.* **up-to-date**) fashionable; current.

■ *n.* **4** time, age, era. **5 a** engagement, rendezvous. **b** escort; sweetheart. ● *v.* **3** (*date from* or *back* to) belong to, come from. **4** show one's *or* its age. **6** have a relationship (with), *colloq.* go steady (with); go out. □ **date rape** acquaintance rape. **out of date** old, ancient, passé, *colloq.* old hat, prehistoric. **up to date** modern, latest, contemporary, *colloq. often derog.* trendy.

date[2] /dayt/ *n.* **1** oval, single-stoned fruit. **2** (in full **date palm**) tall tree native to W. Asia and N. Africa, bearing this fruit.

dat•ed /dáytid/ *adj.* **1** showing or having a date (*dated letter*). **2** old-fashioned; out-of-date.

date•line /dáytlin/ *n.* line at the head of a newspaper article showing the date and place of writing.

da•tive /dáytiv/ *Gram.* ● *n.* case of nouns and pronouns indicating an indirect object or recipient. ● *adj.* of or in the dative.

da•tum /dáytəm, dátəm, daátəm/ *n.* (*pl.* **da•ta**: see DATA as main entry) **1** piece of information. **2** thing known or granted.

daub /dawb/ ● *v.tr.* **1** spread (paint, etc.)

crudely or roughly. **2** coat (a surface) with
paint, etc. **3** [also *absol.*] paint crudely or unskillfully. • *n.* paint, etc., daubed on a surface.

■ *v.* see SMEAR *v.* 1.

daugh•ter /dáwtər/ *n.* **1** girl or woman in relation to her parents. **2** female descendant.
3 [foll. by *of*] female member of a family,
nation, etc. □ **daughter-in-law** (*pl.*
daughters-in-law) wife of one's son.
□□ **daugh•ter•ly** *adj.*

daunt /dawnt/ *v.tr.* discourage; intimidate.
□□ **daunt•ing** *adj.* **daunt•ing•ly** *adv.*

■ dishearten, dispirit, upset, awe, threaten,
frighten.

daunt•less /dáwntlis/ *adj.* intrepid; persevering. □□ **daunt•less•ly** *adv.* **daunt•less•ness**
n.

■ fearless, unflinching, stalwart, brave, courageous, bold, audacious, valorous, daring.

dau•phin /dáwfin, dōfǽn/ *n. hist.* eldest son of
the king of France.

dav•en•port /dávənpawrt/ *n.* large, heavily
upholstered sofa.

daw•dle /dáwd'l/ • *v.* **1** *intr.* **a** walk slowly
and idly. **b** delay; waste time. **2** *tr.* [foll. by
away] waste (time). See synonym study at
LOITER. • *n.* act or instance of dawdling.

■ *v.* **1** linger, straggle, procrastinate,
lounge, *colloq.* dillydally.

dawn /dawn/ • *n.* **1** daybreak. **2** beginning
or incipient appearance of something.
• *v.intr.* **1** (of a day) begin; grow light. **2** begin to appear or develop.

■ *n.* **1** sunrise, crack of dawn, first light,
cockcrow. **2** start, awakening, inception, arrival. • *v.* **1** break; brighten. **2** originate,
arise, emerge, unfold.

dawn• ing /dáwning/ *n.* **1** daybreak. **2** beginning of something.

day /day/ *n.* **1** time between sunrise and sunset. **2 a** 24 hours as a unit of time. **b** corresponding period on other planets. **3** daylight
(*clear as day*). **4** time in a day during which
work is normally done. **5 a** [also *pl.*] period
of the past or present (*the old days*). **b** [prec.
by *the*] present time (*issues of the day*).
6 prime of a person's life (*in my day*). **7 a**
point of time (*will do it one day*). **8** day of a
particular event. **9** a day's endeavor, esp. as
bringing success (*win the day*). □ **all in a
day's work** part of normal routine. **call it a
day** end a period of activity. **day after day**
without respite. **day and night** all the time.
day by day gradually. **day care** supervision
and care, esp. of young children, during the
day. **day in, day out** routinely; constantly.
day laborer unskilled laborer hired by the
day. **day of rest** Sabbath. **day-to-day** mundane; routine. **day trader** one who trades
stocks (usu. over the Internet) attempting to
profit by short-term changes in the value of
stocks. **not one's day** of successive misfortunes for a person. **one of these days** before very long. **one of those days** day when
things go badly. **that will be the day** *colloq.*
that will never happen.

■ **3** daytime, broad daylight. **5 a** age, era;

date. **b** see PRESENT[1] *n.* **6** time, lifetime;
hour, heyday. □ **day by day** see *gradually*
(GRADUAL). **day in, day out** see *all the time* 2
(TIME). **day-to-day** see ROUTINE *adj.* 1. **one
of these days** see SOON 1.

day•break /dáybrayk/ *n.* first appearance of
morning light.

■ see DAWN *n.* 1.

day•dream /dáydreem/ • *n.* pleasant fantasy
or reverie. • *v.intr.* indulge in this. □□ **day′
dream•er** *n.*

■ *n.* fancy, musing, pipedream. • *v.* fantasize; (*daydream about*) imagine, fancy, envisage, envision. □□ **daydreamer** see DREAMER.

day•light /dáylīt/ *n.* **1** light of day. **2** dawn.
3 visible gap or interval. **4** [usu. in *pl.*] *sl.*
one's life or consciousness, esp. as representing vulnerability to fear, etc. (*scared the day-
lights out of me*). □ **daylight saving** achieving longer evening daylight, esp. in summer,
by setting the time an hour ahead of standard time. **see daylight** begin to understand.

■ **1** sunlight, sun, sunshine. **2** see DAWN *n.*
1. □ **see daylight** see *catch on* 2.

day•time /dáytīm/ *n.* part of the day when
there is natural light.

■ see DAY 3.

daze /dayz/ • *v.tr.* stupefy; bewilder. • *n.* state
of bewilderment (*in a daze*). □□ **daz•ed•ly**
/-zidlee/ *adv.*

■ *v.* stun, blind, shock, stagger, overcome,
sl. knock out; confuse, baffle. • *n.* (*in a daze*)
confused; perplexed, disoriented; startled,
stunned, *colloq.* flabbergasted, floored.

daz•zle /dázəl/ • *v.tr.* **1** blind or confuse temporarily by an excess of light. **2** impress or
overpower with knowledge, ability, etc. • *n.*
bright confusing light. □□ **daz′zling** *adj.*
daz′zling•ly *adv.*

■ *v.* **1** stun, stupefy, overpower. **2** bewitch,
enchant, charm. □□ **dazzling** brilliant, radiant, splendid.

dB *abbr.* decibel(s).

DBMS *abbr. Computing* database management system.

DC *abbr.* **1** (also **d.c.**) direct current. **2** District of Columbia.

DD *abbr.* doctor of divinity.

D.D.S. *abbr.* **1** doctor of dental science.
2 doctor of dental surgery.

DDT *abbr.* dichlorodiphenyltrichloroethane, a
colorless chlorinated hydrocarbon used as an
insecticide.

DE *abbr.* Delaware (in official postal use).

de- /dee, di/ *prefix* **1** forming verbs and their
derivatives: **a** down; away (*descend*). **b** completely (*denude*). **2** added to form verbs and
nouns implying removal or reversal (*decen-
tralize*).

dea•con /déekən/ *n.* assistant to a priest, minister, etc.

de•ac•ti•vate /deeáktivayt/ *v.tr.* make inactive
or less reactive. □□ **de•ac•ti•va•tion**
/-váyshən/ *n.* **de•ac′ti•va•tor** *n.*

■ see STOP *v.* 1a.

dead /ded/ • *adj.* **1** no longer alive. **2** *colloq.*
extremely tired or unwell. **3** benumbed (*my
fingers are dead*). **4** [foll. by *to*] insensitive to.
5 no longer effective or in use; extinct.

6 inanimate. **7 a** lacking force or vigor. **b** (of sound) not resonant. **8 a** quiet; lacking activity. **b** motionless; idle. **9 a** (of a microphone, etc.) not transmitting sound, esp. because of a fault. **b** (of a circuit, etc.) carrying no current; not connected to a source of electricity. **10** (of the ball in a game) out of play. **11** abrupt; complete; exact (*come to a dead stop, dead certainty*). • *adv.* **1** absolutely; exactly (*dead on target*). **2** *colloq.* very; extremely (*dead easy*). • *n.* [prec. by *the*] **1** [treated as *pl.*] those who have died. **2** time of silence or inactivity (*dead of night*). □ **dead end 1** closed end of a road, passage, etc. **2** [often (with hyphen) *attrib.*] situation offering no prospects of progress or advancement. **dead heat 1** race in which two or more competitors finish in a tie. **2** result of such a race. **dead letter 1** law or practice no longer observed or recognized. **2** letter that is undeliverable and unreturnable, esp. one with an incorrect address. **dead reckoning** *Naut.* calculation of a ship's position from the log, compass, etc. **dead to the world** *colloq.* fast asleep; unconscious.

■ *adj.* **1** extinct, gone, departed, lifeless, *formal* deceased. **2** exhausted, worn out, fatigued, *colloq.* all in, done in, bushed, pooped, *sl.* beat. **3** insensible, numb, unfeeling, senseless. **4** unconscious; indifferent, uninterested; hardened. **5** obsolete, perished, outmoded, expired. **6** lifeless, inert, inorganic. **7 a** dull, lusterless, flat, vapid, empty, bland, colorless, gray; boring, tedious, monotonous. **b** dull, muffled, deadened. **8 b** stagnant, still, standing, static, inert, inactive, quiet, calm. **11** entire, total, absolute, downright, thorough, utter; categorical, outright; profound, deep; sudden; precise. • *adv.* **1** completely, totally, utterly, categorically, thoroughly, unconditionally, unqualifiedly; precisely. **2** see VERY *adv.* □ **dead heat** tie, stalemate, draw, deadlock. **dead to the world** out, *colloq.* (out) cold.

dead•beat /dédbéet/ *n.* **1** *colloq.* penniless person. **2** *sl.* person constantly in debt.

dead•en /déd'n/ *v.* **1** *tr. & intr.* deprive of or lose vitality, force, brightness, sound, feeling, etc. **2** *tr.* [foll. by *to*] make insensitive.

■ **1** weaken, tire (out), diminish, reduce; drain, tax, exhaust, dull, break, dispirit; moderate, soothe, soften, blunt; languish, falter, slump, fall off, sink, lag, *colloq.* let up. **2** numb, paralyze, anesthetize.

dead•line /dédlìn/ *n.* time limit.

dead•lock /dédlok/ • *n.* situation, esp. one involving opposing parties, in which no progress can be made. • *v.* bring or come to a standstill.

■ *n.* impasse, stalemate, draw, standoff. • *v.* stall, stop.

dead•ly /dédlee/ • *adj.* (**dead•li•er, dead•li•est**) **1** causing or able to cause fatal injury or serious damage. **2** intense; extreme. **3** (of aim, etc.) extremely accurate or effective. **4** deathlike. **5** *colloq.* dreary; dull. • *adv.* **1** as if dead. **2** extremely; intensely (*deadly serious*). □ **deadly nightshade** = BELLADONNA.

■ *adj.* **1** lethal; dangerous, poisonous. **2** see

INTENSE 1, 3. **3** exact, precise. **4** pallid, ghostly. **5** boring, tiresome, humdrum, lackluster.

dead•pan /dédpán/ *adj. & adv.* lacking expression or emotion.

dead•wood /dédwo͝od/ *n.* **1** dead trees or branches. **2** *colloq.* useless people or things.

deaf /def/ *adj.* **1** wholly or partly without hearing. **2** [foll. by *to*] refusing to listen or comply. □ **fall on deaf ears** be ignored. **turn a deaf ear** be unresponsive. □□ **deaf′ness** *n.*

■ **1** hard of hearing, stone-deaf. **2** impervious, indifferent, oblivious, unresponsive. □ **turn a deaf ear** see IGNORE 2.

deal /deel/ • *v.* (*past* and *past part.* **dealt** /delt/) **1** *intr.* **a** [foll. by *with*] take measures concerning (a problem, etc.), esp. to resolve. **b** [foll. by *with*] do business with; associate with. **c** [foll. by *with*] discuss or treat (a subject) **d** behave in a specified way (*dealt honorably by them*). **2** *intr.* [foll. by *in*] to sell or be concerned with commercially. **3** *tr.* [often foll. by *out*] distribute to several people, etc. **4** *tr.* [also *absol.*] distribute (cards) to players. **5** *tr.* administer (*dealt a heavy blow*). • *n.* **1** (usu. **a good** or **great deal**) *colloq.* large amount. **2** *colloq.* business arrangement. **3** specified treatment (*gave them a bad deal*). **4 a** distribution of cards by dealing. **b** player's turn to do this. **c** set of hands dealt to players.

■ *v.* **1 a** (*deal with*) treat, handle. **b** see ASSOCIATE *v.* 5. **c** (*deal with*) see TREAT *v.* 4. **d** act, conduct oneself. **2** (*deal in*) handle, trade in. **3, 4** dole out, allot, apportion; dispense. • *n.* **1** (**a good** or **great deal**) see LOT *n.* 1. **2** transaction, contract. **3** see TREATMENT 1.

deal•er /déelər/ *n.* **1** person or business dealing in (esp. retail) goods. **2** player dealing in a card game. **3** person who sells illegal drugs. □□ **deal′er•ship** *n.* (in sense 1).

■ **1, 3** businessman, businesswoman, merchant, retailer, vendor; wholesaler, distributor, jobber, broker, agent.

deal•ings /déelingz/ *n.pl.* contacts or transactions, esp. in business. □ **have dealings with** associate with.

■ commerce, trade, negotiations; relationships, affairs. □ **have dealings with** see ASSOCIATE *v.* 5.

dealt *past* and *past part.* of DEAL.

dean /deen/ *n.* **1 a** college or university official. **b** head of a university faculty or department or of a medical school. **2** head of a cathedral or collegiate church.

dear /deer/ • *adj.* **1** beloved or esteemed. **2** as a formula of address, esp. beginning a letter (*Dear Sir*). **3** precious; cherished. **4** [usu. in *superl.*] earnest; deeply felt. **5** high-priced. • *n.* (esp. as a form of address) dear person. • *adv.* at great cost. • *int.* expressing surprise, dismay, pity, etc. (*oh dear!*). □ **for dear life** see LIFE. □□ **dear′ly** *adv.* (esp. in sense 3 of *adj.*).

■ *adj.* **1** adored, favored, admired. **3** prized, valued. **4** see EARNEST *adj.* **5** expensive, costly, *colloq.* pricey. • *n.* darling, sweetheart, pet, *colloq.* sweetie, *sl.* baby. • *adv.* at a high *or* excessive price. □□ **dearly** greatly, indeed; lovingly, tenderly; expensively, punitively.

dearth /dɔrth/ *n.* scarcity or lack, esp. of food. See synonym study at LACK.

■ want, need, deficiency, sparseness, insufficiency, inadequacy, shortage, paucity, exiguity, poverty; absence.

death /deth/ *n.* **1** irreversible ending of life. **2** event that terminates life. **3 a** being killed or killing. **b** being dead. **4 a** destruction or permanent cessation (*the death of our hopes*). **b** *colloq.* something terrible or appalling. **5** (usu. **Death**) personification of death, usu. a skeleton. □ **at death's door** close to death. **be the death of 1** cause the death of. **2** be very harmful to. **death trap** *colloq.* dangerous or unhealthy building, vehicle, etc. **fate worse than death** *colloq.* disastrous misfortune or experience. □□ **death'less** *adj.* **death'like** *adj.*

■ **1** demise, dying, exit, *euphem.* passing (away). **4 a** end, termination; extinction, extermination, liquidation; ruin, downfall. □□ **deathless** eternal, immortal, permanent, unending, timeless.

death•bed /déthbed/ *n.* bed where a person dies or has died.

death•blow /déthblō/ *n.* **1** blow or other action that causes death. **2** event, etc., that ends an activity, enterprise, etc.

■ see KILL *v.* 1.

death•ly /déthlee/ • *adj.* (**death•li•er, death• li•est**) suggestive of death (*deathly silence*). • *adv.* in a deathly way (*deathly pale*).

■ *adj.* see DEADLY *adj.* 4.

deb /deb/ *n. colloq.* debutante.

de•ba•cle /daybaákəl, –baíkel, dɔ–/ *n.* (also **dé•bâ'cle**) utter defeat, failure, or collapse.

■ RUIN *n.* 2.

de•bar /dibaár/ *v.tr.* (**de•barred, de•bar• ring**) exclude; prohibit. □□ **de•bar'ment** *n.*

■ see BAN *v.*

de•bark /dibaárk/ *v.* land from a ship. □□ **de• bar•ka•tion** /–káyshən/ *n.*

■ see LAND *v.* 1, 3.

de•base /dibáys/ *v.tr.* lower in quality, value, or character. See synonym study at HUMBLE. □□ **de•based** *adj.* **de•base'ment** *n.* **de•bas'• er** *n.* See synonym study at DEPRAVED

■ degrade, devalue, depreciate, depress, demote, belittle.

de•bat•a•ble /dibáytəbəl/ *adj.* **1** questionable; subject to dispute. **2** capable of being debated. □□ **de•bat'a•bly** *adv.*

■ **1** controversial, arguable, doubtful, dubious, problematic, open to doubt *or* question, polemic; uncertain, undecided.

de•bate /dibáyt/ • *v.* **1** *tr.* [also *absol.*] discuss or dispute, esp. formally. **2 a** *tr.* consider (a matter). **b** *intr.* consider different sides of a question. • *n.* **1** *formal* discussion, esp. in a legislature, etc. **2** discussion. □□ **de•bat'er** *n.*

■ *v.* **1** argue about, contest; question. **2 a** deliberate, reflect on, ponder (over),

weigh, think through. • *n.* **1** argument, dispute, polemic. **2** argument, dispute, contention.

de•bauch /dibáwch/ • *v.tr.* **1** corrupt; pervert. **2** make intemperate or sensually indulgent. • *n.* bout of sensual indulgence.

■ *n.* see ORGY 1.

deb•au•chee /díbawcheé, –sheé, déb–/ *n.* person addicted to excessive sensual indulgence.

de•bauch•er•y /dibáwchɔree/ *n.* excessive sensual indulgence.

■ see DISSIPATION 1.

de•ben•ture /dibénchɔr/ *n.* (in full **de•ben' ture bond**) fixed-interest bond of a company or corporation, backed by general credit rather than specified assets.

de•bil•i•tate /dibílitayt/ *v.tr.* enfeeble; enervate. □□ **de•bil•i•tat•ed** *adj.* **de•bil•i•ta• tion** /–táyshən/ *n.* See synonym study at WEAK

de•bil•i•ty /dibílitee/ *n.* feebleness, esp. of health.

■ see *infirmity* (INFIRM).

deb•it /débit/ • *n.* **1** entry in an account recording a sum owed. **2** sum recorded. **3** total of such sums. **4** debit side of an account. • *v.tr.* enter on the debit side of an account.

■ *n.* see CHARGE *n.* 1b. • *v.* bill, charge, invoice.

deb•o•nair /débənáir/ *adj.* **1** carefree; self-assured. **2** having pleasant manners.

■ **1** insouciant, nonchalant, dashing, charming. **2** elegant, urbane, refined, genteel.

de•brief /deebreéf/ *v.tr. colloq.* interrogate (a diplomat, pilot, etc.) about a mission or undertaking. □□ **de•brief'ing** *n.*

de•bris /dɔbreé, day–, débree/ *n.* scattered fragments, esp. of something wrecked or destroyed.

■ see WRECKAGE 1, 2, WASTE *n.* 2.

debt /det/ *n.* **1** something owed, esp. money. **2** state of owing (*in debt*).

■ **2** obligation; liability, responsibility, accountability; (*in debt*) owing, beholden; in arrears, in the red, *colloq.* in hock.

debt•or /détɔr/ *n.* person who owes a debt, esp. money.

de•bug /deebúg/ *v.tr. colloq.* (**de•bugged, de•bug• ging**) **1** *colloq.* remove concealed listening devices from (a room, etc.). **2** *colloq.* identify and remove defects from (a computer program, etc.).

de•bunk /deebúngk/ *v.tr. colloq.* expose the falseness of (a claim, etc.). □□ **de•bunk'er** *n.*

de•but /daybyōō, dáybyōō/ • *n.* (also **dé•but'**) **1** first public appearance of a performer, show, etc. **2** first appearance of a debutante in society. • *v.* **1** *intr.* make a debut. **2** *tr.* introduce, esp. a performance, etc.

■ *n.* **1** premiere, first night, opening (night). **2** coming out.

deb•u•tante /débyətaant, dáybyōō–/ *n.* (usu. wealthy) young woman making her social debut.

Dec. *abbr.* December.

deca- /déka/ *comb. form* (also **dec-** before a vowel) ten or tenfold (*decagon, decaliter*).

dec•ade /dékayd/ *n.* **1** period of ten years. **2** set, series, or group of ten.

dec•a•dence /dékəd'ns/ *n.* **1** moral or cultural deterioration. **2** immoral behavior.
■ **1** see DECAY *n.* 2.

dec•a•dent /dékədənt/ • *adj.* in a state of moral or cultural deterioration. • *n.* decadent person. □□ **dec'a•dent•ly** *adv.*
■ *adj.* debased; corrupt, degenerate, debauched; see also DISSOLUTE, SELF-INDULGENT. • *n.* see DEGENERATE *n.*

de•caf•fein•at•ed /deekáfinaytid/ *adj.* with caffeine removed or reduced.

dec•a•gon /dékəgon/ *n.* plane figure with ten sides and angles. □□ **de•cag•o•nal** /dikágənəl/ *adj.*

de•cal /déekal/ *n.* = DECALCOMANIA 2.

de•cal•co•ma•ni•a /deekálkəmáyneeə/ *n.* **1** process of transferring designs from specially prepared paper to the surface of glass, porcelain, etc. **2** picture or design using this process.

Dec•a•logue /dékəlawg, –log/ *n.* Ten Commandments.

de•camp /dikámp/ *v.intr.* **1** break up or leave a camp. **2** depart suddenly; abscond.
■ *v.* **1** see LEAVE[1] *v.* 1b, 3.

de•cant /dikánt/ *v.tr.* gradually pour off (liquid, esp. wine), esp. without disturbing the sediment.

de•cant•er /dikántər/ *n.* stoppered glass container for wine.
■ see JUG *n.* 1.

de•cap•i•tate /dikápitayt/ *v.tr.* behead (esp. as a form of capital punishment). □□ **de•cap•i•ta•tion** /–táyshən/ *n.*
■ see BEHEAD.

de•cath•lon /dikáthlon, –lən/ *n.* athletic contest in which each competitor takes part in ten events. □□ **de•cath•lete** /–leet/ *n.*

de•cay /dikáy/ • *v.* **1 a** *intr.* rot; decompose. **b** *tr.* cause to rot or decompose. **2** *intr. & tr.* decline or cause to decline in quality, power, etc. **3** *intr. Physics* [usu. foll. by *w*] (of a substance, etc.) undergo change by radioactivity. • *n.* **1** rotten state. **2** decline in health, quality, etc. **3** *Physics* change by radioactivity.
■ *v.* **1 a** putrefy, spoil; turn, go bad. **2** degenerate, waste away, atrophy; see also DETERIORATE. • *n.* **1** decomposition, mold. **2** deterioration, decadence, collapse; downfall.

de•ceased /diseest/ *formal* • *adj.* dead. • *n.* [usu. prec. by *the*] person who has died, esp. recently.
■ *adj.* see DEAD *adj.* 1.

de•ceit /diseet/ *n.* **1** deception, esp. by concealing the truth. **2** dishonest trick or stratagem. **3** willingness to deceive.
■ **1** fraud, cheating, chicanery, misrepresentation, double-dealing, hypocrisy, treachery, guile, cunning, *colloq.* monkey business, *sl.* hanky-panky. **2** cheat, hoax, swindle, double cross, sham, confidence game, *colloq.* ploy, *sl.* con, scam.

de•ceit•ful /diseetfool/ *adj.* using deceit. □□ **de•ceit'ful•ly** *adv.* **de•ceit'ful•ness** *n.*
■ dishonest, underhand(ed), misleading, insincere, fraudulent, counterfeit, lying; wily, crafty, sly, sneaky, two-faced, hypocritical. □□ **deceitfulness** see DECEIT 1.

de•ceive /diseev/ *v.* **1** *tr.* make (a person) believe what is false; mislead purposely. **2** *tr.* be unfaithful to, esp. sexually. **3** *intr.* use deceit. □ **deceive oneself** persist in a mistaken belief. □□ **de•ceiv'er** *n.*
■ **1** delude, fool, trick, cheat, swindle, betray, double-cross, *colloq.* bamboozle, two-time. **2** cuckold, *colloq.* cheat on.

de•cel•er•ate /deesélərayt/ *v.* begin or cause to begin to reduce speed. □□ **de•cel•er•a•tion** /–ráyshən/ *n.*
■ see SLOW *v.* 1, BRAKE *v.* 2.

De•cem•ber /disémbər/ *n.* twelfth month of the year.

de•cen•cy /déesənsee/ *n.* (*pl.* –**cies**) **1** correct and tasteful behavior. **2** [in *pl.*] the requirements of correct behavior.
■ **1** see PROPRIETY 2.

de•cen•ni•al /diséneeəl/ *adj.* **1** lasting ten years. **2** recurring every ten years. □□ **de•cen'ni•al•ly** *adv.*

de•cent /déesənt/ *adj.* **1 a** conforming with current standards of behavior or propriety. **b** avoiding obscenity. **2** respectable. **3** acceptable; good enough. **4** kind; obliging. □□ **de'cent•ly** *adv.*
■ **1** proper, suitable, appropriate. **b** clean, inoffensive. **2** proper, well-bred, mannerly. **3** adequate, passable, satisfactory, tolerable, *colloq.* OK, not bad. **4** courteous, friendly, gracious. □□ **decently** see PROPERLY 4.

de•cen•tral•ize /deeséntrəliz/ *v.tr.* **1** transfer (power, etc.) from central to local authority. **2** reorganize (a centralized institution, etc.) to give greater local autonomy. □□ **de•cen•tral•i•za•tion** *n.*

de•cep•tion /disépshən/ *n.* **1** deceiving or being deceived. **2** thing that deceives; trick or sham.
■ **1** see DECEIT 1. **2** see DECEIT 2.

de•cep•tive /diséptiv/ *adj.* apt to deceive; misleading. □□ **de•cep'tive•ly** *adv.* **de•cep'tive•ness** *n.*
■ false, illusory; fraudulent, dishonest, fake, *colloq.* shifty; tricky, evasive, elusive, slippery.

deci- /désee/ *comb. form* one-tenth, esp. of a metric unit (*deciliter, decimeter*).

dec•i•bel /désibel/ *n.* unit (one-tenth of a bel) used to measure electrical signals or sound intensities. ¶Abbr.: **dB**.

de•cide /disíd/ *v.* **1 a** *intr.* resolve after consideration. **b** *tr.* resolve or settle (an issue, etc.). **2** *intr.* give a judgment. □□ **de•cid'a•ble** *adj.* **de•cid'ing** *adj.* See synonym study at CRUCIAL.
■ **1** determine, conclude; (*decide on*) choose, select, pick (out), elect, opt for; arbitrate, judge; see also SETTLE 5–7, 8.

de•cid•ed /disídid/ *adj.* **1** [usu. *attrib.*] definite; unquestionable. **2** (of a person) resolute, not vacillating.
■ **1** pronounced, certain, absolute, obvious, unconditional. **2** fixed, firm, adamant, unhesitating, definite, assertive.

de•cid•ed•ly /disídidlee/ *adv.* undoubtedly; undeniably.

de•cid•u•ous /disíjooəs/ *adj.* **1** (of a tree)

shedding leaves annually. **2** (of leaves, horns, teeth, etc.) shed periodically.

dec•i•mal /désiməl/ • *adj.* (of a system of numbers, measures, etc.) based on the number ten. • *n.* decimal fraction. □ **decimal fraction** fraction whose denominator is a power of ten, esp. when expressed positionally by units to the right of a decimal point. **decimal point** period placed before a numerator in a decimal fraction.

dec•i•mate /désimayt/ *v.tr.* destroy a large proportion of. □□ **dec•i•ma•tion** /-máyshən/ *n.*

■ see MASSACRE *v.* 2.

de•ci•pher /disífər/ *v.tr.* **1** convert (text written in code) into an intelligible language. **2** determine the meaning of (anything unclear). □□ **de•ci'pher•a•ble** *adj.*

■ **1** decode, decrypt. **2** unravel, unscramble, translate, solve, figure out, interpret; understand.

de•ci•sion /disízhən/ *n.* **1** act or process of deciding. **2** conclusion or resolution reached after consideration. **3** [often foll. by *of*] **a** settlement of a question. **b** *formal* judgment.

■ **1** settlement, determination, resolution, arbitration. **2, 3** verdict, sentence, ruling, finding, decree.

de•ci•sive /disísiv/ *adj.* **1** that decides an issue; conclusive. **2** (of a person, esp. as a characteristic) able to decide quickly and effectively. See synonym study at RESOLUTE. □□ **de•ci'sive•ly** *adv.* **de•ci'sive•ness** *n.*

■ **2** see FIRM[1] *adj.* 2a.

deck /dek/ • *n.* **1** flooring on a ship. **2** anything resembling a ship's deck, e.g., the floor of a bus. **3** component for playing (disks, tapes, etc.) in sound-reproduction equipment. **4** pack of cards. **5** *sl.* the ground. **6 a** any floor or platform, esp. of a pier for sunbathing. **b** platformlike structure, usu. made of lumber, attached to a house, etc. • *v.tr.* **1** [often foll. by *out*] decorate; adorn. **2** furnish with or cover as a deck.

■ *n.* **1, 2** story, level. **4** set, stack. • *v.* **1** see DECORATE 1, 3.

-deck•er /dékər/ *comb. form* having a specified number of decks or layers (*double-decker*).

de•claim /dikláym/ *v.* **1** *intr. & tr.* speak rhetorically or affectedly. **2** *intr.* practice oratory or recitation. □□ **de•claim'er** *n.* **dec•la•ma•tion** /dékləmáyshən/ *n.* **de•clam•a•to•ry** /diklámətawree/ *adj.*

■ **1** see RANT *v.*

dec•la•ra•tion /dékləráyshən/ *n.* **1** declaring. **2** formal, emphatic, or deliberate statement.

■ assertion, deposition, affirmation, avowal, announcement, proclamation, pronouncement.

de•clare /diklá ir/ *v.tr.* **1** announce openly or formally. **2** pronounce (*declared it invalid*). **3** assert emphatically. **4** acknowledge possession of (dutiable goods, etc.). **5** (as **declared** *adj.*) admit to being (*a declared atheist*). **6** *Cards* **a** [also *absol.*] name (the trump suit). **b** announce that one holds (certain combinations of cards, etc.). See synonym

study at ANNOUNCE. □□ **de•clar'a•ble** *adj.* **de•clar•a•tive** /-klárətiv/ *adj.* **de•clar'a•tive•ly** *adv.* **de•clar•a•to•ry** /-klárətawree/ *adj.* **de•clar'er** *n.*

■ **1, 2** decree, proclaim, herald. **3** affirm, state, avow, swear; confirm, certify. **5** (**declared**) avowed, professed, proclaimed. □□ **declarative, declaratory** see ASSERTIVE 1.

dé•clas•sé /dayklasáy/ *adj.* (*fem.* **dé•clas•sée'**) that has fallen in social status.

de•clas•si•fy /deeklásifi/ *v.tr.* (**–fies, –fied**) declare (information, etc.) to be no longer secret. □□ **de•clas•si•fi•ca•tion** /-fikáyshən/ *n.*

de•clen•sion /diklénshən/ *n.* **1** *Gram.* **a** form of a noun, pronoun, or adjective, by which its grammatical case, number, and gender are identified. **b** class of nouns, etc., with the same inflections. **2** deterioration; declining.

dec•li•na•tion /déklináyshən/ *n.* **1** downward bend or turn. **2** *Astron.* angular distance of a star, etc., north or south of the celestial equator. **3** *Physics* deviation of a compass needle from true north. □□ **dec•li•na'tion•al** *adj.*

de•cline /diklín/ • *v.* **1** *intr.* deteriorate; lose strength or vigor. **2 a** *tr.* refuse, esp. formally and courteously. **b** *tr.* turn away from (a challenge, discussion, etc.). **c** *intr.* give or send a refusal. **3** *intr.* slope downward. **4** *intr.* bend down; droop. **5** *tr.* *Gram.* state the forms of (a noun, pronoun, or adjective). • *n.* **1** gradual loss of vigor or excellence. **2** decay; deterioration. **3** setting; the last part of the course (of the sun, of life, etc.).

■ *v.* **1** degenerate, worsen; go down, wane, subside, ebb. **2** turn down, say no to. **3** descend, drop *or* fall off. **4** see DROOP *v.* 1. • *n.* **1** diminution, decrease, downturn. **2** degeneration, weakening, debility.

de•cliv•i•ty /diklívitee/ *n.* (*pl.* **–ties**) downward slope, esp. a piece of sloping ground. □□ **de•cliv'i•tous** *adj.*

de•coc•tion /dikókshən/ *n.* **1** boiling down to extract some essence. **2** resulting liquid.

de•code /deekód/ *v.tr.* decipher. □□ **de•cod'er** *n.*

■ see DECIPHER 1, 2.

dé•col•le•tage /dáykawltaázh/ *n.* low neckline of a woman's dress, etc.

dé•col•le•té /dáykawltáy/ • *adj.* **1** (of a dress, etc.) having a low neckline. **2** (of a woman) wearing a dress with a low neckline. • *n.* low neckline.

de•com•mis•sion /deékəmíshən/ *v.tr.* **1** close down (a nuclear reactor, etc.). **2** take (a ship) out of service.

de•com•pose /deékəmpóz/ *v.* **1** *intr.* decay; rot. **2** *tr.* separate (a substance, light, etc.) into its elements. □□ **de•com•po•si•tion** /deékompəzíshən/ *n.*

■ **1** disintegrate, putrefy, break down; spoil. **2** break up *or* down, dissect, analyze. □□ **decomposition** see DECAY *n.* 1.

de•com•pres•sion /deékəmpréshən/ *n.* **1** release from compression. **2** gradual reduction of air pressure on a deep-sea diver. □□ **de•com•press'** *v.*

de•con•ges•tant /deekənjéstənt/ • adj. that relieves (esp. nasal) congestion. • n. medicinal agent that relieves congestion.

de•con•struc•tion /deekənstrúkshən/ n. method of critical analysis of philosophical and literary language. □□ de•con•struc'tion•ism n. de•con•struc'tion•ist adj. & n.

de•con•tam•i•nate /deekəntáminayt/ v.tr. remove contamination from. □□ de•con•tam•i•na•tion /-náyshən/ n.

■ see DISINFECT.

de•cor /daykáwr, dáykawr/ n. (also dé•cor') furnishing and decoration of a room, stage, etc.

dec•o•rate /dékərayt/ v.tr. 1 adorn, beautify. 2 paint, wallpaper, etc. 3 serve as an adornment to. 4 confer an award or distinction on. □□ dec•o•ra•tive /dékərətiv, dékrə-, -əray-/ adj. dec'o•ra•tive•ly adv. dec'o•ra•tive•ness n.

■ 1, 3 deck (out), trim, dress (up), spruce up; ornament, garnish; see also EMBELLISH 1 2 refurbish, renovate, fix up.

dec•o•ra•tion /dékəráyshən/ n. 1 decorating. 2 thing that decorates. 3 honorary medal, etc. 4 [in pl.] flags, etc., put up for a public celebration. □ Decoration Day = Memorial Day.

■ 2 garnish, trim, trimming, adornment, embellishment, ornament. 3 laurel, award, badge, colors, order, ribbon.

dec•o•ra•tor /dékəraytər/ n. person who decorates, esp. one who paints or papers houses professionally.

dec•o•rous /dékərəs/ adj. having or showing decorum. □□ dec'o•rous•ly adv. dec'o•rous•ness n.

■ dignified, decent, proper, refined, polite, well-behaved, well-bred, joc. couth. □□ dec•orousness see DECORUM.

de•co•rum /dikáwrəm/ n. appropriate or dignified behavior.

■ seemliness, propriety, correctness, primness, principles; courtesy, politeness, etiquette, dignity, gentility, good manners.

de•cou•page /dáykōopaazh/ n. (also dé•cou•page') decoration of surfaces with paper cutouts.

de•coy • n. /deekoy, dikóy/ person or thing used as a lure, bait, or enticement. • v.tr. /dikóy/ allure or entice, esp. using a decoy.

■ n. trap, attraction, inducement; stool pigeon, shill. • v. attract, induce, coax, seduce, trick.

de•crease • v. /dikrees/ make or become smaller or fewer. • n. /deekrees/ 1 decreasing. 2 amount by which a thing decreases. □□ de•creas'ing•ly adv.

■ v. diminish, decline, lessen, go down, abate, fall (off), shrink, contract, dwindle, ebb, wane, taper off; reduce, lower, curtail, mark down, roll back; colloq. knock down. • n. reduction, lowering, abatement, slackening, curtailment, cut, cut-back.

de•cree /dikree/ • n. 1 official order. 2 legal judgment or decision, esp. in matrimonial cases. • v.tr. ordain by decree.

■ n. 1 mandate, directive, ordinance, edict, law, statute, regulation, enactment, act, ruling. 2 see JUDGMENT 4. • v. order, command, direct, rule, dictate, charge, pronounce.

de•crep•it /dikrépit/ adj. 1 weakened or worn out by age or infirmity. 2 dilapidated. See synonym study at WEAK. □□ de•crep'i•tude n.

■ 1 old, elderly, ancient, feeble, weak, frail, wasted, debilitated, disabled, incapacitated. 2 crumbling, decayed, tumbledown, broken-down, rickety, shaky, creaking, run-down. □□ decrepitude feebleness, weakness, frailty, debilitation, incapacitation, old age; deterioration, decay, ruin.

de•crim•i•nal•ize /deekríminəliz/ v.tr. cease to treat (an action, etc.) as criminal. □□ de•crim•i•nal•i•za'tion n.

de•cry /dikrí/ v.tr. (–cries, –cried) disparage; belittle.

■ see DISPARAGE 1.

ded•i•cate /dédikayt/ v.tr. 1 devote (esp. oneself) to a special task or purpose. 2 address (a book, etc.) as a compliment to a friend, patron, etc. 3 devote (a building, etc.) to an honored person, cause, etc. 4 (as dedicated adj.) a (of a person) devoted single-mindedly to a goal, etc. b (of equipment) designed for a specific purpose. □□ ded•i•ca•tor n. ded•i•ca•to•ry /-kətáwree/ adj.

■ 1 consecrate, surrender, commit, pledge, assign. 2 inscribe; assign. 4 a (dedicated) see DEVOTED.

ded•i•ca•tion /dédikáyshən/ n. 1 dedicating; being dedicated. 2 words with which a book, etc., is dedicated.

■ 1 devotion, commitment, allegiance, loyalty, single-mindedness, fealty; consecration. 2 inscription.

de•duce /didóos, –dyóos/ v.tr. infer logically. □□ de•duc'i•ble adj.

■ conclude, understand, gather, assume, presume, derive.

de•duct /didúkt/ v.tr. subtract, take away, withhold (an amount, portion, etc.).

■ remove, withdraw, knock off.

de•duct•i•ble • adj. that may be deducted, esp. from taxable income. • n. part of an insurance claim to be paid by the insured.

de•duc•tion /didúkshən/ n. 1 a deducting. b amount deducted. 2 a inferring of particular instances from a general law (cf. INDUCTION). b conclusion deduced.

■ 1 a subtraction, withdrawal. 2 b inference, assumption, finding, reasoning, result; guess, conjecture.

de•duc•tive /didúktiv/ adj. of or reasoning by deduction. □□ de•duc'tive•ly adv.

■ see LOGICAL 1.

deed /deed/ • n. 1 thing done intentionally or consciously. 2 brave, skillful, or conspicuous act. 3 action. 4 Law document used for transferring ownership of property. • v.tr. convey or transfer by legal deed.

■ n. 1 see ACT n. 1. 2 exploit, feat. 4 title deed, contract.

deem /deem/ v.tr. formal regard; consider; judge.

deep /deep/ • *adj.* **1** extending far down or in. **2 a** to or at a specified depth (6 *feet deep*). **b** in a specified number of ranks (*soldiers drawn up six deep*). **3** situated or coming from far down, back, or in (*deep in his pockets, deep sigh*). **4** low-pitched; full-toned (*deep voice*). **5** intense; extreme (*deep disgrace*). **6** heartfelt; absorbing (*deep affection*). **7** fully absorbed or overwhelmed (*deep in debt*). **8** profound; difficult to understand (*deep thought*). • *n.* **1** [prec. by *the*] *poet.* the sea. **2** abyss, pit, or cavity. • *adv.* deeply; far down or in (*read deep into the night*). □ **deep freeze 1** refrigerator in which food can be quickly frozen and kept for long periods. **2** suspension of activity. **deep-freeze** *v.tr.* freeze or store (food) in a deep freeze. **deep-fry** (**-fries, -fried**) fry (food) in fat or oil sufficient to cover it. □ **deep'ly** *adv. n.*

■ *adj.* **1** extensive, bottomless, profound; yawning. **4** resonant, booming. **5** rich, strong; see also INTENSE 1, 3, VIVID 1. **6** intense, sincere, earnest, ardent, fervent; see also ABSORBING. **7** rapt, engrossed, occupied, intent. **8** weighty, heavy, arcane, abstruse; obscure, incomprehensible; mysterious; wise, learned, sage, astute, acute, intense. • *n.* **1** (*the deep*) the ocean, the high seas. **2** see ABYSS 1. • *adv.* see *deeply* below, *profoundly* (PROFOUND). □ **deep freeze 2** see PAUSE *n.* □□ **deeply** (far) downward *or* inward, way down, deep down; profoundly, intensely, strongly, acutely, greatly, extremely, severely, unreservedly; passionately.

deep•en /deepən/ *v.* make or become deep or deeper.

■ dig out; intensify, magnify, extend.

deer /deer/ *n.* (*pl.* same) four-hoofed grazing animal, the males of which usu. have antlers.

deer•skin /deerskin/ • *n.* leather from a deer's skin. • *adj.* made from a deer's skin.

de•es•ca•late /dee-éskəlayt/ *v.tr.* reduce the level or intensity of. □□ **de•es•ca•la•tion** /-láyshən/ *n.*

■ see DECREASE *v.*

de•face /difáys/ *v.tr.* disfigure. □□ **de•face′ment** *n.*

■ mar, spoil, ruin, blemish, damage, mutilate.

de fac•to /di fáktō, day/ • *adv.* in fact, whether by right or not. • *adj.* existing in fact (*de facto ruler*). • *n.* (in full **de facto wife** *or* **husband**) person living with another as if married.

■ *adv.* see REALLY 1.

de•fal•ca•tion /deefalkáyshən, –fawl–/ *n. Law* **1** misappropriation of money. **2** amount misappropriated.

de•fame /difáym/ *v.tr.* libel; slander. See synonym study at MALIGN. □□ **def•a•ma•tion** /défəmáyshən/ *n.* **de•fam•a•to•ry** /difámə-tawree/ *adj.*

de•fault /difáwlt/ • *n.* **1** failure to appear, pay, or act in some way. **2** preselected option adopted by a computer program when no alternative is specified. • *v.intr.* fail to fulfill an obligation, esp. to pay money or to appear in court. □ **by default** because of a lack of an alternative or opposition.

■ *n.* **1** negligence, dereliction, lapse, nonperformance, delinquency, inaction. • *v.* lapse, fall short; (*default on*) neglect.

de•feat /diféet/ • *v.tr.* **1** overcome in battle, contest, etc. **2** frustrate; baffle. **3** reject (a motion, etc.) by voting. • *n.* defeating or being defeated.

■ *v.* **1** conquer, subdue, overpower, triumph over, bring down, trounce, whip, crush, *sl.* whop; see also BEAT[1] *v.* 2a. **2** thwart, disappoint, finish; see also FOIL *v.* • *n.* conquest, overthrow, beating, frustration, end.

de•feat•ism /diféetizəm/ *n.* excessive readiness to accept defeat. □□ **de•feat′ist** *n. & adj.*

■ see *desperation* (DESPERATE).

def•e•cate /défikayt/ *v.intr.* discharge feces from the body. □□ **def•e•ca•tion** /–káyshən/ *n.*

■ move the bowels, excrete, void, relieve oneself, *colloq.* mess.

de•fect • *n.* /deefekt, difékt/ imperfection, shortcoming, blemish. See synonym study at FAULT. • *v.intr.* /difékt/ leave one's country or cause for another. □□ **de•fec′tion** *n.* **de•fec′tor** *n.*

■ *n.* deficiency, inadequacy, shortfall, failing, weakness, frailty, flaw, fault, mark. • *v.* desert, turn traitor. □□ **defector** turncoat, renegade, rat.

de•fec•tive /diféktiv/ • *adj.* having a defect or defects; imperfect; faulty. • *n.* often *offens.* mentally defective person. □□ **de•fec′tive•ly** *adv.* **de•fec′tive•ness** *n.*

■ *adj.* flawed, deficient, broken, impaired, marred, *sl.* on the blink.

de•fend /difénd/ *v.tr.* [also *absol.*] **1** resist an attack made on; protect. **2** support or uphold by argument. **3** conduct the defense in a lawsuit. □□ **de•fend′er** *n.*

■ **1** fortify, arm, secure; guard, shield; fight for. **2, 3** plead for, stand up for, stand by, champion.

de•fend•ant /diféndənt, –ant/ *n.* person, etc., sued or accused in a court of law.

■ see LITIGANT *n.*

de•fense /diféns/ *n.* **1** defending from or resisting attack. **2** means of resisting attack. **3** justification; vindication. **4** defendant's case or counsel in a lawsuit. □ **defense mechanism 1** body's reaction against disease. **2** usu. unconscious mental process to avoid anxiety. □□ **de•fense′less** *adj.* **de•fense′less•ly** *adv.* **de•fense′less•ness** *n.*

■ **2** guard, shield; see also PROTECTION 1b. **3** excuse, apology, reason; argument. □□ **defenseless** unprotected, exposed; helpless. **defenselessness** susceptibility; helplessness.

de•fen•si•ble /difénsibəl/ *adj.* **1** justifiable; supportable by argument. **2** able to be easily defended militarily. □□ **de•fen•si•bil′i•ty** *n.* **de•fen′si•bly** *adv.*

■ **1** see TENABLE.

de•fen•sive /difénsiv/ *adj.* **1** done or intended for defense. **2** overreacting to criticism. □□ **de•fen′sive•ly** *adv.* **de•fen′sive•ness** *n.*

■ **1** protective, preservative.

de•fer[1] /difór/ v.tr. (**de•ferred, de•fer•ring**) postpone. See synonym study at POSTPONE. □□ **de•fer′ment** n. **de•fer′ral** n.

■ put off, delay, stay, table, hold over. □□ **deferment, deferral** see *postponement* (POSTPONE[1]), STAY n. 2.

de•fer[2] /difór/ v.intr. (**de•ferred, de•fer•ring**) yield or make concessions. □□ **de•fer′ rer** n.

■ give in, give ground or way, submit, acquiesce; comply.

def•er•ence /défərəns, défrəns/ n. **1** courteous regard; respect. **2** compliance. See synonym study at HONOR. □ **in deference to** out of respect for.

■ **1** politeness, civility, courtesy. **2** obeisance, submission.

def•er•en•tial /défərénshəl/ adj. showing deference; respectful. □□ **def•er•en′tial•ly** adv.

■ see RESPECTFUL.

de•fi•ance /difíəns/ n. open disobedience; bold resistance.

■ resistance, opposition

de•fi•ant /difíənt/ adj. **1** showing defiance. **2** openly disobedient. □□ **de•fi′ant•ly** adv.

■ **1** challenging, bold, brazen, daring; see also AUDACIOUS 2. **2** rebellious, recalcitrant, obstinate, refractory, insubordinate.

de•fi•cien•cy /difíshənsee/ n. (pl. **–cies**) **1** being deficient. **2** lack or shortage. **3** thing lacking.

■ **1, 2** see ABSENCE 3. **3** see DEFECT n.

de•fi•cient /difíshənt/ adj. **1** incomplete. **2** insufficient.

■ **1** wanting, lacking; see also INCOMPLETE. **2** impaired, inadequate, incomplete; sparse, sketchy, skimpy, scarce.

def•i•cit /défisit/ n. **1** amount by which a thing (esp. money) is too small. **2** excess of liabilities over assets.

■ **1** shortfall, shortage, default, loss, deficiency.

de•file[1] /difíl/ v.tr. **1** make dirty; pollute; befoul. **2** corrupt. **3** desecrate; profane. See synonym study at POLLUTE. □□ **de•file′ment** n.

■ **1** see FOUL v. 1. **2** see POISON v. 4. **3** see DESECRATE.

de•file[2] /difíl/ • n. also /déefil/ narrow gorge or pass. • v.intr. march in file.

■ n. see GORGE n. 1.

de•fine /difín/ v.tr. **1** give the meaning of (a word, etc.). **2** describe or explain the scope of. **3** outline. □□ **de•fin′a•ble** adj.

■ **1** explain. **2** spell out, detail, delineate, expand on, characterize; see also CLARIFY 1. **3** demarcate, delimit, circumscribe.

def•i•nite /définit/ adj. **1** having exact and discernible limits. **2** clear and distinct; not vague. □ **definite article** see ARTICLE 4. □□ **def′i•nite•ly** adv.

■ **1** specific, pronounced, explicit; firm. **2** plain, well-defined, unambiguous, obvious.

def•i•nite•ly /définitlee/ • adv. **1** in a definite manner. **2** certainly; without doubt. • int. colloq. yes, certainly.

■ adv. **1** see expressly (EXPRESS[2]). **2** positively, absolutely, surely, to be sure, assuredly, indubitably, undoubtedly, unequivocally,

unquestionably, clearly, patently. int. see ABSOLUTELY 4.

def•i•ni•tion /définishən/ n. **1 a** defining. **b** meaning of a word or nature of a thing. **2** distinctness in outline of an image.

■ **1** description, explanation, explication, clarification. **2** delineation; resolution, focus, precision.

de•fin•i•tive /difínitiv/ adj. **1** (of an answer, verdict, etc.) decisive; unconditional; final. **2** (of a book, etc.) most authoritative. □□ **de•fin′i•tive•ly** adv.

■ **1** clarifying, absolute; see also FINAL adj. 2. **2** consummate, reliable, complete; see also AUTHORITATIVE 1, 3.

de•flate /difláyt/ v. **1 a** tr. let air or gas out of (a tire, balloon, etc.). **b** intr. be emptied of air or gas. **2** tr. & intr. lose or cause to lose confidence. **3** Econ. **a** tr. subject (a currency or economy) to deflation. **b** intr. pursue a policy of deflation. □□ **de•fla′tor** n.

■ **2** see MORTIFY 1.

de•fla•tion /difláyshən/ n. **1** deflating or being deflated. **2** Econ. reduction of money in circulation to increase its value. □□ **de•fla′tion•ar•y** adj.

de•flect /diflékt/ v. **1** tr. & intr. bend or turn aside from a course or purpose. **2** a tr. cause to deviate. **b** intr. deviate. □□ **de•flec•tion** /diflékshən/ n. **de•flec′tor** n.

■ avert, divert, sidetrack, fend off; swerve, veer, bend.

de•flow•er /diflówr/ v.tr. **1** deprive of virginity. **2** ravage; spoil.

de•fo•li•ate /deefóleeayt/ v.tr. remove leaves from, esp. as a military tactic. □□ **de•fo′li•ant** n. & adj. **de•fo•li•a•tion** /-áyshən/ n.

de•form /difáwrm/ v. **1** tr. make ugly; deface; misshape. **2** intr. undergo deformation. □□ **de•form′a•ble** adj. **de•for•ma•tion** /déefawrmáyshən/ n. **de•formed′** adj. **de•for′mi•ty** n. (pl. **–ties**)

■ **1** see DEFACE, DISTORT 1.

de•fraud /difráwd/ v.tr. cheat by fraud.

■ swindle, trick, fool, fleece, deceive, hoodwink, put one over on, rip off, gyp, con.

de•fray /difráy/ v.tr. pay (a cost or expense). □□ **de•fray′al** n.

■ settle, meet, cover; (defray the cost) foot the bill, colloq. pick up the tab or check.

de•frost /difráwst, fróst/ v. **1** tr. remove frost or ice from (esp. a refrigerator, windshield, etc.). **2** tr. unfreeze (frozen food). **3** intr. become unfrozen. □□ **de•frost′er** n.

■ see THAW v. 1, 4.

deft /deft/ adj. neat; dexterous; adroit. □□ **deft′ly** adv. **deft′ness** n.

■ see DEXTEROUS.

de•funct /difúngkt/ adj. **1** no longer existing or used. **2** dead or extinct.

■ **1** inoperative, inapplicable, invalid, expired, obsolete, passé, outmoded, out. **2** see DEAD adj.

de•fuse /deefyóōz/ v.tr. **1** remove the fuse from (a bomb, etc.). **2** reduce tensions in (a crisis, difficulty, etc.).

■ **2** see MODERATE v. 1.

de•fy /difí/ v.tr. (**–fies, –fied**) **1** resist openly;

refuse to obey. **2** (of a thing) present insuperable obstacles to (*defies solution*). **3** challenge (a person) to do or prove something.
■ **1** disobey, flout, go against. **2** frustrate, thwart, baffle, confound; resist, withstand. **3** dare; invite, summon.

deg. *abbr.* degree.

de•gen•er•ate • *adj.* /dijénərət/ fallen from former normality or goodness. See synonym study at DEPRAVED. • *n.* /dijénərət/ degraded person. • *v.intr.* /dijénərayt/ become degenerate. □□ **de•gen•er•a•cy** *n.* **de•gen′er•ate•ly** *adv.*
■ *adj.* debased, corrupt, decadent; ignoble, base, inferior. • *n.* reprobate, rake; pervert, deviate. • *v.* decline, deteriorate; backslide, regress, *sl.* go to the dogs.

de•gen•er•a•tion /dijénəráyshən/ *n.* **1** becoming degenerate. **2** *Med.* morbid deterioration of tissue. □□ **de•gen•er•a•tive** /dijénərətiv/ *adj.*
■ **1** see DECAY *n.* 2.

de•grade /digráyd/ *v.tr.* **1** reduce to a lower rank. **2** dishonor; humiliate. See synonym study at HUMBLE. □□ **de•grad′a•ble** *adj.* **deg•ra•da•tion** /dégrədáyshən/ *n.* **de•grad′er** *n.*
■ **1** see DOWNGRADE *v.* 1. **2** debase, demean, disgrace, shame; belittle, deprecate, cheapen. □□ **degradation** degeneracy, deterioration, corruption; disrepute, shame, humiliation.

de•grad•ing /digráyding/ *adj.* humiliating; causing a loss of self-respect. □□ **de•grad′ing•ly** *adv.*
■ demeaning, debasing, menial.

de•gree /digreé/ *n.* **1** stage in scale, series, or process. **2** stage in intensity or amount (*to a degree*). **3** *Math.* unit of measurement of angles or arcs, with 360 degrees comprising a circle. ¶Symb.: °. **4** *Physics* unit of temperature, hardness, etc. **5** *Med.* extent of burns. **6** academic rank. **7** grade of crime. ■ **by degrees** gradually. **to a degree** *colloq.* considerably.
■ **1** see STAGE *n.* 1. **2** magnitude, extent, limit. ■ **by degrees** little by little, piecemeal, slowly. **to a degree** substantially, quite, decidedly.

de•hu•man•ize /deehyoõmənīz/ *v.tr.* **1** deprive of human characteristics. **2** make impersonal. □□ **de•hu′man•i•za′tion** *n.*

de•hu•mid•i•fy /deéhyoõmídifī/ *v.tr.* (**-fies**, **-fied**) reduce the degree of humidity of; remove moisture from (a gas, esp. air). □□ **de•hu•mid•i•fi•ca•tion** /–fikáyshən/ *n.* **de•hu•mid′i•fi•er** *n.*

de•hy•drate /deéhīdráyt/ *v.* **1** *tr.* **a** remove water from (esp. foods). **b** make dry. **2** *intr.* lose water. □□ **de•hy′drat•ed** *adj.* **de•hy•dra•tion** /–dráyshən/ *n.* **de•hy′dra•tor** *n.* See synonym study at DRY
■ see DRY *v.*

de•ice /deéis/ *v.tr.* **1** remove ice from. **2** prevent the formation of ice on. □□ **de•ic′er** *n.*
■ **1** see THAW *v.* 1, 5.

de•i•fy /deéifī/ *v.tr.* (**-fies**, **-fied**) **1** make a god of. **2** regard or worship as a god. □□ **de•i•fi•ca•tion** /–fikáyshən/ *n.*

deign /dayn/ *v.intr.* think fit; condescend.
■ stoop, lower oneself, *formal* vouchsafe.

de•ism /deéizəm, dáy–/ *n.* reasoned belief in the existence of a god (cf. THEISM). □□ **de′ist** *n.* **de•is′tic** *adj.* **de•is′ti•cal** *adj.*

de•i•ty /deéitee, dáy–/ *n.* (*pl.* **-ties**) **1** god or goddess. **2** divine status, quality, or nature. **3** (**the Deity**) God.
■ **1** creator, divinity; see also GOD *n.* 1. **3** the Creator, the Supreme Being.

dé•jà vu /dáyzhaa voõ/ *n.* feeling of having already experienced a situation.

de•ject /dijékt/ *v.tr.* (usu. as **dejected** *adj.*) make sad or dispirited; depress. □□ **de•ject′ed•ly** *adv.* **de•jec′tion** *n.*
■ (**dejected**) downcast, downhearted, discouraged, crestfallen; melancholy, unhappy, gloomy, blue, low-spirited, sorrowful, *colloq.* down in the dumps.

de ju•re /dee joõree, day joõray/ • *adj.* rightful. • *adv.* rightfully; by right.
■ *adj.* see LEGITIMATE 1, 2.

Del. *abbr.* Delaware.

Del•a•ware /déləwair/ *n.* **1** N. American people native to the northeastern US. **2** language of this people (Also called **Lenape** or **Lenni Lenape**).

de•lay /diláy/ *v.* **1** *tr.* postpone; defer. **2** *tr.* make late. **3** *intr.* be late. See synonym study at POSTPONE. • *n.* **1** delaying. **2** time lost by inaction. **3** hindrance. ■ **delayed-action** [*attrib.*] (of a bomb, etc.) operating some time after being primed or set. □□ **de•lay′er** *n.*
■ *v.* **1** put off or aside, break off, suspend, *colloq.* put on the back burner. **2** detain, retard, impede, hinder. **3** loiter, procrastinate, hesitate, mark time, *colloq.* dillydally. • *n.* **1**, **2** postponement, deferral, holdup, snag. **3** see HINDRANCE.

de•lec•ta•ble /diléktəbəl/ *adj.* esp. *literary* delightful; pleasant. □□ **de•lec•ta•bil•i•ty** /–bilitee/ *n.* **de•lec′ta•bly** *adv.*
■ see PLEASANT.

del•e•gate • *n.* /déligət/ **1** elected representative sent to a conference. **2** member of a committee or deputation. • *v.tr.* /déligayt/ **1 a** commit (authority, etc.) to an agent or deputy. **b** entrust (a task) to another. **2** send or authorize (a person) as a representative.
■ *n.* envoy, agent, ambassador, minister, emissary, commissioner, go-between. • *v.* **1** assign, transfer. **2** depute, designate, nominate, accredit, empower, mandate.

del•e•ga•tion /déligáyshən/ *n.* **1** body of delegates; deputation. **2** delegating or being delegated.
■ **1** see MISSION 3.

de•lete /dileét/ *v.tr.* remove (written or printed matter), esp. by striking out. □□ **de•le•tion** /–leéshən/ *n.*
■ erase, cancel, expunge, efface, eliminate, obliterate, wipe out, eradicate, strike out, cut or edit (out), blue-pencil.

del•e•te•ri•ous /délitee̊reeəs/ *adj.* harmful (to mind or body).
■ see HARMFUL.

delft /delft/ *n.* (also **delft′ware** /délftwair/) glazed, usu. blue and white, earthenware, made in Delft in Holland.

del•i /délee/ n. (pl. **del•is**) colloq. a delicatessen.

de•lib•er•ate • adj. /dilíbərət/ **1 a** intentional. **b** fully considered. **2** slow in deciding; cautious. **3** (of movement, etc.) leisurely and unhurried. • v. /dilíbərayt/ **1** intr. think carefully. **2** tr. consider; discuss carefully. □□ **de•lib•er•ate•ly** /dilíbərətlee/ adv. **de•lib′er•ate•ness** n. **de•lib′er•a•tive** adj. **de•lib′er•a•tive•ly** adv. **de•lib′er•a•tive•ness** n. **de•lib′er•a•tor** n.

■ adj. **1 a** planned, willful, calculated, purposeful. **1 b, 2** confident, prudent, painstaking, thorough. **3** slow, careful. • v. **1** ponder, take counsel, reflect. **2** weigh, debate, study. □□ **deliberately** intentionally, on purpose, consciously.

de•lib•er•a•tion /dilibəráyshən/ n. **1** careful consideration. **2** discussion. **3 a** caution and care. **b** (of action or behavior) purposefulness. **c** (of movement) slowness or ponderousness.

■ **1** see CONSIDERATION 1. **2** see discussion (DISCUSS).

del•i•ca•cy /délikəsee/ n. (pl. **-cies**) **1** (esp. in craftsmanship or beauty) fineness or intricacy of structure or texture. **2** susceptibility to injury or disease. **3** quality of requiring discretion or sensitivity. **4** choice food.

■ **1** grace, gracefulness, daintiness; see also BEAUTY 1. **2** fragility, frailty, frailness, weakness, infirmity, feebleness. **3** difficulty, ticklishness, awkwardness. **4** luxury, treat, morsel.

del•i•cate /délikət/ adj. **1 a** fine in texture, quality, etc. **b** slender or slight. **c** subtle or subdued. **2 a** (of a person) susceptible to injury or illness. **b** (of a thing) easily spoiled or damaged. **3 a** requiring care; tricky. **b** (of an instrument) highly sensitive. □□ **del′i•cate•ly** adv.

■ **1 a** exquisite, dainty, graceful. **c** faint, pastel; see SUBTLE 2. **2 a** feeble, weak, frail. **b** fragile, flimsy. **3 a** ticklish, sensitive, awkward, colloq. sticky, sl. hairy.

del•i•ca•tes•sen /délikətésən/ n. **1** store selling cooked meats, cheeses, prepared foods, etc. **2** (often attrib.) such foods.

De•li•cious /dilishəs/ n. red or yellow variety of apple.

de•li•cious /dilíshəs/ adj. highly enjoyable to the taste or smell. □□ **de•li′cious•ly** adv.

■ luscious, ambrosial, savory, flavorful, tasty, appetizing, palatable, colloq. scrumptious, yummy.

de•light /dilít/ • v. **1** tr. please greatly. **2** intr. take great pleasure. • n. **1** great pleasure. **2** something giving pleasure. □□ **de•light′ed** adj. **de•light′ed•ly** adv.

■ v. **1** gladden, cheer, amuse, entertain, captivate. **2** (delight in) relish, revel in, love, enjoy, colloq. get a kick out of. • n. **1** joy, bliss, ecstasy, rapture. □□ **delighted** pleased, happy, charmed, thrilled, colloq. tickled pink or to death.

de•light•ful /dilítfool/ adj. causing delight. □□ **de•light′ful•ly** adv.

■ pleasing, enjoyable, amusing, entertaining, congenial, winning, charming, engaging; captivating, fascinating.

de•lim•it /dilímit/ v.tr. fix the limits or boundary of. □□ **de•lim•i•ta•tion** /–táyshən/ n.

■ see RESTRICT.

de•lin•e•ate /dilíneeayt/ v.tr. portray by drawing, etc., or in words. □□ **de•lin•e•a•tion** /–áyshən/ n.

de•lin•quent /dilíngkwənt/ • n. offender. • adj. **1** guilty of a minor crime or a misdeed. **2** failing in one's duty. **3** in arrears. □□ **de•lin•quen•cy** /dilíngkwənsee/ n. **de•lin′quent•ly** adv.

■ n. wrongdoer, criminal, miscreant; hooligan, ruffian. • adj. **1** negligent, derelict, remiss. **3** overdue, late, unpaid.

del•i•quesce /délikwés/ v.intr. become liquid, esp. by absorbing water from the air. □□ **del•i•ques′cence** n. **del•i•ques′cent** adj.

de•lir•i•ous /dilíreeəs/ adj. **1** affected with delirium. **2** wildly excited; ecstatic. □□ **de•lir′i•ous•ly** adv.

■ **1** hysterical, incoherent, irrational, ranting, crazed, disturbed; mad, colloq. crazy. **2** thrilled; see also ecstatic (ECSTASY).

de•lir•i•um /dilíreeəm/ n. **1** disorder involving incoherence, hallucinations, etc., caused by intoxication, fever, etc. **2** great excitement; ecstasy. □ **delirium tremens** /tréemənz, –menz/ psychosis of chronic alcoholism involving tremors and hallucinations.

de•liv•er /diliver/ v.tr. **1 a** distribute (letters, goods, etc.) to the addressee or purchaser. **b** hand over. **2** save, rescue, or set free. **3 a** give birth to. **b** assist at the birth of. **4 a** utter or recite (an opinion, speech, etc.). **b** (of a judge) pronounce (a judgment). **5** abandon; resign; hand over (delivered his soul up to God). **6** launch or aim (a blow, ball, or attack).

■ **1 a** carry, bring, convey, transport. **2** liberate, extricate, release, emancipate. **3 a** bring forth, bear. **4 a** give, present, read, broadcast; set forth, publish. **b** set forth, express, promulgate, hand down. **5** give, surrender, cede, yield, relinquish. **6** give, administer, inflict, send, throw, cast, fire.

de•liv•er•ance /dilívərəns/ n. rescuing or being rescued.

■ liberation, release, emancipation; relief; salvation.

de•liv•er•y /dilívəree/ n. (pl. **-ies**) **1 a** delivering of letters, etc. **b** regular distribution of letters, etc. **c** something delivered. **2** childbirth. **3** deliverance. **4** act or style of throwing, esp. a ball. **5** manner or style of giving a speech, etc.

■ **1 a** distribution, conveyance. **3** see DELIVERANCE. **4** see THROW n. 1. **5** presentation, performance; enunciation, expression.

dell /del/ n. small usu. wooded hollow or valley.

del•phin•i•um /delfíneeəm/ n. garden plant with tall spikes of usu. blue flowers.

del•ta /déltə/ n. **1** triangular tract of earth, alluvium, etc., at the mouth of a river. **2** fourth letter of the Greek alphabet (Δ, δ).

del•toid /déltoyd/ • adj. triangular; like a river delta. • n. (in full **deltoid muscle**) thick triangular muscle covering the shoulder joint.

de•lude /dilŏŏd/ v.tr. deceive or mislead.
 ■ see DECEIVE 1.

del•uge /délyŏŏj, –yoozh/ • n. **1** great flood. **2** (**the Deluge**) biblical Flood (Gen. 6–8). **3** great outpouring (of words, paper, etc.). **4** heavy fall of rain. • v.tr. **1** flood. **2** inundate with a great number or amount.
 ■ n. **1** see FLOOD n. 1. **3** see FLOOD n. 2b. **4** see DOWNPOUR. • v. **1** see FLOOD v. 1. **2** see DROWN.

de•lu•sion /dilŏŏzhən/ n. **1** false belief or impression. **2** Psychol. this as a symptom or form of mental disorder. □ **delusions of grandeur** false idea of oneself as being important, noble, famous, etc. □□ **de•lu'sion•al** adj.
 ■ **1** misapprehension, illusion, misconception, hallucination.

de•luxe /dəlúks, lŏŏks/ adj. **1** luxurious or sumptuous. **2** of a superior kind.
 ■ see LUXURIOUS 1.

delve /delv/ v.intr. search or research energetically or deeply.
 ■ see ROOT² v. 2a.

Dem. abbr. Democrat.

de•mag•net•ize /deemágnitiz/ v.tr. remove the magnetic properties of. □□ **de•mag•ne•ti•zation** /–tizáyshən/ n. **de•mag'net•iz•er** n.

dem•a•gogue /démədgog, –gawg/ n. (also **–gog**) political agitator appealing to mob instincts. □□ **dem•a•gog•ic** /–gójik, –gógik, –gŏ–/ adj. **dem•a•gogu•er•y** /–gógəree, –gáwg–/ n. **dem•a•go•gy** /–gójee, –gáw–/ n.
 ■ see agitator (AGITATE).

de•mand /dimánd/ • n. **1** insistent and peremptory request. **2** Econ. desire for a commodity. **3** urgent claim. • v.tr. **1** ask for (something) insistently and urgently. **2** require or need. **3** insist on. **4** (as **demanding** adj.) requiring skill, effort, etc. □ **in demand** sought after. **on demand** as soon as a demand is made (a check payable on demand). □□ **de•mand'ing•ly** adv.
 ■ n. **1** order, command, call, bidding. **2** market. **3** see CLAIM n. 1. • v. **1** require, order; command; requisition. **2** call for, want. **4** (**demanding**) insistent; difficult, hard, exacting, trying, taxing. □ **in demand** coveted, popular. **on demand** on call; at once, immediately.

de•mar•ca•tion /deemaarkáyshən/ n. marking a boundary or limits. □□ **de•mar•cate** /dímaárkayt, deémaar–/ v.tr. **de•mar'ca•tor** n.
 ■ see DEFINITION 2.

de•mean¹ /dimeén/ v.tr. [usu. refl.] lower the dignity of. See synonym study at HUMBLE.
 ■ see LOWER 3.

de•mean² /dimeén/ v.refl. behave (demeaned himself well).
 ■ (demean oneself) see BEHAVE 2.

de•mean•or /dimeénər/ n. behavior or bearing.
 ■ see BEARING 1.

de•ment•ed /diméntid/ adj. mad; crazy.

□□ **de•ment'ed•ly** adv. **de•ment'ed•ness** n.
 ■ see MAD adj. 1.

de•men•tia /diménshə/ n. Med. chronic or persistent insanity marked by memory disorders, impaired reasoning, etc., due to brain disease or injury.

de•mer•it /dimérit/ n. **1** fault. **2** mark given to an offender.

de•mesne /dimáyn, –meén/ n. territory; domain. □ **held in demesne** (of an estate) occupied by the owner.

demi- /démee/ prefix **1** half. **2** partially or imperfectly such.

dem•i•god /démeegod/ n. (fem. **–god•dess** /–godis/) **1** partly divine being. **2** colloq. person of compelling beauty, powers, or personality.

de•mil•i•ta•rize /deemílitəriz/ v.tr. remove military forces from (a frontier, zone, etc.). □□ **de•mil•i•ta•ri•za'tion** n.

dem•i•monde /démeemond, –máwND/ n. **1** class of women considered to be of doubtful social standing and morality. **2** any semirespectable group.

de•mise /dimíz/ • n. **1** death; termination. **2** Law transfer (of property, title, etc.) by demising. • v.tr. Law **1** convey or grant (an estate) by will or lease. **2** transmit (a title, etc.) by death.
 ■ n. **1** see DEATH 1. • v. **1** see LEASE v., make over 1.

de•mi•tasse /démeetas, –taas/ n. small coffee cup, esp. for strong coffee.

de•mo /démō/ n. (pl. **–os**) colloq. = DEMONSTRATION 3.

de•mo•bi•lize /deemōbilíz/ v.tr. disband (troops, ships, etc.). □□ **de•mo•bi•li•za'tion** n.
 ■ see DISBAND.

de•moc•ra•cy /dimókrəsee/ n. (pl. **–cies**) **1** government by the whole population, usu. through elected representatives. **2** nation or organization so governed.

dem•o•crat /déməkrat/ n. **1** advocate of democracy. **2** (**Democrat**) member of the Democratic party.

dem•o•crat•ic /déməkrátik/ adj. **1** of, like, practicing, advocating, or constituting democracy. **2** favoring social equality. □ **Democratic party** US political party, considered to support social reform and greater federal powers. (cf. Republican party). □□ **dem•o•crat'i•cal•ly** adv.
 ■ **1** representative, popular; elected. **2** egalitarian.

de•moc•ra•tize /dimókrətiz/ v.tr. make (a nation, institution, etc.) democratic. □□ **de•moc•ra•ti•za'tion** n.

de•mod•u•late /deemójəlayt/ v.tr. Physics extract (a modulating signal). □□ **de•mod•u•la•tion** /–láyshən/ n. **de•mod'u•la•tor** n.

de•mog•ra•phy /dimógrəfee/ n. study of statistics of births, deaths, disease, etc. □□ **de•mog'ra•pher** n. **dem•o•graph•ic** /démagráfik/ adj. **dem•o•graph'i•cal** adj. **dem•o•graph'i•cal•ly** adv.

de•mol•ish /dimólish/ v.tr. **1 a** pull down (a building). **b** destroy or break. **2** overthrow (an institution). **3** refute. See synonym study at DESTROY. □□ **de•mol′ish•er** *n.* **dem•o•li•tion** /démǝlíshǝn/ *n.* **dem•o•li′tion•ist** *n.*

■ **1 a** tear *or* knock down, dismantle, raze, level. **b** see DESTROY 1. **2** bring to an end; see also OVERTHROW *v.* **3** disprove, dispose of; crush, defeat.

de•mon /déemǝn/ *n.* **1** evil spirit or devil. **2** malignant supernatural being; the Devil. **3** [often *attrib.*] forceful, fierce, or skillful performer. □ **a demon for work** *colloq.* person who works strenuously. □□ **de•mon•ic** /dimónik/ *adj.* **de•mon•ize** /déemǝnīz/ *v.*

■ **1** fiend; monster, ogre, beast. **2** see DEVIL *n.* 1, 2. **3** expert, master, genius, virtuoso, *sl.* ace; (*attrib.*) see *first-rate adj.*

de•mo•ni•ac /dimóneeak/ • *adj.* **1** fiercely energetic or frenzied. **2** of or like demons. • *n.* person possessed by an evil spirit. □□ **de•mo•ni•a•cal** /dèemǝníǝkǝl/ *adj.* **de•mo•ni•a•cal•ly** *adv.*

de•mon•stra•ble /dimónstrǝbǝl/ *adj.* capable of being shown or proved. □□ **de•mon′stra•bly** *adv.*

■ provable, verifiable; evident, obvious, undeniable, apparent, indisputable, unquestionable, conclusive.

dem•on•strate /démǝnstrayt/ *v.* **1** *tr.* show (feelings, etc.). **2** *tr.* describe and explain (a proposition, machine, etc.) by experiment, use, etc. **3** *tr.* logically prove or be proof of. **4** *intr.* take part in or organize a public demonstration. □□ **dem′on•stra•tor** *n.*

■ **1, 3** make evident, establish, exhibit; see also PROVE 1. **2** display, illustrate; see also EXPLAIN 1. **4** march, rally, protest.

dem•on•stra•tion /démǝnstráyshǝn/ *n.* **1** showing of feeling, etc. **2** public meeting, march, etc., for political or moral purpose. **3** exhibition or explanation of specimens or experiments as a method of esp. scientific teaching or proof by logic, argument, etc. □□ **dem•on•stra′tion•al** *adj.*

■ **1** display. **2** protest, rally, sit-in. **3** presentation, display, *colloq.* demo. **4** evidence, testimony, confirmation, substantiation.

de•mon•stra•tive /dimónstrǝtiv/ • *adj.* **1** showing feelings readily; affectionate. **2** logically conclusive; giving proof (*the work is demonstrative of their skill*). **3** *Gram.* (of an adjective or pronoun) indicating the person or thing referred to (*e.g., this, that, those*). • *n.* *Gram.* demonstrative adjective or pronoun. □□ **de•mon′stra•tive•ly** *adv.* **de•mon′stra•tive•ness** *n.*

■ *adj.* **1** expressive, expansive, emotional. **2** illustrative, representative, evidential.

de•mor•al•ize /dimáwrǝlīz, –mór–/ *v.tr.* destroy (a person's) morale; make hopeless. □□ **de•mor•al•i•za′tion** *n.* **de•mor′al•iz•ing** *adj.* **de•mor′al•iz•ing•ly** *adv.*

■ dispirit, daunt, dishearten, discourage, demotivate, defeat; devitalize, depress, subdue, crush.

de•mote /dimốt/ *v.tr.* reduce to a lower rank or class. □□ **de•mo′tion** /–mṓshǝn/ *n.*

■ see DOWNGRADE *v.*

de•mur /dimǝ́r/ • *v.intr.* (**de•murred, de•mur•ring**) **1** raise objections. **2** *Law* put in a demurrer. • *n.* (also **de•mur•ral** /dimǝ́rǝl/)

[*usu. in neg.*] objection (*agreed without demur*). See synonym study at QUALM.

■ *v.* **1** see PROTEST *v.* 1. • *n.* see OBJECTION.

de•mure /dimyŏŏr/ *adj.* (**de•mur•er, de•mur•est**) **1** composed, quiet, and reserved; modest. **2** coy. **3** decorous. □□ **de•mure′ly** *adv.* **de•mure′ness** *n.*

■ **1** see MODEST 1, 2. **2** see COY 1, *prudish* (PRUDE). **3** see DECOROUS, SEEMLY.

de•mur•rer /dimárǝr, –mŭr–/ *n.* *Law* objection raised or exception taken.

de•mys•ti•fy /deemístifī/ *v.tr.* (**–fies, –fied**) **1** clarify (obscure beliefs or subjects, etc.). **2** reduce or remove the mystery from. □□ **de•mys•ti•fi•ca•tion** /–fikáyshǝn/ *n.*

den /den/ *n.* **1** wild animal's lair. **2** place of crime or vice. **3** homey, informal room.

■ **1** see LAIR *n.* 1. **3** see SANCTUM 2.

de•na•ture /deenáychǝr/ *v.tr.* **1** change the properties of (a protein, etc.) by heat, acidity, etc. **2** make (alcohol) unfit for drinking. □□ **de•na′tur•ant** *n.* **de•na•tur•a′tion** /deenaychǝráyshǝn/ *n.*

den•drite /déndrīt/ *n.* **1 a** stone or mineral with natural treelike or mosslike markings. **b** such marks. **2** *Zool. & Anat.* branching process of a nerve cell conducting signals to a cell body. □□ **den•drit•ic** /dendrítik/ *adj.*

den•drol•o•gy /dendrólǝjee/ *n.* the scientific study of trees. □□ **den•dro•log•i•cal** /–drǝlójikǝl/ *adj.* **den•drol′o•gist** *n.*

den•gue /dénggay, –gee/ *n.* infectious tropical viral disease.

de•ni•al /diníǝl/ *n.* **1** denying the truth or existence of. **2** refusal of a request or wish. **3** disavowal of a person as one's leader, etc. **4** = SELF-DENIAL.

■ **1** contradiction, repudiation, disavowal, disclaimer. **2** rejection, rebuff.

de•nier /dényǝr, dǝnyáy, dǝneér/ *n.* unit of weight measuring the fineness of silk, nylon, etc.

den•i•grate /dénigrayt/ *v.tr.* defame or disparage the reputation of (a person); blacken. □□ **den•i•gra•tion** /–gráyshǝn/ *n.*

■ see VILIFY.

den•im /dénim/ *n.* **1** [often *attrib.*] usu. blue, hard-wearing, cotton twill fabric used for jeans, overalls, etc. **2** [in *pl.*] *colloq.* clothing made of this.

den•i•zen /dénizǝn/ *n.* **1** inhabitant or occupant. **2** foreigner admitted to certain rights in an adopted country.

■ **1** dweller, frequenter, resident. **2** see ALIEN *n.* 1.

de•nom•i•nate /dinóminayt/ *v.tr.* **1** give a name to. **2** call or describe (a person or thing).

de•nom•i•na•tion /dinóminiáyshǝn/ *n.* **1** church or religious sect. **2** class of units of numbers, weights, money, etc. (*money of small denominations*). **3 a** name or designation, esp. characteristic or class name. **b** class or kind having a specific name. □□ **de•nom•i•na′tion•al** *adj.*

■ **1** persuasion, school, church, order. **2** size, value; see also CLASS *n.* 1. **3 a** identification, style, title. **b** sort, type, nature, vari-

denominator ~ dependent 204

ety; grade, genus, species, order, classification.

de•nom•i•na•tor /dinóminaytər/ n. Math. number below the line in a fraction; divisor. □ **common denominator 1** common multiple of the denominators of several fractions. **2** common feature of members of a group. **least** (or **lowest**) **common denominator** lowest common multiple as above.

de•note /dinót/ v.tr. **1** be a sign of; indicate. **2** stand as a name for; signify. □□ **de•no•ta•tion** /deenōtáyshən/ n. **de•no•ta•tive** /deékh nōtáytiv, dinótətiv/ adj.
■ **1** specify, signify; see also INDICATE 2. **2** symbolize, represent.

de•noue•ment /daynōōmón/ n. (also **dé•noue•ment**′) final unraveling of a plot or complicated situation.

de•nounce /dinówns/ v.tr. **1** accuse; condemn. **2** inform against. □□ **de•nounce**′**ment** n. **de•nounc**′**er** n.
■ **1** brand, stigmatize, charge, blame, incriminate; criticize, decry, denunciate, attack, assail, censure. **2** betray, report, reveal; see also INFORM 2. □□ **denouncement** see ACCUSATION.

dense /dens/ adj. **1** closely compacted; thick. **2** crowded together. **3** colloq. stupid. □□ **dense**′**ly** adv. **dense**′**ness** n.
■ **1** compressed, solid. **2** packed, congested, populous. **3** slow, thickheaded, colloq. dumb; see also STUPID adj. 1.

den•si•ty /dénsitee/ n. (pl. **-ties**) **1** degree of compactness of a substance. **2** Physics degree of consistency measured by the quantity of mass per unit volume. **3** crowded state. **4** stupidity.

dent /dent/ • n. **1** slight hollow made by a blow or pressure. **2** noticeable effect (lunch made a dent in our funds). • v.tr. mark with a dent.
■ n. **1** see IMPRESSION[1] 4. • v. see MARK v. 1a.

dent. abbr. **1** dental. **2** dentist. **3** dentistry.

den•tal /déntl/ adj. **1** of the teeth or dentistry. **2** Phonet. (of a consonant) produced with the tongue's tip against the upper front teeth (as th) or the ridge of the teeth (as n, s, t). □ **dental floss** thread used to clean between the teeth. **dental hygienist** person trained to clean and examine teeth.

den•ti•frice /déntifris/ n. paste or powder for cleaning teeth.

den•tin /dént'n/ n. (also **den•tine** /-teen/) dense, bony tissue forming the bulk of a tooth.

den•tist /déntist/ n. person qualified to treat diseases and conditions that affect the mouth, jaws, teeth, and their supporting tissues, and to repair and extract teeth. □□ **den**′**tist•ry** n.

den•ti•tion /dentíshən/ n. **1** type, number, and arrangement of teeth. **2** teething.

den•ture /dénchər/ n. removable artificial tooth or teeth.

de•nude /dinōōd, -nyōōd/ v.tr. make naked or bare. □□ **den•u•da•tion** /deenōōdáyshən, -nyōō-/, dényōō-/ n.
■ see BARE v. 1.

de•nun•ci•a•tion /dinúnsee-áyshən, -shee-/ n. denouncing (a person, policy, etc.); public condemnation. □□ **de•nun•ci•ate** /-seeayt/ v. **de•nun**′**ci•a•tor** n.
■ see ACCUSATION.

de•ny /diní/ v.tr. (**-nies, -nied**) **1** declare untrue or nonexistent. **2** repudiate or disclaim. **3** refuse (a person or thing, or something to a person). □ **deny oneself** be abstinent.
■ **1** contradict, dispute, challenge; negate, rebut. **2** disavow, renounce, disown. **3** reject, withhold, forbid; recall, revoke.

de•o•dor•ant /deeódərənt/ n. substance applied to the body or sprayed into the air to remove or conceal unpleasant smells.

de•o•dor•ize /deeódəriz/ v.tr. remove or destroy the smell of. □□ **de•o•dor•i•za**′**tion** n. **de•o**′**dor•iz•er** n.
■ see FRESHEN 1.

de•ox•y•ri•bo•nu•cle•ic ac•id /deéokseeríbōnōōkleeik, -kláyik, -nyōō-/ n. see DNA.

de•part /dipáart/ v. **1** intr. **a** go away; leave. **b** start; set out. **2** intr. diverge; deviate. **3 a** intr. die. **b** tr. formal or literary leave by death (departed this life).
■ **1** go, exit; check out, retire, retreat. **2** turn (aside or away), differ, break away; (depart from) leave, abandon. **3 a** see DIE[1] 1.

de•part•ed /dipáartid/ • adj. bygone. • n. [prec. by the] euphem. dead person or people (mourn the departed).

de•part•ment /dipáartmənt/ n. **1** separate part of a complex whole, esp.: **a** branch of municipal or federal administration. **b** division of a university, school, etc., by subject. **c** section of a large store. **2** colloq. area of special expertise. □ **department store** retail store stocking many varieties of goods by departments. □□ **de•part•men•tal** /deepaartmént'l/ adj. **de•part•men•tal•i**′**ze** v. **de•part•men•tal•ly** adv.
■ **1 a** division, office, bureau, section. **2** responsibility, concern, worry, sphere, domain, colloq. thing, joc. bailiwick.

de•par•ture /dipáarchər/ n. **1** departing. **2** deviation (from the truth, a standard, etc.). **3** [often attrib.] starting of a train, aircraft, etc. **4** new course of action or thought.
■ **1** see EXIT n. 2. **3** see TAKEOFF 1.

de•pend /dipénd/ v.intr. **1** be controlled or determined by. **2 a** be unable to do without. **b** rely on.
■ **1** (depend on or upon) turn on, hinge on, be subject to, be influenced by. **2 b** (depend on or upon) trust (in), count on.

de•pend•a•ble /dipéndəbəl/ adj. reliable. □□ **de•pend•a•bil**′**i•ty** n. **de•pend**′**a•ble•ness** n. **de•pend**′**a•bly** adv.
■ see RELIABLE.

de•pend•ence /dipéndəns/ n. **1** state of being dependent, esp. financially. **2** reliance; trust; confidence.
■ **2** see TRUST n. 1.

de•pen•den•cy /dipéndənsee/ n. (pl. **-cies**) **1** country or province controlled by another. **2** addiction.
■ **1** see PROVINCE 1.

de•pen•dent /dipéndənt/ • adj. **1** depending, conditional, or subordinate. **2** unable to do without (esp. a drug). **3** Gram. (of a clause, phrase, or word) subordinate to a sentence or word. • *n.* person who relies on another, esp. for financial support.

■ *n.* see WARD *n.* 3.

de•pict /dipíkt/ *v.tr.* **1** represent in a drawing, painting, etc. **2** portray in words; describe. □□ **de•pict'er** *n.* **de•pic•tion** /-píkshən/ *n.* **de•pic'tive** *adj.* **de•pic'tor** *n.*

■ **2** see CHARACTERIZE 1, 2.

de•pil•a•to•ry /dipílətawree/ • *adj.* that removes unwanted hair. • *n.* (*pl.* **–ries**) depilatory substance.

de•plane /deepláyn/ *v.* disembark from an airplane.

de•plete /dipleét/ *v.tr.* [esp. in *passive*] **1** reduce in numbers or quantity. **2** exhaust. □□ **de•ple•tion** /-pleéshən/ *n.*

■ **1** see DIMINISH 1. **2** see CONSUME 4.

de•plor•a•ble /diplháwrəbəl/ *adj.* exceedingly bad. □□ **de•plor'a•bly** *adv.*

■ execrable, *colloq.* terrible, appalling; see also AWFUL 1a, b.

de•plore /dipláwr/ *v.tr.* **1** grieve over; regret. **2** find exceedingly bad. □□ **de•plor'ing•ly** *adv.*

■ **1** see MOURN. **2** see DISAPPROVE.

de•ploy /diplóy/ *v.* **1** *Mil.* **a** *tr.* cause (troops) to spread out from a column into a line. **b** *intr.* (of troops) spread out in this way. **2** *tr.* use (arguments, forces, etc.) effectively. □□ **de•ploy'ment** *n.*

de•pop•u•late /deepópyəlayt/ *v.* **1** *tr.* reduce the population of. **2** *intr.* decline in population. □□ **de•pop•u•la•tion** /-láyshən/ *n.*

■ **1** see DESOLATE *v.* 1.

de•port /dipáwrt/ *v.tr.* **1** remove or exile to another country. **2** *refl.* behave (in a specified manner). □□ **de•por•ta•tion** /-táyshən/ *n.*

■ **1** see BANISH 1. **2** (*deport oneself*) see ACT *v.* 1.

de•por•tee /deepawrteé/ *n.* deported person.

■ see EXILE *n.* 3.

de•port•ment /dipáwrtmənt/ *n.* bearing or manners.

■ see CONDUCT *n.* 1.

de•pose /dipóz/ *v.* **1** *tr.* remove from office, esp. dethrone. **2** *intr. Law* bear witness, esp. on oath in court.

■ **1** see OVERTHROW *v.* 2. see ATTEST 1, 3.

de•pos•it /dipózit/ • *n.* **1 a** money in a bank account. **b** anything stored for safekeeping. **2 a** payment made as a first installment or as a pledge for a contract. **b** returnable sum paid on a short-term rental. **3** natural layer of accumulated matter. • *v.tr.* **1** put or lay down. **2** pay (a sum) into a bank account. **3** pay (a sum) as a first installment or as a pledge.

■ *n.* **2 a** down or partial payment. **3** sediment, alluvium, *Chem.* precipitate. • *v.* **1** place, leave; see PUT[1] *v.* 1. **2** entrust; save, set aside, put away, *colloq.* stash (away).

dep•o•si•tion /dépəzíshən/ *n.* **1** deposing, esp. a monarch; dethronement. **2** *Law* **a** process of giving sworn evidence. **b** evidence given under oath; testimony.

■ **1** see removal (REMOVE). **2** see ALLEGATION, TESTIMONY 1, 2.

de•pos•i•to•ry /dipózitawree/ *n.* (*pl.* **–ries**)

1 storehouse for furniture, etc. **2** store (of wisdom, knowledge, etc.).

■ **1** see STOREHOUSE[2]. **2** see MINE *n.* 2.

de•pot /deépo, dépo/ *n.* **1** storehouse, esp. for military supplies. **2** railroad or bus station.

■ **1** see WAREHOUSE *n.*

de•prave /diprávv/ *v.tr.* corrupt, esp. morally. □□ **de•pra•va•tion** /déprəváyshən/ *n.* **de•praved'** *adj.* **de•prav•i•ty** /diprávitee/ *n.*

■ see CORRUPT[1] *v.* 1. □□ **depravity** see VICE 1.

SYNONYM STUDY: **depraved**

CORRUPT, DEBASED, DEGENERATE, PERVERTED, VILE. There are many terms to describe the dark side of human nature. Someone who preys on young children would be considered **depraved**, a term that means totally immoral and implies a warped character or a twisted mind (*a depraved man who stole money from his own mother and eventually murdered her*). While *depraved* suggests an absolute condition, **degenerate** is a relative term that implies deterioration from a mental, moral, or physical standard (*her degenerate habits eventually led to her arrest for possession of drugs*). **Corrupt** also suggests a deterioration or loss of soundness, particularly through a destructive or contaminating influence. But unlike *depraved*, which usually applies to the lower end of the human spectrum, people in high positions are often referred to as *corrupt* (*a corrupt politician from a prominent family*). To say that someone or something is **debased** suggests a lowering in quality, value, dignity, or character (*debased by having to spend time in prison*). **Perverted** and **vile** are the strongest of these words describing lack of moral character. *Perverted* suggests a distortion of someone or something from what is right, natural, or true; in a moral sense, it means to use one's appetites or natural desires for other ends than those which are considered normal or natural (*a perverted individual who never should have been left alone with young children*). Most people find criminals who prey on either very old or very young victims to be **vile**, a more general term for whatever is loathsome, repulsive, or utterly despicable (*a vile killer who deserved the maximum sentence*).

---

dep•re•cate /déprikayt/ *v.tr.* express disapproval of or a wish against; deplore. □□ **dep're•cat•ing•ly** *adv.* **dep•re•ca•tion** /-káyshən/ *n.* **dep•re•ca•to•ry** /-kətawree/ *adj.*

■ see DISAPPROVE.

de•pre•ci•ate /dipreésheeayt/ *v.* **1** *tr. & intr.* diminish in value. **2** *tr.* disparage; belittle.

■ **1** reduce, depress, cheapen; decrease. **2** deride, decry, underrate, undervalue, slight, deprecate, *formal* derogate.

de•pre•ci•a•tion /dipreésheeáyshən/ *n.* **1** amount of wear and tear (of a property, etc.) for which a reduction may be made in valuation. **2** *Econ.* decrease in the value of a currency. **3** belittlement.

■ **2** see SLUMP *n.* **3** see MOCKERY 1, *humiliation* (HUMILIATE).

dep·re·da·tion /dépridáyshən/ *n.* [usu. in *pl.*] despoiling, ravaging, or plundering.

■ pillaging, sacking, devastation; ransacking, robbery, looting.

de·press /diprés/ *v.tr.* **1** push or pull down; lower. **2** make dispirited or dejected. **3** *Econ.* reduce the activity of (esp. trade). □ **depressed area** area suffering from economic depression. □□ **de·press'ing** *adj.* **de·press'ing·ly** *adv.*

■ **1** press (down). **2** oppress, sadden, dishearten, discourage. **3** weaken, dull; depreciate; lower, bring down. □□ **depressing** see OPPRESSIVE 1, 2, SAD 2.

de·pres·sant /diprésənt/ • *adj.* **1** that depresses. **2** *Med.* sedative. • *n.* **1** *Med.* agent, esp. a drug, that sedates. **2** influence that depresses.

■ *n.* **1** see SEDATIVE *n.*

de·pres·sion /dipréshən/ *n.* **1 a** *Psychol.* extreme melancholy, often with physical symptoms. **b** reduction in vitality, vigor, or spirits. **2 a** long period of financial and industrial decline. **b** (**the Depression**) the economic decline of the 1930s. **3** *Meteorol.* lowering of atmospheric pressure. **4** hollow on a surface. **5** pressing down.

■ **1 b** dejection, despair, gloom, sadness, the blues; see also MELANCHOLY *n.* **2** recession, slump, (economic) decline. **3** cyclone. **4** indentation, dent, dimple.

de·pres·sive /diprésiv/ • *adj.* **1** tending to depress. **2** *Psychol.* involving or characterized by depression. • *n.* *Psychol.* person suffering or with a tendency to suffer from depression.

de·prive /diprív/ *v.tr.* **1** strip, dispossess; debar from enjoying. **2** (as **de·prived** *adj.*) **a** (of a child, etc.) suffering from the effects of a poor or loveless home. **b** (of an area) with inadequate housing, facilities, employment, etc. □□ **de·priv'a·ble** *adj.* **de·priv'al** *n.* **dep·ri·va·tion** /déprivάyshən/ *n.*

■ **1** deny, refuse; see DIVEST 2. **2** (**deprived**) needy, in want, impoverished, destitute, underprivileged, disadvantaged.

Dept. *abbr.* department.

depth /depth/ *n.* **1 a** deepness. **b** measurement from the top down, surface inward, or front to back. **2** difficulty; abstruseness. **3** intensity of emotion, color, etc. **4** [in *pl.*] **a** abyss. **b** low, depressed state. **c** lowest or inmost part (*depths of the country*). **5** middle (*in the depth of winter*). □ **depth charge** antisubmarine bomb capable of exploding under water. **in depth** comprehensively, thoroughly, or profoundly. **in-depth** *adj.* thorough. **out of one's depth 1** in water over one's head. **2** engaged in a task or on a subject too difficult for one.

■ **1** profundity; profoundness; see also MEASUREMENT 2. **2** obscurity, complexity, intricacy. **3** strength; vividness, brilliance; see also INTENSITY 5. **4 a, c** (*depths*) deep(s), chasm, nethermost regions, nadir. **5** see MIDDLE *n.* 1. □ **in depth** in detail, exten-

sively, intensively. **in-depth** see THOROUGH 1.

dep·u·ta·tion /dépyŏŏtáyshən/ *n.* delegation.

■ see MISSION 3.

de·pute *v.tr.* /dipyŏŏt/ [often foll. by *to*] **1** appoint as a deputy. **2** delegate (a task, authority, etc.).

■ **2** see DELEGATE *v.* 1.

dep·u·tize /dépyətiz/ *v.intr.* create as a deputy.

■ see COVER *v.* 8b.

dep·u·ty /dépyətee/ *n.* (*pl.* **–ties**) person appointed to act for another.

■ substitute, replacement, stand-in; agent, representative, go-between, intermediary, delegate, emissary, envoy.

de·rail /diráyl/ *v.tr.* [usu. in *passive*] cause (a train, etc.) to leave the rails. □□ **de·rail' ment** *n.*

de·rail·leur /dəráylər/ *n.* gear-shifting mechanism on a bicycle.

de·range /diráynj/ *v.tr.* **1** throw into confusion; disorganize. **2** (esp. as **deranged** *adj.*) make insane (*deranged by tragic events*). □□ **de·range'ment** *n.*

■ **1** see UPSET *v.* 3. **2** (**deranged**) mad, demented, lunatic, unhinged, unbalanced, berserk, *colloq.* touched, dotty, *sl.* out of one's head, cracked, bats, nutty.

der·by /dárbee/ *n.* (*pl.* **–bies**) **1** any of several annual horse races, esp. for three-year-olds. **2** sporting contest. **3** bowler hat. □ **Derby Day** day on which the Kentucky Derby is run.

de·reg·u·late /dee-régyəlàyt/ *v.tr.* remove regulations or restrictions from. □□ **de·reg· u·la·tion** /–láyshən/ *n.*

■ decontrol, derestrict.

der·e·lict /dérilikt/ • *adj.* **1** abandoned; ownerless (esp. of a ship at sea or an empty decrepit property). **2** (esp. of property) ruined; dilapidated. **3** negligent of duty, etc.). • *n.* **1** social outcast; person without a home, job, or property. **2** abandoned property, esp. a ship.

■ *adj.* **1** deserted, neglected. **2** run-down, tumbledown. **3** remiss, delinquent, lax, irresponsible. • *n.* **1** vagrant, tramp, pariah, loafer, malingerer, vagabond, hobo, *sl.* bum.

der·e·lic·tion /dérilíkshən/ *n.* **1** neglect; failure to carry out obligations. **2** abandoning; being abandoned.

■ **1** see NEGLECT *n.* 1.

de·ride /diríd/ *v.tr.* mock. □□ **de·rid'ing·ly** *adv.*

■ ridicule, scoff at, jeer at, laugh at, tease, taunt, scorn, disdain, belittle, disparage, rally, *sl.* knock.

de ri·gueur /də rigŏr/ *predic.adj.* required by custom or etiquette (*evening dress is de rigueur*).

■ see CORRECT *adj.* 2.

de·ri·sion /dirízhən/ *n.* ridicule; mockery (*bring into derision*).

de·ri·sive /dirísiv/ *adj.* scoffing; ironical; scornful (*derisive cheers*). □□ **de·ri'sive·ly** *adv.* **de·ri'sive·ness** *n.*

■ mocking, disdainful, taunting, insulting, jeering, sarcastic.

de·ri·so·ry /dirísəree, –zə–/ *adj.* **1** = DERISIVE.

2 so small or unimportant as to be ridiculous (*derisory offer*).

der•i•va•tion /dérɪváyshən/ *n.* **1** deriving or being derived. **2** formation or tracing of a word from another or from a root. **3** extraction; descent. □□ **der•i•va'tion•al** *adj.*
■ **2, 3** origin, source, ancestry, genealogy; etymology.

de•riv•a•tive /dɪrívətɪv/ • *adj.* derived from another source; not original. • *n.* derived word or thing. □□ **de•riv'a•tive•ly** *adv.*
■ *adj.* borrowed, secondhand, copied, imitative, plagiarized. • *n.* derivation; spin-off, by-product, offshoot.

de•rive /dɪrív/ *v.* **1** *tr.* get, obtain, or form. **2** *intr.* arise from, originate in, be descended or obtained from. **3** *tr.* gather or deduce. **4** *tr.* **a** trace the descent of (a person). **b** show the origin of (a thing). □□ **de•riv'a•ble** *adj.*
■ **1** draw, extract, acquire, procure, receive, gain. **2** (*derive from*) arrive from, issue from, develop from, spring from, be traceable to. **3** elicit, educe, infer; see also DEDUCE.

der•ma•ti•tis /dɔ́rmətítis/ *n.* inflammation of the skin.

der•ma•tol•o•gy /dɔ́rmətóləjee/ *n.* the study of skin disorders. □□ **der•ma•to•log•i•cal** /-təlójikəl/ *adj.* **der•ma•tol'o•gist** *n.*

der•mis /dɔ́rmis/ *n.* **1** (in general use) skin. **2** *Anat.* thick layer of living tissue below the epidermis. □□ **der'mal** *adj.*

der•o•gate /dérəgayt/ *v.intr.* (foll. by *from*) formal detract from (a merit, a right, etc.). □□ **de•rog•a•tive** /dɪrógətiv/ *adj.*
■ (*derogate from*) see DETRACT.

de•rog•a•to•ry /dɪrógətawree/ *adj.* involving disparagement; insulting. □□ **de•rog•a•to'ri•ly** *adv.*
■ offensive, debasing, denigrating, belittling, demeaning.

der•rick /dérik/ *n.* **1** pivoting crane for moving or lifting heavy weights. **2** framework over an oil well, etc., holding the drilling machinery.

der•ri•ere /déreeáir/ *n. colloq. euphem.* (also **der•ri•ère'**) buttocks.

der•rin•ger /dérinjər/ *n.* concealable large-bore pistol.

der•vish /dɔ́rvish/ *n.* member of an ascetic Muslim fraternity. □ **whirling dervish** dervish performing a wild dance as a religious observance.

de•sal•i•nate /deesálinayt/ *v.tr.* remove salt from (esp. sea water). □□ **de•sal•i•na•tion** /-náyshən/ *n.*

des•cant • *n.* /déskant/ *Mus.* melody usu. sung or played above a basic melody. • *v.intr.* /diskánt/ **1** (foll. by *on, upon*) talk lengthily, esp. in praise of. **2** *Mus.* sing or play a descant.

de•scend /disénd/ *v.* **1** *tr. & intr.* go or come down (a hill, etc.). **2** *intr.* (of a thing) sink; fall (*rain descended heavily*). **3** slope downward. **4** *intr.* usu. foll. by *on* **a** attack. **b** make an unexpected and usu. unwelcome visit. **5** *intr.* usu. foll. by *from, to* (of property, rights, etc.) be passed by inheritance. **6** *intr.* **a** sink in rank, quality, etc. **b** (foll. by *to*) degrade oneself morally to (an unworthy act). □ **be descended from** have as an ancestor. □□ **de•scend'ent** *adj.*
■ **1** move down, get down. **2** see SINK *v.* 1, FALL *v.* 1. **3** decline, slant down. **4 a** (*descend on*) assault, invade. **6 b** sink, stoop, lower or humble oneself.

de•scend•ant /diséndənt/ *n.* person or thing descended from another (*a descendant of John Adams*).
■ heir, scion; offshoot; (*descendants*) offspring, progeny.

de•scent /disént/ *n.* **1** act or way of descending. **2** downward slope. **3** lineage; family origin. **4** decline; fall.
■ **1** see DROP *n.* 2a, b. **2** see SLOPE *n.* 1–3. **3** see LINEAGE. **4** see DECREASE *n.*

de•scribe /diskríb/ *v.tr.* **1 a** state the characteristics, appearance, etc., of. **b** (foll. by *as*) assert to be (*described him as a habitual liar*). **2** outline; delineate. □□ **de•scrib'a•ble** *adj.* **de•scrib'er** *n.*
■ **1 a** tell (of), recount, report; detail. **b** characterize, portray, identify, label. **2** mark out, draw; see also TRACE[1] *v.* 3.

de•scrip•tion /diskrípshən/ *n.* **1 a** describing or being described. **b** representation (of a person, object, etc.), esp. in words. **2** sort, kind, or class (*no food of any description*). □ **answers** (or **fits**) **the description** has the qualities specified. □□ **de•scrip•tive** /-tiv/ *adj.*
■ **1 a** see *narration* (NARRATE). **b** account, report; explanation; characterization, depiction; chronicle, history, record. **2** nature, character, type, variety, category, genre.

de•scry /diskrí/ *v.tr.* (**-scries, -scried**) *literary* catch sight of; discern. See synonym study at DISTINGUISH.
■ see SIGHT *v.* 1, 2.

des•e•crate /désikrayt/ *v.tr.* violate (a sacred place or thing) with violence, profanity, etc. □□ **des•e•cra•tion** /-kráyshən/ *n.* **des'e•cra•tor** *n.*
■ profane, dishonor, degrade, debase, pollute, corrupt.

de•seg•re•gate /deeségrigayt/ *v.tr.* abolish racial segregation in (schools, etc.). □□ **de•seg•re•ga•tion** /-gáyshən/ *n.*
■ see INTEGRATE *v.*

de•sen•si•tize /deesénsitīz/ *v.tr.* reduce or destroy the sensitiveness of (an allergic person, etc.). □□ **de•sen•si•ti•za'tion** *n.*
■ see DEADEN 2.

des•ert[1] /dizɔ́rt/ *v.* **1** *tr.* give up; leave (*deserted the sinking ship*). **2** *tr.* forsake or abandon (a cause, person, etc.) (*deserted his children*). **3** *intr. Mil.* run away (esp. from military service). □□ **de•sert'er** *n.* (in sense 3 of *v.*). **de•ser•tion** /-zɔ́rshən/ *n.*
■ **1** forsake, abandon. **2** leave, give up; jilt, throw over; strand, walk out on, *colloq.* dump, *sl.* ditch. **3** quit, defect, *colloq.* go AWOL. □□ **deserter** runaway, fugitive, defector; traitor.

des•ert[2] /dézərt/ • *n.* dry, barren, often sandcovered area of land; uninteresting or barren subject, period, etc. (*a cultural desert*). • *adj.*

1 uninhabited; desolate. **2** uncultivated; barren.

■ *n.* wilderness, wasteland, dust bowl; badlands; emptiness, void. ● *adj.* lonely, deserted; arid, bare, vacant, empty.

de•sert³ /dizért/ *n.* **1** [in *pl.*] acts or qualities deserving reward or punishment. **2** such reward or punishment (*his just deserts*).

■ **2** (*deserts*) due, right; retribution, justice, *colloq.* comeuppance.

de•serve /dizérv/ *v.tr.* **1** be worthy of (reward, punishment, etc.) (*deserves to be imprisoned*). **2** (as **deserved** *adj.*) rightfully merited or earned (*a deserved win*). □□ **de•serv•ed•ly** /–vidlee/ *adv.* **de•serv•ing** /dizérving/ *adj.*

■ **1** merit, be entitled to, rate, warrant, justify. **2** (**deserved**) merited, earned, well-deserved, just, rightful, fitting.

des•ic•cate /désikayt/ *v.tr.* dry out (esp. food for preservation). □□ **des•ic•cat•ed** *adj.* **des•ic•ca•tion** /–káyshən/ *n.* **des•ic•ca•tive** *adj.* **des•ic•ca•tor** *n.* See synonym study at DRY.

de•sid•er•a•tum /disídəráytəm, –ráatəm/ *n.* (*pl.* **de•sid•er•a•ta** /–tə/) something lacking but needed or desired.

de•sign /dizín/ ● *n.* **1** plan or sketch for making a building, machine, garment, etc. **2** lines or shapes forming a pattern or decoration. **3** plan, purpose, or intention. **4** arrangement or layout. ● *v.* **1** *tr.* produce a design for. **2** *tr.* intend, plan, or propose. **3** *absol.* be a designer. See synonym study at INTEND. □ **by design** on purpose. **have designs on** plan to harm or appropriate.

■ *n.* **1** scheme, conception; blueprint, draft, model, pattern, drawing, prototype. **2**, **4** form, configuration, style, motif, composition. **3** aim, objective, goal. ● *v.* **1** plan, invent, create, devise, originate, visualize, sketch out, develop, organize, frame. **2** mean, hope, aim; (*designed for*) see INTEND **4**.

des•ig•nate ● *v.tr.* /dézignayt/ **1** appoint (*designated him as postmaster general*). **2** specify. **3** describe as; style. ● *adj.* /dézignət/ appointed but not yet installed (*bishop designate*). □ **designated driver** member of a group who abstains from alcohol in order to drive the others safely. **designated hitter** *Baseball* batter in the lineup who hits for the pitcher ¶Abbr.: **DH**. □□ **des•ig•na•tion** /dézignáyshən/ *n.* **des•ig•na•tor** *n.*

■ *v.* **1** nominate, name, identify, select, assign. **2** indicate, pinpoint, identify. **3** call, name, term, label, dub.

de•sign•ing /dizíning/ *adj.* crafty or scheming. □□ **de•sign•ing•ly** *adv.*

■ conniving, calculating, wily, cunning, sly, underhanded, shrewd, Machiavellian, deceitful, devious, unscrupulous.

de•sir•a•ble /dizírəbəl/ *adj.* **1** worth having or doing. **2** sexually attractive. □□ **de•sir•a•bil•i•ty** *n.* **de•sir•a•ble•ness** *n.* **de•sir•a•bly** *adv.*

■ **1** sought-after, wanted, coveted, longed-for; profitable, worthwhile, advantageous. **2** seductive, alluring, fetching.

de•sire /dizír/ ● *n.* **1 a** longing or craving. **b** expression of this. **2** lust. **3** something desired. ● *v.tr.* **1** long for; crave. **2** request.

■ *n.* **1 a** yearning, hankering, hunger, *colloq.* yen. **b** wish, request, urge. **2** passion, libido, lustfulness. **3** desideratum, whim; see also WISH *n.* ● *v.* **1** want, fancy, covet, *sl.* have the hots for. **2** ask for, order, demand.

de•sir•ous /dizírəs/ *predic.adj.* **1** ambitious; desiring. **2** wishful; hoping.

■ **1** see INTENT *adj.* **1a.** **2** longing, yearning, hopeful.

de•sist /dizíst/ *v.intr.* [often foll. by *from*] *literary* abstain; cease (*desist from interrupting*).

■ see CEASE *v.*

desk /desk/ *n.* **1** piece of furniture with a writing surface and often drawers. **2** counter in a hotel, bank, etc., which separates the customer from the assistant.

■ **1** writing desk. **2** table, bar.

desk•top /désktop/ *n.* **1 a** working surface of a desk. **b** *Computing* working area on a screen for manipulating windows, icons, etc. **2** [*attrib.*] (esp. of a microcomputer) suitable for use at an ordinary desk. □ **desktop publishing** production of printed matter with a desktop computer and printer.

des•o•late ● *adj.* /désələt/ **1** left alone; solitary. **2** (of a building or place) uninhabited; ruined; dreary. **3** forlorn; wretched. ● *v.tr.* /désəlayt/ **1** devastate; lay waste to. **2** (esp. as **desolated** *adj.*) make wretched. □□ **des•o•late•ly** /–lətlee/ *adv.* **des•o•late•ness** *n.*

■ *adj.* **1** lonely, isolated, deserted. **2** neglected, empty, remote. **3** dreary, forsaken, miserable, disconsolate, sad, woebegone, inconsolable, hopeless. ● *v.* **1** depopulate; destroy, ravage. **2** dismay, dishearten, devastate, discourage; (**desolated**) see WRETCHED **1.**

des•o•la•tion /désəláyshən/ *n.* **1** desolating or being desolated. **2** loneliness, grief, etc. **3** neglected, ruined, barren, or empty state.

■ **2** sorrow, dreariness, despair, melancholy. **3** destruction, ruin, devastation, waste.

de•spair /dispáir/ ● *n.* complete loss or absence of hope. ● *v.intr.* **1** [often foll. by *of*] lose or be without hope. **2** [foll. by *of*] lose hope about. □□ **de•spair•ing•ly** *adv.*

■ *n.* desperation, discouragement, disheartenment, dejection, depression, gloominess, misery. ● *v.* **1** give up hope.

des•per•a•do /déspəráadō/ *n.* (*pl.* **–does** or **–dos**) desperate or reckless person, esp. a criminal.

■ see CRIMINAL *n.*

des•per•ate /déspərət, –prit/ *adj.* **1** reckless or dangerous from despair. **2 a** extremely dangerous or serious. **b** staking all on a small chance. **3** [usu. foll. by *for*] needing or desiring very much. □□ **des•per•ate•ly** *adv.* **des′per•ate•ness** *n.* **des•per•a•tion** /–ráyshən/ *n.*

■ **1** foolhardy, rash, impetuous, frantic. **2 a** urgent, compelling, grave, critical; precarious, perilous. **3** anxious, craving, hungry, desirous, aching, pining. □□ **desperately** see AWFULLY **2. desperation** recklessness, impetuosity, rashness; despair, anguish.

des•pi•ca•ble /déspikəbəl, dispík–/ *adj.* vile; contemptible, esp. morally. □□ **des′pi•ca•bly** *adv.*

■ mean, detestable, low, sordid; shameless.

de•spise /dispíz/ *v.tr.* look down on as inferior, worthless, or contemptible.

■ disdain, scorn, spurn; hate, loathe, detest, abhor.

de•spite /dispít/ *prep.* in spite of.

■ notwithstanding, regardless of, ignoring.

de•spoil /dispóyl/ *v.tr. literary* plunder; rob; deprive (*despoiled the roof of its lead*). See synonym study at RAVAGE. □□ **de•spoil′er** *n.* **de•spo′li•a•tion** /dispóleeáyshən/ *n.*

de•spond•ent /dispóndənt/ *adj.* in low spirits; dejected. □□ **de•spond•ence** /–dəns/ *n.* **de•spond′en•cy** *n.* **de•spond′ent•ly** *adv.*

■ sad, sorrowful, unhappy, melancholy, blue, depressed, down, downcast, downhearted, low, miserable.

des•pot /déspət/ *n.* **1** absolute ruler. **2** tyrant. □□ **des•pot′ic** /–spótik/ *adj.* **des•pot′i•cal•ly** *adv.* **des•pot•ism** /–izəm/ *n.*

■ **1** dictator, autocrat, overlord. **2** oppressor, bully. □□ **despotic** dictatorial, tyrannical, oppressive, authoritarian.

des•sert /dizárt/ *n.* sweet course of a meal, served at or near the end.

des•ti•na•tion /déstináyshən/ *n.* place to which a person or thing is going.

■ journey's end, stopping place; goal, end, objective, target.

des•tine /déstin/ *v.tr.* preordain; intend (*destined then for the navy*). □ **be destined to** be fated or preordained to

■ fate, predetermine; doom; appoint, earmark. □ **be destined to** (*destined*) meant, intended, fated, doomed; bound.

des•ti•ny /déstinee/ *n.* (*pl.* **–nies**) **1** predetermined course of events; fate. **2** particular person's fate or lot.

■ **1** fortune. **2** fate, doom, fortune, portion, kismet.

des•ti•tute /déstitoot, –tyoot/ *adj.* **1** completely impoverished. **2** lacking. □□ **des′ti•tu′tion** /–tŏoshən, –tyŏo–/ *n.*

■ **1** in want, poor, indigent, needy, penniless, hard up, bankrupt, *colloq.* broke. **2** (*destitute of*) bereft of, deficient in, deprived of, devoid of.

de•stroy /distróy/ *v.tr.* **1** pull or break down; demolish. **2** end the existence of; kill (esp. an animal). **3** make useless; spoil utterly. **4** defeat (*destroyed the enemy*).

■ **1** raze, wipe out; annihilate, eradicate; *colloq.* trash. **2** ruin, do away with, terminate, finish; put away, exterminate. **3** negate, overturn, ruin, demolish. **4** see DEFEAT *v.* 1.

SYNONYM STUDY: destroy

ANNIHILATE, DEMOLISH, ERADICATE, EXTERMINATE, EXTIRPATE, RAZE. If you're interested in getting rid of something, you've got a number of options at your disposal. **Destroy** is a general term covering any force that wrecks, ruins, kills, etc. (*to destroy an ant hill by pouring boiling water on it*). If it's a building, you'll want to **demolish** or **raze** it, two words that are generally applied only to very large things. *Raze* is used almost exclusively with

structures; it means to bring something down to the level of the ground (*they razed the apartment building to make way for the new hospital*). **Demolish** implies pulling or smashing something to pieces; when used with regard to buildings, it conjures up a vision of complete wreckage and often a heap of rubble (*their new house was demolished by the first hurricane of the season*). But unlike *raze*, *demolish* can also be applied to nonmaterial things (*to demolish the theory with a few simple experiments*). If you *eradicate* something, you eliminate it completely, literally; you pull it out by the roots (*to eradicate smallpox with a vaccine*) and prevent its reappearance. Likewise, **extirpate** means to destroy something by uprooting it (*the species was extirpated from the park by the flooding*), though the word is used of animal species as well as plant and, figuratively, of ideas, movements, and the like (*it was his duty as a Christian monarch to extirpate the rule of the infidel*). If you're dealing with cockroaches, you'll probably want to **exterminate** them, which means to wipe out or kill in great numbers. Or better yet, you'll want to **annihilate** them, which is the most extreme word in this group and literally means to reduce to nothingness.

---

de•stroy•er /distróyər/ *n.* **1** person or thing that destroys. **2** *Naut.* fast warship used to protect other ships.

de•struct /distrúkt/ *Astronaut.* ● *v.* **1** *tr.* destroy (one's own rocket, etc.) deliberately, esp. for safety reasons. **2** *intr.* be destroyed in this way. ● *n.* act of destructing.

de•struc•tion /distrúkshən/ *n.* **1** destroying or being destroyed. **2** cause of ruin. □□ **de•struct•i•bil•i•ty** /–ibílitee/ *n.* **de•struct′i•ble** *adj.* **de•struc′tive** *adj.* **de•struc′tive•ly** *adv.* **de•struc′tive•ness** *n.*

■ **1** demolition, ruin, devastation, laying waste; slaughter, annihilation, killing; breakdown, collapse. **2** undoing, end; see also RUIN *n.* 2. □□ **destructive** harmful, injurious, hurtful, malignant, damaging, detrimental, deleterious; negative, adverse, opposed, contrary, critical.

des•ue•tude /déswitŏod, –tyŏod/ *n.* state of disuse.

des•ul•to•ry /désəltáwree, déz–/ *adj.* **1** going from one subject to another, esp. halfheartedly. **2** disconnected; superficial. □□ **des′ul•to•ri•ly** *adv.* **des′ul•to•ri•ness** *n.*

■ shifting, unsteady, unmethodical, disorderly, haphazard, erratic; see also SUPERFICIAL 2.

de•tach /ditách/ *v.tr.* **1** unfasten or disengage and remove. **2** (as **detached** *adj.*) impartial; unemotional (*a detached viewpoint*). □□ **de•tach′a•ble** *adj.* **de•tach•ed•ly** /ditáchidlee/ *adv.*

■ **1** separate, uncouple, part, disconnect, free, undo, cut off. **2** (**detached**) disinterested, aloof, uninvolved, indifferent, objective.

de•tach•ment /ditáchmənt/ *n.* **1 a** aloofness;

indifference. **b** impartiality. **2** detaching or being detached. **3** *Mil.* troops, etc., used for a specific purpose.

■ **1 a** unconcern, nonchalance; see DISTANCE *n.* 4. **b** see *objectivity* (OBJECTIVE). **2** separation, disconnection. **3** see SQUAD.

de•tail /dítáyl, dée'tayl/ • *n.* **1** small particular; item; minor element. **2 a** these collectively (*has an eye for detail*). **b** treatment of them (*the detail was insufficient*). **3** *Mil.* small detachment. • *v.tr.* **1** give particulars or circumstances of. **2** *Mil.* assign for special duty. **3** (as **detailed** *adj.*) itemized. □ **in detail** item by item, minutely.

■ *n.* **1** factor, point, technicality; aspect; (*details*) minutiae, fine points, specifics. **3** party, unit; see SQUAD. • *v.* **1** specify, spell out, list, enumerate; describe. **2** appoint, delegate. **3** (**detailed**) exhaustive, thorough; intricate, complex. □ **in detail** specifically, particularly, inside out.

de•tain /dítáyn/ *v.tr.* **1** keep (a person) in custody. **2** keep waiting; delay. □□ **de•tain′ee** *n.* **de•tain′ment** *n.*

■ **1** see IMPRISON 2. **2** see DELAY *v.* 2.

de•tect /dítékt/ *v.tr.* discover or perceive. □□ **de•tect′a•ble** *adj.* **de•tect′a•bly** *adv.* **de•tec′tion** /dítékshən/ *n.*

■ uncover, find (out), locate, learn of, ascertain, determine, dig up, unearth; note, notice, identify, spot, observe, sense.

de•tec•tive /dítéktiv/ • *n.* [often *attrib.*] person who investigates crime. • *adj.* serving to detect. □ **private detective** detective carrying out investigations for a private employer.

■ *n.* (private) investigator, policeman, operative, *colloq.* private eye, sleuth, *sl.* dick, cop, copper, gumshoe, shamus.

dé•tente /daytóNt/ *n.* easing of tension, esp. between nations.

■ see *reconciliation* (RECONCILE).

de•ten•tion /diténshən/ *n.* detaining or being detained.

■ custody, confinement, imprisonment, captivity.

de•ter /dítór/ *v.tr.* (**de•terred, de•ter•ring**) discourage or prevent (a person), esp. through fear. □□ **de•ter′ment** *n.*

■ dissuade, inhibit, intimidate; prevent, stop, obstruct.

de•ter•gent /dítórjənt/ • *n.* cleaning agent. • *adj.* cleansing.

de•te•ri•o•rate /ditéereeərayt/ *v.* make or become bad or worse. □□ **de•te•ri•o•ra•tion** /-ráyshən/ *n.*

■ decline, degenerate, spoil, slide, *colloq.* go to pot, go downhill, *sl.* go to the dogs; decay, disintegrate.

de•ter•mi•nant /dítórminənt/ • *adj.* serving to determine or define. • *n.* determining factor, element, word, etc.

■ *n.* see FACTOR *n.* 1.

de•ter•mi•nate /dítórminət/ *adj.* **1** limited. **2** of definite scope or nature.

■ fixed, exact, precise, distinct; limited.

de•ter•mi•na•tion /dítórmináyshən/ *n.* **1** firmness of purpose. **2** process of deciding, determining, or calculating.

■ **1** resoluteness, resolution, resolve, steadfastness, tenacity, perseverance, fortitude, *colloq.* grit, guts. **2** fixing, settling, decision making, ascertainment.

de•ter•mine /dítórmin/ *v.tr.* **1** find out or establish precisely. **2** decide or settle. **3** be a decisive factor in regard to (*demand determines supply*). □ **be determined** be resolved (*was determined not to give up*). □□ **de•ter′min•a•ble** *adj.*

■ **1** ascertain, decide, discover, detect. **2** choose, resolve; see DECIDE 1. **3** affect, influence, shape, dictate.

de•ter•mined /dítórmind/ *adj.* **1** showing determination; resolute; unflinching. **2** fixed in scope or character; determinate. See synonym study at RESOLUTE. □□ **de•ter′mined•ly** *adv.* **de•ter′mined•ness** *n.*

■ **1** decided, resolved, strong-willed, tenacious, unwavering, persistent, stubborn, adamant. **2** see DETERMINATE.

de•ter•rent /dítórənt, -túr-/ • *adj.* that deters. • *n.* dissuading thing or factor. □□ **de•ter•rence** /-rəns/ *n.*

■ *n.* hindrance, discouragement, check, hitch, obstacle, obstruction, stumbling block; catch, snag, rub, drawback.

de•test /dítést/ *v.tr.* hate; loathe. □□ **de•test′a•ble** *adj.* **de•test′er** *n.* See synonym study at OFFENSIVE.

■ despise, abhor, execrate, abominate, be nauseated by.

de•throne /deethrón/ *v.tr.* remove from the throne; depose. □□ **de•throne′ment** *n.*

■ see OVERTHROW *v.* 1–3.

det•o•nate /dét′nayt/ *v.* explode with a loud noise. □□ **det•o•na•tion** /dét′náyshən/ *n.* **det′o•na•tive** *adj.* **det•o•na•tor** /dét′naytər/ *n.*

■ see EXPLODE 1.

de•tour /deé'toŏr, ditŏŏr/ • *n.* divergence from a direct or intended route. • *v.* make or cause to make a detour.

■ *n.* deviation, circuitous route, roundabout way, bypass. • *v.* turn away (from), divert (from); see also BYPASS *v.*

de•tox•i•fy /deetóksifí/ *v.tr.* remove the poison from. □□ **de•tox•i•fi•ca•tion** /-fikáy-shən/ *n.*

de•tract /ditrákt/ *v.tr.* take away (a part of something); reduce (*self-interest detracted nothing from their victory*). □□ **de•trac•tion** /-trákshən/ *n.* **de•trac′tive** *adj.* **de•trac′tor** *n.*

■ (*detract from*) diminish, subtract from, lessen, disparage.

det•ri•ment /détrimənt/ *n.* **1** harm; damage. **2** something causing this. □□ **det•ri•men•tal** /détrimént′l/ *adj.*

■ disadvantage, drawback; ill, impairment, injury, hurt, loss. □□ **detrimental** disadvantageous, injurious, damaging, deleterious, pernicious.

de•tri•tus /ditrítəs/ *n.* **1** gravel, sand, etc., from erosion. **2** debris.

deuce /dŏŏs, dyŏŏs/ *n.* **1** two on dice or playing cards. **2** *Tennis* score of 40 all, at which two consecutive points are needed to win.

deu•te•ri•um /dŏŏtéereeəm, dyŏŏ-/ *n. Chem.* stable isotope of hydrogen.

deutsche mark /dóychmaark/ n. (also **Deut‧sche‧mark** /dóychə maark/) chief monetary unit of Germany.

de‧val‧ue /deevályoō/ v.tr. (**de‧val‧ues, de‧val‧ued, de‧val‧u‧ing**) reduce the value of. □□ **de‧val‧u‧a'tion** n.
  ■ see DEBASE.

dev‧as‧tate /dévəstayt/ v.tr. **1** cause great destruction to. **2** [often in *passive*] overwhelm with shock or grief. See synonym study at RAVAGE. □□ **dev'as‧tat‧ing** adj. **dev'as‧tat‧ing‧ly** adv. **dev‧as‧ta‧tion** /–táyshən/ n. **dev'as‧ta‧tor** n.
  ■ **1** lay waste, ravage, destroy, sack, raze, ruin, obliterate. **2** disconcert, take aback, shatter, see also SHOCK[1] v. 1. □□ **devastating** overpowering, powerful, potent, awesome; keen, incisive, penetrating, savage.

de‧vel‧op /divéləp/ v. **1** tr. & intr. **a** make or become bigger or fuller, etc. **b** bring or come to an active, visible, or mature state. **2 a** tr. begin to exhibit or suffer from. **b** intr. come into existence; originate; emerge. **3** tr. **a** build on (land). **b** convert (land) to a new use. **4** tr. treat (film, etc.) to make the image visible. See synonym study at MATURE. □ **de‧veloping country** poor or undeveloped country that is becoming more advanced economically and socially. □□ **de‧vel'op‧er** n.
  ■ **1** advance, broaden, evolve, reveal, disclose; cultivate, strengthen; ripen, age; flower. **2 a** show, manifest; come down with; see also CONTRACT v. 3. **b** arise, appear, begin, result. □ **developing country** third world country. □□ **developer** builder, construction company.

de‧vel‧op‧ment /divéləpmənt/ n. **1** developing or being developed. **2** thing that has been developed, esp. an event or circumstance (*the latest developments*). **3** full-grown state. **4** developed area of land. □□ **de‧vel‧op‧men‧tal** /divéləpmént'l/ adj. **de‧vel‧op‧men'tal‧ly** adv.
  ■ **1** evolution, growth, maturation, enlargement; progress; improvement; building, construction (work). **2** occurrence, happening, phenomenon.

de‧vi‧ant /déeveeənt/ ● adj. that deviates from normal, esp. sexually. ● n. deviant person or thing. □□ **de‧vi‧ance** /–veeəns/ n. **de'vi‧an‧cy** n.
  ■ adj. divergent, different, strange, uncommon, odd, peculiar, curious; perverse, colloq. kinky. ● n. see ECCENTRIC n.

de‧vi‧ate v.intr. /déeveeayt/ turn aside or diverge (from a course of action, rule, truth, etc.); digress. ● n. /déeveeət/ deviant, esp. a sexual pervert. □□ **de‧vi‧a‧tion** /–áyshən/ n. **de'vi‧a‧tor** n. **de‧vi‧a‧to‧ry** /–veeətawree/ adj.
  ■ v. veer, wander, stray, drift, divert. ● n. pervert, degenerate.

de‧vice /divís/ n. **1** thing made or adapted for a particular purpose. **2** plan, scheme, or trick. **3** emblematic or heraldic design. □ **leave a person to his or her own devices** leave a person to do as he or she wishes.
  ■ **1** contrivance, machine, utensil, instrument, tool, gadget, colloq. widget, doodad, derog. or joc. contraption, sl. gizmo. **2** plot,

strategy, colloq. ploy; see also SCHEME n. 2. **3** figure, Heraldry charge; insignia, seal, crest; drawing, colloq. logo.

dev‧il /dévəl/ ● n. **1** (usu. **the Devil**) (in Christian and Jewish belief) supreme spirit of evil; Satan. **2 a** evil spirit; demon. **b** personified evil. **3 a** wicked or cruel person. **b** mischievous person. **4** colloq. person of a specified nature (*lucky devil*). **5** mischievousness (*the devil is in him tonight*). ● v.tr. (**dev‧iled, dev‧il‧ing;** dev‧illed, dev‧il‧ling) **1** prepare (food) with hot seasoning **2** harass; worry. □ **between the devil and the deep blue sea** in a dilemma. **devil-may-care** cheerful and reckless. **a devil of** colloq. considerable, difficult, or remarkable (*a devil of a time*). **devil's advocate** person who tests a proposition by arguing against it. **devil's own** colloq. very difficult or unusual (*the devil's own job*). **the devil to pay** trouble to be expected. **go to the devil 1** be damned. **2** [in imper.] depart at once. **like the devil** with great energy. **speak of the devil** said when a person appears just after being mentioned. □□ **dev'il‧ish** adj. & adv.
  ■ n. **1**, Lucifer, Beelzebub, Prince of Darkness, colloq. Old Nick; fiend. **3 a** brute, beast, villain. **b** imp, colloq. scamp, often joc. rascal. **4** fellow, colloq. guy, sl. bastard. **5** see MISCHIEF 1–3. ● v. **2** see WORRY v. 2. □ **devil-may-care** see RECKLESS. **a devil of** see CONSIDERABLE 1, 2, DIFFICULT 1, REMARKABLE 1. **devil's own** fiendish, colloq. beastly; see also DIFFICULT 1, UNUSUAL 2. **go to the devil 2** see beat it. **like the devil** rapidly, colloq. like a house on fire, like a bat out of hell; see vigorously (VIGOR).

dev‧il‧ment /dévəlmənt/ n. mischief; wild spirits.
  ■ see MISCHIEF 1–3.

dev‧il‧ry /dévilree/ n. (also **dev‧il‧try** /–tree/) (pl. **–ries**) wickedness; reckless mischief.
  ■ devilishness, evil, cruelty, malice, viciousness; naughtiness, knavery, often joc. rascality.

de‧vi‧ous /déeveeəs/ adj. **1** (of a person, etc.) not straightforward; underhand. **2** winding; circuitous. □□ **de'vi‧ous‧ly** adv. **de'vi‧ous‧ness** n.
  ■ **1** deceitful, misleading, sneaky, furtive, slick, slippery, crafty, colloq. shifty. **2** indirect, evasive, crooked, rambling

de‧vise /divíz/ v.tr. **1** plan or invent carefully. **2** Law leave (real estate) by will (cf. BEQUEATH). ● n. **1** devising. **2** Law such a clause in a will. □□ **de‧vis'a‧ble** adj. **de‧vi‧see** /–zeé/ n. (in sense 2 of v.). **de‧vis'er** n. **de‧vi'sor** n. (in sense 2 of v.).
  ■ v. **1** concoct, conceive, contrive, design, work out, colloq. cook up. **2** bequeath, convey, give, assign, bestow.

de‧void /divóyd/ predic.adj. [foll. by of] lacking or free from (a devoid of all interest).

de‧volve /divólv/ v. [foll. by on, upon, etc.] **1** tr. pass (work or duties) to (a deputy, etc.). **2** intr. (of work or duties) pass to (a deputy, etc.). □□ **de‧volve'ment** n.

De‧vo‧ni‧an /divóneeən/ ● adj. Geol. of or

relating to the fourth period of the Paleozoic era. • *n.* this period or system.

de•vote /divṓt/ *v.tr. & refl.* [foll. by *to*] apply or give over (resources, etc., or oneself) to (a particular activity, purpose, or person) (*devoted himself to his guests*).

■ assign, allocate, dedicate, consecrate; pledge.

de•vot•ed /divṓtid/ *adj.* very loving or loyal (*a devoted husband*). □□ **de•vot′ed•ly** *adv.* **de•vot′ed•ness** *n.*

■ faithful, true, dedicated, devout, constant; ardent, caring.

dev•o•tee /dévətée, –táy/ *n.* **1** [usu. foll. by *of*] zealous enthusiast or supporter. **2** zealously pious or fanatical person.

■ **1** fan, aficionado, adherent, addict, *colloq.* buff, sl. nut. **2** fanatic, visionary, cultist.

de•vo•tion /divṓshən/ *n.* **1** enthusiastic loyalty (to a person or cause); great love. **2** [in *pl.*] prayers. □□ **de•vo′tion•al** *adj.*

■ **1** zeal, ardor, fervor, intensity, fanaticism, eagerness, willingness; passion, infatuation, fondness, affection, allegiance; dedication.

de•vour /divówr/ *v.tr.* **1** eat hungrily or greedily. **2** (of fire, etc.) engulf; destroy. □□ **de•vour′ing•ly** *adv.*

■ **1** wolf (down), gulp (down), bolt, swallow (up). **2** consume, ravage, annihilate, demolish, ruin, obliterate; overcome.

de•vout /divówt/ *adj.* **1** earnestly religious. **2** earnestly sincere (*devout hope*). □□ **de•vout′ly** *adv.* **de•vout′ness** *n.*

■ **1** devoted, pious, reverent, faithful; holy, godly, saintly, pure; reverential. **2** genuine, heartfelt, ardent, true.

dew /dōo, dyōo/ • *n.* **1** atmospheric vapor condensing on cool surfaces at night. **2** moisture resembling this, e.g., tears. • *v.tr.* wet with or as with dew. □ **dew point** the temperature at which dew forms. □□ **dew•y** /dōo-ee, dyōo-ee/ *adj.* (**dew•i•er, dew•i•est**).

■ *v.* bedew, damp, dampen, moisten; see also WET *v.*

dew•ber•ry /dóoberee, dyōo–/ *n.* (*pl.* **–ries**) bluish fruit like the blackberry.

dew•claw /dóoklaw, dyōo–/ *n.* **1** rudimentary inner toe found on some dogs. **2** false hoof on a deer, etc.

dew•drop /dóodrop, dyōo–/ *n.* drop of dew.

dew•lap /dóolap, dyōo–/ *n.* loose fold of skin hanging from the throat of cattle, dogs, etc.

dex•ter•i•ty /dekstéritee/ *n.* **1** skill in handling. **2** manual or mental adroitness.

■ **1** touch, nimbleness, adroitness, facility; sleight of hand. **2** cleverness, ingenuity, astuteness, sharpness, shrewdness.

dex•ter•ous /dékstrəs, –stərəs/ *adj.* (also **dex•trous**, /–strəs/) having or showing dexterity. □□ **dex′ter•ous•ly** *adv.*

■ deft, lithe, nimble, supple, agile; clever, ingenious, astute.

dex•trose /dékstrōs/ *n. Chem.* form of glucose.

DH *abbr. Baseball* designated hitter.

dho•ti /dṓtee/ *n.* (*pl.* **dho•tis**) loincloth worn by male Hindus.

di-[1] /dī/ *comb. form* twice, two–, double.

di-[2] /dī, dee/ *prefix* form of DIS-before *l, m, n, r, s* (foll. by a consonant), *v*, usu. *g,* and sometimes *j*.

di-[3] /dī/ *prefix* form of DIA-before a vowel.

dia. *abbr.* diameter.

dia- /díə/ *prefix* (also **di-** before a vowel) **1** through (*diaphanous*). **2** apart (*diacritical*). **3** across (*diameter*).

di•a•be•tes /díəbéetis, –teez/ *n.* any disorder of the metabolism with excessive thirst, increased urine production, and high blood sugar. □□ **di•a•bet•ic** /díəbétik/ *adj. & n.*

di•a•bol•ic /díəbólik/ *adj.* (also **di•a•bol•i•cal** /–bólikəl/) **1** of the Devil. **2** devilish; inhumanly cruel or wicked. **3** fiendishly clever or cunning or annoying. □□ **di•a•bol′i•cal•ly** *adv.*

■ **1** devilish, satanic, Mephistophelian, demonic, fiendish. **2** iniquitous, evil, inhuman, hideous, monstrous, odious, vile, base, heinous, malicious, malevolent, sinister.

di•a•crit•ic /díəkrítik/ *n.* sign (e.g., an accent, cedilla, etc.) indicating different sounds or values of a letter. □□ **di•a•crit•i•cal** /díəkrítikəl/ *adj.*

di•a•dem /díədem/ *n.* crown or ornamental headband.

■ see CROWN *n.* 1.

di•aer•e•sis /dī-érəsis/ *n.* (also **di•er′e•sis**) (*pl.* **–ses** /–seez/) mark (as in *naïve*) over a vowel to indicate that it is sounded separately.

diag. *abbr.* **1** diagonal. **2** diagram.

di•ag•nose /díəgnōs, –nōz/ *v.tr.* make a diagnosis of (a disease, fault, etc.) from its symptoms. □□ **di•ag•nos′a•ble** *adj.*

■ identify, determine, recognize, interpret; analyze.

di•ag•no•sis /díəgnṓsis/ *n.* (*pl.* **di•ag•no•ses** /–seez/) **1** identification of a disease, mechanical fault, etc. **2** instance or formal statement of this. □□ **di•ag•nos•tic** /díəgnóstik/ *adj.* **di•ag•nos′ti•cal•ly** *adv.* **di•ag•nos•ti•cian** /–nostishən/ *n.*

■ see *interpretation* (INTERPRET).

di•ag•nos•tics /díəgnóstiks/ *n.* **1** [treated as *pl.*] *Computing* programs used to identify faults in hardware or software. **2** [treated as *sing.*] science or study of diagnosing disease.

di•ag•o•nal /díágənəl/ • *adj.* **1** crossing a straight-sided figure from corner to corner. **2** slanting; oblique. • *n.* straight line joining two nonadjacent corners. □□ **di•ag′o•nal•ly** *adv.*

■ *adj.* see OBLIQUE *adj.* 1.

di•a•gram /díəgram/ • *n.* drawing showing the general scheme or outline of an object and its parts. • *v.tr.* (**di•a•gramed, di•a•gram•ing; di•a•grammed, di•a•gram•ming**) represent by means of a diagram. □□ **di•a•gram•mat•ic** /–grəmátik/ *adj.* **di•a•gram•mat′i•cal•ly** *adv.*

■ *n.* see PLAN *n.* 2.

di•al /díəl/ • *n.* **1** face of a clock or watch, marked to show the hours, etc. **2** flat plate with a scale for measuring weight, volume, etc., indicated by a pointer. **3** movable disk on a telephone, with finger holes and numbers for making a call. **4** adjustment control on a radio, appliance, etc. • *v. tr.* [also *absol.*]

select (a telephone number) by means of a dial or set of buttons (*dialed 911*). □ **dial tone** sound indicating that a telephone is ready for dialing. □□ **di′al•er** *n.*

■ *n.* **1, 2** see INDICATOR 2, 3. **4** see CONTROL *n.* 5. • *v.* see CALL *v.* 2.

di•a•lect /díǝlekt/ *n.* **1** regional form of speech. **2** variety of language with nonstandard vocabulary, pronunciation, or grammar. □□ **di•a•lec•tal** /-lékt'l/ *adj.* **di•a•lec•tol•o•gy** /-tólǝjee/ *n.* **di•a•lec•tol•o•gist** /-tólǝjist/ *n.*

■ **1** speech (pattern), phraseology, idiom, accent. **2** jargon, cant, slang, argot, tongue, *colloq.* lingo.

di•a•lec•tic /díǝléktik/ • *n.* (often in *pl.*) art of investigating the truth of opinions; testing of truth by discussion. • *adj.* of or relating to logical disputation.

■ *n.* (dialectics) see LOGIC.

di•a•logue /díǝlawg, -log/ *n.* (also **di′a•log**) **1** conversation. **2** conversation in written form. See synonym study at CONVERSATION.

■ **1** discussion, meeting, conference, com-

213   **dialect ~ diatom**

munication; parley, talk, chat, bull session, *colloq.* confab, *sl.* rap (session), chin-wag, see also CONVERSATION.

di•al•y•sis /díǝlísis/ *n.* (*pl.*) **di•al•y•ses** /-seez/) separation of particles in a liquid by use of a membrane, esp. for purification of blood.

diam. *abbr.* diameter.

di•am•e•ter /díámitǝr/ *n.* **1** straight line through the center of a circle or sphere. **2** length of this line. □□ **di•am′e•tral** *adj.*

■ see WIDTH 1.

di•a•met•ri•cal /díǝmétrikǝl/ *adj.* (also **di•a•met′ric**) **1** of or along a diameter. **2** (of opposites, etc.) absolute. □□ **di•a•met′ri•cal•ly** *adv.*

di•a•mond /dímǝnd, díǝ-/ • *n.* **1** precious stone of pure carbon crystallized in octahedrons, etc., the hardest naturally occurring substance. **2** figure shaped like the cross section of a diamond; rhombus. **3 a** playing card of a suit denoted by a red rhombus. **b** [in *pl.*] this suit. **4** *Baseball* the playing field, esp. the infield. • *adj.* **1** made of or set with diamonds or a diamond. **2** rhombus-shaped.

di•a•mond•back /dímǝndbak, díǝ-/ *n.* **1** edible freshwater terrapin, native to N. America, with diamond-shaped markings on its shell. **2** rattlesnake, native to N. America, with diamond-shaped markings.

di•a•per /dípǝr, díǝpǝr/ *n.* absorbent material wrapped around a baby to retain urine and feces. □ **diaper rash** inflammation of a baby's skin, caused by prolonged contact with a damp diaper.

di•aph•a•nous /díáfǝnǝs/ *adj.* (of fabric, etc.) light and delicate, and almost transparent. □□ **di•aph′a•nous•ly** *adv.*

di•a•phragm /díǝfram/ *n.* **1** muscular partition separating the thorax from the abdomen in mammals. **2** vibrating disk that produces sound in acoustic systems, etc. **3** device for varying the aperture of a camera lens. **4** contraceptive cap fitting over the cervix. □□ **di•a•phrag•mat•ic** /-fragmátik/ *adj.*

di•a•rist /díǝrist/ *n.* person who keeps a diary. □□ **di•a•ris′tic** *adj.*

di•ar•rhe•a /díǝréǝ/ *n.* condition of excessively frequent and loose bowel movements. □□ **di•ar•rhe′al** *adj.* **di•ar•rhe′ic** *adj.*

di•a•ry /díǝree/ *n.* (*pl.* **-ries**) **1** daily record of events or thoughts. **2** book for this.

■ **1** journal, chronicle, log. **2** appointment book, calendar.

Di•as•po•ra /díáspǝrǝ/ *n.* **1** [prec. by *the*] dispersion of the Jews among the Gentiles mainly in the 8th–6th c. BC. **2** (also **diaspora**) any group of people widely dispersed.

di•a•stase /díǝstays, -stayz/ *n. Biochem.* enzyme converting starch to sugar. □□ **di•a•sta•sic** /-stáysik, -zik/ *adj.* **di•a•stat•ic** /-státik/ *adj.*

di•as•to•le /díástǝlee/ *n. Physiol.* normal rhythmic expansion of the heart's chambers as they fill with blood (cf. SYSTOLE). □□ **di•as•tol•ic** /díǝstólik/ *adj.*

di•a•tom /díǝtom/ *n.* unicellular alga found as

plankton and forming fossil deposits. □□ **di‧a‧to‧ma‧ceous** /-máyshəs/ *adj.*

di‧a‧tom‧ic /díətómik/ *adj.* consisting of two atoms.

di‧a‧ton‧ic /díətónik/ *adj. Mus.* relating to a standard major or minor scale of eight notes.

di‧a‧tribe /díətrīb/ *n.* forceful verbal attack or bitter criticism.

■ see HARANGUE *n.*

dib‧ble /díbəl/ *n.* hand tool for making holes in the ground for seeds or young plants.

dibs /dibz/ *n.pl. sl.* rights; claim (*I have dibs on that apple*).

dice /dīs/ • *n.pl.* **1 a** small cubes with faces bearing 1–6 spots used in games of chance. **b** [treated as *sing.*] use of these cubes (see note at DIE[2]). **2** game played with dice. • *v.tr.* cut (food) into small cubes. □ **no dice** *sl.* no success or prospect of it.

■ *v.* see CHOP[1] *v.* 2.

dic‧ey /dísee/ *adj.* (**dic‧i‧er, dic‧i‧est**) *sl.* risky; unreliable.

■ tricky, chancy, *colloq.* iffy, *sl.* hairy; see also UNRELIABLE.

di‧chot‧o‧my /dīkótəmee/ *n.* (*pl.* **-mies**) division into two, esp. a sharply defined one. □□ **di‧cho‧tom‧ic** /-kátómik/ *adj.* **di‧chot'o‧mize** *v.* **di‧chot'o‧mous** *adj.*

dick /dik/ *n. sl.* detective.

■ see DETECTIVE *n.*

dick‧er /díkər/ *v.* **1** *intr.* bargain; haggle. **2** *tr.* barter; exchange. □□ **dick'er‧er** *n.*

■ deal, negotiate, trade, exchange.

dick‧ey /díkee/ *n.* (also **dick‧y**) (*pl.* **-eys** or **-ies**) *colloq.* false shirtfront.

dict. *abbr.* **1** dictionary. **2** dictation.

dic‧ta *pl.* of DICTUM.

dic‧tate • *v.* /díktayt, diktáyt/ **1** *tr.* say or read aloud (words to be written down or recorded). **2 a** *tr.* prescribe or lay down authoritatively (terms, etc.). **b** *intr.* lay down the law; give orders. • *n.* /díktayt/ [usu. in *pl.*] authoritative instruction (*dictates of conscience*). □□ **dic‧ta‧tion** /diktáyshən/ *n.*

■ *v.* **2** ordain, decree, demand, command, order. • *n.* demand, command, order, direction, edict, fiat, mandate.

dic‧ta‧tor /díktaytər, diktáy-/ *n.* **1** ruler with unrestricted authority. **2** person with supreme authority in any sphere. □□ **dic‧ta‧tor‧ship** /diktáytərship/ *n.*

■ autocrat, despot, overlord, tyrant, Big Brother.

dic‧ta‧to‧ri‧al /díktətáwreeəl/ *adj.* **1** of or like a dictator. **2** imperious; overbearing. □□ **dic‧ta‧to'ri‧al‧ly** *adv.*

■ **1** absolute, totalitarian. **2** despotic, iron-handed, *colloq.* bossy.

dic‧tion /díkshən/ *n.* **1** manner of enunciation in speaking or singing. **2** choice of words.

■ **1** articulation, pronunciation. **2** language, style, expression, usage, terminology, vocabulary, phraseology, phrasing.

dic‧tion‧ar‧y /díkshəneree/ *n.* (*pl.* **-ies**) **1** publication that lists (usu. alphabetically) and explains the words of a language or gives equivalents in another language. **2** reference

publication on any subject, arranged alphabetically (*dictionary of architecture*). **3** *Computing* ordered list of words, codes, etc., used by a program.

■ **1** lexicon, glossary, thesaurus. **2** encyclopedia, reference (book), compendium, thesaurus.

dic‧tum /díktəm/ *n.* (*pl.* **dic‧ta** /-tə/ or **dic'tums**) **1** *formal* utterance or pronouncement. **2** saying or maxim.

did *past* of DO[1].

di‧dac‧tic /dīdáktik/ *adj.* **1** meant to instruct. **2** (of a person) tediously pedantic. □□ **di‧dac'ti‧cal‧ly** *adv.* **di‧dac‧ti‧cism** /-tisizəm/ *n.*

■ **1** see INSTRUCTIVE. **2** see *pedantic* (PEDANT).

did‧dle /díd'l/ *v. colloq.* **1** *tr.* cheat; swindle. **2** *intr.* waste time. □□ **did'dler** *n.*

■ **1** see CHEAT *v.* 1a.

did‧dly /dídlee/ *n.* (also **did‧dly squat**) *sl.* slightest amount (*he hasn't done diddly to help us out*).

did‧n't /díd'nt/ *contr.* did not.

die[1] /dī/ *v.* (**dies, died, dy‧ing** /dí-ing/) **1** *intr.* (of a person, animal, or plant) cease to live; expire. **2** *intr.* **a** come to an end; fade away. **b** cease to function. **c** (of a flame) go out. **3** *intr.* be exhausted or tormented (*nearly died of boredom*). **4** *tr.* suffer (a specified death). □ **be dying** wish for longingly or intently (*am dying to see you*). **die down** become less loud or strong. **die hard** die reluctantly (*old habits die hard*). **die off** die one after another. **die out** become extinct. **never say die** keep up courage, not give in.

■ **1** perish, be no more, drop dead, exit, *euphem.* pass away or on, *formal or literary* depart (this life), *sl.* bite the dust, kick the bucket, croak. **2** expire, end, stop; dwindle, diminish, wither (away), deteriorate **b** break down, fail. **c** see *go out* 3 (GO[1]). **3** see SUFFER 1. □ **be dying** pine, yearn, hunger, ache; (*be dying for*) desire, crave. **die out** perish. **never say die** (keep a) stiff upper lip, be brave, *colloq.* chin up.

die[2] /dī/ *n.* **1** *sing.* of DICE *n.* 1a. ¶*Dice* is now standard in general use in this sense. **2** (*pl.* **dies**) engraved stamping device. □ **the die is cast** an irrevocable step has been taken.

die‧hard /díhaard/ *n.* conservative or stubborn person.

■ see REACTIONARY *adj.*

di‧er‧e‧sis *var.* of DIAERESIS.

die‧sel /déezəl/ *n.* **1** (in full **die‧sel engine**) internal combustion engine that burns fuel ignited by compression. **2** vehicle driven by a diesel engine. **3** fuel for a diesel engine. □ **diesel oil** heavy petroleum product used as fuel in diesel engines.

di‧et[1] /díət/ • *n.* **1** kinds of food that a person or animal habitually eats. **2** food to which a person is restricted, esp. for medical reasons or to control weight. • *v.* **1** *intr.* restrict oneself to small amounts or special kinds of food, esp. to control weight. **2** *tr.* restrict (a person or animal) to a special diet. □□ **di‧et‧ar‧y** /díəteree/ *adj.* **di'et‧er** *n.*

■ *n.* **1** intake, consumption; fare, nourishment, sustenance, victuals. **2** regime, *Med.*

regimen. • *v.* **1** fast, starve (oneself); be on a diet.

di•et² /díət/ *n.* legislative assembly in certain countries.

■ council, congress, parliament, senate, legislature, house, chamber, assembly.

di•e•tet•ic /díətétik/ *adj.* of or relating to diet. □□ **di•e•tet'i•cal•ly** *adv.*

di•e•tet•ics /díətétiks/ *n.pl.* [usu. treated as *sing.*] the scientific study of diet and nutrition.

di•e•ti•tian /díətíshən/ *n.* (also **di•e•ti•cian**) expert in dietetics.

dif- /dif/ *prefix* assim. form of DIS- before *f.*

dif•fer /dífər/ *v.intr.* **1** be unlike or distinguishable. **2** disagree; be at variance (with a person).

■ **1** diverge, deviate, contrast; depart. **2** conflict, take issue, part company, fall out, quarrel, argue.

dif•fer•ence /dífrəns/ *n.* **1** being different or unlike. **2** distinction. **3** quantity by which amounts differ; deficit (*will have to make up the difference*). **4 a** disagreement, quarrel, or dispute. **b** grounds of disagreement (*put aside their differences*).

■ **1** dissimilarity, discrepancy, disagreement, diversity, variation, inequality, contrast. **2** contrast, disparity. **3** see DEFICIT. **4** argument, conflict; see also QUARREL *n.* 1.

dif•fer•ent /dífrənt/ *adj.* **1** unlike. ¶*Different from* is generally regarded as most acceptable; *than* is established in US use, esp. when followed by a clause, e.g., *I am a different person than I was a year ago.* **2** distinct; separate. **3** *colloq.* unusual (*wanted to do something different*). **4** of various kinds; assorted; several; miscellaneous (*available in different colors*). □□ **dif'fer•ent•ly** *adv.*

■ **1, 2** dissimilar, conflicting; opposite, contrary, distinguishable. **3** unique, singular, distinctive, individual, alternative; original. **4** numerous, abundant, many.

dif•fer•en•tial /dífərénshəl/ • *adj.* **1** of, exhibiting, or depending on a difference. **2** varying according to circumstances. • *n.* **1** difference between individuals or examples of the same kind. **2** (in full **differential gear**) gear allowing a vehicle's driven wheels to revolve at different speeds when in a turn. □ **differential calculus** *Math* method of calculating rates of change, maximum or minimum values, etc. (cf. INTEGRAL). □□ **dif•fer•en'tial•ly** *adv.*

dif•fer•en•ti•ate /dífərénsheeáyt/ *v.* **1** *tr.* constitute a difference between or in. **2** *tr. & intr.* find differences (between); discriminate. **3** *tr. & intr.* make or become different while growing or developing (species, word forms, etc.). See synonym study at DISTINGUISH. □□ **dif•fer•en•ti•a•tion** /-sheeáyshən/ *n.*

■ **2** distinguish, separate, contrast, tell apart. **3** modify, specialize, change, transform, adapt, adjust.

dif•fi•cult /dífikult, -kəlt/ *adj.* **1 a** needing much effort or skill. **b** troublesome; perplexing. **2** (of a person): **a** not easy to please. **b** uncooperative; troublesome. **3** characterized by hardships or problems (*a difficult period in his life*).

215 **diet ~ digest**

■ **1 a** hard, tough, burdensome. **b** puzzling, baffling, complex, thorny; *colloq.* sticky. **2** intractable, obstructive, stubborn, unmanageable, *sl.* feisty; ill-behaved; fussy, demanding. **3** troubled, trying, hard.

dif•fi•cul•ty /dífikultee, -kəl-/ *n.* (pl. **–ties**) **1** being difficult. **2 a** difficult thing; problem; hindrance. **b** [often in *pl.*] distress or hardship (*in financial difficulties*).

■ **1** strain, hardship; toughness; awkwardness, complexity. **2 a** obstacle, pitfall, predicament. **b** (*difficulties*) embarrassment, plight, problems, *colloq.* hot water, pickle, fix.

dif•fi•dent /dífidənt/ *adj.* shy; lacking self-confidence. □□ **dif•fi•dence** /-dəns/ *n.* **dif'fi•dent•ly** *adv.*

■ see SHY *adj.* 1.

dif•fuse • *adj.* /difyóos/ **1** (of light, inflammation, etc.) spread out; not concentrated. **2** (of prose, speech, etc.) not concise; long-winded; verbose. • *v.* /difyóoz/ **1** disperse or be dispersed. **2** spread or be spread widely; reach a large area. See synonym study at SCATTER. □□ **dif•fuse'ly** /difyóoslee/ *adv.* **dif•fuse'ness** *n.* **dif•fus•i•ble** /difyóozibəl/ *adj.* **dif•fu•sion** /difyóozhən/ *n.* **dif•fu'sive** *adj.*

■ *adj.* **1** scattered, dispersed, widespread. **2** wordy, loquacious, rambling, meandering. • *v.* circulate, distribute, dispense, dispel, scatter, sow.

dig /dig/ • *v.* (**dig•ging**; *past* and *past part.* **dug** /dug/) **1** *intr.* break up and remove or turn over soil, etc. **2** *tr.* break up the soil of. **3** *tr.* make (a hole, grave, tunnel, etc.) by digging. **4** *tr.* **a** obtain or remove by digging. **b** find or discover after searching. **5** *tr. sl.* like, appreciate, or understand. **6** *tr. & intr.* thrust or drive into or down into. **7** *intr.* [usu. foll. by *into*] investigate or study closely; probe. • *n.* **1** piece of digging. **2** thrust or poke (*a dig in the ribs*). **3** *colloq.* [often foll. by *at*] pointed or critical remark. **4** archaeological excavation. **5** [in *pl.*] *colloq.* living quarters. □ **dig one's feet** (or **heels** or **toes**) **in** be obstinate; dig in *colloq.* begin eating. **dig oneself in 1** prepare a defensive trench or pit. **2** establish one's position. □□ **dig'ger** *n.*

■ *v.* **1** see EXCAVATE³ 1, BURROW *v.* 1, 2. **2** (*dig up*) work; see PLOW *v.* 1. **3** dig out, excavate. **4** (*dig out* or *up*) unearth, exhume, bring to light, expose. **5** enjoy, go for, *colloq.* be into; see also LIKE *v.* 1. **6** jab, prod, nudge. **7** (*dig into*) inquire into, explore, research. • *n.* **2** jab, stab, elbow. **3** insult, insinuation, slur, *colloq.* crack. **5** (*digs*) see ACCOMMODATION 1. □ **dig in** help oneself, set to, *colloq.* dive in.

di•gest • *v.tr.* /dijést, dī-/ **1** assimilate (food) in the stomach and bowels. **2** understand and assimilate mentally. **3** reduce to a systematic or convenient form; classify; summarize. • *n.* /díjest/ **1** compendium or summary of information; résumé. **2** periodical synopsis of current literature or news. □□ **di•gest'i•ble** *adj.* **di•gest•i•bil'i•ty** *n.*

■ *v.* **2** take in, swallow; comprehend, grasp. **3** abbreviate, condense, abridge, shorten.

• *n.* **1** condensation, abridgment, abbreviation. **2** survey, outline; see also SUMMARY *n.*
□□ **digestible** palatable, easy to understand; see also INTELLIGIBLE.

di•ges•tion /dijés-chən, dī-/ *n.* **1** process of digesting. **2** capacity to digest food. □□ **di•ges•tive** /dijéstiv, dī-/ *adj. & n.*

dig•it /dijit/ *n.* **1** any numeral from 0 to 9. **2** *Anat. & Zool.* finger, thumb, or toe.
■ **1** see FIGURE *n.* 4a.

dig•i•tal /dijit'l/ *adj.* **1** of or using a digit or digits. **2** (of a clock, watch, etc.) that gives a reading by displayed digits. **3** (of a computer) operating on data represented by digits. **4** (of a recording) with sound electronically represented by digits. □ **digital video disc** disc on which video images (such as a movie) are digitally stored for playback by laser reflection. □□ **dig'it•al•ly** *adv.*

dig•i•tal•is /dijitális/ *n.* drug prepared from the foxglove, used to stimulate the heart muscle.

dig•i•tize /dijitīz/ *v.tr.* convert (data, etc.) into digital form, esp. for a computer. □□ **dig•i•ti•za'tion** *n.*

dig•ni•fied /dignifīd/ *adj.* having or expressing dignity; noble or stately in appearance or manner.
■ majestic, solemn, distinguished, honorable, elegant; regal.

dig•ni•fy /dignifī/ *v.tr.* (**–fies, –fied**) **1** give dignity or distinction to. **2** ennoble. **3** give the appearance of dignity to (*dignified the house with the name of mansion*).
■ distinguish, exalt, glorify, uplift, enhance.

dig•ni•tar•y /digníteree/ *n.* (*pl.* **–ies**) person of high rank or office.
■ official, notable, magnate, VIP, *colloq.* bigwig, big shot, *sl.* big cheese, Mr. Big; celebrity, lion, luminary.

dig•ni•ty /dignítee/ *n.* (*pl.* **–ties**) **1** composed and serious manner or style. **2** worthiness; excellence. **3** high or honorable rank or position. **4** high regard. **5** self-respect. □ **beneath one's dignity** not considered worthy enough for one to do.
■ **1** stateliness, formality, nobility, composure, control. **2** worth, nobility, honor, respectability, importance. **3** standing, station, status. **5** self-regard, pride.

di•graph /dígraf/ *n.* two letters representing one sound, as in *ph* and *ey*. □□ **di•graph•ic** /–gráfik/ *adj.*

di•gress /dīgrés/ *v.intr.* depart from the main subject in speech or writing. □□ **di•gres'sion** /–gréshən/ *n.*
■ go off the track, get sidetracked, ramble, drift. □□ **digression** aside, deviation, detour.

dike /dīk/ (also **dyke**) • *n.* **1** embankment built to prevent flooding. **2** ditch. **3** causeway. **4** barrier or obstacle; defense. • *v.tr.* provide or defend with a dike or dikes.

di•lap•i•dat•ed /dilápidaytid/ *adj.* in disrepair or ruin.
■ broken-down, wrecked, destroyed, falling apart, decrepit, derelict, battered, ramshackle, crumbling, *colloq.* beat-up.

dil•a•ta•tion /dilətáyshən, dī-/ *n.* widening or expansion of a hollow organ or cavity. □ **dilatation and curettage** operation in which the cervix is expanded and the womb lining scraped off with a curette.

di•late /dīláyt, dīlayt/ *v.* **1** *tr. & intr.* make or become wider or larger (*dilated pupils*). **2** *intr.* [often foll. by *on, upon*] speak or write at length. □□ **di•la•tion** /–láyshən/ *n.*
■ see EXPAND 1.

di•la•to•ry /dílətawree/ *adj.* given to or causing delay. □□ **dil'a•to•ri•ly** *adv.* **dil'a•to•ri•ness** *n.*
■ see TARDY 1.

di•lem•ma /dílémə/ *n.* situation in which a choice has to be made between two equally undesirable alternatives.
■ double bind, predicament, quandary, impasse, deadlock; *colloq.* catch-22, fix, jam, pickle.

dil•et•tante /dílitaänt/ • *n.* (*pl.* **dil'et•tantes** or **dil•et•tan'ti** /–tee/) **1** person who studies a subject or area of knowledge superficially. **2** person who enjoys the arts. • *adj.* not thorough; amateurish. □□ **dil•et•tan'tish** *adj.* **dil•et•tan'tism** *n.*
■ *n.* **1** dabbler, trifler, amateur, tinkerer. **2** see AESTHETE. • *adj.* see SUPERFICIAL 1, 4, AMATEUR *adj.*

dil•i•gent /dílijənt/ *adj.* **1** hardworking. **2** showing care and effort. See synonym study at BUSY. □□ **dil•i•gence** /dílijəns/ *n.* **dil'i•gent•ly** *adv.*
■ industrious, attentive, conscientious, painstaking, careful, thorough, scrupulous, meticulous.

dill /dil/ *n.* herb with aromatic seeds and leaves, used for flavoring and medicinal purposes. □ **dill pickle** pickled cucumber, etc., flavored with dill.

dil•ly•dal•ly /díleedálee/ *v.intr.* (**–lies, –lied**) *colloq.* **1** dawdle; loiter. **2** vacillate.
■ **1** see DELAY *v.* 3.

di•lute /dīlōot, dī-/ • *v.tr.* **1** reduce the strength of (a fluid) by adding water, etc. **2** weaken or reduce in effect. • *adj.* also /dī-/ (esp. of a fluid) diluted; weakened. □□ **di•lut'er** *n.* **di•lu•tion** /–lōoshən/ *n.*
■ *v.* lessen, diminish, decrease, *colloq.* split. • *adj.* weak, watered down, thinned out.

dim /dim/ • *adj.* (**dim•mer, dim•mest**) **1 a** faintly luminous or visible; not bright. **b** obscure; ill-defined. **2** not clearly perceived or remembered. **3** *colloq.* stupid; slow to understand. • *v.* (**dimmed, dim•ming**) *tr. & intr.* make or become dim. □ **dim-witted** *colloq.* stupid. **take a dim view of** *colloq.* disapprove of. □□ **dim'ly** *adv.* **dim'mish** *adj.* **dim'ness** *n.*
■ *adj.* **1 a** weak, imperceptible; dark, shadowy. **b** vague, fuzzy, foggy, clouded. **2** obtuse, doltish, dull, *colloq.* thick, dense; see also STUPID *adj.* 1, 3. • *v.* obscure, dull; darken; weaken.

dime /dīm/ *n. US & Can.* ten-cent coin. □ **a dime a dozen** very cheap or commonplace. **dime novel** cheap popular novel. **turn on a dime** *colloq.* make a sharp turn in a vehicle.

di•men•sion /diménshən, dī-/ *n.* **1** measurable extent, as length, breadth, etc. **2** [in *pl.*]

size; scope; extent. **3** aspect or facet of a situation, etc. □□ **di•men'sion•al** adj. [also in comb.]. **di•men'sion•less** adj.

■ n. **1** see MEASUREMENT 2.

di•min•ish /dimínish/ v. **1** tr. & intr. make or become smaller or less. **2** tr. lessen the reputation or influence of (a person). □ **law of diminishing returns** Econ. fact that the increase of expenditure, investment, taxation, etc., beyond a certain point ceases to produce a proportionate yield. □□ **di•min'ish•a•ble** adj.

■ **1** decrease, decline, abate; reduce, lower, curtail; wane, fade, dwindle. **2** belittle, disparage, degrade, discredit.

di•min•u•en•do /dimínyōō-éndō/ Mus. • adv. gradual decrease in loudness. • n. (pl. –dos) passage played in this way.

dim•i•nu•tion /dímino͞oshon, -nyōō-/ n. **1** act or instance of diminishing. **2** amount by which something diminishes.

■ **1** see DECREASE n.

di•min•u•tive /dimínyotiv/ • adj. **1** remarkably small; tiny. **2** Gram. (of a word or suffix) implying smallness or affection (e.g., –let, –kins). See synonym study at SMALL. • n. Gram. diminutive word or suffix.

■ adj. **1** little, miniature, petite, minute, minuscule, mini-, compact, colloq. teeny.

dim•ple /dímpəl/ • n. small hollow, esp. in the cheeks or chin. • v. **1** intr. produce or show dimples. **2** tr. produce dimples in (a cheek, etc.). □□ **dim'ply** adj.

■ n. depression, indentation.

dim sum /dim súm/ n. (also **dim sim** /sím/) meal or course of savory Cantonese-style snacks, esp. steamed or fried filled dumplings.

dim•wit /dímwit/ n. colloq. stupid person.

■ see FOOL n.

din /din/ n. prolonged loud and distracting noise.

■ clamor, uproar, shouting, babel, commotion, racket, hullabaloo, colloq. row.

dine /din/ v. **1** intr. eat dinner. **2** tr. give dinner to. □ **dine out** dine away from home. **dining room** room in which meals are eaten.

■ **1** have dinner, banquet, feast, colloq. feed.

din•er /dínər/ n. **1** person who dines, esp. in a restaurant. **2** railroad dining car. **3** small restaurant.

■ **3** see CAFÉ 1.

di•nette /dínét/ n. **1** small room or part of a room used for eating meals. **2** (in full **dinette set**) table and chairs designed for such a room.

ding¹ /ding/ • v.intr. make a ringing sound. • n. ringing sound.

ding² /ding/ • v.tr. cause surface damage; dent. • n. nick; minor surface damage; dent.

din•ghy /díngee, dínggee/ n. (pl. –ghies) small boat for rowing or sailing.

din•go /dínggō/ n. (pl. –goes) wild Australian dog.

din•gy /dínjee/ adj. (**din•gi•er**, **din•gi•est**) dirty-looking; drab; dull-colored. □□ **din'gi•ly** adv. **din'gi•ness** n.

■ dark, gloomy, dim, lackluster, faded, discolored; grimy.

din•ky /díngkee/ adj. (**din•ki•er**, **din•ki•est**) colloq. small.

din•ner /dínər/ n. **1** main meal of the day, either at midday or in the evening. **2** formal evening meal or banquet. □ **dinner dance** formal dinner followed by dancing. **dinner jacket** man's, usu. black, formal jacket for evening wear. **dinner service** set of usu. matching dishes, etc., for serving a meal.

■ **1** see MEAL¹. **2** see BANQUET n.

din•ner•ware /dínərwair/ n. tableware, as plates, glassware, etc.

di•no•saur /dínosawr/ n. **1** extinct reptile of the Mesozoic era, often of enormous size. **2** large, unwieldy system or organization. □□ **di•no•sau'ri•an** adj. & n.

dint /dint/ n. □ **by dint of** by force or means of.

di•o•cese /díəsis, –sees, –seez/ n. district administered by a bishop. □□ **di•oc•e•san** /díóisəsən/ adj.

di•ode /díōd/ n. Electronics semiconductor allowing current flow in one direction only and having two terminals.

di•o•ram•a /díorámə, –ráəmə/ n. three-dimensional scenic display with a painted backdrop, viewed through a window, etc. □□ **di•o•ram'ic** /–rámik/ adj.

di•ox•ide /díóksīd/ n. Chem. oxide containing two atoms of oxygen which are not linked together (carbon dioxide).

DIP /dip/ n. Computing form of integrated circuit. □ **DIP switch** arrangement of miniature switches on an electronic device for selecting various modes of operation.

dip /dip/ • v. (**dipped**, **dip•ping**) **1** tr. put or let down briefly into liquid, etc.; immerse. **2** intr. **a** go below a surface or level. **b** (of a level of income, activity, etc.) decline slightly. **3** intr. extend or slope downward. **4** intr. [foll. by into] **a** read briefly from (a book, etc.). **b** take a cursory interest in (a subject). **5** [foll. by into] **a** intr. put a hand, ladle, etc., into a container to take something out. **b** tr. put (a hand, etc.) into a container to do this. **6** tr. & intr. lower or be lowered, esp. in salute. • n. **1** dipping or being dipped. **2** liquid or sauce into which something is dipped. **3** brief swim. **4** brief downward slope in a road, skyline, etc. **5** sl. pickpocket.

■ v. **1** plunge. **2 b** drop, fall. **4** (dip into) a skim (through), scan. b dabble in. **6** let down, drop; be put down, be dropped. • n. **1** lowering, fall. **3** plunge. **4** see SLOPE n. 1–3.

diph•the•ri•a /diftheéreeə, dip–/ n. acute infectious bacterial disease with inflammation, esp. of the throat. □□ **diph•the'ri•al** adj. **diph•the•rit•ic** /–thəritik/ adj. **diph•the•roid** /difthəroyd, díp–/ adj.

diph•thong /dífthawng, –thong, díp–/ n. speech sound in one syllable in which the articulation begins as for one vowel and moves as for another (as in coin, loud, and side). □□ **diph•thon•gal** /–tháwnggəl, –thóng–/ adj.

dip•lod•o•cus /diplódəkəs, di–/ n. giant plant-eating dinosaur with a long neck and tail.

di•plo•ma /dɪplṓmə/ n. (pl. **di•plo•mas**) certificate of qualification awarded by a college, etc. □□ **di•plo•maed** /-məd/ adj.

di•plo•ma•cy /dɪplṓməsee/ n. **1** management of international relations. **2** adroitness in personal relations; tact.

■ **1** foreign affairs, statesmanship, negotiation. **2** discretion, delicacy, discernment.

dip•lo•mat /dɪpləmat/ n. **1** official representing a country abroad; member of a diplomatic service. **2** tactful person. □□ **dip•lo•mat•ic** /dɪpləmátik/ adj.

■ **1** see AMBASSADOR. **2** see PEACEMAKER.

di•pole /dɪpōl/ n. **1** Physics two equal and oppositely charged or magnetized poles separated by a distance. **2** Chem. molecule charged in this way. **3** aerial consisting of a horizontal metal rod with a connecting wire at its center.

dip•so•ma•ni•a /dɪpsəmáyneeə/ n. alcoholism. □□ **dip•so•ma•ni•ac** /-máyneeak/ n.

dip•stick /dɪpstik/ n. rod for measuring the depth of a liquid, esp. in a vehicle's engine.

dip•tych /dɪptik/ n. **1** painting, esp. an altarpiece, on two hinged, usu. wooden panels which may be closed like a book. **2** ancient writing tablet consisting of two hinged leaves with waxed inner sides.

dire /dɪr/ adj. **1 a** calamitous; dreadful. **b** ominous. **2** urgent. □□ **dire•ly** adv. **dire•ness** n.

■ **1 a** see calamitous (CALAMITY). **b** see FEARFUL 2. **2** see SORE adj. 4.

di•rect /dɪrékt, dī-/ • adj. **1** extending or moving in a straight line or by the shortest route. **2 a** straightforward. **b** frank. **3** without intermediaries (direct rule). **4** (of descent) lineal; not collateral. **5** exact; complete; greatest possible (esp. where contrast is implied) (the direct opposite). • adv. in a direct way or manner (dealt with them direct). • v.tr. **1** control; guide; govern the movements of. **2** order or command. **3** tell or show (a person) the way to. **4** [foll. by at, to, toward] **a** point, aim, or cause (a blow or missile) to move in a certain direction. **b** point or address (one's attention, a remark, etc.). **5 a** [also absol.] supervise the performing, staging, etc., of (a movie, play, etc.). **b** supervise the performance of (an actor, etc.). □ **direct access** facility of retrieving data immediately from any part of a computer file. **direct current** electric current flowing in one direction only. ¶Abbr.: **DC, d.c. direct object** Gram. primary object of the action of a transitive verb. □□ **di•rect•ness** n.

■ adj. **1** unswerving, undeviating. **2** honest, uninhibited; tactless; clear, to the point; see also BLUNT adj. 2. **3** without interference, unobstructed; straight. **4** unbroken. **5** polar, diametrical. • v. **1** manage, handle, steer. **2** rule, require, dictate. **3** guide, lead, point (the way); usher, escort. **4** focus, level, target; address.

di•rec•tion /dɪrékshən, dī-/ n. **1** directing; supervision. **2** [usu. in pl.] order or instruction. **3** course or line of movement, sight,

etc. **4** tendency or scope of a theme, subject, or inquiry. □□ **di•rec'tion•al** adj. **di•rec•tion•al•i•ty** /-álitee/ n. **di•rec'tion•al•ly** adv. **di•rec'tion•less** adj.

■ **1** guidance, management, administration, leadership. **2** (directions) information, guidelines. **3** bearing, route, avenue; see also COURSE n. 2, WAY n. 1, 2.

di•rec•tive /dɪréktiv, dī-/ • n. instruction from an authority. • adj. serving to direct.

■ n. see INSTRUCTION 1.

di•rect•ly /dɪréktlee, dī-/ adv. **1 a** at once; without delay. **b** presently; shortly. **2** exactly; immediately (directly opposite, directly after lunch). **3** in a direct manner.

■ **1 a** immediately, promptly, instantly. **b** soon, in a (little) while. **2** precisely, completely; diametrically. **3** straight; frankly, openly, bluntly; tactlessly.

di•rec•tor /dɪréktər, dī-/ n. **1** person who directs or controls something, esp. a member of the board of a corporation. **2** person who directs a movie, play, etc. □□ **di•rec•to•ri•al** /-táwreeəl/ adj. **di•rec'tor•ship** n.

■ **1** guide, leader; pilot, commander; executive, administrator, official, head, chief, manager, supervisor, colloq. top dog, sl. big cheese, honcho; see also BOSS[1] n.

di•rec•tor•ate /dɪréktərət, dī-/ n. **1** board of directors. **2** office of director.

di•rec•to•ry /dɪréktəree, dī-/ n. (pl. **-ries**) alphabetical or thematic listing of a particular group of individuals (e.g., telephone subscribers) or organizations.

■ see INDEX n. 1.

dirge /dərj/ n. lament for the dead. □□ **dirge'ful** adj.

■ see LAMENT n. 2.

dir•i•gi•ble /dírijibəl, diríj-/ n. rigid-frame airship.

dirk /dərk/ n. long dagger.

dirndl /dɔrnd'l/ n. **1** Alpine dress with close-fitting bodice, tight waistband, and full skirt. **2** skirt of this kind.

dirt /dərt/ n. **1** unclean matter that soils. **2** earth; soil. **3 a** foul or malicious words or talk. **b** scurrilous information; scandal; gossip; the lowdown. **4** person or thing considered worthless. □ **dirt bike** motorcycle designed for use on unpaved roads and tracks. **dirt cheap** colloq. extremely cheap. **dirt poor** extremely poor. **dirt track** course made of rolled cinders, soil, etc., for motorcycle racing or flat racing. **treat like dirt** treat (a person) contemptuously; abuse.

■ **1** mud, grime, dust, filth, colloq. muck. **2** loam, ground, clay. **3** indecency, obscenity, smut; rumor, colloq. dope, scuttlebutt. **4** trash; colloq. scum.

dirt•y /dɔrtee/ • adj. (**dirt•i•er, dirt•i•est**) **1** soiled; unclean. **2** causing dirtiness (a dirty job). **3** sordid; lewd; morally illicit or questionable (dirty joke). **4** unpleasant; nasty. **5** dishonest; dishonorable; unfair (dirty play). **6** (of weather) rough; stormy. **7** (of a color) not pure nor clear; dingy. • v. (**-ies, -ied**) make or become dirty. □ **dirty dog** colloq. scoundrel; despicable person. **dirty linen** (or **laundry**) colloq. intimate secrets, esp. of a scandalous nature. **dirty look** colloq. look

of disapproval, anger, or disgust. **dirty trick**
1 dishonorable and deceitful act. **2** [in *pl.*]
underhand political activity. **dirty word**
1 offensive or indecent word. **2** word for
something that is disapproved of (*profit is a
dirty word*). **dirty work 1** unpleasant tasks.
2 dishonorable or illegal activity, esp. done
clandestinely. □□ **dirt′i•ly** *adv.* **dirt′i•ness**
n.

■ *adj.* **1** foul, muddy, filthy, polluted, impure, unsanitary, *sl.* grotty, grungy. **3** smutty, indecent, obscene, coarse. **4** horrible; bitter, malicious, angry; sordid, mean.
5 unscrupulous, underhanded, unsports-
manlike. **6** bad, foul, nasty. • *v.* stain, soil,
pollute, smear.

dis- /dis/ *v.tr. sl.* var. of DISS.

dis- /dis/ *prefix* forming nouns, adjectives, and
verbs indicating: **1** negation (*dishonest*).
2 reversal or absence of an action or state
(*disengage, disbelieve*). **3** removal of a thing or
quality (*dismember, disable*). **4** separation
(*distinguish, dispose*). **5** completeness or intensification (*disembowel, disgruntled*) **6** expulsion from (*disbar*).

dis•a•bil•i•ty /dísəbílitee/ *n.* (*pl.* **–ties**)
1 physical or mental incapacity. **2** lack of
some asset, quality, or attribute, preventing
action.

■ **1** handicap, impairment. **2** inability, incapacity.

dis•a•ble /disáybəl/ *v.tr.* render unable to
function; deprive of an ability. □□ **dis•a′ble•
ment** *n.*

■ (**disabled**) handicapped, incapacitated,
crippled, lame.

dis•a•buse /dísəbyóoz/ *v.tr.* **1** [foll. by *of*]
free from a mistaken idea. **2** disillusion; un-
deceive.

■ *see* DISILLUSION *v.*

dis•ad•van•tage /dísədvántij/ • *n.* unfavorable circumstance or condition. • *v.tr.* cause
disadvantage to. □ **at a disadvantage** in
an unfavorable position or aspect. □□ **dis•
ad•van•ta•geous** /disàdvəntáyjəs, disàd–/
adj.

■ *n.* setback, liability, handicap; problem.

dis•ad•van•taged /dísədvántijd/ *adj.* placed
in unfavorable circumstances (esp. of a person lacking normal opportunities).

■ *see* deprived (DEPRIVE 2).

dis•af•fect•ed /dísəféktid/ *adj.* **1** disloyal,
esp. to one's superiors. **2** estranged; no
longer friendly, discontented. □□ **dis•af•
fect′ed•ly** *adv.* **dis•af•fec•tion** /dísəfékshən/
n.

dis•a•gree /dísəgreé/ *v.intr.* (**–a•grees, –a•
greed, –a•gree•ing**) **1** hold a different
opinion. **2** quarrel. **3** (of factors or circumstances) not correspond. **4** have an adverse
effect upon (a person's health, digestion,
etc.). □□ **dis•a•gree′ment** *n.*

■ **1** dissent, diverge; see also DIFFER 2.
2 dispute, argue. □□ **disagreement** difference, discrepancy; dissent; opposition; quarrel, debate, *sl.* rhubarb.

dis•a•gree•a•ble /dísəgreéəbəl/ *adj.* **1** unpleasant. **2** rude or bad-tempered. □□ **dis•
a•gree′a•ble•ness** *n.* **dis•a•gree′a•bly** *adv.*

■ **1** offensive, distasteful, disgusting, repul-

sive, objectionable, odious. **2** quarrelsome,
uncooperative, unfriendly, curt, discourteous, *colloq.* grouchy.

dis•al•low /dísəlów/ *v.tr.* refuse to allow or
accept as valid; prohibit. See synonym study
at PROHIBIT. □□ **dis•al′low′ance** *n.*

■ *see* PROHIBIT 1.

dis•ap•pear /dísəpeér/ *v.intr.* **1** cease to be
visible. **2** cease to exist or be in circulation
or use. □□ **dis•ap•pear′ance** *n.*

■ **1** vanish, evaporate, vaporize. **2** die (out
or off).

dis•ap•point /dísəpóynt/ *v.tr.* **1** [also *absol.*]
fail to fulfill a desire or expectation of.
2 frustrate (hopes, plans, etc.). □ **be disappointed** fail to have one's expectation, etc.,
fulfilled (*was disappointed in you, am disappointed to be last*). □□ **dis•ap•point′ed** *adj.*
dis•ap•point′ing *adj.* **dis•ap•point′ingly**
adv. **dis•ap•point′ment** *n.*

■ **1** let down, dissatisfy. **2** foil, thwart; *see
also* FRUSTRATE *v.* 2. □□ **disappointed** frustrated, discouraged; saddened, unhappy.
disappointing discouraging, unsatisfactory;
colloq. pathetic. **disappointment** setback,
letdown, *colloq.* washout; frustration, vexation, discouragement, distress, regret.

dis•ap•pro•ba•tion /dísəprobáyshən/ *n.*
strong disapproval.

dis•ap•prove /dísəpr-óov/ *v.* **1** *intr.* have or
express an unfavorable opinion. **2** *tr.* be displeased with. □□ **dis•ap•prov′al** *n.* **dis•ap•
prov′ing** *adj.* **dis•ap•prov′ingly** *adv.*

■ **1** (*disapprove of*) condemn, criticize, belittle, *sl.* knock; see also CRITICIZE 1. □□ **disapproval** condemnation, censure, criticism.
disapproving see CRITICAL 1.

dis•arm /disaárm/ *v.* **1** *tr.* take weapons away
from (a person, nation, etc.). **2** *intr.* (of a nation, etc.) disband or reduce its armed
forces. **3** *tr.* remove the fuse from (a bomb,
etc.). **4** *tr.* render harmless. **5** *tr.* charm;
mollify; placate. □□ **dis•arm′ing** *adj.* (esp.
in sense 5). **dis•arm′ing•ly** *adv.*

■ **3, 4** deactivate, defuse, incapacitate.
5 win over, appease. □□ **disarming** conciliatory; see also *enchanting* (ENCHANT).

dis•ar•ma•ment /disaárməmənt/ *n.* reduction by a nation of its military forces and
weapons.

dis•ar•range /dísəráynj/ *v.tr.* bring into disorder. □□ **dis•ar•range′ment** *n.*

dis•ar•ray /dísə ráy/ • *n.* [often prec. by *in,
into*] disorder; confusion (esp. among people). • *v.tr.* throw into disorder. See synonym study at JUMBLE.

■ *n.* see DISORDER *n.* 1. • *v.* see DISORDER *v.*

dis•as•so•ci•ate /dísəsṓsheeayt, –seeayt/ *v.* =
DISSOCIATE. □□ **dis•as•so•ci•a•tion** /–áy-
shən/ *n.*

dis•as•ter /dizástər/ *n.* **1** great or sudden
misfortune. **2** complete failure. □□ **dis•as′
trous** *adj.* **dis•as′trous•ly** *adv.*

■ **1** catastrophe, calamity, accident. **2** debacle, collapse, *colloq.* washout, dead loss.
□□ **disastrous** cataclysmic, tragic, devastating, *colloq.* awful; unlucky.

dis•a•vow /dísəvów/ *v.tr.* disclaim knowledge

of, responsibility for, or belief in. □□ **dis•a•vow'al** n.
■ see DENY 2.

dis•band /disbánd/ v. **1** intr. (of an organized group, etc.) cease to work or act together. **2** tr. cause (such a group) to disband. □□ **dis•band'ment** n.
■ disperse, scatter, break up, dissolve, retire; demobilize.

dis•bar /disbaár/ v.tr. (**dis•barred, dis•bar•ring**) deprive (an attorney) of the right to practice. □□ **dis•bar'ment** n.

dis•be•lieve /dísbileév/ v. **1** tr. be unable or unwilling to believe (a person or statement). **2** intr. have no faith. □□ **dis•be•lief** /-leéf/ n. **dis•be•liev'ing** adj. **dis•be•liev'ing•ly** adv.
■ **1** see DISTRUST v.

dis•burse /disbórs/ v. **1** tr. expend (money). **2** intr. pay money. □□ **dis•burs'al** n. **dis•burse'ment** n.
■ **1** see SPEND 1.

disc var. of DISK.

dis•card • v.tr. /diskaárd/ **1** reject as unwanted. **2** [also absol.] Cards remove (a card) from one's hand. • n. /dískaard/ [often in pl.] discarded item, esp. a card in a card game.
■ v. **1** get rid of, dispense with, colloq. trash, sl. ditch. **2** n. reject; (discards) scraps.

dis•cern /disó rn/ v.tr. perceive clearly with the mind or the senses. See synonym study at DISTINGUISH. □□ **dis•cern'i•ble** adj. **dis•cern'i•bly** adv.
■ see PERCEIVE. □□ **discernible** visible, apparent, clear, conspicuous, recognizable, tangible.

dis•cern•ing /disórning/ adj. having or showing good judgment or insight. □□ **dis•cern'ing•ly** adv. **dis•cern•ment** /disórnmənt/ n.
■ see JUDICIOUS.

dis•charge • v. /dischaárj/ **1** tr. release, esp. from a duty, commitment, or confinement. **2** tr. dismiss from office, employment, etc. **3** tr. **a** fire (a gun, etc.). **b** (of a gun, etc.) fire (a bullet, etc.). **4 a** tr. [also absol.] pour out or cause to pour out (pus, liquid, etc.) (the wound was discharging). **b** intr. [foll. by into] (of a river, etc.) flow into (esp. the sea). **5** tr. **a** carry out; perform (a duty). **b** relieve oneself of (a financial commitment) (discharged his debt). **6** tr. Physics release an electrical charge from. • n. /díschaarj, dischaárj/ **1** discharging or being discharged. **2** dismissal, esp. from the armed services. **3** written certificate of release, etc. **4** an act of firing a gun, etc. **5** matter (pus, liquid, etc.) discharged. **6** Physics release of an electric charge. □□ **dis•charge'a•ble** adj. **dis•charg'er** n. (in sense 6 of v.).
■ v. **1** let out, dismiss; liberate; see also RELEASE v. 1. **2** expel, oust, colloq. sack, sl. fire; see also DISMISS 2. **3** shoot; detonate, explode. **4 a** emit, exude; ooze. **5 a** fulfill, accomplish. **b** pay, settle. ■ n. **2** expulsion. **3** acquittal, exoneration; see also exemption (EXEMPT), RELEASE n. 1. **4** shooting, salvo; burst. **5** emission, seepage; ooze.

dis•ci•ple /dísípəl/ n. **1** follower of a leader, teacher, philosophy, etc. (a disciple of Zen Buddhism). **2** early believer in Christ, esp. one of the twelve Apostles.
■ **1** apprentice, student, proselyte; adherent, devotee.

dis•ci•pli•nar•i•an /dísiplináireeən/ n. person who upholds or practices firm discipline.
■ (hard) taskmaster, slave driver; tyrant, despot, dictator.

dis•ci•pline /dísiplin/ • n. **1 a** control or order exercised over people or animals, esp. children, prisoners, military personnel, church members, etc. **b** rules used to maintain this control. **c** behavior of groups subjected to such rules (poor discipline in the ranks). **2** mental, moral, or physical training. **3** branch of learning. **4** punishment. • v.tr. **1** punish. **2** train in obedience; drill. □□ **dis'ci•plin•a•ble** adj. **dis'ci•pli•nal** /dísiplin'l, disíplin'l/ adj. **dis•ci•plin•ar•y** /dísiplínéree/ adj.
■ n. **1 a** direction, rule, authority. **b** see CODE 2. **c** conduct, attitude. **2** drilling, exercise, practice. **3** subject, course, specialty. **4** chastisement; see also PUNISHMENT 1, 2. ■ v. **1** chastise, correct; see also CASTIGATE. **2** break in, exercise, coach; check, curb.

dis•claim /diskláym/ v. **1** deny or disown. **2** [often absol.] Law renounce legal claim to (property, etc.).
■ see DENY 1, 2.

dis•claim•er /diskláymər/ n. renunciation or disavowal, esp. of responsibility.
■ see DENIAL 1.

dis•close /disklóz/ v.tr. **1** make known. **2** expose to view. □□ **dis•clos'er** n. **dis•clo•sure** /disklózhər/ n.
■ **1** reveal, divulge, release, report, betray. **2** bare, reveal.

dis•co /dískō/ colloq. • n. (pl. **-cos**) = DISCOTHEQUE. • v.intr. (**-coes, -coed**) **1** attend a discotheque. **2** dance to disco music (discoed the night away). □ **disco music** popular dance music characterized by a heavy bass rhythm.

dis•cog•ra•phy /diskógrəfee/ n. (pl. **-phies**) **1** descriptive catalog of recordings, esp. of a particular performer or composer. **2** the study of recordings. □□ **dis•cog'ra•pher** n.

dis•col•or /diskúlər/ v. spoil or cause to spoil the color of; stain; tarnish. □□ **dis•col•or•a'tion** n.
■ see STAIN v. 1.

dis•com•fit /diskúmfit/ v.tr. **1** disconcert or baffle. **2** thwart. □□ **dis•com'fi•ture** n.
■ **1** embarrass, disturb, fluster, colloq. rattle; confuse. **2** frustrate, foil, outdo, colloq. trump; see also THWART v.

dis•com•fort /diskúmfərt/ • n. **1** lack of ease; slight pain. **2** lack of comfort. • v.tr. make uneasy.
■ n. **1** soreness, irritation; bother. ■ v. see DISCOMFIT 1.

dis•com•mode /dískəmód/ v.tr. inconvenience (a person, etc.). □□ **dis•com•mo'di•ous** adj.

dis•com•pose /dískəmpóz/ v.tr. disturb the composure of; agitate; disturb. □□ **dis•com•po•sure** /-pózhər/ n.
■ see UPSET v. 2.

dis•con•cert /dískənsórt/ v.tr. **1** (often as

disconcerted *adj.*) discompose; agitate; fluster. 2 spoil or upset (plans, etc.). □□ dis•con•cert'ing *adj.*

▪ 1 see AGITATE. 2 see UPSET *v.* 3. □□ dis•concerting awkward, upsetting; confusing, bewildering, perplexing.

dis•con•nect /dískənékt/ *v.tr.* [often foll. by *from*] break the connection or functioning of (things, ideas, etc.). □□ dis•con•nec•tion /dískənékshən/ *n.*

▪ separate, uncouple, detach, part, divide, sever; turn off, switch off, stop, deactivate.

dis•con•nect•ed /dískənéktid/ *adj.* 1 separated, not functioning. 2 (of speech, writing, etc.) incoherent and illogical.

▪ 1 apart, detached, unattached; split. 2 unconnected, confused, garbled, rambling, disjointed, mixed-up, jumbled.

dis•con•so•late /dískónsələt/ *adj.* 1 forlorn. 2 unhappy or disappointed. □□ dis•con'so•late•ly *adv.*

dis•con•tent /dískəntént/ ▪ *n.* lack of contentment; restlessness, dissatisfaction. ▪ *adj.* dissatisfied. ▪ *v.tr.* (esp. as discontented *adj.*) dissatisfy. □□ dis•con•tent'ment *n.*

▪ *n.* displeasure, uneasiness; malaise. ▪ *adj.* see discontented. ▪ *v.* (discontented) displeased, annoyed, fed up.

dis•con•tin•ue /dískəntínyoo/ *v.* 1 *intr. & tr.* come or bring to an end. 2 *tr.* give up; cease from. □□ dis•con•tin'u•ance *n.* dis•con•tin•u•a'tion *n.*

▪ 1 stop, put an end to; interrupt; see also STOP *v.* 1c.

dis•con•tin•u•ous /dískəntínyoôəs/ *adj.* lacking continuity in space or time; intermittent. □□ dis•con•ti•nu'i•ty /-kontinoô-itee, -nyoô-/ *n.* dis•con•tin'u•ous•ly *adv.*

▪ see INTERMITTENT.

dis•cord ▪ *n.* /dískawrd/ 1 disagreement; strife. 2 harsh noise. 3 *Mus.* lack of harmony. ▪ *v.intr.* /dískáwrd/ 1 [usu. foll. by *with*] disagree; clash. □□ dis•cord'ance *n.* dis•cor'dan•cy *n.* dis•cord•ant /dískáwrd'nt/ *adj.* dis•cord'ant•ly *adv.*

▪ *n.* 1 dissension, conflict, disharmony. 2 see NOISE *n.* 1. ▪ *v.* grate, jar, disharmonize; see also DISAGREE.

dis•co•theque /dískətèk/ *n.* club, etc., for dancing to recorded popular music.

dis•count ▪ *n.* /dískownt/ amount deducted from a customary price. ▪ *v.tr.* /dískównt/ 1 disregard as unreliable or unimportant (*discounted his story*). 2 detract from; lessen; deduct (esp. an amount from a bill, etc.). □ at a discount 1 below the nominal or usual price (cf. PREMIUM). 2 not in demand; depreciated. discount rate minimum lending rate. discount storestore, etc., that sells goods at less than the normal retail price. □□ dis'count•a•ble *adj.* dis'count•er *n.*

▪ *n.* reduction, markdown; rebate, allowance. ▪ *v.* 1 omit, dismiss, ignore. 2 lower, knock down; diminish.

dis•coun•te•nance /dískówntinəns/ *v.tr.* 1 [esp. in *passive*] disconcert (*was discountenanced by his abruptness*). 2 refuse to countenance; show disapproval of.

▪ 1 see DISCOMFIT 1. 2 see FROWN *v.* 2.

dis•cour•age /dískórij, –kúr–/ *v.tr.* 1 deprive

---

221   **disconnect ~ discrete**

of courage, confidence, or energy. 2 dissuade (*discouraged her from going*). 3 show disapproval of; oppose (*smoking is discouraged*). □□ dis•cour'age•ment *n.* dis•cour'ag•ing•ly *adv.*

▪ 1 dispirit, dishearten; see also DEMORALIZE. 2 deter; put off, advise against. 3 inhibit, hinder; see also OPPOSE 1.

dis•course ▪ *n.* /dískáwrs/ *literary* 1 conversation; talk. 2 dissertation or treatise on an academic subject. 3 lecture or sermon. ▪ *v.intr.* /dískórs/ 1 talk, converse. 2 *intr.* speak or write learnedly or at length (on a subject).

▪ *n.* 1 see CONVERSATION[1]. 3 a, 3 see LECTURE *n.* 1. ▪ *v.* 1 see CONVERSE. 2 see LECTURE *v.* 1.

dis•cour•te•ous /dískórteeəs/ *adj.* impolite; rude. □□ dis•cour'te•ous•ly *adv.* dis•cour'te•ous•ness *n.* dis•cour•te•sy /dískórtəsee/ *n.*

▪ uncivil, unmannerly, disrespectful, boorish, abrupt, curt.

dis•cov•er /dískúvər/ *v.tr.* 1 find out or become aware of (*discovered a new entrance*). 2 be the first to find or find out (*who discovered America?*). 3 devise or plan (*discover new techniques*). □□ dis•cov'er•a•ble *adj.* dis•cov'er•er *n.*

▪ 1 locate, unearth, uncover; determine, detect; realize, notice, perceive. 2 originate, conceive (of), design. □□ discoverer explorer, voyager, see also PIONEER *n.* 2.

dis•cov•er•y /dískúvəree/ *n.* (*pl.* –ies) 1 discovering or being discovered. 2 person or thing discovered.

▪ finding, uncovering; disclosure, identification, revelation; realization. 2 find, catch; see also INVENTION 2.

dis•cred•it /dískrédit/ ▪ *n.* 1 harm to reputation. 2 person or thing causing this (*he is a discredit to his family*). 3 doubt; disbelief. ▪ *v.tr.* 1 harm the good reputation of. 2 cause to be disbelieved. 3 refuse to believe.

▪ *n.* 1 dishonor, degradation, shame, scandal, defamation; damage, blot, tarnish. 3 suspicion, skepticism, incredulity. ▪ *v.* 1 disparage, defame, dishonor, disgrace, devalue; slander, sully, malign, libel, slur. 2 *colloq.* debunk; see also EXPLODE 4. 3 deny, dispute, doubt; reject; ridicule.

dis•cred•it•a•ble /dískréditəbəl/ *adj.* bringing discredit; shameful. □□ dis•cred'it•a•bly *adv.*

▪ see *shameful* (SHAME).

dis•creet /dískréet/ *adj.* (dis•creet•er, dis•creet•est) 1 a circumspect in speech or action. b tactful; trustworthy. 2 unobtrusive. □□ dis•creet'ly *adv.* dis•creet'ness *n.*

▪ 1 careful, cautious, prudent; judicious. 2 see UNOBTRUSIVE.

dis•crep•an•cy /dískrépənsee/ *n.* (*pl.* –cies) difference; failure to correspond; inconsistency. □□ dis•crep'ant *adj.*

▪ disparity, dissimilarity, deviation, incompatibility, conflict, discordance, contradiction; gap.

dis•crete /dískréet/ *adj.* individually distinct;

separate; discontinuous. □□ **dis•crete′ly**
adv. **dis•crete′ness** *n.*

■ disconnected, unattached; see also DIS-
TINCT 1a.

dis•cre•tion /diskréshən/ *n.* 1 being discreet.
2 freedom to act and think as one wishes,
usu. within legal limits (*it is within his discretion to leave*). □□ **dis•cre′tion•ary** *adj.*

■ 1 tact, diplomacy, delicacy, sound judgment, good sense. 2 choice, judgment, volition, wish, will, inclination.

dis•crim•i•nate /diskríminayt/ *v.intr.* 1 make
or see a distinction. 2 treat unfavorably, esp.
on the basis of race, color, or sex. 3 (esp. as
discriminating *adj.*) observe distinction
carefully; have good judgment. See synonym
study at DISTINGUISH. □□ **dis•crim•i•nate•ly**
/-nətlee/ *adv.* **dis•crim•i•na′tion** *n.* **dis•**
crim•i•na•to•ry /-nətáwree/ *adj.*

■ 1 distinguish, separate, discern. 2 show
favor *or* prejudice. 3 be thoughtful, show diplomacy; (**discriminating**) see DISCRIMI-
NATING. □□ **discrimination** (in sense 2 of
DISCRIMINATE) bigotry, prejudice, bias, intolerance, unfairness.

dis•crim•i•nat•ing /diskríminayting/ *adj.* 1
able to discern, esp. distinctions. 2 having
good taste.

■ perceptive, keen, particular, refined, cultivated.

dis•cur•sive /diskórsiv/ *adj.* rambling or digressive. □□ **dis•cur′sive•ly** *adv.* **dis•cur′**
sive•ness *n.*

■ extensive, long, lengthy, wandering, circuitous, *colloq.* windy.

dis•cus /dískəs/ *n.* (*pl.* **dis′cus•es**) heavy disk
thrown in competition.

dis•cuss /diskús/ *v.tr.* talk or write about;
debate. □□ **dis•cuss′a•ble** *adj.* **dis•cus′sant**
n. **dis•cuss′er** *n.* **dis•cus•sion** /diskúshən/
n.

■ converse about, deliberate (over), review,
colloq. kick around; argue; see also DEBATE *v.*
□□ **discussion** conversation, talk, chat, dialogue, colloquy; debate, argument.

dis•dain /disdáyn/ • *n.* scorn; contempt.
• *v.tr.* 1 regard with disdain. 2 think oneself
superior to; reject (*disdained to enter, disdained answering*). □□ **dis•dain′ful** *adj.*

■ *n.* see CONTEMPT 1. • *v.* see DESPISE.

dis•ease /dizéez/ *n.* 1 unhealthy condition of
the body or the mind; illness; sickness.
2 corresponding condition of plants. 3 particular kind of illness.

■ 1 affliction, ailment, malady, complaint,
disorder. 2 blight, infestation. 3 cancer, virus, plague; infection.

dis•em•bark /disimbaárk/ *v.* put or go ashore
or land from a ship or an aircraft. □□ **dis•**
em•bar•ka′tion *n.*

■ alight, leave; debark, detrain, deplane.

dis•em•bow•el /disimbówəl/ *v.tr.* remove the
bowels or entrails of. □□ **dis•em•bow′el•**
ment *n.*

dis•en•chant /disinchánt/ *v.tr.* disillusion.
□□ **dis•en•chant′ing•ly** *adv.* **dis•en•chant′**
ment *n.*

■ see DISILLUSION *v.*

dis•en•cum•ber /dísinkúmbər/ *v.tr.* free
from encumbrance.

dis•en•fran•chise var. of DISFRANCHISE.

dis•en•gage /dísingáyj/ *v.* 1 a *tr.* detach,
free, loosen, or separate (parts, etc.) (*disengaged the clutch*). b *refl.* detach oneself; get
loose (*disengaged ourselves from their company*). 2 *tr. Mil.* remove (troops) from battle.
3 *intr.* become detached. 4 *intr.* (as **disengaged** *adj.*) a unoccupied; free; vacant.
b uncommitted, esp. politically. □□ **dis•en•**
gage′ment *n.*

■ *v.* 1 unfasten, release, disconnect, unlock, untie; (set) free, liberate; divide, part;
throw off, cut loose; (*disengage oneself*) get
out, get away. 3 separate, part, divide.
4 (**disengaged**) a see FREE *adj.* 3. b see
NEUTRAL *adj.* 1.

dis•en•tan•gle /dísintánggəl/ *v.* 1 *tr.* a unravel; untwist. b free from complications;
extricate. 2 *intr.* become disentangled.
□□ **dis•en•tan′gle•ment** *n.*

■ see STRAIGHTEN, EXTRICATE.

dis•fa•vor /disfáyvər/ *n.* 1 disapproval or dislike. 2 being disliked (*fell into disfavor*).

■ 1 displeasure, dissatisfaction. 2 low esteem *or* regard, dishonor; see also DISCREDIT
n. 1.

dis•fig•ure /disfígyər/ *v.tr.* spoil the appearance of; deform; deface. □□ **dis•fig′ure•**
ment *n.*

■ mar, damage, scar, mutilate, impair, distort, ruin.

dis•fran•chise /disfránchīz/ *v.tr.* (also **dis•**
en•fran•chise /disinfránchīz/) deprive of the
right to vote, be represented, etc. □□ **dis•**
fran′chise•ment *n.*

dis•gorge /disgáwrj/ *v.tr.* 1 vomit. 2 pour
forth; discharge (contents, ill-gotten gains,
etc.). □□ **dis•gorge′ment** *n.*

■ 1 see REGURGITATE 1.

dis•grace /disgráys/ • *n.* 1 shame; ignominy.
2 dishonorable, inefficient, or shameful person, thing, state of affairs, etc. • *v.tr.* bring
shame or discredit on. □ **in disgrace** having
lost respect or reputation; out of favor.
□□ **dis•grace′ful** *adj.* **dis•grace′ful•ly** *adv.*

■ *n.* 1 humiliation, embarrassment, dishonor. • *v.* humiliate, embarrass; degrade,
defame, scandalize. □ **in disgrace** *sl.* in the
doghouse; see also UNPOPULAR. □□ **dis•**
graceful shameful, humiliating, embarrassing, dishonorable, degrading, scandalous,
improper, unseemly.

dis•grun•tled /disgrúnt′ld/ *adj.* discontented; moody; sulky. □□ **dis•grun′tle•ment** *n.*

■ displeased, unhappy, dissatisfied, irritated, vexed, sullen, crotchety, *colloq.* fed up,
peeved, grouchy.

dis•guise /disgíz/ • *v.tr.* alter the appearance,
sound, smell, etc., of, so as to conceal the
identity; make unrecognizable (*disguised herself as a police officer, disguised the taste by
adding sugar*). • *n.* 1 costume, makeup, action, etc., used to conceal or deceive. 2 act
or practice of disguising; concealment of reality. □ **in disguise** 1 wearing a concealing
costume, etc. 2 appearing to be the opposite
(*a blessing in disguise*).

■ *v.* camouflage, cover up; misrepresent,

falsify. • n. 1 false identity, camouflage. 2 pretense, deception; cover-up, façade; see also DECEIT 1, MASQUERADE n. 1.

dis•gust /disgúst/ • n. [usu. foll. by at, for] strong aversion; repugnance. • v.tr. cause disgust in (their behavior disgusts me). □ in disgust as a result of disgust (left in disgust). □□ dis•gust'ed•ly adv. dis•gust'ing adj.

■ n. loathing, contempt, hatred; outrage, indignation. • v. sicken, offend, nauseate, repel, sl. gross out; outrage.

dish /dish/ • n. 1 a shallow, flat-bottomed container for cooking or serving food. b food served in a dish (all the dishes were delicious). 2 [in pl.] plates, cooking pots, etc., used for a meal. 3 a dish-shaped receptacle, object, or cavity. b = satellite dish. 4 sl. sexually attractive person. • v.tr. put (food) into a dish for serving. □ dish out sl. distribute, esp. carelessly or indiscriminately. dish up 1 serve or prepare to serve (food). 2 colloq. seek to present (facts, argument, etc.) attractively. □□ dish'ful n. (pl. ~fuls). dish•like adj.

■ n. 1 a see PLATE n. 1a. b see PLATE n. 1b.

dis•har•mo•ny /dis-haármənee/ n. lack of harmony; discord. □□ dis•har•mo•ni•ous /-mōneeas/ adj.

■ see DISCORD n. 1.

dis•heart•en /dis-haart'n/ v.tr. cause to lose courage or confidence. □□ dis•heart'en•ing•ly adv.

■ see DISCOURAGE 1.

di•shev•eled /dishévəld/ adj. (of the hair, a person, etc.) untidy; ruffled; disordered. □□ di•shev'el v. di•shev'el•ment n.

■ see UNTIDY.

dis•hon•est /disónist/ adj. fraudulent or insincere. □□ dis•hon'est•ly adv. dis•hon•es•ty /disónistee/ n.

■ untrustworthy, underhanded, shady, deceptive, deceitful, unprincipled, colloq. crooked, two-faced, hypocritical.

dis•hon•or /disónər/ • n. 1 shame or disgrace; discredit. 2 something that causes dishonor (a dishonor to her profession). • v.tr. 1 treat without honor or respect. 2 disgrace.

■ n. 1 disrespect, indignity, loss of face. 2 disgrace, insult. • v. 1 insult, abuse. 2 degrade, shame, see also DISGRACE v. 1.

dis•hon•or•a•ble /disónərəbəl/ adj. 1 causing disgrace. 2 unprincipled. □□ dis•hon'or•a•ble•ness n. dis•hon'or•a•bly adv.

■ 1 degrading, ignominious, shameful. 2 unscrupulous, untrustworthy, treacherous, traitorous, disloyal.

dish•pan /dishpan/ n. large, deep pan for washing dishes.

dish•wash•er /dishwoshər, -wawshər/ n. 1 machine for automatically washing dishes. 2 person employed to wash dishes.

dis•il•lu•sion /disilóōzhən/ • n. freedom from illusions; disenchantment. • v.tr. rid of illusions; disenchant. □□ dis•il•lu'sion•ment n.

■ n. disappointment. • v. disabuse, disappoint, enlighten, set straight, put right.

dis•in•cline /disinklín/ v.tr. 1 make reluctant. 2 (as disinclined adj.) unwilling; averse.

■ 2 (disinclined) reluctant, hesitant, loath, opposed.

dis•in•fect /dísinfékt/ v.tr. cleanse (a wound, a room, clothes, etc.) of infection. □□ dis•in•fect•ant /dísinféktənt/ n. & adj. dis•in•fec•tion /-fékshən/ n.

■ clean, purify, sanitize, fumigate, decontaminate, sterilize.

dis•in•for•ma•tion /dísinfərmáyshən/ n. false information, intended to mislead.

■ see LIE[2] n.

dis•in•gen•u•ous /dísinjényōōəs/ adj. having secret motives; insincere. □□ dis•in•gen'u•ous•ly adv. dis•in•gen'u•ous•ness n.

■ false, dishonest, tricky, devious, deceitful, underhanded, calculating, colloq. shifty.

dis•in•her•it /dísinhérit/ v.tr. reject as one's heir; deprive of the right of inheritance. □□ dis•in•her'i•tance n.

■ disown, cut off, reject.

dis•in•te•grate /disíntigrayt/ v. 1 separate into component parts or fragments. 2 lose or cause to lose cohesion. □□ dis•in•te•gra'tion n. dis•in•te•gra•tor n.

■ 1 break up or apart, shatter, crumble.

dis•in•ter /dísintér/ v.tr. (dis•in•terred, dis•in•ter•ring) remove (esp. a corpse) from the ground; unearth; exhume. □□ dis•in•ter'ment n.

dis•in•ter•est•ed /disíntristid, -intəri-/ adj. 1 not influenced by one's own advantage; impartial. 2 disp. uninterested. □□ dis•in'ter•est n. dis•in'ter•est•ed•ly adv. dis•in'ter•est•ed•ness n.

■ 1 unbiased, objective, fair, open-minded, detached, impersonal. 2 see INDIFFERENT 1, 2.

dis•joint /disjóynt/ • v.tr. 1 take apart at the joints. 2 (as disjointed adj.) (esp. of conversation) incoherent; desultory. • adj. (of two or more sets) having no elements in common. □□ dis•joint'ed•ly adv. dis•joint'ed•ness n.

■ v. 1 separate, disconnect, divide. 2 (disjointed) loose, confused, aimless, rambling, disorganized, unsystematic.

disk /disk/ n. (also disc) 1 a flat thin object. b round, flat or apparently flat surface (the sun's disk). 2 layer of cartilage between vertebrae. 3 a phonograph record. b = compact disc. 4 a (in full magnetic disk) round, flat computer storage device. b (in full optical disk) smooth nonmagnetic disk with large storage capacity for data recorded and read by laser. ■ disk (often disc) brake brake employing the friction of pads against a disk. disk drive Computing mechanism for reading or writing data from a disk on which it is stored digitally. disk (also disc) jockey presenter of a selection of phonograph records, compact discs, etc., of popular music, esp. in a broadcast.

■ 1 a see COUNTER[1] 2a, b. 3 see RECORD n. 3.

disk•ette /diskét/ n. Computing = floppy disk.

dis•like /dislík/ • v.tr. have an aversion to; not like. • n. 1 feeling of repugnance or not liking. 2 object of dislike. □□ dis•lik'a•ble adj. (also dis•like'a•ble).

■ *v.* mind, turn from; loathe, detest, *colloq.* hate. • *n.* **1** aversion; animosity; disgust; hostility. **2** see AVERSION 2.

dis•lo•cate /díslōkayt, dislō-/ *v.tr.* **1** disturb the normal connection of (esp. a joint in the body). **2** disrupt; put out of order. **3** displace. □□ **dis•lo•ca•tion** /díslōkáyshən/ *n.*
■ **1** see DISJOINT *v.* 1. **2, 3** see DISRUPT 1, DISPLACE.

dis•lodge /dislój/ *v.tr.* disturb or move. □□ **dis•lodg'ment** *n.* (also **dis•lodge'ment**).
■ see EXPEL 2.

dis•loy•al /dislóyəl/ *adj.* not loyal; unfaithful. □□ **dis•loy'al•ist** *n.* **dis•loy'al•ly** *adv.* **dis•loy'al•ty** *n.*
■ faithless, untrue, false, untrustworthy; treasonable, treacherous, unpatriotic, subversive; renegade.

dis•mal /dízməl/ *adj.* **1** gloomy; miserable. **2** dreary or somber (*dismal brown walls*). **3** *colloq.* feeble or inept (*a dismal performance*). □□ **dis'mal•ly** *adv.*
■ **1, 2** depressing, cheerless, melancholy; lugubrious, mournful, forlorn. **3** see FEEBLE 2.

dis•man•tle /dismánt'l/ *v.tr.* take to pieces; pull down.
■ see DEMOLISH 1a.

dis•may /dismáy/ • *v.tr.* discourage or depress; reduce to despair. • *n.* **1** anxiety. **2** depression or despair.
■ *v.* alarm, frighten, disconcert, unsettle. • *n.* consternation, agitation, fear. **2** see DEPRESSION 1b, DESPAIR *n.*

dis•mem•ber /dismémbər/ *v.tr.* **1** remove the limbs from. **2** partition or divide up. □□ **dis•mem'ber•ment** *n.*
■ **1** see MUTILATE 1. **2** see PARTITION *v.* 1.

dis•miss /dismís/ *v.* **1 a** *tr.* send away; cause to leave one's presence. **b** *intr.* (of an assembly, etc.) disperse; break ranks. **2** *tr.* discharge from employment, etc., esp. dishonorably. **3** *tr.* put out of one's thoughts. **4** *tr.* treat (a subject) summarily (*dismissed his application*). **5** *tr. Law* refuse further hearing to (a case). See synonym study at EJECT. □□ **dis•mis'sal** *n.*
■ **1** disband; release, discharge, let go. **2** oust, release, give notice, lay off, boot (out), *colloq.* sack, *sl.* fire. **3** reject, discount, scorn; belittle, pooh-pooh. □□ **dismissal** discharge, expulsion, *colloq.* walking papers, *sl.* the (old) heave-ho, release.

dis•mis•sive /dismísiv/ *adj.* disdainful. □□ **dis•mis'sive•ly** *adv.* **dis•mis'sive•ness** *n.*

dis•mount /dismównt/ *v.* **1** *intr.* alight from a horse, bicycle, etc. **2** *tr.* [usu. in *passive*] throw from a horse; unseat. • *n.* /dismównt, dís-/ dismounting.

dis•o•be•di•ent /dísəbeedeeənt/ *adj.* disobeying; rebellious. □□ **dis•o•be'di•ence** /-deeəns/ *n.* **dis•o•be'di•ent•ly** *adv.*
■ insubordinate, unruly, naughty, mischievous, bad, obstreperous, unmanageable, wayward, defiant.

dis•o•bey /dísəbáy/ *v.tr.* [also *absol.*] fail or

refuse to obey; disregard (orders) (*disobeyed his mother*). □□ **dis•o•bey'er** *n.*
■ defy, flout, ignore, resist, oppose, violate; mutiny, rebel, revolt.

dis•o•blige /dísəblíj/ *v.tr.* **1** refuse to consider the convenience or wishes of. **2** (as **disobliging** *adj.*) uncooperative.

dis•or•der /disáwrdər/ • *n.* **1** lack of order; confusion. **2** riot; commotion. **3** *Med.* ailment or disease. • *v.tr.* throw into confusion; disarrange.
■ *n.* **1** disarray, chaos, untidiness; mess, clutter, *colloq.* shambles. **2** tumult, disturbance, pandemonium. **3** illness, sickness, complaint. • *v.* upset, muddle, confuse.

dis•or•der•ly /disáwrdərlee/ *adj.* **1** untidy; confused. **2** irregular; unruly; riotous. □□ **dis•or'der•li•ness** *n.*
■ **1** chaotic, scrambled, messy, disorganized, cluttered, haphazard. **2** uncontrolled, undisciplined, rebellious, violent, rowdy, ungovernable.

dis•or•gan•ize /disáwrgəníz/ *v.tr.* **1** destroy the system or order of; throw into confusion. **2** (as **disorganized** *adj.*) lacking organization or system. □□ **dis•or•gan•i•za'tion** *n.*
■ **1** see JUMBLE *v.* 1.

dis•o•ri•ent /disáwreeənt/ *v.tr.* **1** confuse (a person) as to his or her bearings. **2** (often as **disoriented** *adj.*) confuse (a person).
■ (**disoriented**) bewildered, lost, adrift.

dis•own /disōn/ *v.tr.* **1** repudiate; disclaim. **2** renounce one's connection with or allegiance to.
■ see REPUDIATE 1a.

dis•par•age /dispárij/ *v.tr.* **1** criticize; belittle. **2** bring discredit on. □□ **dis•par'age•ment** *n.* **dis•par'ag•ing•ly** *adv.*
■ **1** diminish, depreciate, cheapen, run down, speak ill of. **2** slander, libel, dishonor, defame, malign, vilify, insult.

dis•pa•rate /díspərət, dispár-/ • *adj.* essentially different; without comparison or relation. • *n.* [in *pl.*] things so unlike that there is no basis for their comparison. □□ **dis'pa•rate•ly** *adv.* **dis'pa•rate•ness** *n.*

dis•par•i•ty /dispáritee/ *n.* (*pl.* **-ties**) inequality; difference; incongruity.
■ discrepancy, gap, unevenness, imbalance, dissimilarity.

dis•pas•sion•ate /dispáshənət/ *adj.* free from passion; calm; impartial. □□ **dis•pas'sion•ate•ly** *adv.* **dis•pas'sion•ate•ness** *n.*
■ cool, composed, self-possessed, unemotional, unmoved, serene, *colloq.* unflappable; fair, neutral, evenhanded.

dis•patch /dispách/ (also **des•patch'**) • *v.tr.* **1** send off to a destination or for a purpose. **2** perform (business, a task, etc.) promptly; finish off. **3** kill; execute. See synonym study at KILL. • *n.* **1** sending (a messenger, letter, etc.). **2** killing; execution. **3** also /díspach/ **a** official message on state or esp. military affairs. **b** news report. **4** promptness; efficiency (*done with dispatch*). □□ **dis•patch'er** *n.*
■ *v.* **1** mail, transmit, forward, ship. **2** get done, complete, *colloq.* knock off. **3** murder, dispose of, eliminate, *colloq.* polish off, *sl.* bump off; see also KILL *v.* 1a. • *n.* **1** see

TRANSMISSION 1. **2** murder, assassination. **3 b** communiqué, bulletin, story. **4** haste, speed, quickness.

dis•pel /dispél/ *v.tr.* **(dis•pelled, dis•pel•ling)** dissipate; disperse; scatter. See synonym study at SCATTER. □□ **dis•pel′er** *n.*

■ shed.

dis•pen•sa•ble /dispénsəbəl/ *adj.* **1** able to be done without; unnecessary. **2** that can be given out. □□ **dis•pen•sa•bil′i•ty** *n.*

■ **1** disposable, nonessential, unneeded, expendable.

dis•pen•sa•ry /dispénsəree/ *n.* (*pl.* **–ries**) place where medicines, etc., are dispensed.

■ see PHARMACY 1, INFIRMARY.

dis•pen•sa•tion /díspensáyshən/ *n.* **1 a** dispensing or distributing. **b** [foll. by *with*] the state of doing without (a thing). **c** something distributed. **2** exemption from a penalty or duty. **3** the ordering or management of the world by providence. □□ **dis•pen•sa′tion•al** *adj.*

■ **1 a** see ADMINISTRATION 4. **c** see SHARE *n.* **1**. **2** see *exemption* (EXEMPT).

dis•pense /dispéns/ *v.* **1** *tr.* distribute; deal out. **2** *tr.* administer (a sacrament, justice, etc.). **3** *tr.* make up and give out (medicine, etc.). **4** *intr.* [foll. by *with*] **a** do without; render needless. **b** give exemption from (a rule). □□ **dis•pens′er** *n.*

■ **1** give out, supply, provide, issue, apportion, allocate, *sl.* dish out. **2** discharge, apply, implement, enforce. **4 a** (*dispense with*) forgo, give up, relinquish, waive, forswear; do away with, get rid of, eliminate.

dis•perse /dispərs/ *v.* **1** *intr. & tr.* go, send, drive, or distribute in different directions or widely. **2** *intr.* (of people at a meeting, etc.) leave and go their various ways. **b** *tr.* cause to do this. **3** *tr.* put in circulation; disseminate. See synonym study at SCATTER. □□ **dis•pers′a•ble** *adj.* **dis•pers′al** *n.* **dis•pers′i•ble** *adj.* **dis•per′sion** *n.* **dis•per′sive** *adj.*

■ **1** spread, scatter; diffuse, break up. **2 a** disband, scatter. **b** dismiss, rout. **3** broadcast, send; see also CIRCULATE 2.

dis•pir•it /dispírit/ *v.tr.* **1** (esp. as **dispiriting** *adj.*) make despondent; discourage. **2** (as **dispirited** *adj.*) dejected; discouraged. □□ **dis•pir′it•ed•ly** *adv.* **dis•pir′it•ed•ness** *n.* **dis•pir′it•ing•ly** *adv.*

■ **1** see DEMORALIZE. **2** (**dispirited**) see MISERABLE 1.

dis•place /displáys/ *v.tr.* **1** shift from its accustomed place. **2** remove from office. **3** take the place of; oust. See synonym study at REPLACE. □ **displaced person** refugee because of war, persecution, etc.

■ **1** move, transfer; disturb, unsettle. **2** expel, unseat, eject, *colloq.* kick out, sack, *sl.* fire; see also DISMISS 2. **3** supplant, replace, succeed. □ **displaced person** see REFUGEE.

dis•place•ment /displáysmənt/ *n.* **1** displacing; being displaced. **2** *Physics* amount of a fluid displaced by a solid floating or immersed in it (*ship with a displacement of 11,000 tons*).

dis•play /displáy/ • *v.tr.* **1** expose to view; exhibit; show. **2** show ostentatiously. **3** allow

---

225 dispel ~ disproportionate

to appear; reveal; betray. • *n.* **1** displaying. **2** exhibition or show. **3** ostentation; flashiness. **4** mating rituals of some birds, fish, etc. **5 a** presentation of signals or data on a visual display unit, etc. **b** information so presented. □□ **dis•play′er** *n.*

■ *v.* **1** air, present; advertise, publicize. **2** flaunt, parade, flourish, *colloq.* flash. **3** unveil, disclose, demonstrate. • *n.* **1** show, demonstration, exposition. **2** presentation, array, spectacle, parade. **3** showiness, ceremony, pageantry.

dis•please /displéez/ *v.tr.* make indignant or angry; offend; annoy. □□ **dis•plea•sure** /displézhər/ *n.*

■ put out, dissatisfy, ruffle, *colloq.* miff, *sl.* bug; see also IRK.

dis•port /dispáwrt/ *v.* frolic; gambol; enjoy oneself (*disported on the beach, disported themselves in the ocean*).

■ see PLAY *v.* 1.

dis•pos•a•ble /dispózəbəl/ • *adj.* **1** intended to be used once, then thrown away. **2** that can be disposed of. • *n.* thing designed to be thrown away after one use. □ **disposable income** income after taxes, etc., available for spending.

■ *adj.* **1** throwaway, nonreturnable; paper, plastic. **2** usable.

dis•pos•al /dispózəl/ *n.* **1** disposing of something. **2** arrangement, disposition, or placing of something. □ **at one's disposal 1** available. **2** subject to one's orders or decisions.

■ **2** see DISPOSITION 2b.

dis•pose /dispóz/ *v.* **1** *tr.* **a** make willing; incline (*was disposed to release them*). **b** give a tendency to (*the wheel was disposed to buckle*). **2** *tr.* (as **disposed** *adj.*) have a specified mental inclination (*usu. in comb.*: *ill-disposed*). **3** *intr.* determine the course of events (*man proposes, God disposes*). □ **dispose of 1 a** deal with. **b** get rid of. **c** finish. **d** kill. **e** distribute; dispense; bestow. **2** sell.

■ **1** influence, persuade, induce, (*be disposed*) be inclined; tend, be willing. □ **dispose of 1 a, c** settle, sort out, conclude, complete. **b** discard, dump, scrap, junk, *colloq.* trash. **d** see KILL *v.* 1a. **e** give out, deal out, apportion, transfer. **2** see SELL *v.* 1.

dis•po•si•tion /díspəzíshən/ *n.* **1 a** natural tendency; inclination. **b** temperament or attitude. **2 a** setting in order. **b** arrangement.

■ **1 a** predisposition, susceptibility, preference. **b** character, attitude, nature. **2 b** organization, placement, disposal, grouping.

dis•pos•sess /díspəzés/ *v.tr.* **1** dislodge; oust (a person). **2** [usu. foll. by *of*] deprive. □□ **dis•pos•ses•sion** /–zéshən/ *n.*

■ **1** evict, expel, boot out. **2** deny, disallow; see also DIVEST 2.

dis•pro•por•tion /díprəpáwrshən/ *n.* lack of proportion. □□ **dis•pro•por′tion•al** *adj.* **dis•pro•por′tion•al•ly** *adv.*

■ inequality, unevenness, imbalance, asymmetry.

dis•pro•por•tion•ate /díprəpáwrshənət/ *adj.* **1** lacking proportion. **2** relatively too large or small, long or short, etc. □□ **dis•**

pro·por'tion·ate·ly adv. **dis·pro·por'tion·ate·ness** n.

■ unbalanced, asymmetrical, irregular; inconsistent; unfair, unequal, uneven.

dis·prove /dispróōv/ v.tr. prove false; refute.

■ invalidate, contradict, negate, rebut, discredit.

dis·put·a·ble /dispyōōtəbəl/ adj. open to question; uncertain. □□ **dis·put'a·bly** adv.

■ debatable, moot, doubtful, dubious, controversial.

dis·pu·ta·tion /díspyətáyshən/ n. **1 a** disputing; debating. **b** argument; controversy. **2** formal debate.

dis·pu·ta·tious /díspyətáyshəs/ adj. argumentative.

■ see ARGUMENTATIVE 1.

dis·pute /dispyōōt/ • v. **1** intr. **a** debate; argue. **b** quarrel. **2** tr. discuss, esp. heatedly. **3** tr. question the truth or correctness or validity of (a statement, alleged fact, etc.). **4** tr. contend for; strive to win (disputed the crown). • n. **1** controversy; debate. **2** quarrel. See synonym study at QUARREL. □ **beyond** (or **past** or **without**) **dispute 1** certainly; indisputably. **2** certain; indisputable. **in dispute 1** being argued about. **2** (of a workforce) involved in industrial action. □□ **dis·pu·tant** /-spyōōt'nt/ n. **dis·put'er** n.

■ v. **1** see ARGUE 1. **2** argue about, debate, wrangle over; see also DISCUSS. **3** challenge, impugn, deny. **4** see AIM v. 1, 4. • n. argument, disagreement, difference (of opinion), conflict.

dis·qual·i·fy /diskwólifī/ v.tr. (**-fies, -fied**) **1** debar or pronounce ineligible (disqualified from the race for taking drugs). **2** make or pronounce ineligible or unsuitable (his age disqualifies him for the job). **3** pronounce unqualified (disqualified from practicing as a doctor). □□ **dis·qual·i·fi·ca·tion** /diskwólifikáyshən/ n.

■ reject, exclude, bar, rule out, outlaw.

dis·qui·et /diskwíət/ • v.tr. deprive of peace; worry. • n. anxiety; unrest. □□ **dis·qui'et·ing** adj. **dis·qui'et·ing·ly** adv.

■ v. see PERTURB 2. • n. see ANXIETY 1, 2.

dis·qui·si·tion /diskwizíshən/ n. long or elaborate treatise or discourse on a subject.

■ see LECTURE n. 1.

dis·re·gard /dísrigaárd/ • v.tr. **1** pay no attention to; ignore. **2** treat as of no importance. See synonym study at NEGLECT. • n. indifference; neglect. □□ **dis·re·gard'ful** adj. **dis·re·gard'ful·ly** adv.

■ v. **1** overlook, pay no heed to, pass over. **2** make light of, underrate, dismiss. • n. inattention, nonobservance; disrespect, contempt, disdain.

dis·re·pair /dísripáir/ n. poor condition due to neglect.

■ decay, ruin, collapse, deterioration, ruination.

dis·rep·u·ta·ble /dísrépyətəbəl/ adj. **1** of bad reputation. **2** not respectable in appearance; dirty; untidy. □□ **dis·rep'u·ta·bly** adv.

■ **1** low, base, abject, unworthy, discredita-

ble. **2** disheveled, unkempt, slovenly, shabby, disordered.

dis·re·pute /dísripyōōt/ n. lack of good reputation or respectability; discredit (esp.fall into disrepute).

dis·re·spect /dísrispékt/ n. lack of respect; discourtesy. □□ **dis·re·spect'ful** adj. **dis·re·spect'ful·ly** adv.

■ rudeness, impoliteness; irreverence; see also impertinence (IMPERTINENT). □□ **disrespectful** unmannerly, impudent, colloq. fresh; see also IMPERTINENT.

dis·robe /disrṓb/ v.tr. & refl. [also absol.] divest (oneself or another) of a garment; undress.

■ bare oneself; see also STRIP[1] v. 1, 2.

dis·rupt /disrúpt/ v.tr. **1** interrupt the flow or continuity of (a meeting, speech, etc.). **2** separate forcibly; shatter. □□ **dis·rup·tion** /-rúpshən/ n. **dis·rup'tive** adj. **dis·rup'tive·ly** adv.

■ **1** disorder, upset; break in on. **2** see SEVER 2, SHATTER 1, 2. □□ **disruptive** see UNRULY.

diss /dis/ v.tr. sl. put (a person) down verbally; bad-mouth.

dis·sat·is·fy /dísátisfī/ v.tr. (**-fies, -fied**) (often as **dissatisfied** adj.) make discontented; fail to satisfy. □□ **dis·sat·is·fac·tion** /-fákshən/ n.

■ see DISPLEASE; (**dissatisfied**) unsatisfied, disgruntled. □□ **dissatisfaction** discontent, nonfulfillment, annoyance.

dis·sect /disékt, dī-/ v.tr. **1** cut up, esp. a plant or animal, to examine its parts, structure, etc., or a corpse for a post mortem. **2** analyze; criticize in detail. □□ **dis·sec·tion** /-sékshən/ n.

■ see ANALYZE 1, 2b.

dis·sem·ble /disémbəl/ v. **1** intr. conceal one's motives; talk or act hypocritically. **2** tr. **a** disguise or conceal (a feeling, intention, act, etc.). **b** simulate (dissembled grief in public).

dis·sem·i·nate /disémminayt/ v.tr. scatter about; spread (esp. ideas) widely. See synonym study at SCATTER. □□ **dis·sem·i·na·tion** /-náyshən/ n.

dis·sen·sion /disénshən/ n. disagreement.

■ dissent, discord, contention, strife, conflict.

dis·sent /disént/ • v.intr. **1** disagree. **2** differ, esp. from established or official opinion. • n. **1** difference of opinion. **2** refusal to accept established opinion; nonconformity. □□ **dis·sent'er** n. **dis·sent'ing** adj. **dis·sent'ing·ly** adv.

■ v. **1** see DIFFER 2. • n. **1** see DISSENSION.

dis·ser·ta·tion /dísərtáyshən/ n. detailed discourse, esp. one submitted toward a degree or diploma.

■ see ESSAY n. 1.

dis·serv·ice /dis-sə́rvis/ n. ill turn; injury.

■ wrong, unkindness, disfavor, injustice; harm, damage.

dis·si·dent /dísid'nt/ • adj. disagreeing, esp. with an established government, system, etc. • n. dissident person. □□ **dis'si·dence** n.

■ adj. dissenting, conflicting, unorthodox; see also REBELLIOUS 1. • n. dissenter, protester, rebel; revolutionary, insurgent.

dis•sim•i•lar /disímilər/ *adj.* unlike; not similar. □□ **dis•sim•i•lar•i•ty** /–láritee/ *n.* (*pl.* **–ties**).

■ different, distinct, contrasting. □□ **dissimilarity** disparity, distinction, discrepancy.

dis•si•pate /dísipayt/ *v.* **1 a** *tr.* cause (a cloud, vapor, fear, darkness, etc.) to disappear or disperse. **b** *intr.* disperse; scatter; disappear. **2** *tr.* squander (money, energy, etc.). See synonym study at SCATTER.

■ **1 a** scatter, dispel; shed. **b** spread out, be dispelled; evaporate, vanish. **2** waste, fritter away.

dis•si•pa•tion /dísipáyshən/ *n.* **1** intemperate, dissolute, or debauched living. **2** wasteful expenditure (*dissipation of resources*).

■ **1** intemperance, dissoluteness, dissolution, self-indulgence, overindulgence, hedonism, *dolce vita*, excess(es). **2** waste, wastefulness, profligacy, recklessness, extravagance, prodigality.

dis•so•ci•ate /dísósheeayt, –seeayt/ *v.* disconnect or become disconnected; separate (*dissociated her from their guilt*). □ **dissociate oneself from 1** declare oneself unconnected with. **2** decline to support or agree with (a proposal, etc.). □□ **dis•so•ci•a•tive** /–sheeətiv, –seeətiv/ *adj.*

■ cut off, sever, disjoin, disengage, detach, isolate.

dis•so•lute /dísəlळॊt/ *adj.* lax in morals; licentious.

■ debauched, corrupt, degenerate; see also IMMORAL 3.

dis•so•lu•tion /dísəlळॊshən/ *n.* **1** disintegration; decomposition. **2** undoing or relaxing of a bond, esp.: **a** marriage. **b** partnership. **c** alliance. **3** dismissal or dispersal of an assembly, esp. of a parliament. **4** death. **5** bringing or coming to an end; fading away; disappearance.

■ **1** separation, breakup; decay, ruin. **2** annulment, rescission; divorce. **3** adjournment, dissolving. **4** see DEATH 4a. **5** termination, conclusion; recess.

dis•solve /dizólv/ *v.* **1** *tr. & intr.* make or become liquid, esp. by dispersion in a liquid. **2** *intr. & tr.* disappear or cause to disappear gradually. **3 a** *tr.* dismiss (an assembly, esp. parliament). **b** *intr.* (of an assembly) be dissolved (cf. DISSOLUTION 3). **4** *tr.* annul or put an end to (a partnership, marriage, etc.). **5** *intr.* (of a person) become enfeebled or emotionally overcome (*dissolved into tears*). □□ **dis•solv•a•ble** *adj.*

■ **1** melt, disperse. **2** vanish, fade (away); see also ERODE. **3 a** break up, disperse. **b** adjourn, disband. **4** see CANCEL *v.* **5** collapse.

dis•so•nant /dísənənt/ *adj.* **1** *Mus.* harsh-toned; inharmonious. **2** incongruous; clashing. □□ **dis•so•nance** /–nəns/ *n.*

■ see INCONGRUOUS.

dis•suade /diswáyd/ *v.tr.* discourage (a person); persuade against (*was dissuaded from his belief*). □□ **dis•sua•sion** /–swáyzhən/ *n.* **dis•sua•sive** *adj.*

■ see DISCOURAGE 2.

dis•taff /dístaf/ *n.* **1** stick holding wool or flax

for spinning by hand. **2** corresponding part of a spinning wheel.

dis•tance /dístəns/ • *n.* **1** being far off; remoteness. **2** space or interval between two things. **3** distant point or place (*came from a distance*). **4** avoidance of familiarity; aloofness; reserve (*there was a certain distance between them*). • *v.tr.* [often *refl.*] **1** place far off (*distanced the painful memory*). **2** leave far behind in a race or competition. □ **go the distance 1** *Boxing* complete a fight without being knocked out. **2** complete, esp. a hard task; endure an ordeal. **keep one's distance** maintain one's reserve.

■ *n.* **2** gap, mileage, footage. **4** detachment, coolness, haughtiness • *v.* **1** separate, detach, set apart.

dis•tant /dístənt/ *adj.* **1 a** far away in space or time. **b** [usu. *predic.*] at a specified distance (*three miles distant from them*). **2** remote in position, time, resemblance, etc. (*a distant prospect, a distant relation, a distant likeness*). **3** not intimate; reserved; cool (*a distant stare*). **4** remote; abstracted (*a distant stare*). □□ **dis•tant•ly** *adv.*

■ **1 a** far-off, remote, outlying. **b** away, off. **3** aloof, detached, cold. **4** distracted, absent, detached.

dis•taste /dístáyst/ *n.* dislike; repugnance; aversion, esp. slight (*a distaste for polite company*). □□ **dis•taste'ful** *adj.* **dis•taste•ful•ly** *adv.* **dis•taste•ful•ness** *n.*

■ disfavor, antipathy; dissatisfaction, displeasure. □□ **distasteful** nasty, disagreeable; disgusting; revolting.

dis•tem•per /distémpər/ *n.* disease of some animals, esp. dogs, causing fever, coughing, and catarrh.

dis•tend /disténd/ *v.* swell out by pressure from within (*distended stomach*). □□ **dis•ten•sion** /–ténshən/ *n.*

■ see SWELL *v.* 3, INFLATE 1, 2.

dis•till /distíl/ *v.* **1** *tr. Chem.* purify (a liquid) by vaporizing it and condensing it. **2** *tr.* **a** *Chem.* extract the essence of (a plant, etc.) usu. by heating. **b** extract the essential meaning or implications of (an idea, etc.). **3** *tr.* make (whiskey, essence, etc.) by distilling raw materials. **4** *tr. Chem.* drive (the volatile constituent) off or out by heat. **5** *tr. & intr.* come as or give forth in drops; exude. **6** *intr.* undergo distillation. □□ **dis•til•late** /distilit, –áyt/ *n.* **dis•til•la•tion** /dístiláyshən/ *n.* **dis•till'er** *n.*

■ **2 b** see EXTRACT *v.* 5.

dis•till•er•y /distíləree/ *n.* (*pl.* **–ies**) place where alcoholic liquor is distilled.

dis•tinct /distíngkt/ *adj.* **1** not identical; separate; different. **2** clearly perceptible; definite. **3** unmistakable, decided (*had a distinct impression of being watched*). □□ **dis•tinct'ly** *adv.*

■ **1** discrete, distinguishable, unique; dissimilar, contrasting. **2** plain, vivid, evident, apparent, explicit. **3** see DEFINITE 2.

dis•tinc•tion /distíngkshən/ *n.* **1 a** discriminating or distinguishing. **b** difference made by distinguishing. **2** thing that differentiates.

3 honor, award, title, etc. 4 distinguished character; excellence; eminence (*a film of distinction*).

■ 1 a differentiation, separation. b see CONTRAST *n.* 2 distinctiveness; uniqueness, individuality. 3 see HONOR *n.* 1, PRESTIGE. 4 prominence, superiority, greatness, quality.

dis•tinc•tive /distíngktiv/ *adj.* distinguishing; characteristic. □□ **dis•tinc′tive•ly** *adv.* **dis• tinc′tive•ness** *n.*

■ unique, singular, individual, personal, peculiar.

dis•tin•guish /distínggwish/ *v.* 1 *tr.* see or draw distinctions between; differentiate. 2 *tr.* be a mark or property of; characterize (*distinguished by her greed*). 3 *tr.* discern (*could distinguish two voices*). 4 *tr.* make prominent or noteworthy (*distinguished himself by winning*). 5 *intr.* make or point out a difference between. □□ **dis•tin′guish•a•ble** *adj.*

■ 1 tell apart, separate; single out. 2 individualize, identify; define, designate. 3 sense, perceive, detect. 4 (*distinguish oneself*) see *stand out* 1. 5 differentiate, judge, decide.

SYNONYM STUDY: distinguish

DESCRY, DIFFERENTIATE, DISCERN, DISCRIMINATE. What we **discern** we see apart from all other objects (*to discern the lighthouse beaming on the far shore*). **Descry** puts even more emphasis on the distant or unclear nature of what we're seeing (*the lookout was barely able to descry a man approaching in the dusk*). To **discriminate** is to perceive the differences between or among things that are very similar; it may suggest that some aesthetic evaluation is involved (*to discriminate between two painters' styles*). **Distinguish** requires making even finer distinctions between or among things that resemble each other (*unable to distinguish the difference between the two shades of pink*), although *distinguish* can also mean recognizing by some special mark or outward sign (*the sheriff could be distinguished by his silver badge*). **Differentiate**, on the other hand, suggests the ability to perceive real, though often subtle, differences between things (*only constant practice enables the radar watcher to differentiate the different blips on the screen*). **Differentiate** is also widely used in medical contexts (*bone biopsies are necessary to differentiate osteoporosis from osteomalacia*). If you have trouble *differentiating* among these closely related verbs, you're not alone.

---

dis•tin•guished /distínggwisht/ *adj.* 1 eminent; famous. 2 dignified, elegant. □ **Distinguished Flying Cross** US military decoration for heroism or extraordinary achievement in aerial flight. **Distinguished Service Cross** US Army decoration for extraordinary heroism in combat. **Distinguished Service Medal** US military decoration for exceptionally meritorious service in a duty of great responsibility.

■ 1 celebrated, illustrious, noted. 2 noble, grand, stately.

dis•tort /distáwrt/ *v.tr.* 1 put out of shape. 2 misrepresent (motives, facts, statements, etc.). □□ **dis•tor′tion** *n.*

■ 1 twist, warp, deform; alter. 2 slant, color, misstate.

distr. *abbr.* 1 distribution. 2 distributor. 3 district.

dis•tract /distrákt/ *v.tr.* 1 draw away the attention of (a person, the mind, etc.). 2 bewilder; perplex. 3 amuse, esp. to take attention from pain or worry. □□ **dis•tract′ ed** *adj.* **dis•tract′ed•ly** *adv.* **dis•tract′ing** *adj.*

■ 1 divert, deflect, sidetrack, (*be distracted*) lose concentration. 2 confuse, confound, puzzle. 3 divert, occupy.

dis•trac•tion /distrákshən/ *n.* 1 a distracting, esp. the mind. b thing that distracts; interruption. 2 relaxation; amusement. 3 confusion; madness. □ **to distraction** almost to a state of madness.

■ 1 b see *interruption* (INTERRUPT). 2 diversion, entertainment, pastime, *colloq.* breather. 3 perplexity, bewilderment; disorder; see also *madness* (MAD), FRENZY *n.* 1.

dis•trait /distráy/ *adj.* (*fem.* **dis•traite** /–stráyt/) not paying attention; absentminded; distraught.

dis•traught /distráwt/ *adj.* extremely agitated.

■ distracted, upset, at wit's end; mad, insane, berserk.

dis•tress /distrés/ • *n.* 1 severe pain, sorrow, anguish, etc. 2 poverty. • *v.tr.* 1 subject to distress; exhaust; afflict. 2 cause anxiety to; make unhappy; vex. □ **distress signal** signal from a ship, aircraft, etc., in danger. **in distress** 1 suffering or in danger. 2 (of a ship, aircraft, etc.) in danger or damaged. □□ **dis•tress′ful** *adj.*

■ *n.* 1 anxiety, misery, suffering; desolation. 2 misfortune, difficulty. • *v.* bother, torment; see also TIRE[1] 1.

dis•tressed /distrést/ *adj.* 1 suffering from distress. 2 (of furniture, leather, etc.) aged, damaged, etc., artificially. □ **distressed area** 1 region needful of food, shelter, government aid, etc., due to flood, earthquake, hurricane, etc.

■ 1 see WORRY *v.* 4.

dis•trib•ute /distríbyoot/ *v.tr.* 1 give shares of; deal out. 2 spread about; scatter (*distributed the seeds evenly over the garden*). 3 divide into parts; arrange; classify. □□ **dis•tri•bu• tion** /distribyoóshən/ *n.*

■ 1 dispense, apportion, issue, *sl.* dish out. 2 disperse, strew, disseminate. 3 sort, class; see also DIVIDE *v.* 3c.

dis•trib•u•tor /distríbyətər/ *n.* 1 person or thing that distributes, esp. from a manufacturer to retailers. 2 *Electr.* device in an internal combustion engine for passing current to spark plugs.

dis•trict /distrikt/ • *n.* 1 [often *attrib.*] territory marked off for special administrative purposes. 2 area that has common characteristics; region (*wine-growing district*). • *v.tr.* divide into districts. □ **districts** prosecuting officer of a district. **district court 1** (in several US states) court of general jurisdiction. **2** federal trial court in each federal judicial district.

■ *n.* locality; section, precinct, community, ward.

dis·trust /distrúst/ • *n.* lack of trust; doubt; suspicion. • *v.tr.* have no trust in. □□ **dis·trust'ful** *adj.* **dis·trust'ful·ly** *adv.*

■ *n.* doubtfulness, uncertainty, skepticism. ● *v.* doubt, question, be skeptical of, suspect. □□ **distrustful** incredulous, skeptical, doubtful.

dis·turb /distúrb/ *v.tr.* **1** break the rest, calm, or quiet of. **2 a** agitate; worry. **b** irritate. **3** move from a settled position. □□ **dis·turb'ing** *adj.*

■ **1** agitate, unsettle, upset; interrupt; inconvenience. **2 a** trouble, disconcert, alarm. **b** irk, bother, pester, *colloq.* hassle. **3** disorder, disarrange, confuse. □□ **disturbing** upsetting, troubling, worrying, distressing.

dis·turb·ance /distúrbəns/ *n.* **1** disturbing; being disturbed. **2** tumult; uproar. **3** agitation; worry.

■ **1** disruption, upset, disorder; upheaval, interruption; turbulence, trouble. **2** commotion, outburst, hubbub, fracas, *colloq.* rumpus. **3** see ANXIETY 1, 2.

dis·use • *n.* /disyóōs/ **1** lack of use or practice; discontinuance. **2** disused state. • *v.tr.* /disyóōz/ (esp. as **disused** *adj.*) cease to use. ● **fall into disuse** cease to be used.

■ *v.* (**disused**) neglected; see also ABANDONED 1.

ditch /dich/ • *n.* **1** long, narrow excavated channel, esp. for drainage. **2** watercourse, stream, etc. • *v.* **1** *intr.* make or repair ditches. **2** *tr.* provide with ditches; drain. **3** *tr. sl.* leave in the lurch; abandon. ● **last ditch** see LAST[1].

■ *n.* see CHANNEL[1] 5a. ● *v.* **3** see DESERT 2.

dith·er /díthər/ • *v.intr.* **1** hesitate; be indecisive. **2** *dial.* tremble; quiver. • *n. colloq.* **1** state of agitation or apprehension. **2** state of hesitation, indecisiveness. □□ **dith'er·er** *n.*

■ *v.* **1** see HESITATE 1. **2** see FLUTTER *v.* 4.

dit·sy /dítsee/ *adj.* (also **dit·zy**; **dit·si·er**, **dit·si·est**; **dit·zi·er**, **dit·zi·est**) *colloq.* silly; scatterbrained. □□ **ditz** *n.*

dit·to /dítō/ • *n.* (*pl.* **-tos**) **1** (in accounts, inventories, lists, etc.) aforesaid; same. **2** *colloq.* (replacing a word or phrase to avoid repetition) the same (*came in late last night and ditto the night before*). • *v.tr.* (**-toes**, **-toed**) repeat (another's action or words). □ **ditto marks** quotation marks representing 'ditto.'

dit·ty /dítee/ *n.* (*pl.* **-ties**) short simple song.

■ see SONG.

di·u·ret·ic /díərétik/ • *adj.* causing increased output of urine. • *n.* diuretic drug.

di·ur·nal /dī-úrnəl/ *adj.* **1** of or during the day; not nocturnal. **2** daily; of each day. □□ **di·ur'nal·ly** *adv.*

div. *abbr.* division.

di·va /déevə/ *n.* (*pl.* **di·vas** or **di·ve** /-vay/) woman opera singer; prima donna.

■ see STAR *n.* 6.

di·van /diván, dī-/ *n.* long, low, backless sofa, often used as a bed.

■ see COUCH *n.*

dive /dīv/ • *v.* (**dived** or **dove** /dōv/) **1** *intr.* plunge head first into water. **2** *intr.* **a** *Aeron.* (of an aircraft) plunge steeply downward. **b** *Naut.* (of a submarine) submerge. **c** (of a person) plunge downward. **3** *intr.* [foll. by *into*] *colloq.* occupy oneself suddenly and enthusiastically with (a subject, meal, etc.). **4** *tr.* [foll. by *into*] plunge (a hand, etc.) into. • *n.* **1** diving; plunge. **2 a** submerging of a submarine. **b** steep descent of an aircraft. **3** sudden darting movement. **4** *colloq.* disreputable nightclub, bar, etc. □ **dive-bomb** bomb (a target) while diving in an aircraft. **diving bell** open-bottomed box or bell, supplied with air, in which a person can descend into deep water. **diving board** elevated board used for diving from. □□ **div'er** *n.*

■ *v.* **1, 2** jump, leap, plummet; go under, sink. **3** plunge; immerse oneself. • *n.* **1, 2** nosedive. **3** see DASH *n.* 1. **4** saloon, nightspot, *colloq.* honky-tonk, *sl.* joint.

di·verge /divúrj/ *v.* **1** *intr.* **a** spread out from a point (*diverging rays*). **b** take a different course. **2** *intr.* **a** depart from a set course (*diverged from his parents' wishes*). **b** differ. **3** *tr.* cause to diverge; deflect. □□ **di·ver'gence** *n.* **di·ver'gen·cy** *n.* **di·ver'gent** *adj.* **di·ver'gent·ly** *adv.*

■ **1** divide, fork, split. **b** see PART *v.* 1. **2 a** deviate, wander, diverge.

di·vers /dívərz/ *adj.* more than one; sundry; several.

■ various; miscellaneous, varied, assorted.

di·verse /dívórs, dī-/ *adj.* unlike; varied. □□ **di·verse'ly** *adv.*

■ divergent, miscellaneous, assorted; distinctive, different.

di·ver·si·fy /divúrsifī, dī-/ *v.* (**-fies, -fied**) **1** *tr.* make diverse; vary. **2** *tr. Commerce* spread (investment) over several enterprises or products, esp. to reduce risk. **3** *intr. esp. Commerce* (of a firm, etc.) expand the range of products handled. □□ **di·ver·si·fi·ca·tion** /-fikáyshən/ *n.*

■ **1** variegate, change, mix. **2** extend, branch out.

di·ver·sion /divúrzhən, dī-/ *n.* **1** diverting; deviation. **2 a** diverting of attention deliberately. **b** stratagem for this purpose (*created a diversion to secure their escape*). **3** recreation or pastime. □□ **di·ver'sion·ar·y** *adj.*

■ **1** redirection, deflection; modification. **2 b** distraction, interruption. **3** amusement, distraction, game; relaxation.

di·ver·si·ty /divúrsitee, dī-/ *n.* (*pl.* **-ties**) variety.

■ diverseness; difference, disparity; individuality.

di·vert /divúrt, dī-/ *v.tr.* **1 a** turn aside; deflect. **b** distract (attention). **2** (often as **di·verting** *adj.*) entertain; amuse.

■ **1 a** switch, redirect, sidetrack. **2** distract, occupy, absorb.

di·ver·tic·u·li·tis /dívertikyəlítis/ *n. Med.* inflammation of a diverticulum.

di·ver·tic·u·lum /dívertikyələm/ *n.* (*pl.* **di·ver·tic·u·la** /-lə/) *Anat.* blind tube forming at weak points in a cavity or passage, esp. of the alimentary tract.

di•vest /divést, dī–/ v. tr. **1** unclothe; strip (*divested himself of his jacket*). **2** deprive; dispossess; free; rid (*cannot divest herself of the idea*). □□ **di•vest′i•ture** n. **di•vest′ment** n.
   ■ **1** (*divest oneself of*) take or put off, remove. **2** strip, relieve, disencumber.

di•vide /divíd/ • v. **1** tr. & intr. separate or be separated into parts; break up; split (*the road divides, divided them into three groups*). **2** tr. & intr. distribute; deal; share. **3** tr. a cut off; separate (*divide the sheep from the goats*). **b** mark into parts (*ruler divided into inches*). **c** specify different kinds of; classify (*people can be divided into two types*). **4** tr. cause to disagree (*religion divided them*). **5** Math. a tr. find how many times a (number) contains another (*divide 20 by 4*). **b** intr. (of a number) be contained in a (number) without a remainder (*4 divides into 20*). • n. **1** dividing or boundary line. **2** watershed. □ **divided against itself** formed into factions. **the Great Divide 1** vast continental watershed between two drainage systems, esp. the Rocky Mountains of N. America. **2** boundary between life and death.
   ■ v. **1, 3** a partition, segregate; disconnect, detach. **2** parcel out, allocate, dispense. **3 c** categorize, sort, group. **4** alienate, set at odds, estrange. • n. **1** see BOUNDARY.

div•i•dend /dívidend/ n. **1** money to be divided among a number of persons, esp. that paid by a company to shareholders. **2** Math. number to be divided. **3** benefit (*their long training paid dividends*).
   ■ **1** see CUT n. 8.

div•i•na•tion /dívináyshən/ n. supposed supernatural insight into the future.
   ■ see PROPHECY 2.

di•vine /divín/ • adj. (**di•vin•er**, **di•vin•est**) **1 a** of, from, or like God or a god. **b** sacred. **2 a** more than humanly excellent. **b** colloq. excellent; delightful. v. **1** tr. discover by guessing, intuition. **2** tr. predict. **3** intr. practice divination. • See synonym study at PREDICT. • n. **1** theologian or clergyman. **2** (**the Divine**) God. □ **divine right of kings** doctrine that kings derive their authority from God. **divining rod** see DOWSE. □□ **di•vine′ly** adv.
   ■ adj. **1 a** godly, holy; heavenly. **b** sanctified. **2** superhuman, saintly. **b** marvelous, colloq. great, super, sl. awesome. • v. **1, 2** imagine, conjecture, foretell, foresee. • n. **1** priest, minister. **2** the Creator.

di•vin•i•ty /divínitee/ n. (pl. **–ties**) **1** being divine. **2 a** god; divine being. **b** (as **the Divinity**) God. **3** theology.
   ■ **1** see SANCTITY. **2 a** see GOD n. 1a.

di•vis•i•ble /divízibəl/ adj. capable of being divided, physically or mentally. □□ **di•vis•i•bil•i•ty** /–bílitee/ n.
   ■ see SEPARABLE.

di•vi•sion /divízhən/ n. **1** dividing; being divided. **2** Math. dividing one number by another (see also **long division** (see LONG¹), **short division**). **3** disagreement or discord (*division*

of opinion*). **4 a** one of two or more parts into which a thing is divided. **b** point at which a thing is divided. **5** unit of administration or organization. □ **division sign** sign (÷) indicating that one quantity is to be divided by another. □□ **di•vi′sion•al** adj.
   ■ **1** splitting, separation, segmentation. **3** conflict, breakup, split; see also DISSOLUTION 2. **2** see SEPARATION. • v. **2** cut off, break off, divide, part.

di•vi•sive /divísiv/ adj. tending to divide, esp. in opinion; causing disagreement. □□ **di•vi′sive•ly** adv. **di•vi′sive•ness** n.

di•vi•sor /divízər/ n. Math. number by which another is divided.

di•vorce /diváwrs/ • n. **1** legal dissolution of a marriage. **2** severance or separation (*divorce between thought and feeling*). • v. **1 a** tr. legally dissolve the marriage of. **b** intr. separate by divorce. **c** tr. end one's marriage with. **2** tr. detach; separate (*divorced from reality*).
   ■ n. **1** separation, breakup, split; see also DISSOLUTION 2. **2** see SEPARATION. • v. **2** cut off, break off, divide, part.

di•vor•cé /diváwrsáy/ n. divorced man.
di•vor•cée /diváwrsáy/ n. divorced woman.
div•ot /dívət/ n. piece of turf cut out by a golf stroke.

di•vulge /divúlj, dī–/ v. tr. disclose; reveal (a secret, etc.). □□ **di•vul′gence** n.
   ■ see DISCLOSE 1.

div•vy /dívee/ v. tr. colloq. (**–vies**, **–vied**) share out; divide up.

Dix•ie /díksee/ n. southern states of the US.

Dix•ie•land /díkseeland/ n. **1** = DIXIE. **2** jazz with a strong, two-beat rhythm and collective improvisation.

diz•zy /dízee/ • adj. (**diz•zi•er**, **diz•zi•est**) **1 a** giddy. **b** confused. **2** causing giddiness (*dizzy heights, dizzy speed*). • v. tr. **1** make dizzy. **2** bewilder. □□ **diz′zi•ly** adv. **diz′zi•ness** n.
   ■ adj. **1 a** unsteady, faint, colloq. woozy. **b** silly, scatterbrained; see also *in a daze* (DAZE n.). • v. **2** see BEWILDER, DISORDER v.

DJ abbr. **1** disk jockey. **2** district judge.

djel•la•ba /jəlaábə/ n. (also **djel•la′bah**, **jel′la′ba**) loose, hooded, usu. woolen cloak worn or as worn by Arab men.

DM abbr. (also **D-mark**) deutsche mark.

D.M.D. abbr. doctor of dental medicine.

DNA abbr. deoxyribonucleic acid, the material that carries genetic information in chromosomes. □ **DNA fingerprinting** identification, esp. in a legal case, by analysis of DNA from body tissue, hair, blood, etc.

do¹ /doo/ • v. (3rd sing. present **does** /duz/; past **did** /did/; past part. **done** /dun/) **1** tr. perform; carry out; complete (work, etc.) (*did his homework, there's a lot to do*). **2** tr. a produce; make (*I did a translation*). **b** provide (*do you do lunches?*). **3** tr. bestow; grant (*do me a favor*). **4** intr. act; behave; proceed (*do as I do*). **5** tr. work at; study (*what does your father do?*). **6 a** intr. be suitable or acceptable; suffice (*this dress won't do for a wedding*). **b** tr. satisfy; be suitable for (*that hotel will do me nicely*). **7** tr. deal with; put in order (*the barber will do you next*). **8** intr. **a** fare (*the patients were doing* *well*). **b** perform (*could do better*). **9** *tr.* **a** solve; work out (*we did the puzzle*). **b** [prec. by *can* or *be able to*] be competent at (*can you do cartwheels?*). **10** *tr.* **a** traverse (a certain distance) (*we did fifty miles today*). **b** travel at a specified speed (*he overtook us doing about eighty*). **11** *tr. colloq.* act or behave like (*did a Houdini*). **12** *intr.* **a** *colloq.* finish (*I'm done in the bathroom*). **b** (as **done** *adj.*) be over (*the day is done*). **13** *tr.* produce or give a performance of (*we've never done* Pygmalion). **14** *tr. colloq.* visit; see the sights of (*we did all the art galleries*). **15** *tr. colloq.* **a** (often as **done** *adj.*); [often foll. by *in*] exhaust; tire out (*the climb has completely done me in*). **b** beat up; defeat; kill. **c** ruin (*now you've done it*). **16** *tr. sl.* undergo (a specified term of imprisonment) (*he did two years for fraud*). **17** *tr. sl.* take (a drug). • *v.aux.* **1** [except with *be, can, may, ought, shall, will*] in questions and negative statements or commands (*do you understand?, I don't smoke, don't be silly*). **2** ellipt. or in place of verb (*you know her better than I do*). **3** forming emphasis (*I do want to, they did go*). • *n.* (*pl.* **dos** or **do's**) *colloq.* elaborate event, party, or operation. □ **do away with** *colloq.* **1** abolish. **2** kill. **do in 1** *sl.* **a** kill. **b** ruin; do injury to. **2** *colloq.* exhaust; tire out. **do-it-yourself** *adj.* (of work, esp. building, painting, decorating, etc.) done or to be done by an amateur at home. □ *n.* such work. **do over** *colloq.* redecorate, refurbish. **dos and don'ts** rules of behavior. **do up 1** fasten; secure. **2** *colloq.* **a** refurbish; renovate. **b** adorn; dress up. **do with** [prec. by *could*] would be glad to have; would profit by (*I could do with a rest*). **do without** manage without; forgo (-also *absol.*: *we shall just have to do without*). □□ **do•a•ble** *adj.*

do² /dō/ *n.* (also **doh**) *Mus.* (in tonic sol-fa) the first and eighth notes of a major scale.
DOA *abbr.* dead on arrival (at a hospital, etc.).
DOB *abbr.* date of birth.
Do•ber•man /dōbərmən/ *n.* (in full **Do'herman pin'scher** /pinshər/) large dog of a smooth-coated German breed.
doc /dok/ *n. colloq.* doctor.
do•cent /dōsənt/ *n.* well-informed guide, as in a museum.
doc•ile /dōsəl/ *adj.* submissive, easily managed. □□ **doc'ile•ly** *adv.* **do•cil•i•ty** /–silitee/ *n.*
 ■ see SUBMISSIVE.
dock¹ /dok/ • *n.* **1** waterway for loading, unloading, and repair of ships. **2** [in *pl.*] docks with wharves and offices; dockyard. **3** ship's berth, wharf. **4** = dry dock. • *v.* **1** *tr. & intr.* bring or come into a dock. **2 a** *tr.* join (spacecraft) together in space. **b** *intr.* (of spacecraft) be joined.
 ■ *n.* **2, 3** pier, jetty, quay; (*docks*) harbor. • *v.* **1** (drop) anchor, berth, moor.
dock² /dok/ *n.* enclosure in a criminal court for the accused. □ **in the dock** on trial.
dock³ /dok/ • *v.tr.* **1** cut short (an animal's tail). **2** deduct (a part) from wages, supplies, etc. • *n.* solid, bony part of an animal's tail.
dock•et /dókit/ *n.* **1** schedule of cases in a court of law. **2** list of things to be done.
dock•hand /dókhand/ *n.* longshoreman.

231   **do ~ dodge**

dock•side /dóksīd/ *n.* area adjacent to a dock.
dock•yard /dókyaard/ *n.* area with docks and equipment for building and repairing ships.
doc•tor /dóktər/ • *n.* **1 a** qualified practitioner of medicine; physician. **b** qualified dentist or veterinarian. **2** person who holds a doctorate. • *v. colloq.* **1 a** *tr.* treat medically. **b** *intr.* (esp. as **doctoring** *n.*) practice as a physician. **2** *tr.* fix up (machinery, etc.); mend. **3** *tr.* adulterate. **4** *tr.* tamper with; falsify. □ **Doctor of Philosophy** doctorate in a discipline other than education, law, medicine, or sometimes theology.
 ■ *n.* **1 a** MD, general practitioner, GP, *colloq. medic, sawbones.* • *v.* **1** attend, cure, heal. **2** repair, patch (up). **3** dilute; spike, drug, poison. **4** meddle with, disguise, change.
doc•tor•al /dóktərəl/ *adj.* of or for a degree of doctor.
doc•tor•ate /dóktərət/ *n.* highest university degree, often honorary.
doc•tri•naire /dóktrináir/ • *adj.* applying theory or doctrine dogmatically; theoretical and impractical. • *n.* pedantic theorist.
 ■ *adj.* see *pedantic* (PEDANT).
doc•trine /dóktrin/ *n.* **1** what is taught; body of instruction. **2 a** religious or political, etc., belief. **b** such principles, dogma. □□ **doc'trinal** *adj.*
doc•u•dra•ma /dókyōōdraamə, –dramə/ *n.* television movie based on real events.
doc•u•ment /dókyəmənt/ *n.* written evidence of events, agreement, ownership, etc. • *v.tr.* /dókyəment/ **1** prove by or support with documents. **2** record in a document.
 ■ *n.* paper, certificate, instrument. • *v.* chronicle, detail, describe; verify, certify, substantiate.
doc•u•men•ta•ry /dókyəméntəree/ • *adj.* **1** consisting of documents (*documentary evidence*). **2** providing a factual record or report. • *n.* (*pl.* **-ries**) documentary film, etc.
doc•u•men•ta•tion /dókyəmentáyshən/ *n.* **1** accumulation, classification, and dissemination of information. **2** material collected or disseminated. **3** collection of documents relating to a process or event, as instructions accompanying a computer program.
DOD *abbr.* Department of Defense.
dod•der /dódər/ *v.intr.* tremble or totter, esp. from age. □□ **dod'der•ing** *adj.*
 ■ see TOTTER *v.* □□ **doddering** feeble, shaky.
do•dec•a•gon /dōdékəgon/ *n.* plane figure with twelve sides.
do•dec•a•he•dron /dōdekəheédrən/ *n.* solid figure with twelve faces. □□ **do•dec•a•he'dral** *adj.*
dodge /doj/ • *v.* **1** *intr.* move quickly to elude a pursuer, blow, etc. (*dodged behind the chair*). **2** *tr.* evade by cunning or trickery. • *n.* **1** quick movement to avoid something. **2** clever trick or expedient. □□ **dodg'er** *n.*
 ■ *v.* **1** dart, sidestep, duck. **2** evade, escape from. • *n.* **2** subterfuge, scheme, ruse, *colloq.* ploy.

do•do /dṓdō/ *n.* (*pl.* **–does** or **–dos**) **1** extinct flightless bird. **2** old-fashioned, stupid, or inactive person. □ **as dead as a dodo 1** completely or unmistakably dead. **2** entirely obsolete.

DOE *abbr.* Department of Energy.

doe /dō/ *n.* female deer, reindeer, hare, or rabbit.

do•er /dṓǝr/ *n.* **1** person who does something. **2** one who acts rather than merely talking or thinking.

does *3rd sing. present* of DO[1].

does•n't /dúznt/ *contr.* does not.

dog /dawg, dog/ • *n.* **1** four-legged, flesh-eating animal of many breeds domesticated and wild, kept as pets or for work or sport. **2 a** *colloq.* despicable person. **b** *colloq.* person or fellow of a specified kind (*lucky dog*). **c** *sl. derog.* unattractive or slovenly woman. **3** mechanical device for gripping. • *v.tr.* (**dogged, dog•ging**) **1** follow closely and persistently; pursue; track. **2** *Mech.* grip with a dog. □ **dog days** hottest period of the year. **dog-eared** (of a book, etc.) with the corners worn or battered with use. **dog-eat-dog** *colloq.* ruthlessly competitive. **dog paddle** elementary swimming stroke like that of a dog. **Dog Star** chief star of the constellation Canis Major or Minor, esp. Sirius. **dog tag 1** usu. metal plate attached to a dog's collar, giving owner's address, etc. **2** identification tag, esp. as worn by a member of the military. **go to the dogs** *sl.* deteriorate, be ruined. **hair of the dog** further alcoholic drink to cure hangover from that drink. **put on the dog** *colloq.* behave pretentiously.

　■ *n.* **2 a** see VILLAIN. • *v.* **1** see PURSUE 1.

dog•catch•er /dáwgkachǝr, dóg–/ *n.* official who rounds up and impounds stray dogs in a community.

dog•fight /dáwgfīt, dóg–/ *n.* **1** close combat between fighter aircraft. **2** uproar; rough fight.

dog•fish /dáwgfish, dóg–/ *n.* (*pl.* same or **dog•fish•es**) kind of small shark.

dog•ged /dáwgid, dóg–/ *adj.* tenacious; grimly persistent. See synonym study at STUBBORN. □□ **dog′ged•ly** *adv.* **dog′ged•ness** *n.*

dog•ger•el /dáwgǝrǝl, dóg–/ *n.* poor or trivial verse.

dog•gy /dáwgee, dógee/ • *adj.* of or like a dog. • *n.* (also **dog•gie**) (*pl.* **–gies**) pet name for a dog. □ **doggy** (or **doggie**) **bag** bag for putting leftovers in to take home. □□ **dog′gi•ness** *n.*

dog•house /dáwghows, dóg–/ *n.* dog's shelter. □ **in the doghouse** *sl.* in disgrace or disfavor.

do•gie /dṓgee/ *n.* motherless or neglected calf.

dog•ma /dáwgmǝ, dóg–/ *n.* **1** principle, tenet, or creed, esp. of a church or political party. **2** arrogant declaration of opinion.

　■ **1** see PRINCIPLE 1, CODE *n.* 3.

dog•mat•ic /dawgmátik, dog–/ *adj.* **1 a** (of a person) asserting or imposing opinions; arrogant. **b** intolerantly authoritative. **2** of or in the nature of dogma; doctrinal. □□ **dog•mat′i•cal•ly** *adv.*

　■ **1** arbitrary, dictatorial, pontifical, imperious, *colloq.* pushy.

dog•ma•tism /dáwgmǝtizǝm, dóg–/ *n.* tendency to be dogmatic. □□ **dog′ma•tist** *n.*

　■ see *intolerance* (INTOLERANT).

do-good•er /dṓgŏŏdǝr/ *n.* well-meaning but unrealistic philanthropist or reformer.

dog•wood /dáwgwŏŏd, dóg–/ *n.* type of flowering tree or shrub.

doi•ly /dóylee/ *n.* (also **doy•ley**) (*pl.* **–lies** or **–leys**) small ornamental mat of paper, lace, etc., on a plate for cakes, etc.

do•ing /dṓing/ *n.* **1** [usu. in *pl.*] action; performance of a deed (*it was my doing*). **2** activity; effort (*it takes a lot of doing*).

Dol•by /dólbee/ *n. propr.* electronic noise-reduction system used esp. in tape recording to reduce hiss.

dol•drums /dóldrǝmz/ *n.pl.* [usu. prec. by *the*] **1** low spirits. **2** period of inactivity. **3** equatorial ocean region of calms, sudden storms, and light winds.

　■ **1** see GLOOM *n.* 2.

dole /dōl/ • *n.* **1** [usu. prec. by *the*] unemployment benefits. **2** charitable distribution. • *v.tr.* [usu. foll. by *out*] deal out sparingly. □ **on the dole** *colloq.* receiving welfare, etc., payments from the government.

　■ *n.* **2** apportionment, allocation, dispensation. • *v.* distribute, hand out, dispense, *sl.* dish out.

dole•ful /dólfŏŏl/ *adj.* **1** mournful; sad. **2** dreary; dismal. See synonym study at GLUM. □□ **dole′ful•ly** *adv.* **dole′ful•ness** *n.*

　■ **1** sorrowful, melancholy, gloomy. **2** cheerless, joyless, somber; see also DISMAL 1, 2.

doll /dol/ • *n.* **1** small model of a human figure, as a child's toy. **2** *sl.* young woman, esp. an attractive one. • *v.* [foll. by *up*; often *refl.*] dress up smartly.

dol•lar /dólǝr/ *n.* chief monetary unit in the US, Canada, and Australia, etc. □ **dollar sign** sign ($) used to indicate currency in dollars.

doll•house /dólhows/ *n.* miniature toy house for dolls.

dol•lop /dólǝp/ • *n.* shapeless lump of food, etc. • *v.tr.* [usu. foll. by *out*] serve in large, shapeless quantities.

dol•ly /dólee/ • *n.* (*pl.* **–lies**) **1** child's name for a doll. **2** movable platform for a movie camera. **3** small cart for freight. • *v.* (**–lies, –lied**) *intr.* move a motion-picture or television camera about while shooting.

dol•men /dólmǝn/ *n.* megalithic tomb with a large, flat stone laid on upright ones.

do•lo•mite /dólǝmīt, dól–/ *n.* mineral or rock of calcium magnesium carbonate.

dol•phin /dólfin/ *n.* porpoiselike sea mammal having a slender, beaklike snout.

dolt /dōlt/ *n.* stupid person. □□ **dolt′ish** *adj.*

　■ fool, ass, blockhead, *colloq.* moron, imbecile, *sl.* jerk, dope, dumbbell.

-dom /dǝm/ *suffix* forming nouns denoting: **1** state or condition (*freedom*). **2** rank or status (*earldom*). **3** domain (*kingdom*). **4** class of people (or their attitudes, etc.) (*officialdom*).

do•main /dōmáyn/ *n.* **1** area under one rule; realm. **2** sphere of control or influence.

■ **1** dominion, territory, kingdom, empire. **2** province, field, specialty.

dome /dōm/ • *n.* **1** rounded vault as a roof; large cupola. **2** natural vault or canopy (of the sky, trees, etc.). **3** *Geol.* dome-shaped structure. **4** *sl.* the head. • *v.tr.* (usu. as **domed** *adj.*) cover with or shape as a dome. □□ **dome′like** *adj.*

■ *n.* **4** see HEAD *n.* 1.

do•mes•tic /dōméstik/ • *adj.* **1** of the home, household, or family affairs. **2 a** of one's own country. **b** homegrown or homemade. **3** (of an animal) tamed. • *n.* household servant. □ **domestic partner** person who is living with another in a close personal and sexual relationship. □□ **do•mes′ti•cal•ly** *adv.*

■ *adj.* **1** private, residential. **2 a** native, indigenous. **3** tame, housebroken, trained. ■ *n.* housekeeper, cleaner.

do•mes•ti•cate /dōméstikayt/ *v.tr.* **1** tame (an animal) to live with humans. **2** accustom to home life and management. □□ **do•mes′ti•ca•tion** /-káyshən/ *n.*

■ **1** see TAME *v.* 1.

do•mes•tic•i•ty /dōməstisítee/ *n.* **1** being domestic. **2** domestic or home life.

dom•i•cile /dómisil, -sīl, dō-/ (also **dom•i•cil** /-sil/) • *n.* dwelling place; one's home; residence. • *v.tr.* (usu. as **domiciled** *adj.*) establish or settle in a place.

■ *n.* abode, house, (living) quarters, *colloq.* pad, digs. • *v.* house, locate, lodge; (**domiciled**) see RESIDENT *adj.* 1.

dom•i•nant /dóminənt/ • *adj.* dominating; prevailing; most influential. • *n. Mus.* fifth note of the diatonic scale of any key. □□ **dom′i•nance** *n.* **dom′i•nant•ly** *adv.*

■ *adj.* commanding, authoritative, controlling, predominant, chief, principal.

dom•i•nate /dóminayt/ *v.* **1** *tr. & intr.* command; control (*fear dominated them, dominates over his friends*). **2** *intr.* (of a person, sound, feature of a scene, etc.) be the most influential or conspicuous. **3** *tr. & intr.* (of a building, etc.) have a commanding position over; overlook. □□ **dom•i•na′tion** *n.* **dom′i•na•tor** *n.*

■ **1** govern, rule, direct, *colloq.* run the show. **2** preponderate, stand out, stick out. **3** rise above, overshadow. □□ **domination** authority, control, rule, power, influence, supremacy, ascendancy, hegemony; subjection, suppression, enslavement.

dom•i•neer /dómineer/ *v.intr.* (often as **domineering** *adj.*) behave in an arrogant and overbearing way. □□ **dom•i•neer′ing•ly** *adv.*

■ tyrannize over; (**domineering**) arrogant, autocratic, authoritarian, *colloq.* bossy, pushy.

do•min•ion /dəmínyən/ *n.* **1** sovereignty; control. **2** territory of a sovereign or government; domain. See synonym study at JURISDICTION.

■ **1** rule, authority, dominance. **2** region, area, country.

dom•i•no /dómino/ *n.* (*pl.* **–noes** or **–nos**) **1 a** small oblong piece marked with 0–6 dots

in each half. **b** [in *pl.*, usu. treated as *sing.*] game played with these. **2** mask for the eyes. □ **domino theory** theory that one event will cause similar events, like a row of falling dominoes.

don[1] /don/ *n.* **1** university teacher, esp. a senior member of a college at Oxford or Cambridge. **2** (**Don**) Spanish title of respect.

don[2] /don/ *v.tr.* (**donned, don•ning**) put on (clothing).

■ see *put on* 1 (PUT[1]).

do•nate /dṓnayt, dōnáyt/ *v.tr.* give (money, etc.), esp. voluntarily to charity. See synonym study at GIVE. □□ **do′na•tor** *n.*

■ provide, contribute, pledge, bestow, bequeath.

do•na•tion /dōnáyshən/ *n.* **1** donating. **2** thing, esp. money, donated.

■ **1** giving, contribution. **2** gift, contribution, bequest.

done /dun/ *past part.* of DO[1]. *adj.* **1** completed. **2** cooked. **3** *colloq.* socially acceptable (*the done thing*). **4** [often with *in, up*] *colloq.* tired out. □ **be done with** be finished with. **done for** *colloq.* in serious trouble.

Don Juan /don waan, hwaan, jǒŏan/ *n.* seducer of women.

don•key /dóngkee, dúng–, dáwng–/ *n.* (*pl.* **–keys**) **1** domestic ass. **2** *colloq.* stupid or foolish person.

don•ny•brook /dóneebrŏŏk/ *n.* uproar; wild fight.

do•nor /dṓnər/ *n.* **1** person who gives or donates something (e.g., to a charity). **2** one who provides blood for a transfusion, semen for insemination, or an organ or tissue for transplantation.

■ **1** supplier, benefactor, contributor, supporter, patron.

don't /dōnt/ • *contr.* do not. • *n.* prohibition (*dos and don'ts*).

do•nut var. of DOUGHNUT.

doo•dad /dōōdad/ *n.* **1** fancy article or ornament. **2** gadget.

doo•dle /dōōd'l/ • *v.intr.* scribble or draw, esp. absentmindedly. • *n.* scrawl or drawing made. □□ **doo′dler** *n.*

doom /dōōm/ • *n.* **1 a** grim fate or destiny. **b** death or ruin. **2** condemnation; judgment or sentence. • *v.tr.* **1** [usu. foll. by *to*] condemn or destine (*city doomed to destruction*). **2** (esp. as **doomed** *adj.*) consign to misfortune or destruction.

■ *n.* **1** fortune, lot; downfall, destruction. **2** see SENTENCE *n.* 1. • *v.* **1** see DESTINE. **2** (**doomed**) fated, cursed, damned; ill-fated, bewitched.

dooms•day /dōōmzday/ *n.* day of the Last Judgment.

door /dawr/ *n.* **1 a** movable barrier for closing and opening an entrance to a building, room, cupboard, etc. **b** this as representing a house, etc. (*lives two doors away*). **2 a** entrance or exit; doorway. **b** means of access. □ **door prize** prize awarded usu. by lottery at a dance, charity event, etc. **door-to-door** (of selling, etc.) done at each house in turn. □□ **doored** *adj.* [also in *comb.*].

■ **1 a, 2** see ENTRY 3.

door•bell /dáwrbel/ *n.* bell in a house, etc., rung by visitors outside to signal their arrival.

door•knob /dáwrnob/ *n.* knob turned to open a door.

door•man /dáwrman, –mən/ *n.* (*pl.* **–men**) person on duty at the door to a large building.

door•mat /dáwrmat/ *n.* **1** mat at an entrance for wiping shoes. **2** submissive person.

door•step /dáwrstep/ *n.* step leading up to the outer door of a house, etc. □ **on one's** (or **the**) **doorstep** very close.

■ see THRESHOLD 1.

door•stop /dáwrstop/ *n.* device for keeping a door open or to prevent it from striking a wall, etc., when opened.

door•way /dáwrway/ *n.* opening filled by a door.

doo•zy /dóozee/ *n.* (*pl.* **doo•zies**) (also **doo′ zie**) *colloq.* one that is outstanding of its kind (*a mistake that was a doozy*).

dope /dōp/ • *n.* **1** varnish. **2** thick liquid used as a lubricant, etc. **3** substance added to gasoline, etc., to increase its effectiveness. **4 a** *sl.* narcotic; stupefying drug. **b** drug, etc., given to a horse, athlete, etc., to affect performance. **5** *sl.* stupid person. **6** *sl.* information. • *v.* **1** *tr.* administer dope to; drug. **2** *tr.* smear; daub; apply dope to. **3** *intr.* take addictive drugs.

■ *n.* **4 a** opiate, hallucinogen, *sl.* upper, downer. **5** see DOLT. **6** data, news, *colloq.* lowdown. • *v.* **2** see SMEAR *v.* 1.

dope•y /dópee/ *adj.* (also **dop′y**) (**dop•i•er**, **dop•i•est**) *colloq.* **1 a** half asleep. **b** stupefied by or as if by a drug. **2** stupid; silly. □□ **dop′i•ly** *adv.* **dop′i•ness** *n.*

■ **1 b** see GROGGY. **2** see STUPID *adj.* 1.

Dop•pler ra′dar /dóplər/ *n.* radar system to determine velocity and location, as of storm clouds, etc.

Dor•ic /dáwrik, dór–/ *Archit. adj.* of the oldest, sturdiest, and simplest of the Greek architectural styles. • *n.* Doric order or style.

dork /dawrk/ *n. sl.* dull, slow-witted, or oafish person. □□ **dork′y** *adj.*

dor•mant /dáwrmənt/ *adj.* **1** inactive; sleeping. **2 a** (of a volcano, etc.) temporarily inactive. **b** (of faculties, etc.) in abeyance. **3** (of plants) alive but not growing. See synonym study at LATENT. □□ **dor′man•cy** *n.*

■ **1** resting, quiet, still, motionless, hibernating. **2 b** latent, potential, hidden; see also ABEYANCE.

dor•mer /dáwrmər/ *n.* (in full **dor′mer win′ dow**) projecting upright window in a sloping roof.

dor•mi•to•ry /dáwrmitáwree/ *n.* (*pl.* **–ries**) group sleeping area or building, esp. in a school or institution.

dor•mouse /dáwrmows/ *n.* (*pl.* **dor•mice**) small, mouselike hibernating rodent having a long, bushy tail.

dor•sal /dáwrsəl/ *adj. Anat., Zool. & Bot.* of, on, or near the back (cf. VENTRAL). □□ **dor′ sal•ly** *adv.*

do•ry /dáwree/ *n.* (*pl.* **–ries**) flat-bottomed fishing boat with high bow and flaring sides.

DOS /dos, daws/ *n. Computing* software operating system for personal computers.

dos•age /dósij/ *n.* **1** giving of a dose. **2** size of a dose.

dose /dōs/ • *n.* **1** single portion of medicine. **2** quantity of something experienced (e.g., work, praise, punishment, etc.). **3** amount of radiation received. **4** *sl.* venereal infection. • *v.tr.* **1** treat (a person or animal) with doses of medicine. **2** give a dose or doses to.

■ *n.* **2** portion, amount, measure. • *v.* **1** see TREAT *v.* 3.

dos•si•er /dósee-ay, dáw–/ *n.* file of specific information about a person, event, or subject.

DOT *abbr.* Department of Transportation.

dot /dot/ • *n.* **1 a** small spot, speck, or mark. **b** such a mark as part of an *i* or *j*, as a diacritical mark, as one of a series of marks to signify omission, or as a period. **c** decimal point. **2** shorter signal of the two in Morse code (cf. DASH *n.* 8). **3** tiny or apparently tiny object (*a dot on the horizon*). • *v.tr.* (**dot•ted**, **dot•ting**) **1 a** mark with a dot or dots. **b** place a dot over (a letter). **2** partly cover as with dots (*an ocean dotted with ships*). □ **dot the i's and cross the t's** *colloq.* **1** be minutely accurate. **2** add final touches to a task, exercise, etc. **dot-matrix printer** *Computing* printer with characters formed from dots. **dotted line** line of dots on a document, esp. to show a place for a signature. **on the dot** exactly on time.

■ *n.* **3** spot, speck, fleck. • *v.* **1 a, 2** spot, speckle.

dot•age /dótij/ *n.* feeble-minded senility (*in his dotage*).

do•tard /dótərd/ *n.* senile person.

dot-com /dótkom / • *n.* company whose primary business is conducted over the Internet (with reference to the ".com" at the end of many Internet addresses). • *adj.* of or relating to such a company.

dote /dōt/ *v.intr.* be excessively fond of. □□ **dot′ing•ly** *adv.*

■ love, idolize, adore; pamper, spoil.

dou•ble /dúbəl/ • *adj.* **1** consisting of two parts, things, levels, etc. **2** twice as much or many. **3** twice the usual size, quantity, strength, etc. **4** designed for two people (*double bed*). • *adv.* **1** at or to twice the amount, etc. **2** two together. • *n.* **1** double quantity. **2** counterpart; person who looks exactly like another. **3** [*pl.*] game between two pairs of players. • *v.* **1** *tr.* make or become double; multiply by two. **2** *tr.* amount to twice as much as. **3 a** *tr.* fold or bend (paper, cloth, etc.) over on itself. **b** *intr.* become folded. **4** *intr.* play a twofold role. □ **double agent** one who spies simultaneously for two rival countries, etc. **double back** turn back in the opposite direction. **double-blind** (of a test or experiment) in which neither the tester nor the subject has knowledge of identities, etc., that might lead to bias. **double-cross** deceive or betray (a person one is supposedly helping). **double cross** act of double-crossing. **double-**

double-dealing n. deceit, esp. in business. adj. deceitful; practicing deceit. **double-decker** colloq. anything consisting of two layers. **double Dutch** synchronized jump-rope game using two ropes. **double eagle** Golf score of three strokes under par at any hole. **double play** Baseball putting out two runners. **double standard** rule or principle applied more strictly to some people than to others (or to oneself). **double take** delayed reaction to a situation, etc., immediately after one's first reaction. **double-talk** verbal expression that is (usu. deliberately) ambiguous or misleading. **double up 1** be overcome with pain or laughter. **2** share or assign to a room, quarters, etc., with another or others. **on the double** running; hurrying. □□ **dou'bler** n. **dou'bly** adv.
■ adj. **1** paired, coupled, duplicate(d), doubled; twofold; dual. ■ n. **2** twin, duplicate, copy, replica, facsimile, clone, look-alike, colloq. spitting image.

dou·ble en·ten·dre /dúbəl aantaándrə, dŏŏblaan taáNDrə/ n. **1** word or phrase open to two interpretations, one usu. risqué or indecent. **2** humor using such.

dou·blet /dúblit/ n. **1** one of a pair of similar things. **2** hist. man's short, close-fitting jacket.

dou·bloon /dublŏŏn/ n. hist. Spanish gold coin.

doubt /dowt/ ● n. **1** uncertainty; undecided state of mind. **2** inclination to disbelieve. **3** uncertain state of things. **4** lack of full proof. ● v. **1** tr. feel uncertain or undecided about. **2** tr. hesitate to believe or trust. **3** intr. feel uncertain or undecided. **4** tr. call in question. □ **doubting Thomas** skeptical person (after John 20:24–29). **no doubt** certainly, probably. **without doubt** (or a doubt) certainly. □□ **doubt'er** n. **doubt'ing·ly** adv.
■ n. **1** hesitation, misgiving, reservation(s), qualm(s), anxiety, worry, apprehension, disquiet, fear; indecision. **2** distrust, mistrust, suspicion, incredulity, skepticism. ● v. **2** disbelieve, discredit, mistrust, distrust, have misgivings about, question, suspect. **3** hesitate, have reservations. □ **no doubt** see undoubtedly (UNDOUBTED), probably (PROBABLE). **without doubt** see undoubtedly (UNDOUBTED).

doubt·ful /dówtfŏŏl/ adj. **1** feeling doubt. **2** causing doubt. **3** unreliable. □□ **doubt'ful·ly** adv.
■ **1** skeptical, unconvinced, distrustful, suspicious, uncertain, unsure. **2** in doubt, dubious, questionable, debatable; unsettled, unresolved; indefinite, unclear, anybody's guess, up in the air. **3** see UNRELIABLE.

SYNONYM STUDY: **doubtful**

AMBIGUOUS, DUBIOUS, ENIGMATIC, EQUIVOCAL, PROBLEMATIC, QUESTIONABLE. If you are **doubtful** about the outcome of a situation, you might be understandably **dubious** about getting involved in it. While all of these adjectives express suspicion, indecision, or a lack of clarity, **doubtful** carries such strong connotations of uncertainty that the thing

being described is as good as worthless, unsound, invalid, unlikely, or doomed to fail (it was doubtful that the plane could land safely). **Dubious** is not quite as strong, suggesting suspicion, mistrust, or hesitation (a dubious reputation). It can also mean inclined to doubt or full of hesitation. If you're **doubtful** about the outcome of a particular situation, it means that you are fairly certain it will not turn out well. If you're **dubious**, on the other hand, it means that you're wavering or hesitating in your opinion. **Questionable** may merely imply the existence of doubt (a questionable excuse), but like **dubious**, it also has connotations of dishonesty and immorality (a place where questionable activities were going on). **Problematic**, in contrast to both **dubious** and **questionable**, is free from any suggestion of moral judgment or suspicion. It is applied to things that are genuinely uncertain, and to outcomes that are as likely to be positive as negative (getting everyone in the family to agree could be problematic). **Ambiguous** and **equivocal** refer to lack of clarity. But while **ambiguous** can refer to either an intentional or unintentional lack of clarity (her ambiguous replies to our questions), **equivocal** suggests an intentional wish to remain unclear (his equivocal responses indicated that he wasn't keen to cooperate). It can also mean capable of different interpretations (an equivocal statement that could be taken to mean opposite things). Something that is **enigmatic** is likely to be intentionally unclear as well (an enigmatic statement designed to provoke controversy), although **enigmatic** can also mean perplexing or mysterious.

---

doubt·less /dówtlis/ adv. **1** certainly, no doubt. **2** probably. □□ **doubt'less·ly** adv.
■ **1** undoubtedly, indubitably, indisputably, unquestionably, surely, for certain, naturally, without (a) doubt, beyond or without (a shadow of) a doubt. **2** most or very likely, in all probability or likelihood.

douche /dŏŏsh/ ● n. **1** jet of liquid applied to a body part for cleansing or medicinal purposes. **2** device for producing this. ● v. **1** tr. treat with a douche. **2** intr. use a douche.

dough /dō/ n. **1** thick mixture of flour, etc., and liquid for baking. **2** sl. money. □□ **dough'y** adj.
■ **2** see MONEY 1.

dough·boy /dóboy/ n. United States infantryman, esp. in World War I.

dough·nut /dónut/ n. (also **do'nut**) small fried cake of sweetened dough, usu. ring-shaped.

dough·ty /dówtee/ adj. (**dough·ti·er**, **dough·ti·est**) literary valiant; stouthearted. □□ **dough'ti·ly** adv. **dough'ti·ness** n.

Doug·las fir /dúgləs/ n. large N. American conifer.

dour /dŏŏr,dowr/ adj. severe, stern, or sullenly obstinate in manner or appearance. See synonym study at GLUM. □□ **dour'ly** adv. **dour'ness** n.
■ sour, unfriendly, forbidding, obstinate,

stubborn; *colloq.* hard-nosed; gloomy, morose, grim.

douse /dows/ *v.tr.* **1 a** throw water over. **b** plunge into water. **2** extinguish (a light).

■ *v.* **1** see DRENCH *v.*

dove[1] /duv/ *n.* **1** bird with short legs, small head, and large breast. **2** gentle person; advocate of peace.

dove[2] *past* and *past part.* of DIVE.

dove•tail /dúvtayl/ • *n.* mortise and tenon joint shaped like a dove's spread tail. • *v.* **1** *tr.* join by means of a dovetail. **2** *tr. & intr.* fit readily together; combine neatly.

■ *v.* **2** see COMBINE[1] *v.* 1, FIT *v.* 1a.

dow•a•ger /dówəjər/ *n.* **1** widow with a title or property from her late husband. **2** dignified elderly woman.

dow•dy /dówdee/ *adj.* (**dow•di•er, dow•di•est**) **1** (of clothes) unattractively dull. **2** dressed dowdily. □□ **dow′di•ly** *adv.* **dow′di•ness** *n.*

■ **1** drab, unbecoming, *colloq.* tacky; old-fashioned. **2** frowzy, frumpy, frumpish.

dow•el /dówəl/ • *n.* headless peg for holding together components, hanging clothes on, etc. • *v.tr.* fasten with a dowel.

dow•er /dówər/ *n.* **1** widow's share for life of her husband's estate. **2** dowry.

down[1] /down/ • *adv.* (*superl.* **down•most**) **1** into or toward a lower place, esp. to the ground. **2** in a lower place or position (*blinds were down*). **3** to or in a place regarded as lower, esp. southward. **4** in or into a low or weaker position, mood, or condition (*many down with colds*). **5** (of a computer system) not operating. **6** from an earlier to a later time (*customs handed down*). **7** to a finer or thinner consistency or a smaller amount or size. **8** lower in price or value. **9** into a more settled state. **10** in or into recorded or listed form (*copy it down*). **11** (of part of a larger whole) paid. • *prep.* **1** downward along, through, or into. **2** from top to bottom of. **3** along (*cut down the middle*). • *adj.* (*superl.* **down•most**) **1** directed downward. **2** *colloq.* unhappy; depressed. • *v.tr.* **1** knock or bring down. **2** swallow. • *n.* **1** act of putting down. **2** reverse of fortune. **3** *Football* one of a series of plays. □ **be down on** *colloq.* disapprove. **down-and-out** destitute. **down-at-the-heels** shabby; slovenly. **down in the mouth** looking unhappy. **down on one's luck** *colloq.* dispirited by misfortune.

down payment partial payment at time of purchase. **down-to-earth** practical; realistic. **Down Under** Australia. **down with** *int.* expressing rejection.

■ *adv.* **1** see DOWNWARD *adv.* **8** cheaper, reduced. • *adj.* **2** see MISERABLE 1. • *v.* **1** see *knock down* 1 (KNOCK). • *n.* **2** nadir, low point; (*downs*) bad times, hard times; misfortunes; see also DEPRESSION 1b. □ **down-and-out** indigent, poverty-stricken, poor, penniless, impoverished, *colloq.* on the skids, on skid row; see also BROKE.

down[2] /down/ *n.* **1** fine, soft feathers or hair. **2** fluffy substance. □□ **down′y** *adj.* (**down•i•er, down•i•est**).

■ see FLUFF *n.* 1.

down[3] /down/ *n.* open rolling land.

down•beat /dównbeet/ • *n.* *Mus.* accented beat, usu. the first of the bar. • *adj.* pessimistic; gloomy.

■ *n.* see RHYTHM 2.

down•cast /dównkast/ *adj.* **1** (of eyes) looking downward. **2** dejected.

■ **2** see *dejected* (DEJECT).

down•er /dównər/ *n. sl.* **1** depressant or tranquilizing drug. **2** depressing person or experience; failure.

■ **1** see TRANQUILIZER.

down•fall /dównfawl/ *n.* **1** fall from prosperity or power. **2** cause of this.

■ collapse; ruin, undoing, debacle, breakdown.

down•grade • *v.tr.* /dówngráyd/ **1** reduce in rank or status. **2** speak disparagingly of. • *n.* /dówngrayd/ **1** descending slope. **2** deterioration.

■ *v.* **1** demote, dethrone, humble, lower, displace, depose, dispossess, *colloq.* bring *or* take down a peg (or two). **2** belittle, minimize, play down; see also DISPARAGE 1. • *n.* **1** descent, decline, gradient. **2** see DECLINE *n.* 2.

down•heart•ed /dównha'artid/ *adj.* dejected; in low spirits. □□ **down′heart′ed•ly** *adv.*

■ see SAD 1.

down•hill • *adv.* /dównhíl/ toward the bottom of an incline. • *adj.* /dównhil/ sloping down; descending. □ **go downhill** *colloq.* decline; deteriorate (in health, state of repair, moral state, etc.).

■ □ **go downhill** see DETERIORATE.

down•load /dównlōd/ *v.tr.* *Computing* transfer (data) from one storage device or system to another.

down•play /dównpláy/ *v.tr.* minimize the importance of.

■ see MINIMIZE 2.

down•pour /dównpawr/ *n.* heavy fall of rain.

■ rainstorm, deluge, inundation, torrent.

down•right /dównrit/ • *adj.* **1** plain; straightforward; blunt. **2** utter; complete (*a downright lie*). • *adv.* thoroughly.

■ *adj.* **1** direct, explicit, outspoken, unabashed, bold. **2** out-and-out, outright, absolute; see also COMPLETE *adj.* 3. • *adv.* completely, totally, certainly, (most) assuredly, positively, definitely, absolutely, unequivocally; see also *profoundly* (PROFOUND).

down•shift /dównshift/ *v.* shift (a vehicle) into a lower gear.

down•size /dównsiz/ *v.tr.* (**down-sized, down•siz•ing**) (esp. of personnel) reduce in size.

Down's syn•drome /downz/ *n. Med.* (also **Down′ syn′drome**) congenital disorder with mental retardation and physical abnormalities.

down•stairs • *adv.* /dównstáirz/ **1** down a flight of stairs. **2** to or on a lower floor. • *adj.* /dównstairz/ situated downstairs. • *n.* /dównstáirz/ a lower floor.

■ *adv.* see BELOW *adv.* 2a.

down•state /dównstáyt/ • *adj.* of or in a southern part of a state. • *n.* downstate area. • *adv.* in a downstate area.

down•stream /dównstreém/ • *adv.* in the direction of the flow of a stream, etc. • *adj.* moving downstream.

down•time /dówntīm/ *n.* time during which a machine, esp. a computer, is out of action or unavailable for use.

down•town /dówntówn/ • *adj.* of esp. the central part of a town or city. • *n.* downtown area. • *adv.* in or into a downtown area.

down•trod•den /dówntród'n/ *adj.* oppressed; badly treated.
  ■ subjugated, burdened, afflicted, exploited, overwhelmed, beaten, abused, mistreated.

down•turn /dówntərn/ *n.* decline, esp. economic.
  ■ see DECLINE *n.* 1, 2.

down•ward /dównwərd/ • *adv.* (also **down′wards**) toward what is lower, inferior, etc. • *adj.* moving, extending, or leading downward. □□ **down′ward•ly** *adv.*
  ■ *adv.* below, lower. • *adj.* declining, descending.

down•wind /dównwínd/ *adj. & adv.* in the direction in which the wind is blowing.

dow•ry /dówree/ *n.* (*pl.* **–ries**) property or money brought by a bride to her husband.
  ■ dot; dower.

dowse /dowz/ *v. intr.* search for underground water, etc., using a rod that dips when over the right spot. □□ **dows′er** *n.*

dox•ol•o•gy /doksóləjee/ *n.* (*pl.* **–gies**) liturgical formula of praise to God. □□ **dox•o•log•i•cal** /–səlójikəl/ *adj.*

doz. *abbr.* dozen.

doze /dōz/ • *v. intr.* sleep lightly; be half asleep. • *n.* short, light sleep. □ **doze off** fall lightly asleep. □□ **doz′er** *n.*
  ■ *v.* (take or have a) nap, catnap, drowse, *colloq.* snooze. • *n.* lie-down, forty winks, shut-eye. □ **doze off** drop or nod off; see also NOD *v.* 2.

doz•en /dúzən/ *n.* 1 (*pl.* **doz′en**) twelve, regarded collectively (*two dozen eggs*). 2 set of twelve. 3 [in *pl.*] *colloq.* very many (*made dozens of mistakes*). □ **by the dozen** in large quantities.

DP *abbr.* 1 data processing. 2 displaced person.

DPT *abbr.* (vaccination for) diphtheria, pertussis, and tetanus.

Dr. *abbr.* 1 Doctor. 2 Drive. 3 debtor.

drab /drab/ *adj.* (**drab•ber, drab•best**) 1 dull; uninteresting. 2 of a dull brownish color. □□ **drab′ly** *adv.* **drab′ness** *n.*
  ■ 1 dreary, lackluster, dismal.

drach•ma /drákmə/ *n.* (*pl.* **drach′mas** or **drach•mai** /–mī/ or **drach•mae** /–mee/) 1 chief monetary unit of Greece. 2 silver coin of ancient Greece.

dra•co•ni•an /drəkṓneeən, dray–/ *adj.* (also **dra•con•ic** /–kónik/) very harsh or severe (esp. of laws and their application).

draft /draft/ • *n.* 1 preliminary written version of a speech, document, etc. 2 a written order for payment by a bank. b drawing of money by means of this. 3 military conscription. 4 current of air. 5 pulling; traction. 6 depth of water needed to float a ship. 7 drawing of liquor from a cask, etc. 8 a single act of drinking. b amount thus drunk.

c a dose of liquid medicine. 9 a drawing in of a fishing net. b the fish taken at one drawing. • *v.tr.* 1 prepare a draft of (a document, etc.). 2 select for a special duty or purpose. 3 conscript for military service. □ **draft horse** horse used for pulling heavy loads. □□ **draft•ee** /–tée/ *n.* **draft′er** *n.*
  ■ *n.* 1 plan, sketch, drawing, diagram. 2 a check, money order. 3 call-up. 4 breeze, breath (of air), (light) wind. 8 swallow, sip, gulp, *colloq.* swig. • *v.* 1 sketch (out), outline, design, plan, frame, draw (up). 2 see APPOINT 1. 3 recruit, call up, induct.

drafts•man /dráftsmən/ *n.* (*pl.* **–men**) person who makes drawings, plans, or sketches. □□ **drafts′man•ship** *n.*

draft•y /dráftee/ *adj.* (**–i•er, –i•est**) (of a room, etc.) letting in sharp currents of air. □□ **draft′i•ly** *adv.* **draft′i•ness** *n.*
  ■ see BREEZY 1.

drag /drag/ • *v.* (**dragged, drag•ging**) 1 *tr.* pull along with effort. 2 a *tr.* allow to trail along the ground. b *intr.* trail along the ground. c *intr.* (of time, etc.) pass slowly or tediously. 3 a *intr.* use a grapnel or drag (to find a drowned person or lost object). b *tr.* search the bottom of (a river, etc.) with grapnels, nets, or drags. 4 *tr. colloq.* take (an unwilling person to a place, etc.). 5 *intr.* draw on (a cigarette, etc.). • *n.* 1 obstruction to progress. 2 *colloq.* tiresome person, party, performance, etc. 3 inhalation. 4 *sl.* women's clothes worn by men. 5 *sl.* (in full **drag race**) acceleration race between cars usu. for a short distance. 6 *sl.* street or road (*the main drag*). □ **drag out** protract. **drag queen** *sl.* male transvestite. **drag strip** straight stretch of road for drag racing. **drag up** *colloq.* deliberately mention (an unwelcome subject).
  ■ *v.* 1 haul, tow, tug, trail, lug. • *n.* 2 bore, nuisance, annoyance, aggravation; see also BOTHER *n.* 1.

drag•net /drágnet/ *n.* 1 net drawn through water or across land to trap fish or game. 2 systematic hunt for criminals, etc.

drag•on /drágən/ *n.* mythical monster, usu. depicted as a fire-breathing, winged reptile.

drag•on•fly /drágənflī/ *n.* (*pl.* **–flies**) insect with a long body and two pairs of transparent wings.

dra•goon /drəgōn/ • *n.* 1 cavalryman. 2 rough, fierce fellow. • *v.tr.* [foll. by *into*] coerce; bully.

drain /drayn/ • *v.* 1 *tr.* draw off liquid from. 2 *tr.* draw off (liquid). 3 *intr.* flow or trickle away. 4 *intr.* become dry as liquid flows away. 5 *tr.* exhaust. 6 *tr.* drink all of; empty. • *n.* 1 a channel or pipe carrying off liquid. b tube for drawing off discharge, etc. 2 constant outflow or expenditure. □ **down the drain** *colloq.* lost; wasted. □□ **drain′er** *n.*
  ■ *v.* 1 tap, extract, remove, take away, withdraw, pump off or out. 3 seep, drip, ebb, leach (away). 5 sap, deplete; weaken, debilitate, impair; see also DEPRIVE 1. • *n.* 1 a ditch, trench, culvert, conduit; sewer. 2 depletion, reduction; withdrawal.

drain•age /dráynij/ *n.* **1** draining. **2** system of drains. **3** what is drained off.

drain•pipe /dráynpīp/ *n.* pipe for carrying off water, etc.

drake /drayk/ *n.* male duck.

dram /dram/ *n.* **1** small drink of liquor. **2** measure of weight (apothecaries' one-eighth ounce; avoirdupois one-sixteenth ounce).

dra•ma /drámə, draámə/ *n.* **1** play for stage or broadcasting. **2** art of writing and presenting plays. **3** exciting or emotional event, circumstances, etc. **4** dramatic quality. □□ **dra•mat′ic** *adj.*

■ **1** (theatrical) piece, (stage) production. **2** dramatics, theater, dramatic art(s). **4** histrionics, theatrics. □□ **dramatic** theatrical; sensational; flamboyant, melodramatic, colorful, stirring; see also EXCITING.

dra•mat•ics /drəmátiks/ *n.pl.* [often treated as *sing.*] **1** performance of plays. **2** exaggerated behavior.

■ **1** see THEATER 2. **2** see DRAMA 4.

dram•a•tist /drámətist, draámə–/ *n.* writer of dramas.

■ playwright, screenwriter, scriptwriter.

dram•a•tize /drámətiz, draámə–/ *v.tr.* **1** adapt (a novel, etc.) to a stage play. **2** make a dramatic scene of. **3** express or react to in a dramatic way. □□ **dram•a•ti•za′tion** *n.*

■ **3** exaggerate, overplay, *colloq.* make a (big) thing (out) of, make a song and dance about; make a mountain out of a molehill.

drank *past of* DRINK.

drape /drayp/ • *v.tr.* **1** hang, cover loosely, or adorn with cloth, etc. **2** arrange in folds. • *n.* [in *pl.*] curtains.

■ *v.* **1** festoon, swathe, deck, array, bedeck. • *n.* drapery.

dra•per•y /dráypəree/ *n.* (*pl.* **–ies**) clothing or hangings (esp. curtains) arranged in folds.

dras•tic /drástik/ *adj.* having a far-reaching effect; severe. □□ **dras′ti•cal•ly** *adv.*

■ serious, violent, extreme, sweeping, radical.

draught /draft/ *esp. Brit.* = DRAFT.

draw /draw/ • *v.* (*past* **drew** /drōō/; *past part.* **drawn** /drawn/) **1** *tr.* pull or cause to move toward or after one. **2** *tr.* pull (a thing) up, over, or across. **3** *tr.* pull (curtains, etc.) open or shut. **4** *tr.* attract; bring; take in (*drew a deep breath*). **5** *intr.* suck smoke from (a cigarette, pipe, etc.). **6** *tr.* take out; remove. **7** *tr.* obtain or take from a source (*draw a salary*). **8** *tr.* produce (a picture) by tracing lines and marks. **9** *tr.* [also *absol.*] finish (a contest or game) with equal scores. **10** *tr.* infer (a conclusion). **11** *tr.* elicit; evoke. **12** *tr.* bring out or extract (liquid). **13** *intr.* (of a chimney, etc.) promote or allow a draft. **14** *intr.* [foll. by *on*] call on (a person, a person's skill, etc.). **15** *tr.* write out or compose (a check, document, etc.). **16** *tr.* formulate or perceive (a comparison or distinction). • *n.* **1** act of drawing. **2** attraction. **3** raffle, lottery, etc. **4** game ending in a tie. **5** act of removing a gun from its holster in order to shoot (*quick on the draw*). □ **draw**

the line set a limit (of tolerance, etc.). **draw out 1** prolong. **2** elicit. **draw up 1** draft (a document, etc.). **2** come to a halt.

■ *v.* **1** tug, tow, drag, haul, lug. **4** allure, lure; bring out *or* forth, elicit. **5** take in, inhale. **6** extract; unsheathe. **7** draw out, withdraw; receive, secure, procure. **8** sketch, paint; depict, portray, delineate, design. **10** (*draw the conclusion*) see INFER 1. **11** see ELICIT. **14** (*draw on*) employ, use, make use of, exploit. **15** see *draw up* 1 below. **16** see PERCEIVE 2. • *n.* **1** pull, tug, drag. **2** magnetism, lure, enticement, *colloq.* pull. **4** stalemate, dead heat, deadlock. □ **draw out 1** extend, drag out, lengthen. **2** see ELICIT. **draw up 1** prepare, compile, formulate, devise. **2** stop, pull up *or* over.

draw•back /dráwbak/ *n.* disadvantage.

■ hindrance, stumbling block, obstacle, impediment, hurdle, problem, difficulty, hitch, catch.

draw•bridge /dráwbrij/ *n.* bridge that may be raised or moved aside.

draw•er *n.* **1** /dráwər/ person or thing that draws. **2** /drawr/ lidless, boxlike storage compartment, sliding in and out of a desk, table, etc. **3** [in *pl.*] /drawrz/ underpants. □□ **draw•er′ful** *n.* (*pl.* **–fuls**).

draw•ing /dráwing/ *n.* **1** the art of representing by line with pencils, crayons, etc. **2** picture produced in this way. □ **back to the drawing board** *colloq.* back to begin afresh (after earlier failure).

■ **2** depiction, representation, sketch, outline, design.

draw•ing room /dráwingrōōm, –rōōm/ *n.* **1** room for receiving guests in a private house. **2** private compartment in a train.

drawl /drawl/ • *v.* **1** *intr.* speak with drawn-out vowel sounds. **2** *tr.* utter in this way. • *n.* drawling utterance.

drawn /drawn/ *past part.* of DRAW. *adj.* **1** looking strained and tense. **2** (of butter) melted.

■ **1** haggard, worn out, tired, fatigued, exhausted.

draw•string /dráwstring/ *n.* string that can be pulled to tighten the mouth of a bag, the waist of a garment, etc.

dray /dray/ *n.* low cart without sides for heavy loads.

dread /dred/ • *v.tr.* **1** fear greatly. **2** look forward to with great apprehension. • *n.* great fear; apprehension. • *adj.* dreaded.

■ *v.* **2** flinch from, shrink *or* recoil from, cringe at. • *n.* fright, fearfulness, trepidation, awe, uneasiness, dismay, anxiety, distress; terror, panic. • *adj.* feared, terrifying, terrible.

dread•ful /drédfŏŏl/ *adj.* **1** terrible; inspiring fear or awe. **2** *colloq.* very bad. □□ **dread′ful•ly** *adv.*

■ **1** grievous, dire, horrible, horrendous, appalling, hideous, ghastly. **2** *colloq.* lousy, *sl.* rotten; see also AWFUL 1a, b, TROUBLESOME. □□ **dreadfully** see AWFULLY.

dread•locks /drédloks/ *n.pl.* hair twisted into tight braids hanging down on all sides.

dream /dreem/ • *n.* **1** pictures or events in the mind of a sleeping person. **2** daydream or fantasy. **3** ideal; aspiration. **4** beautiful or ideal person or thing. • *v.* (*past* and *past part.*

dreamed or **dreamt** /dremt/) **1** *intr.* experience a dream. **2** *tr.* imagine as in a dream. **3** [usu. with *neg.*] **a** *intr.* contemplate the possibility of (*would not dream of it*). **b** *tr.* think of as a possibility (*never dreamed that he would come*). □ **dream up** imagine; invent. **like a dream** *colloq.* easily; effortlessly. □□ **dream'like** *adj.*

■ *n.* **2** reverie, delusion, fantasy. **3** ambition, vision; see also ASPIRATION. • *v.* **1**, **2** fancy, conjure up, hallucinate. **3 a** (*dream of*) entertain the thought of. □ **dream up** see *think up.* **like a dream** like a charm; wonderfully, perfectly, successfully. □□ **dreamlike** unreal, fantastic, unbelievable, phantasmagorical, surreal, illusional, fanciful.

dream·er /dreemər/ *n.* romantic or unpractical person.

■ fantasizer, idealist, romantic, Utopian.

dream·land /dreemland/ *n.* ideal or imaginary land.

dream·y /dreemee/ *adj.* (**dream·i·er, dream·i·est**) **1** given to daydreaming; fanciful. **2** dreamlike; vague. **3** *colloq.* delightful; marvelous. □□ **dream'i·ly** *adv.* **dream'i·ness** *n.*

■ **1** absentminded, faraway, thoughtful; musing, occupied; see also *idealistic* (IDEALISM). **2** indistinct, misty, shadowy, faint. **3** see DELIGHTFUL.

drear·y /dreeree/ *adj.* (**drear·i·er, drear·i·est**) dismal, dull, gloomy. □□ **drear'i·ly** *adv.* **drear'i·ness** *n.*

■ joyless, cheerless, bleak, somber, doleful, depressing, melancholy, miserable; boring, lifeless, colorless, drab, prosaic, tedious, tiresome, wearisome, banal.

dredge[1] /drej/ • *v.* **1** *tr.* **a** bring up (lost or hidden material) as if with a dredge. **b** bring up (mud, etc.) from a river, harbor, etc., with a dredge. **2** *intr.* use a dredge. • *n.* apparatus used to scoop from a riverbed or seabed.

dredge[2] /drej/ *v. tr.* sprinkle with flour, sugar, etc.

■ powder, dust, flour.

dregs /dregz/ *n.pl.* **1** sediment; grounds. **2** worthless part.

■ **1** lees, deposit, draff, residue, remains; precipitate. **2** outcasts, pariahs, losers; riffraff, scum.

drench /drench/ *v.tr.* wet thoroughly, soak.

■ saturate, inundate, immerse, drown.

dress /dres/ • *v.* **1 a** *tr.* clothe; array. **b** *intr.* wear clothes, esp. in a specified way (*dresses well*). **2** *intr.* **a** put on clothes. **b** put on formal clothes. **3** *tr.* decorate or adorn. **4** *tr. Med.* treat (a wound) with ointment, etc. **5** *tr.* **a** clean and prepare (poultry, etc.) for cooking or eating. **b** add a dressing to (salad, etc.). **6** *tr.* finish the surface of (fabric, building stone, etc.). **7** *tr.* curry (leather, etc.). **8** *Mil.* **a** *tr.* align (troops, etc.). **b** *intr.* (of troops) come into alignment. • *n.* **1** woman's garment of a bodice and skirt. **2** clothing, esp. a whole outfit. □ **dress code** set of rules for acceptable dress, as at a school, restaurant, etc. **dress down** *colloq.* **1** reprimand or scold. **2** dress casually. **dress out** attire conspicuously. **dress re-**

239   **dreamer ~ drill**

hearsal final rehearsal of a play, etc., wearing costume. **dress up 1** dress in fancy dress. **2** disguise (unwelcome facts) by embellishment.

■ *v.* **1 a** robe, outfit, fit out. **2** get dressed. **4** medicate, *colloq.* doctor; bandage. • *n.* **1** frock, gown. **2** costume, garb, garments, vestments, attire, apparel. □ **dress down 1** berate, rebuke, reprove, upbraid, chew out; see also CASTIGATE.

dres·sage /drisaazh, dre-/ *n.* training of a horse in obedience and deportment.

dress·er /dresər/ *n.* **1** chest of drawers. **2** person who assists actors to dress. **3** person who dresses in a specified way (*a snappy dresser*).

■ **1** see BUREAU 1.

dress·ing /dresing/ *n.* **1** in senses of DRESS *v.* **2 a** sauce for salads. **b** stuffing, esp. for poultry. **3** bandage or ointment for a wound. **4** stiffening used to finish fabrics.

■ **3** see SALVE *n.* 1.

dress·y /dresee/ *adj.* (**dress·i·er, dress·i·est**) (of clothes or a person) stylish; elaborate. □□ **dress'i·ness** *n.*

■ formal, dressed-up; elegant, smart, chic, fashionable, *colloq.* ritzy.

drew *past of* DRAW.

drib·ble /dribəl/ • *v.* **1** *intr.* allow saliva to flow from the mouth. **2** *intr. & tr.* flow or allow to flow in drops. **3** *tr. Sports* move (a ball, etc.) with slight touches or taps. • *n.* **1** act of dribbling. **2** trickling flow. □□ **drib'bler** *n.* **drib'bly** *adj.*

■ *v.* **1** see SLAVER[2] *v.* **2** see TRICKLE[2] *v.* • *n.* **1** see SLAVER *n.* 1. **2** see TRICKLE *n.*

dribs and drabs /dribz and drabz/ *n.pl. colloq.* small scattered amounts (*did the work in dribs and drabs*).

dried *past and past part.* of DRY.

dri·er[1] *compar.* of DRY.

dri·er[2] /drīer/ *n.* (also **dry'er**) machine for drying hair, laundry, etc.

dri·est *superl.* of DRY.

drift /drift/ • *n.* **1 a** slow movement or variation. **b** such movement caused by a current. **2** intention, meaning, etc., of what is said, etc. **3** mass of windblown snow, etc. **4** deviation of a ship, aircraft, etc., from its course. • *v.* **1** *intr.* be carried by or as if by a current. **2** *intr.* progress passively or aimlessly (*drifted into teaching*). **3** *tr. & intr.* pile or be piled into drifts. □ **drift net** large fishing net allowed to drift with the tide. □□ **drift'age** *n.*

■ *n.* **1** see CURRENT *n.* **2** trend, tendency, direction, course, current, bias, inclination, flow; essence, gist, purpose; tenor, tone, spirit, color. **3** accumulation, pile, heap, mass, bank, mound. **4** see TURN *n.* 2. • *v.* **1**, **2** coast, float, waft, bob; wander, roam, meander, stray, rove, ramble, *sl.* mosey.

drift·er /driftər/ *n.* aimless or rootless person.

■ rambler, wanderer, itinerant, rover, vagrant, tramp, vagabond, hobo.

drift·wood /driftwood/ *n.* wood afloat or washed ashore.

drill[1] /dril/ • *n.* **1** tool or machine for boring holes. **2 a** military marching. **b** rigorous discipline or methodical instruction. **c** routine procedure in an emergency (*fire drill*). • *v.* **1** *tr.* [also *absol.*] **a** make a hole with a drill through or into. **b** make (a hole) with a drill. **2** *tr. & intr.* undergo discipline by drill. **3** *tr.* impart (knowledge, etc.) by drill. □ **drill press** machine tool for drilling.

■ *n.* **1** auger, (brace and) bit, gimlet, bradawl. **2** training, instruction, exercise; procedure, practice. • *v.* **1 a** penetrate, pierce, perforate. **b** bore. **2** train, teach, instruct, indoctrinate. **3** drive, force.

drill² /dril/ • *n.* **1** machine for making furrows, sowing, and covering seed. **2** small furrow. **3** row of plants so sown. • *v.tr.* plant in drills.

drill³ /dril/ *n.* W. African baboon related to the mandrill.

drill⁴ /dril/ *n.* coarse twilled cotton or linen fabric.

dri·ly var. of DRYLY.

drink /dringk/ • *v.* (*past* **drank** /drangk/; *past part.* **drunk** /drungk/) **1 a** *tr.* swallow (liquid). **b** *tr.* swallow the liquid contents of (a vessel). **c** *intr.* swallow liquid. **2** *intr.* take alcohol, esp. to excess. • *n.* **1** liquid for drinking. **2 a** alcoholic liquor. **b** portion, glass, etc., of this. **c** excessive use of alcohol. **3** (as **the drink**) *colloq.* the sea. □ **drink in** listen to eagerly. **drink to** toast (a person, event, etc.). **drink a person under the table** remain sober longer than one's drinking companion. **drink up** drink the whole of it. **strong drink** alcoholic liquor. □□ **drink'a·ble** *adj.* **drink'er** *n.*

■ *v.* **1** sip, gulp, lap (up), *literary* quaff; imbibe. **2** tipple, indulge, have a few. • *n.* **1** potation, beverage. **2 a** spirits, *colloq.* booze, firewater, hooch, *sl.* rotgut. **b** nip, draft, jigger, dram, *colloq.* snort. **3** (**the drink**) *poet.* the main, the deep, *sl.* Davy Jones's locker. □ **drink to** salute, celebrate.

drip /drip/ • *v.* (**dripped, drip·ping**) **1** *intr. & tr.* fall or let fall in drops. **2** *intr.* be so wet as to shed drops. • *n.* **1 a** dripping (*steady drip of rain*). **b** drop of liquid. **c** sound of dripping. **2** *colloq.* dull or ineffective person. □ **drip-dry** *v.* (**-dries, -dried**) **1** *intr.* (of fabric, etc.) dry crease-free when hung up to drip. **2** *tr.* leave (a garment, etc.) hanging up to dry. *adj.* able to be drip-dried.

■ *v.* **1** see TRICKLE *v.* **2** be soaked, be sopping, be saturated, be wet through, be drenched, be dripping wet. • *n.* **1** dribble, trickle. **2** milksop, bore, *colloq.* wimp, cream puff, *sl.* dud.

drive /driv/ *v.* (*past* **drove** /drōv/; *past part.* **driv·en** /drivən/) **1** *tr.* urge in some direction, esp. forcibly. **2** *tr.* **a** compel. **b** force into a specified state. **c** urge to overwork. **3 a** *tr.* operate and direct (a vehicle, etc.). **b** *tr. & intr.* convey or be conveyed in a vehicle. **c** *tr.* be competent to drive (a vehicle). **4** *tr.* (of wind, water, etc.) carry along, propel, or cause to go in some direction. **5** *tr.* force (a stake, nail, etc.) into place. **6** *tr.* effect or conclude forcibly (*drove a hard bargain*). **7** *tr.* set or keep (machinery) go-

ing. **8** *tr.* hit a ball hard, making it go fast or a great distance. • *n.* **1** journey or excursion in a vehicle. **2 a** motivation and energy. **b** inner urge. **3 a** usu. landscaped street or road. **b** driveway. **4** *Sports* driving stroke of a bat, club, etc. **5** organized effort (*famine-relief drive*). **6** the transmission of power to machinery, wheels, etc. □ **drive at** intend; mean (*what is he driving at?*). **drive-by** (of a crime, etc.) carried out from a moving vehicle. **drive-in** *attrib.adj.* (of a bank, movie theater, etc.) used while sitting in one's car. *n.* such a bank, movie theater, etc. **driving rain** excessive downpour. **driving range** area for golfing practice. □□ **driv'a·ble** *adj.*

■ *v.* **1** force, push, propel, thrust; herd. **2 a** coerce, pressure, press; goad, incite. **3 a** conduct, maneuver, manipulate, handle, steer, control; pilot. **b** take, bring, give a person a lift; ride, travel. **5** plunge, thrust, sink, ram. **7** see ACTIVATE. • *n.* **1** ride, trip, outing, *colloq.* spin. **2 a** effort, impetus, vigor, vim, enterprise, industry, initiative, ambition, determination, persistence, zeal, enthusiasm, *colloq.* spunk, pep, zip. **b** see URGE *n.* **3** approach, avenue, boulevard, lane, route. **5** campaign, appeal, crusade. □ **drive at** hint (at), suggest, imply, intimate, allude *or* refer to, have in mind.

driv·el /drivəl/ • *n.* silly nonsense; twaddle. • *v.* *intr.* talk drivel. □□ **driv'el·er** *n.*

■ *n.* gibberish, rubbish, balderdash, claptrap, *colloq.* hogwash, tripe, malarkey, *sl.* hooey, bull, rot, bunk. • *v.* prate, prattle, gibber, jabber, blather; see also BABBLE *v.* 1a, b.

driv·en *past part.* of DRIVE.

driv·er /drivər/ *n.* **1** person who drives a vehicle. **2** *Golf* club for driving from the tee. □ **in the driver's seat** in charge.

■ **1** see OPERATOR 1.

drive·way /drivway/ *n.* usu. private road from a public street, etc., to a house, garage, etc.

driz·zle /drizəl/ • *n.* very fine rain. • *v.intr.* (esp. of rain) fall in very fine drops. □□ **driz'zly** *adj.*

droll /drōl/ *adj.* **1** quaintly amusing. **2** odd; surprising. □□ **droll'er·y** *n.* (*pl.* **-ies**). **drol'ly** *adv.* **droll'ness** *n.*

■ **1** see COMIC *adj.*

-drome /drōm/ *comb. form* forming nouns denoting: **1** place for running, racing, etc. (*aerodrome, hippodrome*). **2** thing that runs or proceeds in a certain way (*palindrome, syndrome*).

drom·e·dar·y /drómider ee, drúm-/ *n.* (*pl.* **-ies**) one-humped camel, bred for riding and racing.

drone /drōn/ • *n.* **1** nonworking male of certain bees. **2** idler. **3** deep humming sound. **4** monotonous speech or speaker. • *v.* **1** *intr.* make a deep humming sound. **2** *intr. & tr.* speak or utter monotonously.

drool /drool/ • *v.intr.* **1** drivel; slobber. **2** show much pleasure or infatuation. • *n.* slobbering; driveling.

droop /droop/ • *v.* **1** *intr. & tr.* sag; hang down; languish. **2** *intr.* lose heart; be dejected. • *n.* **1** drooping. **2** loss of spirit or enthusiasm. □□ **droop'y** *adj.*

■ *v.* **1** wilt, dangle; weaken, flag, decline, wither, slump, sag.

drop /drop/ • *n.* **1 a** globule of liquid. **b** very small amount of liquid. **2 a** abrupt slope. **b** degree of this. **c** act of falling or dropping. **d** fall in prices, temperature, etc. **e** deterioration. **3** globular gemstone, piece of candy, etc. **4** curtain or scenery let down on to a stage. **5** [in *pl.*] liquid medicine used in drops. • *v.* (**dropped, drop•ping**) **1** *intr. & tr.* fall or let fall in drops. **2** *intr. & tr.* relinquish. **3 a** *intr. & tr.* sink from exhaustion, a wound, etc. **b** *intr.* die. **4 a** *intr. & tr.* cease or cause to cease; lapse or let lapse; abandon. **b** *tr. colloq.* cease to associate with. **5** *tr.* deposit (a passenger, etc.). **6** *tr. & intr.* utter or be uttered casually. **7** *tr.* send casually (*drop me a postcard*). **8 a** *intr. & tr.* fall or allow to fall in direction, amount, condition, degree, pitch, etc. (*his voice dropped*). **b** *intr.* (of a person) jump down lightly. **9** *tr. colloq.* lose (money, esp. in gambling). **10** *tr.* **a** omit (*drop this article*). **b** omit (a letter, esp. 'h,' a syllable, etc.) in speech. **11** *tr.* (as **dropped** *adj.*) in a lower position than usual (*dropped waist*). **12** *tr.* give birth to (esp. a lamb, a kitten, etc.). **13** *tr.* lose (a game, point, etc.). **14** *tr. colloq.* dismiss or exclude (*was dropped from the team*). □ **at the drop of a hat** given the slightest excuse. **drop in** (or **by**) *colloq.* visit casually. **drop-leaf** (of a table, etc.) having a hinged flap. **drop off 1** decline gradually. **2** *colloq.* fall asleep. **3** = (sense 5 of *v.*). **drop out** *colloq.* cease to participate. **ready to drop** extremely tired. □□ **drop′let** *n.*

■ *n.* **1 a** bead, drip, droplet, tear. **b** bit, spot, taste, dram, sip, nip. **2 a, b** descent, fall; decline, drop-off. **d** see DECREASE[1] *n.* **e** see DECLINE *n.* **1.** • *v.* **1** drip, trickle, dribble. **2** release, let go (of). **3 a** collapse, go down. **b** see DIE **1.** **4** desert, forsake, jilt, discard, reject, *sl.* ditch. **5** drop off, set down, let off *or* out. **8 a** descend, dive, plunge, plummet, collapse, decrease, diminish, subside, lessen. **9** see WASTE *v.* **1.** **10** leave out, exclude, eliminate, delete. **13** concede, let slip. **14** let go, discharge, oust, *colloq.* sack, *sl.* fire; see also DISMISS **2,** OMIT **1.**

drop•out /drópowt/ *n. colloq.* a person who has dropped out, esp. from school.

drop•per /drópər/ *n.* device for administering liquid, esp. medicine, in drops.

drop•pings /drópingz/ *n.pl.* animal dung.

drop•sy /drópsee/ *n.* (*pl.* **-sies**) = EDEMA.

dro•soph•i•la /drəsófilə/ *n.* fruit fly used extensively in genetic research.

dross /draws, dros/ *n.* **1** refuse. **2** scum from melted metals.

drought /drowt/ *n.* **1** prolonged absence of rain. **2** prolonged lack of something. □□ **drought′y** *adj.*

drove[1] *past of* DRIVE.

drove[2] /drōv/ *n.* **1 a** large number (of people, etc.) moving together. **b** [in *pl.*] *colloq.* great number. **2** herd or flock driven or moving together.

■ see THRONG *n.*

drown /drown/ *v.* **1** *tr. & intr.* kill or be killed by submersion in liquid. **2** *tr.* submerge;

flood; drench (*drowned the fields in six feet of water*). **3** *tr.* deaden (grief, etc.) with drink (*drowned his sorrows in drink*). **4** *tr.* make a (sound) inaudible by means of a louder sound.

■ **2** inundate, swamp, deluge, immerse, submerge, engulf; overwhelm, overcome, overpower.

drowse /drowz/ • *v.intr.* be lightly asleep. • *n.* nap.

drow•sy /drówzee/ *adj.* (**drow•si•er, drow•si•est**) **1** half asleep; dozing. **2** sluggish. □□ **drow′si•ly** *adv.* **drow′si•ness** *n.*

■ sleepy, groggy, somnolent; tired, weary, listless, lethargic, lazy.

drub /drub/ *v.tr.* (**drubbed, drub•bing**) **1** thump; belabor. **2** beat in a fight. □□ **drub′bing** *n.*

■ **1** see BEAT *v.* **1.** **2** see OVERCOME *v.* **1.**

drudge /druj/ • *n.* servile worker, esp. at menial tasks. • *v.intr.* work slavishly. □□ **drudg′er•y** *n.* See synonym study at LABOR

■ *n.* hack, plodder, toiler; see also MENIAL *n.* **1.** • *v.* see SLAVE *v.* **1,** LABOR *v.* **1, 2.** □□ **drudgery** toil, labor, *colloq.* grind, sweat.

drug /drug/ • *n.* **1** medicinal substance. **2** (esp. addictive) narcotic, hallucinogen, or stimulant. • *v.* (**drugged, drug•ging**) **1** add a drug to (food or drink). **2** *tr.* **a** administer a drug to. **b** stupefy with a drug. **3** *intr.* take drugs as an addict.

■ *n.* **1** medicine, pharmaceutical, remedy, cure. **2** opiate, *sl.* dope, downer, upper. • *v.* **2 a** dose, medicate, treat. **b** anesthetize, dope, knock out, sedate; dull; poison.

drug•gist /drúgist/ *n.* pharmacist.

drug•store /drúgstawr/ *n.* pharmacy also selling miscellaneous items.

■ see PHARMACY **2.**

Dru•id /dróoid/ *n.* member of an ancient Celtic religion. □□ **Dru′id•ism** *n.* **Dru•id′ic**

drum /drum/ • *n.* **1 a** hollow, cylindrical percussion instrument covered at one or both ends. **b** percussion section. **c** sound made by or like that of a drum. **2** thing resembling a drum, esp. a container. • *v.* (**drummed, drum•ming**) **1** *intr. & tr.* play a drum. **2** *tr. & intr.* beat, tap, or thump (fingers, etc.) continuously (on something). **3** *intr.* (of a bird or an insect) make a loud, hollow noise with quivering wings. □ **drum into** drive (a lesson) into (a person) by persistence. **drum major** leader of a marching band. **drum majorette** female member of a baton-twirling parading group. **drum out** expel for wrongdoing. **drum up** summon, gather, or call up. □□ **drum′mer** *n.*

drum•stick /drúmstik/ *n.* **1** stick for beating a drum. **2** lower leg of a dressed fowl.

drunk /drungk/ • *adj.* **1** rendered incapable by alcohol. **2** overcome with joy, success, power, etc. • *n.* **1** drunkard. **2** *sl.* drinking bout.

■ *adj.* **1** intoxicated, inebriated, besotted, tipsy, pixilated, *colloq.* soused, tight, stewed, tanked (up), loaded, stoned, pickled, sloshed, plastered, smashed, blotto. **2** inspired, exhilarated, exuberant, invigorated, ecstatic; elated. • *n.* **1** drinker, tippler, sot; dipsomaniac, alcoholic, boozer, *sl.* wino, lush. **2** see BENDER.

drunk•ard /drúngkərd/ *n.* person who is habitually drunk.
  ■ see DRUNK *n.* 1.

drunk•en /drúngkən/ *adj.* **1** = DRUNK. **2** caused by or exhibiting drunkenness. □□ **drunk′en•ly** *adv.* **drunk′en•ness** *n.*
  ■ **1** see DRUNK *adj.* 1. □□ **drunkenness** intoxication, insobriety; alcoholism.

drupe /drōōp/ *n.* fleshy stone fruit, e.g., olive or peach. □□ **dru•pa•ceous** /-páyshəs/ *adj.*

dry /drī/ • *adj.* (**dri•er** /drīər/; **dri•est** /drī-ist/) **1** free from moisture, esp.: **a** with moisture having evaporated, drained away, etc. **b** (of the eyes) free from tears. **c** (of a climate, etc.) with insufficient rain. **2** (of wine, etc.) not sweet. **3 a** meager; plain (*dry facts*). **b** uninteresting. **4** (of humor) subtle; ironic. **5** prohibiting the sale of alcohol. • *v.* (**dries**, **dried**) make or become dry. □ **dry cell** battery cell in which the electrolyte is dry. **dry-clean** clean (clothes, etc.) with solvents and no water. **dry dock** enclosure for the building or repairing of ships. **dry goods** fabric, thread, clothing, etc., esp. as distinct from hardware, groceries, etc. **dry ice** solid carbon dioxide. **dry out 1** become fully dry. **2** (of a drug addict, alcoholic, etc.) undergo treatment for addiction. **dry rot** decay of wood caused by certain fungi. **dry run** *colloq.* rehearsal. **dry up 1** make or become utterly dry. **2** *colloq.* cease talking. **3** (of supplies) run out. □□ **dry′ly, dri′ly** *adv.* **dry′ness** *n.*
  ■ *adj.* **1 a** dehydrated, desiccated. **c** arid, parched. **3 a** unadorned, unembellished; see also PLAIN *adj.* 1, BARE *adj.* 4. **b** dreary, boring, dull, stale, uninspired; see also TEDIOUS. **4** droll, wry, cynical, biting, sarcastic. • *v.* dehydrate, desiccate, parch; wither, shrivel, wilt.

SYNONYM STUDY: dry

ARID, DEHYDRATED, DESICCATED, PARCHED. Almost anything lacking in moisture (in relative terms)—whether it's a piece of bread, the basement of a house, or the state of Arizona—may be described as **dry**, a word that also connotes a lack of life or spirit (*a dry lecture on cell division*). **Arid**, on the other hand, applies to places or things that have been deprived of moisture and are therefore extremely or abnormally *dry* (*one side of the island was arid*); it is most commonly used to describe a desertlike region or climate that is lifeless or barren. **Desiccated** is used as a technical term for something from which moisture has been removed, and in general use it suggests lifelessness, although it is applied very often to people who have lost their vitality (*a desiccated old woman who never left her house*) or to animal and vegetable products that have been completely deprived of their vital juices (*desiccated oranges hanging limply from the tree*). **Dehydrated** is very

close in meaning to *desiccated* and is often the preferred adjective when describing foods from which the moisture has been deliberately extracted (*they lived on dehydrated fruit*). *Dehydrated* may also refer to an unwanted loss of moisture (*the virus had left him seriously dehydrated*), as may the less formal term **parched**, which refers to an undesirable or uncomfortable lack of water in either a human being or a place (*parched with thirst; the parched landscape*).

---

dry•ad /drīad, drīəd/ *n.* wood nymph.
dry•wall /drīwawl/ *n.* = PLASTERBOARD.
DSM *abbr.* Distinguished Service Medal.
DST *abbr.* daylight saving(s) time.
DT *abbr.* (also **DT's** /deetéez/) delirium tremens.

du•al /dōōəl, dyōōəl/ *adj.* **1** of two; twofold. **2** double (*dual ownership*). □□ **du•al•i•ty** /-álitee/ *n.* **du′al•ize** *v.tr.* **du′al•ly** *adv.*
  ■ **1** see DOUBLE *adj.* 4.

dub¹ /dub/ *v.tr.* (**dubbed, dub•bing**) **1** make (a person) a knight by touching his shoulders with a sword. **2** give (a person) a name, nickname, etc.
  ■ **2** see NAME *v.* 1.

dub² /dub/ *v.tr.* (**dubbed, dub•bing**) **1** provide (a movie, etc.) with an alternative soundtrack. **2** add (sound effects or music) to a movie or broadcast. **3** copy (a soundtrack).

du•bi•ous /dōōbeeəs, dyōō-/ *adj.* **1** hesitating; doubting. **2** questionable. **3** unreliable; suspicious. See synonym study at DOUBTFUL. □□ **du′bi•ous•ly** *adv.*
  ■ **1** see *skeptical* (SKEPTIC). **2** see DEBATABLE. **3** see UNRELIABLE, SHADY 3.

du•cal /dōōkəl, dyōō-/ *adj.* of or like a duke.
du•cat /dúkət/ *n.* *hist.* former gold coin of Europe.
duch•ess /dúchis/ *n.* **1** duke's wife or widow. **2** woman holding the rank of duke.
duch•y /dúchee/ *n.* (*pl.* **-ies**) territory of a duke or duchess.
duck¹ /duk/ *n.* (*pl.* same or **ducks**) **1** swimming bird, esp. the domesticated mallard or wild duck. **2** its flesh as food. □ **duck soup** *sl.* easy task. **like a duck to water** adapting very readily. **like water off a duck's back** *colloq.* (of remonstrances, etc.) producing no effect.

duck² /duk/ • *v.* **1** plunge, dive, or dip under water and emerge. **2** bend quickly, esp. to avoid a blow or being seen. **3** *colloq.* avoid or dodge (*ducked the meeting*). • *n.* quick lowering of the head, etc.
  ■ *v.* **1** dunk, push under, submerge, immerse. **2** bob, stoop, bow, crouch. **3** sidestep, evade, elude, shun, steer clear of, shirk.

duck³ /duk/ *n.* **1** strong linen or cotton fabric. **2** [in *pl.*] pants made of this (*white ducks*).
duck•bill /dúkbil/ *n.* (also **duck′-billed plat′ ypus**) = PLATYPUS.
duck•ling /dúkling/ *n.* **1** young duck. **2** its flesh as food.
duck•y /dúkee/ *adj. sl.* sweet; pretty; splendid.
duct /dukt/ *n.* channel or tube for conveying fluid, cable, etc.

■ *n.* see PIPE *n.* 1.

duc•tile /dúktəl, -tíl/ *adj.* **1** (of metal) capable of being drawn into wire; pliable. **2** (of a substance) easily molded. □□ **duc•til•i•ty** /-tílitee/ *n.*

■ **2** see PLASTIC *adj.*

dud /dud/ *n. sl.* **1** futile or ineffectual person or thing. **2** shell, etc., that fails to explode. **3** [in *pl.*] clothes.

■ **1** failure, *colloq.* washout, *sl.* flop. **3** (*duds*) see CLOTHES.

dude /dood, dyood/ *n. sl.* **1** dandy. **2** vacationer on a ranch. **3** fellow; guy.

■ **1** fop, man about town. **3** see FELLOW *n.* 1.

dudg•eon /dújən/ *n.* resentment. □ **in high dudgeon** very angry or angrily.

due /doo, dyoo/ • *adj.* **1** owing or payable. **2** merited; appropriate. **3** rightful; proper. **4** *predic.* to be ascribed to (a cause, an agent, etc.) (*the discovery was due to Edison*). **5** intended to arrive or occur at a certain time. • *n.* **1** what is owed to a person. **2** [in *pl.*] what one owes. • *adv.* (of a direction) exactly; directly. □ **due process** legal procedures to ensure individual rights. **due to** because of. **in due course 1** at about the appropriate time. **2** in the natural order.

■ *adj.* **1** unpaid, outstanding, in arrears. **2**, **3** fitting, correct, apropos, suitable, apt; justified; necessary. **4** (*due to*) owing to. **5** expected, anticipated. • *n.* **1** see PREROGATIVE. **2** (*dues*) (membership) fee, charge(s), toll. • *adv.* precisely, straight. □ **due to** owing to, on account of, by reason of, thanks to, as a result of, by virtue of. **in due course 1** see PRESENTLY 1.

du•el /dóoəl, dyóoəl/ • *n.* **1** armed contest between two people, usu. to settle a point of honor. **2** any contest between two. • *v.intr.* fight a duel. □□ **du'el•er** *n.* **du'el•ist** *n.*

■ *n.* **2** see BATTLE *n.* 2. • *v.* see COMBAT *v.* 1.

du•et /dŏō-ét, dyōō-/ *n. Mus.* **1** performance by two performers. **2** composition for two performers. □□ **du•et'tist** *n.*

duf•fel /dúfəl/ *n.* (also **duf'fle**) coarse woolen cloth with a thick nap. □ **duffel bag** cylindrical canvas, etc., bag used as luggage.

duf•fer /dúfər/ *n. sl.* inefficient, useless, or stupid person.

■ incompetent, blunderer, bungler, oaf.

dug *past* and *past part.* of DIG.

du•gong /dóogawng, -gong/ *n.* (*pl.* same or **du•gongs**) marine mammal of Asian seas and coasts. (Also called **sea cow**).

dug•out /dúgowt/ *n.* **1** roofed shelter, esp. for troops or at a baseball field. **2** canoe made from a tree trunk.

duke /dook, dyook/ *n.* **1 a** person holding the highest hereditary title of nobility. **b** prince ruling a duchy. **2** [usu. in *pl.*] *sl.* hand; fist (*put up your dukes!*).

duke•dom /dóokdəm, dyóok-/ *n.* territory ruled by a duke.

dul•cet /dúlsit/ *adj.* (esp. of sound) sweet and soothing.

dul•ci•mer /dúlsimər/ *n.* stringed musical instrument played by being struck with hammers.

dull /dul/ • *adj.* **1** slow to understand; stupid. **2** tedious; boring. **3** (of the weather) overcast; gloomy. **4 a** (esp. of a knife edge, etc.) blunt. **b** (of color, light, sound, etc.) not bright, vivid, or keen. **5** (of pain, etc.) not acute. **6 a** (of a person, an animal, trade, etc.) sluggish; slow-moving. **b** (of a person) listless; depressed. • *v.* make or become dull. □□ **dull'ness** *n.* **dul'ly** *adv.*

■ *adj.* **1** dull-witted, slow-witted, obtuse, doltish; *colloq.* thick, dumb; see also STUPID *adj.* 1,3. **2** tiresome, monotonous, uninspired, humdrum; see also TEDIOUS. **3** dismal, dreary. **4 a** see BLUNT *adj.* 1. **b** hazy, blurry, opaque; drab, dingy, lackluster. **5** numbing, muted. **6** stagnant, lifeless, indifferent, unresponsive, inactive, torpid, down; see also LISTLESS. • *v.* allay, assuage, relieve, mitigate, lessen, reduce; dim, tarnish, obscure, blur, cloud; numb, desensitize.

dull•ard /dúlərd/ *n.* stupid person.

du•ly /dóolee, dyóo-/ *adv.* **1** in due time or manner. **2** rightly; properly; fitly.

■ **1** punctually; see also *promptly* (PROMPT). **2** deservedly, appropriately, suitably, correctly, accordingly.

dumb /dum/ *adj.* **1** unable to speak; mute. **2** silenced by surprise, shyness, etc. **3** *colloq.* stupid; ignorant. □□ **dumb'ly** /dúmlee/ *adv.* **dumb'ness** *n.*

■ **1, 2** speechless, voiceless, wordless; silent, quiet, *colloq.* mum; inarticulate. **3** dull, *colloq.* thick, dense, dim; see also STUPID *adj.* 1, 3.

dumb•bell /dúmbel/ *n.* **1** short bar with a weight at each end, used for muscle-building, etc. **2** *sl.* stupid person.

■ **2** see FOOL *n.* 1.

dumb•found /dúmfównd/ *v.tr.* (also **dum•found'**) strike dumb; confound; nonplus.

■ make speechless, amaze, shock, surprise, startle, take aback, astonish, astound, bewilder, stun, confuse, *colloq.* flabbergast, floor, bowl over, *sl.* knock out, (*be dumbfounded*) be at a loss for words.

dumb•wait•er /dúmwaytər/ *n.* small elevator for carrying food, plates, etc., between floors.

dum•my /dúmee/ • *n.* (*pl.* **-mies**) **1** model of a human, esp.: **a** ventriloquist's doll. **b** figure used to model clothes. **2** imitation or stand-in object. **3** *colloq.* stupid person. **4** *Bridge* partner of the declarer, whose cards are exposed after the first lead. • *adj.* sham; counterfeit. □ **dummy run** trial run; rehearsal. **dummy up** *sl.* keep quiet; give no information.

■ *n.* **1 b** mannequin. **2** copy, reproduction, likeness, mock-up, simulation. **3** idiot, dunce, blockhead, ninny, ass, dolt, numskull, simpleton, *colloq.* dimwit; see also FOOL *n.* 1. • *adj.* see SHAM *adj.*

dump /dump/ • *n.* **1** place for depositing trash, garbage, etc. **2** *colloq.* unpleasant or dreary place. **3** temporary store of ammunition, etc. • *v.tr.* **1** put down firmly or clumsily. **2** deposit or dispose of (rubbish, etc.). **3** *colloq.* abandon; desert. **4** *Mil.* leave (ammunition, etc.) in a dump. **5** *Econ.* send (excess goods) to a foreign market at a low price. **6** *Computing* copy (stored data) to a different location. □ **dump on** *sl.* criticize or abuse; get the better of. **dump truck** truck with a body that tilts or opens at the back for unloading. □□ **dump′ing** *n.*

■ *n.* **2** see HOLE[1] *n.* 3a. • *v.* **1** unload, offload, drop, throw *or* fling down. **2** get rid of, throw away, scrap, discard, jettison, toss out *or* away, junk, *colloq.* chuck (out), *colloq.* trash, *sl.* ditch. **3** see DESERT 1, 2. □ **dump on** see CRITICIZE 1, DEFEAT *v.* 1.

dump•ling /dúmpling/ *n.* **1** ball of boiled or steamed dough, usu. eaten with stew, etc. **2** dough filled with fruit, etc.

dumps /dumps/ *n.pl. colloq.* depression (*in the dumps*).

■ (*in the dumps*) see DESPONDENT.

Dump•ster /dúmpstər/ *n. propr.* large trash receptacle designed to be hoisted and emptied into a truck.

dump•y /dúmpee/ *adj.* (**dump•i•er, dump•i•est**) short and stout. □□ **dump′i•ness** *n.*

■ stocky, squat, chunky, chubby, heavy, tubby, plump, portly, fat, thickset, *colloq.* pudgy.

dun[1] /dun/ • *adj.* dull grayish brown. • *n.* dun color.

dun[2] /dun/ • *n.* demand for payment. • *v.tr.* (**dunned, dun•ning**) importune for payment of a debt; pester.

■ *v.* press, solicit; nag, harass; see also PESTER.

dunce /duns/ *n.* ignorant person; dullard.

■ see FOOL *n.* 1.

dune /doon, dyoon/ *n.* bank of sand formed by the wind.

dung /dung/ *n.* excrement of animals; manure.

■ muck, droppings, guano, feces.

dun•ga•ree /dúnggəree/ *n.* **1** coarse cotton cloth. **2** [in *pl.*] pants or overalls made of this.

dun•geon /dúnjən/ *n.* underground prison cell.

■ oubliette.

dunk /dungk/ *v.tr.* **1** dip (food) into liquid before eating. **2** immerse. □ **dunk shot** basketball shot made by jumping up and thrusting the ball down through the basket.

■ see DIP *v.* 1.

du•o /doo-o, dyoo-o/ *n.* (*pl.* **-os**) **1** pair of performers. **2** duet.

■ see PAIR *n.* 1.

du•o•dec•i•mal /doo-ōdésiməl, dyoo-/ *adj.* relating to a system of numerical notation that has 12 as a base.

du•o•de•num /dooədeénəm, dyoo-, dood-ód′nəm, dyoo-/ *n.* first part of the small intestine below the stomach. □□ **du•o•de′nal** *adj.*

dupe /doop, dyoop/ • *n.* victim of deception. • *v.tr.* make a fool of; cheat.

■ *n.* fool, pigeon, pawn, puppet, *colloq.* stooge, *sl.* fall guy, sucker, sap, mark, patsy. • *v.* deceive, outwit, trick, take in, defraud, humbug, hoax, swindle, flimflam, rook, delude, *colloq.* bamboozle, rip off, put one over on, pull a fast one on, *sl.* con, bilk, snow; see also CHEAT *v.* 1.

du•ple /doopəl, dyoo-/ *adj.* of two parts.

du•plex /doopleks, dyoo-/ • *n.* **1** apartment on two levels. **2** house subdivided for two families. • *adj. Computing* (of a circuit) allowing the transmission of signals in both directions simultaneously.

du•pli•cate • *adj.* /doopliket, dyoo-/ **1** identical. **2 a** having two identical parts. **b** doubled. • *n.* /dooplikət, dyoo-/ identical thing, esp. a copy. • *v.tr.* /dooplikayt, dyoo-/ **1** make or be an exact copy of. **2** repeat (an action, etc.), esp. unnecessarily. □□ **du•pli•ca•ble** /dooplikəbəl, dyoo-/ *adj.* **du•pli•ca•tion** /-káyshən/ *n.* **dup′li•ca•tor** *n.*

■ *adj.* **1** twin, matching; copied. • *n.* (exact or carbon) copy, double, clone, look-alike, reproduction, replica, facsimile, replication; photocopy. • *v.* **1** replicate, imitate, reproduce; copy, photocopy. **2** see REPEAT *v.* 1, REPRODUCE 1, 2.

du•plic•i•ty /dooplísitee, dyoo-/ *n.* deceitfulness. □□ **du•plic′i•tous** *adj.*

■ see DECEIT 1.

du•ra•ble /doorəbəl, dyoo-/ *adj.* lasting; hard-wearing. □□ **du•ra•bil′i•ty** *n.*

■ wear-resistant, heavy-duty, sturdy, tough, stout, strong, firm, sound, dependable, reliable, substantial.

du•ra ma•ter /doorə máytər, maa–, dyoorə/ *n.* outermost membrane of the brain and spinal cord.

du•ra•tion /dooráyshən, dyoor-/ *n.* length of time for which something continues. □ **for the duration** until the end of something obstructing normal activities, as a war. □□ **du•ra′tion•al** *adj.*

■ see TIME *n.* 4, 6.

du•ress /doorés, dyoo-/ *n.* **1** coercive circumstances. **2** forcible restraint or imprisonment.

■ **1** coercion, constraint, compulsion, force. **2** confinement, incarceration, captivity; see also *imprisonment* (IMPRISON).

dur•ing /dooring, dyoor-/ *prep.* throughout or at some point in.

■ see THROUGHOUT *prep.*

du•rum /doorəm, dyoo-/ *n.* hard-seeded wheat used in the manufacture of pasta, etc.

dusk /dusk/ *n.* darker stage of twilight.

■ sundown, nightfall, evening, sunset, eventide.

dusk•y /dúskee/ *adj.* (**dusk•i•er, dusk•i•est**) shadowy; dim; darkish. □□ **dusk′i•ly** *adv.* **dusk′i•ness** *n.*

■ shady, dull, murky, obscure; fuscous.

dust /dust/ • *n.* **1** finely powdered earth, dirt, etc. **2** dead person's remains. • *v.tr.* **1** clear (furniture, etc.) of dust. **2** sprinkle with powder, dust, sugar, etc. □ **dust bowl** area denuded of vegetation by drought or erosion. **dust devil** whirlwind visible as a column of dust. **dusting powder** talcum powder. **dust jacket** paper cover on a book. **dust off** use and enjoy after a long period of neglect. **when the dust settles** when things quiet down.

■ *n.* **1** see DIRT 1. • *v.* **1** see CLEAN *v.* **2** dredge, flour.

dust•pan /dústpan/ *n.* receptacle for (brushed up) dust.

dust•y /dústee/ *adj.* (dust•i•er, dust•i•est) **1** full of, covered with, or resembling dust. **2** (of a color) dull or muted. □□ **dust′i•ly** *adv.* **dust′i•ness** *n.*

Dutch /duch/ • *adj.* of the Netherlands. • *n.* **1** language of the Netherlands. **2** [prec. by *the*; treated as *pl.*] people of the Netherlands. □ **Dutch door** door horizontally divided allowing one part to be shut and the other open. **Dutch elm disease** fungus disease affecting elms. **Dutch oven** covered cooking pot for braising, etc. **Dutch treat** outing, etc., at which people pay for themselves. **Dutch uncle** kind but firm adviser. **go Dutch** share expenses.

du•ti•ful /dóotifool, dyóo-/ *adj.* doing one's duty; obedient. □□ **du′ti•ful•ly** *adv.*

  ■ *responsible, diligent, attentive, compliant,* conscientious.

du•ty /dóotee, dyóo-/ *n.* (*pl.* **-ties**) **1** moral or legal obligation; responsibility. **2** tax on certain imports, etc. **3** job or function. □ **on** (or **off**) **duty** engaged (or not engaged) in one's work.

  ■ **1** see OBLIGATION 2, RESPONSIBILITY 1a. **2** excise, tariff, impost, levy, customs. **3** role, task, chore. □ **off duty** free, on leave.

du•vet /doováy/ *n.* thick, soft quilt with a detachable cover.

  ■ see SPREAD *n.* 8.

DVD • *abbr.* digital video disc.

D.V.M. *abbr.* doctor of veterinary medicine.

dwarf /dwawrf/ • *n.* (*pl.* **dwarfs** or **dwarves** /dwawrvz/) **1 a** *offens.* person of abnormally small stature. **b** animal or plant much below ordinary size. **2** small mythological being with supernatural powers. **3** (in full **dwarf star**) small usu. dense star. • *v.tr.* **1** stunt in growth. **2** cause to seem small or insignificant. □□ **dwarf′ish** *adj.*

  ■ *v.* **1** see STUNT¹ 2. **2** overshadow, dominate; diminish, minimize, lessen.

dweeb /dweeb/ *n. sl.* socially inept person.

dwell /dwel/ • *v.intr.* (*past and past part* **dwelled** or **dwelt**) live; reside. • *n.* slight, regular pause in the motion of a machine. □ **dwell on** (or **upon**) linger over; write, brood, or speak at length on. □□ **dwell′er** *n.*

  ■ *v.* lodge, stay, remain, rest. □ **dwell on** (or **upon**) harp on, belabor, focus on, brood on *or* over, *colloq.* go on about.

dwell•ing /dwéling/ *n.* house; residence.

  ■ habitation, domicile; see also ABODE¹.

DWI *abbr.* driving while intoxicated.

dwin•dle /dwínd'l/ *v.intr.* become gradually less or smaller.

  ■ diminish, decrease, shrink, lessen, wane, fade, peter out, waste away, die down, ebb, decline, subside, taper off; see also DEGENERATE *v.*

Dy *symb. Chem.* dysprosium.

dye /dī/ • *n.* **1** substance used to change the color of hair, fabric, wood, etc. **2** color produced by this. • *v.tr.* (**dye•ing**) color with dye. □ **dyed-in-the-wool** out-and-out; unchangeable. □□ **dye′a•ble** *adj.*

  ■ *n.* see COLOR *n.* 3. • *v.* see COLOR *v.* 1.

dy•ing /dí-ing/ *adj.* of, or at the time of, death. □ **to one's dying day** for the rest of one's life.

  ■ at death's door, on one's deathbed, with one foot in the grave, on one's last legs. □ **to one's dying day** see ALWAYS 1.

dy•nam•ic /dīnámik/ *adj.* **1** energetic; active. **2** *Physics* **a** of motive force. **b** of force in actual operation. **3** of dynamics. □□ **dy•nam′i•cal•ly** *adv.*

  ■ **1** *vigorous, forceful, potent, powerful,* lively, spirited; see also *energetic* (ENERGY).

dy•nam•ics /dīnámiks/ *n.pl.* **1** [usu. treated as *sing.*] the study of motion and its causes. **2** motive forces in any sphere.

dy•na•mism /dínəmizəm/ *n.* energy; dynamic power. □□ **dy′na•mist** *n.*

  ■ vigor, vitality, liveliness, spirit, vim, drive, initiative, *colloq.* get-up-and-go, pep; see also ENERGY 1.

dy•na•mite /dínəmīt/ • *n.* **1** high explosive containing nitroglycerin. **2** potentially dangerous person, situation, etc. • *v.tr.* charge or shatter with dynamite.

  ■ *n.* **1** see EXPLOSIVE *n.* • *v.* see BLAST *v.* 1.

dy•na•mo /dínəmō/ *n.* (*pl.* **-mos**) **1** electric generator. **2** *colloq.* energetic person.

dy•nas•ty /dínəstee/ *n.* (*pl.* **-ties**) **1** line of hereditary rulers. **2** succession of leaders in any field. □□ **dy•nas•tic** /-nástik/ *adj.* **dy•nas′ti•cal•ly** *adv.*

  ■ **1** ancestry, family, house.

dyne /dīn/ *n. Physics* unit of force that, upon a mass of one gram, increases its velocity by one centimeter per second.

dys- /dis/ *comb. form* bad; difficult.

dys•en•ter•y /dísənteree/ *n.* inflammation of the intestines, causing severe diarrhea. □□ **dys•en•ter′ic** *adj.*

dys•func•tion /dísfúngkshən/ *n.* abnormality or impairment of function. □□ **dys•func′tion•al** *adj.*

dys•lex•i•a /disléksee.ə/ *n.* abnormal difficulty in reading and spelling. □□ **dys•lex′ic** *adj. & n.*

dys•pep•sia /dispépsee.ə/ *n.* indigestion. □□ **dys•pep′tic** *n.*

dys•pro•si•um /disprózeeəm/ *n. Chem.* metallic element of the lanthanide series. ¶Symb.: **Dy.**

dys•tro•phy /dístrəfee/ *n.* defective nutrition. □ **muscular dystrophy** hereditary progressive weakening of the muscles. □□ **dys•troph•ic** /distrófik, -trő-/ *adj.*

dz. *abbr.* dozen.

Ee

E[1] /ee/ *n.* (also **e**) (*pl.* **Es** or **E's**; **e's**) **1** fifth letter of the alphabet. **2** *Mus.* third note of the diatonic scale of C major.

E[2] *abbr.* (also **E.**) **1** east; eastern. **2** English. **3** energy.

e- /ee, e/ *prefix* form of EX-[1] 1 before some consonants.

ea. *abbr.* each.

each /eech/ • *adj.* every one of two or more persons or things, regarded separately. • *pron.* each person or thing. □ **each and every** every single. **each other** one another (*they wore each other's hats*).

ea•ger /eegər/ *adj.* enthusiastic; keen. □□ **ea´ger•ly** *adv.* **ea´ger•ness** *n.*

■ avid, zealous, ardent, earnest, hungry, fervent, fervid, passionate, spirited, energetic; impatient, anxious. □□ **eagerness** zeal, fervor, gusto, verve; desire.

SYNONYM STUDY: eager

ARDENT, AVID, ENTHUSIASTIC, FERVENT, KEEN, ZEALOUS. You've heard of the "eager beaver"? Anyone who has a strong interest or an impatient desire to pursue or become involved in something is called *eager* (*eager to get started; an eager learner*). Someone who is especially *eager* might be called *avid*, a word that implies strong enthusiasm or even insatiable desire (*an avid golfer, he was never at home on weekends*). **Ardent** combines eagerness with intense feelings of passion or devotion (*an ardent lover; an ardent theatergoer*), while *fervent* suggests an eagerness that is ready, at least figuratively, to boil over (*their fervent pleas could not be ignored*). Anyone who is deeply interested in something or who shows a spirited readiness to act is called *keen* (*he was keen on bicycling*), while *zealous* implies the kind of eagerness that pushes all other considerations aside (*a zealous environmentalist*). **Enthusiastic** may connote participation rather than expectation: One can be *eager* to take a trip to Switzerland, an *ardent* student of Swiss history, and an *avid* outdoorsperson who is *keen* on hiking, but one is usually called *enthusiastic* about a trip to Switzerland when it is under way or is over; *enthusiastic* also very often applies to someone who outwardly and forcefully expresses eagerness (*she was enthusiastic about our plans to redecorate the apartment*).

---

ea•gle /eegəl/ *n.* **1 a** large bird of prey with keen vision and powerful flight. **b** this as a symbol, esp. of the US. **2** *Golf* score of two strokes under par at a hole. **3** gold US coin worth ten dollars. □ **eagle-eyed** keensighted, watchful. **Eagle Scout** highest Boy Scout rank.

■ □ **eagle-eyed** sharp-sighted; perceptive, discerning, vigilant; see also ALERT *adj.* 1.

ea•glet /eeglit/ *n.* young eagle.

-ean /eeən/ *suffix* var. of -AN.

ear[1] /eer/ *n.* **1** organ of hearing, esp. its external part. **2** faculty for discriminating sounds (*an ear for music*). **3** listening; attention. □ **all ears** listening attentively. **have a person's ear** receive a favorable hearing. **have (or keep) an ear to the ground** be alert to rumors or the trend of opinion. **in one ear and out the other** heard but disregarded or quickly forgotten. **out on one's ear** dismissed ignominiously. **up to one's ears** *colloq.* deeply involved or occupied. □□ **eared** *adj.*

■ **2** sensitivity, appreciation, taste. **3** heed, notice, regard, consideration. □ **all ears** intent, heedful; see also OBSERVANT 1. **have (or keep) an ear to the ground** watch out, keep one's eyes open *or* peeled. **up to one's ears** see ENGAGED 2a.

ear[2] /eer/ *n.* seed-bearing head of a cereal plant.

ear•ache /eerayk/ *n.* pain in the ear.

ear•drum /eerdrum/ *n.* membrane of the middle ear.

ear•ful /eerfool/ *n.* (*pl.* **-fuls**) *colloq.* **1** prolonged amount of talking. **2** strong reprimand.

earl /ərl/ *n.* British nobleman ranking between marquess and viscount. □□ **earl´dom** *n.*

ear•lobe /eerlōb/ *n.* lower, soft external part of the ear.

ear•ly /ərlee/ *adj. & adv.* (**ear•li•er, ear•li•est**) **1** before the usual or expected time. **2 a** not far on in the day or night, or in time. **b** prompt. **3** not far on in a period or process. □ **early bird** *colloq.* one who arrives, gets up, etc., early. □□ **ear´li•ness** *n.*

■ *adj. & adv.* **1** beforehand, ahead (of time), in advance, prematurely; in good time. **2 a** at (the crack *or* break of) dawn, at daybreak. **b** see PROMPT *adj.* **3** initially, originally; primeval, primitive, ancient, old, prehistoric; antique, antiquated.

ear•mark /eermaark/ • *n.* identifying mark. • *v.tr.* **1** set aside for a special purpose. **2** mark (sheep, etc.) with an earmark.

■ *n.* stamp. • *v.* **1** see ASSIGN *v.* 1a. **2** see LABEL *v.* 1.

ear•muff /eermuf/ *n.* cover for the ears, protecting them from cold.

earn /ərn/ *v.tr.* **1** bring in as interest or income. **2** deserve; be entitled to; obtain as reward.

■ **1** make, receive, take home; yield. **2** merit, be worthy of, win, warrant, have a claim *or* right to.

ear•nest /ərnist/ *adj.* intensely serious. □ **in (or in real) earnest** serious(ly), not joking(ly); with determination. □□ **ear´nest•ly** *adv.* **ear´nest•ness** *n.*

■ solemn, grave, sober, steady, resolute, resolved, firm, diligent, industrious, hardworking, sincere, dedicated, committed, devoted, thoughtful, conscientious; zealous, ardent, eager, keen, fervent, fervid, enthusiastic, passionate.

earn•ings /órningz/ *n.pl.* money earned.

■ wages, salary, income, pay, stipend, emolument; proceeds, return, revenue, yield, take.

ear•phone /éerfōn/ *n.* device applied to the ear to receive radio, etc., communications.

ear•ring /éering/ *n.* jewelry worn on the ear.

ear•shot /éershot/ *n.* hearing range.

■ reach, call.

ear•split•ting /éerspliting/ *adj.* excessively loud.

■ see SHRILL *adj.*, LOUD *adj.* 1.

earth /orth/ *n.* **1 a** (also **Earth**) the planet on which we live. **b** land and sea, as distinct from sky. **2 a** the ground. **b** soil. **3** *Relig.* this world, as distinct from heaven or hell. □ **come back** (or **down**) **to earth** return to realities. **earth-shattering** *colloq.* having a traumatic or devastating effect. **on earth** *colloq.* **1** existing anywhere (*the happiest man on earth*). **2** as an intensifier (*what on earth?*). □□ **earth'ward** *adj. & adv.* **earth'wards** *adv.*

■ **1 a** globe, mother earth, world. **2 b** dirt, loam, sod, clay.

earth•en /órthən/ *adj.* **1** made of earth. **2** made of baked clay.

earth•en•ware /órthənwair/ • *n.* pottery, vessels, etc., made of fired clay. • *adj.* made of fired clay.

■ *n.* see POTTERY.

earth•ling /órthling/ *n.* inhabitant of earth, esp. in science fiction.

■ terrestrial, tellurian, mortal, human.

earth•ly /órthlee/ *adj.* **1 a** of the earth; terrestrial. **b** of human life. **2** [usu. with *neg.*] *colloq.* remotely possible (*no earthly use*).

■ **1 b** physical, material, worldly, nonspiritual, sensual, carnal, corporeal, natural, temporal, mortal. **2** conceivable, imaginable, feasible, possible.

earth•quake /órthkwayk/ *n.* convulsion of the earth's surface due to underground faults or volcanic action.

■ quake, tremor.

earth•work /órthwork/ *n.* **1** artificial bank of earth in fortification, road building, etc. **2** process of excavating soil in civil engineering work.

earth•worm /órthworm/ *n.* common worm living and burrowing in the ground.

earth•y /órthee/ *adj.* (**earth•i•er**, **earth•i•est**) **1** of or like earth or soil. **2** somewhat coarse or crude; unrefined (*earthy humor*). **3** down-to-earth. □□ **earth'i•ness** *n.*

■ **2** vulgar, rough; see also CRUDE *adj.* 2a. **3** see PRACTICAL *adj.*

ear•wig /éerwig/ *n.* small elongate insect with a pair of terminal appendages in the shape of forceps.

ease /eez/ • *n.* **1** facility; effortlessness. **2** freedom or relief from pain, anxiety, hardship, etc. • *v.* **1** *tr.* **a** relieve from pain, anxiety, etc. **b** help; facilitate. **2** *intr.* **a** become less painful or burdensome. **b** relax. **3 a** *tr.* slacken. **b** *tr. & intr.* move or be moved carefully into place.

■ *n.* **1** easiness, simplicity. **2** comfort, re-

pose, well-being, relaxation, leisure, rest, contentment, calmness, tranquillity, serenity, peacefulness; informality; casualness, affluence, wealth, prosperity. • *v.* **1 a** comfort, calm, tranquilize, quiet, still, pacify, soothe; mitigate, allay, alleviate, assuage, mollify, appease. **b** expedite, simplify, smooth, further, clear, assist, aid. **2 a** lessen, diminish, abate, decrease. **b** see RELAX 1. **3 b** maneuver, manipulate, inch, guide, steer, slip.

ea•sel /éezəl/ *n.* frame to hold an artist's work, a blackboard, etc.

ease•ment /éezmənt/ *n.* *Law* right of way or a similar right over another's land.

eas•i•ly /éezilee/ *adv.* **1** without difficulty. **2** by far (*easily the best*). **3** very probably (*it could easily snow*).

■ **1** effortlessly, simply; hands down, without even trying, with one's eyes closed, with one's hands tied behind one's back; without a hitch, like a charm *or* dream. **2** indisputably, indubitably, undoubtedly, unquestionably, clearly, far and away, definitely, certainly, surely. **3** most *or* very likely, well.

east /eest/ • *n.* **1 a** point of the horizon where the sun rises at the equinoxes. **b** compass point corresponding to this. **c** direction in which this lies. **2** (usu. **the East**) **a** Asia. **b** formerly Communist nations of eastern Europe. **3** eastern part of a country, town, etc. • *adj.* **1** toward, at, near, or facing the east. **2** from the east (*east wind*). • *adv.* **1** toward, at, or near the east. **2** [foll. by *of*] further east than.

east•bound /éestbownd/ *adj.* traveling or leading eastward.

Eas•ter /éestər/ *n.* festival (held on a Sunday in March or April) of Christ's resurrection.

east•er•ly /éestərlee/ • *adj. & adv.* **1** in an eastern position or direction. **2** (of a wind) from the east. • *n.* (*pl.* **-lies**) such a wind.

east•ern /éestərn/ *adj.* of or in the east. □ **eastern hemisphere** (also **Eastern Hemisphere**) the half of the earth containing Europe, Asia, and Africa. **Eastern (standard) time** standard time used in the eastern US and eastern Canada or in eastern Australia. □□ **east'ern•most** *adj.*

east'ern•er /éestərnər/ (also **East'ern•er**) *n.* native or inhabitant of the east, esp. in the US.

east•ward /éestwərd/ *adj. & adv.* (also **east' wards**) toward the east.

eas•y /éezee/ • *adj.* (**eas•i•er**, **eas•i•est**) **1** not difficult; achieved without great effort. **2 a** free from pain, discomfort, anxiety, etc. **b** affluent. **3** relaxed and pleasant. **4** compliant. • *adv.* with ease; in an effortless or relaxed manner. • *int.* go carefully; move gently. □ **easy chair** large comfortable chair. **easy come easy go** *colloq.* what is easily obtained is soon lost or spent. **easy does it** *colloq.* go carefully. **easy on the eye** (or **ear**, etc.) *colloq.* pleasant to look at (or listen to, etc.). **easy street** *colloq.* situation of ease or affluence. **go easy** [foll. by *with*, *on*] be sparing or cautious. **I'm easy** *colloq.* I have no preference. **of easy virtue** sexually promiscuous. **take it easy 1** proceed carefully. **2** relax. □□ **eas'i•ness** *n.*

■ *adj.* **1** simple, basic, uncomplicated; child's play. **2 a** carefree, easygoing, untroubled, quiet, tranquil, peaceful, undisturbed, comfortable. **3** moderate, unhurried; affable, friendly, amiable, agreeable. **4** tolerant, flexible; obliging, amenable, accommodating. ● *adv.* calmly, serenely.

eas•y•go•ing /éezeegóing/ *adj.* placid and tolerant.

■ relaxed, casual, mellow, carefree, undemanding, *colloq.* laid-back; see also EASY *adj.* 3.

eat /eet/ *v.* (*past* **ate** /ayt/; *past part.* **eat•en** /éet'n/) **1 a** *tr.* take into the mouth, chew, and swallow. **b** *intr.* consume food; have a meal. **2** *intr.* **a** destroy gradually. **b** begin to consume or diminish (resources, etc.). **3** *tr. colloq.* trouble; vex (*what's eating you?*). □ **eat one's heart out** suffer from excessive longing or envy. **eat out** have a meal away from home, esp. in a restaurant. **eat up 1** consume completely. **2** use rapidly or wastefully (*eats up time*). **3** encroach upon. **eat one's words** admit that one was wrong. □□ **eat'a•ble** *adj.* **eat'er** *n.*

■ **1 a** devour, ingest, munch, nibble, put away, gobble, partake of, *sl.* nosh, pig out. **b** dine, have a bite. **2 a** see ERODE. **3** see TROUBLE *v.* 1, 2.

eat•er•y /éetoree/ *n.* (*pl.* **-ies**) *colloq.* informal restaurant.

■ see CAFÉ 1.

eats /eets/ *n.pl. colloq.* food.

eau de co•logne /ódəkəlón/ *n.* alcohol-based perfume.

eaves /eevz/ *n.pl.* underside of a projecting roof.

eaves•drop /éevzdrop/ *v.intr.* (**-dropped,** **-drop•ping**) listen secretly to a private conversation. □□ **eaves'drop•per** *n.*

■ spy, pry, *colloq.* snoop; tap, *sl.* bug.

ebb /eb/ ● *n.* movement of the tide out to sea. ● *v.intr.* **1** flow out to sea; recede. **2** decline. □ **ebb and flow** continuing process of decline and upturn in circumstances.

■ *v.* **1** flow back, subside. **2** flag, decay, wane, diminish, decrease, lessen, drop, slacken, fade (away), dwindle, peter out, waste away, deteriorate, die down, run low.

eb•on•y /ébənee/ ● *n.* (*pl.* **-ies**) heavy, hard, dark wood. **2** any of various trees producing this. ● *adj.* **1** made of ebony. **2** black like ebony.

■ *adj.* **2** see BLACK *adj.* 1.

e•bul•lient /ibúlyant, ibóbl-/ *adj.* exuberant. □□ **e•bul'lience** *n.* **e•bul'lien•cy** *n.* **e•bul'lient•ly** *adv.*

■ high-spirited, buoyant, enthusiastic, zestful, effervescent, excited, elated, animated, ecstatic.

EC *abbr.* European Community.

ec•cen•tric /ikséntrik, ek-/ ● *adj.* **1** odd or capricious in behavior or appearance. **2** not quite concentric nor circular. ● *n.* **1** eccentric person. **2** *Mech.* disk for changing rotatory into backward-and-forward motion.

□□ **ec•cen'tri•cal•ly** *adv.* **ec•cen•tric•i•ty** /éksentrísitee/ *n.* (*pl.* **-ties**).

■ *adj.* **1** unconventional, unusual, peculiar, strange, curious, bizarre, outlandish, queer, quaint, far-out, quirky, offbeat, kinky, uncommon, abnormal, idiosyncratic, unorthodox, whimsical, out of the ordinary, irregular, atypical, errant, aberrant, exceptional, individual, singular, unique, *colloq.* weird. ● *n.* **1** individualist, nonconformist, crank, *colloq.* character, freak, oddball, weirdo. □□ **eccentricity** oddness, nonconformity; idiosyncrasy, peculiarity.

eccl. *abbr.* **1** ecclesiastic. **2** ecclesiastical.

ec•cle•si•as•tic /ikleézeeástik/ ● *n.* clergyman. ● *adj.* = ECCLESIASTICAL.

■ *n.* see CLERGYMAN.

ec•cle•si•as•ti•cal /ikleézeeástikal/ *adj.* of the church or the clergy. □□ **ec•cle•si•as'ti•cal•ly** *adv.*

■ see CLERICAL 1.

ECG *abbr.* electrocardiogram.

ech•e•lon /éshəlon/ *n.* **1** level in an organization, in society, etc.; those occupying it. **2** formation of troops, ships, aircraft, etc., in staggered parallel rows.

■ **1** see GRADE *n.* 1a, CATEGORY.

ech•e•ve•ri•a /échəvəreéə/ *n.* succulent plant of the Americas.

e•chi•no•derm /ikínədərm/ *n.* usu. spiny marine invertebrate, e.g., starfish and sea urchins.

ech•o /ékō/ ● *n.* (*pl.* **-oes** or **-os**) **1 a** repetition of a sound by reflection of sound waves. **b** sound so produced. **2** reflected radio or radar beam. **3** close imitation or repetition of something already done. ● *v.* (**-oes, -oed**) **1** *intr.* **a** (of a place) resound with an echo. **b** (of a sound) be repeated; resound. **2** *tr.* repeat (a sound) by an echo. **3** *tr.* **a** repeat (another's words). **b** imitate the words, opinions, or actions (of a person). □ **echo sounder** apparatus for determining the depth of the sea by measuring the time taken to receive an echo.

■ *n.* **1** reverberation, repercussion, reiteration. **3** copy, replica, replication, duplication, reproduction; reflection, mirror image. ● *v.* **1 a** reverberate, ring. **3** ape, parrot, mimic, simulate, emulate.

e•cho•ic /ekóik/ *adj. Phonet.* (of a word) imitating the sound it represents; onomatopoeic. □□ **ech'o•ism** *n.*

ech•o•lo•ca•tion /ékōlōkáyshən/ *n.* location of objects by reflected sound.

é•clair /aykláir/ *n.* small, elongated light pastry filled with whipped cream or custard, etc.

é•clat /aykláa/ *n.* **1** brilliant display; dazzling effect. **2** conspicuous success.

■ **1** see PANACHE. **2** see RENOWN.

ec•lec•tic /ikléktik/ ● *adj.* deriving ideas, style, etc., from various sources. ● *n.* eclectic person. □□ **ec•lec'ti•cal•ly** *adv.* **ec•lec•ti•cism** /-tisizəm/ *n.*

e•clipse /iklíps/ ● *n.* **1** obscuring of light from one celestial body by another. **2** loss of light, importance, or prominence. ● *v.tr.* **1** (of a celestial body) obscure the light from or to (another). **2** outshine; surpass.

■ *n.* **2** downturn, slump; see also PLUNGE *n.*

- *v.* **1** blot out, veil, shroud, cover. **2** overshadow, top.

ec•clip•tic /iklíptik/ *n.* sun's apparent path among the stars during the year.

ec•logue /éklawg, –log/ *n.* short pastoral poem.

■ idyll.

eco- /ékō, eékō/ *comb. form* ecology, ecological.

ecol. *abbr.* **1** ecological. **2** ecologist. **3** ecology.

e•col•o•gy /ikóləjee/ *n.* **1** study of the relations of organisms to one another and to their physical surroundings. **2** study of the interaction of people with their environment. □□ **ec•o•log•i•cal** /ékəlójikəl, eékə–/ *adj.* **ec•o•log′i•cal•ly** *adv.* **e•col′o•gist** *n.*

econ. *abbr.* **1** economics. **2** economy.

ec•o•nom•ic /ékənómik, eékə–/ *adj.* **1** of economics. **2** profitable; cost effective. **3** considered or studied with regard to human needs (*economic geography*).

■ **1** financial, fiscal, monetary; commercial. **2** moneymaking, remunerative, productive.

ec•o•nom•i•cal /ékənómikəl, eékə–/ *adj.* sparing in the use of resources; avoiding waste. □□ **ec•o•nom′i•cal•ly** *adv.*

■ cost-effective, money saving; cheap, inexpensive, reasonable; thrifty, prudent, conservative, frugal.

SYNONYM STUDY: economical

FRUGAL, MISERLY, PARSIMONIOUS, PROVIDENT, PRUDENT, SPARING, THRIFTY. If you don't like to spend money unnecessarily, you may simply be *economical*, which means that you manage your finances wisely and avoid any unnecessary expenses. If you're *thrifty*, you're both industrious and clever in managing your resources (*a thrifty shopper who never leaves home without her coupons*). **Frugal**, on the other hand, means that you tend to be sparing with money—sometimes getting a little carried away in your efforts—by avoiding any form of luxury or lavishness (*too frugal to take a taxi, even at night*). If you're *sparing*, you exercise such restraint in your spending that you sometimes deprive yourself (*sparing to the point where she allowed herself only one new item of clothing a season*). If you're *provident*, however, you're focused on providing for the future (*never one to be provident, she spent her allowance the day she received it*). **Miserly** and **parsimonious** are both used to describe frugality in its most extreme form. But while being *frugal* might be considered a virtue, being *parsimonious* is usually considered to be a fault or even a vice (*they could have been generous with their wealth, but they chose to lead a parsimonious life*). And no one wants to be called *miserly*, which implies being stingy out of greed rather than need (*so miserly that he reveled in his riches while those around him were starving*).

ec•o•nom•ics /ékənómiks, eékə–/ *n.pl.* [often treated as *sing.*] **1** science of the production and distribution of wealth. **2** application of this to a particular subject.

■ **2** see FINANCE *n.* 1.

e•con•o•mist /ikónəmist/ *n.* expert in or student of economics.

e•con•o•mize /ikónəmīz/ *v.intr.* **1** be economical. **2** [foll. by *on*] use sparingly; spend less on. □□ **e•con•o•mi•za′tion** *n.* **e•con′o•miz•er** *n.*

■ **1** tighten one's belt, cut costs, scrimp (and save), pinch pennies. **2** save, cut back, skimp.

e•con•o•my /ikónəmee/ *n.* (*pl.* **–mies**) **1 a** wealth and resources of a community. **b** particular kind of this (*capitalist economy*). **2 a** careful management of (esp. financial) resources; frugality. **b** instance of this. **3** sparing or careful use.

■ **2 a** thrift, conservation. **b** saving, cutback, reduction. **3** brevity, briefness, succinctness, terseness, conciseness.

ec•o•sys•tem /ékōsistəm, eékō–/ *n.* biological community of interacting organisms and their physical environment.

■ see ENVIRONMENT.

ec•ru /ékroo, áykroo/ *n.* color of unbleached linen.

ec•sta•sy /ékstəsee/ *n.* (*pl.* **–sies**) overwhelming joy or rapture. See synonym study at RAPTURE. □□ **ec•stat′ic** *adj.* **ec•stat′i•cal•ly** *adv.*

■ delight, bliss, thrill, elation, pleasure; heaven on earth. □□ **ecstatic** exhilarated, euphoric, overjoyed, beside oneself, in seventh heaven, *colloq.* on cloud nine.

ecto- /éktō/ *comb. form* outside.

ec•to•morph /éktəmawrf/ *n.* person with a lean body type. □□ **ec•to•mor′phic** *adj.*

ec•top•ic /ektópik/ *adj. Med.* in an abnormal position. □ **ectopic pregnancy** pregnancy occurring outside the uterus.

ec•to•plasm /éktəplazəm/ *n.* outer layer of the cytoplasm.

ec•u•men•i•cal /ékyōōménikəl/ *adj.* **1** of or representing the whole Christian world. **2** seeking worldwide Christian unity. See synonym study at UNIVERSAL. □□ **ec•u•men′i•cal•ism** or **ec′u•me•nism** *n.* **ec•u•men′i•cal•ly** *adv.*

ec•ze•ma /éksimə, égzi–, igzée–/ *n.* inflammation of the skin, with itching and discharge.

ed. *abbr.* **1** edited by. **2** edition. **3** editor. **4** education.

-ed[1] /əd, id/ *suffix* forming adjectives: **1** from nouns, meaning 'having, wearing, affected by, etc.' (*talented, trousered, diseased*). **2** from phrases of adjective and noun (*good-humored, three-cornered*).

-ed[2] /əd, id/ *suffix* forming: **1** the past tense and past participle of weak verbs (*needed, risked*). **2** participial adjectives (*escaped prisoner, a pained look*).

E•dam /eédəm, eédam/ *n.* round Dutch cheese, usu. pale yellow with a red rind.

ed•dy /édee/ • *n.* (*pl.* **–dies**) **1** circular movement of water causing a small whirlpool. **2** similar movement of wind, smoke, etc. • *v.* (**–dies, –died**) whirl around in eddies.

■ *n.* vortex; whirlwind, dust devil; waterspout, twister. • *v.* swirl, whirl, turn, spin.

e•del•weiss /áyd'lvīs/ *n.* white-flowered Alpine plant.

e•de•ma /idéemə/ *n.* accumulation of excess fluid in body tissues. □□ **e•dem•a•tose** /idémətōs, idée–/ *adj.* **e•dem'a•tous** *adj.*

E•den /ēedən/ *n.* (also **Garden of Eden**) place of great happiness; paradise (with reference to the abode of Adam and Eve in the biblical account of Creation).

edge /ej/ • *n.* **1** boundary line or margin of an area or surface. **2** narrow surface of a thin object. **3** meeting line of surfaces. **4 a** sharpened side of the blade. **b** sharpness. **5** area close to a steep drop. **6** edgelike thing. **7** effectiveness, force. **8** advantage. See synonym study at BORDER. • *v.* **1** *tr. & intr.* advance gradually or furtively. **2** *tr.* **a** provide with an edge or border. **b** form a border to. □ **on edge 1** tense and irritable. **2** eager; excited. **set a person's teeth on edge** (of a taste, sound, etc.) cause an unpleasant nervous sensation. **take the edge off** make less effective or intense. □□ **edge'less** *adj.* **edg'er** *n.*

■ *n.* **1** brink, verge, border, side, rim, lip, brim; fringe, limit, perimeter, periphery. **4 b** acuteness, keenness. **7** urgency; incisiveness. **8** head start, upper hand. • *v.* **1** inch, sidle, crawl, creep, steal, worm, work one's way. **2 b** see BORDER *v.* 1, 2.

edge•wise /éjwiz/ *adv.* **1** with edge uppermost or toward the viewer. **2** edge to edge. □ **get a word in edgewise** interject in a conversation dominated by another.

edg•ing /éjing/ *n.* thing forming an edge or border.

■ see BORDER *n.* 3.

edg•y /éjee/ *adj.* (**edg•i•er, edg•i•est**) irritable; nervously anxious. □□ **edg'i•ly** *adv.* **edg'i•ness** *n.*

■ see ANXIOUS 1, TESTY.

ed•i•ble /édibəl/ • *adj.* fit or suitable to be eaten. • *n.* [in *pl.*] food. □□ **ed•i•bil'i•ty** *n.*

■ *adj.* palatable, wholesome, comestible.

e•dict /ēedikt/ *n.* order proclaimed by authority.

ed•i•fice /édifis/ *n.* building, esp. an imposing one.

ed•i•fy /édifī/ *v.tr.* (**–fies, –fied**) improve morally or intellectually. □□ **ed•i•fi•ca'tion** *n.*

■ see EDUCATE 1, 2. □□ **edification** enlightenment, improvement, guidance, education, information, tuition, teaching, schooling, instruction.

ed•it /édit/ *v.tr.* **1** assemble, prepare, or modify (written material) for publication. **2** be editor of (a newspaper, etc.). **3** take extracts from and collate (movies, etc.) to form a unified sequence. **4** reword; correct.

■ **1** redact, copyedit; reorganize; modify, alter, adapt, change, revise; cut, condense. **4** rewrite, rephrase, emend; expurgate; bluepencil, delete.

e•di•tion /idíshən/ *n.* **1** edited or published form of a book, etc. **2** copies of a book, newspaper, etc., issued at one time. **3** particular version or instance of a broadcast. **4** person or thing resembling another.

■ **1, 2** issue; printing; version.

ed•i•tor /éditər/ *n.* **1** person who edits. **2** person who directs preparation of a newspaper or periodical (or section of one) or a news program. **3** person who selects or commissions material for publication. □□ **ed'i•tor•ship** *n.*

■ **1** columnist, journalist; copy editor, reviser. **3** compiler; publisher.

ed•i•to•ri•al /éditáwreeəl/ • *adj.* of editing or editors. • *n.* article giving a newspaper's opinion on a topical issue. □□ **ed•i•to'ri•al•ize** *v.intr.* **ed•i•to'ri•al•ly** *adv.*

■ *n.* essay, column.

-edly /idlee/ *suffix* forming adverbs from verbs, meaning 'in a manner characterized by performance of or undergoing of the verbal action' (*allegedly, disgustedly, hurriedly*).

EDT *abbr.* eastern daylight time.

ed•u•cate /éjəkayt/ *v.tr.* [also *absol.*] **1** give intellectual, moral, or social instruction to. **2** provide education for. □□ **ed•u•ca•ble** /–kəbəl/ *adj.* **ed•u•ca•bil'i•ty** *n.* **ed'u•ca•tive** *adj.* **ed'u•ca•tor** *n.*

■ teach, train, instruct, edify, tutor, school, inform, enlighten.

ed•u•cat•ed /éjəkaytid/ *adj.* **1** having had an (esp. good) education. **2** resulting from (good) education. **3** based on experience or study (*educated guess*).

■ **1** erudite, well-read, lettered, literary, scholarly, learned, well-informed, knowledgeable; cultured, enlightened. **2** refined, polished, cultivated.

ed•u•ca•tion /éjəkáyshən/ *n.* **1** systematic instruction, schooling, etc. **2** particular kind of or stage in education. **3** development of character or mental powers; formative experience. □□ **ed•u•ca'tion•al** *adj.* **ed•u•ca'tion•al•ly** *adv.*

■ **1** teaching, training, tutelage; learning. □□ **educational** academic, scholastic, instructional; informative, instructive, enlightening, edifying.

e•duce /idóos, idyóos/ *v.tr.* bring out or develop; elicit. □□ **e•duc'i•ble** *adj.* **e•duc•tion** /idúkshen/ *n.* **e•duc'tive** *adj.*

■ see DERIVE 1.

EEC *abbr.* European Economic Community.

EEG *abbr.* electroencephalogram.

eel /eel/ *n.* **1** snakelike fish. **2** evasive person or thing. □□ **eel'like** *adj.* **eel'y** *adj.*

EEOC *abbr.* Equal Employment Opportunity Commission.

e'er /air/ *poet.* var. of EVER.

ee•rie /éeree/ *adj.* (**ee•ri•er, ee•ri•est**) gloomy and strange; weird. □□ **ee'ri•ly** *adv.* **ee'ri•ness** *n.*

■ frightening, uncanny, unearthly, mysterious, *colloq.* creepy, spooky.

ef- /if, ef/ *prefix* assim. form of EX-1 1 before *f.*

ef•face /ifáys/ *v.* **1** *tr.* rub or wipe out. **2** *refl.* treat or regard oneself as unimportant (*self-effacing*). □□ **ef•face'ment** *n.*

■ **1** see ERASE 1.

ef•fect /ifékt/ • *n.* **1** result; consequence. **2** efficacy. **3** impression produced on a spectator, hearer, etc. **4** [in *pl.*] property. **5** [in *pl.*] lighting, sound, etc., used to accompany a movie, etc. **6** physical phenomenon

(*Doppler effect*). • *v.tr.* bring about. □ **in effect** for practical purposes; in reality. **take effect** become operative.

■ *n.* **1** outcome, conclusion, upshot; significance, essence, drift, purpose, intention, objective. **2** effectiveness, influence, impact, *colloq.* punch. **4** (*effects*) belongings, possessions, stuff, *colloq.* gear; baggage, luggage. • *v.* cause, make happen, execute, carry out, produce, create. □ **in effect** virtually, more or less; in (point of) fact, really, truly, to all intents and purposes.

ef·fec·tive /iféktiv/ *adj.* **1** having a definite or desired effect. **2** impressive. **3** actual; existing. **4** operative. □□ **ef·fec'tive·ly** *adv.* **ef·fec'tive·ness** *n.*

■ **1** effectual, efficacious, productive; capable, useful, competent. **2** outstanding, striking, powerful. **3** real, true; realizable, usable. **4** operational, in operation, functioning.

SYNONYM STUDY: effective

EFFECTUAL, EFFICACIOUS, EFFICIENT. All of these adjectives mean producing or capable of producing a result, but they are not interchangeable. Use **effective** when you want to describe something that produces a definite effect or result (*an effective speaker who was able to rally the crowd's support*) and **efficacious** when it produces the desired effect or result (*an efficacious remedy that cured her almost immediately*). If something produces the desired effect or result in a decisive manner, use **effectual** (*an effectual recommendation that got him the job*), an adjective that is often employed when looking back after an event is over (*an effectual strategy that finally turned the tide in their favor*). Reserve the use of **efficient** for when you want to imply skill and economy of energy in producing the desired result (*so efficient in her management of the company that layoffs were not necessary*). When applied to people, *efficient* means capable or competent (*an efficient homemaker*) and places less emphasis on the achievement of results and more on the skills involved.

ef·fec·tu·al /ifékchŏŏəl/ *adj.* **1** producing the required result or effect. **2** valid. See synonym study at EFFECTIVE. □□ **ef·fec'tu·al·ly** *adv.*

■ **1** efficient, productive, useful, influential, powerful, adequate. **2** in force, legal, lawful, binding, sound.

ef·fec·tu·ate /ifékchoo-ayt/ *v.tr.* effect. □□ **ef·fec·tu·a·tion** /-áyshən/ *n.*

■ bring about, cause, make happen, carry out, implement, accomplish, do, execute, realize, achieve.

ef·fem·i·nate /iféminət/ *adj.* (of a man) feminine in appearance or manner. □□ **ef·fem·i·na·cy** /-nəsee/ *n.* **ef·fem'i·nate·ly** *adv.*

■ unmanly, womanish, womanly, unmasculine, emasculate, epicene, effete; affected.

ef·fer·vesce /éfərvés/ *v.intr.* **1** give off bubbles of gas. **2** be lively. □□ **ef·fer·ves'cence** *n.* **ef·fer·ves'cent** *adj.*

■ **1** see FIZZ *v.* 2. □□ **effervescent** fizzy, carbonated, sparkling; frothy, bubbly; high-spirited, sparkling, vivacious, lively, exuberant, buoyant, animated, enthusiastic.

ef·fete /iféet/ *adj.* **1 a** feeble. **b** effeminate. **2** exhausted of its essential quality or vitality. □□ **ef·fete'ness** *n.*

ef·fi·ca·cious /éfikáyshəs/ *adj.* producing the desired effect. See synonym study at EFFECTIVE. □□ **ef·fi·ca'cious·ly** *adv.* **ef·fi·ca·cy** /éfikəsee/ *n.*

■ effective, effectual, productive, competent, successful, efficient, useful, serviceable.

ef·fi·cient /ifíshənt/ *adj.* **1** productive with minimum waste or effort. **2** capable; acting effectively. See synonym study at EFFECTIVE. □□ **ef·fi·cien·cy** *n.* **ef·fi'cient·ly** *adv.*

■ **1** economic, thrifty; effective, efficacious, effectual. **2** competent, proficient; see also CAPABLE 1.

ef·fi·gy /éfijee/ *n.* (*pl.* **–gies**) sculpture or model of a person.

■ see IMAGE *n.* 1.

ef·flu·ence /éflōoəns/ *n.* **1** flowing out (of light, electricity, etc.). **2** that which flows out.

■ see STREAM *n.* 2.

ef·flu·ent /éflōoənt/ • *adj.* flowing forth or out. • *n.* waste discharged into a river, etc.

ef·flu·vi·um /iflōoveeəm/ *n.* (*pl.* **ef·flu·vi·a** /-veeə/) unpleasant or noxious odor or vapor.

■ see SMELL *n.* 3.

ef·fort /éfərt/ *n.* **1** physical or mental exertion. **2** determined attempt. **3** force exerted. □□ **ef'fort·less** *adj.* **ef'fort·less·ly** *adv.* **ef'fort·less·ness** *n.*

■ **1** energy, striving, pains, work. **2** endeavor, try, venture; see also ATTEMPT *n.* □□ **effortless** simple, painless, smooth, trouble-free, uncomplicated; see also EASY *adj.* 1.

ef·fron·ter·y /ifrúntəree/ *n.* (*pl.* **–ies**) impudent audacity. See synonym study at TEMERITY.

■ insolence, impertinence, presumption, arrogance, cheek, *colloq.* brass, nerve, *sl.* gall, chutzpah.

ef·fuse /ifyŏoz/ *v.tr.* **1** pour forth (liquid, light, etc.). **2** give out (ideas, etc.). □□ **ef·fu'sive** *adj.* **ef·fu'sive·ly** *adv.* **ef·fu'sive·ness** *n.*

■ □□ **effusive** demonstrative, gushing, enthusiastic, exuberant.

ef·fu·sion /ifyŏozhən/ *n.* **1** outpouring. **2** unrestrained verbiage.

e.g. *abbr.* for example.

e·gal·i·tar·i·an /igálitáireeən/ • *adj.* of or advocating the principle of equal rights and opportunities for all. • *n.* egalitarian person. □□ **e·gal·i·tar'i·an·ism** *n.*

■ *adj.* democratic, classless.

egg¹ /eg/ *n.* **1 a** spheroidal reproductive body produced by females of animals such as birds, reptiles, fish, etc., enclosed in a protective layer and capable of developing into a new individual. **b** egg of the domestic hen, used for food. **2** *Biol.* ovum. **3** *colloq.* person or thing qualified in some way (*a tough egg*). □ **have** (or **put**) **all one's eggs in one basket** *colloq.* risk everything on a single venture. **with egg on one's face** *colloq.* made to look foolish. □□ **egg'y** *adj.* (**egg·i·er, egg·i·est**).

■ **2** see SEED *n.* 1a.

egg[2] /eg/ v.tr. [foll. by on] urge.
■ see MOTIVATE.

egg•head /éghed/ n. colloq. intellectual.
■ see INTELLECTUAL n.

egg•nog /égnog/ n. drink made with eggs, cream, and often alcohol.

egg•plant /égplant/ n. plant bearing edible purple or white egg-shaped fruit.

egg•shell /égshel/ n. 1 shell of an egg. 2 pale off-white color.

e•go /eegō/ n. (pl. **–gos**) 1 the part of the mind that has self-awareness. 2 self-esteem. □ **ego trip** colloq. activity, etc., devoted entirely to one's own interests or feelings.

e•go•cen•tric /éegōséntrik, égō–/ adj. self-centered. □□ **e•go•cen'tri•cal•ly** adv. **e•go•cen•tric•i•ty** /–trisitee/ n.

e•go•ism /éegōizəm, égō–/ n. 1 self-interest as the foundation of morality. 2 = EGOTISM. □□ **e'go•ist** n. **e•go•is'tic** adj. **e•go•is'ti•cal** adj.

e•go•ma•ni•a /éegōmáyneeə, égō–/ n. morbid egotism. □□ **e•go•ma'ni•ac** n. **e•go•ma•ni•a•cal** /–mənīəkəl/ adj.

e•go•tism /éegətizəm, égə–/ n. 1 self-conceit. 2 selfishness. See synonym study at PRIDE. □□ **e'go•tist** n. **e•go•tis'tic** adj. **e•go•tis'ti•cal** adj. **e•go•tis'ti•cal•ly** adv.
■ 1 self-obsession, self-absorption, self-love, self-centeredness, egocentricity, egomania. 2 egoism. □□ **egotistic, egotistical** conceited, proud, arrogant, boastful, vain, egocentric.

e•gre•gious /igréejəs/ adj. outstandingly bad; shocking. □□ **e•gre'gious•ly** adv. **e•gre'gious•ness** n.

e•gress /éegres/ n. exit. □□ **e•gres•sion** /–gréshən/ n.

e•gret /éegrit/ n. heron with long white feathers.

E•gyp•tian /ijípshən/ • adj. of Egypt. • n. 1 native of Egypt. 2 language used in ancient Egypt.

eh /ay/ int. colloq. 1 expressing surprise. 2 asking for something to be repeated or explained.

ei•der /ídər/ n. any of various large northern ducks.

ei•der•down /ídərdown/ n. 1 down from the eider duck. 2 quilt stuffed with this.

eight /ayt/ n. 1 one more than seven. 2 symbol for this (8, viii, VIII).

eight•een /áyteen/ n. 1 one more than seventeen. 2 symbol for this (18, xviii, XVIII). □□ **eight'eenth'** adj. & n.

eighth /ayt–th, ayth/ • n. 1 next after seventh. 2 each of eight equal parts of a thing. • adj. that is the eighth.

eight•y /áytee/ n. (pl. **–ies**) 1 eight times ten. 2 symbol for this (80, lxxx, LXXX). 3 [in pl.] numbers from 80 to 89, esp. as years. □ **eighty-first, -second,** etc. ordinal numbers between eightieth and ninetieth. **eighty-one, -two,** etc., cardinal numbers between eighty and ninety. □□ **eight'i•eth** adj. & n.

ein•stein•i•um /īnstíneeəm/ n. artificial radioactive metallic element. ¶Symb.: **Es**.

ei•ther /éethər, íthər/ • adj. & pron. 1 one or the other of two. 2 each of two. • adv. & conj. 1 as one possibility or alternative. 2 [with neg. or interrog.] any more than the other (I didn't like it either). □ **either-or** unavoidable choice between alternatives. **either way** in either case.

e•jac•u•late • v.tr. /ijákyəlayt/ 1 exclaim. 2 eject (fluid, etc., esp. semen) from the body. • n. /ijákyələt/ ejaculated semen. □□ **e•jac•u•la•tion** /–láyshən/ n. **e•jac'u•la•tor** n. **e•jac•u•la•to•ry** /–lətáwree/ adj.
■ v. 1 see EXCLAIM.

e•ject /ijékt/ v.tr. 1 expel; compel to leave. 2 a cause (the pilot, etc.) to be propelled from an aircraft, etc., in an emergency. b [absol.] (of the pilot, etc.) be ejected in this way (they both ejected at 1,000 feet). 3 cause to be removed. □□ **e•jec'tion** n. **e•jec'tor** n.
■ 1 force or drive out, cast out, oust, get rid of, evict, throw out, boot out; discharge, dismiss, send packing. □□ **ejection** expulsion, discharge, emission; banishment, deportation, removal, eviction; dismissal.

SYNONYM STUDY: **eject**

DISMISS, EVICT, EXPEL, OUST. Want to get rid of someone? You can **eject** him or her, which means to throw or cast out (he was ejected from the meeting room). If you hope the person never comes back, use **expel**, a verb that suggests driving someone out of a country, an organization, etc., for all time (to be expelled from school); it can also imply the use of voluntary force (to expel air from the lungs). If you exercise force or the power of law to get rid of someone or something, **oust** is the correct verb (ousted after less than two years in office). If as a property owner you are turning someone out of a house or a place of business, you'll want to **evict** the person (she was evicted for not paying the rent). **Dismiss** is by far the mildest of these terms, suggesting that you are rejecting or refusing to consider someone or something (to dismiss a legal case). It is also commonly used of loss of employment (dismissed from his job for excessive tardiness).

eke /eek/ v.tr. [foll. by out] contrive to make (a livelihood) or support (an existence).

EKG abbr. electrocardiogram.

e•lab•o•rate • adj. /iláberət/ 1 minutely worked out. 2 complicated. • v. /ilábərayt/ 1 tr. work out or explain in detail. 2 intr. go into details (I need not elaborate). □□ **e•lab'o•rate•ly** adv. **e•lab'o•rate•ness** n. **e•lab•o•ra•tion** /–ráyshən/ n. **e•lab'o•ra•tive** adj. **e•lab'o•ra•tor** n.
■ adj. 1 detailed, painstaking, meticulous, thorough, complete, exhaustive, intricate, involved, precise, exact. 2 complex, convoluted, ornate, fancy. • v. enlarge, expand (upon or on), amplify, flesh out, enhance, develop; go into detail; see also EMBELLISH. □□ **elaboration** enlargement, development, expansion, embellishment.

é•lan /aylón, aylón/ n. vivacity; dash.
■ see VERVE.

e•land /éeland/ n. large African antelope.

e•lapse /iláps/ v.intr. (of time) pass by.
■ go (by), slip by or away, pass away, slide by, glide by.

e•las•tic /ilástik/ • *adj.* **1** able to resume its normal bulk or shape after contraction, dilatation, or distortion. **2** springy. See synonym study at ELASTIC. • *n.* elastic cord or fabric. □□ **e•las'ti•cal•ly** *adv.* **e•las•tic•i•ty** /ilástísi-tee, eelas-/ *n.* **e•las'ti•cize** /ilástisīz/ *v.tr.*

■ *adj.* **1, 2** flexible, stretchable, stretchy, bendable, pliable. □□ **elasticity** flexibility, resilience, plasticity, give; adaptability, tolerance.

e•late /iláyt/ *v.tr.* (esp. as **elated** *adj.*) inspirit; stimulate. □□ **e•lat'ed•ly** *adv.* **e•lat'ed•ness** *n.* **e•la•tion** /–láyshən/ *n.*

■ see INTOXICATE 2; (*elated*) exhilarated, uplifted, joyful, joyous, exultant, ecstatic, delighted, euphoric, overjoyed, in seventh heaven, on cloud nine. □□ **elation** see JOY 1.

el•bow /élbō/ • *n.* **1** joint between the fore arm and the upper arm. **2** elbow-shaped bend. • *v.tr.* thrust or jostle (a person or oneself). □ **elbow grease** *colloq.* vigorous polishing; hard work.

el•bow•room /élbōrōōm/ *n.* plenty of room to move or work in.

el•der[1] /éldər/ • *adj.* (of persons, esp. when related) senior; of a greater age. • *n.* **1** older of two (esp. related) persons. **2** [in *pl.*] persons older and usu. venerable. **3** church official. ■ *adj.* older; venerable, veteran. • *n.* **2** (*elders*) superiors, seniors; patriarchs, matriarchs.

el•der[2] /éldər/ *n.* tree with white flowers and dark berries.

el•der•ber•ry /éldərberee/ *n.* (*pl.* **–ries**) berry of the elder.

eld•er•ly /éldərlee/ • *adj.* rather old; past middle age. • *n.* [*collect.*] [prec. by *the*] elderly people.

■ *adj.* advanced in years, aging, aged. • *n.* (*the elderly*) senior citizens, *colloq.* old-timers.

eld•est /éldist/ *adj. & n.* first-born; oldest.

elec. *abbr.* **1** electric. **2** electrical. **3** electricity.

elect /ilékt/ • *v.tr.* **1** choose. **2** choose by vote. • *adj.* **1** chosen. **2** select; choice. **3** [after a noun designating office] chosen but not yet in office (*president elect*).

■ *v.* select, pick, determine, designate; see also CHOOSE 1, 3, VOTE *v.* 1. • *adj.* **2** see CHOICE *adj.*

e•lec•tion /ilékshən/ *n.* **1** electing or being elected. **2** instance of this.

■ **1** selection, choice, nomination, designation, appointment. **2** poll, vote, referendum, plebiscite.

e•lec•tion•eer /ilékshəneer/ • *v.intr.* take part in an election campaign. • *n.* person who electioneers.

e•lec•tive /iléktiv/ • *adj.* **1** derived from election. **2** (of a body) having the power to elect. **3** optional. • *n.* elective course of study. □□ **e•lec'tive•ly** *adv.*

■ *adj.* **3** see OPTIONAL.

e•lec•tor /iléktər/ *n.* **1** person who has the right of voting. **2** member of the electoral college.

e•lec•tor•al /iléktərəl/ *adj.* relating to electors. □ **electoral college** ad hoc assembly that casts votes for the election of the US president and vice president. □□ **e•lec'tor•al•ly** *adv.*

e•lec•tor•ate /iléktərət/ *n.* body of electors.

e•lec•tric /iléktrik/ *adj.* **1** of, worked by, or charged with electricity; producing electricity. **2** causing or charged with excitement. □ **electric blue** brilliant light blue. **electric chair** electrified chair used for capital punishment. **electric eel** eellike fish of S. America that stuns prey by electric shock. **electric eye** photoelectric cell operating a relay when light is obscured. □□ **e•lec'tri•cal** *adj.* **e•lec'tri•cal•ly** *adv.*

■ **2** alive, buzzing, energized, stimulating, exciting, thrilling, electrifying, moving, stirring, dynamic.

e•lec•tri•cian /iléktríshən, éélek-/ *n.* person who installs or maintains electrical equipment.

e•lec•tric•i•ty /iléktrísitee, éélek-/ *n.* **1** form of energy resulting from the existence of charged particles (electrons, protons, etc.). **2** science of electricity. **3** supply of electric current. **4** excitement.

■ **4** verve, energy, tension, intensity, ardor.

e•lec•tri•fy /iléktrifī/ *v.tr.* (**–fies, –fied**) **1** charge with electricity. **2** convert to the use of electric power. **3** cause sudden excitement in. □□ **e•lec•tri•fi•ca'tion** *n.* **e•lec'tri•fi•er** *n.*

■ **3** animate, move, rouse, stir, stimulate, vitalize, fire, thrill, arouse, charge, energize.

electro- /iléktrō/ *comb. form* of, relating to, or caused by electricity (*electrocute, electromagnet*).

e•lec•tro•car•di•o•gram /iléktrōkaárdeeəgram/ *n.* record of the heartbeat traced by an electrocardiograph.

e•lec•tro•car•di•o•graph /iléktrōkaárdeeəgraf/ *n.* instrument recording electric currents generated by a heartbeat.

e•lec•tro•cute /iléktrəkyōōt/ *v.tr.* kill by electric shock. □□ **e•lec•tro•cu•tion** /–kyōōshən/ *n.*

e•lec•trode /iléktrōd/ *n.* conductor through which electricity enters or leaves an electrolyte, gas, vacuum, etc.

e•lec•tro•en•ceph•a•lo•gram /iléktrōinséf-ələgram/ *n.* record of the brain's activity traced by an electroencephalograph.

e•lec•tro•en•ceph•a•lo•graph /iléktrōinséf-ələgraf/ *n.* instrument recording electrical activity of the brain.

e•lec•trol•y•sis /iléktrólisis, éélek-/ *n.* **1** *Chem.* decomposition by electric current. **2** destruction of tumors, hair roots, etc., by this process. □□ **e•lec•tro•lyt•ic** /iléktrōlítik/ *adj.* **e•lec•tro•lyt'i•cal** *adj.* **e•lec•tro•lyt'i•cal•ly** *adv.*

elec•tro•lyte /iléktrəlīt/ *n.* **1** substance that conducts electricity when molten or in solution, esp. in a battery. **2** solution of this.

e•lec•tro•mag•net /iléktrōmágnit/ *n.* soft metal core made into a magnet by the passage of electricity through a surrounding coil. □□ **e•lec•tro•mag•net'ic** *adj.* **e•lec•tro•mag'net•ism** *n.*

e•lec•tron /iléktron/ *n.* stable elementary particle with a charge of negative electricity.

e•lec•tron•ic /iléktrónik, éélek-/ *adj.* **1 a** pro-

duced by or involving the flow of electrons.
b of electrons or electronics. **2** (of a device) using electronic components. **3 a** (of music) produced by electronic means. **b** (of a musical instrument) producing sounds by electronic means. □ **electronic mail** messages distributed by electronic means. (Also called **E-mail**).

e•lec•tron•ics /ilektróniks, eélek–/ *n.pl.* [usu. treated as *sing.*] science concerned with the behavior and movement of electrons.

e•lec•tro•plate /iléktrəplayt/ • *v.tr.* coat by electrolytic deposition with chromium, silver, etc. • *n.* electroplated articles. □□ **e•lec´tro•plat•er** *n.*

e•lec•tro•shock /iléktrōshok/ *adj.* (of medical treatment) by means of electric shocks.

el•ee•mos•y•nar•y /éləmósineree, –móz–, éleeə–/ *adj.* **1** of or dependent on alms. **2** charitable. **3** gratuitous.
■ **2** see CHARITABLE 1.

el•e•gant /éligənt/ *adj.* **1** graceful. **2** tasteful; refined. **3** ingeniously simple. □□ **el´e•gance** *n.* **el´e•gant•ly** *adv.*
■ **1, 2** exquisite, handsome, dignified, genteel, sophisticated, polished, urbane, suave, debonair. **3** apt, clever, ingenious, neat. □□ **elegance** gentility, polish; luxury, plushness, splendor.

el•e•gi•ac /élijîək, ileéjeeak/ • *adj.* **1** used for elegies. **2** mournful. • *n.* [in *pl.*] elegiac verses. □□ **el•e•gi´a•cal•ly** *adv.*

el•e•gy /élijee/ *n.* (*pl.* **–gies**) song or poem of lament, esp. for the dead.
■ see LAMENT *n.* 2.

elem. *abbr.* elementary.

el•e•ment /élimənt/ *n.* **1** component part; contributing factor or thing. **2** *Chem.* & *Physics* any of the substances that cannot be resolved by chemical means into simpler substances. **3 a** any of the four substances (earth, water, air, and fire) in ancient and medieval philosophy. **b** any of these as a being's natural environment. **4** *Electr.* wire that heats up in an electric appliance. **5** [in *pl.*] atmospheric agencies, esp. wind and storm. **6** [in *pl.*] rudiments of learning. □ **in** (or **out of**) **one's element** in (or out of) one's accustomed or preferred surroundings.
■ **1** constituent, ingredient, unit, piece, segment, feature, particular; group. **3 b** surroundings, atmosphere, situation, locale, territory, sphere, habitat, medium, domain. **6** (*elements*) basics, fundamentals, foundations, essentials, principles.

el•e•men•tal /élimént'l/ *adj.* **1** of the elements. **2** of the powers of nature. **3** essential.
■ **2** primal, original, primordial, primitive. **3** basic, fundamental, key, main; see also INTRINSIC.

el•e•men•ta•ry /éliméntəree, –tree/ *adj.* rudimentary; simple. □ **elementary school** school in which elementary subjects are taught to young children. □□ **el•e•men•tar•i•ly** /–tərəlee/ *adv.*
■ basic, fundamental; straightforward, uncomplicated, plain; see also EASY *adj.* 1. □ **elementary school** grade school.

el•e•phant /élifənt/ *n.* (*pl.* same or **el•e•phants**) largest living land animal, with a trunk and ivory tusks.

el•e•phan•ti•a•sis /élifəntîəsis/ *n.* gross enlargement of the body, esp. the limbs, due to lymphatic obstruction.

el•e•phan•tine /élifánteen, –tīn, éləfən–/ *adj.* **1** of elephants. **2 a** huge. **b** clumsy; unwieldy.

elev. *abbr.* elevation.

el•e•vate /élivayt/ *v.tr.* **1** bring to a higher position. **2** exalt in rank, etc. **3** (usu. as **elevated** *adj.*) **a** raise the spirits of; elate. **b** raise morally or intellectually.
■ **1** raise, lift (up). **2** see EXALT 1. **3 a** (**elevated**) cheerful, happy, exhilarated, joyful, glad. **b** see CIVILIZE; (**elevated**) uplifted, noble, dignified.

el•e•va•tion /éliváyshən/ *n.* **1 a** elevating or being elevated. **b** angle with the horizontal. **c** height above a given level, esp. sea level. **d** raised area. **2** loftiness; grandeur; dignity. **3** diagram showing one side of a building.
■ **1 a** advancement, promotion, advance; uplifting, raising. **c** altitude. **d** hill, rise. **2** exaltation, distinction, refinement, cultivation.

el•e•va•tor /élivaytər/ *n.* **1** hoisting machine. **2** *Aeron.* device on an airplane's tail for changing pitch. **3** platform or compartment for raising and lowering persons or things between floors.

e•lev•en /ilévən/ *n.* **1** one more than ten. **2** symbol for this (11, xi, XI).

e•lev•enth /ilévənth/ • *n.* **1** next after tenth. **2** each of eleven equal parts of a thing. • *adj.* that is the eleventh. □ **eleventh hour** last possible moment.

elf /elf/ *n.* (*pl.* **elves** /elvz/) mythological being, esp. one that is small and mischievous. □□ **elf´in** *adj.* **elf´ish** *adj.* **elv´ish** *adj.*
■ sprite, fairy, puck; see also GOBLIN. □□ **elfin** impish, playful; dainty; small, tiny.

e•lic•it /ilísit/ *v.tr.* **1** draw out; evoke (a response, etc.). **2** draw forth (what is latent). □□ **e•lic•i•ta´tion** *n.* **e•lic´i•tor** *n.*
■ **1** call forth, bring out *or* forth, bring to light.

e•lide /ilīd/ *v.tr.* omit (a vowel or syllable) by elision.

el•i•gi•ble /élijibəl/ *adj.* **1** fit or entitled to be chosen. **2** desirable or suitable, esp. for marriage. □□ **el•i•gi•bil´i•ty** *n.*
■ worthy, qualified, appropriate, fitting.

e•lim•i•nate /ilíminayt/ *v.tr.* **1 a** remove; get rid of. **b** kill; murder. **2** exclude from consideration. **3** excrete. □□ **e•lim•i•na•tion** /–náyshən/ *n.* **e•lim´i•na•tor** *n.*
■ **1 a** dispose of, erase, eradicate, expunge, obliterate; delete, edit (out). **b** assassinate, exterminate, *sl.* bump off, rub out. **2** rule out, drop, leave out, omit.

e•li•sion /ilizhən/ *n.* **1** omission of a vowel or syllable in pronouncing. **2** omission of a passage in a book, etc.

e•lite /ayleét, əleét/ • *n.* **1** choice part of a body or group. **2** size of letter in typewriting (12 per inch). • *adj.* exclusive.
■ *n.* **1** best, crème de la crème; cream, gen-

try, aristocracy, upper classes, *colloq.* upper crust. • *adj.* aristocratic, privileged, blue-blooded.

e•lit•ism /ayleéetizəm, əleet–/ *n.* advocacy of or reliance on leadership or dominance by a select group. □□ **e•lit′ist** *n. & adj.*

e•lix•ir /iliksər/ *n.* **1** *Alchemy* **a** preparation supposedly able to change metals into gold or prolong life. **b** supposed remedy for all ills. **2** *Pharm.* aromatic medicinal solution. **3** quintessence of a thing.

■ **1 b** panacea, cure-all, wonder drug, miracle drug. **3** pith, core, heart, essence, basis, soul.

E•liz•a•be•than /ilízəbeéthən/ • *adj.* of the time of England's Queen Elizabeth I or II. • *n.* person of the time of Queen Elizabeth I.

elk /elk/ *n.* (*pl.* same or **elks**) large deer of N. Europe and Asia.

elk•hound /élkhownd/ *n.* large Scandinavian hunting dog.

ell /el/ *n.* **1** right-angled extension to a building. **2** L-shaped thing.

el•lipse /ilíps/ *n.* closed symmetrical oval figure. □□ **el•lip•tic** /ilíptik/ (also **el•lip′ti•cal**) *adj.* **el•lip′ti•cal•ly** *adv.*

el•lip•sis /ilípsis/ *n.* (*pl.* **el•lip•ses** /–seez/) **1** omission of words within or at the end of a construction or sense. **2** set of three dots, etc., indicating such.

elm /elm/ *n.* **1** tall shade tree with rough serrated leaves. **2** its wood.

el•o•cu•tion /éləkyóoshən/ *n.* art of clear and expressive speech. □□ **el•o•cu′tion•ar•y** *adj.* **el•o•cu′tion•ist** *n.*

e•lon•gate /iláwnggayt, –long–/ • *v.tr.* lengthen; prolong. • *adj.* long in proportion to width. □□ **e•lon•ga•tion** /–gáyshən/ *n.*

e•lope /ilóp/ *v.intr.* run away to wed secretly. □□ **e•lope′ment** *n.*

el•o•quence /éləkwəns/ *n.* fluent and effective use of language. □□ **el′o•quent** *adj.* **el′o•quent•ly** *adv.*

■ see RHETORIC 1. □□ **eloquent** articulate, silver-tongued, well-spoken, persuasive, incisive; smooth, oratorical, rhetorical.

else /els/ *adv.* **1** besides (*someone else*). **2** instead (*what else could I say?*). **3** otherwise; if not (*or else you will be late*).

else•where /éls-hwair, –wáir/ *adv.* in or to some other place.

■ somewhere else, abroad; absent, away.

e•lu•ci•date /ilóosidáyt/ *v.tr.* throw light on; explain. See synonym study at CLARIFY. □□ **e•lu•ci•da•tion** /–dáyshən/ *n.* **e•lu′ci•da•tive** *adj.* **e•lu′ci•da•tor** *n.*

e•lude /ilóod/ *v.tr.* **1** escape adroitly; dodge. **2** avoid compliance with. □□ **e•lu•sion** /ilóozhən/ *n.* **e•lu•so•ry** /–lóosəree/ *adj.*

■ **1** evade, avoid, slip away from, give the slip; bewilder, frustrate; thwart. **2** see SIDESTEP *v.*

e•lu•sive /ilóosiv/ *adj.* **1** difficult to find or catch. **2** difficult to remember. **3** (of an answer, etc.) avoiding the point raised. □□ **e•lu′sive•ly** *adv.* **e•lu′sive•ness** *n.*

■ **1** evasive, slippery. **3** equivocal, indirect.

el•ver /élvər/ *n.* young eel.

elves *pl.* of ELF.

em /em/ *n.* *Printing* unit of measurement equal to the width of an M.

em– /im, em/ *prefix* assim. form of EN-[1], EN-[2] before *b, p.*

'em /əm/ *pron. colloq.* them (*let 'em all come*).

e•ma•ci•ate /imáysheeayt/ *v.tr.* (esp. as **emaciated** *adj.*) make abnormally thin or feeble. □□ **e•ma•ci•a•tion** /–áyshən/ *n.*

■ waste away, shrink, get thin; (**emaciated**) shriveled, shrunken, haggard, gaunt, drawn, pinched, bony, withered, scrawny, starved.

E-mail /éemayl/ *n.* (also **e-mail**) = *electronic mail.*

em•a•nate /émənayt/ *v.* **1** *intr.* issue; originate. **2** *tr.* emit; send forth. □□ **em•a•na•tion** /–náyshən/ *n.*

■ **1** emerge, proceed, flow, ooze, exude; radiate, disperse. **2** give off or out, disseminate, discharge, put out. □□ **emanation** see AURA 1.

e•man•ci•pate /imánsipayt/ *v.tr.* **1** free from restraint, esp. social or political. **2** cause to be less inhibited. **3** free from slavery. □□ **e•man•ci•pa•tion** /–páyshən/ *n.* **e•man′ci•pa•tor** *n.* **e•man′ci•pa•to•ry** *adj.*

■ release, liberate, deliver, loose, let loose, let go, set free; unfetter, unchain, unshackle.

e•mas•cu•late • *v.tr.* /imáskyəlayt/ **1** deprive of force or vigor. **2** castrate. • *adj.* /imáskyəlät/ effeminate. □□ **e•mas•cu•la•tion** /–láyshən/ *n.* **e•mas′cu•la•tor** *n.* **e•mas′cu•la•to•ry** /–lətáwree/ *adj.*

■ *v.* **1** see WEAKEN 1. **2** see NEUTER *v.*

em•balm /embáam, im/ *v.tr.* preserve (a corpse) from decay. □□ **em•balm′er** *n.*

em•bank•ment /embángkmənt, im–/ *n.* earth or stone bank for keeping back water, or for carrying a road or railroad.

em•bar•go /embáargō/ • *n.* (*pl.* **–goes**) **1** order forbidding foreign ships access to ports. **2** official suspension of commerce. • *v.tr.* (**–goes, –goed**) place under embargo.

■ *n.* restraint, proscription, prohibition, interdiction, restriction. • *v.* block, bar, ban, prevent, hold back.

em•bark /embáark, im–/ *v.* **1** *tr. & intr.* put or go on board a ship or aircraft (to a destination). **2** *intr.* [foll. by *on, upon*] engage in an undertaking. □□ **em•bar•ka′tion** *n.*

■ **2** (*embark on*) begin, undertake, initiate, start, go into, set about, take up *or* on, assume, tackle.

em•bar•rass /embárəs, im–/ *v.tr.* **1 a** cause (a person) to feel awkward or ashamed. **b** (as **embarrassed** *adj.*) expressing a feeling of awkwardness or self-consciousness. **2** (as **embarrassed** *adj.*) encumbered with debts. **3** encumber. □□ **em•bar′rass•ing** *adj.* **em•bar′rass•ing•ly** *adv.* **em•bar′rass•ment** *n.*

■ **1 b** (**embarrassed**) uncomfortable, red-faced. □□ **embarrassing** humiliating. **embarrassment** mortification, chagrin.

em•bas•sy /émbəsee/ *n.* (*pl.* **–sies**) **1 a** residence or offices of an ambassador. **b** ambassador and staff. **2** deputation to a foreign country.

em•bat•tle /embát′l, im–/ *v.tr.* **1** set (an

army, etc.) in battle array. **2** provide with battlements. **3** (as **embattled** *adj.*) **a** prepared or arrayed for battle. **b** involved in a conflict or difficult undertaking.

em•bed /embéd, im–/ *v.tr.* (also **im•bed'**) (**–bed•ded, –bed•ding**) fix firmly in; implant.

■ see IMPLANT *v.* 1.

em•bel•lish /embélish, im–/ *v.tr.* **1** beautify; adorn. **2** add interest to (a narrative) with fictitious additions. □□ **em•bel'lish•ment** *n.*

■ **1** dress (up), enhance, garnish, decorate, trim. **2** elaborate, exaggerate. □□ **embellishment** ornamentation, embroidery, garnishment, beautification.

em•ber /émbər/ *n.* **1** small piece of glowing coal or wood in a dying fire. **2** almost extinct residue of a past activity, feeling, etc.

■ **2** remains, remnant; see also VESTIGE 1.

em•bez•zle /embézəl, im–/ *v.tr.* divert (money, etc.) fraudulently to one's own use. □□ **em•bez'zle•ment** *n.* **em•bez'zler** *n.*

■ misappropriate, misuse, make off with; *colloq.* have one's hand in the till.

em•bit•ter /embítər, im–/ *v.tr.* arouse bitter feelings in.

■ sour, poison, pain, dispirit.

em•bla•zon /embláyzən, im–/ *v.tr.* **1** portray or adorn conspicuously. **2** adorn (a heraldic shield).

■ **1** see ILLUMINATE 3.

em•blem /émbləm/ *n.* **1** symbol. **2** heraldic device. □□ **em•blem•at'ic** *adj.* **em•blem•at'i•cal** *adj.* **em•blem•at'i•cal•ly** *adv.*

■ badge, representation, seal, crest, token, sign; trademark, logo.

SYNONYM STUDY: emblem

ATTRIBUTE, IMAGE, SIGN, SYMBOL, TOKEN, TYPE. When it comes to representing or embodying the invisible or intangible, you can't beat a **symbol**. It applies to anything that serves as an outward sign of something immaterial or spiritual (*the cross as a symbol of salvation; the crown as a symbol of monarchy*), although the association between the symbol and what it represents does not have to be based on tradition or convention and may, in fact, be quite arbitrary (*the annual gathering at the cemetery became a symbol of the family's long and tragic history*). An **emblem** is a visual symbol or pictorial device that represents the character or history of a family, a nation, or an office (*the eagle is an emblem of the United States*). It is very close in meaning to **attribute**, which is an object that is conventionally associated with either an individual, a group, or an abstraction (*the spiked wheel as an attribute of St. Catherine; the scales as an attribute of Justice*). An **image** is also a visual representation or embodiment, but in a much broader sense (*veins popping, he was the image of the angry father*). **Sign** is often used in place of *symbol* to refer to a simple representation of an agreed-upon meaning (*the upraised fist as a sign of victory; the white flag as a sign of surrender*), but a *symbol* usually em-

bodies a wider range of meanings, while a *sign* can be any object, event, or gesture from which information can be deduced (*her faltering voice was a sign of her nervousness*). A **token**, on the other hand, is something offered as a symbol or reminder (*he gave her his class ring as a token of his devotion*) and a **type**, particularly in a religious context, is a symbol or representation of something not present (*Jerusalem as the type of heaven; the paschal lamb as the type of Christ*).

---

em•bod•y /embódee, im–/ *v.tr.* (**–ies, –ied**) **1** give a concrete or discernible form to (an idea, concept, etc.). **2** (of a thing or person) be an expression of (an idea, etc.). **3** include; comprise. □□ **em•bod'i•ment** *n.*

■ **1** realize, materialize; manifest, express, personify, demonstrate, epitomize. **2** typify, represent; see also EXEMPLIFY. **3** incorporate; see also INCLUDE 1. □□ **embodiment** incarnation, personification, epitome.

em•bold•en /embóldən, im–/ *v.tr.* make bold; encourage. See synonym study at ENCOURAGE.

em•bol•ism /émbəlizəm/ *n.* obstruction of an artery by a clot of blood, air bubble, etc.

em•boss /embós, im–/ *v.tr.* carve or mold in relief.

em•brace /embráys, im–/ • *v.tr.* **1 a** hold closely in the arms. **b** [of two people] hold each other closely. **2** clasp; enclose. **3** accept eagerly. **4** adopt (a course of action, etc.). **5** include; comprise. • *n.* act of embracing. □□ **em•brace'a•ble** *adj.*

■ *v.* **1** hug, grasp, enfold, cuddle. **2** see CLASP *v.* 2. **3** see ACCEPT 2. **4** espouse, support, welcome, advocate. **5** embody, incorporate. • *n.* hug, squeeze.

em•broi•der /embróydər, im–/ *v.tr.* **1** decorate (cloth, etc.) with needlework. **2** embellish (a narrative). □□ **em•broi'der•er** *n.*

■ **1** see ORNAMENT *v.* **2** see EMBELLISH 2.

em•broi•der•y /embróydəree, im–/ *n.* (*pl.* **–ies**) **1** art of embroidering. **2** embroidered work. **3** embellishment.

■ **3** see ORNAMENT *n.* 1, 2.

em•broil /embróyl, im–/ *v.tr.* involve (a person) in conflict or difficulties. □□ **em•broil'ment** *n.*

■ see ENTANGLE 3.

em•bry•o /émbreeō/ *n.* (*pl.* **–os**) **1 a** unborn or unhatched offspring. **b** human offspring in the first eight weeks from conception. **2** rudimentary plant in a seed. **3** thing in a rudimentary stage. □□ **em•bry•on•ic** /émbreeónik/ *adj.*

■ **3** see GERM 3.

em•bry•ol•o•gy /émbreeólajee/ *n.* study of embryos. □□ **em•bry•ol'o•gist** *n.*

em•cee /émseé/ • *n.* master of ceremonies. • *v.* (**em•cees, em•ceed**) act as an emcee.

■ *n.* see MODERATOR[2]. • *v.* see PRESENT *v.* 4.

e•mend /iménd/ *v.tr.* edit (a text, etc.) to make corrections. □□ **e•men•da'tion** *n.*

■ see REVISE *v.* 1.

em•er•ald /émərəld, émrəld/ *n.* **1** bright-green precious stone, a variety of beryl. **2** color of this.

e•merge /imérj/ *v.intr.* **1** come up or out into

view. **2** come to light; become known, esp. as a result of inquiry, etc. **3** become recognized or prominent. □□ **e•mer'gence** *n.* **e•mer' gent** *adj.*

■ **1** appear, come forth, rise; arise, surface. **2** be revealed, become apparent, transpire. □□ **emergence** materialization, manifestation; see also APPEARANCE 1.

e•mer•gen•cy /imə́rjənsee/ *n.* (*pl.* **–cies**) sudden state of danger, etc., requiring immediate action.

■ crisis, exigency, predicament, difficulty.

e•mer•i•tus /iméritəs/ *adj.* retired and retaining one's title as an honor (*emeritus professor*, *professor emeritus*).

em•er•y /éməree/ *n.* coarse corundum for polishing metal, etc. □ **emery board** emery-coated strip of thin wood, etc., used as a nail file.

e•met•ic /imétik • *adj.* that causes vomiting. • *n.* emetic medicine.

em•i•grate /émigrayt/ *v.intr.* leave one's own country to settle in another. □□ **em'i•grant** *n.* **em•i•gra'tion** / -gráyshən/ *n.*

■ migrate, move, relocate, resettle. □□ **emigrant** émigré, expatriate, refugee, exile.

é•mi•gré /émigray/ *n.* (also **e'mi•gré**) emigrant, esp. a political exile.

■ see EXILE *n.* 3.

em•i•nence /éminəns/ *n.* **1** distinction; recognized superiority. **2** piece of rising ground. **3** (**Eminence**) title of address to a cardinal.

■ **1** see DISTINCTION *n.* 4. **2** see RISE *n.* 2.

em•i•nent /éminənt/ *adj.* distinguished; notable; remarkable in degree. □ **eminent domain** right of government to purchase private property for public. □□ **em'i•nent•ly** *adv.*

■ esteemed, exalted, respected, revered, honored, noteworthy, important, noted, outstanding, prominent, preeminent, conspicuous, superior, great, illustrious, famous, renowned, well-known, celebrated. □□ **eminently** very, exceedingly, extremely, exceptionally, singularly.

e•mir /emeér/ *n.* title of various Muslim rulers. □□ **e•mir'ate** /imeérit, -ayt, aymeér-, émərit/ *n.*

em•is•sar•y /émiseree/ *n.* (*pl.* **–ies**) person sent on a diplomatic mission.

■ see ENVOY.

e•mit /imít/ *v.tr.* (**e•mit•ted, e•mit•ting**) send out (heat, sound, light, etc.), discharge. □□ **e•mis•sion** /imíshən/ *n.*

■ eject, expel, emanate, give off *or* out, vent, radiate; exude, ooze; see also VOICE *v.* □□ **emission** see DISCHARGE *n.* 5.

e•mol•lient /imólyənt/ • *adj.* that softens or soothes the skin. • *n.* emollient agent. □□ **e•mol'lience** *n.*

e•mol•u•ment /imólyəmənt/ *n.* fee from employment.

■ see SALARY *n.*

e•mote /imót/ *v.intr.* show excessive emotion.

e•mo•tion /imóshən/ *n.* strong mental or instinctive feeling such as love or fear.

■ passion, sentiment, sensation.

e•mo•tion•al /imóshənəl/ *adj.* **1** of or relating to emotions. **2** liable to excessive emotion.

3 likely to excite emotion. □□ **e•mo'tion•al•ism** *n.* **e•mo'tion•al•ly** *adv.*

■ **2** excitable, high-strung. **3** moving, poignant, stirring, touching.

em•pa•thize /émpəthīz/ *v.intr.* exercise empathy.

■ identify, sympathize.

em•pa•thy /émpəthee/ *n.* capacity to identify with a person or object. □□ **em•pa•thet•ic** /-thétik/ *adj.* **em•pa•thet'i•cal•ly** *adv.*

em•per•or /émpərər/ *n.* sovereign of an empire.

em•pha•sis /émfəsis/ *n.* (*pl.* **em•pha•ses** /-seez/) **1** importance or prominence given to a thing. **2** stress laid on a word or words to indicate special meaning or importance.

■ **1** significance, attention, prominence.

em•pha•size /émfəsīz/ *v.tr.* put emphasis on.

■ stress, underscore, point up, underline, call *or* draw attention to, highlight, play up.

em•phat•ic /emfátik/ *adj.* **1** forcibly expressive. **2** of words: **a** bearing the stress. **b** used to give emphasis. □□ **em•phat'i•cal•ly** *adv.*

■ **1** demonstrative, pronounced, strong, clear, definite; firm, uncompromising, determined, decided, resolute; earnest, unequivocal, unambiguous, distinct, categorical, explicit; forceful, vigorous, energetic, assertive, intense.

em•phy•se•ma /émfiseémə, -zeémə/ *n.* disease of the lungs causing breathlessness.

em•pire /émpīr/ *n.* **1** extensive group of lands or countries under a single authority. **2** supreme dominion. **3** large commercial organization, etc., directed by one person or group.

■ **1** see DOMAIN 1.

em•pir•i•cal /empirikəl, im-/ *adj.* (also **em•pir'ic**) based on observation or experiment, not on theory. □□ **em•pir'i•cal•ly** *adv.* **em•pir•i•cism** /-sizəm/ *n.* **em•pir'i•cist** *n.*

■ observed, pragmatic, experimental.

em•place•ment /émplaysmənt, im-/ *n.* **1** putting in position. **2** platform for a gun. **3** situation; position.

■ **1, 3** see *placement* (PLACE).

em•ploy /emplóy, im-/ *v.tr.* **1** use the services of (a person) in return for payment. **2** use to good effect. **3** keep (a person) occupied. □□ **em•ploy'a•ble** *adj.* **em•ploy•a•bil'i•ty** *n.* **em•ploy'er** *n.*

■ **1** hire, engage, enlist, recruit, enroll, sign (up), take on; contract; keep, retain. **2** utilize, apply. **3** involve, engross. □□ **employer** proprietor, manager, director, chief, boss; company, firm, corporation.

em•ploy•ee /émployée, -ployée/ *n.* (also **em•ploy'e**) person employed for wages.

■ worker; (*employees*) staff, workforce.

em•ploy•ment /emplóymənt, im-/ *n.* **1** employing or being employed. **2** occupation.

■ **2** job, trade, work, business, profession, vocation.

em•po•ri•um /empáwreeəm/ *n.* (*pl.* **–ums** or **em•po•ri•a** /-reeə/) store selling a wide variety of goods.

em•pow•er /empówǝr, im–/ v.tr. **1** authorize, license. **2** give power to; make able. □□ **em•pow′er•ment** n.

em•press /émpris/ n. **1** wife or widow of an emperor. **2** woman emperor.

emp•ty /émptee/ • adj. (**emp•ti•er, emp•ti•est**) **1** containing nothing. **2** unoccupied; uninhabited; deserted; unfurnished. **3 a** hollow; insincere. **b** without purpose. **c** vacuous. • v. (**-ties, –tied**) **1** tr. remove the contents of. **2** intr. become empty. **3** intr. (of a river) discharge itself (into the sea, etc.). • n. (pl. **–ties**) colloq. empty bottle, etc. □□ **emp′ti•ly** adv. **emp′ti•ness** n.

■ adj. **1** void, unfilled, hollow, bare, barren, vacant, blank; clean, new, unused, clear; drained, spent, exhausted. **2** vacant; desolate, forsaken. **3 a** trivial, shallow, meaningless, insignificant. **b** see purposeless (PURPOSE). **c** fatuous, stupid, foolish, inane. • v. **1** clear (out), vacate, evacuate; drain, exhaust; void; see also DIVEST 2. □□ **emptiness** vacancy; senselessness, pointlessness, aimlessness, futility, uselessness.

EMT abbr. emergency medical technician.

e•mu /eemyōō/ n. large flightless bird of Australia.

em•u•late /émyǝlayt/ v.tr. **1** try to equal or excel. **2** imitate. □□ **em•u•la•tion** /–láyshǝn/ n. **em′u•la•tive** adj. **em′u•la•tor** n.

e•mul•si•fi•er /imúlsifīǝr/ n. substance that stabilizes an emulsion, esp. a food additive used to stabilize processed foods.

e•mul•si•fy /imúlsifī/ v.tr. (**–fies, –fied**) convert into an emulsion. □□ **e•mul•si•fi•ca′tion** n. **e•mul′si•fi•er** n.

e•mul•sion /imúlshǝn/ n. fine dispersion of one liquid in another, esp. as paint, medicine, etc. □□ **e•mul•sive** /–siv/ adj.

en /en/ n. Printing unit of measurement equal to half an em.

en-[1] /en, in/ prefix (also **em-** before b, p) forming verbs, = IN-[1]: **1** from nouns, meaning 'put into or on' (engulf, entrust, embed). **2** from nouns or adjectives, meaning 'bring into the condition of' (enslave). **3** from verbs: **a** in the sense 'in, into, on' (enfold). **b** as an intensifier (entangle).

en-[2] /en, in/ prefix (also **em-** before b, p) in; inside (energy).

-en[1] /ǝn/ suffix forming verbs: **1** from adjectives, usu. meaning 'make or become so or more so' (deepen, fasten, moisten). **2** from nouns (happen, strengthen).

-en[2] /ǝn/ suffix (also **–n**) forming adjectives from nouns, meaning: **1** made or consisting of (often with extended and figurative senses) (wooden). **2** resembling; of the nature of (golden, silvern).

-en[3] /ǝn/ suffix (also **–n**) forming past participles of strong verbs: **1** as a regular inflection (spoken, sworn). **2** with restricted sense (drunken).

-en[4] /ǝn/ suffix forming the plural of a few nouns (children, brethren, oxen).

-en[5] /ǝn/ suffix forming diminutives of nouns (chicken, maiden).

en•a•ble /enáybǝl/ v.tr. **1** give (a person, etc.)

the means or authority. **2** make possible. □□ **en•a′bler** n.

■ **1** qualify, authorize, entitle, permit, allow, sanction, empower; facilitate, help, aid, assist.

en•act /enákt, in–/ v.tr. **1 a** ordain; decree. **b** make (a bill, etc.) law. **2** play (a part). □□ **en•act′ment** n. **en•ac′tor** n.

■ **1 a** command, order, authorize. **b** pass, ratify; see also APPROVE. **2** act (out), portray, depict, perform, appear as.

e•nam•el /ináməl/ • n. **1** glasslike opaque coating for metal, etc. **2 a** smooth, hard coating. **b** hard gloss paint. **3** hard coating of a tooth. • v.tr. inlay or encrust with enamel.

■ n. see GLAZE n.

en•am•or /ináмǝr/ v.tr. [usu. in passive, foll. by of] inspire with love or delight for.

■ see CAPTIVATE.

en•camp /enkámp/ v. **1** settle in a military camp. **2** lodge in the open in tents. □□ **en•camp′ment** n.

en•cap•su•late /enkápsǝlayt, –syōō–, in–/ v.tr. **1** enclose in or as in a capsule. **2** summarize; express briefly. □□ **en•cap•su•la•tion** /–láyshǝn/ n.

■ **2** see sum up 1 (SUM).

en•case /enkáys, in–/ v.tr. **1** put into a case. **2** surround as with a case. □□ **en•case′ment** n.

-ence /ǝns/ suffix forming nouns expressing: **1** quality or state or instance of one (patience). **2** action (reference).

en•ceph•a•li•tis /énséfǝlītis/ n. inflammation of the brain. □□ **en•ceph•a•lit•ic** /–lítik/ adj.

en•ceph•a•lo•gram /enséfǝlōgram/ n. X-ray of the brain.

en•ceph•a•lo•graph /enséfǝlōgraf/ n. = ELECTROENCEPHALOGRAPH.

en•chant /enchánt, in–/ v.tr. **1** charm; delight. **2** bewitch. □□ **en•chant′ed•ly** adv. **en•chant′ing** adj. **en•chant′ing•ly** adv. **en•chant′ment** n.

■ **1** fascinate, beguile, captivate, enthrall, enrapture, attract, allure, entrance. **2** cast a spell on, spellbind, hypnotize, mesmerize, bedevil. □□ **enchanting** charming, fascinating, intriguing, appealing, ravishing, seductive. **enchantment** witchcraft, sorcery, magic, wizardry.

en•chi•la•da /énchiláadǝ/ n. rolled tortilla filled with meat, etc.

en•cir•cle /ensúrkǝl, in–/ v.tr. **1** surround. **2** form a circle around. See synonym study at CIRCUMSCRIBE. □□ **en•cir′cle•ment** n.

■ **1** enclose, ring, encompass, gird; confine, hem or hold in. **2** see CIRCLE v. 2.

en•clave /énklayv, ón–/ n. **1** territory surrounded by foreign territory. **2** group of people who are culturally, intellectually, or socially distinct from those surrounding them.

en•close /enklṓz, in–/ v.tr. **1 a** surround with a wall, fence, etc. **b** shut in. **2** put in a receptacle (esp. an envelope). See synonym study at CIRCUMSCRIBE.

■ **1** pen, encircle, encompass, bound, envelop, corral; confine, close or hem in. **2** insert, include.

en•clo•sure /enklṓzhər, in–/ *n.* **1** act of enclosing. **2** enclosed space or area. **3** thing enclosed with a letter. **4** enclosing fence, etc. ■ **4** wall, railing, barrier, hedge, barricade, boundary.

en•code /enkṓd, in–/ *v.tr.* put into code. □□ **en•cod′er** *n.* ■ encipher, encrypt.

en•com•pass /enkúmpəs, in–/ *v.tr.* **1** surround. **2** contain. See synonym study at CIRCUMSCRIBE. □□ **en•com′pass•ment** *n.* ■ **1** see CIRCLE *v.* 2. **2** see INCLUDE 1.

en•core /óngkawr/ • *n.* **1** call by an audience for continuation of performance, usu. by applause. **2** such a continuation. • *int.* also /–kór/ again; once more.

en•coun•ter /enkównter, in–/ • *v.tr.* **1** meet unexpectedly. **2** meet as an adversary. **3** meet with, experience (problems, opposition, etc.). • *n.* **1** meeting by chance. **2** meeting in conflict. □ **encounter group** group of persons seeking psychological benefit through contact with one another. ■ *v.* **1** come upon, run into *or* across, stumble upon, *colloq.* bump into. **2** contend with, cross swords with, confront. **3** face, wrestle with. • *n.* **2** confrontation, dispute, run-in.

en•cour•age /enkə́rij, –kúr–, in–/ *v.tr.* **1** give courage, confidence, or hope to. **2** urge; advise. **3** promote. □□ **en•cour′age•ment** *n.* **en•cour′ag•ing** *adj.* **en•cour′ag•ing•ly** *adv.* ■ **1** hearten, reassure, inspire. **2** see URGE *v.* 2, ADVISE. **3** advance, support, foster, boost.

SYNONYM STUDY: encourage

EMBOLDEN, FOSTER, HEARTEN, INSPIRE, INSTIGATE, STIMULATE. To **encourage** is to give active help or to raise confidence to the point where one dares to do what is difficult (*encouraged by her teacher, she set her sights on attending Harvard*). **Embolden** also entails giving confidence or boldness, but it implies overcoming reluctance or shyness (*success as a public speaker emboldened her to enter politics*). To **hearten** is to put heart into or to renew someone's spirit (*heartened by the news of his recovery*), and to **inspire** is to infuse with confidence, resolution, or enthusiasm (*inspired by her mother's example, she started exercising regularly*). To **foster** is to encourage by nurturing or extending aid (*to foster the growth of small businesses by offering low-interest loans*); in some contexts, *foster* suggests an unwise or controversial kind of help (*to foster rebellion among local farmers*). **Instigate** also implies that what is being encouraged is not necessarily desirable (*to instigate a fight*), while **stimulate** is a more neutral term meaning to rouse to action or effort (*to stimulate the growth of crops; to stimulate an interest in literature*).

---

en•croach /enkrṓch, in–/ *v.intr.* [foll. by *on*, *upon*] intrude. □□ **en•croach′ment** *n.* ■ trespass, make inroads; (*encroach on or upon*) invade, infringe; infiltrate; enter, advance.

en•crust /enkrúst, in–/ *v.* **1** *tr.* cover with a crust. **2** *intr.* form a crust. □□ **en•crust′ment** *n.* ■ cake.

en•crypt /enkrípt, in–/ *v.tr.* **1** convert (data) into code, esp. to prevent unauthorized access. **2** conceal by this means. □□ **en•cryp′tion** /–krípshən/ *n.*

en•cum•ber /enkúmbər, in–/ *v.tr.* **1** be a burden to. **2** hamper; impede. See synonym study at HINDER. □□ **en•cum′brance** *n.* ■ **1** weigh down, overburden, strain, oppress. **2** hinder, handicap, inconvenience. □□ **encumbrance** onus, load, millstone; impediment, hindrance, obstacle.

ency. *abbr.* (also **encyc.**) encyclopedia.

-ency /ənsee/ *suffix* forming nouns denoting a quality (*efficiency, fluency*) or state (*presidency*).

en•cyc•li•cal /ensíklikəl/ • *n.* papal letter to bishops. • *adj.* (of a letter) for wide circulation.

en•cy•clo•pe•di•a /ensíkləpeédeeə/ *n.* (also **en•cy•clo•pae′di•a**) publication giving information on many subjects, or on many aspects of one subject.

en•cy•clo•pe•dic /ensíkləpeédik/ *adj.* (also **en•cy•clo•pae′dic**) (of knowledge or information) comprehensive. ■ inclusive, broad, extensive, universal, thorough, exhaustive, wide-ranging, complete.

end /end/ • *n.* **1 a** extreme limit. **b** extremity. **2** extreme part or surface of a thing. **3 a** conclusion; finish. **b** latter or final part. **c** death; destruction. **d** result; outcome. **4** goal; purpose. **5** piece left over. **6** [prec. by *the*] *colloq.* limit of endurability. **7** part with which a person is concerned (*no problem at my end*). **8** *Football* player at the extremity of the offensive or defensive line. • *v.* **1** *tr. & intr.* bring or come to an end. **2** *tr.* destroy. **3** *intr.* [foll. by *in*] result. □ **end it all** (or **end it**) *colloq.* commit suicide. **end of the road** point at which hope has to be abandoned. **end result** final outcome. **end up** reach a specified state, action, or place eventually (*ended up a drunk*). **in the end** finally; after all. **keep one's end up** do one's part. **make ends** (or **both ends**) **meet** live within one's income. **on end 1** upright. **2** continuously (*for three weeks on end*). **put an end to 1** stop (an activity, etc.). **2** abolish; destroy. ■ *n.* **1** extent, bounds, endpoint, terminus. **3 a, b** termination, completion; close, finale, ending, windup. **c** expiration, ruin; see also DEATH 4a. **d** consequence, effect, upshot. **4** aim, intention, objective; destination. **5** see REMNANT. **6** (*the end*) the last straw, the final blow, too much. • *v.* **1** terminate, conclude, stop, halt, cease, wind up *or* down, discontinue. **2** annihilate, extinguish. **3** culminate.

en•dan•ger /endáynjər, in–/ *v.tr.* place in danger. □□ **en•dan′ger•ment** *n.* ■ imperil, jeopardize, threaten; risk.

en•dear /endeér, in–/ *v.tr.* make dear to. □□ **en•dear′ing** *adj.* **en•dear′ing•ly** *adv.* **en•dear′ment** *n.* ■ □□ **endearing** attractive, engaging, likable, appealing, pleasing, captivating, winning, lovable.

en•deav•or /endévər, in–/ • *v. tr.* try earnestly. • *n.* earnest attempt.

■ *v.* strive, make an effort, struggle, do one's best; *colloq.* take a stab at, have a go *or* crack at; aim, aspire. • *n.* effort, pains, venture.

en•dem•ic /endémik/ *adj.* regularly or only found among a particular people or in a certain region. See synonym study at NATIVE. □□ **en•dem′i•cal•ly** *adv.*

■ native, indigenous, local.

end•ing /énding/ *n.* **1** end or final part, esp. of a story. **2** inflected final part of a word.

■ **1** see END *n.* 3a, b. **2** termination, suffix.

en•dive /éndiv, óndeev/ *n.* curly-leaved salad green.

end•less /éndlis/ *adj.* **1** infinite; without end. **2** continual. **3** innumerable. **4** (of a belt, chain, etc.) having the ends joined for continuous action over wheels, etc. □□ **end′less•ly** *adv.* **end′less•ness** *n.*

■ **1** immeasurable, limitless, unlimited, boundless, unbounded; eternal, perpetual, everlasting, perennial. **2** incessant, unceasing, constant, never-ending, interminable, nonstop, continuous, uninterrupted, unremitting, relentless, persistent. **3** countless, numerous, untold. □□ **endlessness** eternity, perpetuity.

end•most /éndmōst/ *adj.* nearest the end.

endo- /éndō/ *comb. form* internal.

en•do•crine /éndōkrin, –kreen, –krīn/ *adj.* (of a gland) secreting directly into the blood; ductless.

en•do•cri•nol•o•gy /éndōkrinóləjee/ *n.* study of endocrine glands. □□ **en•do•crin•o•log•i•cal** /–nəlójikəl/ *adj.* **en•do•cri•nol•o•gist** /–nól–/ *n.*

en•do•morph /éndōmawrf/ *n.* person with a heavy, rounded body. □□ **en•do•mor′phic** *adj.* **en•do•mor′phy** *n.*

en•dor•phin /endáwrfin/ *n.* peptide neurotransmitter occurring in the brain and having pain-relieving properties.

en•dorse /endáwrs, in–/ *v. tr.* **1** approve. **2** sign or write on (a document), esp. the back of (a bill, check, etc.). See synonym study at APPROVE. □□ **en•dors′a•ble** *adj.* **en•dor•see** /éndorsée/ *n.* **en•dorse′ment** *n.* **en•dors′er** *n.*

■ **1** confirm, ratify, support; sanction, authorize, advocate, give the go-ahead to, *colloq.* OK, okay, give the green light to. **2** ratify, countersign. □□ **endorsement** approval, backing, consent.

en•dow /endów, in–/ *v. tr.* **1** bequeath or give a permanent income to (a person, institution, etc.). **2** provide with talent, ability, etc. □□ **en•dow′er** *n.* **en•dow′ment** *n.*

■ **1** see AWARD *v.* **2** see BLESS 5. □□ **endowment** bestowal, allocation; bequeathal; grant, (financial) aid, award, funding, subsidy, allowance, donation, gift; bequest, inheritance; (*endowments*) talent(s), gift(s), abilities, strengths, qualities.

en•due /endóo, –dyóo, in–/ *v. tr.* [foll. by *with*] invest or provide (a person) with qualities, powers, etc.

en•dur•ance /endóorəns, –dyóor–, in–/ *n.*

1 power or habit of enduring. **2** ability to withstand prolonged strain.

■ **2** stamina, resilience, staying power, hardiness; perseverance, persistence, fortitude, tenacity; durability, longevity.

en•dure /endóor, –dyóor, in–/ *v.* **1** *tr.* undergo (a difficulty, etc.). **2** *tr.* tolerate. **3** *intr.* last. □□ **en•dur′a•bil′i•ty** *n.* **en•dur′a•ble** *adj.* **en•dur′ing•ly** *adv.*

■ **1** face, brave, survive, stand, bear, withstand, weather. **2** put up with, submit to, stomach, handle. **3** remain, stay, persist, linger; live (on).

end•ways /éndwayz/ *adv.* **1** with end uppermost or foremost. **2** end to end.

en•e•ma /énimə/ *n.* injection of liquid into the rectum, esp. to expel its contents.

en•e•my /énəmee/ *n.* (*pl.* **–mies**) **1** person or group actively hostile to another. **2 a** hostile nation or army. **b** member of this.

■ opponent, antagonist, rival, opposition, other side, adversary, foe.

en•er•gize /énərjīz/ *v. tr.* **1** infuse energy into. **2** provide energy for the operation of (a device). □□ **en′er•giz•er** *n.*

■ stimulate, enliven, animate, invigorate, vitalize, inspire, stir, arouse, awaken, rally, excite, enthuse; drive, motivate, spark, electrify.

en•er•gy /énərjee/ *n.* (*pl.* **–gies**) **1** force, vigor; capacity for activity. **2** capacity of matter or radiation to do work. □□ **en•er•get′ic** *adj.* **en•er•get′i•cal•ly** *adv.*

■ **1** power, strength, might, forcefulness; drive, *colloq.* get-up-and-go, pep; vitality, liveliness, vivacity, spirit, exuberance, zest, gusto, enthusiasm, verve, zeal. □□ **energetic** lively, active, vigorous, dynamic, alive, animated, spirited, vibrant, zealous, enthusiastic, eager, ambitious; invigorating, high-powered.

en•er•vate /énərvayt/ *v. tr.* deprive of vigor or vitality. □□ **en•er•va•tion** /–váyshən/ *n.*

■ weaken, tire (out), weary, drain, tax, exhaust, sap, debilitate, enfeeble, fatigue, wear out.

en•fee•ble /enféebəl, in–/ *v. tr.* make feeble. □□ **en•fee′ble•ment** *n.*

■ see WEAKEN 1.

en•fi•lade /énfiláyd, –laád/ *n.* gunfire directed along a line from end to end.

en•fold /enfóld, in–/ *v. tr.* **1** wrap; envelop. **2** clasp; embrace.

en•force /enfáwrs, in–/ *v. tr.* **1** compel observance of (a law, etc.). **2** impose (an action, conduct, one's will). □□ **en•force′a•ble** *adj.* **en•force•a•bil′i•ty** *n.* **en•forc′ed•ly** *adv.* **en•force′ment** *n.* **en•forc′er** *n.*

■ **1** implement, put into effect, carry out. □□ **enforcement** see *imposition* (IMPOSE).

en•fran•chise /enfránchīz, in–/ *v. tr.* **1** give (a person) the right to vote. **2** free (a slave, etc.). □□ **en•fran′chise•ment** *n.*

en•gage /en-gáyj, in–/ *v.* **1** *tr.* hire. **2** *tr.* **a** [usu. in *passive*] occupy. **b** hold fast. **3** *tr.* [usu. in *passive*] bind by a promise, esp. of marriage. **4** *tr.* reserve (a room, seat, etc.). **5 a** *tr.* interlock (parts of a gear, etc.). **b** *intr.* (of a part, gear, etc.) interlock. **6 a** *tr. & intr.* come into battle. **b** *tr.* bring (troops) into

battle. **7** *intr.* take part (*engage in politics*).
□□ **en•gage'** *adj.*

■ **1** employ, recruit, take on, sign up *or* on, retain, enlist. **2 a** keep busy, absorb, involve, preoccupy. **b** capture, draw; interest, intrigue, engross, fascinate. **3** betroth. **4** book, secure. **6 a** contend (with), wage war (against), take up arms (against). **7** (*engage in*) participate in, get involved in, join *or* partake in, enter into.

en•gaged /en-gáyjd, in-/ *adj.* **1** under a promise to marry. **2 a** occupied; busy. **b** reserved; booked. See synonym study at BUSY.

■ **1** betrothed, pledged; spoken for. **2 a** -busy, occupied, tied up, involved.

en•gage•ment /en-gáyjmənt, in-/ *n.* **1** engaging or being engaged. **2** appointment. **3** betrothal. **4** battle. □ **engagement ring** ring given to a woman by her fiancé.

■ **1** employment, recruitment, enlistment. **2** meeting, rendezvous, commitment, date. **4** fight, war, conflict, clash, encounter.

en•gag•ing /en-gáyjing, in-/ *adj.* attractive; charming. □□ **en•gag'ing•ly** *adv.*

■ pleasant, sociable, delightful, enchanting, endearing, winsome, appealing, winning, agreeable.

en•gen•der /enjéndər, in-/ *v.tr.* give rise to; bring about.

■ see CREATE 1.

en•gine /énjin/ *n.* **1** mechanical contrivance, esp. as a source of power. **2** locomotive.

■ **1** motor, machine, mechanism, appliance, apparatus.

en•gi•neer /únjinéer/ • *n.* **1** person qualified in a branch of engineering. **2 a** person in charge of engines. **b** operator of an engine, esp. a railroad locomotive. **3** [foll. by *of*] contriver. • *v.* **1** *tr.* contrive; bring about. **2** *intr.* act as an engineer.

■ *n.* **2 b** driver. **3** designer, inventor, creator, architect. • *v.* **1** plan, organize, manage, set up, effect.

en•gi•neer•ing /énjinéering/ *n.* application of science to the design, building, and use of machines, etc.

Eng•lish /ínglish/ • *adj.* of England or its people or language. • *n.* **1** language of England, now used in the UK, US, Canada, etc. **2** [prec. by *the*; treated as *pl.*] the people of England. **3** spin given to a ball. □ **English horn** alto woodwind instrument of the oboe family. **English muffin** flat round bread-dough muffin, usu. served sliced and toasted.

Eng•lish•man /ínglishmən/ *n.* (*pl.* **–men**; *fem.* **Eng•lish•wom•an** /ínglishwʊʊmən/ *pl.* **–wom•en**) person who is English by birth or descent.

en•gorge /en-gáwrj, in-/ *v.tr.* **1** [in *passive*] **a** be crammed. **b** *Med.* be congested with blood. **2** devour greedily. □□ **en•gorge'ment** *n.*

■ **2** see DEVOUR 1.

engr. *abbr.* **1** engineer. **2** engraved. **3** engraver. **4** engraving.

en•grave /en-gráyv, in-/ *v.tr.* **1** carve (a text or design) on a hard surface. **2** inscribe (a surface) in this way. **3** impress deeply on a person's memory, etc. □□ **en•grav'er** *n.*

■ **1, 2** cut, chisel, incise, score, etch. **3** stamp, imprint, fix, embed.

en•grav•ing /en-gráyving, in-/ *n.* print made from an engraved plate, block, or other surface.

■ impression, etching, lithograph; woodcut.

en•gross /en-grós, in-/ *v.tr.* absorb the attention of; occupy fully (*engrossed in studying*). □□ **en•gross'ing** *adj.*

■ see OCCUPY 5.

en•gulf /en-gúlf, in-/ *v.tr.* flow over and swamp; overwhelm. □□ **en•gulf'ment** *n.*

■ see DROWN.

en•hance /enháns, in-/ *v.tr.* intensify (qualities, value, etc.); improve (something already of good quality). □□ **en•hance'ment** *n.* **en•hanc'er** *n.*

■ heighten, raise, increase, augment, add to, deepen, strengthen, reinforce, sharpen, amplify, magnify, enlarge, expand, maximize, lift, swell, *colloq.* boost; refine, better, polish, upgrade, enrich.

e•nig•ma /inígmə/ *n.* **1** puzzling thing or person. **2** riddle; paradox. See synonym study at RIDDLE. □□ **en•ig•mat•ic** /énigmátik/ *adj.* **en•ig•mat'i•cal** *adj.* **en•ig•mat'i•cal•ly** *adv.* See synonym study at DOUBTFUL.

■ **1** mystery, problem. **2** conundrum. □□ **enigmatic** see *puzzling* (PUZZLE *v.* 3).

en•join /enjóyn, in-/ *v.tr.* **1** command; order (a person). **2** *Law* prohibit (a person) by order. See synonym study at PROHIBIT. □□ **en•join'ment** *n.*

en•joy /enjóy, in-/ *v.tr.* **1** take pleasure in. **2** have the use or benefit of. **3** experience. □ **enjoy oneself** experience pleasure. □□ **en•joy'a•ble** *adj.* **enjoy'er** *n.* **en•joy'ment** *n.*

■ **1** like, be partial to, appreciate, cherish, be fond of, savor, *sl.* dig; love, adore. **2** profit from, take advantage of. **3** have, possess; suffer with *or* from. □ **enjoy oneself** have a good *or* great time, have fun, live it up, have a ball. □□ **enjoyable** see PLEASANT. **enjoyment** joy, gratification, satisfaction.

en•large /enláarj, in-/ *v.* **1** *tr. & intr.* make or become larger or wider. **2** *tr.* describe in greater detail. **3** *tr.* reproduce on a larger scale. □□ **en•large'ment** *n.*

■ **1, 3** magnify, add to; expand, increase, extend, widen, broaden, lengthen, stretch. **2** expound, embellish; elaborate.

en•larger /enláarjər, in-/ *n.* apparatus for enlarging photographs.

en•light•en /enlít'n, in-/ *v.tr.* **1 a** inform (a person) about a subject. **b** (as **enlightened** *adj.*) knowledgeable. **2** (esp. as **enlightened** *adj.*) free from prejudice or superstition.

■ **1 a** instruct, educate, teach, illuminate, edify. **b** (**enlightened**) well-informed, aware, literate. **2** (**enlightened**) sensible, rational, reasonable, broad-minded, open-minded, liberal.

en•light•en•ment /enlít'nmənt, in-/ *n.* **1** enlightening; being enlightened. **2** (**the Enlightenment**) the 18th-c. philosophy of reason and individualism.

■ **1** see *illumination* (ILLUMINATE 1).

en•list /enlíst, in–/ v. **1** intr. & tr. enroll in the armed services. **2** tr. secure as a means of help or support. □ **enlisted man** soldier or sailor below the rank of officer. □□ **en•list′ ment** n.

■ **1** join up, volunteer; sign up or on, register; recruit, call up, conscript, draft. **2** obtain, get, procure, employ, rally, drum up; retain.

en•liv•en /enlívən, in–/ v.tr. **1** give life or spirit to. **2** make cheerful; brighten (a picture or scene). See synonym study at QUICKEN. □□ **en•liv′en•ment** n.

■ **1** invigorate, stimulate, energize, breathe life into, electrify, activate, refresh. **2** liven up, (up)lift.

en masse /on más/ adv. **1** all together. **2** in a mass.

en•mesh /enmésh, in–/ v.tr. entangle in or as in a net. □□ **en•mesh′ment** n.

en•mi•ty /énmitee/ n. (pl. **–ties**) **1** state of being an enemy. **2** feeling of hostility.

en•ne•ad /éneead/ n. group of nine.

en•no•ble /enṓbal, in–/ v.tr. make noble; elevate. □□ **en•no′ble•ment** n.

en•nui /onweé/ n. mental weariness; boredom.

e•nol•o•gy /eenólajee/ n. the study of wines. □□ **e•no•log•i•cal** /ēēnəlójikəl/ adj. **e•nol′o• gist** n.

e•nor•mi•ty /ináwrmitee/ n. (pl. **–ties**) **1** extreme wickedness. **2** great size.

■ **1** evil, monstrousness, brutality, barbarity, savagery; atrocity, horror, outrage. **2** see SIZE[1] n. 1.

e•nor•mous /ináwrməs/ adj. very large; huge. □□ **e•nor′mous•ly** adv. **e•nor′mous•ness** n.

■ big, immense, vast, massive, gigantic, mammoth, colossal, great, giant; gargantuan, monstrous, monumental, titanic; jumbo; tremendous, stupendous.

e•nough /inúf/ • adj. as much or as many as required. • n. amount or quantity that is enough. • adv. **1** adequately. **2** quite (oddly enough). □ **have had enough of** want no more of; be tired of.

■ adj. sufficient, adequate, ample. • n. plenty; abundance. • adv. **1** sufficiently, reasonably, fairly, satisfactorily. **2** very, perfectly, full.

en•quire var. of INQUIRE.

en•quir•y var. of INQUIRY.

en•rage /enráyj, in–/ v.tr. make furious. □□ **en•rage′ment** n.

■ anger, infuriate, madden, incense, provoke, drive crazy or mad or up the wall; sl. burn up.

en•rap•ture /enrápchər, in–/ v.tr. give intense delight to.

■ thrill, electrify; enchant, bewitch, enthrall, captivate, beguile, fascinate.

en•rich /enrích, in–/ v.tr. **1** make rich or richer. **2** increase the strength, value, or contents of. □□ **en•rich′ment** n.

■ enhance, improve, upgrade, intensify; add to, expand; elaborate, develop.

en•roll /enrṓl, in–/ v. (also **en•rol′**) (en•

rolled, en•rol•ling) **1** intr. enlist. **2** tr. **a** write the name of (a person) on a list. **b** incorporate as a member. □□ **en•roll•ee** /–leé/ n. **en•roll′er** n. **en•roll′ment** n. **en•rol′ ment** n.

■ **1** register, sign up or on, join. **2** register, sign up or on or in. □□ **enrollment** see initiation (INITIATE).

en route /on rōot/ adv. on the way.

Ens. abbr. ensign.

en•sconce /enskóns, in–/ v.tr. establish or settle comfortably.

■ see ESTABLISH 1.

en•sem•ble /onsómbəl/ n. **1 a** thing viewed as the sum of its parts. **b** general effect of this. **2** set of clothes worn together. **3** group of performers working together.

■ **1** composite, aggregate; collection, set, body, group. **2** outfit, costume, suit, colloq. getup. **3** band, orchestra, chorus, sl. combo; company, troupe, cast.

en•shrine /enshrín, in–/ v.tr. **1** enclose in a shrine. **2** preserve or cherish. □□ **en•shri• ne′ment** n.

■ **2** see REVERE.

en•shroud /enshrówd, in–/ v.tr. **1** cover with or as with a shroud. **2** cover completely; hide from view.

en•sign /énsin, –sīn/ n. **1** banner or flag, esp. the military or naval flag of a nation. **2** lowest commissioned officer in the US Navy or US Coast Guard.

en•slave /ensláyv, in–/ v.tr. make (a person) a slave. □□ **en•slave′ment** n. **en•slav′er** n.

■ bind, yoke, fetter, shackle; oppress, dominate. □□ **enslavement** see SLAVERY 1.

en•snare /ensnáir, in–/ v.tr. catch in or as in a snare; entrap. □□ **en•snare′ment** n.

en•sue /ensōo, in–/ v.intr. happen afterward or as a result.

en•sure /enshōor, in–/ v.tr. **1** make certain. **2** make safe.

■ **1** make sure, guarantee; insure. **2** protect, guard, shelter, shield, safeguard, secure.

-ent /ənt, ent/ suffix **1** forming adjectives denoting attribution of an action (consequent) or state (existent). **2** forming nouns denoting an agent (coefficient, president).

en•tail /entáyl, in–/ v.tr. **1 a** necessitate or involve unavoidably. **b** give rise to; involve. **2** Law bequeath (property, etc.) so that it remains within a family. □□ **en•tail′ment** n.

■ **1 a** require, call for. **b** lead to, cause, create.

en•tan•gle /entánggəl, in–/ v.tr. **1** cause to get caught in a snare or among obstacles. **2** cause to become tangled. **3** involve in difficulties. **4** complicate. □□ **en•tan′gle•ment** n.

■ **1, 2** tangle (up), enmesh, snarl, entwine, intertwine, snag, entrap. **3** embroil, mix up, draw or drag in, implicate. **4** confuse, confound.

en•tente /aantaánt/ n. friendly relationship between nations.

en•ter /éntər/ v. **1 a** intr. go or come in. **b** tr. go or come into. **c** intr. come on stage. **2** tr. penetrate. **3** tr. write (a name, details, etc.) in a list, book, etc. **4 a** intr. register or announce oneself as a competitor. **b** tr. be•

come a competitor in (an event). **5** *tr.* **a** become a member of (a society, etc.). **b** enroll in a society, school, etc. **6** *tr.* present for consideration (*entered a protest*). **7** *intr.* [foll. by *into*] **a** engage in (conversation, an undertaking, etc.). **b** bind oneself by (an agreement, etc.). **8** *intr.* [foll. by *on, upon*] undertake; begin to deal with (a subject).

■ **1 c** make an entrance. **2** pierce, bore (into), puncture; spread through(out); infiltrate. **3** make a note of, inscribe, jot down; record, log, document. **5** join, sign up for; admit, let in. **6** submit, tender, offer, put forward, propose. **7** (*enter into*) **a** participate in. **b** subscribe to, be (a) party to. **8** (*enter on* or *upon*) start, set about, commence; embark on.

en•ter•prise /éntərprīz/ *n.* **1** undertaking, esp. a bold or difficult one **2** initiative. **3** business firm.

■ **1** project, venture, program, activity, endeavor, concern. **2** resourcefulness, nerve, spirit, drive, ambition, determination, resolve, motivation, enthusiasm. **3** company, establishment, outfit.

en•ter•pris•ing /éntərprīzing/ *adj.* **1** ready to engage in enterprises. **2** resourceful; imaginative. □□ **en´ter•pris•ing•ly** *adv.*

■ venturesome, daring, courageous, bold, creative, resolute, purposeful. □□ **enterprisingly** adventurously, energetically.

en•ter•tain /éntərtáyn/ *v.tr.* **1** amuse; occupy agreeably. **2 a** receive as a guest. **b** receive guests (*they entertain a great deal*). **3** consider (an idea, feeling, etc.). □□ **en•ter•tain´er** *n.* **en•ter•tain´ing** *adj.*

■ **1** delight, please; interest, engage. **2 a** accommodate. **b** have people over, have visitors *or* guests. **3** contemplate, ponder; foster, encourage. □□ **entertaining** funny, humorous, comical, witty; engaging, enjoyable, pleasing.

en•ter•tain•ment /éntərtáynmənt/ *n.* **1** act or instance of entertaining; process of being entertained. **2** public performance or show. **3** diversions or amusements for guests, etc.

■ amusement, pleasure, sport; recreation; production.

en•thrall /enthráwl, in-/ *v.tr.* captivate, please greatly. □□ **en•thrall´ment** *n.*

en•throne /enthrón, in-/ *v.tr.* place on a throne. □□ **en•throne´ment** *n.*

en•thuse /enthóoz, in-/ *v. colloq.* be or make enthusiastic.

■ see ENERGIZE.

en•thu•si•asm /enthóozeeazəm, in-/ *n.* strong interest; great eagerness. □□ **en•thu´si•ast** *n.* **en•thu•si•as´tic** *adj.* **en•thu•si•as´ti•cal•ly** *adv.* See synonym study at EAGER. See synonym study at ZEALOT

■ passion, fascination, obsession, devotion; keenness, appetite, fervor, excitement. □□ **enthusiast** fan, devotee, aficionado, *colloq.* buff. **enthusiastic** eager, avid; spirited, enthused, excited; devoted, zealous, fanatical, wild.

en•tice /entís, in-/ *v.tr.* persuade by the offer of pleasure or reward. □□ **en•tice´ment** *n.* **en•tic´er** *n.* **en•tic´ing•ly** *adv.*

■ lure, tempt, allure, attract, seduce, charm, coax, induce, beguile, wheedle, *colloq.* sweet-

talk, soft-soap. □□ **enticement** temptation, seduction, persuasion; inducement, attraction, *colloq.* come-on.

en•tire /entír, in-/ *adj.* whole; complete; unbroken.

■ total, full, undivided; uncut, unabridged; intact, perfect; in one piece; continuous, uninterrupted.

en•tire•ly /entírlee, in-/ *adv.* **1** wholly; completely. **2** solely.

■ **1** altogether, fully, perfectly, totally, utterly, thoroughly, absolutely, quite; unequivocally; from start to finish. **2** exclusively, only.

en•tire•ty /entírətee, in-/ *n.* (*pl.* **–ties**) **1** completeness. **2** sum total.

■ **1** totality, whole(ness). **2** whole, aggregate.

en•ti•tle /entítəl, in-/ *v.tr.* **1** give just claim or right. **2** give a title to. □□ **en•ti´tle•ment** *n.*

■ **1** allow, permit; make eligible, qualify; authorize, empower. **2** name, call.

en•ti•ty /éntitee/ *n.* (*pl.* **–ties**) **1** thing with distinct existence. **2** existence or essential nature of a thing regarded distinctly.

■ **1** object, element, unit, being; organism, specimen, creature, individual, body. **2** life, being; essence, quintessence.

en•tomb /entóom, in-/ *v.tr.* place in or as in a tomb. □□ **en•tomb´ment** *n.*

en•to•mol•o•gy /éntəmóləjee/ *n.* study of insects. □□ **en•to•mo•log´i•cal** /-məlójikəl/ *adj.* **en•to•mol´o•gist** *n.*

en•tou•rage /óntoorázh/ *n.* people attending an important person.

■ see RETINUE.

en•trails /éntraylz, trəlz/ *n.pl.* **1** bowels; intestines. **2** innermost parts.

en•trance[1] /éntrəns/ *n.* **1** going or coming in. **2** door, passage, etc., by which one enters. **3** right of admission. **4** coming of an actor on stage.

■ **1, 4** arrival, appearance. **2** entry, entranceway, entryway, doorway, ingress; opening. **3** access, admittance.

en•trance[2] /entrans, in-/ *v.tr.* **1** enchant; delight. **2** put into a trance. □□ **en•trance´ment** *n.* **en•tranc´ing** *adj.* **en•tranc´ing•ly** *adv.*

■ **1** bewitch, spellbind, fascinate, enrapture, thrill, electrify, charm, beguile, captivate. **2** hypnotize, mesmerize.

en•trant /éntrənt/ *n.* person who enters (esp. a competition, profession, etc.).

en•trap /entráp, in-/ *v.tr.* (**en•trapped, en•trap•ping**) **1** catch in or as in a trap. **2** beguile or trick. □□ **en•trap´per** *n.*

■ **1** see TRAP *v.* 2. **2** see BEGUILE 3, SEDUCE 2.

en•trap•ment /entrápmənt, in-/ *n.* **1** act or instance of entrapping; process of being entrapped. **2** *Law* inducement to commit a crime, esp. to secure a prosecution.

en•treat /entréet, in-/ *v.tr.* ask earnestly; beg. See synonym study at BEG. □□ **en•treat´ing•ly** *adv.* **en•treat´y** *n.* (*pl.* **–ies**)

en•trée /óntray/ *n.* (also **en´tree**) **1** main dish of a meal. **2** right of admission.

■ **2** see ADMISSION 2a.

en•trench /entrénch, in–/ v. **1** tr. establish firmly (in a position, office, etc.). **2** intr. [foll. by *upon*] encroach; trespass. □□ **en•trench′ ment** n.

■ **1** fix, root, embed, plant, set. **2** intrude, make inroads; (*entrench upon*) invade, infringe.

en•tre•pre•neur /óntrəprənŏŏr/ n. person who undertakes a commercial risk for profit. □□ **en•tre•pre•neur′i•al** adj. **en•tre•pre′ neur′i•al•ly** adv. **en•tre•pre•neur′ship** n.

■ adventurer, opportunist.

en•tro•py /éntrəpee/ n. *Physics* measure of the disorganization or degradation of the universe. □□ **en•tro′pic** /–trópik/ adj. **en•tro′ pi•cal•ly** adv.

en•trust /entrúst, in–/ v.tr. give into the care of another. □□ **en•trust′ment** n.

■ assign, delegate, leave, commit; trust, charge.

en•try /éntree/ n. (pl. **–tries**) **1** going or coming in. **2** liberty to go or come in. **3** place of entrance. **4** item entered (in a diary, list, etc.). **5** registered competitor.

■ **1** arrival, appearance. **2** access, admittance, admission. **3** entranceway, door, doorway, gate, access, ingress. **4** note, point, recording, listing. **5** entrant, contestant, participant, player, candidate.

en•twine /entwín, in–/ v. **1** tr. & intr. twine together. **2** tr. interweave.

■ interlace, braid, weave, intertwine, twist.

e•nu•mer•ate /inŏŏmərayt, inyŏŏ–/ v.tr. **1** specify (items) one by one. **2** count. □□ **e• nu′mer•a•ble** adj. **e•nu•mer•a•tion** /–ráy-shən/ n. **e•nu′mer•a•tive** /–raytiv, –rətiv/ adj. **e•nu′mer•a•tor** n.

■ **1** mention, name, identify, cite, list, itemize. **2** calculate, figure (up), compute, tally, quantify.

e•nun•ci•ate /inúnseeayt/ v.tr. **1** pronounce clearly. **2** express in definite terms. □□ **e• nun•ci•a•tion** /–áyshən/ n. **e•nun′ci•a•tive** /–seeətiv/ adj. **e•nun′ci•a•tor** n.

■ **1** articulate, speak. **2** see EXPRESS¹ 1, 2. □□ **enunciation** see SPEECH 1.

en•u•re•sis /ényŏŏréesis/ n. bedwetting.

en•vel•op /envélap, in–/ v.tr. **1** wrap up or cover completely. **2** completely surround. See synonym study at CIRCUMSCRIBE. □□ **en• vel′op•ment** n.

■ **1** enfold, clothe, sheathe, conceal, hide, shroud.

en•ve•lope /énvəlōp, ón–/ n. **1** folded paper container, usu. with a sealable flap, for a letter, etc. **2** wrapper; covering.

■ see WRAPPER 1.

en•vi•a•ble /énveeəbəl/ adj. likely to excite envy. □□ **en′vi•a•bly** adv.

■ desirable, desired, sought-after, coveted.

en•vi•ous /énveeəs/ adj. feeling or showing envy. See synonym study at JEALOUS. □□ **en′ vi•ous•ly** adv.

■ jealous, green-eyed, covetous, desirous, resentful.

en•vi•ron•ment /envírənmənt, –víərn–, in–/ n. **1** surroundings, esp. as affecting lives. **2** conditions or circumstances of living.

□□ **en•vi•ron•men′tal** adj. **en•vi•ron•men′ tal•ly** adv.

■ environs, ambiance, atmosphere, climate; habitat, element, territory; sphere, setting; biosphere, ecosystem.

en•vi•ron•men•tal•ist /envírənméntəlist, –víərn–, in–/ n. person concerned with the protection of the natural environment. □□ **en•vi•ron•men′tal•ism** n.

■ ecologist, conservationist, Green, naturalist.

en•vi•rons /énvírənz, –víərnz, in–/ n.pl. surrounding district, esp. around an urban area.

■ see NEIGHBORHOOD.

en•vis•age /envízij, in–/ v.tr. have a mental picture of (a thing or conditions not yet existing).

■ visualize, imagine, envision, conceive (of), dream up; contemplate, look forward to, fantasize about.

en•vi•sion /envízhən, in–/ v.tr. envisage; visualize.

en•voy /énvoy, ón–/ n. **1** messenger or representative. **2** diplomat ranking below ambassador. □□ **en′voy•ship** n.

■ **1** emissary, agent, ambassador, minister, delegate, spokesperson, attaché, diplomat.

en•vy /énvee/ • n. (pl. **–vies**) **1** discontent aroused by another's better fortune, etc. **2** object of this feeling. • v.tr. (**–vies, –vied**) feel envy of (a person, etc.) (*I envy you your position*). □□ **en′vi•er** n.

■ n. **1** jealousy, resentment, bitterness; desire. • v. resent, begrudge; covet.

en•wrap /enráp, in–/ v.tr. (**–wrapped, –wrap•ping**) wrap or enfold.

en•zyme /énzīm/ n. protein catalyst in a specific biochemical reaction. □□ **en•zy•mat′ic** adj.

e.o.m. abbr. (also **E.O.M.**) end of month.

e•on /éeon/ n. (also **ae•on**) **1** very long or indefinite period. **2** age of the universe. **3** an eternity.

■ **1** see AGE n. 2a.

-eous /eeəs/ suffix forming adjectives meaning 'of the nature of' (*erroneous, gaseous*).

EPA abbr. Environmental Protection Agency.

ep•au•let /épəlét/ n. (also **ep′au•lette**) ornamental shoulder piece, esp. on a uniform.

é•pée /aypáy, épay/ n. dueling sword, used (with the end blunted) in fencing. □□ **é•pée′ ist** n.

e•phem•er•al /ifémərəl/ adj. lasting for only a short time; transitory. See synonym study at TEMPORARY. □□ **e•phem•er•al•i•ty** /–álitee/ n. **e•phem′er•al•ly** adv.

■ see TRANSIENT adj. 1.

epi- /épi–/ prefix (usu. **ep-** before a vowel or h) **1** upon (*epidermis*). **2** above (*epicenter*). **3** in addition (*epilogue*).

ep•ic /épik/ • n. **1** long narrative poem of heroic deeds. **2** grand or extended story, film, etc. • adj. **1** of or like an epic. **2** grand; heroic. □□ **ep′i•cal** adj. **ep′i•cal•ly** adv.

ep•i•cene /épiseen/ adj. **1** *Gram.* denoting either sex without change of gender. **2** having characteristics of both sexes or neither sex.

ep•i•cen•ter /épisentər/ n. **1** *Geol.* point at

which an earthquake reaches the earth's surface. **2** central point of a difficulty. □□ **ep•i•cen•tral** /-séntrəl/ adj.

ep•i•cure /épikyŏŏr/ n. person with refined tastes, esp. in food and drink.
■ gourmet, connoisseur, gourmand.

Ep•i•cu•re•an /épikyŏŏréeən, –kyŏŏree–/ • n. **1** disciple of Greek philosopher Epicurus (d. 270 BC), who taught that the highest good is personal happiness. **2 (epicurean)** devotee of (esp. sensual) enjoyment. • adj. **(epicurean)** characteristic of an epicurean. □□ **Ep•i•cu're•an•ism** n.
■ n. **2** see SYBARITE n. • adj. pleasure-seeking, hedonistic, carnal, overindulgent, self-indulgent.

ep•i•dem•ic /épidémik/ • n. **1** widespread occurrence of a disease at a particular time. **2** such a disease. • adj. in the nature of an epidemic. □□ **ep•i•dem'i•cal•ly** adv.
■ n. plague, pestilence; outbreak; scourge. • adj. widespread, rampant, rife, prevalent.

ep•i•de•mi•ol•o•gy /épideemeeólǝjee/ n. study of epidemic diseases and their control. □□ **ep•i•de•mi•o•log•i•cal** /–meeǝlójikǝl/ adj. **ep•i•de•mi•ol'o•gist** n.

ep•i•der•mis /épidérmis/ n. outer layer of the skin. □□ **ep•i•der'mal** adj. **ep•i•der'mic** adj. **ep•i•der'moid** adj.

ep•i•du•ral /épidŏŏrǝl, –dyŏŏr–/ • adj. (of an anesthetic) injected around the dura mater of the spinal cord. • n. epidural anesthetic, used esp. in childbirth.

ep•i•glot•tis /épiglótis/ n. flap of cartilage at the root of the tongue, depressed during swallowing to cover the windpipe. □□ **ep•i•glot'tal** adj. **ep•i•glot'tic** adj.

ep•i•gram /épigram/ n. pointed or witty saying. See synonym study at SAYING. □□ **ep•i•gram•mat•ic** /–grǝmátik/ adj. **ep•i•gram•mat'i•cal•ly** adv. **ep•i•gram'ma•tist** /–grámǝtist/ n.
■ proverb, aphorism, maxim, saw, adage, byword, catchphrase, motto, slogan; quip, witticism, pun; wisecrack. See **epigrammatic** pithy, terse, succinct, witty.

ep•i•graph /épigraf/ n. inscription. See synonym study at SAYING. □□ **ep•i•graph•ic** /épigráfik/ adj. **ep•i•graph'i•cal** adj. **e•pig•ra•phy** /ipígrǝfee/ n.

ep•i•lep•sy /épilepsee/ n. nervous disorder with convulsions and often loss of consciousness.

ep•i•lep•tic /épiléptik/ • adj. relating to epilepsy. • n. person with epilepsy.

ep•i•logue /épilawg, –og/ n. (also **epi'i•log**) concluding narrative part, speech, etc.
■ see SUPPLEMENT n. 1, 2.

ep•i•neph•rine /épinéfrin/ n. (also **ep•i•neph'rin**) **1** hormone secreted by the adrenal glands, affecting circulation and muscular action. **2** natural or synthetic form of this, used as a stimulant. (Also called **adrenaline**).

e•piph•a•ny /ipífǝnee/ n. (pl. **–nies**) **1 (Epiphany) a** manifestation of Christ to the Magi. **b** festival of this on January 6. **2** moment of profound insight. □□ **ep•i•phan•ic** /épifánik/ adj.

ep•i•phyte /épifīt/ n. nonparasitic plant grow-

---

ing on another, e.g., a moss. □□ **ep•i•phyt•ic** /–fítik/ adj.

e•pis•co•pa•cy /ipískǝpǝsee/ n. (pl. **–cies**) **1** government by bishops. **2** [prec. by the] the bishops.

e•pis•co•pal /ipískǝpǝl/ adj. of or headed by a bishop or bishops. □□ **e•pis'co•pal•ism** n.
■ see CLERICAL 1.

E•pis•co•pa•lian /ipískǝpáyleeǝn/ • adj. of or belonging to the Episcopal Church. • n. member of the Episcopal Church. □□ **E•pis•co•pa'lian•ism** n.

e•pis•co•pate /ipískǝpǝt/ n. **1** office or tenure of a bishop. **2** [prec. by the] bishops collectively.

e•pis•i•ot•o•my /ipeezeeótǝmee/ n. (pl. **–mies**) incision made at the opening of the vagina to ease childbirth.

ep•i•sode /épisōd/ n. **1** event or period as part of a sequence. **2** dramatic installment. **3** incident or set of incidents in a narrative. □□ **ep•i•sod'ic** /–sódik/ adj. **ep•i•sod'i•cal•ly** adv.
■ **1, 3** occurrence, happening, circumstance, occasion, affair, matter. **2** part, chapter. □□ **episodic** see OCCASIONAL 1.

e•pis•tle /ipísǝl/ n. **1** formal or joc. letter, esp. a long one on a serious subject. **2 (Epistle)** any of the letters of the apostles in the New Testament.

e•pis•to•lar•y /ipístǝleree/ adj. in the style or form of a letter or letters.

ep•i•taph /épitaf/ n. words written in memory of a person who has died, esp. as a tomb inscription.

ep•i•the•li•um /épitheéleeǝm/ n. (pl. **ep•i•the•li•a** /–leeǝ/ or **ep•i•the•li•ums**) tissue forming the outer layer of the body and lining many hollow structures. □□ **ep•i•the'li•al** adj.

ep•i•thet /épithet/ n. **1** characterizing adjective, etc. **2** such a word as a term of abuse. □□ **ep•i•thet'ic** adj. **ep•i•thet'i•cal** adj. **ep•i•thet'i•cal•ly** adv.
■ **1** see TITLE n. 5. **2** see EXPLETIVE n. 1.

e•pit•o•me /ipítǝmee/ n. **1** person or thing embodying a quality, etc. **2** thing representing another in miniature.
■ **1** embodiment, personification, essence, standard.

e•pit•o•mize /ipítǝmīz/ v.tr. perfectly exemplify. □□ **e•pit•o•mi•za'tion** n.

ep•och /épǝk, éepok/ n. **1** notable period of history. **2** beginning of an era. □□ **ep'och•al** adj.

ep•o•nym /épǝnim/ n. **1** person after whom a discovery, place, etc., is named. **2** the name given.

ep•ox•y /ipóksee/ adj. designating a resin used in adhesives, insulation, coatings, etc.

ep•si•lon /épsilon/ n. fifth letter of the Greek alphabet (E, ε).

Ep•som salts /épsǝm/ n. magnesium sulfate used as a purgative, etc.

equ•a•ble /ékwǝbǝl/ adj. even; not varying; uniform. □□ **eq•ua•bil'i•ty** n. **eq'ua•bly** adv.
■ stable, steady, regular, unchanging,

constant, invariable, consistent; even-tempered, easygoing, calm, levelheaded.

e•qual /ēékwəl/ • *adj.* **1** the same in quantity, quality, size, degree, level, etc. **2** evenly balanced. **3** having the same rights or status. See synonym study at SAME. • *n.* person or thing equal to another. • *v.tr.* **1** be equal to. **2** achieve something that is equal to. □ **equal opportunity** [often in *pl.*] opportunity to be employed, paid, etc., without discrimination on grounds of sex, race, etc. **equal** (or **equals**) **sign** the symbol =. □□ **e•qual′i•ty** /ikwólitee/ *n.* **e′qual•ly** *adv.*

■ *adj.* **1**, **3** identical, mirror-image, fifty-fifty, on a par; equivalent. **2** corresponding, symmetrical; even, proportionate; tied. • *n.* peer, match, fellow. • *v.* **1** see AMOUNT *v.* 1. **2** rival, challenge, compare with, parallel, be in the same league *or* class as *or* with; hold a candle to. □□ **equality** parity, sameness, uniformity, similarity; impartiality, fairness, justice. **equally** see ALIKE *adv.*

e•qual•ize /ēékwəlīz/ *v.* make or become equal. □□ **e•qual′i•za′tion** *n.*

■ counterbalance, offset; even up, match (up); catch up.

e•qua•nim•i•ty /ēékwənímitee, ékwə–/ *n.* mental composure; evenness of temper.

■ see TEMPER *n.* 4.

e•quate /ikwáyt/ *v.* **1** *tr.* regard as equal or equivalent. **2** *intr.* be equal or equivalent to. □□ **e•quat′a•ble** *adj.*

■ **1** see IDENTIFY 3. **2** see PARALLEL *v.* 1.

e•qua•tion /ikwáyzhən/ *n.* **1** equating or making equal; being equal. **2** statement that two mathematical expressions are equal. □□ **e•qua′tion•al** *adj.*

e•qua•tor /ikwáytər/ *n.* imaginary line around the earth or other body, equidistant from the poles. □□ **e•qua•to′ri•al** *adj.*

e•ques•tri•an /ikwéstreeən/ • *adj.* **1** of horses and horseback riding. **2** on horseback. • *n.* (*fem.* **e•ques•tri•enne** /–tree-én/) rider or performer on horseback. □□ **e•ques′tri•an•ism** *n.*

equi- /ēékwee, ékwi/ *comb. form* equal.

e•qui•dis•tant /ēékwidístənt, ékwi–/ *adj.* at equal distances. □□ **e•qui•dis′tant•ly** *adv.*

e•qui•lat•er•al /ēékwilátərəl, ékwi–/ *adj.* having all sides equal in length.

e•qui•lib•ri•um /ēékwilibreeəm, ékwi–/ *n.* (*pl.* **e•qui•lib•ri•ums** or **e•qui•lib•ri•a** /–reeə/) **1** state of physical balance. **2** state of composure.

■ **1** see BALANCE *n.* 3.

e•quine /ēékwīn, ékwīn/ *adj.* of or like a horse.

e•qui•nox /ēékwinoks, ékwi–/ *n.* time or date (about March 20 (*vernal equinox*) and September 22 (*autumnal equinox*) each year) at which the sun crosses the celestial equator, when day and night are of equal length. □□ **e•qui•noc′tial** /ēékwinókshəl, ékwi–/ *adj. & n.*

e•quip /ikwíp/ *v.tr.* (**e•quipped, e•quip′ping**) supply with what is needed. □□ **e•quip′per** *n.*

■ furnish, provide, stock (up), outfit.

e•quip•ment /ikwípmənt/ *n.* **1** necessary articles, clothing, etc., for a purpose. **2** equipping or being equipped.

■ **1** gear, apparatus, paraphernalia, kit, outfit, rig; baggage, luggage.

e•qui•poise /ēékwipoyz, ékwi–/ *n.* **1** equilibrium. **2** counterbalancing thing.

eq•ui•ta•ble /ékwitəbəl/ *adj.* fair; just. □□ **eq′ui•ta•bly** *adv.*

■ right, square, decent, good, correct, impartial, objective, unbiased, nonpartisan; judicious, ethical, moral, honest, honorable; on the up and up.

eq•ui•ta•tion /ékwitáyshən/ *n.* horsemanship.

eq•ui•ty /ékwitee/ *n.* (*pl.* **–ties**) **1** fairness. **2** net value of property after the deduction of any debts. **3** ownership, as in shares of stock, etc.

■ **1** justice, rightfulness, fair play, objectivity, impartiality, judiciousness.

e•quiv•a•lent /ikwívələnt/ • *adj.* **1** equal in value, amount, importance, etc. **2** corresponding. See synonym study at SAME. • *n.* equivalent thing, amount, word, etc. □□ **e•quiv′a•lence** *n.* **e•quiv′a•len•cy** *n.* **e•quiv′a•lent•ly** *adv.*

■ *adj.* **1** one and the same, identical, comparable, analogous, similar, parallel; alike; tantamount. **2** see COORDINATE *adj.* • *n.* match, counterpart, coordinate, twin; equal, peer.

e•quiv•o•cal /ikwívəkəl/ *adj.* **1** of double or doubtful meaning. **2** uncertain; questionable. See synonym study at DOUBTFUL. □□ **e•quiv•o•cal•i•ty** /–kálitee/ *n.* **e•quiv′o•cal•ly** *adv.*

■ dubious; ambiguous, vague, obscure, uncertain; mysterious, cryptic; see SUSPECT *adj.*

e•quiv•o•cate /ikwívəkayt/ *v.intr.* use ambiguity to conceal the truth. □□ **e•quiv′o•ca•cy** *n.* **e•quiv•o•ca•tion** /–káyshən/ *n.* **e•quiv′o•ca•tor** *n.* **e•quiv′o•ca•to•ry** *adj.*

■ prevaricate, quibble, hedge, double-talk. □□ **equivocacy, equivocation** see ambiguity (AMBIGUOUS).

ER *abbr.* **1** emergency room. **2** Elizabeth Regina (Queen Elizabeth).

Er *symb. Chem.* erbium.

-er¹ /ər/ *suffix* forming nouns from nouns, adjectives, and many verbs, denoting: **1** person, animal, or thing that performs a specified action or activity (*cobbler, lover, computer*). **2** person or thing that has a specified attribute or form (*foreigner*). **3** person concerned with a specified thing or subject (*geographer*). **4** person belonging to a specified place or group (*villager*).

-er² /ər/ *suffix* forming the comparative of adjectives (*wider*) and adverbs (*faster*).

-er³ /ər/ *suffix* used in slang formations usu. distorting the root word (*rugger, soccer*).

-er⁴ /ər/ *suffix* forming iterative and frequentative verbs (*blunder, glimmer, twitter*).

-er⁵ /ər/ *suffix* **1** forming nouns and adjectives through OF or AF, corresponding to: **a** L –*aris* (*sampler*) (cf. -AR¹). **b** L –*arius*, –*arium* (*butler, carpenter, danger*). **c** (through OF –*eûre*) L –*atura* or (through OF –*eōr*) L –*atorium*. **2** = -OR¹, -OR².

-er⁶ /ər/ *suffix* esp. *Law* forming nouns denoting verbal action or a document effecting this (*disclaimer, misnomer*). ¶The same ending occurs in *dinner* and *supper*.

ERA *abbr.* **1** *Baseball* earned run average. **2** Equal Rights Amendment.

e•ra /éerə, érə/ *n.* **1** period reckoning from a noteworthy event (*the Christian era*). **2** large distinct period of time, esp. regarded historically (*the pre-Roman era*).

■ age, epoch; eon.

e•rad•i•cate /irádikayt/ *v.tr.* root out; destroy completely. See synonym study at DESTROY. □□ **e•rad'i•ca•ble** *adj.* **e•rad•i•ca•tion** /–káyshən/ *n.* **e•rad'i•ca•tor** *n.*

■ see REMOVE *v.* 2.

e•rase /iráys/ *v.tr.* **1** rub out; obliterate. **2** remove recorded material from (a magnetic tape or medium). □□ **e•ras'a•ble** *adj.* **e•ra'sure** *n.*

■ **1** wipe out, delete, cancel, scratch out, cross *or* rule out, strike out *or* off, expunge; eradicate, eliminate, get rid of.

e•ras•er /iráysər/ *n.* thing that erases, esp. a piece of rubber or plastic used for removing pencil and ink marks.

er•bi•um /árbeeəm/ *n.* soft, silvery, metallic element of the lanthanide series. ¶Symb.: **Er**.

ere /air/ *prep. & conj. poet.* before (of time) (*ere noon*).

e•rect /irékt/ • *adj.* **1** upright; vertical. **2** enlarged and rigid. • *v.tr.* **1** raise; set upright. **2** build. □□ **e•rect'a•ble** *adj.* **e•rec'tion** *n.* **e•rect'ly** *adv.* **e•rect'ness** *n.* **e•rec'tor** *n.*

■ *adj.* **1** standing (up), upstanding, straight. **2** swollen, stiff, hard. • *v.* assemble, put together, fabricate, manufacture, frame, make, construct; establish, found.

e•rec•tile /iréktə̌l, til/ *adj.* that can be erected or become erect.

erg /ərg/ *n. Physics* unit of work or energy, equal to the work done by a force of one dyne when its point of application moves one centimeter in the direction of the force.

er•go /árgō, ér-/ *adv.* therefore.

er•go•nom•ics /árgənómiks/ *n.* study of the efficiency of persons in their working environment. □□ **er•go•nom'ic** *adj.* **er•gon•o•mist** /ergónəmist/ *n.*

er•got /árgət, –got/ *n.* fungal disease of rye and other cereals.

Er•in /érin/ *n. poet.* Ireland.

er•mine /ármin/ *n.* (*pl.* same or **er•mines**) **1** stoat, esp. when in its white winter fur. **2** its white fur.

erne /ern/ *n.* (also **ern**) *poet.* sea eagle.

e•rode /iród/ *v.* wear away; destroy or be destroyed gradually. □□ **e•rod'i•ble** *adj.*

■ eat away (at), consume, devour, corrode; diminish.

e•rog•e•nous /irójinəs/ *adj.* (of a part of the body) sensitive to sexual stimulation.

e•ro•sion /irózhən/ *n.* **1** wearing away of the earth's surface by the action of water, wind, etc. **2** eroding; process of being eroded. □□ **e•ro'sive** *adj.*

■ eating away, corrosion, washing away, abrasion, wear (and tear), damage, weathering.

---

e•rot•ic /irótik/ *adj.* of or causing sexual desire or excitement. □□ **e•rot'i•cal•ly** *adv.*

■ sensual, suggestive, titillating, risqué, seductive, lustful, sexy; sexual, erogenous, carnal, arousing, libidinous, prurient, lascivious, lewd, salacious, obscene, indecent, pornographic, dirty, filthy, blue.

e•rot•i•ca /irótikə/ *n.pl.* erotic literature or art.

e•rot•i•cism /irótisizəm/ *n.* **1** erotic nature or character. **2** use of or reponse to erotic images or stimulation.

err /ər, er/ *v.intr.* **1** be mistaken or incorrect. **2** do wrong; sin. □ **err on the right side** act in favor of the least harmful possibility. **err on the side of** act with a specified bias (*errs on the side of generosity*).

■ **1** be wrong, be in error, be inaccurate, be in the wrong, go astray, make a mistake, miscalculate, (make a) blunder, *colloq.* slip (up). **2** misbehave, lapse, fall.

er•rand /érənd/ *n.* short outing for a specific purpose.

■ see JOURNEY *n.*

er•rant /érənt/ *adj.* **1** deviating from an accepted standard. **2** *literary* traveling in search of adventure (*knight errant*). □□ **er•ran•cy** /–ənsee/ *n.* (in sense 1). **er'rant•ry** *n.* (in sense 2).

er•rat•ic /irátik/ *adj.* **1** inconsistent in conduct, opinions, etc.; unpredictable; eccentric. **2** uncertain in movement. □□ **er•rat'i•cal•ly** *adv.*

■ **1** variable, irregular, random, haphazard, unreliable, unstable; peculiar, abnormal, odd, strange, unusual, weird, unconventional. **2** wandering, meandering, aimless.

er•ra•tum /iraátəm, irát-/ *n.* (*pl.* **er•ra•ta** /–tə/) error in printing or writing.

er•ro•ne•ous /iróneeəs/ *adj.* incorrect; arising from error. □□ **er•ro'ne•ous•ly** *adv.* **er•ro'ne•ous•ness** *n.*

■ wrong, mistaken, false, untrue, faulty, misleading, inaccurate.

er•ror /érər/ *n.* **1** mistake. **2** moral transgression. □□ **er'ror•less** *adj.*

■ **1** inaccuracy, fault, flaw, slip, blunder, gaffe, goof. **2** sin, indiscretion, wrongdoing, misconduct, iniquity.

er•satz /érzaats, –saats, erzaáts, –saáts/ *adj.* substitute; imitation. See synonym study at SPURIOUS.

■ see IMITATION *adj.*

Erse /ers/ • *adj.* Gaelic. • *n.* the Gaelic language.

erst•while /árst-hwīl, –wīl/ *adj.* former; previous.

e•ruc•ta•tion /iruktáyshən, eéruk-/ *n.* belching.

er•u•dite /éryədīt, érə–/ *adj.* **1** learned. **2** showing great learning. □□ **er'u•dite•ly** *adv.* **er•u•di'tion** /–dishən/ *n.* See synonym study at KNOWLEDGE.

e•rupt /irúpt/ *v.intr.* **1** break out suddenly or dramatically. **2** (of a volcano) become active and eject lava, etc. **3** (of a rash, boil, etc.) appear on the skin. □□ **e•rup•tion** /–rúpshən/ *n.* **e•rup'tive** *adj.*

■ **2** spout, gush, explode, blow up, vomit,

spit. **3** come out, appear, flare up. □□ **eruption** outbreak, outburst, discharge, emission, explosion, spouting.

-ery /əree/ *suffix* forming nouns denoting: **1** class or kind (*greenery, machinery*). **2** employment; state or condition (*dentistry, slavery*). **3** place of work or cultivation or breeding (*brewery, rookery*). **4** behavior (*mockery*). **5** often *derog.* all that has to do with (*knavery*).

e•ryth•ro•cyte /iríthrəsít/ *n.* red blood cell.

Es *symb. Chem.* einsteinium.

es•ca•late /éskəlayt/ *v.* **1** *intr. & tr.* increase or develop (usu. rapidly) by stages. **2** *tr.* cause to become more intense. □□ **es•ca•la•tion** –láyshən/ *n.*

■ see INTENSIFY.

es•ca•la•tor /éskəlaytər/ *n.* moving staircase consisting of a circulating belt forming steps.

es•ca•pade /éskəpáyd/ *n.* daring or reckless caper.

■ see ADVENTURE *n.* 2.

es•cape /iskáyp/ • *v.* **1** *intr.* get free of restriction, control, a person, etc. **2** *intr.* (of a gas, liquid, etc.) leak. **3** *intr.* succeed in avoiding danger, punishment, etc. **4** *tr.* avoid. **5** *tr.* (of words, etc.) issue unawares from (a person, a person's lips). • *n.* **1** act or instance of escaping. **2** temporary relief from reality or worry. □□ **es•cap'er** *n.*

■ *v.* **1** get away, break out *or* free *or* loose, bolt, flee, fly, run away *or* off, slip away, take off, scram. **2** seep, discharge, emanate. **4** elude, evade, dodge. • *n.* **1** getaway, flight, departure, break, breakout. **2** distraction, diversion, recreation.

es•cap•ee /iskaypeé/ *n.* person who has escaped.

■ see RUNAWAY 1.

es•cape•ment /iskáypmənt/ *n.* part of a clock, etc., that connects and regulates the motive power.

es•cap•ism /iskáypizəm/ *n.* tendency to seek distraction and relief from reality, esp. in the arts or through fantasy. □□ **es•cap'ist** *n. & adj.*

es•car•got /eskaargó/ *n.* snail, esp. as prepared for food.

es•carp•ment /iskaárpmənt/ *n.* (also **es•carp'**) *Geol.* long, steep slope at the edge of a plateau, etc.

-esce /es/ *suffix* forming verbs, usu. initiating action (*effervesce, fluoresce*).

-escent /ésənt/ *suffix* forming adjectives denoting the beginning of a state or action (*effervescent, fluorescent*). □ **–escence** *suffix* forming nouns

es•cheat /ischeét/ • *n.* reversion of property to the state on the owner's dying without legal heirs. • *v.* **1** *tr.* hand over (property) as an escheat. **2** *intr.* revert by escheat.

es•chew /eschóo/ *v.tr.* avoid; abstain from. □□ **es•chew'al** *n.*

es•cort • *n.* /éskawrt/ **1** one or more persons, vehicles, etc., accompanying a person, vehicle, etc., for protection or as a mark of status. **2** person accompanying a person of the opposite sex socially. • *v.tr.* /iskáwrt/ act as an escort to.

■ *n.* **1** guard, bodyguard, convoy; chaperon, retinue, entourage. **2** companion, boyfriend, partner, date. • *v.* accompany, usher, conduct, guide, attend; guard, watch over.

es•cri•toire /éskritwaár/ *n.* writing desk with drawers, etc.

es•crow /éskrō/ *n. Law* **1** money, property, or written bond, kept in the custody of a third party until a specified condition has been fulfilled. **2** status of this (*in escrow*).

es•cutch•eon /iskúchən/ *n.* **1** shield or emblem bearing a coat of arms. **2** protective plate around a keyhole or door handle. □□ **es•cutch'eoned** *adj.*

ESL *abbr.* English as a second language.

e•soph•a•gus /isófəgəs, ee–/ *n.* (*pl.* **e•soph•a•gi** /–gī, –jī/) passage for food from the mouth to the stomach; gullet. □□ **e•soph•a•ge•al** /isófəjeéəl, eesəfájeeəl/ *adj.*

es•o•ter•ic /ésətérik/ *adj.* intelligible only to those with special knowledge. □□ **es•o•ter'i•cal** *adj.* **es•o•ter'i•cal•ly** *adv.* **es•o•ter'i•cism** /–rəsizəm/ *n.* **es•o•ter'i•cist** *n.*

■ see OCCULT *adj.* 2.

ESP *abbr.* extrasensory perception.

es•pa•drille /éspədríl/ *n.* light canvas shoe with a braided fiber sole.

es•pal•ier /ispályər, –yay/ *n.* **1** latticework for training branches of a tree or shrub. **2** tree or shrub so trained.

es•pe•cial /ispéshəl/ *adj.* notable; exceptional.

es•pec•ial•ly /ispéshəlee, espésh–/ *adv.* chiefly; much more than in other cases.

■ mainly, predominantly, primarily, principally, first, first and foremost; particularly, notably.

Es•pe•ran•to /éspərántō, –raán–/ *n.* artificial universal language intended for international use.

es•pi•o•nage /éspeeənaazh/ *n.* spying or use of spies.

es•pla•nade /ésplənaàd, –náyd/ *n.* long, open level area for walking.

■ see PROMENADE *n.* 2.

es•pous•al /ispówzəl, –səl/ *n.* **1** espousing of a cause, etc. **2** *archaic* marriage; betrothal.

■ 1 see promotion (PROMOTE).

es•pouse /ispówz/ *v.tr.* **1** adopt or support (a cause, doctrine, etc.). **2** *archaic* (usu. of a man) marry. □□ **es•pous'er** *n.*

es•pres•so /esprésō/ *n.* (also **ex•pres•so** /eksprésō/) (*pl.* **–sos**) strong black coffee made under steam pressure.

es•prit /espreé/ *n.* sprightliness; wit. □ **esprit de corps** /də káwr/ devotion to and pride in one's group.

es•py /ispí/ *v.tr.* (**–pies, –pied**) *literary* catch sight of; perceive.

Esq. *abbr.* esquire.

-esque /esk/ *suffix* forming adjectives meaning 'in the style of' or 'resembling' (*Schumannesque, statuesque*).

es•quire /éskwir, iskwír/ *n.* **1** title appended to a man's surname, esp. as a form of address for letters. **2** title placed after the name of an attorney.

es•say • *n.* /ésay/ **1** short piece of writing on

a given subject. **2** *formal* attempt. • *v.tr.* /esáy/ *formal* attempt. □□ **es'say•ist** *n.*

■ *n.* **1** composition, article, paper, theme. **2** effort, endeavor, venture. • *v.* try, undertake, tackle, take a stab at.

es•sence /ésəns/ *n.* **1** fundamental nature, inherent characteristics. **2 a** extract obtained by distillation, etc. **b** perfume. □ **in essence** fundamentally. **of the essence** indispensable; vital.

■ **1** quintessence, substance, core, heart, soul, *colloq.* bottom line. **2 a** concentrate, elixir. **b** see PERFUME *n.* 2. □ **in essence** essentially, basically, in the final analysis. **of the essence** essential, critical, crucial, requisite, important.

es•sen•tial /isénshəl/ • *adj.* **1** necessary; indispensable. **2** of or constituting the essence of a person or thing. See synonym study at INHERENT. See synonym study at NECESSARY. • *n.* [esp. in *pl.*] basic or indispensable element or thing. □ **essential oil** volatile oil of a plant, etc., with its characteristic odor. □□ **es•sen•ti•al•i•ty** /-sheeálitee/ *n.* **es•sen'tial•ly** *adv.* **es•sen'tial•ness** *n.*

■ *adj.* **1** imperative, vital, requisite, required, important, material. **2** see INTRINSIC. • *n.* see NECESSITY 1a.

EST *abbr.* **1** eastern standard time. **2** electroshock treatment.

est. *abbr.* **1** established. **2** estimate. **3** estimated.

-est /ist/ *suffix* forming the superlative of adjectives (*widest, nicest, happiest*) and adverbs (*soonest*).

es•tab•lish /istáblish/ *v.tr.* **1** set up on a permanent basis. **2** achieve permanent acceptance for (a custom, belief, etc.). **3** validate; place beyond dispute.

■ **1** found, create, form, inaugurate; constitute; introduce. **3** prove, verify, certify, confirm, affirm, demonstrate, show, substantiate, support, back up.

es•tab•lish•ment /istáblishmənt/ *n.* **1** establishing; being established. **2 a** business organization or public institution. **b** site of such. **3** (**the Establishment**) social group or authority exerting influence and resisting change.

■ **1** foundation, founding, formation, construction, inauguration, creation. **2 a** concern, firm, company, enterprise. **b** office, workplace, premises, shop, store, market. **3** (**the Establishment**) the government, the authorities, the ruling class, the powers that be.

es•tate /istáyt/ *n.* **1** property consisting of much land usu. with a large house. **2** person's assets and liabilities, esp. at death.

■ **1** domain, manor. **2** property, holding(s), resources, wealth, fortune; belongings, possessions.

es•teem /istéem/ • *v.tr.* **1** have a high regard for. **2** *formal* consider. • *n.* high regard; respect; favor.

■ *v.* **1** respect, value, treasure, prize, cherish, hold dear, appreciate, admire, look up to, venerate, revere, honor. **2** view as, judge, regard as, deem. • *n.* (high) opinion; admiration; approval.

SYNONYM STUDY: esteem

ADMIRE, APPRECIATE, PRIZE, REGARD, RESPECT. If you're a classical music aficionado, you might **appreciate** a good symphony orchestra, **admire** someone who plays the oboe, and **esteem** the works of Beethoven above all other classical composers. All three of these verbs are concerned with recognizing the worth of something, but in order to *appreciate* it, you have to understand it well enough to judge it critically. If you *admire* something, you appreciate its superiority, although not necessarily with any degree of understanding being implied (*to admire the view from the balcony; admire her ability to do calculus*). *Esteem* goes one step further, implying that your admiration is of the highest degree (*a musician esteemed throughout the music world*). You **prize** what you value highly or cherish, especially if it is a possession (*she prized her Stradivarius violin*), while **regard** is a more neutral term meaning to look at or to have a certain mental view of something, either favorable or unfavorable (*to regard him as a great musician; to regard her as a ruthless competitor*). To **respect** is to have a deferential regard for someone or something because of its worth or value (*to respect the conductor's interpretation of the music*).

es•ter /éstar/ *n.* chemical produced by replacing the hydrogen of an acid by an organic radical.

es•ti•ma•ble /éstiməbəl/ *adj.* worthy of esteem. □□ **es'ti•ma•bly** *adv.*

■ esteemed, respected, admired, valued, worthy, honored, excellent, good; respectable, admirable, valuable, honorable, praiseworthy, commendable.

es•ti•mate • *n.* /éstimət/ **1** approximate judgment, esp. of cost, value, size, etc. **2** statement of approximate charge for work to be undertaken. • *v.tr.* /éstimayt/ **1** form an estimate or opinion of. **2** make a rough calculation. □□ **es•ti•ma•tion** /-máyshən/ *n.* **es'ti•ma•tor** *n.*

■ *n.* reckoning, calculation; guess, ballpark figure; evaluation, assessment, appraisal. • *v.* **1** consider, think, believe, judge. **2** guess, calculate, reckon; determine; assess, appraise, value, evaluate. □□ **estimation** approximation; judgment; see also VIEW *n.* 4.

Es•to•ni•an /estóneeən/ • *n.* **1 a** native of Estonia. **b** person of Estonian descent. **2** language of Estonia. • *adj.* of Estonia, its people, or language.

es•trange /istráynj/ *v.tr.* cause (a person or group) to turn away; alienate. □□ **es•trange'ment** *n.*

■ (*estranged*) separated, driven apart; see also ALIENATE.

es•tro•gen /éstrəjən/ *n.* female sex hormone controlling estrus, etc.

es•trus /éstrəs/ *n.* recurring period of sexual receptivity in many female mammals; heat. □□ **es'trous** *adj.*

es•tu•ar•y /és-chŏoeree/ *n.* (*pl.* **–ies**) tidal course or mouth of a river.

ETA *abbr.* estimated time of arrival.

e•ta /áytə, ée'tə/ *n.* seventh letter of the Greek alphabet (H, η).

et al. /et ál/ *abbr.* and others.

etc. *abbr.* = ET CETERA.

et cet•er•a /et sétərə, sétrə/ *adv.* and the rest; and so on.

etch /ech/ *v.* **1 a** *tr.* reproduce (a picture, etc.) by engraving it on a metal plate with acid. **b** *tr.* engrave (a plate) in this way. **2** *intr.* practice this craft. **3** *tr.* impress deeply (esp. on the mind). □□ **etch'er** *n.*
■ *v.* **1 b** carve, incise, inscribe, cut, score. **3** imprint, engrave.

etch•ing /éching/ *n.* **1** print made from an etched plate. **2** art of producing these plates.
■ see ENGRAVING.

ETD *abbr.* estimated time of departure.

e•ter•nal /itúrnəl/ *adj.* **1** existing always. **2** essentially unchanging (*eternal truths*). □ **Eternal City** Rome. **eternal triangle** relationship of three people involving sexual rivalry. □□ **e•ter'nal•ly** *adv.*
■ **1** everlasting, timeless, infinite, endless, limitless, immortal. **2** invariable, permanent, fixed, constant, enduring, lasting. □□ **eternally** see ALWAYS 3.

e•ter•ni•ty /itúrnitee/ *n.* (*pl.* **–ties**) **1** infinite (esp. future) time. **2** endless life after death. **3** being eternal.
■ **1, 3** infinity, endlessness, perpetuity, everlastingness. **2** see *immortality* (IMMORTAL).

eth•ane /éthayn/ *n.* Chem. gaseous hydrocarbon of the alkane series, occurring in natural gas.

eth•a•nol /éthənawl, –nol/ *n.* Chem. = ALCOHOL 1.

e•ther /éethər/ *n.* **1** Chem. colorless volatile organic liquid used as an anesthetic or solvent. **2** clear sky; upper regions of air beyond the clouds. **3** medium formerly assumed to permeate space. □□ **e•ther•ic** /eethérik/ *adj.*
■ **2, 3** see SKY *n.*

e•the•re•al /itheéreeəl/ *adj.* **1** light; airy. **2** highly delicate, esp. in appearance. **3** heavenly. □□ **e•the're•al•ly** *adv.*

eth•ic /éthik/ *n.* set of moral principles.

eth•i•cal /éthikəl/ *adj.* **1** relating to morals, esp. as concerning human conduct. **2** morally correct. **3** (of a drug) available only on prescription. See synonym study at MORAL. □□ **eth'i•cal•ly** *adv.*
■ **2** right, proper, just, righteous; honorable, decent, upright, principled, fair, honest, good, virtuous.

eth•ics /éthiks/ *n.pl.* [also treated as *sing.*] **1** science of morals in human conduct. **2 a** moral principles. **b** set of these. □□ **eth'i•cist** /éthisist/ *n.*

eth•nic /éthnik/ *adj.* **1** having a common national or cultural tradition. **2** denoting origin by birth or descent rather than nationality. **3** relating to race or culture. □ **ethnic cleansing** *euphem.* mass expulsion or killing of people from opposing ethnic groups. □□ **eth'ni•cal•ly** *adv.* **eth•nic•i•ty** /–nísitee/ *n.*
■ *adj.* **1** see RACIAL. **3** see NATIVE *adj.* 2, 4.

eth•no•cen•tric /éthnōséntrik/ *adj.* evaluating other races and cultures by criteria specific to one's own. □□ **eth•no•cen'tri•cal•ly** *adv.* **eth•no•cen•tric'i•ty** /–trísitee/ *n.* **eth•no•cen'trism** *n.*

eth•nol•o•gy /ethnóləjee/ *n.* comparative study of peoples. □□ **eth•no•log•ic** /–nəlójik/ *adj.* **eth•no•log'i•cal** *adj.* **eth•nol'o•gist** *n.*

e•thos /éethos/ *n.* characteristic spirit or attitudes of a community, etc.

eth•yl /éthil/ *n.* [*attrib.*] Chem. radical derived from ethane by removal of a hydrogen atom (*ethyl alcohol*).

eth•yl•ene /éthileen/ *n.* Chem. gaseous hydrocarbon occurring in natural gas and used in the manufacture of polyethylene.

e•ti•ol•o•gy /éeteeóləjee/ *n.* the science of the causes of disease. □□ **e•ti•o•log•ic** /–teeəlójik/ *adj.* **e•ti•o•log'i•cal** *adj.* **e•ti•o•log'i•cal•ly** *adv.*

et•i•quette /étiket, –kit/ *n.* conventional rules of social behavior or professional conduct.
■ code (of behavior), form, convention, protocol, formalities, custom(s), decorum, (good) manners, propriety, politeness, courtesy, civility.

E•trus•can /itrúskən/ • *adj.* of ancient Etruria in Italy. • *n.* **1** native of Etruria. **2** language of Etruria.

et seq. *abbr.* (also **et seqq.**) and the following (pages, etc.).

-ette /et/ *suffix* forming nouns meaning: **1** small (*kitchenette*). **2** imitation or substitute (*leatherette*). **3** often *offens.* female (*suffragette*).

é•tude /áytood, –tŏŏd/ *n.* musical composition designed to improve the technique of the player.

e•tui /etweé/ *n.* small case for needles, etc.

etym. *abbr.* **1** etymological. **2** etymology.

et•y•mol•o•gy /étimóləjee/ *n.* (*pl.* **–gies**) **1 a** verifiable sources of the formation and development of a word. **b** account of these. **2** study of etymologies. □□ **et•y•mo•log•i•cal** /–mólójikəl/ *adj.* **et•y•mo•log'i•cal•ly** *adv.* **et•y•mol'o•gist** *n.*
■ **1a** see DERIVATION.

Eu *symb.* Chem. europium.

eu- /yŏŏ/ *comb. form* well; easily.

eu•ca•lyp•tus /yŏŏkəlíptəs/ *n.* (*pl.* **eu•ca•lyp•ti** /–tī/ or **eu•ca•lyp•tus•es**) **1** tree of Australasia, cultivated for its wood and the oil from its leaves. **2** this oil used as an antiseptic, etc.

Eu•cha•rist /yŏŏkərist/ *n.* **1** Christian sacrament commemorating the Last Supper, in which bread and wine are consecrated and consumed. **2** consecrated elements, esp. the bread. □□ **Eu•cha•ris'tic** *adj.*
■ **1** (Holy) Communion, (Blessed or Holy) Sacrament.

eu•chre /yŏŏkər/ *n.* card game for two, three, or four players in which a hand is won by taking three tricks.

eu•clid•e•an /yŏŏklídeeən/ *adj.* (also **Eu•clid'e•an**) relating to Euclid, 3rd-c. BC Greek mathematician, esp. his system of geometry.

eu•gen•ics /yŏŏjéniks/ *n.pl.* [also treated as *sing.*] science of improving the (esp. human) population by controlling inherited characteristics. □□ **eu·gen'ic** adj. **eu·gen'i·cal·ly** adv. **eu·gen'i·cist** /yōōjénisist/ n. **eu'ge·nist** /yōōjinist/ n.

eu·kar·y·ote /yōōkáreeōt/ n. organism consisting of cells in which the genetic material is within a distinct nucleus. □□ **eu·kar·y·ot·ic** /-reeótik/ adj.

eu·lo·gize /yōō ləjīz/ v.tr. praise in speech or writing. See synonym study at PRAISE. □□ **eu·lo·gist** /-jist/ n. **eu·lo·gis'tic** adj. **eu·lo·gis'ti·cal·ly** adv.

■ extol, laud, compliment, sing the praises of, acclaim. □□ **eulogistic** see COMPLIMENTARY 1.

eu·lo·gy /yōōləjee/ n. (pl. **–gies**) speech or writing in praise of a person.

■ encomium, accolade, tribute, homage; see also ORATION.

eu·nuch /yōōnək/ n. castrated man.

eu·phe·mism /yōōfimizəm/ n. 1 mild or vague expression substituted for a harsher more direct one (e.g., pass over for die). 2 use of such expressions. □□ **eu'phe·mist** n. **eu·phe·mis'tic** adj. **eu·phe·mis'ti·cal·ly** adv. **eu'phe·mize** v.

eu·pho·ny /yōōfənee/ n. (pl. **–nies**) pleasantness of sound, esp. of a word or phrase; harmony. □□ **eu·phon'ic** /-fónik/ adj. **eu·pho·ni·ous** /-fónee-/ adj. **eu·pho'ni·ous·ly** adv.

■ see MELODY 2. □□ **euphonious** see MELODIOUS 2.

eu·pho·ri·a /yōō fáwreeə/ n. intense feeling of well-being. See synonym study at RAPTURE. □□ **eu·phor'ic** /-fáwrik, fōr-/ adj. **eu·phor'i·cal·ly** adv.

■ see RAPTURE.

Eur·a·sian /yōōráyzhən/ • adj. 1 of mixed European and Asian parentage. 2 of Europe and Asia. • n. Eurasian person.

eu·re·ka /yōōreekə/ int. I have found it! (announcing a discovery, etc.).

Euro- /yōōrō/ comb. form Europe; European.

Eu·ro·pe·an /yōōrəpeeən/ • adj. 1 of or in Europe. 2 a descended from natives of Europe. b originating in or characteristic of Europe. • n. 1 native or inhabitant of Europe. 2 person descended from natives of Europe. □ **European Community** (or **European Economic Community**) confederation of certain European countries as a unit with internal free trade and common external tariffs. **European Union** official name of the European Community from November 1993.

eu·ro·pi·um /yōōrópeeəm/ n. soft, silvery metallic element of the lanthanide series. ¶Symb.: **Eu**.

Eu·sta·chian tube /yōōstáyshən, –keeən/ n. Anat. tube from the pharynx to the middle ear.

eu·tha·na·sia /yōōthənáyzhə/ n. bringing about of a gentle death in the case of incurable and painful disease.

e·vac·u·ate /iváikyōō-ayt/ v.tr. 1 a remove (people) from a place of danger. b empty or leave (a place). 2 make empty. 3 withdraw from (a place). 4 empty (the bowels, etc.). □□ **e·vac'u·ant** n. & adj. **e·vac·u·a'tion** /-áyshən/ n. **e·vac'u·a·tor** n.

■ 1 a move, relocate, transfer. b vacate, depart (from), abandon, desert. 2 see EMPTY v. 1. 3 pull out from or of. 4 drain, purge; discharge, excrete, void.

e·vade /iváyd/ v.tr. 1 escape from; avoid, esp. by guile or trickery. 2 avoid doing, answering, etc. □□ **e·vad'a·ble** adj. **e·vad'er** n.

■ get away from, elude, dodge, get out of, sidestep, duck (out of), circumvent, shirk.

e·val·u·ate /ivályōō-ayt/ v.tr. 1 assess; appraise. 2 determine the number or amount of. □□ **e·val·u·a'tion** /-áyshən/ n. **e·val'u·a·tive** adj. **e·val'u·a·tor** n.

■ 1 value. 2 estimate, gauge, calculate, figure, reckon, compute, judge; rate, rank; quantify. □□ **evaluation** appraisal, valuation, assessment; judgment.

ev·a·nes·cent /évənésənt/ adj. (of an impression or appearance, etc.) quickly fading. See synonym study at TEMPORARY. □□ **ev·a·nes'cence** n. **ev·a·nes'cent·ly** adv.

■ see FLEETING.

e·van·gel·i·cal /éevanjélikəl, évən-/ • adj. 1 of or according to the teaching of the gospel or the Christian religion. 2 maintaining the doctrine of salvation by faith. • n. believer in this. □□ **e·van·gel'i·cal·ism** n. **e·van·gel'i·cal·ly** adv.

e·van·ge·list /iivánjəlist/ n. 1 any of the writers of the four Gospels (Matthew, Mark, Luke, John). 2 preacher of the gospel. □□ **e·van'ge·lism** n. **e·van·ge·lis'tic** adj.

e·van·ge·lize /iivánjəliz/ v.tr. 1 preach the gospel to. 2 convert to Christianity. □□ **e·van·ge·li·za'tion** n. **e·van'ge·liz·er** n.

e·vap·o·rate /ivápərayt/ v. 1 intr. turn from solid or liquid into vapor. 2 intr. & tr. lose or cause to lose moisture as vapor. 3 intr. & tr. disappear or cause to disappear (our courage evaporated). □□ **e·vap'o·ra·ble** adj. **e·vap·o·ra·tion** /-áyshən/ n. **e·vap·o·ra·tive** /-váparativ, –raytiv/ adj. **e·vap·o·ra·tor** n.

■ 1 vaporize; steam. 2 dehydrate, desiccate. 3 vanish, evanesce, fade (away).

e·va·sion /iváyzhən/ n. 1 evading. 2 evasive answer.

■ 1 escape, avoidance, shirking, dodging. 2 subterfuge, deceit, deception, chicanery, trickery.

e·va·sive /iváysiv/ adj. 1 seeking to evade. 2 not direct in one's answers, etc. □□ **e·va'sive·ly** adv. **e·va'sive·ness** n.

■ 1 equivocal, ambiguous; devious, cunning, tricky, deceitful, colloq. shifty. 2 indirect, oblique; colloq. cagey; misleading.

eve /eev/ n. 1 evening or day before a holiday, etc. 2 time just before anything (eve of the election). 3 archaic evening.

e·ven[1] /éevən/ • adj. (**e·ven·er**, **e·ven·est**) 1 level; flat and smooth. 2 a uniform in quality; constant. b equal in amount or value, etc. c equally balanced. 3 in the same plane or line. 4 (of a person's temper, etc.) equable; calm. 5 a (of a number) divisible by two without a remainder. b bearing such a number (no parking on even days). • adv. 1 not so much as (never even opened the letter). 2 used to introduce an extreme case (it might *even cost $100*). **3** in spite of; notwithstanding (*even with the delays, we arrived on time*). • *v.* make or become even. □ **even now 1** now as well as before. **2** at this very moment. **even so** nevertheless. **even-steven** (or **Steven**) *colloq.* equal. **get even with** have one's revenge on. **on an even keel 1** (of a ship or aircraft) not listing. **2** (of a plan or person) untroubled. □□ **e'ven•ly** *adv.*

■ *adj.* **1** straight. **2 a** regular, steady, consistent; unvarying, unchanging, set, stable. **b** balanced, the same, identical, fifty-fifty; on a par, tied. **3** coextensive, flush, parallel. **4** - even-tempered, composed, placid, serene, peaceful, cool. • *adv.* **3** despite, disregarding. ■ *v.* smooth, flatten, level; align; equalize, balance (out).

e•ven[2] /ˈeevən/ *n. poet.* evening.

e•ven•hand•ed /ˈeevənhándid/ *adj.* impartial; fair. □□ **e'ven•hand'ed•ly** *adv.* **e'ven•hand'ed•ness** *n.*

eve•ning /ˈeevning/ • *n.* close of the day, esp. from about 6 p.m. to bedtime. • *int.* courteous greeting or farewell. □ **evening star** planet, esp. Venus, conspicuous in the west after sunset.

■ *n.* nightfall, dusk, twilight, sunset, sundown, night, *poet.* eventide. *int.* good evening.

e•ven•song /ˈeevənsawng, -song/ *n.* service of evening prayer.

e•vent /iˈvént/ *n.* **1** thing that happens, esp. one of importance. **2** fact or outcome of a thing's occurring. **3** item in a competitive program. □ **in any event** (or **at all events**) whatever happens. **in the event** as it turns (or turned) out. **in the event of** if (a specified thing) happens. **in the event that** if it happens that.

■ **1** occurrence, incident, episode, occasion, circumstance, affair, experience. **2** result, consequence, upshot, effect, end. **3** see HEAT *n.* 6, CONTEST *n.* 1.

e•vent•ful /iˈvéntfŏŏl/ *adj.* marked by noteworthy events. □□ **e•vent'ful•ly** *adv.* **e•vent'ful•ness** *n.*

■ busy, active, exciting, interesting; important, significant, signal, notable, momentous, memorable.

e•ven•tide /ˈeevəntīd/ *n. archaic* or *poet.* = EVENING.

e•ven•tu•al /iˈvénchŏŏəl/ *adj.* occurring in due course; ultimate. □□ **e•ven'tu•al•ly** *adv.*

■ expected, unavoidable, inevitable, likely, probable, anticipated; final, last, concluding, resulting. □□ **eventually** finally, in the end or long run, sooner or later, at last, when all is said and done, in the final analysis.

e•ven•tu•al•i•ty /iˈvénchŏŏ-álitee/ *n.* (*pl.* -**ties**) possible event or outcome.

■ possibility, likelihood, chance, probability; circumstance, occurrence, happening, case.

e•ven•tu•ate /iˈvénchŏŏ-ayt/ *v.intr. formal* turn out in a specified way; result. □□ **e•ven'tu•a'tion** /-áyshən/ *n.*

■ see *turn out* 5 (TURN).

ev•er /ˈévər/ *adv.* **1** at all times; always. **2** at any time. **3** (as an emphatic word) in any way; at all. **4** [in *comb.*] constantly (*ever-present*). **5** [foll. by *so*] very; very much. □ - **ever since** throughout the period since.

■ **1** eternally, perpetually, endlessly, everlastingly, constantly, continuously, continually, till the end of time; yet, still, even. **2** at all, by any chance.

ev•er•green /ˈévərgreen/ • *adj.* retaining green leaves year round. • *n.* evergreen plant.

ev•er•last•ing /ˈévərlásting/ *adj.* lasting forever or for a long time. □□ **ev•er•last'ing•ly** *adv.*

■ eternal, perpetual, immortal, undying, infinite, timeless; never-ending, continual, continuous, permanent, endless.

ev•er•more /ˈévərmáwr/ *adv.* forever; always.

e•vert /iˈvórt/ *v.tr.* turn outward or inside out. □□ **e•ver'sion** /-vórzhən/ *n.*

eve•ry /ˈévree/ *adj.* **1** each single. **2** each at a specified interval. **3** all possible; the utmost degree of. □ **every now and again** (or **now and then**) from time to time. **every other** each second in a series. **every so often** occasionally. **every which way** *colloq.* **1** in all directions. **2** in a disorderly manner.

eve•ry•bod•y /ˈévreebodee, -budee/ *pron.* every person.

■ see EVERYONE.

eve•ry•day /ˈévreeday/ *adj.* **1** occurring every day. **2** used on ordinary days. **3** commonplace; usual. **4** mundane.

■ **1** daily, day-to-day. **2, 3** customary, familiar, regular, habitual, routine, run-of-the-mill; unexceptional. **4** prosaic, dull, mediocre, inferior.

eve•ry•one /ˈévreewun/ *pron.* every person; everybody.

■ all, one and all, each and every one *or* person, the whole world, everybody under the sun.

eve•ry•thing /ˈévreething/ *pron.* **1** all things; all the things of a group or class. **2** essential consideration (*speed is everything*).

■ **1** the (whole *or* entire) lot, *sl.* the whole (kit and) caboodle, the whole shooting match. **2** see ESSENTIAL *adj.*

eve•ry•where /ˈévreewhair, -wair/ *adv.* **1** in every place. **2** *colloq.* in many places.

■ in every nook and cranny, high and low, far and wide, near and far; universally, globally; all over.

e•vict /iˈvíkt/ *v.tr.* expel (a tenant, etc.) by legal process. See synonym study at EJECT. □□ **e•vic•tion** /-víkshən/ *n.* **e•vic'tor** *n.*

■ turn out, oust, remove, eject, dispossess, put out, kick *or* throw *or* boot out. □□ **eviction** expulsion, removal.

ev•i•dence /ˈévidəns/ • *n.* **1** available facts, circumstances, etc., determining truth or validity. **2** statements, information, etc., admissible as testimony in a court of law. • *v.tr.* be evidence of; attest.

■ *n.* **1** proof, grounds, data, documentation, support; indication, sign(s), marks, suggestion(s), clue(s). **2** attestation, deposition, affidavit. ■ *v.* demonstrate, show, manifest, evince, display, signify, exhibit, reveal, denote, prove, testify, bear witness to.

ev•i•dent /évidənt/ *adj.* **1** plain or obvious; manifest. **2** seeming; apparent (*his evident anxiety*).

■ clear, patent; perceptible, discernible, noticeable, conspicuous; unmistakable.

ev•i•dent•ly /évidəntlee, –déntlee/ *adv.* **1** as shown by evidence. **2** seemingly; as it appears.

■ **1** clearly, obviously, plainly, undoubtedly, without a doubt, undeniably, unquestionably, certainly. **2** apparently, it would seem (so), so it seems, ostensibly.

e•vil /éevəl/ • *adj.* **1** morally bad; wicked. **2** harmful. **3** disagreeable. • *n.* **1** evil thing. **2** wickedness. □□ **e′vil•ly** *adv.* **e′vil•ness** *n.*

■ *adj.* **1** awful, wrong, immoral, sinful, nefarious, iniquitous, heinous, base, corrupt, vile, abominable, infamous, atrocious, horrible, horrid, depraved, vicious, malevolent. **2** hurtful, destructive, pernicious, injurious, mischievous, detrimental, ruinous, disastrous, catastrophic; malignant, dangerous, deadly, lethal, toxic; treacherous, insidious, unscrupulous, unprincipled, dishonest, dishonorable. **3** unpleasant, bad, disgusting, repulsive, awful, nasty, foul, vile, offensive, noxious; putrid. • *n.* **1** sin, vice, iniquity, crime. **2** wrongdoing, iniquity.

e•vil•do•er /éevəldóoər/ *n.* person who does evil. □□ **e′vil•do•ing** *n.*

e•vince /ivíns/ *v.tr.* **1** indicate or make evident **2** show that one has (a quality). □□ **e•vin′ci•ble** *adj.* **e•vin′cive** *adj.*

■ see DEMONSTRATE 3.

e•vis•cer•ate /ivísərayt/ *v.tr.* disembowel □□ **e•vis•cer•a′tion** /–ráyshən/ *n.*

ev•o•ca•tive /ivókətiv/ *adj.* tending to evoke (esp. feelings or memories). □□ **e•voc′a•tive•ly** *adv.* **e•voc′a•tive•ness** *n.*

■ see SUGGESTIVE 1.

e•voke /ivōk/ *v.tr.* **1** inspire or draw forth (memories, feelings, a response, etc.). **2** summon (a supposed spirit from the dead). □□ **ev•o•ca•tion** /évəkáyshən, eevō–/ *n.* **evok′er** *n.*

■ **2** call up or forth, conjure (up); invoke; waken, rouse, raise, reawaken.

ev•o•lu•tion /évəlóoshən/ *n.* **1** gradual development. **2** development of species from earlier forms, as an explanation of origins. **3** unfolding of events, etc. □□ **ev•o•lu′tion•ar•y** *adj.*

■ growth, advance, progress, progression, maturation.

ev•o•lu•tion•ist /évəlóoshənist/ *n.* person who believes in evolution as explaining the origin of species. □□ **ev•o•lu′tion•ism** *n.* **ev•o•lu•tion•is′tic** *adj.*

e•volve /ivólv/ *v.* **1** *intr. & tr.* develop gradually and naturally. **2** *tr.* devise (a theory, plan, etc.). **3** *intr. & tr.* unfold. □□ **e•volv′a•ble** *adj.* **e•volve′ment** *n.*

ewe /yoo/ *n.* female sheep.

ew•er /yóoər/ *n.* water jug with a wide mouth.

ex /eks/ *n. colloq.* former husband or wife.

ex-[1] /eks/ *prefix* (also **e-** before some consonants, **ef-** before *f*) **1** forming verbs meaning: **a** out; forth (*exclude*). **b** upward (*extol*). **c** thoroughly (*excruciate*). **d** bring into a state (*exasperate*). **e** remove or free from (*ex-*

patriate). **2** forming nouns meaning 'former' (*ex-convict*).

ex-[2] /eks/ *prefix* out (*exodus*).

ex•ac•er•bate /igzásərbayt/ *v.tr.* **1** make (pain, etc.) worse. **2** irritate. □□ **ex•ac•er•ba′tion** /–báyshən/ *n.*

■ **1** see AGGRAVATE 1. **2** see AGGRAVATE 2.

ex•act /igzákt/ • *adj.* **1** accurate; correct in all details. **2** precise. • *v.tr.* **1** enforce payment of (money, etc.). **2** demand; insist on. □□ **ex•ac′ti•tude** *n.* **ex•act′ness** *n.* **ex•ac′tor** *n.*

■ *adj.* faithful, true, identical, literal, perfect; meticulous, scrupulous, thorough, painstaking. • *v.* extort; compel.

ex•act•ing /igzáktíng/ *adj.* **1** making great demands. **2** calling for much effort. □□ **ex•act′ing•ly** *adv.* **ex•act′ing•ness** *n.*

■ demanding, challenging, hard, tough, severe, rigorous; difficult, burdensome, taxing; oppressive, tyrannical.

ex•ac•tion /igzákshən/ *n.* **1** exacting; being exacted. **2 a** illegal or exorbitant demand. **b** sum or thing exacted.

ex•act•ly /igzáktlee/ *adv.* **1** accurately; precisely (*worked it out exactly*). **2** in exact terms (*exactly when did it happen?*). **3** (said in reply) quite so. **4** just; in all respects. □ **not exactly** *colloq.* **1** by no means. **2** not precisely.

■ **1** faultlessly, to the letter, word for word, verbatim; absolutely, undeniably.

ex•ag•ger•ate /igzájərayt/ *v.tr.* **1** give an impression of (a thing) that makes it seem larger or greater. **2** overdo. □□ **ex•ag′ger•at•ed•ly** *adv.* **ex•ag′ger•at•ing•ly** *adv.* **ex•ag•ger•a•tion** /–ráyshən/ *n.* **ex•ag′ger•a•tor** *n.*

■ **1** overstate, magnify, inflate, overdraw, stretch, enlarge, overemphasize, overstress, overplay; *colloq.* lay it on thick, pile (it) on. **2** see AMPLIFY 2. □□ **exaggeration** extravagance, hyperbole, excess; *sl.* hot air, bull.

ex•alt /igzáwlt/ *v.tr.* **1** raise in rank or power, etc. **2** praise highly. **3** (usu. as **exalted** *adj.*) **a** make lofty or noble. **b** make rapturously excited. □□ **ex•al•ta•tion** /égzawltáyshən/ *n.* **ex•alt′ed•ly** *adv.* **ex•alt′ed•ness** *n.* **ex•alt′er** *n.*

■ **1** elevate, lift (up *or* on high), upraise, uplift, upgrade, promote, advance, *colloq.* boost **2** honor, extol, glorify, idolize, dignify, revere, venerate, pay homage *or* tribute to, celebrate. **3** (**exalted**) **a** grand, high-flown, inflated, heightened, superior. **b** elated, excited, ecstatic, overjoyed, happy, joyous; noted, prominent, famous, distinguished, prestigious.

ex•am /igzám/ *n.* = EXAMINATION 3.

ex•am•i•na•tion /igzáminááyshən/ *n.* **1** examining; being examined. **2** detailed inspection. **3** test. **4** *formal* questioning in court.

■ **1, 2** investigation, study, analysis, exploration, research, appraisal, assessment; scrutiny; probe, search, survey, checkup. **3** quiz, exam, trial. **4** interrogation, inquiry, cross-examination.

ex•am•ine /igzámin/ *v.tr.* **1** inquire into the nature or condition, etc., of. **2** look closely at. **3** test by examination. **4** check the health of (a patient). ▫▫ **ex•am′in•a•ble** *adj.* **ex•am•i•nee** /–née/ *n.* **ex•am′in•er** *n.*

■ **1, 2** investigate, look over *or* into, inspect, go over *or* through *or* into, scrutinize, analyze, pore over, probe, search, explore, check out. **3** interrogate, cross-examine, question; see also TEST *v.* 1.

ex•am•ple /igzáampəl/ *n.* **1** thing characteristic of its kind *or* illustrating a rule. **2** model. **3** circumstance *or* treatment seen as a warning to others. **4** illustrative problem *or* exercise. See synonym study at MODEL. ▫ **for example** by way of illustration.

■ **1** sample, specimen. **2** standard, prototype, pattern, norm. **3** admonition; see also LESSON 4. **4** illustration, application. ▫ **for example** for instance, as a case in point, to illustrate, e.g.

ex•as•per•ate /igzáaspərayt/ *v.tr.* irritate intensely. ▫▫ **ex•as′per•at•ing•ly** *adv.* **ex•as•per•a′tion** /–ráyshən/ *n.*

■ irk, annoy, bother, harass, provoke, pester, torment, rub the wrong way, *sl.* bug; anger, infuriate, enrage, incense, rile, drive mad; see also AGGRAVATE 2.

ex ca•the•dra /éks kətheédrə/ *adj. & adv.* with full authority (esp. of a papal pronouncement).

ex•ca•vate /ékskəvayt/ *v.tr.* **1 a** make (a hole or channel) by digging. **b** dig out material from (the ground). **2** reveal or extract by digging. ▫▫ **ex•ca•va′tion** /–váyshən/ *n.* **ex′ca•va•tor** *n.*

■ **1** hollow *or* gouge (out), scoop out, burrow. **2** unearth, uncover, expose. ▫▫ **excavation** cavity, pit, crater, ditch, trench, trough; shaft, tunnel.

ex•ceed /ikseéd/ *v.tr.* **1** be more *or* greater than. **2** go beyond *or* do more than is warranted. **3** surpass; excel.

■ **1, 3** be superior to, beat, better, outdistance, overtake, outrank, outrun, outdo; top, pass; transcend, overshadow, eclipse. **2** overstep; overdo.

ex•ceed•ing•ly /ikseéding-lee/ *adv.* extremely.

■ very, exceptionally, remarkably; excessively, greatly, enormously; see also *preeminently* (PREEMINENT).

ex•cel /iksél/ *v.* (**ex•celled, ex•cel•ling**) **1** *tr.* be superior to. **2** *intr.* be preeminent.

■ surpass, beat, exceed, go beyond, outdo, eclipse, top. **2** dominate, shine, stand out.

ex•cel•lence /éksələns/ *n.* outstanding merit or quality.

■ superiority, distinction, greatness, prominence, eminence, preeminence, supremacy; value, worth.

Ex•cel•len•cy /éksələnsee/ *n.* (*pl.* –**cies**) title used in addressing or referring to certain high officials.

ex•cel•lent /éksələnt/ *adj.* extremely good. ▫▫ **ex′cel•lent•ly** *adv.*

■ superb, splendid, great, marvelous, remarkable, sterling, exceptional, superior, supreme, superlative, prime, choice, select, super, terrific, fantastic; distinguished, note-

worthy, notable, admirable; preeminent, outstanding, capital, first-class, first-rate.

ex•cel•si•or /iksélseeər/ *n.* soft wood shavings used for stuffing, packing, etc.

ex•cept /iksépt/ • *v.tr.* exclude. • *prep.* not including; other than. • *conj.* unless.

■ *v.* omit, leave out, excuse. • *prep.* not counting, barring, with the exception of, apart from, excluding.

ex•cept•ing /iksépting/ *prep.* = EXCEPT *prep.*

ex•cep•tion /iksépshən/ *n.* **1** excepting; being excepted. **2** thing to be excepted. **3** instance that does not follow a rule. ▫ **take exception** object. **with the exception of** except; not including.

■ **3** special case, departure; oddity, rarity, peculiarity, quirk. ▫ **take exception (to)** find fault (with), take offense (at), be offended (by); challenge, oppose, disagree (with).

ex•cep•tion•a•ble /iksépshənəbəl/ *adj.* open to objection. ▫▫ **ex•cep′tion•a•bly** *adv.*

■ objectionable, unsatisfactory.

ex•cep•tion•al /iksépshənəl/ *adj.* **1** forming an exception. **2** unusual. **3** outstanding. ▫▫ **ex•cep′tion•al•ly** *adv.*

■ **1, 2** special, especial; out of the ordinary, atypical, uncommon, rare, extraordinary, singular, strange, odd, peculiar. **3** gifted, talented, above average, excellent, superior, extraordinary.

ex•cerpt • *n.* /éksərpt/ extract from a book, film, etc. • *v.tr.* /iksérpt/ take excerpts from (a book, etc.). ▫▫ **ex•cerpt′i•ble** *adj.* **ex•cerp′tion** /–sə́rpshən/ *n.*

■ *n.* passage, quotation, selection, citation. • *v.* extract, select; quote, cite; take, cull.

ex•cess /iksés, ékses/ • *n.* **1** exceeding. **2** amount by which one thing exceeds another. **3 a** overstepping of accepted limits. **b** [in *pl.*] immoderate behavior. • *attrib.adj.* usu. /ékses/ that exceeds a prescribed amount (*excess weight*). ▫ **in** (or to) **excess** exceeding the proper amount or degree. **in excess of** more than; exceeding. ▫▫ **ex•ces′sive** *adj.* **ex•ces′sive•ly** *adv.* **ex•ces′sive•ness** *n.*

■ *n.* **1** overabundance, overflow, redundancy; surplus; overkill. **2** difference, discrepancy. **3** (*excesses*) debauchery, overindulgence, intemperance, extravagance. • *attrib.adj.* surplus, extra, superfluous; see also SUPPLEMENTARY. ▫▫ **excessive** immoderate, inordinate, exorbitant, undue, extreme, unreasonable.

ex•change /ikscháynj/ • *n.* **1** giving of one thing and receiving of another in its place. **2** giving of money for its equivalent in a different currency. **3** part of a telephone number designating a local region. **4** place where merchants, bankers, etc., transact business. **5** short conversation. • *v.* **1** *tr.* give *or* receive (one thing) in place of another. **2** *tr.* give and receive as equivalents. **3** *intr.* make an exchange. ▫ **in exchange** as a thing exchanged (for). ▫▫ **ex•change′a•ble** *adj.* **ex•change•a•bil′i•ty** *n.* **ex•chang′er** *n.*

■ *n.* **1** trade, transfer, switch, swap. **4** market, stock market, stock exchange. • *v.* **1, 2** trade, barter, switch, change, swap.

ex•cheq•uer /ikschékər/ n. royal or national treasury.

ex•cise[1] /éksīz/ n. **1** tax levied on goods produced or sold within the country of origin. **2** tax levied on certain licenses.

ex•cise[2] /iksīz/ v.tr. remove; cut out. □□ **ex•ci•sion** /iksízhən/ n.

ex•cit•a•ble /iksítəbəl/ adj. easily excited. □□ **ex•cit•a•bil'i•ty** n. **ex•cit'a•bly** adv.
■ emotional, nervous, jumpy, restless, fidgety, edgy, touchy, testy, high-strung, volatile, quick-tempered.

ex•cite /iksít/ v.tr. **1 a** rouse the emotions of (a person). **b** arouse (feelings, etc.). **2** provoke. □□ **ex•cit'ant** /iksít'nt, iksīt'nt/ adj. & n. **ex•ci•ta•tion** /−sītáyshən/ n. **ex•cit'ed•ly** adv. **ex•cit'ed•ness** n. **ex•cite'ment** n.
■ **1** stir (up), awaken, inspire; ignite; elicit; electrify, motivate. **2** stimulate, call forth; bring about, incite, instigate, generate. □□ **excitedness**, **excitement** agitation, restlessness, jumpiness, unrest; activity, turmoil, stir, commotion; eagerness, enthusiasm.

ex•cit•ing /iksítíng/ adj. arousing great interest or enthusiasm; stirring. □□ **ex•cit'ing•ly** adv.
■ stimulating, inspiring, moving; seductive, captivating, titillating; thrilling, exhilarating.

ex•claim /ikskláym/ v. **1** intr. cry out suddenly. **2** tr. utter by exclaiming.
■ **1** call (out), shout, yell, blurt out, colloq. holler. **2** proclaim, declare.

ex•cla•ma•tion /ékskləmáyshən/ n. **1** exclaiming. **2** words exclaimed. ■ **exclamation point** punctuation mark (!) indicating exclamation.
■ call, cry, utterance, shout.

ex•clam•a•to•ry /iksklámətawree/ adj. of or serving as an exclamation.

ex•clude /iksklóod/ v.tr. **1** keep out (a person or thing) from a place, group, privilege, etc. **2** remove from consideration. □□ **ex•clud'a•ble** adj. **ex•clud'er** n. **ex•clu'sion** n.
■ **1** shut or lock out, ban, bar, prohibit, forbid; evict, oust, get rid of. **2** eliminate, reject, omit. □□ **exclusion** ban, prohibition; expulsion, eviction; rejection, omission.

ex•clu•sive /iksklóosiv/ • adj. **1** excluding other things. **2** [predic.; foll. by of] not including; except for. **3** tending to exclude others, esp. socially; select. **4** high class. **5** not obtainable or published elsewhere. • n. article, etc., published by only one newspaper, etc. □□ **ex•clu'sive•ly** adv. **ex•clu'sive•ness** n. **ex•clu•siv'i•ty** n.
■ adj. **1** (exclusive of) not counting, excluding, omitting, ignoring, apart from, barring. **3, 4** closed, restricted, private, snobbish; fashionable, upper-class, colloq. classy. **5** unique, limited. • n. scoop.

ex•com•mu•ni•cate /ékskəmyóonikayt/ v.tr. officially exclude (a person) from membership in and sacraments of the church. □□ **ex•com•mu•ni•ca•tion** /−káyshən/ n. adj. **ex•com•mu'ni•ca•tor** n.
■ banish.

ex•con /ékskón/ n. colloq. ex-convict; former prison inmate.

ex•co•ri•ate /ekskáwreeayt/ v.tr. **1** strip or

peel off (skin). **2** censure severely. □□ **ex•co•ri•a•tion** /−áyshən/ n.

ex•cre•ment /ékskrimənt/ n. [in sing. or pl.] feces. □□ **ex•cre•men•tal** /−mént'l/ adj.

ex•cres•cence /ikskrésəns/ n. **1** abnormal or morbid outgrowth. **2** ugly addition. □□ **ex•cres•cent** /−sənt/ adj.
■ **1** see GROWTH 4.

ex•cre•ta /ikskréetə/ n.pl. feces and urine.

ex•crete /ikskréet/ v.tr. (of an animal or plant) expel (waste matter). □□ **ex•cre•tion** /−kréeshən/ n. **ex•cre'tive** adj. **ex•cre•to•ry** /ékskrətawree/ adj.
■ see DEFECATE.

ex•cru•ci•ate /ikskróosheeayt/ v.tr. (esp. as **excruciating** adj.) torment acutely. □□ **ex•cru'ci•at•ing•ly** adv.
■ (excruciating) torturing, agonizing, painful, intense, unbearable, insufferable, harrowing, distressing.

ex•cul•pate /ékskulpayt, ikskúl−/ v.tr. formal free from blame; clear of a charge. □□ **ex•cul•pa•tion** /−páyshən/ n. **ex•cul•pa•to•ry** /−kúlpətawree/ adj.
■ see VINDICATE 1.

ex•cur•sion /ikskárzhən/ n. **1** short pleasure trip. **2** digression. See synonym study at JOURNEY. □□ **ex•cur'sion•al** adj. **ex•cur'sion•ar•y** adj. **ex•cur'sion•ist** n.
■ **1** journey, tour, outing; jaunt. **2** deviation, diversion.

ex•cur•sive /ikskársiv/ adj. digressive; diverse. □□ **ex•cur'sive•ly** adv. **ex•cur'sive•ness** n.

ex•cuse • v.tr. /ikskyóoz/ **1** attempt to lessen the blame attaching to (a person, act, or fault). **2** (of a fact or circumstance) serve in mitigation of (a person or act). **3** obtain exemption for (a person or oneself). **4** [foll. by from] release (a person) from a duty, etc. **5** forgive. • n. /ikskyóos/ **1** reason put forward to justify an offense, fault, etc. **2** apology. **3** [foll. by for] poor or inadequate example of. □□ **ex•cus'a•ble** adj. **ex•cus'a•bly** adv.
■ v. **1** condone, justify, defend; explain, rationalize. **2** see explain away. **4** (excuse from) let off, relieve of. **5** overlook, pardon, disregard. • n. **1, 2** explanation, story, argument; defense.

ex•e•cra•ble /éksikrəbəl/ adj. abominable; detestable. □□ **ex'e•cra•bly** adv.

ex•e•crate /éksikrayt/ v. **1** tr. express or feel abhorrence for. **2** tr. curse (a person or thing). □□ **ex'e•cra•tive** adj. **ex•e•cra•to•ry** /−krətawree/ adj.

ex•e•cute /éksikyōot/ v.tr. **1** carry out a death sentence on. **2** carry out; perform. **3** carry out a design for (a product of art or skill). **4** make valid by signing, sealing, etc. See synonym study at KILL. □□ **ex'e•cut•a•ble** adj. **ex•e•cu'tion** n.
■ **1** put to death, kill; assassinate, murder. **2** effect, fulfill, accomplish, do. **3** complete, finish, deliver; present. **4** ratify, countersign. □□ **execution** killing; murder; performance, accomplishment, doing, discharge, dispatch;

fulfillment, achievement; rendering, delivery, production.

ex•e•cu•tion•er /éksikyŏŏshənər/ *n.* official who carries out a death sentence.

ex•ec•u•tive /igzékyətiv/ • *n.* **1** person or body with managerial or administrative responsibility. **2** branch of government concerned with executing laws, agreements, etc. • *adj.* concerned with executing laws, agreements, etc., or with other administration or management. □□ **ex•ec′u•tive•ly** *adv.*

■ *n.* **1** chairman (of the board), chairperson, chairwoman, director, chief, president, manager, head, leader, principal, administrator; supervisor, superintendent. **2** administration, management, directorship, directorate, leadership. • *adj.* administrative, managerial, supervisory.

ex•ec•u•tor /igzékyətər/ *n.* (*fem.* **ex•ec•u•trix** /-triks/, *pl.* **–tri•ces** /-tríseez/ or **–trix•es**) person appointed to fulfill provisions of a will. □□ **ex•ec•u•to•ri•al** /-táwreeəl/ *adj.*

ex•e•ge•sis /éksijéesis/ *n.* (*pl.* **ex•e•ge•ses** /-seez/) critical explanation of a text, esp. of Scripture. □□ **ex•e•gete** /éksijeet/ *n.* **ex•e•get•ic** /-jétik/ *adj.* **ex•e•get′i•cal** *adj.*

■ see GLOSS[1] *n.* 2.

ex•em•plar /igzémplər, -plaar/ *n.* **1** model. **2** typical instance.

■ **1** see EXAMPLE *n.* 2. **2** see EPITOME 1.

ex•em•pla•ry /igzémpləree/ *adj.* **1** fit to be imitated; outstandingly good. **2** serving as a warning. **3** illustrative; representative. □□ **ex•em′pla•ri•ness** *n.*

■ **1** model; excellent, admirable, commendable. **2** cautionary, admonitory. **3** typical, characteristic.

ex•em•pli•fy /igzémplifī/ *v.tr.* (**–fies, –fied**) **1** illustrate by example. **2** be an example of. □□ **ex•em•pli•fi•ca′tion** *n.*

■ illustrate, typify, represent, epitomize; embody, personify; demonstrate, depict.

ex•empt /igzémpt/ • *adj.* free from an obligation imposed on others. • *v.tr.* [usu. foll. by *from*] free from an obligation. See synonym study at ABSOLUTE. □□ **ex•emp•tion** /-zémpshən/ *n.*

■ *adj.* excused, immune, *colloq.* off the hook. • *v.* spare, let off, (*exempt from*) excuse or relieve from, absolve from or of. □□ **ex•emption** exception, immunity, exclusion.

ex•er•cise /éksərsīz/ • *n.* **1** activity requiring physical effort, done to sustain or improve health. **2** mental or spiritual activity, esp. to develop a skill. **3** task devised as exercise. **4** use or application of a mental faculty, right, etc. **5** [often in *pl.*] military drill or maneuvers. • *v.* **1** *tr.* use or apply (a faculty, right, etc.). **2** *tr.* perform (a function). **3** *a* *intr.* do exercises. *b* *tr.* provide with exercise. **4** *tr.* a tax the powers of. *b* perplex; worry. □□ **ex′er•cis•er** *n.*

■ *n.* **1** movement, working out; see also PRACTICE *n.* 3. **2** see PRACTICE *n.* 3. **3** workout; calisthenics, aerobics. **4** utilization, operation, performance. **5** see MANEUVER *n.* 2. • *v.* **1** employ, put to or into use; exert, wield, execute. **2** see PERFORM 1. **3 a** work out, lim-

ber up, warm up, train. **b** see WALK *v.* 4, TRAIN *v.* 1a. **4 b** concern, distress, trouble, disturb.

ex•ert /igzə́rt/ *v.tr.* **1** exercise; bring to bear (a quality, force, etc.). **2** *refl.* strive. □□ **ex•er•tion** /-zə́rshən/ *n.*

■ **1** use, utilize, put to use, wield, expend. **2** (*exert oneself*) try, make an effort, apply oneself, toil. □□ **exertion** effort, strain, work, struggle, drive, push.

ex•hale /eks-háyl/ *v.* **1** *tr.* breathe out. **2** *tr. & intr.* give off or be given off in vapor. □□ **ex•ha•la′tion** *n.*

■ discharge, emit, give forth; emanate, issue (forth). □□ **exhalation** expiration, breath; respiration; emission, emanation.

ex•haust /igzáwst/ • *v.tr.* **1** consume or use up the whole of. **2** (often as **exhausted** *adj.*) or (**exhausting** *adj.*) tire out. **3** study or expound on (a subject) completely. See synonym study at TIRED. • *n.* **1** waste gases, etc., expelled from an engine after combustion. **2** (also **ex′haust′ pipe**) pipe or system by which these are expelled. □□ **ex•haust′i•ble** *adj.* **ex•haust•i•bil′i•ty** *n.* **ex•haus′ti•bly** *adv.*

■ *v.* **1** expend, deplete, spend. **2** use up, sap; (**exhausted**) (dead) tired, fatigued, weary, worn out, drained, taxed, burned-out; (**exhausting**) tiring, debilitating; arduous, backbreaking, strenuous, grueling. **3** see AMPLIFY 2. • *n.* **1** fumes, emissions; waste.

ex•haus•tion /igzáwschən/ *n.* **1** exhausting; being exhausted. **2** total loss of strength. **3** establishing of a conclusion by eliminating alternatives.

■ **1** emptying, draining, evacuation, depletion. **2** tiredness, fatigue, weariness. **3** elimination, rejection, exclusion.

ex•haus•tive /igzáwstiv/ *adj.* thorough; comprehensive. □□ **ex•haus′tive•ly** *adv.* **ex•haus′tive•ness** *n.*

■ complete, all-inclusive, all-embracing, all-encompassing, extensive, far-reaching, sweeping, full-scale, in-depth.

ex•hib•it /igzíbit/ • *v.tr.* **1** show or reveal publicly. **2** display (a quality, etc.). • *n.* **1** thing or collection displayed. **2** item produced in court as evidence. □□ **ex•hib′i•tor** *n.*

■ *v.* present, offer, demonstrate; manifest, expose, disclose. • *n.* **1** see DISPLAY *n.* 2. **2** see EVIDENCE 2.

ex•hi•bi•tion /éksibíshən/ *n.* **1** display (esp. public) of works of art, etc. **2** exhibiting; being exhibited.

■ **1** exposition, fair, show, showing, presentation. **2** see DEMONSTRATION 3.

ex•hi•bi•tion•ism /éksibíshənizəm/ *n.* **1** tendency toward display or extravagant behavior. **2** *Psychol.* compulsion to display one's genitals in public. □□ **ex•hi•bi′tion•ist** *n.* **ex•hi•bi•tion•is′tic** *adj.* **ex•hi•bi•tion•is′ti•cal•ly** *adv.*

ex•hil•a•rate /igzílərayt/ *v.tr.* (often as **exhilarating** *adj.* or **exhilarated** *adj.*) enliven; raise the spirits of. □□ **ex•hil′a•rant** *adj. & n.* **ex•hil′a•rat•ing•ly** *adv.* **ex•hil•a•ra′tion** /-ráyshən/ *n.* **ex•hil′a•ra•tive** *adj.*

■ (**exhilarating**) invigorating, bracing,

stimulating, refreshing, vitalizing, fortifying; cheering, uplifting, gladdening, heartening, comforting, reassuring; **(exhilarated)** see *ecstatic* (ECSTASY).

ex•hort /igzáwrt/ *v.tr.* urge strongly or earnestly. See synonym study at INCITE. □□ **ex•hor•ta•tion** /táyshən/ *n.* **ex•hort′a•tive** *adj.* **ex•hort•a•to•ry** /–tətáwree/ *adj.* **ex•hort′er** *n.*

■ see URGE *v.* 2. □□ **exhortation** inducement, persuasion; encouragement.

ex•hume /igzóm, –zyóom, eks-hyóom/ *v.tr.* dig out; unearth (esp. a buried corpse). □□ **ex•hu•ma′tion** *n.*

■ see DIG *v.* 4.

ex•i•gen•cy /éksijənsee, igzíj–/ *n.* (*pl.* **–cies**) (also **ex′i•gence** /éksijəns/) **1** urgent need or demand. **2** emergency. □□ **ex′i•gent** *adj.*

■ **1** see NEED *n.* 3, 4. **2** see EMERGENCY. □□ **exigent** see SEVERE 1, URGENT 1.

ex•ig•u•ous /igzígyōos, iksíg–/ *adj.* scanty; small. □□ **ex•i•gu•i•ty** /éksigyōoitee′/ *n.* **ex•ig′u•ous•ly** *adv.* **ex•ig′u•ous•ness** *n.*

■ see MEAGER 1.

ex•ile /éksīl, égzīl/ • *n.* **1** expulsion from one's native land. **2** long absence abroad. **3** exiled person. • *v.tr.* [foll. by *from*] send into exile. • *n.* **1** expatriation, banishment, deportation. **3** expatriate, émigré, deportee. • *v.* expel, deport, banish, oust, eject, drive or cast out.

ex•ist /igzíst/ *v.intr.* **1** have a place in objective reality. **2** occur; be found. **3** continue in being; live.

■ **1** be, prevail, endure, breathe. **2** be present; prevail. **3** survive, subsist, *colloq.* get by; see also LIVE¹ 1–4.

ex•is•tence /igzístəns/ *n.* **1** fact or condition of being or existing. **2** the manner of one's existing or living. **3** all that exists. □□ **ex•ist′ent** *adj.*

■ **1** being, presence, actuality, essence. **2** continuation, persistence, endurance. **3** see WORLD 2.

ex•is•ten•tial /égzisténshəl/ *adj.* **1** of or relating to existence. **2** *Philos.* concerned with human existence as viewed by existentialism. □□ **ex•is•ten′tial•ly** *adv.*

ex•is•ten•tial•ism /égzisténshəlizəm/ *n.* philosophical theory emphasizing the existence of the individual as a free and self-determining agent. □□ **ex•is•ten′tial•ist** *n.*

ex•it /égzit, éksit/ • *n.* **1** passage or door by which to leave a room, etc. **2** act or right of going out. **3** place to leave a highway. **4** actor's departure from the stage. • *v.intr.* **1** go out of a room, etc. **2** leave the stage. □ **exit poll** survey of voters leaving voting booths, used to predict an election's outcome, etc.

■ *n.* **1** way out, egress, gate. **2** departure, leave-taking, withdrawal; flight, exodus, escape. **3** turnoff. • *v.* **1** (take one's) leave, depart, withdraw, walk out; take off, vanish, disappear.

exo– /éksō/ *comb. form* external.

ex•o•dus /éksədəs/ *n.* **1** mass departure. **2** (**Exodus**) *Bibl.* **a** departure of the Israelites from Egypt. **b** the book of the Old Testament relating this.

■ **1** see FLIGHT².

ex of•fi•cio /eksəfisheeó/ *adv. & adj.* by virtue of one's office.

ex•on•er•ate /igzónərayt/ *v.tr.* **1** free or declare free from blame, etc. **2** release from a duty, etc. See synonym study at ABSOLVE. □□ **ex•on•er•a•tion** /–ráyshən/ *n.* **ex•on′er•a•tive** *adj.*

■ **1** see VINDICATE 1.

ex•or•bi•tant /igzáwrbit′nt/ *adj.* (of a price, etc.) grossly excessive. □□ **ex•or′bi•tance** *n.* **ex•or′bi•tant•ly** *adv.*

■ outrageous, extortionate, unreasonable, immoderate, extreme, inordinate, disproportionate, preposterous, unwarranted, unjustifiable, unjustified.

ex•or•cize /éksawrsīz, –sər–/ *v.tr.* **1** expel (a supposed evil spirit) by invocation, etc. **2** free (a person or place) of a supposed evil spirit. □□ **ex•or•cism** /–sizəm/ *n.* **ex′or•cist** *n.*

ex•o•skel•e•ton /éksōskélit′n/ *n.* rigid body covering in certain animals, esp. arthropods. □□ **ex•o•skel′e•tal** *adj.*

ex•o•sphere /éksōsfeer/ *n.* furthermost layer of earth's atmosphere.

ex•ot•ic /igzótik/ • *adj.* **1** introduced from a foreign country. **2** attractively strange or unusual. • *n.* exotic person or thing. □ **exotic dancer** striptease dancer. □□ **ex•ot′i•cal•ly** *adv.* **ex•ot′i•cism** /–tisizəm/ *n.*

■ *adj.* **1** alien, imported. **2** unique, singular; bizarre, extraordinary, remarkable, odd, peculiar. • *n.* see WONDER *n.* 2.

ex•pand /ikspánd/ *v.* **1** *tr. & intr.* increase in size or importance. **2** *intr.* give a fuller account. **3** *tr.* set or write out in full. **4** *tr. & intr.* spread out flat. □□ **ex•pand′a•ble** *adj.* **ex•pand′er** *n.* **ex•pan•si•ble** /ikspánsibəl/ *adj.* **ex•pan•si•bil′i•ty** *n.*

■ **1** enlarge, extend, stretch, inflate; broaden, widen, augment, heighten. **2** (*expand on* or *upon*) develop, amplify, elaborate (on). **4** see SPREAD *v.* 1a.

ex•panse /ikspáns/ *n.* wide continuous area.

■ area, space, stretch, extent, range, sweep, reach, spread.

ex•pan•sion /ikspánshən/ *n.* **1** expanding; being expanded. **2** enlargement of the scale or scope of (esp. commercial) operations. □□ **ex•pan′sion•ism** *n.* **ex•pan′sion•ist** *n.* **ex•pan•sion•is′tic** *adj.* (all in sense 2).

■ development, increase, extension, growth, spread; inflation, swelling.

ex•pan•sive /ikspánsiv/ *adj.* **1** able or tending to expand. **2** extensive. **3** (of a person, etc.) effusive; open. □□ **ex•pan′sive•ly** *adv.* **ex•pan′sive•ness** *n.*

■ **1** expandable, extendable. **2** wide-ranging, broad, far-reaching, widespread. **3** free, easy, genial, amiable, friendly, warm, affable, sociable, outgoing.

ex•pa•ti•ate /ikspáysheeayt/ *v.intr.* speak or write at length. □□ **ex•pa•ti•a•tion** /–áyshən/ *n.* **ex•pa′ti•a•to•ry** /–sheeətáwree/ *adj.*

■ (*expatiate on*) see EXPLAIN 1.

ex•pa•tri•ate • *adj.* living abroad. **2** exiled. • *n.* /ekspáytreeət/ expatriate person. • *v.tr.* /ekspáytreeayt/ expel (a person) from his or her native country. □□ **ex•pa•tri•a•tion** /–áyshən/ *n.*

ex•pect /ikspékt/ *v.tr.* **1 a** regard as likely. **b** look for as appropriate or one's due. **2** *colloq.* think; suppose. □ **be expecting** *colloq.* be pregnant.
■ **1 a** look forward *or* ahead to, contemplate, foresee, envision, anticipate; watch *or* look for, wait for. **b** want, require, need, demand, count upon, hope for. **2** guess, assume, presume, imagine, believe, trust.

ex•pec•tan•cy /ikspéktənsee/ *n.* (*pl.* **–cies**) **1** state of expectation. **2** prospect.
■ **1** anticipation.

ex•pec•tant /ikspéktənt/ *adj.* **1** expecting. **2** [*attrib.*] expecting a baby. □□ **ex•pec′tant•ly** *adv.*
■ **1** waiting, ready, anxious, hopeful, watchful.

ex•pec•ta•tion /ékspektáyshən/ *n.* **1** expecting or looking forward. **2** thing expected. **3** [foll. by *of*] probability of an event.
■ **1** expectancy; anticipation. **2** belief, assumption, presumption, hope; wish, desire. **3** see PROBABILITY.

ex•pec•to•rant /ikspéktərənt/ • *adj.* causing the coughing out of phlegm, etc. • *n.* expectorant medicine.

ex•pec•to•rate /ikspéktərayt/ *v.tr.* cough or spit out (phlegm, etc.). □□ **ex•pec•to•ra•tion** /–ráyshən/ *n.* **ex•pec′to•ra•tor** *n.*

ex•pe•di•ent /ikspéedeeənt/ • *adj.* advantageous; advisable. • *n.* means of attaining an end. □□ **ex•pe•di•ence** /–əns/ *n.* **ex•pe′di•en•cy** *n.* **ex•pe′di•ent•ly** *adv.*
■ *adj.* beneficial, useful, practical, desirable; prudent. • *n.* recourse; resource.

ex•pe•dite /ékspidīt/ *v.tr.* **1** assist the progress of. **2** accomplish (business) quickly. □□ **ex′pe•dit•er** *n.*
■ **1** enable, facilitate; hasten. **2** dispatch; see also COMPLETE *v.* 1.

ex•pe•di•tion /é kspidíshən/ *n.* **1** journey or voyage for a particular purpose, esp. exploration. **2** personnel undertaking this. **3** promptness. See synonym study at JOURNEY. □□ **ex•pe•di′tion•ar•y** *adj.* **ex•pe•di′tion•ist** *n.*
■ **1** (field) trip, excursion; mission. **2** see PARTY *n.* 2. **3** speed, dispatch, haste.

ex•pe•di•tious /ékspidíshəs/ *adj.* acting or done with speed and efficiency. □□ **ex•pe•di′tious•ly** *adv.* **ex•pe•di′tious•ness** *n.*
■ ready, quick, rapid, swift, fast, brisk, speedy, efficient.

ex•pel /ikspél/ *v.tr.* (**ex•pelled, ex•pel•ling**) **1** deprive of membership, etc. **2** force out; eject. See synonym study at EJECT. □□ **ex•pel′la•ble** *adj.* **ex•pel•lee** /–leé/ *n.* **ex•pel′ler** *n.*
■ **1** ban, bar, dismiss, exclude. **2** throw *or* cast out, remove, evict.

ex•pend /ikspénd/ *v.tr.* spend or use up (money, time, etc.).
■ finish (off), consume, exhaust; disburse.

ex•pend•a•ble /ikspéndəbəl/ *adj.* that may be sacrificed or dispensed with; not worth saving. □□ **ex•pend•a•bil′i•ty** *n.* **ex•pend′a•bly** *adv.*

■ disposable, nonessential, unnecessary, replaceable; unimportant, insignificant.

ex•pen•di•ture /ikspéndichər/ *n.* **1** spending or using up. **2** thing (esp. money) expended.
■ **2** outlay, disbursement, expense, cost; price.

ex•pense /ikspéns/ *n.* **1** cost incurred. **2** amount paid to reimburse this. **3** thing that is a cause of expense. □ **at the expense of** so as to cause damage, discredit, etc., to.
■ **1** payment, outlay; price, charge, fee. **2** expenditure. **3** see BURDEN *n.* 1, 2.

ex•pen•sive /ikspénsiv/ *adj.* costing or charging much. □□ **ex•pen′sive•ly** *adv.*
■ costly, dear, high-priced; see also EXTRAVAGANT.

ex•pe•ri•ence /ikspeéreeəns/ • *n.* **1** observation of or practical acquaintance with facts or events. **2** knowledge or skill resulting from this. **3** activity participated in or observed. • *v.tr.* **1** have experience of; undergo. **2** feel. □□ **ex•pe•ri•en•tial** /–énshəl/ *adj.*
■ *n.* **1** participation, involvement, exposure; familiarity. **2** know-how, judgment. **3** event, incident, affair, encounter; trial, test, ordeal. • *v.* **1** live or go through, endure, encounter. **2** sense, be familiar with.

ex•pe•ri•enced /ikspeéreeənst/ *adj.* **1** having had much experience. **2** skilled from experience (*an experienced driver*).
■ **1** mature, seasoned, sophisticated. **2** accomplished, proficient, knowledgeable, qualified.

ex•per•i•ment /ikspérimənt/ • *n.* procedure for testing a hypothesis, etc. • *v.intr.* make an experiment. □□ **ex•per•i•men•ta′tion** *n.* **ex•per′i•ment•er** *n.*
■ *n.* trial, investigation, examination. • *v.* test, try, research.

ex•per•i•men•tal /ikspériméntˈl/ *adj.* **1** based on or making use of experiment. **2** used in experiments. □□ **ex•per•i•men′tal•ism** *n.* **ex•per•i•men′tal•ist** *n.* **ex•per•i•men′tal•ly** *adv.*
■ **1** empirical; experiential.

ex•pert /ékspərt/ • *adj.* **1** having special knowledge or skill. **2** resulting or derived from this. • *n.* person having special knowledge or skill. □□ **ex′pert•ly** *adv.* **ex′pert•ness** *n.*
■ *adj.* **1** skillful, trained, qualified, adept, accomplished; see also KNOWLEDGEABLE. **2** see *first-rate*. • *n.* authority, professional, specialist.

ex•per•tise /ékspərteéz/ *n.* expert skill, knowledge, or judgment.
■ dexterity, adroitness, know-how, mastery.

ex•pi•ate /ékspeeayt/ *v.tr.* **1** pay the penalty for (wrongdoing). **2** make amends for. □□ **ex′pi•a•ble** *adj.* **ex•pi•a•to•ry** /–peeatawree/ *adj.* **ex•pi•a•tion** /–áyshən/ *n.* **ex′pi•a•tor** *n.*
■ **2** see COMPENSATE 2.

ex•pire /ikspír/ *v.* **1** *intr.* (of a period of time, validity, etc.) come to an end. **2** cease to be valid. **3** *intr.* die. **4** *tr.* exhale. □□ **ex•pi•ra′tion** *n.* **ex•pi′ra•to•ry** *adj.* (in sense 4). **ex•pi′ry** *n.*
■ **1, 2** cease, finish, terminate; run out. **3** perish, pass away; see also DIE[1] 1.

4 breathe out, expel. □□ **expiration** exhalation; termination, conclusion.

ex•plain /ikspláyn/ v.tr. **1** make clear or intelligible. **2** say by way of explanation. **3** account for (one's conduct, etc.). See synonym study at CLARIFY. □ **explain away** minimize the significance of by explanation. **explain oneself** give an account of one's meaning, motives, etc. □□ **ex•plain'a•ble** adj. **ex•plain'er** n.
■ **1** get across, clarify, interpret, describe. □ **explain away** justify, rationalize.

ex•pla•na•tion /éksplənáyshən/ n. **1** explaining. **2** statement or circumstance that explains something.
■ **1** interpretation, description, account. **2** cause, motive, reason; justification.

ex•plan•a•to•ry /iksplánətawree/ adj. serving or intended to serve to explain.
■ elucidative, interpretive, interpretative, expository.

ex•ple•tive /éksplətiv/ n. swearword or exclamation.
■ oath, obscenity, epithet, dirty word.

ex•pli•ca•ble /éksplikəbəl, iksplík–/ adj. that can be explained.

ex•pli•cate /éksplikayt/ v.tr. **1** develop the meaning of (an idea, etc.). **2** explain (esp. a text). See synonym study at CLARIFY. □□ **ex•pli•ca•tion** /–káyshən/ n. **ex•pli•ca•tive** /éksplikaytiv, iksplíkətiv/ adj. **ex•pli•ca•tor** n. **ex•pli•ca•to•ry** /éksplikətawree, iksplík–/ adj.

ex•plic•it /iksplísit/ adj. **1** expressly stated; not merely implied. **2** definite; clear. **3** outspoken. □□ **ex•plic'it•ly** adv. **ex•plic'it•ness** n.
■ **1** plain, overt, unmistakable; precise, exact. **2** see DEFINITE. **3** unreserved, open; unrestrained.

ex•plode /ikspló d/ v. **1 a** intr. expand suddenly with a loud noise owing to a release of internal energy. **b** tr. cause (a bomb, etc.) to explode. **2** intr. give vent suddenly to emotion, esp. anger. **3** intr. increase suddenly or rapidly. **4** tr. show (a theory, etc.) to be false or baseless. **5** tr. (as **exploded** adj.) (of a drawing, etc.) showing the components of a mechanism somewhat separated. □□ **ex•plod'er** n.
■ **1** blow up, erupt, burst. **2** lose one's temper, rant, rave, rage, blow one's top, hit the ceiling. **3** see GROW 1. **4** discredit, disprove, repudiate, refute.

ex•ploit • n. /éksployt/ daring feat. • v.tr. /iksplóyt/ **1** make use of (a resource, etc.). **2** take advantage of (esp. a person) for one's own ends. □□ **ex•ploi•ta'tion** n. **ex•ploit'a•tive** adj. **ex•ploit'er** n. **ex•ploit'ive** adj.
■ n. achievement, deed. • v. utilize, profit from; manipulate.

ex•plore /ikspláwr/ v.tr. **1** travel through (a country, etc.) to learn about it. **2** inquire into. □□ **ex•plo•ra'tion** n. **ex•plor'a•tive** adj. **ex•plor'a•to•ry** adj. **ex•plor'er** n.
■ **1** tour; survey. **2** examine, look into, search, investigate; research, study. □□ **ex•ploration** investigation, inspection, observation; expedition; research. **exploratory** see PRELIMINARY adj. **explorer** see PIONEER n. 2.

ex•plo•sion /iksplózhən/ n. **1** exploding. **2** loud noise caused by this. **3** sudden outbreak of feeling. **4** rapid or sudden increase.
■ **1** burst, eruption. **2** blast, bang, report, boom, clap, crack, crash. **3** outburst, flareup, colloq. fit. **4** expansion, mushrooming, blossoming.

ex•plo•sive /iksplósiv/ • adj. **1** able, tending, or likely to explode. **2** dangerously tense. • n. explosive substance. □□ **ex•plo'sive•ly** adv. **ex•plo'sive•ness** n.
■ adj. **2** volatile, flammable, hazardous, unstable, uncertain, unpredictable. • n. dynamite, gunpowder, TNT.

ex•po•nent /ikspónənt/ n. **1** person who promotes an idea, etc. **2** practitioner of an activity, profession, etc. **3** type or representative. **4** Math. raised symbol beside a numeral indicating how many times it is to be multiplied by itself (e.g., $2^3 = 2 \times 2 \times 2$).
■ **1** see PROPONENT n.

ex•po•nen•tial /ékspənénshəl/ adj. **1** of or indicated by a mathematical exponent. **2** (of an increase, etc.) more and more rapid. □□ **ex•po•nen'tial•ly** adv.

ex•port • v.tr. /ikspáwrt, éks–/ sell or send to another country. • n. /ékspawrt/ **1** exporting. **2** exported article or service. □□ **ex•port'a•ble** adj. **ex•port•a•bil'i•ty** n. **ex•por•ta'tion** n. **ex•port'er** n.

ex•pose /ikspóz/ v.tr. **1** leave uncovered or unprotected. **2** (foll. by to) put in the way of. **b** introduce to (exposed to the arts). **3** Photog. subject (film) to light. **4** reveal. **5** exhibit; display. □ **expose oneself** display one's body publicly and indecently. □□ **ex•pos'er** n.
■ **2 a** see SUBJECT v. **b** (expose to) acquaint with. **4** disclose, divulge, bring to light. **5** show, reveal, bare, uncover.

ex•po•sé /ekspōzáy/ n. revelation of something discreditable.
■ see REVELATION.

ex•po•si•tion /ékspəzíshən/ n. **1** explanatory account. **2** explanation or commentary. **3** large public exhibition. □□ **ex•po•si'tion•al** adj.
■ **1, 2** statement; interpretation; theme, article, essay, thesis. **3** show, showing; presentation.

ex•pos•tu•late /ikspóschəlayt/ v.intr. make a protest; remonstrate. □□ **ex•pos•tu•la'tion** /–láyshən/ n.

ex•po•sure /ikspózhər/ n. **1** exposing; being exposed. **2** condition of being exposed to the elements. **3** Photog. **a** exposing film to light. **b** duration of this. □ **exposure meter** Photog. a device for measuring the strength of the light to determine the correct duration of exposure.
■ **1** disclosure, unveiling.

ex•pound /ikspównd/ v.tr. **1** set out in detail. **2** explain or interpret. □□ **ex•pound'er** n.

ex•press¹ /iksprés/ v.tr. **1** represent or make known in words or by gestures, conduct, etc. **2** communicate. **3** represent by symbols. **4** squeeze out (liquid or air). □□ **ex•press'er** n. **ex•press'i•ble** adj.

■ **1, 2** articulate, verbalize; say; show, demonstrate, convey. **3** symbolize, represent. **4** wring *or* force out, extract, expel.

ex·press² /iksprés/ • *adj.* **1** operating at high speed. **2** also /ékspres/ definitely stated. **3 a** done, made, or sent for a special purpose. **b** delivered by a special service. • *adv.* **1** at high speed. **2** by express shipment. • *n.* **1** fast train, etc. **2** service for rapid package delivery. □□ **ex·press'ly** *adv.*

■ *adj.* **1** speedy, quick, swift, fast, rapid, prompt, direct. **2** explicit, straightforward, outright. **3 a** specific, particular; customized. • *adv.* **1** see *promptly* (PROMPT). □□ **expressly** definitely, explicitly, plainly, clearly; especially, specifically.

ex·pres·sion /ikspréshən/ *n.* **1** expressing; being expressed. **2 a** word or phrase expressed. **b** manner of expressing. **3** *Math.* collection of symbols expressing a quantity. **4** person's facial appearance, indicating feeling. **5** depiction or conveyance of feeling, movement, etc., in art. □□ **ex·pres'sion·less** *adj.* **ex·pres'sion·less·ly** *adv.*

■ **1** verbalization, representation, pronouncement; voicing; airing; evidence. **2 a** term, idiom, saying. **b** wording, phraseology, style, diction, usage. **4** look, air, appearance. **5** tone, touch; spirit, depth, intensity.

ex·pres·sion·ism /ikspréshənizəm/ *n.* style of painting, music, drama, etc., seeking to express emotion rather than the external world. □□ **ex·pres'sion·ist** *n. & adj.* **ex·pres·sion·is'tic** *adj.* **ex·pres·sion·is'ti·cal·ly** *adv.*

ex·pres·sive /iksprésiv/ *adj.* **1** full of expression. **2** serving to express. □□ **ex·pres'sive·ly** *adv.* **ex·pres'sive·ness** *n.* **ex·pres'siv·i·ty** *n.*

■ **1** vivid, striking, moving, poignant, explicit, telling, meaningful. **2** indicative, suggestive, revealing.

ex·press·way /iksprésway/ *n.* high-speed highway.

ex·pro·pri·ate /eksprópreeayt/ *v.tr.* take away (property) from its owner. □□ **ex·pro·pri·a·tion** /-áyshən/ *n.* **ex·pro'pri·a·tor** *n.*

■ see APPROPRIATE *v.* 1.

ex·pul·sion /ikspúlshən/ *n.* expelling; being expelled. □□ **ex·pul·sive** /-púlsiv/ *adj.*

■ ejection; removal, dismissal; eviction.

ex·punge /ikspúnj/ *v.tr.* erase; remove. □□ **ex·punc·tion** /ikspúngkshən/ *n.* **ex·pung'er** *n.*

ex·pur·gate /ékspərgayt/ *v.tr.* remove objectionable matter from (a book, etc.). □□ **ex·pur·ga'tion** /-gáyshən/ *n.* **ex'pur·ga·tor** *n.*

ex·qui·site /ékskwizit, ikskwízit/ *adj.* **1** extremely beautiful or delicate. **2** keenly felt. **3** highly discriminating (*exquisite taste*). □□ **ex·quis'ite·ly** *adv.* **ex·quis'ite·ness** *n.*

■ **1** lovely, attractive; striking, elegant; fine, graceful, refined. **2** acute, sharp, agonizing, intense. **3** superb, outstanding, excellent, perfect, wonderful, splendid; acute.

ex·tant /ékstənt, ekstánt/ *adj.* still existing.

■ actual, existent, present.

ex·tem·po·ra·ne·ous /ikstémpəráyneeəs/ *adj.* spoken or done without preparation. □□ **ex·tem·po·ra'ne·ous·ly** *adv.*

■ impromptu, improvised, spontaneous, unrehearsed.

ex·tem·po·re /ikstémpəree/ *adj. & adv.* without preparation.

■ see EXTEMPORANEOUS.

ex·tem·po·rize /ikstémpəriz/ *v.tr.* improvise. □□ **ex·tem·po·ri·za'tion** *n.*

ex·tend /iksténd/ *v.* **1** *tr. & intr.* lengthen or make larger in space or time. **2 a** *tr.* stretch or lay out at full length. **b** *tr. & intr.* (cause to) stretch or span over a period of time. **3** *intr. & tr.* [foll. by *over*] reach or encompass. **4** *intr.* [foll. by *to*] have a certain scope. **5** *tr.* offer (an invitation, hospitality, etc.). □ **extended family** family that includes nearby relatives. □□ **ex·tend'a·ble** *adj.* **ex·tend·a·bil'i·ty** *n.* **ex·tend'i·ble** *adj.* **ex·tend·i·bil'i·ty** *n.* **ex·ten·si·ble** /-sténsibəl/ *adj.* **ex·ten·si·bil'i·ty** *n.*

■ **1** elongate, increase; widen, enlarge. **2 a** see SPREAD *v.* 1a. **b** last, continue; drag out, prolong. **3** range; carry on. **4** (*extend to*) see INCLUDE 1. **5** bestow, accord, impart.

ex·ten·sion /iksténshən/ *n.* **1** extending; being extended. **2** part enlarging or added on. **3** additional part of anything.

■ **1** enlargement, expansion, increase, broadening, lengthening. **2** annex, wing, addition. **3** appendage, adjunct, supplement.

ex·ten·sive /iksténsiv/ *adj.* **1** covering a large area. **2** far-reaching. □□ **ex·ten'sive·ly** *adv.* **ex·ten'sive·ness** *n.*

■ **1** big, great, huge, considerable, sizable, immense, vast. **2** broad; wide-ranging, sweeping, widespread.

ex·ten·sor /iksténsər/ *n.* (in full **extensor muscle**) *Anat.* muscle that extends or straightens part of the body (cf. FLEXOR).

ex·tent /ikstént/ *n.* **1** space over which a thing extends. **2** degree; scope.

■ **1** magnitude, range, scale, sweep; expanse, area, region. **2** limits, lengths; see also RANGE *n.* 1.

ex·ten·u·ate /ikstényōō-ayt/ *v.tr.* (often as **extenuating** *adj.*) lessen the seeming seriousness of (guilt or an offense). □□ **ex·ten·u·a'tion** /-áyshən/ *n.*

■ (**extenuating**) mitigating, tempering, qualifying.

ex·te·ri·or /iksteéreeər/ • *adj.* **1** of or on the outer side. **2** coming from outside. • *n.* **1** outward aspect or surface. **2** outward demeanor.

■ *adj.* **1** external; surface, superficial. **2** extraneous, foreign, alien. • *n.* **1** front, face, façade; skin, shell. **2** see BEARING 1.

ex·ter·mi·nate /ikstérminayt/ *v.tr.* destroy utterly (esp. a living thing). See synonym study at DESTROY. □□ **ex·ter·mi·na'tion** /-náyshən/ *n.* **ex·ter'mi·na·tor** *n.*

■ eradicate, annihilate, eliminate, obliterate, terminate.

ex·ter·nal /ikstérnəl/ • *adj.* **1 a** of or on the outside or visible part. **b** coming from or derived from the outside or an outside source. **2** foreign. **3** outside the conscious subject (*the ex-*

ternal world). **4** for use on the outside of the body. • *n.* [in *pl.*] **1** outward features or aspect. **2** external circumstances. **3** inessentials. □□ **ex·ter′nal·ly** *adv.*

■ *adj.* **1a, 3** outward, exterior, visible, apparent. **1 b** extraneous. **2** international, overseas. • *n.* (*externals*) **1** see ASPECT 2. **2** see ENVIRONMENT. **3** see ACCESSORY *n.* 2.

ex·ter·nal·ize /ikstərnəlīz/ *v.tr.* give or attribute external existence to. □□ **ex·ter·nal·i·za′tion** *n.*

ex·tinct /ikstíngkt/ *adj.* **1** that has died out. **2** (of a volcano) that no longer erupts.

■ **1** dead, vanished; defunct, gone. **2** inactive, dormant.

ex·tinc·tion /ikstíngkshən/ *n.* **1** making extinct; becoming extinct. **2** extinguishing; being extinguished. **3** annihilation.

ex·tin·guish /ikstínggwish/ *v.tr.* **1** cause (a flame, light, etc.) to die out. **2** destroy. □□ **ex·tin′guish·a·ble** *adj.* **ex·tin′guish·er** *n.*

■ **1** put *or* snuff *or* blow out, quench. **2** annihilate, exterminate, eliminate, *colloq.* do away with.

ex·tir·pate /é kstərpayt/ *v.tr.* root out; destroy completely. See synonym study at DESTROY. □□ **ex·tir·pa·tion** /-páyshən/ *n.* **ex′tir·pa·tor** *n.*

ex·tol /ikstốl/ *v.tr.* (**ex·tolled, ex·tol·ling**) praise enthusiastically. See synonym study at PRAISE. □□ **ex·tol′ler** *n.* **ex·tol′ment** *n.*

■ laud, sing the praises of, glorify, honor.

ex·tort /ikstáwrt/ *v.tr.* obtain by coercion.

■ exact, extract, force, wring, wrest.

ex·tor·tion /ikstáwrshən/ *n.* act of extorting, esp. money. □□ **ex·tor′tion·ate** *adj.* **ex·tor′tion·er** *n.* **ex·tor′tion·ist** *n.*

ex·tra /ékstrə/ • *adj.* additional; more than usual, necessary, or expected • *adv.* **1** more than usually. **2** additionally (*was charged extra*). • *n.* **1** extra thing. **2** thing for which an extra charge is made. **3** performer in a minor role.

■ *adj.* added, further, supplementary; auxiliary • *adv.* **1** unusually, exceptionally, remarkably. **2** more. • *n.* **1** see ADDITION 2. **2** markup, surcharge. **3** walk-on.

extra- /ékstrə/ *comb. form* **1** outside; beyond (*extragalactic*). **2** beyond the scope of (*extracurricular*).

ex·tract • *v.tr.* /ikstrákt/ **1** remove or take out. **2** obtain (money, an admission, etc.) by pressure. **3** obtain (a natural resource) from the earth. **4** select (a passage of writing, music, etc.). **5** obtain (juice, etc.) by pressure, distillation, etc. **6** derive (pleasure, etc.). • *n.* /ékstrakt/ **1** short passage from a book, etc. **2** concentrated ingredient. □□ **ex·tract′a·ble** *adj.* **ex·tract·a·bil′i·ty** *n.*

■ *v.* **1** draw *or* pull (out), withdraw, extricate. **2** wrench, extort, extricate. **3** see MINE² *v.* 1, 2. **4** choose, glean, cull, quote, cite. **6** see DERIVE 1. • *n.* **1** excerpt, quotation, selection. **2** essence, distillate.

ex·trac·tion /ikstrákshən/ *n.* **1** extracting; being extracted. **2** lineage; descent.

■ **1** removal, uprooting, withdrawal. **2** origin, birth, ancestry, derivation, parentage.

ex·tra·cur·ric·u·lar /ékstrəkəríkyələr/ *adj.*

(of a subject of study) not included in the normal curriculum.

ex·tra·dite /ékstrədīt/ *v.tr.* hand over (a person accused or convicted of a crime) to the country, state, etc., in which the crime was committed. □□ **ex·tra·di·tion** /ékstrədíshən/ *n.*

■ see BANISH 1.

ex·tra·mar·i·tal /ékstrəmárit′l/ *adj.* (esp. of sexual relations) occurring outside marriage. □□ **ex·tra·mar′i·tal·ly** *adv.*

ex·tra·ne·ous /ikstráyneeəs/ *adj.* **1** of external origin. **2** separate; irrelevant; unrelated. □□ **ex·tra′ne·ous·ly** *adv.* **ex·tra′ne·ous·ness** *n.*

■ **2** inappropriate; out of place; superfluous, unnecessary.

ex·tra·or·di·nar·y /ikstráwrd′neree, ékstrəáwr-/ *adj.* **1** unusual or remarkable. **2** unusually great. **3** (of a meeting, official, etc.) additional; special. □□ **ex·tra·or·di·nar′i·ly** *adv.*

■ **1, 2** outstanding, rare, singular, unique; peculiar, odd, bizarre, strange; amazing, astonishing, astounding, fantastic, incredible, impressive.

ex·trap·o·late /ikstrápəlayt/ *v.tr.* calculate or derive approximately from known data, etc. □□ **ex·trap·o·la·tion** /-láyshən/ *n.*

ex·tra·sen·so·ry /ékstrəsénsəree/ *adj.* outside the known senses.

■ see PSYCHIC *adj.* 1.

ex·tra·ter·res·tri·al /ékstrətərésstreeəl/ • *adj.* outside the earth or its atmosphere. • *n.* (in science fiction) being from outer space.

■ *n.* alien, ET, martian.

ex·trav·a·gant /ikstrávəgənt/ *adj.* **1** spending (esp. money) excessively. **2** costing much. **3** unreasonable; absurd. See synonym study at PROFUSE. □□ **ex·trav′a·gance** *n.* **ex·trav′a·gant·ly** *adv.*

■ **1** lavish, immoderate, wasteful, reckless. **2** exorbitant, expensive, overpriced. **3** wild, outrageous; flamboyant, exaggerated; unjustified. □□ **extravagance** excess, squandering; irrationality.

ex·trav·a·gan·za /ikstrávəgánzə/ *n.* spectacular theatrical production.

■ spectacle, pageant, show.

ex·treme /ikstréem/ • *adj.* **1** of a high or the highest degree (*in extreme danger*). **2** severe. **3** outermost. **4** *Polit.* on the far left or right of a party. **5** risking life or injury (*extreme sports*). • *n.* **1** one or other of two opposite things. **2** highest degree. **3** *Math.* first or last term of a ratio or series. □ **go to extremes** take an extreme course of action. **go to the other extreme** take an opposite course of action. □□ **ex·treme′ly** *adv.* **ex·treme′ness** *n.*

■ *adj.* **1** exceptional, remarkable, outstanding; see also GREAT *adj.* 1a. **2** acute, intense; strict, harsh; excessive; radical, eccentric. **3** farthest, very. • *n.* **2** limit, bounds, maximum.

ex·trem·ist /ikstréemist/ *n.* person with radical views. See synonym study at ZEALOT. □□ **ex·trem′ism** *n.*

■ revolutionary, fanatic, zealot, militant, ultra(ist).

ex•trem•i•ty /ikstrémitee/ *n.* (*pl.* **–ties**) 1 extreme point; end. 2 [in *pl.*] the hands and feet. 3 extreme adversity.

■ 1 limit, edge, boundary; maximum. 2 (*extremities*) fingers, fingertips, toes; limbs.

ex•tri•cate /ékstrikayt/ *v.tr.* free or disentangle from a difficulty, etc. □□ **ex'tri•ca•ble** *adj.* **ex•tri•ca•tion** /–káyshən/ *n.*

■ disengage, liberate, release, rescue, save, deliver.

ex•trin•sic /ekstrínsik, –zik/ *adj.* 1 not inherent or intrinsic. 2 extraneous. 3 from without. □□ **ex•trin'si•cal•ly** *adv.*

■ 1 see IRRELEVANT. 2, 3 outside, external; unrelated.

ex•tro•vert /ékstrəvərt/ *n.* outgoing or sociable person. □□ **ex•tro•ver'sion** /–vɔ́rzhən/ *n.* **ex'tro•vert•ed** *adj.*

ex•trude /ikstro͞od/ *v.tr.* thrust or force out as through a die. □□ **ex•tru'sion** /–tro͞ozhən/ *n.* **ex•tru'sive** /–tro͞osiv/ *adj.*

ex•u•ber•ant /igzo͞obərənt/ *adj.* 1 lively; high-spirited. 2 (of a plant, etc.) prolific. □□ **ex•u'ber•ance** *n.* **ex•u'ber•ant•ly** *adv.*

■ 1 buoyant, spirited, vivacious, energetic. 2 prolific. □□ **exuberance** vitality, zeal, zest; flamboyance.

ex•ude /igzo͞od, ikso͞od/ *v.* 1 *tr. & intr.* ooze out. 2 *tr.* display (an emotion, etc.) freely. □□ **ex•u•date** /ékso͞odayt, éksə–/ *n.* **ex•u•da'tion** *n.* **ex•u'da•tive** *adj.*

■ 1 see EMANATE 1.

ex•ult /igzúlt/ *v.intr.* be joyful. □□ **ex•ul•ta'tion** *n.* **ex•ult'ant** *adj.* **ex•ult'ant•ly** *adv.*

■ rejoice, revel, jump for joy; celebrate. □□ **exultant** delighted, elated, ecstatic.

eye /ī/ • *n.* 1 organ of sight. 2 eye characterized by the color of the iris. 3 region around the eye (*eyes red from crying*). 4 [in *sing.* or *pl.*] sight. 5 particular visual faculty. 6 leaf bud of a potato. 7 calm region at the center of a hurricane. 8 hole of a needle, etc. • *v.tr.* (**eyes, eyed, eye•ing** or **ey•ing**) watch or observe closely. □ **all eyes** 1 watching intently. 2 general attention (*all eyes were on us*). **before one's** (or **one's very**) **eyes** right in front of one. **eye-catching** *colloq.* striking; attractive. **eye for an eye** retaliation in kind. **eye-opener** *colloq.* 1 enlightening experience. 2 bracing drink, etc. **eye shadow** cosmetic applied to the skin around the eyes. **have one's eye on** wish or plan to procure. **have an eye for** be partial to. **hit a person between the eyes** *colloq.* be very obvious or impressive. **keep an eye on** 1 pay attention to. 2 take care of. **keep an eye open** (or **out**) watch carefully. **make eyes at** look flirtatiously at. **my eye** *sl.* nonsense. **open a person's eyes** be enlightening. **see eye to eye** be in agreement.

■ *n.* 1 eyeball, *poet.* orb. 4 vision. 5 discernment, perception, taste, judgment, discrimination. 7 see HEART 5. 8 slit, slot; see also APERTURE. • *v.* study, look *or* gaze upon, regard, view, inspect, examine.

eye•ball /íbawl/ • *n.* ball of the eye within the lids and socket. • *v. sl.* 1 *tr.* look or stare at. 2 *intr.* look or stare.

eye•brow /íbrow/ *n.* line of hair on the ridge above the eye socket. □ **raise one's eyebrows** show surprise, disbelief, or disapproval.

eye•ful /ífo͞ol/ *n.* (*pl.* **–fuls**) *colloq.* 1 long, steady look. 2 visually striking person or thing.

eye•glass /íglas/ *n.* 1 lens for correcting defective sight. 2 [in *pl.*] pair of these, set into a frame.

■ 2 (*eyeglasses*) see SPECTACLES.

eye•lash /ílash/ *n.* each of the hairs growing on the edges of the eyelids. □ **by an eyelash** by a very small margin.

eye•let /ílit/ *n.* 1 small hole for string or rope, etc., to pass through. 2 metal ring reinforcement for this.

eye•lid /ílid/ *n.* either of the skin folds closing to cover the eye.

eye•lin•er /ílīnər/ *n.* cosmetic applied as a line around the eye.

eye•piece /ípees/ *n.* lens or lenses at the end of a microscope, telescope, etc., to which the eye is applied.

eye•sight /ísīt/ *n.* faculty or power of seeing.

■ see SIGHT *n.* 1a.

eye•sore /ísawr/ *n.* visually offensive or ugly thing.

eye•tooth /íto͞oth/ *n.* canine tooth in the upper jaw.

eye•wash /íwosh, íwawsh/ *n.* 1 lotion for the eye. 2 *sl.* nonsense; insincere talk.

eye•wit•ness /íwitnis/ *n.* person who saw thing happen.

■ observer, spectator; bystander, onlooker.

ey•rie var. of AERIE.

Ff

F¹ /ef/ *n.* (also **f**) (*pl.* **Fs** or **F's; f's**) 1 sixth letter of the alphabet. 2 *Mus.* fourth note of the diatonic scale of C major. 3 grade indicating failure.

F² *abbr.* (also **F.**) 1 Fahrenheit. 2 farad(s). 3 female.

F³ *symb. Chem.* fluorine.

f *abbr.* (also **f.**) 1 female. 2 feminine. 3 following page, etc. 4 *Mus.* forte. 5 folio. 6 focal length (cf. F-NUMBER). 7 filly.

fa /faa/ *n. Mus.* fourth note of a major scale.

FAA *abbr.* Federal Aviation Administration.

fa•ble /fáybəl/ *n.* 1 **a** story, esp. a supernatural one, not based on fact. **b** tale, esp. with

animals as characters, conveying a moral. **2** lie. □□ **fa•bler** /fáyblər/ *n*.
  ■ **1** see MYTH 4. **2** see FABRICATION 2.

fab•ric /fábrik/ *n*. **1** woven material; textile. **2** essential structure.
  ■ **1** cloth. **2** constitution, construction, makeup; essence, core; see also STRUCTURE *n*. 1b.

fab•ri•cate /fábrikayt/ *v.tr.* **1** construct, esp. from prepared components. **2** invent (a story, etc.). □□ **fab′ri•ca•tor** *n*.
  ■ **1** manufacture, build, erect, frame, raise, put *or* set up, assemble, fashion, form, make, produce. **2** concoct, create, originate, devise, make up, manufacture.

fab•ri•ca•tion /fábrikáyshən/ *n*. **1** action or process of manufacturing or constructing something. **2** invention of a lie, etc.
  ■ **1** construction, manufacture, building, constructing, erection, framing, putting together, assembly. **2** concoction, creation, origination, contrivance, falsehood, lie, tale, fable, untruth, fiction.

fab•u•lous /fábyələs/ *adj*. **1** incredible; exaggerated; absurd. **2** *colloq*. marvelous (*looking fabulous*). **3** legendary. □□ **fab′u•lous•ly** *adv*. **fab′u•lous•ness** *n*.
  ■ **1** unbelievable, inconceivable, astounding, astonishing, amazing. **2** wonderful, *colloq*. superb, terrific, great, super; *sl*. far-out, hot, groovy, ace, cool. **3** fabled, mythic, mythical, fictional, imaginary, fanciful.

ta•çade /fəsaád/ *n*. **1** face of a building, esp. its principal front. **2** outward appearance or front, esp. a deceptive one.

face /fays/ ● *n*. **1** front of the head from the forehead to the chin. **2 a** expression of the facial features (*had a happy face*). **b** grimace (*make a face*). **3 a** surface; side. **b** dial of a clock, etc. **4** outward appearance or aspect (*the harsh face of capitalism*). ● *v*. **1** *tr. & intr.* look or be positioned toward or in a certain direction (*facing the window*). **2** *tr*. be opposite (*facing page 20*). **3** *tr*. meet resolutely or defiantly; confront (*face one's critics*). **4** *tr*. cover the surface of (a thing) with a coating, extra layer, etc. □ **face-lift 1** (also **face-lifting**) cosmetic surgery to remove wrinkles, etc. **2** procedure to improve the appearance of a thing. **face the music** *colloq*. put up with or stand up to unpleasant consequences, esp. criticism. **face up to** accept bravely, confront; stand up to. **in the face of 1** despite. **2** confronted by. **put one's face on** *colloq*. apply makeup to one's face. **save face** preserve esteem; avoid humiliation. □□ **faced** *adj*. [also in *comb*.]. **fac′ing** *adj*. [also in *comb*.].
  ■ *n*. **1** countenance, physiognomy, *literary* visage, *sl*. mug, pan. **2 a** look, appearance, aspect. **3 a** façade, exterior, front, outside; cover, facing. **4** front, guise, look, exterior; mask, veneer, façade. ● *v*. **1** give (out) onto, front on *or* to *or* toward *or* upon, overlook. **2** see FRONT *v*. 1. **3** encounter, brave, deal *or* cope with, face up to. **4** coat, overlay; finish, surface, veneer. □ **face up to** admit, acknowledge, allow, confess; deal *or* cope with, brave, go up against; bite the bullet. **in the face of 1** in spite of, notwithstanding.

face•less /fáyslis/ *adj*. **1** without identity; purposely not identifiable. **2** lacking character. **3** without a face. □□ **face′less•ly** *adv*. **face′less•ness** *n*.

fac•et /fásit/ *n*. **1** particular aspect of a thing. **2** one side of a cut gem. □□ **fac′et•ed** *adj*. [-also in *comb*.].

fa•ce•tious /fəseéshəs/ *adj*. **1** characterized by flippant or inappropriate humor. **2** (of a person) intending to be amusing, esp. inappropriately. □□ **fa•ce′tious•ly** *adv*. **fa•ce′tious•ness** *n*.

fa•cial /fáyshəl/ ● *adj*. of or for the face. ● *n*. beauty treatment for the face. □□ **fa′cial•ly** *adv*.

fac•ile /fásəl, -sīl/ *adj*. usu. *derog*. **1** easily achieved but of little value. **2** fluent; ready; glib. □□ **fac′ile•ly** *adv*. **fac′ile•ness** *n*.

fa•cil•i•tate /fəsílitayt/ *v.tr.* ease (a process, etc.). □□ **fa•cil•i•ta•tion** /-táyshən/ *n*. **fa•cil′i•ta•tive** *adj*. **fa•cil′i•ta•tor** *n*.
  ■ expedite, smooth, assist, aid, help, further.

fa•cil•i•ty /fəsílitee/ *n*. (*pl*. **-ties**) **1** ease. **2** fluency; dexterity; aptitude. **3** [esp. in *pl*.] opportunity, equipment, or resources for doing something. **4** plant, installation, or establishment. **5** *euphem*. [in *pl*.] (public) toilet.
  ■ **1, 2** effortlessness, skill, skillfulness, deftness, adroitness, ability, efficiency, smoothness, quickness. **3** (*facilities*) potential, capacity; see also APPARATUS. **4** system, buildings, structure, complex. **5** (*facilities*) lavatory, men's room, ladies' room, rest room, *sl*. john.

fac•ing /fáysing/ *n*. **1** garment lining. **2** outer layer covering the surface of a wall, etc.
  ■ **2** façade, surface, front, cladding.

fac•sim•i•le /faksímilee/ *n*. **1** exact copy, esp. of writing, printing, etc. **2 a** production of an exact copy of a document, etc., by electronic scanning and transmission of the resulting data (see also FAX). **b** copy produced in this way. □ **in facsimile** as an exact copy.
  ■ **1** reproduction, carbon copy, duplicate. **2** photocopy, duplicate, fax, *propr*. Xerox.

fact /fakt/ *n*. **1** thing that is known to have occurred, to exist, or to be true. **2** truth; reality. □ **the facts of life** information about sexual functions and practices.
  ■ **1** occurrence, event, happening, incident, experience. **2** actuality, certainty.

fac•tion /fákshən/ *n*. small organized dissenting group within a larger one.
  ■ cabal, cadre, camp, splinter group, circle, clique, set, coterie, lobby, pressure group.

fac•tious /fákshəs/ *adj*. of, characterized by, or inclined to faction. □□ **fac′tious•ly** *adv*. **fac′tious•ness** *n*.
  ■ divisive, conflicting, discordant, contentious, disputatious, argumentative, quarrelsome, seditious.

fac•ti•tious /faktíshəs/ *adj*. **1** contrived. **2** artificial. □□ **fac•ti′tious•ly** *adv*. **fac•ti′tious•ness** *n*.
  ■ manufactured, fabricated, engineered, unauthentic; insincere, unreal, fake, false, bogus, falsified.

fac•toid /fáktoyd/ n. 1 simulated or imagined fact. 2 trivial fact or news item.

fac•tor /fáktər/ • n. 1 circumstance, fact, or influence contributing to a result. 2 Math. whole number, etc., that when multiplied with another produces a given number or expression. • v.tr. Math. resolve into factors or components. □□ **fac′tor•a•ble** adj.
■ n. 1 ingredient, element, consideration, particular, aspect, determinant, cause.

fac•to•ri•al /faktáwreeəl/ Math. • n. product of a number and all the whole numbers below it (four factorial = 4 × 3 × 2 × 1). ¶Symb.: ! (as in 4!). • adj. of a factor or factorial. □□ **fac•to′ri•al•ly** adv.

fac•to•ry /fáktəree/ n. (pl. **–ries**) 1 building or buildings containing equipment for manufacturing machinery or goods. 2 [usu. derog.] place producing mass quantities or a low quality of goods, etc. □ **factory farming** system of rearing livestock using industrial or intensive methods. **factory ship** fishing ship with facilities for immediate processing of the catch.
■ 1 plant, mill, works, workshop.

fac•to•tum /faktótəm/ n. employee who does all kinds of work.

fac•tu•al /fákchōōəl/ adj. based on or concerned with fact. □□ **fac•tu•al•i•ty** /–chōō-álitee/ n. **fac′tu•al•ly** adv.
■ real, true, actual, authentic; faithful, bona fide, accurate; objective, unbiased, unprejudiced.

fac•ul•ty /fákəltee/ n. (pl. **–ties**) 1 aptitude or ability for a particular activity. 2 inherent mental or physical power. 3 teaching staff. 4 personnel, members.
■ 1, 2 capacity, capability, skill, talent, flair, knack, gift, genius; potential. 3 personnel, members.

fad /fad/ n. craze; short-lived fashion. □□ **fad′dish** adj. **fad′dish•ly** adv. **fad′dist** n.
■ mania, rage, trend, vogue.

fade /fayd/ • v. 1 intr. & tr. lose or cause to lose color, light, or sound. 2 intr. lose freshness or strength; (of flowers, etc.) droop; wither. 3 tr. [foll. by in, out] Cinematog. & Broadcasting cause (a photographic image, recorded sound, etc.) to appear or disappear gradually. • n. action or an instance of fading. □ **fade away** colloq. languish; grow thin. □□ **fade′less** adj. **fad′er** n. (in sense 3 of v.)
■ v. 1 (grow) dim or pale, cloud (over); grow faint, blanch, discolor. 2 ebb, flag, fade away, wane, decline, languish, droop, wilt, wither, shrivel, perish. 3 see MERGE[1]. • n. see DECREASE n. □ **fade away** see FLAG v. 1a, WASTE v. 3.

fag•got /fágət/ n. sl. derog. male homosexual.

fag•ot /fágət/ • n. 1 bundle of sticks or twigs bound together as fuel. 2 bundle of iron rods for heat treatment. • v.tr. bind in or make into fagots.

Fahr•en•heit /fárənhīt/ adj. of a scale of temperature on which water freezes at 32° and boils at 212°.

fa•ience /fī-óNs, fay–/ n. decorated and glazed earthenware and porcelain, e.g., delft or majolica.

fail /fayl/ v. 1 intr. not succeed (failed to qualify). 2 a tr. & intr. be unsuccessful in (an examination, test, interview, etc.). b tr. not pass; reject. 3 intr. be unable to; neglect to; choose not to (he failed to appear). 4 tr. disappoint. 5 intr. (of supplies, crops, etc.) be or become lacking or insufficient. 6 intr. become weaker; cease functioning (her health is failing). 7 intr. a (of an enterprise) collapse; come to nothing. b become bankrupt. □ **fail-safe** reverting to a safe condition in the event of a breakdown, etc. **without fail** for certain; whatever happens.
■ 1, 2 a come to grief; fall through, founder, run aground, miscarry, abort, go wrong, misfire, sl. flop; colloq. flunk; be or prove inadequate. 2 b see REJECT v. 1. 4 let down, dissatisfy. 5 see run out 1. 6 weaken, decline, wane, diminish, deteriorate, dwindle, flag, ebb, sink; give out, peter out, stop. 7 a see COLLAPSE v. b crash, go out of business, go under, go into receivership, become insolvent, close up.

fail•ing /fáyling/ • n. fault; weakness. See synonym study at FAULT. • prep. in default of; if not.
■ n. shortcoming, flaw, defect, foible, weak point. • prep. in the absence of, without.

fail•ure /fáylyər/ n. 1 lack of success; failing. 2 unsuccessful person, thing, or attempt. 3 nonperformance; nonoccurrence. 4 breaking down or ceasing to function (heart failure). 5 running short of supply, etc. 6 bankruptcy; collapse.
■ 1 see IMPERFECTION 2. 2 incompetent, colloq. lemon; also-ran, loser, sl. flop, dud; washout, lead balloon. 3 neglect, dereliction; default, remissness. 4 breakdown, collapse, decline, failing. 6 ruin, insolvency, crash.

fain /fayn/ archaic • predic.adj. [foll. by to + infin.] willing under the circumstances to. • adv. gladly (esp. would fain).

faint /faynt/ • adj. 1 indistinct; pale; dim; quiet; not clearly perceived. 2 (of a person) weak or dizzy; inclined to faint. 3 slight; remote; inadequate (a faint chance). 4 feeble; halfhearted (faint praise). 5 timid (a faint heart). • v.intr. lose consciousness. • n. sudden loss of consciousness; fainting. □ **faint-hearted** cowardly; timid. □□ **faint′ly** adv. **faint′ness** n.
■ adj. 1 feeble, weak, subdued, flickering, blurred; faded; imperceptible, unclear; low, soft, slight, hushed. 2 giddy, light-headed, unsteady, colloq. woozy. 3 see REMOTE 4. 4 see FEEBLE 2. 5 see TIMID. • v. pass out, black out, collapse. □ **faint-hearted** weak, feeble, timorous, afraid, frightened, scared.

fair[1] /fair/ • adj. 1 just; unbiased; equitable; in accordance with the rules. 2 blond; light or pale. 3 a (of only) moderate quality or amount; average. b considerable; satisfactory (a fair chance of success). 4 (of weather) fine and dry; (of the wind) favorable. 5 beautiful; attractive. • adv. in a fair manner (play fair). □ **fair game** thing or person one may legitimately pursue, exploit, etc. **fair play** reasonable treatment or behavior. □□ **fair′ish** adj. **fair′ness** n.

■ *adj.* **1** fair-minded, unprejudiced, objective, disinterested, evenhanded; honest, straightforward, aboveboard, upright. **2** fair-haired, flaxen-haired; light-complexioned. **3 a** see MEDIOCRE 1. **b** adequate, respectable, pretty good, tolerable, passable, average, decent. **4** sunny, bright, clear, cloudless, pleasant; benign. **5** pretty, lovely, good-looking, handsome. ■ *adv.* see FAIRLY 1. □ **fair play** see JUSTICE 1–3.

fair² /fair/ *n.* **1** gathering of stalls, amusements, etc., for public (usu. outdoor) entertainment. **2** periodic market, often with entertainments. **3** exhibition, esp. commercial.
■ **1** fête, festival, carnival. **2** fête, bazaar, mart, kermis. **3** exposition, show, exhibit.

fair•ly /fáirlee/ *adv.* **1** in a fair manner. **2** moderately; rather.
■ **1** justly, equitably, properly, honestly, impartially, objectively. **2** acceptably, tolerably, passably, quite.

fair•way /fáirway/ *n.* part of a golf course between a tee and its green, kept free of rough grass.

fair•y /fáiree/ ■ *n.* (*pl.* **–ies**) small imaginary being with magical powers. ■ *adj.* of fairies; fairylike; delicate; small (*fairy wren*). □ **fairy godmother** benefactress. **fairy tale** (or **story**) **1** tale about fairies or other fantastic creatures. **2** incredible story; fabrication. □□ **fairy'like** *adj.*
■ *n.* see IMP n. 2.

fait ac•com•pli /fet aakawnplée, –komplée/ *n.* thing that has been done and is past arguing about or altering.

faith /fayth/ *n.* **1** complete trust or confidence. **2** firm belief, esp. without logical proof. **3 a** system of religious belief. **b** belief in religious doctrines. **4** duty or commitment to fulfill a trust, promise, etc.; allegiance (*keep faith*).
■ **1, 2** certainty, conviction, certitude. **3 a** religion, creed; teaching, doctrine, dogma. **b** see BELIEF.

faith•ful /fáythfool/ *adj.* **1** showing faith. **2** loyal; trustworthy; constant. **3** accurate; true to fact. See synonym study at RESOLUTE. □□ **faith'ful•ly** *adv.* **faith'ful•ness** *n.*
■ **2** true, devoted; reliable, dependable. **3** close, exact, precise, perfect; literal; valid.

faith•less /fáythlis/ *adj.* **1** false; unreliable; disloyal. **2** being without religious faith. □□ **faith'less•ly** *adv.* **faith'less•ness** *n.*
■ **1** insincere, hypocritical, untrustworthy, crooked, inconstant, fickle. **2** skeptical, doubting, unbelieving, disbelieving, agnostic, atheistic, atheistical.

fa•ji•tas /faaheétas, fə–/ *n.pl. Mexican Cookery* thin strips of fried or broiled meat, usu. seasoned.

fake /fayk/ ■ *n.* **1** thing or person that is not genuine. **2** trick. **3** *Sport* feint. ■ *adj.* counterfeit; not genuine. ■ *v.tr.* make a fake or imitation. □□ **fak'er** *n.* **fak'er•y** *n.*
■ *n.* **1** forgery, imitation, counterfeit; faker, impostor, charlatan, fraud, *colloq.* phony. **2** see HOAX *n.* ■ *adj.* forged, fraudulent; imitation; bogus; sham, *colloq.* phony. ■ *v.* forge, counterfeit, fabricate, manufacture; doctor, tamper with, falsify, alter.

fal•con /fálkən, fáwl–/ *n.* diurnal bird of prey having long pointed wings, and sometimes trained to hunt small game for sport.

fall /fawl/ ■ *v.intr.* (*past* **fell** /fel/; *past part.* **fall•en** /fáwlən/) **1** go or come down freely; descend. **2** cease to stand; come to the ground. **3 a** (of hair, clothing, etc.) hang down. **b** (of ground, etc.) slope. **4 a** sink lower. **b** subside. **5** occur (*darkness fell*). **6** decline; diminish (*standards have fallen*). **7** (of the face) show dismay or disappointment. **8** lose power, status, esteem, etc. **9** yield to temptation. **10** take or have a particular direction or place (*the accent falls on the first syllable*). **11** [foll. by *under*, *within*] be classed among. **12** come by chance or duty (*it fell to me to answer*). **13** pass into a specified condition (*fall into decay*). **14** be captured; be defeated. **15** die. **16** [foll. by *on*, *upon*] **a** attack. **b** meet with. **c** embark on. **17** begin (*fell to wondering*). ■ *n.* **1** act or instance of falling. **2** that which falls or has fallen, e.g., snow, rocks, etc. **3** decline in price, value, demand, etc. **4** overthrow; downfall (*the fall of Rome*). **5 a** succumbing to temptation. **b** (**the Fall**) the biblical sin of Adam and its consequences. **6** (also **Fall**) autumn. **7** [*esp.pl.*] waterfall or cascade. **8** a throw in wrestling. ■ **fall apart** (or **to pieces**) **1** break into pieces. **2** be reduced to chaos. **3** lose one's capacity to cope. **fall back retreat. fall back on** have recourse to in difficulty. **fall for** *colloq.* **1** be captivated or deceived by. **2** yield to the charms or merits of. **fall guy** *sl.* **1** easy victim. **2** scapegoat. **fall in 1 a** take one's place in military formation. **b** [as *int.*] the order to do this. **2** collapse inward. **falling star** meteor. **fall into place** begin to make sense or cohere. **fall in with 1** meet or become involved with by chance. **2** agree with. **fall short** be or become deficient or inadequate. **fall short of** fail to reach or obtain. **fall through** fail; come to nothing.
■ *v.* **1** plummet, plunge, dive, nosedive; drop (down), come down. **2** tumble, topple (over or down), keel over; trip, stumble; collapse, slump, drop. **3 b** fall away. **5** see OCCUR¹ 1, 6, come or go down, (become) lower, drop, sink; fall or drop off, decrease, dwindle, subside. **9** see SIN *v.* 1. **14** be overthrown; be taken, be conquered; be lost, be destroyed; succumb, surrender, yield, give up or in, capitulate. **15** perish, be killed, *literary or joc.* be slain. **16** (*fall on* or *upon*) **a** assault, assail, set upon. **c** see EMBARK¹ 2. **17** (*fall to*) see COMMENCE. ■ *n.* **1** descent, drop, dive, nosedive, plunge, tumble. **2** covering, coating, layer. **3** diminution, decrease, downturn, drop, drop-off, lowering, sinking, slump, collapse; depreciation. **4** capture, taking, seizure, defeat, conquest, destruction; surrender, capitulation, submission; decline, collapse. **5 a** see SIN *n.* 1. ■ **fall apart** (or **to pieces**) **1** disintegrate, break apart, fragment, shatter. **2** collapse, break up; see also DISINTEGRATE. **3** disintegrate, crumble, go to pieces, collapse. **fall back** withdraw, draw

back; retire. **fall back on** rely *or* depend on, rely *or* depend upon, return to, count on *or* upon, resort to, call on *or* upon, make use of, use, employ. **fall for** 1 be fooled *or* duped *or* taken in by, swallow, *sl.* be a sucker for. 2 fall in love with, become infatuated with. **fall guy** 1 see FOOL *n.* 3. 2 see SCAPEGOAT *n.* **fall in** 2 sink inward; buckle, cave in. **fall into place** see *add up* 3. **fall in with** 1 become associated *or* allied with, befriend, join, associate with. 2 go along with, concur with, support, accept. **fall short** prove deficient, prove inadequate, prove insufficient, be *or* prove lacking, be *or* prove disappointing; disappoint. **fall through** come to naught, miscarry, die, *colloq.* fizzle (out); see also FAIL *v.* 1, 2a.

fal•la•cy /fáləsee/ *n.* (*pl.* **–cies**) 1 mistaken belief. 2 faulty reasoning; misleading or unsound argument. □□ **fal•la•cious** /fəláyshəs/ *adj.* **fal•la′cious•ly** *adv.*

■ misconception, mistake, error; non sequitur. □□ **fallacious** see UNSOUND 3a.

fal•li•ble /fálibəl/ *adj.* 1 capable of making mistakes. 2 liable to be erroneous. □□ **fal•li•bil′i•ty** *n.* **fal′li•bly** *adv.*

Fal•lo•pi•an tube /fəlópeeən/ *n. Anat.* either of two tubes along which ova travel from the ovaries to the uterus.

fall•out /fáwlowt/ *n.* radioactive nuclear debris.

fal•low /fálō/ *adj.* 1 (of land) plowed and harrowed but left unsown. 2 uncultivated. □□ **fal′low•ness** *n.*

false /fawls/ *adj.* 1 wrong; incorrect. 2 a spurious; sham; artificial (*false gods*). b acting as such; appearing to be such, esp. deceptively (*a false lining*). 4 deceptive. 5 (foll. by *to*) deceitful, treacherous, or unfaithful. □□ **false′ly** *adv.* **false′ness** *n.* **fal′si•ty** *n.* (*pl.* **–ties**)

■ 1 untrue, inaccurate, inexact, imprecise; mistaken, fallacious, erroneous. 2 a feigned, affected, insincere, fake, simulated, synthetic, pseudo, factitious, unnatural, bogus. b deceptive, misleading, untrue, untrustworthy, fraudulent. 4 see DECEPTIVE. 5 see DISLOYAL.

false•hood /fáwls-hood/ *n.* 1 state of being false, esp. untrue. 2 false or untrue thing. 3 a act of lying. b a lie or lies.

■ 2, 3b untruth, fiction, fabrication, distortion; fib, tale, story, fairy tale.

fal•set•to /fawlsétō/ *n.* (*pl.* **–tos**) male singing voice above the normal range.

fal•si•fy /fáwlsifī/ *v.tr.* (**–fies, –fied**) 1 fraudulently alter or make false (a document, evidence, etc.). 2 misrepresent. □□ **fal′si•fi•a•ble** *adj.* **fal•si•fi•a•bil′i•ty** *n.* **fal•si•fi•ca′tion** *n.*

■ 1 *colloq.* massage, cook. 2 distort, twist; see also MISREPRESENT.

fal•ter /fáwltər/ *v.* 1 *intr.* stumble; stagger; go unsteadily. 2 *intr.* waver; lose courage. 3 *tr. & intr.* stammer; speak hesitatingly. □□ **fal′ter•er** *n.* **fal′ter•ing•ly** *adv.*

■ 1 see HOBBLE *v.* 1. 2 see HESITATE 1, DOUBT *v.* 3. 3 see STAMMER *v.*

fame /faym/ *n.* renown; state of being famous.

■ reputation, celebrity, stardom, name, illustriousness, (pre)eminence, prominence, repute.

famed /faymd/ *adj.* much spoken of (*famed for its good food*).

fa•mil•ial /fəmílyəl, –leeəl/ *adj.* of a family or its members.

fa•mil•iar /fəmílyər/ • *adj.* 1 a well known. b often encountered or experienced. 2 well acquainted. 3 excessively informal; impertinent. 4 unceremonious; informal. • *n.* close friend. □□ **fa•mil•i•ar•i•ty** /–eeáritee, –yár–/ *n.* **fa•mil′iar•ly** *adv.*

■ *adj.* 1 commonplace, common, usual, customary, habitual, routine; see also *well-known* 2 (WELL[1]). 2 up on *or* in, (well-)versed in; aware *or* conscious *or* cognizant of, no stranger to; friendly, close, *colloq.* chummy; see also INTIMATE[1] *adj.* 1. 3 overfriendly, free, unrestrained, bold, forward, insolent. 4 casual, relaxed. • *n.* see ASSOCIATE *n.* 2, FRIEND *n.* 1. □□ **familiarity** informality, unceremoniousness; overfamiliarity, boldness, impudence, insolence.

fa•mil•iar•ize /fəmílyərīz/ *v.tr.* make conversant or well acquainted; make well known. □□ **fa•mil•iar•i•za′tion** *n.*

■ accustom to, make familiar *or* acquaint with, initiate in, teach about, educate *or* instruct *or* tutor in; see also PUBLICIZE.

fam•i•ly /fámilee/ *n.* (*pl.* **–lies**) 1 set of parents and children, *or* of relations. 2 descendants of a common ancestor. 3 brotherhood of persons or nations united by political or religious ties. 4 group of objects distinguished by common features. 5 *Biol.* group of related genera of organisms. □ **family planning** birth control. **family tree** chart showing relationships and lines of descent. **in the** (or a) **family way** *colloq.* pregnant.

■ 1 (kith and) kin, kinsmen, kindred, kinfolk, kinsfolk, next of kin, relatives, folks. 2 ancestry, parentage, descent, extraction, derivation, lineage, pedigree, genealogy, family tree, house, line, bloodline, dynasty; blood, stock, strain. 3 see BROTHERHOOD 2. 4 see GROUP *n.* 1.

fam•ine /fámin/ *n.* extreme scarcity, esp. of food.

■ shortage, dearth, paucity, exiguity, lack.

fam•ish /fámish/ *v.* (usu. in *passive*) 1 reduce or be reduced to extreme hunger. 2 *colloq.* (esp. as **famished** *adj.*) feel very hungry.

■ 2 (**famished**) ravenous, empty, *colloq.* starved.

fa•mous /fáyməs/ *adj.* 1 celebrated; well known. 2 *colloq.* excellent. □□ **fa′mous•ly** *adv.* **fa′mous•ness** *n.*

■ 1 renowned, famed, prominent, illustrious, noted, notable, acclaimed; legendary. 2 see EXCELLENT.

fan[1] /fan/ • *n.* 1 apparatus, usu. with rotating blades, for ventilation, etc. 2 wide, flat device, waved to cool oneself. • *v.* (**fanned, fan′ning**) 1 *tr.* blow a current of air on, with or as with a fan. 2 *intr. & tr.* spread out in the shape of a fan. □□ **fan′like** *adj.* **fan′ner** *n.*

fan[2] /fan/ *n.* devotee; follower. □□ **fan′dom** *n.*

■ admirer, enthusiast, lover, adherent, supporter, aficionado, fanatic, zealot, *colloq.* buff, *sl.* fiend, bug, nut.

fa·nat·ic /fənátik/ • *n.* person filled with excessive and often misguided enthusiasm for something. See synonym study at ZEALOT. • *adj.* excessively enthusiastic. □□ **fa·nat·i·cal** *adj.* **fa·nat·i·cal·ly** *adv.* **fa·nat·i·cism** /-tisizəm/ *n.*

■ *n.* extremist, maniac, zealot, *sl.* nut. • *adj.* see *enthusiastic* (ENTHUSIASM). □□ **fanatical** fanatic, extreme, maniacal, mad, rabid, compulsive. **fanaticism** extremism, hysteria, franticness, frenzy, zeal; obsessiveness.

fan·ci·er /fánseeər/ *n.* connoisseur.

fan·ci·ful /fánsifool/ *adj.* **1** existing only in the imagination. **2** indulging in fancies. □□ **fan·ci·ful·ly** *adv.* **fan·ci·ful·ness** *n.*

■ **1** extravagant, fantastic, chimerical, fabulous, unreal. **2** capricious, impulsive, fickle; see also WHIMSICAL 1.

fan·cy /fánsee/ • *n.* (*pl.* **–cies**) **1** individual taste or inclination. **2** whim. **3** supposition. **4 a** faculty of imagination. **b** mental image. • *adj.* [usu. *attrib.*] (**fan·ci·er, fan·ci·est**) **1** ornamental; not plain. **2** capricious; whimsical; extravagant (*at a fancy price*). • *v.tr.* (**–cies, –cied**) **1** be inclined to suppose. **2** *colloq.* feel a desire for (*do you fancy a drink?*). □ **catch** (or **take**) **the fancy of** please; appeal to. **fancy-free** without (esp. emotional) commitments. □□ **fan·ci·ly** *adv.* **fan·ci·ness** *n.*

■ *n.* **1** penchant, preference, partiality, predilection, liking, fondness, attraction. **2** caprice, idea, whimsy, notion. **3** see SUPPOSITION. **4 a** inventiveness, creativity, creativeness. **b** see IMAGE *n.* 7. • *adj.* **1** decorative, ornate, decorated, ornamented, elaborate, embellished, embroidered. **2** fanciful, fantastic, far-fetched, visionary, grandiose; exorbitant. • *v.* **1** think, guess, conjecture, presume, surmise, assume, take it. **2** see WANT *v.* 1a.

fan·dan·go /fandánggō/ *n.* (*pl.* **–goes** or **–gos**) **1** lively Spanish dance for two. **2** music for this.

fan·fare /fánfair/ *n.* **1** short showy or ceremonious sounding of trumpets, bugles, etc. **2** elaborate display.

■ **1** flourish, fanfaronade, blast, blare. **2** fuss, commotion, stir, ado, to-do, hubbub, brouhaha.

fang /fang/ *n.* **1** canine tooth, esp. of a dog or wolf. **2** tooth of a venomous snake, by which poison is injected. □□ **fanged** *adj.* [also in *comb.*]. **fang·less** *adj.*

fan·ny /fánee/ *n.* (*pl.* **–nies**) *sl.* the buttocks. □ **fanny pack** pouch worn on a belt around the waist or hips.

fan·ta·size /fántəsiz/ *v.* **1** *intr.* have a fantasy or fanciful vision. **2** *tr.* imagine; create a fantasy about. □□ **fan·ta·sist** *n.*

■ **1** dream, daydream, speculate. **2** see IMAGINE 1.

fan·tas·tic /fantástik/ *adj.* (also **fan·tas·ti·cal**) **1** *colloq.* excellent; extraordinary. **2** extravagantly fanciful. **3** grotesque. □□ **fan·tas·ti·cal·ly** *adv.*

■ **1** marvelous, spectacular, splendid, won-

derful, tremendous, overwhelming, *colloq.* great; see also EXCELLENT. **2** extravagant, imaginary, illusory, imagined, illusive, unreal, irrational; capricious, eccentric, extraordinary, unbelievable. **3** eccentric, outlandish, fanciful, remarkable, strange, peculiar, odd, queer, bizarre, quaint, exotic.

fan·ta·sy /fántəsee, -zee/ *n.* (*pl.* **–sies**) **1** faculty of inventing images, esp. extravagant or visionary ones. **2** fanciful mental image; daydream. **3** fiction genre that features supernatural, magical, or otherworldly elements.

■ **1** imagination, fancy, creativity, inventiveness, originality. **2** vision, hallucination, mirage, illusion, delusion, chimera; dream, (flight of) fancy.

far /faar/ (**far·ther, far·thest** or **fur·ther, fur·thest**) • *adv.* **1** at or to or by a great distance (*far off*). **2** a long way (off) in space or time (*are you traveling far?*). **3** to a great extent or degree; by much (*far better*). • *adj.* **1** remote, distant (*a far cry*). **2** more distant (*the far end of the hall*). **3** extreme (*far right militants*). □ **as far as 1** to the distance of (a place). **2** to the extent that (*travel as far as you like*). **by far** by a great amount. **far cry** a long way. **the Far East** China, Japan, and other countries of E. Asia. **far-fetched** strained; unconvincing. **far-flung 1** extending far; widely distributed. **2** remote; distant. **so far 1** to such an extent or distance; to this point. **2** until now. **so far so good** progress has been satisfactory up to now.

■ *adv.* **1, 2** far away, far off; afar, far out. **3** (very) much, considerably, decidedly, incomparably. • *adj.* **1** faraway, far-off. **2** extreme, farthest, further; other, opposite. □ **by far** much, considerably, incomparably, immeasurably; easily, definitely, undoubtedly, indubitably, unquestionably. **far-fetched** forced, unbelievable, incredible, improbable, implausible, unlikely, doubtful, dubious. **far-flung 1** see EXTENSIVE 2. **2** see REMOTE 1. **so far 1** to a certain extent or limit or point. **2** until or till or up to the present, until or till or up to this or that point, to date, to this or that point in time, *formal* thus far; see also YET *adv.* 2.

far·ad /fárəd, -ad/ *n. Electr.* unit of capacitance, such that one coulomb of charge causes a potential difference of one volt. ¶Abbr.: F.

far·a·way /fáarəwáy/ *adj.* **1** remote; long past. **2** (of a look) dreamy. **3** (of a voice) sounding as if from a distance.

■ **1** distant, far-off, far-flung; see also REMOTE 1, 2. **2** detached, absent, absent-minded. **3** see FAINT *adj.* 1.

farce /faars/ *n.* **1 a** broadly comic dramatic work based on ludicrously improbable events. **b** this branch of drama. **2** absurdly futile proceedings; pretense; mockery.

■ **2** see MOCKERY 2.

far·ci·cal /fáarsikəl/ *adj.* **1** extremely ludicrous or futile. **2** of or like farce. □□ **far·ci·cal·i·ty** /-kálitee/ *n.* **far·ci·cal·ly** *adv.*

■ **1** laughable, ridiculous, absurd, risible, funny.

fare /fair/ • n. **1 a** price a passenger has to pay to be conveyed by bus, train, etc. **b** passenger paying to travel in a public vehicle. **2** food. • v.intr. progress; get on.

■ n. **1 a** see CHARGE n. 1a. **b** see PASSENGER. **2** meals, victuals, provisions, eatables. • v. manage, do, make one's way, survive, colloq. make out.

fare•well /fáirwél/ • int. good-bye; adieu. • n. leave-taking.

■ int. adios, au revoir, colloq. toodle-oo, so long, ciao, bye, bye-bye, see you, see you later. • n. departure, congé, parting, send-off, good-bye.

fa•ri•na /fəreénə/ n. flour or meal of cereal, nuts, or starchy roots. □□ **far•i•na•ceous** /fárináyshəs/ adj.

farm /faarm/ • n. **1** area of land and its buildings used under one management for growing crops, rearing animals, etc. **2** place or establishment for breeding a particular type of animal, growing fruit, etc. (trout farm). • v. **1 a** tr. use (land) for growing crops, rearing animals, etc. **b** intr. be a farmer; work on a farm. **2** tr. [often foll. by out] delegate or subcontract (work) to others. □ **farm hand** worker on a farm. □□ **farm′a•ble** adj. **farm′er** n. **farm′ing** n.

■ n. **1** farmstead, grange; see also SPREAD n. 10. • v. **1 a** cultivate, work, till. **b** work the land. **2** subcontract, give; see also DELEGATE v. 1.

farm•house /faarmhows/ n. house attached to a farm.

farm•land /faarmland/ n. land used or suitable for farming.

far•ra•go /fəraágō, –ráy–/ n. (pl. **–goes**) medley or hodgepodge. See synonym study at JUMBLE. □□ **far•rag•i•nous** /–raájinəs/ adj.

far•ri•er /fáreeər/ n. smith who shoes horses.

far•row /fárō/ • n. **1** litter of pigs. **2** birth of a litter. • v.tr. [also absol.] (of a sow) produce (pigs).

far•see•ing /faarseéing/ adj. shrewd in judgment; prescient.

far•sight•ed /faarsítid/ adj. **1** having foresight; prudent. **2** able to see clearly only what is comparatively distant. □□ **far′sight′ed•ly** adv. **far′sight′ed•ness** n.

■ **1** foresighted, farseeing; wise, sensible; see also SHREWD. **2** longsighted, hypermetropic, hyperopic.

fart /faart/ coarse • v.intr. emit intestinal gas from the anus. • n. emission of intestinal gas from the anus.

far•ther /faarthər/ (also **fur•ther** /fúrthər/) • adv. **1** to or at a more advanced point in space or time (unsafe to proceed farther). **2** at a greater distance (nothing was farther from his thoughts). • adj. more distant or advanced (on the farther side). □□ **far′ther•most** adj.

far•thest /faarthist/ (also **furth•est** /fúrthist/) • adj. most distant. • adv. to or at the greatest distance.

■ adj. see ULTIMATE adj. 1, 2.

far•thing /faarthing/ n. (in the UK) former coin and monetary unit worth a quarter of an old penny.

fas•ces /fáseez/ n.pl. Rom.Hist. bundle of rods with a projecting ax blade, symbol of a magistrate's power.

fas•cia /fáyshə/ n. **1** Archit. long flat surface on the architrave in classical architecture. **2** flat surface, usu. of wood, covering the ends of rafters.

fas•ci•nate /fásinayt/ v.tr. **1** capture the interest of; attract irresistibly. **2** (esp. of a snake) paralyze (a victim) with fear. □□ **fas′ci•nat•ed** adj. **fas′ci•nat•ing** adj. **fas′ci•nat•ing•ly** adv. **fas•ci•na•tion** /–náyshən/ n. **fas′ci•na•tor** n.

■ **1** intrigue, beguile, absorb, engross, enthrall, captivate, spellbind, bewitch, enchant, charm, hypnotize; see also ENTICE. **2** see PARALYZE. □□ **fascination** enchantment, entrancement, attraction, attractiveness, draw.

Fas•cism /fáshizəm/ n. extreme totalitarian right-wing nationalist movement or philosophy, as instituted in Italy (1922–43). □□ **Fas′cist** n. & adj. (also **fas′cist**). **Fa•scis′tic** adj. (also **fa•scis′tic**).

fash•ion /fáshən/ • n. **1** current popular custom or style, esp. in dress. **2** manner or style of doing something. • v.tr. make or form. □ **after** (or **in**) **a fashion** as well as is practicable, though not satisfactorily. □□ **fash′ion•er** n.

■ n. **1** mode, vogue, trend, look, fad. **2** mode, way. • v. model, style, shape, mold, forge, create.

fash•ion•a•ble /fáshənəbəl/ adj. **1** following, suited to, or influenced by the current fashion. **2** characteristic of or favored by those who are leaders of social fashion. □□ **fash′ion•a•bly** adv.

■ in fashion, chic, à la mode, modish, voguish, in vogue, in, colloq. with it, all the go, colloq. often derog. trendy.

fast[1] /fast/ • adj. **1** rapid; quick-moving. **2** capable of or intended for high speed (a fast car). **3** ahead of the correct time. **4** (of a photographic film) needing only a short exposure. **5** firmly fixed or attached. **6** (of a color) not fading. **7** immoral; dissipated. • adv. **1** quickly; in quick succession. **2** firmly; fixedly; tightly; securely. **3** soundly; completely (fast asleep). □ **fast food** food that can be prepared and served quickly and easily, esp. in a snack bar or restaurant.

■ adj. **1, 2** quick, swift, speedy, brisk, colloq. zippy; hurried, hasty, high-speed, express. **5** fastened, secured, tied, bound, connected; firm, secure, stable, steadfast, staunch. **7** loose, profligate, dissolute, unrestrained, wild, promiscuous, lecherous. • adv. **1** quick, swiftly, rapidly, speedily, briskly, hastily, hurriedly. **2** soundly, tight, immovably, solidly, unshakably. **3** see completely (COMPLETE).

fast[2] /fast/ • v.intr. abstain from all or some kinds of food or drink. • n. act or period of fasting. □□ **fast′er** n.

■ v. go hungry, deny oneself, diet, starve (oneself). • n. diet; hunger strike; sacrifice.

fast•en /fásən/ v.tr. **1** make or become fixed or secure. **2** lock securely; shut in. **3 a** direct (a look, thoughts, etc.) fixedly or intently. **b** focus or direct the attention fixedly upon. □□ **fas′ten•er** n.

■ **1** fix, attach, bind, bond, stick, affix, anchor; tie, lock, secure; join, connect, link, fuse, cement, clamp. **2** see LOCK¹ v. 1.

3 a fix, rivet, focus, aim, point.

fast•en•ing /fásəning/ n. device that fastens something; fastener.

■ catch, clasp, clip, lock, tie.

fas•tid•i•ous /fastídeeəs/ adj. **1** very careful in matters of choice or taste; fussy. **2** easily disgusted; squeamish. □□ **fas•tid′i•ous•ly** adv. **fas•tid′i•ous•ness** n.

■ **1** meticulous, finicky, particular, difficult, critical, colloq. picky. **2** see SQUEAMISH 1.

fast•ness /fástnis/ n. **1** stronghold or fortress. **2** state of being secure.

fat /fat/ ● n. **1** natural oily or greasy substance occurring esp. in animal bodies. **2** part of anything containing this. **3** overabundance or excess. ● adj. (**fat•ter**, **fat•test**) **1** corpulent; plump. **2** containing much fat. **3** (of land or resources) fertile; yielding abundantly. **4** thick; substantial. **5** colloq. iron. very little; not much (fat chance). □ **fat cat** sl. **1** wealthy person, esp. as a benefactor. **2** highly paid executive or official. □□ **fat′less** adj. **fat′ly** adv. **fat′ness** n. **fat′tish** adj.

■ adj. **1** obese, stout, overweight, chubby, pudgy, paunchy. **3** fruitful, profitable; rich. **4** see BULKY, SUBSTANTIAL 1. □ **fat cat 1** see TYCOON. **2** see DIGNITARY. □□ **fatness** obesity, stoutness, corpulence, embonpoint, portliness, plumpness, chubbiness, rotundity, pudginess.

fa•tal /fáytəl/ adj. **1** causing or ending in death (fatal accident). **2** ruinous (made a fatal mistake). □□ **fa′tal•ly** adv.

■ **1** deadly, lethal, mortal, murderous, final, terminal. **2** destructive, fateful, calamitous, disastrous, catastrophic, devastating, cataclysmic, dreadful.

fa•tal•ism /fáytlizəm/ n. **1** belief that all events are predetermined and therefore inevitable. **2** submissive acceptance. □□ **fa′tal•ist** n. **fa•tal•is′tic** adj. **fa•tal•is′ti•cal•ly** adv.

fa•tal•i•ty /fōtálətee, fay-/ n. (pl. **-ties**) **1** occurrence of death by accident or in war, etc. **2** fatal influence.

■ **1** casualty, killing.

fate /fayt/ ● n. **1** a power regarded as predetermining events unalterably. **2 a** the future regarded as determined by such a power. **b** an individual's appointed lot. **3** death; destruction. ● v.tr. preordain.

■ n. **1** fortune, luck, chance, life, destiny, providence, kismet. **2** future, end, outcome; see also DESTINY. **3** doom, downfall, undoing, ruin, disaster, nemesis, end, finish. ● v. predestine, destine, ordain, doom.

fate•ful /fáytfool/ adj. **1** important; decisive. **2** controlled as if by fate. □□ **fate′ful•ly** adv. **fate′ful•ness** n.

■ **1** significant, consequential, momentous, critical, crucial, portentous, earthshaking, pivotal.

fa•ther /fáathər/ ● n. **1** male parent. **2** [usu. in pl.] progenitor or forefather. **3** originator, designer, or early leader. **4** (also **Father**) (often as a title or form of address) priest. **5** (**the Father**) (in Christian belief) first person of the Trinity. **6** [usu. in pl.] elders (city fathers). ● v.tr. **1** beget; be the father of. **2** originate (a scheme, etc.). □ **father figure** older man who is respected like a father.

father-in-law (pl. **fa•thers-in-law**) father of one's husband or wife. □□ **fa′ther•hood** n. **fa′ther•less** adj. **fa′ther•like** adj. & adv.

■ n. **1** paterfamilias, old-fashioned papa, colloq. dad, daddy, old man, pa, pop. **2** forebear, ancestor, primogenitor. **3** creator, founder, initiator, inventor. **4** confessor, minister, pastor, parson, chaplain, padre. **5** see CREATOR¹ 2. **6** (fathers) see ELDER n. ● v. **1** procreate, sire, engender. **2** found, invent, establish, initiate.

fa•ther•land /fáathərland/ n. one's native country.

■ native land, motherland, homeland, birthplace.

fa•ther•ly /fáathərlee/ adj. like or of a father. □□ **fa′ther•li•ness** n.

■ fatherlike, paternal, protective, kindly, kind, warm.

fath•om /fáthəm/ ● n. (pl. often **fath•om** when prec. by a number) measure of six feet, esp. used in taking depth soundings. ● v.tr. **1** grasp or comprehend. **2** measure the depth of. □□ **fath′om•a•ble** adj. **fath′om•less** adj.

■ v. **1** understand, penetrate, divine, determine, ascertain, work out, sound out. **2** gauge, plumb, sound

fa•tigue /fəteeg/ ● n. **1** extreme tiredness. **2** weakness in materials, esp. metal. **3 a** nonmilitary duty in the army. **b** [in pl.] clothing worn for this. ● v.tr. (**fa•tigues**, **fa•tigued**, **fa•tigu•ing**) cause fatigue in. See synonym study at TIRED. □□ **fat•i•ga•ble** /-gəbəl/ adj. **fat•i•ga•bil′i•ty** n. **fa•tigue′less** adj.

■ n. **1** weariness, exhaustion, lassitude, weakness, enervation, lethargy. **2** see WEAKNESS 1, 2. ● v. tire, weary, exhaust, weaken, drain, enervate.

fat•ten /fát'n/ v. make or become fat.

fat•ty /fátee/ adj. (**fat•ti•er**, **fat•ti•est**) like or containing fat. □ **fatty acid** Chem. organic compound that bonds to glycerol to form a fat molecule. □□ **fat′ti•ly** adv. **fat′ti•ness** n.

fat•u•ous /fáchōōəs/ adj. vacantly silly; purposeless; idiotic. □□ **fa•tu•i•ty** /fətóoitee, -tyóo-/ n. (pl. **-ties**). **fat′u•ous•ly** adv. **fat′u•ous•ness** n.

fat•wa /fátwaa/ n. (in Islamic countries) authoritative ruling on a religious matter.

fau•cet /fáwsit/ n. device by which a flow of liquid from a pipe or vessel can be controlled.

■ spigot, cock, spout, valve.

fault /fawlt/ ● n. **1** defect or imperfection. **2** transgression, offense. **3** Tennis service of the ball not in accordance with the rules. **4** responsibility for wrongdoing, error, etc. **5** Geol. extended break in the continuity of strata or a vein. See synonym study at SIN. ● v.tr. find fault with; blame. □ **at fault** guilty; to blame. **find fault** [often foll. by with] make an adverse criticism; complain. **to a fault** excessively.

■ *n.* **1** blemish, flaw, deficiency, shortcoming; frailty, foible. **2** sin, trespass, misdeed, misdemeanor, vice, indiscretion; mistake, error, lapse, failure, oversight, gaffe, blunder. **4** blame, culpability, accountability, liability; responsibility, guilt. **5** see BREAK *n.* 1. ● *v.* censure, criticize; call to account, accuse. □ **at fault** culpable, in the wrong, blamable; responsible, liable. **find fault** (*find fault with*) criticize, censure, take exception to, pick on. **to a fault** extremely, to an extreme, exceedingly, unduly.

SYNONYM STUDY: fault

BLEMISH, DEFECT, FAILING, FLAW, FOIBLE, SHORTCOMING. No one is perfect. But when it comes to cataloging your own imperfections, it's best to start with your **foibles**—the slight weaknesses or eccentricities for which you will be most quickly forgiven. You also have a good chance of being forgiven for your **shortcomings**, which are not necessarily damaging to others (*his inability to analyze his own actions was one of his shortcomings*). **Failing** suggests a more severe shortcoming, usually with more serious consequences (*chronic tardiness was one of her failings*), but a *failing* can also be a weakness of character that you're not responsible for and perhaps not even aware of (*pride is a common failing among those who have met with great success early in life*). **Fault** also implies failure—but not necessarily a serious failure—to reach moral perfection (*his major fault was his outspokenness*). While *fault* usually indicates something inherent in your nature rather than external to it, a **flaw** can be either superficial (*a flaw in his otherwise immaculate appearance*) or profound (*a personality flaw that made her impossible to work with*), and it can refer to things as well as people (*a flaw in the table's finish*). A **blemish** is usually a physical flaw (*a facial blemish*), although it can be anything that disfigures or mars the perfection of someone or something (*a blemish on her otherwise spotless academic record*). You can get rid of a blemish and even overcome your shortcomings, but a **defect** is a flaw so serious that you may never be able to get rid of it (*a defect in his hearing*).

---

fault•find•ing /fáwltfīnding/ *n.* continual criticism.

■ censure, carping, caviling, captiousness.

fault•less /fáwltlis/ *adj.* without fault; free from defect or error. □□ **fault′less•ly** *adv.* **fault′less•ness** *n.*

■ flawless, immaculate; perfect, ideal, exemplary.

fault•y /fáwltee/ (**fault•i•er, fault•i•est**) *adj.* having faults; imperfect; defective. □□ **fault′i•ly** *adv.* **fault′i•ness** *n.*

■ flawed, unsound; impaired; out of order; damaged.

faun /fawn/ *n.* Roman rural deity with a human face and torso and a goat's horns, legs, and tail.

fau•na /fáwnə/ *n.* (*pl.* **fau•nas** or **fau•nae** /-nee/) animal life of a region or geological

period. □□ **fau′nal** *adj.* **fau′nist** *n.* **fau•nis′tic** *adj.*

faux /fō/ *adj.* imitation; counterfeit (*faux emeralds*).

faux pas /fō paá/ *n.* (*pl.* same, *pronunc.* /paáz/) **1** tactless mistake; blunder. **2** social indiscretion.

fa•vor /fáyvər/ ● *n.* **1** act of kindness. **2** esteem; liking; approval; goodwill; friendly regard (*gained their favor*). **3** partiality. **4** small present or token given out, as at a party. ● *v.tr.* **1** regard or treat with favor or partiality. **2** give support or approval to; promote; prefer. **3 a** be to the advantage of (a person). **b** facilitate (a process, etc.). **4** *colloq.* resemble in features. □□ **fa′vor•er** *n.*

■ *n.* **1** courtesy, good *or* kind deed, good turn. **2** (good) opinion, consideration, grace; approbation. **3** favoritism, preference, bias, prejudice; leniency. ● *v.* **1, 2** have a liking *or* preference for, be partial to, like, side with; incline to, go for, opt for; support, back, approve. **3 a** see BENEFIT *v.* 1. **b** help, benefit, aid, assist, expedite. **4** see RESEMBLE.

fa•vor•a•ble /fáyvərəbəl/ *adj.* **1 a** well-disposed; propitious. **b** commendatory; approving. **2** giving consent (*a favorable answer*). **3** promising; auspicious. **4** helpful; suitable. □□ **fa′vor•a•ble•ness** *n.* **fa′vor•a•bly** *adv.*

■ **1 a, 3** fair, encouraging; satisfactory, advantageous, beneficial. **1 b** laudatory, enthusiastic, eager, good, positive, encouraging. **2** see WILLING *adj.* **4** see *advantageous* (ADVANTAGE). □□ **favorably** enthusiastically, positively, sympathetically, agreeably.

fa•vor•ite /fáyvərit, fáyvrit/ ● *adj.* preferred to all others (*my favorite book*). ● *n.* **1** particularly favored person. **2** *Sports* competitor thought most likely to win.

■ *adj.* beloved, best-liked, most-liked. ● *n.* **1** darling, pet, apple of one's eye, ideal, preference.

fa•vor•it•ism /fáyvəritizəm, fáyvri–/ *n.* unfair partiality.

■ bias, prepossession, prejudice, partisanship.

fawn[1] /fawn/ ● *n.* **1** young deer in its first year. **2** light yellowish brown. ● *adj.* fawn colored.

fawn[2] /fawn/ *v.intr.* **1** (of a person) behave servilely; cringe. **2** (of an animal, esp. a dog) show extreme affection. □□ **fawn′er** *n.* **fawn′ing** *adj.* **fawn′ing•ly** *adv.*

fax /faks/ ● *n.* **1** facsimile transmission (see FACSIMILE 2). **2** copy produced by this. ● *v.tr.* transmit in this way.

faze /fayz/ *v.tr.* (often as **fazed** *adj.*) *colloq.* disconcert; perturb; disorient.

FBI *abbr.* Federal Bureau of Investigation.

FCC *abbr.* Federal Communications Commission.

FDA *abbr.* Food and Drug Administration.

FDIC *abbr.* Federal Deposit Insurance Corporation.

Fe *symb. Chem.* iron.

fe•al•ty /fée∂ltee/ *n.* (*pl.* **–ties**) **1** *hist.* feudal tenant's or vassal's fidelity to a lord. **2** allegiance.

fear /feer/ ● *n.* **1** panic or distress caused by

exposure to danger, expectation of pain, etc. **2** cause of fear (*all fears removed*). **3** danger. • *v.* **1 a** *tr.* feel fear about or toward (a person or thing). **b** *intr.* feel fear. **2** *intr.* [foll. by *for*] feel anxiety about. □□ **fear′less** *adj.* **fear′less•ly** *adv.* **fear′less•ness** *n.*

■ *n.* **1** dread, terror, horror; fright, timidity; alarm, trepidation, apprehension. **2** horror, specter, nightmare, bogey, phobia. **3** see DANGER. • *v.* **1 a** be afraid or scared or fearful or frightened of; dread. **b** be afraid or scared or fearful or frightened; tremble, shudder. **2** see WORRY *v.* **1.** □□ **fearless** courageous, brave, bold, intrepid, daring, audacious.

fear•ful /féerfŏŏl/ *adj.* **1** afraid. **2** terrible, awful. □□ **fear′ful•ly** *adv.* **fear′ful•ness** *n.*

■ **1** scared, frightened, terrified, alarmed, intimidated, jumpy, nervous, edgy, cowardly, timid, *colloq.* yellow, jittery. **2** dire, dreadful, frightful, appalling, ghastly, atrocious; terrifying, frightening, horrifying, fearsome. □□ **fearfully** anxiously, edgily, nervously, hesitantly; frightfully, awfully, terribly.

fear•some /féersəm/ *adj.* appalling or frightening, esp. in appearance. □□ **fear′some•ly** *adv.* **fear′some•ness** *n.*

■ terrifying, menacing, terrible, dreadful, awesome.

fea•si•ble /féezibəl/ *adj.* practicable, possible. □□ **fea•si•bil•i•ty** /féezibilitee/ *n.* **fea′si•bly** *adv.*

■ workable, doable, viable, realizable, achievable, attainable, realistic.

feast /feest/ • *n.* **1** large or sumptuous meal, esp. with entertainment. **2** gratification to the senses or mind. **3** religious festival. • *v.intr.* partake of a feast; eat and drink sumptuously. □ **feast one's eyes** on take pleasure in beholding. □□ **feast′er** *n.*

■ *n.* **1** banquet, *colloq.* spread. **2** treat, delight, pleasure; see also *gratification* (GRATIFY). **3** celebration, feast day, holy day, saint's day. • *v.* dine, wine and dine; gorge (oneself); indulge.

feat /feet/ *n.* noteworthy act or achievement.

■ accomplishment, exploit, deed, act, tour de force.

feath•er /féthər/ • *n.* any of the appendages growing from a bird's skin, with a horny hollow stem and fine strands. • *v.tr.* **1** cover or line with feathers. **2** *Rowing* turn (an oar) so that it passes through the air edgewise. **3** *Aeron.* & *Naut.* cause (propeller blades) to rotate in such a way as to lessen the air or water resistance. □ **feather in one's cap** achievement to one's credit. **feather one's nest** enrich oneself. **in fine** (or **high**) **feather** *colloq.* in good spirits. □□ **feath′ered** *adj.* [also in *comb.*]. **feath′er•less** *adj.* **feath′er•y** *adj.* **feath′er•i•ness** *n.*

feath•er•weight /féthərwayt/ *n.* **1** any of various weight classes in certain sports intermediate between bantamweight and lightweight. **2** very light person or thing.

fea•ture /féechər/ • *n.* **1** distinctive or characteristic part of a thing. **2** [usu. in *pl.*] (a distinctive part of) the face. **3** distinctive or regular article in a newspaper or magazine. **4** (in full **fea′ture film**) full-length movie intended as the main attraction at a showing.

291

fearful ~ feed

• *v.* **1** *tr.* make a special display or attraction of; give special prominence to. **2** *tr.* & *intr.* star. □□ **fea′tured** *adj.* [also in *comb.*]. **fea′ture•less** *adj.*

■ *n.* **1** characteristic, attribute, trait, mark, character, quality. **2** (*features*) face, countenance, looks, *literary* visage. **3** column, article, piece. **4** see FILM *n.* **3.** • *v.* **1** promote, publicize, advertise, *sl.* hype; spotlight. **2** (*intr.*) act, perform, take a role or part; have a role or part, be involved.

Feb. *abbr.* February.

fe•brile /fébral, fée–/ *adj.* of or relating to fever; feverish. □□ **fe•bril•i•ty** /fibrílitee/ *n.*

Feb•ru•ar•y /fébrŏŏeree, fébyŏŏ–/ *n.* (*pl.* **–ies**) second month of the year.

fe•ces /féeseez/ *n.pl.* waste matter discharged from the bowels. □□ **fe•cal** /féekəl/ *adj.*

feck•less /féklis/ *adj.* **1** feeble; ineffective. **2** unthinking; irresponsible. □□ **feck′less•ly** *adv.* **feck′less•ness** *n.*

fe•cund /féekənd, fek–/ *adj.* **1** prolific; fertile. **2** fertilizing. See synonym study at FERTILE. □□ **fe•cun•di•ty** /fikúnditee/ *n.*

fed past and past part. of FEED. □ **fed up** [often foll. by *with*] discontented; bored.

fed•er•al /fédərəl/ *adj.* **1** of a system of government in which several states or provinces, etc., form a union but remain independent in internal affairs. **2** of such a federation (*federal laws*). □ **Federal Reserve System** national system of reserve cash available to banks. □□ **fed′er•al•ism** *n.* **fed′er•al•ist** *n.* **fed•er•al•ize** *v.tr.* **fed•er•al•i•za′tion** *n.* **fed′er•al•ly** *adv.*

■ see NATIONAL *adj.*

fed•er•ate /fédərayt/ *v.* unite on a federal basis. □□ **fed•er•a•tive** /fédəraytiv, –rətiv/ *adj.*

fed•er•a•tion /fédəráyshən/ *n.* **1** federal system or group. **2** the act or an instance of federating. □□ **fed•er•a′tion•ist** *n.*

■ **1** confederacy, confederation, society, association, league. **2** amalgamation, alliance, union.

fe•do•ra /fidáwrə/ *n.* soft felt hat with a curled brim.

fee /fee/ *n.* **1** payment made for professional advice or services. **2** entrance or access charge.

■ **1** wage, rate, stipend, salary; pay. **2** price, cost, bill, payment.

fee•ble /féebəl/ *adj.* **1** weak; infirm. **2** lacking energy, effectiveness, etc. See synonym study at WEAK. □□ **fee′ble•ness** *n.* **fee′blish** *adj.* **fee′bly** *adv.*

■ **1** frail, puny, slight; debilitated, enfeebled; sickly, ailing. **2** weak, effete, half-baked, lame, flimsy, unconvincing, shoddy, thin, ineffectual, feckless.

fee•ble•mind•ed /féebəlmíndid/ *adj.* mentally deficient. □□ **fee′ble•mind′ed•ly** *adv.* **fee′ble•mind′ed•ness** *n.*

■ unintelligent, stupid, simple, dull, dullwitted, witless, simpleminded, imbecile, mentally defective, weak-minded, retarded, halfwitted, softheaded, moronic, idiotic.

feed /feed/ • *v.* (*past* and *past part.* **fed** /fed/) **1** *tr.* **a** supply with food. **b** put food into the mouth of. **2** *tr.* give as food, esp. to animals. **3** *intr.* (esp. of animals, or *colloq.* of people) take food; eat. **4** *tr.* nourish; make grow. **5 a** *tr.* maintain supply of raw material, fuel, etc., to (a fire, machine, etc.). **b** *tr.* supply or send (an electronic signal) for broadcast, etc. **c** *intr.* flow into. **6** *tr.* [foll. by *on*] be nourished by. **b** derive benefit from. **7** *tr.* gratify (vanity, etc.). **8** *tr.* provide (advice, information, etc.) to. • *n.* food, esp. for animals. □□ **feed′a•ble** *adj.* **feed′er** *n.*

■ *v.* **1 a** provision, cater *or* provide for; maintain, board. **3** graze, pasture; see also EAT *v.* 1b; (*feed on*) see EAT *v.* 1a. **4** nurture; sustain; see also NOURISH 1. **5 a** fuel; stoke. **6** (*feed on*) **a** subsist *or* survive *or* depend on. **b** thrive on *or* upon. **7** see PANDER *v.* **8** see ADVISE 3. • *n.* fodder, provender, forage, silage.

feed•back /féedbak/ *n.* **1** information about the result of an experiment, etc.; response. **2** *Electronics* return of a fraction of the output signal to the input.

feel /feel/ • *v.* (*past* and *past part.* **felt** /felt/) **1** *tr.* **a** examine or search by touch. **b** [*absol.*] have the sensation of touch. **2** *tr.* perceive or ascertain by touch. **3** *tr.* experience, exhibit, or be conscious of (an emotion, conviction, etc.). **4** *tr.* have a vague or unreasoned impression. **5** *tr.* consider; think. **6** *intr.* seem. **7** *intr.* be consciously; consider oneself (*I feel happy*). **8** *intr.* have sympathy or pity. • *n.* **1** feeling; testing by touch. **2** attendant sensation. **3** sense of touch. □ **feel like** have a wish for; be inclined toward. **feel up to** be ready to face or deal with. **feel one's way** proceed carefully; act cautiously.

■ *v.* **1 a** touch, handle, manipulate, finger. **2** note; see also SENSE *v.* **3** undergo, suffer, bear, endure, withstand; sense. **4, 5** sense, believe, perceive, judge, know, discern, intuit. **6** appear; give an impression of being. **7** seem to be, regard *or* characterize oneself as. **8** sympathize *or* empathize with, commiserate with, be sorry for. • *n.* **2** texture, touch; feeling, air, atmosphere, climate. □ **feel like** wear, desire, crave, *colloq.* fancy.

feel•er /féelər/ *n.* **1** organ in certain animals for sensing or for searching for food. **2** tentative proposal.

■ **1** antenna, tentacle, palp.

feel•ing /féeling/ • *n.* **1 a** capacity to feel; sense of touch. **b** physical sensation. **2 a** emotional reaction. **b** [in *pl.*] emotional susceptibilities or sympathies (*hurt my feelings*). **3** particular sensitivity. **4 a** intuition or notion. **b** general sentiment. **5** readiness to feel sympathy or compassion. **6** emotional commitment or sensibility. • *adj.* sensitive; sympathetic; heartfelt. □□ **feel′ing•less** *adj.* **feel′ing•ly** *adv.*

■ *n.* **1** sensibility, sensitivity, sensation, sense; feel. **2 a** mood, atmosphere, climate; see also EMOTION[1]. **b** (*feelings*) sympathies, emotions, sensibilities. **3** appreciation, sympathy, empathy, identification, compassion. **4 a** opinion, view; idea, instinct, inkling. **b** see ATTITUDE 1. **5, 6** see *sensitivity* (SENSI-

TIVE), IMPRESSION 1. • *adj.* tenderhearted, compassionate; see also TENDER 5.

feet *pl.* of FOOT.

feign /fayn/ *v.tr.* simulate; pretend.

feint /faynt/ • *n.* **1** sham attack or diversionary blow. **2** pretense. • *v.intr.* make a feint.

■ *n.* **1** mock attack, distraction, diversion; see also MANEUVER *n.* 1, 3. **2** bluff, ruse, subterfuge, deception. • *v.* see MANEUVER *v.* 3.

feld•spar /féldspaar/ *n.* (also **felspar** /félspaar/) *Mineral.* group of aluminum silicates of potassium, sodium, or calcium. □□ **feld•spath•ic** /–spáthik/ *adj.* **feld•spath•oid** /féldspəthoyd, félspə–/ *n.*

fe•lic•i•tate /fəlísitayt/ *v.tr.* congratulate. □□ **fe•lic•i•ta•tion** /–táyshən/ *n.* [usu. in *pl.*].

fe•lic•i•tous /fəlísitəs/ *adj.* strikingly apt; pleasantly ingenious. □□ **fe•lic′i•tous•ly** *adv.* **fe•lic′i•tous•ness** *n.*

■ see APPROPRIATE *adj.*

fe•lic•i•ty /fəlísitee/ *n.* (*pl.* **–ties**) **1** intense happiness. **2 a** capacity for apt expression. **b** well-chosen phrase.

fe•line /féelin/ • *adj.* **1** of the cat family. **2** catlike. • *n.* animal of the cat family. □□ **fe•lin•i•ty** /filínitee/ *n.*

fell[1] *past* of FALL *v.*

fell[2] /fel/ *v.tr.* **1** cut down (esp. a tree). **2** strike or knock down (a person or animal). □□ **fell′er** *n.*

■ **1** hew (down). **2** cut *or* knock down, floor.

fell[3] /fel/ *adj. poet.* or *rhet.* ruthless; destructive. □ **at** (or **in**) **one fell swoop** in a single (orig. deadly) action.

fel•low /félō/ *n.* **1** *colloq.* man or boy. **2** [usu. in *pl.*] comrade. **3** counterpart or match; other of a pair. **4** holder of a fellowship. **5** member of a learned society. **6** [*attrib.*] belonging to the same class or activity.

■ **1** gentleman, person, individual, *colloq.* guy. **2** associate, companion, colleague, ally; see also COMRADE. **3** complement, mate, partner. **6** associate(d), affiliate(d), allied, related.

fel•low•ship /félōship/ *n.* **1** companionship; friendliness. **2** participation; sharing; community of interest. **3** body of associates. **4** financial grant to a scholar.

■ **1** friendship, amity, comradeship; friendliness, amicability, sociability. **2** see RAPPORT. **3** company, circle, community, order, organization, society, club; see also ASSOCIATION 1.

fel•on /félən/ *n.* person who has committed a felony.

■ criminal, outlaw, lawbreaker, offender, miscreant.

fe•lo•ni•ous /fəlṓneeəs/ *adj.* **1** criminal. **2** *Law* **a** of or involving felony. **b** who has committed a felony. □□ **fe•lo′ni•ous•ly** *adv.*

■ **1, 2a** see ILLEGAL 2. **2 b** see MISCREANT *adj.*

fel•o•ny /félənee/ *n.* (*pl.* **–nies**) serious, often violent, crime.

felt[1] /felt/ • *n.* cloth of matted and pressed fibers of wool, etc. • *v.tr.* make into felt. □□ **felt′y** *adj.*

felt[2] *past* and *pastpart.* of FEEL.

FEMA /féemə/ *abbr.* Federal Emergency Management Agency.

fe•male /féemayl/ • adj. **1** of the sex that can bear offspring or produce eggs. **2** (of plants) fruit-bearing. **3** of women or female animals or female plants. **4** (of a screw, socket, etc.) hollow to receive an inserted part. • n. female person, animal, or plant. □□ **fe′male•ness** n.

fem•i•nine /féminin/ • adj. **1** of women. **2** having womanly qualities. **3** *Gram.* of or denoting the gender proper to women's names. • n. *Gram.* feminine gender or word. □□ **fem′i•nine•ly** adv. **fem′i•nine•ness** n. **fem•i•nin•i•ty** /–nínitee/ n.

■ adj. **1** female, womanlike, womanly, ladylike.

fem•i•nism /féminizəm/ n. advocacy of women's rights on the ground of the equality of the sexes. □□ **fem′i•nist** n.

femme fa•tale /fém fətál, –taál, fay–/ n. (pl. **femmes fa•tales** pronunc. same) seductively attractive woman.

fe•mur /féemər/ n. (pl. **fe•murs** or **fem•o•ra** /fémərə/) *Anat.* thigh bone. □□ **fem•o•ral** /fémərəl/ adj.

fen /fen/ n. low marshy or flooded land.

fence /fens/ • n. **1** barrier, railing, etc., enclosing an area of ground. **2** sl. receiver of stolen goods. • v. **1** tr. surround with or as with a fence. **2** tr. enclose, separate or confine with or as with a fence. **3** tr. [also absol.] sl. deal in (stolen goods). **4** intr. practice the sport of fencing; use a sword. **5** intr. evade answering. □□ **fence′less** adj. **fenc′er** n.

■ n. **1** palisade, enclosure; confine, wall. • v. **1** enclose, encircle, circumscribe, hedge, bound. **2** coop (up or in), confine, hedge in. **5** hedge; (fence with) parry, avoid, dodge; see also DUCK[1] v. **3**.

fenc•ing /fénsing/ n. **1** set or extent of fences. **2** material for making fences. **3** art or sport of swordplay.

fend /fend/ v. **1** intr. [foll. by for] look after (esp. oneself). **2** tr. [usu. foll. by off] keep away; ward off (an attack, etc.).

■ **1** (fend for oneself) get along (on one's own), make do, shift for oneself, colloq. get by. **2** (fend off) keep at bay, fight off, parry, resist.

fend•er /féndər/ n. **1** low frame bordering a fireplace. **2** shieldlike device or enclosure over or around the wheel of a motor vehicle, bicycle, etc.

feng shui /fúng shwáy, –shwé/ • n. Asian system of building construction and interior design to increase positive energy flow.

fen•nel /fénəl/ n. yellow-flowered fragrant umbelliferous plant used as flavoring.

fen-phen /fénfen/ • n. drug combining fenfluramine and phentermine, formerly prescribed for weight loss.

fe•ral /féerəl, férəl/ adj. **1** (of an animal or plant) wild; untamed; uncultivated. **2** savage; brutal.

■ **1, 2** see WILD adj. **1**. **2** see VICIOUS **1**.

fer•ment • n. /fórment/ **1** agitation; excitement; tumult. **2 a** fermentation. **b** fermenting agent or leaven. • v. /fərmént/ **1** intr. & tr. undergo or subject to fermentation. **2** intr. & tr. effervesce or cause to effervesce.

3 tr. excite; stir up; foment. □□ **fer•ment′a•ble** adj. **fer•ment′er** n.

■ v. **1** leaven, brew; stir up, simmer, seethe. **2** bubble, foam, froth; boil, seethe. **3** agitate, inflame, rouse; foment, incite, instigate.

fer•men•ta•tion /fórmentáyshən/ n. **1** breakdown of a substance by microorganisms, such as yeasts and bacteria, usu. in the absence of oxygen, esp. of sugar in making alcohol. **2** agitation; excitement. □□ **fer•men•ta•tive** /–méntətiv/ adj.

fer•mi•um /fórmeeəm, fér–/ n. *Chem.* transuranic radioactive metallic element produced artificially. ¶Symb.: **Fm**.

fern /fərn/ n. (pl. same or **ferns**) flowerless plant reproducing by spores and usu. having feathery fronds. □□ **fern′er•y** n. (pl. **–ies**). **fern′less** adj. **fern′y** adj.

fe•ro•cious /fəróshəs/ adj. fierce; savage; wildly cruel. □□ **fe•ro′cious•ly** adv. **fe•ro′cious•ness** n.

■ wild, feral, vicious, brutal, bestial, merciless, ruthless, pitiless, inhuman, barbaric, murderous.

fe•roc•i•ty /fərósitee/ n. (pl. **–ties**) ferocious nature or act.

■ see VIOLENCE **1**.

-ferous /fərəs/ comb. form (usu. **–iferous**) forming adjectives with the sense 'bearing,' 'having' (auriferous). □□ **–ferously** suffix forming adverbs. **–ferousness** suffix forming nouns.

fer•ret /férit/ • n. **1** small semidomesticated polecat, used in catching rabbits, rats, etc. • v. **1** intr. hunt with ferrets. **2** intr. rummage; search out. □□ **fer′ret•er** n. **fer′ret•y** adj.

fer•ric /férik/ adj. of iron.

Fer•ris wheel /téris/ n. carnival ride consisting of a tall revolving vertical wheel with passenger cars.

ferro- /férō/ comb. form *Chem.* **1** iron, esp. in ferrous compounds (ferrocyanide). **2** (of alloys) containing iron.

fer•rous /férəs/ adj. containing iron.

fer•rule /férōōl/ n. ring or cap on the end of a stick or tube.

fer•ry /féree/ • n. (pl. **–ries**) **1** boat or aircraft, etc., for conveying passengers and goods, esp. across water. **2** the service itself or the place where it operates. • v. (**–ries**, **–ried**) **1** tr. & intr. convey or go in a ferry. **2** tr. transport from one place to another, esp. as a regular service. □□ **fer′ry•man** /–man/ n. (pl. **–men**)

fer•tile /fórt'l/ adj. **1 a** (of soil) producing abundant vegetation or crops. **b** fruitful. **2 a** (of a seed, egg, etc.) capable of becoming a new individual. **b** (of animals and plants) able to reproduce. **3** inventive. □□ **fer•til•i•ty** /–tilitee/ n.

■ **1** productive; see also FRUITFUL **1**. **2 b** fecund; productive, prolific. **3** teeming, prolific, rich.

SYNONYM STUDY: fertile

FECUND, FRUITFUL, PROLIFIC. A **fertile** woman is one who has the power to produce offspring, just as *fertile* soil produces crops and a *fertile* imagination produces ideas. This adjective pertains to anything in which seeds (or thoughts) can take root and grow. A woman with ten children might be described as **fecund**, which means that she is not only capable of producing many offspring but has actually done it. A woman can be *fertile*, in other words, without necessarily being *fecund*. **Fruitful**, whose meaning is very close to that of *fecund* when used to describe plants and may replace *fertile* in reference to soil or land, pertains specifically to something that promotes fertility or fecundity (*a fruitful downpour*). It can also apply in a broader sense to anything that bears or promotes results (*a fruitful idea; a fruitful discussion*). When applied to people, though, it generally has Biblical overtones (*be fruitful and multiply*). While it's one thing to call a woman with a large family *fecund*, **prolific** is more usually applied to animals or plants in the literal sense of fertility, and suggests reproducing in great quantity or with rapidity. Figuratively, *prolific* is often used of highly productive creative efforts (*a prolific author with 40 titles published*).

fer•til•ize /fórt'līz/ *v.tr.* **1** make (soil, etc.) fertile or productive. **2** cause (an egg, female animal, or plant) to develop or gestate by mating. □□ **fer'ti•liz•a•ble** *adj.* **fer•ti•li•za'tion** *n.*

■ **1** manure, mulch, feed, nourish, compost. **2** impregnate, inseminate, fecundate, fructify, pollinate.

fer•til•iz•er /fórt'līzər/ *n.* chemical or natural substance added to soil to make it more fertile.

fer•vent /fórvənt/ *adj.* **1** ardent; impassioned; intense (*fervent hatred*). **2** hot; glowing. See synonym study at EAGER. □□ **fer'ven•cy** *n.* **fer'vent•ly** *adv.*

■ **1** eager, earnest, enthusiastic, zealous, animated, passionate, fiery; rapturous. **2** inflamed, burning.

fer•vid /fórvid/ *adj.* ardent; intense. □□ **fer'vid•ly** *adv.*

fer•vor /fórvər/ *n.* vehemence; passion; zeal.

■ fervency, ardor, eagerness, earnestness, enthusiasm.

fes•tal /fést'l/ *adj.* **1** joyous; merry. **2** engaging in holiday activities. **3** of a feast.

fes•ter /féstər/ *v.* **1** *tr. & intr.* make or become septic. **2** *intr.* cause continuing annoyance. **3** *intr.* rot; stagnate.

■ **1** suppurate, decompose; see also ROT *v.* 1. **2** see RANKLE. **3** putrefy, mortify, decay, decompose.

fes•ti•val /féstivəl/ *n.* **1** day or period of celebration, religious or secular. **2** series of cultural events.

■ **1** holiday, holy day, fête, fiesta, feast, carnival.

fes•tive /féstiv/ *adj.* **1** of or characteristic of a festival. **2** joyous. **3** fond of feasting; jovial. □□ **fes'tive•ly** *adv.* **fes'tive•ness** *n.*

■ **1** see GALA *adj.* 1. **2** see JOLLY *adj.* 1, 2.

fes•tiv•i•ty /festívitee/ *n.* (*pl.* **–ties**) **1** gaiety; rejoicing. **2 a** festive celebration. **b** [in *pl.*] festive proceedings.

■ **1** mirth, jubilation, conviviality, merriment, revelry. **2** festival, party; see also *celebration* (CELEBRATE).

fes•toon /festoon/ • *n.* chain of flowers, leaves, ribbons, etc., hung in a curve as a decoration. • *v.tr.* adorn with or form into festoons; decorate elaborately. □□ **fes•toon'er•y** *n.*

fet•a /fétə/ *n.* crumbly white Greek-style cheese made of sheep's or goat's milk.

fetch /fech/ *v.tr.* **1** go for and bring back (a person or thing). **2** be sold for; realize (a price). □□ **fetch'er** *n.*

■ **1** retrieve, obtain; summon, call, bring *or* draw forth. **2** sell for, go for, bring in, yield, earn, make.

fetch•ing /féching/ *adj.* attractive. □□ **fetch'ing•ly** *adv.*

■ alluring, taking, winsome, winning, *colloq.* cute.

fête /fayt, fet/ • *n.* **1** great entertainment; festival. **2** saint's day. • *v.tr.* honor or entertain lavishly.

■ *n.* **1** celebration, party, frolic, festivities, reception, *colloq.* get-together, social, shindig, jamboree, carnival. • *v.* celebrate, lionize, make a fuss of *or* over.

fet•id /fétid, féetid/ *adj.* (also **foet'id**) stinking. □□ **fet'id•ly** *adv.* **fet'id•ness** *n.*

fe•tish /fétish/ *n.* **1** *Psychol.* thing abnormally stimulating or attracting sexual desire. **2 a** inanimate object worshiped as magic. **b** thing evoking irrational devotion or respect. □□ **fet'ish•ism** *n.* **fet'ish•ist** *n.* **fet•ish•is'tic** *adj.*

■ **2 a** charm, amulet, talisman, totem. **b** obsession, mania, compulsion, fixation, *idée fixe.*

fet•lock /fétlok/ *n.* **1** part of the back of a horse's leg above the hoof where a tuft of hair grows. **2** such a tuft of hair.

fet•ter /fétər/ • *n.* **1 a** shackle for holding a prisoner by the ankles. **b** any shackle or bond. **2** [in *pl.*] captivity. **3** restraint or check. • *v.tr.* **1** put into fetters. **2** restrict.

■ *n.* **1, 3** see TETHER *n.* • *v.* see CHAIN *v.*

fet•tle /fét'l/ *n.* condition or trim (*in fine fettle*).

fe•tus /féetəs/ *n.* unborn or unhatched offspring of a mammal, esp. a human one more than eight weeks after conception. □□ **fe'tal** *adj.*

feud /fyood/ • *n.* prolonged mutual hostility, esp. between two families, tribes, etc. See synonym study at QUARREL. • *v.intr.* conduct a feud.

■ *n.* vendetta, blood feud; quarrel, dispute. • *v.* quarrel, fall out, dispute, disagree, clash.

feu•dal /fyood'l/ *adj.* of, according to, or resembling the feudal system. □ **feudal system** medieval social system whereby a vassal held land from a superior in exchange for allegiance and service. □□ **feu'dal•ism** *n.* **feu'dal•ist** *n.* **feu•dal•is'tic** *adj.* **feu'dal•ly** *adv.*

fe•ver /féevər/ *n.* **1 a** abnormally high body temperature, often with delirium, etc. **b** disease characterized by this (*scarlet fever*).

2 nervous excitement; agitation. □ **fever pitch** state of extreme excitement. □□ **fe′vered** adj.

■ **2** see FRENZY n. 1. □□ **fevered** see IMPASSIONED.

fe•ver•ish /feevərish/ adj. **1** having the symptoms of a fever. **2** excited; restless. □□ **fe′ver•ish•ly** adv. **fe′ver•ish•ness** n.

■ **1** flushed, hot; febrile, pyretic, Med. pyrexic. **2** frenzied; fitful, ardent, fervent, passionate, burning, fiery, heated, hot, inflamed; flushed.

few /fyoō/ • adj. not many. • n. [as pl.] **1** [prec. by a] some but not many. **2** not many. **3** [prec. by the] **a** the minority. **b** the elect. □ **not a few** considerable number.

■ adj. hardly or scarcely any; infrequent, occasional ■ n. **1, 2** one or two; a handful, a scattering, a small number.

fey /fay/ adj. **1** strange; otherworldly; elfin; whimsical. **2** clairvoyant. □□ **fey′ly** adv. **fey′ness** n.

fez /fez/ n. (pl. **fez•zes**) flat-topped conical red cap, worn by men in some Muslim countries. □□ **fezzed** adj.

fi•an•cé /feeonsáy, feeónsay/ n. (fem. **fi•an•cée** pronunc. same) person to whom another is engaged to be married.

■ betrothed, wife to be, bride to be, husband to be.

fi•as•co /feeáskō/ n. (pl. **–cos**) ludicrous or humiliating failure or breakdown; ignominious result.

■ disaster, muddle, mess, botch, sl. flop.

fi•at /féeat, –aat, fíat, fíət/ n. **1** authorization. **2** decree or order.

fib /fib/ • n. trivial or venial lie. • v.intr. (**fibbed, fib•bing**) tell a fib. □□ **fib′ber** n. **fib′ster** n.

■ n. (little) white lie, tale, untruth, falsehood, fabrication, invention, story, fiction. • v. see LIE² v. 1a.

fi•ber /fíbər/ n. **1** Biol. threads or filaments forming tissue or textile. **2** piece of glass in the form of a thread. **3** substance formed of fibers or able to be spun, woven, or felted. **4** structure; character. □ **fiber optics** optics employing thin glass fibers, usu. for the transmission of light, esp. modulated to carry signals. [also in comb.]. **fi′ber•less** adj. **fi•bri•form** /fíbrifawrm/ adj.

■ **1** strand. **4** texture, mold, cast, composition, constitution, makeup, grain.

fi•ber•board /fíbərbawrd/ n. building material made of wood or other plant fibers compressed into boards.

fi•ber•glass /fíbərglas/ n. **1** textile fabric made from woven glass fibers. **2** plastic reinforced by glass fibers.

fi•broid /fíbroyd/ adj. of, like, or containing fibrous tissue, as some benign tumors.

fi•bro•sis /fíbrósis/ n. Med. thickening and scarring of connective tissue. □□ **fi•brot•ic** /–brótik/ adj.

fib•u•la /fíbyələ/ n. (pl. **fib•u•lae** /–lee/ or **fib•u•las**) Anat. smaller and outer of the two bones between the knee and the ankle in terrestrial vertebrates. □□ **fib′u•lar** adj.

-fic /fik/ suffix (usu. as **–ific**) forming adjec-

tives meaning 'producing,' 'making' (prolific, pacific). □□ **–fically** suffix forming adverbs.

FICA /fíkə/ abbr. Federal Insurance Contributions Act.

-fication /fikáyshən/ suffix (usu. as **–ification** /ifikáyshən/) forming nouns of action from verbs in **–fy** (acidification).

fiche /feesh/ n. (pl. same or **fiches**) microfiche.

fick•le /fíkəl/ adj. inconstant or changeable, esp. in loyalty. □□ **fick′le•ness** n. **fick′ly** adv.

■ unfaithful, faithless, disloyal, changeful, unsteady, unsteadfast, wavering, indecisive, uncertain, unsure.

fic•tion /fíkshən/ n. **1** invented idea, thing, etc. **2** literature, esp. novels, describing imaginary events and people. □□ **fic′tion•al** adj. **fic′tion•al•ize** v.tr. **fic•tion•al•i•za′tion** n. **fic′tion•al•ly** adv.

■ **1** see INVENTION 3. **2** see WRITING 3. □□ **fictional** unreal, imaginary, invented, made-up, fanciful.

fic•ti•tious /fiktíshəs/ adj. **1** imaginary; unreal. **2** counterfeit; not genuine. □□ **fic•ti′tious•ly** adv. **fic•ti′tious•ness** n.

■ **1** imagined, fictive, fanciful, fictional, fancied. **2** false, bogus, spurious, made-up, invented

fid•dle /fíd′l/ • n. stringed instrument played with a bow, esp. a violin. • v. **1** intr. **a** [often foll. by with] play restlessly. **b** [often foll. by about] move aimlessly. **c** act idly or frivolously. **d** [usu. foll. by with] make minor adjustments; tinker. **2** tr. play the fiddle. **b** tr. play (a tune, etc.) on the fiddle. □ **as fit as a fiddle** in very good health. **play second** (or **first**) **fiddle** take a subordinate (or leading) role.

■ n. viola, viol, cello. • v. **1 a** (fiddle with) twiddle; see also TOY v. 1. **b** see FIDGET v. **c** fool or fuss or mess about or around, trifle. **d** see TINKER v.

fid•dler /fídlər/ n. **1** fiddle player. **2** small N. American crab.

fid•dle•stick /fíd′lstik/ n. [in pl.; as int.] nonsense!.

■ (fiddlesticks!) rubbish, moonshine, rot, colloq. hogwash, sl. baloney, humbug, bull.

fi•del•i•ty /fidélitee/ n. **1** faithfulness; loyalty. **2** strict accuracy. **3** precision in reproduction of sound or video.

fidg•et /fíjit/ v.intr. move or act restlessly or nervously. □□ **fid′get•y** adj. **fidg′et•i•ness** n.

■ squirm, twitch, shuffle, wriggle, fiddle, fuss.

fi•du•ci•ar•y /fidōóshee-eree, –shəree, –dyōō-, fi–/ • adj. **1** of a trust, trustee, or trusteeship. **2** held or given in trust. • n. (pl. **–ies**) trustee.

fie /fī/ int. expressing disgust, shame, etc.

fief /feef/ n. land held under the feudal system or in fee.

fief•dom /féefdəm/ n. fief.

field /feeld/ • n. **1** area of open land, esp. one used for pasture or crops. **2** area rich in some natural product (gas field). **3** piece of land for a specified purpose, esp. **a** an area marked out for a game or sport (*football field*), or. **b** an airfield. **4** participants in a contest, race, or sport. **5** expanse of ice, snow, sea, sky, etc. **6** area of activity or study. **7** region in which a force is effective (*magnetic field*). **8** range of perception (*field of view*). **9** [*attrib.*] **a** (of an animal or plant) found in the countryside; wild (*field mouse*). **b** carried out or working in the natural environment (*field test*). **10** background of a picture, coin, flag, etc. • *v.* **1** *Baseball, etc.* **a** *intr.* act as a fielder. **b** *tr.* catch (and return) (the ball). **2** *tr.* deal with (a succession of questions, etc.). □ **field glasses** binoculars for outdoor use. **play the field** *colloq.* avoid exclusive attachment to one person or activity, etc.

■ *n.* **1** pasture, meadow, grassland, clearing. **3** playing field, court, ground, gridiron. **4** competitors, players, entrants, contestants. **6** domain, realm, territory, sphere, line, province, subject, division, department, discipline. • *v.* **1 b** stop, retrieve. **2** cope with, handle, answer, reply to, respond *or* react to.

field•er /féeldər/ *n. Baseball* member of the team that is fielding.

field•work /féeldwərk/ *n.* practical work of a surveyor, collector of scientific data, sociologist, etc., conducted in the natural environment. □□ **field′work•er** *n.*

fiend /feend/ *n.* **1** evil spirit; demon. **2** very wicked or cruel person. **3** *sl.* devotee. □□ **fiend′ish** *adj.* **fiend′ish•ly** *adv.* **fiend′ish•ness** *n.* **fiend′like** *adj.*

■ **1** see DEVIL *n.* 1, 2. **3** fan, enthusiast, *colloq.* buff, freak, *sl.* nut. □□ **fiendish** wicked, cruel, malignant, malevolent, malicious, evil, bad.

fierce /feers/ *adj.* (**fierc•er, fierc•est**) **1** vehemently aggressive or frightening. **2** eager; intense; ardent. **3** unpleasantly strong or intense. □□ **fierce′ly** *adv.* **fierce′ness** *n.*

■ **1** ferocious, savage, wild, truculent, violent, brutal, barbaric, barbarous. **2** fiery, vehement, furious. **3** intense, frenzied, stormy; severe, keen, dire. □□ **fiercely** very, extremely, exceedingly, intensely.

fi•er•y /fíree/ *adj.* (**fi•er•i•er, fi•er•i•est**) **1** consisting of or flaming with fire. **2** like fire in appearance; bright red. **3** hot; burning. **4** spirited. □□ **fi′er•i•ly** *adv.* **fi′er•i•ness** *n.*

■ **1** burning, blazing; afire, on fire, ablaze. **2** glowing, incandescent, glaring, gleaming. **3** red-hot, white-hot, overheated. **4** eager, pugnacious, passionate, excited, excitable, peppery, irritable, fierce, see also ARDENT, BRIGHT *adj.*

fi•es•ta /fee-éstə/ *n.* **1** holiday or festivity. **2** religious festival.

fife /fif/ *n.* kind of small shrill flute used with the drum in military music. □□ **fif′er** *n.*

fif•teen /fiftéen/ • *n.* **1** one more than fourteen. **2** symbol for this (15, xv, XV). **3** size, etc., denoted by fifteen. • *adj.* that amount to fifteen. □□ **fif′teenth** *adj. & n.*

fifth /fifth/ • *n.* **1** next after fourth. **2** any of

five equal parts of a thing. **3** *Mus.* interval or chord spanning five consecutive notes in the diatonic scale (e.g., C to G). **4** (the Fifth) Fifth Amendment to the US Constitution. • *adj.* that is the fifth. □ **take the Fifth** exercise the right guaranteed by the Fifth Amendment to the Constitution of refusing to answer questions in order to avoid incriminating oneself. □□ **fifth′ly** *adv.*

fif•ty /fíftee/ • *n.* (*pl.* **–ties**) **1** product of five and ten. **2** symbol for this (50, l, L). **3** [in *pl.*] numbers from 50 to 59, esp. the years of a century or of a person's life. • *adj.* that amount to fifty. □ **fifty–fifty** *adj.* equal. *adv.* equally. □□ **fif′ti•eth** *adj. n. & adv.*

fig /fig/ *n.* **1** soft pear-shaped fruit with many seeds, eaten fresh or dried. **2** (in full **fig tree**) deciduous tree having broad leaves and bearing figs.

fig. *abbr.* figure.

fight /fit/ • *v.* (*past* and *past part.* **fought** /fawt/) **1** *intr.* **a** contend or struggle in war, battle, single combat, etc. **b** [often foll. by *with*] argue; quarrel. **2** *tr.* contend with (an opponent) in this way. **3** *tr.* engage in (a battle, war, duel, etc.). **4** *tr.* contend about (an issue, an election); maintain (a lawsuit, cause, etc.) against an opponent. **5** *intr.* campaign or strive determinedly to achieve something. **6** *tr.* strive to overcome (disease, fire, fear, etc.). • *n.* **1 a** combat. **b** boxing match. **c** battle; conflict; struggle. **d** argument. **2** power or inclination to fight. □ **fighting chance** opportunity to succeed by great effort. **fight off** repel with effort.

■ *v.* **1 a** battle, conflict, war, engage, clash, feud, combat. **b** dispute, bicker, have words, wrangle, squabble. **2** contend, encounter, engage; see also TACKLE *v.* 2, 4. **3** see ENGAGE 6. **4** argue about *or* against, dispute, question, challenge; contest. **5** rise up, struggle, take up arms. **6** oppose, defy, resist, withstand, confront. • *n.* **1 a** brawl, fray, riot, fracas, tussle, scuffle. **b** see BOUT 2a. **c** clash, war; engagement, encounter. **d** altercation, quarrel, feud, dispute, run-in, disagreement. **2** pugnacity, militancy, belligerence, spirit. □ **fight off** see REPULSE *v.* 1.

fight•er /fítər/ *n.* **1** person or animal that fights. **2** fast military aircraft designed for attacking other aircraft.

■ **1** see BRUISER 2, SOLDIER *n.*

fig•ment /fígmənt/ *n.* invented or imaginary thing.

■ see ILLUSION 4.

fig•u•ra•tive /fígyərətiv/ *adj.* **1** metaphorical, not literal. **2** characterized by or addicted to figures of speech. **3** of pictorial or sculptural representation. □□ **fig′u•ra•tive•ly** *adv.* **fig′u•ra•tive•ness** *n.*

fig•ure /fígyər/ • *n.* **1** external form or bodily shape. **2 a** person as seen in outline but not identified. **b** person as contemplated mentally. **3** *Geom.* a two-dimensional space enclosed by a line or lines, or a three-dimensional space enclosed by a surface or surfaces; any of the classes of these, e.g., the triangle, the sphere. **4 a** numerical symbol or number, esp. any of the ten in Arabic notation. **b** an amount of money; a value. **5** (in full **figure of speech**) recognized form of rhetorical expression giving variety, force, etc., esp. metaphor or hyperbole. • *v.* **1** *intr.* appear or be mentioned, esp. prominently. **2 a** *tr.* calculate. **b** *intr.* do arithmetic. **3 a** *tr.* understand; ascertain; consider. **b** *intr.* *colloq.* be likely or understandable. □ **figure on** count on; expect. **figure out 1** work out by arithmetic or logic. **2** estimate. **3** understand. **figure skater** person who practices figure skating. **figure skating** sport of performing jumps, spins, patterns, etc., while ice skating. □□ **fig′ure•less** *adj.*

■ *n.* **1** outline, silhouette; cut, cast; form, physique, build. **2 a** form, individual, being. **b** personality, presence, character, individual. **4 a** numeral, cipher, digit; character, sign • *v.* **1** feature, have a place, take or play a part, take or play a role. **2 a** figure out, compute, reckon; count, tally, sum. □ **figure on** rely or depend on, trust in; plan on or upon, consider. **figure out 1** calculate, reckon, compute; see also SOLVE. **3** decipher, interpret, translate, grasp, solve.

fig•ure•head /fígyərhed/ *n.* **1** nominal leader. **2** carving, usu. a bust or a full-length figure, at a ship's prow.

■ **1** puppet, dummy, mouthpiece, front man.

fig•u•rine /fígyəréen/ *n.* statuette.

fil•a•ment /fíləmənt/ *n.* **1** threadlike body or fiber. **2** conducting wire or thread with a high melting point in an electric bulb. □□ **fil•a•men•ta•ry** /-méntəree/ *adj.* **fil′a•ment•ed** *adj.* **fil•a•men•tous** /-méntəs/ *adj.*

fil•bert /fílbərt/ *n.* **1** cultivated hazel, bearing edible ovoid nuts. **2** this nut.

filch /filch/ *v.tr.* pilfer; steal. □□ **filch′er** *n.*

file[1] /fil/ • *n.* **1** folder, box, etc., for holding loose papers. **2** set of papers kept in this. **3** *Computing* collection of (usu. related) data stored under one name. • *v.tr.* **1** place (papers) in a file or among (esp. public) records. **2** submit a petition, application, etc. □□ **fil′er** *n.*

■ *n.* **1** portfolio, case. **2** document, dossier. • *v.* **1** classify, organize, systematize, categorize, alphabetize, order, arrange. **2** send in, complete, fill out.

file[2] /fil/ • *n.* line of persons or things one behind another. • *v.intr.* walk in a file.

■ *n.* column, row, rank. • *v.* march, troop.

file[3] /fil/ • *n.* tool with a roughened surface or surfaces, usu. of steel, for smoothing or shaping wood, fingernails, etc. • *v.tr.* smooth or shape with a file. □□ **fil′er** *n.*

fi•let /fílay, fílit/ *n.* fillet of meat. □ **filet mignon** /fílay minyón/ small tender piece of beef from the end of the tenderloin.

fil•i•al /fíleeəl/ *adj.* **1** of or due from a son or daughter. **2** *Biol.* bearing the relation of offspring. □□ **fil′i•al•ly** *adv.*

■ **1** see DUTIFUL.

fil•i•bus•ter /fílibustər/ • *n.* **1** obstruction of progress in a legislative assembly by prolonged speaking. **2** person who engages in this. • *v.* **1** *intr.* act as a filibuster. **2** *tr.* act in this way against (a motion, etc.).

fil•i•gree /fíligree/ *n.* (also **fil•a•gree** /fíla-/) **1** fine ornamental work of gold or silver or

copper wire. **2** anything delicate resembling this. □□ **fil′i•greed** *adj.*

fil•ing /fíling/ *n.* [usu. in *pl.*] particle rubbed off by a file.

Fil•i•pi•no /filipéenō/ • *n.* (*pl.* **–nos**; *fem.* **Fil•i•pi•na** /-nə/, *pl.* **–n s**) native or inhabitant of the Philippines, a group of islands in the SW Pacific. • *adj.* of the Philippines or the Filipinos.

fill /fil/ • *v.* **1** *tr. & intr.* make or become full. **2** *tr.* occupy completely; spread over or through; pervade. **3** *tr.* drill and put a filling into (a decayed tooth). **4** *tr.* appoint a person to hold (a vacant post). **5** *tr.* hold (a position). **6** *tr.* carry out or supply (an order, commission, etc.). **7** *tr.* occupy (vacant time). **8** *tr.* (usu. as **filling** *adj.*) (esp. of food) satisfy; satiate. • *n.* **1** as much as one wants or can bear. **2** enough to fill something. □ **fill in 1** add information to complete. **2** fill (a hole, etc.) completely. **3** act as a substitute. **4** *colloq.* inform (a person) more fully. **fill out 1** enlarge to the required size. **2** become enlarged or plump. **3** add information to complete (a document, etc.).

■ *v.* **1** fill up. **2** crowd (into), stuff, cram (into), pack (into), squeeze into; jam, load; abound in, overflow. **3** block, stop (up), seal, plug, fill in. **5** occupy, take over; discharge, carry out. **8** bloat, sate, gorge, stuff. □ **fill in 1** answer, fill out, make out. **2** see FILL[1] *v.* 3 above. **3** take the place of, take a person's place; see also SUBSTITUTE *v.* 1. **4** tell, advise, let in on, bring up to date. **fill out 1** see PAD *v.* 2. **2** swell, expand, grow; distend, stretch. **3** see *fill in* 1 above.

fill•er /fílər/ *n.* **1** material or an object used to fill a cavity or increase bulk. **2** item filling space in a newspaper, etc.

fil•let /fílit/ • *n.* **1** (usu. *filet* /fíláy/) a fleshy boneless piece of meat from near the loins or the ribs. **b** (in full *fillet steak*) tenderloin. **c** boned longitudinal section of a fish. **2** strip; band. • *v.tr.* (also *filáy, filay*/) remove bones from (fish or meat). □□ **fil′let•er** *n.*

fill•ing /fíling/ *n.* material that fills a cavity, sandwich, pie, etc.

■ filler, stuffing, padding, wadding; contents.

fil•lip /fílip/ • *n.* **1** stimulus or incentive. **2** flick with finger or thumb. • *v.* (**fil•liped**, **fil•lip•ing**) flick.

fil•ly /fílee/ *n.* (*pl.* **–lies**) young female horse.

film /film/ • *n.* **1** thin coating or covering layer. **2** *Photog.* strip or sheet of plastic or other flexible base coated with light-sensitive emulsion for exposure in a camera. **3** story, episode, etc., on a film, with the illusion of movement; movie. **4** slight veil or haze, etc. • *v.* **1** *tr.* [also *absol.*] make a movie or television film of (a book, etc.). **2** *tr. & intr.* cover or become covered with or as with a film.

■ *n.* **1** covering, sheet; skin, coat, membrane. **3** picture, moving picture, motion picture; videotape, video. **4** dusting, murkiness, blur, mist. • *v.* **1** photograph, shoot,

filmmaker ~ find

take. **2** (*film over*) become coated *or* veiled *or* dimmed.

film•mak•er /fílmaykər/ *n.* person who makes motion pictures.

film•y /fílmee/ *adj.* (**film•i•er, film•i•est**) **1** thin and translucent. **2** covered with or as with a film. □□ **film'i•ly** *adv.* **film'i•ness** *n.*
■ **1** gauzy, sheer, gossamer(-like), cobwebby, diaphanous, delicate, flimsy, light, insubstantial. **2** murky, blurry, cloudy, hazy, misty, bleary, blurred.

fil•ter /fíltər/ • *n.* **1** porous device for removing impurities or solid particles from a liquid or gas passed through it. **2** screen or attachment for absorbing or modifying light, X rays, etc. **3** device for suppressing electrical or sound waves of frequencies not required. • *v.* **1** *tr. & intr.* pass or cause to pass through a filter. **2** *intr.* [foll. by *through, into*, etc.] make way gradually.
■ *n.* **1** strainer, sieve, riddle. • *v.* **1** filtrate, run through; percolate, leach; clarify, refine, purify, clean.

filth /filth/ *n.* **1** repugnant or extreme dirt; excrement; refuse. **2** vileness; corruption; obscenity. □□ **filth'i•ly** *adv.* **filth'i•ness** *n.* **filth'y** *adj.* (**filth•i•er, filth•i•est**)
■ **1** slime, filthiness, *colloq.* muck, *sl.* crud, grunge; feces, excreta, manure, dung, sewage; rubbish, garbage. **2** baseness, foulness; perversion, degradation; vulgarity, indecency, grossness, pornography. □□ **filthy** dirty, unclean, begrimed, soiled, stained, grimy, putrid, fetid; obscene, indecent, immoral, gross, impure, smutty, coarse, bawdy, ribald, depraved, corrupt, dirty, lewd; see also *disgraceful* (DISGRACE), VILE 1.

fil•trate /fíltrayt/ • *v.tr.* filter. • *n.* filtered liquid. □□ **fil•tra•tion** /-tráyshən/ *n.*

fin /fin/ *n.* **1** organ on various parts of the body of many aquatic vertebrates and some invertebrates, including fish and cetaceans, for propelling, steering, etc. **2** similar projection on an aircraft, car, etc. **3** swimmer's flipper. □□ **fin'less** *adj.* **finned** *adj.* [also in *comb.*].

fi•na•gle /fináygəl/ *v. colloq.* act or obtain dishonestly or deviously. □□ **fi•na'gler** *n.*
■ see CHEAT *v.* 2.

fi•nal /fínəl/ • *adj.* **1** situated at the end; coming last. **2** conclusive; decisive. • *n.* **1** (also in *pl.*) last or deciding heat or game. **2** examination at the end of an academic course. □□ **fi'nal•ly** *adv.*
■ *adj.* **1** last, closing, concluding, finishing, terminating, ultimate. **2** definitive, unalterable, unchangeable; incontrovertible, irrefutable; absolute, certain, sure. □□ **finally** lastly; at (long) last, eventually, in the end, ultimately, at length; decisively, irrevocably, completely.

fi•na•le /fínaalee, -nálee/ *n.* last movement or section of a piece of music or drama, etc.

fi•nal•ist /fínəlist/ *n.* competitor in a final.

fi•nal•i•ty /fínálitee, fə–/ *n.* (*pl.* **–ties**) **1** quality or fact of being final. **2** belief that something is final.
■ **1** conclusiveness, decisiveness, unalter-

ability, unchangeability, immutability, irreversibility.

fi•na•lize /fínəlīz/ *v.tr.* **1** put into final form. **2** bring to an end. **3** approve the final form of. □□ **fi•na•li•za'tion** *n.*
■ **2** complete, conclude, settle, decide, wrap up, *colloq.* sew up.

fi•nance /fínáns, fī–, fínəns/ • *n.* **1** management of (esp. public) money. **2** monetary support for an enterprise. **3** [in *pl.*] money resources. • *v.tr.* provide capital for. □□ **fi•nan•cial** /-shəl, fī–/ *adj.* **fi•nan'cial•ly** *adv.*
■ *n.* **1** financial affairs, business, commerce, economics. **2** see SUPPORT *n.* 1. **3** (*finances*) capital, cash, funds, assets, holdings. • *v.* fund, invest in, back, capitalize, underwrite, *colloq.* bankroll. □□ **financial** monetary, pecuniary.

SYNONYM STUDY: financial

MONETARY, PECUNIARY, FISCAL. What's the difference between a **financial** crisis and a **fiscal** one? It all depends on who's having trouble with money and the scale of the difficulties. *Financial* usually applies to money matters involving large sums or transactions of considerable importance (*the auction was a financial success; many families had been having financial problems following layoffs at the factory*). *Fiscal* refers specifically to the financial affairs of a government, organization, or corporation (*the end of the company's fiscal year*), while **pecuniary** refers to money matters of a more personal or practical nature and is preferred to *financial* when money is being discussed on a smaller scale (*pecuniary motives; pecuniary assistance; pecuniary difficulties*). Of all these words, **monetary** refers most directly to money as such and is often used when discussing the coinage, distribution, and circulation of money (*the European monetary system; the monetary unit of a country*).

---

fi•nan•cier /fínənseér, fənan–, fīnən–/ *n.* capitalist.
■ banker, backer, moneyman.

finch /finch/ *n.* any small seed-eating passerine bird, including crossbills, canaries, and chaffinches.

find /fīnd/ • *v.tr.* (*past* and *past part.* **found** /fownd/) **1 a** discover by chance or effort (*found a key*). **b** become aware of. **2** succeed in obtaining. **3** seek out and provide or supply. **4** *Law* (of a jury, judge, etc.) decide and declare (*found him guilty*). **5** reach by a natural or normal process (*water finds its own level*). • *n.* **1** discovery of treasure, minerals, etc. **2** thing or person discovered, esp. when of value. □ **find out 1** discover or detect (a wrongdoer, etc.). **2** get information. **3** discover. □□ **find'a•ble** *adj.*
■ *v.* **1a, 2** come across, happen on *or* upon, come on *or* upon, hit on *or* upon, chance on *or* upon, recover, get back; secure, get, procure, acquire; command, gather (up). **3** see SUPPLY *v.* 1, 2. **4** judge, determine to be, pronounce, *formal* deem. ■ *n.* catch; bargain. □ **find out 1** lay one's hand(s) on, track down, turn up, identify. **2** see LEARN 4.

3 light on *or* upon, catch sight of, see, detect, learn, spot, locate.

find•ing /fínding/ • *n.* 1 [often in *pl.*] conclusion reached by an inquiry. 2 [in *pl.*] small parts or tools used by artisans.
■ 1 (*findings*) judgment, verdict, decree, decision.

fine[1] /fín/ • *adj.* 1 of high quality (*they sell fine fabrics*). 2 a excellent; of notable merit (*a fine painting*). b good; satisfactory (*that will be fine*). 3 pure; refined. 4 in good health. 5 (of weather, etc.) bright and clear. 6 a thin; sharp. b in small particles. • *adv.* 1 finely. 2 *colloq.* very well (*suits me fine*). □ **fine arts** poetry, music, and esp. painting, sculpture, and architecture. **fine-tune** make small adjustments to. □□ **fine'ly** *adv.* **fine'ness** *n.*
■ *adj.* 1 superior, supreme, first-class, first-rate, prime, choice, select. 2 a magnificent, marvelous, exquisite, splendid, admirable, super; enjoyable, entertaining; (*of an artist or a performance*) masterly, virtuoso. b pleasant, nice, *colloq.* out of this world, great, OK, *sl.* cool, neat. 3 see PURE 1, 2. 4 well, all right, healthy, *colloq.* OK. 5 sunny, fair, cloudless, pleasant, dry. 6 a diaphanous, gauzy, sheer; keen, pointed. b powdery, powdered, pulverized.

fine[2] /fín/ • *n.* sum of money exacted as a penalty. • *v.tr.* punish by a fine (*fined him $5*). □□ **fin•a•ble** /fínəbəl/ *adj.*
■ *n.* charge, fee, mulct, forfeiture, *Law* amercement. • *v.* penalize, charge, mulct, *Law* amerce.

fin•er•y /fínəree/ *n.* showy dress or decoration.
■ ornaments, trappings, trinkets, frippery, showy dress, best bib and tucker, *colloq.* glad rags, *joc.* Sunday best.

fi•nesse /finés/ • *n.* 1 refinement. 2 subtle or delicate manipulation. 3 artfulness, esp. in handling a difficulty tactfully. • *v.* use or achieve by finesse.
■ *n.* 1 grace, tact, diplomacy, discretion, elegance. 2 trick(s), artifice(s), stratagem(s), wile(s), ruse(s), scheme(s). 3 subtlety, cunning, craftiness, cleverness; style, dash; skillfulness, adroitness. • *v.* see MANEUVER *v.* 3.

fin•ger /fínggər/ • *n.* 1 any of the terminal projections of the hand (esp. other than the thumb). 2 part of a glove, etc., intended to cover a finger. 3 finger-like object or structure. • *v.tr.* 1 touch, feel, or handle with the fingers. 2 *Mus.* a play (a passage) with fingers used in a particular way. b play upon (an instrument) with the fingers. □ **put one's finger on** locate or identify exactly. □□ **fin'gered** *adj.* [also in *comb.*]. **fin'ger•less** *adj.*
■ *n.* 1 digit. • *v.* 1 toy *or* play *or* fiddle with. □ **put one's finger on** find, discover, unearth, track down; indicate, point to, pin down; recall, remember, recollect.

fin•ger•ing /fínggəring/ *n.* 1 manner or technique of using the fingers, esp. to play an instrument. 2 indication of this in a musical score.

fin•ger•nail /fínggərnayl/ *n.* nail at the tip of each finger.

299   **finding ~ fire**

fin•ger•print /fínggərprint/ • *n.* impression made on a surface by the fine ridges on the fingertips, esp. as used for identifying individuals. • *v.tr.* record the fingerprints of.

fin•ger•tip /fínggərtip/ *n.* tip of a finger. □ **have at one's fingertips** be thoroughly familiar with (a subject, etc.).

fin•i•al /fíneeəl/ *n. Archit.* ornamental top or end of a roof, pediment, gable, tower corner, canopy, etc.

fin•ick•y /fínikee/ *adj.* 1 overly particular; fastidious. 2 detailed. □□ **fin'ick•i•ness** *n.*
■ 1 overnice, fussy, nice, critical, precise, punctilious, *colloq.* choosy, picky. 2 fussy, elaborate, fine.

fi•nis /fínis, féenée, fíinís/ *n.* the end (used esp. at the end of a book, movie, etc.).

fin•ish /fínish/ • *v.* 1 *tr.* a bring to an end; come to the end of; complete. b *colloq.* kill; overcome completely. c consume or get through the whole or the remainder of (food or drink) (*finish your dinner*). 2 *intr.* a come to an end; cease. b reach the end, esp. of a race. 3 *tr.* treat the surface of (cloth, woodwork, etc.). • *n.* 1 end; last stage; completion. 2 method, material, or texture used for surface treatment of wood, cloth, etc. □ **finish with** have no more to do with; complete one's use of or association with. □□ **fin'ish•er** *n.*
■ *v.* 1 a accomplish, perfect, achieve, carry out, fulfill. b exterminate, finish off, annihilate, destroy, get rid of, dispose of. c dispose of, eat *or* drink (up), use (up), devour, drain. 2 a end, stop, conclude, close; culminate. • *n.* 1 conclusion, termination, close, closing, ending, finale; death, killing, annihilation. 2 surface, polish; see also TEXTURE 1.

fi•nite /fíinít/ *adj.* 1 limited; not infinite. 2 *Gram.* (of a part of a verb) having a specific number and person. □□ **fi'nite•ly** *adv.* **fi'nite•ness** *n.* **fin•i•tude** /fínitood, -tyood/ *n.*
■ 1 bounded, restricted, delimited, numerable.

Finn /fin/ *n.* native or inhabitant of Finland; person of Finnish descent.

Finn•ish /fínish/ • *adj.* of the Finns or their language. • *n.* language of the Finns.

fiord var. of FJORD.

fir /fər/ *n.* 1 (in full **fir tree**) evergreen coniferous tree with needles borne singly on the stems (cf. PINE[1]). 2 wood of the fir.

fire /fír/ • *n.* 1 a combustion of substances with oxygen, giving out bright light and heat. b flame or incandescence. 2 conflagration; destructive burning (*forest fire*). 3 burning fuel in a fireplace, furnace, etc. 4 fervor; spirit; vivacity. 5 burning heat; fever. • *v.* 1 a *tr.* discharge (a gun, etc.). b *tr.* propel (a missile) from a gun, etc. c *tr.* propel (a ball) with force or high speed. d *intr.* fire a gun or missile. e *tr.* produce (a broadside, salute, etc.) by discharge of guns. f *intr.* (of a gun, etc.) be discharged. 2 *tr.* deliver or utter in rapid succession (*fired insults at us*). 3 *tr. sl.* dismiss (an employee). 4 *intr.* (of an engine) undergo ignition. 5 *tr.* stimulate. 6 *tr.* a bake *or* dry (pottery, bricks, etc.). b cure (tea or tobacco) by artificial heat. □ **catch fire** begin to burn. **fire department** organized body of firefighters trained and employed to extinguish fires. **fire drill** rehearsal of the procedures to be used in case of fire. **fire engine** vehicle carrying equipment for fighting large fires. **fire escape** emergency staircase or apparatus for escape from a building on fire. **fire extinguisher** apparatus with a jet for discharging liquid chemicals, water, or foam to extinguish a fire. **fire power** destructive capacity of guns, etc. **fire storm** high wind or storm following a very intense fire. **under fire 1** being shot at. **2** being rigorously criticized or questioned. □□ **fire′less** adj. **fir′er** n.

■ n. **1 b** blaze; see also *incandescence* (IN-CANDESCENT). **2** holocaust, inferno, blaze. **4** feeling, passion, ardor, ardency, fervency, intensity, vigor, energy, animation, enthusiasm; inspiration, imagination. **5** torridity, fieriness, feverishness. ● v. **1 a** see DISCHARGE v. 3. **b** launch; throw, catapult, hurl. **d** open fire, shoot, blaze away, *colloq.* blast. **3** discharge, oust, give a person notice, boot out, show a person the door, ax, *colloq.* sack, *sl.* bounce. **5** see also STIMULATE. □ **catch fire** kindle, ignite, take fire.

fire•arm /fíraarm/ n. [usu. in pl.] gun, esp. a pistol or rifle.

■ see REVOLVER.

fire•ball /fírbawl/ n. **1** large meteor. **2** ball of flame, esp. from an explosion. **3** energetic person.

fire•bomb /fírbom/ n. incendiary bomb.

fire•brand /fírbrand/ n. **1** piece of burning wood. **2** cause of trouble, esp. a person causing unrest.

■ **2** see *agitator* (AGITATE).

fire•break /fírbrayk/ n. obstacle to the spread of fire in a forest, etc., esp. an open space.

fire•crack•er /fírkrakər/ n. explosive firework.

fire•fight•er /fírfítər/ n. person employed to extinguish fires.

fire•fly /fírflī/ n. (pl. **–flies**) soft-bodied beetle that emits phosphorescent light.

fire•man /fírmən/ n. (pl. **–men**) **1** member of a fire department. **2** person who tends a furnace.

fire•place /fírplays/ n. Archit. **1** place for a domestic fire, esp. a grate or hearth at the base of a chimney. **2** structure surrounding this. **3** area in front of this.

fire•plug /fírplug/ n. hydrant for a fire hose.

fire•proof /fírprōof/ ● adj. able to resist fire or great heat. ● v.tr. make fireproof.

fire•side /fírsīd/ n. **1** area around a fireplace. **2** a person's home or home life. □ **fireside chat** informal talk.

fire•wa•ter /fírwawtər/ n. colloq. strong alcoholic liquor.

fire•wood /fírwŏŏd/ n. wood for use as fuel.

fire•work /fírwərk/ n. **1** device containing combustible chemicals that cause explosions or spectacular effects. **2** [in pl.] outburst of passion, esp. anger.

fir•ing /fíring/ n. **1** discharge of guns. **2** fuel. **3** heating process that hardens clay into pot-

tery. □ **firing line 1** front line in a battle. **2** leading part in an activity, etc.

firm¹ /fərm/ ● adj. **1 a** of solid or compact structure. **b** fixed; stable. **2 a** resolute; determined. **b** steadfast; constant. **3** (of an offer, etc.) not liable to cancellation after acceptance. ● adv. firmly. ● v. make or become firm, secure, compact, or solid. □□ **firm′ly** adv. **firm′ness** n.

■ adj. **1 a** solid, compact, dense, compressed, rigid, stiff. **b** fast, secure, tight, stationary; steady, strong. **2 a** persistent, dogged, definite, positive. **b** staunch, unshaken, unshakable, unwavering; see also STEADFAST. ● v. secure, settle, establish, consolidate. □□ **firmly** solidly, strongly; securely, tightly, rigidly; resolutely, steadfastly, determinedly.

firm² /fərm/ n. business concern or its partners.

■ company, organization, business, enterprise, house.

fir•ma•ment /fə́rməmənt/ n. literary the sky regarded as a vault or arch.

■ skies, (vault of) heaven, empyrean.

first /fərst/ ● adj. **1** earliest in time or order. **2** foremost in position, rank, or importance. **3** most willing or likely. **4** basic or evident. ● n. **1** person or thing first mentioned or occurring. **2** first gear. **3** first place in a race. ● adv. **1** before any other person or thing. **2** before someone or something else. **3** for the first time. □ **at first** at the beginning. **first aid** emergency medical treatment. **first-born** adj. eldest. n. eldest child of a person. **first class 1** set of persons or things grouped together as the best. **2** best accommodation in a train, ship, etc. **3** mail given priority. **first-class** adj. **1** belonging to or traveling by first class. **2** of the best quality; very good. adv. by the first class. **first cousin** see COUSIN. **first gear** see GEAR. **First Lady** wife of the US President. **first name** personal name other than a family name. **first person** see PERSON. **first-rate** adj. of the highest class; excellent. adv. colloq. very well. **2** excellently.

■ adj. **1** oldest, original; initial, maiden, opening. **2** leading, principal, preeminent, primary, chief, head, premier, prime. **4** fundamental, elementary, primary, cardinal, key, essential. ● n. **3** gold (medal); see also WIN n. ● adv. **1** in front, earliest, foremost; firstly, in the first place. **2** beforehand, ahead, sooner. □ **at first** in the beginning, initially, at the start. **first-class 2** see EXCELLENT. **first-rate** (adj.) first-class, high-grade, prime, superior, superb, great, remarkable.

first•hand /fə́rst-hánd/ attrib. adj. & adv. from the original source; direct.

first•ly /fə́rstlee/ adv. in the first place; first (cf. FIRST adv.).

firth /fərth/ n. esp. Sc. (also **frith** /frith/) **1** narrow inlet of the sea. **2** estuary.

fis•cal /fískəl/ adj. of public revenue; of financial matters. See synonym study at FINANCIAL. □ **fiscal year** year as reckoned for taxing or accounting. □□ **fis′cal•ly** adv.

■ financial, economic, budgetary, monetary.

fish /fish/ ● n. (pl. same or **fish•es**) **1** vertebrate cold-blooded animal with gills and fins living wholly in water. **2** any animal living wholly in water, e.g., cuttlefish, shellfish, jellyfish. **3** flesh of fish as food. **4** (**the Fish** or **Fishes**) zodiacal sign or constellation Pisces. • v. **1** *intr.* try to catch fish, esp. with a line or net. **2** *tr.* fish for (a certain kind of fish) or in (a certain stretch of water). **3** *intr.* [foll. by *for*] **a** search for in water or a concealed place. **b** seek by indirect means (*fishing for compliments*). **4** *tr.* [foll. by *up*, *out*, etc.] retrieve with careful or awkward searching. □ **drink like a fish** drink alcoholic beverages excessively. **fish story** *colloq.* exaggerated account. **other fish to fry** other matters to attend to. □□ **fish'like** *adj.*

fish•er•man /fishǝrmǝn/ *n.* (*pl.* **-men**) **1** person who catches fish as a livelihood or for recreation. **2** fishing boat.

fish•er•y /fishǝree/ *n.* (*pl.* **-ies**) **1** place where fish are caught or reared. **2** industry of catching or rearing fish.

fish•hook /fish-hook/ *n.* barbed hook for catching fish.

fish•ing /fishing/ *n.* activity of catching fish, esp. for food or as recreation. □ **fishing rod** long tapering, usu. jointed rod to which a fishing line is attached.

fish•net /fishnet/ *n.* [often *attrib.*] open-meshed fabric.

fish•tail /fishtayl/ • *n.* device, etc., shaped like a fish's tail. • *v. intr.* move the tail of a vehicle from side to side.

fish•y /fishee/ *adj.* (**fish•i•er**, **fish•i•est**) **1** of or like fish. **2** *sl.* of dubious character; questionable; suspect. □□ **fish'i•ly** *adv.* **fish'i•ness** *n.*

■ **1** piscine, fishlike. **2** dubious, doubtful, suspicious, not kosher, shady, funny; improbable.

fis•sile /fisǝl, –īl/ *adj.* **1** capable of undergoing nuclear fission. **2** cleavable; tending to split. □□ **fis•sil•i•ty** /–sĭlitee/ *n.*

fis•sion /fishǝn/ *n.* **1** *Physics* splitting of a heavy atomic nucleus with a release of energy. **2** *Biol.* division of a cell as a mode of reproduction.

fis•sure /fishǝr/ *n.* opening, usu. long and narrow, made esp. by cracking, splitting, or separation of parts.

■ see CRACK *n.* 3

fist /fist/ *n.* **1** tightly closed hand. **2** *sl.* handwriting. □□ **fist'ed** *adj.* [also in *comb.*]. **fist' ful** *n.* (*pl.* **-fuls**)

fist•i•cuffs /fistikufs/ *n.pl.* fighting with the fists.

■ boxing, pugilism, prizefighting.

fis•tu•la /fischǝlǝ/ *n.* (*pl.* **fis•tu•las** or **fis•tu•lae** /–lee/) abnormal or surgically made passage, as between a hollow organ and the body surface. □□ **fis'tu•lar** *adj.* **fis'tu•lous** *adj.*

fit¹ /fit/ • *adj.* (**fit•ter**, **fit•test**) **1 a** well adapted or suited. **b** qualified; competent; worthy. **c** in a suitable condition; ready. **d** good enough. **2** in good health or athletic condition. **3** proper; becoming; right (*it is fit that*). • *v. tr.* (**fit•ted**, **fit•ting**) **1 a** [also *absol.*] be of the right shape and size for (*the dress fits her*). **b** make the right size or shape. **2** [usu. foll. by *with*] supply; furnish; equip.

3 be in harmony with; befit; become (*it fits the occasion*). • *n.* way in which a garment, component, etc., fits. □ **fit in 1** be (esp. socially) compatible or accommodating. **2** find space or time for. **fit out** (or **up**) equip. □□ **fit'ly** *adv.* **fit'ness** *n.* **fit'ter** *n.*

■ *adj.* **1 a** suitable, appropriate, fitted; apt. **b** prepared to, ready to, able to, adequate to. **c** see READY *adj.* 1, 2. **2** healthy, well, hale, vigorous, strong, sturdy, robust. **3** correct, fitting, applicable, apropos. • *v.* **2** provide, fit out or up, install, rig out. **3** suit, be suited to; answer, satisfy. □ **fit in 1** harmonize, find one's place or niche; (*fit in with*) see CONFORM 1, **fit out** (or **up**) see EQUIP. □□ **fit'ness** aptness, appropriateness, pertinence; competence, eligibility, adequacy; health, vigor, well-being; wholesomeness.

fit² /fit/ *n.* **1** sudden seizure of epilepsy, hysteria, apoplexy, fainting, or paralysis, with unconsciousness or convulsions. **2** sudden short bout or burst. □ **by** (or **in**) **fits and starts** spasmodically. **have a fit** *colloq.* be greatly surprised or outraged. **in fits** laughing uncontrollably.

■ **1** attack, convulsion, paroxysm, spasm. **2** outburst, outbreak, paroxysm, spell, period. □ **by** (or **in**) **fits and starts** sporadically, occasionally, fitfully, intermittently.

fit•ful /fitfool/ *adj.* active or occurring spasmodically or intermittently. □□ **fit'ful•ly** *adv.* **fit'ful•ness** *n.*

■ spasmodic, intermittent, sporadic, occasional, periodic, irregular; varying, fluctuating, variable.

fit•ting /fiting/ • *n.* **1** process or an instance of having a garment, etc., fitted (*needed several fittings*). **2** [in *pl.*] fixtures and furnishings of a building. • *adj.* proper; becoming; right. □□ **fit'ting•ly** *adv.* **fit'ting•ness** *n.*

■ *n.* **2** (*fittings*) fitments, attachments, pieces, parts, units, furniture, appointments, accessories. • *adj.* fit, befitting, suitable, appropriate, seemly, apt.

five /fīv/ • *n.* **1** one more than four. **2** symbol for this (5, v, V). • *adj.* that amount to five.

fix /fiks/ • *v.* **1** *tr.* make firm or stable; fasten; secure. **2** *tr.* decide; specify (a price, date, etc.) **3** *tr.* repair **4** *tr.* implant (an idea or memory) in the mind. **5** *tr.* [foll. by *on*, *upon*] direct (one's eyes, attention, etc.). **6** *tr.* place definitely or permanently. **7** *tr.* determine the exact nature, position, etc., of. **8 a** *tr.* make (eyes, features, etc.) rigid. **b** *intr.* become rigid. **9** *tr. colloq.* prepare (food or drink). **10** *tr. colloq.* punish; deal with. **11** *tr. colloq.* secure or arrange fraudulently. **12** *tr.* castrate or spay (an animal). • *n.* **1** *colloq.* dilemma or predicament. **2** position found by bearings or astronomical observations. **3** *sl.* dose of a narcotic drug. **4** *sl.* bribery. □ **fixed income** income deriving from a pension, investment at fixed interest, etc. **fix up 1** arrange; organize; prepare. **2** accommodate. **3** provide (a person) with. **4** restore; refurbish. □□ **fix'a•ble** *adj.* **fix•ed•ly** /fiksidlee/ *adv.* **fix•ed•ness** /fiksidnis/ *n.* **fix'er** *n.*

■ v. **1** affix, anchor, retain, attach, make fast, set. **2** resolve, settle, establish, set, agree on, organize, arrange. **3** mend, patch up, remedy, rectify, correct, emend, adjust, regulate, straighten out, *colloq.* doctor. **4** see IMPLANT v. 2. **5** (*fix on* or *upon*) fasten on or, upon, focus on, rivet on, concentrate on; attract, hold, rivet. **6** establish, station, settle, install, situate, position. **7** specify, establish, identify, locate; assign, allocate, attribute, ascribe, specify. **9** see PREPARE 2. **10** take care of, see to, sort out; retaliate against, wreak vengeance on, hit or strike or get back at, get even with, even the score with, make reprisals against, avenge oneself against, take revenge on, repay, pay back. **11** bribe, buy, *colloq.* grease the palm of; rig; set up. **12** see STERILIZE 2. ■ n. **1** difficulty, corner, quandary, mess, bad situation, dire or desperate straits, *colloq.* pickle, catch-22, jam, hole, tight spot, tough spot, bind. **4** bribery, subornation. □ **fix up 1** see ARRANGE 1, 2. **2** see ACCOMMODATE 1. **3** provide, furnish, supply, accommodate, set up.

fix•ate /fíksáyt/ *v.tr.* **1** direct one's gaze on. **2** *Psychol.* cause (a person) to become abnormally attached to persons or things.

fix•a•tion /fiksáyshən/ *n.* **1** act or an instance of being fixated. **2** obsession; concentration on a single idea.

■ mania, compulsion, fixed idea, *idée fixe*, monomania.

fix•a•tive /fíksətiv/ • *adj.* tending to fix or secure. • *n.* substance used to fix colors, hair, perfume, microscopic specimens, etc.

fix•ings /fíksingz/ *n.pl.* **1** apparatus or equipment. **2** trimmings for a dish. **3** trimmings of a dress, etc.

fix•i•ty /fíksitee/ *n.* **1** fixed state. **2** stability; permanence.

fix•ture /fíkschər/ *n.* something fixed in position.

fizz /fiz/ • *v.intr.* **1** make a hissing or spluttering sound. **2** (of a drink) effervesce. • *n.* effervescence.

■ *v.* **1** hiss, sputter, sizzle, splutter, fizzle. **2** bubble, sparkle, froth. • *n.* sparkle, carbonation, bubbling.

fiz•zle /fízəl/ • *v.intr.* make a feeble hissing or spluttering sound. • *n.* such a sound. □ **fizzle out** end feebly.

■ *v.* see FIZZ v. 1. □ **fizzle out** die (out or away), expire, peter out, come to nothing or naught, fail, fall through.

fizz•y /fízee/ *adj.* (**fizz•i•er, fizz•i•est**) effervescent; carbonated. □□ **fizz′i•ly** *adv.* **fizz′i•ness** *n.*

fjord /fyawrd/ *n.* (also **fiord**) long narrow inlet of sea between high cliffs, as in Norway.

FL *abbr.* Florida (in official postal use).

fl. *abbr.* **1** floor. **2** floruit. **3** fluid.

Fla. *abbr.* Florida.

flab /flab/ *n. colloq.* fat; flabbiness.

flab•ber•gast /flábərgast/ *v.tr.* (esp. as **flabbergasted** *adj.*) *colloq.* overwhelm with astonishment; dumbfound.

flab•by /flábee/ *adj.* (**flab•bi•er, flab•bi•est**) **1** (of flesh, etc.) hanging down; limp; flaccid.

2 (of language or character) feeble. □□ **flab′bi•ly** *adv.* **flab′bi•ness** *n.*

■ **1** loose, slack, sagging. **2** feeble, weak, spineless.

flac•cid /flásid, fláksid/ *adj.* limp; flabby; drooping. □□ **flac•cid•i•ty** /–síditee/ *n.* **flac′cid•ly** *adv.*

flag¹ /flag/ • *n.* piece of cloth, usu. oblong or square, used as a country's emblem or as a standard, signal, etc. • *v.* (**flagged, flagging**) **1** *intr.* **a** grow tired; lose vigor; lag. **b** hang down; droop; become limp. **2** *tr.* **a** inform (a person) by flag signals. **b** communicate (information) by flagging. □ **flag down** signal to stop. □□ **flag′ger** *n.*

■ *n.* banner, ensign, pennant, pennon, streamer. • *v.* **1 a** tire, weaken, languish, falter, fail, dwindle, fade, deteriorate, waste away, degenerate, decline, diminish. **b** sag, dangle, swag. **2** see SIGNAL *v.* 1, 2a. □ **flag down** hail, stop.

flag² /flag/ *n.* (also **flag′stone**) **1** flat, usu. rectangular stone slab used for paving. **2** [in *pl.*] pavement made of these.

flag³ /flag/ *n.* plant with a bladed leaf, esp. the iris.

flag•el•late /flájəlayt/ *v.tr.* scourge; flog. □□ **flag•el•la•tion** /–láyshən/ *n.* **flag′el•la•tor** *n.*

flag•el•lum /fləjéləm/ *n.* (*pl.* **fla•gel•la** /–lə/) *Biol.* long lashlike appendage found principally on microscopic organisms. □□ **fla•gel•lar** /–lər/ *adj.* **fla•gel•li•form** /–lifawrm/ *adj.*

flag•on /flágən/ *n.* large vessel usu. with a handle, spout, and lid, to hold wine, etc.

flag•pole /flágpōl/ *n.* pole on which a flag may be hoisted.

■ staff.

fla•grant /fláygrənt/ *adj.* glaring; notorious; scandalous. □□ **fla•gran•cy** /–grənsee/ *n.* **fla′grant•ly** *adv.*

■ blatant, conspicuous, gross, obvious, out-and-out; infamous, arrant, outrageous, shocking, egregious.

flag•ship /flágship/ *n.* **1** ship having an admiral on board. **2** best or most important member, office, etc., of its kind.

flag•stone /flágstōn/ *n.* = FLAG².

flail /flayl/ • *n.* threshing tool consisting of a wooden staff with a short heavy stick swinging from it. • *v.* **1** *tr.* beat. **2** *intr.* wave or swing wildly or erratically.

■ *v.* **1** see LASH *v.* 2. **2** see FLAP *v.* 1.

flair /flair/ *n.* **1** instinct for selecting or performing what is excellent, useful, etc.; a talent (*has a flair for languages*). **2** talent or ability, esp. artistic or stylistic.

■ ability, aptitude, feel, forte, knack, genius, brilliance, skill, mind, gift, faculty; see also STYLE *n.* 4a, VERVE.

flak /flak/ *n.* (also **flack**) **1** antiaircraft fire. **2** adverse criticism; abuse.

■ **2** censure, disapproval, condemnation, blame.

flake /flayk/ • *n.* **1 a** small thin light piece of snow. **b** similar piece of another material. **2** thin broad piece of material peeled or split off. **3** *sl.* crazy or eccentric person. • *v.* take off or come away in flakes.

■ *n.* **1 a** snowflake. **b** chip, bit, scrap, scale. • *v.* scale (off), chip (off); see also PEEL *v.* 1, 2.

flak•y /fláykee/ *adj.* (**flak•i•er, flak•i•est**) **1** of, like, or in flakes. **2** *sl.* crazy; eccentric. □□ **flak′i•ly** *adv.* **flak′i•ness** *n.*

flam•boy•ant /flambóyənt/ *adj.* **1** ostentatious; showy. **2** floridly decorated. **3** gorgeously colored. □□ **flam•boy′ance** *n.* **flam•boy′an•cy** *n.* **flam•boy′ant•ly** *adv.*

■ **1** extravagant, gaudy, flashy, dazzling; dashing, rakish. **2** florid, elaborate, ornamented, ornate.

flame /flaym/ • *n.* **1 a** ignited gas. **b** [usu. in *pl.*] visible combustion. **2** brilliant orange-red color. **3** a strong passion, esp. love. **b** *colloq.* boyfriend or girlfriend. • *v.* burn; blaze. □□ **flame′less** *adj.* **flame′like** *adj.*

■ *n.* **2** see *incandescence* (INCANDESCENT). **3 a** fervor, ardor, zeal, enthusiasm, eagerness, feverishness. **b** lover, sweetheart, beau. • *v.* see BURN *v.* 2.

fla•men•co /fləméngkō/ *n.* (*pl.* **-cos**) **1** style of Spanish gypsy guitar music. **2** dance performed to this music.

flame•proof /fláymproōf/ *adj.* (esp. of a fabric) treated so as to be nonflammable.

flame•throw•er /fláymthrōər/ *n.* weapon for throwing a spray of flame.

flam•ing /fláyming/ *adj.* **1** emitting flames. **2** bright colored.

■ **1** see ABLAZE *adj.* 1. **2** see BRIGHT *adj.* 2.

fla•min•go /fləmínggō/ *n.* (*pl.* **-gos** or **-goes**) tall, long-necked, web-footed wading bird with crooked bill and pink, scarlet, and black plumage.

flam•ma•ble /flámabəl/ *adj.* easily set on fire; inflammable. □□ **flam•ma•bil′i•ty** *n.*

■ combustible, ignitable.

flan /flan/ *n.* **1** open pastry case with a savory or sweet filling. **2** custard topped with caramel glaze.

flange /flanj/ *n.* *Engin.* projecting flat rim, etc., used for strengthening or attachment

flank /flangk/ • *n.* **1** side of the body between the ribs and hip. **2** side of a mountain, building, etc. **3** side of an array of troops. • *v. tr.* be situated at both sides of.

■ *n.* **1** loin. **2** see SIDE *n.* 1. • *v.* edge, border, line.

flan•nel /flánəl/ *n.* **1** woven wool fabric, usu. napless. **2** [in *pl.*] flannel garments, esp. trousers. □□ **flan′nel•ly** *adj.*

flan•nel•ette /flánəlét/ *n.* napped cotton fabric similar to flannel.

flap /flap/ • *v.* (**flapped, flap•ping**) **1 a** move (wings, the arms, etc.) up and down when flying, or as if flying. **b** *intr.* move up and down; beat. **2** *intr.* swing or sway about; flutter. • *n.* **1** piece of cloth, wood, paper, etc., hinged or attached by one side only, e.g., the folded part of an envelope or a table leaf. **2** one up-and-down motion of a wing, an arm, etc. **3** *colloq.* agitation; panic. **4** hinged or sliding section of a wing used to control lift and drag. □□ **flap′py** *adj.*

• *v.* **1** flail, wave, wag, flutter, thrash. **2** see SWING *v.* 1, 3. • *n.* **1** fold, fly, lappet, lap. **2** beat, flutter, wave, wag. **3** upset, to-do, commotion, fuss.

flap•jack /flápjak/ *n.* pancake.

flap•per /flápər/ *n.* **1** person or thing that flaps. **2** *sl.* (in the 1920s) young unconventional or lively woman.

flare /flair/ • *v.* **1** *intr. & tr.* widen, esp. toward the bottom. **2** *intr. & tr.* burn suddenly with a bright unsteady flame. **3** *intr.* burst into anger; burst forth. • *n.* **1 a** dazzling irregular flame or light. **b** sudden outburst of flame. **2** signal light, bright light, or firework used as a signal. **3** gradual widening, esp. of a skirt or trousers. □ **flare up** burst into a sudden blaze, anger, activity, etc. **flare-up** *n.* sudden outburst.

■ *v.* **1** spread (out *or* outward), broaden, expand, increase, enlarge. **2** blaze *or* flame (up), flare up, flash; see also BURN *v.* 1, 2. **3** explode, erupt, lose one's temper, flare up, *colloq.* blow up. • *n.* **1** blaze, flash, glare, dazzle. **2** beacon, torch. **3** broadening, spread, expansion, increase. □ **flare up** blaze, flame, flash, burn, flare.

flash /flash/ • *v.* **1** *intr. & tr.* emit or reflect or cause to emit or reflect light briefly, suddenly, or intermittently; gleam or cause to gleam. **2** *tr.* send or reflect like a sudden flame. **3** *intr.* a burst suddenly into view or perception. **b** move swiftly **4** *tr.* a send (news, etc.) by radio, telegraph, etc. **b** signal to (a person) by shining lights or headlights briefly. **5** *tr. colloq.* show ostentatiously. • *n.* **1** sudden bright light or flame, e.g., of lightning. **2** very brief time, an instant. **3 a** brief, sudden burst of feeling (*a flash of hope*). **b** sudden display (of wit, understanding, etc.). **4** breaking news story. **5** *Photog.* = FLASHLIGHT. **6** bright patch of color. □ **flash point 1** temperature at which vapor from oil, etc., will ignite in air. **2** point at which anger, indignation, etc., becomes uncontrollable.

■ *v.* **1, 2** scintillate, sparkle, dazzle, glitter, coruscate, twinkle, flicker, shimmer, glimmer; gleam, beam. **3 b** rush, race, speed, dash, streak, tear, hurry, hasten, flick, fly, zoom. **5** see FLAUNT *v.* • *n.* **1** flare, burst, blaze, dazzle, spark, sparkle, coruscation, glitter, twinkle. **2** moment, (split) second, twinkle, twinkling (of an eye), trice, minute. **3 a** outbreak; see also OUTBURST. **b** stroke, flicker, spark.

flash•back /fláshbak/ *n.* scene in a movie, novel, etc., set in a time earlier than the main action.

flash•ing /fláshing/ *n.* usu. metallic strip used to prevent water penetration at the junction of a roof with a wall, etc.

flash•light /fláshlīt/ *n.* battery-operated portable light.

flash•y /fláshee/ *adj.* (**flash•i•er, flash•i•est**) showy; gaudy; cheaply attractive. □□ **flash′i•ly** *adv.* **flash′i•ness** *n.*

■ ostentatious; loud, garish, glaring; cheap, vulgar, tawdry, tasteless, tacky, *sl.* glitzy.

flask /flask/ *n.* **1** narrow-necked bulbous bottle for wine, etc., or as used in chemistry. **2** pocket-sized beverage container.

flat¹ /flat/ • *adj.* (**flat•ter, flat•test**) **1 a** horizontally level (*a flat roof*). **b** even; smooth;

unbroken; (*a flat stomach*). **c** level, shallow (*a flat cap*). **2** unqualified; plain; downright (*a flat denial*). **3** dull; lifeless; monotonous (*spoke in a flat tone*). **4** (of a carbonated drink) having lost its effervescence; stale. **5** *Mus.* **a** below true or normal pitch (*the violins are flat*). **b** half step lower. **6** (of a tire) punctured; deflated. • *adv.* **1** lying at full length; spread out (*lay flat on the floor*). **2** *colloq.* **a** completely; absolutely (*flat broke*). **b** exactly (*five minutes flat*). **3** *Mus.* below the true or normal pitch. • *n.* **1** flat part of anything; something flat (*flat of the hand*). **2** level ground, esp. a plain or swamp. **3** *Mus.* **a** a note lowered a half step below natural pitch. **b** sign ( ) indicating this. **4** *Theatr.* flat section of scenery mounted on a frame. **6** *colloq.* flat tire. □ **flat foot** foot with a less than normal arch. **flat out 1** at top speed. **2** without hesitation or delay. **3** using all one's strength, energy, or resources. □□ **flat′ly** *adv.* **flat′ness** *n.* **flat′tish** *adj.*

■ *adj.* **1 a** horizontal, plane. **b** uninterrupted. **2** unreserved, unconditional, absolute, categorical; plain, direct; downright, outright. **3** insipid, bland, spiritless, lackluster, prosaic, uninteresting. **4** noneffervescent, decarbonated, dead. **6** blown out. • *adv.* **1** prostrate, prone, supine, stretched out. **2 a** categorically, utterly, wholly, uncompromisingly. **b** precisely. • *n.* **2** lowland, tundra, steppe; marsh, bog; mudflat. □ **flat out 1** at maximum *or* full *or* breakneck speed, speedily, quickly, rapidly. **2** unhesitatingly, directly, at once, immediately; plainly, openly.

flat² /flat/ *n.* = APARTMENT.

flat•fish /flátfish/ *n.* any marine fish having both eyes on one side of a flattened body, including sole, turbot, plaice, etc.

flat•foot /flátfŏŏt/ *n.* (*pl.* **–foots** *or* **–feet**) *sl.* police officer.

flat-foot•ed /flátfŏŏtid/ *adj.* **1** having flat feet. **2** *colloq.* unprepared; off guard.

flat•i•ron /flátiərn/ *n.* iron heated externally and used for pressing clothes, etc.

flat•ten /flát′n/ *v.* **1** *tr. & intr.* make or become flat. **2** *tr. colloq.* **a** humiliate. **b** knock down. □□ **flat′ten•er** *n.*

■ **1** level (off *or* out), even (off *or* out). **2 b** knock out, floor, fell; level, raze (to the ground).

flat•ter /flátər/ *v.tr.* **1** compliment unduly; overpraise, esp. for gain or advantage. **2** please, congratulate, or delude (oneself, etc.). **3** make (a person) appear to the best advantage (*that blouse flatters you*). **4** make (a person) feel honored. □□ **flat′ter•er** *n.* **flat′ter•ing** *adj.* **flat′ter•ing•ly** *adv.*

■ **1** toady (to), truckle to, fawn (on *or* upon), *colloq.* butter up, soft-soap. **2** see FOOL *v.* 1, 3. **3** see SUIT *v.* 1. □□ **flatterer** toady, sycophant, fawner, backscratcher. **flattering** becoming, enhancing; complimentary, adulatory, laudatory, fulsome.

flat•ter•y /flátəree/ *n.* (*pl.* **–ies**) **1** exaggerated or insincere praise. **2** act or an instance of flattering.

■ adulation, cajolery, blandishment, toadying.

flat•u•lent /fláchələnt/ *adj.* **1** having or producing intestinal gas. **2** (of speech, etc.) inflated; pretentious. □□ **flat′u•lence** *n.* **flat′u•len•cy** *n.* **flat′u•lent•ly** *adv.*

flat•ware /flátwair/ *n.* **1** forks, knives, spoons, etc. **2** plates, saucers, etc.

flat•worm /flátwərm/ *n.* worm with a flattened body.

flaunt /flawnt/ *v.* display ostentatiously; show off; parade. ¶Often confused with *flout.* □□ **flaunt′er** *n.* **flaunt′y** *adj.*

■ flourish, exhibit, sport, spotlight.

flau•tist /fláwtist, flów–/ *n.* flute player.

fla•vor /fláyvər/ • *n.* **1** distinctive mingled sensation of smell and taste. **2** indefinable characteristic quality. • *v.tr.* give flavor to; season. □□ **fla′vor•ful** *adj.* **fla′vor•less** *adj.* **fla′vor•some** *adj.*

■ *n.* **1** taste, tastiness, savor, tang, piquancy, zest, sapor. **2** character, spirit, nature, property, mark, stamp, style, taste, feel, tinge, aroma, air. • *v.* season, spice.

fla•vor•ing /fláyvəring/ *n.* substance used to flavor food or drink.

flaw /flaw/ • *n.* **1** imperfection; blemish. **2** crack or similar fault. See synonym study at FAULT. • *v.* crack; damage; spoil. □□ **flawed** *adj.* **flaw′less** *adj.* **flaw′less•ly** *adv.* **flaw′less•ness** *n.*

■ *n.* **1** fault, defect, error, mistake, blot, stain, taint, failing, weakness. **2** break, chip, fracture; split, cleft, slit, cut; puncture, hole. • *v.* harm, ruin, mark; discredit, stigmatize. □□ **flawed** damaged, harmed; tainted; defective, imperfect. **flawless** perfect, pristine, pure, uncorrupted, chaste, virgin, clean, immaculate; undamaged, intact; unassailable, unimpeachable.

flax /flaks/ *n.* **1** blue-flowered plant, cultivated for its textile fiber and its seeds. **2** dressed or undressed flax fibers.

flax•en /fláksən/ *adj.* **1** of flax. **2** (of hair) pale yellow.

flay /flay/ *v.tr.* **1** strip the skin or hide off, esp. by beating. **2** criticize severely. □□ **flay′er** *n.*

■ **1** see FLOG. **2** see LAMBASTE 2.

flea /flee/ *n.* small wingless jumping insect that feeds on human and other blood. □ **flea market** market selling secondhand goods, etc.

fleck /flek/ • *n.* **1** small particle or speck, esp. of dust. **2** spot. • *v.tr.* mark with flecks.

■ *n.* see SPOT *n.* 1. • *v.* (*flecked*) dappled, spotted, pied, speckled, dotted, freckled.

fled past and past part. of FLEE.

fledg•ling /fléjling/ *n.* **1** young bird. **2** inexperienced person.

■ **2** see NOVICE.

flee /flee/ *v.* (*past* and *past part.* **fled** /fled/) **1** *intr.* [often foll. by *from, before*] run away. **2** *tr.* run away from; leave abruptly. **3** *intr.* vanish; cease; pass away. □□ **fle•er** /fleeər/ *n.*

■ **1** escape, get away, fly, bolt, go (away), decamp, *colloq.* show a clean pair of heels, make tracks. **2** quit, *colloq.* skip; avoid, evade, shun. **3** see DISAPPEAR.

fleece /flees/ • *n.* **1** woolly covering of a sheep or a similar animal. **2** soft warm fabric. • v.tr. **1** strip (a person) of money, valuables, etc.; swindle. **2** shear (a sheep, etc.). □□ **fleece′a•ble** adj. **fleeced** adj. [also in comb.].

  ■ v. **1** cheat, defraud, overcharge, plunder, milk, rob, rook, soak, flimflam, bleed, pluck, colloq. rip off, sl. bilk, skin, take, gyp. **2** shave, crop, strip, clip.

fleec•y /flēesee/ adj. (**fleec•i•er, fleec•i•est**) **1** of or like a fleece. **2** covered with a fleece. □□ **fleec′i•ly** adv. **fleec′i•ness** n.

fleet[1] /fleet/ n. **1** warships under one commander. **2** number of vehicles operating under one proprietor.

  ■ **1** armada, flotilla, naval task force, squadron, convoy.

fleet[2] /fleet/ adj. swift; nimble. □□ **fleet′ly** adv. **fleet′ness** n.

  ■ rapid, fast, speedy, quick, expeditious.

fleet•ing /fleeting/ adj. transitory; brief. See synonym study at TEMPORARY. □□ **fleet′ing•ly** adv.

  ■ fugitive, transient, temporary, passing, ephemeral.

Flem•ish /flémish/ • adj. of or relating to Flanders. • n. language of Flanders.

flesh /flesh/ n. **1 a** soft, esp. muscular, substance between the skin and bones of an animal or human. **b** plumpness; fat. **2** the body as opposed to the mind or the soul, esp. considered as sinful. **3** pulpy substance of a fruit or a plant. **4** (also **flesh′ col•or**) yellowish pink color. **5** animal or human life. □ **flesh and blood** n. **1** the body or its substance. **2** humankind. **3** human nature, esp. as being fallible. adj. actually living, not imaginary or supernatural. **flesh out** make or become substantial. **in the flesh** in bodily form, in person. **one's own flesh and blood** near relatives; descendants. □□ **flesh′less** adj.

  ■ n. **1 a** muscle, tissue. **b** see FAT n. **2** corporality; flesh and blood. □ **flesh out** give or lend substance to, fill out, enlarge or expand on, develop, amplify. **in the flesh** in propria persona, personally, really, physically, alive, living. **one's own flesh and blood** kin, kinfolk, family, stock, blood, kith and kin, relations.

flesh•ly /fléshlee/ adj. (**flesh•li•er, flesh•li•est**) **1** bodily; sensual. **2** mortal; not divine. **3** worldly. □□ **flesh′li•ness** n.

flesh•y /fléshee/ adj. (**flesh•i•er, flesh•i•est**) **1** plump; fat. **2** of flesh; without bone. **3** pulpy. **4** like flesh. □□ **flesh′i•ness** n.

fleur-de-lis /flőrdəlee/ n. (also **fleur-de-lys**) (pl. **fleurs-** pronunc. same) lily-like emblem used on the former royal arms of France.

flew past of FLY[1].

flex /fleks/ v. **1** tr. & intr. bend (a joint, limb, etc.) or be bent. **2** tr. & intr. move (a muscle) or (of a muscle) be moved to bend a joint. **3** tr. Geol. bend (strata).

  ■ **1** see BEND[1] v. 1. **2** exercise, tense, tighten.

flex•i•ble /fléksibəl/ adj. **1** able to bend without breaking; pliable. **2** adaptable; variable. □□ **flex•i•bil′i•ty** n. **flex′i•bly** adv.

  ■ **1** pliant, elastic, resilient, supple, bendable, limber, lithe, stretchy, stretchable,

305 fleecy ~ flier

springy. **2** versatile; variable; see also adaptable (ADAPT). □□ **flexibility** pliability, pliancy, elasticity, resilience, resiliency, suppleness, flexibleness, limberness, give; manageability, compliance, tractability; docility, obedience.

SYNONYM STUDY: flexible

ELASTIC, LIMBER, PLIABLE, PLIANT, RESILIENT, SUPPLE. If you can bend over and touch your toes, you are **flexible**. But a dancer or gymnast is **limber**, an adjective that specifically applies to a body that has been brought into condition through training (to stay limber, she did yoga every day). Flexible applies to whatever can be bent without breaking whether or not it returns to its original shape (a flexible plastic hose; a flexible electrical conduit); it does not necessarily refer, as limber does, to the human body. Flexible is also used more broadly to describe attitudes (I'm flexible about when we leave, I just want to be back by five) or anything that can easily be modified (flexible hours; flexible spending plans). Unlike flexible, **resilient** implies the ability to spring back into shape after being bent or compressed, or to recover one's health or spirits quickly (so young and resilient that she was back at work in a week). **Elastic** is usually applied to substances or materials that are easy to stretch or expand and that quickly recover their shape or size (pants with an elastic waist); while **supple** is applied to whatever is easily bent, twisted, or folded without breaking or cracking (a soft, supple leather). When applied to the human body, supple suggests the ability to move effortlessly. **Pliant** and **pliable** may be used to describe either people or things that are easily bent or manipulated. Pliant suggests a tendency to bend without force or pressure from the outside, while pliable suggests the use of force or submission to another's will. A pliant person is merely adaptable, but a pliable person is easy to influence and eager to please.

---

flex•or /fléksər/ n. (in full **flex′or mus′cle**) muscle that bends part of the body.

flex•time /flékstīm/ n. (also **flex•i•time** /fléksitīm/) system of flexible working hours.

flick /flik/ • n. **1 a** light, sharp, quickly retracted blow with a whip, etc. **b** sudden release of a bent finger or thumb. **2** sudden movement or jerk, esp. of the wrist. **3** colloq. **a** a movie. **b** [in pl.; prec. by the] the movies. • v. **1** tr. strike or move off with a flick. **2** intr. make a flicking movement or sound.

  ■ n. **2** see WHISK n. 1. **3 a** see FILM n. 3. • v. **1** flip, brush, sweep, toss.

flick•er /flíkər/ • v.intr. **1** (of light or flame) shine or burn unsteadily. **2** flutter; quiver; vibrate. **3** (of hope, etc.) waver. • n. flickering movement, light, thought, etc.

  ■ v. **1** glimmer, shimmer, twinkle; waver, flare. **2** flap; tremble, fluctuate, oscillate. • n. glimmer, glimmering, twinkle, twinkling, sparkle.

fli•er /flíər/ n. (also **fly′er**) colloq. **1** aviator. **2** thing that flies in a specified way (poor *flier*). **3** (usu. **fly'er**) small handbill or circular.

■ **3** see LEAFLET *n.*

flight[1] /flīt/ *n.* **1 a** act or manner of flying. **b** swift movement or passage through the air. **2 a** journey made through the air or in space. **b** timetabled journey made by an airline. **3** series, esp. of stairs. □ **flight attendant** airline employee who attends to passengers' safety and comfort during flights.

■ **1 a** soaring; winging. **2 a** (air *or* space) voyage, (air *or* space) trip.

flight[2] /flīt/ *n.* fleeing; hasty retreat.

■ escape, departure, exit, exodus, getaway, bolting.

flight•less /flītlis/ *adj.* (of a bird, etc.) naturally unable to fly.

flight•y /flītee/ *adj.* (**flight•i•er, flight•i•est**) **1** frivolous; fickle; changeable. **2** slightly crazy. □□ **flight'i•ly** *adv.* **flight'i•ness** *n.*

■ **1** inconstant, capricious, fanciful, variable. **2** mad, silly, harebrained, reckless, irresponsible.

flim•sy /flimzee/ *adj.* (**flims•i•er, flims•i•est**) **1** insubstantial; easily damaged. **2** (of an excuse, etc.) unconvincing. **3** (of clothing) thin. □□ **flim'si•ly** *adv.* **flim'si•ness** *n.*

■ **1** makeshift, jerry-built, rickety, ramshackle, dilapidated; slight, unsubstantial, fragile. **2** feeble, weak, lame, implausible, unbelievable, unsatisfactory, poor. **3** delicate, light; gauzy, transparent.

flinch /flinch/ *v.intr.* draw back in fear, etc.; wince. See synonym study at WINCE. □□ **flinch'er** *n.* **flinch'ing•ly** *adv.*

■ cower, withdraw, cringe, recoil, start, quail.

fling /fling/ • *v.tr.* (*past* and *past part.* **flung** /flung/) **1** throw, rush, or let go of forcefully or hurriedly. **2** put or send suddenly or violently. • *n.* **1** act or instance of flinging; throw; plunge. **2** spell of indulgence or wild behavior (*he's had his fling*). **3** brief or casual romance. **4** impetuous, whirling Scottish dance. □□ **fling'er** *n.*

■ *v.* **1** toss, pitch, cast, heave, sling, *colloq.* lob, chuck. **2** see THROW *v.* 1, 2. • *n.* **1** see THROW *n.* 1. **2** debauch, spree, *sl.* binge.

flint /flint/ *n.* **1 a** hard gray stone of nearly pure silica. **b** piece of this, esp. as a primitive tool or weapon. **2** piece of hard alloy used to give an igniting spark. □□ **flint'y** *adj.* (**flint•i•er, flint•i•est**). **flint'i•ly** *adv.* **flint'i•ness** *n.*

flip /flip/ • *v.tr.* (**flipped, flip•ping**) **1** flick or toss (a coin, ball, etc.) with a quick movement so that it spins in the air. **2** turn or turn over; flick. • *n.* act of flipping. • *adj. colloq.* glib; flippant. □ **flip one's lid** *sl.* **1** lose self-control. **2** go crazy. **flip through 1** turn over (cards, pages, etc.). **2** look cursorily through (a book, etc.).

■ *v.* **1** spin. **2** see TURN *v.* 2. • *adj.* see FLIPPANT. □ **flip one's lid** become angry *or* furious, go berserk, go out of one's head, *colloq.* go mad. **flip through** see BROWSE *v.* 1.

flip-flop /flipflop/ • *n.* **1** usu. rubber sandal with a thong between the toes. **2** esp. sudden change of direction, attitude, policy, etc. • *v.intr.* (**–flopped, –flop•ping**) change direction, attitude, policy, etc., esp. suddenly.

flip•pant /flipənt/ *adj.* treating serious things lightly; disrespectful. □□ **flip'pan•cy** *n.* **flip'pant•ly** *adv.*

■ frivolous, facetious, lighthearted; impudent, impertinent, irreverent, saucy, *colloq.* flip. □□ **flippancy** frivolousness, facetiousness, levity, lightheartedness.

flip•per /flipər/ *n.* **1** broadened limb of a tortoise, penguin, etc., used in swimming. **2** attachment worn on the foot for underwater swimming.

flirt /flərt/ • *v.intr.* **1** behave in a frivolously amorous or sexually enticing manner. **2 a** superficially interest oneself (with an idea, etc.). **b** trifle (with danger, etc.). • *n.* person who indulges in flirting. □□ **flir•ta'tion** *n.* **flir•ta'tious** *adj.* **flir•ta'tious•ly** *adv.* **flirt'y** *adj.* (**flirt•i•er, flirt•i•est**).

■ *v.* **1** play or act the coquette, philander, play the field, womanize. **2** (*flirt with*) play with, entertain, think about *or* of; see also TOY *v.* 1. • *n.* coquette, tease; playboy. □□ **flirtatious** coquettish, seductive, flirty, philandering.

flit /flit/ *v.intr.* (**flit•ted, flit•ting**) move lightly, softly, or rapidly (*flitted from one room to another*). □□ **flit'ter** *n.*

■ go, fly, skip, hop, dart, flick, whisk, flash.

float /flōt/ • *v.* **1** *intr. & tr.* rest or move on or cause (a buoyant object) to rest or move on the surface of a liquid. **2** *intr. colloq.* move in a leisurely or casual way (*floated about humming quietly*). **3** *tr.* **a** bring (a company, scheme, etc.) into being; launch. **b** offer (stock, shares, etc.) on the stock market. **4** *intr. & tr.* circulate or cause (a rumor or idea) to circulate. • *n.* **1** thing that floats, esp.: **a** a raft. **b** cork or other buoyant object on a fishing line. **c** floating device on the surface of water, fuel, etc., controlling the flow. **2** platform mounted on a truck or trailer and carrying a display in a parade, etc. □□ **float'a•ble** *adj.* **float•a•bil'i•ty** /-təbilitee/ *n.*

■ *v.* **1** hover, bob, waft, hang, be suspended *or* poised. **3 a** establish, set up, organize, found, initiate. **4** see SPREAD *v.* 3. • *n.* **1 a** pontoon.

float•ing /flōting/ *adj.* not settled in a definite place; fluctuating; variable. □ **floating kidney** abnormal condition in which the kidneys are unusually movable. **2** such a kidney. **floating point** *Computing* decimal, etc., point that does not occupy a fixed position in the numbers processed. **floating rib** any of the lower ribs, which are not attached to the breastbone. □□ **float'ing•ly** *adv.*

■ see VARIABLE *adj.* 2.

flock[1] /flok/ • *n.* **1 a** number of animals of one kind, esp. birds, feeding or traveling together. **b** number of domestic animals, esp. sheep, goats, or geese, kept together. **2** large crowd of people. **3** Christian congregation or body of believers, esp. in relation to one minister. • *v.intr.* **1** congregate; mass. **2** go together in a crowd; troop.

■ *n.* **1** flight, gaggle, bevy, covey; pride,

pack, troop, school, swarm, horde, host; herd, drove, mob. **2** body, company, group, band, bunch, troop, set, collection, assembly, gathering, mass, mob, throng. • v. **1** assemble, meet, collect, gather, mob. **2** crowd, throng, herd, band together; pour, flood, swarm.

floe /flō/ n. sheet of floating ice.

flog /flawg, flog/ v.tr. (**flogged**, **flog·ging**) beat with a whip, stick, etc. □□ **flog'ger** n.
■ whip, lash, horsewhip, strap, flagellate; chastise.

flood /flud/ • n. **1 a** overflowing or influx of water, esp. over land; inundation. **b** the water that overflows. **2 a** outpouring of water; torrent (*flood of rain*). **b** something resembling a torrent (*flood of tears*). **c** abundance or excess. **3** inflow of the tide (also in *comb.: flood tide*). • v. **1** tr. **a** cover with or overflow in a flood. **b** overflow as if with a flood. **2** tr. irrigate, deluge, or overfill. **3** intr. arrive in great quantities (*complaints flooded in*).
■ n. **1** inundation, deluge, overflow. **2 a** cataract, stream, spate; freshet. **b** surge, outpouring, stream, rush, flow, deluge. **c** glut, surfeit, satiety, profusion. • v. **1** pour over or into or through(out); inundate, deluge, submerge, swamp. **2** inundate, water. **4** sweep, flow, pour, surge, rush.

flood·gate /flúdgayt/ n. **1** gate opened or closed to admit or exclude water, esp. the lower gate of a lock. **2** [usu. in *pl.*] last restraint holding back tears, rain, anger, etc.

flood·light /flúdlīt/ • n. large powerful light to illuminate a building, stage, etc. • v.tr. illuminate with floodlights.

flood·plain /flúdplayn/ n. flat terrain alongside a river that is subject to inundation when the river floods.

flood·wa·ter /flúdwawtər, -wo-/ n. water overflowing as the result of a flood.

floor /flawr/ • n. **1** lower surface of a room. **2 a** bottom of the sea, a cave, etc. **b** any level area. **3** one level of a building; story. **4 a** (in a legislative assembly) the part of the house where members meet. **b** right to speak next in debate (*gave him the floor*). **5** minimum of prices, wages, etc. • v.tr. **1** furnish with a floor. **2** bring or knock (a person) down. **3** colloq. confound; baffle. **4** colloq. overcome. □ **floor show** entertainment presented at a nightclub, etc. **take the floor 1** begin to dance on a dance floor, etc. **2** speak in a debate, at a meeting, etc. □□ **floor'less** adj.
■ n. **2 a** see BOTTOM n. 4. **3** deck. **5** base, lower limit, bottom. • v. **1** see PAVE. **2** bring to the ground, bowl over, fell. **3** stump, bewilder, dumbfound, confuse. **4** beat, defeat, conquer, destroy, rout, overwhelm. □ **take the floor 2** debate; see also LECTURE v. 1.

floor·ing /fláwring/ n. material to make or cover a floor.
■ floor, parquet, planking.

flop /flop/ • v.intr. (**flopped**, **flop·ping**) **1** sway about heavily or loosely. **2** sit, kneel, lie, or fall awkwardly or suddenly. **3** sl. fail; collapse. **4** make a dull sound as of a soft body landing, or of a flat thing slapping water. • n. **1** flopping movement or sound. **2** sl. failure.

• v. **1** dangle, hang (down), droop; swing, wave. **2** collapse, drop or tumble (down), topple, plop down. **3** fall flat, sl. bomb; see also FAIL v. 1, 2a. • n. **2** fiasco, disaster, nonstarter, colloq. lemon, bomb, sl. dud, turkey.

flop·py /flópee/ • adj. (**flop·pi·er, flop·pi·est**) tending to flop; not firm or rigid. • n. (pl. **-pies**) (in full **flop'py disk**) Computing removable disk on flexible magnetic medium for the storage of data. □□ **flop'pi·ly** adv. **flop'pi·ness** n.
■ adj. see LIMP² 1.

flo·ra /fláwrə/ n. (pl. **flo·ras** or **flo·rae** /-ree/) plants of a particular region, geological period, or environment.

flo·ral /fláwrəl/ adj. **1** of flowers. **2** decorated with or depicting flowers. **3** of flora or floras. □□ **flo'ral·ly** adv.

Flor·en·tine /fláwrənteen, -tīn, flór-/ • adj. **1** of or relating to Florence in Italy. **2** (**florentine** /-tccn/) (of a dish) served on a bed of spinach. • n. native or citizen of Florence.

flor·id /fláwrid, flór-/ adj. **1** ruddy; flushed (a *florid complexion*). **2** elaborately ornate; ostentatious; showy. □□ **flo·rid'i·ty** n. **flor'id·ly** adv. **flor'id·ness** n.
■ **1** see ROSY 1. **2** see ORNATE.

flor·ist /fláwrist, flór-/ n. person who deals in or grows flowers. □□ **flo'ris·try** n.

floss /flaws, flos/ • n. **1** rough silk enveloping a silkworm's cocoon. **2** silk thread used in embroidery. **3** = *dental floss*. • v.tr. [also *absol.*] clean (teeth) with dental floss.

floss·y /fláwsee, flósee/ adj. (**floss·i·er, floss·i·est**) **1** of or like floss. **2** colloq. fancy; showy.

flo·ta·tion /flōtáyshən/ n. (also **float·a'tion**) **1** process of launching or financing a commercial enterprise. **2** capacity to float.

flo·til·la /flōtílə/ n. small fleet of boats or naval vessels.

flot·sam /flótsəm/ n. wreckage floating at sea. □ **flotsam and jetsam 1** odds and ends; rubbish. **2** vagrants, etc.

flounce¹ /flowns/ • v.intr. go or move with an agitated, violent, or impatient motion. • n. flouncing movement.
■ v. strut, march, storm, stamp, stomp, bounce; fling.

flounce² /flowns/ n. wide ornamental strip of material gathered and sewn to a skirt, dress, etc.; frill.
■ valance, furbelow, peplum; ruffle.

floun·der¹ /flówndər/ v.intr. **1** struggle in mud, or as if in mud, or when wading. **2** perform a task badly or without knowledge. □□ **floun'der·er** n.
■ grope, blunder, stumble, tumble, stagger.

floun·der² /flówndər/ n. type of edible flatfish.

flour /flowr/ n. **1** meal or powder obtained by grinding grain, esp. wheat. **2** any fine powder. □□ **flour'y** adj. (**flour·i·er, flour·i·est**). **flour'i·ness** n.

flour·ish /flórish, flúr-/ • v. **1** intr. **a** grow vigorously; thrive. **b** prosper; be successful. **c** be in one's prime. **2** tr. wave (a weapon,

flout ~ flunky 308

one's limbs, etc.) vigorously. • *n.* **1** ostentatious gesture with a weapon, a hand, etc. (*removed his hat with a flourish*). **2** ornamental curving decoration of handwriting. **3** fanfare or ornate musical passage. □□ **flour′ish•er** *n.* **flour′ish•y** *adj.*

■ *v.* **1 a** bloom, blossom, flower. **b** boom, succeed, get ahead, do well. **c** mature, develop, ripen, mellow. **2** wield, brandish, wag, swing, twirl, flaunt. • *n.* **1** gesturing, wave; show, display. **2** curl, curlicue. **3** see FANFARE 1.

flout /flowt/ • *v.tr.* express contempt for (the law, rules, etc.) by word or action; mock; insult. ¶ Often confused with *flaunt*. • *n.* flouting speech or act.

■ *v.* deride, scorn, jeer, disdain, spurn, ridicule, disparage, decry, denigrate, belittle; affront.

flow /flō/ • *v.intr.* **1** glide along as a stream. **2** gush out; spring; be spilled. **3** circulate. **4** move smoothly or steadily. **5** (of a garment, hair, etc.) hang easily or gracefully. **6** [often foll. by *from*] result from; be caused by. • *n.* **1 a** flowing movement in a stream. **b** flowing liquid. **c** copious outpouring; stream (*a continuous flow of complaints*). **d** hardened mass that formerly flowed. **2** rise of a tide or a river (*ebb and flow*). □ **flow chart** (or **diagram** or **sheet**) diagram of the movement or action of things or persons engaged in a complex activity.

■ *v.* **1** run, course, stream, trickle; go; purl. **2** rush (out), surge, stream (out), spout, spurt, cascade; issue, originate; (*flow over* or *on to*) spread over or on to, overspread, cover. **3** see CIRCULATE[1] 1. **6** see STEM *v.* 1. • *n.* **1 a** current, course, stream, drift. **b, c** rush, gush, surge, outpouring; flood; see also STREAM *n.* 2.

flow•er /flowʹər/ • *n.* **1** part of a plant from which the fruit or seed is developed. **2** blossom, esp. on a stem and used in bunches for decoration. **3** plant cultivated or noted for its flowers. • *v.intr.* **1** bloom or blossom. **2** reach a peak. □ **the flower of** the best or best part of. □□ **flow′ered** *adj.* [also in *comb.*]. **flow′er•less** *adj.* **flow′er•like** *adj.*

■ *n.* **2** bloom, efflorescence. • *v.* **1** come out, open, efflorescence, unfold. **2** see PEAK[1] *v.* □ **the flower of** the cream or pick or élite of.

flow•er•pot /flowʹərpot/ *n.* pot for growing a plant.

flow•er•y /flowʹəree/ *adj.* **1** florally decorated. **2** (of style, speech, etc.) highly embellished; ornate. □□ **flow′er•i•ness** *n.*

■ **2** high-flown, florid, fancy, showy, grandiloquent; elaborate(d), decorated, ornamented, overwrought.

flow•ing /flōʹing/ *adj.* **1** (of literary style, etc.) fluent; easy. **2** smoothly continuous; not abrupt. **3** (of hair, a garment, a sail, etc.) unconfined. □□ **flow′ing•ly** *adv.*

■ **1** see FLUENT 1. **3** see LOOSE *adj.* 3, 4.

flown *past part.* of FLY[1].

fl. oz. *abbr.* fluid ounce(s).

flu /flōō/ *n. colloq.* influenza.

fluc•tu•ate /flúkchōō-ayt/ *v.intr.* vary irregu-

larly; be unstable; vacillate; rise and fall. □□ **fluc•tu•a•tion** /-áyshən/ *n.*

■ change, shift, alternate, seesaw, yo-yo, swing. □□ **fluctuation** variation(s), change(s), alternation(s), swing(s), vacillation(s); instability, unsteadiness.

flue /flōō/ *n.* **1** smoke duct in a chimney. **2** channel for conveying heat, esp. a hot-air passage in a wall.

■ see VENT[1] *n.* 1.

flu•ent /flōōʹənt/ *adj.* **1** flowing naturally and readily. **2** verbally facile, esp. in a foreign language. □□ **flu′en•cy** *n.* **flu′ent•ly** *adv.*

■ **1** natural, facile, effortless, ready. **2** articulate, eloquent, well-spoken, felicitous. □□ **fluency** flow, articulateness, eloquence, control, command, ease.

fluff /fluf/ • *n.* **1** soft, light, feathery material coming off blankets, etc. **2** soft fur or feathers. **3** *sl.* mistake in a performance, etc. • *v.* **1** shake into or become a soft mass. **2** *colloq.* make a mistake in; blunder (*fluffed his opening line*).

■ *n.* **1** down, fuzz, lint, dust. **3** error, slip; *colloq.* howler, blooper. • *v.* **1** puff up; aerate. **2** ruin, make a mess of, spoil, bungle, botch, foul up.

fluff•y /flúfee/ *adj.* (**fluff•i•er**, **fluff•i•est**) **1** of or like fluff. **2** covered in fluff. **3** superficial. □□ **fluff′i•ly** *adv.* **fluff′i•ness** *n.*

■ **1** downy, soft, puffy, light. **2** downy, woolly, linty.

flu•gel•horn /flōōgəlhawrn/ *n.* valved brass wind instrument like a cornet but with a broader tone.

flu•id /flōōid/ • *n.* substance, esp. a gas or liquid, whose shape is determined by its container. • *adj.* **1** able to flow and alter shape freely. **2** constantly changing. □ **fluid ounce** see OUNCE. □□ **flu•id•i•fy** /-idifi/ *v.tr.* (**-fies**, **-fied**) **flu•id′i•ty** *n.* **flu′id•ly** *adv.* **flu′id•ness** *n.*

■ *n.* solution, liquor; ichor; vapor. • *adj.* **1** liquid, flowing, runny, watery, aqueous. **2** changeable, variable, flexible, adjustable, unfixed, nonstatic, liquid.

fluke[1] /flōōk/ *n.* lucky accident. □□ **fluk′y** *adj.* (**fluk•i•er, fluk•i•est**).

■ stroke of (good) luck, quirk or twist of fate.

fluke[2] /flōōk/ *n.* **1** parasitic flatworm including liver flukes and blood flukes. **2** flatfish, esp. a flounder.

fluke[3] /flōōk/ *n.* **1** *Naut.* broad triangular plate on the arm of an anchor. **2** *Zool.* either of the lobes of a whale's tail.

flume /flōōm/ *n.* **1 a** artificial channel conveying water, etc. **b** water slide into a swimming pool, etc. **2** ravine with a stream.

flum•mox /flúməks/ *v.tr. colloq.* bewilder; disconcert.

■ confound, confuse, baffle, perplex, stump.

flung *past* and *past part.* of FLING.

flunk /flungk/ *colloq.* • *v.* **1** *tr.* **a** fail (an examination, etc.). **b** fail (an examination candidate). **2** *intr.* [often foll. by *out*] fail utterly; give up. • *n.* instance of flunking.

■ *v.* see FAIL *v.* 1, 2a.

flun•ky /flúngkee/ *n.* (also **flun′key**) (*pl.*

–kies or –keys) usu. *derog.* **1** liveried servant. **2** toady. **3** underling.
■ **1** lackey, footman, menial, subordinate. **2** hanger-on, sycophant; see also *yes-man.*

fluo•resce /flŏŏrés, flaw–/ *v.intr.* be or become fluorescent.

fluo•res•cence /flŏŏrésəns, flaw–/ *n.* **1** light radiation from certain substances. **2** property of absorbing light of short (invisible) wavelength and emitting light of longer (visible) wavelength.

fluo•res•cent /flŏŏrésənt, flaw–/ *adj.* having or showing fluorescence. □ **fluorescent lamp** (or **bulb**) esp. tubular lamp or bulb giving light by fluorescence.

fluo•ri•date /flŏŏridayt, flaw–/ *v.tr.* add fluoride to (drinking water, etc.). □□ **fluo•ri•da•tion** /flŏŏridáyshən, flaw–/ *n.*

fluo•ride /flŏŏrīd, flaw–/ *n.* any binary compound of fluorine.

fluo•rine /flŏŏreen, flaw–/ *n.* poisonous pale yellow gaseous element of the halogen group. ¶Symb.: **F**.

fluo•rite /flŏŏrīt, flaw–/ *n.* mineral form of calcium fluoride.

fluo•ro•car•bon /flŏŏrōkaarbən, flaw–/ *n.* compound of a hydrocarbon with fluorine atoms.

flur•ry /flúree, flúree/ • *n.* (*pl.* **ries**) **1** gust or squall (esp. of snow). **2** sudden burst of activity. **3** commotion. • *v.tr.* (**–ries, –ried**) confuse by haste or noise; agitate.
■ *n.* **2** see STIR[1] *n.* 2. **3** to-do, fuss, upset, stir, disturbance, tumult; excitement, activity, agitation. • *v.* bewilder, put out, disturb, excite, fluster.

flush[1] /flush/ • *v.* **1** *intr.* blush; redden. **2** *tr.* (usu. as **flushed** *adj.*) cause to glow, blush, or be elated. **3** *tr.* **a** cleanse (a drain, toilet, etc.) by a rushing flow of water. **b** dispose of (an object) in this way. **4** *intr.* rush out; spurt. • *n.* **1 a** blush. **b** glow of light or color. **2 a** rush of water. **b** cleansing by flushing. **3 a** rush of emotion. **b** elation produced by a victory, etc. **4** freshness; vigor. **5 a** (also **hot flush**) = *hot flash.* **b** feverish temperature. **c** facial redness, esp. caused by fever, alcohol, etc. □□ **flush•er** *n.*
■ *v.* **1** crimson, burn, color (up); glow. **2** (**flushed**) glowing; delighted, thrilled. **3 a** rinse, flush out, wash (out or away). **b** wash away, sluice away. **4** see SPURT *v.* 1a. • *n.* **1** redness, pinkness; radiance, rosiness. **2 a** gush or surge of water, stream, flow. **b** euphoria, thrill, excitement, delight, tingle. **4** see VIGOR 1.

flush[2] /flush/ *adj.* **1** in the same plane; even. **2** *colloq.* having plenty of money. See synonym study at WEALTHY. □□ **flush•ness** *n.*
■ *adj.* **1** level, square, true. **2** wealthy, rich, prosperous, affluent, moneyed, well-to-do, *colloq.* well-heeled.

flush[3] /flush/ *n.* hand of cards all of one suit, esp. in poker.

flush[4] /flush/ *v.* **1** *tr.* cause (esp. a game bird) to fly up. **2** *intr.* fly up and away. □ **flush out 1** reveal. **2** drive out.

flus•ter /flústər/ • *v.* make or become nervous or confused. • *n.* confused or agitated state.

■ *v.* flurry, agitate, stir up, discompose, discomfit, discomfort, disconcert, upset; confuse, baffle, confound, puzzle, perplex. • *n.* agitation, upset, nervousness, discomfort, disquiet; confusion, bafflement.

flute /floot/ *n.* **1** high-pitched wind instrument of metal or wood, having holes along it stopped by the fingers or keys. **2** cylindrical groove. □□ **flute•like** *adj.* **flut•ing** *n.* **flut•ist** *n.* (cf. FLAUTIST). **flut•y** *adj.* (in sense 1 of *n.*)

flut•ter /flútər/ • *v.* **1 a** *intr.* flap the wings in flying or trying to fly (*butterflies fluttered in the sunshine*). **b** *tr.* flap (the wings). **2** *intr.* fall with a quivering motion. **3** *intr.* & *tr.* move or cause to move irregularly or tremblingly. **4** *intr.* go about restlessly; flit; hover. **5** *tr.* agitate; confuse. **6** *intr.* (of a pulse or heartbeat) beat feebly or irregularly. • *n.* **1** act of fluttering. **2** tremulous state of excitement. □□ **flut•ter•er** *n.* **flut•ter•y** *adj.*
■ *v.* **3** flop, wave, oscillate. **4** flicker, flitter; dance about; fuss. **5** see AGITATE 3. • *n.* **1** flapping, flopping, wave, waving, oscillation. **2** flurry, stir, whirl; see also SENSATION 2a.

flux /fluks/ *n.* **1** process of flowing or flowing out. **2** continuous change (*in a state of flux*). **3** *Metallurgy* substance mixed with a metal, etc., to promote fusion.
■ **2** fluctuation, instability, unrest, swing, swinging, wavering, movement; see also CHANGE *n.* 1.

fly[1] /flī/ • *v.* (**flies**; *past* **flew** /flōō/; *past part.* **flown** /flōn/) **1** *intr.* move through the air under control, esp. with wings. **2** (of an aircraft or its occupants): **a** *intr.* travel through the air or through space. **b** *tr.* traverse (a region or distance) (*flew the Pacific*). **3** *tr.* operate a flying vehicle. **4** *tr.* & *intr.* wave or flutter. **5** *intr.* **a** flee. **b** *colloq.* depart hastily. **6** *intr.* hasten or spring violently. **7** *tr.* flee from. **8** *intr. Baseball* hit a fly ball. • *n.* (*pl.* **–ies**) **1 a** flap on a garment, esp. trousers, to contain or cover a fastening. **b** this fastening. **2** flap at the entrance of a tent. **3** [*in pl.*] space over the proscenium in a theater. **4** *Baseball* batted ball hit high in the air. □ **fly-by-night** *adj.* **1** unreliable. **2** short-lived. *n.* unreliable person. □ **fly off the handle** *colloq.* lose one's temper suddenly and unexpectedly. □□ **fly•a•ble** *adj.*
■ *v.* **1** take wing, take to the air, wing, soar. **3** see PILOT *v.* **4** see FLAP *v.* 1. **5** see FLEE 1. **7** see FLEE 2. • *n.* **1** fly front, zipper. □ **fly-by-night**(*adj.*) **1** untrustworthy, irresponsible; disreputable, shady, dubious. **2** temporary, transitory, fugitive, ephemeral, transient.

fly off the handle fly into a rage or fury or temper or passion, go berserk, explode, get worked up, *colloq.* have a fit or tantrum.

fly[2] /flī/ *n.* (*pl.* **flies**) **1** insect with two usu. transparent wings. **2** natural or artificial fly used as bait in fishing. □ **fly-fish** *v.intr.* fish with a fly. **fly in the ointment** minor irritation that spoils enjoyment.
■ **fly in the ointment** hitch, snag, impediment, obstacle, obstruction, problem, difficulty, drawback.

fly•ing /flī-ing/ • *adj.* **1** fluttering or waving

in the air; hanging loose. **2** hasty; brief (*a flying visit*). **3** designed for rapid movement. **4** (of an animal) able to make very long leaps by using winglike membranes, etc. • *n.* flight, esp. in an aircraft. □ **flying buttress** buttress slanting from a separate column, usu. forming an arch with the wall it supports. **flying fish** tropical fish with winglike pectoral fins for gliding through the air. **flying saucer** any unidentified, esp. circular, flying object, popularly supposed to have come from space.

■ *n.* see FLIGHT[1] *n.* 1a.

fly•leaf /flíleef/ *n.* (*pl.* **–leaves**) blank leaf at the beginning or end of a book.

fly•pa•per /flípaypər/ *n.* sticky treated paper for catching flies.

fly•trap /flítrap/ *n.* any of various plants that catch flies, esp. the Venus flytrap.

fly•weight /flíwayt/ *n.* weight class between light flyweight and bantamweight for competitors in certain sports.

fly•wheel /flíhweel, –weel/ *n.* heavy wheel on a revolving shaft used to regulate machinery or accumulate power.

FM *abbr.* **1** frequency modulation. **2** Field Marshal.

Fm *symb. Chem.* fermium.

FNMA /fáneemáy/ *n.* Federal National Mortgage Association.

f-num•ber /éf numbər/ *n.* (also **f-stop**) *Photog.* ratio of the focal length to the effective diameter of a lens.

foal /fōl/ • *n.* young of a horse or related animal. • *v.tr.* (of a mare, etc.) give birth to (a foal).

foam /fōm/ • *n.* **1** mass of small bubbles formed on or in a liquid. **2** froth of saliva or sweat. **3** substance resembling these, e.g., rubber or plastic in a cellular mass. • *v.intr.* **1** emit foam; froth. **2** run with foam. □□ **foam′less** *adj.* **foam′y** *adj.* (**foam•i•er, foam•i•est**).

■ *n.* **1** froth, spume, lather; bubbles, suds; head. • *v.* bubble, froth, spume, lather, suds.

fob[1] /fob/ *n.* **1** (in full **fob chain**) chain of a pocket watch. **2** small pocket. **3** tab on a key ring.

fob[2] /fob/ *v.tr.* (**fobbed, fob•bing**) cheat; deceive. □ **fob off** deceive into accepting something inferior.

fo•cal /fōkəl/ *adj.* of, at, or in terms of a focus. □ **focal distance** (or **length**) distance between the center of a mirror or lens and its focus. **focal point** = FOCUS *n.* 1.

fo′c•s′le var. of FORECASTLE.

fo•cus /fōkəs/ • *n.* (*pl.* **fo•cus•es** or **fo•ci** /fōsī/) **1** *Physics* **a** point at which rays or waves meet after reflection or refraction. **b** the point from which diverging rays or waves appear to proceed. (Also called **focal point**). **2 a** *Optics* point at which an object must be situated for an image of it given by a lens or mirror to be well defined (*bring into focus*). **b** adjustment of the eye or a lens necessary to produce a clear image. **c** state of clear definition. **2** center of interest or activity. • *v.* (**fo•cused, fo•cus•ing** or **fo•cussed,**

fo•cus•sing) **1** *tr.* bring into focus. **2** *tr.* adjust the focus of (a lens, the eye, etc.). **3** *tr. & intr.* concentrate or be concentrated on. □ **focus group** group that meets to discuss a particular problem, issue, etc. □□ **fo′cus•er** *n.*

■ *n.* **2 c** (*in focus*) clear, distinct, sharp, well-defined. **3** focal point, heart, core, hub. • *v.* **3** center, direct, bring to bear; be centered, be directed.

fod•der /fódər/ *n.* dried hay, straw, etc., for cattle, horses, etc.

■ see FEED *n.*

foe /fō/ *n.* enemy or opponent.

fog /fawg, fog/ • *n.* **1** thick cloud of water droplets or smoke suspended in the atmosphere at or near the earth's surface. **2** uncertain or confused position or state. • *v.* (**fogged, fog•ging**) **1** *tr.* cover with or confuse as if with a fog. **2** *intr.* become covered with fog or condensed vapor. □ **in a fog** puzzled; at a loss.

■ *n.* **1** mist, haze, vapor, cloud, smog, *colloq.* pea soup. **2** see DISTRACTION 3. • *v.* fog up, mist up *or* over; bewilder, confuse, obscure, cloud, becloud, muddle. □ **in a fog** see DAZE *n.*

fo•gey var. of FOGY.

fog•gy /fáwgee, fógee/ *adj.* (**fog•gi•er, fog•gi•est**) **1** (of the atmosphere) thick or obscure with fog. **2** of or like fog. **3** vague; confused; unclear. □□ **fog′gi•ly** *adv.* **fog′gi•ness** *n.*

■ **1** see MISTY. **3** see VAGUE 1.

fog•horn /fáwghawrn, fóg–/ *n.* horn warning ships in fog.

fo•gy /fōgee/ *n.* (also **fo′gey**) (*pl.* **–gies** or **–geys**) dull old-fashioned person (esp. *old fogy*). □□ **fo′gy•ish** *adj.*

■ conservative, *colloq.* fossil, stick-in-the-mud.

foi•ble /fóybəl/ *n.* minor weakness or idiosyncrasy. See synonym study at FAULT.

■ imperfection, weak point, fault, frailty, shortcoming, flaw; peculiarity, quirk, crotchet, eccentricity.

foil[1] /foyl/ *v.tr.* frustrate; baffle; defeat. See synonym study at THWART.

■ outwit, thwart, offset, balk, check, impede.

foil[2] /foyl/ *n.* **1** metal hammered or rolled into a thin sheet. **2** person or thing setting off another by contrast.

foil[3] /foyl/ *n.* light blunt sword used in fencing.

foist /foyst/ *v.tr.* [foll. by *on, upon*] impose (an unwelcome person or thing).

■ thrust, force, press, *often joc.* inflict.

fold[1] /fōld/ • *v.* **1** *tr.* **a** bend or close (a flexible thing) over upon itself. **b** [foll. by *back, over, down*] bend a part of (a flexible thing) in the manner specified (*fold down the flap*). **2** *intr.* become or be able to be folded. **3** *tr.* [foll. by *away, up*] make compact by folding. **4** *intr. colloq.* **a** collapse; disintegrate. **b** (of an enterprise) fail; go bankrupt. **5** *tr. poet.* embrace. **6** *tr.* clasp (the arms); wrap; envelop. • *n.* **1** line made by or for folding. **2** folded part. □□ **fold′a•ble** *adj.*

■ *v.* **1** double (over *or* up), crease, pleat, gather. **4 a** see *give way* 2 (WAY). **b** go out of business, go under, close down. **5, 6** hug; gather, enfold, enclose. • *n.* **2** crease, pleat, gather, crimp.

fold[2] /fōld/ • *n.* **1** = SHEEPFOLD. **2** body of believers or members of a church. • *v.tr.* enclose (sheep) in a fold.

-fold /fōld/ *suffix* forming adjectives and adverbs from cardinal numbers, meaning: **1** in an amount multiplied by (*repaid tenfold*). **2** consisting of so many parts (*threefold blessing*).

fold•er /fōldər/ *n.* **1** folding cover or holder for loose papers. **2** folded leaflet.

fo•li•age /fōleeij/ *n.* leaves; leafage.

fo•lic ac•id /fōlik, fól-/ *n.* vitamin of the B complex, found in leafy green vegetables, liver, and kidney.

fo•li•o /fōleeō/ *n.* (*pl.* **-os**) **1** leaf of paper, etc., esp. one numbered only on the front. **2 a** leaf number of a book. **b** page number of a book. **3** sheet of paper folded once, making two leaves of a book. **4** book made of such sheets.

folk /fōk/ *n.* (*pl.* **folk** or **folks**) **1** [treated as *pl.*] people in general or of a specified class (*rich and poor folks alike*). **2** [in *pl.*] (usu. **folks**) one's parents or relatives. **3** [treated as *sing.*] a people. **4** [*attrib.*] of popular origin; traditional (*folk art*). □ **folk dance** dance of traditional origin. **folk singer** singer of folk songs. **folk song** song of popular or traditional origin or style. **folk tale** popular or traditional story.
■ **1** society, the nation, the public, the populace. **2** (*folks*) see FAMILY 1. **3** tribe, (ethnic) group, clan, race.

folk•lore /fōklawr/ *n.* traditional beliefs and stories of a people; the study of these. □□ **folk•lor•ic** *adj.* **folk•lor•ist** *n.* **folk•lor•is•tic** *adj.*

folk•sy /fōksee/ *adj.* (**folk•si•er, folk•si•est**) **1** friendly; informal. **2** of or like folk art, culture, etc. □□ **folk•si•ness** *n.*
■ **1** see INFORMAL.

fol•li•cle /fōlikəl/ *n.* **1** small sac or vesicle. **2** small sac-shaped secretory gland or cavity. □□ **fol•lic•u•lar** /fəlíkyələr/ *adj.* **fol•lic•u•late** /fōlikyəlat, -layt/ *adj.*

fol•low /fōlō/ *v.* **1** *tr.* & *intr.* go or come after (a person or thing proceeding ahead). **2** *tr.* go along (a route, path, etc.). **3** *tr.* & *intr.* come after in order or time (*dessert followed the main course*). **4** *tr.* take as a guide or leader. **5** *tr.* conform to. **6** *tr.* practice (a trade or profession). **7** *tr.* undertake (a course of study, etc.). **8** *tr.* understand. **9** *tr.* maintain awareness of the current state or progress of (events, etc., in a particular sphere). **10** *tr.* provide with a sequel or successor. **11** *intr.* **a** be necessarily true as a result of something else. **b** be a result of. □ **follow through 1** continue (an action, etc.) to its conclusion. **2** *Sports* continue the movement of a stroke after the ball has been struck. **follow-through** *n.* action of following through. **follow up 1** [foll. by *with*] pursue; develop; supplement. **2** make further investigation of. **follow-up** *n.* subsequent or continued action.
■ **1** go or walk or tread or move behind; go or

311   **fold ~ fool**

come next. **2** trace, keep to, pursue. **5** adhere to, comply with, obey, be guided by. **7** see UNDERTAKE 1. **8** fathom, comprehend, grasp, see. **9** keep up with, keep abreast of, take an interest in. **11 b** (*follow from*) be a consequence of, result or develop from. □ **follow through 1** persist or persevere with, conclude, pursue, carry out. **follow-through** see *execution* (EXECUTE). **follow up 1** reinforce, consolidate, support, buttress. **2** pursue, investigate, check (out), check up, inquire about. **follow-up** reinforcement, support, backup, consolidation.

fol•low•er /fōlōər/ *n.* **1** adherent or devotee. **2** person or thing that follows.
■ **1** disciple, student, pupil; supporter, fan.

fol•low•ing /fōlōing/ • *prep.* after in time; as a sequel to. • *n.* adherents or devotees. • *adj.* that follows or comes after.
■ *prep.* see SUBSEQUENT. • *n.* see RETINUE. • *adj.* see ATTENDANT *adj.* 1.

fol•ly /fōlee/ *n.* (*pl.* **-lies**) **1** foolishness; lack of good sense. **2** foolish act, behavior, idea, etc.
■ **1** nonsense, absurdity, silliness, preposterousness, *colloq.* dumbness, *sl.* nuttiness. **2** absurdity, blunder, gaffe, *sl.* goof.

fo•ment /fōmént/ *v.tr.* instigate or stir up (trouble, sedition, etc.). See synonym study at INCITE. □□ **fo•men•ta•tion** /fōməntáyshən/ *n.* **fo•ment'er** *n.*
■ whip up, provoke, incite, initiate, prompt, start, inspire, work up, inflame, fan the flames of, kindle.

fond /fond/ *adj.* **1** [foll. by *of*] having affection or a liking for. **2** affectionate; loving; doting. **3** (of beliefs, etc.) foolishly optimistic or credulous; naive. □□ **fond'ly** *adv.* **fond'ness** *n.*
■ **1** partial to, affectionate toward, attached to. **2** tender, warm, adoring. **3** foolish, see also NAÏVE. □□ **fondly** affectionately, lovingly; foolishly, credulously.

fon•dle /fónd'l/ *v.tr.* caress. □□ **fon'dler** *n.*
■ stroke, pet, pat, touch, feel, cuddle.

fon•due /fondōō, -dyōō/ *n.* dish of flavored melted cheese

font[1] /font/ *n.* **1** receptacle in a church for baptismal water. **2** reservoir for oil in a lamp. □□ **font'al** *adj.* (in sense 1).

font[2] /font/ *Printing* set of type of one face or size.

fon•ta•nel /fóntənél/ *n.* (also **fon•ta•nelle'**) membranous space in an infant's skull at the angles of the parietal bones.

food /fōōd/ *n.* **1** nutritious substance, esp. solid in form, ingested to maintain life and growth. **2** mental stimulus. □ **food chain** *Ecol.* series of organisms each dependent on the next for food. **food processor** machine for chopping and mixing food.
■ **1** nourishment, nutriment, sustenance; foodstuffs, edibles, eatables. **2** ideas; inspiration, stimulation.

food•stuff /fōōdstuf/ *n.* any substance suitable as food.

fool /fōōl/ • *n.* **1** person who acts unwisely or imprudently; stupid person. **2** *hist.* jester;

clown. **3** dupe. • *v.* **1** *tr.* deceive. **2** *tr.* trick; dupe. **3** *intr.* act in a joking or teasing way. **4** *intr.* behave in a playful or silly way.

■ *n.* **1** simpleton, ninny, nincompoop, ass, jackass, dunce, dolt, halfwit, *colloq.* pinhead, silly, loon, goose, idiot, *sl.* twerp, sap, dope. **2** comic, comedian, comedienne, entertainer, zany, buffoon. **3** butt, gull, victim, *colloq.* stooge, *sl.* sucker. • *v.* **1, 2** take in, hoax, hoodwink, bluff, gull, humbug, make a fool of; delude, mislead, *colloq.* kid, *sl.* con. **3** joke, jest, banter, tease, *colloq.* kid. **4** play around *or* about, mess around *or* about, frolic, cavort.

fool•har•dy /foolhaardee/ *adj.* (**fool•har•di•er, fool•har•di•est**) rashly or foolishly bold; reckless. □□ **fool'har•di•ly** *adv.* **fool'har•di•ness** *n.* See synonym study at TEMERITY.

■ rash, imprudent, impetuous, brash, venturesome, daring, audacious, adventurous, daredevil.

fool•ish /foolish/ *adj.* lacking good sense or judgment; unwise. See synonym study at ABSURD. □□ **fool'ish•ly** *adv.* **fool'ish•ness** *n.*

■ senseless, incautious, imprudent, impolitic, indiscreet, unwise, absurd, preposterous, ridiculous, ludicrous, rash, brash, reckless, stupid, asinine, *colloq.* dumb, *sl.* boneheaded, balmy, nuts.

fool•proof /foolproof/ *adj.* (of a procedure, mechanism, etc.) incapable of misuse or mistake.

■ safe, certain, sure, trustworthy, dependable, reliable.

foot /foot/ • *n.* (*pl.* **feet** /feet/) **1 a** lower extremity of the leg below the ankle. **b** part of a sock, etc., covering the foot. **2** lowest or endmost part. **3** step, pace, or tread (*fleet of foot*). **4** (*pl.* **feet** or **foot**) unit of linear measure equal to 12 inches (30.48 cm). **5** *Prosody* **a** group of syllables (one usu. stressed) constituting a metrical unit. **b** similar unit of speech, etc. • *v.tr.* pay (a bill). □ **foot-and-mouth disease** contagious viral disease of cattle, etc. **have one's** (or **both**) **feet on the ground** be practical. **my foot!** *int.* expressing strong contradiction. **on foot** walking; not riding, etc. **put one's foot down** *colloq.* **1** be firmly insistent or repressive. **2** accelerate a motor vehicle. □□ **foot'ed** *adj.* [also in *comb.*]. **foot'less** *adj.*

foot•age /footij/ *n.* **1** length or distance in feet. **2** amount of film made for showing, broadcasting, etc.

foot•ball /footbawl/ *n.* **1** team game played with an inflated oval ball. **2** ball used in this. □□ **foot'ball•er** *n.*

foot•bridge /footbrij/ *n.* bridge for use by pedestrians.

foot•fall /footfawl/ *n.* sound of a footstep.

■ step, footstep, tread.

foot•hill /foot-hil/ *n.* [often in *pl.*] any of the low hills around the base of a mountain.

foot•hold /foot-hōld/ *n.* **1** place, esp. in climbing, where a foot can be supported securely. **2** secure initial position.

■ **1** footing, toehold. **2** see OPENING *n.* 2.

foot•ing /footing/ *n.* **1** foothold; secure position (*lost his footing*). **2** basis on which an enterprise is established or operates; relative position or status.

■ **1** toehold. **2** foundation, base; level, position; terms.

foot•lights /footlīts/ *n.pl.* row of lights along the front of a stage at the level of the actors' feet.

foot•lock•er /footlokər/ *n.* small trunk usu. kept at the foot of a soldier's or camper's bunk.

foot•loose /footloos/ *adj.* free to act as one pleases.

foot•note /footnōt/ *n.* note printed at the foot of a page.

foot•path /footpath/ *n.* trail or path for pedestrians.

foot•print /footprint/ *n.* **1** impression left by a foot or shoe. **2** *Computing* area of desk space, etc., occupied by a computer or other piece of hardware.

foot•race /foot-rays/ *n.* race run by people on foot.

foot•step /footstep/ *n.* **1** step taken in walking. **2** sound of this. □ **follow** (or **tread**) **in a person's footsteps** do as another person did before.

■ **1** tread, pace, stride. **2** footfall, step, tread. □ **follow** (or **tread**) **in a person's footsteps** follow a person's example *or* way of life *or* tradition.

foot•stool /footstool/ *n.* stool for resting the feet on when sitting.

foot•wear /footwair/ *n.* shoes, socks, etc.

foot•work /footwərk/ *n.* use of the feet, esp. skillfully, in sports, dancing, etc.

fop /fop/ *n.* affectedly elegant or fashionable man; dandy. □□ **fop'per•y** *n.* **fop'pish** *adj.* **fop'pish•ly** *adv.* **fop'pish•ness** *n.*

for /fawr, fər/ • *prep.* **1** in the interest or to the benefit of; intended to go to. **2** in defense, support, or favor of. **3** suitable or appropriate to. **4** regarding. **5** representing or in place of. **6** in exchange against. **7** at the price of. **8** as a consequence of. **9 a** with a view to; in the hope or quest of. **b** on account of. **10** to reach; toward (*ran for home*). **11** through or over (a distance or period). **12** as being (*for the last time*). **13** in spite of. **14** considering or making due allowance in respect of. • *conj.* because; since.

■ *prep.* **1** for the sake of, on *or* in behalf of. **2** on the side of, pro, on behalf of. **3** suited to, proper for; for the treatment of. **4** in respect of, as a replacement for, on *or* in behalf of. **9 a** in search *or* pursuit of, seeking, looking for. **b** because of, by reason of, owing to. **10** in the direction of, to, into; to go to. **11** for the duration of, during, in the course of. **13** despite, allowing for. • *conj.* as, inasmuch as, seeing that.

for- /fawr, fər/ *prefix* forming verbs and their derivatives meaning: **1** away; off; (*forget*). **2** prohibition (*forbid*). **3** abstention or neglect (*forgo*). **4** excess or intensity (*forlorn*).

for•age /fawrij, fór-/ • *n.* **1** food for horses and cattle. **2** act or an instance of searching for food. • *v.* **1** *intr.* go searching; rummage (esp. for food). **2** *tr.* obtain food from; plunder. □□ **for'ag•er** *n.*

■ *n.* **1** see FEED *n.* 1. • *v.* **1** see LOOK *v.* 2a, 3a.

for•ay /fáwray, fór–/ *n.* sudden attack; raid or incursion. • *v.intr.* make or go on a foray.

■ *n.* see INROAD 2.

for•bade (also **for•bad'**) *past* of FORBID.

for•bear[1] /fawrbáir/ *v.* (*past* **for•bore** /–báwr/; *past part.* **for•borne** /–báwrn/) *literary* abstain or desist (from) (*forbore to mention it*).

for•bear[2] var. of FOREBEAR.

for•bear•ance /fawrbáirəns/ *n.* patient self-control; tolerance. See synonym study at AB-STINENCE.

for•bid /fərbíd, fawr–/ *v.tr.* (**for•bid•ding**; *past* **for•bade** / bád, báyd/ *or* **forbad** /–bád/; *past part.* **for•bid•den** /–bíd'n/) **1** [foll. by *to* + infin.] order not (*I forbid you to go*). **2** refuse to allow. See synonym study at PROHIBIT. □□ **for•bid'dance** /–dəns/ *n.*

■ **1** (*forbid to*) prohibit *or* ban *or* debar from, hinder *or* stop *or* prevent from. **2** prohibit, ban, outlaw, interdict.

for•bid•ding /fərbíding, fawr–/ *adj.* uninviting; repellent; stern. □□ **for•bid'ding•ly** *adv.*

■ repulsive, odious; hostile, unfriendly, harsh.

for•bore *past* of FORBEAR[1].

for•borne *past part.* of FORBEAR[1].

force /fawrs/ • *n.* **1** power; exerted strength or impetus; intense effort. **2** coercion; compulsion. **3 a** military strength. **b** organized body of soldiers, police, etc. **4** binding power; validity. **5** effect; precise significance. **6** mental or moral strength; efficacy. **7** *Physics* influence tending to cause the motion of a body. **8** person or thing regarded as exerting influence. • *v.tr.* **1** compel or coerce (a person). **2** break open or into by force. **3** drive or propel violently or against resistance. **4** impose or press (on a person). **5** cause, produce, or attain by effort (*forced a smile*). **6** strain or increase to the utmost; overstrain. See synonym study at COMPEL. □ **in force 1** valid; effective. **2** in great strength or numbers. □□ **force'a•ble** *adj.* **forc'er** *n.*

■ *n.* **1** might, energy, potency, strain, exertion. **2** pressure, constraint, duress, *colloq.* arm-twisting. **3** weight, persuasiveness, cogency. **5** meaning, import; see also *significance* (SIGNIFICANT). **6** influence; see also STRENGTH 1. **8** see INFLUENCE *n.* • *v.* **1** make, oblige, require, constrain. **2** pry *or* wrench open, jimmy. **3** push, thrust. **4** see THRUST *v.* 1a. **5** see WRENCH *v.* 3, *insist on*. **6** see STRETCH *v.* 6. □ **in force 1** in effect, in operation, operative, binding, current.

forced /fawrst/ *adj.* **1** obtained or imposed by force (*forced entry*). **2** (of a gesture, etc.) affected; unnatural.

■ **2** artificial, contrived, stilted, labored, strained.

force•ful /fáwrsfŏŏl/ *adj.* **1** vigorous; powerful. **2** (of speech) compelling; impressive. □□ **force'ful•ly** *adv.* **force'ful•ness** *n.*

■ **1** energetic, dynamic, aggressive, potent. **2** effective, efficacious, cogent, telling, convincing.

for•ceps /fáwrseps/ *n.* (*pl.* same) surgical pincers.

for•ci•ble /fáwrsibəl/ *adj.* done by or involving force; forceful. □□ **for'ci•ble•ness** *n.* **for'ci•bly** *adv.*

■ drastic, coercive, severe.

ford /fawrd/ • *n.* shallow water crossing, as in a river. • *v.tr.* cross (water) at a ford. □□ **ford'a•ble** *adj.* **ford'less** *adj.*

■ *v.* see WADE *v.* 4.

fore /fawr/ • *adj.* situated in front. • *n.* front part, esp. of a ship; bow. • *int. Golf* warning to a person in the path of a ball. □ **fore-and-aft** *adj.* (of a sail or rigging) set lengthwise, not on the yards.

■ *n.* see FRONT *n.* 1.

fore- /fawr/ *prefix* forming: **1** verbs meaning: **a** in front (*foreshorten*). **b** beforehand (*forewarn*). **2** nouns meaning: **a** situated in front of (*forecourt*). **b** front part of (*forehead*).

fore•arm[1] /fáwraarm/ *n.* part of the arm from the elbow to the wrist or the fingertips.

fore•bear /fáwrbair/ *n.* (also **for'bear**) [usu. in *pl.*] ancestor.

fore•bode /fawrbṓd/ *v.tr.* **1** betoken; be an advance warning of. **2** have a presentiment of (usu. evil).

fore•bod•ing /fawrbṓding/ *n.* expectation of trouble or evil; presage or omen. □□ **fore•bod'ing•ly** *adv.*

■ premonition, presentiment; omen, sign; apprehension, apprehensiveness, misgiving.

fore•cast /fáwrkast/ • *v.tr.* (*past* and *past part.* **–cast** or **–cast•ed**) predict. See synonym study at PREDICT. • *n.* calculation or estimate of something future, esp. coming weather. □□ **fore'cast•er** *n.*

■ *v.* foretell, prophesy, prognosticate, foresee. • *n.* estimate, prediction, prophecy, prognosis.

fore•cas•tle /fṓksəl/ *n.* (also **fo'c's'le**) *Naut.* forward part of a ship where the crew has quarters.

fore•close /fawrklṓz/ *v.tr.* **1** repossess mortgaged property when a loan is not duly repaid. **2** exclude. □□ **fore•clo'sure** /–klṓzhər/ *n.*

fore•fa•ther /fáwrfaathər/ *n.* [usu. in *pl.*] ancestor.

fore•fin•ger /fáwrfinggər/ *n.* finger next to the thumb.

fore•foot /fáwrfŏŏt/ *n.* (*pl.* **–feet**) front foot of an animal.

fore•front /fáwrfrunt/ *n.* **1** foremost part. **2** leading position.

■ **2** see FRONT *n.* 6.

fore•go[1] /fáwrgṓ/ (**–goes**; *past* **–went** /–wént/; *past part.* **–gone** /–gón/) precede in place or time.

fore•go[2] var. of FORGO.

fore•go•ing /fáwrgṓing/ *adj.* preceding; previously mentioned.

■ former, previous, precedent; above, aforementioned, aforesaid.

fore•gone /fáwrgawn, –gón/ *past part.* of FOREGO[1]. • *attrib.adj.* previous; preceding; completed. □ **foregone conclusion** easily foreseen or predictable result.

fore•ground /fáwrgrownd/ n. **1** part of a view that is nearest the observer. **2** most conspicuous position.

fore•hand /fáwrhand/ n. Tennis, etc. **1** stroke played with the palm of the hand facing the opponent. **2** [attrib.] (also **fore'hand'ed**) of or made with a forehand.

fore•head /fáwrid, –hed, fór–/ n. part of the face above the eyebrows.

for•eign /fáwrin, fór–/ adj. **1** of, from, in, or characteristic of a country or a languáge other than one's own. **2** dealing with other countries (foreign service). **3** unfamiliar; strange. **4** coming from outside (foreign body). □□ **for'eign•ness** n.
■ **1** alien, imported, nonnative; overseas. **2** external, international, overseas. **3** outlandish, peculiar, odd, uncharacteristic. **4** see EXTERNAL adj. 1b.

for•eign•er /fáwrinər, fór–/ n. person born in or coming from a foreign country or place.
■ alien, nonnative, immigrant, outsider, outlander.

fore•leg /fáwrleg/ n. each of the front legs of a quadruped.

fore•lock /fáwrlok/ n. lock of hair just above the forehead.

fore•man /fáwrmən/ n. (pl. **–men**) **1** worker supervising others. **2** presiding juror in a legal trial.
■ **1** superintendent, supervisor, overseer, colloq. boss.

fore•mast /fáwrmast, –məst/ n. forward mast of a ship.

fore•most /fáwrmōst/ • adj. **1** chief or most notable. **2** first; front. • adv. most importantly (first and foremost).
■ adj. first, primary, prime, leading, preeminent. • adv. first, firstly, primarily, in the first place.

fo•ren•sic /fərénsik, –zik/ adj. **1** of or used in courts of law. **2** disp. of or involving forensic science. □□ **fo•ren'si•cal•ly** adv.

fore•play /fáwrplay/ n. stimulation preceding sexual intercourse.

fore•run•ner /fáwr-runər/ n. **1** predecessor. **2** herald.
■ **1** precursor, foregoer, ancestor, progenitor. **2** harbinger, envoy; see also MESSENGER.

fore•see /fáwrseé/ v.tr. (past **–saw** /–sáw/; past part. **–seen** /–seén/) see or be aware of beforehand. □□ **fore•see'a•ble** adj. **fore•se•er** /–seéər/ n.
■ presage, foretell, envisage, forecast, predict, prophesy.

fore•shad•ow /fáwrshádō/ v.tr. be a warning or indication of (a future event). See synonym study at PREDICT.
■ presage, foretoken, portend, augur, indicate, bode.

fore•short•en /fáwrsháwrt'n/ v.tr. show or portray (an object) with the apparent shortening due to visual perspective.

fore•sight /fáwrsīt/ n. **1** regard or provision for the future. **2** process of foreseeing. □□ **fore•sight•ed** /–sítid/ adj. **fore'sight•ed•ly** adv. **fore'sight•ed•ness** n.
■ **1** providence. **2** prevision, foreknowledge.

fore•skin /fáwrskin/ n. fold of skin covering the end of the penis. (Also called **prepuce**).

for•est /fáwrist, fór–/ • n. large area of trees and undergrowth. • v.tr. **1** plant with trees. **2** convert into a forest. □□ **for'est•er** n.
■ n. see WOOD 2.

fore•stall /fáwrstáwl/ v.tr. **1** act in advance of in order to prevent. **2** anticipate. □□ **fore•stall'er** n. **fore•stall'ment** n.
■ **1** anticipate, obstruct, hinder, thwart, frustrate, avert, ward off. **2** see ANTICIPATE 3.

for•est•ry /fáwristree, fór–/ n. **1** science or management of forests. **2** wooded country; forests.

fore•taste • n. /fáwrtayst/ partial enjoyment or suffering in advance. • v.tr. /fáwrtáyst/ taste beforehand.
■ n. earnest, token; anticipation.

fore•tell /fáwrtél/ v.tr. (past and past part. **–told** /–tóld/) **1** predict; prophesy. **2** presage. See synonym study at PREDICT. □□ **fore•tell'er** n.

fore•thought /fáwrthawt/ n. **1** care or provision for the future. **2** previous thinking or devising. **3** deliberate intention.
■ **1** farsightedness, longsightedness; preparation, planning, organization. **2** premeditation, preplanning.

for•ev•er /fərévər, fawr–/ adv. continually; persistently.
■ constantly, continuously, always, all the time.

fore•warn /fáwrwáwrn/ v.tr. warn beforehand. □□ **fore•warn'er** n.

fore•went past of FOREGO[1], FOREGO[2].

fore•wom•an /fáwrwôomən/ n. (pl. **–wom•en**) **1** female worker supervising others. **2** jury spokeswoman.

fore•word /fáwrwərd/ n. introductory remarks at the beginning of a book, often by a person other than the author.
■ preface, prologue, preamble, proem, introduction.

for•feit /fáwrfit/ • n. **1** penalty. **2** something surrendered as a penalty. • adj. lost or surrendered as a penalty. • v.tr. lose the right to; have to pay as a penalty. □□ **for'feit•a•ble** adj. **for'feit•er** n. **for•fei•ture** /–fichər/ n.
■ n. **1** fine, fee, charge, damages. • v. yield, give up or over, relinquish, concede, surrender, cede.

for•gath•er /fáwrgátðər/ v.intr. (also **fore•gath'er**) assemble; meet together; associate.

for•gave past of FORGIVE.

forge[1] /fawrj/ • v.tr. **1** make or write in fraudulent imitation. **2** shape (esp. metal) by heating in a fire and hammering. • n. **1** furnace or workshop for melting or refining metal. □□ **forge'a•ble** adj. **forg'er** n.
■ v. **1** falsify, fake, fabricate. **2** make, construct, fashion, fabricate, manufacture, beat.

forge[2] /fawrj/ v.intr. move forward gradually or steadily. □ **forge ahead 1** take the lead. **2** strive and progress.

forg•er•y /fáwrjəree/ n. (pl. **–ies**) **1** act or an instance of forging. **2** forged or spurious document, signature, etc.
■ **1** falsification, counterfeiting. **2** counterfeit, fake, fraud.

for•get /fərgét/ v. (**for•get•ting**; past **for•got**

/–gŏt/; *past part.* **for•got•ten** /–gŏt'n/ or **for• got) 1** *tr. & intr.* lose the remembrance of. **2** *tr.* overlook; neglect. **3** *tr.* [also *absol.*] cease to think of (*forgive and forget*). □ **forget-me-not** plant with small yellow-eyed bright blue flowers. □□ **for•get'ta•ble** *adj.* **for•get'ter** *n.*

■ **1** fail to remember *or* recall, fail to think of, lose sight of. **2** omit, fail (in); leave (behind); miss, fail to notice. **3** ignore, disregard; put out of one's mind.

for•get•ful /fərgĕtfool/ *adj.* **1** apt to forget; absent-minded. **2** forgetting; neglectful. □□ **for•get'ful•ly** *adv.* **for•get'ful•ness** *n.*

■ **1** distrait, thoughtless, inattentive, lax; amnesic. **2** negligent, heedless, remiss, careless, thoughtless.

for•give /fərgĭv/ *v.tr.* (*past* **for•gave**; *past part.* **for•giv•en**) cease to feel angry or resentful toward; pardon. See synonym study at AB-SOLVE. □□ **for•giv'a•ble** *adj.* **for•giv'a•bly** *adv.* **for•give'ness** *n.* **for•giv'er** *n.*

■ excuse; overlook, condone, clear, acquit, absolve. □□ **forgiveness** pardon, absolution, exoneration; reprieve, remission, acquittal, vindication, indulgence, allowance, *archaic* shrift; mercy, clemency; *formal* exculpation.

for•giv•ing /fərgĭving/ *adj.* inclined readily to forgive. □□ **for•giv'ing•ly** *adv.*

■ tolerant, lenient, forbearing, charitable, merciful.

for•go /fawrgō/ *v.tr.* (also **fore•go'**) (–goes; *past*—went /–wĕnt/; *past part.* **gone** / gawn, –gŏn/) go without; relinquish.

■ abstain from, sacrifice, cede, waive, decline, yield.

for•got *past* of FORGET.

for•got•ten *past part.* of FORGET.

fork /fawrk/ • *n.* **1** instrument with two or more prongs used in eating or cooking. **2** similar much larger instrument used for digging, lifting, etc. **3 a** divergence of anything, e.g., a stick, road, or river, into two parts. **b** place where this occurs. **c** either of the two parts. • *v.* **1** *intr.* diverge into two parts. **2** *tr.* dig or lift, etc., with a fork. □ **fork out** (or **over** or **up**) *sl.* hand over or pay, usu. reluctantly.

forked /fawrkt/ *adj.* **1** having a fork or forklike end or branches. **2** divergent; cleft. **3** [in *comb.*] having so many prongs (*three-forked*).

fork•lift /fawrklĭft/ *n.* vehicle with a horizontal fork in front for lifting and carrying loads.

for•lorn /fawrláwrn/ *adj.* **1** sad and abandoned or lonely. **2** in a pitiful state. □□ **for• lorn'ly** *adv.* **for•lorn'ness** *n.*

■ **1** lonesome, forsaken, deserted; desolate, inconsolable, despairing, woeful, cheerless, joyless. **2** miserable, wretched, pitiable, pathetic.

form /fawrm/ • *n.* **1** shape; arrangement of parts. **2** person or animal as visible or tangible. **3** mode in which a thing exists or manifests itself. **4** species, kind, or variety. **5** document to be filled in. **6** correct procedure. **7** (of an athlete, horse, etc.) condition of health and training. **8** general state or disposition (*in great form*). **9** *Gram.* one of the

ways in which a word may be spelled or pronounced or inflected. **10** arrangement; style. • *v.* **1** *tr.* make or fashion. **2** *intr.* take a certain shape; be formed. **3** *tr.* make up or constitute. **4** *tr.* train or instruct. **5** *tr.* develop or establish. **6** *tr.* embody; organize. □□ **form' less** *adj.* **form'less•ly** *adv.*

■ *n.* **1** figure; configuration, conformation; structure, build. **2** silhouette, figure, shape, image. **3** style, character, manner, fashion; aspect, look. **4** type, version, sort, breed, make, class. **5** protocol, practice, routine; see also PROCEDURE 1–3. **7** state, order, shape, trim, fettle, health. **8** condition, shape, health; mood, temper. • *v.* **1** fabricate, forge, shape, mold. **2** develop, grow, arise, appear, materialize. **3** serve as, function as, act as. **4** see INSTRUCT 1. **5** create, originate, generate, devise, invent, design. **6** arrange, assemble. □□ **formless** see *shapeless* (SHAPE), *chaotic* (CHAOS).

-form /fawrm/ *comb. form* (usu. as **-iform**) forming adjectives meaning having the form of (*cruciform, cuneiform*).

for•mal /fáwrməl/ • *adj.* **1** in accordance with rules, convention, or ceremony. **2** precise or symmetrical (*formal garden*). **3** prim; stiff in manner. **4** explicit or official (*formal agreement*). • *n.* **1** evening dress. **2** occasion on which evening dress is worn. □□ **for' mal•ly** *adv.*

■ *adj.* **1** correct, proper, set, prescribed, conventional, customary; stately, courtly, dignified. **2** orderly. **3** rigid, exact, punctilious; impersonal, reserved. **4** formalized, authorized, valid; express, definite, exact, specific.

SYNONYM STUDY: formal

CEREMONIAL, CEREMONIOUS, POMPOUS, PROPER, PUNCTILIOUS. **Formal** suggests a suit-and-tie approach to certain situations—reserved, conventional, obeying all the rules (*an engraved invitation to a formal dinner requiring black tie or evening gown*). **Proper**, in this regard, implies scrupulously correct behavior that observes rules of etiquette (*the proper way to serve a guest; the proper spoon for dessert*). **Punctilious** behavior observes all the proper formalities (*a "punctilio" is a detail or fine point*), but may verge on the annoying (*her punctilious attention to the correct placement of silverware made setting the table an ordeal*). Someone (usually a man) who likes to show off self-importantly just how *formal* and *proper* he can be runs the risk of becoming the most dreaded dinner guest of all: the **pompous** ass. *Pompous* individuals may derive more than the normal amount of pleasure from participating in **ceremonial** acts or events, which are those performed according to set rules, and in which one demonstrates **ceremonious** behavior (*the Japanese woman could not have been more ceremonious than when she was carrying out the ceremonial serving of tea*). **Ceremonial** is also used to describe items used in formal ceremonies (*ceremonial robes*).

form•al•de•hyde /fawrmáldihīd/ n. colorless pungent gas used as a disinfectant and preservative. ¶Chem. formula: CH₂O. (Also called **methanal**).

for•mal•ism /fáwrməlizəm/ n. 1 excessive adherence to prescribed forms. 2 derog. an artist's concentration on form at the expense of content. □□ **for'mal•ist** n. **for•mal•is'tic** adj.

for•mal•i•ty /fawrmálitee/ n. (pl. **–ties**) 1 a formal, esp. meaningless, procedure or custom. b thing done simply to comply with a rule. 2 rigid observance of rules or conventions.
   ■ 1 form, convention, practice, observance, ritual. 2 formalness, strictness, punctilio, exactness.

for•mal•ize /fáwrməlīz/ v.tr. 1 give definite shape or legal formality to. 2 make formal. □□ **for•mal•i•za•tion** /–lizáyshən/ n.

for•mat /fáwrmat/ • n. 1 shape and size of a book, periodical, etc. 2 style or arrangement. • v.tr. (**for•mat•ted, for•mat•ting**) arrange or put into a format.
   ■ n. 1 form, dimension(s), appearance, look, design, style. 2 structure, method, plan, organization, composition, makeup. • v. see STRUCTURE v.

for•ma•tion /fawrmáyshən/ n. 1 forming. 2 thing formed. 3 particular arrangement, e.g., of troops. □□ **for•ma'tion•al** adj.
   ■ 1, 2 foundation, development, appearance, production, establishment, institution, founding. 3 configuration, pattern, display, array.

form•a•tive /fáwrmətiv/ adj. serving to form or fashion; of formation. □□ **form'a•tive•ly** adv.

for•mer /fáwrmər/ attrib.adj. 1 of the past; earlier; previous. 2 [prec. by the] the first or first mentioned of two.
   ■ 1 old, past, prior; ex–, one-time.

for•mer•ly /fáwrmərlee/ adv. in the past; in former times.
   ■ once, before, previously, long ago, at one time.

for•mi•da•ble /fáwrmidəbəl/ disp. formídəbəl/ adj. 1 inspiring fear or dread. 2 inspiring respect or awe. 3 hard to overcome or deal with. □□ **for'mi•da•ble•ness** n. **for'mi•da•bly** adv.
   ■ 1 dreadful, fearful, fearsome, frightful, daunting. 2 impressive, awesome, awe-inspiring; b breathtaking, amazing. 3 arduous, difficult, daunting.

for•mu•la /fáwrmyələ/ n. (pl. **for•mu•las** or (esp. in senses 1, 2) **for•mu•lae** /–lee/) 1 Chem. chemical symbols showing the constituents of a substance. 2 Math. mathematical rule expressed in symbols. 3 fixed form, esp. of words used on social or ceremonial occasions. 4 a list of ingredients. b infant's liquid food preparation. □□ **for•mu•la•ic** /–láyik/ adj. **for•mu•lar•ize** /–lərīz/ v.tr. **for'mu•lize** v.tr.
   ■ 3 liturgy, rubric; rite; rule, protocol, convention; plan, routine, pattern, system. 4 a recipe, prescription.

for•mu•late /fáwrmyəlayt/ v.tr. 1 express in a formula. 2 express clearly and precisely. □□ **for•mu•la•tion** /–láyshən/ n.
   ■ 1 program, systematize, codify, shape, draft, develop. 2 define, specify, particularize, articulate, vocalize.

for•ni•cate /fáwrnikayt/ v.intr. (of people not married or not married to each other) have sexual intercourse voluntarily. □□ **for•ni•ca•tion** /–kayshən/ n. **for'ni•ca•tor** n.

for•sake /fərsáyk, fawr–/ v.tr. (past **for•sook** /–so̅o̅k/; past part. **for•sak•en** /–sáykən/) 1 give up; break off from; renounce. 2 desert; abandon. □□ **for•sak'en•ness** n. **for•sak'er** n.
   ■ 1 abstain from, relinquish, yield, forgo; reject; abandon. 2 leave, maroon, jilt, reject, rebuff, snub.

for•sooth /fərso̅o̅th, fawr–/ adv. archaic or joc. truly; in truth.

for•swear /fáwrswáir/ v.tr. (past **for•swore** /–swáwr/; past part. **for•sworn** /–swáwrn/) 1 renounce. 2 commit perjury.

for•syth•i•a /fawrsítheeə/ n. ornamental shrub bearing bright yellow flowers in early spring.

fort /fawrt/ n. fortified building or position.

forte¹ /fawrt, fáwrtay/ n. person's strong point; a thing in which a person excels.
   ■ strength, métier, specialty; talent, gift.

for•te² /fórtay/ Mus. • adj. performed loudly. • adv. loudly.

forth /fawrth/ adv. archaic except in set phrases and after certain verbs, esp. bring, come, go, and set. 1 forward; into view. 2 [often in comb.] onward in time (henceforth).

forth•com•ing /fáwrthkúming/ attrib. adj. 1 coming or available soon. 2 (often in comb.) produced when wanted. 3 (of a person) informative; responsive.
   ■ 1 impending, approaching, coming, imminent; likely, probable, possible, in the cards. 3 outgoing, open, frank.

forth•right /fáwrthrīt/ adj. direct and outspoken; straightforward. □□ **forth•right'ly** adv. **forth'right•ness** n.
   ■ straight, blunt, candid; unreserved.

forth•with /fáwrthwith, –with/ adv. without delay.

for•ti•fy /fáwrtifī/ v.tr. (**–fies, –fied**) 1 provide or equip with military defense. 2 strengthen or invigorate physically, mentally, or morally. 3 strengthen (wine) with alcohol. 4 increase the nutritive value of (food, esp. with vitamins). □□ **for'ti•fi•a•ble** adj. **for•ti•fi•ca'tion** n. **for'ti•fi•er** n.
   ■ 1 arm, make ready; defend, secure, protect. 2 brace, stimulate, animate; steel, harden, support. 3, 4 supplement, enhance, enrich, augment, lace.

for•tis•si•mo /fawrtísimō/ Mus. • adj. performed very loudly. • adv. very loudly.

for•ti•tude /fáwrtito̅o̅d, –tyo̅o̅d/ n. courage in pain or adversity.
   ■ bravery, daring, valor, boldness, intrepidity, pluck.

fort•night /fáwrtnīt/ n. period of fourteen days; two weeks. □□ **fort'night•ly** adj. & adv.

for•tress /fáwrtris/ n. fortified building or town.

■ see STRONGHOLD 1.

for•tu•i•tous /fawrtō̏oitəs, –tyoō̏–/ *adj.* due to or characterized by chance; accidental; casual. See synonym study at ACCIDENTAL. □□ **for•tu'i•tous•ly** *adv.* **for•tu'i•tous•ness** *n.* **for•tu'i•ty** *n.*

for•tu•nate /fáwrchənət/ *adj.* **1** favored by fortune; lucky; prosperous. **2** auspicious; favorable. □□ **for'tu•nate•ly** *adv.*

■ **1** blessed, charmed. **2** advantageous, promising, propitious. □□ **fortunately** see *happily* (HAPPY).

for•tune /fáwrchən/ *n.* **1 a** chance or luck as a force in human affairs. **b** person's destiny. **2** [in *sing.* or *pl.*] good or bad luck that befalls a person or an enterprise. **3** good luck. **4** prosperity; riches. □ **fortune-teller** person who claims to predict future events in a person's life. **fortune-telling** practice of this.

■ **1 a** fate, destiny, hazard. **b** lot, fate, portion. **2** circumstance(s), experience(s). **3** fluke, stroke of luck, *colloq.* break. **4** wealth, money, affluence, opulence. □ **fortune-teller** clairvoyant, soothsayer, psychic, oracle.

for•ty /fáwrtee/ • *n.* (*pl.* **-ties**) **1** product of four and ten. **2** symbol for this (40, xl, XL). **3** [in *pl.*] numbers from 40 to 49, esp. as years. • *adj.* that amount to forty. □□ **for'ti•eth** *adj. & n.* *adj. & adv.*

fo•rum /fáwrəm/ *n.* **1** place, agency, or meeting for public discussion. **2** *hist.* public square in an ancient Roman city.

for•ward /fáwrwərd/ • *adj.* **1** lying in one's line of motion. **2** onward or toward the front. **3** precocious; bold in manner; presumptuous. **4** *Commerce* relating to the future (*forward contract*). • *n.* attacking player positioned near the front of a team in football, hockey, etc. • *adv.* **1** to the front; into prominence. **2** in advance; ahead (*sent them forward*). **3** onward. **4** (also **for'wards**) **a** toward the front in the direction one is facing. **b** in the normal direction of motion. • *v.tr.* **1** send (a letter, etc.) on to a further destination. **2** help to advance; promote. □□ **for'ward•er** *n.* **for'ward•ly** *adv.* **for'ward•ness** *n.* (esp. in sense 3 of *adj.*).

■ *adj.* **1** (up) ahead, in front, *colloq.* up front. **2** advance, front, head, fore, foremost. **3** presuming, familiar, confident. • *adv.* **1** ahead, in front, frontward(s), to the fore, up. **2** in front, in the lead *or* vanguard, before, to the fore. **3, 4** along, onward(s), ahead; in front. • *v.* **2** further, back, champion, favor, foster, support; propose, move, submit.

for•went *past* of FORGO.

fos•sil /fósəl/ • *n.* **1** remains or impression of a (usu. prehistoric) plant or animal hardened in rock. **2** *colloq.* antiquated or unchanging person or thing. • *adj.* **1** of or like a fossil. **2** antiquated; out of date. □ **fossil fuel** natural fuel such as coal or gas. □□ **fos'sil•ize** *v.* **fos•sil•i•za'tion** *n.*

■ *n.* **2** see FOGY. • *adj.* **2** see ANCIENT *adj.* 2.

fos•ter /fáwstər, fós–/ • *v.tr.* **1 a** promote the growth or development of. **b** encourage or harbor (a feeling). **2** (of circumstances) be

favorable to. **3** bring up (a child that is not one's own by birth). See synonym study at ENCOURAGE. • *adj.* **1** having a family connection by fostering (*foster child*). **2** concerned with fostering a child (*foster care*). □□ **fos'ter•age** *n.* (esp. in sense 3 of *v.*). **fos'ter•er** *n.*

■ *v.* **1 a** encourage, stimulate, favor, further. **b** nurture; stimulate, arouse, awaken. **2** create, produce, generate, cultivate. **3** rear, raise, take care of.

fought *past* and *past part.* of FIGHT.

foul /fowl/ • *adj.* **1** offensive; loathsome; stinking. **2** dirty; soiled; filthy. **3** *colloq.* revolting; disgusting. **4** noxious. **5** disgustingly abusive or offensive. **6** against the rules. **7** rough; stormy. • *n.* *Sports* unfair or invalid stroke or action. • *adv.* unfairly. • *v.* **1** *tr. & intr.* make or become foul or dirty. **2 a** *tr. Sports* commit a foul against (a player). **b** *intr.* commit a foul. **3 a** *tr.* cause to become entangled or blocked. **b** *intr.* become entangled. **4** *tr.* bungle. □ **foul mouth** person who uses offensive language. **foul play 1** unfair play in games. **2** treacherous or violent activity, esp. murder. **foul-up** muddle or bungle. □□ **foul'ly** *adv.* **foul'ness** *n.*

■ *adj.* **1** vile, obnoxious, revolting, repulsive; stinking, fetid, rancid. **2** grimy, unclean, squalid, sordid, *sl.* yucky. **3** detestable, hateful, abominable, hideous, horrid, *sl.* gross. **4** tainted, adulterated, contaminated, polluted, poisonous. **5** vile, bad, base, depraved, reprobate, corrupt; dirty, obscene, filthy, scatological, coarse, crude. **6** dirty, dishonest, fraudulent, two-faced, dishonorable, unfair; illegal, forbidden. **7** wet, nasty, violent; adverse. • *n.* violation, breach, infringement, infraction. • *adv.* foully, meanly, dishonestly, fraudulently; in violation. • *v.* **1** dirty, defile, soil, besmirch, pollute, contaminate. **3** tangle, entangle, catch (up), snare, snarl (up); jam, block, impede, obstruct. **4** spoil, ruin, mismanage, mishandle, botch (up). □ **foul play 1** cheating, unfairness, dirty tricks, dirty work. **2** trickery, perfidy, guile; conspiracy. **foul-up** see BLUNDER *n.*

found¹ *past* and *past part.* of FIND.

found² /fownd/ *v.* **1** *tr.* establish; originate; initiate. **2 a** *tr.* construct or base (a story, theory, rule, etc.) on. **b** *intr.* have a basis in. □□ **found'er** *n.* **found'er•ship** *n.*

■ **1** constitute, set up, institute, launch, organize. **2 a** ground, build; rest; see also BASE¹ *v.* **1**. □□ **founder** originator, creator, progenitor, author, framer, father.

found³ /fownd/ *v.tr.* **1 a** melt and mold (metal). **b** fuse (materials for glass). **2** make by founding. □□ **found'er** *n.*

foun•da•tion /fowndáyshən/ *n.* **1 a** solid ground or base on which a building rests. **b** [usu. in *pl.*] lowest load-bearing part of a building. **2** material base. **3** basis or underlying principle. **4 a** establishment (esp. of an endowed institution). **b** such an institution, e.g., a college or hospital. □□ **foun•da'tion•al** *adj.*

■ **1** substructure. **2** background, body, ground. **3** base, starting point, fundamental(s), grounds, rationale. **4** founding, instituting, creation, origination.

found•er /fówndər/ v. **1 a** intr. (of a ship) fill with water and sink. **b** tr. cause (a ship) to founder. **2** intr. (of a plan, etc.) fail. **3** intr. (of a horse or its rider) fall to the ground, fall from lameness, stick fast in mud, etc.
■ **1 a** go down or under; be wrecked or destroyed. **2** miscarry, collapse, fall through, abort, break down. **3** trip, stumble, lurch, topple, collapse; go lame.

found•ling /fównɗling/ n. abandoned infant of unknown parentage.

found•ry /fównɗree/ n. (pl. **–ries**) workshop for or a business of casting metal.

fount /fownt/ n. poet. spring or fountain; source.

foun•tain /fówntin/ n. **1** a jet or jets of water made to spout for ornamental purposes or for drinking. **b** structure provided for this. **2** natural spring of water. **3** source. □ **fountain pen** pen with a reservoir or cartridge holding ink. □□ **foun′tained** adj. [also in comb.].
■ **1, 2** spring, spout, spray. **3** see SPRING n. 6, ORIGIN 1.

four /fawr/ • n. **1** one more than three. **2** symbol for this (4, iv, IV, iiii, IIII). • adj. that amount to four. □ **four-letter word** any of several short words referring to sexual or excretory functions, regarded as coarse or offensive. **four-wheel drive** drive powering all four wheels of a vehicle. **on all fours** on hands and knees.

four•fold /fáwrfōld/ adj. & adv. **1** four times as much or as many. **2** consisting of four parts. **3** amounting to four.

401(k) • n. retirement plan in which employees invest before-tax income and earn tax-deferred interest (named for the relevant section of the Internal Revenue Code).

four•some /fáwrsəm/ n. group of four persons.

four•square /fáwrskwáir/ • adj. **1** solidly based. **2** steady; resolute. **3** square shaped. • adv. steadily; resolutely.

four•teen /fáwrteén/ • n. **1** one more than thirteen. **2** symbol for this (14, xiv, XIV). • adj. that amount to fourteen. □□ **four′teenth′** adj. & n.

fourth /fawrth/ • n. **1** next after third. **2** each of four equal parts of a thing; a quarter. **3** (**Fourth**) the Fourth of July. • adj. that is the fourth. □ **fourth dimension 1** postulated dimension additional to those determining area and volume. **2** time regarded as equivalent to linear dimensions. **fourth estate** the press; journalism. □□ **fourth′ly** adv.

fowl /fowl/ n. (pl. same or **fowls**) **1** domestic birds, esp. chickens, kept for eggs and flesh. **2** flesh of these birds as food. **3** [in comb. or collect.] bird (guineafowl). □□ **fowl′er** n.

Fox /foks/ n. **1 a** N. American people native to the northeastern US. **b** member of this people. **2** language of this people.

fox /foks/ • n. **1 a** canine animal with a bushy tail and red or gray fur. **b** fur of a fox. **2** cunning or sly person. **3** sl. an attractive young woman or man. • v. **1 a** intr. act craftily. **b** tr. deceive; trick. **2** tr. (usu. as **foxed** adj.) discolor (the leaves of a book, engraving, etc.) with brownish marks. □ **fox terrier** kind of short-haired terrier. □□ **fox′ing** n. (in sense 2 of v.). **fox′like** adj.
■ n. **2** see DEVIL n. 3b. • v. **1 b** see FLUMMOX.

fox•glove /fóksgluv/ n. tall plant with erect spikes of purple or white flowers like glove fingers.

fox•hole /fóks-hōl/ n. Mil. hole in the ground used as a shelter against enemy fire or as a firing point.

fox•hound /fóks-hownd/ n. hound bred and trained to hunt foxes.

fox•trot /fókstrot/ • n. **1** ballroom dance with slow and quick steps. **2** music for this. • v. intr. (**fox•trot•ted, fox•trot•ting**) perform this dance.

fox•y /fóksee/ adj. (**fox•i•er, fox•i•est**) **1** foxlike; sly; cunning. **2** sl. sexually attractive. □□ **fox′i•ly** adv. **fox′i•ness** n.
■ **1** vulpine; clever, wily, crafty, tricky, guileful. **2** attractive, alluring, seductive, vampish, sexy.

foy•er /fóyər, fóyay, fwaáyay/ n. entrance hall or other large area in a hotel, theater, etc.

FPO abbr. **1** field post office. **2** fleet post office.

fps abbr. (also **f.p.s.**) **1** feet per second. **2** foot-pound-second.

Fr symb. Chem. francium.

Fr. abbr. (also **Fr**) **1** Father. **2** French.

fr. abbr. franc(s).

fra•cas /fráykəs/ n. (pl. same, pronunc. /–kaaz/) noisy disturbance or quarrel.
■ commotion, fuss, hubbub, hullabaloo, uproar; argument, disagreement, dispute, discord, wrangle.

frac•tion /frákshən/ n. **1** numerical quantity that is not a whole number (e.g., 0.5, $\frac{1}{2}$). **2** small part, piece, or amount. See synonym study at FRAGMENT. □□ **frac′tion•al** adj. **frac′tion•ar•y** adj. **frac′tion•ize** v. tr.
■ **2** see SECTION n. 2. □□ **fractional** see LITTLE adj. 1, 2.

frac•tious /frákshəs/ adj. **1** irritable; peevish. **2** unruly. □□ **frac′tious•ly** adv. **frac′tious•ness** n.

frac•ture /frákchər/ • n. breakage, esp. of a bone. • v. Med. undergo or cause to undergo a fracture.
■ n. break, breaking, separation, division. • v. break, rupture, crack, split, breach, separate, literary cleave.

frag•ile /frájil, –jīl/ adj. **1** easily broken; weak. **2** delicate; not strong. □□ **frag′ile•ly** adv. **fra•gil•i•ty** /frəjílitee/ n.
■ **1** breakable, brittle, rickety, frail; tenuous, shaky. **2** dainty, thin, slight; frail, weak; see also FEEBLE 1.

frag•ment • n. /frágmənt/ **1** part broken off; a detached piece. **2** isolated or incomplete part (of a book, etc.). • v. /fragmént/ break or separate into fragments. □□ **frag•men•tal** /–mént′l/ adj. **frag•men•ta′tion** n. **frag′ment•ize** v. tr.

■ *n.* **1, 2** portion, chip, shard, splinter, sliver, scrap, bit, speck, snippet. ● *v.* split (up), shatter, splinter; come apart. ● **fragmentation** see SEPARATION.

SYNONYM STUDY: fragment
FRACTION, PART, PIECE, PORTION, SECTION, SEGMENT. The whole is equal to the sum of its **parts**—*part* being a general term for any of the components of a whole. But how did the whole come apart? **Fragment** suggests that breakage has occurred (*fragments of pottery*) and often refers to a brittle substance such as glass or pottery, though it is also used to refer to words or thoughts (*a fragment of a poem; she remembered only a fragment of the dream*). **Segment** suggests that the whole has been separated along natural or pre-existing lines of division (*a segment of an orange*), and **section** suggests a substantial and clearly separate *part* that fits closely with other parts to form the whole (*a section of a bookcase*). **Fraction** usually suggests a less substantial but still clearly delineated *part* (*a fraction of her income*), and a **portion** is a *part* that has been allotted or assigned to someone (*her portion of the program*). Finally, the very frequently used **piece** is any *part* that is separate from the whole.

frag•men•tar•y /frágmənteree/ *adj.* **1** consisting of fragments. **2** disconnected. □□ **frag'men•tar•i•ly** *adv.*
■ **1** piecemeal, incomplete, sketchy, bitty. **2** disconnected, scattered, disjointed; see also INCOHERENT 2.

fra•grance /fráygrəns/ *n.* **1** sweetness of smell. **2** sweet scent. See synonym study at SMELL. □□ **fra'gran•cy** *n.* **fra'grant** *adj.* **fra'grant•ly** *adv.*
■ **1** redolence, perfume. **2** aroma, perfume; bouquet. □□ **fragrant** aromatic, redolent, perfumed, odoriferous, ambrosial.

frail /frayl/ *adj.* **1** fragile; delicate. **2** in weak health. **3** morally weak. See synonym study at WEAK. □□ **frail'ly** *adv.* **frail'ness** *n.*
■ **1** see FRAGILE 1. **2** ailing, unwell, ill, sick, sickly. **3** susceptible, weak, venal, corruptible; bribable.

frail•ty /fráyltee/ *n.* (*pl.* **–ties**) **1** condition of being frail. **2** liability to err or yield to temptation. **3** weakness; foible.
■ **1** frailness, weakness, infirmity, feebleness. **2** susceptibility, impressionability, vulnerability; fallibility. **3** flaw, fault, defect, imperfection.

frame /fraym/ ● *n.* **1** case or border enclosing a picture, window, door, etc. **2** basic rigid supporting structure of anything, e.g., of a building, motor vehicle, or aircraft. **3** [in *pl.*] structure of spectacles holding the lenses. **4** human or animal body structure. **5 a** established order, plan, or system. **b** construction; structure. **6** single image on film, tape, etc. **7** round of play in bowling, etc. ● *v.tr.* **1 a** set in a frame. **b** serve as a frame for. **2** construct; devise. **3** adapt; fit. **4** *colloq.* concoct a false charge or evidence against; devise a plot with regard to. **5** articulate (words). □ **frame-up** *colloq.* conspiracy, esp. to make an innocent person appear guilty.

□□ **fram'a•ble** *adj.* (also **frame'a•ble**).). **frame'less** *adj.* **fram'er** *n.*
■ *n.* **1** casing, mount, edge; setting. **2** framework, framing, body, fabric, shell; chassis; fuselage. **4** physique, build, body, skeleton, figure. **5 a** form, pattern, scheme, schema. **b** build, arrangement, blueprint. ● *v.* **1** enclose, box (in). **2** build, put together, erect; make, fashion, form, mold, carve out, forge. **3** see ADAPT 1. □ **frame-up** see CONSPIRACY 1.

frame•work /fráymwərk/ *n.* **1** essential supporting structure. **2** basic system.
■ **1** see STRUCTURE *n.* 1b. **2** see FORMAT *n.* 2.

franc /frangk/ *n.* chief monetary unit of France, Belgium, Switzerland, Luxembourg, and several other countries.

fran•chise /fránchīz/ ● *n.* **1** right to vote in elections; citizenship. **2** authorization granted by a company to sell its goods or services in a particular way. ● *v.tr.* grant a franchise to. □□ **fran•chi•see** /-zee/ *n.* **fran'chis•er** *n.* (also **fran'chi•sor**).
■ *n.* **1** see SUFFRAGE. **2** see LICENSE 1. ● *v.* see CHARTER *v.* 1.

fran•ci•um /fránseeəm/ *n. Chem.* radioactive metallic element. ¶Symb.: Fr.

Franco- /frángkō/ *comb. form* French.

fran•gi•ble /fránjibəl/ *adj.* breakable; fragile.

Frank /frangk/ *n.* member of the Germanic nation or coalition that conquered Gaul in the 6th c. □□ **Frank'ish** *adj.*

frank /frangk/ ● *adj.* **1** candid; outspoken (*frank opinion*). **2** undisguised; avowed. ● *v.tr.* stamp (a letter) with an official mark to record the payment of postage. ● *n.* franking signature or mark. □□ **frank'a•ble** *adj.* **frank'er** *n.* **frank'ly** *adv.* **frank'ness** *n.*
■ *adj.* **1** direct, blunt, forthright, *colloq.* upfront; explicit, truthful. **2** open, free, unreserved, uninhibited.

Frank•en•stein /frángkənstīn/ *n.* (in full **Frank'en•stein's mon'ster**) thing that becomes terrifying to its maker; monster.

frank•furt•er /frángkfərtər/ *n.* seasoned smoked sausage.

frank•in•cense /frángkinsens/ *n.* aromatic gum resin used for burning as incense.

Frank•lin stove /fránglin/ *n.* often freestanding cast-iron stove having the general shape of an open fireplace.

fran•tic /frántik/ *adj.* **1** wildly excited. **2** hurried or anxious; desperate. □□ **fran'ti•cal•ly** *adv.* **fran'tic•ly** *adv.*
■ **1** frenzied, frenetic, hectic, hysterical, wild. **2** violent; upset, agitated, perturbed; overwrought.

frappé /frapáy/ *n.* drink made with shaved ice.

frat /frat/ *n. colloq.* student fraternity.

fra•ter•nal /frətərnəl/ *adj.* **1** of a brother or brothers. **2** brotherly. **3** (of twins) developed from separate ova and not necessarily closely similar. □□ **fra•ter'nal•ism** *n.* **fra•ter'nal•ly** *adv.*
■ **2** friendly, comradely; see also *brotherly* (BROTHER).

fra•ter•ni•ty /frətərnitee/ *n.* (*pl.* **–ties**) **1** male students' society. **2** group or company with common interests, or of the same professional class. **3** being fraternal; brotherliness.

■ **2** community, brotherhood, crowd, set, clique, coterie, circle, society. **3** fellowship, camaraderie, comradeship, friendship, companionship.

frat•er•nize /frátərnīz/ *v.intr.* **1** associate with. **2** (of troops) enter into friendly relations with enemy troops or the inhabitants of an occupied country. □□ **frat•er•ni•za′tion** *n.*

■ **1** consort, hobnob, mingle, socialize with, go around with, spend time with, *sl.* hang out (with).

frat•ri•cide /frátrisīd/ *n.* **1** killing of one's brother or sister. **2** person who does this. □□ **frat•ri•cid•al** /-síd′l/ *adj.*

Frau /frow/ *n.* (*pl.* **Frau•en** /frówən/) (often as a title) married or widowed German woman.

fraud /frawd/ *n.* **1** criminal deception. **2** dishonest artifice or trick. **3** impostor.

■ **1** trickery, cheating, subterfuge, deceit, swindling, duplicity. **2** hoax, swindle, scam, deception, cheat, wile. **3** deceiver, trickster, cheat(er), swindler, charlatan.

fraud•u•lent /fráwjələnt/ *adj.* of, involving, or guilty of fraud. □□ **fraud′u•lence** *n.* **fraud′u•lent•ly** *adv.*

■ fake, counterfeit, forged, false, falsified, spurious, deceitful, dishonest, deceptive, tricky, artful, crafty.

fraught /frawt/ *adj.* **1** filled or attended with. **2** *colloq.* causing or affected by great anxiety or distress.

■ **1** charged with, packed with, loaded with. **2** tense, taut, stressed, strained, fretful, anxious; stressful, trying.

Fräu•lein /fróylīn, fröw-/ *n.* (often as a title or form of address) unmarried (esp. young) German woman.

fray[1] /fray/ *v.* **1** *tr. & intr.* wear through or become worn, esp. (of woven material) unweave at the edges. **2** *intr.* (of nerves, temper, etc.) become strained; deteriorate.

■ **1** shred, wear thin, become threadbare, rub, unravel. •

fray[2] /fray/ *n.* brawl.

■ conflict, fight, fighting; see also FRACAS.

fraz•zle /frázəl/ *colloq.* • *n.* worn or exhausted state. • *v.tr.* (usu. as **frazzled** *adj.*) wear out; exhaust.

freak /freek/ • *n.* **1** (also **freak of nature**) monstrosity; abnormally developed individual or thing. **2** *colloq.* **a** unconventional person. **b** fanatic (*health freak*). • *v.* [often foll. by *out*] *colloq.* **1** *intr. & tr.* become or make very angry. **2** *intr. & tr.* undergo or cause to undergo hallucinations or a strong emotional experience, esp. from use of narcotics. **3** *intr.* adopt a wildly unconventional lifestyle. □□ **freak′ish** *adj.* **freak′ish•ly** *adv.* **freak′ish•ness** *n.*

■ *n.* **1** mutant, see also MONSTER 3, 4. **2 b** enthusiast, fan, devotee, aficionado. • *v.* **1** see RAGE *v.*, ANGER *v.* □□ **freakish** see GROTESQUE *adj.* 1, BIZARRE.

freak•y /fréekee/ *adj.* (**freak•i•er**, **freak•i•**

est) **1** of or like a freak. **2** bizarre; unconventional. □□ **freak′i•ly** *adv.* **freak′i•ness** *n.*

freck•le /frékəl/ • *n.* [often in *pl.*] light brown spot on the skin. • *v.* **1** *tr.* (usu. as **freckled** *adj.*) spot with freckles. **2** *intr.* be spotted with freckles. □□ **freck′ly** /fréklee/ *adj.*

free /free/ • *adj.* (**fre•er** /frée•ər/; **fre•est** /fréeist/) **1** not under the control of another; at liberty. **2** autonomous; democratic. **3 a** unrestricted; not restrained or fixed. **b** not imprisoned. **c** released from duties, etc. **d** independent. **4** [foll. by *of, from*] **a** exempt from. **b** not containing (*free of preservatives*). **5** permitted to choose (*free to choose*). **6 a** costing nothing. **b** not subject to tax, duty, etc. **7** not occupied or in use (*the bathroom is free*). **8** lavish. **9** frank; unreserved. **10** (of literary style) not observing the strict laws of form. **11** (of a translation) not literal. • *adv.* **1** in a free manner. **2** without cost or payment. • *v.tr.* **1** make free; liberate. **2** relieve. **3** disengage; disentangle. □ **free enterprise** system of private business operating free from government control. **free fall 1** part of a parachute descent before the parachute opens. **2** movement of a spacecraft in space without thrust from the engines. **free-for-all** chaotic fight, unrestricted discussion, etc. **free hand** freedom to act at one's own discretion (see also FREEHAND). **free-handed** generous. **free-handedly** generously. **free-handedness** generosity. **free market** market with unrestricted competition. **free speech** right to express opinions freely. **free-standing** not supported by another structure. **free trade** international trade without import or export restrictions. **free verse** verse without a fixed metrical pattern. **free will** power of acting at one's own discretion. □□ **free′ly** *adv.* **free′ness** *n.*

■ *adj.* **1** freeborn. **2** independent, self-governing, self-ruling, sovereign. **3 a** unimpeded, untrammeled, unconstrained. **b** at liberty, at large, loose, unconfined. **c** liberated, set free, let go, let off, emancipated. **d** unattached, unconstrained, loose. **4** (*free of* or *from*) rid of, relieved of, safe from, immune from. **5** able, allowed, within one's rights. **6** cost-free, free of charge, complimentary, gratis, on the house. **7** vacant, empty, spare, extra; uninhabited, untenanted. **8** generous, open, liberal, munificent. **9** candid, plain, open, direct. • *adv.* **1** freely, openly, at will. **2** gratis, free of charge. • *v.* **1** set at liberty, release, let go, liberate; unloose, unchain. **2** rid, unburden; rescue, redeem. **3** untie, unbind, unfasten, undo. □ **free hand** see CARTE BLANCHE. **free-handed** see GENEROUS 1. **free will** see VOLITION. □□ **freely** unrestrainedly, unrestrictedly; easily, smoothly; willingly, spontaneously, readily; liberally, lavishly, unreservedly, generously.

-free /free/ *comb. form* free of or from (*duty-free, trouble-free*).

free•bie /fréebee/ *n. colloq.* thing provided free of charge.

free•boot•er /fréebōōtər/ *n.* pirate. □□ **free′boot** *v.intr.*

free•born /free'bawrn/ *adj.* inheriting a citizen's rights and liberty.

freed•man /freed'mən/ *n.* (*pl.* **-men**) emancipated slave.

free•dom /free'də m/ *n.* **1** condition of being free or unrestricted. **2** personal or civic liberty; absence of slave status. **3** power of self-determination; quality of not being controlled by fate or necessity. **4** state of being free to act. **5** condition of being exempt from. **6** unrestricted use of (facilities, etc.). See synonym study at LIBERTY.
■ **1, 2** freeness; release, deliverance, liberation, emancipation, independence. **3** independence. **4** ability, facility, license, permission, right, privilege. **5** exemption, immunity, deliverance, liberation, relief. **6** range, latitude, scope, play, run.

free•hand /free'hand/ • *adj.* (of a drawing, etc.) done by hand without special instruments. • *adv.* in a freehand manner.

free•hold /free'hōld/ *n.* **1** complete ownership of property for life. **2** such land or property. □□ **free'hold•er** *n.*

free•lance /free'lans/ • *n.* (also **free'lanc•er**) person, usu. self-employed, offering services on a temporary basis, esp. to several businesses, etc., for particular assignments. • *v.intr.* act as a freelance. • *adv.* as a freelance.

free•load•er /free'lōdər/ *n. sl.* person who eats, drinks, or lives at others' expense; sponger. □□ **free'load** /-lōd/ *v.intr.*
■ see PARASITE.

free•style /free'stīl/ *adj.* (of a race or contest) in which all styles are allowed, esp.: **1** *Swimming* in which any stroke may be used. **2** *Wrestling* with few restrictions on the holds permitted.

free•think•er /free'thingkər/ *n.* person who rejects dogma or authority, esp. in religious belief. □□ **free'think'ing** *n. & adj.*

free•way /free'wā/ *n.* **1** express highway, esp. with controlled access. **2** toll-free highway.

freeze /freez/ • *v.* (*past* **froze** /frōz/; *past part.* **fro•zen** /frō'zən/) **1** *tr. & intr.* **a** turn or be turned into ice or another solid by cold. **b** make or become rigid from the cold. **2** *intr.* be or feel very cold. **3** *tr. & intr.* cover or become covered with ice. **4** *tr.* preserve (food) by refrigeration below the freezing point. **5** *tr. & intr.* make or become motionless or powerless through fear, surprise, etc. **6** *tr.* make (credits, assets, etc.) temporarily or permanently unrealizable. **7** *tr.* fix or stabilize (prices, wages, etc.) at a certain level. **8** *tr.* arrest (a movement in a movie, video, etc.). • *n.* **1** period or state of frost. **2** fixing or stabilization of prices, wages, etc. **3** film shot in which movement is arrested by the repetition of a frame. □ **freeze-dry** (**-dries**, **-dried**) freeze and dry by the sublimation of ice in a high vacuum. **freezing point** temperature at which a liquid, esp. water, freezes. □□ **freez'a•ble** *adj.* **fro'zen•ly** *adv.*
■ *v.* **1** ice; solidify, congeal, harden, stiffen. **2** be icy or chilled to the bone. **5** fix, immobilize, paralyze, stop (dead), pin. • *n.* **1** freeze-up. **2** immobilization.

freez•er /free'zər/ *n.* refrigerated compartment, cabinet, or room for freezing and preserving food.

freight /frāt/ • *n.* **1** transport of goods. **2** goods transported; cargo. **3** charge for transportation of goods. • *v.tr.* **1** transport (goods) as freight. **2** load with freight.
■ *n.* **1** transportation, carriage, conveyance, shipping. **2** load, shipload, truckload, consignment. **3** tonnage. • *v.* **1** see TRANSPORT *v.* 1. **2** see LOAD *v.* 1.

freight•er /frā'tər/ *n.* ship designed to carry freight.

French /french/ • *adj.* **1** of France or its people or language. **2** having the characteristics attributed to the French people. • *n.* **1** language of France. **2** [prec. by *the;* treated as *pl.*] the people of France. □ **French bread** white bread in a long crisp loaf. **French Canadian** *n.* Canadian whose principal language is French. *adj.* of French-speaking Canadians. **French cuff** double cuff formed by turning back a long cuff and fastening it. **French door** door with glass panes throughout its length. **French dressing 1** creamy orange salad dressing. **2** salad dressing of vinegar and oil, usu. seasoned. **French fries** (also **French fried potatoes**) strips of potato, deep fried. **French horn** coiled brass wind instrument with a wide bell. **French kiss** openmouthed kiss. **French window** pair of casement windows extending to the floor in an outside wall, serving as both window and door. □□ **French'man** *n.* (*pl.* **-men**) **French'wom•an** *n.* (*pl.* **-wom•en**) **French'ness** *n.*

fre•net•ic /frənet'ik/ *adj.* **1** frantic, frenzied. **2** fanatic. □□ **fre•net'i•cal•ly** *adv.*
■ **1** see HECTIC *adj.* 1. **2** see *fanatical* (FANATIC).

fren•zy /fren'zee/ • *n.* (*pl.* **-zies**) wild or delirious excitement, agitation, or fury. • *v.tr.* (**-zies, -zied**) (usu. as **frenzied** *adj.*) drive to frenzy; infuriate. □□ **fren'zied•ly** *adv.*
■ *n.* fever, passion, turmoil, distraction; paroxysm, outburst, furor. • *v.* (**frenzied**) see FEVERISH 2.

fre•quen•cy /free'kwənsee/ *n.* (*pl.* **-cies**) **1** commonness of occurrence. **2** frequent occurrence. **3** *Physics* rate of recurrence of a vibration, etc. □ **frequency modulation** *Electronics* modulation in which the frequency of the carrier wave is varied. ¶Abbr.: **FM.**

fre•quent /free'kwənt/ • *adj.* **1** occurring often or in close succession. **2** habitual; constant. • *v.tr.* /also frikwent'/ attend or go to habitually. □□ **fre•quen•ta'tion** *n.* **fre•quent•er** /frikwent'ər/ *n.* **fre•quent•ly** /free'kwəntlee/ *adv.*
■ *adj.* **1** reiterative, continual. **2** continual, continuing, recurrent, recurring, regular; persistent. • *v.* haunt, patronize, go to or attend regularly, *sl.* hang out at. □□ **frequently** often, regularly, continually, repeatedly, over and over (again); habitually, customarily, regularly.

fres•co /fres'kō/ *n.* (*pl.* **-cos** or **-coes**) paint-

ing done in watercolor on wet plaster.
□□ **fres'coed** adj.

fresh /fresh/ • adj. **1** newly made or obtained. **2 a** other; different; new (start a fresh page). **b** additional (fresh supplies). **3** lately arrived. **4** not stale or musty or faded (fresh flowers). **5** (of food) not preserved. **6** not salty (fresh water). **7** pure; untainted; refreshing. **8** (of the wind) brisk. **9** colloq. impudent. **10** inexperienced. • adv. newly; recently (esp. in comb.: fresh-cut). □□ **fresh'ly** adv. **fresh'ness** n.

■ adj. **1** new, today's, most recent, latest. **2 a** modern, up-to-date; novel, original, unusual. **b** additional, renewed, extra. **4** new, recent. **7** clean, clear, invigorating, unpolluted; wholesome. **8** fair, strong; see also BRISK 2. **9** bold, impertinent, brazen, brassy, forward, disrespectful; see also NAUGHTY 1. **10** young, raw, green, naive, callow, immature. □□ **freshly** newly, recently, just now.

fresh•en /fréshən/ v. **1** make or become fresh. **2** [foll. by up] wash, change clothes, etc.
■ **1** ventilate, air out, deodorize, purify.

fresh•man /fréshmən/ n. (pl. **-men**) first-year student at a high school, college, or university.

fresh•wa•ter /fréshwawtər, -wotər/ adj. not of the sea.

fret[1] /fret/ v. (**fret•ted, fret•ting**) **1** intr. be worried or distressed. **2** tr. **a** cause anxiety or distress to. **b** irritate; annoy. **3** tr. wear or consume by gnawing or rubbing.
■ **1** worry, agonize, grieve, brood, be concerned, be upset. **2 a** worry, concern; see also DISTRESS v. **b** vex, torment, provoke, rankle. **3** see WEAR v. 5.

fret[2] /fret/ n. ornamental pattern made of straight lines joined usu. at right angles.

fret[3] /fret/ n. each of a sequence of bars or ridges on the fingerboard of a guitar, etc. □□ **fret'less** adj.

fret•ful /frétfool/ adj. visibly anxious, distressed, or irritated. □□ **fret'ful•ly** adv. **fret' ful•ness** n.
■ nervous, on edge, edgy, troubled, bothered, vexed.

fret•work /frétwərk/ n. ornamental work of interlacing lines.

Freud•i•an /fróydeeən/ Psychol. • adj. of or relating to Sigmund Freud or his methods of psychoanalysis. • n. follower of Freud or his methods. □ **Freudian slip** unintentional error regarded as revealing subconscious feelings. □□ **Freud'i•an•ism** n.

F.R.G. abbr. Federal Republic of Germany.

Fri. abbr. Friday.

fri•a•ble /fríəbəl/ adj. easily crumbled. □□ **fri•a•bil'i•ty** n.

fri•ar /fríər/ n. member of any of certain religious orders of men, esp. the four mendicant orders. □□ **fri'ar•ly** adj.
■ see MONK.

fric•as•see /fríkəseé/ • n. dish of stewed or fried pieces of meat served in a thick white sauce. • v.tr. (**fric•as•sees, fric•as•seed**) make a fricassee of.

fric•a•tive /fríkətiv/ Phonet. • adj. made by the friction of breath in a narrow opening. • n. consonant made in this way, e.g., f and th.

fric•tion /fríkshən/ n. **1** rubbing of one object against another. **2** the resistance encountered in moving an object. **3** clash of wills, temperaments, or opinions. □□ **fric'tion•al** adj. **fric'tion•less** adj.
■ **1** scraping, grating, chafing; abrasion. **3** discord, conflict, contention, argument, dispute.

Fri•day /fríday, -dee/ n. day of the week following Thursday.

fridge /frij/ n. colloq. = REFRIGERATOR.

friend /frend/ n. **1** person with whom one enjoys mutual affection and regard. **2** sympathizer, helper. □□ **friend'less** adj.
■ **1** companion, partner, comrade, crony, familiar, confidant, confidante.

friend•ly /fréndlee/ • adj. (**friend•li•er, friend•li•est**) **1** well-disposed; kindly; cordial. **2** on amicable terms. • adv. in a friendly manner. □□ **friend'li•ness** n.
■ adj. **1** kind, kindhearted, warmhearted, warm, affectionate, amiable, amicable, genial, sociable. **2** congenial, companionable, comradely, convivial, familiar, close, on good terms.

friend•ship /fréndship/ n. **1** being friends; relationship between friends. **2** friendly disposition felt or shown.
■ **1** amity, harmony, alliance, companionability, comradeship, fellowship. **2** friendliness, amiability, amicability, congeniality, conviviality, sociability.

fri•er var. of FRYER.

frieze /freez/ n. horizontal decorative or sculpted band, esp. along a wall near the ceiling.

frig•ate /frígit/ n. naval vessel between a destroyer and a cruiser in size.

fright /frit/ n. **1 a** sudden or extreme fear. **b** instance of this (gave me a fright). **2** person or thing looking grotesque or ridiculous.
■ **1 a** alarm, terror, horror, panic, trepidation. **b** scare, shock, surprise, start. **2** eyesore, mess, disaster.

fright•en /frítən/ v. **1** tr. fill with fright. **2** tr. drive or force by fright. □□ **fright'en•ing** adj. **fright'en•ing•ly** adv.
■ **1** terrify, scare, alarm, intimidate, panic, petrify. **2** scare, terrify; see also INTIMIDATE. □□ **frightening** terrifying, alarming, startling, shocking, petrifying.

fright•ful /frítfool/ adj. **1 a** dreadful; shocking; revolting. **b** ugly; hideous. **2** colloq. colloq. extreme. □□ **fright'ful•ly** adv.
■ **1** awful, dreadful, terrible, disagreeable, atrocious, abhorrent, loathsome, grisly, ghastly. □□ **frightfully** very, extremely, colloq. awfully; amazingly, surprisingly.

frig•id /fríjid/ adj. **1 a** lacking friendliness or enthusiasm. **b** chilling. **2** cold. **3** sexually unresponsive. □□ **fri•gid'i•ty** /-jíditee/ n. **frig'id•ly** adv. **frig'id•ness** n.
■ **1 a** cold, cool, cold-hearted, forbidding, austere, unemotional; apathetic, unenthusiastic; forced. **2** frosty, frozen, glacial, icy, freezing, wintry.

fri•jo•les /freehólays/ *n.pl.* beans, esp. in Mexican-style cooking.

frill /fril/ *n.* **1** strip of material with one side gathered or pleated, used as an ornamental edging. **2** [in *pl.*] unnecessary embellishments. □□ **frilled** *adj.* **frill'er•y** /–ləree/ *n.* **frill'i•ness** *n.* **frill'y** *adj.* (**frill•i•er, frill•i•est**)

■ **1** trimming, edging, ruffle, decoration. **2** extras, additions, trimmings; ornamentation.

fringe /frinj/ • *n.* **1** ornamental bordering of threads left loose or formed into tassels or twists. **2** outer edge or margin; outer limit of an area, population, etc. (often *attrib.*: *fringe theater*). **3** thing, part, or area of secondary or minor importance. • *v.tr.* adorn with or serve as a fringe. □ **fringe benefit** employee benefit supplementing a money wage or salary. □□ **fringe'less** *adj.* **fring'y** *adj.*

■ *n.* **1** trimming, edge, edging, border, frill, flounce. **2** border, perimeter, boundary, periphery, bounds. • *v.* **1** bind, purfle, trim, edge, border; surround, ring.

frip•per•y /frípəree/ *n.* (*pl.* **–ies**) showy, tawdry, or unnecessary finery or ornament, esp. in dress.

■ see FINERY, ORNAMENT *n.* 1.

Fris•bee /frízbee/ *n. propr.* molded plastic disk for sailing through the air as an outdoor game.

frisk /frisk/ *v.tr. sl.* feel over or search (a person) for a weapon, etc. (usu. rapidly). □□ **frisk'er** *n.*

■ inspect, check, examine, go over, check out.

frisk•y /frískee/ *adj.* (**frisk•i•er, frisk•i•est**) lively; playful. □□ **frisk'i•ly** *adv.* **frisk'i•ness** *n.*

■ frolicsome, rollicking, active, animated, spirited.

frit•ter¹ /frítər/ *v.tr.* waste (money, time, etc.) triflingly.

■ squander, trifle away, idle away.

frit•ter² /frítər/ *n.* piece of fruit, meat, etc., coated in batter and deep-fried (*apple fritter*).

friv•o•lous /frívələs/ *adj.* **1** paltry; trifling; trumpery. **2** lacking seriousness; given to trifling; silly. □□ **fri•vol•i•ty** /–vólitee/ *n.* (*pl.* **–ties**) **friv'o•lous•ly** *adv.* **friv'o•lous•ness** *n.*

■ **1** inconsequential, unimportant, trivial, nugatory, insignificant. **2** scatterbrained, featherbrained, irresponsible, flighty, giddy, puerile, flippant.

frizz /friz/ • *v.tr.* form (hair, etc.) into a mass of small curls. • *n.* **1 a** frizzed hair. **b** row of curls. **2** frizzed state. □□ **friz'zi•ness** *n.* **friz'zy** *adj.* (**friz•zi•er, friz•zi•est**)

friz•zle¹ /frízəl/ *v.tr.* **1** fry, toast, or grill, with a sputtering noise. **2** [often foll. by *up*] burn or shrivel.

friz•zle² /frízəl/ • *v.* **1** *tr.* form (hair) into tight curls. **2** *intr.* [often foll. by *up*] (of hair, etc.) curl tightly. • *n.* frizzled hair.

fro /frō/ *adv.* back (now only in *to and fro*: see TO).

frock /frok/ *n.* **1** woman's or girl's dress. **2** monk's or priest's long gown with loose sleeves. **3** smock.

frog¹ /frawg, frog/ *n.* small amphibian having a tailless smooth-skinned body with legs developed for jumping. □ **frog in the** (or **one's**) **throat** *colloq.* hoarseness.

frog² /frawg, frog/ *n.* ornamental coat fastening of a spindle-shaped button and loop. □□ **frogged** *adj.* **frog'ging** *n.*

frog•man /fráwgman, fróg–, –mən/ *n.* (*pl.* **–men**) person equipped with a rubber suit, flippers, and an oxygen supply for underwater swimming.

frol•ic /frólik/ • *v.intr.* (**frol•icked, frol•ick•ing**) play cheerfully. • *n.* **1** cheerful play. **2** merriment. □□ **frol'ick•er** *n.*

■ *v.* frisk, caper, skylark, gambol, rollick, romp, play, skip, sport. • *n.* **1** horseplay, skylarking. **2** merrymaking, gaiety, sport, fun (and games).

frol•ic•some /fróliksəm/ *adj.* merry; playful. □□ **frol'ic•some•ly** *adv.*

■ frisky, sportive, gay, lively, sprightly, animated.

from /frum, from, frəm/ *prep.* expressing separation or origin, followed by: **1** person, place, time, etc., that is the starting point (*rain comes from the clouds*). **2** place, object, etc., whose distance or remoteness is reckoned or stated (*ten miles from Los Angeles*). **3 a** source (*dig gravel from a pit*). **b** giver or sender (*presents from their parents*). **4** person or thing avoided, deprived, etc. (*took his gun from him*). **5** reason, cause, or motive (*died from fatigue*). **6** thing distinguished or unlike (*know black from white*). **7** lower limit (*saw from 10 to 20 boats*). **8** state changed for another (*raised the penalty from a fine to imprisonment*). **9** adverb or preposition of time or place (*from long ago, from under the bed*).

frond /frond/ *n. Bot.* foliage leaf in various flowerless plants, esp. ferns and palms. □□ **frond'age** *n.* **fron'dose** *adj.*

front /frunt/ • *n.* **1** side or part normally nearer or turned toward the spectator or the direction of motion. **2** any face of a building, esp. that of the main entrance. **3** *Mil.* **a** foremost line or part of an army, etc. **b** line of battle. **4** sector of activity regarded as resembling a military front. **5** demeanor; bearing (*show a bold front*). **6** forward or conspicuous position (*come to the front*). **7** *a* bluff. **b** pretext. **8** person, etc., serving to cover subversive or illegal activities. **9** *Meteorol.* forward edge of an advancing mass of cold or warm air. • *attrib.adj.* **1** of the front. **2** situated in front. • *v.* **1** *intr.* have the front facing or directed toward. **2** *intr. sl.* act as a front or cover for. **3** *tr.* furnish with a front (*fronted with stone*). □ **front office** executives or executive branch of an organization. **2** main office. **front runner** contestant most likely to succeed. **front-wheel drive** automobile drive system in which power is transmitted to the front wheels. **in front of** **1** ahead of; in advance of. **2** in the presence of; confronting. □□ **front'less** *adj.* **front'ward** *adj. & adv.* **front'wards** *adv.*

■ *n.* **1** face, forepart, fore; obverse. **2** frontage, façade. **3** vanguard, van, *Mil.* front line.

5 air, face, expression, countenance. **6** head, forefront, fore. **7** disguise, guise, cover, show. **8** cover. • *attrib.adj.* **2** first, advance, leading, head. • *v.* **1** overlook, face, look out on *or* over. **2** act for, represent; cover for, replace.

front•age /frúntij/ *n.* **1** front of a building. **2** land abutting on a street or on water.

fron•tal /frúnt'l/ *adj.* **1** of, at, or on the front (*frontal attack*). **2** of the forehead. □□ **front′al•ly** *adv.*

fron•tier /frúnteér/ *n.* **1 a** the border between two countries. **b** district on each side of this. **2** limits of attainment or knowledge in a subject. **3** borders between settled and unsettled country. □□ **fron•tier′less** *adj.*
  ■ **1** boundary, bound(s), pale. **2** bound(s), extreme(s).

fron•tiers•man /frúnteérzmən/ *n.* (*pl.* **-men**) person living in the region of a frontier.
  ■ see PIONEER *n.* 2.

fron•tis•piece /frúntispees/ *n.* illustration facing the title page of a book or of one of its divisions.

frost /frawst, frost/ • *n.* **1** white frozen dew. **2** consistent temperature below freezing point causing frost to form. • *v.* **1** *intr.* become covered with frost. **2** *tr.* **a** cover with or as if with frost, powder, etc. **b** give a roughened or finely granulated surface to (glass, metal). **3** *tr.* decorate (a cake, etc.) with icing. □□ **frost′less** *adj.*
  ■ *n.* **2** see FREEZE *n.* 1.

frost•bite /fráwstbīt, fróst–/ *n.* injury to skin due to freezing and often resulting in gangrene.

frost•ing /fráwsting, fróst–/ *n.* icing.

frost•y /fráwstee, fróstee/ *adj.* (**frost•i•er, frost•i•est**) **1** cold with frost. **2** covered with or as with hoarfrost. **3** unfriendly in manner. □□ **frost′i•ly** *adv.* **frost′i•ness** *n.*
  ■ **1** see COLD *adj.* 1. **3** see COLD *adj.* 4.

froth /frawth, froth/ • *n.* **1** foam. **2 a** idle talk or ideas. **b** anything unsubstantial or of little worth. • *v.intr.* emit or gather froth. □□ **froth′i•ly** *adv.* **froth′i•ness** *n.* **froth′y** *adj.* (**froth•i•er, froth•i•est**).
  ■ *n.* **1** spume, suds, lather, bubbles; head. **2** trivia, rubbish, nonsense, twaddle, babble, gibberish. • *v.* foam, spume, bubble, fizz, effervesce; lather.

frown /frown/ • *v.intr.* **1** wrinkle one's brows, esp. in displeasure or deep thought. **2** express disapproval. • *n.* look expressing severity, disapproval, or deep thought. □□ **frown′er** *n.* **frown′ing•ly** *adv.*
  ■ *v.* **1** scowl, glower, glare, knit one's brows. **2** disapprove of, disfavor, discountenance, look askance at. • *n.* scowl, glower, glare, grimace.

frow•zy /frówzee/ *adj.* (also **frow′sy**) (**–zi•er, –zi•est**) slatternly; unkempt; dingy. □□ **frow′zi•ness** *n.*

froze *past* of FREEZE.

fro•zen *past part.* of FREEZE.

fruc•ti•fy /frúktifī, fro͞ok–/ *v.* (**–fies, –fied**) **1** *intr.* bear fruit. **2** *tr.* make fruitful; impregnate.

fruc•tose /frúktōs, fro͞ok–/ *n. Chem.* simple sugar found in honey and fruits. (Also called **levulose, fruit sugar**).

fru•gal /fro͞ogəl/ *adj.* **1** sparing; thrifty. **2** meager; slight; costing little. See synonym study at ECONOMICAL. □□ **fru•gal′i•ty** /–gáli-tee/ *n.* **fru′gal•ly** *adv.* **fru′gal•ness** *n.*
  ■ **1** economical, careful, prudent; abstemious. **2** paltry, poor, skimpy, scanty, scant, small.

fruit /fro͞ot/ • *n.* **1 a** usu. sweet and fleshy edible product of a plant or tree, containing seed. **b** [in *sing.*] these in quantity (*eats fruit*). **2** seed of a plant or tree with its covering, e.g., an acorn, pea pod, cherry, etc. **3** [usu. in *pl.*] vegetables, grains, etc., used for food (*fruits of the earth*). **4** [usu. in *pl.*] the result of action, etc., esp. as financial reward. • *v.* bear or cause to bear fruit. □□ **fruit′ed** *adj.* [also in *comb.*].
  ■ *n.* **4** product(s), revenue(s), outcome, consequence(s), return(s), advantage(s), benefit(s).

fruit•cake /fro͞otkayk/ *n.* cake containing dried fruit.

fruit•ful /fro͞otfool/ *adj.* **1** producing much fruit; abundant. **2** successful; remunerative. See synonym study at FERTILE. □□ **fruit′ful•ly** *adv.* **fruit′ful•ness** *n.*
  ■ **1** fertile, plentiful, abundant, fecund, copious. **2** effective, profitable, remunerative, productive.

fru•i•tion /fro͞o-íshən/ *n.* **1 a** bearing of fruit. **b** production of results. **2** realization of aims or hopes. **3** enjoyment.
  ■ **1b, 2** completion; achievement, success, attainment, accomplishment. **3** see *enjoyment* (ENJOY).

fruit•less /fro͞otlis/ *adj.* **1** not bearing fruit. **2** useless; unsuccessful; unprofitable. □□ **fruit′less•ly** *adv.* **fruit′less•ness** *n.*
  ■ **1** barren, unfruitful, unproductive, sterile, infertile. **2** worthless, futile, pointless, vain, unavailing.

fruit•y /fro͞otee/ *adj.* (**fruit•i•er, fruit•i•est**) **1** of fruit. **2** tasting or smelling like fruit, esp. (of wine) tasting of the grape. □□ **fruit′i•ly** *adv.* **fruit′i•ness** *n.*
  ■ **2** see ROBUST 2.

frump /frump/ *n.* dowdy, unattractive, old-fashioned woman. □□ **frump′ish** *adj.* **frump′ish•ly** *adv.*

frump•y /frúmpee/ *adj.* (**frump•i•er, frump•i•est**) dowdy; unattractive. □□ **frump′i•ly** *adv.* **frump′i•ness** *n.*
  ■ see DOWDY *adj.* 2.

frus•trate /frústrayt/ *v.tr.* **1** make (efforts) ineffective. **2** prevent (a person) from achieving a purpose. **3** (as **frustrated** *adj.*) **a** discontented because unable to achieve one's desire. **b** sexually unfulfilled. **4** disappoint (a hope). See synonym study at THWART. □□ **frus•trat•ed•ly** /–strátidlee/ *adv.* **frus′trat•er** *n.* **frus′trat•ing** *adj.* **frus′trat•ing•ly** *adv.* **frus•tra•tion** /–tráyshən/ *n.*
  ■ **1** counteract, neutralize, nullify, negate. **2** defeat, forestall, stop, halt, cripple, hinder. **3** (**frustrated**) **a** see *discontented* (DISCONTENT). **b** dissatisfied. **4** discourage, foil, thwart, defeat, balk.

fry[1] /frī/ • v. (**fries, fried**) cook or be cooked in hot fat. • n. (pl. **fries**) **1** a French fried potato. **2** social gathering serving fried food.

fry[2] /frī/ n.pl. **1** young or newly hatched fishes. **2** young of other creatures produced in large numbers, e.g., bees or frogs. □ **small fry** people of little importance; children.

fry•er /frīər/ n. (also **fri'er**) **1** person who fries. **2** vessel for frying, esp. deep frying. **3** young chicken for frying.

FSLIC abbr. Federal Savings and Loan Insurance Corporation.

ft. abbr. foot, feet.

FTC abbr. Federal Trade Commission.

fuch•sia /fyōosha/ n. shrub with drooping red, purple, pink, or white flowers.

fud•dle /fúd'l/ • v.tr. confuse or stupefy, esp. with alcoholic liquor. • n. **1** confusion. **2** intoxication.

fud•dy-dud•dy /fúdeedúdee/ sl. • adj. old-fashioned or quaintly fussy. • n. (pl. **–dies**) fuddy-duddy person.
■ adj. see SQUEAMISH 2, STUFFY 3. • n. see FOGY.

fudge /fuj/ • n. soft toffee-like candy made with milk, sugar, butter, etc. • v. **1** tr. put together in a makeshift or dishonest way; fake. **2** tr. deal with incompetently. **3** intr. practice such methods.

fueh•rer var. of FÜHRER.

fu•el /fyōol/ • n. **1** material burned or used as a source of heat or power. **2** food as a source of energy. **3** anything that sustains or inflames emotion or passion. • v. (**fu•eled, fu•el•ing**) **1** tr. supply with fuel. **2** intr. take in or get fuel. □ **fuel injection** direct introduction of fuel into the combustion units of an internal combustion engine. **fuel oil** oil used as fuel in an engine or furnace.
■ n. **2** nourishment, sustenance, nutriment, nutrition. **3** incitement, stimulus, stimulation, provocation; see also SPUR n. 2.

fu•gi•tive /fyōojitiv/ • adj. **1** fleeing. **2** transient; fleeting; of short duration. • n. person who flees, esp. from justice, an enemy, danger, or a master. □□ **fu'gi•tive•ly** adv.
■ adj. **1** escaped, running away, runaway. **2** passing, short-lived, transitory, transient, ephemeral, evanescent.

fugue /fyōog/ n. **1** Mus. contrapuntal composition in which a short melody or phrase is introduced by one part and successively taken up and developed by others. **2** Psychol. loss of awareness of one's identity, often coupled with flight from one's usual environment. □□ **fu'gal** adj.

füh•rer /fyōorər/ n. (also **fueh'rer**) tyrannical leader.

-ful /fōol/ comb. form forming: **1** adjectives from nouns, meaning: **a** full of (beautiful). **b** having the qualities of (masterful). **2** adjectives from adjectives or Latin stems (direful). **3** adjectives from verbs, meaning 'apt to,' (forgetful). **4** nouns (pl. **–fuls**) meaning 'the amount needed to fill' (handful).

ful•crum /fōolkrəm, fúl–/ n. (pl. **ful•cra** /–rə/ or **ful•crums**) point against which a lever is placed to get a purchase or on which it turns or is supported.
■ see PIVOT n. 1.

ful•fill /fōolfil/ v.tr. (**ful•filled, ful•fill•ing**) **1** carry out (a prophecy or promise). **2** satisfy (a desire or prayer). **3** perform; carry out (a task). **4** bring to an end; finish; complete. □□ **ful•fill'a•ble** adj. **ful•fill'er** n. **ful•fill'ment** n.
■ **1** bring about, consummate; see also REALIZE 4, KEEP v. 7. **2** see also ACHIEVE 2. **3** do, bring or carry off, see to, accomplish, effect, effectuate; implement. **4** discharge, carry through, bring or carry to completion. □□ **fulfillment** completion, realization, implementation, execution; performance, achievement.

full[1] /fōol/ • adj. **1** holding all its limits will allow (full of water). **2** having eaten to one's limits or satisfaction. **3** abundant; copious; satisfying; sufficient. **4** having or holding an abundance of. **5** complete (full daylight). **6** (of tone or color) deep and clear. **7** plump; rounded; protuberant (full figure). **8** (of clothes) made of much material arranged in folds or gathers. • adv. **1** very (you know full well). **2** quite; fully (full six miles). □ **full-blooded 1** vigorous; hearty; sensual. **2** not hybrid. **full-blown** fully developed; complete. **full-fledged 1** fully developed. **2** of full rank or standing. **full house 1** maximum or large attendance at a theater, etc. **2** Poker hand with three of a kind and a pair. **full moon** moon with its whole disk illuminated. **full-scale** not reduced in size; complete. **full-time** adj. occupying or using the whole of the available working time. **in full 1** without abridgment. **2** to or for the full amount (paid in full). **in full swing** at the height of activity. **in full view** entirely visible. □□ **full'ness** n.
■ adj. **1** filled, replete, brimming, brimful, chock-full, packed, loaded. **2** gorged, sated, satiated, stuffed, replete. **3** complete, thorough, detailed, broad, extensive, comprehensive, all-inclusive, all-encompassing, exhaustive, plenary. **4** see TEEM 2. **5** maximum, top, unrestricted; entire, whole, unconditional, unqualified; greatest, highest, utmost; perfect. **6** bright, vivid, shining, brilliant, intense. **7** well-rounded, ample, shapely, buxom, busty, voluptuous, well-built, robust, colloq. curvaceous. **8** wide, ample, generous; see also LOOSE adj. 2. • adv. **1** exceedingly, extremely, perfectly, quite, colloq. damned. **2** completely, entirely, wholly, thoroughly, altogether, quite. □ **full-blooded 1** see vigorous (VIGOR). **2** pedigree, thoroughbred, pure-bred. **in full 1** see UNABRIDGED. **2** completely, fully, entirely, wholly, thoroughly, in its entirety, totally, in toto. **in full swing** in (full) operation, under way, in progress, in business, animated, lively, on the move. □□ **fullness** see BODY n. 3, ENTIRETY 1.

full[2] /fōol/ v.tr. cleanse and thicken (cloth).

full•back /fōolbak/ n. **1** offensive player in the backfield in football. **2** defensive player, or a position near the goal, in soccer, field hockey, etc.

ful•mi•nate /fúlminayt, fōol–/ v.intr. **1** express censure loudly and forcefully. **2** explode violently; flash like lightning (*fulminating mercury*). □□ ful•mi•na•tion /–náyshən/ *n.* ful•mi•na•to•ry /–nátawree/ *adj.*

■ 1 see RAIL².

ful•some /fŏolsəm/ *adj.* excessive; cloying. □□ ful'some•ly *adv.* ful'some•ness *n.*

■ see *excessive* (EXCESS).

fum•ble /fúmbəl/ • *v.* 1 *intr.* use the hands awkwardly; grope about. 2 *tr.* handle or deal with clumsily or nervously. • *n.* act of fumbling. □□ fum'bler *n.* fum'bling•ly *adv.*

■ *v.* 1 feel (about); search for, feel for, fish for. 2 mishandle, muff, bungle, botch, *colloq.* flub. • *n.* grope, feel.

fume /fyŏom/ • *n.* [usu. in *pl.*] exuded gas or smoke or vapor, esp. when harmful or unpleasant. • *v.* 1 a *intr.* emit fumes. b *tr.* give off as fumes. 2 *intr.* be affected by (esp. suppressed) anger (*was fuming at their inefficiency*). □□ fume'less *adj.* fum'ing•ly *adv.*

■ *n.* odor; exhalation, exhaust, pollution, smog. • *v.* 1 smoke, reek, steam. 2 seethe, smolder, chafe, rage.

fu•mi•gate /fyŏomigayt/ *v.tr.* 1 disinfect or purify with fumes. 2 apply fumes to. □□ fu•mi•gant /–gənt/ *n.* fu•mi•ga•tion /–gáyshən/ *n.* fu'mi•ga•tor *n.*

■ 1 sanitize, sterilize, *usu. formal* cleanse; fume.

fun /fun/ • *n.* 1 amusement, esp. lively or playful. 2 source of this. 3 (in full fun and games) exciting or amusing goings-on. • *adj. disp. colloq.* amusing; entertaining; enjoyable (*a fun thing to do*). □ make fun of tease; ridicule.

■ *n.* 1 enjoyment, merriment, *colloq.* whoopee; joy, pleasure, gaiety, glee, jollity, playfulness, mirth, cheer, delight. 2 joy, pleasure, delight. 3 sport, recreation, entertainment; festivity, frolic, diversion, pastime. □ make fun of poke fun at, deride, scoff at, lampoon, parody, satirize, *colloq.* kid, rib.

fu•nam•bu•list /fyŏonámbyəlist/ *n.* tightrope walker.

func•tion /fúngkshən/ • *n.* 1 a activity proper to a person or institution. b mode of action or activity by which a thing fulfills its purpose. c official or professional duty. 2 public or social occasion. 3 *Math.* quantity whose value depends on the varying values of others. • *v.intr.* fulfill a function; operate; be in working order. □□ func'tion•less *adj.*

■ *n.* 1 a, b task, chore, assignment; purpose, aim. c job, occupation, work, employment; responsibility, mission, charge. 2 reception, gathering, party, gala, ceremony. • *v.* serve, act; perform, behave, work.

func•tion•al /fúngkshənəl/ *adj.* 1 of or serving a function. 2 practical rather than attractive; utilitarian. 3 *Physiol.* (esp. of disease) of or affecting only the functions of an organ, etc., not structural or organic. □□ func'tion•al•i•ty /–nálitee/ *n.* func'tion•al•ly *adv.*

■ 1 working, functioning, operating, running, going; operational. 2 useful, serviceable, usable.

func•tion•ar•y /fúngkshəneree/ *n.* (*pl.* –ies)

person who has to perform official functions or duties; an official.

■ commissioner, bureaucrat, officeholder, officer.

fund /fund/ • *n.* 1 permanently available supply. 2 stock of money, esp. for a specific purpose. 3 [in *pl.*] money resources. • *v.tr.* 1 provide with money. 2 make (a debt) permanent at fixed interest. □ fund-raiser 1• person who seeks financial support for a cause, enterprise, etc. 2 activity, event, etc., to raise money, as for charity, etc. fund-raising seeking of financial support.

■ *n.* 1 stock, reserve, store, pool, reservoir. 2 nest egg, endowment; see also CACHE *n.* 2. 3 assets, means, wealth, resources, capital, savings; money, (hard) cash. • *v.* 1 finance, pay for, support, endow, subsidize, back.

fun•da•men•tal /fúndəmént'l/ • *adj.* of, affecting, or serving as a base or foundation; essential; primary. • *n.* [usu. in *pl.*] principle. □□ fun•da•men'tal•ly *adv.*

■ *adj.* inherent, intrinsic, rudimentary, elementary; main, prime. • *n.* 1 axiom, essential, law, rule.

fun•da•men•tal•ism /fúndəméntəlizəm/ *n.* (also Fun•da•men'tal•ism) strict maintenance of traditional religious beliefs. □□ fun•da•men'tal•ist *n.*

fu•ner•al /fyŏonərəl/ *n.* burial or cremation of a dead person with its ceremonies. □ funeral director undertaker. funeral parlor (also home) establishment where the dead are prepared for burial or cremation. □□ fu'ner•ar•y *adj.*

■ interment, entombment, inhumation; obsequies.

fu•ne•re•al /fyŏonéereeəl/ *adj.* 1 of or appropriate to a funeral. 2 gloomy; dismal; dark. □□ fu•ne're•al•ly *adv.*

■ 2 morose, somber, lugubrious, mournful, doleful, sorrowful, grave, solemn, sad, melancholy.

fun•gi•cide /fúnjisīd, fúnggi–/ *n.* fungus-destroying substance. □□ fun•gi•cid•al /–síd'l/ *adj.*

fun•gus /fúnggəs/ *n.* (*pl.* fun•gi /–gī, –jī/ or fun•gus•es) any of a group of nonphotosynthetic organisms feeding on organic matter, which include molds, yeast, mushrooms, and toadstools. □□ fun•gal /fúnggəl/ *adj.* fun•gi•form /fúnjifawrm, fúnggi–/ *adj.* fun•giv•or•ous /fúnjívərəs, funggiv–/ *adj.* fun'gous *adj.*

■ see MOLD².

fu•nic•u•lar /fyŏoníkyələr, fə–/ • *adj.* (of a railway, esp. on a mountainside) operating by cable with ascending and descending cars counterbalanced. • *n.* funicular railway.

funk¹ /fungk/ *n.* fear; panic. □ in a funk dejected.

funk² /fungk/ *n. sl.* 1 funky music. 2 strong smell.

funk•y /fúngkee/ *adj.* (funk•i•er, funk•i•est) *sl.* 1 (esp. of jazz or rock music) earthy, bluesy, with a heavy rhythmical beat. 2 fashionable. 3 odd; unconventional. 4 having a strong smell. □□ funk'i•ly *adv.* funk'i•ness *n.*

fun•nel /fúnəl/ • *n.* 1 narrow tube or pipe widening at the top, for pouring liquid, powder, etc., into a small opening. **2** metal chimney on a steam engine or ship. • *v.* (**fun·neled, fun·nel·ing; fun·nelled, fun·nel·ling**) guide or move through or as through a funnel. □□ **fun′nel·like** *adj.*

fun·ny /fúnee/ *adj.* (**fun·ni·er, fun·ni·est**) **1** amusing; comical. **2** strange; perplexing; hard to account for. □ **funny bone** part of the elbow over which the ulnar nerve passes. **funny money** *colloq.* **1** counterfeit money. **2** foreign currency. **3** inflated currency. □□ **fun′ni·ness** *n.*

■ **1** humorous, jocular, jocose, comic, droll; entertaining, diverting, sidesplitting, hilarious. **2** peculiar, odd, queer, weird, bizarre, curious.

fur /fər/ *n.* **1 a** short fine soft hair of certain animals. **b** skin of such an animal with the fur on it; pelt. **2** coat of certain animals as material for making, trimming, or lining clothes. □ **make the fur fly** *colloq.* cause a disturbance; stir up trouble. □□ **fur′less** *adj.*

■ *n.* **1b, 2** see PELT².

fur·be·low /fárbilō/ *n.* **1** gathered strip or pleated border of a skirt or petticoat. **2** [in *pl.*] *derog.* showy ornaments.

fur·bish /fárbish/ *v.tr.* **1** remove rust from; polish. **2** give a new look to; renovate. □□ **fur′bish·er** *n.*

■ **1** see POLISH *v.* 1. **2** see DECORATE 2.

fu·ri·ous /fyŏŏreeəs/ *adj.* **1** extremely angry. **2** full of fury. **3** raging; violent; intense. □□ **fu′ri·ous·ly** *adv.*

■ **1, 2** cross, irate, mad, enraged, infuriated, incensed, maddened, provoked, fuming, beside oneself. **3** fierce, wild, savage; unrestrained.

furl /fərl/ *v.* **1** *tr.* roll up and secure (a sail, umbrella, flag, etc.). **2** *intr.* become furled. □□ **furl′a·ble** *adj.*

■ fold *or* wind up; see also WIND² *v.* 4.

fur·long /fárlawng, -long/ *n.* unit of measurement equal to an eighth of a mile or 220 yards.

fur·lough /fárlō/ • *n.* leave of absence, esp. granted to a member of the armed services. • *v.tr.* grant furlough to.

■ *v.* see FREE *v.* 1.

furn. *abbr.* **1** furnished. **2** furniture.

fur·nace /fárnis/ *n.* enclosed structure for intense heating.

fur·nish /fárnish/ *v.tr.* **1** provide with furniture. **2** [foll. by *with*] cause to have possession or use of. **3** provide; afford; yield. □□ **fur′nished** *adj.*

■ **1** see EQUIP. **2** equip, rig (out *or* up); outfit, provision. **3** see PROVIDE *v.* 1a.

fur·nish·ings /fárnishingz/ *n.pl.* furniture and utensils, etc., in a house, room, etc.

■ see FURNITURE.

fur·ni·ture /fárnichər/ *n.* movable equipment of a house, room, etc., e.g., tables, chairs, and beds. □ **part of the furniture** *colloq.* person or thing taken for granted.

■ furnishings; goods, movables, chattels, effects.

fu·ror /fyŏŏrawr, -ər/ *n.* **1** uproar; outbreak of fury. **2** wave of enthusiastic admiration; craze.

■ **1** outburst, commotion, to-do, hubbub,

stir, fuss; tumult, turmoil. **2** rage, mania, vogue, fad.

fur·ri·er /fóreeər/ *n.* dealer in or dresser of furs.

fur·row /fárō, fúr–/ • *n.* **1** narrow trench made in the ground by a plow. **2** rut, groove, or deep wrinkle. **3** ship's track. • *v.tr.* **1** plow. **2 a** make furrows, grooves, etc., in. **b** mark with wrinkles. □□ **fur′row·less** *adj.* **fur′row·y** *adj.*

■ *n.* **2** channel, trench, track, ditch, gutter; crinkle, crease. • *v.* **1** harrow, till, cultivate, rib. **2 a** groove, channel, flute, score. **b** wrinkle, crease, corrugate.

fur·ry /fóree, fúree/ *adj.* (**fur·ri·er, fur·ri·est**) **1** of or like fur. **2** covered with or wearing fur. □□ **fur′ri·ness** *n.*

■ **1** see SOFT *adj.* 2, WOOLLY *adj.* 1.

fur·ther /fárthər/ • *adv.* **1** = FARTHER. **2** to a greater extent; more. **3** in addition. • *adj.* **1** = FARTHER. **2** more; additional (*threats of further punishment*). • *v.tr.* promote; favor (a scheme, etc.). □□ **fur′ther·er** *n.* **fur′ther·most** *adj.*

■ *adv.* **3** furthermore, besides; moreover, too, also, additionally. • *adj.* **2** other, new, supplemental, extra, spare. • *v.* advance, forward, foster, help.

fur·ther·ance /fárthərəns/ *n.* furthering or being furthered.

■ promotion, advancement, championship, advocacy, patronage, backing, fostering, championing.

fur·ther·more /fárthərmáwr/ *adv.* in addition; besides.

■ see *in addition* (ADDITION).

fur·thest *var.* of FARTHEST.

fur·tive /fártiv/ *adj.* **1** done by stealth. **2** sly; stealthy. □□ **fur′tive·ly** *adv.* **fur′tive·ness** *n.*

■ **1** secret, secretive, clandestine, conspiratorial. **2** foxy, cunning, crafty, wily, slinky, skulking.

fu·ry /fyŏŏree/ *n.* (*pl.* **–ries**) **1 a** wild and passionate anger; rage. **b** fit of rage (*in a blind fury*). **c** impetuosity in battle, etc. **2** violence of a storm, disease, etc. **3** (**Fury**) [usu. in *pl.*] *Gk. mythol.* each of three avenging goddesses.

■ **1 a** *literary* ire, wrath; see also ANGER *n.* **b** see TEMPER *n.* 2. **c** vehemence; see also VIOLENCE 1. **2** ferocity, savagery, fierceness, tempestuousness.

fuse¹ /fyŏŏz/ • *v.* **1** melt with intense heat. **2** blend or amalgamate into one whole by or as by melting. • *n.* device or component for protecting an electric circuit when an excessive current passes through.

■ *v.* **2** merge, unite, combine, mix, mingle; compound.

fuse² /fyŏŏz/ *n.* (also **fuze**) device of combustible matter for igniting an explosive. □□ **fuse′less** *adj.*

fu·se·lage /fyŏŏsəlaazh, –lij, –zə–/ *n.* the body of an airplane.

■ see BODY *n.* 3a.

fus·i·ble /fyŏŏzibəl/ *adj.* that can be easily fused or melted. □□ **fu·si·bil′i·ty** *n.*

fu•sil•ier /fyoōziler'/ n. (also **fu•si•leer'**) hist. soldier armed with a light musket.

fu•sil•lade /fyoōsiláyd, –laàd, –zi–/ n. **1** continuous discharge of firearms. **2** wholesale execution by this means.

fu•sion /fyoōzhən/ n. **1** act or instance of fusing or melting. **2** fused mass. **3** blending of different things into one. **4** coalition. **5** Physics = nuclear fusion. □□ **fu′sion•al** adj.

■ **1–4** see amalgamation (AMALGAMATE).

fuss /fus/ • n. **1** excited commotion; bustle. **2** excessive concern about a trivial thing. **3** sustained protest or dispute. • v.intr. **1** make a fuss. **2** busy oneself restlessly with trivial things. □ **make a fuss** complain vigorously. **make a fuss over** treat (a person or animal) with great or excessive attention. □□ **fuss′er** n.

■ n. **1, 2** bother, fluster, flurry, to-do, furor, stir. • v. **1** kick up a fuss; see also COMPLAIN 1, 2b. □ **make a fuss** see COMPLAIN 1, 2b.

fuss•budg•et /fúsbujit/ n. person who habitually frets over minor matters.

fuss•y /fúsee/ adj. (**fuss•i•er, fuss•i•est**) **1** inclined to fuss. **2** full of unnecessary detail or decoration. **3** fastidious. □□ **fuss′i•ly** adv. **fuss′i•ness** n.

■ **1** see CHOOSY. **2** fancy, elaborate, overdecorated, rococo, ornate. **3** particular, finicky, finical, dainty, colloq. picky, choosy, persnickety, nitpicking.

fus•ty /fústee/ adj. (**fus•ti•er, fus•ti•est**) **1** musty; moldy. **2** stuffy; close. **3** antiquated. □□ **fus′ti•ly** adv. **fus′ti•ness** n.

■ **1** see MUSTY¹ 1, 2. **2** see CLOSE adj. 8.

fu•tile /fyoōt'l, –til/ adj. **1** useless; ineffectual, vain. **2** frivolous; trifling. □□ **fu′tile•ly** adv. **fu•til•i•ty** /–tilitee/ n.

■ **1** unavailing, unsuccessful, unprofitable, abortive, profitless. **2** see WORTHLESS.

fu•ton /foōton/ n. Japanese quilted mattress rolled out on the floor for use as a bed.

fu•ture /fyoōchər/ • adj. **1** going or expected to happen or be or become. **2 a** of time to come (future years). **b** Gram. (of a tense or participle) describing an event yet to happen. • n. **1** time to come. **2** what will happen in the future. **3** future condition of a person, country, etc. **4** prospect of success, etc. (there's no future in it). **5** Gram. future tense. □ **future perfect** Gram. tense giving the sense 'will have done'. **future shock** inability to cope with rapid progress. □□ **fu′ture•less** adj.

■ adj. **1** see PROSPECTIVE. **2 a** tomorrow's, coming; subsequent; to be, to come; see also PROSPECTIVE. • n. **1** days to come; tomorrow; futurity. **3** see PROSPECT n. 1a.

fu•tur•ist /fyoōchərist/ n. [often attrib.] **1** believer in human progress. **2** student of the future.

fu•tur•is•tic /fyoōchəristik/ adj. suitable for the future; ultramodern. □□ **fu•tur•is′ti•cal•ly** adv.

fu•tu•ri•ty /fyootooritee, –tyoor–, choor–/ n. (pl. **–ties**) **1** future time. **2** [in sing. or pl.] future events.

fuze var. of FUSE².

fuzz /fuz/ n. **1** fluff. **2** fluffy or frizzled hair. **3** sl. the police.

■ **1** see FLUFF n. 1. **3** see POLICE n., police officer.

fuzz•y /fúzee/ adj. (**fuzz•i•er, fuzz•i•est**) **1** like fuzz; fluffy. **2** blurred; indistinct. □□ **fuzz′i•ly** adv. **fuzz′i•ness** n.

■ **1** woolly, furry, downy, flocculent, linty; see also HAIRY 1. **2** dim, faint, hazy, foggy, misty, blurry, unclear.

FY abbr. fiscal year.

-fy /fī/ suffix forming: **1** verbs from nouns, meaning: **a** make; produce (pacify). **b** make into (deify). **2** verbs from adjectives, meaning 'bring or come into such a state' (solidify). **3** verbs in causative sense (horrify).

FYI abbr. for your information.

Gg

G¹ /jee/ n. (also g) (pl. **Gs** or **G's; g's**) **1** seventh letter of the alphabet. **2** Mus. fifth note in the diatonic scale of C major.

G² abbr. (also **G.**) **1** gauss. **2** giga–. **3** gravitational constant.

g abbr. (also **g.**) **1** gelding. **2** gram(s). **3** gravity.

GA abbr. Georgia (in official postal use).

Ga symb. Chem. gallium.

Ga. abbr. Georgia (US).

gab /gab/ colloq. • n. talk; chatter. • v.intr. talk incessantly, inconsequentially, or indiscreetly; chatter. □□ **gab′ber** n. **gab′by** adj. (**gab•bi•er, gab•bi•est**)

■ n. prattle, jabber, blather, gossip, colloq. chitchat; cackle, drivel, twaddle, colloq. hogwash, sl. poppycock, bunk, eyewash. v.

jabber, gabble, chatter, gibber, blather, prate.

gab•ar•dine /gábərdeén/ n. (also **gab′er•dine**) smooth durable twilled cloth, esp. of worsted or cotton.

gab•ble /gábəl/ • v.intr. talk inarticulately or too fast. • n. fast unintelligible talk. □□ **gab′bler** n.

■ v. see PRATTLE v. n. see PRATTLE n..

ga•ble /gáybəl/ n. triangular upper part of a wall at the end of a ridged roof. □□ **ga′bled** adj. [also in comb.].

gad /gad/ v.intr. (**gad•ded, gad•ding**) [foll. by about] go about idly or in search of pleasure.

■ run around, flit; see also IDLE v. 2, PHILANDER.

gad•a•bout /gádəbowt/ *n.* person who gads about.

gad•fly /gádflī/ *n.* (*pl.* **–flies**) **1** cattle-biting fly. **2** irritating or harassing person.

■ **2** see TROUBLEMAKER.

gadg•et /gájit/ *n.* mechanical or electronic device or tool. □□ **gadg•e•teer** /-teér/ *n.* **gadg′et•ry** *n.* **gadg′et•y** *adj.*

■ contrivance, appliance, apparatus, mechanism, machine, instrument, implement, utensil, *colloq.* thingamajig, thingy, doohickey. □□ **gadgetry** see APPARATUS.

gad•o•lin•i•um /gád'líneeəm/ *n. Chem.* soft silvery metallic element of the lanthanide series. ¶Symb.: **Gd.**

Gael•ic /gáylik, gálik/ • *n.* any of the Celtic languages spoken in Ireland, Scotland, and the Isle of Man. • *adj.* of or relating to the Celts or the Celtic languages.

gaff /gaf/ *n.* **1** stick with an iron hook for landing large fish. **2** spar to which the head of a fore-and-aft sail is bent.

gaffe /gaf/ *n.* blunder; indiscreet act or remark.

■ see BLUNDER *n.*

gaf•fer /gáfər/ *n.* **1** old fellow; elderly rustic. **2** *colloq.* chief electrician in a movie or television production unit.

gag /gag/ • *n.* **1** piece of cloth, etc., thrust into or held over the mouth to prevent speaking. **2** a joke. **3** thing or circumstance restricting free speech. • *v.* (**gagged, gag•ging**) **1** *tr.* apply a gag to. **2** *tr.* silence; deprive of free speech. **3** a *intr.* choke or retch. **b** *tr.* cause to do this.

■ *n.* **1** muzzle. **2** witticism, jest, quip, pun; hoax, prank, trick; scream, hoot, laugh. **3** restriction, ban, proscription; embargo, boycott. • *v.* **2** curb, put a lid on, suppress, repress, check.

ga•ga /gaágaa/ *adj. sl.* **1** infatuated; overly fond. **2** fatuous; slightly crazy.

gage[1] /gayj/ *n.* **1** pledge; thing deposited as security. **2 a** a challenge to fight. **b** symbol of this, esp. a glove thrown down.

■ **1** see PLEDGE *n.* 2. **2** see CHALLENGE *n.* 1.

gage[2] var. of GAUGE.

gag•gle /gágəl/ • *n.* **1** flock of geese. **2** *colloq.* disorderly group of people. • *v.intr.* (of geese) cackle.

gai•e•ty /gáyətee/ *n.* (also **gay′e•ty**) **1** state of being lighthearted or merry. **2** merrymaking. **3** bright appearance.

■ **1** lightheartedness, cheerfulness, cheeriness, happiness, elation, glee, felicity, delight, pleasure, joy, joyfulness. **2** amusement, festivity, celebration, revelry. **3** brightness, brilliance; see also SPLENDOR 2.

gai•ly /gáylee/ *adv.* in a gay or lighthearted manner.

■ lightheartedly, happily, cheerfully, cheerily, gleefully.

gain /gayn/ • *v.* **1** *tr.* obtain or secure. **2** *tr.* acquire; earn. **3** *tr.* obtain as an increment or addition. **4** *intr.* (foll. by *in*) make a specified advance or improvement. **5** *intr. & tr.* (of a clock, etc.) display a later time. **6** *tr.* come closer to. **7** *tr.* reach or arrive at (a desired place). See synonym study at GET. • *n.* **1** something gained, achieved, etc. **2** increase of possessions, etc.; profit, advance, or improvement. **3** acquisition of wealth. **4** increase in amount. □□ **gain′a•ble** *adj.* **gain′er** *n.* **gain′ings** *n.pl.*

■ *v.* **1** get, acquire, procure, attain, achieve, earn, win. **2** make, get, realize, clear; see also EARN 1. **3** gather, acquire, pick up; put on. **4** improve, progress, advance, increase. **6** gain ground, narrow the gap; get nearer to, close in on. **7** get to, come to; see also REACH *v.* 4. • *n.* **1** achievement, attainment, acquisition; see also ACCOMPLISHMENT 3, ADVANTAGE *n.* 1, 3. **2** yield, return, dividend; proceeds, revenue. **3** increment, rise, addition, advance; progress.

gain•ful /gáynfööl/ *adj.* **1** (of employment) paid. **2** lucrative; remunerative. □□ **gain′ful•ly** *adv.* **gain′ful•ness** *n.*

■ **2** moneymaking, profitable, fruitful.

gain•say /gáynsáy/ *v.tr.* (*past* and *past part.* **gain•said** /-séd/) deny; contradict. □□ **gain′say•er** *n.*

gait /gayt/ *n.* manner of running or walking.

■ see WALK *n.* 1.

gai•ter /gáytər/ *n.* covering of cloth, leather, etc., for the leg below the knee. □□ **gait′ered** *adj.*

gal /gal/ *n. sl.* girl.

■ see GIRL 1.

gal. *abbr.* gallon(s).

ga•la /gáylə, gaálə, gálə/ *n.* [often *attrib.*] festive or special occasion (*a gala performance*).

■ fête, festival, festivity, feast, celebration, holiday.

ga•lac•tic /gəláktik/ *adj.* of or relating to a galaxy or galaxies.

gal•ax•y /gáləksee/ *n.* (*pl.* **–ies**) **1** any of many independent systems of stars, gas, dust, etc., held together by gravitational attraction. **2** (often **the Galaxy**) the Milky Way.

gale /gayl/ *n.* **1** very strong wind. **2** *Naut.* storm. **3** outburst, esp. of laughter.

■ **2** see STORM *n.* 1. **3** burst, explosion, eruption; peal, roar, scream, shout, howl, shriek, hoot.

gall[1] /gawl/ *n.* **1** *sl.* impudence. **2** asperity; rancor. **3** bitterness; anything bitter (*gall and wormwood*). **4** bile. See synonym study at TEMERITY.

■ **1** insolence, impertinence, audacity, brashness, brazenness, *colloq.* brass, nerve, guts. **2, 3** acerbity, causticity, harshness; see also *bitterness* (BITTER).

gall[2] /gawl/ • *n.* sore made by chafing. • *v.tr.* **1** rub sore. **2** vex; annoy; humiliate. □□ **gall′ing•ly** *adv.*

■ *n.* **1** abrasion, scrape, graze, scratch, chafe. • *v.* **1** irritate, chafe, abrade, fret, scrape, scratch. **2** bother, irritate, irk; anger, enrage, inflame.

gall[3] /gawl/ *n.* growth produced by insects or fungus, etc., on plants and trees, esp. on oak.

gal•lant • *adj.* /gálənt/ **1** brave; chivalrous. **2** grand; fine; stately. **3** /gálənt, gəlánt, -laánt/ markedly attentive to women. • *n.* /gálənt, gəlánt, -laánt/ ladies′ man. □□ **gal•lant•ly** /gáləntlee/ *adv.*

■ *adj.* **1** courageous, bold, valiant, daring, dauntless, intrepid, plucky; chivalrous, gracious, honorable. **2** elegant, imposing, noble, dignified, glorious, splendid. ● *n.* lover, Romeo, seducer, sweetheart, beloved, boyfriend.

gal•lant•ry /gálǝntree/ *n.* (*pl.* **–ries**) **1** bravery; dashing courage. **2** courtliness; devotion to women. **3** polite act or speech.

■ **1** see *bravery* (BRAVE). **2** see CHIVALRY 2.

gall•blad•der /gáwlbladǝr/ *n.* (also **gall' blad•der**) *Anat.* organ that stores bile.

gal•le•on /gáleeǝn/ *n. hist.* **1** ship of war (usu. Spanish). **2** large Spanish merchant ship.

gal•ler•i•a /gálǝreeǝ / *n.* collection of small shops under a single roof; arcade.

gal•ler•y /gálǝree/ *n.* (*pl.* **–ies**) **1** room or building for showing works of art. **2** balcony, esp. in a church, hall, etc. **3 a** highest balcony in a theater. **b** its occupants. **4** portico or colonnade. **5** long narrow room, passage, or corridor. **6** group of spectators. □ **play to the gallery** seek to win approval by appealing to popular taste. □□ **gal'ler•ied** *adj.*

■ **4** see PORTICO.

gal•ley /gálee/ *n.* (*pl.* **–leys**) **1** *hist.* low flat single-decked vessel using sails and oars, and usu. rowed by slaves or criminals. **2** ship's or aircraft's kitchen. **3** *Printing* (in full **galley proof**) typeset copy before division into pages. □ **galley slave 1** *hist.* person condemned to row in a galley. **2** drudge.

Gal•lic /gálik/ *adj.* **1** French or typically French. **2** of the Gauls; Gaulish. □□ **Gal•li•cize** /–lisiz/ *v.*

gal•li•um /gáleeǝm/ *n. Chem.* soft bluish white metallic element. ¶Symb.: **Ga**.

gal•li•vant /gálivant/ *v.intr. colloq.* **1** gad about. **2** flirt.

■ **1** see JOURNEY *v.* **2** see PHILANDER.

gal•lon /gálǝn/ *n.* **1** measure of capacity equivalent to four quarts (3.785 liters), used for liquids. **2** [usu. in *pl.*] *colloq.* large amount. □□ **gal'lon•age** *n.*

gal•lop /gálǝp/ ● *n.* fastest pace of a horse or other quadruped, with all the feet off the ground together in each stride. ● *v.intr.* (**gal•loped, gal•lop•ing**) **1** (of a horse, etc., or its rider) go at the pace of a gallop. **2** move, talk, etc., very rapidly. □□ **gal'lop•er** *n.*

■ *v.* see RUN *v.* 1, 3.

gal•lows /gálōz/ *n.pl.* [usu. treated as *sing.*] structure, usu. of two uprights and a crosspiece, for the hanging of criminals. □ **gallows humor** grim and ironic humor.

■ gibbet, *hist.* scaffold.

gall•stone /gáwlstōn/ *n.* small hard mass forming in the gallbladder.

ga•lore /gǝláwr/ *adv.* in abundance (*decorated with flowers galore*).

■ aplenty, in large quantity *or* quantities *or* number(s) *or* amounts, in profusion; everywhere, all over.

ga•losh /gǝlósh/ *n.* [usu. in *pl.*] high, waterproof overshoe, usu. of rubber.

ga•lumph /gǝlúmf/ *v.intr. colloq.* move noisily or clumsily.

gal•van•ic /galvánik/ *adj.* **1 a** sudden and remarkable (*had a galvanic effect*). **b** stimulating. **2** of or producing an electric current by chemical action. □□ **gal•van'i•cal•ly** *adv.*

gal•va•nize /gálvǝnīz/ *v.tr.* **1** rouse forcefully, esp. by shock or excitement. **2** coat (iron) with zinc as a protection against rust. □□ **gal•va•ni•za'tion** *n.* **gal'va•niz•er** *n.*

■ **1** see ROUSE 2a.

gal•va•nom•e•ter /gálvǝnómitǝr/ *n.* instrument for detecting and measuring small electric currents. □□ **gal•va•no•met'ric** /–nǝmétrik/ *adj.*

gam•bit /gámbit/ *n.* **1** chess opening in which a player sacrifices a piece or pawn to secure an advantage. **2** opening move in a discussion, etc. **3** trick or device.

■ **3** see DEVICE 2.

gam•ble /gámbǝl/ ● *v.* **1** *intr.* play games of chance for money, esp. for high stakes. **2** *tr.* bet (a sum of money). **3** *intr.* take great risks in the hope of substantial gain. **4** *intr.* act in the hope or expectation of (*gambled on fine weather*). ● *n.* risky undertaking or attempt. □□ **gam'bler** *n.*

■ *v.* **1, 3** game, wager, bet. **2** risk, venture, hazard, wager; place. **4** take a chance on, count on, bargain on, rely on. ● *n.* risk, venture, chance; uncertainty, speculation.

gam•bol /gámbǝl/ ● *v.intr.* (**gam•boled, gam•bol•ing; gam•bolled, gam•bol•ling**) skip or frolic playfully. ● *n.* playful frolic.

gam•brel /gámbrǝl/ *n.* (in full **gam'brel roof**) gabled roof with each face having two slopes, the lower one steeper.

game¹ /gaym/ ● *n.* **1 a** form or spell of play or sport, esp. a competitive one played according to rules. **b** specific instance of playing such a game; a match. **2** single portion of play forming a scoring unit in some contests. **3** [in *pl.*] meeting for athletic, etc., contests (*Olympic Games*). **4 a** fun; jest. **b** [in *pl.*] jokes; tricks (*none of your games!*). **5** scheme. **6 a** policy or line of action. **b** occupation or profession. **7** [*collect.*] **a** wild animals or birds hunted for sport or food. **b** flesh of these. ● *adj.* spirited; eager and willing. ● *v.intr.* play at games of chance for money; gamble. □ **the game is up** the scheme is revealed or foiled. **game plan 1** winning strategy worked out in advance. **2** plan of campaign, esp. in politics. □□ **game'ly** *adv.* **game'ster** *n.*

■ *n.* **1 a** amusement, pastime, diversion, distraction; recreation. **2** round, bout; see also HEAT¹ *n.* 6. **3** (*games*) contest, competition, meeting, meet, tournament, tourney. **4 a** see PRANK. **b** dodges, ruses, ploys; mischief, horseplay. **5** undertaking, plan, plot, design, stratagem. **6 a** approach. **b** line of work), field, business, trade, *colloq.* racket. ● *adj.* adventurous, plucky, daring, brave, bold. □ **game plan 2** see POLICY 1.

game² /gaym/ *adj.* (of a leg, arm, etc.) lame; crippled.

game•cock /gáymkok/ *n.* (also **game•fowl** /–fowl/) cock bred and trained for cockfighting.

game•keep•er /gáymkeepǝr/ *n.* person employed to care for and protect game.

games•man•ship /gáymzmənshíp/ *n.* art or practice of gaining a psychological advantage over an opponent.

ga•mete /gámeet, gəmeét/ *n. Biol.* mature germ cell able to unite with another in sexual reproduction. □□ **ga•met•ic** /gəmétik/ *adj.*

gam•in /gámin/ *n.* 1 street urchin. 2 impudent boy.

■ 1 see GUTTERSNIPE. 2 see DEVIL *n.* 3b.

ga•mine /gámeen/ *n.* 1 girl gamin. 2 girl with mischievous or boyish charm.

gam•ma /gámə/ *n.* third letter of the Greek alphabet (Γ, γ). □ **gamma radiation** (or **rays**) electromagnetic radiation of very short wavelength.

gam•ut /gámət/ *n.* whole series or range or scope of anything (*the whole gamut of crime*). (See synonym study at RANGE.)

■ scale, spectrum, compass, spread, sweep, field.

gam•y /gáymee/ *adj.* (**gam•i•er, gam•i•est**) 1 having the flavor or scent of game. 2 scandalous; sensational. □□ **gam'i•ly** *adv.* **gam'i•ness** *n.*

gan•der /gándər/ *n.* 1 male goose. 2 *sl.* a look; a glance.

■ 2 see GLANCE *n.* 1.

gang /gang/ *n.* 1 a band of persons associating, esp. for criminal purposes. b *colloq.* such a band pursuing antisocial purposes. 2 set of workers, slaves, or prisoners. □ **gang up** *colloq.* 1 act in concert. 2 combine against.

■ 1 group, pack, mob; crowd, set. □ **gang up** 1 join together, join forces, unite. 2 conspire *or* plot against, unite *or* unify against, join forces against.

gang•land /gángland, -lənd/ *n.* the world of organized crime.

gang•ling /gánggling/ *adj.* (of a person) loosely built; lanky.

■ see LANKY.

gan•gli•on /gánggleeən/ *n.* (*pl.* **gan•gli•a** /-ə/ or **gan•gli•ons**) structure containing an assemblage of nerve cells. □□ **gan•gli•ar** /-gleeər/ *adj.* **gan•gli•on•ic** /-leeónik/ *adj.*

gang•ly /gángglee/ *adj.* (**gan•gli•er, gan•gli•est**) = GANGLING.

gang•plank /gángplangk/ *n.* movable plank usu. with cleats nailed on it for boarding or disembarking from a ship, etc.

gan•grene /gánggreen/ *n. Med.* death and decomposition of a part of the body tissue, usu. resulting from obstructed circulation. □□ **gan•gre•nous** /gánggrinəs/ *adj.*

gang•ster /gángstər/ *n.* member of a gang of violent criminals. □□ **gang'ster•ism** *n.*

■ Mafioso, racketeer, *sl.* mobster, goon, hood, gunsel; see also CRIMINAL *n.*

gang•way /gángway/ *n.* 1 opening in a ship's bulwarks. 2 bridge laid from ship to shore.

gan•net /gánit/ *n.* sea bird that catches fish by plunge-diving.

gant•let var. of GAUNTLET².

gan•try /gántree/ *n.* (*pl.* **-tries**) 1 overhead structure supporting a traveling crane, or railroad or road signals. 2 structure supporting a space rocket prior to launching.

GAO *abbr.* General Accounting Office.

gap /gap/ *n.* 1 unfilled space or interval;

blank; break in continuity. 2 breach in a hedge, fence, or wall. 3 wide divergence in views, etc. □ **fill** (or **close**, etc.) **a gap** make up a deficiency. □□ **gapped** *adj.* **gap'py** *adj.*

■ 1 void, gulf; lull, pause; stop, disruption. 2 opening, space, aperture, hole, cavity, crevice. 3 difference, distinction, disparity, discrepancy, division.

gape /gayp/ • *v.intr.* 1 a open one's mouth wide. b be or become wide open. 2 [foll. by *at*] gaze curiously or wonderingly. 3 split. • *n.* 1 openmouthed stare. 2 yawn. 3 open mouth or beak. 4 a rent or opening. □□ **gap'ing•ly** *adv.*

■ *v.* 1 a yawn, open (wide). 2 stare, goggle, *colloq.* gawk, rubberneck. 3 see SPLIT *v.* 1a. • *n.* 1 goggle, gaze. 4 see SPLIT *n.* 2.

ga•rage /gəraazh, -raáj/ *n.* 1 building or shed for the storage of motor vehicles. 2 establishment selling gasoline, etc., or repairing and selling motor vehicles. • *v.tr.* put or keep (a motor vehicle) in a garage.

garb /gaarb/ • *n.* clothing, esp. of a distinctive kind. • *v.tr.* 1 put (esp. distinctive) clothes on (a person). 2 attire.

■ *n.* see DRESS *n.* 2. • *v.* see CLOTHE 1, 2.

gar•bage /gáarbij/ *n.* 1 a refuse; filth. b domestic waste, esp. food wastes. 2 foul or inferior literature, etc. 3 nonsense.

■ 1 a dross, rubbish, junk, litter, debris, waste. 2 rubbish, trash, *colloq.* tripe. 3 see NONSENSE.

gar•ble /gáarbəl/ *v.tr.* unintentionally distort or confuse (facts, messages, etc.). □□ **gar'bler** *n.*

■ mix up, misconstrue, misunderstand, misread, jumble (up).

gar•den /gáard'n/ • *n.* 1 piece of ground used for growing esp. flowers or vegetables. 2 [esp. in *pl.*] ornamental grounds laid out for public enjoyment (*botanical gardens*). • *v.intr.* cultivate or work in a garden. □□ **gar'den•er** *n.* **gar'den•ing** *n.*

gar•de•nia /gaardéenyə/ *n.* tree or shrub with large white or yellow flowers and usu. a fragrant scent.

gar•gan•tu•an /gaargánchōōən/ *adj.* enormous; gigantic.

■ see GIGANTIC.

gar•gle /gáargəl/ • *v.tr.* wash (one's mouth and throat), esp. for medicinal purposes, with a liquid kept in motion by breathing through it. • *n.* liquid used for gargling.

gar•goyle /gáargoyl/ *n.* grotesque carved human or animal face or figure, esp. as a spout from the gutter on a building.

gar•ish /gáirish/ *adj.* 1 obtrusively bright; showy. 2 gaudy; over-decorated. □□ **gar'ish•ly** *adv.* **gar'ish•ness** *n.*

■ 1 florid, flashy, harsh, loud, obtrusive. 2 tawdry, raffish, meretricious, brummagem, *sl.* glitzy.

gar•land /gáarlənd/ • *n.* wreath of flowers, leaves, etc. • *v.tr.* 1 adorn with garlands. 2 crown with a garland.

■ *n.* crown, chaplet, circlet; festoon. • *v.* wreathe, festoon, decorate; encircle, ring, circle.

gar·lic /gaárlik/ *n.* plant of the onion family with pungent bulb, used as a flavoring in cooking. □□ **gar'lick·y** *adj.*

gar·ment /gaármənt/ *n.* article of dress.
■ item *or* piece of clothing.

gar·ner /gaárnər/ *v.tr.* **1** collect. **2** store; deposit.
■ **1** gather, assemble, amass, accumulate, heap up, pile up. **2** stock (up), lay in *or* up *or* down, put away, put by, stow (away), cache.

gar·net /gaárnit/ *n.* vitreous silicate mineral, esp. a transparent deep red kind used as a gem.

gar·nish /gaárnish/ • *v.tr.* **1** decorate or embellish (esp. food). **2** *Law* serve notice on (a person) for the purpose of legally seizing money belonging to a debtor or defendant. • *n.* (also **gar'nish·ing**) decoration or embellishment, esp. to food. □□ **gar'nish·ment** *n.* (in sense 2).
■ *v.* **1** see DECORATE 1, 3. • *n.* see DECORATION 2.

gar·nish·ee /gaárnisheé/ *Law n.* a person garnished. • *v.tr.* (**gar·nish·ees, gar·nish·eed**) **1** garnish (a person). **2** attach (money, etc.) by way of garnishment.

ga·rotte var. of GARROTE.

gar·ret /gárit/ *n.* **1** top floor or attic room. **2** attic.

gar·ri·son /gárisən/ • *n.* **1** troops stationed in a fortress, town, etc., to defend it. **2** the building occupied by them. • *v.tr.* provide (a place) with or occupy as a garrison.
■ *n.* **2** see STRONGHOLD 1. • *v.* see OCCUPY 4.

gar·rote /gərót/ (also **ga·rotte'**; **gar·rotte'**) • *v.tr.* execute or kill by strangulation, esp. with an iron or wire collar, etc. • *n.* apparatus used for this.

gar·ru·lous /gárələs, gáryə-/ *adj.* **1** talkative, esp. on trivial matters. **2** loquacious; wordy. □□ **gar·ru·li·ty** /gərŏŏlitee/ *n.* **gar'ru·lous·ly** *adv.* **gar'ru·lous·ness** *n.*
■ see TALKATIVE.

gar·ter /gaártər/ *n.* band worn to keep a sock or stocking or shirt sleeve up.

gas /gas/ • *n.* (*pl.* **gas·es**) **1** any airlike substance which moves freely to fill any space available, irrespective of its quantity. **2** such a substance used as fuel (also *attrib.*: *gas stove*). **3** nitrous oxide or another gas used as an anesthetic. **4** poisonous gas. **5** *colloq.* **a** gasoline. **b** motor vehicle's accelerator. **6** enjoyable, attractive, or amusing thing or person. • *v.* (**gas·es, gassed, gas·sing**) **1** *tr.* expose to gas, esp. to kill or make unconscious. **2** *tr. colloq.* fill (the tank of a motor vehicle) with gasoline. □ **gas chamber** room for execution by gas. **gas mask** respirator used as a defense against poison gas.
■ *n.* **1** see FUME *n.*

gas·e·ous /gáseeəs, gáshəs/ *adj.* of or like gas. □□ **gas'e·ous·ness** *n.*

gash /gash/ • *n.* long and deep slash, cut, or wound. • *v.tr.* make a gash in; cut.
■ *n.* incision, laceration. • *v.* slash, lacerate, wound; score, incise, slit, groove, split, *literary* cleave.

gas·ket /gáskit/ *n.* sheet or ring of rubber,

etc., shaped to seal the junction of metal surfaces.

gas·o·line /gásəleén/ *n.* volatile flammable liquid made from petroleum and used as a fuel.

gasp /gasp/ • *v.* **1** *intr.* catch one's breath with an open mouth as in exhaustion or astonishment. **2** *intr.* [foll. by *for*] strain to obtain by gasping (*gasped for air*). **3** *tr.* utter with gasps. • *n.* convulsive catching of breath. □ **at one's last gasp 1** at the point of death. **2** exhausted.
■ *v.* **1** pant, puff, huff, heave, wheeze. **2** gulp for, fight for, strain for. • *n.* snort, puff, gulp, huff, heave, wheeze. □ **at one's last gasp 1** at death's door, on one's deathbed, with one foot in the grave, on one's last legs, *in extremis*. **2** see *exhausted* (EXHAUST *v.* 2).

gas·sy /gásee/ *adj.* (**gas·si·er, gas·si·est**) **1** of or like gas. **2** full of gas. □□ **gas'si·ness** *n.*

gas·tric /gástrik/ *adj.* of the stomach.

gas·tri·tis /gastrítis/ *n.* inflammation of the stomach.

gastro- /gástrō/ *comb. form* (also **gastr-** before a vowel) stomach.

gas·tron·o·my /gastrónəmee/ *n.* the practice, study, or art of eating and drinking well. □□ **gas·tro·nom·ic** /gástrónómik/ *adj.* **gas·tro·nom'i·cal** *adj.* **gas·tro·nom'i·cal·ly** *adv.*

gas·tro·pod /gástrəpod/ *n.* mollusk that moves along by means of a large muscular foot, e.g., a snail, slug, etc.

gate /gayt/ • *n.* **1** barrier, usu. hinged, used to close an entrance through a wall, fence, etc. **2** gateway. **3** means of entrance or exit. **4** numbered place of access to aircraft at an airport. **5** device regulating the passage of water in a lock, etc. **6 a** number of people entering by payment at the gates of a sports stadium, etc. **b** (in full **gate money**) proceeds taken for admission. • *v.tr.* (as **gated** *adj.*) (of a road) having a gate or gates to control the movement of traffic or animals.
■ *n.* **2, 3** opening, access; see also MOUTH *n.* 2a, b. **6 a** admission(s), attendance, crowd, audience, assemblage. **b** see TAKE *n.*

-gate /gayt/ *suffix* forming nouns denoting an actual or alleged scandal comparable in some way to the Watergate scandal of 1972 (*Irangate*).

gate·crash·er /gáytkrashər/ *n.* uninvited guest at a party, etc. □□ **gate'crash** *v.*

gate·fold /gáytfōld/ *n.* page in a book or magazine, etc., that folds out to be larger than the page format.

gate·house /gáyt-hows/ *n.* house standing by a gateway, esp. to a large house or park.

gate·way /gáytway/ *n.* **1** entrance with or opening for a gate. **2** entrance or exit.

gath·er /gáthər/ • *v.* **1** *tr. & intr.* bring or come together; assemble; accumulate. **2** *tr.* acquire by gradually collecting; amass. **3** *tr.* harvest. **4** *tr.* infer or understand. **5** *tr.* increase (*gather speed*). **6** *tr.* [often foll. by *up*] summon up (one's thoughts, energy, etc.) for a purpose. **7** *tr.* gain or recover (one's breath). **8** *tr.* draw (material, or one's brow) together in folds or wrinkles. • *n.* [in *pl.*] part of a garment that is gathered or drawn in. □□ **gath'er•er** n.

■ v. **1** collect, muster, convene, meet, congregate, group; heap or pile (up), stockpile, stock, amass. **2** collect, accumulate, garner, glean. **3** collect, reap, glean. **4** deduce, conclude, be led to believe, take it; hear. **5** gain, acquire, accumulate, pick up. **8** pull together, contract, pleat, tuck, fold; see also WRINKLE v. 1. ● n. (gathers) pleats, folds, ruffles, tucks.

SYNONYM STUDY: **gather**

ASSEMBLE, COLLECT, CONGREGATE, CONVENE, MARSHAL, MUSTER. **Gather** is the most general of these terms meaning to come or bring together. It implies bringing widely scattered things or people to one place but with no particular arrangement (to gather shells at the beach; to gather the family in the living room). **Collect**, on the other hand, implies both selectivity (to collect evidence for the trial) and organization (to collect butterflies as a hobby). To **gather** one's thoughts means to bring them together because they have been previously scattered; to **collect** one's thoughts is to organize them. **Assemble** pertains to objects or people who are brought together for a purpose (to assemble data for a report; to assemble Congress so that the bill could be debated), while **congregate** is more spontaneous, describing a gathering as a result of free choice (people congregated in front of the palace, hoping to catch a glimpse of the queen). **Convene** is a formal word meaning to assemble or meet in a body (to convene an international conference on the subject of global warming). **Marshal** and **muster** are usually thought of as military terms. **Muster** implies bringing together the parts or units of a force (troops mustered for inspection), and **marshal** suggests a very orderly and purposeful arrangement (to marshal the allied forces along the battle front).

gath•er•ing /gáthəring/ n. assembly or meeting.

■ convocation, convention, congress, assemblage, rally, conclave, meet, conference, colloq. get-together.

ga•tor /gáytər/ n. (also **ga'ter**) colloq. alligator.

GATT /gat/ abbr. (also **Gatt**) General Agreement on Tariffs and Trade.

gauche /gōsh/ adj. **1** lacking ease or grace; socially awkward. **2** tactless. □□ **gauche'ly** adv. **gauche'ness** n.

■ **1** see AWKWARD 2. **2** see TACTLESS.

gau•che•rie /gōshəree/ n. gauche manners or action.

gau•cho /gówchō/ n. (pl. **–chos**) cowboy from the S. American pampas.

gaud•y /gáwdee/ adj. (**gaud•i•er**, **gaud•i•est**) tastelessly or extravagantly bright or showy. □□ **gaud'i•ly** adv. **gaud'i•ness** n.

■ garish, flashy, loud, ostentatious, tawdry, sl. glitzy.

gauge /gayj/ (also **gage**) ● n. **1** standard measure to which certain things must conform, esp.: **a** measure of the capacity or contents of a barrel. **b** fineness of a textile. **c** diameter of a bullet. **d** thickness of sheet metal. **2** instrument for measuring. **3** distance between a pair of rails or the wheels on one axle. **4** means of estimating; criterion or test. ● v.tr. **1** measure exactly. **2** estimate or form a judgment of (a person, temperament, situation, etc.). □□ **gauge'a•ble** adj. **gaug'er** n.

■ n. **1** yardstick, benchmark, rule, pattern, guide. **4** standard, yardstick, measure, touchstone, model, guideline, guide, rule, norm, example. ● v. **1** calculate, compute, figure, reckon, determine, weigh. **2** judge, evaluate, appraise, assess, rate; guess.

Gaul /gawl/ n. native or inhabitant of ancient Gaul.

Gaul•ish /gáwlish/ ● adj. of or relating to the ancient Gauls. ● n. their language.

gaunt /gawnt/ adj. **1** lean; haggard. **2** grim or desolate in appearance. See synonym study at THIN. □□ **gaunt'ly** adv. **gaunt'ness** n.

■ **1** thin, scrawny, skinny, scraggy, rawboned, bony. **2** dreary, dismal, bleak, deserted, forlorn, bare.

gaunt•let¹ /gáwntlit/ n. **1** stout glove with a long loose wrist. **2** hist. armored glove. **3** the part of a glove covering the wrist. **4** challenge (esp. in **throw down the gauntlet**).

gaunt•let² /gáwntlit/ n. (also **gant•let** /gánt-/) □ **run the gauntlet 1** be subjected to harsh criticism. **2** pass between two rows of people and receive punishing blows.

gauze /gawz/ n. thin transparent fabric of silk, cotton, etc.

gauz•y /gáwzee/ adj. (**gauz•i•er**, **gauz•i•est**) **1** like gauze. **2** flimsy; delicate. □□ **gauz'i•ly** adv. **gauz'i•ness** n.

■ see FILMY 1.

gave past of GIVE.

gav•el /gávəl/ n. small hammer used by an auctioneer, or for calling a meeting, courtroom, etc., to order.

ga•votte /gəvót/ n. **1** old French dance. **2** music for this.

gawk /gawk/ v.intr. colloq. stare stupidly. □□ **gawk'ish** adj.

■ goggle, gape, colloq. rubberneck.

gawk•y /gáwkee/ adj. (**gawk•i•er**, **gawk•i•est**) awkward or ungainly. □□ **gawk'i•ly** adv. **gawk'i•ness** n.

gay /gay/ ● adj. **1** lighthearted and carefree; mirthful. **2** characterized by cheerfulness or pleasure. **3 a** homosexual. **b** intended for or used by homosexuals (gay bar). **4** brightly colored. ● n. homosexual, esp. male. □□ **gay'ness** n.

■ adj. **1** happy, jovial, debonair, cheerful, gleeful, bright, joyful, jubilant, high-spirited. **2** see PLEASANT. **4** colorful, showy, bright, brilliant, vivid.

gay•e•ty var. of GAIETY.

gaze /gayz/ ● v.intr. look fixedly. ● n. intent look. □□ **gaz'er** n.

■ v. gape; contemplate, regard, scrutinize, observe; see also STARE v. ● n. stare, goggle, fixed or blank look.

ga•ze•bo /gəzeebō/ n. (pl. **–bos** or **–boes**)

open-sided structure designed to give a wide view.

ga•zelle /gəzél/ *n.* any of various graceful soft-eyed antelopes of Asia or Africa.

ga•zette /gəzét/ *n.* **1** newspaper, esp. the official one of an organization or institution (*University Gazette*). **2** *hist.* news'sheet; periodical publication giving current events.

■ see JOURNAL 1.

gaz•et•teer /gázɪteér/ *n.* geographical index or dictionary.

gaz•pa•cho /gəspaáchō/ *n.* (*pl.* **–chos**) Spanish soup made with tomatoes, oil, garlic, onions, etc., and served cold.

GB *abbr.* Great Britain.

Gd *symb. Chem.* element gadolinium.

GDP *abbr.* gross domestic product.

Ge *symb. Chem.* germanium.

gear /geer/ • *n.* **1** [often in *pl.*] set of toothed wheels that work together, as in a vehicle. **2** particular setting of these (*low gear*). **3** equipment or tackle for a special purpose. **4** *colloq.* **a** clothing, esp. when modern or fashionable. **b** possessions in general. • *v.* **1** *tr.* adjust or adapt to. **2** *tr.* [foll. by *up*] make ready or prepared. □ **be geared** (or **all geared**) **up** *colloq.* be ready or enthusiastic. • *n.* **1** (*gears*) cogwheels. **3** apparatus, mechanism, outfit, appliance; machinery, material. **4 a** clothes, garments, *colloq.* togs, *formal* apparel, attire. **b** belongings, things, effects, chattels, goods. • *v.* **1** tailor, fit, accommodate, suit, alter. **2** ready, get ready, set, equip, *colloq.* psych up; see also PREPARE 3a. □ **be geared** (or **all geared**) **up** see READY *adj.* 1, 2.

gear•shift /geérshift/ *n.* lever used to engage or change gear.

gear•wheel /geérhweel, –weel/ *n.* **1** toothed wheel in a set of gears. **2** (in a bicycle) cogwheel driven directly by the chain.

geck•o /gékō/ *n.* (*pl.* **–os** or **–oes**) tropical lizard.

gee /jee/ *int.* (also **gee whiz** /wiz/) *colloq.* mild expression of surprise, discovery, etc.

geek /geek/ *n. sl.* **1** socially inept person. **2** carnival performer of sensational but disgusting acts.

geese *pl.* of GOOSE.

gee•zer /geézər/ *n. sl.* person, esp. an old man.

Gei•ger count•er /gígər/ *n.* device for measuring radioactivity by detecting and counting ionizing particles.

gei•sha /gáyshə, gée–/ *n.* (*pl.* same or **gei•shas**) Japanese hostess trained in entertaining men with dance and song.

gel /jel/ • *n.* **1** semisolid colloidal suspension or jelly. **2** gelatinous hairstyling preparation. • *v.intr.* (**gelled, gel•ling**) form a gel. □□ **ge•la'tion** *n.*

■ *v.* see SET[1] *v.* 6, 7.

gel•a•tin /jélətin/ *n.* (also **gel•a•tine** /–teen/) transparent water-soluble protein derived from collagen and used in food preparation, photography, etc. □□ **ge•lat•i•nize** /jilát'nīz/ *v.* **ge•lat'i•ni•za•tion** *n.*

ge•lat•i•nous /jilát'nəs/ *adj.* **1** of or like gela-

tin. **2** of a jelly-like consistency. □□ **ge•lat'i•nous•ly** *adv.*

■ **2** see THICK *adj.* 5a.

geld /geld/ *v.tr.* castrate or spay.

geld•ing /gélding/ *n.* gelded animal, esp. a male horse.

gem /jem/ *n.* **1** precious stone, esp. when cut and polished. **2** object or person of great beauty or worth. □□ **gem'like** *adj.* **gem'my** *adj.*

■ **1** gemstone, jewel, *sl.* rock. **2** pearl, marvel, treasure; nonpareil, ideal, prize, masterpiece.

Gem•i•ni /jéminī, –nee/ *n.* **1** constellation and third sign of the zodiac (the Twins). **2** person born when the sun is in this sign.

gem•stone /jémstōn/ *n.* precious stone used as a gem.

Gen. *abbr.* **1** General. **2** Genesis (Old Testament).

-gen /jən/ *comb. form* **1** *Chem.* that which produces (*hydrogen, antigen*). **2** *Bot.* growth (*endogen, exogen, acrogen*).

gen•darme /zhondaárm/ *n.* police officer, esp. in France.

gen•der /jéndər/ *n.* **1 a** grammatical classification corresponding to the two sexes and sexlessness. **b** each of these classes of nouns. **2** *colloq.* a person's sex.

gene /jeen/ *n.* unit of heredity composed of DNA or RNA and forming part of a chromosome, etc., that determines a particular characteristic of an individual.

ge•ne•al•o•gy /jéeneeáləjee/ *n.* (*pl.* **–gies**) **1** descent traced continuously from an ancestor. **2** study of family descent. □□ **ge•ne•a•log•i•cal** /jéeneeəlójikəl/ *adj.* **ge•ne•a•log'i•cal•ly** *adv.* **ge•ne•al'o•gist** *n.*

■ **1** see LINEAGE.

gen•er•al /jénərəl/ • *adj.* **1 a** completely or almost universal. **b** including or affecting all or nearly all parts or cases of things. **2** prevalent; widespread; usual. **3** not partial, particular, local, or sectional. **4** not limited in application; relating to whole classes or all cases. **5** not restricted, specialized, or detailed (*a general idea*). See synonym study at UNIVERSAL. • *n.* **1 a** army officer ranking next above lieutenant general. **b** = *brigadier general, lieutenant general, major general.* **2** commander of an army. **3** tactician or strategist of specified merit (*a great general*). □ **general practitioner** nonspecialist doctor working in the community. **in general 1** as a normal rule; usually. **2** for the most part. □□ **gen•er•al•ist** /jénərəlist/ *n.* **gen'er•al•ness** *n.*

■ *adj.* **1** extensive, comprehensive, worldwide, global, ubiquitous; accepted, public, popular, shared; see also UNIVERSAL *adj.* **2** common, normal, regular, prevailing, customary, habitual. **3** mixed, assorted, heterogeneous; see also MISCELLANEOUS. **4** inclusive, all-inclusive, nonexclusive, unrestricted; overall, across-the-board. **5** unspecialized, nonspecialized, encyclopedic, broad, comprehensive, catholic; sweeping, panoramic; vague, indefinite. □ **general practitioner** see DOCTOR *n.* 1a. **in general** see *usually* (USUAL).

gen•er•a•lis•si•mo /jénərəlísimō/ n. (pl. –mos) commander of combined military forces in some countries.

gen•er•al•i•ty /jénərálitee/ n. (pl. –ties) 1 statement or principle, etc., having general validity or force. 2 applicability to a whole class of instances. 3 vagueness; lack of detail. 4 [foll. by of] the main body or majority.

■ 1 law; generalization. 2 see *prevalence* (PREVALENT). 4 (*the generality of*) the great majority of, the vast majority of, the greater part of, most of.

gen•er•al•ize /jénərəlīz/ v. 1 intr. speak in general or indefinite terms. 2 tr. reduce to a general statement. 3 tr. infer (a law or conclusion) by induction. □□ **gen•er•al•i•za′ tion** n, **gen′er•al•iz•er** n.

gen•er•al•ly /jénərəlee/ adv. 1 usually; in most cases. 2 in a general sense; without regard to particulars or exceptions.

■ 1 commonly, ordinarily, customarily, habitually; on average, as a rule, by and large, in general. 2 roughly, broadly, loosely, approximately.

gen•er•ate /jénərayt/ v.tr. 1 bring into existence; produce; evolve. 2 produce (electricity). □□ **gen•er•a•ble** /-rəbəl/ adj.

■ 1 create, originate, initiate, invent, devise, coin; develop, form; give rise to, bring about.

gen•er•a•tion /jénəráyshən/ n. 1 all the people born at a particular time, regarded collectively (*my generation*). 2 single step in descent or pedigree. 3 stage in (esp. technological) development (*fourth-generation computers*). 4 average time for a new human generation (about 30 years). 5 production, as of electricity or heat. 6 procreation. □ **Generation X** term used for people born from about 1965 to 1975. □□ **gen•er•a′tion•al** adj.

■ 1 age (group), cohort; contemporaries, peers. 6 propagation, production, reproduction; breeding.

gen•er•a•tive /jénərətiv, -raytiv/ adj. 1 of or concerning procreation. 2 able to produce; productive.

■ 2 see FERTILE 3.

gen•er•a•tor /jénəraytər/ n. 1 machine for converting mechanical into electrical energy. 2 apparatus for producing gas, steam, etc. 3 person who generates an idea, etc.

ge•ner•ic /jinérik/ adj. 1 characteristic of or relating to a class; general, not specific or special. 2 Biol. characteristic of or belonging to a genus. 3 (of goods, esp. a drug) having no trade or brand name. See synonym study at UNIVERSAL. □□ **ge•ner′i•cal•ly** adv.

gen•er•ous /jénərəs/ adj. 1 giving or given freely. 2 magnanimous; noble-minded; unprejudiced. 3 ample; abundant. □□ **gen•er•os′i•ty** /-rósitee/ n. **gen′er•ous•ly** adv.

■ 1 bountiful, charitable, lavish, open-handed, free, liberal, unstinting. 2 benevolent, charitable, unselfish, forgiving, humanitarian, philanthropic; disinterested, unbiased, broad-minded, tolerant. 3 copious, plentiful, full, lavish; large, substantial, sizable.

gen•e•sis /jénisis/ n. 1 origin, or mode of

formation or generation, of a thing. 2 (**Genesis**) first book of the Old Testament.

■ 1 see ORIGIN 1.

gene-splic•ing /jeen splísing/ • n. method of using enzymes to split genes and recombine them.

ge•net•ic /jinétik/ adj. 1 of genetics or genes. 2 of or in origin. □ **genetic code** Biochem. arrangement of genetic information in chromosomes. **genetic engineering** manipulation of DNA to modify hereditary features. **genetic fingerprinting** (or **profiling**) identifying individuals by DNA patterns from tissue samples. □□ **ge•net′i•cal•ly** adv.

■ 1 see HEREDITARY 1.

ge•net•ics /jinétiks/ n.pl. [usu. treated as sing.] the study of heredity and the variation of inherited characteristics. □□ **ge•net•i•cist** /-isist/ n.

gen•i•al /jéeneeəl/ adj. 1 jovial; sociable; kindly; cheerful. 2 (of climate) mild and warm; conducive to growth. 3 cheering; enlivening. □□ **ge•ni•al•i•ty** /-neeálitee/ n. **ge′nial•ly** adv.

■ 1 good-humored, cheery, convivial, affable, amiable, cordial. 2 see MILD 3. 3 good, heartening, reassuring, uplifting, comforting.

-genic /jénik/ comb. form forming adjectives meaning: 1 producing (*carcinogenic*, *pathogenic*). 2 well suited to (*photogenic*, *radiogenic*). 3 produced by (*iatrogenic*). □□ **-geni•cally** suffix forming adverbs.

ge•nie /jéenee/ n. (pl. usu. **ge•ni•i** /jéenee-ī/) jinni, goblin, or familiar spirit of Arabian folklore.

gen•i•tal /jénit′l/ • adj. of or relating to animal reproduction. • n. [in pl.] external reproductive organs.

■ adj. see SEXUAL. ■ n. (*genitals*) genitalia, sex organs, private parts, colloq. privates.

gen•i•ta•li•a /jénitáyleeə/ n.pl. genitals.

gen•i•tive /jénitiv/ Gram. • n. case indicating possession or close association. • adj. of or in the genitive. □□ **gen•i•ti•val** /-tívəl/ adj. **gen•i•ti′val•ly** adv.

ge•nius /jéenyəs/ n. (pl. **gen•ius•es** or **ge•ni•i** /-nee-ī/) 1 (pl. **gen•ius•es**) a exceptional intellectual or creative power or other natural ability or tendency. b person having this. 2 the tutelary spirit of a person, place, institution, etc.

■ 1 a intellect, intelligence, brilliance; ingenuity, wit, brain(s); talent, gift, knack, flair; faculty, capacity. b mastermind, master, great; virtuoso, maestro; colloq. brain, whiz, whiz kid, Einstein, maven.

genl. abbr. general.

gen•o•cide /jénəsīd/ n. deliberate extermination of a people or nation. □□ **gen•o•ci′dal** /-síd′l/ adj.

-genous /jénəs/ comb. form forming adjectives meaning 'produced' (*endogenous*).

gen•re /zhónrə/ n. 1 kind or style of art, etc. 2 (in full **gen′re paint′ing**) painting of scenes from ordinary life.

■ 1 genus, sort, type, class, category, variety, brand.

gent /jent/ *n. colloq.* (often *joc.*)gentleman.

gen·teel /jenteel/ *adj.* **1** affectedly or ostentatiously refined or stylish. **2** well-bred; refined; upper-class. See synonym study at UR-BANE. □□ **gen·teel'ly** *adv.* **gen·teel'ness** *n.*

■ **1** overpolite, overrefined, pretentious, affected, pompous, snobbish, *colloq.* posh, la-di-da, snooty. **2** high-class, aristocratic, patrician, gracious, polished, cultivated, elegant; courtly, polite, civil, well-mannered, proper, respectable.

gen·tian /jénshən/ *n.* mountain plant usu. with vivid blue flowers.

Gen·tile /jéntīl/ • *adj.* not Jewish; heathen. • *n.* person who is not Jewish.

gen·til·i·ty /jentílitee/ *n.* **1** social superiority. **2** good manners; habits associated with the upper class.

■ **2** see PROPRIETY 2.

gen·tle /jént'l/ *adj.* (**gen·tler**, **gen·tlest**) **1** not rough; mild or kind, esp. in temperament. **2** moderate; not severe or drastic (*gentle rebuke*). **3** (of birth, pursuits, etc.) honorable; refined. □□ **gen'tle·ness** *n.* **gen'tly** *adv.*

■ **1** kindly, tender, thoughtful, patient, indulgent, benign, gracious, compassionate, humane; quiet, calm, still, temperate. **2** soft, light; balmy. **3** noble, high.

gen·tle·man /jént'lmən/ *n.* (*pl.* **–men**) **1** man (in polite or formal use). **2** chivalrous or well-bred man. **3** man of good social position. **4** [in *pl.*] form of address to men in an audience. □□ **gen'tle·man·li·ness** *n.* **gen'tle·man·ly** *adj.*

■ **1** see MAN *n.* **1**. **3** see NOBLE *n.*

gen·tri·fi·ca·tion /jéntrifikáyshən/ *n.* social advancement of an urban area by the refurbishing of buildings and arrival of affluent residents who displace poorer inhabitants. □□ **gen·tri·fy** /–fī/ *v.tr.* (**–fies, –fied**)

gen·try /jéntree/ *n.pl.* **1** (in aristocratic societies) people next below the nobility in position and birth. **2** people, esp. a specific group of people (*these gentry*).

■ **1** landowners, squirearchy. **2** see PEOPLE *n.* 2.

gen·u·flect /jényəflekt/ *v.intr.* bend the knee, esp. in worship. □□ **gen·u·flec·tion** /–flékshən/ *n.* **gen'u·flec·tor** *n.*

gen·u·ine /jényōō-in/ *adj.* **1** really coming from its stated, advertised, or reputed source. **2** properly so called; not sham. **3** sincere. □□ **gen'u·ine·ly** *adv.* **gen'u·ine·ness** *n.*

■ **1, 2** authentic, veritable, real, bona fide, legitimate. **3** candid, frank, open, honest; decent, honorable.

SYNONYM STUDY: genuine

ACTUAL, AUTHENTIC, BONA FIDE, LEGITIMATE, VERITABLE. A car salesperson might claim that the seats of that pricey sedan you're considering are made from **genuine** leather, a word that applies to anything that is really what it is claimed or represented to be. If you're in the market for a Model T Ford, however, you'll want to make sure that the car is **authentic**, which emphasizes formal proof or documentation that an object is what it is claimed to be. Use **bona fide** when sincerity is involved (*a bona fide offer*), and **legitimate** when you mean lawful or in accordance with established rules, principles, and standards (*a legitimate business*). **Veritable** implies correspondence with the truth but not necessarily a literal or strict correspondence with reality (*a veritable supermarket for car-buyers*). How will it feel to drive that Mercedes out of the showroom? You won't know until you're the **actual** owner of the car—a word that means existing in fact rather than in the imagination.

---

ge·nus /jéenəs/ *n.* (*pl.* **gen·er·a** /jénərə/) **1** *Biol.* taxonomic grouping of organisms, usu. of several species, with common structural characteristics. **2** kind; class.

■ see SORT *n.* 1.

geo- /jee-ō/ *comb. form* earth.

ge·o·cen·tric /jéeōséntrik/ *adj.* **1** considered as viewed from the center of the earth. **2** having or representing the earth as the center; not heliocentric. □□ **ge·o·cen'tri·cal·ly** *adv.*

ge·ode /jée-ōd/ *n.* **1** small cavity lined with crystals. **2** rock containing such a cavity. □□ **ge·o·dic** /jee-ódik/ *adj.*

ge·o·de·sic /jéeōdéezik, –désik/ *adj.* (also **ge·o·det·ic** /–détik/) of or relating to geodesy. □ **geodesic dome** dome constructed as a framework of interlocked polygons.

ge·od·e·sy /jee-ódisee/ *n.* branch of mathematics dealing with the shape and area of the earth. □□ **ge·od'e·sist** *n.*

ge·o·graph·ic /jéeōgráfik/ *adj.* (also **ge·o·graph·i·cal** /–gráfikəl/) of or relating to geography. □ **geographic information system(s)** computerized system utilizing precise locational data for mapping, navigation, etc. Abbr.: **GIS.** □□ **ge·o·graph'i·cal·ly** *adv.*

ge·o·graph·i·cal var. of GEOGRAPHIC.

ge·og·ra·phy /jee-ógrəfee/ *n.* **1** the study of the earth's physical features, resources, and climate, and the physical aspects of its population. **2** main physical features of an area. □□ **ge·og'ra·pher** *n.*

geol. *abbr.* **1** geologic. **2** geological. **3** geologist. **4** geology.

ge·ol·o·gy /jee-óləjee/ *n.* science of the earth, including the composition, structure, and origin of its rocks. □□ **ge·o·log·ic** /jèeəlójik/ *adj.* **ge·o·log'i·cal** *adj.* **ge·o·log'i·cal·ly** *adv.* **ge·ol·o·gist** /–óləjist/ *n.*

geom. *abbr.* **1** geometric. **2** geometrical. **3** geometry.

ge·o·met·ric /jéeōmétrik/ *adj.* (also **ge·o·met'ri·cal**) **1** of, according to, or like geometry. **2** (of a design, architectural feature, etc.) characterized by or decorated with regular lines and shapes. □ **geometric progression** progression of numbers with a constant ratio between each number and the one before (as 1, 3, 9, 27, 81). □□ **ge·o·met'ri·cal·ly** *adv.*

ge·om·e·try /jee-ómitree/ *n.* the study of the properties and relations of points, lines, surfaces, and solids. □□ **ge·om·e·tri·cian** /jēˈəmitríshən/ n.

ge·o·phys·ics /jēˈə-ōfíziks/ n. the physics of the earth. □□ **ge·o·phys′i·cal** adj. **ge·o·phys·i·cist** /-zísist/ n.

Geor·gian[1] /jáwrjən/ • adj. of or relating to the state of Georgia. • n. native of Georgia.

Geor·gian[2] /jáwrjən/ • adj. of or relating to Georgia in the Caucasus. • n. 1 native of Georgia; person of Georgian descent. 2 language of Georgia.

ge·o·syn·chro·nous /jēˈə-ōsíngkrənəs/ adj. (of an artificial satellite of the earth) moving in an orbit equal to the earth's period of rotation such as to remain in a fixed position above a point on the earth's surface. (Also called **geostationary**)

ge·ra·ni·um /jəráyneeəm/ n. 1 herb or shrub bearing fruit shaped like the bill of a crane. 2 (in general use) widely cultivated garden plant with red, white, or pink flowers.

ger·bil /jərbil/ n. mouselike desert rodent with long hind legs.

ger·i·at·ric /jéreeátrik/ adj. 1 of old people. 2 colloq. old.

ger·i·at·rics /jéreeátriks/ n.pl. [usu. treated as sing.] branch of medicine or social science dealing with the health and care of old people. □□ **ger·i·a·tri·cian** /-ətríshən/ n.

germ /jərm/ n. 1 microorganism, esp. one that causes disease. 2 seed. 3 original idea, etc., from which something may develop; elementary principle. □□ **germ′y** adj.
  ■ 1 microbe, bacterium, virus, sl. bug. 3 embryo, seed, source, root, origin, start, base, basis, rudiments.

Ger·man /jərmən/ • n. 1 native or inhabitant of Germany; person of German descent. 2 language of Germany. • adj. of Germany or its people or language. □ **German measles** contagious disease, rubella, with symptoms like mild measles. **German shepherd** breed of large dog bred from the wolfhound.

ger·mane /jərmáyn/ adj. [usu. foll. by to] relevant (to a subject under consideration). □□ **ger·mane′ly** adv. **ger·mane′ness** n.
  ■ see RELEVANT.

Ger·man·ic /jərmánik/ • adj. 1 having German characteristics. 2 hist. of the Germans. 3 of the Scandinavians, Anglo-Saxons, or Germans. 4 of the languages or language group called Germanic. • n. 1 branch of Indo-European languages including English, German, Dutch, and the Scandinavian languages. 2 the (unrecorded) early language from which other Germanic languages developed.

ger·ma·ni·um /jərmáyneeəm/ n. Chem. lustrous brittle semimetallic element. ¶Symb.: **Ge**.

ger·mi·cide /jərmisīd/ n. substance destroying germs, esp. those causing disease. □□ **ger·mi·cid·al** /-síd′l/ adj.

ger·mi·nal /jərminəl/ adj. 1 relating to or of the nature of a germ or germs. 2 in the earliest stage of development. 3 productive of new ideas. □□ **ger′mi·nal·ly** adv.
  ■ 2 see PRIMARY adj. 2.

ger·mi·nate /jərminayt/ v. 1 a intr. sprout, bud, or put forth shoots. b tr. cause to

337

geophysics ~ get

sprout or shoot. 2 tr. cause (ideas, etc.) to originate or develop. □□ **ger·mi·na·tion** /-náyshən/ n. **ger′mi·na·tor** n.
  ■ 1 a see SPROUT v. 2.

ger·on·tol·o·gy /jərontóləjee/ n. the study of old age and aging. □□ **ge·ron·to·log·i·cal** /-təlójikəl/ adj. **ger·on·tol′o·gist** n.

ger·ry·man·der /jérimándər/ • v.tr. manipulate the boundaries of (a constituency, etc.) for political advantage. • n. this practice. □□ **ger·ry·man′der·er** n.

ger·und /jérənd/ n. Gram. verbal noun, in English ending in -ing (e.g., do you mind my asking you?, swimming is my favorite exercise).

Ge·sta·po /gestáapō, -shtáa-/ n. German secret police under Nazi rule.

ges·tate /jéstayt/ v.tr. 1 carry (a fetus) in gestation. 2 develop (an idea, etc.).

ges·ta·tion /jestáyshən/ n. 1 a process of carrying or being carried in the womb between conception and birth. b this period. 2 private development of a plan, idea, etc.

ges·tic·u·late /jestíkyəlayt/ v. 1 intr. use gestures instead of or in addition to speech. 2 tr. express with gestures. □□ **ges·tic·u·la·tion** /-láyshən/ n. **ges·tic′u·la·tive** adj. **ges·tic′u·la·tor** n. **ges·tic·u·la·to·ry** /-lətáwree/ adj.
  ■ see SIGNAL v. 1, 2a.

ges·ture /jés-chər/ • n. 1 significant movement of a limb or the body. 2 use of such movements, esp. to convey feeling or as a rhetorical device. 3 action to evoke a response or convey intention, usu. friendly. • v. gesticulate. □□ **ges′tur·al** adj. **ges′tur·er** n.
  ■ n. 1 motion, gesticulation, action, move. 2 gesturing, gesticulation, body language. 3 token, signal, indication; gambit, device. • v. motion, signal, sign, indicate.

ge·sund·heit /gəzóont-hīt/ int. expressing a wish of good health, esp. to a person who has sneezed.

get /get/ • v. (**get·ting**; past **got** /got/; past part. **got** or [and in comb.] **got·ten** /gót′n/) 1 tr. come into the possession of; receive or earn. 2 tr. a fetch; procure. b get hold of (a person). 3 tr. go to catch (a bus, train, etc.). 4 tr. prepare (a meal, etc.). 5 intr. & tr. reach or cause to reach a certain state; become or cause to become (get rich, got them ready). 6 tr. contract (a disease, etc.). 7 tr. establish contact by telephone or radio. 8 tr. experience or suffer; have inflicted on one (got four years in prison). 9 a tr. succeed in bringing, placing, etc. (get it onto the agenda). b intr. & tr. succeed or cause to succeed in coming or going (get you there somehow). 10 tr. [prec. by have] a possess. b [foll. by to + infin.] be bound or obliged (have got to see you). 11 tr. induce; prevail upon (got them to help me). 12 tr. colloq. understand (a person or an argument) (have you got that?). 13 tr. colloq. punish; retaliate (I'll get you for that). 14 tr. colloq. a annoy. b affect emotionally. c attract. 15 tr. develop an inclination (getting to like it). 16 intr. begin (get going). 17 tr. conceive (an idea, etc.). • n. 1 a act of begetting

(of animals). **b** an offspring (of animals).
□ **get about** (or **around**) **1** travel extensively or fast. **2** manage to walk, etc. (esp. after illness). **3** (of news) be circulated, esp. orally. **get at 1** reach; **get hold of. 2** *colloq.* imply. **get away with 1** escape blame or punishment for. **2** steal. **get back at** *colloq.* retaliate against. **get by** *colloq.* just manage. **get off 1** *colloq.* be acquitted; escape with little or no punishment. **2** leave. **3** alight from (a bus, etc.). **get on 1** make progress. **2** enter (a bus, etc.). **get out 1** leave or escape. **2** manage to go outdoors. **3** alight from a vehicle. **4** become known. **get out of** avoid or escape (a duty, etc.). **get over** recover from (an illness, upset, etc.). **get through 1** pass or assist in passing (an examination, etc.). **2** manage; survive. **3** make contact. **4** [foll. by *to*] succeed in making (a person) listen or understand. **get-together** *n. colloq.* social gathering. **get-up** *n. colloq.* style or arrangement of dress, etc., esp. an elaborate one.
□□ **get·ta·ble** *adj.*
■ *v.* **1** obtain, secure, acquire; make, gross, clear, net. **2 a** obtain; go and get, pick up; retrieve; buy. **b** capture, seize, arrest. **3** take, make, come *or* go by. **5** fall, turn, grow; put, place, manipulate; manage; contrive. **6** catch, have, come down with. **7** reach, get in touch with, communicate with. **8** receive; endure, go through. **9 b** transport, carry, bring, move; reach. **10 a** have, own, be provided with. **b** (*have got to*) have to, must, need to. **11** persuade, coax, influence, cajole. **12** appreciate, see, grasp, apprehend. **13** get even with, revenge oneself on, take vengeance on, pay back. **14 a** get at, irritate, vex, irk, nettle, provoke, anger, exasperate. **b** stir, move, touch. **c** see ATTRACT 1, OBSESS. **15** start, begin, come. **16** see BEGIN 2, 4.
□ **get about** (or **around**) **1** be active; gad about. **3** spread, leak (out). **get at 1** gain access to, access, get to. **2** intend, mean, suggest. **get back at** see GET *v.* 13 above. **get by 1** make ends meet, keep the wolf from the door, make do; see also MANAGE *v.* 2, 3, 4. **get off 1** be set free *or* released, escape, get away. **2** depart, set out *or* off, make a start. **3** disembark, dismount, descend (from); climb off, get down from. **get on 1** manage, cope, survive; proceed. **get out 1** depart, go away, retire; be released. **4** see TRANSPIRE 1. **get out of** evade, sidestep, shirk. **get over** recuperate from, get better from, convalesce from. **get through 1** succeed in, complete. **3** (*get through to*) reach, get in touch with. **4** (*get through to*) make oneself clear to. **get-together** see PARTY *n.* 1. **get-up** see OUTFIT *n.* 1.

ACQUIRE, ATTAIN, GAIN, OBTAIN, PROCURE, SECURE. **Get** is a very broad term meaning to come into possession of. You can *get* something by fetching it (*get some groceries*), by receiving it (*get a birthday gift*), by earning it (*get interest on a bank loan*), or by any of a dozen other familiar means. It is such a common, overused word that many writers try to substitute **obtain** for it whenever possible, perhaps because it sounds less colloquial. But it can also sound pretentious (*all employees were required to obtain an annual physical exam*) and should be reserved for contexts where the emphasis is on seeking something out (*to obtain blood samples*). **Acquire** often suggests a continued, sustained, or cumulative acquisition (*to acquire poise as one matures*), but it can also hint at deviousness (*to acquire the keys to the safe*). Use **procure** if you want to emphasize the effort involved in bringing something to pass (*procure a mediated divorce settlement*) or if you want to imply maneuvering to possess something (*procure a reserved parking space*). But beware: *procure* is so often used to describe the act of obtaining partners to gratify the lust of others (*to procure a prostitute*) that it has acquired somewhat unsavory overtones. **Gain** also implies effort, usually in *getting* something advantageous or profitable (*gain entry; gain victory*). In a similar vein, **secure** underscores the difficulty involved in bringing something to pass and the desire to place it beyond danger (*secure a permanent peace; secure a lifeline*). **Attain** should be reserved for achieving a high goal or desirable result (*if she secures the summit of Mt. Everest, she will secure for herself a place in mountaineering history*).

---

get·a·way /gétəway/ *n.* escape, esp. after a crime.
■ flight, retreat; see also ESCAPE *n.* 1.

gew·gaw /gyóōgaw, góō–/ *n.* gaudy plaything or ornament.
■ bauble, gimcrack, trifle, bagatelle, kickshaw, trinket.

gey·ser /gízər/ *n.* intermittently gushing hot spring.
■ see STREAM *n.* 2.

Gha·na·ian /gáaneeən/ • *adj.* of Ghana in W. Africa. • *n.* native or inhabitant of Ghana; person of Ghanaian descent.

ghast·ly /gástlee/ *adj.* (**ghast·li·er, ghast·li·est**) **1** horrible; frightful. **2** *colloq.* objectionable; unpleasant. **3** deathlike; pallid.
□□ **ghast'li·ness** *n.*
■ **1** horrendous, horrid, horrifying, shocking, appalling. **2** *sl.* gross; see also AWFUL 1a, b. **3** livid, ashen, wan, pale, pasty(-faced), ill, sick.

ghee /gee/ *n.* clarified butter, esp. from the milk of a buffalo or cow.

gher·kin /gárkin/ *n.* small variety of cucumber, or a young green cucumber, used for pickling.

ghet·to /gétō/ *n.* (*pl.* **-tos**) **1** part of a city, esp. a slum area, occupied by a minority group or groups. **2** *hist.* Jewish quarter in a city. **3** segregated group or area.

ghost /gōst/ • *n.* **1** supposed apparition of a dead person or animal; disembodied spirit. **2** shadow or mere semblance. **3** secondary or duplicated image produced by defective television reception or by a telescope. • *v.* **1** *intr.* act as ghost writer. **2** *tr.* act as ghost writer of (a work). □ **ghost town** deserted town with few or no remaining inhabitants. □□ **ghost'like** *adj.*

■ *n.* **1** phantom, specter, phantasm, wraith, doubleganger, doppelgänger, ghoul, *colloq.* spook. **2** suggestion, hint, trace, scintilla, glimmer.

ghost•ly /góstlee/ *adj.* (**ghost•li•er, ghost•li•est**) like a ghost; spectral. □□ **ghost'li•ness** *n.*

■ wraithlike, phantasmal; eerie, unearthly.

ghost•write /góstrīt/ *v.* write on behalf of the credited author of a work. □□ **ghost'writ•er** *n.*

ghoul /gōōl/ *n.* **1** person morbidly interested in death, etc. **2** evil spirit in Muslim folklore preying on corpses. □□ **ghoul'ish** *adj.* **ghoul'ish•ly** *adv.* **ghoul'ish•ness** *n.*

■ □□ **ghoulish** devilish, demonic, satanic, diabolic(al), fiendish, morbid, macabre, grisly.

GI /jée-í/ *n.* soldier in the US armed forces, esp. the army.

■ see SOLDIER *n.*

gi•ant /jíənt/ • *n.* **1** imaginary or mythical being of human form but superhuman size. **2** abnormally tall or large person, animal, or plant. **3** person of exceptional ability, integrity, courage, etc. • *attrib.adj.* very large. □□ **gi'ant•ism** *n.* **giant'like** *adj.*

■ *n.* **1** superhuman, colossus, ogre, Goliath; amazon. **2** leviathan, monster; see also JUMBO *n.* ■ *attrib.adj.* see GIGANTIC *adj.*

gib•ber /jíbər/ *v.intr.* speak fast and inarticulately.

■ see PRATTLE *v.*

gib•ber•ish /jíbərish/ *n.* unintelligible or meaningless speech; nonsense.

■ gibber, gabble, jabber, blather, babble; drivel, rubbish, twaddle, *colloq.* gobbledegook.

gib•bet /jíbit/ *n. hist.* **1** gallows. **2** post with an arm on which the bodies of executed criminals were hung up.

gib•bon /gíbən/ *n.* small ape native to SE Asia, having a slender body and long arms.

gib•bous /gíbəs/ *adj.* **1** convex. **2** (of a moon or planet) appearing greater than a semicircle and less than a circle. □□ **gib•bos•i•ty** / bósitee/ *n.* **gib'bous•ly** *adv.* **gib'bous•ness** *n.*

gibe /jīb/ (also **jibe**) • *v.intr.* [often foll. by *at*] jeer; mock. • *n.* instance of gibing; taunt. □□ **gib'er** *n.*

■ *v.* scoff, sneer, make fun, poke fun; tease, ridicule, taunt. • *n.* jeer, sneer, scoff, *colloq.* dig, crack.

gib•lets /jíblits/ *n.pl.* liver, gizzard, neck, etc., of a bird.

gid•dy /gídee/ *adj.* (**gid•di•er, gid•di•est**) **1** having a sensation of whirling and a tendency to fall, stagger, or spin around. **2 a** mentally intoxicated. **b** excitable; frivolous. **3** tending to make one giddy. □□ **gid'di•ly** *adv.* **gid'di•ness** *n.*

■ **1** dizzy, reeling, lightheaded, vertiginous, unsteady, *colloq.* woozy. **2 a** see OVERWROUGHT 1. **b** volatile, impulsive, capricious, whimsical; silly, scatterbrained.

gift /gift/ *n.* **1** thing given; a present. **2** natural ability or talent. **3** act or instance of giv-

ing. □ **gift wrap** (**wrapped, wrap•ping**) wrap attractively as a gift.

■ **1** donation, benefaction, offering; premium, bonus, handout. **2** aptitude, facility, capability, capacity, flair.

gift•ed /gíftid/ *adj.* exceptionally talented or intelligent. □□ **gift'ed•ly** *adv.* **gift'ed•ness** *n.*

■ capable, able, skilled, skillful; outstanding, masterful, virtuoso, first-class, first-rate, topflight.

gig[1] /gig/ *n.* **1** light two-wheeled one-horse carriage. **2** light ship's boat for rowing or sailing.

gig[2] /gig/ *n. colloq.* engagement to play music, etc.

■ see PERFORMANCE 2.

giga- /gígə, jígə/ *comb. form* denoting a factor of 10[9].

gig•a•bit /gígəbit, jígə–/ *n. Computing* unit of information equal to one billion (10[9]) bits.

gig•a•byte /gígəbīt, jígə–/ *n. Computing* unit of information equal to one billion (10[9]) bytes.

gi•gan•tic /jīgántik/ *adj.* **1** enormous. **2** like or suited to a giant. □□ **gi•gan•tesque** /–tésk/ *adj.* **gi•gan'ti•cal•ly** *adv.*

■ huge, massive, immense, towering, vast, giant, colossal, mammoth, titanic, gargantuan.

gig•gle /gígəl/ • *v.intr.* laugh in half-suppressed spasms, esp. in an affected or silly manner. • *n.* such a laugh. □□ **gig'gler** *n.* **gig'gly** *adj.* (**gig•gli•er, gig•gli•est**) **gig'gli•ness** *n.*

■ *v.* chuckle, titter, cackle, snicker, snigger, *colloq.* chortle. • *n.* chuckle, chortle, titter, snicker, snigger.

GIGO /gígō/ *n. Computing abbr.* for *garbage in, garbage out,* an informal rule stating that the quality of the data input determines the quality of the results.

gig•o•lo /jígəlō, zhíg–/ *n.* (*pl.* **–los**) young man paid by an older woman to be her escort or lover.

■ see PARAMOUR.

gild /gild/ *v.tr.* (*past part.* **gild•ed** or as *adj.* in sense 1 **gilt**) **1** cover thinly with gold. **2** give a specious or false brilliance to. □□ **gild'er** *n.* **gild'ing** *n.*

■ **1** see EMBELLISH 1. □□ **gilding** see *embellishment* (EMBELLISH).

gill[1] /gil/ *n.* [usu. in *pl.*] respiratory organ in fishes and other aquatic animals. □□ **gilled** *adj.* [also in *comb.*].

gill[2] /jil/ *n.* unit of liquid measure, equal to a quarter of a pint.

gilt /gilt/ • *adj.* **1** covered thinly with gold. **2** gold-colored. • *n.* gilding. □ **gilt-edged** (of securities, stocks, etc.) very reliable.

■ *adj.* see GOLDEN 1a.

gim•bals /gímbəlz, jím–/ *n.pl.* contrivance, usu. of rings and pivots, for keeping a stove or instruments such as a compass and chronometer horizontal at sea, in the air, etc.

gim•crack /jímkrak/ • *adj.* showy but flimsy and worthless. • *n.* cheap showy ornament; knickknack. □□ **gim'crack•er•y** *n.* **gim' crack•y** *adj.*

gim·let /gímlit/ *n.* **1** small tool with a screw tip for boring holes. **2** cocktail, usu. of gin and lime juice.

gim·mick /gímik/ *n. colloq.* trick or device, esp. to attract attention or publicity. □□ **gim'mick·ry** *n.* **gim'mick·y** *adj.*

■ stratagem, ruse, wile, dodge; contrivance, gadget, *colloq.* ploy; see also GADGET, TRICK *n.* 1.

gin¹ /jin/ *n.* distilled alcoholic spirit flavored with juniper berries. □ **gin rummy** form of the card game rummy.

gin² /jin/ • *n.* **1** machine for separating cotton from its seeds. **2** snare or trap. **3** kind of crane and windlass. • *v.tr.* (**ginned, gin·ning**) treat (cotton) in a gin. □□ **gin'ner** *n.*

■ *n.* **2** see TRAP *n.* 1.

gin·ger /jínjər/ • *n.* **1 a** hot spicy root used as a spice or flavoring. **b** plant having this root. **2** light reddish yellow color. **3** spirit; mettle. • *adj.* of a ginger color. □ **ginger ale** carbonated nonalcoholic clear drink flavored with ginger extract. **ginger beer** carbonated sometimes mildly alcoholic cloudy drink, made from ginger and syrup. □□ **gin'ger·y** *adj.*

gin·ger·bread /jínjərbred/ *n.* **1** cake made with molasses or syrup and flavored with ginger. **2** [often *attrib.*] gaudy, lavish, or superfluous decoration or ornament.

gin·ger·ly /jínjərlee/ • *adv.* in a careful or cautious manner. • *adj.* showing great care or caution. □□ **gin'ger·li·ness** *n.*

■ *adv.* cautiously, carefully, charily, tentatively, warily. • *adj.* careful, cautious, wary, chary, tentative, timid.

ging·ham /gíng-əm/ *n.* plain-woven cotton cloth, esp. striped or checked.

gin·gi·va /jínjívə, jínjivə/ *n.* (*pl.* **gin·gi·vae** /-vee/) the gum. □□ **gin·gi·val** /-jívəl, -jivəl/ *adj.*

gin·gi·vi·tis /jínjivítis/ *n.* inflammation of the gums.

gink·go /gíngkgō/ *n.* (also **ging'ko**) (*pl.* **-gos** or **-goes**) tree with fan-shaped leaves and yellow flowers.

gin·seng /jínseng/ *n.* **1** medicinal plant found in E. Asia and N. America. **2** root of this.

Gip·sy var. of GYPSY.

gi·raffe /jiráf/ *n.* (*pl.* same or **gi·raffes**) ruminant African mammal, with a long neck and forelegs.

gird /gərd/ *v.tr.* (*past* and *past part.* **gird·ed** or **girt**) **1** encircle or secure with a belt or band. **2** enclose or encircle.

■ **1** see BAND¹ *v.* 1. **2** see ENCIRCLE 1.

gird·er /gɔ́rdər/ *n.* large iron or steel support beam.

■ see BEAM *n.* 1.

gir·dle /gɔ́rd'l/ • *n.* **1** belt or cord worn around the waist. **2** woman's corset. **3** thing that surrounds. • *v.tr.* surround with a girdle.

■ *n.* **1** see BELT *n.* 1.

girl /gɔ́rl/ *n.* **1** female child or youth. **2** *colloq.* young (esp. unmarried) woman. **3** *colloq.* girlfriend or sweetheart. **4** *derog.* female

servant. □ **Girl Scout** member of an organization of girls, esp. the Girl Scouts of America, that promotes character, skills, etc. □□ **girl'hood** *n.* **girl'ish** *adj.* **girl'ish·ly** *adv.* **girl'ish·ness** *n.* girlish see YOUNG *adj.* 3.

girl·friend /gɔ́rlfrend/ *n.* **1** regular female companion or lover. **2** female friend.

girt *past part.* of GIRD.

girth /gɔrth/ *n.* **1** distance around a thing. **2** band around the body of a horse to secure the saddle, etc.

■ **1** circumference, ambit, periphery, circuit. **2** belt, girdle, cinch, *literary* cincture.

GIS *abbr.* geographic information system(s).

gist /jist/ *n.* substance or essence of a matter.

■ pith, meat, marrow, core, heart; import; drift.

give /giv/ • *v.* (*past gave* /gayv/; *past part.* **giv·en** /gívən/) **1** *tr.* transfer the possession of freely; hand over as a present. **2** *tr.* **a** bequeath. **b** transfer temporarily; provide with. **c** administer (medicine). **d** deliver (a message). **3** *tr.* **a** pay (*gave him $30 for the bicycle*). **b** sell (*gave him the bicycle for $30*). **4** *tr.* **a** confer; grant. **b** bestow. **c** award. **d** pledge (*gave his word*). **5** *tr.* **a** perform; execute. **b** utter (*gave a shriek*). **6** *tr.* yield as a product or result. **7** *intr.* **a** yield to pressure. **b** collapse (*the roof gave under the pressure*). **8** *tr.* devote; dedicate. **9** *tr.* offer; show. **10** *tr.* impart; be a source of. • *n.* capacity to yield; elasticity. □ **give and take** *v.tr.* exchange (words, blows, or concessions). *n.* exchange of words, etc.; compromise. **give away** **1** transfer as a gift. **2** hand over (a bride) ceremonially to a bridegroom. **3** betray or expose to ridicule or detection. **give in** cease fighting; yield. **give off** emit (vapor, etc.). **give or take** *colloq.* more or less. **give out** **1** announce; emit. **2** break down from exhaustion, etc. **3** run short. **give rise to** cause. **give up** **1** resign; surrender. **2** part with. **3** deliver (a wanted person, etc.). **4** renounce hope of. **5** renounce or cease (an activity). **give way** see WAY. □□ **giv'a·ble, give'a·ble** *adj.* **giv'er** *n.*

■ *v.* **1, 2 a** provide, supply, present; make over, contribute, donate; see also BEQUEATH¹. **2 b** supply with, furnish with; transfer, hand over. **d** impart, pass on, transmit. **3 b** exchange, trade, barter. **4** accord, offer. **5 b** - emit, give out. **6** produce, make, furnish, provide. **7 b** give way, fail, buckle. **8** sacrifice, yield. (up), surrender. **9** see SHOW *v.* 3. **10** cause, lead, induce; allow, provide with; lend. • *n.* flexibility, stretch, play, leeway. □ **give and take** (*n.*) interaction, reciprocity, cooperation. **give away** **3** inform on; reveal, let out; (*give it away*) let the cat out of the bag, give the game *or* show away. **give in** submit, give ground; give up, capitulate, surrender. **give off** give out, exude, discharge; exhale. **give out** **1** publish, make public, broadcast; impart, reveal, disseminate; distribute, hand out. **2** become exhausted, fail, collapse; see also FLAG *v.* 1a. **3** become depleted; see also *run out* 1. **give rise to** start, engender, generate, begin, produce; see also CAUSE *v.* 1. **give up** **1** capitulate, yield, cede, concede. **5** abandon, stop, quit; forgo, forsake.

SYNONYM STUDY: give

AFFORD, AWARD, BESTOW, CONFER, DONATE, GRANT. You **give** a birthday present, **grant** a favor, **bestow** charity, and **confer** an honor. While each of these verbs mean to convey something or transfer it from one's own possession to that of another, the circumstances surrounding that transfer dictate which word is the best one. *Give* is the most general, meaning to pass over, deliver, or transmit something (*give him encouragement*). *Grant* implies that a request or desire has been expressed, and that the receiver is dependent on the giver's discretion (*grant permission for the trip*). *Award* suggests that the giver is in some sense a judge, and that the thing given is deserved (*award a scholarship*), while *bestow* implies that something is given as a gift and may imply condescension on the part of the giver (*bestow a large sum of money on a needy charity*). To *confer* is to give an honor, a privilege, or a favor; it implies that the giver is a superior (*confer a knighthood; confer a college degree*). *Donate* implies that the giving is to a public cause or charity (*donate a painting to the local art museum*), and to *afford* is to give or bestow as a natural consequence (*the window afforded a fine view of the mountains*).

giv•en /gívən/ • *adj.* assumed; granted; specified (*a given number of people*). • *n.* known fact or situation.

∎ *adj.* understood, acknowledged; stated, delineated, set, confirmed. • *n.* assumption, donnée; certainty, reality, actuality.

giz•mo /gízmō/ *n.* (also **gis'mo**) (*pl.* **–mos**) *sl.* gadget.

∎ see GADGET.

giz•zard /gízərd/ *n.* second part of a bird's stomach, for grinding food usu. with grit.

gla•cé /glasáy/ *adj.* **1** (of fruit, esp. cherries) candied. **2** (of cloth, leather, etc.) smooth, polished.

gla•cial /gláyshəl/ *adj.* **1** of ice; icy. **2** *Geol.* characterized or produced by ice. **3** *colloq.* exceptionally slow. □ **glacial epoch** period when ice-sheets were exceptionally extensive. □□ **gla'cial•ly** *adv.*

∎ **1** see ICY 1, 2.

gla•cier /gláyshər/ *n.* mass of land ice formed by the accumulation of snow on high ground.

glad /glad/ *adj.* (**glad•der, glad•dest**) **1** [*predic.*] pleased; willing (*he'll be glad to come*). **2 a** marked by, filled with, or expressing, joy (*a glad expression*). **b** (of news, events, etc.) giving joy (*glad tidings*). □ **glad-hand** *v.tr.* greet cordially or welcome, esp. insincerely. **glad rags** *colloq.* best clothes; evening dress. □□ **glad'ly** *adv.* **glad'ness** *n.*

∎ **1** ready, eager; thrilled, tickled; see also HAPPY 1. **2 a** contented, gratified; delighted. **b** satisfying, cheering. □□ **gladly** cheerfully, readily; see *willingly* (WILLING).

glad•den /gládʼn/ *v.* make or become glad.

∎ cheer (up), delight, hearten, exhilarate, elate.

glade /glayd/ *n.* open space in a wood or forest.

glad•i•a•tor /gládee-aytər/ *n. hist.* trained fighter at ancient Roman shows. □□ **glad•i•a•tor•i•al** /–deeətáwreeəl/ *adj.*

gla•di•o•lus /gládeeōləs/ *n.* (*pl.* **gla•di•o•li** /–lī/ or **gla•di•o•lus•es**) plant of the lily family with sword-shaped leaves and flower spikes.

Glad•stone bag /gládstōn, –stən/ *n.* suitcase that opens flat into two equal compartments.

glam•or•ize /glámərīz/ *v.tr.* (also **glam'our•ize**) make glamorous or attractive. □□ **glam•or•i•za'tion** *n.*

glam•our /glámər/ (also **glam'or**) *n.* **1** physical or cosmetic attractiveness. **2** excitement; adventure (*the glamour of New York*). □ **glamour girl** (or **boy**) attractive young woman (or man), esp. a model, etc. □□ **glam'or•ous** *adj.* **glam'or•ous•ly** *adv.*

∎ **1** see *elegance* (ELEGANT), BEAUTY 1. **2** allure, fascination, charm, charisma, enchantment, magic. □ **glamour girl** (or **boy**) sex symbol, *sl.* dish. □□ **glamorous** alluring, fascinating; chic, smart.

glance /glans/ • *v.intr.* **1** cast a momentary look. **2** (esp. of a weapon) glide or bounce (off an object). **3** (of talk or a talker) pass quickly over a subject(s) (*glanced over the bill*). **4** (of a bright object or light) flash, dart, or gleam; reflect (*the sun glanced off the knife*). • *n.* **1** brief look (*took a glance at the paper*). **2 a** flash or gleam (*a glance of sunlight*). **b** sudden movement producing this. □ **at a glance** immediately upon looking. □□ **glanc'ing•ly** *adv.*

∎ *v.* **1** peek, look briefly; see PEEP[1] *v.* 1. **2** ricochet, rebound. **3** see *pass over* 1 (PASS[1]). **4** glint, sparkle, flicker. • *n.* **1** peek, peep, *sl.* gander. **2** glint, twinkle, glitter.

gland /gland/ *n.* **1** organ in an animal that secretes substances. **2** *Bot.* secreting cells on the surface of a plant.

glan•du•lar /glánjələr/ *adj.* of a gland or glands.

glare /glair/ • *v.* **1** *intr.* look fiercely or fixedly. **2** *intr.* shine dazzlingly. **3** *tr.* express (hate, defiance, etc.) by a look. **4** *intr.* be overly conspicuous. • *n.* **1 a** strong fierce light. **b** oppressive public attention (*the glare of fame*). **2** fierce or fixed look (*a glare of defiance*). □□ **glar'y** *adj.*

∎ *v.* **1** frown, scowl, stare. **2** dazzle, be blinding. **4** look out of place, stick out like a sore thumb. • *n.* **1 a** brilliance, brightness, radiance. **2** stare, frown, glower.

glar•ing /gláiring/ *adj.* **1** obvious; conspicuous (*a glaring error*). **2** shining oppressively. □□ **glar'ing•ly** *adv.*

∎ **1** obtrusive, prominent, blatant. **2** dazzling, brilliant.

glas•nost /gláàsnəst, –nawst/ *n.* (in the former Soviet Union) policy of more open government.

glass /glas/ • *n.* **1** [often *attrib.*] hard, brittle, usu. transparent substance, made by fusing sand with soda and lime, etc. **2** [often *collect.*] object made from glass, esp. a drinking vessel. **3** [in *pl.*] **a** eyeglasses. **b** binoculars; opera glasses. **4** liquid in a glass; a drink (*he likes a glass*). • *adj.* (usu. as **glassed** *adj.*) fit with glass; glaze. • *adj.* of or made from glass. □ **glass case** exhibition display case made mostly from glass. **glass ceiling** barrier hindering promotion, esp. of women and minorities, to executive positions. **glass cutter 1** worker who cuts glass. **2** tool used for cutting glass. □□ **glass′ful** *n.* (*pl.* **–fuls**). **glass′like** *adj.*

■ *n.* **2** glassware; tumbler, flute, goblet. **3** (*glasses*) **a** spectacles, *colloq.* specs, goggles. **4** see DRINK *n.* 1, 2b.

glass•ware /glás wair/ *n.* articles made from glass, esp. drinking glasses, tableware, etc.

glass•y /glásee/ • *adj.* (**glas•si•er, glas•si•est**) **1** of or resembling glass. **2** (of the eye, expression, etc.) abstracted; dull; fixed (*fixed her with a glassy stare*). • *n.* (also **glas′sie**) glass playing marble. □□ **glass′i•ly** *adv.* **glass′i•ness** *n.*

■ *adj.* **1** smooth, shining, slippery; icy. **2** staring, vacant, dazed, lifeless.

glau•co•ma /glawkṓmə, glou–/ *n.* eye condition with increased pressure in the eyeball, causing gradual loss of sight.

glaze /glayz/ • *v.* **1** *tr.* **a** fit (a window, picture, etc.) with glass. **b** provide (a building) with windows. **2** *tr.* cover (pottery, etc.) with a clear, shiny finish. **3** *tr.* cover (pastry, meat, etc.) with a glaze. **4** *intr.* (of the eyes) become fixed or glassy (*his eyes glazed over*). • *n.* **1** vitreous substance used to glaze pottery. **2** shiny coating. □□ **glaz′er** *n.* **glaz′y** *adj.*

■ *v.* **4** see MIST *v.* • *n.* **2** covering; polish, shine, gloss, luster.

gla•zier /gláyzhər/ *n.* person whose trade is glazing windows, etc. □□ **gla′zier•y** *n.*

gleam /gleem/ • *n.* faint or brief light or show (*a gleam of sunlight, not a gleam of hope*). • *v.intr.* **1** emit gleams. **2** shine.

■ *n.* glimmer, glow, glint; beam, ray, shaft; hint, indication, trace. • *v.* **2** glint, shimmer, twinkle, glitter, glisten.

glean /gleen/ *v.tr.* **1** collect (news, facts, gossip, etc.) in small quantities. **2** [also *absol.*] gather (grain, etc.) after the harvest. □□ **glean′er** *n.* **glean′ings** *n.*

■ **1** see EXTRACT *v.* 4. **2** see HARVEST *v.* 1.

glee /glee/ *n.* mirth; delight (*watched the enemy's defeat with glee*). □ **glee club** group that sings choral compositions.

■ merriment, gaiety, high spirits, cheerfulness, exuberance, exhilaration, elation, exultation, joy, jubilation.

glee•ful /gleéfool/ *adj.* joyful. □□ **glee′ful•ly** *adv.* **glee′ful•ness** *n.*

■ delighted, merry, mirthful, exuberant, cheerful.

glen /glen/ *n.* narrow valley.

■ see VALLEY.

glide /glīd/ • *v.* **1** *intr.* (of a stream, snake, skater, etc.) move with a smooth continuous motion. **2** *intr.* (of an aircraft, esp. a glider) fly without engine power. **3** *intr.* pass gently and imperceptibly (*night glided into day*).

4 *intr.* move quietly or stealthily. **5** *tr.* cause to glide. • *n.* **1** gliding. **2** *Phonet.* gradually changing sound made in passing from one position of the speech organs to another. **3** gliding dance. **4** flight in a glider. □□ **glid′ing•ly** *adv.*

■ *v.* **1** slide, flow, coast. **3** slide by, disappear. **4** see SLITHER *v.*

glid•er /glīdər/ *n.* **1** aircraft that flies without an engine. **2** porch swing with a gliding motion.

glim•mer /glímər/ • *v.intr.* shine faintly or intermittently. • *n.* **1** feeble or wavering light. **2** faint gleam (of hope, understanding, etc.). □□ **glim′mer•ing•ly** *adv.*

■ *v.* see FLICKER *v.* 1. • *n.* **1** see FLICKER *n.* **2** see GLEAM *n.*

glimpse /glimps/ • *n.* **1** momentary or partial view. **2** faint transient appearance (*glimpses of the truth*). • *v.* **1** *tr.* see faintly or partly (*glimpsed his face in the crowd*). **2** *intr.* cast a passing glance.

■ *n.* **1** see SIGHT *n.* 1b. • *v.* **1** see SIGHT *v.*

glint /glint/ • *v.* flash or cause to flash; glitter; sparkle; reflect (*eyes glinted with amusement*). • *n.* flash; sparkle.

■ *v.* see SPARKLE *v.* 1a. • *n.* see FLASH *n.* 1.

glis•san•do /glisaándō/ *n.* (*pl.* **glis•san•di** /–dee/ or **–dos**) *Mus.* continuous slide of adjacent notes upward or downward.

glis•ten /glísən/ • *v.intr.* shine, esp. like a wet object, snow, etc.; glitter. • *n.* glitter; sparkle.

■ *v.* gleam, glint; see also SHINE *v.* 1. • *n.* see GLEAM *n.*

glitch /glich/ *n.* *colloq.* sudden irregularity or malfunction.

■ see BUG *n.* 4.

glit•ter /glítər/ • *v.intr.* **1** shine, esp. with a bright reflected light; sparkle. **2** be showy or ostentatious. • *n.* **1** gleam; sparkle. **2** showiness; splendor. **3** sparkling material as decoration. □□ **glit′ter•y** *adj.*

■ *v.* **1** see GLISTEN *v.* • *n.* **1** see GLEAM *n.* **2** flashiness, brilliance, *colloq.* razzmatazz.

glitz /glits/ *n.* *sl.* showy glamour. □□ **glitz′y** *adj.* (**glitz•i•er, glitz•i•est**).

■ see GLITTER *n.* 2.

gloam•ing /glṓming/ *n.* *poet.* twilight; dusk.

gloat /glōt/ • *v.intr.* consider with lust, greed, malice, triumph, etc. • *n.* **1** gloating. **2** expression of satisfaction. □□ **gloat′ing•ly** *adv.*

■ *v.* (*gloat over*) exult in, glory in, relish, revel in, crow over.

glob /glob/ *n.* soft mass or lump.

glob•al /glṓbəl/ *adj.* **1** worldwide (*global conflict*). **2** all-embracing; total. □ **global warming** increase in temperature of the earth's atmosphere caused by the greenhouse effect. □□ **glob′al•ly** *adv.*

■ **1** universal, international. **2** broad, wide-ranging, far-reaching, see also EXTENSIVE 2.

globe /glōb/ *n.* **1 a** [prec. by *the*] the earth. **b** planet, star, or sun. **c** spherical body. **2** spherical representation of earth with a map on the surface. □ **globe-trotter** person who travels widely. **globe-trotting** such travel. □□ **globe′like** *adj.*

■ **1 a** world, mother earth. **b** see STAR *n.* 1. **c** sphere, orb.

glob·u·lar /glóbyələr/ *adj.* **1** globe-shaped; spherical. **2** composed of globules. See synonym study at ROUND. □□ **glob'u·lar·ly** *adv.*
■ **1** see *spherical* (SPHERE).

glob·ule /glóbyo͞ol/ *n.* small round particle; drop.
■ see DROP *n.* 1a.

glock·en·spiel /glókənspeel, –shpeel/ *n.* musical instrument with metal bars, tubes, or bells, played with hammers.

gloom /glo͞om/ • *n.* **1** darkness; obscurity. **2** melancholy; despondency. • *v.* **1** *intr.* be melancholy; frown. **2** *intr.* (of the sky, etc.) be dull or threatening. **3** *tr.* make dark or dismal.
■ *n.* **1** dusk, shadow(s), murkiness. **2** sadness, despair; blues, *colloq.* dumps. • *v.* **2** darken, menace, lower.

gloom·y /glo͞omee/ *adj.* (**gloom·i·er, gloom·i·est**) **1** dark; unlighted. **2** depressed; sullen. **3** dismal; depressing. □□ **gloom'i·ly** *adv.* **gloom'i·ness** *n.*
■ **1** black, shadowy, shaded, obscure; dull, overcast. **2** dejected, morose, glum, joyless, dispirited, despairing. **3** cheerless, dreary.

glo·ri·fy /gláwrifī/ *v.tr.* (**–fies, –fied**) **1** exalt; make glorious. **2** transform into something more splendid. **3** extol; praise. **4** (as **glorified** *adj.*) seeming or pretending to be better than in reality (*just a glorified office boy*). □□ **glo·ri·fi·ca'tion** *n.*
■ **2** elevate, enhance, dignify. **3** applaud, commend, hail. **4** (**glorified**) exalted, high flown, high-sounding.

glo·ri·ous /gláwreeəs/ *adj.* **1** possessing glory; illustrious. **2** conferring glory; honorable. **3** *colloq.* splendid; magnificent; delightful (*a glorious day*). □□ **glo'ri·ous·ly** *adv.*
■ **1** famous, distinguished, excellent. **2** outstanding, admirable. **3** superb, marvelous, wonderful, fine, excellent, *colloq.* heavenly, great, fabulous; see also BRILLIANT *adj.* 2.

glo·ry /gláwree/ • *n.* (*pl.* **–ries**) **1** renown or fame; honor. **2** adoring praise and thanksgiving (*glory to the Lord*) **3** resplendent majesty, beauty, etc. (*the glory of Versailles*). **4** thing that brings renown or praise; distinction. **5** heavenly bliss and splendor. • *v.intr.* pride oneself; exult (*glory in their skill*) □ **glory be!** **1** a devout ejaculation. **2** *colloq.* an exclamation of surprise or delight. **go to glory** *sl.* die; be destroyed.
■ *n.* **1** dignity, prestige, celebrity. **2** worship, gratitude. **3** magnificence, excellence, splendor. **4** merit, quality, credit; see also ACCOMPLISHMENT 3. • *v.* revel, relish, rejoice. □ **glory be!** 2 see INDEED *int.*

gloss¹ /glaws, glos/ • *n.* **1** surface shine or luster. **2** deceptively attractive appearance. **3** (in full **gloss paint**) paint formulated to give a hard glossy finish. • *v.tr.* make glossy. □ **gloss over** **1** seek to conceal beneath a false appearance. **2** conceal or evade by mentioning briefly or misleadingly.
■ *n.* **1** sheen, gleam; glaze, polish, brightness. **2** façade, mask, veneer. • *v.* glaze, polish, burnish. □ **gloss over** veil, cover up, explain away, whitewash.

gloss² /glaws, glos/ • *n.* **1** explanatory comment inserted between the lines or in the margin of a text. **2** comment, explanation, interpretation, or paraphrase. **3** glossary. • *v.* **1** *tr.* add a gloss to (a text, word, etc.). **2** *intr.* make (esp. unfavorable) comments.
■ *n.* **1** footnote; annotation, analysis; explanation, interpretation. • *v.* **1** explain, interpret, comment on, annotate, criticize, analyze; translate.

glos·sa·ry /gláwsəree, -glós/ *n.* (*pl.* **–ries**) (also **gloss**) alphabetical list of terms relating to a specific subject or text; brief dictionary.
■ word list, wordbook.

glos·so·la·li·a /gláwsəláyleeə, glós / *n.* = *gift of tongues* (see TONGUE).

gloss·y /gláwsee, glós / • *adj.* (**gloss·i·er, gloss·i·est**) **1** shiny; smooth. **2** printed on such paper; expensive and attractive, but sometimes lacking in content. • *n.* (*pl.* **–ies**) *colloq.* glossy magazine or photograph. □□ **gloss'i·ly** *adv.* **gloss'i·ness** *n.*
■ *adj.* **1** lustrous, glistening; polished. **2** showy, *sl.* glitzy.

glot·tal /glót'l/ *adj.* of the glottis. □ **glottal stop** sound produced by the sudden opening or shutting of the glottis.

glot·tis /glótis/ *n.* space between the vocal cords, affecting voice modulation through expansion or contraction.

glove /gluv/ • *n.* **1** hand covering, worn esp. for protection against cold or dirt, usu. with separate fingers. **2** padded protective glove, esp.: **a** a boxing glove. **b** *Baseball* fielder's glove. • *v.tr.* cover or provide with a glove(s). □ **glove compartment** recess or cabinet for small articles in the dashboard of a motor vehicle. **throw down** (or **take up**) **the glove** issue (or accept) a challenge. **with the gloves off** mercilessly; unfairly.

glow /glō/ • *v.intr.* **1** emit light and heat without flame; be incandescent. **2 a** (of the body) be heated; sweat. **b** express or feel strong emotion (*glowed with pride*). **3** show a warm color (*the painting glow with warmth*). **4** (as **glowing** *adj.*) expressing pride or satisfaction (*a glowing report*). • *n.* **1** glowing state. **2** bright warm color. **3** feeling of satisfaction or well-being. □□ **glow'ing·ly** *adv.*
■ *v.* **1** shine, gleam, radiate. **4** (**glowing**) complimentary, enthusiastic, favorable. • *n.* **1** luminosity, luster, radiance. **2** flush, blush; radiance, bloom. **3** (good) health.

glow·er /glowər/ • *v.intr.* stare or scowl, esp. angrily. • *n.* glowering look. □□ **glow'er·ing·ly** *adv.*
■ *v.* see SCOWL *v.* • *n.* see GLARE *n.* 2.

glow·worm /glówwərm/ *n.* beetle whose wingless female emits light from the end of the abdomen.

glu·cose /glo͞okōs/ *n.* **1** simple sugar found in blood, fruit juice, etc. (see DEXTROSE). ¶Chem. formula: $C_6H_{12}O_6$. **2** syrup containing glucose sugars.

glue /glo͞o/ • *n.* adhesive substance. • *v.tr.* (**glues, glued, glu·ing** or **glue·ing**) **1** fasten or join with glue. **2** keep or put very close (*an eye glued to the keyhole*). □□ **glue'like** *adj.*

glue′y /glōō-ee/ *adj.* (**glu•i•er, glu•i•est**). **glu′ey•ness** *n.*

■ *n.* paste, cement. • *v.* **1** paste, affix; see STICK² 4.

glum /glum/ *adj.* (**glum•mer, glum•mest**) dejected; sullen; displeased. □□ **glum′ly** *adv.* **glum′ness** *n.*

■ gloomy, dispirited, miserable, crestfallen; see also SAD 1.

SYNONYM STUDY: glum

DOLEFUL, DOUR, LUGUBRIOUS, MELANCHOLY, SATURNINE, SULLEN. All happy people are alike, to paraphrase Tolstoy, but each unhappy person is unhappy in his or her own way. A **sullen** person is gloomy, untalkative, and ill-humored by nature; a **glum** person is usually silent because of low spirits or depressing circumstances (*to be glum in the face of a plummeting stock market*). **Melancholy** suggests a more or less chronic sadness (*her melancholy was the result of an unhappy childhood*), while a person who is **saturnine** has a forbiddingly gloomy and taciturn nature (*his request was met with a saturnine and scornful silence*). **Dour** refers to a grim and bitter outlook or disposition (*a dour old woman who never smiled*), and **doleful** implies a mournful sadness (*the child's doleful expression as his parents left*). Someone or something described as **lugubrious** is mournful or gloomy in an affected or exaggerated way (*lugubrious songs about lost love*).

glut /glut/ • *v.tr.* (**glut•ted, glut•ting**) **1** feed (a person, one's stomach, etc.) to the full; satiate. **2** fill to excess. • *n.* **1** *Econ.* supply exceeding demand (*a glut in the market*). **2** full indulgence.

■ *v.* **1** gorge, stuff, cram; sicken, cloy. **2** overload, overstock; flood, saturate; clog, choke up. • *n.* **1** surplus, excess, surfeit.

glu•ten /glōōtən/ *n.* mixture of proteins in cereal grains.

glu•te•us /glōōteeəs/ *n.* (*pl.* **glu•te•i** /–teeī/) any of the three muscles in each buttock. □□ **glu′te•al** *adj.*

glu•ti•nous /glōōt′nəs/ *adj.* sticky; like glue. □□ **glu′ti•nous•ly** *adv.* **glu′ti•nous•ness** *n.*

■ see STICKY *adj.* 2.

glut•ton /glút′n/ *n.* **1** greedy eater. **2** *colloq.* insatiably eager person (*a glutton for work*). □ **glutton for punishment** person eager to take on hard or unpleasant tasks. □□ **glut′ton•ous** *adj.* **glut′ton•ous•ly** *adv.* See synonym study at GREEDY

■ **1** gourmand, overeater, *colloq.* hog, pig. **2** see ADDICT *n.* 2. ■ **glutton for punishment** see SUCKER *n.* 1. □□ **gluttonous** voracious, *colloq.* piggish, hoggish.

glut•ton•y /glút′nee/ *n.* habitual greed or excess in eating.

■ gourmandism, voracity, insatiability, *colloq.* pigginess.

glyc•er•in /glísərin/ *n.* (also **glyc•er•ol** /glísərawl, –rol/, **glyc′er•ine**) colorless sweet viscous liquid used as medicine, ointment, etc., and in explosives.

gly•co•gen /glíkəjən/ *n.* polysaccharide substance in animal tissues that is converted to glucose for energy. □□ **gly•co•gen•ic** /–jénik/ *adj.*

GM *abbr.* **1** General Motors. **2** general manager.

gm *abbr.* gram(s).

G-man /jéeman/ *n.* (*pl.* **G-men**) *US colloq.* federal officer, esp. an FBI agent.

■ government man, fed.

GMT *abbr.* Greenwich Mean Time.

gnarled /naarld/ *adj.* (also **gnarl′y** /naárlee/) (of a tree, hands, etc.) knobbly; twisted; rugged.

■ knotty, knotted, lumpy, bumpy, bent, crooked.

gnash /nash/ *v.* **1** *tr.* grind (the teeth). **2** *intr.* (of the teeth) strike together; grind.

■ see GRIND *v.* 2b.

gnat /nat/ *n.* **1** small two-winged biting fly. **2** insignificant annoyance.

■ **2** see PEST 1.

gnaw /naw/ *v.* (*past part.* **gnawed** or **gnawn**) **1 a** *tr.* bite persistently; wear away by biting. **b** *intr.* bite; nibble. **2 a** *intr.* (of pain, fear, etc.) corrode; waste away; consume; torture. **b** *tr.* corrode, consume, torture, etc., with pain, fear, etc. (*was gnawed by doubt*). □□ **gnaw′ing** *adj.* **gnaw′ing•ly** *adv.*

■ **1** chew, nibble, munch. **2 a** (*gnaw at*) worry, haunt, trouble, distress, plague, torment.

gneiss /nīs/ *n.* usu. coarse-grained metamorphic rock.

gnoc•chi /nyáwkee/ *n.pl.* small Italian dumplings.

gnome /nōm/ *n.* dwarfish legendary creature or goblin, living under ground.

■ see GOBLIN.

gnom•ic /nṓmik/ *adj.* of, consisting of, or using aphorisms; sententious.

GNP *abbr.* gross national product.

gnu /nōō, nyōō/ *n.* antelope, native to S. Africa, with brown stripes on the neck and shoulders. (Also called **wildebeest**.)

go¹ /gō/ • *v.intr.* (*3rd sing. present* **goes** /gōz/; *past* **went** /went/; *past part.* **gone** /gon/) **1 a** start moving or be moving; travel; proceed. **b** *colloq.* expressing annoyance (*they've gone and broken it*). **2** make a special trip for; participate in; proceed to do (*went skiing, often goes running*). **3** lie or extend to; lead to (*the road goes to the shore, where does that door go?*). **4 a** leave; depart (*they had to go*). **b** *colloq.* disappear (*my bag is gone*). **5** move, act, work, etc. (*the clock doesn't go*). **6 a** make a specified movement (*go like this with your foot*). **b** make a sound (*the gun went bang*). **c** *colloq.* say (*so he goes to me "Why didn't you like it?"*). **7** be in a specified state (*go hungry*). **8 a** pass into a specified condition (*went mad*). **b** *colloq.* die. **c** proceed or escape in a specified condition (*the crime went unnoticed*). **9** (of time or distance) pass; elapse; be traversed (*ten days to go*). **10 a** (of a document, verse, song, etc.) have a specified content or wording; run (*the tune goes like this*). **b** be suitable; fit; match (*the shoes don't go with the hat*). **c** be regularly kept or put (*the forks go here*). **d** find room; fit (*it goes* in the cupboard). **11 a** turn out; proceed in a certain way (things went well). **b** be successful (make the party go). **c** progress (a long way to go). **12 a** be sold (went cheap). **b** (of money) be spent ($200 went for a new jacket). **13 a** be relinquished, dismissed, or abolished (the car will have to go). **b** fail; decline; give way; collapse (his sight is going). **14** be acceptable or permitted; be accepted without question (what I say goes). **15** be guided by; judge or act on or in harmony with (have nothing to go on, a good rule to go by). **16** attend regularly (goes to church). **17** colloq. proceed (often foolishly) to do (don't go making him angry). **18** act or proceed to a certain point (will go so far and no further). **19** (of a number) be capable of being contained in another (6 goes into 12 twice). **20** be allotted or awarded; pass (first prize went to her). **21** be known or called (goes by the same name). **22** apply to; have relevance for (that goes for me, too). • n. (pl. **goes**) **1** act or instance of going. **2** mettle; spirit; dash; animation (she has a lot of go in her). **3** vigorous activity (it's all go). **4** colloq. success (made a go of it). **5** colloq. turn; attempt (I'll have a go at it). **6** permission; approval; go-ahead (gave us a go on the new project). • adj. colloq. functioning properly (all systems are go). □ **go about 1** busy oneself with; set to work at. **2** make a habit of doing (goes about telling lies). **3** Naut. change to an opposite tack. **go ahead** proceed without hesitation. **go-ahead** n. permission to proceed. adj. enterprising. **go along with** agree to. **go back on** fail to keep (one's word, promise, etc.). **go-between** intermediary. **go down 1 a** (of an amount) become less (your weight has gone down). **b** subside (the flood went down). **c** decrease in price; lose value. **2 a** (of a ship) sink. **b** (of the sun) set. **3** (usu. foll. by to) be continued to a specified point. **4** deteriorate; fail; (of a computer, etc.) cease to function. **5** be recorded in writing. **6** be swallowed. **7** (often foll. by with) be received (in a specified way). **go for 1** go to fetch. **2** be accounted as or achieve (went for nothing). **3** prefer; choose (that's the one I go for). **4** colloq. strive to attain (go for it!). **5** colloq. attack (the dog went for him). **go in for** take as one's object, style, pursuit, principle, etc. **go into 1** enter (a profession, etc.). **2** take part in; be a part of. **3** investigate. **go off 1** explode. **2 a** leave the stage. **b** leave; depart. **3** sound, as an alarm, siren, etc. **go on 1** continue; persevere (decided to go on with it). **2** colloq. a talk at great length. **b** admonish (went on and on at him). **3** proceed (went on to become a star). **go out 1** leave a room, house, etc. **2** be broadcast. **3** be extinguished. **4** be courting. **5** cease to be fashionable. **6** (of workers) strike. **go over 1** inspect; rehearse; retouch. **2** (often foll. by to) change one's allegiance or religion. **3** (of a play, etc.) be received in a specified way (went over well in Dallas). **go through 1** be dealt with or completed. **2** discuss in detail; scrutinize in sequence. **3** perform (a ceremony, a recitation, etc.). **4** undergo. **5** colloq. use up; spend (money, etc.). **6** make holes in. **go under**

sink; fail; succumb. **on the go** colloq. **1** in constant motion. **2** constantly working.

■ v. **1 a** advance, pass, voyage, set off, start off. **3** open to, give access to, run. **4 a** withdraw, retreat, take off; see also LEAVE[1] v. 1b. **b** see DISAPPEAR[1] 1. **5** function, operate, run. **6 c** say, utter. **7** live, continue, survive. **8 a** become, turn, grow, get, fall. **b** see DIE 1. **c** pass, continue. **9** slip or tick away, fly, glide by. **10 b** agree or conform, harmonize, blend, be appropriate, complement each other; (go with) set off. **c** belong, live. **11 b** swing, colloq. be a hit. **c** see PROGRESS[1] v. 1. **13 a** be disposed of or discarded or thrown away, be given up, be cast or set or put aside, be done with. **b** fade, weaken, deteriorate, worsen, wear out; fall or go to pieces, break, disintegrate, crack. **15** see JUDGE v. 2, BEHAVE 1. **16** (go to) see ATTEND 1a, 2a, VISIT v. 1. **22** see APPLY 2. • n. **2** see ENERGY 1. **3** action; change; see also STIR n. 2. **4** see TRIUMPH[1] n. 1b. **5** chance, opportunity, try, colloq. crack, whirl, shot, stab. □ **go about 1** approach, tackle, undertake, begin, start. **go ahead** continue, move forward, advance, progress. **go-ahead** (n.) approval, authorization, say-so, colloq. OK, green light, nod. (adj.) ambitious, progressive, resourceful, colloq. go. **go along with** concur with, acquiesce to or in, assent to. **go back on** renege (on), break, retract, fail to keep. **go-between** middleman, mediator, negotiator, agent; messenger. **go down 1** decrease, decline, drop, sink. **2 a** go under, founder, become submerged, drown. **4** crash; see also DETERIORATE, FAIL v. 1, 2a. **5** be remembered or memorialized or recalled. **7** (go down well) find favor or acceptance or approval, be accepted. **go for 1** get, run for, go after. **3** fancy, favor, like, admire. **4** target, try for, set one's sights on. **5** assault, assail, set upon. **go in for** pursue, take up, embrace, undertake, follow, adopt; like, fancy, favor. **go into 3** delve into, examine, analyze, probe; discuss, mention, talk about. **go off 1** blow up, detonate, erupt; fire, be discharged. **2 a** exit, walk off. **b** go (away), set out, exit, quit. **go on 1** proceed, keep (on), carry on; persist, last, endure. **2 a** chatter, drone on, colloq. natter; see also CHATTER v. 1. **b** (go on at) see CRITICIZE 1. **go out 1** depart, exit, leave, go off; see also LEAVE v. 1b. **3** fade or die (out), expire, cease functioning. **4** go together, see (one another), colloq. date. **6** see STRIKE v. 16. **go over 1** review, skim (through or over), scan, read, study; examine, scrutinize, inspect; repeat, reiterate; redo. **2** convert, switch; (go over to) become, turn into. **go through 1** be accepted or approved, pass (muster). **2** see go over 1 above. **4** experience, suffer, bear, tolerate, put up with, endure. **5** see use up. **go under** collapse, subside, go bankrupt, go to the wall, colloq. fold, go belly up.

go² /gō/ n. Japanese board game of territorial possession and capture.

goad /gōd/ • n. **1** spiked stick used for urging cattle forward. **2** anything that incites. • v. tr.

1 urge on with a goad. **2** irritate; stimulate (*goaded him into retaliating*).

■ *n.* **2** see SPUR *n.* 2. • *v.* **2** see SPUR *v.*

goal /gōl/ *n.* **1** object of a person's ambition or effort; destination; aim (*fame is his goal, Washington was our goal*). **2 a** *Sports* receiving structure or area at which the ball, puck, etc., is directed for a score. **b** point(s) won (*scored 3 goals*).

■ **1** purpose, end, objective, target; ideal, aspiration.

goal•keep•er /gólkeepər/ *n.* player defending the goal in various sports. □□ **goal′ie** *n.*

goat /gōt/ *n.* **1** hardy, agile short-haired domesticated mammal, having horns and (in the male) a beard, and kept for its milk and meat. **2** lecherous man. **3** (**the Goat**) zodiacal sign or constellation Capricorn. **4** scapegoat. □ **get a person's goat** *colloq.* irritate a person.

goa•tee /gōtée/ *n.* small pointed beard like that of a goat.

goat•herd /gót-hərd/ *n.* person who tends goats.

goat•skin /gótskin/ *n.* **1** skin of a goat. **2** garment or bottle made of goatskin.

gob /gob/ *sl. n.* **1** lump or clot of slimy matter. **2** [in *pl.*] large amounts (*gobs of cash*).

■ **1** blob, morsel, chunk, piece, fragment.

gob•ble[1] /góbəl/ *v.* eat hurriedly and noisily. □□ **gob′bler** *n.*

gob•ble[2] /góbəl/ *v.intr.* **1** (of a male turkey) make a characteristic swallowing sound in the throat. **2** make such a sound when speaking, esp. when excited, angry, etc.

gob•ble•dy•gook /góbəldeegóok/ *n.* (also **gob′ble•de•gook**) *colloq.* pompous or unintelligible jargon.

■ mumbo jumbo, humbug, nonsense, gibberish, *colloq.* hogwash, *sl.* bull, poppycock.

gob•let /góblit/ *n.* drinking vessel with a foot and a stem, usu. of glass.

■ see GLASS *n.* 2a.

gob•lin /góblin/ *n.* mischievous, ugly, dwarflike creature of folklore.

■ elf, gnome, hobgoblin, imp, leprechaun, demon.

god /god/ *n.* **1 a** (in many religions) superhuman being or spirit worshiped as having power over nature, human fortunes, etc.; deity. **b** image, idol, animal, or other object worshiped as divine or symbolizing a god. **2** (**God**) (in Christian and other monotheistic religions) creator and ruler of the universe; supreme being. **3 a** adored, admired, or influential person. **b** something worshiped like a god (*makes a god of success*). □□ **god′less** *adj.* **god′less•ness** *n.* **god′like** *adj.*

■ **1 a** demigod, divinity, power; (*gods*) immortals. **b** see IDOL 1. **2** (**God**) the Deity, the Godhead; Allah, Jehovah, Yahweh. **3 a** see IDOL 2. □□ **godless** wicked, sinful; profane; atheistic, agnostic, unbelieving. **godlike** divine; sainted; holy, ungodly.

god•child /gódchild/ *n.* person in relation to a godparent.

god•daugh•ter /góddawtər/ *n.* female godchild.

god•dess /gódis/ *n.* **1** female deity. **2** adored woman.

god•fa•ther /gódfaathər/ *n.* **1** male godparent. **2** person directing an illegal organization, esp. the Mafia.

god•for•sak•en /gódfərsaykən/ *adj.* (also **God′for•sak•en**) devoid of all merit; dismal; dreary.

■ see DISMAL 1, 2, BLEAK.

god•head /gódhed/ *n.* (also **God′head**) **1 a** state of being God or a god. **b** divine nature. **2** deity. **3** (**the Godhead**) God.

■ **1 a** divinity. **3** (**the Godhead**) see GOD *n.* 2.

god•ly /gódlee/ *adj.* religious; pious; devout. □□ **god′li•ness** *n.*

■ God-fearing, holy, saintly, faithful, righteous, good.

god•mo•ther /gódmuthər/ *n.* female godparent.

god•par•ent /gódpairənt/ *n.* person who sponsors a child at baptism.

god•send /gódsend/ *n.* unexpected but welcome event or acquisition.

■ gift, blessing, boon, windfall, bonanza, piece of luck.

god•son /gódsun/ *n.* male godchild.

go•fer /gófər/ *n. sl.* person who runs errands, esp. on a movie set or in an office.

gog•gle /gógəl/ • *v.* **1** *intr.* **a** look with wide-open eyes. **b** (of the eyes) be rolled about; protrude. **2** *tr.* turn (the eyes) sideways or from side to side. • *adj.* [usu. *attrib.*] (of the eyes) protuberant or rolling. • *n.* [in *pl.*] eyeglasses for protecting the eyes from glare, dust, water, etc.

■ *v.* **1 a** see GAPE *v.* 2. **b** see PROTRUDE. • *adj.* see PROTUBERANT. • *n.* (**goggles**) *colloq.* specs, shades.

go•ing /góing/ • *n.* **1 a** act or process of going. **b** instance of this; departure. **2 a** condition of the ground for walking, riding, etc. **b** progress affected by this (*found the going hard*). • *adj.* **1** in or into action (*set the clock going*). **2** current; prevalent (*the going rate*). □ **get going** start steadily talking, working, etc. (*can't stop him when he gets going*). **going concern** thriving business. **going on fifteen**, etc., approaching one's fifteenth, etc., birthday. **going to** intending or intended to; about to; likely to (*it's going to sink!*).

■ *n.* **1** leaving; see also RETREAT *n.* 1a. • *adj.* **2** present, accepted, prevailing, usual. □ **going concern** booming business; growth industry.

gold /gōld/ • *n.* **1** yellow, malleable, ductile, high density metallic element resistant to chemical reaction, occurring naturally in quartz veins and gravel, and precious as a monetary medium, in jewelry, etc. ¶Symb.: **Au**. **2** color of gold. **3 a** coins or articles made of gold. **b** wealth. • *adj.* **1** made wholly or chiefly of gold. **2** colored like gold. □ **gold leaf** gold beaten into a very thin sheet. **gold medal** medal of gold, usu. awarded as first prize. **gold mine 1** place where gold is mined. **2** *colloq.* source of wealth. **gold standard** system valuing currency in terms of gold, for which the currency may be exchanged.

gold•en /góldən/ adj. **1 a** made or consisting of gold (*golden coin*). **b** yielding gold. **2** colored or shining like gold (*golden hair*). **3** precious; valuable; excellent; important (*a golden memory, a golden opportunity*). □ **golden age 1** supposed past age when people were happy and innocent. **2** period of a nation's greatest prosperity, literary merit, etc. **golden goose** continuing source of wealth or profit. **golden handshake** *colloq.* payment given on layoff or early retirement. **golden jubilee** fiftieth anniversary. **golden mean** principle of moderation, as opposed to excess. **golden parachute** executive's contract that provides substantial severance pay, etc., upon termination. **golden retriever** retriever with a thick, golden-colored coat. **golden rule** basic principle of action, esp. "do unto others as you would have them do unto you." **golden wedding** fiftieth anniversary of a wedding.

■ **1 a** gilded, gilt. **2** blond, yellow, flaxen; bright, gleaming, lustrous. **3** outstanding; happy, blissful; flourishing, prosperous; advantageous, promising, rosy. □ **golden age 2** see PRIME[1] *n.* 1. **golden rule** see MOTTO.

gold•en•rod /góldənrod/ *n.* plant with a rodlike stem and small, bright yellow flower heads.

gold•finch /góldfinch/ *n.* songbird with a yellow band across each wing.

gold•fish /góldfish/ *n.* small reddish golden Chinese carp kept for ornament. □ **goldfish bowl 1** globular glass container for goldfish. **2** situation lacking privacy.

gold•smith /góldsmith/ *n.* worker in gold.

go•lem /góləm/ *n.* clay figure supposedly brought to life in Jewish legend.

golf /golf, gawlf/ • *n.* game played on a course set in open country, in which a small hard ball is driven with clubs into a series of 18 or 9 holes with the fewest possible strokes. • *v.intr.* play golf. □ **golf club 1** club used in golf. **2** premises used by a golf club. □□ **golf•er** *n.*

gol•ly /gólee/ *int.* expressing surprise.

go•nad /gónad/ *n.* animal organ producing gametes, e.g., the testis or ovary. □□ **go•nad•al** /-nád'l/ *adj.*

gon•do•la /góndələ, gondólə/ *n.* **1** flat-bottomed boat used on Venetian canals, with a high point at each end, worked by one oar at the stern. **2** car suspended from an airship, balloon, or cable.

gon•do•lier /góndəleer/ *n.* oarsman on a gondola.

gone /gawn, gon/ *adj.* **1** departed; left. **2 a** lost; hopeless. **b** dead. **3** *sl.* completely enthralled or entranced, esp. by rhythmic music, drugs, etc.

■ **2 b** see DEAD *adj.* 1.

gon•er /gáwnər, gón-/ *n.* *sl.* person or thing that is doomed, ended, irrevocably lost, etc.; dead person.

gong /gawng, gong/ • *n.* **1** metal disk giving a resonant note when struck. **2** saucer-shaped bell. • *v.tr.* summon with a gong.

gon•or•rhea /gónəreeə/ *n.* venereal disease

with inflammatory discharge. □□ **gon•or•rhe'al** *adj.*

goo /goo/ *n.* **1** sticky or viscous substance. **2** sickening sentiment.

good /good/ • *adj.* (**bet•ter, best**) **1** having the right or desired qualities; satisfactory; adequate. **2 a** (of a person) efficient; competent (*a good driver*). **b** (of a thing) reliable; efficient (*good brakes*). **c** (of health, etc.) strong (*good eyesight*). **3 a** kind; benevolent (*good of you to come*). **b** morally excellent; virtuous (*a good deed*). **c** charitable (*good works*). **d** well-behaved. **4** enjoyable, agreeable (*a good party*). **5** thorough; considerable (*gave it a good wash*), not less than (*waited a good hour*). **7** valid; sound (*a good reason*). • *n.* **1** [only in *sing.*] that which is good; what is beneficial or morally right (*only good can come of it, did it for your own good*). **2** [in *pl.*] **a** movable property or merchandise. **b** [prec. by *the*] *colloq.* what one has undertaken to supply (esp. *deliver the goods*). **3** proof, esp. of guilt. • *adv. colloq.* well (*doing pretty good*). □ **as good as** practically (*he as good as told me*). **for good (and all)** finally; permanently. **good for 1** beneficial to; having a good effect on. **2** able to perform; inclined for (*good for a ten-mile walk*). **3** able to be trusted to pay (*is good for $100*). **to the good** having as profit or benefit.

■ *adj.* **1** commendable, acceptable, fair; see also SATISFACTORY[2]. **2 a** capable, accomplished, proficient, skilled, talented. **b** safe, secure, sound; see also RELIABLE. **c** see SOUND *adj.* 1, HEALTHY 1. **3 a** gracious, gentle, nice, considerate, friendly. **b** righteous, noble, honorable, ethical, upstanding, worthy; esteemed, respected. **c** obedient, well-mannered; angelic. **4** fine, choice, *sl.* neat; welcome, favorable. **5** complete; penetrating, careful; see also THOROUGH 2. **7** genuine, legitimate, authentic, sensible, well-founded; credible, compelling; reliable, secure. • *n.* **1** virtue, merit, worth; advantage, profit, use; avail; see also BENEFIT *n.* 1. **2** (*goods*) **a** commodities, wares, assets; stock, produce. □ **for good (and all)** see *finally* (FINAL). **good for 1** wholesome; see BENEFICIAL.

good-bye /goodbí/ (also **good-'bye'**, **good-by'** or **good-by'**) • *int.* expressing good wishes on parting, ending a telephone conversation, etc., or said with reference to a thing gotten rid of or irrevocably lost. • *n.* (*pl.* **good-byes**) parting; farewell.

■ *int.* farewell, adios, adieu, au revoir, *colloq.* ciao, see you (later), bye, bye-bye. • *n.* see FAREWELL.

good-hu•mored /goodhyoomərd/ *adj.* genial; cheerful; amiable. □□ **good'-hu'mored•ly** *adv.*

good•ly /goodlee/ *adj.* (**good•li•er, good•li•est**) **1** comely; handsome. **2** of imposing size, etc. □□ **good'li•ness** *n.*

■ **1** see COMELY. **2** considerable, sizable, substantial.

good-na•tured /goodnáychərd/ *adj.* kind; patient; easygoing. □□ **good'-na'tured•ly** *adv.*

■ kindhearted, charitable, tolerant, generous, agreeable, pleasant, mellow, considerate, nice, courteous, warm.

good•ness /gŏodnis/ • n. 1 virtue; excellence, esp. moral. 2 kindness (*had the goodness to wait*). 3 what is beneficial in a thing (*the goodness of fresh air*). • int. expressing surprise, anger, etc. (*goodness me!*).

■ n. 1 see VIRTUE 1. 2 see KINDNESS 1. int. see INDEED int.

SYNONYM STUDY: goodness

MORALITY, PROBITY, RECTITUDE, VIRTUE. Of all these words denoting moral excellence, **goodness** is the broadest in meaning. It describes an excellence so well established that it is thought of as inherent or innate and is associated with kindness, generosity, helpfulness, and sincerity (*she has more goodness in her little finger than most people have in their whole body*). **Morality**, on the other hand, is moral excellence based on a code of ethical conduct or religious teaching (*his behavior was kept in line by fear of punishment rather than morality*). Although it is often used as a synonym for *goodness*, **virtue** suggests moral excellence that is acquired rather than innate and that is consciously or steadfastly maintained, often in spite of temptations or evil influences (*her virtue was as unassailable as her noble character*). **Rectitude** is used to describe strict adherence to the rules of just or right behavior and carries strong connotations of sternness and self-discipline (*he had a reputation for rectitude and insisted on absolute truthfulness*). **Probity** describes an honesty or integrity that has been tried and proved (*as mayor, she displayed a probity that was rare in a politician*).

---

good•will /gŏodwil/ n. 1 kindly feeling. 2 established reputation of a business, etc., as enhancing its value.

■ 1 see AFFECTION 1.

good•y /gŏodee/ • n. (also **good'ie**) (*pl.* –ies) 1 [usu. in *pl.*] something good or attractive, esp. to eat. 2 = *goody-goody* n. • int. expressing childish delight. □ **goody-goody** n. smug or obtrusively virtuous person. *adj.* obtrusively or smugly virtuous.

■ □ **goody-goody** see PRIG, PHARISEE. • adj. sanctimonious, self-righteous, *colloq.* holier-than-thou.

goo•ey /gŏo-ee/ adj. (**goo•i•er**, **goo•i•est**) *sl.* 1 viscous; sticky. 2 sentimental. □□ **goo'ey•ness** n. (also **goo'i•ness**).

■ 1 tacky, gummy. 2 sweet, sugary, mushy; maudlin.

goof /gŏof/ *sl.* • n. 1 foolish or stupid person. 2 mistake. • v. 1 tr. bungle; mess up. 2 intr. blunder; make a mistake. 3 intr. [often foll. by *off*] idle; waste time.

■ n. 1 see SILLY n. 2 see MISTAKE n. • v. 1, 2 see FOUL v. 4. 3 see IDLE v. 2.

goof•ball /gŏofbawl/ n. *sl.* 1 pill containing a barbiturate or tranquilizer. 2 silly, ridiculous, or inept person.

goof•y /gŏofee/ adj. (**goof•i•er**, **goof•i•est**) *sl.* stupid; silly. □□ **goof'i•ness** n.

■ see CRAZY 1.

goon /gŏon/ n. *sl.* 1 stupid or playful person. 2 person hired by racketeers, etc.

■ 1 see FOOL n. 1. 2 see THUG.

goose /gŏos/ • n. (*pl.* **geese** /gees/) 1 a large water bird with short legs, webbed feet, and a broad bill. **b** female of this (opp. GANDER). **c** flesh of a goose as food. 2 *colloq.* simpleton. • v.tr. *sl.* poke (a person) between the buttocks. □ **goose bumps** (also **goose flesh** or **pimples** or **skin**) bristling state of the skin produced by cold or fright. **goose egg** zero score in a game. **goose step** military marching step in which the knees are kept stiff.

■ n. 2 see FOOL n. 1.

goose•ber•ry /gŏosberee, –bəree, gŏoz–/ n. (*pl.* –ries) 1 edible yellowish green berry with thin skin enclosing seeds in a juicy flesh. 2 thorny shrub bearing this fruit.

GOP abbr. Grand Old Party (Republican Party).

go•pher /gŏfər/ n. (in full **pock'et go•pher**) burrowing rodent, native to N. America, having external cheek pouches and sharp front teeth; ground squirrel.

Gor•di•an knot /gáwrdeeən/ n. 1 intricate knot. 2 difficult problem or task. □ **cut the Gordian knot** solve a problem by force or by evasion.

gore[1] /gawr/ n. 1 blood shed and clotted. 2 slaughter.

■ 2 carnage, butchery, bloodshed, killing, murder, violence.

gore[2] /gawr/ v.tr. pierce with a horn, tusk, etc.

■ stab, poke, penetrate, puncture, spear, gouge, impale.

gore[3] /gawr/ • n. wedge-shaped piece in a garment, umbrella, etc. • v.tr. shape with a gore.

gorge /gawrj/ • n. 1 narrow opening between hills or a rocky ravine. 2 act of gorging; feast. 3 contents of the stomach. • v. 1 intr. feed greedily. 2 tr. **a** [often *refl.*] satiate; glut. **b** swallow; devour greedily.

■ n. 1 canyon, defile, pass, chasm. 3 vomit, *sl.* puke, upchuck. • v. 1 overindulge, gobble, eat one's fill, *sl.* nosh. 2 **a** fill, stuff, overfeed; (*gorge oneself*) gluttonize, *colloq.* make a hog of oneself; see also OVEREAT. **b** gulp (down), gobble (up *or* down).

gor•geous /gáwrjəs/ adj. 1 richly colored; sumptuous; magnificent. 2 *colloq.* very pleasant; splendid (*gorgeous weather*). 3 *colloq.* strikingly beautiful. □□ **gor'geous•ly** adv.

■ 1 dazzling, brilliant, splendid, glorious, exquisite. 2 wonderful, marvelous, glorious, *colloq.* great, terrific, fantastic. 3 see BEAUTIFUL 1.

gor•gon /gáwrgən/ n. 1 *Gk. mythol.* each of three snake-haired sisters (esp. Medusa) with the power to turn anyone who looked at them to stone. 2 frightening or repulsive woman. □□ **gor•go•ni•an** /gawrgŏneeən/ adj.

■ 2 see HAG 2.

Gor•gon•zo•la /gáwrgənzŏlə/ n. rich cheese with bluish veins.

go•ril•la /gərílə/ n. largest anthropoid ape, native to Central Africa.

gorse /gawrs/ *n.* spiny yellow-flowered shrub native to Europe.

gor•y /gáwree/ *adj.* (**gor•i•er, gor•i•est**) **1** involving bloodshed; bloodthirsty (*a gory film*). **2** covered in gore. □□ **gor'i•ly** *adv.* **gor'i•ness** *n.*

■ **1** bloody; gruesome, grisly. **2** bloody, blood-soaked.

gosh /gosh/ *int.* expressing surprise.

gos•ling /gózling/ *n.* young goose.

gos•pel /góspəl/ *n.* **1** teaching of Christ. **2** (**Gospel**) **a** record of Christ's life in the first four books of the New Testament. **b** each of these books. **c** portion from one of them read at a service. **3** thing regarded as absolutely true (*take my word as gospel*). **4** (in full **gos'pel mu•sic**) African-American evangelical religious singing. □ **gospel truth** something considered to be unquestionably true.

■ **3** fact, certainty, reality.

gos•sa•mer /gósəmər/ • *n.* **1** filmy substance of small spiders' webs. **2** delicate filmy material. • *adj.* light and flimsy.

■ *adj.* see FLIMSY 3.

gos•sip /gósip/ • *n.* **1 a** unconstrained talk or writing, esp. about persons or social incidents. **b** idle talk; groundless rumor. **2** person who indulges in gossip. • *v.intr.* (**gos'siped, gos'sip•ing**) talk or write gossip. □□ **gos'sip•mon•ger** *n.* **gos'sip•y** *adj.*

■ *n.* **1** small talk, prattle, *colloq.* chitchat; see also CHATTER *n.* **2** rumormonger, scandalmonger, busybody, tattletale, *colloq.* bigmouth, Nosy Parker. • *v.* tattle, blab, tell tales, *colloq.* name names; see also *spill the beans* (SPILL), BABBLE *v.* 1a, b. □□ **gossipy** see INDISCREET 1.

got *past* and *past part.* of GET.

Goth /goth/ *n.* **1** member of a Germanic tribe that invaded the Roman Empire in the 3rd–5th c. **2** uncivilized or ignorant person.

Goth•ic /góthik/ • *adj.* **1** of the Goths. **2** in the style of architecture prevalent in W. Europe in the 12th–16th c., characterized by pointed arches. **3** (of a novel, etc.) with supernatural or horrifying events. **4** barbarous; uncouth. • *n.* **1** Gothic language. **2** Gothic architecture.

got•ten *past part.* of GET.

gouache /gwaash, gōo-aásh/ *n.* **1** painting in opaque pigments ground in water and thickened with a glue. **2** these pigments. **3** picture painted this way.

Gou•da /gōoda, gów-/ *n.* mild Dutch cheese.

gouge /gowj/ • *n.* **1 a** chisel with a concave blade, used in woodworking, sculpture, and surgery. **b** indentation made with or as with this. **2** *colloq.* swindle. • *v.tr.* **1** cut with or as with a gouge. **2** brutally scoop out. **3** *colloq.* swindle; extort money from.

■ *n.* **1 b** groove, scratch, gash. **2** see SWINDLE *n.* • *v.* **1** chisel, gash, groove; hollow out. **3** defraud, blackmail, cheat, squeeze, fleece, *sl.* skin, bilk.

gou•lash /gōolaash, -lash/ *n.* highly seasoned Hungarian dish of meat and vegetables, usu. flavored with paprika.

gourd /gōord/ *n.* **1 a** fleshy usu. large fruit with a hard skin, often used as containers, ornaments, etc. **b** climbing or trailing plant bearing this fruit. **2** hollow gourd shell used as a drinking vessel, etc. □□ **gourd'ful** *n.* (*pl.* –**fuls**).

gour•mand /gōormaand/ • *n.* glutton. • *adj.* gluttonous; fond of eating, esp. to excess. □□ **gour'mand•ism** *n.*

■ *n.* see GLUTTON 1.

gour•met /gōormáy/ *n.* connoisseur of good or delicate food.

■ epicure, gastronome, bon vivant.

gout /gowt/ *n.* inflammation of the smaller joints, esp. the big toe. □□ **gout'y** *adj.*

gov•ern /gúvərn/ *v.* **1 a** *tr.* rule or control (a nation, subject, etc.) with authority; conduct the affairs of. **b** *intr.* be in government. **2 a** *tr.* influence or determine (a person or a course of action). **b** *intr.* be the predominating influence. **3** *tr.* be a standard or principle for; constitute a law for; serve to decide (a case). **4** *tr.* check or control (esp. passions and machinery). □□ **gov'ern•a•ble** *adj.*

■ **1 a** direct, manage, run, lead, command. **b** wield power, be in charge, *colloq.* run the show; reign, sit on the throne. **2 a** see INFLUENCE *v.*, DETERMINE 3. **b** dominate, hold sway. **3** see DETERMINE 3. **4** curb, master, subdue, restrain.

gov•er•nance /gúvərnəns/ *n.* act or manner of governing.

■ see MANAGEMENT 1.

gov•er•ness /gúvərnis/ *n.* woman employed to teach children in a private household.

■ see TEACHER.

gov•ern•ment /gúvərnmənt/ *n.* **1** act, manner, or system of governing. **2** body of persons governing a nation. □□ **gov•ern•ment•al** /–mént'l/ *adj.*

■ rule, governance, command, regulation, control, management, administration, leadership, regime.

gov•er•nor /gúvərnər/ *n.* **1** person who governs; ruler. **2** executive head of each state of the US. **3** *Mech.* automatic regulator controlling the speed of an engine, etc. □□ **gov'er•nor•ship** *n.*

■ **1, 2** see LEADER 1.

govt. *abbr.* government.

gown /gown/ • *n.* **1** loose flowing garment, esp. a woman's long dress or nightgown. **2** official or academic robe. **3** members of a university as distinct from the permanent residents of the university town. • *v.tr.* (usu. as **gowned** *adj.*) attire in a gown.

goy /goy/ *n.* (*pl.* **goy•im** /góyim/ or **goys**) *sl.* somtimes *derog.* Jewish name for a non-Jew. □□ **goy'ish** *adj.* (also **goy'isch**).

GP *abbr.* **1** general practitioner. **2** Grand Prix.

GPO *abbr.* **1** General Post Office. **2** Government Printing Office.

grab /grab/ • *v.* (**grabbed, grab•bing**) **1** *tr.* **a** seize suddenly. **b** capture; arrest. **2** *tr.* take greedily or unfairly. **3** *tr. sl.* attract the attention of; impress. **4** *intr.* snatch at. • *n.* sudden clutch or attempt to seize. □ **grab bag 1** container from which one removes a mystery gift, as at a party. **2** miscellaneous items.

up for grabs *sl.* easily obtainable. □□ **grab´ber** *n.*

■ *v.* **1 a** snatch, grasp, catch, snag. **b** seize, catch, collar, apprehend, *sl.* nab, pinch. **2** appropriate, seize, commandeer; usurp. **3** see IMPRESS *v.* 1a. **4** (*grab at*) make a grab for, *colloq.* go for. ● *n.* **1** snatch; grasp, grip. □ **up for grabs** see *on sale* (SALE).

grace /grays/ ● *n.* **1** attractiveness in proportion, manner, movement; elegance. **2** courteous good will (*had the grace to apologize*). **3** attractive feature; accomplishment (*social graces*). **4 a** (in Christian belief) favor of God; divine saving and strengthening influence. **b** state of receiving this. **5** goodwill; favor (*fall from grace*). **6** delay granted as a favor (*a year's grace*). **7** short thanksgiving before or after a meal. **8** (**Grace**) [prec. by *His*, *Her*, *Your*] forms of description or address for a duke, duchess, or archbishop. ● *v.tr.* **1** lend or add grace to; enhance or embellish. **2** confer honor or dignity on (*graced us with his presence*).

■ *n.* **1** gracefulness, finesse, polish, poise; culture, etiquette. **2** (good) manners, decency, tact; kindness, generosity. **3** skill, talent, gift, ability. **4 a** forgiveness, mercy, compassion, charity. **7** prayer; blessing. ● *v.* **1** adorn, decorate, beautify. **2** enhance, distinguish, honor.

grace•ful /gráysfŏŏl/ *adj.* having or showing grace or elegance. □□ **grace´ful•ly** *adv.* **grace´ful•ness** *n.*

■ fluid, flowing, lissome, agile; elegant, polished, suave.

grace•less /gráyslis/ *adj.* lacking grace or elegance or charm.

gra•cious /gráyshəs/ ● *adj.* **1** kind; indulgent and beneficent to others. **2** (of God) merciful; benign. **3** elegant; luxurious. ● *int.* expressing surprise. □□ **gra´cious•ly** *adv.* **gra´cious•ness** *n.*

■ *adj.* **1** benevolent, warmhearted, cordial, amiable, affable, considerate; courteous, polite, tactful. **2** see MERCIFUL. *int.* (upon) my word, by Jove, well I (do) declare, (my) goodness, (good) Lord, good heavens, *colloq.* my stars; see also GOD *int.*

gra•date /gráydayt/ *v.* **1** *intr. & tr.* pass or cause to pass by gradations from one shade to another. **2** *tr.* arrange in steps or grades of size, etc.

■ **1** see BLEND *v.* 3a.

gra•da•tion /gráydáyshən/ *n.* [usu. in *pl.*] **1** stage of transition or advance. **2 a** certain degree in rank, intensity, merit, divergence, etc. **b** arrangement in such degrees. **3** (of paint, etc.) gradual passing from one shade, tone, etc., to another. □□ **gra•da´tion•al** *adj.*

■ **1, 2** see GRADE *n.* 1a.

grade /grayd/ ● *n.* **1 a** certain degree in rank, merit, proficiency, quality, etc. **b** class of persons or things of the same grade. **2** mark indicating the quality of a student's work. **3** class in school, concerned with a particular year's work and usu. numbered from the first upward. **4 a** gradient or slope. **b** rate of as-

cent or descent. ● *v.* **1** *tr.* arrange in or allocate to grades; class; sort. **2** *intr.* [foll. by *up*, *down*, *off*, *into*, etc.] pass gradually between grades, or into a grade. **3** *tr.* give a grade to (a student). **4** *tr.* reduce (a road, etc.) to easy gradients. □ **grade crossing** crossing of a roadway, etc., with a railroad track at the same level. **grade point average** scholastic average obtained by dividing the number of earned grade points by the number of credits taken.

■ *n.* **1 a** position, stage; status. **b** see CATEGORY. **2** rating, score; result. **4 a** rise, incline, decline. ● *v.* **1** classify, organize, group. **3** mark, evaluate, assess; rank.

gra•di•ent /gráydeeənt/ *n.* **1** stretch of road, railroad, etc., that slopes. **2** amount of such a slope.

grad•u•al /grájŏŏəl/ *adj.* **1** progressing by degrees. **2** not rapid, steep, or abrupt. □□ **grad´u•al•ly** *adv.*

■ **1** piecemeal, steady; see SLOW *adj.* 2. **2** easy, even. □□ **gradually** slowly, evenly, step by step; cautiously, carefully.

grad•u•al•ism /grájŏŏəlizəm/ *n.* policy of gradual reform. □□ **grad´u•a•list** *n.* **grad•u•al•is´tic** *adj.*

grad•u•ate ● *n.* /grájŏŏət/ **1** person who has been awarded an academic degree (also *attrib.*: *graduate student*). **2** person who has completed a course of study. ● *v.* /grájŏŏ-áyt/ **1 a** *intr.* take an academic degree. **b** *tr.* grant an academic degree or certificate of completion of school studies. **2** *intr.* **a** [foll. by *from*] be a graduate of a specified university. **b** be a graduate in a specified subject. **3** *intr.* **a** [foll. by *to*] move up to (a higher status, etc.). **b** [foll. by *as*, *in*] gain specified qualifications. **4** *tr.* mark out in degrees or parts. **5** *tr.* arrange in gradations; apportion (e.g., tax) according to a scale. □ **graduate school** division of a university for advanced work by graduates. □□ **grad•u•a•tion** /-áyshən/ *n.*

■ *v.* **3 a** see ADVANCE *v.* 1, 2. **b** qualify, get a degree. **4** see CALIBRATE 1, 2. **5** scale, apportion; see also GRADE *v.* 1.

graf•fi•ti /grəféetee/ *n.pl.* (*sing.* **graf•fi•to**) writing or drawing scribbled, scratched, or sprayed on a surface.

graft[1] /graft/ ● *n.* **1** *Bot.* shoot or scion inserted into a slit of stock, from which it receives sap. **2** *Surgery* tissue, organ, etc., transplanted surgically. ● *v.* **1** *tr.* insert (a scion) as a graft. **2** *intr.* insert a graft. **3** *tr.* *Surgery* transplant (tissue). **4** *tr.* insert or fix (a thing) permanently to another.

■ *n.* **1** bud; see SHOOT *n.* **2** implant. ● *v.* **1** implant, splice, join. **4** affix, join, fasten; see also ATTACH 1.

graft[2] /graft/ *colloq.* ● *n.* practices, esp. bribery, used to secure illicit gains in politics or business. ● *v.intr.* seek or make such gains.

■ *n.* corruption, payola; *colloq.* kickback; see BLACKMAIL *n.* 1.

gra•ham crack•er /gram, gráyəm/ *n.* crisp, slightly sweet whole-wheat cracker.

Grail /grayl/ *n.* (in full **Ho´ly Grail´**) (in medieval legend) cup or platter used by Christ at the Last Supper.

grain /grayn/ • *n.* **1** fruit or seed of a cereal. **2 a** [*collect.*] wheat or related grass used as food. **b** [*collect.*] their fruit. **c** any cereal crop. **3** small hard particle of salt, sand, etc. **4** smallest unit of weight in the troy system (equivalent to $^1/_{480}$ of an ounce) and in the avoirdupois system (equivalent to $^1/_{437.5}$ of an ounce). **5** smallest possible quantity (*not a grain of truth in it*). **6 a** roughness of surface. **b** *Photog.* granular appearance on a photograph or negative. **7** texture. **8** pattern of lines of fiber in wood or paper. • *v.tr.* **1** paint in imitation of the grain of wood or marble. **2** give a granular surface to. □ **against the grain** contrary to one's natural inclination or feeling. □□ **grain'y** *adj.*

■ *n.* **1** kernel; see also SEED *n.* 1a. **2** cereal, grist; wheat, barley, rice, oats. **3** bit, fragment, crumb. **5** iota, scrap, trace, *colloq.* smidgen. **6** graininess; see also INEQUALITY 3. **7** pattern, fiber, weave, nap. □ **against the grain** see ALIEN *adj.* 1a.

gram /gram/ *n.* metric unit of mass equal to one-thousandth of a kilogram.

-gram /gram/ *comb. form* forming nouns denoting a thing written or recorded (often in a certain way) (*monogram, telegram*). □□ **-grammatic** /grəmátik/ *comb. form* forming adjectives.

gram•mar /grámər/ *n.* **1** study or rules of a language's inflections, forms, etc. **2** observance or application of such rules (*bad grammar*) **3** book on grammar. □ **grammar school** elementary school. □□ **gram•mar'i•an** *n.* **gram•mat'i•cal** *adj.* **gram•mat'i•cal•ly** *adv.*

gram•o•phone /gráməfōn/ *n.* = PHONOGRAPH.

gran•a•ry /gránəree, gráy-/ *n.* (*pl.* **-ries**) storehouse for threshed grain.

grand /grand/ • *adj.* **1 a** magnificent; imposing; dignified. **b** noble. **2** main; of chief importance (*grand staircase, grand entrance*). **3** (**Grand**) of the highest rank (*Grand Cross, Grand Inquisitor*). **4** *colloq.* excellent; enjoyable (*had a grand time*). **5** belonging to high society; wealthy (*the grand folk at the manor*). **6** [in *comb.*] in names of family relationships, denoting the second degree of ascent or descent (*granddaughter*). • *n.* **1** = grand piano. **2** (*pl.* same) *sl.* thousand dollars. □ **grand jury** *Law* jury selected to examine the validity of an accusation prior to trial. **grand master 1** chess player of the highest class. **2** head of a military order of knighthood, of Freemasons, etc. **grand piano** large full-toned piano standing on three legs, with horizontal strings. **grand slam 1** *Sports* winning of all of a group of major championships. **2** *Bridge* winning of all 13 tricks. **3** *Baseball* home run with bases loaded. □□ **grand'ly** *adv.* **grand'ness** *n.*

■ *adj.* **1 a** splendid, impressive, majestic, stately, lavish, *colloq.* posh; respected, eminent. **b** solemn, lofty; see also NOBLE *adj.* 3, 4. **2** principal, leading, foremost. **4** marvelous, wonderful, *colloq.* great, smashing, terrific; see also SUPERB. **5** see POSH *adj.* 2, RICH 1.

grand•child /gránchīld, gránd-/ *n.* (*pl.* **-chil•dren**) child of one's son or daughter.

grand•dad•dy /grándadee/ *n.* (also **gran'dad•dy**) (*pl.* **-dies**) **1** *colloq.* grandfather. **2** original and usu. most venerated of its kind (*the granddaddy of symphony orchestras*).

grand•daugh•ter /grándawtər/ *n.* female grandchild.

gran•dee /grandée/ *n.* **1** highest Spanish or Portuguese nobleman. **2** person of high rank or eminence.

gran•deur /gránjər, -jōōr/ *n.* **1** majesty; splendor. **2** nobility of character.

■ **1** magnificence, pomp; see also SPLENDOR 2. **2** see NOBILITY 1.

grand•fa•ther /gránfaathər, gránd-/ *n.* male grandparent. □ **grandfather clock** floorstanding pendulum clock in a tall wooden case. □□ **grand'fa•ther•ly** *adj.*

gran•dil•o•quent /grandíləkwənt/ *adj.* pompous or inflated in language. □□ **gran•dil•o•quence** /-kwəns/ *n.* **gran•dil•o•quent•ly** *adv.*

■ see POMPOUS 2.

gran•di•ose /grándeeōs/ *adj.* **1** producing or meant to produce an imposing effect. **2** ambitious in scale. □□ **gran'di•ose•ly** *adv.* **gran•di•os•i•ty** /-deeósitee/ *n.*

■ **1** grand, monumental; see IMPRESSIVE. **2** lofty, flamboyant, showy, extravagant, *colloq.* highfalutin, flash.

grand•mo•ther /gránmuthər, gránd-/ *n.* female grandparent. □□ **grand'moth•er•ly** *adj.*

grand•pa•rent /gránpairənt, gránd-/ *n.* parent of one's father or mother.

grand•son /gránsun, gránd-/ *n.* male grandchild.

grand•stand /gránstand, gránd-/ *n.* main stand for spectators at a racecourse, etc.

grange /graynj/ *n.* **1** country house with farm buildings. **2** (**Grange**) farmer's social organization.

gran•ite /gránit/ *n.* granular crystalline igneous rock of quartz, mica, etc., used for building.

gran•ny /gránee/ *n.* (also **gran'nie**) (*pl.* **-nies**) *colloq.* grandmother.

Gran•ny Smith /gránee smith/ *n.* green variety of apple.

gra•no•la /grənōlə/ *n.* breakfast or snack food consisting of a mixture of rolled oats, nuts, dried fruits, etc.

grant /grant/ • *v.tr.* **1 a** consent to fulfill (a request, wish, etc.) (*granted all he asked*). **b** allow (a person) to have (a thing) (*granted me my freedom*). **2** give (rights, property, etc.) formally; transfer legally. **3** admit as true; concede, esp. as a basis for argument. See synonym study at GIVE. • *n.* **1** process of granting or thing granted. **2** sum of money officially given, esp. to finance education. □ **take for granted 1** assume something to be true or valid. **2** cease to appreciate through familiarity. □□ **gran•tee** /-tée/ *n.* (esp. in sense 2 of *v.*). **grant'er** *n.* **gran'tor** /-tór/ *n.* (esp. in sense 2 of *v.*).

■ *v.* **1 a** agree to, concur with, admit, allow. **b** permit; give, award, offer; donate, assign. **2** see *make over* 1. **3** see CONCEDE 1a. • *n.* **1**,

2 gift, endowment, donation, contribution; subsidy.

gran•u•lar /grányələr/ adj. of or like grains or granules. □□ **gran•u•lar•i•ty** /–láritee/ n.

■ grainy, granulated, sandy, gritty.

gran•u•late /grányəlayt/ v. form into grains (*granulated sugar*). □□ **gran•u•la•tion** /–láyshən/ n.

gran•ule /grányool/ n. small grain.

■ see GRAIN n. 3.

grape /grayp/ n. **1** berry (usu. green, purple, or black) growing in clusters on a vine, used as fruit and in making wine. **2** [prec. by *the*] *colloq.* wine. □ **grape hyacinth** liliaceous plant with clusters of usu. blue flowers.

grape•fruit /gráypfroot/ n. (*pl.* same) **1** large round yellow citrus fruit. **2** tree bearing this fruit.

grape•vine /gráypvīn/ n. **1** vine. **2** *colloq.* means of transmission of rumor (*heard it through the grapevine*).

■ **2** *sl.* network.

graph /graf/ • n. **1** diagram showing the relation between variable quantities, usu. along two axes. **2** *Math.* collection of points whose coordinates satisfy a given relation. • v.tr. plot or trace on a graph. □ **graph paper** paper printed with a network of lines as a basis for drawing graphs.

■ n. **1** see CHART n. 2.

-graph /graf/ *comb. form* forming nouns and verbs meaning: **1** thing written, drawn, etc., in a specified way (*autograph*). **2** instrument that records (*seismograph, telegraph*).

graph•ic /gráfik/ • adj. **1** of or relating to the visual or descriptive arts, esp. writing and drawing. **2** vividly descriptive; conveying all (esp. unwelcome or unpleasant) details; unequivocal. • n. product of the graphic arts (cf. GRAPHICS). □ **graphic arts** visual and technical arts involving design, writing, drawing, printing, etc. □□ **graph′i•cal•ly** adv.

■ adj. **1** representational, pictorial. **2** lifelike, explicit, realistic, photographic; precise; clear, unambiguous.

-graphic /gráfik/ *comb. form* (also **–graphical** /gráfikəl/) forming adjectives corresponding to nouns in *–graphy*. □□ **–graphically** /gráfiklee/ *comb. form* forming adverbs

graph•ics /gráfiks/ n.pl. [usu. treated as *sing.*] **1** products of the graphic arts. **2** use of diagrams in calculation and design. **3** (in full **com•pu′ter graph′ics**) *Computing* mode of processing and output in which information is in pictorial form.

graph•ite /gráfīt/ n. crystalline allotropic form of carbon used as a lubricant, in pencils, etc.

gra•phol•o•gy /grəfóləjee/ n. the study of handwriting, esp. as a supposed guide to character. □□ **graph•ol′o•gist** n.

-graphy /grəfee/ *comb. form* forming nouns denoting: **1** descriptive science (*geography*). **2** technique of producing images (*photography*). **3** style or method of writing, drawing, etc. (*calligraphy*).

grap•nel /grápnəl/ n. **1** device with iron claws, for dragging or grasping. **2** small anchor with several flukes.

grap•ple /grápəl/ • v. **1** *intr.* fight at close quarters or in close combat. **2** *intr.* try to manage a difficult problem, etc. **3** *tr.* **a** grip with the hands. **b** seize with or as with a grapnel; grasp. • n. **1** a hold or grip in or as in wrestling. **b** contest at close quarters. **2** clutching instrument; grapnel. □ **grappling iron** (or **hook**) = GRAPNEL.

■ v. **1** wrestle, tussle; see FIGHT v. 1a. **2** (*grapple with*) struggle with, tackle, take on. **3** hold, clasp; grab. • n. **1 a** grasp, clutch. **b** see BOUT 2a.

grasp /grasp/ • v. **1** *tr.* **a** clutch at; seize greedily. **b** hold firmly; grip. **2** *intr.* [foll. by *at*] try to seize. **3** *tr.* understand or realize (a fact or meaning). • n. **1** firm hold; grip. **2 a** mastery or control (*a grasp of the situation*). **b** mental hold or understanding (*a grasp of the facts*). **3** mental agility (*a quick grasp*).

■ v. **1 a** grab, snatch. **b** clutch, clasp. **2** (*grasp at*) grab at, reach for; see *jump at*. **3** comprehend, catch, follow, *colloq.* get, *sl.* dig; see. • n. **1** clasp, lock; clutches. **2 a** (*grasp of*) possession of, power over. **b** comprehension, awareness. **3** see INTELLIGENCE 1b.

grasp•ing /grásping/ adj. avaricious; greedy.

■ acquisitive, rapacious.

grass /gras/ • n. **1 a** small plants with green blades that are eaten by cattle, horses, sheep, etc. **b** plant that includes cereals, reeds, and bamboos. **2** pasture land. **3** lawn (*keep off the grass*). **4** *sl.* marijuana. • v.tr. **1** cover with turf. **2** provide with pasture. □ **grass roots 1** fundamental level or source. **2** ordinary people, esp. as voters; rank and file of an organization, esp. a political party. □□ **grass′y** adj. (**gras•si•er, gras•si•est**)

■ n. **2** see PASTURE[1] n. **3** see LAWN. **4** cannabis, hemp, *colloq.* hash, *sl.* pot, green, dope. □ **grass roots 1** see BOTTOM n. 4. **2** see PEOPLE n. 2.

grass•hop•per /grás-hoppər/ n. jumping and chirping plant-eating insect.

grass•land /grásland/ n. large open area covered with grass, esp. used for grazing.

■ see PLAIN[1] n.

grate[1] /grayt/ v. **1** *tr.* reduce to small particles by rubbing on a serrated surface. **2** *intr.* rub with a harsh scraping sound. **3** *tr.* utter in a harsh tone. **4** *intr.* **a** sound harshly or discordantly. **b** have an irritating effect. □□ **grat′er** n.

■ **1** shred, rasp, scrape. **2** rasp, grind, scratch. **3** croak, rasp, growl; see also BAWL[2] 1. **4 a** see JAR v. 1, 2. **b** jar, *colloq.* get on a person's nerves; (*grate on*) annoy, irk, irritate.

grate[2] /grayt/ n. metal frame confining fuel in a fireplace.

grate•ful /gráytfool/ adj. **1** thankful; feeling or showing gratitude (*am grateful to you for helping*). **2** pleasant, acceptable. □□ **grate′ful•ly** adv. **grate′ful•ness** n.

■ **1** appreciative; see also INDEBTED. **2** see PLEASANT.

grat•i•fy /grátifī/ v.tr. (**–fies, –fied**) **1 a** please; delight. **b** please by compliance. **2** indulge in or yield to (a feeling or desire). □□ **grat•i•fi•ca′tion** n.

■ **1 a** cheer, gladden; see also PLEASE 1. **1b, 2** see SATISFY 2, 3. □□ **gratification** satisfaction, fulfillment; reward.

grat•ing¹ /gráyting/ *adj.* **1** sounding harsh or discordant (*a grating laugh*). **2** irritating. □□ **grat′ing•ly** *adv.*

■ **1** jarring, raucous, shrill; screeching, croaking. **2** offensive, irksome.

grat•ing² /gráyting/ *n.* **1** framework of parallel or crossed metal bars. **2** *Optics* set of parallel wires, lines ruled on glass, etc., for producing spectra by diffraction.

■ **1** grate, grid, grille. **2** reticulation.

grat•is /grátis, graá–/ *adv. & adj.* free, without charge.

■ see FREE *adj.* 6.

grat•i•tude /grátirood, –ryōod/ *n.* being thankful; appreciation.

■ acknowledgment, recognition, thanksgiving.

gra•tu•i•tous /grətōoitəs, tyōō–/ *adj.* **1** given or done free of charge. **2** uncalled-for (*a gratuitous insult*). □□ **gra•tu′i•tous•ly** *adv.* **gra•tu′i•tous•ness** *n.*

■ **1** see FREE *adj.* 6. **2** unprovoked, unsolicited, baseless.

gra•tu•i•ty /grətōoitee, –tyōō–/ *n.* (*pl.* **–ties**) money given for service; tip.

■ see TIP³ *n.* 1.

grave¹ /grayv/ *n.* **1 a** trench for the burial of a corpse. **b** mound or memorial stone placed over this. **2** [prec. by *the*] death, esp. as indicating mortal finality. **3** something compared to or regarded as a grave.

■ **1 b** crypt, sepulcher, tomb, vault, mausoleum; gravestone, headstone. **2** (*the grave*) see DEATH 1.

grave² /grayv/ • *adj.* **1 a** serious; weighty; important (*a grave matter*). **b** solemn; somber (*a grave look*). **2** critical or threatening (*grave danger*). • *n.* /graav/ = **grave accent**. □ **grave accent** /graav, grayv/ mark (`) placed over a vowel to denote pronunciation, length, etc. □□ **grave′ly** *adv.*

■ *adj.* **1 a** critical; see also SERIOUS 2, 3. **b** dignified, earnest, gloomy. **2** vital, urgent; perilous, dangerous.

grav•el /grávəl/ • *n.* mixture of coarse sand and small stones, used for paths, roads, etc. • *v.tr.* lay or strew with gravel.

grav•el•ly /grávəlee/ *adj.* **1** of or like gravel. **2** (of a voice) deep and rough sounding.

■ **1** see *gritty* (GRIT). **2** see STRIDENT.

grave•stone /gráyvstōn/ *n.* stone marking a grave.

■ see MONUMENT 1.

grave•yard /gráyvyaard/ *n.* burial ground, esp. by a church. □ **graveyard shift** work shift beginning late at night.

■ churchyard, cemetery, potter's field, *sl.* boneyard.

grav•i•tate /grávitayt/ *v.* **1** *intr.* move or be attracted to. **2** *tr. & intr.* move or tend by force of gravity toward.

■ see LEAN¹ *v.*

grav•i•ta•tion /grávitáyshən/ *n. Physics* **1** force of attraction between particles of matter in the universe. **2** effect of this, esp. the falling of bodies to the earth. □□ **grav•i•ta′tion•al** *adj.*

grav•i•ty /grávitee/ *n.* **1 a** force that attracts a body to the center of the earth or other celestial body. **b** degree of this measured by acceleration. **2** property of having weight. **3 a** importance; seriousness. **b** solemnity; serious demeanor.

■ **1** gravitation; attraction. **2** see WEIGHT *n.* 2, 3. **3 a** significance, magnitude, urgency. **b** dignity, sobriety.

gra•vy /gráyvee/ *n.* (*pl.* **–vies**) **1 a** juices exuding from meat during and after cooking. **b** sauce for food, made from these. **2** *sl.* unearned or unexpected gains, esp. money. □ **gravy boat** vessel for serving gravy. **gravy train** *sl.* source of easy financial benefit.

gray /gray/ (also **grey**) • *adj.* **1** of a color intermediate between black and white. **2 a** (of the weather, etc.) dull; dismal; overcast. **b** bleak; (of a person) depressed. **3 a** (of hair) turning white with age, etc. **b** (of a person) having gray hair. **4** anonymous; unidentifiable. • *n.* **1 a** gray color or pigment. **b** gray clothes or material (*dressed in gray*). **2** gray or white horse. • *v.* make or become gray. □ **gray area** situation or topic not clearly defined. **gray matter 1** darker tissues of the brain and spinal cord. **2** *colloq.* intelligence. □□ **gray′ish** *adj.* **gray′ness** *n.*

■ *adj.* **1** pearly, smoky, grizzly. **2** dark, foggy, cloudy; cheerless, gloomy, glum; see also MISERABLE 3. **4** colorless; see NONDESCRIPT *adj.* □ **gray matter 2** see BRAIN *n.* 3.

graze¹ /grayz/ *v.* **1** *intr.* (of cattle, sheep, etc.) eat growing grass. **2** *tr.* feed (cattle, etc.) on growing grass.

■ **1** see FEED *v.* 3.

graze² /grayz/ • *v.* **1** *tr.* rub or scrape (part of the body, esp. the skin). **2 a** *tr.* touch lightly in passing. **b** *intr.* move with a light passing contact. • *n.* abrasion.

■ *v.* **1** see SCRAPE *v.* 3b. **2 a** see KISS *v.* 3. • *n.* see SCRAPE *n.* 2.

grease /grees/ • *n.* **1** oily or fatty matter esp. as a lubricant. **2** melted animal fat. **3** oily matter in unprocessed wool. • *v.tr.* also /greez/ smear or lubricate with grease. □ **grease the palm of** *colloq.* bribe.

■ *n.* see OIL *n.* • *v.* see OIL *v.*

grease•paint /gréespaynt/ *n.* stage makeup for actors.

greas•y /gréesee, gréezee/ *adj.* (**greas•i•er, greas•i•est**) **1 a** of or like grease. **b** smeared or covered with grease. **c** having too much grease. **2 a** slippery. **b** (of a person or manner) unctuous; smooth. **c** objectionable. □□ **greas′i•ly** *adv.* **greas′i•ness** *n.*

■ **1** oily, fatty, buttery. **2 a** see SLIPPERY 1, 2. **b** oily, fawning, slick, toadying, sycophantic, obsequious, *colloq.* smarmy.

great /grayt/ • *adj.* **1 a** of a size, amount, extent, or intensity considerably above the normal or average (*made a great hole, take great care*). **b** reinforcing other words denoting size, quantity, etc. (*a great big hole, a great many*). **2** important; preeminent; worthy. **3** grand; imposing (*a great occasion, the great hall*). **4 a** (esp. of a public or historic figure) distinguished; prominent. **b** (**the Great**) as a title denoting the most important of the name (*Alexander the Great*). **5 a** (of a person) remarkable in ability, character, achievement, etc. (*a great thinker*). **b** (of a thing) outstanding of its kind (*the Great Depression*). **6** [foll. by *at*] competent; skilled; well-informed. **7** *colloq.* **a** very enjoyable or satisfactory; attractive; fine (*had a great time*). **b** (as an exclam.) fine; very good. **8** [in *comb.*] (in names of family relationships) denoting one degree further removed upward or downward (*great-uncle*, *great-great-grandmother*). • *n.* great or outstanding person or thing. □ **Great Britain** England, Wales, and Scotland. **great circle** see CIR-CLE. **Great Dane** see DANE. □□ **great′ly** *adv.* **great′ness** *n.*

■ *adj.* **1 a** big, large, huge, immense, extreme, considerable; marked, extraordinary, *colloq.* terrific; significant, profound. **2** critical, crucial, vital, major. **3** fine, lofty, exalted, momentous, significant. **4 a** important, celebrated, famous, notable, influential. **5 a** gifted, talented, accomplished, skilled, remarkable, exceptional. **b** extraordinary. **6** (*great at* or *on*) expert at *or* in; talented at. **7** outstanding, first-class, superior, wonderful, *colloq.* super(-duper), smashing, A1, fantastic, terrific, A-OK, *sl.* cracking, ace, groovy, awesome, bad; see also SUPERB.

grebe /greeb/ *n.* diving bird with a long neck, lobed toes, and almost no tail.

Gre•cian /greeshən/ *adj.* (of architecture or facial outline) following Greek models or ideals.

Gre•co-Ro•man /greekō-rṓmən, grékō-/ *adj.* **1** of or relating to the Greeks and Romans. **2** *Wrestling* denoting a style attacking only the upper part of the body.

greed /greed/ *n.* excessive desire, esp. for food or wealth.

■ greediness, avarice; gluttony, piggishness, voracity.

greed•y /greedee/ *adj.* (**greed•i•er, greed•i•est**) **1** having or showing an excessive appetite for food or drink. **2** wanting wealth or pleasure to excess. **3** very keen or eager (*greedy for affection, greedy to learn*). □□ **greed′i•ly** *adv.* **greed′i•ness** *n.*

■ **1** voracious, gluttonous, *colloq.* piggish. **2** avaricious, covetous; materialistic, mercenary. **3** see EAGER.

SYNONYM STUDY: greedy

ACQUISITIVE, COVETOUS, AVARICIOUS, RAPACIOUS, GLUTTONOUS. The desire for money and the things it can buy is often associated with Americans. But not all Americans are **greedy**, which implies an insatiable desire to possess or acquire something, beyond what one needs or deserves (*greedy for profits*). Someone who is *greedy* for food might be called **gluttonous**, which emphasizes consumption as well as desire (*a gluttonous appetite for sweets*), but *greedy* is a derogatory term only when the object of longing is itself evil or when it cannot be possessed without harm to oneself or others (*a reporter greedy for information*). A *greedy* child may grow up to be an **avaricious** adult, which implies a fanatical greediness for money or other valuables. **Rapacious** is an even stronger term, with an emphasis on taking things by force (*so rapacious in his desire for land that he forced dozens of families from their homes*). **Acquisitive**, on the other hand, is a more neutral word suggesting a willingness to exert effort in acquiring things (*an acquisitive woman who filled her house with antiques and artwork*), and not necessarily material things (*a probing, acquisitive mind*). **Covetous**, in contrast to *acquisitive*, implies an intense desire for something as opposed to the act of acquiring or possessing it. It is often associated with the Ten Commandments (*Thou shalt not covet thy neighbor's wife*) and suggests a longing for something that rightfully belongs to another.

Greek /greek/ • *n.* **1 a** native or inhabitant of Greece; person of Greek descent. **b** native or citizen of any of the ancient nation-states of Greece. **2** language of Greece. • *adj.* of Greece or its people or language; Hellenic.

green /green/ • *adj.* **1** of the color between blue and yellow in the spectrum; colored like grass, emeralds, etc. **2** covered with leaves or grass. **3** (of fruit, etc., or wood) unripe or unseasoned. **4** not dried, smoked, or tanned. **5** inexperienced; naive; gullible. **6 a** (of the complexion) pale; sickly-hued. **b** jealous; envious. **7** young; flourishing. **8** vegetable (*green salad*). **9** (also **Green**) concerned with or supporting protection of the environment. • *n.* **1** green color or pigment. **2** green clothes or material (*dressed in green*). **3 a** piece of public or common grassy land (*village green*). **b** grassy area used for a special purpose (*putting green, bowling green*). **4** [in *pl.*] green vegetables. • *v.* make or become green. □ **green** (or **string**) **bean** the green pods of a young kidney bean, eaten as a vegetable. **green belt** area of open land around a city, designated for preservation. **Green Beret** *Mil.* member of the US Army Special Forces. **green card** work and residence permit issued to permanent resident aliens in the US. **green-eyed** jealous. **green-eyed monster** jealousy. **green light 1** signal to proceed on a road, railroad, etc. **2** *colloq.* permission to go ahead with a project. **green pepper** unripe bell or sweet pepper, eaten green as a vegetable. **green thumb** skill in growing plants. □□ **green′ish** *adj.* **green′ly** *adv.* **green′ness** *n.*

■ *adj.* **1** emerald, jade, lime. **2** verdant, fresh; rural, pastoral; see also *leafy* (LEAF[1]). **3** immature, unready. **5** callow, untested, new, raw, *colloq.* wet behind the ears; amateur, unskilled. **6 a** see PALE *adj.* 1. **b** see ENVIOUS[1]. **7** youthful, blooming, thriving. **9** (-also **Green**) environmental, conservational, ecological. • *n.* **3 a** common, grassland; lawn(s). **b** lawn, turf. □ **green-eyed** see ENVIOUS. **green-eyed monster** see ENVY *n.* **green light 2** see *go-ahead n.* (GO).

green•back /greenbak/ *n.* bill of US paper currency.

green•er•y /gréenəree/ n. green foliage or growing plants.

green•gro•cer /gréengrōsər/ n. retailer of fruit and vegetables.

green•horn /gréenhawrn/ n. inexperienced person.
■ beginner, novice, tenderfoot, (new) recruit, *sl.* rookie.

green•house /gréenhows/ n. structure with sides and roof mainly of glass, for growing plants. □ **greenhouse effect** trapping of the sun's warmth in the earth's lower atmosphere caused by an increase in carbon dioxide.

green•room /gréenrōom/ n. room in a theater for actors and actresses who are off stage.

greens•keep•er /gréenzkeepər/ n. keeper of a golf course.

green•sward /gréenswawrd/ n. *archaic or literary* expanse of grassy turf.

Green•wich Mean Time /grénich, grínij/ n. (also **Green'wich Time**) local time on the meridian of Greenwich, England, used as an international basis for reckoning time.

green•y /gréenee/ adj. greenish (*greeny-yellow*).

greet /greet/ v.tr. **1** address politely or welcomingly on meeting or arrival. **2** receive or acknowledge in a specified way (*was greeted with derision*). **3** (of a sight, sound, etc.) become apparent to or noticed by. □□ **greet'er** n.
■ **1, 2** welcome, hail, salute, meet.

greet•ing /gréeting/ n. **1** act or instance of welcoming or addressing politely. **2** words, gestures, etc., used to greet a person. **3** (often in *pl.*) expression of goodwill.
■ **1** salutation, reception. **3** (*greetings*) regards, respects.

gre•gar•i•ous /grigáireeəs/ adj. **1** fond of company. **2** living in flocks or communities. □□ **gre•gar'i•ous•ly** adv. **gre•gar'i•ous•ness** n.
■ **1** see SOCIABLE.

Gre•go•ri•an cal•en•dar /grigáwreeən/ n. calendar now in use, introduced in 1582 by Pope Gregory XIII, as a correction of the Julian calendar.

Gre•go•ri•an chant /grigáwreeən/ n. plainsong ritual music.

grem•lin /grémlin/ n. *colloq.* imaginary mischievous sprite regarded as responsible for mechanical faults, esp. in aircraft.

gre•nade /grináyd/ n. small bomb thrown by hand (**hand' gre•nade'**) or shot from a rifle.

grew *past of* GROW

grey var. of GRAY.

grey•hound /gráyhownd/ n. dog of a tall slender breed that is capable of high speed, used in racing and coursing.

grid /grid/ n. **1** framework of spaced parallel bars; grating. **2** system of squares printed on a map for reference. **3** network of lines, electrical power connections, gas supply lines, etc. **4** wire network between the filament and the anode of a vacuum tube, etc. **5** arrangement of city streets in a rectangular pattern. □□ **grid'ded** adj.
■ **1** see GRATING² 1. **3** see NETWORK n. 2.

grid•dle /gríd'l/ n. circular iron plate placed

over a fire or otherwise heated for baking, toasting, etc.

grid•i•ron /grídiərn/ n. **1** cooking utensil of metal bars for broiling or grilling. **2** football field (with parallel lines marking the area of play). **3** = GRID 5.

grid•lock /grídlok/ n. **1** traffic jam in which vehicular movement is blocked by stoppage of cross traffic. **2** complete standstill in action or progress. □□ **grid'locked** adj.

grief /greef/ n. **1** deep or intense sorrow or mourning. **2** cause of this. □ **come to grief** meet with disaster.
■ **1** anguish, suffering, agony, misery, distress. **2** ordeal, affliction, calamity, adversity. □ **come to grief** fail, miscarry, fall apart or to pieces, *colloq.* come unstuck.

griev•ance /gréevəns/ n. cause for complaint.
■ objection, charge, allegation, grudge, *colloq.* gripe, *sl.* beef; injustice, disservice, injury, insult; wrong, ill, damage.

grieve /greev/ v. **1** tr. cause grief or great distress to. **2** intr. suffer grief, esp. at another's death.
■ **1** see DISTRESS v. **2** mourn, sorrow; weep, cry, moan, keen; (*grieve over*) bemoan, lament, deplore, regret, rue.

griev•ous /gréevəs/ adj. **1** (of pain, etc.) severe. **2** causing grief. **3** flagrant; heinous. □□ **griev'ous•ly** adv.
■ **1** grave, serious; see ACUTE adj. 1a. **2** distressing, hurtful; injurious, damaging. **3** egregious, outrageous, atrocious, *colloq.* awful, appalling, terrible, shocking, dreadful.

grif•fin /grífin/ n. (also **gryph'on**, **grif'fon**) mythical creature with an eagle's head and wings and a lion's body.

grill /gril/ • n. **1** = GRIDIRON 1. **2** food cooked on a grill. **3** (in full **grill' room**) restaurant serving grilled food. • v. **1** tr. & intr. cook or be cooked under a broiler or on a gridiron. **2** tr. & intr. subject or be subjected to extreme heat, esp. from the sun. **3** tr. subject to severe questioning or interrogation. □□ **grill'ing** n. (in sense 3 of v.)
■ v. **1** see BROIL 1. **3** see QUESTION v. 1.

grille /gril/ n. (also **grill**) **1** grating or latticed screen. **2** metal grid protecting the radiator of a motor vehicle.
■ **1** see GRATING² 1.

grill•work /grílwərk/ n. metal fashioned to form a grille.

grim /grim/ adj. (**grim•mer**, **grim•mest**) **1** of stern or forbidding appearance. **2 a** harsh, merciless; severe. **b** resolute (*grim determination*). **3** joyless; sinister (*has a grim truth in it*). **4** unpleasant; unattractive. □□ **grim'ly** adv. **grim'ness** n.
■ **1** see FORBIDDING. **2 a** unrelenting, stony, formidable. **b** unyielding, adamant, determined, stubborn. **3** dreadful, frightful, hideous, horrible. **4** see AWFUL 1a, b.

grim•ace /gríməs, grimáys/ • n. distortion of the face made in disgust, etc., or to amuse. • v.intr. make a grimace.
■ n. see FROWN n. • v. see FROWN v. 1.

grime /grīm/ • n. soot or dirt ingrained in a surface. • v.tr. blacken with grime; befoul.

■ *n.* filth, *colloq.* muck; see DIRT 1. ● *v.* dirty, soil, besmirch.

grin /grin/ ● *v.* (**grin·ned, grin·ning**) 1 *intr.* smile broadly, showing the teeth. 2 *tr.* express by grinning (*grinned his satisfaction*). ● *n.* act of grinning. □ **grin and bear it** take pain or misfortune stoically.

grind /grīnd/ ● *v.* (*past* and *past part.* **ground** /grownd/) 1 a *tr.* reduce to particles or powder by crushing. b *intr.* (of a mill, machine, etc.) move with a crushing action. 2 a *tr.* reduce, sharpen, or smooth by friction. b *tr. & intr.* rub or rub together gratingly (*grind one's teeth*). 3 *tr.* oppress. 4 *intr.* a work or study hard. b produce with effort (*grinding out verses*). c (of a sound) continue gratingly. ● *n.* 1 act or instance of grinding. 2 *colloq.* hard dull work (*the daily grind*). 3 size of ground particles. See synonym study at LABOR.

■ *v.* 1 a pound, pulverize, mill. 2 a whet; file, polish. b gnash, grate. 3 (*grind down*) crush, wear down, persecute. 4 a labor, toil, slave; burn the midnight oil, cram. b (*grind out*) generate, crank out. ● *n.* 2 toil, labor, drudgery; chores.

grind·er /grīndər/ *n.* 1 person or thing that grinds, esp. a machine. 2 molar tooth. 3 *US dial.* submarine sandwich.

■ 1 see MILL¹ *n.* 1b, 2.

grind·stone /grīndstōn/ *n.* 1 thick revolving disk used for grinding, sharpening, and polishing. 2 kind of stone used for this. □ **keep one's nose to the grindstone** work hard and continuously.

grip /grip/ ● *v.* (**gripped, grip·ping**) 1 a *tr.* grasp tightly. b *intr.* take a firm hold. 2 *tr.* (of a feeling or emotion) deeply affect (a person) (*was gripped by fear*). 3 *tr.* compel the attention of (*a gripping story*). ● *n.* 1 firm hold; tight grasp. 2 power of holding attention. 3 a intellectual control. b control of a situation or one's behavior, etc. (*lose one's grip*). 4 a part of a machine that grips. b handle. 5 traveling bag. □ **come to grips with** approach purposefully; begin to deal with.

■ *v.* 1 a clutch, clasp, hold. b hold, stay; see STICK² 6. 2 see SEIZE 4, POSSESS 3. 3 engross, fascinate, entrance, spellbind. ● *n.* 1 clutch, handgrip. 2 control, mastery; authority, influence. 3 a grasp, comprehension, awareness. b see SELF-CONTROL. 5 valise, carryall; see also SUITCASE. □ **come to grips with** tackle, confront, handle, address.

gripe /grīp/ ● *v.* 1 *intr. colloq.* complain. 2 *tr.* affect with gastric pain. ● *n.* 1 [usu. in *pl.*] colic. 2 *colloq.* a complaint. 3 act of griping.

■ *v.* 1 grumble, whine, *colloq.* grouse, bitch, *sl.* beef, bellyache. ● *n.* 1 stomachache, cramp. 2 grievance, objection, *sl.* beef; carping, grousing, *colloq.* bitching.

gris·ly /grizlee/ *adj.* (**gris·li·er, gris·li·est**) causing horror, disgust, or fear. □□ **gris·li·ness** *n.*

■ gruesome, grim, abhorrent, hideous, dreadful, repulsive.

grist /grist/ *n.* grain to grind.

gris·tle /grisəl/ *n.* tough flexible animal tissue; cartilage. □□ **gris·tly** /grislee/ *adj.*

grit /grit/ ● *n.* 1 particles of stone or sand, esp. as irritating or hindering. 2 coarse sandstone. 3 *colloq.* pluck endurance. ● *v.* (**grit·ted, grit·ting**) 1 *tr.* clench (the teeth). 2 *intr.* make or move with a grating sound. □□ **grit·ty** *adj.* (**grit·ti·er, grit·ti·est**). **grit·ti·ness** *n.*

■ *n.* 3 courage, valor, fortitude, spirit, *colloq.* guts, gutsiness, spunk, *sl.* moxie. □□ **gritty** sandy, grainy; rough, abrasive; courageous, resolute, tough, game, determined, *colloq.* gutsy, spunky.

grits /grits/ *n.pl.* coarsely ground hulled grain, esp. hominy.

griz·zled /grizəld/ *adj.* having, or streaked with, gray hair.

griz·zly /grizlee/ ● *adj.* (**griz·zli·er, griz·zli·est**) gray; grayish; gray-haired. ● *n.* (*pl.* **-zlies**) (in full **griz·zly bear**) variety of large brown bear found in N. America.

groan /grōn/ ● *v.* 1 a *intr.* make a deep sound expressing pain, grief, or disapproval. b *tr.* utter with groans. 2 *intr.* complain inarticulately. 3 *intr.* [usu. foll. by *under, beneath, with*] be loaded or oppressed. ● *n.* sound made in groaning. □□ **groan·er** *n.* **groan·ing·ly** *adv.*

■ *v.* 1 moan, sigh, wail. 2 grumble, moan, *colloq.* gripe, grouse, *sl.* beef. 3 be weighed down, be overloaded; be burdened *or* pressured, be overwhelmed. ● *n.* moan, sigh.

gro·cer /grōsər/ *n.* dealer in food and household provisions.

gro·cer·y /grōsəree/ *n.* (*pl.* **-ies**) 1 grocer's trade or store. 2 [in *pl.*] provisions, esp. food, sold by a grocer.

■ 2 see PROVISION *n.* 2.

grog /grog/ *n.* drink of liquor (orig. rum) and water.

grog·gy /grōgee/ *adj.* (**grog·gi·er, grog·gi·est**) unsteady; dazed. □□ **grog·gi·ly** *adv.* **grog·gi·ness** *n.*

■ shaky, weak, dizzy, confused, *colloq.* dopey, woozy.

groin /groyn/ ● *n.* 1 depression between the belly and the thigh. 2 *Archit.* a edge formed by intersecting vaults. b arch supporting a vault. ● *v.tr. Archit.* build with groins.

grom·met /grómit/ *n.* (also **grum·met** /grúmit/) metal, plastic, or rubber eyelet placed in a hole to protect or insulate a rope or cable, etc., passed through it.

groom /grōōm/ ● *n.* 1 = BRIDEGROOM. 2 caretaker of horses. ● *v.tr.* 1 a curry or tend (a horse). b give a neat appearance to (a person, etc.). 2 (of an ape, etc.) clean and comb the fur of (its fellow). 3 prepare or train (a person) for a particular purpose (*was groomed for the top job*).

■ *n.* 2 stableboy, stable girl, stableman, stable lad. ● *v.* 1 spruce up, dress, preen. 2 see CLEAN *v.* 1. 3 fit, coach, tutor.

groove /grōōv/ ● *n.* 1 channel or hollow. 2 established routine or habit. ● *v.* 1 *tr.* make a groove or grooves in. 2 *intr. sl.* a enjoy oneself. b [often foll. by *with*] get on well.

■ *n.* **1** slot, cut, track, channel, furrow. **2** rut, grind, treadmill. • *v.* **1** furrow, flute; see SCORE *v.* 3. **2 a** see *enjoy oneself*.

groov•y /gróōvee/ *adj.* (**groov•i•er, groov•i•est**) *sl.* or *joc.* fashionable and exciting; enjoyable; excellent. □□ **groov'i•ness** *n.*

■ see MARVELOUS 2.

grope /grōp/ • *v.* **1** *intr.* feel about or search blindly or uncertainly with the hands. **2** *intr.* [foll. by *for, after*] search mentally (*was groping for the answer*). **3** *tr.* feel (one's way) toward something. • *n.* process or instance of groping.

■ *v.* **1** fumble; (*grope for*) feel for, fish for. **2** (*grope for*) seek, look for, pursue. • *n.* feel, fumble; searching.

gros•grain /grógrayn/ *n.* corded fabric of silk, rayon, etc.

gross /grōs/ • *adj.* **1** overfed; bloated; repulsively fat. **2** (of a person, manners, or morals) coarse, unrefined, or indecent. **3** flagrant (*gross negligence*). **4** total; without deductions; not net (*gross tonnage*). **5** *sl.* repulsive; disgusting. • *v.tr.* produce or earn as gross profit or income. • *n.* (*pl.* same) amount equal to twelve dozen things. □ **gross domestic product** total value of goods produced and services provided in a country in one year. **gross national product** gross domestic product plus the total of net income from abroad. **gross out** *sl.* disgust, esp. by repulsive or obscene behavior. □□ **gross'ly** *adv.* **gross'ness** *n.*

■ *adj.* **1** overweight, bulky; see also OBESE. **2** vulgar, inappropriate, rude, obscene, **3** outrageous, blatant, obvious. **4** entire, overall, pretax. **5** revolting, nauseating, *sl.* yucky. • *v.* bring in, make; see also EARN 1. □ **gross out** see DISGUST *v.*

gro•tesque /grōtésk/ • *adj.* **1** comically or repulsively distorted. **2** incongruous; absurd. • *n.* decorative form interweaving human and animal features. □□ **gro•tesque'ly** *adv.* **gro•tesque'ness** *n.*

■ *adj.* **1** deformed, unnatural, monstrous. **2** ludicrous, bizarre, outlandish, *colloq.* crazy, insane. • *n.* gargoyle; cartoon.

grot•to /grótō/ *n.* (*pl.* **-toes** or **-tos**) **1** small, esp. picturesque cave. **2** artificial ornamental cave.

■ see CAVE *n.* 1.

grouch /growch/ *colloq.* • *v.intr.* grumble. • *n.* discontented person. □□ **grouch'y** *adj.*

■ *v.* see COMPLAIN 1, 2b. • *n.* see KILLJOY.

ground¹ /grownd/ • *n.* **1 a** surface of the earth. **b** part of this specified in some way (*low ground*). **2** substance of the earth's surface; soil; earth (*stony ground, dug deep into the ground*). **3 a** position, area, or distance on the earth's surface. **b** extent of activity, etc., achieved or of a subject dealt with (*the book covers a lot of ground*). **4** [often in *pl.*] foundation, motive, or reason (*there is ground for concern*). **5** designated area (*often in comb.: fishing-grounds*). **6** [in *pl.*] land attached to a house, etc. **7** area or basis for consideration, agreement, etc. (*common ground*). **8** [in *pl.*] solid particles, esp. of coffee, forming a residue. **9** *Electr.* connection to the ground that completes an electrical circuit. • *v.* **1** *tr.*

a refuse authority for (a pilot or an aircraft) to fly. **b** restrict (esp. a child) from certain activities, places, etc., esp. as a form of punishment. **2 a** *tr.* run (a ship) aground; strand. **b** *intr.* (of a ship) run aground. **3** *tr.* instruct thoroughly (in a subject). **4** *tr.* (often as **grounded** *adj.*) base (a principle, conclusion, etc.) on. **5** *tr. Electr.* connect to the ground. □ **break new** (or **fresh**) **ground** treat a subject previously not dealt with. **get off the ground** *colloq.* make a successful start. **ground control** personnel directing the landing, etc., of aircraft or spacecraft. **ground cover** plants covering the surface of the soil, esp. low-growing spreading plants that inhibit the growth of weeds. **ground floor** floor of a building at ground level. **ground speed** aircraft's speed relative to the ground. **ground swell 1** heavy sea caused by a storm or earthquake. **2** = GROUND-SWELL. **hold one's ground** not retreat or give way. **on the grounds of** because of.

■ *n.* **1 a** (dry) land, solid ground, terra firma. **b** land, terrain, country, territory. **2** sod, loam, clay, dirt. **3** range, scope, territory. **4** justification, rationale, argument, cause, excuse. **7** foundation, footing, position. **8** (*grounds*) dregs, settlings; sediment, deposit. • *v.* **3** teach, train, coach, prepare. **4** establish, found, organize; see also BASE¹ *v.* 1. □ **get off the ground** see START *v.* 1, 2. **hold one's ground** stand firm, stand pat, *colloq.* stick to one's guns; see also PERSEVERE. □□ **ground'less** see GROUNDLESS.

ground² *past* and *past part.* of GRIND.

ground•break•ing /grówndbrayking/ *adj.* innovative in character; pioneering (*groundbreaking techniques in communication*).

ground•ing /grównding/ *n.* basic training or instruction.

■ see BACKGROUND 3.

ground•less /grówndlis/ *adj.* without motive or foundation.

■ baseless, unsupported; hypothetical, imaginary; unsound, unjustified, unreasonable.

grounds•keep•er /grówndzkeepər, grównz-/ *n.* person who maintains the grounds of a property, as a golf course or park.

ground•swell /grówndswel/ *n.* surge of feeling or support.

ground•water /grówndwáwtər, -wotər/ *n.* water found in soil or in pores, crevices, etc., in rock.

ground•work /grówndwork/ *n.* **1** preliminary or basic work. **2** foundation or basis.

■ **1** spadework, preparation(s). **2** underpinning(s), cornerstone; see also FOUNDATION 3, BASIS 1, 2.

group /groōp/ • *n.* persons or things located close together, or considered or classed together. • *v.* **1** *tr. & intr.* form or be formed into a group. **2** *tr.* place in a group or groups. **3** *tr.* classify. □ **group therapy** therapy in which patients with a similar condition are brought together to assist one another psychologically. □□ **group'ing** *n.*

■ *n.* batch, set, collection, assortment; assembly, gathering, congregation, crowd, *colloq* hunch. • *v.* **1, 2** collect, assemble, gather; arrange, organize, bring together. **3** class, sort, rank, categorize, catalog.

group•ie /gróopee/ *n. sl.* ardent follower of touring pop- or rock-music groups, celebrities, or activities.

grouse[1] /grows/ *n.* (*pl.* same) game bird with a plump body and feathered legs.

grouse[2] /grows/ *colloq.* • *v.intr.* grumble or complain pettily. • *n.* complaint.
 ■ *v.* see COMPLAINT 1, 2b. • *n.* see COMPLAINT 2.

grout /growt/ • *n.* thin mortar for filling gaps in tiling, etc. • *v.tr.* provide or fill with grout.
 □□ **grout'er** *n.*

grove /gröv/ *n.* small wood or group of trees.
 ■ see THICKET.

grov•el /gróvəl/ *v.intr.* (**grov•eled, grov•el•ing; grov•elled, grov•el•ling**) **1** behave obsequiously. **2** lie prone in abject humility.
 □□ **grov'el•er** *n.* **grov'el•ing** *adj.*
 ■ **1** see TRUCKLE *v.* **2** see PROSTRATE *v.* 2.
 □□ **groveling** fawning, submissive, cringing, sniveling, *colloq.* bootlicking.

grow /grō/ *v.* (*past* **grew** /grōo/; *past part.* **grown** /grōn/) **1** *intr.* increase in size, height, quantity, degree, etc. **2** *intr.* **a** develop or exist as a living plant or natural product. **b** develop in a specific way or direction (*began to grow sideways*). **c** germinate; sprout; spring up. **3** *intr.* be produced; come naturally into existence; arise. **4** *intr.* [foll. by *on*] become gradually more favored by. **5** *tr.* **a** produce (plants, fruit, wood, etc.) by cultivation. **b** bring forth. **c** cause (a beard, etc.) to develop. **6** *tr.* [in *passive*; foll. by *over, up*] be covered with a growth. □ **grown-up** *adj.* adult. *n.* adult person. **grow up 1** mature. **2** [esp. in *imper.*] begin to behave sensibly.
 □□ **grow'er** *n.*
 ■ **1** develop, enlarge, expand, extend, spread, lengthen, multiply, intensify. **2 a,** **b** blive. **c** see SPRING *v.* 4. **3** develop, evolve, spring (up), begin; see also OCCUR 1. **4** (*grow on*) become accepted by, become more pleasing to. **5 a** plant, sow; breed, raise, propagate. **6** (*be grown over*) be overgrown.
 □ **grown-up** (*adj.*) see MATURE *adj.* 1.

growl /growl/ • *v.* **1** *intr.* **a** (esp. of a dog) make a low guttural sound, usu. of anger. **b** murmur angrily. **2** *intr.* rumble. **3** *tr.* [often foll. by *out*] utter with a growl. • *n.* **1** growling sound. **2** angry murmur; complaint. **3** rumble.
 ■ *v.* **1, 3** see ROAR *v.*

growth /grōth/ *n.* **1** act or process of growing. **2** increase in size or value. **3** something that has grown or is growing. **4** *Med.* abnormal mass of tissue, as a tumor, wart, etc.
 ■ **1** development, evolution; increase, expansion, proliferation, flowering. **2** advance, appreciation, improvement. **3** vegetation; see also SPREAD *n.* 1. **4** lump, swelling.

grub /grub/ • *n.* **1** larva of an insect. **2** *colloq.* food. • *v.* (**grubbed, grub•bing**) **1** *tr.* & *intr.* dig superficially. **2** *tr.* extract (information, etc.) by searching in books, etc.
 ■ *n.* **2** see FOOD 1.

grub•by /grúbee/ *adj.* (**grub•bi•er, grub•bi•est**) dirty. □□ **grub'bi•ly** *adv.* **grub'bi•ness** *n.*

grub•stake /grúbstayk/ • *n.* material or provisions supplied to an enterprise in return for a share in the profits (orig. in prospecting for ore). • *v.tr.* provide with a grubstake.

grudge /gruj/ • *n.* persistent feeling of ill will or resentment (*bears a grudge against me*). • *v.tr.* be resentfully unwilling to give, grant, or allow (a thing). □□ **grudg'ing** *adj.*
 ■ *n.* bitterness, rancor, hard feelings, animosity, malice; grievance, aversion. • *v.* see BEGRUDGE 1, 2, MIND *v.* 1.

gru•el /gróoəl/ *n.* liquid food of oatmeal, etc., chiefly for invalids.

gruel•ing /gróoəling/ *adj.* extremely demanding, severe, or tiring. □□ **gruel'ing•ly** *adv.*
 ■ see ARDUOUS.

grue•some /gróosəm/ *adj.* horrible; grisly; disgusting. □□ **grue'some•ly** *adv.* **grue'some•ness** *n.*
 ■ ghastly, repugnant, hideous, revolting, repulsive, grotesque, shocking, terrible, *colloq.* awful.

gruff /gruf/ *adj.* **1 a** (of a voice) low and harsh. **b** (of a person) having a gruff voice. **2** surly. See synonym study at BRUSQUE.
 □□ **gruff'ly** *adv.* **gruff'ness** *n.*
 ■ **1** throaty, hoarse, husky. **2** grumpy, cantankerous, rude, irritable, cross, abrupt, short-tempered, *colloq.* grouchy.

grum•ble /grúmbəl/ • *v.* **1** *intr.* complain peevishly; be discontented. **2** *intr.* **a** murmur; growl faintly. **b** rumble. **3** *tr.* [often foll. by *out*] utter complainingly. • *n.* **1** complaint. **2** rumble. □□ **grum'bler** *n.* **grum'bling** *adj.* **grum'bling•ly** *adv.*
 ■ *v.* **1, 3** see COMPLAIN 1, 2b. • *n.* **1** see COMPLAINT 2.

grump•y /grúmpee/ *adj.* (**grump•i•er, grump•i•est**) morosely irritable; surly.
 □□ **grump'i•ly** *adv.* **grump'i•ness** *n.*
 ■ see SURLY.

grunge /grunj/ *n. sl.* **1** grime; dirt. **2** aggressive style of rock music characterized by a raucous guitar sound. **3** style of youthful clothing and appearance marked by studied dishevelment. □□ **grun'gy** *adj.*

grunt /grunt/ • *n.* **1** low guttural sound made by a pig. **2** similar sound. • *v.* **1** *intr.* (of a pig) make a grunt or grunts. **2** *intr.* (of a person) make a low inarticulate sound resembling this, esp. to express discontent, dissent, fatigue, etc. **3** *tr.* utter with a grunt.

Gru•yère /gröo-yáir, gree-/ *n.* firm pale cheese made from cow's milk.

gr. wt. *abbr.* gross weight.

Gt. Brit. *abbr.* Great Britain.

gua•ca•mo•le /gwaäkəmólee/ *n.* dip or garnish of mashed avocado mixed with chopped onion, tomatoes, chili peppers, and seasoning.

gua•no /gwaänō/ (*pl.* **–nos**) *n.* excrement of sea birds, bats, etc., used as fertilizer.
 ■ see DUNG *n.*

Gua•ra•ni /gwaäränee/ *n.* **1 a** member of a S. American Indian people. **b** language of this people. **2** (**guarani**) monetary unit of Paraguay.

guar•an•tee /gárəntee/ • n. **1 a** formal promise or assurance, esp. of quality or performance. **b** document assuring this. **2** = GUARANTY. • v.tr. (**guar•an•tees, guar•an•teed**) **1 a** give or serve as a guarantee for. **b** assure the permanence, etc., of. **c** provide with a guarantee. **2** give a promise or assurance.

■ n. pledge; warranty, bond, security. • v. **1** vouch for, stand behind; ensure, certify. **2** pledge, swear, attest.

guar•an•tor /gárəntáwr, –tər/ n. person who gives a guarantee or guaranty.

guar•an•ty /gárəntee/ n. (pl. **–ties**) **1** written or other undertaking to answer for the payment of a debt or for the performance of an obligation by another person liable in the first instance. **2** thing serving as security for a guaranty.

guard /gaard/ • v. **1** tr. watch over and defend or protect. **2** tr. supervise (prisoners, etc.) and prevent from escaping. **3** tr. keep (thoughts or speech) in check. **4** tr. provide with safeguards. **5** intr. take precautions. • n. **1** state of vigilance. **2** person who protects or keeps watch. **3** soldiers, etc., protecting a place or person; escort. **4** part of an army detached for some purpose (advance guard). **5** thing that protects or defends. **6** in some sports. **a** protective or defensive player. **b** defensive posture or motion.

■ v. **1** shield; safeguard, supervise. **2** see SUPERVISE. **3** see CONTROL v. **2. 5** see PREPARE 1. • n. **1** watch, alert, lookout. **2** sentry, security guard; guardian; bodyguard. **3** convoy, patrol, see also ESCORT n. 1. **4** see SQUAD. **5** shield, screen, cover. **6 a** back, defender; collect. defense; see also BACK n. 4.

guard•ed /gáardid/ adj. (of a remark, etc.) cautious; avoiding commitment □□ **guard'ed•ly** adv.

■ careful, prudent, wary; colloq. cagey.

guard•i•an /gáardeeən/ n. **1** defender, protector, or keeper. **2** person having legal custody of another, esp. a minor. □□ **guard'i•an•ship** n.

■ preserver, custodian, ward; trustee. □□ **guardianship** see CARE n. 4.

guard•rail /gáardrayl/ n. rail, e.g., a handrail, fitted as a support or to prevent an accident.

gua•va /gwáavə/ n. **1** small tropical American tree bearing an edible pale yellow fruit with pink juicy flesh. **2** this fruit.

gu•ber•na•to•ri•al /góobərnətáwreeəl, gyóo–/ adj. of or relating to a governor.

guer•ril•la /gərílə/ n. (also **gue•ril'la**) member of a small, independent (usu. political) group taking part in irregular fighting.

■ partisan, freedom fighter, resistance or underground fighter; insurgent, revolutionary, saboteur, terrorist.

guess /ges/ • v. **1** tr. [often absol.] estimate without calculation or measurement, or on the basis of inadequate data. **2** tr. form a hypothesis or opinion about; conjecture; think likely (cannot guess how you did it). **3** tr. conjecture or estimate correctly (you have to guess the weight). **4** intr. make a conjecture about. • n. estimate or conjecture.

■ v. **1, 4** colloq. make a stab (at). **2** surmise,

infer, deduce, conclude; believe, reckon, feel, speculate. • n. assumption, supposition, shot in the dark, colloq. guesstimate.

guess•work /géswərk/ n. process of or results got by guessing.

guest /gest/ • n. **1** person invited to visit, have a meal, etc., at the expense of the inviter. **2** person lodging at a hotel, boardinghouse, etc. **3 a** outside performer invited to take part with regular performers. **b** person who takes part by invitation in a radio or television program (often attrib.: guest artist). • v.intr. be a guest on a radio or television show or in a theatrical performance, etc.

■ n. **1** caller; (guests) company. **2** patron, customer, roomer. **3b** (attrib.) visiting; outside, external.

guff /guf/ n. sl. empty talk; nonsense.

guf•faw /gufáw/ • n. loud or boisterous laugh. • v. **1** intr. utter a guffaw. **2** tr. say with a guffaw.

■ n. see LAUGH n. 1. • v. see LAUGH v. 1.

guid•ance /gíd'ns/ n. **1 a** advice or helpful direction. **b** leadership or direction. **2** guiding or being guided.

■ **1 a** information, counsel, instruction. **b** management, control. **2** counseling, preparation; see INSTRUCTION 2.

guide /gīd/ • n. **1** person who leads or shows the way. **2** person who conducts tours, etc. **3** adviser. **4** directing principle (one's feelings are a bad guide). **5** book with essential information on a subject, esp. = GUIDEBOOK. **6** thing marking a position. • v.tr. **1** act as guide to. **2** be the principle, motive, or ground of (an action, judgment, etc.). **3** direct the affairs of (a government, etc.). □ **guided missile** missile directed to its target by remote control or by equipment within itself. **guide dog** dog trained to guide a blind person.

■ n. **1–2** leader, conductor, director. **3** mentor, counselor, teacher. **4** standard, model, criterion, ideal. **5** handbook, manual. **6** beacon, guiding light, signal, sign, landmark, signpost. • v. **1, 3** lead, conduct, steer; instruct, train, counsel; supervise, oversee, manage. **2** steer, influence; see also MOTIVATE.

guide•book /gídbŏŏk/ n. book of information about a place for visitors, tourists, etc.

guide•line /gídlīn/ n. principle directing action.

■ see STANDARD n. 1.

guild /gild/ n. **1** association of people for mutual aid or the pursuit of a common goal. **2** medieval association of craftsmen or merchants.

■ see ASSOCIATION 1.

guild•er /gíldər/ n. chief monetary unit of the Netherlands.

guile /gīl/ n. deceit; cunning or sly behavior. □□ **guile'ful** adj. **guile'less** adj.

■ see DECEIT 1.

guil•lo•tine /gíləteen, geeə–/ • n. machine with a heavy knife blade that drops vertically, used for beheading. • v.tr. use a guillotine on.

guilt /gilt/ n. **1** fact of having committed a specified or implied offense. **2 a** culpability. **b** feeling of this. □□ **guilt'less** adj.
■ **1** sinfulness, wrongdoing, misconduct. **2 a** blame; responsibility. **b** remorse, regret, contrition, shame.

guilt•y /giltee/ adj. (**guilt•i•er, guilt•i•est**) **1** responsible for a wrong. **2** affected by guilt (a guilty conscience). **3** concerning guilt (a guilty secret). **4** having committed a (specified) offense. □□ **guilt'i•ly** adv. **guilt'i•ness** n.
■ **1, 4** culpable, blameworthy; answerable; at fault. **2** shamefaced, red-faced; remorseful, sorry. **3** see SORDID 2.

guin•ea /ginee/ n. former British gold coin worth 21 shillings, first coined for the African trade. □ **guinea fowl** African fowl with slate-colored, white-spotted plumage. **guinea pig 1** domesticated S. American rodent, kept as a pet or for research in biology, etc. **2** subject used in an experiment.

guise /giz/ n. **1** assumed appearance; pretense (in the guise of, under the guise of). **2** garb.
■ **1** disguise, pretense; see MASK n. 3. **2** see DRESS n. 2.

gui•tar /gitaar/ n. usu. six-stringed musical instrument played with the fingers or a plectrum. □□ **gui•tar'ist** n.

Gu•ja•ra•ti /goֹbjəraàtee/ • n. (pl. **Gu•ja•ra•tis**) **1** language of Gujarat in W. India. **2** native of Gujarat. • adj. of or relating to Gujarat or its language.

gulch /gulch/ n. ravine, esp. one in which a torrent flows.
■ see RAVINE.

gulf /gulf/ • n. **1** deep ocean inlet with a narrow mouth. **2** (the Gulf) **a** Gulf of Mexico. **b** Persian Gulf. **3** deep hollow; chasm or abyss. **4** wide difference of feelings, opinion, etc. • v.tr. engulf; swallow up. □ **Gulf Stream** warm ocean current flowing from the Gulf of Mexico toward Europe.
■ n. **1** cove, firth, fiord; bay. **3** depths; rift, gap; void, breach. **4** rift, gap; difference, conflict. • v. see SWALLOW[1] v. 5.

gull[1] /gul/ n. long-winged, web-footed sea bird usu. having white plumage with a mantle varying from pearly gray to black, and a bright bill.

gull[2] /gul/ v.tr. [usu. in passive; foll. by into] dupe; fool.
■ see DUPE n.

gul•let /gúlit/ n. **1** esophagus. **2** throat.

gul•li•ble /gúlibəl/ adj. easily persuaded or deceived; credulous. □□ **gul•li•bil'i•ty** n. **gul'lib•ly** adv.
■ unsuspecting, unwary; innocent, green, unsophisticated.

CALLOW, CREDULOUS, INGENUOUS, NAÏVE, TRUSTING, UNSOPHISTICATED. Some people will believe anything. Those who are truly **gullible** are the easiest to deceive, which is why they so often make fools of themselves. Those who are merely **credulous** might be a little too quick to believe something, but they usually aren't stupid enough to act on it. **Trusting** suggests the same willingness to believe (a trusting child), but it isn't necessarily a bad way to be (a person so trusting he completely disarmed his enemies). No one likes to be called **naïve** because it implies a lack of street smarts (she's so naïve, she'd accept a ride from a stranger), but when applied to things other than people, it can describe a simplicity and absence of artificiality that is quite charming (the naïve style in which 19th-century American portraits were often painted). Most people would rather be thought of as **ingenuous**, meaning straightforward and sincere (an ingenuous confession of the truth), because it implies the simplicity of a child without the negative overtones. **Callow**, however, comes down a little more heavily on the side of immaturity and almost always goes hand-in-hand with youth. Whether young or old, someone who is **unsophisticated** suffers because of lack of experience.

gull•y /gúlee/ • n. (pl. **–ies**) **1** waterworn ravine. **2** deep artificial channel; gutter or drain. • v.tr. (**–ies, –ied**) **1** form (channels) by water action. **2** make gullies in.
■ n. **1** channel, gorge, canyon, gulch. **2** see DRAIN n. 1a. • v. see FURROW v. 2a.

gulp /gulp/ • v. **1** tr. swallow hastily or greedily. **2** intr. swallow with difficulty. **3** tr. [foll. by down, back] stifle; suppress (esp. tears). • n. **1** act of gulping (drained it at one gulp). **2** large mouthful of a drink.
■ v. **1** gobble, wolf, devour. **2** choke, gasp (for breath). **3** see STIFLE 1. • n. **1** slurp, sip, colloq. swig. **2** swallow.

gum[1] /gum/ • n. **1 a** viscous secretion of some trees and shrubs that hardens on drying but is soluble in water (cf. RESIN). **b** adhesive substance. **2** chewing gum. • v.tr. (**gummed, gum•ming**) **1** smear or cover with gum. **2** fasten with gum. □ **gum arabic** gum exuded by some kinds of acacia and used as glue and in incense. **gum up 1** (of a mechanism, etc.) become clogged or obstructed with stickiness. **2** colloq. interfere with the smooth running of (gum up the works). □□ **gum'my** adj. (**gum•mi•er, gum•mi•est**).
■ n. **1 b** see GLUE n. • v. **2** see GLUE v.

gum[2] /gum/ n. [usu. in pl.] firm flesh around the roots of the teeth.

gum•bo /gúmbō/ n. (pl. **–bos**) soup thickened with okra pods.

gum•drop /gúmdrop/ n. soft, flavored candy made with gelatin or gum arabic.

gump•tion /gúmpshən/ n. colloq. **1** resourcefulness; initiative. **2** common sense.
■ **1** enterprise, backbone, courage, nerve, spirit, colloq. grit, spunk, guts. **2** shrewdness, cleverness, colloq. horse sense.

gum•shoe /gúmshoō/ n. sl. detective.

gun /gun/ • n. **1** weapon consisting of a metal tube and with a grip at one end, from which bullets, etc., are propelled with explosive force. **2** device imitative of this, e.g., a starting pistol. **3** device for discharging insecticide, grease, electrons, etc. **4** gunman.

• v. (**gunned, gun•ning**) **1** tr. **a** shoot (a person) with a gun. **b** shoot at with a gun. **2** tr. colloq. accelerate (an engine or vehicle). **3** intr. [foll. by *for*] seek out determinedly to attack or rebuke. □ **go great guns** colloq. proceed vigorously or successfully. **stick to one's guns** colloq. maintain one's position under attack.

■ n. **1** see REVOLVER. **4** sl. hit man, gunslinger. • v. **2** speed up; (*gun it*) colloq. step on it, step on the gas. □ **stick to one's guns** see PERSEVERE.

gun•boat /gúnbōt/ n. small vessel with heavy guns.

gun•fight /gúnfīt/ n. fight with firearms. □□ **gun'fight•er** n.

gun•fire /gúnfīr/ n. **1** firing of a gun or guns. **2** the noise from this.

gung-ho /gúnghō/ adj. enthusiastic, eager.

gunk /gungk/ n. sl. viscous or liquid material.

■ see MUCK n. 1, 2.

gun•man /gúnmən/ n. (*pl.* **-men**) man armed with a gun, esp. in committing a crime.

gun•met•al /gúnmetəl/ n. **1** dull bluish gray color. **2** alloy of copper and tin or zinc (formerly used for guns).

gun•nel var. of GUNWALE.

gun•ner /gúnər/ n. **1** artillery soldier. **2** Naut. warrant officer in charge of a battery, magazine, etc. **3** member of an aircraft crew who operates a gun.

gun•ner•y /gúnəree/ n. **1** construction and management of large guns. **2** firing of guns.

gun•ny /gúnee/ n. (*pl.* **-nies**) **1** coarse sacking, usu. of jute fiber. **2** sack made of this.

gun•pow•der /gúnpowdər/ n. explosive made of saltpeter, sulfur, and charcoal, used in cartridges, fireworks, etc.

gun•run•ner /gúnrunər/ n. person engaged in smuggling firearms. □□ **gun'run•ning** n.

gun•shot /gúnshot/ n. **1** shot fired from a gun. **2** range of a gun (*within gunshot*).

gun•smith /gúnsmith/ n. person who makes, sells, and repairs small firearms.

gun•wale /gúnəl/ n. (also **gun'nel**) upper edge of the side of a boat or ship.

gup•py /gúpee/ n. (*pl.* **-pies**) freshwater fish of the W. Indies and S. America, frequently kept in aquariums, and giving birth to live young.

gur•gle /gárgəl/ • v. **1** intr. make a bubbling sound as of water. **2** tr. utter with such a sound. • n. gurgling sound.

■ v. **1** babble, ripple, splash. • n. burble, bubble, glug.

gu•ru /gŏorŏo/ n. **1** Hindu spiritual teacher or head of a religious sect. **2 a** influential teacher. **b** revered mentor.

■ see TEACHER.

gush /gush/ • v. **1** tr. & intr. emit or flow in a sudden and copious stream. **2** intr. speak or behave effusively. • n. **1** sudden or copious stream. **2** effusive or sentimental manner. □□ **gush'ing** adj. **gush'y** adj.

■ v. **1** cascade, rush, flood. **2** effervesce, bubble over, colloq. enthuse. • n. **1** rush, flood, flow; outburst. **2** animation; see *exuberance* (EXUBERANT).

gush•er /gúshər/ n. **1** oil well from which oil

flows without being pumped. **2** effusive person.

gus•set /gúsit/ n. piece inserted into a garment, etc., to strengthen or enlarge it. □□ **gus'set•ed** adj.

gust /gust/ • n. **1** sudden strong rush of wind. **2** burst of rain, fire, smoke, or sound. **3** passionate outburst. • v.intr. blow in gusts. □□ **gust'y** adj.

■ n. **1** blast, blow; see also BREEZE n. 1. **2** spurt, wave; see also OUTBURST. **3** see OUTBURST. • v. puff, waft, blast.

gus•to /gústō/ n. (*pl.* **-toes**) zest; enjoyment or vigor.

■ zeal, eagerness, delight, satisfaction; relish, appetite, liking.

gut /gut/ • n. **1** intestine. **2** [in *pl.*] the bowel or entrails. **3** [in *pl.*] colloq. personal courage. **4** colloq. stomach; belly. **5** [in *pl.*] **a** contents. **b** essence, e.g., of an issue or problem. **6 a** material for violin or racket strings or surgical use. **b** material for fishing lines. **7** [*attrib.*] **a** instinctive (*gut reaction*). **b** fundamental (*a gut issue*). • v.tr. (**gut•ted, gut•ting**) **1** remove or destroy the interior of (a house, etc.). **2** take out the guts of (a fish, etc.). **3** extract the essence of (a book, etc.).

■ n. **1, 2** alimentary canal; (*guts*) viscera, vitals, colloq. innards. **3** (*guts*) backbone, bravery, spirit, colloq. grit, spunk. **4** (*guts*) abdomen, beer belly, colloq. tummy; see also STOMACH n. 2. **5** (*guts*) see SUBSTANCE 1. **7** (*attrib.*) **a** basic, heartfelt, intuitive. **b** see FUNDAMENTAL adj. • v. **1** devastate, ravage; strip, empty, sl. clean out. **2** disembowel, dress, clean. **3** see DIGEST v. 3.

gut•less /gútlis/ adj. colloq. lacking courage.

■ see SPINELESS 2.

gut•sy /gútsee/ adj. (**gut•si•er, gut•si•est**) colloq. courageous. □□ **gut'si•ness** n.

■ see BRAVE adj. 1.

gut•ter /gútər/ • n. **1** shallow trough along the eaves of a house, or channel at the side of a street, to carry off rainwater. **2** [*prec. by the*] poor or degraded background or environment. • v. **1** intr. flow in streams. **2** tr. furrow; channel. **3** intr. (of a candle) melt away rapidly.

■ n. **1** see DRAIN n. 1a.

gut•ter•snipe /gútərsnīp/ n. street urchin.

■ waif, ragamuffin, gamin.

gut•tur•al /gútərəl/ • adj. **1** throaty, harsh sounding. **2 a** Phonet. (of a consonant) produced in the throat or by the back of the tongue and palate. **b** of the throat. • n. Phonet. guttural consonant (e.g., *k*, *g*). □□ **gut'tur•al•ly** adv.

■ adj. **1** see GRUFF 1a.

guy[1] /gī/ n. **1** colloq. man; fellow. **2** [usu. in *pl.*] person of either sex.

■ **1** colloq. chap, dude, sl. geezer. **2** individual, human (being), (*guys*) people, folk(s).

guy[2] /gī/ • n. rope or chain to secure a tent or steady a load, etc. • v.tr. secure with a guy or guys.

guz•zle /gúzəl/ v. eat or drink greedily. □□ **guz'zler** n.

■ see SCOFF[2] v.

gybe /jīb/ var. of JIBE[2].

gym /jim/ *n. colloq.* **1** gymnasium. **2** physical education.

gym•na•si•um /jimnáyzeeəm/ *n.* (*pl.* **gym•na•si•ums** or **gym•na•si•a** /–zeeə/) room or building equipped for indoor sports or training.

gym•nas•tics /jimnástiks/ *n.pl.* [also treated as *sing.*] **1** exercises developing or displaying physical agility and coordination, usu. in competition. **2** other forms of physical or mental agility. □□ **gym′nast** *n.* **gym•nas′tic** *adj.* **gym•nas′ti•cal•ly** *adv.*

■ **1** see EXERCISE *n.* 3.

gym•no•sperm /jímnəspərm/ *n.* plants having seeds unprotected by an ovary, including conifers, ginkgos, etc. (opp. ANGIOSPERM).

gyn. *abbr.* (also **gynecol.**) **1** gynecological. **2** gynecologist. **3** gynecology.

gy•ne•col•o•gy /gínikóləjee, jínə–/ *n.* the science and medical specialty of the physiological functions and diseases of women and girls, esp. those affecting the reproductive system. □□ **gy•ne•co•log′i•cal** *adj.* **gy•ne•col′o•gist** *n.*

gyp /jip/ *sl.* • *v.tr.* (**gypped, gyp•ping**) cheat; swindle. • *n.* act of cheating; swindle.

gyp•sum /jípsəm/ *n.* form of calcium sulfate used to make plaster of Paris and in the building industry.

Gyp•sy /jípsee/ *n.* (also **Gip′sy**) (*pl.* **–sies**) **1** member of a nomadic people of Hindu origin with dark skin and hair. **2** (**gypsy**) person resembling or living like a Gypsy. □ **gypsy moth** tussock moth of which the larvae are very destructive to foliage.

■ **1** Romany. **2** (**gypsy**) see MIGRANT *n.*

gy•rate /jírayt/ *v.intr.* (also /jīráyt/) go in a circle or spiral; revolve; whirl. □□ **gy•ra•tion** /–ráyshən/ *n.* **gy′ra•tor** *n.* **gy•ra•to•ry** /–rətáwree/ *adj.*

■ rotate, spin, twirl, pirouette; swivel, turn.

gy•ro /jírō/ *n.* (*pl.* **–ros**) **1** Greek-style roasted lamb served in pita bread. **2** *colloq.* = GYROSCOPE.

gyro– /jírō/ *comb. form* rotation.

gy•ro•scope /jírəskōp/ *n.* rotating wheel whose axis is free to turn but maintains a fixed direction despite change of position, esp. used for stabilization or with the compass in an aircraft, ship, etc. □□ **gy•ro•scop•ic** /–skópik/ *adj.* **gy•ro•scop′i•cal•ly** *adv.*

Hh

H[1] /aych/ *n.* (also **h**) (*pl.* **Hs** or **H's**; **h's**) **1** eighth letter of the alphabet (see AITCH). **2** anything having the form of an H (esp. in *comb.*: *H-girder*).

H[2] *symb. Chem.* hydrogen.

h. *abbr.* **1** hecto–. **2** height. **3** horse. **4** hot. **5** hour(s). **6** husband. **7** Planck's constant. **8** *Baseball* hit; hits.

Ha *symb. Chem.* hahnium.

ha /haa/ *int.* (also **hah**) expressing surprise, suspicion, triumph, etc. (cf. HA HA).

ha•be•as cor•pus /háybeeəs káwrpəs/ *n.* writ requiring a person to be brought before a court, esp. to investigate the lawfulness of the detention.

hab•er•dash•er /hábərdashər/ *n.* dealer in men's clothing. □□ **hab′er•dash•er•y** *n.* (*pl.* **–ies**)

ha•bil•i•ment /həbílimənt/ *n.* [usu. in *pl.*] clothes.

hab•it /hábit/ *n.* **1** settled or regular tendency or practice (*has a habit of ignoring me*). **2** practice that is hard to give up. **3** mental constitution or attitude. **4** *colloq.* addiction. **5 a** dress, esp. of a religious order. **b** (in full **rid′ing hab•it**) woman's riding dress. □ **habit-forming** addictive.

■ **1** disposition, inclination, bent; custom, routine, ritual; way, mannerism. **2, 4** compulsion, obsession, vice; dependence. **3** see ATTITUDE 1. **5 a** costume, uniform, livery; *colloq.* gear, getup; clothes, garments. □ **habit-forming** compulsive, (*of a drug*) hard; see *obsessive* (OBSESS).

hab•it•a•ble /hábitəbəl/ *adj.* suitable for living in. □□ **hab•it•a•bil′i•ty** *n.*

■ livable, inhabitable.

hab•i•tat /hábitat/ *n.* natural home of an organism.

■ domain, range, environment; habitation; see ABODE[1].

hab•i•ta•tion /hábitáyshən/ *n.* **1** inhabiting. **2** house or home.

■ **2** see HOME *n.* 1.

ha•bit•u•al /həbíchōōəl/ *adj.* **1** done constantly or as a habit. **2** regular; usual. **3** given to a (specified) habit. □□ **ha•bit′u•al•ly** *adv.*

■ **1** persistent, continual; automatic, obsessive. **2** settled, ingrained, routine. **3** inveterate, confirmed, compulsive.

ha•bit•u•ate /həbíchōō-ayt/ *v.tr.* accustom; make used to something. □□ **ha•bit•u•a•tion** /–áyshən/ *n.*

ha•bit•u•é /həbíchōō-áy/ *n.* habitual visitor or resident.

■ frequent visitor, patron, *colloq.* regular; resident.

ha•ček /haáchek/ *n.* (also **há•ček**) diacritic (ˇ) placed over letters to modify the sound in Slavic and Baltic languages.

ha•ci•en•da /haásee-éndə/ *n.* in Spanish-speaking countries, an estate, or specifically the main house of an estate.

hack[1] /hak/ • *v.* **1** *tr.* cut or chop roughly. **2** *intr.* deliver cutting blows. **3** *tr.* cut (one's way) through foliage, etc. **4** *tr.* *colloq.* gain unauthorized access to (data in a computer).

5 *tr. sl.* **a** manage. **b** tolerate. **c** (as **hacked off** *adj.*) annoy; disconcert. • *n.* gash or wound, esp. from a kick. □ **hacking cough** short dry frequent cough.

■ *v.* **1** carve; butcher; (*hack off*) sever. **2** (*hack at*) stab (at); cut. **3** chop, hew. **5 b** see TOLERATE 2, 3. **c** (**hacked off**) see *discontented* (DISCONTENT *v.*). □ **hacking cough** bark.

hack² /hak/ • *n.* **1 a** horse for ordinary riding. **b** horse let out for hire. **2** person hired to do dull routine work, esp. writing. **3** taxi. • *attrib.adj.* **1** used as a hack. **2** typical of a hack. • *v.* **1 a** *intr.* ride on horseback on a road at an ordinary pace. **b** *tr.* ride (a horse) in this way. **2** *tr.* make common. **3** drive a taxi.

■ *n.* **1** mount, hackney, *colloq.* nag. **2** drudge, plodder, slave; see WRITER. **3** see TAXI. ■ *attrib. adj.* **2** commonplace, hackneyed, trite; *colloq.* old hat. • *v.* **2** see PROSTITUTE *v.* 2.

hack•er /hákər/ *n.* **1** person or thing that hacks or cuts roughly. **2** *colloq.* **a** person adept at working with computers. **b** person who gains unauthorized access to computer data. **3** golfer who plays poorly.

hack•le /hákəl/ *n.* **1** feather(s) on the neck of a domestic fowl, etc. **2** [in *pl.*] erectile hairs on an animal's back, which rise when it is angry or alarmed. □ **raise one's hackles** cause a person to be angry or indignant.

hack•ney /háknee/ *n.* (*pl.* **–neys**) **1** horse for ordinary riding. **2** [*attrib.*] designating any of various vehicles kept for hire.

hack•neyed /hákneed/ *adj.* (of a phrase, etc.) made commonplace or trite by overuse.

■ see STALE 2.

hack•saw /háksaw/ *n.* saw with a narrow blade set in a frame, for cutting metal.

had *past* and *past part.* of HAVE.

had•dock /hádək/ *n.* (*pl.* same) N. Atlantic marine fish used as food.

Ha•des /háydeez/ *n.* Gk. *mythol.* the underworld; abode of the spirits of the dead. □□ **Ha•de•an** /–deeən/ *adj.*

haf•ni•um /háfneeəm/ *n.* Chem. silvery lustrous metallic element, used in tungsten alloys for filaments, etc. ¶Symb.: **Hf.**

haft /haft/ • *n.* handle of a dagger, knife, etc. • *v.tr.* provide with a haft.

hag /hag/ *n.* **1** ugly old woman. **2** witch.

■ **1** crone, shrew, *sl. derog.* (old) bag. **2** fury, harpy, sorceress

Hag•ga•dah /həgaádə, –gáwdə, haagaadaá/ *n.* **1** legend, etc., used to illustrate a point of the Law in the Talmud. **2** book recited at the Passover Seder service.

hag•gard /hágərd/ *adj.* looking exhausted and distraught, esp. from fatigue, worry, privation, etc. □□ **hag′gard•ness** *n.*

■ gaunt, drawn, pinched, run-down, weary (-looking), spent, worn out; see also *emaciated* (EMACIATE).

hag•gis /hágis/ *n.* Scottish dish of a sheep's or calf's offal mixed with suet, oatmeal, etc., and boiled in a bag made from the animal's stomach or in an artificial bag.

hag•gle /hágəl/ • *v.intr.* [often foll. by *about, over*] dispute or bargain persistently. • *n.* dispute or wrangle. □□ **hag′gler** *n.*

■ *v.* wrangle, bicker; negotiate, barter. • *n.* see ARGUMENT 1.

hagio- /hágeeō, háyjeeō/ *comb. form* of saints or holiness.

hah var. of HA.

ha ha /haáhaá/ *int.* words representing laughter.

hah•ni•um /haániəm/ *n.* Chem. artificially produced radioactive element. ¶Symb.: **Ha.**

hai•ku /híkoo/ *n.* (*pl.* same) Japanese three-line poem of usu. 17 syllables.

hail¹ /hayl/ • *n.* **1** pellets of frozen rain. **2** [foll. by *of*] barrage or onslaught (of missiles, curses, etc.). • *v.* **1** *intr.* [prec. by *it* as subject] shower down hail (*it is hailing, if it hails*). **2 a** *tr.* pour down (blows, words, etc.). **b** *intr.* come down forcefully.

■ *n.* **1** sleet. **2** volley, storm. • *v.* **1** sleet. **2** rain, shower; pelt.

hail² /hayl/ • *v.* **1** *tr.* greet enthusiastically. **2** *tr.* signal to or attract the attention of (*hailed a taxi*). **3** *tr.* acclaim (*hailed him king, was hailed as a prodigy*). **4** *intr.* originate or come (*she hails from Mexico*). • *n.* greeting or act of hailing.

■ *v.* **1** salute; welcome, receive. **2** call, flag down, stop. **3** acknowledge; cheer, applaud. **4** (*hail from*) be from, be a native of. • *n.* salutation; welcome, reception.

hail•stone /háylstōn/ *n.* pellet of hail.

hail•storm /háylstorm/ *n.* period of heavy hail.

■ see STORM *n.* 1.

hair /hair/ *n.* **1 a** fine threadlike strands growing from the skin of mammals, esp. from the human head. **b** these collectively (*his hair is falling out*). **2** anything resembling a hair. **3** elongated cell growing from a plant. **4** very small extent (also *attrib.: a hair crack*). □ **get in a person's hair** *colloq.* annoy a person. **hair-raising** alarming; terrifying. **hair's breadth** very small amount or margin. **let one's hair down** *colloq.* abandon restraint; behave wildly or freely. **make a person's hair stand on end** alarm or horrify a person. □□ **hair′less** *adj.* **hair′like** *adj.*

■ **1 b** tresses, locks, head of hair, mop, *colloq.* mane. **2** fiber, thread, strand. **4** trifle, fraction, *colloq.* whisker; hair's breadth. □ **get in a person's hair** see ANNOY 1. **hair-raising** see *terrifying* (TERRIFY). **hair's breadth** see HAIR 4 above. **let one's hair down** see REVEL *v.* 1, *enjoy oneself*. **make a person's hair stand on end** see SCARE *v.* 1. □□ **hairless** bald, bald-headed, see also SMOOTH *adj.* 3, *v.*

hair•ball /háirbawl/ *n.* (also **hair′ ball**) ball of hair that accumulates in the stomach of a cat, etc., that grooms itself by licking its fur.

hair•brush /háirbrush/ *n.* brush for arranging the hair.

hair•cut /háirkut/ *n.* style or act of cutting the hair.

hair•do /háirdōō/ *n.* (*pl.* **–dos**) *colloq.* style or act of styling hair.

■ hairstyle, haircut, coiffure, hair, cut.

hair•dress•er /háirdresər/ *n.* person who cuts

and styles hair, esp. professionally. □□ **hair′ dress•ing** n.

hair•line /háirlīn/ n. **1** edge of a person's hair, esp. on the forehead. **2** very thin line or crack, etc.

hair•net /háirnet/ n. piece of netting for confining the hair.

hair•piece /háirpees/ n. quantity or switch of detached hair used to augment a person's natural hair.

hair•pin /háirpin/ n. U-shaped pin for fastening the hair. □ **hairpin turn** sharp U-shaped bend in a road.

hair•split•ting /háirspliting/ adj. & n. quibbling.

■ fussy, hypercritical, petty, finicky, colloq. nitpicking.

hair•style /háirstīl/ n. particular way of arranging or dressing the hair. □□ **hair′styl•ing** n. **hair′styl•ist** n.

hair•y /háiree/ adj. (**hair•i•er, hair•i•est**) **1** made of or covered with hair. **2** having the feel of hair. **3** sl. alarmingly unpleasant or difficult. □□ **hair′i•ness** n.

■ **1** hirsute, shaggy, woolly; whiskered, unshaven. **2** downy, fluffy; rough, bristly. **3** dangerous, risky, uncertain, frightening, colloq. scary; tricky, knotty.

hajj /haj/ n. Islamic pilgrimage to Mecca.

hake /hayk/ n. marine food fish resembling a cod.

hal•berd /hálbərd/ n. (also **hal•bert** /–bərt/) hist. combined spear and battle-ax.

hal•cy•on /hálseeən/ adj. **1** calm; peaceful (halcyon days). **2** (of a period) happy; prosperous. See synonym study at CALM.

■ **1** see CALM adj. 1.

hale /hayl/ adj. strong and healthy (esp. in **hale and hearty**).

■ hearty, fit, sound, hardy, robust, colloq. in the pink.

half /haf/ • n. (pl. **halves** /havz/) **1** either of two equal or corresponding parts or groups into which a thing is or might be divided. **2** Sports either of two equal periods of play. • adj. **1** of an amount or quantity equal to a half, or loosely to a part thought of as a half (take half the men, spent half the time reading, half a pint, a half pint, half-price). **2** forming a half (a half share). • adv. **1** [often in comb.] to the extent of half; partly (only half cooked, half-frozen). **2** to a certain extent; somewhat (esp. in idiomatic phrases: half dead, am half inclined to agree). **3** (in reckoning time) by the amount of half (an hour, etc.) (half past two). □ **half-and-half** being half one thing and half another, esp. a liquid of half cream and half milk. **half-baked 1** incompletely considered or planned. **2** (of enthusiasm, etc.) only partly committed. **3** foolish. **half breed** often offens. person of mixed race. **half brother** brother with only one parent in common. **half-life** Physics & Biochem., etc.,time taken for the radioactivity or some other property of a substance to fall to half its original value. **half-mast** position of a flag halfway down the mast, as a mark of respect for a person who has died. **half sister**

sister with only one parent in common. **half-time** n. **1** time at which half of a game or contest is completed. **2** short interval at this time. adj. working half the usual hours. **half-truth** statement that (esp. deliberately) conveys only part of the truth. **not half 1** not nearly (not half long enough). **2** colloq. not at all (not half bad).

half•back /háfbak/ n. (in some sports) player between the linemen and fullbacks, or behind the forward line.

half•heart•ed /háfhaártid/ adj. lacking enthusiasm. □□ **half•heart′ed•ly** adv. **half′heart′ed•ness** n.

■ feeble, lukewarm, indifferent, unconcerned, uninterested.

half•pen•ny /háypnee/ n. (also **ha′penny**) (pl. **–pen•nies** or **–pence** /háypəns/) (in the UK) former coin worth half a penny. ¶Withdrawn in 1984(cf. FARTHING).

half•tone /háftōn/ n. **1** reproduction printed from a block (produced by photographic means) in which the various tones of gray are produced from small and large black dots. **2** Mus. (**half tone**) semitone.

half•way /háfwáy/ • adv. **1** at a point equidistant between two others (we were halfway to Chicago). **2** to some extent; more or less (is halfway decent). • adj. situated halfway (reached a halfway point). □ **halfway house** facility for assisting ex-prisoners, mental patients, etc., in readjusting to society.

■ adj. see INTERMEDIATE adj.

half•wit /háfwit/ n. colloq. extremely foolish or stupid person. □□ **half′wit′ted** adj.

■ dunce, idiot, simpleton, colloq. moron, imbecile. □□ **halfwitted** silly, inane, feebleminded, colloq. thick, dotty, dumb.

hal•i•but /hálibət/ n. (pl. same) large marine flatfish used as food.

hal•i•to•sis /hálitōsis/ n. bad breath.

hall /hawl/ n. **1 a** space or passage into which the front entrance of a house, etc., opens. **b** corridor or passage in a building. **2** large room or building for meetings, meals, concerts, etc. **3** university residence for students.

■ **1** hallway; entrance (hall), entry(way), lobby, vestibule; foyer. **2** auditorium, theater; lecture hall, concert hall, ballroom; assembly rooms. **3** see ACCOMMODATION 1.

hal•le•lu•jah var. of ALLELUIA.

hall•mark /háwlmaark/ • n. **1** mark of purity, as stamped into gold, silver, and platinum. **2** distinctive feature. • v.tr. **1** stamp with a hallmark. **2** designate as excellent.

■ n. **1** sign, symbol; plate mark, assay mark. **2** stamp, mark.

hal•low /hálō/ v.tr. **1** make holy; consecrate. **2** honor as holy.

■ **1** bless, sanctify; dedicate. **2** venerate, worship, revere.

Hal•low•een /hálōwéen/ n. (also **Hal•low•e′en′**) eve of All Saints' Day, Oct. 31, esp. as celebrated by children dressing in costumes and collecting treats door-to-door.

hal•lu•ci•nate /həlóoʊsinayt/ v. **1** tr. produce illusions in the mind of (a person). **2** intr. experience hallucinations.

hal•lu•ci•na•tion /həlóoʊsináyshən/ n. perception of sights, sounds, etc., not actually present. □□ **hal•lu•ci•na•to•ry** /–sinətáwree/ *adj.*

■ mirage, illusion, apparition. □□ **hallucinatory** dreamlike, visionary; fantastic, illusory, imaginary.

hal•lu•ci•no•gen /həlóosinəjən/ *n.* drug causing hallucinations. □□ **hal•lu•ci•no•gen•ic** /–jénik/ *adj.*

hall•way /háwlway/ *n.* entrance hall or corridor.

■ see HALL 1.

ha•lo /háylō/ • *n.* (*pl.* **–loes, –los**) **1** disk or circle of light shown in art surrounding the head of a sacred person. **2** circle of light around a luminous body, esp. the sun or moon. **3** circle or ring. • *v.tr.* (**–loes, –loed**) surround with a halo.

■ *n.* **1, 2** nimbus, aura; corona, radiance. **3** disk, loop, wheel.

hal•o•gen /háləjən/ *n. Chem.* any of the nonmetallic elements: fluorine, chlorine, bromine, iodine, and astatine, which form a salt (e.g., sodium chloride) by simple union with a metal. □□ **ha•lo•gen•ic** /–jénik/ *adj.*

halt[1] • *n.* stop (usu. temporary) (*come to a halt*). • *v.* stop; come or bring to a halt.

■ *n.* standstill, interruption, break; end, close. • *v.* end, finish, cease, conclude, check; see also STOP *v.* 1, 2.

halt[2] /hawlt/ *v.intr.* **1** (esp. as **halting** *adj.*) lack smooth progress. **2** hesitate (*halt between two opinions*). **3** walk hesitatingly. □□ **halt•ing•ly** *adv.*

■ **1** (**halting**) wavering, uneven, faltering; stuttering. **2** see HESITATE 1. **3** dawdle, drag one's feet, scuff, shuffle.

halt•er /háwltər/ • *n.* **1** bridle and rope for leading or tying up a horse, etc. **2 a** strap around the back of a woman's neck holding her dress top or blouse and leaving her shoulders and back bare. **b** garment held by this. • *v.tr.* put a halter on (a horse, etc.).

■ *n.* **1** see TETHER *n.*

halve /hav/ *v.tr.* **1** divide into two halves. **2** reduce by half.

■ see SPLIT *v.* 1a.

halves *pl.* of HALF.

hal•yard /hályərd/ *n. Naut.* rope or tackle for raising or lowering a sail, flag, etc.

ham /ham/ • *n.* **1** upper part of a pig's leg salted and dried or smoked for food. **2** back of the thigh. **3** *sl.* [often *attrib.*] inexpert or unsubtle actor or piece of acting. **4** (in full **ra•di•o ham**) *colloq.* amateur radio operator. • *v.* (**hammed, ham•ming**) *sl.* overact.

■ *n.* **1, 2** see LEG *n.* 1, 3. **3** see THESPIAN *n.* • *v.* see DRAMATIZE.

ham•burg•er /hámbərgər/ *n.* patty of ground beef, usu. fried or grilled and eaten in a soft bread roll.

ham•let /hámlit/ *n.* small village.

■ see SETTLEMENT 2b.

ham•mer /hámər/ • *n.* **1 a** tool with a heavy metal head used for driving nails, etc. **b** similar contrivance, as for exploding the charge in a gun, striking the strings of a piano, etc. **2 a** metal ball attached to a wire for throwing in an athletic contest. **b** sport of throwing the hammer. **3** bone of the middle ear;

malleus. • *v.* **1 a** *tr. & intr.* hit or beat with or as with a hammer. **b** *intr.* strike loudly; knock violently (esp. on a door). **2** *tr.* **a** drive in (nails). **b** fasten or secure by hammering (*hammered the lid down*). **3** *tr.* inculcate (ideas, knowledge, etc.) forcefully or repeatedly. **4** *tr. colloq.* utterly defeat; inflict heavy damage on. **5** *intr.* [foll. by *at, away at*] work hard or persistently at. □ **hammer and sickle** symbols of the industrial worker and peasant used as the emblem of the former USSR and of international communism. **hammer out 1** make flat or smooth by hammering. **2** work out the details of (a plan, agreement, etc.) laboriously. **3** play (a tune, esp. on the piano) loudly or clumsily.

■ *v.* **1, 2a** see POUND[2] *v.* 1.

ham•mer•head /hámərhed/ *n.* **1** striking head of a hammer. **2** shark with a flattened head and eyes in lateral extensions of it.

ham•mer•toe /hámərtō/ *n.* deformed toe bent permanently downward.

ham•mock /hámək/ *n.* bed of canvas or rope network, suspended by cords at the ends.

ham•per[1] /hámpər/ *n.* basket, often with a hinged lid, for laundry, etc.

ham•per[2] /hámpər/ *v.tr.* restrict the free movement or activity of. **2** impede, hinder. See synonym study at HINDER.

■ encumber, obstruct, prevent; balk, thwart, delay, check.

ham•ster /hámstər/ *n.* rodent having a short tail and large cheek pouches, kept as a pet or laboratory animal.

ham•string /hámstring/ *Anat.* • *n.* **1** each of five tendons at the back of the knee in humans. **2** great tendon at the back of the hock in quadrupeds. • *v.tr.* (*past* and *past part.* **ham•strung** or **ham•stringed**) **1** cripple by cutting the hamstrings of (a person or animal). **2** prevent the activity or efficiency of (a person or enterprise).

■ *v.* **1** see LAME *v.* **2** see FRUSTRATE *v.* 2.

hand /hand/ • *n.* **1 a** end part of the human arm beyond the wrist, including the fingers and thumb. **b** in other primates, end part of a forelimb, also used as a foot. **2 a** [often in *pl.*] control; management; custody; disposal (*in good hands*). **b** active support. **3** thing compared with a hand or its functions, esp. the pointer of a clock or watch. **4** right or left side or direction. **5 a** skill (*a hand for making pastry*). **b** person skillful in some respect. **6** individual's writing or the style of this; signature (*a legible hand, in one's own hand*). **7** source of information, etc. (*at first hand*). **8** pledge of marriage. **9** person as a source of manual labor, esp. in a factory, on a farm, or on board ship. **10 a** playing cards dealt to a player. **b** round of play. **11** *colloq.* applause (*got a big hand*). **12** unit of measure of a horse's height, equal to 4 inches (10.16 cm). **13** [*attrib.*] held or done by hand. • *v.tr.* deliver; transfer by hand or otherwise. □ **at hand 1** close by. **2** about to happen. **by hand 1** by a person and not a machine. **2** delivered personally. **hand down 1** pass ownership or use of to another. **2 a** transmit (a decision) from a higher court, etc. **b** express (an opinion or verdict). **hand grenade** see GRENADE. **hand in glove** in collusion or association. **hand in hand** in close association. **hand it to** *colloq.* acknowledge the merit of (a person). **hand-me-down** article of clothing, etc., passed on from another person. **hands down** with no difficulty. **hand-to-hand** (of fighting) at close quarters. **on hand** available. **on the one** (or **the other**) **hand** from one (or another) point of view. **out of hand 1** out of control. **2** peremptorily (*refused out of hand*).

■ *n.* **1 a** fist, *colloq.* paw, *sl.* mitt, flipper. **b** paw. **2 a** (*hands*) hold, possession, authority. **b** part; involvement; see also SUPPORT *n.* 1. **3** indicator. **5 a** touch; see also TALENT 1. **b** see EXPERT *n.* **6** handwriting. **9** worker, drudge, employee. **11** ovation, clap. ● *v.* (*hand in*) submit, present, offer; (*hand to*) pass to, give to, present to or with; (*hand over*) submit, yield, give up, turn over. □ **at hand 1** nearby, handy, (readily) available, within reach, accessible. **2** imminent, approaching, upcoming. **hand down 1** see BEQUEATH. **2 b** see DELIVER 4. **hand in glove** hand in hand, in league, *sl.* in cahoots. **hand in hand** side by side, hand in glove. **hand it to** see RESPECT *v.* 1. **hand-me-down** secondhand, used. **hands down** readily, effortlessly; see EASILY 1. **on hand** see *at hand* 1 above. **out of hand 1** messy; see also *chaotic* (CHAOS). **2** categorically, flat(ly); see also ABSOLUTELY 1.

hand·bag /hándbag/ *n.* small bag carried esp. by a woman and used to hold a wallet, cosmetics, etc.

■ see BAG *n.* 2b.

hand·ball *n.* /hándbawl/ game in which a ball is struck with an open hand against a wall.

hand·bill /hándbil/ *n.* printed notice distributed by hand.

hand·book /hándbŏŏk/ *n.* short manual or guidebook.

hand·cart /hándkaart/ *n.* small cart pushed or drawn by hand.

hand·cuff /hándkuf/ ● *n.* [in *pl.*] lockable linked metal rings for securing a person's wrists. ● *v.tr.* put handcuffs on.

■ *n.* (*handcuffs*) manacles, *colloq.* cuffs. ● *v.* see SHACKLE *v.*

hand·ful /hándfŏŏl/ *n.* (*pl.* **–fuls**) **1** quantity that fills the hand. **2** small number or amount. **3** *colloq.* troublesome person or task.

■ **1** fistful. **2** sprinkling, scattering; a few. **3** see BOTHER *n.* 1.

hand·gun /hándgun/ *n.* small firearm fired with one hand.

hand·i·cap /hándeekap/ ● *n.* **1 a** disadvantage imposed on a superior competitor to make chances more equal. **b** race, etc., in which this is imposed. **2** number of strokes by which a golfer normally exceeds par for the course. **3** thing that makes progress or success difficult. **4** physical or mental disability. ● *v.tr.* (**hand·i·capped, hand·i·cap·ping**) **1** impose a handicap on. **2** place (a

person) at a disadvantage. □□ **hand·i·capped** *adj.*

■ *n.* **3** hindrance, encumbrance, restriction, limitation. ● *v.* hinder, hamper, impede, bar, block.

hand·i·craft /hándeekraft/ *n.* work requiring manual and artistic skill.

hand·i·work /hándeewərk/ *n.* work done or a thing made by hand, or by a particular person.

hand·ker·chief /hángkərchif, –cheef/ *n.* (*pl.* **hand·ker·chiefs** or **–chieves** /–cheevz/) cloth for wiping one's nose, etc.

han·dle /hánd'l/ ● *n.* **1** part by which a thing is held, carried, or controlled. **2** *colloq.* personal title or nickname. ● *v.tr.* **1** touch, feel, operate, or move with the hands. **2** manage or deal with (*knows how to handle people, unable to handle the situation*). **3** deal in (goods). **4** discuss or write about (a subject).

■ *n.* **1** grip; knob, switch, pull. ● *v.* **1** finger; caress; hold, use. **2** run, direct, control; cope with, use; tackle, treat. **3** trade in, traffic in; market. **4** see TREAT *v.* 4.

han·dle·bar /hánd'lbaar/ *n.* [often in *pl.*] steering bar of a bicycle, etc., with a handgrip at each end.

han·dler /hándlər/ *n.* **1** person who deals in certain commodities. **2** person who trains and looks after an animal (esp. a working or show dog).

hand·made /hándmáyd/ *adj.* made by hand, not by machine.

hand·out /hándowt/ *n.* **1** something given free to a needy person. **2** statement given to the press, printed information given to a lecture audience, etc.

■ **1** see GIFT *n.* 1. **2** communiqué.

hand·rail /hándrayl/ *n.* narrow rail for holding as a support.

hand·set /hándset/ *n.* telephone mouthpiece and earpiece forming one unit.

hand·shake /hándshayk/ *n.* clasping of a person's hand as a greeting, etc.

hand·some /hánsəm/ *adj.* (**hand·som·er, hand·som·est**) **1** (of a person) good-looking. **2** (of an object, etc.) imposing; attractive. **3 a** generous; liberal (*a handsome present*). **b** (of a price, fortune, etc.) considerable. □□ **hand·some·ly** *adv.*

■ **1** attractive; see also BEAUTIFUL 1. **2** see IMPRESSIVE 1. **3 a** see GENEROUS 1. **b** sizable, large, substantial.

hand·spring /hándspring/ *n.* acrobatic flip in which one lands first on the hands and then on the feet.

hand·stand /hándstand/ *n.* balancing on one's hands with the feet in the air or against a wall.

hand·work /hándwərk/ *n.* work done with the hands, esp. as opposed to machinery. □□ **hand·worked** *adj.*

hand·writ·ing /hándrīting/ *n.* **1** writing with a pen, pencil, etc. **2** individual's style of writing. □□ **hand·writ·ten** /–ritən/ *adj.*

■ longhand, penmanship, printing, script, calligraphy.

hand·y /hándee/ *adj.* (**hand·i·er, hand·i·est**) **1** convenient to handle or use; useful. **2** placed or occurring conveniently. **3** clever with the hands. □□ **hand′i•ly** adv. **hand′i• ness** n.

■ **1** helpful, practical; serviceable. **2** nearby, accessible, on hand. **3** deft, adroit, skilled. □□ **handily** conveniently; skillfully.

hand•y•man /hándeeman/ n. (pl. **–men**) person who does odd jobs.

hang /hang/ • v. (past and past part. **hung** /hung/ except in sense 7) **1** tr. secure or cause to be supported from above, esp. with the lower part free. **2** tr. set up (a door, gate, etc.) on hinges. **3** tr. place (a picture) on a wall or in an exhibition. **4** tr. attach (wallpaper) to a wall. **5** tr. colloq. blame (a thing) on (a person) (can't hang that on me). **6** tr. [foll. by with] decorate by hanging pictures, etc. (a hall hung with tapestries). **7** tr. & intr. (past and past part. **hanged**) suspend or be suspended by the neck, usu. with a noosed rope, until dead. **8** tr. let droop (hang one's head). **9** intr. remain static in the air. **10** intr. [often foll. by over] be present or imminent (a hush hung over the room). • n. way a thing hangs or falls. □ **get the hang of** colloq. understand the technique or meaning of. **hang around 1** loiter or dally. **2** [foll. by with] associate with (a person, etc.). **hang back 1** show reluctance. **2** remain behind. **hang glider** kitelike glider controlled in flight by a person suspended beneath it. **hang in** colloq. persist; persevere. **hang on** colloq. **1** continue or persevere. **2** cling; retain. **3 a** wait for a short time. **b** (in telephoning) continue to listen during a pause in the conversation. **hang out 1** hang from a clothesline, etc. **2** protrude or cause to protrude downward. **3** lean out of (a window, etc.). **4** sl. spend time; frequent. **5** [foll. by with] sl. accompany; be friends with. **6** loiter; dally. **hang together 1** make sense. **2** remain associated. **hang up 1** hang from a hook, etc. **2** end a telephone conversation, esp. abruptly (then he hung up on me). **3** cause delay or difficulty to. **4** sl. be a psychological or emotional obsession or problem to (is really hung up on her teacher). **hang-up** n. sl. emotional problem or inhibition. **hung jury** jury unable to reach a verdict.

■ v. **1** suspend, sling; attach. **3** put up, show. **5** see FLAME v. 1, 2. **6** see DECORATE 1, 3. **7** string up; lynch. **8** drop. **9** hover, be suspended, float. **10** fall, descend, come down. • n. drape. □ **get the hang of** see GRASP v. 3. **hang around 1** wait (around), linger. **2** socialize with, hobnob with, rub elbows with, sl. hang out with. **hang back 1** hesitate, think twice. **2** see LINGER 1. **hang in** see PERSEVERE. **hang on 1** persist, carry on, endure. **2** (hang on to) cling, grip, grasp; see also RETAIN 1. **3** stay (here); hold on, hold the line. **hang out 1** put out, suspend, swing. **2** see PROTRUDE. **3** bend out. **4** live, be present; (hang out at) haunt, visit. **5** (hang out with) see ASSOCIATE v. 5. **hang together 1** be logical, be consistent. **2** be or remain united, stick together; unite, cooperate. **hang up 1** see SUSPEND 1. **2** break the connection, put down the receiver; (hang up on) cut off. **4** (be hung up on) be obsessed by,

Psychol. have a complex about, be fixated on, colloq. have a thing about. **hang-up** difficulty, Psychol. complex, colloq. thing; see also INHIBITION 1, 2.

hang•ar /hángər/ n. building for housing aircraft, etc.

hang•dog /hángdawg, –dog/ adj. dejected; shamefaced.

hang•er /hángər/ n. **1** person or thing that hangs. **2** (in full **coat′ hang•er**) shaped piece of wood or plastic, etc., from which clothes may be hung. □ **hanger-on** (pl. **hang•ers-on**) follower or dependent, esp. an unwelcome one.

■ □ **hanger-on** supporter, fan, parasite, toady; sl. groupie, wanna-be; see also yesman, scrounger (SCROUNGE).

hang•ing /hánging/ • n. **1 a** executing by hanging a person. **b** [attrib.] meriting or causing this (hanging offense). **2** [usu. in pl.] draperies hung on a wall, etc. • adj. that hangs or is hung; suspended.

■ n. **2** see DRAPERY.

hang•man /hángmən/ n. (pl. **–men**) **1** executioner who hangs condemned persons. **2** word game for two players, in which the tally of failed guesses is kept by drawing a representation of a figure hanging from a gallows.

hang•nail /hángnayl/ n. torn skin near a fingernail.

hang•out /hángowt/ n. sl. place frequented by a person.

hang•over /hángōvər/ n. **1** headache, upset stomach, etc., caused by drinking too much alcohol. **2** survival from the past.

hank /hangk/ n. **1** coil or skein of yarn or thread, etc. **2** measure of cloth or yarn, e.g., 840 yds. for cotton yarn and 560 yds. for worsted.

han•ker /hángkər/ v.intr. long for; crave. □□ **han′ker•ing** n.

■ (hanker after or for or to) fancy, want (to), yearn for or to, thirst after or for, pine for, colloq. yen for; itch to.

han•ky-pan•ky /hángkeepángkee/ n. sl. **1** naughtiness, esp. sexual misbehavior. **2** dishonest dealing; trickery.

■ **1** mischief, tomfoolery, colloq. monkey business. **2** deception, duplicity, legerdemain, sl. funny business.

han•som /hánsəm/ n. (in full **han′som cab**) hist. two-wheeled horse-drawn carriage, with the driver seated behind.

Ha•nuk•kah /khaanəkə, haa–/ n. (also **Cha′ nuk•kah**) Jewish festival of lights, commemorating the purification of the Temple in 165 BC.

hap•haz•ard /hápházərd/ • adj. done, etc., by chance; random. • adv. at random. □□ **hap′ haz′ard•ly** adv.

■ adj. arbitrary, accidental, fortuitous, serendipitous.

hap•less /háplis/ adj. unlucky. □□ **hap′less• ly** adv. **hap′less•ness** n.

■ see UNHAPPY 2.

hap•pen /hápən/ v.intr. **1** occur. **2** have (good or bad) fortune (I happened to meet *her*). **3** be the (esp. unwelcome) fate or experience of (*what happened to you?*). **4** [foll. by *on*] meet or discover by chance. □ **as it happens** in fact; in reality (*as it happens, it turned out well*).

■ **1** take place, arise; develop, materialize. **2** chance. **3** (*happen to*) become of, come of. **4** (*happen on*) come upon, find; encounter.

SYNONYM STUDY: happen
BEFALL, CHANCE, OCCUR, TRANSPIRE. When things **happen**, they come to pass either for a reason or by chance (*it happened the day after school started; she happened upon the scene of the accident*), but the verb is more frequently associated with chance (*it happened to be raining when we got there*). **Occur** can also refer either to something that comes to pass either accidentally or as planned, but it should be used interchangeably with *happen* only when the subject is a definite or actual event (*the tragedy occurred last winter*). Unlike *happen*, *occur* also carries the implication of something that presents itself to sight or mind (*it never occurred to me that he was lying*). **Transpire** is a more formal (and some would say undesirable) word meaning to *happen* or *occur*, and it conveys the sense that something has leaked out or become known (*he told her exactly what had transpired while she was away*). While things that *happen*, *occur*, or *transpire* can be either positive or negative, when something **befalls** it is usually unpleasant (*he had no inkling of the disaster that would befall him when he got home*).

hap•pen•ing /hápəning/ • *n.* **1** event or occurrence. **2** improvised or spontaneous performance. • *adj. sl.* exciting; trendy.
■ *n.* **1** incident, occasion; phenomenon. **2** see *improvisation* (IMPROVISE). • *adj.* see TRENDY *adj.*

hap•py /hápee/ *adj.* (**hap•pi•er, hap•pi•est**) **1** feeling or showing pleasure or contentment. **2 a** fortunate; lucky. **b** (of words, behavior, etc.) apt; pleasing. **3** [in *comb.*] *colloq.* inclined to use excessively or at random (*trigger-happy*). □ **happy-go-lucky** cheerfully casual. **happy hour** period of the day when drinks are sold at reduced prices in bars, hotels, etc. □□ **hap′pi•ly** *adv.* **hap′pi•ness** *n.*
■ **1** glad, delighted, joyful, gleeful, ecstatic; pleased as Punch, in seventh heaven, *colloq.* on cloud nine, tickled pink. **2 a** favorable, blessed. **b** felicitous; see also APPROPRIATE *adj.* □ **happy-go-lucky** see CAREFREE. □□ **happily** joyfully, gleefully, cheerfully, gaily, with pleasure, luckily, propitiously. **happiness** pleasure, delight, enjoyment, joy, gladness, high spirits.

ha•ra-ki•ri /hárəkéeree, háaree-/ *n.* (also **ha′ri-ka′ri**) ritual suicide by disembowelment.

ha•rangue /həráng/ • *n.* lengthy and earnest speech. • *v.tr.* lecture or make a harangue to.
■ *n.* address, oration. • *v.* preach, sermonize; see also LECTURE *v.* 2.

ha•rass /hərás, hárəs/ *v.tr.* **1** trouble and an-

noy continually. **2** make repeated attacks on.
□□ **ha•rass′ment** or **har′ass•ment** *n.*
■ **1** badger, torment, bother, hound, persecute, pester, *colloq.* hassle, plague, *sl.* bug, ride. **2** see MOLEST 2.

har•bin•ger /háarbinjər/ *n.* **1** person or thing that announces or signals the approach of another. **2** forerunner.
■ omen, sign; herald, precursor.

har•bor /háarbər/ • *n.* **1** place of shelter for ships. **2** shelter; place of refuge or protection. • *v.tr.* **1** give shelter to (esp. a criminal or wanted person). **2** keep in one's mind, esp. resentfully (*harbor a grudge*).
■ *n.* **1** port, seaport, haven. **2** haven, asylum; see also SHELTER *n.* 1. • *v.* **1** protect, guard; hide. **2** foster, cherish, retain.

hard /haard/ • *adj.* **1** firm and solid. **2 a** difficult to understand or explain (*hard problem*). **b** difficult to accomplish (*hard decision*). **c** not easy (*hard to believe*). **3** difficult to bear (*a hard life*). **4** (of a person) unfeeling; severely critical. **5** severe; harsh (*hard winter, hard frost*). **6 a** enthusiastic; intense (*hard worker, hard fight*). **b** severe; uncompromising (*hard blow, hard bargain*). **7 a** (of liquor) strongly alcoholic. **b** (of drugs) potent and addictive. **8** (of water) containing mineral salts that make lathering difficult. **9** not disputable; reliable (*hard facts, hard data*). **10** *Stock Exch.* (of currency, prices, etc.) not likely to fall in value. **11** *Phonet.* (of a consonant) guttural (as *c* in *cat*, *g* in *go*). • *adv.* **1** strenuously; intensely; copiously; with one's full effort (*try hard, look hard at, hardworking*). **2** so as to be hard or firm (*hard-baked, the jelly set hard*). **3** *Naut.* fully; to the extreme (*hard to starboard*). □ **be hard on 1** be difficult for. **2** be severe in one's treatment or criticism of. **hard and fast** (of a rule or a distinction made) definite; unalterable; strict. **hard-boiled 1** (of an egg) boiled until the white and yolk are solid. **2** (of a person) tough; shrewd. **hard by** near; close by. **hard copy** printed material produced by computer, usu. on paper. **hard core 1** irreducible nucleus. **2** *colloq.* **a** most active or committed members of a society, etc. **b** conservative or reactionary minority. **hard-core** *adj.* blatant; uncompromising, esp.: **1** (of pornography) explicit; obscene. **2** (of drug addiction) relating to hard drugs, esp. heroin. **hard disk (drive)** *Computing* large-capacity, rigid, usu. magnetic storage disk. **hard hat 1** protective helmet worn on building sites, etc. **2** *colloq.* reactionary person. **hard line** unyielding adherence to a firm policy. **hard-liner** person who adheres rigidly to a policy. **hard-nosed** *colloq.* realistic; uncompromising. **hard-pressed 1** closely pursued. **2** burdened with urgent business. **hard sell** aggressive salesmanship or advertising. **hard up 1** short of money. **2** [foll. by *for*] at a loss for; lacking. □□ **hard′ness** *n.*
■ *adj.* **1** rigid, stiff, inflexible, tough, stony, steely, unyielding. **2 a** perplexing, puzzling, complex, involved; see also DIFFICULT[1] 1b. **b** thorny, tough, awkward, tricky; see also DIFFICULT 3. **c** difficult, tough, awkward,

tricky. **3** laborious, backbreaking, burdensome, tiring, strenuous, bad, grievous, grim, painful, *colloq.* tough. **4** stern, cold, callous, strict, hardhearted, severe, tyrannical, cruel, heartless, harsh, unkind. **5** see SEVERE 3, 4. **6 a** strenuous, diligent, industrious. **b** searching, critical, businesslike, realistic, *colloq.* tough; see also HARD *adj.* 4 above. **7 a** potent; see also STRONG *adj.* 7. **b** habit-forming, hard-core. **9** established, real, strict, straight, bare, unvarnished, undeniable. • *adv.* **1** vigorously, forcefully, energetically, actively, eagerly, persistently, *colloq.* mightily. **2** see FIRM *adj.* 1a. □ **be hard on 1** see DIFFICULT 1a, 3. **2** keep in line, *colloq.* sit on; see also SEVERE 1. **hard and fast** see STRICT 2b FIRM¹ *adj.* 1 hard, firm, set, **2** see TOUGH *adj.* 4a, SHREWD. **hard by** see NEAR *adj.* 1. **hard-core 1** see OBSCENE 1. **2** potent, addictive, habit-forming. **hard line** tough stance, firm position. **hard-liner** stickler, bigot, partisan, *colloq.* stick in the mud. **hard-nosed** see REALISTIC 2, INFLEXIBLE 2. **hard-pressed 1** see TRACK *v.* 1. **2** - busy, occupied, engaged, tied up. **hard up 1** poor, indigent, needy, *colloq.* broke. **2** (*hard up for*) see DESTITUTE 2.

hard•back /haárdbak/ • *adj.* (of a book) bound in stiff covers. • *n.* hardback book.
hard•ball /haárdbawl/ • *n.* **1** = BASEBALL. **2** *sl.* uncompromising methods or dealings, esp. in politics or business (*play hardball*). • *v.tr. sl.* pressure or coerce politically.
hard•bit•ten /haárdbitən/ *adj. colloq.* tough and cynical.
■ severe, calculating; hard-nosed; critical.
hard•cov•er /haárdkəvər/ • *adj.* bound between rigid boards covered in cloth, paper, leather, or film (*hardcover edition of the novel*). • *n.* hardcover book.
hard•en /haárdən/ *v.* **1** make or become hard or harder. **2** become, or make (one's attitude, etc.), uncompromising or less sympathetic. □□ **hard'en•ing** *n.*
■ **1** set, solidify, freeze. **2** intensify, strengthen, reinforce.
hard-head•ed /haárdhédid/ *adj.* practical; not sentimental. □□ **hard'head'ed•ly** *adv.* **hard'head'ed•ness** *n.*
■ systematic, searching, realistic; tough; hard-nosed.
hard-heart•ed /haárdhaártid/ *adj.* unfeeling; unsympathetic. □□ **hard'-heart'ed•ly** *adv.* **hard'-heart'ed•ness** *n.*
■ see HARD *adj.* 4.
har•di•hood /haárdeehŏŏd/ *n.* boldness; daring.
hard•ly /haárdlee/ *adv.* **1** scarcely; only just (*we hardly knew them*). **2** only with difficulty (*could hardly speak*).
■ barely; seldom, rarely; with effort.
hard•ship /haárdship/ *n.* **1** severe suffering or privation. **2** circumstance causing this.
■ want, misery, trouble; adversity, bad luck; misfortune.
hard•top /haárdtop/ *n.* **1** automobile without roof supports between the front and back windows. **2** automobile with a rigid (usu. detachable) roof.

hard•ware /haárdwair/ *n.* **1** tools and household articles of metal, etc. **2** heavy machinery or armaments. **3** mechanical and electronic components of a computer, etc. (cf. SOFTWARE).
■ **1** equipment, utensils, implements, *colloq.* gear. **2** equipment; arms, munitions. **3** equipment; parts.
hard•wood /haárdwŏŏd/ *n.* wood from a deciduous broad-leaved tree as distinguished from that of conifers.
hard•work•ing /haárdwórking/ *adj.* diligent.
■ see DILIGENT.
hard•y /haárdee/ *adj.* (**hard•i•er, hard•i•est**) **1** robust; enduring. **2** (of a plant) able to grow in the open air all year. □□ **har'di•ly** *adv.* **har'di•ness** *n.*
■ **1** strong, tough, vigorous, fit, healthy, sturdy, sound.
hare /hair/ *n.* **1** mammal like a large rabbit, with long ears, short tail, and hind legs longer than forelegs, inhabiting fields, hills, etc. **2** (in full **e•lec'tric hare**) dummy hare propelled by electricity, used in greyhound racing.
hare•brained /háirbraynd/ *adj.* rash; foolish; wild.
■ stupid, silly, inane, mindless; reckless, *colloq.* crackpot.
hare•lip /háirlip/ *n.* congenital fissure of the upper lip.
har•em /háirəm, hár-/ *n.* **1** women of a Muslim household, living in a separate part of the house. **2** their quarters.
hark /haark/ *v.intr. archaic* listen attentively. □ **hark back** revert to a topic discussed earlier.
■ see LISTEN 1, 2.
har•le•quin /haárlikwin/ • *n.* (**Harlequin**) mute character in pantomime, usu. masked and dressed in a diamond-patterned costume. • *adj.* in varied colors.
■ *n.* see FOOL *n.* 2. • *adj.* see VARIEGATED.
har•lot /haárlət/ *n. archaic* prostitute. □□ **har'lot•ry** *n.*
■ see PROSTITUTE *n.*
harm /haarm/ • *n.* hurt; damage. • *v.tr.* cause harm to. □ **out of harm's way** in safety.
■ *n.* injury, abuse; see also SIN¹ *n.* 1, GRIEVANCE. • *v.* hurt, damage, injure. □ **out of harm's way** see SAFE *adj.* 4.
harm•ful /haármfŏŏl/ *adj.* causing or likely to cause harm. □□ **harm'ful•ly** *adv.* **harm'ful•ness** *n.*
■ dangerous, destructive, detrimental, injurious; unhealthy, toxic, poisonous, malignant.
harm•less /haármlis/ *adj.* **1** not able or likely to cause harm. **2** inoffensive. □□ **harm'less•ly** *adv.* **harm'less•ness** *n.*
■ **1** benign, innocuous, gentle, mild, safe. **2** see INOFFENSIVE.
har•mon•ic /haarmónik/ • *adj.* of or characterized by harmony; harmonious. • *n. Mus.* overtone accompanying at a fixed interval (and forming a note with) a fundamental. □□ **har•mon'i•cal•ly** *adv.*
har•mon•i•ca /haarmónikə/ *n.* small rectan-

harmonious ~ hat 370

gular wind instrument with reeds played by
blowing or sucking air through.

har•mo•ni•ous /haarmṓneeəs/ *adj.* **1** pleasant sounding; tuneful. **2** forming a pleasing
or consistent whole. **3** free from disagreement or dissent. □□ **har•mo′ni•ous•ly** *adv.*

■ **1** see TUNEFUL. **2** compatible, complementary; congenial, sympathetic. **3** see
PEACEFUL 1.

har•mo•nize /haármənīz/ *v.* **1** *tr.* add notes
to (a melody) to produce harmony. **2** *tr. &
intr.* bring into or be in harmony. **3** *intr.*
make or form a pleasing or consistent whole.
□□ **har•mo•ni•za′tion** *n.*

■ **2** see AGREE 3a. **3** see COORDINATE *v.* 1.

har•mo•ny /haármənee/ *n.* (*pl.* **–nies**)
1 combination of simultaneously sounded
musical notes to produce chords. **2** apt or
aesthetic arrangement of parts. **3** agreement; concord.

■ **1** melodiousness, tunefulness. **2** see
UNITY 1. **3** consonance, balance, accord; see
also UNITY 2.

har•ness /haárnis/ • *n.* **1** equipment of
straps and fittings by which a horse is fastened to a cart, etc., and controlled. **2** similar arrangement for fastening a thing to a
person's body, for restraining a young child,
etc. • *v.tr.* **1 a** put a harness on (esp. a
horse). **b** attach by a harness. **2** make use of
(natural resources), esp. to produce energy.

■ *n.* **1** see TACK². • *v.* **1** see HITCH *v.* 1.

harp /haarp/ • *n.* upright stringed instrument
plucked with the fingers. • *v.intr.* [foll. by *on*]
talk repeatedly and tediously about.
□□ **harp′ist** *n.*

har•poon /haarpṓn/ • *n.* barbed spear with
a rope attached, for killing whales, etc. • *v.tr.*
spear with a harpoon.

harp•si•chord /haárpsikawrd/ *n.* keyboard
instrument in which strings are plucked mechanically. □□ **harp′si•chord•ist** *n.*

har•py /haárpee/ *n.* (*pl.* **–pies**) **1** *Gk. & Rom.
mythol.* monster with a woman's head and
body and bird's wings and claws. **2** grasping
unscrupulous person.

har•ri•dan /hárid'n/ *n.* bad-tempered
woman.

■ see HAG.

har•ri•er /háreeər/ *n.* **1** hound used for hunting hares. **2** cross-country runner.

har•row /hárō/ • *n.* heavy frame with iron
teeth dragged over plowed land to break up
clods, remove weeds, cover seed, etc. • *v.tr.*
1 draw a harrow over (land). **2** (usu. as **harrowing** *adj.*) distress greatly.

■ *v.* **1** see PLOW *v.* 1. **2** (**harrowing**) disturbing, alarming.

har•ry /háree/ *v.tr.* (**–ries, –ried**) **1** ravage or
despoil. **2** harass; worry.

■ **1** see OVERRUN *v.* 2 see WORRY *v.* 2.

harsh /haarsh/ *adj.* **1** unpleasantly rough or
sharp, esp. to the senses. **2** severe; cruel.
□□ **harsh′ly** *adv.* **harsh′ness** *n.*

■ **1** coarse; grating, raucous; bitter, sour.
2 stern, merciless, unkind, brutal; punitive;
austere, grim, stark, inhuman.

har•um-scar•um /háirəmskáirəm/ *colloq.*

• *adj.* wild and reckless. • *adv.* in a reckless
way.

har•vest /haárvist/ • *n.* **1 a** process of gathering in crops, etc. **b** season of this. **2** season's yield or crop. **3** product or result of any
action. • *v.tr.* gather as harvest; reap. □ **harvest moon** full moon nearest to the autumnal equinox (Sept. 22 or 23). □□ **har′ves•
ter** *n.*

■ *n.* **1 a** reaping, gleaning. **b** autumn, harvest home. **2** produce, fruit; vintage. **3** see
OUTCOME. • *v.* pick, collect, garner, take in;
glean; earn, take in, receive, procure.

has *3rd sing. present* of HAVE.

has-been /házbin/ *n. colloq.* person or thing
that has lost a former importance or usefulness.

hash¹ /hash/ • *n.* **1** dish of cooked meat and
potatoes cut into small pieces and recooked.
2 a mixture; jumble. **b** mess. • *v.tr.* [often
foll. by *out*] settle by conferring or debating.

■ *n.* **2 a** hodgepodge, medley. **b** confusion,
sl. snafu.

hash² /hash/ *n. colloq.* hashish.

hash•ish /hásheesh, hasheésh/ *n.* resinous
product of hemp, smoked or chewed as a
narcotic.

has•n't /házənt/ *contr.* has not.

hasp /hasp/ • *n.* hinged metal clasp that fits
over a staple and can be secured by a padlock. • *v.tr.* fasten with a hasp.

■ *n.* see LOCK¹ *n.* 1.

has•si•um /háseeəm/ *n.* radioactive element.
¶Symb.: **Hs.**

has•sle /hásəl/ *colloq.* • *n.* **1** trouble or inconvenience. **2** argument. • *v.* **1** *tr.* harass; annoy. **2** *intr.* argue; quarrel.

■ *n.* **1** see BOTHER *n.* 1. • *v.* **1** see BOTHER *v.* 1a.

has•sock /hásək/ *n.* **1 a** thick firm cushion
for kneeling on, esp. in church. **b** similar
cushion used as a footrest, etc. **2** tuft of matted grass, etc.

haste /hayst/ *n.* **1** urgency of movement or
action. **2** excessive hurry. □ **make haste**
hurry; be quick.

■ **1** rapidity, quickness, speed. **2** rush, rashness, (hustle and) bustle, impetuousness.
□ **make haste** see HURRY *v.* 1.

hasten /háysən/ *v.* **1** *intr.* make haste; hurry.
2 *tr.* bring about sooner.

■ **1** rush, fly, race, scurry, speed. **2** hurry
(up), expedite.

hast•y /háystee/ *adj.* (**hast•i•er, hast•i•est**)
1 hurried; acting quickly or hurriedly.
2 said, made, or done too quickly or too
soon; rash. See synonym study at SUPERFI-
CIAL. □□ **hast′i•ly** *adv.* **hast′i•ness** *n.*

■ **1** rushed, speedy; swift, brisk. **2** cursory,
superficial, precipitate, impulsive. □□ **hastily** quickly, posthaste; precipitately, impetuously, see also *immediately* (IMMEDIATE).

hat /hat/ *n.* **1** covering for the head, often
with a brim. **2** *colloq.* person's occupation or
capacity, esp. one of several (*wearing his managerial hat*). □ **hat trick** *Sports*scoring of
three goals, etc., in a single game, etc. **keep it
under one's hat** *colloq.* keep it secret. **pass
the hat** collect contributions of money. **take
one's hat off to** *colloq.* acknowledge admiration for.

hatch[1] /hach/ n. **1** opening or door in an aircraft, spacecraft, etc. **2** *Naut.* **a** = HATCH-WAY. **b** cover for this (often in *pl.*: *batten the hatches*).

hatch[2] /hach/ • v. **1** *intr.* **a** (of a young bird, fish, etc.) emerge from the egg. **b** (of an egg) produce a young animal. **2** *tr.* incubate (an egg). **3** *tr.* devise (a plot, etc.). • n. **1** act or instance of hatching. **2** brood hatched. □□ **hatch'er•y** n.

■ v. **2** brood, sit on. **3** contrive, design, *colloq.* cook up.

hatch•back /háchbak/ n. car with a sloping back hinged at the top to form a door.

hatch•et /háchit/ n. light short-handled ax. □ **hatchet job** *colloq.* fierce destructive critique of a person. **hatchet man** *colloq.* person employed to harm or dismiss another.

hatch•way /háchway/ n. opening in a ship's deck for cargo.

hate /hayt/ • v.tr. **1** dislike intensely. **2** *colloq.* **a** dislike. **b** be reluctant (to do something) (*I hate to disturb you*). • n. **1** hatred. **2** *colloq.* hated person or thing.

■ v. **1** loathe, detest, despise. **2 a** see DIS-LIKE v. **b** dislike, resist; (*hate to*) be disinclined to. • n. **1** abhorrence, loathing; hostility. **2** enemy; see AVERSION 2.

hate•ful /háytfŏŏl/ adj. arousing hatred. □□ **hate'ful•ly** adv. **hate'ful•ness** n.

■ loathsome, abhorrent, obnoxious, repugnant, revolting, vile.

ha•tred /háytrid/ n. intense dislike or ill will

■ n. see DISLIKE n. 1.

hat•ter /hátər/ n. maker or seller of hats.

haugh•ty /háwtee/ adj. (**haugh•ti•er**, **haugh•ti•est**) arrogant and disdainful. □□ **haugh'ti•ly** adv. **haugh'ti•ness** n.

■ proud, superior, self-important, pretentious, pompous, *colloq.* highfalutin, stuck-up, high and mighty, snotty.

haul /hawl/ • v.tr. **1** pull or drag forcibly. **2** transport by truck, cart, etc. • n. **1** act or instance of hauling. **2** amount gained or acquired. **3** distance to be traversed (*a short haul*). □□ **haul'er** n.

■ v. **1** tug, tow, lug. **2** carry, convey, move. • n. **1** pull, tug, drag. **2** catch, take, yield. **3** see DISTANCE n. 2.

haunch /hawnch/ n. **1** fleshy part of the buttock with the thigh, esp. in animals. **2** leg and loin of a deer, etc., as food.

■ see LEG n. 2.

haunt /hawnt/ • v. **1** *tr.* (of a ghost) visit (a place) regularly. **2** *tr.* (of a person or animal) frequent (a place). **3** *tr.* (of a memory, etc.) be persistently in the mind of. **4** *intr.* stay habitually. **5** *tr.* trouble; distress (*their shady financial dealings came back to haunt them*). • n. [often in *pl.*] place frequented by a person or animal.

■ v. **2** spend time at, *sl.* hang out at. **3** obsess, preoccupy, torment. • n. stamping ground, domain, *sl.* hangout, turf.

haunt•ing /háwnting/ adj. (of a memory, melody, etc.) poignant; wistful; evocative. □□ **haunt'ing•ly** adv.

Hau•sa /hówzə/ n. (*pl.* same or **Hau•sas**) **1** people of W. Africa and Sudan. **2** Hamitic

language of this people. • adj. of or relating to this people or language.

haute cui•sine /ót kwizeén/ n. cooking of a high standard, esp. of the French traditional school.

have /hav/ • v. (3rd sing. present **has** /haz/; past and past part. **had** /had/) **1** tr. own or be able to use (*has a car, had no time to read, has nothing to wear*). **2** tr. hold in a certain relationship (*has a sister*). **3** tr. contain as a part or quality (*house has two floors, has green eyes*). **4** tr. **a** experience (*had a good time, has a headache*). **b** be subjected to a specified state (*had my car stolen, the book has a page missing*). **c** cause (a person or thing) to be in a particular state or take a particular action (*had him dismissed, had us worried, had my hair cut*). **5** tr. **a** engage in (an activity) (*had an argument*). **b** hold (a meeting, party, etc.). **6** tr. eat or drink (*had a beer*). **7** tr. [usu. in *neg.*] accept or tolerate; permit to (*I won't have it, will not have you say such things*). **8** tr. **a** let (a feeling, etc.) be present (*have no doubt, has a lot of sympathy for me*). **b** show or feel (mercy, pity, etc.) (*have pity on him, have mercy!*). **9** tr. **a** give birth to (offspring). **b** conceive mentally (an idea, etc.). **10** tr. receive; obtain (*not a ticket to be had*). **11** tr. *sl.* **a** get the better of (*I had him there*). **b** [usu. in *passive*] cheat; deceive (*you were had*). **12** aux. [with *past part.* or *ellipt.*, to form the perfect, pluperfect, and future perfect tenses, and the conditional mood] (*have worked, had seen, will have been, had I known, I would have gone, have you met her? yes, I have*). • n. [usu. in *pl.*] *colloq.* person who has wealth or resources. □ **have it in for** *colloq.* be hostile or ill-disposed toward. **have it out** [often foll. by *with*] *colloq.* attempt to settle a dispute by discussion or argument. **have-not** [usu. in *pl.*] *colloq.* person lacking wealth or resources. **have to** be obliged to; must.

■ v. **1** possess, hold, keep. **3** possess, bear, include. **4 a** undergo, suffer, enjoy. **c** instruct to do *or* be, invite to do *or* be, force to do *or* be. **5 a** see ENGAGE 7. **b** give, plan, throw. **6** partake of, consume. **7** see ALLOW 1. **8 b** see SHOW 3. **9 a** bear, deliver; procreate, sire. **b** see CONCEIVE 3. **10** get, acquire; take, accept. **11 a** see BEAT v. 2. **b** see DECEIVE 1. • n. (*haves*) winners, fortunate ones, the rich *or* affluent *or* well-to-do. □ **have it in for** see DISLIKE v. **have it out** see NEGOTIATE 1. **have-not** (*have-nots*) losers, the poor *or* needy *or* hard up. **have on** wear, be dressed in. **have to** see MUST v.

ha•ven /háyvən/ n. **1** harbor or port. **2** place of refuge.

■ **1** see HARBOR n. 1. **2** see REFUGE 1, 2.

have•n't /hávənt/ contr. have not.

hav•er•sack /hávərsak/ n. stout bag for provisions, etc., carried on the back or over the shoulder.

■ see PACK[1] n. 1.

hav•oc /hávək/ n. widespread destruction; great confusion or disorder.

■ devastation, damage, (rack and) ruin, chaos, mayhem.

Ha•wai•ian /həwīʼən/ • *n.* **1 a** native or inhabitant of Hawaii, an island or island group (comprising a US state) in the N. Pacific. **b** person of Hawaiian descent. **2** the Malayo-Polynesian language of Hawaii. • *adj.* of or relating to Hawaii or its people or language.

hawk¹ /hawk/ • *n.* **1** diurnal bird of prey having a curved beak, rounded short wings, and a long tail. **2** *Polit.* person who advocates an aggressive or warlike policy, esp. in foreign affairs. • *v.* **1** *intr.* hunt game with a hawk. **2** *intr. & tr.* attack, as a hawk does. **3** *intr.* (of a bird) hunt on the wing for food. □ **hawk-eyed** keen-sighted. □□ **hawk'ish** *adj.* **hawk'ish•ly** *adv.* **hawk'ish•ness** *n.*

■ *n.* **2** see BELLIGERENT *n.*

hawk² /hawk/ • *v.tr.* carry about or offer (goods) for sale. □□ **hawk'er** *n.*

■ see SELL *v.* 2.

hawk³ /hawk/ • *v.* **1** *intr.* clear the throat noisily. **2** *tr.* bring (phlegm, etc.) up from the throat.

haw•ser /hawʼzər/ *n. Naut.* thick rope or cable for mooring or towing a ship.

haw•thorn /hawʼthawrn/ *n.* thorny shrub or tree with white, red, or pink blossoms and small dark red fruit.

hay /hay/ • *n.* grass mown and dried for fodder. • *v.* **1** *intr.* make hay. **2** *tr.* put (land) under grass for hay. **3** *tr.* make into hay. □ **hay fever** common allergy with respiratory symptoms, caused by pollen or dust. **make hay (while the sun shines)** seize opportunities for profit or enjoyment.

hay•stack /hayʼstak/ *n.* packed pile of hay.

hay•wire /hayʼwīr/ *adj. colloq.* **1** badly disorganized; out of control. **2** (of a person) badly disturbed; erratic.

■ **1** see *out of order* 1 (ORDER).

haz•ard /hazʼərd/ • *n.* **1** danger or risk. **2** source of this. **3** *Golf* obstruction in playing a shot, e.g., a bunker, water, etc. • *v.tr.* **1** venture on (*hazard a guess*). **2** risk. □□ **haz'ard•ous** *adj.*

■ *n.* **1, 2,** peril, threat, jeopardy; pitfall. • *v.* **1** dare, wager; make, (take the) risk (of). **2** stake, chance, gamble on.

haze¹ /hayz/ *n.* **1** thin atmospheric vapor. **2** mental obscurity or confusion.

■ **1** see FOG *n.* 1.

haze² /hayz/ *v.tr.* humiliate (fraternity initiates, etc.).

ha•zel /hayʼzəl/ *n.* **1** shrub or small tree bearing round brown edible nuts. **2** greenish brown color (esp. of the eyes).

ha•zel•nut /hayʼzəlnut/ *n.* fruit of the hazel.

haz•mat /hazʼmat/ • *n. abbr.* hazardous materials.

haz•y /hayʼzee/ *adj.* (**haz•i•er, haz•i•est**) **1** misty. **2** vague; indistinct. **3** confused; uncertain. □□ **ha'zi•ly** *adv.* **ha'zi•ness** *n.*

■ **1** foggy. **2** unclear, blurred, murky, obscure. **3** indefinite, muddled.

H-bomb /aychbom/ *n.* = hydrogen bomb.

hdbk. *abbr.* handbook.

HDTV *abbr.* high-definition television.

He *symb. Chem.* helium.

he /hee/ • *pron.* (*obj.* **him** /him/; *poss.* **his** /hiz/; *pl.* **they** /thay/) **1** the man or boy or male animal previously named or in question. **2** person, etc., of unspecified sex. • *n.* **1** male; man. **2** [in *comb.*] male (*he-goat*). □ **he-man** (*pl.* **-men**) masterful or virile man.

head /hed/ • *n.* **1** upper part of the human body, or foremost or upper part of an animal's body, containing the brain, mouth, and sense organs. **2 a** seat of intellect. **b** mental aptitude or tolerance (*good head for business, no head for heights*). **3** thing like a head in form or position; top. **4** person in charge. **5** front or forward part of something, e.g., a line. **6** upper end of something, e.g., a table or bed. **7** top or highest part of something, e.g., a page, stairs, etc. **8** individual person or animal regarded as a numerical unit (*$10 per head, 20 head of cattle*). **9 a** side of a coin bearing the image of a head. **b** [usu. in *pl.*] this side as a choice in a coin toss. **10** source of a river, etc. **11** height or length of a head as a measure. **12** promontory (esp. in place-names) (*Diamond Head*). **13** *Naut.* **a** bow of a ship. **b** ship's latrine. **14** culmination, climax, or crisis. **15** *sl.* habitual taker of drugs; drug addict. • *attrib.adj.* chief or principal (*head gardener, head office*). • *v.* **1** *tr.* be at the head or front of. **2** *tr.* be in charge of (*headed a small team*). **3 a** *intr.* face or move in a specified direction or toward a specified result (*is heading for trouble*). **b** *tr.* direct in a specified direction. □ **come to a head** reach a crisis. **go to one's head 1** (of liquor) make one dizzy or slightly drunk. **2** (of success) make one conceited. **head off 1** get ahead of so as to intercept. **2** forestall. **head-on 1** with the front foremost (*a head-on crash*). **2** in direct confrontation. **head over heels 1** turning over completely in forward motion as in a somersault, etc. **2** topsy-turvy. **3** utterly; completely (*head over heels in love*). **head shrinker** *sl.* psychiatrist. **head start** advantage granted or gained at an early stage. **head wind** wind blowing from directly in front. **keep one's head** remain calm. **lose one's head** lose self-control; panic. **off the top of one's head** *colloq.* impromptu; without careful thought or investigation. **over one's head 1** beyond one's ability to understand. **2** to a higher authority without one's knowledge or involvement, esp. when one has a right to this.

■ *n.* **1** *sl.* dome, coconut, noggin, *sl.* bean, skull. **2** mind, brain(s), mentality, *colloq.* gray matter; aptitude, talent. **3** see TIP¹ *n.* 1. **4** chief, leader, director, president, *colloq.* boss, *sl.* (big) cheese, (chief) honcho. **5** vanguard, forefront. **7** see TOP¹ *n.* 1. **10** origin, fountainhead, wellspring. **12** headland; see also CLIFF¹. **14** (critical) point, (fever) pitch; peak. • *attrib.adj.* first, leading, main; superior. • *v.* **1** top; see also LEAD *v.* 5. **2** direct, supervise, oversee, govern, manage. **3 a** go, turn, steer, point, (*head for*) make a beeline for. **b** see DIRECT *v.* 3b. □ **come to a head** peak, culminate, *colloq.* climax. **go to one's head 1** see INTOXICATE 1. **head off 1** divert.

2 stop, cut off, block, prevent. **head-on** adj. **2.** see BLUNT adj. **2. head over heels 3** entirely, deeply, wholly, *colloq.* madly. **head shrinker** see *therapist* (THERAPY). **head start** see ADVANTAGE n. 1, 3. **keep one's head** stay cool or calm and collected, *colloq.* not bat an eyelid. **lose one's head** see PANIC v. **off the top of one's head** see OFFHAND adv. 2.

head•ache /hédayk/ n. **1** continuous pain in the head. **2** *colloq.* worrying problem or person. □□ **head'ach•y** adj.

■ **2** bother, inconvenience, nuisance, annoyance, trouble, *colloq.* hassle, pain (in the neck), *sl.* pain in the butt.

head•board /hédbawrd/ n. upright panel at the head of a bed.

head•dress /héd dres/ n. ornamental covering for the head

head•er /hédər/ n. **1** *colloq.* headlong fall or dive. **2** *Computing* line(s) of information printed at the top of the page throughout a document.

■ **1** see TUMBLE n. 1.

head•hunt•ing /hédhunting/ n. **1** practice among some peoples of collecting heads of dead enemies as trophies. **2** practice of recruiting staff by approaching a person employed elsewhere. □□ **head'hunt** v.tr. [also *absol.*]. **head'hunt•er** n.

head•ing /héding/ n. **1 a** title at the head of a page, chapter, etc. **b** section of a subject of discourse, etc. **2** course of an aircraft, ship, etc.

■ **1 b** see CATEGORY.

head•land /hédlənd/ n. promontory.

■ see CAPE³.

head•light /hédlīt/ n. **1** strong light at the front of a motor vehicle or train engine. **2** beam from this.

■ **1** see LIGHT¹ n. 2.

head•line /hédlīn/ • n. **1** heading at the top of an article or page, esp. in a newspaper. **2** [in *pl*] most important items in a news bulletin. • v.tr. star as a performer. □□ **head'lin•er** n.

■ n. **1** see TITLE n. 2.

head•long /hédlawng, –lóng/ adv. & adj. **1** with head foremost. **2** in a rush.

■ **2** see IMPULSIVE.

head•mas•ter /hédmástər/ n. (*fem.* **head•mis•tress** /–místris/) (esp. in private schools) person in charge of a school.

■ see PRINCIPAL n. 2.

head•phone /hédfōn/ n. [usu. in *pl.*] pair of earphones fitting over the head.

head•quar•ters /hédkwáwrtərz/ n. [as *sing.* or *pl.*] administrative center of an organization.

■ see SEAT n. 6.

head•rest /hédrest/ n. support for the head, esp. on a seat.

head•room /hédrōōm, –rŏŏm/ n. **1** space or clearance between the top of a vehicle and the underside of a bridge, etc. **2** space above an occupant's head in a vehicle.

head•set /hédset/ n. headphones, often with a microphone attached, used esp. in telephone and radio communications.

head•stone /hédstōn/ n. stone set up at the head of a grave.

■ see TOMBSTONE.

head•strong /hédstrawng, –strong/ adj. self-willed, obstinate.

■ see SELF-WILLED.

head•wa•ter /hédwawtər, –woter/ n. [in *sing.* or *pl.*] streams flowing at the sources of a river.

head•way /hédway/ n. **1** progress. **2** ship's rate of progress.

■ **1** improvement; see ADVANCE n. 1, 2. **2** speed; knots.

head•word /hédwərd/ n. word forming a heading, e.g., of an entry in a dictionary or encyclopedia.

head•y /hédee/ adj. (**head•i•er**, **head•i•est**) **1** (of alcohol) potent; intoxicating. **2** (of success, etc.) apt to cause conceit. □□ **head'i•ly** adv. **head'i•ness** n.

heal /heel/ v. **1** *intr.* become sound or healthy again. **2** *tr.* cause to heal or be healed. **3** *tr.* put right (differences, etc.). □□ **heal'er** n.

■ **1** mend, improve, get better. **2** cure, restore (to health); mend. **3** reconcile, settle, patch up.

health /helth/ n. **1** state of being well in body or mind. **2** person's mental or physical condition (*in poor health*). **3** soundness, esp. financial or moral (*the health of the nation*). □ **health food** food thought to have health-giving or -sustaining qualities. **health maintenance organization** organization that provides medical care to subscribers who have paid in advance, usu. through a health insurance plan.

■ **1** healthiness, fitness, vitality, well-being. **2** fitness, trim; constitution. **3** see STRENGTH 1.

health•ful /hélthfŏŏl/ adj. conducive to good health; beneficial. See synonym study at SANITARY. □□ **health'ful•ly** adv. **health'ful•ness** n.

health•y /hélthee/ adj. (**health•i•er**, **health•i•est**) **1** having, showing, or promoting good health. **2** indicative of (esp. moral or financial) health. **3** substantial (*a healthy margin*). □□ **health'i•ly** adv. **health'i•ness** n.

■ **1** well, fit, trim, *colloq.* in the pink; wholesome, nourishing.

heap /heep/ • n. **1** disorderly pile. **2** [esp. *pl.*] *colloq.* large number or amount (*there's heaps of time, a heap of chores to finish*). **3** *sl.* old or dilapidated thing, esp. a motor vehicle or building. • v. **1** *tr.* & *intr.* collect or be collected in a heap. **2** *tr.* load copiously. **3** *tr.* accord or offer copiously to (*heaped insults on them*).

■ n. **1** collection, stack. **2** abundance, *colloq.* great deal; (*heaps*) lots, plenty, *colloq.* loads. **3** see WRECK n. 3. • v. **1** gather. **2** see LOAD v. 3–5. **3** pile; see also HURL v.

hear /heer/ v. (*past* and *past part.* **heard** /herd/) **1** *tr.* [also *absol.*] perceive with the ear. **2** *tr.* listen to (*heard them on the radio*). **3** *tr.* judge (a case, etc.). **4** *intr.* be told or informed. **5** *intr.* be contacted by, esp. by letter or telephone. **6** *tr.* grant (a prayer). □ **hear a person out** listen to all that a person says. □□ **hear'er** n.

■ **1** catch. **3** see JUDGE *v.* 1a. **4** learn, discover, be advised; (*hear of*) get wind of, pick up rumors of, *colloq.* hear on the grapevine. **6** heed, answer.

hear•ing /héering/ *n.* **1** faculty of perceiving sounds. **2** range of audible sounds (*within hearing*). **3** opportunity to state one's case. **4** preliminary appearance before a court. □ **hearing aid** device to amplify sound, worn by a partially deaf person.

■ **3** see CHANCE *n.* 2. **4** see TRIAL 1.

hear•ken /háarkən/ *v.intr.* archaic or literary listen (to).

hear•say /héersay/ *n.* rumor; gossip.

■ see RUMOR *n.* 1.

hearse /hərs/ *n.* vehicle for conveying the coffin at a funeral.

heart /haart/ *n.* **1** hollow muscular organ maintaining the circulation of blood by rhythmic contraction and dilation. **2** region of the heart; the breast. **3 a** center of thought, feeling, and emotion (esp. love). **b** capacity for feeling emotion (*has no heart*). **4 a** courage or enthusiasm (*take heart*). **b** mood or feeling (*change of heart*). **5** central or essential part of something. **6 a** heart-shaped thing. **b** conventional representation of a heart with two equal curves meeting at a point at the bottom and a cusp at the top. **7 a** playing card of a suit denoted by a red figure of a heart. **b** [in *pl.*] this suit. **c** [in *pl.*] card game in which players avoid taking tricks containing a card of this suit. □ **at heart 1** in one's inmost feelings. **2** basically; essentially. **break a person's heart** overwhelm a person with sorrow. **by heart** from memory. **heart attack** sudden occurrence of coronary thrombosis usu. resulting in the death of part of a heart muscle. **heart-rending** very distressing. **heart-to-heart** *adj.* (of a conversation, etc.) candid; intimate. *n.* candid or personal conversation. **take to heart** be much affected or distressed by.

■ **1** *colloq.* ticker. **2** chest. **3 a** core, heart of hearts, interior; see also SOUL¹ 1, 2. **b** humanity, sympathy, compassion. **4 a** stomach, bravery, determination, *colloq.* guts, spunk; spirit, verve. **b** see MOOD 1, FEELING 4. **5** kernel, core, nucleus; crux, basics, *colloq.* bottom line, *sl.* nitty-gritty. □ **at heart 1** see INSIDE *adv.* 1. **2** see PRINCIPALLY. **heart-rending** agonizing, heartbreaking, tragic.

heart•ache /háartayk/ *n.* mental anguish or grief.

■ see GRIEF 1.

heart•beat /háartbeet/ *n.* pulsation of the heart.

heart•break /háartbrayk/ *n.* overwhelming distress. □□ **heart′break•er** *n.* **heart′break•ing** *adj.* **heart′bro•ken** *adj.*

■ see GRIEF 1. □□ **heartbroken** unhappy, grief-stricken, crushed, devastated.

heart•burn /háartbərn/ *n.* burning sensation in the chest resulting from indigestion; pyrosis.

■ see INDIGESTION.

heart•en /háart'n/ *v.* make or become more cheerful. See synonym study at ENCOURAGE.

□□ **heart′en•ing** *adj.*

■ see CHEER *v.* 3.

heart•felt /háartfelt/ *adj.* sincere; deeply felt.

■ genuine, earnest, profound, ardent, fervent, passionate.

hearth /haarth/ *n.* **1 a** floor of a fireplace. **b** area in front of a fireplace. **2** this symbolizing the home.

heart•land /háartland/ *n.* central or vital part of an area.

heart•less /háartlis/ *adj.* unfeeling; pitiless. □□ **heart′less•ly** *adv.*

■ cruel, callous, inhuman, brutal, cold, merciless, ruthless.

heart•sick /háartsik/ *adj.* very despondent.

■ see SAD 1.

heart•throb /háart-throb/ *n.* **1** beating of the heart. **2** *colloq.* person for whom one has (esp. immature) romantic feelings.

■ **2** see PASSION 3.

heart•warm•ing /háartwawrming/ *adj.* emotionally rewarding or uplifting.

■ moving, touching; gratifying, pleasing, comforting.

heart•y /háartee/ *adj.* (**heart•i•er**, **heart•i•est**) **1** strong; vigorous. **2** spirited. **3** (of a meal or appetite) large. **4** warm; friendly. **5** genuine; sincere. □□ **heart′i•ly** *adv.* **heart′i•ness** *n.*

■ **1** healthy, robust, active. **2** enthusiastic, vigorous, eager. **3** (of a meal) abundant, substantial, solid, satisfying, strengthening; (of appetite) healthy, robust, good. **4** genial, kindhearted, affectionate. **5** authentic, warm, honest.

heat /heet/ *n.* **1** condition of being hot. **2** Physics **a** energy arising from the motion of molecules. **b** amount of this needed to cause a specific process, or evolved in a process (*heat of formation*, *heat of solution*). **3** hot weather (*succumbed to the heat*). **4 a** warmth of feeling. **b** anger or excitement (*the heat of the argument*). **5** [foll. by *of*] most intense part or period of an activity (*in the heat of battle*). **6** (usu. preliminary or trial) round in a race or contest. **7** *sl.* criticism. • *v.* **1** *tr. & intr.* make or become hot or warm. **2** *tr.* inflame; excite or intensify. □ **heat lightning** flashes of lightning without thunder, as from a distant summer storm. **heat wave** period of very hot weather. **in heat** (of mammals, esp. females) sexually receptive. □□ **heat′ing** *n.*

■ *n.* **1** warmth; fever, temperature. **4** passion, ardor, zeal, exhilaration; fury, vehemence; see also ANGER *n.* **5** see CLIMAX *n.* **6** qualifier; game, stage, level. • *v.* **1** see WARM *v.* 1, THAW *v.* 1, 4. **2** impassion; kindle, ignite, rouse, stimulate.

heat•ed /héetid/ *adj.* **1** (of a person, discussion, etc.) angry; impassioned. **2** made hot. □□ **heat′ed•ly** *adv.*

■ **1** furious, stormy, fiery, excited, inflamed, vehement, intense.

heat•er /héetər/ *n.* device for supplying heat.

heath /heeth/ *n.* **1** area of flattish uncultivated land with low shrubs. **2** plant growing on a heath, esp. heather.

■ **1** see MOOR[1] 1.

hea•then /hée_th_ən/ • *n.* **1** person who does not belong to a widely held religion as regarded by those that do. **2** person regarded as lacking culture or moral principles. • *adj.* **1** of or relating to heathens. **2** having no religion.

■ *n.* **1** unbeliever, infidel, gentile, pagan. **2** barbarian, savage, brute. • *adj.* **1** infidel, *hist.* heretical; savage, barbarian, unenlightened. **2** pagan, atheistic, godless.

hea•ther /hé_th_ər/ *n.* **1** evergreen shrub with purple bell-shaped flowers. **2** any of various shrubs growing esp. on moors and heaths **3** a fabric or yarn of mixed hues supposed to resemble heather. **b** color of this. □□ **hea′ther•y** *adj.*

heat•stroke /héetstrōk/ *n.* severe feverish condition caused by excessive exposure to high temperature.

heat•wave /héetwayv/ *n.* period of abnormally hot weather.

heave /heev/ • *v.* (*past* and *past part.* **heaved** or esp. *Naut.* **hove** /hōv/) **1** *tr.* lift or haul (a heavy thing) with great effort. **2** *tr.* utter with effort or resignation (*heaved a sigh*). **3** *tr. colloq.* throw. **4** *intr.* rise and fall rhythmically or spasmodically. **5** *tr. Naut.* haul by rope. **6** *intr.* retch. • *n.* **1** instance of heaving. **2** [in *pl.*] respiratory disease of horses.

■ *v.* **1** hoist; pull, tug. **2** breathe **3** hurl, toss; *colloq.* sling. **5** vomit, *colloq.* throw up, *sl.* puke. • *n.* **1** pull, wrench.

heav•en /hévən/ *n.* **1** place regarded in some religions as the abode of God and of the good after death. **2** place or state of supreme bliss. **3** *colloq.* something delightful. **4** (**the heav′ens**) the sky as seen from the earth, esp. at night. □□ **heav′en•ward** *adj. & adv.*

■ **1** paradise, kingdom (of heaven); Canaan, Zion, Valhalla. **2** paradise, nirvana, Elysium, Eden, Utopia, happiness, joy. **3** see DELIGHT *n.* **4** (**the heavens**) the blue.

heav•en•ly /hévənlee/ *adj.* **1** of heaven; divine. **2** of the heavens or sky. **3** *colloq.* very pleasing; wonderful.

■ **1** celestial, ethereal, holy, blessed. **2** celestial. **3** delightful, marvelous, sublime, paradisaical, glorious, *colloq.* fantastic.

heav•y /hévee/ • *adj.* (**heav•i•er, heav•i•est**) **1** of great or exceptionally high weight; difficult to lift. **2** of great density; abundant; considerable (*heavy crop*). **3** severe; intense (*heavy fighting*). **4** doing something to excess (*heavy drinker*). **5** (of machinery, artillery, etc.) very large of its kind; large in caliber, etc. **6** needing much physical effort (*heavy work*). **7** a (of a person, writing, music, etc.) serious or somber in tone or attitude; dull; tedious. **b** (of an issue, etc.) grave; important; weighty. **8** a (of food) hard to digest. **b** (of a literary work, etc.) hard to read or understand. **9** oppressive; hard to endure (*a heavy fate, heavy demands*). • *n.* (*pl.* **-ies**) **1** *colloq.* large violent person; thug. **2** villainous role or actor in a play, etc. • *adv.* heavily (esp. in *comb.*: *heavy-laden*). □ **heavy-duty** *adj.* **1** intended to withstand hard use. **2** serious; grave. **heavy going** slow or difficult prog-

375 · **heathen ~ Hebrew**

ress. **heavy-hearted** sad; doleful. **heavy industry** industry producing metal, machinery, etc. **heavy metal 1** metal of high density. **2** *colloq.* [often *attrib.*] highly amplified rock music with a strong beat. □□ **heav′i•ly** *adv.* **heav′i•ness** *n.* **heav′y•ish** *adj.*

■ *adj.* **1** weighty, massive; overweight, obese. **2** solid; copious, ample. **3** concentrated, extensive, excessive. **4** see IMMODERATE. **5** see LARGE *adj.* 1, 2. **6** see HARD *adj.* 3. **7** a grave, ponderous; dry, monotonous; leaden, stodgy. **b** serious, crucial, critical; see also WEIGHTY 2. **8** a see STODGY 1. **b** difficult, complex, esoteric. **9** burdensome, onerous; see also OPPRESSIVE 1, 2. ■ *n.* **1** see THUG. □ **heavy-duty 1** see TOUGH *adj.* 1. **heavy-hearted** see SAD 1.

SYNONYM STUDY: heavy

BURDENSOME, CUMBERSOME, MASSIVE, PONDEROUS, WEIGHTY. Trying to move a refrigerator out of a third-floor apartment is difficult because it is **cumbersome**, which means that it is so heavy and bulky that it becomes unwieldy or awkward to handle. Cartons filled with books, on the other hand, are merely **heavy**, which implies greater density and compactness than the average load. A huge oak dining table might be described as **massive**, which stresses largeness and solidity rather than weight, while something that is **ponderous** is too large or too *massive* to move, or to be moved quickly (*a ponderous printing press*). Most of these terms can be used figuratively as well. *Heavy*, for example, connotes a pressing down on the mind, spirits, or senses (*heavy with fatigue*; *a heavy heart*) and *ponderous* implies a dull and labored quality (*a novel too ponderous to read*). **Burdensome**, which refers to something that is not only *heavy* but must be carried or supported, is even more likely to be used in an abstract way to describe something that is difficult but can, with effort, be managed (*a burdensome task*). Both a package and a problem may be described as **weighty**, meaning actually (as opposed to relatively) heavy; but it is more commonly used to mean very important or momentous (*weighty matters to discuss*).

---

heav•y-hand•ed /hévihándid/ *adj.* **1** clumsy. **2** overbearing; oppressive. □□ **heav′y-hand′ed•ly** *adv.* **heav′y-hand′ed•ness** *n.*

■ **1** awkward, inept, ungraceful. **2** domineering, autocratic.

heav•y•set /héveesét/ *adj.* stocky; thickset.

■ see STOCKY.

heav•y•weight /héveewayt/ *n.* **1 a** weight class in certain sports, esp. boxing, wrestling, weightlifting, etc. **b** sports participant of this weight. **2** person, animal, or thing of above average weight. **3** *colloq.* person of influence or importance.

He•bra•ic /hibráyik/ *adj.* of Hebrew or the Hebrews.

He•brew /héebroō/ • *n.* **1** member of a Semitic people orig. centered in ancient Palestine. **2 a** language of this people. **b** modern form of this used esp. in Israel. • *adj.* **1** of or in Hebrew. **2** of the Hebrews or the Jews.

heck /hek/ *int. colloq.* mild exclamation of surprise or dismay.

heck•le /hékəl/ *v.tr.* interrupt and harass (a public speaker, entertainer, etc.); badger. □□ **heck′ler** *n.*

■ pester, bother, taunt, *colloq.* hassle, plague.

hec•tare /héktair/ *n.* metric unit of square measure, equal to 100 ares (2.471 acres or 10,000 square meters).

hec•tic /héktik/ *adj.* **1** busy and confused; excited. **2** feverish. □□ **hec′ti•cal•ly** *adv.*

■ **1** agitated, bustling, rushed, frantic. **2** flushed, hot.

hecto- /héktə/ *comb. form* hundred, esp. of a unit in the metric system. ¶Abbr.: **h**.

hec•tor /héktər/ • *v.tr.* bully; intimidate. • *n.* bully.

■ *v.* see BULLY *v.* 1. • *n.* see BULLY *n.*

he'd /heed/ *contr.* **1** he had. **2** he would.

hedge /hej/ • *n.* **1** fence or boundary of dense bushes or shrubs. **2** protection against possible loss. • *v.* **1** *tr.* surround or bound with a hedge. **2** *tr.* enclose. **3 a** *tr.* reduce one's risk of loss on (a bet or speculation) by compensating transactions. **b** *intr.* avoid a definite decision or commitment.

■ *n.* **1** see ENCLOSURE 4. • *v.* **1, 2** see EN-CLOSE 1. **3 b** see EQUIVOCATE.

hedge•hog /héjhawg, -hog/ *n.* **1** small nocturnal insect-eating mammal having a piglike snout and a coat of spines, and rolling itself into a ball for defense. **2** porcupine or other animal similarly covered with spines.

he•do•nism /héed′nizəm/ *n.* **1** belief in pleasure as the highest good and the proper aim of humans. **2** behavior based on this. □□ **he′don•ist** *n.* **he•don•is′tic** *adj.*

■ **2** see DISSIPATION 1.

heed /heed/ • *v.tr.* attend to; take notice of. • *n.* careful attention. □□ **heed′ful** *adj.* **heed′less** *adj.* **heed′less•ly** *adv.*

■ *v.* pay attention to, take note of, mark; take, follow, obey. • *n.* notice, consideration, thought. □□ **heedless** unobservant; (*heedless of*) unmindful of, regardless of.

hee-haw /héehaw/ • *n.* bray of a donkey. • *v.intr.* emit a braying sound, esp. a braying laugh.

heel[1] /heel/ • *n.* **1** back part of the foot below the ankle. **2 a** part of a sock, etc., covering the heel. **b** part of a shoe or boot supporting the heel. **3** thing like a heel in form or position. **4** crust end of a loaf of bread. **5** *colloq.* person regarded with contempt or disapproval. **6** [as *int.*] command to a dog to walk close to its owner's heel. • *v.* **1** *tr.* fit or renew a heel on (a shoe or boot). **2** *intr.* touch the ground with the heel, as in dancing. **3** *intr.* (of a dog) follow closely. □ **at** (or **on**) **the heels of** following closely after (a person or event). **down at (the) heel** see DOWN[1]. **kick up one's heels** run or go on a spree. **take to one's heels** run away.

■ *n.* **4** tail end, stump. **5** cad, scoundrel, *colloq.* swine, *sl.* bastard. □ **take to one's**

heels flee, run off, *colloq.* skedaddle, *sl.* split; see also RUN *v.* 2.

heel[2] /heel/ • *v.* **1** *intr.* (of a ship, etc.) lean over. **2** *tr.* cause (a ship, etc.) to do this. • *n.* act or amount of heeling.

■ *v.* **1** list, tip, incline; see also TILT *v.* 1. • *n.* see TILT *n.* 2.

heft•y /héftee/ *adj.* (**heft•i•er**, **heft•i•est**) **1** (of a person) big and strong. **2** (of a thing) large; heavy; powerful. □□ **heft′i•ly** *adv.* **heft′i•ness** *n.*

■ **1** powerful, beefy, *colloq.* hunky. **2** enormous, substantial.

he•ge•mo•ny /hijémənee, héjəmōnee/ *n.* leadership, esp. by one nation over another.

■ see *leadership* (LEADER).

he•gi•ra /hijírə, héjirə/ *n.* (also **he•ji′ra**) **1** (**Hegira**) **a** Muhammad's flight from Mecca to Medina in AD 622. **b** Muslim era reckoned from this date. **2** general exodus or departure.

heif•er /héfər/ *n.* young cow, esp. one that has not had a calf.

height /hīt/ *n.* **1** measurement from base to top or from head to foot. **2** elevation above ground or a recognized level. **3** considerable elevation. **4 a** high place or area. **b** rising ground. **5** top of something. **6 a** most intense part or period. **b** extreme example.

■ **1** tallness, size. **2, 3** altitude. **4** hill, cliff, bluff. **5** crest, apex; see also TOP[1] *n.* 1. **6** acme, zenith, climax; extreme.

height•en /hītən/ *v.* make or become higher or more intense.

■ raise, elevate, lift; strengthen, amplify, magnify, enhance, supplement; see also RISE *v.* 2, INCREASE *v.* 1.

Heim•lich ma•neu•ver /hímlik/ *n.* emergency procedure to aid a choking victim by applying sudden pressure against the victim's upper abdomen to dislodge the object.

hei•nous /háynəs/ *adj.* utterly odious or wicked.

■ see WICKED 1.

heir /air/ *n.* person entitled to property or rank as the legal successor of its former owner (*heir to the throne*). □ **heir apparent** heir whose claim cannot be set aside by the birth of another heir.

■ beneficiary, inheritor, successor.

heir•ess /áiris/ *n.* female heir, esp. to great wealth or high title.

heir•loom /áirlōōm/ *n.* **1** piece of personal property that has been in a family for several generations. **2** piece of property received as part of an inheritance.

■ **1** see ANTIQUE *n.*

heist /hīst/ *sl.* • *n.* robbery. • *v.tr.* rob.

■ *n.* see *robbery* (ROB). • *v.* see STEAL *v.* 1.

held *past* and *past part.* of HOLD.

he•li•cal /hélikəl, héeli-/ *adj.* having the form of a helix.

■ see SPIRAL *adj.*

hel•i•ces *pl.* of HELIX.

he•li•cop•ter /hélikoptər/ • *n.* aircraft without fixed wings, obtaining lift and propulsion from horizontally revolving overhead blades, and capable of moving vertically and horizontally. • *v.* transport or fly by helicopter.

helio- /he´eleeō/ *comb. form* sun.

he•li•o•cen•tric /heˈeleeōséntrik/ *adj.* **1** regarding the sun as center. **2** considered as viewed from the sun's center.

he•li•o•trope /heˈeleeətrōp/ *n.* **1 a** plant with fragrant purple flowers. **b** scent of these. **2** light purple color. **3** bloodstone.

hel•i•port /hélipawrt/ *n.* place where helicopters take off and land.

he•li•um /heˈeleeəm/ *n. Chem.* light, inert, gaseous element used in airships and balloons and as a refrigerant. ¶Symb.: **He**.

he•lix /heˈeliks/ *n.* (*pl.* **he•li•ces** /–seez, hél–/) spiral curve (like a corkscrew) or a coiled curve (like a watch spring).

■ see SPIRAL *n.*

hell /hel/ *n.* **1** place regarded in some religions as the abode of the dead, or of condemned sinners and devils. **2** place or state of misery or wickedness. □ **come hell or high water** no matter what the difficulties. **hell of a** *colloq.* very much of a; extremely (*hell of a hot day*).

■ **1** underworld, inferno, Hades, lower world. **2** purgatory, torment, agony.

he'll /heel/ *contr.* he will; he shall.

hel•la•cious /heláyshəs/ *adj. sl.* **1** impressive; terrific; tremendous; remarkable. **2** overwhelmingly powerful, severe, or difficult.

hel•le•bore /hélibawr/ *n.* evergreen plant having large white, green, or purplish flowers, e.g., the Christmas rose.

Hel•le•nism /hélinizəm/ *n.* Greek character or culture (esp. of ancient Greece). □□ **Hel•len•ic** /lénik/ *adj.* **Hel´len•ist** *n.*

Hel•len•is•tic /hélinístik/ *adj.* of or relating to Greek history, language, and culture from the death of Alexander the Great to the time of Augustus (4th–1st c. BC).

hell•hole /hélhōl/ *n. colloq.* oppressive or unbearable place.

hel•lish /hélish/ *adj.* **1** of or like hell. **2** *colloq.* extremely difficult or unpleasant. □□ **hel´lish•ly** *adv.* **hel´lish•ness** *n.*

■ **1** see INFERNAL 1. **2** see ATROCIOUS 1.

hel•lo /helō, hə–/ *int.* **1 a** expression of informal greeting. **b** used to begin a telephone conversation. **2** cry used to call attention. • *n.* (*pl.* **–los**) cry of "hello".

■ *int.* hi, how do you do?, howdy, *colloq.* ciao, hiya.

helm /helm/ *n.* tiller or wheel for controlling a ship's rudder. • *v.tr.* steer or guide as if with a helm. □ **at the helm** in control; at the head (of an organization, etc.).

■ *n.* steering gear. • *v.* see STEER¹ *v.* 1. □ **at the helm** in command, in the driver's seat; directing, presiding.

hel•met /hélmit/ *n.* protective head covering worn by soldiers, police officers, firefighters, cyclists, etc. □□ **hel´met•ed** *adj.*

helms•man /hélmzmən/ *n.* (*pl.* **–men**) person who steers a vessel.

■ see PILOT *n.* 2, 6, *navigator* (NAVIGATE).

help /help/ • *v.tr.* **1** provide with the means toward what is needed or sought (*helped me with my work*). **2** [often *absol.*] be of use or service to (a person) (*does that help?*). **3** contribute to alleviating (a pain or difficulty). **4** prevent or remedy (*it can't be helped*).

---

5 [usu. with *neg.*] **a** *tr.* refrain from (*can't help it*). **b** *refl.* refrain from acting (*couldn't help himself*). **6** *tr.* serve (a person with food) (*shall I help you to more rice?*). • *n.* **1** helping or being helped (*we need your help*). **2** person or thing that helps. **3** domestic servant or employee, or several collectively. **4** remedy or escape. □ **help oneself 1** serve oneself (with food). **2** take without seeking help; take without permission; steal. □□ **help´er** *n.*

■ *v.* **1** assist, give a hand; support. **2** aid, be useful (to). **3, 4** relieve, cure; avoid. **5 a** stop, resist, keep from. **b** stop, control oneself. • *n.* **1** aid, support, assistance. **2** support; prop, aide. **3** worker(s), hand(s), laborer(s), staff. **4** relief; cure, balm. □ **help oneself 2** appropriate, *colloq.* lift, *sl.* pinch.

help•ful /hélpfŏŏl/ *adj.* giving help; useful. □□ **help´ful•ly** *adv.* **help´ful•ness** *n.*

■ serviceable, practical, beneficial; supportive, reassuring.

help•ing /hélping/ *n.* portion of food, esp. at a meal.

■ serving, ration, plateful, dollop.

help•less /hélplis/ *adj.* **1** lacking help or protection; defenseless. **2** unable to act without help. □□ **help´less•ly** *adv.* **help´less•ness** *n.*

■ **1** vulnerable, dependent; see also *defenseless* (DEFENSE). **2** weak; confused.

help•mate /hélpmayt/ *n.* helpful companion or partner.

hel•ter-skel•ter /héltərskéltər/ • *adv.* in disorderly haste; confusedly. • *adj.* disorderly.

■ *adv.* recklessly, pell-mell, headlong, *colloq.* every which way. • *adj.* confused, haphazard, topsy-turvy, higgledy-piggledy.

hem¹ /hem/ • *n.* border of cloth, esp. a cut edge turned under and sewn down. • *v.tr.* (**hemmed, hem•ming**) turn and sew the edge of (cloth, etc.). □ **hem in** confine; restrict.

■ *n.* see BORDER¹ *n.* 3. • *v.* see SEW. □ **hem in** see BOX *v.* 2.

hem² /hem, həm/ • *int.* (also **a•hem**) calling attention or expressing hesitation by a slight cough or clearing of the throat. • *n.* utterance of this. • *v.intr.* (**hemmed, hem•ming**) say *hem*; hesitate in speech. □ **hem and haw** hesitate, esp. in speaking.

he•ma•tol•o•gy /heˈemətóləjee, hém–/ *n.* the study of the physiology of the blood. □□ **he•ma•tol´o•gist** *n.*

hemi- /hémee/ *comb. form* half.

hem•i•sphere /hémisfeer/ *n.* **1** half a sphere. **2** half of the earth, esp. as divided by the equator (into *northern* and *southern hemisphere*) or by a line passing through the poles (into *eastern* and *western hemisphere*). **3** either lateral half of the brain. □□ **hem•i•spher•ic** /–sféerik, –sférik/ *adj.* **hem•i•spher´i•cal** *adj.*

hem•line /hémlīn/ *n.* lower edge of a skirt, dress, or coat.

hem•lock /hémlok/ *n.* **1** poisonous plant with fernlike leaves and small white flowers. **2** poison made from this.

he•mo•glo•bin /heˈeməglóbin, hém–/ *n.* oxygen-carrying substance containing iron in red blood cells.

he•mo•phil•i•a /ˌheeməfileeə, hém–/ *n. Med.* hereditary disorder with a tendency to bleed severely from even a slight injury, through the failure of the blood to clot normally. □□ **he•mo•phil′ic** *adj.*

he•mo•phil•i•ac /ˌheeməfileeak, –feelee–, hém–/ *n.* person suffering from hemophilia.

hem•or•rhage /hémərij, hémrij/ • *n.* **1** profuse loss of blood from a ruptured blood vessel. **2** extensive damaging loss suffered by a government, organization, etc., esp. of people or assets. • *v.intr.* undergo a hemorrhage.

hem•or•rhoid /héməroyd/ *n.* [usu. in *pl.*] swollen veins at or near the anus; piles. □□ **hem•or•rhoi′dal** *adj.*

hemp /hemp/ *n.* **1** (in full **In′di•an hemp**) herbaceous plant, native to Asia. **2** its fiber used to make rope and strong fabrics. **3** narcotic drug made from the hemp plant.

hem•stitch /hémstich/ • *n.* decorative stitch used in sewing hems. • *v.tr.* hem with this stitch.

hen /hen/ *n.* female bird, esp. of a domestic fowl.

hence /hens/ *adv.* **1** from this time (*two years hence*). **2** for this reason (*hence we seem to be wrong*).

  ■ **1** in the future. **2** therefore, consequently, as a result.

hence•forth /hénsfáwrth/ *adv.* (also **hence•for•ward** /–fáwrwərd/) from this time onward.

  ■ hereafter, from now on, in the future.

hench•man /hénchmən/ *n.* (*pl.* **–men**) **1** trusted supporter or attendant. **2** often *derog.* political supporter; partisan.

  ■ **1** associate, partisan, right-hand man, *colloq.* sidekick.

hen•na /hénə/ *n.* **1** tropical shrub having small pink, red, or white flowers. **2** reddish hair dye made from this.

hen•peck /hénpek/ *v.tr.* (of a woman) constantly harass (a man, esp. her husband).

  ■ nag, pester, torment, carp at, *colloq.* go on at.

hep var. of HIP³.

he•pat•ic /hipátik/ *adj.* of or relating to the liver.

hep•a•ti•tis /hépətítis/ *n.* inflammation of the liver.

hepta- /héptə/ *comb. form* seven.

hep•ta•gon /héptəgən/ *n.* plane figure with seven sides and angles. □□ **hep•tag•o•nal** /–tágənəl/ *adj.*

hep•tath•lon /heptáthlon, –lən/ *n. Sports* seven-event track and field competition, esp. for women.

her /hər/ • *pron.* **1** objective case of SHE (*I like her*). **2** *colloq.* she (*it's her all right, am older than her*). • *poss.pron.* [*attrib.*] of or belonging to her or herself (*her house, her own business*).

her•ald /hérəld/ • *n.* **1** official messenger bringing news. **2** forerunner (*spring is the herald of summer*). • *v.tr.* proclaim the approach of; usher in (*the storm heralded trouble*). □□ **her•ald•ic** /heráldik/ *adj.*

■ *n.* **1** see MESSENGER. **2** see FORERUNNER 2.
• *v.* see ANNOUNCE 1.

her•ald•ry /hérəldree/ *n.* art or knowledge of coats of arms, genealogies, etc.

herb /ərb, hərb/ *n.* **1** any nonwoody seed-bearing plant. **2** plant with leaves, seeds, or flowers used for flavoring, food, medicine, scent, etc. **3** *sl.* marijuana. □□ **her•ba•ceous** /hərbáyshəs/ *adj.* **herb′al** *adj.* **herb′al•ist** *n.*

■ **2** see SPICE *n.* 1.

her•bi•cide /hˊərbisīd, ˊər–/ *n.* poison used to destroy unwanted vegetation.

her•bi•vore /hˊərbivawr, ˊər–/ *n.* animal that feeds on plants. □□ **her•biv•o•rous** /–bívə-rəs/ *adj.*

Her•cu•le•an /hˊərkyəleéən, –kyóoleeən/ *adj.* having or requiring great strength or effort.

■ see SUPERHUMAN 1.

Her•cu•les /hˊərkyəleez/ *n. GK. & Rom. mythol.* man of exceptional strength and size.

herd /hərd/ • *n.* **1** a number of animals, esp. cattle, feeding, traveling, or kept together. **2** [often prec. by *the*] *derog.* large number of people; crowd; mob (*prefers not to follow the herd*). **3** [esp. in *comb.*] keeper of herds; herdsman (*cowherd*). • *v.* **1** *intr. & tr.* go or cause to go in a herd (*herded the cattle into the field*). **2** *tr.* tend (sheep, cattle, etc.) (*he herds the goats*). □□ **herd′er** *n.*

■ *n.* **1** see FLOCK² *n.* 1. **2** group, throng, *usu. derog.* masses, hoi polloi, riffraff. • *v.* **1** gather (together), assemble; round up, corral. **2** shepherd, look after; see also TEND 1.

herds•man /hˊərdzmən/ *n.* (*pl.* **–men**) owner or keeper of herds (of domesticated animals).

here /heer/ • *adv.* **1** in or at or to this place or position (*put it here*). **2** indicating a person's presence or a thing offered (*here is your coat, my son here*). **3** at this point (*here I have a question*). • *n.* this place (*get out of here, lives near here*). • *int.* **1** calling attention: short for *come here, look here*, etc. (*here, where are you going with that?*). **2** indicating one's presence in a roll call: short for *I am here.* □ **neither here nor there** of no importance.

here•a•bouts /ˌheerəbówts/ *adv.* (also **here′a•bout**) near this place.

here•af•ter /heeráftər/ • *adv.* from now on; in the future. • *n.* **1** the future. **2** life after death.

here•by /heerbí/ *adv.* by this means; as a result of this.

he•red•i•tar•y /hiréditeree/ *adj.* **1** (of disease, instinct, etc.) able to be passed down genetically. **2 a** descending by inheritance. **b** holding a position by inheritance.

■ **1** inheritable; innate. **2 a** ancestral, inherited, handed down.

he•red•i•ty /hiréditee/ *n.* **1 a** passing on of physical or mental characteristics genetically. **b** these characteristics. **2** genetic constitution.

here•in /heerín/ *adv.* formal in this matter, book, etc.

her•e•sy /hérəsee/ *n.* (*pl.* **–sies**) **1** belief or practice contrary to orthodox doctrine, esp. of the Christian church. **2** nonconforming opinion (*it's heresy to suggest that instant coffee is as good as the real thing*).

■ 1 see SACRILEGE.

her•e•tic /hérətik/ n. 1 holder of an unorthodox opinion. 2 person believing in or practicing religious heresy. □□ he•ret•i•cal
/hirétikəl/ adj.

■ 1 see NONCONFORMIST. 2 see INFIDEL n.
□□ heretical unorthodox, freethinking, agnostic, atheistic, infidel, heathen, blasphemous, impious.

here•to•fore /héertəfáwr/ adv. formal before
this time.

■ see previously (PREVIOUS).

here•up•on /héerəpón, –páwn/ adv. after
this; in consequence of this.

here•with /héerwíth, –wíth/ adv. with this
(esp. of an enclosure in a letter, etc.).

her•i•tage /héritij/ n. 1 anything that is or
may be inherited. 2 inherited circumstances, benefits, etc. (heritage of confusion).
3 historic buildings, traditions, etc., deemed
valuable.

■ 1 bequest, legacy, birthright. 2 legacy, inheritance.

herk•y-jerk•y /hórkeejórkee/ adj. marked by
fitful, spastic, or unpredictable movement or
manner.

her•maph•ro•dite /hərmáfrədìt/ • n. person,
animal, or plant having both male and female reproductive organs. • adj. combining
aspects of both sexes. □□ her•maph•ro•dit•
ic /-dítik/ adj.

■ n. & adj. see BISEXUAL n. • adj. see BISEXUAL adj.

her•met•ic /hərmétik/ adj. 1 with an airtight
closure. 2 protected from outside agencies.
□□ her•met•i•cal•ly adv.

■ 1 sealed; see also TIGHT adj. 4. 2 enclosed, secured, safe.

her•mit /hórmit/ n. 1 early Christian recluse.
2 any person living in solitude. ■ hermit
crab crab that lives in a cast-off mollusk
shell. □□ her•mit•ic adj.

■ eremite, anchorite, anchoress.

her•mit•age /hórmitij/ n. 1 hermit's dwelling. 2 monastery. 3 solitary dwelling.

her•ni•a /hórneeə/ n. (pl. her•ni•as or her•
ni•ae /-nee-ee/) protrusion of part of an organ through the wall of the cavity containing
it, esp. of the abdomen. □□ her•ni•at•ed adj.

he•ro /héerō/ n. (pl. –roes) 1 a person noted
or admired for nobility, courage, outstanding
achievements, etc. (Newton, a hero of science).
b great warrior. 2 chief male character in a
poem, play, story, etc. 3 dial. = submarine
sandwich.

■ 1 a champion, exemplar, celebrity, star,
idol. b knight. 2 protagonist; (male) lead,
principal.

he•ro•ic /hiróik/ • adj. 1 a (of an act or a
quality) of or fit for a hero. b (of a person)
like a hero. 2 a (of language) grand; high-
flown; dramatic. b (of a work of art) heroic
in scale or subject; unusually large or impressive. • n. [in pl.] 1 high-flown language or
sentiments. 2 unduly bold behavior.
□□ her•o•i•cal•ly adv.

■ adj. 1 brave, courageous, bold, valiant,
noble, honorable, gallant, daring, majestic.
2 a bombastic, exaggerated, extravagant. b -
epic, Homeric, prodigious, larger than life. •
n. 2 (heroics) see BRAVADO.

her•o•in /héroin/ n. highly addictive white
crystalline analgesic drug derived from morphine, often used as a narcotic.

her•o•ine /héroin/ n. 1 woman noted or admired for nobility, courage, outstanding
achievements, etc. 2 chief female character
in a poem, play, story, etc.

■ 1 see HERO 1a. 2 protagonist; (female)
lead; diva.

her•o•ism /héroizəm/ n. heroic conduct or
qualities.

■ see bravery (BRAVE).

her•on /héron/ n. large wading bird with long
legs and a long S-shaped neck.

her•pes /hórpeez/ n. virus disease causing
skin blisters. □ herpes zos•ter /zóstər/ =
SHINGLES.

her•pe•tol•o•gy /hórpitólojee/ n. the study of
reptiles. □□ her•pe•to•log•i•cal /-təlójikəl/
adj. her•pe•tol•o•gist n.

her•ring /héring/ n. N. Atlantic fish used for
food.

her•ring•bone /héringbōn/ n. 1 stitch with a
zigzag pattern. 2 this pattern, or cloth woven
in it.

hers /hərz/ poss.pron. the one(s) belonging to
or associated with her (it is hers, hers are over
there). □ of hers of or belonging to her
(friend of hers).

her•self /hərsélf/ pron. 1 a emphat. form of
SHE or HER (she herself will do it). b refl. form of
HER (she has hurt herself). 2 in her normal
state of body or mind (does not feel quite herself).

hertz /herts/ n. (pl. same) unit of frequency,
equal to one cycle per second. ¶Abbr.: Hz.

he's /heez/ contr. 1 he is. 2 he has.

hes•i•tant /hézit'nt/ adj. 1 hesitating; irresolute. 2 (of speech) stammering; faltering.
□□ hes•i•tance /-təns/ n. hes•i•tan•cy n.
hes•i•tant•ly adv.

■ 1 undecided, uncertain, ambivalent; see
also CAUTIOUS. 2 halting, stuttering.

hes•i•tate /hézitayt/ v.intr. 1 show or feel indecision or uncertainty; pause in doubt.
2 be reluctant (hesitate to say). 3 stammer or
falter in speech. □□ hes•i•ta•tion /-táyshən/
n.

■ 1 vacillate, waver, colloq. dillydally.
2 hang back, think twice; (hesitate to) hold
back from, shrink from. 3 stutter, hem and
haw.

hetero- /hétərō/ comb. form other; different.

het•er•o•dox /hétərədoks/ adj. (of a person,
opinion, etc.) not orthodox. □□ het•er•o•
dox•y n.

het•er•o•ge•ne•ous /hétərōjéeneeəs, –nyəs/
adj. 1 diverse in character. 2 varied in content. □□ het•er•o•ge•ne•i•ty /-jíneeitee/ n.

■ see DIVERSE.

het•er•o•sex•u•al /hétərōsékshōoəl/ • adj.
feeling or involving sexual attraction to persons of the opposite sex. • n. heterosexual
person. □□ het•er•o•sex•u•al•i•ty /-álitee/
n. het•er•o•sex•u•al•ly adv.

■ adj. see STRAIGHT adj. 6b. • n. see
STRAIGHT n. 3b.

heu•ris•tic /hyŏoóristik/ • adj. 1 allowing or

assisting to discover. **2** *Computing* proceeding to a solution by trial and error. • *n.* **1** science of heuristic procedure. **2** heuristic process or method. □□ **heu•ris´ti•cal•ly** *adv.*

hew /hyōō/ *v.* (*past part.* **hewn** /hyōōn/ or **hewed**) **1** *tr.* **a** chop or cut (a thing) with an ax, sword, etc. **b** cut (a block of wood, etc.) into shape. **2** *intr.* strike cutting blows.

■ see CHOP¹ *v.*

hex /heks/ • *v.* **1** *intr.* practice witchcraft. **2** *tr.* cast a spell on; bewitch. • *n.* magic spell; curse.

■ *v.* **2** see BEWITCH 2. • *n.* see JINX *n.*

hexa- /héksə/ *comb. form* six.

hex•a•dec•i•mal /héksədésiməl/ (also **hex**) esp. *Computing* • *adj.* of a system of numerical notation that has 16 rather than 10 as a base. • *n.* hexadecimal system or notation.

hex•a•gon /héksəgən/ *n.* plane figure with six sides and angles. □□ **hex•ag•o•nal** /–ságə-nəl/ *adj.*

hex•a•gram /héksəgram/ *n.* figure formed by two intersecting equilateral triangles.

hex•am•e•ter /heksámitər/ *n.* line of verse of six metrical feet.

hey /hay/ *int.* calling attention or expressing joy, surprise, inquiry, enthusiasm, etc.

hey•day /háyday/ *n.* time of one's greatest strength, vigor, prosperity, etc.

■ see PRIME¹ *n.* 1.

HF *abbr.* high frequency.

Hf *symb. Chem.* hafnium.

Hg *symb. Chem.* mercury.

hgt. *abbr.* height.

hgwy. *abbr.* highway.

HHS *abbr.* (Department of) Health and Human Services.

HI *abbr.* Hawaii (in official postal use).

hi /hī/ *int.* expression of greeting or to call attention.

hi•a•tus /hīáytəs/ *n.* (*pl.* **hi•a•tus•es**) break or gap, esp. in a series, account, or chain of proof.

■ see SPACE *n.* 4.

hi•ba•chi /həbáachee/ *n.* portable charcoal-burning grill.

hi•ber•nate /híbərnayt/ *v.intr.* (of some animals) spend the winter in a dormant state. □□ **hi•ber•na´tion** /–náyshən/ *n.*

Hi•ber•ni•an /hībárneeən/ *archaic poet.* • *adj.* of Ireland. • *n.* native of Ireland.

hi•bis•cus /hībískəs/ *n.* cultivated tree or shrub with large bright-colored flowers.

hic•cup /híkup/ (also **hic´cough**) • *n.* **1** involuntary spasm of the diaphragm causing a coughlike sound. **2** temporary or minor stoppage or difficulty. • *v.* **1** *intr.* make a hiccup. **2** *tr.* utter with a hiccup.

hick /hik/ *n. colloq.* country dweller; provincial.

■ see PROVINCIAL *n.*

hick•o•ry /híkəree/ *n.* (*pl.* **–ries**) **1** N. American tree yielding wood and nutlike edible fruits. **2** the wood of these trees.

hid *past* of HIDE¹.

hid•den *past part.* of HIDE¹.

hide¹ /hīd/ *v.* (*past* **hid** /hid/; *past part.* **hid•den** /hídən/) **1** *tr.* put or keep out of sight (*hid it under the cushion*). **2** *intr.* conceal oneself. **3** *tr.* keep secret (*hid his real motive from her*). **4** *tr.* conceal (*trees hid the house*). □ **hidden agenda** secret motivation; ulterior motive. **hide-and-seek** children's game in which players hide and another searches for them. **hide-out** *colloq.* hiding place. □□ **hid´den** *adj.* **hid´er** *n.*

■ **1** conceal, secrete, squirrel away. **2** take cover, lie low, go into hiding, *colloq.* hole up. **3** conceal, cover (up), disguise. **4** blot out; see also OBSCURE *v.* □ **hide-out** see HIDEAWAY. □□ **hidden** concealed, secret, covert.

hide² /hīd/ *n.* **1** skin of an animal, esp. when tanned or dressed. **2** *colloq.* human skin (*I'll tan your hide*).

■ **1** pelt.

hide•a•way /hídəway/ *n.* hiding place or place of retreat.

■ refuge, haven, retreat, sanctuary, hiding place, *colloq.* hide-out.

hide•bound /hídbownd/ *adj.* **1** narrow-minded; bigoted. **2** (of the law, rules, etc.) constricted by tradition.

■ **1** intolerant; strait-laced, conventional, conservative. **2** bound, limited, hemmed in.

hid•e•ous /hídeeəs/ *adj.* frightful, repulsive, or revolting (*hideous monster*). □□ **hid´e•ous•ly** *adv.* **hid´e•ous•ness** *n.*

■ grotesque, ugly, disgusting, horrible, gruesome, horrifying, outrageous, hateful, atrocious, damnable.

hi•er•ar•chy /híəraarkee/ *n.* (*pl.* **–chies**) **1** system in which grades of status are ranked one above the other (*ranks third in the hierarchy*). **2** hierarchical system (of government, management, etc.). □□ **hi•er•ar•chi•cal** /–raárkikəl/ *adj.*

■ **1** see ORDER *n.* 4.

hi•er•o•glyph•ic /híərəglífik/ • *adj.* depicted with pictures representing words or sounds, as used for ancient Egyptian. • *n.* [*in pl.*] **1** hieroglyphic writing. **2** *joc.* writing difficult to read.

hi-fi /hífī/ *colloq.* • *adj.* of high fidelity. • *n.* (*pl.* **hi-fis**) set of equipment for high fidelity sound reproduction.

hig•gle•dy-pig•gle•dy /hígəldeepígəldee/ • *adv. & adj.* in confusion or disorder. • *n.* state of disordered confusion.

■ *adv. & adj.* see chaotic (CHAOS). • *n.* see CHAOS 1a.

high /hī/ • *adj.* **1 a** of great vertical extent (*high building*). **b** [*predic.*; often in *comb.*] of a specified height (*one inch high, water was waist-high*). **2** far above ground or sea level, etc. (*high altitude*). **3** above the normal level (*high boots, sweater with a high neck*). **4** of exalted, esp. spiritual, quality (*high principles, high art*). **5 a** of exalted rank (*in high society, is high in the government*). **b** important; serious; grave. **6 a** great; intense; extreme; powerful (*high praise, high temperature*). **b** greater than normal (*high prices*). **7** *colloq.* intoxicated. **8** (of a sound or note) of high frequency; shrill; at the top end of the scale. **9** (of a period, an age, a time, etc.) at its peak (*high noon, high summer, High Renaissance*). • *n.*

1 high, or the highest, level or figure. 2 area of high barometric pressure. 3 *sl.* euphoric drug-induced state. • *adv.* 1 far up; aloft (*flew the flag high*). 2 in or to a high degree. 3 at a high price. 4 (of a sound) at or to a high pitch (*sang high*). □ **high and low** everywhere (*searched high and low*). **high beam** full, bright illumination from a motor vehicle's headlight. **high chair** infant's chair with long legs and a tray for meals. **high-class** 1 of high quality. 2 characteristic of the upper class. **high fidelity** reproduction of sound with little distortion, giving a result very similar to the original. **high five** gesture in which two people slap each other's raised palm, esp. out of elation. **high-flown** (of language, etc.) extravagant; bombastic. **high frequency** frequency, esp. in radio, of 3 to 30 megahertz. **high jinks** boisterous joking or merrymaking. **high-level** 1 (of negotiations, etc.) conducted by high-ranking people. 2 *Computing* (of a programming language) that is not machine-dependent and is usu. at a level of abstraction close to natural language. **high-occupancy vehicle** commuter vehicle carrying several (or many) passengers. ¶Abbr.: HOV. **high-pitched** 1 (of a sound) high. 2 (of a roof) steep. 3 at a high level of energy; intense. **high-powered** 1 having great power or energy. 2 important or influential. **high pressure** 1 high degree of activity or exertion. 2 condition of the atmosphere with the pressure above average. **high priest** 1 chief priest, esp. in early Judaism. 2 head of any cult. **high-rise** 1 (of a building) having many stories. 2 such a building. **high school** secondary school. **high sea** (or **seas**) open seas not within any country's jurisdiction. **high-spirited** vivacious; cheerful. **high-strung** very sensitive or nervous. **high tech** *n.* = *high technology. adj.* 1 (of interior design, etc.) imitating styles more usual in industry, etc., esp. using steel, glass, or plastic in a functional way. 2 employing, requiring, or involved in high technology. **high technology** advanced technological development, esp. in electronics. **high tide** time or level of the tide at its peak. **high wire** high tightrope.

■ *adj.* 1 a tall, elevated, towering. 4 lofty, superior; high-class. 5 a chief, leading, important; see also SUPERIOR[1] *adj.* 1. b consequential, weighty, momentous. 6 a huge, considerable, strong. b extreme, excessive; exorbitant, (*predic.*) *colloq.* stiff, steep. 7 inebriated, drunk, drugged, *colloq.* turned-on, on a trip, *sl.* loaded, stoned. 8 high-pitched, squeaky, sharp, piercing; treble, soprano. 9 mid–; late. • *n.* 1 peak, record, maximum. 3 see TRANCE *n.* • *adv.* 1 see ABOVE *adv.* 1. 2 well, far, greatly. 3 dear, sky-high, *colloq.* through the roof. □ **high and low** see EVERYWHERE. **high-class** first-rate, superior, *colloq.* top-drawer, tiptop, A1; aristocratic, elite, exclusive, *colloq.* classy, tony. **high-flown** see *bombastic* (BOMBAST). **high jinks** see FROLIC *n.* 2. **high-pitched** 1 see HIGH *adj.* 8 above. 2 see STEEP *adj.* 1. **high-powered** 1 see POWERFUL. 2 see POWERFUL. **high-spirited** see VIVACIOUS. **high-strung** see NERVOUS 1–3.

high•ball /híbawl/ *n.* drink of liquor (esp. whiskey) and soda, etc., served with ice in a tall glass.

high•boy /híboy/ *n.* tall chest of drawers on legs.

high•brow /híbrow/ *colloq.* • *adj.* intellectual; cultural. • *n.* intellectual or cultured person.
■ *adj.* scholarly, cultivated. • *n. colloq.* brain; see INTELLECTUAL *n.*

high•fa•lu•tin /hífəlóot'n/ (also **high•fa•lu•ting** /–ing/) *colloq. adj.* absurdly pompous or pretentious.
■ see POMPOUS 1.

high-hand•ed /híhándid/ *adj.* overbearing. □□ **high'-hand'ed•ly** *adv.* **high' hand'ed•ness** *n.*
■ see OVERBEARING.

high•land /hílənd/ • *n.* 1 [usu. in *pl.*] 1 area of high land. 2 (**the Highlands**) mountainous part of Scotland. • *adj.* of or in a highland or the Highlands. □□ **high'land•er** *n.* (also **High'land•er**).
■ *n.* 1 see RISE *n.* 2.

high•light /hílīt/ • *n.* 1 (in a painting, etc.) light area, or one seeming to reflect light. 2 moment or detail of vivid interest; outstanding feature. • *n. tr.* 1 bring into prominence; draw attention to. 2 mark with a highlighter pen.
■ *n.* 2 see PIÈCE DE RÉSISTANCE. • *v.* see EMPHASIZE.

high•ly /hílee/ *adv.* 1 in or to a high degree (*highly amusing, commend it highly*). 2 honorably; favorably (*think highly of him*).
■ 1 greatly, tremendously, warmly; extremely, exceptionally; very, much, well. 2 enthusiastically, approvingly.

high-mind•ed /hímíndid/ *adj.* having high moral principles. □□ **high'-mind'ed•ly** *adv.* **high'-mind'ed•ness** *n.*
■ see MORAL *adj.* 2.

high•ness /hínis/ *n.* 1 state of being high (cf. HEIGHT). 2 title used of a prince or princess.

high•way /híway/ *n.* 1 a public road. b main route (by land or water). 2 direct course of action (*highway to success*).
■ 1 see ROAD 1.

high•way•man /híwaymən/ *n.* (*pl.* **-men**) *hist.* robber of passengers, travelers, etc.
■ see *robber* (ROB).

hi•jack /híjak/ • *v.tr.* 1 seize control of (an aircraft in flight, etc.), esp. to force it to a different destination. 2 seize (goods) in transit. • *n.* instance or act of hijacking. □□ **hi'jack•er** *n.*
■ *v.* 2 see STEAL *v.* 1.

hike /hīk/ • *n.* 1 long walk, esp. in the country with backpacks, etc. 2 increase (of prices, etc.). • *v.* 1 *intr.* go for a hike. 2 *tr.* pull up (clothing, etc.). 3 *tr.* increase (prices, etc.). □□ **hik'er** *n.*
■ *n.* 1 see WALK[1] *n.* 2b. 2 see JUMP *n.* 3. • *v.* 1 see WALK *v.* 1, 2. 3 see *mark up* 1 (MARK).

hi•lar•i•ous /hiláireeəs/ *adj.* 1 exceedingly funny. 2 boisterously merry. □□ **hi•lar'i•ous•ly** *adv.* **hi•lar'i•ty** *n.*
■ 1 sidesplitting, uproarious; *colloq.* hysteri-

cal. **2** jolly, mirthful, rollicking. □□ **hilarity** exuberance, glee, jubilation.

hill /hil/ *n.* **1** naturally raised area of land, lower than a mountain. **2** [often in *comb.*] heap; mound (*anthill, dunghill*). **3** sloping piece of road. □□ **hill'i•ness** *n.* **hill'y** *adj.*
■ **1** elevation, rise, mound, knoll, (*hills*) highlands. **2** pile, stack. **3** incline, gradient.

hill•bil•ly /hilbilee/ *n.* (*pl.* **–lies**) *colloq.*, often *derog.* person from a remote or mountainous area, esp. in the Appalachian mountains of the eastern US.
■ see RUSTIC *n.*

hill•side /hilsīd/ *n.* sloping side of a hill.

hill•top /hiltop/ *n.* summit of a hill.

hilt /hilt/ *n.* handle of a sword, dagger, tool, etc. □ **up to the hilt** completely.

him /him/ *pron.* **1** objective case of HE (*I saw him*). **2** *colloq.* he (*it's him again, taller than him*).

Him•a•lay•an /himəláyən/ *adj.* of or relating to the Himalaya mountains in Nepal.

him•self /himsélf/ *pron.* **1 a** *emphat. form* of HE or HIM (*he himself will do it*). **b** *refl. form* of HIM (*he has hurt himself*). **2** in his normal state of body or mind (*does not feel quite himself*).

hind /hīnd/ *adj.* (esp. of parts of the body) at the back (*hind leg*).
■ see POSTERIOR *adj.* 2.

hin•der /híndər/ *v.tr.* [also *absol.*] impede; delay; prevent. See synonym study at PROHIBIT.
■ hamper; thwart, frustrate, stop, check.

SYNONYM STUDY: hinder

ENCUMBER, HAMPER, IMPEDE, OBSTRUCT, PREVENT. If you're about to set off on a cross-country trip by car and wake up to find that a foot of snow has fallen overnight, it would be correct to say that the weather has **hindered** you. But if you're trying to drive through a snowstorm and are forced to creep along at a snail's pace behind a snowplow, it would be correct to say you were **impeded**. To *hinder* is to delay or hold something back, especially something that is under way or is about to start (*she entered college but was hindered by poor study habits*); it connotes a thwarting of progress, either deliberate or accidental. *Impede*, on the other hand, means to slow the progress of someone or something by a deliberate act; it implies that the obstacles are more serious and suggests that movement or progress is so slow that it is painful or frustrating (*the shoes were so tight they impeded his circulation*). Both **hamper** and **encumber** involve hindering by outside forces. To *hamper* is to impede by placing restraints on someone or something so as to make action difficult (*hampered by family responsibilities*), while **encumber** means to hinder by the placing of a burden (*encumbered with several heavy suitcases*). To **obstruct** is to place obstacles in the way, often bringing progress or movement to a complete halt (*obstruct traffic; obstruct justice*). **Prevent** suggests precautionary or restraining measures (*the police prevented him from en-*

tering the burning building) and is also used to describe a nonhuman agency or cause that hinders something (*the snow prevented us from leaving that day*).

Hin•di /hindee/ • *n.* **1** group of spoken dialects of N. India. **2** literary form of Hindustani, an official language of India. • *adj.* of or concerning Hindi.

hind•most /hindmōst/ *adj.* farthest behind; most remote.
■ see LAST[1] *adj.* 1, 5.

hind•quar•ters /hindkwáwrtərz/ *n.pl.* hind legs and adjoining parts of a quadruped.

hin•drance /hindrəns/ *n.* **1** hindering; being hindered. **2** thing that hinders.
■ **2** obstruction, barrier, obstacle; drawback, hitch.

hind•sight /hindsīt/ *n.* wisdom after the event (*realized with hindsight that they were wrong*).

Hin•du /hindoo/ • *n.* follower of Hinduism.
• *adj.* of or concerning Hindus or Hinduism.

Hin•du•ism /hindooizəm/ *n.* main religious and social system of India.

Hin•du•sta•ni /hindoostaanee, –stánee/ • *n.* language based on Western Hindi, a lingua franca in much of India. • *adj.* of or relating to Hindustan, its people, or its language.

hinge /hinj/ • *n.* **1** movable joint on which a door, lid, etc., turns or swings. **2** central point or principle on which everything depends. • *v.* **1** *intr.* **a** depend (on a principle, event, etc.) (*all hinges on his acceptance*). **b** (of a door, etc.) hang and turn (on a post, etc.). **2** *tr.* attach with or as if with a hinge.
■ *n.* **1** see PIVOT *n.* 1. • *v.* **1 a** (*hinge on*) see DEPEND 1.

hint /hint/ • *n.* **1** slight or indirect indication or suggestion (*took the hint and left*). **2** bit of practical information (*handy hints on cooking*). **3** trace; suggestion (*a hint of perfume*). • *v.tr.* suggest slightly (*hinted that they were wrong*).
■ *n.* **1** clue, tip-off; intimation, allusion. **2** clue, suggestion, *colloq.* pointer; (*hints*) help, advice. **3** breath, tinge; touch, dash. • *v.* imply, indicate.

hin•ter•land /hintərland/ *n.* **1** deserted or uncharted areas beyond a coast or a river's banks. **2** remote area.
■ **1** see INTERIOR *n.* 2.

hip[1] /hip/ *n.* **1** projection of the pelvis and upper thigh bone on each side of the body in human beings and quadrupeds. **2** [often in *pl.*] circumference of the body at the buttocks.

hip[2] /hip/ *n.* (also **hep** /hep/) fruit of a rose.

hip[3] /hip/ *adj.* (also **hep** /hep/) (**hip•per, hip•pest**) *sl.* **1** trendy; stylish. **2** understanding; aware.
■ **1** see STYLISH 1. **2** informed, *colloq.* with it; (*hip to*) alert to.

hip•bone /hipbōn/ *n.* bone forming the hip, esp. the ilium.

hip•pie /hípee/ *n.* (also **hip'py**) (*pl.* **–pies**) *colloq.* (esp. in the 1960s) person of unconventional appearance, typically with long hair, jeans, beads, etc., often associated with hallucinogenic drugs and a rejection of conventional values.

■ bohemian, longhair, flower person, *colloq.* dropout.

hip•po /hípō/ *n.* (*pl.* **–pos**) *colloq.* hippopotamus.

hip•po•cam•pus /hípəkámpəs/ *n.* (*pl.* **hip•po•cam•pi** /–pī/) **1** marine fish that swims vertically and with a head suggestive of a horse; sea horse. **2** *Anat.* elongated ridges on the floor of each lateral ventricle of the brain, thought to be the center of emotion and the autonomic nervous system.

Hip•po•crat•ic oath /hípəkrátik/ *n.* oath taken by doctors affirming their obligations and proper conduct.

hip•po•pot•a•mus /hipəpótəməs/ *n.* (*pl.* **hip•po•pot•a•mus•es** or **hip•po•pot•a•mi** /–mī/) large thick-skinned four-legged mammal, native to Africa, inhabiting rivers, lakes, etc.

hip•py var. of HIPPIE.

hire /hīr/ • *v.tr.* **1** employ (a person) for wages or a fee. **2** pay for the temporary use of (a thing); rent or lease. • *n.* hiring or being hired. □□ **hir'a•ble** *adj.* (also **hire'a•ble**). **hir'er** *n.*

■ *v.* **1** engage, enlist, take on. **2** hire out; charter. • *n.* rent, lease; charter.

hire•ling /hírling/ *n.* usu. *derog.* person who works for hire.

■ see SUBORDINATE *n.*

hir•sute /hársōōt/ *adj.* **1** hairy; shaggy. **2** untrimmed. □□ **hir•sut'ism** *n.*

■ **1** see HAIRY 1. **2** see SHAGGY.

his /hiz/ *poss. pron.* **1** [*attrib.*] of or belonging to him or himself (*his house, his own business*). **2** the one or ones belonging to or associated with him (*it is his, his are over there*). □ **of his** of or belonging to him (*friend of his*).

His•pan•ic /hispánik/ • *adj.* **1** of or being a person of Latin-American or Spanish or Portuguese descent in the US. **2** of or relating to Spain or to Spain and Portugal. **3** of Spanish-speaking countries. • *n.* person of Spanish descent living in the US.

hiss /his/ • *v.* **1** *intr.* make a sharp sibilant sound, esp. as a sign of disapproval or derision (*audience booed and hissed, water hissed on the hotplate*). **2** *tr.* express disapproval of by hisses. • *n.* sharp sibilant sound as of the letter *s*.

■ *v.* **1** sizzle, spit; whistle. **2** catcall; see also JEER *v.* 1. • *n.* jeer, boo, hoot, *colloq.* raspberry.

hist *abbr.* **1** historian. **2** historical. **3** history.

his•ta•mine /hístəmin, –meen/ *n.* *Biochem.* organic compound released by body tissues, etc., as in allergic reactions.

his•tol•o•gy /históləjee/ *n.* the study of the structure of tissues.

his•to•ri•an /histáwreeən/ *n.* **1** writer of history, esp. a critical analyst, rather than a compiler. **2** person learned in or studying history (*English historian, ancient historian*).

his•tor•ic /histáwrik, –stór–/ *adj.* famous or important in history or potentially so (*a historic moment*).

■ momentous, noteworthy; celebrated, distinguished, great.

his•tor•i•cal /histáwrikəl, –stór–/ *adj.* **1** of or concerning history (*historical evidence*). **2** (of

383   hippo ~ hit

the study of a subject) showing its development. **3** belonging to the past, not the present. **4** (of a novel, movie, etc.) dealing or professing to deal with historical events. □□ **his•tor'i•cal•ly** *adv.*

■ **1** factual, true, recorded. **2** period; chronological. **3** see PAST *adj.* 1. **4** period.

his•to•ric•i•ty /histərísitee/ *n.* historical genuineness of an event, etc.

his•to•ri•og•ra•phy /histáwreeógrəfee/ *n.* **1** writing of history. **2** the study of historical writing. □□ **his•to•ri•og'ra•pher** *n.* **his•to•ri•o•graph'ic** *adj.* **his•to•ri•o•graph'i•cal** *adj.*

his•to•ry /hístaree/ *n.* (*pl.* **–ries**) **1** continuous record of important or public events. **2 a** study of past events. **b** accumulation of past events (*our nation's history, history of astronomy*). **c** past in general; antiquity. **3** eventful past (*this house has a history*). **4** account of or research into a past event or events, etc. □ **make history 1** influence the course of history. **2** do something memorable.

■ **1** account, chronicle; annals. **2 b** tale, experience(s); biography; see also STORY¹ 2, 4. **c** ancient history, yesterday. **3** reputation, background, life. **4** report; see also INQUIRY 1.

his•tri•on•ic /histreeónik/ • *adj.* theatrical; dramatic. • *n.* [in *pl.*] insincere and dramatic behavior designed to impress.

■ *adj.* see DRAMATIC (DRAMA).

hit /hit/ • *v.* (**hit•ting**; *past* and *past part.* **hit**) **1** *tr.* **a** strike with a blow or missile. **b** (of a moving body) strike. **2** *tr.* cause to suffer or affect adversely. **3** *intr.* [often foll. by *at, against, upon*] direct a blow. **4** *tr.* knock (*hit his head on the door frame*). **5** *tr.* light upon; get at (a thing aimed at) (*he's hit the truth at last*). **6** *tr. colloq.* **a** encounter (*hit a snag*). **b** arrive at (*hit town*). **c** indulge in, esp. liquor, etc. (*hit the bottle*). **7** *tr.* occur forcefully to (*the seriousness of the situation hit him later*). **8** *tr. Sports* **a** propel (a ball, etc.) with a bat, etc. **b** score (runs, etc.) in this way. • *n.* **1 a** blow; stroke. **b** collision. **2** shot, etc., that hits its target. **3** *colloq.* popular success in entertainment. □ **hit and run 1** cause damage and escape or leave the scene before being discovered. **2** *Baseball* play in which a base runner begins running to the next base as the pitcher delivers the ball and the batter then tries to hit the thrown ball. **hit it off** agree or be congenial. **hit man** (*pl.* **hit men**) *sl.* hired assassin. **hit the nail on the head** state the truth exactly. **hit-or-miss** aimed or done carelessly. **hit the road** (or **trail**) *sl.* depart. **hit the spot** *colloq.* be satisfying.

■ *v.* **1 a** cuff, knock, punch, slap, beat, batter, *colloq.* whack, sock, *sl.* belt, wallop, bludgeon, club. **b** collide with, crash into, bump into. **2** hurt, touch; see also AFFECT¹ 2. **3** lash out; (*hit at*) swing at, *colloq.* swipe at. **4** see BEAT *v.* 2a. **5** discover; see also FIND *v.* 1a, 2. **6 a** meet (with); see also FACE *v.* 3. **b** reach, attain. **7** dawn on, occur to. **8 a** drive, *colloq.* swipe. • *n.* **1 a** punch, swat, smack, *colloq.* whack, sock, *sl.* conk. **b** impact, bump, bang; see also COLLISION 1. **2** bull's-eye. **3** triumph, coup, *colloq.* sellout. □ **hit man** see THUG. **hit the nail on the head** put one's finger on it. **hit-or-miss** see CASUAL *adj.* 3a, CARELESS 1, 2. **hit the road** (or **trail**) see *beat it.*

hitch /hich/ • *v.* **1 a** *tr.* fasten with a loop, hook, etc.; tether (*hitched the horse to the cart*). **b** *intr.* become fastened in this way (*the rod hitched in to the bracket*). **2** *tr.* move (a thing) with a jerk; shift slightly (*hitched the pillow to a comfortable position*). **3** *colloq.* **a** *intr.* = HITCHHIKE. **b** *tr.* obtain (a ride) by hitchhiking. • *n.* **1** temporary obstacle. **2** abrupt pull or push; jerk. **3 a** noose or knot of various kinds. **b** connector assembly between a vehicle and something being towed. **4** *colloq.* free ride in a vehicle. **5** *sl.* period of military service. □ **get hitched** *colloq.* marry.

■ *v.* **1** connect, join, hook (up); harness. **2** tug, wrench, *colloq.* yank. • *n.* **1** impediment, snag, difficulty. **2** see JERK¹ *n.* 1, 2. **3** see LOOP *n.* 4 lift. □ **get hitched** see MARRY 1, 2a.

hitch•hike /hích-hik/ *v.intr.* travel by seeking free rides in passing vehicles. □□ **hitch′ hiker** *n.*

■ thumb a lift or ride, *sl.* bum a ride.

hith•er /híthər/ usu. *formal* or *literary adv.* to or toward this place. □ **hither and yon** in various directions; to and fro.

hith•er•to /híthərtoõ/ *adv.* until this time; up to now.

■ see *previously* (PREVIOUS).

Hit•ler /hítlər/ *n.* person who embodies the authoritarian characteristics of Adolf Hitler, Ger. dictator d. 1945.

Hit•tite /hítit/ • *n.* **1** member of an ancient people of Asia Minor and Syria. **2** extinct language of the Hittites. • *adj.* of or relating to the Hittites or their language.

HIV *abbr.* human immunodeficiency virus, any of several retroviruses causing AIDS.

hive /hiv/ • *n.* **1 a** beehive. **b** bees in a hive. **2** busy swarming place. **3** thing shaped like a hive in being domed. • *v.* **1** *tr.* **a** place (bees) in a hive. **b** house (people, etc.) snugly. **2** *intr.* **a** enter a hive. **b** live together like bees.

hives /hivz/ *n.pl.* allergic skin eruption.

HMO *abbr.* health maintenance organization.

Ho *symb. Chem.* holmium.

hoa•gie /hógee/ *n.* (also **hoa′gy**) (*pl.* **–gies**) = *submarine sandwich.*

hoard /hawrd/ • *n.* **1** stock or store (esp. of money or food) laid by. **2** amassed store of facts, etc. • *v.* **1** *tr.* amass and put away; store. **2** *intr.* accumulate more than one's current requirements of food, etc., in a time of scarcity. **3** *tr.* store in the mind. □□ **hoard′er** *n.* **hoard′ing** *n.*

■ *n.* **1** supply, stockpile; reserve, cache. • *v.* **1** collect, lay in; squirrel away, *colloq.* stash (away). **3** see MEMORIZE.

hoarse /hawrs/ *adj.* **1** (of the voice) rough and deep; husky; croaking. **2** having such a voice. □□ **hoarse′ly** *adv.* **hoarse′ness** *n.*

■ see HUSKY¹ 1.

hoar•y /háwree/ *adj.* (**hoar•i•er**, **hoar•i•est**) **1 a** (of hair) gray or white with age. **b** having such hair; aged. **2** old and trite (*hoary joke*).

■ **1 a** see WHITE *adj.* 1. **b** see AGED 2. **2** see MUSTY 2.

hoax /hóks/ • *n.* humorous or malicious deception; practical joke. • *v.tr.* deceive (a person) with a hoax.

■ *n.* swindle, trick, *sl.* con, gyp, snow job; deception, flimflam. • *v.* defraud, cheat, trick, *colloq.* bamboozle.

hob•ble /hóbəl/ • *v.* **1** *intr.* **a** walk lamely; limp. **b** proceed haltingly (*hobbled lamely to his conclusion*). **2** *tr.* **a** tie the legs of (a horse, etc.) to prevent it from straying. **b** tie (a horse's, etc., legs). **3** *tr.* cause (a person, etc.) to limp. • *n.* **1** uneven or infirm gait. **2** rope, etc., for hobbling a horse, etc.

■ *v.* **1** stumble, shuffle, falter. **2, 3** shackle, fetter, restrain; see also HINDER¹. • *n.* **1** shuffle, totter; see also LIMP *n.*

hob•by /hóbee/ *n.* (*pl.* **–bies**) leisure time activity pursued for pleasure. □□ **hob′by•ist** *n.*

■ pastime, sideline, recreation, diversion.

hob•by•horse /hóbeehawrs/ *n.* **1** child's toy consisting of a stick with a horse's head. **2** favorite topic of conversation. **3** rocking horse.

hob•gob•lin /hóbgoblin/ *n.* mischievous imp; bogy.

■ see IMP *n.* 2.

hob•nail /hóbnayl/ *n.* heavy-headed nail used for boot soles.

hob•nob /hóbnob/ *v.intr.* (**hob•nobbed**, **hob•nob•bing**) mix socially or informally.

■ associate, keep company; (*hobnob with*) rub shoulders with.

ho•bo /hóbō/ *n.* (*pl.* **–boes** or **–bos**) tramp; vagrant.

■ see TRAMP *n.* 1.

hock¹ /hok/ *n.* **1** joint of a quadruped's hind leg between the knee and fetlock. **2** knuckle of pork; lower joint of a ham.

hock² /hok/ *colloq.* *v.tr.* pawn; pledge. □ **in hock 1** in pawn. **2** in debt.

■ see PAWN² *v.*

hock•ey /hókee/ *n.* team sport played on skates or on a field, with angled sticks and a puck (when played on ice) or ball.

ho•cus-po•cus /hókəspókəs/ *n.* **1** deception; trickery. **2 a** typical verbal formula used in conjuring. **b** language intended to mystify. • *v.* (**-po•cused**, **–po•cus•ing**; **–po•cussed**, **–po•cus•sing**) **1** *intr.* play tricks. **2** *tr.* play tricks on; deceive.

■ *n.* **1** legerdemain, chicanery, mischief, *sl.* hanky-panky; sleight of hand. **2 a** abracadabra. **b** mumbo-jumbo, gibberish, *colloq.* gobbledygook. • *v.* **2** see DECEIVE 1.

hod /hod/ *n.* **1** V-shaped trough on a pole used for carrying bricks, etc. **2** portable receptacle for coal.

hodge•podge /hójpoj/ *n.* confused mixture; jumble. See synonym study at JUMBLE.

■ miscellany, mishmash, medley, mixed bag, ragbag.

Hodg•kin's dis•ease /hójkinz/ *n.* malignant disease usu. characterized by enlargement of the lymph nodes.

hoe /hō/ • *n.* long-handled tool with a thin metal blade, used for weeding, etc. • *v.* (**hoes, hoed, hoe•ing**) **1** *tr.* weed (crops); loosen (earth) with a hoe. **2** *intr.* use a hoe.

■ *v.* see TILL[3].

hog /hawg, hog/ • *n.* **1 a** domesticated pig, esp. reared for slaughter. **b** other pig, e.g., warthog. **2** *colloq.* greedy person. • *v.* (**hogged, hog•ging**) *tr. colloq.* take greedily; hoard selfishly. □ **go whole hog** *colloq.* do something completely or thoroughly. □□ **hog'gish** *adj.*

■ *n.* **2** see GLUTTON 1. • *v.* see TAKE *v.* 1, MONOPOLIZE. □□ **hoggish** greedy; gluttonous, selfish.

hogs•head /háwgz-hed, hógz-/ *n.* **1** large cask. **2** liquid or dry measure, usu. about 63 gallons.

hog•wash /háwgwosh, -wawsh, hóg-/ *n. colloq.* nonsense; rubbish.

■ see NONSENSE.

hoi pol•loi /hóy palóy/ *n.* [often prec. by *the:* see note below] the masses; the common people. ¶Use with *the* is unnecessary, since *hoi* = 'the,' but is very common

■ herd, riffraff, rabble, crowd, rank and file, silent majority, *derog.* populace, *derog.* proletariat, *usu. derog.* mob.

hoist /hoyst/ • *v.tr.* raise or haul up, esp. with ropes, pulleys, etc. • *n.* **1** act of hoisting; lift. **2** apparatus for hoisting.

■ *v.* lift (up), elevate; winch. • *n.* **2** crane, winch, tackle.

hoi•ty-toi•ty /hóyteetóytee/ • *adj.* haughty; petulant; snobbish. • *int.* expressing surprised protest at presumption, etc.

■ *adj.* arrogant, disdainful, conceited, self-important, *colloq.* high and mighty, stuck-up, snooty, uppity, snotty.

hok•ey /hókee/ *adj.* (also **hok'y**) (**hok•i•er, hok•i•est**) *sl.* sentimental, melodramatic; artificial. □□ **hok'ey•ness** *n.*

ho•kum /hókəm/ *n.* **1** sentimental, popular, sensational, or unreal situations, dialogue, etc., in a movie or play, etc. **2** bunkum; rubbish.

■ **2** see RUBBISH *n.* 3.

hold[1] /hōld/ • *v.* (*past* and *past part.* **held** /held/) **1** *tr.* **a** keep fast; grasp (esp. in the hands or arms). **b** [also *refl.*] keep or sustain in a particular position (*held himself erect*). **c** grasp so as to control (*hold the reins*). **2** *tr.* contain or be capable of containing (*holds two pints*). **3** *tr.* possess, gain, or have, esp.: **a** be the owner or tenant of (land, property, etc.). **b** gain or have gained (a degree, record, etc.). **c** have the position of (a job or office). **d** keep possession of (a place, a person's thoughts, etc.) esp. against attack. **4** *intr.* remain intact (*the roof held under the storm*). **5** *tr.* observe; celebrate; conduct (a meeting, festival, conversation, etc.). **6** *tr.* **a** keep (a person, etc.) in a specified condition, place, etc. (*held her prisoner, held him at arm's length*). **b** detain, esp. in custody. **7** *tr.* **a** engross (*the book held him for hours*). **b** dominate (*held the stage*). **8** *tr.* make (a person, etc.) adhere to (a promise, etc.). **9** *intr.* (of weather) continue as is. **10** *tr.* think; believe (*held that the earth was flat*). **11** *tr.* regard with a specified feeling (*held him in contempt*). **12** *tr.* **a** cease; restrain (*hold your fire*). **b** *colloq.* withhold; not use (*a burger please, and hold the onions!*). **13** *tr.* be able to drink (liquor) without effect. **14** *tr.* (of a judge, a court, etc.) lay down; decide. • *n.* **1** grasp (*catch hold of him*). **2** [often in *comb.*] thing to hold by (*seized the handhold*). **3** [foll. by *on, over*] influence over (*has a strange hold over them*). □ **hold (a thing) against (a person)** regard it as discreditable to. **hold forth** usu. *derog.* speak at length or tediously. **hold the line 1** not yield. **2** maintain a telephone connection. **hold off 1** delay; not begin. **2** keep one's distance. **hold on 1** keep one's grasp on something. **2** wait a moment. **3** (when telephoning) not hang up. **hold out 1** stretch forth (a hand, etc.). **2** offer (an inducement, etc.). **3** maintain resistance. **4** persist or last. **hold out on** *colloq.* refuse something to (a person). **hold up 1 a** support; sustain. **b** maintain (the head, etc.) erect. **c** last; endure. **2** exhibit; display. **3** arrest the progress of; obstruct. **4** stop and rob by force. **hold water** (of reasoning) be sound; bear examination. **take hold** (of a custom or habit) become established. **with no holds barred** with no restrictions; all methods being permitted. □□ **hold'er** *n.*

■ *v.* **1 a, c** seize, grip, *colloq.* hang on to; carry, cradle. **b** maintain, put. **2** accommodate, support, carry. **3** achieve; maintain, sustain. **4** stay, survive. **5** call, assemble; run, participate in, have. **6** confine, restrain; keep; imprison, jail. **7 a** possess, absorb, occupy. **9** see *carry on* 1 **10, 11** judge, consider, take, assume; maintain. **12 a** see CEASE[1] *v.* **b** see WITHHOLD 1. **14** rule; see also *lay down* 2 (LAY). • *n.* **1** grip, clasp, clutch. **3** dominance, mastery, authority; leverage, sway, *colloq.* clout. □ **hold forth** lecture, sermonize, pontificate, *colloq.* go on. **hold off 1** defer, postpone, avoid; (*hold off from*) refrain from. **hold on 1** (*hold on to*) grip, clutch (on to), cling to. **2** see WAIT *v.* 1a. **hold out 1, 2** extend, present, hold up. **3** see RESIST *v.* 1, 2. **4** carry on, persevere, stand firm. **hold up 1 a, b** see SUPPORT *v.* 1, 2. **c** survive, bear up, hold out. **2** present, show, hold out. **3** delay, impede, hinder, set back. **4** waylay, mug, *colloq.* stick up. **hold water** be logical or valid or sensible or consistent, be believable or defensible or workable; make sense, ring true; hold up under scrutiny, bear scrutiny.

hold[2] /hōld/ *n.* cargo area in a ship or aircraft.

hold•ing /hólding/ *n.* **1 a** land held by lease. **b** tenure of land. **2** stocks, property, etc., held. □ **holding company** company created to hold the shares of other companies, which it then controls.

■ **1 a** see FARM *n.* **b** see TENURE 1, 2.

hold•up /hóldəp/ *n.* **1** stoppage or delay. **2** robbery, esp. by the use of threats or violence.

■ **1** setback, hitch, snag. **2** mugging, *colloq.* stickup, *sl.* heist.

hole ~ home

hole ~ home 386

hole /hōl/ • *n.* **1 a** empty space in a solid body. **b** aperture in or through something. **c** flaw; weakness; gap. **2** animal's burrow. **3 a** *colloq.* small, mean, or dingy abode. **b** dungeon; prison cell. **4** *colloq.* awkward situation. **5** *Golf* **a** receptacle in the ground into which the ball is to be hit. **b** one complete playing area from tee to hole. • *v.tr.* **1** make a hole or holes in. **2** put into a hole. □ **hole up** *colloq.* hide oneself. □□ **hol'ey** *adj.*

• *n.* **1 a** cavity, pit, pocket, recess. **b** opening, puncture, rip, break. **2** warren; den, lair. **3 a** shack, hovel, slum, *colloq.* dump. **b** keep, jail, brig. **4** difficulty, fix, mess, *colloq.* scrape; *colloq.* hot water, trouble. • *v.* **1** puncture, pierce, perforate. □ **hole up** see HIDE¹ *v.* 2.

-holic *comb. form* person with a powerful obsession or craving, as *chocoholic*, one who craves chocolate.

hol•i•day /hóliday/ *n.* day of festivity or recreation when no work is done, esp. a national or religious festival, etc.

• feast, celebration, fête, fiesta, gala, red-letter day.

ho•li•ness /hóleenis/ *n.* **1** sanctity; being holy. **2 (Holiness)** title used when referring to or addressing the pope.

• **1** see SANCTITY 1, 2.

ho•lism /hólizəm/ *n.* **1** *Philos.* theory that certain wholes are greater than the sum of their parts. **2** *Med.* treating of the whole person rather than just the symptoms of a disease. □□ **ho•lis'tic** *adj.* **ho•lis'ti•cal•ly** *adv.*

hol•lan•daise sauce /hólǝndáyz/ *n.* creamy sauce of butter, egg yolks, and lemon juice or vinegar, etc.

hol•ler /hólǝr/ *colloq.* • *v.* **1** *intr.* make a loud cry or noise. **2** *tr.* shout. • *n.* loud cry, noise, or shout.

• *v.* see BAWL 1. • *n.* see BELLOW *n.*

hol•low /hóló/ • *adj.* **1 a** having a cavity. **b** sunken (*hollow cheeks*). **2** (of a sound) echoing, low, or muffled. **3** empty; hungry. **4** meaningless (*hollow triumph*). **5** insincere (*hollow laugh, hollow promises*). • *n.* **1** hollow place; hole. **2** valley; basin. • *v.tr.* make hollow; excavate. □□ **hol'low•ly** *adv.* **hol'low•ness** *n.*

• *adj.* **1 a** vacant, void, unfilled; see also EMPTY *adj.* 1. **b** concave, indented, recessed. **3** ravenous, starved. **4** empty, futile, pyrrhic. **5** false, cynical, hypocritical. • *n.* **1** crater, trough, dent; excavation. **2** depression, dip, dale, glen. • *v.* dig, gouge, furrow; (*hollow out*) scoop out.

hol•low•ware /hólōwair/ *n.* hollow articles of metal, china, etc., such as pots, kettles, pitchers, etc.

hol•ly /hólee/ *n.* (*pl.* **-lies**) evergreen shrub with glossy green leaves and red berries.

hol•ly•hock /hóleehok/ *n.* tall plant with large showy flowers of various colors.

Hol•ly•wood /hóleewŏŏd/ *n.* American movie industry or its products, with its center at Hollywood, California.

hol•mi•um /hólmeeǝm/ *n.* *Chem.* soft silvery metallic element of the lanthanide series. ¶Symb.: **Ho.**

ho•lo•caust /hólǝkawst/ *n.* **1** large-scale destruction, esp. by fire or nuclear war. **2 (the Holocaust)** mass murder of Jews by the Nazis in World War II.

• **1** devastation; slaughter, genocide, pogrom; inferno, fire.

ho•lo•gram /hólǝgram/ *n.* *Physics* three-dimensional photographic image made with laser technology.

ho•lo•graph /hólǝgraf/ • *adj.* wholly written by hand by its author. • *n.* holograph document.

ho•log•ra•phy /hǝlógrǝfee/ *n.* *Physics* study or production of holograms. □□ **hol•o•graph•ic** /hólǝgráfik/ *adj.*

hol•ster /hólstǝr/ *n.* leather case for a pistol or revolver, worn on a belt, etc.

ho•ly /hólee/ *adj.* (**ho•li•er, ho•li•est**) **1** morally and spiritually excellent or perfect, and to be revered. **2** belonging to, devoted to, or empowered by, God. **3** consecrated; sacred. □ **holier-than-thou** *colloq.* self-righteous. **Holy Communion** see COMMUNION. **Holy Father** the Pope. **Holy Ghost** = *Holy Spirit.* **Holy Grail** see GRAIL. **Holy Land 1** W. Palestine, esp. Judaea. **2** region similarly revered in non-Christian religions. **Holy See** the papacy or papal court. **Holy Spirit** third person of the Christian Trinity. **holy war** war waged in support of a religious cause. **Holy Week** the week before Easter.

• **1, 2** godly, godlike, saintly, pious, devout; chaste, pure; sacred, divine, heavenly. **3** sanctified, blessed, hallowed. □ **holier-than-thou** see SELF-RIGHTEOUS.

hom•age /hómij/ *n.* acknowledgment of superiority; respect; dutiful reverence (*pay homage to, do homage to*). See synonym study at HONOR.

• obeisance, deference, veneration; honor, tribute.

Hom•burg /hómbǝrg/ *n.* man's felt hat with a narrow curled brim and a lengthwise dent in the crown.

home /hōm/ • *n.* **1 a** place where one lives; fixed residence. **b** dwelling house. **2** members of a family collectively; one's family background (*comes from a good home*). **3** native land. **4** institution caring for people or animals. **5** place where a thing originates or is native or most common. **6** *Baseball* home plate. • *attrib.adj.* **1** of or connected with one's home. **2** carried on or produced in one's own country (*home industries, the home market*). **3** *Sports* played on one's own field, etc. (*home game, home win*). • *adv.* **1 a** to one's home or country (*go home*). **b** arrived at home (*is he home yet?*). **c** at home (*stay home*). **2 a** to the point aimed at (*the thrust went home*). **b** as far as possible (*drove the nail home, pressed his advantage home*). • *v.* **1** *intr.* (esp. of a trained pigeon) return home. **2** *intr.* (of a vessel, missile, etc.) be guided toward a destination or target. □ **at home 1** in one's own house or native land. **2** at ease as if in one's own home (*make yourself at home*). **3** familiar or well informed. **4** available to callers. **home economics** the study of household management. **home plate** *Baseball* plate beside which the batter stands and which the runner must cross to score a run. □□ **home′like** *adj.*

■ *n.* **1** address, (living) quarters; residence, abode, house. **2** household. **3** country, territory, homeland. **4** rest home; refuge, shelter. **5** ENVIRONMENT 1, 2. • *attrib.adj.* **1** family, domestic. **2** native, national. • *v.* **2** (*home in on*) zero in on, head for. □ **at home 2** comfortable, relaxed. **3** (*at home with* or *in*) knowledgeable about, proficient in, *sl.* clued in on. **4** in, welcoming.

home•boy /hómboy/ *n. colloq.* person from one's own town or neighborhood.

home•com•ing /hómkəming/ *n.* **1** arrival at home. **2** annual reunion of alumni held by some high schools, colleges, etc.

home•grown /hómgrōn/ *adj.* grown or produced at home.

home•land /hómland/ *n.* one's native land.

■ see COUNTRY 3.

home•less /hómlis/ • *adj.* lacking a home. • *n.* [prec. by *the*] homeless people. □□ **home′less•ness** *n.*

■ *adj.* on the streets, dispossessed.

home•ly /hómlee/ *adj.* (**home•li•er, home•li•est**) **1** (of people or their features) not attractive in appearance; ugly. **2 a** simple; plain. **b** unpretentious. **c** primitive. □□ **home′li•ness** *n.*

■ **1** plain, unattractive. **2 a** basic, natural; see also SIMPLE *adj.* 2. **b** modest, unassuming, familiar.

home•made /hómmayd/ *adj.* made at home.

home•maker /hómmaykər/ *n.* person who manages a household, esp. as a full-time occupation.

ho•me•op•a•thy /hómeeópəthee/ *n.* treatment of disease by minute doses of drugs that in a healthy person would produce symptoms of the disease. □□ **ho•me•o•path** /-ápáth/ *n.,* **ho•me•o•path•ic** /-meeəpáthik/ *adj.*

Ho•mer•ic /hómérik/ *adj.* **1** of, or in the style of, Homer. **2** of Bronze Age Greece as described in these poems.

■ **1** see HEROIC *adj.* 2b.

home•sick /hómsik/ *adj.* longing for home. □□ **home′sick•ness** *n.*

■ pining, lonely, lonesome; nostalgic, wistful.

home•spun /hómspun/ • *adj.* **1** made or spun at home. **2** plain; simple. • *n.* **1** homespun cloth. **2** anything plain or homely.

■ *adj.* **2** rustic, unrefined, unsophisticated, down-to-earth.

home•stead /hómsted/ *n.* house and adjoining land.

■ see HOUSE *n.* 1a.

home•style /hómstīl/ *adj.* (esp. of food) made at home.

home•ward /hómwərd/ • *adv.* (also **home′wards** /-wərdz/) toward home. • *adj.* going toward home.

home•work /hómwərk/ *n.* **1** work to be done at home, esp. by a student. **2** preparatory work or study.

hom•ey /hómee/ *adj.* (also **hom′y**) (**hom•i•**

er, hom•i•est) suggesting home; cozy. □□ **hom′ey•ness** *n.* (also **hom′i•ness**).

ho•mi•cide /hómisīd, hó-/ *n.* **1** killing of a human being by another. **2** person who kills a human being. □□ **ho•mi•ci′dal** *adj.*

■ **1** see MURDER *n.* 1. **2** see *murderer, murderess* (MURDER). □□ **homicidal** murderous, bloodthirsty, ferocious.

hom•i•ly /hómilee/ *n.* (*pl.* **–lies**) **1** sermon. **2** moralizing discourse. □□ **hom•i•let•ic** /-létik/ *adj.*

■ see SERMON 1.

hom•i•nid /hóminid/ • *n.* member of the primate family including humans and their fossil ancestors. • *adj.* of this family.

ham•i•noid /hóminoyd/ • *adj.* like a human. • *n.* animal resembling a human.

■ *adj.* see HUMAN *adj.* 1–3.

hom•i•ny /hóminee/ *n.* coarsely ground corn kernels, usu. boiled for food.

homo- /hómō/ *comb. form* same (often opp. HETERO-).

ho•mo•ge•ne•ous /hóməjéeneeəs, -yəs/ *adj.* **1** of the same kind. **2** consisting of parts all of the same kind; uniform. □□ **ho•mo•ge•ne•i•ty** /-jineeitee/ *n.* **ho•mo•ge′ne•ous•ly** *adv.*

■ **1** identical, alike, similar. **2** constant, consistent, unvarying.

ho•mog•en•ize /həmójiniz/ *v.* **1** *tr. & intr.* make or become homogeneous. **2** *tr.* treat (milk) so that the fat droplets are emulsified and the cream does not separate.

hom•o•graph /hóməgraf, hó-/ *n.* word spelled like another but of different meaning or origin (e.g., POLE[1], POLE[2]).

ho•mol•o•gous /həmóləgəs/ *adj.* **1 a** having the same relation, relative position, etc. **b** corresponding. **2** *Biol.* (of organs, etc.) similar in position and structure but not necessarily in function.

■ see LIKE[1] *adj.* 1a.

hom•o•nym /hómənim/ *n.* **1** word of the same spelling or sound as another but of different meaning; homograph or homophone. **2** namesake.

ho•mo•pho•bi•a /hómətəbeeə/ *n.* hatred or fear of homosexuals. □□ **ho•mo•phobe** /-əfōb/ *n.* **ho•mo•pho′bic** *adj.*

ho•mo•phone /hóməfōn, hó-/ *n.* word sounding the same as another but of different meaning or origin (e.g., *pair, pear*).

Ho•mo sa•pi•ens /hómō sáypee-enz/ *n.* modern humans regarded as a species.

ho•mo•sex•u•al /hóməséksho͞oəl/ • *adj.* feeling or involving sexual attraction only to persons of the same sex. • *n.* homosexual person. □□ **ho•mo•sex•u•al•i•ty** /-sho͞oálitee/ *n.*

hom•y var. of HOMEY.

hon•cho /hónchō/ *sl. n.* (*pl.* **–chos**) leader or manager; person in charge.

■ see BOSS[1] *n.*

hone /hōn/ • *n.* **1** whetstone, esp. for razors. **2** any stone used for this. • *v.tr.* sharpen on or as on a hone.

■ *v.* see SHARPEN.

hon•est /ónist/ • *adj.* **1** fair and just. **2** free of deceit and untruthfulness; sincere. **3** fairly earned (*an honest living*). **4** (with patronizing effect) blameless but undistinguished. • *adv.* *colloq.* genuinely; really. □□ **hon'es•ty** *n.*

■ *adj.* **1** trustworthy, honorable, decent. **2** candid, frank, open, *colloq.* upfront. **3** aboveboard, straight, square, *colloq.* on the up and up. • *adv.* see REALLY 1.

hon•est•ly /ónistlee/ *adv.* **1** in an honest way. **2** really (*I don't honestly know, honestly, the nerve of them!*).

■ **1** truthfully, honorably, decently, morally, justly, fairly; *colloq.* on the level; candidly, sincerely. **2** see REALLY 1.

hon•ey /húnee/ *n.* (*pl.* **–eys**) **1** sweet sticky yellowish fluid made by bees from nectar. **2** color of this. **3** sweetness. **4** person or thing excellent of its kind. **5** (usu. as a form of address) darling; sweetheart.

■ **5** see DEAR *n.*

hon•ey•comb /húneekōm/ • *n.* **1** structure of hexagonal cells of wax, made by bees to store honey and eggs. **2** pattern arranged hexagonally. • *v.tr.* **1** fill with cavities or tunnels; undermine. **2** mark with a honeycomb pattern.

■ *v.* **1** see RIDDLE[2] *v.* 1.

hon•ey•dew /húneedoō, –dyoō/ *n.* **1** melon with smooth pale skin and sweet green flesh. **2** sweet sticky substance found on plants, excreted by aphids, fungi, etc.

hon•eyed /húneed/ *adj.* (also **hon'ied**) **1** of or containing honey. **2** sweet.

hon•ey•moon /húneemoōn/ • *n.* **1** vacation taken by a newly married couple. **2** initial period of enthusiasm or goodwill. • *v.intr.* spend a honeymoon. □□ **hon'ey•moon•er** *n.*

hon•ey•suck•le /húneesukəl/ *n.* climbing shrub with fragrant yellow, pink, or red flowers.

honk /hawngk, hongk/ • *n.* **1** cry of a wild goose. **2** sound of a car horn. • *v.* **1** *intr.* emit a honk. **2** *tr.* cause to do this.

honk•y-tonk /háwngkeetawngk, hóngkeetongk/ *n.* *colloq.* **1** ragtime piano music. **2** cheap or disreputable nightclub, bar, dancehall, etc.

■ **2** see DIVE *n.* 4.

hon•or /ónər/ • *n.* **1** high respect; reputation. **2** adherence to what is right or accepted conduct. **3** nobleness of mind (*honor among thieves*). **4** official award. **5** privilege; special right (*had the honor of being invited*). **6 a** exalted position. **b** (**Honor**) title of a judge, mayor, etc. **7** person or thing that brings honor (*she is an honor to her profession*). **8 a** (of a woman) chastity. **b** reputation for this. **9** [in *pl.*] **a** special distinction in academics. **b** specialized course of degree studies. • *v.tr.* **1** respect highly. **2** confer honor on. **3** accept or pay (a bill or check) when due. **4** acknowledge. □ **do the honors** perform the duties of a host to guests, etc.

■ *n.* **1** esteem, regard, celebrity, distinction, *colloq.* kudos. **2, 3** uprightness, decency, virtue; integrity, fairness, justness, goodness. **4** see AWARD *n.* 1a. **5** distinction; blessing.

6 a see DIGNITY 3. **8** virginity, virtue, innocence. • *v.* **1** esteem, revere, prize, value. **2** praise, salute, acclaim. **3** redeem, clear, settle. **4** carry out, discharge, fulfill.

SYNONYM STUDY: honor

DEFERENCE, HOMAGE, OBEISANCE, REVERENCE. The Ten Commandments instruct us to "**Honor** thy father and mother." But what does *honor* entail? While all of these nouns describe the respect or esteem that one shows to another, *honor* implies acknowledgment of a person's right to such respect (*honor one's ancestors; honor the dead*). **Homage** is honor with praise or tributes added, and it connotes a more worshipful attitude (*pay homage to the king*). **Reverence** combines profound respect with love or devotion (*he treated his wife with reverence*), while **deference** suggests courteous regard for a superior, often by yielding to the person's status or wishes (*show deference to one's elders*). **Obeisance** is a show of honor or reverence by an act or gesture of submission or humility, such as a bow or a curtsy (*the schoolchildren were instructed to pay obeisance when the queen arrived*).

hon•or•a•ble /ó nərəbəl/ *adj.* **1 a** worthy of honor. **b** bringing honor to its possessor. **c** showing honor; not base. **d** consistent with honor. **2** (**Honorable**) title indicating eminence or distinction, given to certain government officials, members of Congress, etc. See synonym study at MORAL. □□ **hon'or•a•bly** *adv.*

■ **1 a, b, c** upstanding, trustworthy, honest, just, fair, principled, noble, virtuous. **d** right, appropriate, ethical, respectable, decent.

hon•o•rar•i•um /ónəráireeəm/ *n.* (*pl.* **hon•o•rar•i•ums** or **hon•o•rar•i•a** /–reeə/) fee, esp. a voluntary payment for professional services rendered without the normal fee.

■ pay, remuneration; emolument.

hon•or•ar•y /ónəreree/ *adj.* **1 a** conferred as an honor (*honorary degree*). **b** holding such a title or position (*honorary colonel*). **2** (of an office or its holder) unpaid (*honorary treasurer*).

■ **1** see NOMINAL 1.

hon•or•if•ic /ónərifik/ *adj.* **1** conferring honor. **2** (esp. of forms of speech) implying respect. □□ **hon•or•if•i•cal•ly** *adv.*

hooch /hoōch/ *n.* *colloq.* inferior or illicit whiskey.

■ see DRINK *n.* 2a.

hood[1] /hoōd/ • *n.* **1 a** covering for the head and neck, as part of a garment. **b** separate hoodlike garment worn over a university gown to indicate the wearer's degree. **2** cover over the engine of a motor vehicle. **3** canopy to protect users of machinery or to remove fumes, etc. **4** hoodlike part of a cobra, seal, etc. **5** leather covering for a hawk's head. • *v.tr.* cover with a hood.

hood[2] /hoōd/ *n.* *sl.* gangster or gunman.

■ see GANGSTER.

-hood /hoōd/ *suffix* forming nouns: **1** of condition or state (*childhood, falsehood*). **2** indicating a collection or group (*sisterhood, neighborhood*).

hood•lum /hōŏdləm, hōŏd–/ *n.* **1** street hooligan. **2** gangster.

■ **1** thug, ruffian, tough, *colloq.* roughneck; see also BARBARIAN *n.* 1. **2** racketeer, desperado, crook, *sl.* mobster, goon, hood.

hood•wink /hōŏdwingk/ *v.tr.* deceive; delude.

■ fool, trick, defraud, flimflam, pull the wool over a person's eyes, *colloq.* bamboozle, rip off, put one over on, *sl.* take for a ride, cross, bilk, con, gyp, take to the cleaners.

hoo•ey /hōŏ-ee/ *n. & int. sl.* nonsense; humbug.

■ see NONSENSE.

hoof /hōŏf, hōŏf/ *n.* (*pl.* **hoofs** or **hooves** /hōŏvz/) horny part of the foot of a horse, antelope, etc. • *v.* **1** *tr.* walk. **2** *tr. sl.* kick or shove. □ **hoof it** *sl.* **1** go on foot. **2** dance.

hook /hōŏk/ *n.* **1** a bent or curved piece of metal, etc., for catching or hanging things on. **b** fishhook. **2** sharp bend, e.g., in a river. **3 a** *Golf* hooking stroke (see sense 4 of *v.*). **b** *Boxing* short swinging blow with the elbow bent and rigid. • *v.* **1** *tr.* grasp or secure with a hook or hooks. **2 a** *tr.* attach with or as with a hook. **b** *intr.* be or become attached with a hook. **3** *tr.* catch with or as with a hook (*he hooked a fish, she hooked a husband*). **4** *tr.* [also *absol.*] *Golf* strike (the ball) so that it deviates toward the striker. **5** *tr. Boxing* strike (one's opponent) with the elbow bent and rigid. □ **by hook or by crook** by one means or another. **off the hook 1** *colloq.* no longer in difficulty or trouble. **2** (of a telephone receiver) not on its rest, and so preventing incoming calls.

■ *n.* **1 a** peg, holder; fastener, catch. • *v.* **3** trap, snare, bag, land; grab, capture, *sl.* nab. □ **by hook or by crook** come what may, by fair means or foul. **off the hook 1** acquitted, exonerated, cleared.

hoo•kah /hōŏkə/ *n.* tobacco pipe with a long tube passing through water to cool the smoke.

■ see PIPE *n.* 2a.

hooked /hōŏkt/ *adj.* **1** hook-shaped (*hooked nose*). **2** in senses of HOOK *v.* **3** (of a rug or mat) made by pulling woolen yarn through canvas with a hook. **4** *sl.* captivated or addicted.

hook•er /hōŏkər/ *n. sl.* prostitute.

■ see PROSTITUTE *n.*

hook•up /hōŏkəp/ *n.* connection, esp. electronic.

hook•worm /hōŏkwərm/ *n.* **1** nematode worm, with hooklike mouthparts, infesting humans and animals. **2** a disease caused by one of these, often resulting in severe anemia.

hook•y /hōŏkee/ *n.* (also **hook´ey**) □ **play hooky** *sl.* play truant.

hoo•li•gan /hōŏligən/ *n.* hoodlum; ruffian. □□ **hoo´li•gan•ism** *n.*

■ see THUG.

hoop /hōŏp/ *n.* **1** circular band of metal, wood, etc., esp. as part of a framework. **2** arch through which the balls are hit in croquet; wicket. **3** (*pl.*) game of basketball. • *v.tr.* **1** bind with a hoop or hoops. **2** encircle with or as with a hoop.

■ *n.* **1** see RING¹ *n.* 2. • *v.* **2** see CIRCLE *v.* 2.

hoop•la /hōŏplaa/ *n.* **1** *sl.* commotion; excitement. **2** noisy publicity; ballyhoo.

hoo•ray /hōŏráy/ *int.* = HURRAH.

hoot /hōŏt/ *n.* **1** owl's cry. **2** sound made by a vehicle's horn or a steam whistle. **3** shout expressing scorn or disapproval. **4** *colloq.* **a** laughter. **b** cause of this. **5** (also **two hoots**) *sl.* anything at all (*don't give a hoot, doesn't matter two hoots*). • *v.* **1** *intr.* **a** utter or make a hoot. **b** [often foll. by *at*] make loud sounds, esp. of scorn or disapproval or *colloq.* merriment (*hooted with laughter*). **2** *tr.* greet or drive away by hooting. **3** *tr.* sound (a vehicle horn or steam whistle).

■ *n.* **1** see DOWNFALL *n.* 1; **3** see JEER *n.* **4 a** see LAUGH *n.* 1. **5** see DAMN *n.* 2. • *v.* **1 b** see LAUGH *v.* 1. **2** see SQUAWK *v.*

hooves *pl.* of HOOF.

hop¹ /hop/ • *v.* (**hopped, hop•ping**) **1** *intr.* (of a bird, frog, etc.) spring with two or all feet at once. **2** *intr.* (of a person) jump on one foot. **3** *intr. colloq.* **a** make a quick trip. **b** make a quick change of position or location. **4** *tr. colloq.* **a** jump into (a vehicle). **b** obtain (a ride) in this way. • *n.* **1** hopping movement. **2** *colloq.* informal dance. **3** short journey, esp. a flight.

■ *v.* **1** jump, leap, bound. **3 a** pop, run, travel. • *n.* **1** jump, bound, spring. **2** *colloq.* disco; see also DANCE *n.* **3** (short) trip.

hop² /hop/ *n.* **1** climbing plant cultivated for its cones. **2** [in *pl.*] ripe cones of this, used to flavor beer.

hope /hōp/ • *n.* **1** expectation and desire combined, e.g., for a thing (*hope of getting the job*). **2 a** person, thing, or circumstance that gives cause for hope. **b** ground of hope; promise. **3** what is hoped for. • *v.* **1** *intr.* feel hope. **2** *tr.* expect and desire. **3** *tr.* feel fairly confident.

■ *n.* **1, 3** wish; ambition, dream; craving, longing; see also AMBITION 2. **2 b** prospect, confidence, anticipation. • *v.* **1, 2** trust; anticipate, contemplate; (*hope for*) wish, want, seek. **3** (*hope to*) count on, expect to, see also TRUST *v.* 1.

hope•ful /hōpfŏŏl/ • *adj.* **1** feeling hope. **2** causing or inspiring hope. **3** likely to succeed. • *n.* person likely to succeed.

■ *adj.* **1** wishful, desirous; confident, assured; see also *optimistic* (OPTIMISM). **2, 3** promising, bright, rosy, encouraging.

hope•ful•ly /hōpfŏŏlee/ *adv.* **1** in a hopeful manner. **2** it is to be hoped (*hopefully, the car will be ready by then*).

■ **1** expectantly, optimistically. **2** with (any) luck, all being well.

hope•less /hōplis/ *adj.* **1** feeling no hope. **2** admitting no hope (*a hopeless case*). **3** incompetent (*am hopeless at tennis*). □□ **hope´less•ly** *adv.* **hope´less•ness** *n.*

■ **1** despairing, forlorn, gloomy, sad. **2** desperate, beyond hope, beyond repair, lost. **3** bad, poor, inept, unqualified, *colloq.* useless; dud.

Ho•pi /hōpee/ *n.* **1 a** N. American people native to northeastern Arizona. **b** member of this people. **2** language of this people.

hop•per /hópər/ *n.* 1 hopping insect. 2 a container tapering downward (orig. having a hopping motion) through which grain passes into a mill. b similar device in various machines.

hop•scotch /hópskoch/ *n.* children's game of hopping over squares marked on the ground to retrieve a stone.

horde /hawrd/ *n.* 1 usu. *derog.* large group. 2 moving swarm or pack (of insects, wolves, etc.).

hore•hound /háwrhownd/ *n.* 1 plant with a white cottony covering on its stem and leaves. 2 its bitter aromatic juice used against coughs, etc.

ho•ri•zon /hərízən/ *n.* 1 line at which earth and sky appear to meet. 2 limit of mental perception, experience, interest, etc. □ **on the horizon** (of an event) just imminent or becoming apparent.

■ 2 view, range, scope. □ **on the horizon** see *in the pipeline* (PIPELINE).

hor•i•zon•tal /háwrizónt'l, hór-/ • *adj.* 1 parallel to the plane of the horizon; at right angles to the vertical (*horizontal plane*). 2 a combining firms engaged in the same stage of production (*horizontal integration*). b involving social groups of equal status, etc. • *n.* horizontal line, plane, etc. □□ **hor•i•zon'tal•ly** *adv.*

■ *adj.* 1 level, flat; prone, prostrate.

hor•mone /háwrmōn/ *n.* 1 *Biochem.* substance produced in an organism and transported in tissue fluids such as blood or sap to stimulate cells or tissues into action. 2 similar synthetic substance. □□ **hor•mon'al** *adj.*

horn /hawrn/ • *n.* 1 hard outgrowth, often curved and pointed, on the head of cattle, rhinoceroses, giraffes, and other esp. hoofed mammals, found singly, in pairs, or one in front of another. 2 hornlike projection, or thing shaped like a horn. 3 substance of which horns are made. 4 *Mus.* a = *French horn.* b brass wind instrument. c horn player. 5 [often in *comb.*] device sounding a warning (*car horn, foghorn*). • *v.tr.* 1 (esp. as **horned** *adj.*) provide with horns. 2 gore with horns. □ **horn in** *sl.* 1 [usu. foll. by *on*] intrude. 2 interfere. **horn of plenty** cornucopia. **horn-rimmed** (esp. of eyeglasses) having rims made of horn or a similar substance.

■ *n.* 5 see ALARM² *n.* 2a. • *v.* 2 see GORE.

horn•blende /háwrnblend/ *n.* dark brown, black, or green mineral found in rock, and composed of calcium, magnesium, and iron silicates.

hor•net /háwrnit/ *n.* large wasp with a brown and yellow striped body, and capable of inflicting a serious sting.

horn•pipe /háwrnpīp/ *n.* 1 lively dance, usu. by one person (esp. associated with sailors). 2 music for this.

horn•y /háwrnee/ *adj.* (**horn•i•er, horn•i•est**) 1 of or like horn. 2 hard; callused (*horny-handed*). 3 *sl.* sexually excited or frustrated. □□ **horn'i•ness** *n.*

■ 3 see *lustful* (LUST).

ho•rol•o•gy /hawróləjee/ *n.* art of measuring time or making clocks, watches, etc. □□ **ho•ro•log'i•cal** *adj.*

hor•o•scope /háwrəskōp, hór-/ *n.* *Astrol.* 1 forecast of a person's future based on a diagram showing the relative positions of the stars and planets at that person's birth. 2 such a diagram (*cast a horoscope*).

hor•ren•dous /həréndəs/ *adj.* horrifying. □□ **hor•ren'dous•ly** *adv.*

■ see HORRIBLE 1.

hor•ri•ble /háwribəl, hór-/ *adj.* 1 causing or likely to cause horror. 2 *colloq.* unpleasant; excessive (*horrible weather, horrible noise*). □□ **hor'ri•bly** *adv.*

■ 1 hideous, dreadful, gruesome, shocking. 2 disagreeable, offensive, *colloq.* awful, dreadful, ghastly, frightful; see also REVOLTING.

hor•rid /háwrid, hór-/ *adj.* 1 horrible; revolting. 2 *colloq.* unpleasant; disagreeable (*horrid weather, horrid children*).

■ see HORRIBLE.

hor•rif•ic /hawrífik, hór-/ *adj.* horrifying. □□ **hor•rif'i•cal•ly** *adv.*

■ see HORRIBLE 1.

hor•ri•fy /háwrifī, hór-/ *v.tr.* (**-fies, -fied**) arouse horror in; shock. □□ **hor'ri•fy•ing** *adj.*

■ startle, outrage, dismay, scandalize; see also SHOCK¹ *v.* 1.

hor•ror /háwrər, hór-/ • *n.* 1 painful feeling of loathing and fear. 2 intense dislike. 3 person or thing causing horror. • *attrib. adj.* (of literature, movies, etc.) designed to attract by arousing pleasurable feelings of horror.

■ *n.* 1 dread, fright, alarm, panic, terror. 2 repugnance, dread, hatred, revulsion.

hors d'oeuvre /awrdɔ́rvrə, –dɔ́rv/ *n.* (*pl.* same or **hors d'oeuvres**) appetizer served at the beginning of a meal or (occasionally) in place of or during a meal.

■ antipasto.

horse /hawrs/ • *n.* 1 a solid-hoofed plant-eating quadruped with flowing mane and tail, used for riding and to carry and pull loads. b other related four-legged mammals, including asses and zebras. 2 gymnastic apparatus for vaulting. 3 supporting frame esp. with legs (*clothes-horse*). 4 *sl.* heroin. • *v. intr.* [foll. by *around*] fool around. □ **from the horse's mouth** (of information, etc.) from the person directly concerned or another authoritative source. **horse chestnut** 1 large ornamental tree with upright conical clusters of white or pink or red flowers. 2 dark brown fruit of this (like an edible chestnut, but with a coarse bitter taste). **horse race** 1 race between horses with riders. 2 *colloq.* close contest. **horse sense** *colloq.* plain common sense.

horse•back /háwrsbak/ *n.* back of a horse, esp. as sat on in riding. □ **on horseback** mounted on a horse.

horse•fly /háwrsflī/ *n.* (*pl.* **-flies**) any of various biting dipterous insects troublesome esp. to horses.

horse•hair /háwrs-hair/ *n.* hair from the mane or tail of a horse, used for padding, etc.

horse•man /háwrsmən/ *n.* (*pl.* **-men**) skilled rider of horses.

horse•play /háwrsplay/ *n.* boisterous play.
■ see PLAY *n.* 1.

horse•power /háwrspowər/ *n.* (*pl.* same) **1** unit of power equal to 550 foot-pounds per second (about 750 watts). ¶Abbr.: **h.p. 2** power of an engine, etc., measured in terms of this.

horse•rad•ish /háwrsradish/ *n.* **1** plant with long, lobed leaves. **2** pungent root of this scraped or grated as a condiment, often made into a sauce.

horse•shoe /háwrs-shoō/ *n.* **1** U-shaped iron plate nailed to a horse's hoof for protection. **2** thing of this shape. **3** (*pl.*) game in which horseshoes are tossed to encircle a stake.

horse•tail /háwrstayl/ *n.* **1** horse's tail. **2** plant like a horse's tail, with a hollow jointed stem and scale-like leaves.

horse•whip /háwrs-hwip, –wip/ • *n.* whip for driving horses. • *v.tr.* (**–whipped, –whip•ping**) beat with a horsewhip.

horse•wom•an /háwrswōomən/ *n.* (*pl.* **–wom•en**) skilled woman rider of horses.

hors•y /háwrsee/ *adj.* (also **hors'ey**) (**hors•i•er, hors•i•est**) **1** of or like a horse. **2** concerned with or devoted to horses or horse racing. **3** *colloq.* large; clumsy.

hor•ti•cul•ture /háwrtikúlchər/ *n.* art of garden cultivation. □□ **hor•ti•cul'tur•al** *adj.* **hor•ti•cul'tur•ist** *n.*

ho•san•na /hōzánə/ *n. & int.* shout of adoration to God.

hose /hōz/ • *n.* **1** flexible tube for conveying a fluid. **2** [*collect. as pl.*] stockings and socks. • *v.tr.* water or spray or drench with a hose.
■ *n.* **1** see PIPE *n.* 1. • *v.* see WATER *v.* 1.

ho•sier•y /hózhəree/ *n.* stockings and socks.

hosp. *abbr.* **1** hospital. **2** hospice.

hos•pice /hóspis/ *n.* **1** home for people who are terminally ill. **2** lodging for travelers, esp. one kept by a religious order.
■ **1** see HOME *n.* 4. **2** see MONASTERY.

hos•pi•ta•ble /hóspitabəl, hospit–/ *adj.* giving hospitality. □□ **hos'pi•ta•bly** *adv.*
■ welcoming, courteous, friendly, warm, congenial, generous.

hos•pi•tal /hóspit'l/ *n.* institution providing medical and surgical treatment and nursing care for ill or injured people.
■ medical center, infirmary, sanitarium.

hos•pi•tal•i•ty /hóspitálitee/ *n.* friendly and generous reception and entertainment of guests or strangers.
■ cordiality, warmth, congeniality, sociability, generosity.

hos•pi•tal•ize /hóspit'líz/ *v.tr.* send or admit (a patient) to a hospital. □□ **hos•pi•tal•i•za'tion** *n.*

host¹ /hōst/ *n.* **1** large number of people or things. **2** (in full **heav'en•ly host'**) *Bibl.* **a** sun, moon, and stars. **b** angels.
■ army, crowd, horde, multitude, mob, pack, herd, legion.

host² /hōst/ • *n.* **1** person who receives or entertains another as a guest. **2** *Biol.* animal or plant having a parasite. **3** person who introduces and often interviews guests on a show, esp. a television or radio program. • *v.tr.* act as host to (a person) or at (an event).

■ *n.* **3** master of ceremonies, MC, *colloq.* emcee, announcer. • *v.* entertain, play host to; have, hold.

host³ /hōst/ *n.* bread consecrated in the Eucharist.

hos•tage /hóstij/ *n.* person seized or held as security for the fulfillment of a condition.
■ see CAPTIVE *n.*

hos•tel /hóst'l/ *n.* inexpensive lodging esp. for travelers, hikers, etc.

hos•tel•ry /hóst'lree/ *n.* (*pl.* **–ries**) inn.

host•ess /hóstis/ *n.* **1** woman who receives or entertains a guest. **2** woman employed to welcome customers at a restaurant, etc.

hos•tile /hóstəl, –tīl/ *adj.* **1** of an enemy. **2** unfriendly; opposed. □□ **hos'tile•ly** *adv.*
■ **1** warring, combative, opposing. **2** antagonistic, contrary, averse; unsympathetic, inhospitable, see also COLD *adj.* 4.

SYNONYM STUDY: hostile
ADVERSE, BELLICOSE, BELLIGERENT, INIMICAL. Few people have trouble recognizing hostility when confronted with it. Someone who is **hostile** displays an attitude of intense ill will and acts like an enemy (*the audience grew hostile after waiting an hour for the show to start*). Both **bellicose** and **belligerent** imply a readiness or eagerness to fight, but the former is used to describe a state of mind or temper (*after drinking all night, he was in a bellicose mood*), while the latter is normally used to describe someone who is actively engaged in hostilities (*the belligerent brothers were at it again*). While **hostile** and **belligerent** usually apply to people, **adverse** and **inimical** are used to describe tendencies or influences. *Inimical* means having an antagonistic tendency (*remarks that were inimical to everything she believed in*), and *adverse* means turned toward something in opposition (*an adverse wind; under adverse circumstances*). Unlike *hostile*, *adverse* and *inimical* need not connote the involvement of human feeling.

hos•til•i•ty /hostílitee/ *n.* (*pl.* **–ties**) **1** being hostile; enmity. **2** [in *pl.*] acts of warfare.
■ **1** antagonism, ill will, malice, hatred; see also ANIMOSITY. **2** (*hostilities*) war, fighting, combat, action, bloodshed.

hot /hot/ *adj.* (**hot•ter, hot•test**) **1** having a relatively high temperature. **2** producing the sensation of heat (*hot fever, hot flash*). **3** (of pepper, spices, etc.) pungent; piquant. **4** (of a person) feeling heat. **5 a** ardent; passionate; excited. **b** eager; keen (*in hot pursuit*). **6** (of news, etc.) fresh; recent. **7** (of a competitor) strongly favored to win (*a hot favorite*). **8** *sl.* (of goods) stolen, esp. easily identifiable and hence difficult to dispose of. **9** live, at a high voltage. □ **hot air** *sl.* empty, boastful, or excited talk. **hot-blooded** ardent; passionate. **hot dog** *n.* **1 a** = FRANKFURTER. **b** frankfurter sandwiched in a soft roll. **2** *sl.* person who is showy or shows off skills. **hot line** direct exclusive line of communication, esp. for emergencies. **hot plate** heated metal plate for cooking food or keeping it hot. **hot potato** *colloq.* controversial or awkward matter or situation. **hot rod** motor vehicle modified to have extra power and speed. **hot seat** *sl.* **1** position of difficult responsibility. **2** electric chair. **hot-tempered** impulsively angry. **hot tub** tub of heated, circulating water for therapy or recreation, usu. able to accommodate several people. **hot under the collar** angry, resentful, or embarrassed. **hot-water bottle** container, usu. made of rubber, filled with hot water, esp. to warm the feet, a bed, etc. □□ **hot′ly** *adv.* **hot′ness** *n.*

■ **1** fiery, burning, torrid, *colloq.* scorching, sizzling, boiling. **3** spicy, peppery, sharp. **5 a** intense, fervent, zealous. **b** avid, anxious, burning. **6** new, latest. **9** electrified, charged, powered. □ **hot air** bluff, bluster, pomposity, *sl.* bosh, gas; see also DRIVEL *n.* **hot-blooded** see PASSIONATE. **hot-tempered** see IRRITABLE 1. **hot under the collar** see ANGRY 1. □□ **hotly** intensively, energetically, persistently, enthusiastically.

hot•bed /hótbed/ *n.* **1** environment promoting the growth of something, esp. something unwelcome (*hotbed of vice*). **2** bed of earth heated by fermenting manure.

■ **1** breeding ground, fertile source, hothouse.

hot•cake /hótkayk/ *n.* pancake. □ **like hot-cakes** (be sold, etc.) quickly (*the new CD is selling like hotcakes*).

ho•tel /hōtél/ *n.* establishment providing accommodation and meals for payment.

■ inn; motel, bed and breakfast, guesthouse, hostelry.

ho•tel•ier /ótelyáy, hōt′lér/ *n.* hotel-keeper.

■ see PROPRIETOR 2.

hot•head /hót-hed/ *n.* impetuous person. □□ **hot′head′ed** *adj.* **hot′head′ed•ness** *n.*

■ □□ **hotheaded** impetuous, excitable, volatile, rash, hasty, wild, reckless, precipitate, thoughtless.

hot•house /hót-hows/ • *n.* **1** heated building for rearing plants out of season or in a climate colder than is natural for them. **2** environment that encourages the rapid growth or development of something. • *adj.* [*attrib.*] characteristic of something reared in a hothouse; sheltered; sensitive.

■ *n.* **1** hotbed, greenhouse, conservatory. **2** see HOTBED 2. • *adj.* dainty, delicate, pampered, overprotected.

Hou•di•ni /hōōdeénee/ *n.* **1** ingenious escape. **2** person skilled at escaping (for H. Houdini, noted escape artist).

hound /hownd/ • *n.* **1** dog used for hunting. **2** person keen in pursuit of something (usu. in *comb.*: *newshound*). • *v.tr.* **1** harass or pursue relentlessly. **2** chase or pursue with a hound.

■ *v.* **1** persecute, chase, annoy, *colloq.* hassle; see also HARASS 1.

hour /owr/ *n.* **1** twenty-fourth part of a day and night; 60 minutes. **2** time of day; point in time (*a late hour*). **3** period set aside for some purpose (*lunch hour, keep regular hours*). **4** present time (*question of the hour*). **5** time for action, etc. (*the hour has come*). **6** each

time o'clock of a whole number of hours (*buses leave on the hour, on the half hour, at quarter past the hour*). □ **after hours** after closing time.

■ **2** see MOMENT 2.

hour•glass /ówrglas/ • *n.* reversible device with two connected glass bulbs containing sand that takes a specified time to pass from the upper to the lower bulb. • *adj.* hourglass-shaped.

hour•ly /ówrlee/ • *adj.* **1** done or occurring every hour. **2** reckoned hour by hour (*hourly wage*). • *adv.* **1** every hour. **2** frequently; continually.

house • *n.* /hows/ (*pl.* /hówziz/, –siz/) **1 a** building for human habitation. **b** [*attrib.*, often in *comb.*] (of an animal) kept in, frequenting, or infesting houses (*house cat, housefly*). **2** building for a special purpose (*opera house, summer house*). **3** [often in *comb.*] building for keeping animals or goods (*henhouse*). **4** royal family or dynasty (*House of York*). **5** business or institution. **6 a** legislative or deliberative assembly. **b** building where it meets. **c** (**the House**) the House of Representatives. **7 a** audience in a theater, movie theater, etc. **b** theater. **8** *Astrol.* sign of the zodiac. • *v.tr.* /howz/ **1** provide (a person, a population, etc.) with a house or other accommodation. **2** store (goods, etc.). **3** enclose or encase (a part or fitting). □ **House of Lords** (in the UK) chamber of Parliament composed of peers and bishops. **House of Representatives** lower house of the US Congress and other legislatures. **like a house on fire 1** vigorously; fast. **2** successfully; excellently. **on the house** at the management's expense; free.

■ *n.* **1 a** residence, home, homestead, domicile; building, structure. **4** line, lineage, clan. **5** establishment, firm, company, *colloq.* outfit. **6 a** legislature, congress, parliament, assembly, council, diet. **7 c** auditorium, concert hall. • *v.* ₁**1** shelter, accommodate, put up, board. **2** see STORE¹ *v.* **1. 3** see ENCLOSE 1. □ **like a house on fire 1** see FAST *adv.* 1. **2** see WELL¹ *adv.* 5. **on the house** gratis, for nothing, without charge.

house•boat /hówsbōt/ *n.* boat fitted for living in.

house•break•ing /hówsbrayking/ *n.* breaking into a building, esp. in daytime, to commit a crime. □□ **house′break•er** *n.*

house•bro•ken /hówsbrōkən/ *adj.* (of pets) trained to excrete only outdoors or only in proper places.

■ see DOMESTIC *adj.* 3.

house•coat /hówskōt/ *n.* woman's informal indoor robe.

■ see ROBE *n.* 1.

house•dress /hówsdres/ *n.* inexpensive dress of simple design suitable for wear while doing housework.

house•fly /hówsfli/ *n.* common fly.

house•hold /hóws-hōld/ *n.* **1** occupants of a house regarded as a unit. **2** house and its affairs. □ **household word** (or **name**) familiar name, person, or thing. □□ **house′hold•er** *n.*

■ **1** family, ménage.

house•hus•band /hóws-həzbənd/ *n.* married man whose main job is managing household duties.

house•keep•er /hówskeepər/ *n.* person employed to manage a household.
- see SERVANT 1.

house•keep•ing /hówskeeping/ *n.* **1** management of household affairs. **2** operations of maintenance, record keeping, etc., in an organization.

house•maid /hówsmayd/ *n.* female servant in a house.

house•plant /hówsplant/ *n.* plant grown indoors.

house•wares /hówswairz/ *n.pl.* small articles for furnishing a home, such as dishware, glassware, and small appliances.

house•warm•ing /hówswawrming/ *n.* party celebrating a move to a new home.

house•wife /hówswíf/ *n.* (*pl.* **–wives**) woman (usu. married) managing a household. □□ **house'wife•ly** *adj.*

house•work /hówswərk/ *n.* regular housekeeping chores.

hous•ing /hówzing/ *n.* **1 a** dwellings collectively. **b** provision of these. **2** shelter; lodging. **3** rigid casing, esp. for machinery, etc.
- **1, 2** homes, houses, quarters, accommodations; shelter, protection. **3** case, cover, container, box, shield.

HOV *abbr.* high-occupancy vehicle.

hove *past of* HEAVE.

hov•el /húvəl, hóv–/ *n.* small miserable dwelling.
- shack, shanty, hut; pigsty, pigpen, *colloq.* dump.

hov•er /húvər, hóvər/ *v.intr.* **1** (of a bird, helicopter, etc.) remain in one place in the air. **2** wait close at hand; linger.
- **1** float, hang, poise. **2** loiter, wait, hang around.

hov•er•craft /húvərkraft, hóv–/ *n.* (*pl.* same) vehicle that travels over land or water on a cushion of air provided by a downward blast.

how /how/ • *interrog. adv.* **1** by what means; in what way (*how do you do it?*). **2** in what condition, esp. of health (*how is the patient?*). **3** to what extent (*how far is it?, how did they play?*). • *rel. adv.* in whatever way. • *conj. colloq.* that (*told us how he'd been in Canada*). □ **how about** would you like (*how about a game of chess?*). **how do you do?** formal greeting.

how•dah /hówdə/ *n.* seat for riding on an elephant or camel.

how•ev•er /hówévər/ *adv.* **1 a** in whatever way (*do it however you can*). **b** to whatever extent (*must go however inconvenient*). **2** nevertheless.
- **1 a** no matter how, to whatever extent, anyhow, how. **b** no matter how, regardless (of) how. **2** nonetheless, despite that, still, though, yet, even so, at any rate, anyway, anyhow.

how•itz•er /hówitsər/ *n.* short cannon for high-angle firing of shells at low velocities.

howl /howl/ • *n.* **1** long, doleful cry of a dog, wolf, etc. **2** prolonged wailing noise, e.g., as made by a strong wind. **3** loud cry of pain or rage. **4** yell of derision or merriment. • *v.*

1 *intr.* make a howl. **2** *intr.* weep loudly. **3** *tr.* utter (words) with a howl.
- *n.* **1** yowl, yelp. **3** shout, scream, roar. • *v.* **1** yowl, cry, wail, bay; yell, bellow, scream, *colloq.* holler. *See* CRY *v.* 2a.

howl•er /hówlər/ *n. colloq.* glaring mistake.
- blunder, error, *colloq.* slipup, *sl.* boner, goof, screwup, boo-boo.

how•so•ev•er /hówsō-évər/ *adv.* **1** in whatever way. **2** to whatever extent.

hoy•den /hóyd'n/ *n.* boisterous girl.

h.p. *abbr.* (also **hp**) horsepower.

HQ *abbr.* headquarters.

HR *abbr.* (also **H.R.**) **1** House of Representatives. **2** home run.

hr. *abbr.* hour.

HS *abbr.* high school.

Hs *symb. Chem.* hassium.

HST *abbr.* **1** Hawaii(an) Standard Time.

http *abbr.* (also **HTTP**) *Computing* hypertext transfer protocol, the standard for hypertext data distributed on the World Wide Web.

hub /hub/ *n.* **1** central part of a wheel, rotating on or with the axle. **2** center of interest, activity, etc.
- **2** focus, pivot, heart, core, nucleus.

hub•bub /húbub/ *n.* **1** confused noise. **2** disturbance.
- **1** see NOISE *n.* **2** see DISTURBANCE 2.

hub•by /húbee/ *n.* (*pl.* **–bies**) *colloq.* husband.

hu•bris /hyóóbris/ *n.* arrogant pride or presumption. □□ **hu•bris'tic** *adj.*
- see PRIDE *n.* 2.

huck•le•ber•ry /húkəlberee/ *n.* (*pl.* **–ries**) **1** low-growing N. American shrub. **2** blue or black fruit of this.

huck•ster /húkstər/ • *n.* **1** peddler or hawker. **2** publicity agent, esp. for broadcast material. • *v.* **1** *intr.* bargain; haggle. **2** *tr.* carry on a petty traffic in.
- *n.* **1** see PEDDLER (PEDDLE). • *v.* **1** see BARGAIN *v.* **2** see PEDDLE.

HUD /hud/ *abbr.* (Department of) Housing and Urban Development.

hud•dle /húd'l/ • *v.* **1** *tr. & intr.* crowd together. **2** *intr. & refl.* coil one's body into a small space. • *n.* **1** confused or crowded mass. **2** *colloq.* close or secret conference (esp. in **go into a huddle**). **3** *Football* gathering of the players of one team to receive instructions about the next play.
- *v.* **1** cluster, gather. • *n.* **1** group, bunch, throng. **2** meeting, discussion.

hue /hyóó/ *n.* **1** a color or tint. **b** variety or shade of color. **2** attribute of a color by virtue of which it is discernible as red, green, etc.
- **1** shade, tinge, tone.

hue and cry /hyóó/ *n.* loud clamor or outcry.
- see RACKET² 1.

huff /huf/ • *v.intr.* **1** give out loud puffs of air, steam, etc. **2** bluster loudly or threateningly (*huffing and puffing*). • *n.* fit of petty annoyance. □ **in a huff** annoyed and offended. □□ **huff'y** *adj.*
- *v.* **1** see PUFF *v.* 4. **2** puff, storm about; see also RAGE *v.* • *n.* see TANTRUM. □ **in a**

huff piqued, irritated, furious, *colloq.* peeved, in a stink; see also ANGRY 1.

hug /hug/ • *v.tr.* (**hugged, hug•ging**) **1** squeeze tightly in one's arms, esp. with affection. **2** keep close to (the shore, curb, etc.). • *n.* **1** strong clasp with the arms. **2** squeezing grip in wrestling.

■ *v.* **1** clasp, cuddle; see also EMBRACE *v.* 1. **2** follow closely, cling to. • *n.* **1** embrace, squeeze, *colloq.* clinch. **2** clinch.

huge /hyōōj/ *adj.* **1** extremely large. **2** (of immaterial things) very great (*a huge success*). □□ **huge'ly** *adv.*

■ **1** great, enormous, gigantic, immense, vast, *colloq.* jumbo, *sl.* whopping. **2** tremendous, stupendous, enormous, massive, *colloq.* terrific.

Hu•gue•not /hyōōgənot/ *n. hist.* French Protestant.

huh /hə/ *int.* expressing disgust, surprise, etc.

hu•la /hōōlə/ *n.* (also **hu'la-hu'la**) Polynesian dance with flowing arm and rhythmic hip movements.

hulk /hulk/ *n.* **1** body of a dismantled ship. **2** unwieldy vessel. **3** *colloq.* large clumsy-looking person or thing.

■ **1** shipwreck, shell. **3** oaf, lout, *colloq.* galoot, *sl.* klutz.

hulk•ing /húlking/ *adj. colloq.* bulky; large and clumsy.

■ awkward, ungainly, ungraceful, see also MASSIVE 1, 2.

hull¹ /hul/ *n.* body of a ship, airship, flying boat, etc.

■ framework, skeleton, frame, structure.

hull² /hul/ • *n.* **1** outer covering of a fruit, esp. the pod of peas and beans, husk of grain, or calyx of a strawberry. **2** covering. • *v.tr.* remove the hulls from (fruit, etc.).

■ *n.* shell, skin, peel, rind; casing. • *v.* shell, peel, skin.

hul•la•ba•loo /húləbəlōō/ *n.* (*pl.* **hul•la•ba•loos**) uproar; clamor.

■ see UPROAR.

hum /hum/ • *v.* (**hummed, hum•ming**) **1** *intr.* make a low steady buzzing sound. **2** *tr.* sing (a wordless tune) with closed lips. **3** *intr. colloq.* be active (*really made things hum*). • *n.* humming sound.

■ *v.* **1** drone, whir, vibrate. **3** bustle, stir. • *n.* buzz, drone.

hu•man /hyōōmən/ • *adj.* **1** of or belonging to the genus *Homo.* **2** consisting of human beings (*the human race*). **3** of or characteristic of people, esp. as being fallible (*is only human*). **4** showing (esp. the better) qualities of man (*proved to be very human*). • *n.* human being. □ **human being** man or woman or child of the species *Homo sapiens.* **human nature** general characteristics and feelings of human beings. **human rights** rights held to be justifiably belonging to any person.

■ *adj.* **1–3** mortal, manlike; vulnerable. **4** kind, considerate, gentle, forgiving, generous, understanding, good-natured, humane, sensitive. • *n.* person, individual, mortal, soul. □ **human being** see HUMAN *n.* above.

hu•mane /hyōōmáyn/ *adj.* **1** benevolent; compassionate. **2** inflicting the minimum of pain. **3** (of learning) tending to civilize. □□ **hu•mane'ly** *adv.* **hu•mane'ness** *n.*

■ **1** see BENEVOLENT 1.

hu•man•ism /hyōōmənizəm/ *n.* **1** progressive nonreligious philosophy emphasizing human values. **2** (often **Humanism**) literary culture, esp. that of the Renaissance. □□ **hu'man•ist** *n.* **hu•man•is'tic** *adj.*

hu•man•i•tar•i•an /hyōōmánitáireeən/ • *n.* person who seeks to promote human welfare. • *adj.* pertaining to humanitarians. □□ **hu•man•i•tar'i•an•ism** *n.*

■ *n.* good Samaritan, philanthropist. • *adj.* see HUMAN *adj.* 4.

hu•man•i•ty /hyōōmánitee/ *n.* (*pl.* **–ties**) **1 a** the human race. **b** being human. **2** humaneness; benevolence. **3** [in *pl.*] learning or literature concerned with human culture.

■ **1 a** human beings, people, society. **b** humanness, human nature. **2** kindness, consideration, good will, mercy, generosity, sympathy.

hu•man•ize /hyōōmənīz/ *v.tr.* **1** make human. **2** make humane. □□ **hu•man•i•za'tion** *n.*

■ **1** personify, personalize.

hu•man•kind /hyōōmənkínd/ *n.* human beings collectively.

hu•man•ly /hyōōmənlee/ *adv.* **1** by human means (*I will do it if it is humanly possible*). **2** in a human manner.

hum•ble /húmbəl/ • *adj.* **1** having or showing low self-esteem. **2** of low social or political rank (*humble origins*). **3** (of a thing) of modest pretensions, size, etc. • *v.tr.* **1** make humble; abase. **2** lower the rank or status of. □ **eat humble pie** make a humble apology; accept humiliation. □□ **hum'ble•ness** *n.* **hum'bly** *adv.*

■ *adj.* **1** modest, self-effacing, unassuming; meek, deferential. **2** lowly, inferior, mean; low-born. **3** unpretentious, small; see also MODEST 4. • *v.* **1** chasten, subdue, shame. **2** degrade, demote, downgrade; see also REDUCE 6.

SYNONYM STUDY: humble

ABASE, DEBASE, DEGRADE, DEMEAN, HUMILIATE. While all of these verbs mean to lower in one's own estimation or in the eyes of others, there are subtle distinctions among them. **Humble** and **humiliate** sound similar, but *humiliate* emphasizes shame and the loss of self-respect and usually takes place in public (*humiliated by her tearful outburst*), while *humble* is a milder term implying a lowering of one's pride or rank (*to humble the arrogant professor by pointing out his mistake*). **Abase** suggests groveling or a sense of inferiority and is usually used reflexively (*got down on his knees and abased himself before the king*), while **demean** is more likely to imply a loss of dignity or social standing (*refused to demean herself by marrying a common laborer*). When used to describe things, **debase** means a deterioration in the quality or value of something (*a currency debased by the country's political turmoil*), but in reference to people it connotes a weakening of moral standards or character (*debased himself by accepting bribes*). **Degrade** is even stronger, suggesting the destruction of a person's character through degenerate or shameful behavior (*degraded by long association with criminals*).

hum•bug /húmbug/ • *n.* **1** deception or lying. **2** impostor. • *v.* (**hum•bugged, hum•bug•ging**) **1** *intr.* be or behave like an impostor. **2** *tr.* deceive; hoax.
■ **1** deception or lying. **2** impostor.

hum•ding•er /húmdingər/ *n. sl.* excellent or remarkable person or thing.

hum•drum /húmdrum/ *adj.* **1** commonplace; dull. **2** monotonous.
■ boring, tedious, tiresome, routine, ordinary, banal, dry.

hu•mer•us /hyōōmərəs/ *n.* (*pl.* **hu•mer•i** /-rī/) bone of the upper arm. □□ **hu'mer•al** *adj.*

hu•mid /hyōōmid/ *adj.* (of the air or climate) warm and damp.
■ muggy, clammy, sticky, steamy, sultry, wet.

hu•mid•i•fy /hyōōmídifī/ *v.tr.* (**–fies, –fied**) make (air, etc.) humid. □□ **hu•mid•i•fi•ca'tion** *n.* **hu•mid'i•fi•er** *n.*

hu•mid•i•ty /hyōōmíditee/ *n.* (*pl.* **–ties**) **1** humid state. **2** degree of moisture, esp. in the atmosphere.
■ see DAMP *n.*

hu•mil•i•ate /hyōōmílee-ayt/ *v.tr.* injure the dignity or self-respect of. See synonym study at HUMBLE. □□ **hu•mil'i•at•ing** *adj.* **hu•mil'i•a•tion** /-áyshən/ *n.*
■ disgrace, shame, humble, *colloq.* put down; see also HUMBLE *v.* 1. □□ **humiliation** dishonor, loss of face, embarrassment.

hu•mil•i•ty /hyōōmílitee/ *n.* humbleness; meekness.
■ modesty, self-effacement, shyness, submissiveness.

hum•ming•bird /húmingbərd/ *n.* tiny nectar-feeding bird that makes a humming sound with its wings.

hum•mock /húmək/ *n.* hillock, knoll, or hump.
■ see MOUND *n.*

hum•mus /hōōməs/ *n.* dip or appetizer made from ground chickpeas and sesame oil flavored with lemon and garlic.

hu•mon•gous /hyōōmónggəs, –múng-/ *adj.* (also **hu•mun'gous**) *sl.* extremely large or massive.

hu•mor /hyōōmər/ • *n.* **1 a** condition of being amusing. **b** expression of humor in literature, speech, etc. **2** (in full **sense of humor**) ability to perceive or express humor or take a joke. **3** mood or state of mind (*bad humor*). **4** (in full **cardinal humor**) *hist.* each of the four chief fluids (blood, phlegm, choler, melancholy), thought to determine a person's physical and mental qualities. See synonym study at WIT. • *v.tr.* gratify or indulge (a person or taste, etc.). □□ **hu'mor•ist** *n.* **hu'mor•less** *adj.* **hu'mor•less•ly** *adv.* **hu'mor•less•ness** *n.*
■ *n.* **1 a** funniness, comedy, facetiousness. **b** comedy, jokes, *colloq.* wisecracks, gags.

3 temper, spirits, attitude. • *v.* soothe, placate, please, baby, spoil.

hu•mor•ous /hyōōmərəs/ *adj.* **1** showing humor or a sense of humor. **2** facetious; comic. □□ **hu'mor•ous•ly** *adv.*
■ **1** amusing, witty, droll. **2** funny, comical, laughable, hilarious, *colloq.* hysterical, killing.

hump /hump/ • *n.* **1** rounded protuberance on a camel's back, or as an abnormality on a person's back. **2** rounded raised mass of earth, etc. • *v.tr.* **1** *colloq.* lift or carry (heavy objects, etc.) with difficulty. **2** make hump-shaped. □ **over the hump** over the worst; well begun.
■ *n.* **1** bulge, lump, swelling. **2** mound, hummock, hillock. • *v.* **1** drag, haul, heave, *colloq.* schlepp. **2** arch, curve, crook, bend.

hump•back /húmpbak/ *n.* **1 a** deformed back with a hump. **b** person having this. **2** baleen whale with a dorsal fin forming a hump. □□ **hump'backed** *adj.*

hu•mus /hyōōməs/ *n.* organic constituent of soil, usu. formed by decayed vegetation.
■ see SOIL[1] 1.

Hun /hun/ *n.* **1** member of a warlike Asiatic nomadic people who ravaged Europe in the 4th–5th c. **2** vandal.

hunch /hunch/ • *v.* **1** *tr.* bend or arch into a hump. **2** *intr.* sit with the body hunched. • *n.* **1** *colloq.* intuitive feeling or conjecture. **2** hump.
■ *v.* **1** see HUMP *v.* 2. • *n.* **1** impression, suspicion, premonition, idea. **2** see HUMP *n.* 1.

hunch•back /húnchbak/ *n.* = HUMPBACK. □□ **hunch'backed** *adj.*

hun•dred /húndrəd/ • *n.* (*pl.* **hun•dreds** or (in sense 1) **hun•dred**) [in *sing.*, prec. by *a* or *one*] **1** product of ten and ten. **2** symbol for this (100, c, C). **3** set of a hundred things. **4** [in *pl.*] the years of a specified century (*the seventeen hundreds*). • *adj.* that amount to a hundred. □□ **hun'dred•fold** *adj. & adv.* **hun'dredth** *adj. & n.*

hun•dred•weight /húndrədwayt/ *n.* (*pl.* same or **–weights**) **1** (in full **short hundredweight**) unit of weight equal to 100 lb. (about 45.4 kg). **2** (in full **metric hundredweight**) unit of weight equal to 50 kg.

hung *past* and *past part.* of HANG.

Hun•gar•i•an /hunggáireeən/ • *n.* **1 a** native or inhabitant of Hungary. **b** person of Hungarian descent. **2** Finno-Ugric language of Hungary. • *adj.* of Hungary or its people or language.

hun•ger /húnggər/ • *n.* **1** pain, discomfort, or exhaustion caused by lack of food. **2** strong desire. • *v.intr.* **1** crave or desire. **2** feel hunger. □□ **hun'gry** *adj.* (**hun•gri•er, hun•gri•est**). **hun'gri•ly** *adv.*
■ *n.* **1** emptiness, famine. **2** yearning, craving, longing, *colloq.* yen. • *v.* **1** (*hunger for* or *after*) long for, want, *colloq.* have a yen for. **2** have an empty stomach, feel starving. □□ **hungry** famished, ravenous, starving, starved; craving, yearning, desirous, longing, hungering, hankering.

hunk /hungk/ *n.* **1** large piece cut off (*hunk of*

bread). **2** *colloq.* sexually attractive man.
□□ **hunk′y** *adj.* (**hunk•i•er, hunk•i•est**).

hunt /hunt/ • *v.* **1** *tr.* [also *absol.*] **a** pursue
and kill (wild animals, esp. game) for sport
or food. **b** (of an animal) chase (its prey).
2 *intr.* seek; search (*hunting for a pen*). • *n.*
1 practice or instance of hunting. **2** search.
□□ **hunt′er** *n.* **hunt′ress** *n.* **hunt′ing** *n.*
hunts•man /–mən/ *n.* (*pl.* **-men**)

■ *v.* **1** stalk, trail; shoot. **2** (*hunt for or after*)
look (high and low) for, go in quest of; (*hunt
through*) see SEARCH *v.* 1, 3. • *n.* **1** chase,
pursuit, tracking, stalking, search, quest.

hur•dle /hôrd′l/ • *n.* **1** *Track & Field* **a** each
of a series of light frames to be cleared by
athletes in a race. **b** [in *pl.*] a hurdle race.
2 obstacle or difficulty. • *v.* **1** *Track & Field*
a *intr.* run in a hurdle race. **b** *tr.* clear (a hurdle). **2** *tr.* overcome (a difficulty). □□ **hur′
dler** *n.*

■ *n.* **2** barrier, impediment, hindrance, obstruction, snag, complication. • *v.* **1 b** leap
(over), jump (over). **2** surmount, get over;
see also SOLVE.

hur•dy-gur•dy /hôrdeegôrdee/ *n.* (*pl.* **–dies**)
1 musical instrument with a droning sound,
played by turning a handle, esp. one with a
rosined wheel turned by the right hand to
sound the drone strings, and keys played by
the left hand. **2** *colloq.* barrel organ.

hurl /hôrl/ • *v.tr.* **1** throw with great force.
2 utter (abuse, etc.) vehemently. • *n.*
1 forceful throw. **2** act of hurling.

■ *v.* **1** sling, pitch, cast, fire, propel, *colloq.*
chuck, heave. • *n.* **1** see THROW *n.* 1.

hur•ly-bur•ly /hôrleebôrlee/ *n.* boisterous activity; commotion.

■ see DISTURBANCE 2.

Hu•ron /hyŏŏrən, –on/ *n.* **1 a** N. American
people native to the northeastern U.S.
b member of these people. **2** language of
this people.

hur•rah /hŏŏraá/ (also **hur•ray** /hŏŏráy/) *int.*
& n. exclamation of joy or approval.

■ see CHEER *n.* 1.

hur•ri•cane /hôrikayn, húr–/ *n.* **1** storm with
a violent wind, esp. a cyclone in the W. Atlantic. **2** violent commotion. □ **hurricane
lamp** oil lamp designed to resist a high
wind.

■ **1** typhoon, whirlwind, gale. **2** see STIR[1] *n.*
2.

hur•ry /hôree, húree/ • *n.* (*pl.* **–ries**) **1 a** great
haste. **b** [with *neg.* or *interrog.*] need for haste
(*there is no hurry, what's the hurry?*). **2** eagerness to get a thing done quickly. • *v.* (**–ries,
–ried**) **1** *intr.* move or act hastily. **2** *tr.* cause
to move or proceed in this way. **3** *tr.* (as **hurried** *adj.*) hasty; done rapidly owing to lack
of time. □□ **hur′ried•ly** *adv.*

■ *n.* **1 a** rush. **b** pressure; see also *urgency*
(URGENT). **2** see *eagerness* (EAGER). • *v.*
1 rush, hasten, hotfoot (it), *colloq.* get a move
on, hightail (it); speed, race, dash, hustle, *colloq.* tear, scoot. **2** push, drive, urge, spur
(on). **3** (**hurried**) frantic, hectic, rushed,
speedy; brief, short; superficial, cursory.

hurt /hôrt/ • *v.* (*past* and *past part.* **hurt**) **1** *tr.*

[also *absol.*] cause pain or injury to. **2** *tr.*
cause mental pain or distress to. **3** *intr.* suffer pain or harm (*my arm hurts*). • *n.* **1** injury. **2** harm; wrong. • *adj.* expressing emotional pain.

■ *v.* **1** harm, wound. **2** grieve, afflict, depress. **3** ache, throb, be sore; smart, burn. •
n. **1** wound, damage; see also INJURY 1. **2** injury, damage; see also GRIEVANCE. • *adj.* unhappy, distressed, aggrieved, sad, wretched,
sorrowful, mournful.

hurt•ful /hôrtfŏŏl/ *adj.* causing (esp. mental)
hurt. □□ **hurt′ful•ly** *adv.*

■ nasty, cruel, malicious; harmful, injurious.

hur•tle /hôrt′l/ *v.* move or hurl rapidly or
noisily.

■ rush (headlong), plunge; tear, shoot, race,
speed.

hus•band /húzbənd/ • *n.* married man, esp.
in relation to his wife. • *v.tr.* manage thrift-
ily; use (resources) economically.

■ *n.* spouse, partner, *colloq.* mate, old man.
• *v.* budget.

hus•band•ry /húzbəndree/ *n.* **1** farming.
2 management of resources.

■ **2** see ECONOMY 2a.

hush /hush/ • *v.* **1** *tr. & intr.* (often as
hushed *adj.*) make or become silent or
quiet. **2** *tr.* calm; soothe. • *int.* calling for silence. • *n.* expectant stillness or silence.
□ **hush puppy** deep-fried ball of cornmeal
dough.

■ *v.* **1** shush, still; (**hushed**) muted, soft.
2 quiet, pacify, placate. *int.* shush, quiet, *colloq.* shut up, clam up, *sl.* shut your face, button your lip, put a sock in it. • *n.* quiet,
peace, tranquillity.

hush-hush /húsh-húsh/ *adj. colloq.* highly secret.

■ see SECRET *adj.* 1.

husk /husk/ • *n.* **1** dry outer covering of
some fruits or seeds. **2** worthless outside
part of a thing. • *v.tr.* remove husk(s) from.

■ *n.* **1** see SKIN *n.* 3. • *v.* see SHELL *v.* 1.

husk•y[1] /húskee/ *adj.* (**husk•i•er, husk•i•est**)
1 (of a person or voice) dry in the throat;
hoarse. **2** strong; hefty. □□ **husk′i•ly** *adv.*
husk′i•ness *n.*

■ **1** gruff, rasping, raucous. **2** brawny,
strapping, sturdy, burly.

husk•y[2] /húskee/ *n.* (*pl.* **–ies**) dog of a powerful breed used in the Arctic for pulling sleds.

hus•sy /húsee, –zee/ *n.* (*pl.* **–sies**) *derog.* impudent or immoral girl or woman.

hus•tings /hústingz/ *n.* political campaigning, esp. appearances and activities involved
with a campaign.

hus•tle /húsəl/ • *v.* **1** *tr.* push roughly; jostle.
2 *tr.* force, coerce, or deal with hurriedly or
unceremoniously (*hustled them out of the
room*). **3** *intr.* push one's way; hurry; bustle.
4 *tr. sl.* **a** obtain by forceful action. **b** swindle. **5** *intr. sl.* engage in prostitution. • *n.*
1 a act or instance of hustling. **b** forceful or
strenuous activity. **2** *colloq.* fraud or swindle.
□□ **hus′tler** *n.*

■ *v.* **1** shove, elbow, force. **2** (*hustle into or
out of*, etc.) drive *or* push into *or* out of *or*
through, eject from; *sl.* bounce out of.

3 rush, run, sprint, dash. **4 b** see SWINDLE *v.* **5** walk the streets. • *n.* **1 a** pushing, jostling, buffeting. **b** action, activity, stir. **2** see SWINDLE *n.*

hut /hut/ *n.* small simple or crude house or shelter.

■ cabin, shack, shanty.

hutch /huch/ *n.* **1** box or cage, usu. with a wire mesh front, for keeping rabbits, etc. **2** cupboard.

■ **1** see CAGE *n.*

hwy. *abbr.* highway.

hy•a•cinth /hísinth/ *n.* **1** bulbous plant with clusters of usu. purplish blue, pink, or white bell-shaped fragrant flowers. **2** purplish blue.

hy•brid /híbrid/ • *n.* **1** *Biol.* offspring of two plants or animals of different species or varieties. **2** thing composed of diverse elements, e.g., a word with parts taken from different languages. • *adj.* **1** bred as a hybrid. **2** *Biol.* heterogeneous. **3** of mixed character; derived from incongruous elements or unlike sources. □□ **hy′brid•ism** *n.*

■ *n.* **1** crossbreed, cross, mongrel. **2** mixture, composite, combination, compound, blend. • *adj.* **3** see DIVERSE.

hy•brid•ize /híbridiz/ *v.* **1** *tr.* subject (a species, etc.) to cross-breeding. **2** *intr.* **a** produce hybrids. **b** (of an animal or plant) interbreed. □□ **hy•brid•i•za′tion** *n.*

hy•dra /hídrə/ *n.* **1** freshwater polyp with tubular body and tentacles around the mouth. **2** something hard to destroy.

hy•dran•gea /hídráynjə, –dran–/ *n.* shrub with globular clusters of white, pink, or blue flowers.

hy•drant /hídrənt/ *n.* pipe (esp. in a street) with a nozzle for a hose, for drawing water from a main.

■ standpipe, fireplug.

hy•drate /hídrayt/ • *n. Chem.* compound of water combined with another compound or an element. • *v.tr.* **1 a** combine chemically with water. **b** (as **hydrated** *adj.*) chemically bonded to water. **2** cause to absorb water. □□ **hy•dra′tion** /dráyəhən/ *n.*

hy•drau•lic /hídráwlik, –drólik/ *adj.* **1** (of water, oil, etc.) conveyed through pipes or channels usu. by pressure. **2** (of a mechanism, etc.) operated by liquid moving in this manner (*hydraulic brakes*). **3** of or concerned with hydraulics (*hydraulic engineer*). □□ **hy•drau′li•cal•ly** *adv.*

hy•drau•lics /hídráwliks, –dróliks/ *n.pl.* [usu. treated as *sing.*] the science of the conveyance of liquids through pipes, etc., esp. as motive power.

hydro- /hídrō/ *comb. form* (also **hydr–** before a vowel) **1** having to do with water (*hydroelectric*). **2** *Chem.* combined with hydrogen (*hydrochloric*).

hy•dro•car•bon /hídrəkaárbən/ *n. Chem.* compound of hydrogen and carbon.

hy•dro•chlo•ric ac•id /hídrəkláwrik/ *n. Chem.* solution of the colorless gas hydrogen chloride in water. ¶Chem. formula: HCl.

hy•dro•dy•nam•ics /hídrōdīnámiks/ *n.* the science of forces acting on or exerted by fluids (esp. liquids). □□ **hy•dro•dy•nam′ic** *adj.*

hy•dro•e•lec•tric /hídrōiléktrik/ *adj.* **1** generating electricity by waterpower. **2** (of electricity) generated in this way. □□ **hy•dro•e•lec′tric•i•ty** /–trísitee/ *n.*

hy•dro•foil /hídrəfoyl/ *n.* **1** boat with finlike members on struts for lifting its hull out of the water to increase speed. **2** this device.

hy•dro•gen /hídrəjən/ *n. Chem.* colorless gaseous element, without taste or odor, the lightest element and occurring in water and all organic compounds. ¶Symb.: **H.** □ **hydrogen bomb** immensely powerful bomb utilizing the explosive fusion of hydrogen nuclei. (Also called **H bomb**). **hydrogen peroxide** colorless liquid used as an antiseptic and bleach. ¶Chem. formula: H_2O_2. □□ **hy•dro•gen•ous** /–drójinəs/ *adj.*

hy•drog•e•nate /hídrójinayt, hídrəjənayt/ *v.tr.* charge with or cause to combine with hydrogen. □□ **hy•drog•en•a•tion** /–áyshən/ *n.*

hy•drol•o•gy /hídróləjee/ *n.* the science of the properties of water, esp. of its movement in relation to land. □□ **hy•drol′o•gist** *n.*

hy•drol•y•sis /hídrólisis/ *n.* chemical reaction of a substance with water, usu. resulting in decomposition.

hy•dro•lyze /hídrəliz/ *v.* decompose by hydrolysis.

hy•drom•e•ter /hídrómitər/ *n.* instrument for measuring the density of liquids.

hy•dro•pho•bi•a /hídrəfóbeeə/ *n.* **1** morbid aversion to water. **2** rabies, esp. in humans. □□ **hy•dro•pho•bic** /–bik/ *adj.*

hy•dro•plane /hídrəplayn/ • *n.* **1** light fast motorboat designed to skim over water. **2** seaplane. • *v.intr.* **1** (of a boat) skim over the surface of water with its hull lifted. **2** (of a vehicle) glide uncontrollably on a wet road surface.

hy•dro•pon•ics /hídrəpóniks/ *n.* growing plants in sand, gravel, or liquid, without soil and with added nutrients. □□ **hy•dro•pon′ic** *adj.* **hy•dro•pon′i•cal•ly** *adv.*

hy•dro•sphere /hídrəsfeer/ *n.* waters of the earth's surface.

hy•dro•ther•a•py /hídrəthérəpee/ *n.* use of water, esp. swimming, in the treatment of arthritis, paralysis, etc.

hy•drous /hídrəs/ *adj. Chem. & Mineral.* containing water.

hy•e•na /hí-eenə/ *n.* doglike flesh-eating mammal with hind limbs shorter than forelimbs. □ **laughing hyena** *n.* hyena whose howl is compared to a fiendish laugh.

hy•giene /híjeen/ *n.* **1** conditions or practices, esp. cleanliness, conducive to maintaining health. **2** sanitary science. □□ **hy•gi•en•ic** /híjénik, –jéenik/ *adj.* **hy•gi•en′i•cal•ly** *adv.* See synonym study at SANITARY

hy•gien•ist /híjénist, –jee–, –híjeenist/ *n.* specialist in cleanliness for the preservation of health, esp. (**dental hygienist**) a dental assistant who cleans the teeth.

hy•grom•e•ter /hígrómitər/ *n.* instrument for measuring humidity.

hy•men /hímən/ *n. Anat.* membrane at the opening of the vagina.

hymn /him/ • *n.* **1** song of praise, esp. to God in Christian worship. **2** song of praise in honor of a god or other exalted being or thing. • *v.* **1** *tr.* praise or celebrate in hymns. **2** *intr.* sing hymns.
■ *n.* see SONG.

hym•nal /hímnəl/ • *n.* book of hymns. • *adj.* of hymns.

hype /hīp/ *sl.* • *n.* **1** extravagant or intensive publicity promotion. **2** cheating; trick. • *v.tr.* **1** promote (a product) with extravagant publicity. **2** cheat; trick.
■ *n.* **1** see ADVERTISEMENT. • *v.* **1** see PROMOTE 3.

hy•per /hípər/ *adj. sl.* excessively excited, nervous, stimulated, etc.

hyper- /hípər/ *prefix* meaning: **1** over; beyond; above (*hyperphysical*). **2** exceeding (*hypersonic*). **3** excessively; above normal (*hyperbole, hypersensitive*).

hy•per•ac•tive /hìpəráktiv/ *adj.* (of a person, esp. a child) abnormally active. □□ **hy•per•ac•tiv•i•ty** /-tívitee/ *n.*
■ see ACTIVE *adj.* 1a.

hy•per•bo•la /hīpərbələ/ *n.* (*pl.* **hy•per•bo•las** or **hy•per•bo•lae** /-lee/) *Geom.* plane curve produced when a cone is cut by a plane that makes a larger angle with the base than the side of the cone (cf. ELLIPSE).
□□ **hy•per•bol•ic** /-bólik/ *adj.*

hy•per•bo•le /hīpárbəlee/ *n. Rhet.* exaggerated statement not meant to be taken literally.
□□ **hy•per•bol•ic** /hípərbólik/ *adj.* **hy•per•bol•i•cal** *adj.*
■ see *exaggeration* (EXAGGERATE).

hy•per•crit•i•cal /hípərkritikəl/ *adj.* excessively critical, esp. of small faults. □□ **hy•per•crit•i•cal•ly** *adv.*

hy•per•gly•ce•mi•a /hípərglìseémeeə/ *n.* excess of glucose in the bloodstream, often associated with diabetes mellitus.

hy•per•sen•si•tive /hípərsénsitiv/ *adj.* abnormally or excessively sensitive. □□ **hy•per•sen•si•tiv•i•ty** /-tívitee/ *n.*
■ see SENSITIVE *adj.* 2.

hy•per•ten•sion /hípərténshən/ *n.* **1** abnormally high blood pressure. **2** state of great emotional tension. □□ **hy•per•ten•sive** /-ténsiv/ *adj.*

hy•per•text /hípərtekst/ *n. Computing* computer software that links topics on the screen to related information, graphics, etc., usu. by a point-and-click method.

hy•per•ther•mi•a /hípərthórmeeə/ *n. Med.* abnormally high body temperature. □□ **hy•per•ther′mic** *adj.*

hy•per•thy•roid•ism /hípərthíroydizəm/ *n. Med.* overactivity of the thyroid gland, resulting in an increased rate of metabolism. □□ **hy•per•thy′roid** *n. & adj.*

hy•per•ven•ti•la•tion /hípərvént′láyshən/ *n.* abnormally rapid breathing, resulting in an increased loss of carbon dioxide.

hy•phen /hífən/ • *n.* sign (-) used to join words semantically or syntactically (as in *pick-me-up, rock-forming*), to indicate the division of a word at the end of a line, or to indicate a missing or implied element (as in *man- and womankind*). • *v.tr.* **1** write (a compound word) with a hyphen. **2** join (words) with a hyphen.

hy•phen•ate /hífənayt/ *v.tr.* = HYPHEN *v.* □□ **hy•phen•a•tion** /-náyshən/ *n.*

hyp•no•sis /hipnṓsis/ *n.* state like sleep in which the subject acts only on external suggestion.

hyp•no•ther•a•py /hípnōthérəpee/ *n.* treatment of disease by hypnosis.

hyp•not•ic /hipnótik/ • *adj.* **1** of or producing hypnosis. **2** (of a drug) soporific. • *n.* **1** thing, esp. a drug, that produces sleep. **2** person under or open to hypnotism. □□ **hyp•not′i•cal•ly** *adv.*
■ *adj.* **1** see *enchanting* (ENCHANT). **2** see NARCOTIC *adj.* • *n.* **1** see NARCOTIC *n.*

hyp•no•tism /hípnətizəm/ *n.* study or practice of hypnosis. □□ **hyp′no•tist** *n.*

hyp•no•tize /hípnətīz/ *v.tr.* **1** produce hypnosis in. **2** fascinate.
■ **2** mesmerize, entrance, enchant, charm.

hy•po /hípō/ *n.* (*pl.* **-pos**) *colloq.* = HYPODERMIC *n.*

hypo- /hípō/ *prefix* (usu. **hyp-** before a vowel or *h*) **1** under (*hypodermic*). **2** below normal (*hypoxia*).

hy•po•al•ler•gen•ic /hìpōalərjénik/ *adj.* having little likelihood of causing an allergic reaction (*hypoallergenic foods*).

hy•po•chon•dri•a /hípəkóndreeə/ *n.* abnormal anxiety about one's health. □□ **hy•po•chon•dri•ac** /-ak/ *n.* **hy•po•chon•dri•a•cal** /hìpəkondríəkəl/ *adj.*

hy•poc•ri•sy /hipókrisee/ *n.* (*pl.* **-sies**) **1** false claim to virtue; insincerity; pretense. **2** instance of this.
■ **1** deceit, duplicity, playacting, *colloq.* phoniness. **2** see DECEIT 2.

hyp•o•crite /hípəkrit/ *n.* person given to hypocrisy. □□ **hyp•o•crit′i•cal** *adj.* **hyp•o•crit′i•cal•ly** *adv.*
■ double-dealer, pretender, *sl.* creeping Jesus. □□ **hypocritical** deceiving, two-faced, dishonest; see also INSINCERE.

hy•po•der•mic /hípədórmik/ • *adj. Med.* **1** of or relating to the area beneath the skin. **2** **a** (of a drug, etc., or its application) injected beneath the skin. **b** (of a needle, syringe, etc.) used to do this. • *n.* hypodermic injection or syringe.

hy•po•gly•ce•mi•a /hípōglìseémeeə/ *n.* deficiency of glucose in the bloodstream. □□ **hy•po•gly•ce•mic** /-mik/ *adj.*

hy•po•ten•sion /hípəténshən/ *n.* abnormally low blood pressure. □□ **hy•po•ten′sive** *adj.*

hy•pot•e•nuse /hipót′nōos, -nyōos/ *n.* side opposite the right angle of a right triangle.

hy•po•thal•a•mus /hípətháləməs/ *n.* (*pl.* **-mi** /-mī/) *Anat.* region of the brain that controls body temperature, thirst, hunger, etc. □□ **hy•po•thal•a•mic** /-thəlámik/ *adj.*

hy•po•ther•mi•a /hípōthórmeeə/ *n. Med.* abnormally low body temperature.

hy•poth•e•sis /hīpóthisis/ *n.* (*pl.* **hy•poth•e•ses** /-seez/) **1** proposition made as a basis for reasoning, without the assumption of its truth. **2** supposition made as a starting point for further investigation from known facts

(cf. THEORY). **3** groundless assumption.
□□ **hy•poth•e•size** /-sɪz/ v.

hy•po•thet•i•cal /hípəthétikəl/ adj. **1** of or based on or serving as a hypothesis. **2** supposed but not necessarily real or true.
□□ **hy•po•thet′i•cal•ly** adv.

■ assumed, presumed, conjectured, surmised, imaginary.

hy•po•thy•roid•ism /hípōthíroydizəm/ n. Med. subnormal activity of the thyroid gland, resulting in cretinism in children, and mental and physical slowing in adults.
□□ **hy•po•thy′roid** n. & adj.

hys•ter•ec•to•my /hístəréktəmee/ n. (pl. **-mies**) surgical removal of the uterus.

hys•te•ri•a /histéreeə, –steer–/ n. **1** wild uncontrollable emotion or excitement. **2** func-

tional disturbance of the nervous system, of psychoneurotic origin.
■ **2** see MANIA 1.

hys•ter•ic /histérik/ • n. **1** [in pl.] **a** a fit of hysteria. **b** colloq. overwhelming mirth or laughter (we were in hysterics). **2** hysterical person. • adj. = HYSTERICAL.

hys•ter•i•cal /histérikəl/ adj. **1** of or affected with hysteria. **2** morbidly or uncontrolledly emotional. **3** colloq. extremely funny.
□□ **hys•ter′i•cal•ly** adv.

■ **1** see MAD adj. 1. **2** irrational, distracted, frantic; beside oneself. **3** hilarious, sidesplitting, uproarious, comic(al).

Hz abbr. hertz.

Ii

I¹ /ī/ n. (also **i**) (pl. **Is** or **I's**; **i's**) ninth letter of the alphabet.

I² /ī/ pron. (obj. **me**; poss. **my, mine**; pl. **we**) used by a speaker or writer to refer to himself or herself.

I³ symb. Chem. iodine.

I⁴ abbr. (also **I.**) **1** independent. **2** interstate. **3** Island(s). **4** Isle(s). **5** (as a Roman numeral) 1.

i abbr. (also **i.**) **1** incisor. **2** interest. **3** intransitive. **4** island. **5** isle.

IA abbr. Iowa (in official postal use).

Ia. abbr. Iowa.

-ial /eeəl, (ch)əl/ var. of -AL.

i•amb /íamb/ n. Prosody foot consisting of one short (or unstressed) followed by one long (or stressed) syllable.

i•am•bic /íambik/ Prosody • adj. of or using iambs. • n. [usu. in pl.] iambic verse.

-ian /eeən/ suffix var. of -AN.

i•bex /íbeks/ n. (pl. same or **i•bex•es**) wild mountain goat of Europe, N. Africa, and Asia, with a chin beard and curved ridged horns.

ibid. /íbid/ abbr. (also **ib.**) in the same book or passage, etc.

-ibility /ibílitee/ suffix forming nouns from, or corresponding to, adjectives in -ible (possibility).

i•bis /íbis/ n. (pl. same or **i•bis•es**) wading bird with a curved bill, long neck, and long legs.

-ible /ibəl/ suffix forming adjectives meaning 'that may or may be' (see -ABLE) (terrible).

-ibly /íblee/ suffix forming adverbs corresponding to adjectives in -ible.

i•bu•pro•fen /íbyōōprṓfən/ n. anti-inflammatory medication used to relieve pain and reduce fever.

-ic /ik/ suffix forming adjectives (Arabic) and nouns (critic).

-ical /íkəl/ suffix **1** forming adjectives corresponding to nouns or adjectives, usu. in -ic

(classical). **2** forming adjectives corresponding to nouns in -y (pathological).

-ically /iklee/ suffix forming adverbs corresponding to adjectives in -ic or -ical (comically).

ICBM abbr. intercontinental ballistic missile.

ICC abbr. **1** Interstate Commerce Commission. **2** International Claims Commission.

ice /īs/ • n. **1 a** frozen water. **b** sheet of this. **2** sl. diamonds. • v. **1** tr. mix with or cool in ice. **2** tr. & intr. [often foll. by over, up] **a** cover or become covered with ice. **b** freeze. **3** tr. cover (a cake, etc.) with icing. □ **ice cap** permanent covering of ice, e.g., in polar regions. **ice cream** sweet creamy frozen food, usu. flavored. **ice cube** small block of ice made in a refrigerator. **ice hockey** form of hockey played on ice. **ice skate** boot with a blade beneath, for skating on ice. **ice-skate** v.intr. skate on ice. **ice-skater** person who skates on ice. **on ice 1** performed by skaters. **2** colloq. held in reserve; awaiting further attention. **on thin ice** in a risky situation.

■ v. **1** chill, refrigerate. **2** see FREEZE v. 1. □ **on ice 2** see ABEYANCE.

ice•berg /ísbarg/ n. large floating mass of ice. □ **iceberg lettuce** type of various crisp roundheaded lettuces. **the tip of the iceberg** small perceptible part of something (esp. a difficulty) the greater part of which is hidden.

ice•box /ísboks/ n. refrigerator.

ice•break•er /ísbraykər/ n. something that serves to relieve inhibitions, start a conversation, etc.

Ice•land•er /ísləndər/ n. **1** native or national of Iceland, an island in the N. Atlantic. **2** person of Icelandic descent.

Ice•land•ic /íslándik/ • adj. of or relating to Iceland. • n. language of Iceland.

i•chor /íkawr, íkər/ n. **1** Gk. mythol. fluid flowing like blood in the veins of the gods. **2** poet. bloodlike fluid.

ich•thy•ol•o•gy /ˌiktheeólɔjee/ *n.* the study of fishes. □□ **ich•thy•o•log•i•cal** /-theeɔlójikɔl/ *adj.* **ich•thy•ol•o•gist** *n.*

-ician /íshɔn/ *suffix* forming nouns denoting persons skilled in or concerned with subjects having nouns (usu.) ending in *-ic* or *-ics* (*magician, politician*).

i•ci•cle /ísikɔl/ *n.* hanging tapering piece of ice, formed by the freezing of dripping water.

ic•ing /ísing/ *n.* **1** sweet coating on a cake or cookie. **2** formation of ice on a ship or aircraft. □ **icing on the cake** attractive though inessential addition or enhancement.

-icist /ísist/ *suffix* = -ICIAN (*classicist*).

-icity /ísitee/ *suffix* forming abstract nouns, esp. from adjectives in *-ic* (*authenticity*).

ick•y /íkkee/ *adj. colloq.* **1** sickly. **2** (as a general term of disapproval) nasty; repulsive.

i•con /íkon/ *n.* **1** (also **i′kon**) devotional painting of Christ or a saint; esp. in the Eastern Church. **2** image or statue. **3** *Computing* symbol or graphic representation that appears on the monitor in a program, option, or window, esp. one of several for selection. □□ **i•con′ic** *adj.*

■ **2** see IMAGE *n.* 1.

i•con•o•clast /íkónɔklast/ *n.* person who attacks cherished beliefs. □□ **i•con′o•clasm** *n.* **i•con•o•clas′tic** *adj.* **i•con•o•clas′ti•cal•ly** *adv.*

■ see NONCONFORMIST.

i•co•nog•ra•phy /íkɔnógrɔfee/ *n. (pl.* **–phies**) **1** illustration of a subject by drawings or figures. **2 a** the study of portraits, esp. of an individual. **b** the study of artistic images or symbols. **3** treatise on pictures or statuary. □□ **i•co•nog′ra•pher** *n.* **i•con•o•graph•ic** /-nɔgráfik/ *adj.* **i•con•o•graph′i•cal** *adj.* **i•con•o•graph′i•cal•ly** *adv.*

-ics /iks/ *suffix* [treated as *sing.* or *pl.*] forming nouns denoting arts or sciences or branches of study or action (*athletics, politics*).

ICU *abbr.* intensive care unit.

i•cy /ísee/ *adj.* (**i•ci•er, i•ci•est**) **1** very cold. **2** covered with or abounding in ice. **3** (of a tone or manner) unfriendly; hostile (*an icy stare*). □□ **i′ci•ly** *adv.* **i′ci•ness** *n.*

■ **1** ice-cold, frigid, glacial, freezing, frozen, gelid. **2** frozen (over), glacial, icebound; glazed. **3** cold, cool, chilly, distant, aloof, remote. □□ **icily** coldly, frostily, forbiddingly. **iciness** coldness, slipperiness; frigidity.

ID *abbr.* **1** identification (*ID card*). **2** Idaho (in official postal use).

I'd /īd/ *contr.* **1** I had. **2** I should; I would.

id /id/ *n. Psychol.* inherited instinctive impulses of the individual as part of the unconscious.

i.d. *abbr.* inside diameter.

-ide /īd/ *suffix* (also **-id**) *Chem.* forming nouns denoting: **1** binary compounds of an element (the suffix *-ide* being added to the abbreviated name of the more electronegative element, etc.) (*sodium chloride, lead sulfide, calcium carbide*). **2** various other compounds (*amide, anhydride, peptide, saccharide*). **3** elements of a series in the periodic table (*actinide, lanthanide*).

i•de•a /īdéeɔ/ *n.* **1** conception or plan formed by mental effort. **2 a** mental impression or notion; concept. **b** vague belief or fancy. **c** opinion; outlook or point of view. **3** intention, purpose, or essential feature. **4** archetype or pattern. □ **have no idea** *colloq.* **1** not know at all. **2** be completely incompetent. □□ **i•de′a•less** *adj.*

■ **1** construct, thought, notion, plan, design. **2 a, b** impression, picture, (mental) image; perception, understanding, awareness. **c** belief, opinion, hypothesis, theory. **3** aim, goal, objective. **4** see IDEAL *n.* 2a.

SYNONYM STUDY: idea

CONCEPT, CONCEPTION, IMPRESSION, NOTION, THOUGHT. If you have an **idea** it might refer to something perceived through the senses (*I had no idea it was so cold out*), to something visualized (*the idea of a joyous family Christmas*), or to something that is the product of the imagination (*a great idea for raising money*). *Idea* is a comprehensive word that applies to almost any aspect of mental activity. A **thought**, on the other hand, is an idea that is the result of meditation, reasoning, or some other intellectual activity (*she hadn't given much thought to the possibility of losing*). A **notion** is a vague or capricious idea, often without any sound basis (*he had a notion that he could get there by hitchhiking*). A widely held idea of what something is or should be is a **concept** (*the concept of loyalty was beyond him*), while a **conception** is a concept that is held by an individual or small group and that is often colored by imagination and feeling (*her conception of marriage as a romantic ideal*). An idea that is triggered by something external is an **impression**, a word that suggests a half-formed mental picture or superficial view (*he made a good impression; she had the impression that everything would be taken care of*).

---

i•de•al /īdéeɔl/ • *adj.* **1 a** answering to one's highest conception. **b** perfect or supremely excellent. **2 a** existing only in idea. **b** visionary. • *n.* **1** perfect type, or a conception of this. **2 a** actual thing as a standard for imitation. **b** [often in *pl.*] moral principle or standard of behavior. See synonym study at MODEL. □□ **i•de′al•ly** *adv.*

■ *adj.* **1** faultless, excellent, supreme, best, consummate; see also PERFECT *adj.* 2a. **2** conceptual, imagined, imaginary, unreal, abstract, notional. • *n.* **1** acme, epitome, paragon, nonpareil, (standard of) perfection. **2 a** model, criterion. **b** cause; (*ideals*) morals, morality, (code of) ethics; see also IDEOLOGY. □□ **ideally** under *or* in the best of circumstances, at best, in a perfect world.

i•de•al•ism /īdéeɔlizɔm/ *n.* **1** forming or following after ideals, esp. unrealistically (cf. REALISM). **2** representation of things in ideal or idealized form. □□ **i•de′al•ist** *n.* **i•de•al•is′tic** *adj.* **i•de•al•is•ti•cal•ly** *adv.*

■ **1** utopianism, quixotism, quixotry, romanticism. □□ **idealist** idealizer, romantic, optimist; see also VISIONARY *n.* **idealistic** romantic, utopian, optimistic. **idealistically** unrealistically; romantically.

i•de•al•ize /īdéeɔlīz/ *v.tr.* **1** regard or represent in ideal form or character. **2** exalt in thought to ideal perfection or excellence. □□ **i•de•al•i•za'tion** *n.*

■ elevate, glorify, worship, ennoble, deify. □□ **idealization** See PERFECTION 3.

i•dée fixe /eedáy feéks/ *n.* (*pl.* **i•dées fixes** *pronunc.* same) idea that dominates the mind; an obsession.

i•den•ti•cal /idéntikəl/ *adj.* **1** (of different things) agreeing in every detail. **2** (of one thing viewed at different times) one and the same. **3** (of twins) developed from a single fertilized ovum. See synonym study at SAME. □□ **i•den'ti•cal•ly** *adv.*

■ **1** twin, duplicate, matching; (*identical with*) the same as, interchangeable. **2** (very) same, selfsame. □□ **identically** see MADLY 1 *adv.*

i•den•ti•fi•ca•tion /idéntifikáyshən/ *n.* **1 a** identifying; recognition; pinpointing. **b** association of oneself with the feelings, etc., of another person or group. **2** means of identifying. **3** (*attrib.*) serving to identify (esp. the bearer) (*identification card*).

■ **1 a** classification, classifying; authentication, verification. **b** empathy, sympathy, involvement, rapport. **2** passport, driver's license, credentials. **3** (*attrib.*) identity, ID.

i•den•ti•fy /idéntifī/ *v.tr.* (**-fies, -fled**) **1** establish the identity of; recognize. **2** establish or select. **3** (foll. by *with*) associate inseparably or very closely (with a party, policy, etc.). □□ **i•den•ti•fi'a•ble** *adj.*

■ **1, 2** classify, categorize, name, label, tag, place, mark, single out, point out. **3** connect, link, equate. □□ **identifiable** see discernible (DISCERN).

i•den•ti•ty /idéntitee/ *n.* (*pl.* **-ties**) **1 a** condition of being a specified person or thing. **b** individuality; personality. **2** identification or the result of it (*mistaken identity*). **3** absolute sameness.

■ **1** distinctiveness, uniqueness, particularity, singularity, selfhood. **2** see IDENTIFICATION 1a. **3** oneness, unity, equality; indistinguishability.

id•e•o•gram /ídeeəgram/ *n.* character symbolizing a thing without indicating the sounds in its name (e.g., a numeral, Chinese characters).

■ see SIGN *n.* 2.

id•e•o•logue /ídeeəlawg, -log, ídee-/ *n.* **1** theorist; visionary. **2** adherent of an ideology.

id•e•ol•o•gy /ídeeóləjee, idee-/ *n.* (*pl.* **-gies**) **1** ideas at the basis of an economic or political theory. **2** the manner of thinking characteristic of a class or individual. □□ **id•e•o•log•i•cal** /-əlójikəl/ *adj.* **id•e•o•log'i•cal•ly** *adv.* **id•e•ol'o•gist** /-deeól-/ *n.*

■ belief(s), convictions, tenets, credo, philosophy, principles, canons, creed; see also IDEAL *n.* 2b.

ides /īdz/ *n.pl.* eighth day after the nones in the ancient Roman calendar (the 15th day of March, May, July, October; the 13th of other months).

id•i•o•cy /ídeeəsee/ *n.* (*pl.* **-cies**) utter foolishness; idiotic behavior or an idiotic action.

■ see *stupidity* (STUPID).

id•i•om /ídeeəm/ *n.* **1** phrase established by

401   idée fixe ~ idyllic

usage whose meaning is not deducible from the individual words (e.g., *at the drop of a hat*). **2** form of expression peculiar to a language, group, etc. **3 a** language of a people or country. **b** specific character of this. **4** characteristic mode of expression in music, art, etc. □□ **id•i•o•mat•ic** /ídeeəmátik/ *adj.* **id•i•o•mat'i•cal•ly** *adv.*

■ **1** expression, (set) phrase, cliché, saying. **2, 3** idiolect, phraseology, vernacular, dialect; speech.

id•i•o•syn•cra•sy /ídeeōsíngkrəsee/ *n.* (*pl.* **-sies**) **1** mental constitution, opinion, or mode of behavior peculiar to a person. **2** anything highly individualized. □□ **id•i•o•syn•crat•ic** /-krátik/ *adj.* **id•i•o•syn•crat'i•cal•ly** *adv.*

■ **1** see CHARACTERISTIC *n.* **2** see *eccentricity* (ECCENTRIC).

id•i•ot /ídeeət/ *n.* **1** *colloq.* stupid person. **2** mentally deficient person incapable of rational conduct. □ **idiot box** *colloq.* television set. □□ **id•i•ot•ic** /ídeeótik/ *adj.* **id•i•ot'i•cal•ly** *adv.*

■ **1** see FOOL[1] *n.* 1. □□ **idiotic** see STUPID *adj.* 1, 2. **idiotically** see MADLY 1.

i•dle /íd'l/ • *adj.* (**i•dler, i•dlest**) **1** lazy; indolent. **2** not in use; not working; unemployed. **3** (of time, etc.) unoccupied. **4** having no special reason or purpose. **5** useless **6** (of an action, thought, or word) ineffective; worthless; vain. • *v.* **1 a** *intr.* (of an engine) run slowly. **b** *tr.* cause (an engine) to idle. **2** *intr.* be idle. **3** *tr.* (foll. by *away*) pass (time, etc.) in idleness. See synonym study at LOITER. □□ **i'dle•ness** *n.* **i'dler** *n.* **i'dly** *adv.*

■ *adj.* **1** listless, lethargic, slothful. **2** unused, inactive; out of work. **3** free, empty, vacant. **4** aimless; baseless; offhand. **5, 6** pointless, insignificant, meaningless; unavailing • *n.* **2** laze (about), loiter, kill or mark time. **3** (*idle away*) waste, fritter away, kill. □□ **idleness** inactivity, unemployment; laziness, lethargy, torpor; indolence. **idler** loafer, lounger, slacker, shirker, drone, clockwatcher. **idly** lazily, listlessly, indolently, unproductively.

i•dol /íd'l/ *n.* **1** image of a deity, etc., as an object of worship. **2** the object of excessive or supreme adulation (*movie idol*).

■ **1** (graven) image, icon, effigy, symbol, fetish, totem. **2** god, hero or heroine, star, celebrity.

i•dol•a•try /īdólətree/ *n.* **1** the worship of idols. **2** great adulation.

i•dol•ize /íd'līz/ *v.* **1** *tr.* venerate or love excessively. **2** *tr.* make an idol of. **3** *intr.* practice idolatry. □□ **i•dol•i•za'tion** *n.* **i'dol•iz•er** *n.*

■ **1, 2** deify, worship, apotheosize, adore, revere.

i•dyll /íd'l/ *n.* (also **i'dyl**) **1** short description in verse or prose of a picturesque scene or incident, esp. in rustic life. **2** episode suitable for such treatment, usu. a love story. □□ **i'dyl•list** *n.* **i'dyl•lize** *v.tr.*

i•dyl•lic /īdílik/ *adj.* **1** blissfully peaceful and happy. **2** of or like an idyll. □□ **i•dyl'li•cal•ly** *adv.*

■ **1** blissful, heavenly; halcyon; pastoral. □□ **idyllically** blissfully, perfectly; pastorally.

IE *abbr.* **1** Indo-European. **2** industrial engineer(ing).

i.e. *abbr.* that is to say.

-ie /ee/ *suffix* **1** var. of -Y² (*dearie, nightie*). **2** *archaic* var. of -Y¹, -Y³ (*litanie, prettie*).

if /if/ • *conj.* **1** introducing a conditional clause: **a** on the condition or supposition that; in the event that (*if he comes I will tell him*). **b** [with past tense] implying that the condition is not fulfilled (*if I knew I would say*). **2** even though (*I'll finish it, if it takes me all day*). **3** whenever (*if I am not sure I ask*). **4** whether (*see if you can find it*). **5 a** expressing wish or surprise (*if I could just try!*). **b** expressing a request (*if you wouldn't mind opening the door?*). **6** with implied reservation; perhaps not (*very rarely if at all*). • *n.* condition or supposition (*too many ifs about it*). □ **if only** **1** even if for no other reason than (*I'll come if only to see her*). **2** expression of regret (*if only I could swim!*).

if•fy /ifee/ *adj.* (**if•fi•er, if•fi•est**) *colloq.* uncertain; doubtful.

ig•loo /iglóo/ *n.* dome-shaped Eskimo dwelling, esp. one built of blocks of snow.

ig•ne•ous /ignee-əs/ *adj.* **1** of fire; fiery. **2** *Geol.* (esp. of rocks) produced by volcanic or magmatic action.

ig•nite /ignít/ *v.* **1** *tr.* set fire to. **2** *intr.* catch fire. **3** *tr.* provoke or excite (feelings, etc.). □□ **ig•nit′a•ble** *adj.* **ig•nit•a•bil′i•ty** *n.* **ig•nit′i•ble** *adj.* **ig•nit•i•bil′i•ty** *n.*

■ **1** see FIRE *v.* 5. **2** kindle, catch fire, burst into flame. **3** see EXCITE 1a, b.

ig•ni•tion /igníshən/ *n.* **1** mechanism for, or action of, starting an internal combustion engine. **2** igniting or being ignited.

ig•no•ble /ignóbəl/ *adj.* (**ig•no•bler, ig•no•blest**) **1** dishonorable; mean; base. **2** of low birth, position, or reputation. □□ **ig•no•bil′i•ty** *n.* **ig•no′bly** *adv.*

■ **1** see BASE² 1. **2** see HUMBLE *adj.* 2.

ig•no•min•i•ous /ignəmíneeəs/ *adj.* **1** causing or deserving ignominy. **2** humiliating. □□ **ig•no•min′i•ous•ly** *adv.*

ig•no•mi•ny /ignəminee/ *n.* dishonor.

■ see *infamy* (INFAMOUS).

ig•no•ra•mus /ignəráyməs/ *n.* (*pl.* **ig•no•ra•mus•es** or **ig•no•ra•mi**) ignorant person.

ig•no•rance /ignərəns/ *n.* [often foll. by *of*] lack of knowledge. □□ **ig′no•rant** *adj.* **ig′no•rant•ly** *adv.*

■ unawareness, unfamiliarity; inexperience. □□ **ignorant** unknowing, unaware, uneducated, uninformed.

ig•nore /ignáwr/ *v.tr.* **1** refuse to take notice of or accept. **2** intentionally disregard. See synonym study at NEGLECT. □□ **ig•nor′er** *n.*

■ **1** reject, snub, cold-shoulder, turn one's back on. **2** overlook, skip; turn a blind eye to, turn a deaf ear to.

i•gua•na /igwáänə/ *n.* any of various large lizards native to tropical America and the Pacific islands, with a dorsal crest.

IL *abbr.* Illinois (in official postal use).

il- /il/ *prefix* assim. form of IN-¹, IN-² before *l*.

il•e•os•to•my /ileeóstəmee/ *n.* (*pl.* **–mies**) surgical operation in which the ileum is brought through the abdominal wall to create an artificial opening for the evacuation of the bowels.

il•e•um /ileeəm/ *n.* (*pl.* **il•e•a** /ileeə/) *Anat.* third and last portion of the small intestine. □□ **il′e•ac** *adj.*

il•i•um /ileeəm/ *n.* (*pl.* **il•i•a** /ileeə/) bone forming the upper part of each half of the pelvis.

ilk /ilk/ *n.* family, class, or set (*not of the same ilk as you*).

■ see TYPE *n.* 1.

Ill. *abbr.* Illinois.

ill. *abbr.* **1** illustrated. **2** illustration. **3** illustrator.

I'll /īl/ *contr.* I shall; I will.

ill /il/ • *adj.* **1** [usu. *predic.*] out of health; sick (*ill with pneumonia*). **2** (of health) unsound; disordered. **3** wretched; unfavorable (*ill fortune, ill luck*). **4** harmful (*ill effects*). **5** hostile; unkind (*ill feeling*). • *adv.* **1** badly; wrongly. **2 a** imperfectly (*ill-provided*). **b** scarcely (*can ill afford to do it*). **3** unfavorably (*it would have gone ill with them*). • *n.* **1** injury; harm. **2** evil. □ **ill-advised** **1** (of a person) foolish or imprudent. **2** (of a plan, etc.) not well formed or considered. **ill at ease** embarrassed; uneasy. **ill-bred** badly brought up; rude. **ill-fated** destined to or bringing bad fortune. **ill-favored** unattractive. **ill humor** irritability. **ill-mannered** having bad manners; rude. See synonym study at RUDE. **ill-natured** churlish; unkind. **ill-tempered** morose; irritable. **ill-treat** (or **-use**) treat badly; abuse. **ill will** bad feeling; animosity.

■ *adj.* **1** unwell, unhealthy, ailing. **2** bad, poor, mediocre. **3** bad, adverse, unpropitious; disturbing, ominous. **4** hurtful, injurious, detrimental. **5** unfriendly, antagonistic, belligerent. • *adv.* **1** incorrectly, mistakenly, falsely, erroneously. **2 a** badly, insufficiently, unsatisfactorily. **b** hardly, barely. **3** badly, adversely, disastrously. • *n.* **1** damage, hurt, mischief, trouble. **2** wrong, injustice, transgression. □ **ill-advised 1** foolhardy, unwise, reckless. **2** injudicious, misguided. **ill-bred** see *ill-mannered* below. **ill-gotten** see UNLAWFUL. **ill humor** ill temper, irascibility, crossness, grumpiness; volatility. **ill-mannered** discourteous, impolite, ill-bred. **ill-treat** (or **-use**) maltreat, persecute, wrong; misuse, mishandle. **ill will** resentment, dislike, hatred, hate, loathing.

il•le•gal /ileegəl/ *adj.* **1** not legal. **2** contrary to law. □□ **il•le•gal•i•ty** /–gálitee/ *n.* (*pl.* **–ties**) **il•le′gal•ly** *adv.*

■ **1** unlawful, unofficial, unsanctioned, unlicensed. **2** unlawful, illegitimate, criminal, felonious, illicit; see also CROOKED 2, LAWLESS 2. □□ **illegality** unlawfulness, illegitimacy. **illegally** unlawfully, criminally, feloniously.

il•leg•i•ble /iléjibəl/ *adj.* not legible. □□ **il•leg•i•bil′i•ty** *n.* **il•leg′i•bly** *adv.*

■ unreadable, indecipherable; scrawled, scribbled.

il•le•git•i•mate • *adj.* /ilijítimət/ **1** (of a child) born of parents not married to each other. **2** unlawful. **3** improper. • *n.* /iliijítimət/ person whose position is illegitimate, esp. by birth. • *v.tr.* /ilijítimayt/ declare or pronounce illegitimate. □□ **il•le•git•i•ma•cy** /-məsee/ *n.* **il•le•git•i•mate•ly** *adv.*

■ *adj.* **1** bastard, natural, fatherless, born out of wedlock. **2** see ILLEGAL. **3** irregular, incorrect, nonstandard. • *n.* bastard, love child, natural child.

il•lib•er•al /ilíbərəl/ *adj.* **1** intolerant; narrow-minded. **2** not generous; stingy. **3** vulgar; sordid. □□ **il•lib•er•al•i•ty** /-álitee/ *n.* (*pl.* -**ties**) **il•lib•er•al•ly** *adv.*

■ **1** see INTOLERANT. **2** see SELFISH. □□ **illiberality** see *intolerance* (INTOLERANT).

il•lic•it /ilísit/ *adj.* **1** unlawful; forbidden. **2** secret; furtive. □□ **il•lic•it•ly** *adv.* **il•lic•it•ness** *n.*

■ **1** see ILLEGAL 2. **2** underhand, underhanded, sneaky. □□ **illicitly** see *illegally* (ILLEGAL), *secretly* (SECRET).

il•lit•er•ate /ilítərət/ *adj.* **1** unable to read. **2** uneducated. • *n.* illiterate person. □□ **il•lit•er•a•cy** *n.*

■ *adj.* **1** unlettered. **2** unschooled, untaught, benighted, ignorant, unenlightened. • *n.* nonreader; lowbrow, ignoramus.

ill•ness /ílnis/ *n.* **1** disease. **2** being ill.

■ **1** sickness, infection, affliction, ailment. **2** ill health, bad health, indisposition.

il•log•i•cal /ilójikəl/ *adj.* devoid of or contrary to logic. □□ **il•log•i•cal•i•ty** /-kálitee/ *n.* (*pl.* -**ties**) **il•log•i•cal•ly** *adv.*

■ see UNREASONABLE 2. □□ **illogicality** see *absurdity* (ABSURD).

il•lu•mi•nate /ilóominayt/ *v.tr.* **1** light up; make bright. **2** decorate with lights. **3** decorate (a manuscript, etc.) with gold, silver, etc. **4** help to explain. **5** enlighten spiritually or intellectually. **6** shed luster on. □□ **il•lu•mi•nat•ing** *adj.* **il•lu•mi•na•tion** /-náyshən/ *n.* **il•lu•mi•na•tive** /-náyṭiv, -nātiv/ *adj.* **il•lu•mi•na•tor** *n.*

■ **1** brighten, lighten. **2** emblazon, deck out. **3** adorn, embellish, ornament. **4** clarify, shed light on, elucidate. **5** see ENLIGHTEN 1a. **6** enhance, enrich, highlight. □□ **illumination** lighting, brightness, radiance; enlightenment, insight.

il•lu•mi•na•ti /ilóominaátee/ *n.pl.* persons claiming to possess special knowledge or enlightenment.

il•lu•mine /ilóomin/ *v.tr. literary* **1** light up; make bright. **2** enlighten spiritually.

il•lu•sion /ilóoʒhən/ *n.* **1** deception; delusion. **2** misapprehension of the true state of affairs. **3 a** faulty perception of an external object. **b** instance of this. **4** figment of the imagination. **5** = *optical illusion*. □□ **il•lu•sion•al** *adj.* **il•lu•sive** /ilóosiv/ *adj.*

■ **1** deceiving, deceit, trick; fancy. **2** misconception, misunderstanding. **3** hallucination, delusion. **4** fantasy, chimera, mirage. □□ **illusional** see ILLUSORY.

il•lu•sion•ist /ilóoʒhənist/ *n.* person who produces illusions; magician.

il•lu•so•ry /ilóosəree; -zəree/ *adj.* **1** deceptive (esp. as regards value or content). **2** having

the character of an illusion. See synonym study at OSTENSIBLE. □□ **il•lu'so•ri•ly** *adv.* **il•lu'so•ri•ness** *n.*

■ misleading, illusive, fanciful, imaginary.

il•lus•trate /íləstrayt/ *v.tr.* **1 a** provide (a book, etc.) with pictures. **b** elucidate by drawings or pictures. **2** serve as an example of. **3** explain or make clear, esp. by examples. □□ **il'lus•tra•tor** *n.*

■ **1 b** see ILLUMINATE 4. **2** exemplify, typify, represent, epitomize. **3** explicate, elucidate, clarify.

il•lus•tra•tion /íləstráyshən/ *n.* **1** drawing or picture in a book, magazine article, etc. **2** explanatory example. **3** act or instance of illustrating. □□ **il•lus•tra'tion•al** *adj.*

■ **1** painting, sketch, diagram; engraving, etching, woodcut. **2** case (in point), instance; sample. **3** depiction, representation; explanation.

il•lus•tra•tive /ilústrətiv, íləstray-/ *adj.* [often foll. by *of*] serving as an explanation or example. □□ **il•lus'tra•tive•ly** *adv.*

■ see EXEMPLARY 3.

il•lus•tri•ous /ilústreeəs/ *adj.* distinguished; renowned. □□ **il•lus'tri•ous•ly** *adv.* **il•lus'tri•ous•ness** *n.*

■ famous, noted, eminent.

I'm /īm/ *contr.* I am.

im- /im/ *prefix* assim. form of IN-[1], IN-[2] before *b*, *m*, *p*.

image /ímij/ • *n.* **1** representation of an object, e.g., a statue. **2** character or reputation of a person or thing as generally perceived. **3** appearance in a mirror, refracted through a lens, etc. **4** semblance; likeness. **5** person or thing that closely resembles another (*is the image of his father*). **6** simile or metaphor. **7 a** mental representation. **b** idea or conception. See synonym study at EMBLEM. • *v.tr.* make an image of; portray.

■ *n.* **1** picture, sculpture, effigy; idol, fetish, totem. **2** (public) face, persona, appearance. **3** reflection, impression. **4** appearance, aspect, guise; form. **5** double, copy, counterpart, facsimile, chip off the old block. **6** figure (of speech), trope, word painting. **7** impression, perception, thought.

im•age•ry /ímiiree/ *n.* **1** figurative illustration, esp. as used by an author. **2** images collectively. **3** statuary; carving. **4** mental images collectively.

■ **1** figurativeness, word painting, symbolism; metaphor(s), simile(s). **2** artwork, graphics, design; pictures, images, paintings. **4** (visual) perception, visualization; ideas, (mental) pictures, impressions.

i•mag•i•nar•y /imájinéree/ *adj.* **1** existing only in the imagination. **2** *Math.* being the square root of a negative quantity. □□ **i•mag'i•nar•i•ly** *adv.*

■ **1** fictitious, fictive, fanciful, imagined; untrue, nonexistent; illusory, illusive. □□ **imaginarily** fictitiously, fancifully, unreally, illusorily, fallaciously.

i•mag•i•na•tion /imájináyshən/ *n.* **1** mental faculty forming images or concepts of external objects not present to the senses. **2** ability of the mind to be creative or resourceful. 3 process of imagining.

■ 1 fantasy, mind's eye, fancy. 2 imaginativeness, creativity, inventiveness, ingenuity; lateral thinking, originality. 3 visualization, vision.

i•mag•i•na•tive /imájinətiv/ adj. having or showing imagination. See synonym study at CREATIVE. □□ i•mag′i•na•tive•ly adv. i•mag′i•na•tive•ness n.

■ creative, original, ingenious, inventive, innovative. □□ imaginatively creatively, originally, ingeniously.

i•mag•ine /imájin/ v.tr. 1 a form a mental image or concept of. b picture to oneself. 2 think or conceive (imagined them to be soldiers). 3 guess. 4 suppose. □□ i•mag′in•a•ble adj. i•mag′in•er n.

■ 1 envision, ponder; think up. 2 understand, suppose, believe, assume. 3 conjecture, estimate. 4 expect, believe, think, be of the opinion.

i•mag•in•ings /imájiningz/ n.pl. fancies; fantasies.

i•ma•go /imáygō, imaá–/ n. (pl. –goes or i•ma•gi•nes /imájineez/) adult insect.

i•mam /imaám/ n. 1 leader of prayers in a mosque. 2 title of various Islamic leaders. □□ i•mam•ate /–mayt/ n.

im•bal•ance /imbáləns/ n. 1 lack of balance. 2 disproportion.

im•be•cile /imbisil, –səl/ • n. 1 person of abnormally weak intellect, esp. an adult with a mental age of about five. 2 colloq. stupid person. • adj. mentally weak; stupid; idiotic. □□ im•be•cil′ic adj. im•be•cil′i•ty n. (pl. –ties)

■ n. see FOOL n. 1. • adj. see STUPID adj. 1, 5. □□ imbecilic see STUPID adj. 1, 5. imbecility see stupidity (STUPID).

im•bed var. of EMBED.

im•bibe /imbíb/ v.tr. 1 drink (esp. alcoholic liquor). 2 a absorb or assimilate (ideas, etc.). b absorb (moisture, etc.). □□ im•bib′er n.

■ 1 see DRINK v. 1.

im•bro•glio /imbrólyō/ n. (pl. –os) 1 confused or complicated situation. 2 confused heap.

im•bue /imbyō͞o/ v.tr. (im•bues, im•bued, im•bu•ing) 1 inspire or permeate (with feelings, opinions, or qualities). 2 saturate. 3 dye.

■ 1 see PERMEATE. 2 see SATURATE 1, 3.

IMF abbr. International Monetary Fund.

im•i•tate /ímitayt/ v.tr. 1 follow the example of; copy. 2 mimic. 3 make a copy of. 4 be like. □□ im′i•ta•ble adj. im′i•ta•tor n.

■ 1 emulate, match, echo, mirror; take after. 2 copy, affect, ape, emulate. 3 reproduce, duplicate; counterfeit, fake. 4 mirror, reflect, match, take after. □□ imitable copiable, reproducible; easy to impersonate. imitator emulator, simulator; faker; see also MIMIC n.

APE, COPY, IMPERSONATE, MIMIC, MOCK. A young girl might **imitate** her mother by an-

swering the phone in exactly the same tone of voice, while a teenager who deliberately imitates the way her mother talks for the purpose of irritating her would more accurately be said to mimic her. Imitate implies following something as an example or model (he imitated the playing style of his music teacher), while mimic suggests imitating someone's mannerisms for fun or ridicule (they liked to mimic the teacher's southern drawl). To copy is to imitate or reproduce something as closely as possible (he copied the style of dress and speech used by the other gang members). When someone assumes another person's appearance or mannerisms, sometimes for the purpose of perpetrating a fraud, he or she is said to impersonate (arrested for impersonating a police officer; a comedian well known for impersonating political figures). Ape and mock both imply an unflattering imitation. Someone who mimics in a contemptuous way is said to ape (he entertained everyone in the office by aping the boss's phone conversations with his wife), while someone who imitates with the intention of belittling or irritating is said to mock (the students openly mocked their teacher's attempt to have a serious discussion about sex).

im•i•ta•tion /ímitáyshən/ • n. 1 imitating or being imitated. 2 a copy. • adj. counterfeit; fake.

■ n. 1 reproduction, simulation; parody, caricature. 2 replica, facsimile; counterfeit. • adj. synthetic, artificial, simulated.

im•i•ta•tive /ímitaytiv/ adj. 1 imitating; following a model or example. 2 counterfeit. □□ im′i•ta•tive•ly adv.

■ 2 see COUNTERFEIT adj.

im•mac•u•late /imákyələt/ adj. 1 pure; perfectly clean. 2 perfect. 3 faultless; innocent. □ Immaculate Conception RC Ch. doctrine that God preserved the Virgin Mary from the taint of original sin from the moment she was conceived. □□ im•mac′u•late•ly adv. im•mac′u•late•ness n.

■ 1 spotless, stainless, unblemished, pure, untarnished, unsullied, unsoiled, untainted. 2 faultless, flawless; definitive, authoritative; exemplary; accurate. 3 pure, blameless, sinless; chaste; pristine, undefiled, untainted.

im•ma•nent /ímənənt/ adj. 1 indwelling; inherent. 2 (of the Supreme Being) omnipresent (cf. transcendent (TRANSCEND)). □□ im′ma•nence n. im′ma•nen•cy n.

■ 1 see INHERENT 1.

im•ma•te•ri•al /ímətéereeəl/ adj. 1 unimportant. 2 incorporeal. □□ im•ma•te′ri•al•ly adv.

■ 1 inconsequential, insignificant, nugatory, trivial, trifling, petty, paltry, negligible, minor. 2 airy, insubstantial, intangible.

im•ma•ture /ímachŏŏr, –tŏŏr, –tyŏŏr/ adj. 1 not mature. 2 emotionally undeveloped. 3 unripe. See synonym study at YOUTHFUL. □□ im•ma•ture′ly adv. im•ma•tu′ri•ty n.

■ 1 undeveloped, pubescent, youthful; rudimentary, half-grown, unformed; unfinished, incomplete. 2 babyish, childish, puerile, juvenile, callow. 3 unripened, undeveloped, green; unready. □□ **immaturity** see YOUTH 1, INEXPERIENCE.

im·mea·sur·a·ble /iméʒ̱ərəbəl/ *adj.* not measurable; immense. □□ **im·mea·sur·a·bil'i·ty** *n.* **im·mea'sur·a·bly** *adv.*

■ measureless, limitless, illimitable, indeterminable, boundless; vast, immense, huge, enormous; see also GREAT 1a.

im·me·di·ate /iméedeeət/ *adj.* 1 occurring or done at once. 2 nearest; next; not separated by others. 3 most pressing or urgent. 4 (of a relation or action) having direct effect. 5 (of knowledge, reactions, etc.) gained or exhibited without reasoning. □□ **im·me'di·a·cy** *n.* **im·me'di·ate·ly** *adv. & conj.* **im·me'di·ate·ness** *n.*

■ 1 instantaneous, instant, prompt; unhesitating, spontaneous. 2 closest, adjacent, proximate. 3 critical, compelling, vital. 4 proximate. 5 intuitive, spontaneous, instinctive. □□ **immediately** *adv.* at once, without delay, instantly. • *conj.* as soon as.

im·me·mo·ri·al /imimáwrcceəl/ *adj.* 1 beyond memory or record. 2 very old.

im·mense /iméns/ *adj.* 1 immeasurably large; huge. 2 very great; considerable (*made an immense difference*). 3 *colloq.* very good. □□ **im·mense'ly** *adv.* **im·mense'ness** *n.* **im·men'si·ty** *n.*

■ 1 enormous, extensive, vast, massive, voluminous; see also GREAT 1a. 2 see CONSIDERABLE 1, 2.

im·merse /imárs/ *v.tr.* 1 a dip; plunge. b submerge (a person). 2 absorb or involve deeply (in). □□ **im·mer'sion** /imárzhən/ *n.*

■ 1 sink, dunk, duck, drown. 2 engross, engage, occupy, plunge; (*immersed*) preoccupied, wrapped up, engrossed.

im·mi·grant /imigrant/ • *n.* person who immigrates. • *adj.* 1 immigrating. 2 of or concerning immigrants.

■ *n.* newcomer, migrant, settler; alien, foreigner. • *adj.* 1 immigratory, migrant. 2 (ethnic) minority, alien, foreign.

im·mi·grate /imigrayt/ *v.* 1 *intr.* come as a permanent resident into a country. 2 *tr.* bring in (a person) as an immigrant. □□ **im·mi·gra·tion** /–gráyshən/ *n.*

im·mi·nent /iminənt/ *adj.* impending; about to happen. □□ **im'mi·nence** *n.* **im'mi·nent·ly** *adv.*

■ looming, threatening, menacing; at hand. □□ **imminence** nearness, immediacy; threat. **imminently** threateningly, menacingly; see also SOON *adv.* 1.

im·mo·bile /imóbəl, –beel, –bīl/ *adj.* 1 not moving. 2 not able to move or be moved. □□ **im·mo·bil·i·ty** /–bílitee/ *n.*

■ 1 see STATIC *adj.*

im·mo·bi·lize /imóbiltz/ *v.tr.* 1 make or keep immobile. 2 keep (a limb or patient) still for healing purposes. □□ **im·mo·bi·li·za'tion** *n.*

■ 1 see FREEZE *v.* 5, ARREST *v.* 2. 2 see INCAPACITATE 1.

im·mod·er·ate /imódərət/ *adj.* excessive; lacking moderation. □□ **im·mod'er·ate·ly** *adv.* **im·mod'er·a'tion** /–ráyshən/ *n.*

■ extreme, exorbitant, unreasonable. □□ **immoderately** see OVERLY. **immoderation** see EXCESS *n.* 3.

im·mod·est /imódist/ *adj.* 1 lacking modesty; impudent. 2 indecent. □□ **im·mod'est·ly** *adv.* **im·mod'es·ty** *n.*

■ 1 brazen, forward, bold, impertinent, brash. 2 shameless, shameful, indecorous, wanton.

im·mo·late /iməlayt/ *v.tr.* kill or offer as a sacrifice. □□ **im·mo·la·tion** /–láyshən/ *n.*

im·mor·al /imáwrəl, imór–/ *adj.* 1 not conforming to accepted morality (cf. AMORAL). 2 morally wrong (esp. in sexual matters). 3 depraved, dissolute. □□ **im·mo·ral·i·ty** /–álitee/ *n.* (*pl.* **–ties**) **im·mor'al·ly** *adv.*

■ 1 unacceptable, unethical, unprincipled, disgraceful. 2 corrupt, bad, wicked, evil, iniquitous, unprincipled. 3 unprincipled, debauched, indecent. □□ **immorality** unacceptability, amorality, reprehensibility; see also VICE[1] 1, 2. **immorally** see BADLY[1] 1, FAST *adv.* 7.

im·mor·tal /imáwrt'l/ • *adj.* 1 a living forever. b divine. 2 unfading. 3 likely or worthy to be famous for all time. • *n.* 1 a immortal being. b [*pl.*] gods of antiquity. 2 person (esp. an author) of enduring fame. □□ **im·mor·tal·i·ty** /–tálitee/ *n.* **im·mor'tal·ize** *v.tr.*

■ *adj.* 1 a undying, eternal, deathless, everlasting. b godlike, deiform, heavenly, celestial, supernal, unearthly; spiritual, superhuman. 2 perpetual, lasting, constant; perennial, evergreen, stable, steady. 3 glorious, renowned, legendary. • *n.* 1 a god, goddess, deity, divinity; demigod; spirit, angel. b (*immortals*) gods, Olympians, *collect.* pantheon; *Rom. Hist.* lares, penates. 2 legend, genius, luminary, giant. □□ **immortality** deathlessness, imperishability; divinity, deity; see also GLORY *n.* 1. **immortalize** make immortal, apotheosize, deify; exalt, glorify.

im·mov·a·ble /imɵɵvəbəl/ *adj.* 1 not able to be moved. 2 steadfast; unyielding. 3 emotionless. 4 not subject to change. 5 motionless. □□ **im·mov·a·bil·i·ty** *n.* **im·mov'a·bly** *adv.*

■ *adj.* 1 unmovable, fixed, fast, rooted. 2 staunch, unshakable, unswerving, firm. 3 unemotional, unfeeling, impassive, unresponsive 4 unchangeable, immutable, unalterable, changeless, inflexible. 5 unmoving, stationary; jammed, wedged.

im·mune /imyoon/ *adj.* 1 a protected against infection through inoculation or inherited or acquired resistance. b relating to immunity (*immune mechanism*). 2 [foll. by *from, to*] exempt from (*some undesirable factor or circumstance*).

■ 1 a vaccinated, immunized; resistant. 2 (*immune to or from*) free from, safe from, protected against; not liable to, excused from.

im·mu·ni·ty /imyɵɵnitee/ *n.* (*pl.* **–ties**) 1 *Med.* ability of an organism to resist infection by means of antibodies and white blood cells. 2 freedom or exemption from an obligation, penalty, etc.

■ 1 resistance, insusceptibility, protection.

2 nonliability, invulnerability, indemnity, amnesty.

im•mu•nize /ímyəníz/ *v.tr.* make immune, esp. to infection, usu. by inoculation. □□ **im•mu•ni•za'tion** *n.* **im'mu•niz•er** *n.*

im•mu•nol•o•gy /ímyənóləjee/ *n.* scientific study of immunity. □□ **im•mu•no•log'ic** /-nəlójik/ adj. **im•mu•no•log'i•cal** adj. **im•mu•nol•o•gist** /-nóləjist/ *n.*

im•mu•no•sup•pressed /ímyənōsəprést, imyŏ̄-/ *adj.* (of an individual) rendered partially or completely unable to react immunologically.

im•mu•no•sup•pres•sion /ímyənōsəpréshən, imyŏ̄-/ *n.* Biochem. partial or complete suppression of the immune response of an individual, esp. to maintain the survival of an organ after a transplant operation. □□ **im•mu•no•sup•pres'sant** /-présənt/ *n.* **im•mu•no•sup•pres'sive** adj. & tr.

im•mu•no•ther•a•py /ímyənōthérəpee, imyŏ̄-/ *n.* Med. prevention or treatment of disease with substances that simulate the immune response.

im•mure /imyŏ̄r/ *v.tr.* enclose within walls; imprison.

im•mu•ta•ble /imyŏ̄təbəl/ *adj.* unchangeable. □□ **im•mu•ta•bil'i•ty** *n.* **im•mu'ta•bly** adv.

imp /imp/ *n.* **1** mischievous child. **2** small devil or sprite.
■ *n.* **1** urchin, gamin, gamine, mischiefmaker. **2** demon, elf, gnome, leprechaun; hobgoblin.

im•pact • *n.* /ímpakt/ **1** forceful contact. **2** strong effect or influence. • *v.* /impákt/ **1** *tr.* press or fix firmly. **2** *tr.* (as **impacted** adj.) (of a tooth) wedged between another tooth and the jaw. **3** *intr.* **a** [foll. by *against, on*] come forcibly into contact with a (larger) body or surface. **b** [foll. by *on*] have a pronounced effect. □□ **im•pac'tion** /-pákshən/ *n.*
■ *n.* **1** collision, percussion, crash, smash. **2** impression, import, meaning, bearing. • *v.* **1** compress, push in, wedge in. **2** (**impacted**) compressed, forced in.

im•pair /impáir/ *v.tr.* damage or weaken. □□ **im•pair'ment** *n.*
■ cripple, harm, injure, spoil, wreck; lessen, debilitate. □□ **impairment** harm, injury; debilitation, deterioration; reduction.

im•pa•la /impáalə, -pálə/ *n.* (pl. same) small antelope of S. and E. Africa.

im•pale /impáyl/ *v.tr.* transfix or pierce with a sharp instrument. □□ **im•pale'ment** *n.*
■ spear, skewer; stab, puncture.

im•pal•pa•ble /impálpəbəl/ *adj.* **1** not easily grasped by the mind; intangible. **2** imperceptible to the touch. □□ **im•pal•pa•bil'i•ty** *n.* **im•pal'pa•bly** adv.

im•pan•el /impán'l/ *v.tr.* officially establish a jury. □□ **im•pan'el•ment** *n.*

im•part /impáart/ *v.tr.* [often foll. by *to*] **1** communicate (news, etc.). **2** give a share of (a thing). □□ **im•part'a•ble** adj.
■ **1** tell, relate; report; reveal, divulge; mention. **2** donate, bestow, grant, cede.

im•par•tial /impáarshəl/ *adj.* unprejudiced; fair. □□ **im•par•ti•al•i•ty** /-sheeálitee/ *n.* **im•par'tial•ly** adv.
■ equitable, evenhanded, unbiased; disinterested. □□ **impartiality** see *objectivity* (OBJECTIVE). **impartially** see FAIRLY 1.

im•pass•a•ble /impásəbəl/ *adj.* that cannot be traversed. □□ **im•pass•a•bil'i•ty** *n.* **im•pass'a•bly** adv.

im•passe /ímpas/ *n.* deadlock.
■ dead end, stalemate; dilemma; standstill.

im•pas•si•ble /impásibəl/ *adj.* **1** impassive. **2** incapable of feeling or emotion. **3** incapable of suffering any injury. □□ **im•pas•si•bil'i•ty** *n.* **im•pas'si•bly** adv.

im•pas•sioned /impáshənd/ *adj.* deeply felt; ardent.
■ passionate, soulful, vehement; intense, animated, fiery, inflamed.

im•pas•sive /impásiv/ *adj.* **1 a** deficient in or incapable of showing emotion. **b** serene. **2** without sensation. **3** not subject to suffering. □□ **im•pas'sive•ly** adv. **im•pas'sive•ness** *n.* **im•pas•siv'i•ty** *n.*
■ **1 a** unfeeling, emotionless, unemotional, stolid. **b** dispassionate, passionless; imperturbable, stolid. **2** insensible, unfeeling; numb. **3** anesthetized, numb, benumbed.

im•pas•to /impástō, -páas-/ *n.* Art **1** process of laying on paint thickly. **2** this technique of painting.

im•pa•tient /impáyshənt/ *adj.* **1 a** lacking patience or tolerance. **b** (of an action) showing a lack of patience. **2** [often foll. by *for*, or *to* + infin.] restlessly eager. **3** [foll. by *of*] intolerant. □□ **im•pa•tience** /-shəns/ *n.* **im•pa'tient•ly** adv.
■ **1 a** curt, short, abrupt; irritable, irascible, testy. **b** hasty, precipitate, abrupt, rash. **2** uneasy, nervous, fidgety, agitated; anxious. **3** (*impatient of*) prejudiced against, biased against. □□ **impatience** curtness, shortness, abruptness; irritability, irascibility, testiness, temper; haste, rashness, impetuosity; restlessness, uneasiness, nervousness; anxiousness, anxiety, longing; prejudice, bias. **impatiently** curtly, shortly, abruptly; hastily, rashly; unforgivingly, disapprovingly.

im•peach /impéech/ *v.tr.* **1** charge (a public official) with misconduct. **2** call in question; disparage. □□ **im•peach'a•ble** adj. **im•peach'ment** *n.*
■ **1** accuse, arraign, indict, incriminate, implicate. **2** challenge, question, attack, assail, denounce. □□ **impeachable** chargeable, indictable, censurable; questionable, assailable. **impeachment** see ACCUSATION.

im•pec•ca•ble /impékəbəl/ *adj.* faultless; exemplary. □□ **im•pec'ca•bly** adv.
■ flawless, perfect, errorless, unerring; proper, spotless, immaculate.

im•pe•cu•ni•ous /impikyŏ̄neeəs/ *adj.* having little or no money. □□ **im•pe•cu'ni•ous•ness** *n.*

im•ped•ance /impéed'ns/ *n.* Electr. total effective resistance of a circuit, etc., to alternating current.

im•pede /impéed/ *v.tr.* retard by obstructing; hinder. See synonym study at HINDER.

■ obstruct, bar, block, thwart, check, hinder, balk.

im•ped•i•ment /impédimənt/ n. 1 hindrance or obstruction. 2 defect in speech. □□ **im•ped•i•men•tal** /–mént'l/ adj.

■ 1 obstacle, inhibition, bar, barrier, check.

im•ped•i•men•ta /impédiméntə/ n.pl. 1 encumbrances. 2 traveling equipment, esp. of an army.

im•pel /impél/ v.tr. (**im•pelled, im•pel•ling**) 1 drive, force, or urge. 2 propel. □□ **im•pel′lent** adj. & n. **im•pel′ler** n.

■ 1 see FORCE v. 1. 2 see PROPEL 1.

im•pend /impénd/ v.intr. 1 be about to happen. 2 a (of a danger) be threatening. b hang. □□ **im•pend′ing** adj.

■ 1 be imminent, be close or near (at hand), be forthcoming. 2 a threaten, loom, menace. b overhang, dangle, be suspended. □□ **impending** imminent, approaching, in view.

im•pen•e•tra•ble /impénitrəbəl/ adj. 1 not able to be penetrated. 2 inscrutable. 3 inaccessible to ideas, influences, etc. □□ **im•pen•e•tra•bil•i•ty** n. **im•pen′e•tra•ble•ness** n. **im•pen′e•tra•bly** adv.

■ 1 see DENSE 1, resistant (RESIST).

im•pen•i•tent /impénit'nt/ adj. not repentant or penitent. □□ **im•pen′i•tence** n. **im•pen′i•tent•ly** adv.

im•per•a•tive /impérətiv/ • adj. 1 urgent. 2 obligatory. 3 commanding; peremptory. 4 Gram. (of a mood) expressing a command (e.g., come here!). • n. 1 Gram. the imperative mood. 2 command. □□ **im•per•a•ti•val** /–ətíval/ adj. **im•per′a•tive•ly** adv.

■ adj. 1 pressing, exigent; important, compelling. 2 mandatory, compulsory. 3 imperious, magisterial, lordly, high-handed. • n. 2 see COMMAND n. 1.

im•per•cep•ti•ble /impərséptibəl/ adj. 1 not perceptible. 2 very slight, gradual, or subtle. □□ **im•per•cep•ti•bil•i•ty** n. **im•per•cep′ti•bly** adv.

■ 1 indiscernible, unnoticeable, invisible, inaudible, ill-defined, obscure. 2 inconsiderable, insignificant; minute, tiny, minuscule.

im•per•fect /impərfikt/ • adj. 1 faulty; incomplete. 2 Gram. (of a tense) denoting action in progress but not completed (e.g., they were singing). • n. imperfect tense. □□ **im•per′fect•ly** adv.

■ adj. 1 unfinished, unformed, undeveloped; deficient. □□ **imperfectly** see sketchily (SKETCHY), WRONG adv.

im•per•fec•tion /impərfékshən/ n. 1 incompleteness. 2 a faultiness. b fault or blemish.

■ 1 patchiness, rudimentariness; insufficiency, inadequacy. 2 fault, fallibility, failing, error, deficiency.

im•pe•ri•al /impéereeəl/ adj. 1 of or characteristic of an empire or comparable sovereign state. 2 a of or characteristic of an emperor. b supreme in authority. c majestic. □□ **im•pe′ri•al•ly** adv.

■ adj. 1 sovereign, crown, monarchal, monarchic, royal. 2 a imperatorial, royal, regal, majestic. b absolute, commanding, preeminent, predominant. c stately, dignified, exalted. □□ **imperially** magnificently, splen-

didly, grandly, superbly; imposingly, impressively.

im•pe•ri•al•ism /impéereeəlizəm/ n. 1 imperial rule or system. 2 usu. derog. policy of acquiring dependent territories or extending a country's influence through foreign trade, etc. □□ **im•pe′ri•al•ist** n. & adj. **im•pe•ri•al•is′ti•cal•ly** adv.

im•per•il /impéril/ v.tr. bring or put into danger.

■ see ENDANGER.

im•pe•ri•ous /impéereeəs/ adj. overbearing; domineering. □□ **im•pe′ri•ous•ly** adv. **im•pe′ri•ous•ness** n.

■ see domineering (DOMINEER).

im•per•ish•a•ble /impérishəbəl/ adj. that cannot perish. □□ **im•per•ish•a•bil′i•ty** n. **im•per′ish•a•bly** adv.

■ see IMMORTAL adj. 2, PERMANENT.

im•per•ma•nent /impərmənənt/ adj. not permanent; transient. □□ **im•per′ma•nence** n. **im•per′ma•nen•cy** n. **im•per′ma•nent•ly** adv.

■ see TRANSIENT adj.

im•per•me•a•ble /impərmeeəbəl/ adj. that cannot be penetrated by fluids. □□ **im•per•me•a•bil′i•ty** n.

■ impenetrable, impassable; closed, sealed. □□ **impermeability** impenetrability, impassability, imperviousness.

im•per•mis•si•ble /impərmísibəl/ adj. not allowable.

im•per•son•al /impərsənəl/ adj. 1 having no personality. 2 having no personal feeling or reference. 3 Gram. a (of a verb) used esp. with it as a subject (e.g., it is snowing). b (of a pronoun) = INDEFINITE. □□ **im•per′son•al•ly** adv.

■ 1 mechanical, wooden, rigid, cold, unfriendly. 2 disinterested, dispassionate, detached, objective, fair.

im•per•son•ate /impərsənayt/ v.tr. 1 pretend to be (another person). 2 act (a character). See synonym study at IMITATE. □□ **im•per•son•a•tion** /–náyshən/ n. **im•per′son•a•tor** n.

■ 2 see ACT v. 4. □□ **impersonation** see IMPRESSION 3. **impersonator** see MIMIC n.

im•per•ti•nent /impərt'nənt/ adj. rude or insolent. □□ **im•per′ti•nence** n. **im•per′ti•nent•ly** adv.

■ presumptuous, impudent, disrespectful; see also TACTLESS. □□ **impertinence** presumption, impudence, insolence, disrespect.

SYNONYM STUDY: impertinent

IMPUDENT, INSOLENT, INTRUSIVE, MEDDLESOME, OBTRUSIVE. The easiest way to distinguish **impertinent** from these other adjectives that mean exceeding the bounds of propriety is to think of its root: Impertinent behavior is not pertinent—in other words, inappropriate or out of place. The impertinent individual has a tendency to be rude or presumptuous toward those who are entitled to deference or respect (it was an impertinent question to ask a woman who had just lost her husband). The **intrusive** person is unduly curious about other people's affairs (*her constant questions about the state of their marriage were intrusive and unwelcome*), while **obtrusive** implies objectionable actions rather than an objectionable disposition. The *obtrusive* person has a tendency to thrust himself or herself into a position where he or she is conspicuous and apt to do more harm than good (*they tried to keep him out of the meeting because his presence would be obtrusive*). To be **meddlesome** is to have a prying or inquisitive nature and a tendency to interfere in an annoying way in other people's affairs (*a meddlesome neighbor*). **Impudent** and **insolent** are much stronger words for inappropriate behavior. Young people are often accused of being *impudent*, which means to be *impertinent* in a bold and shameless way (*an impudent young man who had a lot to learn about tact*). Anyone who is guilty of insulting and contemptuously arrogant behavior might be called *insolent* (*he was so insolent to the arresting officer that he was handcuffed*).

im•per•turb•a•ble /ímpərtárbəbəl/ *adj.* not excitable; calm. □□ **im•per•turb•a•bil'i•ty** *n.* **im•per•turb'a•bly** *adv.*
  ■ see CALM *adj.* 2. □□ **imperturbability** see SELF-CONTROL.

im•per•vi•ous /impárveeəs/ *adj.* **1** not responsive to argument, etc. **2** not affording passage to a fluid. □□ **im•per'vi•ous•ly** *adv.* **im•per'vi•ous•ness** *n.*
  ■ **1** see UNAFFECTED 1. **2** impermeable, watertight, waterproof.

im•pe•ti•go /ímpitígō/ *n.* contagious skin infection forming pustules.

im•pet•u•ous /impéchōōəs/ *adj.* **1** acting or done rashly or with sudden energy. **2** moving forcefully or rapidly. □□ **im•pet•u•os'i•ty** /-ósitee/ *n.* **im•pet'u•ous•ly** *adv.* **im•pet'u•ous•ness** *n.* See synonym study at TEMERITY
  ■ **1** hasty, abrupt, quick, precipitate. □□ **impetuosity, impetuousness** see HASTE *n.* 2. **impetuously** see HASTY 1.

im•pe•tus /ímpitəs/ *n.* **1** force or energy with which a body moves. **2** driving force or impulse.
  ■ **1** momentum; propulsion, impulsion. **2** drive, thrust, stimulus; see also SPUR *n.* 2.

im•pi•e•ty /impíətee/ *n.* (*pl.* **-ies**) **1** lack of piety or reverence. **2** an act, etc., showing this.

im•pinge /impínj/ *v.tr.* **1** make an impact; have an effect. **2** encroach. □□ **im•pinge'ment** *n.* **im•ping'er** *n.*

im•pi•ous /impeeəs, impí-/ *adj.* **1** not pious. **2** wicked; profane. □□ **im'pi•ous•ly** *adv.* **im'pi•ous•ness** *n.*
  ■ **1** irreligious, irreverent, unholy; sacrilegious. **2** godless, sinful; see also IMMORAL[1] 2. □□ **impiousness** ungodliness, unholiness; see also SIN *n.* 1.

imp•ish /ímpish/ *adj.* of or like an imp; mischievous. □□ **imp'ish•ly** *adv.* **imp'ish•ness** *n.*
  ■ see MISCHIEVOUS 1, 2. □□ **impishness** see MISCHIEF 1, 2.

im•pla•ca•ble /implákəbəl/ *adj.* unable to be appeased. □□ **im•pla•ca•bil'i•ty** *n.* **im•plac'a•bly** *adv.*
  ■ unappeasable, irreconcilable, unforgiving, inexorable; see also MORTAL *adj.* 4.

im•plant • *v.tr.* /implánt/ **1** insert or fix. **2** instill (an idea, etc.) in a person's mind. **3** plant. **4** *Med.* **a** insert (tissue, etc.) in a living body. **b** (of a fertilized ovum) become attached to the wall of the womb. • *n.* /implant/ thing implanted. □□ **im•plan•ta'tion** *n.*
  ■ *v.* **1** inlay, embed, fasten, introduce, put. **2** introduce, sow, plant; indoctrinate, impress. **3** transplant, root, embed. • *n.* insert, inlay, graft, transplant. □□ **implantation** insertion; injection, inoculation; transplantation.

im•plau•si•ble /impláwzibəl/ *adj.* not plausible. □□ **im•plau•si•bil'i•ty** *n.* **im•plau'si•bly** *adv.*
  ■ improbable, unlikely, doubtful, dubious.

im•ple•ment • *n.* /implimənt/ **1** tool, instrument, or utensil. **2** [in *pl.*] equipment; articles of furniture, etc. See synonym study at TOOL. • *v.tr.* /impliment/ **1 a** put (a decision, plan, etc.) into effect. **b** fulfill (an undertaking). **2** complete (a contract, etc.). **3** fill up; supplement. □□ **im•ple•men•ta'tion** *n.*
  ■ *n.* **1** apparatus, device, appliance. **2** (*implements*) machinery, paraphernalia, gear. • *v.* **1, 2** carry out, execute, accomplish. **3** add to, augment; see also FILL *v.* 1. □□ **implementation** see *execution* (EXECUTE), *fulfillment* (FULFILL).

im•pli•cate • *v.tr.* /implikayt/ **1** show (a person) to be involved (in a crime, etc.). **2** [in *passive*; often foll. by *in*] be affected or involved. • *n.* /implikət/ thing implied.
  ■ *v.* **1** incriminate, inculpate, connect; inform on. **2** (*be implicated*) be included, be connected, be associated. • *n.* see IMPLICATION.

im•pli•ca•tion /implikáyshən/ *n.* **1** thing implied. **2** act of implicating or implying.
  ■ consequence, import, purport; incrimination.

im•plic•it /implísit/ *adj.* **1** implied though not plainly expressed. **2** absolute; unquestioning; unreserved. □□ **im•plic'it•ly** *adv.* **im•plic'it•ness** *n.*
  ■ **1** indirect, inferable, understood. **2** unquestioned, unqualified, total. □□ **implicitly** indirectly, by implication, tacitly.

im•plode /implṓd/ *v.* burst or cause to burst inward. □□ **im•plo•sion** /-plṓzhən/ *n.* **im•plo'sive** /-plṓsiv/ *adj.*

im•plore /impláwr/ *v.tr.* **1** entreat (a person). **2** beg earnestly for. See synonym study at BEG. □□ **im•plor'ing** *adj.* **im•plor'ing•ly** *adv.*
  ■ see BEG 2.

im•ply /implí/ *v.tr.* (**-plies, -plied**) **1** strongly suggest the truth or existence of (a thing not expressly asserted). **2** insinuate; hint (*what are you implying?*). **3** signify. □□ **im•plied'** *adj.*
  ■ **1** entail, point to, indicate. **2** intimate; allude to. **3** signal, indicate, mean. □□ **implied** see IMPLICIT 1.

im•po•lite /impəlít/ *adj.* ill-mannered; uncivil; rude. □□ **im•po•lite′ly** *adv.* **im•po•lite′ness** *n.*

■ discourteous, disrespectful, impudent, insolent. □□ **impoliteness** see DISRESPECT.

im•pol•i•tic /impólitik/ *adj.* **1** inexpedient; unwise. **2** not politic. □□ **im•pol′i•tic•ly** *adv.*

■ **1** see FOOLISH. **2** see TACTLESS.

im•pon•der•a•ble /impóndərəbəl/ • *adj.* not able to be estimated. • *n.* [usu. in *pl.*] something difficult to assess. □□ **im•pon•der•a•bil′i•ty** *n.* **im•pon′der•a•bly** *adv.*

■ *adj.* immeasurable, inestimable, inconceivable. • *n.* see INTANGIBLE.

im•port • *v.tr.* /impáwrt, im–/ **1** bring in (goods) to a country. **2 a** indicate; signify. **b** make known. • *n.* /ímpawrt/ **1** process of importing. **2 a** imported article. **b** [in *pl.*] amount imported (*imports exceeded $50 billion*). **3** meaning. **4** importance. □□ **im•port′a•ble** *adj.* **im•por•ta′tion** *n.* **im•port′er** *n.* (all in sense 1 of *v.*).

■ *v.* **1** convey (in), introduce; buy from abroad. **2** imply, mean, convey. • *n.* **1** introduction. **2 b** (*imports*) foreign goods. **3** sense, denotation, signification. **4** significance.

im•por•tant /impáwrt'nt/ *adj.* **1** of great effect or consequence; momentous. **2** having high rank or great authority. □□ **im•por′tance** *n.* **im•por′tant•ly** *adv.*

■ **1** significant, consequential, critical. **2** leading, prominent, notable, eminent. □□ **importance** momentousness, weightiness, gravity; significance; distinction, esteem.

im•por•tu•nate /impáwrchənət/ *adj.* making persistent requests. □□ **im•por′tu•nate•ly** *adv.* **im•por•tu′ni•ty** /–tōōnatee, –tyōō–/ *n.*

■ see INSISTENT 1. □□ **importunity** see *urgency* (URGENT).

im•por•tune /ímpawrtōōn, –tyōōn, impáwrchoon/ *v.tr.* solicit (a person) pressingly. See synonym study at BEG.

■ see SOLICIT 1, 2.

im•pose /impóz/ *v.* **1** *tr.* lay (a tax, duty, charge, or obligation) on. **2** *tr.* enforce compliance with. **3** *intr. & refl.* [foll. by *on, upon,* or *absol.*] demand the attention or commitment of (a person) (*I do not want to impose on you any longer*). □□ **im•po•si′tion** *n.*

■ **1, 2** enjoin, prescribe, dictate; administer, set; (*impose a tax*) exact *or* levy *or* raise a tax. **3** (*impose on or upon*) take advantage of, exploit, force *or* foist oneself (up)on. □□ **imposition** infliction; demand, burden, onus.

im•pos•ing /impózing/ *adj.* impressive or formidable, esp. in appearance. □□ **im•pos′ing•ly** *adv.*

■ see IMPRESSIVE.

im•pos•si•ble /impósibəl/ *adj.* **1** not possible. **2** (loosely) not easy, convenient, or believable. **3** *colloq.* (of a person) outrageous; intolerable. □□ **im•pos•si•bil′i•ty** *n.* **im•pos′si•bly** *adv.*

■ **1** unrealizable, unattainable, impracticable; paradoxical, illogical. **2** difficult, problematic; implausible, far-fetched. **3** unbearable, unendurable, insufferable. □□ **impossibly** paradoxically, illogically, un-

reasonably; unattainably; problematically, awkwardly; unbelievably, implausibly; intolerably, unbearably.

im•post /impóst/ *n.* tax; duty; tribute.

im•pos•tor /impóstər/ *n.* (also **im•pos′ter**) **1** person who pretends to be someone else. **2** swindler.

■ **1** impersonator, humbug, fraud. **2** deceiver, trickster, cheat.

im•pos•ture /impós-chər/ *n.* fraudulent deception.

im•po•tent /ímpət'nt/ *adj.* **1 a** powerless. **b** helpless. **c** ineffective. **2 a** (esp. of a male) unable to achieve an erection or orgasm. **b** *colloq.* unable to procreate; infertile. □□ **im′po•tence** *n.* **im•po•ten•cy** *n.* **im′po•tent•ly** *adv.*

■ **1 a, b** weak, enervated, enfeebled; helpless, feeble. **c** inadequate, inept, incompetent. **2 b** sterile, barren. □□ **impotence, impotency** weakness, powerlessness, helplessness, frailty, feebleness; sterility.

im•pound /impównd/ *v.tr.* **1** confiscate. **2** take possession of. **3** shut up (animals) in a pound. □□ **im•pound′a•ble** *adj.* **im•pound′er** *n.* **im•pound′ment** *n.*

■ **1, 2** see CONFISCATE[2]. **3** see PEN *v.*

im•pov•er•ish /impóvərish/ *v.tr.* (often as **impoverished** *adj.*) **1** make poor. **2** exhaust the strength or natural fertility of. □□ **im•pov′er•ish•ment** *n.*

■ **1** see RUIN *v.* 1; (**impoverished**) destitute, poverty-stricken, needy. **2** see WEAKEN 1; (**impoverished**) stripped, barren, desolate. □□ **impoverishment** see LOSS 3.

im•prac•ti•ca•ble /imprákticabəl/ *adj.* impossible in practice. □□ **im•prac•ti•ca•bil′i•ty** *n.* **im•prac′ti•ca•bly** *adv.*

■ see IMPOSSIBLE 1.

im•prac•ti•cal /impráktikəl/ *adj.* **1** not practical. **2** not practicable. □□ **im•prac•ti•cal•i•ty** /–kálitee/ *n.* **im•prac′ti•cal•ly** *adv.*

■ **1** theoretical, idealistic, abstract; unworldly. **2** see IMPOSSIBLE. □□ **impracticality** idealism, speculativeness, unworldliness, romanticism.

im•pre•ca•tion /imprikáyshən/ *n.* a curse; malediction.

im•pre•cise /ímprisís/ *adj.* not precise. □□ **im•pre•cise′ly** *adv.* **im•pre•ci′sion** /–sízhən/ *n.*

■ inexact, inaccurate, inexplicit, indefinite, ill-defined. □□ **imprecision** inexactitude, inaccuracy, indefiniteness, indistinctness.

im•preg•na•ble /imprégnabəl/ *adj.* **1** (of a fortified position) that cannot be taken by force. **2** resistant to attack or criticism. □□ **im•preg•na•bil′i•ty** /–bílitee/ *n.* **im•preg′na•bly** *adv.*

■ impenetrable, unassailable, well-fortified; thick-skinned, watertight, resistant, tenable. □□ **impregnability** impenetrability, unassailability; inviolability, invulnerability.

im•preg•nate /imprégnayt/ *v.tr.* **1** fill or saturate. **2** imbue with (feelings, moral qualities, etc.). **3 a** make (a female) pregnant. **b** *Biol.* fertilize an ovum. □□ **im•preg•na•tion** /–náyshən/ *n.*

■ **1, 2** drench, soak, steep, permeate. **3** fertilize, inseminate.

im•pre•sa•ri•o /imprisaáreeō, –sáir–/ *n.* (*pl.* **–os**) organizer of public entertainments, esp. a theatrical, etc., manager.

im•press • *v.tr.* /imprés/ **1 a** affect or influence deeply. **b** affect (a person) favorably. **2** emphasize (an idea, etc.). **3 a** imprint or stamp. **b** apply (a mark, etc.) with pressure. **4** make a mark or design on (a thing) with a stamp, seal, etc. • *n.* /impres/ **1** instance of impressing. **2** mark made by a seal, stamp, etc. **3** characteristic mark or quality. **4** = IMPRESSION. □□ **im•press′i•ble** *adj.*

■ *v.* **1 a** touch, move, reach, stir. **b** (*impressed with*) struck by or with, taken with. **2** stress, emphasize. **3, 4** print, engrave, emboss. • *n.* **1** see IMPRESSION 4. **2** see STAMP *n.* 2. **3** see STAMP *n.* 5a. □□ **impressible** see IMPRESSIONABLE.

im•pres•sion /impréshən/ *n.* **1** effect produced (esp. on the mind or feelings). **2** vague notion or belief. **3** imitation of a person or sound, esp. done to entertain. **4 a** impressing of a mark. **b** mark impressed. See synonym study at IDEA.

■ **1** sensation, feeling, perception; impact. **2** idea, feeling, suspicion. **3** impersonation, parody, satire. **4** stamp, brand; dent, indentation.

im•pres•sion•a•ble /impréshənəbəl/ *adj.* easily influenced. □□ **im•pres•sion•a•bil′i•ty** *n.* **im•pres′sion•a•bly** *adv.*

■ suggestible, susceptible, persuadable; soft, pliable, malleable, moldable.

im•pres•sion•ism /impréshənizəm/ *n.* style or movement in art, music, etc., that seeks to convey a brief impression or emotion without close, realistic detail. □□ **im•pres′sion•ist** *n.* **im•pres•sion•is′tic** /impréshənístik/ *adj.*

im•pres•sive /imprésiv/ *adj.* causing approval or admiration. □□ **im•pres′sive•ly** *adv.* **im•pres′sive•ness** *n.*

■ imposing, formidable, awe-inspiring; grand, august, magnificent. □□ **impressively** imposingly, formidably, awesomely; evocatively, movingly, affectingly. **impressiveness** formidableness, awesomeness, power, dignity; evocativeness, provocativeness, emotion.

im•pri•ma•tur /imprimáatər, –máytər, –tŏōr/ *n.* **1** *RC Ch.* official license to print (a religious book, etc.). **2** official approval.

im•print • *v.tr.* /imprínt/ **1** impress or establish firmly, esp. on the mind. **2 a** make a stamp or impression of (a figure, etc.) on a thing. **b** make an impression on (a thing) with a stamp, etc. • *n.* /imprint/ **1** impression or stamp. **2** printer's or publisher's name, etc., printed in a book.

■ *v.* **2** see STAMP *v.* 2. • *n.* **1** see IMPRESSION 4.

im•pris•on /imprízən/ *v.tr.* **1** put into prison. **2** confine; shut up. □□ **im•pris′on•ment** *n.*

■ **1** incarcerate, detain, remand, jail. **2** box in or up, hem in, circumscribe, intern. □□ **imprisonment** incarceration, detention, custody.

im•prob•a•ble /impróbəbəl/ *adj.* **1** unlikely. **2** difficult to believe. □□ **im•prob•a•bil′i•ty** *n.* **im•prob′a•bly** *adv.*

■ **1** doubtful, dubious, questionable. **2** see IMPLAUSIBLE.

im•promp•tu /imprómptōō, –tyōō/ • *adj.* & *adv.* extempore; unrehearsed. • *n.* extempore performance.

■ *adj.* & *adv.* see EXTEMPORANEOUS *adj.*

im•prop•er /imprópər/ *adj.* **1 a** unseemly; indecent. **b** not in accordance with accepted rules of behavior. **2** inaccurate; wrong. □□ **im•prop′er•ly** *adv.*

■ **1 a** unbecoming, untoward; indecorous, immodest, impolite. **b** impolite, unacceptable, unsuitable. **2** mistaken, erroneous, false.

im•pro•pri•e•ty /imprəprī́ətee/ *n.* (*pl.* **–ties**) **1** indecency. **2** instance of this. **3** incorrectness. **4** unfitness.

■ **1** unseemliness, indecorousness, bad or poor taste. **2** gaffe, gaucherie, faux pas, slip. **3** erroneousness, falsity, inaccuracy. **4** unsuitableness, inappropriateness, inaptness.

im•prove /imprōōv/ *v.* **1 a** *tr.* & *intr.* make or become better. **b** *intr.* (foll. by *on, upon*) produce something better than. **2** (as **improving** *adj.*) giving moral benefit. □□ **im•prov′a•ble** *adj.* **im•prove′ment** *n.*

■ **1 a** upgrade, enhance, refine; amend, repair; redress, rectify; recover, recuperate. **b** (*improve on* or *upon*) surpass, beat, exceed. **2** (*improving*) edifying, instructive. □□ **improvement** betterment, enhancement; amendment; recovery, recuperation; change (for the better).

im•prov•i•dent /impróvid′nt/ *adj.* **1** lacking foresight. **2** wasteful. **3** heedless; incautious. □□ **im•prov′i•dence** /–d′ns/ *n.* **im•prov′i•dent•ly** *adv.*

■ **1, 3** imprudent, injudicious, indiscreet. **2** thriftless, spendthrift, uneconomical, profligate. □□ **improvidence** see *imprudence* (IMPRUDENT), *extravagance* (EXTRAVAGANT).

im•pro•vise /imprəvīz/ *v.tr.* [also *absol.*] **1** compose or perform (music, verse, etc.) extempore. **2** provide or construct (a thing) extempore. □□ **im•pro•vi•sa′tion** /–izáyshən/ *n.* **im•pro•vi•sa′tion•al** *adj.* **im′pro•vi•ser** *n.*

■ **1** ad lib, extemporize, vamp, scat, play (it) by ear. **2** invent, concoct, devise, contrive. □□ **improvisation** ad lib, impromptu; invention, concoction; makeshift. **improvisational** ad lib, extempore, impromptu, unrehearsed; made-up, thrown together.

im•pru•dent /improōd′nt/ *adj.* rash; indiscreet. See synonym study at IMPERTINENT. □□ **im•pru′dence** /–d′ns/ *n.* **im•pru′dent•ly** *adv.*

■ hasty, reckless, heedless, precipitate, unthinking. □□ **imprudence** indiscretion, injudiciousness, incautiousness, unguardedness, unwariness.

im•pu•dent /impyəd′nt/ *adj.* impertinent. □□ **im•pu′dence** /–d′ns/ *n.* **im′pu•dent•ly** *adv.*

■ insolent, disrespectful, saucy, brassy; arrogant, presumptuous. □□ **impudence** insolence, disrespect, contempt, contumely, incivility.

im•pugn /impyōōn/ v.tr. challenge or call in question (a statement, action, etc.). □□ **im•pugn'a•ble** adj.

im•pulse /impuls/ n. **1** act of impelling; a push. **2** impetus. **3** *Electr.* surge in current or flow. **4** mental incitement. **5** sudden desire or tendency to act without reflection (*did it on impulse*).

■ **1** see PUSH n. 1. **2** see IMPETUS 2. **4** see *incitement* (INCITE). **5** see FANCY n. 2.

im•pul•sion /impúlshən/ n. **1** impelling. **2** mental impulse. **3** impetus.

im•pul•sive /impúlsiv/ adj. **1** apt to act on impulse. **2** tending to impel. □□ **im•pul'sive•ly** adv. **im•pul'sive•ness** n.

■ **1** impetuous, spontaneous, spur-of-the-moment, snap; unpredictable; quick, precipitate. □□ **impulsively** impetuously, instinctively, spontaneously; see also *hastily* (HASTY). **impulsiveness** impetuousness, impetuosity; unpredictableness, capriciousness; see also HASTE n. 2.

im•pu•ni•ty /impyōōnitee/ n. exemption from punishment, bad consequences, etc. □ **with impunity** without punishment.

■ see *exemption* (EXEMPT).

im•pure /impyōōr/ adj. **1** adulterated. **2 a** dirty. **b** ceremonially unclean. **3** unchaste. □□ **im•pure'ly** adv. **im•pure'ness** n.

■ **1** mixed, alloyed, base, debased. **2 a** see DIRTY adj. 1. **b** unhallowed, forbidden. **3** immoral, sinful, wicked, evil, vile. □□ **impureness** see IMPURITY 1.

im•pu•ri•ty /impyōōritee/ n. (pl. **-ties**) **1** being impure. **2** impure thing or constituent.

■ **1** impureness, baseness, adulteration; uncleanness, dirtiness; unchasteness, immorality, sinfulness. **2** adulterant, admixture, contaminant; see also DIRT n. 1.

im•pute /impyōōt/ v.tr. (**foll. by** *to*) attribute (a fault, etc.) to. □□ **im•put'a•ble** adj. **im•pu•ta'tion** n. **im•pu'ta•tive** adj.

■ (*impute to*) ascribe to, blame on, assign to. □□ **imputable** assignable, attributable, ascribable. **imputation** ascription, attribution, blame.

411

IN abbr. Indiana (in official postal use).

In symb. Chem. indium.

in /in/ • prep. **1** expressing inclusion or position within limits of space, time, circumstance, etc. (*in Nebraska, in bed, in the rain*). **2** during the time of. **3** within the time of (*will be back in two hours*). **4 a** with respect to (*blind in one eye*). **b** as a kind of (*the latest thing in luxury*). **5** as a proportionate part of (*one in three failed*). **6** with the form or arrangement of (*packed in tens*). **7** as a member of (*in the army*). **8** concerned with (*is in politics*). **9** as the content of (*there is something in what you say*). **10** within the ability of (*does he have it in him?*). **11** having the condition of; affected by (*in bad health*). **12** having as a purpose (*in reply to*). **13** by means of or using as material (*drawn in pencil*). **14 a** using for expression (*written in French*). **b** (of music) having as its key (*symphony in C*). **15** (of a word) having as a part (*words beginning in un-*). **16** wearing (*in a suit*). **17** with the identity of (*found a friend in Mary*). **18** into (with a verb of motion or change; *put it in the box*). • adv. expressing position within limits, or motion to such a position: **1** into a room, house, etc. (*come in*). **2** at home, in one's office, etc. (*is not in*). **3** so as to be enclosed or confined (*locked in*). **4** in a publication (*is the advertisement in?*). **5** in or to the inward side (*rub it in*). **6** in fashion or season (*long shirts are in*). **7** exerting favorable action or influence (*their luck was in*). **8** (of a season, harvest, order, etc.) having arrived or been received. **9** (of the tide) at the highest point. • adj. **1** internal; inside. **2** fashionable. **3** confined to a small group (*in-joke*). □ **in on** privy to (a secret, etc.). **ins and outs** all the details. **in that** because; in so far as. **in with** on good terms with

■ prep. **16** see WEAR v. 1. • adv. **6 a** see FASHIONABLE. ■ **in on** see PRIVY adj. 1. **ins and outs** see ROPE n. 3. **in with** en rapport with, tuned in to

in. abbr. inch(es).

in-[1] /in/ prefix (also **il-, im-, ir-**) added to:

1 adjectives, meaning 'not' (*inedible, insane*).
2 nouns, meaning 'without; lacking' (*inaction*).

in-² /in/ *prefix* (also **il-** before *l*, **im-** before *b*, *m*, *p*, **ir-** before *r*) in, on, into, toward, within (*induce, influx, insight, intrude*).

in ab•sen•tia /in absénshə/ *adv.* in (his, her, or their) absence.

in•ad•ver•tent /ínədvə́rt'nt/ *adj.* **1** (of an action) unintentional. **2 a** not properly attentive. **b** negligent. □□ **in•ad•ver'tence** /-t'ns/ *n.* **in•ad•ver'ten•cy** *n.* **in•ad•ver'tent•ly** *adv.*
 ■ **1** unintended, unpremeditated, unthinking. **2** inattentive, unobservant; see also ABSENTMINDED. □□ **inadvertently** see *absentmindedly* (ABSENTMINDED).

in•a•lien•a•ble /ínáyleeənəbəl/ *adj.* that cannot be transferred to another. □□ **in•a'lien•a•bly** *adv.*
 ■ untransferable, nonnegotiable; inviolable, sacrosanct, unchallengeable, absolute.

in•am•o•ra•to /ináməráàtó/ *n.* (*pl.* **-os**) (*fem.* **in•am•o•ra•ta** /-tə/) lover.

in•ane /ináyn/ *adj.* **1** silly; senseless. **2** empty; void. □□ **in•ane'ly** *adv.* **in•an•i•ty** /-ánitee/ *n.* (*pl.* **-ties**)
 ■ **1** asinine, vacuous, absurd, fatuous, empty-headed, foolish, witless. **2** vacant, unfilled, hollow.

in•ar•tic•u•late /ínaartíkyələt/ *adj.* **1** unable to express oneself clearly. **2** (of speech) indistinctly pronounced. **3** mute. □□ **in•ar•tic'u•late•ly** *adv.* **in•ar•tic'u•late•ness** *n.*
 ■ **1** unclear, incomprehensible, unintelligible, incoherent, confused, muddled, mixed-up, jumbled, wild. **2** mumbled, muttered, unintelligible, muffled. **3** voiceless, silent; speechless, tongue-tied.

in•as•much as /ínəzmúch/ *adv.* [foll. by *as*] **1** since; because. **2** to the extent that.
 ■ **1** (*inasmuch as*) see BECAUSE.

in•au•gu•ral /ináwgyərəl/ • *adj.* **1** of inauguration. **2** (of a lecture, etc.) given by a person being inaugurated. • *n.* an inaugural speech, etc.
 ■ *adj.* see INTRODUCTORY.

in•au•gu•rate /ináwgyərayt/ *v.tr.* **1** admit formally to office. **2** initiate the public use of (a building, etc.). **3** begin; introduce. □□ **in•au•gu•ra•tion** /-ráyshən/ *n.* **in•au'gu•ra•tor** *n.* **in•au•gu•ra•to•ry** /-rətáwree/ *adj.*
 ■ **1** install, induct, invest, crown. **2** open, declare open, establish. **3** initiate, start, originate, set up, launch, institute. □□ **inauguration** installation, induction, investiture, instatement.

in•board /ínbawrd/ • *adv.* within the sides of or toward the center of a ship, aircraft, or vehicle. • *adj.* situated inboard.

in•born /ínbáwrn/ *adj.* existing from birth. See synonym study at INHERENT.
 ■ innate, congenital, inherent, hereditary, inbred.

in•bred /ínbréd/ *adj.* **1** inborn. **2** produced by inbreeding.

in•breed•ing /ínbréeding/ *n.* breeding from closely related animals or persons. □□ **in'breed** *v.* (*past* and *past part.* **in•bred**).

inc. *abbr.* **1** (esp. **Inc.**) Incorporated. · **2** incomplete.

In•ca /íngkə/ *n.* member of a Native American people in Peru before the Spanish conquest. □□ **In'can** *adj.*

in•cal•cu•la•ble /inkálkyələbəl/ *adj.* **1** too great for calculation. **2** unpredictable. □□ **in•cal•cu•la•bil'i•ty** *n.* **in•cal'cu•la•bly** *adv.*
 ■ **1** see IMMEASURABLE.

in•can•des•cent /inkandésənt/ *adj.* **1** glowing with heat. **2** shining brightly. **3** (of artificial light) produced by a glowing filament. □□ **in•can•des'cence** *n.* **in•can•des'cent•ly** *adv.*
 ■ **1, 2** aglow, fervent, red-hot; alight, ablaze, aflame, ardent. □□ **incandescence** glow, fervor; fire, blaze, flame; see also *radiance* (RADIANT).

in•can•ta•tion /ínkantáyshən/ *n.* **1 a** magical formula. **b** the use of this. **2** spell or charm. □□ **in•can•ta'tion•al** *adj.*
 ■ **1a, 2** see SPELL² 1.

in•ca•pac•i•tate /ínkəpásitayt/ *v.tr.* **1** render incapable or unfit. **2** disqualify. □□ **in•ca•pac•i•ta•tion** /-táyshən/ *n.*
 ■ **1** immobilize, inactivate, deactivate; disable, cripple, paralyze. **2** see DISQUALIFY.

in•ca•pac•i•ty /ínkəpásitee/ *n.* (*pl.* **-ties**) **1** inability. **2** legal disqualification.

in•car•cer•ate /inkáarsərayt/ *v.tr.* imprison or confine. □□ **in•car•cer•a•tion** /-ráyshən/ *n.* **in•car'cer•a•tor** *n.*
 ■ see IMPRISON. □□ **incarceration** see *imprisonment* (IMPRISON).

in•car•nate • *adj.* /ínkáarnət, -nayt/ **1** embodied in human form (*is the devil incarnate*). **2** represented in a recognizable or typical form (*folly incarnate*). • *v.tr.* /ínkáarnayt/ **1** embody in flesh. **2** put (an idea, etc.) into concrete form; realize. **3** (of a person, etc.) be the living embodiment of (a quality).
 ■ *adj.* **1** see PHYSICAL *adj.* 1. **2** see PHYSICAL *adj.* 2. • *v.* **1** flesh. **2** see EMBODY 1, 3. **3** see PERSONIFY 2.

in•car•na•tion /ínkaarnáyshən/ *n.* **1 a** embodiment in (esp. human) flesh. **b** (**the Incarnation**) *Theol.* the embodiment of God the Son in human flesh as Jesus Christ. **2** living type (of a quality, etc.).

in•cen•di•ar•y /ínséndee-eree/ • *adj.* **1** (of a bomb) designed to cause fires. **2** of or relating to the malicious setting on fire of property. **3** tending to stir up strife. • *n.* (*pl.* **-ies**) **1** fire bomb or device. **2** arsonist. □□ **in•cen'di•ar•ism** *n.*
 ■ *adj.* **3** see INFLAMMATORY 1. • *n.* **3** see *agitator* (AGITATE).

in•cense¹ /ínsens/ • *n.* **1** gum or spice producing a sweet smell when burned. **2** the smoke of this. • *v.tr.* **1** treat or perfume (a person or thing) with incense. **2** burn incense to (a deity, etc.).

in•cense² /inséns/ *v.tr.* [often foll. by *at, with, against*] enrage; make angry.
 ■ see ENRAGE.

in•cen•tive /inséntiv/ • *n.* **1** motive or incitement to action. **2** payment or concession to stimulate greater output by workers. • adj. serving to motivate or incite.

■ n. 1 encouragement, promotion, motivation, inducement. 2 bonus, reward, extra, perquisite. • adj. motivational, promotional.

in•cep•tion /insépshən/ n. beginning. See synonym study at ORIGIN.

■ see BEGINNING 1, 2.

in•ces•sant /insésənt/ adj. unceasing; continual; repeated. □□ in•ces′san•cy n. in•ces′sant•ly adv. in•ces′sant•ness n.

■ see CONTINUAL.

in•cest /insest/ n. sexual intercourse between persons regarded as too closely related to legally marry each other.

in•ces•tu•ous /inséschōōəs/ adj. 1 involving or guilty of incest. 2 (of human relations generally) excessively restricted or resistant to wider influence. □□ in•ces′tu•ous•ly adv.

inch /inch/ • n. 1 unit of linear measure equal to one-twelfth of a foot (2.54 cm). 2 small amount (usu. with neg.: would not yield an inch). • v. move gradually (inched forward). □ every inch 1 entirely (every inch a judge). 2 the whole distance or area (combed every inch of the garden). within an inch of almost to the point of.

■ v. crawl, creep, edge, work one's way; see also EASE v. 5b.

in•cho•ate /inkóit/ adj. 1 just begun. 2 undeveloped; rudimentary; unformed. □□ in•cho′ate•ly adv. in•cho′ate•ness n. in•cho′ative adj.

in•ci•dence /insidəns/ n. 1 fact, manner, or rate of occurrence or action. 2 range, scope, or extent of influence of a thing. 3 Physics the falling of a line, or of a thing moving in a line, upon a surface.

■ 1 frequency, degree; quantity, amount. 2 see RANGE n. 1.

in•ci•dent /insidənt/ • n. 1 a occurrence. b minor event attracting general attention. 2 hostile clash, esp. of warring troops. • adj. 1 [often foll. by to] apt or liable to happen; naturally attaching. 2 (of light, etc.) falling on or upon.

■ n. 1 occasion, happening, episode. 2 confrontation, disturbance, skirmish, fight. • adj. 1 (incident to) pertinent to; dependent on.

in•ci•den•tal /insidéntəl/ adj. 1 a having a minor role in relation to a more important thing, event, etc. b not essential. c casual. 2 [foll. by to] liable to happen. See synonym study at ACCIDENTAL.

■ 1 a secondary, subordinate, subsidiary. b nonessential, unnecessary, dispensable. c chance, fortuitous, random. 2 (incidental to) see INCIDENT adj.

in•ci•den•tal•ly /insidént′lee/ adv. 1 by the way; as an unconnected remark. 2 in an incidental way.

■ 1 by the by, apropos, parenthetically. 2 secondarily, subordinately; coincidentally.

in•cin•er•ate /insínərayt/ v.tr. burn to ashes. □□ in•cin•er•a′tion /-ráyshən/ n. in•cin′er•a•tor n.

in•cip•i•ent /insípeeənt/ adj. 1 beginning. 2 in an initial stage. □□ in•cip′i•ence n. in•cip′i•en•cy n. in•cip′i•ent•ly adv.

■ see INITIAL adj.

in•cise /insíz/ v.tr. 1 make a cut in. 2 engrave.

in•ci•sion /insízhən/ n. 1 a cut, esp. by a surgeon. 2 act of cutting into a thing.

■ 1 slit, gash, slash, cleft.

in•ci•sive /insísiv/ adj. 1 mentally sharp. 2 clear and effective. 3 penetrating. □□ in•ci′sive•ly adv. in•ci′sive•ness n.

■ 1 keen, acute, razor-sharp, piercing. 2 concise, succinct, terse, laconic; crisp, straightforward. 3 cutting, biting, mordant; pungent, acrid.

in•ci•sor /insízər/ n. cutting tooth, esp. at the front of the mouth.

in•cite /insít/ v.tr. urge or stir up. □□ in•cite′ment n. in•cit′er n.

■ exhort, encourage, rally, rouse; foment. □□ incitement exhortation, encouragement, motivation, instigation, persuasion; rabble-rousing; see also INCENTIVE n. 1. inciter see arouser (AROUSE), rabble-rouser (RABBLE).

in•clem•ent /inklémənt/ adj. (of the weather) severe; stormy. □□ in•clem′en•cy n. (pl. -cies). in•clem′ent•ly adv.

■ extreme, intemperate; rainy, squally; see also BAD adj. 2a. □□ inclemency see severity (SEVERE).

in•cli•na•tion /inklináyshən/ n. 1 disposition or propensity. 2 liking or affection. 3 leaning, slope, or slant.

■ 1 predisposition, tendency, bent, bias; see also WISH n. 2 fondness, love, penchant, weakness. 3 angle, bend, tilt, nod; see also INCLINE n.

in•cline • v. /inklín/ 1 tr. a make (a person, etc.) willing (am inclined to think so). b have a tendency (the door is inclined to bang). 2 intr. a be disposed (I incline to think so). b tend. 3 intr. & tr. lean or slope. • n. /ínklin/ slope. □□ in•clin′er n.

■ *v.* **1** lead, get, persuade, convince, influence; (*inclined*) see WILLING *adj.*, LIKELY *adj.* 2. **2** predisposed, have a mind; tend, be prone. **3** bend, bow, nod, stoop, slant; (*inclined*) see OBLIQUE *adj.* 1. • *n.* pitch, grade, gradient, slant.

in•clude /inklóŏd/ *v.tr.* **1** comprise or reckon in as part of a whole; place in a class or category. **2** (as **including** *prep.*) if we include (*six members, including the chairperson*). **3** treat or regard as so included. □□ **in•clud′a•ble** *adj.* **in•clud•i•ble** *adj.* **in•clu′sion** /-kloŏzhən/ *n.*

■ **1** incorporate, embody, encompass; classify, categorize, group; see also SELECT *v.* **2** (**including**) see INCLUSIVE 1. **3** count, number, allow for, take into account, involve. □□ **inclusion** incorporation, involvement; admission, categorization, selection; enclosure, insertion, encompassment.

in•clu•sive /inklóŏsiv/ *adj.* **1** often foll. by *of*) including; comprising. **2** including the limits stated (*pages 7 to 26 inclusive*). **3** including all the normal services, etc. (*a hotel offering inclusive terms*). □ **inclusive language** language that is deliberately nonsexist, esp. avoiding the use of masculine pronouns to cover both men and women. □□ **in•clu′sive•ly** *adv.* **in•clu′sive•ness** *n.*

■ **1** (*inclusive of*) embracing, taking in, covering, incorporating, embodying. **2** comprehensive, overall, full, thorough; general, extensive.

in•cog•ni•to /inkognéŏtó, –kógni-/ • *adj. & adv.* with one's name or identity kept secret. • *n.* (*pl.* **-os**) **1** person who is incognito. **2** pretended identity of such a person.

■ *adj. & adv.* in disguise, under cover; disguised, unidentified, unrecognized; anonymous(ly), covert(ly); (*adj.*) plainclothes, unrecognizable, mysterious; (*adv.*) on the sly. • *n.* **1** mystery man *or* woman. **2** false identity, alias, pseudonym, nom de guerre; masquerade; act, charade.

in•co•her•ent /inkóhéerənt/ *adj.* **1** unable to speak intelligibly. **2** lacking logic or consistency. □□ **in•co•her′ence** *n.* **in•co•her′en•cy** *n.* (*pl.* **-cies**) **in•co•her′ent•ly** *adv.*

■ **1** inarticulate, unintelligible, incomprehensible. **2** illogical, irrational, wild, disordered, confused; rambling, discursive.

in•come /inkum/ *n.* money received from one's work, investments, etc.

■ earnings, revenue(s), receipts, proceeds; see also PROFIT *n.* 2.

in•com•ing /inkuming/ • *adj.* **1** coming in (*incoming telephone calls*). **2** succeeding another (*incoming tenant*). • *n.* **1** [usu. in *pl.*] revenue; income. **2** act of arriving or entering.

■ *n.* **1** see INCOME. **2** see ARRIVAL 1.

in•com•mu•ni•ca•do /inkəmyóŏnikaádó/ *adj.* **1** without means of communication. **2** in solitary confinement.

in•com•pa•ra•ble /inkómpərəbəl/ *adj.* without an equal. □□ **in•com′pa•ra•bil′i•ty** *n.* **in•com′pa•ra•ble•ness** *n.* **in•com′pa•ra•bly** *adv.*

■ beyond compare, unequaled, matchless.

in•com•pat•i•ble /inkəmpátibəl/ *adj.* **1** opposed in character; discordant. **2** inconsistent. **3** unable to live together in harmony. □□ **in•com•pat•i•bil′i•ty** *n.* **in•com•pat′i•bly** *adv.*

■ **1, 3** mismatched, unsuited, clashing; antithetical, hostile. **2** see UNLIKE *adj.* 1. □□ **incompatibility** mismatch, discord, conflict, irreconcilability; disagreement, dissent, opposition.

in•com•pe•tent /inkómpit′nt/ • *adj.* **1** not able to perform a particular task (*incompetent builder*). **2** showing a lack of skill (*incompetent performance*). • *n.* incompetent person. □□ **in•com•pe′tence** /-t′ns/ *n.* **in•com′pe•ten•cy** *n.* **in•com′pe•tent•ly** *adv.*

■ *adj.* **1** unqualified, inexpert, unfit, unable, incapable. **2** unskilled, inept, maladroit, inexpert, awkward, clumsy. • *n.* bungler, botcher, blunderer, flounderer, bumbler, oaf. □□ **incompetence, incompetency** inability, incapability; lack of skill, ineptitude, ineptness, maladroitness; uselessness, hopelessness.

in•com•plete /inkəmpleét/ *adj.* not complete. □□ **in•com•plete′ly** *adv.* **in•com•plete′ness** *n.*

■ unfinished, imperfect, undone, partial. □□ **incompleteness** see IMPERFECTION 1.

in•con•ceiv•a•ble /inkənseévəbəl/ *adj.* **1** unimaginable. **2** *colloq.* very remarkable. □□ **in•con•ceiv′a•bly** *adv.*

■ **1** unthinkable, impossible, unrealistic, improbable; overwhelming. **2** see MIRACULOUS 1, 3.

in•con•clu•sive /inkənklóŏsiv/ *adj.* (of an argument, evidence, or action) not decisive or convincing. □□ **in•con•clu′sive•ly** *adv.* **in•con•clu′sive•ness** *n.*

■ indecisive, indefinite, unsettled, undemonstrated, unproved, unproven.

in•con•gru•ous /inkónggrōŏəs/ *adj.* **1** out of place; absurd. **2** disagreeing; out of keeping. □□ **in•con•gru′i•ty** *n.* (*pl.* **-ties**) **in•con′gru•ous•ly** *adv.*

■ inharmonious, disharmonious, discordant, dissonant; inconsistent; contradictory, paradoxical.

in•con•se•quen•tial /inkónsikwénshəl, inkon-/ *adj.* unimportant. □□ **in•con•se•quen′tial•i•ty** /-sheeálitee/ *n.* (*pl.* **-ties**). **in•con•se•quen′tial•ly** *adv.*

■ insignificant, trivial, trifling, nugatory, minor, little.

in•con•sid•er•a•ble /inkənsídərəbəl/ *adj.* **1** of small size, value, etc. **2** not worth considering. □□ **in•con•sid′er•a•bly** *adv.*

■ see INSIGNIFICANT 1.

in•con•sid•er•ate /inkənsídərət/ *adj.* **1** thoughtless; rash. **2** lacking regard for others. □□ **in•con•sid′er•ate•ly** *adv.* **in•con•sid′er•a•tion** /-ráyshən/ *n.*

■ **1** see IMPRUDENT. **2** thoughtless, uncaring, selfish, callous, tactless.

in•con•sist•ent /inkənsístənt/ *adj.* **1** acting at variance with one's own principles or former conduct. **2** not in keeping; incompatible. **3** (of a single thing) incompatible or discordant; having self-contradictory parts.

□□ in·con·sist'en·cy n. (pl. –cies). in·con·sist'ent·ly adv.

■ 1, 3 inconstant, irregular, changeable, variable, capricious, fickle, erratic; self-contradictory.

in·con·sol·a·ble /ĭnkənsṓləbəl/ adj. (of a person, grief, etc.) that cannot be comforted. □□ in·con·sol'a·bly adv.

■ unconsolable, disconsolate, broken-hearted, forlorn.

in·con·spic·u·ous /ĭnkənspíkyo͞oəs/ adj. not easily noticed. □□ in·con·spic'u·ous·ly adv. in·con·spic'u·ous·ness n.

■ 1 unnoticeable, unobtrusive; unseen; modest, unassuming.

in·con·stant /ĭnkónstənt/ adj. 1 fickle; changeable. 2 variable; irregular. □□ in·con'stan·cy n. (pl. –cies). in·con'stant·ly adv.

■ capricious, mercurial, volatile, flighty, moody; see also INCONSISTENT 1, 3. □□ inconstancy changeableness, changeability, irregularity, variability; fickleness, capriciousness; unfaithfulness.

in·con·test·a·ble /ĭnkəntéstəbəl/ adj. that cannot be disputed. □□ in·con·test·a·bil'i·ty n. in·con·test'a·bly adv.

■ see INCONTROVERTIBLE. □□ incontestably see undoubtedly (UNDOUBTED).

in·con·ti·nent /ĭnkóntinənt/ adj. 1 unable to control the bowels or bladder. 2 lacking self-restraint (esp. in sexual desire). □□ in·con·ti·nence /–nəns/ n. in·con'ti·nent·ly adv.

■ 1 wet, Med. enuretic. 2 unrestrained, unconstrained, unrestricted, uncontrolled; lecherous, libidinous, lascivious, promiscuous □□ incontinence bedwetting, Med. enuresis; unrestrainedness, uncontrollableness, lechery, libidinousness, lasciviousness.

in·con·tro·vert·i·ble /ĭnkóntrəvə́rtibəl/ adj. indisputable; indubitable. □□ in·con·tro·vert'i·bly adv.

■ uncontrovertible, indisputable, undeniable. □□ incontrovertibly see undoubtedly (UNDOUBTED).

in·con·ven·ience /ĭnkənvéenyəns/ • n. 1 lack of comfort or ease. 2 cause or instance of this. • v.tr. cause inconvenience to.

■ n. 1 troublesomeness, cumbersomeness, unwieldiness. 2 trouble, nuisance, bother, annoyance, irritation. • v. discommode, trouble, disturb, upset.

in·con·ven·ient /ĭnkənvéenyənt/ adj. 1 unfavorable to ease or comfort; not convenient. 2 awkward; troublesome. □□ in·con·ven'ient·ly adv.

■ disadvantageous, troublesome, bothersome, annoying; onerous, awkward.

in·cor·po·rate • v. /ĭnkáwrpərayt/ 1 tr. unite; form into one body. 2 intr. become incorporated. 3 tr. combine (ingredients) into one substance. 4 tr. admit as a member of a company, etc. 5 tr. a constitute as a legal corporation. b (as incorporated adj.) forming a legal corporation. • adj. /ĭnkáwrpərət/ (of a company, etc.) formed into a legal corporation. □□ in·cor·po·ra·tion /–áyshən/ n. in·cor'po·ra·tor n.

■ v. 1, 3 unify, integrate, associate; assimilate, merge. 2 unite, integrate, amalgamate,

combine. 4 see INCLUDE 1. □□ incorporation union, unification, integration, association; see also inclusion (INCLUDE).

in·cor·po·re·al /ĭnkawrpáwreeəl/ adj. 1 not composed of matter. 2 of immaterial beings. □□ in·cor·po·re·al'i·ty /–reeálitee/ n. in·cor·po're·al·ly adv.

in·cor·ri·gi·ble /ĭnkáwrijibəl, –kór–/ adj. 1 (of a person or habit) incurably bad or depraved. 2 not readily improved. □□ in·cor·ri·gi·bil'i·ty n. in·cor'ri·gi·ble·ness n. in·cor'ri·gi·bly adv.

■ 1 evil, immoral, wicked, vicious; naughty, mischievous. 2 inveterate, ingrained, hardened.

in·cor·rupt·i·ble /ĭnkərúptibəl/ adj. 1 that cannot be corrupted, esp. by bribery. 2 that cannot decay; everlasting. □□ in·cor·rupt·i·bil'i·ty n. in·cor·rupt'i·bly adv.

■ 1 moral, noble, upright, righteous, pure, upstanding; see also TRUSTWORTHY. 2 lasting, enduring; see also IMMORTAL adj. 2. □□ incorruptibility see INTEGRITY 1.

in·crease • v. /ĭnkrées/ 1 tr. & intr. make or become greater or more numerous. 2 intr. advance (in quality, attainment, etc.). 3 tr. intensify (a quality). • n. /ĭnkrees/ 1 growth; enlargement. 2 multiplication. 3 amount or extent of an increase. □□ in·creas'a·ble adj. in·creas'er n. in·creas'ing·ly adv.

■ v. 1 (tr. & intr.) multiply, propagate, breed; augment, build up, enlarge, amplify, expand; escalate, accelerate; inflate, swell; (tr.) add to, maximize, raise, lift, step up; (intr.) grow, jump, soar, shoot up, rocket, explode. 2 appreciate, improve, get better. 3 enhance, sharpen, strengthen. • n. 1, 2 propagation, proliferation, explosion; augmentation, increment, addition; acceleration, escalation, jump; appreciation; magnification. 3 increment, gain, rise, growth, jump. □□ increasingly progressively, more and more; constantly, ever, still.

in·cred·i·ble /ĭnkrédibəl/ adj. 1 not believable. 2 colloq. amazing. □□ in·cred'i·ble·ness n. in·cred'i·bly adv.

■ 1, 2 unbelievable, inconceivable, unimaginable, unthinkable; impossible, absurd, preposterous; see also amazing (AMAZE).

in·cred·u·lous /ĭnkréjələs/ adj. (often foll. by of) unwilling to believe. □□ in·cre·du·li·ty /ĭnkridóolitee, –dyóo–/ n. in·cred'u·lous·ly adv.

■ disbelieving, mistrustful, distrustful, dubious, doubtful, skeptical. □□ incredulity see DISTRUST n.

in·cre·ment /ĭnkrimənt/ n. 1 a increase or addition, esp. one of a series on a fixed scale. b amount of this. 2 Math. a small amount by which a variable quantity increases. □□ in·cre·men'tal /–mént'l/ adj.

■ 1 a see INCREASE n. 1, 2. b see INCREASE n. 3.

in·crim·i·nate /ĭnkríminayt/ v.tr. 1 tend to prove the guilt of (incriminating evidence). 2 charge with a crime. □□ in·crim·i·na·tion /–náyshən/ n. in·crim'i·na·to·ry /–nətawree/ adj.

■ **1** inculpate, point to, blame. **2** accuse, indict, arraign, impeach, inculpate. □□ **in·crimination** see IMPLICATION, ACCUSATION.

in·crus·ta·tion /ínkrustáyshən/ n. **1** encrusting. **2** crust or hard coating. **3** concretion or deposit on a surface.

■ **2** see SKIN n. 3. **3** see DEPOSIT n. 3.

in·cu·bate /íngkyəbayt/ v. **1** tr. sit on or artificially heat (eggs) in order to hatch them. **2** tr. cause to develop. **3** intr. sit on eggs; brood.

■ **2** breed, grow, raise, nurse.

in·cu·ba·tion /íngkyəbáyshən/ n. **1 a** incubating. **b** brooding. **2** Med. period between infection and the appearance of the first symptoms.

in·cu·ba·tor /íngkyəbaytər/ n. warming apparatus for protecting a premature baby, hatching eggs, etc.

in·cu·bus /íngkyəbəs/ n. (pl. **in·cu·bi** /-bī/ or **in·cu·bus·es**) **1** evil spirit supposed to descend on sleeping women. **2** nightmare. **3** person or thing that oppresses like a nightmare.

in·cul·cate /inkúlkayt/ v.tr. urge or impress (a fact, habit, or idea) persistently. □□ **in·cul·ca·tion** /-káyshən/ n. **in·cul·ca·tor** n.

in·cum·ben·cy /inkúmbənsee/ n. (pl. **-cies**) office, tenure, or sphere of an incumbent.

■ place, position; see also TENURE 1, 2.

in·cum·bent /inkúmbənt/ • adj. **1** [foll. by on, upon] resting as a duty (incumbent on you to warn them). **2** currently holding office. • n. holder of an office or post.

■ adj. **1** obligatory, necessary, required; (incumbent on) expected of. **2** sitting, reigning, presiding; current. • n. officeholder, occupant; official.

in·cu·nab·u·lum /ínkyənábyələm/ n. (pl. **in·cu·nab·u·la** /-lə/) **1** book printed before 1501. **2** [in pl.] early stages of a thing.

in·cur /inkór/ v.tr. (**in·curred**, **in·cur·ring**) suffer or experience (something unpleasant) as a result of one's own behavior, etc. (incurred huge debts). □□ **in·cur·ra·ble** adj.

■ undergo, face, sustain; bring upon or on (oneself), draw, attract.

in·cu·ri·ous /inkyŏoreeəs/ adj. lacking curiosity. □□ **in·cu·ri·os·i·ty** /-reeósitee/ n. **in·cu·ri·ous·ly** adv. **in·cu·ri·ous·ness** n.

in·cur·sion /inkórzhən, -shən/ n. invasion or attack, esp. when sudden or brief. □□ **in·cur·sive** /-kórsiv/ adj.

■ see ATTACK n. 1.

Ind. abbr. **1** Independent. **2** Indiana. **3 a** India. **b** Indian.

in·debt·ed /indétid/ adj. owing gratitude or money. □□ **in·debt'ed·ness** n.

■ obliged, beholden, bound, in a person's debt; liable, responsible; grateful, thankful; in debt, encumbered; insolvent, bankrupt. □□ **indebtedness** see DEBT.

in·de·cent /indéesənt/ adj. **1** offending decency. **2** unbecoming (indecent haste). □□ **in·de'cen·cy** n. (pl. **-cies**). **in·de'cent·ly** adv.

■ **1** shameless, shameful, offensive, outrageous, repellent. **2** unseemly, indecorous, indelicate, immodest; in bad taste. □□ **inde-**

cency shamelessness, shamefulness, offensiveness, outrageousness; see also IMPROPRIETY 1.

in·de·ci·pher·a·ble /indisífərəbəl/ adj. that cannot be deciphered.

in·de·ci·sion /indisízhən/ n. lack of decision; hesitation.

■ indecisiveness, irresolution, irresoluteness, uncertainty, incertitude, doubt, ambivalence, tentativeness.

in·de·ci·sive /indísísiv/ adj. **1** not decisive; hesitating. **2** not conclusive. □□ **in·de·ci'sive·ly** adv. **in·de·ci'sive·ness** n.

■ **1** indefinite, indeterminate, undecided, undetermined, unresolved. **2** undecided, irresolute, uncertain, ambivalent, doubtful.

in·deed /indéed/ • adv. **1** in truth; really; yes; that is so (they are, indeed, a remarkable family). **2** expressing emphasis or intensification (I shall be very glad indeed). **3** admittedly (there are indeed exceptions). **4** in point of fact (if indeed such a thing is possible). • int. expressing irony, contempt, incredulity, etc.

■ adv. **1** truly, truthfully, in reality, in fact; (that's) right, that's true. **2** certainly, surely, to be sure, assuredly. **3** undeniably, granted; of course, no doubt. **4** as a matter of fact, in reality, to be realistic. int. is that so or a fact?, really.

indef. abbr. indefinite.

in·de·fat·i·ga·ble /indifátigəbəl/ adj. unwearying; unremitting. □□ **in·de·fat'i·ga·bil·i·ty** n. **in·de·fat'i·ga·bly** adv.

in·de·fen·si·ble /indifénsibəl/ adj. that cannot be defended or justified. □□ **in·de·fen·si·bil'i·ty** n. **in·de·fen'si·bly** adv.

■ see INEXCUSABLE.

in·def·i·nite /indéfinit/ adj. **1** vague; undefined. **2** unlimited. **3** Gram. not determining the person, etc., referred to. □ **indefinite article** see ARTICLE 4. □□ **in·def'i·nite·ly** adv. **in·def'i·nite·ness** n.

■ **1** uncertain, unsure, ambiguous; unspecified, general; see also INDECISIVE 1. **2** unrestricted, unbounded, indeterminate; unknown, uncounted; uncountable, endless, infinite.

in·del·i·ble /indélibəl/ adj. **1** that cannot be erased or (in abstract senses) removed. **2** (of ink, etc.) that makes indelible marks. □□ **in·del·i·bil'i·ty** n. **in·del'i·bly** adv.

■ **1** ineradicable, ineffaceable; permanent, enduring; imperishable, indestructible.

in·del·i·cate /indélikət/ adj. **1** coarse; unrefined. **2** tactless. **3** tending to indecency. □□ **in·del'i·ca·cy** n. (pl. **-cies**). **in·del'i·cate·ly** adv.

■ **1** rough, crude, vulgar; rude, boorish, loutish, ill-bred. **2** undiplomatic, insensitive, unfeeling; crude, gruff, bluff, blunt, brusque. **3** see INDECENT 2.

in·dem·ni·fy /indémnifī/ v.tr. (**-fies**, **-fied**) **1** protect or secure from harm, a loss, etc. **2** secure against legal responsibility for actions. **3** compensate for a loss. □□ **in·dem·ni·fi·ca'tion** n. **in·dem'ni·fi·er** n.

■ **3** see COMPENSATE 1. □□ **indemnification** see INSURANCE 1, RESTITUTION 2.

in·dem·ni·ty /indémnitee/ n. (pl. **-ties**) **1 a** compensation for loss incurred. **b** sum paid for this, esp. exacted by a victor in war, etc. **2** security against loss. **3** legal exemption from penalties.

■ **1** consideration, restitution, reparation(s); atonement; indemnification, guarantee fund; recompense, repayment, reimbursement. **2** protection, safety, insurance. **3** see *exemption* (EXEMPT).

in•dent /indént/ • *v.tr.* **1** start (a line of print or writing) further from the margin than other lines, e.g., to mark a new paragraph. **2** make or impress marks, notches, etc., in. • *n.* also /índent/ **1** indented line. **2** indentation. □□ **in•dent′er** *n.*

■ *n.* **1** see INDENTATION 2.

in•den•ta•tion /índentáyshən/ *n.* **1** indenting or being indented. **2** notch. **3** a zigzag **4** deep recess in a coastline, etc.

■ **2** nick, snick, groove, joggle, gouge, cut, score; serration, dentil. **3** scalloping, herringbone, stagger.

in•den•tion /indénshən/ *n.* **1** the indenting of a line in printing or writing. **2** = INDENTATION.

in•den•ture /indénchər/ • *n.* **1** [usu. in *pl.*] sealed agreement or contract. **2** formal list, certificate, etc. • *v.tr. hist* bind by indentures, esp. as an apprentice. □□ **in•den′ture•ship** *n.*

in•de•pend•ence /índipéndəns/ *n.* state of being independent. See synonym study at LIBERTY. □ **Independence Day** day celebrating the anniversary of national independence; in the US July 4.

■ freedom, liberty, autonomy, self-determination.

in•de•pen•dent /índipéndənt/ • *adj.* **1 a** not subject to authority or control. **b** self-governing. **2 a** not depending on another person for one's opinion or livelihood. **b** (of income or resources) making it unnecessary to earn one's living. **3** unwilling to be under an obligation to others. **4** *Polit* (usu **Independent**) not belonging to or supported by a party. • *n.* (usu. **Independent**) person who is politically independent. □□ **in•de•pen′dent•ly** *adv.*

■ *adj.* **1 a** unregulated, uncontrolled; unrestrained, unrestricted. **b** self-determined; freelance. **2a, 3** self-reliant, self-contained, self-sufficient; self-willed. **4** nonparty, unaffiliated, nonpartisan, nonaligned. • *n.* individual, nonconformist, maverick, loner. □□ **independently** freely, unrestrictedly, voluntarily; substantively, absolutely; self-reliantly, self-sufficiently.

in•des•crib•a•ble /índiskríbəbəl/ *adj.* **1** too unusual or extreme to be described. **2** vague; indefinite. □□ **in•des•crib′a•bly** *adv.*

■ **1** see INEXPRESSIBLE. **2** see NONDESCRIPT *adj.*

in•de•struc•ti•ble /índistrúktibəl/ *adj.* unable to be destroyed. □□ **in•de•struc•ti•bil′i•ty** *n.* **in•de•struc′ti•bly** *adv.*

■ everlasting, eternal, endless, undying, immortal; unbreakable, shatterproof; see also DURABLE.

in•de•ter•min•a•ble /índitərmínəbəl/ *adj.* that cannot be ascertained or settled. □□ **in•de•ter′min•a•bly** *adv.*

■ see INDEFINITE 1.

in•de•ter•mi•nate /índitərminət/ *adj.* **1** not fixed in extent, character, etc. **2** left doubtful; vague. □□ **in•de•ter′mi•nate•ly** *adv.*

■ **1** see INDEFINITE. **2** see VAGUE 1.

in•dex /índeks/ • *n.* (*pl.* **in•dex•es** or esp. in technical use **in•di•ces** /índiseez/) **1** alphabetical list of names, subjects, etc., with references, usu. at the end of a book. **2** (in full **card′ in′dex**) index with each item entered on a separate card. **3** (in full **in′dex num′ber**) number showing the variation of prices or wages as compared with a chosen base period (*Dow-Jones index*). **4 a** pointer, esp. on an instrument. **b** indicator. **c** sign. • *v.tr.* **1** provide with an index. **2** enter in an index. **3** relate (wages, etc.) to a price index. □ **index finger** the forefinger. □□ **in•dex•a′tion** *n.* **in′dex•er** *n.*

■ *n.* **1** table of contents, directory, catalog, register, inventory, itemization. **3** ratio, quotient, factor, measure. **4** needle, gnomon, guide, marker, *Computing* cursor; mark.

in•di•a ink /índeeə/ *n.* (also **In′dia ink**) black liquid ink.

In•di•an /índeeən/ • *n.* **1 a** native or national of India. **b** person of Indian descent. **2** (in full **A•mer′i•can In′di•an**, also called **Na′tive A•mer′i•can**) member of the aboriginal peoples of America or their descendants. **3** any of the languages of the aboriginal peoples of America. • *adj.* **1** of or relating to India, or to the subcontinent comprising India, Pakistan, and Bangladesh. **2** of or relating to the aboriginal peoples of America. □ **Indian file** = *single file*. **Indian Ocean** ocean between Africa and Australia. **Indian summer** dry, warm weather in late autumn after a frost.

in•di•cate /índikayt/ *v.tr.* **1** point out; make known; show. **2** express the presence of. **3** suggest; call for; require. **4** state briefly. **5** (of a gauge, etc.) give as a reading. □□ **in•di•ca•tion** /índikáyshən/ *n.* See synonym study at SIGN.

■ **1, 4** designate, point to or at, mark, specify; manifest, demonstrate, make clear. **2** signify, betoken, denote, manifest, imply, suggest. **3** demand, need, recommend; hint (at). **5** read, register, show, display, record. □□ **indication** identification, exhibition, signal; *Computing* prompt; omen, portent, warning.

in•dic•a•tive /indíkətiv/ • *adj.* **1** serving as an indication. **2** *Gram.* (of a mood) stating a fact. • *n. Gram.* indicative mood. □□ **in•dic′a•tive•ly** *adv.*

■ *adj.* **1** suggestive, symptomatic; characteristic, typical.

in•di•ca•tor /índikaytər/ *n.* **1** person or thing that indicates. **2** device indicating the condition of a machine, etc. **3** recording instrument attached to an apparatus, etc. **4** flashing light on a vehicle to show that it is about to change direction; turn signal.

■ **1** pointer, designator, marker; signaler; displayer; needle, *Computing* cursor. **2, 3** gauge, recorder; flight recorder, black box; dial, display, panel.

in•di•ces pl. of INDEX.

in•dict /indít/ v.tr. accuse (a person) formally by legal process. □□ in•dict′a•ble adj. in•dict′er n. in•dict′ment n.

■ charge, arraign, impeach, incriminate; denounce, blame. □□ indictee (the) accused, defendant; correspondent. indicter see accuser (ACCUSE). indictment see ACCUSATION.

in•dif•fer•ent /indífrənt/ adj. 1 having no partiality for or against; having no interest in or sympathy for. 2 neither good nor bad; average. 3 inferior. □□ in•dif′fer•ence n. in•dif′fer•ent•ly adv.

■ 1 impartial, neutral, evenhanded, objective, fair; unconcerned, apathetic, uninterested; unsympathetic, insensitive. 2 mediocre, fair (to middling), ordinary; undistinguished, colorless; tolerable, passable, acceptable. 3 second-rate, so-so, mediocre. □□ indifferenceunconcern, apathy; nonchalance, disregard; dispassion, disinterest; see also absentmindedness (ABSENTMINDED).

in•dig•e•nous /indíjinəs/ adj. 1 (esp. of flora or fauna) originating naturally in a region. 2 (of people) born in a region. See synonym study at NATIVE. □□ in•dig′e•nous•ly adv.

■ native, local, endemic; aboriginal, autochthonous.

in•di•gent /indíjənt/ adj. needy; poor. □□ in′di•gence n.

■ see POOR 1. □□ indigence see POVERTY 1.

in•di•gest•i•ble /indijéstibəl/ adj. difficult or impossible to digest. □□ in•di•gest′i•bly adv.

in•di•ges•tion /indijés-chən/ n. 1 difficulty in digesting food. 2 pain or discomfort caused by this. □□ in•di•ges′tive adj.

■ dyspepsia, acidity, heartburn; upset stomach; wind, flatulence.

in•dig•nant /indígnənt/ adj. feeling or showing indignation. □□ in•dig′nant•ly adv.

■ disgruntled, vexed, displeased, resentful; piqued, irritated, irked; see also ANGRY 1.

in•dig•na•tion /indignáyshən/ n. scornful anger at supposed unjust or unfair conduct or treatment.

■ vexation, irritation, annoyance, exasperation, displeasure, resentment; see also ANGER n.

in•dig•ni•ty /indígnitee/ n. (pl. –ties) 1 humiliating treatment. 2 a slight or insult. 3 humiliating quality of something (indignity of my position).

■ 1, 2 injustice, mistreatment; dishonor, embarrassment, disrespect; offense, injury, abuse. 3 abjectness, wretchedness.

in•di•go /índigō/ n. (pl. –os) 1 natural blue dye obtained from the indigo plant. 2 (in full in′di•go blue) color between blue and violet in the spectrum.

in•di•rect /indirékt, –dī–/ adj. 1 not going straight to the point. 2 (of a route, etc.) not straight. 3 not directly sought (indirect result). 4 (of lighting) from a concealed source and diffusely reflected. □ indirect object Gram. person or thing affected by a verbal action but not primarily acted on (e.g., him in

give him the book). □□ in•di•rect′ly adv. in•di•rect′ness n.

■ 1, 2 oblique, circuitous, devious, tortuous, twisty; circumlocutory, digressive, excursive. 3 secondary, ancillary, collateral, incidental.

in•dis•creet /indiskréet/ adj. 1 revealing secrets. 2 injudicious; unwary. □□ in•dis•creet′ly adv.

■ 1 garrulous, loquacious, talkative, gossipy, chattery. 2 imprudent, incautious, unguarded, rash, reckless; thoughtless, insensitive.

in•dis•cre•tion /indiskréshən/ n. 1 lack of discretion; indiscreet conduct. 2 indiscreet action, remark, etc. See synonym study at SIN.

■ 1 garrulousness, loquaciousness, talkativeness; see also imprudence (IMPRUDENT). 2 gaffe, faux pas, misstep, blunder, error.

in•dis•crim•i•nate /indiskrímínət/ adj. 1 making no distinctions. 2 confused; promiscuous. □□ in•dis•crim′i•nate•ly adv.

■ 1 undiscriminating, unselective, uncritical, arbitrary, random. 2 haphazard, chaotic, erratic, disorganized; casual, unmethodical.

in•dis•pens•a•ble /indispénsəbəl/ adj. necessary. See synonym study at NECESSARY. □□ in•dis•pen•sa•bil′i•ty n. in•dis•pen′sa•bly adv.

■ obligatory, compulsory, mandatory, imperative, needful, requisite, essential, vital.

in•dis•posed /indispózd/ adj. 1 slightly unwell. 2 averse or unwilling. □□ in•dis•po•si′tion n.

■ 1 see ILL adj. 1. 2 disinclined, loath, reluctant, hesitant.

in•dis•sol•u•ble /indisólyəbəl/ adj. 1 that cannot be dissolved. 2 lasting. □□ in•dis•sol•u•bil′i•ty n. in•dis•sol′u•bly adv.

■ □□ indissolubly see inextricably (INEXTRICABLE).

in•dite /indít/ v.tr. formal or joc. put into words; write.

in•di•um /índeeəm/ n. Chem. soft, silvery-white metallic element in zinc ores. ¶Symb.: In.

in•di•vid•u•al /indivíjōōəl/ • adj. 1 single. 2 particular; special; not general. 3 having a distinct character. 4 characteristic of a particular person. 5 designed for use by one person. • n. 1 single member of a class. 2 single human being. ■ individual retirement account savings account that allows tax owed on interest to be deferred.

■ adj. 1 sole, solitary, only, lone. 2, 3 singular, specific, separate, discrete; peculiar, distinctive, unique. 4 typical, distinctive, idiosyncratic. 5 single, one-man; personal, custom-built. • n. person, (living) soul, mortal, man, woman, child.

in•di•vid•u•al•ism /indivíjōōəlizəm/ n. 1 being independent and self-reliant. 2 social theory favoring the free action of individuals. □□ in•di•vid•u•al•ist n. in•di•vid•u•al•is′tic adj. in•di•vid•u•al•is′ti•cal•ly adv.

■ □□ individualist independent, freethinker, nonconformist, maverick.

in•di•vid•u•al•i•ty /indivijōō-álitee/ n. (pl. –ties) 1 individual character, esp. when strongly marked. **2** [in *pl.*] individual tastes, etc. **3** separate existence.

■ **1** see *eccentricity* (ECCENTRIC). **2** (*individualities*) see DIVERSITY.

in•di•vid•u•al•ize /indivíjŏŏəlīz/ *v.tr.* **1** give an individual character to. **2** specify. □□ **in•di•vid•u•al•i•za′tion** *n.*

■ **1** see DISTINGUISH 2. **2** see SPECIFY.

in•di•vid•u•al•ly /indivíjŏŏəlee/ *adv.* **1** in an individual capacity. **2** distinctively. **3** one by one; not collectively.

■ **1** see PERSONALLY 2, ALONE 1. **3** one at a time, singly.

Indo- /índŏ/ *comb. form* Indian; Indian and (*Indo-Iranian*).

in•doc•tri•nate /indóktrinayt/ *v.tr.* teach to accept (esp. partisan or tendentious) ideas uncritically. □□ **in•doc•tri•na•tion** /-náyshən/ *n.* **in•doc′tri•na•tor** *n.*

■ train, instruct, discipline; brainwash, propagandize.

In•do-Eu•ro•pe•an /índŏ-yŏŏrəpéeən/ • *adj.* **1** of or relating to the family of languages spoken over the greater part of Europe and Asia as far as N. India. **2** of or relating to the hypothetical parent language of this family. • *n.* **1** Indo-European family of languages. **2** hypothetical parent language of all languages belonging to this family. **3** [usu. in *pl.*] speaker of an Indo-European language.

in•do•lent /índələnt/ *adj.* lazy. □□ **in′do•lence** *n.* **in′do•lent•ly** *adv.*

■ slothful, sluggish, idle, lethargic, shiftless. □□ **indolence** laziness, slothfulness, listlessness, torpor.

in•dom•i•ta•ble /indómitəbəl/ *adj.* **1** that cannot be subdued; unyielding. **2** stubbornly persistent. □□ **in•dom•i•ta•bil′i•ty** *n.* **in•dom′i•ta•bly** *adv.*

■ **1** unconquerable, unbeatable, irrepressible. **2** resolute, resolved, determined, undaunted.

In•do•ne•sian /índənéezhən, -shən/ • *n.* **1 a** native or national of Indonesia in SE Asia. **b** person of Indonesian descent. **2** member of the chief pre-Malay population of the E. Indies. **3** language of the group spoken in the E. Indies, esp. the official language of the Indonesian Republic. • *adj.* of or relating to Indonesia or its people or language.

in•door /índawr/ *adj.* situated, carried on, or used within a building or under cover (*indoor antenna, indoor games*).

in•doors /indáwrz/ *adv.* into or within a building.

in•dorse var. of ENDORSE.

in•du•bi•ta•ble /indŏŏbitəbəl, -dyŏŏ-/ *adj.* that cannot be doubted. □□ **in•du′bi•ta•bly** *adv.*

■ see CERTAIN *adj.* 1b. □□ **indubitably** see *undoubtedly* (UNDOUBTED).

in•duce /indŏŏs, -dyŏŏs/ *v.tr.* **1** prevail on; persuade. **2** bring about. **3** *Med.* bring on (labor) artificially. **4** *Electr.* produce (a current) by induction. **5** infer; deduce. □□ **in•duc′er** *n.* **in•duc′i•ble** *adj.*

■ **1** lead, influence, sway, convince. **2** cause, produce, give rise to, engender; effect, occasion.

in•duce•ment /indŏŏsmənt, -dyŏŏs-/ *n.*

1 attraction that leads one on. **2** thing that induces.

■ **1** lure, incentive, stimulus, enticement, bait. **2** lure, bait, carrot, spur; see also INCENTIVE *n.*

in•duct /indúkt/ *v.tr.* **1** install into a room, office, etc. **2** enlist (a person) for military service. □□ **in•duc•tee** /induktée/ *n.*

■ **1** move in, establish. **2** call up, conscript, enroll, recruit, register, draft.

in•duc•tance /indúktəns/ *n. Electr.* property of an electric circuit that causes an electromotive force to be generated by a change in the current flowing.

in•duc•tion /indúkshən/ *n.* **1** act or an instance of inducting or inducing. **2** *Med.* the process of bringing on (esp. labor) by artificial means. **3** *Logic* inference of a general law from particular instances (cf. DEDUCTION). **4** *Electr.* **a** production of an electric or magnetic state by the proximity (without contact) of an electrified or magnetized body. **b** production of an electric current in a conductor by a change of magnetic field. **5** enlistment for military service.

in•due var. of ENDUE.

in•dulge /indúlj/ *v.* **1** *intr.* [often foll. by *in*] take pleasure freely. **2** *tr.* yield freely to (a desire, etc.). **3** *tr.* gratify the wishes of. **4** *intr. colloq.* take alcoholic liquor. □□ **in•dulg′er** *n.*

■ **1** wallow, luxuriate, be (self-)indulgent; *feast, banquet*; (*indulge in*) yield to, succumb to. **2** give in to, allow, gratify. **3** humor, oblige, cater to; favor, pamper. **4** see DRINK *v.* 2.

in•dul•gence /indúljəns/ *n.* **1 a** indulging. **b** state of being indulgent. **2** thing indulged in. **3** *RC Ch.* remission of punishment for sins after absolution. **4** privilege granted.

■ **1 a** self-indulgence, self-gratification; allowance, acceptance. **b** luxury, extravagance, profligacy; tolerance, sufferance, understanding.

in•dul•gent /indúljənt/ *adj.* **1** ready to overlook faults, etc. **2** indulging or tending to indulge. □□ **in•dul′gent•ly** *adv.*

■ tolerant, permissive, patient, understanding, lenient.

in•dus•tri•al /indústreeəl/ • *adj.* **1** of or relating to industry. **2** designed or suitable for industrial use (*industrial alcohol*). **3** having developed industries (*the industrial nations*). • *n.* [in *pl.*] shares in industrial companies. □ **industrial park** area of land developed for a complex of factories and other businesses, usu. separate from an urban center. □□ **in•dus′tri•al•ly** *adv.*

■ *adj.* **1** see TECHNICAL 1.

in•dus•tri•al•ism /indústreeəlizəm/ *n.* social or economic system in which manufacturing industries are prevalent.

in•dus•tri•al•ist /indústreeəlist/ *n.* person engaged in the management of industry.

■ see *manufacturer* (MANUFACTURE).

in•dus•tri•al•ize /indústreeəlīz/ *v.* **1** *tr.* introduce industries to (a country or region, etc.). **2** *intr.* become industrialized. □□ **in•dus•tri•a•li•za′tion** *n.*

in•dus•tri•ous /indústreeəs/ adj. diligent;hardworking. See synonym study at BUSY. □□ **in•dus'tri•ous•ly** adv. **in•dus'tri•ous•ness** n.

■ sedulous, assiduous; conscientious, painstaking; persistent, dogged; busy, energetic. □□ **industriousness** see INDUSTRY 2, 3.

in•dus•try /índəstree/ n. (pl. **–tries**) 1 a a branch of trade or manufacture. b these collectively. 2 concerted or copious activity (the building was a hive of industry). 3 diligence. 4 habitual employment in useful work.

■ 1 business, enterprise, commerce; production, fabrication. 2 busyness, industriousness; work, labor. 3 industriousness, assiduity; conscientiousness; persistence.

-ine[1] /in, in/ suffix forming adjectives, meaning 'belonging to, of the nature of' (Alpine, asinine).

-ine[2] /in, een/ suffix forming feminine nouns (heroine).

in•e•bri•ate • v.tr. /inéebreeayt/ 1 make drunk. 2 excite. • adj. /inéebreeət/ tending to drink; drunken. • n. /inéebreeət/ drunkard. □□ **in•e•bri•a•tion** /–áyshən/ n. **in•e•bri•e•ty** /ínibríətee/ n.

■ v. 1 see INTOXICATE 1. 2 see INTOXICATE 2.

in•ef•fa•ble /inéfəbəl/ adj. 1 unutterable; too great for description in words. 2 that must not be uttered. □□ **in•ef•fa•bil'i•ty** n. **in•ef'fa•bly** adv.

■ 1 inexpressible, indefinable, indescribable. 2 unmentionable, taboo.

in•ef•fec•tu•al /inifékchooəl/ adj. 1 a without effect. b not producing the desired effect. 2 (of a person) lacking the ability to achieve results. □□ **in•ef•fec•tu•al•i•ty** /–álitee/ n. **in•ef•fec'tu•al•ly** adv. **in•ef•fec'tu•al•ness** n.

■ 2 incapable, incompetent; weak, feeble.

in•ef•fi•cient /inifíshənt/ adj. 1 not efficient. 2 (of a person) not fully capable. □□ **in•ef•fi'cien•cy** n. **in•ef•fi'cient•ly** adv.

■ 1 uneconomical, wasteful; unproductive, ineffective; unprofessional, disorganized. 2 ineffective, ineffectual, unqualified, inept. □□ **inefficiency** wastefulness, extravagance; amateurishness, disorganization. **inefficiently** uneconomically, wastefully; unproductively, unprofitably; unprofessionally, sloppily.

in•el•e•gant /inéligənt/ adj. 1 ungraceful. 2 a unrefined. b unpolished. □□ **in•el'e•gance** n. **in•el'e•gant•ly** adv.

in•e•luc•ta•ble /inilúktəbəl/ adj. 1 unavoidable. 2 inescapable. □□ **in•e•luc'ta•bly** adv.

■ 2 see INEVITABLE 1. □□ **ineluctably** see necessarily (NECESSARY).

in•ept /inépt/ adj. 1 unskillful. 2 absurd; silly. 3 out of place. □□ **in•ept'i•tude** n. **in•ept'ly** adv. **in•ept'ness** n.

■ 1 unskilled, inapt, inexpert, amateurish. 2 ridiculous, preposterous, nonsensical, outlandish. 3 out of keeping, inappropriate, inapt. □□ **ineptitude, ineptness** unskillfulness, inaptitude, inefficiency, incompetence.

in•e•qual•i•ty /ínikwólitee/ n. (pl. **–ties**) 1 a lack of equality. b instance of this. 2 state of being variable. 3 (of a surface) irregularity.

■ 1 disparity, difference; inequity, unfairness, bias. 2 see dissimilarity (DISSIMILAR). 3 unevenness, bumpiness, lumpiness, coarseness.

in•ert /inə́rt/ adj. 1 without inherent power of action, motion, or resistance. 2 without active chemical or other properties. 3 sluggish; slow. □□ **in•ert'ly** adv. **in•ert'ness** n.

■ 1 motionless, immobile, static, stationary, still. 2 inactive, unreactive, unresponsive, neutral. 3 torpid, dull, inactive, leaden, listless. □□ **inertness** see INERTIA.

in•er•tia /inə́rshə/ n. 1 Physics property of matter by which it continues in its existing state of rest or motion unless an external force is applied. 2 inertness; sloth. □□ **in•er'tial** adj.

■ 2 immobility, motionlessness, stasis; neutrality; apathy, sluggishness, slowness, torpor.

in•es•cap•a•ble /iniskáypəbəl/ adj. that cannot be escaped or avoided. □□ **in•es•cap•a•bil'i•ty** n. **in•es•cap'a•bly** adv.

■ □□ **inescapably** see necessarily (NECESSARY).

-iness /eenis/ suffix forming nouns corresponding to adjectives in -y (drowsiness; manliness; see -Y[1], -LY[2]).

in•es•ti•ma•ble /inéstiməbəl/ adj. too great, intense, precious, etc., to be estimated. □□ **in•es'ti•ma•bly** adv.

■ priceless, invaluable, above or beyond or without price; incalculable, innumerable; immeasurable, unfathomable, limitless.

in•ev•i•ta•ble /inévitəbəl/ adj. 1 a unavoidable. b bound to occur. 2 colloq. tiresomely familiar. See synonym study at NECESSARY. □□ **in•ev•i•ta•bil'i•ty** n. **in•ev'i•ta•ble•ness** n. **in•ev'i•ta•bly** adv.

■ 1 inescapable, ineluctable, inexorable, destined; assured, guaranteed. 2 usual, commonplace, everyday, routine.

in•ex•cus•a•ble /ínikskyóozəbəl/ adj. (of a person, action, etc.) that cannot be excused or justified. □□ **in•ex•cus'a•bly** adv.

■ unpardonable, unforgivable; unjustifiable, unjustified, indefensible, unwarrantable.

in•ex•haust•i•ble /inigzáwstibəl/ adj. 1 that cannot be exhausted or used up. 2 that cannot be worn out. □□ **in•ex•haust'i•bly** adv.

■ 1 limitless, boundless, unlimited; renewable. 2 tireless, indefatigable, unflagging, unfailing.

in•ex•o•ra•ble /inéksərəbəl/ adj. 1 relentless. 2 (of a person or attribute) that cannot be persuaded by request or entreaty. □□ **in•ex•o•ra•bil'i•ty** n. **in•ex'o•ra•bly** adv.

■ 1 see RELENTLESS 1. 2 see OBSTINATE. □□ **inexorably** see necessarily (NECESSARY).

in•ex•pe•ri•ence /ínikspeéreeəns/ n. lack of experience, or of the resulting knowledge or skill. □□ **in•ex•pe'ri•enced** adj.

■ immaturity, innocence, callowness, naïveté, greenness. □□ **inexperienced** untrained, unschooled, uninformed; immature, callow, unsophisticated, unworldly, innocent, naive.

in•ex•pert /inékspərt/ adj. unskillful; lacking expertise. □□ in•ex′pert•ly adv.

in•ex•pi•a•ble /inékspeeəbəl/ adj. (of an act or feeling) that cannot be expiated or appeased. □□ in•ex′pi•a•bly adv.

in•ex•pli•ca•ble /iniksplikəbəl, inéks–/ adj. that cannot be explained. □□ in•ex′pli•ca•bly adv.

■ unexplainable, unaccountable, unintelligible, incomprehensible; enigmatic, cryptic, puzzling.

in•ex•press•i•ble /iniksprésibəl/ adj. that cannot be expressed in words. □□ in•ex•press′i•bly adv.

■ unutterable, ineffable, indefinable, indescribable.

in•ex•tin•guish•a•ble /inikstínggwishəbəl/ adj. 1 not quenchable; indestructible. 2 (of laughter, etc.) irrepressible.

■ 1 unquenchable; imperishable, inexpungible, ineffaceable, ineradicable, permanent. 2 see IRREPRESSIBLE.

in ex•tre•mis /in ekstréemis, tré–/ adj. 1 at the point of death. 2 in great difficulties.

in•ex•tri•ca•ble /inékstrikəbəl, iniktrík–/ adj. 1 inescapable. 2 (of a knot, problem, etc.) that cannot be unraveled or solved. 3 intricately confused. □□ in•ex′tri•ca•bly adv.

■ 1 many, labyrinthine; tricky, thorny, difficult; impossible. 2, 3 intricate, complex, complicated; insoluble, unresolvable, insurmountable. □□ inextricably inescapably, ineluctably, unavoidably; intricately; totally, completely.

Inf. abbr. 1 infantry. 2 inferior. 3 infinitive.

in•fal•li•ble /infálibəl/ adj. 1 incapable of error. 2 unfailing, sure to succeed. □□ in•fal•li•bil′i•ty n. in•fal′li•bly adv.

■ impeccable, perfect, incontestable; unerring, faultless, flawless; dependable, reliable.

in•fa•mous /infəməs/ adj. notoriously bad. □□ in′fa•mous•ly adv. in′fa•my n. (pl. –mies)

■ disreputable, discreditable, dishonorable; awful, wicked, evil, iniquitous, villainous. □□ infamy notoriety, ill repute, disrepute, shame, ignominy; wickedness, evil.

in•fan•cy /infənsee/ n. (pl. –cies) 1 early childhood; babyhood. 2 early state in the development of an idea, undertaking, etc. 3 Law the state of being a minor.

■ 2 inception, early or initial stage(s); beginning(s), start, outset, formal commencement; birth, nascency, emergence, dawn, cradle. 3 minority.

in•fant /infənt/ n. 1 child during the earliest period of its life. 2 [esp. attrib.] thing in an early stage of its development.

■ 1 see CHILD 1b.

in•fan•ti•cide /infántisíd/ n. 1 killing of an infant. 2 such a practice. 3 person who kills an infant. □□ in•fan•ti•cid•al /–síd′l/ adj.

in•fan•tile /infántíl/ adj. 1 a like or characteristic of a child. b childish; immature. 2 in its infancy. □ infantile paralysis poliomyelitis. □□ in•fan•til•i•ty /–tílitee/ n. (pl. –ties)

■ 1 childlike, babyish, puerile, juvenile.

2 incipient, emergent, budding; embryonic, rudimentary.

in•fan•try /infantree/ n. (pl. –tries) body of foot soldiers; foot soldiers collectively. □□ in•fan•try•man /infəntreemən/ n. (pl. –men)

in•farct /infaarkt/ n. Med. area of dead tissue caused by an inadequate blood supply. □□ in•farc•tion /–faarkshən/ n.

in•fat•u•ate /infáchoo-ayt/ v.tr. inspire with intense, usu. transitory fondness or admiration. □□ in•fat′u•at•ed adj. in•fat•u•a•tion /–áyshən/ n.

■ see CAPTIVATE. □□ infatuated fascinated, spellbound, besotted, possessed, obsessed; (infatuated with) fond of, mad about.

in•fect /infékt/ v.tr. 1 contaminate or affect with harmful organisms or noxious matter. 2 instill bad feeling or opinion into (a person). □□ in•fec′tor n.

■ 1 see CONTAMINATE, ATTACK v. 4.

in•fec•tion /infékshən/ n. 1 infecting or being infected. 2 instance of this; disease.

■ 2 see DISEASE 1, 3.

in•fec•tious /infékshəs/ adj. 1 infecting with disease. 2 transmissible by infection. 3 (of emotions, etc.) quickly affecting others. □□ in•fec′tious•ly adv.

■ 1 infective, malignant, virulent; poisonous, toxic. 2, 3 contagious, catching, taking, communicable.

in•fe•lic•i•ty /infilísitee/ n. (pl. –ties) 1 inapt expression, etc. 2 instance of this.

in•fer /infər/ v.tr. (in•ferred, in•fer•ring) 1 deduce or conclude. 2 disp. imply. □□ in•ter′a•ble adj.

■ 1 derive, draw the (or a) conclusion, take it; surmise, understand, gather. 2 see IMPLY 1.

in•fer•ence /infərəns/ n. 1 act of inferring. 2 thing inferred. □□ in•fer•en•tial /–rénshəl/ adj. in•fer•en′tial•ly adv.

■ deduction, conclusion, implication, implicate, derivation; understanding, surmise.

in•fe•ri•or /infeereeər/ • adj. 1 a in a lower position. b of lower rank, quality, etc. 2 poor in quality. • n. person inferior to another. □□ in•fe•ri•or•i•ty /infeeree-áwritee, –ór–/ n.

■ adj. 1 lesser, junior, minor, smaller; second, subordinate. 2 second-rate; mean, bad, mediocre. • n. subordinate, junior; menial.

in•fer•nal /infórnəl/ adj. 1 a of hell. b hellish. 2 colloq. detestable. □□ in•fer′nal•ly adv.

■ 1 hell-like, Hadean, Stygian; fiendish, devilish, diabolic; damnable, execrable, wicked.

in•fer•no /infórnō/ n. (pl. –nos) 1 raging fire. 2 scene of horror or distress. 3 hell.

■ 1 blaze, conflagration, holocaust. 3 see HELL 1.

in•fest /infést/ v.tr. (esp. vermin) overrun (a place). □□ in•fes•ta′tion n.

■ invade, plague, take over; swarm over, pervade.

in•fi•del /infid′l, –del/ • n. unbeliever in a particular religion. • adj. 1 that is an infidel. 2 of unbelievers.

■ *n.* heathen, heretic, pagan, agnostic, atheist. ● *adj.* unbelieving, heathen, heretic; gentile.

in·fi·del·i·ty /ínfidélitee/ *n.* (*pl.* –ties) 1 unfaithfulness, esp. adultery. 2 instance of this.

■ 1 faithlessness, disloyalty, deceit; duplicity, treachery, falseness. 2 cuckoldry, (love) affair.

in·field /ínfeeld/ *n.* 1 *Baseball* area enclosed by the three bases and home plate. 2 the four fielders stationed near the bases. □□ **in′field·er** *n.*

in·fight·ing /ínfīting/ *n.* 1 hidden conflict within an organization. 2 boxing within arm's length. □□ **in′fight·er** *n.*

in·fil·trate /ínfiltrayt/ *v.* 1 *tr.* a gain entrance or access surreptitiously and by degrees (as spies, etc.). b cause to do this. 2 *tr.* permeate by filtration. □□ **in·fil·tra′tion** /–tráyshən/ *n.* **in′fil·tra·tor** *n.*

■ 1 a see ENTER 2. 2 see PERMEATE. □□ **infiltration** see INVASION. **infiltrator** see INTRUDER.

in·fi·nite /ínfinit/ *adj.* 1 boundless; endless. 2 very great or many (*infinite resources*). □□ **in′fi·nite·ly** *adv.* **in′fi·nite·ness** *n.*

■ unbounded, limitless, unlimited, innumerable.

in·fin·i·tes·i·mal /ínfinitésimǝl/ *adj.* infinitely or very small. □□ **in·fin·i·tes′i·mal·ly** *adv.*

■ see MINUTE[2] 1.

in·fin·i·tive /infínitiv/ *Gram. n.* form of a verb without a particular subject, tense, etc. (e.g., *see* in *we came to see, let him see*). ● *adj.* having this form. □□ **in·fin·i·tiv·al** /–tívǝl/ *adj.*

in·fin·i·tude /infínitŏŏd, –tyŏŏd/ *n.* 1 = INFINITY 1. 2 = INFINITY 2.

in·fin·i·ty /infínitee/ *n.* (*pl.* –ties) 1 being infinite. 2 infinite number or extent. 3 infinite distance. 4 *Math.* infinite quantity. ¶Symb.: ∞.

■ 1 see ETERNITY 1, 3. 2 see LOT *n.* 1. 3 see ETERNITY 1, 3.

in·firm /infárm/ *adj.* 1 physically weak, esp. through age. 2 (of a person, mind, judgment, etc.) weak; irresolute. See synonym study at WEAK. □□ **in·firm′i·ty** *n.* (*pl.* –ties). **in·firm′ly** *adv.*

■ 1 frail, decrepit, feeble; shaky, wobbly; see also ILL *adj.* 1. 2 hesitant, undecided, uncertain. □□ **infirmity** weakness, feebleness, frailty; instability, unstableness; irresoluteness, hesitancy; illness, affliction.

in·fir·ma·ry /infármǝree/ *n.* (*pl.* –ries) 1 hospital. 2 place for those who are ill, as at school, etc.

■ 1 health center, polyclinic, clinic. 2 sick bay, first-aid post *or* station; dispensary.

in fla·gran·te de·lic·to /in flǝgrántee dilíktō/ *adv.* in the very act of committing an offense.

in·flame /infláym/ *v.* 1 *tr. & intr.* provoke or become provoked to strong feeling, esp. anger. 2 *Med.* a become hot, reddened, and sore. b *tr.* (esp. as **inflamed**) cause inflammation or fever in (a body, etc.); make hot. 3 *tr.* aggravate.

■ 1 incense, enrage, infuriate; arouse, incite, ignite. 2 a burn, redden, chafe. b irritate,

make sore, nettle; (**inflamed**) irritated, sore, hot, fevered, infected, septic. 3 exacerbate, intensify, deepen, heighten.

in·flam·ma·ble /inflámǝbǝl/ ● *adj.* 1 easily set on fire. 2 easily excited. ● *n.* [usu. in *pl.*] flammable substance. □□ **in·flam·ma·bil′i·ty** *n.* **in·flam′ma·bly** *adv.*

■ *adj.* combustible, flammable, ignitable, explosive, fiery. 2 combustible, explosive, irascible, choleric.

in·flam·ma·tion /ínflǝmáyshǝn/ *n.* 1 act or instance of inflaming. 2 *Med.* localized physical condition with heat, swelling, redness, and usu. pain.

■ 1 provocation, enragement; arousal, excitement. 2 irritation, redness, soreness, tenderness.

in·flam·ma·to·ry /inflámǝtáwree/ *adj.* 1 tending to cause anger, etc. 2 of inflammation.

■ 1 excitatory, provocative. 2 irritating, caustic.

in·flat·a·ble /infláytǝbǝl/ ● *adj.* that can be inflated. ● *n.* inflatable object.

in·flate /infláyt/ *v.tr.* 1 distend with air or gas. 2 puff up (with pride, etc.). 3 a bring about inflation (of currency). b raise (prices) artificially. 4 (as **inflated** *adj.*) (esp. of language, sentiments, etc.) bombastic. □□ **in·flat′ed·ly** *adv.* **in·flat′ed·ness** *n.* **in·flat′er** *n.* **in·fla′tor** *n.*

■ 1 blow up, pump up, swell. 2 swell; balloon, expand. 4 (**inflated**) grandiloquent, high-flown; exaggerated.

in·fla·tion /infláyshǝn/ *n.* 1 a act or condition of inflating. b instance of this. 2 *Econ.* a general increase in prices and fall in the purchasing value of money. b increase in available currency regarded as causing this. □□ **in·fla′tion·ar·y** *adj.*

■ 1 see *exaggeration* (EXAGGERATE), EXPANSION. 2 a see INCREASE *n.* 1, 2.

in·flect /inflékt/ *v.* 1 *tr.* change the pitch of (the voice, etc.). 2 *Gram.* a *tr.* change the form of (a word) to express tense, gender, number, mood, etc. b *intr.* undergo such change. □□ **in·flec′tive** *adj.*

in·flec·tion /inflékshǝn/ *n.* 1 a act or condition of inflecting. b instance of this. 2 *Gram.* a process or practice of inflecting words. b inflected form of a word. □□ **in·flec′tion·al** *adj.*

in·flex·i·ble /infléksibǝl/ *adj.* 1 unbendable. 2 immovable; obstinate. 3 inexorable. □□ **in·flex·i·bil′i·ty** *n.* **in·flex′i·bly** *adv.*

■ 1 unbending, stiff, rigid, inelastic, hard. 2 stiff, unbending, rigid; obdurate. 3 unchangeable, intractable, immutable, unadaptable.

in·flict /inflíkt/ *v.tr.* 1 deal (a stroke, wound, etc.). 2 [also *refl.*] often *joc.* impose (suffering, oneself, etc.) on.

■ 1 administer, serve, impose, apply, visit, levy.

in·flo·res·cence /ínflǝrésǝns/ *n.* 1 *Bot.* a complete flower head of a plant. b arrangement of this. 2 flowering.

in·flu·ence /ínflŏŏǝns/ ● *n.* 1 effect a person or thing has on another. 2 moral ascendancy or power. 3 thing or person exercising such power. • *v.tr.* exert influence on. □ **under the influence** *colloq.* affected by alcoholic drink. □□ **in•flu•enc•er** *n.*

■ *n.* impact, impression; force; hold, sway, control. ■ *v.* affect, act *or* play *or* work on; sway, change; move, drive, impel; persuade, motivate.

in•flu•en•tial /inflŏo-énshəl/ *adj.* having great influence or power. □□ **in•flu•en'tial•ly** *adv.*

■ powerful, weighty, strong; authoritative, important; dominant; effective.

in•flu•en•za /inflŏo énzə/ *n.* highly contagious virus infection often occurring in epidemics.

In•flux /ínfluks/ *n.* continual stream of people or things.

in•fo /ínfō/ *n. colloq.* information.

in•fo•mer•cial /ínfōmórshəl/ *n.* television program promoting a commercial product.

in•form /infáwrm/ *v.* 1 *tr.* tell. 2 *intr.* [usu. foll. by *against, on*] make an accusation □□ **in•form'ant** *n.* **in•form'er** *n.*

■ 1 notify, apprise, enlighten, advise, brief. 2 turn informer; (*inform against* or *on*) accuse, incriminate. ■ **informant, informer** stool pigeon, tattletale; source, reporter, correspondent.

in•for•mal /infáwrməl/ *adj.* 1 without formality. 2 (of language, clothing, etc.) not formal; everyday; normal. □□ **in•for•mal•i•ty** /-málitee/ *n.* (*pl.* **-ties**). **in•for'mal•ly** *adv.*

■ unceremonious, unstructured, casual; ordinary, simple. □□ **informality** see EASE *n.* 2.

in•for•ma•tics /ínfərmátiks/ *n.pl.* [usu. treated as *sing.*] the science of processing data for storage and retrieval; information science.

in•for•ma•tion /ínfərmáyshən/ *n.* 1 a something told; knowledge. b news. 2 *Computing* data stored or generated by a program. See synonym study at KNOWLEDGE. □ **information (super)highway** worldwide computer network offering information, shopping, and other services. □□ **in•for•ma'tion•al** *adj.*

■ 1 data, report(s), communication, advice, intelligence.

in•for•ma•tive /infáwrmətiv/ *adj.* (also **in•for•ma•to•ry** /infáwrmətáwree/) giving information; instructive. □□ **in•for'ma•tive•ly** *adv.*

■ communicative, educational, edifying; explanatory.

in•formed /infáwrmd/ *adj.* knowledgeable.

■ aware, in touch; acquainted (with); educated, erudite; intelligent.

in•fo•tain•ment /ínfōtáynmənt/ *n.* 1 factual information presented in dramatized form on television. 2 television program mixing news and entertainment.

in•fra /ínfrə/ *adv.* (in a book or writing) below; further on.

infra- /ínfrə/ *comb. form* below (opp. SUPRA-).

in•frac•tion /infrákshən/ *n.* esp. *Law* violation or infringement. □□ **in•fract** /-frákt/ *v.tr.* **in•frac'tor** *n.*

in•fra dig /ínfrə díg/ *predic.adj. colloq.* beneath one's dignity.

in•fra•red /ínfrəréd/ *adj.* of or using a wavelength just greater than the red end of the visible spectrum.

in•fra•struc•ture /ínfrəstrukchər/ *n.* basic structural foundations, esp. roads, bridges, sewers, etc.

in•fre•quent /infréekwənt/ *adj.* not frequent. □□ **in•fre'quen•cy** *n.* **in•fre'quent•ly** *adv.*

■ occasional, rare, seldom; uncommon; irregular. □□ **infrequently** occasionally, rarely, seldom; irregularly, sporadically.

in•fringe /infrínj/ *v.* 1 *tr.* a violate (a law, an oath, etc.). b act in defiance of (another's rights, etc.). 2 *intr.* [usu. foll. by *on, upon*] encroach, trespass. □□ **in•fringe'ment** *n.* **in•fring'er** *n.*

■ 1 contravene, break, disobey, transgress; flout. 2 (*infringe on* or *upon*) impinge on *or* upon, intrude on *or* upon, break in on, butt in on. □□ **infringement** violation, breach, contravention, infraction; interruption.

in•fu•ri•ate /infyŏoreeayt/ *v.tr.* fill with fury; enrage. □□ **in•fu'ri•at•ing** *adj.* **in•fu'ri•at•ing•ly** *adv.*

■ anger, madden, incense, make a person's blood boil.

in•fuse /infyŏoz/ *v.tr.* 1 imbue; pervade. 2 steep (herbs, tea, etc.) in liquid to extract the content. 3 instill (grace, spirit, life, etc.). □□ **in•fus'er** *n.* **in•fu'sion** /infyŏozhən/ *n.* **in•fu'sive** /-fyŏosiv/ *adj.*

■ 1 see SUFFUSE. 2 brew, soak. 3 see INSTILL 1.

-ing[1] /ing/ *suffix* forming gerunds and nouns from verbs denoting: 1 a verbal action or its result (*asking*). b verbal action as described or classified in some way (*tough going*). 2 material associated with a process, etc. (*piping*). 3 occupation or event (*banking*). 4 set or arrangement of (*coloring*).

-ing[2] /ing/ *suffix* 1 forming the present participle of verbs (*asking*), often as adjectives (*charming*). 2 forming adjectives from nouns (*hulking*) and verbs (*balding*).

in•ge•nious /injeenyəs/ *adj.* 1 clever at inventing, organizing, etc. 2 (of a machine, etc.) cleverly contrived. See synonym study at CREATIVE. □□ **in•ge'ni•ous•ly** *adv.* **in•ge'ni•ous•ness** *n.*

■ skillful, skilled, adept, apt, adroit; resourceful.

in•ge•nue /ánzhənŏo/ *n.* (also **in'gé•nue**) 1 unsophisticated young woman. 2 *Theatr.* a such a part in a play. b actress who plays this part.

■ 1 see INNOCENT *n.*

in•ge•nu•i•ty /ínjinŏoitee, -nyŏo-/ *n.* inventiveness; cleverness.

■ ingeniousness, skill, craft, art, artfulness; resourcefulness, creativity; canniness; talent, flair.

in•gen•u•ous /injényŏoəs/ *adj.* 1 innocent; artless. 2 open; frank. See synonym study at GULLIBLE. □□ **in•gen'u•ous•ly** *adv.* **in•gen'u•ous•ness** *n.*

■ 1 naive, simple, unsophisticated, natural. 2 candid, transparent, straightforward, plain.

in•gest /injést/ *v.tr.* 1 take in (food, etc.); eat.

2 absorb (facts, knowledge, etc.). □□ **in•ges•tion** /injés-chən/ n. **in•ges'tive** adj.

in•glo•ri•ous /in-gláwreeəs/ adj. **1** shameful; ignominious. **2** not famous. □□ **in•glo'ri•ous•ly** adv.

-ingly /inglee/ suffix forming adverbs esp. denoting manner of action or nature or condition (charmingly).

in•got /inggət/ n. bar of cast metal, esp. of gold, etc.

in•grained /in-gráynd/ adj. **1** deeply rooted; inveterate. **2** thorough. **3** (of dirt, etc.) deeply embedded. See synonym study at IN-HERENT.

■ **1** engrained, established, fixed, deep-seated; inherent. **2** see THOROUGH 3. **3** engrained, ground-in; indelible, ineradicable.

in•grate /in-grayt/ formal or literary • n. ungrateful person. • adj. ungrateful.

in•gra•ti•ate /in-gráysheeayt/ v.refl. [usu. foll. by with] bring oneself into favor. □□ **in•gra'ti•at•ing** adj. **in•gra'ti•at•ing•ly** adv. **in•gra•ti•a•tion** /-áyshən/ n.

■ (ingratiate oneself with) flatter, adulate, cultivate, curry favor with, dance attendance on, fawn on or upon. □□ **ingratiating** flattering, adulatory, fawning, groveling, toadyish, servile, obsequious, sycophantic.

in•grat•i•tude /in-grátitood, -tyood/ n. lack of due gratitude.

■ unthankfulness, thanklessness; snakiness.

in•gre•di•ent /in-greedeeənt/ n. component part or element in a recipe, mixture, or combination.

■ constituent, component, factor, admixture; (ingredients) contents, makings.

in•gress /in-gres/ n. **1** act or right of going in or entering. **2** means of entrance. □□ **in•gres'sion** /-gréshən/ n.

in•grow•ing /in-gróing/ adj. growing inward, esp. (of a toenail) growing into the flesh. □□ **in'grown** adj.

in•gui•nal /inggwinəl/ adj. of the groin. □□ **in'gui•nal•ly** adv.

in•hab•it /in-hábit/ v.tr. (of a person or animal) dwell in; occupy (a region, town, house, etc.). □□ **in•hab'i•ta•ble** adj. **in•hab'it•ant** n.

■ reside in, live in, be domiciled in; populate, people; colonize. □□ **inhabitant** resident, tenant, occupant; citizen, native.

in•hal•ant /in-háylənt/ n. medicinal preparation for inhaling.

in•hale /in-hául/ v.tr. [often absol.] breathe in (air, gas, tobacco smoke, etc.). □□ **in•ha•la•tion** /-həláyshən/ n.

■ inspire, breathe, draw (in), suck in, take a breath of; sniff (up), sl. snort.

in•hal•er /in-háylər/ n. device for administering an inhalant.

in•here /in-heer/ v.intr. be inherent.

in•her•ent /in-heerənt, inhér-/ adj. **1** existing in something, esp. as a permanent or characteristic attribute. **2** vested in (a person, etc.) as a right or privilege. □□ **in•her'ence** n. **in•her'ent•ly** adv.

■ **1** innate, connate, inborn, congenital, in-

herited; essential, intrinsic, implicit, basic, fundamental. **2** fundamental, basic; inalienable, inviolable, sacrosanct.

SYNONYM STUDY: inherent

CONGENITAL, ESSENTIAL, INBORN, INGRAINED, INNATE, INTRINSIC. A quality that is **inherent** is a permanent part of a person's nature or essence (an inherent tendency to fight back). If it is **ingrained**, it is deeply wrought into his/her substance or character (ingrained prejudice against women). **Inborn** and **innate** are nearly synonymous, sharing the basic sense of existing at the time of birth, but **innate** is usually preferred in an abstract or philosophical context (innate defects; innate ideas), while **inborn** is reserved for human characteristics that are so deep-seated they seem to have been there from birth (an inborn aptitude for the piano). **Congenital** also means from the time of one's birth, but it is primarily used in medical contexts (congenital color-blindness) and refers to problems or defects (a congenital tendency toward schizophrenia). **Intrinsic** and **essential** are broader terms that can apply to things as well as people. Something that is **essential** is part of the essence or constitution of something (an essential ingredient; essential revisions in the text), while **intrinsic** suggests an irreducible minimum, without regard to less **essential** considerations or properties (her intrinsic fairness; an intrinsic weakness in the design).

---

in•her•it /in-hérit/ v. **1** tr. receive (property, rank, etc.) by legal succession. **2** tr. derive (a quality or characteristic) genetically from one's ancestors. **3** succeed as an heir (a younger son rarely inherits). □□ **in•her'it•a•ble** adj. **in•her'i•tor** n.

■ **1** come into, succeed to, fall or be or become heir to. **3** take over, become heir, receive an inheritance. □□ **inheritor** see HEIR.

in•her•i•tance /in-hérit'ns/ n. **1** thing inherited. **2 a** act of inheriting. **b** instance of this.

■ **1** patrimony, heritage, legacy, bequest, birthright. **2** endowment, succession, bequeathal.

in•hib•it /in-híbit/ v.tr. **1** hinder, restrain, or prevent. **2** (as **inhibited** adj.) subject to inhibition. **3** [usu. foll. by from + verbal noun] forbid or prohibit. See synonym study at THWART. □□ **in•hib'i•tive** adj. **in•hib'i•tor** n. **in•hib•i•to•ry** /-itawree/ adj.

■ **1** hamper, impede, obstruct, interfere with. **2** (**inhibited**) pent up, repressed, restrained, suppressed; shy, reticent, reserved. **3** (inhibit from) interdict from, bar from, ban from, keep from.

in•hi•bi•tion /inhibíshən/ n. **1** Psychol. restraint on the direct expression of an instinct. **2** colloq. emotional resistance to a thought, action, etc. **3 a** act of inhibiting. **b** process of being inhibited.

■ **1, 2** bar, barrier, defense mechanism, blockage; self-consciousness, shyness, reticence, embarrassment. **3** prohibition, interdiction, bar; prevention.

in•hos•pi•ta•ble /inhospítəbəl, inhóspi-/ adj. **1** not hospitable. **2** (of a region, coast, etc.)

not affording shelter, etc. □□ **in•hos′pi•ta•bly** *adv.*

■ **1** unwelcoming, unreceptive, uninviting, unsociable. **2** uninviting, bleak, grim, harsh; forbidding; unfavorable.

in-house • *adj.* /ínhóws/ done or existing within an institution, company, etc. (*an in-house project*). • *adv.* /ínhóws/ internally, without outside assistance.

in•hu•man /inhyōōmən/ *adj.* **1** (of a person, conduct, etc.) brutal; unfeeling; barbarous. **2** not of a human type. □□ **in•hu•man′i•ty** /ínhyōōmánitee/ *n.* (*pl.* **–ties**). **in•hu′man•ly** *adv.*

■ **1** savage, barbaric, beastly; vicious, merciless. **2** nonhuman, animal, bestial; brutish; devilish, fiendish.

in•im•i•cal /inímikəl/ *adj.* [usu. foll. by *to*] **1** hostile. **2** harmful. See synonym study at HOSTILE. □□ **in•im′i•cal•ly** *adv.*

■ **1** see HOSTILE 2. **2** see *detrimental* (DETRIMENT).

in•im•i•ta•ble /inímitəbəl/ *adj.* impossible to imitate. □□ **in•im•i•ta•bil′i•ty** *n.* **in•im′i•ta•bly** *adv.*

■ see UNPARALLELED. □□ **inimitability** see SUPERIORITY. **inimitably** see *perfectly* (PERFECT).

in•iq•ui•ty /iníkwitee/ *n.* (*pl.* **–ties**) **1** wickedness; unrighteousness. **2** gross injustice. □□ **in•iq′ui•tous** *adj.* **in•iq′ui•tous•ly** *adv.*

■ see SIN[1] 1. **2** see SCANDAL 1.

in•i•tial /iníshəl/ • *adj.* of, existing, or occurring at the beginning. • *n.* **1** = *initial letter*. **2** [usu. in *pl.*] the first letter(s) of a (esp. a person's) name or names. • *v.tr.* mark or sign with one's initials. □ **initial letter** letter at the beginning of a word. □□ **in•i′tial•ly** *adv.*

■ *adj.* first, prime, primary, original; aboriginal; incipient; opening, starting, introductory. • *n.* **2** (*initials*) monogram. • *v.* endorse.

in•i•tial•ism /iníshəlizəm/ *n.* group of initial letters used as an abbreviation for a name or expression (cf. ACRONYM).

in•i•tial•ize /iníshəliz/ *v.tr.* set or prepare for the start of an operation. □□ **in•i•tial•i•za′tion** *n.*

in•i•ti•ate • *v.tr.* /iníshee-ayt/ **1** begin; set going. **2 a** admit (a person) into a society, an office, a secret, etc., esp. with a ritual. **b** instruct (a person) in science, etc. • *n.* /iníshee-ət/ initiated person. • *adj.* /iníshee-ət/ (of a person) recently initiated. □□ **in•i•ti•a•tion** /-sheeáyshən/ *n.* **in•i′ti•a•tor** *n.* **in•i′ti•a•to•ry** /iníshee-ətáwree/ *adj.*

■ *v.* **1** start, originate, pioneer, introduce; create, generate, sow, cause, give rise to, trigger. **2 a** accept, introduce, induct; familiarize. **b** teach, train, tutor. • *n.* novice, beginner, apprentice, recruit. • *adj.* new, novice. □□ **initiation** beginning, start, inception, origination; admittance, acceptance; education, teaching, instruction.

in•i•ti•a•tive /iníshətiv, iníshee-ətiv/ • *n.* **1** ability to initiate things; enterprise. **2** origination. **3** right of citizens outside the legislature to originate legislation. • *adj.* beginning; originating.

■ **1** leadership, resourcefulness, self-

motivation. **2** (first) move, (first) step, lead, opening move *or* gambit, *démarche*; see also *initiation* (INITIATE).

in•ject /injékt/ *v.tr.* **1** *Med.* **a** [usu. foll. by *into*] drive (a solution, medicine, etc.) by or as if by a syringe. **b** [usu. foll. by *with*] fill (a cavity, etc.) by injecting. **2** place (an object, quality, etc.) into something. See synonym study at INSERT. □□ **in•ject′a•ble** *adj. & n.* **in•jec′tor** *n.*

■ **1** force *or* shoot in, insert, introduce, transfuse; inoculate. **2** introduce, insert, instill, bring in, interject.

in•jec•tion /injékshən/ *n.* **1 a** act of injecting. **b** instance of this. **2** liquid *or* solution (to be) injected (*prepare a morphine injection*).

■ shot, inoculation, vaccination.

in•junc•tion /injúnkshən/ *n.* **1** authoritative warning or order. **2** *Law* judicial order restraining *or* compelling some action. □□ **in•junc′tive** *adj.*

■ **1** prohibition, interdiction, restriction; admonition.

in•jure /ínjər/ *v.tr.* **1** harm; damage. **2** impair. **3** do wrong to. □□ **in′jured** *adj.* **in′jur•er** *n.*

■ **1** hurt, wreck, maim; assault, molest, beat up; wound. **2** damage, ruin, cripple, mar; vitiate, tarnish. **3** offend, abuse, insult, malign.

in•ju•ri•ous /injŏoreeəs/ *adj.* **1** hurtful. **2** (of language) insulting. **3** wrongful. □□ **in•ju′ri•ous•ly** *adv.* **in•ju′ri•ous•ness** *n.*

■ **1** malicious, nasty; damaging, deleterious, detrimental; harmful, unhealthy. **2** abusive, offensive, scathing; slanderous, libelous, defamatory. **3** unfair, unjust, underhand(ed).

in•ju•ry /ínjəree/ *n.* (*pl.* **–ries**) **1 a** physical harm *or* damage. **b** instance of this. **2** esp. *Law* **a** wrongful action. **b** instance of this. **3** damage to one's good name, etc.

■ **1** hurt, impairment, disablement; break, fracture; bruise, contusion. **2** wrong, abuse; injustice, unjustness, wrongdoing. **3** insult, abuse, calumny, slander, libel, defamation.

in•jus•tice /injústis/ *n.* **1** lack of fairness. **2** unjust act.

■ **1** unfairness, inequity, inequality; discrimination, bias. **2** wrong, injury, outrage.

ink /ingk/ • *n.* **1** colored fluid *or* paste used for writing, printing, etc. **2** *Zool.* black liquid ejected by a cuttlefish, octopus, etc. • *v.tr.* **1** mark with ink. **2** cover (type, etc.) with ink before printing. **3** apply ink to. □ **ink-jet printer** computer-controlled printer in which minute droplets of ink are projected onto the paper.

ink•ling /íngkling/ *n.* slight knowledge or suspicion; hint.

■ clue, (the faintest *or* foggiest) idea, glimmering; intimation.

ink•well /íngkwel/ *n.* pot for ink usu. in a hole in a desk.

ink•y /íngkee/ *adj.* (**ink•i•er, ink•i•est**) of, as black as, or stained with ink. □□ **ink′i•ness** *n.*

in•laid *past* and *past part.* of INLAY.

in•land /ínlənd, ínland/ • *adj.* situated in the interior of a country. • *n.* interior parts of a country. • *adv.* in or toward the interior of a country. □□ **in'land•er** *n.*

■ *n.* see INTERIOR *n.* 2.

in-law /ínlaw/ *n.* [often in *pl.*] relative by marriage.

in•lay • *v.tr.* /ínláy/ (*past* and *past part.* **inlaid** /ínláyd/) **1 a** embed (a thing in another) so that the surfaces are even. **b** ornament (a thing with inlaid work). **2** (as **inlaid** *adj.*) (of a piece of furniture, etc.) ornamented by inlaying. • *n.* /ínlay/ **1** inlaid work. **2** material inlaid. **3** filling shaped to fit a tooth cavity. □□ **in'lay•er** *n.*

■ *v.* **1 a** see IMPLANT *v.* 1.

in•let /ínlet, –lit/ *n.* **1** small arm of the sea, lake, or river. **2** way of entry.

■ **1** see CREEK. **2** see ENTRY 3.

in-line /ínlín/ *adj.* **1** having parts arranged in a line. **2** constituting an integral part of a continuous sequence of operations or machines.

in lo•co pa•ren•tis /in lókō pəréntis/ *adv.* in the place or position of a parent.

in•mate /ínmayt/ *n.* [usu. foll. by *of*] occupant of a prison, etc.

■ prisoner, convict, captive, internee, detainee, patient.

in me•mo•ri•am /in mimáwreeəm/ • *prep.* in memory of (a dead person). • *n.* obituary.

in•most /ínmōst/ *adj.* **1** most inward. **2** most intimate.

inn /in/ *n.* **1** small hotel. **2** restaurant or tavern.

■ **1** see HOTEL.

in•nards /ínərdz/ *n.pl. colloq.* **1** entrails. **2** works (of an engine, etc.).

in•nate /ináyt, ínayt/ *adj.* inborn; natural. See synonym study at INHERENT. □□ **in•nate'ly** *adv.* **in•nate'ness** *n.*

■ see INBORN. □□ **innately** see NATURALLY 1.

in•ner /ínər/ *adj.* **1** inside; interior. **2** (of thoughts, feelings, etc.) deeper; more secret. □ **inner city** central most densely populated area of a city (also (with hyphen) *attrib.*: *inner-city housing*). **inner tube** separate inflatable tube inside a pneumatic tire. □□ **in'ner•most** *adj.*

■ **1** see INTERIOR *adj.* 1. **2** see INTERIOR *adj.* 5.

in•ning /íning/ *n.* **1** *Baseball* division of a game during which both teams bat. **2** single turn at bat for a team.

inn•keep•er /ínkeepər/ *n.* person who keeps an inn.

in•no•cent /ínəsənt/ • *adj.* **1** free from moral wrong. **2** not guilty (of a crime, etc.). **3 a** simple; guileless. **b** pretending to be guileless. **4** harmless. • *n.* innocent person, esp. a young child. □□ **in'no•cence** *n.* **in'no•cen•cy** *n.* **in'no•cent•ly** *adv.*

■ *adj.* **1** virtuous, moral, righteous, good, pure, chaste. **2** guiltless, blameless, (in the) clear. **3 a** unsuspecting, unsuspicious, ingenuous, trusting; naive. **b** demure, coy, meek. **4** well-intentioned, safe, tame. • *n.* infant, babe, child; ingénue, virgin.

in•noc•u•ous /inókyōōəs/ *adj.* **1** harmless.

2 inoffensive. □□ **in•noc'u•ous•ly** *adv.* **in•noc'u•ous•ness** *n.*

■ **1** see HARMLESS 1. **2** see INOFFENSIVE.

in•no•vate /ínəvayt/ *v.intr.* **1** bring in new methods, ideas, etc. **2** make changes. □□ **in•no•va'tion** /–váyshən/ *n.* **in•no•va'tion•al** *adj.* **in'no•va•tor** *n.* **in'no•va•tive** *adj.* **in'no•va•tive•ness** *n.*

■ **1** break new ground, pioneer, blaze a trail. **2** make alterations, modernize, remodel. □□ **innovation** originality, inventiveness; novelty; modernization, alteration. **innovative** see ORIGINAL *adj.* 2.

in•nu•en•do /ínyōō-éndō/ *n.* (*pl.* **–dos** or **–does**) **1** allusive remark or hint, usu. disparaging. **2** remark with a double meaning, usu. suggestive.

■ **1** allusion, insinuation, imputation, slur, suggestion. **2** double entendre; pun, play on words.

in•nu•mer•a•ble /inóōmərəbəl, inyōō–/ *adj.* too many to be counted. □□ **in•nu'mer•a•bly** *adv.*

■ see MANY *adj.*

in•nu•mer•ate /inóōmərət, inyōō–/ *adj.* having no knowledge of or feeling for mathematical operations; not numerate. □□ **in•nu'mer•a•cy** *n.*

in•oc•u•late /inókyəlayt/ *v.tr.* **1** treat with a vaccine or serum to promote immunity against disease. **2** implant (a disease) by means of vaccine. □□ **in•oc'u•la•ble** *adj.* **in•oc•u•la'tion** /–láyshən/ *n.*

■ **1** see INJECT 1. □□ **inoculation** shot, vaccination, injection.

in•of•fen•sive /ínəfénsiv/ *adj.* not objectionable; harmless. □□ **in•of•fen'sive•ly** *adv.* **in•of•fen'sive•ness** *n.*

■ unobjectionable, innocuous, neutral, safe; mild.

in•op•er•a•ble /inópərəbəl/ *adj.* **1** *Surgery* that cannot successfully be operated on. **2** that cannot be operated; inoperative. □□ **in•op•er•a•bil'i•ty** *n.* **in•op'er•a•bly** *adv.*

■ **2** useless, unworkable, broken.

in•op•er•a•tive /inópərətiv/ *adj.* not working or taking effect.

■ see *out of order* 1 (ORDER).

in•or•di•nate /ináwrd'nət/ *adj.* **1** excessive. **2** intemperate. **3** disorderly. □□ **in•or'di•nate•ly** *adv.*

■ **1, 2** immoderate, unrestrained, unbridled; extreme, excessive; outrageous, preposterous. **3** see DISORDERLY 1.

in•or•gan•ic /ínawrgánik/ *adj. Chem.* (of a compound) not organic, usu. of mineral origin (opp. ORGANIC). □ **inorganic chemistry** chemistry of inorganic compounds. □□ **in•or•gan'i•cal•ly** *adv.*

in•pa•tient /ínpayshənt/ *n.* patient who stays in the hospital while under treatment.

in•put /ínpŏŏt/ • *n.* **1** what is put in or taken in, or operated on by any process or system. **2** *Electronics* **a** place where, or a device through which, energy, information, etc., enters a system. **b** energy supplied to a device or system; electrical signal. **3** information fed into a computer. **4** action or process of putting in or feeding in. **5** contribution of information, etc. • *v.tr.* (**in•put•ting**; *past* and *past part.* **in•put** or **in•put•ted** 1 put in. 2 *Computing* supply (data, programs, etc., to a computer, program, etc.). □ **in•put-** (or **in'put/**) **out'put** *Computing, etc.* of, relating to, or for input and output. □□ **in'put•ter** *n.*

in•quest /inkwest, íng–/ *n. Law* inquiry by a coroner into the cause of a death.

■ see INQUIRY 1.

in•qui•e•tude /inkwí-itōōd, –tyōōd/ *n.* uneasiness.

in•quire /inkwír, ing–/ *v.* 1 *intr.* make a formal investigation. 2 *tr.* ask for information as to (*inquired whether we were coming*). 3 *tr.* [foll. by *into*] look into. □□ **in•quir'er** *n.*

■ 1 ask questions, make inquiries; (*inquire into*) investigate, research, explore, probe, look into. 2 query, question; request, seek; ask about *or* after. 3 (*inquire into*) see INVESTIGATE 1.

in•qui•ry /inkwíree, ing–, ínkwəree, ing–/ *n.* (*pl.* **–ries**) 1 investigation, esp. an official one. 2 act of asking.

■ 1 probe, examination, research, search, inspection. 2 question, query, interrogation; request, demand.

in•qui•si•tion /inkwizíshən, ing–/ *n.* 1 usu. *derog.* intensive search or investigation. 2 judicial or official inquiry. 3 (**the Inquisition**) *RC Ch. hist.* ecclesiastical tribunal for the violent suppression of heresy, esp. in Spain. □□ **in•qui•si'tion•al** *adj.* **in•qui•si'tor** /inkwízitər, ing–/ *n.*

■ 1 see *investigation* (INVESTIGATE). 2 see INQUIRY 1.

in•qui•si•tive /inkwízitiv, ing–/ *adj.* 1 unduly curious. 2 seeking knowledge. □□ **in•qui'si•tive•ly** *adv.* **in•qui'si•tive•ness** *n.*

■ 1 prying, curious; intrusive, meddlesome. 2 inquiring, curious. □□ **inquisitiveness** see INTEREST *n.* 1a.

in re /in ree, ráy/ *prep.* = RE¹.

in•road /ínrod/ *n.* 1 [often in *pl.*] a encroachment. b progress. 2 hostile attack.

■ 1 a invasion, incursion, intrusion. b advance, breakthrough. 2 raid, foray; penetration.

INS *abbr.* Immigration and Naturalization Service.

in•sane /insáyn/ *adj.* 1 not of sound mind; mad. 2 *colloq.* extremely foolish. □□ **in•sane'ly** *adv.* **in•san•i•ty** /–sánitee/ *n.* (*pl.* **–ties**)

■ 1 psychotic, neurotic; demented, out of one's mind *or* wits, manic, maniacal; (*be insane*) have bats in the belfry; (*go insane*) take leave of one's senses. 2 silly, fatuous, asinine, inane, stupid. □□ **insanity** madness, dementedness, lunacy; absurdity, nonsense, ridiculousness.

in•sa•tia•ble /insáyshəbəl/ *adj.* 1 unable to be satisfied. 2 extremely greedy. □□ **in•sa•tia•bil'i•ty** *n.* **in•sa'tia•bly** *adv.*

■ 2 see GREEDY 1. □□ **insatiability** see GREED.

in•scribe /inskríb/ *v.tr.* 1 write or carve (words, etc.) on stone, paper, etc. 2 write an informal dedication (to) in (a book, etc.). 3 enter the name of (a person) on a list or in a book. □□ **in•scrib'a•ble** *adj.* **in•scrib'er** *n.*

■ 1 see WRITE 2, 3. 2 address, assign. 3 see ENTER 3.

in•scrip•tion /inskrípshən/ *n.* 1 words inscribed. 2 a act of inscribing. b instance of this. □□ **in•scrip'tion•al** *adj.* **in•scrip'tive** *adj.*

■ 1 dedication, address, message.

in•scru•ta•ble /inskrōōtəbəl/ *adj.* mysterious; impenetrable. □□ **in•scru•ta•bil'i•ty** *n.* **in•scru'ta•ble•ness** *n.* **in•scru'ta•bly** *adv.*

■ see MYSTERIOUS. □□ **inscrutability** see MYSTERY 2.

in•sect /ínsekt/ *n.* 1 any arthropod having a head, thorax, abdomen, two antennae, three pairs of thoracic legs, and usu. one or two pairs of thoracic wings. 2 (loosely) any other small segmented invertebrate animal. □□ **in•sec•tile** /–séktəl, –tíl/ *adj.*

■ 1 see BUG *n.* 1.

in•sec•ti•cide /inséktisīd/ *n.* substance used for killing insects. □□ **in•sec•ti•cid'al** *adj.*

in•sec•ti•vore /inséktivawr/ *n.* any animal or plant feeding on insects. □□ **in•sec•ti•vor•ous** /–tívərəs/ *adj.*

in•se•cure /insikyóor/ *adj.* 1 lacking confidence. 2 a unsafe. b (of a surface) liable to give way. c lacking security. □□ **in•se•cure'ly** *adv.* **in•se•cur'i•ty** *n.*

■ 1 uncertain, unsure, irresolute, hesitant; unsound, unreliable, untrustworthy; diffident, nervous. 2 a, b dangerous, perilous, precarious; unsound; rocky, shaky, wobbly. c unprotected, vulnerable, unguarded.

in•sem•i•nate /insémináyt/ *v.tr.* 1 introduce semen into. 2 sow. □□ **in•sem•i•na•tion** /–náyshən/ *n.* **in•sem'i•na•tor** *n.*

■ 1 see FERTILIZE 2.

in•sen•sate /insénsayt/ *adj.* 1 without physical sensation. 2 unfeeling. 3 stupid. □□ **in•sen'sate•ly** *adv.*

■ 1 see SENSELESS 1, 4. 2 see *thick-skinned* (THICK).

in•sen•si•ble /insénsibəl/ *adj.* 1 a unconscious. b (of the extremities, etc.) numb. 2 [usu. foll. by *of, to*] unaware. 3 callous. 4 too small or gradual to be perceived. □□ **in•sen•si•bil'i•ty** *n.* **in•sen'si•bly** *adv.*

■ 1 insensate, insentient, dead; senseless, dead to the world; benumbed, anesthetized. 2 (*insensible of* or *to*) unmindful of, oblivious to, blind *or* deaf to. 3 unfeeling, emotionless, impassive; cold-hearted, hard-hearted. 4 see IMPERCEPTIBLE 2. □□ **insensibility** see OBLIVION.

in•sen•si•tive /insénsitiv/ *adj.* 1 unfeeling; boorish; crass. 2 not sensitive to physical stimuli. □□ **in•sen'si•tive•ly** *adv.* **in•sen'si•tive•ness** *n.* **in•sen•si•tiv'i•ty** *n.*

■ 1 see THOUGHTLESS 1. □□ **insensitivity** see *imprudence* (IMPRUDENT).

in•sen•ti•ent /insénshənt/ *adj.* not sentient; inanimate. □□ **in•sen•tience** /–shəns/ *n.*

■ see INSENSIBLE 1.

in•sep•a•ra•ble /insépərəbəl/ • *adj.* 1 (esp. of friends) unable or unwilling to be separated. 2 *Gram.* unable to be used as a separate word, e.g., *dis-*, *mis-*, *un-*. • *n.* [usu. in *pl.*]

inseparable person or thing, esp. a friend.
□□ **in•sep′a•ra•bly** adv.
■ adj. **1** see CLOSE¹ adj. 2a, b, ONE adj. 5.
□□ **inseparably** see *inextricably* (INEXTRICA-
BLE).

in•sert • v.tr. /insért/ place, fit, or thrust (a
thing) into another. • n. /insərt/ something
inserted, e.g., a loose page in a magazine.
□□ **in•sert′a•ble** adj. **in•sert′er** n.

■ v. inset, inlay, feed, load; interpolate, interject, interpose. • n. inset, inlay; interpolation, interjection; insertion.

SYNONYM STUDY: insert

INJECT, INTERJECT, INTERPOLATE, INTRODUCE,
MEDIATE. If you want to put something in a
fixed place between or among other things,
you can **insert** it (*insert a new paragraph in
an essay; insert photographs in the text of a
book*). If it's a liquid, you'll probably want to
inject it (*inject the flu vaccine*), although *inject* can also mean to bring in something new
or different (*inject some humor into an otherwise dreary speech*). If it's a person, you'd better **introduce** him or her, which suggests
placing the individual in the midst of a
group so as to become part of it. You can
also *introduce* things (*introduce a new subject
into the curriculum*), but if the thing you're
introducing does not really belong, you may
have to **interpolate** it, which pertains to
things that are extraneous and often *introduced* without authorization (*to interpolate
editorial comments*). If you have something to
introduce in an abrupt or forced manner,
you'll have to **interject**, which usually applies to remarks, statements, or questions (*in
the midst of his speech, she interjected what she
felt were important details*). If you *interject* too
often, however, you risk offending the speaker and may have to ask someone to **mediate**, which means to settle a dispute or bring
about a compromise by taking a stand midway between extremes.

---

in•ser•tion /insórshən/ n. **1** act or instance of
inserting. **2** amendment, etc., inserted in
writing or printing.

in•set • n. /inset/ **1** an insert. **2** small map,
etc., inserted within the border of a larger
one. • v.tr. /inset/ (**in•set•ting**; *past* and *past
part.* **in•set**) **1** put in as an inset. **2** decorate
with an inset.

in•shore /inshawr/ adv. & adj. at sea but
close to the shore.

in•side • n. /ínsíd/ **1 a** inner side. **b** inner
part; interior. **2** [usu. in *pl.*] *colloq.* **a** stomach and bowels. **b** operative part of a machine, etc. • adj. /ínsíd/ situated on or in the
inside; (of information, etc.) available only to
those on the inside. • adv. /ínsíd/ **1** on, in, or
to the inside. **2** *sl.* in prison. • prep. /ínsíd/
1 on the inner side of; within. **2** in less than
(*inside an hour*). □ **inside out** with the inner
surface turned outward. **know a thing inside out** know a thing thoroughly.

■ n. **1** inner surface; lining, reverse; center,
middle, core, heart. **2** (*insides*) **a** entrails,
viscera, gut(s). • adj. internal; indoor; pri-

vate, secret, confidential. • adv. **1** indoors;
centrally, at heart, fundamentally. **2** in jail,
behind bars. • prep. **2** *colloq.* inside of; in under. □ **inside out** outside in, wrong side out,
reversed.

in•sid•er /insídər/ n. **1** person who is within a
society, organization, etc. (cf. OUTSIDER).
2 person privy to a secret. □ **insider trading** *Stock Exch.* illegal practice of trading
while having access to confidential information.

in•sid•i•ous /insídeeəs/ adj. **1** proceeding in-
conspicuously but harmfully. **2** treacherous.
□□ **in•sid′i•ous•ly** adv. **in•sid′i•ous•ness** n.
■ **2** see SINISTER 2. □□ **insidiousness** see
PERFIDY.

in•sight /ínsīt/ n. **1** capacity of understanding hidden truths, etc. **2** instance of this.
□□ **in•sight′ful** adj. **in•sight′ful•ly** adv.
■ perception, percipience, sensitivity, perspicacity.

in•sig•ni•a /insígneeə/ n. [treated as *sing.* or
pl.] **1** badge. **2** distinguishing mark.
■ **1** see SYMBOL n.

in•sig•nif•i•cant /insignifikənt/ adj. **1** unimportant; trifling. **2** (of a person) undistinguished. **3** meaningless. □□ **in•sig•ni′fi•
cance** n. **in•sig′ni′fi•cant•ly** adv.
■ **1** paltry, petty, trivial, nugatory. **2** unexceptional, unremarkable; ordinary, mediocre. **3** senseless, pointless, irrelevant.

in•sin•cere /insinseer/ adj. not sincere; not
candid. □□ **in•sin•cere′ly** adv. **in•sin•cer′i•
ty** /-séritee/ n. (*pl.* **-ties**)
■ dishonest, deceitful, untruthful; synthetic, artificial; two-faced. □□ **insincerity**
see AFFECTATION¹ 1, CANT n. 1.

in•sin•u•ate /insinyóō-ayt/ v.tr. **1** convey indirectly. **2** [often *refl.*; usu. foll. by *into*] introduce (oneself, a person, etc.) into favor,
etc., by subtle manipulation. □□ **in•sin•u•a•
tion** /-áyshən/ n. **in•sin•u•a•tive** /-yóōətiv/
adj. **in•sin′u•a•tor** n.
■ **1** suggest, hint, intimate. **2** (*insinuate oneself*) worm *or* work (one's way), insert oneself. □□ **insinuation** see IMPLICATION, INNU-
ENDO n. 1.

in•sip•id /insípid/ adj. **1** lacking vigor; dull.
2 lacking flavor. □□ **in•sip′id•i•ty** n. **in•sip′
id•ly** adv. **in•sip′id•ness** n.
■ **1** see TEDIOUS. **2** see TASTELESS 1.

in•sist /insíst/ v.tr. maintain or demand assertively. □□ **in•sist′er** n. **in•sist′ing•ly** adv.
■ require; importune, urge, exhort; argue;
swear.

in•sis•tent /insístənt/ adj. **1** insisting.
2 compelling attention; demanding notice.
□□ **in•sis′tence** n. **in•sis′ten•cy** n. **in•sis′
tent•ly** adv.
■ **1** emphatic, firm; assertive; dogged. **2** obtrusive; importunate; loud, noisy.

in si•tu /in seetōō, sī-/ adv. **1** in its place. **2** in
its original place.

in•so•bri•e•ty /insəbrī-itee/ n. intemperance,
esp. in drinking.
■ see *drunkenness* (DRUNKEN).

in•so•far as /insəfaàr az/ adv. to the extent
that.

in•sole /insōl/ n. inner sole of a boot or shoe.

in•so•lent /insələnt/ adj. offensively contemptuous or arrogant; insulting. □□ **in'so• lence** n. **in'so•lent•ly** adv.

■ disrespectful, rude, uncivil, offensive. □□ **insolence** see BRASS n. 5, *impudence* (IM-PUDENT).

in•sol•u•ble /insólyəbəl/ adj. **1** incapable of being solved. **2** incapable of being dissolved. □□ **in•sol•u•bil'i•ty** n. **in•sol'u•bly** adv.

■ **1** see MYSTERIOUS.

in•sol•vent /insólvənt/ • adj. **1** unable to pay one's debts. **2** relating to insolvency (*insol-vent laws*). See synonym study at IMPERTI-NENT. • n. debtor. □□ **in•sol'ven•cy** n.

■ **1** bankrupt, in receivership, ruined, failed. □□ **insolvency** see FAILURE 6, POV-ERTY 1.

in•som•ni•a /insómneeə/ n. habitual sleep-lessness; inability to sleep. □□ **in•som•ni•ac** /-neeak/ n. & adj.

□□ **insomniac** (adj.) see *sleepless* (SLEEP).

in•so•much /ìnsōmúch/ adv. **1** to such an extent. **2** [foll. by *as*] inasmuch.

in•sou•ci•ant /insōōseeənt, aNsōōsyaaN/ adj. carefree; unconcerned. □□ **in•sou'ci•ance** n. **in•sou'ci•ant•ly** adv.

insp. abbr. **1** inspected. **2** inspector.

in•spect /inspékt/ v.tr. **1** look closely at or into. **2** examine (a document, etc.) officially. □□ **in•spec'tion** /-spékshən/ n.

■ look into or over or around; observe, study; scrutinize; investigate. □□ **inspection** see EXAMINATION 1, 2.

in•spec•tor /inspéktər/ n. **1** person who in-spects. **2** police officer usu. ranking just be-low a superintendent. □□ **in•spec'tor•ate** n. **in•spec•to•ri•al** /-táwreeəl/ adj. **in•spec' tor•ship** n.

in•spi•ra•tion /inspiráyshən/ n. **1 a** creative force or influence stimulating creativity. **b** divine influence, esp. on the writing of Scripture, etc. **2** sudden brilliant idea. **3** in-halation. □□ **in•spi•ra'tion•al** adj.

■ **1 a** genius, oracle; stimulus, impetus; spirit. **2** revelation, vision, stroke of genius. **3** sniff, gasp.

in•spire /inspír/ v.tr. **1** stimulate creative ac-tivity, esp. by supposed divine agency. **2 a** animate (a person) with a feeling. **b** in-still (a feeling) into a person, etc. **3** prompt; give rise to. **4** (as **inspired** adj.) **a** (of a work of art, etc.) as if prompted by a supernatural source. **b** (of a guess) intuitive but accurate. **5** inhale. See synonym study at ENCOURAGE. □□ **in•spir•a•to•ry** /-rətáwree/ adj. **in•spir' ed•ly** /-ridlee/ adv. **in•spir'er** n. **in•spir'ing** adj. **in•spir'ing•ly** adv.

■ **1, 2** move, arouse, awaken; uplift, encour-age; invigorate, energize. **3** activate, actuate, instigate. **4** (**inspired**) creative, original, vi-sionary; ingenious. **5** see INHALE.

inst. abbr. **1** instance. **2** institute. **3** institu-tion. **4** instrument.

in•sta•bil•i•ty /ìnstəbílitee/ n. (pl. **-ties**) **1** lack of stability. **2** *Psychol.* unpredictability in behavior, etc.

in•stall /instáwl/ v.tr. (**in•stalled**, **in•stall-ing**) **1** place (equipment, etc.) in position ready for use. **2** place (a person) in an office or rank with ceremony. **3** establish in a place. □□ **in•stal•la'tion** n. **in•stall'er** n.

■ **1** fit, set up, mount; connect (up). **2** in-vest, inaugurate, induct, swear in. **3** place, put, seat. □□ **installation** installing, fitting, setting up, mounting; plant, factory, depot, station, establishment; investiture, inaugura-tion, induction, swearing-in, initiation, es-tablishment.

in•stall•ment /instáwlmənt/ n. **1** any of sev-eral usu. equal payments. **2** any of several parts, as of a television or radio serial. □ **in-stallment plan** payment by installments.

■ **2** episode, part, chapter.

in•stance /instəns/ • n. **1** example or illus-tration of. **2** particular case. • v.tr. cite (a fact, etc.) as an instance. □ **for instance** as an example.

■ n. **1** case (in point), exemplar. **2** situa-tion, event, occasion. • v. adduce, quote, al-lude to. □ **for instance** for example, e.g., like, (such) as.

in•stant /instənt/ • adj. **1** occurring immedi-ately. **2 a** (of food, etc.) processed for quick preparation. **b** prepared hastily and with lit-tle effort (*I have no instant solution*). **3** ur-gent; pressing. • n. **1** precise moment. **2** short space of time. □ **instant replay** im-mediate repetition of part of a videotaped sports event.

■ adj. **1** instantaneous, immediate, direct; abrupt, precipitate. **2 a** ready, ready-made, ready to serve. **3** compelling, critical, imper-ative. • n. **1** second, point (in time), flash.

in•stan•ta•ne•ous /ìnstəntáyneeəs/ adj. oc-curring or done in an instant. □□ **in•stan-ta'ne•ous•ly** adv.

■ immediate, direct, unhesitating, sponta-neous; abrupt. □□ **instantaneously** in-stantly, immediately, at once. **instanta-neousness** see *rapidity* (RAPID).

in•stant•ly /instəntlee/ adv. immediately; at once.

■ see *immediately* (IMMEDIATE).

in•stead /instéd/ adv. **1** [foll. by *of*] as an al-ternative to (*instead of this one*). **2** as an alter-native (*took me instead*) (cf. STEAD).

■ **1** (*instead of*) in place of, in lieu of; rather than, in preference to. **2** rather; by contrast.

in•step /instep/ n. **1** inner arch of the foot be-tween the toes and the ankle. **2** part of a shoe, etc., over or under this.

in•sti•gate /instigayt/ v.tr. **1** bring about by incitement or persuasion. **2** urge on; incite. See synonym study at ENCOURAGE. See syno-nym study at INCITE. □□ **in•sti•ga'tion** /-gáyshən/ n. **in•sti'ga•tive** adj. **in•sti'ga•tor** n.

■ **1** see PROVOKE 2. **2** see INDUCE 1. □□ **in-stigation** see *incitement* (INCITE). **instigator** see TROUBLEMAKER.

in•still /instíl/ v.tr. (**in•stilled**, **in•still•ing**) **1** introduce (a feeling, idea, etc.) gradually. **2** put (a liquid) into drops. □□ **in•stil•la' tion** n. **in•still'er** n. **in•still'ment** n.

■ **1** insinuate, implant, sow. **2** drip, dribble.

in•stinct • n. /instingkt/ **1 a** innate pattern of behavior, esp. in animals. **b** innate impul-sion. **2** unconscious skill; intuition. • predic.adj. /instíngkt/ [foll. by *with*] imbued;

filled (with life, beauty, etc.). □□ **in·stinc′ tive** *adj.* **in·stinc·tu·al** /–stingkchŏŏəl/ *adj.* **in·stinc′tu·al·ly** *adv.*

■ *n.* **1** drive, (unconditional) reflex; nature, tendency; subconscious. **2** bent, talent, flair; knack.

in·sti·tute /ínstitŏŏt, –tyŏŏt/ • *n.* **1** society or organization for the promotion of science, education, etc. **2** building used by an institute. • *v.tr.* **1** establish; found. **2** initiate (an inquiry, etc.). **3** appoint (a person) as a cleric in a church, etc.

■ *n.* **1** establishment, institution, foundation, society; school, college, academy, university; medical *or* health center. • *v.* **1** create, form, set up, inaugurate. **2** start, begin, launch. **3** install, induct, appoint.

in·sti·tu·tion /ínstitŏŏshən, –tyŏŏ–/ *n.* **1** act or an instance of instituting. **2 a** society or organization founded esp. for a particular purpose. **b** building used by an institution. **3** established law, practice, or custom. **4** *colloq.* (of a person, a custom, etc.) familiar object. **5** establishment of a cleric, etc., in a church. □□ **in·sti′tu′tion·al** *adj.* **in·sti·tu′ tion·al·ism** *n.* **in·sti·tu′tion·al·ly** *adv.*

■ **1** establishment, formation, creation, foundation. **2** see INSTITUTE *n.* 1. **3** tradition, habit, usage, routine. **4** fixture, regular, habitué. **5** installation, induction.

in·sti·tu·tion·al·ize /ínstitŏŏshənəlīz, –tyŏŏ–/ *v.tr.* **1** place or keep (a person) in an institution. **2** convert into an institution. □□ **in· sti·tu·tion·al·i·za′tion** *n.*

in·struct /ínstrúkt/ *v.tr.* **1** teach (a person) a subject, etc. **2** direct; command. **3** inform (a person) of a fact, etc.

■ **1** tutor; educate, train; prepare. **2** counsel, advise, tell, order. **3** see INFORM *v.* 1.

in·struc·tion /ínstrúkshən/ *n.* **1** [often in *pl.*] direction; order. **2** teaching; education. □□ **in·struc′tion·al** *adj.*

■ **1** directive, bidding, advice, guidance, counsel. **2** tuition, schooling; lesson(s); guidance.

in·struc·tive /ínstrúktiv/ *adj.* tending to instruct; enlightening. □□ **in·struc′tive·ly** *adv.* **in·struc′tive·ness** *n.*

■ didactic, prescriptive, educational; informative.

in·struc·tor /ínstrúktər/ *n.* (*fem.* **in·struc· tress** /–strúktris/) **1** teacher. **2** university teacher below assistant professor.

■ **1** educator, preceptor, tutor; mentor, adviser.

in·stru·ment /ínstrəmənt/ • *n.* **1** tool or implement, esp. for delicate or scientific work. **2** (in full **mu′si·cal in′stru·ment**) device for producing musical sounds. **3 a** thing used in performing an action. **b** person made use of. **4** measuring device, as in an airplane. **5** formal document. See synonym study at TOOL. • *v.tr.* **1** arrange (music) for instruments. **2** equip with instruments (for measuring, recording, controlling, etc.).

■ *n.* **1** device, apparatus, utensil, appliance. **3 a** agency, means, way. **b** pawn, puppet,

tool. **4** gauge, meter, dial, indicator. **5** contract, legal document. • *v.* **1** score, orchestrate. **2** fit out, kit out, rig out.

in·stru·men·tal /ínstrəment′l/ • *adj.* **1** serving as an instrument or means. **2** (of music) performed on instruments (cf. VOCAL). • *n.* piece of music performed by instruments. □□ **in·stru·men′tal·ist** *n.* **in·stru·men·tal· i·ty** /–mentálitee/ *n.* **in·stru·men′tal·ly** *adv.*

■ *adj.* **1** of service, influential, contributory; helpful.

in·stru·men·ta·tion /ínstrəmentáyshən/ *n.* **1 a** arrangement of music for instruments. **b** instruments used in a piece of music. **2 a** design, provision, or use of instruments in industry, etc. **b** instruments collectively.

in·sub·or·di·nate /ínsəbáwrd′nət/ *adj.* disobedient; rebellious. □□ **in·sub·or′din·ate· ly** *adv.* **in·sub·or·di·na′tion** /–náyshən/ *n.*

■ recalcitrant, defiant, uncooperative; stubborn.

in·sub·stan·tial /ínsəbstánshəl/ *adj.* **1** lacking solidity or substance. **2** not real. □□ **in· sub·stan·ti·al·i·ty** /–sheeálitee/ *n.* **in·sub· stan′tial·ly** *adv.*

■ **1** unsubstantial, flimsy, frail, weak, feeble, fragile. **2** unreal, false, empty, illusory, imaginary.

in·suf·fer·a·ble /ínsúfərəbəl/ *adj.* **1** intolerable. **2** unbearable.

■ **1** insupportable; unendurable; unacceptable. **2** arrogant, conceited, objectionable, obnoxious.

in·su·lar /ínsələr, ínsyə–/ *adj.* **1 a** of or like an island. **b** separated or remote. **2** narrow-minded. □□ **in·su·lar·ism** *n.* **in·su·lar′i·ty** /–láritee/ *n.* **in·su·lar·ly** *adv.*

■ **2** see PROVINCIAL *adj.* 2. □□ insularity see *provincialism* (PROVINCIAL).

in·su·late /ínsəlayt, ínsyə–/ *v.tr.* **1** prevent the passage of electricity, heat, or sound by interposing nonconductors. **2** isolate. □□ **in·su· la·tion** /–láyshən/ *n.* **in′su·la·tor** *n.*

■ **1** protect, shield; wrap. **2** detach, separate.

in·su·lin /ínsəlin/ *n.* *Biochem.* hormone regulating the amount of glucose in the blood, the lack of which causes diabetes.

in·sult • *v.tr.* /ínsúlt/ **1** speak to or treat with scornful abuse. **2** offend the self-respect or modesty of. • *n.* /ínsult/ insulting remark or action. □□ **in·sult′er** *n.* **in·sult′ing·ly** *adv.*

■ *v.* **1** malign, revile, calumniate, defame, vilify. **2** give offense, affront, outrage, scandalize. • *n.* offense, affront, indignity, discourtesy.

in·su·per·a·ble /ínsŏŏpərəbəl/ *adj.* **1** (of a barrier) impossible to surmount. **2** (of a difficulty, etc.) impossible to overcome. □□ **in· su·per·a·bil′i·ty** *n.* **in·su′per·a·bly** *adv.*

■ **1** see INVINCIBLE.

in·sup·port·a·ble /ínsəpáwrtəbəl/ *adj.* **1** unable to be endured. **2** unjustifiable. □□ **in· sup·port′a·bly** *adv.*

■ **1** see INSUFFERABLE 1. **2** see UNTENABLE.

in·sur·ance /ínshŏŏrəns/ *n.* **1** insuring. **2 a** sum paid for this. **b** sum paid out as compensation for theft, damage, loss, etc. **3** = *insurance policy*. □ **insurance policy** contract of insurance.

■ **1** indemnity, indemnification, guarantee, guaranty. **2** premium; charge; outlay **b** compensation, damages, reparation.

in•sure /inshoŏr/ *v.tr.* purchase or issue an insurance policy. □□ **in•sur′a•ble** *adj.* **in•sur′a•bil′i•ty** *n.*

■ see UNDERWRITE 1.

in•sured /inshoŏrd/ ● *adj.* covered by insurance, ● *n.* [usu. prec. by *the*] person, etc., covered by insurance.

in•sur•er /inshoŏrər/ *n.* person or company offering insurance policies.

in•sur•gent /insúrjənt/ ● *adj.* rising in active revolt. ● *n.* rebel. □□ **in•sur′gence** *n.* **in•sur′gen•cy** *n.* (*pl.* **–cies**) See synonym study at UPRISING.

■ *adj.* see REBELLIOUS 1. ● *n.* see REBEL. □□ **insurgence, insurgency** see REBELLION.

in•sur•rec•tion /insərékshən/ *n.* rebellion. See synonym study at UPRISING. □□ **in•sur•rec′tion•ar•y** *adj.* **in•sur•rec′tion•ist** *n.*

■ see REBELLION. □□ **insurrectionary** see REBELLIOUS 1. **insurrectionist** see REBEL.

in•tact /intákt/ *adj.* **1** entire. **2** untouched. □□ **in•tact′ness** *n.*

■ **1** whole, complete, integral, unimpaired, sound. **2** inviolate, unblemished, unscathed.

in•ta•glio /intályō, –tál–/ ● *n.* (*pl.* **–glios**) **1** gem with an incised design (cf. CAMEO). **2** engraved design. ● *v.tr.* (**–glioes, –glioed**) engrave (material) with an incised pattern.

in•take /íntayk/ *n.* **1 a** action of taking in. **b** instance of this. **2** number or amount taken in. **3** place where water, fuel, or air is taken in.

in•tan•gi•ble /intánjibəl/ ● *adj.* **1** unable to be touched. **2** unable to be grasped mentally. ● *n.* thing that cannot be precisely measured or assessed. □□ **in•tan•gi•bil′i•ty** *n.* **in•tan′gi•bly** *adv.*

■ *adj.* **1** untouchable, abstract, unsubstantial. **2** incomprehensible, inconceivable; subtle. ● *n.* abstract; abstraction.

in•te•ger /íntijər/ *n.* whole number.

in•te•gral /íntigrəl, intégrəl/ *adj.* **1 a** of or necessary to a whole. **b** forming a whole. **c** complete. **2** *Math.* of or denoted by an integer. □□ **in•teg′ral•ly** *adv.*

■ **1 a** essential, indispensable; basic, elemental. **b, c** entire, intact, (all) in one piece.

in•te•grate ● *v.* /íntigrayt/ **1** *tr.* combine (parts) into a whole. **b** complete by the addition of parts. **2** *tr. & intr.* bring or come into equal participation in society, a school, etc. **3** *tr.* desegregate, esp. racially (a school, etc.). ● *adj.* /íntigrət/ **1** made up of parts. **2** whole; complete. □ **integrated circuit** *Electronics* small chip, etc., of material replacing several separate components in a conventional electrical circuit. □□ **in•teg•ra•ble** /íntigrəbəl/ *adj.* **in•te•gra•bil′i•ty** *n.* **in•te•gra•tion** /íntigráyshən/ *n.*

■ *v.* unite, unify, bring *or* put together; merge, mix; amalgamate.

in•teg•ri•ty /intégritee/ *n.* **1** moral uprightness; honesty. **2** wholeness; soundness.

431   insure ~ intend

■ **1** rectitude, decency, honor; probity. **2** entirety, totality.

in•teg•u•ment /intégyəmənt/ *n.* natural outer covering, as a skin, husk, rind, etc. □□ **in•teg•u•ment•al** /–mént′l/ *adj.* **in•teg•u•men′ta•ry** *adj.*

■ see SKIN *n.*

in•tel•lect /íntilekt/ *n.* **1 a** faculty of reasoning, knowing, and thinking, as distinct from feeling. **b** understanding. **2** clever or knowledgeable person.

■ **1** rationality, reason, insight; intelligence. **2** see INTELLECTUAL *n.*

in•tel•lec•tu•al /íntilékchooəl/ ● *adj.* **1** of or appealing to the intellect. **2** possessing a high level of intelligence. **3** requiring the intellect. ● *n.* person possessing a highly developed intellect. □□ **in•tel•lec•tu•al•i•ty** /–chooálitee/ *n.* **in•tel•lec′tu•a•lize** *v.* **in•tel•lec′tu•al•ly** *adv.*

■ *adj.* **1** mental, cerebral, rational; abstract, theoretical. **2** intelligent, insightful, analytical; thoughtful, scholarly. **3** profound, abstract, thought provoking, deep. ● *n.* thinker, intellect; scholar, polymath.

in•tel•li•gence /intélijəns/ *n.* **1 a** intellect; understanding. **b** quickness of understanding. **2 a** collection of information, esp. of military or political value. **b** people employed in this. **c** information; news. □ **intelligence quotient** number denoting the ratio of a person's intelligence to the normal or average.

■ **1 a** see INTELLECT 1. **b** cleverness, astuteness; brightness; wisdom, sagacity. **2 a** espionage, spying. **b** secret service, CIA. **c** see INFORMATION 1.

in•tel•li•gent /intélijənt/ *adj.* **1** having or showing intelligence, esp. of a high level. **2** clever. **3 a** (of a device or machine) able to vary its behavior in response to varying situations, requirements, and past experience. **b** (esp. of a computer terminal) having its own data-processing capability; incorporating a microprocessor. □□ **in•tel′li•gent•ly** *adv.*

■ **1** rational, cerebral, intellectual, analytical, logical. **2** bright, brilliant, smart, astute, quick; wise.

in•tel•li•gent•si•a /intélijéntseeə/ *n.* intellectuals, considered as a class.

■ intellectuals, literati, brain trust; see also INTELLECTUAL *n.*

in•tel•li•gi•ble /intélijibəl/ *adj.* able to be understood. □□ **in•tel•li•gi•bil′i•ty** *n.* **in•tel′li•gi•bly** *adv.*

■ understandable, comprehensible; decipherable; (*be intelligible*) make sense, fall into place.

in•tem•per•ate /intémpərət/ *adj.* **1** immoderate. **2** given to excessive indulgence in alcohol, etc. □□ **in•tem′per•ance** *n.* **in•tem′per•ate•ly** *adv.* **in•tem′per•ate•ness** *n.*

■ **1** see IMMODERATE. **2** see SELF-INDULGENT. □□ **intemperance** see EXCESS *n.* 3. **intemperateness** see *prodigality* (PRODIGAL).

in•tend /inténd/ *v.tr.* **1** have as one's purpose. **2** design or destine for. **3** mean. **4** [foll. by *for*] be meant for a person to have or use, etc. **5** (as **intending** *adj.*) who intends to be.

■ **1, 2** have (it) in mind, be going, plan, set out, aim, purpose. **3** signify, indicate, express, imply, suggest. **4** (*intended for*), for, designed for, supposed to be for. **5** (**intending**) prospective, aspirant, aspiring.

SYNONYM STUDY: intend

AIM, DESIGN, MEAN, PLAN, PROPOSE, PURPOSE. If you **intend** to do something, you may or may not be serious about getting it done (*I intend to clean out the garage some day*). but at least you have a goal in mind. Although **mean** can also imply either a firm resolve (*I mean to go, with or without her permission*) or a vague intention (*I've been meaning to write her for weeks*), it is a less formal word that usually connotes a certain lack of determination or a weak resolve. **Plan**, like *mean* and *intend*, may imply a vague goal (*I plan to tour China some day*), but it is often used to suggest that you're taking active steps (*I plan to leave as soon as I finish packing*). **Aim** indicates that you have an actual goal or purpose in mind (*I aim to be the first woman president*) and that you're putting some effort behind it, without the hint of failure conveyed by *mean*. If you **propose** to do something, you declare your intention ahead of time (*I propose that we set up a meeting next week*), and if you **purpose** to do it, you are even more determined to achieve your goal (*I purpose to write a three-volume history of baseball in America*). **Design** suggests forethought and careful planning in order to bring about a particular result (*to design a strategy that will keep everyone happy*).

in•tend•ed /inténdid/ • *adj.* **1** done on purpose. **2** designed; meant. • *n. colloq.* one's fiancé or fiancée.
■ *adj.* **1** see INTENTIONAL. **2** see *destined* (DESTINE). • *n.* see FIANCÉ.

in•tense /inténs/ *adj.* (**in•tens•er, in•tens•est**) **1** existing in a high degree; violent; forceful. **2** very emotional. **3** (of a feeling, etc.) extreme. □□ **in•tense′ly** *adv.* **in•tense′ness** *n.*
■ **1, 3** excessive, immoderate, intemperate; strong, fierce. **2** passionate, impassioned, vehement; hysterical; temperamental, highstrung. □□ **intenseness** see INTENSITY 1.

in•ten•si•fy /inténsifī/ *v.* (**-fies, -fied**) make or become intense or more intense. □□ **in•ten•si•fi•ca′tion** *n.*
■ strengthen, deepen; increase, inflate; enhance, heighten, sharpen.

in•ten•si•ty /inténsitee/ *n.* (*pl.* **-ties**) **1** intenseness. **2** esp. *Physics* measurable amount of some quality, e.g., force, brightness, etc.
■ **1** extremeness, acuteness; passion, devotion. **2** concentration, strength, force; brilliance, richness.

in•ten•sive /inténsiv/ *adj.* **1** thorough; vigorous; directed to a single point, area, or subject. **2** serving to increase production in relation to costs. **3** *Gram.* (of an adjective, adverb, etc.) expressing intensity, as *really* in *my feet are really cold*. □ **intensive care** med-

ical treatment with constant monitoring, etc., of a dangerously ill patient (also (with hyphen) *attrib.*: *intensive-care unit*). □□ **in•ten′sive•ly** *adv.* **in•ten′sive•ness** *n.*
■ **1** thoroughgoing, concentrated, in-depth; energetic, dynamic, rigorous.

in•tent /intént/ • *n.* intention; purpose. • *adj.* **1** [usu. foll. by *on*] **a** resolved; determined. **b** attentively occupied. **2** (esp. of a look) earnest; eager. □ **to** (or **for**) **all intents and purposes** practically; virtually. □□ **in•tent′ly** *adv.* **in•tent′ness** *n.*
■ *n.* see INTENTION 1. • *adj.* **1 a** bent, set, resolute; keen. **b** rapt, engrossed. **2** sincere, serious; diligent; meaningful. □ **to** (or **for**) **all intents and purposes** for all practical purposes, effectively. □□ **intently** avidly, eagerly, keenly; unflinchingly, doggedly.

in•ten•tion /inténshən/ *n.* **1** thing intended; aim or purpose. **2** intending. □□ **in•ten′ tioned** *adj.* [usu. in *comb.*].
■ **1** intent, motive, design, goal, end. **2** premeditation, contemplation; meaning.

in•ten•tion•al /inténshənəl/ *adj.* done on purpose. □□ **in•ten′tion•al•ly** *adv.*
■ intended, deliberate, willful; calculated, planned. □□ **intentionally** deliberately, on purpose, purposely, willfully, consciously, wittingly.

in•ter /intér/ *v.tr.* (**in•terred, in•ter•ring**) bury (a corpse, etc.).

inter- /intər/ *comb. form* **1** between; among (*intercontinental*). **2** mutually; reciprocally (*interbreed*).

in•ter•act /intərákt/ *v.intr.* act reciprocally; act on each other. □□ **in•ter•ac′tant** *adj. & n.* **in•ter•ac•tion** /intərákshən/ *n.*
■ see COOPERATE. □□ **interaction** see INTERCOURSE 1. '

in•ter•ac•tive /intəráktiv/ *adj.* **1** reciprocally active. **2** (of a computer or other electronic device) allowing a two-way flow of information between it and a user. □□ **in•ter•ac′ tive•ly** *adv.*
■ **1** see MUTUAL 1, 2.

in•ter a•li•a /intər áyleeə, áaleeə/ *adv.* among other things.

in•ter•breed /intərbreed/ *v.* (*past* and *past part.* **–bred** /–bréd/) **1** *intr. & tr.* breed or cause to breed with members of a different race or species to produce a hybrid. **2** *tr.* breed within one family, etc. (cf. CROSSBREED).

in•ter•cede /intərseed/ *v.intr.* intervene on behalf of another; plead. □□ **in•ter•ced′er** *n.*

in•ter•cept /intərsépt/ *v.tr.* **1** seize, catch, or stop (a person or thing) going from one place to another. **2** cut off (light, etc.). □□ **in•ter•cep•tion** /–sépshən/ *n.* **in•ter• cep•tive** /–séptiv/ *adj.* **in•ter•cep′tor** *n.*
■ halt, interrupt, arrest; check, block, bar; snatch, grab; appropriate, commandeer; deflect, reroute. □□ **interception** see *prevention* (PREVENT).

in•ter•ces•sion /intərséshən/ *n.* **1** interceding. **2** instance of this. **3** prayer. □□ **in•ter• ces′sion•al** *adj.* **in•ter•ces′sor** *n.* **in•ter• ces′so•ry** *adj.*

in•ter•change • *v.tr.* /intərcháynj/ **1** (of two people) exchange (things) with each other.

2 put each of (two things) in the other's place; alternate. • *n.* /ɪntərchaynj/ **1** reciprocal exchange between two people, etc. **2** alternation. **3** road junction designed so that traffic streams do not intersect. □□ **in•ter•change′a•ble** *adj.* **in•ter•change′a•bly** *adv.* See synonym study at MUTUAL

■ *v.* **1** see EXCHANGE *v.* **2** see ALTERNATE *v.* 2. • *n.* **1** see EXCHANGE *n.* 1. **3** see JUNCTION 2. □□ **interchangeable** see COORDINATE *adj.*, SYNONYMOUS 1.

in•ter•com /ɪntərkom/ *n. colloq.* system of intercommunication by radio or telephone.

in•ter•con•nect /ɪntərkənékt/ *v.* connect with each other. □□ **in•ter•con•nec•tion** /-nékshən/ *n.*

in•ter•con•ti•nen•tal /ɪntərkóntinént′l/ *adj.* connecting or traveling between continents. □□ **in•ter•con•ti•nen′tal•ly** *adv.*

in•ter•course /ɪntərkawrs/ *n.* **1** communication or dealings between individuals, nations, etc. **2** = *sexual intercourse.*

■ **1** interaction, contact; relations, trade.

in•ter•de•nom•i•na•tion•al /ɪntərdinómináyshənəl/ *adj.* concerning more than one (religious) denomination. □□ **in•ter•de•nom•i•na′tion•al•ly** *adv.*

in•ter•de•part•men•tal /ɪntərdeepaartméntʹl/ *adj.* concerning more than one department. □□ **in•ter•de•part′men•tal•ly** *adv.*

in•ter•de•pend /ɪntərdipénd/ *v.intr.* depend on each other. □□ **in•ter•de•pend′ence** *n.* **in•ter•de•pend′en•cy** *n.* **in•ter•de•pend′ent** *adj.*

in•ter•dict • *n.* /ɪntərdikt/ formal or authoritative prohibition. • *v.tr.* /ɪntərdíkt/ **1** prohibit (an action). **2** forbid the use of. **3** restrain (a person). **4** [usu. foll. by *to*] forbid (a thing) to a person. See synonym study at PROHIBIT □□ **in•ter•dic•tion** /-díkshən/ *n.* **in•ter•dic′to•ry** /-díktəree/ *adj.*

■ *n.* see PROHIBITION. • *v.* **1** see PROHIBIT 1. **4** see FORBID 2. □□ **interdiction** see PROHIBITION.

in•ter•dis•ci•pli•nar•y /ɪntərdísiplinéree/ *adj.* of or between more than one branch of learning.

in•ter•est /ɪntərist, -trist/ • *n.* **1 a** curiosity; concern. **b** quality exciting curiosity, etc. **c** noteworthiness; importance (*findings of no particular interest*). **2** subject, hobby, etc., in which one is concerned. **3** advantage or profit. **4** money paid for the use of money lent. **5 a** financial stake (in an undertaking, etc.). **b** legal concern, title, or right (in property). **6** party or group having a common interest. **7** self-interest. • *v.tr.* **1** excite the curiosity or attention of. **2** cause (a person) to take a personal interest. **3** (as **interested** *adj.*) not impartial or disinterested (*an interested party*). □□ **in′ter•est•ed•ly** *adv.*

■ *n.* **1 a** inquisitiveness, fascination, attention. **b** appeal, excitement, attraction. **c** significance, weight, note. **2** pastime, recreation, diversion, avocation. **3** gain, benefit, good, use. **4** charge, fee; percentage, rate. **5 a** participation, involvement, investment. **b** entitlement, claim, stake. **6** industry, business, field. **7** egoism, egotism, selfishness. • *v.* **1** engage, absorb, engross, fascinate. **2** in-

fluence, induce, persuade. **3** (**interested**) concerned, involved, partial, biased.

in•ter•est•ing /ɪntristing, -təresting/ *adj.* causing curiosity; holding the attention. □□ **in′ter•est•ing•ly** *adv.*

■ fascinating, intriguing; provocative, stimulating; absorbing.

in•ter•face /ɪntərfays/ • *n.* **1** esp. *Physics* surface forming a boundary between two regions. **2** point where interaction occurs between two systems, etc. (*interface between psychology and education*). **3** *Computing* apparatus for connecting two pieces of equipment so that they can be operated jointly. **b** means by which a user interacts with a program or utilizes an application. • *v.* connect with.

in•ter•fere /ɪntərfeer/ *v.intr.* **1** [usu. foll. by *with*] **a** (of a person) meddle; obstruct a process, etc. **b** (of a thing) be a hindrance. **2** intervene, esp. without invitation or necessity. **3** [foll. by *with*] *euphem.* molest or assault sexually. □□ **in•ter•fer′er** *n.* **in•ter•fer′ing** *adj.* **in•ter•fer′ing•ly** *adv.*

■ **1** (*interfere with*) hinder, get in the way of, impede, hamper. **2** intrude, interrupt, barge in; pry, meddle. **3** (*interfere with*) see MOLEST 2. □□ **interfering** see INTRUSIVE.

in•ter•fer•ence /ɪntərfeerəns/ *n.* **1** [usu. foll. by *with*] **a** act of interfering. **b** instance of this. **2** fading or disturbance of received radio signals.

■ **1** hindrance, obstruction; interruption; meddlesomeness. **2** static, noise, atmospherics.

in•ter•fer•on /ɪntərfeeron/ *n. Biochem.* any of various proteins that can inhibit the development of a virus in a cell, etc.

in•ter•fuse /ɪntərfyooz/ *v.* **1** *tr.* **a** mix (a thing) with; intersperse. **b** blend (things). **2** *intr.* (of two things) blend with each other. □□ **in•ter•fu•sion** /-fyoozhən/ *n.*

in•ter•im /ɪntərim/ • *n.* intervening time. • *adj.* provisional; temporary.

■ *n.* meanwhile, meantime, interval. • *adj.* see PROVISIONAL *adj.*

in•ter•i•or /ɪnteereeər/ • *adj.* **1** inner (opp. EXTERIOR). **2** inland. **3** internal; domestic (opp. FOREIGN). **4** situated further in or within. **5** inward. **6** coming from inside. • *n.* **1** interior part; inside. **2** interior part of a country or region. **3** domestic affairs of a country. **4** inner nature; the soul. □□ **in•te′ri•or•ize** *v.tr.* **in•te′ri•or•ly** *adv.*

■ *adj.* **1** inside, internal, inward. **2** upcountry, high, midland. **3** national, civil, home. **4** inner, inside. **5** inner, innermost; mental; secret. • *n.* **1** center, heart, core, depths. **2** center; inland, heartland. **3** internal affairs. **4** see SOUL 1, 2.

interj. *abbr.* interjection.

in•ter•ject /ɪntərjékt/ *v.tr.* **1** utter (words) abruptly or parenthetically. **2** interrupt with. See synonym study at INSERT. □□ **in•ter•jec′to•ry** /-jéktəree/ *adj.*

in•ter•jec•tion /ɪntərjékshən/ *n. Gram.* exclamation, esp. as a part of speech (e.g., *ah!*, *dear me!*). □□ **in•ter•jec′tion•al** *adj.*

■ ejaculation, cry, utterance; interruption.

in•ter•lace /íntərláys/ v. **1** tr. bind intricately together. **2** intr. cross each other intricately. □□ **in•ter•lace′ment** n.

■ **1** see WEAVE[1] v.

in•ter•lard /íntərláard/ v.tr. mix (writing or speech) with unusual words or phrases.

in•ter•leave /íntərléev/ v.tr. insert (usu. blank) leaves between the leaves of (a book, etc.).

in•ter•lin•ing /íntərlíning/ n. material used between the fabric (of a garment) and its lining.

in•ter•lock /íntərlók/ v. **1** intr. engage with each other by overlapping. **2** tr. lock or clasp within each other. □□ **in•ter•lock′er** n.

in•ter•loc•u•tor /íntərlókyətər/ n. person who takes part in a conversation. □□ **in•ter•lo•cu′tion** /-ləkyŏŏshən/ n.

in•ter•loc•u•to•ry /íntərlókyətawree/ adj. **1** of dialogue. **2** Law (of a decree, etc.) given provisionally.

in•ter•lop•er /íntərlópər/ n. **1** intruder. **2** person who interferes in others' affairs, esp. for profit. □□ **in′ter•lope** v.intr.

■ **1** see INTRUDER. ■ **interlope** see MEDDLE.

in•ter•lude /íntərlŏŏd/ n. **1 a** pause between the acts of a play. **b** something performed during this pause. **2** intervening time, space, or event that contrasts with what goes before or after.

■ interval, intermission, pause; breathing space, rest, spell.

in•ter•mar•ry /íntərmáree/ v.intr. (–ries, –ried) (of races, castes, families, etc.) become connected by marriage. □□ **in•ter•mar′riage** /íntərmárij/ n.

in•ter•me•di•ar•y /íntərmeédee-eree/ • n. (pl. –ies) intermediate person or thing, esp. a mediator. • adj. acting as mediator; intermediate.

■ n. go-between, middleman; peacemaker, arbitrator. • adj. mediatory; see also INTERMEDIATE adj.

in•ter•me•di•ate • adj. /íntərmeédeeət/ coming between two things in time, place, order, character, etc. • n. /íntərmeédeeət/ intermediate thing. • v.intr. /íntərmeédeeáyt/ act as intermediary. □□ **in•ter•me′di•a•cy** n. **in•ter•me′di•ate•ly** adv. **in•ter•me•di•a•tion** /-deeáyshən/ n. **in•ter•me•di•a•tor** /-deeáytər/ n.

■ adj. middle, medial, midway, halfway, transitional. • n. compromise, middle course. • v. mediate, arbitrate.

in•ter•ment /íntórmənt/ n. burial of a corpse.

■ see BURIAL 1.

in•ter•mez•zo /íntərmétsó/ n. (pl. **in•ter•mez•zi** /-see/ or **–zos**) **1** short instrumental movement in a musical work. **2** short, light dramatic or other performance inserted between the acts of a play.

in•ter•mi•na•ble /íntórminəbəl/ adj. **1** endless. **2** tediously long. □□ **in•ter′mi•na•bly** adv.

■ **1** see ENDLESS 2. **2** see LENGTHY 2. □□ **interminably** see NONSTOP adv.

in•ter•min•gle /íntərmínggəl/ v. [often foll. by with] mix together; mingle.

■ see MIX v. 1, 3, 4a.

in•ter•mis•sion /íntərmíshən/ n. **1** pause or cessation. **2** interval between parts of a play, concert, etc.

■ **1** stop, halt, break, hiatus; rest. **2** interlude, entr'acte.

in•ter•mit•tent /íntərmít′nt/ adj. occurring at intervals. □□ **in•ter•mit′tence** /-mít′ns/ n. **in•ter•mit′ten•cy** n. **in•ter•mit′tent•ly** adv.

■ sporadic, occasional, irregular, random, spasmodic; periodic, cyclic(al), rhythmic(al), seasonal.

in•tern • n. /íntərn/ recent graduate or advanced medical student living in a hospital and acting as an assistant physician or surgeon. • v. **1** tr. /intérn/ confine; oblige (a prisoner, alien, etc.) to reside within prescribed limits. **2** intr. /íntərn/ serve as an intern. □□ **in•tern′ment** n. **in′tern•ship** n.

■ v. **1** see IMPRISON. □□ **internment** see captivity (CAPTIVE).

in•ter•nal /intórnəl/ • adj. **1** of or situated in the inside. **2** of the inside of the body (internal injuries). **3** of a nation's domestic affairs. **4** used or applying within an organization. **5 a** intrinsic. **b** of the mind or soul. • n. [in pl.] intrinsic qualities. □ **internal combustion engine** engine powered by the explosion of gases or vapor with air in a cylinder. □□ **in•ter•nal′i•ty** /-nálitee/ n. **in•ter′nal•ize** v.tr. **in•ter•nal•i•za′tion** n. **in•ter′nal•ly** adv.

■ adj. **1, 2** interior, inner; unseen, invisible. **3** interior, national, civil. **4** in-house, intramural. **5** see INTRINSIC.

in•ter•na•tion•al /íntərnáshənəl/ adj. **1** existing, involving, or carried on between or among nations. **2** agreed on or used by all or many nations (international date line). □□ **in•ter•na•tion•al′i•ty** /-nálitee/ n. **in•ter•na′tion•al•ize** v.tr. **in•ter•na′tion•al•ly** adv.

■ worldwide, intercontinental, multinational; supranational; foreign.

in•ter•na•tion•al•ism /íntərnáshənəlizəm/ n. the advocacy of a community of interests among nations. □□ **in•ter•na′tion•al•ist** n.

in•ter•ne•cine /íntərneéseen, -néseen/ adj. mutually destructive.

In•ter•net /íntərnét/ n. communications network enabling the linking of computers worldwide for data interchange.

in•tern•ist /intórnist/ n. Med. specialist in internal medicine.

in•ter•per•son•al /íntərpórsənəl/ adj. (of relations) occurring between persons, esp. reciprocally. □□ **in•ter•per′son•al•ly** adv.

in•ter•plan•e•tar•y /íntərplániteree/ adj. between planets.

in•ter•play /íntərplay/ n. reciprocal action.

In•ter•pol /íntərpól/ n. International Criminal Police Organization.

in•ter•po•late /intórpəlayt/ v.tr. **1 a** insert (words) in a book. **b** make such insertions in (a book, etc.). **2** estimate (values) from known ones in the same range. See synonym study at INSERT. □□ **in•ter•po•la′tion** /-láyshən/ *n.* in•ter′po•la•tive *adj.* in•ter′po•la•tor *n.*

■ 1 see INSERT *v.* □□ **interpolation** see IN-SERT *n.,* INTERJECTION.

in•ter•pose /íntərpōz/ *v.* **1** *tr.* place or insert (a thing) between others. **2** *tr.* say (words) as an interruption. **3** *tr.* exercise or advance (a veto or objection) so as to interfere. **4** *intr.* intervene (between parties). □□ **in•ter•po•si′tion** *n.*

■ 1 see INSERT *v.* 2 interject, interpolate, put *or* throw in. 4 see INTERFERE 2.

in•ter•pret /intérprit/ *v.* **1** *tr.* explain the meaning of (words, a dream, etc.). **2** *tr.* make out or bring out the meaning of (creative work). **3** *intr.* act as an interpreter. **4** *tr.* explain or understand (behavior, etc.) in a specified manner. See synonym study at CLARIFY. □□ **in•ter′pret•a•ble** *adj.* **in•ter•pret•a•bil′i•ty** *n.* **in•ter•pre•ta′tion** *n.* **in•ter•pre•ta′tion•al** *adj.* **in•ter′pre•ta•tive** /-táytiv/ *adj.* **in•ter′pre•tive** *adj.* **in•ter′pre•tive•ly** *adv.*

■ 1, 2 explicate, clarify; define; paraphrase; decipher. 3 translate. 4 construe, take (to mean), analyze, diagnose. □□ **interpretation** explanation, explication, exegesis, clarification.

in•ter•pret•er /intérpritər/ *n.* person who interprets, esp. one who translates speech orally.

in•ter•ra•cial /intəráyshəl/ *adj.* existing between or affecting different races. □□ **in•ter•ra′cial•ly** *adv.*

in•ter•reg•num /intərégnəm/ *n.* (*pl.* **in•ter•reg•nums** or **in•ter•reg•na** /-nə/) interval, esp. when normal government is suspended between successive reigns or regimes.

in•ter•re•late /intərilàyt/ *v.tr.* relate (two or more things) to each other. □□ **in•ter•re•la′tion** /-láyshən/ *n.* **in•ter•re•la′tion•ship** *n.*

in•ter•ro•gate /intérəgayt/ *v.tr.* ask questions of (a person) esp. closely, thoroughly, or formally. □□ **in•ter•ro•ga′tion** /intèrəgáyshən/ *n.* **in•ter′ro•ga•tor** *n.*

■ see QUESTION *v.* 1 □□ **interrogation** questioning, examination, cross-examination.

in•ter•rog•a•tive /intərógətiv/ *adj.* of, like, or used in questions. □□ **in•ter•rog′a•tive•ly** *adv.*

in•ter•rog•a•to•ry /intərógətawree/ *adj.* of a questioning nature.

in•ter•rupt /intərúpt/ *v.tr.* **1** break the continuous progress of (an action, speech, a person speaking, etc.). **2** break or suspend the continuity of. □□ **in•ter•rupt′er** *n.* **in•ter•rup′tion** /-rúpshən/ *n.* **in•ter•rup′tive** *adj.*

■ 1 intrude into, butt in on; heckle; disturb, disrupt. 2 discontinue, suspend, break off. □□ **interruption** intrusion, disturbance, interference; obstruction, blockage.

in•ter•sect /intərsékt/ *v.* **1** *tr.* divide (a thing) by crossing it. **2** *intr.* (of lines, roads, etc.) cross each other.

■ 1 see CROSS *v.* 1. 2 see CROSS *v.* 2a.

in•ter•sec•tion /intərsékshən/ *n.* **1** act of intersecting. **2** place where two roads intersect. □□ **in•ter•sec′tion•al** *adj.*

■ 1 see MEETING 1. 2 see JUNCTION 2.

in•ter•sperse /intərspérs/ *v.tr.* **1** scatter. **2** [foll. by *with*] diversify (a thing or things with others so scattered). □□ **in•ter•sper′sion** /-pérzhən/ *n.*

in•ter•state • *adj.* /íntərstáyt/ existing or carried on between states, esp. of the US. • *n.* /íntərstayt/ highway that is part of the US Interstate Highway System.

in•ter•stel•lar /intərstélər/ *adj.* between stars.

in•ter•stice /intérstis/ *n.* **1** intervening space. **2** chink or crevice. □□ **in•ter•sti′tial** /intərstíshəl/ *adj.*

in•ter•twine /intərtwín/ *v.* **1** *tr.* [often foll. by *with*] entwine (together). **2** *intr.* become entwined.

■ see ENTWINE 1, 2.

in•ter•val /íntərvəl/ *n.* **1** intervening time or space. **2** difference in pitch between two sounds. □ **at intervals** here and there; now and then. □□ **in•ter•val•lic** /-válik/ *adj.*

■ 1 meanwhile, meantime, interim; gap, blank; lacuna, hiatus. □ **at intervals** (all) around; (every) now and again, periodically.

in•ter•vene /intərvéen/ *v.intr.* **1** occur in time between events. **2** interfere; prevent or modify events. **3** be situated between things. □□ **in•ter•ven′er** *n.* **in•ter•ve′nor** *n.*

■ 2 meddle, intrude; interrupt; intercede, mediate.

in•ter•ven•tion /intərvénshən/ *n.* **1** intervening. **2** interference, esp. by a state in another's affairs. **3** mediation.

■ 1, 2 see INTERFERENCE 1. 3 see AGENCY 2b.

in•ter•view /íntərvyōō/ • *n.* **1** usu. in-person examination of an applicant. **2** conversation between a reporter, etc., and a person of public interest, used as a basis of a broadcast or publication. **3** meeting face to face, esp. for consultation. • *v.tr.* hold an interview with. □□ **in•ter•view•ee** /-vyōō-ée/ *n.* **in′ter•view•er** *n.*

■ *n.* **1** evaluation, appraisal, assessment. **2** discussion, talk; press conference. **3** conference, discussion. • *v.* examine, appraise, evaluate, assess. □□ **interviewee** see CANDIDATE.

in•ter•weave /intərwéev/ *v.tr.* (*past* **–wove** /-wōv/; *past part.* **–wo•ven** /-wōvən/) **1** [often foll. by *with*] weave together. **2** blend intimately.

in•tes•tate /intéstayt/ • *adj.* not having made a will before death. • *n.* person who has died intestate. □□ **in•tes′ta•cy** *n.*

in•tes•tine /intéstin/ *n.* [in *sing.* or *pl.*] lower part of the alimentary canal. □□ **in•tes′tin•al** *adj.*

■ see BOWEL 1.

in•ti•mate¹ /íntimət/ • *adj.* **1** closely acquainted; familiar. **2** private and personal. **3** having sexual relations. **4** (of knowledge) detailed; thorough. • *n.* very close friend. □□ **in′ti•mate•ly** *adv.*

□□ *adj.* **1** close, attached, inseparable, devoted, friendly. **2** interior, secret, confidential. **4** deep, profound, extensive, comprehensive. • *n.* (best) friend, (boon) companion, confidant, crony.

in•ti•mate² /íntimayt/ *v.tr.* **1** state or make

known. **2** imply; hint. □□ **in·ti·mat·er** *n.* **in·ti·ma·tion** /–máyshən/ *n.*

■ **1** announce, say, assert; maintain, claim. **2** suggest, insinuate; indicate. □□ **intimation** see HINT *n.* 1.

in·tim·i·date /intímidayt/ *v.tr.* frighten or overawe, esp. to subdue or influence. □□ **in·tim·i·da·tion** /–dáyshən/ *n.* **in·tí′mi·da·tor** *n.*

■ terrify, petrify, scare, unnerve; daunt, tyrannize. □□ **intimidation** see TERROR 1, THREAT 1.

in·to /intoo/ *prep.* **1** expressing motion or direction to a point on or within (*ran into the house*). **2** expressing direction of attention. **3** expressing a change of state (*separated into groups*). **4** *colloq.* interested in; knowledgeable about (*is really into art*).

in·tol·er·a·ble /intólərəbəl/ *adj.* that cannot be endured. □□ **in·tol′er·a·bly** *adv.*

■ see UNBEARABLE.

in·tol·er·ant /intólərənt/ *adj.* not tolerant, esp. of views, beliefs, or behavior differing from one's own. □□ **in·tol′er·ance** *n.* **in·tol′er·ant·ly** *adv.*

■ impatient, unforgiving, uncompromising, inflexible; biased, prejudiced, bigoted. □□ **intolerance** impatience; narrowmindedness; bias, prejudice, bigotry.

in·to·na·tion /intənáyshən/ *n.* **1** modulation of the voice; accent. **2** intoning. **3** accuracy of musical pitch. □□ **in·to·na′tion·al** *adj.*

■ **1** accentuation, (tonal) inflection, cadence. **2** chanting; articulation, pronunciation. **3** (perfect *or* absolute) pitch.

in·tone /intón/ *v.tr.* **1** recite (prayers, etc.) with prolonged sounds, esp. in a monotone. **2** utter with a particular tone. □□ **in·ton′er** *n.*

in to·to /in tótó/ *adv.* completely.

in·tox·i·cant /intóksikənt/ • *adj.* intoxicating. • *n.* intoxicating substance.

■ *n.* see LIQUOR *n.* 1.

in·tox·i·cate /intóksikayt/ *v.tr.* **1** make drunk. **2** excite or elate beyond self-control. □□ **in·tox·i·ca·tion** /–káyshən/ *n.*

■ **1** inebriate, stupefy, befuddle, fluster, mellow. **2** arouse, overwhelm, exhilarate, delight. □□ **intoxication** see *drunkenness* (DRUNKEN).

in·tox·i·cat·ing /intóksikayting/ *adj.* **1** liable to cause intoxication; alcoholic. **2** exhilarating; exciting. □□ **in·tox′i·cat·ing·ly** *adv.*

■ **1** spirituous, inebriant. **2** invigorating, thrilling, heady, stimulating, electrifying, entrancing, fascinating.

intr. *abbr.* intransitive.

intra- /íntrə/ *prefix* forming adjectives usu. from adjectives, meaning 'on the inside, within' (*intramural*).

in·trac·ta·ble /intráktəbəl/ *adj.* **1** hard to control. **2** stubborn. See synonym study at STUBBORN. □□ **in·trac·ta·bil′i·ty** *n.* **in·trac′ta·ble·ness** *n.* **in·trac′ta·bly** *adv.*

■ see STUBBORN. □□ **intractability** see *obstinacy* (OBSTINATE).

in·tra·mu·ral /íntrəmyóórəl/ *adj.* **1** situated or done within walls. **2** forming part of normal university or college studies. □□ **in·tra·mu′ral·ly** *adv.*

in·tra·mus·cu·lar /íntrəmúskyələr/ *adj.* in or into a muscle or muscles.

in·tran·si·gent /intránsijənt, –tránz–/ • *adj.* uncompromising; stubborn. • *n.* intransigent person. □□ **in·tran′si·gence** *n.* **in·tran′si·gen·cy** *n.* **in·tran′si·gent·ly** *adv.*

■ *adj.* see STUBBORN. □□ **intransigence** see *obstinacy* (OBSTINATE).

in·tran·si·tive /intránsitiv, –tránz–/ *adj.* *Gram.* (of a verb or sense of a verb) that does not take a direct object (whether expressed or implied), e.g., *look* in *look at the sky* (opp. TRANSITIVE). □□ **in·tran′si·tive·ly** *adv.* **in·tran·si·tiv′i·ty** /–tívitee/ *n.*

in·tra·u·ter·ine /íntrəyóótərin, –rīn/ *adj.* within the uterus. □ **intrauterine device** device inserted into the uterus that provides birth control by preventing implantation. ¶Abbr.: **IUD.**

in·tra·ve·nous /íntrəveenəs/ *adj.* in or into a vein or veins. □□ **in·tra·ve′nous·ly** *adv.*

in·trep·id /intrépid/ *adj.* fearless; very brave. See synonym study at BOLD. □□ **in·tre·pid·i·ty** /–trəpíditee/ *n.* **in·trep′id·ly** *adv.*

■ unafraid, undaunted; courageous, valiant; bold, daring, audacious.

in·tri·cate /intrikit/ *adj.* very complicated; perplexingly detailed or obscure. □□ **in′tri·ca·cy** /–kəsee/ *n.* (*pl.* **–cies**). **in′tri·cate·ly** *adv.*

■ complex, involved, convoluted; elaborate, Byzantine; puzzling. □□ **intricacy** see *subtlety* (SUBTLE).

in·trigue • *v.* /intreeg/ (**in·trigues, in·trigued, in·trigu·ing**) **1** *intr.* **a** carry on an underhand plot. **b** use secret influence. **2** *tr.* arouse the curiosity of. • *n.* /intreeg, in–/ **1** underhand plot or plotting. **2** secret arrangement. See synonym study at PLOT. □□ **in·tri′guer** *n.* **in·tri′guing** *adj.* (esp. in sense 2 of *v.*). **in·tri′guing·ly** *adv.*

■ *v.* **1** conspire, plot, machinate, scheme. **2** interest, engross; fascinate, beguile. • *n.* **1** conspiracy, scheme, machination. □□ **intriguing** see INTERESTING.

in·trin·sic /intrínzik/ *adj.* inherent; essential; belonging naturally (*intrinsic value*). See synonym study at INHERENT. □□ **in·trin′si·cal·ly** *adv.*

■ implicit, basic, fundamental, elemental.

intro- /íntró/ *comb. form* into (*introgression*).

intro. *abbr.* **1** introduction. **2** introductory.

in·tro·duce /íntrədóós, –dyóós/ *v.tr.* **1** [foll. by *to*] make (a person or oneself) known by name to another, esp. formally. **2** announce or present. **3** bring (a custom, idea, etc.) into use. **4** bring (legislation) for consideration. **5** [foll. by *to*] initiate (a person) to a subject. **6** insert. **7** bring in; usher in; bring forward. See synonym study at INSERT. □□ **in·tro·duc′er** *n.* **in·tro·duc′i·ble** *adj.*

■ **1** (*introduce to*) acquaint with, present to, make known to. **2** give, offer. **3** inaugurate, initiate, instigate; establish. **4** put forward, propose, move. **5** (*introduce to*) acquaint with, familiarize with. **6** see INSERT *v.* **7** bring forward *or* up, advance, present, raise.

in·tro·duc·tion /ìntrədúkshən/ n. 1 introducing or being introduced. 2 formal presentation of one person to another. 3 explanatory section at the beginning of a book, etc.
■ 1 see INSTITUTION 1. 2 knockdown. 3 see PREAMBLE.

in·tro·duc·to·ry /ìntrədúktəree/ adj. serving as an introduction; preliminary.
■ opening, initial, inaugural; prefatory; first, primary.

in·tro·spec·tion /ìntrəspékshən/ n. examination or observation of one's own mental and emotional processes, etc. □□ **in·tro·spec'tive** adj. **in·tro·spec'tive·ly** adv. **in·tro·spec'tive·ness** n.

in·tro·vert • n. /íntrəvərt/ 1 Psychol. person predominantly concerned with his or her own thoughts. 2 shy, thoughtful person. • adj. /íntrəvərt/ (also **in·tro·vert'ed** /-tid/) typical or characteristic of an introvert. • v.tr. /ìntrəvərt/ Psychol. direct (one's thoughts or mind) inward. □□ **in·tro·ver·sion** /-várzhən, -shən/ n. **in·tro·ver·sive** /-vársiv/ adj. **in'tro·vert·ed** adj. **in·tro·ver·tive** /-vártiv/ adj.
■ adj. (introverted) see SHY adj. 1a.

in·trude /intró͞od/ v. [foll. by on, upon, into] 1 intr. come uninvited or unwanted; force oneself abruptly on others. 2 tr. thrust or force (something unwelcome) on a person. □□ **in·trud'ing·ly** adv. **in·tru·sion** /-trō͞ozhən/ n.
■ 1 encroach, impinge, obtrude, trespass; interfere, meddle; intervene; (intrude on or into) break in on, interrupt. 2 see THRUST v. 2.

in·trud·er /intró͞odər/ n. person who intrudes, esp. into a building with criminal intent.
■ housebreaker, (cat) burglar, thief, robber; trespasser; gatecrasher; interferer, meddler, busybody.

in·tru·sive /intró͞osiv/ adj. 1 that intrudes or tends to intrude. 2 characterized by intrusion. See synonym study at IMPERTINENT. □□ **in·tru'sive·ly** adv. **in·tru'sive·ness** n.
■ interfering, interruptive, obtrusive, invasive; meddlesome, prying, inquisitive, colloq. nosy, snoopy; importunate, forward, presumptuous, colloq. pushy.

in·trust var. of ENTRUST.

in·tu·bate /íntə͞obayt, -tyō͞o-/ v.tr. Med. insert a tube into the trachea for ventilation, usu. during anesthesia. □□ **in·tu·ba·tion** /-báyshən/ n.

in·tu·i·tion /ìntō͞o-íshən, -tyō͞o-/ n. immediate insight or understanding without conscious reasoning. □□ **in·tu·i'tion·al** adj.
■ instinct, inspiration, sixth sense; presentiment, premonition, foreboding.

in·tu·i·tive /intó͞o-itiv, -tyō͞o-/ adj. of, characterized by, possessing, or perceived by intuition. □□ **in·tu'i·tive·ly** adv. **in·tu'i·tive·ness** n.

In·u·it /íny͞o-it/ n. (also **In'nu·it**) (pl. same or **In·u·its**) N. American Eskimo.

in·un·date /ínəndayt/ v.tr. 1 flood. 2 overwhelm. □□ **in·un·da·tion** /-dáyshən/ n.
■ 1 see FLOOD v. 2. 2 see GLUT v. 2. □□ **inundation** see FLOOD n. 1.

in·ure /inyó͞or/ v.tr. accustom (a person) to something esp. unpleasant. □□ **in·ure'ment** n.

in u·ter·o /in y͞otərō/ adv. in the womb; before birth.

in va·cu·o /in vákyō͞o-ō/ adv. in a vacuum.

in·vade /inváyd/ v.tr. 1 enter (a country, etc.) with hostility. 2 swarm into. 3 (of a disease) attack. 4 encroach upon. □□ **in·vad'er** n.
■ 1 see OCCUPY 4. 2 see INFEST. 3 see ATTACK v. 4. 4 see ENCROACH 1. □□ **invader** see INTRUDER.

in·val·id¹ /ínvəlid/ • n. 1 person enfeebled or disabled by illness or injury. 2 [attrib.] **a** of or for invalids. **b** being an invalid (caring for her invalid mother). • v. 1 tr. disable (a person) by illness. 2 intr. become an invalid. □□ **in'va·lid·ism** n.
■ n. 1 valetudinarian, convalescent, patient. 2 a disabled. **b** disabled, handicapped, incapacitated, lame; see also ILL adj. 1. • v. 1 incapacitate, indispose, immobilize. 2 take to one's bed, become housebound.

in·val·id² /inválid/ adj. not valid. □□ **in·val'id·ly** adv.
■ (null and) void, worthless, lapsed; false; illegitimate, illegal; untrue.

in·val·i·date /inválidayt/ v.tr. 1 make (esp. an argument, etc.) invalid. 2 remove the validity or force of (a treaty, contract, etc.). □□ **in·val·i·da·tion** /-dáyshən/ n.
■ 1 see DISPROVE. 2 see REVOKE v. □□ **invalidation** see REPEAL n.

in·val·u·a·ble /invályō͞oəbəl/ adj. above valuation; inestimable. □□ **in·val'u·a·bly** adv.
■ priceless, precious; irreplaceable, unique.

in·va·sion /ináyzhən/ n. invading or being invaded. □□ **in·va·sive** /-váysiv/ adj.
■ occupation, incursion, intrusion, infiltration, encroachment, infringement, transgression, violation. □□ **invasive** see INTRUSIVE.

in·vec·tive /invéktiv/ n. 1 **a** strongly attacking words. **b** use of such words. 2 abusive rhetoric.
■ see ABUSE n. 2.

in·veigh /inváy/ v.intr. [foll. by against] speak or write with strong hostility.

in·vei·gle /inváygəl, -vée-/ v.tr. entice; persuade by guile. □□ **in·vei'gle·ment** n.
■ see ENTICE. □□ **inveiglement** see cajolery (CAJOLE).

in·vent /invént/ v.tr. 1 create by thought; originate (a new method, instrument, etc.). 2 concoct (a false story, etc.). □□ **in·vent'a·ble** adj. **in·ven'tor** n.
■ 1 devise, contrive, think up, dream up, hatch; coin, mint; strike, hit upon. 2 fabricate, make up. □□ **inventor** see CREATOR 1.

in·ven·tion /invénshən/ n. 1 process of inventing. 2 thing invented. 3 fictitious story. 4 inventiveness.
■ 1 creation, conception, contrivance, concoction. 2 creation, design, discovery. 3 fiction, fabrication, fib. 4 originality, creativeness, ingenuity; cleverness.

in·ven·tive /invéntiv/ adj. 1 able to invent; original in devising. 2 showing ingenuity of devising. See synonym study at CREATIVE.

□□ in•ven'tive•ly *adv.* in•ven'tive•ness *n.*

■ see ORIGINAL 2. □□ **inventiveness** see *originality* (ORIGINAL), INVENTION 4.

in•ven•to•ry /ínvəntáwree/ • *n.* (*pl.* –ries) 1 complete list of goods, etc. 2 goods listed in this. 3 the total of a firm's commercial assets. • *v.tr.* (–ries, –ried) 1 make an inventory of. 2 enter (goods) in an inventory.

■ *n.* 1 see LIST[1] *n.*

in•verse /ínvərs, –və́rs/ • *adj.* inverted in position, order, or relation. • *n.* 1 state of being inverted. 2 thing that is the opposite or reverse of another. □ **inverse proportion** (or **ratio**) relation between two quantities such that one increases in proportion as the other decreases. □□ in•verse'ly *adv.*

■ *adj.* see REVERSE *adj.*

in•ver•sion /ínvə́rzhən, –shən/ *n.* 1 turning upside down or inside out. 2 reversal of a normal order, position, or relation. □□ in•ver'sive /-və́rsiv/ *adj.*

in•vert /ínvə́rt/ *v.tr.* 1 turn upside down. 2 reverse the position, order, or relation of. □□ in•vert'er *n.* in•vert'i•ble *adj.* in•vert•i•bil'i•ty *n.*

■ see REVERSE *v.* 1.

in•ver•te•brate /ínvə́rtibrət, –brayt/ • *adj.* 1 (of an animal) not having a backbone. 2 lacking firmness of character. • *n.* invertebrate animal.

■ *adj.* 1 spineless. 2 see SPINELESS 2.

in•vest /ínvést/ *v.* 1 *tr.* apply or use (money), esp. for profit. 2 *intr.* [foll. by *in*] **a** put money for profit (into stocks, etc.). **b** *colloq.* buy. 3 *tr.* **a** provide or endue (a person) with qualities, insignia, or rank. **b** attribute or entrust (qualities or feelings to a person). □□ in•vest'a•ble *adj.* in•vest'i•ble *adj.* in•ves'tor *n.*

■ 1 allot, contribute; venture, risk. 2 **a** speculate; (*invest in*) buy into, back, finance. **b** (*invest in*) purchase. 3 **a** endow, furnish, supply; install, inaugurate. **b** assign, trust. □□ **investor** see *backer* (BACK).

in•ves•ti•gate /ínvéstigayt/ *v.* 1 *tr.* **a** inquire into; examine. **b** make an official inquiry into. 2 *intr.* make a systematic inquiry or search. □□ in•ves•ti•ga•tion /ínvéstigáyshən/ *n.* in•ves'ti•ga•tive *adj.* in•ves'ti•ga•tor *n.* in•ves•ti•ga•to•ry /-gətáwree/ *adj.*

■ make inquiries into, check (up) on, probe, delve into, explore. □□ **investigation** inquiry, check, probe.

in•ves•ti•ture /ínvéstichŏŏr, –chər/ *n.* formal investing of a person with honors or rank.

in•vest•ment /ínvéstmənt/ *n.* 1 investing. 2 money invested. 3 property, etc., in which money is invested.

■ 2 see STAKE[2] *n.* 2. 3 see STOCK *n.* 5.

in•vet•er•ate /ínvétərət/ *adj.* 1 (of a person) confirmed in a habit, etc. 2 **a** (of a habit, etc.) long-established. **b** (of an activity, esp. an undesirable one) habitual. □□ in•vet'er•a•cy /-rəsee/ *n.* in•vet'er•ate•ly *adv.*

■ 1 see INCORRIGIBLE 2. 2 **b** see INGRAINED 1. □□ **inveterately** see *usually* (USUAL).

in•vid•i•ous /invídeeəs/ *adj.* likely to excite

resentment or indignation. □□ in•vid'i•ous•ly *adv.* in•vid'i•ous•ness *n.*

in•vig•o•rate /invígərayt/ *v.tr.* give vigor or strength to. See synonym study at QUICKEN. □□ in•vig'or•at•ing *adj.* in•vig•or•a•tion /-ráyshən/ *n.* in•vig'or•a•tive *adj.* in•vig'or•a•tor *n.*

■ fortify, strengthen, reinforce; exhilarate, refresh. □□ **invigorating** bracing, stimulating, exhilarating. **invigoration** see REFRESHMENT 1.

in•vin•ci•ble /invínsibəl/ *adj.* unconquerable. □□ in•vin•ci•bil'i•ty *n.* in•vin'ci•ble•ness *n.* in•vin'ci•bly *adv.*

■ unbeatable, indomitable; invulnerable, indestructible.

in•vi•o•la•ble /invíələbəl/ *adj.* not to be violated or profaned. □□ in•vi•o•la•bil'i•ty *n.* in•vi'o•la•bly *adv.*

in•vi•o•late /invíələt/ *adj.* not violated or profaned. □□ in•vi'o•late•ly *adv.*

■ see SACRED 2b.

in•vis•i•ble /invízibəl/ *adj.* 1 not visible to the eye. 2 artfully concealed so as to be imperceptible. □□ in•vis•i•bil'i•ty *n.* in•vis'i•bly *adv.*

■ 1 unseeable, imperceptible, undetectable; microscopic, infinitesimal, minuscule. 2 veiled, covert, secret, masked; camouflaged; faint.

in•vi•ta•tion /invitáyshən/ *n.* 1 **a** inviting or being invited. **b** spoken or written form in which a person is invited. 2 enticing.

■ 1 summons, request, call. 2 inducement, allure, enticement.

in•vite • *v.* /invít/ 1 *tr.* ask (a person) courteously to come or to do something. 2 *tr.* make a formal courteous request for. 3 *tr.* tend to call forth unintentionally (something unwanted). 4 **a** *tr.* attract. **b** *intr.* be attractive. • *n.* /ínvit/ *colloq.* (**introverted**) invitation. □□ in•vit'er *n.*

■ *v.* 1 ask, summon, *archaic or literary* bid. 3 see INCUR. 4 see TEMPT 2. • *n.* see INVITATION 1.

in•vit•ing /invíting/ *adj.* 1 attractive. 2 enticing; tempting. □□ in•vit'ing•ly *adv.*

■ appealing, winsome, captivating, fascinating; alluring.

in vi•tro /in véetrō/ *adv. Biol.* taking place in a test tube or other laboratory environment.

in•vo•ca•tion /invəkáyshən/ *n.* 1 invoking, esp. in prayer. 2 summoning a source of inspiration, e.g., the Muses. 3 *Eccl.* the words "In the name of the Father," etc., used as the preface to a sermon, etc. □□ in•vo•ca•to•ry /invókətáwree/ *adj.*

■ intercession, petition, prayer, supplication, entreaty.

in•voice /ínvoys/ • *n.* itemized bill for goods or services. • *v.tr.* 1 make an invoice of (goods and services). 2 send an invoice to (a person).

■ *n.* see BILL[1] *n.* 1. • *v.* bill, charge, debit.

in•voke /invók/ *v.tr.* 1 call on (a deity, etc.) in prayer or as a witness. 2 appeal to (the law, a person's authority, etc.). 3 summon (a spirit) by charms. 4 ask earnestly for (vengeance, help, etc.). □□ in•vo'ca•ble *adj.* in•vok'er *n.*

■ 1, 2, 4 see APPEAL v. 1.

in•vol•un•tar•y /invólantéree/ adj. 1 done without the exercise of the will; unintentional. 2 (of a limb, muscle, or movement) not under conscious control. □□ in•vol•un•tar•i•ly adv.

■ unconscious, unthinking, unpremeditated; impulsive, instinctive.

in•vo•lu•tion /invòlōoshan/ n. 1 process of involving. 2 entanglement. 3 intricacy. 4 curling inward. □□ in•vo•lu•tion•al adj.

in•volve /invólv/ v.tr. 1 cause (a person or thing) to participate, or share the experience or effect (in a situation, activity, etc.). 2 imply; entail; make necessary. 3 implicate (a person in a charge, crime, etc.). 4 include or affect in its operations. 5 (as involved adj.) a [often foll. by in] concerned or interested. b complicated in thought or form. □□ in•volve'ment n.

■ 1 include, engage, engross, occupy. 2 necessitate, require, presuppose. 3 incriminate, inculpate; connect. 4 concern, touch; comprise; number among. 5 (involved) a included, implicated, affected; engaged, absorbed. b complex, intricate. □□ involvement see TIE n. 3.

in•vul•ner•a•ble /invúlnərəbəl/ adj. that cannot be wounded or hurt, physically or mentally. □□ in•vul•ner•a•bil•i•ty n. in•vul'ner•a•bly adv.

■ see INVINCIBLE. □□ invulnerability see IMMUNITY 2.

in•ward /inward/ • adj. 1 directed toward the inside; going in. 2 situated within. 3 mental; spiritual. • adv. (also in'wards) 1 toward the inside. 2 in the mind or soul.

■ adj. 1, 2 interior, inside, internal, inner.

in•ward•ly /inwardlee/ adv. 1 on the inside. 2 in the mind or soul. 3 (of speaking) not aloud; inaudibly.

I/O abbr. Computing input/output.

i•o•dide /íadid/ n. Chem. any compound of iodine with another element or group.

i•o•dine /íadin, –din, –deen/ n. 1 Chem. element forming black crystals and a violet vapor when heated. ¶Symb.: I. 2 solution of this as a mild antiseptic.

i•on /ían, íon/ n. atom or group of atoms that has lost one or more electrons (= CATION), or gained one or more electrons (= ANION). □□ i•on•ic /íónik/ adj.

-ion suffix (usu. as –sion, –tion, –xion); see -ATION, -ITION, -UTION forming nouns denoting: 1 verbal action (excision). 2 instance of this (suggestion). 3 resulting state or product (vexation, concoction).

I•on•ic /íónik/ adj. of the order of Greek architecture characterized by a column with scroll shapes on either side of the capital.

i•on•ize /íaniz/ v. convert or be converted into an ion or ions. □□ i•on•iz'a•ble adj. i•on•i•za'tion n. i'on•iz•er n.

i•on•o•sphere /íónəsfeer/ n. ionized region of the atmosphere above the stratosphere, reflecting radio waves (cf. TROPOSPHERE). □□ i•on•o•spher•ic /–sfeerik, –sfér–/ adj.

i•o•ta /í-ōta/ n. 1 ninth letter of the Greek alphabet (I, ι). 2 [usu. with neg.] smallest possible amount.

IOU /í-ō-yōō/ n. signed document acknowledging a debt.

ip•e•cac /ípikak/ n. root of a S. American shrub used as an emetic and purgative.

ips abbr. (also i.p.s.) inches per second.

ip•so fac•to /ípsō fáktō/ adv. 1 by that very fact or act. 2 thereby.

IQ abbr. intelligence quotient.

Ir symb. Chem. iridium.

ir- /ir/ prefix assim. form of IN-1, IN-2 before r.

IRA abbr. 1 individual retirement account. 2 Irish Republican Army.

I•ra•ni•an /iráyneeən/ • adj. 1 of or relating to Iran (formerly Persia) in the Middle East. 2 of the Indo-European group of languages including Persian, Pashto, Avestan, and Kurdish. • n. native or national of Iran.

I•ra•qi /iráakee/ • adj. of or relating to Iraq in the Middle East. • n. (pl. I•ra•qis) 1 native or national of Iraq. 2 form of Arabic spoken in Iraq.

i•ras•ci•ble /irásibəl/ adj. irritable; hot-tempered. □□ i•ras•ci•bil'i•ty n. i•ras'ci•bly adv.

■ see IRRITABLE 1. □□ irascibility see TEMPER n. 3.

i•rate /iráyt/ adj. angry; enraged. □□ i•rate'ly adv. i•rate'ness n.

■ see ANGRY 1.

ire /ir/ n. literary anger. □□ ire'ful adj.

■ see ANGER n. □□ ireful see ANGRY 1.

ir•i•des•cent /iridésənt/ adj. 1 showing rainbowlike luminous colors. 2 changing color with position. □□ ir•i•des'cence n. ir•i•des'cent•ly adv.

i•rid•i•um /irídeeəm/ n. Chem. hard, white metallic element of the transition series, used esp. in alloys. ¶Symb.: Ir.

i•ris /íris/ n. 1 flat, circular colored membrane behind the cornea of the eye, with a circular opening (pupil) in the center. 2 herbaceous plant of a family with tuberous roots, sword-shaped leaves, and showy flowers.

I•rish /írish/ • adj. of or relating to Ireland; of or like its people. • n. 1 Celtic language of Ireland. 2 [prec. by the; treated as pl.] the people of Ireland. □ Irish coffee coffee mixed with Irish whiskey and served with cream on top. Irish Sea sea between England and Wales and Ireland.

irk /ərk/ v.tr. irritate; bore; annoy.

■ anger, enrage, madden, infuriate, incense.

irk•some /ə́rksəm/ adj. tedious; annoying; tiresome. □□ irk'some•ly adv. irk'some•ness n.

■ irritating, maddening, infuriating, vexing.

i•ron /íərn/ • n. 1 Chem. gray metallic element used for tools and implements, and found in some foods. ¶Symb.: Fe. 2 symbol of strength or firmness. 3 implement with a flat base which is heated to smooth clothes, etc. 5 golf club with a metal sloping face. 6 [pl.] fetters. • adj. 1 made of iron. 2 robust. 3 unyielding; merciless. • v.tr. smooth (clothes, etc.) with an iron. □ Iron Age Archaeol. period following the Bronze Age when iron replaced bronze in the making of implements and weapons. **Iron Curtain** *hist.* notional barrier to the passage of people and information between the former Soviet bloc and the West. ▫▫ **i′ron•er** *n.* **i′ron•ing** *n.* (in sense 1 of *v.*). **i′ron•less** *adj.* **i′ron•like** *adj.*

■ *n.* **6** (*irons*) see MANACLE *n.* 1. • *adj.* **3** see GRIM 2. • *v.* press.

i•ron•clad • *adj.* /íərnklád/ **1** clad or protected with iron. **2** impregnable; rigorous. • *n.* /íərnklad/ *hist.* 19th-c. warship protected by iron plates.

i•ron•ic /írónik/ *adj.* (also **i•ron′i•cal**) using or displaying irony. ▫▫ **i•ron′i•cal•ly** *adv.*

■ ▫▫ **ironically** see *tongue-in-cheek* (TONGUE).

i•ron•stone /íərnstōn/ *n.* kind of hard, white, opaque stoneware.

i•ron•ware /íərnwair/ *n.* articles made of iron.

i•ro•ny /írənee/ *n.* (*pl.* **–nies**) **1** humorous or sarcastic use of language of a different or opposite meaning. **2** ill-timed arrival of an event or circumstance that is in itself desirable. See synonym study at WIT.

■ **1** see SATIRE 1.

Ir•o•quois /írəkwoy/ • *n.* (*pl.* same) **1 a** Native American confederacy of five (later six) peoples formerly inhabiting New York State. **b** member of any of these peoples. **2** any of the languages of these peoples. • *adj.* of or relating to the Iroquois or their languages. ▫▫ **Ir•o•quoi•an** /írəkwóyən/ *n.* & *adj.*

ir•ra•di•ate /iráydee-áyt/ *v.tr.* **1** subject to radiation. **2** shine upon; light up. **3** throw light on (a subject). ▫▫ **ir•ra•di•a•tion** /iráydee-áyshən/ *n.* **ir•ra•di•a•tive** /–deeətiv/ *adj.*

ir•ra•tion•al /iráshənəl/ *adj.* **1** illogical; unreasonable. **2** not endowed with reason. ▫▫ **ir•ra•tion•al•i•ty** /–álitee/ *n.* **ir•ra′tion•al•ly** *adv.*

■ see UNREASONABLE 2. ▫▫ **irrationality** see *absurdity* (ABSURD). **irrationally** see MADLY 1.

ir•rec•on•cil•a•ble /irékənsíləbəl/ *adj.* **1** implacably hostile. **2** (of ideas, etc.) incompatible. ▫▫ **ir•rec•on•cil′a•bly** *adv.*

■ **1** see IMPLACABLE. **2** see INCOMPATIBLE 1, 3.

ir•re•cov•er•a•ble /irikúvərəbəl/ *adj.* that cannot be recovered or remedied. ▫▫ **ir•re•cov′er•a•bly** *adv.*

■ see IRRETRIEVABLE.

ir•re•deem•a•ble /irideéməbəl/ *adj.* **1** that cannot be redeemed. **2** hopeless; absolute. ▫▫ **ir•re•deem′a•bly** *adv.*

ir•re•duc•i•ble /iridóosibəl, –dyóo–/ *adj.* that cannot be reduced or simplified. ▫▫ **ir•re•duc′i•bly** *adv.*

ir•re•fut•a•ble /iréfyətəbəl, írifyóo–/ *adj.* that cannot be refuted. ▫▫ **ir•re•fut•a•bil′i•ty** *n.* **ir•re′fut•a•bly** *adv.*

■ see INCONTROVERTIBLE. ▫▫ **irrefutability** see FINALITY. **irrefutably** see *undoubtedly* (UNDOUBTED).

ir•re•gard•less /irigaárdlis/ *disp.* = REGARDLESS. ¶Though in widespread use, this word should be avoided in favor of *regardless*.

ir•reg•u•lar /irégyələr/ *adj.* **1** not regular; unsymmetrical; varying in form. **2** (of a surface) uneven. **3** contrary to a rule, moral principle, or custom; abnormal. **4** uneven in duration, order, etc. ▫▫ **ir•reg•u•lar•i•ty** /–láritee/ *n.* (*pl.* **–ties**). **ir•reg′u•lar•ly** *adv.*

■ **1, 2** unequal, inequable, asymmetric(al), free-form; bumpy, bulgy. **3** illegitimate, improper; peculiar, unusual, uncommon. **4** sporadic, episodic, random, erratic, spasmodic. ▫▫ **irregularity** inequality, unevenness, bumpiness; anomaly, mistake; see also BUMP *n.* 2.

ir•rel•e•vant /irélivənt/ *adj.* not relevant. ▫▫ **ir•rel′e•vance** *n.* **ir•rel′e•van•cy** *n.* **ir•rel′e•vant•ly** *adv.*

■ inappropriate, inapplicable, beside the question. ▫▫ **irrelevance, irrelevancy** impertinence, intrusiveness, inapplicability, inappropriateness.

ir•re•li•gious /irilíjəs/ *adj.* **1** indifferent or hostile to religion. **2** lacking a religion. ▫▫ **ir•re•li′gious•ly** *adv.*

ir•re•me•di•a•ble /irimeédeeəbəl/ *adj.* that cannot be remedied. ▫▫ **ir•re•me′di•a•bly** *adv.*

■ see HOPELESS 2.

ir•rep•a•ra•ble /irépərəbəl/ *adj.* that cannot be rectified or made good. ▫▫ **ir•rep′a•ra•bly** *adv.*

■ see HOPELESS 2.

ir•re•place•a•ble /iripláysəbəl/ *adj.* **1** that cannot be replaced. **2** of which the loss cannot be made good. ▫▫ **ir•re•place′a•bly** *adv.*

■ **2** see INVALUABLE.

ir•re•press•i•ble /iriprésibəl/ *adj.* that cannot be repressed or restrained. ▫▫ **ir•re•press•i•bil′i•ty** *n.* **ir•re•press′i•bly** *adv.*

■ unrestrainable, uncontrollable; incorrigible.

ir•re•proach•a•ble /iripróchəbəl/ *adj.* faultless; blameless. ▫▫ **ir•re•proach•a•bil′i•ty** *n.* **ir•re•proach′a•bly** *adv.*

■ unimpeachable, beyond reproach; unblemished; honest.

ir•re•sist•i•ble /irizístibəl/ *adj.* **1** too strong or convincing to be resisted. **2** delightful; alluring. ▫▫ **ir•re•sist•i•bil′i•ty** *n.* **ir•re•sist′i•bly** *adv.*

■ **1** unstoppable, indomitable; irrepressible. **2** attractive, appealing; charming.

ir•res•o•lute /irézəloot/ *adj.* **1** hesitant; undecided. **2** lacking in resoluteness. ▫▫ **ir•res•o•lute′ly** *adv.* **ir•res•o•lute′ness** *n.* **ir•res•o•lu•tion** /–lóoshən/ *n.*

■ **1** undetermined, unresolved, indecisive, uncertain. **2** unstable, inconstant; weak, spineless.

ir•re•spec•tive /irispéktiv/ *adj.* [foll. by *of*] not taking into account; regardless of. ▫▫ **ir•re•spec′tive•ly** *adv.*

■ (*irrespective of*) notwithstanding, despite; apart from, ignoring, discounting.

ir•re•spon•si•ble /irispónsibəl/ *adj.* **1** acting or done without due sense of responsibility. **2** not responsible for one's conduct. ▫▫ **ir•re•spon•si•bil′i•ty** *n.* **ir•re•spon′si•bly** *adv.*

■ **1** careless, reckless; rash, unthinking; unreliable. **2** unaccountable. ▫▫ **irresponsibility** see *stupidity* (STUPID).

ir•re•triev•a•ble /iritreévəbəl/ *adj.* that cannot be retrieved or restored. □□ **ir•re•triev′a•bly** *adv.*

■ irrecoverable, irreclaimable, ireparable; hopeless.

ir•rev•er•ent /irévərənt/ *adj.* lacking reverence. □□ **ir•rev′er•ence** *n.* **ir•rev′er•ent•ly** *adv.*

■ blasphemous, impious, profane; disrespectful.

ir•re•vers•i•ble /irivórsibəl/ *adj.* not reversible or alterable. □□ **ir•re•vers•i•bil′i•ty** *n.* **ir•re•vers′i•bly** *adv.*

■ irrevocable, unchangeable, fixed; settled.

ir•re•vo•ca•ble /irévəkəbəl, irivók-/ *adj.* 1 unalterable. 2 gone beyond recall. □□ **ir•re•vo•ca•bil′i•ty** *n.* **ir•re′vo′ca•bly** *adv.*

■ 1 irreversible, unchangeable; permanent. 2 irrecoverable, irretrievable, irreclaimable, lost; desperate, hopeless.

ir•ri•gate /irigayt/ *v.tr.* 1 water (land) by means of channels. 2 *Med.* clean (a wound, etc.) with a constant flow of liquid. □□ **ir′ri•ga•ble** *adj.* **ir•ri•ga•tion** /-gáyshən/ *n.* **ir′ri•ga•tor** *n.*

ir•ri•ta•ble /irítəbəl/ *adj.* 1 easily annoyed. 2 (of an organ, etc.) very sensitive to contact. □□ **ir•ri•ta•bil′i•ty** *n.* **ir′ri•ta•bly** *adv.*

■ 1 irascible, testy, touchy, oversensitive, peevish. 2 delicate. □□ **irritability** see *impatience* (IMPATIENT).

ir•ri•tant /írit′nt/ • *adj.* causing irritation. • *n.* irritant substance. □□ **ir′ri•tan•cy** *n.*

ir•ri•tate /íritayt/ *v.tr.* 1 excite to anger; annoy. 2 stimulate discomfort in (a part of the body). □□ **ir′ri•tat•ed•ly** *adv.* **ir′ri•tat•ing** *adj.* **ir′ri•tat•ing•ly** *adv.* **ir•ri•ta•tion** /-táyshən/ *n.* **ir′ri•ta•tive** *adj.* **ir′ri•ta•tor** *n.*

■ 1 enrage, infuriate, madden; exasperate; bother. 2 hurt, pain, sting, nettle. □□ **irritating** see IRKSOME. **irritation** see BOTHER *n.* 1, INFLAMMATION 2.

ir•rupt /irúpt/ *v.intr.* (foll. by *into*) enter forcibly or violently. □□ **ir•rup•tion** /irúpshən/ *n.*

IRS *abbr.* Internal Revenue Service.

Is. *abbr.* 1 a Island(s). b Isle(s). 2 (also **Isa.**) Isaiah (Old Testament).

is *3rd sing. present of* BE.

ISBN *abbr.* international standard book number.

is•chi•um /ískeeəm/ *n.* (*pl.* **is•chi•a** /-keeə/) curved bone forming the base of each half of the pelvis. □□ **is′chi•al** *adj.*

-ise /īz, eez/ *suffix* forming nouns of quality, state, or function (*exercise, expertise, franchise, merchandise*).

-ish¹ /ish/ *suffix* forming adjectives: 1 from nouns, meaning: a having the qualities or characteristics of (*boyish*). b of the nationality of (*Danish*). 2 from adjectives, meaning 'somewhat' (*thickish*). 3 *colloq.* denoting an approximate age or time of day (*fortyish, sixthirtyish*).

-ish² /ish/ *suffix* forming verbs (*vanish, finish*).

i•sin•glass /ízinglas/ *n.* 1 gelatin obtained from fish, esp. sturgeon, and used in making jellies, glue, etc. 2 mica.

isl. *abbr.* island.

Is•lam /isláam, iz-, isláam, iz-/ *n.* 1 religion of the Muslims, a monotheistic faith regard-

441   irretrievable ~ isotope

ed as revealed by Muhammad as the Prophet of Allah. 2 the Muslim world. □□ **Is•lam′ic** *adj.*

is•land /íland/ *n.* 1 land surrounded by water. 2 anything compared to an island, esp. in being surrounded in some way. 3 detached or isolated thing.

■ 1 islet, cay, key, atoll, ait.

is•land•er /íləndər/ *n.* native or inhabitant of an island.

isle /īl/ *n. poet.* island or peninsula, esp. a small one.

is•let /ílit/ *n.* 1 small island. 2 *Anat.* portion of tissue structurally distinct from surrounding tissues.

ism /izəm/ *n. colloq.* usu. *derog.* any distinctive but unspecified doctrine or practice with a name ending in *-ism*.

-ism /izəm/ *suffix* forming nouns, esp. denoting: 1 an action or its result (*baptism*). 2 system, principle, or ideological movement (*feminism*). 3 state or quality (*heroism, barbarism*). 4 basis of prejudice or discrimination (*racism, sexism*). 5 peculiarity in language (*Americanism*). 6 pathological condition (*alcoholism*).

isn′t /íznt/ *contr.* is not.

iso- /ísō/ *comb. form* equal (*isometric*).

i•so•bar /ísəbaar/ *n.* line on a map connecting positions having the same atmospheric pressure. □□ **i•so•bar•ic** /-bárik/ *adj.*

i•so•late /ísəlayt/ *v.tr.* 1 a place apart or alone; cut off from society. b place in quarantine. 2 a identify and separate for attention. b *Chem.* separate (a substance) from a mixture. □□ **i•so•lat′a•ble** *adj.* **i′so•lat•ed** *adj.* **i•so•la′tion** *n.* **i′so•la•tor** *n.*

■ 1 separate, detach, insulate, segregate; shun, cut, ostracize. 2 see IDENTIFY 1, 2. □□ **isolated** lonesome, lonely, solitary, forlorn; alone, secluded, remote, sequestered, cut off; unique, single, solitary, singular; exceptional

i•so•la•tion•ism /ísəláyshənizəm/ *n.* policy of holding aloof from the affairs of other countries or groups esp. in politics. □□ **i•so•la′tion•ist** *n.*

i•so•mer /ísəmər/ *n. Chem.* one of two or more compounds with the same molecular formula but a different arrangement of atoms and different properties. □□ **i•so•mer•ic** /-mérik/ *adj.* **i•som•er•ism** /ísómərizəm/ *n.* **i•som′er•ize** *v.*

i•so•met•ric /ísəmétrik/ *adj.* 1 of equal measure. 2 *Physiol.* (of muscle action) developing tension while the muscle is prevented from contracting. □□ **i•so•met′ri•cal•ly** *adv.*

i•so•met•rics /ísəmétriks/ *n.pl.* system of physical exercises in which muscles act against each other or a fixed object.

i•sos•ce•les /ísósileez/ *adj.* (of a triangle) having two sides equal.

i•so•ton•ic /ísətónik/ *adj.* 1 having the same osmotic pressure. 2 *Physiol.* (of muscle action) taking place with normal contraction. □□ **i•so•ton′i•cal•ly** *adv.*

i•so•tope /ísətōp/ *n. Chem.* one of two or more forms of an element differing from each other in atomic mass. □□ **i•so•top•ic** /–tópik/ *adj.* **i•so•top′i•cal•ly** *adv.*

Is•rae•li /izráylee/ • *adj.* of or relating to the modern state of Israel in the Middle East. • *n.* native or national of Israel.

Is•ra•el•ite /ízreeəlīt, –rəlīt/ *n. hist.* native of ancient Israel.

is•sue /íshoō/ • *n.* **1 a** giving out or circulation of notes, stamps, etc. **b** quantity of coins, copies of a book, etc., circulated or put on sale at one time. **c** item or amount given out or distributed. **d** each of a regular series of a magazine, etc. (*the May issue*). **2 a** an outgoing. **b** exit; outlet. **3** point in question; important subject of debate. **4** result. **5** *Law* children. • *v.* (**is•sues, is•sued, is•su•ing**) **1** *intr. literary* go or come out. **2** *tr.* **a** publish; put into circulation. **b** supply, esp. officially. **3** *intr.* **a** be derived or result. **b** end; result. **4** *intr.* emerge from a condition. □ **at issue 1** in dispute. **2** at variance. **take issue** disagree. □□ **is′su•a•ble** *adj.* **is′su•ance** *n.* **is′su•er** *n.*

■ *n.* **1 a** output, production, publication, distribution. **b** printing, run, edition. **c** dividend, bonus, yield. **d** copy, edition. **2 a** outflow, flux, discharge. **3** topic; problem, dispute. **4** event, outcome, upshot. **5** descendants, heirs. • *v.* **1** go forth, come forth, emerge. **2 a** send out *or* forth, make known, make public. **b** provide, furnish; equip. **3 a** arise, originate. **b** end up, finish, conclude. **4** come out, appear, surface. □ **at issue** under discussion; in contention. **take issue** argue, contend; dispute, question.

-ist /ist/ *suffix* forming personal nouns (and in some senses related adjectives) denoting: **1** an adherent of a system, etc., in *–ism*: see -ISM 2 (*Marxist*). **2 a** a member of a profession (*pathologist*). **b** a person concerned with something (*pharmacist*). **3** a person who uses a thing (*violinist*). **4** a person who does something expressed by a verb in *–ize* (*plagiarist*). **5** a person who subscribes to a prejudice or practices discrimination (*racist*).

isth•mus /ísməs/ *n.* narrow piece of land connecting two larger bodies of land.

-istic /ístik/ *suffix* forming adjectives from nouns and other stems generally denoting: of, pertaining to, referring to, or characteristic of that which is denoted by the noun or stem (*stylistic*).

it /it/ *pron.* (*poss.* **its**; *pl.* **they**) **1** thing (or occas. the animal or child) previously named or in question (*took a stone and threw it*). **2** person in question (*Who is it?*). **3** as the subject of an impersonal verb (*it is raining*). **4** as a substitute for a deferred subject or object (*it is silly to talk like that*). **5** as a substitute for a vague object (*run for it!*). **6** as the antecedent to a relative word (*it was an owl I heard*). **7** (in children's games) player who has to catch the others. □ **that's it** *colloq.* that is: **1** what is required. **2** the difficulty. **3** the end; enough.

I•tal•ian /itályən/ • *n.* **1** native or national of Italy. **2** language of Italy. • *adj.* of or relating to Italy or its people or language.

I•tal•ian•ate /itályənayt/ *adj.* of Italian style or appearance.

i•tal•ic /itálik/ • *adj.* **1** *Printing* slanting type used esp. for emphasis and in foreign words. • *n.* **1** a letter in italic type. **2** this type.

i•tal•i•cize /itálisīz/ *v.tr.* print in italics. □□ **i•tal•i•ci•za′tion** *n.*

itch /ich/ • *n.* **1** irritation in the skin. **2** impatient desire. • *v.intr.* **1** feel an irritation in the skin. **2** (of a person) feel a desire to do something (*itching to tell you*).

■ *n.* **1** itchiness, tickle, tingle, prickle. **2** craving, hankering, hunger, thirst. • *v.* **1** tickle; tingle, prickle. **2** crave, hanker, hunger; want, need.

itch•y /íchee/ *adj.* (**itch•i•er, itch•i•est**) having or causing an itch. □ **have itchy feet** *colloq.* **1** be restless. **2** have a strong urge to travel. □□ **itch′i•ness** *n.*

■ see RESTLESS 2, 3. □□ **itchiness** see PRICKLE *n.* 3.

it'd /itəd/ *contr. colloq.* **1** it had. **2** it would.

-ite[1] /īt/ *suffix* forming nouns meaning 'a person or thing connected with': (*Israelite, Trotskyite, dynamite*).

-ite[2] /īt, it/ *suffix* **1** forming adjectives (*erudite, favorite*). **2** forming nouns (*appetite*). **3** forming verbs (*expedite, unite*).

i•tem /ítəm/ *n.* **1 a** any of a number of enumerated things. **b** entry in an account. **2** article, esp. one for sale. **3** piece of news, etc.

■ **1, 2** object; point, detail. **3** article, feature, note.

i•tem•ize /ítəmīz/ *v.tr.* state or list item by item. □□ **i•tem•i•za′tion** *n.* **i′tem•iz•er** *n.*

■ enumerate, particularize, detail; recite, rattle off; check off.

it•er•ate /ítərayt/ *v.tr.* repeat; state repeatedly. □□ **it•er•a′tion** /–áyshən/ *n.* **it′er•a•tive** *adj.*

-itic /ítik/ *suffix* forming adjectives and nouns corresponding to nouns in *–ite*, *–itis*, etc. (*Semitic, arthritic, syphilitic*).

i•tin•er•ant /ītínərənt, itín–/ • *adj.* traveling from place to place. • *n.* itinerant person.

i•tin•er•ar•y /ītínəreree, itín–/ *n.* (*pl.* **–ies**) **1** detailed route. **2** record of travel. **3** guidebook.

■ **1** see ROUTE.

-ition /íshən/ *suffix* forming nouns, = -ATION (*admonition, perdition, position*).

-itious[1] /íshəs/ *suffix* forming adjectives corresponding to nouns in *–ition* (*ambitious, supposititious*).

-itious[2] /íshəs/ *suffix* forming adjectives meaning 'related to, having the nature of' (*adventitious*).

-itis /ítis/ *suffix* forming nouns, esp.: **1** names of inflammatory diseases (*appendicitis*). **2** *colloq.* with ref. to conditions compared to diseases (*electionitis*).

-itive /itiv/ *suffix* forming adjectives, = -ATIVE (*positive, transitive*).

it'll /ít'l/ *contr. colloq.* it will; it shall.

-itous /itəs/ *suffix* forming adjectives corresponding to nouns in *–ity* (*calamitous, felicitous*).

its /its/ *poss.pron.* of it; of itself (*can see its advantages*).

it's /its/ *contr.* **1** it is. **2** it has.

it•self /itsélf/ *pron.* emphatic and refl. form of

IT. □ **in itself** viewed in its essential qualities (*not in itself a bad thing*).

it•ty-bit•ty /itee̅bitee̅/ *adj.* (also **it•sy-bit•sy** /itseebitsee̅/) *colloq.* usu. *derog.* tiny; insubstantial; slight.

-ity /itee̅/ *suffix* forming nouns denoting: **1** quality or condition (*purity*). **2** instance of this (*humidity*).

IUD *abbr.* intrauterine (contraceptive) device.

IV /ī-vee̅/ *abbr.* intravenous(ly).

I've /īv/ *contr.* I have.

-ive /iv/ *suffix* forming adjectives meaning 'tending to, having the nature of,' and corresponding nouns (*suggestive, corrosive, palliative, coercive, talkative*). □□ **-ively** *suffix* forming adverbs. **-iveness** *suffix* forming nouns.

i•vo•ry /ī̅vəree, ī̅vree/ *n.* (*pl.* **-ries**) **1** hard substance of the tusks of an elephant, etc. **2** color of this. **3** [usu. in *pl.*] piano key or tooth. □ **ivory tower** seclusion or separation from the harsh realities of life. □□ **i'vo•ried** *adj.*

i•vy /ī̅vee̅/ *n.* (*pl.* **-vies**) climbing evergreen shrub with dark-green, shining five-angled leaves.

-ize /īz/ *suffix* forming verbs, meaning: **1** make or become such (*Americanize, realize*). **2** treat in such a way (*monopolize, pasteurize*). **3 a** follow a special practice (*economize*). **b** have a specified feeling (*sympathize*). □□ **-ization** /-īzáyshən/ *suffix* forming nouns. **-izer** *suffix* forming agent nouns.

Jj

J¹ /jay/ *n.* (also **j**) (*pl.* **Js** or **J's; j's**) **1** tenth letter of the alphabet.

J² *abbr.* (also **J.**) **1** *Cards* jack. **2** Jewish. **3** joule(s). **4** Judge. **5** Justice.

jab /jab/ • *v.tr.* (**jabbed, jab•bing**) **1 a** poke roughly. **b** stab. **2** thrust (a thing) hard or abruptly. • *n.* abrupt blow with one's fist or pointed implement.

■ *v.* **1 a** dig, punch; nudge, elbow. **b** stick; spear, skewer. **2** push, shove, drive, ram. • *n.* **1** poke, dig, stab; punch.

jab•ber /jábər/ • *v.* **1** *intr.* chatter volubly. **2** *tr.* utter (words) in this way. • *n.* meaningless jabbering.

■ *v.* **1** babble, burble, gibber, gabble, drivel. **2** gabble, babble; prate. • *n.* chatter, blather, babble; gibberish, twaddle, nonsense.

ja•bot /zhabō, ja-/ *n.* ornamental frill or ruffle of lace, etc., on the front of a shirt or blouse.

jack /jak/ • *n.* **1** device for lifting heavy objects, esp. vehicles. **2** playing card with a picture of a soldier, page, etc. **3** ship's flag, esp. showing nationality. **4** device to connect an electrical circuit. **5 a** small piece of metal, etc., used with others in tossing games. **b** [in *pl.*] game with a ball and jacks. **6** (**Jack**) familiar form of *John*, esp. typifying the common man or the male of a species. • *v.tr.* **1** raise with or as with a jack (in sense 1). **2** *colloq.* raise, e.g., prices. □ **Jack Frost** frost personified. **jack-in-the-box** toy figure that springs out of a box. **jack-in-the-pulpit** N. American plant having an upright flower spike and an over-arching hoodlike spathe. **jack-of-all-trades** person who can do many different kinds of work. **jack-o'-lantern** lantern made from a pumpkin with holes for facial features.

jack•al /jákəl/ *n.* any of various wild doglike mammals found in Africa and S. Asia.

jack•a•lope /jákəlōp/ • imaginary animal that is half jackrabbit and half antelope.

jack•ass /jákas/ *n.* **1** male ass. **2** stupid person.

jack•daw /jákdaw/ *n.* small gray-headed crow.

jack•et /jákit/ *n.* **1 a** sleeved, short outer garment. **b** thing worn esp. around the torso for protection or support (*life jacket*). **2** casing or covering. **3** = *dust jacket*.

■ **1 a** see COAT • *n.* 1. **2** see WRAPPER 1, 2.

jack•ham•mer /ják-hamər/ *n.* pneumatic hammer or drill.

jack•knife /jáknī̅f/ • *n.* (*pl.* **-knives**) **1** large pocket knife. **2** dive in which the body is first bent at the waist and then straightened. • *v.intr.* (**-knifed, -knif•ing**) (of an articulated vehicle) fold against itself in an accidental skidding movement.

jack•pot /jákpot/ *n.* large prize, esp. accumulated in a game or lottery, etc. □ **hit the jackpot** *colloq.* **1** win a large prize. **2** have remarkable luck or success.

■ see WINDFALL.

jack•rab•bit /jákrabit/ *n.* large prairie hare.

Jac•quard /jəkaárd, jókaárd/ *n.* **1** apparatus using perforated cards that record a pattern and are fitted to a loom to mechanize the weaving of figured fabrics. **2** (in full **Jacquard loom**) loom fitted with this. **3** fabric or article made with this.

Ja•cuz•zi /jəkōōzee̅/ *n. propr.* large bath with underwater jets of water to massage the body.

jade¹ /jayd/ *n.* **1** hard, usu. green stone used for ornaments, etc. **2** green color of jade.

jade² /jayd/ *n.* **1** inferior or worn-out horse. **2** *derog.* disreputable woman.

■ **1** nag, hack. **2** trollop, slattern, hussy.

jad•ed /jáydid/ *adj.* tired or worn out; surfeited. □□ **jad'ed•ly** *adv.* **jad'ed•ness** *n.*

■ exhausted, weary; trite; sated; dull, bored.

jag¹ /jag/ • *n.* sharp projection of rock, etc. • *v.tr.* (**jag•ged, jag•ging**) **1** cut or tear unevenly. **2** make indentations in. □□ **jag′ger** *n.*

jag² /jag/ *n. sl.* **1** drinking bout; spree. **2** period of indulgence in an activity, emotion, etc.
■ **1** carousal, orgy, bacchanal, *sl.* binge. **2** fit, spell, burst, stint, bout.

jag•ged /jágid/ *adj.* **1** unevenly cut or torn. **2** deeply indented; with sharp points. □□ **jag′ged•ly** *adv.* **jag′ged•ness** *n.*
■ **1** rough, uneven, ragged, coarse; chipped. **2** jaggy, serrated, crenellated.

ja•guar /jágwaar/ *n.* large, flesh-eating spotted feline of Central and S. America.

jai a•lai /hí lí, ălí/ *n.* indoor court game similar to handball played with large curved wicker rackets.

jail /jayl/ • *n.* **1** place to which persons are committed by a court for detention. **2** confinement in a jail. • *v.tr.* put in jail.
■ *n.* **1** prison, coop, pen, lockup. **2** imprisonment, incarceration, internment, detention. • *v.* imprison, incarcerate, detain, remand.

jail•break /jáylbrayk/ *n.* escape from jail.

jail•er /jáylər/ *n.* person in charge of a jail or of the prisoners in it.

ja•la•pe•ño /halapáynyō, -peén-/ *n.* hot pepper commonly used in Mexican cooking.

ja•lop•y /jəlópee/ *n.* (*pl.* **-ies**) *colloq.* dilapidated old car.

jal•ou•sie /jálosee/ *n.* blind or shutter made of rows of angled slats to keep out rain, etc., and control the influx of light.

jam¹ /jam/ • *v.* (**jammed, jam•ming**) **1 a** *tr.* squeeze or wedge into a space. **b** *intr.* become wedged. **2 a** *tr.* cause to become wedged or immovable so that it cannot work. **b** *intr.* become jammed in this way. **3** *tr.* push or cram together in a compact mass. **4** *intr.* push or crowd (*they jammed onto the bus*). **5** *tr.* **a** block (a passage, road, etc.) by crowding or obstructing. **b** obstruct the exit of (*we were jammed in*). **6** *tr.* [usu. foll. by *on*] apply (brakes, etc.) forcefully or abruptly. **7** *tr.* make (a radio transmission) unintelligible by interference. **8** *intr. colloq.* (in jazz, etc.) extemporize with other musicians. • *n.* **1** a squeeze or crush. **2** crowded mass (*traffic jam*). **3** *colloq.* predicament. **4** stoppage due to jamming. **5** (in full **jam′ ses•sion**) *colloq.* improvised playing by a group of jazz musicians. □ **jam-packed** *colloq.* full to capacity. □□ **jam′mer** *n.*
■ *v.* **1, 3, 4** force, thrust, wedge; compact. **2** lock, seize; immobilize. **5** congest, fill up, clog, plug. **6** (*jam on*) slam on, ram on. **8** see IMPROVISE 1. • *n.* **1** squash, press. **2** pack, swarm, horde; bottleneck. **3** trouble, difficulty, crisis. **4** blockage, seizure. **5** see *improvisation* (IMPROVISE). □ **jam-packed** replete, brimful, packed.

jam² /jam/ *n.* preserve of fruit and sugar.

jamb /jam/ *n. Archit.* side post or surface of a doorway, window, or fireplace.

jam•ba•lay•a /júmbəlíə/ *n.* dish of rice with shrimp, chicken, etc.

jam•bo•ree /jámbəree/ *n.* **1** celebration or merrymaking. **2** large rally of Boy Scouts or Girl Scouts.
■ **1** party, gathering, fête, fair, festival.

Jan. *abbr.* January.

jan•gle /jánggəl/ • *v.* **1** *intr. & tr.* cause (a bell, etc.) to make a harsh metallic sound. **2** *tr.* irritate (the nerves, etc.) by discord, etc. • *n.* harsh metallic sound.
■ *v.* **1** ring; clang, clank, clatter. **2** see JAR² *v.* 1, 2. • *n.* jingle; rattle, clash, crash, clangor.

jan•i•tor /jánitər/ *n.* caretaker of a building. □□ **jan•i•to•ri•al** /–táwreeəl/ *adj.*

Jan•u•ar•y /jányooeree/ *n.* (*pl.* **-ies**) first month of the year.

ja•pan /jəpán/ • *n.* hard, usu. black varnish, orig. from Japan. • *v.tr.* (**ja•panned, ja•pan•ning**) **1** varnish with japan. **2** make black and glossy.

Jap•a•nese /jápənéez/ • *n.* (*pl.* same) **1 a** native or national of Japan. **b** person of Japanese descent. **2** language of Japan. • *adj.* of or relating to Japan, its people, or its language. □ **Japanese beetle** iridescent green and brown beetle that is a garden and crop pest.

jape /jayp/ *n.* practical joke. • *v.intr.* play a joke. □□ **jap′er•y** *n.*

jar¹ /jaar/ *n.* **1** container of glass, plastic, etc., usu. cylindrical. **2** contents of this. □□ **jar′ful** *n.* (*pl.* **-fuls**).
■ **1** receptacle, vessel, container, bottle, glass.

jar² /jaar/ • *v.* (**jarred, jar•ring**) **1** *intr.* (of sound, manner, etc.) sound discordant or grating (on the nerves, etc.). **2 a** *tr.* strike or cause to strike with vibration or shock. **b** *intr.* (of a body affected) vibrate gratingly. **3** *tr.* send a shock through (a part of the body). **4** *intr.* be at variance; be in conflict. • *n.* **1** jarring sound or sensation. **2** physical shock or jolt. **3** lack of harmony; disagreement.
■ *v.* **1, 2** jangle; rattle, clatter; rasp, scratch. **3** jolt, jounce, jerk. **4** disagree, clash, be at odds. • *n.* **1** discord, cacophony, dissonance. **2** lurch, bump, jerk. **3** disharmony, discord, conflict.

jar•di•niere /jaárd′néer, zhaárdinyáir/ *n.* (also **jar′di•nière**) **1** ornamental pot or stand for plants. **2** dish of mixed vegetables.

jar•gon /jaárgən/ *n.* **1** words or expressions used by a particular group or profession (*medical jargon*). **2** barbarous or debased language. **3** gibberish. See synonym study at DI- ALECT. □□ **jar•gon•is′tic** *adj.* **jar′gon•ize** *v.*
■ **1, 2** cant, argot, idiom, terminology; patois, dialect. **3** twaddle, nonsense, drivel, rubbish, gobbledygook.

jas•mine /jázmin/ *n.* (also **jes•sa•mine** /jésəmin/) any of various fragrant ornamental shrubs usu. with white or yellow flowers.

jas•per /jáspər/ *n.* opaque quartz, usu. red, yellow, or brown.

jaun•dice /jáwndis/ • *n.* **1** *Med.* yellowing of the skin or whites of the eyes, often caused by obstruction of the bile duct or by liver disease. **2** envy. • *v.tr.* **1** affect with jaundice. **2** (esp. as **jaundiced** *adj.*) affect (a person) with envy, resentment, or jealousy.
■ *n.* **2** jealousy, resentment, resentfulness.

• *v.* **2** see PREJUDICE *v.* 1; (**jaundiced**) envious, jealous, resentful.

jaunt /jawnt/ • *n.* short excursion for enjoyment. See synonym study at JOURNEY.
• *v.intr.* take a jaunt.
■ *n.* see EXCURSION 1.

jaunt•y /jáwntee/ *adj.* (**jaunt•i•er, jaunt•i•est**) **1** cheerful and self-confident. **2** sprightly. □□ **jaunt'i•ly** *adv.* **jaunt'i•ness** *n.*
■ buoyant, high-spirited, jovial, jolly, merry.

Jav•a•nese /jávənéez, jaà—/ • *n.* (*pl.* same) **1 a** native of Java in Indonesia. **b** person of Javanese descent. **2** language of Java. • *adj.* of or relating to Java, its people, or its language.

jav•e•lin /jávəlin, jávlin/ *n.* **1** light spear thrown in a competitive sport or as a weapon. **2** such an athletic event.
■ **1** see LANCE *n.* 1.

jaw /jaw/ • *n.* **1 a** upper or lower bony structure in vertebrates forming the framework of the mouth and containing the teeth. **b** corresponding parts of certain invertebrates. **2 a** [in *pl.*] mouth with its bones and teeth. **b** narrow mouth of a valley, channel, etc. **c** gripping parts of a tool or machine. • *v. colloq.* **1** *intr.* speak, esp. at tedious length. **2** *tr.* **a** persuade by talking. **b** admonish or lecture.
■ *n.* **2 a** (*jaws*) see MOUTH *n.* 1. • *v.* **1** see PRATTLE *v.*

jaw•bone /jáwbōn/ *n.* lower jaw in most mammals.

jaw•break•er /jáwbraykər/ *n.* **1** *colloq.* word that is very long or hard to pronounce. **2** round, very hard candy.

jay /jay/ *n.* noisy chattering bird of the crow family with vivid pinkish-brown, blue, black, and white plumage.

jay•walk /jáywawk/ *v.intr.* cross or walk in the street or road without regard for traffic. □□ **jay'walk•er** *n.*

jazz /jaz/ • *n.* **1** music of American origin characterized by improvisation, syncopation, and usu. a regular or forceful rhythm **2** *sl.* pretentious talk or behavior. • *v.intr.* play or dance to jazz. □ **jazz up** brighten or enliven. □□ **jazz'er** *n.*

jazz•y /jázee/ *adj.* (**jazz•i•er, jazz•i•est**) **1** of or like jazz. **2** vivid; unrestrained; showy. □□ **jazz'i•ly** *adv.* **jazz'i•ness** *n.*

JCS *abbr.* (also **J.C.S.**) Joint Chiefs of Staff.

jct. *abbr.* junction.

jeal•ous /jéləs/ *adj.* **1** fiercely protective (of rights, etc.). **2** afraid, suspicious, or resentful of rivalry in love. **3** envious or resentful (of a person, etc.): **4** (of inquiry, supervision, etc.) vigilant. □□ **jeal'ous•ly** *adv.*
■ **1** possessive, defensive. **2** distrustful, mistrustful; anxious, insecure. **3** bitter, jaundiced; green (with envy), covetous. **4** watchful, alert, sharp, observant. □□ **jealously** protectively, possessively; suspiciously; enviously; vigilantly, watchfully.

SYNONYM STUDY: jealous
COVETOUS, ENVIOUS. A young man who is **jealous** of his girlfriend's admirers cannot tolerate their rivalry and is afraid of being

displaced. While *jealous* may merely imply an intense effort to hold on to what one possesses (*jealous of what little time she has to herself*), it is more often associated with distrust, suspicion, anger, and other negative emotions (*a jealous wife*). **Envious**, on the other hand, implies wanting something that belongs to another and to which one has no particular right or claim (*envious of her good fortune*). While jealousy may be either good or bad, depending upon its object, envy is usually bad and often implies a malicious desire to deprive someone else of whatever it is that has made one *envious*. Someone who is covetous has fallen prey to an inordinate or wrongful desire, usually for a person or thing that rightfully belongs to another. In other words, a young man might be *jealous* of the other men who flirt with his girlfriend, while they might be *envious* of her obvious preference for him. But if the young man is married, he'd better not be *covetous* of his neighbor's wife.

---

jeal•ou•sy /jéləsee/ *n.* (*pl.* **–sies**) **1** jealous state or feeling. **2** instance of this.
■ **1** see ENVY *n.*

jeans /jeenz/ *n.pl.* casual pants made of denim.

Jeep /jeep/ *n. propr.* rugged, all-purpose motor vehicle incorporating four-wheel drive.

jeer /jeer/ • *v.* **1** *intr.* [usu foll. by *at*] scoff derisively. **2** *tr.* scoff at; deride. • *n.* a scoff or taunt. □□ **jeer'ing•ly** *adv.*
■ *v.* **1** mock, sneer, gibe, tease; (*jeer at*) ridicule, deride. **2** laugh at, make fun or sport of. • *n.* gibe, fleer, flout, sneer.

je•had var. of JIHAD.

Je•ho•vah /jəhóvə/ *n.* Hebrew name of God in the Old Testament.

je•june /jijóōn/ *adj.* **1** intellectually unsatisfying; shallow. **2** puerile. □□ **je•june'ly** *adv.*
■ **1** see BANAL. **2** see IMMATURE 2.

je•ju•num /jijóōnəm/ *n. Anat.* small intestine between the duodenum and ileum.

jell /jel/ *v.intr. colloq.* **1 a** set, as jelly. **b** (of ideas, etc.) take a definite form. **2** (of two different things) cohere.
■ **1** congeal, coagulate, thicken; crystallize. **2** hang together, bond, connect.

jel•ly /jélee/ • *n.* (*pl.* **–lies**) **1** gelatinous preparation of fruit juice, etc., for use as a jam or a condiment (*grape jelly*). **2** any similar substance. • *v.* (**–lies, –lied**) **1** *intr. & tr.* set or cause to set as a jelly; congeal. **2** *tr.* set (food) in a jelly (*jellied eggs*). □ **jelly roll** rolled sponge cake with a jelly filling. □□ **jel'ly•like** *adj.*

jel•ly•fish /jéleefish/ *n.* (*pl.* usu. same) **1** marine coelenterate with a jellylike body and stinging tentacles. **2** *colloq.* feeble person.

jeop•ar•dize /jépərdīz/ *v.tr.* endanger; put into jeopardy.
■ imperil, threaten, menace, expose; risk.

jeop•ar•dy /jépərdee/ *n.* danger, esp. of severe harm or loss.
■ peril; threat, menace; risk, hazard, chance.

jer•e•mi•ad /jérimíad/ n. doleful complaint or lamentation.

Jer•e•mi•ah /jérimíə/ n. dismal prophet; denouncer of the times.
 ■ see PIER 1.

jerk[1] /jərk/ • n. **1** sharp sudden pull, twist, twitch, start, etc. **2** spasmodic muscular twitch. **3** *sl.* fool. • v. **1** *intr.* move with a jerk. **2** *tr.* pull, thrust, twist, etc., with a jerk. □□ **jerk′er** n.
 ■ n. **1, 2** wrench, tug; lurch; spasm, shudder. **3** *sl.* creep, nerd, dweeb; see also DOLT.
 • v. **1** lurch, jolt, jump. **2** wrench, tug, whip, shove.

jerk[2] /jərk/ *v.tr.* cure (beef, etc.) by cutting it in long slices and drying it in the sun.

jer•kin /jórkin/ n. sleeveless jacket, often of leather.

jerk•y[1] /jórkee/ adj. (**jerk•i•er, jerk•i•est**) **1** having sudden abrupt movements. **2** spasmodic. □□ **jerk′i•ly** adv. **jerk′i•ness** n.
 ■ **1** see *bumpy* (BUMP). **2** see SPASMODIC 2.

jerk•y[2] /jórkee/ n. meat, esp. beef, cured by jerking.

jer•sey /jórzee/ n. (pl. **–seys**) **1 a** knitted, usu. woolen sweater. **b** knitted fabric. **2** (**Jersey**) light brown dairy cow from Jersey.

jest /jest/ • n. **1 a** joke. **b** fun. **2 a** raillery; banter. **b** object of derision (*a standing jest*). • v.intr. **1** joke; make jests. **2** fool about; play or act triflingly. □ **in jest** in fun. □□ **jest′ful** adj.
 ■ n. **1 a** see JOKE n. 1. **b** see SPORT n. 2. **2 a** see BANTER n. • v. see JOKE v. 1. □ **in jest** see *in fun* (FUN).

jest•er /jéstər/ n. professional clown at a medieval court, etc.
 ■ see FOOL n. 2.

Jes•u•it /jézhŏoit, jézŏo–, jézyŏo–/ n. member of the Society of Jesus, a Roman Catholic order.

Je•sus /jeezəs/ n. the name of the source of the Christian religion, d. *c.* AD 30.

jet[1] /jet/ • n. **1** stream of water, steam, gas, flame, etc., shot out esp. from a small opening. **2** spout or nozzle for this purpose. **3 a** jet engine. **b** jet plane. • v. (**jet•ted, jet•ting**) **1** *intr.* spurt out in jets. **2** *tr. & intr. colloq.* send or travel by jet plane. □ **jet lag** extreme tiredness after a long flight across time zones. **jet propulsion** propulsion by the backward ejection of a high-speed jet of gas, etc. **jet set** *colloq.* wealthy people frequently traveling by air, esp. for pleasure. **jet-setter** *colloq.* member of the jet set.
 ■ n. **1** see GUSH[1] n. 1. **3 b** see PLANE n. 3. • v. **1** see GUSH v. 1. □ **jet-setter** see *traveler* (TRAVEL).

jet[2] /jet/ n. **1 a** hard black variety of lignite capable of being carved and highly polished. **b** [*attrib.*] made of this. **2** (in full **jet-black**) deep glossy black color.

jet•sam /jétsəm/ n. discarded material washed ashore, esp. that thrown overboard to lighten a ship, etc. (cf. FLOTSAM).

jet•ti•son /jétisən, –zən/ • v.tr. **1 a** throw (esp. heavy material) overboard to lighten a ship, etc. **b** drop (goods) from an aircraft. **2** abandon; get rid of. • n. act of jettisoning.
 ■ **2** see *throw away* 1.

jet•ty /jétee/ n. (pl. **–ties**) **1** pier or breakwater constructed to protect or defend a harbor, coast, etc. **2** landing pier.
 ■ see PIER 1.

Jew /jŏo/ n. person of Hebrew descent or whose religion is Judaism. □ **Jew's (or Jews') harp** small lyre-shaped musical instrument held between the teeth and struck with the finger.

jew•el /jŏoəl/ • n. **1 a** precious stone. **b** this used in watchmaking. **2** jeweled personal ornament. **3** precious person or thing. • v.tr. (esp. as **jeweled** adj.) adorn or set with jewels. □ **jewel box 1** small box in which jewelry is kept. **2** plastic case for a compact disc or CD-ROM. □□ **jew′el•like** adj.
 ■ n. **1 a** gem, gemstone, brilliant. **3** treasure, gem, pearl; marvel, godsend; blessing; masterpiece. • v. ornament, bedeck, embellish.

jew•el•er /jŏoələr/ n. maker of or dealer in jewels or jewelry.

jew•el•ry /jŏoəlree/ n. jewels esp. for personal adornment, regarded collectively.
 ■ gems, precious stones, ornaments, adornments.

Jew•ish /jŏoish/ adj. **1** of or relating to Jews. **2** of Judaism. □□ **Jew′ish•ness** n.

Jew•ry /jŏoree/ n. (pl. **–ries**) Jews collectively.

Jez•e•bel /jézəbel/ n. shameless or immoral woman.

jg abbr. (also **J.G.**) US Navy junior grade.

jib[1] /jib/ • n. **1** triangular staysail. **2** projecting arm of a crane. • v. (**jibbed, jib•bing**) (of a sail, etc.) pull or swing around from one side of the ship to the other; jibe.

jibe[1] /jīb/ • v. **1** *intr.* (of a fore-and-aft sail or boom) swing across the vessel. **2** *tr.* cause (a sail) to do this. **3** *intr.* (of a ship or its crew) change course so that this happens. • n. change of course causing jibing.

jibe[2] /jīb/ *v.intr.* [usu. foll. by *with*] *colloq.* agree; be in accord.
 ■ see AGREE 3a.

jif•fy /jifee/ n. *colloq.* short time; moment (*in a jiffy*).

jig /jig/ • n. **1 a** lively leaping dance. **b** music for this. **2** device that holds a piece of work and guides the tools operating on it. • v. (**jigged, jig•ging**) **1** *intr.* dance a jig. **2** *tr. & intr.* move quickly and jerkily up and down. **3** *tr.* work on or equip with a jig or jigs.

jig•ger /jigər/ n. **1** measure of spirits, etc. **2** small glass holding this.

jig•gle /jigəl/ v. **1** *tr.* shake lightly; rock jerkily. **2** *intr.* fidget. □□ **jig′gly** adj.
 ■ **1** jog, joggle, jig, agitate, wriggle. **2** see FIDGET.

jig•saw /jigsaw/ n. **1** (in full **jig′saw puz•zle**) picture on board or wood, etc., cut into irregular interlocking pieces to be reassembled. **2** machine saw with a fine blade for cutting on a curve.

ji•had /jihaad/ n. (also **je•had′**) Muslim holy war.

jil•lion /jilyən/ n. *colloq.* very large indefinite number.

jilt /jilt/ *v.tr.* abruptly reject or abandon (a lover, etc.).

■ throw over, discard, desert, break (up) with.

jim crow /jim krō/ *n. hist.* (also **Jim Crow**) practice of segregating blacks. □□ **jim crow′ ism** *n.*

jim•my /jímee/ • *n.* (*pl.* **-mies**) burglar's short crowbar, usu. made in sections. • *v.tr.* (**-mies, -mied**) force open with a jimmy.

jin•gle /jínggəl/ • *n.* **1** mixed noise as of bells or light metal objects being shaken together. **2 a** repetition of the same sound in words, esp as an aid to memory or to attract attention. **b** short verse of this kind used in advertising, etc. • *v.* make or cause to make a jingling sound. □□ **jin′gly** *adj.* (**jin•gli•er, jin•gli•est**).
■ *n.* **1** tintinnabulation, clink, chink, chime, jangle. **2 a** tautophony, alliteration. **b** tune, ditty; slogan. • *v.* tinkle, ring, clink.

jin•go /jínggō/ *n.* (*pl.* **-goes**) supporter of policy favoring war; blustering patriot. □ **by jingo!** a mild oath. □□ **jin′go•ism** *n.* **jin′go•ist** *n.* **jin•go•is′tic** *adj.*

jin•ni /jínee, jínee/ *n.* (also **jinn** /jin/) (*pl.* **jinn** or **jinns**) (in Muslim mythology) intelligent being lower than the angels, able to appear in human and animal forms, and having power over people.

jinx /jingks/ *colloq.* • *n.* person or thing that seems to cause bad luck. • *v.tr.* subject (a person) to an unlucky force.
■ *n.* (evil) spell, curse, (unlucky) charm, evil eye, voodoo. • *v.* curse, bewitch, cast a spell on, damn.

jit•ter /jítər/ • *n. colloq.* (**the jitters**) extreme nervousness. • *v.intr.* be nervous; act nervously. □□ **jit′ter•y** *adj.* **jit′ter•i•ness** *n.*
■ *n.* (the jitters) jitteriness, tension, anxiety, apprehension. □□ **jittery** see NERVOUS 1–3, 5. **jitteriness** see JITTER *n.* above.

jit•ter•bug /jítərbug/ • *n.* **1** nervous person. **2** fast acrobatic dance popular in the 1940s. • *v.intr.* (**-bugged, -bug•ging**) dance the jitterbug.

jive /jīv/ • *n.* **1** jerky lively style of dance esp. popular in the 1950s. **2** music for this. **3** *sl.* talk or conversation, esp. when misleading or pretentious. • *v.intr.* **1** dance the jive. **2** play jive music. □□ **jiv′er** *n.*

job /job/ • *n.* **1** piece of work to be done. **2** paid position of employment. **3** *colloq.* anything one has to do. **4** *colloq.* difficult task (had a job to find them). **5** *sl.* crime, esp. a robbery. • *v.* (**jobbed, job•bing**) **1 a** *intr.* do jobs; do piecework. **b** *tr.* [usu. foll. by out] subcontract. **2 a** *intr.* deal in stocks. **b** *tr.* buy and sell (stocks or goods) as a middleman. □ **job action** any action, esp. a strike, taken by employees as a protest. **job lot** miscellaneous group of articles, esp. bought together. **job-sharing** sharing of a full-time job by several part-time employees.
■ *n.* **1, 3** task, assignment, chore; business. **2** occupation, career, profession. **4** problem, difficulty, hardship. **5** felony; burglary. • *v.* **1 a** work; freelance. **b** (job out) let out, assign, apportion, farm out. **2** trade.

job•ber /jóbər/ *n.* **1** wholesaler. **2** *derog.* broker (see BROKER 2). **3** person who jobs.

jock /jok/ *n. sl.* **1** = JOCKSTRAP. **2** athlete.

jock•ey /jókee/ • *n.* (*pl.* **-eys**) rider in horse races, esp. professional. • *v.* **1** *tr.* **a** trick or cheat (a person). **b** outwit. **2** *tr.* draw (a person) by trickery. **3** *intr.* cheat.
■ *v.* **1, 2** see BEGUILE 3.

jock•strap /jókstrap/ *n.* support or protection for the male genitals, worn esp. by athletes.

jo•cose /jōkṓs/ *adj.* **1** playful in style. **2** fond of joking; jocular. □□ **jo•cose′ly** *adv.* **jo•cos′ i•ty** /-kósitee/ *n.* (*pl.* **-ties**).

joc•u•lar /jókyələr/ *adj.* **1** merry; fond of joking. **2** humorous. □□ **joc•u•lar•i•ty** /-láritee/ *n.* (*pl.* **-ties**). **joc′u•lar•ly** *adv.*
■ see HUMOROUS 1. □□ **jocularity** see HUMOR *n.* 1. **jocularly** see tongue-in-cheek (TONGUE).

jo•cund /jókənd, jṓ-/ *adj. literary* merry; cheerful; sprightly. □□ **jo•cun′di•ty** /jəkúnditee/ *n.* (*pl.* **-ties**). **jo•cund′ly** *adv.*

jodh•purs /jódpərz/ *n.pl.* long breeches for riding, etc., close-fitting from the knee to the ankle.

Joe Blow /jō blō/ *n. colloq.* hypothetical average man.

jog /jog/ • *v.* (**jogged, jog•ging**) **1** *intr.* run slowly, esp. as exercise. **2** *intr.* (of a horse) move at a jog trot. **3** *intr.* proceed laboriously; trudge. **4** *intr.* move up and down with an unhurried motion. **5** *tr.* nudge (a person), esp. to arouse attention. **6** *tr.* shake with a push or jerk. **7** *tr.* stimulate (a person's or one's own memory). • *n.* **1** a shake, push, or nudge. **2** slow walk or trot. □□ **jog′ger** *n.*
■ *v.* **1** trot, lope. **3** plod, labor, toil, slog, drag. **4, 6** bounce, jolt, joggle. **5** prod, push; poke. **7** arouse, stir; refresh. • *n.* **1** prod, poke, shove. **2** jogtrot; stroll

john /jon/ *n. sl.* toilet or bathroom.

John Bull /jon bŏŏl/ *n.* personification of England or the typical Englishman.

joie de vivre /zhwaa də veevrə/ *n.* feeling of healthy and exuberant enjoyment of life.

join /joyn/ • *v.* **1** *tr.* put together; fasten; unite (one or several things or people). **2** *tr.* connect (points) by a line, etc. **3** *tr.* become a member of (an association, organization, etc.). **4** *tr.* take one's place with or in (a company, group, etc.). **5** *tr.* **a** come into the company of (a person). **b** [foll. by *in*] take part with (others) in an activity, etc. **c** share the company of for a specified occasion (may I join you for lunch?). **6** *intr.* [often foll. by *in*] take part with others in an activity, etc. • *n.* point, line, or surface at which things are joined. □ **join battle** begin fighting. **join forces** combine efforts. **join hands 1 a** clasp hands. **b** clasp one's hands together. **2** combine in an action. **join up 1** enlist for military service. **2** unite; connect. □□ **join′a•ble** *adj.*
■ *v.* **1, 2** unify, combine; merge. **3, 4** enter, enlist in; associate oneself with, fall in with. **5** accompany, tag along with, team up with. **6** (join in) participate, share, become involved. • *n.* see JOINT *n.* 1. □ **join forces** see JOIN *v.* 6 above. **join up 1** see ENLIST 1.

join•er /jóynər/ *n.* **1** person who makes furniture and light woodwork. **2** *colloq.* person who readily joins societies, etc. □□ **join′er•y** *n.* (in sense 1).

joint /joynt/ • *n.* **1 a** place at which two or more things are joined. **b** point at which, or a contrivance by which, two parts of an artificial structure are joined. **2** point at which two bones fit together. **3 a** any of the parts into which an animal carcass is divided for food. **b** any of the parts of which a body is made up. **4** *sl.* place of meeting for drinking, etc. **5** *sl.* marijuana cigarette. **6** *Geol.* fissure in a rock. • *adj.* **1** held or done by, or belonging to, two or more persons, etc. (*joint action*). **2** sharing with another (*joint author*). See synonym study at MUTUAL. • *v.tr.* **1** connect by joints. **2** divide (a body or member) at a joint or into joints. □ **out of joint 1** (of a bone) dislocated. **2** out of order. □□ **joint′less** *adj.* **joint′ly** *adv.*

■ *n.* **1** join, union, juncture, connection, linkage, articulation; link. **4** bar, (night)club, watering hole. **5** *sl.* reefer, spliff. • *adj.* **1, 2** shared, common, communal, collective; mutual, reciprocal. • *v.* **1** articulate, hinge; link, couple.

joist /joyst/ *n.* supporting beams in floors, ceilings, etc. □□ **joist′ed** *adj.*

jo•jo•ba /hōhṓbə/ *n.* plant with seeds yielding an oily extract used in cosmetics, etc.

joke /jōk/ • *n.* **1 a** thing said or done to excite laughter. **b** witticism or jest. **2** ridiculous thing, person, or circumstance. • *v.* **1** *intr.* make jokes. **2** *tr.* poke fun at; banter. • **no joke** *colloq.* serious matter. □□ **jok′ing•ly** *adv.* **jok′i•ly** *adv.*

■ *n.* **1** quip, gag; story, anecdote. **2** farce, mockery, absurdity; laughingstock, figure of fun, fool. • *v.* **1** jest, tease. **2** SEE BANTER *v.* 1. □□ **jokingly** see *tongue-in-cheek* (TONGUE).

jok•er /jṓkər/ *n.* **1** person who jokes. **2** *sl.* fellow; man. **3** playing card usu. with a figure of a jester, used in some games.

■ **1** comic, (stand-up) comedian or comedienne; trickster, prankster. **2** see FELLOW 1.

jol•li•ty /jṓlitē/ *n.* (*pl.* **-ties**) merrymaking; festiveness.

jol•ly /jṓlee/ • *adj.* (**jol•li•er, jol•li•est**) **1** cheerful; merry. **2** festive; jovial. **3** slightly drunk. • *v.tr.* (**-lies, -lied**) **1** *colloq.* coax or humor in a friendly way. **2** chaff; banter. □ **Jolly Roger** pirates' black flag, usu. with the skull and crossbones. □□ **jol′li•ly** *adv.* **jol′li•ness** *n.*

■ *adj.* **1, 2** cheery, happy, joyful, joyous; exuberant, high-spirited; light-hearted, buoyant. **3** tipsy; see also DRUNK *adj.* 1. • *v.* **1** appease, cajole, wheedle. **2** see BANTER *v.* 1.

jolt /jōlt/ • *v.* **1** *tr.* disturb or shake (esp. in a moving vehicle) with a jerk. **2** *tr.* shock; perturb. **3** *intr.* move along with jerks. • *n.* **1** such a jerk. **2** surprise; shock.

■ *v.* **1** jar, jerk, bump, knock, nudge, jog, rock, bounce. **2** shake (up), disturb, rattle, agitate, unnerve; surprise, startle, stun. **3** lurch, stagger.

Jo•nah /jṓnə/ *n.* person who seems to bring bad luck.

jon•quil /jóngkwil/ *n.* narcissus with small fragrant yellow or white flowers.

josh /josh/ *sl.* • *n.* good-natured or teasing joke. • *v.* **1** *tr.* tease; banter. **2** *intr.* indulge in ridicule. □□ **josh′er** *n.*

jos•tle /jósəl/ • *v.* **1** *tr.* push against; elbow. **2** *intr.* [foll. by *with*] struggle roughly. • *n.* jostling.

■ *v.* **1** see PUSH *v.* 4. **2** see STRUGGLE *v.* 3.

jot /jot/ • *v.tr.* (**jot•ted, jot•ting**) write briefly or hastily. • *n.* very small amount (*not one jot*).

■ *v.* (*jot down*) make a note of, write or note (down). • *n.* bit, scrap, grain, speck, mite, iota, whit.

joule /jōōl/ *n.* unit of work or energy equal to the force of one newton when its point of application moves one meter in the direction of action of the force. ¶Symb.: **J**.

jour•nal /jṓrnəl/ *n.* **1** newspaper or periodical. **2** daily record of events. **3** book in which transactions are entered. **4** part of a shaft or axle that rests on bearings.

■ **1** paper, magazine, gazette, newsletter; daily, weekly, monthly. **2** diary, chronicle, log(book); almanac. **3** daybook, ledger.

jour•nal•ism /jṓrnəlizəm/ *n.* business or practice of writing and producing newspapers. □□ **jour′nal•ist** *n.* **jour•nal•is′tic** *adj.*

■ □□ **journalist** reporter, newsman, newswoman, columnist, correspondent, *colloq.* stringer; (*journalists*) the press, the fourth estate.

jour•ney /jṓrnee/ • *n.* (*pl.* **-neys**) **1** act of going from one place to another. **2** distance traveled in a specified time (*day's journey*). • *v.intr.* (**-neys, -neyed**) make a journey.

■ *n.* voyage, expedition, trek; trip, excursion; cruise, flight, passage; pilgrimage. • *v.* travel, go (abroad or overseas), take a trip, make one's way.

SYNONYM STUDY: journey

EXCURSION, EXPEDITION, JAUNT, PILGRIMAGE, TRIP, VOYAGE. While all of these nouns refer to a course of travel to a particular place, usually for a specific purpose, there is a big difference between a **jaunt** to the nearest beach and an **expedition** to the rain forest. While a **trip** may be either long or short, for business or pleasure, and taken at either a rushed or a leisurely pace (*a ski trip; a trip to Europe*), a **journey** suggests that a considerable amount of time and distance will be covered and that the travel will take place over land (*a journey into the Australian outback*). A long **trip** by water or through air or space is a **voyage** (*a voyage to the Galapagos; a voyage to Mars*), while a short, casual **trip** for pleasure or recreation is a **jaunt** (*a jaunt to the local shopping mall*). **Excursion** also applies to a brief pleasure trip, usually no more than a day in length, that returns to the place where it began (*an afternoon excursion to the zoo*). Unlike the rest of these nouns, *expedition* and **pilgrimage** apply to *journeys* that are undertaken for a specific purpose. An *expedition* is usually made by an organized group or company (*a scientific expedition; an expedition to locate new sources of oil*), while a *pilgrimage* is a *journey* to a place that has religious or emotional significance (*the Muslims' annual pilgrimage to Mecca; a pilgrimage to the place where her father died*).

jour•ney•man /jərneemən/ n. (pl. **-men**) **1** qualified mechanic or artisan who works for another. **2** reliable but not outstanding worker.

joust /jowst/ hist. • n. combat between two knights on horseback with lances. • v.intr. engage in a joust. □□ **joust'er** n.

Jove /jōv/ n. (in Roman mythology) Jupiter. □ **by Jove!** exclamation of surprise or approval.

jo•vi•al /jōveeəl/ adj. merry; convivial. □□ **ju•vi•al•i•ty** /-álitee/ n. **jo'vi•al•ly** adv.
  ■ see MERRY 1. □□ **joviality** see MERRIMENT.

jowl[1] /jowl/ n. **1** jaw or jawbone. **2** cheek.

jowl[2] /jowl/ n. loose skin on the throat or neck. □□ **jowl'y** adj.

joy /joy/ n. **1** pleasure; extreme gladness. **2** thing that causes joy. □□ **joy'less** adj. **joy'less•ly** adv. **joy'ous** adj. **joy'ous•ly** adv.
  ■ **1** delight, elation, ecstasy; bliss; gladness, happiness, enjoyment; gaiety, glee. **2** treat; blessing, treasure, godsend. □□ **joyless** sad, unhappy, miserable, depressed, downhearted, downcast; despondent; gloomy, disheartening, dreary, dismal.

joy•ful /jóyfŏŏl/ adj. full of, showing, or causing joy. □□ **joy'ful•ly** adv. **joy'ful•ness** n.
  ■ happy, merry, jolly, sunny; glad, pleased, rapt, in seventh heaven, on cloud nine.

joy•ride /jóyrīd/ colloq. • n. a ride for pleasure in a car, usu. recklessly. • v.intr. (past **-rode** /-rōd/, past part. **-rid•den** /-rid'n/) go for a joy ride. □□ **joy'rid•er** n.

joy•stick /jóystik/ n. **1** colloq. control column of an aircraft. **2** lever controlling movement of a computer image.

JP abbr. **1** justice of the peace. **2** jet propulsion.

Jr. abbr. junior.

ju•bi•lant /jōōbilənt/ adj. exultant; rejoicing. □□ **ju'bi•lance** n. **ju'bi•lant•ly** adv.
  ■ see JOYFUL.

ju•bi•lee /jōōbilee/ n. **1** time of rejoicing. **2** anniversary, esp. the 25th or 50th.

Ju•da•ism /jōōdeeizəm, -day-/ n. religion of the Jews, with a belief in one god and a basis in Mosaic and rabbinical teachings. □□ **Ju•da•ic** /-dáyik/ adj. **Ju'da•ist** n.

Ju•das /jōōdəs/ n. traitor.

judge /juj/ • n. **1** public officer appointed to hear and try legal cases. **2** person appointed to decide a dispute or contest. **3 a** person who decides a question. **b** person regarded as qualified to decide or pronounce. • v.tr. **1 a** try a legal case. **b** pronounce sentence on. **2** form an opinion about; appraise. **3** act as a judge of. **4** conclude; consider. □□ **judge'like** adj. **judge'ship** n.
  ■ n. **1** justice, magistrate, jurist. **2** arbitrator, arbiter, umpire, referee, mediator. **3 b** connoisseur, expert, authority, specialist. • v. **1 a** hear, adjudge; weigh. **b** pass judgment on. **2** reckon, estimate, assess, evaluate; determine. **4** regard, hold, believe, perceive.

judg•ment /júɉmənt/ n. (also **judge'ment**) **1** critical faculty; discernment (*an error in judgment*). **2** good sense. **3** opinion or estimate. **4** sentence of a court of justice. □ **against one's better judgment** contrary to what one really feels to be advisable. **judgment by default** see DEFAULT. **Judgment Day** day of the Last Judgment. **Last Judgment** judgment of mankind said to take place at the end of the world.
  ■ **1, 2** discretion, discrimination, perception, insight, reasoning. **3** (point of) view, belief, conviction, feeling, sentiment, idea; evaluation, appraisal, assessment; criticism, critique, review. **4** decision, ruling, verdict, decree. □ **against one's better judgment** reluctantly, unwillingly, grudgingly. **Judgment Day** doomsday, doom.

judg•men•tal /juɉmént'l/ adj. (also **judge'men'tal**) **1** making judgments. **2** condemning; critical. □□ **judg•men'tal•ly** adv.
  ■ **2** see CRITICAL 1.

ju•di•ca•ture /jōōdikəchər/ n. **1** administration of justice. **2** jurisdiction. **3** judges collectively.

ju•di•cial /jōōdíshəl/ adj. **1** of, done by, or proper to a court of law. **2** having the function of judgment (*judicial assembly*). **3** impartial. □□ **ju•di'cial•ly** adv.
  ■ **1, 2** legal, official. **3** equitable, objective, fair, just.

ju•di•ci•ar•y /jōōdíshee-eree, -dishəree/ n. (pl. **-ies**) judges of a judicial branch collectively.

ju•di•cious /jōōdíshəs/ adj. sensible; wise; prudent. □□ **ju•di'cious•ly** adv. **ju•di'cious•ness** n.
  ■ reasonable, logical, sound; wise, astute.

ju•do /jōōdō/ n. sport derived from jujitsu. □□ **ju'do•ist** n.

jug /jug/ n. **1** vessel for liquids, with a handle and an opening for pouring. **2** sl. prison. □□ **jug'ful** n. (pl. **-fuls**).
  ■ **1** pitcher, ewer, jar; carafe, bottle. **2** see PRISON n. 1.

jug•ger•naut /júgərnawt/ n. overwhelming force or object.

jug•gle /júgəl/ v. **1 a** intr. toss objects in the air and catch them, keeping several in the air at the same time. **b** tr. perform such feats with. **2** tr. deal with (several activities) at once. **3** intr. [foll. by with] & tr. **a** deceive or cheat. **b** rearrange or misrepresent (facts) □□ **jug'gler** n.
  ■ **3 a** see DECEIVE 1. **b** distort, falsify; shuffle, switch.

jug•u•lar /júgyələr/ • adj. of the neck or throat. • n. = jugular vein. □ **jugular vein** any of several large veins of the neck, which carry blood from the head.

juice /jōōs/ n. **1** liquid part of plants or fruits. **2** fluid of animal tissue. **3** essence or spirit of anything. **4** colloq. fuel or electricity. **5** sl. alcoholic liquor. □□ **juice'less** adj.
  ■ **1** sap. **3** see ESSENCE 1. **4** gasoline, gas; current, power.

juic•er /jōōsər/ n. **1** device for extracting juice from fruits and vegetables. **2** sl. alcoholic.

juic•y /jo͞osee/ *adj.* (**juic•i•er, juic•i•est**) 1 full of juice; succulent. 2 *colloq.* interesting; racy; scandalous. 3 *colloq.* profitable. □□ **juic'i•ly** *adv.* **juic'i•ness** *n.*
   ■ 1 lush, ripe, luscious. 2 substantial; intriguing, fascinating, sensational, lurid, provocative, spicy, risqué. 3 see *profitable* (PROFIT).

ju•jit•su /jo͞ojitso͞o/ *n.* (also **jiu•jit'su**) Japanese system of unarmed combat and physical training.

ju•jube /jo͞ojo͞ob/ *n.* flavored jellylike lozenge or candy.

juke•box /jo͞okboks/ *n.* coin-operated machine for playing selected music.

Jul. *abbr.* July.

ju•lep /jo͞olip/ *n.* sweet drink, esp. one medicated or with alcohol.

ju•li•enne /jo͞olee-én/ *adj.* [esp. of vegetables] cut into thin strips.

Ju•ly /jo͞olī/ *n.* (*pl.* **Ju•lys**) seventh month of the year.

jum•ble /júmbəl/ • *v.* 1 *tr.* confuse; mix up. 2 *intr.* move about in disorder. • *n.* confused state or heap. □□ **jumb'ly** *adj.*
   ■ *v.* 1 confound, muddle, disarrange, mess (up), scramble. 2 see MILL[1] *v.* 4. • *n.* tangle, clutter; melee; chaos; hodgepodge, mishmash, medley, miscellany.

SYNONYM STUDY: jumble

CONFUSION, CONGLOMERATION, DISARRAY, FARRAGO, HODGEPODGE, MÉLANGE, MUDDLE. **Confusion** is a very broad term, applying to any indiscriminate mixing or mingling that makes it difficult to distinguish individual elements or parts (*a confusion of languages*). The typical teenager's bedroom is usually a **jumble** of books, papers, clothing, CDs, and soda cans—a word that suggests physical disorder and a mixture of dissimilar things. If the disorder exists on a figurative level, it is usually called a **hodgepodge** (*a hodgepodge of ideas, opinions, and quotations, with a few facts thrown in for good measure*). **Conglomeration** refers to a collection of dissimilar things, but with a suggestion that the collection is random or inappropriate (*a conglomeration of decorating styles*). **Mélange** carries even stronger connotations of incongruity and is often used in a contemptuous or derogatory way (*a mélange of drug addicts, petty criminals, and single mothers on welfare*). A **farrago** is an irrational or confused mixture of elements and is usually worse than a *conglomeration* (*a farrago of doubts, fears, hopes, and desires*), while a **muddle** is less serious and suggests confused thinking and lack of organization (*their bank records were in a complete muddle*). **Disarray** implies disarrangement and is most appropriately used when order or discipline has been lost (*his unexpected appearance threw the meeting into disarray*).

---

jum•bo /júmbō/ *colloq.* • *n.* (*pl.* **–bos**) large animal, person, or thing. • *adj.* very large.
   ■ *n.* giant, monster, colossus, behemoth, leviathan. • *adj.* huge, immense, gigantic, enormous, colossal; king-size, queen-size; see also BIG *adj.* 1a.

jump /jump/ • *v.* 1 *intr.* move off the ground by sudden muscular effort in the legs. 2 *intr.* move suddenly or hastily. 3 *intr.* jerk; twitch. 4 *intr.* undergo a rapid change, esp. an advance in status. 5 *intr.* change the subject, etc., rapidly. 6 a *intr.* rise suddenly (*prices jumped*). b *tr.* cause to do this. 7 *tr.* a pass over (an obstacle, etc.) by jumping. b pass over (an intervening thing) to a point beyond. 8 *tr.* pounce on or attack (a person) unexpectedly. • *n.* 1 act of jumping. 2 sudden jerk caused by shock or excitement. 3 abrupt rise in amount, value, status, etc. 4 obstacle to be jumped. 5 a sudden transition. b gap in a series, logical sequence, etc. □ **get** (or **have**) **the jump on** *colloq.* get (or have) an early advantage. **jump at** accept eagerly. **jump down a person's throat** *colloq.* reprimand or contradict a person fiercely. **jump the gun** see GUN. **jump-start** *v.tr.* start (a motor vehicle) by pushing it or with jumper cables. *n.* jump-starting. **jump to it** *colloq.* act promptly and energetically.
   ■ *v.* 1, 2 leap, bound, spring; vault; prance. 3 start, lurch, jolt, wince, flinch. 4, 6 increase, progress; climb, surge, escalate. 5 skip, shift, switch. 7 hurdle, vault, hop, leapfrog; skip (over *or* past), bypass. 8 see ATTACK *v.* 1. • *n.* 1 leap, bound, hop; prance. 2 start, lurch, jolt, shudder. 3 increase, surge, escalation. 4 hurdle, fence, barricade. 5 switch, shift, change; break, interval, hiatus, interruption. □ **get** (or **have**) **the jump on** get *or* have the upper hand. **jump at** snatch, grab (at), pounce on. **jump down a person's throat** oppose, *colloq.* bite a person's head off; rebuke, upbraid. **jump to it** look sharp, get on with it, *colloq.* get cracking, look lively.

jump•er[1] /júmpər/ *n.* 1 sleeveless one-piece dress worn over a blouse. 2 loose jacket.

jump•er[2] /júmpər/ *n.* 1 person or animal that jumps. 2 *Electr.* short wire used to make or break a circuit. □ **jumper cables** pair of cables attached to a battery and used to start a motor vehicle with a weak or discharged battery.

jump•suit /júmpso͞ot/ *n.* one-piece garment for the whole body.

jump•y /júmpee/ *adj.* (**jump•i•er, jump•i•est**) 1 nervous; easily startled. 2 making sudden movements. □□ **jump'i•ly** *adv.* **jump'i•ness** *n.*
   ■ 1 tense, agitated, anxious, edgy, fidgety, flustered, jittery; excitable, skittish. 2 twitchy, jerky, fluttery.

Jun. *abbr.* 1 June. 2 Junior.

jun•co /júngkō/ *n.* (*pl.* **–cos** or **–coes**) small American finch.

junc•tion /júngkshən/ *n.* 1 joint; joining point. 2 place where railroad lines or roads meet or cross. 3 joining. □ **junction box** box containing a junction of electric cables, etc.
   ■ 1 union, juncture, connection; link, bond; brace, hinge. 2 intersection, crossing, convergence; crossroad(s). 3 unification, conjunction, combination, coupling, merger, alliance.

junc•ture /júngkchər/ n. **1** critical convergence of events; critical point of time (*at this juncture*). **2** place where things join. **3** joining.

■ **1** situation, *colloq.* crunch; moment (in time). **2** see JUNCTION 1. **3** see JUNCTION 3.

June /jōōn/ n. sixth month of the year. □ **June bug** large brown scarab beetle.

jun•gle /júnggəl/ n. **1 a** land with dense vegetation, esp. in the tropics. **b** area of such land. **2** place of bewildering complexity or confusion, or of struggle. □ **jungle gym** playground structure with bars, ladders, etc., for climbing.

■ **1** rain forest.

jun•ior /jōōnyər/ • adj. **1** [foll. by *to*] inferior in age, standing, or position. **2** the younger (esp. appended to the name of a son with his father's name). • n. **1** junior person. **2** one's inferior in length of service, etc. **3** third-year high school or college student. □ **junior college** two-year college. **junior high school** school for grades seven, eight, and sometimes nine.

■ adj. **1** (*junior to*) younger than; lower than, subordinate to, secondary to, beneath, under, behind. ■ n. **1, 2** subordinate, *derog.* underling; minor, youth, youngster, juvenile, child.

ju•ni•per /jōōnipər/ n. evergreen shrub or tree with prickly leaves and dark purple berrylike cones.

junk[1] /jungk/ • n. **1** discarded articles; rubbish. **2** thing of little value. **3** *sl.* narcotic drug. • v.tr. discard as junk. □ **junk bond** high-interest bond deemed to be a risky investment. **junk food** food with low nutritional value. **junk mail** unsolicited advertising matter sent through the mail.

■ n. **1, 2** waste, refuse, litter, scrap, garbage, debris, trash; stuff; see also NONSENSE. **3** heroin, *sl.* smack, horse. • v. dispose of, dump, get rid of.

junk[2] /jungk/ n. flat-bottomed sailing vessel in the China seas.

junk•er /júngkər/ • n. **1** person who collects junk, often to repair it for use. **2** old, dilapidated automobile considered of little value.

jun•ket /júngkit/ • n. **1** sweetened and flavored curds. **2** pleasure outing. **3** official's tour at public expense. • v.intr. feast, picnic. □□ **jun'ket•ing** n.

junk•ie /júngkee/ n. *sl.* drug addict.

junk•yard /júngkyard/ n. yard in which junk is collected and sometimes resold.

jun•ta /hōōntə, júntə/ n. political or military clique taking power in a coup d'état.

■ faction, band, ring, party.

Ju•pi•ter /jōōpitər/ n. largest planet of the solar system, fifth from the sun.

Ju•ras•sic /jōōrásik/ *Geol.* • adj. of the second period of the Mesozoic era, noted for dinosaurs. • n. this era or system.

ju•rid•i•cal /jōōrídikəl/ adj. of the law or judicial proceedings. □□ **ju•rid'i•cal•ly** adv.

ju•ris•dic•tion /jōōrisdíkshən/ n. **1** legal or other authority. **2** extent of this; territory it extends over. □□ **ju•ris•dic'tion•al** adj.

■ dominion, control, influence; district, range, reach.

SYNONYM STUDY: jurisdiction

AUTHORITY, COMMAND, DOMINION, POWER, SOVEREIGNTY, SWAY. The **authority** of our elected officials— which refers to their *power* (often conferred by rank or office) to give orders, require obedience, or make decisions— is normally limited by their **jurisdiction**, which is a legally predetermined division of a larger whole, within which someone has a right to rule or decide (*the matter was beyond his jurisdiction*). The president of the United States has more **power** than any other elected official, which means that he has the ability to exert force or control over something. He does not, however, have the *authority* to make laws on his own. As commander in chief, he does have **command** over the nation's armed forces, implying that he has the kind of *authority* that can enforce obedience. Back in the days when Great Britain had **dominion**, or supreme *authority*, over the American colonies, it was the King of England who held **sway** over this country's economic and political life—an old-fashioned word that stresses the sweeping scope of one's power. But his **sovereignty**, which emphasizes absolute or autonomous rule over something considered as a whole, was eventually challenged. The rest, as they say, is history.

ju•ris•pru•dence /jōōrisprōōd'ns/ n. science of philosophy of law. □□ **ju•ris•pru•dent** /-dənt/ adj. & n.

ju•rist /jōōrist/ n. expert in law.

ju•ror /jōōrər/ n. member of a jury.

ju•ry /jōōree/ n. (pl. **-ries**) **1** body of persons giving a verdict in a court of justice. **2** body of persons awarding prizes in a competition.

ju•ry-rigged /jōōree-rigd/ adj. having temporary makeshift rigging or repair.

just /just/ • adj. **1** morally right or fair. **2** (of treatment, etc.) deserved (*just reward*). **3** (of feelings, opinions, etc.) valid; well-grounded. **4** right in amount, etc.; proper. • adv. **1** exactly (*just what I need*). **2** a little time ago (*have just seen them*). **3** *colloq.* simply; merely (*just good friends*). **4** barely; no more than (*just a minute*). **5** *colloq.* positively (*just splendid*). **6** quite (*not just yet*). □ **just about** *colloq.* almost exactly; almost completely. **just in case** as a precaution. **just so 1** exactly arranged (*everything just so*). **2** exactly as you say. □□ **just'ly** adv. **just'ness** n.

■ adj. **1** equitable, impartial, objective; righteous, honest, ethical. **2** due, rightful, merited. **3** justified, justifiable, valid, reasonable. **4** fitting, befitting, appropriate, suitable, correct. • adv. **1** precisely, completely, perfectly, entirely, expressly, explicitly. **2** only *or* just now, (just) a moment ago. **3, 4** only, solely, nothing but, at best, at most. **5** absolutely, altogether, categorically; certainly; really, truly, indeed. □ **just about** nearly, virtually, practically, more or less, approximately. **just in case** lest; for fear that. **just so 1** neat, tidy, perfect. **2** that's right, that's it, quite so.

jus•tice /jústis/ *n.* **1** just conduct. **2** fairness. **3** exercise of authority in the maintenance of right. **4** judicial proceedings. **5** magistrate; judge. □ **do justice to** treat fairly; appreciate properly. **do oneself justice** perform in a worthy manner. **justice of the peace** magistrate who hears minor cases, grants licenses, performs marriages, etc.

■ **1–3** uprightness, righteousness, decency, correctness; fair play; lawfulness; equity. **4** court (of law), courtroom; bench. **5** see JUDGE *n.* 1.

jus•ti•fy /jústifī/ *v.tr.* (**–fies**, **–fied**) **1** show the justice or rightness of (a person, act, etc.). **2** demonstrate the correctness of (an assertion, etc.). **3** demonstrate adequate grounds for (conduct, a claim, etc.). **4** vindicate. **5** (as **justified** *adj.*) just; right. **6** *Printing* adjust (a line of type) to fill a space evenly. □□ **jus'ti•fi•a•ble** *adj.* **jus'ti•fi•a•bly** *adv.* **jus'ti•fi•ca'tion** *n.* **jus'ti•fi•er** *n.*

■ **1, 2, 4** legitimize, rationalize, substantiate,

defend, support, validate, account for. **3** excuse, explain. **5** (**justified**) see RIGHT *adj.* 1. □□ **justification** see ARGUMENT 2, BASIS 1, 2.

jut /jut/ • *v.intr.* (**jut•ted, jut•ting**) protrude; project. • *n.* projection.

■ *v.* stick out, extend, overhang.

jute /jōōt/ *n.* **1** rough fiber from the bark of an E. Indian plant, used for sacking, mats, etc. **2** plant yielding this fiber.

ju•ve•nile /jōōvənīl/ • *adj.* **1 a** youthful. **b** of or for young persons. **2** immature. See synonym study at YOUTHFUL. • *n.* **1** young person. **2** *Commerce* book intended for young people. **3** actor playing a youthful person. □ **juvenile delinquency** offenses committed by minors. **juvenile delinquent** such an offender.

■ *adj.* **1 a** young, under-age, teenage(d); childlike. **b** children's. **2** adolescent, childish, unsophisticated, innocent. • *n.* **1** youth, boy, girl, child, adolescent, minor, teenager, youngster.

jux•ta•pose /júkstəpóz/ *v.tr.* **1** place (things) side by side. **2** place (a thing) beside another. □□ **jux•ta•po•si•tion** /–pəzíshən/ *n.*

K k

K¹ /kay/ *n.* (also **k**) (*pl.* **Ks** or **K's**; **k's**) eleventh letter of the alphabet.

K² *abbr.* (also **K.**) **1** kelvin(s). **2** King; King's. **3** *Computing* unit of 1,024 (i.e., 2¹⁰) bytes or bits, or loosely 1,000. **4** 1,000. **5** *Baseball* strikeout.

K³ *symb.* Chem. potassium.

k *abbr.* **1** kilo–. **2** knot(s).

ka•bob /kəbób/ *n.* pieces of meat, vegetables, etc., cooked on a skewer.

ka•bu•ki /kəbōōkee/ *n.* form of traditional Japanese drama.

kai•ser /kízər/ *n. hist.* emperor, esp. of Germany, Austria, or the Holy Roman Empire.

kale /kayl/ *n.* variety of wrinkle-leafed cabbage.

ka•lei•do•scope /kəlídəskōp/ *n.* **1** tube containing mirrors and pieces of colored glass, etc., producing changing patterns when rotated. **2** constantly changing group of bright or interesting objects. □□ **ka•lei•do•scop•ic** /–skópik/ *adj.*

ka•mi•ka•ze /kámikáazee/ • *n. hist.* Japanese aircraft loaded with explosives and deliberately crashed by its pilot onto its target. • *adj.* reckless; dangerous; potentially self-destructive.

Kan. *abbr.* Kansas.

kan•ga•roo /kánggəróō/ *n.* Australian marsupial with a long tail and strong hindquarters enabling it to travel by jumping. □ **kangaroo court** improperly constituted or illegal court held by a mob, etc.

Kans. *abbr.* Kansas.

Kan•sa /káanzə, –sə/ *n.* **1 a** N. American people native to eastern Kansas. **b** member of this people. **2** language of this people.

ka•o•lin /káyəlin/ *n.* fine, soft, white clay used esp. for porcelain. (Also called **china clay**).

ka•pok /káypok/ *n.* fibrous, cottonlike substance from a tropical tree, used for stuffing cushions, etc.

Ka•po•si's sar•co•ma /kápəseez, kapō–/ *n. Med.* malignant disease causing skin lesions, often associated with AIDS.

kap•pa /kápə/ *n.* tenth letter of the Greek alphabet (Κ, κ).

ka•put /kaapŏŏt/ *predic.adj. sl.* broken; ruined; done for.

ka•ra•o•ke /káreeōkee, kárə–/ *n.* entertainment in which people sing against prerecorded popular song tracks.

ka•rat /kárət/ *n.* measure of purity of gold, pure gold being 24 karats.

ka•ra•te /kəráatee/ *n.* Japanese system of unarmed combat using the hands and feet as weapons.

kar•ma /káarmə/ *n. Buddhism & Hinduism* **1** sum of a person's actions in previous lives, viewed as deciding fate in future existences. **2** destiny. □□ **kar'mic** *adj.*

■ **2** see DESTINY 2.

ka•ty•did /káyteedid/ *n.* N. American insect related to the grasshopper.

kay•ak /kíak/ *n.* small, enclosed canoe for one paddler.

ka•zoo /kəzōō/ *n.* toy musical instrument into which the player sings or hums.

kc *abbr.* kilocycle(s).

ke•a /keeə, káyə/ *n.* colorful parrot of New Zealand.

keel /keel/ • *n.* main lengthwise member

along the base of a ship, etc. • v. 1 [often foll. by over] a intr. turn over or fall down. b tr. cause to do this. 2 tr. & intr. turn keel upward.

■ v. 1 see FALL v. 2. 2 see CAPSIZE.

keel·haul /kéelhawl/ v.tr. 1 hist. drag (a person) under the keel of a ship and up on the other side as a punishment. 2 scold or rebuke severely.

keen[1] /keen/ adj. 1 eager; ardent. 2 [foll. by on] fond of; enthusiastic about. 3 (of the senses) sharp. 4 a (of a person) intellectually acute. b (of a remark, etc.) sharp; biting. 5 having a sharp edge or point. 6 (of a sound, light, etc.) penetrating. 7 colloq. excellent. See synonym study at EAGER. □□ **keen'ly** adv. **keen'ness** n.

■ 1 enthusiastic, avid, zealous, passionate; itching, anxious. 2 (keen on) devoted to, intent on. 3 acute, discriminating, fine, discerning, vivid, clear, distinct. 4 a intelligent, astute, smart, shrewd, clever b pointed, cutting, stinging, sarcastic. 5 honed, razor-sharp, knife-edged. 6 piercing; intense. □□ **keenness** see ENTHUSIASM, INTELLIGENCE 1b.

SYNONYM STUDY: keen

ACUTE, ASTUTE, PENETRATING, PERSPICACIOUS, SHARP, SHREWD. A knife can be sharp, even keen, but it can't be astute. While keen and sharp mean having a fine point or edge, they also pertain to mental agility and perceptiveness. You might describe someone as having a keen mind, which suggests the ability to grapple with complex problems, or to observe details and see them as part of a larger pattern (a keen appreciation of what victory would mean for the Democratic Party) or a keen wit, which suggests an incisive or stimulating sense of humor. Someone who is sharp has an alert and rational mind, but is not necessarily well-grounded in a particular field and may in some cases be cunning or devious (sharp enough to see how the situation might be turned to her advantage). An astute mind, in contrast, is one that has a thorough and profound understanding of a given subject or field (an astute understanding of the legal principles involved). Like sharp, **shrewd** implies both practicality and cleverness, but with an undercurrent of self-interest (a shrewd salesperson). **Acute** is close in meaning to keen, but with more emphasis on sensitivity and the ability to make subtle distinctions (an acute sense of smell). While a keen mind might see only superficial details, a **penetrating** mind would focus on underlying causes (a penetrating analysis of the plan's feasibility). **Perspicacious** is the most formal of these terms, meaning both perceptive and discerning (a perspicacious remark; perspicacious judgment).

keen[2] /keen/ • n. Irish funeral song accompanied with wailing. • v. 1 intr. utter the keen. 2 tr. bewail (a person) in this way. 3 tr. utter in a wailing tone. □□ **keen'er** n.

keep /keep/ • v. (past and past part. **kept** /kept/) 1 tr. have continuous charge of; retain possession of. 2 tr. retain or reserve for a fu-

ture occasion. 3 tr. & intr. retain or remain in a specified condition, position, etc. (keep cool, keep off the grass). 4 tr. put or store in a regular place. 5 tr. [foll. by from] hold back. 6 tr. detain (what kept you?). 7 tr. observe, honor, etc. (a law, custom, etc.). 8 tr. own and look after (animals). 9 tr. [foll. by in] maintain with a supply of. 10 tr. manage (business, etc.). 11 tr. maintain (a house, accounts, etc.) regularly and in proper order. 12 tr. have (a commodity) regularly for sale. 13 tr. guard or protect (a person or place). 14 tr. preserve in being (keep order). 15 intr. continue; repeat habitually (keeps saying that). 16 intr. continue to follow (a way or course). 17 intr. remain fresh; not spoil. 18 intr. maintain (a person), esp. in return for sexual favors (a kept woman). • n. 1 maintenance, food, etc. (hardly earn your keep). 2 charge or control (is in your keep). 3 hist. tower or stronghold. □ **for keeps** colloq. (esp. of something received or won) permanently, indefinitely. **keep at** persist or cause to persist with. **keep away** prevent from being near. **keep back** 1 remain at a distance. 2 retard the progress of. 3 conceal. 4 withhold (kept back $50). **keep down** 1 hold in subjection. 2 keep low in amount. 3 lie low; stay hidden. 4 not vomit (food eaten). **keep in mind** take into account having remembered. **keep off** 1 cause to stay away from. 2 ward off. **keep on** 1 do continually (kept on laughing). 2 continue to use or employ. 3 [foll. by at] pester. **keep out** 1 remain outside. 2 exclude. **keep to** 1 adhere to. 2 confine oneself to. **keep to oneself** 1 avoid contact with others. 2 refuse to disclose. **keep up** 1 maintain (progress, morale, etc.). 2 keep in repair, etc. 3 carry on (a correspondence, etc.). 4 prevent from going to bed. 5 [often foll. by with] not fall behind. **keep up with the Joneses** strive to compete socially with one's neighbors.

■ v. 1 hold, hang on to, preserve, have, save, maintain. 3 stay. 4 stow. 5 prevent, restrain, restrict, prohibit, deter, discourage. 6 delay, hold (up). 7 abide by, follow, obey, adhere to, heed, respect, acknowledge, fulfill, carry out. 8 raise, rear. 9 feed, nourish, nurture, provide for, support, sustain. 10 run, have, maintain, be responsible for. 12 stock, carry, deal in. 13 defend, cover, safeguard, shield. 15 go on, carry on, persist in. 16 stick to. 17 last. 18 finance, subsidize. • n. 1 upkeep, support, sustenance, living. 2 care, custody. 3 fortress. □ **for keeps** once and for all, for good, for ever. **keep at** persevere in, stick at, colloq. plug away at. **keep away** (keep away from) see AVOID[1] 1. **keep back** 2 see SUPPRESS 2. 3, 4 see WITHHOLD 1. **keep down** 1, 2 see SUPPRESS 2, TYRANNIZE. 3 see HIDE v. 2. **keep off** 1 see AVOID[1] 1. 2 see hold off (HOLD). **keep on** 1 carry on, persist in. 3 harass.

keep·er /kéepar/ n. 1 person who keeps or looks after something or someone. 2 custodian; guard. 3 colloq. anything worth keeping.

■ **1** guardian, warden, caretaker; attendant.

keep•ing /ke´eping/ n. **1** custody; charge (in safe keeping). **2** observance.

■ **1** see CARE n. 4.

keep•sake /ke´epsayk/ n. souvenir, esp. of the giver.

■ memento, token, reminder, remembrance, relic.

kees•hond /ka´ys-hond/ n. long-haired Dutch breed of dog.

keg /keg/ n. small barrel. □ **keg party** party at which beer is served from a keg.

■ cask, butt, hogshead, tun.

keis•ter /ke´estər/ n. sl. buttocks.

kelp /kelp/ n. brown seaweed used as a food and mineral source.

kel•vin /ke´lvin/ n. unit of thermodynamic temperature, equal in magnitude to the degree celsius. ¶Abbr.: **K**. □ **Kelvin scale** scale of temperature with absolute zero as zero.

kempt /kempt/ adj. combed; neatly kept.

ken /ken/ n. range of sight or knowledge.

ken•do /ke´ndō/ n. Japanese martial art of fencing with bamboo sticks.

ken•nel /ke´nəl/ • n. **1** small shelter for a dog. **2** [often in pl.] breeding or boarding place for dogs. • v. (**ken•neled, ken•nel•ing; ken•nelled, ken•nel•ling**) **1** tr. put into or keep in a kennel. **2** intr. live in or go to a kennel.

Ke•ogh plan /ke´ō/ • n. tax-deferred retirement investment plan for self-employed persons.

kep•i /ke´pee, ka´ypee/ n. (pl. **kep•is**) French military cap with a horizontal peak.

kept past and past part. of KEEP.

ker•a•tin /ke´rətin/ n. fibrous protein in hair, feathers, hooves, claws, horns, etc.

ker•chief /kə´rchif, –cheef/ n. **1** cloth used to cover the head or neck. **2** handkerchief. □□ **ker´chiefed** adj.

kerf /kərf/ n. slit made by cutting, esp. with a saw.

ker•nel /kə´rnəl/ n. **1** center within the hard shell of a nut, fruit stone, seed, etc. **2** whole seed of a cereal. **3** essence of anything.

■ **1, 2** grain, pip; (nut)meat. **3** core, nucleus, heart, substance, gist, pith, crux.

ker•o•sene /ke´rəseen/ n. petroleum distillate used as a fuel, solvent, etc.

kes•trel /ke´strəl/ n. small hovering falcon.

ketch /kech/ n. type of two-masted sailboat.

ketch•up /ke´chup, ka´chup/ n. (also **cat•sup** /ka´tsəp/) spicy tomato-based condiment.

ke•tone /ke´etōn/ n. any of a class of organic compounds, including acetone. □□ **ke•ton´ic** /kitón´ik/ adj.

ke•to•sis /keetō´sis/ n. condition of abnormally high levels of ketones in the body, associated with fat metabolism and diabetes.

ket•tle /ke´t'l/ n. vessel for boiling or cooking. □ **a fine** (or **pretty**) **kettle of fish** awkward state of affairs. □□ **ket´tle•ful** n. (pl. **–fuls**).

ket•tle•drum /ke´t'ldrum/ n. large bowl-shaped drum.

Kew•pie /kyoo´pee/ n. propr. small, chubby doll with a curl or topknot.

key¹ /kee/ • n. (pl. **keys**) **1** instrument, usu. metal, for moving the bolt of a lock to lock or unlock. **2** similar implement for winding a clock, etc. **3** finger-operated button or lever on a piano, flute, typewriter, computer terminal, etc. **4** means of advance, access, etc. **5 a** solution or explanation. **b** word or system for solving a cipher or code. **c** explanatory list of symbols used in a map, table, etc. **6** Mus. system of notes related to each other and based on a particular note (key of C major). • adj. essential; of vital importance. • v. tr. (**keys, keyed**) **1** fasten with a pin, bolt, etc. **2** enter (data) by means of a keyboard. **3** align or link (one thing to another). **4** regulate the pitch of the strings of (a violin, etc.). □ **key up** make nervous or tense; excite.

■ n. **1** latchkey, skeleton key, passkey, opener. **3** (keys) ivories. **5 a** clue, cue, indication. **b** keyword, password. **c** legend, code. **6** scale, mode, pitch. • adj. necessary, crucial, critical, pivotal, central. • v. **2** type, input. □ **key up** see EXCITE v. 1.

key² /kee/ n. low-lying island or reef, esp. off Florida.

key•board /ke´ebawrd/ • n. **1** set of keys on a typewriter, computer, piano, etc. **2** pianolike electronic musical instrument. • v. enter (data) by means of a keyboard. □□ **key´board•er** n. **key´board•ist** n.

■ n. **1** ivories; see also TERMINAL n. 4. **2** synthesizer. • v. key (in), type, typewrite, input.

key•hole /ke´ehōl/ n. hole by which a key is put into a lock.

key•note /ke´enōt/ n. **1** (esp. attrib.) prevailing tone or idea (keynote address). **2** Mus. note on which a key is based.

■ **1** see THEME 1.

key•pad /ke´epad/ n. small keyboard, etc., on a calculator, telephone, etc.

key•punch /ke´epunch/ • n. device for transferring data by means of punched holes or notches on cards or paper tape. • v. tr. transfer (data) thus. □□ **key´punch•er** n.

key•stone /ke´estōn/ n. **1** central principle of a system, policy, etc. **2** central locking stone of an arch.

■ crux, foundation, cornerstone.

key•stroke /ke´estrōk/ n. single depression of a key on a keyboard, esp. as a measure of work.

key•word /ke´ewərd/ n. **1** key to a cipher, etc. **2 a** word of great significance. **b** significant word used in indexing.

kg abbr. kilogram(s).

KGB /ka´yjeebee´/ n. security police of the former USSR.

kha•ki /ka´kee, kaä–/ • adj. dull brownish-yellow. • n. (pl. **kha•kis**) **1 a** khaki fabric of twilled cotton or wool. **b** [in pl.] pants or a military uniform made of this fabric. **2** dull brownish-yellow color.

khan /kaan, kan/ n. title of rulers and officials in Central Asia, Afghanistan, etc. □□ **khan´ate** n.

Khmer /kmair/ • n. **1** native of Cambodia. **2** language of this people. • adj. of the Khmers or their language.

kHz abbr. kilohertz.

kib•ble /kíbəl/ n. coarsely ground pellets of meal, etc., used as pet food.

kib•butz /kibŏŏts/ n. (pl. **kib•but•zim** /-bŏŏtseém/) communal, esp. farming, settlement in Israel.

kib•itz /kíbits/ v.intr. colloq. offer unwanted advice, esp. to card players. □□ **kib′itz•er** n.
■ see MEDDLE. see BUSYBODY 1. □□ **kibitzer**

ki•bosh /kíbosh/ n. sl. nonsense. □ **put the kibosh on** colloq. put an end to; finally dispose of.

kick /kik/ • v. **1** tr. & intr. strike or propel forcibly with the foot or hoof, etc. **2** intr. express annoyance at; rebel against. **3** tr. sl. give up (a habit). **4** tr. expel or dismiss forcibly. **5** refl. be annoyed with oneself. **6** tr. Football score (a goal) by a kick. • n. **1** blow with the foot or hoof, etc. **2** colloq. a sharp stimulant effect, esp. of alcohol. **b** [often in pl.] pleasurable thrill (did it for kicks). **3** colloq. temporary interest (on a jogging kick). **4** recoil of a fired gun. □ **kick about** (or **around**) colloq. **1 a** drift idly from place to place. **b** be unused or unwanted. **2 a** treat roughly or scornfully. **b** discuss (an idea) unsystematically. **kick the bucket** sl. die. **kick in 1** knock down (a door, etc.) by kicking. **2** sl. pay one's share. **kick in the pants** (or **teeth**) colloq. humiliating setback. **kick off 1 a** Football, etc. begin or resume play. **b** colloq. begin. **2** remove (shoes, etc.) by kicking. **kick-start** (a motorcycle, etc.) by the downward thrust of a pedal. **kick up** (or **kick up a fuss**, etc.) create a disturbance. **kick up one's heels** frolic.
■ v. **1** punt, colloq. boot. **2** see PROTEST¹ v. 1. **3** see DISCONTINUE. **4** see turn out 1. ■ n. **1** punt, hit, dropkick. **2** see THRILL n. 1. **3** see FIXATION. **4** backlash, rebound. □ **kick about** (or **around**) **1 a** see knock about 2. **2 a** see knock about 1. **b** debate, talk over. **kick the bucket** see DIE 1. **kick in 1** smash in, demolish. **kick off 1** see START 1, 2. **kick up a fuss** see COMPLAIN 1.

kick•back /kíkbak/ n. colloq. **1** recoil. **2** (usu. illegal) payment for collaboration.
■ **1** see BACKLASH 2. **2** share, cut, compensation; hush money, payola, colloq. graft, pay-off.

kick•off /kíkawf/ n. **1** Football & Soccer kick that starts play. **2** start of a campaign, drive, project, etc.

kick•stand /kíkstand/ n. rod for supporting a bicycle or motorcycle when stationary.

kid¹ /kid/ n. **1** young goat. **2** leather from its skin. **3** colloq. child. □ **handle with kid gloves** treat carefully. **kid brother** (or **sister**) sl. younger brother (or sister).
■ n. **3** see CHILD 1a.

kid² /kid/ v. (**kid•ded, kid•ding**) colloq. **1** tr. & also refl. deceive; trick. **2** tr. & intr. tease (only kidding). □ **no kidding** sl. that is the truth. □□ **kid′der** n. **kid′ding•ly** adv.
■ **1** see FOOL v. 2. **2** see TAUNT v.

kid•die /kídee/ n. (pl. **–dies**) sl. = KID¹ n. 3.

kid•nap /kídnap/ v.tr. (**kid•napped, kid•nap•ping; kid•naped, kid•nap•ing**) **1** abduct (a person, etc.), esp. to obtain a ransom. **2** steal (a child). □□ **kid′nap•per** n.
■ capture, seize, hold as hostage, snatch.

kid•ney /kídnee/ n. (pl. **–neys**) **1** either of two organs in the abdominal cavity of vertebrates that remove wastes from the blood and excrete urine. **2** animal's kidney as food. □ **kidney bean** red-skinned kidney-shaped bean.

kiel•ba•sa /keelbaásə, kib–/ n. smoked Polish-style sausage.

kill /kil/ • v.tr. **1 a** cause the death of. **b** [absol.] cause death (must kill to survive). **2** destroy; put an end to (feelings, etc.). **3** switch off (a light, engine, etc.). **4** pass (time, or a specified period) usu. while waiting. **5** defeat (legislation, etc.). **6 a** Tennis, etc., hit (the ball) so that it cannot be returned. **b** stop (the ball) dead. **7** render ineffective (taste, sound, color, etc.) (thick carpet killed the sound of footsteps). • n. **1** act of killing. **2** animal or animals killed, esp. by a hunter. **3** colloq. destruction or disablement of an enemy aircraft, submarine, etc. □ **dressed to kill** dressed alluringly or impressively. **in at the kill** present at or benefiting from the successful conclusion of an enterprise. **kill two birds with one stone** achieve two aims at once. **kill with kindness** spoil (a person) with overindulgence.
■ v. **1 a** execute, murder, assassinate, put to death, put an end to, exterminate, snuff out, extinguish; colloq. do away with, bump off, rub out. **2** quash, crush, stamp out, eliminate, expunge. **3** see turn off 1. **4** use up, spend, while away, fritter (away), squander. **7** muffle, neutralize, deaden, silence, smother, suppress. • n. **1** death; termination, conclusion. **2** game, prey; quarry; bag.

SYNONYM STUDY: kill

ASSASSINATE, DISPATCH, EXECUTE, MASSACRE, MURDER, SLAUGHTER, SLAY. When it comes to depriving someone of something of life, the options are endless. To **kill** is the most general term, meaning to cause the death of a person, animal, or plant, with no reference to the manner of killing, the agent, or the cause (to be killed in a car accident). Even inanimate things may be killed (Congress killed the project when they vetoed the bill). To **slay** is to kill deliberately and violently; it is used more often in written than in spoken English (a novel about a presidential candidate who is slain by his opponent). **Murder** implies a malicious and premeditated killing of one person by another (a gruesome murder carried out by the son-in-law), while **assassinate** implies that a politically important person has been murdered, often by someone hired to do the job (to assassinate the head of the guerrilla forces). Someone who is put to death by a legal or military process is said to be **executed** (to execute by lethal injection), but if someone is killed primarily to get rid of him or for her, the appropriate verb is **dispatch**, which also suggests speed or promptness (after delivering the secret documents, the informer was dispatched). While **slaughter** is usually associated with the killing of animals for food, it can also apply to a mass killing of humans (*the slaughter of innocent civilians provoked a worldwide outcry*). **Massacre** also refers to the brutal *murder* of large numbers of people, but it is used more specifically to indicate the wholesale destruction of a relatively defenseless group of people (*the massacre of Bethlehem's male children by King Herod is commemorated as Holy Innocents' Day*).

kill•deer /kíldeer/ *n.* large American plover.

kill•er /kílər/ *n.* **1** person, animal, or thing that kills. **2** *colloq.* **a** impressive, formidable, or excellent thing. **b** decisive blow. □ **killer bee** very aggressive honeybee, orig. from Africa. **killer instinct 1** innate tendency to kill. **2** ruthless streak. **killer whale** voracious cetacean with a prominent dorsal fin.
■ **1** murderer, assassin, exterminator. **2 a** wonder, marvel, *sl.* humdinger, beaut, dilly.

kill•ing /kíling/ • *n.* **1 a** causing of death. **b** instance of this. **2** great (esp. financial) success. • *adj. colloq.* exhausting.
■ *n.* **1** murder, carnage, execution, slaughter, massacre, extermination, annihilation; slaying, homicide. **2** coup, bonanza, windfall. • *adj.* devastating, debilitating, wearying, draining, tiring, taxing.

kill•joy /kíljoy/ *n.* gloomy person, esp. at a party, etc.
■ spoilsport, grouch, wet blanket, *sl.* party pooper.

kiln /kiln, kil/ *n.* furnace or oven for burning, baking, or drying, esp. bricks, pottery, etc.

ki•lo /kéelō/ *n.* (*pl.* **-los**) **1** kilogram. **2** kilometer.

kilo- /kílō/ *comb. form* denoting a factor of 1,000 (esp. in metric units). ¶Abbr.: **k**, or **K** in *Computing.*

kil•o•byte /kíləbīt/ *n. Computing* 1,024 (i.e., 2^{10}) bytes as a measure of data storage.

kil•o•cy•cle /kíləsīkəl/ *n.* former measure of frequency, equivalent to 1 kilohertz. ¶Abbr.: **kc.**

kil•o•gram /kíləgram/ *n.* metric unit of mass, approx. 2.205 lb. ¶Abbr.: **kg.**

kil•o•hertz /kíləhərts/ *n.* 1,000 hertz; 1,000 cycles per second. ¶Abbr.: **kHz.**

kil•o•me•ter /kílómitər, kiləmeetər/ *n.* 1,000 meters (approx. 0.62 miles). ¶Abbr.: **km.** □□ **kil•o•met•ric** /kíləmétrik/ *adj.*

kil•o•ton /kílətun/ *n.* unit of explosive power equivalent to 1,000 tons of TNT.

kil•o•watt /kíləwot/ *n.* 1,000 watts. ¶Abbr.: **kW.**

kil•o•watt-hour /kíləwot-ówr/ *n.* measure of electrical energy equivalent to a power consumption of 1,000 watts for one hour. ¶Abbr.: **kWh.**

kilt /kilt/ *n.* **1** knee-length skirt, usu. of pleated tartan, traditionally worn by Scottish Highland men. **2** similar garment worn by women.

kil•ter /kíltər/ *n.* good working order (esp. *out of kilter*).

ki•mo•no /kimónō/ *n.* (*pl.* **-nos**) **1** long,
loose Japanese robe worn with a sash. **2** similar dressing gown.

kin /kin/ • *n.* one's relatives or family. • *predic.adj.* (of a person) related (*we are kin*) see also AKIN). □ **next of kin** see NEXT.
■ *n.* relations, folks, kinfolk, kinsmen, clan, people, blood relations. • *adj.* akin (to), kindred.

-kin /kin/ *suffix* forming diminutive nouns (*catkin, manikin*).

kind[1] /kīnd/ *n.* **1** race, species, or natural group of animals, plants, etc. **2** class; type; sort; variety. ¶In sense 2, *these* (or *those*) *kind* is often encountered when followed by a plural, as in *I don't like these kind of things*, but *this kind* and *these kinds* are usually preferred. □ **kind of** *colloq.* to some extent. **in kind 1** in the same form; likewise (*replied in kind*). **2** (of payment) in goods or labor, not money. **nothing of the kind 1** not at all like the thing in question. **2** (expressing denial) not at all. **of a kind 1** *derog.* scarcely deserving the name (*a choir of a kind*). **2** similar in some respect (*they're two of a kind*).
■ **1** genus, breed, type, order. **2** category, genre, species, set; brand, make.

kind[2] /kīnd/ *adj.* of a friendly, generous, benevolent, or gentle nature.
■ nice, congenial, affable, amiable, thoughtful, considerate, warm, affectionate.

kin•der•gar•ten /kíndərgaart'n/ *n.* school or class for preschool learning.

kind•heart•ed /kíndháartid/ *adj.* of a kind disposition. □□ **kind′heart′ed•ly** *adv.* **kind′heart′ed•ness** *n.*
■ see KIND[2]. □□ **kindheartedly** see KINDLY[1] 1. **kindheartedness** see KINDNESS 1.

kin•dle /kínd'l/ *v.* **1** *tr.* light or set on fire. **2** *intr.* catch fire. **3** *tr.* arouse; inspire. **4** *intr.* become animated, glow with passion, etc. □□ **kin′dler** *n.*
■ **1** ignite. **2** burst into flame. **3** inflame, foment, incite, provoke, stimulate.

kin•dling /kíndling/ *n.* small sticks, etc., for lighting fires.

kind•ly[1] /kíndlee/ *adv.* **1** in a kind manner (*spoke kindly*). **2** please (*kindly leave me alone*).
■ **1** cordially, graciously, politely, thoughtfully, pleasantly. **2** be so kind as to, be good enough to.

kind•ly[2] /kíndlee/ *adj.* (**kind•li•er, kind•li•est**) **1** kind. **2** (of climate, etc.) pleasant. □□ **kind′li•ness** *n.*
■ **1** see KIND[2]. □□ **kindliness** see KINDNESS 1.

kind•ness /kíndnis/ *n.* **1** being kind. **2** kind act.
■ **1** friendliness, goodness, goodwill, decency, gentleness, understanding, thoughtfulness, warmth. **2** favor, good deed *or* turn.

kin•dred /kíndrid/ • *n.* one's relations, collectively. • *adj.* related, allied, or similar. □ **kindred spirit** person whose character, etc., has much in common with one's own.
■ *n.* see KIN *n.* • *adj.* consanguineous; close, like; akin.

ki•ne•mat•ics /kínimátiks/ *n.pl.* [usu. treated as *sing.*] branch of mechanics concerned with the motion of objects without reference to cause. □□ **ki•ne•mat'ic** *adj.* **ki•ne•mat'i•cal•ly** *adv.*

ki•net•ic /kinétik, kī-/ *adj.* of or due to motion. □□ **ki•net'i•cal•ly** *adv.*

ki•net•ics /kinétiks, kī-/ *n.pl.* = DYNAMICS 1.

kin•folk /kínfok/ *n.pl.* (also **kin'folks, kins' folk**) relatives.

king /king/ • *n.* **1** male sovereign, esp. a hereditary ruler. **2** person or thing preeminent in a specified field, etc. (*railroad king*). **3** large (or the largest) kind of plant, animal, etc. (*king penguin*). **4** *Chess* piece that must be checkmated for a win. **5** crowned piece in checkers. **6** playing card depicting a king. • *v.tr.* make (a person) king. □ **king cobra** large and venomous hooded Indian snake. **king of (the) beasts** the lion. **king-size** (or **-sized**) larger than normal; very large. **king's ransom** a fortune. □□ **king'ly** *adj.* **king'li•ness** *n.* **king'ship** *n.*

■ *n.* **1** crowned head, majesty, monarch, regent. **2** see BIGWIG². □ **king-size** see BIG *adj.* 1a. **king's ransom** see MINT *n.* 2.

king•dom /kíngdəm/ *n.* **1** territory subject to a king or queen. **2** spiritual reign or sphere attributed to God. **3** domain; sphere. **4** province of nature (*vegetable kingdom*). □ **kingdom come** *colloq.* eternity; the next world.

■ **1** empire, sovereignty, monarchy, realm; see also DOMINION 2. **3** field, area, province.

king•fish•er /kíngfishər/ *n.* long-beaked, brightly colored bird that dives for fish in rivers, etc.

king•pin /kíngpin/ *n.* **1** main or large bolt in a central position. **2** essential person or thing.

■ **1** see PIVOT *n.* 1. **2** see BIGWIG, LEADER 1.

kink /kingk/ • *n.* **1 a** twist or bend in wire, etc. **b** tight wave in hair. **2** mental twist or quirk. • *v.* form or cause to form a kink.

■ *n.* **1** crimp, tangle, knot, wrinkle. **2** whim, caprice, fancy; flaw, hitch, snag.

kink•y /kíngkee/ *adj.* (**kink•i•er, kink•i•est**) **1** *colloq.* **a** given to or involving abnormal sexual behavior. **b** (of clothing, etc.) bizarre and sexually provocative. **2** eccentric. **3** having kinks. □□ **kink'i•ly** *adv.* **kink'i•ness** *n.*

■ **1** a perverted, deviant. **b** suggestive, sexy. **2** outlandish, peculiar, quirky, strange, offbeat. **3** frizzy, curly, crimped; tangled, twisted. □□ **kinkiness** see PERVERSION 3b, ODDITY 3.

kins•folk var. of KINFOLK.

kin•ship /kínship/ *n.* **1** blood relationship. **2** sharing of characteristics or origins.

■ **1** (family) ties, lineage, flesh and blood. **2** affinity; connection, similarity, alliance.

kins•man /kínzmən/ *n.* (*pl.* **-men;** *fem.* **kins' wom•an,** *pl.* **-wom•en**) blood relation or *disp.* relation by marriage.

ki•osk /kéeosk, -ósk/ *n.* **1** open-fronted booth from which food, newspapers, tickets, etc., are sold. **2** columnar structure for posting notices, etc.

■ **1** stall, stand, cubicle, shop.

Ki•o•wa /kíəwə/ *n.* **1 a** N. American people native to the southwestern US. **b** member of this people. **2** language of this people.

kip•per /kípər/ • *n.* kippered fish, esp. herring. • *v.tr.* cure (herring, etc.) by splitting, salting, and drying.

kirk /kurk/ *n. Sc. & No. of Engl.* church.

kis•met /kízmet/ *n.* destiny; fate.

kiss /kis/ • *v.* **1** *tr.* touch with the lips, esp. as a sign of love, affection, greeting, or reverence. **2** *absol.* (of two persons) touch each others' lips in this way. **3** *tr.* lightly touch. • *n.* **1** touch with the lips. **2** light touch. **3** droplet-shaped piece of candy, etc. □ **kiss and tell** recount one's sexual exploits. **kissing cousin** distant relative (given a kiss upon meeting). **kiss of death** apparently friendly act that causes ruin. □□ **kiss'a•ble** *adj.*

■ *v.* **1** peck (on the cheek), *colloq.* buss. **2** *colloq.* smooch, neck. **3** brush, graze. • *n.* **1** peck, smack.

kit¹ /kit/ *n.* **1** articles, equipment, etc., for a specific purpose. **2** set of parts needed to assemble an item. □ **kit bag** esp. cylindrical bag used for carrying equipment, etc. **the whole kit and caboodle** see CABOODLE.

■ **1** apparatus, gear, rig, outfit, effects, supplies. □ **kit bag** see PACK¹ *n.* 1.

kit² /kit/ *n.* **1** kitten. **2** young fox, badger, etc.

kitch•en /kíchin/ *n.* room or area where food is prepared and cooked. □ **everything but the kitchen sink** everything imaginable. **kitchen cabinet** group of unofficial advisers thought to be unduly influential.

■ cookhouse, scullery.

kitch•en•ette /kíchinét/ *n.* small kitchen or cooking area.

kitch•en•ware /kíchinwair/ *n.* utensils used in the kitchen.

kite /kit/ *n.* **1** light framework with thin covering, flown on a string in the wind. **2** soaring bird of prey with long wings and usu. a forked tail.

kith /kith/ *n.* □ **kith and kin** friends and relations.

kitsch /kich/ *n.* [often *attrib.*] garish, pretentious, or vulgar art.

kit•ten /kít'n/ *n.* young cat, ferret, etc. □ **have kittens** *colloq.* be extremely upset or anxious.

kit•ten•ish /kít'nish/ *adj.* **1** playful; lively. **2** flirtatious. □□ **kit'ten•ish•ly** *adv.*

■ **1** sportive, frisky. **2** coy, seductive.

kit•ty¹ /kítee/ *n.* (*pl.* **-ties**) **1** fund of money for communal use. **2** pool in some card games.

■ **1** reserve, purse, bank. **2** pot, jackpot, stakes.

kit•ty² /kítee/ *n.* (*pl.* **-ties**) pet name for a kitten or cat.

kit•ty-cor•ner var. of CATERCORNERED.

ki•wi /kéewee/ *n.* (*pl.* **ki•wis**) **1** flightless long-billed New Zealand bird. **2** (**Kiwi**) *colloq.* New Zealander. □ **kiwi fruit** fuzzy-skinned, green-fleshed fruit.

KKK *abbr.* Ku Klux Klan.

klep•to•ma•ni•a /kléptəmáyneeə/ *n.* recurrent urge to steal. □□ **klep•to•ma'ni•ac** *n. & adj.*

klutz /kluts/ *n. sl.* **1** clumsy, awkward person. **2** fool. □□ **klutz'y** *adj.*

km *abbr.* kilometer(s).

kmph *abbr.* kilometers per hour.

kmps *abbr.* kilometers per second.

knack /nak/ *n.* **1** acquired faculty of doing a thing. **2** habit of action, speech, etc.
∎ **1** talent, gift, skill; flair; expertise. **2** trick, art, technique.

knap•sack /nápsak/ *n.* bag of supplies, etc., carried on the back.
∎ see PACK¹ *n.* 1.

knave /nayv/ *n.* **1** rogue; scoundrel. **2** = JACK *n.* 2. □□ **knav′er•y** *n.* (*pl.* **-ies**) **knav′ish** *adj.* **knav′ish•ly** *adv.*
∎ **1** see ROGUE *n.* 1. □□ **knavery** see DEVILRY. **knavish** see DISHONEST.

knead /need/ *v.tr.* **1** prepare dough, paste, etc., by pressing and folding. **2** massage (muscles, etc.) as if kneading. □□ **knead′a•ble** *adj.* **knead′er** *n.*
∎ **1** pummel, work. **2** rub (down), manipulate.

knee /nee/ ∎ *n.* **1** joint between the thigh and the lower leg in humans and other animals. **2** part of a garment covering the knee. ∎ *v.tr.* (**knees, kneed, knee•ing**) touch or strike with the knee (*kneed him in the groin*).
□ **bring a person to his** or **her knees** reduce a person to submission. **knee-deep 1** immersed up to the knees. **2** deeply involved. **knee jerk** reflex kick caused by a blow on the tendon just below the knee. **knee-jerk** [*attrib.*] predictable; automatic.
∎ □ **knee-deep 2** (*knee-deep in*). **knee-jerk** see AUTOMATIC *adj.* 2a.

knee•cap /neékap/ *n.* bone in front of the knee joint; patella.

kneel /neel/ *v.intr.* (*past* and *past part.* **knelt** /nelt/ or **kneeled**) fall or rest on the knees or a knee.
∎ genuflect, crouch, bow, stoop.

knell /nel/ ∎ *n.* **1** sound of a bell, esp. for a death or funeral. **2** announcement, event, etc., regarded as an ill omen. ∎ *v.* **1** *intr.* (of a bell) ring solemnly. **2** *tr.* proclaim by or as by a knell.
∎ *n.* **1** see TOLL² *n.* **2** see WARNING². ∎ *v.* **1** see RING *v.* 1.

knelt *past* and *past part.* of KNEEL.

knew *past* of KNOW.

knick•ers /níkərz/ *n.pl.* loose-fitting pants gathered at the knee or calf.

knick•knack /níknak/ *n.* trinket or small, dainty article.
∎ see GEWGAW, ORNAMENT *n.* 1.

knife /nīf/ ∎ *n.* (*pl.* **knives** /nīvz/) **1** cutting tool, usu. with a sharp-edged blade in a handle. **2** cutting blade in a machine. ∎ *v.tr.* cut or stab with a knife. □ **that one could cut with a knife** *colloq.* (of an accent, atmosphere, etc.) very obvious, oppressive, etc. **under the knife** undergoing surgery. □□ **knife′like** *adj.* **knif′er** *n.*
∎ *n.* **1** cutter; penknife, pocket knife; sword, saber, dagger; switchblade, jackknife. ∎ *v.* pierce, slash, slit, wound.

knight /nīt/ ∎ *n.* **1** man awarded a nonhereditary title (*Sir*) by a sovereign. **2** *hist.* **a** man, usu. noble, raised to honorable military rank. **b** military attendant, esp. of a lady. **3** *Chess* piece usu. shaped like a horse's head. □ **knight-errant 1** medieval knight in search of chivalrous adventures. **2** chivalrous or quixotic man. **knight in shining armor** chivalrous rescuer or helper, esp. of a woman. □□ **knight′hood** *n.* **knight′like** *adj.* **knight′ly** *adj.*

knit /nit/ ∎ *v.* (**knit•ting**; *past* and *past part.* **knit•ted** or (esp. in senses 2–4) **knit**) **1** *tr.* [also *absol.*] make (a garment, etc.) by interlocking loops of yarn with knitting needles or a knitting machine. **2 a** *tr.* contract (the forehead) in vertical wrinkles. **b** *intr.* (of the forehead) contract; frown. **3** *tr. & intr.* make or become close or compact (*a close-knit group*). **4** *intr.* (of a broken bone) become joined; heal. ∎ *n.* knitted material or garment. □□ **knit′ter** *n.*
∎ *v.* **2** furrow, crease. **3** interweave, interlace, bind, unite. **4** grow (together), mend.

knit•ting /níting/ *n.* work being knitted.

knives *pl.* of KNIFE.

knob /nob/ *n.* rounded protuberance, esp. at the end or on the surface of a thing as the handle of a door, drawer, etc. □□ **knob′by** *adj.* **knob′like** *adj.*
∎ *n.* swelling, bump, node; button, control.

knock /nok/ ∎ *v.* **1 a** *tr.* strike with an audible sharp blow. **b** *intr.* strike, esp. a door to gain admittance. **2** *tr.* make (a hole, etc.) by knocking. **3** *tr.* drive (a thing, person, etc.) by striking (*knocked her hand away*). **4** *tr. sl.* criticize. **5** *intr.* (of an engine) make a thumping or rattling noise. ∎ *n.* **1** act of knocking. **2** sharp rap, esp. at a door. **3** audible sharp blow. **4** sound of knocking in an engine. □ **knock about** (or **around**) **1** strike repeatedly; treat roughly. **2** wander aimlessly. **3** be present without design (*there's a cup knocking about somewhere*). **knock down 1** strike (esp. a person) to the ground. **2** demolish. **3** (at an auction) sell to a bidder by a knock with a hammer. **4** *colloq.* lower the price of (an article). **knock-kneed** having knock-knees. **knock-knees** condition in which the legs curve inward at the knee. **knock off 1** strike off with a blow. **2** finish work. **3** rapidly produce (a work of art, etc.). **4** deduct (a sum) from a price, etc. **5** *sl.* steal from (*knocked off a liquor store*). **6** *sl.* kill. **knock on** (or **knock**) **wood** knock something wooden with the knuckles to avert bad luck. **knock out 1** make unconscious by a blow on the head. **2** defeat, esp. in competition. **3** *sl.* astonish. **4** [*refl.*] *colloq.* exhaust (*knocked themselves out swimming*). **knock together** assemble hastily or roughly. **knock up 1** make hastily. **2** damage or mar. **3** *coarse sl.* make pregnant.
∎ *v.* **1** hit, rap, thump, tap. **3** disparage, run down, *colloq.* put down. ∎ *n.* **1, 2** banging, pounding, hammering. **3** smack, clout, whack. □ **knock about** (or **around**) **1** beat (up), batter, abuse, *colloq.* manhandle. **2** roam, ramble, rove, gad about. **knock down 1** fell, cut down. **2** raze, destroy, level, tear down. **4** see REDUCE 7. **knock off 2** quit, go home, close down. **3** see *knock up*

1 below. **4** see DEDUCT. **5** thieve, rob, burglarize, *colloq.* hold up. **6** see KILL *v.* 1. **knock out 1** floor, *colloq.* flatten. **3** overwhelm, astound, *colloq.* bowl over. **knock together** see *knock up* 1 below. **knock up 1** whip up, improvise. **3** impregnate.

knock•er /nókər/ *n.* metal or wooden instrument hinged to a door for knocking.

knock•out /nókowt/ *n.* **1** act of making unconscious by a blow. **2** *Boxing*, etc., blow that knocks an opponent out. **3** *colloq.* outstanding or irresistible person or thing.

■ **2** coup de grâce. **3** sensation, triumph, winner, smash.

knock•wurst /naákwərst/ *n.* variety of thick, seasoned sausage.

knoll /nōl/ *n.* small hill or mound

■ hillock, hummock, barrow, elevation, rise.

knot /not/ *n.* **1 a** intertwining of rope, string, hair, etc., with another, itself, or something else to join or fasten together. **b** set method of this (*a reef knot*). **c** ribbon, etc., tied as an ornament. **d** tangle in hair, knitting, etc. **2 a** unit of a ship's or aircraft's speed, equivalent to one nautical mile per hour. **b** *colloq.* nautical mile. **3** cluster (*knot of journalists at the gate*). **4** bond or tie, esp. of wedlock. **5** hard lump of body tissue. **6 a** knob in a stem, branch, or root. **b** hard mass in a tree trunk at the intersection with a branch. **c** round cross-grained piece in lumber where a branch has been cut through. **7** difficulty; problem. **8** central point in a problem, plot, etc. ● *v.tr.* (**knot•ted, knot•ting**) **1** tie in a knot. **2** entangle. **3** unite closely. □ **knot garden** intricately designed formal garden, esp. of herbs. **tie the knot** get married. □□ **knot•ter** *n.*

■ *n.* **1 a** tie, bond, twist. **d** snarl. **3** group, crowd, bunch, gathering. **6 a** protuberance. ● *v.* **1** fasten, bind, secure, lash. **2** see ENTANGLE 1, 2. **3** join, connect, link, bond.

knot•hole /nóthōl/ *n.* hole in lumber where a knot has fallen out.

knot•ty /nótee/ *adj.* (**knot•ti•er, knot•ti•est**) **1** full of knots. **2** puzzling (*knotty problem*). □□ **knot•ti•ly** *adv.* **knot•ti•ness** *n.*

■ **1** see GNARLED. **2** see *perplexing* (PERPLEX), DIFFICULT 1b.

know /nō/ ● *v.tr.* (*past* **knew** /nōō, nyōō/; *past part.* **known** /nōn/) **1 a** have in the mind; have learned; be able to recall (*knows what to do*). **b** [*also absol.*] be aware of (a fact) (*I think she knows*). **c** have a good command of (*knew German*). **2** be acquainted or friendly with. **3 a** recognize; identify (*I knew him at once*). **b** [foll. by *from*] be able to distinguish (*did not know him from Adam*). **4** be subject to (*her joy knew no bounds*). **5** have personal experience of (fear, etc.). **6** (as **known** *adj.*) **a** publicly acknowledged (*a known thief*). **b** *Math.* (of a quantity, etc.) having a value that can be stated. ● *n.* (in phr. **in the know**) *colloq.* well-informed; having special knowledge. □ **all one knows** (or **knows how**) all one can (*did all she knew to stop it*). **before one knows where one is** with baffling speed. **be not to know** be not to be told (*she's not to know about the party*). **don't I know it!** *colloq.* expression of rueful assent.

don't you know *colloq.* or *joc.* expression used for emphasis (*such a bore, don't you know*). **for all I know** so far as my knowledge extends. **have been known to** be known to have done (*they have been known to forget*). **I knew it!** I was sure that this would happen. **I know what** I have a new idea, suggestion, etc. **know best** be or claim to be better informed, etc., than others. **know better than** [foll. by *that*, or to + infin.] be wise, well-informed, or well-mannered enough to avoid (specified behavior, etc.). **know by name** have heard the name of. **know by sight** recognize the appearance (only) of. **know how** know the way to do something. **know-how** *n.* **1** practical knowledge. **2** natural skill or invention. **know-it-all** *colloq.* person who acts as if he or she knows everything. **know of** be aware of (*not that I know of*). **know the ropes** be fully knowledgeable or experienced. **know a thing or two** be experienced or shrewd. **know what's what** have adequate knowledge of the world, life, etc. **not know what hit one** be suddenly injured, killed, disconcerted, etc. **not want to know** refuse to take any notice of. **what do you know** (or **know about that**) ? *colloq.* expression of surprise. **you know** *colloq.* expression implying something generally known (*you know, the store on the corner*). **you-know-what** (or **-who**) thing or person unspecified but understood. **you never know** nothing in the future is certain. □□ **know'a•ble** *adj.* **know'er** *n.*

■ *v.* **1 a** understand, comprehend, grasp, be acquainted with. **b** be cognizant of, have knowledge of. **2** be familiar with. **3 a** place, recall, remember, recollect. **b** separate, differentiate, discriminate. **5** see EXPERIENCE[1] *v.* **2**. **6** (**known**) **a** see *well-known* (WELL). ● *n.* (**in the know**). see *well-informed* (WELL[1]). □ **know-how** (*n.*) see TECHNIQUE[1] **1**. **know-it-all** see *wise guy* (WISE).

know•ing /nóing/ ● *n.* state of being aware or informed of any thing. ● *adj.* **1** *usu. derog.* cunning; sly. **2** showing knowledge; shrewd. □□ **know'ing•ly** *adv.*

■ *n.* see KNOWLEDGE 2. ● *adj.* **1** conspiratorial, secret, private; significant, meaningful; artful, crafty. **2** wise, clever, aware, qualified, astute, perceptive. □□ **knowingly** see *deliberately* (DELIBERATE).

knowl•edge /nólij/ *n.* **1 a** awareness or familiarity (of a person, fact, or thing) (*have no knowledge of their character*). **b** person's range of information. **2 a** understanding of a subject, language, etc. (*good knowledge of Greek*). **b** sum of what is known (*every branch of knowledge*). □ **to (the best of) my knowledge** so far as I know.

■ **1 a** knowing, grasp, understanding, insight. **b** ken, perception. **2 a** acquaintance, familiarity, expertise, proficiency.

---

you know? **Knowledge** applies to any body of facts gathered by study, observation, or experience, and to the ideas inferred from these facts (*an in-depth knowledge of particle physics*). **Information** may be no more than a collection of data or facts (*information about vacation resorts*) gathered through observation, reading, or hearsay, with no guarantee of their validity (*false information that led to the arrest*). **Scholarship** emphasizes academic *knowledge* or accomplishment (*a special award for scholarship*), while **learning** is *knowledge* gained not only by study in schools and universities but by individual research and investigation (*a man of education and learning*), which puts it on a somewhat higher plane. **Erudition** is on a higher plane still, implying bookish *knowledge* that is beyond the average person's comprehension (*to exhibit extraordinary erudition in a doctoral dissertation*). **Pedantry**, on the other hand, is a negative term for a slavish attention to obscure facts or details or an undue display of *learning* (*the pedantry of modern literary criticism*). You can have extensive *knowledge* of a subject and even exhibit *erudition*, however, without attaining *wisdom*, the superior judgment and understanding that is based on both *knowledge* and experience.

knowl•edge•a•ble /nólijəbəl/ *adj.* well-informed; intelligent. □□ **knowl′edge•a•bly** *adv.*
■ aware, (well-)acquainted, cognizant, familiar, enlightened; well-educated, learned.
known *past part.* of KNOW.
knuck•le /núkəl/ • *n.* **1** bone at a finger joint, esp. that adjoining the hand. **2** knee or ankle joint of an animal, used as food. • *v.tr.* strike, press, or rub with the knuckles. □ **knuckle down** [often foll. by *to*] apply oneself seriously (to a task, etc.). **knuckle sandwich** *sl.* punch in the mouth. **knuckle under** give in; submit.
knuck•le•ball /núkəlbawl/ *n.* *Baseball* pitch delivered with the ball held by the knuckles or fingernails such that the ball has minimal spin and moves erratically.
knuck•le•head /núkəlhed/ *n. colloq.* slow-witted or stupid person.
knurl /nərl/ *n.* small projecting knob, ridge, etc. □□ **knurl′ed** /nərld/ *adj.*
KO *abbr.* knockout.
ko•a•la /kō-äälə/ *n.* Australian bearlike marsupial with thick, gray fur.
kohl•ra•bi /kōlraabee/ *n.* (*pl.* -**bies**) cabbage with an edible turniplike swollen stem.
kook /kōok/ *n. sl.* crazy or eccentric person. □□ **kook′i•ness** *n.* **kook′y** *adj.* (**kook•i•er, kook•i•est**).
■ see WEIRDO. □□ **kooky** see MAD *adj.* 1.
kook•a•bur•ra /kóokəbárə, –búrə/ *n.* Australian kingfisher with a strange laughing cry.
ko•peck /kópek, kó–/ *n.* (also **ko′pek, co′**

peck) Russian coin worth one-hundredth of a ruble.
Ko•ran /kərán, –raán, kaw–/ *n.* the Islamic sacred book. □□ **Ko•ran′ic** *adj.*
Ko•re•an /kəreeən, kaw–/ • *n.* **1** native or national of N. or S. Korea in SE Asia. **2** language of Korea. • *adj.* of or relating to Korea or its people or language.
ko•sher /kóshər/ *adj.* **1** (of food, etc.) fulfilling the requirements of Jewish law. **2** *colloq.* correct; genuine; legitimate.
■ **2** see AUTHENTIC, PERMISSIBLE.
kow•tow /kowtów/ • *n. hist.* Chinese custom of kneeling and touching the ground with the forehead in worship or submission. • *v.intr.* [usu. foll. by *to*] act obsequiously.
■ *v.* genuflect, prostrate oneself, bow (down), cringe, fawn, grovel, pander; play up to, lick a person's boots, *colloq.* butter up, suck up to.
KP *n. Mil. colloq.* kitchen police (kitchen duty).
k.p.h. *abbr.* kilometers per hour.
Kr *symb. Chem.* krypton.
kraal /kraal/ *n. S.Afr.* **1** village of huts enclosed by a fence. **2** enclosure for cattle or sheep.
krem•lin /krémlin/ *n.* **1** citadel within a Russian city or town. **2** (**the Kremlin**) **a** citadel in Moscow. **b** Russian or former USSR government housed within it.
krill /kril/ *n.* tiny planktonic crustaceans.
kro•na /krónə/ *n.* **1** (*pl.* **kro•nor** /krónər, –nawr/) chief monetary unit of Sweden. **2** (*pl.* **kro•nur** /krónər/) chief monetary unit of Iceland.
kro•ne /krónə/ *n.* (*pl.* **kro•ner** /krónər/) chief monetary unit of Denmark and of Norway.
Kru•ger•rand /króogərand, –raant/ *n.* (also **kru′ger•rand**) S. African gold coin.
kryp•ton /krípton/ *n. Chem.* inert gaseous element used in fluorescent lamps, etc. ¶Symb.: **Kr**.
KS *abbr.* Kansas (in official postal use).
kt. *abbr.* **1** karat(s). **2** kiloton(s). **3** knots.
ku•dos /kōodōz, –dōs, –dos, kyōo–/ *n. colloq.* glory; renown.
■ praise, acclaim, fame, prestige, honor, applause, admiration, accolade.
Ku Klux Klan /kōo kluks klán, kyōo–/ *n.* secret white supremacist society of the US.
kum•quat /kúmkwot/ *n.* (also **cum′quat**) **1** small orangelike fruit. **2** shrub or small tree yielding this.
kung fu /kung fōo, kōong/ *n.* Chinese martial art similar to karate.
Kurd /kərd/ *n.* Islamic people of Kurdistan (contiguous areas of Iraq, Iran, and Turkey). □□ **Kurd′ish** *adj. & n.*
kvetch /kvech/ *sl.* • *n.* objectionable person, esp. a complainer. • *v.* complain; whine. □□ **kvetch′er** *n.*
kW *abbr.* kilowatt(s).
kWh *abbr.* kilowatt-hour(s).
KY *abbr.* Kentucky (in official postal use).
Ky. *abbr.* Kentucky.

L l

L¹ /el/ *n.* (also l) (*pl.* Ls or L's; l's) **1** twelfth letter of the alphabet. **2** (as a Roman numeral) 50. **3** thing shaped like an L, as a joint connecting two pipes at right angles.

L² *abbr.* (also L.) **1** Lake. **2** Latin. **3** large.

l *abbr.* (also l.) **1** left. **2** line. **3** liter(s). **4** length.

LA *abbr.* **1** Los Angeles. **2** Louisiana (in official postal use).

La *symb. Chem.* lanthanum.

La. *abbr.* Louisiana.

la /laa/ *n. Mus.* sixth note of a major scale.

lab /lab/ *n. colloq.* laboratory.

la•bel /láybəl/ • *n.* **1** usu. small piece of paper, etc., attached to an object to give information about it. **2** short classifying phrase applied to a person, a work of art, etc. • *v.tr.* (**la•beled, la•bel•ing; la•belled, la•bel•ling**) **1** attach a label to. **2** assign to a category (*labeled them as irresponsible*). □□ **la'bel•er** *n.*

■ *n.* **1** ticket, sticker, stamp, imprint, hallmark, earmark, mark, marker, (price) tag, identification, ID. **2** name, designation, classification, epithet; nickname. • *v.* **1** ticket, tag, stamp, earmark, brand, mark. **2** designate, call, classify, describe, identify.

la•bi•al /láybeeəl/ • *adj.* **1 a** of the lips. **b** *Zool.* of, like, or serving as a lip. **2** *Phonet.* requiring partial or complete closure of the lips. • *n. Phonet.* labial sound.

la•bi•um /láybeeəm/ *n.* (*pl.* **la•bi•a** /-beeə/) *Anat.* each fold of skin enclosing the vulva.

la•bor /láybər/ • *n.* **1** physical or mental work; exertion. **2** workers, esp. manual, considered as a class or political force. **3** process of childbirth. **4** particular task. • *v.* **1** *intr.* work hard; exert oneself. **2** *intr.* strive for a purpose. **3** *tr.* a elaborate needlessly (*I will not labor the point*). **b** (as **labored** *adj.*) done with great effort; not spontaneous. **4** *intr.* [often foll. by *under*] suffer (a disadvantage or delusion) (*labored under universal disapproval*). **5** *intr.* proceed with trouble or difficulty. □ **labor camp** prison camp enforcing hard labor. **Labor Day** first Monday in September (or in some countries May 1), celebrated in honor of working people. **labor-intensive** needing a large workforce. **labor of love** task done for pleasure, not reward. **labor union** association of workers formed to protect and further their rights and interests. **lost labor** fruitless effort.

■ *n.* **1** toil, effort, drudgery, *colloq.* grind. **2** workforce, employees, laborers; (the) working class. **3** *literary* travail; contractions; delivery. **4** job, chore, undertaking, trial. • *v.* **1, 2** toil, sweat, slave (away), struggle. **3 a** belabor, dwell on, harp on. **b** (**labored**) strained, forced, difficult; elaborate, contrived. **4** (*labor under*) endure, bear, undergo. **5** struggle, plow, plod, trudge. □ **la-**

bor camp concentration camp. **labor force** see LABOR *n.* 2 above.

lab•o•ra•to•ry /lábrətáwree/ *n.* (*pl.* **-ries**) room or building for scientific experiments, research, etc.

la•bor•er /láybərər/ *n.* **1** person doing unskilled, usu. manual, work for wages. **2** person who labors.

■ **1** worker, workman, blue-collar worker, drudge.

la•bo•ri•ous /ləbáwreeəs/ *adj.* **1** needing hard work or toil. **2** (esp. of literary style) showing signs of toil; not fluent. □□ **la•bo'ri•ous•ly** *adv.*

■ **1** arduous, strenuous, onerous, backbreaking, grueling, exhausting, taxing. **2** strained, forced, artificial, pedestrian, stiff.

Lab•ra•dor /lábrədawr/ *n.* (in full **Lab'ra•dor re•triev'er**) sporting breed of dog with a black, brown, or golden coat.

lab•y•rinth /lábərinth/ *n.* **1** complicated network of passages, etc. **2** intricate or tangled arrangement. □□ **lab•y•rin•thi•an** /-rintheeən/ *adj.* **lab•y•rin•thine** / -rínthin, -thīn/ *adj.*

■ **1** maze; web. **2** snarl, knot; see also TANGLE *n.* □□ **labyrinthian, labyrinthine** mazelike, tortuous, complex, knotty; confusing, perplexing, puzzling.

lac /lak/ *n.* resinous secretion of the SE Asian lac insect, used in varnish and shellac.

lace /lays/ • *n.* **1** fine open fabric, made by weaving thread in patterns. **2** cord, etc., passed through eyelets or hooks for fastening shoes, etc. • *v.* **1** *tr.* fasten or tighten with a lace or laces. **2** *tr.* flavor (a drink) with liquor. **3** *tr. & [foll. by into] intr. colloq.* lash; beat; defeat. **4** *tr.* pass (a shoelace, etc.) through. **5** *tr.* trim with lace.

■ *n.* **1** openwork, filigree, netting, mesh, web; crochet, tatting. **2** shoelace, shoestring, bootlace, string, tie. • *v.* **1** tie (up), do up, secure, knot, truss. **2** spice (up), enliven, *colloq.* spike. **3** (*lace into*) see BEAT *v.* 1, 3. **4** thread, string, weave; loop. **5** decorate, embellish, garnish, elaborate, adorn.

lac•er•ate /lásərayt/ *v.tr.* mangle or tear (esp. flesh or tissue). □□ **lac•er•a•tion** /-áyshən/ *n.*

■ rip, gash, cut, hack, slash, claw, wound. □□ **laceration** see INJURY[1] 1, TEAR *n.* 1.

lach•ry•mal /lákriməl/ *adj.* (also **lac´ri•mal**) of or for tears.

lach•ry•mose /lákrimōs/ *adj. formal* given to weeping; tearful. □□ **lach´ry•mose•ly** *adv.*

lack /lak/ • *n.* [usu. foll. by *of*] want; deficiency (*lack of talent*). • *v.tr.* be without or deficient in (*lacks courage*). □ **for lack of** owing to the absence of (*went hungry for lack of money*). □□ **lack´ing** *adj.*

■ *n.* absence, need, dearth, scarcity, shortage. • *v.* want (for); need, require.

ABSENCE, DEARTH, PRIVATION, SHORTAGE, WANT. To suffer from a *lack* of food means to be partially or totally without it; to be in **want** of food also implies either a partial or complete lack, but with an emphasis on the essential or desirable nature of what is *lacking*; for example, you may experience a complete *lack* of pain following surgery, but you would be in *want* of medication if pain were suddenly to occur. **Absence**, on the other hand, refers to the complete nonexistence of something or someone. A *lack* of dairy products in your diet implies that you're not getting enough; an *absence* of dairy products implies that you're not getting any at all. If the scarcity or *lack* of something makes it costly, or if something is in distressingly low supply, the correct word is **dearth** (*a dearth of water in the desert; a dearth of nylon stockings during the war*). A **shortage** of something is a partial insufficiency of an established, required, or accustomed amount (*a shortage of fresh oranges after the late-season frost*), while **privation** is the negative state or *absence* of a corresponding positive (*they suffered from hunger, cold, and other privations*).

lack•a•dai•si•cal /lákədáyzikəl/ *adj.* **1** unenthusiastic; listless; idle. **2** feebly sentimental. □□ **lack•a•dai´si•cal•ly** *adv.*

■ **1** dull, apathetic, uncaring, casual, indifferent, blasé, cool, unemotional; lethargic, lazy, sluggish, lifeless; indolent, shiftless, slothful. **2** see AFFECTED 2.

lack•ey /lákee/ *n.* (*pl.* **-eys**) **1** servile follower; toady. **2** footman; manservant.

lack•lus•ter /láklustər/ *adj.* **1** lacking in vitality, etc. **2** dull.

■ **1** drab, lifeless, colorless, dismal, dreary; boring, tedious, unimaginative, flat, insipid,

bland, mediocre; flimsy, feeble, lame. **2** see DULL *adj.* 4b.

la•con•ic /ləkónik/ *adj.* terse; using few words; concise. See synonym study at TERSE. □□ **la•con´i•cal•ly** *adv.*

lac•quer /lákər/ • *n.* varnish made of shellac or synthetic substances. • *v.tr.* coat with lacquer.

lac•ri•mal var. of LACHRYMAL.

la•crosse /ləkráws, -krós/ *n.* game like field hockey, but with a ball passed using sticks having a netted pocket.

lac•tate /láktayt/ *v.intr.* (of mammals) secrete milk.

lac•ta•tion /laktáyshən/ *n.* **1** secretion of milk. **2** suckling of young.

lac•te•al /lákteeəl/ *adj.* of milk; milky.

lac•tic /láktik/ *adj. Chem.* of or from milk. □ **lactic acid** clear carboxylic acid formed in sour milk or produced in muscle tissues during strenuous exercise.

lac•tose /láktōs/ *n. Chem.* sugar that occurs in milk.

la•cu•na /ləkyōōnə/ *n.* (*pl.* **la•cu•nae** /-nee/ or **la•cu•nas**) **1** hiatus; gap. **2** missing portion, esp. in a book, etc.

lac•y /láysee/ *adj.* (**lac•i•er, lac•i•est**) of or resembling lace fabric. □□ **lac´i•ly** *adv.* **lac´i•ness** *n.*

lad /lad/ *n.* boy; youth.

■ son, child, youngster, stripling, whippersnapper, *colloq.* kid.

lad•der /ládər/ *n.* **1** set of horizontal bars fixed between two uprights and used for climbing up or down. **2** hierarchical structure, esp. as a means of advancement, promotion, etc.

lade /layd/ *v.* (*past part.* **lad•en** /láyd'n/) **1** *tr.* **a** load (a ship). **b** ship (goods). **2** *intr.* (of a ship) take on cargo. **3** *tr.* (as **laden** *adj.*) loaded; burdened.

la-di-da /laádeedaá/ *adj. colloq.* (also **la´-de-da´**) pretentious or snobbish, esp. in manner or speech.

■ see SUPERCILIOUS.

la•dle /láyd'l/ • *n.* long-handled spoon with a cup-shaped bowl for serving liquids. • *v.tr.* transfer (liquid) with a ladle. □ **ladle out** distribute, esp. lavishly. □□ **la•dle•ful** *n.* (*pl.* **-fuls**). **la´dler** *n.*

■ *n.* see SCOOP *n.* 1. • *v.* see SCOOP *v.* 1.

la•dy /láydee/ *n.* (*pl.* **-dies**) **1 a** woman regarded as being of superior social status or as having refined manners. **b** (**Lady**) title for certain women of noble rank. **2** woman; female. **3** *colloq.* wife; girlfriend. □ **ladies'** (or **lady's**) **man** man fond of female company; seducer. **ladies' room** women's restroom. **lady-in-waiting** lady attending a queen or princess. **lady-killer** man very attractive to women. **lady of the evening** prostitute. **lady's** (or **lady**) **slipper** orchid with a usu. yellow or pink slipper-shaped lip on its flowers. **old lady** *colloq.* **1** mother. **2** wife; girlfriend. **Our Lady** the Virgin Mary.

■ **1** see NOBLE *n.* 1. **2** see WOMAN 1. **3** see WOMAN 1. □ **ladies' man** see *charmer* (CHARM). **ladies' room** see TOILET 1. **lady-in-waiting** see WOMAN 1. **lady-killer** see *charmer* (CHARM).

la•dy•bug /láydeebug/ *n.* small beetle, usu. red-orange, with black spots.

la•dy•fin•ger /láydeefinggər/ *n.* finger-shaped sponge cake.

la•dy•like /láydeelīk/ *adj.* like or befitting a lady.

■ refined, elegant, gracious, courteous, dignified, proper; effeminate, unmanly, womanly, girlish, feminine.

la•dy•ship /láydeeship/ *n.* respectful form of reference or address to a titled lady.

lag /lag/ • *v.intr.* (**lagged, lag•ging**) fall behind; not keep pace. See synonym study at LOITER. • *n.* delay. □□ **lag´ger** *n.*

■ *v.* straggle, trail, hang back, linger. • *n.* interval, gap, hiatus, lull, holdup.

la•ger /láagər/ *n.* dry, light-colored, mild-flavored beer.

lag•gard /lágərd/ • *n.* dawdler; person who lags behind. • *adj.* dawdling; moving slowly. □□ **lag´gard•ly** *adj. & adv.*

■ *n.* straggler, slouch, sluggard, loafer, slowpoke. • *adj.* see SLOW *adj.* 1.

lag•ging /láging/ *n.* material providing heat insulation for a boiler, pipes, etc.

la•goon /ləgoón/ *n.* **1** stretch of salt water separated from the sea by a sandbank, reef, etc. **2** shallow lake near a larger lake or river. **3** artificial pool for sewage, etc.

laid *past and past part.* of LAY[1].

lain *past part.* of LIE[1].

lair /lair/ *n.* **1** wild animal's resting place. **2** person's hiding place.

■ **1** den, burrow, hole, nest, cave, hollow, covert. **2** hideaway, refuge, cover, *colloq.* hideout.

lais•sez-faire /lésayfáir/ *n.* (also **lais•ser-faire´**) policy of non-interference, esp. by a government.

la•i•ty /láy-itee/ *n.* lay people, as distinct from the clergy.

lake /layk/ *n.* large body of water surrounded by land. □ **the Great Lakes** the Lakes Superior, Huron, Michigan, Erie, and Ontario, along the US–Canada border.

lal•ly•gag *var.* of LOLLYGAG.

lam /lam/ *n.* □ **on the lam** *sl.* in flight, esp. from the police.

la•ma /láamə/ *n.* Tibetan or Mongolian Buddhist monk.

la•ma•ser•y /láaməseree/ *n.* (*pl.* **-ies**) monastery of lamas.

La•maze meth•od /ləmáaz/ *n. Med.* method for childbirth in which breathing exercises and relaxation techniques are used to control pain and facilitate delivery.

lamb /lam/ *n.* **1** young sheep. **2** its flesh as food. **3** mild or gentle person. □ **The Lamb of God** a name for Christ.

lam•ba•da /ləmbáadə/ *n.* fast erotic Brazilian dance.

lam•baste /lambáyst/ *v.tr.* (also **lam•bast** /-bást/) *colloq.* **1** thrash; beat. **2** criticize severely.

■ **1** trounce, whip, scourge, flog, lash, horsewhip, *sl.* belt, tan a person's hide; bludgeon, drub, maul, pummel, batter, bash, *sl.* clobber. **2** censure, rebuke, berate, scold, upbraid, chastise, reprimand, admonish, reprove, belabor, attack, take to task, rake over the coals, *colloq.* call a person on the carpet, tell off, lay into, chew out.

lamb•da /lámdə/ *n.* **1** eleventh letter of the Greek alphabet (Λ, λ). **2** (as λ) symbol for wavelength.

lam•bent /lámbənt/ *adj.* **1** (of a flame or a light) playing on a surface with a soft radiance but without burning. **2** (of the eyes, sky, etc.) softly radiant. **3** (of wit, etc.) lightly brilliant. □□ **lam´ben•cy** *n.* **lam´bent•ly** *adv.*

lame /laym/ • *adj.* **1** disabled, esp. in the foot or leg; limping. **2 a** (of an excuse, etc.) unconvincing; weak. **b** (of verse, etc.) halting. • *v.tr.* make lame; disable. □ **lame duck** official in the final period of office, after the election of a successor. □□ **lame´ly** *adv.* **lame´ness** *n.*

■ *adj.* **1** handicapped, game. **2 a** feeble, flimsy, half-baked, poor, ineffective. **b** awkward, uneven, stiff. • *v.* cripple, hamstring, handicap; maim, damage, hurt, injure, impair.

la•mé /lamáy/ *n.* fabric with gold or silver threads interwoven.

lame•brain /láymbrayn/ *n. colloq.* stupid person. □□ **lame´brain** or **lame´brained** *adj.*

la•ment /ləmént/ • *n.* **1** passionate expression of grief. **2** song or poem of mourning or sorrow. • *v.tr.* [also *absol.*] express or feel grief for or about; regret. □□ **la•men•ta´tion** *n.*

■ *n.* **1** ululation. **2** lamentation, dirge, elegy, requiem. • *v.* mourn, bemoan, bewail, wail; rue, deplore.

la•men•ta•ble /ləméntəbəl, lámənt-/ *adj.* (of an event, condition, etc.) deplorable; regrettable. □□ **la•men´ta•bly** *adv.*

■ wretched, miserable, pitiful, pathetic, unfortunate, sad, awful, intolerable.

lam•i•nate • *v.tr.* /láminayt/ **1** overlay with metal plates, a plastic layer, etc. **2** manufacture by placing layer on layer. • *n.* /láminət/ laminated structure, esp. of layers fixed together. • *adj.* /láminət/ in the form of laminae. □□ **lam•i•na•tion** /-náyshən/ *n.* **lam´i•na•tor** *n.*

lamp /lamp/ *n.* **1** device for producing a steady light, esp.: **a** electric bulb, and usu. its holder. **b** oil or gas lamp. **2** device producing esp. ultraviolet or infrared radiation.

■ *n.* **1** see LIGHT[1] *n.* 4a.

lamp•black /lámpblak/ *n.* pigment made from soot.

lam•poon /lampoón/ • *n.* satirical attack on a person, etc. See synonym study at CARICATURE. • *v.tr.* satirize. □□ **lam•poon´er** *n.* **lam•poon´ist** *n.*

■ *n.* burlesque, satire, parody, *colloq.* take-off, send-up. • *v.* mock, poke fun at.

lamp•post /lámp-pōst/ *n.* tall post supporting an outdoor light.

lam•prey /lámpree, -pray/ *n.* (*pl.* **-preys**) eel-like fish with a sucker mouth, horny teeth, and a rough tongue.

lamp•shade /lámpshayd/ *n.* translucent cover for a lamp.

LAN /lan/ *abbr.* local area network.

lance /lans/ • *n.* **1** long spear, esp. one used by a horseman. **2** = LANCET. • *v.tr.* **1** prick or cut open with a lancet. **2** pierce with a lance.

■ *n.* **1** pike, javelin, shaft. • *v.* **1** puncture, incise, slit. **2** impale, run through, skewer, stab, penetrate.

lanc•er /lánsər/ *n. hist.* soldier armed with a lance.

lan•cet /lánsit/ *n.* small, two-edged surgical knife with a sharp point.

land /land/ • *n.* **1** solid part of the earth's surface. **2** expanse of country; ground; soil. **3** country; nation; state. **4** estate. • *v.* **1 a** *tr. & intr.* set or go ashore. **b** *intr.* disembark (*landed at the harbor*). **2** *tr.* bring (an aircraft, etc.) to the ground or another surface. **3** *intr.* alight on the ground, etc. **4** *tr.* bring (a fish) to land. **5** *tr. & intr.* [also *refl.*] *colloq.* bring to, reach, or find oneself in a certain situation, place, or state (*landed in jail*). **6** *tr. colloq.* win or obtain (a prize, job, etc.). □ **land bridge** neck of land joining two large landmasses. **land mine** explosive mine laid in or on the ground.

■ *n.* **1** dry land, terra firma. **2** dirt, turf, sod, loam; tract, lot, allotment. **3** territory, domain, fatherland, motherland, homeland, native land. **4** property; acreage. • *v.* **1, 3** arrive, touch down, come to rest; berth, dock; dismount. **2** bring or take down. **4** catch, hook, net, take, capture. **5** (*tr.*) get, lead; (*intr.*) arrive, turn up, end up. **6** secure, acquire, procure; gain, earn, receive, come into.

land•ed /lándid/ *adj.* **1** owning land (*landed gentry*). **2** consisting of, including, or relating to land (*landed property*).

land•fall /lándfawl/ *n.* approach to land, esp. for the first time on a sea or air journey.

land•fill /lándfil/ *n.* **1** waste material, etc., used to landscape or reclaim land. **2** place where garbage is buried.

land•form /lándfawrm/ *n.* natural feature of the earth's surface.

land•ing /lánding/ *n.* **1 a** coming to land. **b** place where ships, etc., land. **2** platform between two flights of stairs, or at the top or bottom of a flight. □ **landing craft** craft designed for putting troops and equipment ashore. **landing gear** undercarriage of an aircraft. **landing strip** airstrip.

■ **1 a** touchdown, splashdown; arrival. **b** dock, pier, jetty, wharf, quay.

land•la•dy /lándlaydee/ *n.* (*pl.* **–dies**) **1** woman who rents land or premises to a tenant. **2** woman who keeps a boardinghouse, an inn, etc.

■ **1** see LANDLORD 1. **2** proprietress, manageress, hostess, mistress; see also LANDLORD 2.

land•locked /lándlokt/ *adj.* almost or entirely enclosed by land.

land•lord /lándlawrd/ *n.* **1** man who rents land or premises to a tenant. **2** man who keeps a boardinghouse, an inn, etc.

■ **1** (property) owner, lessor, landowner. **2** host, proprietor, innkeeper, hotelier, manager.

land•lub•ber /lándlubər/ *n.* person unfamiliar with the sea.

land•mark /lándmaark/ *n.* **1 a** conspicuous object in a district, etc. **b** object marking a boundary, etc. **2** prominent and critical event, etc. **3** *attrib.* signifying an important development, etc.

■ **1** feature, monument; *Archit.* terminus. **2** turning point, watershed, milestone. **3** (*attrib.*) crucial, pivotal, seminal, important, historic, significant, ground breaking.

land•mass /lándmas/ *n.* large area of land.

land•own•er /lándōnər/ *n.* owner of land. □□ **land′own•ing** *adj. & n.*

land•scape /lándskayp/ • *n.* **1** scenery, as seen in a broad view from one place. **2** picture representing this; this genre of painting. • *v.tr.* [also *absol.*] improve (a piece of land) by planned plantings, etc.

■ *n.* **1** prospect, view, vista; countryside, terrain.

land•slide /lándslīd/ *n.* **1** sliding down of a mass of land from a mountain, cliff, etc. **2** overwhelming victory in an election.

■ **1** avalanche, mud slide.

lane /layn/ *n.* **1** narrow road or path. **2** division of a road for a stream of traffic. **3** path regularly followed by a ship, aircraft, etc.

■ **1** see ROAD 1, WALK *n.* 3.

lan•gous•tine /lóngōosteén, lánggə–/ *n.* any of several varieties of small lobsters, used as food.

lan•guage /lánggwij/ *n.* **1** use of words as a method of human communication. **2** language of a particular community or country, etc. **3 a** faculty of speech. **b** style of expression. **4** system of symbols and rules for writing computer programs. **5** any method of expression (*sign language*). **6** professional or specialized vocabulary. □ **speak the same language** have a similar outlook, manner of expression, etc.

■ **1, 5** intercourse, interaction; speech, talk. **2** tongue, dialect, slang, vernacular, *colloq.* lingo. **3** articulation; diction, phraseology; vocabulary, wording; *colloq.* gift of gab. **6** jargon, parlance; terminology. □ **speak the same language** see eye to eye, be two of a kind, be soul mates, be of one or the same mind, *colloq.* be on the same wavelength.

lan•guid /lánggwid/ *adj.* **1** lacking vigor; idle; inert. **2** (of trade, etc.) slow-moving; sluggish. **3** faint; weak. □□ **lan′guid•ly** *adv.* **lan′guid•ness** *n.*

■ **1** see IDLE *adj.* 1. **2** see LAZY 3. **3** see FEEBLE 1, 2.

lan•guish /lánggwish/ *v.intr.* **1** lose or lack vitality. **2** droop or pine for. **3** suffer under (esp. depression, confinement, etc.).

■ **1** see ROT *v.* 2b.

lan•guor /lánggər/ *n.* **1** lack of energy; idleness. **2** soft or tender mood or effect. □□ **lan′guor•ous** *adj.* **lan′guor•ous•ly** *adv.*

lan•gur /lunggŏŏr/ *n.* long-tailed Asian monkey.

lank /langk/ *adj.* **1** (of hair, grass, etc.) long, limp, and straight. **2** thin and tall.

lank•y /lángkee/ *adj.* (**lank•i•er, lank•i•est**) (of limbs, a person, etc.) ungracefully thin and long or tall. □□ **lank'i•ly** adv. **lank'i•ness** n.

■ spindly, gangling, gangly, rangy; lean, gaunt, skinny, twiggy, scraggy, bony.

lan•o•lin /lánəlin/ n. fat from sheep's wool used for cosmetics, etc.

lan•tern /lántərn/ n. **1** lamp with a transparent case protecting a flame, etc. **2** raised structure on a dome, room, etc., glazed to admit light. □ **lantern fish** marine fish with small light organs on the head and body. **lantern jaws** long thin jaws and cheeks.

■ **1** see LIGHT[1] n. 2.

lan•tha•nide /lánthənīd/ n. Chem. element of the lanthanide series. □ **lanthanide series** series of 15 metallic elements (from lanthanum to lutetium) having similar chemical properties.

lan•tha•num /lánthənəm/ n. Chem. metallic element of the lanthanide series. ¶Symb.: **La**.

lan•yard /lányərd/ n. **1** cord worn around the neck or shoulder to which a knife, etc., may be attached. **2** Naut. short line for securing, tightening, etc.

La•o•tian /lāyṓshən, lóushən/ • n. **1 a** native or national of Laos in SE Asia. **b** person of Laotian descent. **2** language of Laos. • adj. of or relating to Laos or its people or language.

lap[1] /lap/ n. front of the body from the waist to the knees of a sitting person. □ **in** (or **on**) **a person's lap** as a person's responsibility. **in the lap of luxury** in extremely luxurious surroundings. **lap robe** blanket, etc., used for warmth, esp. on a journey. □□ **lap'ful** n. (pl. **-fuls**).

lap[2] /lap/ • n. **1 a** one circuit of a racetrack, etc. **b** section of a journey, etc. **2 a** amount of overlapping. **b** overlapping part. • v.tr. (**lapped, lap•ping**) **1** lead or overtake (a competitor in a race) by one or more laps. **2** coil, fold, or wrap (a garment, etc.) around. **3** enfold or wrap (a person) in clothing, etc. **4** cause to overlap. □ **lap joint** joining of rails, shafts, etc., by halving the thickness of each at the joint and fitting them together. **lap-weld** v.tr. weld with overlapping edges. n. such a weld.

■ n. **1 a** orbit, round, circle, tour, trip, revolution. **2 b** flap, projection, overlap. • v. **3** see SWATHE v. **4** see OVERLAP v. 1, 2, PROJECT v. 1.

lap[3] /lap/ • v. (**lapped, lap•ping**) **1** tr. **a** [also absol.] (usu. of an animal) drink (liquid) with the tongue. **b** consume (gossip, praise, etc.) greedily. **2 a** tr. (of water) move or beat upon (a shore) with a rippling sound. **b** intr. (of waves, etc.) move in ripples; make a lapping sound. • n. **1 a** act of lapping. **b** amount of liquid taken up. **2** sound of wavelets.

■ v. **1 a** lick• up, slurp; swill; soak (up). **b** (lap up) enjoy, bask in; swallow (whole), colloq. fall for, sl. buy. **2 b** wash, splash, break, roll. • n. **1** lick, slurp, gulp, colloq. swig. **2** splash, ripple.

lap•dog /lápdawg/ n. small pet dog.

la•pel /ləpél/ n. part of a coat, jacket, etc., folded back against the front around the neck opening. □□ **la•pelled'** or **la•peled'** adj.

lap•i•dar•y /lápideree/ • adj. **1** concerned with stone(s). **2** engraved upon stone. • n. (pl. **-ies**) cutter, polisher, or engraver of gems.

lap•is laz•u•li /lápis lázoolee, lázyə–, lázhə–/ n. bright blue semiprecious stone.

Lapp /lap/ • n. **1** member of a Mongol people of N. Scandinavia. **2** language of this people. • adj. of or relating to the Lapps or their language.

lapse /laps/ • n. **1** slight error. **2** weak decline into an inferior state. **3** [foll. by of] passage of time (after a lapse of three years). • v.intr. **1** fail to maintain a position or standard. **2** [foll. by into] fall back into (an inferior or previous state). **3** (of a right or privilege, etc.) become invalid due to disuse, failure to renew, etc.

■ n. **1** slip, mistake, oversight, omission; colloq. slipup, sl. goof. **2** deterioration, degeneration, slump, descent. **3** gap, break, interval, interruption, pause. • v. **1, 2** relapse, slip (back); revert; subside. **3** run out, be up, expire, end.

lap•top /láptop/ n. [often attrib.] portable computer suitable for use while resting on the user's legs.

lap•wing /lápwing/ n. plover with black and white plumage, crested head, and a shrill cry.

lar•board /laarbərd/ n. & adj. Naut. archaic = PORT[3].

lar•ce•ny /laarsənee/ n. (pl. **-nies**) theft of personal property. □ **grand larceny** Law larceny in which the value of the stolen property exceeds a certain legally established limit. □□ **lar'ce•nist** n. **lar'ce•nous** adj.

■ see THEFT.

larch /laarch/ n. **1** deciduous coniferous tree with bright foliage and tough wood. **2** (in full **larch'wood**) its wood.

lard /laard/ • n. pig fat used in cooking, etc. • v.tr. **1** insert strips of fat or bacon in (meat, etc.) before cooking. **2** [foll. by with] embellish (talk or writing) with foreign or technical terms.

lar•der /laardər/ n. **1** room or cupboard for storing food. **2** supply of food, esp. for winter.

large /laarj/ • adj. **1** of relatively great size or extent. **2** of the larger kind (large intestine). **3** of wide range; comprehensive. **4** pursuing an activity on a large scale (large farmer). • n. (**at large**) **1** at liberty. **2** as a body or whole (popular with the people at large). **3** without a specific target (scatters insults at large). **4** representing a whole area and not merely a part of it (councilwoman at large). □□ **large'ness** n. **larg'ish** adj.

■ adj. **1, 2** big, wide, broad; roomy, spacious; king-size, sizable, substantial, considerable, ample; bigger, greater, main, principal; bulky, hefty, stout, stocky, beefy, mighty; fat, obese, plump; see also IMMENSE 1. **3** extensive, far-reaching, sweeping, thorough, grand, major; epic. • n. (**at large**) **1** see FREE adj. 3b. **2** collectively, altogether, over all, overall.

large•ly /laárjlee/ *adv.* to a great extent.

■ mostly, chiefly, mainly, principally, by and large; as a rule, in general, on the whole, essentially.

lar•gesse /laarzhés/ *n.* (also **lar•gess'**) **1** money or gifts freely given. **2** generosity; beneficence.

■ **1** grants, bonuses, endowments, handouts, gratuities. **2** munificence, benevolence; philanthropy, charity, support.

lar•go /laárgō/ *Mus.* • *adv. & adj.* in a slow tempo and dignified in style. • *n.* (*pl.* **–gos**) largo passage or movement.

lar•i•at /láreeat/ *n.* **1** lasso. **2** tethering rope.

lark[1] /laark/ *n.* small bird with tuneful song, esp. the skylark.

lark[2] /laark/ *colloq.* • *n.* frolic; amusing incident. • *v.intr.* [foll. by *about*] play tricks; frolic.

■ *n.* escapade, caper, fling, romp, antic, *colloq.* spree; trick, prank. • *v.* (*lark about*) fool (around), mess around, *colloq.* kid; *sl.* cavort.

lark•spur /laárkspur/ *n.* plant with a spur-shaped calyx.

lar•va /laárvə/ *n.* (*pl.* **lar•vae** /-vee/) stage of development of an insect between egg and pupa. □□ **lar'val** *adj.*

lar•yn•gi•tis /lárinjítis/ *n.* inflammation of the larynx.

lar•ynx /láringks/ *n.* (*pl.* **la•ryn•ges** /lərínjeez/ or **lar•ynx•es**) hollow organ in the throat holding the vocal cords.

la•sa•gna /ləzaányə/ *n.* (also **la•sa'gne**) pasta in wide strips, esp. as cooked and served with cheese, tomato sauce, etc.

las•civ•i•ous /ləsíveeəs/ *adj.* **1** lustful. **2** inciting to or evoking lust. □□ **las•civ'i•ous•ly** *adv.* **las•civ'i•ous•ness** *n.*

■ **1** lecherous, lewd, salacious. **2** obscene, indecent, coarse, offensive, suggestive, lurid, risqué.

lase /layz/ *v.intr.* function as or in a laser.

la•ser /láyzər/ *n.* device that generates an intense beam of coherent light (acronym of *l*ight *a*mplification by *s*timulated *e*mission of *r*adiation).

lash /lash/ • *v.* **1** *intr.* make a sudden whip-like movement. **2** *tr.* beat with a whip, etc. **3** *tr.* castigate in words. **4** *tr.* fasten with a cord, etc. **5** *tr.* (of rain, etc.) beat forcefully upon. • *n.* **1** sharp blow by a whip, etc. **2** flexible end of a whip. **3** eyelash. □ **lash out** speak or hit out angrily.

■ *v.* **1, 2** flail, thrash; (*tr.*) flog, switch, lambaste, *sl.* belt, tan a person's hide. **3** see LAMBASTE 2. **4** tie, bind, secure, strap, make fast. **5** crash, pound, dash, batter, pelt. • *n.* **1** stroke, strike, smack, crack, *colloq.* whack. **2** thong, quirt. □ **lash out** (*lash out at*) attack, tear into, *colloq.* lay into; berate, revile, flay, *colloq.* jump on.

lass /las/ *n.* girl or young woman.

■ young lady, miss, *colloq.* lassie, gal, dame.

Las•sa fe•ver /lásə/ *n.* acute febrile viral disease of tropical Africa.

las•sie /lásee/ *n. colloq.* = LASS.

las•si•tude /lásitōōd, -tyōōd/ *n.* **1** languor;

weariness. **2** disinclination to exert or interest oneself.

las•so /lásō, lasṓ/ • *n.* (*pl.* **–sos** or **–soes**) rope with a noose at one end, esp. for catching cattle, etc. • *v.tr.* (**–soes, –soed**) catch with a lasso. □□ **las'so•er** *n.*

■ *n.* lariat. • *v.* snare, rope.

last[1] /last/ • *adj.* **1** after all others; coming at or belonging to the end. **2 a** most recent. **b** preceding (*got on at the last station*). **3** only remaining (*our last chance*). **4** [prec. by *the*] least likely. **5** lowest in rank (*last place*). • *adv.* **1** after all others. **2** on the most recent occasion. **3** lastly. • *n.* **1** person or thing that is last. **2** last mention or sight, etc. (*shall never hear the last of it*). **3** [prec. by *the*] **a** end or last moment. **b** death. □ **at last** (or **long last**) in the end; after much delay. **last-ditch** (of an attempt, etc.) final; desperate. **last name** surname. **last rites** rites for a person about to die. **last straw** slight addition to a burden that makes it finally unbearable. **last word 1** final or definitive statement (*always has the last word*). **2** latest fashion.

■ *adj.* **1, 5** final, concluding, terminal, ultimate, extreme; hindmost, rearmost; conclusive, decisive; bottom, worst. **2 a** latest, newest. **b** previous, prior, former, earlier. **3** surviving, outstanding; see also ONLY *adj.* • *adv.* **3** finally, in conclusion. • *n.* **2** end, finish. **3 a** see END *n.* 3. **b** see DEATH *n.* 1. □ **at last** finally, eventually. **last-ditch** extreme. **last word 2** all the rage, the latest, state of the art.

last[2] /last/ *v.intr.* **1** remain unexhausted or alive for a time. **2** continue for a time.

■ go on, keep on, carry on; survive, persist, hold out, stand up, endure, withstand; suffice.

last[3] /last/ *n.* model for shaping a shoe or boot. □ **stick to one's last** not meddle with what one does not understand.

■ mold, matrix, form.

last•ing /lásting/ *adj.* **1** continuing; permanent. **2** durable. □□ **last'ing•ly** *adv.*

■ constant, perpetual, indestructible, eternal, enduring, persistent, steadfast.

last•ly /lástlee/ *adv.* finally; in the last place.

lat. *abbr.* latitude.

latch /lach/ • *n.* **1** fastening for a gate, etc. **2** lock needing a key to be opened from the outside. • *v.* fasten or be fastened with a latch. □ **latch on** [often foll. by *to*] *colloq.* **1** attach oneself (to). **2** understand.

latch•key /láchkee/ *n.* (*pl.* **–keys**) key of an outer door.

late /layt/ • *adj.* **1** after the due, usual, or proper time (*late for dinner*). **2 a** far on in a specified period. **b** far on in development. **3** no longer alive or functioning. **4** of recent date. **5** (as **latest**, prec. by *the*) fashionable, up to date. • *adv.* **1** after the due or usual time. **2** far on in time. **3** at or till a late hour. □□ **late'ness** *n.*

■ *adj.* **1** tardy, delayed, overdue, belated, past due. **3** dead, departed, deceased; former, past, ex–, one-time, erstwhile. **4** latest, last. **5** (**the latest**) current, modern, stylish, in vogue. • *adv.* **1** belatedly.

late•com•er /láytkumər/ *n.* person who arrives late.

la•teen /lətéen/ *adj.* (of a ship) rigged with a triangular sail on a long yard at an angle 45° to the mast.

late•ly /láytlee/ *adv.* not long ago; recently; in recent times.
■ recently, (of) late; just; hitherto.

la•tent /láyt'nt/ *adj.* 1 concealed; dormant. 2 undeveloped. □□ **la•ten•cy** *n.* **la•tent•ly** *adv.*
■ 1 see DORMANT 2b. 2 see POTENTIAL *adj.*

SYNONYM STUDY: latent
ABEYANT, DORMANT, QUIESCENT, POTENTIAL. All of these words refer to what is not currently observable or showing signs of activity. A **latent** talent is one that has not yet manifested itself, while **potential** suggests a talent that exists in an undeveloped state (*a potential concert violinist*). A child may have certain *latent* qualities of which his or her parents are unaware, but teachers are usually quick to spot a *potential* artist or poet in the classroom. **Dormant** and **quiescent** are less frequently associated with people and more often associated with things. A volcano might be described as *dormant*, which applies to anything that is currently inactive, but has been active in the past and is capable of becoming active again in the future. *Dormant* carries the connotation of *sleeping* (*plants that are dormant in the winter*), while *quiescent* means *motionless* (*a quiescent sea*), emphasizing inactivity without referring to past or future activity. **Abeyant**, like *dormant*, means suspended or temporarily inactive, but it is most commonly used as a noun (*personal rights and privileges kept in abeyance until the danger had passed*).

lat•er•al /látərəl/ *adj.* of, at, toward, or from the side or sides. □ **lateral thinking** solving problems by apparently illogical methods □□ **lat•er•al•ly** *adv.*

la•tex /láyteks/ *n.* (*pl.* **lat•i•ces** /-tiseez/ or **la•tex•es**) 1 milky fluid of esp. the rubber tree. 2 synthetic product resembling this.

lath /lath/ • *n.* (*pl.* **laths** /lathz, lathz/) thin flat strip of wood. • *v.tr.* attach laths to (a wall or ceiling).

lathe /layth/ *n.* machine for shaping wood, metal, etc., by rotating it against a cutting tool.

lath•er /láthər/ • *n.* 1 froth produced by agitating soap, etc., and water. 2 frothy sweat, esp. of a horse. 3 state of agitation. • *v.* 1 *intr.* form a lather. 2 *tr.* cover with lather. 3 *tr. colloq.* thrash. □□ **lath'er•y** *adj.*
■ *n.* 1 foam, suds. 3 fuss, flutter, panic, bother, *colloq.* dither. • *v.* 1 soap (up); foam. 3 see BEAT *v.* 1.

Lat•in /lát'n/ • *n.* 1 language of ancient Rome and its empire. 2 person who speaks a language derived from Latin. • *adj.* 1 of or in Latin. 2 of the countries or peoples using languages developed from Latin. □ **Latin America** the parts of Central and S. America where Spanish or Portuguese is the main language. **Latin American** *n.* native of Latin America. *adj.* of or relating to Latin America.

La•ti•no /ləteénō/ *n.* (*pl.* **La•ti•nos**; *fem.* **La•ti•na** /-nə/, *pl.* **La•ti•nas**) 1 native or inhabitant of Latin America. 2 person of Spanish-speaking or Latin American descent.

lat•ish /láytish/ *adj. & adv.* fairly late.

lat•i•tude /látitōōd, -tyōōd/ *n.* 1 *Geog.* a angular distance on a meridian north or south of the equator. **b** [usu. in *pl.*] regions or climes. 2 freedom of action or opinion (*was allowed much latitude*). See synonym study at RANGE. □□ **lat•i•tu•di•nal** /-tōōd'nəl, -tyōōd-/ *adj.* **lat•i•tu•di•nal•ly** *adv.*
■ 2 see LEEWAY.

la•trine /lətréen/ *n.* communal toilet, esp. in a camp.

lat•ter /látər/ *adj.* 1 second-mentioned of two. 2 nearer to the end (*latter part of the year*). 3 recent. □ **latter-day** modern; newfangled. **Latter-day Saints** the Mormons.
■ □ **latter-day** see MODERN.

lat•tice /látis/ *n.* 1 structure of crossed laths with spaces between, used as a screen, fence, etc. 2 = LATTICEWORK. □□ **lat'ticed** *adj.* **lat'tic•ing** *n.*
■ 1 see MESH *n.* 1, 2, 3a.

lat•tice•work /látiswərk/ *n.* laths arranged in lattice formation.

Lat•vi•an /látveeən/ • *n.* 1 a native of Latvia, a Baltic republic. **b** person of Latvian descent. 2 language of Latvia. • *adj.* of or relating to Latvia or its people or language.

loud /lawd/ *v.tr.* praise or extol. See synonym study at PRAISE.
■ acclaim, exalt, celebrate, sing the praises of, applaud; promote, advance, commend, *colloq.* boost.

laud•a•ble /láwdəbəl/ *adj.* commendable; praiseworthy. □□ **laud•a•bil•i•ty** *n.* **laud'a•bly** *adv.*
■ admirable, worthy; outstanding, notable.

lau•da•num /láwd'nəm/ *n.* solution prepared from opium.

lau•da•to•ry /láwdətáwree/ *adj.* expressing praise.
■ eulogistic, complimentary; flattering.

laugh /laf/ • *v.* 1 *intr.* make sounds and movements in expressing amusement, scorn, etc. 2 *tr.* express by laughing. 3 *intr.* [foll. by *at*] ridicule; make fun of. • *n.* 1 sound, act, or manner of laughing. 2 *colloq.* comical person or thing. □ **have the last laugh** be ultimately the winner. **laugh off** get rid of (humiliation, etc.) with a jest. **laugh track** recorded laughter added to a comedy show. □□ **laugh'er** *n.*
■ *v.* 1 titter, giggle, chuckle, *colloq.* crack up. 3 (*laugh at*) deride, mock (at), jeer (at), poke fun at, make sport of, scoff at, tease; see also LAMPOON *v.* • *n.* 1 titter, giggle, chuckle. 2 joke, *colloq.* scream, riot; prank; farce, nonsense. □ **laugh off** brush aside, shrug off; dismiss, ignore, minimize.

laugh•a•ble /láfəbəl/ *adj.* ludicrous; amusing. □□ **laugh'a•bly** *adv.*

laugh•ing /láfing/ • *n.* laughter. • *adj.* in senses of LAUGH *v.* □ **laughing gas** nitrous oxide as an anesthetic. **no laughing matter** something serious. □□ **laugh'ing•ly** *adv.*

laugh•ing•stock /láfingstok/ n. person or thing ridiculed.

■ fool, exhibition, spectacle.

laugh•ter /láftər/ n. act or sound of laughing.

launch¹ /lawnch/ • v.tr. **1** set (a vessel) afloat. **2** hurl or send forth (a weapon, rocket, etc.). **3** start or set in motion (an enterprise, attack, etc.). **4** formally introduce (a new product). • n. act of launching. □ **launching pad 1** = LAUNCHPAD. **2** = SPRINGBOARD 2.

■ v. **1, 3, 4** get under way; initiate, spearhead, inaugurate, embark upon, commence; establish. **2** shoot, fire, discharge, propel, deliver, release. • n. flotation; initiation, start, début, inauguration, colloq. kickoff; takeoff.

launch² /lawnch/ n. motorboat, used esp. for pleasure.

■ skiff, tender, runabout.

launch•pad /láwnchpad/ n. platform with a supporting structure, from which rockets are launched.

laun•der /láwndər, laán–/ v.tr. **1** wash and iron (clothes, etc.). **2** colloq. transfer (funds) to conceal their origin. □□ **laun′der•er** n.

■ **1** clean, scrub; press. **2** legitimize.

Laun•dro•mat /láwndrəmat, laán–/ n. propr. establishment with coin-operated washing machines and dryers.

laun•dry /láwndree, laán–/ n. (pl. **–dries**) **1** place for washing clothes, etc. **2** clothes or linen for laundering or newly laundered. □ **laundry list** colloq. lengthy list of items.

lau•re•ate /láwreeət, lór–/ • adj. wreathed with laurel as a mark of honor. • n. person honored for outstanding creative or intellectual achievement (Nobel laureate). □□ **lau′re•ate•ship** n.

lau•rel /láwrəl, lór–/ n. **1** [in sing. or pl.] wreath of bay leaves as an emblem of victory or poetic merit. **2** [in pl.] honor or distinction. **3** evergreen plant with dark-green glossy leaves; bay. □ **rest on one's laurels** be complacent with one's success.

■ **2** (laurels) fame, awards, tributes; acclaim, renown, esteem, admiration. □ **rest on one's laurels** be or get self-satisfied or smug or overconfident; sit back, relax, take it easy.

la•va /laávə, lávə/ n. matter flowing from a volcano that solidifies as it cools.

la•vage /ləvaázh, lávij/ n. Med. washing out of a body cavity with water, etc.

lav•a•to•ry /lávətawree/ n. (pl. **–ries**) room or compartment with a toilet and wash basin.

■ ladies' room, men's room, powder room, bathroom, rest room, colloq. can, john.

lave /layv/ v.tr. literary wash; bathe.

lav•en•der /lávindər/ n. **1 a** evergreen shrub with purple aromatic flowers. **b** its flowers and stalks dried and used to scent linen, etc. **2** pale purplish-blue color.

lav•ish /lávish/ • adj. **1** abundant; profuse. **2** generous. **3** excessive. See synonym study at PROFUSE. • v.tr. [often foll. by on] bestow or spend (money, effort, praise, etc.) abundantly. □□ **lav′ish•ly** adv. **lav′ish•ness** n.

■ adj. **1** plentiful, ample, copious, prolific; lush, plush. **2** liberal, munificent, unsparing,

effusive; charitable, magnanimous. **3** immoderate, extravagant; wasteful, wanton; superfluous. • v. disburse, colloq. splurge; squander; shower, heap, sl. dish out.

law /law/ n. **1 a** rule enacted or customary in a community and recognized as enjoining or prohibiting certain actions. **b** body of such rules. **2** respect for laws (law and order). **3** laws collectively as a social system or subject of study. **4** binding force or effect (their word is law). **5** [prec. by the] **a** the legal profession. **b** colloq. the police. **6** regularity in natural occurrences (law of gravity). □ **law-abiding** obedient to the laws. **lay down the law** be dogmatic or authoritarian. **take the law into one's own hands** redress a grievance by one's own means, esp. by force.

■ **1 a** regulation, ordinance, statute, act, measure, decree, order, directive, command, commandment, mandate. **b** constitution, code, charter. **2** justice, right, equity, fairness, order; lawfulness, legitimacy, legality. **4** (predic.) final, definitive; irrevocable. **5 b** see POLICE n. **1, 2. 6** principle, theory; deduction, conclusion, formula. □ **law-abiding** respectful, dutiful, upright. **lay down the law** dictate, command, order.

law•break•er /láwbraykər/ n. person who breaks the law. □□ **law′break•ing** n. & adj.

law•ful /láwfŏŏl/ adj. conforming with or recognized by law; not illegal. □□ **law′ful•ly** adv. **law′ful•ness** n.

■ licit, legitimate, valid; permissible, authorized.

law•giv•er /láwgivər/ n. person who establishes a set of laws.

law•less /láwlis/ adj. **1** having no laws or law enforcement. **2** disregarding laws. **3** unbridled; uncontrolled. □□ **law′less•ly** adv. **law′less•ness** n.

■ **1** anarchic, anarchical, anarchistic, chaotic, disorderly, unregulated. **2** unlawful, criminal, felonious, illegal, illicit, colloq. crooked; dishonest, corrupt. **3** unrestrained, undisciplined, wild, unruly.

law•mak•er /láwmaykər/ n. legislator.

law•man /láwman/ n. (pl. **–men**) law-enforcement officer, esp. a sheriff or policeman.

lawn¹ /lawn/ n. piece of grass kept mown in a yard, garden, park, etc. □ **lawn tennis** usual form of tennis, played with a soft ball on outdoor grass or a hard court. **lawn mower** machine for cutting the grass on a lawn.

■ green, turf, sod, literary sward.

lawn² /lawn/ n. fine linen or cotton fabric.

law•ren•ci•um /lərénseeəm, law–/ n. Chem. artifically made transuranic radioactive metallic element. ¶Symb.: **Lw.**

law•suit /láwsŏŏt/ n. process or instance of making a claim in a court of law.

law•yer /láwyər, lóyər/ n. member of the legal profession. □□ **law′yer•ly** adj.

■ attorney(-at-law), jurist, counselor (-at-law), counsel, advocate, legal practitioner, solicitor.

lax /laks/ adj. **1** lacking care, concern, etc. **2** loose; not compact. □□ **lax′i•ty** n. **lax′ly** adv. **lax′ness** n.

■ **1** careless, devil-may-care, thoughtless,

unthinking, negligent, remiss, inattentive, lackadaisical, casual; permissive, indulgent, lenient, liberal, nonchalant, *colloq.* laid-back. **2** relaxed, open; flexible, slack.

lax•a•tive /láksətiv/ • *adj.* easing evacuation of the bowels. • *n.* laxative medicine.

lay¹ /lay/ • *v.* (*past* and *past part.* **laid** /layd/) **1** *tr.* place on a surface, esp. horizontally or in the proper or specified place. **2** *intr. dial.* or *erron.* lie. ¶ This use, incorrect in standard English, is probably partly encouraged by confusion with *lay* as the past of *lie*, as in *the dog lay on the floor*, which is correct; *the dog is laying on the floor* is not correct. **3** *tr.* [often *absol.*] (of a hen bird) produce (an egg). **4** *tr.* attribute or impute (blame, etc.). **5** *tr.* prepare or make ready (a plan or a trap). **6** *tr.* prepare (a table) for a meal. **7** *tr.* put down as a wager; stake. **8** *tr. sl. offens.* have sexual intercourse with. • *n.* way, position, or direction in which something lies. □ **laid-back** *colloq.* relaxed; unbothered. **lay aside** put to bed or the house. **lay aside 1** put to one side. **2** cease to consider. **3** save (money, etc.) for future needs. **lay bare** expose; reveal. **lay a charge** make an accusation. **lay claim to** claim as one's own. **lay down 1** put on the ground. **2** formulate (a rule or principle). **3** pay or wager (money). **4** store (wine) in a cellar. **5** set down on paper. **6** sacrifice (one's life). **lay one's hands on** obtain; locate. **lay hands on 1** seize or attack. **2** place one's hands on or over, esp. in confirmation, or spiritual healing. **lay hold of** seize or grasp. **lay in** provide oneself with a stock of. **lay into** *colloq.* punish or scold severely. **lay it on thick** (or **with a trowel**) *colloq.* flatter or exaggerate grossly. **lay off 1** discharge (workers) temporarily. **2** *colloq.* desist. **lay of the land** current state of affairs. **lay open 1** break the skin of. **2** [foll. by *to*] expose (to criticism, etc.). **lay out 1** spread out; expose to view. **2** prepare (a corpse) for burial. **3** *colloq.* knock unconscious. **4** prepare a layout. **5** expend (money). **lay to rest** bury in a grave. **lay up 1** store; save. **2** put (a ship, etc.) out of service.

• *v.* **1** put (down), set (down), deposit. **2** see LIE¹ *n.* 1. **4** ascribe, assign, direct. **5** see PREPARE¹ **1**. **6** set, arrange, spread. **7** bet, risk, venture, put up or down. **8** sleep with, go to bed with, make love to, have sex with. • *n.* see POSITION *n.* 1, 2. □ **laid-back** see *relaxed* (RELAX *v.* 3). **laid up** see SICK *adj.* 2. **lay bare** see EXPOSE 4. **lay claim to** see CLAIM *v.* 1. **lay down 1** see LAY *v.* 1 above. **2** set down; insist on, exact. **4** see STORE *v.* 2. **5** put in writing. **6** see SACRIFICE *v.* **lay one's hands on** see OBTAIN 1. **lay hold of** grab, snatch, get, *sl.* nab. **lay in** see *stock up* 2. **lay it on thick** see EXAGGERATE 1, FLATTER 1. **lay off 1** suspend; dismiss, release, let go. **2** see CEASE *v.* **lay of the land** condition, situation; atmosphere, mood, character.

lay² /lay/ *adj.* **1 a** nonclerical. **b** not ordained into the clergy. **2 a** not professionally qualified. **b** of or done by such persons.

■ **1** laic, civil; secular, worldly. **2** amateur, nonspecialist, popular.

lay³ /lay/ *n.* **1** short poem meant to be sung. **2** song.

■ lyric, ballad, *hist.* ode; see also SONG 1.

lay⁴ *past* of LIE¹.

lay•a•bout /láyəbowt/ *n.* habitual loafer or idler.

lay•er /láyər/ • *n.* **1** thickness of matter, esp. one of several, covering a surface. **2** person or thing that lays. **3** hen that lays eggs. • *v.tr.* arrange in layers. □□ **lay'ered** *adj.*

■ *n.* **1** see FILM *n.* 1. **4** see SPREAD *v.* 1b.

lay•ette /layét/ *n.* set of clothing, etc., for a newborn child.

lay•man /láymən/ *n.* (*pl.* **-men**; *fem.* **lay•wom•an**, *pl.* **-wom•en**) **1** nonordained member of a church. **2** person without professional knowledge.

lay•off /láyawf/ *n.* **1** temporary discharge of workers. **2** period when this is in force.

lay•out /láyowt/ *n.* **1** way in which plans, printed matter, etc., are arranged or set out. **2** something arranged or set out in a particular way.

lay•o•ver /láyōvər/ *n.* period of rest before a further stage in a journey, etc.; stopover.

laze /layz/ *v.intr.* spend time lazily or idly.

la•zy /láyzee/ *adj.* (**la•zi•er**, **la•zi•est**) **1** disinclined to work; doing little work. **2** of or inducing idleness. **3** sluggish; slow-moving. □□ **la'zi•ly** *adv.* **la'zi•ness** *n.*

■ **1** indolent, slothful, idle, shiftless, inert, inactive. **2** easy, relaxed, carefree, *colloq.* laid-back. **3** languid, torpid, stagnant, snaillike.

la•zy•bones /láyzeebōnz/ *n.* (*pl.* same) *colloq.* lazy person.

lb. *abbr.* pound (weight).

LC *abbr.* (also **L.C.** or **l.c.**) **1** landing craft. **2** (**LC** or **L.C.**) Library of Congress. **3** lowercase.

LCD *abbr.* **1** liquid crystal display. **2** lowest (or least) common denominator.

LCM *abbr.* lowest (or least) common multiple.

lea /lee, láy/ *n. poet.* (also **ley**) meadow; pasture land.

leach /leech/ *v.* **1** *tr.* make (a liquid) percolate through some material. **2** *tr. & intr.* [foll. by *away*, *out*] remove (soluble matter) or be removed in this way. □□ **leach'er** *n.*

■ see PERCOLATE 1.

lead¹ /leed/ • *v.* (*past* and *past part.* **led** /led/) **1** *tr.* cause to go with one, esp. by guiding or going in front. **2** *tr.* **a** direct the actions or opinions of. **b** guide by persuasion or example. **3** *tr.* [also *absol.*] provide access to (*the road leads to Atlanta*). **4** *tr.* go through (a life, etc., of a specified kind) (*led a miserable existence*). **5** *tr.* **a** have the first place in. **b** [*absol.*] be ahead in a race or game. **c** [*absol.*] be preeminent in some field. **6** *tr.* be in charge of (*leads a team*). **7** *tr.* **a** direct by example. **b** be the principal player of (a group of musicians). **8** *tr.* [also *absol.*] begin a round of play at cards by playing (a card) or a card of (a particular suit). **9** *intr.* [foll. by *to*] result in. **10** *intr.* [foll. by *with*] (of a newspaper) use a particular item as the main story. • *n.* **1** guidance given by going in front; example. **2 a** leading place; leadership. **b** amount by which a competitor is ahead of the others. **3** clue (*first real lead in the case*). **4** leash. **5 a** chief part in a play, etc. **b** person playing this. **6** (in full **lead story**) item of news given the greatest prominence. **7 a** act or right of playing first in a game of cards. **b** card led. • *attrib.adj.* leading; principal; first. □ **lead by the nose** cajole (a person) into compliance. **lead-in 1** introduction, opening, etc. **2** wire leading in from outside, esp. from an aerial to a receiver or transmitter. **lead off 1** begin. **2** *Baseball* be the first batter in the inning. **lead on** entice deceptively. **lead time** time between the initiation and completion of a production process. **lead up to** precede; prepare for.

■ *v.* **1** conduct, take, convey, steer, show (the way), escort, accompany, usher, shepherd. **2** bring, move, induce, cause, influence, prompt, persuade. **3** go, connect with; carry. **4** pass, spend, experience; suffer, bear, endure, undergo. **5** be *or* move *or* go *or* forge ahead; excel, dominate, shine; surpass, exceed, overshadow, outdo, beat. **6, 7a** run, head (up); supervise, manage, govern, command, control, preside. **9** (*lead to*) create, cause, bring on *or* about, produce, give rise to. • *n.* **1** direction, model, standard. **2** front, vanguard, first place; priority, preeminence; advantage, edge. **3** tip, indication, pointer, hint, suggestion, cue; evidence, tip-off. **4** tether, restraint; halter, reins. **5** principal, hero, heroine, leading role, leading lady *or* man, star. • *attrib. adj.* foremost; main, chief, premier. □ **lead-in 1** overture, preamble, preface, prelude, *colloq.* intro. **lead off 1** see BEGIN 1. **lead on** lure, allure, seduce, beguile, *colloq.* sweet-talk, soft-soap; see also MISLEAD. **lead up to** pave *or* clear (the way) for; broach, bring up, work up to.

lead² /led/ • *n.* **1** *Chem.* heavy, bluish-gray soft ductile metallic element. ¶Symb.: **Pb.** **2 a** graphite. **b** thin length of this in a pencil. **3** *colloq.* bullets. **4** *Printing* blank space between lines of print. **5** [*attrib.*] made of lead. • *v.tr.* **1** cover, weight, or frame with lead. **2** *Printing* separate lines of (printed matter) with lead strips. **3** add a lead compound to (gasoline, etc.). □ **lead balloon** failure; unsuccessful venture.

lead•en /léd'n/ *adj.* **1** of or like lead. **2** heavy; slow; burdensome (*leaden limbs*). **3** inert; depressing. **4** lead-colored (*leaden skies*). □□ **lead′en•ly** *adv.* **lead′en•ness** *n.*

■ **2** weighty, massive, dense, sluggish, oppressive. **3** lifeless, inanimate, listless, lethargic. **4** gray, ashen, dull, drab, gloomy, somber, dreary.

lead•er /leédər/ *n.* **1** person or thing that leads. **2** person followed by others. □□ **lead′er•ship** *n.*

■ chief, head, director, chair, principal, manager, *colloq.* boss; king, queen, sovereign, monarch, ruler, governor, president, premier, head of state, prime minister; pioneer, organizer; conductor, pilot, guide. □□ **lead-**

ership direction, guidance, control, management, supervision; rule, government, reign.

lead•ing /leéding/ *adj.* chief; most important. □ **leading lady** actress playing the principal part. **leading man** actor playing the principal part. **leading question** question that prompts the answer wanted.

■ principal, main, foremost, head, premier, top, first, greatest, best, primary, central; outstanding, prominent; peerless, unequaled, unrivaled, unsurpassed. □ **leading lady, leading man** see LEAD¹ *n.* 5.

leaf /leéf/ • *n.* (*pl.* **leaves** /leevz/) **1** each of several flattened usu. green structures of a plant, usu. on the side of a stem or branch. **2** single thickness of paper. **3** very thin sheet of metal, etc. **4** hinged or insertable part of a table, etc. • *v.* **1** *intr.* put forth leaves. **2** *tr.* [foll. by *through*] turn over the pages of (a book, etc.). □□ **leaf′age** *n.* **leafed** *adj.* [also in *comb.*]. **leaf′less** *adj.* **leaf′less•ness** *n.* **leaf′like** *adj.* **leaf′y** *adj.* (**leaf•i•er, leaf•i•est**).

■ *n.* **1** see BLADE¹ 3. **2** see SHEET *n.* • *v.* **2** see THUMB *v.* 2. □□ **leafless** see BARE *adj.* 2. **leafy** foliate; green, verdant, lush.

leaf•let /leéflit/ *n.* **1** young leaf. **2** *Bot.* any division of a compound leaf. **3** sheet of paper giving information.

■ **3** pamphlet, brochure, handbill, circular, handout, flyer.

league¹ /leeg/ • *n.* **1** people, countries, groups, etc., combining for a purpose. **2** group of sports teams that compete for a championship. • *v.intr.* (**leagues, leagued, leagu•ing**) [often foll. by *together*] join in a league. □ **in league** allied; conspiring. **League of Women Voters** nonpartisan organization that promotes voter awareness and participation.

■ *n.* confederation, federation, union, association, coalition, alliance; guild, society. • *v.* ally, unite, associate, affiliate, band together, team up. □ **in league** united, in collusion, *sl.* in cahoots.

league² /leeg/ *n. archaic* measure of distance, usu. about three miles.

leak /leek/ • *n.* **1 a** hole through which matter, esp. liquid or gas, passes accidentally in or out. **b** matter passing through this. **c** act or instance of leaking. **2** disclosure of secret information. • *v.* **1 a** *intr.* (of liquid, gas, etc.) pass through a leak. **b** *tr.* lose or admit (liquid, gas, etc.) through a leak. **2** *tr.* disclose (secret information). **3** *intr.* [often foll. by *out*] (of secret information) become known. □ **take a leak** *sl.* urinate. □□ **leak′y** *adj.* (**leak•i•er, leak•i•est**).

■ *n.* **1 a** fissure, crack, chink, puncture. **b, c** leakage, discharge, seepage, ooze, secretion, flow. **2** revelation, exposure, divulgence. • *v.* **1 a** escape, issue, seep (out), ooze (out). **b** secrete. **2** divulge, reveal, bring to light, tell, report, make known *or* public; let slip, blab. **3** (*leak out*) come to light.

leak•age /leékij/ *n.* **1** action or result of leaking. **2** what leaks in or out. **3** disclosure of secret information.

lean¹ /leen/ • *v.* (*past* and *past part.* **leaned**

/leend, lent/ or **leant** /lent/) **1** *tr. & intr.* [often foll. by *across, back, over,* etc.] be or place in a sloping position; incline from upright. **2** *tr. & intr.* [foll. by *against, on, upon*] rest or cause to rest for support against, etc. **3** *intr.* [foll. by *on, upon*] rely on. **4** *intr.* [foll. by *to, toward*] be partial to. • *n.* inclination (*a decided lean to the right*). □ **lean on** *colloq.* put pressure on (a person) to act in a certain way. **lean-to** (*pl.* **-tos**) **1** building with its roof leaning against a wall. **2** shed with an inclined roof usu. leaning against trees, posts, etc.

■ *v.* slant, tilt, bend, tip. **2** (*tr.*) prop, set, put, lay, place, position; (*intr.*) lie, repose, recline **3** (*lean on*) depend on, count on, bank on. **4** (*lean to* or *toward*) favor, prefer, show *or* have a preference for. • *n.* slope, pitch, cant. □ **lean on** intimidate, railroad, browbeat, *colloq.* put the screws on. **lean-to** see SHED¹.

lean² /leen/ • *adj.* **1** thin; having little fat. **2** meager; of poor quality (*lean crop*) See synonym study at THIN. • *n.* lean part of meat. □ **lean years** years of scarcity. □□ **lean'ly** *adv.* **lean'ness** *n.*

■ *adj.* **1** slim, slender, spare, skinny, scrawny, gaunt, rangy, lanky. **2** scant, skimpy, inadequate, deficient, insufficient, sparse.

lean•ing /leening/ *n.* tendency or partiality.

■ bent, inclination, bias, liking, preference, propensity, affinity.

leap /leep/ • *v.* (*past* and *past part.* **leaped** /leept, lept/ or **leapt** /lept/) **1** *intr.* jump or spring forcefully. **2** *tr.* jump across. • *n.* forceful jump. □ **by leaps and bounds** with startlingly rapid progress. **leap at 1** rush toward; pounce upon. **2** accept eagerly. **leap of faith** accepting something on the basis of trust not reason. **leap year** year, occurring once in four, with 366 days (adding Feb. 29). □□ **leap'er** *n.*

■ *v.* **1** bound, hop, skip; prance, *sl.* cavort. **2** hurdle, vault; rise, surge, soar, shoot up. • *n.* upsurge, escalation, lift, *colloq.* boost. □ **by leaps and bounds** quickly, swiftly, fast, *colloq.* like greased lightning, like a house on fire. **leap at 2** be eager for; seize (on), grasp, *colloq.* sweep up(on).

leap•frog /leepfrawg, -frog/ • *n.* game in which players vault with parted legs over others bending down. • *v.* (**-frogged, -frogging**) **1** *intr.* [foll. by *over*] perform such a vault. **2** *tr.* vault over in this way. **3** *tr. & intr.* (of two or more people, vehicles, etc.) overtake alternately.

learn /lərn/ *v.* (*past* and *past part.* **learned** /lərnd, lərnt/ or **learnt** /lərnt/) **1** *tr.* gain knowledge of or skill in. **2** *tr.* memorize. **3** *intr.* [foll. by *of*] be informed about. **4** *tr.* [foll. by *that, how,* etc.] become aware of. □□ **learn'a•ble** *adj.* **learn'er** *n.*

■ **1** be taught; master, study. **2** learn by heart *or* rote; remember. **3** (*learn of*) find out (about), discover, uncover, determine, ascertain; come across. **4** gather, hear, realize. □□ **learner** student, pupil, apprentice; beginner, novice, *sl.* rookie.

learn•ed /lərnid/ *adj.* **1** having much learn-

ing. **2** showing or requiring learning (*a learned work*). □□ **learn'ed•ly** *adv.* **learn'ed•ness** *n.*

■ **1** knowledgeable, (well-)informed, erudite, (well-)educated, well-read; *colloq.* in the know. **2** scholarly, academic; abstract, theoretical, formal, profound; educational, scholastic.

learn•ing /lərning/ *n.* knowledge acquired by study. See synonym study at KNOWLEDGE. □ **learning curve 1** graph showing time needed to acquire a new skill, knowledge of a subject, etc. **2** time represented by such a graph. **learning disability** disorder that interferes with the learning process.

■ lore, wisdom, schooling, education, instruction; information.

lease /lees/ • *n.* agreement by which the owner of property rents it for a specified time. • *v.tr.* grant or take on a lease. □ **new lease on life** improved prospect of living, or of use after repair. □□ **leas'a•ble** *adj.* **leas'er** *n.*

■ *n.* rental, hire, charter; contract, deal. • *v.* rent (out), let (out), hire (out).

lease•hold /lees-hōld/ *n.* **1** holding of property by lease. **2** property held by lease. □□ **lease'hold•er** *n.*

leash /leesh/ • *n.* strap for holding a dog, etc. • *v.tr.* **1** put a leash on. **2** restrain.

■ *n.* see LEAD¹ *n.* 4. • *v.* see TETHER *v.*

least /leest/ • *adj.* **1** smallest; slightest. **2** (of a species, etc.) very small (*least tern*). • *n.* least amount. • *adv.* in the least degree. □ **at least 1** at any rate. **2** (also **at the least**) not less than. **in the least** [usu. with *neg.*] in the smallest degree (*not in the least offended*). **to say the least** used to imply the moderation of a statement (*that is doubtful to say the least*).

■ *adj.* **1** see MINIMUM *adj.* **2** see LITTLE *adj.* 7. *n.* see MINIMUM *n.*

leath•er /leth̄ər/ • *n.* **1** material made from the skin of an animal by tanning, etc. **2** [*attrib.*] made of leather. • *v.tr.* beat; thrash. □□ **leath'er•y** *adj.*

■ *n.* **1** see HIDE² *n.* 1. • *v.* see BEAT *v.* 1. □□ **leathery** see TOUGH¹ *adj.* 1.

leath•er•back /leth̄ərbak/ *n.* large marine turtle, having a thick leathery carapace.

leath•er•ette /leth̄əret/ *n.* imitation leather.

leath•er•neck /leth̄ərnek/ *n. sl.* US Marine.

leave¹ /leev/ *v.* (*past* and *past part.* **left** /left/) **1 a** *tr.* go away from. **b** *intr.* depart. **2** *tr.* cause to or let remain. **3** *tr.* abandon. **4** *tr.* have remaining after one's death. **5** *tr.* bequeath. □ **leave alone 1** not interfere with. **2** not have dealings with. **leave much** (or **a lot,** etc.) **to be desired** be highly unsatisfactory. **leave off** discontinue. **leave out** omit; not include. **left for dead** abandoned as being beyond rescue. □□ **leav'er** *n.*

■ *v.* **1b** go *or* be on one's way, get going, set off, take off, *colloq.* push off, scram, *sl.* shove off, beat it, split. **2** leave behind; forget, mislay, lose. **3** desert, forsake; walk *or* run out on, leave in the lurch, *colloq.* dump, *sl.* ditch. **5** see BEQUEATH 1, 2. □ **leave alone 1** lay off, leave in peace. **2** avoid, shun, steer clear of. **leave off** see END v. 1. **leave out** see OMIT 1.

leave[2] /leev/ n. **1** permission. **2 a** (in full **leave of absence**) permission to be absent from duty. **b** period for which this lasts. □ **on leave** legitimately absent from duty. **take one's leave** bid farewell. **take one's leave of** bid farewell to.

  ■ **1** authorization, license, consent, approval, blessing, go-ahead, colloq. green light. **2** furlough, time off, vacation.

leav•en /lévən/ • n. **1** substance added to dough to make it ferment and rise. **2** transforming influence. • v.tr. **1** ferment (dough) with leaven. **2 a** permeate and transform. **b** [foll. by with] modify with a tempering element.

leaves pl. of LEAF.

leav•ings /léevingz/ n.pl. things left over, esp. as worthless.

Leb•a•nese /lébənéez/ • adj. of or relating to Lebanon in the Middle East. • n. (pl. same) **1** native or national of Lebanon. **2** person of Lebanese descent.

lech /lech/ colloq. v.intr. = LECHER.

lech•er /léchər/ n. person with excessive sexual desire, esp. a man. □□ **lech′er•ous** adj. **lech′er•ous•ly** adv. **lech′er•ous•ness** n. **lech′er•y** n.

  ■ see LIBERTINE n. 1. □□ **lecherous** lustful, randy, lascivious, lewd, prurient, salacious.

lec•i•thin /lésithin/ n. **1** fatty compound found in egg yolk and other living tissue. **2** preparation of this used to emulsify foods, etc.

lec•tern /léktərn/ n. stand for holding a book for a lecturer, etc.

lec•ture /lékchər/ • n. **1** discourse giving information to a class, etc. **2** long reprimand. • v. **1** intr. deliver a lecture or lectures. **2** tr. reprimand. □□ **lec′tur•er** n.

  ■ n. **1** speech, address, talk, presentation. **2** sermon, scolding, tongue-lashing, rebuke, colloq. talking-to. • v. **1** speak, talk; preach. **2** rebuke, reproach, scold, berate, lambaste; admonish, warn, advise.

LED abbr. light-emitting diode.

led past and past part. of LEAD[1].

ledge /lej/ n. narrow horizontal or shelflike projection. □□ **ledged** adj.

  ■ shelf, ridge, overhang; mantelpiece, windowsill.

led•ger /léjər/ n. principal record of the accounts of a business.

lee /lee/ n. **1** shelter. **2** (in full **lee side**) side away from the wind.

leech /leech/ n. **1** bloodsucking worm formerly used medically. **2** person who imposes on others.

leek /leek/ n. plant of the onion family, with overlapping leaves forming a cylindrical bulb.

leer /leer/ • v.intr. look slyly, lasciviously, or maliciously. • n. leering look. □□ **leer′ing•ly** adv.

  ■ v. (leer at) ogle, eye (up). • n. ogle, colloq. the once-over.

leer•y /léeree/ adj. (**leer•i•er, leer•i•est**) sl. **1** knowing; sly. **2** [foll. by of] wary.

  ■ **1** cunning, crafty, shrewd, colloq. shifty. **2** suspicious, skeptical, distrustful, cautious.

lees /leez/ n.pl. **1** sediment of wine, etc. **2** dregs; refuse.

  ■ **1** see SEDIMENT 1. **2** see RUBBISH n. 2.

lee•ward /léewərd, Naut. lōōərd/ • adj. & adv. on or toward the side sheltered from the wind. • n. leeward region, side, or direction.

lee•way /léeway/ n. **1** sideways drift of a ship to leeward. **2** allowable scope of action.

  ■ **2** latitude, freedom, range, play, (elbow) room.

left[1] /left/ • adj. **1** on or toward the west side of the human body or any object when facing north. **2** (also **Left**) Polit. socialistic. • adv. on or to the left side. • n. **1** left-hand part, region, or direction. **2** (often **Left**) Polit. group or section favoring liberalism, social reform, etc. □ **have two left feet** be clumsy. **left bank** bank of a river on the left facing downstream. **left field** Baseball part of the outfield beyond third base. **left-hand** adj. **1** on or toward the left side of a person or thing (left-hand drive). **2** done with the left hand. **3** (of a screw) = LEFT-HANDED 3b. **left wing** liberal or socialist section of a political party. **left-wing** adj. liberal; socialist; radical. **left-winger** person on the left wing.

  ■ adj. **1** sinistral. **2** progressive, radical, liberal. • n. **1** port; stage left. **2** liberals, democrats; communists.

left[2] past and past part. of LEAVE[1].

left-hand•ed /léft-hándid/ adj. **1** using the left hand by preference. **2** (of a tool, etc.) made to be used with the left hand. **3 a** turning to the left; toward the left. **b** (of a screw) advanced by turning counterclockwise. **4 a** (of a compliment) ambiguous. **b** of doubtful sincerity. □□ **left-hand′ed•ly** adv. **left′-hand′ed•ness** n. **left′-hand′er** n.

  ■ **1** sinistral, colloq. southpaw. **3** counterclockwise. **4** backhanded, equivocal, questionable, doubtful; hollow, empty.

left•ism /léftizəm/ n. Polit. principles or policy of the left. □□ **left′ist** n. & adj.

  ■ □□ **leftist** (n.) see PROGRESSIVE[1] n. (adj.) see LEFT adj. 2.

left•most /léftmōst/ adj. furthest to the left.

left•o•ver /léftōvər/ • adj. remaining over; not used up or disposed of. • n. [in pl.] surplus items (esp. of food).

  ■ adj. residual, extra, excess. • n. (leftovers) remains, remnants, scraps, leavings; odds and ends; debris, refuse.

left•y /léftee/ n. (pl. **–ies**) colloq. left-handed person.

leg /leg/ n. **1** each of the limbs on which a person or animal walks and stands. **2** leg of an animal or bird as food. **3** part of a garment covering a leg. **4** support of a chair, table, etc. **5** section of a journey, relay race, competition, etc. □ **feel** (or **find**) **one's legs** become able to stand or walk. **give a person a leg up** help a person to mount a horse, etc. **leg it** colloq. walk or run fast. **leg-of-mutton sleeve** sleeve that is full and loose on the upper arm but close-fitting on the forearm. **not have a leg to stand on** be unable to support one's argument. **on one's last legs** near death or the end of one's usefulness, etc. □□ **legged** /legd, légid/ adj. [also in comb.].

■ n. **1** calf, thigh; limb, member. **2** shank, ham, drumstick, hock. **3** trouser(s), pants, legging(s), stocking(s); hose. **4** spindle; brace, prop, column, pillar, post. **5** stage, segment, portion, stretch, lap. □ **give a person a leg up** aid, assist, support; push, colloq. boost. **leg it** see RUN v. 1, 3. **on one's last legs** decrepit, worn-out, spent, colloq. all in; run-down, falling apart, broken-down, dilapidated.

leg•a•cy /légəsee/ n. (pl. **–cies**) **1** gift left in a will, **2** thing handed down by a predecessor.
■ **1** see BEQUEST 2.

le•gal /léegal/ adj. **1** of or based on law. **2** appointed or required by law. **3** permitted by law. □ **legal age** age at which a person assumes adult rights and privileges by law. **legal aid** state assistance for legal advice or proceedings. **legal holiday** public holiday established by law. **legal tender** currency that cannot legally be refused in payment of a debt. □□ **le'gal•ly** adv.
■ **1** judicial, jurisprudent, forensic. **2** constitutional, statutory. **3** lawful, legitimate, licit, acceptable, permissible, permitted, admissible, authorized. □ **legal tender** see MONEY 1.

le•gal•ese /leegəleez/ n. colloq. technical language of legal documents.

le•gal•ism /léegəlizəm/ n. excessive adherence to law or formula. □□ **le'gal•ist** n. **le•gal•is'tic** adj. **le•gal•is'ti•cal•ly** adv.
■ strictness, rigidity, fastidiousness. □□ **legistic** literal, pedantic, petty, narrow-minded, hairsplitting, colloq. nitpicking.

le•gal•i•ty /ligálitee, leegál-/ n. (pl. **–ties**) **1** lawfulness. **2** [in pl.] obligations imposed by law.

le•gal•ize /léegalīz/ v.tr. make lawful. □□ **le•gal•i•za'tion** n.
■ see LEGITIMATE adj. 1. □□ **legalization** see SANCTION 2.

leg•ate /légət/ n. **1** member of the clergy representing the Pope. **2** ambassador or delegate. □□ **leg'ate•ship** n.

leg•a•tee /légətee/ n. recipient of a legacy.

le•ga•tion /ligáyshən/ n. **1** office and staff of a diplomatic minister. **2** official headquarters of such.

le•ga•to /ligaátō/ Mus. • adv. & adj. in a smooth flowing manner. • n. (pl. **–tos**) **1** legato passage. **2** legato playing.

le•ga•tor /ligáytər/ n. giver of a legacy.

leg•end /léjənd/ n. **1 a** traditional story; myth. **b** such stories collectively. **2** colloq. famous or remarkable person or event. **3a** inscription. **b** caption. **c** wording on a map, etc., explaining the symbols used.
■ **1** folklore, fable, tradition; (folk) tale, epic, saga. **2** immortal, hero, great, luminary, giant, god, goddess, deity; celebrity, idol, superstar. **3** motto, slogan, wording; key, code, table.

leg•end•ar•y /léjəndəree/ adj. **1** of or connected with legends. **2** colloq. remarkable. □□ **leg'end•ar'i•ly** adv.

■ **1** mythic, mythical, romantic, epic, fabled; fabulous. **2** phenomenal, extraordinary, notable, great, classic; famous, celebrated, renowned.

leg•er•de•main /léjərdəmáyn/ n. **1** sleight of hand. **2** trickery.

leg•ging /léging/ n. **1** [usu. in pl.] covering for the leg from the knee to the ankle. **2** [pl.] close-fitting usu. knitted trousers.

leg•gy /légee/ adj. (**leg•gi•er, leg•gi•est**) **1** long-legged. **2** long-stemmed. □□ **leg'gi•ness** n.

leg•horn /léghawrn, –ərn/ n. (also **Leg'horn**) bird of a small hardy breed of domestic fowl.

leg•i•ble /léjibəl/ adj. clear enough to read; readable. □□ **leg•i•bil'i•ty** n. **leg'i•bly** adv.
■ plain, distinct; decipherable, intelligible.

le•gion /léejən/ • n. **1** division of 3,000–6,000 men in the ancient Roman army. **2** large organized body. • predic.adj. great in number. □ **American Legion** association of US ex-servicemen formed in 1919. **foreign legion** body of foreign volunteers in a modern, esp. French, army.

le•gion•naire /léejənáir/ n. **1** member of a foreign legion. **2** member of the American Legion. □ **legionnaires' disease** form of bacterial pneumonia.

leg•is•late /léjislayt/ v.intr. make laws.

leg•is•la•tion /léjisláyshən/ n. **1** process of making laws. **2** laws collectively.

leg•is•la•tive /léjislaytiv/ adj. of or empowered to make legislation. □□ **leg•is•la'tive•ly** adv.

leg•is•la•tor /léjislaytər/ n. **1** member of a legislative body. **2** lawgiver.

leg•is•la•ture /léjislaychər/ n. legislative body.
■ assembly, congress (or Congress), diet, council, parliament, house (or House), senate (or Senate).

le•git /lijít/ adj. colloq. legitimate.

le•git•i•mate /lijítimət/ adj. **1** (of a child) born of parents married to each other. **2** lawful; proper; regular. **3** logically admissible. **4** relating to serious drama as distinct from musical comedy, revue, etc. See synonym study at GENUINE. □□ **le•git'i•ma•cy** /–məsee/ n. **le•git'i•mate•ly** adv. **le•git'i•ma•tion** /–máyshən/ n.
■ **1, 2** licit, legal; constitutional, permissible, authorized, rightful; established, orthodox; official, authentic, genuine, bona fide, real. **3** justifiable, reasonable, rational, valid, sound, right, correct.

le•git•i•ma•tize /lijítimətīz/ v.tr. = LEGITIMIZE.

le•git•i•mize /lijítimīz/ v.tr. **1** make legitimate. **2** serve as a justification for. □□ **le•git•i•mi•za'tion** n.
■ **1** see AUTHORIZE 1. **2** see JUSTIFY 1, 2, 4. □□ **legitimization** see SANCTION 2.

leg•room /légrōōm/ n. space for the legs of a seated person.

leg•ume /légyōōm/ n. **1** leguminous plant. **2** any edible part of a leguminous plant.

le•gu•mi•nous /ligyōōminəs/ adj. of the family of plants with seeds in pods, including peas and beans.

lei /láy-ee, lay/ *n.* Polynesian garland of flowers.

lei•sure /léezhər, lézh–/ *n.* free time, as for recreation. □ **at leisure 1** not occupied. **2** in an unhurried manner. **at one's leisure** when one has time.

■ spare time, time off; holiday, vacation; respite, rest; enjoyment, diversion; ease, (peace and) quiet, relaxation. □ **at leisure 1** see IDLE *adj.* 2. **2** calmly, steadily; casually, easily. **at one's leisure** see *at leisure* 2 above.

lei•sure•ly /léezhərlee, lézh–/ • *adj.* unhurried; relaxed. • *adv.* deliberately, without hurry. □□ **lei'sure•li•ness** *n.*

■ *adv.* see SLOW *adv.* 1.

lei•sure•wear /léezhərwair, lézh–/ *n.* informal clothes, esp. sportswear.

leit•mo•tiv /lítmōteef/ *n.* (also **leit'mo•tif**) recurrent or main theme.

LEM /lem/ *abbr.* lunar excursion module.

lem•ming /léming/ *n.* small arctic rodent reputed to rush into the sea and drown during mass migration.

lem•on /lémən/ *n.* **1 a** yellow, oval, sour citrus fruit. **b** tree that produces this fruit. **2** pale-yellow color. **3** *colloq.* feeble, unsatisfactory, or disappointing thing, esp. a car. □ **lemon balm** herb with leaves smelling and tasting of lemon. □□ **lem'on•y** *adj.*

lem•on•ade /lémənáyd/ *n.* drink made from lemon juice.

le•mur /léemər/ *n.* long-tailed arboreal primate of Madagascar.

Len•a•pe /lénəpee, lənáapee/ *n.* see DELAWARE.

lend /lend/ *v.tr.* (*past* and *past part.* **lent** /lent/) **1** grant temporary use of (a thing). **2** allow the use of (money) at interest. **3** bestow or contribute (*lend assistance*). □ **lend an ear** (or **one's ears**) listen. **lend itself to** (of a thing) be suitable for. □□ **lend'a•ble** *adj.* **lend'er** *n.* **lend'ing** *n.*

■ **1, 2** loan, advance, put out; rent (out), lease (out). **3** impart, furnish, provide, give, confer. □ **lend an ear** see LISTEN 1, 2. **lend itself to** be appropriate to *or* for, be applicable *or* adaptable to.

length /lengkth, length/ *n.* **1** extent from end to end. **2** extent in or of time. **3** distance a thing extends (*at arm's length*). **4** length of a horse, boat, etc., as a measure of the lead in a race. □ **at length 1** (also **at great,** etc., **length**) in detail. **2** at last.

■ **1, 3** span, reach, stretch; measure, size, dimension. **2** duration, term, period. □ **at length 1** in depth, thoroughly, completely, exhaustively, extensively. **2** finally, ultimately.

length•en /léngkthən, length–/ *v.* make or become longer. □□ **length'en•er** *n.*

■ extend, elongate, stretch, expand; drag out, draw out, prolong; grow, enlarge.

length•wise /léngkthwiz, length–/ • *adv.* in a direction parallel with a thing's length. • *adj.* lying or moving lengthwise.

length•y /léngkthee, léngthee/ *adj.* (**length•i•er, length•i•est**) **1** of unusual length. **2** (of speech, writing, a speaker, etc.) verbose;

tedious. □□ **length'i•ly** *adv.* **length'i•ness** *n.*

■ **1** long, extensive, elongated. **2** boring, dull, wearisome, tiresome, endless, interminable; long-winded.

le•ni•ent /léenyənt/ *adj.* merciful; tolerant; not severe. □□ **le'ni•ence** *n.* **le'ni•en•cy** *n.* **le'ni•ent•ly** *adv.* See synonym study at MERCY

■ compassionate, forgiving, humane, generous, patient, kindhearted; liberal, permissive, easygoing, moderate; soft, mild, gentle, kind, tender.

le•no /léenō/ *n.* (*pl.* **–nos**) openwork fabric with the warp threads twisted in pairs.

lens /lenz/ *n.* **1** piece of a transparent substance with one or (usu.) both sides curved for concentrating or dispersing light rays, esp. in optical instruments. **2** *Physics* device for focusing or otherwise modifying the direction of movement of light, sound, electrons, etc. □□ **lensed** *adj.* **lens'less** *adj.*

Lent /lent/ *n.* *Eccl.* period of fasting and penitence preceding Easter. □□ **Lent'en** *adj.*

lent *past* and *past part.* of LEND.

-lent /lənt/ *suffix* forming adjectives (*pestilent, violent*) (cf. -ULENT).

len•til /léntəl/ *n.* **1** pealike plant. **2** its edible seed.

len•to /léntō/ *Mus.* • *adj.* slow. • *adv.* slowly.

Le•o /lée-ō/ *n.* (*pl.* **–os**) **1** constellation, traditionally regarded as the figure of a lion. **2 a** fifth sign of the zodiac (the Lion). **b** person born under this sign.

le•o•nine /léeənīn/ *adj.* **1** like a lion. **2** of or relating to lions.

leop•ard /lépərd/ *n.* (*fem.* **leop•ard•ess** /–dis/) large African or Asian feline with a black-spotted, yellowish, or all black coat; panther.

le•o•tard /léeətaard/ *n.* **1** close-fitting one-piece garment worn by dancers, acrobats, etc. **2** = TIGHTS.

lep•er /lépər/ *n.* person suffering from leprosy.

lep•i•dop•ter•ous /lépidóptərəs/ *adj.* of the order of insects that includes butterflies and moths. □□ **lep•i•dop'ter•an** *adj.* & *n.* **lep•i•dop'ter•ist** *n.*

lep•re•chaun /léprəkon, –kawn/ *n.* small mischievous sprite in Irish folklore.

lep•ro•sy /léprəsee/ *n.* contagious deforming disease that affects skin and nerves. □□ **lep'rous** *adj.*

les•bi•an /lézbeeən/ • *n.* homosexual woman. • *adj.* of or relating to female homosexuality. □□ **les'bi•an•ism** *n.*

lese-maj•es•ty /leez májistee/ *n.* (also **lèse-maj•es•té** /layz mázhestay/) **1** treason. **2** insult to a sovereign or ruler. **3** presumptuous conduct.

le•sion /léezhən/ *n.* injury to an organ, etc., affecting its function.

less /les/ • *adj.* **1** smaller in extent, degree, duration, number, etc. **2** of smaller quantity. **3** *disp.* fewer (*eat less cookies*). • *adv.* to a smaller extent. • *n.* smaller amount. • *prep.* minus (*made $1,000 less tax*). □ **much less** with even greater force of denial (*do not suspect him of negligence, much less of dishonesty*).

-less /lis/ *suffix* forming adjectives and adverbs: **1** from nouns, meaning 'not having, without, free from' (*doubtless*). **2** from verbs, meaning 'not affected by or doing the action of the verb' (*tireless*). □□ **–lessly** *suffix* forming adverbs. **–lessness** *suffix* forming nouns.

less•ee /lesée/ *n.* person who holds a property by lease.
■ see TENANT *n.* 1.

less•en /lésən/ *v.* make or become less; diminish.
■ see DIMINISH 1.

less•er /lésər/ *adj.* [usu. *attrib.*] not so great as the other or the rest (*lesser evil, lesser egret*).
■ see INFERIOR *adj.* 1.

les•son /lésən/ *n.* **1 a** amount of teaching given at one time. **b** time assigned to this. **2** [in *pl.*; foll. by *in*] systematic instruction (*lessons in French*). **3** thing learned or to be learned by a pupil. **4** experience that serves to warn or encourage (*let that be a lesson to you*). **5** passage from the Bible read aloud during a church service.
■ **1 a** class, session, period. **2** (*lessons*) schooling, classes; course (of study). **3** exercise, drill; assignment, homework, task. **4** example, maxim; admonition; message, moral. **5** reading, text.

les•sor /lésawr/ *n.* person who lets a property by lease.

lest /lest/ *conj.* in order that not; for fear that (*lest we forget*).

let¹ /let/ *v.* (**let•ting**; *past* and *past part.* **let**) **1** *tr.* **a** allow to. **b** cause to (*let me know*). **2** *tr.* [foll. by *into*] **a** allow to enter. **b** make acquainted with (a secret, etc.). **3** *tr.* rent (rooms, land, etc.). **4** *v.* allow or cause (liquid or air) to escape (*let blood*). **5** *tr.* award (a contract for work). **6** *aux.* supplying the first and third persons of exhortations (*let us pray*), commands (*let there be light*), assumptions (*let AB be equal to CD*), and permission or challenge (*let him do his worst*). □ **let alone 1** not to mention (*hasn't got a television, let alone a VCR*), **2** = let be. **let be** not interfere with or do. **let down 1** lower. **2** disappoint. **3** lengthen (a garment). **let go 1** release. **2** lose hold of. **3** cease to think or talk about. **let oneself go 1** give way to enthusiasm, impulse, etc. **2** neglect one's appearance or habits. **let in 1** allow to enter (*let the dog in*). **2** [foll. by *on*] allow (a person) to share privileges, information, etc. **let off 1** allow to alight from a vehicle, etc. **2 a** not punish or compel. **b** [foll. by *with*] punish lightly. **let on** *colloq.* **1** reveal a secret. **2** pretend (*let on that he had succeeded*). **let out 1** release. **2** reveal (a secret, etc.). **3** make (a garment) looser. **4** emit (a sound, etc.). **let up** *colloq.* **1** become less intense or severe. **2** relax one's efforts. **to let** for rent.
■ *v.* **1 a** permit (to), sanction (to), authorize (to). **b** arrange for, enable (to). **2** (*let into*) **a** admit to. **b** inform or notify or apprise of, brief about, bring up to date about, *colloq.* fill in on. **5** farm (out), delegate. □ **let down 1** move or bring or put down, drop. **2** fail, frustrate; dissatisfy, disillusion. **let go**

---

1 see *let out* 1 below. **2** release, drop, unloose; relinquish, surrender, lose. **3** drop, give up, abandon. **let off 2 a** pardon, forgive, excuse, exempt (from), spare (from), let go, exonerate, absolve, clear, acquit, vindicate, *colloq.* let off the hook. **let on 1** talk, tell, blab, let the cat out of the bag, *colloq.* spill the beans, blow the whistle, *sl.* squeal. **2** (*let on that*) make as if, (put on an) act as if. **let out 1** (let) loose, liberate, (set) free. **2** divulge, disclose, confess, admit, leak; announce, publicize. **4** express; give out, produce, issue. **let up 1** decrease, abate, ease (up), diminish, lessen, subside, soften, fade, weaken. **2** have a rest, slow down, *colloq.* take or have a breather.

let² /let/ *n.* (in tennis, squash, etc.) obstruction of a ball or player, requiring the ball to be served again. □ **without let or hindrance** unimpeded.

-let /lit, lət/ *suffix* forming nouns, usu. diminutives (*droplet, leaflet*) or denoting articles of ornament or dress (*anklet*).

let•down /létdown/ *n.* disappointment.
■ see *disappointment* (DISAPPOINT).

le•thal /lée̅thəl/ *adj.* causing death. □□ **le'thal•ly** *adv.*
■ deadly, fatal, mortal, deathly, murderous, life-threatening.

leth•ar•gy /léthərjee/ *n.* **1** lack of energy. **2** *Med.* morbid drowsiness. □□ **le•thar•gic** /lithaárjik/ *adj.* **le•thar'gi•cal•ly** *adv.*
■ **1** sluggishness, sloth, laziness, indolence, idleness, lassitude, listlessness; inactivity, inertia; indifference, apathy. **2** fatigue, exhaustion, sleepiness. □□ **lethargic** sluggish, slow, dull, lazy, idle, listless; weary, tired, weak, exhausted, drowsy, sleepy.

let's /lets/ *contr.* let us (*let's go now*).

let•ter /létər/ • *n.* **1** alphabetic character. **2** written or printed communication, usu. sent by mail. **3** precise terms of a statement. **4** [in *pl.*] **a** literature. **b** erudition. • *v.tr.* inscribe letters on. □ **letter bomb** terrorist explosive device in the form of a mailed package. **letter carrier** one who is employed to deliver mail. **letter-perfect** precise, verbatim. **letter-quality** of the quality of printing suitable for a business letter. **man** (or **woman**) **of letters** scholar or author. **to the letter** with adherence to every detail. □□ **let'ter•er** *n.* **let'ter•less** *adj.*
■ *n.* **1** symbol, sign; (*letters*) initials. **2** note, line, message; postcard; correspondence, mail. **4** (*letters*) (creative) writing, fiction; learning, scholarship. • *v.* mark, initial. □ **to the letter** precisely, literally, exactly, accurately, strictly, word for word, verbatim.

let•tered /létərd/ *adj.* well-read or educated.
■ literate, literary, erudite, scholarly, learned, academic, knowledgeable.

let•ter•head /létərhed/ *n.* **1** printed heading on stationery. **2** stationery with this.

let•ter•ing /létəring/ *n.* **1** process of inscribing letters. **2** letters inscribed.

let•ter•press /létərpres/ *n.* printing from raised type.

let•tuce /létis/ *n.* plant with crisp leaves used in salads.

let•up /létup/ *n. colloq.* **1** reduction in intensity. **2** relaxation of effort.
■ abatement; break, time out, lull, respite, pause, *colloq.* breather.

leu•ke•mi•a /lōōkéemeeə/ *n.* malignant disease in which too many leukocytes are produced. □□ **leu•ke′mic** *adj.*

leu•ko•cyte /lōōkəsit/ *n.* white blood cell. □□ **leu•ko•cyt′ic** /–sitik/ *adj.*

lev•ee /lévee/ *n.* embankment against river floods.

lev•el /lévəl/ • *n.* **1** horizontal line or plane. **2** height or value reached (*eye level, sugar level*). **3** social, moral, or intellectual standard. **4** plane of rank or authority (*discussions at cabinet level*). **5** instrument giving a horizontal line. **6** level surface. **7** floor or story in a building, ship, etc. • *adj.* **1** flat and even. **2** horizontal. **3** even with something else. • *v.* **1** *tr.* make level. **2** *tr.* raze. **3** *tr.* [also *absol.*] aim (a missile or gun). **4** *tr.* [also *absol.*] direct (an accusation, etc.). **5** *intr.* [usu. foll. by *with*] *sl.* be frank or honest. □ **do one's level best** *colloq.* do one's utmost. **level off** make or become level or smooth. **on the level** *colloq. adv.* without deception. *adj.* honest; truthful. **on a level with 1** in the same horizontal plane as. **2** equal with. □□ **lev′el•ly** *adv.* **lev′el•ness** *n.*
■ *n.* **2** position, grade; magnitude; step, station, point, stage; elevation, altitude, depth. **3** class, position, status. **4** see RANK[1] *n.* 1a. **7** tier, deck. • *adj.* **1** smooth, uniform, straight; continuous, true. **2** prone, supine. **3** parallel, flush; equal, on a par. • *v.* **1** smooth (out), iron (out). **2** demolish, destroy, lay waste, tear down, flatten. **3** point, direct; (*absol.*) draw a bead, zero in. **4** (*level at*) aim at, focus on. **5** (*level with*) be or play fair with, be straight *or* open with, *colloq.* be up front with. □ **level off** see LEVEL *v.* 1 above. **on the level** (*adv.*) straight (out), directly, plainly, *colloq.* upfront. (*adj.*) straightforward, sincere, fair, aboveboard, *colloq.* on the up and up.

lev•el•head•ed /lévəlhédid/ *adj.* mentally well-balanced; sensible. □□ **lev•el•head′ed•ly** *adv.* **lev•el•head′ed•ness** *n.*
■ sane, reasonable, rational, even-tempered, composed, calm, cool, *colloq.* unflappable.

lev•er /lévər, leev–/ • *n.* **1** bar used to pry. **2** bar pivoted about a fulcrum (fixed point) acted upon by a force (effort) to move a load. **3** handle moved to operate a mechanism. • *v.* **1** *intr.* use a lever. **2** *tr.* lift, move, or act on with a lever.
■ *v.* **2** see LIFT *v.* 1.

lev•er•age /lévərij, leé–/ *n.* **1** action or power of a lever. **2** means of accomplishing a purpose; power; influence. □ **leveraged buyout** buyout of a company by its management using outside capital.
■ **1** see PURCHASE *n.* 3. **2** see INFLUENCE *n.* 1.

le•vi•a•than /livíəthən/ *n.* **1** *Bibl.* sea monster. **2** anything very large or powerful, esp. a ship.

Le•vis /léeviz/ *n.pl. propr.* type of (orig. blue) denim jeans reinforced with rivets.

lev•i•tate /lévitayt/ *v.* **1** *intr.* rise and float in the air (esp. with reference to spiritualism). **2** *tr.* cause to do this. □□ **lev•i•ta′tion** /–táyshən/ *n.* **lev′i•ta•tor** *n.*

lev•i•ty /lévitee/ *n.* lack of serious thought; frivolity.
■ lightheartedness, lightness, flippancy; inconsistency, flightiness; silliness, foolishness.

lev•y /lévee/ • *v.tr.* (**–ies, –ied**) **1** impose or collect payment, etc. **2** enlist or enroll (troops, etc.). **3** proceed to make (war). • *n.* (*pl.* **–ies**) **1 a** collecting of a tax, etc. **b** contribution, tax, etc., levied. **2 a** act of enrolling troops, etc. **b** [in *pl.*] persons enrolled. □□ **lev′i•a•ble** *adj.*
■ *v.* **1** impose, charge, exact, demand; raise. **2** see MOBILIZE *v.* 1. **3** see INFLICT. • *n.* **1 b** see TAX *n.* 1.

lewd /lōōd/ *adj.* **1** lascivious. **2** indecent; obscene. □□ **lewd′ly** *adv.* **lewd′ness** *n.*
■ **1** lustful, lecherous, licentious, salacious, wanton. **2** smutty, crude, coarse, foul, dirty, filthy, raw, risqué, offensive, (sexually) explicit.

lex•i•cal /léksikəl/ *adj.* **1** of the words of a language. **2** of or as of a lexicon. □□ **lex′i•cal•ly** *adv.*

lex•i•cog•ra•phy /léksikógrəfee/ *n.* compiling of dictionaries. □□ **lex•i•cog′ra•pher** *n.* **lex•i•co•graph•ic** /–kəgráfik/ *adj.* **lex•i•co•graph′i•cal** *adj.* **lex•i•co•graph′i•cal•ly** *adv.*

lex•i•col•o•gy /léksikóləjee/ *n.* study of the form, history, and meaning of words. □□ **lex•i•co•log•i•cal** /–kəlójikəl/ *adj.* **lex•i•co•log′i•cal•ly** *adv.* **lex•i•col•o•gist** /–kóləjist/ *n.*

lex•i•con /léksikon/ *n.* **1** dictionary. **2** vocabulary of a person, language, branch of knowledge, etc.

Li *symb. Chem.* lithium.

li•a•bil•i•ty /líəbilitee/ *n.* (*pl.* **–ties**) **1** being liable. **2** troublesome responsibility; handicap. **3** what a person is liable for, esp. [in *pl.*] debts.
■ **1** answerability, accountability; vulnerability. **2** burden, disadvantage, drawback, snag, hitch, fly in the ointment. **3** (*liabilities*) obligations, arrears.

li•a•ble /líəbəl/ *predic.adj.* **1** legally bound. **2** [foll. by *to*] subject to (a tax or penalty). **3** [foll. by *to* + infin.] under an obligation. **4** *disp.* [foll. by *to* + infin.] apt; likely (*it is liable to rain*).
■ **1** responsible. **3** obligated, (duty-)bound. **4** prone, inclined.

li•aise /lee-áyz/ *v.intr.* [foll. by *with, between*] *colloq.* establish cooperation; act as a link.

li•ai•son /lee-áyzon, leé-ay–/ *n.* **1 a** communication or cooperation. **b** person who initiates such. **2** illicit sexual relationship.
■ **1** connection, contact. **2** (love) affair, entanglement.

li•ar /líər/ *n.* person who tells a lie or lies, esp. habitually.
■ fibber, prevaricator, falsifier.

Lib. *abbr.* Liberal.

lib /lib/ *n. colloq.* liberation (*women's lib*).

li•ba•tion /lībáyshən/ *n.* **1 a** pouring out of a drink offering to a god. **b** such a drink offering. **2** *joc.* drink.

li•bel /líbəl/ • *n. Law* **1 a** published false statement damaging to a person's reputation. **2** act of publishing this. • *v.tr.* (**libeled, li•bel•ing; li•belled, li•bel•ling**) **1** defame by libelous statements. **2** accuse falsely and maliciously. See synonym study at MALIGN. □□ **li'bel•er** *n.* **li'bel•ous** *adj.*

■ *n.* defamation, vilification, slander, misrepresentation; aspersion, slur. • *v.* defame, vilify, belittle, disgrace, dishonor, humiliate; slander, malign, discredit. □□ **libelous** see *slanderous* (SLANDER).

lib•er•al /líbərəl, líbrəl/ • *adj.* **1** ample; full; abundant. **2** generous. **3** open minded **4** not strict or rigorous. **5** broadening (*liberal studies*). **6** favoring political and social reform. • *n.* person of liberal views. □ **liberal arts** arts as distinct from science and technology. □□ **lib'er•al•ism** *n.* **lib'er•al•ist** *n.* **lib'er•al•is'tic** *adj.* **lib•er•al'i•ty** *n.* **lib'er•al•ly** *adv.*

■ *adj.* **1** lavish, plentiful, profuse. **2** bountiful, giving, magnanimous, unselfish, unsparing. **3** fair, broad-minded, unprejudiced, unbiased, tolerant; relaxed, permissive; impartial. **4** flexible, lenient, casual. **5** progressive, freethinking, humanistic. • *n.* progressive, libertarian, reformer, independent, freethinker, leftist, left-winger.

lib•er•al•ize /líbərəlīz, líbrə-/ *v.* make or become more liberal or less strict. □□ **lib•er•al•i•za'tion** *n.*

■ broaden, widen, extend; loosen, relax, modify, moderate, soften.

lib•er•ate /líbərayt/ *v.tr.* set free. □□ **lib•er•a'tion** /-áyshən/ *n.* **lib'er•a•tor** *n.*

■ release, (let) loose, let go or out or off, deliver, rescue, emancipate. □□ **liberation** deliverance, emancipation; freedom, liberty.

lib•er•tar•i•an /líbərtáireeən/ *n.* **1** advocate of liberty. **2** believer in free will. • *adj.* believing in free will. □□ **lib•er•tar'i•an•ism** *n.*

lib•er•tine /líbərteen, -tin/ • *n.* **1** dissolute or licentious person. **2** person who follows his or her own inclinations. • *adj.* **1** licentious. **2** freethinking. □□ **lib'er•tin•ism** *n.*

■ *n.* **1** lecher, reprobate, profligate, rake, roué, playboy; womanizer, philanderer. **2** freethinker, liberal, libertarian. • *adj.* **1** dissolute, degenerate, wanton, lascivious; see also LEWD 1. **2** progressive.

lib•er•ty /líbərtee/ *n.* (*pl.* **-ties**) **1** freedom from captivity, slavery, etc. **2** freedom to do as one pleases. □ **at liberty 1** free. **2** [foll. by *to* + infin.] entitled; permitted. **take liberties 1** behave in an unduly familiar manner. **2** [foll. by *with*] deal freely with rules or facts. **take the liberty** [foll. by *to* + infin., or *of* + verbal noun] presume; venture.

■ **1** independence, sovereignty; emancipation, liberation. **2** license, leave; latitude; free will. □ **at liberty 1** unfettered, unrestricted; see also FREE *adj.* **3**. **2** allowed, authorized, given the go-ahead. **take liberties 1** be forward or impudent or impertinent or improper. **take the liberty** be presumptuous *or* bold, go so far, have the audacity *or* effrontery, *colloq.* have the nerve.

SYNONYM STUDY: **liberty**

FREEDOM, INDEPENDENCE, LICENSE, PERMISSION. The Fourth of July is the day on which Americans commemorate their nation's **independence**, a word that implies the ability to stand alone, without being sustained by anything else. While *independence* is usually associated with states or nations, **freedom** and **liberty** more often apply to individuals. But unlike *freedom*, which implies a total absence of restraint or compulsion (*the freedom to speak openly*), *liberty* implies the power to choose among alternatives rather than merely being unrestrained (*the liberty to select their own form of government*). *Freedom* can also apply to many different types of oppressive influences (*freedom from interruption; freedom to leave the room at any time*), while *liberty* often connotes deliverance or release (*to give the slaves their liberty*). **License** may imply the *liberty* to disobey rules or regulations imposed on others, especially when there is an advantage to be gained in doing so (*poetic license*). But more often it refers to an abuse of *liberty* or the power to do whatever one pleases (*license to kill*). **Permission** is an even broader term than *license*, suggesting the capacity to act without interference or censure, usually with some degree of approval or authority (*permission to be absent from his post*).

li•bid•i•nous /libídənəs/ *adj.* lustful. □□ **li•bid'i•nous•ly** *adv.*

■ see *lustful* (LUST).

li•bi•do /libeedō, -bí-/ *n.* (*pl.* **-dos**) *Psychol.* psychic drive or energy, esp. that associated with sexual desire. □□ **li•bid•i•nal** /libídənəl/ *adj.* **li•bid'i•nal•ly** *adv.*

■ see LUST *n.* 3.

Li•bra /leebrə, lí-/ *n.* **1** constellation, traditionally regarded as the figure of scales. **2 a** seventh sign of the zodiac (the Balance or Scales). **b** person born under this sign.

li•brar•i•an /lībráireeən/ *n.* person in charge of, or an assistant in, a library. □□ **li•brar'i•an•ship** *n.*

li•brar•y /líbreree/ *n.* (*pl.* **-ies**) **1** a collection of books. **b** room or building containing such. **2 a** similar collection of films, records, computer software, etc. **b** place where these are kept.

■ **1b** see STUDY *n.* 3.

li•bret•to /librétō/ *n.* (*pl.* **-tos** or **li•bret•ti** /-tee/) text of an opera, etc. □□ **li•bret'tist** *n.*

Lib•y•an /líbeeən, líbyən/ • *adj.* **1** of or relating to modern Libya in N. Africa. **2** of ancient N. Africa west of Egypt. **3** of or relating to the Berber group of languages. • *n.* **1 a** native or national of modern Libya. **b** person of Libyan descent. **2** ancient language of the Berber group.

lice *pl.* of LOUSE.

li•cense /lísəns/ • *n.* **1** permit or permission to own or use something, do something, or carry on a business. **2** liberty of action, esp. when excessive. **3** deviation from fact, etc., esp. for effect (*poetic license*). See synonym study at LIBERTY. • *v.tr.* **1** grant a license to. **2** authorize. □ **license plate** usu. metal plate of a motor vehicle that attests to its registration. □□ **li'cens•a•ble** *adj.* **li'cens•er** *n.* **li'cen•sor** *n.*

■ *n.* **1** pass, certificate; authorization, leave, entitlement, right, freedom, privilege. **2** lack of control *or* restraint, looseness; immoderation, dissipation. **3** disregard, departure. • *v.* entitle, allow, enable, empower, certify, sanction, approve.

li•cen•see /lisənsée/ *n.* holder of a license.

li•cen•ti•ate /lisénsheeət/ *n.* holder of a professional license.

li•cen•tious /lisénshəs/ *adj.* immoral in sexual relations; promiscuous. □□ **li•cen'tious•ly** *adv.* **li•cen'tious•ness** *n.*

■ see IMMORAL 3. □□ **licentiousness** see *indecency* (INDECENT).

li•chee var. of LITCHI.

li•chen /líkən/ *n.* plant composed of a fungus and an alga, growing on rocks, tree trunks, etc.

lic•it /lísit/ *adj.* not forbidden; lawful. □□ **lic'it•ly** *adv.*

lick /lik/ • *v.* **1** *tr.* pass the tongue over. **2** *tr.* bring into a specified condition by licking (*licked it clean*). **3 a** *tr.* (of a flame, waves, etc.) play lightly over. **b** *intr.* move gently or caressingly. **4** *tr. colloq.* defeat; excel. **5** *tr. colloq.* thrash. • *n.* **1** act of licking with the tongue. **2** = *salt lick.* **3** *colloq.* small amount (*a lick of paint*). □ **lick and a promise** *colloq.* hasty performance of a task. **lick a person's boots** be servile. **lick one's lips** (or **chops**) **1** look forward with relish. **2** show one's satisfaction. **lick one's wounds** be in retirement after defeat. □□ **lick'er** *n.* [also in *comb.*].

■ *v.* **4** see OVERCOME 1.

lick•e•ty-split /líkəteesplit/ *adv. colloq.* at full speed; headlong.

lick•ing /líking/ *n. colloq.* **1** thrashing. **2** defeat.

lic•o•rice /líkərish, –ris/ *n.* **1** black root extract used in candy and medicine. **2** leguminous plant from which it is obtained.

lid /lid/ *n.* **1** hinged or removable cover, esp. for a container. **2** = EYELID. □ **put a lid on** be quiet about; keep secret. **take the lid off** *colloq.* expose (a scandal, etc.). □□ **lid'ded** *adj.* [also in *comb.*]. **lid'less** *adj.*

■ **1** see COVER *n.* 1a.

lie¹ /lī/ • *v.intr.* (**ly•ing** /lī-ing/; *past* **lay** /lay/; *past part.* **lain** /layn/) **1** be in or assume a horizontal position. **2** rest flat on a surface. **3** remain undisturbed or undiscussed, etc. (*let matters lie*). **4 a** be kept or remain or be in a specified state or place (*money is lying in the bank*). **b** (of abstract things) exist; reside (*my sympathies lie with the family*). • *n.* **1 a** way, direction, or position in which a thing lies. **b** *Golf* position of a golf ball when about to be struck. **c** place of cover of an animal or a bird. □ **lie ahead** be going to happen; be in store. **lie down** assume a lying position; have a short rest. **lie heavy** cause

discomfort or anxiety. **lie in state** be laid in a public place of honor before burial. **lie low 1** keep quiet or unseen. **2** be discreet about one's intentions. **take lying down** [usu. with *neg.*] accept (defeat, rebuke, etc.) without resistance or protest, etc.

■ *v.* **1** recline, stretch out; repose, lean. **2** be level. **3** cease, lapse. **4 b** be, remain, belong. □ **lie ahead** see IMPEND¹ 1. **lie down** see LIE *v.* 1 above, REST¹ *v.* 1, 2. **lie low 1** hide, keep out of sight.

lie² /lī/ • *n.* intentionally false statement. • *v.* (**lies, lied, ly•ing** /lī-ing/) **1** *intr.* **a** tell a lie or lies. **b** (of a thing) be deceptive (*the camera cannot lie*). **2** *tr.* get (oneself) into or out of a situation by lying (*lied my way out of danger*). □ **lie detector** instrument for determining whether a person is telling the truth by testing for certain physiological changes.

■ *n.* **1** falsehood, untruth, fib, fabrication, cock-and-bull story, *colloq.* (tall) tale, *sl.* whopper. • *v.* **1 a** prevaricate, twist the evidence *or* facts, commit perjury, exaggerate, fib. **b** misrepresent *or* distort *or* falsify the evidence. □ **lie detector** polygraph.

liege /leej, leezh/ usu. *hist.* • *adj.* (of a superior) entitled to receive or (of a vassal) bound to give feudal service or allegiance. • *n.* **1** (in full **liege lord**) feudal superior. **2** [usu. in *pl.*] vassal; subject.

lien /leen, léeən/ *n. Law* a right over another's property to protect a debt charged on that property.

lieu /loō/ *n.* □ **in lieu 1** instead. **2** [foll. by *of*] in the place of.

lieut. *abbr.* lieutenant.

lieu•ten•ant /loōténənt/ *n.* **1** deputy. **2 a** army officer next in rank below captain. **b** naval officer next in rank below lieutenant commander. **3** police officer next in rank below captain. □ **lieutenant colonel** (or **commander** or **general**) officer ranking next below colonel, commander, or general. **lieutenant governor** elected official next in rank to a state's governor. □□ **lieu•ten'an•cy** *n.* (*pl.* **–cies**)

■ **1** see AIDE, DEPUTY.

life /līf/ *n.* (*pl.* **lives** /līvz/) **1** capacity for growth, functional activity, and continual change until death. **2** living things (*insect life*). **3 a** period during which life lasts; period from birth to the present or from the present to death (*will regret it all my life*). **b** duration of a thing's existence or of its ability to function. **4 a** state of existence as a living individual (*sacrificed their lives*). **b** living person (*many lives were lost*). **5 a** individual's actions or fortunes; manner of one's existence (*start a new life*). **b** particular aspect of this (*love life*). **6** business and pleasures of the world (*best way to see life*). **7** energy; liveliness (*full of life*). **8** biography. **9** *colloq.* sentence of imprisonment for life. □ **come to life 1** emerge from inactivity. **2** (of an inanimate object) assume an imaginary animation. **for dear** (or **one's**) **life** as a matter of extreme urgency (*hanging on for dear life, run for your life*). **for the life of** [foll. by pers. pron.] even if (one's) life depended on it (*can not for the life of me remember*). **large as life**

colloq. in person, esp. prominently (*stood there large as life*). **larger than life 1** exaggerated. **2** (of a person) having an exuberant personality. **life-and-death** vitally important; desperate (*a life-and-death struggle*). **life belt** buoyant belt for keeping a person afloat. **life buoy** buoyant support for keeping a person afloat. **life cycle** series of changes in the life of an organism. **life expectancy** average period that a person at a specified age may expect to live. **life insurance** insurance for a sum to be paid on the death of the insured person. **life jacket** buoyant jacket for keeping a person afloat. **life preserver** life jacket, etc. **life raft** inflatable or log, etc., raft for use in an emergency. **life sciences** biology and related subjects. **life sentence** sentence of imprisonment for life. **life-size** (or **-sized**) of the same size as the person or thing represented. **life-support** *adj.* (of equipment) allowing vital functions to continue during severe disablement. **matter of life and** (or **or**) **death** matter of vital importance. **not on your life** *colloq.* most certainly not. **take one's life in one's hands** take a crucial personal risk.

■ **1** existence, being; sentience, viability. **3** lifetime, days; efficacy. **4 b** mortal, human (being), individual, soul. **5** living, way of life, walk of life, lifestyle; field, line, career; passion, *colloq.* thing, *sl.* bag. **7** animation, vitality, vivacity, sparkle, dash, verve, zest, flair, *colloq.* pep, zing; spirit, bounce. **8** autobiography, memoir(s), (life) story, diary, journal.

life•blood /lífblud/ *n.* **1** blood, as being necessary to life. **2** vital factor or influence.

life•boat /lífbōt/ *n.* small boat for use in an emergency.

life•guard /lífgaard/ *n.* expert swimmer employed to rescue bathers from drowning.

life•less /líflis/ *adj.* **1** dead. **2** lacking movement or vitality. □□ **life′less•ly** *adv.* **life′less•ness** *n.*

■ **1** departed, *formal* deceased. **2** unconscious, insensate, in a faint, inert, unmoving, corpselike, immobile; inactive, dull, boring, stale; lethargic.

life•like /líflīk/ *adj.* closely resembling the person or thing represented.

■ authentic, realistic, natural, true to life, real.

life•line /líflīn/ *n.* **1 a** rope, etc., used for lifesaving. **b** diver's signaling line. **2** sole means of communication or transport. **3** fold in the palm of the hand, regarded as significant in palmistry.

life•long /líflawng, –long/ *adj.* lasting a lifetime.

lif•er /lífər/ *n.* *sl.* **1** person serving a life sentence. **2** person committed to a very long career, esp. in the military.

life•sav•er /lífsayvər/ *n.* person or thing that saves one from serious difficulty. □□ **life′sav•ing** *n. & adj.*

life•style /lífstīl/ *n.* way of life of a person or group.

life•time /líftīm/ *n.* **1** duration of a person's life. **2** duration of a thing or its usefulness. **3** *colloq.* long time.

life•work /lífwórk/ *n.* task, profession, etc., pursued throughout one's lifetime.

lift /lift/ • *v.* **1** *tr.* raise or remove to a higher position. **2** *intr.* go up; be raised. **3** *tr.* elevate to a higher plane of thought or feeling (*the news lifted their spirits*). **4** *intr.* (of a cloud, fog, etc.) rise; disperse. **5** *tr.* remove (a barrier or restriction). **6** *tr.* transport (supplies, troops, etc.) by air. **7** *tr. colloq.* **a** steal. **b** plagiarize (a passage of writing, etc.). • *n.* **1** lifting or being lifted. **2** ride in another person's vehicle. **3 a** *Brit.* = ELEVATOR 3. **b** apparatus for carrying persons up or down a mountain, etc. (see *ski lift*). **4** transport by air (see AIRLIFT *n.*). **5** upward pressure that air exerts on an airfoil. **6** supporting or elevating influence; feeling of elation. **7** layer of leather, etc., in the heel of a shoe, esp. to increase height. □ **lift a finger** (or **hand**, etc.) [in *neg.*] make the slightest effort (*didn't lift a finger to help*). **lift off** (of a spacecraft or rocket) rise from the launching pad. **lift up one's voice** sing out. □□ **lift′a•ble** *adj.* **lift′er** *n.*

■ *v.* **1** elevate; hoist (up), pull up. **2** see RISE *v.* **1**. **3** dignify, uplift, promote, exalt, *colloq.* boost; brighten, enhance. **4** dissipate, vanish, break up, float away. **5** terminate, stop; take away, get rid of, withdraw. **6** airlift. **7 a** appropriate, pocket, take, *sl.* pinch. **b** copy, pirate. • *n.* **1** elevation, rise, increase. **2** *colloq.* hitch. **4** airlift. **6** encouragement, inspiration, reassurance, cheering up, *colloq.* shot in the arm. □ **lift a finger** (or **hand**) make any attempt, make a move, do one's part, do anything, contribute. **lift off** see *take off* 6.

lift•off /líftawf/ *n.* vertical takeoff of a spacecraft or rocket.

lig•a•ment /lígəmənt/ *n.* band of tough, fibrous tissue linking bones.

■ sinew, tendon.

lig•a•ture /lígəchoor/ • *n.* **1** tie, bandage. **2** *Mus.* slur; tie. **3** two or more letters joined, e.g., æ. **4** bond; thing that unites. • *v. tr.* bind or connect with a ligature.

li•ger /lígər/ *n.* offspring of a male lion and a female tiger.

light¹ /līt/ • *n.* **1** electromagnetic radiation that stimulates sight and makes things visible. **2** source of light, e.g., the sun, a lamp, fire, etc. **3** [often in *pl.*] traffic light. **4** a flame or spark serving to ignite. **b** device producing this (*have you got a light?*). **5** aspect in which a thing is regarded (*appeared in a new light*). **6 a** mental or spiritual illumination; enlightenment. **b** hope; happy outcome. **7** eminent person (*leading light*). **8** window or opening in a wall to let light in. • *v.* (*past* **lit** /lit/; *past part.* **lit** or [*attrib.*] **light•ed**) **1** *tr. & intr.* ignite. **2** *tr.* provide with light or lighting. **3** *intr.* [usu. foll. by *up*] (of the face or eyes) brighten with animation. • *adj.* **1** well provided with light; not dark. **2** (of a color) pale (*light blue*). □ **bring** (or **come**) **to light** reveal or be revealed. **in a good** (or **bad**) **light** giving a favorable (or unfavorable) impression. **in light of** having regard to; drawing information from. **light**

meter instrument for measuring light intensity, esp. for correct photographic exposure. **light of one's life** usu. *joc.* a much-loved person. **light up 1** *colloq.* begin to smoke a cigarette, etc. **2** illuminate a scene. **light-year** distance light travels in one year, nearly 6 trillion miles. **lit up** *colloq.* drunk. **out like a light** deeply asleep or unconscious. **throw** (or **shed**) **light on** help to explain. □□ **light′ish** *adj.* **light′ness** *n.*

■ *n.* **1** illumination; daylight, moonlight, sunlight. **2** lightbulb, beacon, lantern, torch, candle, star, flame, headlight, headlamp, streetlight, flashlight. **3** (*lights*) traffic signal(s), stop light(s). **4** match, lighter, ignition. **5** see ASPECT 1b. **6 a** elucidation, edification, insight, explanation. **b** see HOPE *n.* 1, 3, *happiness* (HAPPY). ● *v.* **1** turn on; kindle, set fire to; come on. **2** illuminate, brighten. **3** (*light up*) cheer up, liven up, perk up. ● *adj.* **1** bright, (well-) lit, shining, luminous, brilliant, sunny. **2** light-hued, pastel, subdued. □ **bring** (or **come**) **to light** unearth, find, discover, expose, disclose; appear, turn up, develop, emerge. **in light of** considering, in view of, in consideration of, taking into account, keeping *or* bearing in mind. **out like a light** see UNCONSCIOUS *adj.* **throw** (or **shed**) **light on** elucidate, clarify, clear up.

light² /lɪt/ ● *adj.* **1** not heavy. **2** relatively low in weight, amount, intensity, etc. (*light arms, light traffic*). **3** carrying or suitable for small loads (*light aircraft*). **4** (of food) easy to digest. **5** (of entertainment, music, etc.) intended for amusement only; not profound. **6** (of sleep or a sleeper) easily disturbed. **7** easily borne or done (*light duties*). **8** nimble; quick-moving (*light step*). **9 a** unburdened (*light heart*). **b** giddy (*light in the head*). ● *adv.* **1** in a light manner (*sleep light*). **2** with a minimum load (*travel light*). ● *v.intr.* (*past and past part.* **lit** /lɪt/ *or* **light•ed**) **1** [foll. by *on, upon*] come upon by chance. **2** alight. □ **lighter-than-air** (of an aircraft) weighing less than the air it displaces. **light-fingered** given to stealing. **light-footed** nimble. **light-headed** giddy; delirious. **light-headedness** being light-headed. **light heavyweight** see HEAVYWEIGHT. **light industry** manufacture of small or light articles. **light into** *colloq.* attack. **light touch** delicate or tactful treatment. **make light of** treat as unimportant. **make light work of** do a thing quickly and easily. □□ **light′ish** *adj.* **light′ly** *adv.* **light′ness** *n.*

■ *adj.* **1** lightweight, portable, manageable. **2** slight, delicate; deficient, skinny, gaunt; see also LEAN² *adj.* 1. **4** simple, modest, moderate. **5** amusing, pleasurable; trivial; see also INCONSEQUENTIAL². **7** bearable, tolerable, effortless, *colloq.* cushy. **8** agile, spry, lithe, buoyant, limber. **9 a** cheerful, happy, sunny, merry, untroubled, easygoing. **b** see DIZZY *adj.* 1a. ● *v.* **1** (*light on* or *upon*) chance *or* happen *or* stumble *or* hit (up)on, come across, encounter, find, meet up with. □ **light-fingered** thieving; furtive, crooked. **light-footed** see LIGHT *adj.* 8 above. **light-headed**

see DIZZY *adj.* 1. **light into** assail, assault; *colloq.* lace into; see also ATTACK *v.* 1, 3. **make light of** dismiss, shrug off, brush aside; trivialize; see also DISREGARD *v.* 2, *play down.*

light•bulb /lɪtbʌlb/ *n.* glass bulb containing inert gas and a filament, giving light when an electric current is passed through.

light•en¹ /lɪt′n/ *v.* **1 a** *tr. & intr.* make or become lighter in weight. **b** *tr.* reduce the weight or load of. **2** *tr.* bring relief to (the heart, mind, etc.). **3** *tr.* mitigate (a penalty).

■ **2** relieve, cheer (up), brighten, gladden, comfort. **3** see MITIGATE, TEMPER *v.* 2.

light•en² /lɪt′n/ *v.* **1 a** *tr.* shed light on. **b** *tr. & intr.* make or grow lighter or brighter. **2** *intr.* shine brightly; flash.

■ **1** illuminate, cast light upon, brighten, light up.

light•er¹ /lɪtər/ *n.* device for lighting cigarettes, etc.

light•er² /lɪtər/ *n.* boat for transferring goods from a ship.

light•heart•ed /lɪt-haártíd/ *adj.* **1** cheerful. **2** (unduly) casual; thoughtless. □□ **light′heart•ed•ly** *adv.* **light′heart•ed•ness** *n.*

■ see LIGHT² *adj.* 9a.

light•house /lɪt-hows/ *n.* tower or other structure containing a beacon light to warn or guide ships at sea.

■ see BEACON 1.

light•ing /lɪtɪŋ/ *n.* **1** equipment in a room, street, etc., for producing light. **2** arrangement or effect of lights.

■ **2** see *illumination* (ILLUMINATE).

light•ning /lɪtnɪŋ/ *n.* flash of bright light produced by an electric discharge between clouds or between clouds and the ground. ● *attrib.adj.* very quick (*with lightning speed*). □ **lightning bug** = FIREFLY. **lightning rod** metal rod or wire fixed to a building, mast, etc., to divert lightning.

■ *n.* see BOLT *n.* 3. ● *attrib.adj.* see RAPID *adj.* 1.

light•ship /lɪtʃɪp/ *n.* moored or anchored ship with a beacon light.

light•weight /lɪtwayt/ ● *adj.* **1** of below average weight. **2** of little importance or influence. ● *n.* **1** lightweight person, animal, or thing. **2 a** weight class in certain sports between featherweight and welterweight. **b** sportsman of this weight.

■ *adj.* **1** see LIGHT² *adj.* 1. **2** see INCONSEQUENTIAL. ● *n.* see WEAKLING *n.*

lig•nite /lɪgnɪt/ *n.* soft brown coal showing traces of plant structure, intermediate between bituminous coal and peat. □□ **lig•nit•ic** /-nítik/ *adj.*

like•a•ble /lɪkəbəl/ *adj.* (also **like′a•ble**) pleasant; easy to like. □□ **lik′a•ble•ness** *n.* **lik′a•bly** *adv.*

■ genial, amiable, congenial, agreeable, nice, friendly, good-natured.

like¹ /lɪk/ ● *adj.* (**more like, most like**) having some or all of the qualities of; alike (*in like manner*). ● *prep.* in the manner of; to the same degree as (*acted like an idiot*). ● *conj. colloq. disp.* **1** as (*cannot do it like you do*). **2** as if (*ate like they were starving*). ● *n.* counterpart; equal. □ **and the like** and similar things; et cetera (*music, painting, and the like*). **like-minded** having the same tastes, opinions, etc. **like-mindedness** being likeminded. **like so** *colloq.* like this; in this manner. **the likes of** *colloq.* a person such as. **more like it** *colloq.* nearer what is required.

■ *adj.* similar (to), comparable (to *or* with), identical (to), close (to), (much) the same (as); resembling. ● *prep.* in the same way as, along the same lines as. ● *conj.* **1** in the same way as. **2** as though. ● *n.* match, peer, fellow, twin, equivalent.

like² /līk/ ● *v.tr.* **1** find agreeable or enjoyable. **2 a** choose to have; prefer (*like my coffee black*). **b** wish for (*would like tea*). **3** [prec. by *how*] feel about; regard (*how would you like it if it happened to you?*). ● *n.* [in *pl.*] things one prefers. □ **I like that!** *iron.* as an exclamation expressing affront.

■ *v.* **1** be fond of, approve of, have a fondness for, take pleasure in; love *esp.* a man, *sl.* dig, get a charge out of. **2** go for, want, rather *or* sooner have, desire. ● *n.* (*likes*) preference(s), favorite(s), *colloq.* thing, cup of tea, *sl.* bag; see also WEAKNESS 3.

-like /līk/ *comb. form* forming adjectives from nouns, meaning 'similar to, characteristic of' (*doglike*).

like·a·ble var. of LIKABLE.

like·li·hood /līkleehood/ *n.* probability. □ **in all likelihood** very probably.

■ strong *or* distinct possibility, good chance.

like·ly /līklee/ ● *adj.* **1** probable. **2** reasonably expected (*likely to come*). **3** promising; suitable (*three likely candidates*). ● *adv.* probably. □ **as likely as not** probably. **not likely!** *colloq.* certainly not; I refuse. □□ **like'li·ness** *n.*

■ *adj.* **1** conceivable, reasonable, plausible. **2** apt, inclined, *disp.* liable. **3** fitting, proper, appropriate. ● *adv.* no doubt, in all probability.

lik·en /līkən/ *v.tr.* [foll. by *to*] point out the resemblance of.

■ compare, equate, match, juxtapose, associate.

like·ness /līknis/ *n.* **1** [foll. by *between, to*] resemblance. **2** [foll. by *of*] semblance or guise (*in the likeness of a ghost*). **3** portrait or representation (*is a good likeness*).

■ **1** similarity, closeness, sameness. **2** appearance, image, look, style. **3** copy, replica, facsimile, duplicate, reproduction, double, look-alike, spitting image; portrayal, drawing, print, photograph, sculpture, statue.

SYNONYM STUDY: likeness

AFFINITY, ANALOGY, RESEMBLANCE, SIMILARITY, SIMILITUDE. Two sisters who are only a year apart in age and who are very similar to each other in terms of appearance and personality would be said to bear a **likeness** to one another. **Similarity** applies to people or things that are merely somewhat alike (*there was a similarity between the two women, both of whom were raised in the Midwest*), while **resemblance** suggests a *similarity* only in appearance or in superficial or external ways (*with their short hair and blue eyes, they bore a strong resemblance to each other*). **Affinity** adds to *resemblance* a natural kinship, temperamental sympathy, common experience, or some

---

481   **like ~ lime**

other relationship (*to have an affinity for young children*). **Similitude** is a more literary word meaning *likeness* or *similarity* in reference to abstract things (*a similitude of the truth*). An **analogy** is a comparison of things that are basically unlike but share certain attributes or circumstances (*he drew an analogy between the human heart and a bicycle pump*).

like·wise /līkwīz/ *adv.* **1** also. **2** similarly.

■ **1** moreover, too, as well, furthermore, besides, in addition. **2** the same, in like manner.

lik·ing /līking/ *n.* **1** what one likes; one's taste. **2** regard or fondness (*had a liking for chocolate*).

■ **1** fancy, preference. **2** affinity, partiality, inclination, appreciation, penchant; appetite, weakness.

li·lac /līlək, -lok, -lak/ *n.* **1** shrub with fragrant pinkish-violet or white blossoms. **2** pale pinkish-violet color. ● *adj.* of this color.

li·li·pu·tian /lilipyoshən/ (also **Lil·li·pu'tian**) ● *n.* diminutive person or thing. ● *adj.* diminutive.

lilt /lilt/ ● *n.* **1 a** light springing rhythm. **b** tune marked by this. **2** (of the voice) characteristic cadence. ● *v.intr.* (esp. as **lilting** *adj.*) move or speak, etc., with a lilt (*lilting melody*).

■ *n.* **1 a** see RHYTHM. ● *v.* (**lilting**) see MUSICAL *adj.* 2.

lil·y /lilee/ *n.* (*pl.* -ies) **1** plant with trumpet-shaped flowers on a tall stem. **2** similar plant, as the water lily. □ **lily-livered** cowardly. **lily of the valley** plant with white, bell-shaped, fragrant flowers. **lily pad** floating leaf of a water lily. **lily-white 1** as white as a lily. **2** faultless. □□ **lil'ied** *adj.*

■ **1** see LEG *n.* 1, 3. **2** see BRANCH *n.* 1.

li·ma bean /līmə/ *n.* **1** plant with broad, flat, edible seeds. **2** seed of this plant.

limb¹ /lim/ *n.* **1** arm, leg, or wing **2** large branch of a tree. □ **out on a limb 1** isolated; stranded. **2** at a disadvantage. **tear limb from limb** violently dismember. **with life and limb** (esp. escape) without grave injury. □□ **limbed** *adj.* [also in *comb.*] **limb'less** *adj.*

■ **1** see LEG *n.* 1, 3. **2** see BRANCH *n.* 1.

limb² /lim/ *n.* edge of the sun, moon, etc.

lim·ber /limbər/ ● *adj.* **1** lithe. **2** flexible. See synonym study at FLEXIBLE. ● *v.* **1** *tr.* make limber. **2** *intr.* become limber. □□ **lim'ber·ness** *n.*

■ *adj.* **1** see NIMBLE 1. **2** see FLEXIBLE 1. ● *v.* see EXERCISE *v.* 3a.

lim·bo¹ /limbō/ *n.* (*pl.* -bos) **1** (in some Christian beliefs) abode of the souls of unbaptized infants, and of the just who died before Christ. **2** intermediate state or condition.

■ **2** (*in limbo*) up in the air, suspended, on hold, on the back burner.

lim·bo² /limbō/ *n.* (*pl.* -bos) W. Indian dance in which the dancer bends backward to pass under a horizontal bar that is progressively lowered.

lime¹ /lim/ ● *n.* **1** (in full **quick'lime**) white

substance (calcium oxide) obtained by heating limestone. **2** calcium hydroxide obtained by reacting quicklime with water. • *v.tr.* treat with lime. □□ **lim'y** *adj.* (**lim•i•er, lim•i•est**).

lime[2] /līm/ *n.* **1 a** a citrus fruit like a lemon but green, smaller, and more acid. **b** tree bearing this. **2** pale green color.

lime•light /límlīt/ *n.* **1** intense white light used formerly in theaters. **2** glare of publicity.

lim•er•ick /límərik, límrik/ *n.* humorous five-line stanza with a rhyme scheme *aabba*.

lime•stone /límstōn/ *n.* rock composed mainly of calcium carbonate.

lim•ey /límee/ *n.* (also **Lim'ey**) (*pl.* **–eys**) *sl. offens.* British person (orig. a sailor).

lim•it /límit/ • *n.* **1** point, line, or level beyond which something does not or may not extend. **2** greatest or smallest amount permissible. • *v.tr.* set or serve as a limit to. □ **off limits** out of bounds. □□ **lim'it•a•ble** *adj.* **lim•i•ta'tion** *n.* **lim'it•er** *n.* **lim'it•less** *adj.*

■ *n.* extent, end, restriction; border, edge, boundary; confines. • *v.* check, curb, restrict; set, define, determine, fix. □ **off limits** see TABOO *adj.* □□ **limitation** see CHECK *n.* 2c. **limitless** boundless, extensive, vast; endless, inexhaustible, innumerable, countless, unending.

lim•it•ed /límitid/ *adj.* **1** confined. **2** not great in scope or talents (*limited experience*). **3 a** scanty; restricted. **b** restricted to a few examples (*limited edition*). □□ **lim'it•ed•ness** *n.*

■ **1** fixed, checked, curbed. **2, 3a** narrow, sparing; few, minimal; unimaginative.

limn /lim/ *v.tr. hist.* illuminate (manuscripts). □□ **lim•ner** /–nər/ *n.*

lim•o /límō/ *n.* (*pl.* **–os**) *colloq.* limousine.

lim•ou•sine /líməzeen/ *n.* large, luxurious automobile, esp. with a chauffeur.

limp[1] /limp/ • *v.intr.* walk lamely. • *n.* lame walk.

■ hobble, stagger, totter.

limp[2] /limp/ *adj.* **1** not stiff or firm. **2** without energy or will. □□ **limp'ly** *adv.* **limp'ness** *n.*

■ **1** slack; soft, drooping, floppy; flaccid. **2** exhausted, tired, fatigued, worn out; weak, feeble.

lim•pet /límpit/ *n.* marine gastropod that sticks tightly to rocks.

lim•pid /límpid/ *adj.* clear; transparent. □□ **lim•pid'i•ty** *n.* **lim'pid•ly** *adv.* **lim'pid•ness** *n.*

lin•age /líníj/ *n.* number of lines in printed or written matter.

linch•pin /línchpin/ *n.* **1** pin through the end of an axle to keep a wheel on. **2** person or thing vital to an enterprise, etc.

■ **2** see MAINSTAY 1.

lin•den /líndən/ *n.* tree with heart-shaped leaves and fragrant flowers.

line[1] /līn/ *n.* **1** continuous mark on a surface. **2 a** straight or curved continuous extent of length without breadth. **b** track of a moving point. **3** contour or outline. **4** limit or boundary. **5** row of persons or things.

6 a row of printed or written words. **b** portion of verse written in one line. **7** [in *pl.*] words of an actor's part. **8** short letter or note (*drop me a line*). **9** cord, rope, etc. **10 a** wire or cable for a telephone or telegraph. **b** connection by means of this. **11** branch or route of a railroad system, or a whole system under one management. **12 a** regular succession of buses, ships, aircraft, etc., plying between certain places. **b** company conducting this (*shipping line*). **13** lineage. **14** course or manner of procedure, conduct, thought, etc. (*did it along these lines*). **15** course or channel (*lines of communication*). **16** business or occupation. **17** class of commercial goods (*new line of hats*). **18** *colloq.* false or exaggerated account (*gave me a line about missing the bus*). **19** arrangement of soldiers or ships side by side. • *v.* **1** *tr.* mark with lines. **2** *tr. & intr.* stand at intervals along (*crowds lined the route*). □ **bring into line** make conform. **come into line** conform. **end of the line** point at which further effort is unproductive or one can go no further. **in line for** likely to receive. **in the line of** in the course of (esp. of duty). **in** (or **out of**) **line with** in (or not in) alignment or accordance with. **lay** (or **put**) **it on the line** speak frankly. **line drive** *Baseball* hard-hit ball that travels nearly parallel to the ground. **line printer** machine that prints output from a computer a line at a time. **line up 1** arrange or be arranged in a line or lines. **2** have ready (*had a job lined up*). **on the line 1** at risk (*put my reputation on the line*). **2** speaking on the telephone. **out of line 1** not in alignment. **2** inappropriate. **step out of line** behave inappropriately.

■ *n.* **1** stroke, score; rule; diagonal, slash. **3** silhouette, profile. **4** border, frontier, edge. **5** strip, band, train, column, rank, file. **7** (*lines*) role, script. **8** card, postcard. **9** string, wire, cable. **12b** firm; see also BUSINESS 5. **13** see LINEAGE. **14** direction, path, way, route, tack, game, strategy, tactic(s), approach, plan; see also PLATFORM 2. **16** department, field, area, activity, forte, specialty; profession, *colloq.* racket. **17** stock, brand, make, type, kind, variety. **18** story, (sales) pitch, *sl.* spiel. **19** formation; vanguard, *Mil.* front (line). • *v.* **1** rule, score. **2** edge, border, fringe. □ **in line for** ready for, up for, a candidate for, in the running for. **in** (or **out of**) **line with** (*in line with*) aligned with, true to, plumb or flush with; in agreement or accord or step or harmony with; (*out of line with*) misaligned with; inconsistent with, contrary to. **line up 1** align, straighten; form ranks or columns. **2** set up, put or set in place, arrange (for); secure, obtain; acquire, engage, hire, sign (up).

line[2] /līn/ *v.tr.* cover the inside surface of (a garment, box, etc.). □ **line one's pocket** (or **purse**) make money, usu. by corrupt means.

■ □ **line one's pocket** accept bribes, *colloq.* be on the make.

lin•e•age /línee-ij/ *n.* lineal descent; ancestry; pedigree.

■ extraction, family tree, stock, line, bloodline, parentage, genealogy; forebears, forefathers, family, people, clan, tribe; descendants, succession, progeny, offspring.

lin•e•al /líneeǝl/ *adj.* **1** in the direct line of descent or ancestry. **2** linear; of or in lines. □□ **lin′e•al•ly** *adv.*

lin•e•a•ment /líneeǝmǝnt/ *n.* [usu. in *pl.*] distinctive feature or characteristic, esp. of the face.

lin•e•ar /líneeǝr/ *adj.* **1 a** of or in lines. **b** of length (*linear extent*). **2** long and narrow and of uniform breadth. □ **linear equation** equation between two variables that gives a straight line when plotted on a graph. □□ **lin•e•ar•i•ty** /–neeáritee/ *n.* **lin′e•ar•ize** *v.tr.* **lin′e•ar•ly** *adv.*
 ■ **1a** see STRAIGHT *adj.* 1.

line•man /línmǝn/ *n.* (*pl.* **–men**) **1 a** person who repairs and maintains telephone or power lines. **b** person who tests the safety of railroad lines. **2** *Football* player on the line of scrimmage.

lin•en /línin/ • *n.* **1** cloth woven from flax. **2** [*collect.*] sheets, towels, tablecloths, etc. • *adj.* made of linen. □ **wash one's dirty linen in public** be indiscreet about one's domestic quarrels, etc.
 ■ **2** bedclothes, bed linen(s), pillowcases; napkins; washcloths.

liner[1] /línǝr/ *n.* ship or aircraft, etc., carrying passengers on a regular line.
 ■ boat, vessel; airliner, jet, airplane.

liner[2] /línǝr/ *n.* removable lining. □ **liner notes** printed information packaged with cassette tapes, CDs, etc.

lines•man /línzmǝn/ *n.* (*pl.* **–men**) (in games played on a field or court) official who decides whether a ball has fallen within the playing area.

line•up /línup/ *n.* **1** line of people. **2** list of participants in a game, etc.

-ling /ling/ *suffix* denoting a diminutive (*duckling*).

lin•ger /línggǝr/ *v.intr.* **1** loiter. **2** dally. **3** (esp. of an illness) be protracted. □□ **lin′ger•er** *n.* **lin′ger•ing** *adj.* **lin′ger•ing•ly** *adv.*
 ■ **1** stay (behind), remain. **2** idle, dawdle, *colloq.* dillydally. **3** persist, endure, continue, drag on. □□ **lingering** (long-) drawn-out, persistent, slow.

lin•ge•rie /láánzhǝráy, lánzhǝreé/ *n.* women's underwear and nightclothes.
 ■ see UNDERCLOTHES.

lin•go /línggo/ *n.* (*pl.* **–goes**) *colloq.* **1** foreign language. **2** vocabulary of a special subject or group of people. See synonym study at DIALECT.
 ■ **1** tongue, speech; dialect, vernacular. **2** jargon, argot, slang, idiom; terminology.

lin•gua fran•ca /línggwǝ frángkǝ/ *n.* (*pl.* **lingua fran•cas** or **lin•guae fran•cae** /–gwee frángkee/) common language adopted by speakers with different native languages.

lin•gual /línggwǝl/ *adj.* **1** of or formed by the tongue. **2** of speech or languages. □□ **lin′gual•ly** *adv.*

lin•gui•ca /línggweésǝ/ • *n.* a type of Portuguese smoked pork sausage.

lin•gui•ne /línggweénee/ *n.* (also **lin•gui′ni**) pasta made in slender flattened strips.

lin•guist /línggwist/ *n.* person skilled in languages or linguistics.

lin•guis•tic /línggwístik/ *adj.* of language or the study of languages. □□ **lin•guis′ti•cal•ly** *adv.*

lin•guis•tics /línggwístiks/ *n.* study of language and its structure.

lin•i•ment /línimǝnt/ *n.* medication rubbed into the skin.
 ■ see LOTION.

lin•ing /líning/ *n.* material that covers an inside surface.
 ■ see INSIDE *n.* 1,

link /lingk/ • *n.* **1** loop or ring of a chain. **2 a** connecting part; one in a series. **b** state or means of connection. • *v.* **1** *tr.* connect or join (two things or one to another). **2** *intr.* be joined; attach oneself to (a system, etc.).
 ■ *n.* **2 a** tie, bond, coupling. **b** linkage, tie-in, affiliation. **3** stud. • *v.* **1** couple, fasten (together), unite; intertwine, clasp.

link•age /língkij/ *n.* **1** connection. **2** system of links.
 ■ **1** see CONNECTION *n.* 1. **2** see JOINT *n.* 1.

links /lingks/ *n.pl.* [treated as *sing.* or *pl.*] golf course.

link•up /língkup/ *n.* act or result of linking up.

lin•net /línit/ *n.* finch with brown and gray plumage.

li•no•le•um /linóleeǝm/ *n.* canvas-backed material coated with linseed oil, powdered cork, etc., used esp. as a floor covering.

lin•seed /línseed/ *n.* seed of flax. □ **linseed oil** oil extracted from linseed and used esp. in paint and varnish.

lint /lint/ *n.* fluff. □□ **lint′y** *adj.*
 ■ see FLUFF *n.* 1.

lin•tel /línt'l/ *n. Archit.* horizontal supporting piece of wood, stone, etc., across the top of a door or window.

li•on /líǝn/ *n.* **1** (*fem.* **li•on•ess** /–nis/) large feline of Africa and S. Asia, with a tawny coat and, in the male, a flowing shaggy mane. **2** (**the Lion**) zodiacal sign or constellation Leo. **3** brave or celebrated person. □ **lion's share** largest or best part.

li•on•heart /líǝnhaart/ *n.* courageous and generous person. □□ **li′on•heart•ed** *adj.*

li•on•ize /líǝniz/ *v.tr.* treat as a celebrity. □□ **li•on•i•za′tion** *n.* **li′on•iz•er** *n.*

lip /lip/ *n.* **1** either of the two fleshy parts forming the edges of the mouth opening. **2** edge of a vessel, etc. **3** *colloq.* impudent talk. □ **bite one's lip** repress an emotion. retort, etc. **curl one's lip** express scorn. **lip service** insincere support, etc. **lip-sync** synchronize lip movements to recorded sound so appear to be singing or talking. □□ **lip′less** *adj.* **lip′like** *adj.* **lipped** *adj.* [also in *comb.*].
 ■ **2** see RIM[1] *n.* 1. **3** see *impudence* (IMPUDENT). □ **lip service** see CANT[1] *n.* 1.

lip•gloss /lípglos, –glaws/ *n.* cosmetic preparation for adding shine or color to the lips.

li•pid /lípid/ *n. Chem.* any of a group of fatlike

substances, including fatty acids, oils, waxes, and steroids.

li•po•suc•tion /lípōsúkshən, lí–/ n. surgical removal of excess fat from under the skin by suction.

lip•read•ing /lípreeding/ n. (esp. of a deaf person) practice of understanding (speech) from observing a speaker's lip movements. □□ **lip′read** v. **lip′read•er** n.

lip•stick /lípstik/ n. stick of cosmetic for coloring the lips.

liq•ue•fy /líkwifī/ v. (**–fies, –fied**) Chem. make or become liquid. □□ **li•que•fa•cient** /–fáyshənt/ adj. & n. **li•que•fac•tion** /–fákshən/ n. **li′que•fi•er** n.

■ see DISSOLVE v. 1.

li•queur /likɔ́r, –kyŏŏr/ n. any of several sweet alcoholic liquors, variously flavored.

liq•uid /líkwid/ • adj. **1** having a consistency like that of water or oil. **2** (of sounds) clear and pure; fluent. **3** (of assets) easily converted into cash. • n. **1** liquid substance. **2** Phonet. sound of l or r. □ **liquid crystal** turbid liquid with some order in its molecular arrangement. **liquid crystal display** visual display in electronic devices in which liquid crystals respond to signals. □□ **li•quid′i•ty** n. **liq′uid•ly** adv.

■ adj. **1** fluid; melted; runny, watery; molten. **2** distinct, clarion; flowing, smooth, harmonious, melodious. **3** convertible, disposable; solvent. • n. **1** fluid, liquor, juice, sap, solution.

liq•ui•date /líkwidayt/ v. **1 a** tr. wind up the affairs of (a business) by paying debts and distributing assets. **b** intr. (of a company) be liquidated. **2** tr. pay off (a debt). **3** tr. convert into cash. **4** tr. kill. □□ **liq•ui•da•tion** /–dáyshən/ n. **liq′ui•da•tor** n.

■ **2** see PAY v. 2. **4** see KILL v. 1.

li•quid•i•ty /likwíditee/ n. (pl. **–ties**) **1** the state of being liquid. **2** availability of liquid assets.

liq•uid•ize /líkwidīz/ v.tr. reduce to a liquid state.

liq•uor /líkər/ n. **1** alcoholic (esp. distilled) drink. **2** other liquid, esp. that produced in cooking.

■ n. **1** spirit(s), colloq. booze, firewater, hooch, sl. hard stuff, moonshine. **2** extract, stock, broth, infusion; distillate.

li•ra /léerə/ n. (pl. **li•re** /léere/ or **li•ras**) **1** chief monetary unit of Italy. **2** chief monetary unit of Turkey.

lisle /līl/ n. fine cotton thread for stockings, etc.

lisp /lisp/ • n. speech in which s is pronounced like th in thick and z is pronounced like th in this. • v. speak or utter with a lisp. □□ **lisp′er** n. **lisp′ing•ly** adv.

lis•some /lísəm/ adj. (also **lis′som**) lithe; supple; agile. □□ **lis′some•ly** adv. **lis′some•ness** n.

list[1] /list/ • n. number of items, names, etc., written or printed together as a record. • v.tr. **1 a** make a list of. **b** enumerate. **2** enter in a list. □ **list price** price of something as shown in a published list. □□ **list′ing** n.

■ n. inventory, index, catalog, program, schedule, register, roster. • v. **1 a** itemize. **b** name, recount, recite, rattle off. **2** enroll, log, note, record.

list[2] /list/ • v.intr. (of a ship, etc.) lean over to one side. • n. process or instance of listing.

■ v. tilt, slant, heel, tip, cant. • n. slope, camber.

lis•ten /lísən/ v.intr. **1** make an effort to hear. **2** take notice of; heed. □ **listen in 1** eavesdrop. **2** listen to a radio or television broadcast. □□ **lis′ten•er** n.

■ pay attention, lend an ear, be all ears, colloq. tune in; (listen to) mind; follow, respect, accept. □ **listen in 1** spy, pry, colloq. snoop.

list•less /lístlis/ adj. lacking energy or enthusiasm. □□ **list′less•ly** adv. **list′less•ness** n.

■ sluggish, lethargic, languid, torpid, lifeless, weak, spent, weary, tired, drained, colloq. done in, bushed, pooped; indifferent, apathetic.

lit past and past part. of LIGHT[1], LIGHT[2].

lit•a•ny /lít′nee/ n. (pl. **–nies**) **1** series of petitions to God with set responses. **2** tedious recital (a litany of woes).

■ **1** prayer, invocation, supplication. **2** recitation.

li•tchi /léechee/ n. (also **li′chee, ly′chee**) **1** sweet, fleshy fruit with a thin, spiny skin. **2** tree bearing this.

li•ter /léetər/ n. metric unit of capacity equal to about 1.057 quarts.

lit•er•a•cy /lítərəsee/ n. ability to read and write.

lit•er•al /lítərəl/ adj. **1** taking words in their basic sense without metaphor or allegory. **2** following exactly the original wording (literal translation). **3** prosaic; matter-of-fact. **4** so called without exaggeration (literal extermination). **5** of a letter of the alphabet. □□ **lit′er•al•ize** v.tr. **lit′er•al•ly** adv. **lit′er•al•ness** n.

■ adj. **1** denotative; see also LITERAL adj. 4 below. **2** verbatim; precise, faithful, strict. **3** dull, banal, unimaginative, pedestrian, tedious; down-to-earth. **4** essential, pure, simplistic, true, actual, bona fide; unvarnished, unadulterated. □□ **literally** word for word; exactly; truly; tediously.

lit•er•ar•y /lítəreree/ adj. **1** of, occupied with, or used in formal literature. **2** well informed about literature. □□ **lit•er•ar′i•ness** n.

■ **1** artistic, poetic, dramatic. **2** well-read, lettered, bookish; cultured, refined, learned, knowledgeable, scholarly.

lit•er•ate /lítərət/ • adj. able to read and write. • n. literate person. □□ **lit′er•ate•ly** adv.

■ adj. see LEARNED 1.

lit•e•ra•ti /lítəráatee/ n.pl. learned people.

lit•er•a•ture /lítərəchər, –chŏŏr/ n. **1** written works, esp. those valued for form and style. **2** writings of a country, period, or particular subject. **3** colloq. printed matter, leaflets, etc.

■ **1, 2** books, publications, work(s), texts; poetry, drama, fiction, essays, novels. **3** document(s), paper(s); brochure(s), pamphlet(s), booklet(s), manuals, handout(s), circular(s); information, data, instructions.

-lith /lith/ *suffix* denoting types of stone (*laccolith, monolith*).

lithe /lith/ *adj.* flexible; supple. □□ **lithe'ly** *adv.* **lithe'ness** *n.* **lithe'some** *adj.*

■ see SUPPLE *adj.* 1.

lith•i•um /lítheeəm/ *n. Chem.* soft, silver-white metallic element. ¶ Symb.: **Li.**

lith•o•graph /líthəgraf/ • *n.* lithographic print. • *v.tr.* 1 print by lithography. 2 write or engrave on stone.

li•thog•ra•phy /lithógrəfee/ *n.* process of printing from a plate so treated that ink adheres only to what is to be printed. □□ **li•thog'ra•pher** *n.* **lith•o•graph•ic** /líthəgráfik/ *adj.* **lith•o•graph'i•cal•ly** *adv.*

lith•o•sphere /líthəsfeer/ *n.* layer including the earth's crust and upper mantle. □□ **lith•o•spher•ic** /-sféerik, -stēr-/ *adj*

Lith•u•a•ni•an /líthoō-áyneeən/ • *n.* 1 **a** native of Lithuania. **b** person of Lithuanian descent. 2 language of Lithuania. • *adj.* of or relating to Lithuania or its people or language.

lit•i•gant /lítigənt/ *n.* a party to a lawsuit.

lit•i•gate /lítigayt/ *v.* 1 *intr.* be a party to a lawsuit. 2 *tr.* contest (a point) in a lawsuit. □□ **lit•i•ga'tion** /-gáyshən/ *n.* **lit'i•ga•tor** *n.*

■ 1 go to court, take (legal) action. 2 see CONTEST *v.* 1. □□ **litigation** case; redress.

li•ti•gious /litíjəs/ *adj.* 1 given to litigation. 2 quarrelsome. □□ **li•ti'gious•ly** *adv.* **li•ti'gious•ness** *n.*

lit•mus /lítməs/ *n.* dye that turns red under acid conditions and blue under alkaline conditions. □ **litmus paper** paper stained with litmus, used to test for acids or alkalis. **litmus test** 1 test for acids and alkalis using litmus paper. 2 test to establish true character.

lit•ter /lítər/ • *n.* 1 **a** refuse, esp. paper, discarded in an open or public place. **b** odds and ends lying about. 2 young animals brought forth at a birth. 3 vehicle containing a couch and carried by people or animals. 4 stretcher for the sick and wounded. 5 straw, etc., as bedding for animals. 6 granulated material for a cat's waste. • *v.tr.* 1 make (a place) untidy with litter. 2 scatter carelessly.

■ *n.* 1 rubbish, waste, garbage, trash; debris. 2 brood, offspring. • *v.* 1 clutter (up), mess (up). 2 strew, spread, toss, throw.

lit•ter•bug /lítərbug/ *n.* person who leaves litter in a public place.

lit•tle /lít'l/ • *adj.* (**lit•tler, lit•tlest;** *less* /les/ or *les•ser* /lésər/; *least* /leest/) 1 small in size, amount, degree, etc. 2 **a** short in stature. **b** of short distance or duration. 3 trivial. 4 young or younger (*little boy, my little sister*). 5 paltry; contemptible (*you little sneak*). See synonym study at SMALL. • *n.* 1 not much; only a small amount (*got very little out of it*). 2 [usu. prec. by *a*] **a** a certain but no great amount (*every little bit helps*). **b** short time or distance (*after a little*). • *adv.* (**less, least**) 1 to a small extent only (*little more than speculation*). 2 not at all; hardly (*little thought*). 3 [prec. by *a*] somewhat (*is a little deaf*). □ **Little Bear** = *Little Dipper*. **Little Dipper** constellation in Ursa Minor in the shape of a dipper. **little by little** by degrees; gradually. **little finger** smallest finger, at the outer end of the hand. **no little** considerable; a good deal of (*took no little trouble over it*). **not a little** *n.* much; a great deal. *adv.* extremely (*not a little concerned*). □□ **lit'tle•ness** *n.*

■ *adj.* 1, 2 **a** slight, diminutive, compact, petite; puny; microscopic, infinitesimal, *colloq.* teeny-weeny. 2 **b** brief. 3 trifling, minor, slight, *colloq.* piddling; inconsequential, negligible. 4 youthful; junior. 5 despicable, low, mean, cheap, petty, *colloq.* two-bit. • *n.* 1 hardly *or* scarcely anything; a pittance, *colloq.* peanuts, chicken feed. 2 **a** bit, piece, scrap, drop, dab, touch, hint, *colloq.* smidgen, tad. **b** while. • *adv.* 1, 2 scarcely, barely; seldom; by no means. 3 (*a little*) slightly, rather, quite, fairly, pretty, *colloq.* sort of, kind of, kinda.

lit•to•ral /lítərəl/ • *adj.* of or on the shore. • *n.* region lying along a shore.

lit•ur•gy /lítərjee/ *n.* (*pl.* **-gies**) prescribed form of public worship. □□ **li•tur'gi•cal** *adj.* **li•tur'gi•cal•ly** *adv.*

■ □□ **liturgical** see SOLEMN 2.

liv•a•ble /lívəbəl/ *adj.* (also **live'a•ble**) 1 (of a house, climate, etc.) fit to live in. 2 (of a life) worth living. □□ **liv•a•bil'i•ty** *n.*

■ 1 see HABITABLE.

live[1] /liv/ *v.intr.* 1 have life; be or remain alive. 2 [foll. by *on, off*] subsist or feed (*lives on fruit, lives off the family*). 3 conduct oneself in a specified way (*live quietly*). 4 survive. 5 enjoy life to the fullest. □ **live and let live** condone others' failings so as to be similarly tolerated. **live down** cause (past guilt, embarrassment, etc.) to be forgotten. **live it up** *colloq.* live gaily and extravagantly. **live through** survive. **live to** survive and reach (*lived to a great age*). **live up to** honor; fulfill. **live with** 1 share a home with. 2 tolerate.

■ 1, 2 exist, breathe; thrive, keep going, last, endure; (*live on*) eat, use, consume; depend on. 4 pull *or* come through; emerge, walk away; go on, continue. □ **live it up** see *enjoy oneself*. **live through** see WEATHER *v.* **live to** see REACH *v.* 4. **live up to** see FULFILL 1, 2.

live[2] /liv/ *adj.* 1 [*attrib.*] that is alive; living. 2 (of a broadcast) heard *or* seen at the time of its performance. 3 of current importance (*a live issue*). 4 **a** (of coals) glowing. **b** (of a shell) unexploded. **c** (of a wire, etc.) connected to electrical power. □ **live oak** American evergreen tree. **live wire** energetic and forceful person.

■ 1 breathing, animate; viable. 3 contemporary. 4 **a** burning, aglow, aflame, flaming, red-hot, white-hot. **b** loaded, charged. **c** electrified. □ **live wire** fireball, tiger, demon, *colloq.* dynamo.

live•a•ble var. of LIVABLE.

live•li•hood /lívleehŏŏd/ *n.* means of living; sustenance.

■ see SUSTENANCE 2.

live•long /lívlawng, –long/ *adj.* entire (*the livelong day*).

live•ly /lívlee/ *adj.* (**live•li•er, live•li•est**)

1 full of life; energetic. **2** brisk (*a lively pace*). **3** vivacious; jolly; sociable. **4** bright and vivid. □□ **live′li·ness** n.

■ **1** vital; spry, perky, bouncy, bubbly, exuberant; dynamic. **2** crisp, smart, *colloq.* snappy. **3** jovial, convivial, high-spirited. **4** brilliant, intense, bold, loud, fluorescent; colorful, cheerful.

liv·en /lívən/ v. *colloq.* brighten; cheer.

■ hearten, stimulate, *colloq.* pep up.

liv·er /lívər/ n. **1** large glandular organ in the abdomen of vertebrates. **2** flesh of an animal's liver as food. **3** dark reddish-brown color. □ **liver spots** brownish pigmentation of the skin, esp. of older people.

liv·er·wurst /lívərwərst, –vərst/ n. sausage of ground cooked liver, etc.

liv·er·y /lívəree/ n. (pl. **–ies**) **1** distinctive marking or outward appearance (*birds in their winter livery*). **2 a** place where horses can be hired. **b** company that has vehicles for hire. **3** distinctive uniform of a servant, etc.

lives pl. of LIFE.

live·stock /lívstok/ n. [usu. treated as pl.] animals, esp. on a farm, regarded as an asset.

liv·id /lívid/ adj. **1** *colloq.* furiously angry. **2 a** of a bluish leaden color. **b** discolored as by a bruise. See synonym study at PALE. □□ **li·vid′i·ty** n. **liv′id·ly** adv. **liv′id·ness** n.

■ **1** see ANGRY 1. **2** see GRAY 1.

liv·ing /líving/ • n. **1** livelihood. **2** enjoyment of life. • adj. **1** contemporary; now existent (*greatest living poet*). **2** (of a likeness) exact. **3** (of a language) still in use. □ **living room** room for general day use. **living will** written statement of a person's desire not to be kept alive by artificial means.

■ n. **1** see SUSTENANCE 2. • adj. **1** see ALIVE 1. □ **living room** see PARLOR.

liz·ard /lízərd/ n. slender reptile having usu. a long tail, four legs, movable eyelids, and a rough or scaly hide.

'll v. (usu. after pronouns) shall; will (*I'll, that'll*).

lla·ma /láːmə, yáːa–/ n. S. American ruminant, kept as a beast of burden and for its soft, woolly fleece.

lla·no /láːnō, yáːa–/ n. (pl. **–nos**) grassy plain or steppe, esp. in S. America.

LLB abbr. Bachelor of Laws.

LLD abbr. Doctor of Laws.

lo /lō/ int. archaic look (*lo and behold!*).

load /lōd/ • n. **1** what is carried or is to be carried at one time. **2** burden or commitment of work, responsibility, etc. **3** [in pl.] *colloq.* plenty; a lot. **4** amount of power carried by an electric-circuit. • v. **1** tr. put a load on or aboard. **2** intr. take a load aboard; pick up a load. **3** tr. [often foll. by *with*] **a** add weight to. **b** oppress. **4** tr. insert the required operating medium) in a device, e.g., film in a camera, etc. **5** tr. **a** weight with lead. **b** give a bias to (dice, etc.) with weights. □ **get a load of** sl. listen attentively to; notice.

■ n. **1** cargo, shipment, quantity; load. **2** pressure, strain, stress, encumbrance, millstone; care, anxiety. **3** (*loads*) see LOT n. 1. •

v. **1, 2** lade, freight; fill, pack. **3** saddle; overload, overwhelm, crush, tax. □ **get a load of** pay attention to, lend an ear to, take note of, look at, examine, study, *colloq.* check out.

load·ed /lódid/ adj. **1** sl. **a** wealthy. **b** drunk. **c** drugged. **2** (of dice, etc.) weighted. **3** (of a question or statement) charged with hidden implication.

■ **1 a** see WEALTHY. **b** see DRUNK adj. 1. **c** intoxicated, sl. stoned, spaced (out). **2** biased; crooked. **3** trick; misleading; prejudiced.

load·stone var. of LODESTONE.

loaf¹ /lōf/ n. (pl. **loaves** /lōvz/) **1** unit of baked bread. **2** [often in *comb.*] other food formed in the shape of a bread loaf.

■ **2** brick, cake, block, chunk, hunk, slab.

loaf² /lōf/ v.intr. spend time idly.

■ lounge (about *or* around), hang around, loiter, loll, laze, sl. goof off.

loaf·er /lófər/ n. **1** idle person. **2** (**Loaf′er**) *propr.* leather shoe shaped like a moccasin.

■ **1** layabout, slacker, shirker, sluggard, ne'-er-do-well, *colloq.* lazybones, sl. bum, gold brick.

loam /lōm/ n. fertile soil of clay, sand, and humus. □□ **loam′y** adj. **loam′i·ness** n.

loan /lōn/ • n. **1** thing lent, esp. money. **2** lending or being lent. • v.tr. lend. □ **loan shark** *colloq.* person who lends money at exorbitant rates of interest.

■ n. advance, allowance, credit; lease, charter; mortgage. • v. allow, put out; rent (out).

loath /lōth, lōth/ predic.adj. disinclined; reluctant.

■ unwilling, resistant, averse, opposed.

loathe /lōth/ v.tr. detest. □□ **loath′er** n. **loath′ing** n.

■ hate, dislike, abhor, abominate; despise. □□ **loathing** repugnance, revulsion, disgust, aversion.

loath·some /lóthsəm, lóth–/ adj. arousing hatred or disgust; repulsive. □□ **loath′some·ly** adv. **loath′some·ness** n.

■ detestable, odious, abominable, despicable, contemptible; offensive; hideous, repugnant, revolting; vile, foul.

loaves pl. of LOAF¹.

lob /lob/ • v.tr. (**lobbed, lob·bing**) hit or throw (a ball, etc.) slowly or in a high arc. • n. **1** ball struck in a high arc. **2** stroke producing this result.

■ v. loft, toss; pitch, fling, hurl, launch, cast. • n. **2** hit, shot.

lob·by /lóbee/ • n. (pl. **–bies**) **1** entrance hall. **2** body of persons seeking to influence legislators on behalf of a particular interest (*tobacco lobby*). • v.tr. (**–bies, –bied**) **1** solicit the support of (an influential person). **2** (of members of the public) seek to influence (the members of a legislature). □□ **lob′by·er** n. **lob′by·ist** n.

■ n. **1** porch, anteroom, foyer, vestibule; corridor, hall, passage. **2** pressure group; faction. • v. petition, appeal to, push, press; persuade, sway.

lobe /lōb/ n. **1** roundish and flattish pendulous part, often one of a pair (*lobes of the brain*). **2** = EARLOBE. □□ **lo′bar** adj. **lobed** adj.

lo•bel•ia /lōbe̅elyə/ *n.* plant with profuse blue, scarlet, white, or purple flowers having a deeply cleft corolla.

lo•bot•o•my /ləbótəmee/ *n.* (*pl.* **–mies**) incision into the frontal lobe of the brain.

lob•ster /lóbstər/ • *n.* edible marine crustacean with stalked eyes and two pincerlike claws. • *v.intr.* catch lobsters. □ **lobster pot** basket in which lobsters are trapped.

lo•cal /lókəl/ • *adj.* **1** belonging to, peculiar to, or existing in a particular place. **2** of or affecting only a part. **3** (of a train, bus, etc.) stopping at all stations. • *n.* **1** inhabitant of a particular place. **2** local train, bus, etc. **3** local anesthetic. **4** local branch of a labor union. □ **local area network** *Computing* system for linking telecommunications or computer equipment in several offices, a group of buildings, etc. ¶Abbr.: **LAN**. **local color** characteristics of a place, esp. as depicted in literature, film, etc. □□ **lo'cal•ly** *adv.*

■ *adj.* **1** indigenous, native, endemic; topical; regional, territorial, provincial, divisional; neighboring, nearby. **2** localized, specific; restricted, limited. • *n.* **1** resident, native, national, *poet.* denizen.

lo•cale /lōkál/ *n.* scene or locality of an event or occurrence.

■ site, setting, vicinity; situation, place, venue.

lo•cal•i•ty /lōkálitee/ *n.* (*pl.* **–ties**) **1** district. **2** site or scene of something.

■ **1** see NEIGHBORHOOD 1. **2** see SPOT *n.* 2.

lo•cal•ize /lókəlīz/ *v.tr.* restrict or assign to a particular place. □□ **lo•cal•i•za'tion** *n.*

lo•cate /lókayt, lōkáyt/ *v.tr.* **1** discover the place of. **2** establish in a place. **3** [in *passive*] be situated.

■ **1** detect, identify, ascertain, pinpoint; track down, uncover, lay one's hands on; find, come across. **2, 3** place, put, position, set (up), install.

lo•ca•tion /lōkáyshən/ *n.* **1** place. **2** locating. □ **on location** *Cinematog.* in a natural, not a studio setting.

■ **1** position, spot, site, scene, setting, locale. **2** placement, installation; discovery, detection.

loc. cit. /lók sit/ *abbr.* in the passage already cited.

loch /lok, lokh/ *n.* *Sc.* **1** lake. **2** narrow inlet of the sea.

lo•ci *pl.* of LOCUS.

lock¹ /lok/ • *n.* **1** mechanism for fastening a door, lid, etc., that requires a key or a combination to work it. **2** section of a canal or river within gates for raising and lowering the water level. **3** mechanism for exploding the charge of a gun. • *v.* **1 a** *tr.* fasten with a lock. **b** *tr.* [foll. by *up*] shut and secure by locking. **2** *tr.* [foll. by *up, in, into*] enclose (a person or thing) by locking or as if by locking. **3** *tr. & intr.* make or become rigidly fixed. **4** *tr. & intr.* become or cause to become jammed or caught. **5** *tr.* entangle; interlock. □ **lock out 1** keep (a person) out by locking the door. **2** (of an employer) submit (employees) to a lockout. **lock, stock, and barrel** *n.* the whole of a thing. *adv.* completely. **under lock and key** securely locked up. □□ **lock'a•ble** *adj.*

■ *n.* **1** padlock, deadlock, hasp, bolt. • *v.* **1** fasten, seal, latch. **2** shut up or in or away, put away; imprison, jail, incarcerate, shut, put behind bars. **3** jam, stick, seize (up), freeze. **4** catch, snag, lodge; see also LOCK¹ *v.* 3 above. **5** clasp, clutch; entwine. □ **lock out** exclude, bar, debar. **lock, stock, and barrel** (*adv.*) see *completely* (COMPLETE).

lock² /lok/ *n.* **1** tress of hair. **2** [in *pl.*] the hair of the head.

■ **1** curl, ringlet, strand; cowlick. **2** (*locks*) *colloq.* mane.

lock•er /lókər/ *n.* lockable cupboard or compartment, esp. for public use. □ **locker room** room containing lockers, esp. in a sports facility.

■ see COMPARTMENT *n.* 1, TRUNK 4.

lock•et /lókit/ *n.* small ornamental case holding a portrait, lock of hair, etc., and usu. worn on a necklace.

lock•jaw /lókjaw/ *n.* = TRISMUS. ¶Not in technical use.

lock•out /lókowt/ *n.* employer's exclusion of employees from their workplace until certain terms are agreed to.

lock•smith /lóksmith/ *n.* maker and repairer of locks.

lock•up /lókup/ *n.* holding cell for police suspects.

lo•co /lókō/ • *adj. sl.* crazy. • *n.* (*pl.* **–cos** or **–coes**) *sl.* crazy person.

■ *adj.* see CRAZY 1. • *n.* see MANIAC.

lo•co•mo•tion /lōkəmōshən/ *n.* motion or the power of motion from one place to another.

lo•co•mo•tive /lōkəmōtiv/ • *n.* engine for pulling trains. • *adj.* of, relating to, or effecting locomotion (*locomotive power*).

lo•co•weed /lókōweed/ *n.* poisonous leguminous plant of the southwestern US, causing disease in livestock.

lo•cus /lókəs/ *n.* (*pl.* **lo•ci** /lósī, –kee, –kī/) **1** position. **2** *Math.* curve, etc., formed by all points satisfying certain conditions.

■ **1** see PLACE *n.* 1a, b.

lo•cust /lókəst/ *n.* **1** grasshoppers migrating in swarms and destroying vegetation. **2** cicada. **3** (in full **locust bean**) carob. **4** (in full **locust tree**) N. American flowering tree yielding durable wood.

lo•cu•tion /lōkyōōshən/ *n.* word, phrase, or idiom.

lode /lōd/ *n.* vein of metal ore.

lo•den /lód'n/ *n.* **1** thick, waterproof woolen cloth. **2** dark green color in which this is often made.

lode•star /lódstaar/ *n.* **1** star that a ship, etc., is steered by, esp. the pole star. **2 a** guiding principle. **b** object of pursuit.

■ **1** see GUIDE *n.* 6. **2** see GUIDE *n.* 4.

lode•stone /lódstōn/ *n.* (also **load'stone**) **1** magnetic oxide of iron. **2** thing that attracts.

lodge /loj/ • *n.* **1** small house occupied by a gatekeeper, gardener, etc. **2** house or hotel in a resort. **3** house occupied in the season for skiing, hunting, etc. **4** members or the meeting place of a branch of a society such as the Freemasons. **5** beaver's or otter's lair. • *v.* **1** *tr.* submit a complaint, etc. **2** *tr. & intr.* make or become fixed or caught. **3** *intr.* reside or live, esp. as a paying guest.

■ *n.* **1** gatehouse, cottage. **2** villa. **3** chalet, cabin. **4** chapter, order, fellowship, wing, group. • *v.* **1** bring (forward), put, lay, set forth, register. **2** wedge, embed *or* become embedded; see also STICK² 6. **3** stay, abide, dwell.

lodg•er /lójər/ *n.* person receiving accommodation in another's house for payment.

lodg•ing /lójing/ *n.* **1** temporary accommodation. **2** [in *pl.*] room or rooms rented for lodging.

■ **1** see ACCOMMODATION 1.

lo•ess /lóis, les, lus/ *n.* fertile deposit of fine, wind-blown dust.

loft /lawft, loft/ • *n.* **1** attic. **2** room over a stable, etc. for hay, etc. **3** gallery in a church or hall (*organ loft*). **4** upstairs room. **5** height of an airborne ball. • *v.tr.* send (a ball, etc.) high up.

■ *v.* see LOB *v.* 1.

loft•y /láwftee, lóf-/ *adj.* (**loft•i•er, loft•i•est**) **1** (of things) of imposing height. **2** haughty; aloof. **3** exalted; noble. □□ **loft'i•ly** *adv.* **loft'i•ness** *n.*

■ **1** tall, high, elevated, towering, soaring. **2** arrogant, condescending, patronizing, pompous. **3** imposing, grand, magnificent, distinguished, famous, prominent, illustrious. □□ **loftiness** see *arrogance* (ARROGANT), NOBILITY 1.

log¹ /lawg, log/ • *n.* **1** unhewn piece of a felled tree. **2** device for gauging the speed of a ship. **3** record of events during the voyage of a ship or aircraft. • *v.tr.* (**logged, log•ging**) **1** enter (data) in a logbook. **2** (of a ship, etc.) achieve (a certain distance, speed, etc.). **3** cut into logs. □ **log in** = *log on.* **log on** (or **off**) go through the procedures to begin (or conclude) use of a computer system. **sleep like a log** sleep without stirring.

■ *n.* **3** see RECORD *n.* 1. • *v.* **1** see RECORD *v.* 1.

log² /lawg, log/ *n.* logarithm.

lo•gan•ber•ry /lógənberee/ *n.* (*pl.* **–ries**) **1** hybrid of a blackberry and a raspberry. **2** its dark red fruit.

log•a•rithm /láwgərithəm, lóg–/ *n.* the power to which a number must be raised to produce a given number (*the logarithm of 1,000 to base 10 is 3*). ¶Abbr.: **log.** □□ **log•a•rith•mic** /–ríthmik/ *adj.* **log•a•rith'mi•cal•ly** *adv.*

log•book /láwgbŏŏk, lóg–/ *n.* book containing a detailed record or log.

■ see JOURNAL 2.

loge /lōzh/ *n.* (in a theater, etc.). **1** front section of the first balcony. **2** private box or enclosure.

log•ger /láwgər, lóg–/ *n.* lumberjack.

log•ger•head /láwgərhed, lóg–/ *n.* □ **at loggerheads** disagreeing or disputing; at odds.

log•ging /láwging, lóg–/ *n.* cutting and preparing timber.

log•ic /lójik/ *n.* **1 a** science of reasoning.

b particular scheme of or treatise on this. **2** expected procedure or outcome. □□ **lo•gi•cian** /ləjíshən/ *n.*

■ **1** thinking, argument, rationale; philosophy; sense.

-logic /lójik/ *comb. form* (also **–logical** /lójikəl/) forming adjectives corresponding esp. to nouns in *–logy* (*analogic, theological*).

log•i•cal /lójikəl/ *adj.* **1** of logic or formal argument. **2** correctly reasoned. □□ **log•i•cal•i•ty** /–kálitee/ *n.* **log'i•cal•ly** *adv.*

■ **1** syllogistic, inferential, deductive, inductive. **2** valid, sound, legitimate, reasonable, rational, consistent; correct, right; plausible, credible, believable; sensible, intelligent, practical.

lo•gis•tics /ləjístiks/ *n.pl.* planning for and provision of services and supplies for an operation, program, etc. □□ **lo•gis'tic** *adj.* **lo•gis'ti•cal** *adj.* **lo•gis'ti•cal•ly** *adv.*

log•jam /láwgjam, lóg–/ *n.* **1** crowded mass of logs in a river. **2** deadlock.

lo•go /lógō/ *n.* (*pl.* **–gos**) *colloq.* = LOGOTYPE.

lo•go•type /láwgōtīp, lóg–/ *n.* emblem or trademark of a company, organization, etc.

log•roll•ing /láwgrōling, lóg–/ *n.* **1** *colloq.* exchanging favors, esp. for political gain. **2** sport in which two people stand on and rotate a floating log until one loses by falling off. □□ **log'roll** *v.* **log'roll•er** *n.*

-logy /ləjee/ *comb. form* forming nouns denoting: **1** (usu. as **–ology**) subject of study or interest (*archaeology, zoology*). **2** characteristic of speech or language (*tautology*). **3** discourse (*trilogy*).

loin /loyn/ *n.* **1** [in *pl.*] the part of the body on both sides of the spine between the false ribs and the hipbones. **2** meat from this part of an animal.

■ **1** (*loins*) flanks, sides.

loin•cloth /lóynklawth, –kloth/ *n.* cloth worn around the loins, esp. as a sole garment.

loi•ter /lóytər/ *v.intr.* **1** hang around; linger idly. **2** go slowly, with long pauses. □□ **loi'ter•er** *n.*

SYNONYM STUDY: loiter

DALLY, DAWDLE, IDLE, LAG. Someone who hangs around downtown after the shops are closed and appears to be deliberately wasting time is said to **loiter**, a verb that connotes improper or sinister motives (*the police warned the boys not to loiter*). To **dawdle** is to pass time leisurely or to pursue something halfheartedly (*to dawdle in a stationery shop; to dawdle over a sinful of dishes*). Someone who **dallies** *dawdles* in a particularly pleasurable and relaxed way, with connotations of amorous activity (*he dallied with his girlfriend when he should have been delivering papers*). **Idle** suggests that the person makes a habit of avoiding work or activity (*to idle away the hours of a hot summer day*), while **lag** suggests falling behind or failing to maintain a desirable rate of progress (*she lagged several yards behind her classmates as they walked to the museum*).

loll /lol/ *v.* **1** *intr.* stand, sit, or recline in a lazy attitude. **2** *tr. & intr.* [foll. by *out*] hang loosely. □□ **loll'er** *n.*

■ 1 see LOUNGE v.

lol•li•pop /lólleepop/ n. hard, usu. round candy on a stick.

lol•ly•gag /lóleegag/ v.intr. (also **lal•ly•gag** /láleegag/) (**-gagged, -gag•ging**) sl. loiter.

■ see LOAF².

lone /lōn/ attrib.adj. **1** (of a person) solitary; without a companion. **2** (of a place) unfrequented; uninhabited. □ **lone wolf** person who prefers to act alone.

■ **1** see LONELY 1. **2** see isolated (ISOLATE). □ **lone wolf** see individualist (INDIVIDUALIST).

lone•ly /lónlee/ adj. (**lone•li•er, lone•li•est**) **1** solitary. **2** (of a place) unfrequented. **3** sad because without friends. □ **lonely heart** lonely person (in sense 3). □□ **lone'li•ness** n.

■ **1** sole, lone, single, solo, alone; separate, detached. **2** uninhabited, deserted, desolate, remote, cut off, secluded, isolated. **3** see FORLORN 1. □□ **loneliness** solitude, desolation, isolation, seclusion.

lon•er /lónər/ n. person or animal that prefers to be alone.

lone•some /lónsəm/ adj. **1** solitary. **2** feeling lonely. □ **by** (or **on**) **one's lonesome** all alone. □□ **lone'some•ly** adv. **lone'some•ness** n.

■ see LONELY 1. See FORLORN 1.

long¹ /lawng, long/ • adj. (**long•er** /láwnggər, lóng-/; **long•est** /láwnggist, long-/) **1** measuring much from end to end in space or time. **2** in length or duration (three miles long, two months long). **3** consisting of many items or units. **4** seemingly more than the stated amount; tedious (ten long miles). **5** elongated. **6** lasting much time (long friendship). **7** far-reaching. **8** (of a vowel) having the pronunciation shown in the name of the letter. **9** (of odds or a chance) of low probability. **10** (of stocks) bought with the expectation of a rise in price. **11** [foll. by on] colloq. well supplied with. • n. long interval or period (will not take long). • adv. (**long•er** /lónggər/; **long•est** /lónggist/) **1** by or for a long time (long before). **2** throughout a specified time (all day long). □ **as** (or **so**) **long as** provided that. **before long** soon. **in the long run** eventually. **the long and the short of it 1** all that can or need be said. **2** eventual outcome. **long-distance 1** (of a telephone call, public transport, etc.) between distant places. **2** (of a weather forecast) long-range. **long division** division of numbers with details of the calculations written down. **long-drawn** (or **-drawn-out**) prolonged; esp. unduly. **long face** dismal expression. **long-faced** with a long face. **long haul** prolonged effort or task. **long in the tooth** rather old. **long johns** colloq. = long underwear. **long jump** track-and-field contest of jumping as far as possible along the ground in one leap. **long-lived** having a long life; durable. **long-playing** (of a phonograph record) playing for about 20–30 minutes on each side. **long-range** extending a long distance or time. **long-running** continuing for a long time. **long shot 1** wild guess or venture. **2** bet at long odds. **3** Cinematog. shot including objects at a distance. **long-sleeved** with sleeves reaching to the wrist. **long-standing** that has long existed. **long-suffering** bearing provocation patiently. **long suit** thing at which one excels. **long-term** of or for a long time (long-term plans). **long underwear** warm, close-fitting undergarment with ankle-length legs and often a long-sleeved top. **long wave** radio wave of frequency less than 300 kHz. **not by a long shot** by no means. □□ **long'ish** adj.

■ adj. **1, 3–5, 7** lengthy, extensive, considerable; extended; prolonged; endless, interminable, unending; numerous, innumerable; time-consuming; long-distance. **6** see LASTING. □ **as** (or **so**) **long as** on condition that, (only) if. **before long** see SOON 1. **in the long run** see finally (FINAL). **not by a long shot** no way, in or under no circumstances, never.

long² /lawng, long/ v.intr. [foll. by for or to + infin.] have a strong wish or desire for.

■ crave, want, yearn, hunger, colloq. yen.

long. abbr. longitude.

lon•gev•i•ty /lonjévitee, lawn-/ n. long life.

long•hair /láwnghair, lóng-/ n. person characterized by the associations of long hair, esp. a hippie or intellectual.

long•hand /láwnghand, lóng-/ n. ordinary handwriting.

long•horn /láwnghawrn, lóng-/ n. one of a breed of cattle with long horns.

long•ing /láwnging, lóng-/ • n. intense desire. • adj. having or showing this feeling. □□ **long'ing•ly** adv.

■ n. craving, yearning, hunger. • adj. see DESIROUS 2.

lon•gi•tude /lónjitōod, -tyōod, láwn-/ n. angular distance east or west from the prime meridian.

lon•gi•tu•di•nal /lónjitōod'nəl, -tyōod-, láwn-/ adj. **1** of or in length. **2** running lengthwise. **3** of longitude. □□ **lon•gi•tu'di•nal•ly** adv.

long•shore•man /láwngshawrmən, lóng-/ n. (pl. **-men**) person employed to load and unload ships.

long•time /láwngtīm, lóng-/ adj. that has been such for a long time.

long-wind•ed /láwngwíndid, lóng-/ adj. **1** (of speech or writing) tediously lengthy. **2** able to run a long distance without rest. □□ **long-wind'ed•ly** adv. **long-wind'ed•ness** n.

■ **1** see TEDIOUS. □□ **long-windedness** see TEDIUM, TAUTOLOGY.

loo•fah /lōōfə/ n. (also **luf•fa** /lúfə/) **1** climbing gourdlike plant. **2** its dried fruit fibers used as a sponge.

look /lŏŏk/ • v. **1 a** intr. use one's sight. **b** tr. turn one's eyes on; examine. **2** intr. a make a search. **b** [foll. by at] consider; examine (look at the facts). **3** intr. [foll. by for] **a** search for. **b** expect. **4** intr. have a specified appearance; seem. **5** intr. [foll. by into] investigate. • n. **1** act of looking; glance (scornful look). **2** [in sing. or pl.] appearance of a face; expression. **3** appearance of a thing (has a European look). • int. (also **look**

here!) calling attention, expressing a protest, etc. □ **look after** take care of. **look one's age** appear to be as old as one really is. **look-alike** person or thing closely resembling another. **look alive** (or **lively**) *colloq.* be brisk and alert. **look as if** suggest by appearance the belief that (*it looks as if he's gone*). **look back 1** turn one's thoughts to (something past). **2** [usu. with *neg.*] cease to progress (*have never looked back*). **look down on** (or **upon** or **look down one's nose at**) regard with contempt or superiority. **look forward to** await with specified feelings. **look in** make a short visit. **look like 1** have the appearance of. **2** threaten or promise (*looks like rain*). **look on** regard (*looks on you as a friend*). **look out 1** [often foll. by *for*] be vigilant or prepared. **2** [foll. by *on, over,* etc.] afford a specified outlook. **look over** inspect; examine. **look-see** quick survey or inspection. **look sharp** act promptly. **look through 1** penetrate (a pretense or pretender) with insight. **2** ignore by pretending not to see. **look up 1** search for (esp. information in a book). **2** *colloq.* go to visit (a person). **3** raise one's eyes. **4** improve, esp. in price, prosperity, or well-being (*things are looking up*). **look up to** respect; venerate. **not like the look of** find alarming or suspicious; distrust. □□ **–looking** *adj.* [in comb.].

■ *v.* **1a, 2b** (*look at*) observe, regard, view; study, contemplate, notice; watch. **2a, 3a** hunt, seek. **3b** (*look for*) hope for, aim at; *disp.* anticipate; seek, demand, require. **5** (*look into*) inquire; delve, dig, probe, explore, research, check. ● *n.* **1** gaze, glare, stare. **2, 3** aspect, bearing, manner, air, demeanor; countenance. *int.* (**look here!**) hey, listen to me. ● **look after** care for, attend (to), mind, serve, wait on, nurse, protect, guard. **look-alike** twin, double, exact *or* perfect likeness, clone, (dead) ringer, *colloq.* spitting image. **look down on** disdain, despise, scorn, spurn, sneer at, *colloq.* turn up one's nose at. **look forward to** anticipate, wait for; expect. **look out 1** be careful, be alert, watch out, beware, pay attention, be on (one's) guard. **2** (*look out on* or *over*) have a view over, overlook. **look over** survey; look at, scan, study, check (out *or* over), *sl.* eyeball. **look up 1** seek, hunt for, try to find, track *or* run down. **2** call on, look *or* drop in on, get in touch with. **4** get better, pick up, make headway *or* progress. **look up to** admire, esteem, honor, revere.

look•er /lŏŏkər/ *n. colloq.* an attractive person.

look•ing glass /lŏŏking glas/ *n.* mirror.

look•out /lŏŏkowt/ *n.* **1** watch or looking out. **2 a** post of observation. **b** person or party stationed to keep watch. **3** *colloq.* person's own concern.

■ **1** alert. **2 b** guard, sentry, sentinel, watchman. **3** responsibility, worry, problem, difficulty, *colloq.* headache.

loom¹ /lŏŏm/ *n.* apparatus for weaving.

loom² /lŏŏm/ *v.intr.* **1** appear dimly, esp. as a

threatening shape. **2** (of an event or prospect) be ominously close.

■ **1** emerge, materialize, surface, arise. **2** impend, threaten, hang, hover.

loon /lŏŏn/ *n.* **1** aquatic diving bird. **2** *colloq.* crazy person.

■ **2** see FOOL *n.* 1.

loon•y /lŏŏnee/ *sl.* ● *n.* (*pl.* **–ies**) mad or silly person; lunatic. ● *adj.* (**loon•i•er, loon•i•est**) crazy; silly. □ **loony bin** *sl.* psychiatric hospital. □□ **loo'ni•ness** *n.*

■ *n.* see MADMAN. ● *adj.* see CRAZY 1.

loop /lŏŏp/ ● *n.* **1 a** figure produced by a curve, or a doubled thread, etc., that crosses itself. **b** anything forming this figure. **2** contraceptive coil. **3** endless strip of tape or film allowing continuous repetition. **4** *Computing* sequence of instructions that is repeated until a condition is satisfied. ● *v.* **1** tr. form into a loop. **2** tr. fasten with a loop or loops. **3** intr. **a** form a loop. **b** move in looplike patterns. **4** intr. (also **loop the loop**) *Aeron.* fly in a circle vertically.

■ *n.* **1** noose, ring, eyelet. ● *v.* **1–3** twist, coil, wind, curl.

loop•hole /lŏŏp-hōl/ *n.* means of evading a rule, etc., without infringing it.

■ escape, cop-out; *colloq.* dodge; evasion.

loop•y /lŏŏpee/ *adj.* (**loop•i•er, loop•i•est**) *sl.* crazy.

loose /lŏŏs/ ● *adj.* **1** free from bonds or restraint. **2** not tightly held, fixed, etc. **3** slack; relaxed. **4** not compact or dense. **5** inexact. **6** morally lax. ● *n.* state of freedom, esp. as an escapee (*on the loose*). ● *v.tr.* **1** release; set free. **2** untie (something that constrains). **3** discharge (a missile, etc.). □ **at loose ends** uncertain; disorganized. **loose-leaf** (of a notebook, etc.) with each page separate and removable. **play fast and loose** ignore one's obligations; be unreliable. □□ **loose'ly** *adv.* **loose'ness** *n.*

■ *adj.* **1** unfettered, unshackled; at liberty, at large; (*break loose*) see ESCAPE *v.* 1. **2** unattached, detached, unfastened; movable; untied, unbound, unsecured, unfastened, unpackaged, free; (*of clothing*) baggy, flowing; (*of hair*) down. **3** lax, limp, soft, floppy. **6** wanton, promiscuous, fast, licentious. ● *v.* **1** let go, let *or* set *or* turn loose; liberate, deliver. **2** undo, disengage, release, ease, loosen, slacken; cast off. **3** let go, let fly, fire, shoot, unleash, deliver, emit. □ **at loose ends** aimless, adrift.

loos•en /lŏŏsan/ *v.* make or become loose or looser. □□ **loos'en•er** *n.*

■ ease, undo, unfasten, unhook, unbutton, unlace, untie, unbind, unbuckle; unscrew; soften; separate.

loot /lŏŏt/ ● *n.* **1** spoil; booty. **2** *sl.* money. ● *v.tr.* plunder. □□ **loot'er** *n.*

■ *n.* plunder, prize, haul, *sl.* swag. ● *v.* sack, ransack, rob, pillage, raid, ravage; see also STEAL *v.* 1.

lop¹ /lop/ *v.* (**lopped, lop•ping**) **1** tr. cut or remove (a part or parts) from a whole, esp. branches from a tree. **2** tr. remove (items) as superfluous. **3** intr. [foll. by *at*] make lopping strokes on (a tree, etc.). □□ **lop'per** *n.*

■ **1, 2** chop (off), trim, crop, prune, dock,

snip (off), pare, shorten, hack (off), amputate.

lop² /lop/ v. (**lopped, lop·ping**) hang limply. □ **lop-eared** (of an animal) having drooping ears. □□ **lop'py** adj.

lope /lōp/ • v.intr. run with a long bounding stride. • n. long bounding stride.
  ■ v. see RUN v. 1, 3.

lop·sid·ed /lópsídid/ adj. unevenly balanced. □□ **lop'sid·ed·ly** adv. **lop'sid·ed·ness** n.
  ■ askew, awry, crooked, irregular, colloq. cockeyed; biased, unfair.

lo·qua·cious /lōkwáyshəs/ adj. talkative. □□ **lo·qua'cious·ly** adv. **lo·qua'cious·ness** n. **lo·quac·i·ty** /-kwásitee/ n.
  ■ see TALKATIVE.

lord /lawrd/ • n. **1** master or ruler. **2** hist. feudal superior, esp. of a manor. **3** (in the UK) person with the title Lord, esp. a marquess, earl, viscount, or baron. **4** (**Lord**) [often prec. by the] God or Christ. • int. (**Lord**) expressing surprise, dismay, etc. □ **lord it over** domineer. **lord over** rule over. **Lord's Prayer** prayer taught by Jesus to his disciples. **Lord's Supper** the Eucharist.
  ■ n. **1** monarch, sovereign. **3** nobleman, peer. **4** the Almighty, the Creator, the Supreme Being, Jesus, Jehovah. int. see GOD int. □ **lord it over** pull rank on, colloq. boss (about or around).

lord·ly /láwrdlee/ adj. (**lord·li·er, lord·li·est**) **1** haughty; imperious. **2** suitable for a lord. □□ **lord'li·ness** n.
  ■ **1** see snobbish (SNOB). **2** see NOBLE adj. 1. □□ **lordliness** see snobbery (SNOB).

lord·ship /láwrdship/ n. **1** (usu. **Lordship**) title used in addressing or referring to a lord, etc. **2** dominion; rule; ownership.

lore /lawr/ n. traditions and knowledge on a subject.
  ■ folklore; beliefs; myths; teaching(s), wisdom.

lor·gnette /lawrnyét/ n. [in sing. or pl.] pair of eyeglasses or opera glasses held by a long handle.

lor·i·keet /láwrikeet, lór-/ n. small, brightly colored parrot.

lo·ris /láwris/ n. (pl. same) small, tailless, large-eyed nocturnal lemur of Asia.

lose /lōōz/ v.tr. (past and past part. **lost** /lawst, lost/) **1** be deprived of or cease to have, esp. by negligence. **2** be deprived of (a person, pet, etc.) by death. **3** become unable to follow, grasp, or find. **4** let or have pass from one's control or reach. **5** be defeated in (a game, lawsuit, battle, etc.). **6** evade; get rid of (lost our pursuers). **7** cause (a person) the loss of (will lose you your job). **8** [in passive] disappear; perish. □ **be lost** (or **lose oneself**) **in** be engrossed in. **be lost on** be wasted on; not appreciated by. **be lost without** have great difficulty if deprived of. **get lost** sl. [usu. in imper.] go away. **lose one's cool** colloq. lose one's composure. **lose face** be humiliated. **lose heart** be discouraged. **lose one's nerve** become timid or irresolute. **lose out** [often foll. by on] colloq. not get a fair chance or advantage (in). **lose one's temper** become angry. **losing battle** effort in which failure seems certain.

lost cause 1 enterprise, etc., with no chance of success. **2** person one can no longer hope to influence. □□ **los'a·ble** adj. **los'er** n.
  ■ **1, 2** mislay, misplace; suffer the loss of. **4, 5** give up, forfeit; yield, succumb, be beaten. **6** elude, escape, slip. **8** (be lost) see DISAPPEAR¹, DIE 1. □ **get lost** see beat it. **lose one's cool** see EXPLODE 2. **lose one's nerve** see PANIC v. **lose one's temper** see EXPLODE 2. **lost cause** see DISASTER 2, FAILURE 2.

loss /laws, los/ n. **1** losing; being lost. **2** person, thing, or amount lost. **3** detriment or disadvantage resulting from losing. □ **at a loss 1** (sold, etc.) for less than was paid for it. **2** puzzled; uncertain. **be at a loss for words** not know what to say. **loss leader** item sold at a loss to attract customers.
  ■ **1** deprivation, bereavement; denial, sacrifice; defeat, setback, failure. **2** reduction, depletion; liability; casualty, death. **3** harm, impairment, injury, damage. □ **at a loss 2** confused, perplexed, mystified, bewildered; helpless, disorientated.

lost past and past part. of LOSE.

lot /lot/ n. **1** colloq. [prec. by a or in pl.] **a** large number or amount (a lot of people, lots of fun). **b** colloq. much (a lot warmer). **2 a** each of a set of objects used in making a chance selection. **b** this method of deciding (chosen by lot). **c** share or responsibility resulting from it. **3** destiny, fortune, or condition. **4** plot; allotment of land. **5** article or set of articles for sale at an auction, etc. □ **bad lot** person of bad character. **cast** (or **draw**) **lots** decide by lots. **a whole lot** colloq. very much.
  ■ n. **1** (a lot or lots) a good or great deal, plenty, colloq. oodles, zillions, colloq. scads; (a lot of) many, numerous. **2 b** lottery, raffle; drawing straws. **c** portion, interest, allotment, assignment, ration, allowance. **3** luck, fate, karma, plight, doom, end.

lo·thar·i·o /lōtháireeō/ n. rake or libertine.

lo·tion /lóshən/ n. medicinal or cosmetic liquid preparation applied externally.
  ■ cream, liniment, balm, salve, ointment.

lot·ter·y /lótəree/ n. (pl. **-ies**) **1** game in which numbered tickets are sold and prizes are won by the holders of numbers drawn at random. **2** thing whose success is governed by chance.
  ■ **1** raffle, sweepstakes, drawing, pool.

lot·to /lótō/ n. **1** game of chance involving the drawing of numbers. **2** lottery.

lo·tus /lótəs/ n. **1** mythological plant inducing luxurious languor when eaten. **2** type of water lily. □ **lotus-eater** person given to indolent enjoyment. **lotus position** cross-legged position of meditation with the feet resting on the thighs.

loud /lowd/ • adj. **1** strongly audible; noisy. **2** (of colors, etc.) gaudy; obtrusive. • adv. loudly. □ **out loud** aloud. □□ **loud'ly** adv. **loud'ness** n.
  ■ adj. **1** deafening, earsplitting, booming, blaring, thunderous, piercing; clamorous; loudmouthed, brash; vociferous, raucous;

see also ROWDY adj. **2** garish, flashy, showy, ostentatious, sl. snazzy.

loud•mouth /lówdmowth/ n. colloq. noisily self-assertive, vociferous person. □□ **loud' mouthed** adj.

loud•speak•er /lówdspeékər/ n. apparatus that converts electrical impulses into sound, esp. music and voice.

Lou Gehrig's dis•ease /lōō gérigz/ n. = AMYOTROPHIC LATERAL SCLEROSIS.

lounge /lownj/ • v.intr. **1** recline comfortably; loll. **2** stand or move about idly. • n. **1** place for lounging. **2** waiting room. **3** sofa. □ **lounge lizard** colloq. person who frequents bars, etc. □□ **loung'er** n.

■ v. idle, loaf, laze, languish. • n. **1** lobby, foyer, reception (room).

louse /lows/ n. **1** (pl. **lice** /līs/) parasitic insect. **2** sl. (pl. **lous•es**) contemptible person. □ **louse up** sl. botch.

lous•y /lówzee/ adj. (**lous•i•er**, **lous•i•est**) **1** infested with lice. **2** colloq. very bad; disgusting. **3** colloq. well supplied; teeming (with). □□ **lous'i•ly** adv. **lous'i•ness** n.

■ **2** awful, low, base, despicable, vile, sl. rotten; poor, inferior; shoddy, shabby, miserable. **3** (lousy with) swarming with, crawling with, knee-deep in.

lout /lowt/ n. boorish person. □□ **lout'ish** adj.

■ see ROWDY n. □□ **loutish** see ROUGH adj. 4a.

lou•ver /lōōvər/ n. each of a set of overlapping slats that admit air and light and exclude rain. □□ **lou'vered** adj.

lov•age /lúvij/ n. aromatic herb of the carrot family.

love /luv/ • n. **1** deep affection; fondness. **2** sexual passion. **3** sexual relations. **4** beloved one; sweetheart. **5** (in some games) no score; nil. • v.tr. **1** feel love or deep fondness for. **2** delight in; admire; greatly cherish. **3** colloq. like very much (loves books). □ **fall in love** develop a great (esp. sexual) love (for). **for love** for pleasure not profit. **for the love of** for the sake of. **in love** enamored (of). **love affair** romantic relationship between two people; passion for something. **love apple** archaic tomato. **love child** child born out of wedlock. **love-hate relationship** intense relationship involving ambivalent feelings. **love life** one's amorous or sexual relationships. **love nest** place of intimate lovemaking. **love seat** small sofa for two. **make love 1** have sexual intercourse (with). **2** archaic pay amorous attention (to). **not for love or money** colloq. not in any circumstances. □□ **lov'a•ble** adj. **love'a•ble** adj. **love'less** adj.

■ n. **1** devotion, attraction, friendship, adoration; liking, enjoyment, preference; concern, care. **2** lust, fervor, rapture, infatuation. **4** darling, dear(est), honey, sweetie (pie); lover, mate; girlfriend, boyfriend, beau. • v. **1** adore, idolize, dote on, treasure, hold dear, colloq. have a crush on. **2, 3** take pleasure in, relish, be fond of, enjoy, appreciate, colloq. get a kick out of. □ **love affair** amour, romance; mania. **make love** embrace, cuddle, caress, fondle, colloq. neck, pet; romance; colloq. have sex. □□ **lovable** adorable, darling, dear, endearing, sweet, affectionate, colloq. cute. **loveless** unloving; unloved.

love•bird /lúvbərd/ n. **1** small parrot that seems to be affectionate to its mate. **2** [in pl.] pair of overtly affectionate lovers.

love•lorn /lúvlawrn/ adj. pining from unrequited love.

love•ly /lúvlee/ • adj. (**love•li•er**, **love•li•est**) **1** exquisitely beautiful. **2** colloq. pleasing; delightful. • n. (pl. **–lies**) colloq. pretty woman. □□ **love'li•ness** n.

■ adj. **1** good-looking, pretty, handsome, attractive, bewitching, ravishing, gorgeous. **2** satisfying, enjoyable, nice, pleasant.

love•mak•ing /lúvmayking/ n. **1** amorous sexual activity, esp. sexual intercourse. **2** archaic courtship.

lov•er /lúvər/ n. **1** person in love with another. **2** person with whom another is having sexual relations. **3** [in pl.] couple in love or having sexual relations. **4** person who enjoys something specified (music lover).

■ **1** see LOVE n. 4. **4** see enthusiast (ENTHUSIASM).

love•sick /lúvsik/ adj. languishing with romantic love. □□ **love'sick•ness** n.

lov•ing /lúving/ • adj. feeling or showing love; affectionate. • n. affection; active love. □ **loving cup** two-handled drinking cup. □□ **lov'ing•ly** adv. **lov'ing•ness** n.

■ adj. see AFFECTIONATE. □□ **lovingly** see fondly (FOND).

low¹ /lō/ • adj. **1** not high or tall. **2** not elevated. **3** of or in humble rank. **4** small or less than normal amount or extent or intensity. **5** dejected; lacking vigor. **6** not shrill or loud. **7** commonplace. **8** unfavorable (low opinion). **9** abject; vulgar. • n. **1** low or the lowest level or number. **2** area of low pressure. • adv. **1** in or to a low position or state. **2** in a low pitch or tone. □ **low-ball** n. Cards a type of poker. v. underestimate or underbid a price (usu. for a service) deliberately. **low beam** automobile headlight providing short-range illumination. **low-class** of low quality or social class. **low comedy** comedy that borders on farce. **low-cut** (of a dress, etc.) made with a low neckline. **lowdown** adj. abject; mean; dishonorable. n. colloq. relevant information (about). **lowgrade** of low quality. **low-key** lacking intensity; restrained. **low-level** Computing (of a programming language) close in form to machine language. **lowlying** at low altitude (above sea level, etc.). **low-pitched 1** (of a sound) low. **2** (of a roof) having only a slight slope. **low pressure 1** little demand for activity or exertion. **2** (of atmospheric pressure) below average. **low profile** avoidance of attention or publicity. **low tide** time or level of the tide at its ebb. □□ **low'ish** adj. **low'ness** n.

■ adj. **1** short, small, stubby. **2** low-lying. **3** poor, lowborn, lowly, inferior, ignoble. **4** reduced. **5** weak, frail, feeble; miserable, dismal; unhappy, depressed, sad, despondent. **6** quiet, soft, subdued, muted, muffled. **7** low-grade, mediocre. **8** critical, adverse.

9 contemptible, foul, nasty; coarse, indecent, crude, rude, offensive. □ **low-cut** revealing. **low-down** (*n.*) intelligence, data, facts, inside story *or* information, *sl.* dope. **low-pitched 1** see LOW¹ *adj.* 6 above.

low² /lō/ • *n.* sound made by cattle; moo. • *v.intr.* utter this sound.
■ *v.* bellow.

low•born /lóbawrn/ *adj.* of humble birth.

low•brow /lóbrow/ • *adj.* not intellectual or cultured. • *n.* lowbrow person. □□ **low′browed** *adj.*

low•er /lóər/ • *adj.* (*n.*) (compar. of LOW¹). **1** less high in position or status. **2** situated below another part. **3 a** situated on less high land (*Lower Egypt*). **b** situated to the south (*Lower California*). • *adv.* in *or* to a lower position, status, etc. • *v.* **1** *tr.* let *or* haul down. **2** *tr. & intr.* make or become lower. **3** *tr.* degrade. □ **lower class** working-class people. **lower-class** *adj.* of the lower class. □□ **low′er•most** *adj.*
■ *adj.* **1** further down; see also INFERIOR *adj.* 1. **2, 3a** under. **3 b** southern. • *adv.* see DOWNWARD *adv.* • *v.* **1** bring *or* put down, drop. **2** reduce, decrease, mark down, lessen; turn down, quiet, moderate, soften, tone down. **3** abase, debase, shame, humiliate; (*lower oneself*) see CONDESCEND 1. □ **lower-class** see PLEBEIAN *adj.* 1.

low•er•case /lóərkays/ • *n.* small letters. • *adj.* of or having small letters.

low•land /lóland/ • *n.* low-lying country. • *adj.* of or in lowland. □□ **low′land•er** *n.*
■ *n.* see FLAT¹ *n.* 2.

low•ly /lólee/ *adj.* (**low•li•er, low•li•est**) humble; unpretentious. □□ **low′li•ness** *n.*
■ see HUMBLE *adj.* 2, MODEST 1, 2.

lox¹ /loks/ *n.* liquid oxygen.

lox² /loks/ *n.* smoked salmon.

loy•al /lóyəl/ *adj.* faithful. □□ **loy′al•ly** *adv.* **loy′al•ty** *n.*
■ true, dependable, devoted, trustworthy, reliable. □□ **loyalty** fidelity, allegiance, patriotism, dedication.

loy•al•ist /lóyəlist/ *n.* person who remains loyal to the legitimate sovereign, government, etc. □□ **loy′al•ism** *n.*

loz•enge /lózinj/ *n.* **1** diamond-shaped figure. **2** sweet *or* medicinal tablet, for dissolving in the mouth.

LP *abbr.* long-playing (phonograph record).
■ see RECORD *n.* 3.

LPG *abbr.* liquefied petroleum gas.

LPN *abbr.* licensed practical nurse.

LSD *abbr.* lysergic acid diethylamide.

Lt. *abbr.* lieutenant.

Ltd. *abbr.* limited.

Lu *symb. Chem.* lutetium.

lub•ber /lúbər/ *n.* clumsy person. □□ **lub′ber•ly** *adj. & adv.*

lu•bri•cant /lóobrikənt/ • *n.* substance used to reduce friction. • *adj.* lubricating.

lu•bri•cate /lóobrikayt/ *v.tr.* **1** apply oil *or* grease, etc. **2** make slippery. □□ **lu•bri•ca•tion** /-káyshən/ *n.* **lu′bri•ca•tive** *adj.* **lu′bri•ca•tor** *n.*
■ oil, grease.

lu•cid /lóosid/ *adj.* **1** expressing or expressed clearly. **2** sane. See synonym study at SENSI-

BLE. □□ **lu•cid′i•ty** *n.* **lu′cid•ly** *adv.* **lu′cid•ness** *n.*
■ **1** see CLEAR *adj.* 4. **2** see RIGHT *adj.* 4, SANE 1. □□ **lucidity** see CLARITY.

Lu•ci•fer /lóosifər/ *n.* the devil; Satan.

luck /luk/ *n.* **1** good or bad fortune. **2** circumstances of life (beneficial or not) brought by this. **3** good fortune; success due to chance. □ **no such luck** *colloq.* unfortunately not. □□ **luck′less** *adj.*
■ **1, 2** destiny, fate, accident. **3** serendipity; stroke of luck, *colloq.* break. □□ **luckless** see UNFORTUNATE *adj.* 1.

luck•i•ly /lúkilee/ *adv.* **1** (qualifying a whole sentence or clause) fortunately (*luckily there was enough food*). **2** in a lucky or fortunate manner.

luck•y /lúkee/ *adj.* (**luck•i•er, luck•i•est**) **1** having or resulting from good luck. **2** bringing good luck. □□ **luck′i•ness** *n.*
■ **1** fortunate; charmed; blessed. **2** favorable, auspicious.

lu•cra•tive /lóokrətiv/ *adj.* profitable; yielding financial gain. □□ **lu′cra•tive•ly** *adv.* **lu′cra•tive•ness** *n.*
■ see *profitable* (PROFIT).

lu•cre /lóokər/ *n. derog.* financial profit or gain.

lu•di•crous /lóodikrəs/ *adj.* absurd; ridiculous; laughable. See synonym study at ABSURD. □□ **lu′di•crous•ly** *adv.* **lu′di•crous•ness** *n.*
■ farcical, preposterous, asinine, foolish, silly, crazy.

luff /luf/ *v.tr.* [also *absol.*] steer (a ship) nearer the wind.

luf•fa var. of LOOFAH.

lug /lug/ • *v.* (**lugged, lug•ging**) *tr.* drag or carry with effort. • *n.* nut that fastens a wheel to an axle.
■ *v.* tug, tow, haul, heave, pull; *colloq.* schlep, tote.

luge /loozh/ • *n.* toboggan ridden in a supine position down a chute. • *v.intr.* ride on a luge.

Lu•ger /lóogər/ *n.* type of German automatic pistol.

lug•gage /lúgij/ *n.* traveler's suitcases, bags, etc.
■ baggage, gear, belongings.

lug•ger /lúgər/ *n.* small ship with a quadrilateral sail.

lug•sail /lúgsayl, səl/ *n.* sail for a lugger.

lu•gu•bri•ous /loogóobreeəs, -gyóo-/ *adj.* doleful; mournful; dismal. See synonym study at GLUM. □□ **lu•gu′bri•ous•ly** *adv.* **lu•gu′bri•ous•ness** *n.*

luke•warm /lóokwáwrm/ *adj.* **1** moderately warm; tepid. **2** unenthusiastic; indifferent. □□ **luke′warm′ly** *adv.* **luke′warm′ness** *n.*
■ cool, indifferent, halfhearted.

lull /lul/ • *v.* **1** soothe or send to sleep. **2** *tr.* [usu. foll. by *into*] deceive (a person) into confidence. **3** *intr.* (of noise, a storm, etc.) abate or fall quiet. • *n.* calm period.
■ *v.* **1** pacify, mollify, tranquilize. • *n.* pause, respite, *colloq.* letup; quiet, hush, stillness, peacefulness.

lul•la•by /lúləbī/ *n.* (*pl.* **–bies**) soothing song to send a child to sleep.

lu•lu /lōōlōō/ *n. sl.* remarkable or excellent person or thing.

lum•ba•go /lumbáygō/ *n.* rheumatic pain in the lower back.

lum•bar /lúmbər, –baar/ *adj.* of the lower back area.

lum•ber[1] /lúmbər/ *v.intr.* move clumsily. □□ **lum'ber•ing** *adj.*

lum•ber[2] /lúmbər/ • *n.* **1** timber cut and prepared for use. **2** disused or cumbersome objects. • *v.intr.* cut and prepare forest timber. □□ **lum'ber•er** *n.* **lum'ber•ing** *n.*

■ *n.* **1** wood, beams, planks, boards. **2** odds and ends, junk, clutter.

lum•ber•jack /lúmbərjak/ *n.* (also **lum•ber•man** /–mən/, *pl.* **–men**) one who fells, prepares, or conveys lumber.

lu•mi•nar•y /lōōmineree/ *n.* (*pl.* **–ies**) **1** natural light-giving body. **2** source of intellectual or moral inspiration. **3** celebrity.

■ **2** see INSPIRATION 1. **3** see CELEBRITY 1.

lu•mi•nes•cence /lōōminésəns/ *n.* emission of light without heat. □□ **lu•mi•nes'cent** *adj.*

■ radiance, glow. □□ **luminescent** see LUMINOUS 2.

lu•mi•nous /lōōminəs/ *adj.* **1** shedding light. **2** phosphorescent; visible in darkness (*luminous paint*). □□ **lu•mi•nos•i•ty** /–nósitee/ *n.* **lu'mi•nous•ly** *adv.* **lu'mi•nous•ness** *n.*

■ **1** shining, bright, brilliant, lit (up), illuminated, radiant. **2** glowing, aglow, fluorescent.

lum•mox /lúməks/ *n. colloq.* clumsy or stupid person.

lump[1] /lump/ • *n.* **1** compact shapeless mass. **2** tumor; swelling; bruise. **3** heavy, dull, or ungainly person. • *v.* **1** *tr.* mass together or group indiscriminately. **2** *intr.* become lumpy. □ **lump sum 1** sum covering a number of items. **2** money paid down at once. □□ **lump'y** *adj.*

■ *n.* **1** piece, clod, chunk, wad, clump, hunk; wedge; heap, pile. **2** bump, growth, bulge, knob; cyst, boil. • *v.* **1** (*lump together*) combine, join, consolidate, bunch, throw together. □□ **lumpy** bumpy, uneven, grainy.

lump[2] /lump/ *v.tr. colloq.* put up with ungraciously (*like it or lump it*).

lu•na•cy /lōōnəsee/ *n.* (*pl.* **–cies**) **1** insanity. **2** great folly.

■ **1** madness, dementia, craziness, psychosis, mania. **2** foolishness, senselessness, stupidity; eccentricity.

lu•na moth /lōōnə/ *n.* large N. American moth with crescent-shaped spots on pale green wings.

lu•nar /lōōnər/ *adj.* of, relating to, or determined by the moon. □ **lunar module** small craft for traveling between the moon and an orbiting spacecraft. **lunar month 1** interval between new moons (about 29½ days). **2** (in general use) four weeks.

lu•nate /lōōnayt/ *adj.* crescent-shaped.

lu•na•tic /lōōnətik/ • *n.* **1** insane person. **2** someone foolish or eccentric. • *adj.* mad; foolish. □ **lunatic fringe** extreme or eccentric minority group.

■ *n.* see MADMAN. • *adj.* see MAD *adj.* 1.

lunch /lunch/ • *n.* midday meal. • *v. intr.* eat lunch. □ **out to lunch** *sl.* unaware; incompetent. □□ **lunch'er** *n.*

lunch•box /lúnchboks/ *n.* container for a packed lunch.

lunch•eon /lúnchən/ *n. formal* lunch. □ **luncheon meat** sliced, cold prepared meats used for sandwiches, etc.

lunch•eon•ette /lúnchənét/ *n.* restaurant serving light lunches.

lung /lung/ *n.* either of the pair of respiratory organs in humans and many other vertebrates.

lunge /lunj/ • *n.* **1** sudden movement forward. **2** basic attacking move in fencing. • *v.* **1** *intr.* make or deliver a lunge. **2** *tr.* drive (a weapon, etc.) violently in some direction.

■ *n.* **2** thrust, jab, strike. • *v.* **1** dive, plunge, charge, pounce, dash. **2** thrust, stab.

lu•pine[1] /lōōpin/ *n.* plant with long tapering spikes of blue, purple, pink, white, or yellow flowers.

lu•pine[2] /lōōpīn/ *adj.* of or like a wolf or wolves.

lu•pus /lōōpəs/ *n.* any of various ulcerous skin diseases, esp. tuberculosis of the skin.

lurch[1] /lərch/ • *n.* stagger; sudden unsteady movement. • *v.intr.* stagger; move suddenly and unsteadily.

■ *n.* pitch; list, tilt, toss. • *v.* sway, stumble, reel; veer.

lurch[2] /lərch/ *n.* □ **leave in the lurch** desert (a friend, etc.) in difficulties.

■ □ **leave in the lurch** abandon, forsake; drop, jilt.

lure /lōōr/ • *v.tr.* **1** entice, usu. by baiting. **2** attract with the promise of a reward. • *n.* thing used to entice. □□ **lur'ing** *adj.* **lur'ing•ly** *adv.*

■ *v.* tempt, attract, coax, seduce, draw in, charm, persuade. • *n.* bait, decoy, inducement, magnet, *sl.* come-on.

lu•rid /lōōrid/ *adj.* **1** vivid or glowing in color. **2** sensational; horrifying. **3** ghastly; wan (*lurid complexion*). □□ **lu'rid•ly** *adv.* **lu'rid•ness** *n.*

■ **1** glaring, flaming; fluorescent, loud, garish. **2** shocking, graphic; horrid, grisly, gruesome, frightful. **3** pale, ashen, sallow.

lurk /lərk/ *v.intr.* **1** linger furtively. **2 a** lie in ambush. **b** hide, esp. for sinister purposes. **3** (as **lurking** *adj.*) latent (*a lurking suspicion*). □□ **lurk'er** *n.*

■ *v.* **1, 2** loiter; skulk, prowl, sneak, (lie in) wait. **3** (**lurking**) see *sneaking* (SNEAK *v.* 3).

lus•cious /lúshəs/ *adj.* **1** richly pleasing to the senses. **2** voluptuously attractive. □□ **lus'cious•ly** *adv.* **lus'cious•ness** *n.*

■ **1** delicious, mouthwatering, tasty, *colloq.* scrumptious.

lush[1] /lush/ *adj.* **1** (of vegetation) luxuriant and succulent. **2** luxurious. See synonym study at PROFUSE. □□ **lush'ly** *adv.* **lush'ness** *n.*

■ **1** thick, lavish; juicy, ripe. **2** palatial, elaborate, sumptuous, *colloq.* ritzy, plush.

lush[2] /lush/ *n. sl.* alcoholic; drunkard.

lust /lust/ • *n.* **1** strong sexual desire. **2** passionate desire for. • *v. intr.* have a strong desire. □□ **lust'ful** *adj.* **lust'ful·ly** *adv.* **lust' ful·ness** *n.*

■ *n.* **1** passion, sexual appetite. **2** drive, voracity, avidness, ambition. • *v.* (*lust after*) crave, hunger or thirst for *or* after, ache for. □□ **lustful** libidinous, salacious, *sl.* horny.

lus·ter /lústər/ *n.* **1** gloss; brilliance. **2** shining surface. **3** splendor; glory. □□ **lus'ter·less** *adj.* **lus'trous** *adj.* **lus'trous·ly** *adv.* **lus'trous·ness** *n.*

■ *n.* **1** sheen, radiance, iridescence. **3** attractiveness; renown, honor, distinction. □□ **lustrous** glossy, shiny, polished.

lust·y /lústee/ *adj.* (**lust·i·er, lust·i·est**) **1** healthy and strong. **2** vigorous or lively. □□ **lust'i·ly** *adv.* **lust'i·ness** *n.*

■ energetic, robust, hale and hearty; buxom.

lute /loot/ *n.* guitarlike instrument with a long neck and pear-shaped body.

lu·te·ti·um /looteeshəm/ *n. Chem.* silvery metallic element of the lanthanide series. ¶Symb.: **Lu.**

Lu·ther·an /lóothərən/ • *n.* **1** follower of Martin Luther, German religious reformer d. 1546. **2** member of the Lutheran Church. • *adj.* of or characterized by the theology of Martin Luther. □□ **Lu'ther·an·ism** *n.*

lutz /luts/ *n.* figure skating jump in which the skater jumps from the outside back edge of one skate, rotates in the air, and lands on the outside back edge of the other skate.

Lux·em·bourg·er /lúksəmbərgər/ *n.* **1** native or national of Luxembourg. **2** person who traces descent from Luxembourg.

lux·u·ri·ant /lugzhóoreeənt, lukshóor-/ *adj.* **1** profuse in growth; prolific; exuberant. **2** florid; richly ornate. See synonym study at PROFUSE. □□ **lux·u'ri·ance** *n.* **lux·u'ri·ant· ly** *adv.*

■ **1** abundant, lush, rich; luxurious; lavish, thriving, rife, teeming. **2** elaborate, fancy, flamboyant, showy, ostentatious, flashy.

lux·u·ri·ate /lugzhóoreeayt, lukshóor-/ *v. intr.* **1** [foll. by *in*] enjoy in a luxurious manner. **2** relax in comfort.

■ **1** (*luxuriate in*) wallow in, bask in, delight in, revel in, savor. **2** be *or* live in the lap of luxury, enjoy oneself.

lux·u·ri·ous /lugzhóoreeəs, lukshóor-/ *adj.* **1** supplied with luxuries. **2** extremely comfortable. □□ **lux·u'ri·ous·ly** *adv.* **lux·u'ri· ous·ness** *n.*

■ **1** opulent, sumptuous, grand, lavish, splendid, fancy, *colloq.* ritzy, plushy, posh, swank.

lux·u·ry /lúgzhəree, lúkshəree/ *n.* (*pl.* **–ries**) **1** choice or costly surroundings, possessions, etc. **2** [*attrib.*] providing great comfort; expensive (*luxury apartment*).

■ **1** opulence, splendor, extravagance; indulgence. **2** (*attrib.*) see OPULENT 1, EXPENSIVE 1.

495

Lw *symb. Chem.* lawrencium.

-ly[1] /lee/ *suffix* forming adjectives esp. from nouns, meaning: **1** having the qualities of (*princely*). **2** recurring at intervals of (*daily*).

-ly[2] /lee/ *suffix* forming adverbs from adjectives, denoting esp. manner or degree (*boldly, happily, miserably, deservedly*).

ly·chee var. of LITCHI.

Ly·cra /líkrə/ *n. propr.* elastic fiber or fabric used esp. for close-fitting sports clothing.

lye /lī/ *n.* strong alkaline solution, esp. for washing.

ly·ing[1] /lí-ing/ *pres. part.* of LIE[1]. *n.* a place to lie (*a dry lying*).

ly·ing[2] /lí-ing/ *pres. part* of LIE[2]. *adj.* deceitful; false.

■ untruthful, dishonest, deceptive, duplicitous.

Lyme dis·ease /līm/ *n.* disease transmitted by ticks, characterized by rash, fever, fatigue, and joint pain.

lymph /limf/ *n.* colorless fluid from body tissues. □ **lymph node** (or **gland**) small mass of tissue that conveys lymph. □□ **lym'phoid** *adj.* **lym'phous** *adj.*

lym·phat·ic /limfátik/ *adj.* **1** of, secreting, or conveying lymph. **2** flabby; sluggish.

lym·pho·ma /limfómə/ *n.* (*pl.* **lym·pho·mas** or **lym·pho·ma·ta** /-mətə/) malignant tumor of the lymph nodes.

lynch /linch/ *v. tr.* (of a mob) put (a person) to death without a legal trial. □□ **lynch'er** *n.* **lynch'ing** *n.*

lynx /lingks/ *n.* wild cat with a short tail, spotted fur, and tufted ear tips.

lyre /līr/ *n.* ancient U-shaped harplike instrument.

lyre·bird /lírbərd/ *n.* Australian bird, the male of which has a lyre-shaped tail display.

lyr·ic /lírik/ • *adj.* **1** (of poetry) expressing the writer's emotions. **2** meant to be sung, songlike. • *n.* **1** lyric poem. **2** [in *pl.*] words of a song.

■ *adj.* **1** subjective, sentimental. **2** melodic, musical, melodious; sweet, lilting. • *n.* **2** (*lyrics*) libretto.

lyr·i·cal /lírikəl/ *adj.* **1** = LYRIC *adj.* **1**. **2** *colloq.* highly enthusiastic (*wax lyrical about*). □□ **lyr'i·cal·ly** *adv.*

■ **2** ecstatic, impassioned, emotional, exuberant.

lyr·i·cism /lírisizəm/ *n.* character or quality of being lyric.

lyr·i·cist /lírisist/ *n.* person who writes the words to a song.

ly·ser·gic ac·id /līsórjik/ *n.* crystalline acid. □ **lysergic acid diethylamide** /dī-éthilámīd/ powerful hallucinogenic drug. ¶ Abbr.: **LSD.**

-lysis /lisis/ *comb. form* forming nouns denoting disintegration or decomposition (*electrolysis*).

Mm

M¹ /em/ *n.* (*pl.* **Ms** or **M's; m's**) **1** thirteenth letter of the alphabet. **2** (as a Roman numeral) 1,000.

M² *abbr.* (also **M.**) **1** Master. **2** *Monsieur*. **3** mega–. **4** *Chem.* molar. **5** Mach. **6** *Mus.* major.

m *abbr.* (also **m.**) **1 a** masculine. **b** male. **2** married. **3** mile(s). **4** meter(s). **5** million(s). **6** minute(s). **7** milli–.

MA *abbr.* **1** Master of Arts. **2** Massachusetts (in official postal use).

ma /maa/ *n. colloq.* mother.

ma'am /mam/ *n.* madam.

ma•ca•bre /məkáábər/ *adj.* (also **ma•ca'ber**) grim, gruesome.

  ■ ghastly, grisly, gory, grotesque, ghoulish, fiendish, eerie, fearsome; deathly, ghostly.

mac•ad•am /məkádəm/ *n.* broken stone used for road building. □□ **mac•ad'am•ize** *v.*

mac•a•da•mi•a /mákədáymeeə/ *n.* Australian evergreen tree bearing edible nutlike seeds.

mac•a•ro•ni /mákərónee/ *n.* tubular variety of pasta.

mac•a•roon /mákərōōn/ *n.* small light cake or cookie made with egg white, sugar, and ground almonds or coconut.

ma•caw /məkáw/ *n.* long-tailed brightly colored parrot native to S. and Central America.

Mace /mays/ *n. propr.* aerosol spray used to disable an attacker temporarily. □□ **mace** *v.*

mace¹ /mays/ *n.* **1** heavy spiked club used esp. in the Middle Ages. **2** ceremonial staff of office.

mace² /mays/ *n.* fibrous layer between a nutmeg's shell and its husk, dried and ground as a spice.

mac•er•ate /másərayt/ *v.* **1** *tr. & intr.* make or become soft by soaking. **2** *intr.* waste away, as by fasting. □□ **mac•er•a•tion** /-ráyshən/ *n.* **mac'er•a•tor** *n.*

Mach /maak, mak/ *n.* (in full **Mach number**) ratio of the speed of a body to the speed of sound in the surrounding medium.

ma•chet•e /məshétee, məchétee/ *n.* heavy knife used in Central America and the W. Indies as a tool and weapon.

Mach•i•a•vel•li•an /mákeeəvéleeən/ *adj.* elaborately cunning; scheming, unscrupulous. □□ **Mach•i•a•vel'li•an•ism** *n.*

  ■ deceitful, cunning, shrewd, crafty, wily, foxy.

mach•i•nate /mákinayt, másh-/ *v.intr.* lay plots; intrigue. □□ **mach•i•na•tion** /-náyshən/ *n.* **mach'i•na•tor** *n.* See synonym study at PLOT

  ■ conspire, plot, scheme, collude, connive, maneuver, design. □□ **machination** plot, scheme, intrigue, maneuver, design, stratagem, ruse, trick.

ma•chine /məsheen/ • *n.* **1** apparatus using or applying mechanical power, having several interrelated parts. **2** particular kind of machine, esp. a vehicle or an electrical or electronic apparatus, etc. **3** controlling system of an organization, etc. (*the party machine*). • *v.tr.* make or operate on with a machine. □ **machine gun** automatic gun giving continuous, rapid fire. **machine-readable** in a form that a computer can process. **machine tool** mechanically operated tool.

  ■ *n.* **1** mechanism, device, contrivance, appliance, instrument, implement. **2** engine, motor; car, motor car, automobile. **3** organization; ring, gang, cabal. • *v.* shape, manufacture; sew (up).

ma•chin•er•y /məsheenəree/ *n.* (*pl.* **–ies**) **1** machines collectively. **2** components of a machine; mechanism. **3** means devised or available (*machinery for decision making*).

  ■ **1** see APPARATUS. **2** see WORK *n.* 6.

ma•chin•ist /məsheenist/ *n.* **1** person who operates a machine, esp. a machine tool. **2** person who makes machinery.

ma•chis•mo /məcheezmō, –chízmō/ *n.* exaggeratedly assertive manliness; show of masculinity.

ma•cho /maachō/ *adj.* showily manly or virile.

  ■ masculine; proud, arrogant.

mack•er•el /mákərəl, mákrəl/ *n.* (*pl.* same or **mack•er•els**) N. Atlantic marine fish used for food.

mack•in•tosh /mákintosh/ *n.* (also **mac'in•tosh**) waterproof, esp. rubberized, coat.

mac•ra•mé /mákrəmáy/ *n.* **1** art of knotting cord or string to make decorative articles. **2** articles made in this way.

macro- /mákrō/ *comb. form* **1** long. **2** large; large-scale.

mac•ro•bi•ot•ic /mákrōbīótik/ • *adj.* of a diet intended to prolong life, comprising pure vegetable foods, brown rice, etc. • *n.* [in *pl.*; treated as *sing.*] theory of such a diet.

mac•ro•cosm /mákrōkozəm/ *n.* **1** universe. **2** the whole of a complex structure. □□ **mac•ro•cos•mic** /-kózmik/ *adj.* **mac•ro•cos'mi•cal•ly** *adv.*

ma•cron /máykraan, mák-/ *n.* diacritical mark (‾) over a long or stressed vowel.

mac•ro•scop•ic /mákrəskópik/ *adj.* **1** visible to the naked eye. **2** regarded in terms of large units. □□ **mac•ro•scop'i•cal•ly** *adv.*

mad /mad/ *adj.* (**mad•der, mad•dest**) **1** insane; having a disordered mind. **2** wildly foolish. **3** [often foll. by *about*] wildly excited or infatuated (*is chess-mad*). **4** *colloq.* angry. **5** (of an animal) rabid. □ **like mad** *colloq.* with great energy, intensity, or enthusiasm. □□ **mad'ness** *n.*

  ■ **1** psychotic, neurotic, schizophrenic, schizoid; insane, deranged, certifiable, crazed, demented, lunatic, *colloq.* crazy, *sl.* out of one's head, screwy, cuckoo, nuts. **2** silly, childish, immature, puerile, wild, nonsensical, foolhardy, madcap, heedless. **3** crazy, ardent, enthusiastic, eager, avid, zealous, passionate, *colloq.* dotty, *sl.* nuts. **4** furious, infuriated, incensed, enraged, irate, fuming, raging, berserk. **5** wild, ferocious. □ **like mad** madly, feverishly, in a frenzy, frenziedly, desperately, excitedly; enthusiastically, fervently, ardently. □□ **madness** insanity, lunacy, mania, mental illness; folly, foolishness, nonsense, *colloq.* craziness.

mad•am /mádəm/ *n.* **1** polite or respectful form of address or mode of reference to a woman. **2** woman brothel-keeper.

Mad•ame /mədáam, mádəm/ *n.* **1** (*pl.* **Mes•dames** /maydáam, –dám/) title or form of address corresponding to Mrs. or madam. **2** (**madame**) = MADAM 1.

mad•cap /mádkap/ • *adj.* **1** wildly impulsive. **2** undertaken without forethought. • *n.* wildly impulsive person.

■ *adj.* see IMPULSIVE.

mad•den /mádn/ *v.* **1** *tr. & intr.* make or become mad. **2** *tr.* irritate intensely. □□ **mad′den•ing** *adj.* **mad′den•ing•ly** *adv.*

■ **2** infuriate, anger, enrage, incense, provoke, inflame, vex, pique, gall, annoy, *colloq.* drive a person crazy *or* up the wall, *sl.* bug, burn up, tick off.

mad•der /mádər/ *n.* **1** herbaceous plant with yellowish flowers. **2** red dye obtained from the root of the madder.

made /mayd/ *past and past part.* of MAKE.

Ma•dei•ra /mədeérə/ *n.* amber-colored fortified white wine from the island of Madeira off the coast of N. Africa.

Mad•e•moi•selle /mádəməél, mádmwə–/ *n.* (*pl.* **-s** or **Mes•de•moi•selles** /máydmwə–/) title or form of address used of or to an unmarried woman; Miss.

mad•house /mádhows/ *n.* **1** *archaic* or *colloq.* mental home or hospital. **2** *colloq.* scene of confused uproar.

mad•ly /mádlee/ *adv.* **1** in a mad manner. **2** *colloq.* **a** passionately. **b** extremely.

■ **1** insanely, hysterically, dementedly, wildly, foolishly, stupidly, inanely. **2 a** ardently, fervently, furiously, fervidly, wildly. **b** excessively, desperately, intensely, wildly, exceedingly.

mad•man /mádmən, -man/ *n.* (*pl.* **-men**) man who is insane or who behaves insanely.

■ lunatic, psychopath, psychotic, maniac, crazy.

Ma•don•na /mədónə/ *n. Eccl.* **1** [prec. by *the*] name for the Virgin Mary. **2** picture or statue of the Madonna.

ma•dras /mádrəs, mədrás/ *n.* strong, lightweight cotton fabric with colored or white stripes, checks, etc.

ma•dra•sa /mədrásə/ *n.* (also **madrasah** or **medrese** /-drésə/) a Muslim seminary, consisting of classrooms and dormitories around a mosque.

mad•ri•gal /mádrigəl/ *n.* usu. 16th-c. or 17th-c. part song for several voices, usu. unaccompanied. □□ **mad′ri•gal•ist** *n.*

mad•wom•an /mádwōmən/ *n.* (*pl.* **-wom•en**) woman who is insane or who behaves insanely.

mael•strom /máylstrəm/ *n.* **1** great whirlpool. **2** state of confusion.

■ **1** see WHIRLPOOL. **2** see CHAOS.

maes•tro /místrō/ *n.* (*pl.* **maes•tri** /–stree/ or **–tros**) (often as a respectful form of address) **1** distinguished musician, esp. a conductor or performer. **2** great performer in any sphere.

Ma•fi•a /máafeeə, máf–/ *n.* organized international body of criminals. □□ **Ma•fi•o•so** /–ōsō/ *n.*

mag•a•zine /mágəzeén/ *n.* **1** periodical publication containing articles, stories, etc. **2** chamber for holding a supply of cartridges in a firearm. **3** similar device feeding a camera, slide projector, etc. **4** military store for arms, ammunition, etc.

■ **1** periodical, publication; see also JOURNAL 1. **4** arsenal, ammunition *or* munitions dump, armory.

ma•gen•ta /məjéntə/ • *n.* **1** brilliant crimson shade. **2** aniline dye of this color. • *adj.* of or colored with magenta.

mag•got /mágət/ *n.* soft-bodied larva of certain two-winged insects, esp. the housefly or bluebottle. □□ **mag′got•y** *adj.*

ma•gi *pl.* of MAGUS.

mag•ic /májik/ • *n.* **1 a** supposed art of influencing the course of events supernaturally. **b** witchcraft. **2** conjuring tricks. **3** enchanting quality or phenomenon. • *adj.* **1** of or resulting from magic. **2** producing surprising results. □□ **mag′i•cal** *adj.* **mag′i•cal•ly** *adv.*

■ *n.* **1** sorcery, wizardry, black magic, necromancy, voodoo. **2** legerdemain, prestidigitation, sleight of hand. **3** enchantment, allure, allurement, charm, bewitchment, spell, witchery. • *adj.* **1** magical, miraculous, necromantic, occult, mystic. **2** magical, miraculous, marvelous, amazing. □□ **magical** miraculous, magic, wonderful, enchanting, entrancing, bewitching; see also MAGIC *adj.*, MARVELOUS.

ma•gi•cian /məjíshən/ *n.* person skilled in magic.

■ wizard, sorcerer, sorceress, magus, necromancer, enchanter, enchantress, Houdini, Circe, witch.

mag•is•te•ri•al /májistéereeəl/ *adj.* **1** imperious. **2** of or conducted by a magistrate. □□ **mag•is•te′ri•al•ly** *adv.*

■ **1** see OVERBEARING, POMPOUS.

mag•is•trate /májistrayt, –strət/ *n.* **1** civil officer administering the law. **2** official conducting a court for minor cases and preliminary hearings (*magistrates' court*). □□ **mag•is•tra•cy** /májistrəsee/ *n.*

mag•ma /mágmə/ *n.* (*pl.* **mag•ma•ta** /–mətə/ or **mag•mas**) molten rock under the earth's crust, which forms igneous rock. □□ **mag•mat•ic** /–mátik/ *adj.*

Mag•na Car•ta /mágnə kaártə/ *n.* (also **Mag′na Char′ta**) charter of liberty and political rights obtained from King John of England in 1215.

mag•nan•i•mous /magnániməs/ *adj.* nobly generous; not petty in feelings or conduct. □□ **mag•na•nim•i•ty** /mágnənímitee/ *n.* **mag•nan′i•mous•ly** *adv.*

■ see GENEROUS 2. □□ **magnanimity** see HUMANITY 2.

mag•nate /mágnayt, –nət/ *n.* wealthy and

influential person, esp. in business (*shipping magnate*).

mag•ne•sia /magneˊezhə, –shə, –zyə/ *n.* magnesium oxide used as an antacid and laxative. □□ **mag•ne´sian** *adj.*

mag•ne•si•um /magneˊezeeəm/ *n. Chem.* silvery lightweight metallic element used in alloys. ¶Symb.: **Mg**.

mag•net /mágnit/ *n.* **1** piece of iron, steel, ore, etc., having properties of attracting or repelling iron. **2** lodestone.

mag•net•ic /magnétik/ *adj.* **1 a** having the properties of a magnet. **b** producing, produced by, or acting by magnetism. **2** very attractive or alluring (*a magnetic personality*). □ **magnetic field** region of variable force around magnets, magnetic materials, or current-carrying conductors. **magnetic resonance imaging** noninvasive diagnostic technique employing a scanner to obtain computerized images of internal body tissue. ¶Abbr.: **MRI. magnetic tape** tape coated with magnetic material for recording sound or pictures or for the storage of information. □□ **mag•net´i•cal•ly** *adv.*

■ **2** attracting, engaging, captivating, enthralling, seductive, entrancing, bewitching, beguiling.

mag•net•ism /mágnitizəm/ *n.* **1 a** magnetic phenomena and their study. **b** property of producing these phenomena. **2** attraction; personal charm.

■ **2** appeal, allure, magic, lure, attractiveness, pull, seductiveness, irresistibility, draw, charisma.

mag•net•ize /mágnitīz/ *v.tr.* **1** give magnetic properties to. **2** make into a magnet. **3** attract as or like a magnet. □□ **mag•net´iz•a•ble** *adj.* **mag•net•i•za´tion** *n.* **mag´net•iz•er** *n.*

mag•ne•to /magneˊetō/ *n.* (*pl.* –**tos**) electric generator using permanent magnets and producing high voltage.

mag•nif•i•cent /magnífisənt/ *adj.* **1** splendid, stately. **2** sumptuously or lavishly constructed or adorned. **3** *colloq.* fine, excellent. □□ **mag•nif´i•cence** *n.* **mag•nif´i•cent•ly** *adv.*

■ **1** glorious, grand, impressive, imposing, awe-inspiring, brilliant, commanding, august, noble. **2** sumptuous, lavish, exquisite, gorgeous, resplendent. **3** see SUPERB.

mag•ni•fy /mágnifī/ *v.tr.* (–**fies, –fied**) **1** make (a thing) appear larger than it is, as with a lens. **2** exaggerate. **3** intensify. □□ **mag•ni•fi•ca´tion** *n.* **mag´ni•fi•er** *n.*

■ **1** enlarge, expand, amplify, inflate, increase, augment. **2** overstate, *colloq.* blow up. **3** heighten, build up, *colloq.* boost; aggravate, worsen. □□ **magnification** *n.* enlargement, amplification; buildup, strengthening, enhancement; enlargement, amplification.

mag•ni•tude /mágnitōōd, –tyōōd/ *n.* **1** largeness. **2** size. **3** importance. **4** degree of brightness of a star.

■ **1, 2** greatness, extent, bigness, immensity, enormousness, dimension(s). **3** signifi-

cance, consequence, note; see also *importance* (IMPORTANT).

mag•no•lia /magnōlyə/ *n.* **1** tree with dark-green foliage and large waxlike flowers. **2** pale creamy-pink color.

mag•num /mágnəm/ *n.* (*pl.* **mag•nums**) wine bottle of about twice the standard size.

mag•num o•pus /mágnəm ōpəs/ *n.* **1** great work of art, literature, etc. **2** most important work of an artist, writer, etc.

■ see MASTERPIECE.

mag•pie /mágpī/ *n.* **1** kind of crow with a long pointed tail, black-and-white plumage, and noisy behavior. **2** chatterer. **3** person who collects things indiscriminately.

ma•gus /máygəs/ *n.* (*pl.* **ma•gi** /máyjī/) **1** priest of ancient Persia. **2** (**the Magi**) the 'wise men' from the East who brought gifts to the infant Christ (Matt. 2:1).

Mag•yar /mágyaar/ • *n.* **1** member of a Ural-Altaic people now predominant in Hungary. **2** language of this people. • *adj.* of or relating to this people or language.

ma•ha•ra•ja /ma͞aharáaja, –zha/ *n.* (also **ma•ha•ra´jah**) *hist.* title of some princes of India.

ma•ha•ra•ni /ma͞aharáanee/ *n.* (also **ma•ha•ra´nee**) *hist.* maharaja's wife or widow.

ma•ha•ri•shi /ma͞ahareéshi/ *n.* great Hindu sage.

ma•hat•ma /məháatmə, –hát-/ *n.* **1** (esp. in India) revered person. **2** each of a class of persons in India and Tibet supposed by some to have preternatural powers.

Ma•hi•can /məheˊekən/ *n.* (also **Mo•hi´can**) **1** N. American people native to the upper Hudson River Valley of New York state. **2** member of this people.

mah-jongg /maajóng, –jáwng, –zhóng, –zháwng/ *n.* (also **mah´jong´**) Chinese game for four resembling rummy and played with 136 or 144 pieces called tiles.

ma•hog•a•ny /məhógənee/ *n.* (*pl.* –**nies**) **1 a** reddish-brown wood used for furniture. **b** color of this. **2** tropical tree yielding this wood.

ma•hout /məhówt/ *n.* (esp. in India) elephant driver.

maid /mayd/ *n.* **1** female domestic servant. **2** *archaic* or *poet.* girl or young woman. □ **maid of honor** principal bridesmaid.

■ **1** housemaid, maidservant, domestic, chambermaid, lady's maid, charwoman. **2** young lady, schoolgirl, miss, mademoiselle.

maid•en /máyd'n/ • *n. archaic* or *poet.* girl; young unmarried woman. • *adj.* **1** unmarried (*maiden aunt*). **2** first (*maiden voyage*). □ **maiden name** wife's surname before marriage. □□ **maid´en•hood** *n.* **maid´en•ish** *adj.* **maid´en•like** *adj.* **maid´en•ly** *adj.*

■ *n.* see MAID 2. • *adj.* **2** inaugural, initial.

maid•en•hair /máyd'nhair/ *n.* (in full **maidenhair fern**) fern with fine hairlike stalks and delicate fronds.

maid•en•head /máyd'nhed/ *n.* **1** virginity. **2** hymen.

maid•serv•ant /máydservənt/ *n.* female domestic servant.

mail¹ /mayl/ • *n.* **1** letters and parcels, etc., conveyed by the postal system. **2** postal system. **3** one complete delivery or collection of mail. • v.tr. send by mail. □ **mail carrier** person who delivers mail. **mailing list** list of people to whom advertising matter, information, etc., is to be mailed. **mail order** order for goods sent by mail.

■ n. **1** correspondence. **2** postal service, post office. • v. dispatch.

mail² /mayl/ n. armor made of rings, chains, or plates, joined together flexibly. □□ **mailed** adj.

mail•bag /máylbag/ n. large sack or bag for carrying mail.

mail•box /máylboks/ n. **1** receptacle for pickup and delivery of mail. **2** computer file in which electronic mail is stored.

mail•man /máylmən/ n. (pl. **-men**) mail carrier.

maim /maym/ v.tr. cripple, disable, mutilate.
■ lame, incapacitate, wound, wing, hamstring.

main /mayn/ • adj. **1** chief in size, importance, etc.; principal (the main part). **2** exerted to the full (by main force). • n. **1** principal duct, etc., for water, sewage, etc. (water main). **2** poet. ocean or oceans. □ **in the main** for the most part. **main line 1** chief railway line. **2** sl. principal vein, esp. as a site for a drug injection (cf. MAINLINE).

■ adj. **1** primary, prime, (most) important, capital, cardinal, paramount, first, foremost, leading, outstanding, largest, biggest, necessary, essential. **2** sheer, brute, utter, pure. • n. **1** pipe, channel, line, pipeline, conduit, water or gas main. □ **in the main** see MAINLY.

main•frame /máynfraym/ n. (often attrib.) large-scale computer system.

main•land /máynland, -lənd/ n. large continuous extent of land, excluding neighboring islands, etc. □□ **main'land•er** n.

main•line /máynlīn/ v. sl. **1** intr. take drugs intravenously. **2** tr. inject (drugs) intravenously. □□ **main'lin•er** n.

main•ly /máynlee/ adv. for the most part; chiefly.
■ in the main, principally, predominantly, generally, above all, on the whole, in general, mostly.

main•mast /máynmast, -mest/ n. Naut. principal mast of a ship.

main•sail /máynsayl, -səl/ n. Naut. **1** (in a square-rigged vessel) lowest sail on the mainmast. **2** (in a fore-and-aft rigged vessel) sail set on the after part of the mainmast.

main•spring /máynspring/ n. **1** principal spring of a watch, clock, etc. **2** chief motive power; incentive.

main•stay /máynstay/ n. **1** chief support. **2** Naut. stay from the maintop to the foot of the foremast.
■ **1** (sheet) anchor, bulwark, buttress, pillar.

main•stream /máynstreem/ n. (often attrib.) prevailing trend in opinion, fashion, etc.

main•tain /mayntáyn/ v.tr. **1** cause to continue; keep up (an activity, etc.). **2** support by work, expenditure, etc. **3** assert as true. **4** preserve in good repair. **5** provide means for. □□ **main•tain'er** n. **main•tain'a•ble** adj. **main•tain•a•bil'i•ty** n.
■ **1**, **2** preserve, persevere in, keep going, persist in, carry on; nurture. **3** hold, state,

say, declare, claim, allege, testify, contend. **4** look after, take care of, care for, keep up, service.

main•te•nance /máyntənəns/ n. **1** maintaining or being maintained. **2** provision of the means to support life.
■ **1** upkeep, care, servicing, preservation, conservation; continuation, perpetuation. **2** upkeep, livelihood, subsistence, support, allowance, living, sustenance.

maî•tre d'hô•tel /métrə dōtél, máyt–/ n. (pl. **maî•tres d'hôtel** pronunc. same). (also **maître d'**) headwaiter.

maize /mayz/ n. **1** = CORN¹ n. 1. **2** yellow.

ma•jes•tic /məjéstik/ adj. showing majesty; stately and dignified; grand, imposing. □□ **ma•jes'ti•cal•ly** adv.
■ imperial, regal, royal, kingly, queenly, princely, noble, magnificent, monumental, impressive, striking.

maj•es•ty /májistee/ n. (pl. **-ties**) **1** impressive stateliness, dignity, or authority, esp. of bearing, language, the law, etc. **2** (**Majesty**) part of several titles given to a sovereign or a sovereign's wife or widow or used in addressing them.
■ **1** see DIGNITY 1.

ma•jol•i•ca /məyólika, məjól–/ n. (also **ma•iol'i•ca**) colorfully decorated earthenware.

ma•jor /máyjər/ • adj. **1** important, large, serious, significant. **2** (of an operation) serious. **3** Mus. **a** (of a scale) having intervals of a semitone between the third and fourth, and seventh and eighth degrees. **b** (of an interval) greater by a semitone than a minor interval (major third). **c** (of a key) based on a major scale. • n. **1** army officer next below lieutenant colonel and above captain. **2 a** a student's most emphasized subject or course. **b** student specializing in a specified subject. • v.intr. (foll. by in) study or qualify in as a special subject. □ **major general** officer next below a lieutenant general. □□ **ma'jor•ship** n.
■ adj. **1** vital, critical, crucial, principal, prime, main, big; grave; larger, greater, bigger, chief. • n. **2 a** specialization. **b** specialist. • v. specialize.

ma•jor•do•mo /máyjərdómō/ n. (pl. **-mos**) chief steward of a great household.

ma•jor•i•ty /məjáwritee, -jór–/ n. (pl. **-ties**) **1** [usu. foll. by of] greater number or part. **2** Polit. number by which the votes cast for one party, candidate, etc., exceed those of the next in rank (won by a majority of 151). **3** full legal age (attained his majority). **4** rank of major.
■ **1** bulk, preponderance, mass, better or best part. **3** adulthood, maturity, seniority, womanhood, manhood.

make /mayk/ • v.tr. (past and past part. **made** /mayd/) **1** construct; create; form from parts or other substances. **2** cause or compel. **3 a** bring about (made a noise). **b** cause to become or seem (made him angry). **4** compose; prepare (made her will). **5** constitute; amount to (2 and 2 make 4). **6 a** undertake (made a promise). **b** perform (a bodily movement, a speech, etc.). **7** gain; acquire; procure. **8** prepare. **9 a** arrange bedding neatly on (a bed). **b** arrange and ignite materials for (a fire). **10** *colloq.* **a** arrive at (a place) or in time for (a train, etc.). **b** manage to attend. **c** achieve a place in (*made the first team*). **11** enact (a law, etc.). **12** consider to be; estimate as. **13** secure the success of (*it made my day*). **14** accomplish (a distance, speed, score, etc.). **15** form in the mind; (*I make no judgment*). • *n.* **1** type, origin, brand, etc., of manufacture. **2** kind of mental, moral, or physical structure or composition. □ **make away with** = *make off with*. **make-believe 1** pretense. **2** pretended. **make believe** pretend. **make do** manage with the limited or inadequate means available. **make for 1** tend to result in (happiness, etc.). **2** proceed toward (a place). **make it 1** *colloq.* succeed in reaching, esp. in time. **2** *colloq.* be successful. **make off** (or **away**) **with** steal. **make out 1 a** distinguish by sight or hearing. **b** decipher (handwriting, etc.). **2** understand (*can't make him out*). **3** assert; pretend. **4** *colloq.* make progress; fare. **5** write out. **6** *colloq.* engage in sexual play or petting. **make over 1** transfer the possession of. **2** refashion. **make up 1** act to overcome (a deficiency). **2** complete (an amount, a party, etc.). **3** compensate. **4** be reconciled. **5** concoct. **6** apply cosmetics to. **make up one's mind** decide. **make up to** curry favor with. **make water** *colloq.* urinate. **make way 1** allow room for others to proceed. **2** be superseded by. **make one's way** go; prosper. **on the make** *colloq.* **1** intent on gain. **2** looking for sexual partners. □□ **mak·a·ble** *adj.* **mak'er** *n.*

■ *v.* **1** build, assemble, erect, put together, fashion, form, originate, fabricate, manufacture. **2** force, impel, coerce, provoke. **3** occasion; produce, create; appoint, name. **4** make out *or* up, draw (up), write. **5** represent, add up to, total, come to. **6 a** see UNDERTAKE[1] 1. **b** deliver, present; see also EXECUTE 2. **7** earn, reap, garner, take in, clear, realize, gross, net. **8** cook, *colloq.* fix. **9 a** prepare, arrange, tidy (up). **b** lay, prepare. **10 a** reach, attain, get (to). **c** get on *or* in. **11** pass, frame, establish, set up, organize. **12** judge, think, calculate. **14** reach; do, go *or* travel *or* move at; score, achieve. • *n.* **1** kind, style, sort. **2** see MAKEUP 2. **make-believe 1** see PRETENSE 1. **2** see FICTITIOUS 2. **make believe** fancy, playact, dream, fantasize, imagine. **make do 1** get by *or* along, cope, scrape by, survive. **make for 1** promote, contribute to, be conducive to; see also LEAD *v.* 9. **make it 1** arrive, get there, show up, appear. **2** succeed, prosper, triumph, win. **make off with** rob, filch, pilfer, walk away *or* off with. **make out 1** see, discern, detect, discover. **2** fathom, comprehend, figure out, perceive. **3** suggest, imply, hint, insinuate, intimate; make to appear, make believe. **4** see FARE *v.* **5** complete, fill in, fill out; draw (up). **make over 1** hand over, sign over, convey, assign. **2** do over, remodel, redeco-

rate, alter. **make up 1** redress. **2** fill out, finish (out), flesh out. **3** redress, make good, atone, make amends. **4** make peace, come to terms, bury the hatchet. **make up one's mind** see DECIDE 1. **make up to** see INGRATIATE. **make water** see URINATE. **make way 1** move aside, clear the way, allow to pass. **2** see *get on* 1. **make one's way** see PROCEED 1. **on the make 1** aggressive, assertive, enterprising, *colloq.* pushy. **2** *sl.* cruising.

make·shift /máykshift/ • *adj.* temporary; serving for the time being. • *n.* temporary substitute or device.

■ *adj.* ad interim, stopgap, expedient, emergency, improvised, ad hoc, tentative. • *n.* expedient, improvisation, substitute, jury-rig; see also STOPGAP.

make·up /máykəp/ *n.* **1** cosmetics for the face, etc., either generally or to create an actor's appearance or disguise. **2** person's character, temperament, etc. **3** composition of a thing.

■ **1** maquillage, greasepaint, *colloq.* warpaint. **2** constitution, cast, disposition, personality, make. **3** constitution, arrangement, construction, format, configuration.

mak·ing /máyking/ *n.* [in *pl.*] essential qualities or ingredients (*has the makings of a general*). □ **in the making** in the course of being made or formed.

ma·ko /máykō, maàkō/ *n.* (*pl.* **–kos**) type of shark.

mal- /mal/ *comb. form* **1 a** bad, badly (*malpractice, maltreat*). **b** faulty, faultily (*malfunction*). **2** not (*maladroit*).

mal·ad·just·ed /máləjústid/ *adj.* **1** not correctly adjusted. **2** (of a person) unable to adapt to or cope with the demands of a social environment. □□ **mal·ad·just'ment** *n.*

■ **2** unstable, neurotic, disturbed, unbalanced.

mal·a·droit /málədróyt/ *adj.* clumsy; bungling. □□ **mal·a·droit'ly** *adv.* **mal·a·droit'ness** *n.*

■ see CLUMSY 1. □□ **maladroitly** see *roughly* (ROUGH). **maladroitness** see *ineptitude* (INEPT).

mal·a·dy /málədee/ *n.* (*pl.* **–dies**) ailment; disease.

■ see DISEASE.

Mal·a·gas·y /máləgásee/ • *adj.* of or relating to Madagascar, an island in the Indian Ocean. • *n.* language of Madagascar.

ma·laise /məláyz/ *n.* **1** nonspecific bodily discomfort. **2** feeling of uneasiness.

■ **1** see AILMENT. **2** DISCONTENT *n.*

mal·a·mute /máləmyōōt/ *n.* (also **mal'e·mute**) any of an Alaskan breed of large sled dogs.

mal·a·prop·ism /máləpropizəm/ *n.* (also **mal·a·prop** /máləprop/) use of a word in mistake for one sounding similar, to comic effect, e.g., *allegory* for *alligator*.

ma·lar·i·a /məláireeə/ *n.* recurrent fever caused by a parasite introduced by the bite of a mosquito. □□ **ma·lar'i·al** *adj.* **ma·lar'i·an** *adj.* **ma·lar'i·ous** *adj.*

ma·lar·key /məlaárkee/ *n. colloq.* humbug; nonsense.

Ma·lay /máylay, məláy/ • *n.* **1** member of a

people predominating in Malaysia and Indonesia. **2** language of this people, the official language of Malaysia. • *adj.* of or relating to this people or this language. □□ **Ma•lay'an** *n. & adj.*

Ma•a•ya•lam /málayáaləm/ *n.* language of S. India.

mal•con•tent /málkəntent/ • *n.* discontented person; rebel. • *adj.* discontented or rebellious.

male /mayl/ • *adj.* **1** of the sex that can beget offspring by fertilization or insemination. **2** of men or male animals, plants, etc.; masculine. **3** (of plants or their parts) containing only fertilizing organs. **4** (of parts of machinery, etc.) designed to enter or fill the corresponding female part (*a male plug*). • *n.* male person or animal. □□ **male'ness** *n.*

■ *adj.* **2** masculine, man's; virile, manful, macho; see also MANLY 1. • *n.* see MAN *n.* 1.

SYNONYM STUDY: male

MANFUL, MANLY, MANNISH, MASCULINE, VIRILE. We speak of a *male* ancestor, a *masculine* scent, and a *manly* activity, but only of women as *mannish*. While all of these adjectives apply to what is characteristic of, or like the *male* of the species, particularly the human species, *male* can be used with plants or animals as well as human beings and is used to describe whatever is biologically distinguished from the female sex (*an all-male choir; a male cat; a male holly bush*). *Masculine* refers to the qualities, characteristics, and behaviors associated with or thought to be appropriate to men and boys (*a masculine style of writing; a masculine handshake*). *Manly* emphasizes the desirable qualities that a culture associates with a mature man, such as courage and independence (*the manly virtues; the manly sport of football*), although it may also be applied to boys. **Manful** differs from *manly* primarily in its emphasis on sturdiness and resoluteness (*a manful effort to hold back tears*). *Virile* is a stronger word than *masculine* or *manly* and is applied only to mature men; it suggests the vigor, muscularity, and forcefulness—and especially the sexual potency—associated with mature manhood (*a virile man who looked like a young Charlton Heston*).

mal•e•dic•tion /málidíkshən/ *n.* **1** curse. **2** utterance of a curse. □□ **mal•e•dic•tive** /-tiv/ *adj.* **mal•e•dic•to•ry** /-díktəwree/ *adj.*

mal•e•fac•tor /málifaktər/ *n.* criminal; evildoer. □□ **mal•e•fac'tion** *n.*

ma•lev•o•lent /məlévələnt/ *adj.* wishing evil to others. □□ **ma•lev'o•lence** *n.* **ma•lev'o•lent•ly** *adv.*

■ see EVIL *adj.* 1. □□ **malevolence** see HOSTILITY 1.

mal•fea•sance /malféezəns/ *n. Law* evildoing. □□ **mal•fea'sant** *n. & adj.*

mal•for•ma•tion /málformáyshən/ *n.* faulty formation. □□ **mal'formed** /-fáwrmd/ *adj.*

mal•func•tion /málfúngkshən/ • *n.* failure to function normally. • *v.intr.* fail to function normally.

■ *n.* see TROUBLE *n.* 4. • *v.* fall through, backfire, fail.

mal•ice /mális/ *n.* **1 a** intention to do evil. **b** desire to tease, esp. cruelly. **2** *Law* wrongful intention. □ **malice aforethought** (or **prepense**) *Law* intention to commit a crime, esp. murder.

■ **1** see HOSTILITY 1.

ma•li•cious /məlíshəs/ *adj.* characterized by malice. □□ **ma•li'cious•ly** *adv.* **ma•li'cious•ness** *n.*

■ see VICIOUS 1, 3. □□ **maliciousness** see VENOM 2.

ma•lign /məlín/ • *adj.* **1** (of a thing) injurious. **2** (of a disease) malignant. **3** malevolent. • *v.tr.* speak ill of; slander. □□ **ma•lign'er** *n.* **ma•lig•ni•ty** /məlígnitee/ *n.* (*pl.* –ties) **ma•lign'ly** /-línlee/ *adv.*

■ *adj.* **1, 3** see EVIL *adj.* 2. • *v.* see SLANDER *v.* □□ **malignity** see VENOM 2.

SYNONYM STUDY: malign

CALUMNIATE, DEFAME, LIBEL, SLANDER, VILIFY. Want to ruin someone's life? You can **malign** the person, which is to say or write something evil without necessarily lying (*she was maligned for her past association with radical causes*). To **calumniate** is to make false and malicious statements about someone, often implying that you have seriously damaged that person's good name (*after leaving his job, he spent most of his time calumniating and ridiculing his former boss*). To **defame** is to cause actual injury to someone's good name or reputation (*he defamed her by accusing her of being a spy*). If you don't mind risking a lawsuit, you can **libel** the person, which is to write or print something that *defames* him or her (*the tabloid libeled the celebrity and ended up paying the price*). **Slander**, which is to *defame* someone orally, is seldom a basis for court action but can nevertheless cause injury to someone's reputation (*after a loud and very public argument, she accused him of slandering her*). If all else fails, you can **vilify** the person, which is to engage in abusive name-calling (*even though he was found innocent by the jury, he was vilified by his neighbors*).

ma•lig•nant /məlígnənt/ *adj.* **1 a** (of a disease) very virulent or infectious. **b** cancerous. **2** harmful; feeling or showing intense ill will. □□ **ma•lig'nan•cy** *n.* (*pl.* –cies). **ma•lig'nant•ly** *adv.*

■ **1** pernicious, harmful, injurious, life-threatening, invasive. **2** injurious, malign, malevolent, evil.

ma•lin•ger /məlínggər/ *v.intr.* exaggerate or feign illness in order to escape duty, work, etc. □□ **ma•lin'ger•er** *n.*

mall /mawl/ *n.* **1** sheltered walk or promenade. **2** enclosed shopping center.

mal•lard /málərd/ *n.* (*pl.* same or **mal•lards**) wild duck or drake of the northern hemisphere.

mal•le•a•ble /máleeəbəl/ *adj.* **1** (of metal, etc.) that can be shaped by hammering. **2** adaptable; pliable, flexible. □□ **mal•le•a•bil'i•ty** *n.* **mal'le•a•bly** *adv.*

■ **1** see PLASTIC *adj.* 1. **2** see *adaptable*

(ADAPT). □□ **malleability** see *flexibility* (FLEXIBLE).

mal•let /málit/ *n.* **1** hammer, usu. of wood. **2** long-handled wooden hammer for striking a croquet or polo ball.

mal•low /málō/ *n.* plant with hairy stems and leaves and pink or purple flowers.

mal•nour•ished /málnɔ́risht, –núr–/ *adj.* suffering from malnutrition. □□ **mal•nour′ish•ment** *n.*

mal•nu•tri•tion /málno͞otríshən, –nyo͞o–/ *n.* dietary condition resulting from the absence of healthful foods.

mal•o•dor•ous /malódərəs/ *adj.* having an unpleasant smell.

mal•prac•tice /malpráktis/ *n.* improper, negligent, or criminal professional conduct.

malt /mawlt/ • *n.* **1** barley or other grain that is steeped, germinated, and dried, esp. for brewing or distilling and vinegar making. **2** *colloq.* malt whiskey; malt liquor. • *v. tr.* convert (grain) into malt. □ **malted milk 1** drink combining milk, a malt preparation, and ice cream or flavoring. **2** powdered malt preparation used to make this. **malt liquor** a kind of strong beer.

Mal•tese /máwlte͡ez, -te͡es/ • *n.* **1** (*pl.* same) native or national of Malta, an island in the W. Mediterranean. **2** language of Malta. • *adj.* of or relating to Malta.

mal•treat /máltre͡et/ *v.tr.* ill-treat. □□ **mal•treat′er** *n.* **mal•treat′ment** *n.*

■ see *ill-treat.* □□ **maltreatment** see ABUSE *n.* 4.

ma•ma /máəmə, məmáə/ *n. colloq.* mother.

mam•ba /máəmbə/ *n.* venomous African snake.

mam•bo /máəmbō/ *n.* (*pl.* **–bos**) **1** Latin American dance like the rumba. **2** the music for this.

mam•ma /máəmə/ *n.* (also **mom′ma**) *colloq.* MAMA.

mam•mal /máməl/ *n.* warm-blooded vertebrate of the class secreting milk for the nourishment of its young. □□ **mam•ma•li•an** /–máyleeən/ *adj. & n.* **mam•mal•o•gy** /–mólijee/ *n.*

mam•ma•ry /máməree/ *adj.* of the breasts.

mam•mog•ra•phy /mamógrəfee/ *n. Med.* X-ray technique of diagnosing and locating abnormalities (esp. tumors) of the breasts.

mam•mon /mámən/ *n.* (also **Mam′mon**) wealth regarded as a god or as an evil influence. □□ **mam′mon•ism** *n.* **mam′mon•ist** *n.*

mam•moth /máməth/ • *n.* large extinct elephant with a hairy coat and curved tusks. • *adj.* huge.

■ *adj.* see HUGE 1.

man /man/ • *n.* (*pl.* **men** /men/) **1** adult human male. **2 a** human being; person (*no man is perfect*). **b** the human race (*man is mortal*). **3** person showing characteristics associated with males (*she's more of a man than he is*). **4 a** worker; employee. **b** manservant or valet. **5** [usu. in *pl.*] soldiers, sailors, etc., esp. nonofficers. **6** any one of a set of pieces used in playing chess, checkers, etc. • *v.tr.*

(**manned, man′ning**) **1** supply with a person or people for work or defense, etc. **2** work or service or defend (*man the pumps*). □ **as one man** in unison; in agreement. **man about town** fashionable man of leisure. **man-hour** (or **-day,** etc.) hour (or day, etc.) regarded in terms of the amount of work that could be done by one person within this period. **man in** (*or* **on**) **the street** ordinary average person. **man-made** artificial; synthetic. **man of letters** scholar; author. **man-of-war** armed ship. **to a man** all without exception. □□ **man′less** *adj.*

■ *n.* **1** gentleman, *colloq.* guy, fellow, chap, *sl.* dude. **2 a** mortal. **b** people, human beings, mankind, mortals, *Homo sapiens*, humanity. **4 a** see WORKER. **b** servant, *joc.* retainer; houseboy, houseman. • *v.* **1** staff; crew. □ **as one man** as one, together, harmonious, in harmony. **man about town** see SWELL *n.* 4, TRENDY *n.* **man in** (*or* **on**) **the street** layman, laywoman. **man of letters** see SCHOLAR 1, AUTHOR *n.* 1.

man•a•cle /mánəkəl/ • *n.* [usu. in *pl.*] **1** handcuff. **2** restraint. • *v.tr.* fetter with manacles.

■ *n.* **1** (*manacles*) shackles, fetters, chains; see also RESTRAINT 5. **2** see RESTRAINT 2. • *v.* shackle, handcuff, restrain, put *or* throw *or* clap in irons, chain (up).

man•age /mánij/ *v.* **1** *tr.* organize; regulate; be in charge of. **2** *tr.* succeed in achieving; contrive. **3** *intr.* **a** succeed in one's aim, esp. against heavy odds. **b** meet one's needs with limited resources, etc. **4** *tr.* control.

■ **1** handle, administer, run, supervise, look after, watch over, direct, head, oversee; govern. **2, 3** function, make do, make it, cope. **4** handle, cope or deal with, govern, manipulate.

man•age•a•ble /mánijəbəl/ *adj.* able to be easily managed, controlled, or accomplished, etc. □□ **man•age•a•bil′i•ty** *n.* **man′age•a•bly** *adv.*

■ controllable; tractable, compliant, amenable, docile.

man•age•ment /mánijmənt/ *n.* **1** managing or being managed. **2 a** professional administration of business concerns, public undertakings, etc. **b** people engaged in this.

■ **1** control, supervision, manipulation, handling, direction, directing, directorship, administration, government. **2 b** administration, executive(s), bosses, directors, board (of directors).

man•ag•er /mánijər/ *n.* **1** person controlling or administering a business or part of a business. **2** person controlling the affairs, training, etc., of a person or team in sports, entertainment, etc. □□ **man•a•ge′ri•al** /mánijéereeəl/ *adj.* **man•a•ge′ri•al•ly** *adv.* **man′ag•er•ship** *n.*

■ **1** supervisor, superintendent, director, executive, head, proprietor, overseer, foreman, forewoman. **2** impresario, administrator; see also DIRECTOR 2.

ma•ña•na /mənyáənə/ *adv.* in the indefinite future. • *n.* an indefinite future time.

man•a•tee /mánəte͡e/ *n.* large aquatic planteating mammal.

man•da•la /mánd·lə, mún-/ n. symbolic circular figure representing the universe in various religions.

man•da•rin /mándərin/ n. **1** (**Mandarin**) most widely spoken form of Chinese and official language of China. **2** *hist.* Chinese official in any of nine grades of the pre-Communist civil service. **3 a** party leader. **b** powerful member of the establishment. □□ **man'da•rin•ate** n.

man•date /mándayt/ • n. **1** official command or instruction by an authority. **2** support given by electors to a party course of action, union, etc., for a policy or course of action. **3** commission to act for another. • v.tr. instruct (a delegate) to act or vote in a certain way. □□ **man'da'tor** n.
• n. **1** see COMMAND n. 1. **2** see APPROVAL. • v. see DECREE v.

man•da•to•ry /mándətáwree/ adj. **1** of or conveying a command. **2** compulsory. □□ **man'da•to•ri•ly** adv.
■ **2** obligatory, requisite, required, essential, demanded, necessary, needed.

man•di•ble /mándibəl/ n. **1** jaw, esp. the lower jaw in mammals and fishes. **2** upper or lower part of a bird's beak. **3** either half of the crushing organ in an arthropod's mouthparts. □□ **man•dib'u•lar** adj.

man•do•lin /mándəlin/ n. musical instrument resembling a lute, having paired metal strings plucked with a plectrum. □□ **man'do•lin'ist** n.

man•drake /mándrayk/ n. poisonous plant having emetic and narcotic properties and possessing a root once thought to resemble the human form.

man•drel /mándrəl/ n. **1** shaft in a lathe to which work is fixed while being turned. **2** cylindrical rod around which metal or other material is forged or shaped.

man•drill /mándril/ n. large W. African baboon.

mane /mayn/ n. long hair on the neck of a horse, lion, etc. □□ **maned** adj. [also in comb.] **mane'less** adj.

ma•nège /manézh/ n. (also **ma•nege**) **1** riding school. **2** movements of a trained horse. **3** horsemanship.

ma•neu•ver /mənoovər/ • n. **1** planned and controlled movement or series of moves. **2** [in pl.] large-scale exercise of troops, warships, etc. **3 a** often deceptive planned or controlled action. **b** skillful plan. • v. **1** intr. & tr. perform or cause to perform a maneuver. **2** intr. & tr. perform or cause (troops, etc.) to perform military maneuvers. **3 a** tr. handle adroitly. **b** intr. use artifice. □□ **ma•neu'ver•a•ble** adj. **ma•neu•ver•a•bil•i•ty** /-vrəbílitee, -vərə-/ n. **ma•neu'ver•er** n.
■ n. **1, 3** stratagem, tactic, trick, gambit, subterfuge, ruse, dodge. **2** exercise(s), war game(s). • v. **1** manipulate, run, drive, guide, navigate, steer. **3** manipulate, contrive, plot, scheme, machinate, intrigue.

man•ful /mánfool/ adj. brave; resolute. See synonym study at MALE. □□ **man'ful•ly** adv. **man'ful•ness** n.

man•ga•nese /mánggəneez/ n. *Chem.* gray

metallic transition element used with steel to make alloys. ¶Symb.: **Mn**.

mange /maynj/ n. skin disease in hairy and woolly animals.

man•ger /máynjər/ n. long open box or trough in a stable, etc., for horses or cattle to eat from.

man•gle[1] /mánggəl/ v.tr. **1** hack, cut, or mutilate by blows, etc. **2** spoil; ruin. □□ **man' gler** n.
■ **1** lacerate, chop (up), crush, damage, cripple, maim, destroy. **2** butcher, mutilate, mar, wreck.

man•gle[2] /mánggəl/ n. machine having two or more cylinders between which clothes, etc., are squeezed and pressed.

man•go /mánggō/ n. (pl. **-goes** or **-gos**) **1** fleshy yellowish-red fruit. **2** E. Indian evergreen tree bearing this.

man•grove /mánggrōv/ n. tropical tree or shrub with many tangled roots above ground.

man•gy /máynjee/ adj. (**man•gi•er, man•gi•est**) **1** having mange. **2** squalid; shabby. □□ **man'gi•ly** adv. **man'gi•ness** n.
■ **1** scabious, scabby. **2** scruffy, dirty, sleazy, sorry, slovenly, unkempt, slummy, dingy, seedy, poor.

man•han•dle /mánhánd'l/ v.tr. *colloq.* handle roughly.
■ hustle, jostle, tousle, molest, shove, maul.

man•hat•tan /mənhátən/ n. cocktail made of vermouth and whiskey, usu. flavored with bitters.

man•hole /mánhōl/ n. covered opening in a floor, pavement, sewer, etc., for workers to gain access.

man•hood /mánhŏŏd/ n. **1** state of being a man rather than a child or woman. **2 a** manliness; courage. **b** a man's sexual potency. **3** men of a country, etc.
■ **2 a** masculinity, manfulness, virility, machismo, bravery, pluck, boldness, *colloq.* guts, grit.

man•hunt /mánhunt/ n. search for a person, esp. a criminal.

ma•ni•a /máyneeə/ n. **1** *Psychol.* mental illness marked by periods of great excitement and violence. **2** [often foll. by *for*] excessive enthusiasm; obsession (*has a mania for jogging*).
■ **1** madness, lunacy, insanity, dementia, dementedness, derangement, hysteria, *colloq.* craziness. **2** rage, craze, passion, fad; compulsion, urge.

-mania /máyneeə/ comb. form **1** *Psychol.* denoting a special type of mental abnormality or obsession (*megalomania*). **2** denoting extreme enthusiasm or admiration (*bibliomania*).

ma•ni•ac /máyneeak/ n. **1** *colloq.* person exhibiting extreme symptoms of wild behavior, etc.; madman. **2** *colloq.* obsessive enthusiast. □□ **ma•ni•a•cal** /mənɪákəl/ adj. **ma•ni'a•cal•ly** adv.
■ **1** madwoman, lunatic, psychopath, psychotic, *sl.* crackpot, nut. **2** fanatic, fan, zealot, *colloq.* freak, *sl.* fiend, nut. □□ **mani-**

acal manic, maniac, insane, lunatic, mad, demented; hysterical, berserk, wild.

man•ic /mánik/ • *adj.* of or affected by mania. • *n.* person having such a disorder. □ **manic-depressive** *Psychol. adj. & n.* affected by or relating to a mental disorder with alternating periods of elation and depression. □□ **man′i•cal•ly** *adv.*

man•i•cure /mánikyŏor/ • *n.* cosmetic treatment of the hands and fingernails. • *v.tr.* give a manicure to (the hands or a person). □□ **man′i•cur•ist** *n.*

man•i•fest[1] /mánifest/ • *adj.* clear or obvious. • *v. tr.* show plainly to the eye or mind. □ **Manifest Destiny** 19th c. doctrine asserting that the United States was destined to expand westward to the Pacific. □□ **man•i•fes•ta′tion** *n.* **man′i•fest•ly** *adv.* See synonym study at SIGN

■ *adj.* apparent, evident, plain, patent, blatant, conspicuous. • *v.* demonstrate, exhibit, evince, reveal, disclose. □□ **manifestation** display, exhibition, demonstration, show, disclosure; declaration; materialization. **manifestly** evidently, clearly, obviously, plainly, apparently.

man•i•fest[2] /mánifest/ *n.* cargo or passenger list.

man•i•fes•to /mániféstō/ *n.* (*pl.* –**tos** or –**toes**) public declaration of policy and aims esp. political or social.

■ declaration, platform, program.

man•i•fold /mánifōld/ • *adj. literary* **1** many and various. **2** having various forms, parts, applications, etc. • *n.* **1** manifold thing. **2** *Mech.* pipe or chamber branching into several openings.

■ *adj.* diverse, diversified, multifarious, varied, assorted, multiplex, miscellaneous, sundry. • *n.* **1** composite, amalgam; see also BLEND *n.*

man•i•kin /mánikin/ *n.* (also **man′ni•kin**) **1** little man; dwarf. **2** anatomical model of the body.

Ma•nil•a /mənílə/ *n.* (also **Ma•nil′la**) **1** (in full **Manila hemp**) strong fiber of a Philippine tree. **2** (also **ma•nil′a**) strong brown paper made from Manila hemp or other material.

ma•nip•u•late /mənípyəlayt/ *v.tr.* **1** handle, esp. skillfully. **2** manage (a person, situation, etc.) to one's own advantage, esp. unfairly. **3** manually examine and treat (a part of the body). □□ **ma•nip•u•la•ble** /–ləbəl/ *adj.* **ma•nip•u•la′tion** /–láyshən/ *n.* **ma•nip•u•la•tive** /mənípyələtiv/ *adj.* **ma•nip′u•la•tor** *n.*

■ **1** control, operate, direct, work, use, treat, employ. **2** handle, control, maneuver, orchestrate, choreograph, influence, use, exploit; rig, falsify.

man•kind *n.* **1** /mánkínd/ human species. **2** /mánkínd/ male people, as distinct from female.

man•ly /mánlee/ *adj.* (**man•li•er**, **man•li•est**) **1** having qualities regarded as admirable in a man, such as courage, frankness, etc. **2** befitting a man. See synonym study at MALE. □□ **man′li•ness** *n.*

■ **1** manful, virile, courageous, bold, brave, intrepid, valorous; masculine, male, macho, red-blooded.

man•na /mánə/ *n.* **1** substance miraculously supplied as food to the Israelites in the wilderness (Exod. 16). **2** unexpected benefit (esp. *manna from heaven*).

manned /mand/ *adj.* (of an aircraft, spacecraft, etc.) having a human crew.

man•ne•quin /mánikin/ *n.* **1** fashion model. **2** window dummy.

man•ner /mánər/ *n.* **1** way a thing is done or happens. **2** [in *pl.*] **a** social behavior (*it is bad manners to stare*). **b** polite or well-bred behavior (*he has no manners*). **3** person's outward bearing, way of speaking, etc. **4** style in literature, art, etc. (*in the manner of Rembrandt*). □ **to the manner born** *colloq.* naturally at ease in a specified job, situation, etc. □□ **man′ner•less** *adj.* (in sense 2b).

■ **1** mode, style, technique, procedure, method. **2** etiquette, decorum, (good) form, politeness; social graces. **3** air, behavior, demeanor, deportment.

man•nered /mánərd/ *adj.* **1** [in *comb.*] behaving in a specified way (*ill-mannered*). **2** artificial.

■ **1** (*comb.*) -behaved. **2** contrived, stilted, stiff, affected, insincere, pompous, pretentious, posed.

man•ner•ism /mánərizəm/ *n.* **1** habitual gesture or way of speaking, etc.; idiosyncrasy. **2 a** stylistic trick in art, etc. **b** excessive use of these. □□ **man′ner•ist** *n.* **man•ner•is′tic** *adj.*

■ **1** quirk, peculiarity, trait, characteristic, habit.

man•ner•ly /mánərlee/ • *adj.* well-mannered; polite. • *adv.* politely. □□ **man′ner•li•ness** *n.*

man•ni•kin var. of MANIKIN.

man•nish /mánish/ *adj.* **1** usu. *derog.* (of a woman) masculine in appearance or manner. **2** characteristic of a man. See synonym study at MALE. □□ **man′nish•ly** *adv.* **man′nish•ness** *n.*

ma•nom•e•ter /mənómitər/ *n.* pressure gauge for gases and liquids. □□ **man•o•met′ric** /mánəmétrik/ *adj.*

man•or /mánər/ *n.* (also **man′or house**) large country house with lands. □□ **ma•no•ri•al** /mənáwreeəl/ *adj.*

■ see ESTATE 1, PALACE 2.

man•pow•er /mánpowr/ *n.* number of people available or required for work, service, etc.

man•qué /maaNkáy/ *adj.* [placed after noun] that might have been but is not; unfulfilled (*a comic actor manqué*).

man•sard /mánsaard/ *n.* roof that has four sloping sides, each of which becomes steeper halfway down.

manse /mans/ *n.* house of a minister, esp. a Presbyterian.

man•ser•vant /mánservənt/ *n.* (*pl.* **men•ser•vants**) male servant.

-manship /mənship/ *suffix* forming nouns denoting skill in a subject or activity (*craftsmanship, gamesmanship*).

man•sion /mánshən/ *n.* large house.

man•slaugh•ter /mánslawtər/ *n. Law* unlawful killing of a human being without malice aforethought.

man•tel•piece /mánt'lpees/ *n.* (also **man•tel**) structure of wood, marble, etc., above and around a fireplace.

man•til•la /mantílə, -téeə/ *n.* lace scarf worn by Spanish women over the hair and shoulders.

man•tis /mántis/ *n.* (*pl.* same or **man•tis•es**) (in full **praying mantis**) predatory insect that holds its forelegs in a position suggestive of hands folded in prayer,

man•tis•sa /mantísə/ *n.* part of a logarithm after the decimal point.

man•tle /mánt'l/ • *n.* **1** loose sleeveless cloak. **2** covering (*mantle of snow*), **3** lacelike tube fixed around a gas jet to give an incandescent light. **4** region between the crust and core of the earth. • *v. tr.* clothe; conceal; envelop.
■ *n.* **1** cape, wrap, shawl. **2** cover, sheet, veil, blanket, screen, cloak, shroud, pall, canopy, curtain. • *v.* cover, surround, encircle, shroud, veil, screen.

man•tra /mántrə, maàn–, mún–/ *n.* **1** word or sound repeated to aid concentration in meditation, orig. in Hinduism and Buddhism. **2** Vedic hymn.

man•u•al /mányōōəl/ • *adj.* **1** of or done with the hands (*manual labor*). **2** (of a machine, etc.) worked by hand, not automatically. • *n.* **1** book of instructions. **2** *Mil.* exercise in handling a rifle, etc. □□ **man'u•al•ly** *adv.*
■ *adj.* **1** hand, blue-collar. **2** hand-operated. • *n.* **1** handbook, companion; directions, guide.

man•u•fac•ture /mányəfákchər/ • *n.* making of articles, esp. in a factory, etc. • *v.tr.* **1** make (articles), esp. on an industrial scale. **2** invent or fabricate (evidence, a story, etc.). □□ **man•u•fac'tur•er** *n.*
■ *n.* (*mass*) production, construction, building, assembly, fabrication. • *v.* **1** (*mass-*) produce, construct, build, assemble, fabricate. **2** concoct, create, contrive, make up, think up. □□ **manufacturer** maker, producer, processor, industrialist; fabricator.

man•u•mit /mányəmít/ *v.tr.* (**man•u•mit•ted**, **man•u•mit•ting**) *hist.* set (a slave) free. □□ **man•u•mis•sion** /–míshən/ *n*

ma•nure /mənóōr, –nyóōr/ • *n.* fertilizer, esp. dung. • *v.tr.* [also *absol.*] apply manure to (land, etc.).

man•u•script /mányəskript/ • *n.* **1** handwritten or typed text. **2** handwritten form. • *adj.* written by hand.
■ *adj.* handwritten, holograph.

Manx /mangks/ • *adj.* of the Isle of Man. • *n.* **1** former Celtic language of the Isle of Man. **2** [treated as *pl.*] Manx people. □ **Manx cat** breed of tailless cat.

man•y /ménee/ • *adj.* (**more** /mawr/; **most** /mōst/) great in number; numerous. • *n.* [as *pl.*] a large number (*many went*).
■ *adj.* multitudinous, profuse, innumerable, numberless, uncountable, *literary* myriad. • *n.* a good *or* great deal, hordes *or* a horde, crowds *or* a crowd, swarms *or* a swarm, throngs *or* a throng, masses *or* a mass, moun-

tains *or* a mountain, a profusion, multitudes *or* a multitude, a good *or* great many, an abundance, plenty; *colloq.* lots *or* a lot, hundreds *or* a hundred, oodles, zillions, loads *or* a load, scads.

Mao•ism /mówizəm/ *n.* Communist doctrines of Mao Zedong (d. 1976), Chinese statesman. □□ **Mao'ist** *n. & adj.*

Mao•ri /mówree/ • *n.* (*pl.* same or **Mao•ris**) **1** member of the Polynesian aboriginal people of New Zealand. **2** language of the Maori. • *adj.* of the Maori.

map /map/ • *n.* **1** flat representation of the earth's surface, or part of it. **2** two-dimensional representation of the stars, the heavens, the moon, etc. • *v.tr.* (**mapped**, **map•ping**) represent on a map. □ **map out** arrange in detail; plan. □□ **map'less** *adj.* **map'per** *n.*
■ *n.* see CHART *n.* • *v.* see CHART *v.*

ma•ple /máypəl/ *n.* **1** any of various trees grown for shade, ornament, wood, or its sugar. **2** wood of the maple. □ **maple sugar** sugar produced by evaporating the sap of the sugar maple, etc. **maple syrup** syrup produced from the sap of the sugar maple, etc.

Mar. *abbr.* March

mar /maar/ *v.tr.* (**marred**, **mar•ring**) spoil; disfigure.
■ damage, wreck, ruin, impair; deform, blight, blot.

mar•a•bou /máarəboo/ *n.* (also **mar'a•bout**) **1** large W. African stork. **2** its down as a trimming for hats, etc.

ma•ra•ca /məraákə/ *n.* gourd or gourd-shaped container filled with beans, etc., shaken as a percussion instrument.

mar•a•schi•no /máraskeenō, –shée–/ *n.* (*pl.* **–nos**) sweet liqueur made from a Dalmatian cherry. □ **maraschino cherry** cherry with maraschino flavor.

Ma•ra•thi /məraátee, –rátee/ *n.* (also **Mah•rat'ti**) language of central and W. India.

mar•a•thon /márəthon/ *n.* **1** long-distance running race, usu. of 26 miles 385 yards (42.195 km). **2** long-lasting or difficult task, operation, etc. (often *attrib.: a marathon shopping expedition*). □□ **mar'a•thon•er** *n.*

ma•raud /məráwd/ *v.* **1** *intr.* make a plundering raid. **2** *tr.* plunder (a place) □□ **ma•raud'er** *n.*
■ □□ **marauder** see THIEF.

mar•ble /maárbəl/ • *n.* **1** crystalline limestone capable of taking a polish, used in sculpture and architecture. **2** [often *attrib.*] **a** anything made of marble (*marble clock*). **b** anything resembling marble in hardness, coldness, durability, etc. **3 a** small ball of marble, glass, clay, etc., used as a toy. **b** [in *pl.*; treated as *sing.*] game using these. **4** [in *pl.*] *sl.* one's mental faculties. • *v.tr.* **1** (esp. as **marbled** *adj.*) stain or color (paper, soap, etc.) to look like marble. **2** (as **marbled** *adj.*) (of meat) streaked with alternating layers of lean and fat. □□ **mar'bly** *adj.*
■ *v.* **1** (**marbled**) see MOTTLE).

March /maarch/ *n.* third month of the year.

march[1] /maarch/ • *v.* **1** *intr.* walk in a military manner with a regular tread. **2** *tr.* cause to march or walk (*marched him out of the room*). **3** *intr.* **a** walk or proceed steadily. **b** (of events, etc.) continue unrelentingly (*time marches on*). • *n.* **1 a** act of marching. **b** uniform step of troops, etc. **2** progress or continuity. **3** piece of music composed to accompany a march. □ **marching orders 1** *Mil.* direction for troops to depart for war, etc. **2** dismissal. □□ **march′er** *n.*

■ *v.* **1** parade, step, stride, strut, tread, pace. **3 a** see WALK *v.* 1, 2. • *n.* **1 a** parade, procession, cortege, walk. **2** see PROGRESS *n.* 2. □ **marching orders 2** see *dismissal* (DISMISS).

march² /maarch/ *n. hist.* [usu. in *pl.*] boundary, frontier.

Mar·di Gras /maʼardee graʼa/ *n.* last day before Lent, celebrated in some places, as New Orleans; Shrove Tuesday.

mare¹ /mair/ *n.* female of any equine animal, esp. the horse. □ **mare's nest** illusory discovery.

ma·re² /maʼaray/ *n.* (*pl.* **ma·ri·a** /maʼareea/ or **ma·res**) large dark flat area on the moon.

mar·ga·rine /maʼarjərin/ *n.* butter substitute made from vegetable oils or animal fats with milk, etc.

mar·ga·ri·ta /maargəreeʼta/ *n.* cocktail made with tequila, lime or lemon juice, and orange-flavored liqueur.

mar·gin /maʼarjin/ *n.* **1** edge or border. **2** blank border on each side of the print on a page, etc. **3** amount (of time, money, etc.) by which a thing exceeds, falls short, etc. (*margin of profit*). **4** amount deposited with a stockbroker by the customer when borrowing from the broker to purchase securities. See synonym study at BORDER. □ **margin of error** allowance for miscalculation. □□ **mar′gin·al** *adj.* **mar′gin·al·ly** *adv.*

■ **1** perimeter, bound(s), boundary; rim, lip, side, brink. **3** majority, gap, difference, shortfall, deficit, surplus, excess, profit. □□ **marginal** borderline, minimal, small, slight, negligible.

mar·gi·na·li·a /maʼarjináyleeə/ *n.pl.* marginal notes.

mar·gin·al·ize /maʼarjinəlīz/ *v.tr.* make or treat as insignificant. □□ **mar·gin·al·i·za′tion** *n.*

ma·ri·a·chi /maareeaʼachee, mar–/ *n.* **1** Mexican band of strolling musicians. **2** music played by such a band.

mar·i·gold /maʼrigōld/ *n.* plant with bright yellow, orange, or maroon flowers.

mar·i·jua·na /maʼriwaʼanə/ *n.* (also **ma·ri·hua′na**) dried leaves, etc., of hemp, smoked or ingested as a drug.

■ *slang* pot, grass, weed.

ma·rim·ba /mərimbə/ *n.* **1** xylophone of Africa and Central America. **2** modern instrument derived from this.

ma·ri·na /mərеenə/ *n.* harbor for pleasure yachts, etc.

mar·i·nade /maʼrináyd/ • *n.* **1** mixture of wine, vinegar, oil, spices, etc., in which meat,

fish, etc., is soaked before cooking. **2** meat, fish, etc., so soaked. • *v.tr.* = MARINATE.

ma·ri·na·ra /maarinaʼarə/ *adj.* (of a pasta sauce) made with tomatoes, spices, etc., usu. without meat.

mar·i·nate /maʼrinayt/ *v.tr.* soak (meat, fish, etc.) in a marinade. □□ **mar·i·na·tion** /–náyshən/ *n.*

ma·rine /mərеen/ • *adj.* **1** of, found in, or produced by the sea. **2** of or relating to shipping or naval matters (*marine insurance*). • *n.* **1** country's shipping, fleet, or navy (*merchant marine*). **2 a** member of the US Marine Corps. **b** member of a body of troops trained to serve on land or sea.

■ *adj.* **1** maritime, sea, oceanic, aquatic, saltwater. **2** maritime, nautical, naval, seafaring, seagoing, oceangoing, sea. • *n.* **1** flotilla, naval force, armada.

mar·i·ner /maʼrinər/ *n.* sailor.

mar·i·on·ette /maʼreeənét/ *n.* puppet worked by strings.

mar·i·tal /maʼritəl/ *adj.* of marriage or the relations between husband and wife. □□ **mar′i·tal·ly** *adv.*

mar·i·time /maʼritim/ *adj.* **1** connected with the sea or seafaring (*maritime insurance*). **2** living or found near the sea.

■ **1** see MARINE 2. **2** see MARINE 1.

mar·jo·ram /maʼarjərəm/ *n.* aromatic herb used in cooking.

mark¹ /maark/ • *n.* **1** trace, sign, stain, etc., on a surface, etc. **2** [esp. in *comb.*] a written or printed symbol (*question mark*). **b** number or letter denoting excellence, conduct, proficiency, etc. (*black mark*). **3** sign or indication of quality, character, feeling, etc. **4** target, object, goal, etc. **5** line, etc., indicating a position; marker. **6** (usu. **Mark**) (followed by a numeral) particular design, model, etc., of a car, aircraft, etc. **7** runner's starting point in a race. • *v.tr.* **1 a** make a mark on (a thing or person), esp. by writing, cutting, scraping, etc. **b** put an identifying mark, initials, name, etc., on. **2** allot marks to; correct (a student's work, etc.). **3** attach a price to. **4** notice or observe (*she marked his agitation*). **5** characterize (*day was marked by storms*). □ **beside** (or **off** or **wide of**) **the mark 1** not to the point; irrelevant. **2** not accurate. **make one's mark** attain distinction. **mark down 1** mark (goods, etc.) at a lower price. **2** make a written note of. **mark time** *Mil.* march on the spot, without moving forward. **2** wait. **mark up 1** mark (goods, etc.) at a higher price. **2** mark or correct (text, etc.).

■ *n.* **1** spot, scar, blemish, smear, smudge, impression, dent, nick. **2 a, 3** emblem, device, hallmark, seal, earmark, fingerprint, badge, characteristic, token, brand, stamp, label. **2 b** rating, grade, grading, score. **4** objective, aim, purpose, end. **5** indicator, guide, signpost, landmark. • *v.* **1** spot, stain, blemish, smear, smudge, streak, dent, trace, pockmark, nick, scratch, cut, chip, pit, bruise. **2** grade, evaluate, assess, appraise. **3** label; price, tag. **4** pay attention to, attend (to), pay heed to, note, take notice of, heed, watch. **5** brand, stamp, identify, distinguish. □ **beside** (or **off** or **wide of**) **the mark 1** see

make one's mark succeed, get ahead, triumph, distinguish oneself. **mark down 1** reduce, devalue, discount. **2** write (down), record, register, note (down). **mark time 2** see WAIT v. 1a. **mark up 1** increase, hike, colloq. up.

mark² /maark/ n. = DEUTSCHE MARK.

mark•down /maarkdown/ n. reduction in price.

marked /maarkt/ adj. **1** having a visible mark. **2** clearly noticeable; evident (a marked difference). **3** (of playing cards) having distinctive marks on their backs to assist cheating. □□ **mark•ed•ly** /-kidlee/ adv. **mark'ed•ness** n.

■ **1** see SPOTTY 1. **2** conspicuous, decided, pronounced, considerable, remarkable, significant.

mark•er /maarkər/ n. **1** stone, post, etc., used to mark a position, etc. **2** person or thing that marks. **3** sl. IOU.

mar•ket /maarkit/ • n. **1** gathering of people for the purchase and sale of provisions, livestock, etc. **2** open space or covered building used for this. **3** demand for a commodity. **4** place or group providing such a demand. **5** conditions as regards, or opportunity for, buying or selling. **6** [prec. by the] trade in a specified commodity (the grain market). • v. tr offer for sale. □ **market research** study of consumers' needs and preferences. □□ **mar•ket•a•bil'i•ty** n. **mar'ket•a•ble** adj. **mar'ket•er** n.

■ n. **1** marketplace, exchange. **2** shop, store, bazaar, supermarket, superstore. **3**, **4** call, trade; outlet; clientele. **6** see TRADE n. 1a, b. • v. sell, merchandise, retail, vend, peddle, hawk, make available, furnish.

mar•ket•ing /maarkiting/ n. **1** selling or buying in a market. **2** activity or process involving research, promotion, sales, and distribution of a product or service.

mar•ket•place /maarkitplays/ n. **1** open space where a market is held in a town. **2** scene of actual dealings. **3** forum or sphere for the exchange of ideas, etc.

mark•ing /maarking/ n. [usu. in pl.] **1** identification mark, esp. a symbol on an aircraft. **2** coloring of an animal's fur, feathers, skin, etc.

marks•man /maarksmən/ n. (pl. **-men**; fem. **-wom•an**, pl. **-wom•en**) person skilled in shooting, esp. with a pistol or rifle. □□ **marks'man•ship** n.

mark•up /maarkup/ n. amount added to cost for profit.

mar•lin /maarlin/ n. large long-nosed marine fish.

mar•ma•lade /maarməlayd/ n. preserve of citrus fruit, usu. bitter oranges, made like jam.

mar•mo•set /maarməset, -zet/ n. small tropical American monkey having a long bushy tail.

mar•mot /maarmət/ n. burrowing rodent with a heavyset body and short bushy tail.

ma•roon¹ /məroon/ adj. & n. brownish-crimson.

ma•roon² /məroon/ v.tr. leave (a person) isolated in a desolate place (esp. an island).

■ abandon, cast away, desert, strand, forsake; isolate.

marque /maark/ n. make of a product, as a sports car.

mar•quee /maarkee/ n. projecting roof over an entry.

mar•quess /maarkwis/ n. British nobleman ranking between duke and earl.

mar•que•try /maarkitree/ n. (also **mar'que•te•rie**) inlaid work in wood, ivory, etc.

mar•quis /maarkwis, -kee/ n. nobleman ranking between duke and count.

mar•quise /maarkeez, -kee/ n. **1** wife or widow of a marquis. **2** woman holding the rank of marquis.

mar•riage /marij/ n. **1** legal union of a man and a woman. **2** wedding. **3** intimate union (marriage of true minds). □□ **mar•riage•a•bil'i•ty** n. **mar'riage•a•ble** adj.

■ **1** matrimony, wedlock. **2** nuptials. **3** association, alliance, connection, coupling, merger.

mar•ried /mareed/ • adj. **1** united in marriage. **2** of or relating to marriage (married life). • n. [usu. in pl.] married person (young marrieds).

■ adj. **2** see matrimonial (MATRIMONY).

mar•row /maro/ n. soft fatty substance in the cavities of bones.

mar•ry /maree/ v. (**-ries, -ried**) **1** tr. a take as one's wife or husband in marriage. **b** join or give in marriage. **2** tr. a unite intimately. **b** correlate (things) as a pair. □ **marry off** find a wife or husband for.

■ **1 a** get married to, lead down the aisle or to the altar, colloq. get hitched or spliced to. **b** join in wedlock or (holy) matrimony; give away, marry off. **2 a** fit (together), unify, bond, weld, fuse, put together, couple, join, link; ally, amalgamate, combine. **b** match (up).

Mars /maarz/ n. reddish planet, fourth in order of distance from the sun and next beyond the earth.

marsh /maarsh/ n. low land flooded in wet weather and usu. watery at all times. □ **marsh gas** methane. □□ **marsh'y** adj. (**marsh•i•er, marsh•i•est**). **marsh'i•ness** n.

■ swamp, bog, wetland(s), marshland, fen, slough.

mar•shal /maarshəl/ • n. **1** officer of a judicial district, similar to a sheriff. **2** head of a fire department. **3** high-ranking officer in the armed forces of certain countries (air marshal). **4** officer arranging ceremonies, controlling procedure at races, etc. • v.tr. arrange (soldiers, facts, one's thoughts, etc.) in due order. See synonym study at GATHER. □□ **mar'shal•er** n.

marsh•mal•low /maarshmelo, -malo/ n. spongy confection made of sugar, albumen, gelatin, etc.

mar•su•pi•al /maarsoopeeəl/ • n. mammal characterized by being born incompletely developed and usu. carried and suckled in a pouch. • adj. of or like a marsupial.

mart /maart/ n. market.

mar•ten /maárt'n/ n. weasellike carnivore having valuable fur.

mar•tial /maárshəl/ adj. **1** of or appropriate to warfare. **2** warlike; brave; fond of fighting. □ **martial arts** fighting sports such as judo and karate. **martial law** military government, involving the suspension of ordinary law. □□ **mar′tial•ly** adv.
■ **1** military, soldierly, naval, fighting, service. **2** belligerent, bellicose, pugnacious, militant; courageous, valorous.

Mar•tian /maárshən/ • adj. of the planet Mars. • n. hypothetical inhabitant of Mars.

mar•tin /maárt'n/ n. a kind of swallow.

mar•ti•net /maárt'nét/ n. strict (esp. military or naval) disciplinarian.

mar•ti•ni /maarteénee/ n. cocktail made of gin and dry vermouth, often garnished with a green olive, lemon peel, etc.

mar•tyr /maártər/ • n. **1** person who suffers or is put to death for refusing to renounce a faith or belief. **2** constant sufferer. • v.tr. **1** put to death as a martyr. **2** torment. □□ **mar′tyr•dom** n.
■ n. **1** see VICTIM 1, 2. • v. see PERSECUTE 1. □□ **martyrdom** see PASSION 4a.

mar•vel /maárvəl/ • n. **1** wonderful thing or person. • v.intr. feel surprise or wonder. □□ **mar′vel•er** n.
■ n. miracle, phenomenon; see also WONDER n. 2. • v. wonder, be awed or amazed or astonished, gape.

mar•vel•ous /maárvələs/ adj. **1** astonishing. **2** excellent. □□ **mar′vel•ous•ly** adv.
■ **1** wonderful, amazing, astounding, surprising, remarkable, extraordinary, phenomenal, miraculous, unbelievable, incredible. **2** glorious, splendid, superb, spectacular, wonderful, sensational, unparalleled, colloq. terrific, great, fantastic.

Marx•ism /maárksizəm/ n. anticapitalist political and economic theories of Karl Marx, advocating communism and socialism. □□ **Marx′ist** n. & adj.

mar•zi•pan /maárzipan/ n. paste of ground almonds, sugar, etc., used in confectionery.

mas•car•a /maskárə/ n. cosmetic for darkening the eyelashes.

mas•cot /máskot/ n. person, animal, or thing that is supposed to bring good luck.

mas•cu•line /máskyəlin/ • adj. **1** of or characteristic of men. **2** manly; vigorous. **3** Gram. of or denoting the male gender. See synonym study at MALE. • n. Gram. masculine gender; masculine word. □□ **mas′cu•line•ly** adv. **mas•cu•lin′i•ty** n.
■ adj. **2** see MANLY 1.

ma•ser /máyzər/ n. device for amplifying or generating coherent monochromatic electromagnetic radiation in the microwave range (acronym of microwave amplification by stimulated emission of radiation; (cf. LASER)).

MASH /mash/ abbr. Mobile Army Surgical Hospital.

mash /mash/ • n. **1** soft mixture. **2** mixture of boiled grain, bran, etc., given warm to horses, etc. **3** mixture of malt and hot water used in brewing. **4** soft pulp. • v.tr. reduce (potatoes, etc.) to a uniform mass by crushing. □□ **mash′er** n.
■ v. see CRUSH v. 1.

mask /mask/ • n. **1** covering for all or part of the face as a disguise or for protection. **2** likeness of a person's face, esp. one made by taking a mold from the face (death mask). **3** disguise or pretense (throw off the mask). • v.tr. **1** cover (the face, etc.) with a mask. **2** disguise or conceal (a taste, one's feelings, etc.). **3** protect from a process. □□ **mask′er** n.
■ n. **3** guise, camouflage, show, semblance, cover, facade, veil. • v. **1** see VEIL v. **2** camouflage, cover (up), hide, cloak, obscure, veil, screen, shroud.

mas•och•ism /másəkizəm/ n. **1** form of (esp. sexual) perversion involving one's own pain or humiliation. **2** colloq. enjoyment of what appears to be painful or tiresome. □□ **mas′och•ist** n. **mas•och•is′tic** adj. **mas•och•is′ti•cal•ly** adv.

ma•son /máysən/ n. **1** person who builds with stone or brick. **2** (**Mason**) Freemason.

Ma•son-Dix•on line /máysən-díksən/ n. boundary between Maryland and Pennsylvania, taken as the northern limit of the slave-owning states before the abolition of slavery.

Ma•son•ic /məsónik/ adj. of or relating to Freemasons.

ma•son•ry /máysənree/ n. **1 a** work of a mason. **b** stonework; brickwork. **2** (**Masonry**) Freemasonry.

masque /mask/ n. dramatic and musical entertainment esp. of the 16th and 17th c. □□ **mas′quer** n.

mas•quer•ade /máskəráyd/ • n. **1** false show or pretense. **2** masked ball. • v.intr. [often foll. by as] appear in disguise, assume a false appearance. □□ **mas•quer•ad′er** n.
■ n. **1** disguise, deception, pose, dissimulation, bluff, subterfuge, fakery, imposture. • v. pretend to be, pass oneself off as, impersonate, simulate, pose as.

Mass. abbr. Massachusetts.

mass[1] /mas/ • n. **1** coherent body of matter of indefinite shape. **2** dense aggregation of objects (a mass of fibers). **3** large number or amount. **4** [prec. by the] **a** the majority. **b** [in pl.] ordinary people. **5** Physics quantity of matter a body contains. **6** [attrib.] on a large scale (mass action). • v. assemble into a mass. □ **mass-market** see MARKET. **mass media** = MEDIA 2. **mass noun** Gram.noun that is not countable and cannot be used with the indefinite article or in the plural (e.g., happiness). **mass-produce** produce by mass production. **mass production** production of large quantities of a standardized article by a standardized mechanical process. □□ **mass′less** adj.
■ n. **1, 2** pile, heap, mountain, load, stack, mound, bunch, bundle, lot, batch, quantity, hoard, store, collection; block, concretion, chunk, lump, hunk, nugget. **3** abundance, quantity, profusion, multitude, horde, host, mob, colloq. bunch, ton, mountain. **4 a** best or better or greater part, bulk, body, preponderance, lion's share. **b** (the masses) the common people, the plebeians, (the) hoi polloi, the lower class(es), derog. the proletariat. • v.

amass, pile or heap up, gather, aggregate, accumulate, collect; meet, get or come together.

mass² /mas/ n. (often **Mass**) celebration of the Eucharist, esp. in the Roman Catholic Church.

mas•sa•cre /másəkər/ • n. general slaughter (of persons, occasionally of animals). • v.tr. **1** make a massacre of. **2** murder (esp. a large number of people) cruelly or violently. See synonym study at KILL.

■ n. carnage, annihilation, blood bath, killing, extermination, butchery, (mass) murder. • v. **1** see DEFEAT v. 1, wipe out 1a. **2** slaughter, annihilate, kill, execute, exterminate, butcher, liquidate, destroy.

mas•sage /məsáazh, –saáj/ • n. rubbing, kneading, etc., of the body with the hands for therapeutic benefit. • v.tr. apply massage to. □□ **mas•sag•er** n.

■ n. rub, rubdown, manipulation. • v. rub (down), manipulate, knead.

mas•seur /masŕr/ n. (fem. **masseuse** /masŏz/) person who provides massage professionally.

mas•sive /másiv/ adj. **1** large and heavy or solid. **2** exceptionally large. **3** substantial; impressive (a massive reputation). See synonym study at HEAVY. □□ **mas•sive•ly** adv. **mas•sive•ness** n.

■ **1, 2** big, oversized, huge, bulky, enormous, immense, gigantic, towering, mammoth, colossal, titanic, vast, tremendous. **3** see IMPRESSIVE.

mast¹ /mast/ n. **1** long upright post for supporting a ship's sails. **2** post or latticework upright for supporting a radio or television antenna. **3** flagpole (half-mast). □□ **mast'ed** adj. [also in comb.]. **mas'ter** n. [also in comb.].

mast² /mast/ n. fruit of the beech, oak, chestnut, and other forest trees, esp. as food for pigs.

mas•tec•to•my /mastéktəmee/ n. (pl. **-mies**) Surgery removal of all or part of a breast.

mas•ter /mástər/ • n. **1** person having control or ownership (master of the house). **2** Naut. captain of a merchant ship. **3** person who has or gets the upper hand (we shall see which of us is master). **4** skilled practitioner (often attrib.: master carpenter). **5** holder of a university degree orig. giving authority to teach in the university (Master of Arts, Master of Science). **6** great artist. **7** Chess, etc. player of proven ability at international level. **8** original version (e.g., of a film or audio recording) from which a series of copies can be made. **9** (**Master**) title prefixed to the name of a boy not old enough to be called Mr. • adj. **1** commanding; superior (a master spirit). **2** main; principal (master bedroom). **3** controlling others (master plan). • v.tr. **1** overcome; defeat. **2** acquire complete knowledge of or skill in. □ **master key** key that opens several locks, each of which also has its own key. **Master of Ceremonies** see CEREMONY. □□ **mas'ter•dom** n. **mas'ter•hood** n. **mas'ter•less** adj.

■ n. **1** owner, head, chief, leader, chieftain, commander, lord, governor, director, controller, employer, manager, overseer, supervisor, colloq. boss, bigwig, top dog. **3** chief, leader, colloq. boss. **4** expert, authority, craftsman, adept, maestro, mastermind. • adj. **1** controlling. **2** biggest, chief; see also MAIN adj. 1. **3** commanding, superior, prime, basic, chief, overall. • v. **1** control, repress, suppress, subdue, subjugate, bridle, check, quell, get the better of, conquer. **2** learn, grasp, become expert in, know a thing inside out, know, understand.

mas•ter•ful /mástərfŏol/ adj. **1** imperious; domineering. **2** masterly. □□ **mas'ter•ful•ly** adv. **mas'ter•ful•ness** n.

■ **1** authoritarian, dictatorial, tyrannical, despotic, arbitrary, overbearing, arrogant, peremptory. **2** adept, expert, excellent, superior, superb, adroit, exquisite, superlative, supreme, consummate.

mas•ter•ly /mástərlee/ adj. very skillful. □□ **mas'ter•li•ness** n.

■ see SKILLFUL. □□ **masterliness** see FACILITY 1, 2.

mas•ter•mind /mástərmīnd/ • n. **1** person with an outstanding intellect. **2** person directing an intricate operation. • v.tr. plan and direct (a scheme or enterprise).

■ n. genius, mind, intellect, brain; planner, contriver. • v. devise, conceive, think up, engineer, generate.

mas•ter•piece /mástərpees/ n. **1** outstanding piece of artistry or workmanship. **2** person's best work.

■ masterwork, magnum opus, tour de force, jewel, work of art, pièce de résistance; chef-d'œuvre.

mas•ter•stroke /mástərströk/ n. outstandingly skillful act of policy, etc.

mas•ter•work /mástərwork/ n. masterpiece.

mas•ter•y /mástəree/ n. **1** dominion, sway. **2** comprehensive knowledge or skill.

■ **1** see SWAY n. 1. **2** see SKILL, COMMAND n. 2.

mast•head /mást-hed/ n. **1** highest part of a ship's mast. **2 a** title of a newspaper, etc., at the head of the front or editorial page. **b** printed notice in a newspaper, magazine, etc., giving details of staff, ownership, etc.

mas•ti•cate /mástikayt/ v.tr. grind or chew (food) with one's teeth. □□ **mas•ti•ca•tion** /–káyshən/ n. **mas'ti•ca•tor** n.

mas•tiff /mástif/ n. large strong breed of dog.

mas•to•don /mástədon/ n. large extinct mammal resembling the elephant.

mas•toid /mástoyd/ • adj. shaped like a woman's breast. • n. conical prominence on the temporal bone behind the ear.

mas•tur•bate /mástərbayt/ v. arouse oneself sexually or cause (another person) to be aroused by manual stimulation of the genitals. □□ **mas•tur•ba•tion** /–báyshən/ n. **mas'tur•ba•tor** n.

■ □□ **masturbation** onanism, self-gratification, Psychol. autoeroticism, old-fashioned self-abuse.

mat¹ /mat/ • n. **1** piece of coarse material for wiping shoes on, esp. a doormat. **2** piece of cork, rubber, plastic, etc., for protecting a surface. **3** piece of resilient material for landing on in gymnastics, wrestling, etc. • v. (**mat•ted, mat•ting**) **1** tr. (esp. as **matted** adj.) entangle in a thick mass (*matted hair*). **2** intr. become matted.

mat² var. of MATTE.

mat³ /mat/ n. = MATRIX.

mat•a•dor /mátədawr/ n. bullfighter whose task is to kill the bull.

match¹ /mach/ • n. **1** contest or game of skill. **2 a** equal contender. **b** person or thing exactly like or corresponding to another. **3** marriage. • v. **1 a** tr. be equal to or harmonious with; correspond to. **b** intr. correspond; harmonize. **2** tr. place in conflict, contest, or competition with. **3** tr. find material, etc., that matches (another). **4** tr. find a person or thing suitable for another (*matching unemployed workers to available jobs*). □ **match point 1** Tennis, etc. **a** the state of a game when one side needs only one more point to win the match. **b** this point. **2** Bridge unit of scoring in matches and tournaments. □□ **match'a•ble** adj.

■ n. **1** competition, meet, tourney, tournament, bout, duel, trial. **2 a** equal, equivalent, like, peer, fellow, mate. **b** parallel, replica, copy, double, twin, look-alike, facsimile, counterpart. **3** betrothal, alliance, combination, compact, contract. • v. **1** fit, suit; accord, agree, go (together), coordinate, blend. **2** pit or set or put against, play off against. **4** match up, join, marry, unite, link, combine, put together, pair up or off, conjoin.

match² /mach/ n. short thin piece of flammable material tipped with a composition that can be ignited by friction.

match•box /máchboks/ n. box for holding matches.

match•less /máchlis/ adj. without an equal, incomparable. □□ **match'less•ly** adv.

■ unique, original, peerless, unequaled, unparalleled.

match•mak•er /máchmaykər/ n. person who tries to arrange an agreement or relationship between two parties, esp. a marriage partnership. □□ **match'mak•ing** n.

match•stick /máchstik/ n. stem of a match.

mate¹ /mayt/ • n. **1** friend or fellow worker. **2 a** each of a pair, esp. of animals, birds, or socks. **b** colloq. partner in marriage. **c** [in comb.] fellow member or joint occupant of (*roommate*). **3** Naut. officer on a merchant ship subordinate to the master. • v. **1** tr. bring together for marriage or breeding. **2** intr. come together for marriage or breeding. □□ **mate'less** adj.

■ n. **1** companion, associate, colleague, co-worker, comrade, crony, ally, alter ego. **2 a** fellow, twin, counterpart. **b** spouse, helpmate, consort, husband, wife, colloq. better half, hubby. • v. **1** pair (up), match (up), marry, join, unite, couple, link (up), usu. formal or literary wed. **2** breed, couple, copulate, pair (up).

mate² /mayt/ n. & v.tr. Chess = CHECKMATE.

ma•te•ri•al /mətéereeəl/ • n. **1** matter from which a thing is made. **2** cloth; fabric. **3** [in

pl.] things needed for an activity (*building materials*). **4** [in sing. or pl.] information, etc., to be used in writing a book, etc. (*experimental material*). • adj. **1** of matter; corporeal. **2** concerned with bodily comfort, etc. (*material well-being*). **3** important; essential; relevant (*at the material time*). □□ **ma•te•ri•al•i•ty** /–reeálitee/ n.

■ n. **1** substance, fabric; stuff. **2** textile, stuff. **3** constituents, elements, components. **4** data, facts, statistics, figures, documents, documentation. • adj. **1** physical, tangible, concrete, solid, real, substantial, palpable, bodily. **2** physical, corporeal. **3** consequential, significant.

ma•te•ri•al•ism /mətéereeəlizəm/ n. **1** tendency to prefer material possessions and physical comfort to spiritual values. **2** Philos. theory that nothing exists but matter and its movements and modifications. □□ **ma•te'ri•al•ist** n. **ma•te•ri•al•is'tic** adj. **ma•te•ri•al•is'ti•cal•ly** adv.

■ □□ **materialistic** greedy, acquisitive, selfish, commercial, sybaritic, colloq. usu. derog. yuppie.

ma•te•ri•al•ize /mətéereeəlīz/ v. **1** intr. become actual fact. **2** intr. colloq. appear or be present when expected. **3** tr. represent or express in material form. □□ **ma•te•ri•al•i•za'tion** n.

■ **1** happen, come to pass, take place, occur. **2** turn up; take shape or form, form, emerge.

ma•te•ri•al•ly /mətéereeəlee/ adv. substantially, considerably.

■ palpably, significantly, seriously, essentially.

ma•ter•nal /mət́rnəl/ adj. **1** of or like a mother. **2** motherly. **3** related through the mother (*maternal uncle*). □□ **ma•ter'nal•ism** n. **ma•ter•nal•is'tic** adj. **ma•ter'nal•ly** adv.

■ **1, 2** warm, nurturing, caring, understanding, affectionate, tender, kind; maternalistic; matriarchal.

ma•ter•ni•ty /mət́rnitee/ n. **1** motherhood. **2** [attrib.] for women during and just after childbirth (*maternity hospital*).

math /math/ n. colloq. mathematics.

math•e•mat•i•cal /máthimátikəl/ adj. **1** of mathematics. **2** rigorously precise; exact. □□ **math•e•mat'i•cal•ly** adv.

■ **1** arithmetical. **2** exact, rigorous.

math•e•mat•ics /máthimátiks/ n.pl. **1** [also treated as sing.] abstract science of number, quantity, and space. **2** [as pl.] use of mathematics in calculation, etc. □□ **math•e•ma•ti•cian** /–mətíshən/ n.

mat•i•née /mat'náy/ n. (also **mat•i•nee'**) afternoon performance in a theater, etc. □ **matinée idol** handsome actor admired esp. by women.

mat•ins /mát'nz/ n. [as sing. or pl.] service of morning prayer in churches of the Anglican communion.

ma•tri•arch /máytreeaark/ n. female head of a family or tribe. □□ **ma•tri•ar•chal** /–aárkəl/ adj. **ma•tri•ar•chy** /–aárkee/ n.

ma•tri•ces pl. of MATRIX.

mat•ri•cide /mátrisid, máy–/ n. **1** killing of

one's mother. **2** person who does this. □□ **mat•ri•cid′al** adj.

ma•tric•u•late /mətríkyəlàyt/ v. **1** intr. be enrolled at a college or university. **2** tr. admit (a student) to membership of a college or university. □□ **ma•tric•u•la•tion** /–láyshən/ n.

mat•ri•mo•ny /mátrimōnee/ n. (pl. **–nies**) **1** rite of marriage. **2** state of being married. □□ **mat•ri•mo•ni•al** /–mōneeəl/ adj. **mat•ri•mo•ni•al•ly** adv.

■ **1** wedding service. **2** marriage, wedlock. □□ **matrimonial** marital, marriage, wedding, conjugal, nuptial; married, wedded, connubial.

ma•trix /máytriks/ n. (pl. **ma•tri•ces** /–triseez/ or **ma•trix•es**) mold in which a thing is cast or shaped.

ma•tron /máytrən/ n. **1** married woman, esp. a dignified and sober one. **2** woman supervisor, as in an institution. □ **matron of honor** married woman attending the bride at a wedding. □□ **ma′tron•ly** adj.

matte /mat/ (also **matt** or **mat**) • adj. (of a color, surface, etc.) dull, without luster. • n. (in full **matte paint**) paint formulated to give a dull flat finish.

mat•ter /mátər/ • n. **1 a** physical substance in general, as distinct from mind and spirit. **b** that which has mass and occupies space. **2** particular substance (coloring matter). **3** thing that is amiss (what is the matter?). **4** content as distinct from its manner of form. **5** affair or situation being considered, esp. in a specified way (a serious matter). **6** Physiol. **a** any substance in or discharged from the body. **b** pus. • v.intr. **1** be of importance; have significance. □ **as a matter of fact** in reality (esp. to correct a falsehood or misunderstanding). **no matter 1** regardless of. **2** it is of no importance.

■ n. **1, 2** material, stuff. **3** problem, difficulty, trouble; complication, worry. **4** essentials, pith, theme, argument, purport, implication; signification, meaning, import. **5** issue, question, business, subject, topic; occurrence, episode; event. **6** see DISCHARGE n. **5.** • v. be important, count, be of consequence, make a difference.

mat•ter-of-fact /mátərəfákt/ adj. (see also MATTER). **1** unimaginative; prosaic. **2** unemotional. □□ **mat′ter-of-fact′ly** adv. **mat′ter-of-fact′ness** n.

■ **1** straightforward, direct, forthright, factual, unvarnished, unadorned; sober, unartistic, unpoetic, dry, dull. **2** see DISINTERESTED 1, HONEST adj. 2.

mat•ting /máting/ n. fabric for mats.

mat•tock /mátək/ n. agricultural tool shaped like a pickax, with an adze and a chisel edge as the ends of the head.

mat•tress /mátris/ n. fabric case stuffed with soft, firm, or springy material, or a similar case filled with air or water, used on or as a bed.

ma•ture /məchŏŏr, –tyŏŏr, –tŏŏr/ • adj. (**ma•tur•er, ma•tur•est**) **1** with fully developed powers of body and mind; adult. **2** complete in natural development; ripe. **3** (of thought, intentions, etc.) duly careful and adequate. **4** (of a bond, etc.) due for payment. • v. **1** tr.

& intr. develop fully; ripen. **2** intr. (of a bond, etc.) become due for payment. □□ **ma•ture′ly** adv. **ma•ture′ness** n. **ma•tu′ri•ty** n.

■ adj. **1** grown (up), full-grown, of age, experienced, knowledgeable, sophisticated. **2** ready, ripened, mellow, aged, seasoned. **3** see MEASURED 2. • v. **1** age; grow up, come of age; mellow, season, come to maturity. □□ **maturity** adulthood, majority; ripeness, readiness, mellowness; perfection, completion, fullness.

SYNONYM STUDY: mature

AGE, DEVELOP, MELLOW, RIPEN. Most of us would prefer to **mature** rather than simply to **age**. *Mature* implies gaining wisdom, experience, or sophistication as well as adulthood; when applied to nonhuman living things, it indicates fullness of growth and readiness for normal functioning (a mature crop of strawberries). *Age*, on the other hand, refers to the changes that result from the passage of time, often with an emphasis on the negative or destructive changes that accompany growing old (the tragedy aged him five years). **Develop** is like *mature* in that it means to go through a series of positive changes to attain perfection or effectiveness, but it can refer to a part as well as a whole organism (the kitten's eyesight had begun to develop at three weeks). **Ripen** is a less formal word meaning to *mature*, but it usually applies to fruit (the apples ripened in the sun). **Mellow** suggests the tempering, moderation, or reduction in harshness that comes with time or experience. With its connotations of warmth, mildness, and sweetness, it is a more positive word than *mature* or *age* (to mellow as one gets older).

---

mat•zo /mátsə/ n. (also **mat′zoh**; pl. **–zos** or **–zohs** or **mat•zoth** /–sōt/) unleavened bread, served esp. at Passover.

maud•lin /máwdlin/ adj. weakly or tearfully sentimental, esp. in a tearful and effusive stage of drunkenness.

■ (over)emotional, mawkish, tearful, weepy, mushy, romantic, colloq. soupy, slushy.

maul /mawl/ • v.tr. **1** beat and bruise. **2** handle roughly or carelessly. • n. heavy hammer. □□ **maul′er** n.

maun•der /máwndər/ v.intr. talk in a rambling manner.

mau•so•le•um /máwsəlee′əm/ n. large and grand tomb.

mauve /mōv/ • adj. pale purple. • n. **1** this color. **2** bright but delicate pale purple dye. □□ **mauv′ish** adj.

mav•er•ick /mávərik, mávrik/ n. **1** unbranded calf or yearling. **2** unorthodox or independent-minded person.

■ **2** see *individualist* (INDIVIDUALISM).

maw /maw/ n. **1** stomach of an animal. **2** jaws or throat of a voracious animal.

mawk•ish /máwkish/ adj. sentimental in a feeble or sickly way. □□ **mawk′ish•ly** adv. **mawk′ish•ness** n.

max. abbr. maximum.

max•i /máksee/ n. (pl. **max•is**) colloq. maxiskirt or other garment with a long skirt.

maxi- /máksee/ comb. form very large or long (maxicoat).

max•il•la /maksílə/ n. (pl. **max•il•lae** /-lee/ or **max•il•las**) 1 jaw or jawbone, esp. the upper jaw in most vertebrates. □□ **max•il•lar•y** /máksəléeree/ adj.

max•im /máksim/ n. general truth or rule of conduct expressed in a sentence. See synonym study at SAYING.

■ saying, proverb, axiom, aphorism, adage, byword, saw.

max•i•mize /máksimīz/ v.tr. increase or enhance to the utmost. □□ **max•i•mi•za′tion** n. **max′i•miz•er** n.

■ broaden, improve, magnify, augment, add to, expand, build up, enlarge; embroider, embellish, elaborate; inflate, overplay, overdo, overstate.

max•i•mum /máksiməm/ • n. (pl. **max•i•ma** /-mə/) highest possible or attainable amount. • adj. that is a maximum. □□ **max′i•mal** adj. **max′i•mal•ly** adv.

■ n. utmost, uttermost, greatest, most, highest, extreme, extremity, limit, peak, pinnacle. • adj. maximal, greatest, most, utmost, uttermost, superlative.

May /may/ n. 1 fifth month of the year. 2 (**may**) hawthorn or its blossom. □ **May Day** May 1, esp. as a festival with dancing, or as an international holiday in honor of workers.

may /may/ v.aux. (3rd sing. present **may**; past **might** /mīt/) 1 expressing possibility (it may be true). 2 expressing permission (may I come in?). ¶Both can and may are used to express permission; in more formal contexts may is usual since can also denotes capability (can I move? = am I physically able to move?; may I move = am I allowed to move?). 3 expressing a wish (may he live to regret it). 4 expressing uncertainty or irony in questions (who may you be?).

Ma•ya /máayə/ n. 1 (pl. same or **Ma•yas**) member of an ancient native people of Central America. 2 language of this people. □□ **Ma′yan** adj. & n.

may•be /máybee/ adv. perhaps; possibly.

May•day /máyday/ n. international radio distress signal.

may•flow•er /máyflowər/ n. any of various flowers that bloom in May.

may•fly /máyflī/ n. (pl. **–flies**) insect with four delicate wings, the adult of which lives briefly in spring.

may•hem /máyhem/ n. violent or damaging action.

■ violence, havoc, destruction, devastation.

may•on•naise /máyənáyz/ n. thick creamy dressing made of egg yolks, oil, vinegar, etc.

may•or /máyər, mair/ n. chief executive of a city or town. □□ **may′or•al** adj.

may•or•al•ty /máyərəltee, máir–/ n. (pl. **–ties**) 1 office of mayor. 2 mayor's period of office.

may•pole /máypōl/ n. (also **Maypole**) deco-

rated pole for dancing around on May Day.

maze /mayz/ n. 1 network of paths and hedges designed as a puzzle for those who try to penetrate it. 2 complex network of paths or passages; labyrinth. 3 confusion, confused mass, etc. □□ **ma′zy** adj. (**ma•zi•er, ma•zi•est**).

■ 2 complex, warren. 3 see TANGLE n.

ma•zur•ka /məzúrkə/ n. 1 lively Polish dance in triple time. 2 music for this.

MB abbr. Computing megabyte(s).

MBA abbr. Master of Business Administration.

MC abbr. 1 master of ceremonies. 2 Member of Congress.

MD abbr. 1 Doctor of Medicine. 2 Maryland (in official postal use). 3 Managing Director. 4 muscular dystrophy.

Md symb. Chem. mendelevium.

Md. abbr. Maryland.

ME abbr. 1 Maine (in official postal use). 2 Middle East.

Me. abbr. Maine.

me /mee/ pron. objective case of I² (he saw me).

mead /meed/ n. alcoholic drink of fermented honey and water.

mead•ow /médō/ n. 1 piece of grassland, esp. one used for hay. 2 piece of low well-watered ground, esp. near a river. □□ **mead′ow•y** adj.

■ 1 field, pasture, poet. lea, poet. mead.

mea•ger /méegər/ adj. 1 lacking in amount or quality (a meager salary). 2 (of a person or animal) lean; thin. □□ **mea′ger•ly** adv. **mea′ger•ness** n.

■ 1 scanty, poor, paltry, inadequate, skimpy, scrimpy, sparse, insufficient, bare, puny, trifling, niggardly. 2 spare, skinny, scrawny, bony, emaciated, gaunt.

meal¹ /meel/ n. 1 occasion when food is eaten. 2 the food eaten on one occasion. □ **meal ticket** 1 ticket entitling one to a meal, esp. at a specified place with reduced cost. 2 person or thing that is a source of food or income.

■ spread, collation; dinner, supper, breakfast, lunch, brunch; formal luncheon; victuals, nourishment.

meal² /meel/ n. grain or pulse ground to powder.

meal•y /méelee/ adj. (**meal•i•er, meal•i•est**) 1 a of or like meal; soft and powdery. b containing meal. 2 (of a complexion) pale. 3 (of a horse) spotty. 4 (in full **mealy-mouthed**) afraid to use plain expressions. □□ **meal′i•ness** n.

■ 2 see PALE¹ adj. 1. 3 see SPOTTY 1. 4 mincing, reticent, reluctant, hesitant, equivocal; see also OBSEQUIOUS.

mean¹ /meen/ v.tr. (past and past part. **meant** /ment/) 1 have as one's purpose or intention. 2 design or destine for a purpose. 3 intend to convey or indicate or refer to. 4 be of some specified importance to. See synonym study at INTEND. □ **mean it** not be joking or exaggerating. **mean well** have good intentions.

■ 1, 2 intend, purpose, plan, aim, have in mind, contemplate, have in view; want, wish, expect, hope.

mean² /meen/ • adj. **1** not generous or liberal. **2** (of an action) ignoble; small-minded. **3** (of a person's capacity, understanding, etc.) inferior; poor. **4** shabby. **5 a** malicious; ill-tempered. **b** vicious or aggressive in behavior. **6** colloq. skillful; formidable. □□ **mean'ly** adv. **mean'ness** n.

■ **1** stingy, miserly, tight, close, near, parsimonious, tightfisted, closefisted, uncharitable, ungenerous. **2** low, base, abject; mean-spirited, small, petty. **3** low. **4** inferior, poor, lowly, abject, modest, humble, run-down, seedy, squalid, mangy, wretched, sordid. **5** unkind, cruel, unaccommodating, disobliging; cantankerous, churlish. **6** excellent, wonderful, marvelous, great, exceptional, effective, skilled, sl. bad.

mean³ /meen/ • n. **1** term midway between extremes. **2** Math. quotient of the sum of several quantities and their number, the average. • adj. **1** (of a quantity) equally far from two extremes. **2** calculated as a mean. ■ n. middle, norm, (happy) medium; balance. • adj. middle, center, intermediate, medial, medium, median, average, middling.

me•an•der /meeándər/ • v.intr. **1** wander at random. **2** (of a stream) wind about. □□ **me•an'drous** adj.
■ ramble, zigzag, snake, coil, twist; stroll, amble.

mean•ie /meenee/ n. (also **mean'y**) (pl. **-ies**) colloq. mean, niggardly, or small-minded person.

mean•ing /meening/ • n. **1** what is meant. **2** significance. • adj. expressive; significant. □□ **mean'ing•ly** adv.
■ n. sense, import, content, signification, denotation; purport, implication, tenor, drift; interpretation, explanation. • adj. see EXPRESSIVE 1.

mean•ing•ful /meeningfool/ adj. **1** full of meaning; significant. **2** Logic able to be interpreted. □□ **mean'ing•ful•ly** adv. **mean'ing•ful•ness** n.
■ **1** important, consequential, serious, sober, deep, substantial, pithy, telling; suggestive, pregnant, telltale.

mean•ing•less /meeninglis/ adj. having no meaning or significance. □□ **mean'ing•less•ly** adv. **mean'ing•less•ness** n.
■ empty, hollow, vacuous, insubstantial, unsubstantial; puny, paltry, worthless, irrelevant, insignificant.

means /meenz/ n.pl. **1** [often treated as sing.] that by which a result is brought about. **2 a** money resources. **b** wealth. □ **by all means** (or **all manner of means**) certainly. **by means of** by the agency or instrumentality of. **by no means** (or **no manner of means**) not at all; certainly not.
■ **1** instrument, agency, method, process, technique, avenue, medium, vehicle. **2** funds, cash, capital, finances. □ **by all means** (or **all manner of means**) absolutely, definitely, surely, of course, positively. **by means of** by dint of, via, through, by way of, using, utilizing. **by no means** (or **no manner of means**) in no way, definitely or absolutely not, on no account, not conceivably.

meant past and past part. of MEAN¹.

mean•time /meentim/ • adv. = MEANWHILE. • n. intervening period.

mean•while /meenwil, –hwil/ • adv. **1** in the intervening period. **2** at the same time. • n. intervening period.
■ adv. in the meanwhile, meantime, in the meantime; temporarily. • n. interim, meantime, interval.

mean•y var. of MEANIE.

mea•sles /meezəlz/ n.pl. [also treated as sing.] acute infectious viral disease marked by red spots on the skin.

mea•sly /meezlee/ adj. (**mea•sli•er, mea•sli•est**) colloq. inferior, contemptible; meager.
■ sparse, scanty, worthless; see also WRETCHED 2.

mea•sure /mézhər/ • n. **1** size or quantity found by measuring. **2** system of measuring (liquid measure). **3** instrument for measuring. **4** standard used for valuing. **5** [usu. in pl.] suitable action to achieve some end. **6** legislative act. **7** poetical rhythm; meter. **8** Mus. bar or the time content of a bar. • v. **1** tr. ascertain the extent or quantity of (a thing) by comparison with a standard. **2** intr. be of a specified size (it measures six inches). **3** tr. mark (a line, etc., of a given length). **4** tr. [foll. by out] deal or distribute (a thing) in measured quantities. □ **beyond measure** excessively. **for good measure** as a finishing touch. **measure up** have the necessary qualifications (for). □□ **meas'ur•a•ble** adj. **meas'ur•a•bly** adv. **meas'ure•less** adj.
■ n. **1** amount, magnitude, amplitude, bulk, mass, extent, reach, dimension(s), capacity, volume. **2, 3** scale, gauge, yardstick, rule; standard, criterion, method. **4** gauge, rank, rating, measurement, estimation. **5** step(s), course (of action); plan(s), method, means, avenue. **6** bill, resolution, legislation, statute, law. **7** beat, cadence, time; bar. • v. **1** rank, rate, gauge, meter, weigh, calculate, reckon. **3** measure off, mark off or out, limit, delimit. **4** dole out, ration (out), parcel out, apportion, allot, share out. □ **beyond measure** see unduly (UNDUE). **for good measure** to boot, as well, in addition, moreover, furthermore. **measure up** qualify (for), be suitable (for); meet, equal, fulfill, match, reach, attain, be equal to.

meas•ured /mézhərd/ adj. **1** rhythmical; regular. **2** (of language) carefully considered. □□ **meas'ured•ly** adv.
■ **1** regulated, steady, uniform, even, monotonous. **2** careful, cautious, prudent, calculated, studied, considered, deliberate, systematic, sober, intentional.

meas•ure•ment /mézhərmənt/ n. **1** measuring. **2** amount determined by measuring. **3** [in pl.] detailed dimensions.
■ **1** ascertainment, determination, assessment, estimation, appraisal, evaluation, valuation, judgment. **2** dimension, extent, size, amount, measure; length, breadth, height, width, depth; area; volume, capacity.

meat /meet/ n. **1** flesh of animals (esp.

mammals) as food. **2** [foll. by *of*] essence or chief part of. **3** edible part of nuts, shellfish, etc. □□ **meat′i•ness** *n.* **meat′less** *adj.* **meat′y** *adj.* (**meat•i•er, meat•i•est**)

■ **2** pith, core, heart, marrow, kernel, gist, substance.

Mec•ca /méka/ *n.* **1** place one aspires to visit. **2** birthplace of a faith, policy, pursuit, etc.

me•chan•ic /mikánik/ *n.* skilled worker, esp. one who makes or uses or repairs machinery.

me•chan•i•cal /mikánikəl/ *adj.* **1** of machines or mechanisms. **2** working or produced by machinery. **3** (of a person or action) like a machine; automatic; lacking originality. □□ **me•chan′i•cal•ly** *adv.*

■ **2** automatic, automated, machine-driven, robotic. **3** reflex, involuntary, instinctive, routine, habitual.

me•chan•ics /mikániks/ *n.pl.* [usu. treated as *sing.*] **1** branch of applied mathematics dealing with motion and tendencies to motion. **2** science of machinery. **3** method of construction or routine operation of a thing.

■ **1** machinery, workings, works, system. **2** movement, action, moving parts, gears; device, apparatus. **3** way, means, method, procedure, approach.

mech•a•nize /mékəniz/ *v.tr.* **1** give a mechanical character to. **2** introduce machines in. **3** *Mil.* equip with tanks, armored cars, etc. □□ **mech′a•ni•za′tion** *n.* **mech′a•niz•er** *n.*

med•al /méd′l/ *n.* piece of metal, usu. in the form of a disk, struck or cast with an inscription or device to commemorate an event, etc., or awarded as a distinction to a soldier, athlete, etc. □□ **med′aled** *adj.* **me•dal•lic** /midálik/ *adj.*

med•al•ist /méd′list/ *n.* recipient of a (specified) medal.

me•dal•lion /midályən/ *n.* **1** large medal. **2** thing shaped like this, e.g., a decorative panel or tablet, portrait, etc.

■ **1** see PENDANT. **2** see PLAQUE.

med•dle /méd′l/ *v.intr.* [often foll. by *with, in*] interfere in or busy oneself unduly with others' concerns. □□ **med′dler** *n.*

■ intrude, butt in, thrust one's nose in, pry, intervene.

med•dle•some /méd′lsəm/ *adj.* fond of meddling; interfering. See synonym study at IM-PERTINENT. □□ **med′dle•some•ly** *adv.* **med′dle•some•ness** *n.*

■ see NOSY *adj.* □□ **meddlesomeness** interference, interruption, intrusiveness, obtrusiveness, invasiveness.

me•di•a /méedeeə/ *n.pl.* **1** *pl.* of MEDIUM. **2** [usu. prec. by *the*] main means of mass communication (esp. newspapers and broadcasting) regarded collectively. ¶Use as a mass noun with a singular verb is common (e.g., *the media is on our side*), but is generally disfavored (cf. AGENDA, DATA).

me•di•al /méedeeəl/ *adj.* **1** situated in the middle. **2** of average size. □□ **me′di•al•ly** *adv.*

■ **1** see MIDDLE *adj.* 1, 2. **2** see MEDIUM *adj.*

me•di•an /méedeeən/ • *adj.* situated in the middle. • *n.* **1** *Geom.* straight line drawn from any vertex of a triangle to the middle of the opposite side. **2** *Math.* middle value of a series. **3** (also **median strip**) center divider separating opposing lanes on a divided highway. □□ **me′di•an•ly** *adv.*

■ *adj.* see CENTRAL 1.

me•di•ate /méedeeayt/ *v.* **1** *intr.* intervene (between parties in a dispute) to produce agreement or reconciliation. **2** *tr.* act as an intermediary. See synonym study at INSERT. □□ **me•di•a′tion** /-áyshən/ *n.* **me′di•a•tor** *n.* **me•di•a•to•ry** /méedeeətáwree/ *adj.*

■ **1** arbitrate, referee, umpire, moderate, liaise; see also NEGOTIATE 1, 2. □□ **mediator** arbitrator, arbiter, referee, umpire, judge.

med•ic /médik/ *n. colloq.* medical practitioner or student, esp. a member of a military medical corps.

Med•i•caid /médikayd/ *n.* federal system of health insurance for those requiring financial assistance.

med•i•cal /médikəl/ *adj.* of medicine. □ **medical examination** examination to determine a person's physical fitness. □□ **med′i•cal•ly** *adv.*

Med•i•care /médikair/ *n.* federal government program of health insurance for persons esp. over 65 years of age.

med•i•cate /médikayt/ *v.tr.* **1** treat medically. **2** impregnate with a medicinal substance. □□ **med•i•ca•tion** /médikáyshən/ *n.* **med•i•ca•tive** /médikáytiv/ *adj.*

■ **1** see TREAT *v.* 3. □□ **medication** see MEDICINE 2.

me•dic•i•nal /mədísinəl/ *adj.* (of a substance) having healing properties. □□ **me•dic′i•nal•ly** *adv.*

■ remedial, therapeutic, curative, restorative.

med•i•cine /médisin/ *n.* **1** science or practice of the diagnosis, treatment, and prevention of disease. **2** drug or preparation used for the treatment or prevention of disease. □ **medicine man** person believed to have magical powers of healing, esp. among Native Americans.

■ **2** medication, medicament, remedy, pharmaceutical, prescription; panacea, cure-all. □ **medicine man** healer, witch doctor, shaman.

me•di•e•val /méedee-éevəl, méd–, míd–/ *adj.* **1** of the Middle Ages. **2** *colloq.* old-fashioned; archaic. □□ **me•di•e′val•ism** *n.* **me•di•e′val•ist** *n.* **me•di•e′val•ly** *adv.*

me•di•o•cre /méedeeókər/ *adj.* **1** of middling quality; neither good nor bad. **2** second-rate. □□ **me•di•oc•ri•ty** /-ókritee/ *n.*

■ **1** indifferent, ordinary, commonplace, average, medium, everyday, run-of-the-mill, pedestrian, tolerable. **2** third-rate, inferior, poor, *colloq.* nothing to write home about, no great shakes.

med•i•tate /méditayt/ *v.* **1** *intr.* engage in deep thought; reflect. **2** *tr.* plan mentally.

□□ **med•i•ta•tion** /–táyshən/ *n.* **med′i•ta•tor** *n.*

■ **1** reflect, think, ponder, study, ruminate, cogitate, contemplate, cerebrate. **2** consider, contemplate, scheme, devise, contrive, design, conceive, frame.

med•i•ta•tive /méditaytiv/ *adj.* inclined to meditate. □□ **med′i•ta•tive•ly** *adv.* **med′i•ta•tive•ness** *n.*

■ thoughtful, pensive, contemplative, reflective, studious, cogitative, abstracted, rapt, engrossed.

Med•i•ter•ra•ne•an /méditəráyneeən/ • *n.* large landlocked sea bordered by S. Europe, SW Asia, and N. Africa. • *adj.* of or characteristic of the Mediterranean or its surrounding region (*Mediterranean climate*).

me•di•um /méedeeəm/ • *n.* (*pl.* **me•di•a** or **me•di•ums**) **1** middle quality, degree, etc., between extremes. **2** means by which something is communicated. **3** intervening substance through which impressions are conveyed to the senses, etc. **4** material or form used by an artist, composer, etc. **5** (*pl.* **me•di•ums**) person claiming to communicate with the dead. • *adj.* between two qualities, degrees, etc. □□ **me•di•um•is′tic** *adj.* (in sense 5 of *n.*). **me′di•um•ship** *n.* (in sense 5 of *n.*).

■ *n.* **1** average, middle, midpoint, compromise, center, mean, norm. **2, 4** method, mode, approach, instrument, device, mechanism, intermediation. **3** atmosphere, environment, ambiance, milieu. **5** see PSYCHIC *n.* • *adj.* average, middle, middling, mild, medial, median, normal.

med•ley /médlee/ *n.* (*pl.* **–leys**) **1** varied mixture. **2** collection of tunes, etc., played as one piece.

■ **1** assortment, combination, miscellany, mélange, collection, conglomeration, agglomeration, mixed bag, jumble, mess, farrago, stew, goulash.

me•dul•la /midúlə/ *n.* inner region of certain organs, e.g., the kidney. □ **medulla oblongata** /óblonggaatə/ continuation of the spinal cord within the skull, forming the lowest part of the brain stem.

meek /meek/ *adj.* **1** humble and submissive. **2** piously gentle in nature. □□ **meek′ly** *adv.* **meek′ness** *n.*

■ modest, unassuming, unambitious, unpretentious, mild, bland, patient, deferential, shy, retiring, lowly, tame, timid, weak, docile, compliant.

meer•schaum /méershəm, –shawm/ *n.* **1** soft white claylike substance. **2** tobacco pipe with the bowl made from this.

meet /meet/ • *v.* (*past* and *past part.* **met** /met/) **1 a** *tr.* encounter; come face to face with. **b** *intr.* (of two or more people) come into each other's company. **2** *tr.* be present at the arrival of (a person, train, etc.). **3 a** *tr.* come together or into contact with (*where the road meets the river*). **b** *intr.* come together or into contact (*where the sea and the sky meet*). **4 a** *tr.* make the acquaintance of. **b** *intr.* (of two or more people) make each other's acquaintance. **5** *intr. & tr.* come together or come into contact with for the purposes of

conference, worship, etc. (*the committee meets every week*). **6** *tr.* **a** deal with or answer (*met the proposal with hostility*). **b** satisfy or conform with. **7** *tr.* pay (a bill, etc.). **8** *tr. & f* [foll. by *with*] *intr.* experience, encounter, or receive (*met their death*). **9** *tr.* oppose in battle, etc. • *n.* assembly of competitors, etc. □ **meet the eye** (or **the ear**) be visible (or audible). **meet a person halfway** make a compromise. **meet with** receive (a reaction) (*met with the committee's approval*). □□ **meet′er** *n.*

■ *v.* **1** come across, chance on or upon, happen on or upon, stumble on or into, see. **3** link up, join, unite, touch, intersect. **4** be introduced to. **5** convene, assemble, gather, get together, collect. **6** handle, satisfy, fulfill, take care of, dispose of. **7** settle, defray, liquidate. **8** be met by; undergo, endure, suffer, have, go through. **9** see FIGHT *v.* 1a. • *n.* competition, contest, meeting, match, tourney, tournament, rally. □ **meet with** see RECEIVE 4.

meet•ing /méeting/ *n.* **1** coming together. **2** assembly of people; gathering.

■ **1** rendezvous, encounter, assignation; convergence, converging, confluence, joining. **2** convention, conference, gathering, congress, conclave, session.

mega- /mégə/ *comb. form* **1** large. **2** one million. ¶Abbr.: **M**.

meg•a•bucks /mégəbuks/ *n. colloq.* great sums of money.

meg•a•byte /mégəbīt/ *n.* Computing 1,048,576 (i.e., 2²⁰) bytes as a measure of data capacity, or loosely 1,000,000 bytes. ¶Abbr.: **MB**.

meg•a•hertz /mégəhərts/ *n.* one million hertz. ¶Abbr.: **MHz**.

meg•a•lith /mégəlith/ *n.* Archaeol. large stone, esp. a prehistoric monument. □□ **meg•a•lith′ic** *adj.*

meg•a•lo•ma•ni•a /mégəlōmáyneeə/ *n.* **1** mental disorder producing delusions of grandeur. **2** passion for grandiose schemes. □□ **meg•a•lo•ma′ni•ac** *adj. & n.* **meg•a•lo•ma•ni•a•cal** /–mənīəkəl/ *adj.*

meg•a•lop•o•lis /mégəlópəlis/ *n.* urban area of great extent. □□ **meg•a•lo•pol•i•tan** /–ləpólit′n/ *adj. & n.*

meg•a•phone /mégəfōn/ *n.* large funnel shaped device for amplifying the sound of the voice.

meg•a•ton /mégətun/ *n.* unit of explosive power equal to one million tons of TNT.

meg•a•watt /mégəwot/ *n.* one million watts. ¶Abbr.: **MW**.

mei•o•sis /mīósis/ *n. Biol.* cell division that results in daughter cells with half the chromosome number of the parent cell. □□ **mei•ot•ic** /mīótik/ *adj.* **mei•ot′i•cal•ly** *adv.*

meit•ne•ri•um /mītnəreeəm/ *n. Chem.* artificially produced chemical element. ¶Symb.: **Mt**.

mel•a•mine /méləmeen/ *n.* **1** white crystalline compound producing resins. **2** (in full **melamine resin**) plastic made from this and used esp. for laminated coatings.

mel•an•cho•li•a /mélənkóleeə/ n. depression; anxiety.

mel•an•chol•y /mélənkolee/ • n. (pl. **–ies**) 1 pensive sadness. 2 depression. • adj. sad; depressing; expressing sadness. See synonym study at GLUM. □□ **mel•an•chol'ic** adj.

■ n. sorrow, misery, gloom, unhappiness, the blues, moroseness, melancholia, dejection, dejectedness, despondence, despondency. • adj. morose, depressed, unhappy, dejected, despondent, blue, downhearted, glum, gloomy, woeful, woebegone, lugubrious, disconsolate, downcast; saddening.

Mel•a•ne•sian /mélənéezhən, –shən/ • adj. 1 member of the dominant Negroid people of Melanesia, an island group in the W. Pacific. 2 language of this people. • adj. of or relating to this people or their language.

mé•lange /maylónzh/ n. mixture; medley. See synonym study at JUMBLE.

mel•a•nin /mélənin/ n. dark-brown to black pigment occurring in the hair, skin, and iris of the eye.

mel•a•no•ma /mélənómə/ n. malignant tumor of melanin-forming cells, usu. in the skin.

Mel•ba /mélbə/ n. □ **Melba toast** very thin crisp toast.

meld /meld/ v. merge; blend; combine.

■ see BLEND v.

mel•lif•lu•ous /məliflōōəs/ adj. (of a voice or words) pleasing; musical; flowing. □□ **mel•lif'lu•ence** n. **mel•lif'lu•ent** adj. **mel•lif'lu•ous•ly** adv. **mel•lif'lu•ous•ness** n.

mel•low /mélō/ • adj. 1 (of sound, color, light) soft and rich; free from harshness. 2 (of character) softened or matured by age or experience. 3 genial; jovial. 4 partly intoxicated. 5 (of wine) well-matured; smooth. See synonym study at MATURE. • v. make or become mellow. □□ **mel'low•ly** adv. **mel'low•ness** n.

■ adj. 1 softened, subtle, muted, pastel; musical; melodious, full, pure, rich. 2, 3 easygoing, gentle, good-natured, easy, cordial, friendly, warm. 4 see DRUNK adj. 1. • v. mature, ripen, age, season, sweeten.

me•lod•ic /məlódik/ adj. 1 of or relating to melody. 2 having or producing melody. □□ **me•lod'i•cal•ly** adv.

me•lo•di•ous /məlódeeəs/ adj. 1 of, producing, or having melody. 2 sweet-sounding. □□ **me•lo'di•ous•ly** adv. **me•lo'di•ous•ness** n.

■ 1 see TUNEFUL. 2 dulcet, tuneful, euphonious, harmonious, melodic, lyrical, musical, mellifluous.

mel•o•dra•ma /mélədraamə, –dramə/ n. 1 sensational dramatic piece with crude appeals to the emotions. 2 genre of drama of this type. 3 language, behavior, or an occurrence suggestive of this. □□ **mel•o•dra•mat'ic** /–drəmátik/ adj. **mel•o•dra•mat'i•cal•ly** adv. **mel•o•dram•a•tist** /–drámətist/ n. **mel•o•dram'a•tize** v.t.

■ 2 fantasy, Gothic horror. 3 see DRAMA 4. □□ **melodramatic** sensational, sensationalistic, dramatic, stagy, theatrical, (over)sentimental.

mel•o•dy /mélədee/ n. (pl. **–dies**) 1 arrangement of single notes in a musically expressive succession. 2 principal part in harmonized music; tune.

■ song, air, strain, measure, theme, refrain.

mel•on /mélən/ n. sweet fruit of various gourds.

melt /melt/ v. 1 intr. become liquefied by heat. 2 tr. change to a liquid condition by heat. 3 a intr. & tr. dissolve. b intr. (of food) be easily dissolved in the mouth. 4 intr. be softened as a result of pity, love, etc. 5 tr. soften (a person, feelings, the heart, etc.). 6 intr. change or merge imperceptibly into. 7 intr. leave or disappear unobtrusively. □ **melting point** temperature at which any given solid will melt. **melting pot** place where races, theories, etc., are mixed. □□ **melt'a•ble** adj. & n. **melt'er** n. **melt'ing•ly** adv.

■ 1–3 soften, thaw, liquefy, fuse; liquidize; deliquesce. 4, 5 thaw; mollify, assuage, touch, move. 6 blend, fade, disappear, dissolve, shrink. 7 dissolve, vanish, evaporate, go away, fade, pass, shrink.

melt•down /méltdown/ n. 1 melting of a structure, esp. the overheated core of a nuclear reactor. 2 disastrous event.

mem•ber /mémbər/ n. 1 person, animal, plant, etc., belonging to a society, team, taxonomic group, etc. 2 constituent portion of a complex structure. 3 a any part or organ of the body, esp. a limb. b = PENIS. □□ **mem'bered** adj. [also in comb.]. **mem'ber•less** adj.

■ 1 associate, fellow. 2 see ELEMENT 1.

mem•ber•ship /mémbərship/ n. 1 being a member. 2 number of members. 3 body of members.

■ 1 see BELONGING 2.

mem•brane /mémbrayn/ n. 1 any pliable sheetlike structure acting as a boundary, lining, or partition in an organism. 2 thin pliable sheet or skin of various kinds. □□ **mem•bra•nous** /–brənəs/ adj.

me•men•to /miméntó/ n. (pl. **–tos** or **–toes**) object kept as a reminder or a souvenir of a person or an event.

■ keepsake, remembrance, relic.

me•men•to mo•ri /məméntó máwree, –rī/ n. (pl. same) warning or reminder of death (e.g., a skull).

mem•o /mémó/ n. (pl. **–os**) colloq. memorandum.

mem•oir /mémwaar/ n. 1 historical account or biography written from personal knowledge or special sources. 2 [in pl.] autobiography. □□ **mem'oir•ist** n.

■ 1 report, reportage, narrative, journal, record, life. 2 reminiscences, recollections, memories, diary, journal.

mem•o•ra•bil•i•a /mémərəbileeə, –bílyə/ n.pl. souvenirs of memorable events.

■ remembrances, reminders, relics, trophies, tokens.

mem•o•ra•ble /mémərəbəl/ adj. 1 worth remembering, not to be forgotten. 2 easily remembered. □□ **mem•o•ra•bil'i•ty** n. **mem'o•ra•bly** adv.

unforgettable, catchy; noteworthy, notable, remarkable.

mem•o•ran•dum /mémərándəm/ *n.* (*pl.* **mem•o•ran•da** /-də/ or **mem•o•ran•dums**) **1** note or record made for future use. **2** informal written message, esp. in business, etc.

■ minute, reminder, message, *colloq.* memo.

me•mo•ri•al /məmáwreeəl/ • *n.* object, institution, or custom established in memory of a person or event. • *adj.* intending to commemorate a person or thing (*memorial service*). □ **Memorial Day** holiday on which those who died in war are remembered, usu. the last Monday in May.

■ *n.* monument, marker, plaque, cenotaph, statue; remembrance, reminder. • *adj.* commemorative.

mem•o•rize /mémərīz/ *v.tr.* commit to memory. □□ **mem•o•ri•za'tion** *n.* **mem'o•riz•er** *n.*

■ learn by heart *or* rote, learn word for word; retain.

mem•o•ry /mémərce/ *n.* (*pl.* **-ries**) **1** mental faculty by which things are recalled. **2** store of things remembered. **3** recollection or remembrance. **4** storage capacity of a computer, etc. **5** reputation of a dead person. **6** length of time over which the memory or memories of any given person or group extends. **7** act of remembering (*deed worthy of memory*). □ **from memory** without verification in books, etc.

■ **1** recall, recollection, retention. **3** reminiscence, thought. **4** RAM (random access memory), ROM (read-only memory), memory bank. **5** see NAME *n.* 4. **7** remembrance, recollection.

men *pl.* of MAN.

men•ace /ménis/ • *n.* **1** threat. **2** *joc.* pest, nuisance. • *v.* threaten, esp. in a malignant or hostile manner. □□ **men'ac•er** *n.* **men'ac•ing** *adj.* **men'ac•ing•ly** *adv.*

■ *n.* **1** danger, peril; intimidation, scare, warning. **2** see PEST 1. • *v.* intimidate, daunt, terrorize, terrify, cow, bully, frighten, scare, alarm. □□ **menacing** threatening, ominous, minatory, baleful, black, dark.

mé•nage /maynáazh/ *n.* members of a household.

me•nag•er•ic /mənájərce/, -náazh-/ *n.* small zoo.

men•ar•che /menáarkee/ *n.* onset of first menstruation.

mend /mend/ • *v.* **1** *tr.* restore to a sound condition; repair. **2** *intr.* regain health. **3** *tr.* improve. • *n.* darn or repair. □ **mend one's ways** reform; improve one's habits. **on the mend** recovering. □□ **mend'a•ble** *adj.* **mend'er** *n.*

■ *v.* **1** fix, patch (up), rectify, correct, remedy. **2** heal, improve, recover, convalesce. **3** correct, better, reform, revise, rectify. • *n.* patch.

men•da•cious /mendáyshəs/ *adj.* lying; untruthful. □□ **men•da'cious•ly** *adv.* **men•da'cious•ness** *n.* **men•dac•i•ty** /-dásitee/ *n.* (*pl.* **-ties**)

men•de•le•vi•um /méndəleéveeəm/ *n. Chem.*

---

artificial transuranic radioactive metallic element. ¶Symb.: **Md**.

Men•del•ism /méndəlizəm/ *n.* theory of heredity based on the recurrence of certain inherited characteristics transmitted by genes. □□ **Men•de•li•an** /-deéleeən/ *adj. & n.*

men•di•cant /méndikənt/ • *adj.* **1** begging. **2** (of a friar) living solely on alms. • *n.* **1** beggar. **2** mendicant friar. □□ **men•di•can•cy** /-kənsee/ *n.* **men•dic•i•ty** /-dísitee/ *n.*

men•folk /ménfōk/ *n.pl.* **1** men in general. **2** the men of one's family.

me•ni•al /meéneeəl/ • *adj.* degrading; servile. • *n.* domestic servant. □□ **me'ni•al•ly** *adv.*

■ *adj.* lowly, humble, subservient, base, low, mean, slavish; routine, unskilled, domestic. • *n.* lackey, serf, drudge, slave, hireling, gofer, underling.

men•in•gi•tis /méninjítis/ *n.* infection and inflammation of the meninges. □□ **men•in•git•ic** /-jítik/ *adj.*

me•ninx /meéningks/ *n.* (*pl.* **me•nin•ges** /məninjeez/) [usu. in *pl.*] any of the three membranes that enclose the brain and spinal cord. □□ **me•nin•ge•al** /minínjeeəl/ *adj.*

me•nis•cus /məniskəs/ *n.* (*pl.* **me•nis•ci** /-nísī/ or **me•nis•cus•es**) **1** *Physics* curved upper surface of a liquid in a tube. **2** lens that is convex on one side and concave on the other. □□ **me•nis'coid** *adj.*

men•o•pause /ménəpawz/ *n.* ceasing of menstruation. □□ **men•o•pau'sal** *adj.*

mo•nor•ah /mənáwrə, nórə/ *n.* seven- or nine-armed candelabrum used in Jewish worship, esp. as a symbol of Judaism.

men•ses /ménseez/ *n.pl.* flow of blood in menstruation.

men•stru•al /ménstrooəl/ *adj.* of or relating to the menses or menstruation. □ **menstrual cycle** process of ovulation and menstruation in female primates.

men•stru•ate /ménstroo-ayt/ *v.intr.* discharge blood and other materials from the uterus, usu. at monthly intervals. □□ **men•stru•a'tion** /ménstroo-áyshən/ *n.*

men•su•ra'tion /ménshəráyshən/ □□ / *n.* measuring.

mens•wear /ménzwair/ *n.* clothes for men.

-ment /mənt/ *suffix* **1** forming nouns expressing the means or result of the action of a verb (*abridgment*, *embankment*). **2** forming nouns from adjectives (*merriment*, *oddment*).

men•tal / mént'l/ *adj.* **1** of, in, or done by the mind. **2** *colloq.* **a** insane. **b** crazy; wild; eccentric (*is mental about pop music*). □ **mental age** degree of mental development compared to chronological age. □□ **men'tal•ly** *adv.*

■ **1** intellectual, cognitive, cerebral, comprehensive, perceptual, rational, conceptual, theoretical, noetic, abstract. **2 a** lunatic, mad, psychotic, demented, mentally ill; (*often derog.*) *colloq.* crazy, certifiable, dotty, *sl.* off one's rocker, nutty, batty.

men•tal•i•ty /mentálitee/ *n.* (*pl.* **-ties**) **1** mental character or disposition. **2** kind or degree of intelligence.

■ **1** inclination, attitude, bent, mind-set, temperament. **2** intelligence, brain, capacity, intellect, wit, sense, judgment, acuity, acumen, IQ, rationality.

men•thol /ménthawl/ n. mint-tasting organic alcohol found in oil of peppermint, etc., used as a flavoring and to relieve local pain. □□ **men•tho•lat•ed** /–thəlaytid/ adj.

men•tion /ménshən/ • v.tr. **1** refer to briefly. **2** reveal or disclose. • n. reference. □ **not to mention** and also. □□ **men'tion•a•ble** adj.

■ v. **1** speak or write about, allude to, touch on or upon, make mention of, talk of, bring up or in, introduce; point out, indicate, make known. **2** divulge, intimate, impart, suggest, hint at, imply, insinuate. • n. referral, allusion, note, citation, mentioning; announcement, remark.

men•tor /méntawr/ n. experienced and trusted adviser.

■ see adviser (ADVISE).

men•u /ményōō/ n. **1 a** list of dishes available in a restaurant, etc. **b** list of items to be served at a meal. **2** Computing list of options showing the commands or facilities available.

me•ow /mee-ów/ • n. characteristic cry of a cat. • v.intr. make this cry.

■ n. mew; caterwaul. • v. meow, mew, miaul.

mer•can•tile /mə́rkəntil/ adj. **1** of trade; trading. **2** commercial. **3** mercenary; fond of bargaining.

■ **1, 2** business, trade, marketing, market.

mer•ce•nar•y /mə́rsəneree/ • adj. primarily concerned with money or other reward (mercenary motives). • n. (pl. **–ies**) hired soldier in foreign service.

■ adj. grasping, greedy, acquisitive, covetous, predatory. • n. soldier of fortune, usu. derog. hireling.

mer•cer•ize /mə́rsəriz/ v.tr. treat (cotton) with caustic alkali to strengthen and impart luster. □□ **mer•cer•i•za'tion** n.

mer•chan•dise /mə́rchəndiz/ • n. goods for sale. • v. **1** intr. trade; traffic. **2** tr. trade or traffic in. **3** tr. **a** put on the market; promote. **b** advertise; publicize (an idea or person). □□ **mer'chan•dis•a•ble** adj. **mer' chan•dis•er** n.

■ n. commodities, products, stock, staples. • v. **1, 2** deal, distribute, retail, (buy and) sell. **3** market.

mer•chant /mə́rchənt/ n. retail trader; dealer; storekeeper. □ **merchant marine** a nation's commercial shipping. **merchant ship** = MERCHANTMAN.

■ retailer, seller, store owner, tradesman, tradeswoman, vendor.

mer•chant•man /mə́rchəntmən/ n. (pl. **–men**) ship conveying merchandise.

mer•ci•ful /mə́rsifool/ adj. having, showing, or feeling mercy. □□ **mer'ci•ful•ly** adv. **mer'ci•ful•ness** n.

■ compassionate, sympathetic, forgiving, kind, kindly, clement, kindhearted, forbearing, sparing, lenient, tender. □□ **mercifully** see happily (HAPPY).

mer•ci•less /mə́rsilis/ adj. **1** pitiless. **2** show-ing no mercy. □□ **mer'ci•less•ly** adv. **mer'ci•less•ness** n.

■ cruel, ruthless, heartless, unmerciful, inhumane, inhuman, brutal, savage, barbarous, callous, hard, hard-hearted, tyrannical, stony hearted.

mer•cu•ri•al /mərkyŏŏreeəl/ adj. **1** (of a person) sprightly; ready-witted; volatile. **2** of or containing mercury. □□ **mer•cu'ri•al•ism** n. **mer•cu•ri•al•i•ty** /–reeálitee/ n. **mer•cu' ri•al•ly** adv.

■ **1** see VOLATILE adj. 2. □□ **mercuriality** see inconstancy (INCONSTANT).

mer•cu•ry /mə́rkyəree/ n. **1** Chem. silvery-white heavy liquid metallic element used in barometers, thermometers, etc. ¶Symb.: **Hg**. **2 (Mercury)** planet nearest to the sun. □□ **mer•cu'ric** /–kyŏŏrik/ adj. **mer•cu'rous** adj.

mer•cy /mə́rsee/ n. (pl. **–cies**) **1** compassion or forbearance shown to enemies or offenders in one's power. **2** quality of compassion. **3** act of mercy. **4** something to be thankful for. □ **at the mercy of** wholly in the power of.

■ **1, 2** pity, quarter, tolerance, sympathy, favor, forgiveness, kindness, kindliness, leniency, tenderness, humanity, humaneness. **3** errand of mercy, kindness, favor. **4** see LUCK 3. □ **at the mercy of** under a person's thumb.

SYNONYM STUDY: mercy

BENEVOLENCE, CHARITY, CLEMENCY, COMPASSION, LENIENCY. If you want to win friends and influence people, it's best to start with **benevolence**, a general term for goodwill and kindness (a grandfather's benevolence). **Charity** is even better, suggesting forbearance and generous giving (to feed someone out of charity; to view selfish behavior with charity), but also meaning tolerance and understanding of others. **Compassion**, which is a feeling of sympathy or sorrow for someone else's misfortune, will put you one step closer to sainthood (to show compassion for the homeless), and showing **mercy** will practically guarantee it. Aside from its religious overtones, mercy means compassion or kindness in our treatment of others, especially those who have offended us or who deserve punishment (the jury's mercy toward the accused). **Clemency** is mercy shown by someone whose duty or function it is to administer justice or punish offenses (the judge granted clemency), while **leniency** emphasizes gentleness, softness, or lack of severity, even if it isn't quite deserved (a father's leniency in punishing his young son).

---

mere /meer/ attrib.adj. (**mer•est**) that is solely or no more or better than what is specified. □□ **mere'ly** adv.

■ bare, basic, sheer, simple, very; least, nothing but. □□ **merely** only, simply, solely, purely; barely.

mer•e•tri•cious /méritríshəs/ adj. showily but falsely attractive. □□ **mer•e•tri'cious•ly** adv. **mer•e•tri'cious•ness** n.

mer•gan•ser /mərgánsər/ n. diving fish-eating duck.

merge /mərj/ v. **1 a** combine or be combined. **b** join or blend gradually. **2** lose or cause to lose character and identity in (something else).

■ **1** coalesce, unite, join, amalgamate, consolidate, blend, mix, mingle, fuse, conflate.

merg•er /mórjər/ n. combining, esp. of two commercial companies, etc., into one.

■ combination, coalescence, union, amalgamation, consolidation, coalition, merging, pooling, blending.

me•rid•i•an /mərídeeən/ n. **1 a** circle of constant longitude, passing through a given place and the terrestrial poles. **b** corresponding line on a map. **2** prime; full splendor.

me•ringue /məráng/ n. confection of sugar, egg whites, etc., baked crisp.

me•ri•no /məréenō/ n. (pl. **-nos**) **1** (in full **merino sheep**) variety of sheep with long fine wool. **2** wool of this sheep, or cloth made from this.

mer•it /mérit/ • n. **1** quality of deserving well. **2** excellence; worth. **3** [usu. in pl.] **a** thing that entitles one to reward or gratitude. **b** esp. Law intrinsic rights and wrongs. • v.tr. deserve or be worthy of.

■ n. **1, 2** worthiness, value, quality, virtue, good. **3 a** assets, advantage(s). • v. earn, warrant, rate, have a right or claim to.

mer•i•toc•ra•cy /méritókrəsee/ n. (pl. **-cies**) **1** government by persons selected according to merit. **2** group of persons selected in this way. **3** society governed by meritocracy.

mer•i•to•ri•ous /méritáwreeəs/ adj. praiseworthy. □□ **mer•i•to′ri•ous•ly** adv. **mer•i•to′ri•ous•ness** n.

■ honorable, laudable, commendable, creditable, admirable, estimable, excellent, exemplary, outstanding.

mer•maid /mórmayd/ n. imaginary sea creature, with the head and trunk of a woman and the tail of a fish.

mer•ri•ment /mérimənt/ n. **1** being merry. **2** mirth; fun.

■ jollity, joviality, merrymaking, revelry, gaiety, high or good spirits, mirth, mirthfulness, joyfulness, felicity.

mer•ry /méree/ adj. (**mer•ri•er, mer•ri•est**) **1** joyous. **2** full of laughter or gaiety. □ **make merry** be festive; enjoy oneself. □□ **mer′ri•ly** adv. **mer′ri•ness** n.

■ cheerful, happy, gay, cheery, jolly, jovial, in high or good spirits, mirthful, joyful, hilarious. □ **make merry** celebrate, carouse, frolic; see also REVEL v. 1.

mer•ry-go-round /méreegōrownd/ n. **1** revolving machine with wooden horses or other animals, etc., for riding on at an amusement park, etc. **2** cycle of bustling activities.

mer•ry•mak•ing /méreemayking/ n. festivity; fun. □□ **mer′ry•mak•er** n.

mes•cal /méskal/ n. peyote cactus.

mes•ca•line /méskəleen, –lin/ n. (also **mes•ca•lin** /–lin/) hallucinogenic alkaloid present in mescal.

mes•dames pl. of MADAME.

mes•de•moi•selles pl. of MADEMOISELLE.

mesh /mesh/ • n. **1** network fabric or struc-

ture. **2** each of the open spaces or interstices between the strands of a net or sieve, etc. **3** [in pl.] **a** network. **b** snare. • v.intr. **1** (of the teeth of a wheel) be engaged (with others). **2** be harmonious.

■ n. **1–3a** meshwork, netting, net, web, webbing, lattice, latticework, screen, screening, interlacing, lacework, grid, grate, grating, trellis. **3 b** grip, clutch(es), grasp, web, trap, entanglement. • v. **1** fit (together), dovetail, knit, enmesh, match, interlock. **2** see JELL 2.

mes•mer•ize /mézməriz/ v.tr. **1** Psychol. hypnotize. **2** fascinate; spellbind. □□ **mes•mer•ic** /mezmérik/ adj. **mes•mer•ism** /–izəm/ n. **mes′mer•ist** n. **mes•mer•i•za′tion** n. **mes′mer•iz•er** n. **mes′mer•iz•ing•ly** adv.

■ **2** see FASCINATE 1.

meso- /mésō, méz–/ comb. form middle; intermediate.

mes•o•morph /mézəmawrf, més–/ n. person with a compact and muscular body. □□ **mes•o•mor′phic** adj.

me•son /mézon, més–, méezon, –son/ n. Physics any of a class of elementary particles believed to participate in the forces that hold nucleons together in the atomic nucleus. □□ **me•son′ic** /mézik, més–, méezik, sik/ adj. **me′son′ic** adj.

mes•o•sphere /mésəsfeer, méz–/ n. region of the atmosphere extending in altitude from 20 to 50 miles

Mes•o•zo•ic /mésəzō-ik, méz–/ Geol. • adj. of or relating to an era of geological time marked by the development of dinosaurs, and with evidence of the first mammals, birds, and flowering plants. • n. this era.

mes•quite /méskéet/ n. **1** thorny N. American leguminous tree. **2** wood of the mesquite, as used in grilling food.

mess /mes/ • n. **1** dirty or untidy state. **2** state of confusion, embarrassment, or trouble. **3** something causing a mess, e.g., spilled liquid, etc. **4 a** soldiers, etc., dining together. **b** = mess hall. **c** meal taken there. **5** derog. disagreeable concoction. **6** portion of liquid or pulpy food. • v. **1** tr. [often foll. by up] make a mess of; dirty; muddle. **2** intr. [foll. by with] interfere with. □ **mess about** (or **around**) act desultorily. **mess hall** communal, esp. military, dining area. **mess kit** soldier's cooking and eating utensils.

■ n. **1** chaos, disorder, disarray, disorganization, muddle; untidiness. **2** predicament, difficulty, plight, trouble, quandary, imbroglio, foul-up, colloq. stew, fix. **3** mixture, miscellany, hash, hodgepodge. • v. **1** clutter up, make untidy, turn upside down, pull to pieces, upset; ruin, destroy, wreck, bungle, botch. **2** intervene in, meddle with or in, intrude in, butt in or into, tinker with. □ **mess about** (or **around**) fool or play (about or around), poke or fiddle about or around; dally, waste time, dawdle. **mess hall** mess, canteen, refectory.

mes•sage /mésij/ n. **1** oral or written communication sent by one person to another. **2** central import or meaning of an artistic work, etc. □ **get the message** *colloq.* understand what is meant.

■ **1** bulletin, report, communiqué, news, dispatch, information. **2** idea, point, essence, implication.

mes•sen•ger /mésinjər/ *n.* person who carries a message.

■ envoy, emissary, nuncio; page, courier, *sl.* gofer.

Mes•si•ah /misíə/ *n.* **1** (also **mes•si′ah**) liberator of an oppressed people or country. **2 a** promised deliverer of the Jews. **b** [usu. prec. by *the*] Christ regarded as this. □□ **Mes•si′ah•ship** *n.* **Mes•si•an•ic** /méseeánik/ *adj.* **Mes•si•a•nism** /mésíənizəm/ *n.*

■ **1** deliverer, emancipator, savior, redeemer.

mes•sieurs pl. of MONSIEUR.

messrs. /mésərz/ pl. of MR.

mess•y /mésee/ *adj.* (**mess•i•er**, **mess•i•est**) **1** untidy or dirty. **2** causing or accompanied by a mess. **3** difficult to deal with. □□ **mess′i•ly** *adv.* **mess′i•ness** *n.*

met *past and past part.* of MEET.

meta- /métə/ *comb. form* (usu. **met-** before a vowel or *h*) **1** denoting change of position or condition (*metabolism*). **2** denoting position: **a** behind. **b** after or beyond (*metaphysics*). **c** of a higher or second-order kind (*metalanguage*).

me•tab•o•lism /mətábəlizəm/ *n.* all the chemical processes that occur within a living organism, resulting in energy production and growth. □□ **met•a•bol•ic** /métəbólik/ *adj.* **met•a•bol′i•cal•ly** *adv.*

me•tab•o•lize /mətábəliz/ *v.* process or be processed by metabolism. □□ **me•tab′o•liz•a•ble** *adj.*

met•a•car•pus /métəkáarpəs/ *n.* (*pl.* **met•a•car•pi** /–pī/) **1** set of five bones of the hand that connects the wrist to the fingers. **2** this part of the hand. □□ **met•a•car′pal** *adj.*

met•al /mét′l/ • *n.* **1** any of a class of chemical elements such as gold, silver, iron, and tin, usu. lustrous ductile solids and good conductors of heat and electricity. **2** alloy of any of these. • *adj.* made of metal.

met•a•lan•guage /métəlanggwij/ *n.* language or system used to discuss or analyze another language or system.

me•tal•lic /mətálik/ *adj.* **1** of, consisting of, or characteristic of metal or metals. **2** sounding like struck metal. **3** having the sheen or luster of metals. □□ **me•tal′li•cal•ly** *adv.*

met•al•lur•gy /mét′lərjee/ *n.* science concerned with the production, purification, and properties of metals and their application. □□ **met•al•lur•gic** /mét′lərjik/ *adj.* **met•al•lur′gi•cal** *adj.* **met•al•lur′gi•cal•ly** *adv.* **met•al•lur′gist** *n.*

met•a•mor•phic /métəmáwrfik/ *adj.* **1** of metamorphosis. **2** *Geol.* (of rock) transformed by natural agencies such as heat and pressure. □□ **met•a•mor′phism** *n.*

met•a•mor•phose /métəmáwrfōz/ *v.tr.* **1** change in form. **2 a** turn (into a new form). **b** change the nature of.

■ see CHANGE *v.* 1.

met•a•mor•pho•sis /métəmáwrfəsis / *n.* (*pl.* **met•a•mor•pho•ses** /–seez/) **1** change of character, conditions, etc. **2** change of form in an animal, e.g., from a pupa to an insect, etc.

■ see CHANGE *n.* 1.

met•a•phor /métəfawr/ *n.* application of a name or descriptive term or phrase to an object or action to which it is not literally applicable (e.g., *killing him with kindness*). □□ **met•a•phor•ic** /–fáwrik, –fórik/ *adj.* **met•a•phor•i•cal** /–fáwrikəl, –fórikəl/ *adj.* **met•a•phor•i•cal•ly** /–fáwriklee, –fóriklee/ *adv.*

■ figure (of speech), analogy, analog, image, trope. □□ **metaphoric, metaphorical** nonliteral, analogical, analogous, figurative, symbolic, tropological.

met•a•phys•i•cal /métəfizikəl/ *adj.* **1** of metaphysics. **2** excessively subtle or theoretical. □□ **met•a•phys′i•cal•ly** *adv.*

■ **2** see ABSTRACT *adj.* 1a, SUBTLE 1, THEORETICAL.

met•a•phys•ics /métəfiziks/ *n.pl.* [usu. treated as *sing.*] **1** theoretical philosophy of being and knowing. **2** philosophy of mind. **3** *colloq.* abstract or subtle talk; mere theory. □□ **met•a•phy•si•cian** /–zíshən/ *n.*

me•tas•ta•sis /mətástəsis/ *n.* (*pl.* **me•tas•ta•ses** /–seez/) *Physiol.* transference of a bodily function, disease, etc., from one part or organ to another. □□ **me•tas′ta•size** *v.intr.* **met•a•stat•ic** /métəstátik/ *adj.*

■ see TRANSITION. □□ **metastasize** see SPREAD *v.* 2.

met•a•tar•sus /métətáarsəs/ *n.* (*pl.* **met•a•tar•si** /–sī/) **1** part of the foot between the ankle and the toes. **2** set of bones in this. □□ **met•a•tar′sal** *adj.*

met•a•the•sis /mitáthisis/ *n.* (*pl.* **me•tath•e•ses** /–seez/) **1** *Gram.* transposition of sounds or letters in a word. **2** *Chem.* interchange of atoms or groups of atoms between two molecules. **3** instance of either of these. □□ **met•a•thet•ic** /métəthétik/ *adj.* **met•a•thet′i•cal** *adj.*

mete /meet/ *v.tr. literary* apportion or allot.

■ deal (out), distribute, dole (out), assign, allocate, parcel out, share (out), ration (out), measure out.

me•te•or /méeteear, –eeawr/ *n.* **1** small body of matter from outer space that becomes incandescent as a result of friction with the earth's atmosphere. **2** streak of light emanating from a meteor.

me•te•or•ic /méeteeáwrik, –ór–/ *adj.* **1** of meteors. **2** rapid like a meteor; dazzling; transient. □□ **me•te•or′i•cal•ly** *adv.*

■ **2** brief, short-lived, temporary, transitory, ephemeral; brilliant, flashing, spectacular.

me•te•or•ite /méeteeərīt/ *n.* fallen meteor that reaches the earth's surface from outer space. □□ **me•te•or•it•ic** /–rítik/ *adj.*

me•te•or•oid /méeteeəróyd/ *n.* any small body moving in the solar system that becomes visible as it passes through the earth's atmosphere as a meteor.

me•te•or•ol•o•gy /méeteeəróləjee/ *n.* the study of the processes and phenomena of the atmosphere, esp. as a means of forecasting the weather. □□ **me•te•or•o•log•i•cal**

/-rəlójikəl/ adj. me•te•or•o•log'i•cal•ly adv. me'te•or•ol'o•gist n.

521   meter ~ mfg.

me•ter[1] /méetər/ n. basic metric measure of length, equal to about 39.4 inches. □□ **me' ter•age** n.

me•ter[2] /méetər/ n. **1** poetic rhythm, determined by the number and length of feet in a line. **2** basic pulse and rhythm of a piece of music.

me•ter[3] /méetər/ • n. instrument that measures, esp. one for recording a quantity of gas, electricity, postage, etc., supplied, present, or needed. • v.tr. measure by means of a meter.

  ■ n. see INDICATOR 2, 3. • v. see MEASURE v. 1.

-meter /mitər, méetər/ comb. form **1** forming nouns denoting measuring instruments (barometer). **2** Prosody forming nouns denoting lines of poetry with a specified number of measures (pentameter).

meth•a•done /méthədōn/ n. potent narcotic analgesic drug used esp. as a substitute for morphine or heroin.

meth•ane /méthayn/ n. Chem. colorless, odorless, flammable gas, the main constituent of natural gas.

meth•a•nol /méthənawl, -nol/ n. Chem. colorless, volatile, flammable liquid, used as a solvent. (Also called **methyl alcohol**).

me•thinks /mithíngks/ v.intr. (past **me•thought** /mitháwt/) archaic it seems to me.

meth•od /méthəd/ n. **1** special form of procedure esp. in any branch of mental activity. **2** orderliness; regular habits.

  ■ **1** way, means, approach, route, avenue, road, mode, manner, technique; plan, scheme, program; methodology. **2** arrangement, order, system, structure, organization, design, pattern, neatness.

me•thod•i•cal /məthódikəl/ adj. (also **me• thod'ic**) characterized by method or order. □□ **me•thod'i•cal•ly** adv.

  ■ organized, ordered, systematic, structured, businesslike, orderly, neat, tidy, regular, routine; deliberate; plodding, labored.

Meth•od•ist /méthədist/ n. member of any of several Protestant religious bodies (now united) originating in the teachings of John Wesley. □□ **Meth'od•ism** n. **Meth•od•is' tic** adj.

meth•od•ol•o•gy /méthədóləjee/ n. (pl. **-gies**) system or science of methods. □□ **meth•od•o•log'i•cal** /-dəlójikəl/ adj. **meth•od•o•log'i•cal•ly** adv. **meth•od•ol'o• gist** n.

  ■ see SYSTEM 3.

meth•yl /méthil/ n. Chem. univalent hydrocarbon radical CH_3, present in many organic compounds. □ **methyl alcohol** = METHANOL. □□ **me•thyl'ic** adj.

me•tic•u•lous /mətíkyələs/ adj. **1** giving great or excessive attention to details. **2** very careful and precise. □□ **me•tic'u•lous•ly** adv. **me•tic'u•lous•ness** n.

  ■ accurate, exact, fastidious, scrupulous, thorough.

mé•tier /métyáy/ n. (also **me'tier**) **1** one's trade, profession, or department of activity. **2** one's forte.

me•ton•y•my /mitónimee/ n. substitution of the name of an attribute or adjunct for that of the thing meant (e.g., White House for president). □□ **met•o•nym•ic** /métənímik/ adj. **met•o•nym'i•cal** adj.

met•ric /métrik/ adj. of or based on the meter. □ **metric system** decimal measuring system with the meter, liter, and gram (or kilogram) as units of length, volume, and mass. **metric ton** (or **tonne**) 1,000 kilograms (2,205 lb.).

-metric /métrik/ comb. form (also **-metrical**) forming adjectives corresponding to nouns in -meter and -metry (geometric). □□ **-metri• cally** comb. form forming adverbs.

met•ri•cal /métrikəl/ adj. **1** of, relating to, or composed in meter (metrical psalms). **2** of or involving measurement (metrical geometry). □□ **met'ri•cal•ly** adv.

  ■ **1** see POETIC 1.

met•ro /métrō/ n. (pl. **-ros**) subway system, esp. in Paris.

met•ro•nome /métrənōm/ n. Mus. instrument marking time at a selected rate by giving a regular tick. □□ **met•ro•nom•ic** /-nómik/ adj.

me•trop•o•lis /mitrópəlis/ n. chief city of a country; capital city. □□ **met•ro•pol•i•tan** /métrəpólit'n/ adj.

  ■ megalopolis, municipality. □□ **metro• politan** see MUNICIPAL.

-metry /mitree/ comb. form forming nouns denoting procedures and systems corresponding to instruments in -meter (calorimetry, thermometry).

met•tle /mét'l/ n. strength of character; spirit; courage. □ **on one's mettle** incited to do one's best. □□ **met'tled** adj. [also in comb.]. **met'tle•some** adj.

  ■ see DISPOSITION 1b, SPIRIT n. 5c. □□ **mettlesome** see SPIRITED.

mew /myoo/ • v.intr. (of a cat, gull, etc.) utter its characteristic cry. • n. this sound, esp. of a cat.

mewl /myool/ v.intr. **1** cry feebly; whimper. **2** mew like a cat.

  ■ **1** see CRY v. 2a.

mews /myooz/ n. esp. Brit. set of stables around an open yard or along a lane, now often converted into dwellings.

Mex•i•can /méksikən/ • n. **1** native or national of Mexico, a country in southern N. America. **2** language spoken in Mexico. • adj. of or relating to Mexico or its people.

me•zu•zah /mezóōzə, -zóōzáá/ n. (also **me• zu'za**; pl. **-zas**; also **me•zu•zot** or **me•zu• zoth** /-zoōzót/) parchment inscribed with religious texts, inserted into a small case, and attached to the doorpost of a Jewish house as a sign of faith.

mez•za•nine /mézəneen/ n. low story between two others (usu. between the first and second floors).

mez•zo /métsō/ Mus. • adv. half; moderately. • n. (in full **mezzo-soprano**) **1** female singing voice between soprano and contralto. **2** singer with this voice.

M.F.A. abbr. Master of Fine Arts.

mfg. abbr. manufacturing.

m.f.n. *abbr.* most favored nation.

mfr. *abbr.* **1** manufacture. **2** manufacturer.

Mg *symb. Chem.* magnesium.

mg *abbr.* milligram(s).

Mgr. *abbr.* **1** Manager. **2** Monseigneur. **3** Monsignor.

MHz *abbr.* megahertz.

MI *abbr.* Michigan (in official postal use).

mi /mee/ *n. Mus.* third tone of the diatonic scale.

mi. *abbr.* mile(s).

MIA *abbr.* missing in action.

mi•ca /míkə/ *n.* any of a group of silicate minerals with a layered structure, esp. muscovite. □□ **mi•ca•ceous** /–káyshəs/ *adj.*

mice *pl.* of MOUSE.

Mich. *abbr.* **1** Michigan. **2** Michaelmas.

Mich•ael•mas /míkəlməs/ *n.* feast of St. Michael, September 29.

Mick•ey Finn /míkee fin/ *n.* (often **Mickey**) *sl.* alcoholic drink adulterated with a narcotic or laxative.

micro- /míkrō/ *comb. form* **1** small (*microchip*). **2** denoting a factor of one millionth (10^{-6}) (*microgram*). ¶Symb.: **μ**.

mi•crobe /míkrōb/ *n.* minute living being; microorganism (esp. bacteria causing disease and fermentation). □□ **mi•cro•bi•al** /–krōbeeəl/ *adj.* **mi•cro•bic** /–krōbik/ *adj.*
■ germ, bacterium, *sl.* bug.

mi•cro•bi•ol•o•gy /míkrōbīóləjee/ *n.* scientific study of microorganisms. □□ **mi•cro•bi•o•log•i•cal** /–bīəlójikəl/ *adj.* **mi•cro•bi•o•log'i•cal•ly** *adv.* **mi•cro•bi•ol'o•gist** *n.*

mi•cro•brew•er•y /míkrōbrŏŏaree/ *n.* limited-production brewery, often selling only locally.

mi•cro•chip /míkrōchip/ *n.* small piece of semiconductor (usu. silicon) used to carry electronic circuits.

mi•cro•com•put•er /míkrōkəmpyŏŏtər/ *n.* small computer that contains a microprocessor as its central processor.

mi•cro•cosm /míkrəkozəm/ *n.* **1** miniature representation. **2** mankind viewed as the epitome of the universe. **3** any community or complex unity viewed in this way. □□ **mi•cro•cos•mic** /–kózmik/ *adj.* **mi•cro•cos'mi•cal•ly** *adv.*

mi•cro•dot /míkrōdot/ *n.* microphotograph of a document, etc., reduced to the size of a dot.

mi•cro•ec•o•nom•ics /míkrō-ĕekənómiks, –ék–/ *n.* branch of economics dealing with individual commodities, producers, etc.

mi•cro•e•lec•tron•ics /míkrō-ilektróniks/ *n.* design, manufacture, and use of microchips and microcircuits.

mi•cro•fiche /míkrōfeesh/ *n.* (*pl.* same or **mi•cro•fich•es**) flat rectangular piece of film bearing miniaturized photographs of a printed text or document.

mi•cro•film /míkrōfilm/ • *n.* length of film bearing miniaturized photographs of documents, etc. • *v.tr.* photograph (a document, etc.) on microfilm.

mi•cro•light /míkrōlīt/ *n.* kind of motorized hang glider.

mi•crom•e•ter /mīkrómitər/ *n.* gauge for accurately measuring small distances, thicknesses, etc. □□ **mi•crom'e•try** *n.*

mi•cron /míkron/ *n.* one-millionth of a meter.

Mi•cro•ne•sian /míkrəneézhən/ • *adj.* of Micronesia, an island group in the W. Pacific. • *n.* native of Micronesia.

mi•cro•or•gan•ism /míkrō-áwrgəniz(ə)m/ *n.* microscopic organism, e.g., algae, bacteria, fungi, protozoa, and viruses.
■ see MICROBE.

mi•cro•phone /míkrəfōn/ *n.* instrument for converting sound waves into electrical currents. □□ **mi•cro•phon•ic** /–fónik/ *adj.*

mi•cro•proc•es•sor /míkrōprósesər/ *n.* integrated circuit that contains all the functions of a central processing unit of a computer.

mi•cro•scope /míkrəskōp/ *n.* instrument magnifying small objects by means of a lens or lenses.

mi•cro•scop•ic /míkrəskópik/ *adj.* **1** visible only with a microscope. **2** extremely small. **3** of the microscope. □□ **mi•cro•scop'i•cal** *adj.* (in sense 4). **mi•cro•scop'i•cal•ly** *adv.*
■ **1, 2** see TINY.

mi•cros•co•py /mīkróskəpee/ *n.* use of the microscope. □□ **mi•cros'co•pist** *n.*

mi•cro•sec•ond /míkrōsekənd/ *n.* one-millionth of a second.

mi•cro•sur•ger•y /míkrōsúrjəree/ *n.* intricate surgery performed using microscopes. □□ **mi•cro•sur•gi•cal** /–súrjikəl/ *adj.*

mi•cro•wave /míkrəwayv/ • *n.* **1** electromagnetic wave with a wavelength in the range 0.001–0.3m. **2** (in full **microwave oven**) oven that uses microwaves to cook or heat food quickly. • *v.tr.* cook in a microwave oven.

mid /mid/ *attrib.adj.* [usu. in *comb.*] that is the middle.

Mi•das touch /mídəs/ *n.* knack for money-making.

mid•day /míd-dáy/ *n.* middle of the day; noon.
■ noontide, twelve noon, 1200 hours, high noon.

mid•dle /míd'l/ • *attrib.adj.* **1** at an equal distance from the extremities of a thing. **2** (of a member of a group) so placed as to have the same number of members on each side. **3** intermediate in rank, quality, etc. **4** average (*of middle height*). • *n.* **1** the middle point or position or part. **2** waist. □ **middle age** period between youth and old age, about 45 to 60. **middle-aged** in middle age. **Middle Ages** period of European history between ancient times and the Renaissance, from *c.* 476 to 1453. **Middle America 1** middle class in the US, esp. as a conservative political force. **2** US Middle West. **middle class** class of society between the upper and the lower socially, economically, etc. **middle-class** *adj.* of the middle class. **middle ear** cavity of thxe central part of the ear behind the eardrum. **Middle East** area covered by countries from Egypt to Iran inclusive. **Middle English** the English language from *c.* 1150 to 1500. **middle-of-the-road** moderate; avoiding extremes. **middle**

school school for children usu. in grades 5 to 8. **Middle West** = MIDWEST.

■ *adj.* **1, 2** central, center, medial, median; midway, mid, halfway; inner, inside. **3** see INTERMEDIATE *adj.* **4** normal, mean; see also AVERAGE *adj.* 1a. ■ *n.* **1** center, midpoint, midst, halfway point; heart, bull's-eye. **2** midriff, stomach. □ **middle class** (petty *or* petite) bourgeoisie; Middle America. **middle-class** see BOURGEOIS *adj.* **middle-of-the-road** see MODERATE *adj.* 1a.

mid•dle•brow /mídˈbrów/ *colloq. adj.* claiming to be or regarded as only moderately intellectual.

mid•dle•man /mídˈlmán/ *n.* (*pl.* **-men**) **1** any of the traders who handle a commodity between its producer and its consumer. **2** intermediary.

■ see INTERMEDIARY *n.*

mid•dle•weight /mídˈlwáyt/ *n.* weight class in certain sports intermediate between welterweight and light heavyweight.

mid•dling /mídling/ • *adj* moderately good (esp. *fair* to *middling*). • *adv.* fairly or moderately. □□ **mid′dling•ly** *adv.*

■ *adj.* see MODERATE *adj.* 2, 4.

midge /mij/ *n. colloq.* gnatlike insect.

midg•et /mijit/ *n.* extremely small person or thing.

mid•land /mídlənd/ • *n.* middle part of a country. • *adj.* of or in the midland. □□ **mid′land•er** *n.*

mid•night /mídnīt/ *n.* 12 o'clock at night.

mid•riff /mídrif/ *n.* **1** region of the front of the body between the thorax and abdomen. **2** diaphragm.

■ **1** see MIDDLE *n.* 2.

mid•ship•man /mídshípmən/ *n.* (*pl.* **-men**) cadet in the US Naval Academy.

mid•ships /mídshíps/ *adv.* = AMIDSHIPS.

midst /mídst/ • *prep. poet.* amidst. • *n.* middle (now only in phrases as below). □ **in the midst of** among; in the middle of. **in four (or your or their) midst** among us (or you or them).

■ □ **in the midst of** halfway *or* midway through; during; see also AMONG 1

mid•sum•mer /mídsúmər/ *n.* period of or near the summer solstice, around June 21.

mid•way /mídwáy/ • *n.* area for concessions and amusements at a carnival, fair, etc. • *adv.* in or toward the middle of the distance between two points.

Mid•west /mídwést/ *n.* region of northern US states from Ohio west to the Rocky Mountains.

mid•wife /mídwíf/ *n.* (*pl.* **-wives** /-wívz/) person trained to assist at childbirth. □□ **mid′wife•ry** /-wíferee/ *n.*

mid•win•ter /mídwintər/ *n.* period of or near the winter solstice, around Dec. 22.

mien /meen/ *n. literary* person's look or bearing.

■ see LOOK *n.* 2, 3.

miff /mif/ *v.tr. colloq.* [usu. in *passive*] offend.

might¹ /mīt/ *past* of MAY, used esp.: **1** in reported speech, expressing possibility (*said he might come*) or permission (*asked if I might leave*) (cf. MAY 1, 2). **2** expressing a possibil-

ity based on a condition not fulfilled (*if you'd looked you might have found it*). **3** expressing complaint that an obligation or expectation is not or has not been fulfilled (*they might have asked*). **4** expressing a request (*you might call in at the butcher's*). **5** *colloq.* **a** = MAY 1 (*it might be true*). **b** (in tentative questions) = MAY 2 (*might I have the pleasure of this dance?*). **c** = MAY 4 (*who might you be?*).

might² /mīt/ *n.* strength; power. □ **with might and main** see MAIN.

■ energy, force, muscle, mightiness; influence, authority, weight, sway, dominion, ascendancy.

might•y /mítee/ • *adj.* (**might•i•er**, **might•i•est**) **1** powerful; strong. **2** massive; bulky. **3** *colloq.* great; considerable. • *adv. colloq.* very. □□ **might′i•ly** *adv.* **might′i•ness** *n.*

■ *adj.* **1** potent, influential, dominant, predominant, ascendant; muscular, robust, strapping, sturdy, brawny. **2** big, large, huge, grand, great, enormous, gargantuan. **3** see CONSIDERABLE 1, 2. • *adv.* see VERY *adv.*

mi•graine /mígrayn/ *n.* intense headache that often affects vision.

mi•grant /mígrənt/ • *adj.* that migrates. • *n.* migrant person or animal.

■ *adj.* transient, migratory, itinerant, peripatetic, nomadic, gypsy, vagrant. • *n.* wanderer, rover, drifter, gypsy, nomad, itinerant, transient, migrator, wayfarer.

mi•grate /mígrayt/ *v.intr.* **1** (of people) move from one place of abode to another, esp. in a different country. **2** (of a bird or fish) change its area of habitation with the seasons. □□ **mi•gra•tion** /-gráyshən/ *n.* **mi•gra′tion•al** *adj.* **mi′gra•tor** *n.* **mi•gra•to•ry** /-grətawree/ *adj.*

■ go, travel, settle, resettle, relocate, move house; emigrate, immigrate; wander, roam, voyage, rove, drift

mi•ka•do /mikaádō/ *n.* (*pl.* **-dos**) *hist.* emperor of Japan.

mike /mīk/ *n. colloq.* microphone.

mil /mil/ *n.* one-thousandth of an inch.

mi•la•dy /miláydee/ *n.* (*pl.* **-dies**) noblewoman or great lady.

Mil•an•ese /milneez/ • *adj.* of or relating to Milan in N. Italy. • *n.* (*pl.* same) native of Milan.

milch /milch/ *adj.* (of a domestic mammal) giving or kept for milk. □ **milch cow** = *milk cow.*

mild /mīld/ *adj.* **1** gentle and conciliatory. **2** moderate; not severe. **3** (of food, tobacco, etc.) not sharp or strong in taste, etc. **4** tame; feeble; lacking energy or vivacity. □□ **mild′ish** *adj.* **mild′ly** *adv.* **mild′ness** *n.*

■ **1** placid, peaceful, calm, tranquil, tolerant, mellow, inoffensive, serene, good-natured, affable, amiable. **2** clement, balmy, warm, fair; see also LENIENT. **4** see TAME *adj.* 3.

mil•dew /míldō, -dyōo/ • *n.* destructive growth of minute fungi on plants, damp paper, leather, etc. • *v.* taint or be tainted with mildew. □□ **mil′dew•y** *adj.*

■ *n.* see MOLD². • *v.* see SPOIL *v.* 3. □□ **mildewy** see MOLDY 1.

mild•ly /mĭldlee/ *adv.* in a mild fashion. □□ **to put it mildly** as an understatement (implying the reality is more extreme.).

mile /mīl/ *n.* (also **statute mile**) unit of linear measure equal to 1,760 yards (approx. 1.609 kilometers).

mile•age /mīlij/ *n.* **1 a** number of miles traveled, used, etc. **b** number of miles traveled by a vehicle per unit of fuel. **2** traveling expenses (per mile). **3** *colloq.* use; advantage.
■ **1 a** see DISTANCE *n.* 2.

mile•post /mīlpōst/ *n.* post or sign giving distance in miles, as along a highway.

mil•er /mīlər/ *n. colloq.* person or horse qualified or trained specially to run a mile.

mile•stone /mīlstōn/ *n.* **1** stone marking a distance in miles. **2** significant event or stage in a life, history, project, etc.
■ **2** see LANDMARK 2.

mi•lieu /mĭlyō, meelyō/ *n.* (*pl.* **mi•lieus** or **mi•lieux** /–lyōz/) one's environment or social surroundings.
■ climate, environs, background, neighborhood, precincts; ambiance, sphere, setting.

mil•i•tant /mĭlit'nt/ • *adj.* **1** combative; aggressively active, esp. in support of a (usu. political) cause. **2** engaged in warfare. • *n.* militant person. □□ **mil'i•tan•cy** *n.* **mil'i•tant•ly** *adv.*
■ *adj.* **1** aggressive, pugnacious, belligerent, hostile, contentious. **2** warring, fighting, combatant, embattled. • *n.* activist, fighter; aggressor, combatant.

mil•i•ta•rism /mĭlitərĭzəm/ *n.* **1** military spirit. **2** undue prevalence of the military spirit or ideals. □□ **mil'i•ta•rist** *n.* **mil•i•ta•ris'tic** *adj.* **mil•i•ta•ris'ti•cal•ly** *adv.*
■ □□ **militaristic** see WARLIKE 1.

mil•i•ta•rize /mĭlitərīz/ *v.tr.* **1** equip with military resources. **2** make military or warlike. □□ **mil•i•ta•ri•za'tion** *n.*

mil•i•tar•y /mĭlitéree/ • *adj.* of, relating to, or characteristic of soldiers or armed forces. • *n.* [as *sing.* or *pl.*; prec. by *the*] members of the armed forces, as distinct from civilians and the police. □ **military police** corps responsible for police and disciplinary duties in the army. □□ **mil•i•tar•i•ly** /–táirəlee/ *adv.* **mil'i•tar•i•ness** *n.*
■ *adj.* martial, soldierly, army, fighting, service. • *n.* (armed) services, army, air force, soldiery.

mil•i•tate /mĭlitayt/ *v.intr.* (of facts or evidence) have force or effect (against). ¶Often confused with *mitigate.*
■ work *or* go *or* operate against, foil, counter, countervail (against), cancel (out); resist, oppose.

mi•li•tia /mĭlishə/ *n.* military force, esp. one raised from the civil population and supplementing a regular army in an emergency. □□ **mi•li'tia•man** *n.* (*pl.* **-men**).

milk /mĭlk/ • *n.* **1** opaque white fluid secreted by female mammals for the nourishment of their young. **2** milk of cows, goats, or sheep as food. **3** milklike juice of plants, e.g., in the coconut. • *v.tr.* **1** draw milk from (a cow, ewe, goat, etc.). **2** exploit (a person or situa-

tion). □ **milk cow 1** cow raised for its milk. **2** profitable venture. **milk run** routine expedition or service journey. **milk shake** drink of milk, flavoring, and usu. ice cream, mixed by shaking or blending. **milk tooth** temporary tooth in young mammals. □□ **milk'er** *n.*
■ *n.* **3** latex; juice, sap. • *v.* **2** bleed, drain, take advantage of.

milk•maid /mĭlkmayd/ *n.* girl or woman who milks cows or works in a dairy.

milk•man /mĭlkman/ *n.* (*pl.* **-men**) person who sells or delivers milk.

milk•sop /mĭlksop/ *n.* spiritless or meek person, esp. a man.
■ coward, weakling, namby-pamby, crybaby, *colloq.* sissy.

milk•y /mĭlkee/ *adj.* (**milk•i•er, milk•i•est**) **1** of, like, or mixed with milk. **2** (of a gem or liquid) cloudy; not clear. □ **Milky Way** faintly luminous band of light emitted by countless stars encircling the heavens; the Galaxy. □□ **milk'i•ness** *n.*
■ **2** see FILMY 2.

mill¹ /mĭl/ • *n.* **1 a** building fitted with a mechanical apparatus for grinding grain. **b** such an apparatus. **2** apparatus for grinding any solid substance to powder or pulp (*pepper mill*). **3** factory. • *v.* **1** *tr.* grind (grain), produce (flour), or hull (seeds) in a mill. **2** *tr.* produce regular ribbed markings on the edge of (a coin). **3** *tr.* cut or shape (metal) with a rotating tool. **4** *intr.* move aimlessly (around). □ **go** (or **put**) **through the mill** undergo (or cause to undergo) intensive work or training, etc. □□ **mill'a•ble** *adj.*
■ *n.* **1b, 2** grinder, quern, crusher, roller. **3** plant, works, workshop, shop, foundry. • *v.* **1** crush, powder, pulverize, granulate. **4** crowd, throng, swarm.

mill² /mĭl/ *n.* one-thousandth of a US dollar.

mil•len•ni•um /mĭléneeəm/ *n.* (*pl.* **mil•len•ni•a** /–neeə/ or **mil•len•ni•ums**) **1** one-thousandth anniversary. **2** a period of 1,000 years. **3** the 1000-year period of Christ's prophesied reign in person on earth (Rev. 20:1–5). □□ **mil•len'ni•al** *adj.* **mil•len'ni•al•ist** *n. & adj.*

mill•er /mĭlər/ *n.* person who works or owns a mill.

mil•let /mĭlit/ *n.* **1** cereal plant bearing a large crop of small nutritious seeds. **2** seed of this.

milli- /mĭlee, –i, –ə/ *comb. form* one thousandth.

mil•li•gram /mĭligram/ *n.* one-thousandth of a gram.

mil•li•li•ter /mĭlileetər/ *n.* one-thousandth of a liter.

mil•li•me•ter /mĭlimeetər/ *n.* one-thousandth of a meter.

mil•li•ner /mĭlinər/ *n.* person who makes or sells women's hats. □□ **mil•li•ner•y** /–eree/ *n.*

mil•lion /mĭlyən/ *n.* a thousand thousand. □□ **mil'lion•fold** *adj. & adv.* **mil'lionth** *adj. & n.*

mil•lion•aire /mĭlyənáir/ *n.* (*fem.* **mil•lion•air•ess** /–ris/) person who has over one million dollars, pounds, etc.

mil•li•pede /míləpeed/ n. (also **mil'le•pede**) small crawling invertebrate with many legs.

mil•li•sec•ond /mílisekənd/ n. one-thousandth of a second.

mill•race /mílrays/ n. current of water that drives a mill wheel.

mill•stone /mílstōn/ n. **1** each of two circular stones used for grinding grain. **2** heavy burden or responsibility.

mill•wright /mílrīt/ n. person who designs, builds, or operates a mill or milling machinery.

mi•lord /miláwrd/ n. hist. English nobleman.

milt /milt/ n. reproductive gland or sperm of a male fish.

mime /mīm/ • n. **1** acting using only gestures. **2** (also **mime artist**) practitioner of mime. • v. tr. [also absol.] convey by gesture without words. □□ **mim'er** n.

mim•e•o•graph /mímeeəgraf/ • n. **1** [often attrib.] machine that produces copies from a stencil. **2** copy produced in this way. • v. tr. reproduce by this process.

mi•met•ic /mimétik/ adj. relating to or habitually practicing imitation or mimicry. □□ **mi•met'i•cal•ly** adv.

mim•ic /mímik/ • v. tr. (**mim•icked**, **mim•ick•ing**) **1** imitate (a person, gesture, etc.) esp. to entertain or ridicule. **2** copy minutely or servilely. **3** (of a thing) resemble closely. See synonym study at IMITATE. • n. person skilled in imitation. • adj. having an aptitude for mimicry; imitating. □□ **mim'ick•er** n.

mim'ic•ry n. See synonym study at CARICATURE

■ v. **1** mock, satirize, caricature, parody; ape, copy, simulate. **2** reproduce, duplicate; see also IMITATE 3. **3** mirror, echo; see also RESEMBLE. • n. impersonator, imitator, impressionist, caricaturist, parodist; colloq. copycat. • adj. imitative, mimetic; imitation, mock, simulated. □□ **mimicry** see IMITATION n. 1.

mi•mo•sa /mimṓsə, -zə/ n. **1** shrub having globular usu. yellow flowers. **2** acacia plant with showy yellow flowers. **3** cocktail of champagne and orange juice.

min. abbr. **1** minute(s) **2** minimum.

min•a•ret /mínərét/ n. slender turret connected to a mosque. □□ **min•a•ret'ed** adj.

min•a•to•ry /mínətáwree/ adj. threatening; menacing.

mince /mins/ v. **1** tr. cut up or grind into very small pieces. **2** intr. (usu. as **mincing** adj.) speak or walk with an affected delicacy. □ **mince words** [usu. with neg.] use polite expressions, etc. □□ **minc'er** n. **minc'ing•ly** adv. (in sense 2 of v.).

■ **1** see cut up 1, GRIND v. 1a. **2** (**mincing**) effeminate, dainty, delicate, foppish, dandyish, affected, precious.

mince•meat /mínsmeet/ n. mixture of currants, raisins, sugar, apples, candied peel, spices, often suet, and sometimes meat. □ **make mincemeat of** utterly defeat.

mind /mīnd/ • n. **1 a** seat of consciousness, thought, volition, and feeling. **b** attention; concentration. **2** intellect; reason. **3** remembrance; memory. **4** one's opinion (we're of the same mind). **5** way of thinking or feeling (shocking to the Victorian mind). **6** sanity. • v. tr. **1** [usu. with neg. or interrog.] object to (do you mind if I smoke?). **2** remember; heed; take care to (mind you come on time). **3** have charge of temporarily (mind the house while I'm away). **4** apply oneself to; concern oneself with. □ **have (it) in mind** intend. **mind-boggling** colloq. overwhelming; startling. **mind-read** discern the thoughts of (another person). **mind reader** person capable of mind reading. **never mind 1** expression used to comfort or console. **2** (also **never you mind**) expression used to evade a question. **3** disregard (never mind the cost). **out of one's mind** crazy.

■ n. **1 b** consciousness, awareness; thoughts, attentiveness; see also PERCEPTION, sensitivity (SENSITIVE). **2** intelligence, wit(s), mentality, brain, brains, brainpower, sense, sagacity, wisdom, perception, percipience, reason; aptitude, head, perception, capacity. **3** recollection. **4** sentiment, attitude, (point of) view, feeling, judgment, belief, viewpoint. **5** intention, disposition, temper, temperament, humor, fancy, tendency, bent. **6** see SANITY 1. • v. **1** resent, take offense at, be offended by, dislike, be troubled or annoyed by. **2** not forget to, make sure to, be sure to; attend to, pay attention to, obey, listen to. **3** watch over, take care of, care for, look after, sit with, baby-sit, guard. **4** attend to, apply oneself to, take care of, see also mind one's own business (BUSINESS). □ **have (it) in mind** see INTEND 1, 2. **mind-read** read a person's mind. **never mind 2** see mind one's own business (BUSINESS). **3** ignore, forget, pay no attention to, do not think twice about, do not give a second thought to. **out of one's mind** see CRAZY 1.

mind•ed /míndid/ adj. **1** [in comb.] having a specified kind of mind or interest. **2** disposed or inclined.

mind•ful /míndfŏŏl/ adj. [often foll. by of] taking heed or care; being conscious. □□ **mind'ful•ly** adv. **mind'ful•ness** n.

■ aware, alert, attentive, alive, heedful, careful, conscientious, watchful, vigilant.

mind•less /míndlis/ adj. **1** lacking intelligence; stupid. **2** not requiring thought or skill (totally mindless work). **3** heedless of (advice, etc.). □□ **mind'less•ly** adv. **mind'less•ness** n.

■ **1** asinine, obtuse, idiotic, thoughtless, witless, senseless. **2** perfunctory, unthinking; see also MECHANICAL 3. **3** unaware.

mind•set /míndset/ n. **1** mental attitude that can influence one's interpretation of events or situations. **2** inclination or a fixed way of thinking.

mine¹ /mīn/ poss.pron. the one or ones of or belonging to me (it is mine). □ **of mine** of or belonging to me.

mine² /mīn/ • n. **1** excavation in the earth for extracting metal, coal, salt, etc. **2** abundant source (of information, etc.). **3** military explosive device placed in the ground or in the water. • v. tr. **1** obtain (metal, coal, etc.) from a mine. **2** dig in (the earth, etc.) for ore, etc. **3** tunnel. **4** lay explosive mines under or in. □□ **min'ing** *n.*

■ *n.* **1** pit, excavation; colliery, coalfield. **2** quarry, store, storehouse, supply, deposit, depository; fund, mint, treasury. • *v.* **1**, **2** excavate, quarry, extract, scoop out *or* up, remove, unearth; derive, extract, draw. **3** dig *or* burrow in; gouge (out), scoop (out).

mine•field /mínfeeld/ *n.* **1** area planted with explosive mines. **2** subject or situation presenting unseen hazards.

min•er /mínər/ *n.* person who works in a mine.

min•er•al /mínərəl/ *n.* **1** any of the species into which inorganic substances are classified. **2** substance obtained by mining. □ **mineral oil** *Pharm.* colorless, odorless, oily liquid obtained from petroleum and used as a laxative, in manufacturing cosmetics, etc. **mineral water** natural or processed water containing some dissolved salts.

min•er•al•o•gy /mínərólájee/ *n.* scientific study of minerals. □□ **min•er•al•og•i•cal** /-rəlójikəl/ *adj.* **min•er•al'o•gist** *n.*

min•e•stro•ne /mínistrónee/ *n.* thick vegetable soup.

mine•sweep•er /mínsweepər/ *n.* ship for clearing away floating and submerged mines.

min•gle /mínggəl/ *v.* **1** *tr. & intr.* mix; blend. **2** *intr.* [often foll. by *with*] (of a person) move about; associate. □□ **min'gler** *n.*

■ **1** intermingle, intermix, combine, amalgamate, merge, compound, marry. **2** mix, socialize, associate, fraternize, hobnob, consort, spend time.

min•i /mínee/ *n.* (*pl.* **min•is**) *colloq.* miniskirt, minidress, etc.

mini- /mínee/ *comb. form* miniature.

■ micro-.

min•i•a•ture /míneeəchər, mínichər/ • *adj.* **1** much smaller than normal. **2** represented on a small scale. See synonym study at SMALL. • *n.* **1** any object reduced in size. **2** small-scale minutely finished portrait. □□ **min'i•a•tur•ist** *n.* (in sense 2 of *n.*).

■ *adj.* small, small-scale, little, tiny, diminutive, minute.

min•i•a•tur•ize /míneeəchəriz, mínichə-/ *v.tr.* produce in a smaller version; make small. □□ **min•i•a•tur•i•za'tion** *n.*

min•i•bike /míneebik/ *n.* motorbike designed for off-road use, esp. with elevated handlebars.

min•i•cam /míneekam/ *n.* portable lightweight video camera.

min•i•com•put•er /míneekəmpyōótər/ *n.* computer of medium power.

min•i•ma *pl.* of MINIMUM.

min•i•mal /mínimǝl/ *adj.* **1** very minute; smallest; least. **2** *Art,* etc. characterized by the use of simple or primary forms or structures, etc. □□ **min'i•mal•ism** *n.* (in sense 2). **min'i•mal•ist** *n.* (in sense 2). **min'i•mal•ly** *adv.* (in sense 1).

■ minutest, littlest; minimum.

min•i•mize /mínimiz/ *v.* **1** *tr.* reduce to, or estimate at, the smallest possible amount or degree. **2** *tr.* estimate or represent at less

than the true value or importance. **3** *intr.* attain a minimum value. □□ **min•i•mi•za'tion** *n.* **min'i•miz•er** *n.*

■ **1** shrink, lessen, diminish, prune, abbreviate. **2** belittle, de-emphasize, downplay, play down, make little *or* light of, disparage, decry.

min•i•mum /mínimǝm/ *n.* (*pl.* **min•i•ma** /-mǝ/) • *n.* least possible or attainable amount. • *adj.* that is a minimum. □ **minimum wage** lowest wage permitted by law.

■ *n.* (rock) bottom, base, floor, lower limit. • *adj.* minimal, minutest, littlest, least, slightest, lowest.

min•ion /mínyǝn/ *n. derog.* servile agent; slave.

min•i•ser•ies /míneeseereez/ *n.* short series of television programs on a common theme.

min•i•skirt /míneeskǝrt/ *n.* very short skirt.

min•is•ter /mínistǝr/ • *n.* **1** member of the clergy. **2** head of a government department (in some countries). **3** diplomatic agent, usu. ranking below an ambassador. • *v. intr.* render aid or service to. □□ **min•is•te'ri•al** /-ísteéreeǝl/ *adj.* **min•is•te'ri•al•ly** *adv.*

■ *n.* **1** cleric, clergyman, clergywoman, ecclesiastic, pastor, reverend, churchman. **2**, **3** envoy, delegate, diplomat, emissary. • *v.* attend (to *or* on *or* upon), wait on, care for, look after, see to; aid, help, assist, support.

min•is•tra•tion /mínistráyshǝn/ *n.* **1** [usu. in *pl.*] aid or service. **2** supplying (of help, justice, etc.). □□ **min•is•trant** /mínistrǝnt/ *adj. & n.*

min•is•try /mínistree/ *n.* (*pl.* **–tries**) **1** [prec. by *the*] vocation office, tenure, or profession of a religious minister. **2** [prec. by *the*] body of ministers of a government or of a religion. **3** government department headed by a minister. **4** ministering; ministration.

■ **1**, **2** priesthood, the church, the pulpit; clergy; see also CABINET 2. **3** office, bureau, agency; see also DEPARTMENT 1a.

min•i•van /míneevan/ *n.* vehicle, smaller than a full-sized van, for passengers, cargo, etc.

mink /mingk/ *n.* **1** semiaquatic stoatlike animal bred for its thick brown fur. **2** this thick brown fur. **3** coat made of this.

Minn. *abbr.* Minnesota.

min•now /mínō/ *n.* small freshwater fish.

Mi•no•an /minóǝn/ *Archaeol.* • *adj.* of or relating to the Bronze Age civilization centered on Crete (*c.* 3000–1100 BC). • *n.* inhabitant of Minoan Crete or the Minoan world.

mi•nor /mínǝr/ • *adj.* **1** lesser or comparatively small in size or importance (*minor poet*). **2** *Mus.* less by a semitone than a corresponding major. • *n.* **1** person under the legal age limit or majority. **2** student's subsidiary subject or course. • *v.intr.* [foll. by *in*] (of a student) undertake study in a (subject) as a subsidiary. □ **minor scale** *Mus.* scale with half steps between the second and third, fifth and sixth, and seventh and eighth degrees.

■ *adj.* **1** smaller, secondary, subordinate, subsidiary; insignificant, obscure, inconsequential, unimportant, trifling, trivial, negligible. • *n.* **1** child, youngster, youth, stripling, teenager, adolescent.

mi•nor•i•ty /mɪnáwritee, –nór–/ *n.* (*pl.* **–ties**) **1** smaller number or part, esp. within a political party or structure; less than half. **2** relatively small group of people differing from others in race, religion, language, political persuasion, etc. **3** being under full legal age. □ **minority leader** leader of the minority political party in a legislature.

■ **3** see CHILDHOOD.

min•ox•i•dil /mənóksədil/ *n.* drug taken orally to treat hypertension or applied topically to stimulate hair growth.

min•strel /mínstrəl/ *n.* **1** medieval singer or musician. **2** [usu. in *pl.*] member of a band of public entertainers with blackened faces, etc., performing songs and music ostensibly of African American origin.

■ **1** troubadour, balladeer, minnesinger, bard.

mint¹ /mint/ *n.* **1** aromatic plant used for flavoring. **2** peppermint or spearmint candy or lozenge. □ **mint julep** sweet iced alcoholic drink of bourbon flavored with mint. □□ **mint'y** *adj.* (**mint•i•er, mint•i•est**)

mint² /mint/ • *n.* **1** place where money is coined. **2** vast sum of money. • *v.tr.* **1** make (coin) by stamping metal. **2** invent or coin (a word, phrase, etc.). □ **in mint condition** as new. □□ **mint'age** *n.*

■ *n.* **2** (small) fortune, king's ransom, millions, billions, wad(s), *colloq.* pile, heap(s), packet, pot(s), loads. • *v.* **1** stamp, coin, produce. **2** see COIN *v.* 1.

min•u•et /mɪnyoo-ét/ *n.* **1** slow stately dance for two in triple time. **2** *Mus.* music for this.

mi•nus /mínəs/ • *prep.* **1** with the subtraction of (*7 minus 4 equals 3*). ¶Symb.: –. **2** (of temperature) below zero (*minus 2°*). **3** *colloq.* lacking; deprived of (*returned minus their dog*). • *adj.* negative. • *n.* **1** = *minus sign.* **2** *Math.* negative quantity. **3** disadvantage. □ **minus sign** the symbol (-) indicating subtraction or a negative value.

mi•nus•cule /mínəskyōol/ *adj.* *colloq.* extremely small or unimportant. □□ **mi•nus'cu•lar** /mɪnúskyōolər/ *adj.*

■ see MINUTE² 1.

min•ute¹ /mínit/ *n.* **1** sixtieth part of an hour. **2** distance covered in one minute (*twenty minutes from the station*). **3** moment. **4** sixtieth part of an angular degree. **5** [in *pl.*] official memorandum or brief summary of a meeting, etc. □ **up-to-the-minute** completely up to date.

■ **3** instant, (split) second, flash, trice, *colloq.* sec, jiff, mo. **5** log, record, journal, transcript, notes, résumé, proceedings; see also MEMORANDUM. □ **up-to-the-minute** latest, newest, modern, up to date, fashionable, smart, all the rage, in vogue, stylish.

mi•nute² /mínoōt, –yōōt/ *adj.* (**mi•nut•est**) **1** very small. **2** accurate; detailed. See synonym study at SMALL. □□ **min'ute•ly** *adv.*

■ **1** little, tiny, minuscule, minimal, miniature, infinitesimal, microscopic, mini–, *colloq.* pint-sized. **2** see PRECISE 2.

min•ute•man /mínitman/ *n.* (*pl.* **–men**) *US hist.* (also **Min'ute•man**) American militiaman of the Revolutionary War period (ready to march at a minute's notice).

mi•nu•ti•a /minoōsheeə, –shə, –nyōō–/ *n.* (*pl.* **–ti•ae** /–shee-ee/) [usu. in *pl.*] precise, trivial, or minor detail.

■ see *refinement* (REFINE).

minx /mingks/ *n.* pert, sly, or playful girl.

mir•a•cle /mírəkəl/ *n.* **1** extraordinary event attributed to some supernatural agency. **2** remarkable occurrence. **3** remarkable specimen (*the plan was a miracle of ingenuity*).

■ see WONDER *n.* 2.

mi•rac•u•lous /mirákyələs/ *adj.* **1** of the nature of a miracle. **2** supernatural. **3** remarkable; surprising. □□ **mi•rac'u•lous•ly** *adv.* **mi•rac'u•lous•ness** *n.*

■ **1, 3** marvelous, wonderful, incredible, unbelievable, inexplicable, unexplainable, extraordinary, spectacular, amazing, astounding. **2** magical, preternatural, superhuman; see also SUPERNATURAL *adj.*

mi•rage /mɪráazh/ *n.* **1** optical illusion caused by atmospheric conditions. **2** illusory thing.

■ see ILLUSION 3.

mire /mɪr/ • *n.* **1** stretch of swampy or boggy ground. **2** mud; dirt. • *v.* **1** *tr.* & *intr.* plunge or sink in a mire. **2** *tr.* involve in difficulties.

■ *n.* **1** swamp, bog, fen, marsh, quagmire. **2** ooze, muck, slime. • *v.* **1** bog down, entangle, tangle, enmesh, mesh, involve.

mir•ror /mírər/ • *n.* **1** polished surface, usu. of amalgam-coated glass or metal, which reflects an image. **2** anything reflecting truly or accurately. • *v.tr.* reflect as in a mirror.

■ *n.* **1** looking glass, glass, speculum, reflector. **2** reflection, reproduction, picture, representation. • *v.* reproduce, represent, depict, repeat, echo.

mirth /mərth/ *n.* merriment; laughter. □□ **mirth'ful** *adj.* **mirth'ful•ly** *adv.* **mirth' ful•ness** *n.* **mirth'less** *adj.* **mirth'less•ly** *adv.* **mirth'less•ness** *n.*

■ merrymaking, jollity, gaiety, fun, amusement, frolic, joviality, joyousness, revelry, rejoicing.

MIS *abbr. Computing* management information system.

mis- /mis/ *prefix* added to verbs, verbal derivatives, and nouns, meaning 'amiss,' 'badly,' 'wrongly,' 'unfavorably,' or having negative force (*mislead, misshapen, mistrust, misadventure*).

mis•ad•ven•ture /mísədvénchər/ *n.* bad luck; misfortune.

mis•a•lign /mísəlín/ *v.tr.* give the wrong alignment to. □□ **mis•a•lign'ment** *n.*

mis•an•thrope /mísənthrōp, míz–/ *n.* (also **mis•an•thro•pist** /misánthrəpist/) person who hates or avoids human society. □□ **mis•an•throp•ic** /–thrópik/ *adj.* **mis•an•throp'i•cal** *adj.* **mis•an•throp'i•cal•ly** *adv.* **mis•an•thro•py** /misánthrəpee/ *n.*

■ loner, hermit, recluse, anchorite, lone wolf. □□ **misanthropic** antisocial, unsocial, unsociable.

mis•ap•ply /mísəplí/ *v.tr.* (**–plies, –plied**) apply (esp. funds) wrongly. □□ **mis•ap•pli•ca•tion** /mísəplikáyshən/ *n.*

■ see MISUSE v. 1. □□ **misapplication** see
MISUSE n.

mis•ap•pre•hend /mísaprihénd/ v.tr. misunderstand. □□ **mis•ap•pre•hen•sion**
/-hénshən/ n. **mis•ap•pre•hen'sive** adj.

mis•ap•pro•pri•ate /mísəprŏpreeayt/ v.tr.
take for one's own use; embezzle. □□ **mis•
ap•pro•pri•a•tion** /-áyshən/ n.

■ steal, filch, pilfer, pocket, peculate.

mis•be•got•ten /mísbigót'n/ adj. 1 illegitimate; bastard. 2 contemptible; disreputable.

mis•be•have /mísbiháyv/ v.intr. & refl. (of a
person or machine) behave badly. □□ **mis•
be•hav'ior** n.

■ behave improperly, be bad or naughty,
cause trouble, colloq. carry on, act up.
□□ **misbehavior** naughtiness, badness, misconduct, delinquency.

misc. abbr. miscellaneous.

mis•car•riage /mískárij/ n. 1 spontaneous
premature abortion. 2 failure (of a plan, system, etc.).

■ 2 abortion, collapse, breakdown, failing;
defeat.

mis•car•ry /mískáree/ v.intr. (-ries, -ried)
1 have a miscarriage. 2 (of a business, plan,
etc.) fail; be unsuccessful.

■ 2 abort; fail, fall through, break down, go
wrong, founder, come to nothing or naught,
go awry.

mis•cast /mískást/ v.tr. (past and past part.
-cast) allot an unsuitable part to (an actor).

mis•ce•ge•na•tion /mísèjináyshən, mísəjə-/
n. interbreeding of races, esp. of whites and
nonwhites.

mis•cel•la•ne•ous /mísəláyneeəs/ adj. 1 of
mixed composition or character. 2 [foll. by
pl. noun] of various kinds. □□ **mis•cel•la'
ne•ous•ly** adv.

■ varied, heterogeneous, diverse, mixed, diversified, motley, sundry, assorted, various,
varying, multifarious.

mis•cel•la•ny /mísəláynee/ n. (pl. -nies)
mixture; medley, esp. a varied literary collection.

■ assortment, variety, diversity, mixed bag,
job lot, ragbag, mélange, potpourri, gallimaufry, motley.

mis•chance /míscháns/ n. 1 bad luck. 2 instance of this.

mis•chief /míschif/ n. 1 pranks; scrapes.
2 playful malice; archness. 3 harm; injury.
4 person or thing responsible for harm or annoyance.

■ 1, 2 misbehavior, naughtiness, impishness, roguishness, mischievousness,
playfulness, devilment. 3 damage, detriment, trouble, hurt, wrong, difficulty.
4 trouble, worry, bother, colloq. hassle; see
also NUISANCE.

mis•chie•vous /míschivəs/ adj. 1 (of a person) disposed to mischief. 2 (of conduct)
playfully malicious. 3 (of a thing) harmful.
□□ **mis'chie•vous•ly** adv. **mis'chie•vous•
ness** n.

■ 1, 2 naughty, impish, roguish, devilish,
elfish, puckish. 3 injurious, hurtful, damaging; pernicious, detrimental.

mis•ci•ble /mísibəl/ adj. [often foll. by with]
capable of being mixed. □□ **mis•ci•bil'i•ty**
n.

mis•con•ceive /mískənseev/ v. 1 intr. [often
foll. by of] have a wrong idea or conception.
2 tr. (as **misconceived** adj.) badly planned,
organized, etc. □□ **mis•con•ceiv'er** n. **mis•
con•cep'tion** /-sépshən/ n.

■ 1 misunderstand, misconstrue, misjudge,
miscalculate, mistake, misapprehend, misinterpret. 2 (**misconceived**) ill-organized; ill-
judged, ill thought out. □□ **misconception**
false or wrong notion or idea, error, mistake,
delusion.

mis•con•duct /mískóndukt/ n. 1 improper
or unprofessional behavior. 2 bad management.

■ 1 see misbehavior (MISBEHAVE).

mis•con•strue /mískənstrōō/ v.tr. interpret
wrongly. □□ **mis•con•struc'tion** /-strúk-
shən/ n.

mis•count /mískównt/ • v.tr. [also absol.]
count wrongly. • n. a wrong count.

mis•cre•ant /mískreeənt/ n. vile wretch; villain.

■ criminal, wrongdoer, felon, malefactor,
rogue, reprobate, scoundrel, knave, thug, colloq. scamp, crook, baddy, often joc. rascal, sl.
hood, mug.

mis•deal /mísdeel/ • v.tr. [also absol.] (past
and past part. -dealt /-délt/) make a mistake
in dealing (cards). • n. 1 mistake in dealing
cards. 2 misdealt hand.

mis•deed /mísdeed/ n. evil deed; wrongdoing; crime.

■ offense, felony, misdoing, transgression,
misdemeanor, fault, misconduct, sin, trespass.

mis•de•mean•or /mísdimeenər/ n. 1 offense; misdeed. 2 Law indictable offense,
less heinous than a felony.

■ see OFFENSE 1.

mis•di•rect /mísdirékt, -dī-/ v.tr. direct (a
person, letter, blow, etc.) wrongly. □□ **mis•
di•rec'tion** /-rékshən/ n.

■ misguide, misadvise; misaddress; see also
MISINFORM.

mis•do•ing /mísdōoing/ n. misdeed.

mi•ser /mízər/ n. person who hoards wealth
greedily. □□ **mi'ser•li•ness** n. **mi'ser•ly**
adj. See synonym study at ECONOMICAL.

■ skinflint, hoarder, niggard, penny-
pincher, colloq. money-grubber. □□ **miserly**
stingy, niggardly, penny-pinching, parsimonious, mean, cheeseparing, tightfisted,
close.

mis•er•a•ble /mízərəbəl/ adj. 1 wretchedly
unhappy or uncomfortable. 2 inadequate
(miserable hovel); contemptible. 3 causing
wretchedness or discomfort (miserable weather). 4 stingy; mean. □□ **mis'er•a•ble•ness**
n. **mis'er•a•bly** adv.

■ 1 wretched, depressed, woeful, woebegone, sad, dejected, forlorn, disconsolate, despondent. 2 unworthy, poor, sorry, pitiful,
pathetic, squalid. 3 unpleasant, inclement,
untoward, bad, awful. 4 see MEAN² 1.

mis•er•y /mízəree/ n. (pl. -ies) 1 wretched
state of mind, or of outward circumstances.
2 thing causing this.

■ **1** unhappiness, distress, discomfort, wretchedness, sadness, melancholy, sorrow, heartache, grief, anguish; squalor, poverty, destitution, privation. **2** hardship, suffering, calamity, disaster, curse, misfortune, ordeal, trouble, catastrophe, trial, tribulation.

mis•fire /mísfír/ • *v.intr.* **1** (of a gun, motor engine, etc.) fail to go off or start or function regularly. **2** (of an action, etc.) fail to have the intended effect. • *n.* such a failure.

■ *v.* **2** abort, miscarry, go wrong, fizzle out, fall through. • *n.* miscarriage, malfunction, *sl.* dud.

mis•fit /mísfít/ *n.* **1** person unsuited to an environment, occupation, etc. **2** garment, etc., that does not fit.

■ **1** eccentric, individual, nonconformist, maverick.

mis•for•tune /misfáwrchən/ *n.* bad luck.

■ ill luck, ill fortune, hard luck, infelicity, adversity; accident, misadventure, mishap, calamity, catastrophe.

mis•giv•ing /misgíving/ *n.* [usu. in *pl.*] feeling of mistrust or apprehension. See synonym study at QUALM.

■ worry, concern, anxiety, qualm, scruple, disquiet; dread, premonition.

mis•gov•ern /mísgúvərn/ *v.tr.* govern (a state, a nation, etc.) badly. □□ **mis•gov′ern•ment** *n.*

mis•guide /mísgíd/ *v.tr.* **1** (as **misguided** *adj.*) mistaken in thought or action. **2** mislead; misdirect. □□ **mis•guid′ance** *n.* **mis•guid′ed•ly** *adv.* **mis•guid′ed•ness** *n.*

■ **1** (misguided) wrong, misdirected, foolish, unreasoning, erroneous, misled, misplaced. **2** see MISLEAD.

mis•han•dle /mís-hánd′l/ *v.tr.* **1** deal with incorrectly or ineffectively. **2** handle roughly or rudely; ill-treat.

■ **1** mismanage, bungle, botch, misconduct, mess up. **2** abuse, mistreat, maltreat, brutalize, maul.

mis•hap /mís-háp/ *n.* unlucky accident.

■ see MISFORTUNE.

mis•hear /mis-heér/ *v.tr.* (*past* and *past part.* **–heard** /-hérd/) hear incorrectly or imperfectly.

mish•mash /míshmash, –maash/ *n.* confused mixture.

■ mess, medley, hash, gallimaufry, farrago, potpourri.

mis•in•form /misinfórm/ *v.tr.* give wrong information to; mislead. □□ **mis•in•for•ma′tion** *n.*

■ misguide, misadvise, misdirect, delude, deceive, dupe, fool, gull, lead astray. □□ **misinformation** disinformation; (*piece of misinformation*) red herring, false trail, false scent.

mis•in•ter•pret /mísintórprit/ *v.tr.* **1** interpret wrongly. **2** draw a wrong inference from. □□ **mis•in•ter•pre•ta′tion** *n.* **mis•in•ter′pret•er** *n.*

■ misunderstand, misconstrue, misconceive, misread.

mis•judge /mísjúj/ *v.tr.* [also *absol.*] **1** judge wrongly. **2** have a wrong opinion of. □□ **mis•judg′ment** *n.*

mis•lay /mísláy/ *v.tr.* (*past* and *past part.* **–laid** /-láyd/) unintentionally put (a thing) where it cannot readily be found.

■ misplace, lose.

mis•lead /misleéd/ *v.tr.* (*past* and *past part.* **–led** /-léd/) **1** cause (a person) to go wrong, in conduct, belief, etc. **2** lead astray or in the wrong direction. □□ **mis•lead′er** *n.*

■ misinform, misguide, misdirect, fool, outwit, bluff, hoodwink, trick, humbug, deceive, dupe.

mis•lead•ing /mísleéding/ *adj.* causing to err or go astray; imprecise. □□ **mis•lead′ing•ly** *adv.*

■ see FALSE *adj.* 2b.

mis•man•age /mismánij/ *v.tr.* manage badly or wrongly. □□ **mis•man′age•ment** *n.*

mis•match • *v.tr.* /mísmách/ (usu. as **mismatched** *adj.*) match unsuitably or incorrectly. • *n.* /mísmach/ bad match.

■ *v.* (mismatched) mismated, ill-matched, incompatible, unfit, inappropriate, unsuited, unsuitable, incongruous.

mis•no•mer /misnómər/ *n.* name or term used wrongly.

mi•sog•y•ny /misójinee/ *n.* hatred of women. □□ **mi•sog′y•nist** *n.* **mi•sog′y•nous** *adj.*

mis•place /mispláys/ *v.tr.* **1** put in the wrong place. **2** bestow (affections, confidence, etc.) on an inappropriate object. **3** mislay (words, actions, etc.) badly. □□ **mis•place′ment** *n.*

■ **1** see LOSE 1, 2.

mis•print • *n.* /mísprint/ mistake in printing. • *v.tr.* /mísprínt/ print wrongly.

■ *n.* error, erratum, typographical error, *colloq.* typo.

mis•pri•sion /mísprízhən/ *n. Law* wrong action or omission.

mis•pro•nounce /mísprənówns/ *v.tr.* pronounce (a word, etc.) wrongly. □□ **mis•pro•nun•ci•a•tion** /-nunseeáyshən/ *n.*

mis•quote /mískwót/ *v.tr.* quote wrongly. □□ **mis•quo•ta′tion** *n.*

mis•read /mísreéd/ *v.tr.* (*past* and *past part.* **–read** /-réd/) read or interpret (text, a situation, etc.) wrongly.

■ see MISINTERPRET.

mis•rep•re•sent /mísreprizént/ *v.tr.* represent wrongly; give a false or misleading account or idea of. □□ **mis•rep•re•sen•ta′tion** *n.* **mis•rep•re•sen′ta•tive** *adj.*

■ distort, twist, pervert, garble, misstate, mangle; falsify.

mis•rule /mísroól/ • *n.* bad government; disorder. • *v.tr.* govern badly.

Miss. *abbr.* Mississippi.

miss¹ /mis/ • *v.* **1** *tr.* [also *absol.*] fail to hit, reach, find, catch, see, meet, hear, etc. **2** *tr.* fail to seize (an opportunity, etc.) (*I missed my chance*). **3** *tr.* notice or regret the loss or absence of. **4** *tr.* avoid (*go early to miss the traffic*). **5** *intr.* (of an engine, etc.) fail; misfire. • *n.* failure to hit, reach, attain, connect, etc. □□ **miss′a•ble** *adj.*

■ *v.* **3** long for, yearn for, pine for, want, need, wish for. **4** see AVOID 1.

miss² /mis/ *n.* **1** girl or unmarried woman. **2** (**Miss**) **a** respectful title of an unmarried woman or girl. **b** title of a beauty queen (*Miss World*).

■ **1** (young) lady, (young) woman, bachelor girl, mademoiselle, Fräulein, signorina, señorita; schoolgirl, teenager, coed, *colloq.* teenybopper; spinster.

mis•sal /mísəl/ *n. RC Ch., Anglican Ch.* **1** book containing the texts used in the service of the Mass. **2** book of prayers, esp. an illuminated one.

mis•shap•en /mis-sháypən/ *adj.* ill-shaped, deformed, distorted. □□ **mis•shap′en•ly** *adv.* **mis•shap′en•ness** *n.*

■ twisted, contorted, crooked, crippled, warped.

mis•sile /mísəl/ *n.* object or weapon suitable for throwing or propelling, esp. one directed by remote control or automatically. □□ **mis′sile•ry** /-əlree/ *n.*

■ projectile; brickbat.

miss•ing /mísing/ *adj.* lost; not present.

■ see ABSENT *adj.* 1.

mis•sion /míshən/ *n.* **1** particular task or goal assigned to or assumed by a person or group. **2** military or scientific operation or expedition. **3** body of persons sent to conduct negotiations, etc., or to propagate a religious faith. **4** missionary post.

■ **1** duty, function, purpose, job, office, work, assignment, errand, calling, occupation, vocation. **2** see EXPEDITION 1. **3** delegation, legation, deputation, commission.

mis•sion•ar•y /míshəneree/ • *adj.* of, concerned with, or characteristic of, religious missions. • *n.* (*pl.* **–ies**) person doing missionary work.

■ *n.* evangelist, preacher, proselytizer.

mis•sis var. of MISSUS.

mis•sive /mísiv/ *n.* letter; message.

■ communication, dispatch, *formal* or *joc.* epistle.

mis•spell /mís-spél/ *v.tr.* (*past* and *past part.* **–spelled** or **–spelt**) spell wrongly.

mis•spend /mís-spénd/ *v.tr.* (*past* and *past part.* **–spent** /–spént/) (esp. as **misspent** *adj.*) spend amiss or wastefully.

■ see WASTE *v.* 1; **(misspent)** wasted, squandered, idle, dissipated, thrown away, profitless, prodigal.

mis•state /mís-stáyt/ *v.tr.* state wrongly or inaccurately. □□ **mis•state′ment** *n.*

■ see TWIST *v.* 5. □□ **misstatement** falsification, misreport, misquotation, distortion; error, inaccuracy.

mis•step /mís-stép/ *n.* **1** wrong step or action. **2** faux pas.

■ **1** false step, blunder, mistake, error, bad *or* wrong *or* false move, slip. **2** indiscretion, lapse, oversight, gaffe, *colloq.* slipup.

mis•sus /mísəz/ *n.* (also **mis′sis**) *sl.* or *joc.* **1** form of address to a woman. **2** a wife. □ **the missus** my or your wife.

mist /mist/ • *n.* **1 a** water vapor near the ground in minute droplets limiting visibility. **b** condensed vapor obscuring glass, etc. **2** anything resembling or obscuring like mist. • *v.* cover or become covered with mist or as with mist. □□ **mist′like** *adj.*

■ *n.* fog, haze, smog, cloud; drizzle, mizzle.
• *v.* cloud (up *or* over), fog, dim, blur, film, steam up.

mis•take /mistáyk/ • *n.* **1** incorrect idea or opinion; thing incorrectly done or thought. **2** error of judgment. • *v.tr.* (*past* **mis•took** /–tŏŏk/; *past part.* **mis•tak•en** /–táykən/) **1** misunderstand. **2** wrongly take or identify. **3** choose wrongly. □□ **mis•tak′a•ble** *adj.* **mis•tak′a•bly** *adv.*

■ *n.* misconception, misapprehension, miscalculation; fault, slip, erratum; bad move, blunder. • *v.* **1** misinterpret, misjudge, misconstrue, get wrong, misread. **2** mix up with, confuse with, take for, misidentify as.

mis•tak•en /mistáykən/ *adj.* **1** wrong. **2** misunderstood; incorrect. □□ **mis•tak′en•ly** *adv.*

■ erroneous, fallacious, false, inaccurate, misconceived; flawed, warped.

mis•ter /místər/ *n.* title or form of address for a man.

mis•time /mís-tím/ *v.tr.* say or do at the wrong time.

mis•tle•toe /mísəltō/ *n.* parasitic plant growing on apple and other trees and bearing white glutinous berries.

mis•took *past* of MISTAKE.

mis•treat /mistréet/ *v.tr.* treat badly. □□ **mis•treat′ment** *n.*

■ abuse, maltreat, wrong; damage, harm; molest. □□ **mistreatment** abuse, maltreatment, ill use; molestation, brutalization, *sl.* roughing-up.

mis•tress /místris/ *n.* **1** female head of a household. **2** woman in authority. **3** woman (other than his wife) with whom a married man has a (usu. prolonged) sexual relationship.

■ **3** lover, girlfriend, kept woman, the other woman, inamorata.

mis•tri•al /mís-tríəl/ *n.* trial rendered invalid by procedural error.

mis•trust /mís-trúst/ • *v.tr.* **1** be suspicious of. **2** feel no confidence in. • *n.* **1** suspicion. **2** lack of confidence.

■ *v.* suspect, distrust, doubt, misdoubt, question. • *n.* distrust, doubt, skepticism, wariness, reservation.

mis•trust•ful /mís-trústfŏŏl/ *adj.* **1** suspicious. **2** lacking confidence. □□ **mis•trust′ful•ly** *adv.* **mis•trust′ful•ness** *n.*

mist•y /místee/ *adj.* (**mist•i•er, mist•i•est**) **1** of or covered with mist. **2** obscure; vague; dim. □□ **mist′i•ly** *adv.* **mist′i•ness** *n.*

■ cloudy, foggy, hazy; fuzzy, blurred; unclear.

mis•un•der•stand /mísundərstánd/ *v.tr.* (*past* and *past part.* **–un•der•stood** /–stŏŏd/) **1** fail to understand correctly. **2** (usu. as **misunderstood** *adj.*) misinterpret.

■ misconceive, misconstrue, misapprehend, get wrong, misread, misjudge, miscalculate, miss the point of.

mis•un•der•stand•ing /mísundərstánding/ *n.* **1** failure to understand correctly. **2** slight disagreement or quarrel.

■ **1** misconception, misconstruction, misinterpretation, misapprehension, misreading.

2 discord, dispute, argument, difference, dissension, controversy, rift.

mis•use • *v.tr.* /mísyóoz/ **1** use wrongly; apply to the wrong purpose. **2** ill-treat. • *n.* /mísyóos/ wrong or improper use or application. □□ **mis•us′er** *n.*

■ *v.* **1** abuse, misapply, misemploy, misappropriate; pervert. **2** see MISTREAT. • *n.* misapplication, misusage, perversion; corruption, solecism, malapropism, barbarism; see also *mistreatment* (MISTREAT).

mite¹ /mīt/ *n.* small, often parasitic arachnid. □□ **mit′y** *adj.*

mite² /mīt/ *n.* **1** small sum of money. **2** small object or person.

■ **2** see PARTICLE 2.

mi•ter /mítər/ *n.* **1** tall deeply-cleft headdress worn by bishops, esp. as a symbol of office. **2** joint of two pieces of wood or other material at an angle of 90°. • *v.* join with a miter. □□ **mi′tered** *adj.*

mit•i•gate /mítigayt/ *v.tr.* make milder or less intense or severe (*your offer certainly mitigated their hostility*). See synonym study at ALLEVIATE. □□ **mit′i•ga•ble** *adj.* **mit•i•ga•tion** /-gáyshən/ *n.* **mit′i•ga•tor** *n.* **mit•i•ga•to•ry** /-gótawree/ *adj.*

■ moderate, temper, reduce, abate, lessen, decrease, calm, tranquilize, soothe, placate, still, soften, dull.

mi•to•sis /mītósis/ *n. Biol.* type of cell division that results in two nuclei each having the full number of chromosomes. □□ **mi•tot•ic** /-tótik/ *adj.*

mi•tral /mítrəl/ *adj.* of or like a miter. ▫ **mitral valve** two-cusped valve between the left atrium and the left ventricle of the heart.

mitt /mit/ *n.* **1** baseball glove with mittenlike finger section. **2** = MITTEN. **3** *sl.* hand or fist. **4** glove leaving the fingers and thumb-tip exposed.

mit•ten /mít'n/ *n.* glove with two sections, one for the thumb and the other for all four fingers. □□ **mit′tened** *adj.*

mix /miks/ • *v.* **1** *tr.* combine; blend; put together. **2** *tr.* prepare by combining the ingredients. **3** *intr.* **a** join, be mixed, or combine, esp. readily. **b** be compatible. **c** be sociable (*must learn to mix*). **4** *intr.* [foll. by *in*] participate in. • *n.* **1** a mixing; mixture. **b** proportion of materials, etc., in a mixture. **2** ingredients prepared commercially for making a cake, concrete, etc. **3** merging of film pictures or sound. ▫ **be mixed up in** (or **with**) be involved in or with (esp. something undesirable). **mix up 1** mix thoroughly. **2** confuse; mistake the identity of. **mix-up** *n.* confusion, misunderstanding, or mistake. □□ **mix′a•ble** *adj.*

■ *v.* merge, unite, alloy, mingle, intermingle; incorporate, put together, stir, mix up. **2** see PREPARE 2. **3 a** blend, merge, unite, mingle, intermingle. **b** go together. **3c, 4** socialize; fraternize, consort, hobnob, go around or about, associate. • *n.* **1 a** see MIXTURE. ▫ **be mixed up in** (or **with**) be implicated in, be embroiled in, be connected with, be drawn into. **mix up 1** see MIX *v.* 1, 3 above. **2** confound, bewilder, muddle, perplex; snarl, ensnarl, tangle; misidentify; inter-

change, exchange. **mix-up** mess, muddle, hodgepodge, tangle, *sl.* screwup, snafu.

mixed /mikst/ *adj.* **1** of diverse qualities or elements. **2** containing persons from various backgrounds, both genders, etc. ▫ **mixed bag** diverse assortment of things or persons. **mixed blessing** thing having advantages and disadvantages. **mixed-up** *colloq.* mentally or emotionally confused; socially ill-adjusted.

■ **1** diversified, assorted, heterogeneous, sundry; (*of ancestry, etc.*) hybrid, half-bred, mongrel; (*of feelings, etc.*) confused, muddled, conflicting.

mix•er /míksər/ *n.* **1** device for mixing foods, etc. **2** drink to be mixed with another. **3** *Broadcasting & Cinematog.* device for merging two or more audio or video input signals.

mix•ture /míks-chər/ *n.* **1** process of mixing or being mixed. **2** result of mixing; something mixed; combination of ingredients, qualities, characteristics, etc.

■ amalgamation, combination, blend, association, synthesis. **2** assortment, amalgam, amalgamation, medley, compound, alloy, composite, blend, jumble, mix, miscellany.

miz•zen•mast /mízənmast/ *n.* mast next aft of a ship's mainmast.

ml *abbr.* milliliter(s).

Mlle. *abbr.* (*pl.* **Mlles.**) Mademoiselle.

mm *abbr.* millimeter(s).

MM. *abbr.* Messieurs.

Mme. *abbr.* (*pl.* **Mmes.**) Madame.

MN *abbr.* Minnesota (in official postal use).

Mn *symb. Chem.* manganese.

mne•mon•ic /nimónik/ • *adj.* of or designed to aid the memory. • *n.* mnemonic device. □□ **mne•mon′i•cal•ly** *adv.*

MO *abbr.* **1** Missouri (in official postal use). **2** money order.

Mo *symb. Chem.* molybdenum.

Mo. *abbr.* Missouri.

moan /mōn/ • *n.* **1** long, low plaintive sound. **2** complaint; grievance. • *v.intr.* **1** make a moan or moans. **2** *colloq.* complain or grumble. □□ **moan′er** *n.* **moan′ing•ly** *adv.*

■ *n.* **1** lament, lamentation, groan, wail, ululation, sigh, sob, cry; sough. **2** grumble, *colloq.* grouse, gripe, *sl.* beef. • *v.* **1** sigh, cry, wail, sob; mourn, lament, bemoan, weep. **2** lament, groan, wail, whine.

moat /mōt/ *n.* deep defensive ditch around a castle, town, etc., usu. filled with water.

mob /mob/ • *n.* **1** disorderly crowd; rabble. **2** [prec. by *the*] usu. *derog.* the populace. **3** = MAFIA. • *v.tr.* (**mobbed, mob•bing**) crowd around in order to attack or admire. □□ **mob′ber** *n.*

■ *n.* **1** horde, host, legion, press, throng, pack, herd, swarm, crush. **2** (*the mob*) the rabble, the riffraff, the proletariat, the (general) public, the masses. • *v.* jostle, throng, surround, beset, clamor over.

mo•bile /móbəl, -beel, -bīl/ • *adj.* **1** movable; able to move easily. **2** readily changing its expression. **3** transportable in a motor vehicle. **4** (of a person) able to change his or her social status. • *n.* /-beel/ decorative structure that may be hung so as to turn freely. □ **mobile home** transportable structure usu. parked and used as a residence. □□ **mo•bil•i•ty** /mōbílitee/ n.

■ adj. **1, 3** nonstationary; portable; motorized, traveling; agile, versatile. **2** expressive, sensitive, animated, plastic. □□ **mobility** see MOTION n. 1.

mo•bi•lize /mốbilíz/ v. **1** tr. organize for service or action (esp. troops in time of war). **2** intr. be organized in this way. □□ **mo′bi•liz•a•ble** adj. **mo•bi•li•za′tion** n. **mo′bi•liz•er** n.

■ **1** assemble, marshal, conscript, enroll, enlist.

mob•ster /móbstər/ n. sl. gangster.

moc•ca•sin /mókəsin/ n. soft, flat-soled leather slipper or shoe.

mo•cha /mốkə/ n. **1** coffee of fine quality. **2** beverage or flavoring made with this, often with chocolate added.

mock /mok/ • v.tr. **1** ridicule; scoff at. **2** mimic contemptuously. **3** jeer, defy, or delude contemptuously. See synonym study at IMITATE. ■ attrib.adj. sham; imitation; pretended. □ **mock-up** experimental model or replica of a proposed structure, etc. □□ **mock′a•ble** adj. **mock′er** n. **mock′ing•ly** adv.

■ v. **1, 3** deride, make fun of, tease, taunt, tantalize, gibe (at), chaff, laugh at, colloq. rib, kid. **2** ape, imitate, caricature, lampoon, satirize, colloq. spoof, take off. • adj. substitute, artificial, simulated, fake, synthetic, false, ersatz, feigned.

mock•er•y /mókəree/ n. (pl. **-ies**) **1** derision; ridicule. **2** absurdly inadequate or futile action, etc.

■ **1** disdain, taunting, disparagement, abuse, scorn. **2** travesty, farce, absurdity; see also JOKE n. 2.

mock•ing•bird /mókingbərd/ n. bird that mimics the notes of other birds.

mod /mod/ colloq. adj. modern, esp. in style of dress.

mod•al /mốd′l/ adj. **1** of mode or form. **2** Gram. **a** of the mood of a verb. **b** (of an auxiliary verb, e.g., would) used to express the mood of another verb. **3** Mus. denoting a style of music using a particular mode. □□ **mod′al•ly** adv.

mode /mōd/ n. **1** way or manner in which a thing is done; method of procedure. **2** prevailing fashion or custom. **3** Mus. any of several types of scale. **4** Gram. = MOOD².

■ **1** method, approach, form, course, fashion, procedure. **2** style, look, vogue; trend, rage, craze, fad.

mod•el /mód′l/ • n. **1** representation in three dimensions of an existing person or thing or of a proposed structure, esp. on a smaller scale (often attrib.: model train). **2** simplified description of a system, etc., to assist calculations and predictions. **3** particular design or style, esp. of a car. **4** exemplary person or thing. **5** person employed to pose for an artist or photographer or to display clothes, etc., by wearing them. • v. **1** tr. fashion,

shape, or form a model. **2 a** intr. act or pose as a model. **b** tr. display (a garment). □□ **mod′el•er** n.

■ n. **1** replica, mock-up, maquette, miniature, dummy; image, likeness. **3** kind, type, version; variety, sort; brand. **4** original, archetype, prototype, pattern, paragon, ideal, exemplar, example. **5** subject, sitter, poser. • v. **1** mold, sculpt, design; make, fabricate; (model after or on) imitate, copy. **2** sit; display, show (off), exhibit; wear, sport.

SYNONYM STUDY: model

ARCHETYPE, EXAMPLE, IDEAL, PARADIGM, PATTERN, PROTOTYPE. Most parents try to set a good **example** for their children, although they may end up setting a bad one. An example, in other words, is a precedent for imitation, either good or bad. Most parents would do better to provide a **model** for their children, which refers to a person or thing that is to be followed or imitated because of its excellence in conduct or character; model also connotes a physical shape to be copied closely (a ship's model; a model airplane). Not all children regard their parents as an **ideal** to which they aspire, a word that suggests an imagined perfection or a standard based upon a set of desirable qualities (the ideal gentleman; the ideal of what an artist should be); but young people's lives often end up following the **pattern** established by their parents, meaning that their lives follow the same basic configuration or design. While **prototype** and **archetype** are often used interchangeably, they really mean quite different things. An archetype is a perfect and unchanging form that existing things or people can approach but never duplicate (the archetype of a mother), while a prototype is an early, usually unrefined version that later versions reflect but may depart from (the prototype for today's gas-guzzling cars). **Paradigm** can refer to an example that serves as a model, but today its use is primarily confined to a grammatical context, where it means a set giving all the various forms of a word, such as the conjugation of a verb.

---

mo•dem /mốdem/ n. device for transmitting data between computers, esp. over a telephone line.

mod•er•ate • adj. /módərət/ **1** avoiding extremes; temperate in conduct or expression. **2** fairly or tolerably large or good. **3** calm. • n. /módərət/ person who holds moderate views. • v. /módərayt/ **1** tr. & intr. make or become moderate. **2** tr. [also absol.] act as a moderator or to. □□ **mod′er•ate•ly** adv. **mod′er•ate•ness** n. **mod•er•a•tion** /módəráyshən/ n. See synonym study at ABSTINENCE.

■ adj. **1** calm, reasonable, cool, judicious, rational, balanced; center, middle-of-the-road, mainstream. **2** fair, middling, average, ordinary, medium. • n. nonradical, nonreactionary, Polit. often derog. centrist. • v. **1** abate, calm, mollify, soothe, ease, relax, alleviate, pacify, mitigate. **2** mediate, arbitrate, referee, judge, chair, supervise. □□ **moderately** somewhat, rather, quite, fairly, com-

paratively, slightly, passably, more or less.
moderation see TEMPERANCE 1.

mod•er•a•tor /módərraytər/ n. **1** arbitrator or mediator. **2** presiding officer.

■ **1** arbiter, judge, referee, umpire. **2** chair, chairperson, chairman, chairwoman, president, coordinator.

mod•ern /módərn/ • adj. **1** of the present and recent times. **2** in current fashion; not antiquated. • n. [usu. in pl.] person living in modern times. □ **modern English** English from about 1500 onward. □□ **mo•der•ni•ty** /-dérnitee/ n. **mod′ern•ly** adv. **mod′ern•ness** n.

■ adj. up-to-date, current, contemporary, today's, new, fresh, novel, brand-new, up to the minute, present-day.

mod•ern•ism /módərnizəm/ n. modern ideas, methods, or practices. □□ **mod′ern•ist** n. **mod•ern•is′tic** adj. **mod•ern•is′ti•cal•ly** adv.

mod•ern•ize /módərnīz/ v. **1** tr. make modern; adapt to modern needs or habits. **2** intr. adopt modern ways or views. □□ **mod•ern•i•za′tion** n. **mod′ern•iz•er** n.

■ **1** renovate, streamline, redecorate, refurbish. □□ **modernization** see improvement (IMPROVE), DEVELOPMENT 1.

mod•est /módist/ adj. **1** humble; not vain. **2** diffident; bashful; retiring. **3** decorous. **4** restrained; not excessive or exaggerated, unpretentious. □□ **mod′est•ly** adv. **mod′es•ty** n.

■ **1, 2** unassuming, unpresuming, unpretentious, unobtrusive, reserved. **3** see DECOROUS. **4** moderate, limited, understated, unexaggerated; humble, simple, plain; inconspicuous, unobtrusive.

mod•i•cum /módikəm/ n. [foll. by of] small quantity.

■ bit, trifle, jot, tittle, atom, scintilla, spark, iota.

mod•i•fi•er /módifīər/ n. **1** person or thing that modifies. **2** Gram. a word, esp. an adjective or noun used attributively, that qualifies the sense of another word (e.g., good and family in a good family house).

mod•i•fy /módifī/ v.tr. (-fies, -fied) **1** make less severe or extreme. **2** make partial changes in. **3** Gram. qualify or expand the sense of (a word, etc.). □□ **mod′i•fi•a•ble** adj. **mod•i•fi•ca′tion** n.

■ **1** reduce, decrease, diminish, lessen, moderate, temper; qualify, limit, restrict. **2** adjust, adapt, change, vary, transform, alter.

mod•ish /módish/ adj. fashionable; stylish. □□ **mod′ish•ly** adv. **mod′ish•ness** n.

mod•u•late /mójəlayt/ v. **1** tr. **a** regulate or adjust. **b** moderate. **2** tr. adjust or vary the tone or pitch of (the speaking voice). **3** tr. alter the amplitude or frequency of (a wave). **4** intr. & tr. Mus. change or cause to change from one key to another. □□ **mod•u•la′tion** /-láyshən/ n. **mod′u•la•tor** n.

■ **1, 2** set, tune, balance, temper, modify, vary; lower, tune or tone down, turn down, soften.

mod•ule /mójool/ n. **1** standardized part or independent unit used in construction. **2** in-

533 **moderator ~ mold**

dependent self-contained unit of a spacecraft. **3** unit or period of training or education. □□ **mod•u•lar** /-jələr/ adj. **mod•u•lar•i•ty** /-jəláritee/ n.

mo•dus op•e•ran•di /módəs ópərándee, -dī/ n. (pl. **mo•di op•e•ran•di** /módee, -dī/) method of working.

mo•dus vi•ven•di /módəs vivéndee, -dī/ n. (pl. **mo•di vi•ven•di** /módee, -dī/) **1** way of living or coping. **2** arrangement between people who agree to differ.

mo•gul /mógəl/ n. colloq. important or influential person.

■ magnate, tycoon, baron, mandarin, nabob, VIP.

mo•hair /móhair/ n. **1** hair of the angora goat. **2** yarn or fabric from this, either pure or mixed with wool or cotton.

Mo•hawk /móhawk/ n. **1 a** member of a Native American people of New York State. **b** language of this people. **2** (of a hairstyle) with the head shaved except for a strip of hair from the middle of the forehead to the back of the neck.

Mo•he•gan /móheegən/ • n. member of a Native American people of Connecticut. • adj. of or relating to this people.

Mo•hi•can var. of MAHICAN.

moi•e•ty /móyətee/ n. (pl. -ties) Law or literary **1** half. **2** each of the two parts into which a thing is divided.

moire /mwaar, mawr/ n. (in full **moire an•tique**) watered fabric, orig. mohair, now usu. silk.

moist /moyst/ adj. **1** slightly wet; damp. **2** (of the season, etc.) rainy. □□ **moist′ly** adv. **moist′ness** n.

■ **1** wettish, dampish, dewy, dank, humid, soggy, moisture-laden, clammy, muggy. **2** damp, wet, drizzly.

moist•en /móysən/ v. make or become moist.

mois•ture /móys-chər/ n. water or other liquid causing slight dampness. □□ **mois′ture•less** adj.

■ see WET n. 1.

mois•tur•ize /móys-chərīz/ v.tr. make less dry (esp. the skin by use of a cosmetic). □□ **mois′tur•iz•er** n.

mo•lar /mólər/ • adj. (usu. of a mammal's back teeth) serving to grind. • n. molar tooth.

mo•las•ses /məlásiz/ n.pl. [treated as sing.] uncrystallized syrup extracted from raw sugar during refining.

mold¹ /mōld/ • n. **1** hollow container into which a substance is poured or pressed to harden into a required shape. **2** form; shape. **3** Archit. molding or group of moldings. **4** frame or template. **5** character or disposition (in heroic mold). • v.tr. **1** make (an object) in a required shape or from certain ingredients. **2** give a shape to. **3** influence. □□ **mold′a•ble** adj. **mold′er** n.

■ n. **1, 4** cast, matrix, die; pattern, frame. **2** pattern, format, structure, build, construction, design. **5** nature, stamp, type, kind, kidney, sort. • v. **1, 2** shape, form, work, fashion, configure, sculpture; forge, cast, stamp, die-cast. **3** shape, form, affect, make, control, direct.

mold[2] /mōld/ *n.* woolly or furry growth of minute fungi occurring esp. in moist warm conditions.

■ mildew, fungus, must, mustiness; blight, smut.

mold[3] /mōld/ *n.* loose earth, when rich in organic matter.

mold•er /mōldər/ *v.intr.* decay to dust; deteriorate.

mold•ing /mōldiŋ/ *n.* ornamentally shaped plaster or woodwork as an architectural feature.

mold•y /mōldee/ *adj.* (**–i•er, –i•est**) **1** covered with mold. **2** stale; out of date. □□ **mold′i•ness** *n.*

■ **1** musty, mildewy, mildewed; decaying, carious. **2** aged, ancient, outdated, old-fashioned, antediluvian.

mole[1] /mōl/ *n.* **1** small burrowing insect-eating mammal with dark velvety fur. **2** *colloq.* spy established deep within an organization in a position of trust.

mole[2] /mōl/ *n.* small often dark blemish on the skin.

mole[3] /mōl/ *n.* pier, breakwater, or causeway.

mole[4] /mōl/ *n. Chem.* SI unit of amount of substance equal to the quantity containing as many elementary units as there are atoms in 0.012 kg of carbon 12. □□ **mo′lar** *adj.* **mo•lar•i•ty** /məláritee/ *n.*

mol•e•cule /mólikyōōl/ *n.* **1** *Chem.* smallest fundamental unit of an element or compound. **2** small particle. □□ **mo•lec•u•lar** /məlékyələr/ *adj.*

mole•hill /mólhil/ *n.* small mound thrown up by a mole in burrowing.

mole•skin /mólskin/ *n.* **1** skin of a mole used as fur. **2** kind of cotton fustian with its surface shaved before dyeing.

mo•lest /məlést/ *v.tr.* **1** annoy or pester in a hostile or injurious way. **2** attack or interfere with (a person), esp. sexually. See synonym study at ATTACK. □□ **mo•les•ta•tion** /mólestáyshən, mól–/ *n.* **mo•lest′er** *n.*

■ **1** irritate, vex, disturb, badger, provoke, nettle, tease. **2** accost, meddle with, abuse, assault, ill-treat.

mol•li•fy /mólifī/ *v.tr.* (**–fies, –fied**) **1** appease. **2** reduce the severity of. See synonym study at PACIFY. □□ **mol•li•fi•ca′tion** *n.* **mol′li•fi•er** *n.*

■ **1** see CALM *v.* **2** see MODERATE *v.* 1.

mol•lusk /móləsk/ *n.* invertebrate with a soft body and usu. a hard shell, e.g., a snail or oyster. □□ **mol•lus•kan** or **mol•lus•can** /məlúskən/ *n. & adj.* **mol′lusk•like** *adj.*

mol•ly•cod•dle /móleekodəl/ • *v.tr.* coddle; pamper. • *n.* effeminate man or boy; milksop.

molt /mōlt/ *v.* **1** *intr.* shed feathers, hair, a shell, etc., in the process of renewing plumage, a coat, etc. **2** *tr.* (of an animal) shed (feathers, hair, etc.). □□ **molt′er** *n.*

■ see SHED[2].

mol•ten /mōltən/ *adj.* melted, esp. made liquid by heat.

mo•lyb•de•num /məlíbdinəm/ *n. Chem.* silver-white brittle metallic transition element used in steel. ¶Symb.: **Mo**.

mom /mom/ *n. colloq.* mother. □ **mom-and-pop store** of or pertaining to a small retail business, as a grocery store, owned and operated by members of a family.

mo•ment /mōmənt/ *n.* **1** very brief portion of time. **2** exact or particular point of time (*at last the moment arrived*). **3** importance. **4** product of force and the distance from its line of action to a point.

■ **1** instant, second, minute, flash. **2** instant, time, second, minute; point (in time), juncture, stage. **3** weight, consequence, significance, import, gravity.

mo•men•tar•y /mōmənteree/ *adj.* lasting only a moment. □□ **mo•men•tar•i•ly** /–táirilee/ *adv.* **mo•men•tar′i•ness** *n.*

■ fleeting, temporary, ephemeral, evanescent, impermanent, fugitive, passing, transitory, brief.

mo•men•tous /mōméntəs/ *adj.* having great importance. □□ **mo•men′tous•ly** *adv.* **mo•men′tous•ness** *n.*

■ important, weighty, consequential, significant, grave.

mo•men•tum /mōméntəm/ *n.* (*pl.* **mo•men•ta** /–tə/) **1** *Physics* quantity of motion of a moving body, the product of its mass and velocity. **2** the impetus gained by movement. **3** strength or continuity derived from an initial effort.

■ energy, force, drive, power, impulse, thrust, push.

mom•ma /mómə/ *n.* var. of MAMMA.

mom•my /mómee/ *n.* (*pl.* **–mies**) *colloq.* mother.

Mon. *abbr.* Monday.

mon•arch /mónərk, –aark/ *n.* **1** ruler of a country, esp. hereditary, as a king, queen, etc. **2** large orange and black butterfly. □□ **mo•nar•chic** /mənáarkik/ *adj.* **mo•nar′chi•cal** *adj.*

■ **1** sovereign, potentate; emperor, empress.

mon•ar•chism /mónərkizəm/ *n.* advocacy of or the principles of monarchy. □□ **mon′ar•chist** *n.*

mon•ar•chy /mónərkee/ *n.* (*pl.* **–chies**) **1** form of government with a monarch at the head. **2** a nation with this. □□ **mo•nar•chi•al** /mónáarkeeəl/ *adj.*

■ **1** monocracy, autocracy; royalism, monarchism. **2** kingdom, empire, domain, principality.

mon•as•ter•y /mónəsteree/ *n.* (*pl.* **–ies**) residence of a religious community, esp. of monks living in seclusion.

■ abbey, cloister, priory, friary, *Ind.* ashram.

mo•nas•tic /mənástik/ *adj.* of or relating to monasteries or monks, nuns, etc. □□ **mo•nas′ti•cal•ly** *adv.* **mo•nas•ti•cism** /–tisizəm/ *n.*

Mon•day /múnday, –dee/ *n.* second day of the week, following Sunday.

mon•e•tar•y /móniteree, –mún/ *adj.* **1** of the currency in use. **2** of or consisting of money. See synonym study at FINANCIAL. □□ **mon•e•tar•i•ly** /–táirəlee/ *adv.*

■ **2** pecuniary, fiscal, financial, capital, cash.

mon•ey /múnee/ *n.* **1** current medium of exchange in the form of coins and paper currency. **2** (*pl.* **–eys** or **–ies**) [in *pl.*] sums of money. **3** wealth. □ **for my money** in my opinion or judgment; for my preference. **in the money** *colloq.* having or winning a lot of money. **money-grubber** *colloq.* person greedily intent on amassing money. **money-grubbing** *n.* this practice. *adj.* given to this. **money market** *Stock Exch.* trade in short-term stocks, loans, etc. **money order** order for payment of a specified sum, issued by a bank or post office. □□ **mon′ey•less** *adj.*

■ **1** currency, legal tender, specie, (hard) cash, ready money, paper money, coin(s), (small) change, bills, greenbacks, *colloq.* shekels, *sl.* loot, dough, bread, bucks. **3** resources, fortune, funds, finance(s), capital. □ **for my money** in my view, to my mind, as I see it; for my liking. **in the money** rich, wealthy, affluent, moneyed, well off, well-to-do, *colloq.* flush, well-heeled, rolling in it, filthy rich, *sl.* loaded. **money grubber** see *miserly* (MISER). **money-grubbing** see *miserly* (MISER).

mon•ey•bags /múneebagz/ *n.pl.* [treated as *sing.*] *colloq.* usu. *derog.* wealthy person.

mon•eyed /múneed/ *adj.* having much money; wealthy.

■ see WEALTHY.

mon•ey•mak•er /múneemaykər/ *n.* **1** person who earns much money. **2** thing, idea, etc., that produces much money. □□ **mon′ey•mak•ing** *n. & adj.*

mon•ger /múnggər, móng–/ *n.* [usu. in *comb.*] dealer; trader; promoter (*warmonger*).

Mon•go•li•an /monggṓleeən/ • *n.* native, inhabitant, or language of Mongolia. • *adj.* of or relating to Mongolia.

mon•gol•ism /mónggəlizəm/ *n.* = DOWN′S SYNDROME. ¶The term *Down's syndrome* is now preferred.

Mon•gol•oid /mónggəloyd/ • *adj.* **1** characteristic of the Mongolians, esp. in having a broad flat yellowish face. **2** (**mongoloid**) *often offens.* having the characteristic symptoms of Down's syndrome. • *n.* Mongoloid or mongoloid person.

mon•goose /mónggōōs/ *n.* (*pl.* **mon•goos•es** or **mon•geese**) small flesh-eating civetlike mammals.

mon•grel /múnggrəl, móng–/ • *n.* dog or other animal or plant of mixed breed. • *adj.* of mixed origin, nature, or character. □□ **mon′grel•ism** *n.* **mon′grel•ize** *v.tr.* **mon′grel•i•za′tion** *n.*

■ *n.* crossbreed, mixed breed, half-breed, *Biol.* hybrid.

mon•i•ker /mónikər/ *n.* (also **mon′ick•er**) *sl.* name.

mon•i•tor /mónitər/ • *n.* **1** any of various persons or devices for checking or warning about a situation, operation, etc. **2** school pupil with disciplinary or other special duties. **3** cathode-ray tube used as a television receiver or computer display device. • *v.tr.* **1** act as a monitor of. **2** maintain regular surveillance over; check. □□ **mon•i•to•ri•al** /–táwreeəl/ *adj.*

■ *n.* **1** watchdog, supervisor, sentinel,

guard, guardian, custodian; proctor. • *v.* watch, oversee, observe, audit, supervise, superintend, scan, examine.

monk /mungk/ *n.* member of a religious community of men living under vows. □□ **monk′ish** *adj.*

■ brother, religious, cenobite, monastic, friar.

mon•key /múngkee/ • *n.* (*pl.* **–keys**) **1** any of various primates, including marmosets, baboons, apes, etc. **2** mischievous person, esp. a child (*young monkey*). • *v.* (**–keys, –keyed**) **1** *tr.* mimic or mock. **2** *intr.* tamper; fool around. □ **monkey business** *colloq.* mischief. **monkey wrench** wrench with an adjustable jaw. □□ **mon′key•ish** *adj.*

■ *n.* **1** simian, ape. **2** imp, devil, mischief-maker, *archaic or joc.* rapscallion, *colloq.* scamp, *often joc.* rascal. • *v.* **1** imitate, impersonate, copy, ape; see also MOCK *v.* **2**. **2** play, fiddle, meddle, interfere, mess (about or around). □ **monkey business** see MISCHIEF 1–3.

mon•key•shine /múngkeeshīn/ *n.* [usu. in *pl.*] *colloq.* = *monkey business*.

mono¹ /mónō/ *n. colloq.* infectious mononucleosis.

mono² /mónō/ *colloq. adj.* monophonic.

mono– /mónō/ *comb. form* (usu. **mon–** before a vowel) one; alone; single (*monorail*).

mon•o•chro•mat•ic /mónəkrəmátik/ *adj.* **1** *Physics* (of light or other radiation) of a single wavelength or frequency. **2** containing only one color. □□ **mon•o•chro•mat′ic•al•ly** *adv.*

mon•o•chrome /mónəkrōm/ • *n.* photograph or picture done in one color or different tones of this, or in black and white only. • *adj.* having or using only one color or in black and white only. □□ **mon•o•chro•mic** /–krómik/ *adj.*

mon•o•cle /mónəkəl/ *n.* single eyeglass. □□ **mon′o•cled** *adj.*

mon•o•clo•nal /mónəklṓnəl/ *adj.* cloned from one cell.

mon•o•cot•y•le•don /mónəkótəleed′n/ *n. Bot.* any flowering plant with a single cotyledon. □□ **mon•o•cot•y•le′don•ous** *adj.*

mon•oc•u•lar /mənókyələr/ *adj.* with or for one eye. □□ **mon•oc′u•lar•ly** *adv.*

mo•nog•a•my /mənógəmee/ *n.* practice or state of being married to one person at a time. □□ **mo•nog′a•mist** *n.* **mo•nog′a•mous** *adj.* **mo•nog′a•mous•ly** *adv.*

mon•o•gram /mónəgram/ *n.* two or more letters, esp. a person's initials, interwoven into a device. □□ **mon•o•gram•mat•ic** /–grəmátik/ *adj.* **mon′o•grammed** *adj.*

mon•o•graph /mónəgraf/ *n.* separate treatise on a single subject. □□ **mo•nog•ra•pher** /mənógrəfər/ *n.* **mon•o•graph•ic** /mónəgráfik/ *adj.*

mon•o•lin•gual /mónōlínggwəl/ *adj.* speaking or using only one language.

mon•o•lith /mónəlith/ *n.* **1** single block of stone, esp. shaped into a pillar or monument. **2** massive, immovable, or solidly uniform person or thing. □□ **mon•o•lith′ic** *adj.*

■ □□ **monolithic** massive, huge, enormous, monumental; featureless, uniform; rigid, impenetrable, invulnerable.

mon•o•logue /mónəlawg, –log/ n. **1 a** soliloquy. **b** dramatic composition for one performer. **2** long speech by one person in a conversation, etc. □□ **mon•o•log•ic** /–lójik/ adj. **mon•o•log'i•cal** adj. **mon•o•log•ist** /mənólǝjist/ n. (also **–logu•ist**).

mon•o•ma•ni•a /mónəmáyneeə/ n. obsession of the mind by one idea or interest. ·□□ **mon•o•ma'ni•ac** n. & adj. **mon•o•ma•ni•a•cal** /–mǝníǝkǝl/ adj.

mon•o•nu•cle•o•sis /mónónōōkleeósis, –nyōō–/ n. abnormally high proportion of monocytes in the blood.

mon•o•phon•ic /mónəfónik/ adj. **1** (of sound reproduction) using only one channel of transmission (cf. STEREOPHONIC). **2** Mus. homophonic. □□ **mon•o•phon'i•cal•ly** adv.

mo•nop•o•list /mənópəlist/ n. person who has or advocates a monopoly. □□ **mo•nop•o•lis'tic** adj.

mo•nop•o•lize /mənópəliz/ v.tr. **1** obtain exclusive possession or control of. **2** dominate or prevent others from sharing in. □□ **mo•nop•o•li•za'tion** n. **mo•nop'o•liz•er** n.

■ corner, control, colloq. hog.

mo•nop•o•ly /mənópəlee/ n. (pl. **–lies**) **1 a** exclusive possession or control of the trade in a commodity or service. **b** this conferred as a privilege by the government. **2** commodity or service that is subject to a monopoly.

mon•o•rail /mónōrayl/ n. railway with a single track.

mon•o•so•di•um glu•ta•mate /mónəsódiəm glōōtəmayt/ n. Chem. white crystalline powder used to flavor food. ¶Abbr.: **MSG**.

mon•o•syl•la•ble /mónəsiləbəl/ n. word of one syllable. □□ **mon•o•syl•lab•ic** /–silábik/ adj. **mon•o•syl•lab'i•cal•ly** adv.

mon•o•the•ism /mónəthéeizəm/ n. doctrine that there is only one God. □□ **mon'o•the•ist** n. **mon•o•the•is'tic** adj. **mon•o•the•is'ti•cal•ly** adv.

mon•o•tone /mónətōn/ • n. **1** sound or utterance continuing or repeated on one note without change of pitch. **2** sameness of style in writing. • adj. without change of pitch.

mo•not•o•nous /mənótʼnəs/ adj. lacking in variety; tedious through sameness. □□ **mo•not'o•nous•ly** adv. **mo•not'o•nous•ness** n.

■ boring, dull, tiresome, humdrum, sleep-inducing, soporific; unvaried, unvarying, unchanging.

mo•not•o•ny /mənótʼnee/ n. **1** state of being monotonous. **2** dull or tedious routine.

■ **1** see TEDIUM.

Mon•sieur /məsyö/ n. (pl. **Mes•sieurs** /mesyö/) **1** French title corresponding to Mr. or sir. **2** Frenchman.

Mon•si•gnor /monséenyər/ n. (pl. **Mon•si•gnors** or **Mon•si•gno•ri** /–sēnyawree/) title of various Roman Catholic prelates, officers of the papal court, etc.

mon•soon /monsōōn, món–/ n. **1** seasonal

wind in S. Asia, esp. in the Indian Ocean. **2** rainy season accompanying the summer monsoon. □□ **mon•soon'al** adj.

mon•ster /mónstər/ n. **1** imaginary creature, usu. large and frightening. **2** inhumanly cruel or wicked person. **3** large, usu. ugly or misshapen animal or thing. **4** [attrib.] huge.

■ **1** beast, fiend, ogre, giant, dragon, brute. **2** see DEVIL n. 3a. **3** mutant, mutation, freak; monstrosity, eyesore. **4** (attrib.) see HUGE 1, GIGANTIC.

mon•strance /mónstrəns/ n. RC Ch. vessel in which the consecrated Host is displayed for veneration.

mon•strous /mónstrəs/ adj. **1** like a monster; abnormally formed. **2** huge. **3 a** outrageously wrong or absurd. **b** atrocious. □□ **mon•stros•i•ty** /–strósitee/ n. **mon'strous•ly** adv. **mon'strous•ness** n.

■ **1** awful, horrible, horrid, horrific, horrendous, horrifying, hideous, ugly. **2** gigantic, giant, vast, enormous, colossal, monster, gargantuan. **3** outrageous, shocking, scandalous, atrocious, appalling, wicked, villainous, evil, ugly, vile, insensitive, cruel. □□ **monstrosity** monstrousness, heinousness, horribleness, horridness, hideousness.

Mont. abbr. Montana.

mon•tage /montáazh, mawn–/ n. **1** technique of producing a new composite whole from fragments of pictures, words, music, etc. **2** a composition produced in this way.

month /munth/ n. **1** (in full **calendar month**) **a** each of usu. twelve periods into which a year is divided. **b** period of time between the same dates in successive calendar months. **3** = lunar month.

month•ly /múnthlee/ • adj. done, produced, or occurring once a month. • adv. once a month; from month to month. • n. (pl. **–lies**) monthly periodical.

mon•u•ment /mónyəmənt/ n. **1** anything enduring that serves to commemorate or make celebrated, esp. a structure or building. **2** ancient building or site. **3** typical or outstanding example (a monument of indiscretion).

■ **1** marker, memorial, tablet; sepulcher, gravestone, tombstone. **3** model, archetype, pattern, paragon, nonpareil, perfect specimen, exemplar.

mon•u•men•tal /mónyəméntʼl/ adj. **1 a** extremely great; stupendous (a monumental achievement). **b** (of a literary work) massive and permanent. **2** of or serving as a monument. □□ **mon•u•men•tal•i•ty** /–tálitee/ n. **mon•u•men'tal•ly** adv.

■ **1 a** staggering, awe-inspiring, outstanding, prominent, immense, colossal, vast, awesome, epoch-making. **b** huge, gigantic, enormous, prodigious, colossal, immense, vast, tremendous. **2** commemorative, memorial.

-mony /mōnee/ suffix forming nouns, esp. denoting an abstract state or quality (acrimony, testimony).

moo /mōō/ • v.intr. (**moos, mooed**) make

the vocal sound of cattle; = LOW² v. • n. (pl. moos) this sound.

mooch /mooch/ v.tr. colloq. beg; impose upon. □□ **mooch′er** n.

■ see BEG 1b.

mood¹ /mood/ n. **1** state of mind or feeling. **2** [in pl.] fits of melancholy or bad temper. ■ **1** humor, attitude, inclination, disposition, nature, temper, feeling. **2** (moods) see TEMPER n. 2.

mood² /mood/ n. Gram. form or set of forms of a verb serving to indicate whether it is to express fact, command, wish, etc. (subjunctive mood).

mood·swing /moodswing/ n. marked change in temperament, as from euphoria to depression.

mood·y /moodee/ • adj. (mood·i·er, mood·i·est) given to changes of mood; gloomy; sullen. • n. colloq. bad mood; tantrum. □□ **mood′i·ly** adv. **mood′i·ness** n.

■ adj. fickle, volatile, capricious, mercurial, unstable; testy, crotchety, short-tempered; glum, moping.

moon /moon/ • n. **1** the natural satellite of the earth, orbiting it monthly. **2** satellite of any planet. • v. intr. behave dreamily or listlessly. □□ **moon′less** adj.

moon·beam /moonbeem/ n. ray of moonlight.

moon·light /moonlit/ • n. light of the moon. • v.intr. (–lighted) colloq. have two paid occupations, esp. one by day and one by night. □□ **moon′light·er** n.

moon·lit /moonlit/ adj. lighted by the moon.

moon·scape /moonskayp/ n. **1** surface or landscape of the moon. **2** area resembling this; wasteland.

moon·shine /moonshin/ n. **1** foolish talk or ideas. **2** sl. illicitly distilled or smuggled alcoholic liquor. **3** moonlight.

■ **1** nonsense, rubbish, humbug, drivel, twaddle, balderdash. **2** colloq. hooch. **3** moonbeams.

moon·shot /moonshot/ n. launching of a spacecraft to the moon.

moon·stone /moonstōn/ n. feldspar of pearly appearance.

moon·struck /moonstruk/ adj. slightly mad.

Moor /moor/ n. member of a Muslim people inhabiting NW Africa. □□ **Moor′ish** adj.

moor¹ /moor/ n. tract of open uncultivated upland, esp. when covered with heather. □□ **moor′ish** adj.

■ heath, moorland, wasteland.

moor² /moor/ v.tr. attach (a boat, buoy, etc.) to a fixed object. □□ **moor′age** n.

■ secure, tie up, make fast, dock, berth, anchor; fix.

moor·ing /mooring/ n. **1** [often in pl.] place where a boat, etc., is moored. **2** [in pl.] set of permanent anchors and chains laid down for ships to be moored to.

■ **2** sheet anchor.

moose /moos/ n. (pl. same) largest variety of N. American deer.

moot /moot/ • adj. [orig. the noun used attrib.] debatable; undecided. • n. Law discussion of a hypothetical case as an academic exercise.

■ adj. arguable, undetermined, controversial, doubtful, disputable, open to debate, at issue, indefinite.

mop /mop/ • n. **1** wad or bundle of cotton or synthetic material fastened to the end of a stick, for cleaning floors, etc. **2** similarly shaped large or small implement for various purposes. **3** thick mass of hair. • v.tr. (mopped, mop·ping) wipe or clean with or as with a mop. □ **mop up 1** wipe up with or as with a mop. **2** dispatch; make an end of. **3** Mil. complete the occupation of (a district, etc.) by capturing or killing enemy troops left there.

■ v. see WIPE v. 1.

mope /mōp/ v.intr. be gloomily depressed or listless; behave sulkily. □□ **mop′er** n. **mop′i·ly** adv. **mop′i·ness** n. **mop′y** adj. (mop·i·er, mop·i·est).

■ see SULK v. □□ **mopy** see MOODY adj.

mo·ped /mōped/ n. lightweight motorized bicycle with pedals.

mo·raine /mərayn/ n. area covered by rocks and debris carried down and deposited by a glacier. □□ **mo·rain′al** adj.

mor·al /mawrəl, mor–/ • adj. **1 a** concerned with the distinction between right and wrong. **b** concerned with accepted rules and standards of human behavior. **2** virtuous; capable of moral action. **3** founded on moral law. **4** concerned with or leading to a psychological effect associated with confidence in a right action (moral courage). • n. **1** moral lesson (esp. at the end) of a fable, story, event, etc. **2** [in pl.] moral behavior, e.g., in sexual conduct. □□ **mor′al·ly** adv.

■ adj. **1** ethical; moralizing, moralistic, deontic, prescriptive. **2** ethical, right, good, pure, honest, proper, upright, honorable, decent, respectable. • n. **1** homily, teaching, point, message; aphorism, maxim. **2** conduct, mores, beliefs, habits, customs.

ETHICAL, HONORABLE, RIGHTEOUS, SANCTIMONIOUS, VIRTUOUS. You can be an **ethical** person without necessarily being a **moral** one, since ethical implies conformity with a code of fair and honest behavior, particularly in business or in a profession (an ethical legislator who didn't believe in cutting deals), while moral refers to generally accepted standards of goodness and rightness in character and conduct—especially sexual conduct (the moral values she'd learned from her mother). In the same way, you can be **honorable** without necessarily being **virtuous**, since honorable suggests dealing with others in a decent and ethical manner, while virtuous implies the possession of moral excellence in character (many honorable businesspeople fail to live a virtuous private life). **Righteous** is similar in meaning to virtuous but also implies freedom from guilt or blame (righteous anger), but the righteous person can also be somewhat intolerant and narrow-minded, in which case "self-righteous" might be a better adjective. Someone who makes a hypocritical show of being *righteous* is often described as **sanctimonious**—in other words, acting like a saint without having a saintly character.

mo•rale /mərál/ *n.* mental attitude or bearing of a person or group, esp. as regards confidence, discipline, etc.
■ dedication, spirit(s), unity, esprit de corps; disposition.

mor•al•ist /máwrəlist, mór–/ *n.* person who practices or teaches morality. □□ **mor•al•is´ tic** *adj.* **mor•al•is´ti•cal•ly** *adv.*

mo•ral•i•ty /mərálitee/ *n.* (*pl.* **–ties**) 1 degree of conformity to moral principles. 2 right moral conduct. 3 particular system of morals (*commercial morality*). See synonym study at GOODNESS.
■ 1, 2 ethics, morals, principle(s), mores, standards, ideals; honesty, right, rightness. 3 behavior, conduct, habit(s), custom(s); see also ETIQUETTE.

mor•al•ize /máwrəlīz, mór–/ *v.* 1 *intr.* [often foll. by *on*] indulge in moral reflection or talk. 2 *tr.* interpret morally. □□ **mor•al•i• za´tion** *n.* **mor´al•iz•er** *n.* **mor´al•iz•ing•ly** *adv.*

mo•rass /mərás/ *n.* 1 entanglement; disordered situation, esp. one impeding progress. 2 *literary* bog or marsh.
■ 1 confusion, muddle, mess, quagmire, tangle. 2 swamp, fen, quag, mire, quagmire, slough.

mor•a•to•ri•um /máwrətáwreeəm, mór–/ *n.* (*pl.* **mor•a•to•ri•ums** or **mor•a•to•ri•a** /–reeə/) 1 temporary prohibition or suspension (of an activity). 2 a legal authorization to debtors to postpone payment. b period of this postponement.
■ 1 halt, freeze, stay, postponement, delay.

mor•bid /máwrbid/ *adj.* 1 unwholesome; macabre. 2 *Med.* of the nature of or indicative of disease. □□ **mor•bid´i•ty** *n.* **mor´bid•ly** *adv.* **mor´bid•ness** *n.*
■ 1 unhealthy, disordered, unsound, sick, sickly; grim, ghoulish, monstrous, ghastly, grotesque.

mor•dant /máwrd'nt/ • *adj.* 1 caustic; biting. 2 serving to fix dye. • *n.* mordant substance (in sense 2 of *adj.*). □□ **mor´dan•cy** *n.* **mor´ dant•ly** *adv.*

more /mawr/ • *adj.* greater in quantity or degree; additional. • *n.* greater quantity, number, or amount. • *adv.* 1 to a greater degree or extent. 2 forming the comparative of some adjectives and adverbs. □ **more or less** 1 in a greater or less degree. 2 approximately; as an estimate.
■ □ **more or less** 1 see SOMEWHAT *adv.* 2 see *approximately* (APPROXIMATE).

more•o•ver /máwróvər/ *adv.* further; besides.
■ furthermore, not only that, more than that, what is more; to boot, into the bargain, in addition.

mo•res /máwrayz, –reez/ *n.pl.* customs or conventions regarded as essential to or characteristic of a community.

morgue /mawrg/ *n.* 1 mortuary. 2 (in a newspaper office, etc.) room or file of miscellaneous information.

mor•i•bund /máwribund, mór–/ *adj.* 1 at the point of death. 2 lacking vitality. □□ **mor•i• bun´di•ty** *n.*
■ 1 dying, in extremis, at death's door, failing, fading, with one foot in the grave. 2 see LIFELESS 2.

Mor•mon /máwrmən/ *n.* member of the Church of Jesus Christ of Latter-day Saints. □□ **Mor´mon•ism** *n.*

morn /mawrn/ *n. poet.* morning.

morn•ing /mawrning/ *n.* early part of the day, esp. from sunrise to noon. □ **morning glory** twining plant with trumpet-shaped flowers. **morning sickness** nausea felt in the morning in pregnancy.
■ a.m., *Naut.* or *Law* forenoon, *poet.* morn.

Mo•roc•can /mərókən/ • *n.* 1 native or national of Morocco in N. Africa. 2 person of Moroccan descent. • *adj.* of or relating to Morocco.

mo•roc•co /mərókō/ *n.* (*pl.* **–cos**) fine flexible leather made (orig. in Morocco) from goatskins tanned with sumac.

mo•ron /máwron/ *n.* 1 *colloq.* very stupid person. 2 adult with a mental age of about 8–12. □□ **mo•ron´ic** *adj.* **mo•ron´i•cal•ly** *adv.*
■ 1 see FOOL *n.* 1.

mo•rose /mərós/ *adj.* sullen and ill-tempered. □□ **mo•rose´ly** *adv.* **mo•rose´ness** *n.*
■ see SULLEN *adj.* 1.

morph /mawrf/ *v.intr. Cinematog.* change form or appearance, as from person to animal, by computer-controlled special effects. □□ **morph´ing** *n.*

mor•pheme /máwrfeem/ *n. Linguistics* smallest meaningful morphological unit of a language. □□ **mor•phe´mic** *adj.* **mor•phe´mi• cal•ly** *adv.*

mor•phine /máwrfeen/ *n.* narcotic drug from opium used to relieve pain.

mor•phol•o•gy /mawrfóləjee/ *n.* the study of the forms or structures of things. □□ **mor• pho•log•i•cal** /mawrfəlójikəl/ *adj.* **mor•pho• log´i•cal•ly** *adv.* **mor•phol´o•gist** *n.*

mor•row /máwrō, mór–/ *n. literary* the following day.

Morse /mawrs/ *n.* (in full **Morse code**) alphabet or code in which letters are represented by combinations of long and short light or sound signals.

mor•sel /máwrsəl/ *n.* mouthful; small piece (esp. of food).
■ bite, gobbet, spoonful, taste, sample; crumb, fragment.

mor•tal /mawrt'l/ • *adj.* 1 subject to death. 2 causing death; fatal. 3 associated with death. 4 intense; very serious; implacable. • *n.* human being. □□ **mor´tal•ly** *adv.*
■ *adj.* 1 human; physical, bodily, corporeal, corporal; transitory, temporal. 2 deadly, lethal, terminal. 4 relentless, unrelenting, bitter, deadly, unappeasable, abject, extreme, awful, great. • *n.* man, woman, person, soul, individual, creature.

mor•tal•i•ty /mawrtálitee/ *n.* (*pl.* **–ties**) 1 being subject to death. 2 loss of life on a large scale. 3 death rate.

mor•tar /máwrtər/ *n.* 1 mixture of lime with

cement, sand, and water, used in building to bond bricks or stones. **2** short large-bore cannon for firing shells at high angles. **3** vessel in which ingredients are pounded with a pestle. □□ **mor'tar•less** *adj.* (in sense 1).

■ **1** see CEMENT *n.*

mor•tar•board /máwrtərbawrd/ *n.* **1** academic cap with a stiff, flat square top. **2** flat board for holding mortar.

mort•gage /máwrgij/ • *n.* **1 a** conveyance of property to a creditor as security for a debt. **b** deed effecting this. **2 a** debt secured by a mortgage. **b** loan resulting in such a debt. • *v.tr.* **1** convey (a property) by mortgage. **2** pledge (oneself, one's powers, etc.). □□ **mort'gage•a•ble** *adj.*

■ *n.* **2** see LOAN *n.* • *v.* see PAWN *v.*

mort•ga•gee /máwrgijée/ *n.* creditor in a mortgage.

mort•ga•gor /máwrgijər/ *n.* (also **mort'gag•er** /-jər/) debtor in a mortgage.

mor•ti•cian /mawrtíshən/ *n.* = UNDERTAKER.

mor•ti•fy /máwrtifī/ *v.* (**-fies, -fied**) **1** *tr.* shame; humiliate. **2** *tr.* bring (the body, the flesh, the passions, etc.) into subjection by self-denial or discipline. **3** *intr.* (of flesh) be affected by gangrene or necrosis. □□ **mor•ti•fi•ca'tion** *n.* **mor'ti•fy•ing** *adj.* **mor'ti•fy•ing•ly** *adv.*

■ **1** abase, humble, embarrass, abash, chagrin, rebuff. **2** punish, castigate, discipline, control, subdue, restrain, subjugate. **3** gangrene, fester, putrefy, rot, decompose.

mor•tise /máwrtis/ (also **mor'tice**) • *n.* hole in a framework designed to receive another part, esp. a tenon. • *v.tr.* **1** join securely, esp. by mortise and tenon. **2** cut a mortise in.

mor•tu•ar•y /máwrchoo-eree/ • *n.* (*pl.* **-ies**) room or building in which dead bodies may be kept until burial or cremation. • *adj.* of or concerning death or burial.

Mo•sa•ic /mōzáyik/ *adj.* of Moses (in the Old Testament). □ **Mosaic Law** laws attributed to Moses.

mo•sa•ic /mōzáyik/ *n.* **1 a** picture or pattern produced by an arrangement of small variously colored pieces of glass or stone, etc. **2** [*attrib.*] **a** of or like a mosaic. **b** diversified. □□ **mo•sa•i•cist** /-záyisist/ *n.*

mo•sey /mōzee/ *v.intr.* (**-seys, -seyed**) [often foll. by *along*] *sl.* walk in a leisurely or aimless manner.

Mos•lem var. of MUSLIM.

mosque /mosk/ *n.* Muslim place of worship.

mos•qui•to /məskéetō/ *n.* (*pl.* **-toes** or **-tos**) insect, the female of which sucks the blood of humans and other animals.

moss /maws/ *n.* small, flowerless plant growing in dense clusters on the surface of the ground, in bogs, on trees, stones, etc. □□ **moss'i•ness** *n.* **moss'like** *adj.* **moss'y** *adj.* (**moss•i•er, moss•i•est**)

most /mōst/ • *adj.* **1** existing in the greatest quantity or degree. **2** the majority of. • *n.* **1** greatest quantity or number. **2** the majority. • *adv.* **1** in the highest degree. **2** forming the superlative of some adjectives and adverbs. **3** *colloq.* almost. □ **at most** no more or better than (*this is at most a make-*

shift). **make the most of** employ to the best advantage.

■ □ **at most** see JUST *adv.* 3, 4.

-most /mōst/ *suffix* forming superlative adjectives and adverbs from prepositions and other words indicating relative position (*foremost, uttermost*).

most•ly /mōstlee/ *adv.* **1** as regards the greater part. **2** usually.

■ **2** see *usually* (USUAL).

mote /mōt/ *n.* speck of dust.

■ see SPECK *n.* 2.

mo•tel /mōtél/ *n.* roadside hotel for motorists.

moth /mawth, moth-/ *n.* **1** nocturnal insect having a stout body and without clubbed antennae. **2** small insect of this type, the larva of which feeds on cloth, etc. □□ **moth-eaten 1** damaged by moths. **2** timeworn. □□ **moth'y** *adj.* (**moth•i•er, moth•i•est**).

moth•ball /máwthbawl, móth-/ *n.* ball of naphthalene, etc., placed in stored clothes to keep away moths.

moth•er /múthər/ • *n.* **1** female parent. **2** quality or condition, etc., that gives rise to another. **3** (in full **Mother Superior**) head of a female religious community. • *v.tr.* **1** give birth to; be the mother or origin of. **2** protect as a mother. □ **Mother Goose rhyme** nursery rhyme. **mother-in-law** (*pl.* **moth•ers-in-law**) mother of one's husband or wife. **mother-of-pearl** smooth iridescent inner layer of the shell of some mollusks. **mother tongue** native language. □□ **moth'er•hood** *n.* **moth'er•less** *adj.* **moth'er•like** *adj. & adv.*

■ *n.* **1** matriarch, materfamilias, *colloq.* ma, mama, mamma, mom; nourisher, nurturer; dam. **2** origin, genesis; see also SOURCE *n.* 1, 2. • *v.* **1** have, deliver, bear, bring forth; see also CAUSE. **2** nurture, nourish, nurse, care for, pamper, baby.

moth•er•board /múthərbawrd/ *n.* computer's main circuit board, into which other boards can be plugged or wired.

moth•er•land /múthərland/ *n.* native country.

moth•er•ly /múthərlee/ *adj.* like or characteristic of a mother in affection, care, etc. □□ **moth'er•li•ness** *n.*

■ see MATERNAL 1, 2.

mo•tif /mōteéf/ *n.* **1** distinctive feature or dominant idea in artistic or literary composition. **2** *Mus.* short succession of notes producing a single impression, out of which longer passages are developed.

■ **1** theme, topic, subject; pattern, figure.

mo•tile /mōt'l, -til, -tīl/ *adj. Zool. & Bot.* capable of motion. □□ **mo•til•i•ty** /-tílitee/ *n.*

mo•tion /mōshən/ • *n.* **1** moving; changing position. **2** gesture. **3** formal proposal put to a committee, legislature, etc. • *v.* **1** *tr.* direct (a person) by a sign or gesture. **2** *intr.* make a gesture directing (*motioned to me to leave*). □ **go through the motions** do something perfunctorily or superficially. **in motion** moving; not at rest. **motion picture** [often (with hyphen) *attrib.*] film or movie with the illusion of movement (see FILM *n.* 3). □□ **mo'tion·less** *adj.*

■ *n.* **1** movement, change, shift, action; activity, commotion, stir, agitation. **2** gesticulation, signal, sign. **3** suggestion, proposition, recommendation, offering. • *v.* gesture, beckon, signal, wave; gesticulate, sign. □□ **motionless** see STILL[1] *adj.* 1.

mo·ti·vate /mótivayt/ *v.tr.* **1** supply a motive to; be the motive of. **2** stimulate the interest of (a person in an activity). □□ **mo·ti·va·tion** /–váyshən/ *n.* **mo·ti·va·tion·al** *adj.* **mo·ti·va·tion·al·ly** *adv.*

■ prompt, activate, move, inspire, incite; excite, egg (on), urge, prod. □□ **motivation** inducement, incentive, stimulus; attraction, lure, enticement.

mo·tive /mótiv/ • *n.* **1** factor or circumstance that induces a person to act in a particular way. **2** = MOTIF. • *adj.* causing or concerned with movement. □□ **mo'tive·less** *adj.*

■ *n.* **1** stimulus, inducement, incentive; cause, reason. • *adj.* driving, impelling, propelling, propulsive.

mot·ley /mótlee/ *adj.* (**mot·li·er**, **mot·li·est**) **1** diversified in color. **2** of varied character (*a motley crew*).

mo·to·cross /mótōkraws, –kros/ *n.* cross-country racing on motorcycles.

mo·tor /mótər/ • *n.* **1** thing that imparts motion. **2** engine, esp. one using electricity or internal combustion. • *adj.* **1** giving, imparting, or producing motion. **2** driven by a motor. **3** of or for motor vehicles. **4** *Anat.* relating to muscular movement or the nerves activating it. □ **motor home** vehicle built on a truck frame and outfitted as a residence. **motor pool** vehicles for use by personnel as needed as for a military installation. **motor vehicle** road vehicle powered by an internal-combustion engine.

■ *n.* **1** see ENGINE.

mo·tor·bike /mótərbīk/ *n.* **1** lightweight motorcycle. **2** motorized bicycle.

mo·tor·bus /mótərbus/ *n.* = BUS 1.

mo·tor·cade /mótərkayd/ *n.* procession of motor vehicles.

mo·tor·cy·cle /mótərsíkəl/ *n.* two-wheeled motor-driven road vehicle without pedal propulsion. □□ **mo'tor·cy·clist** *n.*

mo·tor·ist /mótərist/ *n.* driver of an automobile.

mo·tor·ize /mótərīz/ *v.tr.* **1** equip (troops, etc.) with motor transport. **2** provide with a motor. □□ **mo·tor·i·za'tion** *n.*

mot·tle /mót'l/ *v.tr.* (esp. as **mottled** *adj.*) mark with spots or smears of color.

■ see DAPPLE *v.*; (**mottled**) dappled, brindled, marbled, streaked, splotchy, blotched, blotchy.

mot·to /mótō/ *n.* (*pl.* **–toes** or **–tos**) maxim adopted as a rule of conduct, etc.

■ proverb, saying, adage, saw, aphorism; catchword.

mound /mownd/ *n.* heap or pile of earth, stones, etc.

■ stack; tumulus, (kitchen) midden, *Archaeol.* tell.

mount[1] /mownt/ • *v.* **1** *tr.* ascend; climb on. **2** *tr.* a set on horseback. **b** (as **mounted** *adj.*) serving on horseback (*mounted police*). **3** *intr.* increase; accumulate. **4** *tr.* place (an object) on a support or in a backing, frame, etc. **5** *tr.* arrange; organize; set in motion. • *n.* **1** backing, setting, or other support on which a picture, etc., is set for display. **2** horse for riding. □□ **mount'a·ble** *adj.* **mount'er** *n.*

■ *v.* **1** go up, scale, clamber up, make one's way up. **3** rise (up), ascend, soar; wax, rise, escalate, intensify, multiply. **5** display, exhibit; stage, prepare; coordinate, compose; frame, set off, back. • *n.* **1** mounting, background, set, arrangement, backdrop.

mount[2] /mownt/ *n. archaic* (*except before a name*) mountain; hill (*Mount Everest, Mount of Olives*).

moun·tain /mównt'n/ *n.* **1** large natural elevation of the earth's surface. **2** large heap or pile; huge quantity. □ **mountain bike** bicycle with a light sturdy frame for riding on mountainous terrain. **mountain goat** white goatlike animal of the Rocky Mountains, etc. **mountain lion** puma. **mountain range** line of mountains connected by high ground. **mountain sickness** sickness caused by the rarefaction of the air at great heights. □□ **moun'tain·y** *adj.*

■ **1** height, eminence, prominence, peak, alp. **2** stack, mound, accumulation, abundance, mass, *colloq.* ton(s), heaps, stacks; surplus, surfeit.

moun·tain·eer /mównt'néer/ *n.* person skilled in mountain climbing. □□ **moun'tain·eer·ing** *n.*

moun·tain·ous /mównt'nəs/ *adj.* **1** (of a region) having many mountains. **2** huge.

■ **1** craggy, alpine, hilly. **2** towering, high, steep, enormous, immense, formidable, mighty; see also GIGANTIC.

moun·te·bank /mówntibángk/ *n.* **1** swindler; charlatan. **2** clown.

Moun·tie /mówntee/ *n. colloq.* member of the Royal Canadian Mounted Police.

mount·ing /mównting/ *n.* = MOUNT[1] *n.* 1.

mourn /mawrn/ *v.* feel or show deep sorrow or regret for (a dead person, a lost thing, etc.). □□ **mourn'er** *n.*

■ grieve, lament, sorrow, bemoan, bewail; regret, rue.

mourn·ful /máwrnfŏŏl/ *adj.* **1** doleful; sad; expressing mourning. □□ **mourn'ful·ly** *adv.* **mourn'ful·ness** *n.*

■ sorrowful, sorrowing, dismal, melancholy, blue; grievous, distressing, upsetting, tragic, saddening.

mourn·ing /mawrning/ *n.* **1** expression of deep sorrow, esp. for a dead person. **2** solemn clothes worn in mourning.

■ **1** grief, lament, grieving, lamentation, sorrowing, keening, weeping. **2** black, sackcloth (and ashes).

mouse /mows/ • *n.* (*pl.* **mice** /mīs/) **1** common small rodent. **2** timid or feeble person. **3** *Computing* small hand-held device that controls the cursor on a computer monitor. • *v.intr.* (also /mowz/) hunt for or catch mice. □□ **mouse'like** *adj. & adv.* **mous'er** *n.*

■ *n.* **2** see COWARD *n.*

mousse /moos/ *n.* **1 a** dessert of whipped cream, eggs, etc., usu. flavored with fruit or chocolate. **b** meat or fish purée made with whipped cream, etc. **2** preparation applied to the hair enabling it to be styled more easily.

mous·tache var. of MUSTACHE.

mous·y /mówsee/ *adj.* (**mous·i·er, mous·i·est**) **1** of or like a mouse. **2** shy or timid; ineffectual. **3** nondescript light brown. □□ **mous'i·ly** *adv.* **mous'i·ness** *n.*

■ **2** cowering, timorous, self-effacing, bashful, diffident.

mouth ■ *n.* /mowth/ (*pl.* **mouths** /mowthz/) **1** external opening in the head, through which most animals admit food and emit communicative sounds. **2** opening of a container, cave, trumpet, etc. **3** place where a river enters the sea. ■ *v.* /mowth/ **1** *tr. & intr.* utter or speak solemnly or with affectation; rant; declaim. **2** *tr.* utter very distinctly. **3** *intr.* **a** move the lips silently. **b** grimace. □ **mouth organ** = HARMONICA. □□ **mouthed** /mowthd/ *adj.* [also in *comb.*] **mouth'er** /mówthər/ *n.* **mouth'less** /mówthlis/ *adj.*

■ *n.* **1** lips, jaws, orifice, *sl.* trap, kisser, chops, yap; muzzle, maw, *Zool.* stoma. **2** aperture, doorway, door, gateway, gate, access; passage, passageway, orifice, vent. **3** outfall, debouchment, embouchure, outlet. ■ *v.* **1, 2** say, pronounce, announce, enunciate, articulate.

mouth·ful /mówthfool/ *n.* (*pl.* **–fuls**) **1** quantity, esp. of food, that fills the mouth. **2** small quantity. **3** long or complicated word or phrase.

■ **1** morsel, bite, spoonful, lump, chunk, hunk. **2** see MODICUM. **3** tongue twister.

mouth·piece /mówthpees/ *n.* **1** part of a musical instrument, telephone, etc. placed next to or near the mouth. **2** *colloq.* lawyer.

■ **1** embouchure; receiver, handset. **2** attorney, *colloq.* shyster; see also LAWYER.

mouth·wash /mówthwosh, –wawsh/ *n.* liquid antiseptic, etc., for rinsing the mouth or gargling.

mouth·wa·ter·ing /mówthwawtəring/ *adj.* having a delicious smell or appearance.

mov·a·ble /moovəbəl/ (also **move'a·ble**) *adj.* **1** that can be moved. **2** variable in date from year to year. □□ **mov·a·bil'i·ty** *n.* **mov'a·ble·ness** *n.* **mov'a·bly** *adv.*

■ **1** portable, transportable, transferable. **2** floating, changeable, unfixed.

move /moov/ ■ *v.* **1** *intr. & tr.* change one's position, posture, or place, or cause to do this. **2** *tr. & intr.* put or keep in motion; rouse; stir. **3 a** *intr.* make a move in a board game. **b** *tr.* change the position of (a piece) in a board game. **4** *intr.* go; proceed; make progress. **5** *intr.* [foll. by *in*] live or be socially active in (a specified place or group, etc.). **6** *tr.* affect (a person) with emotion. **7** *tr.* stimulate; provoke; prompt or incline. **8 a** *tr.* cause (the bowels) to be evacuated. **b** *intr.* (of the bowels) be evacuated. **9** *tr.* propose in a meeting, deliberative assembly, etc. **10** *intr.* sell; be sold. ■ *n.* **1** act or instance of moving. **2** change of house, business

541   **mousse ~ mow**

premises, etc. **3** step taken to secure some action or effect; initiative. **4 a** the changing of the position of a piece in a board game. **b** player's turn to do this. □ **get a move on** *colloq.* **1** hurry up. **2** make a start. □□ **mov'er** *n.*

■ *v.* **1, 4** shift, stir, budge, make a move, set off, start off; advance, progress, make headway, pass, travel, voyage, migrate, transfer; see also LEAVE[1] *v.* 1b. **2, 7** arouse, actuate, lead, spur, motivate, influence, impel, inspire, make, excite, stir up; prod, remind. **5** circulate, mix, mingle, socialize, fraternize, keep company, hobnob, associate, *colloq.* hang around *or* about, *sl.* hang out. **6** touch, stir (up), shake (up), agitate, hit (hard), upset, strike, disturb, ruffle, disquiet, have an effect on. **9** put forward *or* forth, forward, advance, submit, suggest, advocate, propound, request. ■ *n.* **1, 2** gesture, gesticulation, action, motion, movement; stirring, change, changeover, relocation, transfer, shift, removal. **3** maneuver, device, trick, caper, dodge, stratagem, artifice, ruse, action, act, deed, gambit, *colloq.* ploy. **4 b** time, opportunity, chance, *colloq.* shot, go. □ **get a move on 1** hasten, make haste, rush, run, *colloq.* step on it *or* on the gas. **2** begin, start, get started, get going, get moving, get under way, stir *or* bestir oneself, *colloq.* get cracking, get *or* set *or* start the ball rolling, get the show on the road, *formal* commence.

move·a·ble var. of MOVABLE.

move·ment /moovmənt/ *n.* **1** moving or being moved. **2** moving parts of a mechanism (esp. a clock or watch). **3 a** body of persons with a common object. **b** campaign undertaken by such a body. **4** [usu. in *pl.*] person's activities and whereabouts, esp. at a particular time. **5** *Mus.* principal division of a longer musical work. **6** progressive development of a poem, story, etc. **7** motion of the bowels.

■ **1** move, motion, relocation, repositioning, migration; maneuver; action, activity; gesture, gesticulation. **2** mechanism, works, workings, machinery, action, gears. **3** front, faction, party, group, wing, lobby; campaign, crusade, drive. **6** unfolding, progression, progress, momentum, advancement.

mov·ie /moovee/ *n.* esp. *colloq.* **1** motion picture. **2** (**the movies**) **a** motion-picture industry or medium. **b** the showing of a movie (*going to the movies*).

■ film, moving picture, *colloq.* flick, talkie; cinema.

mov·ie·dom /mooveedəm/ *n.* the movie industry and its associated businesses, personnel, etc.

mow[1] /mō/ *v.tr.* (*past part.* **mowed** or **mown**) cut down (grass, hay, etc.) with a scythe or machine. □ **mow down** kill or destroy randomly or in great numbers. □□ **mow'a·ble** *adj.* **mow'er** *n.*

■ scythe, trim, shear. □ **mow down** annihilate, massacre, butcher, slaughter, exterminate.

mow[2] /mow/ *n. dial.* **1** stack of hay, wheat,

etc. **2** place in a barn where hay, etc., is heaped.

MP *abbr.* **1** military police. **2** Member of Parliament.

m.p.g. *abbr.* miles per gallon.

m.p.h. *abbr.* miles per hour.

Mr. /místər/ *n.* (*pl.* **Messrs.**) **1** title for a man. **2** title prefixed to a designation of office, etc. (*Mr. President*).

MRI *abbr.* magnetic resonance imaging.

Mrs. /mísiz/ *n.* (*pl.* same or **Mes·dames**) title for a married woman.

MS *abbr.* **1** Mississippi (in official postal use). **2** Master of Science. **3** multiple sclerosis. **4** (also **ms.**) manuscript.

Ms. /miz/ *n.* title for a married or unmarried woman.

M.Sc. *abbr.* Master of Science.

MS-DOS /émesdáws, –dós/ *abbr. propr.* microcomputer disk operating system.

MSG *abbr.* monosodium glutamate.

Msgr. *abbr.* **1** Monseigneur. **2** Monsignor.

MST *abbr.* Mountain Standard Time.

MT *abbr.* Montana (in official postal use).

Mt *abbr.* meitnerium.

Mt. *abbr.* **1** mount. **2** mountain.

mu /myōō, mōō/ *n.* twelfth Greek letter (M, μ).

much /much/ • *adj.* existing or occurring in a great quantity. • *n.* **1** a great quantity. **2** [usu. in *neg.*] noteworthy or outstanding example (*not much to look at*). • *adv.* **1** in a great degree. **2** for a large part of one's time (*is much away from home*). □□ **much'ly** *adv. joc.*

mu·ci·lage /myōōsilij/ *n.* **1** viscous substance obtained from plants. **2** adhesive gum; glue. □□ **mu·ci·lag·i·nous** /–lájinəs/ *adj.*

muck /muk/ • *n.* **1** farmyard manure. **2** *colloq.* dirt or filth; anything disgusting. • *v.tr.* **1** [usu. foll. by *up*] *colloq.* bungle (a job). **2** make dirty or untidy. □□ **muck'i·ness** *n.* **muck'y** *adj.* (**muck·i·er, muck·i·est**).

■ *n.* ordure, dung, excrement; bilge, slime, sludge, ooze. • *v.* **1** muff (up), spoil, make a mess of, botch, mess up, *colloq.* make a muck of, foul up, *sl.* screw up.

muck·rake /múkrayk/ *v.intr.* search out and reveal scandal. □□ **muck'rak·er** *n.* **muck'rak·ing** *n.*

mu·cous /myōōkəs/ *adj.* of or covered with mucus. □ **mucous membrane** mucussecreting epithelial tissue lining many body cavities and tubular organs. □□ **mu·cos·i·ty** /–kósitee/ *n.*

mu·cus /myōōkəs/ *n.* **1** slimy substance secreted by a mucous membrane. **2** gummy substance found in all plants.

mud /mud/ *n.* wet, soft, earthy matter. □ **fling** (or **sling** or **throw**) **mud** speak disparagingly or slanderously. **one's name is mud** one is unpopular or in disgrace.

■ muck, ooze, slime, mire, clay, sludge, silt, dirt.

mud·dle /múd'l/ • *v.* **1** *tr.* [often foll. by *up, together*] bring into disorder. **2** *tr.* bewilder; confuse. • *n.* **1** disorder. **2** muddled condition. See synonym study at JUMBLE.

□ **muddle-headed** stupid; confused. □□ **mud'dler** *n.* **mud'dling·ly** *adv.*

■ *v.* **1** confuse, mix up, jumble, scramble, entangle; bungle, botch, mismanage, muff. **2** confound, mystify, baffle, mix up, disorient(ate). • *n.* mess, confusion, mix-up, jumble, tangle, hodgepodge, mishmash, *colloq.* stew, *sl.* screw-up, snafu. □ **muddle-headed** bewildered, perplexed, puzzled, confused; see also STUPID *adj.* 1.

mud·dy /múdee/ • *adj.* (**mud·di·er, mud·di·est**) **1** like or covered in mud. **2** turbid; not clear; impure. **3** confused; vague. • *v.tr.* (**–dies, –died**) make muddy. □□ **mud'di·ly** *adv.* **mud'di·ness** *n.*

■ *adj.* **1** fouled, muddied, dirty, grubby; oozy, squelchy, squishy. **3** muddled, addled, mixed-up; unclear, obscure. • *v.* dirty, soil, begrime, smirch, besmirch, spatter, bespatter; obscure, dull.

mu·ez·zin /myōō-ézin, mōō–/ *n.* Muslim crier who proclaims the hours of prayer, usu. from a minaret.

muff[1] /muf/ *n.* fur or other covering for keeping the hands or ears warm.

muff[2] /muf/ *v.tr.* **1** bungle. **2** miss (a catch, ball, etc.).

■ **1** see BOTCH *v.* 1.

muf·fin /múfin/ *n.* small cake or quick bread made from batter or dough and baked in a muffin pan.

muf·fle /múfəl/ *v.tr.* **1** wrap or cover for warmth or to deaden sound. **2** (usu. as **muffled** *adj.*) stifle (an utterance, e.g., a curse). **3** prevent from speaking.

■ swathe, swaddle, cloak, envelop, enfold; silence, suppress, subdue, damp (down), dampen.

muf·fler /múflər/ *n.* **1** wrap or scarf worn for warmth. **2** noise-reducing device on a motor vehicle's exhaust system.

■ **1** shawl, stole, boa.

muf·ti /múftee/ *n.* civilian clothes (*in mufti*).

mug /mug/ • *n.* **1 a** drinking vessel, usu. cylindrical with a handle. **b** its contents. **2** *sl.* face. **3** *sl.* hoodlum or thug. • *v.* (**mugged, mug·ging**) **1** *tr.* rob (a person) with violence, esp. in a public place. **2** *intr. sl.* make faces, esp. before an audience, a camera, etc. □ **mug shot** *sl.* photograph of a face, esp. for official purposes. □□ **mug'ger** *n.* (esp. in sense 1 of *v.*). **mug'ful** *n.* (*pl.* **–fuls**). **mug'ging** *n.* (in sense 1 of *v.*).

■ *n.* **1** jug, tankard, stein, toby jug, pot, schooner, beaker, cup. **2** features, countenance, *literary* visage, *sl.* pan, kisser. **3** see THUG. • *v.* **1** set upon, assault; see also ATTACK *v.* 1. **2** pull a face, grimace.

mug·gy /múgee/ *adj.* (**mug·gi·er, mug·gi·est**) oppressively damp and warm; humid. □□ **mug'gi·ness** *n.*

■ sticky, sultry, oppressive, steamy, close; moist, soggy.

mu·ja·hi·din /mōōjaahideen/ *n.pl.* (also **mu·ja·he·din', –deen'**) guerrilla fighters in Islamic countries.

mu·lat·to /moolátō, –laá–, myōō–/ *n.* (*pl.* **–toes** or **–tos**) person of mixed white and black parentage.

mul·ber·ry /múlberee, –bəree/ *n.* (*pl.* **–ries**)

1 deciduous tree bearing edible dark-red or white berries. **2** its fruit. **3** dark-red or purple color.

mulch /mulch/ • *n.* mixture of straw, leaves, etc., spread around or over a plant to enrich or insulate the soil. • *v.tr.* treat with mulch.

mule[1] /myōōl/ *n.* **1** offspring (usu. sterile) of a male donkey and a female horse. **2** stupid or obstinate person. ▫▫ **mul'ish** *adj.* **mul'ish•ly** *adv.* **mul'ish•ness** *n.*

  ■ ▫▫ **mulish** see STUBBORN.

mule[2] /myōōl/ *n.* light shoe or slipper without a back.

mu•le•teer /myōōlitēer/ *n.* mule driver.

mull[1] /mul/ *n.* ponder or consider.

  ■ study, think over *or* about, cerebrate, cogitate, evaluate, turn over, weigh (up), deliberate (on *or* over).

mull[2] /mul/ *v.tr.* warm (wine or cider, etc.) with added sugar, spices, etc.

mul•lah /mŭlə, mool-/ *n.* Muslim learned in Islamic theology and sacred law.

mul•let /mŭlit/ *n.* any of several kinds of marine fish commonly used as food.

mul•li•ga•taw•ny /mŭligətawnee/ *n.* highly seasoned soup orig. from India.

mul•lion /mŭlyən/ *n.* (also **mun•nion** /mŭn–/) vertical bar dividing the panes in a window (cf. TRANSOM). ▫▫ **mul'lioned** *adj.*

multi- /mŭltee, –tī/ *comb. form* many; more than one.

mul•ti•cul•tur•al /mŭlteekŭlchərəl/ *adj.* of or relating to or constituting several cultural or ethnic groups within a society. ▫▫ **mul•ti•cul'tur•al•ism** *n.* **mul•ti•cul'tur•al•ly** *adv.*

mul•ti•far•i•ous /mŭltifáireeəs/ *adj.* **1** many and various. **2** diverse. ▫▫ **mul•ti•far'i•ous•ly** *adv.* **mul•ti•far'i•ous•ness** *n.*

mul•ti•lat•er•al /mŭltilátərəl/ *adj.* **1** (of an agreement, treaty, conference, etc.) in which three *or* more parties participate. **2** having many sides. ▫▫ **mul•ti•lat'er•al•ly** *adv.*

mul•ti•lin•gual /mŭlteelínggwəl, –tī–/ *adj.* in or using several languages. ▫▫ **mul•ti•lin'gual•ly** *adv.*

mul•ti•me•di•a /mŭltimédeeə/ • *attrib. adj.* involving several media. • *n.* combined use of several media, such as film, print, sound, etc.

mul•ti•na•tion•al /mŭlteenáshənəl, –tī–/ • *adj.* **1** operating in several countries. **2** of several nationalities or ethnic groups. • *n.* multinational company. ▫▫ **mul•ti•na'tion•al•ly** *adv.*

mul•ti•ple /mŭltipəl/ • *adj.* **1** having several or many parts, elements, or individual components. **2** many and various. • *n.* number that contains another without a remainder (56 *is a* multiple *of* 7). ▫▫ **multiple-choice** (of a question in an examination) accompanied by several possible answers from which the correct one has to be chosen. **multiple sclerosis** see SCLEROSIS.

mul•ti•plex /mŭltipleks/ • *adj.* **1** manifold; of many elements. **2** involving simultaneous transmission of several messages along a single channel of communication. • *n.* building that houses several movie theaters. ▫▫ **mul'ti•plex•er** *n.* (also **mul'ti•plex•or**).

mul•ti•pli•cand /mŭltiplikánd/ *n.* quantity to be multiplied by a multiplier.

mul•ti•pli•ca•tion /mŭltiplikáyshən/ *n.* multiplying. ▫ **multiplication sign** the symbol $(\mu;)$, to indicate that one quantity is to be multiplied by another, as in $2 \mu; 3 = 6$. ▫▫ **mul•ti•pli•ca•tive** /–plikətiv/ *adj.*

mul•ti•plic•i•ty /mŭltiplísitee/ *n.* (*pl.* **–ties**) **1** manifold variety. **2** [foll. by *of*] great number.

mul•ti•pli•er /mŭltiplīər/ *n.* quantity by which a given number is multiplied.

mul•ti•ply /mŭltiplī/ *v.* (**–plies, –plied**) **1** *tr.* [also *absol.*] obtain from (a number) another that is a specified number of times its value (multiply 6 *by* 4). **2** *intr.* increase in number.

  ■ **2** see INCREASE *v.* 1.

mul•ti•proc•ess•ing /mŭlteeprósesing/ *n.* *Computing* processing using two or more processors.

mul•ti•ra•cial /mŭlteeráyshəl, –tī–/ *adj.* relating to or made up of many human races. ▫▫ **mul•ti•ra'cial•ly** *adv.*

mul•ti•tude /mŭltitōōd, –tyōōd/ *n.* great number; crowd.

  ■ see MANY *n.* 1, CROWD *n.* 1.

mul•ti•tu•di•nous /mŭltitōōd'nəs, –tyōōd–/ *adj.* **1** very numerous. **2** consisting of many individuals or elements. ▫▫ **mul•ti•tu'di•nous•ly** *adv.* **mul•ti•tu'di•nous•ness** *n.*

mum[1] /mum/ *adj. colloq.* silent (keep mum). ▫ **mum's the word** say nothing.

  ■ mute, close-mouthed, quiet, tight-lipped.

mum[2] /mum/ *n.* = CHRYSANTHEMUM.

mum•ble /mŭmbəl/ • *v.* speak or utter indistinctly. • *n.* indistinct utterance. ▫▫ **mum'bler** *n.*

  ■ *v.* murmur, mutter, slur, swallow one's words.

mum•bo jum•bo /mŭmbōjúmbō/ *n.* (*pl.* **jum•bos**) meaningless or ignorant ritual or language.

mum•mer /mŭmər/ *n.* actor in a traditional mime.

mum•mer•y /mŭmərее/ *n.* (*pl.* **–ies**) **1** ridiculous (esp. religious) ceremonial. **2** performance by mummers.

mum•mi•fy /mŭmifī/ *v.tr.* (**–fies, –fied**) preserve (a body) as a mummy. ▫▫ **mum•mi•fi•ca'tion** *n.*

mum•my /mŭmee/ *n.* (*pl.* **–mies**) body of a human being or animal embalmed for burial, esp. in ancient Egypt.

mumps /mumps/ *n.pl.* [treated as *sing.*] infectious viral disease with swelling of the neck and face.

munch /munch/ *v.tr.* eat steadily with a marked action of the jaws.

  ■ chew, crunch, masticate, champ, chomp, scrunch.

munch•ies /mŭncheez/ *n. pl. colloq.* **1** snack foods. **2** urge to snack.

mun•dane /mŭndáyn/ *adj.* **1** dull; routine. **2** of this world; worldly. ▫▫ **mun•dane'ly** *adv.* **mun•dane'ness** *n.*

  ■ **1** see HUMDRUM *adj.* **2** see WORLDLY 1.

mu•nic•i•pal /myoonísipəl/ *adj.* of or concerning a municipality or its self-government. □ **municipal bond** bond issued by a city, county, state, etc., to finance public projects. □□ **mu•nic′i•pal•ize** *v.tr.* **mu•nic′i• pal•ly** *adv.*

■ civic, civil, metropolitan, urban, city, town, borough.

mu•nic•i•pal•i•ty /myo͞onísipálitee/ *n.* (*pl.* **-ties**) town or district having local government.

■ city, metropolis, borough.

mu•nif•i•cent /myo͞onífisənt/ *adj.* splendidly generous; bountiful. □□ **mu•nif′i•cence** *n.* **mu•nif′i•cent•ly** *adv.*

mu•ni•tion /myo͞oníshən/ *n.* [usu. in *pl.*] military weapons, ammunition, equipment, and stores.

mu•on /myo͞o-on/ *n. Physics* unstable elementary particle like an electron, but with a much greater mass.

mu•ral /myo͞orəl/ • *n.* painting executed directly on a wall. • *adj.* **1** of or like a wall. **2** on a wall. □□ **mu′ral•ist** *n.*

mur•der /mə́rdər/ • *n.* **1** unlawful premeditated killing of a human being by another. **2** *colloq.* unpleasant, troublesome, or dangerous state of affairs. • *v.tr.* **1** kill (a human being) intentionally and unlawfully. **2** *colloq.* utterly defeat or spoil by a bad performance, mispronunciation, etc. See synonym study at KILL. □□ **mur′der•er** *n.* **mur′der• ess** *n.*

■ *n.* **1** homicide, manslaughter, slaying, assassination; slaughter, butchery; bloodshed, carnage. **2** see HELL 2. • *v.* **1** assassinate, put to death, destroy, butcher, *sl.* wipe out, bump off. **2** ruin, mar, destroy, wreck, kill, mangle, butcher. □□ **murderer, murderess** killer, assassin, homicide, cutthroat, executioner, butcher.

mur•der•ous /mə́rdərəs/ *adj.* **1** (of a person, weapon, action, etc.) capable of, intending, or involving murder or great harm. **2** *colloq.* extremely troublesome, unpleasant, or dangerous. □□ **mur′der•ous•ly** *adv.*

■ **1** fatal, lethal, deadly, deathly, mortal; destructive, devastating, sanguinary, bloody. **2** strenuous, stressful, difficult, arduous, exhausting.

murk /mərk/ *n.* darkness; poor visibility.

■ see GLOOM *n.* 1.

murk•y /mə́rkee/ *adj.* (**-i•er, -i•est**) **1** dark; gloomy. **2** (of darkness) thick; dirty. **3** suspiciously obscure; shady (*murky past*). □□ **murk′i•ly** *adv.* **murk′i•ness** *n.*

■ **1, 2** threatening, dim, clouded, cloudy, overcast, gray, dismal, dreary, bleak, somber, grim. **3** see SHADY 3.

mur•mur /mə́rmər/ • *n.* **1** subdued continuous sound, as made by waves, a brook, etc. **2** softly spoken or nearly inarticulate utterance. • *v.* **1** *intr.* make a murmur. **2** *tr.* utter (words) in a low voice, esp. as a complaint. □□ **mur′mur•er** *n.* **mur′mur•ing•ly** *adv.* **mur′mur•ous** *adj.*

■ *n.* **1** undercurrent, undertone, background noise or sound, rumble, mumble. **2** see WHISPER *n.* 1. • *v.* mumble, mutter; whisper, drone; complain, grumble.

mus•cat /múskat, -kət/ *n.* **1** (also **mus•ca• tel** /múskətél/) sweet fortified white wine made from musk-flavored grapes. **2** this grape.

mus•cle /músəl/ • *n.* **1** fibrous tissue with the ability to contract, producing movement in or maintaining the position of an animal body. **2** part of an animal body that is composed of muscles. **3** physical power or strength. • *v.intr.* [usu. foll. by *in*] *colloq.* force oneself on others; intrude. □ **muscle-bound** with muscles stiff and inelastic through excessive exercise or training. □□ **mus′cled** *adj.* [usu. in *comb.*]. **mus′cle• less** *adj.*

■ *n.* **3** see STRENGTH 1.

mus•cu•lar /múskyələr/ *adj.* **1** of or affecting the muscles. **2** having well-developed muscles. □ **muscular dystrophy** see DYSTROPHY. □□ **mus•cu•lar•i•ty** /-lárítee/ *n.*

■ **2** sinewy, brawny, burly, powerful, wellbuilt.

mus•cu•la•ture /múskyələchər/ *n.* muscular system of a body or organ.

mus•cu•lo•skel•e•tal /məskyəlōskélət'l/ *adj.* of or involving both the muscles and the skeleton.

Muse /myo͞oz/ *n. Gk. & Rom. mythol.* one of the nine goddesses, the daughters of Zeus and Mnemosyne, who inspire poetry, music, drama, etc.

muse /myo͞oz/ *v. literary* **1** *intr.* [usu. foll. by *on, upon*] ponder; reflect. **2** *tr.* say meditatively.

■ **1** cogitate, meditate, contemplate, ruminate, think; dream, daydream; weigh, evaluate.

mu•se•um /myo͞ozee′əm/ *n.* building used for storing and exhibiting objects of historical, scientific, or cultural interest.

mush¹ /mush/ *n.* **1** soft pulp. **2** feeble sentimentality. **3** boiled cornmeal dish. **4** *sl.* (also /mo͞osh/) mouth; face. □□ **mush′y** *adj.* (**mush•i•er, mush•i•est**). **mush′i•ly** *adv.* **mush′i•ness** *n.*

■ **2** see *sentimentality* (SENTIMENTAL). □□ **mushy** soft, pulpy, doughy, spongy, sloppy, slushy, *colloq.* squishy. **mushiness** see *sentimentality* (SENTIMENTAL).

mush² /mush/ *v.intr.* **1** [in *imper.*] used as a command to encourage sled dogs. **2** travel across snow with a dogsled.

mush•room /múshro͞om, -ro͞om/ • *n.* edible fungus with a stem and domed cap. • *v.intr.* appear or develop rapidly.

■ *v.* see PROLIFERATE.

mu•sic /myo͞ozik/ *n.* **1** art of combining vocal or instrumental sounds (or both) to produce beauty of form, harmony, and expression of emotion. **2** sounds so produced. **3** musical compositions. **4** written or printed score of a musical composition. **5** pleasant natural sounds.

mu•si•cal /myo͞ozikəl/ • *adj.* **1** of or relating to music. **2** melodious; harmonious. **3** fond of or skilled in music. **4** set to or accompanied by music. • *n.* movie or drama that features songs. □□ **mu•si•cal•i•ty** /-kálitee/ *n.* **mu′si•cal•ize** *v.tr.* **mu′si•cal•ly** *adv.* **mu′ si•cal•ness** *n.*

mu·si·cian /myo͞ozíshən/ n. person who plays a musical instrument, esp. professionally, or is otherwise musically gifted. □□ **mu·si′cian·ly** adj. **mu′si·cian·ship** n.

mu·si·col·o·gy /myo͞ozikóləjee/ n. the academic study of music. □□ **mu·si·col′o·gist** n. **mu·si·co·log′i·cal** /-kəlójikəl/ adj.

musk /musk/ n. substance produced by a gland in the male musk deer and used as an ingredient in perfumes. □ **musk deer** small hornless Asian deer. **musk ox** shaggy goat-antelope native to N. America. □□ **musk′y** adj. (**musk·i·er, musk·i·est**). **musk′i·ness** n.

mus·kel·lunge /múskəlunj/ n. large N. American pike.

mus·ket /múskit/ n. hist. smooth-bored light gun.

mus·ket·eer /múskiteér/ n. hist. soldier armed with a musket.

musk·rat /múskrat/ n. **1** large aquatic rodent native to N. America, having a musky smell. **2** fur of this.

Mus·lim /múzlim, mo͝oz–, mo͝os–/ (also **Mos·lem** /mózləm/) • n. follower of the Islamic religion. • adj. of or relating to the Muslims or their religion.

mus·lin /múzlin/ n. strong, woven cotton fabric.

muss /mus/ colloq. • v.tr. [often foll. by up] disarrange; throw into disorder. • n. mess. □□ **muss′y** adj.

■ v. see MESS v. 1. □□ **mussy** see UNTIDY.

mus·sel /músəl/ n. bivalve mollusk often used for food.

must /must/ • v.aux. (3rd sing. present **must**; past **had to** or in indirect speech **must**) **1** be obliged to. **2** be certain to. **3** ought to. • n. colloq. thing that should not be missed.

■ v. **1, 3** should, have to, need to, be required to, be or feel compelled or forced to. • n. necessity, requisite, requirement, obligation, sine qua non, essential.

mus·tache /mústash, məstásh/ n. (also **mous′tache**) hair left to grow on a man's upper lip. □□ **mus′tached** adj.

mus·tang /mústang/ n. small wild horse native to Mexico and California.

mus·tard /mústərd/ n. **1** plant with slender pods and yellow flowers. **2** seeds of this which are crushed, made into a paste, and used as a spicy condiment. **3** brownish-yellow color. □ **mustard gas** colorless oily liquid whose vapor is a powerful irritant.

mus·ter /mústər/ • v. **1** tr. summon. **2** tr. & intr. collect, gather together. See synonym study at GATHER. • n. assembly of persons for inspection. □ **pass muster** be accepted as adequate.

■ v. call together, assemble, convene, mobilize, rally, round up, gather, marshal; muster up, formal convoke; come together. □ **pass muster** come or be up to scratch, measure up, be acceptable or adequate, be good enough, colloq. make the grade.

must·n't /músənt/ contr. must not.

mus·ty /mústee/ adj. (**mus·ti·er, mus·ti·est**) **1** moldy; stale. **2** antiquated. □□ **must′i·ly** adv. **must′i·ness** n.

■ **1** damp, mildewed, mildewy, rancid, spoiled, decayed. **2** stale, old-fashioned, ancient, out-of-date, bygone; hoary, worn out, trite, clichéd, colloq. old hat.

mu·ta·ble /myo͞otəbəl/ adj. literary **1** liable to change. **2** fickle. □□ **mu·ta·bil′i·ty** n.

mu·ta·gen /myo͞otəjən/ n. agent promoting mutation. □□ **mu·ta·gen′ic** /-jénik/ adj. **mu·ta·gen·e·sis** /-jénisis/ n.

mu·tant /myo͞ot′nt/ • adj. resulting from mutation. • n. mutant form.

mu·ta·tion /myo͞otáyshən/ n. **1** change; alteration. **2** genetic, heritable change. **3** mutant. □□ **mu′tate** v. **mu·ta′tion·al** adj. **mu·ta′tion·al·ly** adv.

■ **1** modification, transformation, metamorphosis, evolution, variation. **3** deformity, monstrosity, freak, anomaly. □□ **mutate** see TRANSFORM v.

mute /myo͞ot/ • adj. **1** silent; refraining from speech. **2** (of a person or animal) dumb; speechless. • n. **1** dumb person (a deaf mute). **2** Mus. device for damping the sound of a musical instrument. • v.tr. **1** deaden, muffle, or soften the sound, color, etc., of. **2** (as **muted** adj.) subdued. □□ **mute′ly** adv. **mute′ness** n.

■ adj. voiceless, wordless, tight-lipped, taciturn, tacit. • v. **1** silence, stifle, dampen, damp (down); subdue.

mu·ti·late /myo͞otilayt/ v.tr. **1 a** deprive (a person or animal) of a limb or organ. **b** destroy the use of (a limb or organ). **2** disfigure or destroy, esp. by cutting. □□ **mu·ti·la′tion** /-láyshən/ n. **mu·ti·la′tive** adj. **mu′ti·la·tor** n.

■ **1** maim, disfigure, mangle, cripple; dismember. **2** deface, vandalize, spoil, mar, ruin; bowdlerize.

mu·ti·ny /myo͞otnee/ • n. (pl. **-nies**) open revolt, esp. by soldiers or sailors against their officers. See synonym study at UPRISING. • v.intr. (**-nies, -nied**) revolt; engage in mutiny. □□ **mu·ti·neer** /-eér/ n. **mu′ti·nous** adj. **mu′ti·nous·ly** adv.

■ n. rebellion, revolution, insurgency, insurgence. • v. rebel, rise up; disobey, subvert, agitate. □□ **mutineer** see REBEL. **mutinous** rebellious, revolutionary, subversive, seditious, insurgent.

mutt /mut/ n. **1** dog. **2** sl. ignorant or blundering person.

mut·ter /mútər/ • v. **1** intr. speak low in a barely audible manner. **2** intr. murmur; grumble. • n. **1** muttered words or sounds. **2** muttering. □□ **mut′ter·er** n. **mut′ter·ing·ly** adv.

■ v. **1** mumble, murmur, grunt; see also WHISPER v. **1**. **2** complain, moan, colloq. grouch, grouse, gripe.

mut·ton /mút′n/ n. flesh of sheep as food. □□ **mut′ton·y** adj.

mu·tu·al /myo͞ocho͞oəl/ adj. **1** (of feelings, actions, etc.) experienced or done by each of two or more parties with reference to the other or others (mutual affection). **2** colloq. disp. common to two or more persons. □ **mutual fund** investment program funded by shareholders that trades in diversified holdings and is professionally managed. □□ **mu·tu·al·i·ty** /-chōō-álitee, -tyōō-álitee/ *n.* **mu·tu·al·ly** *adv.*

■ **1** reciprocal, reciprocated; interactive, complementary. **2** shared; see also COMMON *adj.* 2.

SYNONYM STUDY: mutual

COMMON, INTERCHANGEABLE, JOINT, RECIPRO-CAL, SHARED. In the 15th century, **mutual** was synonymous with **reciprocal**; both adjectives suggested—and still do—a relationship between two parties in which the same thing is given and taken on both sides (*mutual admiration; a mutual misunderstanding*). Since the 16th century, however, it has also been used to mean **shared** or having in **common** (*their mutual objective was peace*). Nowadays, *reciprocal* is more commonly used in official or technical contexts (*a reciprocal lowering of taxes by both states; a reciprocal trade agreement*), while *mutual* is used to describe any similarity of interests, opinions, or feelings, even if the relationship is not a reciprocal one (*a mutual interest in bird watching*). **Common** is a much vaguer term, used to describe anything that is *shared* by one or by all members of a group (*a common language*), while **joint** emphasizes the possession of something by two people (*a joint business venture*). **Shared** implies more emotional warmth than *joint*, *mutual*, or *reciprocal* (*a shared passion for classical music*); it is also used to describe something that is actually divided up and used by two or more people (*a shared meal*). Unlike all of the above, **interchangeable** applies to elements that can be used in place of one another (*interchangeable parts; interchangeable terms*); it has more to do with function and less to do with human relationships.

---

muu·muu /mōōmōō/ *n.* woman's loose brightly colored dress.

Mu·zak /myōōzak/ *n.* **1** *propr.* system of music transmission for playing in public places. **2** (**muzak**) recorded light background music.

muz·zle /múzəl/ • *n.* **1** projecting part of an animal's face, including the nose and mouth. **2** guard fitted over an animal's nose and mouth to stop it biting or feeding. **3** open end of a firearm. • *v.tr.* **1** put a muzzle on. **2** impose silence upon. □□ **muz′zler** *n.*

■ *n.* **1** snout, trunk, proboscis. • *v.* **2** see SILENCE *v.*

MVP *abbr. Sports* most valuable player.

MW *abbr.* megawatt(s).

my /mī/ *poss.pron.* [*attrib.*] of or belonging to me or myself.

my·al·gi·a /mīáljə/ *n.* muscular pain. □□ **my·al′gic** *adj.*

My·ce·nae·an /mísineéən/ • *adj. Archaeol.*of or relating to the late Bronze Age civilization in Greece (*c.* 1580–1100 BC), depicted in the Homeric poems. • *n.* inhabitant of Mycenae or the Mycenaean world.

my·col·o·gy /mīkóləjee/ *n.* **1** the study of

fungi. **2** fungi of a particular region. □□ **my·co·log·i·cal** /-kəlójikəl/ *adj.* **my·co·log′i·cal·ly** *adv.* **my·col′o·gist** *n.*

my·e·lin /mī-ilin/ *n.* white substance that forms a sheath around certain nerve fibers. □□ **my·e·li·na′tion** *n.*

my·e·li·tis /mī-ilítis/ *n.* inflammation of the spinal cord.

My·lar /mílaar/ *n. propr.* durable polyester film used for recording tapes, insulation, etc.

my·nah /mínə/ *n.* (also **my′na, mi′na**) any of various SE Asian starlings, esp. those able to mimic the human voice.

my·o·pi·a /mīópeeə/ *n.* **1** nearsightedness. **2** lack of imagination or intellectual insight. □□ **my·op·ic** /mīópik/ *adj.* **my·op′i·cal·ly** *adv.*

■ □□ **myopic** see NEARSIGHTED 1, SMALL-MINDED.

myr·i·ad /míreeəd/ *literary* • *n.* **1** an indefinitely great number. **2** ten thousand. • *adj.* of an indefinitely great number.

■ *n.* **1** see LOT *n.* 1. • *adj.* see UNLIMITED.

myrrh /mər/ *n.* gum resin used, esp. in the Near East, in perfumery, incense, etc. □□ **myrrh′ic** *adj.* **myrrh′y** *adj.*

myr·tle /mɔ́rtəl/ *n.* **1** evergreen shrub with aromatic foliage and white flowers. **2** = PERIWINKLE¹.

my·self /mīsélf/ *pron.* **1** *emphat.* form of I² or ME (*I saw it myself*). **2** *refl.* form of ME (*I was angry with myself*).

mys·te·ri·ous /mistéereeəs/ *adj.* full of or wrapped in mystery. □□ **mys·te′ri·ous·ly** *adv.* **mys·te′ri·ous·ness** *n.*

■ puzzling, enigmatic, baffling, insoluble, unsolvable, bewildering, confounding, confusing, perplexing; cryptic, arcane, secret, inscrutable, covert, hidden.

mys·ter·y /místəree/ *n.* (*pl.* **–ies**) **1** secret, hidden, or inexplicable matter (*the reason remains a mystery*). **2** secrecy or obscurity (*wrapped in mystery*). **3** (in full **mystery story**) fictional work dealing with a puzzling event, esp. a crime. See synonym study at RIDDLE.

■ **1** puzzle, enigma, conundrum, riddle, question. **2** indefiniteness, vagueness, nebulousness, ambiguity, ambiguousness, inscrutability, inscrutableness. **3** detective story or novel, murder story or mystery, thriller, *colloq.* whodunit.

mys·tic /místik/ • *n.* person who seeks spiritual truths or experiences. • *adj.* **1** mysterious and awe-inspiring. **2** spiritually allegorical or symbolic. **3** occult; esoteric. **4** of hidden meaning. □□ **mys·ti·cism** /-tisizəm/ *n.*

■ *adj.* **1** see OCCULT *adj.* 1, 3. **4** see CRYPTIC.

mys·ti·cal /místikəl/ *adj.* of mystics or mysticism. □□ **mys′ti·cal·ly** *adv.*

■ allegorical, symbolic(al), mystic, cabalistic, arcane, unrevealed, secret, occult, supernatural, esoteric.

mys·ti·fy /místifī/ *v.tr.* (**–fies, –fied**) **1** bewilder; confuse. **2** wrap up in mystery. □□ **mys·ti·fi·ca′tion** *n.*

■ **1** confound, mix up, stump, puzzle, baffle, beat, *colloq.* flummox; fool, mislead, hoax, humbug.

mys•tique /misteek/ n. atmosphere of mystery and veneration attending some activity or person.

■ mystery, magic, charisma, aura, inscrutability, charm.

myth /mith/ n. **1** traditional narrative usu. involving supernatural or imaginary persons and embodying popular ideas on natural or social phenomena, etc. **2** such narratives collectively. **3** widely held but false notion. **4** fictitious person, thing, or idea. **5** allegory (*the Platonic myth*). □□ **myth′ic** adj. **myth′i•cal** adj. **myth′i•cal•ly** adv.

■ **1, 2, 5** legend, fable, parable, (folk)tale, (folk)story, *literary* mythus. **3** see *misconception* (MISCONCEIVE). **4** fable, lie, (tall) tale,

fiction, untruth, falsehood, fabrication, fantasy, fairy story *or* tale, cock-and-bull story, *sl.* whopper. □□ **mythic, mythical** mythological, fabled, legendary, traditional, folkloric; allegorical, symbolic, parabolic(al); fanciful, imaginary.

my•thol•o•gy /mithóləjee/ n. (pl. **-gies**) **1** - body of myths (*Greek mythology*). **2** the study of myths. □□ **myth•o•log•ic** /-thəlójik/ adj. **myth•o•log′i•cal** adj. **myth•o•log′i•cal•ly** adv. **my•thol′o•gist** n. **my•thol′o•gize** v.

■ **1** folklore, fable, legend, tradition, lore, stories.

Nn

N¹ /en/ n. (also **n**) (pl. **Ns** or **N's; n's**) fourteenth letter of the alphabet. □ **to the nth** (or **nth degree**) **1** *Math.* to any required power. **2** to any extent; to the utmost.

N² abbr. (also **N.**) **1** north; northern. **2** noon. **3** New.

N³ symb. *Chem.* nitrogen.

n abbr. (also **n.**) **1** born. **2** name. **3** neuter. **4** noon. **5** number. **6** noun.

Na symb. *Chem.* sodium.

N.A. abbr. North America.

n/a abbr. **1** not applicable. **2** not available.

NAACP /endəbəláyseepee/ abbr. National Association for the Advancement of Colored People.

nab /nab/ v.tr. (**nabbed, nab•bing**) sl. **1** arrest, catch in wrongdoing. **2** seize, grab.

■ **1** capture, apprehend, pick up, collar, nail, *colloq.* run in.

na•bob /náybob/ n. wealthy person of influence.

na•cho /náachō/ n. (pl. **-chos**) [usu. in pl.] tortilla chip, usu. topped with melted cheese, peppers, etc.

na•cre /náykrər/ n. mother-of-pearl. □□ **na•cre•ous** /náykreeəs/ adj.

na•dir /náydər, -deer/ n. **1** part of the celestial sphere directly below an observer (opp. ZENITH). **2** lowest point.

■ **2** abyss, rock bottom; depths (of despair), *sl.* the pits.

NAFTA /náftə/ abbr. North American Free Trade Agreement.

nag¹ /nag/ v. **1 a** tr. persistently annoy, irritate, scold, urge, etc., (a person). **b** intr. find fault, complain, or urge, esp. persistently. **2** intr. (of a pain) ache dully but persistently. **3 a** tr. worry or preoccupy (a person, the mind, etc.) (*his mistake nagged him*). **b** intr. [often foll. by at] worry or gnaw. • n. persistently nagging person.

■ v. **1, 3** irk, pester, criticize, henpeck, pick at, goad, pick on. n. pest, shrew.

nag² /nag/ n. colloq. horse, esp. an old or worthless one.

■ hack, pony, dobbin.

Na•hua•tl /náawaat'l/ • n. **1** member of a group of peoples native to southern Mexico and Central America. **2** language of these peoples. • adj. of the Nahuatl peoples or language.

nai•ad /níad/ n. (pl. **nai•ads** or **-ades** /níədeez/) *Mythol.* water nymph.

nail /nayl/ • n. **1** small usu. sharpened metal spike with a broadened flat head, driven in with a hammer to join things or to serve as a peg, protection (cf. HOBNAIL), or decoration. **2** horny covering at the tip of the human finger or toe. • v.tr. **1** fasten with a nail or nails. **2** fix or keep (a person, attention, etc.) fixed. **3 a** secure, catch, or get hold of (a person or thing). **b** expose or discover (a lie or a liar).

■ n. **1** tack, brad; fastener. **2** fingernail, toenail. • v. **1** attach, secure, join, tack. **2** see HOLD¹ v. 7a. **3 a** see CATCH v. 1. **b** see EXPOSE 5.

na•ive /naa-eev/ adj. (also **na•ive′**) **1** innocent; unaffected. **2** credulous; simple see synonym study at GULLIBLE. □□ **na•ive′ly** adv. **na•ive•té** /naa-eevtáy, -eevtáy/ n.

■ unsophisticated, artless, natural, childlike; unsuspecting, trusting.

na•ked /náykid/ adj. **1** without clothes; nude. **2** undisguised (*naked truth*). **3** defenseless. **4** without addition, comment, support, evidence, etc. **5** devoid; without. **6** without leaves, hairs, scales, shell, etc. □□ **na′ked•ly** adv. **na′ked•ness** n.

■ **1** bare, stripped, undressed, in the raw. **2** plain, evident, obvious; blatant, undeniable, glaring, unmistakable. **4** unaided, unsupported; see also BARE adj. 3.

SYNONYM STUDY: naked

BALD, BARE, BARREN, NUDE. Someone who isn't wearing any clothes is **naked**; this adjective is usually associated with revealing a part or all of the body (*They found her naked and weak with hunger*). A naked person who appears in a painting or photograph is called a **nude,** a euphemistic but more socially acceptable term referring to the unclothed human body. **Bare** can describe the branches of a tree as well as human limbs; it implies the absence of the conventional or appropriate covering (*a bare wooden floor; bare legs; four bare walls*). **Bald** also suggests a lack of covering, but it refers particularly to lack of natural covering, esp. hair (*a bald head*). **Barren,** like *bald,* implies a lack of natural covering, especially vegetation, but it also connotes destitution and fruitlessness (*a barren wasteland that could barely support life*). A *bald* artist might paint a *nude* woman whose *bare* arms are extended against a *barren* winter landscape.

---

nam•by-pam•by /námbeepámbee/ • *adj.* lacking vigor or drive; weak. • *n.* (*pl.* **–bies**) timid or weak person.
  ■ *adj.* see WEAK *adj.* 3. • *n.* see WEAKLING.
name /naym/ • *n.* **1 a** a word by which an individual person, animal, place, or thing is known, spoken of, etc. **b** all who go under one name; family, clan, or people in terms of its name (*the Scottish name*). **2** usu. abusive term used of a person, etc. **3** famous person. **4** reputation, esp. a good one. • *v.tr.* **1** give a name to. **2** call (a person or thing) by the right name (*named the man in the photograph*). **3** mention; specify; cite. **4** nominate, appoint, etc. □ **in name** (or **name only**) as a mere formality; hardly at all (*is the leader in name only*). **in the name of** as representing; by virtue of. □□ **name′a•ble** *adj.*
  ■ *n.* **1, 2** designation, label, tag. **3** celebrity, star, hero. **4** honor, distinction, fame. • *v.* **1** label, tag, call; christen, baptize. **3, 4** choose, elect, delegate; identify.
name•less /náymlis/ *adj.* **1** having or showing no name. **2** inexpressible; indefinable. **3** unnamed; anonymous, esp. deliberately. **4** too horrific to be named.
  ■ **1, 3** unidentified, incognito; unknown, unheard-of; obscure. **2** unidentifiable, unspecified. **4** unspeakable, abominable, indescribable, repulsive.
name•ly /náymlee/ *adv.* that is to say; in other words.
  ■ specifically, to wit.
name•sake /náymsayk/ *n.* person or thing having the same name as another.
nan•ny /nánee/ *n.* (*pl.* **–nies**) **1** child's nursemaid. **2** (in full **nan′ny goat**) female goat.
nano- /nánō, náynō/ *comb. form* denoting a factor of 10^{-9} (*nanosecond*).
nap[1] /nap/ • *v.intr.* (**napped, nap•ping**) sleep lightly or briefly. • *n.* short sleep or doze, esp. by day.
  ■ *v.* doze, nod (off), catnap. • *n.* siesta, *colloq.* shut-eye, snooze.
nap[2] /nap/ *n.* **1** raised pile on textiles, esp. velvet. **2** soft downy surface.
  ■ **1** texture, weave, down; see also TEXTURE *n.* 1, 2.
na•palm /náypaam/ • *n.* jellied incendiary substance used in bombs. • *v.tr.* attack with napalm bombs.

nape /nayp/ *n.* back of the neck.
naph•tha /náf-thə, náp-/ *n.* flammable oil obtained by the dry distillation of organic substances such as coal, etc.
naph•tha•lene /náf-thəleen, náp-/ *n.* white crystalline aromatic distillate of coal tar used in mothballs and the manufacture of dyes, etc.
nap•kin /nápkin/ *n.* square piece of linen, paper, etc., used for wiping the lips, fingers, etc., at meals.
narc /nark/ *n.* (also **nark**) *sl.* federal agent or police officer who enforces drug and narcotics laws.
nar•cis•sism /naársisizəm/ *n. Psychol.* excessive or erotic interest in oneself, one's physical features, etc. □□ **nar′cis•sist** *n. & adj.* **nar•cis•sis′tic** *adj.*
  ■ see VANITY 1. □□ **narcissistic** see VAIN 1.
nar•cis•sus /naarsísəs/ *n.* (*pl.* **nar•cis•si** /-sī/ or **nar•cis•sus•es**) any of several bulbous plants bearing a single flower with an undivided corona, as the daffodil.
nar•co•lep•sy /naárkəlepsee/ *n. Med.* disease with fits of sleepiness and drowsiness. □□ **nar•co•lep′tic** /–léptik/ *adj. & n.*
nar•cot•ic /naarkótik/ • *adj.* **1** (of a substance) inducing drowsiness, sleep, or stupor. **2** (of a drug) affecting the mind. • *n.* narcotic substance, drug, or influence.
  ■ *adj.* **1** soporific, sedative, dulling, anesthetic, tranquilizing. • *n.* sedative, opiate, anesthetic, tranquilizer.
Nar•ra•gan•sett /narəgánsət, -gánt-/ *n.* **1 a** N. American people native to Rhode Island. **b** member of this people. **2** language of this people.
nar•rate /nárayt, naráyt/ *v.tr.* [also *absol.*] **1** give a story or account of. **2** provide a spoken accompaniment for (a film, etc.). □□ **nar•ra•tion** /–ráyshən/ *n.* **nar′ra•tor** *n.*
  ■ relate, tell, recount, describe; read. □□ **narration** telling; report, chronicle, tale; reading, voice-over. **narrator** commentator, announcer, reader.
nar•ra•tive /nárətiv/ • *n.* spoken or written account of connected events in order of happening. • *adj.* in the form of, or concerned with, narration (*narrative verse*).
  ■ *n.* story, tale, chronicle, report, history, statement.
nar•row /nárō/ • *adj.* (**nar•row•er, nar•row•est**) **1 a** of small width. **b** confined or confining. **2** of limited scope. **3** with little margin. • *n.* [usu. in *pl.*] narrow part of a strait, river, pass, street, etc. • *v.* **1** *intr.* become narrow; diminish; contract; lessen. **2** *tr.* make narrow; constrict; restrict. □□ **nar′row•ly** *adv.* **nar′row•ness** *n.*
  ■ *adj.* **1 a** slender, slim, thin; tapering. **b** limited, close, tight, constricted, restricted. **2** restricted, circumscribed. **3** close, hairbreadth; lucky. • *n.* channel, passage. • *v.* **1** decrease, reduce. **2** limit, qualify, diminish, focus. □□ **narrowly** barely, (only) just, scarcely, *colloq.* by a whisker; closely, critically.
nar•row-mind•ed /nárōmíndid/ *adj.* rigid or restricted in one's views; intolerant. □□ **nar′row-mind′ed•ness** *n.*

■ bigoted, biased, opinionated, one-sided, conservative, petty, shallow, puritanical, unprogressive, sl. square.

nar•whal /naárwəl/ n. Arctic white whale, the male of which has a long straight tusk.

nar•y /náiree/ adj. colloq. or dial. not any; no (nary a one).

NASA /násə/ abbr. National Aeronautics and Space Administration.

na•sal /náyzəl/ • adj. **1** of, for, or relating to the nose. **2** pronounced or spoken with the breath passing through the nose. • n. Phonet. nasal letter or sound. □□ **na'sal•ize** v. **na•sal•i•za'tion** n. **na'sal•ly** adv.

NASCAR /naskaár/ • abbr. National Association for Stock Car Auto Racing.

nas•cent /násənt, náy-/ adj. **1** in the act of being born. **2** just beginning to be. □□ **nas'cen•cy** /násənsee, náy-/ n.

NASDAQ /názdak, nás-/ abbr. National Association of Securities Dealers Automated Quotations.

nas•ty /nástee/ adj. (**nas•ti•er, nas•ti•est**) **1 a** highly unpleasant. **b** annoying; objectionable. **2** difficult to negotiate; dangerous, serious. **3** (of a person or animal) illnatured; offensive. **4 a** obscene. **b** delighting in obscenity. □□ **nas'ti•ly** adv. **nas'ti•ness** n.

■ **1** disagreeable, unsavory, painful. **2** bad, severe, acute; hard, tricky, problematical. **3** unpleasant, ugly, vicious, surly. **4** dirty, pornographic, blue, crude.

na•tal /náytəl/ adj. of or from one's birth.

■ see INHERENT 1, INBORN.

Natch•ez /náchiz/ n. **1 a** N. American people native to Mississippi. **b** member of this people. **2** language of this people.

na•tion /náyshən/ n. **1** community of people of mainly common descent, history, language, etc., forming a unified government or inhabiting a territory. **2** tribe or confederation of tribes of Native Americans. □□ **na'tion•hood** n.

■ **1** country, state, land, domain.

na•tion•al /náshənəl/ • adj. **1** of or common to a nation or the nation. **2** peculiar to or characteristic of a particular nation. • n. citizen of a specified country. □ **national anthem** patriotic song adopted by a nation. **National Guard** federally subsidized state militia, called into service in cases of emergency. □□ **na'tion•al•ly** adv.

■ adj. countrywide, federal; public. • n. resident; voter.

na•tion•al•ism /náshənəlizəm/ n. **1** patriotic feeling, principles, etc. **2** policy of national independence. □□ **na'tion•al•ist** n. & adj. **na•tion•al•is'tic** adj.

■ □□ **nationalist** (n.) see PATRIOT. **nationalistic** patriotic, xenophobic, isolationist.

na•tion•al•i•ty /náshənálitee/ n. (pl. **-ties**) **1 a** status of belonging to a particular nation. **b** nation (people of all nationalities). **2** ethnic group forming a part of one or more political nations.

■ **1** citizenship. **2** race, ethnic minority, tribe; heritage.

na•tion•al•ize /náshənəlīz/ v.tr. **1** take (industry, land, etc.) into government control

or ownership. **2 a** make national. **b** make into a nation. □□ **na•tion•al•i•za'tion** n.

na•tion•wide /náyshənwíd/ adj. & adv. extending over the whole nation.

na•tive /náytiv/ • n. **1 a** person born in a specified place. **b** local inhabitant. **2** often offens. member of a nonwhite indigenous people, as regarded by the colonial settlers. **3** indigenous animal or plant. • adj. **1** inherent; innate. **2** of one's birth (native dress). **3** belonging to a specified place (the anteater is native to S. America). **4 a** indigenous. **b** of the natives of a place. **5** in a natural state; unadorned; simple. □ **Native American** member of the indigenous peoples of America or their descendants.

■ n. **1** aborigine; citizen, resident; local. • adj. **1** see INHERENT 1, INBORN. **2** domestic, local; aboriginal; national, ethnic. **3** see INDIGENOUS. **5** real, genuine; plain.

SYNONYM STUDY: native

ABORIGINAL, ENDEMIC, INDIGENOUS. A **native** New Yorker is probably not **indigenous**, although both words apply to persons or things that belong to or are associated with a particular place by birth or origin. **Native** means born or produced in a specific region or country (native plants; native dances), but it can also apply to persons or things that were introduced from elsewhere some time ago—which is the case with most New Yorkers who consider themselves natives. **Indigenous**, on the other hand, is more restricted in meaning; it applies only to something or someone that is not only native but was not introduced from elsewhere (the pumpkin is indigenous to America). Generally speaking, native applies to individual organisms, while indigenous applies to races or species. Something that is **endemic** is prevalent in a particular region because of special conditions there that favor its growth or existence (heather is endemic in the Scottish Highlands; malaria is endemic in Central America). There are no longer any **aboriginal** New Yorkers, a word that refers to the earliest known inhabitants of a place or to ancient peoples who have no known ancestors and have inhabited a region since its earliest historical time. Australia is known for its aboriginal culture, which was preserved for centuries through geographical isolation.

---

na•tiv•i•ty /nətívitee, nay-/ n. (pl. **-ties**) **1** (esp. **the Nativity**) **a** the birth of Christ. **b** Christmas. **2** birth.

■ **2** see BIRTH n. 1.

natl. abbr. national.

NATO /náytō/ abbr. North Atlantic Treaty Organization.

nat•ty /nátee/ adj. (**nat•ti•er, nat•ti•est**) colloq. **1** smartly or neatly dressed. **2** trim; smart (a natty blouse). □□ **nat'ti•ly** adv.

nat•u•ral /náchərəl/ adj. **1 a** existing in or caused by nature. **b** uncultivated; wild. **2** in the course of nature; not exceptional. **3** (of human nature, etc.) not surprising; to be expected. **4** (of a person or a person's behavior) unaffected, easy, spontaneous. **5 a** (of

qualities, etc.) inherent; innate. **b** (of a person) having such qualities (*a natural linguist*). **6** not disguised or altered (as by makeup, etc.). **7** likely by its or their nature to be such (*natural enemies*). **8** *Mus.* **a** (of a note) not sharpened or flatted. **b** (of a scale) not containing sharps or flats. See synonym study at NORMAL. ● *n.* **1** *colloq.* person or thing naturally suitable, adept, expert, etc. **2** *Mus.* **a** sign (♮) denoting a return to natural pitch. **b** natural note. □ **natural gas** flammable mainly methane gas extracted from the earth. **natural history 1** study of animals or plants. **2** aggregate of the facts concerning the flora and fauna, etc., of a particular place or class. **natural law** *Philos.* unchanging moral principles common to all people by virtue of their nature as human beings. **natural numbers** integers 1, 2, 3, etc. **natural resources** materials or conditions occurring in nature and capable of economic exploitation. **natural science** sciences used in the study of the physical world. **natural selection** Darwinian theory of the survival and propagation of organisms best adapted to their environment. □□ **nat′u·ral·ness** *n.*
■ *adj.* **1a, 2, 6** ordinary, common, normal; reasonable, accepted; expected; simple, basic, true. **4** unstudied, candid, genuine, ingenuous. **5 a** see INHERENT 1, INBORN. **7** logical, appropriate, expected. □ **natural history 1** ecology, biology, botany, zoology, geology.

nat·u·ral·ism /náchərəlizəm/ *n.* **1** realistic representation in art and literature of nature, character, etc. **2 a** *Philos.* theory of the world that excludes the supernatural or spiritual. **b** moral or religious system based on this theory. □□ **nat·u·ral·is·tic** /-ístik/ *adj.*

nat·u·ral·ist /náchərəlist/ *n.* **1** expert in natural history. **2** adherent of naturalism.
■ **1** ecologist, biologist, botanist, zoologist; wildlife expert, conservationist, environmentalist, ecologist.

nat·u·ral·ize /náchərəlīz/ *v.* **1** *tr.* admit (a foreigner) to citizenship. **2** *tr.* successfully introduce (an animal, plant, etc.) into another region. □□ **nat·u·ral·i·za′tion** *n.*

nat·u·ral·ly /náchərəlee, náchrə-/ *adv.* **1** in a natural manner. **2** as might be expected; of course.
■ **1** normally; inherently, instinctively, easily. **2** needless to say, certainly.

na·ture /náychər/ *n.* **1** innate or essential qualities or character (*is the nature of iron to rust*). **2** (often **Nature**) **a** physical power causing all material phenomena. **b** these physical phenomena. **3** kind, sort, or class (*things of this nature*). **4** natural world. □ **by nature** innately.
■ **1** properties, features, personality, makeup. **2 a** Mother Nature. **b** wildlife, fauna and flora, environment, countryside. **3** variety, description; category, type; constitution. **4** scenery, countryside, wilderness. □ **by nature** see NATURALLY 1.

na·tured /náychərd/ *adj.* [in *comb.*] having a specified disposition (*good-natured*).

naught /nawt/ ● *n.* **1** nothing. **2** zero. ● *adj.* [usu. *predic.*] worthless; useless.
■ *n.* **1** nil, *sl.* zilch.

naugh·ty /náwtee/ *adj.* (**naugh·ti·er, naugh·ti·est**) **1** (esp. of children) disobedient; badly behaved. **2** *colloq. joc.* indecent. □□ **naugh′ti·ly** *adv.* **naugh′ti·ness** *n.*
■ **1** mischievous, devilish; unruly, undisciplined. **2** improper, offensive, vulgar.

nau·se·a /náwzeeə, -zhə, -seeə, -shə/ *n.* **1** feeling of sickness with an inclination to vomit. **2** loathing; revulsion.

nau·se·ate /náwzeeayt, -zhee-, -see-, -shee-/ *v.* **1** *tr.* affect with nausea (*was nauseated by the smell*). **2** *intr.* feel sick. □□ **nau′se·at·ing** *adj.*
■ **1** sicken, disgust, repel.

nau·seous /náwshəs, -zeeəs/ *adj.* **1** affected with nausea; sick. **2** causing nausea; offensive to the taste or smell.
■ **2** loathsome, sickening, disgusting, nasty, foul.

nau·ti·cal /náwtikəl/ *adj.* of sailors or navigation; naval; maritime. □ **nautical mile** unit of approx. 2,025 yards (1,852 meters): (also called **sea mile**). □□ **naut′i·cal·ly** *adv.*
■ marine, seafaring, seagoing; boating, yachting, sailing.

nau·ti·lus /náwt′ləs/ *n.* (*pl.* **nau·ti·lus·es** or **nau·ti·li** /-lī/) cephalopod with a spiral shell, esp. one having a chambered shell.

Nav·a·jo /návəhō, náa-/ *n.* (*pl.* **–jos**) (also **Nav′a·ho**) (*pl.* **-hos**) **1** member of N. American people native to New Mexico and Arizona. **2** language of this people.

na·val /náyvəl/ *adj.* **1** of, in, for, etc., the navy or a navy. **2** of or concerning ships (*a naval battle*).
■ see NAUTICAL.

nave /nayv/ *n.* central part of a church, usu. from the west door to the chancel and excluding the side aisles.

na·vel /náyvəl/ *n.* depression in the center of the belly caused by detachment of the umbilical cord. □ **navel orange** large seedless orange with a navellike formation at the top.
■ *Anat.* umbilicus, *colloq.* belly button.

nav·i·ga·ble /návigəbəl/ *adj.* **1** (of a river, etc.) affording a passage for ships. **2** (of a ship, etc.) seaworthy. **3** (of a balloon, airship, etc.) steerable. □□ **nav·i·ga·bil′i·ty** *n.*
■ **1** passable, negotiable; clear, open. **2, 3** sailable; controllable.

nav·i·gate /návigayt/ *v.* **1** *tr.* manage or direct the course of (a ship, aircraft, etc.). **2** *tr.* **a** sail on (a sea, etc.). **b** fly through (the air). **3** *intr.* assist the driver by map-reading, etc. **4** *intr.* sail a ship; sail in a ship. □□ **nav′i·ga·tor** *n.*
■ **1** maneuver, guide, steer. **2, 4** cruise, journey; cross. □□ **navigator** helmsman, skipper, pilot.

nav·i·ga·tion /návigáyshən/ *n.* **1** act or process of navigating. **2** method of determining a ship's or aircraft's position and course by geometry, astronomy, radio signals, etc.
■ **1** pilotage, seamanship, steering, sailing.

na·vy /náyvee/ *n.* (*pl.* **-vies**) **1** (often **the Navy**) **a** a nation's ships of war, including crews, maintenance systems, etc. **b** officers and enlisted personnel of a navy. **2** (in full **na'vy blue'**) dark-blue color. □ **navy bean** small white kidney bean.

■ **1a** naval force(s); see also FLEET[1] 1.

nay /nay/ • *adv.* or rather; and even; and more than that (*impressive, nay, magnificent*). • *n.* **1** the word 'nay.'. **2** negative vote (*counted 16 nays*). □□ **nay'say•er** *n.*

■ □□ **naysayer** dissenter, dissident.

Na•zi /naatsee, nát–/ • *n.* (*pl.* **Na•zis**) **1** *hist.* member of the German National Socialist party. **2** adherent of this party's tenets. • *adj.* of Nazis, Nazism, etc. □□ **Na'zism** /naatsizəm, nát–/ *n.*

NB *abbr.* **1** New Brunswick. **2** nota bene.

Nb *symb. Chem.* niobium.

NBC *abbr.* National Broadcasting Company.

NC *abbr.* North Carolina (in official postal use).

NCO *abbr.* noncommissioned officer.

ND *abbr.* North Dakota (in official postal use).

Nd *symb. Chem.* neodymium.

n.d. *abbr.* no date.

N.Dak. *abbr.* North Dakota.

NE *abbr.* **1** Nebraska (in official postal use). **2** northeast. **3** northeastern.

Ne *symb. Chem.* neon.

Ne•an•der•thal /neeándərthawl, –tawl, –taal/ *adj.* (also **Ne•an'der•tal**) of the type of early human widely distributed in Paleolithic Europe.

neap /neep/ *n.* (in full **neap tide**) tide just after the first and third quarters of the moon when there is least difference between high and low water.

Ne•a•pol•i•tan /neeəpólitən/ • *n.* native or citizen of Naples in Italy. • *adj.* of Naples. □ **Neapolitan ice cream** ice cream made in layers of different colors and flavors.

near /neer/ • *adv.* **1** to or at a short distance in space or time (*the time drew near, dropped near to them*). **2** closely (*as near as one can guess*). • *prep.* [*compar.* & *superl.* also used] **1** to or at a short distance (in space, time, condition, or resemblance) from. **2** [in *comb.*] **a** that is almost (*near-hysterical*). **b** intended as a substitute for; resembling (*near beer*). • *adj.* **1** [usu. *predic.*] close to, in place or time (*the man nearest you*). **2 a** closely related. **b** intimate **3** close; narrow (*near escape*). • *v.* **1** *tr.* approach; draw near to. **2** *intr.* draw near. □ **the Near East** region comprising the countries of the eastern Mediterranean. **near miss 1** narrowly avoided collision. **2** attempt that is almost but not quite successful. □□ **near'ish** *adj.* **near'ness** *n.*

■ *adv.* **1** close by, not far (off *or* away), nearby, in the vicinity. • *prep.* **1** close to, next to, adjacent to, within reach of. • *adj.* **1** imminent, immediate, impending; nearby, adjacent, next-door. **2 a** intimate, connected, attached. **b** see INTIMATE[1] *adj.* 1. **3** hairbreadth; lucky. • *v.* come close *or* closer to; verge on, lean toward. □ **near miss 1** narrow escape, *colloq.* close shave.

near•by /neerbí/ • *adj.* near, in position. • *adv.* close; not far away.

■ *adj.* close, within reach, handy. • *adv.* about, around.

near•ly /neerlee/ *adv.* **1** almost. **2** closely.

■ **1** not quite, about, just about, practically; barely, hardly.

near•sight•ed /neersitid/ *adj.* unable to see distant objects clearly. □□ **near'sight•ed•ness** *n.*

■ shortsighted, myopic, dim-sighted.

neat /neet/ *adj.* **1** tidy and methodical. **2** elegantly simple. **3** brief, clear, and pointed. **4 a** cleverly executed. **b** deft; dexterous. **5** (of esp. alcoholic liquor) undiluted. **6** *sl.* (as a general term of approval) good, pleasing, excellent. □□ **neat'ly** *adv.* **neat'ness** *n.*

■ **1** orderly, clean, uncluttered, fastidious, **2** unadorned, well-proportioned; regular, precise. **3** distinct, witty, lucid, crisp; see also *epigrammatic* (EPIGRAM). **4** adroit, efficient, expert. **5** straight, unmixed. **6** fine, wonderful, marvelous, first-class.

neat•en /neet'n/ *v.tr.* make neat.

■ tidy (up), straighten (up *or* out), clean (up), spruce up.

Nebr. *abbr.* Nebraska.

neb•u•la /nébyələ/ *n.* (*pl.* **neb•u•lae** /–lee/ or **ne•bu•las**) *Astron.* **1** cloud of gas and dust, glowing or appearing as a dark silhouette against other glowing matter. **2** bright area caused by a galaxy, or a large cloud of distant stars. □□ **neb'u•lar** *adj.*

neb•u•lous /nébyələs/ *adj.* **1** cloudlike **2 a** formless, clouded. **b** hazy, indistinct, vague (*put forward a few nebulous ideas*). **3** *Astron.* of or like a nebula(e).

■ **2** unclear, obscure, fuzzy, ill-defined, shapeless, blurred.

nec•es•sar•y /nésəseree/ • *adj.* **1** requiring to be done, achieved, etc.; requisite; essential. **2** determined, existing, or happening by natural laws, predestination, etc., not by free will; inevitable. • *n.* (*pl.* **-ies**) [usu. in *pl.*] basic requirements. □□ **nec•es•sar'i•ly** *adv.*

■ *adj.* **1** indispensable, compulsory, vital. **2** certain, inexorable; unavoidable, inescapable. • *n.* see NECESSITY 1a. □□ **necessarily** inevitably, naturally, certainly.

SYNONYM STUDY: necessary

ESSENTIAL, INDISPENSABLE, INEVITABLE, REQUISITE. Food is **essential** to human life, which means that we must have it to survive. *Essential* can also apply to something that makes up the *essence*, or necessary qualities or attributes, of a thing (*good brakes are essential to safe driving*). Clothing is **indispensable** in northern climates, which means that it cannot be done without if the specified or implied purpose—in this case, survival—is to be achieved. **Necessary** applies to something without which a condition cannot be fulfilled (*cooperation was necessary to gather the harvest*), although it generally implies a pressing need rather than absolute indispensability. **Requisite** refers to that which is required by the circumstances (*the requisite skills for a botanist*) and generally describes a requirement that is imposed from the outside rather than an inherent need.

ne•ces•si•tate /nisésitayt/ v.tr. make necessary (esp. as a result) (will necessitate some sacrifice). See synonym study at COMPEL.

■ see ENTAIL v.

ne•ces•si•ty /nisésitee/ n. (pl. –ties) 1 a indispensable thing. b indispensability. 2 imperative need. 3 want; poverty; hardship. □ of necessity unavoidably.

■ 1 a requirement, essential, prerequisite. b unavoidability, inevitability. 2 urgency, emergency, crisis. 3 indigence, need, destitution, difficulty. □ of necessity see necessarily (NECESSARY).

neck /nek/ • n. 1 a part of the body connecting the head to the shoulders. b part of a garment around or close to the neck. 2 something resembling a neck, such as the narrow part of a cavity or vessel, a passage, channel, etc. • v. colloq. kiss and caress amorously. □ neck and neck running even in a race, etc. up to one's neck [often foll. by in] colloq. very deeply involved; very busy.

■ n. 2 see CAPE² n. • v. kiss, smooch. □ neck and neck see LEVEL adj. 3.

neck•er•chief /nékərchif, –cheef/ n. square of cloth worn around the neck.

neck•lace /nékləs/ n. chain or string of beads, precious stones, links, etc., worn as an ornament around the neck.

■ beads, chain, choker.

neck•line /néklin/ n. edge or shape of the opening of a garment at the neck.

neck•tie /néktī/ n. = TIE n. 2.

necro- /nékrō/ comb. form corpse.

nec•ro•man•cy /nékrōmansee/ n. 1 prediction of the future by supposed communication with the dead. 2 witchcraft. □□ nec'ro•man•cer n.

■ see MAGIC n. 1. □□ necromancer see MAGICIAN.

nec•ro•phil•i•a /nékrōfileeə/ n. (also nec•ro•phil•y /nikrófilee/) morbid and esp. erotic attraction to corpses. □□ nec•ro•phile /nékrəfīl/ n. nec•ro•phil•ic adj. ne•croph•i•lism /–krófilizəm/ n.

ne•cro•sis /nekrósis/ n. Med. & Physiol. death of tissue caused by disease or injury, esp. as one of the symptoms of gangrene or pulmonary tuberculosis. □□ ne•crot•ic /–krótik/ adj.

nec•tar /néktər/ n. 1 sugary substance produced by plants and made into honey by bees. 2 Gk. & Rom. mythol. the drink of the gods. 3 drink compared to this. □□ nec'tar•ous adj.

nec•tar•ine /nektəreen/ n. variety of peach with a thin brightly colored smooth skin and firm flesh.

née /nay/ adj. (also nee) born (Mrs. Ann Smith, née Jones).

need /need/ • v.tr. 1 stand in want of; require (needs a new coat). 2 be under the necessity or obligation. • n. 1 requirement. 2 circumstances requiring action; necessity. 3 destitution; poverty. 4 crisis; emergency. □ if need be if required.

■ v. 1 demand, call for; lack, miss. 2 (need to) see GET v. 10b. • n. 1, 2 call, demand;

constraint; essential, requisite; shortage, scarcity. 3, 4 distress, difficulty; deprivation, indigence.

need•ful /néedfóol/ adj. requisite; necessary. □□ need'ful•ly adv.

■ see NECESSARY adj. 1.

nee•dle /néed'l/ • n. 1 a very thin small piece of smooth steel, etc., pointed at one end and with a slit (eye) for thread at the other, used in sewing. b larger plastic, wooden, etc., slender stick without an eye, used in knitting. c slender hooked stick used in crochet. 2 pointer on a dial. 3 end of a hypodermic syringe. 4 pointed rock or peak. 5 leaf of a fir or pine tree. • v.tr. colloq. incite or irritate; provoke (the silence needled him).

■ n. 2 see INDICATOR 1. 5 see SPINE 2. • v. see IRRITATE 1.

nee•dle•point /néed'lpoynt/ n. decorative needlework or lace made with a needle.

need•less /néedlis/ adj. 1 unnecessary. 2 uncalled-for; gratuitous. □□ need'less•ly adv. need'less•ness n.

■ nonessential, superfluous, redundant, useless, excessive, dispensable. □□ needlessly unduly, excessively.

nee•dle•work /néed'lwərk/ n. sewing or embroidery.

needs /needz/ adv. archaic of necessity (must needs decide).

need•y /néedee/ adj. (need•i•er, need•i•est) 1 (of a person) poor; destitute. 2 (of circumstances) characterized by poverty. 3 emotionally impoverished or demanding. □□ need'i•ness n.

■ 1 indigent, poverty-stricken, penniless, disadvantaged.

ne'er /nair/ adv. poet. = NEVER. □ ne'er-do-well n. good-for-nothing person. adj. good-for-nothing.

ne•far•i•ous /nifáireeəs/ adj. wicked; iniquitous. □□ ne•far'i•ous•ly adv. ne•far'i•ous•ness n.

■ see EVIL adj. 1. □□ nefariousness see EVIL n. 2.

ne•gate /nigáyt/ v.tr. 1 nullify; invalidate. 2 deny.

■ 1 see NEUTRALIZE.

ne•ga•tion /nigáyshən/ n. 1 absence or opposite of something actual or positive. 2 act of denying. □□ neg•a•to•ry /négətáwree/ adj.

■ 2 see DENIAL 1.

neg•a•tive /négətiv/ • adj. 1 expressing or implying denial, prohibition, or refusal. 2 (of a person or attitude) lacking positive attributes. 3 marked by the absence of qualities (a negative reaction). 4 opposite to a thing regarded as positive (debt is negative capital). 5 Algebra (of a quantity) less than zero, to be subtracted from others or from zero (opp. POSITIVE). 6 Electr. a of the kind of charge carried by electrons (opp. POSITIVE). b containing or producing such a charge. • n. 1 negative statement, reply, or word. 2 Photog. a image with black and white reversed or colors replaced by complementary ones. b developed film or plate bearing such an image. □□ neg'a•tive•ly adv. neg•a•tiv'i•ty n.

■ *adj.* **1** contradictory, anti, opposing. **2** apathetic, cool, uninterested, unresponsive, pessimistic. **3** see INERT 2.

neg•a•tiv•ism /négətivizəm/ *n.* negative position or attitude; extreme skepticism, criticism, etc.

ne•glect /niglékt/ • *v.tr.* **1** fail to care for or to do; be remiss about (*neglected their duty*). **2** not pay attention to; disregard (*neglected the obvious warning*). • *n.* **1** lack of caring; negligence (*the house suffered from neglect*). **2 a** neglecting. **b** being neglected (*the house fell into neglect*). □□ **ne•glect′ful** *adj.* **ne•glect′ful•ly** *adv.*

■ *v.* **1** disregard, let slide *or* pass, forget, shirk; omit. **2** ignore, slight, overlook; pass by, scorn, cold-shoulder. ■ *n.* **1** laxity, dereliction, default, failure.

SYNONYM STUDY: neglect

DISREGARD, IGNORE, OVERLOOK, SLIGHT. One of the most common reasons why people fail to arrive at work on time is that they **neglect** to set their alarm clocks, a verb that implies a failure to carry out some expected or required action, either intentionally or through carelessness. Some people, of course, choose to **disregard** their employers' rules pertaining to tardiness, which implies a voluntary, and sometimes deliberate, inattention. Others hear the alarm go off and simply **ignore** it, which suggests not only a deliberate decision to **disregard** something but a stubborn refusal to face the facts. No doubt they hope their employers will **overlook** their frequent late arrivals, which implies a failure to see or to take action, which can be either intentional or due to haste or lack of care (*to overlook minor errors*). But they also hope no one will **slight** them for their conduct when it comes to handing out raises and promotions, which means to **disregard** or **neglect** in a disdainful way.

---

neg•li•gee /néglizháy/ *n.* (also **neg•li•gée**, **nég•li•gé**) woman's dressing gown of sheer fabric.

neg•li•gence /néglijəns/ *n.* **1** lack of proper care and attention. **2** culpable carelessness. □□ **neg•li•gent** /-jənt/ *adj.* **neg′li•gent•ly** *adv.*

■ **1** inattention, indifference, dereliction, failure, laxness.

neg•li•gi•ble /néglijibəl/ *adj.* not worth considering; insignificant. □□ **neg′li•gi•bly** *adv.*

■ minor, unimportant, trifling, trivial, inconsequential.

ne•go•ti•ate /nigósheeayt, -seeayt/ *v.* **1** *intr.* discuss in order to reach an agreement. **2** *tr.* arrange (an affair) or bring about (a result) by negotiating. **3** *tr.* find a way over, through, etc. (an obstacle, difficulty, etc.). **4** *tr.* convert (a check, etc.) into money. □□ **ne•go′tia•ble** /-shəbəl, -sheeə-/ *adj.* **ne•go•ti•a•tion** /-áyshən/ *n.* **ne•go′ti•a•tor** *n.*

■ **1** deal, bargain, haggle; debate, mediate. **2** organize, conduct; obtain, accomplish. **3** clear, pass, cross. □□ **negotiation** mediation, arbitration, bargaining; deal. **negotiator** arbiter, moderator.

Ne•gro /néegrō/ • *n.* (*pl.* **-groes**) member of

a dark-skinned race orig. native to Africa. • *adj.* **1** of black people. **2** (as **negro**) *Zool.* black or dark (*negro ant*). ¶The term *black* or *African American* is preferred when referring to people. □□ **Ne′groid** /néegroyd/ *adj.*

neigh /nay/ • *n.* high whinnying sound of a horse. • *v.* **1** *intr.* make such a sound. **2** *tr.* say, cry, etc., with such a sound.

neigh•bor /náybər/ • *n.* **1** person or thing near or living next door to or near or nearest another. **2** fellow human being. • *v.* **1** *tr.* border on; adjoin. **2** *intr.* [often foll. by *on*, *upon*] border; adjoin.

■ *v.* see BORDER *v.* 3a.

neigh•bor•hood /náybərhŏod/ *n.* **1 a** district, esp. one forming a community within a town or city. **b** people of a district; one's neighbors. **2** neighborly feeling or conduct. □ **in the neighborhood of** roughly; about (*paid in the neighborhood of $100*).

■ **1** locality, vicinity, precinct(s). **2** neighborliness. □ **in the neighborhood of** approximately, around, nearly.

neigh•bor•ly /náybərlee/ *adj.* characteristic of a good neighbor; friendly; kind. □□ **neigh′bor•li•ness** *n.*

■ cordial, warm, sociable, thoughtful, helpful, courteous.

nei•ther /néethər, nîth / • *adj. & pron.* [foll. by sing. verb] not the one nor the other (of two); not either. • *adv.* **1** not either; not on the one hand (foll. by *nor. neither knowing nor caring*). **2** also not (*if you do not, neither shall I*): *a com. archaic* nor yet, nor.

nel•son /nélsən/ *n.* wrestling hold in which one arm is passed under the opponent's arm from behind and the hand is applied to the neck (**half nelson**), or both arms and hands are applied (**full nelson**).

nem•a•tode /némətōd/ *n.* parasitic or free-living worm with a slender unsegmented cylindrical shape. (Also called **round-worm**.)

nem•e•sis /némisis/ *n.* (*pl.* **nem•e•ses** /-seez/) **1** retributive justice. **2 a** downfall caused by this. **b** agent of such a downfall. **3** something that one cannot conquer, achieve, etc.

neo- /nee-ō/ *comb. form* **1** new; modern. **2** new form of.

ne•o•clas•si•cal /nee-ōklásikəl/ *adj.* (also **ne•o•clas•sic** /-ik/) of or relating to a revival of a classical style in the arts, etc. □□ **ne•o•clas•si•cism** /-sisizəm/ *n.*

ne•o•co•lo•ni•al•ism /nee-ōkəlóneeəlizəm/ *n.* use of economic, political, or other pressures to control or influence other countries, esp. former dependencies.

ne•o•dym•i•um /nee-ōdímeeəm/ *n. Chem.* silver-gray metallic element used in coloring glass, etc. ¶Symb.: **Nd**.

ne•o•lith•ic /nee-əlíthik/ *adj.* of the later Stone Age, when ground or polished stone weapons and implements prevailed.

ne•ol•o•gism /nee-óləjizəm/ *n.* **1** new word or expression. **2** coining or use of new words.

■ coinage.

ne•on /nee-on/ *n.* *Chem.* inert gaseous element giving an orange glow when electricity is passed through it (*neon light, neon sign*). ¶Symb.: **Ne**.

ne•o•phyte /neeəfīt/ *n.* **1** new convert, esp. to a religious faith. **2** beginner; novice.
■ **1** proselyte. **2** see NOVICE.

ne•o•prene /nee-əpreen/ *n.* synthetic rubber-like polymer.

Ne•pal•i /nipawlee/ • *n.* (*pl.* same or **Ne•pal•is**) (also **Ne•pal•ese** /népəleez, -leess/) **1 a** native or national of Nepal in Central Asia. **b** person of Nepali descent. **2** language of Nepal. • *adj.* of Nepal or its language or people.

neph•ew /néfyoō/ *n.* son of one's brother or sister, or of one's brother-in-law or sister-in-law.

ne•phrit•ic /nəfritik/ *adj.* **1** of or in the kidneys; renal. **2** of or relating to nephritis.

ne•phri•tis /nefrítis/ *n.* inflammation of the kidneys. (Also called **Bright's disease**).

ne plus ul•tra /náy plooss oóltraa, nē plus últrə/ *n.* **1** furthest attainable point. **2** culmination, acme, or perfection.

nep•o•tism /népətizəm/ *n.* favoritism to relatives in conferring offices or privileges.
■ see FAVORITISM.

Nep•tune /néptoōn, –tyoōn/ *n.* **1** eighth planet from the sun. **2** *Gk. mythol.* god of the sea.

nep•tu•ni•um /neptoōneeəm, –tyoō–/ *n.* *Chem.* radioactive transuranic metallic element. ¶Symb.: **Np**.

nerd /nərd/ *n.* (also **nurd**) *sl.* **1** foolish, feeble, or uninteresting person. **2** person intellectually talented but socially unskilled. □□ **nerd•y** *adj.*

nerve /nərv/ • *n.* **1** fiber or bundle of fibers that transmits impulses of sensation or motion between the brain or spinal cord and other parts of the body. **2 a** coolness in danger; bravery. **b** *colloq.* impudence. **3** [in *pl.*] heightened nervousness or sensitivity; mental or physical stress. • *v.tr.* give strength, vigor, or courage to. □ **get on a person's nerves** irritate a person. **nerve cell** nerve cell transmitting impulses in nerve tissue. **nerve center** center of control. **nerve gas** poisonous gas affecting the nervous system. **nerve-racking** (also **nerve-wrack•ing**) stressful, frightening.
■ *n.* **1** (*attrib.*) neuro–. **2 a** courage, daring; assurance, will, *colloq.* guts, grit. **b** effrontery, impertinence, insolence. **3** (*nerves*) tension, anxiety, worry, fright. □ **get on a person's nerves** annoy, upset; see also IRK. **nerve-racking** harrowing, agonizing, distressing.

nerve•less /nórvlis/ *adj.* **1** inert; lacking vigor. **2** confident; not nervous. □□ **nerve′less•ly** *adv.* **nerve′less•ness** *n.*

ner•vous /nórvəs/ *adj.* **1** timid or anxious. **2 a** excitable; highly strung. **b** resulting from this (*nervous headache*). **3** affecting or acting on the nerves. □ **nervous breakdown** period of mental illness. **nervous system** the body's network of specialized cells that transmit nerve impulses between parts of the

body (cf. *central nervous system*). □□ **ner′vous•ly** *adv.* **ner′vous•ness** *n.*
■ **1, 2** tense, agitated, flustered, distressed, worried, edgy, uneasy. **3** neurological.

nerv•y /nórvee/ *adj.* (**nerv•i•er, nerv•i•est**) bold; impudent; pushy.
■ see IMPERTINENT.

-ness /nis/ *suffix* forming nouns from adjectives, etc., expressing state or condition, or an instance of this (*happiness*).

nest /nest/ • *n.* **1** structure or place where a bird lays eggs and shelters its young. **2** any creature's breeding place or lair. **3** snug retreat or shelter. **4** group or set of similar objects, often of different sizes and fitting together for storage (*nest of tables*). • *v.* **1** *intr.* use or build a nest. **2** *intr.* (of objects) fit together or one inside another. **3** *tr.* (usu. as **nested** *adj.*) establish in or as in a nest. □ **nest egg** sum of money saved for the future.
■ *n.* **1** roost, perch, aerie. **2, 3** den, refuge, hideaway.

nes•tle /nésəl/ *v.* **1** *intr.* settle oneself comfortably. **2** *intr.* press oneself against another in affection, etc. **3** *tr.* push (a head or shoulder, etc.) affectionately or snugly. **4** *intr.* lie half hidden or embedded.
■ **1, 2** cuddle, snuggle, huddle, curl up, nuzzle.

nest•ling /nésling, nést–/ *n.* bird too young to leave its nest.

net[1] /net/ • *n.* **1** open-meshed fabric of cord, rope, etc. **2** piece of net used esp. to restrain, contain, or delimit, or to catch fish, etc. **3** structure with net used in various games, esp. forming the goal in soccer, hockey, etc., and dividing the court in tennis, etc. **4** = NETWORK. • *v.* (**net•ted, net•ting**) *tr.* cover, confine, or catch with a net.
■ *n.* **1** webbing, openwork, lacework. **2** trammel, trawl, fishnet, butterfly net, mosquito net. • *v.* capture, trap.

net[2] /net/ • *adj.* **1** remaining after all necessary deductions. **2** (of an effect, result, etc.) ultimate, effective. • *v.tr.* (**net•ted, net•ting**) gain or yield as profit, weight, etc. □ **net profit** actual gain after expenses have been paid.
■ *adj.* **1** clear, after taxes, take-home. **2** final, end, concluding. • *v.* make, realize, clear.

neth•er /néthər/ *adj. archaic* = LOWER 2. □ **nether regions** (or **world**) hell; the underworld.
■ □ **nether regions** see HELL 1.

Neth•er•land•er /néthərlandər/ *n.* **1** native or national of the Netherlands. **2** person of Dutch descent.

net•su•ke /nétsoōkee/ *n.* (*pl.* same or **net•su•kes**) carved buttonlike ornament, esp. of ivory or wood.

net•ting /néting/ *n.* **1** netted fabric. **2** piece of this.

net•tle /nét′l/ • *n.* plant with jagged leaves covered with stinging hairs. • *v.tr.* **1** irritate; provoke. **2** sting with nettles.

net•tle•some /nét′lsəm/ *adj.* **1** difficult. **2** annoying.
■ see TROUBLESOME.

net•work /nétwərk/ • *n.* **1** arrangement of intersecting horizontal and vertical lines.

2 complex system of railways, roads, people, computers, etc., that interconnect or communicate. 3 group of broadcasting stations connected for simultaneous broadcast of a program. • v. 1 tr. link (machines, esp. computers) to operate interactively. 2 intr. establish a network. 3 intr. be a member of a network (esp. people).

■ n. 1 see NET[1] n. 1. 2 arrangement, grid, web.

neu•ral /nŏorəl, nyŏor–/ adj. of or relating to a nerve or the central nervous system.

neu•ral•gia /nŏoráljə, nyŏo–/ n. intense intermittent pain along a nerve, esp. in the head or face. □□ **neu•ral′gic** adj.

neu•ri•tis /nŏorítis, nyŏo–/ n. inflammation of a nerve or nerves. □□ **neu•rit′ic** /–rítik/ adj.

neuro- /nŏorō, nyŏorō/ comb. form nerve or nerves.

neu•rol•o•gy /nŏoráaləjee, nyŏo–/ n. study of the nervous system. □□ **neu•ro•log•i•cal** /–rəlójikəl/ adj. **neu•rol′o•gist** n.

neu•ron /nŏoron, nyŏor–/ n. (also **neu•rone** /–ōn/) specialized cell transmitting nerve impulses; nerve cell. □□ **neu•ron′ic** adj.

neu•ro•sis /nŏorósis, nyŏo–/ n. (pl. **neu•ro•ses** /–seez/) mental illness marked by anxiety, obsessions, compulsive acts, etc., caused by a disorder of the nervous system usu. without organic change.

neu•ro•sur•ger•y /nŏorōsórjəree, nyŏor–/ n. surgery performed on the brain or spinal cord. □□ **neu•ro•sur•geon** /–jən/ n. **neu•ro•sur′gi•cal** adj.

neu•rot•ic /nŏorótik, nyŏo–/ • adj. 1 caused by or relating to neurosis. 2 (of a person) suffering from neurosis. 3 colloq. abnormally sensitive or obsessive. • n. neurotic person. □□ **neu•rot′i•cal•ly** adv.

■ adj. 2, 3 unstable, disturbed, irrational, anxious, nervous.

neut. abbr. neuter.

neu•ter /nŏotər, nyŏo–/ • adj. 1 Gram. (of a noun, etc.) neither masculine nor feminine. 2 (of a plant) having neither pistils nor stamen. 3 (of an insect, animal, etc.) sexually undeveloped; castrated or spayed. • n. 1 Gram. neuter word. 2 a nonfertile insect. b castrated animal. • v.tr. castrate or spay.

■ adj. 2 asexual, sexless. 3 asexual, sexless; neutered • v. desex, fix, geld, alter.

neu•tral /nŏotrəl, nyŏo–/ • adj. 1 not helping nor supporting either of two sides; impartial. 2 indistinct; vague; indeterminate. 3 (of a gear) in which the engine is disconnected from the driven parts. 4 (of colors) not strong nor positive; gray or beige. 5 Chem. neither acid nor alkaline. 6 Electr. neither positive nor negative. • n. 1 a neutral nation, person, etc. b subject of a neutral nation. 2 neutral gear. □□ **neu•tral•i•ty** /–trálitee/ n. **neu′tral•ly** adv.

■ adj. 1 nonbelligerent, noncombatant; nonaligned, unaffiliated, unallied; indifferent, unbiased. 2, 4 dull, washed-out, pale, indefinite, taupe, ecru.

neu•tral•ize /nŏotrəliz, nyŏo–/ v.tr. 1 make neutral. 2 counterbalance; render ineffective by an opposite force or effect. □□ **neu′tral•iz•er** n.

■ 2 void, annul, counterbalance, offset, equalize; compensate for.

neu•tri•no /nŏotreenō, nyŏo–/ n. (pl. **–nos**) elementary particle with zero electric charge and probably zero mass.

neu•tron /nŏotron, nyŏo–/ n. uncharged elementary particle of about the same mass as a proton. □ **neutron bomb** bomb producing neutrons and little blast, destroying life but not property.

Nev. abbr. Nevada.

nev•er /névər/ adv. 1 at no time; on no occasion; not ever. 2 not at all. □ **never-never land** imaginary utopian place.

■ 1 not at any time, not at all. 2 by no means, on no account, in no case, not in the least.

nev•er•more /névərmáwr/ adv. at no future time.

nev•er•the•less /névərthəlés/ adv. in spite of that; notwithstanding; all the same.

■ still, yet, nonetheless, regardless, even so, but, anyway.

ne•vus /néevəs/ n. (pl. **ne•vi** /–vī/) 1 raised red birthmark. 2 = MOLE[2].

new /nŏo, nyŏo/ • adj. 1 a of recent origin or arrival. b made, invented, discovered, acquired, or experienced recently or now for the first time. 2 in original condition; not worn or used. 3 a renewed or reformed. b reinvigorated. 4 different from a recent previous one. 5 unfamiliar or strange. 6 a modern. b newfangled. 7 advanced in method or theory. • adv. [usu. in comb.] 1 newly, recently (new-baked). 2 anew, afresh. □ **New Age** set of beliefs intended to replace traditional Western Culture, with alternative approaches to religion, medicine, the environment, music, etc. **new moon** moon when first seen as a crescent after conjunction with the sun. **New Testament** part of the Bible concerned with the life and teachings of Christ and his earliest followers. **New World** N. and S. America. **New Year's Day** January 1. **New Year's Eve** December 31. □□ **new′ish** adj. **new′ness** n.

■ adj. 1 a brand-new, newly arrived. b novel, original, innovative. 2 fresh, mint. 3 revitalized, reborn, changed. 4 fresh, (an)other. 5 unknown, unusual, unexplored; experimental. 6, 7 latest, avant-garde, innovative, contemporary.

new•born /nŏobawrn, nyŏo–/ adj. 1 (of a child, etc.) recently born. 2 spiritually reborn; regenerated.

new•com•er /nŏokumər, nyŏo–/ n. 1 person who has recently arrived. 2 beginner in some activity.

■ 1 alien, immigrant, foreigner. 2 amateur, novice, greenhorn.

new•el /nŏoəl, nyŏo–/ n. 1 supporting central post of winding stairs. 2 top or bottom supporting post of a stair rail.

new•fan•gled /nŏofánggəld, nyŏo–/ adj. derog. different from what one is used to; objectionably new.

■ see MODERN adj.

New•found•land /nŏófəndlənd, noofówndlənd, nyŏ͞o–, –land, –fənd–, nyŏ͞o–/ *n*. (in full **New•found•land dog**) very large dog with a thick, usu. black, coarse coat.

new•ly /nŏ͞olee, nyŏ͞o–/ *adv*. **1** recently. **2** afresh, anew. **3** in a new or different manner.

news /nŏ͞oz, nyŏ͞oz/ *n.pl*. [usu. treated as *sing.*] **1** information about important or interesting recent events, esp. when published or broadcast. **2** [prec. by *the*] broadcast report of news. **3** newly received or noteworthy information.

■ **1, 3** word, advice, *colloq*. info; report, (press) release; rumor, scandal. **2** (*the news*) newscast, telecast; news brief, (news) bulletin.

news•cast /nŏ͞ozkast, nyŏ͞oz–/ *n*. radio or television broadcast of news reports. □□ **news' cast•er** *n*.

news•deal•er /nŏ͞ozdeelər, nyŏ͞oz–/ *n*. person who sells newspapers, magazines, etc.

news•let•ter /nŏ͞ozletər, nyŏ͞oz–/ *n*. concise periodical of news, events, etc., of special interest.

news•pa•per /nŏ͞ozpaypər, nyŏ͞oz–, nŏ͞os–, nyŏ͞os–/ *n*. **1** printed publication (usu. daily or weekly) containing news, advertisements, correspondence, etc. **2** newsprint.

■ **1** see PUBLICATION 1b.

news•print /nŏ͞ozprint, nyŏ͞oz–/ *n*. low-quality paper on which newspapers are printed.

news•stand /nŏ͞ozstand, nyŏ͞oz–/ *n*. stall for the sale of newspapers, magazines, etc.

news•week•ly /nŏ͞ozweeklee, nyŏ͞oz–/ *n*. periodical published weekly that summarizes current events.

news•wor•thy /nŏ͞ozwərthee, nyŏ͞oz–/ *adj*. noteworthy as news.

news•y /nŏ͞ozee, nyŏ͞o–/ *adj*. (**news•i•er, news•i•est**) *colloq*. full of news.

newt /nŏ͞ot, nyŏ͞ot/ *n*. small amphibian having a well-developed tail.

New Test. *abbr*. New Testament.

new•ton /nŏ͞ot'n, nyŏ͞o–/ *n. Physics* SI unit of force that, acting on a mass of one kilogram, increases its velocity by one meter per second every second. ¶Abbr.: **N**.

New Zea•land•er /nŏ͞ozeelandər, nyŏ͞o–/ *n*. **1** native or national of New Zealand, an island group in the Pacific. **2** person of New Zealand descent.

next /nekst/ • *adj*. **1** being or positioned or living nearest. **2** nearest in order of time. • *adv*. **1** in the nearest place or degree (*put it next to mine*). **2** on the first or soonest occasion. • *n*. next person or thing. □ **next door** in the next house or room. **next to** almost (*next to nothing left*).

■ *adj*. **1** see *adjoining* (ADJOIN). **2** see SUBSEQUENT.

nex•us /néksəs/ *n*. (*pl*. same) connected group or series.

Nez Per•cé /náy persáy/ *n*. (also **Nez Per•ce** /néz pérs, nés pérs/) *n*. **1 a** N. American people native to the northwestern US. **b** member of this people. **2** language of this people.

NH *abbr*. New Hampshire (also in official postal use).

Ni *symb. Chem.* nickel.

ni•a•cin /níəsin/ *n*. = NICOTINIC ACID.

nib /nib/ *n*. pen point.

■ cap, tip.

nib•ble /níbəl/ • *v*. **1** *tr. & intr*. **a** take small bites at. **b** eat in small amounts. **c** bite at gently or cautiously or playfully. **2** *intr*. [foll. by *at*] show cautious interest in. • *n*. **1** very small amount of food. **2** *Computing* half a byte, i.e., 4 bits.

■ *v*. **1** see *pick at* (PICK¹). • *n*. **1** see MORSEL.

nibs /nibz/ *n*. □ **his nibs** *joc. colloq*. mock title used for an important or self-important person.

ni•cad /nícad/ • *adj*. nickel and cadmium. • *n*. nickel and cadmium battery.

nice /nis/ *adj*. **1** pleasant, satisfactory. **2** (of a person) kind, good-natured. **3** *iron*. bad or awkward (*a nice mess you've made*). **4** fine or subtle (*nice distinction*). **5** fastidious; delicately sensitive. □□ **nice'ly** *adv*. **nice'ness** *n*.

■ **1, 2** agreeable, commendable; amiable, friendly, gracious. **3** see AWFUL 1a, b. **4, 5** exquisite, flawless; attentive, discriminating, perceptive; complex, intricate.

ni•ce•ty /nísitee/ *n*. (*pl*. **–ties**) **1** subtle distinction or detail. **2** precision, accuracy. **3** [in *pl*.] refinements, trimmings.

niche /nich, neesh/ *n*. **1** shallow recess, esp. in a wall to contain a statue, etc. **2** comfortable or suitable position in life or employment.

■ **1** bay, slot, cell, hole, pigeonhole, cubbyhole; see also NOOK. **2** pigeonhole; see PLACE *n*. 4.

nick /nik/ • *n*. small cut or notch. • *v.tr*. make a nick or nicks in. □ **in the nick of time** only just in time.

■ *n*. chip, gouge, scratch; dent; flaw, mark. • *v*. cut, notch, chip, gouge, gash, scratch, dent, score.

nick•el /níkəl/ • *n*. **1** *Chem*. malleable silver-white metallic element used in special steels, in magnetic alloys, and as a catalyst. ¶Symb.: **Ni**. **2** five-cent coin. • *v.tr*. coat with nickel. □ **nickel-and-dime** *adj*. involving a small amount of money; insignificant; trivial. *v.tr*. weaken (one's financial position) by continued small expenses, bills, etc.

nick•el•o•de•on /níkəlódeeən/ *n. colloq*. **1** early movie theater, esp. one with admission priced at 5 cents. **2** jukebox.

nick•name /níknaym/ • *n*. familiar or humorous name given to a person or thing instead of or as well as the real name. • *v.tr*. give a nickname to.

■ *n*. pet name, *colloq*. handle, tag, *sl*. moniker.

nic•o•tine /níkəteen/ *n*. poisonous alkaloid present in tobacco.

nic•o•tin•ic ac•id /níkətinik/ *n*. vitamin of the B complex, found in milk, liver, and yeast, a deficiency of which causes pellagra. (Also called **niacin**).

nic•ti•tate /níktitayt/ *v.intr*. close and open the eyes; blink or wink. □ **nictitating membrane** transparent third eyelid in amphibians, birds, etc., that protects the eye without loss of vision.

niece /nees/ *n.* daughter of one's brother or sister, or of one's brother-in-law or sister-in-law.

niels•bohr•i•um /neelzbáwreeəm/ *n.* artificially produced radioactive element. ¶Symb.: **Ns**.

nif•ty /niftee/ *adj.* (**nif•ti•er, nif•ti•est**) *colloq.* 1 clever; adroit. 2 smart; stylish.
■ 1 skillful, neat; healthy, apt, suitable; excellent, fine. 2 chic, fashionable, snappy, *colloq.* classy; see also DAPPER 1.

nig•gard•ly /nígərdlee/ • *adj.* 1 stingy; parsimonious. 2 meager; scanty. • *adv.* in a stingy or meager manner. □□ **nig′gard•li•ness** *n.*

nig•gle /nígəl/ *v.intr.* 1 be overattentive to details. 2 find fault in a petty way. □□ **nig′gling** *adj.*
■ moan, nag, complain, *colloq.* grouse, bitch, *sl.* kvetch.

nigh /nī/ *adv., prep., & adj. archaic* or *dial.* near.

night /nīt/ *n.* 1 period of darkness between one day and the next; time from sunset to sunrise. 2 nightfall. 3 darkness of night.
□ **night owl** *colloq.* person active at night.
■ 1, 3 nighttime, evening; gloom. 2 sunset, twilight, dusk.

night•cap /nítkap/ *n.* 1 *hist.* cap worn in bed. 2 hot or alcoholic drink taken at bedtime.

night•club /nítklub/ *n.* club that is open at night and provides refreshment and entertainment.

night•fall /nítfawl/ *n.* onset of night; end of daylight.
■ see DUSK.

night•gown /nítgown/ *n.* woman's or child's loose garment worn in bed.

night•hawk /níthawk/ *n.* nocturnal bird related to the whippoorwill.

night•in•gale /nítn'gayl/ *n.* small reddish-brown bird, of which the male sings melodiously, esp. at night.

night•life /nítlīf/ *n.* entertainment available at night in a town.

night•ly /nítlee/ • *adj.* 1 happening, done, or existing in the night. 2 recurring every night. • *adv.* every night.
■ *adj.* 1 nocturnal, bedtime. • *adv.* night after night; after dark, after sunset; nocturnally.

night•mare /nítmair/ *n.* 1 frightening dream. 2 *colloq.* terrifying or very unpleasant experience or situation. 3 haunting or obsessive fear. □□ **night′mar•ish** *adj.*
■ 2 see ORDEAL. □□ **nightmarish** frightening, terrifying, alarming, *colloq.* creepy, scary.

night•shirt /nítshərt/ *n.* long shirt worn in bed.

night•spot /nítspot/ *n.* nightclub.

night•stick /nítstik/ *n.* policeman's club.

night•time /níttīm/ *n.* time of darkness.

NIH *abbr.* National Institutes of Health.

ni•hil•ism /ní-ilizəm, nee-/ *n.* rejection of all religious and moral principles. □□ **ni′hil•ist** *n.* **ni•hil•is′tic** *adj.*
■ □□ **nihilist** skeptic, doubter, cynic.

-nik /nik/ *suffix* forming nouns denoting a person associated with a specified thing or quality (*beatnik, refusenik*).

nil /nil/ *n.* nothing; no number or amount.
■ zero, love, naught, goose-egg, *sl.* zilch.

nim•ble /nímbəl/ *adj.* (**nim•bler, nim•blest**) 1 quick and light in movement or action; agile. 2 (of the mind) quick to comprehend; clever, versatile. □□ **nim′bly** *adv.*
■ 1 lively, active, energetic, adroit. 2 alert, quick-witted, intelligent.

nim•bus /nímbəs/ *n.* (*pl.* **nim•bi** /-bī/ or **nim•bus•es**) 1 **a** bright cloud or halo investing a deity or person or thing. **b** halo of a saint, etc. 2 *Meteorol.* rain cloud.

NIMBY /nímbee/ *abbr. colloq.* not in my backyard.

nin•com•poop /nínkəmpōōp/ *n.* simpleton; fool.
■ see FOOL *n.* 1.

nine /nīn/ • *n.* 1 one more than eight, or one less than ten. 2 symbol for this (9, ix, IX). • *adj.* that amount to nine. □□ **ninth** /nīnth/ *n. & adj.*

9/11 /nínilévən/ *n. colloq.* September 11, (2001), the date on which the World Trade Center and the Pentagon were attacked by terrorists.

nine•fold /nínfōld/ *adj. & adv.* nine times as much or as many.

nine•teen /nínteén/ • *n.* 1 one more than eighteen, nine more than ten. 2 symbol for this (19, xix, XIX). • *adj.* that amount to nineteen. □□ **nine′teenth** *n. & adj.*

nine•ty /níntee/ *n.* (*pl.* **-ties**) 1 product of nine and ten. 2 symbol for this (90, xc, XC). 3 [in *pl.*] numbers from 90 to 99, esp. years. □□ **nine′ti•eth** *n. & adj.*

nin•ja /nínjə/ *n.* person skilled in a Japanese martial art emphasizing stealth.

nin•ny /nínee/ *n.* (*pl.* **-nies**) foolish or simple-minded person.
■ see FOOL *n.* 1.

ni•o•bi•um /nīóbeeəm/ *n. Chem.* rare gray-blue metallic element used in alloys for superconductors. ¶Symb.: **Nb**.

nip[1] /nip/ • *v.tr.* (**nipped, nip•ping**) 1 pinch, squeeze, or bite sharply. 2 remove by pinching, etc. 3 (of the cold, etc.) cause pain or harm to. • *n.* 1 **a** pinch, sharp squeeze. **b** bite. 2 biting cold. □ **nip and tuck** neck and neck. **nip in the bud** suppress or destroy (esp. an idea) at an early stage.
• *v.* 1, 2 nibble; snip, clip, tweak. 3 sting, bite, hurt. • *n.* 1 tweak, snip; nibble. 2 iciness, frost; sharpness. □ **nip and tuck** tied, equal, *colloq.* even-steven; see also CLOSE[1] *adj.* 5. **nip in the bud** stop, arrest; squelch, put down.

nip[2] /nip/ • *n.* small quantity of liquor. • *v.intr.* (**nipped, nip•ping**) drink liquor.
■ *n.* taste, drop, sip, finger, tot.

nip•per /nípər/ *n.* 1 person or thing that nips. 2 claw of a crab, lobster, etc. 3 [in *pl.*] any tool for gripping or cutting, e.g., forceps or pincers.
■ 3 (*nippers*) tweezers, pliers.

nip•ple /nípəl/ *n.* 1 small projection in which the mammary ducts of either sex of mammals terminate and from which in females milk is secreted for the young. 2 mouthpiece of a feeding bottle or pacifier. 3 device like a nipple in shape or function.

nip•py /nípee/ *adj.* (**nip•pi•er, nip•pi•est**)

colloq. **1** chilly, cold. **2** tending to nip, as a dog.

nir•va•na /nərváanə, neer–/ *n.* (in Buddhism) perfect bliss attained by the extinction of individuality.

■ see PARADISE 2.

ni•sei /néesay, neesáy/ *n.* (also **Ni′sei**) American whose parents were immigrants from Japan.

nit /nit/ *n.* egg or young form of a louse or other parasitic insect.

ni•ter /nítər/ *n.* saltpeter; potassium nitrate.

nit•pick /nítpik/ *v.intr. colloq.* find fault in a petty manner. □□ **nit′pick•er** *n.* **nit′pick•ing** *n.*

■ see QUIBBLE *v.*

ni•trate /nítrayt/ • *n.* **1** any salt or ester of nitric acid. **2** potassium or sodium nitrate as a fertilizer. • *v.tr. Chem.* treat, combine, or impregnate with nitric acid. □□ **ni•tra′tion** /–áyshən/ *n.*

ni•tric /nítrik/ *adj.* of or containing nitrogen. □ **nitric acid** colorless corrosive poisonous liquid. ¶Chem. formula: HNO_3.

nitro– /nítrō/ *comb. form* of or containing nitric acid, niter, or nitrogen.

ni•tro•gen /nítrəjən/ *n. Chem.* colorless, tasteless, odorless gaseous element that forms four-fifths of the atmosphere. ¶Symb.: N. □□ **ni•trog•e•nous** /–trójinəs/ *adj.*

ni•tro•glyc•er•in /nítrōglísərin/ *n.* (also **ni′ tro•glyc•er•ine**) explosive yellow liquid made by reacting glycerol with sulfuric and nitric acids.

ni•trous ox•ide /nítrəs/ *n.* colorless gas used as an anesthetic (= *laughing gas*) and as an aerosol propellant. ¶ Chem. formula: N_2O.

nit•ty-grit•ty /níteegrítee/ *n. sl.* realities or practical details of a matter.

nit•wit /nítwit/ *n. colloq.* stupid person.

■ see FOOL *n.* 1.

nix /niks/ *sl.* • *n.* nothing. • *v.tr.* **1** cancel. **2** reject.

■ *n.* see ZERO *n.* 1. • *v.* **2** see VETO *v.*

NJ *abbr.* New Jersey (in official postal use).

NLRB *abbr.* National Labor Relations Board.

NM *abbr.* New Mexico (in official postal use).

N.Mex. *abbr.* New Mexico.

No *symb. Chem.* nobelium.

No. *abbr.* **1** number. **2** North.

no[1] /nō/ *adj.* **1** not any (*there is no excuse, no two of them are alike*). **2** not a; quite other than (*is no fool, is no part of my plan*). **3** hardly any (*did it in no time*). **4** used elliptically as a slogan, notice, etc., to forbid, reject, or deplore the thing specified (*no parking*). □ **no-brainer** problem, question, examination, etc., that requires very little thought. **no-fault** (of insurance) valid regardless of the allocation of blame for an accident, etc. **no-go** impossible, hopeless. **no man's land 1** *Mil.* space between two opposing armies. **2** area not assigned to any owner. **3** area of uncertainty. **no-no** *colloq.* thing not possible or acceptable. **no-win** of or designating a situation in which success is impossible.

no[2] /nō/ • *adv.* **1** equivalent to a negative sentence: the answer to your question is neg-

ative; your request or command will not be complied with; the statement made or course of action intended or conclusion arrived at is not correct or satisfactory; the negative statement made is correct. **2** [foll. by *compar.*] by no amount; not at all (*no better than before*). • *n.* (*pl.* **noes** or **nos**) **1** utterance of the word *no.* **2** denial or refusal. **3** negative vote.

NOAA /nóə/ *abbr.* National Oceanic and Atmospheric Administration.

No•bel•ist /nōbélist/ *n.* winner of a Nobel prize.

no•bel•i•um /nōbéleeəm/ *n. Chem.* radioactive metallic element. ¶Symb.: **No**.

No•bel prize /nōbél/ *n.* any of six international prizes awarded annually for physics, chemistry, physiology or medicine, literature, economics, and the promotion of peace.

no•bil•i•ty /nōbílitee/ *n.* (*pl.* **–ties**) **1** nobleness of character, mind, birth, or rank. **2** class of nobles; aristocracy.

■ **1** dignity, greatness, glory; integrity, goodness, character; position, class, blue blood. **2** (*the nobility*) the élite, the ruling class(es), *colloq.* the upper crust.

no•ble /nóbəl/ • *adj.* (**no•bler**, **nob•lest**) **1** belonging by rank, title, or birth to the aristocracy. **2** of excellent character; magnanimous. **3** of imposing appearance; splendid. **4** excellent; admirable. • *n.* nobleman or noblewoman. □□ **no′ble•ness** *n.*

■ *adj.* **1** highborn, upper-class, titled, high-ranking, lordly, blue-blood(ed). **2** upright, righteous, honorable, principled. **3, 4** magnificent, impressive, stately; distinguished, honored. • *n.* aristocrat, patrician, lord, lady.

no•ble•man /nóbəlmən/ *n.* (*pl.* **–men**) man of noble rank or birth; peer.

no•blesse o•blige /nóblés ōbléezh/ *n.* privilege entails responsibility.

no•ble•wom•an /nóbəlwŏomən/ *n.* (*pl.* **–wom•en**) woman of noble rank or birth; peeress.

no•bod•y /nóbodee, –budee, –bədee/ • *pron.* no person. • *n.* (*pl.* **–ies**) person of no importance, authority, or position.

■ *pron.* no one; not anyone. • *n.* nonentity, unknown, zero, nothing; see also COG 2.

noc•tur•nal /noktɜ́rnəl/ *adj.* of or in the night; done or active by night.

■ nightly, nighttime.

noc•turne /nóktərn/ *n. Mus.* short romantic composition, usu. for piano.

nod /nod/ • *v.* (**nod•ded**, **nod•ding**) **1** *intr.* incline one's head slightly and briefly in greeting, assent, or command. **2** *intr.* let one's head fall forward in drowsiness. **3** *tr.* incline (one's head). **4** *tr.* signify (assent, etc.) by a nod. • *n.* nodding of the head, esp. as a sign to proceed, etc. □ **nod off** *colloq.* fall asleep.

■ *v.* **1, 4** say yes; consent, agree; (*nod at*) greet, acknowledge. **2** doze (off), nap. **3** see INCLINE *v.* 3, SWAY *v.* 1. • *n.* signal, cue, indication; approval; consent, acquiescence, *colloq.* OK. □ **nod off** see NOD *v.* 2 above.

node /nōd/ *n.* **1** *Bot.* **a** part of a plant stem from which leaves emerge. **b** knob on a root or branch. **2** *Anat.* natural swelling in an organ or part of the body. **3** *Physics* point of minimum disturbance in a standing wave system. **4** component in a computer network. □□ **nod′al** *adj.*

■ **2** see SWELLING.

nod•ule /nójōōl/ *n.* **1** small, rounded lump. **2** small swelling or aggregation of cells, e.g., a small tumor, node, or ganglion. □□ **nod•u•lar** /–jələr/ *adj.*

■ **2** see SWELLING.

No•el /nō-él/ *n.* **1** Christmas. **2** (also **noel**) Christmas carol.

nog•gin /nógin/ *n.* **1** small mug. **2** *sl.* head.

noise /noyz/ • *n.* **1** sound, esp. a loud or unpleasant or undesired one. **2** irregular fluctuations accompanying a transmitted signal but not relevant to it. • *v. tr.* [usu. in *passive*] make public; spread abroad (a person's fame or a fact).

■ *n.* **1** clamor, din, thunder, uproar, racket; discordance, cacophony. • *v.* make known, circulate, rumor.

noise•less /nóyzlis/ *adj.* making little or no noise. □□ **noise′less•ly** *adv.*

■ silent, mute, still, hushed, muffled.

noi•some /nóysəm/ *adj.* **1** harmful; noxious. **2** evil-smelling.

■ **1** see BAD *adj.* 3. **2** see SMELLY.

nois•y /nóyzee/ *adj.* (**nois•i•er, nois•i•est**) **1** full of noise. **2** making much noise. □□ **nois′i•ness** *n.*

■ loud, deafening, ear-splitting, jarring, grating, harsh.

no•mad /nómad/ • *n.* **1** member of a tribe roaming place to place for pasture. **2** wanderer. • *adj.* **1** living as a nomad. **2** wandering. □□ **no•mad′ic** /–mádik/ *adj.*

■ **2** see *rover* (ROVE). □□ **nomadic** see *traveling* (TRAVEL).

nom de plume /nóm də plōōm/ *n.* (*pl.* **noms de plume** *pronunc.* same) pen name.

■ see PSEUDONYM.

no•men•cla•ture /nómənklaychər, nōménkləchər/ *n.* **1** person's or community's system of names for things. **2** terminology of a science, etc.

■ **2** see TERMINOLOGY.

nom•i•nal /nóminəl/ *adj.* **1** existing in name only; not real or actual (*nominal ruler*). **2** (of a sum of money, rent, etc.) virtually nothing; much below the actual value of a thing. **3** of or in names (*nominal and essential distinctions*). **4** of or as or like a noun. □□ **nom′i•nal•ly** *adv.*

■ **1** titular, so-called, self-styled; puppet, figurehead. **2** insignificant, trivial, minor; derisory.

nom•i•nate /nóminayt/ *v. tr.* **1** propose (a candidate) for election. **2** appoint to an office. **3** name or appoint (a date or place). □□ **nom•i•na•tion** /–náyshən/ *n.* **nom′i•na•tor** *n.*

■ select, designate, recommend, present.

nom•i•na•tive /nóminətiv/ • *n. Gram.* **1** case of nouns, pronouns, and adjectives, expressing the subject of a verb. **2** word in this case. • *adj. Gram.* of or in this case.

■ *n.* nominative (case).

nom•i•nee /nóminée/ *n.* person who is nominated for an office or as the recipient of a grant, etc.

■ candidate, appointee; assignee.

non- /non/ *prefix* giving the negative sense of words with which it is combined, esp.: **1** not doing or having or involved with (*nonattendance, nonpayment, nonproductive*). **2 a** not of the kind or class described (*nonalcoholic, non-*

non•a•bra′sive *adj.*
non•ab•sor′bent *adj.*
non•a•bu′sive *adj.*
non•ad•dic′tive *adj.*
non•ad•he′sive *adj.*
non•ad•just′a•ble *adj.*
non•ag•gres′sion *n.*
non•al•co•hol′ic *adj.*
non•al•ler′gic *adj.*
non•be•liev′er *n.*
non•black′ *n.*
non•can′cer•ous *adj.*
non-Chris′tian *adj. & n.*
non•cler′i•cal *adj. & n.*
non•com•bus′ti•ble *adj.*
non•com•pli′ance *n.*
non•con•struc′tive *adj.*
non•con•ta′gious *adj.*
non•con•tro•ver′sial *adj.*
non•de•duct′i•ble *adj.*
non•de•nom•i•na′tion•al *adj.*
non•dry′ing *adj.*
non•ef•fec′tive *adj.*
non•es•sen′tial *adj.*
non•ex•ist′ence *n.*
non•ex•ist′ent *adj.*
non•ex•plo′sive *adj. & n.*
non•fat′ten•ing *adj.*
non•flam′ma•ble *adj.*

non•greas′y *adj.*
non•haz′ard•ous *adj.*
non•he′red′i•tar•y *adj.*
non•his•tor′i•cal *adj.*
non•hu′man *adj.*
non•i•den′ti•cal *adj.*
non•in•clu′sive *adj.*
non•in•fec′tious *adj.*
non•in•flect′ed *adj.*
non•in•flam′ma•to•ry *adj.*
non•in•fla′tion•ar•y *adj.*
non•in•te•grat•ed *adj.*
non•in•ter•change′a•ble *adj.*
non•in•ter•fer′ence *n.*
non•in•tox′i•cat•ing *adj.*
non•ir′ri•tat•ing *adj.*
non•lin′e•ar *adj.*
non•mag•net′ic *adj.*
non•ma•lig′nant *adj.*
non•mem′ber *n.*
non•mi′gra•to•ry *adj.*
non•mil′i•tant *adj.*
non•mil′i•tar•y *adj.*
non•nar•cot′ic *adj. & n.*
non•ne•go′ti•a•ble *adj.*
non•ob•jec′tive *adj.*
non•ob•lig′a•to•ry *adj.*
non•ob•serv′ant *adj.*
non•of•fi′cial *adj.*

non•or•gan′ic *adj.*
non•par′ti•san *adj.*
non•pay′ing *adj.*
non•pay′ment *n.*
non•per′ish•a•ble *adj.*
non•poi′son•ous *adj.*
non•po•lit′i•cal *adj.*
non•pol•lut′ing *adj.*
non•po′rous *adj.*
non•prac′tic•ing *adj.*
non•pro•duc′tive *adj.*
non•pro•fes′sion•al *adj. & n.*
non•prof′it•a•ble *adj.*
non•pub′lic *adj.*
non•ra′cial *adj.*
non•re•ac′tive *adj.*
non•re•cip′ro•cal *adj. & n.*
non•re•cip′ro•cat•ing *adj.*
non•re•cur′ring *adj.*
non•re•deem′a•ble *adj.*
non•re•fill′a•ble *adj.*
non•re•new′a•ble *adj.*
non•rep•re•sen•ta′tion•al *adj.*
non•re•sis′tant *adj.*
non•re•turn′a•ble *adj.*
non•rhyth′mic *adj.*
non•sal′a•ried *adj.*

non•sci•en•tif′ic *adj.*
non•sea′son•al *adj.*
non•sec•tar′i•an *adj.*
non•sex′ist *adj.*
non•sex′u•al *adj.*
non′skid′ *adj.*
non•slip′ *adj.*
non•smok′er *n.*
non•smok′ing *adj.*
non•spe•cif′ic *adj.*
non•stain′ing *adj.*
non•stick′ *adj.*
non•swim′mer *n.*
non•tar′nish•ing *adj.*
non•tax′a•ble *adj.*
non•tech′ni•cal *adj.*
non•think′ing *adj.*
non•threat′en•ing *adj.*
non•tox′ic *adj.*
non•trans•fer′a•ble *adj.*
non•us′er *n.*
non•ven′om•ous *adj.*
non•ver′bal *adj.*
non•vir′u•lent *adj.*
non•vo′cal *adj.*
non•vot′er *n.*
non•white′ *n. & adj.*
non•work′ing *adj.*

member). **b** forming terms used adjectivally (*nonunion, nonparty*). **3** lack of (*nonaccess*). **4** [with adverbs] not in the way described (*nonaggressively*). **5** forming adjectives from verbs, meaning "that does not" or "that is not meant to (or to be)" (*nonskid, noniron*). **6** used to form a neutral negative sense when a form in *in-* or *un-* has a special sense or (usu. unfavorable) connotation (*noncontroversial, noneffective, nonhuman*). ¶The number of words that can be formed with this prefix is unlimited; consequently only a selection, considered the most current or semantically noteworthy, can be given here.

no·na·ge·nar·i·an /nónəjináireeən, nō–/ • *n.* person from 90 to 99 years old. • *adj.* of this age.

no·na·gon /nónəgon/ *n.* plane figure with nine sides and angles.

non·a·ligned /nónəlínd/ *adj.* (of nations, etc.) not aligned with another (esp. major) power. □□ **non·a·lign'ment** *n.*

■ uncommitted, nonallied; neutral, impartial.

non·am·big·u·ous /nónambígyōōəs/ *adj.* not ambiguous. ¶Neutral in sense: see NON-6.

non·bel·lig·er·ent /nónbəlíjərənt/ • *adj.* not engaged in hostilities. • *n.* nonbelligerent nation, etc. □□ **non·bel·lig'er·en·cy** *n.*

nonce /nons/ *n.* □ **for the nonce** for the time being; for the present occasion. **nonce word** word coined for one occasion.

■ □ **for the nonce** see *for the time being* (TIME).

non·cha·lant /nónshəláant/ *adj.* calm and casual, unmoved, indifferent. □□ **non·cha·lance'** *n.* **non·cha·lant'ly** *adv.*

■ cool, unexcited, aloof, blasé, serene; apathetic.

non·com /nónkom/ *n. colloq.* noncommissioned officer.

non·com·ba·tant /nónkəmbát'nt, –kómbət'nt/ *n.* person not fighting in a war, esp. a civilian, army chaplain, etc.

non·com·mis·sioned /nónkəmíshənd/ *adj. Mil.* (of an officer) not holding a commission. ¶Abbr.: NCO.

non·com·mit·tal /nónkəmít'l/ *adj.* avoiding commitment to a definite opinion or course of action.

■ wary, cautious, careful, guarded.

non compos men·tis /nón kompəs méntis/ *adj.* (also **non com'pos**) not in one's right mind.

non·con·duc·tor /nónkəndúktər/ *n.* substance that does not conduct heat or electricity.

non·con·form·ist /nónkənfáwrmist/ *n.* person who does not conform to a prevailing principle. □□ **non·con·form'i·ty** *n.*

■ renegade, maverick, rebel, individualist.

non·de·script /nóndiskript/ *adj.* lacking distinctive characteristics; not easily classified.

■ indescribable; ordinary, common, unremarkable.

non·drink·er /nóndríngkər/ *n.* person who does not drink alcoholic liquor.

■ abstainer, teetotaler.

none /nun/ • *pron.* **1 a** not any of (*none of this concerns me*). **b** not any one of (*none were recovered*). ¶The verb following *none* in this sense can be singular or plural according to the sense. **2** no persons (*none but fools have ever believed it*). • *adj.* [usu. with a preceding noun implied] no; not any (*you have money and I have none*). • *adv.* by no amount; not at all (*am none the wiser*).

■ *pron.* no one, nobody, no person; not one.

non·en·ti·ty /nonéntitee/ *n.* (*pl.* **–ties**) **1** person or thing of no importance. **2** nonexistent thing, figment.

none·the·less /núnthəlés/ *adv.* nevertheless.

non·e·vent /nónivént/ *n.* unimportant or anticlimactic occurrence.

■ lead balloon, *colloq.* non-starter, *sl.* dud.

non·fer·rous /nónférəs/ *adj.* (of a metal) other than iron or steel.

non·fic·tion /nónfíkshən/ *n.* literary work other than fiction, including biography and reference books.

non·in·ter·ven·tion /nónintərvénshən/ *n.* principle or practice of not becoming involved in others' affairs, esp. by one nation in regard to another.

non·pa·reil /nónpərél/ • *adj.* unrivaled or unique. • *n.* **1** such a person or thing. **2** candy made from a chocolate disk, decorated with sugar pellets.

■ *n.* **1** paragon, model, ne plus ultra, ideal.

non·plus /nonplús/ *v.tr.* (**non·plussed**, **non·plus·sing**; **non·plused**, **non·plus·ing**) completely perplex.

■ confound, puzzle, confuse, shock, *colloq.* faze, flummox.

non·prof·it /nónprófit/ *adj.* not involving nor making a profit.

■ self-financing, noncommercial, charitable.

non·pro·lif·er·a·tion /nónprəlífəráyshən/ *n.* prevention of an increase in something, esp. possession of nuclear weapons.

non·res·i·dent /nónrézidənt/ • *adj.* **1** not residing in a particular place, esp. not residing where one works, seeks office, etc. **2** (of a post) not requiring the holder to reside at the place of work. • *n.* nonresident person. □□ **non·res·i·den'tial** /–dénshəl/ *adj.*

non·re·sis·tance /nónrizístəns/ *n.* practice or principle of not resisting authority.

non·sense /nónsens, –səns/ *n.* absurd or meaningless words or ideas; foolish or extravagant conduct. □□ **non·sen·si·cal** /–sénsikəl/ *adj.* **non·sen'si·cal·ly** *adv.*

■ rubbish, drivel, gibberish, garbage, mumbo jumbo; mischief, clowning, antics. □□ **nonsensical** senseless, absurd, laughable, irrational.

non se·qui·tur /non sékwitər/ *n.* conclusion that does not logically follow from the premises.

non·start·er /nónstaartər/ *n.* **1** person or animal that does not start in a race. **2** *colloq.* person or thing that is unlikely to succeed or be effective.

non·stop /nónstóp/ • *adj.* **1** (of a train, etc.) not stopping at intermediate places. **2** (of a journey, performance, etc.) done without a stop or intermission. • *adv.* without stopping or pausing.

■ *adj.* uninterrupted, continuous, direct; unending, interminable, persistent, constant, steady, regular, habitual. • *adv.* endlessly, continually, continuously, relentlessly, constantly, round-the-clock, day in day out.

non•un•ion /nónyōōnyən/ *adj.* **1** not belonging to a labor union. **2** not done or produced by members of a labor union.

non•vi•o•lence /nónvíələns/ *n.* avoidance of violence, esp. as a principle. □□ **non•vi•o•lent** /-lənt/ *adj.*

■ nonresistance; pacifism; passive resistance. □□ **nonviolent** see PEACEABLE 1.

noo•dle[1] /nōōd'l/ *n.* strip or ring of pasta.

noo•dle[2] /nōōd'l/ *n. sl.* head.

nook /nŏŏk/ *n.* corner or recess; secluded place. □ **in every nook and cranny** everywhere.

■ niche, alcove, crevice, crack, opening; retreat, hideaway, nest, *colloq.* hideout.

noon /nōōn/ *n.* twelve o'clock in the day; midday.

■ 1200 hours, twelve noon, high noon.

no one /nó wun/ *n.* no person; nobody.

noose /nōōs/ • *n.* **1** loop with a slip knot, tightening when pulled, esp. in a snare, lasso, or hangman's halter. **2** snare or bond. • *v.tr.* **1** catch with or enclose in a noose; ensnare. **2 a** make a noose on (a cord). **b** (often foll. by *around*) arrange (a cord) in a noose.

■ *n.* **1** see LOOP *n.*

nor /nawr, nər/ *conj.* **1** and not; and not either (*can neither read nor write*). **2** and no more; neither ("*I cannot go*" – "*Nor can I*").

Nor•dic /náwrdik/ • *adj.* **1** of the tall blond Germanic people in northern Europe, esp. in Scandinavia. **2** of or relating to Scandinavia or Finland. • *n.* Nordic person.

nor•east•er /noreéstər/ *n.* northeaster.

norm /nawrm/ *n.* **1** standard or pattern or type. **2** customary behavior, etc.

■ model, criterion, measure, gauge, yardstick; average, mean.

nor•mal /náwrməl/ • *adj.* **1** conforming to a standard; regular; usual; typical. **2** free from mental or emotional disorder. • *n.* **1** normal value of a temperature, etc., esp. that of blood. **2** usual state, level, etc. □□ **nor'mal•cy** *n.* **nor•mal•i•ty** /-málitee/ *n.* **nor•mal•i•za'tion** *n.* **nor'mal•ize** *v.*

■ *adj.* **1** average, conventional, ordinary, universal, orthodox. **2** sane, stable, rational. □□ **normalize** standardize, regulate, control; conform.

SYNONYM STUDY: normal

AVERAGE, NATURAL, ORDINARY, REGULAR, TYPICAL, USUAL. Most of us want to be regarded as **normal**, an adjective that implies conformity with established norms or standards and is the opposite of abnormal (*a normal body temperature; normal intelligence*). **Regular**, like *normal*, is usually preferred to its opposite (irregular) and implies conformity to prescribed standards or established patterns (*their regular monthly meeting; a regular guy*), but *normal* carries stronger connotations of conformity within prescribed limits and

sometimes allows for a wider range of differences. Few of us think of ourselves as **ordinary**, a term used to describe what is commonplace or unexceptional (*an ordinary person wearing ordinary clothes*), although many people are ordinary in some ways and extraordinary in others. **Average** also implies conformity with what is regarded as normal or ordinary (*a woman of average height*), although it tends to emphasize the middle ground and to exclude both positive and negative extremes. **Typical** applies to persons or things possessing the representative characteristics of a type or class (*a typical teenager; a typical suburban mother*). Someone or something described as **natural** behaves or operates in accordance with their inherent nature or character (*his fears were natural for one so young*), while **usual** applies to that which conforms to common or ordinary use or occurrence (*we paid the usual price*).

nor•mal•ly /náwrmalee/ *adv.* **1** in a normal manner. **2** usually.

■ **2** see *usually* (USUAL).

Nor•man /náwrmən/ • *n.* **1** native or inhabitant of medieval or modern Normandy. **2** people established there in the 10th c., who conquered England in 1066. • *adj.* **1** of or relating to the Normans. **2** of or relating to the Norman style of architecture. □ **Norman Conquest** conquest of England by William of Normandy in 1066.

nor•ma•tive /náwrmətiv/ *adj.* of or establishing a norm.

Norse /nawrs/ • *n.* **1 a** Norwegian language. **b** Scandinavian language group. **2** [prec. by *the*; treated as *pl*] **a** Norwegians. **b** Vikings. • *adj.* of ancient Scandinavia, esp. Norway. □□ **Norse'man** *n.* (*pl.* **-men**)

north /nawrth/ • *n.* **1 a** point of the horizon 90° counterclockwise from east. **b** compass point corresponding to this. **2** (usu. **the North**) **a** part of the world or a country or a town lying to the north. **b** the arctic. • *adj.* **1** toward, at, near, or facing north. **2** from the north (*north wind*). • *adv.* **1** toward, at, or near the north. **2** further north than. □ **North American** *adj.* of North America. *n.* native or inhabitant of North America, esp. a citizen of the US or Canada. **north pole** (also **North Pole**) northernmost point of the earth's axis of rotation. **North Star** polestar.

north•east /nawrtheést/ • *n.* **1** point of the horizon midway between north and east. **2** direction in which this lies. • *adj.* of, toward, or coming from the northeast. • *adv.* toward, at, or near the northeast.

north•east•er /náwrtheéstər, nawreéstər/ *n.* (also **nor'east'er**) **1** northeast wind. **2** strong storm from the northeast, esp. in New England.

north•er•ly /náwrthərlee/ *adj. & adv.* **1** in a northern position or direction. **2** (of wind) blowing from the north.

■ *adj.* **1** north, northward, northbound.

north•ern /náwrthərn/ *adj.* **1** of or in the

north; inhabiting the north. **2** lying or directed toward the north. □ **northern hemisphere** (also **Northern Hemisphere**) the half of the earth north of the equator. **northern lights** aurora borealis. □□ **north´ern•most** adj.

■ northerly, north; northward, northbound.

north•er•ner /náwrthərnər/ n. native or inhabitant of the north.

north•west /náwrthwést/ • n. **1** point of the horizon midway between north and west. **2** direction in which this lies. • adj. of, toward, or coming from the northwest. • adv. toward, at, or near the northwest.

Nor•we•gian /nawrwée´jən/ • n. **1 a** native or national of Norway. **b** person of Norwegian descent. **2** language of Norway. • adj. of or relating to Norway.

nose /nōz/ • n. **1** organ above the mouth of a human or animal, used for smelling and breathing. **2 a** sense of smell. **b** ability to detect a particular thing (a nose for scandal). **3** front end or projecting part of a thing, e.g., of a car or aircraft. • v. **1** tr. **a** perceive the smell of, discover by smell. **b** detect. **2** intr. pry or search. **3 a** intr. make one's way cautiously forward. **b** tr. make (one's or its way). □ **by a nose** by a very narrow margin. **keep one's nose clean** sl. stay out of trouble; behave properly. **nose cone** cone-shaped nose of a rocket, etc. **nose job** sl. surgery on the nose, esp. for cosmetic reasons; rhinoplasty. **on the nose** sl. precisely. **put a person's nose out of joint** colloq. embarrass, disconcert, frustrate, or supplant a person. **turn up one's nose** colloq. show disdain. **under a person's nose** colloq. right before a person. **with one's nose in the air** haughtily.

■ v. **2** see ROOT² v. 2a. □ **on the nose** exactly. **put a person's nose out of joint** see OFFEND 1, 2, DISPOSSESS 1.

nose•bleed /nṓzbleed/ n. bleeding from the nose.

nose•dive /nṓzdiv/ • n. **1** steep downward plunge by an airplane. **2** sudden plunge or drop. • v.intr. make a nosedive.

nose•gay /nṓzgay/ n. sweet-scented bunch of flowers.

■ see BOUQUET 1.

nosh /nosh/ sl. • v. eat, esp. between meals. • n. snack.

■ v. snack, nibble, pick; see also EAT v. 1. • n. see SNACK n.

nos•tal•gia /nostáljə, –jeeə, nə–/ n. **1** sentimental yearning for a period of the past. **2** severe homesickness. □□ **nos•tal´gic** adj. **nos•tal´gi•cal•ly** adv.

■ **1** see sentimentality (SENTIMENTAL), LONGING n. □□ **nostalgic** see HOMESICK, WISTFUL.

nos•tril /nóstrəl/ n. either of two openings in the nose.

nos•trum /nóstrəm/ n. **1** quack remedy. **2** panacean plan or scheme, esp. for political or social reform.

■ **1** see MEDICINE 2, ELIXIR 1b.

nos•y /nṓzee/ (also **nos´ey**) adj. (**nos•i•er**, **nos•i•est**) colloq. inquisitive, prying. □□ **nos´i•ly** adv. **nos´i•ness** n.

■ curious, spying, eavesdropping.

not /not/ adv. expressing negation, esp.: **1** (also **n't** joined to a preceding verb) following an auxiliary verb or be or (in a question) the subject of such a verb (she isn't there). ¶Use with other verbs is now archaic (fear not), except with participles and infinitives (not knowing, I cannot say; we asked them not to come). **2** used elliptically for a negative sentence or verb or phrase (Do you want it? – – Certainly not!). **3** used to express the negative of other words (not a single one was left).

no•ta be•ne /nṓtə bénay/ v. note well (that which follows). ¶Abbr.: **NB**.

no•ta•ble /nṓtəbəl/ • adj. worthy of note; striking; remarkable; eminent. • n. eminent person. □□ **no•ta•bil´i•ty** n. **no´ta•bly** adv.

■ adj. distinctive, singular, extraordinary, unmatched, outstanding, unforgettable; famous, important, distinguished. • n. dignitary, VIP; celebrity, colloq. big shot, bigwig, sl. big gun, (big) cheese. □□ **notably** particularly, especially, distinctly, unusually, clearly, curiously, surprisingly; meaningfully, significantly, importantly.

no•ta•rize /nṓtəriz/ v.tr. certify (a document) as a notary.

no•ta•ry /nṓtəree/ n. (pl. **–ries**) (in full **no´ta•ry pub´lic**) person authorized to perform certain legal formalities, esp. to draw up or certify contracts, deeds, etc. □□ **no•tar•i•al** /nōtáireeəl/ adj.

no•ta•tion /nōtáyshən/ n. **1** representation of numbers, quantities, musical notes, etc., by symbols. **2** any set of such symbols.

■ signs, code, characters; symbolism.

notch /noch/ • n. **1** V-shaped indentation on an edge or surface. **2** deep, narrow mountain pass or gap. • v.tr. **1** make notches in. **2** [foll. by up] record or score with or as with notches.

■ n. **1** nick, cut, dent, groove, cleft, mark, gouge, gash. • v. **1** nick, cut, dent, mark. **2** (notch up) gain, win, achieve, tally.

note /nōt/ • n. **1** brief written record as an aid to memory, for use in writing, public speaking, etc. (often in pl.: spoke without notes). **2** observation, usu. unwritten, of experiences, etc. (compare notes). **3** short or informal letter. **4** short annotation or additional explanation in a book, etc.; footnote. **5** written promise of payment. **6 a** notice, attention. **b** distinction, eminence. **7 a** written sign representing the pitch and duration of a musical sound. **b** single musical tone of definite pitch. **8** quality or tone of speaking, expressing mood or attitude, etc.; hint or suggestion (sound a note of warning). • v.tr. **1** observe, notice; give or draw attention to. **2** record as a thing to be remembered or observed. **3** [in passive; often foll. by for] be famous or well known (were noted for their generosity).

■ n. **1** memorandum, reminder, colloq. memo. **2**, **4** comment, remark, explanation, critique, criticism. **3** message, postcard, line, thank-you note. **5** promissory note, letter of credit, (bank) draft. **6 a** heed, regard, respect. **b** consequence, substance, importance. **8** theme, characteristic, motif; signal, cue, suspicion. • v. 1 perceive, see, spot, consider, mention. 2 register, write down, chronicle.

note•book /nótbŏŏk/ n. small book for making notes. □ **notebook computer** lightweight computer that closes to notebook size.

■ see TABLET 3.

note•paper /nótpaypər/ n. paper for writing notes or letters.

note•wor•thy /nótwərthee/ adj. worthy of attention; remarkable.

■ notable; exceptional, extraordinary, unusual, singular.

noth•ing /núthing/ • n. 1 not anything. 2 no thing (can find nothing useful). 3 person or thing of no importance. 4 nonexistence; what does not exist. 5 (in calculations) no amount (a third of nothing is nothing). • adv. not at all, in no way. □ **for nothing** 1 at no cost; without payment. 2 to no purpose. **nothing doing** colloq. 1 a no prospect of success or agreement. b I refuse. 2 nothing is happening.

■ n. 1, 2 nil, sl. nix, zilch. 3 zero, nobody; trifle, colloq. peanuts. 4 nothingness, nonentity, void, emptiness, vacuum. 5 see ZERO n. 1. □ **for nothing** 2 to no avail; see also in vain (VAIN).

noth•ing•ness /núthingnis/ n. 1 nonexistence. 2 worthlessness, triviality, insignificance.

■ see OBLIVION.

no•tice /nótis/ • n. 1 attention; observation. 2 displayed sheet, etc., bearing an announcement. 3 a intimation or warning (give notice). b formal declaration of intention to end an agreement, leave employment, etc. 4 short published review or comment about a new play, book, etc. • v.tr. perceive; observe. □ **take notice of** 1 observe. 2 act upon.

■ n. 1 awareness, perception; regard, consideration. 2 bill, leaflet, flyer; see also SIGN n. 4. 3 notification, announcement. 4 criticism, write-up. • v. note, pay attention to, heed, remark, see, discern, detect, make out, identify, recognize, colloq. spot. □ **take notice of 1** see NOTICE v. above.

no•tice•a•ble /nótisəbəl/ adj. 1 easily seen or noticed; perceptible. 2 noteworthy. □□ **no'tice•a•bly** adv.

■ 1 visible, distinct, evident, clear, clear-cut, conspicuous, obvious; unmistakable. 2 significant, remarkable, important, distinct.

SYNONYM STUDY: noticeable

CONSPICUOUS, OUTSTANDING, PROMINENT, REMARKABLE, STRIKING. A scratch on someone's face might be **noticeable**, while a scar that runs from cheekbone to chin would be **conspicuous**. When it comes to describing the things that attract our attention, *noticeable* means readily noticed or unlikely to escape observation (a noticeable facial tic; a noticeable aversion to cocktail parties), while *conspicuous* implies that the eye (or mind) cannot miss it (her absence was conspicuous). Use **prominent** when you want to describe something that literally or figuratively stands out from

---

its background (a prominent nose). It can also apply to persons or things that stand out so clearly they are generally known or recognized (a prominent citizen; a prominent position on the committee). Something or someone who is **outstanding** rises above or beyond others and is usually superior to them (an outstanding student). **Remarkable** applies to whatever is *noticeable* because it is extraordinary or exceptional (remarkable blue eyes). **Striking** is an even stronger word, used to describe something so out of the ordinary that it makes a deep and powerful impression on the observer's mind or vision (a striking young woman over six feet tall).

---

no•ti•fy /nótifī/ v.tr. (**-fies, -fied**) 1 inform or give notice to (a person). 2 make known. □□ **no•ti•fi•ca'tion** n.

■ 1 tell, advise, alert. 2 announce, report, declare. ■□ **notification** word, warning; see also ADVICE 2.

no•tion /nóshən/ n. 1 a concept or idea. b opinion., c vague view or understanding. 2 inclination, impulse, or intention. 3 [in pl.] small, useful articles, esp. thread, needles, buttons, etc. See synonym study at IDEA.

■ 1 thought, image, (mental) picture; clue. 2 fancy, whim.

no•tion•al /nóshənəl/ adj. 1 hypothetical; imaginary. 2 (of knowledge, etc.) speculative. □□ **no'tion•al•ly** adv.

■ 1 see IMAGINARY.

no•to•ri•ous /nōtáwreeəs/ adj. well-known, esp. unfavorably (notorious criminal). □□ **no•to•ri•e•ty** /-tərīətee/ n. **no•to'ri•ous•ly** adv.

■ infamous, shameful, scandalous; legendary. □□ **notoriety** dishonor, disgrace, scandal.

not•with•stand•ing /nótwithstánding, -with-/ • prep. in spite of. • adv. nevertheless; all the same.

■ prep. despite, regardless of. • adv. nonetheless, still, anyway.

nou•gat /nóōgət/ n. chewy candy made from sugar or honey, nuts, egg white, and often fruit pieces.

nought var. of NAUGHT.

noun /nown/ n. Gram. word (other than a pronoun) used to name a person, place, thing, or concept (common noun), or a particular one of these (proper noun).

nour•ish /nə́rish, núr-/ v.tr. 1 a sustain with food. b enrich. c provide with intellectual or emotional sustenance or enrichment. 2 foster or cherish (a feeling, etc.). □□ **nour'ish•ing** adj.

■ 1 feed, support, nurture; strengthen, encourage, stimulate. 2 nurse, maintain, keep, nurture, sustain.

nour•ish•ment /nə́rishmənt, núr-/ n. sustenance, food.

■ nutriment, nutrition, colloq. grub.

nou•veau riche /nóōvō réesh/ n. (pl. **nou'veaux riches** pronunc. same) person who has recently acquired (usu. ostentatious) wealth.

Nov. abbr. November.

no•va /nóvə/ *n.* (*pl.* **no•vas** or **no•vae** /–vee/) star showing a sudden burst of brightness that then subsides.

nov•el[1] /nóvəl/ *n.* fictitious prose story of book length.

■ romance, fiction; novella, novelette, bestseller.

nov•el[2] /nóvəl/ *adj.* of a new kind or nature; strange.

■ unusual, unfamiliar, fresh, different; untested, unknown.

nov•el•ette /nóvəlét/ *n.* short novel.

nov•el•ist /nóvəlist/ *n.* writer of novels.

■ see WRITER.

no•vel•la /nəvélə/ *n.* (*pl.* **no•vel•las** or **no•vel•le** /–lee, –lay/) short novel or narrative story; tale.

nov•el•ty /nóvəltee/ *n.* (*pl.* **–ties**) **1** newness. **2** new or unusual thing or occurrence. **3** small toy or decoration, etc. **4** [*attrib.*] having novelty (*novelty toys*).

■ **1** originality, freshness. **3** gimcrack, trifle, gewgaw, bauble. **4** (*attrib.*) see NEW *adj.* 1b.

No•vem•ber /nōvémbər/ *n.* eleventh month of the year.

no•ve•na /nōvéenə, nə–/ *n. RC Ch.* devotion consisting of special prayers or services on nine successive days.

nov•ice /nóvis/ *n.* **1 a** probationary member of a religious order. **b** new convert. **2** beginner; inexperienced person.

■ **1, 2** neophyte, novitiate, amateur, apprentice, rookie.

no•vi•ti•ate /nōvísheeət, –ayt/ *n.* (also **no•vi′ci•ate**) **1** period of being a novice. **2** religious novice. **3** novices' quarters.

No•vo•caine /nóvəkayn/ *n.* (also **no′vo•caine**) *propr.* local anesthetic derived from benzoic acid.

now /now/ • *adv.* **1** at the present or mentioned time. **2** immediately. **3** under the present circumstances. **4** on this further occasion. **5** (esp. in a narrative) then, next. • *conj.* as a consequence. • *n.* this time; the present. □ **now and again** (or **then**) from time to time; intermittently.

■ *adv.* **1, 3** at the moment, right now; today, in these times; any more, any longer. **2** at once, right away, promptly. **5** at this or that point. • *conj.* see FOR *conj.* • *n.* the time being, this moment. □ **now and again** occasionally, sometimes, seldom, once in a blue moon.

now•a•days /nówədayz/ • *adv.* at the present time or age; in these times. • *n.* the present time.

no•where /nṓhwair, –wair/ • *adv.* in or to no place. • *pron.* no place. □ **nowhere near** not nearly.

no•wise /nṓwīz/ *adv.* in no manner; not at all.

nox•ious /nókshəs/ *adj.* harmful, unwholesome.

■ see HARMFUL.

noz•zle /nózəl/ *n.* spout on a hose, etc., from which a jet issues.

Np *symb. Chem.* neptunium.

NRC *abbr.* Nuclear Regulatory Commission.

Ns *abbr.* NIELSBOHRIUM.

ns *abbr.* nanosecond.

NSF *abbr.* **1** National Science Foundation. **2** not sufficient funds.

NT *abbr.* New Testament.

–n't /ənt/ *adv.* [in *comb.*] = NOT (*isn't*, *mustn't*).

nth see N[1].

nt. wt. *abbr.* net weight.

nu /nōō, nyōō/ *n.* thirteenth letter of the Greek alphabet (N, ν).

nu•ance /nōō-aans, nyōō–/ *n.* subtle shade of meaning, feeling, color, etc.

■ see SHADE *n.* 4.

nub /nub/ *n.* **1** point or gist (of a matter or story). **2** small lump, esp. of coal. □□ **nub′by** *adj.*

■ **1** essence, core, heart, meat. **2** protuberance, bump, bulge; swelling.

nu•bile /nōōbīl, –bil, nyōō–/ *adj.* (of a woman) marriageable or sexually attractive. □□ **nu•bil•i•ty** /–bílitee/ *n.*

nu•cle•ar /nōōkleeər, nyōō–/ *adj.* **1** of, relating to, or constituting a nucleus. **2** using nuclear energy. □ **nuclear energy** energy obtained by nuclear fission or fusion. **nuclear family** a couple and their children, regarded as a basic social unit. **nuclear fission** nuclear reaction in which a heavy nucleus splits, accompanied by the release of energy. **nuclear fusion** nuclear reaction in which atomic nuclei of low atomic number fuse to form a heavier nucleus with the release of energy. **nuclear medicine** *Med.* specialty that uses radioactive materials for diagnosis and treatment. **nuclear physics** physics of atomic nuclei and their interactions, esp. in the generation of nuclear energy. **nuclear power 1** power generated by a nuclear reactor. **2** country that has nuclear weapons. **nuclear reactor** device in which a nuclear fission chain reaction is used to produce energy.

■ **2** atomic, fission, fusion; atom, hydrogen, neutron. □ **nuclear energy** atomic power, atomic energy.

nu•cle•ate /nōōkleeayt, nyōō–/ • *adj.* having a nucleus. • *v.* form or form into a nucleus.

nu•cle•ic acid /nōōkleeik, –klayik, nyōō–/ *n.* either of two complex organic molecules (DNA and RNA), present in all living cells.

nu•cle•o•lus /nōōkleeələs, nyōō–/ *n.* (*pl.* **nu•cle•o•li** /–lī/) dense spherical structure within a nondividing nucleus.

nu•cle•on /nōōkleeon, nyōō–/ *n. Physics* proton or neutron.

nu•cle•us /nōōkleeəs/ *n.* (*pl.* **nu•cle•i** /–lee-ī/) **1 a** central part or thing around which others are collected. **b** kernel of an aggregate or mass. **2** initial part meant to receive additions. **3** *Physics* positively charged central core of an atom. **4** *Biol.* specialized, often central part of a cell, containing the genetic material.

■ **1** core, heart, center, focus.

nude /nōōd, nyōōd/ • *adj.* naked; bare; unclothed. See synonym study at NAKED. • *n.* **1** painting, sculpture, photograph, etc., of a nude human figure; such a figure. **2** nude person. □□ **nu′di•ty** *n.*

■ *adj.* undressed, stark naked, without a stitch (on).

nudge /nuj/ • *v.tr.* **1** prod gently with the elbow to attract attention. **2** give a reminder or encouragement to (a person). • *n.* prod; gentle push.

■ *v.* jog, poke, bump; prompt. • *n.* poke, elbow, jab; prompt.

nud•ist /nŏŏdist, nyŏŏ–/ *n.* person who advocates or practices going unclothed. □□ **nud′ism** *n.*

nu•ga•to•ry /nŏŏgətawree, nyŏŏ–/ *adj.* **1** futile; trifling; worthless. **2** inoperative; not valid.

nug•get /núgit/ *n.* **1** lump of gold, etc., as found in the earth. **2** something valuable for its size (*nugget of information*).

■ **1** see LUMP[1] *n.* 1.

nui•sance /nŏŏsəns, nyŏŏ–/ *n.* person, thing, or circumstance causing trouble or annoyance.

■ inconvenience, irritation, thorn in one's side, bother; pest, nag.

nuke /nŏŏk, nyŏŏk/ *colloq.* • *n.* nuclear weapon. • *v.tr. colloq.* **1** bomb or destroy with nuclear weapons. **2** to cook (something) in a microwave oven.

null /nul/ *adj.* **1** (esp. **null and void**) invalid. **2** nonexistent; amounting to nothing. **3** without character or expression.

■ **1** see INVALID[2].

nul•li•fy /núlifī/ *v.tr.* (**-fies, -fied**) neutralize; invalidate; cancel. □□ **nul•li•fi•ca′tion** *n.*

■ see NEUTRALIZE. □□ **nullification** see *cancellation* (CANCEL).

num. *abbr.* **1** number. **2** numerical.

numb /num/ • *adj.* deprived of feeling or the power of motion (*numb with cold*). • *v.tr.* **1** make numb. **2** stupefy; paralyze. □□ **numb′ness** *n.*

■ *adj.* deadened, senseless; asleep. • *v.* anesthetize, drug, immobilize, stun. □□ **numbness** paralysis; see also STUPOR.

num•ber /númbər/ • *n.* **1 a** arithmetical value representing a particular quantity used in counting and calculating. **b** word, symbol, or figure representing this; numeral. **c** arithmetical value showing position in a series. **2** total count or aggregate (*the number of accidents has decreased*). **3** [in *pl.*] arithmetic. **4 a** [in *sing.* or *pl.*] quantity or amount; total; count (*large number of people*). **b** [in *pl.*] numerical preponderance (*force of numbers*). **5 a** person or thing having a place in a series, esp. a single issue of a magazine, an item in a program, etc. **b** song, dance, musical item, etc. **6** company, collection, group (*among our number*). **7** *Gram.* classification of words by their singular or plural forms. • *v.tr.* **1** include. **2** assign a number or numbers to. **3** amount to (a specified number). **4 a** count. **b** comprise (*numbering forty thousand men*). □ **do a number on** *sl.* injure, cheat, criticize, or humiliate. **have a person's number** *colloq.* understand a person's real motives, character, etc. **number one** *n. colloq.* oneself (*always takes care of number one*). *adj.* most important (*the number-one priority*).

■ *n.* **1** numeral, integer, figure, digit. **2** see SUM[1] *n.* 1, 2. **3** (*numbers*) see SUM *n.* 3. **5 a** edition, copy. **b** see ACT *n.* 3a. **6** see

GROUP *n.*, COMPANY *n.* 1a. • *v.* **1** see INCLUDE 3. **3** see AMOUNT *v.* 1. **4 a** see COUNT *v.* 1. **b** see INCLUDE 1.

num•ber•less /númbərlis/ *adj.* innumerable.

■ uncountable, countless, numerous, untold, infinite.

numb•skull var. of NUMSKULL.

num•er•a•ble /nŏŏmərəbəl, nyŏŏ–/ *adj.* that can be counted.

num•er•al /nŏŏmərəl, nyŏŏ–/ • *n.* figure or group of figures denoting a number. • *adj.* of or denoting a number.

■ *n.* see NUMBER *n.* 1.

num•er•ate • *v.* /nŏŏmərayt, nyŏŏ–/ = ENUMERATE. • *adj.* /nŏŏmərət, nyŏŏ–/ acquainted with the basic principles of mathematics. □□ **nu•mer•a•cy** /–əsee/ *n.*

num•er•a•tor /nŏŏməraytor, nyŏŏ–/ *n.* number above the line in a common fraction showing how many of the parts indicated by the denominator are taken (e.g., 2 in $^2/_3$).

nu•mer•i•cal /nŏŏmérikəl, nyŏŏ–/ *adj.* (also **nu•mer′ic**) of or relating to a number or numbers. □□ **nu•mer′i•cal•ly** *adv.*

nu•mer•ol•o•gy /nŏŏməróləjee, nyŏŏ–/ *n.* (*pl.* **-gies**) study of the supposed occult significance of numbers.

nu•mer•ous /nŏŏmərəs, nyŏŏ–/ *adj.* **1** [with *pl.*] great in number. **2** consisting of many (*the rose family is a numerous one*).

■ **1** see MANY *adj.*

nu•mi•nous /nŏŏminəs, nyŏŏ–/ *adj.* **1** indicating the presence of a divinity. **2** spiritual. **3** awe-inspiring.

nu•mis•mat•ics /nŏŏmizmátiks, nyŏŏ–/ *n.pl.* [usu. treated as *sing.*] study of coins or medals. □□ **nu•mis•mat′ic** *adj.* **nu•mis•ma′tist** /nŏŏmízmətist, nyŏŏ–/ *n.*

num•skull /númskul/ *n.* stupid or foolish person.

■ see FOOL *n.* 1.

nun /nun/ *n.* member of a community of women living apart under religious vows.

nun•ci•o /núnsheeō/ *n.* (*pl.* **-os**) RC Ch. papal ambassador.

nun•ner•y /núnəree/ *n.* (*pl.* **-ies**) religious house of nuns; convent.

nup•tial /núpshəl/ • *adj.* of or relating to marriage or weddings. • *n.* [usu. in *pl.*] wedding.

■ *adj.* bridal, matrimonial, marital, connubial, conjugal.

nurd var. of NERD.

nurse /nərs/ • *n.* **1** person trained to care for the sick or infirm. **2** (formerly) person employed or trained to take charge of young children. • *v.* **1 a** *intr.* work as a nurse. **b** *tr.* attend to (a sick person). **2** *tr. & intr.* feed or be fed at the breast. **3** *tr.* hold or treat carefully (*sat nursing my feet*). **4** *tr.* **a** foster; promote the development of (the arts, plants, etc.). **b** harbor or nurture (a grievance, hatred, etc.). **5** *tr.* consume slowly. □ **nurse-practitioner** registered nurse with advanced training in diagnosing and treating illness.

■ *n.* **1** attendant. • *v.* **1 b** care for, treat. **2** suckle, breast-feed. **4** cherish, cultivate; coddle, baby, pamper.

nurse•maid /nɔ́rsmayd/ *n.* woman in charge of a child or children.
■ au pair, nanny, mammy.

nur•ser•y /nɔ́rsəree/ *n.* (*pl.* **–ies**) **1 a** room or place equipped for young children. **b** day-care facility for children. **2** place where plants, trees, etc., are reared for sale or transplantation. □ **nursery rhyme** simple traditional song or story in rhyme for children. **nursery school** school for children from the age of about three to five.
■ □ **nursery school** kindergarten, playgroup, day care.

nur•ser•y•man /nɔ́rsəreemən/ *n.* (*pl.* **–men**) owner of or worker in a plant nursery.

nurs•ing /nɔ́rsing/ *n.* practice or profession of caring for the sick as a nurse. □ **nursing home** facility providing residence and nursing care for the elderly, disabled, etc.

nur•ture /nɔ́rchər/ • *n.* **1** process of bringing up or training (esp. children). **2** nourishment. **3** sociological factors as an influence on or determinant of personality (opp. NATURE). • *v.tr.* **1** bring up; rear. **2** nourish. □□ **nur′tur•er** *n.*
■ *n.* **1** see UPBRINGING. • *v.* **1** see *bring up* 1. **2** see NOURISH. □□ **nurturer** see MOTHER *n.* 1.

nut /nut/ *n.* **1 a** fruit consisting of a hard or tough shell around an edible kernel. **b** this kernel. **2** pod containing hard seeds. **3** small usu. hexagonal piece of metal, etc., with a threaded hole through it for securing a bolt. **4** *sl.* **a** crazy or eccentric person. **b** obsessive enthusiast or devotee (*health-food nut*). □ **nuts and bolts** *colloq.* practical details.
■ **1 b** see KERNEL 1, 2. **4** see MADMAN **b** see *enthusiast* (ENTHUSIASM).

nut•case /nútkays/ *n. sl.* crazy or foolish person.

nut•crack•er /nútkrakər/ *n.* device for cracking nuts.

nut•hatch /nút-hach/ *n.* small bird that climbs trees and feeds on nuts, insects, etc.

nut•meg /nútmeg/ *n.* hard aromatic spheroidal seed used as a spice and in medicine.

nu•tri•a /nóōtreeə, nyóō–/ *n.* **1** aquatic beaverlike rodent, native to S. America. **2** its skin or fur.

nu•tri•ent /nóōtreeənt, nyóō–/ • *n.* substance that provides essential nourishment. • *adj.* nutritious.

nu•tri•ment /nóōtrimənt, nyóō–/ *n.* anything nourishing; food.
■ see NOURISHMENT.

nu•tri•tion /nōōtríshən, nyōō–/ *n.* **1** food, nourishment. **2** study of diet and its relation to health. □□ **nu•tri′tion•al** *adj.* **nu•tri′tion•ist** *n.*
■ **1** see NOURISHMENT.

nu•tri•tious /nōōtríshəs, nyōō–/ *adj.* nourishing as food.
■ healthy, wholesome, life-giving, beneficial.

nuts /nuts/ • *adj. sl.* crazy, mad. • *int. sl.* expression of contempt (*nuts to you*). □ **be nuts about** *colloq.* be very fond of.
■ *adj.* see CRAZY 1.

nut•shell /nútshel/ *n.* hard exterior covering of a nut. □ **in a nutshell** in a few words.

nut•ty /nútee/ *adj.* (**nut•ti•er**, **nut•ti•est**) **1 a** full of nuts. **b** tasting like nuts. **2** *sl.* = NUTS *adj.* □□ **nut′ti•ness** *n.*
■ **2** see CRAZY 1. □□ **nuttiness** see FOLLY 1.

nuz•zle /núzəl/ *v.* **1** *tr.* prod or rub gently with the nose. **2** *intr.* [foll. by *into*, *against*, *up to*] press the nose gently. **3** *tr.* [also *refl.*] nestle; lie snug.
■ **1, 2** see CARESS *v.* **3** see NESTLE.

NV *abbr.* Nevada (in official postal use).

NW *abbr.* **1** northwest. **2** northwestern.

NY *abbr.* New York (in official postal use).

NYC *abbr.* New York City.

ny•lon /nílon/ *n.* **1** synthetic polyamide fibers with tough, lightweight, elastic properties, used in industry and for textiles, etc. **2** nylon fabric. **3** [in *pl.*] stockings of nylon.

nymph /nimf/ *n.* **1** mythological female spirit associated with aspects of nature, esp. rivers and woods. **2** *poet.* beautiful young woman. **3** immature form of some insects.

NYSE *abbr.* New York Stock Exchange.

NZ *abbr.* New Zealand.

Oo

O[1] /ō/ *n.* (also **o**) (*pl.* **Os** or **O's**; **o's**) **1** fifteenth letter of the alphabet. **2** human blood type.

O[2] *symb. Chem.* oxygen.

O[3] /ō/ *int.* **1** var. of OH. **2** prefixed to a name in the vocative (*O God*).

o' /ə/ *prep.* of, on (*o'clock*, *will-o'-the-wisp*).

-o /ō/ *suffix* forming usu. *sl.* or *colloq.* variants or derivatives (*weirdo*, *wino*).

oaf /ōf/ *n.* (*pl.* **oafs**) **1** awkward lout. **2** stupid person. □□ **oaf′ish** *adj.* **oaf′ish•ly** *adv.* **oaf′ish•ness** *n.*

oak /ōk/ *n.* **1** tree having lobed leaves and bearing acorns. **2** durable wood of this tree, used esp. for furniture and in building. **3** [*attrib.*] made of oak (*oak table*). □□ **oak′en** *adj.*

oa•kum /ṓkəm/ *n.* loose fiber obtained by picking old rope to pieces and used esp. in caulking.

oar /awr/ *n.* pole with a blade used for rowing or steering a boat by leverage against the water.
■ paddle, scull, sweep.

oar•lock /áwrlok/ *n.* device for holding an oar in position while rowing.

oars•man /áwrzmən/ *n.* (*pl.* **–men**; *fem.* **oars•wom•an**, *pl.* **–wom•en**) rower. □□ **oars′man•ship** *n.*

OAS *abbr.* Organization of American States.

o•a•sis /ō-áysis/ *n.* (*pl.* **o•a•ses** /–seez/) **1** fertile spot in a desert. **2** area or period of calm in the midst of turbulence.

■ **1** water hole. **2** haven, refuge, (safe) harbor, sanctuary.

oat /ōt/ *n.* **1** cereal plant, cultivated in cool climates. **2** [in *pl.*] grain yielded by this, used as food. □□ **oat′en** *adj.*

oat•cake /ótkayk/ *n.* thin oatmeal cake.

oath /ōth/ *n.* (*pl.* **oaths** /ōthz, ōths/) **1** solemn declaration (often naming God) as to the truth of something or as a commitment to future action. **2** profane or blasphemous utterance; curse.

■ **1** vow, pledge, promise, word (of honor). **2** swearword, expletive, four-letter word, obscenity, dirty word.

oat•meal /ótmeel/ *n.* **1** meal made from ground or rolled oats used esp. in cereal, cookies, etc. **2** cooked breakfast cereal made from this. **3** grayish-fawn color flecked with brown.

ob. *abbr.* he or she died.

ob– /ob/ *prefix* (also **oc–** before *c*, **of–** before *f*, **op–** before *p*) meaning: **1** meeting or facing (*occasion, obvious*). **2** opposition, hostility, or resistance (*obstreperous, opponent, obstinate*). **3** finality or completeness (*obsolete, occupy*).

ob•bli•ga•to /óbligáartō/ *n.* (*pl.* **–tos**) Mus. complicated accompaniment forming an integral part of a composition.

ob•du•rate /óbdoorit, –dyoor–/ *adj.* **1** stubborn. **2** hardened against persuasion or influence. See synonym study at STUBBORN. □□ **ob•du•ra•cy** /–doorasee, –dyoor–/ *n.*

■ **1** see OBSTINATE. **2** see DOGMATIC 1. □□ **obduracy** see *obstinacy* (OBSTINATE).

o•be•di•ent /ōbéedeeənt/ *adj.* **1** obeying or ready to obey. **2** submissive; dutiful (*obedient to the law*). □□ **o•be′di•ence** *n.* **o•be′di•ent•ly** *adv.*

■ compliant, respectful, agreeable, subservient, passive.

o•bei•sance /ōbáysəns, ōbée–/ *n.* **1** bow, curtsy, or other respectful or submissive gesture. **2** homage; deference (*pay obeisance*). See synonym study at HONOR. □□ **o•bei′sant** *adj.*

■ **1** see BOW² 2. **2** respect, submission, reverence, honor.

ob•e•lisk /óbəlisk/ *n.* tapering, usu. four-sided stone pillar set up as a monument or landmark, etc. **2** mountain, tree, etc., of similar shape.

■ **1** needle.

o•bese /ōbées/ *adj.* very fat; corpulent. □□ **o•be′si•ty** *n.*

■ overweight, stout, heavy. □□ **obesity** corpulence, plumpness, tubbiness; size, weight.

o•bey /ōbáy/ *v.* **1** *tr.* **a** carry out the command of (*you will obey me*). **b** carry out (a command) (*obey orders*). **2** *intr.* do what one is told to do. **3** *tr.* be actuated by (a force or impulse).

■ comply (with), submit (to), observe, follow, mind; discharge, execute.

ob•fus•cate /óbfuskayt/ *v.tr.* **1** obscure or confuse. **2** stupefy, bewilder. □□ **ob•fus•ca•tion** /–káyshən/ *n.*

■ **1** see OBSCURE *v.*

ob–gyn /ōbée-jeewién/ *abbr.* **1** obstetrician-gynecologist. **2** obstetrics-gynecology.

o•bit•u•ar•y /óbíchoo–eree/ *n.* (*pl.* **–ies**) **1** notice of a death esp. in a newspaper. **2** account of the life of a deceased person.

■ death notice, eulogy, *colloq.* obit.

obj. *abbr.* **1** object. **2** objective. **3** objection.

ob•ject ■ *n.* /óbjikt, –jekt/ **1** material thing that can be seen or touched. **2** person or thing to which action or feeling is directed (*the object of our study*). **3** thing sought or aimed at; purpose. **4** *Gram.* noun or its equivalent governed by an active transitive verb or by a preposition. ■ *v.* /əbjékt/ **1** *intr.* express or feel opposition, disapproval, or reluctance; protest. **2** *tr.* state as an objection. □ **object lesson** striking practical example of some principle. □□ **ob•jec′tor** /əbjéktər/ *n.*

■ *n.* **1** item; reality, entity. **2** focus, target, destination. **3** end, intention, reason, goal. ■ *v.* argue, complain, refuse.

ob•jec•ti•fy /əbjéktifí/ *v.tr.* (**–fies, –fied**) present as an object.

ob•jec•tion /əbjékshən/ *n.* **1** expression or feeling of opposition or disapproval. **2** adverse reason or statement.

■ protest, dislike, exception, argument, challenge, complaint.

ob•jec•tion•a•ble /əbjékshənəbəl/ *adj.* **1** open to objection. **2** unpleasant, offensive. □□ **ob•jec′tion•a•bly** *adv.*

■ **1** see EXCEPTIONABLE. **2** see OFFENSIVE *adj.* 1.

ob•jec•tive /əbjéktiv/ ■ *adj.* **1** external to the mind; actually existing. **2** (of a person, writing, art, etc.) dealing with outward things or exhibiting unbiased facts; not subjective. **3** *Gram.* (of a case or word) constructed as or appropriate to the object of a transitive verb or preposition (cf. ACCUSATIVE). ■ *n.* something sought or aimed at; objective point. □□ **ob•jec′tive•ly** *adv.* **ob•jec′tive•ness** *n.* **ob•jec•tiv′i•ty** *n.*

■ *adj.* **1** manifest, palpable, real; see also FACTUAL, ACTUAL 1. **2** fair, impartial, just, neutral, open-minded. ■ *n.* target, goal, purpose, intention. □□ **objectiveness, objectivity** impartiality, fairness, detachment.

ob•jet d'art /áwbzhay daar/ *n.* (*pl.* **ob•jets d'art** *pronun.* same) small object of artistic worth.

ob•la•tion /əbláyshən, ob–/ *n.* Relig. thing offered to a divine being.

■ see OFFERING.

ob•li•gate /óbligayt/ *v.tr.* [usu. in *passive*; foll. by *to* + infin.] bind (a person) legally or morally.

■ commit; require, compel, force.

ob•li•ga•tion /óbligáyshən/ *n.* **1** constraining power of a law, precept, duty, contract, etc. **2** duty. **3** binding agreement. **4 a** service or benefit (*repay an obligation*). **b** indebtedness for this.

■ **1, 3** compulsion; requirement; promise. **2** responsibility, charge, burden; trust. **4** liability; see also KINDNESS 2.

ob•lig•a•to•ry /əbligətáwree/ *adj.* **1** legally or

morally binding. **2** compulsory. □□ **ob·lig·a·to·ri·ly** adv.

■ required, demanded; incumbent; indispensable, essential.

o·blige /əblíj/ v.tr. **1** constrain; compel. **2** be binding on. **3 a** make indebted by conferring a favor. **b** gratify (*oblige me by leaving*). **c** perform a service for (often *absol.*: *will you oblige?*). **4** [in *passive*; foll. by *to*] be indebted (*am obliged to you for your help*). See synonym study at COMPEL.

■ **1, 2** make, require, demand. **3** accommodate, indulge, please. **4** (*obliged*) thankful, grateful, appreciative.

o·blig·ing /əblíjing/ adj. courteous, accommodating; ready to do a service or kindness. □□ **o·blig·ing·ly** adv.

■ willing, gracious, considerate, helpful, supportive.

ob·lique /əbléek/ • adj. **1 a** slanting. **b** diverging from a straight line or course. **2** not going straight to the point; indirect. • n. oblique muscle. □□ **ob·lique·ly** adv. **o·blique′ness** n.

■ adj. **1** sloping, diagonal, angled, askew. **2** roundabout, circuitous, evasive, sly, clandestine, underhand(ed), deceitful.

ob·lit·er·ate /əblítərayt/ v.tr. **1 a** blot out; destroy. **b** leave no clear traces of. **2** deface (a postage stamp, etc.) to prevent further use. □□ **ob·lit·er·a·tion** /-ráyshən/ n.

■ **1** erase, rub out, eradicate, delete; annihilate, kill.

ob·liv·i·on /əblíveeən/ n. state of having or being forgotten.

■ blankness, darkness, obscurity, anonymity, extinction; unawareness, disregard.

ob·liv·i·ous /əblíveeəs/ adj. **1** [often foll. by *of*] forgetful; unmindful. **2** [foll. by *to, of*] unaware of. □□ **ob·liv·i·ous·ly** adv. **ob·liv′i·ous·ness** n.

■ absentminded; unconscious, insensitive, unconcerned. □□ **obliviousness** disregard, unconsciousness, forgetfulness.

ob·long /óblawng/ • adj. rectangular with adjacent sides unequal. • n. oblong figure or object.

ob·lo·quy /óbləkwee/ n. **1** ill spoken of. **2** abuse, detraction.

■ **1** see *notoriety* (NOTORIOUS). **2** see ABUSE n. 2.

ob·nox·ious /əbnókshəs/ adj. offensive; objectionable; disliked. □□ **ob·nox′ious·ly** adv. **ob·nox′ious·ness** n.

■ revolting, repulsive, disgusting, vile, sickening, abhorrent, hateful, obscene, awful, nasty, *colloq.* beastly.

o·boe /óbō/ n. **1** woodwind double-reed instrument of treble pitch and plaintive tone. **2** its player. □□ **o·bo·ist** /óbō-ist/ n.

ob·scene /əbséen/ adj. **1** offensively indecent, esp. by offending accepted sexual morality. **2** *colloq.* highly offensive. □□ **ob·scene·ly** adv. **ob·scen·i·ty** /-sén-/ n.

■ **1** improper, rude, shameful, risqué, vulgar, immoral, coarse, dirty, pornographic. **2** outrageous, shocking, obnoxious, sickening, despicable.

ob·scu·ran·tism /əbskyŏorántizəm, óbskyŏorán-/ n. opposition to knowledge and enlightenment. □□ **ob·scu′ran·tist** n.

ob·scure /əbskyŏor/ • adj. **1** not clearly expressed nor easily understood. **2** unexplained; doubtful. **3** dark. **4** indistinct. **5** hidden. **6 a** unnoticed. **b** (of a person) undistinguished; hardly known. • v.tr. make obscure, dark, indistinct, or unintelligible. □□ **ob·scure′ly** adv. **ob·scu′ri·ty** n.

■ adj. **1, 2, 4** uncertain, ambiguous, vague, hazy; complex, occult. **3** unlit, gloomy, dim. **5** secret, concealed, remote. **6** unheard-of, anonymous, unimportant, unsung. • v. dim, cloud, dull, shade; hide, disguise.

ob·se·quies /óbsikweez/ n.pl. funeral rites.

ob·se·qui·ous /əbséekweeəs/ adj. servilely obedient or attentive. □□ **ob·se′qui·ous·ly** adv. **ob·se′qui·ous·ness** n.

■ low, cringing, toadying, sycophantic, groveling.

ob·serv·ance /əbzérvəns/ n. **1** keeping or performing of a law, duty, custom, ritual, etc. **2** ceremony; rite.

■ **1** obedience, compliance, adherence, regard, recognition, respect. **2** celebration, ritual, service; form, custom, tradition.

ob·serv·ant /əbzérvənt/ adj. **1** acute or diligent in taking notice. **2** attentive in esp. religious observances (*an observant Jew*). □□ **ob·serv′ant·ly** adv.

■ **1** watchful, alert, attentive, aware; heedful, attentive. **2** obedient, respectful.

ob·ser·va·tion /óbzərváyshən/ n. **1** noticing; being noticed. **2** perception. **3** remark, comment, or statement. **4** accurate watching and noting of phenomena as they occur in nature with regard to cause and effect or mutual relations. □□ **ob·ser·va′tion·al** adj.

■ **1, 2, 4** examination, scrutiny, inspection, viewing, discovery. **3** reflection, opinion, impression, criticism.

ob·ser·va·to·ry /əbzérvətawree/ n. (pl. **-ries**) building for astronomical or other observation.

ob·serve /əbzérv/ v. **1** tr. perceive; become conscious of. **2** tr. watch carefully. **3** tr. **a** follow or adhere to (a law, command, method, principle, etc.). **b** keep or adhere to (an appointed time). **c** maintain (silence). **d** perform (a rite). **e** celebrate (an anniversary). **4** tr. examine and note scientifically. **5** tr. say, esp. by way of comment. **6** intr. remark. □□ **ob·serv′a·ble** adj. **ob·serv′er** n.

■ **1** see NOTICE v. **2, 4** look at, monitor, study, sl. case. **3 a, b** obey, comply with, respect. **c** see MAINTAIN 1, 2. **4, 6** keep, commemorate, recognize. **5** remark, mention; state. □□ **observable** noticeable, recognizable, distinct, obvious.

ob·sess /əbsés/ v. [often in *passive*] preoccupy; haunt. □ **obsessive-compulsive** relating to a neurosis characterized by an obsessive thought and compulsive behavior, such as repeated hand washing. □□ **ob·ses′sive** adj. & n. **ob·ses′sive·ly** adv. **ob·ses′sive·ness** n.

■ take control of, torment, control, possess, *colloq.* plague. □□ **obsessive**(adj.) dominating, addictive; tormenting.

ob•ses•sion /əbséshən/ *n.* **1** obsessing or being obsessed. **2** persistent idea or thought dominating a person's mind. □□ **ob•ses'sion•al** *adj.* **ob•ses'sion•al•ly** *adv.*

■ fixation, preoccupation, passion, mania, *sl.* hang-up.

ob•sid•i•an /əbsídeeən/ *n.* dark glassy rock formed from lava.

ob•so•les•cent /óbsəlésənt/ *adj.* becoming obsolete; going out of use or date. □□ **ob•so'les•cence** /-səns/ *n.*

■ fading, declining, dying; see also OBSOLETE.

ob•so•lete /óbsəleet/ *adj.* disused; discarded; antiquated. See synonym study at OLD.

■ out-of-date, out of fashion, passé, dated.

ob•sta•cle /óbstəkəl/ *n.* person or thing that obstructs progress.

■ impediment, hindrance, hurdle, catch, barrier, bar.

ob•stet•rics /əbstétriks, ob–/ *n.pl.* [usu. treated as *sing.*] branch of medicine concerned with pregnancy and childbirth. □□ **ob•stet'ric** *adj.* **ob•ste•tri•cian** /-stətríshən/ *n.*

ob•sti•nate /óbstinət/ *adj.* stubborn, intractable. See synonym study at STUBBORN. □□ **ob•sti•na•cy** /-nəsee/ *n.* **ob'sti•nate•ly** *adv.*

■ dogged, persistent, mulish, headstrong. □□ **obstinacy** tenacity, intransigence, inflexibility.

ob•strep•er•ous /əbstrépərəs/ *adj.* **1** turbulent; unruly. **2** noisy. See synonym study at VOCIFEROUS. □□ **ob•strep'er•ous•ly** *adv.* **ob•strep'er•ous•ness** *n.*

■ boisterous, rowdy, disorderly, rambunctious, vociferous, raucous.

ob•struct /əbstrúkt/ *v.tr.* **1** block up. **2** prevent or retard the progress of. See synonym study at HINDER. □□ **ob•struc'tive** *adj.* **ob•struc'tive•ness** *n.* **ob•struct'or** *n.*

■ **1** clog, stop (up), bar, blockade. **2** balk, hamper, impede, stall.

ob•struc•tion /əbstrúkshən/ *n.* **1** blocking; being blocked. **2** obstacle or blockage. **3** retarding of progress by deliberate delays. □□ **ob•struc'tion•ist** *n.* (in sense 3).

■ **1** barring; hindering, stalling. **2** barrier, hurdle, hindrance, bottleneck. **3** delaying tactics.

ob•tain /əbtáyn/ *v.* **1** *tr.* acquire; secure. **2** *intr.* be prevalent or established or in vogue. See synonym study at GET. □□ **ob•tain'a•ble** *adj.* **ob•tain'ment** *n.*

■ **1** get, come by, grasp, capture, seize, buy, purchase, earn, gain. **2** prevail, exist, be customary.

ob•trude /əbtroód/ *v.* **1** *intr.* stick out; push forward. **2** *tr.* thrust forward (oneself, one's opinion, etc.) importunately. □□ **ob•tru'sion** /-troózhən/ *n.* **ob•tru•sive** /-siv/ *adj.* **ob•tru'sive•ly** *adv.* **ob•tru'sive•ness** *n.* See synonym study at IMPERTINENT.

■ impinge, trespass, intrude, impose.

ob•tuse /əbtoós, –tyoós/ *adj.* **1** dull-witted. **2** blunt; not sharp. **3** (of an angle) between 90° and 180°. □□ **ob•tuse'ly** *adv.* **ob•tuse'ness** *n.*

■ **1** insensitive, dense, dim-witted. **2** rounded; see also BLUNT *adj.* 1.

ob•verse /óbvərs/ *n.* **1 a** side of a coin or

medal, etc., bearing the head or principal design. **b** this design (cf. REVERSE). **2** front or proper or top side of a thing. **3** counterpart of a fact or truth.

■ **2** see FRONT *n.* 1.

ob•vi•ate /óbveeayt/ *v.tr.* get around or do away with (a need, inconvenience, etc.). □□ **ob•vi•a•tion** /-áyshən/ *n.*

■ see PRECLUDE 2. □□ **obviation** see *prevention* (PREVENT).

ob•vi•ous /óbveeəs/ *adj.* easily seen or recognized or understood. □□ **ob'vi•ous•ly** *adv.* **ob'vi•ous•ness** *n.*

■ clear, plain, apparent, evident, conspicuous, undeniable; see also CERTAIN *adj.* 1b. □□ **obviously** clearly, plainly, apparently.

oc•a•ri•na /ókəreenə/ *n.* small egg-shaped wind instrument.

oc•ca•sion /əkáyzhən/ • *n.* **1 a** special or noteworthy event or happening. **b** time of this (*on the occasion of their marriage*). **2** reason, ground(s), or justification. **3** juncture suitable for doing something; opportunity. **4** subordinate or incidental cause (*the assassination was the occasion of the war*). • *v.tr.* **1** be the cause of. **2** cause (a person or thing to do something). □ **on occasion** now and then; when the need arises.

■ *n.* **1 a** function, affair; observance, ceremony. **2** provocation, stimulus. **3** time, circumstance, chance. ■ *v.* give rise to, bring about, effect, provoke, create, generate. □ **on occasion** see *occasionally* (OCCASIONAL).

oc•ca•sion•al /əkáyzhənəl/ *adj.* **1** happening irregularly and infrequently. **2 a** made or meant for, or associated with, a special occasion. **b** (of furniture, etc.) made or adapted for infrequent and varied use. □□ **oc•ca'sion•al•ly** *adv.*

■ **1** intermittent, periodic, random. **2 a** particular, solemn, official; see also CEREMONIAL *adj.* 1. **b** additional, spare, accessory. □□ **occasionally** sometimes, (every) now and then, periodically, sporadically.

Oc•ci•dent /óksidənt, –dent/ *n. poet.* or *rhet.* **1** [prec. *by the*] West. **2** Europe, America, or both, as distinct from the Orient. □□ **oc•ci•den'tal** *adj.* & *n.*

oc•ci•put /óksiput/ *n.* back of the head. □□ **oc•cip•i•tal** /-sípit'l/ *adj.*

oc•clude /əkloód/ *v.tr.* stop up or close (pores or an orifice). □□ **oc•clu•sion** /əkloózhən/ *n.* **oc•clu•sive** /-siv/ *adj.*

oc•cult /əkúlt, ókúlt/ *adj.* **1** supernatural; mystical. **2** kept secret; esoteric.

■ **1** magical, unexplained, puzzling, mysterious, incomprehensible. **2** dark, private, hidden, obscure, vague, mystical, mysterious.

oc•cu•pant /ókyəpənt/ *n.* person who occupies, resides in, or is in a place, etc. □□ **oc'cu•pan•cy** /-pənsee/ *n.* (*pl.* **-cies**)

■ resident, inhabitant, tenant, renter, owner; incumbent.

oc•cu•pa•tion /ókyəpáyshən/ *n.* **1** what occupies one; means of passing one's time. **2** person's employment. **3 a** act of taking or holding possession of (a country, district, etc.) by military force. **b** state or time of this. □□ **oc•cu•pa′tion•al** *adj.*

■ 2 job, position, career, field, calling, trade, pursuit, skill, profession, business, work. 3 **a** conquest, seizure, takeover.

oc•cu•py /ókyəpī/ *v.tr.* (**–pies, –pied**) 1 reside in. 2 take up or fill (space or time or a place). 3 hold (a position or office). 4 take military possession of (a country, region, town, strategic position). 5 [usu. in *passive*] keep busy or engaged.

■ 1 live in, tenant, inhabit, make one's home in, be located in. 2 cover, extend over, consume, use (up). 3 see HOLD[1] *v.* 3. 4 capture, seize, conquer, invade, dominate, hold. 5 absorb, monopolize; divert, amuse, entertain.

oc•cur /əkár/ *v.intr.* (**oc•curred, oc•cur•ring**) 1 come into being; happen. 2 exist or be encountered. 3 come into the mind of. See synonym study at HAPPEN.

■ 1 take place, arise, appear, surface, materialize. 3 (*occur to*) dawn on, strike, hit, suggest itself to, cross a person's mind.

oc•cur•rence /əkárəns, əkúr–/ *n.* 1 occurring. 2 incident or event.

■ 1 existence, instance, appearance, development; frequency, rate. 2 happening, phenomenon.

o•cean /óshən/ *n.* 1 large expanse of sea, esp. the Atlantic, Pacific, Indian, Arctic, and Antarctic Oceans. 2 [often in *pl.*] very large expanse or quantity of anything (*oceans of time*). □□ **o•ce•an•ic** /ósheeánik/ *adj.*

■ 1 deep blue sea, high sea(s), *colloq.* the drink, *sl.* Davy Jones('s locker). 2 (*oceans*) plenty, an abundance, *colloq.* loads, a lot, tons, oodles.

o•cea•nar•i•um /óshənáireeəm/ *n.* (*pl.* **o•cea•nar•i•ums** or **–ri•a** /–reeə/) large seawater aquarium for keeping sea animals.

o•cea•nog•ra•phy /óshənógrəfee/ *n.* the study of the oceans. □□ **o•cea•nog′ra•pher** *n.* **o•cea•no•graph′ic** *adj.* **o•cea•no•graph′i•cal** *adj.*

o•ce•lot /ósilot, ósi–/ *n.* 1 medium-sized feline native to S. and Central America, having a deep yellow or orange coat with black striped and spotted markings. 2 its fur.

o•cher /ókər/ *n.* 1 mineral of clay and ferric oxide, used as a pigment varying from light yellow to brown or red. 2 pale brownish yellow. □□ **o′cher•ous** *adj.*

o′clock /əklók/ *adv.* of the clock (*6 o'clock*).

OCR *abbr.* optical character recognition.

Oct. *abbr.* October.

octa- /óktə/ *comb. form* (**oct-** before a vowel) eight.

oc•ta•gon /óktəgon, –gən/ *n.* plane figure with eight sides and angles. □□ **oc•tag•o•nal** /–tágənəl/ *adj.*

oc•ta•he•dron /óktəheédrən/ *n.* (*pl.* **oc•ta•he•drons** or **oc•ta•he•dra** /–drə/) solid figure contained by eight (esp. triangular) plane faces. □□ **oc•ta•he′dral** *adj.*

oc•tane /óktayn/ *n.* colorless flammable hydrocarbon present in gasoline. ¶Chem. formula: C_8H_{18}.

oc•tave /óktiv, –tayv/ *n.* 1 *Mus.* **a** eight notes occupying the interval between (and including) two notes, one having twice or half the frequency of vibration of the other. **b** this interval. **c** each of the two notes at the extremes of this interval. 2 group of eight.

oc•ta•vo /oktáyvō, oktaávō/ *n.* (*pl.* **–vos**) 1 size of book or page given by folding a standard sheet three times to form a quire of eight leaves. 2 book or sheet of this size. ¶Abbr.: **8vo.**

oc•tet /oktét/ *n.* (also **oc•tette′**) 1 *Mus.* **a** composition for eight voices or instruments. **b** performers of such a piece. 2 group of eight. 3 first eight lines of a sonnet.

octo- /óktō/ *comb. form* (**oct-** before a vowel) eight.

Oc•to•ber /októbər/ *n.* tenth month of the year.

oc•to•ge•nar•i•an /óktəjináireeən/ • *n.* person from 80 to 89 years old. • *adj.* of this age.

oc•to•pus /óktəpəs/ *n.* (*pl.* **oc•to•pus•es**) cephalopod mollusk having eight suckered arms, a soft saclike body, and strong beaklike jaws.

oc•u•lar /ókyoolər/ *adj.* of or connected with the eyes or sight; visual.

oc•u•list /ókyəlist/ *n. formerly* 1 ophthalmologist. 2 optometrist.

OD[1] *abbr.* 1 doctor of optometry. 2 overdraft.

OD[2] /ódeé/ *sl.* • *n.* overdose, esp. of a narcotic drug. • *v.intr.* (**OD's, OD'd, OD'ing**) take an overdose.

o.d. *abbr.* outside diameter.

odd /od/ *adj.* 1 strange, remarkable, eccentric. 2 casual, occasional (*odd jobs*). 3 not normally noticed or considered; unpredictable. 4 additional; besides the calculated amount (*a few odd cents*). 5 **a** (of numbers) not integrally divisible by two. **b** bearing such a number (*no parking on odd dates*). 6 one item of a pair. 7 (appended to a number, sum, weight, etc.) somewhat more than (*forty-odd people*). 8 by which a round number, given sum, etc., is exceeded (*we have 102 — what shall we do with the odd 2?*). □□ **odd′ly** *adv.* **odd′ness** *n.*

■ 1 peculiar, unusual, different, unexpected, out of the ordinary, unique, singular. 2 part-time, irregular, random. 4, 6, 8 leftover, surplus, extra; uneven, unmatched, unpaired.

odd•ball /ódbawl/ *n. colloq.* 1 eccentric person. 2 [*attrib.*] strange, bizarre.

■ 1 see ECCENTRIC *n.* 1. 2 (*attrib.*) see ODD *adj.* 1.

odd•i•ty /óditee/ *n.* (*pl.* **–ties**) 1 strange person, thing, or occurrence. 2 peculiar trait. 3 state of being odd.

■ 1 peculiarity, curiosity, rarity, freak, character. 2 irregularity, idiosyncrasy, eccentricity, quirk. 3 peculiarity, strangeness, curiosity, individuality, singularity, distinctiveness, anomaly, *colloq.* kinkiness, *sl.* kookiness.

odds /odz/ *n.pl.* 1 ratio between the amounts staked by the parties to a bet, based on the expected probability either way. 2 balance of probability in favor of or against some result (*the odds are that it will rain*). □ **odds and ends** miscellaneous articles or remnants. **odds-on** state when success is more likely than failure, esp. as indicated by the betting odds.

■ chances, likelihood. □ **odds and ends** fragments, leftovers, leavings, bits (and pieces), shreds, scraps.

ode /ōd/ *n.* lyric poem, usu. rhymed and in the form of an address, in varied or irregular meter.

■ see POEM.

o•di•ous /ōdēəs/ *adj.* hateful; repulsive. See synonym study at OFFENSIVE. □□ **o'di•ous•ly** *adv.* **o'di•ous•ness** *n.*

■ see REPULSIVE.

o•di•um /ōdēəm/ *n.* widespread dislike or disapproval.

o•dom•e•ter /ōdómitər/ *n.* instrument for measuring the distance traveled by a wheeled vehicle.

o•dor /ōdər/ *n.* **1** property of a substance that has an effect on the nasal sense of smell **2** quality or trace (*odor of intolerance*). **3** regard, repute (*in bad odor*). See synonym study at SMELL. □□ **o'dor•less** *adj.* (in sense 1).

■ **1** scent, aroma, fragrance, perfume, stench, stink. **2** air, breath, hint, suggestion, tone. **3** standing, esteem.

o•dor•if•er•ous /ōdəriférəs/ *adj.* diffusing a scent, esp. an agreeable one; fragrant.

■ see *fragrant* (FRAGRANCE).

od•ys•sey /ódisee/ *n.* (*pl.* −**seys**) long adventurous journey.

■ see JOURNEY *n.*

OED *abbr.* Oxford English Dictionary.

Oed•i•pus com•plex /édipəs, éedi−/ *n. Psychol.* (according to Freud, etc.) emotions aroused in a young (esp. male) child by a subconscious sexual desire for the parent of the opposite sex. □□ **Oed'i•pal** *adj.*

OEM *abbr.* original equipment manufacturer.

oe•no•phile /éenəfil/ *n.* connoisseur of wines.

o'er /ôr/ *prep. adv. & Poet. poet.* = OVER.

oeu•vre /óvrə/ *n.* works of an author, painter, composer, etc., esp. regarded collectively.

■ see WORK *n.* 5.

of /uv, ov, əv/ *prep.* connecting a noun (often a verbal noun) or pronoun with a preceding noun, adjective, adverb, or verb, expressing a wide range of relations broadly describable as follows: **1** origin or cause (*paintings of Turner, died of malnutrition*). **2** material or substance (*house of cards, built of bricks*). **3** belonging or connection (*thing of the past, articles of clothing*). **4** identity or close relation (*city of Rome, pound of apples*). **5** removal or separation (*north of the city, robbed us of $500*). **6** reference or direction (*beware of the dog, short of money*). **7** partition, classification, or inclusion (*no more of that, part of the story, this sort of book*). **8** description, quality, or condition (*person of tact, girl of ten*). **9** time in relation to the following hour (*quarter of three*).

off /awf, of/ • *adv.* **1** away; at or to a distance (*is three miles off*). **2** out of position; not on or touching or attached (*take your coat off*). **3** so as to be rid of (*sleep it off*). **4** so as to be dis-

continued or stopped (*turn off the radio*). **5** to the end; so as to be clear (*clear off, pay off*). **6** situated as regards money, supplies, etc. (*is not very well off*). **7** (of food, etc.) beginning to decay. • *prep.* **1 a** from; away or down or up from (*fell off the chair*). **b** not on (*was already off the pitch*). **2 a** (temporarily) relieved of or abstaining from (*off duty*). **b** not achieving or doing one's best in (*off one's game*). **3** using as a source or means of support (*live off the land*). **4** leading from; not far from (*a street off 1st Avenue*). • *adj.* far, further (*the off side of the wall*). □ **off and on** intermittently; now and then. **off-color** somewhat indecent. **off-key 1** out of tune. **2** not quite suitable or fitting. **off-limits** prohibited. **off-line** *Computing* (of a computer terminal or process) not directly controlled by or connected to a central processor. **off-load** = UNLOAD. **off-peak** used or for use at times other than those of greatest demand. **off-putting** disconcerting; repellent. **off-road** *attrib.adj.* (of a vehicle, etc.) designed for rough terrain or for cross-country driving. **off-season** time when business, etc., is slack. **off the wall** crazy; absurd. **off-white** white with a gray or yellowish tinge.

■ *adv.* **1** out, elsewhere; afar. **2** away; loose, separate, gone. **4** canceled, postponed. **5** up, entirely; see also THROUGH *adv.* **6** fixed, supplied. **7** sour, moldy, bad, rancid. • *prep.* **1** out of. **2 b** not up to, not on. **3** on, by, from. **4** near, next to, connecting with. • *adj.* see *far adj.* **1** □ **off and on** on and off; see also *by fits and starts* (FIT). **off-color** risqué, ribald, bawdy, suggestive, inappropriate, blue. **off-key 1** tuneless, flat. **2** see INCONGRUOUS. **off putting** see DISAGREEABLE 1.

of•fal /áwfəl, óf−/ *n.* **1** less valuable edible parts of a carcass, esp. the entrails and internal organs. **2** refuse or waste stuff.

■ **2** see RUBBISH 1.

off•beat • *adj.* /áwfbeet, óf−/ **1** not coinciding with the beat. **2** eccentric, unconventional. • *n.* /ófbeet/ any of the unaccented beats in a bar.

■ *adj.* **2** strange, weird, peculiar, odd, unorthodox, unusual, unexpected, *colloq.* kinky, way out, *sl.* off-the-wall, far-out.

of•fend /əfénd/ *v.* **1** *tr.* cause offense to; wound the feelings of. **2** *tr.* displease or anger. **3** *intr.* do wrong; transgress. □□ **of•fend'er** *n.* **of•fend'ing** *adj.*

■ **1, 2** insult, slight, humiliate; annoy, irritate; disgust, sicken, repulse. **3** see TRANSGRESS. □□ **offender** criminal, culprit, sinner, *colloq.* crook.

of•fense /əféns/ *n.* **1** illegal act; transgression or misdemeanor. **2** wounding of the feelings (*no offense was meant*). **3** /áwfens, óf−/ aggressive action. **4** /áwfens, óf−/ *Sports* team in possession of the ball, puck, etc. See synonym study at SIN.

■ **1** violation, crime, felony, infraction, wrong, sin; lapse, slip, error. **2** resentment, annoyance. **3** see AGGRESSION 2.

of•fen•sive /əfénsiv/ • *adj.* **1** giving or meant

or likely to give offense; insulting. **2** disgusting. **3 a** aggressive, attacking. **b** (of a weapon) for attacking. **4** *Sports* designating the team in possession of the ball, puck, etc. • *n.* **1** aggressive action or attitude. **2** attack; offensive campaign. □□ **of•fen′sive•ly** *adv.* **of•fen′sive•ness** *n.*

■ *adj.* **1** rude, disrespectful, impolite, objectionable. **2** obnoxious, repulsive, sickening, rotten. **3 a** antagonistic, hostile, threatening. • *n.* **2** onslaught, drive, assault.

SYNONYM STUDY: offensive

ABHORRENT, ABOMINABLE, DETESTABLE, ODIOUS, REPUGNANT. Looking for just the right word to express your dislike, distaste, disgust, or aversion to something? **Offensive** is a relatively mild adjective, used to describe anyone or anything that is unpleasant or disagreeable (*she found his remarks offensive; the offensive sight of a dirty cat-litter box*). If you want to express strong dislike for someone or something that deserves to be disliked, use **detestable** (*a detestable man who never had a kind word for anyone*). If something is so *offensive* that it provokes a physical as well as a moral or intellectual response, use **odious** (*the odious treatment of women during the war in Bosnia*), and if you instinctively draw back from it, use **repugnant** (*the very thought of piercing one's nose was repugnant to her*). If your *repugnance* is extreme, go one step further and use **abhorrent** (*an abhorrent act that could not go unpunished*). Save **abominable** for persons and things that are truly loathsome or terrifying (*an abominable act of desecration; his abominable taste in clothes; the Abominable Snowman*).

---

of•fer /áwfər, óf–/ • *v.* **1** *tr.* present for acceptance, refusal, or consideration (*offered me a drink*). **2** *intr.* express readiness or show intention (*offered to take the children*). **3** *tr.* provide; give an opportunity for. **4** *intr.* present itself; occur (*as opportunity offers*). **5** *tr.* attempt (*violence, resistance, etc.*). • *n.* **1** expression of readiness to do or give if desired, or to buy or sell. **2** amount offered. **3** proposal (*esp. of marriage*). **4** bid.

■ *v.* **1** propose; see also VENTURE *v.* **3**. **2** volunteer. **3** submit; extend; suggest. • *n.* presentation, proposition.

of•fer•ing /áwfəring, óf–/ *n.* **1** contribution or gift, esp. of money to a church. **2** thing offered as a religious sacrifice or token of devotion.

■ donation, present.

of•fer•to•ry /áwfərtàwree, óf–/ *n.* (*pl.* **–ries**) **1** *Eccl.* offering of the bread and wine at the Eucharist. **2 a** collection of money at a religious service. **b** money collected.

off•hand /áwfhánd, óf–/ • *adj.* curt or casual in manner. • *adv.* without preparation or premeditation. □□ **off′hand′ed** *adj.* **off′hand′ed•ly** *adv.* **off′hand′ed•ness** *n.*

■ *adj.* brusque, ungracious, informal, aloof, easygoing, relaxed. • *adv.* impromptu, extemporaneously, off-the-cuff.

of•fice /áwfis, óf–/ *n.* **1** room or building used

as a place of business, esp. for clerical or administrative work. **2** room or place for a particular kind of business. **3** position with duties attached to it. **4** tenure of an official position, esp. that of government. **5** duty attaching to one's position; task or function. **6** [usu. in *pl.*] kindness or attention; service (esp. *through the good offices of*). **7** *Eccl.* form of worship. **8** ceremonial duty.

■ **1** workplace; headquarters, base, center. **2** department, branch; section, division; organization, firm, company, corporation. **3, 4, 5** obligation, responsibility, service, occupation, appointment, assignment, job. **6** (*offices*) auspices, support, advocacy, help, patronage, backing.

of•fi•cer /áwfisər, óf–/ *n.* **1** person holding a position of authority or trust, esp. one with a commission in the armed services, etc. **2** policeman or policewoman. **3** holder of a post in a society or business (e.g., the president or secretary). **4** holder of a public, civil, or ecclesiastical office.

■ **1, 3, 4** (public) official, dignitary, public servant, appointee, bureaucrat, manager, director. **2** officer of the law, constable, *colloq.* G-man, *sl.* cop, gumshoe, fuzz.

of•fi•cial /əfíshəl/ • *adj.* **1** of or relating to an office (see OFFICE *n.* **3, 4**) or its tenure or duties. **2** characteristic of officials and bureaucracy. **3** properly authorized. • *n.* person holding office or engaged in official duties. □□ **of•fi′cial•dom** *n.* **of•fi′cial•ly** *adv.*

■ *adj.* **1, 2** ceremonial, formal, solemn, proper, bureaucratic. **3** legitimate, legal, authentic, accredited, licensed, recognized, accepted. • *n.* see OFFICER *n.* **1, 3, 4**.

of•fi•ci•ate /əfísheeáyt/ *v.intr.* **1** act in an official capacity. **2** conduct a religious service. □□ **of•fi•ci•a•tion** /–áyshən/ *n.* **of•fi′ci•a•tor** *n.*

■ **1** umpire, referee, judge, adjudicate, mediate; (*officiate at*) preside (over), direct, chair, lead, supervise.

of•fi•cious /əfíshəs/ *adj.* **1** asserting one's authority aggressively; domineering. **2** intrusive; meddlesome. □□ **of•fi′cious•ly** *adv.* **of•fi′cious•ness** *n.*

■ dictatorial, persistent, demanding, bold.

off•ing /áwfing, óf–/ *n.* more distant part of the sea in view. □ **in the offing** likely to appear or happen soon.

off•screen /áwfskréen, óf–/ • *adj.* not appearing on a movie, television, or computer screen. • *adv.* outside the view presented by a filmed scene.

off•set • *n.* /áwfset, óf–/ **1** compensation; consideration or amount neutralizing the effect of a contrary one. **2** [often *attrib.*] method of printing in which ink is transferred from a plate or stone to a rubber surface and from there to paper, etc. (*offset lithography*). • *v.tr.* /áwfsét, óf–/ (**–set•ting**; *past* and *past part.* **–set**) **1** counterbalance, compensate. **2** print by the offset process.

■ *n.* **1** counterbalance, counteraction, check. • *v.* **1** counteract, balance (out), equalize, make up (for), repay, make good, reimburse.

off•shoot /áwfshoot, óf–/ *n.* **1 a** side shoot or

branch. **b** descendant of a family. **2** something derivative.

■ **1 a** spur; limb, twig, stem. **b** relative, kin. **2** outgrowth, development, spin-off, by-product.

off•shore /áwfsháwr, óf–/ *adj.* **1** at sea some distance from the shore. **2** (of the wind) blowing seaward. **3** (of goods, funds, etc.) made or registered abroad.

off•side /áwfsíd, óf–/ *adj. Sports* (of a player in a field game or ice hockey) in a position, usu. ahead of the ball, that is not allowed if it affects play.

off•spring /áwfspring, óf–/ *n.* (*pl.* same) children; descendant(s).

■ youngster(s), brood, young, successor(s), heir(s).

off•stage /áwfstáyj, óf–/ *adj. & adv. Theatr.* not on the stage and so not visible to the audience.

oft /awft, oft/ *adv. archaic* or *literary* often (usu. in *comb.*: *oft-recurring*).

of•ten /áwfən, áwftən, óf–/ *adv.* (**of•ten•er**, **of•ten•est**) **1** frequently; many times. **2** at short intervals.

■ regularly, much, usually, ordinarily, continually.

o•gle /ógəl/ • *v.* **1** *tr.* eye amorously or lecherously. **2** *intr.* look amorously. • *n.* amorous or lecherous look. □□ **o′gler** *n.*

■ *v.* **1** make eyes at, leer at, *colloq.* look a person over. **2** leer, gaze, *colloq.* gawk. • *n.* leer, stare, gape, *colloq.* glad eye.

o•gre /ógər/ *n.* (*fem.* **o•gress** /ógris/) **1** human-eating giant in folklore, etc. **2** terrifying person. □□ **o′gre•ish** *adj.*

■ monster, fiend, troll, brute, sadist.

OH *abbr.* Ohio (in official postal use).

oh /ō/ *int.* (also **O**) expressing surprise, pain, entreaty, etc.

ohm /ōm/ *n. Electr.* unit of resistance, transmitting a current of one ampere when subjected to a potential difference of one volt. ¶Symb.: Ω.

oho /ōhṓ/ *int.* expressing surprise or exultation.

-oid /oyd/ *suffix* forming adjectives and nouns, denoting form or resemblance (*asteroid*, *rhomboid*, *thyroid*). □□ **-oidal** *suffix* forming adjectives. **-oidally** *suffix* forming adverbs.

oil /oyl/ • *n.* **1** any of various thick, viscous, usu. flammable liquids insoluble in water (see also *mineral oil*). **2** petroleum. **3 a** [usu. in *pl.*] = *oil paint*. **b** *colloq.* picture painted in oil paints. • *v.* **1** *tr.* apply oil to; lubricate. **2** *tr.* impregnate or treat with oil. **3** *tr. & intr.* supply with or take on oil as fuel. □ **oil paint** mix of ground color pigment and oil. **oil painting 1** art of painting in oil paints. **2** picture painted in oil paints. **oil slick** patch of oil, esp. on the sea.

■ *n.* **1, 2** lubricant, grease; fuel. • *v.* **1** grease; see also SLICK *v.*

oil•cloth /óylklawth, –kloth/ *n.* **1** fabric waterproofed with oil. **2** canvas coated with oil and used to cover a table or floor.

oil•skin /óylskin/ *n.* **1** cloth waterproofed with oil. **2** [often *pl.*] garment or suit made of this.

oil•stone /óylstōn/ *n.* fine-grained flat stone used with oil for sharpening flat tools, e.g., chisels, planes, etc. (cf. WHETSTONE).

oil•y /óylee/ *adj.* (**oil•i•er**, **oil•i•est**) **1** of, like, or containing oil. **2** covered or soaked with oil. **3** (of a manner, etc.) fawning, insinuating, unctuous. □□ **oil′i•ness** *n.*

■ **1, 2** greasy, soapy, buttery; slippery; slimy, smooth. **3** glib, smooth, servile, bootlicking, *colloq.* smarmy; suave, sophisticated.

oint•ment /óyntmənt/ *n.* greasy healing or cosmetic preparation for the skin.

■ unguent, balm, salve; *propr.* Vaseline; lotion, cream.

O•jib•wa /ōjíbway/ • *n.* **1 a** N. American people native to Canada and the eastern and central northern US. **b** member of this people. **2** language of this people. • *adj.* of or relating to this people or their language. (Also called **Chippewa**).

OK[1] /ōkáy/ (also **o•kay**) *colloq.* • *adj.* [often as *int.*] all right; satisfactory. • *adv.* well; satisfactorily (*that worked out OK*). • *n.* (*pl.* **OKs**) approval, sanction. • *v.tr.* (**OK's**, **OK'd**, **OK'ing**) approve, sanction.

■ *adj.* acceptable, correct, suitable; well, sound; adequate, mediocre, not bad. • *adv.* all right, reasonably; see also WELL[1] *adv.* 1. • *n.* ratification, authorization, endorsement, agreement. • *v.* ratify, authorize, endorse, support, allow.

OK[2] *abbr.* Oklahoma (in official postal use).

o•key-doke /ōkeedṓk/ *adj. & adv.* (also **o•key-do•key** /–dṓkee/) *sl.* = OK[1].

Okla. *abbr.* Oklahoma.

o•kra /ókrə/ *n.* **1** plant yielding long ridged seed pods. **2** seed pods eaten as a vegetable and used to thicken soups and stews.

old /ōld/ *adj.* (**old•er**, **old•est**) (cf. (ELDER[1], ELDEST).) **1 a** advanced in age. **b** not young or near its beginning. **2** made long ago. **3** long in use. **4** worn or dilapidated or shabby from age or use. **5** having the characteristics (experience, feebleness, etc.) of age. **6** practiced, inveterate. **7** belonging to the past; lingering on; former (*old times*). **8** dating from far back; ancient, primeval (*old friends*). **9** (appended to a period of time) of age (*is four years old*). □ **old age** later part of normal life. **old-boy network** preferment in employment of those from a similar social background, college, etc. **the old country** native country of immigrants, etc. **Old English** English language up to *c.* 1150. **old-fashioned** in or according to a fashion or tastes no longer current; antiquated. **Old Glory** US national flag. **old guard** original or past or conservative members of a group. **old hat** *colloq. adj.* hackneyed. **old lady** *colloq.* one's mother or wife. **old maid 1** *derog.* elderly unmarried woman. **2** prim and fussy person. **3** card game in which players try not to be left with an unpaired queen. **old man** *colloq.* one's husband or father. **old master 1** great artist of former times, esp. of the 13th–17th c. in Europe. **2** painting by such a painter. **Old Norse** Germanic language from which the Scandinavian languages were derived. **old school 1** traditional attitudes. **2** people having such attitudes. **Old Testament** part of the Christian Bible containing the scriptures of the Hebrews. **old-time** belonging to former times. **old-timer** person with long experience or standing. **old wives' tale** foolish or unscientific tradition or belief. **Old World** Europe, Asia, and Africa. □□ **old′ish** adj.

■ **1** elderly, long-lived, getting on (in years), colloq. over-the-hill. **2, 3** ancient, prehistoric, antique, dated, archaic, colloq. antediluvian. **4** decayed, ramshackle, disintegrated; cast-off. **6** experienced, veteran, proficient. **7** previous, onetime. **8** long-standing, enduring, former; early, primitive. □ **old age** see AGE n. 3. **old-fashioned** antique, outdated, stale, colloq. old hat. **old hat** (adj.) see old-fashioned above.

SYNONYM STUDY: old

AGED, ANCIENT, ANTEDILUVIAN, ANTIQUATED, ARCHAIC, OBSOLETE. No one likes to be thought of as **old**, which means having been in existence or use for a relatively long time (an old washing machine). But those who are **aged**, indicating a longer life span than old and usually referring to persons of very advanced years, are often proud of the fact that they have outlived most of their peers. Children may exaggerate and regard their parents as **ancient**, which very often means dating back to the remote past, specifically the time before the end of the Roman Empire (ancient history), and their attitudes as **antediluvian**, which literally means dating back to the period before the biblical Great Flood and Noah's ark (an antediluvian transportation system), even though the parents in question have barely reached middle age. Some people seem older than they really are, simply because their ideas are **antiquated**, which means out of vogue or no longer practiced (antiquated ideas about dating). Things rather than people are usually described as **archaic**, which means having the characteristics of an earlier, sometimes primitive, period (archaic words like "thou" and "thine"). **Obsolete** also refers to things, implying that they have gone out of use or need to be replaced by something newer (an obsolete textbook; a machine that will be obsolete within the decade).

old•en /ốldən/ adj. archaic of old (esp. in olden times).

old•ie /ốldee/ n. colloq. old person or thing.
■ senior citizen; retiree, colloq. old-timer.

o•le•ag•i•nous /ốleeájinəs/ adj. like or producing oil.

o•le•an•der /ốleeándər/ n. evergreen poisonous shrub native to the Mediterranean and bearing clusters of white, pink, or red flowers.

o•le•o•mar•ga•rine /ốleeōmáarjərin/ n. margarine made from vegetable oils.

ol•fac•to•ry /olfáktəree, ōl–/ adj. of or relating to the sense of smell.

ol•i•garch /óligaark, óli–/ n. member of an oligarchy.

ol•i•gar•chy /óligaarkee, óli–/ n. (pl. **–chies**) **1** government or nation governed by a small group of people. **2** members of such a government. □□ **ol•i•gar•chic** /–gaárkik/ adj. **ol•i•gar′chi•cal** adj.

ol•ive /óliv/ • n. **1** (in full **ol′ive tree**) evergreen tree having dark-green, lance-shaped leathery leaves with silvery undersides. **2** small oval fruit of this, having a hard stone and bitter flesh, green when unripe and bluish-black when ripe. **3** grayish-green color of an unripe olive. **4** wood of the olive tree. • adj. **1** colored like an unripe olive. **2** (of the complexion) yellowish-brown, sallow. □ **olive branch 1** branch of an olive tree as a symbol of peace. **2** gesture of reconciliation or friendship. **olive oil** oil extracted from olives, used esp. in cookery.

O•lym•pi•ad /ōlímpeead/ n. **1** period of four years between Olympic games, used by the ancient Greeks in dating events. **2** celebration of the modern or ancient Olympic Games.

O•lym•pi•an /əlímpeeən, ōlím–/ • adj. **1** of or associated with Mount Olympus in NE Greece, traditionally the home of the Greek gods. **2** (of manners, etc.) condescending; superior. **3** = O LYMPIC. • n. **1** any of the Greek gods regarded as living on Olympus. **2** competitor in the Olympic games.

O•lym•pic /əlímpik, ōlím–/ • adj. of ancient Olympia or the Olympic games. • n. pl. (**the O•lym′pics**) Olympic games. □ **Olympic games 1** ancient Greek festival held at Olympia every four years, with athletic, literary, and musical competitions. **2** modern international sports festival usu. held every four years since 1896 in different venues.

O•ma•ha /ốməhaw, –haa/ • n. **1 a** N. American people native to Nebraska. **b** member of this people. **2** language of this people. • adj. of or relating to this people or their language.

OMB abbr. Office of Management and Budget.

om•buds•man /ómbŏŏdzmən/ n. (pl. **–men**) official appointed to investigate complaints against public authorities, etc.

o•me•ga /ōmáygə, ōmeegə, ōméga/ n. **1** last (24th) letter of the Greek alphabet (Ω, ω). **2** last of a series; final development.

om•e•lette /ómlit/ n. (also **om′e•let**) beaten eggs cooked in a frying pan and served plain or with a savory or sweet filling.

o•men /ốmən/ n. occurrence or object regarded as portending good or evil. See synonym study at SIGN.
■ sign, token, indication, forewarning, premonition.

om•i•cron /ómikron, ốmi–/ n. fifteenth letter of the Greek alphabet (O, o).

om•i•nous /óminəs/ adj. **1** threatening. **2** of evil omen. □□ **om′i•nous•ly** adv.
■ foreboding, fateful, menacing, sinister; unfavorable, inauspicious.

o•mis•sion /ōmíshən/ n. **1** omitting or being omitted. **2** something omitted or overlooked.
■ leaving out, deletion, elimination; failure, default, neglect.

o•mit /ōmít/ v.tr. (**o•mit•ted, o•mit•ting**)

1 leave out; not insert or include. **2** leave undone. **3** fail or neglect.

■ **1** exclude, skip, pass over. **2, 3** disregard, forget, overlook.

omni- /ómnee/ *comb. form* **1** all. **2** in all ways or places.

om•ni•bus /ómnibəs/ • *n.* = BUS. • *adj.* **1** serving several purposes. **2** comprising several items.

■ *n.* see COACH *n.* 1.

om•nip•o•tent /omnípət'nt/ *adj.* **1** having great or absolute power. **2** having great influence. □□ **om•nip′o•tence** *n.*

■ **1** see DICTATORIAL 1. □□ **omnipotence** see SUPREMACY.

om•ni•pres•ent /ómniprézənt/ *adj.* **1** present everywhere. **2** widely or constantly encountered. □□ **om•ni•pres′ence** *n.*

■ **1** see UNIVERSAL *adj.* 2 see PREVALENT 1. □□ **omnipresence** see *prevalence* (PREVALENT).

om•nis•cient /omníshənt/ *adj.* knowing everything. □□ **om•ni•science** /–shəns/ *n.*

■ all-knowing.

om•niv•o•rous /omnívərəs/ *adj.* **1** feeding on both plants and flesh. **2** making use of everything available. □□ **om•ni•vore** /ómnivawr/ *n.* **om•niv′o•rous•ly** *adv.*

on /on, awn/ • *prep.* **1** supported by or attached to or covering or enclosing (*sat on a chair, stuck on the wall, rings on her fingers, leaned on his elbow*). **2** (of time) exactly at; during (*on the hour, working on Tuesday*). **3** as a result of (*on further examination I found this*). **4** (so as to be) having membership, etc., of or residence at or in (*she is on the board of directors, lives on the waterfront*). **5** close to (*a house on the sea*). **6** in the direction of. **7** having as a basis or motive (*on good authority, did it on purpose*). **8** concerning (*writes on finance*). **9** using or engaged with (*is on the pill, hero on business*). **10** at the expense of (*drinks are on me*). **11** added to (*disaster on disaster*). **12** in a specified manner or style (*on the cheap, on the run*). • *adv.* **1** (so as to be) wearing (*put your boots on*). **2** in the appropriate direction; toward (*look on*). **3** further forward (*is getting on in years*). **4** with continued action or operation (*went plodding on, light is on*). **5** due to take place as planned (*is the party still on?*). • *adj.* Baseball positioned at a base as a runner. □ **be on to** realize the significance or intentions of. **on and off** intermittently. **on and on** continually; at tedious length. **on-line** *Computing* (of equipment or a process) directly controlled by or connected to a central processor. **on-screen** *adj.* appearing in a movie or on television. *adv.* within the view presented by a filmed scene. **on time 1** punctual; punctually. **2** by means of installment payments (*buying new furniture on time*).

once /wuns/ • *adv.* **1** on one occasion only (*did not once say please, have read it once*). **2** at some time in the past (*could once play chess*). **3** ever or at all (*if you once forget it*). • *conj.* as soon as (*once they have gone we can relax*). • *n.* one time or occasion (*just the once*). □ **at once 1** immediately. **2** simulta-

---

575   **omni- ~ oneness**

neously. **for once** on this (or that) occasion, even if at no other. **once and for all** conclusively; in conclusion. **once** (or **every once**) **in a while** occasionally. **once-over** *colloq.* **1** rapid inspection. **2** appraising glance. **once upon a time** at some vague time in the past.

■ *adv.* **1** one time. **2** formerly, previously, before, some time ago. **3** see EVER 2. • *conj.* when, the moment. □ **at once 1** right away, without delay; in a wink, in no time (at all), in two shakes (of a lamb's tail), *colloq.* before you can say Jack Robinson, in a jiff *or* jiffy. **2** together, at the same time, *colloq.* at one go. **once and for all** finally, positively, definitely. **once** (or **every once**) **in a while** now and then, now and again, periodically, from time to time. **once-over** examination, assessment, check, survey, evaluation; see also SCAN *n.* 1.

on•co•gene /ón̄gkəjeen/ *n.* gene that can transform a cell into a tumor cell.

on•col•o•gy /ón̄gkóləjee/ *n. Med.* study of tumors.

on•com•ing /ónkuming, áwn–/ *adj.* approaching from the front.

■ advancing, arriving, coming, nearing, imminent.

one /wun/ • *adj.* **1** single and integral in number. **2** (with a noun implied) single person or thing of the kind expressed or implied (*one of the best*). **3** particular but undefined, esp. as contrasted with another (*that is one view*). **4** only such (*the one man who can do it*). **5** forming a unity (*one and undivided*). **6** identical; the same. • *n.* **1 a** lowest cardinal number. **b** thing numbered with it. **2** unity; a unit. **3** single thing or person or example (often referring to a noun previously expressed or implied: *the big dog and the small one*). • *pron.* **1** person of a specified kind (*loved ones*). **2** any person. **3** I, me (*one would like to help*). ¶Often regarded as an affectation. □ **at one** in agreement. **one-horse 1** using a single horse. **2** *colloq.* small, poorly equipped. **one-on-one** of or direct person-to-person conflict. **one-sided** unfair; partial. **one-to-one** with one member of one group corresponding to one of another. **one-track mind** mind preoccupied with one subject. **one up** *colloq.* having a particular advantage. **one-way** allowing movement or travel in one direction only.

■ *adj.* **3** a particular, a certain, a given, a specific. **4** single, lone, sole. **5** inseparable, joined, one and the same, harmonious, whole. *pron.* **1, 2** an individual, a man *or* a woman, everybody, anyone; people. □ **at one** agreed, united, in harmony. **one-sided** biased, prejudiced, unjust, narrow-minded. **one up** ahead, in the lead, on top, one step ahead.

O•nei•da /ōnídə/ • *n.* **1 a** N. American people native to New York state. **b** member of this people. **2** language of this people. • *adj.* of or relating to this people or their language.

one•ness /wún-nis/ *n.* **1** singleness. **2** uniqueness. **3** agreement. **4** sameness.

on•er•ous /ónərəs, ốn–/ adj. burdensome. □□ **on'er•ous•ness** n.

■ see *burdensome* (BURDEN). □□ **onerous-ness** see *severity* (SEVERE).

one•self /wunsélf/ pron. reflexive and (in apposition) emphatic form of *one* (*kill oneself, one has to do it oneself*).

one•time /wúntīm/ adj. & adv. former.

on•go•ing /ón-gō̃ing, áwn–/ adj. 1 continuing. 2 in progress (*ongoing discussions*).

■ developing, evolving, growing; unbroken, running.

on•ion /únyən/ n. 1 plant having a short stem and bearing greenish-white flowers. 2 swollen bulb of this with many concentric skins used in cooking, pickling, etc. □□ **on'ion•y** adj.

on•look•er /ónlŏŏkər, áwn–/ n. spectator. □□ **on'look•ing** adj.

■ observer, witness, watcher, viewer; bystander, passerby.

on•ly /ốnlee/ • adv. 1 solely, merely, exclusively. 2 no longer ago than (*saw them only yesterday*). 3 with no better result than (*hurried home only to find her gone*). • attrib.adj. 1 existing alone of its or their kind (*their only son*). 2 best or alone worth knowing (*the only place to eat*). • conj. colloq. except that; but. □ **only too** extremely (*is only too willing*).

■ adv. 1 just, alo1ne; simply, at best, at worst, at most, purely. • attrib.adj. sole, single, lone, exclusive. • conj. however. □ **only too** see *extremely* (EXTREME).

on•o•mas•tics /ónəmástiks/ n.pl. (treated as sing.) study of the origin and formation of (esp. personal) proper names.

on•o•mat•o•poe•ia /ónəmátəpeèə, –maàtə–/ n. formation of a word from a sound associated with what is named (e.g., *cuckoo, sizzle*). □□ **on•o•mat•o•poe'ic** adj. **o•no•mat•o•po•et•ic** /–pŏétik/ adj.

on•rush /ónrush, áwn–/ n. onward rush.

on•set /ónset, áwn–/ n. 1 attack. 2 impetuous beginning.

■ 1 assault, onrush, onslaught, charge. 2 start, inauguration, launch, origin.

on•shore /ónsháwr, áwn–/ adj. 1 on the shore. 2 (of the wind) blowing from the sea toward the land.

on•slaught /ónslawt, áwn–/ n. fierce attack.

■ see ATTACK n. 1.

on•stage /ónstáyj/ adj. & adv. Theatr. on the stage; visible to the audience.

Ont. abbr. Ontario.

on•to /óntoo, óntə/ prep. disp. to a position or state on or in contact with (cf. *on to*).

on•tog•e•ny /ontójənee/ n. life cycle or development of a single organism.

o•nus /ốnəs/ n. (pl. **o•nus•es**) burden, duty, or responsibility.

■ see BURDEN n. 1, 2.

on•ward /ónwərd, áwn–/ • adv. (also **on'wards**) 1 further on. 2 with advancing motion. • adj. directed onward.

■ adv. forward, ahead. • adj. advancing, progressing.

on•yx /óniks/ n. semiprecious variety of agate with colored layers.

oo•dles /ŏŏd'lz/ n.pl. colloq. very great amount.

■ see LOT n. 1.

oops /ŏŏps, ŏŏps/ int. colloq. expressing surprise or apology, esp. on making an obvious mistake.

ooze[1] /ŏŏz/ • v. 1 intr. trickle or leak slowly out. 2 intr. (of a substance) exude. 3 tr. exude or exhibit (a feeling) liberally (*oozed sympathy*). • n. sluggish flow. □□ **ooz'y** adj.

■ v. weep, seep, secrete, bleed, drain; discharge.

ooze[2] /ŏŏz/ n. wet mud or slime, esp. at the bottom of a river, lake, or estuary. □□ **ooz'y** adj.

■ muck, mire, silt, sludge, sediment, sl. gunk, glop.

o•pal /ốpəl/ n. iridescent mineral often used as a gemstone. □□ **o•pal•es•cence** /ốpəléssəns/ n. **o•pal•es•cent** /–sənt/ adj.

o•paque /ốpáyk/ adj. (**o•paqu•er, o•paqu•est**) 1 not transmitting light. 2 impenetrable to sight. 3 obscure; not lucid. 4 obtuse; dull-witted. □□ **o•pac•i•ty** /ốpásitee/ n. **o•paque'ly** adv. **o•paque'ness** n.

■ 1, 2 dark, murky, muddy. 3 unclear, vague, baffling. 4 dense, stupid, blockheaded, slow.

op art /op/ n. colloq. = optical art.

op. cit. abbr. in the work already quoted.

OPEC /ốpek/ abbr. Organization of Petroleum Exporting Countries.

o•pen /ốpən/ • adj. 1 not closed nor locked nor blocked up; allowing access. 2 unenclosed; unconfined; unobstructed. 3 uncovered, exposed. 4 undisguised; public. 5 unfolded or spread out (*had the map open on the table*). 6 (of a fabric) with gaps or intervals. 7 a (of a person) frank and communicative. b (of the mind) accessible to new ideas; unprejudiced. 8 a (of an exhibition, shop, etc.) accessible to visitors or customers. b (of a meeting) admitting all. 9 (of a race, competition, scholarship, etc.) unrestricted as to who may compete. 10 (foll. by *to*) a willing to receive (*is open to offers*). b (of a choice, offer, or opportunity) still available (*there are three courses open to us*). c likely to suffer from or be affected by (*open to abuse*). • v. 1 tr. & intr. make or become open or more open. 2 a tr. change from a closed or fastened position so as to allow access (*opened the door*). b intr. (of a door, lid, etc.) have its position changed to allow access (*the door opened slowly*). 3 intr. [foll. by *into, on to*, etc.] (of a door, room, etc.) afford access as specified (*opened on to a large garden*). 4 a tr. start or establish or get going (a business, activity, etc.). b intr. be initiated; make a start. • n. 1 [prec. by *the*] a open space or country or air. b public notice or view; general attention (esp. *into the open*). 2 open championship, competition, or scholarship. □ **open air** [usu. prec. by *the*] outdoors. **open-and-shut** (of an argument, case, etc.) straightforward and conclusive. **open-ended** having no predetermined limit. **open-faced** designating a sandwich with no covering slice of bread. **open-hearted** frank and kindly. **open-heart surgery** surgery with the heart

exposed and the blood made to bypass it.
open house 1 welcome or hospitality for visitors. **2** time when real estate offered for sale is open to prospective buyers. **open-minded** accessible to new ideas; unprejudiced. **open question** undecided matter.
□□ o'pen•er *n.* o'pen•ly *adv.* o'pen•ness *n.*

■ *adj.* **1–3** ajar, gaping; unbolted, unlatched, yawning, revealed, bare, vulnerable; unprotected; unwrapped, unsealed, unfastened; clear, unobstructed, spacious; treeless, uncrowded, unfenced; unenclosed, unconfined; ice-free, passable; attentive. **4** exposed, well-known; evident, obvious, unconcealed, plain, blatant. **5** extended, outstretched, expanded. **6** loosely woven, rough, coarse. **7 a** candid, outspoken, straightforward, direct, sincere **b** receptive, open-minded, flexible. **8, 9** free, public, available; obtainable; unobstructed, unregulated, unconditional, unqualified; unrestrained, uninhibited. **10 b** accessible; unfilled, vacant. **c** liable, subject, susceptible.
• *v.* **1, 2** unlock, unlatch, unfasten; uncover; unseal; undo, untie, unwrap; unblock, clear. **3** (*open into* or *on to*) lead to, connect with. **4** begin, get under way; launch, put into operation, activate; establish, set up; *colloq.* get *or* start the ball rolling, kick off. □ **open-and-shut** see SIMPLE *adj.* 1. **open-minded** enlightened, undogmatic; see also LIBERAL *adj.* 3, 6. □□ **openness** see CANDOR.

o•pen•hand•ed /ópənhándid/ *adj.* generous.

o•pen•ing /ópəning/ • *n.* **1** aperture or gap, esp. allowing access. **2** opportunity. **3** beginning; initial part. • *adj.* initial; first.
■ *n.* **1** break, breach, crack, split, hole. **2** chance, occasion, *colloq.* break; job, position, vacancy. **3** start, origin, inauguration, launch, début; start-off, start-up. • *adj.* see INITIAL *adj.*

o•pen•work /ópənwərk/ *n.* pattern with intervening spaces in metal, leather, lace, etc.

o•pe•ra[1] /ópərə, óprə/ *n.* **1** dramatic work in one or more acts, set to music for singers (usu. in costume) and instrumentalists. **2** this as a genre. □ **opera glasses** small binoculars for use at the opera or theater. □□ **op•er•at•ic** /ópərátik/ *adj.* **op•er•at•i•cal•ly** *adv.*
■ □ **opera glasses** see GLASS *n.* 3b.

o•pe•ra[2] *pl.* of OPUS.

op•or•a•ble /ópərəbəl/ *adj.* **1** that can be operated. **2** suitable for treatment by surgery.
■ **1** workable, usable, functional, fit, in working condition.

op•er•ate /ópərayt/ *v.* **1** *tr.* manage; work; control. **2** *intr.* be in action; function. **3** *intr.* [often foll. by *on*] **a** perform a surgical operation. **b** conduct a military or naval action. **4** *tr.* bring about; accomplish. □ **operating system** basic software that enables the running of a computer program.
■ **1** run, direct, conduct; drive. **2** go, run, perform; work, serve, act. **4** produce, effect.

op•er•a•tion /ópəráyshən/ *n.* **1 a** action or method of working or operating. **b** being active or functioning (*not yet in operation*). **c** scope or range of effectiveness of a thing's activity. **2** active process. **3** piece of work,

esp. one in a series (often in *pl.*: *begin operations*). **4** surgery performed on a patient. **5** strategic movement of troops, ships, etc., for military action.
■ **1, 2** running, performance, movement; handling, direction, control, management. **3** undertaking, venture, project, deal, task. **5** maneuver, mission, campaign, exercise.

op•er•a•tion•al /ópəráyshənəl/ *adj.* **1 a** of or used for operations. **b** engaged in operations. **2** able or ready to function. □□ **op•er•a'tion•al•ly** *adv.*
■ **2** see FUNCTIONAL 1.

op•er•a•tive /ópərətiv, óprə–/ • *adj.* **1** in operation; having effect. **2** having the principal relevance (*"may" is the operative word*). **3** of or by surgery. • *n.* detective; spy.
■ *adj.* **1** functioning, working, in force, effective. **2** significant, important, vital; see also PERTINENT 1. • *n.* undercover agent, (FBI or CIA) agent, *colloq.* G-man; (private) investigator, P.I., *colloq.* private eye, sleuth, snoop.

op•er•a•tor /ópəraytər/ *n.* **1** person controlling a machine, etc. **2** person engaging in business. **3** *colloq.* person acting in a specified way (*smooth operator*).
■ **1** driver; worker, practitioner. **2** businessman, businesswoman, business person, administrator, manager, supervisor.

op•er•et•ta /ópəretə/ *n.* **1** one-act or short opera. **2** light opera.

oph•thal•mic /ofthálmik, op–/ *adj.* of or relating to the eye and its diseases.

oph•thal•mol•o•gy /ófthalmóləjee, –thó–, op–/ *n.* scientific study of the eye. □□ **oph•thal•mol'o•gist** *n.*

o•pi•ate /ópeeət/ • *adj.* **1** containing opium. **2** narcotic, soporific. • *n.* **1** drug containing opium, usu. to ease pain or induce sleep. **2** thing that soothes or stupefies.
■ *adj.* **2** see NARCOTIC *adj.* 1. • *n.* **1** see NARCOTIC *n.* **2** see SEDATIVE *n.*

o•pine /ōpín/ *v.tr.* hold or express as an opinion.

o•pin•ion /əpínyən/ *n.* **1** unproven belief or assessment. **2** view held as probable. **3** what one thinks about something. **4 a** professional advice. **b** *Law* formal statement of reasons for a judgment given.
■ **1, 3** judgment, thought, (point of) view, conviction, perception, idea.

o•pin•ion•at•ed /əpínyənaytid/ *adj.* conceitedly assertive or dogmatic in one's opinions.
■ stubborn, pigheaded, inflexible; prejudiced, partisan.

o•pi•um /ópeeəm/ *n.* **1** addictive drug prepared from the juice of the opium poppy, used as an analgesic and narcotic. **2** anything regarded as soothing or stupefying.

o•pos•sum /əpósəm/ *n.* tree-living American marsupial having a prehensile tail and hind feet with an opposable thumb.

opp. *abbr.* opposite.

op•po•nent /əpōnənt/ • *n.* person who opposes or belongs to an opposing side. • *adj.* opposing; contrary; opposed.
■ *n.* antagonist, competitor; (*opponents*) opposition, other side.

op•por•tune /ópərtŏŏn, –tyŏŏn/ adj. 1 (of a time) well-chosen or especially favorable. 2 (of an action or event) well-timed. See synonym study at TIMELY.

■ 1 advantageous, appropriate, happy, helpful, fortunate. 2 seasonable, apt, convenient, suitable.

op•por•tu•nism /ópərtŏŏnizəm, –tyŏŏ–/ n. adaptation to circumstances, esp. regardless of principle. □□ **op•por•tun′ist** n. & adj. **op•por•tu•nis′tic** adj. **op•por•tu•nis′ti•cal•ly** adv.

■ □□ **opportunistic** expedient, taking advantage.

op•por•tu•ni•ty /ópərtŏŏnitee, –tyŏŏ–/ n. (pl. –ties) favorable chance or opening offered by circumstances.

■ occasion, possibility, moment, time, colloq. break.

op•pos•a•ble /əpŏzəbəl/ adj. Zool. (of the thumb in primates) capable of touching the other digits on the same hand.

op•pose /əpŏz/ v.tr. [often absol.] 1 resist; argue against. 2 [foll. by to] place in opposition or contrast. □□ **op•pos′er** n.

■ 1 counter, object to, defy, take a stand against; dispute, rebut, challenge. 2 (oppose to) match with, play off against.

op•po•site /ópəzit/ • adj. 1 [often foll. by to] having a position on the other side; facing. 2 [often foll. by to, from] contrary; diametrically different. • n. anything opposite. • adv. 1 in an opposite position (the tree stands opposite). 2 in a complementary role to (another actor, etc.). • prep. in a position opposite to (opposite the house is a tree). □ **opposite number** person holding an equivalent position in another group, etc. **the opposite sex** women in relation to men or vice versa.

■ adj. 1 vis-à-vis. 2 conflicting, contradictory. • n. reverse, contrary. • adv. 1 in front. • prep. facing.

SYNONYM STUDY: opposite

ANTITHETICAL, CONTRADICTORY, CONTRARY, REVERSE. All of these adjectives are usually applied to abstractions and are used to describe ideas, statements, qualities, forces, etc. —that are so far apart as to seem irreconcilable. **Opposite** refers to ideas or things that are symmetrically opposed in position, direction, or character—in other words, that are set against each other in such a way that the contrast or conflict between them is highlighted (they sat opposite each other at the table). **Contradictory** goes a little further, implying that if one of two opposing statements, propositions, or principles is true, the other must be false. Contradictory elements are mutually exclusive; for example, "alive" and "dead" are contradictory terms because logically they cannot both be applied to the same thing. **Antithetical** implies that the two things being contrasted are diametrically opposed—as far apart or as different from each other as is possible (their interests were antithetical). **Contrary** adds connotations of conflict or antagonism (a contrary view of the situation), while **reverse** applies to that which moves or faces in the opposite direction (the reverse side).

op•po•si•tion /ópəzíshən/ n. 1 resistance, antagonism. 2 being hostile or in conflict or disagreement. 3 contrast or antithesis. 4 group or party of opponents or competitors.

■ 1–3 unfriendliness, defiance, adversity; disapproval, criticism. 4 adversaries, antagonists, enemy, other side.

op•press /əprés/ v.tr. 1 keep in subservience. 2 govern or treat harshly. □□ **op•pres•sion** /əpréshən/ n. **op•pres′sor** n.

■ crush, repress, tyrannize (over), overpower. □□ **oppressor** bully, tyrant, despot.

op•pres•sive /əprésiv/ adj. 1 harsh or cruel. 2 (of weather) close and sultry. □□ **op•pres′sive•ly** adv. **op•pres′sive•ness** n.

■ 1 overwhelming, unbearable, intolerable, brutal; disheartening, discouraging. 2 suffocating, stuffy, airless; muggy.

op•pro•bri•ous /əprŏbreeəs/ adj. (of language) severely scornful; abusive.

■ see abusive (ABUSE).

op•pro•bri•um /əprŏbreeəm/ n. 1 disgrace. 2 cause of this.

■ 1 see DISGRACE n.

opt /opt/ v.intr. decide; make a choice. □ **opt out** [often foll. by of] choose not to participate.

■ see CHOOSE 3.

op•tic /óptik/ adj. of or relating to the eye or vision (optic nerve).

op•ti•cal /óptikəl/ adj. 1 of sight; visual. 2 a of or concerning sight or light in relation to each other. b belonging to optics. 3 (esp. of a lens) constructed to assist sight. □ **optical art** style of painting that gives the illusion of movement by the precise use of pattern and color. **optical character recognition** identification of printed characters using photoelectric devices. **optical fiber** thin glass fiber through which light can be transmitted. **optical illusion** image that deceives the eye. □□ **op′ti•cal•ly** adv.

op•ti•cian /optíshən/ n. 1 maker or seller of eyeglasses, contact lenses, etc. 2 person trained in the detection and correction of poor eyesight.

op•tics /óptiks/ n.pl. [treated as sing.] scientific study of sight and the behavior of light.

op•ti•mal /óptiməl/ adj. best or most favorable.

■ see OPTIMUM adj.

op•ti•mism /óptimizəm/ n. 1 inclination to hopefulness and confidence (opp. PESSIMISM). 2 Philos. theory that good must ultimately prevail over evil. □□ **op′ti•mist** n. **op•ti•mis′tic** adj. **op•ti•mis′ti•cal•ly** adv.

■ 1 positiveness, cheerfulness. □□ **optimist** see idealist (IDEALISM). **optimistic** positive, hopeful, confident.

op•ti•mize /óptimiz/ v. 1 tr. make the best or most effective use of. 2 intr. be an optimist. □□ **op•ti•mi•za′tion** n.

op•ti•mum /óptiməm/ • n. (pl. **op•ti•ma** /–mə/ or **op•ti•mums**) 1 most favorable conditions (for growth, reproduction, etc.). **2** best possible compromise. • adj. = OPTIMAL.

■ n. **1** best, finest; ideal, perfection. **2** lesser evil. • adj. finest, choicest; first-class, excellent; extraordinary, unique.

op•tion /ópshən/ n. **1 a** choosing; choice. **b** thing chosen. **2** liberty to choose. **3** *Stock Exch.*, etc., right to buy or sell at a specified price within a set time.

■ **1** selection, alternative. **2** choice, privilege, election.

op•tion•al /ópshənəl/ adj. not obligatory. □□ **op′tion•al•ly** adv.

■ voluntary, discretionary, nonmandatory.

op•tom•e•try /optómitree/ n. practice or profession of testing the eyes for defects in vision and prescribing corrective lenses or exercises □□ **op′tom′e•trist** /optómitrist/ n.

op•u•lent /ópyələnt/ adj. **1** wealthy. **2** luxurious. **3** abundant. See synonym study at WEALTHY. □□ **op′u•lence** n.

■ **1** affluent, rich, prosperous. **2** see PLUSH adj. **3** copious, plentiful, profuse.

o•pus /ópəs/ n. (pl. **op•er•a** /ópərə/ or **op•us•es**) **1** *Mus.* **a** a musical composition. **b** (also **op.**) used before a number given to a composer's work, usu. indicating the order of publication (*Beethoven, op. 15*). **2** any artistic work (cf. MAGNUM OPUS).

■ work, production, creation.

OR abbr. **1** Oregon (in official postal use). **2** operating room.

or /awr, ər/ conj. **1** introducing an alternative (*white or black*). **2** introducing a synonym or explanation of a preceding word, etc (*suffered from vertigo or dizziness*). **3** otherwise (*run or you'll be late*). □ **or else 1** otherwise (*do it now, or else you will have to do it tomorrow*). **2** colloq. expressing a warning or threat (*hand over the money or else*).

-or¹ /ər/ suffix forming nouns denoting an agent (*actor, escalator*) or condition (*error, horror*).

-or² /ər/ suffix forming nouns denoting state or condition (*error, horror*).

or•a•cle /áwrəkəl, ór–/ n. **1** a place at which advice or prophecy was sought from the gods in classical antiquity. **b** response given. **c** prophet or prophetess at an oracle. **2** source of wisdom. □□ **o•rac•u•lar** /awrák-yələr/ adj.

■ **1 b** prophecy, prediction, advice. **c** seer, fortune-teller. **2** authority, guru, mastermind, mentor, wizard.

o•ral /áwrəl/ • adj. **1** by word of mouth; spoken; not written (*the oral tradition*). **2** done or taken by mouth (*oral contraceptive*). • n. colloq. spoken examination, test, etc. □□ **o′ral•ly** adv.

■ adj. **1** verbal, vocal, pronounced. • n. viva voce.

or•ange /áwrinj, ór–/ • n. **1 a** round juicy citrus fruit with a bright reddish-yellow tough rind. **b** tree or shrub bearing fragrant white flowers and yielding this fruit. **2** reddish-yellow color of an orange. • adj. orange-colored; reddish-yellow.

o•rang•u•tan /awrángətàn, əràng–/ n. large red long-haired tree-living ape of Borneo

and Sumatra, with characteristic long arms and hooked hands and feet.

o•rate /awráyt, áwrayt/ v.intr. esp. joc. or derog. speak, esp. pompously or at length.

o•ra•tion /awráyshən, ōráy–/ n. formal speech, etc., esp. when ceremonial.

■ declaration, address, lecture; valedictory, eulogy.

or•a•tor /áwrətər, ór–/ n. **1** person making a speech. **2** eloquent public speaker.

or•a•to•ri•o /àwrətáwreeō/ n. (pl. **–os**) semidramatic work for orchestra and voices, esp. on a sacred theme.

or•a•to•ry /áwrətawree, ór–/ n. (pl. **–ries**) **1** art or practice of formal speaking, esp. in public. **2** exaggerated, eloquent, or highly colored language. □□ **or•a•tor′i•cal** adj.

■ speechmaking, rhetoric, way with words, fluency, colloq. gift of gab.

orb /awrb/ n. **1** globe surmounted by a cross, esp. carried by a sovereign at a coronation. **2** sphere; globe.

■ **2** ball.

or•bit /áwrbit/ • n. **1 a** curved, usu. closed course of a planet, satellite, etc. **b** one complete passage around a body. **2** range or sphere of action. • v. **1** intr. (of a satellite, etc.) go around in orbit. **2** tr. move in orbit around. **3** tr. put into orbit. □□ **or′bit•al** adj. **or′bit•er** n.

■ n. **1 a** circuit, path, revolution. • v. **1, 2** revolve, turn; circle.

or•ca /áwrkə/ n. any of various whales, esp. the killer whale.

or•chard /áwrchərd/ n. piece of land with fruit trees.

or•ches•tra /áwrkəstrə/ n. **1** group of instrumentalists, esp. combining strings, woodwinds, brass, and percussion (*symphony orchestra*). **2 a** (in full **or•ches•tra pit**) part of a theater, etc., where the orchestra plays, usu. in front of the stage. **b** main-floor seating area in a theater. □□ **or•ches′tral** /–késtrəl/ adj.

or•ches•trate /áwrkəstràyt/ v.tr. **1** arrange or compose for an orchestra. **2** arrange (elements of a situation, etc.) for maximum effect. □□ **or•ches•tra′tion** /–áyshən/ n.

■ **1** see ARRANGE 5. **2** see ARRANGE 1. □□ **orchestration** see ARRANGEMENT 5, TACTICS 2.

or•chid /áwrkid/ n. **1** plant bearing flowers in fantastic shapes and brilliant colors, usu. having one petal larger than the others and variously spurred, lobed, pouched, etc. **2** flower of these plants.

or•dain /awrdáyn/ v.tr. **1** confer holy orders on; appoint to the Christian ministry. **2 a** decree (*ordained that he should go*). **b** (of God, fate, etc.) destine; appoint (*has ordained us to die*).

■ **2 a** see DECREE v. **b** see DESTINE.

or•deal /awrdeél/ n. painful or horrific experience; severe trial.

■ test, hardship, trouble, adversity, tragedy.

or•der /áwrdər/ • n. **1 a** condition in which every part, unit, etc., is in its right place; tidiness. **b** specified sequence, succession, etc. (*alphabetical order*). **2** [in *sing.* or *pl.*] authoritative command, direction, etc. **3** state of peaceful harmony under a constituted authority. **4** kind; sort (*talents of a high order*). **5 a** direction to a manufacturer, tradesman, waiter, etc., to supply something. **b** goods, etc., supplied. **6** constitution or nature of the world, society, etc. (*the moral order*). **7** *Biol.* taxonomic rank below a class and above a family. **8** (esp. **Order**) fraternity of monks and friars, or formerly of knights, bound by a common rule of life (*the Franciscan order*). **9 a** any of the grades of the Christian ministry. **b** [in *pl.*] status of a member of the clergy (*Anglican orders*). **10** any of the classical styles of architecture (Doric, Ionic, Corinthian, Tuscan, and Composite). **11** principles of procedure, decorum, etc., accepted by a meeting, legislative assembly, etc., or enforced by its president. • *v.tr.* **1** command; bid; prescribe. **2** command or direct (a person) to a specified destination. **3** direct a manufacturer, waiter, tradesman, etc., to supply (*ordered dinner*). **4** put in order; regulate. □ **in order 1** one after another according to some principle. **2** fit for use. **3** according to the rules (of procedure at a meeting, etc.). **in order that** so that. **in order to** with the purpose of doing. **on the order of** approximately. **on order** (of goods, etc.) ordered but not yet received. **out of order 1** not working properly. **2** not according to the rules (of a meeting, organization, etc.). **3** not in proper sequence.

■ *n.* **1** organization, uniformity, system, pattern; arrangement, grouping, classification, layout. **2** instruction, dictate, request, decree; rule, law, requirement. **3** calm, tranquillity, discipline. **4** style, genre; see also SORT *n.* 1. **5 a** purchase order, requisition. **6** condition, state (of affairs). **8** brotherhood, sisterhood, fellowship, association, society, guild, sect. **11** proceeding(s), conduct; protocol. • *v.* **1, 2** instruct, charge, require; demand, ordain; force. **3** requisition, send (away) for, call for, reserve, commission, contract for. **4** organize, systematize, arrange, classify, prioritize, lay out. □ **in order 1, 2** neat, clean, (well-)organized, ready, arranged. **3** suitable, appropriate, correct; required. **in order that** with the aim *or* purpose *or* intention that. **in order to** to, so as to. **on the order of** roughly, somewhere near, something like; see also NEARLY 1. **out of order 1** out of service, broken, nonfunctioning, broken-down, *colloq.* bust(ed), shot, *sl.* (gone) kaput, on the blink. **2** unseemly, out of place, improper. **3** disordered, nonsequential, unorganized, chaotic.

or•der•ly /áwrd'rlee/ • *adj.* **1** methodically arranged; regular. **2** obedient to discipline; well-behaved. • *n.* (*pl.* **–lies**) **1** hospital attendant with nonmedical duties, esp. cleaning, moving equipment, escorting patients, etc. **2** soldier who carries orders for an officer, etc. □□ **or'der•li•ness** *n.*

■ *adj.* **1** (well-)organized, neat, shipshape, systematic, harmonious. **2** disciplined, law-

abiding, well-mannered, civilized. • *n.* assistant, adjutant, messenger.

or•di•nal /áwrd'nəl/ *n.* (in full **or'di•nal num'ber**) number defining a thing's position in a series, e.g., 'first,' 'second,' 'third,' etc. (cf. CARDINAL).

or•di•nance /áwrd'nəns/ *n.* **1** authoritative order; decree. **2** statute, esp. by a local authority.

■ **1** see DECREE *n.* 1. **2** see LAW 1a.

or•di•nar•y /áwrd'neree/ *adj.* **1** regular; normal; usual (*in the ordinary course of events*). **2** statute, esp. boring; commonplace (*an ordinary man*). See synonym study at NORMAL. □ **out of the ordinary** unusual. □□ **or•di•nar'i•ly** /–áirəlee/ *adv.* **or•di•nar'i•ness** *n.*

■ **1** expected, common, customary, routine; humdrum, conventional, modest, plain. □ **out of the ordinary** extraordinary, strange, unfamiliar, rare. □□ **ordinarily** usually, as a rule, in general.

or•di•nate /áwrd'nit/ *n.* *Math.* straight line from any point parallel to one coordinate axis and meeting the other, usually a coordinate measured parallel to the vertical (cf. ABSCISSA).

or•di•na•tion /áwrd'náyshən/ *n.* **1** conferring holy orders, esp. on a priest or deacon. **2** admission of a priest, etc., to church ministry.

■ see *installation* (INSTALL).

ord•nance /áwrdnəns/ *n.* **1** artillery; military supplies. **2** branch of the armed forces dealing esp. with military stores and materials.

or•dure /áwrjər, –dyŏor/ *n.* **1** dung. **2** obscenity.

Ore. *abbr.* Oregon.

ore /awr/ *n.* naturally occurring solid material from which metal or other valuable minerals may be extracted.

Oreg. *abbr.* Oregon.

o•reg•a•no /ərégənō, awrég–/ *n.* aromatic herb, the fresh or dried leaves of which are used as a flavoring in cooking. (Also called **wild marjoram**) (cf. MARJORAM).

or•gan /áwrgən/ *n.* **1 a** usu. large musical instrument having pipes supplied with air from bellows, sounded by keys, and distributed into sets or stops that form partial organs, each with a separate keyboard. **b** smaller instrument without pipes, producing similar sounds electronically. **2** usu. self-contained part of an organism having a special vital function (*vocal organs, digestive organs*). **3** medium of communication, esp. a newspaper, sectarian periodical, etc. □□ **or'gan•ist** *n.*

■ **2** device, implement; member, structure, process. **3** vehicle, publication.

or•gan•dy /áwrgəndee/ *n.* (also **or'gan•die**) (*pl.* **–dies**) fine translucent cotton muslin, usu. stiffened.

or•gan•elle /áwrgənél/ *n.* *Biol.* any of various organized or specialized structures that form part of a cell.

or•gan•ic /awrgánik/ *adj.* **1 a** *Physiol.* of a bodily organ(s). **b** *Med.* (of a disease) affecting an organ. **2** (of a plant or animal) having organs or an organized physical structure. **3** *Agriculture* produced without the use of chemical fertilizers, pesticides, etc. (*organic* *farming*). **4** *Chem.* (of a compound, etc.) containing carbon (opp. INORGANIC). **5 a** structural; inherent. **b** constitutional; fundamental. **6** organized; systematic (*an organic whole*). □□ **or•gan'i•cal•ly** *adv.*

■ **2** living, natural, biological. **5** basic, elementary, essential, innate, natural. **6** coherent, coordinated, integrated, orderly.

or•gan•ism /áwrgɔnizəm/ *n.* **1** living individual consisting of a single cell or of a group of interdependent parts sharing the life processes. **2** individual live plant or animal.

■ living thing, structure, body; being, entity, creature.

or•ga•ni•za•tion /àwrgɔnizáyshən/ *n.* **1** organizing; being organized. **2** organized body, esp. a business, government department, charity, etc. □□ **or•ga•ni•za'tion•al** *adj.*

■ **1** structuring, coordination; systematization, classification, pattern, design. **2** institution, federation, society, coalition.

or•gan•ize /áwrgɔníz/ *v. tr.* **1** give an orderly structure to; systematize. **2** arrange for or initiate (a plan, etc.). **3** [often *absol.*] **a** enroll (new members) in a labor union, political party, etc. **b** form (a labor union or other political group). □ **organized crime** organization of people who carry out illegal activities for profit. □□ **or'gan•iz•er** *n.*

■ **1** coordinate, arrange, sort (out), categorize. **2** form, found, establish, develop. **3 b** see INSTITUTE *v.* 1, 2.

or•gan•za /awrgánzɔ/ *n.* thin stiff transparent silk or synthetic dress fabric.

or•gasm /áwrgazəm/ *n.* climax of sexual excitement. □□ **or•gas'mic** /-gázmik/ *adj.*

or•gy /áwrjee/ *n.* (*pl.* **-gies**) **1** wild drunken festivity, esp. one at which indiscriminate sexual activity takes place. **2** excessive indulgence in an activity.

■ **1** bacchanalia, debauchery, revel, *sl.* binge, bender. **2** overindulgence, fling, *colloq.* spree.

o•ri•el /áwreeɔl/ *n.* projecting window of an upper story.

o•ri•ent • *n.* /áwreeɔnt/ **(the Orient)** countries E. of the Mediterranean, esp. E. Asia. • *v.* /áwree-ent/ **1** *tr.* **a** find the bearings of. **b** bring (oneself, different elements, etc.) into a clearly understood position or relationship; direct. **2** *tr.* **a** place or build (a church, building, etc.) facing toward the East. **b** bury (a person) with the feet toward the East. **2** *intr.* turn eastward or in a specified direction.

■ *v.* **1** adjust, adapt, accustom, familiarize, acclimate.

o•ri•en•tal /àwree-éntəl/ • *adj.* **1** (often **Oriental**) of or characteristic of Eastern civilization, etc. **2** of or concerning the East, esp. E. Asia. • *n.* (esp. **Oriental**) native of the Orient.

o•ri•en•ta•tion /àwree-entáyshən/ *n.* **1** orienting; being oriented. **2 a** relative position. **b** person's attitude or adjustment in relation to circumstances, esp. politically or psychologically. **3** introduction to a subject or situation; briefing. □□ **o•ri•en•ta'tion•al** *adj.*

■ **1, 2** placement, bearings, adjustment, position. **3** training, initiation, familiarization.

---

o•ri•en•teer•ing /àwree-enteéring/ *n.* cross-country race in which participants use a map and a compass to navigate along an unfamiliar course.

or•i•fice /áwrifis, ór-/ *n.* opening, esp. the mouth of a cavity.

■ see OPENING *n.* 1.

orig. *abbr.* **1** original. **2** originally.

o•ri•ga•mi /áwrigáamee/ *n.* Japanese art of folding paper into decorative shapes.

or•i•gin /áwrijin, ór-/ *n.* **1** beginning or starting point; source. **2** [often in *pl.*] person's ancestry (*what are his origins?*).

■ **1** root, derivation, foundation, basis; birth, dawning, launch. **2** (*origins*) parentage, genealogy, heritage.

SYNONYM STUDY: origin

INCEPTION, PROVENANCE, ROOT, SOURCE. The **origin** of something is the point from which it starts or sets out, or the person or thing from which it is ultimately derived (*the origin of the custom of carving pumpkins at Halloween; the origin of a word*). It often applies to causes that were in operation before the thing itself was brought into being. **Source,** on the other hand, applies to that which provides a first and continuous supply (*the source of the river; an ongoing source of inspiration and encouragement*). **Root,** more often than *source,* applies to what is regarded as the first or final cause of something; it suggests an origin so fundamental as to be the ultimate cause from which something stems (*money is the root of all evil*). **Inception** refers specifically to the beginning of an undertaking, project, institution, or practice (*she was in charge of the organization from its inception*). **Provenance** is similarly restricted in meaning, referring to the specific place, or sometimes the race or people, from which something is derived or by whom it was invented or constructed (*in digging, they uncovered an artifact of unknown provenance*).

---

o•rig•i•nal /ɔríjinəl/ • *adj.* **1** existing from the beginning; innate. **2** inventive; creative. **3** not derivative or imitative; firsthand. See synonym study at CREATIVE. • *n.* **1** original model, pattern, picture, etc., from which another is copied or translated. **2** eccentric or unusual person. □□ **o•rig•i•nal•i•ty** /-nál-/ *n.* **o•rig'i•nal•ly** *adv.*

■ *adj.* **1** initial, first, earliest; native, indigenous. **2** novel, innovative, imaginative; fresh. **3** master, authentic, genuine; prototypic(al). • *n.* **1** prototype, source; master. **2** nonconformist, individualist, *colloq.* character. □□ **originality** creativity, inventiveness, daring, individuality. **originally** (at) first, initially, to begin with, *colloq.* from the word go; creatively, unusually.

o•rig•i•nate /ɔríjinayt/ *v.* **1** *tr.* cause to begin; initiate. **2** *intr.* [usu. foll. by *from, in, with*] have as an origin; begin. □□ **o•rig•i•na•tion** /-náyshən/ *n.* **o•rig'i•na•tive** *adj.* **o•rig'i•na'tor** *n.*

■ **1** create, bring about, give birth to; conceive, start, introduce, establish, invent.

2 arise, rise, spring, emerge, develop, evolve. □□ **origination** emergence, initiation; see also ORIGIN 1.

O-ring /ó-ring/ *n.* gasket in the form of a ring with a circular cross section.

o•ri•ole /áwreeōl/ *n.* American bird with black and orange plumage in the male.

Or•lon /áwrlon/ *n.propr.* synthetic fiber and fabric for textiles and knitwear.

or•mo•lu /áwrməlōō/ *n.* 1 [often *attrib.*] gilded bronze or gold-colored alloy of copper, zinc, and tin used to decorate furniture, make ornaments, etc. 2 articles made of or decorated with these.

or•na•ment • *n.* /áwrnəmənt/ 1 thing used to adorn, esp. a trinket, vase, figure, etc. 2 quality or person conferring adornment, grace, or honor (*an ornament to her profession*). • *v.tr.* /áwrnəment/ adorn; beautify. □□ **or•na•men'tal** *adj.* **or•na•men•ta'tion** *n.*

■ *n.* 1 embellishment, decoration, gingerbread, trimming. • *v.* decorate, enhance, embroider.

or•nate /awrnáyt/ *adj.* elaborately adorned; highly decorated. □□ **or•nate'ly** *adv.* **or•nate'ness** *n.*

■ florid, overdone, lavish, pompous, pretentious.

or•ner•y /áwrnəree/ *adj. colloq.* cantankerous; unpleasant. □□ **or'ner•i•ness** *n.*

■ see TESTY.

or•ni•thol•o•gy /áwrnithóləjee/ *n.* the scientific study of birds. □□ **or•ni•tho•log•i•cal** /–thəlójikəl/ *adj.* **or•ni•thol'o•gist** *n.*

o•ro•tund /áwrətund/ *adj.* 1 (of the voice) round; imposing. 2 (of writing, style, etc.) pompous; pretentious.

or•phan /áwrfən/ • *n.* [often *attrib.*] 1 child whose parents are dead. 2 young animal that has lost its mother. 3 person or thing bereft of previous protection, support, advantages, etc. • *v.tr.* bereave (a child) of its parents.

or•phan•age /áwrfənij/ *n.* residential institution for orphans.

or•rer•y /áwroree, ór–/ *n.* (*pl.* **–ies**) clockwork model of the solar system.

ortho- /áwrthō/ *comb. form* 1 straight; rectangular; upright. 2 right; correct.

or•tho•don•tics /áwrthədóntiks/ *n.pl.* [treated as *sing.*] (also **or•tho•don•tia** /–dónshə/) treatment of irregularities in the teeth and jaws. □□ **or•tho•don'tic** *adj.* **or•tho•don'tist** *n.*

or•tho•dox /áwrthədoks/ *adj.* 1 holding correct or currently accepted opinions, esp. on religious doctrine, morals, etc. 2 not independent-minded; unoriginal; unheretical. □ **Orthodox Church** Eastern Christian Church, separated from the Western Christian Church in the 11th c., having the Patriarch of Constantinople as its head, and including the national churches of Russia, Romania, Greece, etc. □□ **or'tho•dox•y** *n.*

■ conformist, recognized, official, standard, established.

or•thog•ra•phy /awrthógrəfee/ *n.* (*pl.* **–phies**) 1 correct or conventional spelling.

2 spelling with reference to its correctness (*dreadful orthography*). 3 study or science of spelling. □□ **or•tho•graph•ic** /áwrthəgráfik/ *adj.*

or•tho•pe•dics /áwrthəpeediks/ *n.pl.* [treated as *sing.*] branch of medicine dealing with the correction of deformities of bones or muscles. □□ **or•tho•pe'dic** *adj.* **or•tho•pe'dist** *n.*

or•thot•ics /awrtháatiks/ *n.* 1 *Med.* science of treating joint, bone, or muscle disorders with mechanical support, braces, etc. 2 devices, such as inserts for athletic shoes, used for such treatment.

-ory /áwree, əree/ *suffix* forming nouns denoting a place for a particular function (*dormitory, refectory*) or adjectives (and occasionally nouns) relating to or involving a verbal action (*accessory, compulsory, directory*).

OS *abbr.* 1 old style. 2 ordinary seaman. 3 oculus sinister (left eye). 4 outsize. 5 out of stock.

Os *symb. Chem.* osmium.

os•cil•late /ósilayt/ *v.* 1 *tr. & intr.* **a** swing back and forth like a pendulum. **b** move back and forth between points. 2 *intr.* vacillate; vary between extremes of opinion, action, etc. □□ **os•cil•la•tion** /–láyshən/ *n.* **os'cil•la•tor** *n.*

■ fluctuate, waver, seesaw, sway; equivocate, shilly-shally.

os•cil•lo•scope /əsíləskōp/ *n.* device for viewing oscillations in electrical current, etc., by a display on the screen of a cathode-ray tube.

os•cu•late /óskyəlayt/ *v. joc.* kiss.

-ose[1] /ōs/ *suffix* forming adjectives denoting possession of a quality (*grandiose, verbose*). □□ **–ose•ly** *suffix* forming adverbs. **–ose•ness** *suffix* forming nouns(cf. –OSITY).

-ose[2] /ōs/ *suffix Chem.* forming names of carbohydrates (*cellulose, sucrose*).

OSHA /óshə/ *abbr.* Occupational Safety and Health Administration.

o•sier /ózhər/ *n.* willows used in basketwork.

-osis /ósis/ *suffix* (*pl.* **–os•es** /óseez/) denoting a process or condition (*apotheosis, metamorphosis*), esp. a pathological state (*acidosis, neurosis, thrombosis*).

-osity /ósitee/ *suffix* forming nouns from adjectives in *-ose* (see –OSE[1]) and *-ous* (*verbosity, curiosity*).

os•mi•um /ózmeeəm/ *n. Chem.* hard, bluish-white element, the heaviest known metal, occurring naturally and used in certain alloys. ¶ Symb.: **Os**.

os•mo•sis /ozmṓsis, os–/ *n.* 1 *Biochem.* passage of a solvent through a semipermeable partition into a more concentrated solution. 2 any process by which something is acquired by absorption. □□ **os•mot•ic** /–mótik/ *adj.*

os•prey /óspray, –pree/ *n.* (*pl.* **–preys**) large bird of prey, with a brown back and white markings, feeding on fish. (Also called **fish hawk**.).

os•si•fy /ósifī/ *v.* (**–fies, –fied**) 1 turn into bone; harden. 2 make or become rigid, callous, or unprogressive. □□ **os•si•fi•ca'tion** *n.*

■ 1 see PETRIFY 2.

os•so bu•co /áwsō bōōkō/ *n.* (also **os'so buc'co**) shank of veal stewed in wine with vegetables.

os•su•ar•y /óshōōeree, ósyōō–/ *n.* (*pl.* **–ies**) receptacle for the bones of the dead.

os•ten•si•ble /osténsibəl/ *adj.* apparent; professed. □□ **os•ten′si•bly** *adv.*

■ see APPARENT 2, *alleged* (ALLEGE). □□ **ostensibly** see *apparently* (APPARENT).

os•ten•sive /osténsiv/ *adj.* directly demonstrative.

■ see TANGIBLE 2.

os•ten•ta•tion /óstentáyshən/ *n.* pretentious display, esp. of wealth and luxury. □□ **os•ten′ta′tious** *adj.* **os•ten•ta′tious•ly** *adv.*

■ exhibitionism, showing off, flamboyance. □□ **ostentatious** showy, boastful, flaunting, pretentious, theatrical, *colloq.* flash.

osteo- /ósteeō/ *comb. form* bone.

os•te•o•ar•thri•tis /óstecōaarthrítis/ *n.* degenerative disease of joint cartilage. □□ **os•te•o•ar•thrit•ic** /–thrítik/ *adj.*

os•te•op•a•thy /óstecópəthee/ *n.* treatment of disease through manipulation of bones, esp. the spine, displacement of these being the supposed cause. □□ **os•te•o•path** /ósteeəpath/ *n.*

os•te•o•po•ro•sis /ósteeōpərṓsis/ *n.* condition of brittle bones caused by loss of bony tissue, esp. as a result of hormonal changes, or deficiency of calcium or vitamin D.

os•tra•cize /óstrəsīz/ *v.tr.* **1** exclude (a person) from a society, favor, common privileges, etc.; refuse to associate with. **2** banish. □□ **os•tra•cism** /–sizəm/ *n.*

■ **1** blackball, blacklist, boycott, isolate, snub, shun, cold-shoulder. **2** exile.

os•trich /óstrich, áw–/ *n.* **1** large African swift-running flightless bird with long legs and two toes on each foot. **2** person who refuses to accept facts (from the belief that ostriches bury their heads in the sand when pursued).

OT *abbr.* Old Testament.

o.t. *abbr.* (also **O.T.**) **1** occupational therapist. **2** occupational therapy. **3** overtime.

OTB *abbr.* off-track betting.

oth•er /úthər/ • *adj.* **1** not the same as one or some already mentioned or implied; separate in identity or distinct in kind. **2 a** further; additional. **b** alternative of two (*open your other eye*). • *n.* or *pron.* [orig. an ellipt. use of the *adj.*, now with *pl.* in –*s*] **1** additional, different, or extra person, thing, example, etc. (see ANOTHER, *each other*). **2** [in *pl.*; prec. by *the*] the ones remaining (*where are the others?*). • *adv. disp.* otherwise (*cannot react other than angrily*). □ **the other day** (or **night** or **week**, etc.) a few days, etc., ago.

■ *adj.* **2 a** see FURTHER *adj.* 2. **b** see ALTERNATIVE *adj.* 1.

oth•er•wise /úthərwīz/ • *adv.* **1** else; or else; in different circumstances. **2** in other respects (*he is somewhat unkempt, but otherwise very suitable*). **3** in a different way (*could not have acted otherwise*). • *adj.* [*predic.*] in a different state (*the matter is quite otherwise*).

■ *adv.* **1, 2** if not, in another situation, on the other hand; in other respects. **3** in another manner.

oth•er•world•ly /úthərwárldlee/ *adj.* **1** unworldly; impractical. **2** concerned with life after death, etc.

-otic /ótik/ *suffix* forming adjectives and nouns corresponding to nouns in *–osis*, meaning 'affected by or producing or resembling a condition in *–osis*' or 'a person affected with this' (*narcotic, neurotic, osmotic*). □□ **-ot•i•cal•ly** *suffix* forming adverbs.

o•ti•ose /ósheeōs, ótee–/ *adj.* **1** serving no practical purpose; not required. **2** futile.

o•ti•tis /ōtítis/ *n.* inflammation of the ear.

Ot•ta•wa /átawə, –waa, –waw/ • *n.* **1 a** N. American people native to Canada and the Great Lakes region. **b** member of this people. **2** language of this people. • *adj.* of this people or their language.

ot•ter /ótər/ *n.* **1** aquatic fish-eating mammal having strong claws and webbed feet. **2** its fur or pelt.

ot•to•man /ótəmən/ *n.* **1** upholstered seat, usu. square and without back or arms. **2** footstool of similar design.

ouch /owch/ *int.* expressing pain or annoyance.

ought /awt/ *v.aux.* [usu. foll. by *to* + infin.; present and past indicated by the following infin.] **1** expressing duty or rightness (*we ought to love our neighbors*). **2** expressing advisability or prudence (*you ought to go for your own good*). **3** expressing esp. strong probability (*he ought to be there by now*).

■ see MUST *v.* 1, 3.

Oui•ja /weejə, –jee/ *n.* (in full **Oui′ja board**) *propr.* board game purporting to give advice, etc.

ounce /owns/ *n.* **1 a** unit of weight of one-sixteenth of a pound avoirdupois. ¶Abbr.: **oz. b** unit of one-twelfth of a pound troy. **2** small quantity. □ **fluid ounce** unit of capacity equal to one-sixteenth of a pint.

our /owr, aar/ *poss.pron.* [*attrib.*] **1** of or belonging to us or ourselves (*our house, our own business*). **2** of or belonging to all people (*our children's future*).

ours /owrz, aars/ *poss.pron.* the one or ones belonging to or associated with us (*it is ours, ours are over there*).

our•selves /owrsélvz, aar–/ *pron.* **1 a** *emphat. form* of WE or US (*we ourselves did it, made it ourselves*). **b** *refl.* form of US (*are pleased with ourselves*). **2** in our normal state of body or mind (*not quite ourselves today*).

-ous /əs/ *suffix* forming adjectives meaning 'abounding in, characterized by, of the nature of' (*envious, glorious, mountainous, poisonous*). □□ **–ous•ly** *suffix* forming adverbs. **–ous•ness** *suffix* forming nouns.

oust /owst/ *v.tr.* **1** drive out or expel, esp. by forcing oneself into the place of. **2** dispossess. See synonym study at EJECT.

■ **1** see EXPEL 1. **2** see DISPOSSESS 1.

oust•er /ówstər/ *n.* **1** ejection as a result of physical action, judicial process, or political upheaval. **2** expulsion.

out /owt/ • *adv.* **1** away from or not in or at a place, etc. (*keep him out*). **2** [forming part of phrasal verbs] indicating **a** dispersal away from a center, etc. (*hire out*). **b** coming or bringing into the open (*stand out*). **c** need for attentiveness (*look out*). **3 a** not in one's house, office, etc. **b** no longer in prison. **4** to or at an end; completely (*out of bananas*). **5** (of a fire, candle, etc.) not burning. **6** *colloq.* unconscious. **7** (of a party, politician, etc.) not in office. **8** unfashionable. **9** *Sports* (of a batter, base runner, etc.) no longer taking part as such, having been tagged, struck out, caught, etc. **10 a** not worth considering; rejected. **b** not allowed. **11** (of a stain, mark, etc.) not visible; removed. • *prep.* out of (*looked out the window*). • *n.* **1** *colloq.* way of escape; excuse. **2** *Baseball* play in which a batter or base runner is retired from an inning. • *v.* **1** *intr.* come or go out; emerge. **2** *tr. colloq.* expose the homosexuality of (esp. a prominent person). □ **out-and-out** *adj.* thorough; surpassing. *adv.* thoroughly; surpassingly. **out for** having one's interest or effort directed to; intent on. **out of 1** from within (*came out of the house*). **2** not within (*I was never out of the city*). **3** from among (*nine people out of ten*). **4** beyond the range of. **5** without or so as to be without (*out of sugar*). **6** from (*get money out of him*). **7** owing to; because of (*asked out of curiosity*). **8** by the use of (material) (*what did you make it out of?*). **9** at a specified distance from (a town, port, etc.) (*seven miles out of Topeka*). **10** beyond (*something out of the ordinary*). **out to** keenly striving to do.

■ *adv.* **1** abroad, elsewhere, not (at) home, absent. **2a, b, 3a** outside, outdoors; to or into public notice, out of the closet; revealed, exposed, visible, in sight. **3 b** free, at liberty, at large. **4** thoroughly, effectively. **5** extinguished, unlit; doused; exhausted, finished; completed; nonfunctioning. **6** *colloq.* (out) cold, out for the count; see also INSENSIBLE 1. **8** outdated, old-fashioned, antiquated, old hat, obsolete. **10 b** unacceptable, forbidden. • *n.* **1** loophole, evasion, alibi. □ **out-and-out** *adj.* complete, pure, utter, outright;

downright. **out for** interested in, bent on, after, seeking, in search of. **out to** trying or aiming *or* eager to.

out- /owt/ *prefix* added to verbs and nouns, meaning: **1** so as to surpass or exceed (*outdo, outnumber*). **2** external; separate (*outline, outhouse*). **3** out of; away from; outward (*outgrowth*).

out•age /ówtij/ *n.* period of time during which a power supply, etc., is not operating.

out•back /ówtbak/ *n.* esp. *Austral.* remote and us. uninhabited inland districts.

out•bal•ance /ówtbáləns/ *v.tr.* outweigh.

out•board /ówtbawrd/ • *adj.* **1** (of a motor) attachable to the outside of a boat. **2** (of a boat) having an outboard motor. • *n.* **1** outboard engine. **2** boat with an outboard engine.

out•break /ówtbrayk/ *n.* **1** sudden eruption of war, disease, rebellion, etc. **2** outcrop.

■ **1** see *eruption* (ERUPT).

out•build•ing /ówtbilding/ *n.* detached shed, barn, etc., within the grounds of a main building.

out•burst /ówtbərst/ *n.* **1** verbal explosion of anger, etc. **2** bursting out.

■ eruption, blowup; surge, rush; fit, attack, tantrum.

out•cast /ówtkast/ • *n.* person rejected by his or her home, country, society, etc. • *adj.* rejected; homeless; friendless.

■ *n.* pariah, exile, reject; expatriate, refugee.

out•class /ówtklás/ *v.tr.* **1** surpass in quality. **2** defeat easily.

■ **2** see SURPASS 1.

out•come /ówtkum/ *n.* result; visible effect.

■ consequence, effect, upshot, *colloq.* bottom line, *sl.* payoff.

out•crop /ówtkrop/ *n.* **1 a** emergence of a stratum, etc., at the surface. **b** stratum, etc., emerging. **2** noticeable manifestation.

■ **1** see ROCK¹ *n.* 3.

out•cry /ówtkrī/ *n.* (*pl.* **–cries**) strong public protest.

■ complaint, uproar, clamor, commotion, outburst, noise.

out•dat•ed /ówtdáytid/ *adj.* out of date; obsolete.

out•dis•tance /ówtdístəns/ *v.tr.* leave (a competitor) behind completely.

out•do /ówtdóō/ *v.tr.* (*3rd sing. present* **–does**; *past* **–did**; *past part.* **–done**) exceed or excel; surpass.

■ transcend, outstrip, outshine, top, overcome, defeat.

out•door /ówtdawr/ *adj.* done, existing, or used out of doors.

■ alfresco, open-air; see also OUTSIDE *adj.* 1.

out•doors /ówtdáwrz/ • *adv.* in or into the open air. • *n.* the world outside buildings; open air.

■ *adv.* see OUTSIDE *adv.* 1–3.

out•er /ówtər/ *adj.* **1** outside; external (*pierced the outer layer*). **2** farther from the center or inside. □ **outer space** universe beyond the earth's atmosphere. □□ **out'er•most** *adj.*

■ **1** see EXTERNAL *adj.* 1a, 3; 1b. **2** see OUT-LYING.

out•field /ówtfeeld/ *n.* outer part of a playing area, esp. a baseball field. □□ **out'field•er** *n.*

out•fit /ówtfit/ • n. 1 set of clothes esp. designed to be worn together. 2 set of equipment, etc. 3 colloq. group of people regarded as a unit, etc.; team. • v.tr. [also refl.] (–fit•ted, –fit•ting) provide with an outfit, esp. of clothes.

■ n. 1 suit, colloq. getup; dress, colloq. duds, threads. 2 gear, rig, kit, paraphernalia, utensils. 3 firm, business, organization. • v. equip, provision, stock, supply, furnish; dress, clothe.

out•fit•ter /ówtfitər/ n. 1 business that supplies outdoor equipment, arranges tours, etc. 2 retailer of men's clothing.

out•flank /ówtflángk/ v.tr. 1 a extend one's flank beyond that of (an enemy). b outmaneuver (an enemy) in this way. 2 get the better of; confound (an opponent).

out•fox /ówtfóks/ v.tr. colloq. outwit.

out•go•ing /ówtgóing/ adj. 1 friendly. 2 retiring from office. 3 going out or away.

■ 1 genial, easygoing, extrovert. 2, 3 departing, ex-, former.

out•grow /ówtgró/ v.tr. (past –grew; past part. –grown) 1 grow too big for. 2 leave behind (a childish habit, etc.). 3 grow faster or taller than.

out•growth /ówtgróth/ n. 1 offshoot; natural product. 2 the process of growing out.

■ 1 see OFFSHOOT 2.

out•house /ówt-hows/ n. 1 outbuilding used as a toilet, usu. with no plumbing. 2 building, esp. a shed, etc., built next to or on the grounds of a house.

out•ing /ówting/ n. pleasure trip; excursion.

■ jaunt, junket, expedition, drive.

out•land•ish /owtlándish/ adj. bizarre; strange; unfamiliar. □□ **out•land'ish•ly** adv. **out•land'ish•ness** n.

■ odd, exotic, foreign, alien, unheard-of, different, unfamiliar, weird, freakish.

out•last /ówtlást/ v.tr. last longer than.

■ outlive; outwear; weather, endure; see also sit out.

out•law /ówtlaw/ • n. 1 fugitive from the law. 2 hist. person denied protection of the law. • v.tr. declare or make illegal.

■ n. 1 criminal, gangster, robber. • v. forbid, ban, prohibit.

out•lay /ówtlay/ n. what is spent on something.

■ expense, cost, disbursement, payment.

out•let /ówtlet, –lit/ n. 1 means of exit or escape. 2 means of expression (of a talent, emotion, etc.). 3 agency, distributor, or market for goods (a new retail outlet in China). 4 electrical power receptacle.

■ 1 way out, relief, release. 3 retailer, boutique, booth; see also MARKET n. 3, 4.

out•line /ówtlīn/ • n. 1 rough draft of a diagram, plan, proposal, etc. 2 summary of main features. 3 sketch containing only contour lines. 4 [in sing. or pl.] lines enclosing or indicating an object. • v.tr. 1 draw or describe in outline. 2 mark the outline of.

■ n. 1, 2 synopsis, digest, abstract, overview, review. 4 contour, boundary; profile, silhouette. • v. trace, draft, rough out.

out•live /ówtlív/ v.tr. 1 live longer than (an-

---

other person). 2 live beyond (a specified date or time).

out•look /ówtlŏŏk/ n. 1 prospect for the future. 2 mental attitude.

■ 1 forecast, expectation(s), promise; see also FORECAST n. 2 position, point of view, perspective.

out•ly•ing /ówtlī-ing/ adj. situated far from a center; remote.

■ distant, far-off; furthest, farthest.

out•ma•neu•ver /ówtmənŏŏvər/ v.tr. 1 use skill and cunning to secure an advantage over (a person). 2 outdo in maneuvering.

out•mod•ed /ówtmódid/ adj. 1 out of fashion. 2 obsolete.

out•pa•tient /ówtpayshənt/ n. hospital patient whose treatment does not require overnight hospitalization.

out•place•ment /ówtplaysmənt/ n. assistance in finding new employment for workers who have been dismissed.

out•post /ówtpōst/ n. 1 detachment set at a distance from the main body of an army, esp. to prevent surprise. 2 distant branch or settlement.

■ 2 see SETTLEMENT 2.

out•put /ówtpŏŏt/ • n. 1 product of a process, esp. of manufacture, or of mental or artistic work. 2 quantity or amount of this. 3 printout, results, etc., supplied by a computer. 4 power, etc., delivered by an apparatus. • v.tr. (–put•ting; past and past part. –put or –put•ted) 1 put or send out. 2 (of a computer) supply (results, etc.).

■ n. 1, 2 production, yield; achievement; see also WORK n. 3. • v. 1 produce, generate, achieve; print out, transmit.

out•rage /ówt-rayj/ • n. 1 extreme violation of others' rights, sentiments, etc. 2 gross offense or indignity. 3 fierce resentment. • v.tr. 1 subject to outrage. 2 injure, insult, etc., flagrantly.

■ n. 1 violence, atrocity, brutality. 2 see INSULT[1] n. 3 affront, indignation. • v. 1 violate, desecrate; assault, attack. 2 offend, infuriate, enrage, colloq. rile; see also SHOCK v. 1.

out•ra•geous /owt-rάyjəs/ adj. 1 shocking. 2 grossly cruel. 3 immoral, offensive. □□ **out•ra'geous•ly** adv.

■ 1 excessive, unreasonable, preposterous. 2 vicious, heinous, atrocious. 3 indecent, obnoxious, obscene, objectionable, explicit, appalling.

ou•tré /ŏŏtráy/ adj. unconventional; eccentric.

■ unusual, bizarre, strange; outrageous.

out•rid•er /ówt-rīdər/ n. mounted rider ahead of, or with, a procession, etc.

out•rig•ger /ówt-rigər/ n. 1 beam, spar, or framework, rigged out and projecting from or over the side of a boat or canoe to give stability. 2 boat fitted with this.

out•right • adv. /ówt-rít/ 1 altogether; entirely (proved outright). 2 without reservation; openly. • adj. /ówt-rít/ 1 downright; direct; complete. 2 undisputed; clear. □□ **out'right•ness** n.

■ adv. completely, thoroughly; exactly, categorically, candidly; unconditionally; out of hand. • *adj.* **1** undisguised, utter, out-and-out. **2** unqualified, unrestricted, unconditional, definite.

out•run /ówt-rún/ *v.tr.* (**-run•ning**; *past* **–ran**; *past part.* **–run**) **1** run faster or farther than. **2** go beyond.

out•sell /ówtsél/ *v.tr.* (*past* and *past part.* **–sold**) **1** sell more than. **2** be sold in greater quantities than.

out•set /ówtset/ *n.* start; beginning.
■ inauguration, inception, *colloq.* kickoff.

out•shine /ówtshín/ *v.tr.* (*past* and *past part.* **–shone**) shine brighter than; surpass in ability, excellence, etc. •

out•side • *n.* /ówtsíd/ **1** external side or surface; outer parts. **2** external appearance; outward aspect. • *adj.* /ówtsíd/ **1** of, on, or nearer the outside; outer. **2 a** not belonging (*outside help*). **b** not a part of. **3** (of a chance, etc.) remote; very unlikely. **4** (of an estimate, etc.) greatest or highest possible. **5** *Baseball* (of a pitched ball) missing the strike zone by passing home plate on the side away from the batter. • *adv.* /ówtsíd/ **1** on or to the outside. **2** in or to the open air. **3** not within or enclosed or included. • *prep.* /ówtsíd/ **1** not in; to or at the exterior of. **2** external to; not included in; beyond the limits of (*outside the law*).
■ *n.* **1** exterior, face, shell; façade. **2** look, demeanor, face; mask, disguise, false front. • *adj.* **1** exterior; outdoor. **2 a** foreign, alien; excluded, uninvolved, different; private, peripheral; independent, freelance. **3** faint; see also SLENDER 2. **4** maximum, best, worst. • *adv.* externally; out, outdoors.

out•sid•er /ówtsídər/ *n.* **1** nonmember of some circle, party, profession, etc. **2** competitor, applicant, etc., thought to have little chance of success.
■ **1** noninitiate, layman, laywoman, stranger; newcomer, visitor, intruder. **2** dark horse.

out•size /ówtsíz/ *adj.* unusually large.

out•skirts /ówtskərts/ *n.pl.* outer area of a town, etc.
■ periphery, edge, suburb(s), neighborhood, fringe(s).

out•smart /ówtsmaárt/ *v.tr. colloq.* outwit; be cleverer than.
■ outthink, outplay, get the better of, trick, hoodwink, deceive, *colloq.* outfox; swindle, *colloq.* bamboozle, *sl.* con.

out•spo•ken /ówtspókən/ *adj.* frank in stating one's opinions. □□ **out•spo′ken•ly** *adv.* **out•spo′ken•ness** *n.*
■ candid, open, direct, unambiguous, blunt, brash, tactless, crude.

out•spread /ówtspréd/ *adj.* spread out; extended or expanded.

out•stand•ing /ówtstánding/ *adj.* **1 a** conspicuous; eminent, esp. because of excellence. **b** [usu. foll. by *at, in*] remarkable (in a specified field). **2** (esp. of a debt) not yet settled (*$200 still outstanding*). See synonym study at NOTICEABLE. □□ **out•stand′ing•ly** *adv.*

■ **1** prominent, famous, memorable, distinguished, notable, exceptional, *colloq.* smashing, super. **2** unresolved, unpaid, due, receivable, payable; remaining.

out•sta•tion /ówtstayshən/ *n.* remote branch or outpost.

out•strip /ówtstríp/ *v.tr.* (**-stripped**, **-strip•ping**) **1** pass in running, etc. **2** surpass, esp. competitively.
■ overcome, outperform, beat, excel.

out•take /ówt-tayk/ *n.* length of film or tape rejected in editing.

out•vote /ówtvót/ *v.tr.* defeat by a majority of votes.

out•ward /ówt-wərd/ • *adj.* **1** situated on or directed toward the outside. **2** going out. **3** bodily; external; apparent. • *adv.* (also **out′wards**) in an outward direction. • *n.* outward appearance of something; exterior. □□ **out′ward•ly** *adv.*
■ *adj.* **1, 3** exterior, obvious, visible; superficial, surface, false, worldly, secular, material. • *adv.* outside, away. □□ **outwardly** externally, apparently, visibly.

out•wear /ówt-wáir/ *v.tr.* (*past* **–wore**; *past part.* **–worn**) **1** exhaust; wear out; wear away. **2** live or last beyond the duration of. **3** (as **outworn** *adj.*) out of date; obsolete.
■ overcome, tip the scales, surpass, prevail over, compensate for, (more than) make up for.

out•wit /ówt-wít/ *v.tr.* (**-wit•ted**, **-wit•ting**) be too clever or crafty for; deceive by greater ingenuity.
■ see OUTSMART.

o•va *pl.* of OVUM.

o•val /óvəl/ • *adj.* **1** egg-shaped; ellipsoidal. **2** having the outline of an egg; elliptical. • *n.* egg-shaped or elliptical closed curve.
■ *adj.* ovoid, ellipsoid(al).

o•va•ry /óvəree/ *n.* (*pl.* **–ries**) **1** each of the female reproductive organs in which ova are produced. **2** hollow base of the carpel of a flower, containing one or more ovules. □□ **o•var•i•an** /óváireeən/ *adj.*

o•va•tion /óváyshən/ *n.* enthusiastic reception, esp. spontaneous and sustained applause.
■ acclaim, cheers, clapping, praise, *colloq.* (big) hand.

ov•en /úvən/ *n.* **1** enclosed compartment of brick, stone, or metal for cooking food. **2** chamber for heating or drying.

o•ver /óvər/ • *adv.* expressing movement or position or state above or beyond something stated or implied: **1** outward and downward from a brink or an erect position (*knocked the man over*). **2** so as to cover or touch a whole surface (*paint it over*). **3** so as to produce a fold, or reverse a position. **4 a** across a street or other space (*came over from England*). **b** for a visit, etc. (*invited them over*). **5** with change from one hand or part to another (*went over to the enemy*). **6** with motion above something; so as to pass across something (*climb over*). **7 a** from beginning to end (*think it over*). **b** again. **8** in excess; more than is right or required. **9** for or until a later time. **10** at an end; settled. • *prep.* **1** above, in, or to a position higher than; upon. **2** out and down from; down from the edge of. **3** so as to cover (*a hat over his eyes*). **4** above and across (*flew over the North Pole*). **5** concerning; while occupied with (*laughed over a good joke*). **6 a** superior to; in charge of. **b** in preference to. **7** so as to deal with completely (*went over the plans*). **8** during. **9** beyond; more than. □ **over against** in an opposite situation to; adjacent to, in contrast with. **over and over** repeatedly. **over-the-counter 1** (of medicine) sold without a prescription. **2** (of stocks, etc.) not listed on or traded by an organized securities exchange. **over-the-top** *colloq.* excessive.

■ *adv.* **1** to the ground *or* floor. **7 a** see THROUGH *adv.* **b** once more. **8** remaining, outstanding. **10** (of with), finished, concluded. • *prep.* **1** on, on top of. **3, 4** across. **5** see ABOUT *prep.* 1, *in the middle of* (MIDDLE). **7, 8** for, throughout; (all) about, all over. **9** greater than, in excess of, (over and) above; exceeding. □ **over and over** see *repeatedly* (REPEAT).

over- /ōvər/ *prefix* added to verbs, nouns, adjectives, and adverbs, meaning: **1** excessively (*overheat, overdue*). **2** upper, outer, extra (*overcoat, overtime*). **3** 'over' in various senses (*overhang, overshadow*). **4** completely; utterly (*overawe, overjoyed*).

over‧a‧chieve /ōvərəchéev/ *v.* **1** *intr.* do more than might be expected (esp. scholastically). **2** *tr.* achieve more than (an expected goal or objective, etc.). □□ **over‧a‧chieve'ment** *n.* **over‧a‧chiev'er** *n.*

over‧act /ōvərákt/ *v.* act in an exaggerated manner.

■ see OVERDO *v.*

over‧all • *adj.* /ōvəráwl/ **1** from end to end. **2** total; inclusive of all. • *adv.* /ōvəráwl/ in all parts; taken as a whole. • *n.* /ōvərawl/ [in *pl.*] protective trousers, dungarees, or a combination suit, worn by workmen, etc.

■ *adj.* **2** complete, comprehensive, entire.

over‧arm /ōvəraarm/ *adj. & adv.* done or made with the arm above the shoulder (*pitch it overarm*).

over‧awe /ōvər-áw/ *v.tr.* overcome with awe.

■ overwhelm, intimidate, dominate, frighten, disconcert.

over‧bal‧ance /ōvərbálʲəns/ *v.* **1** *tr.* outweigh. **2** *intr.* fall over.

■ **1** see OUTWEIGH.

over‧bear‧ing /ōvərbéring/ *adj.* **1** domineering; masterful. **2** overpowering.

■ repressive, bullying, officious, high and mighty, lordly, haughty, *colloq.* bossy, highfalutin.

over‧bite /ōvərbīt/ *n.* condition in which the teeth of the upper jaw project forward over those of the lower jaw.

over‧blown /ōvərblōn/ *adj.* excessively inflated or pretentious.

■ see IMMODERATE.

over‧board /ōvərbáwrd/ *adv.* from a ship into the water (*fall overboard*). □ **go overboard** behave immoderately; go too far.

over‧book /ōvərbdók/ *v.tr.* [also *absol.*] make too many bookings for (an aircraft, hotel, etc.).

over‧came *past of* OVERCOME.

over‧cast /ōvərkást/ *adj.* **1** (of the sky, weather, etc.) covered with cloud; dull and gloomy. **2** (in sewing) edged with stitching to prevent fraying.

■ **1** sunless, moonless, starless, dark, dreary, threatening.

over‧charge /ōvərchaarj/ • *v.tr.* **1** charge too high a price to (a person) or for (a thing). **2** put exaggerated or excessive detail into (a description, picture, etc.). • *n.* excessive charge (of explosive, money, etc.).

over‧coat /ōvərkōt/ *n.* **1** heavy coat, esp. one worn over indoor clothes for warmth outdoors in cold weather. **2** protective coat of paint, etc.

■ **1** see COAT *n.* 1.

over‧come /ōvərkúm/ *v.* (*past* **–came**; *past part.* **–come**) **1** *tr.* prevail over; master. **2** *tr.* (as **overcome** *adj.*) **a** exhausted; made helpless. **b** [usu. foll. by *with, by*] affected by (emotion, etc.). **3** *intr.* be victorious.

■ **1** defeat, conquer, triumph over, overthrow, *colloq.* lick. **2** (**overcome**) beaten, overwhelmed, speechless, moved, *colloq.* bowled over.

over‧de‧vel‧op /ōvərdivéləp/ *v.tr.* **1** develop too much. **2** *Photog.* treat with developer for too long.

over‧do /ōvərdóo/ *v.tr.* (*3rd sing. present* **–does**; *past* **–did**; *past part.* **–done**) **1** carry to excess; take too far (*I think you overdid the sarcasm*). **2** (esp. as **overdone** *adj.*) overcook. □ **overdo it** (or **things**) exhaust oneself.

■ **1** take to extremes, exaggerate, go overboard with; overindulge in. **2** burn, blacken. □ **overdo it** (or **things**) overwork, overload oneself, bite off more than one can chew, burn the candle at both ends.

o•ver•dose /ŏvərdōs/ • *n.* excessive dose (of a drug, etc.). • *v.* **1** *tr.* give an excessive dose of (a drug, etc.) or to (a person). **2** *intr.* take an excessive dose (of a drug, etc.). **3** *sl.* (usu. foll. by *on*) have or experience an excessive amount of (*we overdosed on movies this weekend*).

o•ver•draft /ŏvərdraft/ *n.* **1** deficit in a bank account caused by drawing more money than is credited to it. **2** amount of this.

o•ver•draw /ŏvərdráw/ *v.* (*past* **–drew**; *past part.* **–drawn**) **1** *tr.* draw a sum of money in excess of the amount credited to (one's bank account). **2** *intr.* overdraw one's account.

o•ver•drive /ŏvərdrīv/ *n.* **1** mechanism in a motor vehicle providing a gear ratio higher than that of the usual gear. **2** state of high activity.

o•ver•dub • *v.tr.* /ŏvərdúb/ (**–dubbed, –dubbing**) [also *absol.*] impose (additional sounds) on an existing recording. • *n.* /ŏvərdub/ overdubbing.

o•ver•due /ŏvərdōō, –dyōō/ *adj.* past the time due for payment, arrival, return, etc.
■ late, tardy, behind, belated, past due.

o•ver•es•ti•mate • *v.tr.* [also *absol.*] /ŏvəréstimayt/ form too high an estimate of (a person, ability, cost, etc.). • *n.* /ŏvəréstimit/ too high an estimate. □□ **o•ver•es•ti•ma•tion** /–áyshən/ *n.*

o•ver•ex•pose /ŏvərikspóz/ *v.tr.* [also *absol.*] **1** expose too much, esp. to the public eye. **2** *Photog.* expose (film) too long. □□ **o•ver•ex•po•sure** /–spózhər/ *n.*

o•ver•flow • *v.* /ŏvərflō/ **1** *tr.* flow over (the brim, limits, etc.). **2** *intr.* **a** (of a receptacle, etc.) be so full that the contents overflow it. **b** (of contents) overflow a container. **3** *tr.* (of a crowd, etc.) extend beyond the limits of (a room, etc.). **4** *tr.* flood (a surface or area). **5** *intr.* (of kindness, a harvest, etc.) be very abundant. • *n.* /ŏvərflō/ [also *attrib.*] **1** what overflows or is superfluous. **2** outlet for excess water, etc.
■ *v.* **1** see *run over* 1. **3** see FILL *v.* 2. **4** see FLOOD *v.* 1. **5** (*overflow with*) see ABOUND 2. • *n.* **1** see EXCESS *n.* 1. **2** see FLOOD *n.* 1.

o•ver•grown /ŏvərgrón/ *adj.* **1** abnormally large (*overgrown eggplant*). **2** wild; grown over with vegetation (*overgrown pond*).
■ **1** see ENORMOUS, TALL *adj.* 1. **2** covered, overrun.

o•ver•hand /ŏvərhand/ *adj. & adv.* **1** (in tennis, baseball, etc.) thrown or played with the hand above the shoulder; overarm. **2** *Swimming* = OVERARM.

o•ver•hang • *v.* /ŏvərháng/ (*past and past part.* **–hung**) project or hang over. • *n.* /ŏvərhang/ **1** overhanging part of a structure or rock formation. **2** amount by which this projects.
■ *v.* protrude, stick out, extend (out). • *n.* ledge; projection.

o•ver•haul • *v.tr.* /ŏvərháwl/ **1** thoroughly

examine and repair as necessary. **2** overtake.
• *n.* /ŏvərhawl/ thorough examination, with repairs if necessary.
■ *v.* **1** recondition, rebuild, repair, service, mend, fix (up). **2** pass, gain on, draw ahead of. • *n.* renovation, servicing, repair, adjustment; see also EXAMINATION 1, 2.

o•ver•head • *adv.* /ŏvərhéd/ **1** above one's head. **2** in the sky or on the floor above. • *adj.* /ŏvərhed/ **1** placed overhead. **2** (of expenses) arising from general operating costs. • *n.* /ŏvərhed/ overhead expenses.
■ *adv.* (up) in the air, high up. • *adj.* **1** elevated, raised, upper. • *n.* (basic or fixed or running) costs, expense(s).

o•ver•hear /ŏvərheer/ *v.tr.* (*past and past part.* **–heard**) [also *absol.*] hear as an eavesdropper or unintentionally.

o•ver•joyed /ŏvərjóyd/ *adj.* filled with great joy.
■ delighted, ecstatic, elated, *colloq.* tickled pink or to death.

o•ver•kill /ŏvərkil/ • *n.* **1** amount by which the capacity for destruction exceeds what is necessary for victory or annihilation. **2** excess. • *v.* kill or destroy to a greater extent than necessary.

o•ver•land /ŏvərland, –lənd/ *adj. & adv.* by land.

o•ver•lap • *v.* /ŏvərláp/ (**–lapped, –lapping**) **1** *tr.* partly cover (another object). **2** *tr.* cover and extend beyond. **3** *intr.* (of two things) partly coincide (*where psychology and philosophy overlap*). • *n.* /ŏvərlap/ **1** extension over. **2** amount of this.
■ *v.* **1, 2** overlie, overlay. **3** correspond, intersect; see also MEET *v.* 3. • *n.* lap, flap.

o•ver•lay • *v.tr.* /ŏvərláy/ (*past and past part.* **–laid**) **1** lay over. **2** [foll. by *with*] cover the surface of (a thing) with (a coating, etc.). • *n.* /ŏvərlay/ **1** thing laid over another. **2** (in printing, map reading, etc.) transparent sheet superimposed on another.
■ *v.* **1** see OVERLAP *v.* 1, 2. **2** see SPREAD *v.* 4a. • *n.* **1** see SKIN *n.* 3, OVERLAP *n.*

o•ver•leaf /ŏvərleef/ *adv.* on the other side of the leaf (of a book).

o•ver•look • *v.tr.* /ŏvərlŏŏk/ **1** fail to notice; ignore, condone (an offense, etc.). **2** have a view from above. **3** supervise. See synonym study at NEGLECT. • *n.* /ŏvərlŏŏk/ commanding position or view.
■ *v.* **1** miss, neglect, disregard; wink at, let ride. **2** command a view of, look over.

o•ver•lord /ŏvərlawrd/ *n.* supreme lord.

o•ver•ly /ŏvərlee/ *adv.* excessively; too.
■ exceedingly, unduly, inordinately, *colloq.* damned.

o•ver•mas•ter /ŏvərmástər/ *v.tr.* master completely; conquer.

o•ver•much /ŏvərmúch/ • *adv.* to too great an extent. • *adj.* excessive.

o•ver•night • *adv.* /ŏvərnít/ **1** for a night. **2** during a night. **3** suddenly; immediately. • *adj.* /ŏvərnit/ **1** for use overnight (*overnight bag*). **2** done, etc., overnight.

o•ver•pass /ŏvərpas/ *n.* road or railroad line that passes over another by means of a bridge.

o•ver•play /ŏvərpláy/ *v.tr.* give undue impor-

tance to; overemphasize. □ **overplay one's hand** be unduly optimistic about one's capabilities.
  ■ see EXAGGERATE 1.

o•ver•pop•u•lat•ed /óvərpópyəlaytid/ *adj.* having too large a population. □□ **o•ver•pop•u•la•tion** /-láyshən/ *n.*

o•ver•pow•er /óvərpówr/ *v.tr.* **1** subdue. **2** (of heat, emotion, etc.) be too intense for; overwhelm. □□ **o•ver•pow•er•ing** *adj.* **o•ver•pow•er•ing•ly** *adv.*
  ■ **1** overcome, conquer, defeat, *colloq.* best. **2** overcome, dumbfound, amaze, stun, *colloq.* floor. □□ **overpowering** overwhelming, irresistible, powerful, oppressive.

o•ver•price /óvərprís/ *v.tr.* price (a thing) too highly.

o•ver•print • *v.tr.* /óvərprínt/ **1** print further matter on (a surface already printed, esp. a postage stamp). **2** [also *absol.*] print too many copies of (a work). • *n.* /óvərprint/ **1** words, etc., overprinted. **2** overprinted postage stamp.

o•ver•pro•duce /óvərprədoos, -dyoos/ *v.tr.* [usu. *absol.*] **1** produce more of (a commodity) than is wanted. **2** produce to an excessive degree. □□ **o•ver•pro•duc•tion** /-dúkshən/ *n.*

o•ver•qual•i•fied /óvərkwólifīd/ *adj.* too highly qualified (esp. for a particular job, etc.).

o•ver•rate /óvəráyt/ *v.tr.* assess too highly.
  ■ overvalue, make too much of.

o•ver•reach /óvərreech/ *v.tr.* outwit; get the better of by cunning or artifice. □ **overreach oneself** strain oneself or fail by attempting too much.

o•ver•re•act /óvəreeákt/ *v.intr.* respond more forcibly, etc., than is justified. □□ **o•ver•re•ac•tion** /-ákshən/ *n.*
  ■ make a mountain out of a molehill, lose one's sense of proportion, go overboard.

o•ver•ride • *v.tr.* /óvərīd/ (*past* **-rode**; *past part.* **-rid•den**) **1** (often as **overriding** *adj.*) have or claim precedence or superiority over (*an overriding consideration*). **2 a** intervene and make ineffective. **b** interrupt the action of (an automatic device), esp. to take manual control. • *n.* /óvərīd/ **1** suspension of an automatic function. **2** device for this.
  ■ *v.* **1** see OUTWEIGH; (**overriding**) dominant, prevailing, primary. **2 a** see REVERSE *v.* 2.

o•ver•rule /óvərool/ *v.tr.* set aside (a decision, etc.) by exercising a superior authority.

o•ver•run • *v.tr.* /óvərún/ (**-run•ning**; *past* **-ran**; *past part.* **-run**) **1** (of pests, weeds, etc.) swarm or spread over. **2** conquer or ravage (territory) by force. **3** (of time, expenditure, etc.) exceed (a fixed limit). • *n.* /óvərun/ excess of produced items.
  ■ *v.* **1, 2** invade, defeat, destroy, scourge, sack, *colloq.* blitz.

o•ver•seas • *adv.* /óvərseez/ abroad (*was sent overseas for training*). • *adj.* /óvərseez/ foreign.
  ■ *adv.* see ABROAD 1. • *adj.* see EXTERNAL *adj.* 2.

o•ver•see /óvərsee/ *v.tr.* (**-sees**; *past* **-saw**; *past part.* **-seen**) officially supervise (workers, work, etc.). □□ **o•ver•se•er** *n.*

  ■ direct, manage, watch (over), administer; handle, control.

o•ver•shad•ow /óvərshádō/ *v.tr.* **1** appear much more prominent or important than. **2** shelter from the sun.
  ■ **1** dominate, outshine, eclipse, steal the limelight from.

o•ver•shoe /óvərshoo/ *n.* shoe of rubber, etc., worn over another as protection from wet, cold, etc.

o•ver•shoot /óvərshoot/ *v.tr.* (*past* and *past part.* **-shot**) **1** pass or send beyond (a target or limit). **2** (of an aircraft) fly or taxi beyond (the runway) when landing or taking off.

o•ver•sight /óvərsīt/ *n.* **1** failure to notice something. **2** inadvertent mistake. **3** supervision.
  ■ **1** carelessness, neglect, dereliction. **2** error, slip, blunder. **3** management, guidance, administration; charge, care, custody.

o•ver•sim•pli•fy /óvərsímplifī/ *v.tr.* (**-fies**, **-fied**) [also *absol.*] distort (a problem, etc.) by stating it in too simple terms. □□ **o•ver•sim•pli•fi•ca•tion** *n.*

o•ver•size /óvərsīz/ *adj.* (also **-sized** /-sīzd/) of greater than the usual size.
  ■ see LARGE *adj.* 1, 2.

o•ver•sleep /óvərsleep/ *v.intr.* & *refl.* (*past* and *past part.* **-slept**) sleep beyond the intended time of waking.

o•ver•spe•cial•ize /óvərspéshəlīz/ *v.intr.* concentrate too much on one aspect or area. □□ **o•ver•spe•cial•i•za•tion** *n.*

o•ver•state /óvərstáyt/ *v.tr.* **1** state (esp. a case or argument) too strongly. **2** exaggerate. □□ **o•ver•state•ment** *n.*
  ■ magnify, hyperbolize, embroider.

o•ver•stay /óvərstáy/ *v.tr.* stay longer than (one's welcome, a time limit, etc.).

o•ver•steer /óvərsteer/ • *v.intr.* (of a motor vehicle) tend to turn more sharply than was intended. • *n.* this tendency.

o•ver•step /óvərstép/ *v.tr.* (**-stepped**, **-step•ping**) **1** pass beyond (a boundary or mark). **2** violate (certain standards of behavior, etc.).
  ■ **1** exceed, transcend, surpass; see also PASS¹ *v.* 4

o•ver•strung /óvərstrúng/ *adj.* (of a person, disposition, etc.) intensely strained; highly strung.

o•ver•stuff /óvərstúf/ *v.tr.* **1** stuff more than is necessary. **2** (as **overstuffed** *adj.*) (of furniture) made soft and comfortable by thick upholstery.
  ■ **1** see CRAM 1.

o•vert /óvərt, óvárt/ *adj.* unconcealed; done openly. □□ **o•vert•ly** *adv.*
  ■ apparent, evident, plain, public. □□ **overtly** (out) in the open, for all to see.

o•ver•take /óvərtáyk/ *v.tr.* (*past* **-took**; *past part.* **-tak•en**) **1** catch up with and pass. **2** (of a storm, misfortune, etc.) come suddenly upon.
  ■ **1** reach, move by or past, leave behind, outdistance. **2** catch (unprepared), strike, hit.

o•ver•tax /óvərtáks/ *v.tr.* **1** make excessive

demands on (a person's strength, etc.). **2** tax too heavily.

o•ver•throw • *v.tr.* /ōvərthrố/ (*past* **–threw**; *past part.* **–thrown**) **1** remove forcibly from power. **2** conquer; overcome. **3** *Baseball* **a** (of a fielder) throw beyond the intended place. **b** (of a pitcher) throw too vigorously. • *n.* /ōvərthrố/ defeat or downfall.

■ *v.* **1** defeat, overpower, bring down, depose, *colloq.* best. • *n.* rout, conquest, ousting, end, collapse.

o•ver•time /ōvərtīm/ • *n.* **1** time worked in addition to regular hours. **2** payment for this. **3** *Sports* additional period of play at the end of a game when the scores are equal. • *adv.* in addition to regular hours.

o•ver•tone /ōvərtōn/ *n.* **1** *Mus.* any tones above the lowest in a harmonic series. **2** subtle quality or implication (*sinister overtones*).

■ **2** undertone, connotation, hint, suggestion, innuendo.

o•ver•ture /ōvərchər, –choŏr/ *n.* **1** orchestral piece opening an opera, etc. **2** [usu. in *pl.*] **a** opening of negotiations. **b** formal proposal or offer (esp. *make overtures to*).

■ (*overtures*) approach, advance, proposition.

o•ver•turn /ōvərtûrn/ *v.* **1** *tr.* cause to turn over; upset. **2** *tr.* reverse; subvert. **3** *intr.* turn over; fall over.

■ **1, 3** capsize, upend, upset, turn upside down. **2** bring down, overthrow, depose; invalidate; see also ABOLISH.

o•ver•use • *v.tr.* /ōvəryōoz/ use too much. • *n.* /ōvəryōos/ excessive use.

o•ver•view /ōvərvyōo/ *n.* general survey.

o•ver•weight /ōvərwayt/ *adj.* beyond an allowed or suitable weight.

■ see FAT *adj.* 1.

o•ver•whelm /ōvərhwélm, –wélm/ *v.tr.* **1** overpower with emotion. **2** overpower with an excess of business, etc. **3** bury or drown beneath a huge mass; submerge utterly. □□ **o•ver•whelm'ing** *adj.*

■ **1** overcome, stagger, astonish, shock, confuse, surprise, *colloq.* bowl over, *joc.* discombobulate, *sl.* blow a person's mind. **2, 3** inundate, overcome, flood; deluge, swamp.

o•ver•work /ōvərwûrk/ • *v.* **1** *intr.* work too hard. **2** *tr.* cause (another person) to work too hard. **3** *tr.* weary or exhaust with too much work. **4** *tr.* make excessive use of. • *n.* excessive work.

■ *v.* **1** do too much, overtax oneself, exhaust oneself. **2–4** overexert, overstrain, overburden. • *n.* overexertion, strain.

o•ver•wrought /ōvəráwt/ *adj.* **1** overexcited; nervous; distraught. **2** too elaborate.

■ **1** tense, edgy, jumpy, distracted. **2** overdone, ornate, fussy, gaudy.

ovi- /ōvee/ *comb. form* egg, ovum.

o•vi•duct /ōvidukt/ *n.* tube through which an ovum passes from the ovary.

o•vine /ōvīn/ *adj.* of or like sheep.

o•vip•a•rous /ōvípərəs/ *adj. Zool.* producing young from eggs expelled from the body before they are hatched (cf. VIVIPAROUS).

o•void /ōvoyd/ • *adj.* (of a solid or of a sur-

face) egg-shaped. • *n.* ovoid body or surface.

■ *adj.* see OVAL *adj.*

o•vo•vi•vip•a•rous /ōvōvīvípərəs/ *adj. Zool.* producing young by means of eggs hatched within the body (cf. OVIPAROUS, VIVIPAROUS). □□ **o•vo•vi•vi•par•i•ty** /–páritee/ *n.*

ov•u•late /ōvyəlayt, óvyə–/ *v.intr.* produce ova or ovules, or discharge them from the ovary. □□ **ov•u•la•tion** /–láyshən/ *n.*

ov•ule /áavyōol, óvyōol/ *n.* part of the ovary of seed plants that contains the germ cell; unfertilized seed. □□ **ov'u•lar** *adj.*

o•vum /ōvəm/ *n.* (*pl.* **o•va** /ōvə/) **1** mature reproductive cell of female animals, produced by the ovary. **2** egg cell of plants.

■ **2** see SEED *n.* 1a.

ow /ow/ *int.* expressing sudden pain.

owe /ō/ *v.tr.* **1 a** be under obligation. **b** [*absol.*, usu. foll. by *for*] be in debt (*still owe for my car*). **2** [often foll. by *to*] be under obligation to render (gratitude, honor, etc.) (*owe grateful thanks to*). **3** [usu. foll. by *to*] be indebted to a person or thing for (*we owe to Newton the principle of gravitation*).

ow•ing /ō-ing/ *predic.adj.* **1** owed; yet to be paid (*the balance owing*). **2** [foll. by *to*] **a** caused by (*the cancellation was owing to ill health*). **b** [as *prep.*] because of (*delayed owing to bad weather*).

■ **1** in arrears; see also OUTSTANDING 2. **2** (*owing to*) on account of, thanks to; through, as a result of.

owl /owl/ *n.* **1** nocturnal bird of prey with large eyes and a hooked beak. **2** *colloq.* person compared to an owl, esp. in looking solemn or wise. □□ **owl'ish** *adj.*

owl•et /ówlit/ *n.* small or young owl.

own /ōn/ • *adj.* [prec. by *possessive*] **1** belonging to oneself or itself. **2** individual; peculiar; particular. • *v.* **1** *tr.* have as property; possess. **2 a** *tr.* confess; admit as valid, true, etc. (*owns he did not know*). **b** *intr.* [foll. by *up to*] confess to (*owned up to a prejudice*). **3** *tr.* acknowledge. □ **hold one's own** maintain one's position; not be defeated or lose strength. **on one's own 1** alone. **2** independently, without help. □□ **–owned** *adj.* [in *comb.*]. **own'er** *n.* **own'er•ship** *n.*

■ *adj.* see INDIVIDUAL *adj.* 2–4. • *v.* **1** see POSSESS 1. **2** see CONFESS 1a. **3** see ACKNOWLEDGE 1.

ox /oks/ *n.* (*pl.* **ox•en** /óksən/) **1** large usu. horned domesticated ruminant used for draft, for supplying milk, and for eating as meat. **2** castrated male of a domesticated species of cattle. .

■ **1** (*oxen*) see CATTLE.

ox•bow /óksbō/ *n.* **1** U-shaped collar of an ox yoke. **2** loop formed by a horseshoe bend in a river.

ox•ford /óksfərd/ *n.* **1** low-heeled shoe that laces over the instep. **2** cotton fabric made in a basket weave, used for shirts and sportswear.

ox•ide /óksīd/ *n.* binary compound of oxygen.

ox•i•dize /óksidīz/ *v.* **1** combine or cause to combine with oxygen. **2** cover (metal) or (of metal) become covered with a coating of oxide; make or become rusty. □□ **ox•i•di•za′ tion** *n.* **ox′i•diz•er** *n.*

ox•y•a•cet•y•lene /ókseeəsét'leen/ *adj.* of or using a mixture of oxygen and acetylene, esp. in cutting or welding metals.

ox•y•gen /óksijən/ *n. Chem.* colorless, tasteless, odorless gaseous element, occurring naturally in air, water, and most minerals and organic substances, and essential to plant and animal life. ¶Symb.: **O**. □ **oxygen tent** tentlike enclosure supplying a patient with air rich in oxygen.

ox•y•gen•ate /óksijənayt/ *v.tr.* **1** supply, treat, or mix with oxygen; oxidize. **2** charge (blood) with oxygen by respiration. □□ **ox•y•gen•a•tion** /-náyshən/ *n.*

ox•y•mo•ron /ókseemáwron/ *n. rhet.* figure of speech in which apparently contradictory terms appear in conjunction (e.g., *faith unfaithful kept him falsely true*).

oys•ter /óystər/ *n.* **1** bivalve mollusk, esp. edible kinds, sometimes producing a pearl. **2** something regarded as containing all that one desires (*the world is my oyster*). **3** (in full **oys•ter white**) white color with a gray tinge.

oz. *abbr.* ounce(s).

o•zone /ózōn/ *n.* **1** *Chem.* colorless unstable gas with a pungent odor and powerful oxidizing properties, used for bleaching, etc. ¶Chem. formula: O_3. **2** *colloq.* **a** invigorating air at the seaside, etc. **b** exhilarating influence. □ **ozone-friendly** (of manufactured articles) containing chemicals that are not destructive to the ozone layer. **ozone hole** area of the ozone layer in which depletion has occurred. **ozone layer** layer of ozone in the stratosphere that absorbs most of the sun's ultraviolet radiation.

P¹ /pee/ *n.* (also **p**) (*pl.* **Ps** or **P's**; **p's**) sixteenth letter of the alphabet.

P² *abbr.* (also **P.**) **1** (on road signs) parking. **2** *Chess* pawn

P³ *symb. Chem.* phosphorus.

p *abbr.* (also **p**) **1** page. **2** piano (softly). **3** pico-.

PA *abbr.* **1** Pennsylvania (in official postal use). **2** public address (esp. *PA system*).

Pa *symb. Chem.* protactinium.

pa /paa/ *n. colloq.* father.

p.a. *abbr.* per annum.

PABA /paabə/ *abbr. Biochem.* PARA-AMINO-BENZOIC ACID.

Pab•lum /pábləm/ *n.* **1** *propr.* bland cereal food for infants. **2** (**pablum**) simplistic or unimaginative writing, ideas, etc.

PAC /pak/ *abbr.* political action committee.

pace /pays/ • *n.* **1 a** single step in walking or running. **b** distance covered in this. **2** speed in walking or running. **3** rate of progression. **4** gait. • *v.* **1** *intr.* **a** walk with a slow or regular pace. **b** (of a horse) = AMBLE. **2** *tr.* traverse or measure by pacing. **3** *tr.* set the pace for. □ **keep pace** advance at an equal rate (as). **put a person through his** (or **her**) **paces** test a person's qualities in action, etc. □□ **paced** *adj.* **pac′er** *n.*

■ *n.* **1 a** footstep, stride, tread. **b** step, stride. **2** rate, tempo, velocity, *colloq.* clip. • *v.* **1 a** stride, tread. **2** walk, stride, tread, perambulate; gauge, judge, rate, estimate, determine. □ **keep pace** keep up, keep in step *or* stride, stay level; compare, contend, compete.

pace•mak•er /páysmaykər/ *n.* **1** device for stimulating heart contractions. **2** competitor who sets the pace in a race.

pace•set•ter /páys-setər/ *n.* leader.

pach•y•derm /pákidərm/ *n.* any thick-skinned mammal, esp. an elephant or rhinoceros.

pach•y•san•dra /pakisándrə/ *n.* low-growing evergreen plant used as a ground cover.

pa•cif•ic /pəsífik/ • *adj.* peaceful; tranquil. • *n.* (**the Pacific**) expanse of ocean between N. and S. America to the east and Asia to the west. □□ **pa•cif′i•cal•ly** *adv.*

pac•i•fi•er /pásifiər/ *n.* **1** person or thing that pacifies. **2** rubber or plastic nipple for a baby to suck on.

pac•i•fism /pásifizəm/ *n.* belief that war and violence are morally unjustified. □□ **pac′i•fist** *n. & adj.*

pac•i•fy /pásifi/ *v.tr.* (**-fies, -fied**) **1** appease. **2** bring (a country, etc.) to a state of peace. □□ **pac•i•fi•ca′tion** *n.*

SYNONYM STUDY: pacify

APPEASE, CONCILIATE, MOLLIFY, PLACATE, PROPITIATE. You might try to **pacify** a crying baby, to **appease** a demanding boss, to **mollify** a friend whose feelings have been hurt, and to **placate** an angry crowd. While all of these verbs have something to do with quieting people who are upset, excited, aroused, or disturbed, each involves taking a slightly different approach. *Pacify* suggests a soothing or calming (*the mother made soft cooing noises in an attempt to pacify her child*). *Appease* implies that you've given in to someone's demands or made concessions in order to please (*she said she would visit his mother just to appease him*), while *mollify* stresses minimizing anger or hurt feelings by taking positive action (*her flattery failed to mollify him*). *Placate* suggests changing a hostile or angry attitude to a friendly or favorable one, usually with a more complete or long-lasting effect than *appease* (*they were able to placate* *their enemies by offering to support them).* You can **propitiate** by allaying or forestalling the anger of a superior or someone who has the power to injure you (*they were able to propitiate the trustees by holding a dinner party in their honor*). **Conciliate** implies the use of arbitration or compromise to settle a dispute or to win someone over (*the company made every effort to conciliate its angry competitor*).

pack[1] /pak/ • *n.* **1 a** collection of things wrapped up or tied together for carrying. **b** = BACKPACK. **2** set of items packaged for use or disposal together. **3** set of playing cards. **4** group or collection, esp. a group of wild animals. • *v.* **1** *tr.* **a** fill (a suitcase, bag, etc.) with clothes and other items. **b** put (things) together in a bag or suitcase. **2** *intr.* & *tr.* crowd or cram; fill tightly. **3** *tr.* cover (a thing) with something pressed tightly around. **4** *tr.* be capable of delivering with force. **5** *intr.* (of animals, etc.) form a pack. □ **pack animal** animal used for carrying packs. **pack ice** area of large crowded pieces of floating ice in the sea. **pack it in** (or **up**) *colloq.* end or stop it. **send packing** *colloq.* dismiss summarily. □□ **pack′a•ble** *adj.* **pack′er** *n.*

■ *n.* **1** parcel, package, bundle, load; knapsack, rucksack, haversack. **2** parcel, package, packet. **3** deck, set, stack. • *v.* **1 b** cram, jam, squeeze; stuff. **2** bundle, jam, press, ram, stuff; crowd, squeeze. □ **pack it in** (or **up**) cease, finish, quit.

pack[2] /pak/ *v.tr.* select (a jury, etc.) or fill (a meeting) so as to secure a decision in one's favor.

pack•age /pákij/ • *n.* **1 a** bundle of things packed. **b** box, parcel, etc., in which things are packed. **2** (in full **pack′age deal**) set of proposals or items offered or agreed to as a whole. • *v.tr.* make up into or enclose in a package. □ **package store** retail store selling alcoholic beverages in sealed containers. □□ **pack′ag•er** *n.*

■ *n.* **1** packet, parcel, pack, box, container, case, carton, bundle. **2** combination, unit; deal, agreement, contract, arrangement, settlement. • *v.* wrap, pack, containerize, case, encase, enclose, include.

pack•ag•ing /pákijing/ *n.* **1** wrapping or container for goods. **2** process of packing goods.

pack•et /pákit/ *n.* **1** small package. **2** (in full **pack′et boat**) *hist.* mail boat or passenger ship.

■ **1** pack, box, container, case, carton.

pack•ing /páking/ *n.* **1** act or process of packing. **2** material used as padding to pack esp. fragile articles.

pact /pakt/ *n.* agreement or a treaty.

■ bargain, alliance, contract, compact, concord.

pad[1] /pad/ • *n.* **1** piece of soft material used to reduce friction or jarring, fill out hollows, hold or absorb liquid, etc. **2** sheets of blank paper fastened together at one edge, for writing or drawing on. **3** fleshy underpart of an animal's foot or of a human finger. **4** flat surface for helicopter takeoff or rocket

launching. **5** *colloq.* apartment or bedroom. **6** floating leaf of a water lily. • *v.tr.* (**pad•ded**, **pad•ding**) **1** provide with a pad or padding; stuff. **2** lengthen or fill out (a book, etc.) with unnecessary material.

■ *n.* **1** cushion, pillow, wad, wadding, stuffing, padding, filling, filler. **2** writing pad, notepad, drawing pad, tablet. **5** room(s), home, place, quarters, lodging(s). • *v.* **1** cushion, wad, fill; upholster. **2** (*pad out*) expand, inflate, stretch, dilate, protract, extend.

pad[2] /pad/ • *v.* (**pad•ded**, **pad•ding**) *intr.* walk with a soft dull steady step. • *n.* sound of soft steady steps.

pad•ding /páding/ *n.* soft material used to pad or stuff with.

pad•dle /pád′l/ • *n.* **1** short broad-bladed oar. **2** paddle-shaped instrument. • *v.* **1** *intr.* & *tr.* move on water or propel a boat by means of paddles. **2** *tr. colloq.* spank. □ **paddle wheel** wheel with radiating paddles around it for propelling a ship. □□ **pad′dler** *n.*

■ *n.* **1** sweep, scull, blade. • *v.* **1** row, scull; propel, move. **2** thrash, beat, whip, flog.

pad•dle•ball /pád′lbawl/ *n.* ball game played on an enclosed court with short-handled perforated paddles.

pad•dock /pádək/ *n.* **1** small field, esp. for keeping horses in. **2** turf enclosure at a racecourse.

pad•dy /pádee/ *n.* (*pl.* **–dies**) field where rice is grown.

pad•dy wag•on /pádee/ *n. colloq.* police van for transporting those under arrest.

pad•lock /pádlok/ • *n.* detachable lock hanging by a pivoted hook on the object fastened. • *v.tr.* secure with a padlock.

pa•dre /paàdray, –dree/ *n.* **1** clergyman, esp. a priest. **2** chaplain in any of the armed services.

pae•an /péeən/ *n.* song of praise or triumph.

pa•el•la /pī-élə, paa-áyaa/ *n.* Spanish dish of rice, saffron, chicken, seafood, etc.

pa•gan /páygən/ • *n.* **1** nonreligious person; pantheist; heathen. **2** person following a polytheistic or pantheistic religion. **3** hedonist. • *adj.* **1 a** of pagans. **b** irreligious. **2** pantheistic. □□ **pa′gan•ish** *adj.* **pa′gan•ism** *n.* **pa′ganize** *v.*

■ *n.* unbeliever, idolater, infidel. • *adj.* **1** idolatrous, gentile; see also HEATHEN *adj.*

page[1] /payj/ • *n.* **1 a** leaf of a book, periodical, etc. **b** each side of this. **2** episode; memorable event. • *v.tr.* paginate.

■ *n.* **1 a** sheet, folio. **b** verso, recto. **2** phase, period, time, epoch, age, record, chapter. • *v.* number.

page[2] /payj/ • *n.* person employed to run errands, attend to a door, etc. • *v.tr.* **1** summon by making an announcement or by sending a messenger. **2** summon by a pager.

■ *n.* attendant, errand boy, messenger; bellboy. • *v.* send for *or* after, call, call for, call out, beep, buzz.

pag•eant /pájənt/ *n.* **1** elaborate parade or spectacle. **2** spectacular procession or play illustrating historical events.

■ **1** display, tableau, show, procession, ceremony, ritual, event, affair, extravaganza.

pag•eant•ry /pájəntree/ n. (pl. **–ries**) spectacular show; pomp.

■ ceremony, display, magnificence, extravagance.

pag•er /páyjər/ n. radio device with a beeper, activated from a central point to alert the person wearing it.

pag•i•nate /pájinayt/ v.tr. assign numbers to the pages of a book, etc. □□ **pag•i•na'tion** /-náyshən/ n.

pa•go•da /pəgṓdə/ n. Hindu or Buddhist temple, esp. a many-tiered tower, in India and the Far East.

paid past and past part. OF PAY.

pail /payl/ n. **1** bucket. **2** amount contained in this. □□ **pail'ful** n. (pl. **–fuls**)

pain /payn/ • n. **1** range of unpleasant bodily sensations produced by illness, accident, etc. **2** mental suffering or distress. **3** [in pl.] careful effort (take pains). **4** (also **pain in the neck**, etc.) colloq. troublesome person or thing; nuisance. • v.tr. cause pain to. □ **on** (or **under**) **pain of** with (death, etc.) as the penalty. □□ **pain'ful** adj. **pain'ful•ly** adv. **pain'ful•ness** n.

■ n. **1** hurt, suffering, discomfort, distress, soreness, ache, aching, pang, spasm, smart, cramp. **2** anguish, agony, affliction, grief, misery, wretchedness, despair, torment. **3** trouble, exertion, toil, labor. **4** irritation, vexation, annoyance, bother, pest, bore, colloq. headache, drag. • v. hurt, distress, grieve, wound, injure; trouble, depress.

pain•kill•er /páynkilər/ n. medicine or drug for alleviating pain. □□ **pain'kill•ing** adj.

■ anodyne, analgesic, anesthetic, sedative, palliative.

pain•less /páynlis/ adj. not causing or suffering pain. □□ **pain'less•ly** adv. **pain'less•ness** n.

■ trouble-free, easy, simple, comfortable, effortless.

pain•stak•ing /páynztayking/ adj. careful, industrious, thorough. □□ **pains'tak•ing•ly** adv.

■ see THOROUGH 2.

paint /paynt/ • n. **1** coloring matter, esp. in liquid form for imparting color to a surface. **2** this as a dried film or coating (the paint peeled off). • v.tr. **1 a** cover with paint. **b** apply paint of a specified color to. **2** depict (an object, scene, etc.) with paint; produce (a picture) by painting. **3** describe vividly. □□ **paint'a•ble** adj.

■ n. **1** color, tint, dye, coloring, pigment, stain. **2** coat, surface; enamel. • v. **1** coat, brush, daub, color, tint, dye, stain, decorate. **2** portray, picture, show, represent, render. **3** depict, portray, picture, draw, characterize.

paint•er[1] /páyntər/ n. person who paints, esp. an artist or decorator.

paint•er[2] /páyntər/ n. rope attached to the bow of a boat for tying it to a pier, dock, etc.

paint•ing /páynting/ n. **1** process or art of using paint. **2** painted picture.

pair /pair/ • n. **1** set of two persons or things used together or regarded as a unit (a pair of gloves). **2** article (e.g., scissors) consisting of two joined or corresponding parts. **3 a** romantically involved couple. **b** mated couple

of animals. **4** two playing cards of the same denomination. • v. **1** arrange or be arranged in couples. **2** mate.

■ n. **1** couple, twosome, two of a kind, set of two, duo, brace. **3** (courting or engaged or married) couple, twosome. • v. **1** match (up), pair off or up, team (up), put together, partner, twin, double. **2** marry; join or be joined in wedlock or (holy) matrimony.

Pais•ley /páyzlee/ n. (also **pais•ley**) [often attrib.] distinctive detailed pattern of curved feather-shaped figures.

Pai•ute /pīyōōt/ n. (also **Piute**) **1 a** N. American people native to the southwestern US. **b** member of this people. **2** language of this people.

pa•ja•mas /pəjaáməz, –jám–/ n.pl. **1** suit of loose pants and jacket for sleeping in **2** loose pants tied at the waist, worn by both sexes in some Asian countries.

Pa•ki•stan•i /pákistánee, paákistaánee/ • n. **1** native or national of Pakistan. **2** person of Pakistani descent. • adj. of or relating to Pakistan.

pal /pal/ n. colloq. friend or comrade.

■ alter ego, crony, mate, companion, playmate, classmate, colloq. chum, sidekick, amigo, buddy.

pal•ace /pális/ n. **1** official residence of a president or sovereign. **2** mansion; spacious building.

■ **2** castle, stately home, manor (house), (country) estate, château, villa.

pal•at•a•ble /pálətəbəl/ adj. **1** pleasant to taste. **2** (of an idea, suggestion, etc.) acceptable; satisfactory. □□ **pal•at•a•bil'i•ty** n. **pal'at•a•ble•ness** n. **pal'at•a•bly** adv.

pal•a•tal /pálət'l/ • adj. **1** of the palate. **2** (of a sound) made by placing the surface of the tongue against the hard palate (e.g., y in yes). • n. palatal sound. □□ **pal'a•tal•ize** v.tr. **pal•a•tal•i•za'tion** n. **pal'a•tal•ly** adv.

pal•ate /pálət/ n. **1** structure closing the upper part of the mouth cavity in vertebrates. **2** taste; liking.

pa•la•tial /pəláyshəl/ adj. (of a building) like a palace, esp. spacious and magnificent. □□ **pa•la'tial•ly** adv.

■ luxurious, deluxe, splendid, stately, sumptuous.

pal•a•tine /pálətīn/ adj. (also **Palatine**) hist. having or subject to authority that elsewhere belongs only to a sovereign.

pa•la•ver /pəlávər, –laávər/ n. tedious fuss and bother.

■ trouble, red tape, commotion, bother, nonsense, colloq. song and dance, carrying-on.

pale[1] /payl/ • adj. **1** diminished in coloration; of a whitish or ashen appearance. **2** of faint luster; dim. • v. **1** intr. & tr. grow or make pale. **2** intr. become feeble in comparison (with). □□ **pale'ly** adv. **pale'ness** n. **pal'ish** adj.

■ adj. **1** colorless, white, wan, sallow, waxen, livid, ashen, ashy, pallid, bloodless, whitish, pasty, whey-faced. **2** faint, light, washed-out, pastel; see also DIM adj. 1a. • v.

1 blanch, dim, whiten. 2 diminish, lessen, fade (away), decrease, abate.

SYNONYM STUDY: pale

ASHEN, LIVID, PALLID, WAN. Someone of fair complexion who usually stays indoors and spends very little time in the sun is apt to be **pale**, referring to an unnaturally white or colorless complexion; one can also become *pale* out of fear or illness. Someone who has lost color from being ill or under stress may be described as **pallid**, which suggests a paleness that is the result of weakness, weariness, faintness, or some other abnormal condition (*his inner torment made him pallid*). **Wan** also connotes an unhealthy condition or sickly *paleness* (*her wan face smiled at him from the hospital bed*). Someone who is **ashen** has skin the *pale* grayish color of ashes (*ashen with fear*), while **livid** can mean bluish to describe loss of normal coloring (*the livid face of a drowned corpse*), or can mean reddish or flushed (*livid with rage*).

pale² /payl/ *n.* 1 pointed piece of wood for fencing, etc.; stake. 2 boundary or enclosed area. □ **beyond the pale** outside the bounds of acceptable behavior.
■ 1 paling, palisade, picket, upright, post, stake. 2 limit(s), restriction, bounds, border(s), confines. □ **beyond the pale** improper, irregular, unseemly, unsuitable; inadmissible, forbidden.

pale•face /páylfays/ *n.* white person.

paleo- /páyleeō/ *comb. form* ancient; old; prehistoric.

pa•le•og•ra•phy /páyleeógrəfee/ *n.* the study of writing and documents from the past. □□ **pa•le•og´ra•pher** *n.* **pa•le•o•graph•ic** /-leeəgráfik/ *adj.* **pa•le•o•graph´i•cal** *adj.* **pa•le•o•graph´i•cal•ly** *adv.*

pa•le•o•lith•ic /páyleeəlíthik/ *adj. Archaeol.* of or relating to the early part of the Stone Age.

pa•le•on•tol•o•gy /páyleeontóləjee/ *n.* the study of life in the geological past. □□ **pa•le•on•to•log•i•cal** /-təlój-/ *adj.* **pa•le•on•tol´o•gist** *n.*

Pa•le•o•zo•ic /páyleeəzóik/ *Geol.* • *adj.* of an era of geological time marked by the appearance of marine and terrestrial plants and animals, esp. invertebrates. • *n.* this era.

Pal•es•tin•i•an /pálistíneeən/ • *adj.* of or relating to Palestine, a region (in ancient and modern times) on the E. Mediterranean coast. • *n.* native of Palestine in ancient or modern times.

pal•ette /pálit/ *n.* 1 thin board or slab or other surface, usu. with a hole for the thumb, on which an artist holds and mixes colors. 2 range of colors, etc., used by an artist.

pal•i•mony /pálimōnee/ *n. colloq.* allowance made by one member of an unmarried couple to the other after separation.

pa•limp•sest /pálimpsest/ *n.* writing material or manuscript on which the original writing has been erased for reuse.

pal•in•drome /pálindrōm/ *n.* word or phrase that reads the same backward as forward

(e.g., *rotator*). □□ **pal•in•drom•ic** /-drómik, -drō/ *adj.* **pa•lin´dro•mist** *n.*

pal•ing /páyling/ *n.* 1 fence of pales. 2 pale.

pal•i•sade /pálisáyd/ *n.* 1 fence or pales or iron railings. 2 [in *pl.*] line of high cliffs.

pall¹ /pawl/ *n.* 1 cloth spread over a coffin, hearse, or tomb. 2 dark covering (*pall of darkness, pall of smoke*).
■ 2 see MANTLE *n.* 2.

pall² /pawl/ *v.* 1 *intr.* (often foll. by *on*) become uninteresting (to). 2 *tr.* satiate; cloy.
■ 1 bore, tire, weary, jade, irk, irritate.

pal•la•di•um /pəláydeeəm/ *n. Chem.* white ductile metallic element occurring naturally in various ores and used in chemistry as a catalyst and for making jewelry. ¶Symb.: **Pd**.

pall•bear•er /páwlbairər/ *n.* person helping to carry or officially escorting a coffin at a funeral.

pal•let¹ /pálit/ *n.* 1 straw mattress. 2 makeshift bed.

pal•let² /pálit/ *n.* 1 = PALETTE. 2 portable platform for transporting and storing loads. □□ **pal´let•ize** *v.tr.* (in sense 2).

pal•li•ate /páleeayt/ *v.tr.* 1 alleviate (disease) without curing it. 2 excuse; extenuate. □□ **pal•li•a•tion** /-áyshən/ *n.* **pal´li•a•tive** *n. & adj.* **pal´li•a•tive•ly** *adv.* **pal´li•a•tor** *n.*

pal•lid /pálid/ *adj.* pale, esp. from illness. See synonym study at PALE. □□ **pal´lid•ly** *adv.* **pal´lid•ness** *n.*

pal•lor /pálər/ *n.* pallidness; paleness.

palm¹ /paam, paw(l)m/ *n.* 1 any usu. tropical tree with no branches and a mass of large leaves at the top. 2 leaf of this tree as a symbol of victory. □ **Palm Sunday** Sunday before Easter, celebrating Christ's entry into Jerusalem. □□ **pal•ma´ceous** *adj.*

palm² /paam, paw(l)m/ • *n.* inner surface of the hand between the wrist and fingers. • *v.tr.* conceal in the hand. □ **palm off** impose on or dispose of fraudulently. □□ **pal´mar** /pálmər, paá-/ *adj.* **palmed** *adj.* **palm´ful** *n.* (*pl.* **-fuls**).

pal•mate /pálmayt, paál-, paámayt/ *adj.* 1 shaped like an open hand. 2 having lobes, etc., like spread fingers.

pal•met•to /palmétō/ *n.* small palm tree.

palm•is•try /páamistree/ *n.* supposed divination from lines and other features on the palm of the hand. □□ **palm´ist** *n.*

palm•y /páamee/ *adj.* (**palm•i•er, palm•i•est**) 1 of or like or abounding in palms. 2 triumphant; flourishing.

pal•o•mi•no /páləmeénō/ *n.* golden or tan-colored horse with a light-colored mane and tail.

pal•pa•ble /pálpəbəl/ *adj.* 1 that can be touched or felt. 2 readily perceived. See synonym study at TANGIBLE. □□ **pal•pa•bil´i•ty** *n.* **pal´pa•bly** *adv.*

pal•pate /pálpayt/ *v.tr.* examine (esp. medically) by touch. □□ **pal•pa•tion** /-páyshən/ *n.*

pal•pi•tate /pálpitayt/ *v.intr.* 1 pulsate; throb. 2 tremble. □□ **pal´pi•tant** *adj.* **pal•pi•ta•tion** /-táyshən/ *n.*

pal•sy /páwlzee/ • *n.* (*pl.* **-sies**) paralysis, esp. with involuntary tremors. • *v.tr.* (**-sies, -sied**) affect with palsy.

pal•try /páwltree/ *adj.* (**pal•tri•er, pal•tri•est**) worthless; contemptible; trifling. □□ **pal′tri•ness** *n.*

■ trivial, petty, small, insignificant, pitiful, pathetic, pitiable, puny, sorry, wretched, miserable.

pam•pas /pámpəs/ *n.pl.* large treeless plains in S. America.

pam•per /pámpər/ *v.tr.* overindulge; spoil. □□ **pam′per•er** *n.*

■ baby, coddle, cosset, mollycoddle, pet.

pam•phlet /pámflit/ • *n.* small, usu. unbound booklet or leaflet. □□ **pam•phlet•eer** /-teér/ *n. & v.*

■ *n.* brochure, tract, circular; handbill, bill, notice.

pan[1] /pan/ • *n.* **1** vessel of metal, earthenware, etc., usu. broad and shallow, used for cooking, heating, etc. **2** any similar shallow container. • *v.tr.* (**panned, pan•ning**) **1** *colloq.* criticize severely. **2** wash (gold-bearing gravel) in a pan. □ **pan out** turn out; work out. □□ **pan′ful** *n.* (*pl.* **–fuls**). **pan′like** *adj.*

■ *n.* **1** saucepan, frying pan, pot, casserole, skillet. • *v.* **1** censure, find fault with, put down, reject, flay, excoriate, roast, *colloq.* trash, *sl.* knock. **2** separate, sift. □ **pan out** result, come out, end (up), conclude, culminate, *formal* eventuate.

pan[2] /pan/ • *v.* (**panned, pan•ning**) **1** *tr.* swing (a video or movie camera) horizontally to give a panoramic effect or to follow a moving object. **2** *intr.* (of a video or movie camera) be moved in this way. • *n.* panning movement.

pan- /pan/ *comb. form* **1** all; the whole of. **2** relating to or comprising the whole. (*pan-American*).

pan•a•ce•a /pánəseeə/ *n.* universal remedy. □□ **pan•a•ce′an** *adj.*

pa•nache /pənásh, –naásh/ *n.* assertiveness or flamboyant confidence of style or manner.

■ flourish, dash, élan, éclat, chic, sophistication, *savoir faire, savoir vivre,* flamboyance, verve, style, vivacity.

pan•a•ma /pánəmaa/ *n.* hat of strawlike material made from the leaves of a palmlike tropical plant.

Pa•na•ma•ni•an /pùnəmáyneeən/ • *n.* **1** native or national of the Republic of Panama in Central America. **2** person of Panamanian descent. • *adj.* of or relating to Panama.

pan•cake /pánkayk/ *n.* **1** thin flat cake of batter usu. fried in a pan or on a griddle. **2** flat cake of makeup, etc.

pan•chro•mat•ic /pánkrōmátik/ *adj. Photog.* (of film, etc.) sensitive to all visible colors of the spectrum.

pan•cre•as /pángkreeəs/ *n.* gland near the stomach supplying the duodenum with digestive fluid and secreting insulin. □□ **pan•cre•at•ic** /-kreeátik/ *adj.* **pan•cre•a•ti•tis** /-kreeátitis/ *n.*

pan•da /pándə/ *n.* **1** (also **gi′ant pan′da**) large bearlike mammal, native to China and Tibet, having characteristic black and white markings. **2** (also **red′ pan′da**) Himalayan raccoon-like mammal with reddish-brown fur.

pan•dem•ic /pandémik/ *adj.* (of a disease) prevalent over a whole country or the world.

pan•de•mo•ni•um /pándimóneeəm/ *n.* **1** uproar; utter confusion. **2** scene of this.

■ bedlam, chaos, turmoil, disorder, tumult, frenzy.

pan•der /pándər/ • *v.intr.* gratify; indulge. • *n.* (also **pan′der•er**) **1** a go-between in illicit love affairs; procurer. **2** person who encourages licentiousness.

■ *v.* satisfy, humor, fulfill, bow to, yield to, truckle to, cater to. • *n.* **1** pimp, solicitor.

Pan•do•ra's box /pandáwrəz/ *n.* process that once activated will generate many unmanageable problems.

pane /payn/ *n.* single sheet of glass in a window or door.

■ panel, windowpane, light, bull's-eye.

pan•e•gyr•ic /pánijírik, –jírik/ *n.* laudatory discourse; eulogy. □□ **pan•e•gyr′i•cal** *adj.*

pan•el /pánəl/ • *n.* **1 a** distinct, usu. rectangular, section of a surface (e.g., of a wall or door). **b** control panel (see CONTROL *n.* 5). **2** strip of material as part of a garment. **3** group of people gathered to form a team in a broadcast game, for a discussion, etc. **4** list of available jurors; jury. • *v.tr.* fit, cover, or decorate with panels. □ **panel truck** small enclosed delivery truck.

pan•el•ing /pánəling/ *n.* **1** paneled work. **2** wood for making panels.

pan•el•ist /pánəlist/ *n.* member of a panel.

pang /pang/ *n.* [often in *pl.*] sudden sharp pain or painful emotion.

■ stab, ache, pinch, prick, twinge; qualm, hesitation.

pan•han•dle /pánhand'l/ • *n.* narrow strip of territory extending from one state into another. • *v. colloq.* beg for money in the street. □□ **pan′han•dler** *n.*

pan•ic /pánik/ • *n.* **1** sudden uncontrollable fear or alarm. **2** infectious apprehension or fright esp. in commercial dealings. • *v.* (**panicked, pan•ick•ing**) affect or be affected with panic. □ **panic-stricken** (or **–struck**) affected with panic. □□ **pan′ick•y** *adj.*

■ *n.* terror, fright, dread, horror, dismay, consternation, hysteria; anxiety, apprehension. • *v.* frighten, scare, alarm, terrify, unnerve; become terrified or alarmed or fearful or frightened, lose one's nerve. □ **panic-stricken** (or **–struck**) terrified, alarmed, horrified, aghast, terror-stricken or terror-struck, panicky, frenzied, in a frenzy, hysterical, beside oneself, fearful, afraid. □□ **panicky** see *panic-stricken* above.

pan•nier /pányər/ *n.* basket, bag, or box, esp. one of a pair for transporting loads.

pan•o•ply /pánəplee/ *n.* (*pl.* **–plies**) **1** complete or magnificent array. **2** complete suit of armor. □□ **pan′o•plied** *adj.*

pan•o•ra•ma /pánərámə, –raá–/ *n.* **1** unbroken view of a surrounding region. **2** complete survey or presentation of a subject, sequence of events, etc. **3** continuous passing scene. □□ **pan•o•ram′ic** *adj.* **pan•o•ram′i•cal•ly** *adv.*

■ **1** see VIEW *n.* 2. **2** see VIEW *n.* 3. □□ **pan-**

oramic sweeping, commanding, extensive, comprehensive, wide, overall, scenic, far-reaching, all-embracing.

pan•sy /pánzee/ *n.* (*pl.* **–sies**) garden plant with flowers of various rich colors.

pant /pant/ • *v.* **1** *intr.* breathe with short quick breaths. **2** *tr.* [often foll. by *out*] utter breathlessly. **3** *intr.* yearn or crave. • *n.* panting breath. □□ **pant'ing•ly** *adv.*

■ *v.* **1, 2** gasp, huff, puff, blow, heave, wheeze. **3** hanker after, hunger or thirst for or after, ache for, want.

pan•ta•loon /pántəloõn/ *n.* [in *pl.*] *hist.* men's close-fitting breeches fastened below the calf or at the foot.

pan•the•ism /pántheeizəm/ *n.* **1** belief that God is identifiable with the forces of nature and with natural substances. **2** worship that admits or tolerates all gods. □□ **pan'the•ist** *n.* **pan•the•is'tic** *adj.* **pan•the•is'ti•cal** *adj.* **pan•the•is'ti•cal•ly** *adv.*

pan•the•on /pántheeon, –ən/ *n.* **1** building in which illustrious dead are buried or have memorials. **2** the deities of a people collectively. **3** temple dedicated to all the gods, esp. the circular one at Rome. **4** group of esteemed persons.

pan•ther /pánthər/ *n.* **1** leopard, esp. with black fur. **2** cougar.

pant•ies /pánteez/ *n.pl. colloq.* short-legged or legless underpants worn by women and girls.

pan•to•mime /pántəmīm/ • *n.* use of gestures and facial expression to convey meaning without speech, esp. in drama and dance. • *v.* convey meaning without speech using only gestures. □□ **pan•to•mim'ic** /–mímik/ *adj.*

pan•try /pántree/ *n.* (*pl.* **–tries**) small room or cupboard for storage of kitchen supplies, groceries, etc.

pants /pants/ *n.pl.* outer garment reaching from the waist usu. to the ankles, divided into two parts to cover the legs.

■ slacks, trousers.

pant•suit /pántsoõt/ *n.* (also **pants suit**) woman's suit with pants and a jacket.

pan•ty hose /pánteehōz/ *n.* [usu. treated as *pl.*] usu. sheer one-piece garment combining panties and stockings.

pap /pap/ *n.* **1** soft or semiliquid food for infants or invalids. **2** light or trivial reading matter; nonsense. □□ **pap'py** *adj.*

pa•pa /páapə, pəpáa/ *n.* father (esp. as a child's word).

pa•pa•cy /páypəsee/ *n.* (*pl.* **–cies**) **1** pope's office or tenure. **2** papal system.

pa•pal /páypəl/ *adj.* of a pope or the papacy. □□ **pa'pal•ly** *adv.*

pa•paw var. of PAWPAW.

pa•pa•ya /pəpíə/ *n.* **1** edible yellow fruit with orange flesh. **2** tropical tree bearing this.

pa•per /páypər/ • *n.* **1** material manufactured in thin sheets from the pulp of wood or other fibrous substances, used for writing or drawing or printing on, or as wrapping material, etc. **2** [*attrib.*] **a** made of or using paper. **b** flimsy like paper. **3** = NEWSPAPER.

4 a printed document. **b** [in *pl.*] identification or other legal documents. **5** = WALLPAPER. **6** essay or dissertation. **7** piece of paper. • *v.tr.* **1** apply paper to, esp. decorate (a wall, etc.) with wallpaper. **2** [foll. by *over*] disguise or try to hide. □ **paper clip** clip of bent wire or of plastic for holding several sheets of paper together. **paper tiger** apparently threatening, but ineffectual, person or thing. **paper trail** documentation of transactions, etc. □□ **pa'per•er** *n.* **pa'per•less** *adj.* **pa'per•y** *adj.*

■ *n.* **3** tabloid, daily, weekly, journal, gazette, publication, periodical, newsletter, organ, *derog.* rag, sheet. **4** instrument, form, certificate, deed; credential(s), identification; docket, file, dossier. **6** article, composition, assignment, report, thesis, study, tract, analysis, critique, monograph. • *v.* **1** wallpaper, line; decorate. **2** cover up; see also COVER *v.* 1.

pa•per•back /páypərbak/ (also **pa'per•bound**) • *adj.* (of a book) bound in stiff paper. • *n.* a paperback book.

pa•per•boy /páypərboy/ *n.* (*fem.* **pa•per•girl** /–gərl/) boy or girl who delivers or sells newspapers.

pa•per•weight /páypərwayt/ *n.* small heavy object for keeping loose papers in place.

pa•per•work /páypərwərk/ *n.* **1** routine clerical or administrative work. **2** documents, esp. for a particular purpose.

pa•pier mâ•ché /páypər məsháy, papyáy/ *n.* paper pulp used for molding into boxes, trays, etc.

pa•pil•la /pəpílə/ *n.* (*pl.* **pa•pil•lae** /–pílee/) small nipplelike protuberance in a part or organ of the body. □□ **pap'il•lar•y** *adj.* **pap'il•lose** *adj.*

pa•poose /papóõs, pə–/ *n.* young Native American child.

pa•pri•ka /pəpréekə, páprika/ *n.* **1** *Bot.* a red pepper. **2** powdery condiment made from it.

Pap smear /pap/ (also **Pap test**) *n.* test for cervical cancer, etc., done by a cervical smear.

pa•py•rus /pəpírəs/ *n.* (*pl.* **pa•py•ri** /–rī/) **1** aquatic plant with dark green stems topped with fluffy inflorescences. **2** writing material prepared in ancient Egypt from the pithy stem of this.

par /paar/ *n.* **1** average or normal amount, degree, condition, etc. (*be up to par*). **2** equality; equal footing. **3** *Golf* number of strokes a skilled player should normally require for a hole or course. **4** *Stock Exch.* face value of stocks and shares, etc. **5** (in full **par of exchange**) recognized value of one country's currency in terms of another's. □ **par for the course** *colloq.* what is normal or to be expected.

■ **1** standard, normal, norm, expectation. **2** level; see also PARITY 1.

par- /pər, par, paar/ *prefix* var. of PARA-before a vowel or *h*; (*paraldehyde, parody, parhelion*).

para- /párə/ *prefix* (also **par-**) **1** beside (*para-military*). **2** beyond (*paranormal*).

par•a•a•mi•no•ben•zo•ic acid /párə-əmeénōbenzóik/ *n.* *Biochem.* compound used in suntan lotions and sunscreens to absorb ultraviolet light. ¶Abbr.: **PABA**.

par•a•ble /párəbəl/ *n.* **1** narrative of imagined events used to illustrate a moral or spiritual lesson. **2** allegory.
■ fable, lesson, morality tale.

pa•rab•o•la /pərábələ/ *n.* open plane curve formed by the intersection of a cone with a plane parallel to its side.

par•a•bol•ic /pàrəbólik/ *adj.* **1** of or expressed in a parable. **2** of or like a parabola. □□ **par•a•bol′i•cal•ly** *adv.*

par•a•chute /párəshoot/ • *n.* rectangular or umbrella-shaped apparatus allowing a slow and safe descent, esp. from an aircraft. • *v.* convey or descend by parachute. □□ **par′a•chut•ist** *n.*

pa•rade /pəráyd/ • *n.* **1** formal or ceremonial muster of troops for inspection. **2** public procession. **3** ostentatious display. • *v.* **1 a** *tr.* march through (streets, etc.) in procession. **b** *intr.* march ceremonially. **2** *tr.* display ostentatiously. □□ **pa•rad′er** *n.*
■ *n.* **2** march, train, file, promenade, cortège; column. **3** exhibition, show, spectacle, array, splash. • *v.* **1** march, pass in review, promenade, walk, file. **2** flaunt, show (off), brandish, wave, air, *literary* vaunt.

par•a•digm /párədim/ *n.* **1** example or pattern. **2** *Gram.* representative set of the inflections of a noun, verb, etc. See synonym study at MODEL. □□ **par•a•dig•mat•ic** /–digmátik/ *adj.* **par•a•dig′mat′i•cal•ly** *adv.*

par•a•dise /párədis/ *n.* **1** heaven. **2** place or state of complete happiness. **3** (in full **earthly paradise**) abode of Adam and Eve; garden of Eden. □□ **par•a•di•si′a•cal** /–dəsízəkəl/ *adj.*
■ **1** Zion, Elysium, Elysian Fields, happy hunting ground, the promised land, Valhalla. **2** heaven on earth, dreamland, seventh heaven, (Garden of) Eden, utopia, Shangri-la; bliss, rapture, heaven.

par•a•dox /párədoks/ *n.* **1 a** seemingly absurd or contradictory statement, even if actually well-founded. **b** self-contradictory or essentially absurd statement. **2** person or thing having contradictory qualities, etc. See synonym study at RIDDLE. □□ **par•a•dox′i•cal** *adj.* **par•a•dox′i•cal•ly** *adv.*
■ contradiction, self-contradiction, incongruity, inconsistency, absurdity, ambiguity, enigma, puzzle. □□ **paradoxical** impossible, improbable, illogical.

par•af•fin /párəfin/ *n.* (also **par′af•fin wax**) waxy mixture of hydrocarbons used in candles, waterproofing, etc.

par•a•gon /párəgon, –gən/ *n.* model of excellence.
■ epitome, archetype, prototype, quintessence, pattern, standard, exemplar, ideal.

par•a•graph /párəgraf/ • *n.* **1** distinct section of a piece of writing, beginning on a new usu. indented line. **2** symbol (usu. ¶) used to mark a new paragraph. **3** short item in a newspaper, usu. of only one paragraph. • *v.tr.* arrange in paragraphs. □□ **par•a•graph•ic** /–gráfik/ *adj.*

par•a•keet /párəkeet/ *n.* small usu. long-tailed parrot.

par•a•le•gal /pàrəléegəl/ • *adj.* of auxiliary aspects of the law. • *n.* person trained in subsidiary legal matters.

par•al•lax /párəlaks/ *n.* apparent difference in the position or direction of an object caused when the observer's position is changed. □□ **par•al•lac•tic** /–láktik/ *adj.*

par•al•lel /párəlel/ • *adj.* **1** side by side and having the same distance continuously between them. **2** precisely similar, analogous, or corresponding; simultaneous. • *n.* **1** person or thing precisely analogous or equal to another. **2** comparison. **3** (in full **parallel of latitude**) *Geog.* **a** each of the imaginary parallel circles of constant latitude on the earth's surface. **b** corresponding line on a map (*the 49th parallel*). • *v.tr.* **1** be parallel to; correspond to. **2** represent as similar; compare. □□ **par•al•lel•ism** *n.*
■ *adj.* **2** congruent, analogical, correspondent, like, matching, homologous, coordinate, equivalent. • *n.* **1** analog, match, homologue, equivalent, counterpart, equal. **2** analogy, parallelism, equivalence, correspondence, symmetry, equality; see also COMPARISON 3. • *v.* **1** match, equate to or with, be likened to, correlate to or with, compare with or to, imitate, repeat, echo; keep pace with, conform to or with, balance, set off, offset. **2** match, equate, liken, juxtapose, associate, correlate.

par•al•lel•o•gram /pàrəléləgram/ *n.* *Geom.* four-sided plane rectilinear figure with opposite sides parallel.

pa•ral•y•sis /pərálisis/ *n.* (*pl.* **pa•ral•y•ses** /–seez/) **1** impairment or loss of esp. the motor function of the nerves. **2** state of utter powerlessness. □□ **par•a•lyt•ic** /pàrəlítik/ *adj. & n.* **par•a•lyt′i•cal•ly** *adv.*

par•a•lyze /párəliz/ *v.tr.* **1** affect with paralysis. **2** render powerless; cripple. □□ **par•a•ly•za′tion** *n.* **par′a•lyz•ing•ly** *adv.*
■ **2** disable, incapacitate; immobilize.

par•a•me•ci•um /pàrəméeseeəm/ *n.* freshwater protozoan of a characteristic slipper-like shape covered with cilia.

par•a•med•ic /párəmédik/ *n.* **1** paramedical worker. **2** person trained in emergency medical procedures.

par•a•med•i•cal /pàrəmédikəl/ *adj.* (of services, etc.) supplementing and supporting medical work.

pa•ram•e•ter /pərámitər/ *n.* **1** *Math.* quantity constant in the case considered but varying in different cases. **2 a** characteristic or feature. **b** (loosely) constant element or factor, esp. serving as a limit or boundary. □□ **par•a•met•ric** /pàrəmétrik/ *adj.* **pa•ram′e•trize** *v.tr.*

par•a•mil•i•tar•y /pàrəmíliteree/ *adj.* (of forces) ancillary to and similarly organized to military forces.

par•a•mount /párəmownt/ *adj.* supreme; requiring first consideration. □□ **par′a•mount•ly** *adv.*
■ preeminent, chief, dominant, main, major, predominant, cardinal, first, prime, primary, principal, essential.

par·a·mour /párəmŏŏr/ n. illicit lover of a married person.

■ love, inamorato, inamorata, mistress, gigolo, concubine, kept woman, (the) other woman.

par·a·noi·a /párənóyə/ n. **1** personality disorder esp. characterized by delusions of persecution and self-importance. **2** abnormal tendency to suspect and mistrust others. □□ **par·a·noi'ac** adj. & n. **par·a·noid** /-noyd/ adj. & n.

par·a·nor·mal /párənórməl/ adj. beyond the scope of normal objective investigation or explanation. □□ **par·a·nor'mal·ly** adv.

par·a·pet /párəpit/ n. **1** low wall at the edge of a roof, balcony, etc., or along the sides of a bridge. **2** defense of earth or stone to conceal and protect troops. □□ **par'a·pet·ed** adj.

par·a·pher·na·li·a /párəfərnáylyə/ n.pl. [also treated as sing.] miscellaneous belongings, equipment, accessories, etc.

■ apparatus, outfit, kit, appliances, utensils, gear, rig, material(s), matériel, things, tackle.

par·a·phrase /párəfrayz/ • n. free rendering or rewording of a passage. • v.tr. express the meaning of (a passage) in other words. □□ **par·a·phras'tic** /-frástik/ adj.

■ n. rephrasing, rewriting, rewrite, rehash, rendition, version. • v. rephrase, metaphrase, reword, restate.

par·a·ple·gi·a /párəpléejə/ n. paralysis of the legs and part or the whole of the trunk. □□ **par·a·ple'gic** adj. & n.

par·a·psy·chol·o·gy /párəsīkóləjee/ n. the study of mental phenomena outside the sphere of ordinary psychology. □□ **par·a·psy·cho·log·i·cal** /-sīkəlójikəl/ adj. **par·a·psy·chol'o·gist** n.

par·a·quat /párəkwot/ n. quick-acting herbicide, becoming inactive on contact with the soil.

par·a·site /párəsīt/ n. **1** organism living in or on another and benefiting at the expense of the other. **2** person who lives off or exploits another or others. □□ **par·a·sit·ic** /-sítik/ adj. **par·a·sit'i·cal** adj. **par·a·sit'i·cal·ly** adv. **par·a·sit·ol·o·gy** /-tóləjee/ n. **par·a·si·tol'o·gist** n.

■ **2** leech, bloodsucker, hanger-on, sponge, cadger.

par·a·sol /párəsawl, -sol/ n. light umbrella used to give shade from the sun.

par·a·sym·pa·thet·ic /párəsimpəthétik/ adj. Anat. relating to the part of the autonomic nervous system that controls the slowing of the heartbeat, constriction of the pupils, etc.

par·a·thy·roid /párəthíroyd/ Anat. • n. gland next to the thyroid, secreting a hormone that regulates calcium levels in the body. • adj. of or associated with this gland.

par·a·troops /párətrŏŏps/ n.pl. troops equipped to be dropped by parachute from aircraft. □□ **par'a·troop·er** n.

par·boil /páarboyl/ v.tr. partly cook by boiling.

par·cel /páarsəl/ • n. **1** goods, etc., wrapped in a package. **2** piece of land. • v.tr. [foll. by out] divide into portions.

■ n. **1** package, packet, carton, box, container, case; bundle, lot, group, batch, collection, pack, set. **2** portion, plot, section, tract, lot, plat. • v. apportion, allot, deal (out), dole (out), hand out.

parch /paarch/ v. make or become hot and dry. □□ **parched** adj. See synonym study at DRY.

■ dry (out or up), desiccate, dehydrate; scorch, sear, burn, bake, roast; shrivel (up), wither.

Par·chee·si /paarcheezee, pər-, -see/ n. propr. board game played with dice.

parch·ment /páarchmənt/ n. **1 a** animal skin, esp. that of a sheep or goat, prepared as a writing or painting surface. **b** manuscript written on this. **2** (in full **vegetable parchment**) high-grade paper made to resemble parchment.

par·don /páard'n/ • n. **1** act of excusing or forgiving an offense, error, etc. **2** (in full **full par·don**) remission of the legal consequences of a crime or conviction. • v.tr. **1** release from the consequences of an offense, error, etc. **2** forgive; excuse. See synonym study at ABSOLVE. □□ **par'don·a·ble** adj. **par'don·a·bly** adv.

■ n. **1** forgiveness, amnesty, remission, release, reprieve, absolution. • v. remit, reprieve, absolve, overlook, let off, condone, exonerate, formal exculpate.

pare /pair/ v.tr. **1** trim by cutting away the surface or edge. **2** diminish little by little. □□ **par'er** n.

■ **1** peel, skin, shave; decorticate, excoriate. **2** reduce, decrease, cut (back or down), curtail, lower.

par·ent /páirənt, pár-/ • n. **1** person who has or adopts a child; a father or mother. **2** animal or plant from which others are derived. **3** source, origin, etc. • v.tr. [also absol.] be a parent of. □ **parent company** company of which other companies are subsidiaries. □□ **par·en·tal** /pərént'l/ adj. **pa·ren'tal·ly** adv. **par'ent·hood** n.

■ n. **1** surrogate mother, progenitor, procreator, materfamilias, paterfamilias, adoptive parent or mother or father, colloq. old lady or woman, old man. **3** originator, wellspring, fountainhead, root.

par·ent·age /páirəntij, pár-/ n. lineage; descent from or through parents (their parentage is unknown).

■ ancestry, line, family, extraction, origin, pedigree.

pa·ren·the·sis /pərénthəsis/ n. (pl. **pa·ren·the·ses** /-seez/) **1 a** explanatory or qualifying word, clause, or sentence. **b** [in pl.] pair of rounded brackets () used for this in writing or printing. **2** interlude or interval.

par·en·thet·ic /párənthétik/ adj. **1** of or by way of a parenthesis. **2** interposed. □□ **par·en·thet'i·cal** adj. **par·en·thet'i·cal·ly** adv.

par·ent·ing /páirənting, pár-/ n. occupation or concerns of parents.

■ rearing, upbringing, raising, nurturing; parenthood.

pa·reve /páarəvə, páarvə/ adj. made without milk or meat and thus suitable for kosher use.

par ex•cel•lence /paár eksəlóns/ *adv.* as having special excellence; being the supreme example of its kind.

par•fait /paarfáy/ *n.* **1** rich frozen custard of whipped cream, eggs, etc. **2** layers of ice cream, meringue, etc., served in a tall glass.

pa•ri•ah /pəríə/ *n.* **1** social outcast. **2** *hist.* member of a low caste or of no caste in S. India.

pa•ri•e•tal /pəríətəl/ *adj. Anat.* of the wall of the body or any of its cavities. □ **parietal bone** either of a pair of bones forming the central part of the sides and top of the skull.

par•i•mu•tu•el /párimyōōchōōəl/ *n.* form of betting in which those backing the first three places divide the losers' stakes.

par•ing /páiring/ *n.* strip or piece cut off.

par•ish /párish/ *n.* **1** area having its own church and clergy. **2** county in Louisiana. **3** inhabitants of a parish.

pa•rish•ion•er /pərishənər/ *n.* inhabitant or member of a parish.

Pa•ri•sian /pəréezhən, –rízhən, –rizeeən/ • *adj.* of or relating to Paris in France. • *n.* native or inhabitant of Paris.

par•i•ty /páritee/ *n.* **1** equality; equal status or pay. **2** equivalence of one currency with another; being at par.
■ **1** equivalence, uniformity, congruity, similitude, conformity, congruence.

park /paark/ • *n.* **1** public land set aside for recreation or as a preserve. **2** gear position or function in an automatic transmission that immobilizes the drive wheels. **3** area devoted to a specified purpose (*industrial park*) • *v.* **1** *tr.* [also *absol.*] leave (a vehicle) usu. temporarily. **2** *tr. colloq.* deposit and leave, usu. temporarily. □ **parking meter** coin-operated meter that receives payment for vehicles parked in the street and indicates the time available.
■ *n.* **1** garden(s), green(s), common(s), reserve, parkland, woodland, estate; playground. • *v.* store, *colloq.* stash, dump; sl. ditch; see also SET[1] *v.*

par•ka /paárkə/ *n.* hooded winter jacket.

Par•kin•son's dis•ease /paárkinsənz/ *n.* (also **Par'kin•son•ism**) progressive disease of the nervous system with tremor, muscular rigidity, and emaciation.

Par•kin•son's law /paárkinsənz/ *n.* facetious notion that work expands so as to fill the time available for its completion.

park•way /paárkway/ *n.* open landscaped highway.

par•lance /paárləns/ *n.* particular idiom.
■ **way** *or* manner of speaking, phrasing, phraseology, speech, wording, language, dialect, jargon.

par•lay /paárlay/ • *v.tr.* use (money won on a bet) as a further stake. • *n.* bet made by parlaying.

par•ley /paárlee/ • *n.* conference for debating points in a dispute, esp. a discussion of terms for an armistice, etc. See synonym study at CONVERSATION. • *v.intr.* hold a parley.
■ *n.* discussion, dialogue, negotiation, deliberation, meeting, colloquy, colloquium. •

v. confer, discuss, deliberate, talk, negotiate, powwow.

par•lia•ment /paárləmənt/ *n.* legislature of various countries, as the United Kingdom.
■ legislature, council, congress, diet, assembly, house, chamber.

par•lia•men•tar•i•an /paárləmentáireeən/ *n.* **1** member of a parliament. **2** person who is well-versed in parliamentary procedures.

par•lia•men•ta•ry /paárləmentəree, –tree/ *adj.* **1** of or relating to a parliament. **2** enacted or established by a parliament.

par•lor /paárlər/ *n.* **1** sitting room in a private house. **2** store providing specified goods or services (*beauty parlor*).
■ **1** living room, drawing room, morning room, reception (room), lounge.

Par•me•san /paármizaán, –zán, –zən/ *n.* a kind of hard dry cheese made orig. at Parma and used esp. in grated form.

pa•ro•chi•al /pərókeeəl/ *adj.* **1** of or concerning a parish. **2** merely local, narrow, or restricted in scope. □ **parochial school** school run or supported by a church. □□ **pa•ro'chi•al•ism** *n.* **pa•ro'chi•al•ly** *adv.*
■ **1** regional, provincial, local. **2** insular, isolated, provincial, limited, narrow-minded, petty, shortsighted, hidebound, conservative, conventional, illiberal.

par•o•dy /párədee/ • *n.* (*pl.* **–dies**) **1** humorous exaggerated imitation of an author, literary work, style, etc. **2** feeble imitation; travesty. See synonym study at CARICATURE. • *v.tr.* (**–dies, –died**) compose a parody of. □□ **par•o•dic•** /pəródik/ *adj.* **par'o•dist** *n.*
■ *n.* **1** burlesque, lampoon, satire, caricature, mockery, *colloq.* takeoff, spoof, send-up; mimicry. **2** mockery; distortion, perversion, corruption. • *v.* burlesque, lampoon, satirize, caricature, mock, mimic, ape, ridicule, deride, *colloq.* take off, spoof, send up.

pa•role /pəról/ • *n.* release of a prisoner temporarily for a special purpose or completely before the fulfillment of a sentence, on the promise of good behavior. • *v.tr.* put (a prisoner) on parole. □□ **pa•rol•ee** /–leé/ *n.*

par•ox•ysm /párəksizəm/ *n.* **1** sudden attack or outburst. **2** fit of disease. □□ **par•ox•ys•mal** /–sízməl/ *adj.*
■ convulsion, spasm, throe, seizure, spell, eruption.

par•quet /paárkáy/ • *n.* **1** flooring of parquetry. **2** main-floor area of a theater. • *v.tr.* furnish (a room) with a parquet floor.

par•quet•ry /paárkitree/ *n.* use of wooden blocks arranged in a pattern to make floors or inlay for furniture.

par•ri•cide /párisīd/ *n.* **1** killing of a near relative, esp. of a parent. **2** act of parricide. **3** person who commits parricide. □□ **par•ri•ci'dal** /–síd'l/ *adj.*

par•rot /párət/ • *n.* **1** mainly tropical bird with a short hooked bill, often vivid plumage, and the ability to mimic the human voice. **2** person who mechanically repeats the words or actions of another. • *v.tr.* repeat mechanically.

■ *n.* 2 imitator, mimic, *colloq.* copycat. • *v.* imitate, mimic, ape; echo, reiterate.

par•ry /páree/ *v.tr.* (**–ries, –ried**) 1 avert or ward off, esp. with a countermove. 2 deal skillfully with (an awkward question, etc.). • *n.* (*pl.* **–ries**) act of parrying.

parse /paars/ *v.tr.* describe the function and forms (of a sentence or a word in context) grammatically. □□ **pars′er** *n.* esp. *Computing*

par•sec /páarsek/ *n.* unit of stellar distance, equal to about 3.25 light years (3.08 x 10^16 meters).

par•si•mo•ny /páarsimōnee/ *n.* stinginess. □□ **par•si•mo•ni•ous** /–mōneeəs/ *adj.* **par•si•mo′ni•ous•ly** *adv.* See synonym study at ECONOMICAL

pars•ley /páarslee/ *n.* biennial herb, with crinkly or flat aromatic leaves, used for seasoning and garnishing food.

pars•nip /páarsnip/ *n.* 1 plant with a large pale yellow tapering root. 2 this root eaten as a vegetable.

par•son /páarsən/ *n.* 1 rector. 2 any (esp. Protestant) member of the clergy. □□ **par•son•i•cal** /–sónikəl/ *adj.*

par•son•age /páarsənij/ *n.* church house provided for a parson.

part /paart/ • *n.* 1 some but not all of a thing or number of things. 2 essential member, constituent, or component. 3 division of a book, broadcast serial, etc. 4 each of several equal portions of a whole (*has 3 parts sugar to 2 parts flour*). 5 a portion allotted; share. b person's share in an action, etc. 6 a character assigned to an actor on stage. b words spoken by an actor on stage. c copy of these. 7 *Mus.* melody, etc., assigned to a particular voice or instrument. 8 each of the sides in an agreement or dispute. 9 [in *pl.*] region or district (*not from these parts*). 10 dividing line in combed hair. See synonym study at FRAGMENT. • *v.* 1 *tr. & intr.* divide or separate into parts. 2 *intr.* leave; say good-bye to. 3 *intr.* [foll. by *with*] give up; hand over. 4 *tr.* comb hair to form a part. • *adv.* to some extent; partly. □ **for one's part** as far as one is concerned. **in part** (or **parts**) to some extent; partly. **part and parcel** an essential part. **part of speech** *n.* each of the categories to which words are assigned in accordance with their grammatical and semantic functions. **part-time** *adj.* occupying or using only part of one's working time. **part-timer** person employed in part-time work. **take part** assist or have a share (in).

■ *n.* 1 some, a few, not all. 2 piece, portion, division, segment, section; element, ingredient, unit. 3 episode, installment, chapter. 4 measure, unit, share. 5 a allotment, percentage, participation, interest, parcel. b interest, participation, say, voice, influence. 6 a role. b, c lines, script. 8 interest, cause, faction, party. 9 neighborhood, quarter, section, area, corner, vicinity. • *v.* 1 split (up); put or pull apart, *literary* put asunder. 2 separate, part company, split (up), go one's way, break up; depart, go. 3 yield, relinquish, re-

lease, sacrifice, forgo, go without, renounce, forsake, let go, surrender. • *adv.* see *in part* (PART) below. □ **in part** partially, part, to some degree, in some measure; relatively, comparatively, somewhat. **take part** participate, join in, be (a) party, play a part or role, be involved or associated, have or take a hand.

par•take /paartáyk/ *v.intr.* (*past* **par•took** /–tŏŏk/; *past part.* **par•taken** /–táykən/) 1 take a share or part. 2 eat or drink something. □□ **par•tak′a•ble** *adj.* **par•tak′er** *n.*

■ 1 share, participate, enter. 2 receive, get, have; see also EAT 1, DRINK *v.* 1.

par•terre /paartáir/ *n.* 1 level space in a garden occupied by flower beds arranged formally. 2 rear seating area of a theater.

par•the•no•gen•e•sis /páarthinōjénisis/ *n. Biol.* reproduction by a female gamete without fertilization. □□ **par•the•no•ge•net•ic** /–jinétik/ *adj.* **par•the•no•ge•net′i•cal•ly** *adv.*

par•tial /páarshəl/ • *adj.* 1 not complete; forming only part. 2 biased; having a liking for. • *n.* denture for replacing one or several, but not all, of the teeth. □□ **par•ti•al•i•ty** /páarsheeálitee/ *n.* **par′tial•ly** *adv.*

■ *adj.* 1 fragmentary, imperfect; see also INCOMPLETE. 2 prejudiced, partisan, inclined, influenced, discriminatory; in favor of, predisposed to or toward, fond of. □□ **partiality** prejudice, bias, inclination; preference, taste, relish. **partially** partly, in part, to some extent or degree, to a certain extent or degree, not totally or wholly or entirely, restrictedly, incompletely.

par•tic•i•pate /paartísipayt/ *v.intr.* take a part or share (in). □□ **par•tic•i•pa•tion** /–páyshən/ *n.* **par•tic′i•pant** *n.* **par•tic′i•pa•tor** *n.* **par•tic•i•pa•to•ry** /–pátəwree/ *adj.*

■ partake, have or take a hand, get or become involved; engage in, join in, enter into, be or become associated with. □□ **participant** participator, partaker, sharer, party. **participation** see VOICE *n.* 2c.

par•ti•ci•ple /páartisipəl/ *n. Gram.* word formed from a verb (e.g., *going, gone, being, been*) and used in compound verb forms (e.g., *is going, has been*) or as an adjective (e.g., *working woman, burned toast*). □□ **par•ti•cip•i•al** /–sípeeəl/ *adj.* **par•ti•cip′i•al•ly** *adv.*

par•ti•cle /páartikəl/ *n.* 1 minute portion of matter. 2 least possible amount (*not a particle of sense*). 3 *Gram.* minor part of speech, esp. a short indeclinable one.

■ 1 atom, molecule. 2 atom, molecule, scintilla, spark, mote, suggestion, hint, suspicion, gleam, bit, crumb.

par•ti•cle•board /páartikəlbŏrd, –bawrd/ *n.* building material made in flat sheets from scrap wood bonded with adhesive.

par•ti-col•ored /páarteekúlərd/ *adj.* of more than one color in patches.

■ motley, variegated, pied, mottled.

par•tic•u•lar /pərtikyəlar, pətik–/ • *adj.* 1 relating to or considered as one thing or person as distinct from others; individual. 2 more than is usual; special. 3 scrupulously exact; fastidious. • *n.* 1 detail; item. 2 [in *pl.*]

points of information; detailed account. □ **in particular** especially; specifically. □□ **par·tic·u·lar·i·ty** /–lárítee/ *n.*

■ *adj.* **1** certain, specific, special, peculiar, singular, single, isolated, distinct, discrete. **2** marked, especial, exceptional, remarkable, noteworthy, notable, outstanding. **3** fussy, meticulous, finicky, finical, discriminating. ● *n.* **1** fine point, specific, element, fact, circumstance. **2** minutiae, details, facts, circumstances. □ **in particular** particularly, precisely, exactly, specially.

par·tic·u·lar·ize /pərtíkyələriz, pətík–/ *v.tr.* [also *absol.*] **1** name specifically or one by one. **2** specify (items). □□ **par·tic·u·lar·i·za′tion** *n.*

par·tic·u·lar·ly /pərtíkyələrlee, pətík–/ *adv.* **1** especially; very. **2** specifically (*they particularly asked for you*).

■ **1** specially, exceptionally, peculiarly, singularly, distinctively, uniquely, unusually. **2** in particular, especially, principally, mainly; only, solely.

par·tic·u·late /pərtíkyəlayt, –lət, paar–/ ● *adj.* in the form of separate particles. ● *n.* matter in this form.

part·ing /paárting/ *n.* **1** leave-taking or departure. **2** division; separating.

■ **1** farewell, saying good-bye, leaving, going (away), making one's adieus *or* adieux; valediction. **2** splitting, dividing, breaking (up *or* apart); separation, split, breakup, rift, rupture, partition.

par·ti·san /paártizən/ (also **par·ti·zan**) ● *n.* **1** strong, esp. unreasoning, supporter of a party, cause, etc. **2** *Mil.* guerrilla. ● *adj.* of or like partisans. □□ **par′ti·san·ship** *n.*

■ *n.* **1** devotee, follower, adherent, backer, champion, enthusiast, fan, zealot. **2** freedom fighter, underground *or* resistance fighter, irregular. ● *adj.* guerrilla, freedom, underground, resistance, irregular.

par·ti·tion /paartíshən/ ● *n.* **1** division into parts. **2** structure dividing a space into two parts, esp. a light interior wall. ● *v.tr.* **1** divide into parts. **2** separate with a partition. □□ **par·ti′tioned** *adj.* **par·ti′tion·er** *n.* **par·ti′tion·ist** *n.*

■ *n.* **1** separation, splitting (up), split-up, breakup, segmentation. **2** (room) divider, barrier, screen, separator. ● *v.* **1** separate, cut up, subdivide, split (up). **2** divide (off), wall off, screen (off), fence off.

part·ly /paártlee/ *adv.* to some extent; not entirely.

■ see *partially* (PARTIAL).

part·ner /paártnər/ ● *n.* **1** person who shares or takes part with another or others. **2** companion in dancing. **3** player on the same side in a game. **4** either member of a married or unmarried couple. ● *v.tr.* be the partner of. □□ **part′ner·less** *adj.* **part′ner·ship** *n.*

■ *n.* **1** sharer, partaker, associate, colleague, participant, accomplice, accessory, confederate, comrade, ally, collaborator, *colloq.* pal, sidekick, buddy. **3** teammate. **4** wife, husband, spouse, helpmate, consort; lover, cohabitant.

par·took *past* of PARTAKE.

par·tridge /paártrij/ *n.* (*pl.* same or **par·**

tridg•es) any of various species of game bird.

par·tu·ri·tion /paártŏŏríshən, -tyŏŏ-, -chŏŏ-/ *n. Med.* act of bringing forth young; childbirth.

par·ty /paártee/ ● *n.* (*pl.* **–ties**) **1** social gathering. **2** body of persons engaged in an activity or traveling together (*search party*). **3** group of people united in a cause, opinion, etc., esp. an organized political group. **4** each side in an agreement or dispute. **5** *Law* accessory (to an action). **6** *colloq.* person. ● *v.* (**–ties, –tied**) entertain at or attend a party. □ **party line 1** policy adopted by a political party. **2** shared telephone line.

■ *n.* **1** celebration, fete, function, reception, soiree, festivity, *colloq.* get-together, shindig. **2** group, company, band, corps, gang, crew, commando, team, squad, troop, *colloq.* bunch, outfit. **3** side, interest, faction, league, club, coalition, bloc, division, lobby, caucus. **4** individual, person, litigant, plaintiff, defendant, part, interest, signer. **5** participant, participator, confederate, associate, ally, accomplice.

par·ve·nu /paárvənŏŏ/ *n.* (*fem.* **par·ve·nue**) **1** person who has recently gained wealth or position. **2** upstart.

■ arriviste, nouveau riche, adventurer, social climber; intruder.

pas·chal /páskəl/ *adj.* **1** of Passover. **2** of Easter.

pa·sha /paáshə/ *n.* (also **pa′cha**) *hist.* title (placed after the name) of a Turkish officer of high rank.

pass¹ /pas/ ● *v.* (*past part.* **passed**) (see also PAST). **1** *intr.* move onward; proceed past. **2** *tr.* **a** go past; leave (a thing, etc.) on one side or behind in proceeding. **b** overtake, esp. in a vehicle. **3** *intr. & tr.* be transferred or cause to be transferred from one person or place to another. **4** *tr.* surpass; exceed. **5** *intr.* get through. **6** *intr.* be accepted as or known as. **7** *tr.* move; cause to go. **8 a** *intr.* be successful (in school, etc.). **b** *tr.* be successful in (school, etc.). **c** *tr.* judge as satisfactory. **9 a** *tr.* (of a bill) be approved by (a parliamentary process). **b** *tr.* cause or allow (a bill) to proceed to further legislative processes. **c** *intr.* (of a bill or proposal) be approved. **10** *intr.* occur; elapse; happen. **11 a** *intr.* circulate; be current. **b** *tr.* put into circulation. **12** *tr.* spend or use (a certain time or period). **13** *tr. Sports* send (the ball) to another player of one's own team. **14** *intr.* forgo one's turn or chance in a game, etc. **15** *intr.* come to an end. **16** *tr.* discharge from the body. **17** *tr.* **a** utter (criticism) about. **b** pronounce (judicial sentence) on. ● *n.* **1** act or instance of passing. **2** permission giving free entry, access, leave, etc. **3** *Sports* transference of the ball to another player on the same side. □ **in passing 1** by the way. **2** in the course of conversation, etc. **make a pass at** *colloq.* make amorous or sexual advances to. **pass around 1** distribute. **2** send or give to each of a number in turn. **pass away 1** *euphem.* die. **2** cease to exist;

come to an end. **pass the buck** *colloq.* deny or shift responsibility. **pass by 1** go past. **2** disregard; omit. **pass on 1** proceed on one's way. **2** *euphem.* die. **3** transmit to the next person in a series. **pass out 1** become unconscious. **2** distribute. **pass over 1** - omit, ignore, or disregard. **2** ignore the claims of (a person). **3** *euphem.* die. **pass up** *colloq.* refuse or neglect (an opportunity, etc.). □□ **pass′er** *n.*

■ *v.* **1** go (ahead), progress, extend, lie; run, flow, fly, roll, course, stream, drift, sweep. **2** proceed *or* move past, go by; cross, go across, traverse. **3, 11, 13** give, hand around *or* along *or* over, pass on *or* over, deliver, convey, slip, hurl, toss, throw, release. **4** outdo, transcend, go beyond, overshoot, outstrip, outrun, surmount, outdistance. **5** go *or* travel *or* voyage *or* make one's way past *or* through *or* by, progress, make headway, advance. **6** be taken for, be mistaken for, be regarded as. **7** see PUT[1] *v.* **1. 8 a** qualify, pass muster, get *or* come through, succeed. **9 b** permit, approve, sanction, enact, accept, authorize, endorse, carry, agree to, confirm. **10** go (by); expire; slip by *or* away, fly; crawl, creep, drag; *formal* eventuate; see also OCCUR 1. **12** devote, expend, employ, occupy, fill, while away; dissipate, waste, fritter away, kill. **13** decline, abstain, go *or* do without. **15** go away, disappear, vanish, evaporate, fade away, cease (to exist), die out. **16** evacuate, void, eliminate, excrete. **17** express, issue, declare, deliver, set forth, offer. ● *n.* **1** maneuver, approach; passage, flight, flyby, transit. **2** authorization, permit, license, approval, safe conduct, protection; freedom, liberty, authority, sanction, clearance, go-ahead, *colloq.* green light. □ **in passing** incidentally, by the by, parenthetically. **pass around 1** see DISTRIBUTE 1. **2** see CIRCULATE 2. **pass away 1** expire, perish, succumb, breathe one's last, *archaic or colloq.* give up the ghost, *euphem.* pass on *or* over, *sl.* croak, kick the bucket, bite the dust. **2** vanish, disappear, go away, stop, cease, end. **pass on 1** see PROCEED 1. **2** see *pass away* 1 above. **3** see PASS *v.* 3, 11, 13 above. **pass out 1** faint, collapse, black out, drop, keel over, *colloq.* conk (out), *literary* swoon. **2** see DISTRIBUTE 1. **pass over 1** let pass, let go (by), overlook, pay no heed to, skip. **3** see *pass away* 1 above. **pass up** reject, decline, waive, turn down, dismiss, spurn, renounce; deny (oneself), skip, give up, forgo, let go (by); abandon, forswear, forsake, let pass, ignore, pay no heed, disregard.

pass² /pas/ *n.* narrow passage through mountains.
■ defile, gorge, col, cut, canyon, notch, gap, gully, couloir; opening, way, route, road.

pass•a•ble /pásəbəl/ *adj.* **1** barely satisfactory; just adequate. **2** (of a road, pass, etc.) that can be passed. □□ **pass′a•bly** *adv.*
■ **1** acceptable, tolerable, all right, admissible, allowable, presentable, average, fair (enough). **2** traversable, navigable, negotiable, open, unblocked. □□ **passably** see FAIRLY 2, PRETTY *adv.*

pas•sage /pásij/ *n.* **1** process or means of passing; transit. **2** = PASSAGEWAY. **3** liberty or right to pass through. **4** journey by sea or air. **5** transition. **6** short extract from a book, piece of music, etc.
■ **1** movement, moving, going, transition, traversal, traverse, progress. **3** safe conduct, protection, permission, right of way, privilege, freedom, visa, authorization, allowance. **4** voyage, trip, cruise, crossing, sail, run, travel, traveling. **5** change, mutation, shift, conversion, progression, passing; progress, flow, march, advance. **6** excerpt, selection, section, part, snippet, portion, text, paragraph, canto, stanza, verse, line, sentence, phrase; citation, quotation.

pas•sage•way /pásijway/ *n.* narrow way for passing along, esp. with walls on either side; corridor.
■ hall, passage, hallway, lobby; route, avenue.

pass•book /pásbŏŏk/ *n.* book issued by a bank, etc., to an account holder for recording deposits and withdrawals.

passé /pasáy/ *adj.* **1** old-fashioned. **2** past its prime.
■ **1** unfashionable, dated, out-of-date, behind the times, outmoded, obsolete, obsolescent, antiquated.

pas•sen•ger /pásinjər/ *n.* traveler in or on a public or private conveyance (other than the driver, pilot, crew, etc.).
■ rider, fare, voyager, commuter.

pas•ser•by /pásərbī/ *n.* (*pl.* **pas′sers•by**) person who goes past, esp. by chance.

pas•sim /pásim/ *adv.* (of allusions or references in a published work) to be found at various places throughout the text.

pass•ing /pásing/ ● *adj.* **1** in sense of PASS[1] *v.* **2** transient; fleeting. **3** cursory; incidental (*a passing reference*). ● *n.* **1** in senses of PASS[1] *v.* **2** *euphem.* death. □□ **pass′ing•ly** *adv.*
■ *adj.* **2** disappearing, ephemeral, brief, going, fading (away), short-lived, expiring. **3** hasty, superficial, casual, quick, fleeting, brief, summary. ● *n.* **2** dying, demise, end, loss, expiry, expiration.

pas•sion /páshən/ *n.* **1** strong emotion or enthusiasm. **2** emotional outburst. **3** object arousing passion. **4** (**the Passion**) *Relig.* suffering of Christ during his last days. □□ **pas′sion•less** *adj.*
■ **1** ardor, ardency, eagerness, intensity, fervor, fervency, fervidness, zeal; infatuation, mania, obsession, craze, craving, lust, thirst, hunger, itch, yearning, longing, desire, love, *colloq.* yen, crush. **2** fit, frenzy, paroxysm, fury, furor. **3** love, beloved, idol, hero, heroine, obsession, infatuation, *colloq.* crush, heartthrob; see also ENTHUSIASM. **4** (**the Passion**) pain, agony, martyrdom.

pas•sion•ate /páshənət/ *adj.* **1** dominated by or easily moved to strong feeling, esp. love or anger. **2** showing or caused by passion. □□ **pas′sion•ate•ly** *adv.*
■ ardent, eager, intense, fervid, zealous, avid, earnest, feverish, fanatic(al), vehement, impassioned; quick-tempered, irascible, hotheaded, fiery, testy, huffy; aroused, lustful, lecherous, erotic, sexual, amorous.

pas•sive /pásiv/ *adj.* **1** suffering action; acted upon. **2** offering no opposition; submissive. **3** not active; inert. **4** *Gram.* designating the voice in which the subject undergoes the action of the verb. □ **passive resistance** nonviolent refusal to cooperate. **passive smoking** involuntary inhaling, of smoke from others' cigarettes, etc. □□ **pas′sive•ly** *adv.* **pas′sive•ness** *n.* **pas•siv′i•ty** *n.*

■ **2** repressed, deferential, yielding, compliant, complaisant, receptive, flexible, malleable, pliable. **3** inactive, nonaggressive, motionless, unresponsive, quiet, calm, tranquil, serene, placid, still, idle.

pass•key /páskee/ *n.* **1** private key to a gate, etc., for special purposes. **2** skeleton key or master key.

Pass•o•ver /pásōvər/ *n.* Jewish spring festival commemorating the liberation of the Israelites from Egyptian bondage.

pass•port /páspawrt/ *n.* **1** official document issued by a government certifying the holder's identity and citizenship, and authorizing travel abroad. **2** [foll. by *to*] thing that ensures admission or attainment (*a passport to success*).

pass•word /páswərd/ *n.* prearranged word or phrase securing recognition, admission, etc.

■ watchword, open sesame, sign, countersign.

past /past/ • *adj.* **1** gone by in time. **2** recently completed or gone by (*the past month*), **3** relating to a former time. **4** *Gram.* expressing a past action or state. • *n.* **1 a** past time. **b** past events. **2** person's past life, esp. if discreditable. **3** past tense or form. • *prep.* **1** beyond in time or place. **2** beyond the range, duration, or compass of. • *adv.* so as to pass by (*hurried past*). □ **past master** expert.

■ *adj.* **1** over, done, finished, (over and) done with. **2** last, recent. **3** late, former, onetime, sometime, previous, prior. • *n.* **1** days *or* years *or* times gone by, old times, former times, the (good) old days, yesterday, yesteryear. **2** history, background, life, career, biography. • *prep.* **1** across, over; after. **2** surpassing, exceeding. • *adv.* on, by, along, away.

pas•ta /paasta/ *n.* **1** dried flour paste used in various shapes in cooking (e.g., spaghetti). **2** cooked dish made from this.

paste /payst/ • *n.* **1** any moist fairly stiff mixture. **2** dough of flour with fat, water, etc. **3** liquid adhesive for sticking paper, etc. **4** hard vitreous composition used in making imitation gems. • *v.tr.* **1** fasten or coat with paste. **2** *sl.* beat or thrash. □□ **past•ing** *n.* (esp. in sense 2 of *v.*).

paste•board /páystbawrd/ *n.* **1** stiff material made by pasting together sheets of paper. **2** [*attrib.*] **a** flimsy. **b** fake.

pas•tel /pastél/ *n.* **1** crayon of powdered pigments bound with a gum solution. **2** work of art in pastel. **3** light and subdued shade of a color. □□ **pas•tel′ist** *n.*

pas•tern /pástərn/ *n.* **1** part of a horse's foot between fetlock and hoof. **2** corresponding part in other animals.

pas•teur•ize /páschəriz, pástyə–/ *v.tr.* steril-

ize (milk, etc.) by heating. □□ **pas•teur•i•za′tion** *n.* **pas′teur•iz•er** *n.*

pas•tiche /pasteésh/ *n.* literary or artistic work from or imitating various sources.

■ mixture, medley, blend, compound, composite, patchwork, olio, olla podrida, potpourri, motley.

pas•time /pástim/ *n.* pleasant recreation or hobby.

■ avocation, diversion, distraction, amusement, entertainment, fun, play, relaxation, leisure.

pas•tor /pástər/ *n.* priest or minister in charge of a church or a congregation. □□ **pas′tor•ate** *n.* **pas′tor•ship** *n.*

■ vicar, clergyman, clergywoman, parson, reverend, father, divine, ecclesiastic, bishop.

pas•tor•al /pástərəl/ • *adj.* **1** of shepherds or flocks and herds. **2** of or portraying country life. **3** of a pastor. • *n.* pastoral poem, play, picture, etc. □□ **pas′to•ral•ism** *n.* **pas′to•ral•ly** *adv.*

■ *adj.* **1** country, rural, rustic, provincial, farming, agricultural, agrarian; humble. **2** bucolic, idyllic, innocent, simple, tranquil, serene, uncomplicated, arcadian. **3** clerical, ministerial, ecclesiastic(al), church(ly). • *n.* idyll, eclogue, pastorale.

pas•tra•mi /pəstraámee/ *n.* seasoned smoked beef.

pas•try /páystree/ *n.* (*pl.* **–tries**) **1** dough of flour, fat, and water baked and used as a base and covering for pies, etc. **2 a** food, made wholly or partly of this. **b** item of this food.

pas•tur•age /páschərij/ *n.* land for pasture.

pas•ture /páschər/ • *n.* **1** grassland suitable for grazing. **2** herbage for animals. • *v. tr.* put (animals) to pasture.

■ *n.* **1** meadow, meadowland, pasturage, grass, range.

past•y /páystee/ *adj.* (**past•i•er**, **past•i•est**) unhealthy pale (esp. in complexion). □□ **past′i•ly** *adv.* **past′i•ness** *n.*

■ wan, pallid, pasty-faced, sallow, pale-faced.

pat[1] /pat/ • *v.tr.* (**pat•ted**, **pat•ting**) **1** strike gently with the hand or a flat surface. **2** flatten or mold by patting. • *n.* **1** light stroke or tap, esp. with the hand in affection, etc. **2** sound made by this. **3** small mass (esp. of butter) formed by patting. □ **pat on the back** gesture of approval or congratulation.

■ *v.* **1** tap, touch, dab; pet, stroke, caress • *n.* **1, 2** tap, touch, dab; stroke, caress. **3** piece, patty, lump, cake, portion. □ **pat on the back** commendation, praise, compliment, flattery.

pat[2] /pat/ • *adj.* **1** prepared or known thoroughly. **2** apposite or opportune, esp. unconvincingly so. • *adv.* in a pat manner. □ **stand pat** stick stubbornly to one's opinion or decision. □□ **pat′ly** *adv.* **pat′ness** *n.*

■ *adj.* **1** see READY *adj.* **1, 2. 2** apt, suitable, ready, appropriate; well-rehearsed; glib, slick. • *adv.* thoroughly, perfectly, exactly, precisely, faultlessly, flawlessly, just so *or* right, readily; off pat; slickly, glibly.

patch /pach/ • *n.* **1** piece of material or

metal, etc., used to mend a hole or as rein-forcement. **2** pad worn to protect an injured eye. **3** dressing, etc., put over a wound. **4** large or irregular distinguishable area on a surface. **5** piece of ground. **6** scrap or remnant. • *v.tr.* **1** repair with a patch or patches. **2** (of material) serve as a patch to. **3** put together, esp. hastily. **4** [foll. by *up*] settle (a quarrel, etc.). □ **patch test** test for allergy by applying to the skin patches containing allergenic substances. □□ **patch'er** *n.*

■ *n.* **1** scrap. **2** eye patch. **3** pad, bandage, plaster. **4** region, zone, stretch, section, segment. **5** plot, tract, ground, parcel, field, plat, lot. **6** piece, shred, snip, snippet, tatter. • *v.* **1, 2** patch up *or* over, mend, vamp, revamp, darn, sew (up), reinforce, cover. **3** patch up, fix (up), improvise, knock together *or* up. **4** straighten out, reconcile, resolve, heal.

patch•ou•li /pɔchŏŏlee, páchŏŏlee/ *n.* perfume obtained from a strongly scented E. Indian plant.

patch•work /páchwɔrk/ *n.* **1** sewn work using small pieces of cloth with different designs, forming a pattern. **2** thing composed of various small pieces or fragments.

■ **2** pastiche, pasticcio, mixture, confusion, mosaic.

patch•y /páchee/ *adj.* (**patch•i•er, patch•i•est**) **1** uneven in quality. **2** having or existing in patches. □□ **patch'i•ly** *adv.* **patch'i•ness** *n.*

pate /payt/ *n. colloq. or joc.* head.

pâ•té /paatáy, pa–/ *n.* rich paste or spread of finely chopped and spiced meat or fish, etc.

pa•tel•la /pɔtélə/ *n.* (*pl.* **pa•tel•lae** /–lee/) kneecap. □□ **pa•tel'lar** *adj.* **pa•tel•late** /–lɔt/ *adj.*

pat•ent /pát'nt/ • *n.* **1** official document conferring a right or title, esp. the sole right to make or use or sell some invention. **2** invention or process so protected. • *adj.* **1** /páyt'nt/ obvious; plain. **2** conferred or protected by patent. • *v.tr.* obtain a patent for. □ **patent leather** glossy leather. **patent medicine** trademarked medicine usu. available without prescription. □□ **pa'ten•cy** *n.* **pat'ent•a•ble** *adj.* **pat'ent•ly** *adv.* (/páytɔntlee/ in sense 1 of *adj.*).

■ *n.* **1** letters patent, trade name, (registered) trademark, copyright, license, permit. **2** see INVENTION 2. • *adj.* **1** clear, transparent, manifest, apparent, evident, self-evident, unmistakable. **2** proprietary.

pa•ter•nal /pɔtɔrnɔl/ *adj.* **1** fatherly. **2** related through the father. **3** (of a government, etc.) limiting freedom and responsibility by well-meaning regulations. □□ **pa•ter'nal•ly** *adv.*

■ **1** kindly, indulgent, solicitous, fond, loving; patriarchal. **2** patrilineal, patrimonial. **3** paternalistic.

pa•ter•nal•ism /pɔtɔrnɔlizɔm/ *n.* policy of governing or behaving in a paternal way. □□ **pa•ter'nal•ist** *n.* **pa•ter•nal•is'tic** *adj.* **pa•ter•nal•is'ti•cal•ly** *adv.*

pa•ter•ni•ty /pɔtɔrnitee/ *n.* **1** fatherhood.

2 one's paternal origin. **3** the source or authorship of a thing.

■ **1** fathership. **2** parentage, descent, heritage, line, lineage, extraction, family, stock, strain, blood.

path /path/ *n.* (*pl.* **paths** /paa_th_z/) **1** way or track made for or by walking. **2** line along which a person or thing moves (*flight path*). **3** course of action. □□ **path'less** *adj.*

■ **1** footpath, pathway, trail, walk, walkway, footway, pavement, sidewalk. **2** way, course, track, route, road, orbit, trajectory. **3** approach, channel, direction, procedure, process, way, avenue, means.

pa•thet•ic /pɔthétik/ *adj.* **1** arousing pity, sadness, or contempt. **2** *colloq.* miserably inadequate. □□ **pa•thet'i•cal•ly** *adv.*

■ **1** moving, stirring, affecting, affective, touching, emotional, emotive, poignant, tragic, heartrending. **2** meager, paltry, feeble, inadequate, poor, petty.

path•o•gen /páthɔjɔn/ *n.* agent causing disease. □□ **path•o•gen•ic** /–jénik/ *adj.*

path•o•log•i•cal /páthɔlójikɔl/ *adj.* **1** of pathology. **2** of or caused by a physical or mental disorder (*a pathological fear of spiders*). □□ **path•o•log'i•cal•ly** *adv.*

pa•thol•o•gy /pɔthólɔjee/ *n.* **1** science of bodily diseases. **2** symptoms of a disease. □□ **pa•thol'o•gist** *n.*

pa•thos /páythos, –thaws, –thōs/ *n.* quality in speech, writing, events, etc., that evokes pity or sadness.

path•way /páthway/ *n.* path or its course.

-pathy /pɔthee/ *comb. form* forming nouns denoting: **1** curative treatment (*allopathy*, *homeopathy*). **2** feeling (*telepathy*).

pa•tience /páyshɔns/ *n.* perseverance; ability to endure; forbearance.

■ tolerance, restraint, toleration, stoicism, fortitude, endurance, sufferance, submission; diligence, tenacity, doggedness, assiduity.

pa•tient /páyshɔnt/ • *adj.* having or showing patience. • *n.* person receiving medical treatment. □□ **pa'tient•ly** *adv.*

■ *adj.* resigned, submissive, stoical, long-suffering, compliant; forbearing, tolerant; diligent, dogged, tenacious, persistent. • *n.* invalid, sufferer, case, client.

pa•ti•na /pɔteenə, pát'nə/ *n.* (*pl.* **pa•ti•nas**) **1** film, usu. green, formed on old bronze. **2** similar film or gloss on other surfaces. □□ **pat•i•nat•ed** /pát'naytid/ *adj.* **pat•i•na'tion** *n.*

pa•ti•o /páteeō/ *n.* **1** paved usu. roofless area adjoining and belonging to a house. **2** roofless inner court.

pa•tois /patwáá, pátwaa/ *n.* (*pl.* same, *pronunc.* /–waaz/) regional dialect of the common people.

pa•tri•arch /páytreeaark/ *n.* **1** male head of a family or tribe. **2** *Eccl.* **a** chief bishop in the Orthodox Church. **b** (in the Roman Catholic Church) bishop ranking immediately below the pope. **3** venerable old man. □□ **pa•tri•ar'chal** *adj.* **pa•tri•ar'chal•ly** *adv.*

pa•tri•arch•ate /páytreeáárkɔt, –kayt/ *n.* office, rank, see, or residence of a patriarch.

pa•tri•ar•chy /páytreeáárkee/ *n.* (*pl.* **–chies**)

system of society, government, etc., ruled by a man or men and with descent through the male line.

pa•tri•cian /pətríshən/ • *n.* **1** *hist.* member of the ancient Roman nobility. **2** aristocrat. • *adj.* aristocratic; well-bred.

pat•ri•mo•ny /pátrimōnee/ *n.* (*pl.* **–nies**) property inherited from one's father or ancestor. □□ **pat•ri•mo′ni•al** *adj.*

pa•tri•ot /páytreeət, –ot/ *n.* person who is devoted to and ready to support or defend his or her country. □□ **pa•tri•ot′ic** /–reeótik/ *adj.* **pa•tri•ot′i•cal•ly** *adv.* **pa′tri•o•tism** *n.*

▪ nationalist, loyalist; flag-waver, chauvinist.

pa•trol /pətról/ • *n.* **1** act of walking or traveling around an area in order to protect or supervise it. **2** guards, police, troops, etc., sent out to watch or protect. • *v.* (**pa•trolled, pa•trol•ling**) **1** *tr.* carry out a patrol of. **2** *intr.* act as a patrol. □ **patrol car** police car used in patrolling roads and streets. □□ **pa•trol′ler** *n.*

▪ *n.* **1** rounds, policing, beat; protection, (safe)guarding, defense. **2** sentry, sentinel, patrolman, *see also* SQUAD. • *v.* **1** police, guard, protect, defend, watch over. **2** walk a beat, make *or* do the rounds, be on *or* stand *or* keep guard, be on *or* stand *or* keep watch, keep vigil. □ **patrol car** squad car, prowl car.

pa•trol•man /pətrólmən/ *n.* (*pl.* **–men**) police officer assigned to or patrolling a specific route.

pa•tron /páytrən/ *n.* (*fem.* **pa•tron•ess**) **1** person who gives financial or other support to a person, cause, work of art, etc. **2** habitual customer. □ **patron saint** protecting or guiding saint of a person, place, etc.

▪ **1** benefactor, philanthropist, Maecenas, protector, supporter, sponsor; backer, *colloq.* booster, *sl.* angel. **2** client, purchaser, buyer, patronizer, habitué.

pa•tron•age /pátrənij/ *n.* **1** patron's *or* customer's support. **2 a** power to appoint others to government jobs. **b**. distribution of such jobs.

▪ **1** sponsorship, backing, promotion, encouragement, trade, business; trading, traffic.

pa•tron•ize /páytrəniz, pát–/ *v.tr.* **1** treat condescendingly. **2** act as a patron toward (a person, cause, artist, etc.); support; encourage. **3** be a customer of. □□ **pa•tron•i•za′tion** *n.* **pa′tron•iz•er** *n.* **pa′tron•iz•ing** *adj.* **pa′tron•iz•ing•ly** *adv.*

▪ **1** look down on, scorn, talk down to; disdain, demean, put down, humiliate. **2** sponsor, back, promote, aid, assist, help, fund. **3** deal with, do business with, buy from, frequent, shop at.

pat•ro•nym•ic /pátrənímik/ *n.* name derived from the name of a father or ancestor, e.g., *Johnson, O'Brien, Ivanovich.*

pat•sy /pátsee/ *n.* (*pl.* **–sies**) person who is deceived, ridiculed, tricked, etc.

pat•ter[1] /pátər/ • *v. intr.* make a rapid succession of taps. • *n.* rapid succession of taps, short light steps, etc.

▪ *v.* spatter, tap; beat, pelt. • *n.* spatter, pitter-patter, pit-a-pat, tapping, tattoo, drum, thrum, beat.

pat•ter[2] /pátər/ • *n.* rapid speech used by a comedian or salesperson. • *v. intr.* talk glibly or mechanically.

▪ *n.* pitch, sales talk, *colloq.* line, *sl.* spiel. • *v.* chatter, prattle, prate, babble, gabble, cackle, jabber, rattle (on).

pat•tern /pátərn/ • *n.* **1** decorative design. **2** regular or logical form, order, etc. **3** model or design, e.g., of a garment, from which copies can be made. **4** example of excellence; ideal; model (*a pattern of elegance*). See synonym study at MODEL. • *v.tr.* **1** model (a thing) on a design, etc. **2** decorate with a pattern.

▪ *n.* **1** figure, motif, device; decoration, ornament. **2** system, arrangement, plan, theme; repetition, consistency, regularity. **3** original, blueprint, diagram, plan, layout, draft, guide. **4** archetype, prototype, exemplar, paragon, standard, yardstick, criterion. • *v.* **1** see IMITATE 1, 2. **2** figure, ornament; see also EMBELLISH 1.

pat•ty /pátee/ *n.* (*pl.* **–ties**) small flat cake of food.

pau•ci•ty /páwsitee/ *n.* smallness of number or quantity.

paunch /pawnch/ *n.* **1** belly or stomach, esp. when protruding. **2** ruminant's first stomach; rumen. □□ **paunch′y** *adj.* (**paunch•i•er, paunch•i•est**). **paunch′i•ness** *n.*

▪ *n.* **1** potbelly, *colloq.* tummy, gut, *sl.* beer belly.

pau•per /páwpər/ *n.* person without means; beggar. □□ **pau′per•ism** /–rizəm/ *n.* **pau′per•ize** *v.tr.* **pau•per•i•za′tion** /–rīzáysh'n/ *n.*

▪ indigent, down-and-out, bankrupt, insolvent.

pause /pawz/ • *n.* temporary stop; silence. • *v.intr.* **1** make a pause; wait. **2** linger over (a word, etc.).

▪ *n.* hesitation, interruption, delay, lull, lapse, moratorium, holdup, wait, break, rest, breathing space. • *v.* **1** delay, break, hesitate, mark time, falter, rest.

pave /payv/ *v.tr.* cover (a street, floor, etc.) with paving, etc. □ **pave the way for** prepare for. □□ **pav′er** *n.* **pav′ing** *n.*

▪ surface, floor; tile, flag, concrete; macadamize, tarmac. □ **pave the way for** facilitate, ease; see also PREPARE 1.

pave•ment /páyvmənt/ *n.* paved path, roadway, etc.

pa•vil•ion /pəvílyən/ *n.* **1** tent, esp. a large one at a show, fair, etc. **2** building or stand used for entertainments, exhibits, etc. **3** detached building that is part of a connected set of buildings, as at a hospital.

Pav•lo•vi•an /pavlṓveeən/ *adj.* of or relating to I. P. Pavlov or his work, esp. on conditioned reflexes.

paw /paw/ • *n.* **1** foot of an animal having claws or nails. **2** *colloq.* person's hand. • *v.* **1** *tr.* strike or scrape with a paw or foot. **2** *intr.* scrape the ground with a paw or hoof. **3** *tr. colloq.* fondle awkwardly or indecently.

pawl /pawl/ *n.* lever with a catch for the teeth of a wheel or bar.

pawn[1] /pawn/ *n.* **1** *Chess* piece of the smallest size and value. **2** person used by others for their own purposes.

■ **2** tool, cat's-paw, puppet, instrument, dupe.

pawn[2] /pawn/ • *v. tr.* **1** deposit an object, esp. with a pawnbroker, as security for money lent. **2** pledge or wager. • *n.* object left as security for money, etc., lent.

■ *v.* mortgage, hypothecate, deposit, *colloq.* hock. • *n.* collateral, guaranty, guarantee, pledge, surety.

pawn•broker /páwnbrókər/ *n.* person who lends money at interest on the security of personal property pawned. □□ **pawn′brok•ing** *n.*

Paw•nee /pawneé, paa–/ *n.* **1 a** N. American people native to Kansas and Nebraska. **b** member of this people. **2** language of this people.

pawn•shop /páwnshop/ *n.* pawnbroker's shop.

paw•paw /páwpaw/ *n.* (also **pa′paw**) N. American tree with purple flowers and edible fruit.

pay /pay/ • *v. tr.* (*past* and *past part.* **paid** /payd/) **1** [also *absol.*] give (a person, etc.) what is due for services done, goods received, debts incurred, etc. **2** give (a sum) for work done, a debt, etc. **3 a** give, bestow, or express. **b** make (a visit). **4** [also *absol.*] be profitable or advantageous. **5** reward or punish. **6** let out (a rope) by slackening it. • *n.* wages. • *adj.* requiring payment of a coin, a set fee, etc., for use. □ **in the pay of** employed by. **pay back 1** repay. **2** punish or be revenged on. **pay dirt 1** *Mineral.* ground worth working for ore. **2** financially promising situation. **pay off 1** dismiss (workers) with a final payment. **2** *colloq.* yield good results; succeed. **3** pay (a debt) in full. **pay phone** coin-operated telephone. □□ **pay•ee** /payeé/ *n.* **pay′er** *n.*

■ *v.* **1** recompense, compensate, remunerate, reward, indemnify, repay, reimburse. **2** repay, refund, reimburse, satisfy, clear, remit, discharge, liquidate, settle, honor, meet. **3** extend, transmit, pass on, deliver; do. **4** benefit, profit, avail, help, advantage; (*absol.*) be worthwhile, yield a return, produce results, show a profit, pay off; see also SUCCEED 1. **5** pay back or out, repay, settle (accounts) with, requite; take *or* get revenge on, chastise, castigate, get even with. **6** (*pay out*) release, loosen, slack *or* slacken off (on). • *n.* remuneration, consideration, reward, money, salary, fee, honorarium, remittance, allowance, stipend; payment, compensation, recompense. □ **pay back** see PAY *v.* 5 above. **pay off** 1 see DISMISS 2. **2** see PAY *v.* 4 above. **3** see PAY *v.* 2 above.

pay•a•ble /páyəbəl/ *adj.* that must or may be paid; due.

■ owed, owing, outstanding, unpaid, receivable.

pay•day /páyday/ *n.* day on which salary or wages are paid.

pay•load /páylōd/ *n.* **1** part of an aircraft's load from which revenue is derived, as paying passengers. **2** explosive warhead carried by an aircraft or rocket.

pay•mas•ter /páymastər/ *n.* official who pays troops, workers, etc.

pay•ment /páymənt/ *n.* **1** act or an instance of paying. **2** amount paid. **3** reward; recompense.

■ **1** remuneration, compensation, settlement. **2** expenditure, disbursement, distribution, outlay, fee, contribution, charge, expense. **3** see PAY *n.*

pay•off /páyawf/ *n. sl.* **1** act of payment. **2** climax. **3** final reckoning. **4** *colloq.* bribe; bribery.

pay•o•la /payólə/ *n.* bribe offered in return for unofficial promotion of a product, etc., in the media.

pay-per-view • *n.* system in which television viewers are charged for watching a specific program (usu. applied to movies or sporting events).

pay•roll /páyrōl/ *n.* list of employees receiving regular pay.

Pb *symb. Chem.* lead.

PBS *abbr.* Public Broadcasting Service.

PC *abbr.* **1** personal computer. **2** politically correct.

PCB *abbr.* **1** *Computing* printed circuit board. **2** *Chem.* polychlorinated biphenyl, any of several toxic aromatic compounds formed as waste in industrial processes.

PCP *n.* **1** *sl.* illicit hallucinogenic drug, phencyclidine hydrochloride (*phenyl cyclohexyl piperidine*). **2** pneumocystis carinii pneumonia.

pct. *abbr.* percent.

PD *abbr.* Police Department.

Pd *symb. Chem.* palladium.

pd. *abbr.* paid.

PDT *abbr.* Pacific Daylight Time.

PE *abbr.* physical education.

pea /pee/ *n.* **1** hardy climbing plant, with seeds growing in pods and used for food. **2** its seed.

peace /pees/ *n.* **1 a** quiet; tranquillity. **b** mental calm; serenity (*peace of mind*). **2** freedom from or the cessation of war. **3** freedom from civil disorder. □ **hold one's peace** keep silent. **peace pipe** tobacco pipe smoked as a token of peace among some Native Americans.

■ **1** serenity, calm, calmness, placidity, placidness. **2** harmony, accord, peacefulness, peacetime; cease-fire, armistice, truce.

peace•a•ble /peésəbəl/ *adj.* **1** disposed to peace. **2** tranquil; peaceful. □□ **peace′a•ble•ness** *n.* **peace′a•bly** *adv.*

■ **1** pacific, inoffensive, dovish, peace-loving, mild, nonviolent, peaceful. **2** see PEACEFUL 1.

peace•ful /peésf͞ool/ *adj.* **1** characterized by peace; tranquil. **2** not infringing peace. See synonym study at CALM. □□ **peace′ful•ly** *adv.* **peace′ful•ness** *n.*

■ **1** peaceable, serene, placid, calm, quiet, quiescent, gentle, restful. **2** see PEACEABLE 1.

peace•mak•er /peʹesmaykər/ n. person who brings about peace. □□ **peaceʹmak•ing** n. & adj.

■ conciliator, pacifier, reconciler, propitiator, placater, pacificator, mediator, arbitrator, intermediator.

peace•time /peʹestim/ n. period when a country is not at war.

peach /peech/ n. **1 a** round juicy fruit with downy cream or yellow skin flushed with red. **b** tree bearing this. **2** yellowish pink color of. **3** colloq. **a** person or thing of superlative quality. **b** often offens. attractive young woman. □□ **peachʹy** adj. (**peach•i•er, peach•i•est**). **peachʹl•ness** n.

■ **3** see BEAUTY 2a.

pea•cock /peʹekok/ n. male peafowl, having brilliant plumage and an erectile fanlike tail (with eyelike markings).

pea•fowl /peʹefowl/ n. peacock or peahen.

pea•hen /peʹehen/ n. female peafowl.

pea jack•et /peʹe jakit/ n. (also **peaʹcoat**) n. sailor's short double-breasted woolen overcoat.

peak¹ /peek/ • n. **1** projecting usu. pointed part, esp.: **a** the pointed top of a mountain. **b** a mountain with a peak. **c** stiff brim at the front of a cap. **2 a** highest point. **b** time of greatest success. • v.intr. reach the highest value, quality, etc. □□ **peaked** adj. **peakʹi•ness** n.

■ n. **1 a, b** pinnacle, crest, ridge, tor, summit; mountain, eminence. **c** visor. **2** top, tip, apex, acme, culmination, pinnacle, apogee; extreme, utmost, consummation, climax. • v. crest, culminate, (reach a) climax, reach a peak, top (out); come to a head.

peak² /peek/ v.intr. **1** waste away. **2** (as **peaked** /peʹekid/ adj.) pale; sickly.

peal /peel/ • n. **1 a** the loud ringing of a bell or bells, esp. a series of changes. **b** set of bells. **2** loud repeated sound, esp. of thunder, laughter, etc. • v. **1** intr. sound forth in a peal. **2** tr. utter sonorously. **3** tr. ring (bells) in peals.

■ n. ring, carillon, chime, toll, tolling, tinkle; changes; clang, clangor; knell; clap, crash, roar, rumble, thunder. • v. toll, chime, clang, reverberate, resonate, resound; knell; boom, crash, roar, roll.

pea•nut /peʹenut/ n. **1** leguminous plant, bearing pods that ripen underground and contain seeds used as food and yielding oil. **2** seed of this plant. **3** [in pl.] colloq. paltry or trivial thing or amount, esp. of money. □ **peanut butter** paste of ground roasted peanuts.

pear /pair/ n. **1** yellowish or brownish green fleshy fruit, tapering toward the stalk. **2** tree bearing it.

pearl /parl/ • n. **1 a** [often attrib.] usu. white or bluish gray hard mass formed within the shell of certain oysters highly prized as a gem for its luster (pearl necklace). **b** imitation of this. **2** precious thing; finest example. **3** anything resembling a pearl, e.g., a dewdrop, tear, etc. • v. intr. fish for pearl oysters. □□ **pearl•er** n. **pearʹly** adj.

■ n. **2** gem, treasure, prize, flower, wonder, nonpareil. □□ **pearly** nacreous, pearl-like, lustrous; mother-of-pearl.

peas•ant /pézənt/ n. **1** small farmer; agricultural worker. **2** derog. boorish or unsophisticated person. □□ **peas•ant•ry** n. (pl. **–ries**).

■ rustic, provincial, (farm) worker, (country) bumpkin, hick, yokel, boor, colloq. hick, hayseed, rube.

peat /peet/ n. **1** vegetable matter decomposed in water and partly carbonized, used for fuel, in horticulture, etc. **2** a cut piece of this. □□ **peatʹy** adj.

peat•bog /peʹetbawg, –bog/ n. bog composed of peat.

peat•moss /peʹetmaws, –mos/ n. dried peat from mosses.

peb•ble /pébəl/ n. small smooth stone worn by the action of water. □□ **pebʹbly** adj.

■ □□ **pebbly** see STONY 1.

pec /pek/ abbr. pectoral (muscle).

pe•can /pikáan, –kán, péekan/ n. **1** pinkish brown smooth nut with an edible kernel. **2** hickory of the southern US, producing this.

pec•ca•dil•lo /pékədílo/ n. (pl. **–loes** or **–los**) trifling offense; venial sin.

■ slip, error, lapse, mistake, infraction, violation,.

peck¹ /pek/ • v.tr. **1** strike or bite (something) with a beak. **2** kiss hastily or perfunctorily. **3 a** make (a hole) by pecking. **b** remove or pluck out by pecking. **4** colloq. [also absol.] eat (food) listlessly; nibble at. ■ n. **1 a** stroke or bite with a beak. **b** mark made by this. **2** hasty or perfunctory kiss. □ **pecking order** social hierarchy.

■ v. **1** see TAP² v. 1, 2. **2** see KISS¹ v. 1. **4** see pick at 1 (PICK). ■ n. **1 a** see TAP² n. 1a. **2** see KISS n. 1.

peck² /pek/ n. dry measure equal to 8 quarts.

pec•tin /péktin/ n. Biochem. any of various soluble gelatinous polysaccharides found in ripe fruits, etc., and used as a gelling agent in jams and jellies. □□ **pecʹtic** adj.

pec•to•ral /péktərəl/ • adj. of or worn on the breast or chest. • n. [esp. in pl.] pectoral muscle or fin.

pec•u•late /pékyəlayt/ v. embezzle (money). □□ **pec•u•la•tion** /–láyshən/ n. **pecʹu•la•tor** n.

pe•cu•liar /pikyōōlyər/ adj. **1** strange; odd; unusual. **2 a** belonging exclusively. **b** belonging to the individual. **3** particular; special. □□ **pe•cuʹliar•ly** adv.

■ adj. **1** curious, queer, bizarre, weird, abnormal, anomalous, aberrant, deviant, eccentric, uncommon, colloq. way-out. **2 a** typical of, characteristic of, characterized by, natural to, symptomatic of, appropriate to or for, distinctive of. **3** see PARTICULAR adj. 1. □□ **peculiarly** see ESPECIALLY.

pe•cu•li•ar•i•ty /pikyōōleeáritee/ n. (pl. **–ties**) **1 a** idiosyncrasy; oddity. **b** instance of this. **2** characteristic or habit.

■ **1** unusualness, eccentricity, abnormality, irregularity, quirk, kink. **2** feature, property, quality, trait, attribute, earmark, hallmark, mark, particularity.

pe•cu•ni•ar•y /pikyŏŏnee-eree/ *adj.* of, concerning, or consisting of, money (*pecuniary aid*). See synonym study at FINANCIAL. □□ pe•cu•ni•ar'i•ly *adv.*

ped•a•gogue /pédəgog, –gawg/ *n.* schoolmaster or teacher, esp. a pedantic one. □□ ped•a•gog•ic /–gójik, –gójik/ *adj.* ped•a•gog'i•cal *adj.* ped•a•gog'i•cal•ly *adv.* ped•a•gog•ism /–gog–/ *n.* (also ped'a•gogu•ism)

ped•a•go•gy /pédəgójee, –gojee/ *n.* science of teaching. □□ ped•a•gog•ics /–gójiks, –gój•iks/ *n.*

ped•al[1] /péd'l/ • *n.* lever or control operated by foot, esp. in a vehicle, on a bicycle, etc. • *v.* 1 *intr.* operate a cycle, organ, etc., by using the pedals. 2 *tr.* work (a bicycle, etc.) with the pedals.

ped•al[2] /péd'l, pée–/ *adj. Zool.* of the foot or feet.

ped•ant /péd'nt/ *n.* person who insists on strict adherence to formal rules or literal meaning at the expense of a wider view. □□ pe•dan•tic /pidántik/ *adj.* pe•dan'ti•cal•ly *adv.* ped'ant•ry *n.* (*pl.* –ries). See synonym study at KNOWLEDGE.

■ see PURIST. □□ **pedantic** didactic, doctrinaire, donnish, pedantical, professorial, pompous, stuffy, perfectionist, scrupulous, overscrupulous.

ped•dle /péd'l/ *v.* 1 *tr.* a sell (goods) while traveling. b advocate or promote. 2 *tr.* sell (drugs) illegally. 3 *intr.* engage in selling. □□ ped•dler /–dlər/ *n.* ped'dler•y *n.*

■ sell, hawk, market, vend, huckster, *colloq.* push. □□ **peddler** hawker, (door-to-door) salesman, cheapjack, vendor, *colloq.* drummer.

ped•er•as•ty /pédərastee/ *n.* anal intercourse esp. between a man and a boy. □□ ped'er•ast *n.*

ped•es•tal /pédistəl/ *n.* 1 base supporting a column or pillar. 2 stone, etc., base of a statue, etc.

■ foundation, platform, stand, substructure, mounting, pier, foot, leg, support, plinth, dado.

pe•des•tri•an /pidéstreeən/ • *n.* [often *attrib.*] person who is walking. • *adj.* prosaic; dull; uninspired. □□ pe•des'tri•an•ism *n.* pe•des'tri•an•ize *v.*

■ *n.* walker, stroller, rambler. • *adj.* boring, banal, tiresome, commonplace, mundane, tedious, unimaginative, uninteresting, monotonous.

pe•di•at•rics /pèedeeátriks/ *n.pl.* [treated as *sing.*] branch of medicine dealing with children and their diseases. □□ pe•di•at'ric *adj.* pe•di•a•tri'cian /–deeətríshən/ *n.*

ped•i•cure /pédikyŏŏr/ *n.* care or treatment of the feet, esp. of the toenails.

ped•i•gree /pédigree/ *n.* 1 [often *attrib.*] recorded line of descent. 2 genealogical table. □□ ped'i•greed *adj.*

■ 1 ancestry, genealogy, blood, bloodline, line, extraction, lineage, stock, heritage. 2 family tree.

ped•i•ment /pédimənt/ *n.* triangular front part of a building, esp. over a doorway, etc. □□ ped•i•men•tal /–mént'l/ *adj.* ped'i•ment•ed *adj.*

pe•dom•e•ter /pidómitər/ *n.* instrument for estimating distance traveled on foot by recording the number of steps taken.

pe•dun•cle /pedúngkəl, pèedung–/ *n. Bot.* stalk of a flower, fruit, or cluster. □□ pe•dun•cu•lar /–kyələr/ *adj.* pe•dun'cu•late /–kyələt/ *adj.*

peek /peek/ • *v.intr.* look slyly; peep. • *n.* quick or sly look.

■ *v.* see PEEP[1] *v.* • *n.* see PEEP[1] *n.*

peel /peel/ • *v.* 1 *tr.* a strip the skin, rind, bark, wrapping, etc., from. b strip (skin, peel, wrapping, etc.) from a fruit, etc. 2 *intr.* a become bare of bark, skin, paint, etc. b flake off. • *n.* outer covering of a fruit, vegetable, shrimp, etc.; rind. □□ peel'er *n.* (in sense 1 of *v.*).

■ *v.* skin, pare, flay, descale; hull, bark, scale, shuck. • *n.* skin, coating, peeling.

peel•ing /péeling/ *n.* strip of the outer skin of a vegetable, fruit, etc. (*potato peelings*).

■ peel, skin, rind.

peen /peen/ *n.* the wedge-shaped or thin or curved end of a hammer head.

peep[1] /peep/ • *v.intr.* 1 look through a narrow opening; look furtively. 2 come slowly into view; emerge. • *n.* furtive or peering glance. □ peeping Tom furtive voyeur.

■ *v.* 1 peer, peek, glimpse, squint. • *n.* look, glimpse, peek, squint, *colloq.* look-see, *sl.* gander.

peep[2] /peep/ • *v.intr.* make a shrill feeble sound as of young birds, mice, etc.; squeak; chirp. • *n.* 1 such a sound; cheep. 2 slightest sound or utterance, esp. of protest, etc.

■ *v.* tweet, cheep, twitter, pipe, chirrup, chirr. • *n.* 1 chirp, tweet, squeak, twitter, pipe. 2 complaint, outcry, protest, protestation, grumble.

peep•hole /péep-hōl/ *n.* tiny hole to look through.

peer[1] /peer/ *v.intr.* look keenly or with difficulty.

■ peep, peek, squint, look; see also EYE *v.*

peer[2] /peer/ *n.* 1 person who is equal in ability, standing, rank, or value; a contemporary (*tried by a jury of his peers*). 2 a (*fem.* peer•ess) member of the British nobility. b noble of any country. □□ peer'age *n.* peer'less *adj.*

■ 1 equal, compeer; like, match; confrère, associate, colleague. 2 noble, nobleman, noblewoman, lord, lady, aristocrat. □□ **peer•less** without equal, unequaled, matchless, unmatched, unrivaled, unique.

peeve /peev/ *colloq.* • *v.tr.* (usu. as peeved *adj.*) annoy; vex; irritate. • *n.* 1 cause of annoyance. 2 vexation.

■ *v.* see IRRITATE 1; (peeved) see DISGRUNTLED.

peev•ish /péevish/ *adj.* querulous; irritable. □□ pee'vish•ly *adv.* pee'vish•ness *n.*

■ testy, touchy, fretful, ill-humored, waspish, petulant, crabbed, churlish, short-tempered, ill-natured, tetchy.

peg /peg/ • *n.* 1 a usu. cylindrical pin or bolt of wood or metal, used for holding, hanging, or supporting things. **2** small peg, matchstick, etc., for calculating the scores at cribbage. • *v.tr.* (**pegged, peg•ging**) **1** fix (a thing) with a peg. **2** *Econ.* stabilize (prices, wages, etc.). **3** throw. □ **peg away** work consistently. **take a person down a peg or two** humble a person.

■ *n.* **1** dowel, rod, stick; thole(pin); hook. • *v.* **1** fasten, secure, make fast, attach, pin. **2** fix, attach, pin, set (by), control (by), limit (by), restrict, confine, freeze. **3** toss, shy, flip, sling, cast. □ **peg away** persevere at *or* with, apply oneself to, persist at *or* with, keep at, stick to, stay with. **take a person down a peg or two** diminish, lower, subdue, downgrade, mortify, humiliate, put down.

peg•board /pégbawrd/ *n.* board having a regular pattern of small holes for pegs, used for displays, games, etc.

pe•jo•ra•tive /pijáwrətiv, –jór–, péjərə–, pée–/ • *adj.* depreciatory. • *n.* depreciatory word. □□ **pe•jo′ra•tive•ly** *adv.*

Pe•king•ese /péekinéez, –ées/ (also **Pe•kin′ ese**) *n.* (*pl.* same) short-legged lapdog with long hair and a snub nose.

pe•koe /péekó/ *n.* superior kind of black tea.

pe•lag•ic /pilájik/ *adj.* of or performed on the open sea.

pelf /pelf/ *n. derog.* or *joc.* money; wealth.

pel•i•can /pélikən/ *n.* large gregarious waterfowl with a large bill and a pouch in the throat for storing fish.

pel•la•gra /pilágrə, –láygrə, –laa–/ *n.* disease caused by deficiency of nicotinic acid, characterized by cracking of the skin and often resulting in insanity. □□ **pel•la′grous** *adj.*

pel•let /pélit/ *n.* **1** small compressed ball of paper, bread, etc. **2** pill. **3** piece of small shot. □□ **pel′let•ize** *v.tr.*

■ **2** see PILL¹ 1a. **3** see SHOT 3b.

pell-mell /pélmél/ *adv.* **1** headlong; recklessly (*rushed pell-mell out of the room*). **2** in disorder or confusion.

■ **1** helter-skelter, heedlessly, slam-bang, slapdash, feverishly, incautiously, wildly. **2** confusedly, chaotically, in disorder; see also HELTER-SKELTER *adv.*

pel•lu•cid /pilóosid/ *adj.* transparent; clear; not confused. □□ **pel•lu′cid•i•ty** *n* **pel•lu′ cid•ly** *adv.*

■ see TRANSPARENT 1,. CLEAR *adj.* 6.

pelt¹ /pelt/ *v.* **1** *tr.* [usu. foll. by *with*] strike repeatedly with thrown objects. **2** *intr.* fall quickly and torrentially.

■ *v.* **1** bombard, shower, bomb, pepper, strafe, batter, shell, assail, assault, attack. **2** come down in sheets *or* buckets, sheet down, pour (down), rain cats and dogs.

pelt² /pelt/ *n.* **1** undressed skin of a fur-bearing mammal. **2** *joc.* human skin. □□ **pelt′ry** *n.*

■ **1** skin, hide, coat, fur, fleece.

pel•vic /pélvik/ *adj.* of or relating to the pelvis. □ **pelvic girdle** bony or cartilaginous structure in vertebrates to which the posterior limbs are attached.

pel•vis /pélvis/ *n.* (*pl.* **pel•vis•es** or **pel•ves** /–veez/) basin-shaped cavity at the lower end of the torso of most vertebrates, formed from the hip bones, sacrum, and other vertebrae.

pen¹ /pen/ • *n.* instrument for writing or drawing with ink. • *v.tr.* (**penned, pen• ning**) write. □ **pen name** literary pseudonym. **pen pal** *colloq.* friend communicated with by letter only.

■ *n.* fountain pen, ballpoint (pen), felt-tip, quill. • *v.* jot down, make a note of, note, put on paper, commit to paper, commit to writing, scribble, scrawl, scratch.

pen² /pen/ • *n.* small enclosure for cows, sheep, poultry, etc. • *v.tr.* (**penned, pen• ning**) [often foll. by *in, up*] enclose or shut in a pen.

■ *n.* coop, hutch, sty, pound, fold, stall, confine, corral. • *v.* confine, coop up, impound, corral.

pen³ /pen/ *n. sl.* = PENITENTIARY *n.*

pe•nal /péenəl/ *adj.* **1** of or concerning punishment or its infliction. **2** (of an offense) punishable, esp. by law. □□ **pe′nal•ly** *adv.*

■ **1** correctional, punitive, disciplinary.

pe•nal•ize /péenəliz/ *v.tr.* subject (a person) to a penalty or comparative disadvantage. □□ **pe•nal•i•za′tion** *n.*

■ discipline, mulct, fine, impose a penalty on, *Law* amerce; see also PUNISH 1.

pen•al•ty /pénəltee/ *n.* (*pl.* **-ties**) **1 a** punishment, esp. a fine, for a breach of law, contract, etc. **b** fine paid. **2** disadvantage, loss, etc., esp. as a result of one's own actions (*paid the penalty for his carelessness*). **3** disadvantage imposed on a competitor or team for a breach of the rules, etc.

■ **1** discipline, penance, sentence; forfeit, toll, exaction. **2** price.

pen•ance /pénəns/ *n.* act of self-punishment as reparation for guilt, sins, etc.

■ (self-)punishment, penalty, repentance, penitence, reparation, atonement, regret, contrition.

pen•chant /pénchənt/ *n.* inclination or liking.

■ bent, proclivity, leaning, bias, predisposition, predilection, partiality, proneness, propensity.

pen•cil /pénsil/ • *n.* [often *attrib.*] instrument for writing or drawing, usu. consisting of a thin rod of graphite, etc., enclosed in a wooden cylinder or metal case. • *v.tr.* (**pen• ciled, pen•cil•ing; pen•cilled, pen•cil• ling**) **1** tint or mark with or as if with a pencil. **2** write, esp. tentatively or provisionally. □□ **pen′cil•er** *n.*

pen•dant /péndənt/ *n.* (also **pend′ent**) hanging jewel, etc., esp. one attached to a necklace, bracelet, etc.

■ ornament, luster, medallion, locket, eardrop.

pen•dent /péndənt/ *adj.* (also **pend′ant**) **1 a** hanging. **b** overhanging. **2** undecided; pending. □□ **pen′den•cy** *n.*

■ **1** see PENDULOUS.

pend•ing /pénding/ • *predic.adj.* awaiting decision or settlement; undecided (*a settlement was pending*). • *prep.* **1** during (*pending these negotiations*). **2** until (*pending his return*).

■ *predic.adj.* unsettled, undetermined, unconfirmed, unfinished, inconclusive, (up) in the air, in the balance, abeyant, on hold. •

prep. **1** see THROUGHOUT *prep.* **2** awaiting, waiting (for), till.

pen•du•lous /pénjələs, péndə–, –dyə–/ *adj.* hanging down; drooping and esp. swinging. □□ **pen′du•lous•ly** *adv.*

■ pendent, sagging, dangling, suspended, pensile.

pen•du•lum /pénjələm, péndə–, –dyə–/ *n.* weight suspended so as to swing freely, esp. a rod with a weighted end regulating the movement of a clock's works.

pen•e•trate /pénitrayt/ *v.* **1** *tr.* **a** find access into or through, esp. forcibly. **b** permeate. **2** *tr.* see into, find out, or discern (a person's mind, the truth, a meaning, etc.). **3** *tr.* see through. **4** *intr.* be absorbed by the mind. **5** *tr.* (as **penetrating** *adj.*) **a** insightful; sensitive. **b** easily heard; piercing. □□ **pen′e•tra•ble** *adj.* **pen•e•tra•bil′i•ty** *n.* **pen′e•trant** *adj. & n.* **pen′e•trat•ing** *adj.* **pen′e•trat•ing•ly** *adv.* **pen•e•tra′tion** /–tráyshən/ *n.* **pen•e•tra′tive** /–trativ/ *adj.* **pen′e•tra•tor** *n.* See synonym study at KEEN

■ **1 a** enter, go through *or* into, pass through *or* into, pierce, bore (into); reach, get to, get at, touch, affect. **b** suffuse, pervade, filter through *or* into, seep through *or* into. **2** understand, sense, become aware *or* conscious of, uncover, discover, comprehend, grasp. **4** sink in, be understood, register, get through, become clear, come across. **5** (**penetrating**) **a** incisive, trenchant, keen, searching, deep, acute, sharp, perceptive, perspicuous. **b** audible; shrill, strident, ear-splitting, ear-shattering, pervasive. □□ **penetration** perforation, incision; insight, keenness, perception, percipience, intelligence, perspicacity, understanding.

pen•guin /pénggwin/ *n.* flightless sea bird of the southern hemisphere, with wings developed into scaly flippers for swimming underwater.

pen•i•cil•lin /pénisilin/ *n.* any of various antibiotics produced naturally by molds or synthetically.

pen•in•su•la /pənínsələ, –syələ/ *n.* piece of land almost surrounded by water. □□ **pen•in′su•lar** *adj.*

pe•nis /péenis/ *n.* (*pl.* **pe•nis•es** or **pe•nes** /–neez/) male organ of copulation and (in mammals) urination. □□ **pe•nile** /–nīl, –nəl/ *adj.*

■ phallus, *esp. joc.* organ.

pen•i•tent /pénitənt/ • *adj.* repentant. • *n.* repentant sinner. □□ **pen′i•tence** *n.* **pen•i•ten′tial** /–ténshəl/ *adj.* **pen•i•ten′tial•ly** *adv.* **pen′i•tent•ly** *adv.*

■ *adj.* regretful, remorseful, sorrowful, sorry, rueful, contrite, apologetic, shamefaced. □□ **penitence** contrition, regret, repentance, regretfulness, compunction, remorse. **penitential** see SORRY 1.

pen•i•ten•tia•ry /péniténshəree/ • *n.* (*pl.* **–ries**) state or federal prison. • *adj.* **1** of or concerning penance. **2** of or concerning reformatory treatment.

pen•knife /pén-nīf/ *n.* pocketknife.

■ knife, jackknife; clasp knife.

pen•light /pénlīt/ *n.* pen-sized flashlight.

pen•man•ship /pénmənship/ *n.* ability in handwriting.

Penn. *abbr.* (also **Penna.**) Pennsylvania.

pen•nant /pénənt/ *n.* **1** *Naut.* long tapering flag. **2 a** flag denoting a sports championship, etc. **b** sports championship.

■ banner, pennon, streamer, banderole, gonfalon, ensign, colors, standard, labarum, jack.

pen•ni•less /pénilis/ *adj.* having no money; destitute. □□ **pen′ni•less•ly** *adv.* **pen′ni•less•ness** *n.*

■ see DESTITUTE 1.

pen•non /pénən/ *n.* long narrow flag; pennant. □□ **pen′noned** *adj.*

Penn•syl•va•nian /pénsilváynyən/ • *n.* **1** native or inhabitant of Pennsylvania. **2** [*prec. by the*] *Geol.* Paleozoic era period from about 310 to 280 million years ago, an age of insect and reptile development. • *adj.* **1** of or relating to Pennsylvania. **2** *Geol.* of or relating to the Pennsylvanian period.

pen•ny /pénee/ *n.* (*pl.* **–nies**) **1** (in the US, Canada, etc.) one-cent coin. **2** British coin equal to one hundredth of a pound. **3** *hist.* former British coin equal to one two-hundred-and-fortieth of a pound. □ **penny-pincher** very frugal person. **penny-pinching** *n.* frugality; cheapness. *adj.* frugal.

■ □ **penny-pinching**(*n.*) miserliness, frugality, cheapness, stinginess. (*adj.*) see MEAN² 1.

pen•ny•weight /péneewayt/ *n.* unit of weight, 24 grains or one twentieth of an ounce troy.

Pe•nob•scot /pənóbskot, –skət/ *n.* **1 a** N. American people native to Maine. **b** member of this people. **2** language of this people.

pe•nol•o•gy /peenóləjee/ *n.* the study of the punishment of crime and of prison management. □□ **pe•no•log′i•cal** /–nəlójikəl/ *adj.* **pe•nol′o•gist** *n.*

pen•sion /pénshən/ • *n.* regular payment made to the disabled, retirees, etc. • *v.tr.* grant a pension to. □□ **pen′sion•a•ble** *adj.* **pen′sion•er** *n.* **pen′sion•less** *adj.*

■ *n.* retirement income, superannuation, social security, *colloq.* golden handshake; benefit, allowance, annuity, subsistence. □□ **pensioner** veteran, senior citizen, retiree, golden-ager, oldster.

pen•sive /pénsiv/ *adj.* **1** deep in thought. **2** sorrowfully thoughtful. □□ **pen′sive•ly** *adv.* **pen′sive•ness** *n.*

■ **1** thoughtful, meditative, musing, cogitative, absorbed, contemplative, reflective, preoccupied, ruminative. **2** brooding, sober, serious, grave; wistful.

pent /pent/ *adj.* closely confined; shut in (*pent-up feelings*).

■ (*pent-up*) restrained, constrained, repressed, stifled, bottled up, held in, checked, held back, curbed.

penta- /péntə/ *comb. form* five.

pen•ta•cle /péntəkəl/ *n.* figure used as a symbol, esp. in magic, e.g., a pentagram.

pen•ta•gon /péntəgon/ *n.* **1** plane figure with five sides and angles. **2** (**the Pentagon**) pentagonal headquarters building of the US

Department of Defense, located near Washington, D.C. ▭▭ **pen•tag•o•nal** /-tágənəl/ *adj.*

pen•ta•gram /péntəgram/ *n.* five-pointed star.

pen•tam•e•ter /pentámitər/ *n.* verse of five feet, e.g., English iambic verse of ten syllables.

Pen•ta•teuch /péntətŏok, –tyŏok/ *n.* first five books of the Old Testament. ▭▭ **pen'ta•teuch•al** *adj.*

pen•tath•lon /pentáthlən, –laan/ *n.* athletic event comprising five different events for each competitor. ▭▭ **pen•tath'lete** /-táthleet/ *n.*

Pen•te•cost /péntikawst, –kost/ *n.* **1 a** Whitsunday. **b** festival celebrating the descent of the Holy Spirit on Whitsunday, fifty days after Easter. **2** Jewish harvest festival, on the fiftieth day after the second day of Passover.

Pen•te•cos•tal /péntikóst'l, –káwst'l/ *adj.* (also **pen'te•cos'tal**) of or designating esp. fundamentalist Christian sects and individuals who emphasize the gifts of the Holy Spirit and express religious feelings by clapping, shouting, dancing, etc. ▭▭ **Pen•te•cos'tal•ism** *n.* **Pen•te•cos'tal•ist** *adj. & n.*

pent•house /pént-hows/ *n.* house or apartment on the roof or the top floor of a tall building.

Pen•to•thal /péntəthawl/ *n. propr.* intravenous anesthetic, thiopental sodium.

pen•ul•ti•mate /pinúltimət/ *adj. & n.* last but one.

pen•um•bra /pinúmbrə/ *n.* (*pl.* **pen•um•brae** /-bree/ or **pen•um•bras**) **1 a** partly shaded region around the shadow of an opaque body, esp. that around the total shadow of the moon or earth in an eclipse. **b** less dark outer part of a sunspot. **2** partial shadow. ▭▭ **pen•um'bral** *adj.*

pe•nu•ri•ous /pinŏoreeəs, pinyŏor–/ *adj.* **1** poor. **2** stingy; grudging. ▭▭ **pe•nu'ri•ous•ly** *adv.* **pe•nu'ri•ous•ness** *n.*
■ **1** poverty-stricken, destitute, impoverished, penniless, indigent, needy; see also BROKE. **2** penny-pinching, miserly, tight, tightfisted, closefisted, cheap.

pen•u•ry /pényəree/ *n.* (*pl.* **-ries**) **1** destitution, poverty. **2** lack, scarcity.

pe•on /péeon, péeən/ *n.* **1** Spanish American day laborer or farm worker. **2** drudge. **3** *hist.* worker held in servitude in the southwestern US. ▭▭ **pe'on•age** *n.*

pe•o•ny /péeənee/ *n.* (*pl.* **-nies**) herbaceous plant with large globular red, pink, or white flowers.

peo•ple /péepəl/ ● *n.* [usu. as *pl.*] **1 a** persons composing a community, tribe, race, nation, etc. (*the American people*). **b** group of persons of a usu. specified kind (*the chosen people*). **2** [prec. by *the*] the mass of people in a country, etc. **3** parents or other relatives. **4** subjects, armed followers, congregation, etc. **5** persons in general (*people do not like rudeness*). ● *v.tr.* populate; inhabit.
■ *n.* **1 a** clan, folk, population, society. **2** masses, (general) public, hoi polloi, multitude, populace, common people; silent majority; electorate, voters, voting public, grass

roots; man in the street. **3** relations, kin, kinsmen, kinsfolk, family, kith and kin; ancestors, forebears. **4** flock. **5** individuals, human beings; living souls, mortals, bodies.
● *v.* colonize, settle, occupy; fill.

pep /pep/ *colloq.* ● *n.* vigor; go; spirit. ● *v.tr.* (**pepped, pep•ping**) [usu. foll. by *up*] fill with vigor. □ **pep talk** usu. short talk intended to enthuse, encourage, etc.
■ *n.* vim (and vigor), animation, vivacity, energy, verve, zest, fire, sprightliness, life. ● *v.* (*pep up*) stimulate, invigorate, animate, enliven, vitalize, vivify, energize, exhilarate, quicken, arouse.

pep•per /pépər/ ● *n.* **1** hot aromatic condiment from the dried berries of certain plants. **2** plant with a red, green, or yellow many-seeded fruit grown as a vegetable. ● *v.tr.* **1** sprinkle or treat with or as if with pepper. **2** pelt with missiles. □ **pepper mill** device for grinding pepper by hand.
■ *v.* **1** scatter, dot, speckle, fleck, spot, spray, spatter, stipple, mottle. **2** see PELT¹ *v.* 1.

pep•per•corn /pépərkawrn/ *n.* dried pepper berry.

pep•per•mint /pépərmint/ *n.* **1 a** mint plant grown for its strong-flavored oil. **b** this oil. **2** candy flavored with peppermint. ▭▭ **pep'per•mint•y** *adj.*

pep•per•o•ni /pépərónee/ *n.* spicy sausage seasoned with pepper.

pep•per•y /pépəree/ *adj.* **1** of, like, or containing much pepper. **2** hot-tempered. **3** pungent, stinging. ▭▭ **pep'per•i•ness** *n.*
■ **2** see PASSIONATE. **3** see PUNGENT 1.

pep•py /pépee/ *adj.* (**pep•pi•er, pep•pi•est**) *colloq.* vigorous; energetic; bouncy. ▭▭ **pep'pi•ly** *adv.* **pep'pi•ness** *n.*

pep•sin /pépsin/ *n.* enzyme contained in the gastric juice.

pep•tic /péptik/ *adj.* concerning or promoting digestion. □ **peptic ulcer** an ulcer in the stomach or duodenum.

Pe•quot /péekwot/ *n.* **1 a** N. American people native to eastern Connecticut. **b** member of this people. **2** language of this people.

por /pər/ *prep.* **1** for each. **2** by means of; by; through (*per rail*). **3** (in full **as per**) in accordance with.

per- /pər/ *prefix* **1** forming verbs, nouns, and adjectives meaning: through; all over. **2** completely; very.

per•ad•ven•ture /pərədvénchər, pér–/ *archaic* or *joc. adv.* perhaps.

per•am•bu•late /parámbyəlayt/ *v.* **1** *tr.* walk through, over, or about. **2** *intr.* walk from place to place. ▭▭ **per•am•bu•la•tion** /-láyshən/ *n.* **per•am•bu•la•to•ry** /-lətáwree/ *adj.*

per an•num /pər ánəm/ *adv.* for each year.

per cap•i•ta /pər kápitə/ *adv. & adj.* for each person.

per•ceive /pərseev/ *v.tr.* **1** apprehend, esp. through the sight; observe. **2** apprehend with the mind; understand; regard. ▭▭ **per•ceiv'a•ble** *adj.* **per•ceiv'er** *n.*
■ **1** see, make out, discern, catch sight of, glimpse, spot, take in, notice, note, discover.

2 gather, comprehend, appreciate, grasp, feel, sense, deduce, view, look on, consider, judge, believe, think.

per•cent /pərsént/ (also **per cent**) • *adv.* in every hundred. • *n.* **1** percentage. **2** one part in every hundred.

per•cent•age /pərséntij/ *n.* **1** rate or proportion percent. **2** proportion. **3** *colloq.* personal benefit or advantage.

■ **2** share, part, portion, interest, piece, *colloq.* cut.

per•cen•tile /pərséntíl/ *n. Statistics* one of 99 values of a variable dividing a population into 100 equal groups as regards the value of that variable.

per•cep•ti•ble /pərséptibəl/ *adj.* capable of being perceived. See synonym study at TANGIBLE. □□ **per•cep´ti•bil´i•ty** *n.* **per•cep´ti•bly** *adv.*

■ discernible, detectable, observable, perceivable, noticeable, distinguishable, recognizable, apparent.

per•cep•tion /pərsépshən/ *n.* **1** act or faculty of perceiving. **2 a** intuitive recognition of a truth, aesthetic quality, etc. **b** instance of this. □□ **per•cep´tu•al** /-chŌōəl/ *adj.* **per•cep´tu•al•ly** *adv.*

■ **2** appreciation, grasp, awareness, consciousness, realization, apprehension, intuition, insight, feeling, sense, impression, idea, notion.

per•cep•tive /pərséptiv/ *adj.* **1** capable of perceiving. **2** sensitive; discerning; observant (*a perceptive remark*). □□ **per•cep´tive•ly** *adv.* **per•cep´tive•ness** *n.* **per•cep•tiv´i•ty** *n.*

■ **2** astute, alert, attentive, quick, alive, quick-witted, intelligent, acute, sharp; see also OBSERVANT 1.

perch[1] /pərch/ • *n.* **1** bar, branch, etc., used by a bird to rest on. **2** high or precarious place for a person or thing to rest on. • *v.* [usu. foll. by *on*] settle or rest, or cause to settle or rest on or as if on a perch, etc.

■ *n.* **2** spot, location, position, site, vantage point. • *v.* roost, sit, nest; place, put, set, situate.

perch[2] /pərch/ *n.* (*pl.* same or **perch•es**) spiny-finned freshwater edible fish.

per•chance /pərcháns/ *adv.* **1** by chance. **2** possibly; maybe.

per•co•late /pérkəlayt/ *v.* **1** *intr.* **a** (of liquid, etc.) filter or ooze gradually. **b** (of an idea, etc.) permeate gradually. **2** *tr.* strain (a liquid, powder, etc.) through a fine mesh, etc. □□ **per•co•la´tion** /-láyshən/ *n.*

■ **1** seep, transfuse, leach, drip, drain, strain, infuse, transude, filtrate, trickle, sink in.

per•co•la•tor /pérkəlaytər/ *n.* machine for making coffee by circulating boiling water through ground beans.

per•cus•sion /pərkúshən/ *n.* **1** *Mus.* **a** [often *attrib.*] playing of music by striking instruments with sticks, etc. (*a percussion band*). **b** such instruments collectively. **2** forcible striking of one esp. solid body against another. □ **percussion cap** small amount of explosive powder contained in metal or paper and exploded by striking. □□ **per•cus´sion•ist** *n.* **per•cus´sive** *adj.* **per•cus´sive•ly** *adv.* **per•cus´sive•ness** *n.*

per di•em /pər dée-em, díem/ • *adv. & adj.* for each day. • *n.* allowance or payment for each day.

per•di•tion /pərdíshən/ *n.* eternal death; damnation.

■ hell, hellfire, doom, ruin, condemnation, destruction.

per•e•gri•nate /périgrinayt/ *v.intr.* travel; journey. □□ **per•e•gri•na´tion** /-náyshən/ *n.* **per´e•gri•na•tor** *n.*

per•e•grine /périgrin, -green/ *n.* (in full **per´e•grine fal´con**) widely distributed falcon used for falconry.

pe•remp•to•ry /pərémptəree/ *adj.* **1** admitting no denial or refusal. **2** dogmatic; imperious; dictatorial. □□ **pe•remp´to•ri•ly** *adv.* **pe•remp´to•ri•ness** *n.*

■ **1** commanding, imperative, emphatic, positive, firm, insistent. **2** authoritative, tyrannical, despotic, autocratic, domineering, *colloq.* bossy.

pe•ren•ni•al /pəréneeəl/ • *adj.* **1** lasting through a year or several years. **2** (of a plant) lasting several years (cf. ANNUAL). **3** lasting a long time or for ever. • *n.* perennial plant. □□ **per•en´ni•al•ly** *adv.*

■ *adj.* **3** continuing, enduring, lifelong, persistent; endless, unending, ceaseless, unceasing, imperishable.

pe•re•stroi•ka /pérestróykə/ *n. hist.* (in the former Soviet Union) reform of the economic and political system.

per•fect • *adj.* /pérfikt/ **1** complete; not deficient. **2 a** faultless (*a perfect diamond*). **b** blameless in morals or behavior. **3 a** very satisfactory (*a perfect evening*). **b** [often foll. by *for*] most appropriate; suitable. **4** exact; precise (*a perfect circle*). **5** entire; unqualified (*a perfect stranger*). **6** *Gram.* (of a tense) denoting a completed action or event in the past. • *v.tr.* /pərfékt/ **1** make perfect; improve. **2** carry through; complete. • *n.* /pérfikt/ *Gram.* the perfect tense. □ **perfect pitch** = absolute pitch. □□ **per•fect´er** *n.* **per´fect´i•ble** *adj.* **per•fect´i•bil´i•ty** *n.* **per´fect•ly** *adv.* **per´fect•ness** *n.*

■ *adj.* **1** absolute, finished, (fully) realized, fulfilled, consummate, pure, entire, whole. **2 a** flawless, sublime, ideal, superb, supreme, superlative, preeminent, excellent. **b** righteous, holy, faultless, flawless, spotless, pure, immaculate. **3 a** see DELIGHTFUL. **b** fitting, (just) right, apt, correct, proper. **4** accurate, correct, unerring, true. **5** utter, complete, thorough, out-and-out, unalloyed; see also ABSOLUTE *adj.* 1. • *v.* **1** refine, polish, cultivate, better; see also IMPROVE 1a. **2** finish, realize, fulfill, consummate, accomplish, achieve. □□ **perfectly** completely, entirely, absolutely; superbly, superlatively, flawlessly; very, full, quite.

per•fec•ta /pərféktə/ *n.* form of betting in which the first two places in a race must be predicted in the correct order.

per•fec•tion /pərfékshən/ *n.* **1** act or process of making perfect. **2** state of being perfect;

faultlessness; excellence. **3** perfect person, thing, or example. □ **to perfection** exactly; completely.

■ **1** refinement, enhancement; improvement, *formal* amelioration. **2** purity, flawlessness, sublimity, superiority; see also EXCELLENCE. **3** ideal, paragon, model, archetype, pattern, mold, standard, idealization, essence. □ **to perfection** see *completely* (COMPLETE).

per•fec•tion•ism /pərfékshənizəm/ *n.* uncompromising pursuit of excellence. □□ **per•fec'tion•ist** *n. & adj.*

■ strictness, fastidiousness, rigorousness, stringency. □□ **perfectionist** (*n.*) purist, pedant, precisian, precisionist, stickler. (*adj.*) meticulous, precise, punctilious, scrupulous, exacting; see also FUSSY 3.

per•fi•dy /pərfídee/ *n.* breach of faith; treachery. □□ **per•fid'i•ous** *adj.* **per•fid'i•ous•ly** *adv.*

■ perfidiousness, deceit, traitorousness, treason, disloyalty, faithlessness, falseness, falsity. □□ **perfidious** treacherous, deceitful, traitorous, treasonous, treasonable, disloyal, faithless, false.

per•fo•rate /pərfərayt/ *v.* **1** *tr.* make a hole or holes through; pierce. **2** *tr.* make a row of small holes in (paper, etc.) so that a part may be torn off easily. □□ **per•fo•ra•tion** /-ráyshən/ *n.* **per'fo•ra•tive** *adj.* **per'fo•ra•tor** *n.*

■ **1** puncture, drill, bore; see also PIERCE 1.

per•force /pərfáwrs/ *adv. archaic* unavoidably; necessarily.

per•form /pərfáwrm/ *v.* **1** *tr.* do; execute. **2** *intr. act in a play*; play an instrument or sing, etc. **3** *intr.* (of a trained animal) execute tricks, etc. **4** *intr.* operate; function. □□ **per•form'a•ble** *adj.* **per•form'er** *n.* **per•form'ing** *adj.*

■ carry out, complete, bring off or about, accomplish, do, fulfill; discharge, dispatch, conduct; present, stage, produce; see also EFFECT *v.* **4** do, act, behave, run, work, go, respond. □□ **performer** actor, actress, thespian, trouper, player, entertainer.

per•form•ance /pərfáwrməns/ *n.* **1 a** act, process, or manner of performing or carrying out. **b** execution (of a duty, etc.). **2** staging or production (of a drama, piece of music, etc.) (*the afternoon performance*).

■ **1** execution, accomplishment, effectuation, discharge, dispatch, conduct, fulfillment, completion. **2** show, showing, play, act; concert, *colloq.* gig.

per•form•ing arts /pərfáwrming/ *n.pl.* drama, music, and dance, etc.

per•fume /pərfyóōm/ • *n.* **1** sweet smell. **2** fluid containing the essence of flowers, etc.; scent. See synonym study at SMELL. • *v.tr.* (also /pərfyóōm/) (usu. as **perfumed** *adj.*) impart a sweet scent to; impregnate with a sweet smell. □□ **per'fum•y** *adj.*

■ *n.* **1** fragrance, aroma, odor, bouquet, nose. **2** eau de cologne, toilet water, fragrance, scent, balm. • *v.* scent; (**perfumed**) see *fragrant* (FRAGRANCE).

per•fum•er /pərfyóōmər/ *n.* maker or seller of perfumes. □□ **per•fum'er•y** *n.* (*pl.* **–ies**).

per•func•to•ry /pərfúngktəree/ *adj.* **1** done merely out of duty; superficial. □□ **per•func'to•ri•ly** *adv.* **per•func'to•ri•ness** *n.*

■ routine, mechanical, automatic, robotlike, unthinking; hasty, hurried, fleeting, rushed; slipshod, slovenly.

per•go•la /pərgələ/ *n.* arbor or covered walk, formed of growing plants trained over a trellis.

per•haps /pərháps/ *adv.* it may be; possibly.

■ maybe, it is possible (that), conceivably, it may be.

peri- /péree/ *prefix* around; about.

per•i•car•di•um /périkaardeeəm/ *n.* (*pl.* **per•i•car•di•a** /-deeə/) membranous sac enclosing the heart. □□ **per•i•car'di•ac** /-deeak/ *adj.* **per•i•car'di•al** *adj.* **per•i•car•di•tis** /-dítis/ *n.*

per•i•gee /périjee/ *n.* point in an orbit where the orbiting body is nearest the center of the body it is orbiting. (opp. APOGEE). □□ **per•i•ge'an** *adj.*

per•i•he•li•on /périheelyən/ *n.* (*pl.* **per•i•he•li•a** /-lyə/) point of a planet's or comet's orbit nearest to the sun's center

per•il /péril/ *n.* serious and immediate danger.

■ threat, risk, jeopardy, exposure, vulnerability.

per•il•ous /périləs/ *adj.* **1** full of risk; dangerous; hazardous. **2** exposed to imminent risk of destruction, etc. □□ **per'il•ous•ly** *adv.* **per'il•ous•ness** *n.*

■ **1** risky, unsafe; see also DANGEROUS. **2** vulnerable, susceptible, exposed, at risk, in danger, in jeopardy.

per•im•e•ter /pərímitər/ *n.* **1 a** circumference or outline of a closed figure. **b** length of this. **2** outer boundary of an enclosed area.

■ **2** border, borderline, margin, periphery, limit(s), bounds, ambit, circumference, edge, verge, fringe(s).

per•i•ne•um /périneeəm/ *n.* region of the body between the anus and the scrotum or vulva. □□ **per•i•ne'al** *adj.*

per•i•od /péereeəd/ • *n.* **1** length or portion of time (*periods of rain*). **2** distinct portion of history, a person's life, etc. (*the Federal period*). **3** *Geol.* time forming part of a geological era. **4** interval between recurrences of an event. **5** time allowed for a lesson in school. **6** occurrence of menstruation. **7 a** punctuation mark (.) used at the end of a sentence or an abbreviation. **b** used at the end of a sentence, etc., to indicate finality. • *adj.* characteristic of some past period (*period furniture*).

■ *n.* **1** interval, term, span, duration, spell, space, stretch, *colloq.* patch; while. **2** time, era, days, epoch, eon, age, years. **5** lesson, class, session.

per•i•od•ic /péereeódik/ *adj.* appearing or occurring at regular intervals. □ **periodic table** arrangement of elements in order of increasing atomic number. □□ **per•i•od'ic•i•ty** *n.*

■ periodical, regular, recurrent, cyclical, cyclic.

pe•ri•od•i•cal /péereeódikəl/ • *n.* newspaper,

magazine, etc., issued at regular intervals, usu. monthly or weekly. • *adj.* periodic; occasional. □□ **pe•ri•od′i•cal•ly** *adv.*

■ *n.* journal, paper, publication, newsletter, organ, serial, weekly, monthly, quarterly. • *adj.* see PERIODIC.

per•i•o•don•tics /péreeədóntiks/ *n.pl.* [treated as *sing.*] branch of dentistry concerned with the structures surrounding and supporting the teeth. □□ **per•i•o•don′tal** *adj.* **per•i•o•don′tist** *n.*

per•i•pa•tet•ic /péripətétik/ *adj.* going from place to place; itinerant. □□ **per•i•pa•tet′i•cal•ly** *adv.* **per•i•pa•tet•i•cism** /–tétəsizəm/ *n.*

■ see *traveling* (TRAVEL).

pe•riph•er•al /pərífərəl/ • *adj.* **1** of minor importance; marginal. **2** of the periphery; on the fringe. **3** (of equipment) used with a computer, etc., but not an integral part of it. • *n.* peripheral device or piece of equipment.

□ **peripheral vision 1** area seen around the outside of one's field of vision. **2** ability to perceive in this area. □□ **pe•riph′er•al•ly** *adv.*

■ *adj.* **1** incidental, unimportant, minor, secondary, inessential; see also IMMATERIAL 1. **2** circumferential, external, perimetric, outside, outer.

pe•riph•er•y /pərífəree/ *n.* (*pl.* **–ies**) **1** boundary of an area or surface. **2** outer or surrounding region.

■ **1** perimeter, circumference, border, edge, rim, brim, margin. **2** see OUTSKIRTS.

pe•riph•ra•sis /pərífrasis/ *n.* (*pl.* **pe•riph•ra•ses** /–seez/) roundabout way of speaking; circumlocution. □□ **per•i•phras′tic** /périfrástik/ *adj.* **per•i•phras′ti•cal•ly** *adv.*

per•i•scope /périskōp/ *n.* apparatus with a tube and mirrors or prisms, by which an observer can see things otherwise out of sight. □□ **per•i•scop′ic** /–skópik/ *adj.* **per•i•scop′i•cal•ly** *adv.*

per•ish /pérish/ *v.intr.* be destroyed; suffer death or ruin.

■ expire, lose one's life, be killed, be lost, meet one's death; see also DIE[1] 1.

per•ish•a•ble /périshəbəl/ • *adj.* liable to perish; subject to decay. • *n.* thing, esp. a foodstuff, subject to speedy decay. □□ **per•ish•a•bil′i•ty** *n.* **per•ish•a•ble•ness** *n.*

per•i•to•ne•um /périt′néeəm/ *n.* (*pl.* **per•i•to•ne•ums** or **per•i•to•ne•a** /–néeə/) serous membrane lining the cavity of the abdomen. □□ **per•i•to•ne′al** *adj.*

per•i•to•ni•tis /périt′nítis/ *n.* inflammatory disease of the peritoneum.

per•i•wig /périwig/ *n.* esp. *hist.* wig. □□ **per•i•wigged** *adj.*

per•i•win•kle[1] /périwingkəl/ *n.* evergreen trailing plant with blue or white flowers.

per•i•win•kle[2] /périwingkəl/ *n.* intertidal saltwater snail.

per•jure /pórjər/ *v.refl. Law* willfully tell an untruth when under oath. □□ **per′jur•er** *n.*

per•ju•ry /pórjəree/ *n.* (*pl.* **–ries**) *Law* act of willfully telling an untruth when under oath. □□ **per•ju•ri•ous** /–jŏoreeəs/ *adj.*

■ lying, mendacity, mendaciousness, falsification, deception, untruthfulness, dishonesty, duplicity.

perk[1] /pərk/ *v.tr.* raise (one's head, etc.) briskly. □ **perk up 1** recover confidence, courage, life, or zest. **2** restore confidence or courage or liveliness in. **3** freshen up.

■ □ **perk up 1** cheer up, become jaunty, brighten, liven up, quicken, revive, *colloq.* buck up. **2** invigorate, revitalize, vitalize, revive, inspirit. **3** see SPRUCE[1] *v.*

perk[2] /pərk/ *n. colloq.* perquisite.

perk[3] /pərk/ *v. colloq.* **1** *intr.* (of coffee) percolate, make a bubbling sound in the percolator. **2** *tr.* percolate (coffee).

perk•y /pórkee/ *adj.* (**perk•i•er**, **perk•i•est**) **1** self-assertive; cocky; pert. **2** lively; cheerful. □□ **perk′i•ly** *adv.* **perk′i•ness** *n.*

■ **1** see PERT. **2** cheery, jaunty, bouncy, bright, perk, vigorous, vitalized, spirited, energetic, zestful.

perm /pərm/ • *n.* permanent wave. • *v.tr.* give a permanent wave to (a person or a person's hair).

per•ma•frost /pórməfrawst, –frost/ *n.* subsoil that remains frozen throughout the year, as in polar regions.

per•ma•nent /pórmənənt/ • *adj.* lasting, or intended to last or function, indefinitely. • *n.* = *permanent wave.* □ **permanent press** process applied to a fabric to make it wrinkle-free. **permanent wave** artificial wave in the hair, intended to last for some time. □□ **per′ma•nence** *n.* **per′ma•nen•cy** *n.* **per′ma•nent•ly** *adv.*

■ *adj.* unchanging, invariable, changeless, fixed, unchangeable, immutable; everlasting, eternal, unending, endless, perpetual, undying, imperishable. □□ **permanence**, **permanency** fixedness, changelessness, unalterableness, immutability, unchangeableness. **permanently** for ever, for good, once and for all, always, eternally.

per•me•a•ble /pórmeeəbəl/ *adj.* capable of being permeated. □□ **per•me•a•bil′i•ty** *n.*

per•me•ate /pórmeeayt/ *v.* **1** *tr.* penetrate throughout; pervade; saturate. **2** *intr.* diffuse itself. □□ **per′me•ance** *n.* **per′me•ant** *adj.* **per•me•a•tion** /–áyshən/ *n.* **per′me•a•tor** *n.*

■ **1** imbue, infiltrate, enter, spread through(out), seep through(out), percolate (through), soak through.

per•mis•si•ble /pərmísibəl/ *adj.* allowable. □□ **per•mis•si•bil′i•ty** *n.* **per•mis′si•bly** *adv.*

■ admissible, acceptable, allowed, permitted, tolerable, legal, licit, lawful, legitimate, authorized, proper.

per•mis•sion /pərmíshən/ *n.* consent; authorization. See synonym study at LIBERTY.

■ assent, leave, license, sanction, acceptance, approval, approbation, countenance, allowance.

per•mis•sive /pərmísiv/ *adj.* **1** tolerant; liberal. **2** giving permission. □□ **per•mis′sive•ly** *adv.* **per•mis′sive•ness** *n.*

■ **1** indulgent, lenient, latitudinarian, lax, easygoing, nonrestrictive, libertarian. **2** assenting, consenting, acquiescent; see also AGREEABLE 2.

per•mit • v. /pərmít/ (**per•mit•ted, per•mit•ting**) **1** tr. give permission or consent to; authorize; allow. **2 a** tr. give an opportunity to. **b** intr. give an opportunity (circumstances permitting). • n. /pérmit/ document giving permission, allowing entry, etc. □□ **per•mit•tee** /pérmitée/ n. **per•mit′ter** n.

■ v. **1** see AUTHORIZE 1, 2a. **2 a** enable, allow, entitle. **b** license, authorization, warrant; pass, passport, visa.

per•mu•ta•tion /pérmyōōtáyshən/ n. **1** one of the possible ordered arrangements or groupings of a set of numbers, items, etc. **2** any combination or selection of a specified number of things from a larger group. □□ **per•mu•ta′tion•al** adj.

per•ni•cious /pərníshəs/ adj. destructive; ruinous; fatal. □□ **per•ni′cious•ly** adv. **per•ni′cious•ness** n.

per•o•ra•tion /pérəráyshən/ n. concluding part of a speech, forcefully summing up what has been said.

per•ox•ide /pəróksíd/ • n. Chem. **1 a** = hydrogen peroxide. **b** [often attrib.] solution of hydrogen peroxide used to bleach the hair or as an antiseptic. **2** compound of oxygen with another element containing the greatest possible proportion of oxygen. • v.tr. bleach (the hair) with peroxide.

per•pen•dic•u•lar /pérpəndíkyələr/ • adj. **1** Geom. at right angles (to a given line, plane, or surface). **2** upright; vertical. **3** (of a slope) very steep. • n. perpendicular line, plane, or direction. □□ **per•pen•dic•u•lar•i•ty** /–dikyōōláritee/ n. **per•pen•dic′u•lar•ly** adv.

■ adj. **1** at 90 degrees to. **2** erect, plumb, straight (up and down).

per•pe•trate /pérpitrayt/ v.tr. commit (a crime, blunder, etc.). □□ **per•pe•tra•tion** /–tráyshən/ n. **per′pe•tra•tor** n.

■ execute, perform, carry out, effect, do; practice.

per•pet•u•al /pərpéchōōəl/ adj. **1** eternal; lasting for ever or indefinitely. **2** continuous; uninterrupted. □□ **per•pet′u•al•ly** adv.

■ **1** everlasting, never-ending, unending, perennial, ageless, timeless, long lived, permanent, indefinite. **2** constant, incessant, persistent, unremitting, unending, nonstop, endless, recurrent.

per•pet•u•ate /pərpéchōō-ayt/ v.tr. **1** make perpetual. **2** preserve from oblivion. □□ **per•pet•u•ance** n. **per•pet•u•a•tion** /–áyshən/ n. **per•pet′u•a•tor** n.

■ **2** continue, maintain, extend, keep (on or up), keep going, memorialize, immortalize, eternalize.

per•pe•tu•i•ty /pérpitōō-itee, –tyōō–/ n. (pl. **–ties**) state or quality of being perpetual. □ **in perpetuity** forever.

■ permanence, constancy, timelessness, everlastingness; eternity; infinity. □ **in perpetuity** for ever, for all time, till the end of time, forevermore.

per•plex /pərpléks/ v.tr. **1** puzzle; bewilder; disconcert. **2** complicate or confuse (a matter). □□ **per•plex′ed•ly** adv. **per•plex′ing** adj. **per•plex′ing•ly** adv.

■ **1** confuse, mystify, distract, baffle, befud-

dle, confound, muddle, colloq. throw, bamboozle. **2** see COMPLICATE 1. □□ **perplexing** confusing, bewildering, puzzling, mystifying, baffling, disconcerting, enigmatic; labyrinthine, complex, complicated, Byzantine.

per•plex•i•ty /pərpléksitee/ n. (pl. **–ties**) **1** bewilderment. **2** thing which perplexes. **3** state of being complicated.

■ **1** confusion, bafflement, befuddlement, puzzlement, bemusement, doubt, difficulty. **2** puzzle, enigma, mystery, problem, paradox, quandary. **3** intricacy, complexity, complicatedness, arcaneness, reconditeness, impenetrability, impenetrableness.

per•qui•site /pérkwizit/ n. **1** extra profit or allowance additional to a main income, etc. **2** customary extra right or privilege. **3** incidental benefit attached to employment, etc.

■ consideration, emolument, bonus, reward, (fringe) benefit, extra, dividend, colloq. perk.

per se /pər sáy/ adv. by or in itself; intrinsically.

per•se•cute /pérsikyōōt/ v.tr. subject to hostility or ill-treatment, esp. on the grounds of political or religious belief. □□ **per•se•cu•tion** /–kyōōshən/ n. **per′se•cu•tor** n. **per•se•cu•to•ry** /–tawree/ adj.

■ oppress, maltreat, ill-treat, abuse, molest, victimize, tyrannize, afflict, punish, martyr, torment, torture. □□ **persecution** oppression, maltreatment, ill-treatment, abuse, hectoring, bullying.

per•se•vere /pérsiveér/ v.intr. continue steadfastly or determinedly; persist. □□ **per•ser′ance** n.

■ be steadfast or staunch or constant, keep going, stand fast or firm, show determination; endure, carry on or through, keep at or on or up, see through, cling to. □□ **perseverance** persistence, steadfastness, determination, resolution, resolve, decision, firmness, purposefulness, pertinacity.

Per•sian /pérzhən, –shən/ • n. **1 a** native or inhabitant of Persia (now Iran). **b** person of Persian descent. **2** language of ancient Persia or modern Iran. **3** (in full **Per′sian cat**) cat of a breed with long silky hair. • adj. of or relating to Persia or its people or language. □ **Persian lamb** tightly curled fur of a young karakul, used in clothing.

per•si•flage /pérsiflaazh/ n. light raillery; banter.

per•sim•mon /pərsímən/ n. **1** tropical evergreen tree bearing edible tomato-like fruits. **2** fruit of this.

per•sist /pərsíst/ v.intr. **1** continue firmly or obstinately. **2** continue in existence; survive.

■ **1** be persistent, insist, stand firm or fast, be steadfast or staunch; persevere; see also PERSEVERE. **2** remain, endure, carry on, keep up or on; see also SURVIVE 1.

per•sist•ent /pərsístənt/ adj. **1** continuing obstinately; persisting. **2** enduring. **3** constantly repeated (persistent nagging). □□ **per•sist′ence** n. **per•sist′en•cy** n. **per•sist′ent•ly** adv.

■ **1** persevering, tenacious, steadfast, firm,

fast, fixed, staunch, resolute, resolved, determined, unfaltering. **2, 3** continuing, lasting, persisting; constant, continuous, continual, unending, interminable. □□ **persistence** perseverance, resolve, determination, resolution, steadfastness, tenacity, constancy.

per•snick•e•ty /pərsníkitee/ *adj. colloq.* **1** fastidious. **2** precise or overprecise.

per•son /pɔ́rsən/ *n.* **1** individual human being. **2** living body of a human being (*hidden somewhere about your person*). **3** *Gram.* any of three classes of personal pronouns, verb forms, etc.: the person speaking (**first person**); the person spoken to (**second person**); the person spoken of (**third person**). **4** [in *comb.*] used to replace *–man* in words referring to either sex (*salesperson*). □ **in person** physically present.

■ **1** individual, being, (living) soul; mortal; (*persons*) people. □ **in person** physically, personally, bodily, actually, in the flesh, *colloq.* large as life; oneself.

per•so•na /pərsɔ́nə/ *n.* (*pl.* **per•so•nae** /–nee/) aspect of the personality as shown to or perceived by others. □ **persona non grata** /non gráatə, grátə/ person not acceptable.

■ face, front, façade, mask, guise, exterior, role; self.

per•son•a•ble /pɔ́rsənəbəl/ *adj.* pleasing in appearance and behavior. □□ **per′son•a•ble•ness** *n.* **per′son•a•bly** *adv.*

per•son•age /pɔ́rsənij/ *n.* **1** person, esp. of rank or importance. **2** character in a play, etc.

■ **1** celebrity, luminary, VIP, name, notable, somebody, personality, star, magnate, mogul; see also BIGWIG.

per•son•al /pɔ́rsənəl/ *adj.* **1** one's own; individual; private. **2** done or made in person (*my personal attention*). **3** directed to or concerning an individual (*personal letter*). **4 a** referring (esp. in a hostile way) to an individual's private life or concerns (*no need to be personal*). **b** close; intimate (*a personal friend*). **5** of the body and clothing (*personal hygiene*). □ **personal computer** computer designed for use by a single individual. **personal pronoun** pronoun replacing the subject, object, etc., of a clause, etc., e.g., *I, we, you, them, us.*

■ **1** particular; see also INDIVIDUAL¹ *adj.* 2–4. **2** physical, bodily, actual, live. **3** private, confidential, intimate; unofficial. **4 a** see FAMILIAR *adj.* 3. **b** see INTIMATE *adj.* 1.

per•son•al•i•ty /pɔ́rsənálitee/ *n.* (*pl.* **–ties**) **1** distinctive character or qualities of a person, often as distinct from others (*an attractive personality*). **2** famous person.

■ **1** nature, temperament, disposition, makeup, persona; identity. **2** celebrity, luminary, star, superstar, name, somebody, headliner.

per•son•al•ize /pɔ́rsənəliz/ *v.tr.* make personal, esp. by marking with one's name, etc. □□ **per•son•al•i•za′tion** *n.*

■ monogram, initial, individualize; sign, autograph.

per•son•al•ly /pɔ́rsənəlee/ *adv.* **1** in person. **2** for one's own part. **3** in a personal manner (*took the criticism personally*).

■ **1** oneself. **2** in one's (own) view *or* opinion, for oneself, as far as one is concerned.

per•son•i•fy /pərsónifi/ *v.tr.* (**–fies, –fied**) **1** represent (an abstraction or thing) as human. **2** (usu. as **personified** *adj.*) embody (a quality) in one's own person; exemplify typically. □□ **per•son•i•fi•ca′tion** *n.* **per•son′i•fi•er** *n.*

■ **1** humanize, personalize, anthropomorphize. **2** typify, epitomize, be the embodiment of, manifest, represent, stand for.

per•son•nel /pɔ́rsənél/ *n.* body of employees, persons involved in a public undertaking, armed forces, etc.

■ see STAFF *n.* 2.

per•spec•tive /pərspéktiv/ *n.* **1 a** art of drawing solid objects on a two-dimensional surface to suggest third dimension. **b** picture drawn in this way. **2** apparent relation between visible objects as to position, distance, etc. **3** mental view of the relative importance of things (*keep the right perspective*). **4** geographical or imaginary prospect. □□ **per•spec′tiv•al** *adj.* **per•spec′tive•ly** *adv.*

■ **3** attitude, position, angle, approach, sentiment, outlook, lookout. **4** (point of) view, viewpoint, standpoint, prospect, vantage point, position, angle.

per•spi•ca•cious /pɔ́rspikáyshəs/ *adj.* having mental penetration or discernment. See synonym study at KEEN. □□ **per•spi•ca′cious•ly** *adv.* **per•spi•cac′i•ty** /–kásitee/ *n.*

per•spic•u•ous /pərspíkyoo͞əs/ *adj.* **1** easily understood; clearly expressed. **2** expressing things clearly. □□ **per•spi•cu•i•ty** /pɔ́rspi-kyoo͞-itee/ *n.* **per•spic′u•ous•ly** *adv.* **per•spic′u•ous•ness** *n.*

per•spi•ra•tion /pɔ́rspiráyshən/ *n.* **1** = SWEAT. **2** sweating. □□ **per•spi′ra•to•ry** /pɔ́rspírətawree, pɔ́rspirə–/ *adj.*

■ **1** dampness, wetness. **2** *Med.* diaphoresis.

per•spire /pərspír/ *v.* sweat.

per•suade /pərswáyd/ *v.tr. & refl.* **1** cause to believe; convince. **2** induce. □□ **per•suad′a•ble** *adj.* **per•suad•a•bil′i•ty** *n.* **per•sua′si•ble** *adj.*

■ **1** bring around, win over, convert; assure. **2** prevail (up)on, exhort, importune, prompt, sway.

per•sua•sion /pərswáyzhən/ *n.* **1** persuading. **2** persuasiveness. **3** belief or conviction, or the group holding it.

■ **1** inducement, influence, exhortation; see also *encouragement* (ENCOURAGE). **3** opinion, creed, faith; sect, denomination, faction; see also BELIEF 1a, b.

per•sua•sive /pərswáysiv, –ziv/ *adj.* able to persuade. □□ **per•sua′sive•ly** *adv.* **per•sua′sive•ness** *n.*

■ convincing, influential, effective, productive, impressive, efficacious, cogent, weighty, compelling.

pert /pərt/ *adj.* saucy; impudent. □□ **pert′ly** *adv.* **pert′ness** *n.*

■ forward, brash, brazen, cheeky, insolent, impertinent, flippant, bold, presumptuous, disrespectful.

pert. *abbr.* pertaining.

per•tain /pərtáyn/ *v.intr.* **1** [foll. by *to*] **a** relate or have reference to. **b** belong to as a part or appendage or accessory. **2** [usu. foll. by *to*] be appropriate to.

■ **1 a** concern, refer to, apply to, include, cover, affect. **2** be fitting for, befit, suit.

per•ti•na•cious /pórt'náyshəs/ *adj.* stubborn; persistent; obstinate (in a course of action, etc.). See synonym study at STUBBORN. □□ **per•ti•na'cious•ly** *adv.* **per•ti•nac'i•ty** /-násitee/ *n.*

per•ti•nent /pórt'nənt/ *adj.* **1** relevant. **2** to the point. □□ **per'ti•nence** *n.* **per'ti•nen•cy** *n.* **per'ti•nent•ly** *adv.*

■ **1** fitting, suitable, apt, germane, apropos, apposite; see also APPROPRIATE *adj.* **2** see INCISIVE 2.

per•turb /pərtórb/ *v.tr.* **1** throw into confusion or disorder. **2** disturb mentally; agitate. □□ **per•turb'a•ble** *adj.* **per•tur•ba'tion** /-báyshən/ *n.* **per•tur•ba•tive** /pərtúrbətiv, pórtərbáytiv/ *adj.* **per•tur'bing•ly** *adv.*

■ **1** see DISORDER *v.* **2** upset, fluster, ruffle, unsettle, disconcert, make uneasy, discomfit, vex.

per•tus•sis /pərtúsis/ *n.* whooping cough.

pe•ruke /pərook/ *n. hist.* wig.

pe•ruse /pərooz/ *v.tr.* read or study carefully. □□ **pe•rus'al** *n.* **pe•rus'er** *n.*

■ scrutinize, examine, inspect, review; scan, run one's eye over; search, explore, survey, appraise. □□ **perusal** reading, scrutiny, check, examination, study.

Pe•ru•vi•an /pərooveeən/ • *n.* **1** native or national of Peru. **2** person of Peruvian descent. • *adj.* of or relating to Peru.

per•vade /pərváyd/ *v.tr.* spread throughout; permeate. □□ **per•va'sion** /-váyzhən/ *n.*

per•va•sive /pərváysiv, -ziv/ *adj.* **1** pervading. **2** able to pervade. □□ **per•va'sive•ly** *adv.* **per•va'sive•ness** *n.*

■ **1** penetrating, permeating, omnipresent, general, inescapable, prevalent, universal, widespread.

per•verse /pərvórs/ *adj.* **1** (of a person or action) deliberately or stubbornly departing from what is reasonable or required. **2** persistent in error. **3** wayward; intractable; peevish. **4** perverted; wicked. See synonym study at STUBBORN. □□ **per•verse'ly** *adv.* **per•verse'ness** *n.* **per•ver'si•ty** *n.* (*pl.* **-ties**)

■ **2** wrong, wrongheaded, awry, contrary, wayward. **3** stubborn, self-willed, wrongheaded, willful, obdurate, obstinate, pigheaded; cantankerous, testy, curmudgeonly, churlish, crusty, crotchety, bad-tempered, awkward, petulant, captious. **4** see ROTTEN 2.

per•ver•sion /pərvórzhən, -shən/ *n.* **1** act of perverting; state of being perverted. **2 a** preference for an abnormal form of sexual activity. **b** such an activity.

■ **1** deviation, diversion, misdirection, corruption, subversion, distortion. **2 b** deviation, deviance, deviancy, abnormality, depravity, debauchery.

per•vert • *v.tr.* /pərvórt/ **1** turn (a person or thing) aside from its proper use or nature.

2 misapply (words, etc.). **3** lead astray from right opinion or conduct. • *n.* /pórvərt/ perverted person, esp. sexually. □□ **per•ver'sive** /-vórsiv/ *adj.* **per•vert'ed** *adj.* **per•vert'ed•ly** *adv.* **per•vert'er** *n.* See synonym study at DEPRAVED

■ *v.* **1, 2** deflect, divert, sidetrack, turn aside or away, subvert, misdirect, distort. **3** degrade, corrupt. • *n.* deviant, degenerate, debauchee, deviate; see also WEIRDO.

pes•ky /péskee/ *adj.* (**pes•ki•er**, **pes•ki•est**) *colloq.* troublesome; annoying. □□ **pesk•i•ly** *adv.* **pesk•i•ness** *n.*

pe•so /páysō/ *n.* chief monetary unit of several Latin American countries and of the Philippines.

pes•si•mism /pésimizəm/ *n.* **1** tendency to be gloomy or expect the worst. **2** *Philos.* belief that all things tend to evil. □□ **pes'si•mist** *n.* **pes•si•mis'tic** *adj.* **pes•si•mis'ti•cal•ly** *adv.*

■ **1** defeatism, negativity, cynicism; discouragement, gloom, melancholy, despair. □□ **pessimist** see MISERY. **pessimistic** gloomy, negative, despairing, depressed, despondent, dejected, downhearted.

pest /pest/ *n.* **1** troublesome or annoying person or thing; nuisance. **2** destructive animal.

■ **1** annoyance, nag, irritant, bother, gadfly, bane, trial

pes•ter /péstər/ *v.tr.* trouble or annoy, esp. with frequent or persistent requests. □□ **pes'ter•er** *n.*

■ nag, irritate, irk, bother, get at or to, badger, plague, vex, fret, hound, harass, harry, heckle, nettle, *colloq.* drive a person up the wall, get under a person's skin.

pes•ti•cide /péstisīd/ *n.* substance used for destroying pests, esp. insects. □□ **pes•ti•cid'al** *adj.*

pes•ti•lence /péstiləns/ *n.* fatal epidemic disease; plague.

■ epidemic, pandemic, black death.

pes•ti•lent /péstilənt/ *adj.* **1** destructive to life; deadly. **2** harmful or morally destructive. **3** *colloq.* troublesome; annoying. □□ **pes•ti•lent•ly** *adv.*

pes•ti•len•tial /péstilénshəl/ *adj.* **1** of or relating to pestilence. **2** dangerous; troublesome, pestilent. □□ **pes•ti•len'tial•ly** *adv.*

pes•tle /pésəl/ *n.* **1** club-shaped instrument for pounding substances in a mortar. **2** appliance for pounding, etc.

pes•to /péstō/ *n.* sauce made of fresh chopped basil, garlic, olive oil, and Parmesan cheese, used for pasta, fish, etc.

pet¹ /pet/ • *n.* **1** domestic or tamed animal kept for pleasure or companionship. **2** darling; favorite. • *attrib.adj.* **1** kept as a pet. **2** of or for pet animals. **3** often *joc.* favorite or particular. **4** expressing fondness or familiarity (*pet name*). • *v.tr.* (**pet•ted**, **pet•ting**) **1** treat as a pet. **2** [also *absol.*] fondle, esp. erotically. □ **pet peeve** *colloq.* something especially annoying to an individual. □□ **pet'ter** *n.*

■ *n.* **2** idol, apple of one's eye, *colloq.* fairhaired boy, *derog.* minion. • *attrib.adj.*

1 tame, trained, domesticated; broken, housebroken. **3** favored, preferred, cherished, special; prized, treasured, precious, dearest, adored, darling. • *v.* **1** pamper, favor, baby, coddle, cosset, mollycoddle, spoil, indulge. **2** caress, stroke, pat; cuddle, snuggle, *colloq.* neck, smooch.

pet[2] /pet/ *n.* feeling of petty resentment or ill-humor.
   ■ (bad *or* ill) temper, fit of pique, sulk, (bad) mood.

peta– /pétə/ *comb. form* denoting a factor of 10^{15}.

pet•al /pét'l/ *n.* each of the parts of the corolla of a flower. □□ **pet•al•ine** /–lin, –lin/ *adj.* **pe′talled** *adj.* [also in *comb.*] **pet′al•like** *adj.* **pet′al•oid** *adj.*

pe•tard /pitaárd/ *n. hist.* **1** small bomb used to blast down a door, etc. **2** kind of firework.

pe•ter /péetər/ *v.intr.* (foll. by *out*) diminish; come to an end.
   ■ evaporate, wane, come to nothing, die out, disappear, fail, fade (out *or* away), dwindle, run out.

pe•tite /pətéet/ *adj.* (of a woman) small and trim. See synonym study at SMALL.
   ■ delicate, dainty, diminutive, little, slight, tiny.

pet•it four /pétee fáwr/ *n.* (*pl.* **pet•its fours** /fórz/) very small fancy frosted cake.

pe•ti•tion /pətíshən/ • *n.* **1** supplication or request. **2** formal written request, esp. one signed by many people. **3** *Law* application to a court for a writ, etc. • *v.* **1** *tr.* make or address a petition to. **2** *intr.* appeal earnestly or humbly. See synonym study at BEG. □□ **pe•ti′tion•a•ble** *adj.* **pe•ti•tion′ar•y** *adj.* **pe•ti′tion•er** *n.*
   ■ *n.* **1** application, solicitation, suit, entreaty, plea, appeal. • *v.* **1** request, ask, apply to, solicit. **2** supplicate, plead; entreat, beseech; pray; see also APPEAL *v*, 1.

pet•rel /pétrəl/ *n.* sea bird, usu. flying far from land.

Pe•tri dish /péetree/ *n.* shallow covered dish used for the culture of bacteria, etc.

pet•ri•fy /pétrifi/ *v.* (**–fies, –fied**) **1** *tr.* (also as **petrified** *adj.*) paralyze with fear, astonishment, etc. **2** *tr.* change (organic matter) into a stony substance. **3** *intr.* become like stone. □□ **pet•ri•fac•tion** /–fákshən/ *n.*
   ■ **1** frighten, scare, horrify, terrify, numb, shock, dumbfound, stun, astonish, astound; *colloq.* flabbergast; (**petrified**) horrified, horror-struck, terrified, terror-stricken, panic-stricken, frightened, afraid; shocked, speechless, dumbfounded, dumbstruck, stunned, thunderstruck, astonished, astounded, stupefied. **2** ossify, fossilize, turn to stone.

pet•ro•chem•i•cal /pétrōkémikəl/ *n.* substance industrially obtained from petroleum or natural gas.

pet•ro•dol•lar /pétrōdolər/ *n.* notional unit of currency earned by a petroleum-exporting country.

pet•rol /pétrəl/ *n. Brit.* gasoline.

pe•tro•le•um /pətrṓleeəm/ *n.* hydrocarbon oil found in the upper strata of the earth, refined for use as fuel, etc. □ **petroleum jelly** (also **pet•ro•la•tum**) translucent solid mixture of hydrocarbons used as a lubricant, ointment, etc.

pet•ti•coat /péteekòt/ *n.* woman's or girl's skirted undergarment hanging from the waist or shoulders. □□ **pet′ti•coat•ed** *adj.* **pet′ti•coat•less** *adj.*

pet•ti•fog /péteefawg/ *v.intr.* (**pet•ti•fogged, pet•ti•fog•ging**) **1** practice legal trickery. **2** quibble or wrangle about petty points. □□ **pet′ti•fog•ger** *n.* **pet•ti•fog′ger•y** *n.* **pet′ti•fog•ging** *adj.*

pet•tish /pétish/ *adj.* peevish; petulant; easily put out. □□ **pet′tish•ly** *adv.* **pet′tish•ness** *n.*

pet•ty /pétee/ *adj.* (**pet•ti•er, pet•ti•est**) **1** unimportant; trivial. **2** mean; small-minded; contemptible. □ **petty cash** money from or for small items of receipt or expenditure. **petty officer** naval NCO. □□ **pet′ti•ly** *adv.* **pet′ti•ness** *n.*
   ■ **1** insignificant, paltry, niggling, trifling, negligible, puny, inessential, nonessential, inconsequential. **2** miserly, stingy, cheeseparing, grudging, cheap, parsimonious, ungenerous, tight, tightfisted, close.

pet•u•lant /péchələnt/ *adj.* peevishly impatient or irritable. □□ **pet′u•lance** *n.* **pet′u•lant•ly** *adv.*
   ■ peevish, pettish, ill-humored, testy, waspish, irascible, choleric, cross, captious, ill-tempered, bad-tempered, splenetic, moody, sour, bilious, crabby, crabbed.

pe•tu•nia /pitṓnyə, –tyṓn–/ *n.* plant with white, purple, red, etc., funnel-shaped flowers.

pew /pyōo/ *n.* (in a church) long bench with a back. □□ **pew′less** *adj.*

pew•ter /pyṓotər/ *n.* **1** gray alloy of tin with lead, copper, antimony, or various other metals. **2** utensils made of this. □□ **pew′ter•er** *n.*

pey•o•te /payṓtee/ *n.* **1** type of Mexican cactus; mescal. **2** hallucinogenic drug prepared from this.

Pfc. *abbr.* (also **PFC**) Private First Class.

PG *abbr.* (of movies) classified as suitable for children subject to parental guidance.

pg. *abbr.* page.

PGA *abbr.* Professional Golfers' Association.

PG-13 *abbr.* (of movies) classified as suitable for children under age 13 subject to parental guidance.

pH /pèe-áych/ *n. Chem.* numerical scale measuring the relative acidity or alkalinity of a solution.

phag•o•cyte /fágəsìt/ *n.* type of cell capable of engulfing and absorbing foreign matter, esp. a leukocyte ingesting bacteria in the body. □□ **phag•o•cyt•ic** /–sítik/ *adj.*

pha•lanx /fálangks/ *n.* (*pl.* **pha•lanx•es** or **pha•lan•ges** /fəlánjeez/) **1** *Gk Antiq.* line of battle, esp. a body of Macedonian infantry drawn up in close order. **2** set of people, etc., forming a compact mass, or banded for a common purpose.

phal•lus /fáls/ *n.* (*pl.* **phal•li** /–lì/ or **phal•lus•es**) **1** (esp. erect) penis. **2** image of this as a symbol of generative power in nature. □□ **phal·lic** /fálik/ *adj.* **phal'li·cal·ly** *adv.* **phal·li·cism** /–lísizəm/ *n.*

phan·tasm /fántazəm/ *n.* illusion; phantom. □□ **phan·tas·mal** /–tázm'l/ *adj.* **phan·tas'mic** /–tázmik/ *adj.*

phan·tas·ma·go·ri·a /fántazməgáwreeə/ *n.* shifting series of real or imaginary figures as seen in a dream. □□ **phan·tas·ma·gor·ic** /–gáwrik, –gór–/ *adj.* **phan·tas·ma·gor'i·cal** *adj.*

phan·tom /fántəm/ • *n.* **1** ghost; apparition; specter. **2** mental illusion. • *adj.* merely apparent; illusory.
 ■ *n.* **1** spirit, phantasm, wraith, revenant, vision, eidolon, *colloq.* spook. **2** figment (of the imagination), delusion, phantasm, chimera, hallucination; see also ILLUSION 3, 4. • *adj* see ILLUSORY.

phar. *abbr.* (also **pharm.** or **Pharm.**) **1** pharmaceutical. **2** pharmacist **3** pharmacy.

Pha·raoh /fáirō, fárō, fáyrō/ *n.* **1** ruler of ancient Egypt. **2** title of this ruler. □□ **Phar·a·on·ic** /fáirayónik/ *adj.*

Phar·i·see /fárisee/ (also **phar'l·see**) *n.* **1** member of an ancient Jewish sect, distinguished by strict observance of the traditional and written law. **2** self-righteous person; hypocrite. □□ **Phar·i·sa·ic** /fárisáyik/ *adj.* **Phar·i·sa'i·cal** *adj.* **Phar'i·sa·ism** *n.*
 ■ **2** pretender, dissembler, humbug, fraud, charlatan, prig. □□ **Pharisaic, Pharisaical** hypocritical, insincere, self-righteous, pretentious, sanctimonious.

phar·ma·ceu·ti·cal /fáarməséotik'l/ • *adj.* of the use or sale of medicinal drugs. • *n.* medicinal drug. □□ **phar·ma·ceu'ti·cal·ly** *adv.* **phar·ma·ceu'tics** *n.*

phar·ma·cist /fáarməsist/ *n.* person qualified to prepare and dispense drugs.
 ■ pharmacologist, druggist.

phar·ma·col·o·gy /fáarməkóləjee/ *n.* the science of the action of drugs on the body. □□ **phar·ma·co·log·i·cal** /–lój–/ *adj.* **phar·ma·co·log'i·cal·ly** *adv.* **phar·ma·col'o·gist** *n.*

phar·ma·co·poe·ia /fáarməkəpeeə/ *n.* **1** book, esp. one officially published, containing a list of drugs with directions for use. **2** stock of drugs. □□ **phar·ma·co·poe'ial** *adj.*

phar·ma·cy /fáarməsee/ *n.* (*pl.* **–cies**) **1** preparation and (esp. medicinal) dispensing of drugs. **2** drugstore.
 ■ **1** pharmaceutics **2** dispensary, druggist.

phar·ynx /fáringks/ *n.* (*pl.* **pha·ryn·ges** /fərínjeez/) cavity behind the nose and mouth, and connecting them to the esophagus. □□ **pha·ryn'gal** /–rínggəl/ *adj.* **pha·ryn·ge·al** /fərinjeeəl, –jəl, fárinjéeəl/ *adj.* **phar·yn·gi'tis** /–rinjítis/ *n.*

phase /fayz/ • *n.* **1** distinct stage in a process of change or development. **2** each of the aspects of the moon or a planet, according to the amount of its illumination. • *v.tr.* carry out (a program, etc.) in phases or stages. □ **phase in** (or **out**) bring gradually into (or out of) use. □□ **pha'sic** *adj.*
 ■ *n.* **1** see STAGE *n.* 1. **2** stage, state, form,

---

shape, appearance, look. □ **phase in** (gradually) introduce, usher in, work in, inject, insert, insinuate, include, incorporate. **phase out** ease off, wind up, put a stop to, (gradually) eliminate, remove, withdraw.

Ph.D. *abbr.* Doctor of Philosophy.

pheas·ant /fézənt/ *n.* long-tailed game birds, orig. from Asia.

phe·no·bar·bi·tal /féenōbáarbitawl, –tal/ *n.* narcotic and sedative barbiturate drug used esp. to treat epilepsy.

phe·nol /féenawl, –nol/ *n. Chem.* monohydroxyl derivative of benzene used in dilute form as an antiseptic and disinfectant. (Also called **carbolic**). □□ **phe·no'lic** /finólik/ *adj.*

phe·nom·e·nal /finóminəl/ *adj.* **1** of the nature of a phenomenon **2** extraordinary; remarkable; prodigious. □□ **phe·nom'e·nal·ly** *adv.*
 ■ **2** outstanding, exceptional, unusual, freakish, rare, uncommon, singular, unorthodox, unprecedented, unheard of, unparalleled, unbelievable, marvelous.

phe·nom·e·non /finóminən/ *n.* (*pl.* **phe·nom·e·na** /–nə/) **1** fact or occurrence that appears or is perceived. **2** remarkable person or thing. **3** *Philos.* object of a person's perception; what the senses or the mind notice.
 ■ **1** event, happening, incident, occasion, experience. **2** wonder, curiosity, spectacle, sight, sensation, marvel, rarity, exception, miracle, standout. **3** *Philos.* percept.

pher·o·mone /férəmōn/ *n.* chemical substance secreted and released by an animal for detection and response by another usu. of the same species. □□ **pher·o·mo'nal** *adj.*

phi /fī/ *n.* twenty-first letter of the Greek alphabet (Φ, φ).

phi·al /fíəl/ *n.* = VIAL.

phil- *comb. form* var. of PHILO-.

-phil *comb. form* var. of -PHILE.

phi·lan·der /filándər/ *v.intr.* [often foll. by *with*] flirt or have casual affairs with women; womanize. □□ **phi·lan'der·er** *n.*
 ■ play about *or* around, carry on, dally, tease, toy, *colloq.* play the field, gallivant. □□ **philanderer** gallant, roué, rake, debauchee, Romeo, womanizer, satyr, lecher, sport, *colloq.* stud; see also FLIRT *n.*

phil·an·throp·ic /fílənthrópik/ *adj.* loving one's fellow people; benevolent. □□ **phil·an'throp·i·cal·ly** *adv.*
 ■ charitable, eleemosynary, generous, magnanimous, munificent, openhanded, ungrudging, unstinting, beneficent, humanitarian, altruistic, humane.

phi·lan·thro·py /filánthrəpee/ *n.* practical benevolence, esp. charity on a large scale. □□ **phi·lan'thro·pist** *n.* **phi·lan'thro·pize** *v.*
 ■ generosity, magnanimity, charitableness, public-spiritedness, bigheartedness, largesse, thoughtfulness, kindheartedness, beneficence. □□ **philanthropist** philanthrope, contributor, donor, benefactor, benefactress, patron, patroness, sponsor.

phi•lat•e•ly /filát′lee/ n. collection and study of postage stamps. □□ **phil•a•tel•ic** /filətélik/ adj. **phil•a•tel′i•cal•ly** adv. **phi•lat′e•list** n.

-phile /fil/ comb. form (also **-phil** /fil/) forming nouns and adjectives denoting fondness for what is specified (bibliophile, Francophile).

phil•har•mon•ic /fílhaarmónik/ adj. fond of music (used characteristically in the names of orchestras, choirs, etc.).

phi•lip•pic /filípik/ n. bitter verbal attack or denunciation.

Phi•lis•tine /filisteen, –stĭn, filístin, –teen/
• n. **1** member of a people opposing the Israelites in ancient Palestine. **2** (usu. **philistine**) person who is hostile or indifferent to culture. □□ **phil′is•tin•ism** n.

■ n. **2** vulgarian, ignoramus, Babbitt, materialist, barbarian, boor, yahoo. • adj. uncultured, uncultivated, unenlightened, unrefined, unread, commonplace, bourgeois, commercial, materialistic.

Phil•lips /filips/ n. [usu. attrib.] propr. denoting a screw with a cross-shaped slot for turning, or a corresponding screwdriver.

philo- /filō/ comb. form (also **phil-** before a vowel or h) denoting a liking for what is specified.

phi•lo•den•dron /filədéndrən/ n. (pl. **philo•den•drons** or **phil•o•den•dra** /–drə/) climbing plant with bright foliage.

phi•lol•o•gy /filóləjee/ n. science of language, esp. in its historical and comparative aspects. □□ **phil•o•lo•gi•an** /–ləlójeeən/ n. **phi•lol′o•gist** n. **phil•o•log•i•cal** /–ləlójikəl/ adj. **phil•o•log′i•cal•ly** adv.

phi•los•o•pher /filósəfər/ n. **1** person engaged or learned in philosophy. **2** person who lives by philosophy.

phil•o•soph•i•cal /fíləsófikəl/ adj. (also **phil•o•soph′ic**) **1** of or according to philosophy. **2** skilled in or devoted to philosophy. **3** calm in adversity. □□ **phil•o•soph′i•cal•ly** adv.

■ **1, 2** rational, logical, reasoned, argued; see also LEARNED[1]. **3** detached, unconcerned, unemotional, unimpassioned, composed, thoughtful, serene, stoical, patient, unruffled, coolheaded, tranquil, unperturbed; see also WISE adj. 1.

phi•los•o•phize /filósəfīz/ v.intr. **1** reason like a philosopher. **2** speculate; theorize. □□ **phi•los′o•phiz•er** n.

phi•los•o•phy /filósəfee/ n. (pl. **–phies**) **1** use of reason and argument in seeking truth and knowledge of reality, esp. of the causes and nature of things and of the principles governing existence. **2** particular system or set of beliefs reached by this; personal rule of life.

■ **1** metaphysics, epistemology, logic, rationalism, reason, thinking; argument. **2** viewpoint, (point of) view, outlook, opinion, attitude, feeling, sentiment, idea, notion, ideology, (set of) beliefs or values, tenets.

phil•ter /fíltər/ n. love potion.

phle•bi•tis /flibítis/ n. inflammation of the walls of a vein. □□ **phle•bit•ic** /–bítik/ adj.

phlegm /flem/ n. **1** thick viscous substance secreted by the mucous membranes of the respiratory passages, discharged by coughing. **2 a** calmness. **b** sluggishness. □□ **phlegm′y** adj.

phleg•mat•ic /flegmátik/ adj. stolidly calm; unexcitable; unemotional. □□ **phleg•mat′i•cal•ly** adv.

■ stoical, stoic, apathetic, uninvolved, unfeeling, uncaring, unresponsive, stolid; self-possessed, self-controlled, controlled, restrained, composed, calm, tranquil, placid; listless, indolent, inactive, passive.

phlo•em /flóem/ n. Bot. tissue conducting food material in plants (cf. XYLEM).

phlox /floks/ n. cultivated plant with scented clusters of esp. white, blue, and red flowers.

-phobe /fōb/ comb. form forming nouns and adjectives denoting a person with a specified fear or dislike (xenophobe).

pho•bi•a /fóbeeə/ n. abnormal or morbid fear or aversion. □□ **pho′bic** adj. & n.

■ horror, terror, dread, hatred, detestation, abhorrence, loathing, execration, revulsion, répugnance.

-phobia /fóbeeə/ comb. form forming abstract nouns denoting a fear or dislike of what is specified (agoraphobia, xenophobia). □□ **-phobic** comb. form forming adjectives.

phoe•nix /féeniks/ n. mythical bird, the only one of its kind, that burned itself on a funeral pyre and rose from the ashes to live through another cycle.

phone /fōn/ n. & v. colloq. = TELEPHONE.

pho•neme /fóneem/ n. any of the units of sound in a specified language that distinguish one word from another (e.g., p, b, d, t as in pad, pat, bad, bat, in English). □□ **pho•ne′mic** adj. **pho•ne′mics** n.

pho•net•ic /fənétik/ adj. **1** representing vocal sounds. **2** (of a system of spelling, etc.) having a direct correspondence between symbols and sounds. **3** of or relating to phonetics. □□ **pho•ne′ti•cal•ly** adv. **pho•net′i•cize** /–nétəsīz/ v.tr.

pho•net•ics /fənétiks/ n.pl. [usu. treated as sing.] **1** vocal sounds. **2** the study of these. □□ **pho•ne•ti•cian** /fónitíshən/ n.

phon•ic /fónik/ • adj. of sound; acoustic; of vocal sounds. • n. [in pl.] method of teaching reading based on sounds. □□ **phon′i•cal•ly** adv.

phono- /fónō/ comb. form denoting sound.

pho•no•graph /fónəgraf/ n. instrument that reproduces recorded sound by a stylus that is in contact with a rotating grooved disk. ¶Now more usually called a record player.

pho•nol•o•gy /fənóləjee/ n. the study of sounds in a language. □□ **pho•no•log•i•cal** /fónəlójikəl/ adj. **pho•no•log′i•cal•ly** adv. **pho•nol•o•gist** /fənóləjist/ n.

■ phonemics; phonetics.

pho•ny /fónee/ (also **pho•ney**) colloq. • adj. (**pho•ni•er, pho•ni•est**) **1** sham; counterfeit. **2** fictitious; fraudulent. • n. (pl. **–nies** or **–neys**) phony person or thing. □□ **pho′ni•ly** adv. **pho′ni•ness** n.

■ adj. unreal, fake, pretend, synthetic, artificial, factitious, false, imitation, bogus, spurious. • n. fake, fraud, imitation, counterfeit; impostor, pretender.

phos•gene /fósjeen, fóz–/ n. colorless poisonous gas (carbonyl chloride), formerly used in warfare.

phos•phate /fósfayt/ n. salt or ester of phosphoric acid, esp. used as a fertilizer. □□ **phos•phat•ic** /–fátik/ adj.

phos•phor /fósfər/ n. synthetic fluorescent or phosphorescent substance esp. used in cathode-ray tubes.

phos•pho•res•cence /fósfərésəns/ n. **1** radiation similar to fluorescence but detectable after excitation ceases. **2** emission of light without combustion or perceptible heat. □□ **phos′pho•resce** v.intr. **phos′pho•res•cent** adj.

phos•pho•rus /fósfərəs/ n. Chem. nonmetallic element existing in allotropic forms, esp. as a poisonous whitish waxy substance burning slowly at ordinary temperatures and so appearing luminous in the dark ¶Symb.: **P**. □□ **phos•phor•ic** /–fórik/ adj. **phos′pho•rous** adj.

pho•to /fótó/ n. = PHOTOGRAPH n. □ **photo finish** close finish of a race or contest, esp. one where the winner is only distinguishable on a photograph. **photo opportunity** (also **pho′to-op**) occasion on which celebrities, etc., pose for photographers by arrangement.

photo– /fótó/ comb. form denoting: **1** light. **2** photography.

pho•to•cop•y /fótōkópee/ n. (pl. **–ies**) photographic copy of printed or written material. • v.tr. (**–ies, –ied**) make a photocopy of. □□ **pho′to•cop•i•er** n.

■ propr. Xerox, Photostat.

pho•to•e•lec•tric /fótóiléktrik/ adj. marked by or using emissions of electrons from substances exposed to light. □ **photoelectric cell** device using this effect to generate current. □□ **pho•to•e•lec•tric•i•ty** /–trisítee/ n.

pho•to•fin•ish•ing /fótōfinishing/ n. process of developing and printing photographic film.

pho•to•gen•ic /fótōjénik/ adj. **1** (esp. of a person) having an appearance that looks pleasing in photographs. **2** Biol. producing or emitting light. □□ **pho•to•gen′i•cal•ly** adv.

pho•to•graph /fótəgraf/ • n. picture taken by means of the chemical action of light or other radiation on sensitive film. • v.tr. [also absol.] take a photograph of (a person, etc.). □□ **pho•tog•ra•pher** /fətógrəfər/ n. **pho•to•graph•i•cal•ly** /–gráfiklee/ adv.

■ n. snapshot, print, snap, photo, shot, colloq. pic. • v. take a picture of, shoot, film, take, snap. □□ **photographer** cameraman, cinematographer, paparazzo.

pho•to•graph•ic /fótəgráfik/ adj. **1** of, used in, or produced by photography. **2** having the accuracy of a photograph.

■ **1** cinematic, filmic; pictorial. **2** vivid, natural, realistic, graphic, accurate, exact, precise, faithful, detailed.

pho•tog•ra•phy /fətógrəfee/ n. taking and processing of photographs.

pho•ton /fóton/ n. quantum of electromagnetic radiation energy, proportional to the frequency of radiation.

pho•to•sen•si•tive /fótōsénsitiv/ adj. react-

ing chemically, electrically, etc., to light. □□ **pho•to•sen•si•tiv•i•ty** /–tívitee/ n.

Pho•to•stat /fótəstat/ • n. propr. **1** type of machine for making photocopies. **2** copy made by this means. • v.tr. (**pho′to•stat**) (**–stat•ted, –stat•ting**) make a Photostat of. □□ **pho•to•stat′ic** adj.

■ n. **1** photocopier. **2** photocopy, copy, stat, propr. Xerox.

pho•to•syn•the•sis /fótōsinthisis/ n. process in which the energy of sunlight is used by organisms, esp. green plants, to synthesize carbohydrates from carbon dioxide and water. □□ **pho•to•syn′the•size** v. **pho•to•syn•thet•ic** /–thétik/ adj. **pho•to•syn•thet′i•cal•ly** adv.

phrase /frayz/ • n. **1** group of words forming a conceptual unit, but not a sentence. **2** idiomatic or short pithy expression. **3** Mus. group of notes forming a distinct unit within a larger piece. • v.tr. express in words. □□ **phras′al** adj. **phras′ing** n.

■ n. **1** clause, word group, collocation, locution. **2** idiom, proverb, motto, slogan, saying, catchphrase, adage, maxim. • v. word, put into words, put, frame, formulate, couch, put or set forth, verbalize, articulate, voice, utter, say, write.

phra•se•ol•o•gy /fráyzeeóləjee/ n. (pl. **–gies**) **1** choice or arrangement of words. **2** mode of expression. □□ **phra•se•o•log•i•cal** /–əlójikəl/ adj.

■ wording, phrasing, language, style, diction.

phre•nol•o•gy /frinóləjee/ n. hist. the study of the shape and size of the cranium as a supposed indication of character and mental faculties. □□ **phren•o•log′i•cal** /–nəlójikəl/ adj. **phre•nol′o•gist** n.

phy•lac•ter•y /fíláktəree/ n. (pl. **–ies**) small leather box containing Hebrew texts, worn by Jewish men at prayer.

phy•lum /fíləm/ n. (pl. **phy•la** /–lə/) Biol. taxonomic rank below kingdom comprising a class or classes and subordinate taxa.

phys•i•cal /fízikəl/ • adj. **1** of or concerning the body (physical exercise). **2** of matter; material (both mental and physical force). **3 a** of, or according to, the laws of nature (a physical impossibility). **b** belonging to physics (physical science). • n. (in full **physical examination**) medical examination. □ **physical science** sciences used in the study of inanimate natural objects. **physical therapy** n. treatment of disease, injury, deformity, etc., by massage, infrared heat treatment, remedial exercise, etc. □□ **phys•i•cal•i•ty** /–kálitee/ n. **phys′i•cal•ly** adv. **phys′i•cal•ness** n.

■ adj. **1** bodily, corporal. **2** corporeal, tangible, palpable, real, actual, true, concrete; fleshly, incarnate, carnal, animal, mortal; non-spiritual.

phy•si•cian /fizíshən/ n. medical doctor; M.D.

■ doctor, medical practitioner, general practitioner, GP, surgeon, colloq. doc, medico, medic.

phys•ics /fíziks/ *n.* science dealing with the properties and interactions of matter and energy. □□ **phys•i•cist** /–zisist/ *n.*

phys•i•og•no•my /fizeeógnəmee, –ónəmee/ *n.* (*pl.* **–mies**) cast or form of a person's features, expression, body, etc. □□ **phys•i•og•nom•ic** /–ognómik, –ənómik/ *adj.* **phys•i•og•nom′i•cal** *adj.* **phys•i•og•nom′i•cal•ly** *adv.* **phys•i•og′no•mist** *n.*

■ see FEATURE *n.* 2.

phys•i•og•ra•phy /fizeeógrəfee/ *n.* description of nature, of natural phenomena, or of a class of objects; physical geography. □□ **phys•i•og′ra•pher** *n.* **phys•i•o•graph•ic** /–zeeəgráfik/ *adj.* **phys•i•o•graph′i•cal** *adj.* **phys•i•o•graph′i•cal•ly** *adv.*

phys•i•o•log•i•cal /fizeeəlójikəl/ *adj.* (also **phys•i•o•log′ic**) of or concerning physiology. □□ **phys•i•o•log′i•cal•ly** *adv.*

phys•i•ol•o•gy /fizeeóləjee/ *n.* **1** science of the functions of living organisms and their parts. **2** these functions. □□ **phys•i•ol′o•gist** *n.*

phys•i•o•ther•a•py /fizeeōthérəpee/ = *physical therapy.*

phy•sique /fizeék/ *n.* bodily structure; build.

■ figure, body, frame, shape, form.

pi /pī/ *n.* **1** sixteenth letter of the Greek alphabet (Π, π). **2** (as π) the symbol of the ratio of the circumference of a circle to its diameter (approx. 3.14159).

pia ma•ter /píə máytər, peéə/ *n. Anat.* delicate innermost membrane enveloping the brain and spinal cord.

pi•a•nis•si•mo /peeənísimō/ *Mus. adj.* performed very softly. • *adv.* very softly. • *n.* (*pl.* **–mos** or **pi•a•nis•si•mi** /–mee/) passage to be performed very softly.

pi•a•nist /peéənist, pee-án–/ *n.* player of a piano.

pi•an•o[1] /peeánō, pyánō/ *n.* (*pl.* **–nos**) large musical instrument played by pressing down keys on a keyboard and causing hammers to strike metal strings.

pi•a•no[2] /pyaánō/ • *adj.* **1** *Mus.* performed softly. **2** subdued. • *adv.* **1** *Mus.* softly. **2** in a subdued manner. • *n.* (*pl.* **–nos**) *Mus.* piano passage.

pi•an•o•forte /pyánófáwrt, –fáwrtee/ *n. Mus.* piano.

pi•az•za /pee-aátsə, –saa/ *n.* **1** public square or marketplace. **2** /peeázə, –aázə/ *dial.* veranda of a house.

pi•broch /peébrokh, –brawkh/ *n.* series of esp. martial or funerary variations on a theme for the bagpipes.

pi•ca /píkə/ *n. Printing* **1** unit of type size (¹/₆ inch). **2** size of letters in typewriting (10 per inch).

pic•a•dor /píkədawr/ *n.* matador's mounted assistant who goads the bull with a lance in a bullfight.

pi•ca•resque /píkərésk/ *adj.* (of a style of fiction) dealing with the episodic adventures of rogues, etc.

pic•a•yune /píkəyóón/ *n. adj.* **1** of little value; trivial. **2** mean; contemptible; petty.

pic•ca•lil•li /píkəlílee/ *n.* (*pl.* **pic•ca•lil•lis**) pickle of chopped vegetables, mustard, and hot spices.

pic•co•lo /píkəlō/ *n.* small flute sounding an octave higher than the ordinary one.

pick[1] /pik/ • *v.tr.* **1** choose (*picked a team*). **2** detach or pluck (a flower, fruit, etc.). **3 a** probe with the finger, an instrument, etc., to remove unwanted matter. **b** clear (a bone, carcass, etc.) of scraps of meat, etc. **4** eat (food, a meal, etc.) in small bits. **5** open (a lock) with an instrument other than a key. **6** steal, as from a person's pocket. • *n.* **1** act or instance of picking. **2 a** selection or choice. **b** the right to select (*had first pick*). **3** the best (*pick of the bunch*). □ **pick and choose** select fastidiously. **pick at 1** eat (food) without interest. **2** = *pick on* 1 (PICK[1]). **pick off 1** pluck (leaves, etc.) off. **2** shoot (people, etc.) one by one. **3** *Baseball* put out a base runner caught off base. **pick on 1** find fault with; nag at. **2** select, as for special attention. **pick up 1 a** grasp and raise (*picked up his hat*). **b** clean up; straighten up. **2** acquire (*picked up a cold*). **3 a** fetch (a person, animal, or thing) left in another person's charge. **b** stop for and take along with one, esp. in a vehicle. **4** make the acquaintance of (a person) casually, esp. as a sexual overture. **5** recover; prosper; improve. **6** arrest. □□ **pick′a•ble** *adj.* **pick′er** *n.*

■ *v.* **1** select, single out, opt for, elect. **2** gather, collect, harvest. **4** pick at, nibble, peck. • *n.* **2 a** option, preference. **3** choicest, crème de la crème. □ **pick at** 1 nibble (at), peck at; play *or* toy with. **pick off 2** kill; see also ELIMINATE[1] 1. **pick on 1** bully, intimidate, abuse, browbeat, tease. **2** see PICK *v.* 1 above. **pick up 1 a** lift (up), take up. **2** learn, become acquainted with, *colloq.* get the hang of. **3** call for, give a lift *or* ride to, collect. **4** meet, introduce oneself to; make advances to; see also APPROACH *v.* 3. **5** get better, make headway, rally. **6** apprehend, detain, take into custody.

pick[2] /pik/ *n.* **1** long-handled tool having a usu. curved iron bar pointed at one or both ends, used for breaking up hard ground, masonry, etc. **2** *colloq.* plectrum.

pick•ax /píkaks/ *n.* (also **pick′axe**) = PICK[2].

pick•et /píkit/ • *n.* **1** person or group of people outside a place of work, intending to persuade esp. workers not to enter during a strike, etc. **2** pointed stake or peg driven into the ground to form a fence, etc. **3** (also **pic•quet, piq•uet**) *Mil.* small body of troops or a single soldier sent out to watch for the enemy. • *v.* **1 a** *tr. & intr.* station or act as a picket. **b** *tr.* beset or guard with a picket or pickets. **2** *tr.* secure with stakes. □ **picket line** boundary established by workers on strike. □□ **pick′et•er** *n.*

■ *n.* **1** picketer, demonstrator, protester, striker. **2** pale, post, stanchion, upright, rod, palisade, paling. **3** guard, patrol, watch; sentry, sentinel, scout. • *v.* **1** protest, demonstrate; blockade; see also STRIKE *v.* 16a. **2** enclose, shut in, wall in, fence in; hem in.

pick•ings /píkingz/ *n.pl.* **1** perquisites; pilferings (*rich pickings*). **2** remaining scraps; gleanings.

pick•le /píkəl/ • n. **1 a** [often in *pl.*] vegetables, esp. cucumbers, preserved in brine, vinegar, mustard, etc. **b** brine, vinegar, etc., in which food is preserved. **2** *colloq.* plight (*a fine pickle we are in!*). • v.tr. **1** preserve in pickle. **2** treat with pickle. **3** (as **pickled** *adj.*) *sl.* drunk.

■ n. **2** see PLIGHT[1]. • v. **3** (**pickled**) see DRUNK *adj.* 1.

pick•pock•et /píkpókit/ n. person who steals from the pockets of others.

pick•up /píkəp/ n. **1** *sl.* person met casually, esp. for sexual purposes. **2** small truck with an enclosed cab and open back. **3 a** part of a record player carrying the stylus. **b** detector of vibrations, etc. **4** act of picking up.

pick•y /píkee/ adj. (**pick•i•er, pick•i•est**) *colloq.* excessively fastidious; choosy. □□ **pick'i•ness** n.

pic•nic /píknik/ • n. **1** outing or excursion including a packed meal eaten out of doors. **2** [usu. with *neg.*] *colloq.* something agreeable or easily accomplished, etc. • v.intr. (**pic•nicked, pic•nick•ing**) take part in a picnic. □□ **pic'nick•er** n. **pic'nick•y** adj. *colloq.*

■ n. **2** child's play, *colloq.* pushover, cinch, piece of cake, breeze; see also BREEZE n. 2; (*no picnic*) torture, agony, *colloq.* a pain in the neck, *sl.* pain in the butt; difficult, arduous, torturous, agonizing, painful.

pico- /peeko, píkó/ comb. form denoting a factor of 10⁻¹² (*picometer*).

pic•to•graph /píktəgraf/ n. (also **pic•to•gram** /píktəgram/) **1** pictorial symbol for a word or phrase. **2** pictorial representation of statistics, etc., on a chart; graph, etc. □□ **pic•to•graph'ic** adj. **pic•tog•ra•phy** /-tógrəfee/ n.

pic•to•ri•al /piktáwreeəl/ adj. **1** of or expressed in a picture or pictures. **2** illustrated. □□ **pic•to'ri•al•ly** adv.

pic•ture /píkchər/ • n. **1** [often *attrib.*] painting, drawing, photograph, etc. **2** total visual or mental impression produced; scene (*the picture looks bleak*). **3** movie. **4** person or thing resembling another closely (*the picture of her aunt*). • v.tr. **1** represent in a picture. **2** imagine. **3** describe graphically. □ **get the picture** *colloq.* grasp the tendency or drift of circumstances, information, etc. **picture tube** cathode-ray tube of a television set. **picture window** very large window consisting of one pane of glass.

■ n. **1** portrait, depiction, representation, illustration, sketch, photo. **2** idea, notion, understanding, image; see also SCENE 6. **3** film, movies, cinema, *colloq.* flick. **4** image, likeness, double, duplicate, twin, (exact) replica, facsimile. • v. **1** depict, draw, portray, paint, show, illustrate. **2** envision, envisage, visualize, fancy, conceive (of), contemplate. □ **get the picture** get the gist or drift; see also EXAMPLE n. 1–2, 4.

pic•tur•esque /píkchərésk/ adj. **1** (of landscape, etc.) beautiful or striking, as in a picture. **2** (of language, etc.) strikingly graphic; vivid. □□ **pic•tur•esque'ly** adv. **pic•tur•esque'ness** n.

■ **1** charming, idyllic, fetching, attractive,

---

pretty, lovely, quaint. **2** colorful, realistic, striking.

pid•dle /píd'l/ v.intr. **1** *colloq.* urinate (used esp. to or by children). **2** work or act in a trifling way. **3** (as **piddling** *adj.*) *colloq.* trivial; trifling. □□ **pid'dler** n.

pid•gin /píjin/ n. simplified language used for communication between people not having a common language.

pie /pí/ n. **1** baked dish of fruit, meat, custard, etc., usu. with a top and base of pastry. **2** anything resembling a pie in form (*mud pie*). □ **easy as pie** very easy. **pie chart** circle divided into sections to represent relative quantities. **pie in the sky** unrealistic prospect of future happiness.

■ **1** see TART[1].

pie•bald /píbawld/ • adj. (usu. of an animal, esp. a horse) having irregular patches of two colors, esp. black and white. • n. piebald animal, esp. a horse.

piece /pees/ • n. **1 a** distinct portion forming part of or broken off from a larger object. **b** each of the parts of something. **2** coin. **3 a** usu. short literary or musical composition; picture. **b** theatrical play. **4** item. **5** object moved in a board game. **6** definite quantity in which a thing is sold. See synonym study at FRAGMENT. • v.tr. [usu. foll. by *together*] form into a whole; put together; join. □ **go to pieces** collapse emotionally. **piece of cake** see CAKE. **piece of one's mind** sharp rebuke or lecture. **piece work** work paid for by the amount produced. □□ **piec'er** n. (in sense 4 of v.).

■ n. **1 a** bit, morsel, scrap, chunk, hunk, sliver, lump, particle, fragment; share, portion, part, segment; serving, helping. **3** work; (short) story, article, essay, poem; piece of music, opus, (musical) number, arrangement, tune, melody; production, drama, sketch, show. **4** instance; see also EXAMPLE n. 1. **5** man, token; chessman, checker. • v. (*piece together*) assemble; fix, unite, mend; make sense of □ **go to pieces** be shattered, have a nervous breakdown, disintegrate, go out of or lose control, break down, *colloq.* crack up. **piece of one's mind** scolding, reprimand, tongue-lashing, telling-off, chiding, rap over or on the knuckles.

pièce de ré•sis•tance /pyés də rayzeestonss/ n. (*pl.* **pièces de ré•sis•tance** *pronunc.* same) **1** most important or remarkable item. **2** most substantial dish at a meal.

■ **1** highlight, (special or main) feature, (special or main) attraction, specialty, masterpiece, chef-d'œuvre.

piece•meal /péesmeel/ • adv. piece by piece; gradually. • adj. partial; gradual; unsystematic.

■ adv. little by little, inch by inch, bit by bit, inchmeal; fitfully, intermittently, sporadically. • adj. inchmeal; disjointed, fragmentary, sporadic.

pied /píd/ adj. parti-colored.

pied-à-terre /pyáydaatáir/ n. (*pl.* **pieds-à-terre** *pronunc.* same) usu. small residence for occasional use.

pier /peer/ *n.* **1** structure of iron or wood raised on piles and leading out to sea, a lake, etc., used as a promenade and landing place. **2 a** support of an arch or of the span of a bridge; pillar. **b** solid masonry between windows, etc.
■ **1** wharf, landing place, jetty, quay. **2 a** column, pile, piling, post, upright; see also BUTTRESS *n.*

pierce /peers/ *v.* **1** *tr.* **a** penetrate the surface of. **b** prick with a sharp instrument, esp. to make a hole in. **2** pass through or into; penetrate. □□ **pierc′er** *n.* **pierc′ing•ly** *adv.*
■ **1** puncture, thrust *or* poke into, lance, spear, spit, run through *or* into, skewer, impale; perforate. **2** (*pierce through* or *into*) see PENETRATE 1a.

pie•ro•gi /pərōgee, pee–/ *n.* (also **pi•ro′gi**) (*pl.* same or **–gies**) small pastry envelopes filled with mashed potatoes, cabbage, or chopped meat.

pi•e•ty /pī-itee/ *n.* (*pl.* **–ties**) **1** quality of being pious. **2** pious act.
■ **1** devotion, devotedness, respect, deference, dedication, dutifulness, loyalty, affection; piousness, reverence, veneration, devoutness, holiness, godliness.

pig /pig/ *n.* **1** omnivorous hoofed bristly mammal, esp. a domesticated kind. **2** flesh of esp. a young or suckling pig as food (*roast pig*). **3** *colloq.* greedy, dirty, obstinate, sulky, or annoying person. **4** oblong mass of metal (esp. iron or lead) from a smelting furnace. □ **buy a pig in a poke** buy, accept, etc., something without knowing its value or esp. seeing it. **pig iron** crude iron from a smelting furnace. **pig out** *sl.* eat gluttonously. □□ **pig′gish** *adj.* **pig′gish•ly** *adv.* **pig′gish•ness** *n.* **pig′let** *n.* **pig′like** *adj.*

pi•geon /pijin/ *n.* large usu. gray and white bird often domesticated and bred and trained to carry messages, etc.; dove. □ **pigeon-toed** (of a person) having the toes turned inward.

pi•geon•hole /píjinhōl/ • *n.* each of a set of compartments in a cabinet or on a wall for papers, letters, etc. • *v.tr.* **1** deposit in a pigeonhole. **2** put aside for future consideration. **3** assign to a preconceived category.

pig•gy /pígee/ • *n.* (also **pig′gie**) *colloq.* little pig. • *adj.* (**pig•gi•er, pig•gi•est**) like a pig. □ **piggy bank** pig-shaped box for coins.

pig•gy•back /pígeebak/ (also **pick′a•back** /píkəbak/) • *n.* ride on the back and shoulders of another person. • *adv.* **1** on the back and shoulders of another person. **2 a** on the back or top of a larger object. **b** in addition to; along with.

pig•head•ed /píg-hédid/ *adj.* obstinate. □□ **pig′head•ed•ly** *adv.* **pig′head•ed•ness** *n.*

pig•ment /pígmənt/ *n.* **1** coloring matter used as paint or dye. **2** natural coloring matter of animal or plant tissue, e.g., chlorophyll, hemoglobin. □□ **pig′men•tar•y** *adj.*

pig•men•ta•tion /pígməntáyshən/ *n.* natural coloring of plants, animals, etc.

pig•my var. of PYGMY.

pig•pen /pígpen/ *n.* = PIGSTY.

pig•skin /pígskin/ *n.* **1** hide of a pig. **2** leather made from this. **3** a football.

pig•sty /pígstī/ *n.* (*pl.* **–sties**) **1** pen or enclosure for a pig or pigs. **2** filthy house, room, etc.

pig•tail /pígtayl/ *n.* braid or gathered hank of hair hanging from the back of the head. □□ **pig•tailed** *adj.*

pike[1] /pīk/ *n.* (*pl.* same) large voracious freshwater fish, with a long narrow snout and sharp teeth.

pike[2] /pīk/ *n.* *hist.* infantry weapon with a pointed steel or iron head on a long wooden shaft.

pi•laf /pilaaf, peelaaf/ *n.* (also **pi•laff′; pi•law, pi•lau** /–láw, –lów/) dish of spiced rice or wheat with meat, fish, vegetables, etc.

pi•las•ter /pilástər/ *n.* rectangular column, esp. one projecting from a wall. □□ **pi•las′ tered** *adj.*

pil•chard /pílchərd/ *n.* small marine fish, of the herring family (see SARDINE).

pile[1] /pīl/ • *n.* **1** heap of things piled or gathered upon one another (*a pile of leaves*). **2** large imposing building (*a stately pile*). **3** *colloq.* large quantity. **b** large amount of money. • *v.* **1** *tr.* **a** heap up. **b** load. **2** *intr.* crowd hurriedly or tightly. □ **pile it on** *colloq.* exaggerate.
■ *n.* **1** mound, stack, accumulation, stockpile, mass, mountain, collection, assemblage, batch. **3 a** large *or* great amount, a lot, *colloq.* great *or* good deal; (*piles*) ocean(s), lots, masses, stack(s), *colloq.* oodles, tons. **b** fortune, wealth, wad; see also MINT[2] *n.* 2. • *v.* **1** stack (up); mound; accumulate, stockpile, amass, collect; load up. **2** pack in, jam in, crush in, cram into, jump in. □ **pile it on** see EXAGGERATE 1.

pile[2] /pīl/ *n.* heavy support beam driven vertically into the bed of a river, soft ground, etc. □ **pile driver** machine for driving piles into the ground.

pile[3] /pīl/ *n.* soft projecting surface on velvet, plush, etc., or esp. on a carpet; nap.
■ shag, plush; fuzz, down, fleece.

piles /pīlz/ *n.pl. colloq.* hemorrhoids.

pile-up /pílup/ *n.* collision of (esp. several) motor vehicles.

pil•fer /pílfər/ *v.tr.* [also *absol.*] steal (objects) esp. in small quantities. □□ **pil′fer•age** *n.* **pil′fer•er** *n.*
■ rob, plunder, thieve, filch, take, snatch, grab, *colloq.* walk off with, lift; see also APPROPRIATE *v.* 1.

pil•grim /pílgrim/ *n.* **1** person who journeys to a sacred place. **2** traveler. **3** (**Pilgrim**) one of the English Puritans who founded the colony of Plymouth, Massachusetts, in 1620.
■ **1** hajji, *hist.* palmer.

pil•grim•age /pílgrimij/ *n.* **1** pilgrim's journey. **2** any journey taken for nostalgic or sentimental reasons. See synonym study at JOURNEY.
■ **1** hajj, holy expedition. **2** expedition, trek, voyage, tour, trip, excursion.

pill /pil/ *n.* **1 a** solid medicine formed into a ball or a flat disk for swallowing whole.

b [usu. prec. by *the*] *colloq.* contraceptive pill. **2** *sl.* difficult or unpleasant person.

■ **1 a** tablet, capsule, caplet, bolus, pellet, pilule; pastille, lozenge, troche. **2** nuisance, bore, pest, *colloq.* pain (in the neck), crank, drag.

pil•lage /pílij/ • *v.tr.* [also *absol.*] plunder; sack (a place or a person). See synonym study at RAVAGE. • *n.* pillaging, esp. in war. □□ **pil'lag•er** *n.*

■ *v.* raid, ravage, rob, loot, ransack, rifle, maraud, vandalize, *literary* despoil. • *n.* plunder, despoliation, looting, robbery, sack, ransacking.

pil•lar /pílər/ *n.* **1** usu. slender vertical structure of wood, metal, or esp. stone used as a support or for ornament. **2** person regarded as a mainstay or support (*a pillar of strength*). **3** upright mass of air, water, rock, etc. □ **from pillar to post** (driven, etc.) from one place to another; to and fro. □□ **pil'lared** *adj.*

■ **1** column, pilaster, pile, piling, pier, upright, post, shaft, prop. **2** supporter, upholder, backbone, linchpin; leader.

pill•box /pílboks/ *n.* **1** small shallow cylindrical box for holding pills. **2** hat of a similar shape. **3** *Mil.* small partly underground enclosed concrete fort used as an outpost.

pil•lo•ry /pílərее/ • *n.* (*pl.* **–ries**) *hist.* wooden framework with holes for the head and hands, enabling the public to assault or ridicule a person so imprisoned. • *v.tr.* (**–ries**, **–ried**) **1** expose to ridicule. **2** *hist.* put in the pillory.

pil•low /pílō/ • *n.* soft support or cushion, as under the head in sleeping. • *v.tr.* **1** rest on or as if on a pillow. **2** serve as a pillow for (*moss pillowed her head*). □□ **pil'low•y** *adj.*

■ *n.* bolster, pad.

pil•low•case /pílōkays/ *n.* washable cover for a pillow.

pi•lot /pílət/ • *n.* **1** person who operates the flying controls of an aircraft. **2** person qualified to take charge of a ship entering or leaving a harbor. **3** [usu. *attrib.*] experimental undertaking or test (*a pilot project*). **4** guide. • *v.tr.* **1** act as a pilot on (a ship) or of (an aircraft). **2** conduct, lead, or initiate as a pilot (*piloted the new scheme*). □ **pilot light** small gas burner kept alight to light another. □□ **pi'lot•age** *n.* **pi'lot•less** *adj.*

■ *n.* **1** captain, aviator, aviatrix, airman, airwoman, *colloq.* flyer. **2** steersman, helmsman, navigator, wheelsman. **3** see TRIAL 2. **4** leader, cicerone, conductor; see also GUIDE *n.* 1–2. • *v.* steer, navigate, drive; fly; guide, run, control; see also DIRECT *v.* 1.

pi•lot•house /pílət-hows/ *n.* enclosed area on a vessel for the helmsman, etc.

pi•mien•to /piméntō, pímyéntō/ *n.* (also **pimen'to**) red, ripe bell pepper.

pimp /pimp/ • *n.* man who lives off the earnings of a prostitute or a brothel; pander. • *v.intr.* act as a pimp.

■ *n.* procurer. • *v.* procure.

pim•ple /pímpəl/ *n.* **1** small hard inflamed spot on the skin. **2** anything resembling a pimple, esp. in relative size. □□ **pim'pled** *adj.* **pim'ply** *adj.*

625

pillage ~ pinch

■ **1** pustule, papula, blackhead, pock, *Med.* comedo, *colloq.* whitehead, *sl.* zit; boil, swelling.

PIN /pin/ *n.* personal identification number.

pin /pin/ • *n.* **1 a** small thin pointed piece of esp. steel wire used (esp. in sewing) for holding things in place, attaching one thing to another, etc. **b** small brooch (*diamond pin*). **c** badge fastened with a pin. **2** peg of wood or metal for various purposes. • *v.tr.* (**pinned**, **pin•ning**) **1 a** fasten with a pin or pins (*pinned up the hem*). **b** transfix with a pin, lance, etc. **2** [usu. foll. by *on*] fix (blame, responsibility, etc.) on a person, etc. **3** seize and hold fast. □ **pin down 1** bind (a person, etc.) to a promise, arrangement, etc. **2** force (a person) to declare his or her intentions. **3** restrict the actions or movement of (an enemy, etc.). **4** specify (a thing) precisely. **pin money** very small sum of money, esp. for spending on inessentials. **pins and needles** tingling sensation in a limb recovering from numbness.

■ *n.* **1a, 2** tack, nail, dowel, bolt, thole, spike, rivet, stud; thumbtack. **1 b, c** clip; tiepin, stickpin. • *v.* **1** secure, tack, hold, staple, clip; attach, fix, affix, stick; see also TRANSFIX 1. **2** blame, hold responsible *or* accountable, point the finger at, accuse. **pin down 1** keep, hold, commit, oblige. **3** confine, hold (down), immobilize, tie down, constrain. **4** pinpoint, name, identify, determine. **pin money** pocket money, spending money; *colloq.* peanuts.

pi•na co•la•da /peenə kəláadə/ *n.* (also **pi•ña co•la•da** /peenyə/) drink made from pineapple juice, rum, and cream of coconut.

pin•a•fore /pínəfawr/ *n.* woman's sleeveless, wraparound, washable covering for the clothes, tied at the back.

pi•ña•ta /peenyáatə/ *n.* decorated container, often of papier mâché, filled with toys, candy, etc., that is used in a game in which attempts are made to break it open with a stick.

pin•ball /pínbawl/ *n.* game in which small metal balls are shot across a board and score points by striking pins with lights, etc.

pince-nez /pánsnáy, píns-/ *n.* (*pl.* same) pair of eyeglasses with a nose clip instead of earpieces.

pin•cers /pínsərz/ *n.pl.* **1** (also **pair of pincers**) gripping tool resembling scissors but with blunt usu. concave jaws. **2** front claws of lobsters and some other crustaceans.

■ **1** pliers, nippers, tweezers.

pinch /pinch/ • *v.* **1** *tr.* a grip tightly, esp. between finger and thumb. **b** [often *absol.*] (of a shoe, garment, etc.) constrict painfully. **2** *tr.* (of cold, hunger, etc.) grip painfully (*she was pinched with cold*). **3** *tr. sl.* a steal. **b** arrest. • *n.* **1** act of pinching. **2** small amount (*pinch of snuff*). **3** stress or pain caused by poverty, cold, hunger, etc. □ **in a pinch** in an emergency; if necessary. **pinch-hit 1** *Baseball* bat instead of another player. **2** fill in as a substitute, esp. at the last minute.

■ *v.* **1** squeeze, nip, tweak, compress,

constrict, crush. **3 a** thieve, rob, take, shoplift, filch, pilfer, snatch, grab, *colloq.* lift, swipe; see also APPROPRIATE[1] *v.* 1. **b** apprehend, take into custody, collar, *colloq.* run in, bust, *sl.* nab. • *n.* **1** squeeze, nip, tweak, twinge. **2** see BIT 1, DASH *n.* 6. □ **in a pinch** in a predicament *or* crisis *or* difficulty, in a ticklish *or* delicate situation, *colloq.* in a pickle *or* jam *or* scrape; if required *or* needed, if all else fails, *faute de mieux.*

pin•cush•ion /pínkŏoshən/ *n.* small cushion for holding pins.

pine[1] /pīn/ *n.* **1** evergreen tree native to northern temperate regions, with needle-shaped leaves. **2** soft timber of this. □ **pine cone** cone-shaped fruit of the pine tree. □□ **pin'er•y** *n.* (*pl.* **-ies**).

pine[2] /pīn/ *v.intr.* **1** decline or waste away, esp. from grief, disease, etc. **2** long eagerly; yearn.

pin•e•al /píneeəl, pī-/ *adj.* shaped like a pine cone. □ **pineal gland** (or **body**) pea-sized conical mass of tissue in the brain, secreting a hormonelike substance.

pine•ap•ple /pínapəl/ *n.* **1** tropical plant with a spiral of sword-shaped leaves and a thick stem bearing a large fruit developed from many flowers. **2** fruit of this, consisting of yellow flesh surrounded by a tough segmented skin.

ping /ping/ • *n.* single short high ringing sound. • *v.intr.* **1** make a ping. **2** = KNOCK 5.

Ping-Pong /píngpong/ *n. propr.* = *table tennis.*

pin•head /pínhed/ *n.* **1** flattened head of a pin. **2** very small thing. **3** *colloq.* stupid or foolish person.

pin•hole /pínhōl/ *n.* hole made by or for a pin.

pin•ion[1] /pínyən/ • *n.* outer part of a bird's wing. • *v.tr.* **1** cut off the pinion of (a wing or bird) to prevent flight. **2** bind the arms of (a person).

pin•ion[2] /pínyən/ *n.* **1** small toothed gear engaging with a larger one. **2** toothed spindle engaging with a wheel.

pink[1] /pingk/ • *n.* **1** pale red color (*decorated in pink*). **2** cultivated plant with sweet-smelling white, pink, crimson, etc., flowers. **3** [prec. by *the*] most perfect condition, etc. (*the pink of health*). • *adj.* **1** [often in *comb.*] of a pale red color. **2** esp. *derog.* tending to socialism. □ **in the pink** *colloq.* in very good health. **pink slip** notice of layoff or termination from one's job. □□ **pink'ish** *adj.* **pink'ly** *adv.* **pink'ness** *n.* **pink'y** *adj.*

■ *adj.* **1** rosy, rose, rose-colored, pinkish, flesh-colored, flesh, salmon, carnation. **2** socialist, left, left-wing, bolshie, *colloq.* 'red. □ **in the pink** at one's best, healthy, (hale and) hearty, in the best of health.

pink[2] /pingk/ *v.tr.* **1** pierce. **2** cut a scalloped or zigzag edge on. □ **pinking shears** (or **scissors**) dressmaker's serrated shears for cutting a zigzag edge.

pin•na•cle /pínəkəl/ *n.* **1** culmination or climax. **2** natural peak. **3** ornamental turret usu. ending in a pyramid or cone, crowning a buttress, roof, etc.

■ **1** peak, apex, acme, summit, zenith, crowning point. **2** top, summit, tip, cap, crest, crown.

pin•nate /pínayt/ *adj.* (of a compound leaf) having leaflets arranged on either side of the stem. □□ **pin'nat•ed** *adj.* **pin'nate•ly** *adv.* **pin•na•tion** /-náyshən/ *n.*

pin•point /pínpoynt/ • *n.* **1** point of a pin. **2** something very small or sharp. • *v.tr.* locate with precision.

pin•prick /pínprik/ *n.* **1** prick caused by a pin. **2** trifling irritation.

pin•stripe /pínstrīp/ *n.* **1** very narrow stripe in cloth. **2** fabric or garment with this.

pint /pīnt/ *n.* measure of capacity for liquids, one half of a quart or 16 fluid ounces (.41 liter). □ **pint-sized** (also **pint-size**) *colloq.* very small, esp. of a person.

pin•up /pínup/ *n.* **1** photograph of a movie star, etc., for display. **2** person in such a photograph.

pin•wheel /pínhweel/ *n.* **1** fireworks device that whirls and emits colored fire. **2** stick with vanes that twirl in the wind.

Pin•yin /pínyin/ *n.* system of romanized spelling for transliterating Chinese.

pi•o•neer /pīəneer/ • *n.* **1** initiator of a new enterprise, inventor, etc. **2** explorer or settler; colonist. • *v.* **1 a** *tr.* initiate or originate (an enterprise, etc.). **b** *intr.* act or prepare the way as a pioneer. **2** *tr. Mil.* open up (a road, etc.) as a pioneer. **3** *tr.* go before, lead, or conduct.

■ *n.* **1** groundbreaker, innovator, leader, trendsetter, pacemaker, pacesetter, trailblazer. **2** pathfinder, frontiersman, trailblazer; navigator, conquistador. • *v.* **1** create, invent, take the first step in, introduce, institute, inaugurate. **3** see LEAD[1] *v.* 1.

pi•ous /pīəs/ *adj.* **1** devout; religious. **2** hypocritically virtuous; sanctimonious. □□ **pi'ous•ly** *adv.* **pi'ous•ness** *n.*

■ **1** reverent, God-fearing, godly, faithful, holy, dedicated, devoted, spiritual, moral, good, virtuous. **2** hypocritical, sanctimonious, self-righteous, pharisaic, *colloq.* goody-goody.

pip[1] /pip/ *n.* seed of an apple, pear, orange, grape, etc.

pip[2] /pip/ *n.* any of the spots on playing cards, dice, or dominos.

pipe /pīp/ • *n.* **1** tube used to convey water, gas, etc. **2 a** (also **tobacco pipe**) narrow wooden or clay, etc., tube with a bowl at one end containing burning tobacco, etc., for smoking. **b** quantity of tobacco held by this. **3** *Mus.* **a** wind instrument consisting of a single tube. **b** any of the tubes by which sound is produced in an organ. **c** [in *pl.*] = BAGPIPES. **4** tubal organ, vessel, etc., in an animal's body. • *v.tr.* **1** [also *absol.*] play (a tune, etc.) on a pipe or pipes. **2** convey (oil, water, gas, etc.) by pipes. **3** transmit (music, a radio program, etc.) by wire or cable. □ **pipe cleaner** piece of flexible covered wire for cleaning a tobacco pipe. **pipe down** *colloq.* be quiet or less insistent. **pipe organ** *Mus.* organ using pipes instead of or as well as reeds. □□ **pipe'ful** *n.* (*pl.* **-fuls**). **pipe'less** *adj.*

■ n. 1 duct, hose, line, main, conduit, pipeline, channel. 2 a brier, meerschaum, chibouk; hookah, narghile, calumet. • v. 1 tootle, skirl, whistle. 2 transmit, deliver, channel, conduct. 3 see BROADCAST v. 1. □ **pipe down** quiet down, make less noise, tone (it) down, hush (up), shush, *colloq.* shut up.

pipe dream /píp dreem/ n. unattainable or fanciful hope or scheme.

pipe•fit•ter /pípfitər/ n. person who installs and repairs pipes.

pipe•fit•ting /pípfiting/ n. 1 coupling, elbow, etc., used as a connector in a pipe system. 2 work of a pipefitter.

pipe•line /píplīn/ n. 1 long, usu. underground, pipe for conveying esp. oil. 2 channel supplying goods, information, etc. □ **in the pipeline** awaiting completion or processing.

■ 1 tube, duct, hose, line, main, conduit, passage, channel. □ **in the pipeline** on the way, under way, in preparation, in the offing, ready, imminent, coming.

pi•pette /pīpét/ n. slender tube for transferring or measuring small quantities of liquids.

pip•ing /píping/ n. 1 thin pipelike fold used to edge hems or frills on clothing, seams on upholstery, etc. 2 lengths of pipe, or a system of pipes, esp. in domestic use. □ **piping hot** very or suitably hot (esp. as required of food, water, etc.).

pip•it /pípit/ n. small bird resembling a lark.

pip•pin /pípin/ n. type of apple.

pip•squeak /pípskweek/ n. *colloq.* insignificant or contemptible person or thing.

pi•quant /péekənt, háant, peekáant/ adj. 1 agreeably pungent, sharp, or appetizing. 2 pleasantly stimulating, or disquieting, to the mind. □□ **pi′quan•cy** n. **pi′quant•ly** adv.

■ 1 see PUNGENT 1. 2 keen, acute, intense, incisive, sharp, stinging, pointed, piercing; see also *stimulating* (STIMULATE), WITTY. □□ **piquancy** see SPICE n. 2.

pique /peek/ • v.tr. (**piques, piqued, piquing**) 1 wound the pride of; irritate. 2 arouse (curiosity, interest, etc.). • n. ill-feeling; enmity; resentment (*in a fit of pique*).

pi•ra•cy /pírəsee/ n. (pl. **–cies**) 1 practice or an act of robbery of ships at sea. 2 similar practice or act in other forms, esp. hijacking. 3 infringement of copyright.

■ 3 see PLAGIARISM 1.

pi•ra•nha /piraánə, –ránə, raányə, –rányə/ n. freshwater predatory fish native to S. America.

pi•rate /pírət/ • n. 1 a person who commits piracy. b ship used by pirates. 2 person who infringes another's copyright or other business rights. • v.tr. reproduce (the work or ideas, etc., of another) without permission. □□ **pi•rat•ic** /–rátik/ adj. **pi•rat•i•cal** adj. **pi•rat′i•cal•ly** adv.

■ n. 1 a buccaneer, rover, corsair, freebooter, sea robber, picaroon. 2 plagiarist, plagiarizer, infringer. • v. plagiarize, copy, steal, appropriate, poach.

pir•ou•ette /pírooét/ • n. dancer's spin on one foot or the point of the toe. • v.intr. perform a pirouette.

■ n. whirl, twirl, turn, revolution. • v. spin, whirl, twirl, turn (around), revolve, pivot.

pis•ca•to•ry /pískətawree/ adj. of fishermen or fishing.

■ piscatorial, fishy, piscine, fishlike.

Pi•sces /píseez/ n. 1 constellation and twelfth sign of the zodiac (the Fishes). 2 person born when the sun is in this sign.

pis•tach•i•o /pistásheeō, –staásheeō/ n. 1 tree bearing small brownish green flowers and ovoid reddish fruit. 2 (in full **pis•tach•i•o nut**) edible pale green seed of this.

pis•til /pístil/ n. female organs of a flower, comprising the stigma, style, and ovary. □□ **pis′til•late** /–lət, –lāyt/ adj.

pis•tol /pístəl/ n. small hand-held firearm. □ **pistol-whip** (**-whipped, -whip•ping**) beat with a pistol.

■ gun, handgun, revolver, six-shooter, *colloq.* shooting iron, *sl.* piece, Saturday night special, gat.

pis•ton /pístən/ n. disk or short cylinder fitting closely within a tube in which it moves up and down, as in an internal combustion engine, pump, etc. □ **piston ring** sealing ring on a piston. **piston rod** rod attached to a piston to impart motion.

pit¹ /pit/ • n. 1 usu. large deep hole in the ground. 2 hollow or indentation on a surface. 3 *Theatr.* = orchestra pit. 4 (**the pits**) *sl.* wretched or the worst imaginable place, situation, person, etc. 5 area at the side of a track where racing cars are serviced and refueled. • v.tr. (**pit•ted, pit•ting**) 1 [usu. foll. by *against*] set (one's wits, strength, etc.) in opposition or rivalry. 2 (usu. as **pitted** adj.) make pits, esp. scars, in. □ **pit bull (terrier)** strong, compact breed of American dog noted for its ferocity. **pit stop 1** brief stop at the pit by a racing car for servicing or refueling. **2** *colloq.* stop, as during a long journey, for food, rest, etc.

■ n. 1 shaft, cavity, mine, well, mine shaft, quarry, working, abyss, chasm, crater. 2 depression, dent, dimple, pockmark, pock. 4 (**the pits**) lowest of the low, rock bottom; the worst, awful, terrible, *sl.* lousy. • v. 1 match; see also OPPOSE 1, 2. 2 dent, pockmark, scar; (**pitted**) pockmarked, defaced, marred, marked.

pit² /pit/ • n. stone of a fruit. • v.tr. (**pit•ted, pit•ting**) remove pits from (fruit)

■ n. see STONE n. 1.

pi•ta /péetə/ n. (also **pit′ta**) flat, hollow, unleavened bread that can be split and filled.

pit-a-pat /pítəpát/ /pítəpátər/ • adv. 1 with a sound like quick light steps. 2 with a faltering sound (*heart went pit-a-pat*). • n. such a sound.

pitch¹ /pich/ • v. 1 tr. [also *absol.*] erect and fix (a tent, camp, etc.). 2 tr. throw. 3 tr. express in a particular style or at a particular level. 4 tr. fall heavily, esp. headlong. 5 intr. (of a ship, aircraft, etc.) plunge in a longitudinal direction (cf. ROLL v. 5a). 6 a tr. *Baseball* deliver (the ball) to the batter. b intr. *Baseball* play at the position of pitcher. • n. 1 height, degree, intensity, etc. (*the pitch* *of despair*). **2** degree of a slope, esp. of a roof. **3** *Mus.* that quality of a sound which is governed by the rate of vibrations producing it; degree of highness or lowness of a tone. **4** pitching motion of a ship, etc. **5** delivery of a baseball by a pitcher. **6** *colloq.* salesman's advertising or selling approach. □ **pitched battle 1** vigorous argument, etc. **2** *Mil.* battle planned beforehand and fought on chosen ground. **pitched roof** sloping roof. **pitch in** *colloq.* **1** set to work vigorously. **2** assist; cooperate.

■ *v.* **1** raise, set *or* put up, position, place. **2** toss, cast, fling, hurl, sling, fire, launch, shoot, send, let fly, lob, *colloq.* chuck. **3** see DIRECT *v.* 4. **4** plunge, dive, drop, plummet, (take a) nosedive. **5** toss about, lurch, go head over heels. ■ *n.* **1** see HEIGHT 6. **2** see SLANT *n.* 1. □ **pitched battle 1** see ARGUMENT 1. **pitch in 1** see SHOULDER *v.* 2. **2** contribute, help, *colloq.* chip in.

pitch² /pich/ • *n.* sticky resinous black or dark brown substance obtained by distilling tar or turpentine, used for caulking the seams of ships, etc. • *v.tr.* coat or smear with pitch. □ **pitch-black** (or **-dark**) very or completely dark.

■ *n.* tar, bitumen, asphalt. • *adj.* **pitch-black** (or **-dark**) black, ebony, inky, coal-black, sooty, jet-black, raven, *esp. poet.* sable; unlit, unlighted, moonless.

pitch•blende /píchblend/ *n.* mineral form of uranium oxide occurring in pitchlike masses and yielding radium.

pitch•er¹ /píchər/ *n.* large jug with a lip and a handle, for holding liquids. □□ **pitch′er•ful** *n.* (*pl.* **-fuls**).

■ see JUG *n.* 1.

pitch•er² /píchər/ *n.* **1** person or thing that pitches. **2** *Baseball* player who delivers the ball to the batter.

pitch•fork /píchfawrk/ *n.* long-handled two-pronged fork for pitching hay, etc.

pitch•man /píchmən/ *n.* **1** salesperson. **2** person who sells goods from a portable stand, as at a fair or on the street.

pit•e•ous /píteeəs/ *adj.* deserving or causing pity; wretched. □□ **pit′e•ous•ly** *adv.* **pit′e•ous•ness** *n.*

■ pitiable, pathetic, pitiful, plaintive, miserable, heartrending, poignant, distressing, grievous, heartbreaking, moving, painful; mournful, sad, doleful.

pit•fall /pítfawl/ *n.* **1** unsuspected snare, danger, or drawback. **2** covered pit for trapping animals, etc.

■ **1** peril, hazard, catch, difficulty, snag; trap. **2** trap.

pith /pith/ *n.* **1** spongy white tissue lining the rind of an orange, lemon, etc. **2** essential part. **3** *Bot.* spongy cellular tissue in the stems and branches of plants. **4 a** physical strength; vigor. **b** force; energy. □□ **pith′less** *adj.*

■ **2** core, heart, kernel, nucleus, crux, focus, focal point, essence, meat, marrow. **4** see VIGOR 1.

pith•y /píthee/ *adj.* (**pith•i•er, pith•i•est**)

1 (of style, speech, etc.) condensed, terse, and forceful. **2** of, like, or containing much pith. See synonym study at TERSE. □□ **pith′i•ly** *adv.* **pith′i•ness** *n.*

pit•i•a•ble /píteeəbəl/ *adj.* **1** deserving or causing pity. **2** contemptible. □□ **pit′i•a•ble•ness** *n.* **pit′i•a•bly** *adv.*

pit•i•ful /pitifool/ *adj.* **1** causing pity. **2** contemptible. □□ **pit′i•ful•ly** *adv.* **pit′i•ful•ness** *n.*

■ **1** see PITEOUS. **2** beggarly, sorry, mean; small, little, insignificant, trifling, pathetic.

pit•i•less /pitilis/ *adj.* showing no pity (*pitiless heat of the desert*). □□ **pit′i•less•ly** *adv.*

pi•ton /péeton/ *n.* peg or spike driven into a rock or crack to support a climber or a rope.

pit•tance /pít′ns/ *n.* **1** scanty or meager allowance, remuneration, etc. **2** small number or amount.

■ **2** *colloq.* peanuts, chicken feed, small potatoes.

pit•ter-pat•ter var. of PIT-A-PAT.

pi•tu•i•tar•y /pitōō-iteree, -tyōō-/ *n.* (*pl.* **-ies**) (also **pi•tu′i•tar•y gland** or **body**) small ductless gland at the base of the brain.

pit•y /pítee/ • *n.* (*pl.* **-ies**) **1** sorrow and compassion aroused by another's condition (*felt pity for the child*). **2** grounds for regret (*what a pity!*). • *v.tr.* (**-ies, -ied**) feel pity for. □□ **pit′y•ing** *adj.* **pit′y•ing•ly** *adv.*

■ *n.* **1** sympathy; commiseration, condolence. **2** (crying) shame; disgrace, sin, sacrilege, *colloq.* crime. • *v.* sympathize with, feel for, commiserate with, feel sorry for, bleed for, weep for, be moved by.

piv•ot /pívət/ • *n.* **1** short shaft or pin on which something turns or oscillates. **2** crucial or essential person, point, etc. • *v.* **1** *intr.* turn on or as if on a pivot. **2** *intr.* hinge on; depend on. **3** *tr.* provide with a pivot. □□ **piv′ot•al** *adj.*

■ *n.* **1** fulcrum, pintle, gudgeon, hinge, swivel, kingpin, spindle. **2** center, heart, hub, crux; see also KEYSTONE. • *v.* **1** rotate, revolve, spin, twirl, whirl, swivel; see also TURN *v.* 1. **2** hang, rely; revolve around. □□ **pivotal** critical, central, focal, crucial, significant.

pix•el /píksəl/ *n.* *Electronics* any of the minute dots, etc., that comprise an image on a display screen.

pix•ie /píksee/ *n.* (also **pix′y**) (*pl.* **-ies**) a being like a fairy.

piz•za /péetsə/ *n.* flat round base of dough baked with a topping of tomatoes, cheese, onions, etc.

piz•ze•ri•a /péetsəréeə/ *n.* place where pizzas are made or sold.

piz•zi•ca•to /pítsikaátō/ *Mus.* • *adv.* plucking the strings of a violin, etc., with the finger. • *adj.* (of a note, passage, etc.) performed pizzicato.

pkg. *abbr.* (also **pkge.**) package.

pl. *abbr.* **1** plural. **2** place. **3** plate. **4** esp. *Mil.* platoon.

plac•ard /plákaard, -kərd/ • *n.* large poster, esp. for advertising. • *v.tr.* set up placards on (a wall, etc.).

pla•cate /pláykayt, plák-/ *v.tr.* pacify; conciliate. See synonym study at PACIFY. □□ **pla′cat·ing·ly** *adv.* **pla·ca′tion** /–áyshən/ *n.* **pla′ca·to·ry** /–kətawree/ *adj.*

■ see CALM *v.* □□ **placation** conciliation, appeasement, propitiation, pacification. **placatory** see PROPITIATORY.

place /plays/ • *n.* **1 a** a particular portion of space. **b** portion of space occupied by a person or thing. **c** proper or natural position (*take your places*). **2** city, town, village, etc. (*was born in this place*). **3** residence; dwelling. **4** rank; status. **5** space, esp. a seat, for a person (*two places in the coach*). **6** building or area for a specific purpose (*fireplace*). **7** point reached in a book, etc. (*lost my place*). **8** particular spot on a surface, esp. of the skin (*sore place on his wrist*). **9** employment or office. **10** position; rank; prerogative. **11** second finishing position, esp. in a horse race. **12** position of a number in a series indicated in decimal or similar notation. • *v.tr.* **1** put (a thing, etc.) in a particular place or state; arrange. **2** identify, classify, or remember correctly. **3** assign to a particular place; locate. **4** find a job, clerical post, etc., for. **5** assign rank, importance, or worth to. **6** make (an order for goods, etc.). **7** (as **placed** *adj.*) second in a race. □ **go places** *colloq.* be successful. **in place of** in exchange for; instead of. **place mat** small mat on a table underneath a person's plate. **place-name** name of a geographic location, as a city, town, hill, lake, etc. **place setting** set of plates, silverware, etc., for one person at a meal. **put a person in his** or **her place** deflate or humiliate a person. **take place** occur. **take the place of** be substituted for; replace. □□ **place′less** *adj.* **place′ment** *n.*

■ *n.* **1 a, b** location, site, position, point, spot, locus, area, locale, scene, setting. **2** locale, area, neighborhood, vicinity, district, section, quarter, region; hamlet. **3** home, house, flat, apartment, room(s), quarters, lodgings. **4** station, standing, grade, position, niche, slot, situation. **5** chair, position, spot. **9** position, job, post, appointment, situation, *colloq.* billet, berth; occupation. • *v.* **1** put (out), position, dispose, order, set (out), lay, lodge, deposit, *colloq.* stick. **2** put one's finger on; recall, recognize; see IDENTIFY 1, 2. **3** station, post; see also SITUATE *v.* **4** see APPOINT 1. **5** class, classify, rank, group, categorize, bracket, grade; regard, view, see. □ **go places** succeed, get ahead, advance, prosper, thrive, flourish. **in place of** in lieu of. **put a person in his** or **her place** humble, mortify, bring down, squelch. **take place** happen, go on, come about; arise; see also OCCUR 1. **take the place of** see REPLACE 2. □□ **placement** arrangement, placing, position, distribution, array, disposition, deployment, positioning, stationing; employment, appointment.

pla·ce·bo /pləseebō/ *n.* **1 a** pill, medicine, etc., prescribed more for psychological reasons than for any physiological effect. **b** placebo used as a control in testing new drugs, etc.

pla·cen·ta /pləséntə/ *n.* (*pl.* **pla·cen·tae** /–tee/ or **pla·cen·tas**) organ in the uterus of

pregnant mammals that nourishes and maintains the fetus. □□ **pla·cen′tal** *adj.*

plac·er /plásər/ *n.* deposit of sand, gravel, etc., in the bed of a stream, etc., containing valuable minerals in particles.

plac·id /plásid/ *adj.* **1** (of a person) not easily aroused or disturbed; peaceful. **2** mild; calm; serene. See synonym study at CALM. □□ **pla·cid·i·ty** /pləsíditee/ *n.* **plac′id·ly** *adv.* **plac′id·ness** *n.*

plack·et /plákit/ *n.* opening or slit in a garment.

pla·gia·rism /pláyjərizəm/ *n.* **1** plagiarizing. **2** something plagiarized. □□ **pla′gia·rist** *n.* **pla·gia·ris′tic** *adj.*

■ **1** plagiary, piracy, theft, stealing, appropriation, thievery, usurpation. **2** borrowing, *colloq.* crib.

pla·gia·rize /pláyjəriz/ *v.tr.* [also *absol.*] **1** take and use (the thoughts, writings, inventions, etc., of another person) as one's own. **2** pass off the thoughts, etc., of (another person) as one's own. □□ **pla′gia·riz·er** *n.*

plague /playg/ • *n.* **1** deadly contagious disease. **2** unusual infestation of a pest, etc. (*a plague of frogs*). **3 a** great trouble. **b** affliction. • *v.tr.* (**plagues**, **plagued**, **plagu·ing**) **1** affect with plague. **2** *colloq.* pester or harass continually. □□ **plague′some** *adj.*

■ *n.* **1** epidemic, pestilence, pandemic. **3** scourge, misfortune, curse, bane, calamity, evil, blight, adversity. • *v.* **2** badger, harry, hound, bother, vex, nag.

plaid /plad/ *n.* **1** any cloth with a tartan pattern. **2** this pattern. □□ **plaid′ed** *adj.*

plain /playn/ • *adj.* **1** clear; evident (*is plain to see*). **2** readily understood; simple (*in plain words*). **3** uncomplicated; unembellished; simple. **4** (esp. of a woman or girl) not good-looking; homely. **5** straightforward. • *adv.* **1** clearly. **2** simply (*that is plain stupid*). • *n.* level tract of treeless country. □□ **plain′ly** *adv.* **plain′ness** *n.*

■ *adj.* **1, 2** distinct, crystal clear, lucid, vivid, transparent, apparent, obvious, patent, self-evident, manifest, unmistakable, unequivocal. **3** unadorned, undecorated, unostentatious, unpretentious, homely, basic, austere, stark; see also SIMPLE *adj.* 2. **4** unattractive, ordinary-looking, unlovely, ugly. **5** open, honest, forthright, plainspoken, direct, frank, candid, blunt, outspoken, unreserved, sincere. • *adv.* **1** see clearly (CLEAR). **2** see SIMPLY 2. • *n.* prairie, grassland, pasture, meadowland, pampas, llano, savanna, steppe, tundra; heath, wold, moor, moorland; plateau, tableland, mesa.

plain·clothes·man /playnklôzmən, klôthz–, –man/ *n.* police officer who wears civilian clothes while on duty.

plain·song /pláynsawng, –song/ *n.* unaccompanied church music sung in unison in medieval modes and in free rhythm.

plaint /playnt/ *n. literary* complaint; lamentation.

plain·tiff /pláyntif/ *n. Law* person who brings a case against another into court (opp. DEFENDANT).

plaint•ive /pláyntiv/ *adj.* **1** expressing sorrow; mournful. **2** mournful-sounding. □□ **plain′tive•ly** *adv.* **plaint′ive•ness** *n.*

plait /playt, plat/ • *n.* **1** = BRAID 2. **2** = PLEAT.
• *v.tr.* = BRAID.
■ *n.* **1** braid, pigtail. • *v.* see BRAID *v.*

plan /plan/ • *n.* **1** method or procedure by which a thing is to be done; design or scheme. **2** drawing or diagram of a structure. **3** map of a town or district. • *v.* **(planned, plan•ning) 1** *tr.* arrange (a procedure, etc.) beforehand; form a plan. **2** *tr.* **a** design (a building, new town, etc.). **b** make a plan of (an existing building, an area, etc.). **3** *tr.* (as **planned** *adj.*) in accordance with a plan. **4** *intr.* make plans. See synonym study at INTEND. □□ **plan′ner** *n.* **plan′ ning** *n.*
■ *n.* **1** system, arrangement, program, project, formula, pattern; see also DESIGN *n.* 1, INTENTION 1. **2** sketch, design, layout, blueprint, chart, map. • *v.* **1** intend, expect, aim, contrive, devise; envisage, envision, foresee, contemplate, propose; see also ARRANGE 2, 3. **2** see DESIGN *v.* 1.

plane[1] /playn/ • *n.* **1** flat surface on which a straight line joining any two points on it would wholly lie. **2** level surface. **3** *colloq.* = AIRPLANE. **4** level of attainment, thought, knowledge, etc. • *adj.* **1** (of a surface, etc.) perfectly level. **2** (of an angle, figure, etc.) lying in a plane.
■ *n.* **2** flat. **3** aircraft, airliner, jet (plane). **4** see DEGREE 1. • *adj.* **1** flat, even, horizontal; smooth.

plane[2] /playn/ • *n.* tool used to smooth a usu. wooden surface by paring shavings from it.
• *v.tr.* smooth (wood, metal, etc.) with a plane.

plane[3] /playn/ *n.* (in full **plane tree**) tree with maple-like leaves and bark which peels in uneven patches.

plan•et /plánit/ *n.* **1** celestial body moving in an elliptical orbit around a star. **2** the earth. □□ **plan•e•tar•y** *adj.* **plan•e•tol•o•gy** /-tóləjee/ *n.*

plan•e•tar•i•um /plánitáireeəm/ *n.* (*pl.* **plan• e•tar•i•ums** or **plan•e•tar•i•a** /-reeə/) **1** domed building in which images of stars, planets, constellations, etc., are projected for public entertainment or education. **2** device for such projection.

plan•gent /plánjənt/ *adj.* **1** (of a sound) loud and reverberating. **2** (of a sound) plaintive; sad. □□ **plan′gen•cy** *n.*

plank /plangk/ • *n.* **1** long flat piece of timber used esp. in building, flooring, etc. **2** item of a political or other program. • *v.tr.* **1** provide, cover, or floor, with planks. **2** *colloq.* **a** put (a thing, person, etc.) down roughly or violently. **b** pay (money) on the spot or abruptly.
■ *n.* **1** board, slab. • *v.* **2 a** slap, slam, dump, fling, toss, throw, sling.

plank•ing /plángking/ *n.* planks as flooring, etc.

plank•ton /plángktən/ *n.* chiefly microscopic organisms drifting or floating in the sea or fresh water. □□ **plank•ton•ic** /-tónik/ *adj.*

plant /plant/ • *n.* **1 a** living organism usu. containing chlorophyll enabling it to live wholly on inorganic substances and lacking specialized sense organs and the power of voluntary movement. **b** small organism of this kind, as distinguished from a shrub or tree. **2 a** machinery, fixtures, etc., used in industrial processes. **b** factory. • *v.tr.* **1** place (a seed, bulb, or growing thing) in the ground so that it may take root and flourish. **2** put or fix in position. **3** cause (an idea, etc.) to be established esp. in another person's mind. **4** deliver (a blow, kiss, etc.) with a deliberate aim. **5** *colloq.* position or conceal (something incriminating or compromising) for later discovery. □□ **plant′a•ble** *adj.* **plant′let** *n.* **plant′like** *adj.*
■ *n.* **2 a** apparatus; gear; see also EQUIPMENT[2]. **b** mill, works, workshop. • *v.* **1** bed (out), sow, seed, set (out). **2** place, position, station, situate, set (out), *colloq.* stick. **3** implant, establish, root, fix, ingrain, lodge, sow, instill, insinuate, introduce, impress, imprint. **5** hide; see also SECRETE.

plan•tain[1] /plántin/ *n.* **1** kind of banana plant widely grown for its fruit. **2** starchy fruit of this.

plan•ta•tion /plantáyshən/ *n.* **1** estate on which cotton, tobacco, etc., is cultivated. **2** area planted with trees, etc.

plant•er /plántər/ *n.* **1** manager or occupier of a coffee, cotton, etc., plantation. **2** large container for decorative plants.
■ **2** flowerpot, plant pot.

plaque /plak/ *n.* **1** ornamental or commemorative tablet. **2** deposit on teeth where bacteria proliferate.
■ **1** medallion, plate, panel, marker, slab, plaquette.

plas•ma /plázmə/ *n.* (also **plasm** /plázəm/) **1** colorless fluid part of blood, lymph, or milk. **2** = PROTOPLASM. **3** gas of positive ions and free electrons in about equal numbers. □□ **plas•mat•ic** /-mátik/ *adj.* **plas′mic** *adj.*

plas•ter /plástər/ • *n.* **1** soft pliable mixture esp. of lime putty with sand or Portland cement, etc., for spreading on walls, ceilings, etc., to form a smooth hard surface when dried. **2** *hist.* curative or protective substance spread on a bandage, etc., and applied to the body (*mustard plaster*). • *v.tr.* **1** cover (a wall, etc.) with plaster or a similar substance. **2** coat thickly or to excess; bedaub. **3** stick or apply (a thing) thickly like plaster. **4** make (esp. hair) smooth with water, gel, etc. □ **plaster of Paris** fine white plaster made of gypsum and used for making plaster casts, etc. □□ **plas′ter•er** *n.* **plas′ter•y** *adj.*
■ *v.* **2** smear, daub, spread, cover, overlay, smother. **3** smear, daub, spread, spread.

plas•ter•board /plástərbawrd/ *n.* type of board with a center filling of plaster, used for partitions, walls, etc.

plas•tic /plástik/ • *n.* **1** any of a number of synthetic polymeric substances that can be given any required shape. **2** [*attrib.*] made of plastic (*plastic bag*); made of cheap materials. **3** *colloq.* credit card, charge card, etc. • *adj.* capable of being molded; pliant; supple. □ **plastic surgery** process of reconstructing or repairing parts of the body by the transfer of tissue, either in the treatment of injury or for cosmetic reasons. □□ **plas'tic•al•ly** *adv.* **plas•tic'i•ty** /-tísitee/ *n.* **plas•ti•cize** /-tisíz/ *v.tr.* **plas•ti•ci•za'tion** *n.* **plas'ti•ciz•er** *n.*

■ *n.* **2** (*attrib.*) cheap, inferior, worthless, pinchbeck, shoddy, chintzy, gaudy, *colloq.* crummy. • *adj.* moldable, pliable, shapable, soft, waxy, malleable, workable, ductile, flexible.

plate /playt/ • *n.* **1 a** shallow vessel from which food is eaten or served. **b** contents of this. **2** similar vessel used esp. for making a collection in a church, etc. **3** [*collect.*] **a** utensils of silver, gold, or other metal. **b** objects of plated metal. **4 a** a piece of metal with a name or inscription for affixing to a door, container, etc. **b** = *license plate.* **5** illustration on special paper in a book. **6** thin sheet of metal, glass, etc., coated with a sensitive film for photography. **7** flat thin usu. rigid sheet of metal, etc., often part of a mechanism. **8 a** smooth piece of metal, etc., for engraving. **b** impression made from this. **9 a** plastic dental device to hold artificial teeth. **b** *colloq.* denture. **10** *Geol.* each of several rigid sheets of rock thought to form the earth's outer crust. **11** *Baseball* base at which the batter stands and which a runner touches to score. • *v.tr.* **1** apply a thin coat esp. of silver, gold, or tin to (another metal). **2** cover (esp. a ship) with plates of metal, esp. for protection. □ **plate glass** thick fine-quality glass for storefront windows, etc., orig. cast in plates. **plate tectonics** *Geol.* study of the earth's surface based on the concept of moving plates (see sense 10 of *n.*) forming its structure. □□ **plate'ful** *n.* (*pl.* **-fuls**). **plate'less** *adj.* **plat'er** *n.*

■ *n.* **1 a** platter, dish, bowl, *hist.* trencher. **b** plateful, serving, portion, dish, platter. **4 a** see PLAQUE 1. **5** picture, print, vignette. **7** layer, leaf, pane, panel, lamina. • *v.* **1** cover, coat, overlay, face, laminate.

pla•teau /platṓ/ *n.* (*pl.* **pla•teaux** /-tṓz/ or **pla•teaus**) **1** area of fairly level high ground. **2** state of little variation after an increase.

■ **1** tableland, table, upland, plain.

plate•let /pláytlit/ *n.* small colorless disk of protoplasm found in blood and involved in clotting.

plat•en /plát'n/ *n.* **1** plate in a printing press which presses the paper against the type. **2** cylindrical roller in a typewriter against which the paper is held.

plat•form /plátfawrm/ *n.* **1** raised level surface, as for a speaker, for freight loading, etc. **2** declared policy of a political party.

■ **1** stand, dais, stage, podium, rostrum. **2** party line, principle(s), tenet(s), program, manifesto.

plat•i•num /plát'nəm/ *n.* *Chem.* ductile malleable silvery-white metallic element unaffected by simple acids and fusible only at a very high temperature. ¶Symb.: **Pt.**

plat•i•tude /plátitōōd, -tyōōd/ *n.* trite or commonplace remark, esp. one solemnly delivered. □□ **plat•i•tu•di•nize** /-tōōd'nīz,

-tyōō-/ *v.intr.* **plat•i•tu•di•nous** /-tōōdənəs/ *adj.*

■ see CLICHÉ. □□ **platitudinous** see BANAL.

Pla•ton•ic /plətónik/ *adj.* **1** of or associated with the Greek philosopher Plato (d. 347 BC) or his ideas. **2** (**platonic**) (of love or friendship) not sexual. □□ **Pla•ton'i•cal•ly** *adv.*

■ **2** (**platonic**) nonphysical, asexual, nonsexual, chaste, dispassionate, detached, spiritual, friendly.

Pla•to•nism /pláyt'nizəm/ *n.* philosophy of Plato or his followers. □□ **Pla'to•nist** *n.*

pla•toon /plətōōn/ *n.* **1** *Mil.* subdivision of a company. **2** group of persons acting together.

■ company, squad, squadron, group, patrol, team, cadre, body, formation, unit, *colloq.* outfit.

plat•ter /plátər/ *n.* large flat dish or plate, esp. for food.

■ serving dish, server, salver, tray.

plat•y•pus /plátipəs/ *n.* Australian aquatic egg-laying mammal having a pliable ducklike bill. (Also called **duckbill**).

plau•dit /pláwdit/ *n.* [usu. in *pl.*] tribute; applause.

■ see APPLAUSE 1, 2.

plau•si•ble /pláwzibəl/ *adj.* **1** (of an argument, statement, etc.) seeming reasonable or probable. **2** (of a person) persuasive but deceptive. □□ **plau•si•bil'i•ty** *n.* **plau'si•bly** *adv.*

■ **1** likely, believable, cogent, convincing, feasible, credible, creditable, tenable, conceivable. **2** specious, mendacious, misleading, deceitful, casuistic, sophistical, smooth; see also DECEPTIVE.

play /play/ • *v.* **1** *intr.* occupy or amuse oneself pleasantly or idly. **2** *intr.* act lightheartedly or flippantly (with feelings, etc.). **3** *tr.* **a** perform on or be able to perform on (a musical instrument). **b** perform (a piece of music, etc.). **c** cause (a record, radio, etc.) to produce sounds. **4 a** *intr.* perform a role in (a drama, etc.). **b** *tr.* perform (a drama or role) on stage, or in a movie or broadcast. **c** *tr.* give a dramatic performance at (a particular theater or place). **5** *tr.* behave or act as (*play the fool*). **6** *tr.* perform (a trick or joke, etc.) on (a person). **7** *tr.* **a** take part in (a game or recreation). **b** compete with (another player or team) in a game. **c** occupy (a specified position) in a team for a game. **d** assign (a player) to a position. • *n.* **1** recreation or amusement, esp. as the spontaneous activity of children and young animals. **2 a** playing of a game. **b** action or manner of this. **3** dramatic piece for the stage, etc. **4** activity or operation (*brought into play*). **5 a** freedom of movement. **b** space or scope for this. □ **play along** pretend to cooperate. **play around** (or **about**) **1** behave irresponsibly. **2** philander. **play back** play (sounds recently recorded), esp. to monitor recording quality, etc. **play-by-play** *adj.* pertaining to a description, esp. of a sports event, with continuous commentary. *n.* such a description (*he called the play-by-play*). **play down**

minimize the importance of. **played out** exhausted of energy or usefulness. **play for time** seek to gain time by delaying. **play off** [usu. foll. by *against*] **1** oppose (one person against another), esp. for one's own advantage. **2** play an extra match to decide a draw or tie. **play-off** *Sports* game played to break a tie. **play on words** pun. **play up to** flatter, esp. to win favor. **play with fire** take foolish risks. □□ **play'a•ble** *adj.* **play•a•bil'i•ty** *n.*

■ *v.* **1** frolic, caper, sport, have fun. **2** see TOY *v.* 1. **3 c** operate; put *or* turn on. **4 a** act; appear. **b** put on, act, take the role of, appear as. **7 a** join in, participate in, engage in; take up. **b** contend with, compete against, challenge. ■ *n.* **1** frivolity, entertainment, fun; tomfoolery, horseplay. **3** show, production. **4** see OPERATION 1, 2. **5** flexibility, looseness, leeway, room. □ **play along** (*play along with*) go along with; see also OBLIGE 3. **play around** or **about 1** fool around, horse around, act up, misbehave; tease. **2** flirt, be unfaithful; womanize; *colloq.* fool around. **play down** belittle, diminish, make light of, brush off. **played out** see *exhausted* (EXHAUST *v.* 2). **play for time** delay, procrastinate, stall, temporize, hesitate. **play up to** curry favor with, toady to, truckle to, fawn on; see also FLATTER 1. **play with fire** imperil *or* endanger a thing, tempt fate, live dangerously.

play•act /playakt/ *v.* **1** *intr.* act in a play. **2** *intr.* behave affectedly or insincerely. **3** *tr.* act (a scene, part, etc.). □□ **play'act•ing** *n.* **play'ac•tor** *n.*

play•back /playbak/ *n.* act or instance of replaying recorded audio or video from a tape, etc.

play•bill /playbil/ *n.* poster or program for a play.

play•boy /playboy/ *n.* irresponsible pleasure-seeking man.
■ man about town, roué, rake, debauchee, womanizer, Don Juan, Casanova, lothario, lady-killer.

play•er /playər/ *n.* **1** person taking part in a sport or game. **2** person playing a musical instrument. **3** actor.
■ **1** contestant, participant, competitor, contender; athlete, sportswoman, sportsman. **2** musician, instrumentalist, performer. **3** actress, performer, entertainer, trouper, thespian.

play•ful /playfool/ *adj.* **1** fond of or inclined to play. **2** done in fun; humorous; jocular. □□ **play'ful•ly** *adv.* **play'ful•ness** *n.*
■ **1** fun-loving, sportive, gamesome, frolicsome, puppyish. **2** jocose, teasing, tongue-in-cheek.

play•go•er /playgōər/ *n.* person who goes often to the theater.

play•ground /playgrownd/ *n.* outdoor area set aside for play.

play•house /playhows/ *n.* **1** theater. **2** toy house for children to play in.

play•ing card /playing/ *n.* each of a set of usu. 52 rectangular cards, divided into four suits and used to play various games.

play•mate /playmayt/ *n.* child's companion in play.
■ playfellow, friend, *colloq.* pal, buddy; see also CHUM.

play•pen /playpen/ *n.* portable enclosure for young children to play in.

play•thing /plaything/ *n.* toy.
■ game, gewgaw.

play•wright /playrīt/ *n.* person who writes plays.
■ dramatist, dramaturge, scriptwriter, screenwriter.

pla•za /plaazə/ *n.* **1** marketplace or open square (esp. in a town). **2** service and rest area on an expressway.
■ see SQUARE *n.* 2.

plea /plee/ *n.* **1** earnest appeal or entreaty. **2** *Law* formal statement by or on behalf of a defendant. **3** excuse. □ **plea bargain** (or **bargaining**) arrangement between prosecutor and defendant whereby the defendant pleads guilty to a lesser charge in the expectation of leniency.
■ **1** petition, request, supplication, suit, cry, solicitation. **2** answer, defense, argument; case. **3** argument, explanation, justification; pretext; see also EXCUSE *n.* 1, 2.

plead /pleed/ *v.* (*past* and *past part.* **plead•ed** or **pled** /pled/) **1** *intr.* make an earnest appeal. **2** *intr. Law* address a court. **3** *tr.* maintain (a cause) esp. in a court. **4** *tr. Law* declare to be one's state as regards guilt in or responsibility for a crime (*plead guilty, plead insanity*). **5** *tr.* offer or allege as an excuse (*pleaded forgetfulness*). See synonym study at BEG. □□ **plead'a•ble** *adj.* **plead'er** *n.* **plead'ing** *n.* **plead'ing•ly** *adv.*
■ **1** request, entreat, appeal to, petition, apply to, implore, beseech, beg, importune; cry for, ask (for), seek, beg (for). **3** argue, put forward.

pleas•ant /plézənt/ *adj.* (**pleas•ant•er,** **pleas•ant•est**) pleasing to the mind, feelings, or senses. □□ **pleas'ant•ly** *adv.* **pleas'ant•ness** *n.*
■ pleasurable, nice, enjoyable, satisfying, good, lovely, attractive, gratifying, delightful, charming; friendly, affable, amiable, amicable, sweet, companionable.

pleas•ant•ry /plézəntree/ *n.* (*pl.* **–ries**) pleasant or amusing remark, esp. made in casual conversation.

please /pleez/ *v.* **1** *tr.* [also *absol.*] be agreeable to; give pleasure to. **2** *tr.* [in *passive*] **a** be glad or willing to. **b** derive pleasure or satisfaction (from). **3** *intr.* think fit; have the will or desire (*take as many as you please*). **4** *tr.* (short for **may it please you**) used in polite requests (*come in, please*). □ **please oneself** do as one likes. □□ **pleased** *adj.* **pleas'ing** *adj.* **pleas'ing•ly** *adv.*
■ **1** delight, gratify, humor, content, cheer, gladden, amuse. **2 a** be content, be happy, be delighted. **3** like, prefer, choose, desire, want, see fit, wish, will. □□ **pleased** happy, delighted, glad, gratified, satisfied.

pleas•ur•a•ble /plézhərəbəl/ *adj.* causing pleasure; agreeable. □□ **pleas'ur•a•ble•ness** *n.* **pleas'ur•a•bly** *adv.*
■ see PLEASANT.

pleas•ure /pléZHər/ *n.* **1** feeling of satisfaction or joy. **2** enjoyment. **3** source of pleasure or gratification. **4** *formal* a person's will or desire (*what is your pleasure?*). **5** sensual gratification.

■ **1, 2** happiness, delight; fulfillment, contentment, gratification. **3** comfort, solace; recreation, amusement, entertainment, diversion. **4** wish, preference, inclination; discretion. **5** hedonism, debauchery, libertinism.

pleat /pleet/ • *n.* fold or crease, esp. a flattened fold in cloth doubled upon itself. • *v.tr.* make a pleat or pleats in.

plebe /pleeb/ *n.* first-year student at a military academy.

ple•be•ian /plibéeən/ • *n.* commoner, esp. in ancient Rome. • *adj.* **1** uncultured. **2** coarse; ignoble. □□ **ple•be'ian•ism** *n.*

■ *n.* proletarian, common man or woman. • *adj.* **1** unrefined, uncultivated, lowbrow, unpolished, provincial, rustic, popular, commonplace, undistinguished. **2** uncouth, crass, vulgar, brutish, barbaric.

pleb•i•scite /plébisīt, -sit/ *n.* direct, popular vote on an issue.

■ popular ballot, referendum, poll.

plec•trum /pléktrəm/ *n.* (*pl.* **plec•trums** or **plec•tra** /-trə/) thin flat piece of plastic or horn, etc., held in the hand and used to pluck a string, esp. of a guitar.

pled *past of* PLEAD.

pledge /plej/ • *n.* **1** solemn promise or undertaking. **2** thing given as security for the fulfillment of a contract, the payment of a debt, etc. **3** thing given as a token. • *v.tr.* **1** deposit as security. **2** promise solemnly by the pledge of (one's honor, word, etc.). **3** [often *refl.*] bind by a solemn promise. □□ **pledge'a•ble** *adj.* **pledg'er** *n.* **pled'gor** *n.*

■ *n.* **1** oath, vow, word (of honor), covenant, bond, agreement, assurance, guaranty, guarantee. **2** gage, bond, guaranty, guarantee; collateral, earnest, surety. • *v.* **2** swear, vow, undertake. **3** see BIND *v.* 5.

ple•na•ry /pléenəree, plén-/ *adj.* **1** entire; unqualified; absolute. **2** (of an assembly) to be attended by all members.

plen•i•po•ten•ti•ar•y /plénipəténshəree, -shee-eree/ • *n.* (*pl.* **-ies**) person (esp. a diplomat) invested with the full power of independent action. • *adj.* having this power.

plen•i•tude /plénitood, -tyood/ *n.* **1** fullness; completeness. **2** abundance.

plen•te•ous /pléntees/ *adj.* plentiful. □□ **plen'te•ous•ly** *adv.* **plen'te•ous•ness** *n.*

plen•ti•ful /pléntifool/ *adj.* abundant; copious. See synonym study at PREVALENT. □□ **plen'ti•ful•ly** *adv.* **plen'ti•ful•ness** *n.*

■ ample, profuse, lavish, bountiful, generous, fruitful, productive, bumper, luxuriant, thriving, prolific, *poet.* bounteous, plenteous.

plen•ty /pléntee/ • *n.* **1** great or sufficient quantity or number. **2** abundance. • *adv. colloq.* fully; entirely.

■ *n.* **1** see LOT *n.* 1. **2** plentifulness, copiousness, wealth, profusion, lavishness, prodigality.

ple•o•nasm /pléeənazəm/ *n.* use of more

---

words than are needed to give the sense (e.g., *see with one's eyes*). □□ **ple•o•nas•tic** /-nástik/ *adj.* **ple•o•nas'ti•cal•ly** *adv.*

pleth•o•ra /pléthərə/ *n.* oversupply; glut; excess. □□ **ple•thor•ic** /plətháwrik, -thór-/ *adj.* **ple•thor'i•cal•ly** *adv.*

pleu•ra /ploorə/ *n.* (*pl.* **pleu•rae** /-ree/) membrane enveloping the lungs. □□ **pleu'ral** *adj.*

pleu•ri•sy /ploorisee/ *n.* inflammation of the pleura, marked by pain in the chest or side, fever, etc. □□ **pleu•rit•ic** /-ritik/ *adj.*

Plex•i•glas /pléksiglas/ *n. propr.* tough, clear thermoplastic used instead of glass.

plex•us /pléksəs/ *n.* (*pl.* same or **plex•us•es**) *Anat.* network of nerves or vessels (*gastric plexus*). □□ **plex'i•form** *adj.*

pli•a•ble /plíəbəl/ *adj.* **1** bending easily; supple. **2** yielding; compliant. See synonym study at FLEXIBLE. □□ **pli•a•bil'i•ty** *n.* **pli'a•ble•ness** *n.* **pli'a•bly** *adv.*

■ **1** flexible, pliant, elastic, plastic, malleable, workable, bendable, ductile, *colloq.* bendy; lithe, limber. **2** tractable, adaptable, flexible, pliant, persuadable.

pli•ant /plíənt/ *adj.* **1** See PLIABLE 1. See synonym study at FLEXIBLE. □□ **pli'an•cy** *n.* **pli'ant•ly** *adv.*

pli•ers /plíərz/ *n.pl.* pincers with parallel flat usu. serrated surfaces for holding small objects, bending wire, etc.

plight[1] /plīt/ *n.* condition or state, esp. an unfortunate one.

■ circumstances, situation, case; difficulty, predicament, quandary, trouble, extremity; mess, bind, *colloq.* hole, jam, pickle, spot, scrape, fix, *disp.* dilemma.

plight[2] /plīt/ *archaic v.tr.* pledge.

plinth /plinth/ *n.* **1** lower square slab at the base of a column. **2** base supporting a vase or statue, etc.

PLO *abbr.* Palestine Liberation Organization.

plod /plod/ *v.intr.* (**plod•ded, plod•ding**) **1** walk doggedly or laboriously; trudge. **2** [often foll. by *at*] work slowly and steadily. □□ **plod'der** *n.* **plod'ding•ly** *adv.*

■ **1** tramp, lumber, labor, *colloq.* galumph. **2** labor, work, drudge, toil, slave (away), grind (away), grub (on or along), peg away (at), *colloq.* plug (along or away).

plop /plop/ • *n.* **1** sound as of a smooth object dropping into water without a splash. **2** act of falling with this sound. • *v.* (**plopped, plop•ping**) fall or drop with a plop.

plot /plot/ • *n.* **1** defined and usu. small piece of ground. **2** interrelationship of the main events in a play, novel, movie, etc. **3** conspiracy or secret plan. • *v.tr.* (**plot•ted, plot•ting**) **1** make a plan or map of. **2** [also *absol.*] plan or contrive secretly (a crime, conspiracy, etc.). **3** mark (a point or course, etc.) on a chart or diagram. □□ **plot'less** *adj.* **plot'ter** *n.*

■ *n.* **1** patch, tract, acreage, area, allotment, lot, plat. **2** story, story line, scenario. **3** scheme, plan, intrigue, machination, cabal, conspiracy, stratagem. • *v.* **1, 3** draw, plan, map (out); diagram, lay down, outline, represent, figure, chart; mark, indicate, designate, label. **2** scheme, intrigue, machinate, cabal, collude, conspire, hatch, devise, design, arrange, organize.

SYNONYM STUDY: plot

CABAL, CONSPIRACY, INTRIGUE, MACHINATION. If you come up with a secret plan to do something, especially with evil or mischievous intent, it's called a **plot** (*a plot to purchase the property before it was put up for sale*). If you get other people or groups involved in your *plot*, it's called a **conspiracy** (*a conspiracy to overthrow the government*). **Cabal** usually applies to a small group of political conspirators (*a cabal of right-wing extremists*), while **machination** (usually plural) suggests deceit and cunning in devising a *plot* intended to harm someone (*the machinations of the enemy*). An **intrigue** involves more complicated scheming or maneuvering than a *plot* and often employs underhanded methods in an attempt to gain one's own ends (*she had a passion for intrigue, particularly where romance was involved*).

plo•ver /plúvər, plṓ–/ *n.* plump-breasted shorebird, e.g., the lapwing, the sandpiper.

plow /plow/ • *n.* **1** implement for cutting furrows in the soil and turning it up. **2** implement resembling this (*snowplow*). • *v.* **1** *tr.* [also *absol.*] turn up (the earth) with a plow, esp. before sowing. **2** *tr.* **a** furrow or scratch (a surface) as if with a plow. **b** move through or break the surface of (water). **3** *tr.* produce (a furrow, line, or wake) in this way. **4** *intr.* advance laboriously, esp. through work, a book, etc. **5** *intr.* move like a plow steadily or violently. □□ **plow′a•ble** *adj.* **plow′er** *n.*

■ *v.* **1** till, cultivate, furrow, harrow, rib. **4** see PROCEED 1. **5** drive, plunge, push, career, bulldoze, lunge, dive.

plow•share /plów′shair/ *n.* cutting blade of a plow.

ploy /ploy/ *n. colloq.* cunning maneuver to gain advantage.

pluck /pluk/ • *v.* **1** *tr.* remove by picking or pulling out or away. **2** *tr.* strip (a bird) of feathers. **3** *intr.* [foll. by *at*] tug or snatch at. **4** *tr.* sound (the string of a musical instrument) with the finger or plectrum, etc. • *n.* **1** courage; spirit. **2** plucking. □□ **pluck′er** *n.* **pluck′less** *adj.*

■ *v.* **1** pick; snatch, grab, yank off, tear (off or away); withdraw, draw out, extract, pull or take out. **3** pull (at), catch (at), clutch (at), jerk, twitch, *colloq.* yank. • *n.* **1** bravery, boldness, intrepidity, backbone, mettle, determination, gameness, resolve, resolution.

pluck•y /plúkee/ *adj.* (**pluck•i•er, pluck•i•est**) brave; spirited. □□ **pluck′i•ly** *adv.* **pluck′i•ness** *n.*

plug /plug/ • *n.* **1** piece of solid material fitting tightly into a hole. **2** device fitting into holes in a socket for making an electrical connection. **3** *colloq.* piece of (often free) publicity for an idea, product, etc. **4** cake or stick of tobacco; piece of this for chewing. • *v.* (**plugged, plug•ging**) **1** *tr.* [often foll.

by *up*] stop up (a hole, etc.) with a plug. **2** *tr. sl.* shoot or hit (a person, etc.). **3** *tr. colloq.* promote (an idea, product, etc.). **4** *intr. colloq.* work steadily away (at). □□ **plug′ger** *n.*

■ *n.* **1** stopper, stopple, bung, cork. **3** mention, promotion, recommendation, puff; advertisement, *colloq.* promo. **4** chew, twist, quid, pigtail. • *v.* **1** close (up *or* off), seal (off *or* up), cork, stopper, stopple, bung, block (up *or* off), dam (up). **2** see SHOOT *v.* 1c. **3** publicize, mention, push, advertise, puff. **4** see PLOD *v.* 2.

plum /plum/ *n.* **1 a** oval fleshy fruit with sweet pulp and a flattish stone. **b** tree bearing this. **2** reddish-purple color. **3** something especially prized (often *attrib.*: *a plum job*).

■ **3** find, catch, coup, prize, treasure; (*attrib.*) esteemed, favored, *often joc.* pet.

plum•age /plṓomij/ *n.* bird's feathers. □□ **plum′aged** *adj.* [usu. in *comb.*].

plumb /plum/ • *n.* ball of lead or other heavy material, esp. one attached to the end of a line for finding the depth of water or determining the vertical on an upright surface. • *adv.* **1** exactly (*plumb in the center*). **2** vertically. **3** *sl.* quite; utterly (*plumb crazy*). • *adj.* vertical. • *v.tr.* **1** sound or test with a plumb. **2** reach or experience in extremes. **3** learn in detail the facts about (a matter).

■ *n.* weight, bob, plummet, sinker. • *adv.* **1** precisely, dead, right, directly, slap. **2** perpendicularly, straight up and down. **3** see DOWNRIGHT *adv.* • *adj.* see PERPENDICULAR. • *v.* **1** fathom, probe; measure, gauge; determine. **2** go through, go into, explore, probe, delve into.

plumb•er /plúmər/ *n.* person who fits and repairs the apparatus of a water supply system.

plumb•ing /plúming/ *n.* **1** system or apparatus of water supply, heating, etc., in a building. **2** work of a plumber.

plume /ploōm/ • *n.* **1** feather, esp. a large one used for ornament. **2** ornament of feathers, etc., attached to a helmet or hat or worn in the hair. **3** something resembling this (*plume of smoke*). • *v.tr.* **1** decorate or provide with a plume or plumes. **2** (of a bird) preen (itself or its feathers). □□ **plume′less** *adj.* **plume′like** *adj.* **plum′er•y** *n.* **plum′y** *adj.* (**plum•i•er, plum•i•est**).

plum•met /plúmit/ • *n.* plumb. • *v.intr.* fall or plunge rapidly.

■ *v.* see PLUNGE *v.* 1b.

plump¹ /plump/ • *adj.* having a full rounded shape; fleshy. • *v.* make or become plump. □□ **plump′ish** *adj.* **plump′ly** *adv.* **plump′ness** *n.*

■ *adj.* chubby, stout, full-bodied, portly, tubby, rotund, round, squat, chunky, buxom, corpulent. • *v.* puff up *or* out; fatten, fill out; see also PAD¹ *v.* 2.

plump² /plump/ • *v.* drop or fall abruptly. • *adv. colloq.* directly; bluntly.

■ *v.* plummet, plunge, dive, sink, collapse, flop (down); deposit, set *or* put (down), plonk, plop, dump. • *adv.* abruptly, suddenly, at once, unexpectedly, without warning, bang; see also STRAIGHT *adv.* 1.

plun•der /plúndər/ • *v.tr.* **1** rob; loot. **2** [also absol.] steal or embezzle (goods). See synonym study at RAVAGE. • n. **1** activity of plundering. **2** property acquired by plundering. □□ **plun'der•er** n.

■ v. **1** pillage, ravage, ransack, rifle (through), pirate, sack, strip, pluck, maraud, lay waste. **2** see STEAL v. 1. • n. **1** pillage, looting, robbery, depredation, spoliation, ransacking, brigandage, piracy, banditry. **2** booty, loot, spoils, takings, sl. boodle, swag.

plunge /plunj/ • v. **1 a** tr. thrust forcefully or abruptly. **b** intr. dive; propel oneself forcibly. **c** intr. & tr. enter or cause to enter or embark impetuously. **2** tr. immerse completely. **3** intr. move suddenly and dramatically downward. • n. plunging action or movement, dive. □ **take the plunge** colloq. commit oneself to a (usu. risky) course of action.

■ v. **1 a** see THRUST¹ v. 1. **b** descend, drop, plummet, fall (headlong); pitch, nosedive, catapult or hurl oneself. **c** see LAUNCH v. 1, 3, 4. **2** submerge, sink; see also IMMERSE 1. • n. nosedive, fall, pitch, drop, descent; submersion, immersion. □ **take the plunge** gamble, wager, bet, risk; give it one's all, colloq. go for it, go all out, sl. go for broke.

plung•er /plúnjər/ n. **1** part of a mechanism that works with a plunging or thrusting movement. **2** rubber cup on a handle for clearing blocked pipes.

plu•ral /plóorəl/ • adj. **1** more than one in number. **2** Gram. (of a word or form) denoting more than one. • n. Gram. plural word or form. □□ **plu'ral•ly** adv.

plu•ral•ism /plóorəlizəm/ n. form of society in which the members of minority groups maintain their independent cultural traditions. □□ **plu'ral•ist** n. **plu•ral•is'tic** adj. **plu•ral•is'ti•cal•ly** adv.

plu•ral•i•ty /plóorálitee/ n. (pl. **-ties**) **1** state of being plural. **2** large or the greater number. **3** majority that is not absolute.

plus /plus/ • prep. **1** Math. with the addition of. ¶Symbol: +. **2** colloq. with; having gained. • adj. **1** (after a number) at least (fifteen plus). **2** (after a grade, etc.) somewhat better than. **3** Math. positive. **4** having a positive electrical charge. **5** [attrib.] additional; extra. • n. **1** = plus sign. **2** Math. additional or positive quantity. **3** advantage. • conj. colloq. disp. also; and furthermore (they arrived late, plus they were hungry). □ **plus sign** symbol +, indicating addition or a positive value.

■ prep. **1** and, added to, increased by, with an increment of, (coupled) with, together with. • adj. **5** added, supplementary. • n. **3** benefit, asset, addition, bonus, extra.

plush /plush/ • n. cloth of silk, cotton, etc., with a long soft nap. • adj. **1** made of plush. **2** luxurious. □□ **plush'ly** adv. **plush'ness** n.

■ adj. **2** costly, deluxe, palatial, lavish, rich, opulent, sumptuous, regal, swanky, colloq. ritzy.

Plu•to /plóotō/ n. outermost known planet of the solar system.

plu•toc•ra•cy /plóotókrəsee/ n. (pl. **-cies**) **1 a** government by the wealthy. **b** nation governed in this way. **2** wealthy élite or ruling class. □□ **plu•to•crat** /plóotəkrat/ n. **plu•to•crat'ic** adj. **plu•to•crat'i•cal•ly** adv.

plu•to•ni•um /plóotóneeəm/ n. Chem. dense silvery radioactive metallic transuranic element. ¶Symb.: **Pu**.

plu•vi•al /plóoveeəl/ adj. **1** of rain; rainy. **2** Geol. caused by rain. □□ **plu'vi•ous** adj. (in sense 1).

ply¹ /plī/ n. (pl. **plies**) **1** thickness or layer of wood, cloth, etc. (three-ply). **2** strand of yarn or rope, etc.

■ **1** leaf, fold.

ply² /plī/ v. (**plies, plied**) **1** tr. use or wield vigorously (a tool, weapon, etc.). **2** tr. work steadily at (one's business or trade). **3** tr. [foll. by with] supply (a person) continuously (with food, drink, etc.). **4** intr. (of a vehicle, etc.) travel regularly (to and fro).

ply•wood /plíwood/ n. strong thin board consisting of two or more layers glued and pressed together.

Pm symb. Chem. promethium.

p.m. abbr. between noon and midnight (Latin post meridiem).

PMS abbr. premenstrual syndrome.

pneu•mat•ic /noomátik, nyoo-/ adj. **1** filled with air or wind. **2** operated by compressed air. □□ **pneu•mat'i•cal•ly** adv. **pneu•ma•tic'i•ty** /nóomətisitee, nyoo-/ n.

pneu•mo•nia /noomónyə, nyoo-/ n. bacterial inflammation of one lung (**single pneumonia**) or both lungs (**double pneumonia**). □□ **pneu•mon'ic** /-mónik/ adj.

PO abbr. **1** Post Office. **2** postal order. **3** Petty Officer.

Po symb. Chem. polonium.

poach¹ /pōch/ v.tr. **1** cook (an egg) without its shell in or over boiling water. **2** cook (fish, etc.) by simmering in a small amount of liquid. □□ **poach'er** n.

poach² /pōch/ v. **1** tr. [also absol.] catch (game or fish) illegally. **2** intr. [often foll. by on] trespass or encroach (on another's property, ideas, etc.). □□ **poach'er** n.

pock /pok/ n. (also **pock•mark**) **1** small pusfilled spot on the skin, esp. caused by chickenpox or smallpox. **2** a mark resembling this. □ **pockmarked** bearing marks resembling or left by such spots. □□ **pock'y** adj.

pock•et /pókit/ • n. **1** small bag sewn into or on clothing, for carrying small articles. **2** pouchlike compartment or holder. **3** isolated group or area (pockets of resistance). **4** [attrib.] **a** of a suitable size and shape for carrying in a pocket. **b** small. • v.tr. **1** put into one's pocket. **2** appropriate, esp. dishonestly. □ **pocket knife** knife with a folding blade or blades, for carrying in the pocket. **pocket veto** executive veto of a legislative bill by allowing it to go unsigned. □□ **pock'et•a•ble** adj. **pock'et•less** adj.

■ n. **1** pouch, sack. **3** island, center, cluster, concentration. **4 b** see SMALL adj. 1. • v. **2** take, keep; filch, embezzle, steal, thieve, pilfer, help oneself to, colloq. swipe, walk off or away with, rip off, lift.

pock•et•book /pókitbook/ n. purse or handbag.

pod /pod/ n. **1** long seed vessel esp. of a leguminous plant, e.g., a pea. **2** cocoon of a silkworm.

■ **1** shell, hull, case, husk, skin, shuck.

po•di•a•try /pədīˈatree/ n. Med. care and
treatment of the foot. □□ **po•di′a•trist** n.

po•di•um /pōˈdeeəm/ n. (pl. **po•di•ums** or
po•di•a /-deeə/) platform or rostrum.

po•em /pōˈəm/ n. metrical composition, usu.
concerned with feeling or imaginative description.

■ verse, lyric, rhyme, song, ode, ballad, sonnet.

po•e•sy /pōˈəzee, -see/ n. archaic poetry.

po•et /pōˈit/ n. (fem. **po′et•ess** /pōˈətis/)
1 writer of poems. **2** person possessing high
powers of imagination or expression, etc.
□ **poet laureate** poet appointed to write
poems for official state occasions.

■ **1** versifier, rhymester, lyricist, lyrist,
rhymer, minstrel.

po•et•ic /pōˈetik/ adj. (also **po•et′i•cal**) **1** of
or like poetry or poets. **2** elevated or sublime
in expression. □ **poetic justice** well-
deserved unforeseen retribution or reward.
poetic license writer's or artist's transgression of established rules for effect. □□ **po•et′
i•cal•ly** adv.

■ **1** artistic, fine, aesthetic, Parnassian.
2 see SUBLIME adj. 1.

po•et•ics /pōˈetiks/ n. **1** art of writing poetry. **2** the study of poetry and its techniques.

po•et•ry /pōˈətree/ n. **1** art or work of a poet.
2 poems collectively. **3** poetic or tenderly
pleasing quality.

■ **1, 2** verse, versification.

po•grom /pōˈgrəm, pəgrúm, -gróm/ n. organized massacre (orig. of Jews in Russia).

poign•ant /pōynyənt/ adj. **1** painfully sharp
to the emotions or senses; deeply moving.
2 arousing sympathy. □□ **poign′ance** n.
poign′an•cy n. **poign′ant•ly** adv.

■ distressing, upsetting, agonizing, grievous, painful, woeful, sad, sorrowful,
heartrending, heartbreaking, excruciating,
pathetic, pitiable, piteous, pitiful.

poin•set•ti•a /pōynsétteeə, -séteə/ n. shrub
with large usu. scarlet bracts surrounding
small yellow flowers.

point /pōynt/ • n. **1** sharp or tapered end of a
tool, weapon, pencil, etc. **2** tip or extreme
end. **3** that which in geometry has position
but not magnitude. **4** particular place or position. **5** precise or critical moment. **6** very
small mark on a surface. **7** dot or other
punctuation mark, esp. = PERIOD. **8** = decimal point. **9** stage or degree in progress or increase. **10** of temperature at which a change
of state occurs (freezing point). **11** single
item; detail or particular. **12** unit of scoring
in games or of measuring value, etc.
13 a significant or essential thing. **b** sense or
purpose; advantage or value. **14** distinctive
feature or characteristic (it has its points).
15 a each of 32 directions marked at equal
distances around a compass. **b** corresponding direction toward the horizon. **16** [usu. in

pl.] electrical contact in the distributor of a
motor vehicle. **17** promontory. **18** Printing
unit of measurement for printed type (in the
US 0.351 mm). • v. **1 a** tr. direct or aim (a
finger, weapon, etc.). **b** intr. direct attention.
2 intr. aim or be directed to. **3** intr. indicate;
be evidence of (it all points to murder). □ **at
(or on) the point of** on the verge of. **beside
the point** irrelevant. **point-blank** adj. **1** (of
a shot) aimed or fired horizontally at a range
very close to the target. **2** blunt; direct. adv.
1 at very close range. **2** directly; bluntly.
point of order parliamentary query as to
correct procedure. **point of view 1** position
from which a thing is viewed. **2** particular
way of considering a matter. **point out** indicate; show; draw attention to. **point up** emphasize; show as important. **to the point** relevant or relevantly. **up to a point** to some
extent but not completely.

■ n. **1** spike, spur, prong. **2** peak, apex.
4 site; location, locale, spot. **5** time, instant,
juncture. **6** speck, spot, fleck. **7** (full) stop.
9 see STAGE n. 1. **11** element, aspect, facet,
matter, issue, subject, question. **13 a** focus,
essence, meat, pith, substance, heart, nucleus, crux, nub, core, bottom, details, sl.
brass tacks, nitty-gritty. **b** intent, intention,
aim, goal, object, objective, sense, thrust,
drift, theme, import; application, applicability, relevancy. **14** attribute, aspect, trait,
quality, property. **17** projection, headland,
cape, peninsula, bluff, ness. • v. **1 a** level,
train. **b** see INDICATE 1, 4. **3** see SUGGEST 2.
□ **at (or on) the point of** on the brink of,
just about to. **beside the point** incidental,
immaterial, unimportant, inconsequential.
point-blank adj. **2** straight, flat, straightforward, abrupt, categorical, explicit, uncompromising, unmitigated, unalloyed, downright. • adv. **2** right away, flatly, abruptly,
categorically, unqualifiedly, explicitly, unreservedly, plainly, frankly. **point of view
1** viewpoint, perspective, approach, position,
angle, slant, orientation. **2** opinion, view, belief, (way of) thinking, principle, doctrine,
tenet. **point out** designate, call attention to,
identify; bring up, mention, emphasize,
stress. **point up** stress, accentuate, underline, underscore, accent, spotlight. **to the
point** pertinent, appropriate, fitting, apropos, germane, apt.

point•ed /pōyntid/ adj. **1** sharpened or tapering to a point. **2** (of a remark, etc.) penetrating; cutting. **3** emphasized; made evident.
□□ **point′ed•ly** adv. **point′ed•ness** n.

■ **1** sharp, barbed, spined, pointy. **2** piercing, sharp, pungent, keen, trenchant, biting,
barbed; see also INCISIVE 3. **3** see EXPLICIT 1.

point•er /pōyntər/ n. **1** thing that points, e.g.,
the index hand of a gauge, etc. **2** rod for
pointing to features on a map, chart, etc.
3 colloq. hint, clue, or indication. **4** dog of a
breed that on scenting game stands rigid
looking toward it.

■ **1** indicator, arrow, hand; cursor. **3** tip,
suggestion, recommendation, piece of advice.

poin•til•lism /pwántilizəm, pōyn-/ n. Art
technique of impressionist painting using

tiny dots of various pure colors, which become blended in the viewer's eye. □□ **poin′til·list** *n. & adj.* **poin·til·list′ic** *adj.*

point·less /póyntlis/ *adj.* lacking force, purpose, or meaning. □□ **point′less·ly** *adv.* **point′less·ness** *n.*

■ purposeless, aimless, worthless, meaningless, futile.

poise /poyz/ • *n.* **1** composure. **2** equilibrium. **3** carriage (of the head, etc.). • *v.* **1** *tr.* balance; hold suspended or supported. **2** *intr.* be balanced; hover in the air, etc.

■ *n.* **1** control, self-possession, aplomb, assurance, dignity. **2** balance, equipoise, counterpoise. • *v.* **1** steady, suspend; equilibrate. **2** balance, hang, float.

poised /poyzd/ *adj.* **1** composed; self-assured. **2** [often foll. by *for*, or *to* + infin.] ready for action.

■ **1** controlled, self-possessed, self-confident, assured. **2** standing by, waiting, prepared, *colloq.* all set.

poi·son /póyzən/ • *n.* **1** substance causing an organism death or injury, esp. in a small quantity. **2** *colloq.* harmful influence. • *v.tr.* **1** administer poison to. **2** kill, injure, or infect with poison. **3** (esp. as **poisoned** *adj.*) treat something with poison. **4** corrupt; pervert; spoil. □ **poison ivy** climbing plant secreting an irritant oil from its leaves. □□ **poi′son·er** *n.* **poi′son·ous** *adj.* **poi′son·ous·ly** *adv.*

■ *n.* **1** toxin, venom, bane; mephitis. **2** cancer, canker, virus, bad influence, blight, contagion. • *v.* **4** vitiate, subvert, warp, degrade, deprave; taint, destroy; see also SPOIL *v.* 1. □□ **poisonous** toxic, virulent, venomous, noxious, mephitic; malicious, malevolent.

poke[1] /pōk/ • *v.* **1 a** *tr.* thrust or push with the hand, point of a stick, etc. **b** *intr.* be thrust forward. **2** *tr.* thrust the end of a finger, etc., against. **3** *tr.* produce (a hole, etc., in a thing) by poking. **4** *intr.* **a** move or act desultorily. **b** [foll. by *about, into*] pry; search casually. • *n.* thrust; jab. □ **poke fun at** ridicule.

■ *v.* **1 a** jab, prod, dig (into), stab, push, elbow, butt, shove, stick; see also PUNCH[1] *v.* 1. **4 a** see *mess about*. **b** nose (about or around), intrude; meddle, interfere; *colloq.* snoop (about); dig into, tamper with, probe into. • *n.* prod, dig, stab, push, nudge, jog, shove; see also PUNCH[1] *n.* 1. □ **poke fun at** tease, mock, make fun of, jeer at, chaff at, taunt.

poke[2] /pōk/ *n. dial.* bag or sack.

pok·er[1] /pókər/ *n.* stiff metal rod for stirring an open fire.

pok·er[2] /pókər/ *n.* card game in which bluff is used as players bet on the value of their hands. □ **poker face 1** impassive countenance appropriate to a poker player. **2** person with this. **poker-faced** having a poker face.

pok·y /pókee/ *adj.* (**pok·i·er, pok·i·est**) **1** (of a room, etc.) small and cramped. **2** slow. □□ **pok′i·ly** *adv.* **pok′i·ness** *n.*

po·lar /pólər/ *adj.* **1** of or near a pole of the earth. **2** having magnetic or electric polarity. **3** directly opposite in character. □ **polar bear** white bear of the Arctic regions.

■ **3** opposed, antithetical, contrary, contradictory.

po·lar·i·ty /pəláritee/ *n.* (*pl.* **–ties**) **1** tendency of a lodestone, magnetized bar, etc., to point with its extremities to the magnetic poles of the earth. **2** condition of having two poles with contrary qualities. **3** state of having two opposite tendencies, opinions, etc. **4** electrical condition of a body (positive or negative).

po·lar·ize /pólərīz/ *v.* **1** *tr.* restrict the vibrations of (a transverse wave, esp. light) to one direction. **2** *tr.* give magnetic or electric polarity. **3** *tr. & intr.* divide into two opposing groups. □□ **po′lar·i·za·ble** *adj.* **po·lar·i·za′tion** *n.* **po′lar·i·zer** *n.*

Pole /pōl/ *n.* **1** native or national of Poland. **2** person of Polish descent.

pole[1] /pōl/ • *n.* long slender rounded piece of wood or metal. • *v.tr.* push or propel (a small boat) with a pole. □ **pole vault** *n.* sport of vaulting over a high bar with the aid of a long flexible pole. *v.intr.* take part in this sport. **pole-vaulter** person who pole vaults.

■ *n.* rod, stick, staff, spar, shaft, mast, upright.

pole[2] /pōl/ *n.* **1** (in full **north pole, south pole**) **a** each of the two points in the celestial sphere about which the stars appear to revolve. **b** each of the extremities of the axis of rotation of the earth or another body. **2** each of the two opposite points on the surface of a magnet at which magnetic forces are strongest. **3** each of two terminals (positive and negative) of an electric cell or battery, etc. □ **be poles apart** differ greatly, esp. in nature or opinion. □□ **pole′ward** *adj.* **pole′wards** *adj. & adv.*

■ □ **poles apart** (very or completely) different, worlds apart, at opposite extremes, at opposite ends of the earth; irreconcilable.

pole·cat /pólkat/ *n.* **1** skunk. **2** small European brownish black, flesh-eating mammal of the weasel family.

po·lem·ic /pəlémik/ • *n.* **1** controversial discussion. **2** *Polit.* verbal or written attack. • *adj.* (also **po·lem′i·cal**) involving dispute; controversial. □□ **po·lem′i·cal·ly** *adv.* **po·lem′i·cist** /–misist/ *n.* **po·lem′i·cize** *v.tr.*

po·lem·ics /pəlémiks/ *n.pl.* art or practice of disputation.

pole·star /pólstaar/ *n.* **1** *Astron.* star now about 1° distant from the celestial north pole. **2** thing serving as a guide.

■ **1** North Star, lodestar. **2** see GUIDE *n.* 6.

po·lice /pəlées/ • *n.* **1** [usu. prec. by *the*] civil force of a government, responsible for maintaining public order. **2** [as *pl.*] its members. **3** force with similar functions (*transit police*). • *v.tr.* **1** control (a country or area) by means of police. **2** provide with police. **3** keep order in; control; monitor. □ **police officer** policeman or policewoman. **police state** totalitarian country controlled by political police supervising the citizens' activities.

■ *n.* **1, 2** constabulary, *colloq.* the law, *sl.* fuzz, pigs, the Man; policemen, policewomen, police officers. • *v.* **1** patrol, guard, watch, protect; see also CONTROL *v.* 2. **3** enforce, regulate, administer, oversee, observe, supervise. □ **police officer** officer (of the law), gendarme, lawman, patrolman, patrolwoman, *sl.* cop, shamus, fuzz, copper, flatfoot, *sl. derog.* pig.

po•lice•man /pəlēesmən/ *n.* (*pl.* **-men**; *fem.* **po•lice•wom•an,** *pl.* **-wom•en**) member of a police force.

pol•i•cy[1] /pólisee/ *n.* (*pl.* **-cies**) **1** course or principle of action adopted or proposed by a government, party, business, or individual, etc. **2** prudent conduct; sagacity.
  ■ **1** approach, procedure, plan, design, scheme, action, strategy, tactic(s). **2** see *prudence* (PRUDENT).

pol•i•cy[2] /pólisee/ *n.* (*pl.* **-cies**) insurance contract.

pol•i•cy•hold•er /póliseehōldər/ *n.* person or body holding an insurance policy.

po•li•o•my•e•li•tis /pōleeōmī-ilítis/ *n.* (also **po•li•o**) *Med.* infectious viral disease that affects the central nervous system and can cause temporary or permanent paralysis.

Po•lish /pólish/ • *adj.* **1** of or relating to Poland. **2** of the Poles or their language. • *n.* language of Poland.

pol•ish /pólish/ • *v.* **1** make or become smooth or glossy esp. by rubbing. **2** (esp. as **polished** *adj.*) refine or improve; add finishing touches to. • *n.* **1** substance used for polishing. **2** smoothness or glossiness produced by friction. **3** refinement; elegance. □ **polish off** finish (esp. food) quickly. □□ **pol•ish′a•ble** *adj.* **pol•ish′er** *n.*
  ■ *v.* **1** shine, brighten, burnish, buff, furbish, wax, clean, gloss. **2** (**polished**) accomplished, finished, masterful, masterly; flawless, faultless, perfect, impeccable; refined, elegant, cultivated. • *n.* **1** wax, beeswax, oil. **2** gloss, shine, luster, sheen, glaze, brilliance, sparkle, gleam. **3** see *refinement* (REFINE). □ **polish off** dispose of, put away, eat up, gobble (up), consume.

po•lite /pəlít/ *adj.* (**po•lit•er, po•lit•est**) **1** having good manners; courteous. **2** cultivated; cultured. **3** refined; elegant (*polite letters*). □□ **po•lite′ly** *adv.* **po•lite′ness** *n.*
  ■ **1** civil, respectful, well-mannered, mannerly, diplomatic, considerate. **2** see *polished* (POLISH).

pol•i•tesse /pólétés/ *n.* formal politeness.

pol•i•tic /pólitik/ • *adj.* **1** (of an action) judicious; expedient. **2** (of a person) prudent; sagacious. • *v.intr.* (**pol•i•ticked, pol•i•tick•ing**) engage in politics.
  ■ *adj.* **1** see JUDICIOUS. **2** tactful, diplomatic, discreet, judicious, wise, sage, sensible, percipient.

po•lit•i•cal /pəlítikəl/ *adj.* **1** of or concerning government, or public affairs generally. **2** taking or belonging to a side in politics. **3** concerned with seeking status, authority, etc. (*political decision*). □ **political action committee** permanent organization that collects and distributes funds for political purposes. ¶Abbr.: **PAC. political correctness** avoidance of forms of expression and action that exclude or marginalize sexual, racial, and cultural minorities; advocacy of this. **politically correct** in conformance with political correctness. **political science** the study of systems of government. □□ **po•lit′i•cal•ly** *adv.*
  ■ **1** governmental, state, public, national; civic, civil. **2** partisan, factional, factious; active, involved.

pol•i•ti•cian /pólitíshən/ *n.* **1** person engaged in politics, esp. as a practitioner. **2** person skilled in politics. **3** *derog.* person with self-interested political concerns.
  ■ **1** legislator, lawmaker, statesman, stateswoman; minister, senator, congressman, congresswoman, representative, public servant, administrator.

po•lit•i•cize /pəlítisīz/ *v.* **1** *tr.* **a** give a political character to. **b** make politically aware. **2** *intr.* engage in or talk politics. □□ **po•lit′i•ci•za′tion** *n.*

po•lit•i•co /pəlítikō/ *n.* (*pl.* **-cos**) *colloq.* politician.

pol•i•tics /pólitiks/ *n.pl.* **1** [treated as *sing.* or *pl.*] **a** art and science of government. **b** public life and affairs. **2** [usu. treated as *pl.*] **a** particular set of ideas, principles, or commitments in politics (*what are their politics?*). **b** activities concerned with seeking power, status, etc.
  ■ **1** political science, government, statecraft, diplomacy, statesmanship. **2 b** manipulation, machination, maneuvering, wire-pulling; see also GOVERNMENT 1.

pol•i•ty /pólitee/ *n.* (*pl.* **-ties**) **1** form or process of civil government or constitution. **2** organized society; state.

pol•ka /pólkə, pṓkə/ • *n.* **1** lively dance of Bohemian origin in duple time. **2** music for this. • *v.intr.* (**pol•kas, pol•kaed** /-kəd/ or **pol•ka'd, pol•ka•ing** /-kəing/) dance the polka. □ **polka dot** round dot as one of many forming a regular pattern on a textile fabric, etc.

poll /pōl/ • *n.* **1 a** voting. **b** result of voting or number of votes recorded. **2** survey of opinion. • *v.tr.* **1 a** take the vote or votes of. **b** (of a candidate) receive (so many votes). **2** record the opinion of (a person or group). □□ **poll′ster** *n.*
  ■ *n.* **1 b** voting, vote, return, tally, figures, ballot, count. **2** canvass, census. • *v.* **1 a** ballot. **b** get, win, register, tally. **2** canvass, ballot, sample, survey.

pol•len /pólən/ *n.* fine dustlike grains discharged from the male part of a flower containing the gamete that fertilizes the female ovule. □ **pollen count** index of the amount of pollen in the air. □□ **pol•len′less** *adj.*

pol•li•nate /pólinayt/ *v.tr.* [also *absol.*] sprinkle (a stigma) with pollen. □□ **pol•li•na′tion** /-náyshən/ *n.* **pol′li•na•tor** *n.*

pol•lute /pəlõot/ *v.tr.* **1** contaminate or defile (the environment). **2** make foul or filthy. **3** destroy the purity or sanctity of. □□ **pol•lu′tant** *adj. & n.* **pol•lut′er** *n.* **pol•lu′tion** *n.*
  ■ **1** poison; see also CONTAMINATE 1. **2** foul, soil, taint, stain; see also DIRTY *v.* **3** corrupt, desecrate, profane, defile, violate. □□ **pollu-**

tion contamination, adulteration; vitiation, corruption; see also SACRILEGE.

ADULTERATE, CONTAMINATE, DEFILE, TAINT. When a factory pours harmful chemicals or wastes into the air or water, it is said to **pollute** the environment. But *pollute* may also refer to impairing the purity, integrity, or effectiveness of something (*a campaign polluted by allegations of sexual impropriety*). To **contaminate** is to spread harmful or undesirable impurities throughout something; unlike *pollute*, which suggests visible or noticeable impurities, **contaminate** is preferred where the change is unsuspected or not immediately noticeable (*milk contaminated by radioactive fallout from a nuclear plant accident*). **Adulterate** often refers to food products to which harmful, low-quality, or low-cost substances have been added in order to defraud the consumer (*cereal adulterated with sawdust*), although this word can apply to any mixture where the inferior or harmful element is included deliberately and in the hope that no one will notice (*a report adulterated with false statistics*). To **defile** is to *pollute* something that should be kept pure or sacred (*a church defiled by vandals*), while **taint** implies that decay or corruption has taken place (*the campaign was tainted by illegal donations*).

po•lo /pólo/ *n.* game of Asian origin played on horseback with a long-handled mallet and wooden ball.

po•lo•naise /pólənáyz, pò–/ *n.* 1 dance of Polish origin in triple time. 2 music for this.

po•lo•ni•um /pəlóneeəm/ *n. Chem.* rare radioactive metallic element, occurring naturally in uranium ores. ¶Symb.: Po

pol•ter•geist /póltərgìst/ *n.* noisy mischievous ghost, esp. one manifesting itself by physical damage.

pol•troon /poltróŏn/ *n.* spiritless coward. □□ **pol•troon'er•y** *n.*

poly-¹ /pólee/ *comb. form* denoting many or much.

poly-² /pólee/ *comb. form Chem.* polymerized (*polyester*).

pol•y•an•dry /póleeandree/ *n.* 1 polygamy in which a woman has more than one husband. 2 *Bot.* state of having numerous stamens. □□ **pol•y•an•drous** /–ándrəs/ *adj.*

pol•y•chro•mat•ic /póleekrōmátik/ *adj.* 1 many-colored. 2 (of radiation) containing more than one wavelength. □□ **pol•y•chro•ma•tism** /–krómətizəm/ *n.*

pol•y•chrome /póleekrōm/ • *adj.* in many colors. • *n.* work of art in several colors, esp. a colored statue. • *n.* **pol•y•chrom'ous** *adj.*

pol•y•es•ter /pólee-éstər/ *n.* type of synthetic fiber or resin.

pol•y•eth•yl•ene /pólee-éthileen/ *n. Chem.* plastic polymer of ethylene used for packaging and insulating materials.

po•lyg•a•my /pəligəmee/ *n.* practice of having more than one spouse at a time. □□ **po•lyg•a•mist** /–gəmist/ *n.* **po•lyg'a•mous** *adj.*

pol•y•glot /póleeglot/ • *adj.* knowing, using, or written in several languages. • *n.* polyglot

---

person. □□ **pol•y•glot'tal** *adj.* **pol•y•glot' tic** *adj.*

pol•y•gon /póleegon/ *n.* plane figure with many (usu. a minimum of three) sides and angles. □□ **po•lyg•o•nal** /pəlígənəl/ *adj.*

pol•y•graph /póleegraf/ *n.* machine designed to detect and record changes in physiological characteristics (e.g., rates of pulse and breathing), used esp. as a lie-detector.

pol•y•he•dron /póleehéedrən/ *n.* (*pl.* **pol•y• he•dra** /–drə/) solid figure with many (usu. more than six) faces. □□ **pol'y•he'dral** *adj.* **pol'y•he'dric** *adj.*

pol•y•math /póleemath/ *n.* 1 person of much or varied learning. 2 great scholar. □□ **pol• y•math'ic** *adj.*

pol•y•mer /pólimər/ *n.* compound composed of one or more large molecules that are formed from repeated units of smaller molecules.

Pol•y•ne•sian /póline´ezhən/ • *adj.* of or relating to Polynesia, a group of Pacific islands including New Zealand, Hawaii, Samoa, etc. • *n.* 1 a native of Polynesia. b person of Polynesian descent. 2 family of languages including Maori, Hawaiian, and Samoan.

pol•y•no•mi•al /pólinómeeəl/ *Math.* • *n.* expression of more than two algebraic terms. • *adj.* of or being a polynomial.

pol•yp /pólip/ *n.* 1 *Zool.* individual coelenterate. 2 *Med.* small usu. benign growth on a mucous membrane.

po•lyph•o•ny /pəlifənee/ *n.* (*pl.* **–nies**) *Mus.* contrapuntal music. □□ **pol•y•phon•ic** /póleefónik/ *adj.* **pol•y•phon'i•cal•ly** *adv.* **po•lyph'o•nous** *adj.*

pol•y•pro•py•lene /póleeprópileen/ *n. Chem.* polymer of propylene used for films, fibers, or molding materials.

pol•y•sac•cha•ride /póleesákərīd/ *n.* any of a group of carbohydrates whose molecules consist of long chains of monosaccharides.

pol•y•sty•rene /póleestireen/ *n.* plastic polymer of styrene used for insulation and in packaging.

pol•y•syl•lab•ic /póleesilábik/ *adj.* 1 (of a word) having many syllables. 2 characterized by the use of words of many syllables. □□ **pol•y•syl•lab'i•cal•ly** *adv.* **pol•y•syl•la•ble** /–sílabal/ *n.*

pol•y•tech•nic /póleetéknik/ • *n.* institution of higher education offering courses in many esp. vocational or technical subjects. • *adj.* dealing with or devoted to various vocational or technical subjects.

pol•y•the•ism /póleetheeizəm/ *n.* belief in or worship of more than one god. □□ **pol•y• the'ist** *n.* **pol•y•the•is'tic** *adj.*

pol•y•un•sat•u•rat•ed /pólecunsáchəraytid/ *adj. Chem.* (of a compound, esp. a fat or oil molecule) containing several double or triple bonds and therefore capable of further reaction.

pol•y•u•re•thane /póleeyŏŏrəthayn/ *n.* any polymer containing the urethane group, used in adhesives, paints, etc.

pol•y•vi•nyl chlo•ride /póleevínil/ *n.* polymer of vinyl chloride, easily colored and used for a wide variety of products including pipes, flooring, etc. ¶Abbr.: **PVC**.

po•made /pomáyd, -màad/ *n.* scented dressing for the hair and the skin of the head.

po•man•der /pómandər, pōmán–/ *n.* **1** ball of mixed aromatic substances. **2** (usu. spherical) container for this.

pome•gran•ate /pómigranit, pómgranit, púm–/ *n.* **1** orange-sized fruit with a tough reddish outer skin and containing many seeds in a red pulp. **2** tree bearing this.

pom•mel /póməl, póm–/ • *n.* **1** knob, esp. at the end of a sword hilt. **2** upward projecting front part of a saddle. • *v.tr.* = PUMMEL.

pomp /pomp/ *n.* **1** splendid display; splendor. **2** [often in *pl.*] vainglory (*pomps and vanities of this wicked world*).

■ **1** glory, grandeur, magnificence, show, pageantry, ceremony, spectacle, brilliance, ceremoniousness. **2** see VANITY 1, OSTENTATION.

pom•pom /pómpom/ *n.* (also **pom•pon** /–pon/) ornamental ball or tuft often worn on hats or clothing.

pomp•ous /pómpə s/ *adj.* self-important; affectedly grand or solemn. See synonym study at FORMAL. □□ **pom•pos•i•ty** /pompósitee/ *n.* (*pl.* **–ties**) **pom•pous•ly** *adv.* **pomp•ous•ness** *n.*

■ vain, proud, arrogant, haughty, overbearing, conceited, egotistical, boastful, braggart, snobbish, magisterial, imperious, *colloq.* uppity, highfalutin, stuck-up.

pon•cho /pónchō/ *n.* (*pl.* **–chos**) blanket-like cloak with a slit in the middle for the head.

pond /pond/ *n.* **1** fairly small body of still water formed naturally or by hollowing or embanking. **2** *joc.* the sea.

■ **1** pool, tarn, lake, *poet.* mere. **2** see SEA 1.

pon•der /póndər/ *v.* **1** *tr.* weigh mentally; think over; consider. **2** *intr.* [usu. foll. by *on*, *over*] think; muse.

■ brood over or upon, mull over, deliberate over, meditate upon or on; contemplate, cogitate.

pon•der•ous /póndərəs/ *adj.* **1** heavy; unwieldy. **2** laborious. **3** (of style, etc.) dull; tedious. See synonym study at HEAVY. □□ **pon'der•ous•ly** *adv.* **pon'der•ous•ness** *n.*

■ **1** weighty, cumbersome, cumbrous, elephantine. **2** tiresome, difficult; see also LABORIOUS 1. **3** labored, turgid, pedestrian, stilted, inflated, wordy, verbose, prolix, pompous, grandiloquent; see also TEDIOUS.

pon•iard /pónyard/ *n.* small slim dagger.

pon•tiff /póntif/ *n. RC Ch.* pope.

pon•tif•i•cal /pontífikəl/ *adj.* **1** *RC Ch.* of or befitting a pontiff; papal. **2** pompously dogmatic. □□ **pon•tif'i•cal•ly** *adv.*

pon•tif•i•cate /pontífikayt/ *v.intr.* **1** be pompously dogmatic. **2** *RC Ch.* officiate as bishop, esp. at Mass.

■ **1** see PREACH 2, RANT *v.*

pon•toon /pontóon/ *n.* **1** flat-bottomed boat. **2** each of several boats, hollow metal cylinders, etc., used to support a temporary bridge. **3** float for a seaplane.

po•ny /pónee/ *n.* (*pl.* **–nies**) **1** horse of any small breed. **2** small drinking glass. **3** [in *pl.*] *sl.* racehorses.

po•ny•tail /póneetayl/ *n.* person's hair drawn back, tied, and hanging down like a pony's tail.

poo•dle /pōōd'l/ *n.* **1** dog of a breed with a curly coat that is usually clipped. **2** this breed.

pooh-pooh /pōōpōō/ *v.tr.* express contempt for; ridicule.

■ see BELITTLE, DISMISS 4.

pool¹ /pōōl/ *n.* **1** small body of still water. **2** small shallow body of any liquid. **3** pool for swimming.

■ **1** pond, lake, tarn, *poet.* mere.

pool² /pōōl/ • *n.* **1 a** [often *attrib.*] common supply of persons, vehicles, commodities, etc., for sharing by a group (*car pool*). **b** group sharing duties, etc. **2** collective amount of players' stakes in gambling, etc. **3 a** joint commercial venture. **b** common funding for this. **4** any of several games similar to billiards played on a pool table with usu. 16 balls. • *v.tr.* **1** put (resources, etc.) into a common fund. **2** share (things) in common.

• *n.* **2** pot, jackpot, kitty, bank, purse. **3 a** syndicate, combine, cartel, trust, group, consortium. • *v.* **1** combine, merge, consolidate, amalgamate.

poop¹ /pōōp/ *n.* stern of a ship; aftermost and highest deck.

poop² /pōōp/ *n. sl.* up-to-date or inside information.

poor /pŏor/ *adj.* **1** lacking adequate money or means to live comfortably. **2 a** deficient in (a possession or quality) (*poor in spirit*). **b** (of soil, ore, etc.) unproductive. **3 a** scanty; inadequate (*a poor crop*). **b** less good than is usual or expected (*poor visibility*). **4** unfortunate (*you poor thing*). □ **poor boy** = *submarine sandwich*.

■ **1** needy, destitute, indigent, penniless, poverty-stricken, impoverished, badly off, necessitous, low-income; see also BROKE. **2 a** low in; lacking (in), wanting. **b** barren, unfruitful, infertile, sterile; depleted, exhausted, impoverished, low-yielding. **3 a** low, skimpy, meager, scant, insufficient, sparse. **b** bad, awful, inadequate, unsatisfactory, unacceptable, inefficient. **4** unlucky, pathetic, luckless, pitiful, pitiable, ill-fated, miserable, wretched, hapless.

poor•ly /pŏorlee/ • *adv.* in a poor manner; badly. • *predic. adj.* unwell.

■ *adv.* defectively, scantily, skimpily, inadequately, unsatisfactorily, incompetently, inexpertly, improperly, crudely. *predic. • adj.* indisposed, ailing, sick, off-color; see also ILL *adj.*

pop¹ /pop/ • *n.* **1** sudden sharp explosive sound as of a cork when drawn. **2** *colloq.* effervescent soft drink. **3** = *pop fly.* • *v.* (**popped**, **pop•ping**) **1** *intr. & tr.* make or cause to make a pop. **2** *intr. & tr.* put or move quickly or suddenly. **3** *intr.* [often foll. by *up*] (of a ball) rise up into the air. □ **pop fly** *Baseball* high fly ball hit esp. to the infield.

pop the question *colloq.* propose marriage.

pop-up *adj.* having parts that spring or extend up automatically (*pop-up book*). *n* = *pop fly.*

■ *n.* **1** explosion, bang, report, crack, snap. **2** fizzy *or* carbonated drink, soda. • *v.* **1** burst; explode, bang, go off. **2** run. □ **pop the question** ask for a person's hand (in marriage).

pop² /pop/ *colloq.* • *adj.* **1** in a popular or modern style. **2** performing popular music, etc. (*pop star*). • *n.* pop music. □ **pop art** art based on modern popular culture and the mass media. **pop culture** commercial culture based on popular taste.

pop³ /pop/ *n. colloq.* father.

pop. *abbr.* population.

pop•corn /pópkawrn/ *n.* **1** corn whose kernels burst open when heated. **2** these kernels when popped.

pope /pōp/ *n.* (as title usu. **Pope**) head of the Roman Catholic Church.

pop•in•jay /pópinjay/ *n.* fop; conceited person.

pop•lar /póplər/ *n.* tree with a usu. rapidly growing trunk and tremulous leaves.

pop•lin /póplin/ *n.* plain woven fabric usu. of cotton, with a corded surface.

pop•o•ver /pópovər/ *n.* light puffy hollow muffin made from an egg-rich batter.

pop•py /pópee/ *n.* (*pl.* **–pies**) plant with showy often red flowers and a milky sap.

pop•py•cock /pópeekok/ *n. sl.* nonsense.

Pop•si•cle /pópsikəl/ *n. propr.* flavored ice confection on a stick.

pop•u•lace /pópyələs/ *n.* the common people.

■ (ordinary) people, masses, commonalty, commonality, (general) public, commoners, multitude, hoi polloi, peasantry, proletariat, common folk, working class, rank and file.

pop•u•lar /pópyələr/ *adj.* **1** liked or admired by many people or by a specified group (*a popular hero*). **2 a** of or carried on by the general public (*popular meetings*). **b** prevalent among the general public (*popular discontent*). **3** adapted to the understanding, taste, or means of the people (*popular science*). □□ **pop′u•lar•ism** *n.* **pop•u•lar•i•ty** /-láritee/ *n.* **pop′u•lar•ly** *adv.*

■ **1** favorite, favored, well-received, well-liked; see also FASHIONABLE. **3** lay, nonprofessional; public, general, universal, average, everyday, ordinary, common. □□ **popular•ity** acceptance, reputation; vogue, trend, stylishness, *colloq. often derog.* trendiness. **popularly** commonly, generally, ordinarily, usually, universally.

pop•u•lar•ize /pópyələrīz/ *v.tr.* **1** make popular. **2** cause (a person, principle, etc.) to be generally known or liked. **3** present (a difficult subject) in a readily understandable form. □□ **pop•u•lar•i•za′tion** *n.* **pop′u•lar•iz•er** *n.*

pop•u•late /pópyəlayt/ *v.tr.* **1** inhabit; form the population of (a town, country, etc.). **2** supply with inhabitants.

■ **1** reside in, live in, occupy, *literary* dwell in. **2** colonize, settle, people.

pop•u•la•tion /pópyəláyshən/ *n.* **1** inhabitants. **2** total number of these or any group of living things.

■ **1** people, populace, residents, natives, citizenry, citizens, folk, *poet.* denizens.

pop•u•list /pópyəlist/ • *n.* member or adherent of a political party seeking support mainly from the ordinary people. • *adj.* of or relating to such a political party. □□ **pop′u•lism** *n.* **pop•u•lis′tic** *adj.*

pop•u•lous /pópyələs/ *adj.* thickly inhabited. □□ **pop′u•lous•ly** *adv.*

■ crowded, heavily populated, teeming, thronged.

por•ce•lain /páwrsəlin, páwrslin/ *n.* **1** hard vitrified translucent ceramic. **2** objects made of this. □□ **por•cel•a•ne•ous** /páwrsəláyneeəs/ *adj.*

porch /pawrch/ *n.* **1** covered shelter for the entrance of a building. **2** veranda. □□ **porched** *adj.* **porch′less** *adj.*

por•cine /páwrsin, -sin/ *adj.* of or like pigs.

por•cu•pine /páwrkyəpīn/ *n.* rodent having defensive spines or quills.

pore¹ /pawr/ *n.* esp. *Biol.* minute opening in a surface through which gases, liquids, or fine solids may pass.

■ orifice, hole, aperture, vent, perforation, *Biol.* spiracle.

pore² /pawr/ *v.intr.* [foll. by *over*] **1** be absorbed in studying (a book, etc.). **2** meditate on; think intently about.

■ (*pore over*) study, examine, scrutinize, peruse, read, go over; see also MEDITATE.

pork /pawrk/ *n.* **1** the (esp. unsalted) flesh of a pig, used as food. **2** = *pork barrel.* □ **pork barrel** *colloq.* government funds as a source of political benefit.

por•ky /páwrkee/ *adj.* (**por•ki•er, por•ki•est**) **1** *colloq.* fleshy; fat. **2** of or like pork.

porn /pawrn/ *n. colloq.* pornography.

por•nog•ra•phy /pawrnógrəfee/ *n.* **1** explicit description or exhibition of sexual activity in literature, films, etc. **2** literature, etc., characterized by this. □□ **por•nog′ra•pher** *n.* **por•no•graph•ic** /nəgráfik/ *adj.* **por•no•graph′i•cal•ly** *adv.*

■ **2** erotica, curiosa, *colloq.* porn, porno; smut, filth, dirt. □□ **pornographic** obscene, lewd, offensive, indecent, prurient, smutty, blue, dirty, salacious, licentious.

po•rous /páwrəs/ *adj.* **1** full of pores. **2** letting through air, water, etc. □□ **po•ros•i•ty** /pórósitee/ *n.* **po′rous•ly** *adv.*

■ spongy, spongelike; permeable, pervious, penetrable.

por•phy•ry /páwrfiree/ *n.* (*pl.* **–ries**) hard rock quarried in ancient Egypt, composed of crystals of white or red feldspar in a red matrix. □□ **por•phy•rit•ic** /-rítik/ *adj.*

por•poise /páwrpəs/ *n.* sea mammal of the whale family with a low triangular dorsal fin and a blunt rounded snout.

por•ridge /páwrij, pór–/ *n.* dish consisting of oatmeal or another cereal boiled in water or milk.

por•rin•ger /páwrinjər, pór–/ *n.* small bowl, often with a handle, for soup, stew, etc.

port¹ /pawrt/ *n.* **1** harbor. **2** town with a harbor. □ **port of call** place where a ship or a person stops on a journey.

■ haven; seaport.

port² /pawrt/ *n.* (in full **port wine**) strong,

sweet, dark red (occas. brown or white) forti-fied wine of Portugal.

port³ /pawrt/ • *n.* left side (looking forward) of a ship, boat, or aircraft. • *v.tr.* [also *absol.*] turn (the helm) to port.

port⁴ /pawrt/ *n.* **1** opening in the side of a ship for entrance, loading, etc. **2** porthole.

por•ta•ble /páwrtəbəl/ • *adj.* easily movable; convenient for carrying. • *n.* portable object, e.g., a radio, typewriter, etc. ▫▫ **por•ta•bil′i•ty** *n.* **por′ta•bly** *adv.*

■ *adj.* transportable, manageable, handy, light, lightweight, compact.

por•tage /páwrtij, –taa͞zh/ • *n.* **1** carrying of boats or goods between two navigable waters. **2** place at which this is necessary. • *v.tr.* convey (a boat or goods) over a portage.

por•tal /páwrt′l/ *n.* doorway or gate, etc., esp. a large and elaborate one.

port•cul•lis /pawrtkúlis/ *n.* strong heavy grat-ing lowered to block a gateway in a fortress, etc.

por•tend /pawrténd/ *v.tr.* **1** foreshadow as an omen. **2** give warning of.

■ see FORESHADOW.

por•tent /páwrtent/ *n.* omen; sign of some-thing to come, esp. something of a momen-tous or calamitous nature.

por•ten•tous /pawrténtəs/ *adj.* **1** like or serv-ing as a portent. **2** pompously solemn. ▫▫ **por•ten′tous•ly** *adv.*

■ **1** ominous, threatening, fateful, menac-ing, foreboding, lowering, unpromising, un-propitious, ill-omened. **2** dignified, stately, courtly, majestic, august.

por•ter¹ /páwrtər/ *n.* **1** person employed to carry luggage, etc., at an airport, hotel, etc. **2** dark brown bitter beer. ▫▫ **por′ter•age** *n.*

■ **1** bearer, (baggage) carrier *or* attendant, redcap.

por•ter² /páwrtər/ *n.* gatekeeper or doorkeep-er.

■ watchman, doorman, concierge; care-taker.

por•ter•house steak /páwrtərhows/ *n.* thick steak cut from the thick end of a sirloin.

port•fo•li•o /pawrtfṓleeṓ/ *n.* (*pl.* **–os**) **1** case for keeping loose sheets of paper, drawings, etc. **2** range of investments held by a person, a company, etc. **3** office of a minister of state. **4** samples of an artist's work.

port•hole /páwrt-hōl/ *n.* (esp. glassed-in) ap-erture in a ship's or aircraft's side for the ad-mission of light.

por•ti•co /páwrtikṓ/ *n.* (*pl.* **–coes** or **–cos**) roof supported by columns usu. attached as a porch to a building.

■ porch, veranda, gallery, colonnade, stoa.

por•tion /páwrshən/ • *n.* **1** part or share. **2** amount of food allotted to one person. **3** one's destiny or lot. See synonym study at FRAGMENT. • *v.tr.* **1** divide (a thing) into por-tions. **2** [foll. by *out*] distribute.

■ *n.* **1** allotment, quota, ration, apportion-ment, allowance; segment, section, division. **2** helping, serving; ration, share; piece. **3** see DESTINY 2. • *v.* **1** partition, split up, carve up, cut up, break up, section. **2** share out, al-

locate, ration, allot, dole out, deal (out), par-cel out.

Port•land ce•ment /páwrtlənd/ *n.* cement manufactured from chalk and clay.

port•ly /páwrtlee/ *adj.* (**port•li•er, port•li•est**) corpulent; stout. ▫▫ **port′li•ness** *n.*

port•man•teau /pawrtmántō, páwrtmantṓ/ *n.* (*pl.* **port•man•teaus** or **port•man•teaux** /–tōz, –tṓz/) leather trunk for clothes, etc., opening into two equal parts. ▫ **portman-teau word** word blending the sounds and combining the meanings of two others, e.g., *motel* from *motor* and *hotel.*

por•trait /páwrtrit, –trayt/ *n.* **1** representation of a person or animal, esp. of the face, made by drawing, painting, photography, etc. **2** verbal picture; graphic description. **3** (in graphic design, etc.) format in which the height of an illustration, etc., is greater than the width (cf. LANDSCAPE).

■ **1** picture, likeness, vignette, image, rendi-tion, portrayal; sketch, drawing, painting. **2** profile, portrayal; account, characteriza-tion.

por•trait•ist /páwrtritist/ *n.* person who makes portraits.

por•trai•ture /páwrtrichər/ *n.* the making of portraits.

por•tray /pawrtráy/ *v.tr.* **1** make a likeness of. **2** describe graphically. ▫▫ **por•tray′a•ble** *adj.* **por•tray′al** *n.* **por•tray′er** *n.*

■ represent, picture, show, depict, render, characterize, delineate. ▫▫ **portrayal** see PORTRAIT 1, 2, *rendering* (RENDER).

Por•tu•guese /páwrchəgeéz, –geés/ • *n.* (*pl.* same) **1 a** native or national of Portugal. **b** person of Portuguese descent. **2** language of Portugal. • *adj.* of or relating to Portugal or its people or language.

pose /pōz/ • *v.* **1** *intr.* assume a certain atti-tude of body, esp. when being photographed or being painted for a portrait. **2** *intr.* [foll. by *as*] pretend to be (another person, etc.) (*posing as a celebrity*). **3** *intr.* behave affect-edly in order to impress others. **4** *tr.* put for-ward or present (a question, etc.). • *n.* **1** an attitude of body or mind. **2** affectation; pre-tense.

■ *v.* **1** sit, model. **2** impersonate, be dis-guised as, masquerade as, profess to be, pass for. **3** attitudinize, posture, put on airs; see also *show off* 2. **4** set, ask, submit, broach, advance, raise. • *n.* **1** position, posture, stance; see also ATTITUDE. **2** act, affected-ness, display, façade, show; attitude.

po•seur /pōzőr/ *n.* (*fem.* **po•seuse** /pōzőz/) person who poses for effect or behaves af-fectedly.

posh /posh/ *colloq. adj.* elegant; stylish. ▫▫ **posh′ly** *adv.* **posh′ness** *n.*

■ smart, upmarket, high-class, deluxe, plush, luxurious, grand, swanky, *colloq.* classy.

pos•it /pózit/ *v.tr.* **1** assume as a fact; postu-late. **2** put in place or position.

■ **1** hypothesize, propound, put *or* set forth, put forward, advance, pose, predicate. **2** see POSITION *v.*

po•si•tion /pəzíshən/ • *n.* **1** place occupied by a person or thing. **2** placement or arrangement. **3** proper place (*in position*). **4** advantage (*jockey for position*). **5** viewpoint. **6** person's situation in relation to others. **7** rank; status. **8** paid employment. • *v.tr.* place in position. □ **in a position to** able to. □□ **po•si′tion•al** *adj.* **po•si′tion•er** *n.*

■ *n.* **1** spot, location, site, situation; whereabouts. **2** posture, attitude, stance, pose; disposition, configuration. **3** see PLACE *n.* **5** point of view, outlook, attitude, stance, vantage, vantage point, stand, standpoint, opinion. **6** condition, state; circumstances. **7** class, place, standing, station. **8** job, occupation, situation, post, office, place. • *v.* put, lay, lie, situate, site, locate, establish, set, fix, settle, pose.

pos•i•tive /pózitiv/ • *adj.* **1** explicit; definite. (*positive proof*). **2** (of a person) convinced, confident, or overconfident in his or her opinion. **3 a** constructive; directional (*positive thinking*). **b** optimistic. **4** marked by the presence rather than absence of qualities or (esp. *Med.*) symptoms. **5** esp. *Philos.* dealing only with matters of fact; practical. **6** tending toward increase or progress. **7** greater than zero. **8** *Electr.* of, containing, or producing the kind of electrical charge produced by rubbing glass with silk; absence of electrons. **9** (of a photographic image) showing lights and shades or colors true to the original. • *n.* positive photograph, quantity, etc. □□ **pos′i•tive•ly** *adv.*, **pos′i•tive•ness** *n.* **pos•i•tiv•i•ty** /pózitívitee/ *n.*

■ *adj.* **1** sure, certain, unequivocal, categorical, absolute, unqualified, unambiguous, unmistakable, clear-cut, clear, firm, express, decisive, indisputable. **2** sure, certain, satisfied, decided; dogmatic, pontifical, opinionated, pigheaded, stubborn. **3 a** productive, useful, practical, functional, pragmatic. **b** beneficial, favorable, complimentary, productive, supportive; promising, encouraging, cheerful, confident. **4** affirmative, confirming. □□ **positively** definitely, absolutely, unquestionably, certainly, assuredly, constructively; see also *utterly* (UTTER[1]).

pos•i•tron /pózitron/ *n.* *Physics* elementary particle with a positive charge equal to the negative charge of an electron and having the same mass as an electron.

poss. *abbr.* **1** possession. **2** possessive. **3** possible. **4** possibly.

pos•se /pósee/ *n.* **1** strong force or company or assemblage. **2** (in full **pos•se co•mi•ta•tus** /kómitáytəs/) summoned body of law enforcers.

pos•sess /pəzés/ *v.tr.* **1** hold as property; own. **2** have a faculty, quality, etc. **3** occupy; dominate the mind of. (*possessed by fear*). □□ **pos•ses′sor** *n.*

■ **1** be in possession of, have, enjoy, be blessed *or* endowed with. **2** hold, contain, embody, embrace, include. **3** take over, take control of, have power over, bedevil, captivate, enchant; control, govern, influence, hold, consume, obsess; see also BEWITCH.

pos•ses•sion /pəzéshən/ *n.* **1** possessing or being possessed. **2** thing possessed. **3** holding or occupancy. **4** [in *pl.*] property, wealth,

subject territory, etc. □□ **pos•ses′sion•less** *adj.*

■ **1, 3** ownership, proprietorship; control, hold, tenure, keeping, care, custody, guardianship, protection. **4** (*possessions*) belongings, effects, chattels, assets, worldly goods, things.

pos•ses•sive /pəzésiv/ • *adj.* **1** a desire to possess or retain what one already owns. **2** jealous and domineering. **3** *Gram.* indicating possession. • *n.* (in full **possessive case**) *Gram.* case of nouns and pronouns expressing possession. □□ **pos•ses′sive•ly** *adv.* **pos•ses′sive•ness** *n.*

■ *adj.* **1** greedy, selfish, ungenerous, stingy, niggardly. **2** overprotective, controlling, overbearing.

pos•si•bil•i•ty /pósibílitee/ *n.* (*pl.* **–ties**) **1** state or fact of being possible. **2** thing that may exist or happen. **3** [usu. in *pl.*] potential (*esp.have possibilities*).

■ **1** conceivability, feasibility, plausibility, admissibility; likelihood, chance, prospect. **3** (*possibilities*) potentiality, promise; capability, capacity.

pos•si•ble /pósibəl/ *adj.* **1** capable of existing, happening, being done, etc. **2** potential (*possible way of doing it*).

■ **1** feasible, plausible, imaginable, conceivable, thinkable, credible, believable, tenable, realizable, achievable, attainable; likely, probable.

pos•si•bly /pósiblee/ *adv.* **1** perhaps. **2** in accordance with possibility (*cannot possibly refuse*).

■ **1** maybe, if possible, *joc.* peradventure. **2** in any way, under any circumstances, at all, by any chance, ever.

pos•sum /pósəm/ *n.* *colloq.* = OPOSSUM □ **play possum 1** pretend to be asleep or unconscious. **2** feign ignorance.

post[1] /pōst/ • *n.* **1** piece of timber or metal set upright in the ground, etc., used as a support, marker, etc. **2** pole, etc., marking the start or finish of a race. • *v.tr.* **1** attach (a paper, etc.) in a prominent place. **2** announce or advertise by placard or in a published text.

■ *n.* **1** pole, stake, upright, column, pillar, pale, picket, shaft, pier, pylon, pile, piling, strut, shore, stanchion. • *v.* **1** put *or* pin *or* tack *or* stick *or* hang up, affix. **2** proclaim, publish, propagate, promulgate.

post[2] /pōst/ • *n.* mail. • *v.tr.* (esp. as **posted** *adj.*) supply a person with information (*keep me posted*). □ **post exchange** *Mil.* store at a military base, etc. **post-haste** with great speed. **Post Office 1** public department or corporation responsible for postal services. **2** (**post office**) room or building where postal business is carried on.

■ *n.* postal service; letters, correspondence. • *v.* **1** send (off), dispatch, mail. **2** (*keep a person posted*) advise, brief, notify, *colloq.* fill in; see also INFORM 1.

post[3] /pōst/ • *n.* **1** place where a soldier is stationed or which he or she patrols. **2** place of duty. **3 a** position taken up by a body of soldiers. **b** force occupying this. **4** job.

• *v.tr.* place or station (soldiers, an employee, etc.).

■ *n.* **4** assignment, appointment, position; employment, work. • *v.* put, position, situate, set, locate.

post- /pōst/ *prefix* after in time or order (*post-war*).

post•age /pṓstij/ *n.* amount charged for sending a letter, etc., by mail. □ **postage stamp** official stamp affixed to a letter, etc., indicating the amount of postage paid.

post•al /pṓst'l/ *adj.* of or by mail.

post•card /pṓstkaárd/ *n.* card for sending by mail.

post•er /pṓstər/ *n.* **1** placard in a public place. **2** large printed picture. □ **poster paint** gummy opaque paint.

■ **1** notice, bill; see also SIGN *n.* 4. **2** print, reproduction.

pos•te•ri•or /posteéreeər, pō–/ • *adj.* **1** later; coming after in series, order, or time. **2** at the back. • *n.* buttocks. □□ **pos•te•ri•or•i•ty** /–áwritee, –ór–/ *n.* **pos•te'ri•or•ly** *adv.*

■ *adj.* **1** ensuing, following, succeeding; see also SUBSEQUENT. **2** hind, rear, back, hinder, rearward. • *n.* rump, seat, backside(s), *colloq.* bottom, *colloq. euphem.* derrière, *sl.* tush, *sl.* ass, butt, can.

pos•ter•i•ty /postéritee/ *n.* **1** all succeeding generations. **2** descendants of a person.

■ **2** successors, heirs, children, offspring, issue.

post•grad•u•ate /pōstgrájōōət/ *adj.* **1** (of a course of study) carried on after taking a high school or college degree. **2** of or relating to postgraduate students.

post•hu•mous /pṓschəməs/ *adj.* **1** occurring after death. **2** (of a child) born after the death of its father. **3** (of a book, etc.) published after the author's death. □□ **post'hu•mous•ly** *adv.*

post•man /pṓstmən/ *n.* (*pl.* **–men;** *fem.* **post•wom•an,** *pl.* **–wom•en**) person employed to deliver and collect letters, etc.

post•mark /pṓstmaark/ • *n.* official dated postage cancellation mark stamped on a letter. • *v.tr.* mark (an envelope, etc.) with this.

post•mas•ter /pṓstmástər/ *n.* person in charge of a post office.

post•mod•ern /pṓstmódərn/ *adj.* (in literature, architecture, the arts, etc.) denoting a movement reacting against modern tendencies, esp. by drawing attention to former deficiencies. □□ **post'mod'ern•ism'** *n.* **post'mod'ern•ist** *n. & adj.*

post•mor•tem /pōstmáwrtəm/ • *n.* **1** (in full **postmortem examination**) examination made after death, esp. to determine its cause. **2** *colloq.* discussion analyzing the course and result of a game, election, etc. • *adv. & adj.* after death.

■ *n.* **1** autopsy, necropsy. **2** see ANALYSIS 1.

post•na•tal /pṓstnáyt'l/ *adj.* characteristic of or relating to the period after childbirth.

post•paid• /pṓstpáyd/ *adj.* on which postage has been paid.

post•pone /pōstpṓn, pəspṓn/ *v.tr.* cause or arrange (an event, etc.) to take place at a later time. □□ **post•pon'able** *adj.* **post•pone'ment** *n.* **post•pon'er** *n.*

■ delay, adjourn, defer, keep in abeyance, put off *or* aside *or* back, lay aside, suspend, shelve. □□ **postponement** delay, adjournment, suspension, deferment, deferral.

SYNONYM STUDY: postpone

ADJOURN, DEFER, DELAY, SUSPEND. All of these verbs have to do with putting things off. **Defer** is the broadest in meaning; it suggests putting something off until a later time (*to defer payment; to defer a discussion*). If you **postpone** an event or activity, you put it off intentionally, usually until a definite time in the future (*we postponed the party until the next weekend*). If you **adjourn** an activity, you postpone it until another day or place; *adjourn* is usually associated with meetings or other formal gatherings that are brought to an end and then resumed (*the judge adjourned the hearing until the following morning*). If you **delay** something, you postpone it because of obstacles (*delayed by severe thunderstorms and highway flooding*) or because you are reluctant to do it (*to delay going to the dentist*). **Suspend** suggests stopping an activity for a while, usually for a reason (*forced to suspend work on the bridge until the holiday weekend was over*).

post•script /pṓstskript, pṓskript/ *n.* additional paragraph or remark, usu. at the end of a letter, introduced by 'P.S.'.

post•tu•late • *v.tr.* /póschəlayt/ **1** assume as a necessary condition, esp. as a basis for reasoning; take for granted. **2** claim. • *n.* /póschəlat/ **1** thing postulated. **2** fundamental prerequisite or condition. □□ **pos•tu•la•tion** /–láyshən/ *n.*

pos•ture /póschər/ • *n.* **1** bodily carriage or bearing. **2** mental or spiritual attitude or condition. **3** condition or state of affairs, etc.) (*in more diplomatic postures*). • *v.* **1** *intr.* assume a mental or physical attitude, esp. for effect. **2** *tr.* pose (a person). □□ **pos'tur•al** *adj.* **pos'tur•er** *n.*

■ *n.* **1** pose, position, attitude, stance; see also CARRIAGE 4. **2** stance, position, feeling, sentiment, outlook, (point of) view, viewpoint, orientation. **3** position, situation, disposition, circumstance, status. • *v.* **1** pose, attitudinize, put on airs, put on a show, do for effect.

po•sy /pṓzee/ *n.* (*pl.* **–sies**) small bunch of flowers.

■ bouquet, nosegay, spray.

pot¹ /pot/ • *n.* **1** vessel, usu. rounded, for holding liquids or solids or for cooking in. **2** contents of a pot. **3** total amount of the bet in a game, etc. **4** *colloq.* large sum (*pots of money*). • *v.tr.* (**pot•ted, pot•ting**) place in a pot. □ **go to pot** *colloq.* deteriorate; be ruined. **pot roast** a piece of meat cooked slowly in a covered dish. **pot-roast** *v.tr.* cook (a piece of meat) in this way. □□ **pot'ful** *n.* (*pl.* **–fuls**).

■ *n.* **1** pan, saucepan, cauldron, casserole, cooking pot, stewpan. **3** jackpot, bank, kitty, stakes, pool. **4** see LOT *n.* 1. □ **go to pot** see DETERIORATE.

pot² /pot/ *n. sl.* marijuana.

po•ta•ble /pótəbəl/ *adj.* drinkable. □□ **po•ta•bil´i•ty** *n.*

pot•ash /pótash/ *n.* alkaline potassium compound.

po•tas•si•um /pətáseeəm/ *n. Chem.* soft silvery white metallic element. ¶Symb.: **K**. □□ **po•tas´sic** *adj.*

po•ta•to /pətáytō/ *n.* (*pl.* **–toes**) 1 starchy plant tuber that is cooked and used for food. 2 plant bearing this.

pot•bel•ly /pótbelee/ *n.* (*pl.* **–lies**) 1 protruding stomach. 2 person with this. 3 small bulbous stove. □□ **pot´bel´lied** *adj.*

pot•boil•er /pótboylər/ *n.* work of literature or art done merely to make the writer or artist a living.

po•tent /pót´nt/ *adj.* 1 powerful; strong. 2 (of a reason) cogent; forceful. 3 (of a male) capable of sexual erection or orgasm. □□ **po´tence** *n.* **po´ten•cy** *n.* **po´tent•ly** *adv.*

■ 1 mighty, vigorous, forceful, formidable, influential. 2 effective, convincing, persuasive, compelling, efficacious, sound, valid. 3 virile, masculine, manly.

po•ten•tate /pót´ntayt/ *n.* monarch or ruler.

po•ten•tial /pəténshəl/ • *adj.* capable of coming into being or action; latent. See synonym study at LATENT. • *n.* 1 capacity for use or development; possibility. 2 usable resources. 3 *Physics* quantity determining the energy of mass in a gravitational field or of charge in an electric field. □□ **po•ten•ti•al•i•ty** /–sheeálitee/ *n.* **po•ten´tial•ly** *adv.*

■ *adj.* possible, likely, implicit, implied, imminent, developing, budding, embryonic, dormant, quiescent, future, unrealized. • *n.* 1 capability, aptitude, potency; (*have potential*) *colloq.* have what it takes.

poth•er /póthər/ *n.* noise; commotion; fuss.

pot•herb /pótərb, –harb/ *n.* any herb grown in a kitchen garden or a pot.

pot•hole /pót-hōl/ *n.* 1 deep hole, as in rock. 2 hole in a road surface.

po•tion /pōshən/ *n.* a liquid medicine, drug, poison, etc.

■ draft, brew, potation, *formal* beverage, *joc.* libation; philter, elixir, tonic, concoction; dose.

pot•luck /pótlək/ *n.* 1 whatever (hospitality, food, etc.) is available. 2 meal to which each guest brings a dish to share.

pot•pour•ri /pópoōree/ *n.* 1 mixture of dried petals and spices used to perfume a room, etc. 2 musical or literary medley.

■ 2 mixture, miscellany, assortment, olla podrida, gallimaufry, salmagundi, patchwork.

pot•sherd /pótshərd/ *n.* shard of pottery, esp. one found on an archaeological site.

pot•shot /pótshót/ *n.* 1 random shot. 2 shot aimed at an animal, etc., within easy reach. 3 shot at a game bird, etc., merely to provide a meal.

pot•tage /pótij/ *n. archaic* soup; stew.

pot•ter /pótər/ *n.* maker of ceramic vessels. □ **potter's field** burial place for paupers, strangers, etc. **potter's wheel** horizontal revolving disk to carry clay for making pots.

pot•ter•y /pótəree/ *n.* (*pl.* **–ies**) 1 vessels, etc., made of fired clay. 2 potter's work. 3 potter's workshop.

■ 1 earthenware, ceramics, terra cotta, crockery, stoneware, porcelain, china.

pot•ty /pótee/ *n.* (*pl.* **–ties**) *colloq.* small pot for toilet-training a child.

pouch /powch/ • *n.* 1 small bag or detachable outside pocket. 2 pocketlike receptacle of kangaroos, etc. • *v.tr.* put or make into a pouch. □□ **pouched** *adj.* **pouch´y** *adj.*

■ *n.* 1 sack, purse, *dial.* poke, *usu. hist.* reticule.

poul•tice /pōltis/ • *n.* soft medicated and usu. heated mass applied to the body for relieving soreness and inflammation. • *v.tr.* apply a poultice to.

poul•try /pōltree/ *n.* domestic fowls (ducks, geese, turkeys, chickens, etc.), esp. as a source of food.

pounce /powns/ • *v.intr.* 1 spring or swoop, esp. as in capturing prey. 2 (often foll. by *on*, *upon*) make a sudden attack. • *n.* act or an instance of pouncing. □□ **pounc´er** *n.*

■ *v.* leap, jump; (*pounce on*) fall upon, take by surprise or unawares, attack, ambush, mug. • *n.* spring, swoop, dive, sweep, leap, jump.

pound¹ /pownd/ *n.* 1 unit of weight equal to 16 oz. avoirdupois or 12 oz. troy. ¶Abbr.: **lb.** 2 (in full **pound sterling**) (*pl.* same or **pounds**) chief monetary unit of the UK and several other countries. □ **pound sign 1** the sign #. 2 the sign £, representing pound sterling. □□ **pound´age** *n.*

pound² /pownd/ *v.* 1 *tr.* crush or beat with repeated heavy blows. 2 *intr.* deliver heavy blows or gunfire. 3 *intr.* (of the heart) beat heavily. □□ **pound´er** *n.*

■ 1 batter, pelt, hammer, pummel; thump, belabor, thrash, bludgeon, cudgel, strike; grind, powder, pulverize. 3 throb, hammer, thump, pulse, pulsate, palpitate.

pound³ /pownd/ *n.* enclosure where stray animals or officially removed vehicles are kept until redeemed.

■ pen, compound, confine, yard, see also ENCLOSURE 4.

pour /pawr/ *v.* 1 *intr. & tr.* flow or cause to flow, esp. downward. 2 *tr.* dispense (a drink) by pouring. 3 *intr.* [of rain, or with *it* as subject] fall heavily. 4 *intr.* come or go in profusion or rapid succession (*letters poured in*). □□ **pour´a•ble** *adj.* **pour´er** *n.*

■ 1 run, gush, rush, flood, stream, course, spout, spurt; discharge, let out, let flow. 3 rain, teem down, come down in buckets, rain cats and dogs, pelt down. 4 stream, swarm, crowd, throng, gush, teem.

pout /powt/ • *v.* 1 *intr.* push the lips forward as an expression of displeasure or sulking. 2 *tr.* push (the lips) forward in pouting. • *n.* 1 such an action or expression. 2 (**the pouts**) a fit of sulking. □□ **pout´er** *n.* **pout´ing•ly** *adv.* **pout´y** *adj.*

■ *v.* 1 make a moue, pull a long face, frown, lower, knit one's brows; mope, brood, sulk. • *n.* 1 moue, (long) face, grimace, mouth, scowl, frown. **2 (the pouts)** sulk, huff, mood; the sulks.

pov•er•ty /póvərtee/ *n.* **1** being poor; need. **2** scarcity or lack. □ **poverty-stricken** extremely poor.

■ **1** want, penury, indigence, destitution, pauperism, impecuniousness, neediness, beggary. **2** scarceness, want, need, insufficiency, shortage, dearth, paucity. □ **poverty-stricken** see POOR 1.

POW *abbr.* prisoner of war.

pow•der /pówdər/ • *n.* **1** substance in the form of fine dry particles. **2** medicine or cosmetic in this form. **3** = GUNPOWDER. • *v.tr.* **1** apply powder to. **2** (esp. as **powdered** *adj.*) reduce to a fine powder (*powdered milk*). □ **powder puff** soft pad for applying powder to the skin. **powder room** women's toilet. □□ **pow'der•y** *adj.*

■ *n.* **1** dust; talc. • *v.* **1** dust; dredge, flour. **2** pulverize, grind, crush, pound, granulate, levigate, triturate. □ **powder room** toilet, lavatory, ladies' room, rest room, bathroom, washroom, comfort station.

pow•er /pówər/ • *n.* **1** the ability to do or act (*will do all in my power*). **2** particular faculty of body or mind (*powers of persuasion*). **3** government, influence, or authority; control (*the party in power*). **4** authorization; delegated authority (*police powers*). **5** influential person, body, government, etc. **6** vigor; energy. **7** active property or function (*heating power*). **8** mechanical or electrical energy as distinct from hand labor (often *attrib.*: *power tools, power steering*). **9 a** public supply of (esp. electrical) energy. **b** particular source or form of energy (*hydroelectric power*). **10** *Physics* rate of energy output. **11** product obtained when a number is multiplied by itself a certain number of times (*2 to the power of 3 = 8*). **12** magnifying capacity of a lens. See synonym study at JURISDICTION. • *v.tr.* supply with mechanical or electrical energy. □ **power of attorney** see ATTORNEY. **power plant 1** facility producing esp. electrical power. **2** source of power, as an engine. **the powers that be** those in authority. □□ **pow'ered** *adj.* [also in *comb.*].

■ *n.* **2** capacity, capability, ability, potential, competence, potentiality, energies; talent, skill, ability, gift, aptitude, genius, knack. **3** dominance, mastery, rule, command, ascendancy, sovereignty, dominion; weight, sway, pull, *colloq.* clout, *sl.* drag. **4** right, warrant; see also LICENSE *n.* 1, PERMISSION. **6** strength, might, force, mightiness, potency, forcefulness, brawn, muscle. **9** electricity. □ **the powers that be** establishment, government, administration, authorities.

pow•er•boat /pówərbōt/ *n.* powerful motor-boat.

pow•er•ful /pówərfŏŏl/ *adj.* having much power or influence. □□ **pow'er•ful•ly** *adv.* **pow'er•ful•ness** *n.*

■ potent, strong, mighty, vigorous, robust, energetic, intense, substantial, great, high; influential, strong, compelling, forceful, weighty; important, impressive, effectual.

pow•er•house /pówərhóws/ *n.* **1** = power plant. **2** *colloq.* person or thing of great energy.

pow•er•less /pówərlis/ *adj.* **1** without power or strength. **2** wholly unable. □□ **pow'er•less•ly** *adv.* **pow'er•less•ness** *n.*

■ **1** helpless, ineffectual, ineffective, incapacitated, weak. **2** not able to, unfit *or* incompetent *or* unqualified to.

pow•wow /pów-wów/ • *n.* a meeting for discussion (orig. among Native Americans). • *v.tr.* hold a powwow.

pox /poks/ *n.* **1** any virus disease producing a rash of pimples that leave pockmarks on healing. **2** *colloq.* = SYPHILIS.

pp *abbr.* pianissimo.

pp. *abbr.* pages.

ppd. *abbr.* **1** postpaid. **2** prepaid.

p.p.m. *abbr.* parts per million.

PPS *abbr.* additional postscript.

PR *abbr.* **1** public relations. **2** Puerto Rico.

Pr *symb. Chem.* praseodymium.

pr. *abbr.* pair.

prac•ti•ca•ble /práktikəbəl/ *adj.* **1** that can be done or used. **2** possible in practice. □□ **prac•ti•ca•bil'i•ty** *n.* **prac'ti•ca•bly** *adv.*

■ feasible, workable, performable, doable, achievable, attainable, accomplishable, viable.

prac•ti•cal /práktikəl/ *adj.* **1** of or concerned with practice or use rather than theory. **2** useful; functional. **3** (of a person) inclined to action rather than speculation; able to make things function well. **4** so in practice or effect. **5** feasible; concerned with what is actually possible (*practical politics*). □ **practical joke** humorous trick played on a person. □□ **prac•ti•cal•i•ty** /-kálitee/ *n.* (*pl.* -ties).

■ **1** empirical, pragmatic, empiric, experimental, applied, field, hands-on. **2** pragmatic, usable, utilitarian, serviceable; appropriate, suitable. **3** down-to-earth, pragmatic, hardheaded, realistic, businesslike, commonsensical, sensible. **4** virtual, effective, essential. □ **practical joke** see PRANK.

prac•ti•cal•ly /práktiklee/ *adv.* **1** virtually; almost (*practically nothing*). **2** in a practical way.

■ **1** (very) nearly, just about, more or less. **2** realistically, in fact, in reality; empirically; sensibly, efficiently.

prac•tice /práktis/ • *n.* **1** habitual action or performance. **2** habit or custom (*has been my regular practice*). **3 a** repeated exercise in an activity requiring the development of skill. **b** session of this. **4** action or execution as opposed to theory. **5** the professional work or business of a doctor, lawyer, etc. • *v.* **1** *tr.* perform habitually; carry out in action. **2** *tr. & intr.* do repeatedly as an exercise to improve a skill; exercise oneself in or on (an activity requiring skill). **3** *tr.* (as **practiced** *adj.*) experienced, expert. **4** *tr.* pursue or be engaged in (a profession, religion, etc.). □□ **prac'tic•er** *n.*

■ *n.* **2** praxis, *formal or joc.* wont; routine, convention, tradition, rule, procedure, mode, style, way. **3** discipline, drill, repetition, rehearsal, training, preparation; work-out. **4** operation, enactment, reality, actuality, fact, truth. • *v.* **1** make a practice of, do, act, put into practice. **2** work out, train, prepare, rehearse, study; run through, go through. **3** (**practiced**) accomplished, proficient, skilled, capable, adept, seasoned, able, qualified, gifted, talented, skillful.

prac•ti•tion•er /praktíshənər/ *n.* person practicing a profession, esp. medicine (*general practitioner*).

prae•to•ri•an guard /preetáwreeən/ (also **pre•to•ri•an**) *Rom.Hist.* bodyguard of the Roman emperor.

prag•mat•ic /pragmátik/ *adj.* dealing with matters with regard to their practical requirements or consequences. □□ **prag•mat′i•cal•ly** *adv.*

prag•ma•tism /prágmətizəm/ *n.* **1** pragmatic attitude or procedure. **2** philosophy that evaluates assertions solely by their practical consequences and bearing on human interests. □□ **prag′ma•tist** *n.* **prag•ma•tis′tic** *adj.*

prai•rie /práiree/ *n.* large area of usu. treeless grassland esp. in central N. America. □ **prairie dog** N. American rodent living in burrows and making a barking sound.
■ see PLAIN *n.*

praise /prayz/ • *v.tr.* **1** express warm approval or admiration of. **2** glorify (God) in words • *n.* praising). □□ **praise′ful** *adj.* **prais′er** *n.*
■ *v.* **1** acclaim, laud, applaud, pay tribute to, compliment, commend, eulogize, extol, honor. **2** worship, revere, reverence, exalt, venerate, hallow. • *n.* acclaim, approval, approbation, applause, plaudits, acclamation, glory, *colloq.* kudos; honor, glorification, adoration, exaltation, worship. □ **sing the praises of** see PRAISE *v.* 1 above.

praise•wor•thy /práyzwərthee/ *adj.* worthy of praise; commendable. □□ **praise′wor•thi•ly** *adv.* **praise′wor•thi•ness** *n.*
■ laudable, admirable, creditable, worthy, meritorious.

pra•line /práaleen, práy-/ *n.* any of several candies made with almonds, pecans, or other nuts and sugar.

prance /prans/ • *v.intr.* **1** (of a horse) raise the forelegs and spring from the hind legs. **2** walk or behave in an arrogant manner. • *adj.* prancing. □□ **pranc′er** *n.*
■ *v.* **1** curvet, capriole, caper, skip, frisk, jump, spring, bound.

prank /prangk/ *n.* practical joke; piece of mischief. □□ **prank′ish** *adj.*
■ trick, frolic, escapade, antic, caper, stunt, jape.

prank•ster /prángkstər/ *n.* person fond of playing pranks.
■ see JOKER 1.

pra•se•o•dym•i•um /práyzeeōdímeeəm, práysee-/ *n. Chem.* soft silvery metallic element of the lanthanide series, occurring naturally in various minerals. ¶Symb.: **Pr**.

prate /prayt/ • *v.* **1** *intr.* chatter; talk too much. **2** *intr.* talk foolishly or irrelevantly. **3** *tr.* tell or say in a prating manner. • *n.* prating; idle talk. □□ **prat′er** *n.* **prat′ing** *adj.*

prat•tle /prát'l/ • *v.* chatter or say in a childish or inconsequential way. • *n.* **1** childish chatter. **2** inconsequential talk. □□ **prat′tler** *n.* **prat′tling** *adj.*
■ *v.* prate, babble, blab, blather, gibber, jabber, palaver, tattle, twaddle, gabble, patter, drivel on, *colloq.* natter, gas, gab, jaw. • *n.* prate, prating, babble, blather, gibber, jabber, palaver, tattle, twaddle

prawn /prawn/ *n.* edible shrimplike shellfish.

pray /pray/ *v.* **1** *intr.* say prayers (to God, etc.); make devout supplication. **2 a** *tr.* entreat, beseech. **b** *tr. & intr.* ask earnestly (*prayed to be released*). **3** *tr.* [*as imper.*] old-fashioned please (*pray tell me*). ■ **praying mantis** see MANTIS.
■ **1** offer a prayer. **2 a** ask, call upon or on, implore, appeal to, plead (with), beg, importune, solicit, petition, supplicate. **b** see ASK 2, BEG 2.

prayer /prair/ *n.* **1 a** solemn request or thanksgiving to God. **b** formula used in praying (*the Lord's prayer*). **c** act of praying (*be at prayer*). **2** entreaty to a person. □ **prayer book** book of set prayers. □□ **prayer′ful** *adj.*
■ **1 a** invocation, intercession; see also LITANY 1. **c** devotion, praying, intercession, worship. **2** petition, supplication, request, plea, suit, appeal. □□ **prayerful** devout.

pre- /pree/ *prefix* before (in time, place, order, degree, or importance).

preach /preech/ *v.* **1 a** *intr.* deliver a sermon. **b** *tr.* deliver (a sermon); proclaim or expound. **2** *intr.* give moral advice in an obtrusive way. **3** *tr.* advocate or inculcate (a quality or practice, etc.). □□ **preach′a•ble** *adj.* **preach′er** *n.*
■ **1 a** sermonize, *colloq.* preachify. **b** teach,

evangelize, propagate, explain; see also INTERPRET 1, 2. **2** moralize, sermonize, lecture, pontificate, *colloq.* preachify; see also RANT *v.* **3** urge, instill, teach; see also CHAMPION *v.* □□ **preacher** orator, rhetorician, speechmaker; minister, clergyman, clergywoman, cleric, reverend.

pre•am•ble /prée-ámbəl/ *n.* **1** preliminary statement or introduction. **2** introductory part of a constitution, statute, or deed, etc.

■ **1** foreword, prologue, preface; proem, exordium.

Pre•cam•bri•an /preekámbreeən/ *Geol.* • *adj.* of or relating to the earliest era of geological time. • *n.* this era.

pre•can•cer•ous /preekánsrəs, –kántsər–/ *adj.* having the tendency to develop into a cancer. □□ **pre•can′cer•ous•ly** *adv.*

pre•car•i•ous /prikáireeəs/ *adj.* **1** uncertain; dependent on chance (*makes a precarious living*). **2** insecure; perilous (*precarious health*). □□ **pre•car′i•ous•ly** *adv.* **pre•car′i•ous•ness** *n.*

■ unreliable, unsure, unpredictable, unstable, unsteady, unsettled, shaky, doubtful, dubious, questionable; risky, hazardous, treacherous, dangerous, difficult.

pre•cau•tion /prikáwshən/ *n.* **1** action taken beforehand to avoid risk or ensure a good result. **2** caution exercised beforehand; prudent foresight. □□ **pre•cau′tion•ary** *adj.*

■ **1** preventive measure, safety measure, safeguard. **2** prudence, providence, forethought, cautiousness, circumspection, care, attention, watchfulness.

pre•cede /priseéd/ *v.tr.* (often as **preceding** *adj.*) come or go before in time, order, importance, etc.

■ go ahead *or* in advance of, lead, pave the way for, herald; foreshadow, antedate; (**preceding**) foregoing, former, previous, prior, earlier, abovementioned.

prec•e•dence /présidəns, priseéd′ns/ *n.* (also **prec′e•den•cy**) priority in time, order, or importance, etc.

■ preeminence, preference, privilege; see also PRIORITY.

prec•e•dent • *n.* /présidənt/ previous case or legal decision, etc., taken as a guide for subsequent cases or as a justification. • *adj.* /priseéd′nt, présidnt/ preceding in time, order, importance, etc.

■ *n.* yardstick, criterion, standard, prototype, model, example, exemplar, pattern, paradigm, lead, guide.

pre•cept /preésept/ *n.* rule or guide, esp. for conduct. □□ **pre•cep′tive** /–séptiv/ *adj.*

■ principle, law, unwritten law, canon, guideline, dictate, code, injunction; maxim, proverb, axiom, motto, slogan, saying, byword, aphorism.

pre•cep•tor /priséptər/ *n.* (*fem.* **pre•cep′tress** /–tris/) teacher or instructor. □□ **pre•cep•to•ri•al** /preéseptawreeəl/ *adj.*

pre•ces•sion /priséshən/ *n.* □ **pre•ces′sion of the e•qui•nox•es 1** slow retrograde motion of equinoctial points along the ecliptic.

2 resulting earlier occurrence of equinoxes in each successive sidereal year.

pre•cinct /preésingkt/ *n.* **1** enclosed or specially designated area. **2** [in *pl.*] environs. **3** official district, esp. for police or electoral purposes.

■ **2** suburbs; purlieus, outskirts; boundaries, borders, bounds, confines.

pre•ci•os•i•ty /présheeósitee/ *n.* overrefinement in art or language, esp. in the choice of words.

pre•cious /préshəs/ *adj.* **1** of great value or worth. **2** beloved; much prized (*precious memories*). **3** affectedly refined. □ **precious metals** gold, silver, and platinum. □□ **pre′cious•ly** *adv.* **pre′cious•ness** *n.*

■ **1** valuable, invaluable, costly, expensive, high-priced, priceless. **2** cherished, esteemed, valued, choice, dear, dearest, adored, loved. **3** precise, overrefined, chichi, overnice, studied, artificial, affected.

prec•i•pice /présipis/ *n.* **1** vertical or steep face of a rock, cliff, mountain, etc. **2** dangerous situation.

■ escarpment, bluff, crag; see also CLIFF.

pre•cip•i•tate • *v.tr.* /prisípitayt/ **1** hasten the occurrence of; cause to occur prematurely. **2** throw down headlong. **3** *Chem.* cause (a substance) to be deposited in solid form from a solution. **4** *Physics* **a** cause (dust, etc.) to be deposited from the air on a surface. **b** condense (vapor) into drops and so deposit it. • *adj.* /prisípitət/ **1** headlong; violently hurried (*precipitate departure*). **2** (of a person or act) hasty; rash; inconsiderate. • *n.* /prisípitət/ *Chem.* substance precipitated from a solution. □□ **pre•cip′i•tate•ly** /–sípitətlee/ *adv.* **pre•cip′i•tate•ness** /–sípitətnəs/ *n.* **pre•cip′i•ta•tor** *n.*

■ *v.* **1** accelerate, speed (up), advance, hurry, quicken, expedite, bring on *or* about, trigger, provoke. **2** catapult, hurl, fling, cast, launch, project. • *adj.* **1** violent, rapid, swift, quick, speedy; sudden, abrupt, unannounced. **2** impetuous, careless, reckless, incautious, injudicious, harum-scarum, foolhardy.

pre•cip•i•ta•tion /prisípitáyshən/ *n.* **1** act of precipitating or the process of being precipitated. **2** rash haste. **3 a** rain or snow, etc., falling to the ground. **b** quantity of this.

■ **2** see HASTE *n.* 2. **3 a** showers, drizzle, rainfall; snowfall, hail, sleet.

pre•cip•i•tous /prisípitəs/ *adj.* **1 a** of or like a precipice. **b** dangerously steep. **2** = PRECIPITATE *adj.* □□ **pre•cip′i•tous•ly** *adv.* **pre•cip′i•tous•ness** *n.*

■ **1** perpendicular, abrupt, sheer, bluff, vertical.

pré•cis /práysee/ *n.* (*pl.* same /–seez/) summary; abstract.

■ outline, synopsis, aperçu, résumé, conspectus, survey, overview, abridgment, digest.

pre•cise /prisís/ *adj.* **1 a** accurately expressed. **b** definite; exact. **2** scrupulous in being exact. □□ **pre•cise′ness** *n.*

■ **1** correct, accurate, unerring, strict, meticulous, faithful, perfect, true. **2** punctilious, strict, meticulous, careful, conscientious, particular.

pre•cise•ly /prisíslee/ *adv.* in a precise manner; exactly.

■ correctly, absolutely, punctiliously, minutely, carefully, meticulously, scrupulously, conscientiously.

pre•ci•sion /prisízhən/ *n.* **1** accuracy. **2** [*attrib.*] marked by or adapted for precision (*precision timing*). □□ **pre•ci'sion•ism** *n.* **pre•ci'sion•ist** *n.*

■ **1** correctness, exactness, exactitude, fidelity, faithfulness, preciseness, perfection, flawlessness.

pre•clude /priklood/ *v.tr.* **1** prevent. **2** make impossible. See synonym study at PROHIBIT. □□ **pre•clu•sion** /-kloozhən/ *n.* **pre•clu•sive** /-kloosiv/ *adj.*

■ **1** bar, stop, exclude, prohibit, debar, obstruct, impede, inhibit. **2** remove, forestall, rule out, obviate, avoid.

pre•co•cious /prikóshəs/ *adj.* **1** (of a person, esp. a child) prematurely developed in some faculty or characteristic. **2** (of an action, etc.) indicating such development. □□ **pre•co'cious•ly** *adv.* **pre•coc•i•ty** /-kósitee/ *n.*

■ **1** advanced, forward, bright, gifted, intelligent, smart.

pre•cog•ni•tion /preekognishən/ *n.* (supposed) foreknowledge, esp. of a supernatural kind. □□ **pre•cog'ni•tive** /-kógnitiv/ *adj.*

pre•con•ceive /preekənseev/ *v.tr.* (esp. as **preconceived** *adj.*) form (an idea or opinion, etc.) beforehand.

■ (**preconceived**) prejudged, predetermined, prejudiced, biased, anticipatory.

pre•con•cep•tion /preekənsépshən/ *n.* **1** preconceived idea. **2** prejudice.

■ prejudgment, presupposition, assumption, presumption, *idée fixe*, preconceived notion; bias.

pre•con•di•tion /preekəndíshən/ *n.* prior condition, that must be fulfilled before other things can be done.

■ prerequisite, stipulation, essential, must, sine qua non, imperative, requirement, proviso, qualification.

pre•cur•sor /prikársər, preékər-/ *n.* **1 a** forerunner. **b** person who precedes in office, etc. **2** harbinger.

■ **1** predecessor, antecedent; progenitor, foregoer. **2** herald, forerunner, envoy, messenger.

pred. *abbr.* predicate.

pre•date /preedáyt/ *v.tr.* exist or occur at a date earlier than.

pred•a•tor /prédətər/ *n.* animal naturally preying on others.

pred•a•to•ry /prédətawree/ *adj.* **1** (of an animal) preying naturally upon others. **2** plundering or exploiting others. □□ **pred•a•to'ri•ly** *adv.*

■ **1** predacious, carnivorous, raptorial. **2** ravenous, piratical, exploitative, parasitic; see also RAPACIOUS.

pre•de•cease /preedisees/ • *v.tr.* die earlier than (another person). • *n.* death preceding that of another.

pre•de•ces•sor /prédisesər, preé-/ *n.* person or thing coming before, as a former holder of an office or position.

■ forerunner, antecedent, precursor; forebear, forefather, ancestor, antecedent.

pre•des•tine /preedéstin/ *v.tr.* **1** determine beforehand. **2** ordain in advance by divine will or as if by fate. □□ **pre•des•ti•na'tion** *n.*

■ see DESTINE. □□ **predestination** destiny; doom, fate, lot, kismet, karma; foreordination; predetermination.

pre•de•ter•mine /preeditórmin/ *v.tr.* **1** determine or decree beforehand. **2** predestine. □□ **pre•de•ter'mi•na•ble** *adj.* **pre•de•ter'mi•nate** *adj.* **pre•de•ter•mi•na'tion** *n.*

■ **1** fix, prearrange, preestablish, preplan, preset, set up; see also ARRANGE 2, 3. **2** fate, doom, destine, predestinate, predoom, ordain, foreordain; see also DESTINE. □□ **predetermination** see *predestination* (PREDESTINE).

pre•dic•a•ment /pridíkəmənt/ *n.* difficult, unpleasant, or embarrassing situation.

■ quandary, difficulty, trial, imbroglio, emergency, crisis, impasse, bind, box, *colloq.* pickle, state, jam, fix.

pred•i•cate • *v.tr.* /prédikayt/ **1** assert or affirm as true or existent. **2** found or base (a statement, etc.) on. • *n.* /-kət/ *Gram. & Logic* what is said about the subject of a sentence or proposition, etc. (e.g., *went home* in *John went home*). □□ **pred'i•ca'tion** /-káyshən/ *n.*

■ *v.* **1** assume, propose, postulate, posit, suppose. **2** see BASE[1] *v.* 1. □□ **predication** hypothesis, thesis, principle, contention, assertion, belief.

pred•i•ca•tive /prédikaytiv/ *adj.* **1** *Gram.* (of an adjective or noun) forming or contained in the predicate, as *old* in *the dog is old.* **2** that predicates. □□ **pred'i•ca•tive•ly** *adv.*

pre•dict /pridíkt/ *v.tr.* foretell; prophesy. □□ **pre•dic'tive** *adj.* **pre•dic'tive•ly** *adv.* **pre•dic'tor** *n.*

■ forecast, foresee, augur, prognosticate, presage, *formal* vaticinate; intimate, hint, suggest.

SYNONYM STUDY: predict

AUGUR, DIVINE, FORECAST, FORESHADOW, FORETELL, PROGNOSTICATE, PROPHESY. While all of these words refer to telling something before it happens, **predict** is the most commonly used and applies to the widest variety of situations. It can mean anything from hazarding a guess (*to predict he'd never survive the year*) to making an astute inference based on facts or statistical evidence (*to predict that the Republicans would win the election*). When a meteorologist tells us whether it will rain or snow tomorrow, he or she is said to **forecast** the weather, a word that means *predict* but is used particularly in the context of weather and other phenomena that cannot be *predicted* easily (*to forecast an influx of women into the labor force*). **Divine** and **foreshadow** mean to suggest the future rather than to *predict* it, especially by giving or evaluating subtle hints or clues. To *divine* something is to perceive it through intuition or insight (*to divine in the current economic situation the disaster that lay ahead*), while *foreshadow* can apply to anyone or anything that gives an indication of what is to come (*her abrupt departure that night foreshadowed the breakdown in their relationship*). **Foretell**, like *foreshadow*, can refer to the clue rather than the person who gives it and is often used in reference to the past (*evidence that foretold the young girl's violent end*). **Augur** means to *divine* or *foreshadow* something by interpreting signs and omens (*the turnout on opening night augured well for the play's success*). **Prophesy** connotes either inspired or mystical knowledge of the future and suggests more authoritative wisdom than *augur* (*a baseball fan for decades, he prophesied the young batter's rise to stardom*). Although anyone who has inside information or knowledge of signs and symptoms can **prognosticate**, it is usually a doctor who does so by looking at the symptoms of a disease to *predict* its future outcome.

---

pre·dict·a·ble /pridíktəbəl/ *adj.* that can be predicted or is to be expected. □□ **pre·dict· a·bil·i·ty** *n.* **pre·dict'a·bly** *adv.*
■ foreseeable, expected, anticipated, imaginable.

pre·dic·tion /pridíkshən/ *n.* **1** art of predicting or process of being predicted. **2** thing predicted; forecast.
■ **2** see FORECAST *n.*

pred·i·lec·tion /prédʼlékshən, prée-/ *n.* [often foll. by *for*] preference or special liking.

pre·dis·pose /prēedispóz/ *v.tr.* **1** influence favorably in advance. **2** [foll. by *to*, or *to* + infin.] render liable or inclined beforehand. □□ **pre·dis·po·si·tion** /‑pəzishən/ *n.*

pre·dom·i·nant /pridóminənt/ *adj.* **1** predominating. **2** being the strongest or main element. □□ **pre·dom'i·nance** *n.* **pre· dom'i·nant·ly** *adv.*
■ **1** dominant, controlling, sovereign, ruling, preeminent, preponderant. **2** main, primary, leading, chief, prevailing, prevalent; see also CHIEF *adj.* 2. □□ **predominance** superiority, influence, dominance, preeminence, preponderance, transcendence.

pre·dom·i·nate /pridómináyt/ *v.intr.* **1** [foll. by *over*] have or exert control. **2** be superior. **3** be the strongest or main element; preponderate (*garden in which dahlias predominate*).
■ **1** control, rule, reign, get *or* have the upper hand, be in charge, hold sway; see also DOMINATE 1. **3** dominate, obtain, prevail, be in the majority; be prevalent *or* widespread *or* current.

pree·mie /prēemee/ *n. colloq.* infant born prematurely.

pre·em·i·nent /prée-éminənt/ *adj.* **1** surpassing others. **2** outstanding. □□ **pre·em' i·nence** *n.* **pre·em'i·nent·ly** *adv.*
■ **2** peerless, excellent, distinguished, eminent, inimitable, superb, unequaled, matchless, incomparable. □□ **preeminence** peerlessness, magnificence, excellence, distinction, eminence, inimitability. **preeminently** manifestly, eminently, notably, conspicuously, prominently, signally, uniquely, primarily, principally, chiefly, mainly.

pre·empt /prée-émpt/ *v.tr.* **1 a** forestall. **b** acquire or appropriate in advance. **2** obtain by preemption. □□ **pre·emp'tor** *n.* **pre·emp'to·ry** *adj.*
■ **1 a** see ANTICIPATE 3. **b** usurp, arrogate, take over, assume, take possession of, seize, take, possess.

pre·emp·tion /prée-émpshən/ *n.* acquisition by one person or party before the opportunity is offered to others.

pre·emp·tive /prée-émptiv/ *adj.* **1** preempting. **2** (of military action) intended to prevent attack by disabling the enemy.

preen /preen/ *v.tr. & refl.* **1** (of a bird) straighten (the feathers or itself) with its beak. **2** (of a person) primp or admire (oneself, one's hair, clothes, etc.). □□ **preen'er** *n.*
■ **1** plume, groom, prink, trim, clean. **2** smarten, dress up, prettify, beautify, prink, spruce up, doll up.

pre·fab /préefáb/ *n. colloq.* prefabricated building.

pre·fab·ri·cate /préefábrikayt/ *v.tr.* manufacture sections of (a building, etc.) prior to their assembly on a site. □□ **pre·fab·ri·ca· tion** /‑brikáyshən/ *n.*

pref·ace /préfəs/ • *n.* introduction to a book. • *v.tr.* **1** [foll. by *with*] introduce or begin (a speech or event). **2** provide (a book, etc.) with a preface. □□ **pre·fa·to·ri·al** /‑fətáwreeəl/ *adj.* **pref'a·to·ry** *adj.*
■ *n.* foreword, prologue, preamble, proem, exordium. • *v.* **1** prefix, prologue, begin, open, start off. □□ **prefatory** see INTRODUCTORY.

pre·fect /préefekt/ *n.* administrator; overseer. □□ **pre·fec·to·ri·al** /‑táwreeəl/ *adj.*

pre·fec·ture /préefekchər/ *n.* administrative district. □□ **pre·fec·tur·al** /prifékchərəl/ *adj.*

pre·fer /prifór/ *v.tr.* (**pre·ferred**, **pre·fer· ring**) **1** choose; like better. **2** submit (information, an accusation, etc.) for consideration. **3** promote or advance (a person).
■ **1** favor, lean *or* incline toward, be inclined toward, be partial to. **2** present, offer, propose, proffer, advance, tender, put forward, file, lodge, enter. **3** see PROMOTE 1.

pref·er·a·ble /préfərəbəl, *disp.* prifér‑/ *adj.* **1** to be preferred. **2** more desirable. □□ **pref'er·a·bly** *adv.*
■ preferred, better, best, advantageous, beneficial.

pref·er·ence /préfərəns, préfrəns/ *n.* **1** act or an instance of preferring or being preferred. **2** thing preferred. **3** favoring of one person, etc., before others. □□ **pref·er·en·tial** /‑énshəl/ *adj.* **pref·er·en'tial·ly** *adv.*
■ **1** partiality, proclivity, predilection, liking; predisposition, bent, inclination, leaning. **2** favorite, choice, selection, pick, desire, option. **3** see FAVORITISM. □□ **preferential** privileged, better, favored, superior, favorable; biased, prejudiced, partial.

pre·fer·ment /prifórmənt/ *n.* promotion to a higher office.

pre·fig·ure /prēefígyər/ *v.tr.* **1** represent beforehand by a figure or type. **2** imagine beforehand. □□ **pre·fig·u·ra'tion** *n.* **pre·fig' ur·a·tive** *adj.*

pre•fix /préefiks/ • *n.* element at the beginning of a word to adjust or qualify its meaning (e.g., *ex-, non-, re-*). • *v.tr.* **1** add as an introduction. **2** join (a word or element) as a prefix. □□ **pre•fix•ion** /–fíkshən/ *n.*

preg•nan•cy /prégnənsee/ *n.* (*pl.* **–cies**) condition or instance of being pregnant.

preg•nant /prégnənt/ *adj.* **1** having a child or young developing in the uterus. **2** full of meaning; significant or suggestive (*a pregnant pause*). □□ **preg'nant•ly** *adv.* (in sense 2).

■ **1** expectant, impregnate, *literary* with child, *literary or Zool* gravid, *colloq.* in the family way; (*be pregnant*) *colloq.* be expecting, *sl.* have a bun in the oven. **2** charged, fraught, loaded, weighty, meaningful, expressive, pointed.

pre•hen•sile /préehénsəl, –síl/ *adj. Zool.* (of a tail or limb) capable of grasping.

pre•his•tor•ic /préehistáwrik, –stór–/ *adj.* **1** of or relating to the period before written records **2** *colloq.* utterly out of date. □□ **pre•his'tor•i•cal•ly** *adv.* **pre•his•to•ry** /–hístəree/ *n.*

■ **1** primordial, primal, primeval, primitive, earliest. **2** outdated, old-fashioned, passé; see also ANTIQUATED.

pre•judge /préejúj/ *v.tr.* form a premature judgment on (a person, issue, etc.). □□ **pre•judg'ment** *n.*

prej•u•dice /préjədis/ • *n.* **1 a** preconceived opinion. **b** bias or partiality. **2** detriment. • *v.tr.* **1** impair the validity or force of (a right, claim, statement, etc.). **2** (esp. as **prejudiced** *adj.*) cause (a person) to have a prejudice.

■ *n.* **1** preconception, prejudgment, preconceived notion; leaning, warp, twist, predisposition, predilection; favoritism, partisanship, prepossession. **2** see DETRIMENT. • *v.* **1** bias, influence, warp, twist, distort, slant; color, jaundice, poison. **2** (**prejudiced**) predisposed, partial, prepossessed; unfair, one-sided, biased, bigoted, intolerant.

prej•u•di•cial /préjədíshəl/ *adj.* causing prejudice; detrimental. □□ **prej•u•di'cial•ly** *adv.*

■ injurious, damaging, harmful, unfavorable, inimical, deleterious, disadvantageous, pernicious.

pre•lim•i•nar•y /prilíminəree/ • *adj.* introductory; preparatory. • *n.* (*pl.* **–ies**) [usu. in *pl.*] **1** preliminary action or arrangement (*dispense with the preliminaries*). **2** preliminary trial or contest.

■ *adj.* initial, opening, prefatory, preceding, precursory, antecedent; exploratory, premonitory. • *n.* **1** introduction, beginning, opening, preparation, prelude, overture, prologue. **2** round; see also HEAT *n.* 6.

pre•lude /prélyood, práylood, prée–/ *n.* [often foll. by *to*] **1** action, event, or situation serving as an introduction. **2** beginning introductory part of a poem, etc. **3 a** introductory piece of music to a fugue, suite, or an act of an opera. **b** short piece of music of a similar type.

pre•ma•ture /preemǝchŏŏr, –tyŏŏr, –tŏŏr/ *adj.* **1** occurring or done before the usual or proper time; too early (*premature decision*). **2** (of a baby) born (esp. three or more weeks)

before the end of the full term of gestation. □□ **pre•ma•ture'ly** *adv.*

■ **1** untimely, unready, unseasonable, too soon, hasty, ill-timed. **2** preterm. □□ **prematurely** preterm, ahead of time, too soon, too early, hastily, overhastily.

pre•med•i•tate /préeméditayt/ *v.tr.* (often as **premeditated** *adj.*) think out or plan (an action) beforehand (*premeditated murder*). □□ **pre•med•i•ta'tion** *n.*

■ (**premeditated**) planned, conscious, intentional, intended, willful, deliberate; contrived, preplanned, calculated, preconceived. □□ **premeditation** planning, preplanning, forethought, intent; criminal intent, mens rea.

pre•men•stru•al /préeménstrooǝl/ *adj.* of, occurring, or experienced before menstruation. □ **premenstrual syndrome** physical and psychological symptoms experienced by some women prior to menstruation. □□ **pre•men'stru•al•ly** *adv.*

pre•mier /prǝméer, –myéer, préemeer/ • *n.* prime minister or other head of government in certain countries. • *adj.* first in importance, order, or time.

■ *n.* PM, chief executive, president, chancellor. • *adj.* premiere, prime, primary, chief, principal, head, main, foremost, top-ranking, high-ranking.

pre•miere /prǝméer, –myáir/ (also **pre•mière**) • *n.* first performance or showing. • *v.tr.* give a premiere of.

■ *n.* first night, opening (night). • *v.* open, launch.

prem•ise /prémis/ *n.* **1** *Logic* previous statement from which another is inferred. **2** [in *pl.*] house or building with its grounds and appurtenances.

■ **1** assumption, proposition, postulate, hypothesis, conjecture, assertion, supposition, thesis; presupposition, proposal, see also PRESUMPTION 2.

pre•mi•um /préemeeəm/ *n.* **1** amount to be paid for a contract of insurance. **2** sum added to interest, wages, price, etc. **3** reward or prize. **4** [*attrib.*] (of a commodity) of best quality and therefore more expensive. □ **at a premium 1** highly valued. **2** scarce and in demand.

■ **2** extra, dividend, perquisite; see also BONUS 2. **3** see REWARD *n.* 1a. **4** see CHOICE *adj.* □ **at a premium 1** costly, expensive, dear, high-priced; valuable, precious. **2** rare, hard to come by, in short supply, thin on the ground.

pre•mo•ni•tion /prémənishən, prée–/ *n.* forewarning; presentiment. □□ **pre•mon•i•to•ry** /primónitawree/ *adj.*

■ foreboding, suspicion, feeling, hunch.

pre•oc•cu•py /prée–ókyəpī/ *v.tr.* (**–pies**, **–pied**) **1** (of a thought, etc.) dominate or engross the mind of (a person). **2** (as **pre-occupied** *adj.*) mentally distracted. **3** occupy beforehand. □□ **pre•oc•cu•pa'tion** *n.*

■ **1** see OCCUPY 5. **2** (**preoccupied**) engrossed, rapt, thoughtful, pensive; abstracted, oblivious, unaware.

pre•or•dain /prēeawrdáyn/ *v.tr.* ordain or determine beforehand.

prep /prep/ *colloq. n.* • *n.* **1** preparation (esp. of a patient before surgery). **2** student in a preparatory school. • *v.tr.* prepare (a person) for an examination, etc. □ **prep school** = *preparatory school*.

prep. *abbr.* preposition.

pre•paid *past* and *past part.* of PREPAY.

prep•a•ra•tion /prépəráyshən/ *n.* **1** preparing; being prepared. **2** [often in *pl.*] something done to make ready. **3** specially prepared substance, esp. a food or medicine.

■ **1** organization, planning; groundwork, spadework; training, education, teaching, instruction, tuition. **2** plans, arrangements, provision(s), measures, program. **3** compound, concoction, mixture, product.

pre•pa•ra•to•ry /pripárətawree, –páir–, prépərə–/ • *adj.* serving to prepare; introductory. • *adv.* in a preparatory manner. □ **preparatory school** usu. private school preparing pupils for college.

■ *adj.* preparative, preliminary, prefatory, initial; see also INTRODUCTORY. • *adv. (preparatory to)* in preparation for, preceding; see also BEFORE *prep.* 1, 2.

pre•pare /pripáir/ *v.* **1** *tr.* make or get ready for use, consideration, etc. **2** *tr.* make ready or assemble (food, a meal, etc.). **3 a** *tr.* make (a person or oneself) ready or disposed in some way. **b** *intr.* get ready (*prepare to jump*). □□ **pre•par′er** *n.*

■ **1** arrange, lay, set, (put in) order, organize, provide for, make provision(s) for. **2** cook (up), make, do, whip up, *colloq.* fix. **3 a** (get) ready, prime, make fit, fit (out), equip, outfit, adapt; brace, steel; train, groom.

pre•par•ed•ness /pripáiridnis/ *n.* readiness, esp. for war.

■ vigilance, alertness, fitness.

pre•pay /prēepáy/ *v.tr.* (*past* and *past part.* **pre•paid**) pay (a charge) in advance. □□ **pre•pay′a•ble** *adj.* **pre•pay′ment** *n.*

pre•pon•der•ant /pripóndərənt/ *adj.* predominant; preponderating. □□ **pre•pon′der•ance** *n.* **pre•pon′der•ant•ly** *adv.*

■ see PREDOMINANT 1. □□ **preponderance** dominance, predominance, primacy, ascendancy, superiority, supremacy; majority, bulk, mass.

pre•pon•der•ate /pripóndərayt/ *v.intr.* [often foll. by *over*] **1** be greater in influence, quantity, or number. **2** predominate.

prep•o•si•tion /prépəzíshən/ *n. Gram.* word governing (and usu. preceding) a noun or pronoun and expressing a relation to another word or element, as in: "the man *on* the platform," "came *after* dinner," "what did you do it *for?*". □□ **prep′o•si′tion•al** *adj.* **prep′o•si′tion•al•ly** *adv.*

pre•pos•sess /prēepəzés/ *v.tr.* **1** [usu. in *passive*] (of an idea, feeling, etc.) take possession of (a person); imbue. **2 a** prejudice (usu. favorably). **b** (as **prepossessing** *adj.*) attractive; appealing. □□ **pre•pos′ses•sion** /–zéshən/ *n.*

■ **2 a** see BIAS *v.* **b** (**prepossessing**) pleasing, engaging, charming, captivating, fascinating, winsome, winning, magnetic, alluring, bewitching, fetching. □□ **prepossession** see OBSESSION, PRECONCEPTION.

pre•pos•ter•ous /pripóstərəs/ *adj.* utterly absurd; outrageous. See synonym study at ABSURD. □□ **pre•pos′ter•ous•ly** *adv.*

■ ridiculous, ludicrous, laughable, risible, senseless, mad, irrational, incredible, weird, bizarre.

prep•py /prépee/ (also **prep′pie**) *colloq.* • *n.* (*pl* **–pies**) person attending an expensive private school. • *adj.* (**prep•pi•er, prep•pi•est**) **1** like a preppy. **2** neat and fashionable.

pre•req•ui•site /prēerékwizit/ • *adj.* required as a precondition. • *n.* prerequisite thing.

■ *adj.* essential, necessary, requisite, imperative, indispensable, obligatory. • *n.* precondition, requirement, requisite, condition, stipulation, sine qua non.

pre•rog•a•tive /prirógətiv/ *n.* right or privilege exclusive to an individual or class.

■ liberty, power, due, advantage, license, authority.

pres•age /présij/ • *n.* **1** omen or portent. **2** presentiment or foreboding. • *v.tr.* (also /prisáyj/) portend; foreshadow.

■ *n.* **1** see OMEN *n.* **2** see FOREBODING. • *v.* see FORESHADOW.

Pres•by•te•ri•an /prézbitéereeən/ • *adj.* (of a church) governed by elders all of equal rank. • *n.* member of a Presbyterian Church. □□ **Pres′by•te′ri•an•ism′** *n.*

pre•school /prēeskōōl/ *adj.* of or relating to the time before a child is old enough to go to school. □□ **pre′school•er** *n.*

pre•scient /préshənt, –eeənt, prē–/ *adj.* having foreknowledge or foresight. □□ **pre′sci•ence** *n.* **pre′scient•ly** *adv.*

■ clairvoyant; see also FARSIGHTED 1. □□ **prescience** clairvoyance, prevision, vision, foresight.

pre•scribe /priskríb/ *v.tr.* **1 a** advise the use of (a medicine, etc.). **b** recommend. **2** lay down or impose authoritatively. □□ **pre•scrib′er** *n.*

■ **1 b** see ADVISE 1, 2. **2** ordain, order, dictate, decree, enjoin, rule, set down, stipulate, specify.

pre•scrip•tion /priskrípshən/ *n.* **1** act or an instance of prescribing. **2 a** doctor's (usu. written) instruction for the preparation and use of a medicine. **b** medicine prescribed.

■ **1** see INSTRUCTION 1. **2 a** formula, recipe. **b** remedy, medication, drug, preparation, medicament.

pre•scrip•tive /priskríptiv/ *adj.* **1** prescribing. **2** *Linguistics* concerned with or laying down rules of usage. □□ **pre•scrip′tive•ly** *adv.* **pre•scrip′tive•ness** *n.* **pre•scrip′tiv•ism** *n.* **pre•scrip′tiv•ist** *n. & adj.*

■ **1** dictatorial, constrictive, didactic, restrictive, dogmatic, authoritarian, overbearing, autocratic.

pres•ence /prézəns/ *n.* **1** being present. **2** place where a person is. **3** person's appearance or bearing, esp. when imposing. **4** person or thing that is present (*there was a presence in the room*). □ **presence of mind**

calmness and self-command in sudden diffi-culty, etc.

■ **1** attendance, company, companionship, society, fellowship, coming; existence. **3** carriage, deportment, air, aspect, aura; personality. **4** being, manifestation; spirit, wraith, specter. □ **presence of mind** self-possession, self-control, self-assurance, coolness, coolheadedness, composure.

pres•ent[1] /prézənt/ • *adj.* **1** [usu. *predic.*] being in the place in question. **2 a** now existing, occurring, or being such. **b** now being considered or discussed, etc. (*in the present case*). **3** *Gram.* expressing an action, etc., now going on or habitually performed. • *n.* [prec. by *the*] **1** the time now passing (*no time like the present*). **2** *Gram.* present tense. □ **at present** now. **present-day** *adj.* of this time; modern.

■ *adj.* **2 a** current, contemporary, present-day, existent. • *n.* **1** the time being, right now, this moment; see also NOW *adv.* 1, 3. □ **at present** right *or* just now, currently, at this point, at this *or* the moment, presently.

pre•sent[2] /prizént/ *v.tr.* **1** introduce, offer, or exhibit. **2 a** offer, give, or award as a gift. **b** make available to; cause to have (*presented them with a new car*). **3** put (a form of entertainment) before the public. **4** introduce (*may I present my fiancé?*). **5** (of an idea, etc.) offer or suggest itself. □ **present arms** hold a rifle, etc., vertically in front of the body as a salute. □□ **present'er** *n.* (in sense 3 of *v.*).

■ **1** bring in or up, proffer, tender, produce, submit, set forth, put forward *or* up; display. **2** bestow, grant, confer, turn *or* hand over; provide, furnish, supply; dispense, distribute, dole out. **3** give, stage, show, exhibit, put on, mount, produce. **4** host, give, offer, *colloq.* emcee; announce; make known, acquaint.

pres•ent[3] /prézənt/ *n.* gift, thing given or presented.

■ donation, offering, bounty, donative.

pre•sent•a•ble /prizéntəbəl/ *adj.* **1** of good appearance; fit to be presented. **2** fit for presentation. □□ **pre•sent•a•bil'i•ty** *n.* **pre•sent'a•bly** *adv.*

■ **1** decent, respectable; see also SMART *adj.* 2. **2** fit, fitting, suitable, acceptable, satisfactory, adequate, passable, tolerable, admissible, all right, allowable.

pre•sen•ta•tion /prèzəntáyshən, prèezen–/ *n.* **1 a** presenting; being presented. **b** thing presented. **2** manner or quality of presenting. **3** demonstration or display; lecture. □□ **pre•sen•ta'tion•al** *adj.*

■ **1** bestowal, donation, conferral, conferment; handover; see also *endowment* (ENDOW). **2** delivery; appearance; production. **3** see DEMONSTRATION 3, LECTURE *n.* 1.

pre•sen•ti•ment /prizéntimənt, –séntimənt/ *n.* vague expectation; foreboding (esp. of misfortune).

pres•ent•ly /prézəntlee/ *adv.* **1** soon; after a short time. **2** at the present time; now.

■ **1** by and by, in a little while, shortly, in due course, after a while *or* time, before long. **2** see NOW *n.*

pres•er•va•tion /prèzərváyshən/ *n.* **1** pre-

653　　　**present ~ press**

serving or being preserved. **2** state of being well or badly preserved.

■ **1** upkeep, maintenance, care, conservation; retention, perpetuation, continuation, safekeeping, safeguarding.

pre•ser•va•tive /prizárvətiv/ • *n.* substance for preserving perishable foods, wood, etc. • *adj.* tending to preserve.

pre•serve /prizárv/ • *v.tr.* **1 a** keep safe or free from harm, decay, etc. **b** keep alive (a name, memory, etc.). **2** maintain or retain. **3** treat or refrigerate (food) to prevent decomposition or fermentation. • *n.* [in *sing.* or *pl.*] **1** preserved fruit; jam. **2** place where game or fish, etc., are preserved. **3** sphere or area of activity regarded as a person's own. □□ **pre•serv'a•ble** *adj.* **pre•serv'er** *n.*

■ *v.* **1 a** protect, guard, safeguard, shield, shelter, defend, spare. **2** keep (up), conserve; sustain, hold; see also MAINTAIN 1, 2, 4. **3** conserve, pickle, cure, smoke, kipper, salt, corn, marinate, can, freeze, freeze-dry, dry, irradiate. • *n.* **1** conserve, jelly, marmalade. **2** (*wildlife*) reserve, sanctuary, park. **3** see SPHERE *n.* 3.

pre•shrunk /préeshrúngk/ *adj.* (of a fabric or garment) treated so that it shrinks during manufacture and not in use.

pre•side /prizíd/ *v.intr.* **1** be chairperson or president of a meeting, etc. **2** exercise control or authority.

■ **1** chair, administer, officiate at; manage, handle, supervise, run, oversee, head (up).

pres•i•den•cy /prézidənsee/ *n.* (*pl.* –**cies**) office, term, or function of president.

■ premiership, leadership, rule, command; *colloq.* driver's seat, saddle; administration.

pres•i•dent /prézidənt/ *n.* **1** elected head of a republican government. **2** head of a college, university, company, society, etc. □□ **pres•i•den'tial** /–dénshəl/ *adj.* **pres•i•den'tial•ly** *adv.*

■ chief, leader, principal, *colloq.* head, *sl.* (big) cheese, (chief *or* head) honcho, Mr. Big.

press[1] /pres/ • *v.* **1** *tr.* apply steady force to (a thing in contact). **2** *tr.* **a** compress or squeeze a thing to flatten, shape, or smooth it. **b** squeeze (a fruit, etc.) to extract its juice. **c** manufacture (a record, etc.) by molding under pressure. **3** *intr.* be urgent; demand immediate action. **4** *intr.* [foll. by *for*] make an insistent demand. **5** *intr.* form a crowd. **6** *intr.* [foll. by *on, forward*, etc.] hasten insistently. **7** *tr.* (of an enemy, etc.) bear heavily on. **8** *tr.* urge or entreat. **9** *tr.* insist on. • *n.* **1** act or instance of pressing. **2** device for compressing, flattening, shaping, extracting juice, etc. **3** = *printing press*. **4** [prec. by *the*] **a** art or practice of printing. **b** newspapers, journalists, etc., generally or collectively. **5** publicity. **6** (**Press**) **a** a printing house or establishment. **b** publishing company. **7 a** crowding. **b** crowd (of people, etc.). **8** the pressure of affairs. □ **be pressed for** have barely enough (time, etc.). **press agent** person employed to obtain publicity. **press conference** interview given to a number of

press ~ pretentious 654

journalists. **press release** official statement issued to newspapers.

■ *v.* **1** squeeze, compress, push; depress. **2 a** iron. **b** crush, compress, mash; purée. **4** (*press for*) cry out for, call for; beck. **5** flock, gather, mill, swarm, throng. **6** (*press on* or *forward*) see HURRY *v.* 1. **8** pressure, pressurize, importune, beseech, beg. **9** pursue; see also LABOR *v.* 3a. • *n.* **1** push, squeeze, nudge, shove, thrust. **4 b** (*the press*) the papers, *joc.* the fourth estate; newsmen, reporters, paparazzi, newshounds. **5** review(s); see also NOTICE *n.* 4. **7 b** throng, swarm, cluster, pack. **8** stress; urgency, haste, hurly-burly. □ **be pressed for** (*be pressed for time*) be busy, be run off one's feet, *colloq.* be up to one's neck.

press[2] /pres/ *v.tr.* **1** *hist.* force to serve in the army or navy. **2** bring into use as a makeshift (*was pressed into service*).

press•ing /présing/ *adj.* urgent. See synonym study at CRUCIAL. □□ **press'ing•ly** *adv.*

■ compelling, pivotal, major, important, vital, critical.

pres•sure /préshər/ • *n.* **1 a** exertion of continuous force on or against a body by another in contact with it. **b** force exerted. **c** amount of this. **2** urgency (*work under pressure*). **3** affliction or difficulty (*under financial pressure*). **4** constraining influence (*if pressure is brought to bear*). • *v.tr.* **1** coerce. **2** persuade. □ **pressure cooker** airtight pot for cooking quickly under steam pressure. **pressure group** group formed to influence public policy.

■ *n.* **1 a, b** compression, tension; weight, power, strength. **2, 3** stress, strain, constraint; demand(s); oppression, press, weight, burden, load. **4** power, sway; insistence, coercion, inducement. • *v.* **1** see FORCE *v.* 1. **2** prevail upon *or* on, induce, get.

pres•sur•ize /préshəriz/ *v.tr.* **1** (esp. as **pressurized** *adj.*) maintain normal atmospheric pressure in (an aircraft cabin, etc.) at a high altitude. **2** raise to a high pressure. □□ **pres•sur•i•za'tion** *n.*

pres•ti•dig•i•ta•tor /préstidijitaytər/ *n. formal* magician. □□ **pres•ti•dig•i•ta'tion** *n.*

pres•tige /prestéezh/ *n.* **1** respect, reputation, or influence derived from achievements, power, associations, etc. **2** [*attrib.*] having or conferring prestige.

■ **1** status, standing, rank, stature, eminence, esteem.

pres•ti•gious /prestéejəs, -stíj-/ *adj.* having or showing prestige. □□ **pres•ti'gious•ly** *adv.* **pres•ti'gious•ness** *n.*

■ prestigeful, distinguished, august, dignified, illustrious, acclaimed, respected, celebrated, renowned, eminent.

pres•to /préstō/ *adv.* **1** *Mus.* in quick tempo. **2** (in a magician's formula in performing a trick) look!.

pre•sum•a•bly /prizōōməblee/ *adv.* as may reasonably be presumed.

■ probably, in all likelihood, (very *or* most) likely.

pre•sume /prizōōm/ *v.* **1** *tr.* suppose to be

true; take for granted. **2** *tr.* [often foll. by *to* + infin.] a dare. **b** venture (*may I presume to ask?*). **3** *intr.* be presumptuous. □□ **pre•sum'a•ble** *adj.* **pre•sum'ed•ly** *adv.*

■ **1** assume, surmise, infer, presuppose, take it; postulate, posit. **2** take the liberty, make so bold as, have the audacity *or* effrontery, go so far as.

pre•sump•tion /prizúmpshən/ *n.* **1** arrogance; presumptuous behavior. **2 a** act of presuming a thing to be true. **b** thing that is or may be presumed to be true.

■ **1** effrontery, hubris, audacity, boldness, brazenness, impudence, impertinence, insolence, temerity. **2** assumption, supposition, presupposition, preconception; belief, thought, feeling.

pre•sump•tive /prizúmptiv/ *adj.* giving reasonable grounds for presumption. □□ **pre•sump'tive•ly** *adv.*

■ likely, plausible, tenable, believable, credible, conceivable, acceptable, justifiable, sensible.

pre•sump•tu•ous /prizúmpchōōəs/ *adj.* unduly or overbearingly confident and presuming. See synonym study at BOLD. □□ **pre•sump'tu•ous•ly** *adv.* **pre•sump'tu•ous•ness** *n.*

■ arrogant, proud, prideful, overconfident, overweening, forward, egotistical, audacious, bold, brazen.

pre•sup•pose /préesəpōz/ *v.tr.* **1** assume beforehand. **2** require as a precondition; imply. □□ **pre•sup•po•si'tion** *n.*

■ **1** see PRESUME 1. **2** see REQUIRE 1.

pre•teen /prétén/ • *adj.* of or relating to a child just under the age of thirteen. • *n.* a child of such an age.

pre•tend /priténd/ *v.* **1** *tr.* claim or assert falsely so as to deceive. **2** *tr.* imagine to oneself in play (*pretended to be monsters*). **3** *intr.* [foll. by *to*] a lay claim to (a right or title, etc.). **b** profess to have (a quality, etc.).

■ **1** see *make believe* (BELIEVE).

pre•tend•er /priténdər/ *n.* **1** person who claims a throne or title, etc. **2** person who pretends.

■ **1** claimant, aspirant, candidate, seeker.

pre•tense /préetens, priténs/ *n.* **1** pretending; make-believe. **2** false show of intentions or motives (*under false pretenses*). **3** [foll. by *to*] claim, esp. a false or ambitious one. **4** display; ostentation.

■ **1** fiction, fabrication, invention. **2** front, façade, appearance, cover, cloak, veil, mask; hoax, artifice, sham, pose. **3** right, title. **4** affectation, ostentation, show, airs; humbuggery, humbug, deception.

pre•ten•sion /priténshən/ *n.* **1 a** assertion of a claim. **b** justifiable claim. **2** pretentiousness.

■ **1 a** claim; aspiration(s), ambitiousness; see also AMBITION 2. **b** right, title. **2** pretense, ostentation, affectation, hypocrisy, show, artifice.

pre•ten•tious /priténshəs/ *adj.* **1** making an excessive claim to great merit or importance. **2** ostentatious. □□ **pre•ten'tious•ly** *adv.* **pre•ten'tious•ness** *n.*

■ **1** pompous, self-aggrandizing, self-important, affected, snobbish, lofty, haughty, hoity-toity. **2** showy, superficial, grandiose, grandiloquent; bombastic, inflated, high-flown, exaggerated, flowery, fustian.

pret•er•it /prétərit/ (also **pret'er•ite**) *Gram.* • *adj.* expressing a past action or state. • *n.* preterit tense or form.

pre•ter•nat•u•ral /préetərnáchərəl/ *adj.* outside the ordinary course of nature; supernatural. □□ **pre•ter•nat'u•ral•ly** *adv.*

pre•text /préetekst/ *n.* **1** ostensible or alleged reason or intention. **2** excuse offered.

■ pretense, guise; rationalization, explanation; see also EXCUSE *n.* 1, 2.

pret•ti•fy /prítifī/ *v.tr.* (**–fies, –fied**) make pretty, esp. in an affected way. □□ **pret'ti•fi•er** *n.*

pret•ty /prítee/ • *adj.* (**pret•ti•er, pret•ti•est**) **1** attractive in a fine or charming way. **2** fine or good of its kind (*a pretty wit*). • *adv. colloq.* fairly; moderately; considerably. • *v.tr.* (**–ties, –tied**) [often foll. by *up*] make pretty or attractive. □□ **pret'ti•ly** *adv.* **pret'ti•ness** *n.* **pret'ty•ish** *adj.*

■ *adj.* **1** comely, good-looking, nice-looking, appealing, lovely, fair; *colloq.* cute; sweet, melodic. **2** see FINE[1] *adj.* 2. • *adv.* rather, quite, reasonably, tolerably, somewhat; very, extremely, unbelievably, incredibly.

pret•zel /prétsəl/ *n.* crisp or chewy knot-shaped or stick-shaped bread, usu. salted.

pre•vail /priváyl/ *v.intr.* **1** be victorious or gain mastery. **2** be the more usual or predominant. **3** exist or occur in general use or experience; be current. **4** [foll. by *on, upon*] persuade. □□ **pre•vail'ing** *adj.* **pre•vail'ing•ly** *adv.* See synonym study at PREVALENT.

■ **1** win (out), succeed, triumph, gain or achieve victory. **2, 3** predominate, preponderate, dominate; be prevalent or widespread. **4** induce, sway, convince, prompt.

prev•a•lent /prévələnt/ *adj.* **1** generally existing or occurring. **2** predominant. □□ **prev'a•lence** *n.* **prev'a•lent•ly** *adv.*

■ **1** current, general, universal, catholic, common, frequent, ubiquitous, pervasive, omnipresent. **2** prevailing, dominant, governing, ruling; see also PREDOMINANT 1. □□ **prevalence** frequency, commonness, currency, universality, ubiquitousness, ubiquity.

SYNONYM STUDY: prevalent

ABUNDANT, COMMON, COPIOUS, PLENTIFUL, PREVAILING, RIFE. Wildflowers might be **prevalent** in the mountains during the spring months, but a particular type of wildflower might be the **prevailing** one. *Prevalent*, in other words, implies widespread occurrence or acceptance in a particular place or time (*a prevalent belief in the nineteenth century*), while *prevailing* suggests that something exists in such quantity it surpasses all others or leads all others in acceptance, usage, or belief (*the prevailing theory about the evolution of man*). Wildflowers might also be **abundant** in the valleys—a word that, unlike *prevalent* and *prevailing*, is largely restricted to observations about a place and may suggest oversupply (*an abundant harvest*). **Plentiful**, on the other hand, refers to a large or full supply without the connotations of oversupply (*a country where jobs were plentiful*). If wildflowers are **rife**, it means that they are not only *prevalent* but spreading rapidly; if they're **copious**, it means they are being produced in such quantity that they constitute a rich or flowing abundance (*to weep copious tears*). What often happens, with wildflowers as well as with other beautiful things, is that they become so *abundant* they are regarded as **common**, a word meaning usual or ordinary (*the common cold*). Like *prevalent*, *common* can apply to a time as well as a place (*an expression common during the Depression*). But neither *abundant* nor *common* connotes dominance as clearly as *prevalent* does.

pre•var•i•cate /privárikayt/ *v.intr.* **1** speak or act evasively or misleadingly. **2** quibble; equivocate. □□ **pre•var•i•ca•tion** /-rikáyshən/ *n.* **pre•var'i•ca•tor** *n.*

pre•vent /privént/ *v.tr.* stop from happening or doing something; hinder; make impossible. See synonym study at HINDER. □□ **pre•vent'a•ble** *adj.* (also **pre•vent'i•ble**). **pre•vent'er** *n.* **pre•ven•tion** /-vénshən/ *n.*

■ put a stop to, arrest, (bring to a) halt; impede, curb, restrain, hamper, obstruct; preclude, forestall, avert; prohibit, ban, bar, debar. □□ **prevention** preclusion, avoidance; prohibition, forbiddance, interdiction; obstruction, stopping, arrest, halt; restraint.

pre•ven•tive /privéntiv/ (also **pre•ven•ta•tive** /privéntativ/) • *adj.* serving to prevent, esp. preventing disease. • *n.* preventive agent, measure, drug, etc. □□ **pre•ven'tive•ly** *adv.*

■ *adj.* inhibitive, inhibitory, restrictive; prophylactic, precautionary, protective; counteractive. • *n.* inhibitor, hindrance, curb, block, barrier, obstacle; prophylactic, protection, shield.

pre•view /préevyoo/ • *n.* showing of a movie, play, exhibition, etc., before it is seen by the general public. • *v.tr.* see or show in advance.

■ *n.* advance showing, private viewing.

pre•vi•ous /préeveeəs/ • *adj.* coming before in time or order. • *adv.* [foll. by *to*] before. □□ **pre'vi•ous•ly** *adv.*

■ *adj.* former, prior, past, earlier, sometime, erstwhile; above, preceding, antecedent, anterior. • *adv.* (*previous to*) previously to, prior to, in advance of; see also BEFORE *prep.* 1, 2. □□ **previously** before, once, formerly, earlier, at one time, then; in the past, in days gone by, in days of old, in days *or* times past.

prey /pray/ • *n.* **1** animal that is hunted or killed by another for food. **2** person or thing that is influenced by or vulnerable to (something undesirable) (*prey to morbid fears*). • *v.intr.* [foll. by *on, upon*] **1** seek or take as prey. **2** (of a disease, emotion, etc.) exert a harmful influence. □□ **prey'er** *n.*

■ *n.* **1** quarry, kill; victim; game. **2** victim,

target, objective; dupe, *colloq.* mark, *sl.* fall guy, pushover. • *v.* **1** live off, feed on *or* upon, eat, consume, devour; stalk, pursue, hunt. **2** oppress, weigh on *or* upon, burden, depress, strain, vex, worry, gnaw (at), plague.

price /prīs/ • *n.* **1** amount of money or goods for which a thing is bought or sold. **2** what is or must be given, done, sacrificed, etc., to obtain or achieve something. • *v.tr.* fix or find the price or value of (a thing for sale). □ **at a price** at a high cost. □□ **priced** *adj.* [also in *comb.*]. **pric′er** *n.*

■ *n.* **1** charge, cost, expense, expenditure, outlay, payment. **2** sacrifice, toll, penalty, cost; see also LOSS 2, 3. • *v.* value, evaluate, rate, cost.

price•less /prīslis/ *adj.* **1** invaluable. **2** *colloq.* very amusing or absurd. □□ **price′less•ly** *adv.* **price′less•ness** *n.*

■ **1** costly, dear, expensive, high-priced, valuable, precious. **2** hilarious, (screamingly) funny, sidesplitting, *colloq.* hysterical; ridiculous, droll, comical.

pric•ey /prīsee/ *adj.* (also **pric′y**) (**pric•i•er, pric•i•est**) *colloq.* expensive. □□ **pric′i•ness** *n.*

prick /prik/ • *v.tr.* **1** pierce slightly; make a small hole in. **2** trouble mentally. • *n.* **1** act or instance of pricking. **2** small hole or mark made by pricking. **3** pain. □ **prick up one's ears 1** (of a dog, etc.) make the ears erect when on the alert. **2** (of a person) become suddenly attentive.

■ *v.* **1** puncture, punch, perforate, penetrate. **2** see TROUBLE *v.* 1, 3. • *n.* **2** pinhole, pinprick; perforation; see also LEAK *n.* 1a. **3** sting, pinch, twinge, prickle, tingle, smart; see also PANG.

prick•er /prikər/ *n.* **1** one that pricks, as an animal or plant. **2** small thorn or other sharp pointed outgrowth.

prick•le /prikəl/ • *n.* **1** small thorn. **2** hard pointed spine of a hedgehog, etc. **3** prickling sensation. • *v.* affect or be affected with a sensation as of pricking.

■ *n.* **1** bristle, barb, needle, spike. **3** prickliness, itch, itchiness, sting, tingling, prick, tingle. • *v.* tingle, sting, itch, smart; jab, prick.

prick•ly /priklee/ *adj.* (**prick•li•er, prick•li•est**) **1** having prickles. **2** (of a person) ready to take offense. □ **prickly heat** itchy inflammation of the skin. **prickly pear 1** cactus bearing large pear-shaped prickly fruits. **2** its fruit. □□ **prick′li•ness** *n.*

■ **1** bristly, thorny, brambly, spiny, barbed, briery, spiky. **2** touchy, irritable, petulant, cantankerous, testy.

pric•y var. of PRICEY.

pride /prīd/ • *n.* **1 a** elation or satisfaction at achievements, qualities, or possessions, etc., that do one credit. **b** object of this feeling. **2** high or overbearing opinion of one's worth or importance. **3** self-respect. **4** group or company (of animals, esp. lions). • *v.refl.* [foll. by *on, upon*] be proud of. □ **take pride** (or **a pride**) **in 1** be proud of. **2** maintain in good condition or appearance. □□ **pride′ful** *adj.* **pride′ful•ly** *adv.* **pride′less** *adj.*

■ *n.* **1 b** boast, prize, treasure, jewel, gem, delight, joy, darling, ideal. **2** self-satisfaction, conceit, proudness, egotism, egocentricity, hauteur, vanity, hubris, arrogance. **3** honor, self-esteem, amour propre, dignity; credit. • *v.* take pride in, plume oneself on, preen oneself on, delight in, revel in, celebrate, glory in. □ **take (a) pride in 1** see PRIZE¹ *v.* **2** see CHERISH 2.

priest /preest/ *n.* **1** ordained minister of hierarchical Christian churches. **2** official minister of a non-Christian religion. □□ **priest′hood** *n.* **priest′like** *adj.*

■ **1** clergyman, clergywoman, ecclesiastic, cleric, churchman, reverend, vicar, divine, man of the cloth.

priest•ess /preestis/ *n.* female priest of a non-Christian religion.

priest•ly /preestlee/ *adj.* of or associated with priests. □□ **priest′li•ness** *n.*

■ clerical, ecclesiastical, pastoral, hieratic, sacerdotal.

prig /prig/ *n.* self-righteous or moralistic person. □□ **prig′gish** *adj.* **prig′gish•ly** *adv.* **prig′gish•ness** *n.*

■ prude, purist, pedant, puritan, moralist. □□ **priggish** prim, demure, prudish, prissy, puristic, moralistic, pedantic, straitlaced, stiff-necked.

prim /prim/ *adj.* (**prim•mer, prim•mest**) **1** stiffly formal and precise. **2** prudish. □□ **prim′ly** *adv.* **prim′ness** *n.*

pri•ma bal•le•ri•na /preemə/ *n.* chief female dancer in a ballet or ballet company.

pri•ma•cy /prīməsee/ *n.* (*pl.* **–cies**) **1** preeminence. **2** office of an ecclesiastical primate.

pri•ma don•na /preemə/ *n.* (*pl.* **pri•ma don•nas**) **1** chief female singer in an opera or opera company. **2** temperamentally self-important person. □□ **pri′ma don′na·ish** *adj.*

pri·ma fa·cie /prímə fáyshee, –shee-ee, shə, préemə/ *adj.* (of evidence) based on the first impression.

pri·mal /príməl/ *adj.* **1** primitive; primeval. **2** chief; fundamental. □□ **pri′mal·ly** *adv.*

pri·ma·ry /prímeree, –məree/ • *adj.* **1 a** of the first importance; chief. **b** fundamental; basic. **2** earliest; original. **3** designating any of the colors red, green, and blue, or (for pigments) red, blue, and yellow. • *n.* (*pl.* **-ies**) **1** thing that is primary. **2** (in full **primary election**) preliminary election to appoint delegates or to select candidates. □ **primary school** = *elementary school.* □□ **pri·mar·i·ly** /prímérilee/ *adv.*

▪ *adj.* **1 a** first, prime, principal, main, leading, preeminent; cardinal. **b** essential, rudimentary, elemental, first, primitive. **2** first, initial, primitive, primeval, germinal, beginning. □□ **primarily** principally, mainly, chiefly, at bottom, first of all, preeminently, basically, essentially.

pri·mate /prímayt/ *n.* **1** member of the highest order of mammals, including lemurs, apes, monkeys, and human beings. **2** archbishop. □□ **pri·ma·tial** /–máyshəl/ *adj.* **pri·ma·tol·o·gy** /mətóləjee/ *n.* (in sense 1).

pri·ma·ver·a /préemavuira/ *adj.* (of pasta, seafood, etc.) made with or containing an assortment of vegetables.

prime[1] /prím/ • *adj.* **1** chief; most important. **2** (esp. of beef) first-rate; excellent. **3** primary; fundamental. **4** *Math.* (of a number) divisible only by itself and 1 (e.g., 2, 3, 5, 7, 11). • *n.* **1** state of the highest perfection (*prime of life*). **2** the best part. □ **prime minister** head of an elected parliamentary government. **prime time** time at which a radio or television audience is largest.

▪ *adj.* **1** see MAIN *adj.* **1.** **2** first-class, choice, select, superior, preeminent, leading, unparalleled, matchless, peerless. **3** original, basic, elemental, elementary, primitive. • *n.* **1** best years, heyday; springtime, *poet.* springtide; pinnacle, acme, peak, zenith. □ **prime minister** see PREMIER *n.*

prime[2] /prím/ *v.tr.* **1** prepare (a thing) for use or action. **2** prepare for firing or detonation. **3** pour (liquid) into a pump to prepare it for working. **4** prepare (wood, etc.) for painting by applying a substance that prevents paint from being absorbed. **5** equip (a person) with information, etc.

▪ **1** see PREPARE 1, 3a. **5** educate, teach, instruct, coach, train, tutor, drill; inform, brief, apprise.

prim·er[1] /prímər/ *n.* substance used to prime wood, etc.

prim·er[2] /prímər, prímər/ *n.* **1** elementary textbook for teaching children to read. **2** introductory book.

pri·me·val /prímeevəl/ *adj.* **1** of or relating to the earliest age of the world. **2** ancient; primitive. □□ **pri·me′val·ly** *adv.*

prim·i·tive /prímitiv/ *adj.* **1** at an early stage of civilization. **2** undeveloped; crude; simple (*primitive methods*). • *n.* primitive per-

son of thing. □□ **prim′i·tive·ly** *adv.* **prim′i·tive·ness** *n.*

▪ *adj.* **1** antediluvian, ancient, aboriginal, early, primordial, primal, primeval, pristine. **2** rude, raw, barbaric, uncultured, barbarian, coarse, rough, uncivilized; basic, naïve, unrefined, unpolished.

pri·mo·gen·i·ture /prímōjénichər/ *n.* **1** fact or condition of being the firstborn child. **2** (in full **right of primogeniture**) right of inheritance of the firstborn. □□ **pri·mo·gen′i·tal** *adj.*

pri·mor·di·al /prímáwrdeeəl/ *adj.* **1** existing at or from the beginning; primeval. **2** original; fundamental. □□ **pri·mor′di·al·ly** *adv.*

primp /primp/ *v.tr.* **1** make (the hair, one's clothes, etc.) neat or overly tidy. **2** *refl.* groom (oneself) painstakingly.

▪ **1** groom, tidy, preen, prink, *colloq.* gussy up, *sl.* dude up. **2** preen *or* prink *or* prettify *or* plume oneself, spruce oneself (up), deck *or* fig oneself out, smarten up.

prim·rose /prímrōz/ *n.* **1 a** plant bearing pale yellow flowers. **b** flower of this. **2 a** pale yellow color. □ **primrose path** pursuit of pleasure, esp. with disastrous consequences.

prince /prins/ *n.* **1** male member of a royal family other than a reigning king. **2** ruler of a small nation. **3** nobleman in some countries. **4** (as a courtesy title in some connections) a duke, marquess, or earl. **5** chief or greatest (*the prince of novelists*). □ **Prince of Wales** the heir apparent to the British throne, as a title. □□ **prince′like** *adj.*

prince·ly /prínslee/ *adj.* (**prince·li·er**, **prince·li·est**) **1** of or worthy of a prince. **2 a** generous; splendid. **b** (of a sum of money) substantial. □□ **prince′li·ness** *n.*

▪ **1** royal, noble, regal, sovereign, majestic, imperial. **2** lavish, bountiful, liberal, ample; magnificent, luxurious, majestic, sumptuous; considerable, large.

prin·cess /prínses/ *n.* **1** wife of a prince. **2** female member of a royal family other than a reigning queen.

prin·ci·pal /prínsipəl/ • *adj.* **1** [usu. *attrib.*] first in rank or importance; chief. **2** main; leading. • *n.* **1** head, ruler, or superior. **2** head of a school. **3** leading performer. **4** capital sum as distinguished from interest or income. □ **principal parts** *Gram.* parts of a verb from which all other parts can be deduced.

▪ *adj.* **1, 2** chief, primary, prime, paramount, foremost, prominent, key, preeminent; starring, important. • *n.* **1** director, president, chief, employer, manager, manageress, superintendent, *colloq.* boss. **2** dean, director, headmaster, headmistress, master, chancellor, president. **3** star, lead, leading lady *or* man, leading role, main part. **4** capital, capital funds, resources, investment, reserves, assets.

prin·ci·pal·i·ty /prínsipálitee/ *n.* (*pl.* **-ties**) **1** nation ruled by a prince. **2** government of a prince.

prin·ci·pal·ly /prínsiplee/ *adv.* for the most part; chiefly.

prin•ci•ple /prínsipəl/ *n.* **1** fundamental truth or law as the basis of reasoning or action. **2 a** personal code of conduct. **b** [in *pl.*] such rules of conduct. **3** general law in physics, etc. **4** law of nature or science. □ **in principle** as regards fundamentals but not necessarily in detail. **on principle** on the basis of a moral attitude (*I refuse on principle*).

■ **1** given, precept, tenet, fundamental, rule, dictum, canon, doctrine, teaching, dogma, proposition. **2** honor, uprightness, honesty, morality, morals, probity, integrity, conscience; (*principles*) philosophy, attitude, (point of) view, viewpoint, sentiment, belief, credo, creed. □ **in principle** in theory, theoretically, ideally; fundamentally, at bottom, in essence.

prin•ci•pled /prínsipəld/ *adj.* based on or having (esp. praiseworthy) principles of behavior.

■ ethical, honorable, proper, correct, right, just.

print /print/ • *n.* **1** indentation or residual mark (*fingerprint*). **2 a** printed lettering or writing. **b** words in printed form. **3** picture or design printed from a block or plate. **4** *Photog.* picture produced on paper from a negative. **5** printed cotton fabric. • *v.tr.* **1** produce or cause (a book, picture, etc.) to be produced by applying inked types, blocks, or plates, to paper, vellum, etc. **2** express or publish in print. **3** [often foll. by *on, in*] impress or stamp. **4** [often *absol.*] write (words or letters) without joining, in imitation of typography. **5** *Photog.* produce (a photograph) from a negative. **6** [usu. foll. by *out*] (of a computer, etc.) produce output in printed form. □ **in print** (of a book, etc.) available from the publisher. **out of print** no longer available from the publisher. □□ **print′a•ble** *adj.* **print′less** *adj.* (in sense 1 of *n.*)

■ *n.* **1** impression; see also MARK¹ *n.* **1. 2** text, printed matter; see also TYPE *n.* **6. 3** reproduction, copy, replica, facsimile; illustration; pattern, motif. **4** see PHOTOGRAPH *n.* • *v.* **1, 2** issue, run off, put out. **3** see STAMP *v.* **2**.

print•er /príntər/ *n.* **1** person who prints books, magazines, advertising matter, etc. **2** owner of a printing business. **3** device that prints, esp. as part of a computer system.

print•ing /prínting/ *n.* **1** production of printed books, etc. **2** single impression of a book. **3** printed letters or writing imitating them. □ **printing press** machine for printing from types or plates, etc.

print•out /príntowt/ *n.* computer output in printed form.

pri•or /príər/ • *adj.* **1** earlier. **2** coming before in time, order, or importance. • *adv.* [foll. by *to*] before. • *n.* superior officer of a religious house or order. □□ **pri•or•ate** /–rət/ *n.* **pri•or•ess** /príəris/ *n.*

■ *adj.* **1** former, previous; see also FOREGO-

ING. • *adv.* previous to, previously to; see also BEFORE *prep.* 2.

pri•or•i•ty /príáwritee, –ór–/ *n.* (*pl.* **–ties**) **1** precedence in rank, etc. **2** interest having prior claim to consideration. □□ **pri•or′i•tize** *v.tr.* **pri•or•i•ti•za′tion** *n.*

■ **1** precedency, preference; primacy, urgency, predominance, preeminence, rank, superiority.

pri•o•ry /príəree/ *n.* (*pl.* **–ries**) monastery governed by a prior or a convent governed by a prioress.

prism /prízəm/ *n.* **1** solid geometric figure whose two ends are similar, equal, and parallel rectilinear figures, and whose sides are parallelograms. **2** transparent body in this form, usu. triangular, that separates white light into a spectrum of colors. □□ **pris•mat•ic** /–mátik/ *adj.* **pris•mat′i•cal•ly** *adv.*

pris•on /prízən/ *n.* **1** place of confinement for convicted criminals or persons awaiting trial. **2** custody; confinement. □ **prison camp 1** camp for prisoners of war or political prisoners. **2** minimum-security prison.

■ **1** jail, lockup, penal institution, guardhouse, penitentiary, brig, calaboose, correctional facility, *sl.* clink, can, cooler, jug, stir, slammer, pokey, pen.

pris•on•er /príznər/ *n.* **1** person kept in prison. **2** person or thing confined by illness, another's grasp, etc.

■ **1** convict, inmate, internee, detainee, jailbird, *sl.* con.

pris•sy /prísee/ *adj.* (**pris•si•er, pris•si•est**) prim; prudish. □□ **pris′si•ly** *adv.* **pris′si•ness** *n.*

■ overnice, straitlaced, old-maidish.

pris•tine /prísteen, prísteén/ *adj.* **1** in its original condition; unspoiled. **2** *disp.* spotless; fresh as if new.

■ **1** uncorrupted, pure, unsullied, undefiled, virginal, virgin, chaste, untouched, unpolluted. **2** clean, gleaming, shiny, polished, unspotted; immaculate, as new; mint.

pri•va•cy /prívəsee/ *n.* **1 a** state of being private and undisturbed. **b** person's right to this. **2** freedom from intrusion or public attention. **3** avoidance of publicity.

■ **1** seclusion, retirement, solitude, isolation, reclusion. **3** secretiveness, confidentiality; see also SECRECY.

pri•vate /prívət/ • *adj.* **1** belonging to an individual; one's own; personal (*private property*). **2** confidential (*private talks*). **3** kept or removed from public knowledge or observation. **4** not open to the public. **5** secluded. **6** (of a person) not holding public office or an official position. • *n.* **1** soldier with a rank below corporal. **2** [in *pl.*] *colloq.* genitals. □ **in private** privately. **private detective** detective engaged privately, outside an official police force. **private enterprise** business or businesses not under government control. **private eye** *colloq.* private detective. **private parts** genitals. **private sector** the part of the economy free of direct government control. □□ **pri′vate•ly** *adv.*

■ *adj.* **1** individual. **2** (top) secret, clandestine, hidden, concealed, covert, surreptitious, *colloq.* hush-hush; unofficial. **3, 5** hid-

ing, undeclared, unspoken. **4** restrictive, restricted, exclusive, special, reserved. • *n.*
1 infantryman, foot soldier, poilu, enlisted
man, GI. **2** (*privates*) private parts, sexual *or*
sex organs, genitalia, pudenda, *euphem.* one's
person. □ **in private** in secret, secretly, sub
rosa, personally, in confidence, confidentially, clandestinely, secretively, furtively, covertly. **private parts** see PRIVATE *n.* 2 above.

pri•va•tion /prīváyshən/ *n.* lack of the comforts or necessities of life (*suffered many privations*). See synonym study at LACK.
■ deprivation, hardship, indigence, poverty,
penury, destitution, pauperism, beggary; distress, misery.

pri•vat•ize /prívatīz/ *v.tr.* make private, esp.
transfer (a business, etc.) to private as distinct from government control or ownership.
□□ **pri•va•ti•za′tion** *n.*

priv•et /prívit/ *n.* deciduous or evergreen
shrub bearing small white flowers and much
used for hedges.

priv•i•lege /prívilij, prívlij/ • *n.* **1** right, advantage, or immunity. **2** special benefit or
honor (*a privilege to meet you*). • *v.tr.* invest
with a privilege. □□ **priv′i•leged** *adj.*
■ *n.* **1** benefit, prerogative, concession,
freedom, liberty, franchise; permission, consent, leave, authorization, sanction, authority, license; exemption, dispensation.
2 pleasure; see also HONOR *n.* 5. □□ **privileged** favored, élite, special, protected, immune; licensed, authorized; wealthy, rich, affluent; powerful, empowered; confidential,
secret, private.

priv•y /prívee/ • *adj.* **1** (foll. by *to*) sharing in
the secret of (a person's plans, etc.). **2** *archaic* hidden; secret. • *n.* (*pl.* **-ies**) toilet, esp. an
outhouse. □□ **priv′i•ly** *adv.*
■ *adj.* **1** aware of, in on, sharing (in), cognizant of, apprised of, informed *or* advised
about *or* of, *colloq.* wise to, *sl.* hip to. **2** see SE-
CRET *adj.* 1. • *n.* bathroom, lavatory, latrine,
sl. can, john, head.

prize¹ /prīz/ • *n.* **1** something that can be
won in a competition, lottery, etc. **2** reward
given as a symbol of victory or superiority.
3 something worth striving for. **4** [*attrib.*] supremely excellent or outstanding of its kind.
• *v.tr.* value highly. See synonym study at ES-
TEEM. □ **prize money** money offered as a
prize.
■ *n.* **2** award, trophy, premium; honor, accolade; winnings, jackpot. **4** (*attrib.*) choice,
excellent, winning, champion, select, superior, superlative, first-rate, first-class. • *v.*
treasure, esteem, cherish, appreciate, rate
highly.

prize² /prīz/ (*also* **prise**) *v.tr.* force open or
out by leverage.

prize•fight /prízfīt/ *n.* boxing match fought
for prize money. □□ **prize′fight′er** *n.*

prize•win•ner /prízwinər/ *n.* winner of a
prize. □□ **prize′win′ning** *adj.*

pro¹ /prō/ *colloq. n.* (*pl.* **pros**) professional.

pro² /prō/ • *adj.* for; in favor. • *n.* (*pl.* **pros**)
reason or argument for or in favor. • *prep.* in
favor of. □ **pro bono** pertaining to a service,
esp. legal work, for which no fee is charged.

pro-choice in favor of the right to legal
abortion. **pro-life** opposed to the right to legal abortion. **pros and cons** reasons for and
against a proposition.

pro- /prō/ *prefix* **1** favoring or supporting
(*pro-government*). **2** acting as a substitute or
deputy for (*proconsul*). **3** forward (*produce*).
4 forward and downward (*prostrate*). **5** onward (*progress*). **6** in front of (*protect*).

pro•ac•tive /prō-áktiv/ *adj.* (of a person, policy, etc.) taking the initiative. □□ **pro•ac′
tion** *n.* **pro•ac′tive•ly** *adv.*

prob. *abbr.* **1** probable. **2** probably. **3** problem.

prob•a•bil•ism /próbəbalizəm/ *n.* **1** *Philos.*
doctrine that probability is the basis for belief and action since certainty is impossible.
2 *RC Ch.* ethical theory that it is allowable to
follow any one of many conflicting opinions
even though an opposing one may be more
probable.

prob•a•bil•i•ty /próbəbilitee/ *n.* (*pl.* **-ties**)
1 being probable. **2** likelihood of something
happening. **3** probable or most probable
event (*probability is that they will come*).
4 *Math.* extent to which an event is likely to
occur, measured by the ratio of the favorable
cases to the whole number of cases possible.
□ **in all probability** most probably.
■ **2, 3** likeliness, odds, (good) chance,
(strong *or* distinct) possibility, good prospect.

prob•a•ble /próbəbəl/ • *adj.* expected to happen or prove true; likely. • *n.* probable candidate, member of a team, etc. □□ **prob′a•bly**
adv.
■ *adj.* possible, plausible, feasible, believable, credible, conceivable. □□ **probably**
(very) likely, in all likelihood, in all probability; presumably.

pro•bate /prōbayt/ *v.tr.* establish the validity
of (a will).

pro•ba•tion /prəbáyshən/ *n.* **1** *Law* system of
suspending the sentence of a criminal offender subject to a period of good behavior
under supervision. **2** period of testing, as
for a new employee. □ **probation officer**
official supervising offenders on probation.
□□ **pro•ba′tion•al** *adj.* **pro•ba′tion•ary**
adj.

pro•ba•tion•er /prəbáyshənər/ *n.* person on
probation, a newly appointed nurse, teacher,
etc.

probe /prōb/ • *n.* **1** penetrating investigation.
2 small device for measuring, testing, etc.
3 blunt surgical exploratory instrument.
4 (in full **space probe**) unmanned exploratory spacecraft. • *v.tr.* **1** examine or inquire
into closely. **2** explore with a probe.
□□ **probe′a•ble** *adj.* **prob′er** *n.* **prob′ing•ly**
adv.
■ *n.* **1** examination, exploration, scrutiny,
search, study, inquiry. • *v.* **1** explore, scrutinize, investigate, search (into), look into, go
into; dig into, delve into.

pro•bi•ty /prōbitee, prób-/ *n.* uprightness;
honesty. See synonym study at GOODNESS.
■ integrity, morality, rectitude, virtue,

problem ~ prodigal   660

goodness, decency, righteousness, right-mindedness, sincerity.

prob•lem /próbləm/ *n.* **1** doubtful or difficult matter requiring a solution (*the problem of ventilation*). **2** something hard to understand, accomplish, or deal with.
■ difficulty, trouble, complication, dilemma, question, (Gordian) knot, hornet's nest, *colloq.* can of worms.

prob•lem•at•ic /próbləmátik/ *adj.* (also **prob•lem•at'i•cal**) **1** difficult; posing a problem. **2** doubtful or questionable. See synonym study at DOUBTFUL. □□ **prob•lem•at'i•cal•ly** *adv.*
■ **1** see DIFFICULT 1. **2** uncertain, debatable, disputable, moot, controversial, tricky.

pro bo•no /prō bónō/ • *adv. & adj.* denoting work undertaken for the public good without charge, esp. legal work for a client with a low income.

pro•bos•cis /prōbósis/ *n.* **1** long flexible trunk or snout of some mammals, e.g., an elephant or tapir. **2** elongated mouth parts of some insects.

pro•ce•dure /prəséejər/ *n.* **1** way of proceeding, esp. a mode of conducting business or a legal action. **2** mode of performing a task. **3** series of actions conducted in a certain order or manner. □□ **pro•ce'dur•al** *adj.* **pro•ce'dur•al•ly** *adv.*
■ conduct, course, action, course of action, process, methodology, form, system, approach; routine, drill.

pro•ceed /prōséed, prə-/ *v.intr.* **1** go forward or on further; make one's way. **2** continue; go on with an activity. **3** (of an action) be carried on or continued. **4** adopt a course of action. **5** go on to say.
■ **1** move on *or* ahead *or* forward, advance, progress, move along, push *or* press on *or* onward(s), forge ahead. **2** pass on; see also *carry on* 1. **4** go on, continue; see also START *v.* 1, 2.

pro•ceed•ing /prōséeding, prə-/ *n.* **1** action or piece of conduct. **2** [in *pl.*] (in full **legal proceedings**) lawsuit. **3** [in *pl.*] published report of discussions or a conference.
■ **1** measure, act, move, step, undertaking, deed, procedure, process, operation, transaction. **2 legal proceedings** suit, action, case, process, cause, trial; litigation. **3** transactions, procès-verbal, minutes, record(s), annals, account(s), archives.

pro•ceeds /prōseedz/ *n.pl.* profits.
■ gain, yield; income, takings, receipts, return(s).

pro•cess¹ /próses, prō-/ • *n.* **1** course of action or proceeding, esp. as a series of stages. **2** progress or course (*in process of construction*). **3** natural evolution or change (*process of growing old*). **4** summons or writ. **5** *Anat., Zool., & Bot.* natural appendage or outgrowth on an organism. • *v.tr.* **1** handle or deal with by a particular process. **2** treat (food, esp. to prevent decay) (*processed cheese*). □□ **pro'cess•a•ble** *adj.*
■ *n.* **1** operation, system, method, approach; see also PROCEDURE. **2** midst, mid-

dle. **4** see ACTION *n.* 8, WARRANT *n.* 2. • *v.* **1** take care of, manage, look after; prepare, make or get ready; answer. **2** prepare.

pro•cess² /prəsés/ *v.intr.* walk in procession.

pro•ces•sion /prəséshən/ *n.* **1** number of people or vehicles, etc., moving forward in orderly or ceremonial succession. **2** movement of such a group.
■ **1** parade, march, cortege, column, line, file, train.

pro•ces•sion•al /prəséshənəl/ *adj.* **1** of processions. **2** used, carried, or sung in processions.

pro•ces•sor /prósesər, prō-/ *n.* machine that processes things, esp.: **1** = *central processor.* **2** = *food processor.*

pro•claim /prōkláym, prə-/ *v.tr.* **1** announce or declare publicly or officially. **2** declare (a person) to be (a king, traitor, etc.). See synonym study at ANNOUNCE. □□ **pro•claim'er** *n.* **proc•la•ma•tion** /prókləmáyshən/ *n.*
■ **1** pronounce, make known, publish, advertise, broadcast; profess, assert. **2** brand, accuse of being, stigmatize as, pronounce, announce, decree. □□ **proclamation** announcement, declaration, publication, promulgation, statement, advertisement.

pro•cliv•i•ty /prōklívitee/ *n.* (*pl.* **-ties**) tendency or inclination.

pro•cras•ti•nate /prōkrástinayt/ *v.* **1** *intr.* defer action. **2** *tr.* defer or delay, esp. intentionally or habitually. □□ **pro•cras•ti•na•tion** /-náyshən/ *n.* **pro•cras'ti•na•tor** *n.*
■ **1** temporize, play for time, dally, delay, stall, take one's time, dillydally; hesitate, pause, waver, vacillate.

pro•cre•ate /prōkreeayt/ *v.tr.* [often *absol.*] produce (offspring) naturally. □□ **pro•cre•ant** /prōkreeənt/ *adj.* **pro•cre•a•tive** *adj.* **pro•cre•a'tion** *n.* **pro•cre•a•tor** *n.*

Pro•crus•te•an /prōkrústeeən/ *adj.* seeking to enforce uniformity by forceful or ruthless methods.

proc•tor /próktər/ *n.* supervisor of students in an examination, etc. □□ **proc•to•ri•al** /-táwreeəl/ *adj.*

pro•cure /prōkyŏŏr, prə-/ *v.tr.* **1** obtain, esp. by care or effort; acquire. **2** bring about. **3** obtain (people) for prostitution. See synonym study at GET. □□ **pro•cur'a•ble** *adj.* **pro•cure'ment** *n.*
■ **1** get, come by, secure, get *or* lay one's hands on; requisition; buy, purchase. **2** accomplish, contrive, effect, cause, produce; see also *bring about.* **3** pander, pimp.

pro•cur•er /prōkyŏŏrər, prə-/ *n.* pimp.
■ pander; madam, procuress, bawd, *sl.* hustler; see also PIMP *n.*

prod /prod/ • *v.tr.* (**prod•ded, prod•ding**) **1** poke with the finger or a pointed object. **2** stimulate to action. • *n.* **1** poke or thrust. **2** stimulus to action. □□ **prod'der** *n.*
■ *v.* **1** jab, dig, nudge, thrust, elbow. **2** spur, urge, impel, push, prompt, rouse, stir, incite; move, goad, pester, harass, hector. • *n.* **1** jab, dig, nudge, push. **2** push, shove, prompt; see also SPUR *n.* 2.

prod•i•gal /pródigəl/ • *adj.* **1** recklessly wasteful. **2** [foll. by *of*] lavish. See synonym study at PROFUSE. • *n.* prodigal person.

□□ **prod•i•gal•i•ty** /–gálitee/ *n.* **prod'i•gal•ly** *adv.*

■ *adj.* **1** extravagant, spendthrift, profligate, immoderate, intemperate, reckless. **2** generous, bountiful, copious, profuse, excessive, liberal, luxuriant, abundant. • *n.* wastrel, spendthrift, squanderer, waster, big spender; see also PROFLIGATE *n.* □□ **prodigality** wastefulness, extravagance, excessiveness, immoderation, intemperateness; lavishness, luxuriousness, luxuriance, abundance, bounty, bountifulness, copiousness, profusion.

pro•di•gious /prədíjəs/ *adj.* **1** marvelous or amazing. **2** enormous. □□ **pro•di'gious•ly** *adv.*

■ **1** astonishing, astounding, startling, *colloq.* fabulous, fantastic, mind-boggling. **2** vast, immeasurable, colossal, tremendous; giant, gigantic, mammoth, monumental, stupendous.

prod•i•gy /pródijee/ *n.* (*pl.* **–gies**) **1** person endowed with exceptional qualities or abilities, esp. a precocious child. **2** marvelous, esp. extraordinary, thing.

■ **1** genius, mastermind, wizard, virtuoso, *colloq.* brain, wunderkind, Einstein, whiz kid. **2** marvel, phenomenon, sensation, miracle; see also WONDER *n.* 2.

pro•duce • *v.tr.* /prədóos, –dyóos/ **1** bring forward for consideration, inspection, or use. **2** manufacture (goods) from raw materials, etc. **3** bear or yield (offspring, fruit, a harvest, etc.). **4** bring into existence. **5** cause or bring about. **6** supervise the production of (a movie, broadcast, etc.). • *n.* /pródos, –dyóos, pró–/ **1** what is produced, esp. agricultural products. **2** fruits and vegetables collectively. □□ **pro•duc•i•ble** /–sib'l/ *adj.*

■ *v.* **1** bring out, introduce, present, offer, show; disclose, reveal. **2** make, fabricate, turn out; construct, assemble. **3** put out *or* forth, generate; see also BEAR[1] 3. **4, 5** give rise to, bring forth, spark off, initiate, occasion; create, generate, give birth to. • *n.* **1** goods, merchandise, commodities, stock, staples, wares.

pro•duc•er /prədóosər, –dyóo–/ *n.* **1** *Econ.* person who produces goods or commodities. **2** person generally responsible for the production of a movie, play, broadcast, etc.

■ **1** maker, manufacturer, fabricator, processor; creator, grower. **2** promoter, impresario, administrator, manager, stage manager, showman.

prod•uct /pródukt/ *n.* **1** thing or substance produced by natural process or manufacture. **2** result. **3** *Math.* quantity obtained by multiplying quantities together.

■ **1** artifact, commodity; (*products*) see PRODUCE *n.* 1. **2** consequence, outcome, issue, effect, yield.

pro•duc•tion /prədúkshən/ *n.* **1** producing or being produced, esp. in large quantities (*go into production*). **2** total yield. **3** thing produced, esp. a movie, broadcast, play, etc. □□ **pro•duc'tion•al** *adj.*

■ **1** manufacture, manufacturing, making, fabrication, preparation; formation, assem-

bly, building. **3** product; show, performance; work, opus.

pro•duc•tive /prədúktiv/ *adj.* **1** of or engaged in the production of goods. **2** producing much. **3** [foll. by *of*] producing or giving rise to. □□ **pro•duc'tive•ly** *adv.* **pro•duc'tive•ness** *n.*

■ **2** fruitful, fertile, rich, fecund, plentiful, abundant.

pro•duc•tiv•i•ty /próduktívitee, prō–/ *n.* **1** capacity to produce. **2** effectiveness of productive effort, esp. in industry. **3** production per unit of effort.

■ **2** efficiency, productiveness.

Prof. *abbr.* Professor.

pro•fane /prōfáyn, prə–/ • *adj.* **1** not sacred; secular. **2 a** irreverent; blasphemous. **b** vulgar; obscene. • *v.tr.* **1** treat (a sacred thing) with irreverence or disregard. **2** violate or pollute (something entitled to respect). □□ **pro•fa•na•tion** /prófənáyshən/ *n.* **pro•fane'ly** *adv.* **pro•fan'er** *n.*

■ *adj.* **1** nonreligious, laic, lay, nonclerical, temporal; unsanctified, unconsecrated, unhallowed. **2 a** sacrilegious, idolatrous, irreligious, unbelieving, disbelieving, impious, godless. **b** impure, unclean, dirty, filthy, smutty, foul, foulmouthed, coarse, uncouth, rude, low, bawdy. • *v.* **2** debase, contaminate, taint, vitiate, degrade, defile, desecrate, pervert.

pro•fan•i•ty /prōfánitee, prə–/ *n.* (*pl.* **–ties**) **1** profane or profane language; blasphemy.

■ **1** see SACRILEGE. **2** obscenity, cursing, swearing, foul *or* bad language.

pro•fess /prəfés, prō–/ *v.tr.* **1** claim openly to have (a quality or feeling). **2** declare (*profess ignorance*). **3** affirm one's faith in or allegiance to.

■ **2** assert, claim, asseverate, state, affirm, confirm, confess, maintain, set forth, put forward, pronounce.

pro•fessed• /prəfést, prō–/ *adj.* **1** self-acknowledged. **2** alleged; ostensible. □□ **pro•fess•ed•ly** /–fésidlee/ *adv.*

■ **1** sworn, acknowledged, confirmed, certified, declared. **2** supposed, apparent, purported, so-called.

pro•fes•sion /prəféshən/ *n.* **1** work that involves some branch of advanced learning or science. **2** people engaged in a profession. **3** declaration or avowal.

■ **1** occupation, calling, field, vocation, employment, specialty, job, position. **3** confession, affirmation, statement, assertion, asseveration; admission.

pro•fes•sion•al /prəféshənəl/ • *adj.* **1** of or belonging to or connected with a profession. **2 a** skillful. **b** worthy of a professional (*professional conduct*). **3** engaged in a specified activity as one's main paid occupation. • *n.* a professional person. □□ **pro•fes'sion•al•ism'** *n.* **pro•fes'sion•al•ly** *adv.*

■ *adj.* **1** trained, practiced, veteran, experienced, qualified, licensed; competent, able, skilled, expert, masterful. • *n.* master, expert, specialist, authority, proficient.

pro•fes•sor /prəfésər/ *n.* **1 a** (often as a title) university academic of the highest rank. **b** university teacher. **2** person who professes a religion. □□ **pro•fes•so•ri•al** /prófisáw-reeəl/ *adj.* **pro•fes•so′ri•al•ly** *adv.* **pro•fes′sor•ship** *n.*

prof•fer /prófər/ *v.tr.* (esp. as **proffered** *adj.*) offer.

pro•fi•cient /prəfíshənt/ *adj.* [often foll. by *in*, *at*] adept; expert. □□ **pro•fi•cien•cy** /–shən-see/ *n.* **pro•fi′cient•ly** *adv.*

▪ skillful, skilled, experienced, practiced, well-versed, trained, professional, qualified, capable, able. □□ **proficiency** skill, adeptness, expertise, expertness, know-how, skillfulness, aptitude, capability.

pro•file /prófïl/ • *n.* **1 a** outline (esp. of a human face) as seen from one side. **b** representation of this. **2** short biographical or character sketch. • *v.tr.* represent or describe by a profile. ▪ **keep a low profile** remain inconspicuous. □□ **pro′fil•er** *n.*

▪ *n.* **1** contour, silhouette, side view. **2** biography, thumbnail sketch, portrait, vignette. • *v.* draw, sketch, characterize, portray, paint, depict, style. ▪ **keep a low profile** keep low *or* down, soft-pedal; see also *dummy up.*

prof•it /prófit/ • *n.* **1** advantage or benefit. **2** financial gain; excess of returns over expenditures. • *v.* **1** *tr.* [also *absol.*] be beneficial to. **2** *intr.* obtain an advantage or benefit. ▪ **at a profit** with financial gain. □□ **prof•it•a•bil′i•ty** *n.* **prof′it•a•ble** *adj.* **prof′it•a•bly** *adv.* **prof′it•less** *adj.*

▪ *n.* **1** avail, good, gain, value, interest, use, usefulness. **2** net profit *or* income, net, return(s), yield, payback, revenue. • *v.* **1** advance, further, be of profit *or* advantage to, benefit, promote, aid, help. **2** take advantage of, turn to advantage *or* account, exploit, utilize, make (good) use of, make capital (out) of. □□ **profitable** productive, lucrative, fruitful, well-paid, cost-effective, gainful, beneficial, helpful, useful, utilitarian.

prof•i•teer /prófitéer/ • *v.intr.* make or seek to make excessive profits, esp. illegally. • *n.* person who profiteers.

▪ *v.* see PROFIT *v.* 2. • *n.* racketeer, exploiter, extortionist, extortioner, black marketer, bloodsucker.

prof•li•gate /prófligət/ • *adj.* **1** licentious; dissolute. **2** recklessly extravagant. • *n.* profligate person. □□ **prof•li•ga•cy** /–gəsee/ *n.* **prof′li•gate•ly** *adv.*

▪ *adj.* **1** degenerate, loose, depraved, debauched, immoral. **2** prodigal, wasteful, reckless, improvident, spendthrift, immoderate, excessive. • *n.* debauchee, degenerate, reprobate, libertine; prodigal, spendthrift, wastrel, waster, squanderer. □□ **profligacy** debauchery, immorality, dissipation, dissoluteness; prodigality, extravagance, wastefulness, recklessness.

pro for•ma /prō fáwrmə/ *adv. & adj.* as or being a matter of form; for the sake of form.

pro•found /prəfównd, prō–/ *adj.* (**pro•found•er, pro•found•est**) **1** having or de-

manding great knowledge or insight. **2** deep; intense; unqualified (*profound indifference*). **3** deeply felt. □□ **pro•found′ly** *adv.* **pro•found′ness** *n.* **pro•fun•di•ty** /–fúnditee/ *n.* (*pl.* **–ties**).

▪ **1** learned, scholarly, intellectual, erudite, discerning, astute; deep, unfathomable, abstruse, recondite, arcane. **2** great; keen, acute, extreme; utter, complete, total. □□ **profoundly** deeply, greatly, very, extremely, keenly. **profoundness, profundity** depth, intensity, abstruseness, reconditeness; erudition, discernment, scholarship.

pro•fuse /prəfyōōs, prō–/ *adj.* **1** lavish; extravagant. **2** exuberantly plentiful; abundant (*a profuse variety*). □□ **pro•fuse′ly** *adv.* **pro•fuse′ness** *n.* **pro•fu•sion** /–fyōōzhən/ *n.*

▪ **1** generous, unsparing, unselfish, unstinting, exuberant, magnanimous. **2** ample, copious, prolific, superabundant, lush; excessive, considerable. □□ **profuseness, profusion** abundance, bounty, plenty, plentifulness, copiousness, superfluity, glut.

SYNONYM STUDY: **profuse**

EXTRAVAGANT, LAVISH, LUSH, LUXURIANT, PRODIGAL. Something that is **profuse** is poured out or given freely, often to the point of exaggeration or excess (*profuse apologies*). **Extravagant** also suggests unreasonable excess, but with an emphasis on wasteful spending (*her gift was much too extravagant for the occasion*). Someone who is **prodigal** is so recklessly extravagant that his or her resources will ultimately be exhausted (*the prodigal heir to the family fortune*). Another way to end up impoverished is through **lavish** spending, a word that combines extravagance with generosity or a lack of moderation (*lavish praise; lavish furnishings*). While *lavish, extravagant,* and *prodigal* are often used to describe human behavior, **lush** and **luxuriant** normally refer to things. What is *luxuriant* is produced in great quantity, suggesting that it is not only *profuse* but gorgeous (*luxuriant auburn hair*). Something described as *lush* is not only *luxuriant* but has reached a peak of perfection (*the lush summer grass*).

pro•gen•i•tor /prōjénitər/ *n.* **1** ancestor. **2** predecessor. □□ **pro•gen•i•to•ri•al** /–táw-reeəl/ *adj.*

▪ **1** see ANCESTOR 1. **2** forerunner, precursor, antecedent, foregoer.

prog•e•ny /prójinee/ *n.* **1** offspring of a person or other organism. **2** descendant or descendants.

▪ **1** children, young, sons and daughters, *derog.* spawn; see also ISSUE *n.* 5. **2** posterity, heirs, scions, successors; see also SUCCESSION 2.

pro•ges•ter•one /prōjéstərōn/ *n.* steroid hormone that stimulates the preparation of the uterus for pregnancy.

prog•no•sis /prognόsis/ *n.* (*pl.* **prog•no•ses** /–seez/) forecast, as of a process or the course of a disease.

▪ prognostication, prediction, prophecy, projection.

prog•nos•tic /prognóstik/ • *n.* **1** advance indication or omen, esp. of the course of a disease, etc. **2** prediction; forecast. • *adj.* fore-telling; predictive. □□ **prog•nos′ti•cal•ly** *adv.*

prog•nos•ti•cate /prognóstikayt/ *v.tr.* fore-tell; foresee; prophesy. See synonym study at PREDICT. □□ **prog•nos•ti•ca•tion** /-káyshən/ *n.* **prog•nos•ti•ca•tive** /-kətiv/ *adj.* **prog•nos′ti•ca•tor** *n.*

■ predict, forecast, presage; betoken, augur, herald.

pro•gram /prógram, -grəm/ • *n.* **1** list of a series of events, performers, etc., at a public function, etc. **2** radio or television broad-cast. **3** plan of future events. **4** course or se-ries of studies, lectures, etc.; syllabus. **5** se-ries of coded instructions to control the operation of a computer or other machine. • *v.tr.* (**pro•grammed, pro•gram•ming; pro•gramed, pro•gram•ing**) **1** make a program of. **2** express (a problem) or in-struct (a computer) by means of a program. □□ **pro•gram′ma•ble** *adj.* **pro•gram′mat•ic** *adj.* **pro•gram•mat′i•cal•ly** *adv.* **pro′gram•mer** (or **pro′gram•er**) *n.*

■ *n.* **1, 3** schedule, agenda, outline, calen-dar. **2** production, show, presentation, tele-cast. **4** curriculum; timetable, schedule. • *v.* **1** prearrange, plan, lay out, map (out), set up, schedule, slate.

prog•ress • *n.* /prógres/ **1** forward or on-ward movement toward a destination. **2** ad-vance; improvement. • *v.intr.* /prəgrés/ **1** move or be moved forward or onward; con-tinue. **2** advance, develop, or improve (*sci-ence progresses*). □ **in progress** developing; going on.

■ *n.* **1** progression, advancement; headway, moving. **2** advancement, promotion, devel-opment, spread; elevation, rise; growth. • *v.* **1** advance, go (forward or onward or on), proceed, forge ahead. **2** get better, grow, ex-pand, increase, evolve, mature. □ **in prog-ress** under way, ongoing, taking place, at work, in operation, in the pipeline.

pro•gres•sion /prəgréshən/ *n.* **1** progressing (*mode of progression*). **2** succession; series. □□ **pro•gres′sion•al** *adj.*

■ **1** forward movement, advance, progress; ascension, rise. **2** order, sequence, train, chain; set.

pro•gres•sive /prəgrésiv/ • *adj.* **1** moving forward. **2** proceeding step-by-step; cumu-lative. **3** a favoring or implementing rapid progress or social reform. **b** modern. **4** (of disease, violence, etc.) increasing in severity or extent. **5** *Gram.* (of an aspect) expressing an action in progress, e.g., *am writing, was writing*. • *n.* (also **Progressive**) advocate of progressive political policies. □□ **pro•gres′ sive•ly** *adv.* **pro•gres′sive•ness** *n.* **pro•gres′siv•ism** *n.*

■ *adj.* **2, 4** continuing, developing, grow-ing, ongoing; step-by-step, gradual. **3 a** forward-looking, advanced, reform, re-formist, left-wing, radical, liberal. **b** new, go-ahead, enterprising, see also CAPABLE 1. • *n.* reformist, reformer, revisionist; leftist, left-winger; see also LIBERAL *n.*

pro•hib•it /prōhíbit/ *v.tr.* **1** forbid. **2** prevent. □□ **pro•hib′it•er, pro•hib′i•tor** *n.*

■ **1** bar, ban, disallow, interdict, outlaw, ta-boo, debar. **2** stop, obstruct, block, impede, hinder, hamper.

<hr>

SYNONYM STUDY: **prohibit**

BAN, DISALLOW, ENJOIN, FORBID, HINDER, IN-TERDICT, PRECLUDE. There are a number of ways to prevent something from happening. You can **prohibit** it, which assumes that you have legal or other authority (*to prohibit smoking*) and are willing to back up your prohibition with force; or you can simply **forbid** it and hope that you've got the nec-essary clout (*to forbid teenagers to stay out after midnight*). **Ban** carries a little more weight—both legal and moral—and **inter-dict** suggests that church or civil authorities are behind the idea. To **enjoin** is to prohibit by legal injunction (*the truckers were enjoined from striking*), which practically guarantees that you'll get what you want. A government or some other authority may **disallow** an act it might otherwise have permitted (*the IRS disallowed the deduction*), but anyone with a little gumption can **hinder** an activity by putting obstacles in its path (*to hinder the thief's getaway by tripping him on his way out the door*) Of course, the easiest way to *pro-hibit* something is to **preclude** it, which means stopping it before it even gets started.

pro•hi•bi•tion /prōhibíshən, prōəbíshən/ *n.* **1** forbidding or being forbidden. **2** *Law* edict or order that forbids. **3** (usu. **Prohibi-tion**) period (1920–33) in the US when the manufacture and sale of alcoholic beverages was prohibited by law. □□ **pro•hi•bi′tion-ist** *n.*

■ **1** forbiddance, banning, disallowance, in-terdiction, outlawry; bar, interdict, injunc-tion, embargo, ban.

pro•hib•i•tive /prōhíbitiv/ *adj.* **1** prohibiting. **2** (of prices, taxes, etc.) extremely high. □□ **pro•hib′i•tive•ly** *adv.* **pro•hib′i•tive-ness** *n.*

■ **1** suppressive, repressive; inhibitory, re-straining. **2** excessive, extortionate, exorbi-tant, outrageous.

proj•ect • *n.* /prójekt/ **1** plan; scheme. **2** ex-tensive undertaking, academic assignment, etc. • *v.* /prəjékt/ **1** *intr.* protrude; jut out. **2** *tr.* throw. **3** *tr.* extrapolate (results, etc.); forecast. **4** *tr.* cause (light, shadow, images, etc.) to fall on a surface. **5** *tr.* cause (a sound, esp. the voice) to be heard at a dis-tance. **6** *tr.* [often *refl.* or *absol.*] express or promote forcefully or effectively. **7** *tr. Psy-chol.* **a** [also *absol.*] attribute (an emotion, etc.) to an external object or person, esp. un-consciously. **b** [*refl.*] project (oneself) into another's feelings, the future, etc.

■ *n.* **1** proposal, idea, program, design. **2** activity, enterprise, venture. • *v.* **1** stick out, overhang, stand out, bulge, ex-tend. **2** cast, hurl, fling, toss, launch, propel, see also THROW *v.* 1, 2. **3** estimate, reckon, calculate, predict; see also FORECAST *v.* **4** re-flect, transmit, cast, throw, shed. **6** see COM-MUNICATE 1a; (*project oneself*) carry on,

conduct oneself, present oneself, see also BE-
HAVE 1. **7 a** see ATTRIBUTE *v.*

pro•jec•tile /prəjéktəl, –tíl/ *n.* **1** missile, esp.
fired by a rocket. **2** bullet, shell, etc.
■ brickbat; cartridge, shot, rocket.

pro•jec•tion /prəjékshən/ *n.* **1** projecting or
being projected. **2** thing that projects or ob-
trudes. **3** presentation of an image, etc., on a
surface or screen. **4** forecast. **5 a** mental image viewed as an objective reality. **b** unconscious transfer of feelings, etc., to external
objects or persons. **6** representation on a
plane surface of any part of the surface of the
earth. □□ **pro•jec'tion•ist** *n.* (in sense 3).
■ **2** protrusion, protuberance, bulge, extension; prominence, spur, outcrop. **4** estimate,
prediction, prognostication; extrapolation.
5 b transference, ascription; see also *attribution* (ATTRIBUTE).

pro•jec•tor /prəjéktər/ *n.* apparatus for projecting slides or movies onto a screen.

pro•lapse /prólaps/ • *n.* (also **pro•lap•sus**
/–lápsəs/) forward or downward displacement of a part or organ. • *v.intr.* undergo
prolapse.

pro•le•tar•i•at /prólitáireeət/ *n.* **1** the working class. **2** esp. *derog.* lowest, esp. uneducated, class. □□ **pro•le•tar'i•an** *adj.* **pro•le•
tar'i•an•ism** *n.*

pro•lif•er•ate /prəlifərayt/ *v.* **1** *intr.* reproduce; increase rapidly in numbers. **2** *tr.* produce (cells, etc.) rapidly. □□ **pro•lif•er•a•
tion** /–fəráyshən/ *n.*
■ **1** grow, multiply, mushroom, snowball;
breed. □□ **proliferation** growth, increase,
escalation, multiplication, expansion,
spread, buildup, rise.

pro•lif•ic /prəlifik/ *adj.* **1** producing many
offspring or much output. **2** [often foll. by
of] abundantly productive. See synonym
study at FERTILE. □□ **pro•lif'i•ca•cy** *n.* **pro•
lif'i•cal•ly** *adv.*
■ **1** productive, creative, fertile, fecund,
fruitful.

pro•lix /próliks, próliks/ *adj.* (of speech, writing, etc.) lengthy; tedious. □□ **pro•lix'i•ty** *n.*
pro•lix'ly *adv.*

pro•logue /prólawg, –log/ (also **pro'log**) *n.*
1 preliminary speech, poem, etc., esp. of a
play. **2** introductory event.

pro•long /prəláwng, –lóng/ *v.tr.* extend in
time or space. □□ **pro•lon•ga'tion** *n.* **pro•
long'ed•ly** *adv.* **pro•long'er** *n.*
■ lengthen, elongate, stretch (out), draw *or*
drag out.

prom /prom/ *n.* *colloq.* school or college formal dance.

prom•e•nade /prómənáyd, –naád/ • *n.*
1 outing for display or pleasure. **2** paved
public walk. • *v.* **1** *intr.* make a promenade.
2 *tr.* make a promenade through (a place).
■ *n.* **1** walk, stroll, saunter, ramble, turn;
ride, drive. **2** esplanade, parade. • *v.* **1** walk,
stroll, saunter, amble, ramble, perambulate,
take a walk *or* stroll.

Pro•me•the•an /prəméetheeən/ *adj.* daring
or inventive.

pro•me•thi•um /prəméetheeəm/ *n.* *Chem.* radioactive metallic element of the lanthanide
series. ¶Symb.: **Pm**.

prom•i•nent /próminənt/ *adj.* **1** jutting out;
projecting. **2** conspicuous. **3** distinguished;
important. See synonym study at NOTICEA-
BLE. □□ **prom'i•nence** *n.* **prom'i•nency** *n.*
prom'i•nent•ly *adv.*
■ **1** protuberant, protruding; bulging;
raised. **2** noticeable, pronounced, obvious,
evident, recognizable. **3** eminent, preeminent, notable, noteworthy, noted, well-
known, famed, significant. □□ **prominence**
celebrity, eminence, fame, distinction, nota-
bility, reputation, preeminence; hill, hillock,
rise, hummock, outcrop; headland, point;
protuberance, projection.

pro•mis•cu•ous /prəmiskyŏoəs/ *adj.* **1** having frequent and diverse sexual relationships,
esp. transient ones. **2** random or indiscriminate. □□ **prom•is•cu•i•ty** /prómiskyŏoitee/
n. **pro•mis'cu•ous•ly** *adv.*
■ **1** lax, loose, wanton, wild, uninhibited, licentious, dissipated, dissolute. **2** undiscriminating; mixed, miscellaneous, heterogeneous.

prom•ise /prómis/ • *n.* **1** assurance that one
will or will not undertake a certain action,
behavior, etc. **2** potential for achievement.
• *v.tr.* **1** make (a person) a promise. **2 a** afford expectations of (*promises to be a good
cook*). **b** seem likely to (*is promising to rain*).
3 *colloq.* assure. □ **the promised land**
1 *Bibl.* Canaan (Gen. 12:7, etc.). **2** any desired place, esp. heaven. □□ **prom'is•er** *n.*
■ *n.* **1** word (of honor), pledge, vow, oath;
agreement, contract. **2** capability, capacity,
aptitude; expectation, likelihood, probability; see also ABILITY. • *v.* **1** give one's word
(of honor), pledge, swear, vow, take an oath,
undertake. **2 a** give (an *or* every) indication
of, hint at, suggest, foretell, augur. **b** show
signs of, look like, appear likely to, bid fair to.
3 swear, confirm. □ **the promised land**
2 see HEAVEN 2.

prom•is•ing /prómising/ *adj.* likely to turn
out well; hopeful; full of promise (*promising
start*). □□ **prom'is•ing•ly** *adv.*
■ encouraging, favorable, auspicious, positive, rosy.

prom•is•so•ry /prómisawree/ *adj.* conveying
a promise. □ **promissory note** signed document containing a written promise to pay a
stated sum.

pro•mo /prómō/ *colloq.* *n.* (*pl.* **–mos**) **1** publicity blurb or advertisement. **2** trailer for a
television program, etc.

pro•mon•to•ry /próməntawree/ *n.* (*pl.* **–ries**)
point of high land jutting out into the sea,
etc.; headland.

pro•mote /prəmót/ *v.tr.* **1** raise (a person) to
a higher office, rank, grade, etc. **2** encourage
(a cause, process, desired result, etc.).
3 publicize and sell (a product). □□ **pro•
mot'able** *adj.* **pro•mot•a•bil'i•ty** *n.* **pro•
mo'tion** /–móshən/ *n.* **pro•mo'tion•al** *adj.*
■ **1** advance, move up, prefer, upgrade, elevate; create. **2** help, further, assist, advance,
support, forward; endorse, sponsor, espouse,
commend. **3** advertise, push, market, beat
the drum for, tout. □□ **promotion** further-

ance, advancement, encouragement, support; advance, rise, preferment; espousal, commendation; advertising, marketing, publicity, advertisement.

pro•mot•er /prəmótər/ *n.* **1** person who promotes. **2** person who finances, organizes, etc., a sporting event, show, etc.

prompt /prompt/ • *adj.* made, done, etc., readily or at once. • *adv.* punctually. • *v.tr.* **1** incite; urge (*prompted them to action*). **2** assist (an actor or hesitating speaker) with a cue or suggestion. **3** give rise to; inspire. • *n.* **1** something that prompts. **2** *Computing* indication or sign on a computer screen to show that the system is waiting for input. □□ **prompt′ing** *n.* **prompt′i•tude** *n.* **prompt′ly** *adv.* **prompt′ness** *n.*

■ *adj.* alert, eager, ready, quick, expeditious; immediate, instantaneous, unhesitating, rapid. • *adv.* on the dot; see also SHARP *adv.* 1. • *v.* **1** egg (on), prod, nudge, spur, induce, impel, provoke. **2** cue, remind, feed lines to. **3** bring about, occasion, elicit, evoke, provoke, call forth. • *n.* **1** reminder, cue, hint, stimulus, refresher, suggestion. □□ **promptly** quickly, at once, straight away, directly, right away, immediately, without delay.

prompt•er /prómptər/ *n.* person or thing that prompts actors, etc.

pro•mul•gate /próməlgayt/ *v.tr.* **1** make known to the public; disseminate; promote. **2** proclaim (a decree, news, etc.). See synonym study at ANNOUNCE. □□ **pro•mul•ga•tion** /-gáyshən/ *n.* **prom′ul•ga•tor** *n.*

prone /prōn/ *adj.* **1 a** lying face downward. **b** lying flat, prostrate. **2** [usu. foll. by *to*, or *to* + infin.] disposed or liable. □□ **prone′ness** /prón-nis/ *n.*

■ **1** face down; reclining, recumbent, horizontal. **2** inclined, apt, predisposed, of a mind, subject, given

prong /prong/ *n.* each of two or more projections at the end of a fork, etc. □□ **pronged** *adj.* [also in comb.].

pro•noun /prónown/ *n. Gram.* word used instead of and to indicate a noun already mentioned or known, esp. to avoid repetition (e.g., *me, their, this, ourselves*).

pro•nounce /prənówns/ *v.tr.* **1** [also *absol.*] utter or speak (words, sounds, etc.) in a certain way. **2** utter or deliver (a judgment, sentence, curse, etc.) officially or formally. **3** state as being one's opinion. □□ **pro•nounce′a•ble** *adj.* **pro•nounce′ment** *n.* **pro•nounc′er** *n.*

■ **1** say, voice, express, articulate, enunciate, vocalize; put into words. **2** declare, proclaim, announce, assert; see also PASS[1] *v.* 17. **3** declare, judge, adjudge, proclaim; accuse of being. □□ **pronouncement** statement, assertion, announcement, proclamation; decree, edict, dictum, order, ordinance.

pro•nounced /prənównst/ *adj.* strongly marked; decided (*pronounced flavor*). □□ **pro•nounc•ed•ly** /-nównsidlee/ *adv.*

■ definite, distinct, unmistakable, strong, clear.

pron•to /próntō/ *adv. colloq.* promptly; quickly.

pro•nun•ci•a•tion /prənúnseeáyshən/ *n.*

1 way in which a word is pronounced, esp. with reference to a standard. **2** act of pronouncing. **3** way of pronouncing words, etc.

■ **1, 3** enunciation, articulation, elocution, diction.

proof /proof/ • *n.* **1** facts, evidence, argument, etc., establishing or helping to establish a fact. **2** demonstration; proving. **3** test or trial (*put them to the proof*). **4** standard of strength of distilled alcoholic spirits. **5** *Printing* trial impression before final printing. **6** stage in the resolution of a mathematical or philosophical problem. **7** photographic print made for selection, etc. • *adj.* impervious to penetration, ill effects, etc. (*proof against the harshest weather*). □□ **proof′less** *adj.*

■ *n.* **1** documentation, data, certification, testimony, ammunition. **2** verification, corroboration, confirmation, validation, authentication, ratification, substantiation. **3** measure; standard, touchstone, criterion. • *adj.* protected, resistant; impenetrable.

proof•read /proofreed/ *v.tr.* (*past* and *past part.* **-read** /-red/) read (esp. printer's proofs) and mark any errors. □□ **proof′read′er** *n.* **proof′read•ing** *n.*

prop[1] /prop/ • *n.* **1** rigid, esp. separate, support. **2** person who supplies support, assistance, comfort, etc. • *v.tr.* (**propped, prop•ping**) [often foll. by *against, up*, etc.] support with or as if with a prop.

■ *n.* **1** brace, stay, buttress, mainstay, upright. **2** see SUPPORT *n.* 2. • *v.* (*prop up*) brace, hold (up), buttress, stay, bolster, uphold, sustain; lean, stand, rest.

prop[2] /prop/ *n. Theatr. colloq.* = PROPERTY 3.

prop[3] /prop/ *n. colloq.* aircraft propeller.

prop•a•gan•da /própəgándə/ *n.* **1** organized program of publicity, selected information, etc., used to propagate a doctrine, etc., (*pamphlets full of propaganda*). **2** usu. *derog.* ideas, etc., so propagated. □□ **prop•a•gan′dist** *n.* **pro•pa•gan′dize** *v.*

■ advertising, promotion, publicity; disinformation, newspeak, rumors, lies.

prop•a•gate /própəgayt/ *v.* **1** *tr.* **a** breed (a plant, animal, etc.) from the parent stock. **b** (of a plant, animal, etc.) reproduce itself. **2 a** *tr.* disseminate (a statement, belief, theory, etc.). **b** *intr.* grow more widespread or numerous. □□ **prop•a•ga•tion** /-gáyshən/ *n.* **prop′a•ga•tive** *adj.* **prop′a•ga•tor** *n.*

■ **1 b** breed, generate, multiply, proliferate. **2 a** publicize, dispense, distribute, spread, publish; proclaim, make known. **b** multiply, increase, spread.

pro•pane /própayn/ *n.* gaseous hydrocarbon of the alkane series used as bottled fuel. ¶ Chem. formula: C_3H_8.

pro•pel /prəpél/ *v.tr.* (**pro•pelled, pro•pel•ling**) **1** drive or push forward. **2** urge on; encourage. □□ **pro•pel′lant** *n.* **pro•pel′lent** *n. & adj.*

■ **1** impel, move, actuate, set in motion, get moving, thrust forward, launch. **2** see SPUR *v.*

pro•pel•ler /prəpélər/ *n.* revolving shaft with blades, esp. for propelling a ship or aircraft.

pro•pen•si•ty /prəpénsitee/ *n.* (*pl.* **–ties**) inclination or tendency (*has a propensity for wandering*).

prop•er /própər/ *adj.* **1 a** accurate; correct. **b** fit; suitable; right (*at the proper time*). **2** decent; respectable, esp. excessively so. **3** belonging or relating (*respect proper to them*). **4** [usu. placed after noun] strictly so called; real; genuine (*this is the crypt, not the cathedral proper*). See synonym study at FORMAL.
□ **proper noun** (or **name**) *Gram.* name used for an individual person, place, animal, country, title, etc., e.g., Jane, London, Everest. □□ **prop′er•ness** *n.*

■ **1 a** exact, true, right, precise, orthodox, formal, accepted. **b** fitting, suited, correct, appropriate, apt, apposite. **2** decorous, dignified, genteel, seemly, correct; gentlemanly, ladylike, polite, refined. **3** own, individual, separate, distinct, correct, specific; characteristic, distinctive; see also DUE *adj.* 2, 3. **4** see REAL *adj.* 2.

prop•er•ly /própərlee/ *adv.* **1** fittingly; suitably. **2** accurately; correctly (*properly speaking*). **3** rightly (*he very properly refused*). **4** with decency; respectably (*behave properly*).

■ **1** duly, appropriately, well, rightly, correctly, aptly. **2** precisely, exactly, strictly, technically. **4** politely, decently, decorously, nicely, courteously.

prop•er•tied /própərteed/ *adj.* having property, esp. land.

prop•er•ty /própərtee/ *n.* (*pl.* **–ties**) **1 a** something owned; a possession, esp. a house, land, etc. **b** possessions collectively. **2** attribute, quality, or characteristic. **3** movable object used on a theater stage, in a movie, etc.

■ **1 b** land, acreage, ground(s), real estate, realty; see also ESTATE 2. **2** feature, trait, mark, hallmark.

proph•e•cy /prófisee/ *n.* (*pl.* **–cies**) **1 a** prophetic utterance, esp. Biblical. **b** prediction of future events. **2** faculty, practice, etc., of prophesying (*the gift of prophecy*).

■ **1 b** see FORECAST *n.* **2** prediction, fortune-telling, divination, soothsaying, augury, prognostication.

proph•e•sy /prófisī/ *v.* (**–sies, –sied**) **1** *tr.* [usu. foll. by *that, who,* etc.] foretell (an event, etc.). **2** *intr.* speak as a prophet; foretell future events. See synonym study at PREDICT. □□ **proph′e•si•er** *n.*

■ **1** predict, forecast, forewarn, prognosticate; augur, presage, foreshadow, portend, bode, harbinger, herald.

proph•et /prófit/ *n.* (*fem.* **proph•et•ess** /–tis/) **1** religious seer or interpreter. **2 a** person who foretells events. **b** spokesman; advocate.

■ **2 a** prophesier, oracle, forecaster, seer, soothsayer, clairvoyant, prognosticator. **b** see ADVOCATE *n.* 1.

pro•phet•ic /prəfétik/ *adj.* **1** [often foll. by *of*] containing a prediction; predicting. **2** of a prophet. □□ **pro•phet′i•cal** *adj.* **pro•phet′i•cal•ly** *adv.*

■ **1** prophetical, predictive, prognostic, divinatory, oracular, inspired, prescient, sibylline, apocalyptic.

pro•phy•lac•tic /prófiláktik, próf–/ • *adj.* tending to prevent disease. • *n.* **1** preventive medicine or action. **2** condom.

■ *adj.* see PREVENTIVE *adj.* • *n.* **1** see PREVENTIVE *n.* **2** sheath, *colloq.* rubber.

pro•phy•lax•is /prófiláksis, próf–/ *n.* (*pl.* **pro•phy•lax•es** /–seez/) preventive treatment against disease.

pro•pin•qui•ty /prəpíngkwitee/ *n.* **1** nearness in space; proximity. **2** close kinship. **3** similarity.

pro•pi•ti•ate /prōpísheeayt/ *v.tr.* appease (an offended person, etc.). See synonym study at PACIFY. □□ **pro•pi•ti•a•tion** /–áyshən/ *n.* **pro•pi′ti•a•tor** *n.*

■ make amends to, placate, answer; see also HUMOR *v.*

pro•pi•ti•a•to•ry /prōpísheeəətawree, –písha–/ *adj.* serving or intended to propitiate.

pro•pi•tious /prəpíshəs/ *adj.* **1** favorable. **2** (of the weather, etc.) suitable. See synonym study at TIMELY. □□ **pro•pi′tious•ly** *adv.* **pro•pi′tious•ness** *n.*

■ **1** auspicious, promising, advantageous, lucky. **2** apt, fitting, timely; fair, favorable; see also OPPORTUNE 2.

prop•jet /própjet/ *n.* jet airplane powered by turboprops.

pro•po•nent /prəpónənt/ *n.* person advocating a motion, theory, or proposal.

■ proposer, promoter, supporter, upholder, backer, subscriber, patron, espouser, adherent, enthusiast.

pro•por•tion /prəpáwrshən/ • *n.* **1 a** comparative part or share. **b** comparative ratio (*proportion of births to deaths*). **2** correct or pleasing relation of things or parts of a thing. **3** [in *pl.*] dimensions; size (*large proportions*). **4** *Math.* equality of ratios between two pairs of quantities, e.g., 3:5 and 9:15. • *v.tr.* make proportional. □□ **pro•por′tioned** *adj.* [also in *comb.*]. **pro•por′tion•less** *adj.* **pro•por′tion•ate** *adj.* **pro•por′tion•ate•ly** *adv.*

■ *n.* **1 a** portion, division, percentage, quota, ration, *colloq.* cut. **b** relation, relationship, comparison, correlation. **2** balance, agreement, concord, harmony, symmetry, congruity. **3** magnitude, measurements, extent; volume, capacity, mass, bulk. • *v.* adjust, modify, regulate, change, modulate, poise.

pro•por•tion•al /prəpáwrshənəl/ *adj.* in due proportion; comparable. □□ **pro•por•tion•al•i•ty** /–nálitee/ *n.* **pro•por′tion•al•ly** *adv.*

■ proportionate, proportioned, analogous, analogical, relative, related, correlated, corresponding.

pro•pos•al /prəpózəl/ *n.* **1 a** act or an instance of proposing something. **b** course of action, etc., so proposed (*the proposal was never carried out*). **2** offer of marriage.

■ **1** offer, presentation, bid, tender, motion, overture, proposition, program, project; plan, scheme, draft.

pro•pose /prəpóz/ *v.* **1** *tr.* [also *absol.*] put forward for consideration or as a plan. **2** *tr.* intend; purpose. **3** *intr.* make an offer of marriage. **4** *tr.* nominate. See synonym study at INTEND. □□ **pro•pos′er** *n.*

■ **1** offer, tender, proffer; submit, advance, set forth, propound, recommend, suggest. **2** mean, plan, resolve, have a mind, expect, aim. **4** see NOMINATE.

prop•o•si•tion /própəzíshən/ • *n.* **1** statement or assertion. **2** scheme proposed; proposal. **3** *Logic* statement subject to proof or disproof. **4** *colloq.* problem (*difficult proposition*). **5** *Math.* formal statement of a theorem or problem. **6** *colloq.* sexual proposal. • *v.tr. colloq.* make a proposal (esp. of sexual intercourse) to. □□ **prop•o•si′tion•al** *adj.*

■ *n.* **1** see STATEMENT 1–3. **2** see SCHEME *n.* 1a. **4** see PROBLEM 1, 2. • *v.* accost, solicit, make advances *or* overtures to, *colloq.* make a pass at.

pro•pound /prəpównd/ *v.tr.* offer for consideration; propose. □□ **pro•pound′er** *n.*

■ put forward, set forth, proffer, suggest.

pro•pri•e•tar•y /prəprīətəree/ *adj.* **1** of, holding, or concerning property, or relating to a proprietor (*proprietary rights*). **2** held in private ownership.

pro•pri•e•tor /prəprīətər/ *n.* (*fem.* **pro•pri•e•tress**) owner of a business, hotel, etc. □□ **pro•pri•e•to•ri•al** /-táwreeəl/ *adj.* **pro•pri•e•to•ri•al•ly** *adv.* **pro•pri′e•tor•ship** *n.*

■ property owner, landlord, landlady, innkeeper, hotelkeeper, hotelier, manager.

pro•pri•e•ty /prəprīətee/ *n.* (*pl.* **–ties**) **1** fitness; rightness. **2** correctness of behavior or morals. **3** [in *pl.*] details or rules of correct conduct.

■ **1** correctness, properness, appropriateness, decorum; advisability, wisdom. **2** decorum, politeness, courtesy, politesse, refinement, sedateness. **3** protocol, good *or* proper form, punctilio, etiquette, social graces, civilities.

pro•pul•sion /prəpúlshən/ *n.* **1** driving or pushing forward. **2** impelling influence. □□ **pro•pul•sive** /-púlsiv/ *adj.*

■ **2** drive, impulse, impetus, thrust, power, driving force.

pro rata /prō ráytə, raatə/ • *adj.* proportional. • *adv.* proportionally.

pro•rate /prórayt/ *v.tr.* allocate or distribute pro rata. □□ **pro•ra′tion** *n.*

pro•sa•ic /prōzáyik/ *adj.* **1** like prose; lacking poetic beauty. **2** unromantic; dull; commonplace (*took a prosaic view of life*). □□ **pro•sa′i•cal•ly** *adv.*

■ **2** banal, tedious, prosy, pedestrian, flat, routine, everyday, bland, characterless, plain, trite, tired, lifeless, insipid, uninteresting, humdrum, monotonous.

pro•sce•ni•um /prōséeneeəm/ *n.* (*pl.* **pro•sce•ni•ums** or **pro•sce•ni•a** /-neeə/) vertical arched opening to the stage.

pro•scribe /prōskríb/ *v.tr.* **1** banish; exile. **2** put (a person) outside the protection of the law. **3** reject or denounce. □□ **pro•scrip•tion** /-skrípshən/ *n.* **pro•scrip•tive** /-skríp-tiv/ *adj.*

prose /prōz/ *n.* ordinary form of the written or spoken language (opp. POETRY, VERSE).

pros•e•cute /prósikyoot/ *v.tr.* **1** [also *absol.*] **a** institute legal proceedings against (a per-

son). **b** institute a prosecution with reference to (a claim, crime, etc.). **2** carry on (a trade, pursuit, etc.). □□ **pros•e•cut′a•ble** *adj.* **pros•e•cu•tion** /-kyóoshən/ *n.* **pros′e•cu•tor** *n.* **pros•e•cu•to•ri•al** /-táwreeəl/ *adj.*

■ **1 a** arraign, indict, charge, put on trial, bring to trial, try. **2** carry out, perform, do, conduct, follow, engage in.

pros•e•lyte /prósilīt/ • *n.* person converted, esp. recently, from one opinion, creed, party, etc., to another. • *v.tr.* = PROSELYTIZE. □□ **pros′e•lyt•ism** /-salitizəm/ *n.*

pros•e•lyt•ize /prósilitīz/ *v.tr.* [also *absol.*] convert (a person or persons) from one belief, etc., to another, esp. habitually. □□ **pros′e•lyt•iz•er** *n.*

pros•o•dy /prósədee/ *n.* versification; study of meter, rhyme, etc. **2** the study of speech rhythms. □□ **pro•sod•ic** /prəsódik/ *adj.* **pros′o•dist** *n.*

pros•pect • *n.* /próspekt/ **1 a** [often in *pl.*] expectation, esp. of success in a career, etc. **b** something anticipated. **2** extensive view of landscape, etc. (*striking prospect*). **3** possible or probable customer, subscriber, etc. • *v.* /próspekt/ [usu. foll. by *for*] explore (a region) for gold, etc. □□ **pros′pec•tor** *n.*

■ *n.* **1 a** future, outlook, chances, hopes, possibilities, opportunities. **2** scene, panorama, landscape, vista, sight, spectacle. • *v.* (*prospect for*) search for, look for, seek, quest after *or* for, pursue, hunt (for), try to find.

pro•spec•tive /prəspéktiv/ *adj.* expected; future (*prospective bridegroom*). □□ **pro•spec′tive•ly** *adv.*

■ forthcoming, coming, approaching, imminent, nearing.

pro•spec•tus /prəspéktəs/ *n.* printed document advertising or describing a school, commercial enterprise, etc.

■ brochure, pamphlet, booklet, leaflet, catalog.

pros•per /próspər/ *v.intr.* succeed; thrive.

■ flourish, progress, get ahead, grow; profit, gain.

pros•per•i•ty /prospéritee/ *n.* state of being prosperous; wealth or success.

■ (good) fortune, riches, affluence, money, plenty.

pros•per•ous /próspərəs/ *adj.* successful; rich; thriving. See synonym study at WEALTHY. □□ **pros′per•ous•ly** *adv.* **pros′per•ous•ness** *n.*

■ wealthy, moneyed, affluent, well-to-do, well-off; fortunate, halcyon; flourishing, booming, thrifty; see also SUCCESSFUL.

pros•tate /próstayt/ *n.* (in full **prostate gland**) gland surrounding the neck of the bladder in male mammals and releasing part of the semen. □□ **pros•tat′ic** /-státik/ *adj.*

pros•the•sis /prósthéesis/ *n.* (*pl.* **pros•the•ses** /-seez/) artificial part supplied to replace a missing body part. □□ **pros•thet′ic** /-thétik/ *adj.* **pros•thet′i•cal•ly** *adv.*

pros•ti•tute /próstitoot, -tyoot/ • *n.* person who engages in sexual activity for payment. • *v.tr.* **1** make a prostitute of (esp. oneself). **2** misuse (one's talents, skills, etc.) for money. □□ **pros•ti•tu•tion** /–tōŏshən/ *n.* **pros'ti•tu•tor** *n.*

■ *n.* whore, call girl, streetwalker, slut, trollop, drab, *sl.* tart, hustler, working girl, hooker; catamite, gigolo. ● *v.* **2** devalue, abuse, corrupt, misemploy, misapply, pervert. □□ **prostitution** whoredom, *colloq. or joc.* the oldest profession; degradation, debasement, profanation, defilement, desecration, misuse, abuse.

pros•trate /próstrayt/ ● *adj.* **1 a** lying face downward, esp. in submission. **b** lying horizontally. **2** overcome, esp. by grief, exhaustion, etc. ● *v.tr.* **1** lay (a person, etc.) flat on the ground. **2** [*refl.*] throw (oneself) down in submission, etc. **3** overcome; make weak. □□ **pros•tra•tion** /prostráyshən/ *n.*

■ *adj.* **1** prone, horizontal, stretched out, procumbent. **2** overwhelmed, overpowered, crushed, brought *or* laid low, paralyzed; exhausted, drained, fatigued, spent, worn-out. ● *v.* **1** see LAY¹ *v.* **1. 2** lie down, kowtow, bow (down), bow and scrape, grovel, kneel. **3** overwhelm, overpower, crush, lay *or* bring low, paralyze, exhaust, fatigue, weary. □□ **prostration** submission, servility; weariness, exhaustion, tiredness, weakness; despair, misery, desolation.

pros•y /prózee/ *adj.* (**pros•i•er, pros•i•est**) tedious; commonplace; dull (*prosy talk*). □□ **pros'i•ly** *adv.* **pros'i•ness** *n.*

Prot. *abbr.* Protestant.

prot•ac•tin•i•um /prótaktíneeəm/ *n. Chem.* radioactive metallic element. ¶Symb.: **Pa**.

pro•tag•o•nist /prótágənist/ *n.* chief person in a drama, story, etc.

■ hero, heroine; principal, lead, leading role, title role.

pro•te•an /próteeən, –teeən/ *adj.* **1** variable; taking many forms. **2** (of an artist, writer, etc.) versatile.

■ **1** ever-changing, multiform, changeable, polymorphous, polymorphic. **2** see VERSATILE 1.

pro•tect /prətékt/ *v.tr.* keep (a person, thing, etc.) safe; defend; guard (*goggles protected her eyes from dust*).

■ safeguard, shield, cover, screen; care for, preserve.

pro•tec•tion /prətékshən/ *n.* **1 a** protecting or being protected; defense. **b** thing, person, or animal that provides protection. **2** *colloq.* **a** immunity from molestation obtained by payment to organized criminals, etc. **b** (in full **protection money**) payment, as bribes, made to police, etc., for overlooking criminal activities. □□ **pro•tec'tion•ist** *n.*

■ **1 a** care, guardianship, custody, charge, safekeeping. **b** defense, screen, shield, barrier, aegis, guard; security, safety, immunity. **2 b** see BLACKMAIL *n.* 1.

pro•tec•tive /prətéktiv/ *adj.* protecting. □□ **pro•tec'tive•ly** *adv.* **pro•tec'tive•ness** *n.*

■ preservative, defensive.

pro•tec•tor /prətéktər/ *n.* **1** person who protects. **2** guardian or patron. □□ **pro•tec'tor•al** *adj.*

■ defender, guardian angel, champion.

pro•tec•tor•ate /prətéktərət/ *n.* **1** nation that is controlled and protected by another. **2** this relation.

pro•té•gé /prótizhay, prótizháy/ *n.* (*fem.* **pro•té•gée** *pronunc.* same) person under the protection, patronage, tutelage, etc., of another.

■ ward, charge, dependent, foster child; student, pupil.

pro•tein /próteen/ *n.* any of a group of organic compounds composed of amino acids and forming an essential part of all living organisms. □□ **pro•tein•a•ceous** /–teenáyshəs/ *adj.*

pro tem /prō tém/ *adj. & adv. colloq.* = PRO TEMPORE.

pro tem•po•re /prō témpəree/ *adj. & adv.* for the time being.

Prot•er•o•zo•ic /prótərəzóik, prō–/ *Geol.* ● *adj.* of or relating to the later part of the Precambrian era. ● *n.* this time.

pro•test ● *n.* /prótest/ statement or act of dissent or disapproval. ● *v.* /prətést, prō–/ **1** *intr.* make a protest. **2** *tr.* affirm (one's innocence, etc.) solemnly. **3** *tr.* object to (a decision, etc.). □ **under protest** unwillingly. □□ **pro•test'er** *n.* **pro•test'ing•ly** *adv.* **pro•tes'tor** *n.*

■ *n.* remonstrance, objection, complaint, outcry, clamor, grumble. ● *v.* **1** object, complain, grumble, dissent, demur. **2** assert, declare, asseverate, announce, profess. □ **under protest** reluctantly, involuntarily, begrudgingly, grudgingly; under duress.

Prot•es•tant /prótistənt/ ● *n.* member or follower of a Christian Church separated from the Roman Catholic Church after the Reformation. ● *adj.* of the Protestant Churches or their members, etc. □□ **Prot'es•tant•ism** *n.* **Prot'es•tant•ize** *v.*

pro•tes•ta•tion /prótistáyshən, prōte–/ *n.* **1** strong affirmation. **2** protest.

proto- /prótō/ *comb. form* first (*prototype*).

pro•to•col /prótəkawl, –kol/ *n.* **1** official formality and etiquette. **2** original draft of a diplomatic document, esp. of the terms of a treaty. **3** formal statement of a transaction.

■ **1** rule(s) *or* code(s) *or* standard(s) of behavior, conventions, customs, form. **2** outline.

pro•to•lan•guage /prótōlanggwij/ *n.* language from which other languages are believed to have been derived.

pro•ton /próton/ *n. Physics* stable elementary particle with a positive electric charge, occurring in all atomic nuclei. □□ **pro•ton•ic** /prətónik/ *adj.*

pro•to•plasm /prótəplazəm/ *n.* material comprising the living part of a cell. □□ **pro•to•plas•mal** /–plazmǝl/ *adj.* **pro•to•plas•mat•ic** /–mátik/ *adj.* **pro'to•plas'mic** *adj.*

pro•to•type /prótətīp/ *n.* **1** original as a pattern for imitations, improved forms, etc. **2** trial model or preliminary version. See synonym study at MODEL. □□ **pro•to•typ•ic** /–típik/ *adj.* **pro•to•typ'i•cal** *adj.* **pro•to•typ'i•cal•ly** *adv.*

■ **1** model, archetype, pattern, exemplar, first, master.

pro•to•zo•an /prótəzóən/ ● *n.* (also **pro•to•**

zo•on /-zō-on/) (pl. pro•to•zo•a /-zōə/ or pro•to•zo•ans) unicellular microscopic organism. • adj. (also pro•to•zo•ic /-zō-ik/) of or this group. □□ pro'to•zo'al adj.

pro•tract /prōtrákt, prə-/ v.tr. 1 prolong or lengthen. 2 (as protracted adj.) of excessive length or duration. 3 draw (a plan, etc.) to scale. □□ pro•tract'ed•ly adv. pro•tract'ed•ness n.
■ 1 see LENGTHEN. 2 (protracted) long, long-drawn-out, interminable, prolonged, overlong, never-ending.

pro•trac•tor /prōtráktər, prə-/ n. instrument for measuring angles, usu. in the form of a graduated semicircle.

pro•trude /prōtōōd/ v. 1 intr. project. 2 tr. thrust or cause to thrust out. □□ pro•tru•sion /-trōōzhən/ n. pro•tru'sive adj.
■ 1 stick out, jut (out), extend, poke out; bulge, balloon, bag (out). □□ protrusion projection, protuberance, prominence, swelling, excrescence, outgrowth.

pro•tu•ber•ant /prōtōōbərənt, –tyōō–, prə-/ adj. bulging out; prominent (protuberant eyes). □□ pro•tu'ber•ance n.
■ protrusive, protruding, gibbous; extrusive, excrescent, extruding, projecting, undefilable.

proud /prowd/ adj. 1 feeling greatly honored or pleased. 2 a haughty; arrogant. b [often in comb.] having a proper pride; satisfied. 3 (of an occasion, etc.) justly arousing pride. (a proud day for us). 4 (of a thing) imposing; splendid. □□ proud'ly adv. proud'ness n.
■ 1 well-pleased, satisfied, contented, glad; gratified. 2 a conceited, self-satisfied, self-important, vain, prideful, complacent. 3 lofty, dignified, lordly, noble, great, respected, honored. 4 stately, majestic, magnificent, grand, impressive.

prove /prōōv/ v. (past part. proved or proven) 1 tr. demonstrate the truth of by evidence or argument. 2 intr. a be found (it proved to be untrue). b emerge as (will prove the winner). 3 tr. Math. test the accuracy of (a calculation). □ prove oneself show one's abilities, courage, etc. □□ prov'a•ble adj prov•a•bil'i•ty n. prov'a•bly adv.
■ 1 verify, authenticate, confirm, make good, corroborate, show; support, sustain, back (up). 2 turn out, be shown, be established; end up.

prov•e•nance /próvinəns/ n. origin or place of origin. See synonym study at ORIGIN.

Pro•ven•çal /prōvonsáal, próv-/ • adj. of Provence, a former province of SE France. • n. 1 native of Provence. 2 language of Provence.

prov•en•der /próvindər/ n. animal fodder.
■ forage, feed.

prov•erb /próvərb/ n. short pithy saying in general use, held to embody a general truth. See synonym study at SAYING.
■ maxim, aphorism, saw, adage, apothegm, axiom.

pro•ver•bi•al /prəvárbeeəl/ adj. 1 as well-known as a proverb; notorious (his proverbial honesty). 2 of or referred to in a proverb (proverbial ill wind). □□ pro•ver'bi•al•ly adv.
■ 1 acknowledged, axiomatic, time-

honored; see also well-known (WELL¹). 2 axiomatic, aphoristic, epigrammatic, apothegmatic, gnomic; well-known.

pro•vide /prəvíd/ v. 1 tr. supply; furnish. 2 intr. a make due preparation. b prepare for the maintenance of a person, etc. 3 tr. stipulate in a will, statute, etc. □□ pro•vid'er n.
■ 1 equip, outfit, fix up with, provision; produce, yield, afford. 2 a make provision(s), arrange, cater, prepare, plan. b look after, care for, support, take care of. 3 lay down, require, demand, specify, state.

pro•vid•ed /prəvídid/ on the condition or understanding (that).
■ providing (that), if (only), only if, as long as.

prov•i•dence /próvidəns/ n. 1 protective care of God or nature. 2 (Providence) God in this aspect. 3 timely care or preparation; foresight; thrift.
■ 1 protection, concern, beneficence, direction. 3 forethought, preparation, frugality, husbandry.

prov•i•dent /próvidənt, –dent/ adj. having or showing foresight; thrifty. See synonym study at ECONOMICAL. □□ prov'i•dent•ly adv.
■ farsighted, longheaded, farseeing, thoughtful, sage; frugal, economical; canny, prudent.

prov•i•den•tial /próvidénshəl/ adj. 1 of or by divine foresight or interposition. 2 opportune; lucky. □□ prov'i•den'tial•ly adv.
■ 2 fortunate, blessed, felicitous, happy, timely.

prov•ince /próvins/ n. 1 principal administrative division of some countries. 2 (the provinces) whole of a country outside major cities. esp. regarded as uncultured, unsophisticated, etc. 3 field, area or sphere of action
■ 1 territory, state, zone, region, area, district. 2 (the provinces) (the) outlying districts, the countryside, the hinterland. 3 responsibility, concern, function;.

pro•vin•cial /prəvínshəl/ • adj. 1 of a province or provinces. 2 unsophisticated or uncultured. • n. 1 inhabitant of a province or the provinces. 2 unsophisticated or uncultured person. □□ pro•vin'cial•ism n. pro•vin•ci•al•i•ty /–sheeálitee/ n. pro•vin'cial•ly adv.
■ adj. 1 see LOCAL adj. 1. 2 uncultivated, limited, uninformed, parochial, insular, narrow-minded, small-town, colloq. hick. • n. 2 rustic, (country) bumpkin, yokel, colloq. hick, hayseed. □□ provincialism narrow-mindedness, insularity, parochialism; unsophisticatedness, simplicity, naïveté.

pro•vi•sion /prəvízhən/ • n. 1 act or an instance of providing (made no provision for his future). 2 [in pl.] food, drink, etc., esp. for an expedition. 3 a legal or formal statement providing for something. b clause of this. • v.tr. supply with provisions. □□ pro•vi'sion•er n.
■ n. 1 preparation(s), arrangement(s), plan(s); equipment; see also STEP n. 3.

2 (*provisions*) supplies, stores, stock(s); foodstuffs, eatables, edibles, victuals, rations, groceries. **3** b term, stipulation, proviso, condition, restriction. • *v.* stock, victual; see also EQUIP.

pro•vi•sion•al /prəvízhənəl/ *adj.* providing for immediate needs only; temporary. □□ **pro•vi´sion•al•ly** *adv.*
■ interim, transitional, stopgap; conditional.

pro•vi•so /prəvízō/ *n.* (*pl.* **–sos**) **1** stipulation. **2** clause of stipulation or limitation in a document.
■ see CONDITION *n.* 1.

prov•o•ca•tion /próvəkáyshən/ *n.* **1** act or instance of provoking; state of being provoked. **2** cause of annoyance.
■ **1** incitement, instigation. **2** insult, offense, taunt, irritation; ground(s), reason, cause, justification.

pro•voc•a•tive /prəvókətiv/ • *adj.* **1** tending to provoke, esp. anger or sexual desire. **2** intentionally annoying. • *n.* provocative thing. □□ **pro•voc´a•tive•ly** *adv.* **pro•voc´a•tive•ness** *n.*
■ *adj.* **1** alluring, seductive, stimulating, suggestive. **2** irritating, galling, irksome, nettlesome, exasperating.

pro•voke /prəvók/ *v.tr.* **1** rouse or incite. **2** call forth; instigate; cause. **3** irritate or anger. See synonym study at INCITE. □□ **pro•vok´a•ble** *adj.* **pro•vok´ing•ly** *adv.*
■ **1** stir, stimulate, move, motivate, prompt, induce, encourage, push, impel. **2** start, incite, produce, foment, kindle, see also CAUSE *v.* **3** annoy, irk, pester, vex, pique, enrage, madden, incense, infuriate, rile, gall.

pro•vo•lo•ne /próvəlónee/ *n.* medium hard Italian cheese.

pro•vost /próvōst, próvəst/ *n.* high administrative officer of a church or university.
□ **provost marshal** /prōvṓ/ head of military police force or detail.

prow /prow/ *n.* bow of a ship adjoining the stem.

prow•ess /prówis/ *n.* **1** skill; expertise. **2** valor; gallantry.
■ **1** ability, skillfulness, aptitude, adroitness, dexterity. **2** bravery, courage, boldness, daring.

prowl /prowl/ • *v.* **1** *tr.* roam (a place) in search or as if in search of prey, plunder, etc. **2** *intr.* move about like a hunter. • *n.* act or an instance of prowling. □□ **prowl´er** *n.*
■ *v.* **1** scour, scavenge, range over, rove, patrol, cruise. **2** lurk, sneak, skulk, steal, slink, creep; lie in wait.

prox•i•mate /próksimət/ *adj.* **1** nearest or next before or after. **2** approximate. □□ **prox´i•mate•ly** *adv.*

prox•im•i•ty /proksímitee/ *n.* nearness in space, time, etc.
■ closeness, adjacency, contiguity, propinquity.

prox•y /próksee/ *n.* (*pl.* **–ies**) [also *attrib.*] **1** authorization given to a substitute or deputy (*a proxy vote*). **2** person authorized to act as a substitute, etc.

■ **2** deputy, agent, delegate, surrogate.

prude /prood/ *n.* person having or affecting an attitude of extreme propriety or modesty, esp. in sexual matters. □□ **prud´er•y** *n.* (*pl.* **–ies**). **prud´ish** *adj.* **prud´ish•ly** *adv.* **prud´ish•ness** *n.*
■ prig, puritan, (Mrs.) Grundy, *colloq.* goody-goody. □□ **prudery, prudishness** priggishness, puritanicalness, puritanism, Grundyism, primness. **prudish** priggish, puritanical, old-maidish, prissy, prim, straitlaced, stiff, overnice, proper, demure.

pru•dent /proód'nt/ *adj.* **1** (of a person or conduct) careful to avoid undesired consequences; circumspect. **2** discreet. See synonym study at ECONOMICAL. □□ **pru´dence** *n.* **pru´dent•ly** *adv.*
■ **1** cautious, watchful, wise, sage, sagacious. **2** politic, judicious, discriminating; see also *tactful* (TACT). □□ **prudence** discretion, wisdom, sagacity, care, tact; foresightedness, forethought, foresight, farsightedness.

pru•den•tial /proodénshəl/ *adj.* of, involving, or marked by prudence (*prudential motives*). □□ **pru•den´tial•ly** *adv.*

prune[1] /proon/ *n.* dried plum.

prune[2] /proon/ *v.tr.* **1** trim (a tree, etc.) by cutting away dead or overgrown branches, etc. **2 a** [often foll. by *off*] clear (a book, etc.) of superfluous matter. **b** remove (superfluous matter). □□ **prun´er** *n.*
■ clip, cut back, pare (down).

pru•ri•ent /proóreeənt/ *adj.* **1** having an unhealthy obsession with sexual matters. **2** encouraging such an obsession. □□ **pru´ri•ence** *n.* **pru´ri•en•cy** *n.* **pru´ri•ent•ly** *adv.*
■ **1** voyeuristic, lubricious, salacious. **2** dirty, lewd, filthy, pornographic, smutty, obscene, foul, scurrilous, vile.

Prus•sian /prúshən/ • *adj.* of or relating to Prussia, a former German kingdom, or relating to its rigidly militaristic tradition. • *n.* native of Prussia.

pry[1] /prī/ *v.intr.* (**pries, pried**) [usu. foll. by *into*] inquire presumptuously. □□ **pry´ing** *adj.* **pry´ing•ly** *adv.*
■ intrude, meddle, interfere, be nosy, peer, peek.

pry[2] /prī/ *v.tr.* (**pries, pried**) = PRIZE[2].

PS *abbr.* **1** postscript. **2** private secretary.

PSA • *abbr.* public service announcement.

psalm /saam/ *n.* (also **Psalm**) sacred songs esp. from the Book of Psalms (Old Testament). □□ **psalm´ist** *n.*

psal•ter /sáwltər/ *n.* **1** the Book of Psalms. **2** copy of the Psalms, esp. for liturgical use.

p's and q's *n.* □ **mind one's p's and q's 1** attend to one's own conduct and manners. **2** attend to one's accuracy in work.

PSAT *abbr.* Preliminary Scholastic Assessment Test.

pseud. *abbr.* pseudonym.

pseudo- /soódō/ *comb. form* (also **pseud-** before a vowel) **1** false; not genuine (*pseudo-intellectual*). **2** resembling or imitating (often in technical applications) (*pseudomalaria*).

pseu•do•nym /soódənim/ *n.* fictitious name, esp. one assumed by an author.

■ nom de plume, nom de guerre, alias, pen name.

psf *abbr.* (also **p.s.f.**) pounds per square foot.

psi /sī, psī/ *n.* twenty-third letter of the Greek alphabet (Ψ, ψ).

p.s.i. *abbr.* pounds per square inch.

pso•ri•a•sis /sərīəsis/ *n.* skin disease marked by red scaly patches.

psst /pst/ *int.* (also **pst**) whispered exclamation seeking to attract a person's attention surreptitiously.

PST *abbr.* Pacific Standard Time.

psych /sīk/ *v.tr. colloq.* (also **psyche**) **1** prepare (oneself or another person) mentally for an ordeal, etc. **2** [often foll. by *out*] influence a person psychologically, esp. negatively; intimidate; frighten.

psych. /sīk/ (also **psychol.**) *abbr.* **1** psychological. **2** psychology.

psy•che /sīkee/ *n.* **1** soul; spirit. **2** mind.

■ **1** life force, anima, (inner) self, subconscious, unconscious, inner man *or* woman. **2** intellect.

psy•che•del•ic /sīkidélik/ • *adj.* **1 a** expanding the mind's awareness, etc., esp. through the use of hallucinogenic drugs. **b** (of a drug) producing hallucinations. **2** *colloq.* hallucinatory in effect, color, design, etc. • *n.* hallucinogenic drug. □□ **psy•che•del′i•cal•ly** *adv.*

psy•chi•a•try /sīkīətree/ *n.* the study and treatment of mental disease. □□ **psy•chi•at′ric** /-keeátrik/ *adj.* **psy•chi•at′ri•cal** *adj.* **psy•chi•at′ri•cal•ly** *adv.* **psy•chi•a•trist** /-kīətrist/ *n.*

psy•chic /sīkik/ • *adj.* **1** (of a person) considered to have occult powers, such as telepathy, clairvoyance, etc. **2** of the soul *or* mind. • *n.* person considered to have psychic powers; medium. □□ **psy′chi•cal** *adj.* **psy′chi•cal•ly** *adv.*

■ *adj.* **1** telepathic, clairvoyant; see also PROPHETIC. **2** psychical, mental, spiritual, psychological, intellectual. • *n.* spiritualist, clairvoyant, mind reader, telepathist; seer, seeress, fortune-teller.

psy•cho /sīkō/ *colloq.* • *n.* (*pl.* **-chos**) psychopath. • *adj.* psychopathic.

psycho- /sīkō/ *comb. form* relating to the mind or psychology.

psy•cho•a•nal•y•sis /sīkōənálisis/ *n.* therapeutic method of treating mental disorders by discussion and analysis of repressed fears and conflicts. □□ **psy•cho•an•a•lyze** /-ánəliz/ *v.* **psy•cho•an•a•lyst** /-ánəlist/ *n.* **psy•cho•an•a•lyt′ic** *adj.* **psy•cho•an•a•lyt′i•cal•ly** *adv.*

psy•cho•bab•ble /sīkōbabəl/ *n. colloq. derog.* jargon used in popular psychology. □□ **psy′cho•bab•bler** *n.*

psy•cho•log•i•cal /sīkəlójikəl/ *adj.* **1** of, or arising in the mind. **2** of psychology. **3** *colloq.* (of an ailment, etc.) imaginary. □ **psychological warfare** campaign directed at reducing an opponent's morale. □□ **psy•cho•log′i•cal•ly** *adv.*

■ **1** mental, nonphysical, psychosomatic, intellectual, psychical, psychic, subconscious. **3** see IMAGINARY.

psy•chol•o•gy /sīkóləjee/ *n.* (*pl.* **-gies**) **1** sci-

entific study of the human mind. **2** treatise on or theory of this. **3** mental characteristics, etc., of a person, group, situation, etc. □□ **psy•chol′o•gist** *n.* **psy•chol′o•gize** *v.*

■ **3** (mental) makeup, constitution, attitude, behavior, thought processes, thinking, psyche, nature, feeling(s).

psy•cho•path /sīkəpath/ *n.* **1** person suffering from chronic mental disorder esp. with abnormal *or* violent social behavior. **2** mentally or emotionally unstable person. □□ **psy•cho•path′ic** *adj.* **psy•cho•path′i•cal•ly** *adv.*

psy•cho•pa•thol•o•gy /sīkōpəthóləjee/ *n.* **1** scientific study of mental disorders. **2** mentally or behaviorally disordered state. □□ **psy•cho•path•o•log•i•cal** /-pathəlójikəl/ *adj.*

psy•cho•sis /sīkósis/ *n.* (*pl.* **psy•cho•ses** /-seez/) severe mental derangement with loss of contact with external reality.

psy•cho•so•mat•ic /sīkōsəmátik/ *adj.* (of an illness, etc.) mental, not physical, in origin. □□ **psy•cho•so•mat′i•cal•ly** *adv.*

psy•cho•ther•a•py /sīkōthérəpee/ *n.* the treatment of mental disorder by psychological means. □□ **psy•cho•ther•a•peu•tic** /-pyốotik/ *adj.* **psy•cho•ther′a•pist** *n.*

psy•chot•ic /sīkótik/ • *adj.* of *or* characterized by a psychosis. • *n.* psychotic person. □□ **psy•chot′i•cal•ly** *adv.*

■ *adj.* mad, insane, psychopathic, deranged, demented, lunatic, unbalanced, (mentally) ill *or* sick, disturbed. • *n.* mental patient, madman, madwoman, maniac, lunatic, psychopath, *colloq.* schizo, mental.

PT *abbr.* **1** physical therapy. **2** physical training.

Pt *symb. Chem.* platinum.

pt. *abbr.* **1** part. **2** pint. **3** point. **4** port.

PTA *abbr.* Parent-Teacher Association.

ptar•mi•gan /taármigən/ *n.* grouse with black or gray plumage in the summer and white in the winter.

pter•o•dac•tyl /térədáktil/ *n.* large extinct flying reptile.

pto•maine /tṓmayn/ *n.* any of various amine compounds, some toxic, in putrefying animal and vegetable matter.

Pu *symb. Chem.* plutonium.

pub /pub/ *n. colloq.* tavern or bar.

■ barroom, saloon, inn, taproom, *sl.* watering hole.

pub. *abbr.* (also **publ.**) **1** public. **2** publication. **3** published. **4** publisher. **5** publishing.

pu•ber•ty /pyṓobərtee/ *n.* period during which adolescents reach sexual maturity.

■ pubescence, sexual maturity, adolescence, teens, young manhood, young womanhood, the awkward age.

pu•bes /pyṓobeez/ *n.* (*pl.* same) **1** lower part of the abdomen at the front of the pelvis. **2** pubic hair.

pu•bes•cence /pyṓobésəns/ *n.* **1** time when puberty begins. **2** *Bot.* soft down on plants. **3** *Zool.* soft down on various parts of animals, esp. insects. □□ **pu•bes′cent** *adj.*

pu•bic /pyo͞obik/ *adj.* of or relating to the pubes or pubis.

pu•bis /pyo͞obis/ *n.* (*pl.* **pu•bes** /–beez/) either of a pair of bones forming the two sides of the pelvis.

pub•lic /públik/ • *adj.* **1** of the people as a whole. **2** open to or shared by all. **3** done or existing openly (*public protest*). **4** (of a service, funds, etc.) provided by, concerning, or serving government (*public records*). • *n.* **1** [as *sing.* or *pl.*] community in general, or members of the community. **2** specified section of the community (*reading public*). □ **go public** become a public company or corporation. **in public** openly; publicly. **public-address system** loudspeakers, microphones, amplifiers, etc., used in addressing large audiences. **public health** provision of adequate sanitation, drainage, etc., by government. **public relations** professional maintenance of a favorable public image, esp. by a company, famous person, etc. **public school 1** *US* free, government-supported school. **2** *Brit.* private boarding school. **public sector** government-controlled part of an economy, industry, etc. **public utility** organization supplying water, gas, etc., to the community. □□ **pub′lic•ly** *adv.*

■ *adj.* **1** communal, community, common, general, collective, universal, popular. **2** accessible, free, unrestricted, nonexclusive, communal. **3** open, known, manifest, visible, viewable, conspicuous, exposed, overt; projected, acknowledged, admitted. **4** government, state, national, federal, civic, civil. • *n.* **1** people (at large *or* in general), citizenry, citizens, nation, populace, population, society, voters; plebeians, proletariat, rank and file, commonalty. **2** sector, segment, group, crowd; see also WORLD 5.

pub•li•can /públikən/ *n.* **1** *Rom.Hist.* & *Bibl.* tax collector. **2** *Brit.* keeper of a pub.

pub•li•ca•tion /públikáyshən/ *n.* **1 a** preparation and issuing of a book, newspaper, etc. **b** book, etc., so issued. **2** making something publicly known.

■ **1 a** booklet, pamphlet, brochure, leaflet, periodical, magazine, journal, newsletter, newspaper, paper. **2** dissemination, promulgation, publicizing, publishing, proclamation, reporting, announcement.

pub•li•cist /públisist/ *n.* publicity or public relations agent.

pub•lic•i•ty /publísitee/ *n.* **1 a** advertising. **b** material or information used for this. **2** public exposure.

■ **1 a** public relations, marketing, promotion; see also ADVERTISEMENT 2. **2** see ATTENTION *n.* 1.

pub•li•cize /públisīz/ *v.tr.* advertise; make publicly known.

■ promote, push, give publicity to; air, broadcast, circulate, announce, put out, release; disclose, reveal.

pub•lish /públish/ *v.tr.* **1** [also *absol.*] prepare and issue (a book, newspaper, etc.) for public sale. **2** make generally known. See synonym study at ANNOUNCE. □□ **pub′lish•a•ble** *adj.*

■ **2** make public, put out, broadcast, circulate, release, spread (about *or* around), advertise; reveal, divulge.

pub•lish•er /públishər/ *n.* **1** person or esp. a company that produces and distributes copies of books, etc., for sale.

puce /pyo͞os/ *adj.* & *n.* dark red or purplish brown.

puck[1] /puk/ *n.* rubber disk used in ice hockey.

puck[2] /puk/ *n.* mischievous or evil sprite. □□ **puck′ish** *adj.* **puck′ish•ly** *adv.*

puck•er /púkər/ • *v.* gather or cause to gather into wrinkles, folds, or bulges (*puckered her eyebrows*). • *n.* such a wrinkle, bulge, fold, etc. □□ **puck′er•y** *adj.*

■ *v.* draw together, compress, purse, crinkle, ruffle, furrow, wrinkle. • *n.* gather, tuck, pleat, ruffle, ruck.

pud•ding /po͞oding/ *n.* any of various dessert dishes, usu. containing flavoring, sugar, milk, etc.

pud•dle /púd′l/ *n.* small pool, esp. of rainwater. □□ **pud′dler** *n.* **pud′dly** *adj.*

pu•den•dum /pyo͞odéndəm/ *n.* (*pl.* **pu•den•da** /–də/) [usu. in *pl.*] genitals, esp. of a woman.

pudg•y /pújee/ *adj.* (**pudg•i•er, pudg•i•est**) *colloq.* (esp. of a person) plump; slightly overweight. □□ **pudge** *n.* **pudg′i•ly** *adv.* **pudg′i•ness** *n.*

pueb•lo /pwéblō/ *n.* (*pl.* **–los**) settlement of multistoried adobe houses built by the Native Americans of the southwestern United States.

pu•er•ile /pyo͞oəril, pyo͞oril, –rīl/ *adj.* trivial; childish; immature. See synonym study at YOUTHFUL. □□ **pu′er•ile•ly** *adv.* **pu•er•il•i•ty** /–rílitee/ *n.* (*pl.* **–ties**)

■ babyish, infantile, juvenile, adolescent; ridiculous,ᵣ shallow, inconsequential, insignificant.

Puer•to Ri•can /pwértō réekən, páwrtə/ • *n.* **1** native of Puerto Rico, an island of the West Indies. **2** person of Puerto Rican descent. • *adj.* of or relating to Puerto Rico.

puff /puf/ • *n.* **1 a** short quick blast of breath, wind, vapor, etc. **b** sound of or like this. **2** draw of smoke from a cigarette, pipe, etc. **3** light pastry containing jam, cream, etc. **4** extravagantly enthusiastic review of a book, etc., esp. in a newspaper. **5** = *powder puff.* • *v.* **1** *intr.* emit a puff of air or breath; blow with short blasts. **2** *intr.* (of a person smoking, a steam engine, etc.) emit or move with puffs. **3** *intr.* breathe hard; pant. **4** *intr.* & *tr.* [usu. foll. by *up, out*] become or cause to become inflated; swell (*his eye was inflamed and puffed up*). **5** *tr.* (usu. as **puffed up** *adj.*) elate; make proud or boastful. **6** *tr.* advertise or promote (goods, a book, etc.) with exaggerated or false praise. □ **puff pastry** light flaky pastry.

■ *n.* **1** blow, breath, wind, whiff, gust. **2** pull, *sl.* drag. • *v.* **1** exhale, breathe (out). **2** draw on, pull at *or* on, smoke, drag on. **3** huff, gasp, wheeze, blow. **4** inflate, distend, bloat, stretch, balloon, expand, pump up. **5** (**puffed up**) see PROUD 2a. **6** publicize, push, trumpet, blow up, ballyhoo.

puff•ball /púfbawl/ n. ball-shaped fungus emitting clouds of spores.

puf•fin /púfin/ n. northern seabird with a large head, brightly colored triangular bill, and black and white plumage.

puff•y /púfee/ adj. (**puff•i•er, puff•i•est**) **1** swollen, esp. of the face, etc. **2** fat. **3** gusty. □□ **puff´i•ly** adv. **puff´i•ness** n.

pug /pug/ n. (in full **pugdog**) dog of a dwarf breed with a broad flat nose and deeply wrinkled face. □ **pug nose** a short squat or snub nose. **pug-nosed** having such a nose.

pu•gil•ist /pyo͞ojilist/ n. boxer, esp. a professional. □□ **pu´gil•ism** n. **pu•gil•is´tic** adj.

pug•na•cious /pugnáyshəs/ adj. quarrelsome; disposed to fight. □□ **pug•na´cious•ly** adv. **pug•nac•i•ty** /-násitee/ n.

■ aggressive, belligerent, combative, bellicose, antagonistic, argumentative, hostile, litigious, contentious.

puke /pyo͞ok/ v. sl. vomit. □□ **puk´ey** adj.

pul•chri•tude /púlkritoōd, -tyoōd/ n. literary beauty. □□ **pul•chri•tu•di•nous** /-toōdinəs, tyoōd-/ adj.

pule /pyo͞ol/ v.intr. cry querulously or weakly; whimper.

pull /po͞ol/ • v. **1** tr. exert force upon (a thing) tending to move it to oneself or the origin of the force (*stop pulling my hair*). **2** tr. cause to move in this way. **3** intr. exert a pulling force. **4** tr. extract; pluck out. **5** tr. damage (a muscle, etc.) by abnormal strain. **6** tr. [foll. by *on*] bring out (a weapon). **7** intr. [foll. by *at*] tear or pluck at. **8** intr. inhale deeply; draw or suck (on a pipe, etc.). **9** tr. remove (a plant) by the root. • n. **1** act of pulling. **2** force exerted by this. **3** influence; advantage. **4** something that attracts or draws attention. **5** deep draft of esp. liquor. □ **pull back** retreat or cause to retreat. **pull in 1 a** arrive, esp. at a destination. **b** restrain; tighten. **2** (of a bus, train, etc.) arrive to take passengers. **3** earn or acquire. **4** colloq. arrest. **pull a person's leg** deceive a person playfully. **pull off 1** remove by pulling. **2** succeed in achieving or winning. **pull out 1** take out by pulling. **2** depart. **3** withdraw from an undertaking. **4** (of a bus, train, etc.) leave with its passengers. **5** (of a vehicle) move onto the road and accelerate. **pull over** (of a vehicle) move to the side of or off the road. **pull one's punches** avoid using one's full force. **pull strings** exert (esp. clandestine) influence. **pull together** work in harmony. **pull up 1** stop or cause to stop moving. **2** pull out of the ground. **3** draw closer to or even with, as in a race. **pull one's weight** do one's fair share of work. □□ **pull´er** n.

■ v. **1** jerk, pull at, pluck, tug. **2** draw, haul, drag; see also TUG[1] v. 1. **4** see EXTRACT v. 1. **5** tear, stretch, strain, rip, sprain. **7** see PLUCK v. 3, 4. **8** drag, puff; see also INHALE. **9** pull out, extract, uproot. • n. **1** see TUG n. 1. **2, 4** magnetism, appeal, pulling power, seductiveness, seduction; attraction, draw, lure. **3** authority, weight, leverage. **5** see DRAFT n. 5. □ **pull back** withdraw, draw back, back off, recoil. **pull in 1** draw up *or* in *or* over; see also ARRIVE 1. **3** see EARN 1, ACQUIRE 1. **4** apprehend, take into custody, col-

---

lar. **pull a person's leg** tease, chaff, rib, twit. **pull off 1** detach, rip *or* tear off; see also SEPARATE v. 1. **2** bring off, accomplish, manage, perform. **pull out 1** uproot, extract, withdraw; pull up, take out. **2, 4** see LEAVE v. 1b, 3, 4. **3** give up; retreat, draw back. **pull strings** use connections, pull wires. **pull together** cooperate, agree. **pull up 1** see STOP v. 3. **pull one's weight** perform, colloq. do one's bit, deliver the goods.

pul•let /po͞olit/ n. young hen, esp. one less than one year old.

pul•ley /po͞olee/ n. (pl. **-leys**) grooved wheel or set of wheels for a rope, etc., to pass over, set in a block and used for changing the direction of a force.

Pull•man /po͞olmən/ n. railroad sleeping car.

pull•o•ver /po͞olōvər/ n. garment put on over the head and covering the top half of the body.

pul•mo•nar•y /po͞olməneree, púl-/ adj. **1** of or relating to the lungs. **2** having lungs or lunglike organs. □□ **pul•mo•nate** /-nayt, -nət/ adj.

pulp /pulp/ • n. **1** soft fleshy part of fruit, etc. **2** soft shapeless mass derived from rags, wood, etc., used in papermaking. • v. **1** tr. reduce to pulp. **2** intr. become pulp. □□ **pulp´er** n. **pulp´less** adj. **pulp´y** adj. **pulp´i•ness** n.

■ n. **1** marrow, flesh. • v. **1** mash, squash, pulverize, triturate, grind down, levigate.

pul•pit /po͞olpit, púl-/ n. **1** raised enclosed platform in a church, etc., from which the preacher delivers a sermon. **2** [prec. by *the*] preachers or preaching collectively.

pul•sar /púlsaar/ n. Astron. cosmic source of regular and rapid pulses of radiation, e.g., a rotating neutron star.

pul•sate /púlsayt/ v.intr. **1** expand and contract rhythmically; throb. **2** vibrate; quiver; thrill. □□ **pul•sa•tion** /-sáyshən/ n. **pul´sa•tor** n. **pul•sa•to•ry** /púlsətawree/ adj.

■ beat, pulse, pound, thrum, drum, thump, thud, reverberate, hammer, palpitate, oscillate.

pulse /puls/ • n. **1 a** rhythmical throbbing of the arteries, esp. as felt in the wrists, temples, etc. **b** each successive beat of the arteries or heart. **2** throb or thrill of life or emotion. **3** latent feeling. **4** single vibration of sound, electric current, light, etc. **5** rhythmical beat, esp. of music. • v.intr. pulsate. □□ **pulse´less** adj.

■ n. **2** see THRILL n. 2. **5** beating, throb, throbbing, pulsation, pounding, drumming, reverberation; rhythm. • v. see PULSATE.

pul•ver•ize /púlvəriz/ v. **1** tr. reduce to fine particles. **2** intr. be reduced to dust. **3** colloq. tr. **a** demolish. **b** defeat utterly. □□ **pul´ver•i•za´tion** n. **pul´ver•iz•er** n.

■ **1, 2** powder, comminute, grind, crush, mill, granulate, crumble. **3** devastate, destroy, crush, smash, shatter, ruin, wreck, annihilate; see also BEAT v. 1a.

pu•ma /pyo͞omə, po͞o-/ n. large American wild cat. (Also called **cougar, panther, mountain lion**).

pum•ice /púmis/ n. (in full **pumice stone**) **1** light porous volcanic rock often used as an abrasive in cleaning or polishing substances. **2** piece of this used for removing callused skin, etc.

pum•mel /púmǝl/ v.tr. (also **pom•mel**) strike repeatedly, esp. with the fist.

pump¹ /pump/ • n. machine for raising or moving liquids, compressing gases, inflating tires, etc. • v. **1** tr. raise or remove (liquid, gas, etc.) with a pump. **2** tr. [often foll. by *up*] fill (a tire, etc.) with air. **3** intr. work a pump. **4** tr. question (a person) persistently to obtain information. **5** tr. move vigorously up and down. □ **pump iron** (also **pump up**) colloq. exercise with weights.

■ v. **1** send, deliver, push; (*pump out*) drive or force out, draw off or out, siphon (out or off), drain, tap, extract, withdraw. **2** see IN‑ FLATE 1. **4** interrogate, quiz, probe, grill.

pump² /pump/ n. low-cut shoe without ties, straps, etc.

pum•per•nick•el /púmpǝrnikǝl/ n. type of dark rye bread.

pump•kin /púmpkin, púng–/ n. rounded orange edible gourd of a vine.

pun /pun/ • n. humorous use of a word to suggest different meanings, or of words of the same sound and different meanings. • v.intr. (**punned, pun•ning**) [foll. by *on*] make a pun or puns with (words). □ **pun′ ning•ly** adv. **pun′ster** n.

■ n. play on words, quibble, double entendre, innuendo, equivoque, paronomasia; wordplay; quip, witticism.

punch¹ /punch/ • v.tr. **1** strike bluntly, esp. with a closed fist. **2 a** pierce a hole in (metal, paper, a ticket, etc.) as or with a punch. **b** pierce (a hole) by punching. • n. **1** blow with a fist. **2** colloq. vigor; momentum. □ **punch-drunk** stupefied from or as though from a series of heavy blows. **punch line** words giving the point of a joke or story. □□ **punch′er** n.

■ v. **1** hit, clip, jab, smack, box, clout, thump. **2 a** puncture, perforate, penetrate, go through, rupture. **b** prick. • n. **1** clip, jab, smack, box, cuff, thump, uppercut, clout. **2** effect, impact, effectiveness, force, impetus, forcefulness, power, vitality, gusto, life.

punch² /punch/ n. tool or machine for punching holes in or impressing a design or stamping a die on a material.

punch³ /punch/ n. drink of fruit juices, sometimes mixed with wine or liquor, served cold or hot.

punch•y /púnchee/ adj. (**punch•i•er, punch•i•est**) **1** having punch or vigor; forceful. **2** = *punch-drunk* (PUNCH¹).

punc•til•i•o /pungktíleeō/ n. (pl. **–os**) **1** delicate point of ceremony or honor. **2** etiquette.

punc•til•i•ous /pungktíleeǝs/ adj. **1** attentive to formality or etiquette. **2** precise in behavior. See synonym study at FORMAL. □□ **punc• til′i•ous•ly** adv. **punc•til′i•ous•ness** n.

punc•tu•al /púngkchōǝl/ adj. observant of the appointed time; prompt. □□ **punc•tu• al•i•ty** /–álitee/ n. **punc′tu•al•ly** adv.

■ on time, timely; on target.

punc•tu•ate /púngkchōō–ayt/ v.tr. **1** insert punctuation marks in. **2** interrupt at intervals. **3** emphasize.

■ **2** break; intersperse, interlard, pepper, sprinkle.

punc•tu•a•tion /púngkchōō–áyshǝn/ n. **1** system or arrangement of marks used to punctuate a written passage. **2** practice or skill of punctuating. □ **punctuation mark** any of the marks (e.g., period and comma) used in writing to separate sentences, etc., and to clarify meaning.

punc•ture /púngkchǝr/ • n. **1** piercing, as of a tire. **2** hole made in this way. • v. **1** tr. make a puncture in. **2** intr. become punctured. **3** tr. prick, pierce, or deflate.

■ n. **1** perforation, holing; prick. **2** see LEAK n. 1a. • v. **1, 3** hole, penetrate, go through, nick, disillusion, discourage.

pun•dit /púndit/ n. often iron. learned expert or teacher. □□ **pun′dit•ry** n.

pun•gent /púnjǝnt/ adj. **1** having a sharp or strong taste or smell. **2** (of remarks) penetrating; biting; caustic. **3** Biol. having a sharp point. □□ **pun′gen•cy** n. **pun′gent•ly** adv.

■ **1** spicy, hot, penetrating, aromatic, seasoned, peppery, piquant, tangy. **2** sharp, stinging, severe, astringent, stern, acrid, harsh, acid, acrimonious.

pun•ish /púnish/ v.tr. **1** cause (an offender) to suffer for an offense. **2** inflict a penalty for (an offense). **3 a** tax severely. **b** hurt, abuse, or treat improperly. □□ **pun′ish•a•ble** adj. **pun′ish•er** n. **pun′ish•ing** adj. (in sense 3a).

■ **1** penalize, chastise, castigate, discipline, chasten, amerce, scold, rebuke, flog, beat, scourge, spank, whip, warm or tan a person's hide. **3 b** maltreat, mistreat, harm, injure, damage. □□ **punishing** grueling, hard, arduous, strenuous, exhausting, tiring.

pun•ish•ment /púnishmǝnt/ n. **1** act or instance of punishing; condition of being punished. **2** loss or suffering inflicted in this. **3** colloq. severe treatment or suffering.

■ **1, 2** chastisement, castigation, discipline, scolding, rebuke, reproof; penance, penalty; flogging, beating, whipping, scourging, spanking. **3** injury, harm, damage, abuse, maltreatment, torture; beating, thrashing.

pu•ni•tive /pyōōnitiv/ adj. (also **pu•ni•to•ry** /–tawree/) inflicting or intended to inflict punishment. □□ **pu′ni•tive•ly** adv.

■ chastening, castigatory, disciplinary, retributive.

punk /pungk/ n. **1 a** worthless person or thing (often as a general term of abuse). **b** nonsense. **2** (in full **punk rock**) loud fast-moving form of rock music with crude and aggressive effects. **3** hoodlum or ruffian. □□ **punk′y** adj.

■ **1 a** see WRETCH 2. **b** see NONSENSE. **3** hooligan, delinquent, tough, thug; see also HOODLUM.

punt¹ /punt/ • n. flat-bottomed boat, square at both ends, propelled by a long pole. • v.

1 *tr.* propel (a punt) with a pole. **2** *intr. & tr.* travel or convey in a punt. □□ **punt'er** *n.*

punt² /punt/ • *v.tr.* kick (a football) after it has dropped from the hands and before it reaches the ground. • *n.* such a kick. □□ **punt'er** *n.*

pu•ny /pyóonee/ *adj.* (**pu•ni•er, pu•ni•est**) **1** undersized. **2** weak; feeble. **3** petty. □□ **pu'ni•ly** *adv.* **pu'ni•ness** *n.*

■ **1, 2** small, little, diminutive, tiny, minute; frail, sickly, weakly, underfed. **3** insignificant, unimportant, inconsequential, paltry, trivial, trifling.

pup /pup/ *n.* **1** young dog. **2** young wolf, rat, seal, etc. □ **pup tent** small two-person tent.
■ **1** puppy, whelp.

pu•pa /pyóopə/ *n.* (*pl.* **pu•pae** /-pee/) insect in the stage of development between larva and imago. □□ **pu'pal** *adj.*

pu•pil¹ /pyóopəl/ *n.* person who is taught by another.
■ student, learner, schoolchild, schoolgirl, schoolboy.

pu•pil² /pyóopəl/ *n.* dark circular opening in the center of the iris of the eye. □□ **pu'pil•lar** *adj.* **pu'pil•lar•y** *adj.*

pup•pet /púpit/ *n.* **1** small figure moved by various means as entertainment. **2** person controlled by another. □□ **pup'pet•ry** *n.*
■ **2** figurehead, cat's-paw, pawn, dupe, tool, instrument.

pup•py /púpee/ *n.* (*pl.* **-pies**) **1** young dog. **2** conceited or arrogant young man. □ **puppy love** infatuation, esp. among adolescents. □□ **pup'py•hood** *n.* **pup'py•ish** *adj.*

pur•blind /pórblind/ *adj.* **1** partly blind. **2** obtuse; dim-witted. □□ **pur'blind•ness** *n.*

pur•chase /pórchis/ • *v.tr.* **1** buy. **2** obtain or achieve at some cost. • *n.* **1** buying. **2** something bought. **3** firm hold on a thing to move it or to prevent it from slipping; leverage. □□ **pur'chas•a•ble** *adj.* **pur'chas•er** *n.*

■ *v.* **1** acquire, procure, obtain, get, secure. **2** win, gain, realize, attain. • *n.* **1** acquisition, purchasing, procurement. **2** acquisition, *colloq.* buy. **3** grip, support, toehold, foothold, grasp; position.

pure /pyoor/ *adj.* **1** unmixed; unadulterated. **2** chaste. **3** not morally corrupt. **4** guiltless. **5** (of a subject of study) abstract; not applied. □□ **pure'ness** *n.*

■ **1** uncontaminated, clear, unalloyed, entire, true, perfect; 24-karat, sterling, solid. **2, 3** virginal, virgin, intact, maidenly, vestal, immaculate, undefiled, uncorrupted, wholesome, virtuous, good, modest, moral, correct. **4** innocent, above suspicion, above reproach, blameless. **5** conceptual, theoretical, hypothetical, conjectural, speculative, notional.

pure•bred /pyóorbred/ • *adj.* belonging to a recognized breed of unmixed lineage. • *n.* purebred animal.

pu•rée /pyooráy, pyooée/ • *n.* smooth pulp of vegetables, fruit, etc. • *v.tr.* (**pu•rées, pu•réed**) make a purée of.

pure•ly /pyóorlee/ *adv.* **1** in a pure manner. **2** merely; solely; exclusively.

---

675   **punt ~ purple**

pur•ga•tive /pórgətiv/ • *adj.* **1** serving to purify. **2** strongly laxative. • *n.* **1** purgative thing. **2** laxative.

■ *adj.* **1** cathartic, depurative, purifying. **2** cathartic, aperient, evacuant. • *n.* **1** purifier, depurative, purge. **2** cathartic, aperient, purge, depurative.

pur•ga•to•ry /pórgətawree/ • *n.* (*pl.* **-ries**) **1** condition or supposed place of spiritual cleansing, esp. (*RC Ch.*) of those dying in the grace of God but having to expiate venial sins, etc. **2** place or state of temporary suffering or expiation. • *adj.* purifying. □□ **pur•ga•to•ri•al** /-táwreeəl/ *adj.*

purge /pórj/ • *v.tr.* **1** make physically or spiritually clean. **2** remove by cleansing. **3** rid (an organization, party, etc.) of persons regarded as undesirable. **4** empty (the bowels). • *n.* **1** act of purging. **2** purgative. □□ **purg'er** *n.*

■ *v.* **1** purify, clean (out), scour (out), depurate, wash (out); clear, exonerate, absolve. **3** free from, clear. **4** see EMPTY *v.* **1.** • *n.* **1** cleansing, purification; ousting, ouster, removal, ejection, expulsion, elimination. **2** see PURGATIVE *n.* **2.**

pu•ri•fy /pyóorifī/ *v.tr.* (**-fies, -fied**) **1** [often foll. by *of, from*] cleanse or make pure. **2** make ceremonially clean. **3** clear of extraneous elements. □□ **pu•ri•fi•ca'tion** *n.* **pu•rif•i•ca•to•ry** /rifəkátawree/ *adj.* **pu'ri•fi•er** *n.*

■ **1** clean, clarify, refine, wash, sanitize, depurate.

pu•rist /pyóorist/ *n.* stickler for or advocate of scrupulous purity, esp. in language or art. □□ **pur'ism** *n.* **pu•ris'tic** *adj.*

■ pedant, precisionist, formalist, stickler, prescriptivist.

pu•ri•tan /pyóoritn/ • *n.* **1** (**Puritan**) *hist.* member of a group of English Protestants who sought to simplify and regulate forms of worship. **2** person practicing extreme strictness in religion or morals. • *adj.* **1** *hist.* of the Puritans. **2** scrupulous and austere in religion or morals. □□ **pu'ri•tan•ism** *n.*

■ *n.* **2** moralist, pietist, purist, religionist, fanatic, zealot; see also PRIG. • *adj.* **2** prudish, puritanical, prim, proper, straitlaced, ascetic, moralistic, pietistic, intolerant, disapproving, bigoted, narrow-minded.

pu•ri•tan•i•cal /pyoóritánikəl/ *adj.* often *derog.* strictly religious or moral in behavior. □□ **pu•ri•tan'i•cal•ly** *adv.*

pu•ri•ty /pyóoritee/ *n.* pureness; cleanness.

■ cleanliness, clarity; healthfulness, wholesomeness; faultlessness, correctness; chastity, innocence.

purl¹ /pərl/ • *n.* **1** type of inverted knitting stitch. **2** chain of minute loops ornamenting edges of lace, etc. • *v.tr.* [also *absol.*] knit with a purl stitch.

purl² /pərl/ *v.intr.* (of a brook, etc.) flow with a swirling motion and babbling sound.

pur•loin /pərlóyn/ *v.tr.* *literary* steal; pilfer. □□ **pur•loin'er** *n.*

pur•ple /pórpəl/ • *n.* **1** color intermediate between red and blue. **2** purple robe, esp. as the dress of an emperor or senior magistrate. **3** [prec. by *the*] position of rank, authority, or privilege. • *adj.* of a purple color. □ **purple passage** (or **prose** or **patch**) overly ornate or elaborate literary passage. □□ **pur'plish** *adj.*

pur•port • *v.tr.* /pərpáwrt/ **1** profess; be intended to seem. **2** (of a document or speech) have as its meaning; state. • *n.* /pórpawrt/ ostensible meaning;. sense or tenor. □□ **pur•port'ed•ly** *adv.*
   ▪ *v.* **1** pretend, claim, make a pretense. • *n.* see MEANING *n.* 1, 2. □□ **purportedly** see *seemingly* (SEEMING).

pur•pose /pórpəs/ • *n.* **1** object to be attained; thing intended. **2** intention to act. **3** resolution; determination. • *v.tr.* have as one's purpose; design; intend. See synonym study at INTEND. □ **on purpose** intentionally. **to no purpose** with no result or effect. □□ **pur'pose•ful** *adj.* **pur'pose•ful•ly** *adv.* **pur'pose•ful•ness** *n.* **pur'pose•less** *adj.* **pur'pose•ly** *adv.*
   ▪ *n.* **1** intention, intent, end, goal, ambition, objective, rationale, reason, motive. **2** intent, scheme, plan, design. **3** firmness, persistence, drive, single-mindedness. • *v.* plan, resolve, mean, aim, contemplate, propose. □ **on purpose** purposely, deliberately, willfully, by design, consciously. □□ **pur'pose•ful** intended, planned, deliberate, willful; resolved, settled, determined, decided, sure, certain. **pur'pose•less** aimless, undirected, directionless; erratic, haphazard.

pur•pos•ive /pórpəsiv, pərpō–/ *adj.* **1** having or serving a purpose. **2** done with a purpose. **3** resolute; purposeful. □□ **pur'pos•ive•ly** *adv.* **pur'pos•ive•ness** *n.*

purr /pór/ • *v.intr.* **1** (of a cat) make a low vibratory sound expressing contentment. **2** (of machinery, etc.) make a similar sound. • *n.* purring sound.

purse /pórs/ • *n.* **1** small pouch for carrying money on the person. **2** handbag. **3** money; funds. **4** sum as a present or prize in a contest. • *v.tr.* pucker or contract (the lips). □ **hold the purse strings** have control of expenditure.
   ▪ *n.* **1** bag, moneybag, wallet, pocketbook. **2** bag, pocketbook. **3** wealth, resources, finances, capital, revenue, income. **4** reward, award, gift. • *v.* wrinkle, compress, press together.

purs•er /pórsər/ *n.* officer on a ship who keeps accounts, esp. the head steward in a passenger vessel.

pur•su•ance /pərsōoəns/ *n.* [foll. by *of*] carrying out or observance (of a plan, idea, etc.).

pur•su•ant /pərsōoənt/ • *adj.* pursuing. • *adv.* [foll. by *to*] conforming to or in accordance with. □□ **pur•su'ant•ly** *adv.*

pur•sue /pərsōo/ *v.tr.* (**pur•sues, pur•sued, pur•su•ing**) **1** follow with intent to overtake or capture or do harm to. **2** continue or proceed along (a route or course of action). **3** follow or engage in (study or other activity). **4** proceed in compliance with (a plan, etc.). **5** seek after; aim at. **6** continue to in-

vestigate or discuss (a topic). **7** seek the attention or acquaintance of (a person) persistently. □□ **pur•su'er** *n.*
   ▪ **1** chase, go *or* run after, hunt (after *or* for), trail, track. **2** follow (on with), keep to; carry on with, persist *or* persevere in, maintain, proceed with. **3** take; see also ENGAGE[1] 7. **5** aspire to, work for *or* toward, try *or* strive for, search for. **7** go after, woo, pay court to, court; follow, hound; see also CHASE *v.* 1, 3.

pur•suit /pərsōot/ *n.* **1** act or an instance of pursuing. **2** occupation or activity pursued. □ **in pursuit of** pursuing.
   ▪ **1** hunt, tracking, stalking, chase; pursuance. **2** work, field, area, business, profession, trade; hobby, pastime.

pu•ru•lent /pyōoərələnt, pyōoryə–/ *adj.* of, containing, or discharging pus. □□ **pu'ru•lence** *n.* **pu'ru•len•cy** *n.* **pu'ru•lent•ly** *adv.*

pur•vey /pərváy/ *v.* **1** *tr.* provide or supply (articles of food) as one's business. **2** *intr.* [often foll. by *for*] **a** make provision. **b** act as supplier. □□ **pur•vey'ance** *n.* **pur•vey'or** *n.*

pur•view /pórvyōo/ *n.* **1** scope or range of a document, scheme, etc. **2** range of physical or mental vision.

pus /pus/ *n.* thick yellowish or greenish liquid produced from infected tissue.

push /pŏosh/ • *v.* **1** *tr.* exert a force on (a thing) to move it or cause it to move away. **2** *intr.* exert such a force (*do not push*). **3** *intr. & tr.* **a** thrust forward or upward. **b** project or cause to project (*pushes out new roots*). **4** *intr.* move forward or make (one's way) by force or persistence. **5** *intr.* exert oneself, esp. to surpass others. **6** *tr.* urge, impel, or press (a person) hard. **7** *tr.* pursue or demand persistently (*pushed for reform*). **8** *tr.* promote. **9** *tr. colloq.* sell (a drug) illegally. • *n.* **1** act or instance of pushing; shove or thrust. **2** force exerted in this. **3** vigorous effort. **4** enterprise; determination to succeed. □ **push around** *colloq.* bully. **push button** button to be pushed esp. to operate an electrical device. **push one's luck** take undue risks. **2** act presumptuously. **push-up** exercise in which the body, extended and prone, is raised upward by pushing down with the hands until the arms are straight.
   ▪ *v.* **1** thrust, shove, drive, move, get moving, propel; press. **3 b** see PROJECT *v.* 2. **4** continue, proceed, advance, press on *or* onward; shove, thrust, elbow, shoulder, force, jostle. **6** encourage, induce, persuade, prod, spur; compel, force, dragoon; badger, hound; see also TAX *v.* 3. **7** see PURSUE 2, 7. **8** publicize, advertise, propagandize, puff. **9** peddle. • *n.* **1** nudge; press. **2** drive, thrust; see also FORCE *n.* 1. **3** see ATTEMPT *n.* **4** ambition, initiative, resourcefulness, energy, dynamism. □ **push around** intimidate, domineer, tyrannize, torment.

push•er /pŏoshər/ *n.* **1** *colloq.* illegal seller of drugs. **2** *colloq.* pushing or pushy person. **3** thing for pushing.

push•ing /pŏoshing/ *adj.* **1** pushy. **2** *colloq.* having nearly reached (a specified age).

push•o•ver /pŏoshōvər/ *n. colloq.* **1** something that is easily done. **2** person easily overcome, persuaded, etc.

■ **1** child's play, *colloq.* piece of cake, picnic, cinch; see also BREEZE *n.* 2. **2** *colloq.* soft touch, *sl.* mark, sucker, sap.

push•y /pŏoshee/ *adj.* (**push•i•er, push•i•est**) *colloq.* excessively self-assertive. □□ **push′i•ly** *adv.* **push′i•ness** *n.*

■ forward, assertive, self-seeking, forceful, aggressive, domineering, overbearing, ambitious, bumptious.

pu•sil•lan•i•mous /pyŏosilánimǝs/ *adj.* lacking courage; timid. □□ **pu•sil•la•nim′i•ty** /-lǝnímitee/ *n.* **pu•sil•lan′i•mous•ly** *adv.*

puss•y /pŏosee/ *n.* (*pl.* **-ies**) (also **puss; puss′y•cat**) *colloq.* cat. □ **pussy willow** willow with furry catkins.

pussy•foot /pŏosefŏot/ *v.intr.* **1** move stealthily or warily. **2** act cautiously or non committally. □□ **puss′y•foot′er** *n.*

■ **1** sneak, creep, slink, prowl, steal, tiptoe. **2** beat about the bush, hem *or* hum and haw, equivocate, be evasive.

pus•tule /pŭschŏol/ *n.* pimple containing pus. □□ **pus′tu•lous** *adj.*

put /pŏot/ • *v.* (**put•ting;** *past* and *past part.* **put**) **1** *tr.* move to or cause to be in a specified place or position. **2** *tr.* bring into a specified condition, relation, or state. **3** *tr.* **a** impose or assign. **b** [foll. by *on, to*] impose or enforce the existence of (*put a stop to it*). **4** *tr.* **a** cause (a person) to go or be, habitually or temporarily (*put them at their ease*). **b** *refl.* imagine (oneself) in a specified situation (*put yourself in my shoes*). **5** *tr.* express in a specified way (*to put it mildly*). **6** *tr.* [foll. by *at*] estimate (an amount, etc.) (*put the cost at $50*). **7** *tr.* [foll. by *into*] express or translate in (words, or another language). **8** *tr.* [foll. by *into*] invest. **9** *tr.* [foll. by *on*] wager **10** *tr.* [foll. by *to*] submit for consideration or attention (*put it to a vote*). **11** *tr.* throw (esp. a shot or weight) as sport. **12** *intr.* (of a ship, etc.) proceed in a specified direction. • *n.* **1** a throw of the shot or weight. **2** *Stock Exch.* option of selling stock or a commodity at a fixed price at a given date. • *adj.* stationary; fixed (*stay put*). □ **put across 1** make acceptable or effective. **2** express in an understandable way. **3** (often in **put it** or **one across**) achieve by deceit. **put away 1** put (a thing) back in the place where it is normally kept. **2** set (money, etc.) aside for future use. **3 a** imprison. **b** commit to a mental institution. **4** consume (food and drink), esp. in large quantities. **put down 1** suppress by force. **2** *colloq.* snub or humiliate. **3** record or enter in writing. **4** enter the name of (a person) on a list. **5** attribute (*put it down to bad planning*). **6** put (an old or sick animal) to death. **7** preserve or store (eggs, etc.) for future use. **8** pay as a deposit. **put off 1** postpone. **2** evade (a person). **3** hinder or dissuade. **put on 1** clothe oneself with. **2** turn on (an electrical device, light, etc.). **3** stage (a play, show, etc.). **4 a** pretend to be affected by (an emotion). **b** assume; take on (a character or appearance). **5** increase one's weight by (a specified amount). **6** [foll. by *to*] make aware of or put in touch with (*put us on to their new accountant*). **put-on** *n. colloq.* deception or hoax. **put

out 1 a** (often as *adj.*) disconcert or annoy. **b** [often *refl.*] inconvenience (*don't put yourself out*). **2** extinguish (a fire or light). **put up 1** build or erect. **2** can; preserve (food) for later use. **3** take or provide accommodation for (*put me up for the night*). **4** engage in (a fight, struggle, etc.) as a form of resistance. **5** offer. **6 a** present oneself for election. **b** propose for election. **7** provide (money) as a backer. **8** display (a notice). **put upon** *colloq.* take advantage of (a person). **put up with** endure; tolerate; submit to. □□ **put′ter** *n.*

■ *v.* **1** situate, set, lay, station, stand. **3** *n.* place, attribute; raise, levy, exact. **4 b** consider, regard, picture, envisage. **5, 7** word, phrase; say, utter. **6** see GAUGE *v.* 2. **9** bet, gamble, stake, chance, risk. **10** (*put to*) present to, set before; refer to; see also SUBMIT 2. **11** heave, toss, fling, cast. • *n.* **1** see THROW *n.* 1. □ **put across 2** make clear, get across, explain. **put away 1** return, replace, put back; store. **3 a** jail, incarcerate, send up. **b** institutionalize. **4** devour, gorge, polish off. **put down 1** quash, quell, topple, crush. **2** abash, crush, silence, mortify; deflate, slight, reject. **3, 4** register, set down, list; log, note (down); enroll. **5** ascribe, assign, impute. **6** destroy, put to sleep. **put off 1** delay, defer, put back. **3** see DETER. **put on 1** don, get dressed in. **2** switch on. **3** mount, produce, present; perform. **4 a** take on, affect, feign. **5** gull, put on. **put out 1** vex, irritate, exasperate, irk, perturb. **b** disturb, trouble, bother; create difficulties. **2** turn off, snuff out. **put up 1** construct, raise, set up, put together **3** accommodate, lodge, board, house. **5** see PRESENT *v.* 1. **7** contribute, give, donate. **8** see DISPLAY *v.* 1. **put up with** take, stand (for), stomach, accept, bear.

pu•ta•tive /pyŏotativ/ *adj.* reputed; supposed (*his putative father*). □□ **pu′ta•tive•ly** *adv.*

pu•tre•fy /pyŏotrifī/ *v.* (**-fies, -fied**) become or make putrid; go bad. □□ **pu•tre•fa′cient** /-fáyshǝnt/ *adj.* **pu•tre•fac′tion** /-fákshǝn/ *n.* **pu•tre•fac′tive** /-fáktiv/ *adj.*

■ rot, decompose, decay, molder, deteriorate, go off.

pu•tres•cent /pyŏotrésǝnt/ *adj.* **1** in the process of rotting. **2** of or accompanying this process. □□ **pu•tres′cence** *n.*

pu•trid /pyŏotrid/ *adj.* **1** decomposed; rotten. **2** foul; noxious. □□ **pu′trid•ly** *adv.*

■ **1** rotting, decomposing, decayed, decaying, moldy. **2** fetid, rank; see also FOUL *adj.* 1, 4a.

putsch /pŏoch/ *n.* sudden revolution; violent uprising. See synonym study at UPRISING.

putt /pŭt/ • *v.tr.* strike (a golf ball) gently on a putting green. • *n.* putting stroke. □ **putting green** (in golf) area of close-cropped grass around a hole. □□ **put′ter** *n.*

put•ter /pŭtǝr/ *v.intr.* **1** work or occupy oneself in a desultory but pleasant manner. **2** go slowly; dawdle; loiter. □□ **put′ter•er** *n.*

■ **1** see *mess about.* **2** amble, saunter, stroll, wander.

put•ty /pŭtee/ • *n.* (*pl.* **-ties**) soft, pliable

mixture used for fixing panes of glass, filling holes in woodwork, etc. • *v.tr.* (**-ties, -tied**) cover, fix, join, or fill up with putty.

putz /puts/ • *n. sl.* simple-minded foolish person. • *v.intr. sl.* [usu. foll. by *around*] move (about) or occupy oneself in an aimless or idle manner.

puz•zle /púzəl/ • *n.* **1** difficult or confusing problem; enigma. **2** problem or toy designed to test knowledge or ingenuity. See synonym study at RIDDLE. • *v.* **1** *tr.* confound or disconcert mentally. **2** *intr.* be perplexed (about). **3** *tr.* (usu. as **puzzling** *adj.*) require much thought to comprehend. □□ **puz′zle•ment** *n.* **puz′zling•ly** *adv.*

■ *n.* **1** question, paradox, poser, mystery. **2** poser, riddle, conundrum, *colloq.* brainteaser. • *v.* **1** baffle, bewilder, confuse, mystify, perplex, nonplus. **2** be confused *or* baffled *or* bewildered; (*puzzle over*) study, ponder (over), mull over, contemplate, meditate on. **3** (**puzzling**) mystifying, enigmatic, bewildering, baffling, perplexing.

puz•zler /púzlər/ *n.* difficult question or problem.

Pvt. *abbr.* private.

PX *abbr.* post exchange.

pyg•my /pígmee/ • *n.* (also **pig′my**) (*pl.* **-mies**) **1** member of a small people of equatorial Africa and parts of SE Asia. **2** very small person, animal, or thing. □□ **pyg•mae•an** /pigmeéən, pígmee-/ *adj.* (also **pyg′me•an**).

■ **2** dwarf, midget, runt.

py•lon /pílon/ *n.* tall structure erected as a support (esp. for electric power cables) or boundary or decoration.

py•or•rhe•a /píəreéə/ *n.* gum disease causing shrinkage of the gums, loosening of the teeth, and discharge of pus.

pyr•a•mid /pírəmid/ *n.* **1** monumental structure, usu. of stone, with a square base and sloping sides meeting centrally at an apex, esp. an ancient Egyptian royal tomb. **2** solid of this type with a base of three or more sides. □□ **py•ram•i•dal** /-rámid'l/ *adj.* **py•ram′i•dal•ly** *adv.* **pyr•a•mid′ic** *adj.* (also **pyr•a•mid′i•cal**). **pyr•a•mid′i•cal•ly** *adv.*

pyre /pīr/ *n.* heap of combustible material, esp. a funeral pile for burning a corpse.

Py•rex /píreks/ *n. propr.* hard heat-resistant type of glass, often used for cookware.

py•rite /pírīt/ *n.* = PYRITES.

py•rites /pīríteez, pírīts/ *n.* (in full **iron pyrites**) yellow lustrous form of iron disulfide. □□ **py•rit•ic** /-rítik/ *adj.* **py•ri•tous** /pírītəs/ *adj.*

pyro- /pírō/ *comb. form* **1** denoting fire. **2** *Mineral.* denoting a mineral, etc., altered by heat or fiery in color.

py•ro•ma•nia /pírōmáyneeə/ *n.* obsessive desire to set fire to things. □□ **py•ro•ma′ni•ac** *n.*

py•ro•tech•nics /pírōtékniks/ *n.pl.* **1** art of making fireworks. **2** display of fireworks. **3** any brilliant display. □□ **py′ro•tech′nic** *adj.* **py•ro•tech′ni•cal** *adj.*

pyr•rhic /pírik/ *adj.* (of a victory) won at too great a cost.

Py•thag•o•re•an the•o•rem /pīthágəreéən/ *n.* theorem that the square of the hypotenuse of a right triangle is equal to the sum of the squares of the other two sides.

py•thon /píthon, -thən/ *n.* large tropical constricting snake.

pyx /piks/ *n.* (also **pix**) *Eccl.* vessel in which the consecrated bread of the Eucharist is kept.

Qq

Q[1] /kyōō/ *n.* (also **q**) (*pl.* **Qs** or **Q's**; **q's**) seventeenth letter of the alphabet.

Q[2] *abbr.* (also **Q.**) **1** question. **2** Queen, Queen's.

qb *abbr.* quarterback.

QED *abbr.* QUOD ERAT DEMONSTRANDUM.

qt. *abbr.* quart(s).

qty. *abbr.* quantity.

qua /kwaa/ *conj.* in the capacity of; as being.

quack[1] /kwak/ • *n.* harsh sound made by ducks. • *v.intr.* **1** utter this sound. **2** *colloq.* talk loudly and foolishly.

quack[2] /kwak/ *n.* unqualified practitioner, esp. of medicine. □□ **quack′er•y** *n.* **quack′ish** *adj.*

■ charlatan, impostor, pretender, faker, fraud.

quad /kwod/ *n. colloq.* quadrangle.

quad•ran•gle /kwódranggəl/ *n.* **1** four-sided plane figure, esp. a square or rectangle. **2**

four-sided courtyard. □□ **quad•ran′gu•lar** *adj.*

quad•rant /kwódrənt/ *n.* **1** quarter of a circle's circumference. **2** quarter of a circle enclosed by two radii at right angles. **3** instrument for taking angular measurements.

qua•drat•ic /kwodrátik/ *adj. Math.* **1** involving the second and no higher power of an unknown quantity or variable (*quadratic equation*). **2** square.

quadri- /kwódree/ (also **quadr-** or **quadru-**) *comb. form* denoting four.

quad•ri•ceps /kwódriseps/ *n. Anat.* four-part muscle at the front of the thigh.

quad•ri•lat•er•al /kwódrilátərəl/ • *adj.* having four sides. • *n.* four-sided figure.

qua•drille /kwodríl/ *n.* **1** square dance containing usu. five figures. **2** music for this.

quad•ri•ple•gia /kwódripleéjeeə, -jə/ *n. Med.* paralysis of all four limbs. □□ **quad•ri•ple′gic** *adj. & n.*

quad•ru•ped /kwódrəped/ *n.* four-footed animal, esp. a mammal. □□ **quad•ru•ped•al** /-roॅopid'l/ *adj.*

qua•dru•ple /kwodroॅopəl, –druॅp–, kwódroॅopəl/ • *adj.* **1** fourfold. **2** having four parts. • *n.* fourfold number or amount. • *v.* multiply by four. □□ **qua•drup'ly** *adv.*

qua•dru•plet /kwodroॅoplit, –druॅp–, kwódroॅoplit/ *n.* each of four children born at one birth.

qua•dru•pli•cate • *adj.* /kwodroॅoplikət/ **1** fourfold. **2** of which four copies are made. • *v.tr.* /-kayt/ multiply by four. □ **in quadruplicate** in four identical copies.

quag•mire /kwágmīr, kwóg–/ *n.* **1** soft boggy or marshy area that gives way underfoot. **2** hazardous situation.

quail[1] /kwayl/ *n.* (*pl.* same or **quails**) small game bird related to the partridge.

quail[2] /kwayl/ *v.intr.* flinch; be apprehensive with fear.

quaint /kwaynt/ *adj.* piquantly or attractively odd or old-fashioned. □□ **quaint'ly** *adv.* **quaint'ness** *n.*

■ outmoded, antiquated, outdated, antique; picturesque, sweet, curious, strange, bizarre, peculiar, unusual, queer, uncommon, singular, eccentric.

quake /kwayk/ • *v.intr.* shake; tremble. • *n.* *colloq.* earthquake. □□ **quak'y** *adj.* (**quak•i•er, quak•i•est**).

■ *v.* quiver, shudder; vibrate. *n.* tremor.

Quak•er /kwáykər/ *n.* member of the Society of Friends, a Christian movement devoted to peaceful principles and eschewing formal ritual. □□ **Quak'er•ish** *adj.* **Quak'er•ism** *n.*

qual•i•fi•ca•tion /kwólifikáyshən/ *n.* **1** act or an instance of qualifying. **2** [often in *pl.*] quality, skill, or accomplishment fitting a person for a position or purpose. **3** thing that modifies or limits.

■ **2** ability, aptitude, competence, capacity, proficiency. **3** limitation, restriction, modification, reservation; prerequisite, requirement.

qual•i•fy /kwóliſī/ *v.* (**-fies, -fied**) **1** *tr.* make competent or fit for a position or purpose. **2** *tr.* make legally entitled. **3** *intr.* satisfy conditions or requirements. **4** *tr.* add reservations to; modify or make less absolute (a statement or assertion). □□ **qual'i•fi•er** *n.*

■ **1** equip, fit, ready, prepare, condition, make eligible. **2** certify. **3** be eligible, have the qualifications, be fit or equipped or ready or prepared. **4** modulate; restrict, limit; see also MODIFY 1. □□ **qualifier** see HEAT *n.* 6.

qual•i•ta•tive /kwólitaytiv/ *adj.* concerned with or depending on quality. □□ **qual'i•ta•tive•ly** *adv.*

qual•i•ty /kwólitee/ *n.* (*pl.* **-ties**) **1** degree of excellence. **2** general excellence. **3** distinctive attribute or faculty. **4** relative nature or kind or character of a thing. □ **quality control** system of maintaining standards in manufactured products.

■ **1** grade, caliber, rank, value, worth. **2** see EXCELLENCE 1. **3** property, feature, characteristic, mark, distinction, trait.

qualm /kwaam, kwawm/ *n.* **1** misgiving; uneasy doubt esp. about one's own conduct.

2 scruple of conscience. **3** momentary faint or sick feeling.

■ **1** second thought(s), uncertainty, hesitation, uneasiness, reluctance, disinclination, queasiness. **2** compunction, twinge, pang.

SYNONYM STUDY: qualm

COMPUNCTION, DEMUR, MISGIVING, SCRUPLE. To have **qualms** is to have an uneasy, often sickening, feeling that you have acted or are about to act against your better judgment (*she had qualms about leaving a nine-year-old in charge of an infant*). **Misgivings** are even stronger, implying a disturbed state of mind because you're no longer confident that what you're doing is right (*his misgivings about letting his 80-year-old mother drive herself home turned out to be justified*). **Compunction** implies a momentary pang of conscience because what you are doing or are about to do is unfair, improper, or wrong (*they showed no compunction in carrying out their devious plans*). **Scruples** suggest a more highly developed conscience or sense of honor; it implies that you have principles, and that you would be deeply disturbed if you thought you were betraying them (*her scruples would not allow her to participate in what she considered antifeminist activities*). **Demur** connotes hesitation to the point of delay, but the delay is usually caused by objections or indecision rather than a sense of conscience (*they accepted his decision without demur*).

quan•da•ry /kwóndəree, dree/ *n.* (*pl.* **-ries**) **1** state of perplexity. **2** difficult situation; practical dilemma.

■ confusion; predicament, plight; see also DILEMMA.

quan•ti•fy /kwóntifī/ *v.tr.* (**-fies, -fied**) **1** determine the quantity of. **2** measure or express as a quantity. □□ **quan'ti•fi•a•ble** *adj.* **quan•ti•fi•ca'tion** *n.* **quan'ti•fi•er** *n.*

■ **1** see COUNT *v.* 1, CALCULATE 1.

quan•ti•ta•tive /kwóntitaytiv/ *adj.* pertaining to quantity. □□ **quan'ti•ta•tive•ly** *adv.*

quan•ti•ty /kwóntitee/ *n.* (*pl.* **-ties**) **1** property of things that is measurable. **2** amount; number. **3** specified or considerable portion or number or amount. **4** [in *pl.*] large amounts or numbers (*quantities of food*). **5** *Math.* value, component, etc., that may be expressed in numbers.

■ **2** extent, volume; sum, total; weight, measure. **3** see BULK *n.* 1a, AMOUNT *n.* 1. **4** see LOT *n.* 1.

quan•tum /kwóntəm/ *n.* (*pl.* **quan•ta** /-tə/) **1** *Physics* discrete quantity of radiant energy. **2** required or allowed amount. □ **quantum jump** (or **leap**) **1** sudden large increase or advance. **2** *Physics* abrupt transition in an atom or molecule from one quantum state to another. **quantum mechanics** (or **theory**) *Physics* system or theory using the assumption that energy exists in discrete units.

quar•an•tine /kwárənteen, kwór–/ • *n.* **1** isolation imposed on persons or animals to prevent infection or contagion. **2** period of this. • *v.tr.* put in quarantine.

quark /kwawrk, kwaark/ *n.* *Physics* any of several postulated components of elementary particles.

quar•rel /kwáwrəl, kwór-/ • *n.* **1** usu. verbal contention or altercation. **2** occasion of complaint or dispute. • *v.intr.* **1** find fault. **2** dispute; break off friendly relations. □□ **quar′rel•er** *n.*

  ■ *n.* **1** dispute, argument, disagreement, debate, controversy, difference (of opinion), falling out. **2** objection, grudge, *colloq.* gripe. • *v.* **1** see OBJECT *v.*, OPPOSE 1, 2. **2** argue, disagree, altercate, have an altercation, differ, wrangle.

SYNONYM STUDY: quarrel

ALTERCATION, DISPUTE, FEUD, ROW, SPAT, SQUABBLE, WRANGLE. Family feuds come in a variety of shapes and sizes. A husband and his wife may have a **quarrel**, which suggests a heated verbal argument, with hostility that may persist even after it is over (*it took them almost a week to patch up their quarrel*). Siblings tend to have **squabbles**, which are childlike disputes over trivial matters, although they are by no means confined to childhood (*frequent squabbles over who would pick up the check*). A **spat** is also a petty *quarrel*, but unlike *squabble*, it suggests an angry outburst followed by a quick ending without hard feelings (*another spat in an otherwise loving relationship*). A **row** is more serious, involving noisy quarreling and the potential for physical violence (*a row that woke the neighbors*). Neighbors are more likely to have an **altercation**, which is usually confined to verbal blows but may involve or threaten physical ones (*an altercation over the location of the fence*). A **dispute** is also a verbal argument, but one that is carried on over an extended period of time (*an ongoing dispute over who was responsible for taking out the garbage*). Two families who have been enemies for a long time are probably involved in a **feud**, which suggests a bitter *quarrel* that lasts for years or even generations (*the feud between the Hatfields and the McCoys*). There is no dignity at all in being involved in a **wrangle**, which is an angry, noisy, and often futile *dispute* in which both parties are unwilling to listen to the other's point of view.

---

quar•rel•some /kwáwrəlsəm, kwór-/ *adj.* given to quarreling. □□ **quar′rel•some•ly** *adv.* **quar′rel•some•ness** *n.*

  ■ argumentative, querulous, contrary, combative, antagonistic, pugnacious; irascible, cross, choleric.

quar•ry[1] /kwáwree, kwór-/ • *n.* (*pl.* -**ries**) place from which stone, etc., may be extracted. • *v.tr.* (**-ries, -ried**) extract (stone) from a quarry.

quar•ry[2] /kwáwree, kwór-/ *n.* (*pl.* -**ries**) **1** object of pursuit by a bird of prey, hunters, etc. **2** intended victim or prey.

  ■ game, prize, target.

quart /kwawrt/ *n.* **1** liquid measure equal to a quarter of a gallon; two pints (.95 liter). **2** -

unit of dry measure, equivalent to one thirty-second of a bushel (1.1 liter).

quar•ter /kwáwrtər/ • *n.* **1** each of four equal parts into which a thing is or might be divided. **2** period of three months. **3 a** 25 cents. **b** coin of this denomination. **4** district or section. **5** source of supply (*help from any quarter*). **6** [in *pl.*] **a** lodgings; abode. **b** *Mil.* living accommodation of troops, etc. **7** mercy offered or granted to an enemy in battle, etc., on condition of surrender. • *v.tr.* **1** divide into quarters. **2 a** put (troops, etc.) into quarters. **b** station or lodge in a specified place.

  ■ *n.* **4** area, region, zone, division, territory, neighborhood. **5** place, location, point, spot, area; direction. **6 a** living quarters, accommodation(s), rooms, residence, habitation, domicile, home, house. **b** billet, barracks, cantonment. **7** compassion, mercifulness, clemency, leniency, forgiveness, favor, humanity, pity. • *v.* **2** billet, accommodate, house, board, shelter, put up; post.

quar•ter•back /kwáwrtərbak/ *Football n.* player who directs offensive play.

quar•ter•deck /kwáwrtərdek/ *n.* part of a ship's upper deck near the stern, usu. reserved for officers.

quar•ter•fi•nal /kwáwrtərfín′l/ *Sports n.* match or round immediately preceding a semifinal.

quar•ter•ly /kwáwrtərlee/ • *adj.* produced, payable, or occurring once every quarter of a year. • *adv.* once every quarter of a year. • *n.* (*pl.* **-lies**) quarterly journal.

quar•ter•mas•ter /kwáwrtərmastər/ *n.* **1** army officer in charge of quartering, rations, etc. **2** naval petty officer in charge of steering, signals, etc.

quar•tet /kwawrtét/ *n.* **1** *Mus.* **a** composition for four performers. **b** the performers. **2** any group of four.

quar•to /kwáwrtō/ *n.* (*pl.* -**tos**) *Printing* **1** size given by folding a (usu. specified) sheet of paper twice. **2** book consisting of sheets folded in this way. ¶Abbr.: **4to.**

quartz /kwawrts/ *n.* mineral form of silica that crystallizes as hexagonal prisms.

qua•sar /kwáyzaar, -zər, -saar, -sər/ *n.* *Astron.* starlike celestial object having a spectrum with a large red shift.

quash /kwosh/ *v.tr.* **1** annul; reject as not valid, esp. by a legal procedure. **2** suppress; crush (a rebellion, etc.).

  ■ **1** nullify, void, declare *or* render null and void, invalidate, revoke, set aside, rescind, cancel. **2** subdue, quell, put down, squelch, stamp on, repress, overthrow.

quasi- /kwáyzī, kwáazee/ *comb. form* **1** seemingly; not really (*quasi-scientific*). **2** almost (*quasi-independent*).

  ■ **1** pseudo-; see also *apparently* (APPARENT). **2** partly, to some extent; virtually; see also ALMOST.

qua•ter•na•ry /kwótərneree, kwətórnəree/ • *adj.* **1** having four parts. **2** (**Quaternary**) *Geol.* of the most recent period in the Cenozoic era. • *n.* (**Quaternary**) *Geol.* this period.

quat•rain /kwótrayn/ *n.* stanza of four lines.

qua•ver /kwáyvər/ • v. **1** intr. (esp. of a voice or musical sound) vibrate; shake; tremble. **2** tr. sing or say with a quavering voice. • n. **1** trill in singing. **2** tremble in speech. □□ **qua'ver•ing•ly** adv. **qua'ver•y** adj.

■ v. **1** quiver, shiver, waver, shudder, oscillate, flutter. • n. **2** trembling, quiver, tremor, shaking, vibration.

quay /kee, kay/ n. solid, stationary, artificial landing place for loading and unloading ships. □□ **quay'age** n.

quea•sy /kwéezee/ adj. (**–si•er, –si•est**) **1 a** (of a person) feeling nausea. **b** (of a person's stomach) easily upset; weak of digestion. **2** (of the conscience, etc.) overscrupulous; tender. □□ **quea'si•ly** adv. **quea'si•ness** n.

■ **1 a** sick, nauseous, nauseated, ill, bilious, queer.

Quech•ua /kéchwə, –waa/ n. **1** member of a central Peruvian native people. **2** S. American native language widely spoken in Peru and neighboring countries. □□ **Quech'uan** adj.

queen /kween/ n. **1** (as a title usu. **Queen**) female sovereign. **2** (in full **queen consort**) king's wife. **3** woman, country, or thing preeminent of its kind (tennis queen). **4** fertile female among ants, bees, etc. **5** most powerful piece in chess. **6** playing card with a picture of a queen. □ **queen bee 1** fertile female in a hive. **2** chief or controlling woman in an organization or social group. □□ **queen'less** adj. **queen'like** adj.

■ **1** monarch, ruler; empress. **3** star; ideal, epitome, paragon, nonpareil.

queen•ly /kwéenlee/ adj. (**queen•li•er, queen•li•est**) **1** fit for or appropriate to a queen. **2** majestic. □□ **queen'li•ness** n.

queer /kweer/ • adj. **1** strange; odd; eccentric. **2** derog. sl. homosexual. • n. derog. sl. homosexual. • v.tr. sl. spoil; put out of order. □□ **queer'ish** adj. **queer'ly** adv. **queer'ness** n.

■ adj. **1** peculiar, funny, curious, uncommon, unconventional, unorthodox, atypical, singular, exceptional, anomalous, extraordinary, unusual, bizarre. • v. ruin, bungle, mess up, botch, muff, wreck, make a mess of, colloq. make a hash of, muck up, fluff, sl. blow.

quell /kwel/ v.tr. **1** crush or put down (a rebellion, etc.). **2** suppress (fear, anger, etc.). □□ **quell'er** n. [also in comb.].

■ **1** suppress, repress, subdue, quash, overcome, squelch, overwhelm, defeat. **2** restrain, control, hold in check; moderate, mollify, soothe; pacify, tranquilize, compose.

quench /kwench/ v.tr. **1** satisfy (thirst) by drinking. **2** extinguish (a fire or light, etc.). **3** cool, esp. with water. □□ **quench'a•ble** adj. **quench'er** n. **quench'less** adj.

■ **1** slake, sate, satiate, allay, appease, assuage, gratify. **2** put out, douse, smother, snuff out.

quer•u•lous /kwérələs, kwéryə–/ adj. complaining; peevish. □□ **quer'u•lous•ly** adv. **quer'u•lous•ness** n.

■ critical, hypercritical, finicky, finical, fussy, overparticular; petulant, testy, carping, touchy, irritable.

que•ry /kweéree/ • n. (pl. **–ries**) **1** question. **2** question mark. • v.tr. (**–ries, –ried**) **1** ask or inquire. **2** call (a thing) in question.

■ n. **1** inquiry; doubt, uncertainty, reservation, problem.

quest /kwest/ n. search or the act of seeking. □□ **quest'er** n. **quest'ing•ly** adv.

■ pursuit, exploration, expedition, voyage (of discovery); chase, hunt.

ques•tion /kwéschən/ • n. **1** sentence worded or expressed so as to seek information. **2** doubt or dispute about a matter. **3** matter to be discussed or decided or voted on. **4** problem requiring an answer or solution. • v.tr. **1** ask questions of; interrogate. **2** throw doubt upon; raise objections to. □ **call in** (or **into**) **question** make a matter of dispute; query. **in question** that is being discussed or referred to. **out of the question** too impracticable, etc., to be worth discussing; impossible. **question mark** punctuation mark (?) indicating a question. □□ **ques'tion•er** n. **ques'tion•ing•ly** adv. **ques'tion•less** adj.

■ n. **2** query, demur, objection; see also DOUBT n. 1. **3** issue, point, concern; see also MATTER n. 7. **4** difficulty, doubt, uncertainty, query. • v. **1** query, interview, sound out, quiz, pump, grill. **2** call in or into question, doubt, query, mistrust, distrust, cast doubt upon. □ **call in** (or **into**) **question** question, doubt, challenge, dispute. **in question 1** under discussion or consideration; at issue. **out of the question** unthinkable, absurd, ridiculous, preposterous, inconceivable, beyond consideration.

ques•tion•a•ble /kwéschənəbəl/ adj. doubtful as regards truth, quality, honesty, wisdom, etc. See synonym study at DOUBTFUL. □□ **ques'tion•a•ble•ness** n. **ques'tion•a•bly** adv.

■ dubious, debatable, moot, disputable, borderline, ambiguous, suspect, shady; see also QUEER adj. 1.

ques•tion•naire /kwéschənáir/ n. written series of questions, esp. for statistical study.

queue /kyoo/ • n. **1** line or sequence of persons, vehicles, etc., awaiting their turn. **2** pigtail or braid of hair. • v.intr. (**queues, queued, queu•ing** or **queue•ing**) esp. Brit. line (up).

■ n. **1** row, file, column, string, train, cortège, procession, chain; tail. **2** ponytail, horse tail; plait. • v. get in or into line, form a line or queue.

quib•ble /kwibəl/ • n. **1** petty objection; trivial point of criticism. **2** play on words; pun. **3** evasion; insubstantial argument which relies on an ambiguity, etc. • v.intr. use quibbles. □□ **quib'bler** n. **quib'bling** adj. **quib'bling•ly** adv.

■ n. **1** cavil, nicety, quiddity; trifle. **2** see PUN n. **3** sophism, quip, equivocation. • v. equivocate, split hairs, evade the issue, be evasive, palter.

quiche /keesh/ n. unsweetened custard pie with a savory filling.

quick /kwik/ • adj. **1** taking only a short time.

2 arriving after a short time; prompt. **3** with only a short interval (*in quick succession*). **4** lively; intelligent; alert. **5** (of a temper) easily roused. **6** *archaic* alive (*the quick and the dead*). • *adv.* quickly. • *n.* **1** soft flesh below the nails, or the skin, or a sore. **2** seat of feeling or emotion (*cut to the quick*). □ - **quick-tempered** quick to lose one's temper; irascible. □□ **quick′ly** *adv.* **quick′ness** *n.*

■ *adj.* **1** rapid, fast, speedy, swift; expeditious, express, high-speed. **2** immediate, timely, instantaneous; see also PROMPT *adj.* 1. **4** vivacious, animated; bright, adept, adroit, dexterous, perceptive, perspicacious, keen, sharp, acute; agile, nimble. **5** short, excitable, touchy, testy, impatient. **6** see ALIVE 3. • *adv.* see *quickly* below. • *n.* **2** see CORE *n.* 2a. □ **quick-tempered** excitable, impulsive, temperamental, hot-tempered, waspish, choleric, splenetic. □□ **quickly** quick, rapidly, swiftly, speedily; fast; posthaste, *tout de suite*, on the double; instantly, promptly, hastily, at once.

quick•en /kwíkən/ *v.* **1** *tr. & intr.* make or become quicker; accelerate. **2** *tr.* give life or vigor to; rouse.

■ **1** hasten, speed up, expedite, hurry, rush. **2** stimulate, arouse, kindle, spark, invigorate, excite, animate.

SYNONYM STUDY: quicken

ANIMATE, ENLIVEN, INVIGORATE, STIMULATE, VITALIZE. While all of these verbs mean to make alive or lively, **quicken** suggests the rousing or renewal of life, especially life that has been inert or suspended (*She felt the baby quicken during her second trimester of pregnancy*). **Animate** means to impart life, motion, or activity to something that previously lacked such a quality (*a discussion animated by the presence of so many young people*). **Stimulate** means to goad into activity from a state of inertia, inactivity, or lethargy (*the professor's constant questions stimulated her students to do more research*), while **enliven** refers to a *stimulating* influence that brightens or makes lively what was previously dull, depressed, or torpid (*A sudden change in the weather enlivened the group's activities*). **Invigorate** and **vitalize** both mean to fill with vigor or energy, but the former refers to physical energy (*invigorated by the climb up the mountain*), while the latter implies that energy has been imparted in a nonphysical sense (*to vitalize an otherwise dull meeting*).

---

quick•ie /kwíkee/ *n. colloq.* thing done or made quickly.
quick•lime /kwíklīm/ *n.* = LIME¹ *n.* 1.
quick•sand /kwíksand/ *n.* **1** loose wet sand that sucks in anything placed or falling into it. **2** bed of this.
quick•sil•ver /kwíksilvər/ *n.* mercury.
quick-wit•ted /kwíkwítid/ *adj.* quick to grasp a situation, make repartee, etc. □□ **quick′-wit′ted•ness** *n.*

■ acute, sharp, clever, smart, nimble-witted, alert, keen.

quid pro quo /kwíd prō kwố/ *n.* **1** thing given as compensation. **2** return made (for a gift, favor, etc.).

■ recompense, payment, requital.

qui•es•cent /kwiésənt, kwee-/ *adj.* **1** inert. **2** silent; dormant. See synonym study at LATENT. □□ **qui•es′cence** *n.* **qui•es′cent•ly** *adv.*

qui•et /kwíət/ • *adj.* (**qui•et•er, qui•et•est**) **1** with little or no sound or motion. **2** of gentle or peaceful disposition. **3** unobtrusive; not overt. **4** undisturbed; uninterrupted. **5** enjoyed in quiet (*a quiet smoke*). **6** tranquil; not anxious or remorseful. • *n.* **1** silence; stillness. **2** undisturbed state; tranquillity. • *v.* **1** *tr.* soothe; make quiet. **2** *intr.* [often foll. by *down*] become quiet or calm. □□ **qui′et•ly** *adv.* **qui′et•ness** *n.*

■ *adj.* **1** silent, soundless, noiseless, hushed; still, smooth, motionless; inactive. **2** see GENTLE *adj.* 1. **3** see UNOBTRUSIVE, PRIVATE *adj.* 2. **4** see PEACEFUL 1. **6** serene, peaceful, unperturbed, calm, placid. ■ *n.* **1** still, soundlessness, noiselessness, hush, quietness, quietude. **2** calmness, serenity, peace; see also CALM *n.* 1. ■ *v.* see CALM *v.* □□ **quietly** silently, soundlessly, noiselessly, inaudibly; peacefully, calmly, serenely; unobtrusively.

qui•e•tude /kwí-itōōd, -tyōōd/ *n.* state of quiet.

qui•e•tus /kwī-eétəs/ *n.* **1** something which quiets or represses. **2** discharge or release from life; death; final riddance.

quill /kwil/ *n.* **1** large feather in a wing or tail. **2** hollow stem of this. **3** (in full **quill pen**) pen made of a quill. **4** [usu. in *pl.*] spine of a porcupine.

quilt /kwilt/ • *n.* bedcovering made of padding enclosed between layers of cloth, etc., and kept in place by patterned stitching. • *v.tr.* make quilts. □□ **quilt′er** *n.* **quilt′ing** *n.*

■ *n.* duvet; bedspread, eiderdown, counterpane.

quince /kwins/ *n.* **1** hard acidic pear-shaped fruit used chiefly in preserves. **2** tree bearing this fruit.

qui•nine /kwínīn, kwin-/ *n.* **1** alkaloid found esp. in cinchona bark. **2** bitter drug containing this, used as a tonic and to reduce fever.

quin•tes•sence /kwintésəns/ *n.* purest and most perfect, or most typical, form, manifestation, or embodiment of some quality or class. □□ **quin•tes•sen′tial** /kwíntisénshəl/ *adj.* **quin•tes•sen′tial•ly** *adv.*

■ epitome, embodiment, incarnation, personification, model, prototype, exemplar, ideal, beau ideal.

quin•tet /kwintét/ *n.* **1** *Mus.* **a** composition for five. **b** the performers. **2** any group of five.

quin•tu•ple /kwintōōpəl, -tyōō-, -túpəl, kwíntəpəl/ • *adj.* fivefold; consisting of five parts. • *n.* fivefold number or amount. • *v.* multiply by five.

quin•tu•plet /kwintúplit, -tōō-, -tyōō-, kwíntə-/ *n.* each of five children born at one birth.

quip /kwip/ • *n.* clever saying; epigram.

• *v.intr.* (**quipped, quip•ping**) make quips. ◻◻ **quip′ster** *n.*

■ *n.* bon mot, witticism, sally, aphorism; jest, joke, gag, *colloq.* one-liner, crack. • *v.* see JOKE *v.* 1.

quire /kwīr/ *n.* 25 (also 24) sheets of paper.

quirk /kwərk/ *n.* **1** peculiarity of behavior. **2** trick of fate; freak. ◻◻ **quirk′ish** *adj.* **quirk′y** *adj.* (**quirk•i•er, quirk•i•est**). **quirk′i•ly** *adv.* **quirk′i•ness** *n.*

■ **1** caprice, vagary, whim, idiosyncrasy, oddity. **2** twist; oddity, aberration; fluke, accident.

quis•ling /kwízling/ *n.* traitorous collaborator.

quit /kwit/ *v.tr.* (**quit•ting**; *past* and *past part.* **quit** or **quit•ted**) **1** [also *absol.*] give up; let go; abandon (a task, etc.). **2** cease; stop (*quit grumbling*). **3** leave or depart from.

■ **1** resign, relinquish, leave, renounce, retire from, withdraw from, forsake. **2** discontinue, leave off, *literary* desist from. **3** go (away) from, get away from, flee; see also LEAVE[1] *v.* 1b, 3.

quite /kwīt/ *adv.* **1** completely; entirely. **2** rather; to some extent. ◻ **quite a few** *colloq.* a fairly large number of.

■ **1** very, totally, utterly, fully, wholly, absolutely. **2** fairly, moderately, somewhat, relatively, to some *or* a certain extent ◻ **quite a few** quite a lot, a fair number *or* few, a good number *or* few.

quits /kwits/ *predic.adj.* on even terms by retaliation or repayment (*then we'll be quits*). ◻ **call it quits** agree not to proceed further in a quarrel, etc.

quit•ter /kwítər/ *n.* **1** person who gives up easily. **2** shirker.

quiv•er[1] /kwívər/ • *v.intr.* tremble or vibrate with a slight rapid motion. • *n.* quivering motion or sound. ◻◻ **quiv′er•ing•ly** *adv.* **quiv′er•y** *adj.*

■ *v.* shake, shiver, quaver, shudder, tremor, oscillate. • *n.* tremble, quaver, shudder, spasm, shake.

quiv•er[2] /kwívər/ *n.* case for holding arrows.

quix•ot•ic /kwiksótik/ *adj.* **1** extravagantly and romantically chivalrous. **2** visionary; pursuing lofty but unattainable ideals. **3** *derog.* foolhardy. ◻◻ **quix•ot′i•cal•ly** *adv.*

■ **1** romantic, gallant; sentimental. **2** idealistic, utopian, impractical, unpractical, unrealistic, romantic. **3** absurd, mad, reckless, wild, preposterous.

quiz /kwiz/ • *n.* (*pl.* **quiz•zes**) **1** quick or informal test. **2** (also **quiz show**) test of knowledge, esp. as a form of entertainment. • *v.tr.* (**quizzed, quiz•zing**) examine by questioning.

■ *n.* examination, exam. • *v.* question, interrogate, ask, interview, ask the opinion of, grill.

quiz•zi•cal /kwízikəl/ *adj.* **1** expressing or done with mild or amused perplexity. **2** strange; comical. ◻◻ **quiz′zi•cal•ly** *adv.*

■ **1** perplexed, bemused, puzzled, inquiring, questioning. **2** curious, queer; see ODD *adj.* 1.

quod erat demonstrandum /kwod érət démənstrándəm, érààt démōnstraàndōōm/ (esp. at the conclusion of a proof, etc.) which was the thing to be proved. ¶Abbr.: **QED**.

quod vide /kwod veéday, vídee/ which see (in cross-references, etc.). ¶Abbr.: **q.v.**

quoin /koyn, kwoin/ *n.* **1** external angle of a building. **2** cornerstone. **3** wedge.

quoit /koyt, kwoit/ *n.* **1** ring of rope or metal, etc., thrown to encircle a peg. **2** [in *pl.*] game using these.

quon•dam /kwóndəm, –dam/ *predic.adj.* that once was, sometime; former.

Quon•set hut /kwónsit/ *n. propr.* prefabricated metal building with a semicylindrical corrugated roof.

quo•rum /kwáwrəm/ *n.* minimum number of members that must be present to constitute a valid meeting.

quo•ta /kwótə/ *n.* **1** share that an individual person, group, or company is bound to contribute to or entitled to receive from a total. **2** number of goods, people etc., stipulated or permitted.

■ **1** apportionment, portion, allotment, allocation, allowance, ration, part, proportion, percentage.

quot•a•ble /kwótəbəl/ *adj.* worth, or suitable for, quoting.

quo•ta•tion /kwōtáyshən/ *n.* **1** act or an instance of quoting or being quoted. **2** passage or remark quoted. **3** *Stock Exch.* amount stated as the current price of stocks or commodities. **4** contractor's estimate. ◻ **quotation mark** raised marks, single (' ') or double (" "), used to mark a quoted passage, for emphasis, etc.

■ **2** citation, reference, extract, excerpt, selection, sound bite, *colloq.* quote. **3** market price, charge, rate, cost, *colloq.* quote; value.

quote /kwōt/ • *v.tr.* **1** cite or appeal to (an author, book, etc.) in confirmation of some view. **2** repeat or copy out a passage from. **3** [as *int.*] (in dictation, reading aloud, etc.) indicate the presence of opening quotation marks (*he said, quote, "I shall stay"*). **4** state the price of. • *n. colloq.* **1** passage quoted. **2** price quoted. **3** [usu. in *pl.*] quotation marks.

■ *v.* **1** refer to. • *n.* **1** see QUOTATION 2. **2** see QUOTATION 3.

quoth /kwōth/ *v.tr.* [only in 1st and 3rd person] *archaic* said.

quo•tid•i•an /kwotídeeən/ *adj.* **1** daily; of every day. **2** commonplace; trivial.

■ **1** diurnal, everyday, *Physiol.* circadian.

quo•tient /kwóshənt/ *n.* result of a division.

q.v. *abbr.* quod vide.

qwerty /kwə́rtee/ *attrib.adj.* denoting the standard keyboard on English-language typewriters, word processors, etc.

Rr

R¹ /aar/ *n.* (also **r**) (*pl.* **Rs** or **R's; r's**) eighteenth letter of the alphabet.

R² *abbr.* **1** (also **R.**) river. **2** *Chess* rook. **3** (of movies) classified as prohibited to children under age 17 unless accompanied by an adult.

r. *abbr.* (also **r**) **1** right. **2** recto. **3** run(s). **4** radius.

Ra *symb. Chem.* radium.

rab•bet /rábit/ • *n.* step-shaped channel, etc., cut into wood, etc., usu. to receive the edge or tongue of another piece. • *v.tr.* **1** join or fix with a rabbet. **2** make a rabbet in.

rab•bi /rábī/ *n.* (*pl.* **rabbis**) **1** Jewish scholar or teacher, esp. of the law. **2** Jewish religious leader. □□ **rab•bin•i•cal** /rəbínikəl/ *adj.*

rab•bit /rábit/ *n.* **1** long-eared, burrowing, plant-eating mammal related to the hare. **2** its fur. □ **rabbit ears** television antenna consisting of two movable rods, usu. on top of the set. **rabbit punch** chopping blow to the nape of the neck.

rab•ble /rábəl/ *n.* **1** disorderly crowd; mob. **2** contemptible or inferior set of people. □ **rabble-rouser** person who stirs up the rabble or a crowd.

  ■ **1** horde, throng, swarm, gang. **2** vermin, dregs (of society). □ **rabble-rouser** agitator, demagogue, inciter, troublemaker, insurrectionist.

ra•bid /rábid/ *adj.* **1** furious; violent. **2** fanatical. **3** affected with rabies; mad. □□ **ra•bid•i•ty** *n.* **ra'bid•ly** *adv.* **ra'bid•ness** *n.*

  ■ **1** raging; see also VIOLENT 2a. **2** unreasonable, extreme, headstrong. **3** crazed, frenzied, maniacal, berserk.

ra•bies /ráybeez/ *n.* contagious and fatal viral disease, esp. of dogs, cats, raccoons, etc., transmissible through saliva to humans; hydrophobia.

rac•coon /rakóŏn/ *n.* **1** N. American nocturnal mammal with a bushy, ringed tail and masklike band across the eyes. **2** its fur.

race¹ /rays/ • *n.* **1** contest of speed between runners, horses, vehicles, etc. **2** contest between persons to be first to achieve something. **3 a** strong sea or river current. **b** channel with a swift current. **4** each of two grooved rings in a ball bearing or roller bearing. • *v.* **1** *intr.* take part in a race. **2** *tr.* have a race with. **3** *tr.* cause to race. **4 a** *intr.* go at full or excessive speed. **b** *tr.* cause to do this. □□ **rac'er** *n.*

  ■ *n.* **1** competition. **3 b** sluice, flume, course. • *v.* **4 a** hurry, hasten, dash, fly, rush, *colloq.* tear, rip, zip, step on it. **b** rush, push, press, drive; urge, egg.

race² /rays/ *n.* **1** each of the major divisions of humankind, having distinct physical characteristics. **2** fact or concept of division into races. **3** genus, species, breed, or variety of animals or plants. □ **race relations** relations between members of different races, usu. in the same country.

  ■ **1** stock, tribe, nation, people, folk, clan, family.

race•horse /ráys-hors/ *n.* horse bred or kept for racing.

ra•ceme /rayseém, rə–/ *n. Bot.* flower cluster with separate flowers attached by short stalks at equal distances along the stem.

race•track /ráystrak/ *n.* track for horse, automobile, etc., racing.

ra•cial /ráyshəl/ *adj.* **1** of or concerning race. **2** on the grounds of or connected with difference in race (*racial discrimination*). □□ **ra'cial•ly** *adv.*

  ■ **1** ethnic, genetic, ethnological, tribal; national.

rac•ism /ráysizəm/ *n.* **1** belief in the superiority of a particular race; prejudice based on this. **2** antagonism toward other races. □□ **rac'ist** *n. & adj.*

  ■ **1** apartheid, bigotry. □□ **racist** (*adj.*) chauvinistic, bigoted.

rack¹ /rak/ • *n.* **1** framework usu. with rails, bars, etc., for holding things. **2** cogged or toothed bar or rail engaging with a wheel or pinion, etc. **3** *hist.* instrument of torture used to stretch the victim's limbs. • *v.tr.* **1** (of disease or pain) inflict suffering on. **2** place in or on a rack. □ **on the rack** in distress or under strain. **rack one's brains** make a great mental effort. **rack up** accumulate or achieve (a score, etc.).

  ■ *n.* **1** support; stand, scaffold. • *v.* **1** torment, torture, agonize, persecute.

rack² /rak/ *n.* destruction (esp. *rack and ruin*).

rack³ /rak/ *n.* cut of lamb, etc., including the front ribs.

rack•et¹ /rákit/ *n.* (also **rac'quet**) hand-held implement with a round or oval frame strung with catgut, nylon, etc., used in tennis, squash, etc.

rack•et² /rákit/ *n.* **1** uproar; din. **2** *sl.* scheme for obtaining money, etc., by fraudulent and often violent means. **3** *colloq.* line of business.

  ■ **1** noise, disturbance, commotion. **2** trick, dodge, swindle, ruse, *sl.* con, scam. **3** profession, occupation, trade, job.

rack•e•teer /rákiteér/ *n.* person who operates an illegal business, as gambling, extortion, etc. □□ **rack•et•eer'ing** *n.*

  ■ gangster, *sl.* mobster; see also *swindler* (SWINDLE).

ra•con•teur /rákontőr/ *n.* (*fem.* **ra•con•teuse** /–tőz/) teller of interesting anecdotes.

  ■ storyteller, taleteller; chronicler, narrator.

rac•quet var. of RACKET¹.

rac•quet•ball /rákətbawl/ *n.* racket game played on a four-walled court.

rac•y /ráysee/ *adj.* (**rac•i•er, rac•i•est**) **1** lively and vigorous in style. **2** risqué; suggestive. **3** of distinctive quality (*racy flavor*). □□ **rac'i•ly** *adv.* **rac'i•ness** *n.*

  ■ **1** fresh, bouncy, vivacious, dynamic.

2 bawdy, lusty, salacious, obscene, off-color. **3** sharp, spicy, piquant, pungent, savory, zesty, tangy.

rad[1] /rad/ *n.* unit of absorbed dose of ionizing radiation.

rad[2] /rad/ • *n. sl.* political radical. • *adj. sl.* wonderful; terrific.

ra•dar /ráydaar/ *n.* system for detecting the direction, range, or presence of objects by reflection of transmitted radio waves (acronym of *radio detecting and ranging*).

ra•di•al /ráydeeəl/ • *adj.* **1** of or in rays. **2 a** arranged like rays or radii. **b** having spokes or radiating lines. **3** (of a tire) having fabric layers laid radially at right angles to the center of the tread. • *n.* radial tire. □□ **ra′di•al•ly** *adv.*

ra•di•ant /ráydeeənt/ *adj.* **1** emitting rays of light or energy. **2** (of eyes or looks) beaming with joy, hope, or love. **3** (of beauty) splendid or dazzling. □ **radiant heat** heat transmitted by radiation. □□ **ra′di•ance** *n.* **ra′di•ant•ly** *adv.*

■ **1** shining, bright, brilliant, luminous, gleaming, glowing. **2** happy, ecstatic, delighted, joyful, elated. **3** see *dazzling* (DAZZLE). □□ **radiance** brightness, brilliance, sparkle, glow; warmth, happiness.

ra•di•ate /ráydeeayt/ *v.* **1** *intr.* **a** emit rays of light, heat, etc. **b** (of light or heat) be emitted in rays. **2** *tr.* emit (light, heat, or sound) from a center. **3** *tr.* transmit or demonstrate (joy, etc.) **4** *intr. & tr.* diverge or cause to diverge or spread from a center.

■ **1 a** shine, gleam, glow, glisten, sparkle. **2** emanate, shed, send out, give off or out. **3** disperse, spread. **4** fan out, spread out, extend, unfurl.

ra•di•a•tion /ráydeeáyshən/ *n.* **1** radiating; being radiated. **2** *Physics* **a** emission of energy as electromagnetic waves or as moving particles. **b** energy thus transmitted. **3** (in full **ra•di•a′tion ther′a•py**) treatment of disease using radiation, such as X rays or ultraviolet light. □□ **ra•di•a′tion•al** *adj.* **ra•di•a′tion•al•ly** *adv.*

■ **1** emanation, diffusion, dispersal.

ra•di•a•tor /ráydeeaytər/ *n.* **1** person or thing that radiates. **2** device through which hot water or steam circulates to heat a room, etc. **3** engine-cooling device in a motor vehicle, etc.

rad•i•cal /rádikəl/ • *adj.* **1** primary; fundamental. **2** far-reaching; thorough. **3** representing or holding extreme political views; revolutionary. **4** *Math.* of the root of a number or quantity. • *n.* **1** person holding radical views or belonging to a radical party. **2** *Chem.* a atom with one or more unpaired electrons. **b** element or atom normally forming part of a compound and remaining unaltered during ordinary chemical changes. **3** *Math.* quantity forming or expressed as the root of another. □ **radical sign** √ , ³√ , etc., indicating the square, cube, etc., root of the number following. □□ **rad′i•cal•ism** *n.* **rad′i•cal•ly** *adv.*

■ *adj.* **1** basic, elementary, inherent, essential. **2** complete, entire, total; drastic. **3** fa-

---

685   **rad ~ raffia**

natical, militant; left-wing. • *n.* **1** extremist, fanatic, zealot; leftist.

ra•dic•chi•o /rədeékeeō/ *n.* (*pl.* **–os**) variety of chicory with dark red leaves.

rad•i•ces *pl.* of RADIX.

ra•di•i *pl.* of RADIUS.

ra•di•o /ráydeeō/ • *n.* (*pl.* **–os**) **1** (often *attrib.*) **a** transmission and reception of sound messages, etc., by electromagnetic waves of radio frequency. **b** apparatus for this. **2** sound broadcasting (*prefers the radio*). • *v.* (**–oed**) **1** *tr.* **a** send (a message) by radio. **b** send a message to (a person) by radio. **2** *intr.* communicate or broadcast by radio. □ **radio frequency** frequency band of telecommunication, ranging from 10^4 to 10^{11} or 10^{12} Hz. **radio star** small star, etc., emitting strong radio waves. **radio telescope** directional aerial system for collecting and analyzing radiation in the radio-frequency range from stars, etc.

radio- /ráydeeō/ *comb. form* **1** denoting radio or broadcasting. **2** connected with radioactivity. **3** connected with rays or radiation.

ra•di•o•ac•tive /ráydeeō-áktiv/ *adj.* of or exhibiting radioactivity. □□ **ra•di•o•ac′tive•ly** *adv.*

ra•di•o•ac•tiv•i•ty /ráydeeō-aktivitee/ *n.* spontaneous disintegration of atomic nuclei, with emission of radiation or particles.

ra•di•ol•o•gy /ráydeeóləjee/ *n.* the study of X rays and other high-energy radiation, esp. as used in medicine. □□ **ra•di•o•log•ic** /-deeəlójik/ *adj.* **ra•di•o•log′i•cal** *adj.* **ra•di•ol′o•gist** *n.*

ra•di•om•e•ter /ráydeeómitər/ *n.* instrument for measuring the intensity or force of radiation. □□ **ra•di•om′e•try** *n.*

ra•di•os•co•py /ráydeeóskopee/ *n.* examination by X rays, etc., of objects opaque to light. □□ **ra•di•o•scop′ic** /-deeəskópik/ *adj.*

ra•di•o•ther•a•py /ráydeeōthérapee/ *n.* radiation therapy (see RADIATION). □□ **ra•di•o•ther′a•peu′tic** /-pyóothik/ *adj.* **ra•di•o•ther′a•pist** *n.*

rad•ish /rádish/ *n.* **1** plant with a fleshy pungent root. **2** this root, eaten esp. raw.

ra•di•um /ráydeeəm/ *n. Chem.* radioactive metallic element orig. obtained from pitchblende, etc. ¶Symb.: **Ra**

ra•di•us /ráydeeəs/ *n.* (*pl.* **ra•di•i** /-dee-ī/ or **ra•di•us•es**) **1** *Math.* **a** straight line from the center to the circumference of a circle or sphere. **b** length of this. **2** distance from a center (*within a radius of 20 miles*). **3 a** thicker and shorter of the two bones in the human forearm. **b** corresponding bone in a vertebrate's foreleg or a bird's wing.

ra•dix /ráydiks/ *n.* (*pl.* **rad•i•ces** /-diseez/ or **ra•dix•es**) *Math.* number or symbol used as the basis of a numeration scale (e.g., ten in the decimal system).

ra•don /ráydon/ *n. Chem.* gaseous radioactive inert element arising from the disintegration of radium. ¶Symb.: **Rn**

RAF *abbr.* (in the UK) Royal Air Force.

raf•fi•a /ráfeeə/ *n.* **1** palm tree native to Madagascar, having very long leaves. **2** fiber from its leaves used for weaving, tying plants, etc.

raf•fish /ráfish/ *adj.* **1** disreputable; rakish. **2** tawdry. □□ **raf′fish•ly** *adv.* **raf′fish•ness** *n.*

raf•fle /ráfəl/ • *n.* fund-raising lottery with prizes. • *v.tr.* [often foll. by *off*] sell by means of a raffle.

■ *n.* draw.

raft[1] /raft/ • *n.* **1** flat floating structure of logs or other materials for conveying persons or things. **2** lifeboat or small (often inflatable) boat. • *v.* **1** *tr.* cross (water) on a raft. **2** *intr.* [often foll. by *across*] work a raft (across water, etc.).

raft[2] /raft/ *n. colloq.* large collection.

raf•ter /ráftər/ *n.* each of the sloping beams forming the framework of a roof.

rag[1] /rag/ *n.* **1** torn, frayed, or worn piece of woven material. **2** [in *pl.*] old or worn clothes. **3** *derog.* newspaper. □ **in rags 1** much torn. **2** in old torn clothes. **rag bag 1** bag for scraps of fabric, etc. **2** miscellaneous collection. **rag doll** stuffed doll made of cloth. **rag paper** made from cotton or linen pulp. **rags to riches** poverty to affluence.

■ **3** periodical, journal, daily, tabloid. □ **in rags 1** see *tattered* (TATTER).

rag[2] /rag/ *v.tr.* (**rag•ged, rag•ging**) **1** tease; play rough jokes on. **2** scold; reprove severely.

■ **1** taunt, make fun of, poke fun at, pull a person's leg, *colloq.* kid; see also TORMENT *v.* 2. **2** see SCOLD *v.* 1.

rag[3] /rag/ *n. Mus.* ragtime composition or tune.

rag•a•muf•fin /rágəmufin/ *n.* child in ragged dirty clothes.

rage /rayj/ • *n.* **1** fierce or violent anger. **2** fit of this. **3** violent action of a natural force. **4** temporary enthusiasm; fad. • *v.intr.* **1** be full of anger. **2** speak furiously or madly. **3** (of wind, battle, fever, etc.) be violent; be at its height; continue unchecked. □ **all the rage** popular; fashionable.

■ *n.* **1** fury, *literary* wrath, ire; see also ANGER *n.* **2** frenzy, hysterics, tantrum. **3** see FORCE *n.* 1. **4** fashion, craze, trend. • *v.* **1**, **2** rant, rave, foam at the mouth, seethe.

rag•ged /rágid/ *adj.* **1** torn; frayed. **2** in ragged clothes. **3** with a broken or jagged outline or surface. **4** lacking finish, smoothness, or uniformity. **5** exhausted (esp. *be run ragged*). □ **run ragged** exhaust; wear out. □□ **rag′ged•ly** *adv.* **rag′ged•ness** *n.* **rag′ged•y** *adj.*

■ **1, 2** shaggy, tattered; shabby, seedy. **3** uneven, irregular, jagged. **4** see ROUGH[1] *adj.* 7. □ **run ragged** see TIRE 1.

rag•lan /ráglən/ *n.* [often *attrib.*] overcoat without shoulder seams, the sleeves running up to the neck.

ra•gout /ragóo/ *n.* meat stewed with vegetables and highly seasoned.

rag•pick•er /rágpikər/ *n.* collector and seller of rags.

rag•tag /rágtag/ *adj.* motley.

rag•time /rágtīm/ *n.* form of highly syncopated early jazz, esp. for the piano.

rag•weed /rágweed/ *n.* any of various plants with allergenic pollen.

rah /raa/ *int. colloq.* expression of encouragement, approval, etc., esp. to a team or a player.

raid /rayd/ • *n.* rapid surprise attack, esp.: **1** in warfare. **2** to commit a crime or do harm. **3** by police, etc., to arrest suspects or seize illicit goods. • *v.tr.* make a raid on. □□ **raid′er** *n.*

■ *n.* **1–3** incursion, invasion, sortie, *colloq.* blitz; *colloq.* bust. • *v.* invade, assault, storm; pillage, ransack.

rail[1] /rayl/ • *n.* **1** level or sloping bar or series of bars: **a** used to hang things on. **b** as the top of a banister. **c** forming part of a fence or barrier. **2** steel bar or continuous line of bars laid on the ground, usu. as a railroad. **3** [often *attrib.*] railroad (*send it by rail*). • *v.tr.* **1** furnish with a rail or rails. **2** enclose with rails.

■ *n.* **1** rod; railing. **3** (*by rail*) by train.

rail[2] /rayl/ *v.intr.* complain using abusive language; rant. □□ **rail′er** *n.* **rail′ing** *n. & adj.*

■ revile, attack, berate, scold, criticize, *colloq.* go on at.

rail[3] /rayl/ *n.* wading bird often inhabiting marshes.

rail•ing /ráyling/ *n.* **1** fence or barrier made of rails. **2** material for these.

rail•ler•y /ráyləree/ *n.* (*pl.* **–ies**) good-humored ridicule.

■ banter, badinage, repartee, joking, jesting, *colloq.* kidding.

rail•road /ráylrōd/ • *n.* **1** track or set of tracks of steel rails upon which trains run. **2** such a system. • *v.tr.* rush or coerce (a person or thing) (*railroaded me into going*).

■ *v.* force, urge, push, pressure, bully.

rail•way /ráylway/ *n.* = RAILROAD.

rai•ment /ráymənt/ *n. archaic* clothing.

rain /rayn/ • *n.* **1 a** condensed atmospheric moisture falling in drops. **b** fall of such drops. **2** [in *pl.*] **a** rainfalls. **b** [prec. by *the*] rainy season. **3** rainlike falling of liquid, particles, objects, etc. • *v.* **1** *intr.* [prec. by *it* as subject] rain falls (*if it rains*). **2 a** *intr.* fall like rain. **b** *tr.* [prec. by *it* as subject] send in large quantities (*it rained blood*). **3** *tr.* lavishly bestow. **4** *intr.* (of the sky, etc.) send down rain. □ **rain check 1** ticket given for later use when an outdoor event is canceled by rain. **2** promise that an offer will be maintained though deferred. **rain date** date on which an event postponed by rain is held. **rain forest** luxuriant tropical forest with heavy rainfall. **rain gauge** instrument measuring rainfall. **rain out** [esp. in *passive*] cause (an event, etc.) to be canceled because of rain. □□ **rain′y** *adj.* (**rain•i•er, rain•i•est**).

■ *n.* **1** precipitation, drizzle. • *v.* **1** pour (down), drizzle. **2 a** trickle, shower, sprinkle; come down. **3** hail. □□ **rainy** see WET *adj.* 2.

rain•bow /ráynbō/ • *n.* arch of colors formed by reflection, refraction, and dispersion of the sun's rays in rain or mist. • *adj.* many-colored. □ **rainbow trout** large Pacific coast trout of N. America.

rain•coat /ráynkōt/ *n.* waterproof or water-resistant coat.

rain•drop /ráyndrop/ *n.* single drop of rain.

rain•fall /ráynfawl/ *n.* **1** fall of rain. **2** quantity of rain falling within a given area in a given time.

■ **1** shower, cloudburst, downpour, rainstorm, deluge, monsoon; see also PRECIPITATION 3a. **2** precipitation.

rain•proof /ráynproof/ *adj.* resistant to rainwater.

rain•storm /ráynstawrm/ *n.* storm with heavy rain.

rain•water /ráynwawtər, -wotər/ *n.* water obtained from collected rain, as distinct from a well, etc.

raise /rayz/ • *v.tr.* **1** put or take into a higher position. **2** cause to rise, stand, or be vertical. **3** increase the amount, value, or strength of. **4** construct or build. **5** levy, collect, or bring together (*raise money*). **6** cause to be heard or considered (*raise an objection*). **7** bring into being; arouse (*raise hopes*). **8** bring up; educate. **9** breed; grow (*raise vegetables*). **10** [foll. by *to*] *Math.* multiply a quantity to a specified power. **11** *Cards* bet more than (another player). **12** remove (a barrier, etc.). ■ **1** *Cards* increase in a stake or bid. **2** increase in salary. □ **raise the devil** *colloq.* make a disturbance. **raise from the dead** restore to life. **raise hell** *colloq.* make a disturbance.

■ *v.* **1** lift (up), elevate; hoist, pull up. **3** advance, *colloq.* jack (up). **4** erect, put up. **5** assemble, gather, round up, recruit. **6** introduce, bring up, put forward, present, suggest, set forth. **7** put or set in motion, prompt, initiate, inspire, give rise to; stimulate, *colloq.* boost. **8** nurture, rear; parent; see also EDUCATE 1. **9** farm, cultivate. **12** lift. • *n.* **2** see INCREASE *n.* 3. □ **raise from the dead** revive, resurrect, recall. **raise hell** raise Cain.

rai•sin /ráyzən/ *n.* partially dried grape. □□ **rai'sin•y** *adj.*

rai•son d'ê•tre /ráyzoN détrə/ *n.* (*pl.* **raisons d'être** *pronunc.* same) purpose or reason for a thing's existence.

■ function, role.

raj /raaj/ *n.* [prec. by *the*] British sovereignty in India.

ra•ja /ráajə/ *n.* (also **ra'jah**) *hist.* **1** Indian king or prince. **2** petty dignitary or noble in India.

rake¹ /rayk/ • *n.* implement consisting of a pole with a toothed crossbar at the end, used for gathering loose material, smoothing soil, etc. • *v.* **1** *tr.* collect or make smooth with or as with a rake. **2** *intr.* use a rake. **3** *tr.* direct gunfire along (a line) from end to end. **4** *tr.* scratch or scrape. □ **rake in** *colloq.* amass (profits, etc.). **rake up** (or **over**) revive the unwelcome memory of. □□ **rak'er** *n.*

■ *v.* **1** gather; scrape up, pick up; see also SMOOTH *v.* 1. **4** grate, graze, rasp. □ **rake in** pull in, accumulate. **rake up** resurrect, bring up, recall; dredge up, dig up.

rake² /rayk/ *n.* dissolute man of fashion.

■ roué, lothario, womanizer, playboy, ladies' man, lady-killer, Don Juan, Casanova, *sl.* wolf; man about town; see also DANDY *n.*

rake³ /rayk/ • *v.* set or be set at a sloping angle. • *n.* raking position or build.

rak•ish /ráykish/ *adj.* dashing; jaunty. □□ **rak'ish•ly** *adv.* **rak'ish•ness** *n.*

■ dapper, debonair, chic, *colloq.* sharp.

rale /raal/ *n.* abnormal rattling sound from the lungs.

ral•ly /rálee/ • *v.* (**-lies, -lied**) **1** *tr. & intr.* bring or come together as support for or for action. **2** *tr.* revive (courage, etc.). **3** *intr.* recover after illness, etc.; revive. **4** *intr.* (of share prices, etc.) increase after a fall. • *n.* (*pl.* **-lies**) **1** rallying or being rallied. **2** mass meeting for a cause. **3** (in tennis, etc.) extended exchange of strokes. □□ **ral'li•er** *n.*

■ *v.* **1** round up, summon, gather; assemble, congregate. **3** improve, get better, recuperate, come to. • *n.* **1** see GATHERING. **2** convention, assembly.

RAM /ram/ *abbr.* *Computing* random-access memory; internally stored software or data that is directly accessible.

ram /ram/ • *n.* **1** male sheep. **2** (**the Ram**) zodiacal sign or constellation Aries. • *v.tr.* (**rammed, ram•ming**) **1** force or squeeze into place by pressure **2** beat or drive by heavy blows. **3** (of a ship, vehicle, etc.) strike violently; crash against. □ **ram home** stress forcefully (an argument, lesson, etc.).

■ *v.* **1** jam, cram, crowd, pack, compress, stuff. **2** pound, hammer. **3** butt, hit, collide with, dash against, slam into. □ **ram home** see STRESS *v.* 1.

Ram•a•dan /ráamədan, ramədáan/ *n.* ninth month of the Muslim year, with strict fasting from sunrise to sunset.

ram•ble /rámbəl/ • *v.intr.* **1** walk for pleasure. **2** talk or write disconnectedly. • *n.* walk taken for pleasure. □□ **ram'bling** *adj.*

■ *v.* **1** amble, stroll, saunter, *sl.* mosey. **2** wander, digress, get off the point; rattle on, *colloq.* go on (and on). • *n.* stroll, hike. □□ **rambling** roving, wandering, nomadic; disjointed, disorganized, aimless, confused, muddled.

ram•bler /rámblər/ *n.* **1** person who rambles. **2** straggling or climbing rose.

ram•bunc•tious /rambúngkshəs/ *adj. colloq.* **1** uncontrollably exuberant. **2** unruly. □□ **ram•bunc'tious•ly** *adv.* **ram•bunc'tious•ness** *n.*

ram•e•kin /rámikin/ *n.* small dish for baking and serving an individual portion of food.

ram•i•fi•ca•tion /rámifikáyshən/ *n.* **1** subdivision of a complex structure or process. **2** consequence.

■ **1** branch, extension, offshoot. **2** result, effect, upshot, implication.

ramp /ramp/ *n.* **1** slope, esp. joining two levels of ground, floor, etc. **2** movable stairs for entering or leaving an aircraft.

■ **1** grade, gradient, incline; rise; dip.

ram•page • *v.intr.* /rámpáyj/ **1** rush wildly or violently about. **2** rage; storm. • *n.* /rámpayj/

wild or violent behavior. □ **on the rampage** rampaging. □□ **ram'pag•er** n.

■ v. **1** charge; see also TEAR[1] v. **5**. **2** rant, rave, run amok; see also RAGE v. ● n. recklessness, frenzy, fury. □ **on the rampage** berserk, out of control.

ram•pant /rámpənt/ adj. **1** unchecked; flourishing excessively. **2** violent or fanatical. □□ **ram'pan•cy** n. **ram'pant•ly** adv.

■ **1** unrestrained, uncontrolled, unbridled, abounding, rife, widespread, prevalent; indiscriminate. **2** wild, frenzied; see also FURIOUS 3.

ram•part /rámpaart/ n. **1** defensive wall with a broad top and usu. a stone parapet. **2** walkway on top of such a wall.

■ **1** fortification, bulwark, barricade.

ram•rod /rámrod/ n. **1** rod for ramming down the charge of a muzzle-loading firearm. **2** thing that is very straight or rigid.

ram•shack•le /rámshakəl/ adj. tumbledown; rickety.

■ dilapidated, crumbling, broken-down, decrepit, flimsy, shaky, unstable, run-down.

ran past of RUN.

ranch /ranch/ ● n. farm where animals are bred, such as cattle, sheep, etc. **2** (in full **ranch house**) single-story or split-level house. ● v.intr. farm on a ranch. □□ **ranch'er** n.

ran•cid /ránsid/ adj. smelling or tasting like rank, stale fat. □□ **ran•cid'i•ty** n.

■ stinking, fetid; rotten, putrid.

ran•cor /rángkər/ n. inveterate bitterness; malignant hate. □□ **ran•cor'ous** adj. **ran'cor•ous•ly** adv. See synonym study at VINDICTIVE.

■ spitefulness, resentment, hostility, malevolence, animosity, spite, malice. □□ **rancor•ous** hateful, malicious, venomous, vindictive.

rand /rand, raant/ n. chief monetary unit of South Africa.

R & B abbr. rhythm and blues.

R & D abbr. research and development.

ran•dom /rándəm/ adj. made, done, etc., without method or conscious choice. □ **at random** without aim or purpose. **random-access** Computing (of a memory or file) having all data directly accessible, so it need not be read sequentially. □□ **ran'dom•ly** adv. **ran'dom•ness** n.

■ haphazard, chance, accidental, incidental, hit-or-miss. □ **at random** haphazardly, by chance, casually.

R and R abbr. **1** rescue and resuscitation. **2** rest and recreation (or recuperation or relaxation).

ran•dy /rándee/ adj. (**ran•di•er, ran•di•est**) lustful. □□ **ran'di•ly** adv. **ran'di•ness** n.

rang past of RING[2].

range /raynj/ ● n. **1 a** region between limits of variation; extent; scope. **b** such limits. **2** distance attainable by a gun or projectile. **3** row, series, etc., esp. of mountains. **4** open or enclosed area with targets for shooting. **5** cooking stove. **6** nonstop distance that can be covered by a vehicle, aircraft, etc. **7** distance between a camera and the subject to be

photographed. **8** large area of open land for grazing or hunting. ● v. **1** lie spread out; extend. **2** tr. [usu. in passive or refl.] place or arrange in a row or ranks or in a specified situation, order, etc. (trees ranged in ascending order of height). **3** intr. rove; wander. □ **range finder** instrument for estimating the distance of an object, esp. one to be shot at or photographed.

■ n. **1** sweep, reach, limit, span, area, stretch, sphere, orbit. **3** tier, rank, line, file, string, chain. ● v. **1** vary, fluctuate; stretch, run, go. **2** line up, align; organize, group. **3** see WANDER v. 1.

SYNONYM STUDY: **range**

COMPASS, GAMUT, LATITUDE, REACH, SCOPE, SWEEP. To say that someone has a wide **range** of interests implies that these interests are not only extensive but varied. Another way of expressing the same idea would be to say that the person's interests run the **gamut** from television quiz shows to nuclear physics, a word that suggests a graduated scale or series running from one extreme to another. **Compass** implies a range of knowledge or activity that falls within very definite limits reminiscent of a circumference (within the compass of her abilities), while **sweep** suggests more of an arc-shaped range of motion or activity (the sweep of the searchlight) or a continuous extent or stretch (a broad sweep of lawn). **Latitude** and scope both emphasize the idea of freedom, although scope implies great freedom within prescribed limits (the scope of the investigation), while latitude means freedom from such limits (she was granted more latitude than usual in interviewing the disaster victims). Even someone who has a wide range of interests and a broad scope of authority, however, will sooner or later come up against something that is beyond his or her **reach**, which suggests the furthest limit of effectiveness or influence.

---

rang•er /ráynjər/ n. **1** keeper of a national park or forest. **2** member of a body of armed men. **3** wanderer.

rang•y /ráynjee/ adj. (**rang•i•er, rang•i•est**) tall and slim.

■ see LANKY.

ra•ni /raanee/ n. (also **ra'nee**) hist. raja's wife or widow; Hindu queen.

rank[1] /rangk/ ● n. **1 a** position in a hierarchy. **b** high social position. **c** place in a scale. **2** row or line. **3** row of soldiers drawn up abreast. **4** order; array. ● v. **1** intr. have rank or place (ranks next to the chief of staff). **2** tr. classify; grade. □ **close ranks** maintain solidarity. **pull rank** use one's superior rank to gain advantage, coerce another, etc. **rank and file** ordinary undistinguished people. **the ranks** the common soldiers, i.e., privates and corporals.

■ n. **1 a** place, level, echelon, grade. **b** standing; nobility, (blue) blood; eminence. **2** string, file, column, tier. ● v. **1** count, arrange. **2** rate, categorize.

rank[2] /rangk/ adj. **1** too luxuriant; choked with or apt to produce weeds or excessive foliage. **2 a** foul-smelling. **b** loathsome; corrupt. **3** flagrant; complete. □□ **rank'ness** *n.*

■ **1** lush, flourishing, profuse, dense, fertile. **2 a** offensive, disgusting, vile, rancid, stinking, reeking, fetid, noxious, rotten, putrid. **b** low, base; indecent, shocking, lurid, outrageous. **3** gross, downright, utter, sheer, absolute, out-and-out, blatant.

ran•kle /rángkəl/ *v.intr.* (of envy, disappointment, etc., or their cause) cause persistent annoyance or resentment.

■ grate, hurt, chafe, smolder, fester; (*rankle with*) vex, plague, nettle, torment, get (to), upset.

ran•sack /ránsak/ *v.tr.* **1** pillage or plunder (a house, country, etc.). **2** thoroughly search. □□ **ran'sack•er** *n.*

■ **1** rob, sack, loot, strip, ravage. **2** examine, go through *or* over, comb, rummage *or* rifle through, scour, scrutinize, turn inside out.

ran•som /ránsəm/ • *n.* **1** money demanded or paid for the release of a captive. **2** liberation of a captive in return for this. • *v.tr.* buy the freedom or restoration of; redeem.

■ *n.* **1** payment, payout, *sl.* payoff. **2** release, freedom; rescue. • *v.* rescue, release, deliver, free, liberate.

rant /rant/ • *v.* speak loudly, bombastically, violently, or theatrically. • *n.* piece of ranting.

■ *v.* declaim, pontificate, trumpet, preach; (*rant and*) rave, bellow, rage. • *n.* tirade, diatribe; rhetoric.

rap /rap/ • *n.* **1** smart, slight blow. **2** sharp tapping sound. **3** *sl.* blame; punishment. **4 a** rhythmic monologue recited to music. **b** (in full **rap' mu•sic**) style of pop music with words recited rather than sung. • *v.* (**rapped, rap•ping**) **1** *tr.* strike smartly. **2** *intr.* knock; make a sharp tapping sound. **3** *tr.* criticize adversely. **4** *intr. sl.* talk. □ **beat the rap** escape punishment. **take the rap** suffer the consequences, esp. for a crime, etc., committed by another. □□ **rap'per** *n.*

■ *n.* **1** hit, crack, stroke. **3** see BLAME *n.* 2. • *v.* **1** see STRIKE *v.* 1. **2** hammer. **3** see REBUKE *v.* **4** chat, *colloq.* gab, *sl.* chew the fat. □ **beat the rap** get off, *sl.* walk.

ra•pa•cious /rəpáyshəs/ *adj.* grasping, predatory. See synonym study at GREEDY. □□ **ra•pa'cious•ly** *adv.* **ra•pa'cious•ness** *n.* **ra•pac•i•ty** /rəpásitee/ *n.*

■ greedy, covetous, avaricious, preying, ravenous, extortionate. □□ **rapacity** greed, cupidity, avarice.

rape[1] /rayp/ • *n.* **1** act of forcing a person to have sexual intercourse. **2** violent assault; forcible interference. • *v.tr.* commit rape on. □□ **rap'ist** *n.*

■ *n.* **1** ravishment, sexual assault. **2** violation, ransacking, defilement. • *v.* violate.

rape[2] /rayp/ *n.* plant grown as food for livestock and for its seed, from which oil is made.

rap•id /rápid/ • *adj.* **1** quick; swift; brief. **2** (of a slope) descending steeply. • *n.* [usu. in *pl.*] steep descent in a riverbed, with a swift current. □ **rapid eye movement** type of jerky movement of the eyes during dreaming. **rapid-fire** [*attrib.*] fired, asked, etc., in quick succession. □□ **ra•pid'i•ty** *n.* **rap'id•ly** *adv.* **rap'id•ness** *n.*

■ *adj.* **1** fast, speedy, expeditious, prompt; hurried, hasty, sudden. □□ **rapidity** quickness, dispatch. **rapidly** *colloq.* in a flash, like a bat out of hell, like (greased) lightning, in (less than) no time.

ra•pi•er /ráypeeər, ráypyər/ *n.* light slender sword for thrusting.

rap•ine /rápin, –īn/ *n. rhet.* plundering; robbery.

rap•port /rapáwr/ *n.* relationship or communication, esp. when useful and harmonious.

■ empathy, affinity, bond, (mutual) understanding.

rap•proche•ment /rapròshmón/ *n.* resumption of harmonious relations, esp. between nations.

rap•scal•lion /rapskályən/ *n.* rascal; scamp; rogue.

rapt /rapt/ *adj.* **1** fully absorbed or intent. **2** carried away with joyous feeling or lofty thought. □□ **rapt'ly** *adv.* **rapt'ness** *n.*

■ **1** enraptured, entranced, fascinated, engrossed, captivated. **2** elated, overjoyed, ecstatic; uplifted, elevated.

rap•tor /ráptər/ *n.* bird of prey, e.g., an owl, falcon, or eagle. □□ **rap•to•ri•al** / táwreeəl/ *adj.*

rap•ture /rápchər/ *n.* **1** ecstatic delight. **2** [in *pl.*] great pleasure or enthusiasm or the expression of it. □□ **rap'tur•ous** *adj.* **rap'tur•ous•ly** *adv.*

■ **1** ecstasy, joy, pleasure, elation, thrill, euphoria. □□ **rapturous** joyous, euphoric.

SYNONYM STUDY: rapture
BLISS, ECSTASY, EUPHORIA, TRANSPORT. Happiness is one thing; **bliss** is another, suggesting a state of utter joy and contentment that verges on the joy of heaven (*marital bliss*). **Ecstasy** is even more extreme, describing a trancelike state in which one loses consciousness of one's surroundings (*the ecstasy of young love*). Although it originally referred to being raised or lifted out of oneself by divine power, nowadays **rapture** is used in much the same sense as *ecstasy* to describe an elevated sensation of *bliss* (*to listen in speechless rapture to her favorite soprano*). **Transport** applies to any powerful emotion by which one is carried away (*a transport of delight*) When happiness is carried to an extreme or crosses over into mania, it is called **euphoria**. **Euphoria** may outwardly resemble *ecstasy* or *rapture*; but upon closer examination, it is usually found to be exaggerated and out of proportion (*the euphoria that came over him whenever he touched alcohol*).

rare[1] /rair/ *adj.* (**rar•er, rar•est**) **1** seldom done or found or occurring; uncommon; unusual. **2** exceptionally good (*had a rare time*). **3** of less than the usual density (*rare atmosphere of the mountain*). □ **rare earth** lanthanide element. □□ **rare'ness** *n.*

■ **1** exceptional, out of the ordinary, extraordinary, atypical; scarce, infrequent, few and far between, sparse; unparalleled, unique, singular.

rare² /rair/ adj. (**rarer, rarest**) (of meat) cooked lightly, so as to be still red inside.
■ underdone, undercooked.

rare•bit /ráirbit/ n. = Welsh rabbit.

rar•e•fy /ráirifī/ v. (**–fies, –fied**) (esp. as **rarefied** adj.) make or become less dense or solid (*rarefied air*). □□ **rar•e•fac•tion** /-fákshən/ n. **rar•e•fac′tive** adj.
■ (**rarefied**) thin, diluted, insubstantial, tenuous.

rare•ly /ráirlee/ adv. **1** seldom; not often. **2** exceptionally.
■ **1** infrequently, hardly (ever), almost never, once in a blue moon.

rar•ing /ráiring/ adj. [foll. by to + infin.] colloq. enthusiastic; eager (*raring to go*).

rar•i•ty /ráiritee/ n. (pl. **–ties**) **1** rareness. **2** uncommon thing.
■ **1** unusualness, uncommonness, uniqueness. **2** curiosity, oddity, collector's item, find; rare bird, rara avis.

ras•cal /ráskəl/ n. dishonest or mischievous person. □□ **ras′cal•ly** adj.
■ imp, devil, scalawag, rogue, knave, rapscallion, colloq. vagabond, scamp.

rash¹ /rash/ adj. reckless; impetuous; hasty. □□ **rash′ly** adv. **rash′ness** n. See synonym study at TEMERITY.
■ impulsive, unthinking, careless, wild, madcap, harebrained.

rash² /rash/ n. **1** eruption of the skin in spots or patches. **2** sudden widespread appearance.
■ **1** see INFLAMMATION 2. **2** outbreak, wave, flood, epidemic.

rash•er /ráshər/ n. thin slice of bacon or ham.

rasp /rasp/ • n. **1** coarse kind of file. **2** rough grating sound. • v. **1** tr. scrape with or as with a rasp. **2 a** intr. make a grating sound. **b** tr. say gratingly. □□ **rasp′ing•ly** adv. **rasp′y** adj.
■ n. **1** grater. **2** scratch, grinding. • v. **1** abrade, grate, file. **3** croak; see also JAR² v. 1, 2.

rasp•ber•ry /rázberee/ n. (pl. **–ries**) **1 a** bramble having stoneless, usu. red berries. **b** this berry. **2** colloq. sound made with the lips expressing dislike, derision, or disapproval.

Ras•ta•far•i•an /ráàstəfaàreeən, rástəfáir–/ • n. member of a sect regarding Ethiopian emperor Haile Selassie (d. 1975, entitled *Ras Tafari*) as God. • adj. of or relating to this sect. □□ **Ras•ta•far′i•an•ism** n.

rat /rat/ • n. **1 a** rodent like a large mouse. **b** any similar rodent. **2** colloq. deserter; turncoat. **3** colloq. unpleasant person. **4** [in pl.] sl. exclamation of contempt, annoyance, etc. • v.intr. (**rat•ted, rat•ting**) colloq. [foll. by on] **1** betray; let down. **2** inform on. □ **rat race** hectic work routine; struggle to succeed.

ra•ta•tou•ille /rátətoŏ-ee, raàtaa–/ n. dish made of stewed eggplant, onions, tomatoes, zucchini, and peppers.

ratch•et /ráchit/ n. **1** set of teeth on the edge of a bar or wheel with a catch permitting motion in one direction only. **2** (in full **ratchet wheel**) wheel with a rim so toothed.

rate¹ /rayt/ • n. **1** numerical proportion expressed in units (*rate of 50 miles per hour*) or as the basis of calculating (*rate of taxation*). **2** fixed or appropriate charge, cost, or value (*postal rates*). **3** pace of movement or change. **4** class or rank (*first-rate*). • v. **1** tr. **a** estimate the worth or value of. **b** assign a value to. **2** tr. consider; regard as. **3** intr. [foll. by as] rank or be rated. **4** tr. be worthy of; deserve. □ **at any rate** in any case; whatever happens. **at this rate** if this example is typical.
■ n. **1** scale; measure, level. **2** price, fee, tariff. **3** gait, speed, colloq. clip. **4** grade, place, position. • v. **1 a** evaluate, judge, assess, appraise. **2** see CONSIDER 6. **3** count, stand, be placed. **4** merit, be entitled to. □ **at any rate** in any event, regardless, notwithstanding.

rate² /rayt/ v.tr. scold angrily.
■ berate, reprimand, rebuke, reproach, colloq. chew out.

rath•er /ráthər/ adv. **1** by preference (*would rather stay*). **2** as a more likely alternative (*is stupid rather than honest*). **3** more precisely (*a book, or rather, a pamphlet*). **4** slightly; to some extent (*rather drunk*).
■ **1** preferably, sooner. **4** quite, somewhat, fairly, colloq. sort of, kind of, pretty.

rat•i•fy /rátifī/ v.tr. (**–fies, –fied**) confirm or accept by formal consent, signature, etc. See synonym study at APPROVE. □□ **rat•i•fi•ca′tion** n. **rat′i•fi•er** n.
■ approve, sanction, endorse, certify, affirm.

rat•ing /ráyting/ n. **1** placing in a rank or class. **2** estimated standing of a person as regards credit, etc. **3** rank on a ship, in the military, etc. **4** relative popularity of a broadcast program as determined by the estimated size of the audience.

ra•ti•o /ráysheeō, ráyshō/ n. (pl. **–os**) quantitative relation between two comparable magnitudes (*a ratio of three to two*).
■ proportion, correlation.

ra•tion /ráshən, ráy–/ • n. **1** official allowance of food, clothing, etc., in a time of shortage. **2** [usu. in pl.] fixed daily allowance of food, esp. in the armed forces. **3** [in pl.] provisions. • v.tr. **1** limit (persons or provisions) to a fixed ration. **2** distribute (food, etc.) in fixed quantities.
■ n. **1** share, quota, allotment, allocation, portion, apportionment. **3** (*rations*) supplies. • v. **1** budget, restrict. **2** (*ration out*) allot, dole (out), dispense.

ra•tion•al /ráshənəl/ adj. **1** of or based on reason. **2** sensible; sane. **3** endowed with reason. **4** Math. (of a quantity or ratio) expressible as a ratio of whole numbers. See synonym study at SENSIBLE. □□ **ra•tion•al•i•ty** /-nálitee/ n. **ra′tion•al•ly** adv.
■ **1** logical, practical, pragmatic. **2** reasonable, sound, clear-headed, sober, moderate. **3** discriminating, thinking, enlightened.

ra•tion•ale /ráshənál/ n. fundamental reason; logical basis.
■ ground(s), principle, theory, thinking.

ra•tion•al•ism /ráshənəlizəm/ n. practice of treating reason as the basis of knowledge and belief. □□ **ra′tion•al•ist** n.

ra•tion•al•ize /ráshənəlīz/ v. offer a rational but specious explanation of (one's) behavior or attitude). □□ **ra•tion•al•i•za′tion** n.

■ make excuses for, account for, justify; reason out.

rat•line /rátlin/ n. (also **rat′lin**) [usu. in pl.] any of the small lines fastened across a ship's shrouds like ladder rungs.

rat•tan /rətán/ n. East Indian climbing palm with long, thin, jointed pliable stems, used for furniture, etc.

rat•tle /rát′l/ • v. **1 a** intr. give out a rapid succession of short, sharp, hard sounds. **b** tr. make (a window, etc.) do this. **2** intr. move with a rattling noise. **3 a** tr. [usu. foll. by off] say or recite rapidly **b** intr. [usu. foll. by on] talk in a lively thoughtless way. **4** tr. colloq. disconcert; alarm. • n. **1** rattling sound. **2** device or plaything made to rattle. **3** set of horny rings in a rattlesnake's tail. □ **rattle the saber** threaten war.

■ v. **1 a** clatter, jangle. **1b, 2** shake, vibrate, jiggle; jounce. **3 a** (rattle off) reel off, run through. **b** chatter, babble, jabber, gibber, prattle, ramble. **4** unnerve, disturb, upset, agitate, fluster. • n. **1** clatter, crackle; rale. **2** noisemaker.

rat•tle•snake /rát′lsnayk/ n. poisonous American snake with rattling horny rings in its tail.

rat•tling /rátling/ • adj. **1** that rattles. **2** brisk; vigorous (rattling pace). • adv. remarkably (rattling good story).

rat•ty /rátee/ adj. (**rat•ti•er, rat•ti•est**) colloq. shabby; seedy. □□ **rat′ti•ness** n.

■ straggly, unkempt; see also SEEDY 3, NASTY 1.

rau•cous /ráwkəs/ adj. harsh sounding; loud and hoarse. □□ **rau′cous•ly** adv. **rau′cous•ness** n.

■ rasping, grating, dissonant, noisy.

raun•chy /ráwnchee/ adj. (**raun•chi•er, raun•chi•est**) colloq. **1** coarse; earthy. **2** grubby. □□ **raun′chi•ly** adv. **raun′chi•ness** n.

rav•age /rávij/ • v. devastate; plunder. • n. **1** the act or an instance of ravaging; devastation; damage. **2** [usu. in pl.] destructive effect (the ravages of winter).

■ v. lay waste, ruin, destroy, demolish, wreak havoc on; pillage, ransack. • n. **1** destruction, ruin. **2** (ravages) see DEPREDATION.

SYNONYM STUDY: ravage

DESPOIL, DEVASTATE, PILLAGE, PLUNDER, SACK, WASTE. **Ravage, pillage, sack,** and **plunder** are all verbs associated with the actions of a conquering army during wartime. *Ravage* implies violent destruction, usually in a series of raids or invasions over an extended period of time (the invading forces ravaged the countryside). *Plunder* refers to the roving of soldiers through recently conquered territory in search of money and goods (they plundered the city and left its inhabitants destitute), while *pillage* describes the act of stripping a conquered city or people of valuables (their churches pillaged by ruthless invaders). *Sack* is even more extreme than *pillage*, implying not only the seizure of all valuables, but total de-

struction as well (The army sacked every village along the coast). *Despoil* also entails the stripping of valuables, but with less violence than *sack*; it is more common in nonmilitary contexts, where it describes a heedless or inadvertent destruction (forests despoiled by logging companies). *Devastate* emphasizes the ruin and desolation that follow *ravaging*, whether it happens to buildings, forests, or crops (fields of corn devastated by flooding). *Waste* comes close in meaning to *devastate*, but it suggests a less violent or more gradual destruction (a region of the country wasted by years of drought and periodic fires).

rave /rayv/ • v. intr. **1** talk wildly or furiously in or as in delirium. **2** speak with rapturous admiration (about). • n. [usu. attrib.] colloq. highly enthusiastic review of a film, play, etc.

■ v. **1** rant (and rave), rage, storm; fume, seethe, **2** (rave about) praise, applaud, go into raptures about, be thrilled about. • n. tribute, testimonial, plaudit, accolade.

rav•el /rávəl/ v. **1** tr. & intr. entangle or become entangled or knotted. **2** tr. confuse or complicate (a question or problem). **3** tr. disentangle; separate into threads.

■ **1** see TANGLE v. 1. **2** see COMPLICATE 1. **3** see FREE v. 3.

ra•ven /ráyvən/ • n. large glossy blue-black crow with a hoarse cry. • adj. glossy black.

rav•en•ing /rávəning/ adj. voraciously seeking prey.

rav•en•ous /rávənəs/ adj. **1** very hungry. **2** voracious. **3** rapacious. □□ **rav′en•ous•ly** adv. **rav′en•ous•ness** n.

■ **1** famished, starving. **2** see VORACIOUS. **3** see RAPACIOUS.

ra•vine /rəveen/ n. deep narrow gorge. □□ **ra•vined′** adj.

■ canyon, pass, cleft, gully, valley, gulch, gap.

rav•ing /ráyving/ • n. [usu. in pl.] wild or delirious talk. • adj. **1** delirious; frenzied. **2** remarkable; intensive (a raving beauty). • adv. wildly (raving mad). □□ **rav′ing•ly** adv.

■ n. (ravings) ranting, blustering; delirium. • adj. **1** mad, insane, crazed, irrational, maniacal, frantic, hysterical, colloq. crazy. **2** rare, extraordinary, colloq. stunning. • adv. completely, totally, absolutely.

rav•i•o•li /ráveeólee/ n. small pasta envelopes containing cheese, ground meat, etc.

rav•ish /rávish/ v.tr. **1** rape (a woman). **2** enrapture. **3** carry off by force. □□ **rav′ish•er** n. **rav′ish•ment** n.

■ **1** see VIOLATE 4. **2** delight, captivate, enthrall, fascinate. **3** seize; see ABDUCT.

rav•ish•ing /rávishing/ adj. entrancing; delightful; very beautiful. □□ **rav′ish•ing•ly** adv.

■ dazzling, gorgeous, striking, radiant, colloq. stunning.

raw /raw/ adj. **1** uncooked. **2** in the natural state; not processed or manufactured. **3** inexperienced; untrained. **4 a** having the flesh exposed. **b** sensitive to the touch from being exposed. **5** (of the atmosphere, day, etc.)

chilly and damp. **6 a** crude; coarse. **b** brutal. □ **in the raw 1** in its natural state. **2** naked. **raw deal** harsh or unfair treatment. **raw material** that from which the process of manufacture makes products. **raw sienna** brownish-yellow earth used as a pigment. **raw umber** umber in its natural state, dark yellow in color. □□ **raw′ish** *adj.* **raw′ly** *adv.* **raw′ness** *n.*

■ **1** fresh. **2** untreated, unrefined, unfinished, crude. **3** new, unseasoned, immature, green. **4** unprotected; sore, tender, inflamed, painful. **5** cold, biting, bitter, *colloq.* nippy. **6 a** see CRUDE *adj.* 1b. **b** frank, candid, blunt. □ **in the raw 2** nude, *colloq.* in the buff, in the altogether, *joc.* in one's birthday suit.

raw•boned /ráwbōnd/ *adj.* gaunt and bony.

■ lean, gangling, skinny, scrawny, hollow-cheeked.

raw•hide /ráwhīd/ *n.* **1** untanned hide. **2** rope or whip of this.

ray[1] /ray/ *n.* **1** narrow beam of light from a small or distant source. **2** straight line in which radiation travels to a given point. **3** [in *pl.*] radiation of a specified type (*X rays*). **4** promising trace (*ray of hope*). **5** any of a set of radiating lines, parts, or things. □□ **rayed** *adj.*

■ **1** shaft, streak, gleam, flash. **4** glimmer, spark.

ray[2] /ray/ *n.* marine fish with a broad flat body and a long slender tail.

ray•on /ráyon/ *n.* textile fiber or fabric made from cellulose.

raze /rayz/ *v.tr.* completely destroy; tear down. See synonym study at DESTROY.

■ bring down, demolish, level, bulldoze.

ra•zor /ráyzər/ *n.* instrument with a sharp blade used in cutting hair, esp. from the skin. □ **razor's edge 1** keen edge. **2** critical situation. **razor wire** wire with sharpened projections, often coiled atop walls for security.

ra•zor•back /ráyzərbak/ *n.* wild hog with a sharp ridged back.

razz /raz/ *v.tr. sl.* tease; ridicule.

raz•zle-daz•zle /rázzldázzl/ *n. sl.* **1** glamorous excitement; bustle. **2** extravagant publicity.

■ **1** see GLITTER *n.* 2, FLURRY *n.* 3. **2** *sl.* (media) hype.

razz•ma•tazz /rázmətaz/ *n.* (also **raz•za•ma•tazz** /rázmə-/) *colloq.* **1** = RAZZLE-DAZZLE. **2** insincere actions; double-talk.

Rb *symb. Chem.* rubidium.

RC *abbr.* Roman Catholic.

RD *abbr.* Rural Delivery.

Rd. *abbr.* Road (in names).

RDA *abbr.* **1** recommended daily allowance. **2** recommended dietary allowance.

Re *symb. Chem.* rhenium.

re[1] /ray, ree/ *prep.* **1** in the matter of (as the first word in a heading). **2** *colloq.* about; concerning.

re[2] /ray/ *n. Mus.* **1** second note of a major scale. **2** the note D in the fixed-do system.

re- /ree, ri, re/ *prefix* **1** attachable to almost any verb or its derivative, meaning: **a** once more; afresh; anew (*readjust*). **b** back; with return to a previous state (*reassemble*). ¶A hyphen is sometimes used when the word begins with *e* (*re-enact*), or to distinguish the compound from a more familiar one-word form (*re-form* = form again). **2** (also **red-** before a vowel, as in *redolent*) in verbs and

re•ab•sorb′ *v.*	re•as•sign′ *v.*	re•es•tab′lish•ment *n.*	re•oc•cur′ *v.*
re•ac•cept′ *v.*	re•as•sign′ment *n.*	re•e•val′u•ate• *v.*	re•o′pen *v.*
re•ac•cus′tom *v.*	re•a•wak′en *v.*	re•ex•am′ine *v.*	re•or′ga•nize• *v.*
re•ac•quaint′ *v.*	re•bind′ *v.*	re•ex•am•i•na′tion *n.*	re•pop′u•late• *v.*
re•ac•quire *v.*	re•build′ *v.*	re•fo′cus *v.*	re•pro′cess *v.*
re•ad•apt′ *v.*	re•charge′ *v. & n.*	re•for′mat *v.*	re•pro′gram *v.*
re•ad•ap•ta′tion *n.*	re•charge′a•ble *adj.*	re•for′mu•late *v.*	re•pro•gram′ma•ble *adj.*
re•ad•dress′ *v.*	re•clas′si•fy *v.*	re•for•mu•la′tion *n.*	re•pub′lish *v.*
re•ad•just′ *v.*	re•clas•si•fi•ca′tion *n.*	re•fur′nish *v.*	re•read′ *v.*
re•ad•just′ment *n.*	re•com•mence′ *v.*	re•grow′ *v.*	re•re•cord′ *v.*
re•ad•mit′ *v.*	re•com•mence′ment *n.*	re•heat′ *v.*	re•re•lease′ *v.*
re•ad•mis′sion *n.*	re•con•nect′ *v.*	re•im•pose′ *v.*	re•route′ *v.*
re•a•dopt′ *v.*	re•con•nec′tion *n.*	re•in•fect′ *v.*	re•sched′ule *v.*
re•af•firm′ *v.*	re•con•vene′ *v.*	re•in•oc′u•late• *v.*	re•seal′ *v.*
re•af•fir•ma′tion *n.*	re•con•vert′ *v.*	re•in•sert′ *v.*	re•seal′a•ble *v.*
re•a•lign′ *v.*	re•con•ver′sion *v.*	re•in•ter′pret *v.*	re•sell′ *v.*
re•a•lign′ment *n.*	re•de•fine′ *v.*	re•in•ter•pre•ta′tion *n.*	re•set′tle *v.*
re•al′lo•cate• *v.*	re•dis•cov′er *v.*	re•in•vest′ *v.*	re•shape′ *v.*
re•al•lo•ca′tion *v.*	re•dis•trib′ute *v.*	re•in•vest′ment *n.*	re•state′ *v.*
re•ap•pear′ *v.*	re•dis•tri•bu′tion *n.*	re•is′sue *v. & n.*	re•stock′ *v.*
re•ap•pear′ance *n.*	re•draft′ *v.*	re•kin′dle *v.*	re•string′ *v.*
re•ap•ply′ *v.*	re•draw′ *v.*	re•learn′ *v.*	re•style′ *v.*
re•ap•pli•ca′tion *v.*	re•e•lect′ *v.*	re•light′ *v.*	re•tell′ *v.*
re•ap•point′ *v.*	re•e•lec′tion *n.*	re•load′ *v.*	re•type′ *v.*
re•ap•point′ment *n.*	re•em•bark′ *v.*	re•name′ *v.*	re•up•hol′ster *v.*
re•arm′ *v.*	re•e•merge′ *v.*	re•ne•go′ti•ate• *v.*	re•use′ *v. & n.*
re•ar′ma•ment *n.*	re•em′pha•size• *v.*	re•ne•go•ti•a′tion *n.*	re•vis′it *v.*
re•as•sem′ble *v.*	re•em•ploy′ *v.*	re•nom′i•nate• *v.*	re•vi′tal•ize• *v.*
re•as•sem′bly *n.*	re•em•ploy′ment *n.*	re•num′ber *v.*	re•wire′ *v.*
re•as•sess′ *v.*	re•en′ter *v.*	re•oc′cu•py *v.*	
re•as•sess′ment *n.*	re•es•tab′lish *v.*	re•oc•cu•pa′tion *n.*	

verbal derivatives denoting: **a** in return; mutually (*react*). **b** opposition (*repel*). **c** behind or after (*remain*). **d** retirement or secrecy (*recluse*). **e** off; away; down (*recede, repress*). **f** frequentative or intensive force (*redouble, refine*). **g** negative force (*recant*).

reach /reech/ • *v.* **1** *intr. & tr.* stretch out; extend. **2** *intr.* stretch out the hand, etc.; make a reaching motion or effort. **3** *tr.* get as far as (*reached Chicago at noon*). **4** *tr.* get to or attain (*temperature reached 90°*). **5** *tr.* make contact with the hand, etc., or by telephone, etc. **6** *tr.* hand; pass (*reach that book for me*). • *n.* **1** extent to which a hand, etc., can be reached out, influence exerted, motion carried out, etc. **2** act of reaching out. **3** continuous extent, esp. of a river. □□ *synonym* study at RANGE. □□ **reach'a•ble** *adj.*

■ *v.* **1, 2** (*reach out*) hold out, outstretch. **3** arrive at, get to, come to, end up at or in, *colloq.* make it to. **4** get up to, climb to, rise to; achieve, accomplish. **5** get in touch with, get through to, get (a) hold of. **6** convey. • *n.* **1** range, scope; capacity.

re•act /reeákt/ *v.intr.* **1** respond (to a stimulus, etc.). **2** tend in a reverse or contrary direction. **3** *Chem. & Physics* (of a substance or particle) be the cause of activity or interaction with another (*nitrous oxide reacts with the metal*).

■ **1** act, behave; retaliate, reciprocate.

re•ac•tion /reeákshən/ *n.* **1** reacting; response. **2** bodily response to a drug, etc. **3** response in a reverse or contrary way. **4** interaction of substances undergoing chemical change. □□ **re•ac'tion•ist** *n. & adj.*

■ **1** reply, answer; reciprocation; see also RESPONSE 1, 2.

re•ac•tion•ar•y /reeákshəneree/ • *adj.* tending to oppose (esp. political) change and advocate return to a former system. • *n.* (*pl.* -ies) reactionary person.

■ ultraconservative, conservative, rightist, traditionalist.

re•ac•ti•vate /reeáktivayt/ *v.tr.* restore to a state of activity; bring into action again. □□ **re•ac•ti•va•tion** /-váyshən/ *n.*

re•ac•tive /reeáktiv/ *adj.* **1** showing reaction. **2** reacting rather than initiating. □□ **re•ac•tiv'i•ty** *n.*

■ **1** see RESPONSIVE.

re•ac•tor /reeáktər/ *n.* **1** person or thing that reacts. **2** (in full **nu'cle•ar re•ac'tor**) apparatus or structure in which a controlled nuclear chain reaction releases energy.

read /reed/ • *v.* (*past* and *past part.* **read** /red/) **1** *tr.* [also *absol.*] reproduce mentally or vocally written or printed words. **2** *tr.* convert or be able to convert (characters, symbols, etc.) into the intended words or meaning. **3** *tr.* interpret mentally. **4** *tr.* find (a thing) stated in print, etc. **5** *tr.* assume as intended or deducible (*read too much into it*). **6** *tr.* (of a recording instrument) show (a specified figure, etc.) (*the thermometer reads 20°*). **7** *intr.* convey meaning in a specified manner when read (*it reads persuasively*). **8** *tr. Computing* access (data), as to copy or display. **9** *tr.* understand or interpret by hearing words or seeing signs, gestures, etc.

• *n.* **1** period of reading. **2** *colloq.* book, etc., as regards its readability (*is a good read*). □ **read a person like a book** understand a person's motives, etc. **read between the lines** look for or find hidden meaning. **read lips** = *lipread* (LIPREADING). **read-only** *Computing*(of a memory) able to be read at high speed but not capable of being changed by program instructions. **read up** make a special study of (a subject). **read-write** *Computing*capable of reading existing data and accepting alterations or further input.

■ *v.* **1** peruse, study, look over, pore over. **2** understand, comprehend; translate, decode. **3** see INTERPRET 1, 2; 4. **5** assign, infer, presume, conclude, find.

read•a•ble /réedəbəl/ *adj.* **1** able to be read, **2** interesting or pleasant to read. □□ **read•a•bil'i•ty** *n.* **read'a•bly** *adv.*

■ **1** legible, intelligible, understandable. **2** entertaining, enjoyable, absorbing, engaging.

read•er /réedər/ *n.* **1** person who reads. **2** book of extracts for learning, esp. a language. **3** person appointed to read aloud, esp. in church.

read•er•ship /réedərship/ *n.* readers of a newspaper, etc.

read•i•ly /réd'lee/ *adv.* **1** without reluctance; willingly. **2** without difficulty or delay.

■ **1** eagerly, freely, gladly, happily, cheerfully. **2** effortlessly, smoothly; promptly, quickly, in no time, immediately.

read•ing /réeding/ *n.* **1 a** act of reading. **b** matter to be read. **2** [in *comb.*] used for reading (*reading room*). **3** literary knowledge. **4** entertainment at which a play, poems, etc., are read. **5** figure, etc., shown by a recording instrument. **6** interpretation.

■ **1 a** see *perusal* (PERUSE), RECITAL 1, 3. **b** see *interpretation* (INTERPRET).

read•out /réedowt/ *n.* **1** display of information, as on a gauge, etc. **2** information displayed.

read•y /rédee/ • *adj.* (**read•i•er, read•i•est**) **1** with preparations complete (*dinner is ready*). **2** in a fit state (*are you ready?*), **3** willing, inclined, or resolved (*ready for anything*). **4** within reach; easily secured (*ready cash*). **5** immediate; unqualified (*found ready acceptance*). **6** [foll. by *to* + *infin.*] about to do something (*a bud just ready to burst*). • *adv.* beforehand; immediately usable (-ready-to-eat). • *v.tr.* (**-ies, -ied**) make ready; prepare. □ **at the ready** ready for action. **ready-made 1** (esp. of clothes) made in a standard size, not to measure. **2** already available; convenient (*ready-made excuse*). □□ **read'i•ness** *n.*

■ *adj.* **1, 2** prepared, (all) set. **3** apt, likely, disposed, given, prone; pleased; content; consenting, agreeable, eager, keen, *colloq.* game. **4** handy, available, at one's fingertips, close at hand, convenient. **5** see IMMEDIATE 1. **6** *disp.* liable; (*ready to*) on the verge of, close to. • *v.* equip, *colloq.* psych up; see also PREPARE 1, 3. □ **at the ready** in position, poised, on deck; see also READY *adj.* 4 above.

ready-made 1 off-the-rack. **2** handy, suitable.

re•a•gent /ree-áyjənt/ *n. Chem.* substance used to cause a reaction, esp. to detect another substance.

re•al /reel/ • *adj.* **1** actually existing or occurring. **2** genuine; rightly so called; not artificial. **3** *Law* consisting of immovable property such as land or houses (*real estate*). **4** appraised by purchasing power (*real value*). • *adv. colloq.* really; very. □ **for real** *colloq.* as a serious or actual concern. **real estate** property, esp. land and buildings. **real life** that lived by actual people, as distinct from fiction, drama, etc. **real time** actual time during which a process or event occurs. **real-time** [*attrib.*] *Computing* (of a system) in which the response is ongoing and occurs during the actual time of an event. □□ **real′ness** *n.*

■ *adj.* **1** natural; physical, tangible. **2** true, actual, authentic, legitimate, bona fide; sincere, honest. • *adv.* see REALLY 2. □ **for real** see *in earnest* (EARNEST).

re•al•ism /ree·əlizəm/ *n.* **1** practice of regarding things in their true nature and dealing with them as they are. **2** fidelity to nature in representation. □□ **re′al•ist** *n.*

re•al•is•tic /ree·əlístik/ *adj.* **1** regarding things as they are. **2** based on facts rather than ideals. □□ **re•al•is′ti•cal•ly** *adv.*

■ **1** natural, lifelike, true to life, graphic. **2** practical, matter-of-fact, down-to-earth, pragmatic, sensible, reasonable, levelheaded, rational, sane, no-nonsense, *colloq.* hard-nosed.

re•al•i•ty /ree·álitee/ *n.* (*pl.* **–ties**) **1** what is real or existent or underlies appearances. **2** the real nature (of). **3** real existence; state of being real. □ **in reality** in fact.

■ **1** actuality, fact, truth, genuineness, authenticity. **2** see NATURE 1, 7. □ **in reality** indeed, actually, to be sure.

re•al•ize /ree·əliz/ *v.tr.* **1** [also *absol.*] be fully aware of; conceive as real. **2** [also *absol.*] understand clearly. **3** present as real. **4** convert into actuality (*realized a childhood dream*). **5** obtain, as profit. □□ **re•al•iz′a•ble** *adj.* **re•al•i•za′tion** *n.* **re′al•iz•er** *n.*

■ **1** appreciate, be conscious (of); see also KNOW *v.* 1b. **2** comprehend, grasp, see, *colloq.* catch on to. **4** make real, effect, bring about, make happen, accomplish, achieve, fulfill, materialize. **5** acquire, gain, clear, make, bring *or* take in, net, produce, get. □□ **realization** conception, understanding, recognition; consummation, accomplishment, achievement.

re•al•ly /ree·əlee, reelee/ *adv.* **1** in reality. **2** positively (*really useful*). **3** indeed; truly. **4** [often in *interrog.*] an expression of mild protest or surprise.

■ **1** in (point of) fact, genuinely, actually, truly, honestly, as a matter of fact. **2** assuredly, undeniably; very, extremely. **3** absolutely; see also DEFINITELY *adv.* 2. **4** well, I declare; well I never, you don't say, is that so, go on; no kidding, come on.

realm /relm/ *n.* **1** kingdom. **2** domain.

■ **1** empire, principality. **2** sphere; territory, area.

Re•al•tor /ree·əltər/ *n. propr.* real estate agent who is a member of the National Association of Realtors.

re•al•ty /ree·əltee/ *n.* real estate.

ream¹ /reem/ *n.* **1** twenty quires (or 500 sheets) of paper. **2** [in *pl.*] large quantity (*wrote reams about it*).

ream² /reem/ *v.tr.* widen (a hole in metal, etc.) with a borer.

■ broaden, extend, drill out, bore out, open up.

re•an•i•mate /ree·ánimayt/ *v.tr.* **1** restore to life. **2** restore to activity or liveliness. □□ **re•an•i•ma•tion** /-máyshən/ *n.*

■ **1** see RESURRECT 2. **2** see REJUVENATE. □□ **reanimation** see REVIVAL 1, 3.

reap /reep/ *v.tr.* **1** cut or gather (esp. grain) as a harvest. **2** harvest the crop of (a field, etc.). **3** receive as the consequence of one's own or others' actions.

■ **1** garner, glean. **3** bring in, procure, acquire, get, take in.

reap•er /reepər/ *n.* **1** person who reaps. **2** machine for reaping. □ **the reaper** (or **grim reaper**) death personified.

rear¹ /reer/ • *n.* **1** back part of anything. **2** space behind, or position at the back of, anything. **3** *colloq.* buttocks. • *adj.* at the back. □ **bring up the rear** come last. **rear admiral** naval officer ranking below vice admiral. **rear guard 1** body of troops detached to protect the rear, esp. in retreats. **2** defensive or conservative element in an organization, etc.

■ *n.* **1** hind part, tail (end), *Naut.* stern. **2** (*at* or *in the rear*) see BEHIND *prep.* 1a, b. **3** seat, hindquarters, posterior, rump, rear end, *colloq.* bottom, behind, backside.

rear² /reer/ *v.* **1** *tr.* **a** bring up and educate (children). **b** breed and care for (animals). **c** cultivate (crops). **2** *intr.* (of a horse, etc.) raise itself on its hind legs. **3** *tr.* set upright; build. □□ **rear′er** *n.*

■ **1** raise; care for, look after, tend, nurture; cultivate. **3** erect, put up, construct.

rear•most /reermōst/ *adj.* furthest back.

■ see LAST¹ *adj.* 1, 5.

re•ar•range /ree·əráynj/ *v.tr.* arrange again in a different way. □□ **re•ar•range′ment** *n.*

■ adjust, alter, shuffle, change; see also TIDY *v.*

rear•ward /reerwərd/ • *adj.* to the rear. • *adv.* (also **rear′wards**) toward the rear.

■ see BACKWARD.

rea•son /reezən/ • *n.* **1** motive, cause, or justification. **2** fact adduced or serving as this. **3** intellectual faculty by which conclusions are drawn from premises. **4** sanity (*has lost his reason*). **5** sense; moderation. • *v.* **1** *intr.* form or try to reach conclusions by connected thought. **2** *intr.* use an argument (with) by way of persuasion. **3** *tr.* conclude or assert in argument. □ **stand to reason** be evident or logical. **listen to reason** be persuaded to act sensibly. □□ **rea′son•ing** *n.*

■ *n.* **1, 2** purpose, aim, intention, objective, goal; argument, case, explanation, rationale, ground(s), pretext, basis, defense; excuse, rationalization. **3** reasoning, logic; intelligence. **4** see SANITY 1. **5** common sense; see also SENSE *n.* 4, 5. • *v.* **1** think rationally *or* logically, use (one's) judgment. **2** *(reason with)* discuss with, talk with, plead with, prevail (up)on. **3** argue, calculate, figure (out), work out, deduce, think out *or* through. □□ **reasoning** thinking, analysis; rationale, explanation.

rea·son·a·ble /réezənəbəl/ *adj.* **1** having sound judgment. **2** not absurd. **3 a** not excessive; inexpensive. **b** tolerable; fair. See synonym study at SENSIBLE. □□ **rea'son·a·ble·ness** *n.* **rea'son·a·bly** *adv.*
■ **1** sensible, rational, sane, logical, sober, moderate, judicious, wise, intelligent. **2** well-grounded, valid. **3** appropriate, suitable, acceptable, within reason; average, equitable.

re·as·sure /réeəshŏŏr/ *v.tr.* **1** restore confidence to; dispel the apprehensions of. **2** confirm in an opinion or impression. □□ **re·as·sur'ance** *n.* **re·as·sur'ing** *adj.* **re·as·sur'ing·ly** *adv.*
■ **1** comfort, encourage, hearten, cheer, uplift, set *or* put a person's mind at rest, set *or* put at ease.

re·bate /réebayt/ • *n.* partial refund. • *v.tr.* pay back as a rebate. □□ **re·bat'a·ble** *adj.* **re·bat'er** *n.*
■ *n.* discount, reduction, deduction, allowance. • *v.* give back.

reb·el • *n.* /rébəl/ person who fights against or resists established authority. • *adj.* /rébəl/ [*attrib.*] **1** rebellious. **2** of rebels. **3** in rebellion. • *v.intr.* /ribél/ (**re·belled, re·bel·ling**) **1** act as a rebel; revolt. **2** feel or display repugnance.
■ *n.* revolutionary, insurgent, insurrectionist, mutineer, freedom fighter, guerrilla; heretic, nonconformist, dissenter. • *adj.* **1** see REBELLIOUS 1. • *v.* **1** revolt, mutiny, rise up, *(rebel against)* defy, disobey.

re·bel·lion /ribélyən/ *n.* open resistance to authority, esp. organized armed resistance to an established government. See synonym study at UPRISING.
■ uprising, revolution, mutiny, insurrection, revolt, insurgence; defiance.

re·bel·lious /ribélyəs/ *adj.* **1** tending to rebel. **2** in rebellion. **3** (of a thing) unmanageable. □□ **re·bel'lious·ly** *adv.* **re·bel'lious·ness** *n.*
■ **1** defiant, mutinous, revolutionary, insurgent, seditious; disobedient. **4** difficult, refractory.

re·birth /réebérth/ *n.* **1** new incarnation. **2** spiritual enlightenment. **3** revival. □□ **re·born** /réebáwrn/ *adj.*
■ **1** see REINCARNATION. **2** see *illumination* (ILLUMINATE). **3** renaissance, renewal, reawakening, resurgence.

re·bound • *v.intr.* /ribównd/ spring back after impact. • *n.* /réebownd/ **1** act of rebounding; recoil. **2** reaction after a strong emotion. □ **on the rebound** while still recovering from an emotional shock, esp. rejection by a lover. □□ **re·bound'er** *n.*
■ *v.* bounce, ricochet. • *n.* **1** return, comeback. **2** see BACKLASH 1.

re·buff /ribúf/ • *n.* **1** rejection of another's advances, help, sympathy, request, etc. **2** repulse; snub. • *v.tr.* give a rebuff to.
■ *n.* discouragement, refusal, dismissal, brush-off. • *v.* reject, repel, drive away, slight, ignore, give a person the cold shoulder.

re·buke /ribyŏŏk/ • *v.tr.* reprove sharply; subject to protest or censure. • *n.* rebuking or being rebuked; reproof. □□ **re·buk'er** *n.* **re·buk'ing·ly** *adv.*
■ *v.* scold, reproach, admonish, reprimand, lecture, berate, castigate, criticize, rake over the coals, *colloq.* bawl out, tell off, chew out. • *n.* castigation, upbraiding; tongue-lashing.

SYNONYM STUDY: rebuke
ADMONISH, CENSURE, CHIDE, REPRIMAND, REPROACH, REPROVE, SCOLD. All of these verbs mean to criticize or express disapproval, but which one you use depends on how upset you are. If you want to go easy on someone, you can **admonish** or **reprove**, both of which indicate mild and sometimes kindly disapproval. To *admonish* is to warn or counsel someone, usually because a duty has been forgotten or might be forgotten in the future *(to admonish her about leaving the key in the lock)*, while *reprove* also suggests mild criticism aimed at correcting a fault or pattern of misbehavior *(he was reproved for his lack of attention in class)*. To **chide** someone is also to express mild disapproval, but often in a nagging way *(he chided her into apologizing)*. If you want to express your disapproval formally or in public, use **censure** or **reprimand**. You can *censure* someone either directly or indirectly *(the judge censured the lawyer for violating courtroom procedures; a newspaper article that censured "deadbeat dads")*, while *reprimand* suggests a direct confrontation *(reprimanded by his parole officer for leaving town without reporting his whereabouts)*. If you're irritated enough to want to express your disapproval quite harshly and at some length, you can **scold** *(to scold a child for jaywalking)*. **Rebuke** is the harshest word of this group, meaning to criticize sharply or sternly, often in the midst of some action *(to rebuke a carpenter for walking across an icy roof)*.

---

re·bus /réebəs/ *n.* representation of a word or phrase by pictures, etc., suggesting its parts.

re·but /ribút/ *v.tr.* (**re·but·ted, re·but·ting**) **1** refute or disprove (evidence or a charge). **2** force or turn back; check. □□ **re·but'ment** *n.* **re·but'ta·ble** *adj.* **re·but'tal** *n.*
■ **1** deny, discredit, contradict, expose, shoot down. **2** see CHECK *v.* 2a. □□ **rebuttal** denial, contradiction; retort, response.

rec. *abbr.* **1** receipt. **2** record. **3** recreation.

re·cal·ci·trant /rikálsitrənt/ • *adj.* **1** obstinately disobedient. **2** objecting to restraint. • *n.* recalcitrant person. □□ **re·cal'ci·trance** *n.* **re·cal'ci·trant·ly** *adv.*
■ *adj.* **1** stubborn, defiant, headstrong, rebellious, unruly, insubordinate. **2** unyielding, immovable, inflexible.

re·call /rikáwl/ • *v.tr.* **1 a** summon to return.

b (of a product) request return to fix a defect. **2** recollect; remember. **3** bring back to memory; serve as a reminder of. **4** revoke or annul (an action or decision). **5** take back (a gift). • *n.* (also /ˈrēˌkawl/) **1** act or instance of recalling. **2** act of remembering. **3** ability to remember. □□ **re•call′a•ble** *adj.*

■ *v.* **1** call back; rally. **2** call to mind. **4** rescind, retract, withdraw, recant, take back. • *n.* **1** withdrawal; summons. **2** recollection; reminiscence.

re•cant /rikánt/ *v.* **1** *tr.* withdraw and renounce (a former belief, etc.) as erroneous or heretical. **2** *intr.* disavow a former opinion. □□ **re•can•ta′tion** *n.* **re•cant′er** *n.*

■ **1** recall, deny, rescind, revoke, retract, take back. **2** see RENEGE 1.

re•cap /ˈrēˌkap/ *colloq.* • *v.* (**re•capped, re•cap•ping**) recapitulate. • *n.* recapitulation.

re•ca•pit•u•late /rēˈkapíchəlayt/ *v.tr.* go briefly through again; summarize. □□ **re•ca•pit•u•la•tive** /-əlātiv/ *adj.* **re•ca•pit•u•la•to•ry** /-lətáwree/ *adj.*

■ sum up; *colloq.* recap; recount, enumerate, recite, relate, list.

re•ca•pit•u•la•tion /rēˈkapíchəláyshən/ *n.* **1** act of recapitulating. **2** *Mus.* section in which themes are restated.

re•cede /riséed/ *v.intr.* **1** go or shrink back or further off. **2** diminish; fade. **3** slope backward (*a receding chin*).

■ **1** ebb, subside, abate, withdraw, retreat. **2** lessen, dwindle, wane; see also DECLINE *v.* 1.

re•ceipt /riséet/ *n.* **1** receiving or being received. **2** written acknowledgment of payment. **3** [usu. in *pl.*] amount of money, etc., received.

■ **1** delivery, acceptance; arrival, appearance. **2** sales slip, ticket, stub, proof of purchase, voucher. **3** (*receipts*) income, proceeds, gate, return, take.

re•ceive /riséev/ *v.tr.* **1** take or accept. **2** acquire; be provided with. **3** accept delivery of (something sent). **4** have conferred or inflicted on one. **5** admit; provide accommodation for (*received many visitors*). **6** (of a receptacle) be able to hold. **7** greet or welcome, esp. in a specified manner. **8** convert (broadcast signals) into sound or pictures. □□ **re•ceiv′a•ble** *adj.*

■ **1, 2** get, obtain, come by, be given, inherit; learn, ascertain, find out; see also EARN[1]. **4** (*of honors*) collect, earn, gain, win; (*of a blow, etc.*) experience, undergo, endure, suffer, bear, sustain, be subjected to, meet with. **5** show in, let in; see also ADMIT 3, ACCOMMODATE 1. **6** see HOLD *v.* 2. **7** meet; respond to, react to.

re•ceiv•er /riséevər/ *n.* **1** person or thing that receives. **2** telephone earpiece. **3** person appointed by a court to receive funds, administer property of a bankrupt, etc. **4** radio or television receiving apparatus. **5** *Football* offensive player eligible to catch a forward pass.

re•ceiv•er•ship /riséevərship/ *n.* state of being dealt with by a receiver.

re•cent /réesənt/ • *adj.* **1** not long past. **2** not long established; lately begun. **3** (**Recent**) *Geol.* of the most recent epoch of the Quaternary period. • *n.* *Geol.* this epoch. □□ **re′cent•ly** *adv.*

■ *adj.* **2** new, current, modern, up-to-date.

re•cep•ta•cle /riséptəkəl/ *n.* containing vessel, place, or space.

■ container; box, tin, can, case, bag, basket.

re•cep•tion /risépshən/ *n.* **1** receiving or being received. **2** manner in which a person or thing is received. **3** social occasion for receiving guests. **4** (also **re•cep′tion desk**) arrival area at a hotel, office, etc. **5 a** receiving of broadcast signals. **b** quality of this.

■ **2** welcome, greeting, treatment; reaction, response. **3** party, function.

re•cep•tion•ist /risépshənist/ *n.* person employed to receive guests, answer the telephone, etc.

re•cep•tive /riséptiv/ *adj.* able or quick to receive impressions or ideas. □□ **re•cep′tive•ly** *adv.* **re•cep•tiv•i•ty** /réeséptivitee/ *n.*

■ open, responsive, amenable, willing, flexible; sharp, alert, perceptive, astute.

re•cess /réeses, risés/ • *n.* **1** space set back in a wall. **2** [often in *pl.*] remote or secret place. **3** temporary cessation from proceedings, school, etc. • *v.* **1** *tr.* make a recess in. **2** *tr.* place in a recess. **3 a** *intr.* take a recess; adjourn. **b** *tr.* order a recess.

■ *n.* **1** alcove, niche, nook, cranny, bay, hollow. **2** (*recesses*) innermost reaches, corners, depths. **3** respite, rest, break, *colloq.* breather; holiday, vacation. • *v.* **3 a** take a break, stop, rest, pause.

re•ces•sion /riséshən/ *n.* **1** temporary decline in economic activity or prosperity. **2** receding or withdrawal from a place or point. □□ **re•ces′sion•ar•y** *adj.*

■ **1** downturn, slump, dip, depression.

re•ces•sion•al /riséshənəl/ *n.* hymn sung while the clergy and choir withdraw after a service.

re•ces•sive /risésiv/ *adj.* **1** tending to recede. **2** *Genetics* appearing in offspring only when not masked by an inherited dominant characteristic. □□ **re•ces′sive•ly** *adv.* **re•ces′sive•ness** *n.*

re•cher•ché /rəsháirsháy/ *adj.* **1** carefully sought out; rare; exotic. **2** far-fetched; obscure.

re•cid•i•vist /risídivist/ *n.* person who relapses into crime, etc. □□ **re•cid′i•vism** *n.* **re•cid•i•vis′tic** *adj.*

rec•i•pe /résipee/ *n.* **1** statement of ingredients and procedure required for preparing cooked food. **2** device for achieving something.

■ **1** formula. **2** expedient; plan, procedure, method, approach, technique, way, means, system.

re•cip•i•ent /risípeeənt/ *n.* person who receives something.

■ receiver, beneficiary, heir, heiress, legatee.

re•cip•ro•cal /risíprəkəl/ • *adj.* **1** in return (*reciprocal greeting*). **2** mutual. See synonym study at MUTUAL. • *n.* *Math.* expression or function so related to another that their product is one (e.g., ½ is the reciprocal of 2).

□□ **re•cip•ro•cal•i•ty** /-kálitee/ *n.* **re•cip′ro•cal•ly** *adv.*

■ *adj.* **2** common, shared, joint.

re•cip•ro•cate /risíprəkayt/ *v.* **1** *tr.* return or requite (affection, etc.). **2** *intr.* [foll. by *with*] offer or give something in return. **3** *tr.* interchange. **4** **a** *intr.* (of a part of a machine) move backward and forward. **b** *tr.* cause to do this. □□ **re•cip•ro•ca•tion** /-káyshən/ *n.* **re•cip′ro•ca•tor** *n.*

■ **1** repay, match, equal. **2** see RESPOND *v.* 2. **3** exchange; swap, trade.

re•ci•proc•i•ty /résiprósitee/ *n.* **1** condition of being reciprocal. **2** mutual action. **3** give and take, esp. of privileges.

re•cit•al /risít'l/ *n.* **1** reciting or being recited. **2** performance by a solo instrumentalist, dancer, or singer or by a small group. **3** detailed account; narrative.

■ **1, 3** narration, recitation, telling, recounting; report. **2** concert.

rec•i•ta•tion /résitáyshən/ *n.* **1** reciting. **2** thing recited.

rec•i•ta•tive /résitətéev/ *n.* musical declamation in the narrative and dialogue parts of opera and oratorio.

re•cite /risít/ *v.* **1** *tr.* repeat aloud or declaim (a poem or passage) from memory. **2** *intr.* give a recitation. **3** *tr.* enumerate. □□ **re•cit′er** *n.*

■ **1** quote, read out or aloud. **2** hold forth, speak. **3** spell out, detail, chronicle, list, recount, relate, report.

reck•less /réklis/ *adj.* heedless; rash. □□ **reck′less•ly** *adv.* **reck′less•ness** *n.*

■ careless, thoughtless, foolhardy, impulsive, negligent, foolish, wild.

reck•on /rékən/ *v.* **1** *tr.* count; compute. **2** *tr.* consider or regard. **3** *tr.* be of the considered opinion. **4** *intr.* [foll. by *with*] take into account. **5** *dial.* think; suppose (*I reckon I'll stay*). □ **to be reckoned with** of considerable importance, not to be ignored.

■ **1** calculate; add (up). **2** judge, look upon, view, estimate, appraise. **3** suppose, think, assume, presume, guess, imagine. **4** (*reckon with*) take into consideration, consider, bear in mind.

reck•on•ing /rékəning/ *n.* **1** counting or calculating. **2** consideration. **3** settlement of an account. □ **day of reckoning** time when something must be atoned for or avenged.

■ **1** computation, enumeration. **2** see OPINION 1, 3. **3** payment, return, *sl.* payoff. □ **day of reckoning** judgment day; retribution.

re•claim /rikláym/ *v.tr.* **1** seek the return of (one's property, rights, etc.). **2** bring under cultivation, esp. after being under water. **3 a** win back. **b** tame; civilize. See synonym study at RECOVER. □□ **re•claim′a•ble** *adj.* **re•claim′er** *n.* **rec•la•ma•tion** /rékləmáyshən/ *n.*

■ **1, 2** take back, recover, redeem, save, retrieve; restore. **3 a** reform; rescue. **b** enlighten, refine, improve.

re•cline /riklín/ *v.* **1** *intr.* assume or be in a horizontal or leaning position. **2** *tr.* cause to recline or move from the vertical. □□ **re•clin′a•ble** *adj.*

■ lie down, lie back, lean back, stretch out, lounge.

re•clin•er /riklínər/ *n.* comfortable chair for reclining in.

re•cluse /réklōōs, riklōōs/ *n.* person given to or living in seclusion or isolation; hermit. □□ **re•clu•sion** /riklōōzhən/ *n.* **re•clu′sive** *adj.*

■ eremite; loner, lone wolf. □□ **reclusive** solitary, lone, secluded, isolated, cloistered, sequestered.

rec•og•ni•tion /rékəgníshən/ *n.* recognizing or being recognized.

■ identification, detection; acknowledgment, acceptance, awareness, perception, admission; honor.

re•cog•ni•zance /rikógnizəns, -kónə-/ *n.* *Law* a charge to observe some condition, e.g., to appear when summoned.

rec•og•nize /rékəgnīz/ *v.tr.* **1** identify as already known. **2** realize or discover the nature of. **3** realize or admit. **4** acknowledge the existence, validity, etc., of. **5** show appreciation of; reward. □□ **rec•og•niz′a•ble** *adj.* **rec•og•niz•a•bil′i•ty** *n.* **rec•og•niz′a•bly** *adv.* **rec′og•niz•er** *n.*

■ **1** detect, place, recall. **2** perceive, understand, be or become aware of, know. **3** see, accept, own, concede. **4** approve, sanction, validate, endorse. **5** honor, salute, pay respect to, pay homage to.

re•coil /rikóyl/ • *v.intr.* **1** suddenly move or spring back in fear, horror, or disgust. **2** shrink mentally in this way. **3** (of a gun) be driven backward by its discharge. For synonym study at WINCE. • *n.* (also /réekoyl/) act or sensation of recoiling.

■ *v.* **1, 2** jerk or jump back, start, flinch, wince, balk, shy away. • *n.* kick, rebound, comeback; backlash.

rec•ol•lect /rékəlékt/ *v.tr.* **1** remember. **2** succeed in remembering; call to mind. □□ **rec•ol•lec•tion** /-lékshən/ *n.*

■ **1** recall, retain. **2** see REMEMBER 2. □□ **recollection** memory, remembrance; reminiscence.

re•com•bi•nant /reekómbinənt/ *Biol.* • *adj.* (of a gene, etc.) formed by recombination. • *n.* recombinant organism or cell. □ **recombinant DNA** DNA that has been recombined using constituents from different sources.

rec•om•mend /rékəménd/ *v.tr.* **1** suggest as fit for some purpose or use. **2** advise as a course of action, etc. **3** make acceptable or desirable. □□ **rec•om•men•da′tion** *n.*

■ **1** endorse, propose, support, promote. **2** urge; advocate. **3** favor, make attractive. □□ **recommendation** counsel, advice, direction, suggestion; endorsement, blessing, approval.

rec•om•pense /rékəmpens/ • *v.tr.* **1** make amends to (a person) or for (a loss, etc.). **2** reward or punish (a person or action). • *n.* **1** reward; requital. **2** retribution.

■ **1** reward, remuneration. **2** retribution.

rec•on•cile /rékənsīl/ *v.tr.* **1** make friendly again after an estrangement. **2** make acquiescent or contentedly submissive to (something disagreeable). **3** settle (a quarrel, etc.). **4** make or show to be compatible. □□ **rec•**

on•cil'a•ble adj. **rec'on•cile•ment** n. **rec'on•cil•er** n. **rec•on•cil•i•a•tion** /–sileeáy-shən/ n. **rec•on•cil•i•a•to•ry** /–síleeətawree/ adj.

■ **1** get or bring (back) together, unite, re-unite, restore harmony between, make peace between. **2** see RESIGN 2. **3** sort out, smooth over. □□ **reconciliation** appeasement, paci-fication, reunion; compromise, agreement.

re•con•dite /rékəndīt, rikón–/ adj. **1** (of a subject or knowledge) abstruse; little known. **2** (of an author or style) obscure. □□ **re'con•dite•ly** adv. **re'con•dite•ness** n.

■ **1** arcane, esoteric, deep, profound, enig-matic.

re•con•di•tion /reekəndíshən/ v.tr. **1** over-haul; refit; renovate. **2** make usable again. □□ **re•con•di'tion•er** n.

■ see OVERHAUL v. 1.

re•con•nais•sance /rikónisəns/ n. survey of a region, esp. to locate an enemy or ascertain strategic features.

■ examination, investigation, inspection.

re•con•noi•ter /reekənóytər, rékə–/ v. make a reconnaissance.

■ survey, examine, scout (out), scan, ex-plore, investigate, inspect, scrutinize, check out.

re•con•sid•er /reekənsídər/ v. consider again, esp. for a possible change of decision. □□ **re•con•sid•er•a'tion** n.

■ see REVIEW v. 2, 5. □□ **reconsideration** see REVIEW n. 3.

re•con•sti•tute /reekónstitoot, –tyoot/ v.tr. **1** reconstruct; reorganize. **2** restore dried food, etc., by adding water. □□ **re•con•sti•tu'tion** /–tooshən/ n.

re•con•struct /reekənstrúkt/ v.tr. **1** build again. **2** recall or reenact past events, etc., by assembling the evidence for them. □□ **re•con•struct'i•ble** adj. (also **re•con•struct'a•ble**). **re•con•struc•tion** /–strúkshən/ n. **re•con•struc'tive** adj.

rec•ord • n. /rékərd/ **1 a** evidence or informa-tion constituting an (esp. official) account of something that has occurred, been said, etc. **b** document preserving this. **2** state of being set down or preserved in writing, etc. **3** (in full **pho'no•graph rec'ord**) disk carrying recorded sound in grooves on each surface, for reproduction by a record player. **4** official report of legal proceedings. **5 a** facts known about a person's past. **b** list of a person's pre-vious criminal convictions. **6** best perfor-mance or most remarkable event of its kind. • v.tr. /rikáwrd/ **1** set down in writing, etc., for later reference. **2** convert (sound, a broad-cast, etc.) into permanent form for later re-production. □ **break** (or **beat**) **the record** outdo all previous performances, etc. for **the record** as an official statement, etc. **go on record** state one's opinion or judgment openly or officially. **off the record** unofficial-ly; confidentially. **record player** apparatus for reproducing sound from phonograph records. □□ **re•cord'a•ble** adj.

■ n. **1** (record or records) documentation; re-port, journal, register, list. **3** album, LP,

forty-five. **5** history, background; résumé. • v. **1** transcribe, take down, report. □ **off the record** between you and me; privately, not for publication. **record player** phonograph.

re•cord•er /rikáwrdər/ n. **1** apparatus for re-cording, esp. a tape recorder. **2** keeper of records. **3** wind instrument like a flute but blown through the end.

■ **2** CD, compact disc; record, tape.

re•cord•ing /rikáwrding/ n. **1** process by which audio or video signals are recorded for later reproduction. **2** material or a program recorded.

re•count¹ /rikównt/ v.tr. **1** narrate. **2** tell in detail.

■ **1** relate, recite. **2** describe, enumerate, go over.

re•count² • v. /reekównt/ tr. count again. • n. /reekownt/ recounting, esp. of votes in an election.

re•coup /rikoōp/ v.tr. recover or regain (a loss). See synonym study at RECOVER. □□ **re•coup'a•ble** adj. **re•coup'ment** n.

■ make good, make up (for), redeem; com-pensate.

re•course /reekawrs, rikáwrs/ n. **1** resorting to a possible source of help. **2** person or thing resorted to. □ **have recourse to** turn to (a person or thing) for help.

■ access; backup, reserve, alternative, reme-dy.

re•cov•er /rikúvər/ v. **1** tr. regain possession, use, or control of. **2** intr. return to health, consciousness, or to a normal state or posi-tion. **3** tr. obtain or secure by legal process. **4** tr. retrieve or make up for (a loss, setback, etc.). **5** tr. retrieve; salvage. □□ **re•cov'er•a•ble** adj. **re•cov•er•a•bil'i•ty** n. **re•cov'er•y** n.

■ **1** reclaim, retake, recapture; rescue, re-store. **2** get well or better, recuperate, im-prove, pull through; survive, live. **4** recoup, redeem. □□ **recovery** recuperation; revival; redemption.

SYNONYM STUDY: recover

RECLAIM, RECOUP, REGAIN, RESTORE, RETRIEVE. If you lose or let go of something and find it either by chance or with effort, you **recover** it (to recover the stolen artwork). Although it is often used interchangeably with recover, **re-gain** puts more emphasis on getting back something of which you have been deprived, usually after a laborious search or effort (to regain one's position as chairperson; to regain one's eyesight). **Recoup** refers to the recovery of something similar or equivalent to what has been lost, usually in the form of compen-sation (he tried to recoup his gambling losses). **Reclaim** and **restore** both involve bringing something back to its original condition or to a better or more useful state. Reclaim is usu-ally associated with land (to reclaim neglected farmlands), while restore is linked to buildings or objects of art (to restore an 18th-century house). **Retrieve** implies that something has slipped beyond reach, and that a concerted effort or search is required to recover it (her desperate efforts to retrieve the family dog from the flooded house).

rec•re•ant /rékreeənt/ *literary* • *adj.* craven; cowardly. • *n.* coward. □□ **rec′re•an•cy** *n.* **rec′re•ant•ly** *adv.*

rec•re•a•tion /rékree-áyshən/ *n.* **1** process or means of refreshing or entertaining oneself. **2** pleasurable activity. □□ **rec•re•a′tion•al** *adj.* **rec•re•a′tion•al•ly** *adv.*
■ amusement, diversion, leisure, sport, play.

re•crim•i•nate /rikríminayt/ *v.intr.* make mutual or counter accusations. □□ **re•crim′i•na•tion** /-náyshən/ *n.* **re•crim•i•na•to•ry** /-nətawree/ *adj.*
■ □□ **recrimination** retaliation, reprisal.

re•cruit /rikróot/ • *n.* **1** newly enlisted serviceman or servicewoman. **2** new member; beginner. • *v.* **1** *tr.* enlist (a person) as a recruit. **2** *tr.* form (an army, etc.) by enlisting recruits. **3** *intr.* get or seek recruits. □□ **re•cruit′ment** *n.*
■ *n.* conscript, trainee, apprentice, *sl.* rookie; newcomer, novice, neophyte, greenhorn. • *v.* **1** induct, enroll. **2** muster, raise; see also MOBILIZE.

rec•ta *pl.* of RECTUM.

rec•tal /réktəl/ *adj.* of or by means of the rectum. □□ **rec′tal•ly** *adv*

rec•tan•gle /réktanggəl/ *n.* plane figure with four straight sides and four right angles. □□ **rec•tan′gu•lar** *adj.*

rec•ti•fy /réktifī/ *v.tr.* (**-fies, -fied**) **1** adjust; make right. **2** convert (alternating current) to direct current. □□ **rec•ti•fi′a•ble** *adj.* **rec•ti•fi•ca′tion** *n.* **rec′ti•fi•er** *n.*
■ **1** correct, amend, remedy, reconcile.

rec•ti•lin•e•ar /réktilíneeər/ *adj.* (also **rec•ti•lin•e•al** /-eeəl/) **1** bounded or characterized by straight lines. **2** in or forming a straight line. □□ **rec•ti•lin•e•ar•i•ty** /-ineárítee/ *n.* **rec•ti•lin′e•ar•ly** *adv.*

rec•ti•tude /réktitood, -tyōod/ *n.* **1** moral uprightness. **2** correctness. See synonym study at GOODNESS.
■ propriety, morality, virtue, decency, honesty, integrity, righteousness, respectability.

rec•to /réktō/ *n.* (*pl.* **-tos**) **1** right-hand page of an open book. **2** front of a printed leaf.

rec•tor /réktər/ *n.* **1** clergy member in charge of a church or religious institution. **2** head of some schools, universities, and colleges.

rec•to•ry /réktəree/ *n.* (*pl.* **-ries**) rector's house.

rec•tum /réktəm/ *n.* (*pl.* **rectums** or **recta** /-tə/) final section of the large intestine, terminating at the anus.

re•cum•bent /rikúmbənt/ *adj.* lying down; reclining. □□ **re•cum′ben•cy** *n.* **re•cum′bent•ly** *adv.*
■ horizontal, reposing, supine, prone, prostrate.

re•cu•per•ate /rikōopərayt/ *v.* **1** *intr.* recover from illness, exhaustion, loss, etc. **2** *tr.* regain (health, a loss, etc.). □□ **re•cu•per•a′tion** /-ráyshən/ *n.* **re•cu•per•a•tive** /-rətiv/ *adj.*
■ **1** improve, convalesce, get better. **2** see RECOVER *v.* 1.

re•cur /rikúr/ *v.intr.* (**re•curred, re•cur′ring**) **1** occur again; be repeated. **2** come back to one's mind.
■ **1** return, reoccur, reappear.

re•cur•rent /rikúrənt, -kúr-/ *adj.* recurring; happening repeatedly. □□ **re•cur′rence** *n.* **re•cur′rent•ly** *adv.*
■ **1** frequent, periodic, regular, persistent.

re•cy•cle /réesíkəl/ *v.tr.* convert (waste) to reusable material. □□ **re•cy′cla•ble** *adj.*
■ reuse, reclaim.

red /red/ • *adj.* **1** of a color like blood. **2** flushed in the face with shame, anger, etc. **3** (of the eyes) bloodshot or red-rimmed. **4** (of the hair) reddish-brown; tawny. **5** *colloq.* communist; socialist. • *n.* **1** red color or pigment. **2** *colloq.* communist; socialist. **3** debit side of an account (*in the red*). □ **red-blooded** virile; vigorous. **red carpet** privileged treatment of a visitor. **red cell** (or **cor′pus•cle**) erythrocyte. **Red Cross** international relief organization. **red dwarf** old, relatively cool star. **red-eye 1** late-night or overnight flight. **2** *sl.* cheap whiskey. **red-faced** embarrassed; ashamed. **red flag** warning of danger. **red giant** relatively cool giant star. **red-handed** in the act of committing a crime, doing wrong, etc. **red herring** misleading clue. **red hot 1** *colloq.* hot dog. **2** small, red candy with a strong cinnamon flavor. **red-hot 1** heated until red. **2** (of news) completely new. **red-letter day** day that is pleasantly noteworthy or memorable. **red light 1** signal to stop on a road, etc. **2** warning or refusal **red-light district** district containing many brothels. **red meat** meat that is red when raw, esp. beef. **red tape** excessive bureaucracy or formality, esp. in public business. □□ **red′dish** *adj.* **red′ness** *n.*
■ *adj.* **1** crimson, scarlet, vermilion, burgundy, cherry, maroon, cardinal, russet, wine, ruby. **2** blushing, embarrassed. **4** orange, ginger, strawberry blonde, auburn. **5** see LEFT[1] *adj.* 2. • *n.* **1** see RED[1] *adj.* 1 above. **2** see *left-winger* (LEFT). **3** (*in the red*) see DEBT[1]. □ **red-blooded** see TOUGH *adj.* 2. **red-eye 2** see LIQUOR *n.* 1. **red-faced** see ASHAMED 2. **red-handed** in flagrante (delicto), *colloq.* with one's hand in the till. **red herring** see *misinformation* (MISINFORM). **red-hot** *adj.* see HOT *adj.* 1. **2** see *brand-new.* **red light 2** see WARNING 1. **red tape** see BUREAUCRACY. □□ **reddish** see ROSY 1. **redness** see FLUSH *n.* 1.

red•cap /rédkap/ *n.* baggage porter.

red•coat /rédkōt/ *n. hist.* British soldier (so called from the scarlet uniform of most regiments).

red•den /réd'n/ *v.* make or become red.

re•dec•o•rate /reedékərayt/ *v.tr.* decorate (a room, etc.) again or differently. □□ **re•dec•o•ra′tion** /-ráyshən/ *n.*

re•deem /rideém/ *v.tr.* **1** recover by a stipulated payment. **2** make a single payment to discharge (a regular charge or obligation). **3** convert (tokens or bonds, etc.) into goods or cash. **4** deliver from sin and damnation. **5** make up for; compensate for. **6** *refl.* save (oneself) from blame. □□ **re•deem′a•ble** *adj.*
■ **1** reclaim, regain, retrieve, get back, buy

back. **2** see PAY v. 2. **3** exchange, trade in. **4** save, rescue, absolve, deliver (from evil). **5** rehabilitate; atone for, offset, make restitution for.

re•deem•er /ridēémər/ n. person who redeems. □ **the Redeemer** Christ.

re•demp•tion /ridémpshən/ n. **1** redeeming; being redeemed. **2** thing that redeems. □□ **re•demp•tive** /–tiv/ adj.

■ **1** see *recovery* (RECOVER). □□ **redemptive** compensatory.

re•de•vel•op /rēédivéləp/ v.tr. develop anew (esp. an urban area). □□ **re•de•vel′op•er** n. **re•de•vel′op•ment** n.

red•head /rédhed/ n. person with red hair.

red•neck /rédnek/ n. derog. working-class, politically conservative or reactionary white person.

re•do /rēédōō/ v.tr. (3rd sing. present **re•does**; past **re•did**; past part. **re•done**) **1** do again or differently. **2** redecorate.

red•o•lent /rédlənt/ adj. **1** strongly suggestive or smelling of. **2** fragrant. □□ **red′o•lence** n. **red′o•lent•ly** adv.

■ **1** (redolent with or of) reminiscent of, similar to; odorous, smelly. **2** aromatic, perfumed, sweet-scented.

re•dou•ble /rēédúbəl/ v. make or grow greater or more intense or numerous.

re•doubt /ridówt/ n. Mil. outwork or fieldwork without flanking defenses.

re•doubt•a•ble /ridówtəbəl/ adj. formidable, esp. as an opponent. □□ **re•doubt′a•bly** adv.

re•dound /ridównd/ v.intr. **1** make a great contribution to (one's credit or advantage, etc.). **2** come back or recoil (upon).

re•dress /idrés/ • v.tr. remedy or rectify (a wrong, grievance, etc.). • n. (also /réédres/) **1** reparation for a wrong. **2** [foll. by of] redressing (a grievance, etc.). □□ **re•dress′er** n. (also **re•dres′sor**).

re•duce /ridōōs, –dyōōs/ v. **1** tr. & intr. make or become smaller or less. **2** tr. bring by force or necessity (to some undesirable state or action) (reduced them to tears). **3** tr. convert to another (esp. simpler) form (reduced it to a powder). **4** tr. convert (a fraction) to the form with the lowest terms. **5** tr. simplify. **6** tr. make lower in status, rank, price, etc. **7** intr. lessen one's weight or size. □ **reduced circumstances** poverty after relative prosperity. □□ **re•duc′er** n. **re•duc′i•ble** adj. **re•duc•i•bil′i•ty** n. **re•duc′tion** n.

■ **1** decrease, diminish, abate, lessen; ease (up on), let up (on), moderate; cut (back), cut down, shorten. **3** turn; break down or up; see also CHANGE v. 1. **6** demote, degrade, downgrade, colloq. bust; lower, drop, mark down. **7** lose weight, slim (down), diet, slenderize.

re•dun•dant /ridúndənt/ adj. **1** superfluous. **2** that can be omitted without any loss of significance. □□ **re•dun′dan•cy** n. (pl. **–cies**). **re•dun′dant•ly** adv.

■ **1** unnecessary, surplus, unneeded, unwanted.

re•du•pli•cate /ridōōplikayt, –dyōō–/ v.tr.

1 make double. **2** repeat. □□ **re•du•pli•ca′tion** /–káyshən/ n.

red•wood /rédwōōd/ n. very large Californian conifer yielding red wood.

reed /reed/ n. **1 a** water or marsh plant with a firm stem. **b** tall straight stalk of this. **2 a** the vibrating, sound-producing part of the mouthpiece of some wind instruments. **b** [esp. in pl.] reed instrument. □ **reed organ** keyboard instrument with the sound produced by metal reeds.

reed•y /réedee/ adj. (**reed•i•er, reed•i•est**) **1** full of reeds. **2** like a reed. **3** (of a voice) like a reed instrument in tone; not full. □□ **reed′i•ness** n.

reef[1] /reef/ n. ridge of rock, coral, etc., at or near the surface of the sea.

reef[2] /reef/ Naut. • n. part of a sail, folded and tied to reduce the surface area in a high wind. • v.tr. take in a reef or reefs of (a sail).

reef•er /réefər/ n. **1** sl. marijuana cigarette. **2** thick close-fitting double-breasted jacket.

reek /reek/ • v.intr. **1** smell strongly and unpleasantly. **2** have unpleasant or suspicious associations (reeks of corruption). • n. foul or stale smell.

■ v. **1** stink. **2** (reek of) suggest, smack of. • n. stench, odor.

reel /reel/ • n. **1** cylindrical device on which film, wire, etc., are wound. **2** quantity wound on a reel. **3** device for winding and unwinding a line as required, esp. in fishing. **4** revolving part in various machines. **5 a** lively folk dance. **b** music for this. • v. **1** tr. wind (fishing line, etc.) on a reel. **2** tr. [foll. by in, up] draw (fish, etc.) with a reel. **3** intr. stand or move unsteadily. **4** intr. be shaken mentally or physically. □ **reel off** say or recite very rapidly and without apparent effort. □□ **reel′er** n.

■ v. **3** stagger, totter, waver; rock, sway, pitch, swing. □ **reel off** rattle off.

re•en•act /rééinákt/ v.tr. act out (a past event). □□ **re•en•act′ment** n.

re•en•try /rée-éntree/ n. (pl. **–tries**) act of entering again, esp. (of a spacecraft, missile, etc.) into the earth's atmosphere.

ref /ref/ n. colloq. referee in sports.

re•fec•to•ry /riféktəree/ n. (pl. **–ries**) dining room, esp. in a monastery or college.

re•fer /rifər/ v. (**re•ferred, re•fer•ring**) **1** tr. send on or direct (a person, or a question for decision). **2** intr. appeal or have recourse (to some authority or source of information) (referred to his notes). **3** tr. send (a person) to a medical specialist, etc. **4** intr. make an allusion or direct the hearer's attention (did not refer to our problems). **5** intr. (of a statement, etc.) pertain (this paragraph refers to last year). □□ **re•fer•a•ble** /riférəbəl, réfər–/ adj. **re•fer′ral** n. **re•fer′rer** n.

■ **1** hand over, assign; point. **2** (refer to) look at, consult, turn to. **4, 5** (refer to) allude to, mention, touch on, indicate.

ref•er•ee /réfərée/ • n. **1** umpire, esp. in football or boxing. **2** person consulted in a dispute, etc. • v. (**ref•er•ees, ref•er•eed**) **1** intr. act as referee. **2** tr. be the referee of (a game, etc.).

ref•er•ence /réfərəns, réfrəns/ • n. **1** referring of a matter to some authority. **2 a** direction to a book, passage, etc. **b** book or passage so cited. **3 a** written testimonial supporting an applicant for employment, etc. **b** person giving this. • *v.tr.* provide (a book, etc.) with references to authorities. □ **reference book** book intended to be consulted for information on individual matters. **with** (or **in**) **reference to** regarding; as regards; about. **without reference to** not taking account of. □□ **ref•er•en•tial** /réfər-énshəl/ *adj.*

■ *n.* **1** referral, *Law* appeal. **2 a** citation, note, notation. **3 a** endorsement, recommendation.

ref•er•en•dum /réfəréndəm/ *n.* (*pl.* **ref•er•en•dums** or **ref•er•en•da** /-də/) direct popular vote on a political question.

re•fill • *v.tr.* /réefíl/ fill again. • *n.* /réefil/ **1** new filling. **2** material for this. □□ **re•fill′a•ble** *adj.*

re•fine /rifín/ *v.* **1** *tr.* free from impurities or defects. **2** *tr. & intr.* make or become more polished, elegant, or cultured. □□ **re•fin′a•ble** *adj.* **re•fined′** *adj.* **re•fine′ment** *n.*

■ **1** see PURIFY. **2** cultivate, civilize; hone, focus; see also ENHANCE. □□ **refined** sophisticated, urbane, genteel, gracious; subtle, discriminating; pure, clean. **refinement** enhancement; purification; culture, polish, elegance; distinction, detail.

re•fin•er•y /rifínəree/ *n.* (*pl.* **-ies**) plant where oil, etc., is refined.

re•fit • *v.* /réefít/ (**re•fit•ted**, **re•fit•ting**) make or become fit or serviceable again by renewal, repairs, etc. • *n.* /réefit/ refitting. □□ **re•fit′ment** *n.*

refl. *abbr.* **1** reflex. **2** reflexive.

re•flect /riflékt/ *v.* **1** *tr.* (of a surface or body) throw back (heat, light, sound, etc.). **2** *tr.* (of a mirror) show an image of. **3** *tr.* testify to (*their behavior reflects a wish to succeed*). **4** *tr.* (of an action, result, etc.) allow or bring (credit, discredit, etc.). **5 a** *intr.* meditate. **b** *tr.* consider.

■ **1** mirror, return; echo. **3** demonstrate, exhibit, illustrate, point to, indicate, suggest. **4** attract, cast, throw. **5 a** (*reflect on* or *upon*) think about, contemplate, mull over. **b** remind oneself, remember.

re•flec•tion /riflékshən/ *n.* **1** reflecting; being reflected. **2 a** reflected light, heat, or color. **b** reflected image. **3** reconsideration (*on reflection*). **4** discredit or thing bringing discredit. **5** idea arising in the mind; comment. □□ **re•flec′tion•al** *adj.*

■ **1** echo. **3** meditation; second thoughts. **4** see DISCREDIT *n.* 1. **5** see THOUGHT 4, COMMENT *n.* 1.

re•flec•tive /rifléktiv/ *adj.* **1** reflecting. **2** (of mental faculties) concerned in reflection or thought. **3** thoughtful; given to meditation. □□ **re•flec′tive•ly** *adv.* **re•flec′tive•ness** *n.*

■ **3** pensive, contemplative, cogitative.

re•flec•tor /rifléktər/ *n.* **1** piece of glass or metal, etc., for reflecting light in a required direction. **2 a** telescope, etc., using a mirror to produce images. **b** the mirror itself.

re•flex /réefleks/ • *adj.* **1** (of an action) independent of will, as an automatic response to

the stimulation of a nerve. **2** (of an angle) exceeding 180°. • *n.* reflex action.

re•flex•ive /rifléksiv/ *Gram.* • *adj.* **1** (of a word or form) referring back to the subject of a sentence (esp. of a pronoun, e.g., *myself*). **2** (of a verb) having a reflexive pronoun as its object (as in *to wash oneself*). • *n.* reflexive word or form, esp. a pronoun. □□ **re•flex′ive•ly** *adv.* **re•flex′ive•ness** *n.*

re•for•est /réefáwrist, fór-/ *v.tr.* replant former forest land with trees. □□ **re•for•es•ta•tion** /-stáyshən/ *n.*

re•form /rifáwrm/ • *v.* **1** *tr. & intr.* make or become better by the removal of faults and errors. **2** *tr.* abolish or cure (an abuse or malpractice). • *n.* **1** removal of faults or abuses, esp. moral, political, or social. **2** improvement. □ **reform school** institution for the reform of youthful offenders. □□ **re•form′a•ble** *adj.*

■ *v.* **1** improve, emend, rectify, correct, remedy. **2** see ABOLISH. • *n.* **1** rehabilitation, modification, reorganization.

ref•or•ma•tion /réfərmáyshən/ *n.* reforming or being reformed, esp. a radical change for the better in political, religious, or social affairs. □ **the Reformation** *hist.* 16th-c. movement for the reform of abuses in the Roman Catholic Church.

re•for•ma•to•ry /rifáwrmətawree/ *n.* (*pl.* **-ries**) = *reform school.*

re•form•er /rifáwrmər/ *n.* person who advocates or brings about (esp. political or social) reform.

re•fract /rifrákt/ *v.tr.* (of water, air, glass, etc.) deflect (a ray of light, etc.) at a certain angle when it enters obliquely from another medium. □□ **re•frac′tion** *n.* **re•frac′tive** *adj.*

re•frac•tor /rifráktər/ *n.* **1** refracting medium or lens. **2** telescope using a lens to produce an image.

re•frac•to•ry /rifráktəree/ *adj.* stubborn; unmanageable; rebellious. □□ **re•frac′to•ri•ly** *adv.*

re•frain¹ /rifráyn/ *v.intr.* [foll. by *from*] avoid doing (an action).

■ (*refrain from*) keep from, abstain from, eschew; stop, give up, discontinue, quit.

re•frain² /rifráyn/ *n.* **1** recurring phrase or lines, esp. at the ends of stanzas. **2** music accompanying this.

■ **1** chorus, burden, reprise, tag.

re•fresh /rifrésh/ *v.tr.* **1** give fresh spirit or vigor to. **2** revive or stimulate (the memory). □□ **re•fresh′er** *n.* **re•fresh′ing** *adj.* **re•fresh′ing•ly** *adv.*

■ **1** enliven, renew, breathe new life into. **2** jog, activate, prod. □□ **refreshing** invigorating, bracing, exhilarating; cool, thirst-quenching.

re•fresh•ment /rifréshmənt/ *n.* **1** refreshing or being refreshed in mind or body. **2** [usu. in *pl.*] food or drink that refreshes.

■ **1** stimulation, restoration, renewal. **2** (*refreshments*) snack(s), *colloq.* grub, eats, *sl.* chow.

re•frig•er•ant /rifríjərənt/ • *n.* substance used for refrigeration. • *adj.* cooling.

re•frig•er•ate /rifríjərayt/ v. 1 tr. & intr. make or become cool or cold. 2 tr. subject (food, etc.) to cold in order to freeze or preserve it. □□ **re•frig•er•a•tion** /-ráyshən/ n. **re•frig•er•a•tive** /-rətiv/ adj.
■ chill, ice, freeze.

re•frig•er•a•tor /rifríjəraytər/ n. cabinet or room in which food, etc., is kept cold.

ref•uge /réfyōōj/ n. 1 shelter from pursuit, danger, or trouble. 2 person or place, etc., offering this.
■ sanctuary, haven, asylum; citadel, hideout.

ref•u•gee /réfyōōjeé/ n. person taking refuge, esp. in a foreign country, from war, persecution, or natural disaster.
■ fugitive, escapee, displaced person, exile, émigré.

re•fund • v. /rifúnd/ tr. [also absol.] 1 pay back (money or expenses). 2 reimburse (a person). • n. /réefund/ 1 act of refunding. 2 sum refunded. □□ **re•fund•a•ble** adj.

re•fur•bish /rifórbish/ v.tr. 1 brighten up. 2 restore and redecorate. □□ **re•fur•bish•ment** n.
■ 2 refurnish, clean (up), polish, renew, renovate, spruce up, remodel, revamp.

re•fuse[1] /rifyōōz/ v.tr. 1 withhold acceptance of or consent to. 2 indicate unwillingness or inability. 3 [often with double object] not grant (a request) made by (a person). □□ **re•fus•a•ble** adj. **re•fus•al** n.
■ 1 decline, spurn, give thumbs down. 3 - deny, deprive (of); reject. □□ **refusal** denial, rejection, rebuff.

re•fuse[2] /réfyōōs/ n. items rejected as worthless; waste.
■ rubbish, litter, garbage, trash, debris, junk.

re•fute /rifyōōt/ v.tr. 1 prove the falsity or error of (a statement, etc.). 2 rebut by argument. □□ **re•fut•a•ble** adj. **re•fu•ta•tion** /réfyōōtáyshən/ n. **re•fut•er** n.
■ confute.

re•gain /rigáyn/ v.tr. obtain possession or use of after loss. See synonym study at RECOVER.

re•gal /réegəl/ adj. 1 royal; of or by a monarch or monarchs. 2 fit for a monarch; magnificent; majestic. □□ **re•gal•ly** adv.
■ 1 kingly, queenly, stately. 2 splendid, grand.

re•gale /rigáyl/ v.tr. 1 entertain lavishly with feasting. 2 entertain or divert (with talk, etc.). □□ **re•gale•ment** n.
■ 1 feast, wine and dine, indulge. 2 amuse, delight, captivate, fascinate, charm.

re•ga•li•a /rigáylyə/ n.pl. 1 insignia of royalty. 2 elaborate clothes, accouterments, etc.; trappings; finery.
■ 1 decorations, emblems, badges. 2 gear, paraphernalia.

re•gard /rigaárd/ • v.tr. 1 gaze on steadily (usu. in a specified way) (regarded them suspiciously). 2 heed; take into account. 3 think of in a specified way (I regard them kindly). See synonym study at ESTEEM. • n. 1 gaze; steady or significant look. 2 attention or care. 3 esteem; kindly feeling. 4 respect; point attended to. 5 [in pl.] expression of friendliness in a letter, etc.; compliments (sent my best regards). □ **as regards** about; concerning; in respect of. **in** (or **with**) **regard to** as concerns; in respect of.
■ v. 1 view, look at or upon or on, contemplate, stare at. 2 esteem, allow for, consider, notice. 3 perceive, judge; (regard highly) respect, value, admire. • n. 1 see GAZE n. 2 concern, thought, notice. 3 reverence, approval, appreciation, admiration, fondness. 4 particular, aspect, matter. 5 (regards) best wishes, greetings. □ **as regards** see CONCERNING. **in** (or **with**) **regard to** with reference to, in relation to.

re•gard•ing /rigaárding/ prep. about; concerning; in respect of.
■ with regard to, with reference to, in the matter of, pertaining to, anent, colloq. re.

re•gard•less /rigaárdlis/ • adj. without regard or consideration for (regardless of cost). • adv. no matter what (carried on regardless). □□ **re•gard•less•ly** adv.
■ adj. (regardless of) despite, notwithstanding, in spite of. • adv. nevertheless, in any event, in any case, anyway.

re•gat•ta /rigátə, –gátə/ n. sporting event consisting of a series of boat or yacht races.

re•gen•cy /réejənsee/ n. (pl. –cies) office of regent.

re•gen•er•ate • v. /rijénərayt/ 1 tr. & intr. generate again. 2 tr. improve the moral condition of. 3 tr. impart new, more vigorous, and spiritually greater life to. 4 intr. & tr. Biol. regrow or cause (new tissue) to regrow. • adj. /rijénərət/ spiritually born again; reformed. □□ **re•gen•er•a•tion** /–jenəráyshən/ n. **re•gen•er•a•tive** /–rətiv/ adj. **re•gen•er•a•tive•ly** adv. **re•gen•er•a•tor** n.

re•gent /réejənt/ • n. 1 person appointed to rule when a monarch is a minor or absent or incapacitated. 2 member of a governing body, as of a university. • adj. [placed after noun] acting as regent (prince regent).

reg•gae /régay/ n. W. Indian style of music with a strongly accented subsidiary beat.

reg•i•cide /réjisid/ n. 1 person who kills or takes part in killing a king. 2 act of killing a king. □□ **reg•i•cid'al** adj.

re•gime /rayzheém/ n. (also **ré•gime'**) 1 a system of government. b derog. particular government. 2 = REGIMEN.
■ 1 rule, administration, leadership.

reg•i•men /réjimen/ n. prescribed course of exercise, way of life, and diet.
■ see DIET[1] n. 2.

reg•i•ment • n. /réjimənt/ 1 military unit below division level. 2 large array or number. • v.tr. /réjiment/ 1 organize (esp. oppressively) in groups or according to a system. 2 form into a regiment. □□ **reg•i•ment'al** adj. **reg'i•ment•ed** adj. **reg•i•men•ta'tion** n.
■ n. 2 see LOT n. 1. • v. 1 discipline, order, regulate, control. □□ **regimented** see UNIFORM adj. 1, 2.

re•gion /réejən/ n. 1 geographical area or division (mountainous region). 2 part of the body (lumbar region). 3 sphere or realm (region of metaphysics). □ **in the region of** approximately. □□ **re'gion•al** adj. **re'gion•al•ly** adv.

■ **1** see AREA 2. **3** domain, province, field, jurisdiction. □ **in the region of** see *approximately* (APPROXIMATE). □□ **regional** see LOCAL *adj.* 1–2.

reg•is•ter /réjistər/ • *n.* **1** official list, e.g., of births, marriages, property transactions, etc. **2** book in which items are recorded for reference. **3 a** range of a voice or instrument. **b** part of this range (*lower register*). **4** machine in a store, etc., usu. with a drawer for money, for recording sales, etc. **5** *Linguistics* each of several forms of a language (colloquial, literary, etc.) used in particular circumstances. • *v.* **1** *tr.* set down (a name, fact, etc.) formally; record in writing. **2** *tr.* make a mental note of. **3** *tr.* enter or cause to be entered in a particular register. **4** *tr.* (of an instrument) record automatically; indicate. **5 a** *tr.* express (an emotion) facially or by gesture (*registered surprise*). **b** *intr.* (of an emotion) show in a person's face or gestures. □ **registered nurse** state-certified nurse. □□ **reg'is•tra•ble** *adj.*

■ *n.* **1** record, annal(s), chronicle, directory, file, index, inventory, listing. • *v.* **1** enter, catalog, log. **2** see NOTICE *v.* **4** mark, measure, show. **5 a** display, reveal, reflect.

reg•is•trar /réjistraar/ *n.* **1** official responsible for keeping a register. **2** enrollment administrator in a university, etc.

reg•is•tra•tion /rejistráyshən/ *n.* **1** registering; being registered. **2** certificate, etc., that attests to this.

reg•is•try /réjistree/ *n.* (*pl.* **-tries**) **1** place where registers or records are kept. **2** registration.

re•gress • *v.* /rigrés/ **1** *intr.* move backward, esp. return to a former state. **2** *intr. & tr. Psychol.* return or cause to return mentally to a former stage of life. • *n.* /réegres/ act or an instance of going back. □□ **re•gres•sion** /-grés-shən/ *n.* **re•gres•sive** *adj.* **re•gres'sive•ly** *adv.*

re•gret /rigrét/ • *v.tr.* (**re•gret•ted, re•gret•ting**) feel or express sorrow, repentance, or distress over (an action or loss, etc.). • *n.* **1** feeling of sorrow, repentance, disappointment, etc., over an action or loss, etc. **2** [often in *pl.*] an (esp. polite or formal) expression of disappointment or sorrow at an occurrence, inability to comply, etc. □ **give** (or **send**) **one's regrets** formally decline an invitation. □□ **re•gret'ful** *adj.* **re•gret'ful•ly** *adv.* **re•gret'ta•ble** *adj.* **re•gret'ta•bly** *adv.*

■ *v.* rue, mourn, repent; repent. • *n.* **1** guilt, remorse, sadness. □ **give** (or **send**) **one's regrets** refuse, say no. □□ **regretful** sorry, sad, contrite. **regrettable** undesirable, unwelcome, unfortunate; wrong, *colloq.* awful.

re•group /reegroop/ *v.* group or arrange again or differently. □□ **re•group'ment** *n.*

reg•u•lar /régyələr/ • *adj.* **1** conforming to a rule or principle; systematic. **2 a** harmonious; symmetrical (*regular features*). **b** (of a surface, etc.) smooth; level; uniform. **3** acting, done, or recurring uniformly or calculably in time or manner; habitual; constant. **4** *Gram.* (of a noun, verb, etc.) following the normal type of inflection. **5** *colloq.* complete;

---

absolute (*a regular hero*). **6** *Geom.* (of a figure) having all sides and all angles equal. **7** (of forces or troops, etc.) proper or full-time (*regular soldiers*). **8** (of a person) defecating or menstruating at predictable times. See synonym study at NORMAL. • *n.* **1** regular soldier. **2** *colloq.* regular customer, visitor, etc. □□ **reg•u•lar•i•ty** /-láritee/ *n.* **reg'u•lar•ize** *v.tr.* **reg•u•lar•i•za'tion** *n.* **reg'u•lar•ly** *adv.*

■ *adj.* **1** scheduled, consistent, uniform. **2 a** uniform, even, well-proportioned, classic. **b** straight, continuous, flat, plumb. **3** routine, customary, normal, usual, standard; periodic. **5** utter, thorough, genuine. **6** equilateral, equiangular. • *n.* **2** fixture, habitué, patron, client, frequenter. □□ **regularity** consistency, balance, order, predictability, reliability, dependability.

reg•u•late /régyəlayt/ *v.tr.* **1** control by rule. **2** subject to restrictions. **3** adapt to requirements. **4** alter the speed of (a machine or clock) so that it may work accurately. □□ **reg•u•la•tive** /-lətiv/ *adj.* **reg'u•la•tor** *n.* **reg•u•la•to•ry** /-lətəwree/ *adj.*

■ **1** monitor; govern, run, direct, manage. **2** see RESTRICT. **3** adjust, modify, set, fix.

reg•u•la•tion /régyəláyshən/ *n.* **1** regulating; being regulated. **2** prescribed rule. **3** [*attrib.*] in accordance with regulations; of the correct type, etc. (*regulation uniform*).

■ **1** adjustment, control. **2** ruling, law, or dict, directive. **3** (*attrib.*) standard, official, proper.

re•gur•gi•tate /rigórjitayt/ *v.* **1** *tr.* bring (swallowed food) up again to the mouth. **2** *tr.* cast or pour out again (*regurgitate the facts*). **3** *intr.* be brought up again; gush back. □□ **re•gur•gi•ta•tion** /-táyshən/ *n.*

■ **1** vomit, *colloq.* throw up, *sl.* puke, barf. **2** reiterate.

re•hab /réehab/ *n. colloq.* rehabilitation.

re•ha•bil•i•tate /reehəbílitayt/ *v.tr.* **1** restore to effectiveness or normal life by training, etc., esp. after imprisonment or illness. **2** restore to former privileges, proper condition, etc. □□ **re•ha•bil•i•ta•tion** /-táyshən/ *n.* **re•ha•bil'i•ta•tive** *adj.*

■ **1** reestablish, reform, straighten out. **2** reinstate; renew, renovate, fix (up); resuscitate.

re•hash • *v.tr.* /reehásh/ put (old material) into a new form without significant change or improvement. • *n.* /réehash/ **1** material rehashed. **2** rehashing.

■ *v.* rework, go over again.

re•hears•al /rihórsəl/ *n.* **1** act or instance of rehearsing. **2** trial performance or practice of a play, recital, etc.

■ **1** repetition. **2** run-through, *colloq.* dry run.

re•hearse /rihórs/ *v.* **1** *tr.* practice (a play, recital, etc.) for later public performance. **2** *intr.* hold a rehearsal. **3** *tr.* train (a person) by rehearsal. **4** *tr.* recite or say over.

■ **1** run through, go through or over. **3** see TRAIN *v.* 1a. **4** repeat.

Reich /rīkh/ *n.* the former German state, esp. the Third Reich (1933–45).

reign /rayn/ • *v.intr.* **1** be king or queen. **2** prevail (*confusion reigns*). **3** (as **reigning** *adj.*) (of a winner, champion, etc.) currently holding the title, etc. • *n.* **1** sovereignty; rule. **2** period during which a sovereign rules.

■ *v.* **1** rule, govern, wear the crown, occupy the throne. **2** predominate, hold sway; *colloq.* run the show, rule the roost, *sl.* call the shots. • *n.* **1** command, jurisdiction, control, domination.

re•im•burse /rèeimbórs/ *v.tr.* **1** repay (a person who has expended money). **2** repay (a person's expenses). □□ **re•im•burs′a•ble** *adj.* **re•im•burse′ment** *n.* **re•im•burs′er** *n.*

■ **1** recompense, pay back, compensate, remunerate.

rein /rayn/ • *n.* [in *sing.* or *pl.*] **1** long narrow strap with each end attached to the bit, used to guide or check a horse, etc. **2** means of control or guidance. • *v.tr.* **1** check or manage with reins. **2** hold (in) as with reins. **3** govern; restrain; control. □ **give free rein to** remove constraints from; allow full scope to. **keep a tight rein on** allow little freedom to.

■ *n.* **2** curb, restraint, harness, leash; (*hold the reins*) see DOMINATE 1. • *v.* **2, 3** (*rein in*) limit, bridle, restrict, hold back.

re•in•car•na•tion /rèeinkaarnáyshən/ *n.* rebirth of a soul in a new body. □□ **re•in•car′nate** /–kaárnayt/ *v.tr.* · **re•in•car′nate** /–kaárnət/ *adj.*

■ transmigration, metempsychosis. □□ **re•incarnate**(*adj.*) reincarnated, reborn, redivivus.

rein•deer /ráyndeer/ *n.* (*pl.* same or **rein-deers**) subarctic deer of which both sexes have large antlers.

re•in•force /rèeinfáwrs/ *v.tr.* strengthen or support, esp. with additional personnel, material, etc. □ **reinforced concrete** concrete with metal bars or wire, etc., embedded to increase its strength. □□ **re•in•force′ment** *n.* **re•in•forc′er** *n.*

■ buttress, bolster, fortify, prop (up), shore up, brace. □□ **reinforcement** strengthener; (*reinforcements*) reserves, auxiliaries; help, aid, backup.

re•in•state /rèeinstáyt/ *v.tr.* **1** replace in a former position. **2** restore (a person, etc.) to former privileges. □□ **re•in•state′ment** *n.*

re•in•sure /rèeinshōŏr/ *v.* insure again (esp. by transferring risk to another insurer). □□ **re•in•sur′ance** *n.* **re•in•sur′er** *n.*

REIT /reet/ *abbr.* real estate investment trust.

re•it•er•ate /rée-ítərayt/ *v.tr.* say or do again or repeatedly. □□ **re•it•er•a•tion** /–ráyshən/ *n.* **re•it•er•a•tive** /–raytiv, –rətiv/ *adj.*

■ repeat, restate, iterate; labor, belabor, dwell on.

re•ject • *v.tr.* /rijékt/ **1** put aside or send back as not to be used or complied with, etc. **2** refuse to accept or believe in. **3** rebuff or snub (a person). **4** cast up again; vomit. **5** *Med.* show an immune response to (a transplanted organ or tissue) so that it fails to survive. • *n.* /réejekt/ thing or person re-

jected as unfit or below standard. □□ **re•ject′er** /rijéktər/ *n.* (also **re•jec′tor**).) **re•jec•tion** /–jékshən/ *n.*

■ *v.* **1** decline, spurn, veto, turn down; throw away *or* out, discard, disown, eliminate. **2** see DISMISS 4, RENOUNCE 2. **3** shun, brush aside, repel, give a person the cold shoulder, turn one's back on, ignore, give a person the brush-off; jilt. • *n.* second, irregular, discard, castoff. □□ **rejection** refusal, denial, turndown.

re•joice /rijóys/ *v.intr.* feel great joy; be glad. □□ **re•joic′ing•ly** *adv.*

■ delight, exult, glory, revel, be happy *or* delighted *or* overjoyed; jump for joy, celebrate.

re•join[1] /reejóyn/ *v.* **1** *tr. & intr.* join together again; reunite. **2** *tr.* join (a companion, etc.) again.

re•join[2] /rijóyn/ *v.* **1** *tr.* say in answer; retort. **2** *intr. Law* reply to a charge or pleading in a lawsuit. □□ **re•join′der** *n.*

re•ju•ve•nate /rijōōvinayt/ *v.tr.* make (as if) young again. □□ **re•ju•ve•na•tion** /–náy-shən/ *n.* **re•ju′ve•na•tor** *n.*

■ restore, refresh, renew, breathe new life into.

rel. *abbr.* **1** relating. **2** relative. **3** religion. **4** religious.

re•lapse /riláps/ • *v.intr.* fall back or sink again (into a worse state after improvement). • *n.* (also /rèelaps/) relapsing, esp. a deterioration in a patient's condition after partial recovery.

■ *v.* decline, weaken, fail, fade, regress. • *n.* degeneration, lapse, retrogression.

re•late /riláyt/ *v.* **1** *tr.* narrate or recount. **2** *tr.* [in *passive*; often foll. by *to*] be connected by blood or marriage. **3** *tr.* connect (two things) in thought or meaning. **4** *intr.* have reference (to). **5** *intr.* **a** bring oneself into relation (to). **b** feel sympathetic (to). □□ **re•lat′a•ble** *adj.*

■ **1** tell, report, describe. **3** associate, link, tie. **4** (*relate to*) apply to, concern, regard, pertain to, refer to. **5 b** (*relate to*) understand, empathize with, identify with.

re•lat•ed /riláytid/ *adj.* connected.

■ kin, akin; associated, affiliated; allied.

re•la•tion /riláyshən/ *n.* **1 a** what one person or thing has to do with another. **b** way in which one person stands or is related to another. **2** relative. **3** [in *pl.*] **a** dealings (with others). **b** sexual intercourse. **4** = RELATIONSHIP. □ **in relation to** as regards. □□ **re•la′tion•al** *adj.*

■ **1 a** relationship, connection, association, link, tie, kinship. **b** see LINK *n.* 2b. **2** kinsman, kinswoman. **3** (*relations*) **a** doings. **b** coitus, sex. ■ **in relation to** concerning, about, regarding, *colloq.* re.

re•la•tion•ship /riláyshənship/ *n.* **1** fact or state of being related. **2** *colloq.* **a** connection or association (*good working relationship*). **b** emotional (esp. sexual) association between two people.

rel•a•tive /rélətiv/ • *adj.* **1** considered in relation to something else (*relative velocity*). **2** implying comparison or contextual relation (*"heat" is a relative word*). **3** comparative (*their relative advantages*). **4** having mutual relations; corresponding in some way; related to each other. **5** [foll. by *to*] having reference or relating (*the facts relative to the issue*). **6** *Gram.* (of a word, esp. a pronoun) referring to an expressed or implied antecedent. • *n.* **1** person connected by blood or marriage. **2** species related to another by common origin. **3** *Gram.* relative word, esp. a pronoun. □□ **rel'a•tive•ly** *adv.*

■ *adj.* **3** see PROPORTIONAL *adj.* **4** allied, affiliated, associated. **5** (*relative to*) pertinent *or* relevant *or* germane *or* applicable to. • *n.* **1** see RELATION 2. □□ **relatively** more or less, somewhat, rather, to some degree, to some extent.

rel•a•tiv•i•ty /rélətívitee/ *n.* **1** being relative. **2** *Physics* **a** (*special theory of relativity*) theory based on the principle that all motion is relative and that light has constant velocity. **b** (*general theory of relativity*) theory extending this to gravitation and accelerated motion.

re•lax /rıláks/ *v.* **1** *tr. & intr.* make or become less stiff, rigid, tense, or formal. **2** *intr.* cease work or effort. **3** *tr.* (as **relaxed** *adj.*) at ease; unperturbed. □□ **re•lax•a'tion** *n.* **re•lax'er** *n.*

■ **1** loosen, ease, slacken; calm down, ease off *or* up, take it easy, unwind; tone down; lighten up (on). **2** slow down, let up, rest. **3** (**relaxed**) easygoing, calm, mellow; *sl.* laid back. □□ **relaxation** recreation, leisure; alleviation, lessening, *colloq.* letup.

re•lax•ant /rıláksənt/ • *n.* drug, etc., that relaxes and reduces tension. • *adj.* causing relaxation.

re•lay /reélay/ • *n.* **1** fresh set of people, material, etc. **2** = *relay race.* **3** device activating an electric circuit, etc., in response to changes affecting itself. **4** device to receive, reinforce, and transmit a message, broadcast, etc. **b** relayed message *or* transmission. • *v.tr.* (also /rıláy/) receive (a message, broadcast, etc.) and transmit it to others. □ **relay race** team race in which each member in turn covers part of the distance.

re•lease /rıleés/ • *v.tr.* **1** set free; liberate. **2** allow to move from a fixed position. **3** make (information, a film, etc.) publicly available. • *n.* **1** liberation from restriction, duty, or difficulty. **2** handle or catch that frees a mechanism. **3** document or item of information made available for publication (*press release*). **4 a** film, record, etc., that is released. **b** releasing or being released in this way. □□ **re•leas'a•ble** *adj.*

■ *v.* **1** let go, (let) loose, untie, deliver. **3** issue, publish; launch. • *n.* **1** freedom, discharge, emancipation. **3** announcement, notice, story, report.

rel•e•gate /réligayt/ *v.tr.* **1** consign or dismiss to an inferior position. **2** banish. □□ **rel•e•ga'tion** /–gáyshən/ *n.*

re•lent /rılént/ *v.intr.* abandon a harsh intention; yield to compassion; relax severity.

■ soften, capitulate, show mercy, come around.

re•lent•less /rıléntlıs/ *adj.* **1** unrelenting. **2** oppressively constant. See synonym study

at SEVERE. □□ **re•lent'less•ly** *adv.* **re•lent' less•ness** *n.*

■ **1** unyielding, unstoppable; rigid, obstinate; uncompromising, ruthless, merciless, cruel. **2** nonstop, persistent, incessant, perpetual, continuous.

rel•e•vant /rélivənt/ *adj.* bearing on or having reference to the matter in hand. □□ **rel'e• vance** *n.* **rel'e•van•cy** *n.* **rel'e•vant•ly** *adv.*

■ pertinent, appropriate, applicable, germane. □□ **relevance, relevancy** connection, tie-in, relation.

re•li•a•ble /rılíəbəl/ *adj.* dependable; of sound and consistent character or quality. □□ **re•li• a•bil'i•ty** *n.* **re•li'a•bly** *adv.*

■ trustworthy, safe; honest, responsible; credible.

re•li•ance /rılíəns/ *n.* trust; confidence. □□ **re•li'ant** *adj.*

■ (*reliance in* or *on*) trust in, faith in, dependence on.

rel•ic /rélık/ *n.* **1** object interesting because of its age or association. **2** part of a deceased holy person's remains, etc., kept out of reverence. **3** surviving custom or belief, etc., from a past age. **4** memento or souvenir. **5** [in *pl.*] fragments, ruins, etc.

■ **4** keepsake, remembrance, token. **5** (*relics*) traces, remnants, wreckage.

re•lief /rıleéf/ *n.* **1 a** alleviation of or deliverance from pain, distress, anxiety, etc. **b** feeling accompanying such deliverance. **2** assistance (esp. financial) given to those in need. **3 a** replacing of a person or persons on duty. **b** person or persons replacing others in this way. **4 a** method of molding, carving, or stamping in which the design stands out from the surface. **b** piece of sculpture, etc., in relief. **5** vividness; distinctness (*in sharp relief*). **6** reinforcement or rescue (of a place). □ **relief map** map indicating hills and valleys by shading, etc.

■ **1 a** easing, abatement, release. **b** see EASE *n.* 2. **2** aid, help, support, backing, subsidy. **3 a** see SUBSTITUTE *n.*, CHANGE *n.* 3. **b** substitute, stand-in. **5** sharpness, focus, precision, clarity.

re•lieve /rıleév/ *v.tr.* **1** bring or give relief to. **2** mitigate the tedium or monotony of. **3** release (a person) from a duty by acting as or providing a substitute. **4** [foll. by *of*] take (a burden or responsibility) away from (a person). See synonym study at ALLEVIATE. □ **re• lieve oneself** urinate or defecate. □□ **re• liev'a•ble** *adj.* **re•lieved'** *adj.* **re•liev'er** *n.*

■ **1** aid, rescue; alleviate, ease, soothe; see also ASSIST *v.* 1. **2** see MITIGATE. **3** stand in for, replace, take over for *or* from. **4** free, rid, unburden.

re•li•gion /rılíjən/ *n.* **1** belief in a personal God or gods entitled to obedience and worship. **2** expression of this in worship. **3** particular system of faith and worship. **4** thing that one is devoted to.

■ **1, 3, 4** creed, faith.

re•lig•i•os•i•ty /rılíjeeósitee/ *n.* condition of being religious or excessively religious.

re•li•gious /rılíjəs/ *adj.* **1** devoted to religion;

pious; devout. **2** of or concerned with religion. **3** of or belonging to a monastic order. **4** scrupulous; conscientious. □□ **re•li′gious•ly** *adv.*

■ **1** churchgoing, God-fearing, holy, spiritual. **2** see SPIRITUAL *adj.* 2. **4** exact, precise, rigorous, meticulous, faithful.

re•lin•quish /rilíngkwish/ *v.tr.* **1** surrender or resign (a right or possession). **2** give up or cease from (a habit, plan, etc.). **3** relax hold of (an object held). □□ **re•lin′quish•ment** *n.*

■ **1, 2** yield, cede, waive; drop, renounce, let go of. **3** release, free.

SYNONYM STUDY: relinquish

ABANDON, CEDE, SURRENDER, WAIVE, YIELD. Of all these verbs meaning to let go or give up, **relinquish** is the most general. It can imply anything from simply releasing one's grasp (*she relinquished the wheel*) to giving up control or possession reluctantly (*After the defeat, he was forced to relinquish his command*). **Surrender** also implies giving up, but usually after a struggle or show of resistance (*The villagers were forced to surrender to the guerrillas*). **Yield** is a milder synonym for *surrender*, implying some concession, respect, or even affection on the part of the person who is *surrendering* (*She yielded to her mother's wishes and stayed home*). **Waive** also suggests a concession, but it seldom implies force or necessity. It means to give up voluntarily a right or claim to something (*She waived her right to have a lawyer present*). To **cede** is to give up by legal transfer or according to the terms of a treaty (*The French ceded the territory that is now Louisiana*). If one *relinquishes* something finally and completely, often because of weariness or discouragement, the correct word is **abandon** (*They were told to abandon all hope of being rescued*).

---

rel•ish /rélish/ • *n.* **1** great liking or enjoyment. **2 a** appetizing flavor. **b** attractive quality. **3** condiment eaten with plainer food to add flavor. • *v.tr.* **1** get pleasure out of; enjoy greatly. **2** anticipate with pleasure.

■ *n.* **1** pleasure, delight, fondness; zest, fancy. **2 a** see TANG 1. **b** see APPEAL *n.* 4. • *v.* **1** delight in, be partial to, savor. **2** look forward to, eagerly await.

re•live /reéliv/ *v.tr.* live (an experience, etc.) over again, esp. in the imagination.

re•lo•cate /reélókayt/ *v.* **1** *tr.* locate in a new place. **2** *intr.* move to a new place. □□ **re•lo•ca•tion** /-káyshən/ *n.*

re•luc•tant /rilúktənt/ *adj.* unwilling or disinclined. □□ **re•luc′tance** *n.* **re•luc′tant•ly** *adv.*

■ unenthusiastic, hesitant; loath; averse, opposed. □□ **reluctance** aversion, dislike, hesitancy.

re•ly /rilí/ *v.intr.* (**–lies, –lied**) [foll. by *on, upon*] depend on with confidence or assurance.

■ (*rely on* or *upon*) count on or upon, trust in, swear by.

REM /rem/ *abbr.* rapid eye movement.

re•main /rimáyn/ *v.intr.* **1** be left over after others or other parts have been removed, used, etc. **2** stay; be left behind (*remained at home*). **3** continue to be (*remained calm*). **4** (as **remaining** *adj.*) left behind; unused.

■ **2** linger; see also STAY[1] *v.* 1. **3** carry on as, persist as. **4** (**remaining**) extant, outstanding, leftover, surviving.

re•main•der /rimáyndər/ • *n.* **1** part remaining or left over. **2** remaining persons or things. **3** number left after division or subtraction. **4** copies of a book left unsold. • *v.tr.* dispose of (a remainder of books) at a reduced price.

■ *n.* **1, 2** rest, balance, residue; remnants; surplus.

re•mains /rimáynz/ *n.pl.* **1** what remains after other parts have been removed or used, etc. **2** relics of antiquity, esp. of buildings. **3** dead body.

■ **1** vestiges, remnants, leftovers, scraps. **2** see RELIC 5. **3** corpse, carcass, cadaver.

re•make • *v.tr.* /reémáyk/ (*past* and *past part.* **re•made**) make again or differently. • *n.* /reémayk/ thing that has been remade, esp. a movie.

re•mand /rimánd/ *v.tr.* return (a prisoner) to custody, esp. to allow further inquiries to be made.

re•mark /rimaárk/ • *v.* **1** *tr.* **a** say by way of comment. **b** take notice of. **2** *intr.* make a comment. • *n.* **1** written or spoken comment; anything said. **2** noticing or noting (*worthy of remark*).

■ *v.* **1 a** mention, state, assert. **b** observe, regard. **2** reflect (on or upon); (*remark on* or *upon*) discuss, review, examine. • *n.* **1** see COMMENT *n.* 1. **2** see COMMENT *n.* 2a.

re•mark•a•ble /rimaárkəbəl/ *adj.* worth notice; exceptional; striking. See synonym study at NOTICEABLE. □□ **re•mark′a•ble•ness** *n.* **re•mark′a•bly** *adv.*

■ extraordinary, unusual, outstanding, noteworthy, notable, distinguished, uncommon, incredible, impressive; strange, different, odd, peculiar; distinctive, special, wonderful, marvelous, rare, memorable, unforgettable.

re•match /reémach/ *n.* return match or game.

re•me•di•al /rimeédeeəl/ *adj.* **1** affording or intended as a remedy. **2** (of teaching) for those in need of improvement in a particular discipline. □□ **re•me′di•al•ly** *adv.*

rem•e•dy /rémidee/ • *n.* (*pl.* **–dies**) **1** medicine or treatment. **2** means of counteracting or removing anything undesirable. • *v.tr.* (**–dies, –died**) rectify; make good.

■ *n.* **1** cure, therapy, restorative. **2** countermeasure, answer, solution. • *v.* correct, reform, improve, redress, repair; restore.

re•mem•ber /rimémbər/ *v.tr.* **1** keep in the memory; not forget. **2** bring back into one's thoughts. **3** convey greetings from (one person) to (another) (*remember me to your mother*).

■ **1** retain, keep or bear in mind, recall, call to mind; think back to. **2** recollect, think back on or to.

re•mem•brance /rimémbrəns/ *n.* **1** remembering; being remembered. **2** memory; rec-

greetings conveyed through a third person.

■ **2** reminiscence, thought. **3** memento, reminder, token, relic. **4** (*remembrances*) regards, best wishes.

re•mind /rimínd/ *v.tr.* cause (a person) to remember or think of (something or someone).

■ jog a person's memory.

re•mind•er /rimíndər/ *n.* **1** thing that reminds, esp. a memo or note. **2** memento.

■ **1** mnemonic; cue. **2** souvenir, keepsake, remembrance.

rem•i•nisce /réminís/ *v.intr.* indulge in reminiscence.

■ remember, recollect, think back, look back.

rem•i•nis•cence /réminísəns/ *n.* **1** remembering things past. **2** [in *pl.*] collection in literary form of incidents and experiences that a person remembers.

■ **1** recollection, memory, remembrance; thought. **2** (*reminiscences*) reflections, memoirs.

rem•i•nis•cent /réminísənt/ *adj.* **1** [foll. by *of*] tending to remind one of or suggest. **2** concerned with reminiscence. □□ **rem•i•nis'cent•ly** *adv.*

■ **1** (*reminiscent of*) suggestive of, similar to.

re•miss /rimís/ *adj.* careless of duty; lax; negligent.

■ slack, neglectful, forgetful.

re•mis•sion /rimíshən/ *n.* **1** forgiveness (of sins, etc.). **2** remitting of a debt or penalty, etc. **3** diminution of force, effect, or degree (esp. of disease or pain). □□ **re•mis•sive** /-mísiv/ *adj.*

■ **1** absolution. **3** abatement, alleviation, easing.

re•mit /rimít/ *v.* (**re•mit•ted, re•mit•ting**) **1** *tr.* cancel or refrain from exacting or inflicting (a debt, punishment, etc.). **2** *intr. & tr.* abate or slacken; cease partly or entirely **3** *tr.* send (money, etc.) in payment. **4** *tr.* refer (a matter for decision, etc.) to some authority. **5** *tr.* pardon (sins, etc.). □□ **re•mit•ta•ble** /mítəbl/ *adj.* **re•mit'tal** *n.* **re•mit'ter** *n.*

■ **2** subside, ebb, ease up or off, diminish, decrease, lessen, alleviate. **3** see PAY *v.* 2. **4** see REFER 1.

re•mit•tance /rimít'ns/ *n.* **1** payment sent, esp. by mail. **2** sending money.

■ **1** see PAY *n.*

rem•nant /rémnənt/ *n.* **1** small remaining quantity. **2** piece of leftover cloth, etc. See synonym study at TRACE.

■ **1** vestige, trace, remains. **2** scrap, fragment, end.

re•mod•el /reemód'l/ *v.tr.* **1** model again or differently. **2** reconstruct.

re•mon•strate /rémənstráyt, rimón-/ *v.* **1** *intr.* [foll. by *with*] make a protest; argue forcibly. **2** *tr.* urge protestingly. □□ **re•mon'strance** *n.* **re•mon'strant** *adj.* **re•mon•stra•tion** /rémənstráyshən/ *n.* **re•mon•stra•tive** /rimónstrətiv/ *adj.* **re•mon'stra•tor** *n.*

re•morse /rimáwrs/ *n.* **1** deep regret for a wrong committed. **2** compassion (esp. in *without remorse*). □□ **re•morse'ful** *adj.* **re•morse'ful•ly** *adv.* **re•morse'less** *adj.*

■ repentance, pangs of conscience, compunction. □□ **remorseful** sorry, guilty, contrite, ashamed. **remorseless** cruel, heartless, callous, merciless, ruthless; relentless.

re•mote /rimót/ *adj.* (**re•mot•er, re•mot•est**) **1** far away in place or time. **2** isolated; secluded. **3** distantly related (*remote ancestor*). **4** slight; faint (*not the remotest chance*). **5** aloof; not friendly. □ **remote control** control of an apparatus from a distance by means of signals transmitted from a radio or electronic device. □□ **re•mote'ly** *adv.* **re•mote'ness** *n.*

■ **1** distant, removed, outlying. **2** lonely, out-of-the-way; *sl.* in the sticks, in the boondocks. **3** far-removed; early, ancient. **4** slim, slender, poor, negligible, improbable, unlikely. **5** detached, standoffish, indifferent.

re•move /rimó͞ov/ *v.tr.* **1** take off or away from the place occupied. **2** get rid of; eliminate (*will remove all doubts*). **3** take away. **4** dismiss (from office, etc.). **5** [in *passive*; foll. by *from*] distant or remote in condition (*not far removed from anarchy*). **6** (as **removed** *adj.*) (esp. of cousins) separated by a specified number of steps of descent (*a first cousin twice removed* = a grandchild of a first cousin). □□ **re•mov'a•ble** *adj.* **re•mov•a•bil'i•ty** *n.* **re•mov'al** *n.*

■ **1** shed, discard, detach, disconnect, undo. **2** eradicate, erase, delete, expunge. **4** discharge, expel, oust, unseat, kick out, *colloq.* sack, *sl.* fire. □□ **removal** transfer, displacement, expulsion.

re•mu•ner•ate /rimyō͞onərayt/ *v.tr.* serve as or provide recompense for (toil, etc.) or to (a person). □□ **re•mu•ner•a•tion** /ráynhən/ *n.* **re•mu•ner•a•tive** /-rətiv, -raytiv/ *adj.*

■ □□ **remuneration** payment, compensation, salary, wages, earnings; income; reimbursement, restitution, reparation.

Ren•ais•sance /rénəsaans, -zaans/ *n.* **1** revival of art and literature in the 14th–16th c. **2** period of this. **3** culture and style of art, architecture, etc., developed during this era. **4** (**renaissance**) any similar revival.

■ **4** (**renaissance**) rebirth, renewal, resurgence.

re•nal /reénəl/ *adj.* of or concerning the kidneys.

re•nas•cent /rinásənt, rináy-/ *adj.* springing up anew; being reborn. □□ **re•nas'cence** *n.*

rend /rend/ *v.* (*past* and *past part.* **rent** /rent/) *tr.* tear or wrench forcibly.

■ split, rip, divide; tear.

rend•er /réndər/ *v.tr.* **1** cause to be or become (*rendered us helpless*). **2** give or pay (money, service, etc.), esp. in return or as a thing due (*render thanks*). **3 a** give (assistance). **b** show (obedience, etc.). **c** do (a service, etc.). **4 a** represent or portray. **b** perform; execute. **5** translate. **6** melt (fat, etc.). □□ **ren'der•ing** *n.*

■ **1** make. **2** reciprocate, return, repay. **3 a** offer, extend, proffer. **c** provide, carry out, fulfill. **4 a** depict, create, produce. **b** see ACT *v.* 4a, PERFORM 2. **5** interpret; transcribe, convert; reword. **6** clarify; extract.

□□ **rendering** interpretation, performance, portrayal, rendition, version.

ren•dez•vous /róndayvōō, –də–/ • *n.* (*pl.* same /–vōōz/) **1** agreed or regular meeting place. **2** meeting by arrangement. • *v.intr.* (**ren•dez•vouses** /–vōōz/; **ren•dez•voused** /–vōōd/; **ren•dez•vous•ing** /–vōōing/) meet at a rendezvous.

ren•di•tion /rendíshən/ *n.* interpretation or rendering, esp. artistic.
■ see *rendering* (RENDER).

ren•e•gade /rénigayd/ • *n.* person who deserts a party or principles. • *adj.* traitorous; heretical.
■ *n.* dissident; turncoat, defector, apostate. • *adj.* treasonous, disloyal.

re•nege /riníg, –nég, –néeg/ *v.* **1** *intr.* go back on one's word, etc. **2** *tr.* deny; renounce. □□ **re•neg′er** *n.*
■ **1** back out, break one's promise, recant. **2** abjure; see also ABANDON *v.* 2.

re•new /rinōō, –nyōō/ *v.tr.* **1** revive; restore. **2** reinforce; resupply; replace. **3** reestablish; resume. **4** [also *absol.*] grant or be granted a continuation of (a license, lease, etc.). □□ **re•new′a•ble** *adj.* **re•new′al** *n.* **re•new′er** *n.*
■ **1** regenerate, refresh, rejuvenate, revitalize; revamp, redo, refurbish, renovate, redecorate, *colloq.* do over. **2** restock, replenish, refill. **3** pick or take up (again), restart, reopen.

ren•net /rénit/ *n.* preparation made from the stomach membrane of a calf or from certain fungi, used in making cheese.

re•nounce /rinówns/ *v.tr.* **1** formally abandon (a claim, right, etc.). **2** repudiate; reject. □□ **re•nounce′a•ble** *adj.* **re•nounce′ment** *n.*
■ **1** give up, surrender, forgo, forsake. **2** spurn, disown, discard.

ren•o•vate /rénəvayt/ *v.tr.* restore to good condition; repair. □□ **ren•o•va′tion** /–váy-shən/ *n.* **ren′o•va•tor** *n.*
■ redecorate, refurbish, revamp, remodel.

re•nown /rinówn/ *n.* fame; high distinction. □□ **re•nowned′** *adj.*
■ celebrity, repute, eminence, note; stardom. □□ **renowned** famous, prominent, well-known, illustrious.

rent¹ /rent/ • *n.* **1** tenant's periodical payment to an owner for the use of land or premises. **2** payment for the use of a service, equipment, etc. • *v.* **1** *tr.* take, occupy, or use at a rent. **2** *tr.* let or hire (a thing) for rent. **3** *intr.* [foll. by *for, at*] be let or hired out at a specified rate. □□ **rent′er** *n.*
■ *n.* **2** charge, lease; fee. • *v.* lease, charter.

rent² /rent/ *n.* **1** large tear in a garment, etc. **2** cleft; fissure.
■ **1** rip, split, gash, slash, hole, slit. **2** see GORGE *n.* 1.

rent³ *past* and *past part.* of REND.

rent•al /rént′l/ *n.* **1** amount paid or received as rent. **2** act of renting. **3** rented house, etc.

re•nun•ci•a•tion /rinúnseeáyshən/ *n.* **1** renouncing or giving up. **2** self-denial.

re•or•i•ent /rée-áwree-ent, –óree-ent/ *v.tr.*

1 give a new direction or outlook to (ideas, a person, etc.); redirect (a thing). **2** help (a person) find his or her bearings again. **3** [*refl.*] adjust oneself to.

re•or•i•en•tate /rée-áwreeəntayt, –óreeən–/ *v.tr.* = REORIENT. □□ **re•or•i•en•ta′tion** /–táyshən/ *n.*

Rep. *abbr.* **1** Representative. **2** Republican. **3** Republic.

rep¹ /rep/ *n. colloq.* representative, esp. a salesperson.

rep² /rep/ *n. colloq.* repertory theater or company.

repaid *past* and *past part.* of REPAY.

re•pair¹ /ripáir/ • *v.tr.* **1** restore to good condition after damage or wear. **2** set right or make amends for (loss, wrong, etc.). • *n.* **1** restoring to sound condition (*in need of repair*). **2** result of this (*the repair is hardly visible*). **3** relative condition for working or using (*in good repair*). □□ **re•pair′a•ble** *adj.* **re•pair′er** *n.*
■ *v.* **1** fix (up), mend, patch (up), adjust. • *n.* **1** restoration, renovation. **3** form, working order, shape.

re•pair² /ripáir/ *v.intr.* [foll. by *to*] resort; have recourse; go (*repaired to Spain*).

re•pair•man /ripáirmən/ *n.* (*pl.* **–men**) person who repairs machinery, etc.

rep•a•ra•ble /répərəbəl, ripárəbəl/ *adj.* (of a loss, etc.) that can be made good. □□ **rep•a•ra•bil′i•ty** *n.* **rep′a•ra•bly** *adv.*

rep•a•ra•tion /répəráyshən/ *n.* **1** making amends. **2** [esp. in *pl.*] compensation for war damage. □□ **re•par•a•tive** /ripáirətiv/ *adj.*
■ **2** badinage, patter, raillery, wordplay.

re•past /ripást/ *n.* **1** food and drink for a meal.

re•pa•tri•ate /réepáytreeayt/ *v.* **1** *tr.* restore (a person) to his or her native land. **2** *intr.* return to one's own native land. • *n.* /–treeət/ person who has been repatriated. □□ **re•pa•tri•a•tion** /–áyshən/ *n.*

re•pay /réepáy/ *v.tr.* (*past* and *past part.* **re•paid**) **1** pay back (money). **2** make repayment to (a person). **3** requite (a service, action, etc.). □□ **re•pay′a•ble** *adj.* **re•pay′ment** *n.*
■ **1** refund, square, give back, return. **2** compensate, reimburse. **3** reciprocate.

re•peal /ripéel/ • *v.tr.* revoke or annul (a law, etc.). • *n.* repealing. □□ **re•peal′a•ble** *adj.*
■ *v.* recall, rescind, reverse, cancel, nullify, abolish.

re•peat /ripéet/ • *v.* **1** *tr.* say or do over again. **2** *tr.* recite, rehearse, report, or reproduce (something from memory). **3 a** *intr.* recur; appear again. **b** *refl.* recur in the same or a similar form (*history repeats itself*). • *n.* **1 a** repeating. **b** thing repeated (often *attrib.*: *repeat performance*). **2** repeated broadcast. □ **repeating decimal** decimal fraction in which the same figures repeat indefinitely. □□ **re•peat′a•ble** *adj.* **re•peat•a•bil′i•ty** *n.* **re•peat′ed•ly** *adv.*
■ *v.* **1** reiterate, restate, retell, *colloq.* recap; echo. **2** quote, replicate. **3 a** see RECUR.

b duplicate. • *n.* **1** copy, replica. **2** rerun, re-broadcast. □□ **repeatedly** again and again, time after time, recurrently, repetitiously.

re•pel /ripél/ *v.tr.* (**re•pelled, re•pel•ling**) **1** drive back; ward off. **2** refuse admission or acceptance to. **3** be repulsive or distasteful to. □□ **re•pel′lent** *adj. & n.* **re•pel′ler** *n.*
  ■ **1** repulse, reject, fend off, resist. **3** revolt, repulse, offend. □□ **repellent** *adj.* repulsive, revolting, disgusting, offensive, repugnant.

re•pent /ripént/ *v.* **1** *intr.* feel deep sorrow about one's actions, etc. **2** *tr.* [also *absol.*] wish one had not done; resolve not to continue (a wrongdoing, etc.). □□ **re•pent′ance** *n.* **re•pent′ant** *adj.* **re•pent′er** *n.*
  ■ regret, lament, rue. □□ **repentant** contrite, remorseful, sorry, ashamed, penitent.

re•per•cus•sion /réepərkúshən, répər–/ *n.* **1** indirect effect or reaction. **2** recoil after impact. **3** echo. □□ **re•per•cus′sive** /–kúsiv/ *adj.*
  ■ **1** consequence, aftereffect, result; outcome, conclusion, upshot. **3** reverberation; boom, peal.

rep•er•toire /répərtwaar/ *n.* stock of pieces, etc., that a performer, etc. is prepared to perform.

rep•er•to•ry /répərtawree/ *n.* (*pl.* **–ries**) **1** = REPERTOIRE. **2** performance of various plays for short periods by one company. **3 a** repertory company. **b** repertory theaters collectively. **4** store or collection, esp. of information, instances, etc. □ **repertory company** theatrical company that performs plays from a repertoire.
  ■ **4** repertoire, reservoir, stock, supply, stockpile.

rep•e•ti•tion /répitíshən/ *n.* **1** repeating or being repeated. **2** thing repeated. □□ **rep•e•ti′tious** *adj.* **rep•e•ti′tious•ly** *adv.* **re•pet′i•tive** *adj.* **re•pet′i•tive•ly** *adv.*
  ■ reiteration, duplication, replication; rerun, echo. □□ **repetitious** tiresome, tedious, redundant. **repetitive** wordy; monotonous.

re•place /ripláys/ *v.tr.* **1** put back in place. **2** take the place of; succeed; be substituted for. **3** provide a substitute for. □□ **re•place′a•ble** *adj.* **re•place′ment** *n.* **re•plac′er** *n.*
  ■ **1** restore, return. **2** take over from.

SYNONYM STUDY: replace

DISPLACE, SUPERSEDE, SUPPLANT. When a light bulb burns out, you **replace** it, meaning that you substitute something new or functioning for what is lost, destroyed, or worn out. If something *replaces* what is obsolete or ineffective with something that is superior, more up-to-date, or more authoritative, the correct verb is **supersede** (*the computer superseded the electric typewriter*). In contrast, **displace** suggests that something or someone has been ousted or dislodged forcibly, without necessarily implying that it was inferior or ineffective (*a growing number of workers were being displaced by machines*). **Supplant** is more restricted in meaning; it suggests that someone or something has been *displaced* by force, fraud, or innovation (*The democratic government had been supplanted by a power-hungry tyrant*). It can also mean uprooted or

---

wiped out (*the English immigrants gradually supplanted the island's native inhabitants*).

---

re•play • *v.tr.* /reepláy/ play (a match, recording, etc.) again. • *n.* /réeplay/ act or instance of replaying a match, recording, or recorded incident in a game, etc.

re•plen•ish /riplénish/ *v.tr.* **1** fill up again. **2** renew (a supply, etc.). □□ **re•plen′ish•ment** *n.*
  ■ restock, refill; reinforce.

re•plete /ripléet/ *adj.* **1** filled or well-supplied. **2** stuffed; gorged; sated. □□ **re•plete′ness** *n.* **re•ple•tion** /–pléeshən/ *n.*
  ■ **1** chock-full, crammed *or* jammed, teeming. **2** satisfied, full.

rep•li•ca /réplikə/ *n.* **1 a** exact copy. **b** (of a person) exact likeness. **2** copy or model, esp. on a smaller scale. □□ **rep′li•cate** *v.* **rep•li•ca′tion** *n.*
  ■ **1 a** duplicate, facsimile, reproduction, replication; carbon copy, photocopy, duplication. **b** twin, clone, (dead) ringer, double, *colloq.* picture, spitting image. **2** see MODEL *n.* 1, 3.

re•ply /riplí/ • *v.* (**–plies, –plied**) **1** *intr.* make an answer; respond in word or action. **2** *tr.* say in answer. • *n.* (*pl.* **–plies**) **1** act of replying. **2** what is replied; response. □□ **re•pli′er** *n.*
  ■ *v.* **1** counter. **2** retort, rejoin, return. • *n.* **1** reaction. **2** *sl.* comeback.

re•port /ripáwrt/ • *v.* **1** *tr.* **a** give an account of. **b** state as fact or news. **c** relate as spoken by another. **2** *tr.* make an official or formal statement about. **3** *tr.* name or specify (an offender or offense). **4** *intr.* present oneself as having returned or arrived. **5** *intr.* make or send in a report. **6** *intr.* be responsible (to a supervisor, etc.). **7** *intr.* [usu. foll. by *on*] act as a journalist. • *n.* **1** account given or opinion formally expressed after investigation or consideration. **2** account of an event, esp. for publication or broadcast. **3** common talk; rumor. **4** way a person or thing is spoken of. **5** periodical statement on (esp. a student's) work, conduct, etc. **6** sound of an explosion. □ **report card** official report of a student's grades, progress, etc. □□ **re•port′ed•ly** *adv.*
  ■ *v.* **1 a, b** relate, recount, describe, narrate, tell of, detail, set forth; document. **c** recite, communicate. **2** publish, publicize, reveal, disclose. **4** make oneself known. **7** (*report on*) investigate, cover, probe, scrutinize. • *n.* **1** see ACCOUNT *n.* 1. **2** story, article, piece, dispatch, *colloq.* write-up. **3** piece of gossip *or* hearsay; see also RUMOR *n.* **5** evaluation, appraisal. **6** bang, boom, shot, gunshot, blast.

re•port•age /ripáwrtij, répawrtáazh/ *n.* **1** reporting of news, etc. **2** factual presentation in a book, etc.

re•port•er /ripáwrtər/ *n.* person employed to report news, etc., for newspapers or broadcasts.
  ■ journalist, correspondent, columnist.

re•pose¹ /ripóz/ • *n.* **1** cessation of activity. **2** sleep. **3** peaceful state; tranquillity. • *v.*

1 *intr. & refl.* lie down in rest. **2** *intr.* lie, be lying, or be laid, esp. in sleep or death.
■ *n.* **1** break, breather. **3** calm, quiet, stillness. ● *v.* **1** see LIE¹ *v.* 1, REST¹ *v.* 1, 2. **2** see REST¹ *v.* 2.

re•pose² /ripóz/ *v.tr.* [foll. by *in*] place (trust, etc.) in.

re•pos•i•to•ry /ripózitawree/ *n.* (*pl.* **–ries**) **1** place where things are stored, esp. a warehouse or museum. **2** receptacle. **3** book, person, etc., regarded as a store of information, etc.
■ **3** mine, storehouse, treasure trove.

re•pos•sess /réepəzés/ *v.tr.* regain possession of (esp. property or goods on which repayment of a debt is in arrears). □□ **re•pos′ses•sion** /-zéshən/ *n.* **re•pos•ses′sor** *n.*

rep•re•hend /réprihénd/ *v.tr.* rebuke; blame; find fault with. □□ **rep•re•hen•sion** /-hénshən/ *n.*

rep•re•hen•si•ble /réprihénsibəl/ *adj.* deserving censure; blameworthy. □□ **rep•re•hen•si•bil′i•ty** *n.* **rep•re•hen′si•bly** *adv.*

rep•re•sent /réprizént/ *v.tr.* **1** stand for or correspond to. **2** be a specimen or example of. **3** symbolize. **4** describe; depict; delineate. **5** be a substitute or deputy for; be entitled to act or speak for. **6** be elected as a member of a legislature, etc. □□ **rep•re•sent′a•ble** *adj.*
■ **1** epitomize. **2** see EXEMPLIFY. **3** see SYMBOLIZE. **4** show, characterize, portray. **5** stand (in) for, replace, act on behalf of.

rep•re•sen•ta•tion /réprizentáyshən/ *n.* **1** representing or being represented. **2** thing that represents another. **3** [esp. in *pl.*] allegation or opinion. □□ **rep•re•sen•ta′tion•al** *adj.*
■ **2** reproduction, replica; image, likeness; depiction, portrayal. **3** deposition; declaration, account.

rep•re•sen•ta•tive /réprizéntətiv/ ● *adj.* **1** typical of a class or as a specimen (*representative sample*). **2 a** consisting of elected deputies, etc. **b** based on representation by such deputies (*representative government*). **3** serving as a portrayal or symbol (of). ● *n.* **1** sample, specimen, or typical embodiment. **2** agent, spokesperson, etc. **3** legislative delegate, deputy, etc.
■ *adj.* **1** characteristic, illustrative, exemplary. **2 b** democratic, popular. **3** (*representative of*) symbolic of, like. ● *n.* **1** see SPECIMEN, *embodiment* (EMBODY). **2** salesman *or* saleswoman, *colloq.* rep; see also AGENT 1a. **3** substitute, ambassador, envoy, emissary; congressman, congresswoman.

re•press /riprés/ *v.tr.* **1** check; restrain; keep under (control); quell. **2** *Psychol.* actively exclude (an unwelcome thought) from conscious awareness. □□ **re•press′er** *n.* (also **re•press′sor**). **re•press′si•ble** *adj.* **re•press′sion** /-préshən/ *n.* **re•pres′sive** *adj.* **re•pres′sive•ly** *adv.*
■ suppress, put down, curb, restrain, hold back *or* in, subdue; discourage. □□ **repression** restraint, control; deterrence. **repressive** tyrannical, oppressive, brutal.

re•prieve /ripréev/ ● *v.tr.* **1** remit or postpone the execution of (a condemned person). **2** give respite to. ● *n.* **1 a** reprieving or being reprieved. **b** warrant for this. **2** respite.
■ *v.* let off, spare, pardon; commute. ● *n.* **1a, 2** stay (of execution), delay, suspension; amnesty.

rep•ri•mand /réprimand/ ● *n.* official or sharp rebuke. ● *v.tr.* administer this. See synonym study at REBUKE.
■ *n.* scolding, reproach, lecture, *colloq.* talking-to. ● *v.* admonish, berate, criticize, take to task, *colloq.* tell off, chew out.

re•print ● *v.tr.* /réeprínt/ print again. ● *n.* /réeprint/ **1** reprinting of a book, etc. **2** book, etc., reprinted.

re•pri•sal /riprízəl/ *n.* (act of) retaliation.
■ requital; revenge, retribution, vengeance, repayment.

re•prise /ripréez/ *n.* **1** repeated passage in music. **2** repeated item in a musical program.

re•proach /ripróch/ ● *v.tr.* express disapproval to (a person) for a fault, etc. See synonym study at REBUKE. ● *n.* **1** rebuke or censure. **2** thing that brings disgrace or discredit. **3** disgraced or discredited state. □ **above** (or **beyond**) **reproach** perfect. □□ **re•proach′a•ble** *adj.* **re•proach′er** *n.* **re•proach′ful** *adj.* **re•proach′ful•ly** *adv.* **re•proach′ing•ly** *adv.*
■ □□ **reproachful** faultfinding, critical, disparaging.

rep•ro•bate /réprəbayt/ ● *n.* unprincipled or immoral person. ● *adj.* immoral.
■ *n.* scoundrel, miscreant, rake, roué, degenerate. ● *adj.* depraved, despicable, shameless, reprehensible.

re•pro•duce /réeprədo͞os, –dyo͞os/ *v.* **1** *tr.* produce a copy or representation of. **2** *tr.* cause to be seen or heard, etc., again (*reproduce the sound exactly*). **3** *intr.* produce further members of the same species by natural means. **4** *refl.* produce offspring. □□ **re•pro•duc′er** *n.* **re•pro•duc′i•ble** *adj.* **re•pro•duc•i•bil′i•ty** *n.*
■ **1, 2** duplicate, replicate, recreate, simulate; imitate. **3** breed, multiply, propagate, procreate, spawn, proliferate.

re•pro•duc•tion /réeprədúkshən/ *n.* **1** reproducing or being reproduced. **2** copy; [*attrib.*] imitation. □□ **re•pro•duc′tive** *adj.* **re•pro•duc′tive•ly** *adv.*
■ **1** duplication; propagation; facsimile, replica.

re•proof /ripro͞of/ *n.* **1** blame. **2** rebuke.
■ **1** see BLAME *n.* 1. **2** see REBUKE *n.*

re•prove /ripro͞ov/ *v.tr.* rebuke (a person, a person's conduct, etc.). See synonym study at REBUKE. □□ **re•prov′er** *n.* **re•prov′ing•ly** *adv.*
■ see REPRIMAND *v.*

rep•tile /réptil/ *n.* **1** cold-blooded scaly animal of the class including snakes, lizards, crocodiles, turtles, tortoises, etc. **2** mean, groveling, or repulsive person. □□ **rep•til•i•an** /–tíleeən, –tílyən/ *adj. & n.*

re•pub•lic /ripúblik/ *n.* nation in which power is held by the people or their elected representatives.

re•pub•li•can /ripúbliken/ • *adj.* **1** of or constituted as a republic. **2** characteristic of a republic. **3** advocating or supporting republican government. • *n.* **1** person advocating or supporting republican government. **2** (**Republican**) supporter of the Republican party. □ **Republican party** one of the two main US political parties, favoring a lesser degree of central power. □□ **re•pub'li•can•ism** *n.*

re•pu•di•ate /ripyŏŏdeeayt/ *v.tr.* **1 a** disown; disavow; reject. **b** refuse dealings with. **c** deny. **2** refuse to recognize or obey (authority or a treaty). **3** refuse to discharge (an obligation or debt). □□ **re•pu•di•a•tion** /-áyshən/ *n.* **re•pu'di•a•tor** *n.*
  ■ **1 a** scorn, renounce, rescind, discard. **2** see DISOWN.

re•pug•nance /ripúgnəns/ *n.* (also **re•pug'nan•cy**) **1** antipathy; aversion. **2** inconsistency or incompatibility of ideas, etc. □□ **re•pug'nant** *adj.* See synonym study at OFFENSIVE
  ■ □□ **repugnant** repulsive, abhorrent, disgusting, offensive, revolting, vile, loathsome, foul, intolerable, obnoxious, sickening.

re•pulse /ripúls/ • *v.tr.* **1** drive back by force of arms. **2 a** rebuff. **b** refuse. **3** be repulsive to. • *n.* repulsing or being repulsed.
  ■ *v.* **1** repel, ward off, fight *or* beat off. **2 a** see REBUFF[1] *v.* **b** see REFUSE[1]. **3** see REPEL 3. • *n.* rejection, denial, snub, cold shoulder.

re•pul•sion /ripúlshən/ *n.* **1** aversion; disgust. **2** *Physics* tendency of bodies to repel each other.

re•pul•sive /ripúlsiv/ *adj.* **1** causing aversion or loathing; disgusting. **2** *Physics* exerting repulsion. □□ **re•pul'sive•ly** *adv.* **re•pul'sive•ness** *n.*
  ■ **1** revolting, abhorrent, loathsome, repugnant, offensive, obnoxious, unpleasant, sickening, vile, hideous, horrible.

rep•u•ta•ble /répyətəbəl/ *adj.* of good repute; respectable. □□ **rep'u•ta•bly** *adv.*
  ■ honorable, respected, trusted, reliable.

rep•u•ta•tion /répyətáyshən/ *n.* **1** what is generally said or believed about a person's or thing's character or standing (*a reputation for dishonesty*). **2** good repute; respectability.
  ■ name, stature, position, status.

re•pute /ripyŏŏt/ • *n.* reputation. • *v.tr.* (as **reputed** *adj.*) be generally considered; be said to be. □ **house of ill repute** brothel. □□ **re•put'ed•ly** *adv.*
  ■ *n.* (**reputed**) rumored, regarded, looked on *or* upon, considered, thought, believed, alleged, purported.

re•quest /rikwést/ • *n.* **1** act of asking for something. **2** thing asked for. **3** demand (*in great request*). • *v.tr.* **1** ask to be given or allowed or favored with. **2** ask a person to do something. **3** ask (that). □ **by** (or **on**) **request** in response to an expressed wish. □□ **re•quest'er** *n.*
  ■ *n.* **1, 2** solicitation, petition, application. • *v.* **1** seek, apply for, insist on. **2** call on, require, appeal to.

re•qui•em /rékweeəm, reékwee-/ *n.* **1** (**Requiem**) [also *attrib.*] esp. *RC Ch.* Mass for

the repose of the souls of the dead. **2** music for this.

re•quire /rikwír/ *v.tr.* **1** need; depend on. **2** lay down as an imperative (*required by law*). **3** command; instruct; insist on. □□ **re•quir'er** *n.* **re•quire'ment** *n.*
  ■ **1** necessitate, demand, ask *or* call for. **2** see DECREE *v.* **3** order, coerce, force, compel, make. □□ **requirement** requisite, prerequisite, condition, stipulation, provision.

req•ui•site /rékwizit/ • *adj.* required by circumstances; necessary. See synonym study at NECESSARY. • *n.* thing needed (for some purpose).

req•ui•si•tion /rékwizíshən/ • *n.* **1** official order for supplies. **2** formal demand or request. **3** being called or put into service. • *v.tr.* demand the use or supply of, esp. by requisition order. □□ **req•ui•si'tion•er** *n.*
  ■ *n.* **2** see ORDER *n.* 2. • *v.* call for, mandate; appropriate, confiscate, take possession of.

re•quite /rikwít/ *v.tr.* **1** make return for (a service). **2** reward or avenge (a favor or injury). □□ **re•quit'al** *n.*
  ■ **1** reciprocate, match, complement. **2** recompense; revenge, pay back for. □□ **requital** payment, quid pro quo; remuneration; retribution, vengeance; retaliation.

re•run • *v.tr.* /reé-rún/ (**re•run•ning**; *past* **re•ran**; *past part.* **re•run**) run (a race, broadcast, etc.) again. • *n.* /reé-run/ **1** act of rerunning. **2** television program, etc., shown again.

re•sale /reésáyl/ *n.* sale of a thing previously bought.

re•scind /risínd/ *v.tr.* abrogate; revoke; cancel. □□ **re•scind'a•ble** *adj.* **re•scind'ment** *n.* **re•scis•sion** /-sízhən/ *n.*

res•cue /réskyŏŏ/ • *v.tr.* (**res•cues**, **res•cued**, **res•cu•ing**) save or set free from danger, harm, etc. • *n.* rescuing or being rescued. □□ **res'cu•a•ble** *adj.* **res'cu•er** *n.*
  ■ *v.* deliver, liberate, let go. • *n.* release, deliverance.

re•search /risárch, reésarch/ • *n.* systematic investigation into and study of materials, sources, etc., in order to establish facts and reach new conclusions. • *v.* **1** *tr.* do research into or for. **2** *intr.* make researches. □ **research and development** work directed toward the innovation, introduction, and improvement of products and processes. □□ **re•search'a•ble** *adj.* **re•search'er** *n.*
  ■ *n.* exploration(s), delving(s), examination(s), inspection(s); analysis, analyses. • *v.* study, check (into), experiment (with).

re•sem•blance /rizémbləns/ *n.* likeness; similarity. See synonym study at LIKENESS.
  ■ correspondence, agreement, comparability.

re•sem•ble /rizémbəl/ *v.tr.* be like; have a similarity to.
  ■ seem *or* look *or* sound *or* taste like, bear (a) resemblance to, correspond to, take after, *colloq.* favor.

re•sent /rizént/ *v.tr.* feel indignation at; be aggrieved by. □□ **re•sent'ful** *adj.* **re•sent'ful•ly** *adv.* **re•sent'ment** *n.*

■ begrudge. □□ **resentful** bitter, envious, jealous, annoyed. **resentment** acrimony, rancor, indignation, ill will, malice.

res•er•va•tion /rézərváyshən/ n. **1** reserving or being reserved. **2** thing booked, e.g., a room in a hotel. **3** express or tacit limitation to an agreement, etc. (*had reservations about the plan*). **4** area of land reserved for a particular group, as a tract federally designated for Native Americans.

■ n. **1, 2** booking, order, arrangement. **3** qualm, scruple; objection; condition; reticence, reluctance, hesitation.

re•serve /rizə́rv/ • v.tr. **1** put aside; keep back for a later occasion or special use. **2** order to be specially retained or allocated for a particular person or at a particular time. **3** retain or secure (*reserve the right to*). • n. **1** thing reserved for future use; extra amount. **2** self-restraint; reticence; lack of cordiality. **3** [in sing. or pl.] assets kept readily available. **4** [in sing. or pl.] standby or supplemental troops. **5** = RESERVIST. **6** substitute player on a team. **7** land reserved for special use, esp. as a habitat. □ **in reserve** unused and available if required. □□ **re•serv'a•ble** adj. **re•serv'er** n.

■ v. **1** hold back, withhold, save, delay, put off, defer; retain, conserve, preserve. **2** book. **3** see RETAIN 1. • n. **1** store, stock, stockpile, supply, reservoir, fund; hoard, cache. **2** formality, coolness, aloofness. **4** backup; (*reserves*) auxiliaries, reinforcements. **7** reservation, sanctuary, national park; preserve. □ **in reserve** ready, on hand, on call, in readiness, in store, *colloq.* on tap.

re•served /rizə́rvd/ adj. **1** reticent; uncommunicative. **2** set apart; destined for some use or fate. □□ **re•serv'ed•ly** adv. **re•serv'ed•ness** n.

■ **1** restrained, silent, taciturn, unresponsive, unemotional, cool, formal, aloof, distant, withdrawn.

re•serv•ist /rizə́rvist/ n. member of the reserve forces.

res•er•voir /rézərvwaar/ n. **1** large lake used as a source of water supply. **2** receptacle for or of fluid. **3** reserve or supply esp. of information.

re•set /réesét/ v.tr. (**re•set•ting**; *past* and *past part.* **re•set**) set (a broken bone, gems, a mechanical device, etc.) again or differently. □□ **re•set'ta•ble** adj.

re•side /rizíd/ v.intr. **1** have one's home; dwell permanently. **2** (of power, a right, etc.) rest or be vested in. **3** [foll. by *in*] (of a quality) be present or inherent in.

res•i•dence /rézidəns/ n. **1** act of residing. **2** place where a person resides; abode. □ **in residence** dwelling at a specified place, esp. for the performance of duties.

■ **1** residency, stay, sojourn; tenancy, occupancy. **2** home, domicile, house, habitation; mansion, manor (house), estate. □ **in residence** see RESIDENT adj. 1.

res•i•den•cy /rézidənsee/ n. (pl. **–cies**) **1** = RESIDENCE 1, 2. **2** period of hospital staff training for a physician.

res•i•dent /rézidənt/ • n. **1** permanent inhabitant. **2** medical graduate engaged in specialized practice under supervision in a hospital. • adj. **1** residing; in residence. **2** having quarters at one's workplace, etc. (*resident housekeeper*). **3** located in; inherent. **4** (of birds, etc.) nonmigratory.

■ n. **1** dweller, citizen, denizen; tenant, occupant. • adj. **1** living, staying, dwelling, abiding. **3** situated *or* positioned, lodged *or* placed, found; see also INHERENT 1.

res•i•den•tial /rézidénshəl/ adj. **1** suitable for or occupied by private houses (*residential area*). **2** pertaining to or used as a residence (*residential hotel*). □□ **res•i•den'tial•ly** adv.

re•sid•u•al /rizíjōōəl/ • adj. **1** left as a residue. **2** *Math.* resulting from subtraction. • n. **1** residual quantity. **2** [in pl.] pay to performers for reruns of taped shows, etc. □□ **re•sid'u•al•ly** adv.

■ adj. **1** remaining, leftover, surplus.

res•i•due /rézidōō, –dyōō/ n. what is left over or remains; remainder.

■ leftovers, rest, excess, dregs.

re•sign /rizín/ v. **1** intr. give up office, one's employment, etc. **2** tr. surrender; hand over (a right, charge, task, etc.). **3** refl. reconcile (oneself) to the inevitable.

■ **1** leave, give notice; retire, quit. **2** abdicate, let go (of); see also RELINQUISH 1, 2. **3** (*resign oneself*) adjust (oneself), adapt (oneself), submit (oneself).

res•ig•na•tion /rézignáyshən/ n. **1** resigning, esp. from one's job or office. **2** document, etc., conveying this. **3** uncomplaining endurance of a sorrow or difficulty.

■ **1** notice; abdication, surrender. **3** submission, acceptance, tolerance.

re•signed /rizínd/ adj. having resigned oneself; submissive, acquiescent. □□ **re•sign•ed'ly** /–zínidlee/ adv. **re•sign'ed•ness** n.

re•sil•ient /rizílyənt/ adj. **1** resuming its original shape after bending, compression, etc. **2** readily recovering from a setback. See synonym study at FLEXIBLE. □□ **re•sil'ience** n. **re•sil'ien•cy** n. **re•sil'ient•ly** adv.

■ **1** see ELASTIC adj. 1, 2. **2** see BUOYANT 2. □□ **resilience** bounce, flexibility, suppleness; buoyancy.

res•in /rézin/ n. **1** adhesive substance secreted by some plants. **2** (in full **syn•thet'ic res'in**) organic compound made by polymerization, etc., and used in plastics, etc. □□ **res'in•ous** adj.

re•sist /rizíst/ • v. **1** tr. withstand the action or effect of. **2** tr. abstain from (pleasure, temptation, etc.). **3** tr. strive against; refuse to comply with (*resist arrest*). **4** intr. offer opposition; refuse to comply. • n. protective coating of a resistant substance. □□ **re•sist'ant** adj. **re•sist'er** n. **re•sist'i•ble** adj. **re•sist•i•bil'i•ty** n.

■ v. **1** hold out against, stand up to *or* against; weather, endure, outlast; hinder, repel, thwart, impede, block. **2** refuse, turn down, decline, forgo, reject. **3** struggle against, combat, oppose, defy. **4** see BATTLE v. 1, PROTEST v. 1. □□ **resistant** stubborn, obstinate, rebellious; (*resistant to*) unaffected by.

re•sis•tance /rizístəns/ *n.* **1** resisting; refusal to comply. **2** power of resisting (*resistance to wear and tear*). **3** ability to withstand disease. **4** impeding or stopping effect exerted by one thing on another. **5** *Physics* property or measure of hindering the conduction of electricity, heat, etc. **6** (in full **re•sist′ance move′ment**) secret organization resisting authority, esp. in an occupied country.

■ **1** opposition, defiance. **3** resilience, hardiness, endurance; immunity, insusceptibility. **4** see OBSTRUCTION 3. **6** see UNDERGROUND *n.* 2.

re•sis•tor /rizístər/ *n. Electr.* device having resistance to the passage of an electrical current.

res•o•lute /rézəlŏot/ *adj.* determined; firm of purpose. □□ **res′o•lute′ly** *adv.* **res′o•lute′ness** *n.*

■ resolved, purposeful, stubborn, adamant, set, decided, inflexible; steadfast, firm, unwavering.

res•o•lu•tion /rézəlŏoshən/ *n.* **1** resolute temper or character. **2** thing resolved on; intention (*New Year's resolutions*). **3** formal expression of opinion or intention by a legislative body, etc. **4** solving of a problem, doubt, or question. **5** separation into components. **6** optical clarity or sharpness.

■ **1** resolve, determination, purpose, obstinacy, perseverance, persistence, tenacity, single-mindedness, dedication. **2** commitment, pledge, promise, obligation. **3** proposal, proposition, plan; motion; verdict,

judgment, decision, ruling. **4** answer, solution. **6** fineness.

re•solve /rizólv/ • *v.* **1** *intr.* make up one's mind; decide firmly. **2** *tr.* (of an assembly or meeting) pass a resolution by vote. **3** *intr. & tr.* separate or cause to separate into constituent parts. **4** *tr.* solve; explain; settle (doubt, argument, etc.). ■ *n.* firm mental decision or intention. □□ **re•solv′a•ble** *adj.* **re•solv•a•bil′i•ty** *n.* **re•solv′er** *n.*

■ *v.* **1** determine, conclude. **2** move; see also RULE *v.* 3. **3** convert, transform, break down, reduce. **4** work out, figure out, clear up, answer. ■ *n.* see RESOLUTION 1, 2, 3.

re•solved /rizólvd/ *adj.* resolute; determined.

res•o•nant /rézənənt/ *adj.* **1** (of sound) echoing; resounding. **2** (of a body, room, etc.) tending to reinforce or prolong sounds. **3** (of a place) resounding. □□ **res′o•nance** *n.* **res′o•nant•ly** *adv.*

■ **1** vibrant, reverberating, ringing, booming, thundering, thunderous, loud.

res•o•nate /rézənayt/ *v.intr.* produce or show resonance; resound. □□ **res′o•na•tor** *n.*

re•sorb /risáwrb, -záwrb/ *v.tr.* absorb again. □□ **re•sorb′ence** *n.* **re•sorb′ent** *adj.* **re•sorp•tion** /-sáwrpshən, -záwrp-/ *n.*

re•sort /rizáwrt/ • *n.* **1** place frequented for recreation, health, etc. **2 a** thing to which one has recourse; expedient; measure. **b** recourse (to). • *v.intr.* turn (to) as an expedient. (*resorted to threats*) ■ **as a last resort** when all else has failed.

■ *n.* **2 a** alternative, backup, reserve, refuge. • *v.* (*resort to*) fall back on.

re•sound /rizównd/ *v.intr.* **1** (of a place) ring or echo. **2** *intr.* produce echoes; go on sounding.

■ resonate, reverberate, boom; thunder (out).

re•sound•ing /rizównding/ *adj.* **1** in senses of RESOUND. **2** unmistakable; emphatic (*a resounding success*). □□ **re•sound′ing•ly** *adv.*

re•source /récsawrs, -zawrs, risáwrs, záwrs/ *n.* **1** expedient or device. **2** [usu. in *pl.*] means available; asset. **3** [in *pl.*] country's collective wealth. **4** [often in *pl.*] skill in devising expedients. □□ **re•source′ful•ly** *adv.* **re•source′ful•ness** *n.* See synonym study at CREATIVE.

■ **1** measure, contrivance. **2** (*resources*) see ASSET 2, MEANS 2, STOCK *n.* 1, 2. **3** (*resources*) prosperity; reserves. **4** initiative, ingenuity, talent, imagination, aptitude. □□ **resourceful** clever, enterprising, creative.

re•spect /rispékt/ • *n.* **1** deferential esteem felt or shown toward a person or quality. **2** heed or regard. **3** aspect, particular, etc. **4** reference; relation (*morality that has no respect to religion*). **5** [in *pl.*] greetings; polite messages (*give them my respects*). • *v.tr.* **1** regard with deference, esteem, or honor. **2 a** avoid interfering with, harming, etc. **b** treat with consideration. See synonym study at ESTEEM. ■ **with all due respect** mollifying formula preceding an expression of one's disagreement with another's views. **with respect to** regarding. □□ **re•spect′er** *n.*

■ *n.* **1** admiration, regard; appreciation, courtesy. **2** see REGARD *n.* 2. **3** detail, point, feature, quality, trait. **4** connection, bearing. **5** (*respects*) good *or* best wishes, compliments, salutations. ● *v.* **1** admire, value, look up to, revere. **2 b** heed, obey, attend to, defer to.

re•spect•a•ble /rispéktəbəl/ *adj.* **1** decent and proper in appearance and behavior. **2** fairly competent (*a respectable effort*). **3** reasonably good in condition, appearance, number, size, etc. (*a respectable salary*). □□ **re•spect•a•bil'i•ty** *n.* **re•spect'a•bly** *adv.*

■ **1** good; sound; upright, honest; reputable, law-abiding. **2** commendable, admirable; passable, not bad. **3** appreciable, fair, considerable, sizable, good-sized, substantial, *colloq.* tidy.

re•spect•ful /rispéktfŏŏl/ *adj.* showing deference (*stood at a respectful distance*). □□ **re•spect'ful•ly** *adv.* **re•spect'ful•ness** *n.*

■ courteous, polite, well-mannered, well-behaved, mannerly, civil, cordial, gracious, accommodating.

re•spect•ing /rispékting/ *prep.* with regard to; concerning.

re•spec•tive /rispéktiv/ *adj.* concerning or appropriate to each of several individually (*go to your respective places*). □□ **re•spec'tive•ly** *adv.*

■ separate, individual, personal, specific. □□ **respectively** singly, severally.

res•pi•ra•tion /réspiráyshən/ *n.* **1 a** breathing. **b** single breath. **2** *Biol.* in organisms, absorption of oxygen and release of energy and carbon dioxide.

res•pi•ra•tor /réspiraytər/ *n.* **1** apparatus worn over the face to purify, warm, etc., inhaled air. **2** *Med.* apparatus for maintaining artificial respiration.

re•spire /rispír/ *v.* **1** *tr. & intr.* breathe. **2** *intr.* inhale and exhale air. **3** *intr.* (of a plant) carry out respiration. □□ **res•pi•ra•to•ry** /résparatawree, rispírə-/ *adj.*

res•pite /réspit/ *n.* **1** interval of rest or relief. **2** delay permitted before discharge of obligation or suffering of penalty.

■ **1** intermission, break, breather. **2** reprieve, stay, postponement, extension.

re•splen•dent /rispléndənt/ *adj.* brilliant; dazzlingly or gloriously bright. □□ **re•splen'dence** *n.* **re•splen'den•cy** *n.* **re•splen'dent•ly** *adv.*

re•spond /rispónd/ *v.* **1** *intr.* answer; reply. **2** *intr.* react. **3** *intr.* show responsiveness (to) by behavior or change (*does not respond to kindness*).

■ **1** (make a) retort; counter. **2** reciprocate; behave, act; retaliate. **3** be responsive, be affected *or* moved *or* touched.

re•spon•dent /rispóndənt/ *n.* defendant, esp. in an appeal or divorce case.

re•sponse /rispóns/ *n.* **1** answer given in word or act; reply. **2** feeling, movement, change, etc., caused by a stimulus or influence. **3** [often in *pl.*] *Eccl.* any part of the liturgy said or sung in answer to the priest.

■ **1** retort, rejoinder, reaction, *sl.* comeback. **2** effect; result, consequence, outcome, upshot.

re•spon•si•bil•i•ty /rispónsibilitee/ *n.* (*pl.* **–ties**) **1 a** being responsible. **b** authority and obligation. **2** person or thing for which one is responsible.

■ **1 a** accountability, liability; blame, guilt. **b** see POWER *n.* 3, 5, INDEPENDENCE. **2** charge, duty, trust.

re•spon•si•ble /rispónsibəl/ *adj.* **1** liable to be called to account (to a person or for a thing). **2** morally accountable for one's actions; capable of rational conduct. **3** of good credit, position, or repute; respectable. **4** being the primary cause. **5** involving responsibility. □□ **re•spon'si•bly** *adv.*

■ **1, 2** answerable, bound. **3** reliable, reputable, trustworthy, dependable, ethical, honest. **4** guilty, to blame, at fault. **5** important, leading.

re•spon•sive /rispónsiv/ *adj.* **1** responding readily (to some influence). **2** sympathetic. **3** answering. □□ **re•spon'sive•ly** *adv.* **re•spon'sive•ness** *n.*

■ **1, 2** alert, alive, receptive, sensitive, impressionable.

rest¹ /rest/ ● *v.* **1** *intr.* cease, abstain, or be relieved from exertion, action, etc. **2** *intr.* be still or asleep, esp. to refresh oneself or recover strength. **3** *tr.* give relief or repose to; allow to rest. **4** *intr.* lie (on); be supported (by). **5** *intr.* depend; be based; rely. **6** *intr.* (of a look) light (upon) or be steadily directed (on). **7** *tr.* place for support. **8** *intr.* be left without further investigation or discussion (*let the matter rest*). **9** *intr.* **a** lie in death. **b** lie buried (in a churchyard, etc.). **10** *tr.* (as **rested** *adj.*) refreshed by resting. ● *n.* **1** repose or sleep. **2** cessation of exertion, activity, etc. **3** period of resting. **4** support for holding or steadying something. **5** *Mus.* **a** interval of silence. **b** sign denoting this. □ **at rest** not moving; not troubled; dead. **lay to rest** inter (a corpse). **rest area** = *rest stop.* **rest one's case** conclude one's argument, etc. **rest** (or **God rest**) **his** (or **her**) **soul** may God grant his (or her) soul repose. **rest home** place where old or frail people can be cared for. **rest room** public toilet. **rest stop** area for travelers to stop for rest, refreshment, etc.

■ *v.* **1** relax, repose, unwind, take it easy. **2** doze, lie down, (take a) nap, *colloq.* snooze. **4** see LIE¹ *v.* 1. **5** see DEPEND 1. **8** drop, cease, end, stop. **10** (**rested**) see REFRESH 1. ● *n.* **1** nap, siesta, *colloq.* shut-eye. **2** relaxation, respite, time off *or* out, leisure. **3** intermission, recess; vacation. **4** prop, holder. □ **at rest** see CALM *adj.* 1, DEAD *adj.* 1. **rest room** see TOILET.

rest² /rest/ ● *n.* [prec. by *the*] the remaining part or parts; the others; the remainder. ● *v.intr.* **1** remain in a specified state (*rest assured*). **2** be left in the hands or charge of (*final arrangements rest with you*).

■ *n.* balance; remains, remnants, leftovers; surplus. ● *v.* **1** (continue to) be, keep on being. **2** reside, be placed, be found.

res•tau•rant /réstərənt, –raant, réstraant/ *n.*

public premises where meals or refreshments may be had.

res•tau•ra•teur /réstərətốr/ n. restaurant owner or manager.

rest•ful /réstfŏŏl/ adj. **1** favorable to quiet or repose. **2** undisturbed. □□ **rest′ful•ly** adv. **rest′ful•ness** n.

■ **1** tranquil, calm, peaceful, still, serene, pacific; relaxed.

res•ti•tu•tion /réstitŏŏshən, –tyŏŏ–/ n. **1** restoring of a thing to its proper owner. **2** reparation.

■ **1** return, recovery, replacement; reinstatement. **2** amends, compensation, redress, remuneration.

res•tive /réstiv/ adj. **1** fidgety; restless. **2** unmanageable; rejecting control. □□ **res′tive•ly** adv. **res′tive•ness** n.

■ **1** see RESTLESS 2, 3. **2** see DISOBEDIENT, UNGOVERNABLE.

rest•less /réstlis/ adj. **1** finding or affording no rest. **2** uneasy; agitated. **3** constantly in motion; fidgety. □□ **rest′less•ly** adv. **rest′less•ness** n.

■ **1** sleepless, wakeful. **2** restive, edgy, on edge, nervous, high-strung, jumpy, jittery, uptight, colloq. antsy. **3** skittish.

res•to•ra•tion /réstəráyshən/ n. **1** restoring or being restored. **2** model or representation of the supposed original form of a thing. **3** (**Restoration**) hist. **a** [prec. by the] reestablishment of England's monarchy in 1660. **b** [often attrib.] literary period following this (Restoration comedy).

■ **1** renovation, repair, reconstruction.

re•stor•a•tive /ristáwrətiv, –stốr–/ • adj. tending to restore health or strength. • n. restorative medicine, food, etc. (needs a restorative). □□ **re•stor′a•tive•ly** adv.

■ analeptic, tonic.

re•store /ristáwr/ v.tr. **1** bring back to the original state by rebuilding, repairing, etc. **2** bring back to health, etc. **3** give back to the original owner. **4** reinstate. **5** replace; put back; bring back. See synonym study at RECOVER. □□ **re•stor′a•ble** adj. **re•stor′er** n.

■ **1** renovate, refurbish, reconstruct, resurrect. **2** make better, cure; see also HEAL 2. **3** return; repay. **4** rehabilitate, reestablish.

re•strain /ristráyn/ v.tr. **1** check or hold in; keep in check or under control or within bounds. **2** repress; keep down. **3** confine; imprison. □□ **re•strain′a•ble** adj. **re•strain′er** n.

■ **1** curb, govern; limit, restrict, inhibit, regulate, curtail, hinder. **2** stifle; see also REPRESS 1. **3** incarcerate, detain, lock up, jail.

re•straint /ristráynt/ n. **1** restraining or being restrained. **2** controlling agency or influence. **3** self-control; moderation. **4** reserve of manner. **5** confinement, esp. because of insanity.

■ **2** rein, restriction, constraint, limit, curtailment. **3, 4** poise, self-discipline. **5** duress, captivity.

re•strict /ristríkt/ v.tr. **1** confine; bound; limit. **2** withhold from general circulation or disclosure. □□ **re•strict′ed•ly** adv. **re•strict′ed•ness** n. **re•stric′tion** n.

■ **1** circumscribe, regulate, restrain, impede. □□ **restriction** restraint; stipulation, condition.

re•stric•tive /ristríktiv/ adj. imposing restrictions. □ **restrictive clause** Gram. relative clause, usu. without surrounding commas. □□ **re•stric′tive•ly** adv. **re•stric′tive•ness** n.

re•sult /rizúlt/ • n. **1** consequence, issue, or outcome of something. **2** satisfactory outcome (gets results). **3** end product of calculation. **4** [in pl.] list of scores or winners, etc., in an examination or sporting event. • v.intr. **1** arise as the actual or follow as a logical consequence. **2** have a specified end or outcome (resulted in a large profit). □□ **re•sult′ant** adj.

■ n. **1** effect; development; conclusion, upshot. • v. **1** develop, emerge, happen, occur, come (about). **2** culminate.

re•sume /rizŏŏm/ • v. **1** tr. & intr. begin again or continue after an interruption. **2** tr. & intr. begin to speak, work, or use again; recommence. **3** tr. get back; take back (resume one's seat). • n. = RÉSUMÉ. □□ **re•sum′a•ble** adj.

■ v. **1** see CONTINUE 2, carry on 1. **2** restart, reopen, resurrect. **3** reoccupy; see also RECOVER v. 1.

ré•su•mé /rézŏŏmay/ n. (also **resumé, resume**) summary, esp. of a person's employment history.

■ abstract, outline; curriculum vitae, biography.

re•sump•tion /rizúmpshən/ n. resuming. □□ **re•sump′tive** /–tiv/ adj.

re•sur•face /reesúrfis/ v. **1** tr. lay a new surface on (a road, etc.). **2** intr. rise or arise again; turn up again.

re•sur•gent /risúrjənt/ adj. **1** rising or arising again. **2** tending to rise again. □□ **re•sur′gence** n.

■ on the rise. □□ **resurgence** renaissance, rebirth, revival, renewal, return, resurrection.

re•sur•rect /rézərékt/ v. **1** tr. colloq. revive the practice, use, or memory of. **2** tr. & intr. raise or rise from the dead.

■ **1** bring back, reintroduce, restore, renew, resuscitate. **2** reincarnate; reawaken.

re•sur•rec•tion /rézərékshən/ n. **1** rising from the dead. **2** (**Resurrection**) **a** Christ's rising from the dead. **b** rising of the dead at the Last Judgment. **3** revival after disuse, inactivity, or decay. □□ **re•sur•rec′tion•al** adj.

re•sus•ci•tate /risúsitayt/ v. **1** revive from unconsciousness or apparent death. **2** restore to vogue, vigor, or vividness. □□ **re•sus•ci•ta′tion** /–táyshən/ n. **re•sus′ci•ta′tive** adj. **re•sus′ci•ta′tor** n.

re•tail /réetayl/ n. • sale of goods in small quantities to the public. • adj. & adv. by retail; at a retail price. • v. (also /rītáyl/) **1** tr. sell (goods) in retail trade. **2** intr. (of goods) be sold in this way (retails at $4.95). □□ **re′tail•er** n.

re•tain /ritáyn/ v.tr. **1 a** keep possession of; not lose. **b** not abolish, discard, nor alter. **2** keep in one's memory. **3** keep in place;

hold fixed. **4** secure the services of (a person, esp. an attorney) with a preliminary payment. □□ **re•tain′a•ble** adj.

■ **1** hold on to, save, preserve, colloq. hang on to. **2** remember, keep in mind. **3** contain, absorb, soak up. **4** engage, hire, commission, take on.

re•tain•er /ritáynər/ n. **1** person or thing that retains. **2** fee for retaining an attorney, etc. **3** faithful servant (esp. old retainer).

re•take • v.tr. /réetáyk/ (past **re′took**; past part. **re•tak′en**) **1** take again. **2** recapture. • n. /réetayk/ **1** act of filming a scene or recording music, etc., again. **2** scene or recording obtained in this way.

re•tal•i•ate /ritáleeayt/ v. repay an injury, insult, etc., in kind; attack in return. □□ **re•tal′i•a•tion** /-áyshən/ n. **re•tal′i•a•tor** n. **re•tal′i•a•to•ry** /-táleeətáwree/ adj.

■ counter, strike back, take revenge, wreak vengeance, reciprocate, settle a score; avenge, requite; get even with.

re•tard /ritaárd/ v.tr. **1** make slow or late. **2** delay the progress or accomplishment of. □□ **re•tard′ant** adj. & n. **re•tar•da•tion** /réetaardáyshən/ n.

■ hold up or back; hinder, impede, keep back.

re•tard•ed /ritaárdid/ adj. backward in mental or physical development.

retch /rech/ v.intr. make a motion of vomiting esp. involuntarily and without effect.

re•ten•tion /riténshən/ n. **1 a** retaining; being retained. **b** memory. **2** failure to evacuate urine or another secretion. □□ **re•ten′tive** /-tiv/ adj. **re•ten′tive•ly** adv.

ret•i•cence /rétisəns/ n. **1** personal hesitancy or avoidance; reluctance. **2** disposition to silence. □□ **ret′i•cent** adj. **ret′i•cent•ly** adv.

■ see RESERVE n. 2. □□ reticent quiet, shy, timid, retiring, reserved; unresponsive, tight-lipped.

re•tic•u•late • v. /ritíkyəlayt/ divide or be divided in fact or appearance into a network. • adj. /-yələt, -layt/ reticulated. □□ **re•tic′u•late•ly** adv. **re•tic•u•la•tion** /-láyshən/ n.

ret•i•na /rét′nə/ n. (pl. **ret′i•nas**, **ret•i•nae** /-nee/) layer at the back of the eyeball sensitive to light. □□ **ret′i•nal** adj.

ret•i•nue /rét′nōō, -yōō/ n. body of attendants accompanying an important person.

■ entourage, escort, convoy, cortège, company, train.

re•tire /ritír/ v. **1 a** intr. leave office or employment, esp. because of age. **b** tr. cause (a person) to do this. **2** intr. withdraw; go away; retreat. **3** intr. seek seclusion or shelter. **4** intr. go to bed. **5** intr. & tr. Baseball (of a batter or side) put out. □□ **re•tired′** adj. **re•tir•ee′** n. **re•tire′ment** n. **re•tir′er** n.

■ **2, 3** hibernate, sequester or cloister oneself. **4** call it a day, colloq. hit the hay or sack, turn in. □□ **retiree**, **retirer** see pensioner (PENSION).

re•tir•ing /ritíring/ adj. fond of seclusion. □□ **re•tir′ing•ly** adv.

■ shy, bashful, coy, demure, modest, diffident, timid, unassuming, humble, self-

effacing; aloof, removed, standoffish, distant, reclusive.

re•took past of RETAKE.

re•tort¹ /ritáwrt/ • n. incisive or witty or angry reply. • v. **1** tr. say by way of a retort. **2** intr. make a retort.

■ n. rejoinder; retaliation, quip, barb, colloq. wisecrack, sl. comeback. • v. fling or hurl (back); counter; requite.

re•tort² /ritáwrt, réetawrt/ n. vessel with a long downward-turned neck used in distilling liquids, etc.

re•touch /réetúch/ v.tr. improve (a picture, photograph, etc.) by minor alterations.

■ touch up, correct; restore, repair, recondition.

re•trace /reetráys/ v.tr. **1** go back over (one's steps, etc.). **2** trace back to a source or beginning.

re•tract /ritrákt/ v. **1** tr. [also absol.] withdraw (a statement or undertaking). **2** tr. & intr. draw or be drawn back or in. □□ **re•tract′a•ble** adj. **re•trac′tion** n. **re•trac′tive** adj.

■ **1** take back, rescind, revoke, repeal, deny, disavow.

re•trac•tile /ritráktil, -tīl/ adj. capable of being retracted. □□ **re•trac•til•i•ty** /-tilitee/ n.

re•tread • v.tr. /réetréd/ (past **re•trod**; past part. **re•trod•den**) **1** tread (a path, etc.) again. **2** put a fresh tread on (a tire). • n. /réetred/ retreaded tire.

re•treat /ritréet/ v. **1** intr. (esp. of military forces) go back; retire. **2** intr. (esp. of features) recede. • n. **1** act of retreating. **b** Mil. signal for this. **2 a** withdrawal into privacy or security. **3** place of shelter, seclusion, or meditation. **4** Mil. bugle call at sunset.

■ v. **1** decamp, flee, take flight, recoil; withdraw, pull out. **2** see RECEDE 1. • n. **1 a** evacuation, rout, flight. **2** retirement, escape, departure. **3** sanctuary, refuge, haven, asylum.

re•trench /ritrénch/ v. **1** tr. reduce the amount of (costs). **2** intr. cut down expenses. □□ **re•trench′ment** n.

ret•ri•bu•tion /rétribyōōshən/ n. requital, usu. for evil done; vengeance. □□ **re•trib•u•tive** /ritríbyətiv/ adj. **re•trib•u•to•ry** /ritríbyətawree/ adj.

■ revenge, reprisal, retaliation, redress; justice.

re•trieve /ritréev/ v.tr. **1 a** regain possession of. **b** recover by investigation or effort of memory. **2** obtain (information stored in a computer, etc.). **3** (of a dog) find and bring in (killed or wounded game, etc.). **4** rescue (esp. from a bad state). See synonym study at RECOVER. □□ **re•triev′a•ble** adj. **re•triev′al** n.

■ **1 a** reclaim; see also RECOVER v. 1. **3** fetch. **4** see DELIVER 2.

re•triev•er /ritréevər/ n. **1** dog of a breed used for retrieving game. **2** this breed.

ret•ro /rétrō/ adj. reviving or harking back to the past.

retro- /rétrō/ comb. form **1** denoting action back or in return. **2** Anat. & Med. denoting location behind.

ret•ro•ac•tive /rétrō-áktiv/ adj. (esp. of legislation) having retrospective effect. □□ **ret•**

ro·ac'tive·ly adv. ret·ro·ac·tiv·i·ty /–tívi-tee/ n.

ret·ro·fit /rétrōfit/ v.tr. (–fit·ted, –fit·ting) modify machinery, vehicles, etc.) to incorporate changes and developments introduced after manufacture.

ret·ro·grade /rétrəgrayd/ • adj. 1 directed backward; retreating. 2 reverting esp. to an inferior state; declining. 3 inverse; reversed (retrograde order). • v.intr. 1 move backward; recede. 2 decline; revert.

ret·ro·gress /rétrəgrés/ v.intr. 1 move backward. 2 deteriorate. □□ ret·ro·gres·sion /–gréshən/ n. ret·ro·gres·sive adj. ret·ro·gres'sive·ly adv.

ret·ro·rock·et /rétrō-rókit/ n. auxiliary rocket for slowing down a spacecraft, etc.

ret·ro·spect /rétrəspekt/ n. regard or reference to previous conditions. □ in retrospect when looked back on. □□ ret·ro·spec·tion /–spékshən/ n.
■ □ in retrospect with hindsight, on reconsideration.

ret·ro·spec·tive /rétrəspéktiv/ • adj. 1 looking back on or dealing with the past. 2 (of an exhibition, recital, etc.) showing an artist's development over his or her lifetime. • n. retrospective exhibition, recital, etc. □□ ret·ro·spec'tive·ly adv.

ret·ro·vi·rus /rétrōvírəs/ n. Biol. any of a group of RNA viruses that form DNA during the replication of their RNA.

re·try /reetrí/ v.tr. (–tries, –tried) try (a defendant or lawsuit) a second or further time. □□ re·tri'al n.

re·turn /ritórn/ • v. 1 intr. come or go back. 2 tr. bring or put or send back. 3 tr. pay back or reciprocate; give in response. 4 tr. yield (a profit). 5 tr. say in reply; retort. 6 tr. (in tennis, etc.) hit or send (the ball) back. 7 tr. reelect to political office, etc. • n. 1 coming or going back. 2 a giving, sending, putting, or paying back. b thing given or sent back. 3 key on a computer or typewriter to start a new line. 4 [in sing. or pl.] proceeds or profit of an undertaking. 5 formal report compiled or submitted by order (tax return). □ in return as an exchange or reciprocal action. many happy returns (of the day) greeting on a birthday, etc. □□ re·turn'a·ble adj.
■ v. 1 reappear, resurface; recur; revert, turn back. 2 replace, restore. 3 requite, repay. 4 earn, gain. 5 see REPLY v. 2. • n. 1 homecoming; recurrence, comeback. 2 a replacement, restoration, reimbursement, reparation, amends. 4 earnings, gain, income, revenue. 5 statement, record.

re·turn·ee /ritərnée/ n. person who returns home from abroad, esp. after war service.

re·un·ion /reeyóonyən/ n. 1 reuniting; being reunited. 2 social gathering of people formerly associated.

Rev. abbr. 1 Reverend. 2 Revelation (New Testament).

rev /rev/ colloq. • n. [in pl.] number of revolutions of an engine per minute. • v. (revved, rev·ving) 1 intr. (of an engine) revolve; turn over. 2 tr. [also absol.; often foll. by up] cause (an engine) to run quickly.

717   retrofit ~ reverie

re·vamp /reevámp/ v.tr. renovate; revise; improve.
■ overhaul, redo, recondition, repair, fix, refit, restore.

re·veal /riveel/ v.tr. 1 display or show; allow to appear. 2 disclose; divulge; betray (revealed his plans). 3 tr. [in refl. or passive] come to sight or knowledge. □□ re·veal'ing·ly adv.
■ 1 expose, present, exhibit, unveil, uncover, lay bare. 2 make known, air, let out, give away, let slip, leak, colloq. let on.

re·veil·le /révəlee/ n. military wake-up signal.

rev·el /révəl/ • v.intr. 1 have a good time; be extravagantly festive. 2 take keen delight (in). • n. [in sing. or pl.] reveling. □□ rev'el·er n. rev'el·ry n. (pl. –ries).
■ v. 1 make merry, celebrate, cut loose, carouse, colloq. live it up, party. 2 (revel in) rejoice in, bask in, savor, relish. • n. romp, fling, colloq. spree, sl. ball; festival, gala. □□ revelry merrymaking, fun, gaiety, festivity.

rev·e·la·tion /révəláyshən/ n. 1 a revealing, esp. by divine or supernatural agency. b knowledge disclosed in this way. 2 striking disclosure. 3 (Revelation) last book of the New Testament. □□ rev·e·la'tion·al adj
■ 2 admission; declaration; discovery, disclosure.

re·venge /rivénj/ • n. 1 retaliation for an offense or injury. 2 desire for this; vindictive feeling. 3 (in games) win after an earlier defeat. • v. tr. [in refl. or passive] inflict retaliation for an offense. 2 intr. take vengeance. □□ re·venge'ful adj. re·venge'ful·ly adv. re·veng'er n.
■ n. 1 reprisal, retribution, satisfaction. 2 see RANCOR. • v. 1 settle a score or an old score with, get even with, even the score; avenge, exact retribution for. 2 give a person a taste of his or her own medicine.

rev·e·nue /révənōō, –nyōō/ n. 1 a income, esp. of a large amount. b [in pl.] items constituting this. 2 government's income from which public expenses are met.
■ 1 proceeds, return(s), profit(s), gain, take.

re·ver·ber·ate /rivórbərayt/ v. 1 a intr. (of sound, light, or heat) be returned, echoed, or reflected repeatedly. b tr. return (a sound, etc.) in this way. 2 intr. (of a story, rumor, etc.) be heard much or repeatedly. □□ re·ver'ber·ant adj. re·ver'ber·ant·ly adv. re·ver·ber·a·tion /–ráyshən/ n. re·ver·ber·a·tive /–rətiv/ adj. re·ver'ber·a·tor n. re·ver·ber·a·to·ry /–rətawree/ adj.

re·vere /riveer/ v.tr. hold in deep or religious respect. □□ rev'er·ence n. rev'er·ent adj. rev·er·en·tial /–énshəl/ adj. rev·er·en'tial·ly adv. See synonym study at HONOR
■ adore, venerate, esteem, admire, worship. □□ reverence honor, awe; homage, obeisance.

rev·er·end /révərənd, révrənd/ • adj. (esp. as the title of a clergyman) deserving reverence. • n. colloq. clergyman.

rev·er·ie /révəree/ n. spell of abstracted musing.
■ daydream; see also FANTASY n. 2.

re•verse /rivə́rs/ • v. **1** tr. turn the other way around or up or inside out. **2** tr. change to the opposite character or effect (reversed the decision). **3** intr. & tr. travel or cause to travel backward. **4** revoke or annul (a decree, etc.). • adj. **1** backward or upside-down. **2** opposite or contrary in character or order; inverted. See synonym study at OPPOSITE. • n. **1** opposite or contrary (the reverse is the case). **2** occurrence of misfortune; defeat. **3** reverse gear or motion. **4** reverse side. □ **reverse the charges** make the recipient of a telephone call responsible for payment. □□ **re•ver′sal** n. **re•vers′er** n. **re•vers′i•ble** adj. **re•vers•i•bil′i•ty** n. **re•vers′i•bly** adv.
■ v. **1** invert, overturn, turn over; transpose, switch. **2** overthrow, quash, nullify, revoke, negate, declare null and void, repeal, rescind, overrule, countermand, undo; renounce, recant. **3** back up, backtrack. • adj. **1** converse; mirror. • n. **1** antithesis. **2** setback, disappointment, mishap, disaster, colloq. washout. **4** verso, underside; colloq. flip side. □□ **reversal** turnabout, turnaround, change, about-face; annulment, cancellation.

re•vert /rivə́rt/ v.intr. **1** [foll. by to] return to a former state, practice, opinion, etc. **2** (of property, an office, etc.) return by reversion.
■ **1** (revert to) come or go back to, relapse into.

re•view /rivyo͞o′/ • n. **1** general survey or assessment of a subject or thing. **2** survey of the past. **3** revision or reconsideration. **4** display and formal inspection of troops, etc. **5** criticism of a book, play, etc. **6** periodical with critical articles on current events, the arts, etc. • v.tr. **1** survey or look back on. **2** reconsider or revise. **3** hold a review of (troops, etc.). **4** write a review of (a book, play, etc.). **5** view again. □□ **re•view′a•ble** adj. **re•view′er** n.
■ n. **1** examination, study, inspection, analysis, consideration, scrutiny. **3** reassessment, reappraisal. **4** parade, procession, array. **5** critique, evaluation, commentary. **6** see PERIODICAL n. • v. **1** examine, regard, study, consider, weigh. **2, 5** reexamine, look at or over again. **4** criticize, give one's opinion of, discuss, judge.

re•vile /rivī́l/ v. **1** tr. abuse; criticize abusively. **2** intr. talk abusively; rail. See synonym study at SCOLD. □□ **re•vile′ment** n. **re•vil′er** n. **re•vil′ing** n.

re•vise /rivī́z/ v.tr. **1** examine and improve or amend (esp. written or printed matter). **2** consider and alter (an opinion, etc.). □□ **re•vis′a•ble** adj. **re•vis′er** n. **re•vi•sion** /–vízhən/ n. **re•vi′so•ry** adj.
■ **1** edit, emend, correct; rework; rewrite. **2** change, modify, adjust.

re•vi•sion•ism /rivízhənizəm/ n. departure from or modification of accepted doctrine, theory, view of history, etc. □□ **re•vi′sion•ist** n. & adj.

re•viv•al /rivī́vəl/ n. **1** reviving; being revived. **2** new production of an old play, etc. **3** reawakening of religious fervor. □□ **re•viv′**

al•ism n. **re•viv′al•ist** n. **re•viv•al•is′tic** adj.
■ **1** resurrection, renewal, restoration, revitalization; comeback. **3** rebirth, resurgence.

re•vive /rivī́v/ v. **1** come or bring back to consciousness, life, or strength. **2** come or bring back to existence, use, notice, etc. □□ **re•viv′a•ble** adj.
■ **1** (re)awaken, wake (up), waken; come around, recover; bring around, resuscitate. **2** resume, reopen; renew, reactivate, recall, breathe new life into.

re•viv•i•fy /rivívifī/ v.tr. (**–fies**, **–fied**) restore to animation, activity, vigor, or life. □□ **re•viv•i•fi•ca′tion** n.

re•voke /rivṓk/ v.tr. rescind, withdraw, or cancel (a decree or promise, etc.). □□ **re•vo′ca•ble** /révəkəbəl/ adj. **re•vo•ca•bil•i•ty** /révəkəbilitee/ n. **rev•o•ca•tion** /révəkáyshən/ n. **re•vok′er** n.
■ invalidate, annul, void, nullify; retract.

re•volt /rivṓlt/ • v. **1** intr. rise in rebellion. **2 a** tr. affect with strong disgust (was revolted by the thought of it). **b** intr. feel strong disgust. • n. act of rebelling.
■ v. **1** mutiny, take up arms; protest. **2 a** repel, offend, repulse, sicken, shock, horrify. • n. revolution, uprising, insurrection, takeover.

re•volt•ing /rivṓlting/ adj. disgusting; horrible. □□ **re•volt′ing•ly** adv.
■ loathsome, abhorrent, nasty, offensive, vile, sl. gross, rotten.

rev•o•lu•tion /révəlo͞oshən/ n. **1** forcible overthrow of a government or social order. **2** any fundamental change or reversal of conditions. **3** revolving. **4** completion of an orbit or rotation. **5** cyclic recurrence. See synonym study at UPRISING. □□ **rev•o•lu′tion•ar•y** adj. & n. **rev•o•lu′tion•ism** n. **rev•o•lu′tion•ist** n.
■ **1** coup, mutiny, uprising, insurrection, takeover. **2** upheaval, cataclysm, transformation. **3, 4** turn, gyration; spin; circle, circuit, lap. **5** cycle, phase, period. □□ **revolutionary** adj. novel, innovative, creative, new, different; radical, seditious, subversive; rebel. • n. rebel, insurgent, extremist.

rev•o•lu•tion•ize /révəlo͞oshənīz/ v.tr. introduce fundamental change to.

re•volve /rivólv/ v. **1** intr. & tr. turn or cause to turn around, esp. on an axis; rotate. **2** intr. move in a circular orbit. **3** tr. ponder (a problem, etc.).
■ **1, 2** spin (around); pivot, gyrate, circle, orbit. **3** turn over (in one's mind), weigh, consider, contemplate.

re•volv•er /rivólvər/ n. pistol with revolving chambers enabling several shots to be fired without reloading.
■ gun, firearm, handgun, side arm, sl. gat, rod, piece.

re•vue /rivyo͞o′/ n. theatrical entertainment of a series of short usu. satirical sketches and songs.

re•vul•sion /rivúlshən/ n. abhorrence; sense of loathing.
■ disgust, repugnance, aversion, hatred.

re•ward /riwáwrd/ • n. **1 a** return or recompense for service or merit. **b** requital for good or evil; retribution. **2** sum offered for the detection of a criminal, restoration of lost property, etc. • *v.tr.* give a reward to (a person) or for (a service, etc.).

■ *n.* **1 a** prize, award, tribute. **b** (just) deserts. **2** see BOUNTY 2. • *v.* compensate, pay, requite.

re•ward•ing /riwáwrding/ *adj.* (of an activity, etc.) worthwhile; satisfying. □□ **re•ward′ing•ly** *adv.*

■ gratifying, enriching, fruitful, profitable, productive.

re•wind /reewínd/ • *v.tr.* (*past* and *past part.* **re•wound**) wind (a film, tape, etc.) back to the beginning. • *n.* function on a tape deck, camera, etc., to rewind (tape, film, etc.). □□ **re•wind′er** *n.*

re•word /reewɔ́rd/ *v.tr.* change the wording of.

■ paraphrase, put another way, express differently.

re•work /reewɔ́rk/ *v.tr.* revise; refashion; remake.

re•write • *v.tr.* /reerít/ (*past* **re•wrote**; *past part.* **re•writ•ten**) write again, esp. differently. • *n.* /reerít/ **1** rewriting. **2** thing rewritten.

Reye's syn•drome /ríz, ráz/ *n. Med.* acute, often fatal brain disease of children, associated with aspirin use.

Rf *symb. Chem.* rutherfordium.

RFD *abbr.* rural free delivery.

Rh[1] *symb. Chem.* rhodium.

Rh[2] see RH FACTOR.

rhap•so•dize /rápsədiz/ *v.intr.* talk or write rhapsodies.

rhap•so•dy /rápsədee/ *n.* (*pl.* **-dies**) **1** enthusiastic, ecstatic, or extravagant utterance or composition. **2** piece of music in one extended movement, usu. emotional in character. □□ **rhap•sod•ic** /rapsódik/ *adj.* **rhap•sod′i•cal** *adj.*

■ □□ **rhapsodic, rhapsodical** elated, overjoyed, effusive, rapturous, thrilled, euphoric; walking on air, in seventh heaven, *colloq.* on top of the world.

rhe•a /réeə/ *n.* small, flightless ostrichlike bird of South America.

rhe•ni•um /réeneeəm/ *n. Chem.* rare metallic element of the manganese group. ¶ Symb.: **Re.**

rhe•o•stat /réeəstat/ *n. Electr.* device used to control a current by varying the resistance. □□ **rhe•o•stat′ic** *adj.*

rhe•sus /réesəs/ *n.* (in full **rhe′sus mon′key**) small monkey common in N India. □ **rhesus factor** = RH FACTOR.

rhet•o•ric /rétərik/ *n.* **1** art of effective or persuasive speaking or writing. **2** language designed to persuade or impress. □ **rhetorical question** question asked not for information but for an effect, e.g., *who cares?* for *nobody cares.* □□ **rhe•tor′i•cal** *adj.* **rhe•tor′i•cal•ly** *adv.*

■ **1** eloquence, way with words, *colloq.* gift of gab. **2** bombast, puffery, *sl.* hot air. □□ **rhetorical** pretentious, inflated; artificial, contrived; stylistic.

rheu•ma•tism /róomətizəm/ *n.* disease marked by inflammation and pain in the joints, muscles, or fibrous tissue, esp. rheu-

matoid arthritis. □□ **rheu•mat′ic** *adj.* **rheu•mat′i•cal•ly** *adv.*

rheu•ma•toid /róomətoyd/ *adj.* having the character of rheumatism. □ **rheumatoid arthritis** chronic progressive disease causing inflammation and stiffening of the joints.

Rh fac•tor *Physiol.* antigen occurring in the red blood cells of most humans.

rhine•stone /rínstōn/ *n.* imitation gemstone.

rhi•ni•tis /rinítis/ *n.* inflammation of the mucous membrane of the nose.

rhi•no /rínō/ *n.* (*pl.* same or **–nos**) *colloq.* rhinoceros.

rhi•noc•er•os /rinósərəs/ *n.* (*pl.* same or **rhi•noc′er•os•es**) large thick-skinned ungulate of Africa and S. Asia, with one or two horns on the nose.

rhi•zome /rízōm/ *n.* underground rootlike stem bearing both roots and shoots.

rho /rō/ *n.* seventeenth letter of the Greek alphabet (Ρ, ρ).

rho•di•um /rṓdeeəm/ *n. Chem.* hard white metallic element of the platinum group. ¶ Symb.: **Rh.**

rho•do•den•dron /rṓdədéndrən/ *n.* evergreen shrub with large clusters of trumpet-shaped flowers.

rhom•boid /rómboyd/ • *adj.* (also **rhom•boid•al** /–bóyd′l/) like a rhombus. • *n.* quadrilateral of which only the opposite sides and angles are equal.

rhom•bus /rómbəs/ *n.* (*pl.* **rhom•bus•es** or **rhom•bi** /–bī/) *Geom.* parallelogram with oblique angles and equal sides.

rhu•barb /róobaarb/ *n.* **1 a** plants producing long fleshy dark-red stalks used cooked as food. **b** stalks of this. **2** *sl.* heated dispute.

rhyme /rīm/ • *n.* **1** identity of sound between words or the endings of words, esp. in verse. **2** [in *sing.* or *pl.*] verse or poem having rhymes. **3** word providing a rhyme. • *v.* **1** *intr.* **a** (of words or lines) produce a rhyme. **b** [foll. by *with*] act as a rhyme (with another). **2** *intr.* make or write rhymes; versify. □ **rhyme or reason** sense; logic. □□ **rhym′er** *n.*

■ □ **rhyme or reason** meaning, wisdom, rationale.

rhythm /ríthəm/ *n.* **1** measured regular flow of verse or prose determined by the length of stress and syllables. **2** pattern of accent and duration of notes in music. □ **rhythm and blues** popular music with a blues theme and a strong rhythm, **rhythm method** birth control by avoiding sexual intercourse when ovulation is likely to occur. □□ **rhyth′mic** *adj.* **rhyth′mi•cal** *adj.* **rhyth′mi•cal•ly** *adv.* **rhythm′less** *adj.*

■ measure, meter; tempo, beat.

RI *abbr.* Rhode Island (also in official postal use).

rib /rib/ • *n.* **1** each of the curved bones joined in pairs to the spine and protecting the chest. **2** supporting ridge, timber, rod, etc. • *v.tr.* (**ribbed**, **rib′bing**) **1** provide with ribs. **2** *colloq.* make fun of; tease. □ **rib cage** wall of bones formed by the ribs. □□ **ribbed** *adj.* **rib′bing** *n.* **rib′less** *adj.*

rib•ald /ríbəld/ *adj.* coarsely or disrespectfully humorous; scurrilous.

rib•bon /ríbən/ *n.* **1** narrow strip or band of fabric, used esp. for trimming or decoration. **2** long, narrow strip of anything (*typewriter ribbon*). **3** [in *pl.*] ragged strips. □□ **rib′boned** *adj.*

ri•bo•fla•vin /ríbōfláyvin/ *n.* vitamin of the B complex, found in liver, milk, eggs, etc. (Also called **vitamin B₂**.)

ri•bo•nu•cle•ic ac•id /ríbənookléeik, –kláyik, –nyoo–/ *n.* nucleic acid in living cells, involved in protein synthesis. ¶Abbr.: **RNA**.

rice /rīs/ • *n.* **1** cereal grass cultivated in marshes, esp. in Asia. **2** grains of this, used as food. • *v.tr.* sieve (cooked potatoes, etc.) into thin strings. □□ **ric′er** *n.*

rich /rich/ • *adj.* **1** having much wealth. **2** splendid; costly; elaborate. **3** copious; abundant; fertile. **4** (of food or diet) containing much fat, spice, etc. **5** (of the fuel mixture in an engine) containing a high proportion of fuel. **6** (of color or sound or smell) mellow and deep; strong and full. **7** highly amusing. • *n.* (**the rich**) [used with a *pl. v.*] wealthy persons, collectively. □□ **rich′ly** *adv.* **rich′ness** *n.*

■ **1** *adj.* wealthy, affluent, prosperous, well-to-do, well-off, *colloq.* on easy street, *sl.* loaded. **2** expensive, dear, valuable, precious, priceless; lavish, lush, luxurious, exquisite, superb, elegant. **3** productive, plentiful, ample, bountiful, fruitful, prolific. **4** fattening, heavy, creamy. **6** intense, dark, warm, vibrant; savory, fragrant, pungent. **7** hilarious; ridiculous, funny, absurd; outrageous. □□ **richly** sumptuously; thoroughly, fully.

rich•es /ríchiz/ *n.pl.* abundant means; valuable possessions.

■ wealth, affluence, opulence, plenty, prosperity.

Rich•ter scale /ríktər/ *n.* scale of 0 to 10 for representing the strength of an earthquake.

rick•ets /ríkits/ *n.* [treated as *sing.* or *pl.*] bone-softening disease of children, caused by a deficiency of vitamin D.

rick•et•y /ríkitee/ *adj.* **1** insecure; shaky. **2** suffering from rickets. □□ **rick′et•i•ness** *n.*

■ **1** wobbly, unsteady, tottering, teetering, precarious; decrepit, flimsy, frail; feeble.

rick•sha /ríkshaw/ *n.* (also **rick′shaw**) light, two-wheeled hooded vehicle drawn by one or more persons.

ric•o•chet /ríkəshay, rikəsháy/ • *n.* action of a projectile, esp. a shell or bullet, in rebounding off a surface. • *v.intr.* (**ric•o•cheted** /–shayd/; **ric•o•chet•ing** /–shaying/) (of a projectile) make a ricochet.

ri•cot•ta /rikótə, –káwtaa/ *n.* soft Italian cheese resembling cottage cheese.

rid /rid/ *v.tr.* (**rid•ding**; *past* and *past part.* **rid**) free (a person or place) of something unwanted. □ **be** (or **get**) **rid of** dispose of.

■ rescue from, save from. □ **be** (or **get**) **rid of** send away, banish, exile, expel, eject, eliminate, reject, dismiss, *colloq.* unload; throw out *or* away.

rid•dance /rídəns/ *n.* getting rid of something. □ **good riddance** welcome relief from an unwanted person or thing.

rid•dle¹ /ríd′l/ • *n.* **1** question or statement testing ingenuity in divining its answer or meaning. **2** puzzling fact, thing, or person. • *v.intr.* speak in riddles. □□ **rid′dler** *n.*

■ *n.* conundrum, puzzle, poser, problem, brainteaser; enigma, mystery.

SYNONYM STUDY: riddle

CONUNDRUM, ENIGMA, MYSTERY, PARADOX, PUZZLE . All of these terms imply something baffling or challenging. A **mystery** is anything that is incomprehensible to human reason, particularly if it invites speculation (*the mystery surrounding her sudden disappearance*). An **enigma** is a statement whose meaning is hidden under obscure or ambiguous allusions, so that we can only guess at its significance; it can also refer to a person of puzzling or contradictory character (*he remained an enigma throughout his long career*). A **riddle** is an *enigma* involving contradictory statements, with a hidden meaning designed to be guessed at (*the old riddle about how many college graduates it takes to change a light bulb*). **Conundrum** applies specifically to a *riddle* phrased as a question, the answer to which usually involves a pun or a play on words, such as "What is black and white and read all over?" A **paradox** is a statement that seems self-contradictory or absurd, but in reality expresses a possible truth (*Francis Bacon's well-known paradox, "The most corrected copies are commonly the least correct"*). A **puzzle** is not necessarily a verbal statement, but it presents a problem with a particularly baffling solution or tests one's ingenuity or skill in coming up with a solution (*a crossword puzzle*).

rid•dle² /ríd′l/ • *v.tr.* **1** make many holes in, esp. with gunshot. **2** [in *passive*] spread through; permeate (*riddled with errors*). **3** pass through a riddle. • *n.* coarse sieve.

■ *v.* **1** perforate, pepper, honeycomb. **2** fill, infest, pervade, infect. • *n.* colander, sifter.

ride /rīd/ • *v.* (*past* **rode** /rōd/; *past part.* **rid•den** /rid′n/) **1** *tr. & intr.* travel or be carried on (a bicycle, etc.) or in (a vehicle). **2** *tr. & intr.* sit on and control or be carried by (a horse, etc.). **3** *tr.* be carried or supported by (*the ship rides the waves*). **4** *tr.* traverse. **5** *intr.* lie at anchor; float buoyantly. **6** *tr.* give a ride to (*rode the child on his back*). **7** (as **ridden** *adj.*) infested or afflicted (often in *comb.*: *rat-ridden cellar*). • *n.* **1** journey or spell of riding. **2** amusement for riding on at a carnival, etc. □ **let ride** leave to a natural course. **ride out** come safely through (a storm, danger, etc.). **ride shotgun** *colloq.* ride in the front passenger seat of a vehicle. **ride up** (of a garment, etc.) work upward out of place. **take for a ride 1** *colloq.* hoax or deceive. **2** *sl.* abduct in order to murder. □□ **rid′a•ble** *adj.*

■ *v.* **1, 2** journey, go, proceed; be borne *or* conveyed; see also DRIVE *v.* 3a, b. **7** (*be ridden by* or *with*) be plagued by, be dominated by, be tormented by. • *n.* **1** drive, trip, excursion, tour, jaunt, outing, *colloq.* spin. □ **let ride** let it be. **ride out** see through, spend, pass; see also ENDURE 1. **take for a ride** 1 delude, swindle, trick, defraud, take in, *colloq.* bamboozle. 2 (kidnap and) kill *or* execute, *sl.* do in, bump off.

rid•er /rídər/ *n.* 1 person who rides (esp. a horse). 2 addition to a document. □□ **rid′er•less** *adj.*

ridge /rij/ • *n.* 1 line of the junction of two surfaces sloping upward toward each other. 2 long, narrow hilltop, mountain range, or watershed. 3 any narrow elevation. • *v.tr.* mark with ridges. □□ **ridg′y** *adj.*
■ *n.* 1 strip; crest, peak. 2 see *prominence* (PROMINENT).

ridge•pole /ríjpōl/ *n.* horizontal roof pole.

rid•i•cule /rídikyōol/ • *n.* derision; mockery.
■ *v.tr.* mock.
■ *n.* jeering, taunting, ribbing. • *v.* tease, laugh at, poke fun at, lampoon, parody, make a laughingstock of, *sl.* josh, razz, rag.

ri•dic•u•lous /ridíkyələs/ *adj.* 1 deserving or inviting ridicule. 2 unreasonable; absurd. See synonym study at ABSURD. □□ **ri•dic′u•lous•ly** *adv.* **ri•dic′u•lous•ness** *n.*
■ laughable, comical, funny, humorous, ludicrous, farcical, droll, amusing, hilarious, preposterous, silly, nonsensical, foolish, outlandish.

rid•ing /rídiŋ/ *n.* 1 in senses of RIDE *v.* 2 practice or skill of riding horses.

rife /rīf/ *predic.adj.* 1 of common occurrence; widespread. 2 (foll. by *with*) abounding in; teeming with. See synonym study at PREVALENT. □□ **rife′ness** *n.*

riff /rif/ *n.* short repeated phrase in jazz, etc.

rif•fle /rífəl/ • *v.* 1 *tr.* a turn (pages) in quick succession. b shuffle (playing cards). 2 *intr.* [often foll. by *through*] leaf quickly (through pages). • *n.* 1 act or instance of riffling. 2 patch of waves or ripples on water.

riff-raff /rífraf/ *n.* rabble; disreputable persons.
■ hoi polloi; *colloq.* scum; dregs (of society).

ri•fle[1] /rífal/ • *n.* gun with a long, rifled barrel, esp. one fired from shoulder level. • *v.tr.* make spiral grooves in (a gun barrel) to make a bullet spin. □ **rifle range** place for rifle practice.

ri•fle[2] /rífal/ *v.tr.* & [foll. by *through*] *intr.* search and rob.
■ plunder, pillage, loot; (*rifle through*) see RANSACK 2.

ri•fle•man /rífalmən/ *n.* (*pl.* **-men**) 1 soldier armed with a rifle. 2 person skilled in shooting a rifle.

ri•fling /rífliŋ/ *n.* grooves in a gun barrel.

rift /rift/ • *n.* 1 crack; split; opening. 2 disagreement; breach. • *v.tr.* tear or burst apart.
■ *n.* 1 tear, rent, hole, chink; fissure, crevice, cleft, gulf, gap. 2 schism, difference; break, discord; distance.

rig[1] /rig/ • *v.tr.* (**rigged, rig•ging**) 1 provide (a sailing ship) with sails, rigging, etc. 2 fit out; equip. 3 [foll. by *up*] set up as a makeshift. 4 assemble. • *n.* 1 arrangement of a vessel's masts, sails, etc. 2 equipment for a special purpose. 3 tractor-trailer. □□ **rigged** *adj.* [also in *comb.*].

■ *v.* 2 set up, outfit, supply, provision. • *n.* 2 gear, tackle, apparatus.

rig[2] /rig/ • *v.tr.* (**rigged, rig•ging**) manage or conduct fraudulently (*rigged the election*). • *n.* trick or dodge. □□ **rig′ger** *n.*
■ *v.* falsify, tamper with, fake, *colloq.* doctor, fix.

rig•ger /rígər/ *n.* 1 person who rigs or who arranges rigging. 2 worker on an oil rig.

rig•ging /rígiŋ/ *n.* vessel's spars, ropes, etc.

right /rīt/ • *adj.* 1 just; morally or socially correct. 2 true; not mistaken. 3 suitable; preferable. 4 sound or normal; healthy; satisfactory. 5 on or toward the east side of the human body or of anything when facing north. 6 (of a side of fabric, etc.) meant for display or use. • *n.* 1 that which is correct or just. 2 justification or fair claim. 3 legal or moral authority to act. 4 right-hand part, region, or direction. 5 (often **Right**) conservative political group. • *v.tr.* 1 [often *refl.*] restore to a proper, straight, or vertical position. 2 correct or avenge (mistakes, wrongs, etc.). • *adv.* 1 straight (*go right on*). 2 *colloq.* immediately (*I'll be right back*). 3 a [foll. by *to, around, through*, etc.] all the way (*sank right to the bottom*). b [foll. by *off, out*, etc.] completely (*came right off its hinges*). 4 exactly; quite (*right in the middle*). 5 properly; correctly; satisfactorily (*if I remember right*). 6 on or to the right side. • *int. colloq.* expressing agreement or assent. □ **as right as rain** perfectly sound and healthy. **in one's own right** through one's own position or effort, etc. **right angle** angle of 90°. **right away** immediately. **right-hand** *adj.* 1 on or toward the right side of a person or thing. 2 done with the right hand. **right-handed** 1 using the right hand by preference. 2 (of a tool, etc.) made to be used with the right hand. **right-minded** (or **-thinking**) having sound views and principles. **right of way** 1 right established by usage to pass over another's ground. 2 right of one vehicle to proceed before another. **right on!** *colloq.* expression of strong approval or encouragement. **right-to-die** pertaining to the avoidance of using artificial life support in case of severe illness or injury. **right-to-life** pertaining to the movement opposing abortion. **right-to-work** pertaining to legislation outlawing obligatory union membership. **right wing** conservative section of a political party or system. **right-wing** *adj.* conservative or reactionary. **right-winger** person on the right wing. □□ **right′a•ble** *adj.* **right′ly** *adv.* **right′ness** *n.*
■ *adj.* 1 good, proper, legal, lawful, honest, ethical, fair. 2 accurate, exact, precise, perfect, valid, *colloq.* on the button. 3 fitting; (of time) favorable, convenient. 4 sane, rational, *colloq.* OK. 5 right-hand, dextral. 6 upper, front; (*right side*) face, surface, top, outside. • *n.* 1 justice, reason, truth, fairness, equity, goodness. 2 see CAUSE[1] *n.* 2. 3 privilege, prerogative, license, liberty; (*right to*) title to. 5 right wing. • *v.* 1 straighten (up or out), set upright. 2 amend, rectify; get even for,

requite. • *adv.* **2** directly, straightaway, promptly. **4** precisely. **5** aptly, favorably. *int.* definitely, absolutely. □ **as right as rain** fine; see also OK *adj.* **right away** see *at once* 1 (ONCE). **right-minded** (or **–thinking**) see CONSCIENTIOUS. **right on!** excellent; see also FABULOUS 2.

right•eous /ríchəs/ *adj.* morally right; virtuous; law-abiding. See synonym study at MORAL. □□ **right'eous•ly** *adv.* **right'eous• ness** *n.*

■ just, upright, good, honest, ethical, honorable, fair, reputable, trustworthy; justified, appropriate.

right•ful /rítfŏol/ *adj.* **1** legitimate. **2** equitable; fair. □□ **right'ful•ly** *adv.*

■ **1** legal, lawful, proper, true; bona fide, valid, authorized. **2** see EQUITABLE.

right•ism /rítizəm/ *n. Polit.* principles or policy of the right. □□ **right'ist** *n. & adj.*

right•most /rítmōst/ *adj.* furthest to the right.

rig•id /ríjid/ *adj.* **1** not flexible; unbendable. **2** inflexible; harsh. □□ **ri•gid'i•ty** *n.* **rig'id• ly** *adv.* **rig'id•ness** *n.*

■ **1** stiff, firm, hard, strong. **2** unyielding, unbending, uncompromising, stringent, severe, strict; obstinate, stubborn, willful, resolute.

rig•ma•role /rígmərōl/ (also **rig•a•ma•role** /rígə–/) *n.* **1** lengthy, complicated procedure. **2** rambling or meaningless talk.

■ **1** ceremony, ritual; bother, *colloq.* hassle. **2** mumbo-jumbo, gobbledygook, *sl.* bunk.

rig•or /rígər/ *n.* severity; strictness. □ **rigor mortis** stiffening of the body after death. □□ **rig'or•ous** *adj.* **rig'or•ous•ly** *adv.* **rig' or•ous•ness** *n.*

■ harshness; rigidity, inflexibility; hardship, austerity, discipline.

rile /rīl/ *v.tr. colloq.* anger; irritate.

rill /ril/ *n.* small stream.

rim /rim/ • *n.* **1 a** edge or border. **b** margin or verge, esp. of something circular. **2** part of eyeglasses frame surrounding the lenses. **3** outer edge of a wheel, holding the tire. See synonym study at BORDER. • *v.tr.* (**rimmed, rim•ming**) provide with a rim; edge. □□ **rim'less** *adj.* **rimmed** *adj.* [also in *comb.*].

■ *n.* **1** brim, lip, perimeter.

rim•rock /rímrok/ *n.* an outcrop of resistant rock forming a margin to a gravel deposit, esp. one forming a cliff at the edge of a plateau.

rime /rīm/ *n.* light covering of frost.

rind /rīnd/ *n.* tough outer skin of fruit, vegetables, cheese, etc.

■ peel, husk, pod, hull, shell.

rin•der•pest /ríndərpest/ *n.* an infectious viral disease of ruminants, esp. cattle, characterized by fever, dysentery, and inflammation of the mucous membranes.

ring¹ /ring/ • *n.* **1** circular band, usu. of metal, worn on a finger. **2** circular band of any material. **3** circular line or band around an object. **4** enclosure for a circus performance, boxing, etc. **5** people or things in a circle. **6** group of people combined illicitly

for profit, etc. • *v.tr.* **1** make or draw a circle around. **2** put a ring through the nose of (a pig, bull, etc.). • □ **ring finger** finger next to the little finger, esp. of the left hand. **run rings around** *colloq.* outclass or outwit (another person). □□ **ringed** *adj.* [also in *comb.*].

■ *n.* **2** loop, circlet, belt; hoop, quoit. **4** rink, arena. **6** gang, band, pack, clan; (secret) society. • *v.* **1** encircle, circumscribe, gird; surround, hem in, compass. □ **run rings around** baffle, nonplus; see also MYSTIFY.

ring² /ring/ • *v.* (*past* **rang** /rang/; *past part.* **rung** /rung/) **1** *intr.* give a clear resonant or vibrating sound of or as of a bell. **2** *tr.* make (esp. a bell) ring. **3** *tr.* call by telephone. **4** *intr.* (of a place) resound with a sound (*theater rang with applause*). **5** *intr.* (of the ears) be filled with a sensation of ringing. **6** *intr.* convey a specified impression (*words rang hollow*). • *n.* **1** ringing sound or tone. **2** act or sound of ringing a bell. **3** telephone call. **4** specified feeling conveyed by words (*a melancholy ring*). □ **ring up** record (an amount, etc.) on a cash register. □□ **ringed** *adj.* [also in *comb.*]. **ring'er** *n.* **ring'ing** *adj.* **ring'ing• ly** *adv.*

■ *v.* **1** peal, chime (out), toll, knell; resonate. **3** phone, *sl.* give a person a buzz. • *n.* **1** clanging, tinkle. **2** chime. **4** see UNDERCURRENT 2.

ring•er /ríngər/ *n. sl.* **1 a** athlete or horse entered in a competition by fraudulent means, esp. as a substitute. **b** person's double, esp. an impostor. **2** bell ringer. □ **be a dead ringer for** resemble (a person) exactly.

ring•lead•er /ríngleedər/ *n.* leading instigator of a crime, etc.

ring•let /rínglit/ *n.* curly lock of hair.

ring•mas•ter /ríngmastər/ *n.* director of a circus performance.

ring•side /ríngsíd/ *n.* [often *attrib.*] area beside a boxing ring, circus ring, etc.

ring•worm /ríngwərm/ *n.* fungous infections of the skin causing circular inflamed patches.

rink /ringk/ *n.* **1** area of ice for skating. **2** enclosed area for roller-skating.

rinse /rins/ • *v.tr.* **1** wash lightly. **2** put (clothes, etc.) through clean water to remove soap or detergent. **3** treat (hair) with a rinse. • *n.* **1** rinsing. **2** solution for cleansing the mouth. **3** temporary hair tint. □□ **rins'er** *n.*

■ *v.* **1** see FLUSH¹ *v.* 3a. **3** highlight; see also TINT *v.* • *n.* **1** washing. **3** dye.

ri•ot /ríət/ • *n.* **1 a** disturbance of the peace by a crowd. **b** [*attrib.*] involved in suppressing riots (*riot police*). **2** uncontrolled revelry. **3** lavish display or sensation (*riot of emotion*). **4** *colloq.* very amusing thing or person. • *v.intr.* engage in a riot. □ **read the Riot Act** put a firm stop to insubordination, etc. **run riot 1** throw off all restraint. **2** (of plants) grow or spread uncontrolled. □□ **ri' ot•er** *n.* **ri'ot•ous** *adj.*

■ *n.* **1 a** uproar, tumult, fray, mêlée. **4** comedian, comedienne; *sl.* gas. • *v.* rebel, revolt, storm, go on a rampage. □□ **riotous** wild, noisy, chaotic, violent; rowdy, boisterous, unruly.

RIP *abbr.* may he or she or they rest in peace (acronym of Latin *requiescat* (pl. *requiescant*) *in pace*).

rip¹ /rip/ • *v.* (**ripped, rip•ping**) **1** *tr.* tear or cut (a thing) quickly or forcibly away or apart. **2** *tr.* make a tear in. **3** *intr.* come violently apart; split. **4** *intr.* rush along. • *n.* **1** long tear. **2** act of ripping. □ **let rip** *colloq.* act or proceed without restraint. **rip cord** cord for releasing a parachute from its pack. **rip into** attack (a person) verbally. **rip off** *colloq.* defraud; steal. **rip-off** *n. colloq.* fraud; swindle.

■ *v.* **1** rend; see also SLIT *v.* **2** slash, cut open, gash. **3** see SPLIT *v.* 1a. • *n.* **1** rent. □ **rip into** see ATTACK *v.* 3. **rip off** rob, cheat, trick, fleece, dupe, *colloq.* bamboozle, *sl.* con, gyp; *colloq.* lift, swipe. **rip-off** deception; *sl.* con job.

rip² /rip/ *n.* stretch of rough water in the sea or in a river, caused by the meeting of currents.

ri•par•i•an /ripáireeən/ *adj.* of or on a riverbank.

ripe /rip/ *adj.* **1** (of grain, fruit, cheese, etc.) ready to be reaped, picked, or eaten. **2** mature; fully developed. **3** (of a person's age) advanced. **4** fit or ready (*land ripe for development*). □□ **ripe•ly** *adv.* **ripe•ness** *n.*

■ **1** fully grown, mellow, aged. **2** seasoned, sage, wise, experienced. **3** adult. **4** right, ideal, suitable.

rip•en /ripən/ *v.* make or become ripe; mature. See synonym study at MATURE.

■ develop; age, season; bring or come to maturity.

ri•poste /ripóst/ *n.* quick retort.

rip•ple /ripəl/ • *n.* **1** ruffling of the water's surface. **2 a** gentle lively sound, e.g., of laughter or applause. **b** brief wave of emotion, etc. (*a ripple of interest*). • *v.* **1 a** *intr.* form or flow in ripples. **b** *tr.* cause to do this. **2** *intr.* show or sound like ripples. □□ **rip'ply** *adj.*

■ *n.* **1** wavelet, wave, riffle. **2 b** flurry, flutter, stir. • *v.* **1** ruffle, undulate. **2** see GURGLE *v.*

rip-roar•ing /ripráwring/ *adj.* **1** wildly noisy or boisterous. **2** excellent; first-rate. □□ **rip-roar'ing•ly** *adv.*

rip•saw /ripsaw/ *n.* saw for sawing wood along the grain.

rip•snort•er /ripsnawrtər/ *n. colloq.* energetic, remarkable, or excellent person or thing. □□ **rip•snort'ing** *adj.* **rip•snort'ing•ly** *adv.*

rip•tide /riptid/ *n.* disturbance in the sea where opposing tidal currents meet.

rise /riz/ • *v.intr.* (*past* **rose** /rōz/; *past part.* **ris•en** /rizən/) **1** come or go up. **2** grow, project, expand, or incline upward; become higher. **3** appear above the horizon. **4 a** get up from lying, sitting, or kneeling. **b** get out of bed. **5** come to life again (*rise from the ashes*). **6** (of dough) swell by the action of yeast, etc. **7** rebel. **8** originate; have as its source. • *n.* **1** rising. **2** upward slope; hill. **3** increase. **4** increase in status or power. **5** origin. □ **get a rise out of** *colloq.* provoke a reaction from (a person). **rise above** **1** be

---

superior to (petty feelings, etc.). **2** show dignity or strength in the face of (difficulty, poor conditions, etc.).

■ *v.* **1** lift, climb, soar, mount. **2** ascend, go uphill. **3** come up, come out. **4 a** stand (up), arise; get to one's feet. **b** wake up. **7** revolt, mutiny, take up arms. **8** start, begin, spring up; occur, happen, take place. • *n.* **1** ascent, ascension, flight, takeoff. **2** knoll, elevation, highland, incline. **3** intensification, amplification, buildup, strengthening; see also INCREASE *n.* 1, 2. **4** see PROGRESS *n.* 2. **5** see ORIGIN 1. □ **get a rise out of** stimulate, incite, instigate, foment, goad, shake up, agitate, stir (up). **rise above** see TRANSCEND 2.

ris•er /rizər/ *n.* **1** person who rises, esp. from bed. **2** vertical section between the treads of a staircase.

ris•i•ble /rizibəl/ *adj.* laughable; ludicrous.

ris•ing /rizing/ • *adj.* **1** increasing (*rising costs*). **2** advancing to maturity or high standing (*rising young lawyer*). • *n.* revolt; insurrection; uprising.

risk /risk/ • *n.* **1** chance or possibility of danger, loss, injury, etc. **2** person or thing regarded in relation to risk (*is a poor risk*) • *v.tr.* **1** expose to risk. **2** accept the chance of. □□ **risk'i•ly** *adv.* **risk'i•ness** *n.* **risk'y** *adj.*

■ *n.* **1** peril; hazard. **2** gamble, liability; threat, menace. • *v.* **1** endanger, imperil, jeopardize. □□ **risky** dangerous, perilous, chancy, precarious, *colloq.* iffy.

ris•qué /riskáy/ *adj.* slightly indecent.

■ indelicate, naughty, spicy, racy, suggestive.

rite /rit/ *n.* religious or solemn observance, act, or procedure. □ **rite of passage** [often in *pl.*] event marking a stage of life, e.g., marriage.

■ solemnity, ceremony, ritual, formality, custom, practice.

rit•u•al /richooəl/ • *n.* **1** prescribed order of performing rites. **2** procedure regularly followed. • *adj.* of or done as a ritual or rites. □□ **rit'u•al•ism** *n.* **rit'u•al•ist** *n.* **rit•u•al•is•tic** *adj.* **rit•u•al•is'ti•cal•ly** *adv.* **rit•u•al•i•za'tion** *n.* **rit'u•al•ize** *v.* **rit'u•al•ly** *adv.*

■ *n.* **1** routine, practice, protocol. **2** see RITE. • *adj.* ceremonious, sacramental; formal, conventional, customary, habitual, prescribed, usual.

ritz•y /ritsee/ *adj.* (**ritz•i•er, ritz•i•est**) *colloq.* **1** high-class; luxurious. **2** ostentatiously smart. □□ **ritz'i•ly** *adv.* **ritz'i•ness** *n.*

riv. *abbr.* river.

ri•val /rivəl/ • *n.* **1** person competing with another. **2** person or thing that equals another in quality. • *v.tr.* **1** be the rival of. **2** seem or claim to be as good as. □□ **ri'val•ry** *n.* (*pl.* **–ries**)

■ *n.* **1** competitor, opponent, contender, challenger, adversary; opposition. **2** match; see also EQUIVALENT *n.* 2. • *v.* compete with, contend with, challenge; measure up to, be a match for. □□ **rivalry** competition, conflict, struggle; contention.

rive /rīv/ *v.tr* (*past* **rived**; *past part.* **riv•en** /rívən/) split or tear apart violently.

ri•ver /rívər/ *n.* **1** copious natural stream of water flowing to the sea, a lake, etc. **2** copious flow (*river of lava*). □ **sell down the river** *colloq.* betray or let down.

■ **1** watercourse, tributary, waterway, creek. **2** flood, torrent. □ **sell down the river** see BETRAY 2.

ri•ver•side /rívərsīd/ *n.* ground along a riverbank.

riv•et /rívit/ • *n.* bolt for joining parts with its headless end being beaten out or pressed down when in place. • *v.tr.* **1 a** join or fasten with rivets. **b** fix; make immovable. **2 a** direct intently (one's eyes or attention, etc.). **b** (esp. as **riveting** *adj.*) engross (a person or the attention). □□ **riv′et•er** *n.*

■ *v.* **1 b** make secure; see also ANCHOR *v.* 1, 2. **2 a** see FIX *v.* 5. **b** (**riveting**) spellbinding, hypnotic, fascinating, gripping, captivating, absorbing.

riv•u•let /rívyəlit/ *n.* small stream.

rm. *abbr.* room.

RN *abbr.* registered nurse.

Rn *symb. Chem.* radon.

RNA *abbr.* ribonucleic acid.

roach /rōch/ *n.* **1** *colloq.* cockroach. **2** *sl.* butt of a marijuana cigarette.

road /rōd/ *n.* **1** path or way with a prepared surface, used by vehicles, pedestrians, etc. **2** one's way or route. **3** [usu. in *pl.*] anchorage near the shore. □ **one for the road** *colloq.* final (esp. alcoholic) drink before departure. **on the road** traveling, esp. as a firm's representative. **road hog** *colloq.* reckless or inconsiderate motorist. **road show** performance given by a touring company. **the road to** way of getting to or achieving (*road to ruin*).

■ **1** thoroughfare, byway, roadway, avenue, boulevard, street, lane, alley, highway, parkway, turnpike, expressway, freeway. **2** see PATH 2.

road•bed /rōdbed/ *n.* foundation of a railroad, road, etc.

road•block /rōdblok/ *n.* barrier on a road, esp. one set up to stop and examine traffic.

road•house /rōdhows/ *n.* inn or club on a major road.

road•run•ner /rōdrunər/ *n.* fast-running species of cuckoo of Mexican and US deserts.

road•side /rōdsīd/ *n.* strip of land beside a road.

road•ster /rōdstər/ *n.* open car without rear seats.

road•way /rōdway/ *n.* road, esp. the part for traffic.

road•work /rōdwərk/ *n.* **1** construction or repair of roads. **2** athletic exercise or training involving running on roads.

roam /rōm/ *v.* **1** *intr.* ramble; wander. **2** *tr.* travel unsystematically over, through, or about. □□ **roam′er** *n.*

■ rove, range, drift, meander; *sl.* mosey.

roan /rōn/ • *adj.* (of esp. a horse) having a coat thickly interspersed with another color. • *n.* roan animal.

roar /rawr/ • *n.* **1** loud, deep, hoarse sound. **2** loud laugh. • *v.* **1** *intr.* utter or make a roar. **2** *intr.* travel in a vehicle at high speed. **3** *tr.* say, sing, or utter in a loud tone. □□ **roar′er** *n.*

■ *n.* **1** bellow, thunder, rumble, boom; cry, yell, yowl, clamor, outcry. **2** guffaw, howl, hoot.

roar•ing /ráwring/ *adj.* in senses of ROAR *v.* □ **roaring forties** stormy ocean tracts between lat. 40° and 50° S. **roaring twenties** decade of the 1920s (with ref. to its postwar buoyancy).

■ see THUNDEROUS.

roast /rōst/ • *v.* **1** *tr.* cook (food, esp. meat) in an oven or by open heat. **2** *tr.* expose to great heat. **3** *tr.* **a** criticize severely. **b** honor at a roast (sense *n.* 4). **4** *intr.* undergo roasting. • *attrib.adj.* roasted. • *n.* **1** roast meat. **2** piece of meat for roasting. **3** party where roasted food is eaten. **4** banquet at which the honoree is subjected to good-natured ridicule.

■ *v.* **3 a** see CRITICIZE 1, TAUNT *v.*

roast•er /rōstər/ *n.* **1** person or thing that roasts. **2** something fit for roasting, e.g., a fowl, a potato, etc.

roast•ing /rōsting/ • *adj.* very hot. • *n.* **1** in senses of ROAST *v.* **2** severe criticism or denunciation.

■ *adj.* see HOT *adj.* 1. • *n.* **2** see REPRIMAND *n.*

rob /rob/ *v.tr.* (**robbed**, **rob•bing**) **1** take unlawfully from, esp. by force or threat. **2** deprive of what is due or normal (*was robbed of my sleep*). **3** [*absol.*] commit robbery. **4** *colloq.* cheat; swindle. □□ **rob′ber** *n.* **rob′ber•y** *n.* (*pl.* **-ies**).

■ **1** loot, rifle, ransack, plunder, raid, pillage, sack; burglarize; hold up, mug, *colloq.* stick up. **2** deny, refuse. **4** defraud, fleece, *colloq.* rip off, *sl.* gyp. □□ **robber** thief, pickpocket; burglar; bandit; pirate; mugger. **robbery** theft, thievery; larceny; *sl.* heist; holdup, *colloq.* stickup; overcharging, exploitation.

robe /rōb/ • *n.* **1** long, loose outer garment. **2** [often in *pl.*] long outer garment worn as an indication of rank, office, profession, etc. • *v.* **1** *tr.* clothe in a robe; dress. **2** *intr.* put on one's robes or vestments.

■ *n.* **1** cloak, mantle, cape, wrap. • *v.* **1** see DRESS *v.* 1a.

rob•in /róbin/ *n.* (also **rob′in red′breast**) red-breasted thrush.

ro•bot /rōbot/ *n.* **1** machine with a human appearance or functioning like a human. **2** person who works mechanically but insensitively. □□ **ro•bot′ic** *adj.* **ro′bot•ize** *v.tr.*

■ **1** android, automaton. **2** drudge.

ro•bot•ics /rōbótiks/ *n.pl.* the study of robots; art or science of their design and operation.

ro•bust /rōbúst/ *adj.* (**ro•bust•er**, **ro•bust•est**) **1** strong and sturdy, esp. in physique or construction. **2** (of wine, etc.) full-bodied. □□ **ro•bust′ly** *adv.* **ro•bust′ness** *n.*

■ **1** sound; healthy, fit, hardy, hearty, stout, strapping, vigorous. **2** flavorful, sapid.

rock¹ /rok/ *n.* **1** hard material of the earth's crust. **2** *Geol.* any natural material, hard or soft (e.g., clay), consisting of one or more minerals. **3** stone of any size. **4** firm and dependable support or protection. □ **between a rock and a hard place** forced to choose between two unpleasant alternatives. **on the rocks** *colloq.* **1** short of money. **2** broken down. **3** (of a drink) served over ice cubes. **rock-bottom** (of prices, etc.) the very lowest. **rock candy** sugar crystallized in large masses onto a string or stick. **rock garden** garden in which rocks are a chief feature. **rock salt** common salt as a solid mineral.

■ **4** pillar *or* tower of strength, mainstay, backbone, *sl.* brick. □ **on the rocks** *see* DESTITUTE **1**. **2** in ruins, beyond repair, *colloq.* in (a) shambles; shattered.

rock² /rok/ • *v.* **1** *tr.* move gently to and fro; set or maintain such motion. **2** *intr.* be in such motion. **3 a** *intr.* sway from side to side; shake; reel. **b** *tr.* cause to do this. • *n.* **1** rocking movement. **2** = *rock and roll.* □ **rock and** (or **rock 'n'**) **roll** popular music originating in the 1950s, characterized by a heavy beat and simple melodies, often with a blues element. **rock the boat** *colloq.* disturb the equilibrium of a situation. **rocking chair** chair mounted on rockers or springs for gently rocking in. **rocking horse** toy horse on rockers or springs for a child to rock on.

■ *v.* **1** swing; lull. **2, 3a** toss; roll, lurch; wobble. **3 b** shudder, rattle.

rock•a•bil•ly /rókəbilee/ *n.* music combining elements of rock and roll and hillbilly music.

rock•er /rókər/ *n.* **1** person or thing that rocks. **2** curved bar, etc., on which something can rock. **3** rocking chair. **4 a** devotee of rock music. **b** performer of rock music. □ **off one's rocker** *sl.* crazy.

rock•et /rókit/ • *n.* **1** cylindrical projectile that can be propelled to a great height or distance by combustion of its contents. **2** engine using a similar principle. **3** rocket-propelled missile, spacecraft, etc. • *v.intr.* **1** move rapidly upward or away. **2** increase rapidly (*prices rocketed*).

■ *v.* **1** *see* SPEED *v.* **2** skyrocket, shoot up, climb, soar, *colloq.* go through the roof.

rock•et•ry /rókitree/ *n.* science or practice of rocket propulsion.

rock•y¹ /rókee/ *adj.* (**rock•i•er, rock•i•est**) **1** of or like rock. **2** full of rock or rocks. □□ **rock•i•ness** *n.*

■ stony, pebbly; craggy; hard, bumpy, uncomfortable.

rock•y² /rókee/ *adj.* (**rock•i•er, rock•i•est**) *colloq.* unsteady; tottering. □□ **rock•i•ly** *adv.* **rock•i•ness** *n.*

■ unstable, teetering, shaky, rickety, unsure, doubtful, questionable, *colloq.* iffy.

ro•co•co /rəkókō/ • *adj.* **1** of a late baroque style of decoration. **2** (of literature, music, architecture, etc.) highly ornamented; florid. • *n.* rococo style.

■ *adj.* **2** *see* ORNATE.

rod /rod/ *n.* **1** slender straight bar, esp. of wood or metal. **2** cane for flogging. **3** = *fishing rod.* **4** measure of length equal to 5¹/₂ yards. □□ **rod•less** *adj.* **rod•like** *adj.*

■ **1** pole, baton, wand, staff, stick. **2** birch, switch.

rode *past* of RIDE.

ro•dent /ród'nt/ *n.* mammal with strong incisors, e.g., rat, mouse, squirrel, beaver, porcupine.

ro•de•o /ródeeō, rōdáyō/ *n.* (*pl.* **-os**) exhibition of cowboys' skills in handling animals.

roe¹ /rō/ *n.* fish eggs.

roe² /rō/ *n.* (*pl.* same or **roes**) (also **roe deer**) small European and Asian deer.

roe•buck /róbuk/ *n.* (*pl.* same or **roe'bucks**) male roe deer.

roent•gen /réntgən, –jən, rúnt–/ *n.* unit of radiation produced by X rays, etc.

rog•er /rójər/ *int.* **1** your message has been received and understood (used in radio communication, etc.). **2** *sl.* I agree.

rogue /rōg/ *n.* **1** dishonest or unprincipled person. **2** *joc.* mischievous person. **3** [usu. *attrib.*] **a** wild animal driven away or living apart from others. **b** stray, irresponsible, or undisciplined person or thing. □ **rogues' gallery** collection of photographs of known criminals, etc., used for identification of suspects. □□ **ro'guer•y** *n.* **ro'guish** *adj.* **ro'guish•ly** *adv.* **ro'guish•ness** *n.*

■ **1** trickster, swindler, cheat, cad, ne'er-do-well, good-for-nothing, scoundrel, *colloq.* scamp. **2** *see* RASCAL. **3** (*attrib.*) uncontrollable, unmanageable, self-willed, unruly, lawless.

roil /royl/ *v.tr.* **1** make (a liquid) turbid by agitating it. **2** = RILE.

■ **1** *see* AGITATE **3**.

roist•er /róystər/ *v.intr.* (esp. as **roistering** *adj.*) be uproarious. □□ **rois'ter•er** *n.* **rois'ter•ing** *n.* **rois'ter•ous** *adj.*

role /rōl/ *n.* (also **rôle**) **1** actor's part in a play, motion picture, etc. **2** function. □ **role model** person looked to by others as an example.

■ **1** character **2** place; duty, task, responsibility.

roll /rōl/ • *v.* **1 a** *intr.* move or go in some direction by turning on an axis. **b** *tr.* cause to do this. **2 a** *intr.* move or advance on or (of time, etc.) as if on wheels, etc. **b** *tr.* cause to do this. **3 a** *tr.* turn over and over on itself to form a more or less cylindrical or spherical shape (*rolled a newspaper*). **b** *tr.* form a cylinder or ball. **4** *intr. & tr.* rotate. **5** *intr.* **a** (of a moving vehicle) sway to and fro sideways. **b** walk unsteadily. **6** *intr.* show or go with an undulating surface (*rolling hills, waves roll in*). **7** *intr. & tr.* sound or utter with a vibratory or trilling effect **8** *tr.* throw (dice). **9** *tr. sl.* rob (esp. a helpless victim). • *n.* **1** rolling motion or gait. **2** rolling. **3** rhythmic sound of thunder, etc. **4** complete revolution of an aircraft, etc. **5** cylinder formed by turning material over and over on itself. **6** small portion of bread individually baked. **7 a** official list or register. **b** total numbers on this. □ **on a roll** *sl.* experiencing a bout of success or progress. **roll back** cause (esp. prices) to decrease. **roll call** calling out a list of names to establish who is present. **rolled gold** thin coating of gold applied to a baser metal by rolling. **rolled into one** combined in one person or thing. **roll in 1** arrive in great numbers or quantity. **2** wallow or luxuriate in. **rolling pin** cylinder for rolling out pastry, dough, etc. **rolling stone** person who is unwilling to settle down. **roll-top desk** desk with a flexible cover sliding in curved grooves. **roll with the punches** withstand adversity, difficulties, etc. □□ **roll′a•ble** adj.

■ v. **1** rotate, cycle; go around, orbit, tumble, somersault. **2 a** cruise, coast; float (by or past), sail (by or past), fly (by or past); elapse, disappear, vanish. **5 b** see STAGGER v. 1a. **6** billow, rise and fall; see also WAVE v. 2. **7** rumble, reverberate, boom, peal, resonate. ● n. **1** wave; spin, toss, whirl, twirl. **3** rumble, reverberation, boom, clap, roar. **5** reel, spool, scroll. **6** bun, bagel. **7 a** record, directory, listing, catalog. □ **roll in 1** pour in, flow in, colloq. show up. **2** revel in, savor, bask in.

roll•a•way /rṓləway/ adj. (of a bed, etc.) that can be removed on wheels or casters.

rol•ler /rṓlər/ n. **1** revolving cylinder for smoothing, spreading, crushing, stamping, hanging a cloth on, etc., used alone or in a machine. **2** small cylinder on which hair is rolled for setting. **3** long, swelling wave. □ **roller bearing** bearing like a ball bearing but with small cylinders instead of balls. **roller coaster** n. amusement ride consisting of an elevated track with cars that rise and plunge steeply. **roller skate** see SKATE[1].

■ **1** drum. **3** see WAVE n. 1, 2.

Rol•ler•blade /rṓlərblayd/ ● n. propr. (usu. pl.) in-line skates. ● v.intr. use Rollerblades.

rol•lick /rṓlik/ v.intr. (esp. as **rollicking** adj.) be jovial or exuberant.

■ see REVEL v. 1.

roll•over /rṓlōvər/ n. Econ. extension or transfer of a debt or other financial relationship.

ro•ly-po•ly /rṓleepṓlee/ adj. pudgy; plump.

■ see PLUMP[1] adj.

ROM /rom/ n. Computing read-only memory; memory not capable of being changed by program instruction.

Rom. abbr. **1** Roman. **2** Romania. **3** Romans (New Testament).

ro•maine /rṓmáyn/ n. long-leafed lettuce.

Ro•man /rṓmən/ ● adj. **1** of ancient or modern Rome, its territory, people, etc. **2** of papal Rome, esp. . = ROMAN CATHOLIC. **3** (**roman**) (of type) plain and upright, used in ordinary print. **4** based on the ancient Roman alphabet. ● n. **1** native or inhabitant of Rome. **2** (**roman**) roman type. □ **Roman candle** firework discharging colored balls and sparks. **Roman Empire** hist. that established by Augustus in 27 BC, including much of Europe, N Africa, and SW Asia. **Roman holiday** enjoyment derived from others' discomfort. **Roman numeral** any of the Roman letters representing numbers: I = 1, V = 5, X = 10, L = 50, C = 100, D = 500, M = 1000.

Ro•man Cath•o•lic /rṓmən/ ● adj. of the part of the Christian Church acknowledging

the pope as its head. ● n. member of this Church. □□ **Ro′man Ca•thol′i•cism** n.

ro•mance /rṓmáns/ ● n. (also disp. /rṓmans/) **1** atmosphere, attitude or tendency characterized by a sense of remoteness from or idealization of everyday life. **2 a** love affair. **b** sentimental or idealized love. **3** literary genre with romantic love or highly imaginative unrealistic episodes. ● adj. (**Romance**) of any of the languages descended from Latin (French, Italian, Spanish, etc.). ● v.tr. court; woo.

■ n. **1** fantasy, mystery, nostalgia; glamour, exoticism. **2 a** amour, liaison. **3** melodrama; love story; Gothic novel or tale, legend. ● v. chase, pursue; flatter, curry favor with, colloq. butter up, soft-soap.

Ro•ma•ni•an /rṓmáyneeən/ (also **Rumanian** /rōō-/) ● n. **1 a** native or national of Romania. **b** person of Romanian descent. **2** language of Romania. ● adj. of Romania, its people, or its language.

Ro•ma•no /rṓmaánō/ n. strong-tasting hard cheese.

Ro•mansh /rṓmánsh, -maánsh/ n. Rhaeto-Romanic dialect, esp. as spoken in Switzerland.

ro•man•tic /rṓmántik/ ● adj. **1** of, characterized by, or suggestive of romance. **2** inclined toward or suggestive of love. **3** (of a person) imaginative; visionary; idealistic. **4 a** (of style in art, music, etc.) concerned more with feeling and emotion than with form and aesthetic qualities. **b** (also **Romantic**) of the 18th–19th-c. movement or style in the European arts. **5** impractical; fantastic. ● n. **1** romantic person. **2** romanticist. □□ **ro•man′ti•cal•ly** adv.

■ adj. **1** imaginary, fictitious, fictional, idealized, fabulous, made-up, dreamed-up, fantasized, fanciful, mythical, idyllic; sentimental, maudlin, mushy. **2** emotional; see also TENDER[1] 4. **3** see IMAGINATIVE, idealistic (IDEALISM). **5** unrealistic, quixotic, absurd, wild. ● n. **1** Don Quixote, idealist; sentimentalist; see also DREAMER.

ro•man•ti•cism /rṓmántisizəm/ n. (also **Romanticism**) adherence to a romantic style in art, music, etc. □□ **ro•man′ti•cist** n. (also **Romanticist**).

ro•man•ti•cize /rṓmántisīz/ v. **1** tr. make or render romantic or unreal (romanticized account of war). **2** intr. indulge in romantic thoughts or actions. □□ **ro•man•ti•ci•za′tion** n.

Rom•a•ny /rṓmənee, rō′-/ n. language of the Gypsies.

Ro•me•o /rṓmeeō/ n. (pl. **-os**) passionate male lover or seducer.

romp /romp/ ● v.intr. play energetically. ● n. **1** spell of romping. **2** colloq. easy win.

■ v. see FROLIC v. ● n. **1** see FROLIC n. 1, 2.

romp•er /rómpər/ n. [usu. in pl.] one-piece garment, esp. for a child, that covers the trunk and has short pants.

rood /rōōd/ n. crucifix.

■ cross.

roof /rōōf, rŏŏf/ ● n. (pl. **roofs**) **1** upper covering of a building. **2** top of any enclosed space. ● v.tr. cover with or as with a roof.

□ **go through the roof** *colloq.* (of prices, etc.) reach extreme or unexpected heights. **hit** (or **go through** or **raise**) **the roof** *colloq.* become very angry. **raise the roof 1** create a noisy racket. **2** protest noisily. □□ **roofed** *adj.* [also in *comb.*]. **roof'er** *n.*

roof•ing /rōōfiŋ, rŏŏf-/ *n.* material for constructing a roof.

roof•top /rōōftop, rŏŏf-/ *n.* top of a house.

rook[1] /rŏŏk/ • *n.* black European and Asiatic bird of the crow family. • *v.tr.* **1** charge (a customer) extortionately. **2** win money from (a person), esp. by swindling.
■ *v.* **1** see FLEECE *v.* 1. **2** see SWINDLE *v.*

rook[2] /rŏŏk/ *n.* chess piece with its top in the shape of a battlement; castle.

rook•er•y /rŏŏkəree/ *n.* (*pl.* **-ies**) colony of certain birds (esp. rooks or penguins) or seals.

rook•ie /rŏŏkee/ *n. sl.* **1** new recruit. **2** *Sports* first-year player.
■ **1** see RECRUIT *n.* 1, 2.

room /rōōm, rŏŏm/ • *n.* **1** space for or occupied by something; capacity. **2** part of a building enclosed by walls, floor, and ceiling. • *v.intr.* lodge; board. □ **rooming house** house with rented rooms for lodging. **room service** (in a hotel, etc.) service of food or drink taken to a guest's room. □□ **-roomed** *adj.* [in *comb.*]. **room'er** *n.* **room'ful** *n.* (*pl.* **-fuls**).
■ *n.* **1** see SPACE *n.* 1c. **2** see CELL 1. • *v.* live, reside, stay. □ **rooming house** boardinghouse; see also HOTEL.

room•mate /rōōm-mayt, rŏŏm-/ *n.* person occupying the same room, apartment, etc., as another

room•y /rōōmee, rŏŏ-/ *adj.* (**room•ier, room•i•est**) having much room; spacious. □□ **room'i•ly** *adv.* **room'i•ness** *n.*
■ capacious, commodious, large, sizable, big, ample.

roost /rōōst/ • *n.* branch or perch for a bird, esp. to sleep. • *v.intr.* settle for rest or sleep. □ **come home to roost** (of a scheme, etc.) recoil unfavorably upon the originator. **rule the roost** be in charge (esp. of others).
■ *v.* perch, sit; *sl.* crash; nest.

roost•er /rōōstər/ *n.* male domestic chicken; cock.

root[1] /rōōt, rŏŏt/ • *n.* **1** part of a plant normally below the ground, conveying nourishment from the soil. **2** [in *pl.*] attachment, esp. to one's place of origin. **3** embedded part of a hair, tooth, nail, etc. **4** basic cause, source, or origin. **5** *Math.* number that when multiplied by itself a specified number of times gives a specified number or quantity (*cube root of eight is two*). **6** core of a word, without prefixes, suffixes, etc. See synonym study at ORIGIN. • *v.* **1 a** *intr.* take root or grow roots. **b** *tr.* cause to do this. **2** *tr.* fix firmly; establish. **3** *tr.* [foll. by *out*] a drag or dig up by the roots. **b** find and get rid of. □ **put down roots** become settled or established. **root beer** carbonated drink made from an extract of roots. **root canal** *Dentistry* surgery to remove the diseased nerve of a tooth. **take root 1** begin to grow and draw nourishment from the soil. **2** become fixed

or established. □□ **root'ed•ness** *n.* **root'less** *adj.* **root'let** *n.*
■ *n.* **1** taproot, rootlet, tuber, radicle, rhizome. **2** (*roots*) heritage; family; ancestors, predecessors; birthplace, native land *or* country *or* soil. **4** basis, foundation, seat, wellspring. • *v.* **1 b** plant, embed, set (out), sow, fix. **2** set; implant, instill. **3 b** uncover, discover, unearth, turn up; eliminate, destroy, exterminate. □ **put down roots** see SETTLE 1, 2a, b. **take root 1** germinate, sprout, develop. **2** catch on, take hold.

root[2] /rōōt, rŏŏt/ • *v.* **1 a** *intr.* (of an animal, esp. a pig) turn up the ground with the snout, beak, etc., in search of food. **b** *tr.* [foll. by *up*] turn up (the ground) by rooting. **2 a** *intr.* rummage. **b** *tr.* find or extract by rummaging. **3** *intr.* [foll. by *for*] *sl.* encourage by applause or support. □□ **root'er** *n.* (in sense 3).
■ **2 a** forage, dig, nose, poke, ferret, burrow, delve, search. **3** (*root for*) cheer (for); encourage, urge on, *colloq.* boost.

rope /rōp/ • *n.* **1** stout cord made by twisting together strands of hemp, nylon, wire, etc. **2** onions, garlic bulbs, pearls, etc., strung together. **3** [in *pl.*, prec. by *the*] conditions in some sphere of action (*show a person the ropes*). • *v.tr.* **1** fasten, secure, or catch with rope. **2** [usu. foll. by *off, in*] enclose with rope. □ **give a person plenty of** (or **enough**) **rope** (**to hang himself** or **herself**) give a person enough freedom of action to bring about his or her own downfall. **rope in** (or **into**) persuade to take part in (*was roped into doing the laundry*).
■ *n.* **1** see CORD *n.* 1. **3** (*the ropes*) the routine, *colloq.* the score. • *v.* tie, bind, lash, hitch, tether. □ **rope in** (or **into**) attract, draw (in), tempt, entice, lure.

Roque•fort /rōkfərt/ *n. propr.* soft blue cheese made from sheep's milk.

ror•qual /ráwrkwəl/ *n.* any of various whales having a dorsal fin. (Also called **finback, fin whale**.)

Ror•schach test /ráwrshaak/ *n. Psychol.* personality test based on interpretation of inkblots.

ro•sa•ceous /rōzáyshəs/ *adj. Bot.* of the large plant family that includes the rose.

ro•sa•ry /rōzəree/ *n.* (*pl.* **-ries**) **1** *RC Ch.* repeated sequence of prayers, usu. said while counting them on a string of beads. **2** string of beads used for this.

rose[1] /rōz/ • *n.* **1** prickly bush or shrub bearing usu. fragrant red, pink, yellow, or white flowers. **2** this flower. **3** light crimson color; pink. • *adj.* rose-colored. □ **rose water** perfume made from roses. **rose window** circular window with roselike tracery. **see** (or **look**) **through rose-colored glasses** regard (circumstances, etc.) with unfounded favor or optimism.

rose[2] *past of* RISE.

ro•sé /rōzáy/ *n.* light pink wine.

ro•se•ate /rōzeeət, -ayt/ *adj.* rose-colored (*roseate tern*).

rose•bud /rōzbud/ *n.* bud of a rose.

rose•mary /rózmairee, –mə̄ree/ n. evergreen fragrant shrub used as an herb.

ro•sette /rōzét/ n. rose-shaped ornament of ribbon.

rose•wood /rózwŏŏd/ n. any of several fragrant close-grained woods used in making furniture.

Rosh Ha•sha•nah /ráwsh həsháwnə, –shaà–, haashaanaà, rósh/ n. (also **Rosh Ha•sha′na**) the Jewish New Year.

ros•in /rózin/ • n. resin, esp. in solid form.
• v.tr. rub (esp. the bow of a violin, etc.) with rosin. □□ **ros′in•y** adj.

ros•ter /róstər/ n. list or plan of turns of duty, players available, etc.
■ docket.

ros•trum /róstrəm/ n. (pl. **ros•tra** /–strə/ or **ros•trums**) platform for public speaking, conducting an orchestra, etc.
■ stage, dais, podium, stand.

ros•y /rózee/ adj. (**ros•i•er, ros•i•est**)
1 pink; red. 2 optimistic; hopeful. □□ **ros′i•ly** adv. **ros′i•ness** n.
■ 1 rose-colored, roseate, reddish, pinkish, cherry; ruddy, flushed, blushing, florid. 2 promising, favorable, auspicious, encouraging, sunny, bright, cheerful.

rot /rot/ • v.intr. (**rot•ted, rot•ting**) 1 decompose; decay. 2 gradually perish; waste away. • n. 1 process or state of rotting. 2 sl. nonsense.
■ v. 1 fester, molder (away); spoil, go bad, be tainted, mold; corrode, disintegrate, deteriorate. 2 degenerate, decline, wither, crumble; languish. • n. 1 putrefaction, blight, corrosion. 2 balderdash, rubbish, drivel, colloq. hogwash, sl. bull, baloney.

ro•ta•ry /rótəree/ • adj. acting by rotation (rotary drill). • n. (pl. **–ries**) 1 rotary machine. 2 traffic circle.
■ adj. rotatory, revolving, spinning.

ro•tate /rótayt/ v. 1 intr. & tr. move around an axis or center; revolve. 2 a tr. take or arrange in rotation. b intr. act or take place in rotation (the chairmanship rotates annually). □□ **ro′tat•a•ble** adj. **ro•ta′tion** n. **ro•ta•tive** /rótaytiv/ adj. **ro′ta•tor** n. **ro•ta•to•ry** /rótətawree/ adj.
■ 1 gyrate, whirl, pivot, reel; turn, spin. 2 change, alternate, switch, swap; exchange; trade places, take turns.

ROTC /rótsee/ abbr. Reserve Officers Training Corps.

rote /rōt/ n. [usu. prec. by by] mechanical or habitual repetition (with ref. to acquiring knowledge).
■ routine, ritual; (by rote) by heart, from memory; automatically, mechanically.

rot•gut /rótgut/ n. inferior whiskey.

ro•tis•ser•ie /rōtísəree/ n. rotating spit for roasting and barbecuing meat.

ro•tor /rótər/ n. 1 rotary part of a machine. 2 rotary airfoil on a helicopter.

ro•to•till•er /rótətilər/ n. machine with a rotating blade for breaking up or tilling the soil. □□ **ro′to•till** v.tr.

rot•ten /rót′n/ adj. (**rot•ten•er, rot•ten•est**)
1 rotting or rotted. 2 morally, socially, or po-

litically corrupt. 3 sl. a disagreeable; unpleasant. b (of a plan, etc.) ill-advised; unsatisfactory (rotten idea). c ill (feel rotten today). □□ **rot′ten•ly** adv. **rot′ten•ness** n.
■ 1 decayed, decomposed, putrid, moldy, spoiled, bad; corroded, deteriorating, disintegrating, crumbling; falling to pieces. 2 immoral, dishonest, deceitful, venal, shameless, degenerate, evil, wicked, vile; base, despicable, wretched, miserable, nasty, contemptible, low-down, mean. 3 a awful, terrible, horrible, lousy, sl. stinking. c sick.

Rott•wei•ler /rótwīlər/ n. 1 dog of a tall black-and-tan breed. 2 this breed.

ro•tund /rōtúnd/ adj. plump; round. □□ **ro•tun′di•ty** n. **ro•tund′ly** adv.
■ spherical; chubby, portly, tubby, stout, fat, obese, overweight, roly-poly.

ro•tun•da /rōtúndə/ n. circular building, hall, or room, esp. one with a dome.

rou•é /rŏŏ-áy/ n. debauchee, esp. an elderly one; rake.
■ playboy, womanizer, lecher, lothario, Don Juan, Casanova, flirt, lady-killer, sl. wolf, dirty old man.

rouge /rŏŏzh/ • n. 1 red cosmetic for coloring the cheeks. 2 reddish metal polish. • v. 1 tr. color with rouge. 2 intr. apply rouge.

rough /ruf/ • adj. 1 uneven; bumpy; not smooth. 2 hairy; shaggy; coarse in texture. 3 not mild, quiet, nor gentle; boisterous; coarse. 4 harsh; insensitive. 5 unpleasant; severe; demanding. 6 hard or unfair toward. 7 incomplete; rudimentary; approximate. See synonym study at RUDE. • adv. in a rough manner. • n. 1 hard aspect of life; hardship (take the rough with the smooth). 2 Golf rough ground. 3 unfinished or natural state. • v.tr. 1 [foll. by up] ruffle (feathers, hair, etc.). 2 [foll. by out] shape, sketch, or plan roughly. □ **rough-and-ready** crude but effective. **rough-and-tumble** irregular; scrambling; disorderly. **diamond in the rough** person of good nature but rough manners. **rough draft** first or original draft (of a story, report, document, etc.). **rough-hewn** uncouth; unrefined. **rough it** do without basic comforts. **rough up** sl. treat (a person) with violence. □□ **rough′ly** adv. **rough′ness** n.
■ adj. 1 irregular, jagged, rugged, lumpy. 2 see HAIRY 1, COARSE 1. 3 brusque, curt, abrupt, discourteous, impolite, disrespectful, rude, uncouth, vulgar, ill-mannered, ill-bred; unrestrained; grating, discordant; rasping, gruff, husky, hoarse. 4 inconsiderate, violent, unfeeling, cruel, tough, brutal. 5 difficult, arduous, laborious. 7 unfinished, imperfect, unpolished, raw; estimated, cursory, colloq. ballpark; preliminary. • adv. violently, savagely, brutally. • v. 2 draft, mock up, outline. □ **rough-and-tumble** see IRREGULAR adj. 4, DISORDERLY 1. **rough up** beat (up), thrash, attack, batter, assault. □□ **roughly** harshly, ruthlessly; clumsily, awkwardly, ineptly; about, nearly, approximately.

rough•age /rúfij/ n. coarse, fibrous material in food.

rough•en /rúfən/ v. make or become rough.

rough•house /rúfhows/ sl. • n. disturbance

or row; boisterous play. • v. **1** tr. handle (a person) roughly. **2** intr. make a disturbance.
  ■ n. rowdiness, disorderly conduct; see also FRACAS. • v. **2** see BRAWL v.

rough•neck /rúfnek/ n. colloq. **1** rough or rowdy person. **2** worker on a drill rig.
  ■ **1** ruffian, thug, yahoo, hooligan.

rough•shod /rúfshod/ adj. (of a horse) having shoes with nail heads projecting to prevent slipping. □ **ride roughshod over** treat inconsiderately or arrogantly.

rou•lette /rŏolét/ n. gambling game in which a ball is dropped on to a revolving numbered wheel.

round /rownd/ • adj. **1** shaped like a circle, sphere, or cylinder; convex; circular; curved. **2** entire; complete. **3** candid; outspoken. **4** [usu. attrib.] (of a number) expressed for convenience as a whole number (spent $297.32, or in round figures $300). • n. **1** round object or form. **2** a recurring series of activities, functions, etc. **b** fixed route for deliveries, etc. **3** single provision of drinks, etc., to each member of a group. **4** a ammunition to fire one shot. **b** act of firing this. **5** set, series, or sequence of actions in turn, esp. **a** one spell of play in a game, etc. **b** one stage in a competition. **6** song overlapping at intervals. • adv. = AROUND adv. 5–12. • prep. = AROUND prep. 5–12. • v. **1** a tr. give a round shape to. **b** intr. assume a round shape. **2** tr. double or pass around (a corner, cape, etc.). **3** tr. express (a number) approximately for brevity [also foll. by down when the number is decreased and up when it is increased]. □ **make one's rounds** take a customary route for inspection, etc. **make the rounds** (of news, etc.) be passed on from person to person, etc. **round robin 1** petition, esp. with signatures written in a circle to conceal the order of writing. **2** tournament in which each competitor plays in turn against every other. **round table** assembly for discussion, esp. at a conference (often attrib.: round-table talks). **round trip** trip to one or more places and back again. **round up** collect or bring together. □□ **round'ish** adj. **round'ness** n.
  ■ adj. **1** disk-shaped; ring-shaped; spherical, ball-shaped, globular; arched. **2** exact, precise, full; continuous. **3** plain, honest, straightforward, direct, unvarnished, genuine, truthful, frank, open, blunt; categorical. **4** approximate, colloq. ballpark. • n. **1** circle, disk; ring, hoop; ball, sphere, globe, orb, bead. **2** a cycle, sequence, succession. **b** circuit, course; beat; see also ROUTE n. **4** a bullet(s), cartridge(s), shell(s). **5** heat, stage, level, turn, bout. • v. **2** orbit, go around. □ **round up** gather, assemble, muster, pull together, herd, marshal, corral.

SYNONYM STUDY: round

ANNULAR, CIRCULAR, GLOBULAR, SPHERICAL. What do a bicycle wheel, a basketball, and a barrel of oil have in common? All are considered to be **round**, an adjective that may be applied to anything shaped like a circle, a sphere, or a cylinder. But of these three objects, only a basketball is **spherical**, which means having a *round* body whose surface is

equally distant from the center at all points. Something that is **globular** is shaped like a ball or a globe but is not necessarily a perfect sphere (globular drops of oil leaking from the seam). A wheel is *circular*, as is a Frisbee; in fact, anything with a round, flat surface in the shape of a ring or a disk may be described as *circular*—whether or not it corresponds to a perfect circle. But the rings of a tree are described as **annular**, a word that usually implies having a series of concentric ringlike forms or structures.

---

round•a•bout /równdəbowt/ adj. circuitous; indirect.
  ■ circular, long; circumlocutory, evasive, oblique.

roun•de•lay /równdilay/ n. short simple song with a refrain.

round•house /równdhows/ n. circular repair shed for railroad locomotives, built around a turntable.

round•ly /równdlee/ adv. **1** bluntly; in plain language (was roundly criticized). **2** in a thoroughgoing manner (go roundly to work).

round•up /równdup/ n. **1** systematic rounding up of people or things. **2** summary of facts or events.
  ■ **1** gathering, assembly, rally, collection, herding, corralling. **2** synopsis, digest, outline, review, colloq. recap.

round•worm /równdwərm/ n. worm, esp. a nematode, with a rounded body.

rouse /rowz/ v. **1** a tr. bring out of sleep; wake. **b** intr. cease to sleep; wake up. **2** a tr. stir up; make active or excited. **b** intr. become active. **3** tr. provoke to anger (is terrible when roused). **4** tr. evoke (feelings). □□ **rous'a•ble** adj. **rous'er** n. **rous'ing** adj. **rous'ing•ly** adv.
  ■ **1** arouse; waken, awaken; get up, arise. **2** a stimulate, inspirit, animate, move. **b** see STIR¹ v. 3. **3** goad, incite, work up, fire up. **4** see EVOKE 2. □□ **rousing** energizing, inspiring, invigorating, electrifying.

roust•a•bout /rówstəbowt/ n. **1** laborer on an oil rig. **2** unskilled or casual laborer, as in a circus.

rout¹ /rowt/ • n. **1** disorderly retreat. **2** heavy defeat. • v.tr. put to flight; defeat utterly.
  ■ n. **1** dispersal, withdrawal; see also RETREAT n. 1a. **2** trouncing, overthrow; debacle, conquest, thrashing, beating, colloq. licking, sl. shellacking. • v. bring down, subdue, suppress, conquer, overwhelm, overpower, crush, destroy, put down, colloq. lick, sl. clobber.

rout² /rowt/ v. **1** intr. & tr. = ROOT². **2** tr. cut a groove, or any pattern not extending to the edges, in (a wooden or metal surface). □ **rout out** force out of bed, a hiding place, etc. □□ **rout'er** n.

route /root, rowt/ • n. way or course taken (esp. regularly). • v.tr. send, forward, or direct by a particular route.
  ■ n. direction, path, road. • v. see FORWARD v. 1.

rou•tine /rooteen/ • n. **1** regular course or

procedure. **2** set sequence in a dance, comedy act, etc. • *adj.* **1** performed as part of a routine. **2** of a customary or standard kind. □□ **rou·tine′ly** *adv.*

■ *n.* **1** way, method; practice, formula; program, schedule, plan. **2** performance, number, part, *sl.* shtick. • *adj.* **1** regular, everyday; boring, tedious, unimaginative; automatic, mechanical. **2** familiar, conventional, usual.

rove /rōv/ *v.* **1** *intr.* wander without a settled destination; roam. **2** *intr.* (of eyes) look in changing directions. **3** *tr.* wander over or through. □□ **rov′er** *n.*

■ □□ **rover** itinerant, traveler, rolling stone, nomad, gypsy, sojourner, drifter, tramp, gadabout, vagabond.

row¹ /rō/ *n.* **1** line of persons or things. **2** line of seats across a theater, etc. **□ hard** (or **tough**) **row to hoe** difficult task. **in a row 1** forming a row. **2** *colloq.* in succession (*two Sundays in a row*).

■ **1** file, column, rank, string. **2** see TIER. □ **in a row 2** consecutively, one after the other.

row² /rō/ • *v.* **1** *tr.* propel (a boat) with oars. **2** *tr.* convey (a passenger) in this way. **3** *intr.* propel a boat in this way. • *n.* excursion in a rowboat. □□ **row′er** *n.*

row³ /row/ *colloq.* • *n.* commotion; quarrel. See synonym study at QUARREL. • *v.intr.* make or engage in a row.

■ *n.* disturbance, clamor, uproar, fuss, turmoil; altercation, argument, dispute, squabble, fracas, *colloq.* spat. • *v.* argue, have words, bicker.

row·boat /rṓbōt/ *n.* small boat propelled by oars.

row·dy /rówdee/ • *adj.* (**row·di·er, row·di·est**) noisy and disorderly. • *n.* (*pl.* **–dies**) rowdy person. □□ **row′di·ly** *adv.* **row′di·ness** *n.* **row′dy·ism** *n.*

■ *adj.* boisterous, loud, unruly. • *n.* ruffian, tough, hooligan, yahoo, brawler, lout, hoodlum, hood. □□ **rowdyism** troublemaking.

row·el /rówəl/ *n.* spiked revolving disk at the end of a spur.

roy·al /róyəl/ • *adj.* **1** of, suited to, or worthy of a king or queen; majestic. **2** in the service or under the patronage of a king or queen. • *n. colloq.* member of the royal family. □ **royal blue** deep vivid blue. **royal family** family to which a sovereign belongs. **royal jelly** substance secreted by honeybee workers and fed by them to future queen bees. □□ **roy′al·ly** *adv.*

■ *adj.* **1** stately, queenly, kingly, regal, imperial, princely.

roy·al·ist /róyəlist/ *n.* supporter of monarchy. □□ **roy′al·ism** *n.*

roy·al·ty /róyəltee/ *n.* (*pl.* **–ties**) **1** office, dignity, or power of a king or queen; sovereignty. **2** royal person(s). **3** percentage of profit from a patent, song, book, etc., paid to the creator.

■ **1** see *sovereignty* (SOVEREIGN). **3** commission, share, payment, compensation.

rpm. *abbr.* (also **r.p.m.**) revolutions per minute.

RR *abbr.* **1** railroad. **2** rural route.

RSV *abbr.* Revised Standard Version (of the Bible).

RSVP *abbr.* (in an invitation, etc.) please answer, (French *répondez s'il vous plaît*).

rt. *abbr.* right.

rte. *abbr.* route.

Ru *symb. Chem.* ruthenium.

rub /rub/ • *v.* (**rubbed, rub·bing**) **1** *tr.* move one's hand or another object with firm pressure over the surface of. **2** *tr.* apply (one's hand, etc.) in this way. **3** *tr.* clean, polish, make dry, chafe, make sore, etc., by rubbing. **4** *tr.* apply (polish, ointment, etc.) by rubbing. **5** *intr.* [foll. by *against, on*] move with contact or friction. • *n.* **1** spell or instance of rubbing. **2** impediment or difficulty (*there's the rub*). □ **rub away** remove by rubbing. **rub elbows with** associate or come into contact with (another person), esp. socially. **rub it in** (or **rub a person's nose in it**) emphasize or repeat an embarrassing fact, etc. **rub off 1** [usu. foll. by *on*] be transferred by contact (*some of his attitudes have rubbed off on me*). **2** remove by rubbing. **rub out 1** erase with an eraser. **2** *sl.* kill; eliminate. **rub the wrong way** irritate.

■ *v.* **1** massage, knead, smooth, stroke. **3** scour, scrub; wipe, shine, buff; see also CHAFE *v.* 1. **4** smear, spread, put. • *n.* **1** rubdown. **2** hindrance, obstacle, problem, trouble; catch, hitch, snag. □ **rub away** see ERODE. **rub elbows with** socialize with, hobnob with, mix with, fraternize with, keep company with. **rub it in** (or **rub a person's nose in it**) make an issue of it, harp on it, dwell on it. **rub off** be passed on or along, be transmitted or communicated or imparted; (*rub off on*) affect. **2** delete, eliminate, eradicate. **rub out** see KILL *v.* 1a. **rub the wrong way** annoy, irk, provoke, anger, *colloq.* get under a person's skin, peeve, *sl.* bug.

rub·ber¹ /rúbər/ *n.* **1** tough elastic substance made from the latex of plants or synthetically. **2** *colloq.* condom. **3** [in *pl.*] galoshes. □ **rubber band** loop of rubber for holding papers, etc., together. **rubber plant 1** evergreen plant with dark-green shiny leaves, often cultivated as a houseplant. **2** (also **rubber tree**) any of various tropical trees yielding latex. **rubber stamp** device for inking and imprinting on a surface. **rubber-stamp** *v.tr.* **1** use a rubber stamp. **2** approve automatically. □□ **rub′ber·y** *adj.* **rub′ber·i·ness** *n.*

■ □□ **rubbery** see YIELDING 2. **rubberiness** see *elasticity* (ELASTIC).

rub·ber² /rúbər/ *adj.* designating the deciding game or match in a series.

rub·ber·ize /rúbəriz/ *v.tr.* treat or coat with rubber.

rub·ber·neck /rúbərnek/ *colloq.* • *n.* person, esp. a tourist, who stares inquisitively or stupidly. • *v.intr.* act in this way.

■ *n.* sightseer. • *v.* gape, gawk.

rub·bish /rúbish/ *n.* **1** waste material; debris; refuse; litter. **2** worthless material or articles; junk. **3** [often as *int.*] nonsense. □□ **rub′bish·y** *adj.*

■ **1** garbage, dross; trash. **2** rejects, dregs. **3** balderdash, colloq. malarkey, hogwash.

rub•ble /rúbəl/ n. rough fragments of stone, brick, etc. □□ **rub′bly** adj.

■ debris.

rube /rōob/ n. colloq. country bumpkin.

ru•bel•la /rōobélə/ n. German measles.

ru•bi•cund /rōobikund/ adj. ruddy; reddish.

■ see ROSY 1.

ru•bid•i•um /rōobídeeəm/ n. Chem. soft silvery metallic element. ¶Symb.: **Rb**.

ru•ble /rōobəl/ n. chief monetary unit of Russia, the USSR (hist.), and some other former republics of the USSR.

ru•bric /rōobrik/ n. **1** heading or passage in red or special lettering. **2** explanatory words. □□ **ru′bri•cal** adj

ru•by /rōobee/ • n. (pl. **–bies**) **1** rare precious stone varying from deep crimson or purple to pale rose. **2** glowing, purple-tinged red color. • adj. of this color.

ruck•sack /rúksak, rōok-/ n. BACKPACK n.

■ knapsack, haversack.

ruck•us /rúkəs/ n. fracas or commotion.

rud•der /rúdər/ n. **1** flat piece hinged vertically to the stern of a ship for steering. **2** vertical airfoil pivoted from the stabilizer of an aircraft, for controlling horizontal movement.

rud•dy /rúdee/ adj. (**rud•di•er, rud•di•est**) **1** (of a person or complexion) freshly or healthily red. **2** reddish. □□ **rud′di•ly** adv. **rud′di•ness** n.

■ see ROSY 1

rude /rōod/ adj. **1** impolite; offensive. **2** roughly made or done (rude shelter). **3** primitive. **4** abrupt; startling (rude awakening). **5** colloq. indecent, lewd. □□ **rude′ly** adv. **rude′ness** n.

■ **1** impertinent, impudent, discourteous; unmannerly, insulting, insolent, disrespectful, colloq. fresh; ill-mannered, uncouth. **2** crude, clumsy, awkward, raw, makeshift, simple, basic. **3** uneducated, coarse, unrefined; uncivilized; unsophisticated. **4** see ABRUPT 1, 5 naughty, vulgar, obscene, dirty, filthy, gross, pornographic.

SYNONYM STUDY: rude

CALLOW, CRUDE, ILL-MANNERED, ROUGH, UNCIVIL, UNCOUTH. Someone who lacks consideration for the feelings of others and who is deliberately insolent is **rude** (it was rude of you not to introduce me to your friends). **Ill-mannered** suggests that the person is ignorant of the rules of social behavior rather than deliberately rude (an ill-mannered child), while **uncivil** implies disregard for even the most basic rules of social behavior among civilized people (his uncivil response resulted in his being kicked out of the classroom). **Rough** is used to describe people who lack polish and refinement (he was a rough but honest man), while **crude** is a more negative term for individuals and behavior lacking culture, civility, and tact (to make a crude gesture). **Uncouth** describes what seems strange, awkward, or unmannerly rather than rude (his uncouth behavior at the wedding). Although individuals of any age

---

may be rude, crude, ill-mannered, or uncouth, **callow** almost always applies to those who are young or immature; it suggests naïveté and lack of sophistication (he was surprisingly callow for a man of almost 40).

ru•di•ment /rōodimənt/ n. **1** [in pl.] elements or first principles of a subject. **2** [in pl.] imperfect beginning of something yet to develop. □□ **ru•di•men′ta•ry** adj.

■ **1** (rudiments) basics, essentials, fundamentals. □□ **rudimentary** elementary, primary, primal; primitive, undeveloped, immature; seminal.

rue[1] /rōo/ v.tr. (**rues, rued, ru•ing**) repent of. □□ **rue′ful** adj. **rue′ful•ly** adv. **rue′ful•ness** n.

■ see REGRET v. □□ **rueful** see regretful (REGRET). **ruefulness** see REGRET n.

rue[2] /rōo/ n. perennial evergreen shrub with bitter strong-scented leaves.

ruff /ruf/ n. **1** projecting, starched, frilly collar of the 16th c. **2** projecting or colored ring of feathers or hair around a bird's or animal's neck.

ruf•fi•an /rúfeeən/ n. violent, lawless person. □□ **ruf′fi•an•ism** n.

■ see THUG.

ruf•fle /rúfəl/ • v.tr. **1** disturb the smoothness or tranquillity of. **2** upset the calmness of (a person). **3** gather (lace, etc.) into a ruffle. • n. frill of lace, etc.

■ v. **1** see DISTURB 1. **2** agitate, disconcert, confuse, stir up, perturb, unnerve, fluster, bother, shake up, trouble, worry. • n. trimming.

ru•foua /rōofəs/ adj. (esp of animals) reddish-brown.

rug /rug/ n. floor covering of shaggy material or thick pile. □ **pull the rug (out) from under** deprive of support; weaken; unsettle.

rug•by /rúgbee/ n. team game played with an oval ball that may be kicked, carried, and passed.

rug•ged /rúgid/ adj. **1** rough; uneven; wrinkled. **2** unpolished; lacking refinement. **3** robust; sturdy. □□ **rug′ged•ly** adv. **rug′ged•ness** n.

■ **1** broken, irregular, bumpy, jagged; craggy; irregular. **2** rude, uncouth, uncivilized, unrefined, crude; austere, harsh. **3** hardy, durable, strong, hale, tough, vigorous.

ru•in /rōoin/ • n. **1** destroyed or wrecked state. **2** utter destruction. **3** [in sing. or pl.] remains of a destroyed building, etc. **4** cause of ruin (will be the ruin of us). • v.tr. **1** bring to ruin. **2** (esp. as **ruined** adj.) reduce to ruins. □□ **ru•in•a′tion** n. **ru′in•ous** adj. **ru′in•ous•ly** adv.

■ n. **1** see DESTRUCTION 1. **2** downfall, collapse, fall, devastation, undoing, disintegration, ruination, wiping out; elimination. **3** (ruins) debris, fragments, rubble. **4** nemesis, curse, end, bane. • v. **1** undo, reduce to nothing, crush; impoverish; spoil, damage, destroy, wreck, harm, hurt, impair, sl. screw up. **2** devastate, demolish, annihilate, wipe out, lay waste, raze, flatten. □□ **ruinous** disastrous, catastrophic, calamitous, crippling, fatal, nasty.

rule /rōōl/ • *n.* **1** principle to which an action conforms or is required to conform. **2** custom; standard. **3** government; dominion. **4** straight measure; ruler. • *v.* **1** *tr.* dominate; keep under control. **2** *tr. & intr.* have sovereign control of. **3** *tr.* pronounce authoritatively. **4** *tr.* make parallel lines across (paper). □ **as a rule** usually. **rule of thumb** rule based on experience or practice rather than theory. **rule out** exclude; pronounce irrelevant or ineligible. **rule the roost** be in control.

■ *n.* **1** regulation, order, law, ordinance, ruling, decree, statute, direction, guide, guideline, precept. **2** benchmark, practice, routine, convention, policy. **3** authority, control, sovereignty, command, supervision. • *v.* **1** direct, guide, manage, lead, preside over, oversee, regulate. **2** run; govern, be in charge (of). **3** decide, resolve, judge, decree, find, declare. □ **as a rule** generally, normally, for the most part, mostly, ordinarily, mainly, chiefly, on the whole, more often than not. **rule out** ban, bar, prohibit, eliminate, forbid, preclude, proscribe, dismiss, disregard. **rule the roost** see DOMINATE 1.

rul•er /rōōlər/ *n.* **1** person exercising government or dominion. **2** straight usu. graduated strip of wood, metal, etc., used to draw lines or measure distance. □□ **rul′er•ship** *n.*

■ **1** see LEADER 1. **2** rule, measure.

rul•ing /rōōling/ • *n.* authoritative decision or announcement. • *adj.* dominant; prevailing (*ruling prices*).

■ *n.* see DECISION 2, 3. • *adj.* see DOMINANT *adj.*

rum /rum/ *n.* spirit distilled from sugar cane or molasses.

Ru•ma•ni•an var. of ROMANIAN.

rum•ba /rúmbə, rŏŏm–/ • *n.* **1** Cuban dance. **2** music for it. • *v.tr.* (**rum•bas, rum•baed** /–bəd/, **rum•ba•ing** /–bə-ing/) dance the rumba.

rum•ble /rúmbəl/ • *v.intr.* **1** make a continuous deep resonant sound as of distant thunder. **2** move with a rumbling noise. **3** engage in a street fight, esp. as part of a gang. • *n.* **1** rumbling sound. **2** *sl.* street fight between gangs. □ **rumble seat** uncovered folding seat in the rear of an automobile. □□ **rum′bler** *n.*

■ *v.* **1** see THUNDER *v.* 2. • *n.* **1** see THUNDER *n.* 1, 2. **2** see FIGHT *n.* 1a.

ru•mi•nant /rōōminənt/ • *n.* cud-chewing animal. • *adj.* **1** of ruminants. **2** contemplative.

ru•mi•nate /rōōminayt/ *v.tr. & [foll. by over, on, etc.] intr.* meditate; ponder. **2** *intr.* (of ruminants) chew the cud. □□ **ru•mi•na•tion** /–náyshən/ *n.* **ru•mi•na•tive** /–nətiv/ *adj.* **ru′mi•na•tive•ly** *adv.* **ru′mi•na•tor** *n.*

■ **1** (*ruminate over, on*) see PONDER.

rum•mage /rúmij/ • *v.tr. & [foll. by in, through, among] intr.* search, esp. unsystematically. • *n.* **1** instance of rummaging. **2** things found by rummaging. □ **rummage**

sale sale of miscellaneous usu. secondhand articles, esp. for charity. □□ **rum′mag•er** *n.*

■ *v.* comb, scour, *colloq.* turn inside out, turn upside down. • *n.* **2** knickknacks, odds and ends.

rum•my¹ /rúmee/ *n.* any of various card games in which the players try to form sets and sequences of cards.

rum•my² /rúmee/ *n. sl.* drunkard or sot.

ru•mor /rōōmər/ • *n.* general talk or hearsay of doubtful accuracy. • *v.tr.* [usu. in *passive*] report by way of rumor (*it is rumored that you are leaving*).

■ *n.* gossip, *colloq.* scuttlebutt, *sl.* poop; see also WORD *n.* 7. • *v.* intimate, suggest, leak, tell.

rump /rump/ *n.* hind part of a mammal or bird, esp. the buttocks.

rum•ple /rúmpəl/ *v.* make or become creased or ruffled. □□ **rum′ply** *adj.*

■ wrinkle, crumple, crush, crinkle, scrunch (up), pucker.

rum•pus /rúmpəs/ *n. colloq.* disturbance; brawl; uproar.

■ commotion, fuss, to-do; fracas, *colloq.* row.

run /run/ • *v.* (**run•ning;** *past* **ran** /ran/; *past part.* **run**) **1** *intr.* go with quick steps on alternate feet. **2** *intr.* flee. **3** *intr.* go hurriedly, briefly, etc. **4** *intr.* **a** advance by or as by rolling or on wheels, or smoothly or easily. **b** be in action or operation (*left the engine running*). **5** *intr.* be current or operative (*the lease runs for 99 years*). **6** *intr.* (of a play, etc.) be staged or presented. **7** *intr.* extend; have a course, order, or tendency. **8 a** *intr.* compete in a race. **b** *intr.* finish a race in a specified position. **c** *tr.* compete in (a race). **9** *intr.* seek election (*ran for president*). **10** *tr.* cause (water, etc.) to flow. **11** *intr.* spread rapidly. **12** *tr.* traverse (a course, race, or distance). **13** *tr.* perform (an errand). **14** *tr.* publish (an article, etc.) in a periodical. **15 a** *tr.* cause (a machine or vehicle, etc.) to operate. **b** *intr.* (of a mechanism, etc.) move or work freely. **16** *tr.* direct or manage (a business, etc.). **17** *tr.* own and use (a vehicle) regularly. **18** *tr.* transport in a vehicle (*shall I run you to the post office?*). **19** *tr.* smuggle (guns, etc.). **20** *intr.* (of a dyed color) spread. **21 a** *intr.* (of a thought, the eye, the memory, etc.) pass quickly (*ideas ran through my mind*). **b** *tr.* cause (one's eye) to look cursorily. **c** *tr.* pass (a hand, etc.) rapidly over. **22** *intr.* (of hosiery) unravel along a line from a snag. **23** *intr.* exude liquid matter. • *n.* **1** running. **2** short excursion. **3** distance traveled. **4** general tendency. **5** regular route. **6** spell or course (*run of bad luck*). **7** high general demand. **8** quantity produced in one period of production. **9** average type or class. **10** *Baseball* point scored by a runner reaching home plate. **11** [foll. by *of*] free use of or access to (*had the run of the house*). **12 a** enclosure for domestic animals. **b** range of pasture. **13** line of unraveled stitches, esp. in hosiery. **14** (**the runs**) *colloq.* attack of diarrhea. □ **on the run 1** escaping. **2** hurrying about. **run across** happen to meet. **run against** oppose, as in an election. **run along** *colloq.* depart. **run around** *sl.* engage in sexual relations (esp. casually or illicitly). **run away with** win (a prize, etc.) easily. **run down 1** knock down. **2** (of an unwound clock, etc.) stop. **3** become feeble from overwork or underfeeding. **4** discover after a search. **5** disparage. **run-down 1** decayed after prosperity. **2** enfeebled through overwork, etc. **run dry** cease to flow; be exhausted. **run for it** seek safety by fleeing. **run in** *colloq.* arrest. **run-in** *n.* quarrel. **run into 1** collide with. **2** encounter. **run into the ground** *colloq.* bring to exhaustion, disrepair, etc. **run its course** follow its natural progress. **run low** (or **short**) become depleted; have too little (*ran short of gas*). **run off 1** flee. **2** produce (copies, etc.) on a machine. **3** flow or cause to flow away. **run off at the mouth** *sl.* talk incessantly. **run-of-the-mill** ordinary. **run on** talk incessantly. **run out 1** come to an end; become used up. **2** [foll. by *of*] exhaust one's stock of. **3** expel; drive out (*ran him out of town*). **run out on** *colloq.* desert (a person). **run over 1** overflow. **2** study or repeat quickly. **3** (of a vehicle or its driver) knock down or crush. **run ragged** exhaust (a person). **run the show** *colloq.* dominate in an undertaking, etc. **run a temperature** be feverish. **run through** examine or rehearse briefly. **run-through** rehearsal. **run up** accumulate (a debt, etc.) quickly. **run up against** meet with (a difficulty or difficulties).

■ *v.* **1, 3** sprint, race, scamper, scurry, dart, dash, rush, hurry, hasten, *colloq.* step on it, get a move on. **2** run away or off, escape, take flight, bolt, abscond, (make a) run for it, take off, *colloq.* clear out, scram, *sl.* beat it. **4 a** see ADVANCE *v.* 1, 2. **b** see WORK *v.* 3. **5** last, be in effect, be in force. **6** show, be on. **7** stretch, reach; amount, total up. **8 a** take part, participate. **b** come (in). **9** be a candidate, vie; contend. **11** flow, pour, stream, flood, gush, spill, dribble, drip, spurt, trickle, seep, cascade, spout; issue. **12** go, cover, sprint. **13** do, fulfill, carry out. **14** print, put out, release, carry. **15 b** operate, function, tick. **16** supervise, conduct, superintend, control, handle, regulate, take care of, look after, administer, be in charge of, coordinate; keep, maintain. **18** convey, give (a person) a lift, drive, take, bring. **19** bootleg, deal or traffic in. **20** diffuse. **21 a** meander, float, drift, flit, fly. ● *n.* **1** sprint, dash, race, jog, trot. **2** trip, outing, jaunt, junket; *colloq.* spin, joyride. **3** way, journey; see also DISTANCE *n.* 2. **5** circuit, round; beat. **6** period, spate, stretch, interval. **7** call, request. **9** category, kind, sort. **11** freedom, liberty. **12 a** pen. **b** paddock, field; pound; see also PASTURE *n.* **14 (the runs)** see DIARRHEA *n.* □ **on the run 1** on the loose, fleeing, in flight, running away, *sl.* on the lam. **2** on the move, in haste, at speed, *colloq.* on the go. **run across** come across, find, stumble (up)on, hit (up)on, chance (up)on, happen (up)on, *colloq.* bump into. **run along** go away, leave, *sl.* get lost. **run around** philander, be unfaithful, *colloq.* gallivant, sleep around, play the field. **run down 1** collide with, strike, hit, smash or

crash into. **2** burn out; see also PETER. **3** weaken, tire, become worn out. **4** trace, track or hunt (down). **5** criticize, decry, defame, vilify, *colloq.* pan, *sl.* knock. **run-down 1** ramshackle, dilapidated, tumbledown, decrepit, rickety, broken-down. **2** weary, exhausted, debilitated, weak, worn out, fatigued, tired, drained, spent, burnt-out. **run in** take into custody, apprehend, pinch, collar, *colloq.* bust, *sl.* nab. **run-in** disagreement, argument, dispute, altercation. **run into 1** see COLLIDE 1. **2** see *run across* above. **run off 1** see RUN *v.* 2 above. **2** duplicate, print, turn out, churn out. **run-of-the-mill** see ORDINARY *adj.* **run out 1** finish, go, peter out; expire, terminate, cease. **2** (*run out of*) use up, consume, eat up, be out of. **run out on** abandon, leave high and dry, forsake, leave in the lurch. **run over 1** spill (over), extend or reach or spread or stretch over or beyond, exceed. **2** rehearse, run through, practice, review, go over. **3** see *run down* 1 above. **run the show** be in charge, *colloq.* be boss; see also *call the shots*. **run through** see *run over* 2 above. **run-through** practice, trial, test.

run•a•bout /rúnəbowt/ *n.* light car, boat, or aircraft.

run•a•round /rúnərownd/ *n.* (esp. as *give a person the runaround*) deceit or evasion.

run•a•way /rúnəway/ *n.* **1** fugitive. **2** animal or vehicle that is running out of control. **3** [*attrib.*] that is running away or out of control (*runaway inflation*).

■ **1** escapee, refugee, deserter, truant. **3** (*attrib.*) wild, uncontrolled, unchecked, rampant; driverless, riderless.

run•down /rúndown/ *n.* summary or brief analysis.

■ runthrough, synopsis, survey, précis, résumé, outline, rough idea.

rune /roon/ *n.* **1** letter of the earliest Germanic alphabet. **2** mark of mysterious or magic significance. □□ **ru′nic** *adj.*

rung[1] /rung/ *n.* **1** step of a ladder. **2** strengthening crosspiece in a chair, etc. □□ **runged** *adj.* **rung′less** *adj.*

rung[2] *past part.* of RING[2].

run•nel /rúnəl/ *n.* brook.

run•ner /rúnər/ *n.* **1** person, horse, etc., that runs, esp. in a race. **2** creeping plant stem that can take root. **3** rod, groove, or blade on which a thing (e.g., a sled) slides. **4** messenger, scout, etc. □ **runner-up** (*pl.* **runners-up**) competitor or team taking second place.

■ **1** sprinter, jogger; *colloq.* miler. **4** courier, errand boy or girl, page, *sl.* gofer; agent, tout.

run•ning /rúning/ ● *n.* **1** action of runners in a race, etc. **2** management; operation. ● *adj.* **1** continuous (*running battle*). **2** consecutive (*three days running*). **3** done with a run (*running jump*). □ **in** (or **out of**) **the running** (of a competitor) with a good (or poor) chance of winning. **running light** navigational light displayed by a ship, aircraft, etc., during darkness. **running mate** candidate for a secondary position in an election.

■ *n.* **2** see OPERATION 1, 2. ● *adj.* **1** ongoing,

perpetual, sustained, constant. **2** see SUC-CESSIVE.

run•ny /rúnee/ *adj.* (**run•ni•er, run•ni•est**) **1** tending to run or flow. **2** excessively fluid.

run•off /rúnawf/ *n.* **1** additional election, race, etc., after a tie. **2** surface water not absorbed by the ground.

runt /runt/ *n.* **1** smallest animal in a litter. **2** weakling; undersized person. □□ **runt′y** *adj.*

■ **2** dwarf, pygmy, midget; see also WEAK-LING.

run•way /rúnway/ *n.* **1** surface along which aircraft take off and land. **2** narrow walkway extending out from a stage into an auditorium.

ru•pee /rōōpée, rōōpee/ *n.* chief monetary unit of India, Pakistan, etc.

rup•ture /rúpchər/ • *n.* **1** breaking; breach. **2** abdominal hernia. • *v.* **1** *tr.* break or burst (a cell or membrane, etc.). **2** *intr.* undergo a rupture. □□ **rup′tur•a•ble** *adj.*

■ *n.* **1** breakup, disagreement, schism; rift. • *v.* **1** split. **2** divide, separate.

ru•ral /rŏŏrəl/ *adj.* in, of, or suggesting the country. □ **rural free delivery** (also **rural delivery service**) postal delivery to mailboxes in rural areas. □□ **ru′ral•ly** *adv.*

■ pastoral, countrified, sylvan, bucolic, rustic; agrarian.

ruse /rōōz/ *n.* stratagem; trick.

■ device, deception, maneuver, dodge, pretense, subterfuge, wile, artifice, *colloq.* ploy.

rush[1] /rush/ • *v.* **1** *intr.* go, move, or act precipitately or with great speed. **2** *tr.* move or transport with great haste. **3** *intr.* [foll. by *at*] **a** move suddenly toward. **b** begin impetuously. **4** *tr.* perform or deal with hurriedly (*don't rush your dinner*). **5** *tr.* force (a person) to act hastily. **6** *tr.* attack or capture by sudden assault. • *n.* **1** rushing. **2** great activity; commotion. **3** [*attrib.*] done with great haste or speed (*a rush job*). **4** sudden migration of large numbers. □ **rush hour** time each day when traffic is heaviest. □□ **rush′er** *n.* **rush′ing•ly** *adv.*

■ *v.* **1** hurry (up), hasten, run, race, bustle, make haste, dash, scurry, hustle, scramble, go like a bat out of hell, shake a leg, *colloq.* scoot, move (it), step on it, make it snappy, get moving, get cracking, hightail (it). **4** push. **6** charge, storm, *colloq.* blitz. • *n.* **1** (hustle and) bustle; surge, charge, advance; see also ATTACK *n.* 1. **2** fuss, excitement, flurry, to-do. **3** (*attrib.*) urgent, pressing, high-priority, top-priority, emergency.

rush[2] /rush/ *n.* marsh plant with slender stems, used for making chair seats, baskets, etc. □□ **rush′y** *adj.*

rusk /rusk/ *n.* slice of bread rebaked as a light biscuit.

rus•set /rúsit/ • *adj.* reddish-brown. • *n.* **1** reddish-brown color. **2** russet-colored fruit (esp. apple) or vegetable (esp. potato). □□ **rus′set•y** *adj.*

Rus•sian /rúshən/ • *n.* **1** native or national of Russia or the former Soviet Union. **2** lan-

guage of Russia. • *adj.* of Russia, its people, or their language. □ **Russian roulette** act of daring in which one squeezes the trigger of a revolver held to one's head with one chamber loaded, having first spun the chamber.

rust /rust/ • *n.* **1** reddish corrosive coating formed on iron, steel, etc., by oxidation, esp. when wet. **2** fungal plant disease with rust-colored spots. **3** impaired state due to disuse or inactivity. • *v.* **1** *tr. & intr.* affect or be affected with rust. **2** *intr.* lose quality or efficiency by disuse or inactivity.

rus•tic /rústik/ • *adj.* **1** having the characteristics of or associations with the country or country life. **2** unsophisticated. **3** rude; rough. • *n.* country person. □□ **rus′ti•cal•ly** *adv.* **rus•tic′i•ty** /–tisitee/ *n.*

■ *adj.* **1** see RURAL. **2** plain, simple, uncomplicated, naïve, unrefined, countrified. • *n.* peasant, bumpkin, yokel, country boy *or* girl, *colloq.* hick, hayseed, *colloq. often derog.* hillbilly.

rus•ti•cate /rústikayt/ *v.* **1** *intr.* retire to or live in the country. **2** *tr.* make rural. □□ **rus•ti•ca•tion** /–káyshən/ *n.*

rus•tle /rúsəl/ • *v.* **1** *intr. & tr.* make or cause to make a gentle sound as of dry, blown leaves. **2** *tr.* [also *absol.*] steal (cattle or horses). • *n.* rustling sound. □ **rustle up** *colloq.* produce quickly when needed. □□ **rus′tler** *n.* (esp. in sense 2 of *v.*).

■ *v.* **1** whisper, swish.

rust•proof /rústprōōf/ • *adj.* not susceptible to corrosion by rust. • *v.tr.* make rustproof.

rust•y /rústee/ *adj.* (**rust•i•er, rust•i•est**) **1** rusted or affected by rust. **2** impaired by neglect. **3** rust-colored. □□ **rust′i•ly** *adv.* **rust′i•ness** *n.*

rut[1] /rut/ • *n.* **1** deep track made by the passage of wheels. **2** established (esp. tedious) procedure. • *v.tr.* (**rut•ted, rut•ting**) mark with ruts. □ **in a rut** following a fixed (esp. tedious or dreary) pattern of behavior. □□ **rut′ty** *adj.*

■ **1** groove, furrow. **2** routine, grind.

rut[2] /rut/ • *n.* periodic sexual excitement of male deer and other animals. • *v.intr.* (**rut•ted, rut•ting**) be affected with rut.

ru•ta•ba•ga /rōōtəbáygə/ *n.* large yellow-fleshed turnip.

ru•the•ni•um /rōōthéeneeəm/ *n. Chem.* rare hard white metallic element. ¶Symb.: **Ru**.

ruth•er•for•di•um /rúthərfáwrdeeəm/ *n. Chem.* artificially made transuranic metallic element. ¶Symb.: **Rf**.

ruth•less /rōōthlis/ *adj.* having no pity nor compassion. □□ **ruth′less•ly** *adv.* **ruth′less•ness** *n.*

■ cruel, merciless, unmerciful, harsh, fierce, vicious, savage, ferocious, hard-hearted, callous, unfeeling, tough, severe, heartless, inhuman, brutal, mean.

RV *abbr.* **1** Revised Version (of the Bible). **2** recreational vehicle.

-ry /ree/ *suffix* = -ERY (*infantry, rivalry*).

rye /rī/ *n.* **1 a** cereal plant. **b** grain of this used for bread and fodder. **2** (in full **rye whis′key**) whiskey distilled from fermented rye.

Ss

S¹ /es/ *n.* (also **s**) (*pl.* **Ss** or **S's**; **s's** /ésiz/)
1 nineteenth letter of the alphabet. 2 S-shaped object or curve.

S² *abbr.* (also **S.**) 1 Saint. 2 society. 3 south, southern.

S³ *symb. Chem.* sulfur.

s. *abbr.* 1 second(s). 2 singular. 3 son. 4 succeeded.

-s' *suffix* denoting the possessive case of plural nouns and sometimes of singular nouns ending in *s* (*the boys' shoes, Charles' book*).

's *abbr.* 1 is; has (*he's*). 2 us (*let's*). 3 *colloq.* does (*what's he say?*).

-s¹ /s; z after a vowel sound or voiced consonant, e.g., *ways, bags/ suffix* denoting the plurals of nouns.

-s² /s; z after a vowel sound or voiced consonant, e.g., *ties, begs/ suffix* forming the 3rd person sing. present of verbs.

-s³ /s; z after a vowel sound or voiced consonant, e.g., *besides/ suffix* 1 forming adverbs (*afterwards, besides, mornings*). 2 forming possessive pronouns (*hers, ours*).

-s⁴ /s; z after a vowel sound or voiced consonant/ *suffix* forming nicknames or pet names (*Fats, Cutes*).

's¹ /s; z/ *suffix* denoting the possessive case of singular nouns and of plural nouns not ending in *-s* (*John's book, book's cover, children's shoes*).

-'s² /s; z after a vowel sound or voiced consonant/ *suffix* denoting the plural of a letter or symbol (*S's, 8's*).

SA *abbr.* 1 Salvation Army. 2 South Africa. 3 South America.

Sab·bath /sábəth/ *n.* religious day of rest kept by Christians on Sunday and Jews on Saturday.

sab·bat·i·cal /səbátikəl/ • *adj.* 1 of the Sabbath. 2 (of leave) granted at intervals from one's usual work, as to a teacher for study or travel. • *n.* period of sabbatical leave.

sa·ber /sáybər/ *n.* 1 curved cavalry sword. 2 tapered fencing sword. □ **saber rattling** display or threat of military force.

Sa·bin vac·cine /sáybin/ *n.* oral vaccine giving immunity against poliomyelitis.

sa·ble /sáybəl/ *n.* 1 small, brown-furred mammal of N. Europe and N. Asia. 2 its skin or fur.

sa·bot /sabó, sábō/ *n.* shoe hollowed out from a block of wood.

sab·o·tage /sábətaazh/ • *n.* deliberate damage to productive capacity, esp. as a political act. • *v.tr.* commit sabotage on. □□ **sab·o·teur'** *n.*

■ *n.* destruction; subversion, treachery, treason. • *v.* incapacitate, disable, cripple; destroy, wreck, spoil, ruin, disrupt; undermine. □□ **saboteur** see SUBVERSIVE *n.*

SAC /sak/ Strategic Air Command.

sac /sak/ *n.* membranous bag in an animal or plant.

sac·cha·rin /sákərin/ *n.* sugar substitute.

sac·cha·rine /sákərin, -reen, -rīn/ *adj.* 1 sugary. 2 unpleasantly overpolite, sentimental, etc.

■ 2 see SENTIMENTAL.

sac·er·do·tal /sásərdótəl, sák-/ *adj.* of priests or the priestly office. □□ **sac·er·do'tal·ly** *adv.*

sa·chem /sáychəm/ *n.* supreme leader of some Native American tribes.

sa·chet /sasháy/ *n.* small bag or packet containing dry perfume, etc.

sack¹ /sak/ • *n.* 1 a large, strong bag for storing or conveying goods. b quantity contained in a sack. 2 [prec. by the] *colloq.* dismissal from employment. 3 [prec. by the] *sl.* bed. • *v.tr.* 1 put into a sack or sacks. 2 *colloq.* dismiss from employment. See synonym study at RAVAGE. □□ **sack'ful** *n.* (*pl.* **-fuls**)

■ *n.* 1 pouch. 2 one's marching orders, *colloq.* one's walking papers, the boot. • *v.* 2 discharge, lay off, ax, *sl.* fire.

sack² /sak/ • *v.tr.* plunder and destroy (a captured town, etc.). • *n.* such sacking.

sack·cloth /sák-klawth, -kloth/ *n.* 1 coarse fabric of flax or hemp. 2 clothing for mourning (esp. *sackcloth and ashes*).

sac·ra·ment /sákrəmənt/ *n.* symbolic Christian ceremony, esp. baptism and the Eucharist. □□ **sac·ra·men·tal** *adj.*

■ □□ **sacramental** see SACRED 1b, 2.

sa·cred /sáykrid/ *adj.* 1 a dedicated to a god. b connected with religion. 2 safeguarded or required by religion, reverence, or tradition. □ **sacred cow** *colloq.* hallowed idea or institution. □□ **sa'cred·ly** *adv.* **sa'cred·ness** *n.*

■ 1 a consecrated; holy, blessed, divine, b religious, spiritual, church; priestly. 2 ritual, ceremonial, solemn, sacramental; sacrosanct.

sac·ri·fice /sákrifīs/ • *n.* 1 a voluntary giving up of something valued. b thing given up. c the loss entailed. 2 a slaughter of an animal or person or surrender of a possession, as an offering to a deity. b animal, person, or thing offered. • *v.tr.* give up (a thing) as a sacrifice. □□ **sac·ri·fi·cial** /-físhəl/ *adj.* **sac·ri·fi'cial·ly** *adv.*

■ *n.* 1 a forfeiture, relinquishment. b see OFFERING. 2 b (burnt) offering; donation, gift. • *v.* forgo, surrender, let go (of), lose, yield; refrain from. □□ **sacrificial** expiatory.

sac·ri·lege /sákrilij/ *n.* violation or misuse of what is regarded as sacred. □□ **sac·ri·le·gious** /-lījəs/ *adj.* **sac·ri·le'gious·ly** *adv.*

■ desecration, debasement, abuse, heresy, irreverence. □□ **sacrilegious** blasphemous, disrespectful.

sac·ro·il·i·ac /sákrōíleeak, sákrō-/ *n.* juncture of the sacrum and the ilium bones of the pelvis.

sac•ro•sanct /sákrōsangkt/ adj. (of a person, place, law, etc.) most sacred; inviolable. □□ **sac•ro•sanc•ti•ty** /-sángktitee/ n.

sac•rum /sáykrəm, sák–/ n. (pl. **sac'ra** /-krə/ or **sac'rums**) Anat. triangular bone formed from fused vertebrae and situated between the two hipbones of the pelvis.

sad /sad/ adj. (**sad•der**, **sad•dest**) **1** unhappy; feeling sorrow or regret. **2** causing sorrow. **3** regrettable. **4** shameful; deplorable. □ **sad sack** colloq. inept person, esp. a soldier. □□ **sad'ly** adv. **sad'ness** n.

■ **1** melancholy, downcast, dejected, depressed, low, sorrowful, morose, blue, brokenhearted, heartbroken, miserable. **2** depressing, gloomy, dreary, dismal, somber, heartbreaking, distressing. **3** see *regrettable* (REGRET). **4** unfortunate, awful, bad, shabby, dirty, sorry, pathetic, pitiful, colloq. lousy, sl. rotten. □□ **sadness** misery, grief, depression, melancholy.

sad•den /sád'n/ v. make or become sad.

■ depress, deject, dishearten, distress, grieve.

sad•dle /sád'l/ • n. **1** seat of leather, etc., fastened on a horse, etc., for riding. **2** seat on a bicycle, etc. **3** cut of meat consisting of the two loins. • v.tr. **1** put a saddle on (a horse, etc.). **2** [foll. by with] burden (a person). □ **in the saddle 1** mounted. **2** in office or control. **saddle shoes** laced shoes with yokes that contrast in color with the rest of the upper. **saddle stitch** stitch of thread or a wire staple passed through a magazine or booklet at its folded spine.

■ v. **2** see BURDEN v.

sad•dle•bag /sád'lbag/ n. **1** each of a pair of bags laid across a horse, etc. **2** bag attached to a bicycle saddle, etc.

Sad•du•cee /sájəsee, sádyə–/ n. member of an ancient fundamentalist Jewish sect. □□ **Sad•du•ce•an** /–seeən/ adj.

sa•dism /sáydizəm, sád–/ n. pleasure derived from inflicting cruelty on others. □□ **sad'ist** n. **sa•dis•tic** /sədístik/ adj. **sa•dis'ti•cal•ly** adv.

■ see *brutality* (BRUTAL). □□ **sadist** brute, beast, savage. **sadistic** cruel, monstrous, ruthless, perverse.

sa•do•mas•och•ism /sáydōmásəkizəm, sádō–/ n. combination of sadism and masochism in one person. □□ **sa•do•mas'o•chist** n. **sa•do•mas•o•chis•tic** /–kístik/ adj.

sa•fa•ri /səfaáree/ n. (pl. **sa•fa•ris**) expedition, esp. in E. Africa, to hunt or observe animals.

safe /sayf/ • adj. **1** free of danger or injury. **2** secure; not risky. **3** reliable; certain. **4** (also **safe and sound**) uninjured. • n. strong, lockable cabinet, etc., for valuables. □ **safe-conduct 1** privilege of immunity from arrest or harm. **2** document securing this. **safe-deposit box** secured box (esp. in a bank vault) for storing valuables. **safe house** place of refuge for spies, etc. **safe sex** sexual activity in which precautions are taken against sexually transmitted diseases. □□ **safe'ly** adv. **safe'ness** n.

■ adj. **1** see HARMLESS 1. **2** protected, sheltered, shielded. **3** sure, sound, risk-free, dependable. **4** unharmed, whole, unhurt, all right, colloq. OK. • n. strongbox; coffer, chest. □ **safe house** see REFUGE.

safe•crack•er /sáyfkrakər/ n. person who breaks open and robs safes.

safe•guard /sáyfgaard/ • n. proviso, stipulation, quality, or circumstance that tends to prevent something undesirable. • v.tr. guard; protect.

■ n. precaution, preventive measure. • v. defend, save, look after, shield.

safe•keep•ing /sáyfkeeping/ n. preservation in a safe place.

■ safety; see also PROTECTION 1a.

safe•ty /sáyftee/ n. (pl. **–ties**) **1** being safe. **2** [attrib.] designating an item for preventing injury (safety lock). □ **safety belt** = seat belt. **safety-deposit box** = safe-deposit box. **safety first** motto advising caution. **safety match** match igniting only on a specially prepared surface. **safety pin** doubled pin with a guarded point. **safety razor** razor with a guard to prevent cutting the skin. **safety valve 1** automatic valve relieving excessive pressure. **2** means of giving harmless vent to excitement, etc.

■ **1** safeness, protection, shelter, security; aegis, cover, refuge, sanctuary; safekeeping.

saf•flow•er /sáflowr/ n. thistlelike plant yielding a red dye and edible oil.

saf•fron /sáfrən/ • n. **1** bright yellow-orange food coloring and flavoring made from dried crocus stigmas. **2** color of this. • adj. saffron-colored.

sag /sag/ • v.intr. (**sagged**, **sag•ging**) **1** sink or subside, esp. unevenly. **2** bulge or curve downward in the middle. **3 a** fall in price. **b** (of a price) fall. • n. state or extent of sagging. □□ **sag'gy** adj.

■ v. **1, 2** droop, slump, bend, dip. **3** drop, go or come down, decrease. • n. droop, sinkage, dip; reduction, slump.

sa•ga /saágə/ n. **1** long, heroic story of achievement, esp. medieval Icelandic or Norwegian. **2** any long, involved story.

■ **1** legend, epic, romance; Edda.

sa•ga•cious /səgáyshəs/ adj. showing insight, good judgment, or wisdom. See synonym study at SENSIBLE. □□ **sa•ga'cious•ly** adv. **sa•gac'i•ty** /səgásitee/ n.

■ see ASTUTE 1. □□ **sagacity** see astuteness (ASTUTE).

sage[1] /sayj/ n. aromatic herb with dull grayish-green leaves. □□ **sag'y** adj.

sage[2] /sayj/ • n. wise person. • adj. of or indicating profound wisdom. □□ **sage'ly** adv.

■ n. philosopher, guru, pundit, oracle, savant, expert, authority. • adj. judicious, prudent; sagacious, discerning, shrewd, intelligent.

sage•brush /sáyjbrush/ n. shrubby aromatic plant of western N. America.

Sag•it•tar•i•us /sájitáireeəs/ n. **1** constellation and ninth sign of the zodiac (the Archer). **2** person born under this sign. □□ **Sag•it•tar'i•an** /-eeən/ adj. & n.

sa•go /sáygō/ n. (pl. **–gos**) **1** edible starch made from the sago palm. **2** (in full **sago**

palm) tropical palm from which sago is made.

sa•gua•ro /səgwaärō, səwaärō/ *n.* (*pl.* **–ros**) giant cactus of Mexico and the SW United States.

sa•hib /saab, saähib/ *n. hist.* (in India) form of address to European men.

said *past* and *past part.* of SAY.

sail /sayl/ • *n.* **1** piece of material extended on rigging to catch the wind and propel a vessel. **2** ship's sails collectively. **3** voyage or excursion in a sailing ship, etc. **4** wind-catching apparatus of a windmill. • *v.* **1** *intr.* travel on water by the use of sails or engine power. **2** *tr.* **a** navigate (a ship, etc.). **b** travel on (a sea). **3** *tr.* set (a toy boat) afloat. **4** *intr.* glide or move smoothly. **5** *intr. colloq.* succeed easily (*sailed through the exams*). □ **sail into** *colloq.* attack physically or verbally. **under sail** with sails set. □□ **sail′a•ble** *adj.* **sailed** *adj.* [also in *comb.*]. **sail′less** *adj.*
■ *n.* **3** journey, trip, cruise. • *v.* **1** go sailing *or* boating *or* yachting. **2 a** pilot, steer. **4** drift, flow, waft, sweep, coast, float.

sail•board /sáylbáwrd/ *n.* board with a mast and sail, used in windsurfing. □□ **sail′board•er** *n.* **sail′board•ing** *n.*

sail•boat /sáylbōt/ *n.* boat driven by sails.

sail•cloth /sáylklawth, –kloth/ *n.* canvas or canvaslike material for sails, upholstery, tents, etc.

sail•fish /sáylfish/ *n.* large marine fish with a large dorsal fin.

sail•or /sáylər/ *n.* **1** seaman or mariner, esp. one below the rank of officer. **2** person who enjoys boating. □□ **sail′or•ly** *adj.*
■ **1** seafarer, (old) salt, sea dog, *colloq.* tar, *sl.* gob.

sail•plane /sáylplayn/ *n.* glider designed for sustained flight.

saint /saynt/ • *n.* **1** holy or (in some churches) canonized person regarded as having a place in heaven. **2** very virtuous person. • *v.tr.* (as **sainted** *adj.*) sacred; of a saintly life. □□ **saint′hood** *n.* **saint′like** *adj.* **saint′ly** (**saint•li•er, saint•li•est**) *adj.*
■ *v.* (**sainted**) see *saintly* below. □□ **saint-like** see HOLY 1, 2. **saintly** blessed, godly, angelic, pure, righteous, virtuous.

St. Ber•nard /bərnaárd/ *n.* very large dog of a breed orig. kept in the Alps for rescue.

sake[1] /sayk/ *n.* **1** benefit; advantage. **2** cause; purpose.

sa•ke[2] /saákee, –ke/ *n.* Japanese rice wine.

sa•laam /səlaám/ *n. esp.* Islamic greeting with a low bow and the right palm on the forehead.

sal•a•ble /sáyləbəl/ *adj.* (also **sale′a•ble**) fit to be sold; finding purchasers. □□ **sal•a•bil′i•ty** *n.*
■ popular, sought-after, commercial, marketable.

sa•la•cious /səláyshəs/ *adj.* **1** lustful; lecherous. **2** (of writings, pictures, talk, etc.) tending to cause sexual desire. □□ **sa•la′cious•ly** *adv.* **sa•la′cious•ness** *n.* **sa•lac′i•ty** /səlásitee/ *n.*

sal•ad /sáləd/ *n.* mixture of usu. cold vegetables, eggs, meats, pasta, etc., often with dressing. □ **salad days** period of youthful

---

inexperience. **salad dressing** mixture of oil, vinegar, etc., used in a salad.

sal•a•man•der /sáləmandər/ *n.* tailed newt-like amphibian.

sa•la•mi /səlaámee/ *n.* (*pl.* **sa•la•mis**) highly seasoned orig. Italian sausage often flavored with garlic.

sal•a•ry /sáləree/ • *n.* (*pl.* **–ries**) fixed regular wages. • *v.tr.* (**–ries, –ried**) (usu. as **salaried** *adj.*) pay a salary to.
■ *n.* income, pay, earnings, emolument, compensation.

sale /sayl/ *n.* **1** exchange of a commodity for money, etc.; act or instance of selling. **2** amount sold. **3** event at which goods are sold, esp. at reduced prices. □ **for** (or **up for**) **sale** offered for purchase. **on sale** available for purchase, esp. at a reduced price.
■ **1** vending, marketing, traffic, trade; transaction. □ **for** (or **up for**) **sale** on the market.

sale•a•ble var. of SALABLE.

sales•clerk /sáylzklərk/ *n.* salesperson in a retail store.

sales•man /sáylzmən/ *n.* (*pl.* **–men;** *fem.* **sales•wom•an,** *pl.* **–wom•en**) person employed to sell goods or services.
■ salesperson, cashier, (sales)clerk.

sales•man•ship /sáylzmənship/ *n.* **1** skill in selling. **2** techniques used in selling.

sales•room /sáylzrōōm, –rōōm/ *n.* room for the display and purchase of items, esp. at an auction.

sal•i•cyl•ic ac•id /sálisilik/ *n.* chemical used as a fungicide and in aspirin and dye. □□ **sa•lic•y•late** /səlísilayt/ *n.*

sa•lient /sáylyənt/ • *adj.* **1** prominent; conspicuous. **2** (of a fortification) pointing outward. • *n.* salient angle or part of a fortification. □□ **sa′li•ence** *n.* **sa′li•en•cy** *n.* **sa′li•ent•ly** *adv.*
■ *adj.* **1** outstanding, pronounced, noticeable, significant, important, marked, striking, remarkable, noteworthy, principal, chief, primary.

sa•line /sáyleen, –līn/ • *adj.* containing or like salt. • *n.* saline solution. □□ **sa•lin•i•ty** /səlínitee/ *n.* **sal•i•ni•za•tion** /sálinizáyshən/ *n.*
■ *adj.* see SALT *adj.*

sa•li•va /səlívə/ *n.* liquid secreted into the mouth by glands. □□ **sal•i•var•y** /sáliveree/ *adj.*
■ see SPIT[1] *n.*

sal•i•vate /sálivayt/ *v.intr.* secrete saliva. □□ **sal•i•va•tion** /–váyshən/ *n.*
■ see SLAVER[2] *v.*

sal•low /sálō/ *adj.* (**sal•low•er, sal•low•est**) (of the skin or complexion, or of a person) of a sickly yellow or pale brown. □□ **sal′low•ness** *n.*
■ see PALE[1] *adj.* 1.

sal•ly /sálee/ (*pl.* **–lies**) • *n.* **1** sudden charge; sortie. **2** going forth; excursion. **3** witticism; piece of banter. • *v.intr.* (**–lies, –lied**) [usu. foll. by *out, forth*] go for a walk, set out on a journey, etc.
■ *n.* **1** see CHARGE *n.* 4a. **3** see WITTICISM.

salm•on /sámən/ • *n.* (*pl.* same or **salm′ons**) edible fish with characteristic pink flesh.

• *adj.* of the color of salmon flesh. □□ **salm′** **on•y** *adj.*

sal•mo•nel•la /sálmənélə/ *n.* (*pl.* **sal•mo•** **nel•lae** /–lee/) bacteríum causing food poisoning.

sa•lon /səlón, saláwN/ *n.* **1** reception room. **2** room or establishment of a hairdresser, beautician, etc. **3** *hist.* meeting of eminent people in the home of a lady of fashion.

 ■ **1** see LOUNGE *n.* 1.

sa•loon /səlốōn/ *n.* bar; tavern.

sal•sa /sáalsə/ *n.* **1** dance music of Cuban origin, with jazz and rock elements. **2** dance performed to this music. **3** spicy sauce made from tomatoes, chilies, onions, etc.

SALT /sawlt/ *abbr.* Strategic Arms Limitation Talks (or Treaty).

salt /sawlt/ • *n.* **1** (also **common salt**) sodium chloride, esp. mined or evaporated from seawater. **2** chemical compound formed from the reaction of an acid with a base. **3** piquancy; pungency; wit. **4** [in *sing.* or *pl.*] a substance resembling salt in taste, form, etc. (*bath salts*). **b** substance used as a laxative. **5** (also **old salt**) experienced sailor. • *adj.* **1** impregnated with, containing, or tasting of salt. **2** (of a plant) growing in the sea or in salt marshes. • *v.tr.* **1** cure or preserve with salt or brine. **2** season with salt. **3** make (a narrative, etc.) piquant. **4** sprinkle (the ground, etc.) with salt, esp. in order to melt snow, etc. □ **salt away** *sl.* stash money, etc.; save. **salt the books** *sl.* show receipts as larger than they really have been. **salt lick** place where animals go to lick salt. **salt a mine** *sl.* introduce extraneous ore, material, etc., to make the source seem rich. **salt of the earth** person or people of great worthiness, reliability, honesty, etc. (Matt. 5:13). **take with a grain of salt** regard as exaggerated; believe only part of. **worth one's salt** efficient; capable.

 ■ *n.* **1** sea salt, rock salt, table salt. **3** sting, spice, zest, vigor, vitality, liveliness, pepper, poignancy, bite, seasoning, zip, *colloq.* pep, zing, punch. **5** see SAILOR. • *adj.* salty, saline, brackish, briny. • *v.* **1** corn; pickle, souse. **2** flavor. □ **salt away** hoard, put or lay away, squirrel (away), store up, stockpile. **salt the books** *colloq.* cook the books. **take with a grain of salt** see DISTRUST *v.* **worth one's salt** see CAPABLE 1.

salt•cel•lar /sáwltselər/ *n.* vessel holding salt for table use.

sal•tine /sawltéen/ *n.* lightly salted, square, flat cracker.

salt•pe•ter /sáwltpeetər/ *n.* potassium nitrate, used in preserving meat and in gunpowder.

salt•shak•er /sáwltshaykər/ *n.* container of salt for sprinkling.

salt•wa•ter /sáwltwawtər/ *adj.* **1** of or living in the sea. **2** pertaining to or made with salt water.

salt•y /sáwltee/ *adj.* (**salt•i•er**, **salt•i•est**) **1** tasting of, containing, or preserved with salt. **2** racy; risqué. □□ **salt′i•ness** *n.*

 ■ **2** see RACY 2.

sa•lu•bri•ous /səlốōbreeəs/ *adj.* **1** health-

giving; healthy. **2** (of surroundings, etc.) pleasant; agreeable. See synonym study at SANITARY. □□ **sa•lu′bri•ous•ly** *adv.* **sa•lu′** **bri•ous•ness** *n.*

 ■ **1** see WHOLESOME 1. **2** see PLEASANT.

sa•lu•ki /səlốōkee/ *n.* (*pl.* **sa•lu•kis**) **1** tall, swift, slender dog of a silky-coated breed. **2** this breed.

sal•u•tar•y /sályəteree/ *adj.* **1** producing good effects; beneficial. **2** health-giving.

sal•u•ta•tion /sályətáyshən/ *n.* expression of greeting, spoken or written. □□ **sal•u•ta′** **tion•al** *adj.*

 ■ greeting, glad hand.

sal•u•ta•to•ry /səlốōtətawree/ • *adj.* of salutation. • *n.* (*pl.* **–ries**) oration, esp. as given by the second-ranking member of a graduating class. □□ **sa•lu•ta•to•ri•an** /–táwreeən/ *n.* (in sense of n.).

sa•lute /səlốōt/ • *n.* **1** gesture of respect, homage, greeting, etc. **2** *Mil.* & *Naut.* prescribed gesture or use of weapons or flags as a sign of respect or recognition. **3** ceremonial discharge of a gun or guns. • *v.* **1 a** *tr.* make a salute to. **b** *intr.* perform a salute. **2** *tr.* greet. □□ **sa•lut′er** *n.*

 ■ *n.* **1** salutation. • *v.* **2** hail, accost; address.

sal•vage /sálvij/ • *n.* **1** rescue of property, from the sea, fire, etc. **2** property saved in this way. **3** a saving and use of waste materials. **b** materials salvaged. • *v.tr.* save from a wreck, fire, adverse circumstances, etc. □□ **sal′vage•a•ble** *adj.* **sal′vag•er** *n.*

 ■ *n.* **1** recovery, retrieval, deliverance, salvation. **3** a reclamation, recycling, reuse, reutilization. • *v.* recover, deliver, retrieve, reclaim; preserve, retain.

sal•va•tion /salváyshən/ *n.* **1** saving or being saved. **2** deliverance from sin and damnation. **3** person or thing that saves.

 ■ **1** see SALVAGE *n.* 1. **2** redemption. **3** see SAVIOR 1.

salve /sav, saav/ • *n.* **1** healing ointment. **2** thing that is soothing or consoling. • *v.tr.* soothe.

 ■ *n.* **1** balm, lotion; dressing; liniment. **2** opiate, narcotic, relief. • *v.* relieve, ease, alleviate, assuage, palliate, mollify, comfort, appease.

sal•ver /sálvər/ *n.* metal serving tray.

sal•vo /sálvō/ *n.* (*pl.* **–voes** or **–vos**) simultaneous firing of artillery.

 ■ see VOLLEY *n.* 1.

Sa•mar•i•tan /səmárit′n/ *n.* (in full **good Sa-maritan**) charitable or helpful person (Luke 10:33, etc.). □□ **Sa•mar′i•tan•ism** *n.*

sa•mar•i•um /səmáireeəm/ *n. Chem.* soft, silvery metallic element of the lanthanide series. ¶Symb.: **Sm**.

sam•ba /sámbə, sáam–/ • *n.* **1** ballroom dance of Brazilian and African origins. **2** music for this. • *v.intr.* (**sam•bas, sam•** **baed** /–bəd/, **sam•ba•ing** /–bə–ing/) dance the samba.

same /saym/ • *adj.* **1** identical; not different. **2** unvarying; uniform. **3** just mentioned. • *pron.* [prec. by *the*] the same person or thing (*asked for the same*). • *adv.* [usu. prec. by *the*] similarly; in the same way (*we all feel the same*). □ **all** (or **just**) **the same**

1 emphatically the same. 2 in spite of changed conditions. **at the same time** 1 simultaneously. 2 notwithstanding. **be all** (or **just**) **the same to** expression of indifference or impartiality (*it's all the same to me what we do*). **same here** *colloq.* the same applies to me. **the same to you!** may you do, have, find, etc., the same thing. □□ **same′ness** *n.*

■ *adj.* 1 exactly *or* just the same; very. 2 unchanging, unaltered, constant, monotonous. 3 aforesaid, aforementioned, abovementioned. • *adv.* (*the same*) see ALIKE *adv.* □ **all** (or **just**) **the same** 2 nevertheless, nonetheless, even so, yet, but, anyway, anyhow, in any case, in any event, at any rate, regardless, still; that (having been) said, having said that, when all is said and done. **at the same time** 1 see *at once* 2 (ONCE). 2 see NOTWITHSTANDING *adv.*, *conj.* □□ **sameness** see *uniformity* (UNIFORM).

Sa•mo•an /səmṓən/ • *n.* 1 native of Samoa, a group of islands in the Pacific. 2 language of this people. • *adj.* of or relating to Samoa or its people or language.

sam•o•var /sáməvaar/ *n.* Russian urn for making tea.

Sam•o•yed /sáməyed, səmóyed/ *n.* 1 dog of a white Arctic breed. 2 this breed.

sam•pan /sámpan/ *n.* small boat used in the Far East.

sam•ple /sámpəl/ • *n.* 1 [also *attrib.*] small representative part or quantity. 2 illustrative or typical example. • *v.tr.* take, give, or try samples of.

■ *n.* 1 specimen, example, representative; (*attrib.*) illustrative, trial, test. 2 see ILLUSTRATION 2. • *v.* test, taste, experience.

sam•pler /sámplər/ *n.* 1 person who samples. 2 collection of representative items, etc. 3 piece of embroidery worked in various stitches as a specimen of proficiency.

■ 2 see SAMPLE *n.* 1.

sam•u•rai /sámoorī, sáa–/ *n.* (*pl.* same) member of a former military caste in Japan.

sanc•ti•fy /sángktifī/ *v.tr.* (**–fies,** **–fied**) 1 treat as holy. 2 free from sin. □□ **sanc•ti•fi•ca′tion** *n.* **sanc′ti•fi•er** *n.*

■ 1 consecrate, hallow, make sacred; glorify, exalt. 2 purify, cleanse; see also PURGE *v.* 1.

sanc•ti•mo•ni•ous /sángktimṓnēəs/ *adj.* making a show of sanctity or piety. See synonym study at MORAL. □□ **sanc•ti•mo′ni•ous•ly** *adv.* **sanc•ti•mo′ni•ous•ness** *n.* **sanc′ti•mo•ny** *n.*

■ self-righteous, *colloq.* holier-than-thou.

sanc•tion /sángkshən/ • *n.* 1 approval or encouragement given to an action, etc., by custom or tradition. 2 confirmation of a law, etc. 3 penalty for disobeying a law or rule. 4 [esp. in *pl.*] esp. economic action by a nation to coerce another to conform to norms of conduct. • *v.tr.* 1 authorize, countenance, or agree to (an action, etc.). 2 ratify; make binding. See synonym study at APPROVE. □□ **sanc′tion•able** *adj.*

■ *n.* 1 acceptance, affirmation, assent, compliance, permission, OK. 2 ratification, validation, certification. 3 see PENALTY 1. • *v.* 1 permit, allow, consent to, support, back, sponsor, favor. 2 second, authorize, legalize, license, certify.

sanc•ti•ty /sángktitee/ *n.* (*pl.* **–ties**) holiness; sacredness; inviolability.

■ piety, saintliness, divinity, godliness; indomitability.

sanc•tu•ar•y /sángkchooeree/ *n.* (*pl.* **–ies**) 1 holy place; church, temple, etc. 2 place of refuge for birds, wild animals, etc. 3 a immunity from arrest. b the right to offer this.

■ 1 sanctum, shrine, chapel, house of worship, house of God; synagogue, mosque, pagoda. 2 reserve, preserve, conservation area, national park. 3 a asylum, protection, shelter, safety.

sanc•tum /sángktəm/ *n.* (*pl.* **sanc•tums** or **sanc•ta** /–tə/) 1 holy place. 2 *colloq.* study; den.

■ 1 see SANCTUARY 1. 2 retreat; hiding place.

sand /sand/ • *n.* 1 loose grains resulting from the erosion of rocks and found on the seashore, riverbeds, deserts, etc. 2 [in *pl.*] grains of sand. 3 [in *pl.*] expanse of sand. • *v.tr.* smooth with sandpaper. □ **sand dollar** round, flat sea urchin. **sand dune** mound or ridge of sand formed by the wind. **sands are running out** allotted time is nearly at an end. □□ **sand′er** *n.*

■ *v.* see SMOOTH *v.* 1.

san•dal /sánd'l/ *n.* shoe with an openwork upper or no upper, attached to the foot usu. by straps.

san•dal•wood /sánd'lwŏŏd/ *n.* scented wood of an Asian tree.

sand•bag /sándbag/ • *n.* bag filled with sand used for fortifications, ballast, etc. • *v.tr.* (**–bagged,** **–bag•ging**) 1 barricade or defend with sandbags. 2 fell with a blow from a sandbag. 3 coerce. □□ **sand′bag•ger** *n.*

sand•bar /sándbaar/ *n.* bank of sand at the mouth of a river or on the coast.

sand•blast /sándblast/ • *v.tr.* roughen, treat,

sandbox ~ sap 740

or clean with a jet of sand driven by compressed air or steam. • *n.* this jet. ▫▫ **sand′blast•er** *n.*

sand•box /sándboks/ *n.* box of sand for children to play in.

sand•hog /sándhawg, -hog/ *n.* person who works underwater laying foundations, constructing tunnels, etc.

sand•lot /sándlot/ *n.* piece of unoccupied sandy land used for children's games.

sand•man /sándman/ *n.* fictional man supposed to make children sleep by sprinkling sand in their eyes.

sand•pa•per /sándpaypər/ • *n.* paper with an abrasive coating for smoothing or polishing. • *v.tr.* smooth with sandpaper.

sand•pip•er /sándpipər/ *n.* wading shore bird with a piping call.

sand•stone /sándstōn/ *n.* sedimentary rock of consolidated sand.

sand•storm /sándstawrm/ *n.* storm of wind with clouds of sand.

sand•wich /sándwich, sán-/ • *n.* two or more slices of bread with a filling of meat, cheese, etc. • *v.tr.* **1** put (a thing, statement, etc.) between two of another character. **2** squeeze in between others (*sat sandwiched in the middle*). ▫ **sandwich generation** generation of people responsible for bringing up their own children and caring for their ageing parents.

sand•y /sándee/ *adj.* (**sand•i•er, sand•i•est**) **1** having the texture of sand. **2** having much sand. **3** yellowish-red. ▫▫ **sand′i•ness** *n.*
■ **1** gritty, grainy, granular. **3** see RED *adj.* 4.

sane /sayn/ *adj.* **1** of sound mind; not mad. **2** (of views, etc.) moderate; sensible. See synonym study at SENSIBLE. ▫▫ **sane′ly** *adv.* **sane′ness** *n.*
■ **1** normal, rational, *colloq.* all there. **2** well-balanced, right-minded, levelheaded, reasonable, judicious.

sang *past of* SING.

sang-froid /saanfrwaá/ *n.* composure, coolness, etc., in danger or under agitating circumstances.
■ indifference, self-possession, self-control, poise, *colloq.* unflappability, *sl.* cool.

san•gri•a /sanggréeə/ *n.* drink of red wine with lemonade, fruit, spices, etc.

san•gui•nar•y /sánggwəneree/ *adj.* bloody; bloodthirsty. ▫▫ **san•gui•nar•i•ly** /-nérolee/ *adv.*
■ gory; homicidal; brutal, brutish, savage, barbarous.

san•guine /sánggwin/ *adj.* **1** optimistic; confident. **2** (of the complexion) florid; ruddy. ▫▫ **san′guine•ly** *adv.* **san′guine•ness** *n.*
■ **1** rosy, hopeful. **2** bright; see also ROSY 1.

san•i•tar•i•um /sánitáireeəm/ *n.* (*pl.* **san•i•tar•i•ums** or **san•i•tar•i•a** /-reeə/) **1** establishment for the restoration of health. **2** health resort.
■ **1** rest home, convalescent home, nursing home.

san•i•tar•y /sániteree/ *adj.* **1** of conditions that affect health, esp. with regard to dirt and infection. **2** hygienic; free from or designed to kill germs, infection, etc. ▫ **sanitary engineer** person dealing with systems needed to maintain public health. **sanitary napkin** absorbent pad used during menstruation. ▫▫ **san•i•tar•i•an** /-áireeən/ *n. & adj.* **san•i•tar′i•ly** *adv.*
■ **2** clean, sterile, antiseptic, disinfected, aseptic, germ-free, bacteria-free.

SYNONYM STUDY: **sanitary**

ANTISEPTIC, HEALTHFUL, HYGIENIC, SALUBRIOUS, STERILE. Americans thrive on cleanliness and the eradication of germs. They try to keep their homes **sanitary**, a term that goes beyond cleanliness to imply that measures have been taken to guard against infections or disease. They demand that their communities provide schools and workplaces that are **hygienic**—in other words, that adhere to the rules or standards promoting public health. But it would be almost impossible to duplicate the conditions found in a hospital, where everything that comes in contact with patients must be **sterile** or free of germs entirely. Most Americans are not so much interested in making their environment **antiseptic**, a word that is similar in meaning to *sterile* but implies preventing infections by destroying germs that are already present (*an antiseptic solution*) as they are in keeping it **healthful**, which means conducive to the health or soundness of the body. Many Americans, as they grow older, choose to move to a more **salubrious** climate, a word that applies primarily to an air quality that is invigorating and that avoids harsh extremes.

san•i•ta•tion /sánitáyshən/ *n.* **1** sanitary conditions. **2** maintenance or improving of these. **3** disposal of sewage and refuse.

san•i•tize /sánitiz/ *v.tr.* **1** make sanitary; disinfect. **2** render (information, etc.) more acceptable by removing improper or disturbing material. ▫▫ **san′i•tiz•er** *n.*
■ **1** see DISINFECT.

san•i•ty /sánitee/ *n.* **1** state of being sane. **2** tendency to avoid extreme views.
■ **1** reason, mental health *or* soundness, normality, rationality, stability.

sank *past of* SINK.

sans /sanz, SON/ *prep.* without.

San•skrit /sánskrit/ • *n.* ancient and sacred language of the Hindus in India. • *adj.* of or in this language.

sans ser•if /sansérif/ (also **sans-ser′if**) *Printing n.* form of type without serifs. • *adj.* without serifs.

San•ta Claus /sántə klawz/ *n.* (also *colloq.* **Santa**) legendary person said to bring children Christmas presents.

sap¹ /sap/ • *n.* **1** vital juice circulating in plants. **2** vigor; vitality. • *v.tr.* (**sapped, sap•ping**) drain of sap.
■ *n.* **2** lifeblood; see also LIFE 7. • *v.* bleed, draw, rob, milk.

sap² /sap/ *v.tr.* (**sapped, sap•ping**) undermine; weaken.
■ devitalize, deplete, drain, debilitate; cripple.

sap³ /sap/ *n. sl.* foolish person.

■ fool, ass, *colloq.* nitwit, dimwit, chump, dupe, *sl.* sucker.

sap•id /sápid/ *adj.* **1** having an agreeable flavor; palatable. **2** (of talk, writing, etc.) not vapid. □□ **sa•pid′i•ty** *n.*
■ **1** see TASTY.

sa•pi•ent /sáypeeənt/ *adj.* wise. □□ **sa′pi•ence** *n.* **sa′pi•ent•ly** *adv.*

sap•ling /sápling/ *n.* **1** young tree. **2** youth.

sap•phire /sáfir/ • *n.* **1** transparent, bright blue precious stone. **2** its color. • *adj.* of sapphire blue.

sap•py /sápee/ *adj.* (**sap•pi•er, sap•pi•est**) **1** full of sap. **2** overly emotional or sentimental. □□ **sap′pi•ly** *adv.* **sap′pi•ness** *n.*

sap•ro•phyte /sáprəfit/ *n.* plant or microorganism living on dead or decayed organic matter. □□ **sap•ro•phyt′ic** /–fítik/ *adj.*

Sar•a•cen /sárəsən/ *hist.* • *n.* Arab or Muslim at the time of the Crusades. • *adj.* of the Saracens.

sar•casm /saárkazəm/ *n.* **1** bitter or wounding remark. **2** taunt, esp. one ironically worded. See synonym study at WIT. □□ **sar•cas•tic** /–kástik/ *adj.* **sar•cas′ti•cal•ly** *adv.*
■ **1, 2** see TAUNT *n.*, DIG *n.* **3.** □□ **sarcastic** scornful, derisive, mocking, ridiculing, scathing.

sar•co•ma /saarkōmə/ *n.* (*pl.* **sar•co•mas** or **sar•co•ma•ta** /–mətə/) malignant tumor of connective tissue. □□ **sar•co•ma•to•sis** /–mətósis/ *n.*

sar•coph•a•gus /saarkófəgəs/ *n.* (*pl.* **sar•coph•a•gi** /–gi, –jī/) stone coffin.

sar•dine /saardéen/ *n.* small, edible fish, usu. sold tightly packed in cans.

sar•don•ic /saardónik/ *adj.* **1** grimly jocular. **2** bitterly mocking or cynical. □□ **sar•don′i•cal•ly** *adv.*
■ **1** ironic, cynical, sarcastic; see also INCISIVE 3. **2** derisive, derisory, mocking, cynical, sarcastic, ironic.

sa•ri /saáree/ *n.* (also **sa′ree**) (*pl.* **sa•ris** or **sa•rees**) length of cloth draped around the body, traditionally worn by women of India.

sa•rong /səráwng, –róng/ *n.* Malay and Javanese garment of a long strip of cloth wrapped around the body and tucked around the waist or under the armpits.

sar•sa•pa•ril•la /sáspərilə, saárs–/ *n.* preparation of the dried roots of various plants, used to flavor a carbonated drink.

sar•to•ri•al /saartáwreeəl/ *adj.* of men's clothes or tailoring. □□ **sar•to′ri•al•ly** *adv.*

s.a.s.e. *abbr.* self-addressed stamped envelope.

sash[1] /sash/ *n.* long strip or loop of cloth, etc., worn over one shoulder or around the waist. □□ **sashed** *adj.*

sash[2] /sash/ *n.* frame holding the glass in a fixed or sliding window. □□ **sashed** *adj.*

sa•shay /sasháy/ *v.intr. colloq.* walk or move ostentatiously, casually, or diagonally.

sass /sas/ *colloq.* • *n.* impudence; disrespectful mannerism or speech. • *v.tr.* be impudent to.

sas•sa•fras /sásəfras/ *n.* **1** small tree native to N. America. **2** medicinal preparation from its leaves or bark.

SAT *abbr. propr.* **1** Scholastic Assessment Test. **2** (formerly) Scholastic Aptitude Test.

Sat. *abbr.* Saturday.

Sa•tan /sáyt'n/ *n.* the Devil; Lucifer.

sa•tan•ic /sətánik, say–/ *adj.* **1** of, like, or befitting Satan. **2** diabolical; hellish. □□ **sa•tan′i•cal•ly** *adv.*
■ diabolic, fiendish, devilish; evil, wicked, iniquitous; monstrous, heinous, atrocious, hideous.

Sa•tan•ism /sáyt'nizəm/ *n.* **1** worship of Satan. **2** pursuit of evil. □□ **Sa′tan•ist** *n.*

satch•el /sáchəl/ *n.* bag, usu. with a shoulder strap, for carrying books, etc.

sate /sayt/ *v.tr.* **1** gratify fully. **2** overfill.

sa•teen /satéen/ *n.* glossy, satinlike cotton fabric.

sat•el•lite /sát′lit/ • *n.* **1** celestial body orbiting the earth or another planet. **2** artificial body placed in orbit around the earth or another planet. **3** small country controlled by another. • *adj.* transmitted by satellite (*satellite communications*). □ **satellite dish** concave dish-shaped antenna for receiving broadcasting signals transmitted by satellite.
■ *n.* **1** moon, planet. **2** sputnik, spacecraft, rocket.

sa•ti•e•ty /sətí-itee/ *n.* **1** being glutted or overfilled. **2** feeling of having too much of something. **3** (foll. by *of*) cloyed dislike of.
■ **1** surfeit, saturation, excess. **3** excess, surfeit; see also DISGUST *n.*

sat•in /sát'n/ • *n.* fabric with a glossy surface on one side. • *adj.* smooth as satin. □□ **sat′in•ized** *adj.* **sat′in•y** *adj.*

sat•in•wood /sát'nwdd/ *n.* kind of yellow, glossy timber.

sat•ire /sátir/ *n.* **1** use of ridicule, irony, sarcasm, etc., to expose folly or vice or to lampoon an individual. **2** work using this. See synonym study at WIT. □□ **sa•tir•ic** /sətirik/ *adj.* **sa•tir′i•cal** *adj.* **sa•tir′i•cal•ly** *adv.* **sat•i•rist** /sátərist/ *n.*
■ **1** mockery, caricature. **2** burlesque, lampoon, parody.

sat•i•rize /sátiriz/ *v.tr.* assail or describe with satire. □□ **sat•i•ri•za′tion** *n.*
■ poke fun at, ridicule, pillory, mock; lampoon, parody; mimic.

sat•is•fac•tion /sátisfákshən/ *n.* **1** satisfying or being satisfied. **2** thing that satisfies. **3** thing that settles an obligation or pays a debt. **4** atonement; compensation.
■ **1** gratification, comfort, delight, joy, pleasure. **2** comfort, delight, joy, pleasure. **4** payment, requital; redress, expiation, amends.

sat•is•fac•to•ry /sátisfáktəree/ *adj.* adequate; causing or giving satisfaction. □□ **sat•is•fac′to•ri•ly** *adv.*
■ sufficient, acceptable, passable; all right, not bad.

sat•is•fy /sátisfi/ *v.* (**–fies, –fied**) **1** *tr.* **a** meet the expectations or desires of; comply with (a demand). **b** be adequate. **2** *tr.* meet (an appetite or want). **3** *tr.* pay (a debt or creditor). **4** *tr.* provide with adequate information or proof; convince. □□ **sat'is•fi•a•ble** *adj.* **sat'is•fy•ing** *adj.*

■ **1 a** see also FULFILL 2, 3. **1 b** gratify, please, fulfill; placate, appease, pacify. **2** slake, quench, satiate; fulfill, gratify, indulge. **3** repay, make good. **4** persuade, assure; reassure; put a person's mind at rest. □□ **satisfying** gratifying, satisfactory, fulfilling; comforting, pleasing.

sa•trap /sátrap, sáy–/ *n.* **1** provincial governor in the ancient Persian empire. **2** subordinate, often despotic ruler.

sat•u•rate /sáchərayt/ *v.tr.* **1** fill with moisture. **2** fill to capacity. **3** cause (a substance, etc.) to absorb, hold, etc., as much as possible of another substance, etc. □□ **sat•u•ra•ble** /–rəbəl/ *adj.* **sat•u•rant** /–rənt/ *n. & adj.* **sat•u•ra•tion** /sáchəráyshən/ *n.*

■ **1** soak, drench, waterlog. **2** steep, fill.

Sat•ur•day /sátərday, –dee/ *n.* seventh day of the week, following Friday.

Sat•urn /sátərn/ *n.* sixth planet from the sun, with a system of broad flat rings circling it. □□ **Sa•tur•ni•an** /satórneeən/ *adj.*

sat•ur•nine /sátərnīn/ *adj.* **1** of a sluggish, gloomy temperament. **2** (of looks, etc.) dark and brooding. See synonym study at GLUM.

sa•tyr /sáytər, sát–/ *n.* **1** *Gk. & Rom. mythol.* woodland god with some manlike and goatlike features. **2** lustful or sensual man.

sauce /saws/ *n.* **1** liquid or semisolid preparation taken as a relish with food; the liquid constituent of a dish. **2** something adding piquancy or excitement. **3** *colloq.* impudence; impertinence. □□ **sauce'less** *adj.*

■ **1** gravy, juice; relish, dressing.

sauce•pan /sáwspan/ *n.* cooking pan, usu. with a lid and a long handle. □□ **sauce'pan•ful** *n.* (*pl.* **–fuls**).

sau•cer /sáwsər/ *n.* shallow circular dish for holding a cup. □□ **sau'cer•ful** *n.* (*pl.* **–fuls**). **sau'cer•less** *adj.*

sau•cy /sáwsee/ *adj.* (**sau•ci•er, sau•ci•est**) impudent. □□ **sau'ci•ly** *adv.* **sau'ci•ness** *n.*

■ see IMPUDENT. □□ **sauciness** see *impudence* (IMPUDENT).

Sau•di /sówdee, sáw–/ (also **Sau•di A•ra•bi•an** /əráybeeən/) • *n.* (*pl.* **Saudis**) **1** native or national of Saudi Arabia. **2** person of Saudi descent. • *adj.* of or relating to Saudi Arabia.

sau•er•kraut /sówərkrowt/ *n.* chopped pickled cabbage.

sau•na /sáwnə, sow–/ *n.* **1** Finnish-style steam bath. **2** building used for this.

saun•ter /sáwntər/ • *v.intr.* walk slowly; stroll. • *n.* a leisurely ramble. □□ **saun'ter•er** *n.*

■ *v.* amble, ramble, wander. • *n.* **1** walk, stroll, amble, wander.

sau•ri•an /sáwreeən/ *adj.* of or like a lizard.

sau•sage /sáwsij/ *n.* seasoned ground meat, often in a tube-shaped edible casing.

sau•té /sōtáy, saw–/ *adj.* quickly cooked or browned in a little hot fat. • *v.tr.* (**sau•téed** or **sau•téd**) cook in this way.

sav•age /sávij/ • *adj.* **1** fierce; cruel. **2** wild; primitive. **3** *colloq.* angry; bad-tempered.

• *n.* **1** *derog.* member of a primitive tribe. **2** cruel or barbarous person. • *v.tr.* **1** (esp. of a dog, wolf, etc.) attack and bite or trample. **2** (of a critic, etc.) attack fiercely. □□ **sav'age•ly** *adv.* **sav'age•ry** *n.* (*pl.* **–ries**).

■ *adj.* **1** vicious, ferocious, beastly, pitiless, merciless. **2** uncivilized, beastly, inhuman; untamed, undomesticated, feral. **3** see NASTY 3. • *n.* **1** wild man *or* woman. **2** see BEAST 2. • *v.* **2** see ATTACK *v.* 3.

sa•van•na /səvánə/ *n.* (also **sa•van'nah**) grassy plain in tropical and subtropical regions.

sa•vant /savaánt, sávənt/ *n.* (*fem.* **sa•vante**) learned person.

save[1] /sayv/ • *v.* **1** *tr.* [often foll. by *from*] rescue, preserve, protect, or deliver from danger, harm, etc. **2** *tr.* keep for future use. **3** *tr.* [often *refl.*] **a** relieve (another person or oneself) from spending (money, time, trouble, etc.). **b** obviate a need. **4** *tr.* preserve from damnation. **5** *tr. & refl.* preserve (one's strength, health, etc.). • *n. Ice hockey, soccer, etc.* prevention of an opponent's scoring, etc. □□ **sav'a•ble** *adj.* (also **save'a•ble**). **sav'er** *n.*

■ *v.* **1** (come to a person's) rescue, deliver; liberate, release, bail out; recover, retrieve, keep, guard, safeguard. **2** put aside, keep; retain, preserve. **3 a** obviate, preclude, spare, prevent. **b** prevent; see also PRECLUDE 2. **4** see REDEEM 4. **5** see CONSERVE *v.* 1.

save[2] /sayv/ *archaic* or *formal* • *prep.* except; but. • *conj.* unless; but; except.

sav•ing /sáyving/ • *adj.* [often in *comb.*] making economical use of (*labor-saving*). • *n.* **1** anything saved. **2** an economy. **3** [usu. in *pl.*] money saved. • *prep.* except. □ **savings and loan association** banking institution that accepts funds deposited at interest and lends funds for mortgages. **savings bank** bank receiving deposits at interest and returning the profits to the depositors.

■ *n.* **3** (*savings*) cache, nest egg; see also HOARD *n.*

sav•ior /sáyvyər/ *n.* (also **sav'iour**) **1** person who saves from danger, destruction, etc. **2** (**Savior**) [prec. by *the, our*] Christ.

■ **1** rescuer, salvation, Good Samaritan, liberator. **2** the Redeemer, Jesus, (the) Messiah.

sa•voir faire /sávwaa fáir/ *n.* the ability to act suitably in any situation; tact.

■ tactfulness, discretion; sophistication, urbanity.

sa•vor /sáyvər/ • *n.* characteristic taste, flavor, etc. • *v.* **1** *tr.* **a** appreciate and enjoy the taste of (food). **b** enjoy or appreciate (an experience, etc.). **2** *intr.* [foll. by *of*] suggest by taste, smell, etc. (*savors of mushrooms*). □□ **sa'vor•less** *adj.*

■ *n.* taste, flavor, zest, tang, piquancy. • *v.* **1** relish; smack one's lips over; indulge in.

sa•vor•y[1] /sáyvəree/ *n.* (*pl.* **–ries**) aromatic herb used esp. in cooking.

sa•vor•y[2] /sáyvəree/ *adj.* **1** having an appetizing taste or smell. **2** pleasant; acceptable. □□ **sa'vor•i•ly** *adv.* **sa'vor•i•ness** *n.*

■ *adj.* **1** palatable, delicious, tasty, toothsome, appetizing. **2** honest, proper, decent, reputable, respectable.

sav•vy /sávee/ • *n.* knowingness; shrewdness; understanding. • *adj.* (**sav•vi•er, sav•vi•est**) knowing; wise.

■ *n.* see UNDERSTANDING *n.* 1. • *adj.* see INTELLIGENT 2.

saw¹ /saw/ • *n.* hand tool having a toothed blade or disk used to cut hard materials. • *v.* (*past part.* **sawed** or **sawn** /sawn/) **1** *tr.* cut (wood, etc.) with a saw. **2** *intr.* use a saw. **3** *intr.* move with a sawing motion. □□ **saw′like** *adj.*

saw² *past of* SEE¹.

saw³ /saw/ *n.* proverb; maxim (*that's just an old saw*).

■ saying, aphorism, axiom, adage, epigram.

saw•dust /sáwdust/ *n.* powdery particles of wood produced in sawing.

saw•horse /sáwhawrs/ *n.* rack supporting wood for sawing.

saw•mill /sáwmil/ *n.* factory in which wood is sawed mechanically into planks or boards.

sawn *past part.* of SAW¹.

saw•tooth /sáwtŏoth/ *adj.* (also **saw•toothed** /-tŏotht/) (esp. of a roof, wave, etc.) shaped like the teeth of a saw.

saw•yer /sáwyər/ *n.* person who saws lumber professionally.

sax /saks/ *n. colloq.* = SAXOPHONE. □□ **sax′ist** *n.*

Sax•on /sáksən/ *n.* **1** *hist.* **a** member of the Germanic people that conquered parts of England in 5th– 6th c. **b** (usu. **Old Sax′on**) language of the Saxons. **2** = ANGLO-SAXON.

sax•o•phone /sáksəfon/ *n.* keyed brass reed instrument. □□ **sax•o•phon•ic** /-fónik/ *adj.* **sax•o•phon•ist** /-səfōnist/ *n.*

say /say/ • *v.* (*3rd sing. present* **says** /sez/; *past and past part.* **said** /sed/) **1** *tr.* utter (specified words); remark. **b** express. **2** *tr.* **a** state; promise. **b** have specified wording; indicate. **3** *tr.* [in *passive*; usu. foll. by *to* + *infin.*] be asserted or described. **4** *tr.* repeat (a lesson, etc.); recite. **5** *tr.* Art, etc., convey (inner meaning or intention). • *n.* **1 a** opportunity for stating one's opinion, etc. **b** stated opinion. **2** share in a decision. □ **say-so 1** power of decision. **2** mere assertion. that is to say 1 in other words. 2 or at least. □□ **say′a•ble** *adj.* **say′er** *n.*

■ *v.* **1 a** state, affirm, declare, maintain, assert. **b** tell, put, verbalize. **2 a** prophesy, predict. **3** (*be said*) be mentioned, be suggested or hinted. **4** utter, speak. **5** signify, denote, symbolize. • *n.* **1 a** turn, chance, moment. **2** voice, authority, influence. □ that is to say 1 see NAMELY.

say•ing /sáying/ *n.* **1** act or instance of saying. **2** maxim, proverb, adage, etc. □ go without saying be too well known or obvious to need mention.

SYNONYM STUDY: saying

ADAGE, APHORISM, APOTHEGM, EPIGRAM, EPIGRAPH, MAXIM, PROVERB. "Once burned, twice shy" is an old **saying** about learning from your mistakes. In fact, *sayings*—a term used to describe any current or habitual expression of wisdom or truth—are a dime a dozen. **Proverbs**—*sayings* that are well known and often repeated, usually expressing metaphorically a truth based on common sense or practical experience—are just as plentiful (*her favorite proverb was "A stitch in time saves nine"*). An **adage** is a time-honored and widely known *proverb*, such as "Where's there's smoke, there's fire." A **maxim** offers a rule of conduct or action in the form of a *proverb*, such as "Neither a borrower nor a lender be." **Epigram** and **epigraph** are often confused, but their meanings are quite separate. An *epigram* is a terse, witty, or satirical statement that often relies on a paradox for its effect (*Oscar Wilde's well-known epigram that "The only way to get rid of temptation is to yield to it"*). An *epigraph*, on the other hand, is a brief quotation used to introduce a piece of writing (*he used a quote from T. S. Eliot as the epigraph to his new novel*). An **aphorism** requires a little more thought than an *epigram*, since it aims to be profound rather than witty (*she'd just finished reading a book of Mark Twain's aphorisms*). An **apothegm** is a pointed and often startling *aphorism*, such as Samuel Johnson's remark that "Patriotism is the last refuge of a scoundrel."

Sb *symb. Chem.* the element antimony.

SBA *abbr.* Small Business Administration.

SC *abbr.* South Carolina (also in official postal use).

Sc *symb. Chem.* the element scandium.

s.c. *abbr.* small capitals.

scab /skab/ • *n.* **1** dry rough crust formed over a healing cut, sore, etc. **2** *colloq. derog.* person who refuses to strike or join a trade union, or who tries to break a strike by working. • *v.intr.* (**scabbed, scab•bing**) **1** act as a scab. **2** form a scab; heal over. □□ **scabbed** *adj.* **scab′by** *adj.* (**scab•bi•er, scab•bi•est**). **scab′bi•ness** *n.* **scab′like** *adj.*

■ *n.* **2** strikebreaker.

scab•bard /skábərd/ *n. hist.* sheath for a sword, etc.

sca•bies /skáybeez/ *n.* contagious skin disease causing severe itching (cf. ITCH).

sca•brous /skábrəs, skáy–/ *adj.* **1** having a rough surface, scaly **2** indecent; salacious. □□ **scab′rous•ly** *adv.* **scab′rous•ness** *n.*

scaf•fold /skáfold, –fōld/ • *n.* **1** *hist.* raised wooden platform for the execution of criminals, esp. by hanging. **2** = SCAFFOLDING • *v.tr.* attach scaffolding to (a building). □□ **scaf′fold•er** *n.*

scaf•fold•ing /skáfolding, –fōlding/ *n.* temporary structure formed of poles, planks, etc., erected by workers and used by them while building or repairing a house, etc.

scal•a•wag /skáləwag/ *n.* (also **scal′ly•wag**) scamp; rascal.

scald /skawld/ • *v.tr.* **1** burn (the skin, etc.) with hot liquid or steam. **2** heat (esp. milk) to near boiling point. **3** clean with boiling water. See synonym study at BURN. • *n.* burn, etc., caused by scalding. □□ **scald′er** *n.*

scale¹ /skayl/ • *n.* **1** each of the small, thin, bony or horny overlapping plates protecting the skin of fish and reptiles. **2** deposit formed in a kettle, boiler, etc. • *v.* **1** *tr.* remove scale(s). **2** *intr.* form, come off in, or drop scales.

▪ *n.* **1** lamina, lamella, scute, scutum.

scale[2] /skayl/ *n.* **1 a** [often in *pl.*] weighing device. **b** (also **scale'pan**) each of the dishes on a simple scale balance. **2** (**the Scales**) zodiacal sign or constellation Libra. □ **tip** (or **turn**) **the scales** be the decisive factor.

▪ *n.* **1 a** see BALANCE *n.*

scale[3] /skayl/ • *n.* **1** graded classification system. **2 a** [often *attrib.*] *Geog. & Archit.* ratio of size in a map, model, picture, etc. **b** relative dimensions or degree (*generosity on a grand scale*). **3** *Mus.* arrangement of all the notes in any system of music in ascending or descending order. **4 a** set of marks on a line used in measuring. **b** piece of metal, apparatus, etc., on which these are marked. • *v.tr.* climb (a wall, height, etc.). □ **scale down** reduce in size. **scale up** increase in size. □□ **scal'er** *n.*

▪ *n.* **1** ranking, graduation, hierarchy, range. **2 a** proportion. • *v.* **1** ascend, clamber up, go up. □ **scale down** decrease, reduce, diminish. **scale up** see ENLARGE 1, 3.

sca•lene /skáyleen/ *adj.* (esp. of a triangle) having unequal sides.

scal•lion /skályən/ *n.* any long-necked onion with a small bulb.

scal•lop /skáləp, skól–/ (also **scol'lop** /skól–/) • *n.* **1** bivalve mollusk much prized as food. **2** (in full **scal'lop shell**) single shell of a scallop, with a toothed edge. **3** [in *pl.*] ornamental edging cut in material in imitation of a scallop edge. • *v.tr.* (**scal•loped, scal•loping**) ornament (an edge or material) with scallops or scalloping. □□ **scal'lop•er** *n.* **scal'lop•ing** *n.* (in sense 3 of *n.*).

▪ *v.* **2** pink, serrate, notch.

scalp /skalp/ • *n.* **1** skin covering the top of the head, with the hair, etc., attached. **2 a** *hist.* scalp of an enemy cut or torn away as a trophy by a Native American. **b** trophy or symbol of triumph, conquest, etc. • *v.tr.* **1** *hist.* take the scalp of (an enemy). **2** *colloq.* resell (shares, tickets, etc.) at a high or quick profit. □□ **scalp'er** *n.*

scal•pel /skálpəl/ *n.* surgeon's sharp knife.

scam /skam/ *n. sl.* trick or swindle; fraud.

▪ see TRICK *n.* 1.

scam•per /skámpər/ • *v.intr.* run quickly. • *n.* act or instance of scampering.

scam•pi /skámpee/ *n.pl.* large shrimp, esp. sautéed in garlic butter.

scan /skan/ • *v.* (**scanned, scan•ning**) **1** *tr.* look at intently or quickly. **2** *intr.* (of a verse, etc.) be metrically correct (*this line doesn't scan*). **3** *tr.* resolve (a picture) into its elements of light and shade in a prearranged pattern. • *n.* **1** scanning. **2** image obtained by scanning or with a scanner. □□ **scan'na•ble** *adj.*

▪ *v.* **1** glance at *or* through, skim, read over, peruse. • *n.* **1** look, survey, inspection, examination, overview. **2** see IMAGE *n.* 3.

scan•dal /skánd'l/ *n.* **1** thing or a person causing general public outrage or indigna-

tion. **2** outrage, etc., so caused. **3** malicious gossip. □□ **scan'dal•ous** *adj.* **scan'dal•ous•ly** *adv.*

▪ **1** disgrace, embarrassment; stigma; smirch, black mark. **2** shame, disgrace; discredit, infamy. **3** slander, libel, calumny; rumor, backbiting. □ **scandalous** shocking, disgraceful, ignominious, outrageous.

scan•dal•ize /skándəlīz/ *v.tr.* offend morally; shock.

▪ appall, outrage, offend, horrify, upset.

scan•dal•mon•ger /skánd'lmɔnggər, –mɔnggər/ *n.* person who spreads malicious scandal.

Scan•di•na•vi•an /skándináyveeən/ • *n.* **1 a** native or inhabitant of Scandinavia (Denmark, Norway, Sweden, and sometimes Finland and Iceland). **b** person of Scandinavian descent. **2** family of languages of Scandinavia. • *adj.* of or relating to Scandinavia or its people or languages.

scan•di•um /skándeeəm/ *n. Chem.* metallic element occurring naturally in lanthanide ores. ¶ Symb.: **Sc**.

scan•ner /skánər/ *n.* **1** device for obtaining an electronic image of something. **2** device for monitoring radio frequencies, esp. police or emergency frequencies.

scan•sion /skánshən/ *n.* metrical scanning of verse.

scant /skant/ *adj.* barely sufficient; deficient. □□ **scant'ly** *adv.* **scant'ness** *n.*

scant•y /skántee/ *adj.* (**scant•i•er, scant•i•est**) **1** of small extent or amount. **2** barely sufficient. □□ **scant'i•ly** *adv.* **scant'i•ness** *n.*

▪ scant, sparse, scarce, meager; limited.

scape•goat /skáypgōt/ • *n.* person blamed for others. • *v.tr.* make a scapegoat of. □□ **scape'goat•er** *n.*

▪ *n.* victim, cat's-paw, whipping boy, straw man, *sl.* fall guy. • *v.* see ACCUSE 1.

scap•u•la /skápyələ/ *n.* (*pl.* **scap•u•lae** /–lee/ or **scap•u•las**) shoulder blade.

scar /skaar/ • *n.* usu. permanent mark on the skin from a healed wound, burn, or sore. • *v.* (**scarred, scar•ring**) **1** *tr.* (esp. as **scarred** *adj.*) mark with a scar. **2** *intr.* form a scar. □□ **scar'less** *adj.*

▪ *n.* blemish, mark, disfigurement, cicatrice. • *v.* **1** blemish, mark, disfigure, mar, wound, injure, damage.

scar•ab /skárəb/ *n.* **1** sacred dung beetle of ancient Egypt. **2** ancient Egyptian gem cut in the form of a beetle.

scarce /skairs/ *adj.* **1** [usu. *predic.*] insufficient for the demand; scanty. **2** rare. □ **make oneself scarce** *colloq.* keep out of the way. □□ **scarce'ness** *n.*

▪ *adj.* **1** scant, inadequate, deficient. **2** at a premium, in short supply; unusual, few and far between.

scarce•ly /skáirslee/ *adv.* **1** hardly; barely; only just. **2** surely not.

▪ **1** not quite, almost not. **2** certainly *or* definitely not, not at all.

scar•ci•ty /skáirsitee/ *n.* (*pl.* **–ties**) lack or inadequacy, esp. of food.

▪ want, need, paucity, dearth, insufficiency.

scare /skair/ • *v.* **1** *tr.* frighten, esp. suddenly.

2 *tr.* (as **scared** *adj.*) frightened; terrified. **3** *tr.* [usu. foll. by *away*, *off*, etc.] drive away by frightening. • *n.* **1** sudden attack of fright. **2** alarm. □□ **scar′er** *n.*

■ *v.* **1** alarm, startle, shock. **2** (**scared**) alarmed, afraid, shocked, horrified, startled. **3** (*scare off*) see SHOO *v.* • *n.* **1** shock, surprise, start.

scare•crow /skáirkrō/ *n.* human figure dressed in old clothes and set up in a field to scare birds away.

scarf[1] /skaarf/ *n.* (*pl.* **scarfs** or **scarves** /skaarvz/) square, triangular, or long, narrow strip of material worn around the neck, over the shoulders, or tied around the head for warmth or ornament. □□ **scarfed** *adj.*

scarf[2] /skaarf/ • *v.tr.* join the beveled ends of lumber, etc., by bolting, gluing, etc. • *n.* joint made by scarfing.

scar•i•fy /skárifī, skáir–/ *v.tr.* (**–fies, –fied**) make superficial incisions in. □□ **scar•i•fi•ca′tion** *n.*

scar•let /skáarlit/ • *n.* brilliant red color tinged with orange. • *adj.* of a scarlet color. □ **scarlet fever** infectious bacterial fever with a scarlet rash.

scarp /skaarp/ *n.* steep slope.

scar•y /skáiree/ *adj.* (**scar•i•er, scar•i•est**) *colloq.* frightening. □□ **scar′i•ly** *adv.*

■ scaring, eerie, terrifying, hair-raising.

scat[1] /skat/ *colloq.* • *v.intr.* (**scat•ted, scat•ting**) depart quickly. • *int.* go!

scat[2] /skat/ • *n.* improvised jazz singing using sounds imitating instruments, instead of words. • *v.intr.* (**scat•ted, scat•ting**) sing scat.

scathe /skayth/ *v.* (as **scathing** *adj.*) witheringly scornful.

■ (**scathing**) searing, damaging, harmful, severe.

scat•ter /skátər/ • *v.* **1** *tr.* throw here and there; strew. **2** *tr.* & *intr.* disperse or cause (hopes, clouds, etc.) to disperse. **3** *tr.* (as **scat•tered** *adj.*) not clustered together. • *n.* (also **scat•ter•ing**) **1** act or instance of scattering. **2** small amount scattered. □□ **scat′ter•er** *n.*

■ *v.* **1** shower, sprinkle, spread. **2** dispel, diffuse; dissipate; see also DISPERSE 1, 2a. **3** (**scattered**) see DIFFUSE *adj.* 1, SPORADIC. • *n.* **2** (**scattering**) smattering, sprinkling; suggestion, hint; see also TOUCH *n.* 3.

something has completely dissolved, disintegrated, or vanished (*early-morning mist dissipated by the sun*). **Broadcast** originally meant to *scatter* seed, but it is also used figuratively to mean make public (*The news of the president's defeat was broadcast the next morning*). **Disseminate** also means to publish or make public, but it implies a wider audience and usually a longer duration. You can spend a lifetime *disseminating* knowledge, in other words, but you would *broadcast* the news of the birth of your first grandchild.

scat•ter•brain /skátərbrayn/ *n.* person lacking concentration. □□ **scat′ter•brained** *adj.*

scav•enge /skávinj/ *v.* **1** *tr.* & *intr.* search for and collect (discarded items). **2** *tr.* feed on carrion, refuse, etc.

scav•en•ger /skávinjər/ *n.* **1** person who seeks and collects discarded items. **2** animal feeding on carrion, refuse, etc.

sce•nar•i•o /sináreeō, –náareeō/ *n.* (*pl.* **–os**) **1** outline of the plot of a play, film, opera, etc. **2** postulated sequence of future events. □□ **sce•nar′ist** *n.* (in sense 1).

■ **1** synopsis, plot (summary); scheme, framework.

scene /seen/ *n.* **1** place where events occur. **2 a** incident in real life, fiction, etc. **b** description or representation of an incident, etc. **3** public display of emotion, temper, etc. **4** portion of a play in a fixed setting. **5** piece of scenery used in a play. **6** landscape or a view. **7** *colloq.* area of action or interest; milieu. □ **behind the scenes 1** *Theatr.* offstage. **2** unknown to the public; secret(ly).

■ **1** location, site, place, setting. **2 a** see INCIDENT *n.* 1. **3** commotion, upset, brouhaha. **6** sight, panorama, vista. **7** see SPECIALTY; see SPHERE *n.* 3. □ **behind the scenes** private(ly), clandestine(ly), confidential(ly), surreptitious(ly), *colloq.* on the q.t.

scen•er•y /séenəree/ *n.* **1** natural features of a landscape. **2** *Theatr.* painted representations of landscape, rooms, etc., used as the background in a play, etc.

■ **1** see LANDSCAPE *n.* **2** see SET 5.

sce•nic /séenik/ *adj.* **1 a** picturesque. **b** of natural scenery. **2** (of a picture, etc.) representing an incident. **3** *Theatr.* of or on the stage. □□ **sce′ni•cal•ly** *adv.*

■ **1 a** beautiful, impressive, grand, striking, spectacular.

scent /sent/ • *n.* **1** distinctive, esp. pleasant, smell. **2 a** perceptible scent trail left by an animal. **b** sense of smell. **3** = PERFUME 2. See synonym study at SMELL. • *v.* **1** *tr.* **a** discern by scent. **b** sense the presence of. **2** *tr.* make fragrant. **3** *tr.* (as **scented** *adj.*) having esp. a pleasant smell (*scented soap*).

■ *n.* **1** fragrance, aroma, perfume, redolence, odor. **2** spoor, track, smell. • *v.* **1 a** smell, sniff (out). **b** discern, perceive, detect. **3** (**scented**) see *fragrant* (FRAGRANCE).

scep•ter /séptər/ *n.* staff as a symbol of sovereignty. □□ **scep′tered** *adj.*

sch. *abbr.* **1** school. **2** scholar.

sched•ule /skéjōōl, –ōōəl/ • *n.* **1 a** list or plan of intended events, times, etc. **b** plan of work. **2** list of rates or prices. **3** timetable. • *v.tr.* include in a schedule. □□ **sched'ul•er** *n.*

■ *n.* **1** program, timetable; calendar, agenda. **2** index. • *v.* **1** program, organize, plan, arrange.

sche•mat•ic /skimátik, skee–/ • *adj.* **1** of or concerning a scheme or diagram. **2** representing objects by symbols, etc. • *n.* diagram, esp. of an electronic circuit. □□ **sche•mat'i•cal•ly** *adv.*

■ *adj.* **2** diagrammatical, representational; symbolic. • *n.* schema; layout, design, plan, pattern.

scheme /skeem/ • *n.* **1 a** systematic plan or arrangement. **b** proposed or operational systematic arrangement (*color scheme*). **2** cunning plot. • *v.* plan, esp. secretly or deceitfully. □□ **schem'er** *n.* **schem'ing** *adj. & v.*

■ *n.* **1 a** design, program, system. **b** pattern, layout, design, blueprint. **2** plan, maneuver, strategy, stratagem, tactic; (*schemes*) games, scheming. • *v.* plan, plot, conspire, machinate, connive; contrive.

scher•zo /skáirtsō/ *n.* (*pl.* **–zos**) *Mus.* vigorous, light, or playful composition, usu. as a movement in a symphony, sonata, etc.

schism /sízəm, skiz–/ *n.* division of a group (esp. religious) into opposing sects or parties usu. over doctrine. □□ **schis•mat•ic** /sizmátik, skiz–/ *adj. & n.*

■ split, rift, break; division, rupture, separation; disunion; faction, camp, set, sect.

schist /shist/ *n.* layered crystalline rock.

schiz•o•phre•ni•a /skítsəfréenēeə, –frénēeə/ *n.* mental disease marked by a breakdown in the relation between thoughts, feelings, and actions, frequently accompanied by delusions and retreat from society. □□ **schiz•o•phren•ic** /–frénik/ *adj. & n.*

schle•miel /shləmeél/ *n. colloq.* foolish or unlucky person.

schlep /shlep/ (also **schlepp**) *colloq.* • *v.* (**schlepped, schlep•ping**) **1** *tr.* carry; drag. **2** *intr.* go or work tediously or effortfully. • *n.* (also **schlep•per**) person or thing that is tedious, awkward, or slow.

schlock /shlok/ *n. colloq.* inferior goods; trash.

schmaltz /shmaalts/ *n. colloq.* sentimentality, esp. in music, etc. □□ **schmaltz'y** *adj.* (**schmaltz•i•er, schmaltz•i•est**).

■ see SENTIMENTAL.

schmuck /shmuk/ *n. sl.* foolish or contemptible person.

schnapps /shnaaps/ *n.* any of various alcoholic drinks, often flavored.

schnau•zer /shnówzər/ *n.* **1** dog of a German breed with a close wiry coat and heavy whiskers around the muzzle. **2** this breed.

schnit•zel /shnítsəl/ *n.* veal cutlet.

schol•ar /skólər/ *n.* **1** learned person; academic. **2** pupil. □□ **schol'ar•ly** *adj.* **schol' ar•li•ness** *n.*

■ **1** authority, expert, pundit, savant, intellectual. **2** student, schoolboy, schoolgirl.

schol•ar•ly learned, erudite, lettered, scholastic, intellectual.

schol•ar•ship /skólərship/ *n.* **1 a** academic achievement; learning of a high level. **b** standards of a good scholar. **2** payment from the funds of a school, university, local government, etc., to maintain a student in full-time education, awarded on the basis of scholarly achievement. See synonym study at KNOWLEDGE.

■ **1 a** erudition, knowledge, know-how, expertise. **2** grant, endowment, award, fellowship.

scho•las•tic /skəlástik/ *adj.* of or concerning schools, education, etc. □□ **scho•las'ti•cal•ly** *adv.* **scho•las•ti•cism** /–tisizəm/ *n.*

■ *adj.* **1** see ACADEMIC *adj.* 1.

school¹ /skōōl/ • *n.* **1** educational institution. **2 a** buildings used by such an institution. **b** pupils, teachers, etc. **c** time of teaching, or the teaching itself (*no school today*). **3** university division. **4 a** group of artists, etc., whose works share distinctive characteristics. **b** group of people sharing a cause, principle, method, etc. (*school of thought*). • *v.tr.* **1** educate. **2** discipline; train; control. **3** (as **schooled** *adj.*) [foll. by *in*] educated or trained (*schooled in humility*).

■ *n.* **1, 2a, b** (educational) institution; institute, college, university, seminary. **4 a** set, circle, coterie, clique, sect. **b** see PERSUASION 3. • *v.* **1** see EDUCATE 1, 2. **2** teach, mold, shape, form. **3** (**schooled**) drilled, indoctrinated, instructed, tutored.

school² /skōōl/ • *n.* group of fish, porpoises, whales, etc. • *v.intr.* form schools.

school•house /skōōlhows/ *n.* building used as a school.

school•ing /skōōling/ *n.* education, esp. at school.

■ teaching, instruction, tutelage, guidance, training.

school•marm /skōōlmaarm/ *n.* **1** *old-fash.* (also **school•ma'am** /–maam/) female schoolteacher. **2** *colloq.* formal, rule-conscious person. □□ **school'marm•ish** *adj.*

■ □□ **schoolmarmish** prim, straitlaced, fussy.

school•room /skōōlrōōm, –rŏŏm/ *n.* room used for lessons.

school•teach•er /skōōlteechər/ *n.* teacher in a school. □□ **school'teach•ing** *n.*

schoo•ner /skōōnər/ *n.* **1** fore-and-aft rigged ship with two or more masts, the foremast being smaller than the other masts. **2** very tall beer glass.

schuss /shŏŏs/ • *n.* straight downhill run on skis. • *v.intr.* make a schuss.

schwa /shwaa/ *n. Phonet.* **1** indistinct unstressed vowel sound as in *a* mom*e*nt ago. **2** symbol /ə/ representing this.

sci•at•ic /sīátik/ *adj.* of the hip or its nerves.

sci•at•i•ca /sīátikə/ *n.* neuralgia of the hip and thigh.

sci•ence /síəns/ *n.* **1** branch of knowledge involving systematized observation and experimentation. **2 a** systematic and formulated knowledge, esp. on a specified subject. **b** pursuit or principles of this. **3** skillful technique. □ **science fiction** fiction based on imagined future scientific discoveries, frequently dealing with space travel, life on other planets, etc.

■ **3** skill, method, system.

sci•en•tif•ic /sīəntifik/ *adj.* **1 a** (of an investigation, etc.) according to the systematic methods of science. **b** systematic; accurate. **2** used in, engaged in, or relating to science. □□ **sci•en•tif•i•cal•ly** *adv.*

■ **1 b** (well-)organized, controlled, orderly, methodical, precise, accurate, meticulous.

sci•en•tist /sīəntist/ *n.* expert in a science.

sci-fi /sīfī/ *n.* [often *attrib.*] *colloq.* science fiction.

scim•i•tar /simitər, –taar/ *n.* Oriental curved sword.

scin•til•la /sintilə/ *n.* **1** trace. **2** spark.

scin•til•late /sintilayt/ *v.intr.* **1** (esp. as **scintillating** *adj.*) talk cleverly or wittily; be brilliant. **2** sparkle; twinkle. □□ **scin•til•la•tion** /–láyshən/ *n.*

■ **1** (scintillating) witty, clever; see also BRILLIANT *adj.* 2. **2** see TWINKLE *v.*

sci•on /sīən/ *n.* **1** descendant. **2** (also **ci•on**) shoot of a plant, etc., esp. for grafting or planting. **2** descendant.

scis•sors /sizərz/ *n.pl.* (also **pair of scissors** *sing.*) manual cutting instrument having two pivoted blades with finger and thumb holes in the handles.

scle•ro•sis /sklərṓsis/ *n.* **1** abnormal hardening of body tissue (see also ARTERIOSCLEROSIS, ATHEROSCLEROSIS). **2** (in full **mul•ti•ple scle•ro•sis**) chronic and progressive disease of the nervous system. □□ **scle•rot•ic** /sklərótik/ *adj. &n.*

scoff /skof/ • *v.intr.* [usu. foll. by *at*] speak derisively; mock; be scornful. • *n.* mocking words, taunt. □□ **scoff•er** *n.* **scoff•ing•ly** *adv.*

■ *v.* tease, sneer (at), poke fun (at); (*scoff at*) deride, belittle, disparage.

scold /skṓld/ • *v.* **1** *tr.* rebuke. **2** *intr.* find fault noisily. See synonym study at REBUKE. • *n.* *archaic* nagging or grumbling woman. □□ **scold•er** *n.* **scold•ing** *n.*

■ *v.* **1** reprimand, reprove, upbraid, criticize, censure. **2** complain, rail, lecture. • *n.* nag, shrew, termagant, virago.

<hr>

SYNONYM STUDY: **scold**

BERATE, CHIDE, REVILE, UPBRAID, VITUPERATE. A mother might *scold* a child who misbehaves, which means to rebuke in an angry, irritated, and often nagging way, whether or not such treatment is justified. **Chide** is more formal than *scold*, and it usually implies disapproval for specific failings (*she was chided by her teacher for using "less" instead of "fewer"*), while **berate** suggests a prolonged *scolding*, usually aimed at a pattern of behavior or way of life rather than a single misdeed and often combined with scorn or contempt for the person being criticized (*he berated his parents for being too protective and ruining his social life*). **Upbraid** also implies a lengthy expression of displeasure or criticism, but usually with more justification than *scold* and with an eye toward encouraging better behavior in the future (*the tennis coach*

upbraided her players for missing so many serves). **Revile** and **vituperate** are reserved for very strong or even violent displays of anger. To *revile* is to use highly abusive and contemptuous language (*to revile one's opponent in the press*), while **vituperate** connotes even more violence in the attack (*the angry hockey players were held apart by their teammates, but they continued to vituperate each other with the foulest possible language*).

<hr>

sconce /skons/ *n.* wall bracket for candles or electric lights.

scone /skon, skōn/ *n.* biscuitlike cake, esp. served with tea.

scoop /skoop/ • *n.* **1** any of various objects resembling a spoon, esp.. **a** short-handled deep shovel used for transferring grain, sugar, etc. **b** long-handled ladle used for transferring liquids. **c** excavating part of a digging machine, etc. **2** quantity taken up by a scoop. **3** scooping movement. **4** exclusive news item. • *v.tr.* **1** [usu. foll. by *out*] hollow out with or as if with a scoop. **2** [usu. foll. by *up*] lift with or as if with a scoop. **3** precede (a rival newspaper, etc.) with news. □□ **scoop•er** *n.* **scoop•ful** *n.* (*pl.* **–fuls**)

■ *n.* **1 b** ladle, dipper, spoon, bailer. **c** bucket. • *v.* **1** (*scoop out*) gouge out, spoon out, dig out, excavate. **2** (*scoop up*) pick up, gather (up).

scoot /skoot/ *colloq.* *v.intr.* dart away quickly.

scoot•er /skṓotər/ *n.* **1** child's toy consisting of a footboard on two wheels and a long steering handle. **2** (in full **motor scooter**) light two-wheeled motorized bicycle with a shieldlike protective front.

scope /skōp/ *n.* **1** range; opportunity. **2** reach of mental activity, observation, or outlook. See synonym study at RANGE.

■ **1** space, room, leeway, elbowroom, reach, extent.

-scopy /skəpee/ *comb. form* indicating viewing or observation, usu. with an instrument ending in -*scope* (*microscopy*).

scor•bu•tic /skawrbyṓotik/ • *adj.* relating to, resembling, or affected with scurvy. • *n.* person affected with scurvy. □□ **scor•bu•ti•cal•ly** *adv.*

scorch /skawrch/ • *v.* **1** *tr.* a burn or discolor the surface of with dry heat. **b** affect with the sensation of burning. **2** *intr.* become discolored, etc., with heat. **3** *tr.* (as **scorch•ing** *adj.*) *colloq.* **a** (of the weather) very hot. **b** (of criticism, etc.) stringent; harsh. See synonym study at BURN. • *n.* mark made by scorching. □ **scorched earth policy** destroying anything that might be of use to an invading enemy force. □□ **scorch•er** *n.* **scorch•ing•ly** *adv.*

■ *v.* **1, 2** sear, roast; singe, char, blacken. **3** (scorching) **a** torrid, boiling, sweltering. **b** critical, caustic, scathing.

score /skawr/ • *n.* **1 a** number of points made by a player, team, etc., in some games. **b** total number of points, etc., at the end of a game. **2** (*pl.* same or **scores**) twenty or a set of twenty. **3** [in *pl.*] a great many. **4 a** reason or motive (*rejected on the score of absurdity*). **b** topic; subject (*no worries on that score*). **5** *Mus.* a copy of a composition showing all the vocal and instrumental parts arranged one below the other. **b** music for a film or play. **6** notch, line, etc., cut or scratched into a surface. • *v.* **1** *tr.* win or gain (a goal, run, success, etc.). **2** *intr.* **a** make a score in a game. **b** keep the tally of points, runs, etc., in a game. **3** *tr.* mark with notches, incisions, lines, etc. **4** *tr. Mus.* orchestrate or arrange (a piece of music).

■ *n.* **1 a, b** tally, sum (total). **4 a** ground(s), basis, rationale. **b** see SUBJECT *n.* 1. **5 a** music, accompaniment; vocal score, *Mus.* full score. **6** nick, groove, mark, stroke. • *v.* **1 a** see GAIN *v.* 1. **2 b** keep (the) score. **3** scratch, nick, cut, groove.

score•board /skáwrbawrd/ *n.* board for publicly displaying the score in a game or match.

scorn /skawrn/ • *n.* **1** disdain; contempt; derision. **2** object of contempt, etc. (*the scorn of all onlookers*). • *v.tr.* **1** hold in contempt. **2** [often foll. by *to* + infin.] abstain from or refuse to do as unworthy. □□ **scorn'er** *n.* **scorn'ful** *adj.* **scorn'ful•ly** *adv.* **scorn'ful•ness** *n.*

■ *n.* **1** contumely, contemptuousness, deprecation, mockery. • *v.* **1** reject, rebuff, disown, disavow, disregard, ignore, shun. **2** (*scorn to*) see REFRAIN[1].

Scor•pi•o /skáwrpee÷/ *n.* (*pl.* **–os**) **1** constellation and eighth sign of the zodiac (the Scorpion). **2** person born under this sign. □□ **Scor'pi•an** *adj. & n.*

scor•pi•on /skáwrpee÷n/ *n.* **1** arachnid with lobsterlike pincers and a jointed stinging tail. **2** (**the Scor•pi•on**) zodiacal sign or constellation Scorpio.

Scot /skot/ *n.* **1 a** native of Scotland. **b** person of Scottish descent. **2** *hist.* member of a Gaelic people that migrated from Ireland to Scotland around the 6th century.

Scotch /skoch/ • *adj.* var. of SCOTTISH or SCOTS. ■ *n.* **1** var. of SCOTTISH or SCOTS. **2** (in full **Scotch whiskey**) whiskey distilled in Scotland, esp. from malted barley. ¶"Scots" or "Scottish" is preferred to "Scotch" when referring to the people of Scotland

scotch /skoch/ *v.tr.* **1** put an end to; frustrate. **2** *archaic* wound without killing.

Scots /skots/ • *adj.* **1** = SCOTTISH *adj.* **2** in the dialect, accent, etc., of (esp. Lowlands) Scotland. • *n.* **1** = SCOTTISH *n.* **2** form of English spoken in (esp. Lowlands) Scotland.

Scots•man /skótsmən/ *n.* (*pl.* **–men**; *fem.* **Scots•wom•an**, *pl.* **–wom•en**) **1** native of Scotland. **2** person of Scottish descent.

Scot•tie /skótee/ *n. colloq.* **1** (also **Scot'tie dog**) = *Scottish terrier.* **2** Scot.

Scot•tish /skótish/ • *adj.* of or relating to Scotland or its inhabitants. ■ *n.* [prec. by *the*; treated as *pl.*] the people of Scotland (see also SCOTS). □ **Scottish terrier 1** small terrier of a rough-haired short-legged breed. **2** this breed. □□ **Scot'tish•ness** *n.*

scoun•drel /skówndrəl/ *n.* unscrupulous villain; rogue.

■ wretch, good-for-nothing, scapegrace, blackguard, cur.

scour[1] /skowr/ • *v.tr.* **1 a** cleanse or brighten by rubbing, esp. with soap, chemicals, sand, etc. **b** [usu. foll. by *away, off,* etc.] clear (rust, stains, reputation, etc.) by rubbing, hard work, etc. **2** clear out (a pipe, channel, etc.) by flushing through. ■ *n.* scouring; state of being scoured, esp. by a swift water current. □□ **scour'er** *n.*

■ *v.* **1 a** scrub, clean, wash, polish, burnish, buff. **b** (*scour away, off,* etc.) scrub or clean or wash or rub off.

scour[2] /skowr/ *v.* **1** *tr.* hasten over (an area, etc.) searching thoroughly (*scoured the newspaper*). **2** *intr.* range hastily, esp. in search or pursuit.

■ **1** rake, comb, search, hunt through.

scourge /skərj/ • *n.* **1** whip used for punishment, esp. of people. **2** anything regarded as a cause of suffering (*scourge of famine*). • *v.tr.* **1** whip. **2** punish harshly; oppress. □□ **scourg'er** *n.*

■ *n.* **1** lash, horsewhip, *hist.* cat-o'-nine-tails. **2** curse, misfortune, bane, evil, affliction. • *v.* **1** flog, beat, lash. **2** castigate, chastise, discipline, afflict.

scout /skowt/ • *n.* **1** person, esp. a soldier, sent ahead to get information about the enemy's position, strength, etc. **2** = *talent scout.* **3** (**Scout**) Boy Scout or Girl Scout. • *v.* **1** *intr.* act as a scout. **2** *intr.* [foll. by *about, around*] make a search. **3** *tr.* [often foll. by *out*] *colloq.* explore to get information about (territory, etc.). □□ **scout'er** *n.* **scout'ing** *n.*

■ *v.* **1** spy, reconnoiter. **2, 3** look (about or around) (for), hunt (about or around) (for); reconnoiter, investigate.

scout•mas•ter /skówtmastər/ *n.* person in charge of a group of Scouts.

scow /skow/ *n.* flat-bottomed boat for freight, etc.

scowl /skowl/ • *n.* frowning or sullen expression. • *v.intr.* make a scowl or frown. □□ **scowl'er** *n.*

■ *n.* grimace, glare, glower, lower. • *v.* glower, frown, grimace, glare, look daggers, lower.

scrab•ble /skrábəl/ • *v.intr.* scratch or grope to find or collect or hold on to something. ■ *n.* act of scrabbling.

scrag•gly /skráglee/ *adj.* sparse and irregular.

scram /skram/ *v.intr.* (**scrammed, scram•ming**) [esp. in *imper.*] *colloq.* go away.

scram•ble /skrámbəl/ • *v.* **1** *intr.* make one's way over rough ground, rocks, etc., by clambering, crawling, etc. **2** *intr.* [foll. by *for, at*] struggle with competitors (for a thing or share). **3** *intr.* move with difficulty or awkwardly. **4** *tr.* **a** mix together indiscriminately. **b** jumble or muddle. **5** *tr.* cook (beaten eggs). **6** *tr.* make (a broadcast transmission or telephone conversation) unintelligible. **7** *intr.* move hastily. **8** *intr.* (of fighter aircraft or their pilots) take off quickly for action. ■ *n.* **1** act of scrambling. **2** difficult climb or walk. **3** [foll. by *for*] eager struggle or competition. **4** emergency takeoff by fighter aircraft.

■ *v.* **1** climb, scrabble, struggle. **2** jostle, tussle, wrestle, grapple. **3** struggle, flounder, blunder. **4** confuse, shuffle, intermingle. **7** rush, hurry, scamper, run, hasten, race, scurry, scuttle. ● *n.* **1** scrabble, scrimmage, struggle, tussle. **2** struggle, pull. **3** (*scramble for*) contest for, race *or* rush for.

scram•bler /skrámblər/ *n.* device for scrambling telecommunications signals.

scrap¹ /skrap/ ● *n.* **1** small detached piece; fragment. **2** rubbish *or* waste material. **3** [in *pl.*] **a** odds and ends. **b** bits of uneaten food. ● *v.tr.* (**scrapped, scrap•ping**) discard as useless.

■ *n.* **1** bit, shred, remnant; see also FRAGMENT *n.* **2** debris, junk; see also RUBBISH *n.* 1. **3** (*scraps*) **a** remnants, leavings, remains; see also *odds and ends*. **b** leftovers, leavings, scrapings, crumbs. ● *v.* throw away, reject, abandon.

scrap² /skrap/ *colloq.* ● *n.* fight or rough quarrel. ● *v.tr.* (**scrapped, scrap•ping**) [often foll. by *with*] have a scrap. □□ **scrap′per** *n.*

■ *n.* brawl, fracas, fray, scuffle, Donnybrook. ● *v.* fight, brawl, scuffle, wrangle, spar.

scrap•book /skrápbook/ *n.* book of blank pages for sticking cuttings, drawings, etc., in.

scrape /skrayp/ ● *v.* **1** *tr.* **a** move a hard or sharp edge across (a surface), esp. to make smooth. **b** apply (a hard or sharp edge) in this way. **2** *tr.* [foll. by *away, off*, etc.] remove (a stain, projection, etc.) by scraping. **3** *tr.* **a** rub (a surface) harshly against another. **b** scratch or damage by scraping. **4** *a tr.* move with a sound of scraping. **b** *intr.* emit or produce such a sound. **c** *tr.* produce such a sound from. **5** *intr.* move or pass along while almost touching close or surrounding obstacles, etc. (*the car scraped through the narrow lane*). **6** *tr.* just manage to achieve (a living, an examination pass, etc.). **7** *intr.* **a** barely manage. **b** pass an examination, etc., with difficulty. **8** *tr.* amass with difficulty. ● *n.* **1** act or sound of scraping. **2** abrasion. **3** *colloq.* awkward predicament. □□ **scrap′er** *n.*

■ *v.* **2** (*scrape away, off,* etc.) rub off or away, scour off or away, scrub off or away. **3 b** graze, abrade, scuff. **5** squeeze. **6** eke out. **7 a** get by, cope, survive. **b** *colloq.* squeak by or through. **8** gather, garner, save (up), scratch together or up. ● *n.* **2** bruise, scratch; injury. **3** difficulty, quandary, mess, tight spot.

scrap•py /skrápee/ *adj.* (**scrap•pi•er, scrap•pi•est**) **1** consisting of scraps. **2** carelessly arranged or put together. **3 a** argumentative. **b** (of a fighter) wiry and aggressive. □□ **scrap′pi•ly** *adv.* **scrap′pi•ness** *n.*

scratch /skrach/ ● *v.tr.* **1** score or mark the surface of with a sharp object. **2** scrape, esp. with the nails to relieve itching. **3** cancel or strike (out) with a pencil, etc. **4** withdraw (a competitor, candidate, etc.). ● *n.* **1** mark or wound made by scratching. **2** sound of scratching. **3** *colloq.* superficial wound. ● *adj.* **1** collected by chance. **2** heterogeneous (*a scratch crew*). □ **from scratch 1** from the beginning. **2** without help or advantage.

up to scratch up to the required standard. □□ **scratch′er** *n.* **scratch′i•ly** *adv.* **scratch′i•ness** *n.* **scratch′y** *adj.*

■ *v.* **1** gouge, claw. **2** chafe, rub. **3** obliterate, cross out, delete. **4** take out, eliminate, remove. ● *n.* **1** gouge; gash, abrasion, scrape. **3** scrape, graze, scuff, bruise. ● *adj.* random, haphazard, casual, makeshift. □ **from scratch 1** from the start or outset, *colloq.* from the word go. **up to scratch** up to par, adequate, sufficient.

scrawl /skrawl/ ● *v.* write in a hurried untidy way. ● *n.* piece of hurried writing. □□ **scrawl′y** *adj.*

■ *v.* scribble; scratch. ● *n.* scribble, squiggle.

scraw•ny /skráwnee/ *adj.* (**scraw•ni•er, scraw•ni•est**) lean; skinny. □□ **scrawn′i•ness** *n.*

■ bony, spare, reedy, lank(y), scraggy, gaunt.

scream /skreem/ ● *n.* **1** loud, high-pitched piercing cry of fear, pain, etc. **2** act of emitting a scream. **3** *colloq.* irresistibly funny occurrence or person. ● *v.* **1** *intr.* emit a scream. **2** *tr.* speak or sing (words, etc.) in a screaming tone. **3** *intr.* laugh uncontrollably.

■ *n.* **1** shriek, screech, squeal, yowl, wail, caterwaul. **3** *colloq.* card, riot, hoot. ● *v.* **1, 2** shriek, screech, squeal, yowl. **3** roar, howl, guffaw.

screech /skreech/ ● *n.* harsh, high-pitched scream. ● *v.* utter with or make a high pitched noise. □□ **screech′er** *n.* **screech′y** *adj.* (**screech•i•er, screech•i•est**).

■ *n.* see SCREAM *n.* 1. ● *v.* see SCREAM *v.* 1, 2.

screed /skreed/ *n.* long usu. tiresome piece of writing or speech.

screen /skreen/ ● *n.* **1** fixed or movable upright partition for separating, concealing, or sheltering. **2** thing used to conceal or shelter. **3 a** blank surface on which a photographic image is projected. **b** [prec. by *the*] movies or the motion-picture industry. **4** frame with fine wire netting to keep out flies, mosquitoes, etc. **5** large sieve or riddle. ● *v.tr.* **1** shelter; hide. **2 a** show (a film, etc.). **b** broadcast (a television program). **3** sift (grain, coal, etc.) through a screen. □ **screen test** audition for a part in a motion picture. □□ **screen′er** *n.*

■ *n.* **1** divider, wall, shield. **2** shelter, shield; see also VEIL *n.* 3. **3 b** cinema, silver screen. **5** strainer, filter, colander. ● *v.* **1** shield, protect, guard, conceal. **2 b** see BROADCAST *v.* 1a.

screen•play /skreenplay/ *n.* script of a motion picture or television show.

screen•writ•er /skreenrítər/ *n.* person who writes screenplays.

screw /skroo/ ● *n.* **1** thin metal cylinder or cone with a spiral ridge or thread running around the outside (**male screw**) or the inside (**female screw**). **2** (in full **screw propeller**) propeller with twisted blades acting like a screw on the water or air. ● *v.* **1** *tr.* fasten or tighten with a screw or screws. **2** *tr.* turn (a screw). **3** *intr.* twist or turn around like a screw. **4** *tr.* [foll. by *out of*] extort (consent, money, etc.) from (a person). □ **have a screw loose** *colloq.* be slightly crazy. **put the screws on** *colloq.* pressure; intimidate. **screw up 1** contract or contort (one's face, etc.). **2** contract and crush into a tight mass (piece of paper, etc.). **3** summon up (one's courage, etc.). **4** *sl.* bungle.

■ *v.* **2, 3** rotate. **4** (*screw out of*) force from. □ **put the screws on** influence, force, constrain, press, coerce. **screw up 1** twist. **2** crumple. **3** raise, stretch, strain, tap. **4** - ruin, spoil, destroy, botch.

screw•ball /skróobawl/ *sl.* • *n.* **1** *Baseball* pitch thrown with spin opposite that of a curveball. **2** crazy or eccentric person. • *adj.* crazy.

screw•driv•er /skróodrīvər/ *n.* tool with a shaped tip to fit into the head of a screw to turn it.

screw•y /skróo-ee/ *adj.* (**screw•i•er, screw•i•est**) *sl.* **1** crazy or eccentric. **2** absurd. □□ **screw'i•ness** *n.*

scrib•ble /skríbəl/ • *v.* write carelessly or hurriedly. • *n.* scrawl. □□ **scrib'bler** *n.* **scrib'bly** *adj.*

■ *v.* scrawl, scratch. □□ **scribbler** see WRITER 1.

scribe /skrīb/ *n.* **1** ancient or medieval copyist of manuscripts. **2** writer, esp. a journalist.

■ **1** copier, transcriber, *hist.* scrivener; amanuensis, clerk. **2** author; columnist, reporter.

scrim /skrim/ *n.* open-weave fabric for lining or upholstery, etc.

scrim•mage /skrímij/ • *n.* **1** rough or confused struggle; brawl. **2** *Football* a single play from the snap of the ball till the ball is dead. **3** *Sports* practice game. • *v. intr.* engage in a scrimmage. □□ **scrim'mag•er** *n.*

■ *n.* **1** skirmish, scuffle, fray, brouhaha, riot. • *v.* see BRAWL *v.*

scrimp /skrimp/ *v.* **1** *intr.* be sparing or parsimonious. **2** *tr.* use sparingly. □□ **scrimp'y** *adj.*

scrip /skrip/ *n.* **1** provisional certificate of money subscribed to a bank or company, etc., entitling the holder to a formal certificate and dividends. **2** [*collect.*] such certificates.

script /skript/ • *n.* **1** handwriting; written characters. **2** type imitating handwriting. **3** alphabet or system of writing (*Russian script*). **4** text of a play, film, or broadcast. • *v.tr.* write a script for (a motion picture, etc.).

■ *n.* **1** handwriting, (cursive) writing, calligraphy. **4** manuscript, book, screenplay, libretto.

scrip•ture /skrípchər/ *n.* **1** sacred writings. **2** (**Scripture** or **the Scriptures**) the Bible.

script•writ•er /skript-rītər/ *n.* person who writes scripts for a motion picture, broadcast, etc. □□ **script'writ•ing** *n.*

scrod /skrod/ *n.* young cod or haddock, esp. as food.

scroll /skrōl/ • *n.* **1** roll of parchment or paper esp. with writing on it. **2** ornamental design or carving imitating a roll of parchment.

• *v.tr.* move (a display on a computer screen) vertically.

scro•tum /skrótəm/ *n.* (*pl.* **scro•ta** /–tə/ or **scro•tums**) pouch of skin containing the testicles. □□ **scro'tal** *adj.*

scrounge /skrownj/ *colloq.* • *v.* **1** *tr.* obtain (things) illicitly or by cadging. **2** *intr.* search about to find something at no cost. • *n.* act of scrounging. □□ **scroung'er** *n.*

■ *v.* **1** beg, sponge, *sl.* bum. **2** sponge, *sl.* freeload. □□ **scrounger** cadger, parasite, sponger, *sl.* freeloader.

scrub[1] /skrub/ • *v.* (**scrubbed, scrub•bing**) **1** *tr.* rub hard so as to clean. **2** *intr.* use a brush in this way. **3** *tr. colloq.* scrap or cancel. **4** *tr.* use a chemical process to remove impurities from (gas, etc.). • *n.* scrubbing or being scrubbed. □□ **scrub'ber** *n.*

■ *v.* **1, 2** scour, scrape. **3** call off, abort, drop, terminate, give up.

scrub[2] /skrub/ *n.* **1 a** brushwood or stunted forest growth. **b** area of land covered with this. **2** *Sports colloq.* team or player not of the first class. □□ **scrub'by** *adj.*

scruff /skruf/ *n.* back of the neck.

scruff•y /skrúfee/ *adj.* (**scruff•i•er, scruff•i•est**) *colloq.* shabby; slovenly; untidy. □□ **scruff'i•ly** *adv.* **scruff'i•ness** *n.*

scrump•tious /skrúmpshəs/ *adj. colloq.* **1** delicious. **2** giving pleasure; delightful. □□ **scrump'tious•ly** *adv.* **scrump'tious•ness** *n.*

■ **1** see DELICIOUS.

scrunch /skrunch/ • *v.* **1** make or become crushed or crumpled. **2** make or cause to make a crunching sound. • *n.* act or instance of scrunching.

scru•ple /skróopəl/ • *n.* [in *sing.* or *pl.*] moral concern; doubt caused by this. See synonym study at QUALM. • *v.intr.* [foll. by *to*] be reluctant because of scruples.

■ *n.* qualm, misgiving, doubt, twinge of conscience. • *v.* (*scruple to*) balk at, hesitate to, have (any) misgivings *or* qualms about *or* over.

scru•pu•lous /skróopyələs/ *adj.* **1** conscientious or thorough. **2** careful to avoid doing wrong. □□ **scru•pu•los•i•ty** /–lósitee/ *n.* **scru'pu•lous•ly** *adv.* **scru'pu•lous•ness** *n.*

■ **1** careful, cautious, meticulous, exacting, precise. **2** ethical, honorable, upstanding, moral, principled.

scru•ti•nize /skróot'nīz/ *v.tr.* look closely at; examine with close scrutiny. □□ **scru'ti•niz•er** *n.*

■ analyze, dissect, investigate, probe, study.

scru•ti•ny /skróot'nee/ *n.* (*pl.* **–nies**) **1** critical gaze. **2** close examination.

■ **2** analysis, investigation, probing, study; check.

scu•ba /skóobə/ *n.* (*pl.* **scu•bas**) gear that provides an air supply from a portable tank for swimming underwater (acronym for *self-contained underwater breathing apparatus*).

scuff /skuf/ • *v.* **1** *tr.* graze or brush against. **2** *tr.* mark or wear down (shoes) in this way. **3** *intr.* walk with dragging feet; shuffle. • *n.* mark of scuffing.

■ *v.* **2** see SCRAPE *v.* 3b. **3** stumble, drag one's feet. • *n.* see SCRAPE *n.* 2.

scuf•fle /skúfəl/ • *n.* confused struggle or disorderly fight at close quarters. • *v.intr.* engage in a scuffle.

scull /skul/ • *n.* **1** either of a pair of small oars used by a single rower. **2** oar placed over the stern of a boat to propel it, usu. by a twisting motion. **3** racing rowboat. • *v.tr.* propel (a boat) with sculls.
■ *n.* **1, 2** paddle, sweep. • *v.* see PADDLE *v.* 1.

scul•ler•y /skúlərее/ *n.* (*pl.* **-ies**) small kitchen or room at the back of a house for washing dishes, etc.

sculpt /skulpt/ *v.* (also **sculp**) sculpture.

sculp•tor /skúlptər/ *n.* (*fem.* **sculp•tress** /-tris/) artist who makes sculptures.

sculp•ture /skúlpchər/ • *n.* **1** art of making three-dimensional or relief forms. **2** work of sculpture. • *v.* **1** *tr.* represent in sculpture. **2** *intr.* practice sculpture. □□ **sculp′tur•al** *adj.* **sculp′tur•al•ly** *adv.* **sculp′tur•esque′** *adj.*
■ *n.* **2** statue, statuette, relief; (*sculptures*) marbles. • *v.* **1** sculpt, model, chisel, carve, cast, form, fashion.

scum /skum/ • *n.* **1** layer of dirt, froth, etc., at the top of liquid. **2** most worthless part of something. **3** *colloq.* worthless person or group. • *v.* (**scummed, scum•ming**) **1** *tr.* remove scum from; skim. **2** *tr.* be or form a scum on. **3** *intr.* (of a liquid) develop scum. □□ **scum′my** *adj.* (**scum•mi•er, scum•mi•est**) *adj.*
■ *n.* **1** see DIRT 1. **3** see RIFF-RAFF. □□ **scummy** see *filthy* (FILTH).

scum•bag /skúmbag/ *n. sl.* worthless despicable person.

scup•per /skúpər/ *n.* hole at the edge of a boat's deck to allow water to run off.

scur•ri•lous /skórilas, skúr-/ *adj.* grossly or indecently abusive. □□ **scur′ril•ous•ly** *adv.* **scur′ril•ous•ness** *n.*
■ foulmouthed, vulgar, obscene; vituperative, offensive, insulting.

scur•ry /skúree, skúree/ • *v.intr.* (**-ries, -ried**) run or move hurriedly; scamper. • *n.* (*pl.* **-ries**) **1** act or sound of scurrying. **2** bustle; haste.
■ *v.* dash, scramble, dart, fly, race, sprint. • *n.* **2** rush, hustle; see also FLURRY *n.* 3.

scur•vy /skúrvee/ *n.* disease caused by a deficiency of vitamin C.

scut•tle¹ /skút′l/ *n.* receptacle for carrying and holding a small supply of coal.

scut•tle² /skút′l/ • *v.intr.* **1** scurry. **2** run away; flee from danger or difficulty. • *n.* hurried gait.

scut•tle³ /skút′l/ • *n.* hole with a lid in a ship's deck or side. • *v.tr.* let water into (a ship) to sink it.

scut•tle•butt /skút′lbut/ *n.* **1** water cask on the deck of a ship, for drinking from. **2** *colloq.* rumor; gossip.

scuz•zy /skúzee/ *adj. sl.* abhorrent or disgusting.

scythe /sīth/ • *n.* mowing and reaping implement with a long curved blade swung over the ground by a long pole with two short handles projecting from it. • *v.tr.* cut with a scythe.

SD *abbr.* South Dakota (in official postal use).

S.Dak. *abbr.* South Dakota.

SE *abbr.* **1** southeast. **2** southeastern.

Se *symb. Chem.* selenium.

sea /see/ *n.* **1** expanse of salt water that covers most of the earth's surface. **2** any part of this. **3** particular (usu. named) tract of salt water partly or wholly enclosed by land (*North Sea*). **4** large inland lake (*Sea of Galilee*). **5** waves of the sea; their motion or state (*choppy sea*). **6** [foll. by *of*] vast quantity or expanse. □ **at sea 1** in a ship on the sea. **2** (also **all at sea**) perplexed; confused. **sea horse** small upright marine fish with a head like that of a horse. **sea legs** ability to keep one's balance and avoid seasickness when at sea. **sea lion** large-eared seal.
■ **1** ocean, high seas(s), blue water. **5** see WAVE *n.* 1, 2. **6** plethora, abundance, surfeit, profusion. □ **at sea 2** disoriented, bewildered, baffled; adrift.

sea•bed /séebed/ *n.* ground under the sea; ocean floor.

sea•board /séebawrd/ *n.* **1** seashore or coastal region. **2** the line of a coast.

sea•borg•i•um /seebáwrgeeəm/ *n. Chem.* artificially produced element, atomic number 106. ¶Symb.: **Sg.**

sea•coast /séekōst/ *n.* land adjacent to the sea.

sea•far•er /séefairər/ *n.* **1** sailor. **2** traveler by sea. □□ **sea′far•ing** *adj. & n.*

sea•food /séefood/ *n.* edible sea fish or shellfish.

sea•go•ing /séegōing/ *adj.* (of ships) fit for crossing the sea.

sea•gull /séegul/ *n.* = GULL¹.

seal¹ /seel/ • *n.* **1** piece of wax, lead, paper, etc., with a stamped design, attached to a document as a guarantee of authenticity or security. **2** engraved piece of metal, gemstone, etc., for stamping a design on a seal. **3** substance or device to close a gap. **4** act or gesture regarded as a guarantee. **5** decorative adhesive stamp. • *v.tr.* **1** close securely. **2** stamp or fasten with a seal. **3** fix a seal to. **4** certify as correct with a seal or stamp. **5** confine or fasten securely. □□ **seal′a•ble** *adj.*
■ *n.* **1** authentication, confirmation, verification. • *v.* **1** seal up, close up, zip up, plug (up), stop (up); cork. **4** authenticate, confirm, verify.

seal² /seel/ • *n.* fish-eating amphibious sea mammal with flippers and webbed feet. • *v.intr.* hunt for seals. □□ **seal′er** *n.*

seal•ant /séelant/ *n.* material for sealing

seal•skin /séelskin/ *n.* **1** skin or prepared fur of a seal. **2** garment made from this.

seam /seem/ • *n.* **1** line where two edges join, esp. of cloth or boards. **2** fissure between parallel edges. **3** wrinkle. **4** stratum of coal, etc. • *v.tr.* join with a seam. □□ **seam′er** *n.* **seam′less** *adj.*
■ *n.* **1** junction, juncture, join, joint. **3** scar, cicatrice. **4** lode, vein, bed, layer.

sea•man /séemən/ *n.* (*pl.* **-men**) sailor, esp. one below the rank of officer. □□ **sea′man•like** *adj.* **sea′man•ly** *adj.*
■ **1** see SAILOR.

sea•man•ship /séemənship/ *n.* skill in managing a ship or boat.

seam•stress /séemstris/ *n.* woman who sews professionally.

seam•y /séemee/ *adj.* (**seam•i•er, seam•i•est**) unpleasant; disreputable. □□ **seam′i•ness** *n.*

■ sordid, nasty, dark, shameful, squalid.

se•ance /sáyons/ *n.* (also **séance**) meeting at which spiritualists attempt to make contact with the dead.

sea•plane /séeplayn/ *n.* aircraft designed to take off from and land and float on water.

sea•port /séepawrt/ *n.* town with a harbor for seagoing ships.

sear /seer/ *v.tr.* **1 a** scorch; cauterize; brand. **b** (as **searing** *adj.*) burning (*searing pain*). **2** brown (meat) quickly at a high temperature. See synonym study at BURN.

search /sərch/ • *v.* **1** *tr.* look through or go over thoroughly to find something. **2** *tr.* examine or feel over (a person) to find anything concealed. **3** *tr.* **a** probe. **b** examine or question (one's mind, conscience, etc.) thoroughly. **4** *intr.* [often foll. by *for*] make a search or investigation. **5** *intr.* (as **searching** *adj.*) (of an examination) thorough. • *n.* **1** searching. **2** investigation. □□ **search′a•ble** *adj.* **search′er** *n.* **search′ing•ly** *adv.*

■ *v.* **1, 3** search through, examine, scrutinize, check. **2** see FRISK *v.* **4** look (about *or* around), cast about, seek. **5** (**searching**) see THOROUGH 2. • *n.* **1** hunt, pursuit; see also QUEST *n.* **2** analysis, exploration, examination, scrutiny, probe, inquiry. □□ **searchingly** penetratingly, piercingly, intently, deeply.

search•light /sórchlīt/ *n.* **1** powerful outdoor electric light with a concentrated directional beam. **2** beam from this.

■ spotlight, arc light, spot; ray, shaft.

sea•scape /séeskayp/ *n.* picture or view of the sea.

sea•shell /séeshel/ *n.* shell of a saltwater mollusk.

sea•shore /séeshawr/ *n.* land next to the sea.

sea•sick /séesik/ *adj.* nauseated from the motion of the sea. □□ **sea′sick•ness** *n.*

sea•side /séesīd/ *n.* seacoast, esp. as a vacation resort.

sea•son /séezən/ • *n.* **1** each of the four divisions of the year (spring, summer, autumn, and winter). **2** time of year characterized by climatic or other features (*dry season*). **3** time of year when something is plentiful, active, etc. **4** proper or suitable time. • *v.* **1** *tr.* flavor (food) with salt, herbs, etc. **2** *tr. & intr.* **a** make or become suitable or in the desired condition, esp. by exposure to the air or weather. **b** (usu. as **seasoned** *adj.*) make or become experienced. □ **in season 1** (of food) available in plenty and in good condition. **2** (of an animal) in heat. **3** timely. **season ticket** ticket entitling the holder to any number of journeys, admittances, etc., in a given period. □□ **sea′son•er** *n.*

■ *n.* **1–3** period. • *v.* **1** spice, salt, flavor, *colloq.* pep up. **2 a** ripen, age, condition, mellow. **b** (**seasoned**) long-standing, practiced, well-versed. □ **in season 1** ripe, ready; seasoned; plentiful. **3** see TIMELY.

sea•son•a•ble /séezənəbəl/ *adj.* **1** suitable to or usual in the season. **2** opportune. **3** meeting the needs of the occasion. See synonym study at TIMELY. □□ **sea′son•a•ble•ness** *n.* **sea′son•a•bly** *adv.*

■ **1** appropriate, apt, opportune, timely, fitting. **2, 3** appropriate, suitable, apt, proper.

sea•son•al /séezənəl/ *adj.* of, depending on, or varying with the season. □□ **sea′son•al•ly** *adv.*

sea•son•ing /séezəning/ *n.* spice or flavoring added to food.

seat /seet/ • *n.* **1** thing made or used for sitting on. **2** buttocks. **3** part of a garment covering the buttocks. **4** part of a chair, etc., on which the sitter's weight directly rests. **5** place for one person to sit. **6** *Polit.* right to occupy a seat, esp. as a member of Congress, etc. **7** site or location of something specified (*seat of learning*). • *v.tr.* **1** cause to sit. **2 a** provide seating for. **b** provide with seats. **3** (as **seated** *adj.*) sitting. **4** put or fit in position. □ **seat belt** belt securing a person in the seat of a car, aircraft, etc.

■ *n.* **1** place, chair; bench, sofa, settee, throne, saddle. **2** bottom, posterior, rump. **6** place, position; incumbency. **7** focus, base, center, heart, hub. • *v.* **2** hold, accommodate, contain, have room *or* capacity *or* space for. **3** (**seated**) sitting down; sedentary. **4** locate, position.

sea•ward /séewərd/ • *adv.* (also **sea′wards** /-wərdz/) toward the sea. • *adj.* going or facing toward the sea. • *n.* such a direction or position.

sea•way /séeway/ *n.* **1** inland waterway open to seagoing ships. **2** ship's progress. **3** ship's path across the sea.

sea•weed /séeweed/ *n.* algae growing in the sea.

sea•wor•thy /séewərthee/ *adj.* (esp. of a ship) fit to put to sea. □□ **sea′wor•thi•ness** *n.*

se•ba•ceous /sibáyshəs/ *adj.* of or relating to oily secretions or fat.

seb•or•rhe•a /sébəreeə/ *n.* excessive discharge from the sebaceous glands.

SEC *abbr.* Securities and Exchange Commission.

Sec. *abbr.* secretary.

sec /sek/ *n. colloq.* (in phrases) a second (of time).

sec. *abbr.* second(s).

se•cant /séekant, -kənt/ *Math. n.* **1** line cutting a curve at one or more points. **2** the ratio of the hypotenuse to the shorter side adjacent to an acute angle (in a right triangle). ¶Abbr.: **sec**.

se•cede /siseed/ *v.intr.* [usu. foll. by *from*] withdraw formally from an organization. □□ **se•ced′er** *n.*

■ break away; (**secede from**) abandon, quit, leave.

se•ces•sion /siséshən/ *n.* **1** act or instance of seceding. **2** (**Secession**) *hist.* the withdrawal of eleven southern states from the US Union in 1860–61, leading to the Civil War. □□ **se•ces′sion•ism** *n.* **se•ces′sion•ist** *n.*

■ **1** withdrawal, defection, break, breaking, separation.

se•clude /siklóod/ *v.tr.* [also *refl.*] **1** keep (a person or place) away from company. **2** (esp. as **secluded** *adj.*) hide or screen from view.

■ **1** see SEGREGATE 1. **2** (**secluded**) private, separated, isolated; off the beaten track.

se•clu•sion /siklóozhən/ *n.* **1** secluded state; retirement. **2** secluded place. □□ **se•clu′sion•ist** *n.* **se•clu′sive** /-klóosiv/ *adj.*

■ **1** privacy, separation, isolation, loneliness, solitude. **2** see RETREAT *n.* 3.

sec•ond¹ /sékənd/ • *n.* **1** position in a sequence corresponding to that of the number 2 in the sequence 1–2. **2** runner-up. **3** second (and next to lowest) in a sequence of gears. **4** another person or thing in addition to one previously mentioned or considered. **5** [in *pl.*] inferior goods. **6** [in *pl.*] *colloq.* a second helping. **7** assistant to a boxer, etc. • *adj.* **1** next after first. **2** additional. **3** subordinate; inferior. • *v.tr.* support; back up. □ **second-guess** *colloq.* judge or criticize with hindsight. **second lieutenant** lowest-ranked commissioned officer of the army, air force, or marines. **second nature** acquired tendency that has become instinctive (*is second nature to him*). **second person** *Gram.* see PERSON. **second-rate** mediocre; inferior. **second string** alternative available in case of need. **second thoughts** revised opinion or resolution. **second wind** **1** recovery of normal breathing during exercise after initial breathlessness. **2** renewed energy to continue an effort.

■ *n.* **5** (*seconds*) rejects. • *adj.* **2** further, other, subsequent. **3** next. • *v.* supplement, aid, help, assist.

sec•ond² /sékənd/ *n.* **1** sixtieth of a minute of time or angular distance. ¶Symb.: ″. **2** *colloq.* very short time (*wait a minute!*). **3** second hand (as in some watches and clocks, recording seconds).

sec•ond•ar•y /sékənderee/ • *adj.* **1** coming after or next below what is primary. **2** derived from or depending on or supplementing what is primary. **3** (of education, a school, etc.) for those who have had primary education, usu. from 11 to 18 years. • *n.* (*pl.* **-ies**) secondary thing. □□ **sec•ond•ar′i•ly** *adv.*

■ *adj.* **1** subsidiary, ancillary, subordinate, inferior, minor. **2** derivative, secondhand, unoriginal.

sec•ond•hand /sékəndhánd/ • *adj.* **1 a** (of goods) having had a previous owner; not new. **b** (of a store, etc.) where such goods can be bought. **2** (of information, etc.) accepted on another's authority and not from original investigation. • *adv.* **1** on a secondhand basis. **2** indirectly.

■ *adj.* **1 a** used, old, worn, *colloq.* hand-me-down.

sec•ond•ly /sékəndlee/ *adv.* **1** furthermore; in the second place. **2** as a second item.

se•cre•cy /séekrisee/ *n.* **1** keeping of secrets as a fact, habit, or faculty. **2** state in which all information is withheld.

■ mystery, concealment, confidentiality, stealth, secretiveness, surreptitiousness, covertness.

se•cret /séekrit/ • *adj.* **1** kept or meant to be kept private, unknown, or hidden. **2** acting or operating secretly. • *n.* **1** thing to be kept secret. **2** thing known only to a few. **3** valid but not commonly known or recognized method of achieving or maintaining something (*what's their secret?*). □ **secret agent** spy. **Secret Service** branch of the US Treasury Department charged with apprehending counterfeitors and with providing security for the president and certain other officials and their families. □□ **se′cret•ly** *adv.*

■ *adj.* **1** concealed, classified. **2** confidential, private, undercover. • *n.* **1, 2** private or confidential matter or affair. □□ **secretly** surreptitiously, quietly, privately, covertly.

sec•re•tar•i•at /sékritáireeət/ *n.* administrative office or department, esp. a governmental one.

sec•re•tar•y /sékriteree/ *n.* (*pl.* **-ies**) **1** employee who assists with correspondence, records, makes appointments, etc. **2** official appointed by a society, etc., to conduct its correspondence, keep its records, etc. □□ **sec•re•tar′i•al** /-táireeəl/ *adj.*

se•crete¹ /sikréet/ *v.tr. Biol.* (of a cell, organ, etc.) produce by secretion. □□ **se•cre′tor** *n.*

se•crete² /sikréet/ *v.tr.* conceal; put into hiding.

■ hide, cache, bury.

se•cre•tion /sikréeshən/ *n.* **1** *Biol.* a process by which substances are produced and discharged from a cell for a function in the organism or for excretion **b** secreted substance. **2** act of instance of concealing.

■ **1** secreting, release, oozing, seeping, seepage, discharge.

se•cre•tive /séekritiv, sikrée-/ *adj.* inclined to make secrets; uncommunicative. □□ **se′cre•tive•ly** *adv.* **se′cre•tive•ness** *n.*

■ cryptic, mysterious, enigmatic; conspiratorial, furtive; reticent, silent, closemouthed, taciturn.

sect /sekt/ *n.* **1** group subscribing to (sometimes unorthodox) religious, political, or philosophical doctrines. **2** religious denomination.

■ **1** denomination, body, cult, persuasion.

sec•tar•i•an /sektáireeən/ • *adj.* **1** of or concerning a sect. **2** bigoted or narrow-minded in following the doctrines of one's sect. • *n.* **1** member of a sect. **2** bigot. □□ **sec•tar′i•an•ism** *n.*

■ *adj.* **1** partisan, factional, cliquish, usu. *derog.* clannish. **2** parochial, narrow, narrow-minded, limited, insular. • *n.* **1** adherent, member, votary, cultist. **2** dogmatist, fanatic, zealot, extremist.

sec•tion /sékshən/ • *n.* **1** part cut off or separated from something. **2** each of the parts into which a thing is divided (actually or conceptually) or divisible or out of which a structure can be fitted together. **3** distinct group or subdivision of a larger body of people. **4** esp. *Surgery* separation by cutting.

5 a cutting of a solid by a plane. **b** resulting figure. See synonym study at FRAGMENT. • *v.tr.* arrange in or divide into sections.

■ *n.* **1** fraction, segment, portion, slice. **2** segment, portion, fraction, division; sample, cross section; stage. **3** part, division, department, branch, sector. • *v.* cut (up), segment, split.

sec·tion·al /sékshənəl/ *adj.* **1** made in sections. **2** local rather than general. □□ **sec'tion·al·ism** *n.* **sec'tion·al·ist** *n. & adj.* **sec'tion·al·ize** *v.tr.* **sec'tion·al·ly** *adv.*

sec·tor /séktər/ *n.* **1** distinct part of an enterprise, society, the economy, etc. **2** *Mil.* subdivision of an area. **3** plane figure enclosed by two radii of a circle, ellipse, etc., and the arc between them.

sec·u·lar /sékyələr/ *adj.* **1** not spiritual nor sacred. **2** (of education, etc.) not concerned with religion nor religious belief. □□ **sec'u·lar·ism** *n.* **sec'u·lar·ize** *v.tr.* **sec·u·lar·i·za'tion** *n.* **sec'u·lar·ly** *adv.*

■ *adj.* **1** worldly, terrestrial, mundane, temporal.

se·cure /sikyŏŏr/ • *adj.* **1** untroubled by danger or fear. **2** safe. **3** reliable; certain not to fail. **4** fixed or fastened. • *v.tr.* **1** make secure or safe. **2** fasten, close, or confine securely. **3** succeed in obtaining. See synonym study at GET. □□ **se·cur'a·ble** *adj.* **se·cure'ly** *adv.* **se·cure'ment** *n.*

■ *adj.* **1** unthreatened, protected, sheltered, safe. **2** shielded, protected, unexposed; impregnable. **3** safe, good, solid, healthy. **4** firm, steady, stable. • *v.* **1** see FORTIFY 1. **2** make fast, fix, affix, attach, anchor. **3** get (hold of), come by, acquire.

se·cu·ri·ty /sikyŏŏritee/ *n.* (*pl.* **–ties**) **1** secure condition or feeling. **2** thing that guards or guarantees. **3** thing deposited or pledged as a guarantee of a loan, etc. **4** [often in *pl.*] certificate attesting credit or the ownership of stock, bonds, etc.

■ **1** confidence, certainty, assurance. **2** refuge, sanctuary, asylum, shelter. **3** collateral, deposit, pledge, insurance.

secy. *abbr.* secretary.

se·dan /sidán/ *n.* enclosed automobile for four or more people.

se·date[1] /sidáyt/ *adj.* tranquil and dignified; equable; serious. □□ **se·date'ly** *adv.* **se·date'ness** *n.*

■ composed, serene, peaceful, calm; dignified.

se·date[2] /sidáyt/ *v.tr.* put under sedation.

se·da·tion /sidáyshən/ *n.* state of rest or sleep, produced by a sedative drug.

sed·a·tive /sédətiv/ • *n.* calming drug, influence, etc. • *adj.* calming; soothing; inducing sleep.

■ *n.* narcotic, tranquilizer, opiate, sleeping pill, soporific. • *adj.* narcotic, tranquilizing, relaxing.

sed·en·tar·y /séd'nteree/ *adj.* **1** sitting. **2** (of work, etc.) done while sitting and with little physical exercise.

■ **1** seated. **2** stationary, immobile, deskbound; seated.

sedge /sej/ *n.* grasslike plant usu. growing in wet areas. □□ **sedg'y** *adj.*

sed·i·ment /sédimənt/ *n.* **1** matter that settles to the bottom of a liquid; dregs. **2** *Geol.* matter deposited by water or wind. □□ **sed·i·men·ta·ry** /-méntəree/ *adj.* **sed·i·men·ta'tion** *n.*

■ **1** lees, deposit, grounds, remains, residue.

se·di·tion /sidíshən/ *n.* conduct or speech inciting to rebellion. □□ **se·di'tious** *adj.* **se·di'tious·ly** *adv.*

■ **1** agitation, rabble-rousing, insubordination; fomentation, incitement. □□ **seditious** rebellious, mutinous, riotous, treacherous, dissident, disloyal; inflammatory, rabble-rousing.

se·duce /sidŏŏs, –dyŏŏs/ *v.tr.* **1** entice into sexual activity or wrongdoing. **2** tempt (*seduced by the smell of coffee*). □□ **se·duc'er** *n.* **se·duc'i·ble** *adj.* **se·duc·tion** /sidúkshən/ *n.* **se·duc'tive** *adj.* **se·duc'tive·ly** *adv.* **se·duc'tress** /sidúktris/ *n.*

■ **1** defile, deflower, violate, ravish; vamp; dishonor. **2** lure, entice, attract, allure. □□ **seducer** rake, libertine, roué, lecher. **seductive** alluring, attractive, tempting, enticing, inviting, tantalizing, appealing, sexy.

sed·u·lous /séjə ləs/ *adj.* persevering; diligent; painstaking. See synonym study at BUSY. □□ **se·du·li·ty** /sidŏŏlitee, –dyŏŏ–/ *n.* **sed'u·lous·ly** *adv.* **sed'u·lous·ness** *n.*

se·dum /séedəm/ *n.* plant with fleshy leaves and star-shaped yellow, pink, or white flowers.

see[1] /see/ *v.* (*past* **saw** /saw/; *past part.* **seen** /seen/) **1** *tr.* discern by use of the eyes. **2** *intr.* have or use the power of discerning objects with the eyes. **3** *tr.* understand. **4** *tr.* learn; find out. **5** *tr.* meet and recognize. **6** *tr.* **a** meet socially. **b** meet regularly as a boyfriend or girlfriend. **7 a** *intr.* wait until one knows more. **b** *tr.* consider; decide (on). **8** *tr.* experience. **9** *intr.* ensure. **10** *tr.* **a** (in gambling, esp. poker) equal (a bet). **b** equal the bet of (a player). □ **see about 1** attend to. **2** consider; look into. **see through 1** not be deceived by; detect the true nature of. **2** penetrate visually. **see-through** *adj.* (esp. of clothing) translucent. **see to** = *see about.*

■ **1** perceive, note, notice, mark, spot, watch, witness. **3** comprehend, apprehend, appreciate. **4** determine, ascertain, establish; investigate, study. **6 a** socialize with, spend time with. **b** court, woo, *colloq.* go out with. **7 a** think, reflect, decide, consider. **b** think (about), mull over, ponder. **8** see MEET *v.* 8, EXPERIENCE *v.* 1. **9** see to it, attend to, make provision for; assure. □ **see about 1** see to, look after, take care of. **2** give some thought to; investigate, study. **see through 1** perceive. **see-through** sheer, diaphanous, gauzy.

see[2] /see/ *n.* office or jurisdiction of a bishop or archbishop.

seed /seed/ • *n.* **1 a** flowering plant's unit of reproduction capable of developing into another such plant. **b** seeds collectively. **2** semen; milt. **3** fundamental or underlying cause. **4** descendants. • *v.* **1** *tr.* place seeds in. **2** *intr.* sow seeds. **3** *intr.* produce or drop seed. □ go (or run) to seed 1 cease flowering as seed develops. 2 become degenerate; unkempt, etc. seed money money allocated to initiate a project. □□ seed'less adj.

■ n. 1 a grain, spore, kernel, pit, bulb, ovum, germ, Biol. egg. 2 spermatozoa, sperm; (soft) roe. 3 germ, beginning, root; reason, basis; grounds. 4 offspring, children, progeny. • v. 1 sow, plant. □ go (or run) to seed 2 become dilapidated, decay, decline, deteriorate.

seed•ling /seedling/ n. plant raised from seed.

seed•y /seedee/ adj. (seed•i•er, seed•i•est) 1 full of seed. 2 going to seed. 3 shabby looking. □□ seed'i•ly adv. seed'i•ness n.

■ 3 dilapidated, worn (out), mangy, grubby.

see•ing /seeing/ conj. considering that; inasmuch as; because.

■ conj. in view of (the fact that), whereas, in the light of.

seek /seek/ v. (past and past part. sought /sawt/) 1 a tr. make a search or inquiry for. b intr. [foll. by for, after] make a search or inquiry. 2 tr. a try or want to find or get. b ask for (sought help from him). 3 tr. endeavor. □□ seek'er n. [also in comb.].

■ 1a, 2a look for, be after, hunt (for). 2 b request, beg; demand. 3 attempt, try, undertake.

seem /seem/ v.intr. 1 give the impression of being (seems ridiculous). 2 appear to be.

■ 1 appear, look; sound, feel, have (all) the hallmarks or earmarks of. 2 look; see also FEEL v. 7.

seem•ing /seeming/ adj. apparent but perhaps not real (with seeming sincerity). See synonym study at OSTENSIBLE. □□ seem'ing•ly adv.

■ see APPARENT 2, OUTWARD 1, 3. □ seemingly evidently; apparently, outwardly, ostensibly superficially, falsely.

seem•ly /seemlee/ adj. (seem•li•er, seem•li•est) conforming to propriety or good taste; decorous; suitable. □□ seem'li•ness n.

■ proper, fitting, appropriate, becoming; comme il faut; decent, dignified.

seen past part. of SEE[1].

seep /seep/ v.intr. ooze out; percolate slowly. □□ seep'age n.

seer /seer, seer/ n. prophet; visionary.

■ soothsayer, fortune-teller, oracle, augur, prophesier.

seer•suck•er /seersukər/ n. material of linen, cotton, etc., with a puckered surface.

see•saw /seesaw/ • n. 1 a long plank balanced on a central support for children to sit on at each end and move up and down by pushing the ground with their feet. b game played on this. 2 up-and-down or to-and-fro motion. • v.intr. 1 play on a seesaw. 2 move up and down as on a seesaw. 3 vacillate in policy, emotion, etc. • adj. & adv. with up-and-down or backward-and-forward motion.

■ v. 3 teeter, waver, vary, fluctuate.

seethe /seeth/ v.intr. 1 boil; bubble over. 2 be very agitated, esp. with anger. □□ seeth'ing•ly adv.

■ 1 simmer, foam. 2 foam at the mouth, fume, burn with anger, rage, rant (and rave).

seg•ment /segmənt/ • n. 1 each part into which a thing is or can be divided. 2 Geom. part of a figure cut off by a line or plane intersecting it, esp.: a part of a circle enclosed between an arc and a chord. b part of a line included between two points. c part of a sphere cut off by any plane not passing through the center. See synonym study at FRAGMENT. • v. (usu. /-mént/) divide into segments. □□ seg•men•tal /-mént'l/ adj. seg•men•tal•ly /-mént'lee/ adv. seg•men•tar•y /ségməntairee/ adj. seg•men•ta•tion /-táyshən/ n.

■ n. 1 section, division, portion; component, element. • v. separate, part, split, fragment.

seg•re•gate /ségrigayt/ v.tr. 1 isolate. 2 enforce racial segregation on (persons) or in (a community, etc.). □□ seg're•ga•ble adj. seg're•ga•tive adj.

■ 1 partition, seclude, sequester, set apart, compartmentalize, exclude, ostracize.

seg•re•ga•tion /ségrigáyshən/ n. 1 enforced separation of racial groups in a community, etc. 2 act or instance of segregating; state of being segregated. □□ seg•re•ga'tion•al adj. seg•re•ga'tion•ist n. & adj.

■ 1 jim crowism, apartheid. 2 separation, segmentation, partition, seclusion, exclusion; ostracism.

se•gue /ségway/ esp. Mus. • v.intr. (se•gues, se•gued, se•gue•ing) go on without a pause. • n. uninterrupted transition from one song or melody to another.

seine /sayn/ n. fishing net for encircling fish, usu. hauled ashore.

seis•mic /sízmik/ adj. of or relating to an earthquake or earthquakes. □□ seis'mal adj. seis'mi•cal adj. seis'mi•cal•ly adv.

seis•mo•graph /sízməgraf/ n. instrument that records the force, direction, etc., of earthquakes. □□ seis•mo•graph'ic adj. seis•mo•graph'i•cal adj.

seis•mol•o•gy /sizmóləjee/ n. the study of earthquakes. □□ seis•mo•log'i•cal /-məlójikəl/ adj. seis•mo•log'i•cal•ly adv. seis•mol'o•gist n.

seize /seez/ v. 1 tr. take hold of forcibly or suddenly. 2 tr. take possession of forcibly. 3 tr. a take possession of (contraband goods, etc.) by warrant or legal right; confiscate; impound. b arrest or apprehend (a person). 4 tr. affect suddenly. 5 tr. take advantage of (an opportunity). 6 tr. comprehend quickly or clearly. 7 intr. a take hold forcibly or suddenly. b take advantage eagerly. 8 intr. (of a moving part in a machine) become jammed. □□ seiz'a•ble adj. seiz'er n. sei'zure n.

■ 1 grab, grasp, snatch. 2 capture, appropriate, commandeer; see also GRAB v. 2. 3 a confiscate, capture, impound. b capture, catch, take into custody. 4 catch, transfix, stop, afflict, beset. 5 make the most of, exploit. 6 see REALIZE 2. 8 stop, stick, freeze (up).

sel•dom /séldəm/ • adv. rarely; not often. • adj. rare.

■ *adv.* infrequently, hardly ever, very occasionally. • *adj.* see RARE[1] 1.

se•lect /silékt/ • *v.tr.* choose, esp. as the best or most suitable. • *adj.* **1** chosen for excellence or suitability; choice. **2** (of a society, etc.) exclusive. □□ **se•lec'ta•ble** *adj.*

■ *v.* pick, prefer, opt for, single out. • *adj.* **1** selected, handpicked, special, preferred, favored. **2** privileged, elite, closed; see also EXCLUSIVE *adj.* 3, 4.

se•lec•tion /silékshən/ *n.* **1** selecting or being selected. **2** selected person or thing. □□ **se•lec'tive** *adj.* **se•lec'tive•ly** *adv.* **se•lec'tiv•i•ty** /silektívitee, sél–, seèl–/ *n.*

■ **1** choosing, picking, singling out; electing, voting; election. **2** choice, pick, preference, option. □□ **selective 1** particular, discerning, discriminating, exacting.

se•le•ni•um /sileèneeəm/ *n. Chem.* nonmetallic element. ¶Symb.: **Se.**

self /self/ • *n.* (*pl.* **selves** /selvz/) **1** individuality; essence; personality. **2** person or thing as the object of introspection or reflexive action (*the consciousness of self*). **3 a** one's own interests or pleasure. **b** concentration on these (*self is a bad guide to happiness*). • *adj.* of the same color as the rest or throughout.

■ *n.* **1** see IDENTITY 1.

self- /self/ *comb. form* expressing reflexive action: **1** of or directed toward oneself or itself (*self-respect*). **2** by oneself or itself, esp. without external agency (*self-evident*). **3** on, in, for, or relating to oneself or itself (*self-confident*).

self-a•base•ment /sélfəbáysmənt/ *n.* self-humiliation; cringing.

self-a•buse /sélfəbyoōs/ *n.* **1** the reviling of oneself. **2** masturbation.

self-ad•dressed /sélfadrést/ *adj.* (of an envelope, etc.) having one's own address on for return communication.

self-ag•gran•dize•ment /sélfəgrándizmənt/ *n.* process of enriching oneself or making oneself powerful. □□ **self-ag'gran•diz•ing** /–grándìzing/ *adj.*

self-ap•point•ed /sélfəpóyntid/ *adj.* designated so by oneself; not authorized by another.

self-a•ware /sélfəwáir/ *adj.* conscious of one's character, feelings, motives, etc. □□ **self'-a•ware'ness** *n.*

self-cen•tered /sélfséntərd/ *adj.* preoccupied with one's own personality or affairs. □□ **self'-cen'tered•ly** *adv.* **self'-cen'tered•ness** *n.*

■ see SELFISH. □□ **self-centeredness** see SELF-ESTEEM 2.

self-clean•ing /sélfkleéning/ *adj.* (esp. of an oven) cleaning itself when heated, etc.

self-con•fessed /sélfkənfést/ *adj.* openly admitting oneself to be (*a self-confessed thief*).

self-con•scious /sélfkónshəs/ *adj.* socially inept through embarrassment or shyness. □□ **self'-con'scious•ly** *adv.* **self'-con' scious•ness** *n.*

■ embarrassed, coy, diffident, shy, self-effacing.

self-con•tained /sélfkəntáynd/ *adj.* **1** (of a person) uncommunicative or reserved; independent, self-possessed. **2** complete in itself. □□ **self'-con•tain'ment** *n.*

■ **1** distant, aloof, withdrawn, reticent, standoffish; unemotional; in control. **2** whole, entire.

self-con•trol /sélfkəntrōl/ *n.* power of controlling one's external reactions, emotions, etc.; equanimity. □□ **self'-con•trolled'** *adj.*

■ self-discipline, self-restraint, forbearance, self-denial, willpower.

self-de•cep•tion /sélfdisépshən/ *n.* deceiving oneself esp. concerning one's true feelings, etc. □□ **self-de•ceit** /–diseét/ *n.* **self-de•ceiv•er** /–diseévər/ *n.* **self-de•ceiv•ing** /–diseéving/ *adj.* **self'-de•cep'tive** *adj.*

self-de•feat•ing /sélfdifeéting/ *adj.* (of an action, etc.) doomed to failure because of internal inconsistencies.

self-de•fense /sélfdiféns/ *n.* **1** aggressive act, speech, etc., intended as defense. **2** skills for defending oneself. □□ **self'-de•fen'sive** *adj.*

self-de•ni•al /sélfdinīal/ *n.* negation of one's interests, needs, or wishes, esp. in favor of those of others; self-control; forbearance. □□ **self'-de•ny'ing** *adj.*

self-de•struct /sélfdistrúkt/ • *v.intr.* (of a spacecraft, bomb, etc.) explode or disintegrate automatically, esp. when preset to do so. • *adj.* enabling a thing to self-destruct.

self-de•ter•mi•na•tion /sélfditərmináyshən/ *n.* **1** nation's right to determine its own government, etc. **2** ability to act with free will. □□ **self-de•ter•mined** /–tórmind/ *adj.* **self-de•ter•min•ing** /–tórmining/ *adj.*

self-dis•ci•pline /sélfdísiplin/ *n.* ability to apply oneself; self-control. □□ **self-dis' ciplined** *adj.*

self-ef•fac•ing /sélfifáysing/ *adj.* retiring; modest; timid. □□ **self'-ef•face'ment** *n.* **self'-ef•fac'ing•ly** *adv.*

self-em•ployed /sélfimplóyd/ *adj.* working for oneself, as a contractor or owner of a business, etc. □□ **self'-em•ploy'ment** *n.*

self-es•teem /sélfisteém/ *n.* **1** good opinion of oneself; self-confidence. **2** unduly high regard for oneself; conceit. See synonym study at PRIDE.

self'-ab•sorp'tion *n.*	self-crit'i•cal *adj.*	self'-im•prove'ment *n.*	self'-pol•i•na'tion *n.*
self'-ab•sorbed' *adj.*	self-crit'i•cism *n.*	self'-in•crim•i•na'tion *n.*	self'-pol'li•nat•ing *adj.*
self'-ad•just'ing *adj.*	self-de•lu'sion *n.*	self'-in•duced' *adj.*	self'-pro•claimed' *adj.*
self-as•ser'tion *n.*	self'-doubt' *n.*	self'-in•flict'ed *adj.*	self'-pro•tec'tion *n.*
self-as•sured' *adj.*	self-ed'u•cat•ed *adj.*	self'-jus•ti•fi•ca'tion *n.*	self'-re•proach' *n.*
self'-as•sur'ance *n.*	self'-fer•ti•li•i•za'tion *n.*	self'-love' *n.*	self'-sus•tain'ing *adj.*
self'-com•pla'cent *adj.*	self'-gov•ern•ment *n.*	self'-mo'ti•vat•ed *adj.*	
self'-con'fi•dence *n.*	self'-gov•ern•ing *adj.*	self'-mo•ti•va'tion *n.*	
self'-con'fi•dent *adj.*	self'-im•posed' *adj.*	self'-per•pet'u•at•ing *adj.*	

■ 2 vanity, egoism, narcissism, self-centeredness, egotism.

self·ev·i·dent /sélfévidənt/ adj. obvious; without the need of evidence or further explanation. □□ **self-ev'i·dence** n. **self-ev'i·dent·ly** adv.
■ evident, patent, clear, incontrovertible, plain.

self·ex·am·i·na·tion /sélfigzáminåyshən/ n. **1** study of one's own conduct, etc. **2** examining of one's body for signs of illness, etc.

self·ex·plan·a·to·ry /sélfiksplánətawree/ adj. easily understood; not needing explanation.

self·ex·pres·sion /sélfikspréshən/ n. artistic or free expression. □□ **self'-ex·pres'sive** adj.

self·ful·fill·ing /sélf-foolfiling/ adj. (of a prophecy, etc.) bound to come true as a result of its being made.

self·help /sélfhélp/ n. theory that individuals should provide for their own support and improvement in society.

self·im·age /sélfímij/ n. one's own idea or picture of oneself.

self·in·dul·gent /sélfindúljənt/ adj. indulging or tending to indulge oneself in pleasure, idleness, etc. □□ **self'-in·dul'gence** n. **self'-in·dul'gent·ly** adv.
■ self-gratifying, selfish, extravagant, intemperate; dissolute, dissipated; gluttonous, greedy.

self·in·ter·est /sélfintrist, -tərist/ n. one's personal interest or advantage. □□ **self-in'ter·est·ed** adj.

self·ish /sélfish/ adj. concerned chiefly with one's own personal profit or pleasure. □□ **self'ish·ly** adv. **self'ish·ness** n.
■ inconsiderate, thoughtless, grudging, uncharitable; self-indulgent; greedy, acquisitive.

self·knowl·edge /sélfnólij/ n. understanding of oneself, one's motives, etc.

self·less /sélflis/ adj. unselfish. □□ **self'less·ly** adv. **self'less·ness** n.
■ charitable, self-denying, generous, altruistic.

self·made /sélfmáyd/ adj. **1** successful or rich by one's own effort. **2** made by oneself.
■ **1** independent, self-reliant, entrepreneurial.

self·pit·y /sélfpítee/ n. extreme sorrow for one's own troubles, etc. □□ **self-pit'y·ing** adj. **self-pit'y·ing·ly** adv.

self·por·trait /sélfpáwrtrit/ n. portrait or description of an artist, writer, etc., by himself or herself.

self·pos·sessed /sélfpəzést/ adj. habitually exercising self-control; poised; composed. □□ **self-pos·ses·sion** /-zéshən/ n.
■ cool, serene, placid, collected, self-assured, calm.

self·pres·er·va·tion /sélfprézərváyshən/ n. **1** preservation of one's own life, safety, etc. **2** this as a basic instinct of human beings and animals.

self·pro·pelled /sélfprəpéld/ adj. (esp. of a motor vehicle, etc.) moving or able to move without external propulsion. □□ **self'-pro·pel'ling** adj.

self·reg·u·lat·ing /sélfrégyəlayting/ adj. regulating oneself or itself without intervention. □□ **self-reg·u·la·tion** /-láyshən/ n. **self-reg·u·la·to·ry** /-lətawree/ adj.

self·re·li·ance /sélfrilíəns/ n. reliance on one's own resources, etc.; independence. □□ **self'-re·li'ant** adj. **self'-re·li'ant·ly** adv.

self·re·spect /sélfrispékt/ n. respect for oneself. □□ **self'-re·spect'ing** adj.
■ honor, dignity, integrity, self-regard, self-esteem, pride.

self·re·straint /sélfristráynt/ n. = SELF-CONTROL. □□ **self'-re·strained'** adj.

self·right·eous /sélfríchəs/ adj. smugly sure of one's rectitude, correctness, etc. □□ **self-right'eous·ly** adv. **self-right'eous·ness** n.
■ Pharisaic(al), sanctimonious, pietistic, hypocritical, complacent, self-satisfied, priggish.

self·sac·ri·fice /sélfsákrifis/ n. negation of one's own interests, wishes, etc., in favor of those of others. □□ **self-sac'ri·fic·ing** adj.

self·same /sélfsaym/ adj. [prec. by the] very same (the selfsame village). See synonym study at SAME.

self·seek·ing /sélfséeking/ adj. & n. seeking one's own welfare before that of others. □□ **self'-seek'er** n.
■ see SELFISH.

self·ser·vice /sélfsórvis/ • adj. **1** (of a store, restaurant, gas station, etc.) where customers serve themselves. **2** (of a machine) serving goods after the insertion of coins. • n. colloq. self-service store, gas station, etc.

self·start·er /sélfstaartər/ n. **1** electric appliance for starting an engine. **2** ambitious person who needs no external motivation.

self·styled /sélfstíld/ adj. called so by oneself.
■ would-be, soi-disant, professed, self-proclaimed.

self·suf·fi·cient /sélfsəfíshənt/ adj. **1 a** needing nothing; independent. **b** (of a person, nation, etc.) able to supply one's own needs. **2** arrogant. □□ **self'-suf·fi'cien·cy** n. **self'-suf·fi'cient·ly** adv.
■ **1** self-reliant, self-supporting, self-sustaining. **2** see SELF-CONTAINED 1, ARROGANT.

self·sup·port·ing /sélfsəpáwrting/ adj. capable of maintaining oneself financially. □□ **self'-sup·port'** n.

self·taught /sélftáwt/ adj. self-educated.

self·willed /sélfwild/ adj. obstinately pursuing one's own wishes. □□ **self-will'** n.
■ headstrong, determined, refractory, stubborn.

self·worth /sélfwórth/ n. = SELF-ESTEEM 1.

sell /sel/ • v. (past and past part. **sold** /sold/) **1** tr. make over or dispose of in exchange for money. **2** tr. offer for sale. **3** intr. (of goods) be purchased (will never sell). **4** intr. have a specified price. **5** tr. cause to be sold (the author's name alone will sell many copies). • n. colloq. manner of selling (soft sell). □ **sell-by date** latest recommended date for sale, esp. of perishable food. **sell off** sell the remainder of (goods) at reduced prices. **sell out 1** sell all one's stock, shares, etc. **2 a** betray. **b** be treacherous or disloyal. □□ **sell′a•ble** *adj.* **sell′er** *n.*

■ *v.* **1** *Law* vend. **2** market, deal in, trade in, handle. **3** go, be sold, move. □ **sell out 2** inform against, give away; see also BETRAY 2. □ **seller** dealer, vendor, merchant, retailer, salesperson.

sell•out /séllowt/ *n.* **1** commercial success, esp. the selling of all tickets for a show. **2** betrayal.

selt•zer /séltsər/ *n.* soda water.

sel•vage /sélvij/ *n.* (also **sel′vedge**) edging that prevents cloth from unraveling.

se•man•tic /simántik/ *adj.* relating to meaning in language; relating to the connotations of words. □□ **se•man′ti•cal•ly** *adv.*

se•man•tics /simántiks/ *n.pl.* [usu. treated as *sing.*] branch of linguistics concerned with meaning. □□ **se•man′ti•cist** /-tisist/ *n.*

sem•a•phore /sémafawr/ • *n.* **1** *Mil.*, etc., system of signaling with the arms or two flags. **2** railroad signaling apparatus consisting of a post with a movable arm or arms, etc. • *v.* signal or send by semaphore. □□ **sem•a•phor′ic** *adj.*

sem•blance /sémbləns/ *n.* **1** outward or superficial appearance of something (*semblance of anger*). **2** resemblance.

■ **1** image, bearing, aspect, air, look. **2** see RESEMBLANCE.

se•men /séemən/ *n.* reproductive fluid of males.

se•mes•ter /siméstər/ *n.* half of an academic year.

sem•i /sémī, sémee/ *n.* (*pl.* **sem•is**) *colloq.* SEMITRAILER.

semi- /sémee, sémī/ *prefix* **1** half (*semicircle*). **2** partly. **3** almost (*a semismile*). **4** occurring or appearing twice in a specified period (*semiannual*).

sem•i•cir•cle /sémeesərkəl, sémī-/ *n.* half of a circle or of its circumference. □□ **sem•i•cir′cu•lar** /sémeesərkyələr, sémī-/ *adj.*

sem•i•co•lon /sémikōlən/ *n.* punctuation mark (;) of intermediate value between a comma and a period.

sem•i•con•duc•tor /sémeekəndúktər, sémī-/ *n.* substance that has conductivity intermediate between insulators and metals. □□ **sem•i•con•duct′ing** *adj.*

sem•i•con•scious /sémeekónshəs, sémī-/ *adj.* partly or imperfectly conscious.

sem•i•fi•nal /sémeefínəl, sémī-/ *n.* match or round immediately preceding the final. □□ **sem•i•fi′nal•ist** *n.*

sem•i•nal /sémīnəl/ *adj.* **1** of seed, semen, or reproduction. **2** germinal. **3** rudimentary; undeveloped. **4** (of ideas, etc.) providing the basis for future development. □ **seminal fluid** semen. □□ **sem′i•nal•ly** *adv.*

■ **2, 3** embryonic, potential, inchoate, unformed. **4** original, basic, creative, primary, formative.

sem•i•nar /sémīnaar/ *n.* **1** small class at a university, etc., for discussion and research. **2** conference of specialists.

sem•i•nar•y /sémineree/ *n.* (*pl.* **–ies**) **1** training college for priests, rabbis, etc. **2** place of education or development. □□ **sem•i•nar•i•an** /–náireeən/ *n.*

Sem•i•nole /sémənōl/ *n.* **1 a** N. American people native to Florida. **b** member of this people. **2** language of this people.

se•mi•ot•ics /seēmeeótiks, sém–/ *n.* study of signs and symbols in various fields, esp. language. □□ **se•mi•ot′ic** *adj.* **se•mi•ot′i•cal** *adj.* **se•mi•o•ti′cian** /–tishən/ *n.*

sem•i•per•me•a•ble /sémeepórmeeəbəl, sémī–/ *adj.* (of a membrane, etc.) allowing certain substances to pass through.

sem•i•pre•cious /sémeepréshəs, sémī–/ *adj.* (of a gem) less valuable than a precious stone.

sem•i•pro•fes•sion•al /sémeeprəféshənəl, sémī–/ • *adj.* **1** receiving payment for an activity but not relying on it for a living. **2** involving semiprofessionals. • *n.* semiprofessional musician, sportsman, etc.

sem•i•skilled /sémeeskild, sémī–/ *adj.* (of work or a worker) having or needing some training.

Sem•ite /sémīt/ *n.* member of the peoples supposed to be descended from Shem, son of Noah (Gen. 10:21 ff.), including esp. the Jews, Arabs, Assyrians, and Phoenicians. □□ **Sem′i•tism** /sémitizəm/ *n.*

Se•mit•ic /simítik/ *adj.* **1** of or relating to the Semites, esp. the Jews. **2** of or relating to the languages of the family including Hebrew and Arabic.

sem•i•tone /sémeetōn, sémī–/ *n. Mus.* half a tone.

sem•i•trail•er /sémeetráylər, sémī–/ *n.* trailer having wheels at the back but supported at the front by a towing vehicle.

sen. *abbr.* **1 a** senator. **b** senate. **2** senior.

sen•ate /sénit/ *n.* **1** legislative body. **2** (**Senate**) upper and smaller assembly in the US, France, and other countries, in the states of the US, etc.

sen•a•tor /sénətər/ *n.* member of a senate. □□ **sen•a•to•ri•al** /–táwreeəl/ *adj.*

send /send/ *v.tr.* (*past* and *past part.* **sent** /sent/) **1 a** order or cause to go or be conveyed. **b** propel; cause to move (*sent him flying*). **c** cause to go or become (*send to sleep*). **d** dismiss with or without force (*sent her away*). **2** *sl.* put into ecstasy. □ **send away for** send an order to a dealer for (goods). **send for 1** summon. **2** order by mail. **send off 1** get (a letter, parcel, etc.) dispatched. **2** attend the departure of (a person) as a sign of respect, etc. **send-off** *n.* demonstration of goodwill, etc., at the departure of a person, the start of a project, etc. □□ **send′a•ble** *adj.* **send′er** *n.*

■ **1 a** communicate, transmit, convey, deliver; broadcast, televise, radio, telegraph. **b** release, discharge, shoot; cast, throw, toss. **d** dispatch, charge. **2** delight, please, charm, enrapture. □ **send for** call for; request, ask for.

Sen•e•ca /sénikə/ *n.* **1 a** N. American people native to western New York. **b** member of this people. **2** language of this people. □□ **Sen′e•can** *adj.*

se•nile /seénil/ • *adj.* **1** of or characteristic of

old age. **2** having the weaknesses or diseases of old age. • *n.* senile person. □□ **se•nil•i•ty** /sinílitee/ *n.*

■ *adj.* **2** decrepit, declining, failing, geriatric; simple, feeble-minded; forgetful. □□ **senility** old age, senescence; dotage.

se•nior /séenyər/ • *adj.* **1** more or most advanced in age or standing. **2** of high or highest position. **3** (placed after a person's name) senior to a relative of the same name. **4** of the final year at a university, high school, etc. • *n.* **1** person of advanced age or comparatively long service, etc. **2** one's elder, or one's superior in length of service, membership, etc. **3** senior student. □ **senior citizen** elderly person, esp. a retiree. □□ **sen•ior•i•ty** /séenyáwritee, -yor-/ *n.*

■ *adj.* **1–3** elder, older; (higher-)ranking, superior; chief. □ **senior citizen** retired person, (old-age) pensioner, golden-ager.

sen•na /sénə/ *n.* **1** cassia tree. **2** laxative prepared from the dried pod of this.

se•ñor /senyáwr/ *n.* (pl. **se•ñor•es** /-rez/) title used of or to a Spanish-speaking man.

se•ño•ra /senyáwrə/ *n.* title used of or to a Spanish-speaking married woman.

se•ño•ri•ta /sényəréetə/ *n.* title used of or to a Spanish-speaking unmarried woman.

sen•sa•tion /sensáyshən/ *n.* **1** feeling in one's body detected by the senses. **2 a** intense interest, etc., esp. among a large group of people. **b** person, event, etc., causing such interest.

■ **1** sense, impression, awareness; foreboding, presentiment; suspicion. **2 a** commotion, stir, thrill; excitement. **b** success, sell-out.

sen•sa•tion•al /sensáyshənəl/ *adj.* **1** causing or intended to cause great public excitement, etc. **2** dazzling; wonderful. □□ **sen•sa'tion•al•ism** *n.* **sen•sa'tion•al•ize** *v.tr.* **sen•sa'tion•al•ly** *adv.*

■ **1, 2** exciting, stimulating, electrifying, galvanizing; incredible, spectacular, great, marvelous, fabulous, fantastic; lurid, vivid, dramatic, extravagant.

sense /sens/ • *n.* **1 a** any of the five bodily faculties by which sensation is roused (*dull sense of smell*). **b** sensitiveness of all or any of these. **2** ability to perceive or feel. **3** consciousness; intuitive awareness. **4** quick or accurate appreciation, understanding, or instinct. **5** common sense. **6 a** meaning of a word. **b** intelligibility or coherence. • *v.tr.* **1** perceive by a sense or senses. **2** be vaguely aware of.

■ *n.* **1** sight, vision, hearing, taste, smell, touch. **2, 3** see UNDERSTANDING *n.* 1. **4, 5** intelligence, perception, quick-wittedness, judgment. **6** drift, gist. • *v.* feel, detect, realize; see also UNDERSTAND 1, 2.

sense•less /sénslis/ *adj.* **1** unconscious. **2** wildly foolish. **3** without meaning or purpose. **4** incapable of sensation. □□ **sense'less•ly** *adv.* **sense'less•ness** *n.*

■ **1, 4** insensible, stunned; unfeeling, benumbed. **2, 3** pointless, purposeless, ridiculous, ludicrous, unintelligent, illogical, irrational, meaningless, absurd.

sen•si•bil•i•ty /sénsibílitee/ *n.* (*pl.* **–ties**)

1 capacity to feel. **2** sensitiveness. **3** [in *pl.*] emotional capacities or feelings.

■ **3** (*sensibilities*) emotions, sentiments, susceptibilities.

sen•si•ble /sénsibəl/ *adj.* **1** having or showing wisdom or common sense. **2 a** perceptible by the senses. **b** great enough to be perceived. **3** (of clothing, etc.) practical and functional. **4** [foll. by *of*] aware. See synonym study at TANGIBLE. □□ **sen'si•ble•ness** *n.* **sen'si•bly** *adv.*

■ **1, 3** reasonable, logical, rational, reasoned, prudent, judicious; well-thought-out. **2** perceivable, detectable, evident, discernible. **4** (*sensible of*) acquainted with, cognizant of, sensitive to, mindful of.

SYNONYM STUDY: sensible

LUCID, RATIONAL, REASONABLE, SAGACIOUS, SANE. A **sensible** person brings an umbrella when rain is forecast. A **rational** one studies the weather map, observes the movement of the clouds across the sky, listens to the forecast on the radio, and then decides whether or not an umbrella is necessary. *Sensible* implies the use of common sense and an appreciation of the value of experience (*a sensible decision not to travel until his injuries had healed*); while *rational* suggests the ability to reason logically and to draw conclusions from inferences (*a rational explanation for why she failed the exam*). **Lucid** and **sane**, like *rational*, are associated with coherent thinking. *Lucid* suggests a mind free of internal pressures or distortions (*lucid intervals during which he was able to recognize his wife and children*), while *sane* indicates freedom from psychosis or mental derangement (*judged to have been sane when she committed the crime*). *Sane* also has a meaning very close to that of *sensible* and *reasonable* (*a sane approach to disciplining problem teenagers*). A **sagacious** person is an extremely shrewd one who is both discerning and practical. He or she can look out the window and tell whether it's going to rain just by studying the facial expressions of passersby as they glance nervously at the sky.

---

sen•si•tive /sénsitiv/ • *adj.* **1** acutely affected by external stimuli or mental impressions; having sensibility. **2** (of a person) easily offended. **3** (of an instrument, film, etc.) responsive to or recording slight changes. **4** (of a topic, etc.) requiring tactful treatment or secrecy. • *n.* person who is sensitive (esp. to supposed occult influences). □□ **sen'si•tive•ly** *adv.* **sen'si•tive•ness** *n.* **sen•si•tiv•i•ty** /sénsitívitee/ *n.*

■ *adj.* **1** delicate, tender, sore, susceptible. **2** touchy, thin-skinned, tender, vulnerable, testy. **3, 4** finely tuned, delicate. □□ **sensitivity** sensitiveness, acuteness, perception, understanding; compassion.

sen•si•tize /sénsitīz/ *v.tr.* make sensitive.

sen•sor /sénsər/ *n.* device for the detection or measurement of a physical property to which it responds.

sen•so•ry /sénsəree/ *adj.* of sensation or the senses. □□ **sen'so•ri•ly** *adv.*

sen•su•al /sénshōōəl/ adj. **1 a** of or depending on the senses only and not on the intellect or spirit; carnal; fleshly. **b** given to the pursuit of sensual pleasures or the gratification of the appetites. **2** of sense or sensation; sensory. □□ **sen′su•al•ism** n. **sen′su•al•ist** n. **sen•su•al•i•ty** /sénshōō-álitee/ n. **sen′su•al•ly** adv.

■ **1** physical, appetitive, voluptuous; erotic, sexual, lustful, unchaste, abandoned. □□ **sensuality** eroticism, sexuality, physicality, carnality.

sent past and past part. of SEND.

sen•tence /séntəns/ • n. **1** set of words complete in itself as the expression of a thought, containing or implying a subject and predicate, and conveying a statement, question, exclamation, or command. **2 a** decision of a court of law, esp. the punishment allotted to a person convicted in a criminal trial. **b** declaration of this. • v.tr. **1** declare the sentence of (a convicted criminal, etc.). **2** [foll. by to] declare (such a person) to be condemned to a specified punishment.

■ n. **2** judgment, ruling, verdict.

sen•ten•tious /senténshəs/ adj. **1** pompously moralizing. **2** affectedly formal. **3** aphoristic; given to the use of maxims. See synonym study at TERSE. □□ **sen•ten′tious•ly** adv. **sen•ten′tious•ness** n.

■ **1** see pedantic (PEDANT). **2** see POMPOUS. **3** see epigrammatic (EPIGRAM).

sen•tient /sénshənt/ adj. having the power of perception by the senses. □□ **sen′tience** n. **sen′tient•ly** adv.

sen•ti•ment /séntimənt/ n. **1** mental feeling. **2 a** what one feels. **b** verbal expression of this. **3** mawkish tenderness.

■ **1** attitude, sensibility, emotion. **2** thought; (sentiments) view, outlook, opinion. **3** sentimentality, sentimentalism.

sen•ti•men•tal /séntiméntl/ adj. **1** of or characterized by sentiment. **2** showing or affected by emotion rather than reason. □□ **sen•ti•men′tal•ism** n. **sen•ti•men′tal•ist** n. **sen•ti•men•tal•i•ty** /-tálitee/ n. **sen•ti•men′tal•ize** v. **sen•ti•men′tal•ly** adv.

■ emotional; sympathetic, compassionate; romantic, nostalgic. □□ **sentimentality** romanticism, nostalgia, pathos, emotionalism, mawkishness.

sen•ti•nel /séntinəl/ n. sentry; lookout.

sen•try /séntree/ n. (pl. **–tries**) soldier standing guard.

se•pal /seepəl/ n. Bot. division or leaf of the calyx.

sep•a•ra•ble /sépərəbəl/ adj. able to be separated. □□ **sep•a•ra•bil′i•ty** n. **sep′a•ra•ble•ness** n. **sep′a•ra•bly** adv.

sep•a•rate • adj. /sépərət, séprət/ forming a unit by itself; physically disconnected, distinct, or individual. • n. /sépərət, séprət/ [in pl.] separate articles of clothing suitable for wearing together in various combinations. • v. /sépərayt/ **1** tr. make separate; sever. **2** tr. prevent union or contact of. **3** intr. go different ways; disperse. **4** tr. divide or sort (milk, ore, fruit, etc.) into constituent parts or sizes.

□□ **sep′a•rate•ly** adv. **sep′a•rate•ness** n. **sep•a•ra•tive** /–rətiv/ adj.

■ adj. divided, separated, disjoined, detached, isolated, discrete; unrelated, other; withdrawn, solitary; shut or closed off or away. • v. **1** sever, disjoin, pull or take or break apart, disassemble, unhook. **3** split (up), break up, divorce; fork, bifurcate, diverge, branch. **4** distinguish, discriminate, analyze, sort (out), classify; group, collate. □□ **separately** individually, independently, singly, one by one.

sep•a•ra•tion /sépəráyshən/ n. **1** separating or being separated. **2** (in full **judicial separation**) or (**legal separation**) arrangement by which a husband and wife remain married but live apart.

■ partition, division, split, schism; disassociation, severance; disintegration, breakup.

sep•a•rat•ist /sépərətist, séprə–/ n. person who favors separation, esp. political independence. □□ **sep′a•ra•tism** n.

sep•a•ra•tor /sépəraytər/ n. machine for separating, e.g., cream from milk.

se•pi•a /seepeeə/ n. **1** dark reddish-brown color or paint. **2** brown tint used in photography.

sep•sis /sépsis/ n. **1** state of being septic. **2** blood poisoning.

Sept. abbr. **1** September. **2** Septuagint.

Sep•tem•ber /septémbər/ n. ninth month of the year.

sep•tet /septét/ n. (also **sep•tette′**) **1** Mus. **a** composition for seven performers. **b** the performers. **2** any group of seven.

sep•tic /séptik/ adj. contaminated with bacteria from a festering wound, etc.; putrefying. □ **septic tank** tank in which the organic matter in sewage is disintegrated through bacterial activity.

sep•ti•ce•mi•a /séptiseemeeə/ n. blood poisoning. □□ **sep•ti•ce′mic** adj.

sep•tu•a•ge•nar•i•an /sépchōōəjinárireeən, –tōō–, –tyōō–/ • n. person from 70 to 79 years old. • adj. of this age.

Sep•tu•a•gint /séptōōəjint, –tyōō–/ n. Greek version of the Old Testament including the Apocrypha.

sep•tum /séptəm/ n. (pl. **sep•ta** /–tə/) Anat. partition such as that between the nostrils.

sep•ul•cher /sépəlkər/ n. (also **sep′ul•chre**) tomb or burial place. □□ **sepulchral** /sipúlkrəl/ adj.

■ mausoleum, burial vault, grave, crypt.

seq. abbr. (pl. **seqq.**) the following.

se•quel /seekwəl/ n. **1** what follows (esp. as a result). **2** novel, motion picture, etc., that continues the story of an earlier one.

se•quence /seekwəns/ • n. **1** succession. **2** order of succession. **3** set of things belonging next to one another. **4** part of a motion picture, etc., dealing with one scene or topic. • v.tr. arrange in a definite order. □□ **se•quen•tial** /sikwénshəl/ adj. **se•quen′tial•ly** adv.

■ n. **1–3** progression, chronology, series, chain, string, course; system. □□ **sequential** successive, ordered, orderly, serial, progressive.

se•ques•ter /sikwéstər/ v.tr. (esp. as **sequestered** adj.) seclude; isolate; set apart.

se•quin /se´kwin/ *n.* circular spangle for attaching to clothing as an ornament. □□ **se´quined** *adj.*

se•quoi•a /sikwóyə/ *n.* Californian evergreen coniferous tree of very great height.

se•ragl•io /sərályō, –raal–/ *n.* (*pl.* **–ios**) harem.

se•ra•pe /sərəápee/ *n.* shawl or blanket worn as a cloak by Spanish Americans.

ser•aph /sérəf/ *n.* (*pl.* **ser•a•phim** /–fim/ or **ser•aphs**) angelic being of the highest order of the celestial hierarchy. □□ **se•raph•ic** /səráfik/ *adj.* **se•raph´i•cal•ly** *adv.*

Ser•bi•an /sórbeeən/ • *n.* **1** dialect of the Serbs (cf. SERBO-CROAT). **2** native or inhabitant of Serbia. • *adj.* of or relating to the Serbs or their dialect.

Ser•bo-Cro•at /sórbōkrốat/ (also **Ser•bo-Cro•a•tian** /–krō-áyshən/) • *n.* main official language of the former Yugoslavia, combining Serbian and Croatian dialects. • *adj.* of or relating to this language.

ser•e•nade /sérənáyd/ • *n.* piece of music sung or played at night, esp. by a lover under his lady's window. • *v.tr.* sing or play a serenade to. □□ **ser•e•nad´er** *n.*

ser•en•dip•i•ty /sérəndípitee/ *n.* faculty of making happy discoveries by accident. □□ **ser•en•dip´i•tous** *adj.* **ser•en•dip´i•tous•ly** *adv.*

se•rene /sirén/ *adj.* (**se•ren•er, se•ren•est**) **1 a** clear and calm. **b** unruffled. **2** placid; tranquil; unperturbed. See synonym study at CALM. □□ **se•rene´ly** *adv.* **se•ren•i•ty** /sirénitee/ *n.*

■ peaceful, pacific, peaceable, restful, halcyon, idyllic; cool, collected, composed.

serf /sərf/ *n. hist.* agricultural laborer not allowed to leave the land. □□ **serf´dom** *n.*

■ *hist.* vassal, villein. **serfdom** see SLAVERY 1.

serge /sərj/ *n.* durable twilled worsted, etc., fabric.

ser•geant /sáarjənt/ *n.* **1** noncommissioned army, marine, or air force officer next below warrant officer. **2** police officer ranking below captain. □ **sergeant major** *Mil.* highest-ranking noncommissioned officer. □□ **ser´gean•cy** *n.* (*pl.* **–cies**).

se•ri•al /séereeəl/ • *n.* **1** story, play, etc., published, broadcast, or shown in regular installments. **2** periodical. • *adj.* **1** of or in or forming a series. **2** (of a story, etc.) in the form of a serial. □ **serial number** number showing the position of an item in a series. □□ **se´ri•al•ly** *adv.*

se•ri•al•ize /séereeəlīz/ *v.tr.* publish or produce in installments. □□ **se•ri•al•i•za´tion** *n.*

se•ries /séereez/ *n.* (*pl.* same) **1** number of things of which each is similar to the preceding or in which each successive pair are similarly related; sequence, succession, order, row, or set. **2** set of successive games between the same teams. **3** set of related but individual programs.

ser•if /sérif/ *n.* slight projection extending from the main part of a letter, as in T contrasted with T (cf. SANS SERIF).

se•ri•ous /séereeəs/ *adj.* **1** thoughtful; earnest;

nest; sober. **2** important; demanding consideration. **3** not slight nor negligible. **4** sincere; not ironic nor joking. □□ **se´ri•ous•ly** *adv.* **se´ri•ous•ness** *n.*

■ **1** grave, solemn, unsmiling, straight-faced, sedate; responsible; humorless, somber, grim, dour. **2, 3** grave, vital, weighty, significant, momentous; acute, critical, life-threatening. **4** straightforward, genuine, (in) earnest, honest. □□ **seriously** soberly, really, honestly, sincerely; gravely, badly, severely.

ser•mon /sórmən/ *n.* **1** spoken or written discourse on a religious or moral subject, esp. a discourse based on a text or passage of Scripture and delivered in church. **2** piece of admonition or reproof; lecture. □□ **ser´mon•ize** *v.* **ser´mon•iz•er** *n.*

■ **1** homily, address, exhortation, lecture, speech, talk. **2** lesson, reprimand, reproach, rebuke.

se•rous /séerəs/ *adj.* of or like or producing serum; watery. □ **serous gland** (or **membrane**) gland (or membrane) with a serous secretion.

ser•pent /sórpənt/ *n.* **1** usu. *literary* **a** snake, esp. large. **b** scaly limbless reptile. **2** sly or treacherous person.

ser•pen•tine /sórpəntīn/ *adj.* **1** of or like a serpent. **2** coiling; tortuous; sinuous; meandering; writhing. **3** cunning; subtle; treacherous.

■ **2** twisting, winding, snaking, roundabout. **3** evil, bad, diabolic(al), wily, cunning.

ser•rate • *v.tr.* /séráyt/ (usu. as **serrated** *adj.*) provide with a sawlike edge. • *adj.* /scráyt/ esp. *Anat., Bot., & Zool.* notched like a saw. □□ **ser•ra•tion** /–ráyshən/ *n.*

■ *v.* (**serrated**) sawtooth(ed), crenellated, notched. □□ **serration** tooth, spike, point, prong; notch.

ser•ried /séreed/ *adj.* (of ranks of soldiers, rows of trees, etc.) pressed together; without gaps.

se•rum /séerəm/ *n.* (*pl.* **se•ra** /–rə/ or **se•rums**) **1** liquid that separates from a clot when blood coagulates used esp. in inoculations. **2** watery fluid in animal bodies.

ser•vant /sórvənt/ *n.* **1** person employed to do domestic duties. **2** devoted follower; person willing to serve another.

■ **1** domestic, help, maid.

serve /sərv/ • *v.* **1** *tr.* do a service for (a person, community, etc.). **2** *tr.* [also *absol.*] be a servant to. **3** *intr.* carry out duties. **4** *intr.* **a** be employed in (an organization, the armed forces, etc.). **b** be a member of the armed forces. **5 a** *tr.* be useful; meet the needs of. **b** *intr.* meet requirements; perform a function. **6** *intr.* act as a waiter. **7** *tr.* attend to (a customer). **8** *tr.* deliver (a subpoena, etc.) to (someone). **9** *tr. Tennis*, etc. deliver (a ball, etc.) to begin or resume play. • *n. Tennis*, etc.act or instance of serving. □ **serve a person right** be a person's deserved punishment or misfortune.

■ *v.* **1, 2, 7** wait on, minister to, look after, assist, help. **3, 4** see WORK *v.* 2a. **5** fulfill, carry out, discharge, work, do, suffice. **6** give out, present, set out, provide. **8** hand out, give, present.

serv•er /sɔ́rvər/ n. **1** person who serves. **2** *Eccl.* person assisting the celebrant at a service, esp. the Eucharist.

serv•ice /sɔ́rvis/ • n. **1** helping or doing work for another or for a community, etc. **2** work done in this way. **3** assistance or benefit given. **4** supplying of a public need, e.g., water, gas, etc. **5** employment as a servant. **6** state or period of employment. **7** public department or organization (*civil service*). **8** [in *pl.*] the armed forces. **9** ceremony of worship. **10** maintenance of a machine, etc. **11** assistance or advice given to customers after the sale of goods. **12** a serving of food, drinks, etc. **b** extra charge nominally made for this. **13** set of dishes, etc., for serving meals. **14** *Tennis*, etc. **a** act or instance of serving. **b** person's turn to serve. • v.tr. **1** provide a service. **2** maintain or repair (a car, machine, etc.). □ **at a person's service** ready to serve a person. **in service 1** employed as a servant. **2** available for use. **service industry** one providing services not goods. **service station** place for servicing cars, selling fuel, etc.

■ n. **1–3, 11** aid, backing, support; use, serving, care, attention. **4** see SYSTEM 1, SUPPLY n. 1. **5, 6** employ; assignment, post, position, appointment. **8** (*services*) army, navy, air force, marines. **9** rite, ritual; liturgy. **10** overhaul, servicing, checking. **14** serve. • v. **1, 2** see MAINTAIN 4.

serv•ice•a•ble /sɔ́rvisəbəl/ adj. **1** useful or usable. **2** able to render service. **3** durable but plain. □□ **serv•ice•a•bil′i•ty** n. **serv′ice•a•bly** adv.

■ **1** workable, working, functional, functioning, operative. **3** hardwearing, long-lasting, practical, functional.

serv•ice•man /sɔ́rvismæn/ n. (pl. **–men**) **1** man serving in the armed forces. **2** man providing service or maintenance.

serv•ice•wom•an /sɔ́rviswŏŏmən/ n. (pl. **–wom•en**) woman serving in the armed forces.

serv•ile /sɔ́rvil/ adj. **1** of or like a slave. **2** slavish; fawning; completely dependent. □□ **serv′ile•ly** adv. **ser•vil•i•ty** /–vílitee/ n.

■ **2** submissive, subservient, menial, craven, acquiescent, abject, cringing, deferential, ingratiating.

serv•ing /sɔ́rving/ n. quantity of food served to one person.

ser•vi•tude /sɔ́rvitŏŏd, –tyŏŏd/ n. **1** slavery. **2** subjection (esp. involuntary); bondage.
■ serfdom, subjugation, enslavement.

ser•vo /sɔ́rvō/ n. (pl. **–vos**) (in full **ser′vo•mech•an•ism**) powered mechanism for automatic control of electrical, hydraulic, etc., devices.

ses•a•me /sésəmee/ n. *Bot.* **1** E. Indian plant with seeds used as food and yielding an edible oil. **2** its seeds.

ses•sion /séshən/ n. **1** assembly of a deliberative or judicial body to conduct its business. **2** single meeting for this purpose. **3** period ·

during which such meetings are regularly held. **4** academic year.

■ **1, 2** sitting, seating, conference, hearing.

set[1] /set/ v. (**set•ting**; *past* and *past part.* **set**) **1** *tr.* put, lay, or stand (a thing) in a certain position or location. **2** *tr.* **a** fix ready or in position. **b** dispose suitably for use, action, or display. **3** *tr.* **a** adjust (a clock or watch) to show the right time. **b** adjust (an alarm clock) to sound at the required time. **4** *tr.* insert (a jewel) in a ring, framework, etc. **5** *tr.* lay (a table) for a meal. **6** *tr.* arrange (the hair) while damp so that it dries in the required style. **7** *intr.* & *tr.* harden or solidify. **8** *intr.* (of the sun, moon, etc.) appear to move below the horizon. **9** *tr.* represent (a story, etc.) as happening in a certain time or place. **10** *tr.* assign (*set them an essay*). **11** *tr.* exhibit as a model. **12** *tr.* initiate; lead. **13** *tr.* establish (a record, etc.). **14** *tr.* **a** put parts of (a broken or dislocated bone, limb, etc.) into the correct position for healing. **b** deal with (a fracture or dislocation) in this way. **15** *tr.* (in full **set to music**) provide (words, etc.) with music for singing. **16** *tr.* [often foll. by *up*] *Printing* **a** arrange or produce (type or film, etc.) as required. **b** arrange the type or film, etc., for (a book, etc.). **17** *tr.* **a** cause (a hen) to sit on eggs. **b** place (eggs) for a hen to sit on. □ **set about** begin. **set down 1** record in writing. **2** land an aircraft. **set forth 1** begin a journey. **2** make known. **set on** (or **upon**) **1** attack violently. **2** cause or urge to attack. **set out 1** begin a journey. **2** [foll. by *to* + infin.] intend. **set up 1** place in position or view. **2** organize or start (a business, etc.). **3** establish.

■ **1, 2** set down, place, situate, locate; prepare; arrange, set out. **3** regulate, turn, synchronize, fix. **5** arrange, spread; prepare. **7** stiffen, freeze; gel, congeal. **8** go down, sink, decline. **9** see SITUATE v. **10** see ASSIGN v. 1a. **12** see INITIATE v. 1. **13** lay down, appoint, impose, stipulate, define, designate. **14** see ATTACH 1, MEND v. 1. □ **set about** get or make ready, start, undertake, launch into. **set down 1** write (down), register, jot down. **2** make a landing, touch down. **set forth 1** set out or off, start (out), get under way. **2** expound, express, voice, propose, propound, state. **set on** (or **upon**) **1** assault, pounce on; ambush, beat up. **set out 1** see *set forth* 1 above. **2** (*set out to*) see AIM v. 1, 4. **set up 1** build, put up, erect, assemble, construct. **2, 3** begin, initiate, found.

set[2] /set/ n. **1** group of linked, related, or similar persons or things. **2** collection of implements, vessels, etc., regarded collectively and needed for a specified purpose. **3** radio or television receiver. **4** (in tennis, etc.) group of games counting as a unit toward a match. **5** setting, including stage furniture, etc., for a play, etc.

■ **1** collection, combination, number, grouping, assortment; order, succession. **2, 3** kit, outfit, rig; equipment, apparatus. **5** scene, mounting, scenery, *mise en scène*.

set[3] /set/ adj. **1** in senses of SET[1]. **2** determined in advance. **3** fixed. **4** prepared for action. □ **set screw** screw for adjusting or clamping parts of a machine.

■ **2, 3** established, scheduled; customary, usual; definite, firm, unvarying; stereotyped, trite, hackneyed, traditional, unchanged, unvaried, invariable. **4** ready, fit, primed.

set•back /sétbak/ n. **1** reversal or arrest of progress. **2** relapse.

■ **1** hindrance, hitch, check.

set•tee /setée/ n. seat (usu. upholstered), with a back and usu. arms, for more than one person.

set•ter /sétər/ n. **1** dog of a large, long-haired breed trained to stand rigid when scenting game. **2** this breed.

set•ting /séting/ n. **1** position or manner in which a thing is set. **2** immediate surroundings (of a house, etc.). **3** surroundings of any object regarded as its framework; the environment of a thing. **4** place and time, scenery, etc., of a story, drama, etc. **5** mounting in which a jewel is set. **6** set of cutlery and other accessories for one person at a table.

■ **1–3** scenery, background, backdrop, locale, location, environment, milieu, frame, context, site, placement.

set•tle /sét'l/ v. **1** tr. & intr. establish or become established in an abode or way of life. **2** intr. & tr. a cease or cause to cease from wandering, disturbance, movement, etc. **b** adopt a regular or secure style of life. **c** apply oneself (to work, etc.). **3 a** intr. sit or come down to stay for some time. **b** tr. cause to do this. **4** tr. & intr. bring to or attain fixity, certainty, composure, or quietness. **5** tr. determine or decide or agree upon. **6** tr. resolve (a dispute, etc.). **7** tr. terminate (a lawsuit) by mutual agreement. **8** tr. pay (a debt, an account, etc.). **9** intr. (as **settled** adj.) not likely to change for a time. **10** tr. colonize. **11** intr. subside. □□ **set'tler** n.

■ **1, 2a, b** (intr.) take up residence, go, come, make one's home, put down roots, locate. **2 c** see APPLY 5. **3** alight, land, put down, set down. **4** calm down, subside; calm, soothe, tranquilize; arrange, order; clarify, clear. **5–7** establish, appoint, set, confirm, affirm; reconcile, resolve. **8** square, dispose of, clear, defray; settle up. **10** populate, people, plant. **11** sink, decline, fall, gravitate. □□ **settler** colonist, pioneer, immigrant.

set•tle•ment /sét'lmənt/ n. **1** settling; being settled. **2 a** colonization of a region. **b** place occupied by settlers. **3** agreement.

■ **1** decision, conclusion, confirmation, establishment. **2 a** settling, populating. **b** colony, outpost, community, encampment; village, hamlet. **3** rapprochement, resolution, adjustment, reconciliation.

set•up /sétup/ n. **1** arrangement or organization. **2** manner, structure, or position of this. **3** colloq. trick or conspiracy, esp. to make an innocent person appear guilty.

■ **1, 2** system, layout, regime, framework; conditions, circumstances. **3** trap, ambush.

sev•en /sévən/ n. **1** one more than six. **2** symbol for this (7, vii, VII). □□ **sev'enth** adj. & n.

sev•en•teen /sévəntéen/ n. **1** one more than sixteen. **2** symbol for this (17, xvii, XVII). □□ **sev'en•teenth'** adj. & n.

sev•en•ty /sévəntee/ n. (pl. **–ties**) **1** seven times ten. **2** symbol for this (70, lxx, LXX). **3** [in pl.] the numbers from 70 to 79, esp. the years of a century or of a person's life. □□ **sev'en•ti•eth** adj. & n.   **sev'en•ty•fold** adj. & adv.

sev•er /sévər/ v. **1** divide, break, or make separate, esp. by cutting. **2** part; divide (severed our friendship). □□ **sev'er•a•ble** adj.

■ **1** lop or chop or hack (off), split, separate. **2** separate, disunite; dissolve, break off, terminate, discontinue.

sev•er•al /sévrəl/ • adj. **1** more than two but not many. **2** separate or respective. • n. some; a few. □□ **sev'er•al•ly** adv.

■ adj. **1** some, a few, a handful. **2** various, sundry, diverse, different.

sev•er•ance /sévərəns, sévrəns/ n. act or instance of severing. □ **severance pay** amount paid to an employee on the early termination of a contract.

se•vere /sivéer/ adj. **1** rigorous, strict, and harsh. **2** serious; critical. **3** vehement or forceful. **4** unadorned; plain in style. □□ **se•vere'ly** adv.   **se•ver•i•ty** /-vérite/ n.

■ **1** austere, hard, stony; despotic, dictatorial; demanding, exacting; stringent. **2** dangerous, grave, life-threatening. **3** harsh, bitter, cold, extreme, intense. **4** stark, bare, austere, Spartan, ascetic. □□ **severely** acutely, seriously, badly; strictly, harshly, rigorously. **severity** strictness, harshness, rigor, austerity, hardness; coldness, aloofness; punitiveness.

SYNONYM STUDY: **severe**

ASCETIC, AUSTERE, RELENTLESS, STERN, STRICT, UNMITIGATED. A storm, a hairdo, and a punishment may all be described as **severe**, which means strict, uncompromising, or restrained, without a hint of softness, mildness, levity, or indulgence. **Austere**, on the other hand, primarily applies to people, their habits, their way of life, and the environments they create; it implies coldness, stark simplicity, and restraint (an austere room with only a table and chair). **Ascetic** implies extreme self-denial and self-discipline, in some cases to the point of choosing what is painful or disagreeable (he had an ascetic approach to life and rejected all creature comforts). **Strict** literally means bound or stretched tight; in extended use, it means strenuously exact (a strict curfew, strict obedience). **Stern** combines harshness and authority with strictness or severity (a stern judge). **Unmitigated** means unmodified and unsoftened in any way (a streak of unmitigated bad luck).

---

sew /sō/ v. tr. (past part. **sewn** /sōn/ or **sewed**) fasten, join, etc., by making stitches with a needle and thread or a sewing machine. □ **sew up 1** join or enclose by sewing. **2** colloq. [esp. in passive] satisfactorily conclude. **3** obtain exclusive use of. □□ **sew'er** n.

■ sew up, stitch, repair; sew on, attach; tack, baste. □ **sew up 2** see CLINCH v. 1.

sew•age /sóoij/ (also **sew•er•age** /sóowərij/) *n.* waste matter conveyed in sewers.

sew•er /sóoər/ *n.* conduit, usu. underground, for carrying off drainage water and sewage.

sew•er•age /sóoərij/ *n.* **1** system of or drainage by sewers. **2** = SEWAGE.

sew•ing /sóing/ *n.* piece of material or work to be sewn.

sew•ing ma•chine /sóing/ *n.* machine for sewing or stitching.

sex /seks/ • *n.* **1** either of the main divisions (male and female) into which living things are placed on the basis of their reproductive functions. **2** sexual instincts, desires, etc., or their manifestation. **3** *colloq.* sexual intercourse. • *adj.* of or relating to sex (*sex education*). • *v.tr.* **1** determine the sex of. **2** (as **sexed** *adj.*) **a** having a sexual appetite (*highly sexed*). **b** having sexual characteristics. □ **sex appeal** sexual attractiveness. **sex chromosome** chromosome determining the sex of an organism. **sex symbol** person widely noted for sex appeal.
■ *n.* **1** gender. • *v.* **2** see (*sexed*) SEXUAL 1.

sex•a•ge•nar•i•an /séksəjináireeən/ • *n.* person from 60 to 69 years old. • *adj.* of this age.

sex•ism /séksizəm/ *n.* prejudice or discrimination, esp. against women, on the grounds of sex. □□ **sex'ist** *adj. & n.*

sex•ol•o•gy /seksólojee/ *n.* study of sexual life or relationships, esp. in human beings. □□ **sex•o•log•i•cal** /séksəlójikəl/ *adj.* **sex•ol'o•gist** *n.*

sex•tant /sékstənt/ *n.* instrument for measuring the angular distance of objects by means of mirrors.

sex•tet /sekstét/ *n.* (also **sex•tette'**) **1** *Mus.* composition for six voices or instruments. **2** performers of such a piece. **3** any group of six.

sex•ton /sékstən/ *n.* person who looks after a church and churchyard.

sex•tu•plet /sekstúplit, –tŏŏ–, –tyŏŏ–, sékstŏŏ–, tyŏŏ–/ *n.* each of six children born at one birth.

sex•u•al /sékshŏŏəl/ *adj.* of or relating to sex, or to the sexes or the relations between them. □ **sexual intercourse** insertion of a man's erect penis into a woman's vagina, usu. followed by the ejaculation of semen. □□ **sex•u•al•i•ty** /–álitee/ *n.* **sex'u•al•ly** *adv.*
■ reproductive, genital, procreative; erotic, carnal, fleshly. • **sexual intercourse** mating; copulation, sexual relations, lovemaking.

sex•y /séksee/ *adj.* (**sex•i•er**, **sex•i•est**) **1** sexually attractive or stimulating. **2** sexually aroused. □□ **sex'i•ly** *adv.* **sex'i•ness** *n.*
■ **1** erotic, arousing, exciting, sensual, sensuous. **2** randy, lustful, lecherous.

Sg *abbr.* SEABORGIUM.

Sgt. (also **SGT**) *abbr.* Sergeant.

shab•by /shábee/ *adj.* (**shab•bi•er**, **shab•bi•est**) **1** in bad repair or condition; faded and worn. **2** contemptible; dishonorable. □□ **shab'bi•ly** *adv.* **shab'bi•ness** *n.*
■ **1** worn (out), dingy, threadbare, frayed; run-down, ramshackle, neglected. **2** unpleasant, nasty, disagreeable, mean; despicable, vile.

shack /shak/ • *n.* roughly built hut or cabin. • *v.intr.* [foll. by *up*] *sl.* cohabit, esp. as lovers.
■ *n.* hovel, shanty, lean-to. • *v.* (*shack up*) live together.

shack•le /shákəl/ • *n.* **1** metal loop or link, closed by a bolt, to connect chains, etc. **2** fetter enclosing the ankle or wrist. **3** [usu. in *pl.*] restraint or impediment. • *v.tr.* fetter; impede; restrain.
■ *n.* **2** leg iron, chain, irons, manacle, handcuff. **3** (*shackles*) restriction, trammels, deterrent, check. • *v.* chain, manacle, handcuff; hold back, check.

shad /shad/ *n.* (*pl.* same or **shads**) *Zool.* edible marine fish spawning in fresh water.

shade /shayd/ • *n.* **1** comparative darkness (and usu. coolness) caused by shelter from direct light. **2** area so sheltered. **3** color, esp. as distinguished from one nearly like it. **4** slight amount. **5** screen excluding or moderating light. **6** [in *pl.*] *colloq.* sunglasses. **7** *literary* ghost. • *v.tr.* **1** screen from light. **2** cover, moderate, or exclude the light of. **3** darken, esp. with parallel pencil lines to represent shadow, etc. □□ **shade'less** *adj.*
■ *n.* **1, 2** shadow, dimness, semidarkness, gloominess, murkiness. **3** tint, tinge, tone, hue; intensity. **4** hint, intimation, tinge, suggestion; fraction. **5** lampshade; window blind, curtain; cover, awning, canopy. **7** specter, apparition, phantom, spirit. • *v.* **1, 2** protect, shield, shelter; dim, shadow; mask. **3** opaque, blacken.

shad•ing /sháyding/ *n.* representation of light and shade, e.g., by penciled lines, on a map or drawing.

shad•ow /shádō/ • *n.* **1** shade; patch of shade projected by a body intercepting light. **2** slightest trace; weak or insubstantial remnant. **3** shaded part of a picture. **4** gloom or sadness. • *v.tr.* **1** cast a shadow over. **2** secretly follow and watch. □□ **shad'ow•er** *n.* **shad'ow•less** *adj.* **shad'ow•y** *adj.*
■ *n.* **1** darkness, gloom, dimness, dusk, obscurity. **2** hint, intimation, suggestion, vestige; remnant. **4** see GLOOM *n.* 2. • *v.* **2** trail, track, tail.

shad•y /sháydee/ *adj.* (**shad•i•er**, **shad•i•est**) **1** giving shade. **2** situated in shade. **3** (of a person or behavior) disreputable; of doubtful honesty. □□ **shad'i•ly** *adv.* **shad'i•ness** *n.*
■ **3** questionable, uncertain, unreliable, suspicious, suspect, dubious, devious.

shaft /shaft/ • *n.* **1 a** arrow or spear. **b** long slender stem of these. **2** remark intended to hurt or provoke. **3** [foll. by *of*] bolt (of lightning). **4** stem or handle of a tool, implement, etc. **5** long narrow space, usu. vertical, for access to a mine, for ventilation, etc. **6** long and narrow part transmitting motion between other parts. **7** central stem of a feather. • *v.tr. colloq.* treat unfairly.
■ *n.* **1 a** see also LANCE *n.* **2** thrust, barb, sting, dart, gibe, taunt. **3** flash, fulmination. **4** pole, rod, staff, stick, shank. **5** mine shaft, tunnel, adit; air shaft, duct, vent; passage, entrance, access.

shag[1] /shag/ *n.* **1** rough growth or mass of hair, carpet pile, etc. **2** coarse kind of cut tobacco.

shag[2] /shag/ *v.tr.* (**shagged, shag·ging**) *Baseball* catch and return (fly balls) during practice.

shag·gy /shágee/ *adj.* (**shag·gi·er, shag·gi·est**) **1** hairy; rough-haired. **2** unkempt. □□ **shag'gi·ly** *adv.* **shag'gi·ness** *n.*
■ woolly, uncut, hirsute, disheveled.

shah /shaa/ *n. hist.* title of the former monarch of Iran.

shake /shayk/ • *v.* (*past* **shook** /shòōk/; *past part.* **shak·en** /sháykən/) **1** *tr. & intr.* move forcefully or quickly up and down or to and fro. **2 a** *intr.* tremble or vibrate markedly. **b** *tr.* cause to do this. **3** *tr.* **a** agitate or shock. **b** *colloq.* upset the composure of. **4** *intr. colloq.* shake hands. • *n.* **1** shaking; being shaken. **2** [in *pl.*; prec. by *the*] fit of or tendency to trembling or shivering. **3** ■ *milk shake.* **4** shingle made by splitting sections of a log. □ **no great shakes** *colloq.* not very good or significant. **shake down 1** settle or cause to fall by shaking. **2** settle down; break in. **3** *sl.* extort money from. **shake hands** [often foll. by *with*] clasp right hands at meeting or parting, in reconciliation or congratulation, etc. **shake off** get rid of (something unwanted). **shake up 1** mix (ingredients) by shaking. **2** make uncomfortable. **3** rouse from lethargy, apathy, conventionality, etc. **shake-up** *n.* upheaval or drastic reorganization. □□ **shak'a·ble** *adj.* (also **shake'a·ble**).
■ *v.* **1, 2** quiver, quake, shudder, jiggle, rock, oscillate. **3** stir (up), mix (up); upset, distress, frighten. • *n.* **1** rattle, quiver, quake, shudder. **2** (*the shakes*) tremors, d.t.'s, *colloq.* the willies. □ **shake down 2** break in, condition, test, prove **3** blackmail, squeeze, threaten. **shake off** discard, dislodge, drop; brush off, elude. **shake up 2** see DISTURB 2a. **3** see ROUSE 2a. **shake-up** rearrangement, overhaul, revamp, restructuring.

SYNONYM STUDY: shake

QUAKE, QUIVER, SHIVER, SHUDDER, TREMBLE. Does a cool breeze make you **shiver, quiver, shudder,** or **tremble**? All of these verbs describe vibrating, wavering, or oscillating movements that, in living creatures, are often involuntary expressions of strain or discomfort. **Shake,** which refers to abrupt forward-and-backward, side-to-side, or up-and-down movements, is different from the others in that it can be done as well as by a person or object (*to shake a can of paint, to shake visibly while lifting a heavy load*). **Tremble** applies specifically to the slight, rapid, shaking motion the human body makes when it is nervous, frightened, or uneasy (*his hands trembled when he picked up the phone*). To **shiver** is to make a similar movement, but the cause is usually cold or fear (*to shiver in the draft from an open door*), while **quiver** suggests a rapid and almost imperceptible vibration resulting from disturbed or irregular surface tension; it refers more often to things (*the lake quivered in the breeze*), although people

---

may *quiver* when they're under emotional tension (*her lower lip quivered and her eyes were downcast*). **Shudder** suggests a more intense *shaking*, usually in response to something horrible or revolting (*to shudder at the thought of eating uncooked meat*). **Quake** implies a violent upheaval or *shaking,* similar to what occurs during an earthquake (*the boy's heart quaked at his father's approach*).

---

shake·down /sháykdown/ *n.* **1** extortion. **2** *sl.* thorough search. **3** [*attrib.*] *colloq.* denoting a voyage, flight, etc., to test a new ship or aircraft and its crew.

shak·er /sháykər/ *n.* **1** person or thing that shakes. **2** container for shaking together the ingredients of cocktails, etc. **3** (**Shaker**) member of an American religious sect living simply, in celibate mixed communities. □□ **Shak'er·ism** *n.* (in sense 3).

Shake·spear·e·an /shaykspéereeən/ (also **Shake·spear'i·an**) • *adj.* **1** of or relating to William Shakespeare, English dramatist d. 1616. **2** in the style of Shakespeare. • *n.* student of Shakespeare's works, etc.

shak·y /sháykee/ *adj.* (**shak·i·er, shak·i·est**) **1** unsteady; trembling. **2** unsound; infirm. **3** unreliable. □□ **shak'i·ly** *adv.* **shak'i·ness** *n.*
■ uncertain, wobbly, unstable, precarious, rickety, insecure, untrustworthy, dubious.

shale /shayl/ *n.* soft rock of consolidated mud or clay that splits easily. □□ **shal'y** *adj.*

shall /shal, shəl/ *v.aux.* (*3rd sing. present* **shall**; *past* **should** /shŏŏd, shəd/) [foll. by infin. without *to,* or *absol.*; present and past only in use] **1** (in the 1st person) expressing the future tense (*I shall return soon*) or (with *shall* stressed) emphatic intention (*I shall have a party*). **2** (in the 2nd and 3rd persons) expressing strong assertion or command rather than a wish (cf. WILL[1]) (*you shall not catch me again*).

shal·lot /shálət, shəlót/ *n.* onionlike plant with a cluster of small edible bulbs.

shal·low /shálō/ • *adj.* **1** of little depth. **2** superficial; trivial. See synonym study at SUPERFICIAL. • *n.* [often in *pl.*] shallow place. □□ **shal'low·ly** *adv.* **shal'low·ness** *n.*
■ *adj.* surface, skin-deep; empty, flimsy. • *n.* shoal, sandbar, shelf.

shalt /shalt/ *archaic* 2nd person sing. of SHALL.

sham /sham/ • *n.* (**shammed, sham·ming**) **1** *intr.* feign; pretend. **2** *tr.* pretend to be. • *n.* **1** imposture; pretense. **2** person or thing pretending or pretended to be what he or she or it is not. • *adj.* counterfeit. □□ **sham'mer** *n.*
■ *v.* **1** fake, dissemble. **2** simulate, feign, fake, affect. • *n.* fake, fraud, counterfeit, imitation, hoax. • *adj.* fake, fraudulent, imitation, paste, simulated.

sham·ble /shámbəl/ • *v.intr.* walk or run with a shuffling or awkward gait. • *n.* shambling gait.

sham·bles /shámbəlz/ *n.pl.* [usu. treated as *sing.*] **1** *colloq.* mess or muddle (*the room was a shambles*). **2** butcher's slaughterhouse. **3** scene of carnage.

■ **1** chaos, devastation, disaster, pigsty, pigpen.

shame /shaym/ • *n.* **1** distress or humiliation caused by consciousness of one's guilt or folly. **2** capacity for experiencing this feeling, esp. as imposing a restraint on behavior (*has no sense of shame*). **3** state of disgrace, discredit, or intense regret. **4 a** person or thing that brings disgrace, etc. **b** thing or action that is wrong or regrettable. • *v.tr.* **1** bring shame on; make ashamed. **2** force by shame. □ **put to shame** disgrace or humiliate by revealing superior qualities, etc. □□ **shame'ful** *adj* **shame'ful•ly** *adv.* **shame'ful•ness** *n.*

■ *n.* **1** embarrassment, mortification, chagrin, ignominy. **2** humility, modesty, (sense of) decency; diffidence, shyness. **3, 4** ignominy, dishonor, disrepute, degradation; pity, disaster; outrage. • *v.* **1** embarrass, humiliate, mortify; disgrace, dishonor. **2** coerce; embarrass, humiliate. □ **put to shame** surpass, eclipse, outclass, show up. □□ **shameful** disgraceful, dishonorable, base, low, mean, vile.

shame•faced /sháymfáyst/ *adj.* **1** showing shame. **2** bashful; diffident.

■ **1** ashamed, shamed, abashed, embarrassed. **2** shy, modest, self-effacing, timid, meek.

shame•less /sháymlis/ *adj.* **1** having or showing no shame. **2** impudent. □□ **shame'less•ly** *adv.* **shame'less•ness** *n.*

■ wild, flagrant, unreserved, uncontrolled, immodest, wanton, indecent, rude, improper, bold.

sham•poo /shampóō/ • *n.* **1** substance used to wash hair, a car, a carpet, etc. **2** act or instance of cleaning with shampoo. • *v.tr.* (**sham•poos, sham•pooed**) wash with shampoo.

sham•rock /shámrok/ *n.* plant with trifoliate leaves; national emblem of Ireland.

shang•hai /shanghí/ *v.tr.* (**shang•hais, shang•haied, shang•hai•ing**) trick or force (a person) into working.

shank /shangk/ *n.* **1 a** the leg. **b** lower part of the leg. **2** lower part of an animal's foreleg, esp. as a cut of meat. **3** shaft or stem. **4** long narrow part of a tool, etc., joining the handle to the working end. □□ **shanked** *adj.* [also in *comb.*].

shan•ty /shántee/ *n.* (pl. **–ties**) hut or cabin.

shape /shayp/ • *n.* **1** total effect produced by the outlines of a thing. **2** external form or appearance. **3** specific form or guise. **4** person or thing as seen, esp. indistinctly (*shape emerged from the mist*). • *v.* **1** *tr.* give a certain shape or form to; fashion. **2** *tr.* adapt or make conform. **3** *intr.* give signs of a future shape or development. □ **shape up** show promise; make good progress. □□ **shap'a•ble** *adj.* (also **shape'a•ble**). **shaped** *adj.* **shape'less** *adj.* [also in *comb.*]. **shape'less•ly** *adv.* **shape'less•ness** *n.* **shap'er** *n.*

■ *n.* **1, 2** pattern, configuration, structure; line(s), profile. **3** disguise, appearance. • *v.* **1** form, mold, cast, make, create, model. **2** change, modify, remodel, fit, adapt, adjust. **3** see *turn out* 5. □ **shape up** improve, move or come along. □□ **shapeless** amorphous, formless, nebulous, unformed, indefinite, vague.

shape•ly /sháyplee/ *adj.* (**shape•li•er, shape•li•est**) **1** well formed. **2** of pleasing shape. □□ **shape'li•ness** *n.*

■ comely, well-proportioned, graceful, neat, well turned out, good-looking, attractive; voluptuous.

shard /shaard/ *n.* **1** broken piece of pottery, etc. **2** = POTSHERD.

share[1] /shair/ • *n.* **1** portion that a person receives from or gives to a common amount. **2 a** part contributed by an individual to an enterprise or commitment. **b** part received by an individual from this. • *v.* **1** *tr.* get or have or give a share of. **2** *tr.* use or benefit from jointly with others. **3** *intr.* have a share; be a sharer (*shall I share with you?*). **4** *intr.* [foll. by *in*] participate. □□ **share'a•ble** *adj.* (also **shar'a•ble**). **shared** *adj.* **shar'er** *n.* See synonym study at MUTUAL.

■ *n.* **1** allotment, division, apportionment, allocation, interest, dividend. **2** interest, piece, stake, equity, slice. • *v.* **1, 2** divide up, allot, apportion.

share[2] /shair/ *n.* = PLOWSHARE.

share•hold•er /sháirhōldər/ *n.* owner of shares in a company.

share•ware /sháirwair/ *n.* *Computing* software distributed free.

shark[1] /shaark/ *n.* large, usu. voracious marine fish with a long body and prominent dorsal fin.

shark[2] /shaark/ *n.* *colloq.* swindler; profiteer.

shark•skin /shaárkskin/ *n.* **1** skin of a shark. **2** smooth, dull-surfaced fabric.

sharp /shaarp/ • *adj.* **1** having an edge or point able to cut or pierce. **2** tapering to a point or edge. **3** abrupt; steep. **4** well-defined; clean-cut. **5 a** severe or intense. **b** (of food, etc.) pungent. **c** (of a frost) severe; hard. **6** (of a voice or sound) shrill and piercing. **7** (of words, etc.) harsh or acrimonious (*had a sharp tongue*). **8** acute; quick to comprehend. **9** quick to take advantage; artful. **10** vigorous or brisk. **11** *Mus.* (C, F, etc., **sharp**) semitone higher than C, F, etc. **12** *colloq.* stylish. See synonym study at KEEN. • *n.* **1** *Mus.* **a** note raised a semitone above natural pitch. **b** the sign (SHRP;) indicating this. **2** *colloq.* swindler; cheat. • *adv.* **1** punctually. **2** suddenly. **3** *Mus.* above true pitch. □ **sharp-witted** keenly perceptive or intelligent. □□ **sharp'ly** *adv.* **sharp'ness** *n.*

■ *adj.* **1, 2** acute, keen; razor-sharp, knife-edged; pointed. **3** sudden, precipitous, sheer, vertical, angular. **4** see DEFINITE 2. **5 a, c** poignant, cutting, sudden, piercing. **b** hot, spicy, piquant. **6** high-pitched, penetrating, strident. **7** acidulous, acerbic, vitriolic, cutting. **8** keen, keen-witted, sharp-witted, shrewd, intelligent. **9** clever, shrewd, crafty, sly, unscrupulous, dishonest. **10** see VIGOROUS 1, 3, 4, BRISK *adj.* 1. **12** chic, dapper, spruce, smart, fashionable. • *adv.* **1** precisely, exactly, on the dot. **2** sharply, abruptly, promptly; see also *suddenly* (SUDDEN). □ **sharp-witted** see INTELLIGENT 2.

□□ **sharply** severely, sternly, harshly; suddenly, quickly, abruptly.

sharp•en /sha̅arpən/ v. make or become sharp. □□ **sharp'en•er** n.
■ hone, grind, strop, whet.

sharp•er /sha̅arpər/ n. swindler, esp. at cards.

sharp•shoot•er /sha̅arpsho̅otər/ n. skilled marksman. □□ **sharp'shoot•ing** n. & adj.

shat•ter /sha̅tər/ v. 1 tr. & intr. break suddenly in pieces. 2 tr. severely damage or utterly destroy. 3 tr. greatly upset. 4 tr. (usu. as **shattered** adj.) exhaust. □□ **shat'ter•ing** adj. **shat'ter•ing•ly** adv. **shat'ter-proof** adj.
■ 1 disintegrate, burst, pulverize, smash, splinter. 2 ruin, devastate, wreck, dash, demolish. 3 disturb, perturb, trouble, discompose. 4 (**shattered**) see *exhausted* (EXHAUST v. 2).

shave /shayv/ • v.tr. (past part. **shaved** or [as adj.] **shav•en**) 1 remove (bristles or hair) with a razor. 2 reduce by a small amount. 3 pass close to without touching; miss narrowly. • n. 1 shaving or being shaved. 2 narrow miss or escape = *close shave* (see CLOSE¹).
■ v. 2 trim, clip, crop; pare; snip off.

shav•er /sha̅yvər/ n. 1 thing that shaves. 2 colloq. young lad.

shav•ing /sha̅yving/ n. 1 thin strip cut off of wood, etc. 2 [attrib.] used in shaving the face (*shaving cream*).

shawl /shawl/ n. piece of fabric, usu. rectangular, worn over the shoulders or head. □□ **shawled** adj.

Shaw•nee /shawne̅e, shaa–/ n. 1 a N. American people native to the central Ohio valley. b member of this people. 2 language of this people.

she /shee/ • pron. (obj. **her**; poss. **her**; pl. **they**) 1 woman or girl or female animal previously named or in question. 2 thing regarded as female, e.g., vehicle or ship. • n. 1 female; woman. 2 [in comb.] female (*she-goat*).

sheaf /sheef/ • n. (pl. **sheaves** /sheevz/) group of things laid lengthwise together and usu. tied, esp. grain stalks, etc. • v.tr. (also **sheave** /sheev/) make into sheaves.

shear /sheer/ • v.tr. (past **sheared**, archaic **shore** /shor/; past part. **shorn** /shorn/ or **sheared**) 1 cut with scissors or shears, etc. 2 remove by cutting. 3 clip the wool off (a sheep, etc.). • n. [in pl.] (also **pair of shears** sing.) large clipping or cutting instrument shaped like scissors. □□ **shear'er** n.

sheath /sheeth/ n. (pl. **sheaths** /sheethz, sheeths/) 1 close-fitting cover for the blade of a knife or sword. 2 condom. 3 Bot., Anat., & Zool. enclosing case or tissue. 4 woman's close-fitting dress. □□ **sheath'less** adj.

sheathe /sheeth/ v.tr. 1 put into a sheath. 2 encase; protect with a sheath.

she•bang /shibáng/ n. sl. (esp. *the whole shebang*) everything.

shed¹ /shed/ n. one-story structure usu. of wood for storage or shelter for animals, etc., or as a workshop.
■ hut, shack, stall, booth, cote, hutch.

shed² /shed/ v.tr. (**shed•ding**; past and past

part. **shed**) 1 let or cause to fall off (*trees shed their leaves*). 2 take off (clothes). 3 cause to fall or flow (*shed blood*). 4 disperse; diffuse; radiate (*shed light*). □□ **shed'der** n.
■ 1 drop, spill; molt, cast. 2 remove, strip. 3 spill, drop, pour out or forth, discharge, emit. 4 dissipate, spread; emanate, emit.

she'd /sheed/ contr. 1 she had. 2 she would.

sheen /sheen/ n. 1 gloss or luster. 2 radiance; brightness.
■ shine, gleam, polish, shininess, glow, shimmer.

sheep /sheep/ n. (pl. **same**) 1 ruminant mammal with a thick woolly coat, esp. kept in flocks for its wool or meat. 2 bashful, timid, or silly person.

sheep•dog /sheepdawg, –dog/ n. 1 dog trained to guard and herd sheep. 2 a dog of various breeds suitable for this. b any of these breeds.

sheep•ish /sheepish/ adj. 1 bashful; shy; reticent. 2 embarrassed through shame. □□ **sheep'ish•ly** adv. **sheep'ish•ness** n.
■ 1 timid, withdrawn, passive, docile. 2 see SHAMEFACED 1.

sheep•skin /sheepskin/ n. 1 garment or rug of sheep's skin with the wool on. 2 leather from a sheep's skin used in bookbinding.

sheer¹ /sheer/ • adj. 1 unqualified; absolute (*sheer luck*). 2 (of a cliff or ascent, etc.) perpendicular. 3 (of a textile) diaphanous. • adv. 1 directly; outright. 2 perpendicularly. □□ **sheer'ly** adv. **sheer'ness** n.
■ adj. 1 unmitigated, downright, out-and-out, unadulterated. 2 steep, precipitous, abrupt, vertical. 3 transparent, see-through, thin.

sheer² /sheer/ • v.intr. swerve or change course. • n. Naut. deviation from a course.

sheet¹ /sheet/ n. 1 large rectangular piece of cotton or other fabric, used for bedclothes. 2 a broad usu. thin flat piece of material (e.g., paper or metal). b [attrib.] made in sheets (*sheet iron*). 3 wide continuous surface or expanse of water, ice, flame, falling rain, etc. 4 set of unseparated postage stamps. □ **sheet metal** metal formed into thin sheets. **sheet music** music published on unbound pages.
■ 2a, 3 pane, panel, plate, slab; lamina, layer; area, stretch, film, coat, coating, covering, blanket, cover, surface, skin.

sheet² /sheet/ n. rope attached to the lower corner of a sail for securing or controlling it.

sheikh /sheek, shayk/ n. (also **sheik**) chief or head of an Arab tribe, family, or village. □□ **sheikh'dom** n.

shek•el /shékəl/ n. 1 chief monetary unit of modern Israel. 2 hist. silver coin and unit of weight in ancient Israel, etc. 3 [in pl.] colloq. money; riches.

shelf /shelf/ n. (pl. **shelves** /shelvz/) 1 flat piece of wood or metal, etc., projecting from a wall, or as part of a unit, used to support books, etc. 2 flat-topped recess in a wall, etc., used for supporting objects. □ **on the shelf** postponed, as a plan or project. **shelf life** amount of time for which a stored item of medicine, food, etc., remains usable. □□ **shelved** /shelvd/ *adj.* **shelf′ful** *n.* (*pl.* **-fuls**).

shell /shel/ • *n.* **1** hard outer case of many marine mollusks, tortoises, eggs, nuts, etc. **2** explosive projectile for use in a gun or mortar. **3** any of several things resembling a shell in being an outer case, esp.: **a** a light racing boat. **b** walls of an unfinished or gutted building, ship, etc. • *v.* **1** *tr.* remove the shell or pod from. **2** *tr.* bombard with shells. **3** *intr.* (of a seed, etc.) be released from a shell. □ **shell out** *colloq.* pay out (money). **shell shock** nervous breakdown resulting from exposure to battle. **shell-shocked** suffering from shell shock. □□ **shelled** *adj.* **shell′-less** *adj.* **shell′-like** *adj.*

■ *n.* **1** cover, shield; armor, carapace, integument, cocoon; shuck, husk, rind, crust, pod. **2** cartridge, shot, bomb; case, casing. **3** façade, framework, chassis, skeleton, hull. • *v.* **1** husk, peel, hull, shuck. **2** fire on, cannonade. □ **shell out** give out, disburse, spend; hand over.

she′ll /sheel, shil/ *contr.* she will; she shall.

shel•lac /shəlák/ • *n.* lac resin used for making varnish. • *v.tr.* (**shel•lacked, shel•lack•ing**) **1** varnish with shellac. **2** *sl.* defeat or thrash soundly.

shell•fish /shélfish/ *n.* **1** edible aquatic shelled mollusk, e.g., oyster, mussel, etc. **2** crustacean, e.g., crab, shrimp, etc.

shel•ter /shéltər/ • *n.* **1** protection from danger, bad weather, etc. **2 a** place of refuge. **b** animal sanctuary. • *v.* **1** *tr.* serve as shelter to; protect. **2** *intr. & refl.* find refuge; take cover.

■ *n.* **1** cover, shield, refuge, asylum, sanctuary, haven, safety, security; covering. **2 a** habitation, home, housing, accommodation, hostel. • *v.* **1** screen, shield, defend, safeguard, guard, keep, secure, harbor, conceal. **2** seek or take refuge or shelter, lie low.

shelve /shelv/ *v.tr.* **1** put (books, etc.) on a shelf. **2 a** abandon or defer (a plan, etc.). **b** remove (a person) from active work, etc. **3** fit (a cupboard, etc.) with shelves. □□ **shelv′er** *n.* **shelv′ing** *n.*

■ **2 a** postpone, put off or aside, pigeonhole, table.

shelves *pl.* of SHELF.

she•nan•i•gan /shinánigən/ *n.* [esp. in *pl.*] *colloq.* high-spirited or dubious behavior.

shep•herd /shépərd/ • *n.* **1** (*fem.* **shep•herd•ess** /shépərdis/) person employed to tend sheep. **2** member of the clergy, etc., who cares for and guides a congregation. • *v.tr.* **1 a** tend (sheep, etc.) as a shepherd. **b** guide (followers, etc.). **2** marshal or drive (a crowd, etc.) like sheep.

■ *v.* **1** see TEND² 1. **1b, 2** lead, convoy, escort, conduct.

sher•bet /shárbət/ *n.* fruit-flavored ice confection.

sher•iff /shérif/ *n.* civil law-enforcement officer.

Sher•pa /shárpə/ *n.* (*pl.* same or **Sher•pas**) **1** a Himalayan people living on the borders

of Nepal and Tibet, and skilled in mountaineering. **2** member of this people.

sher•ry /shéree/ *n.* (*pl.* **-ries**) fortified wine orig. from S. Spain.

she′s /sheez/ *contr.* **1** she is. **2** she has.

Shi•a /sheeə/ *n.* one of the two main branches of Islam.

shib•bo•leth /shibəleth/ *n.* long-standing formula, doctrine, phrase, etc., held to be true by a party or sect.

shield /sheeld/ • *n.* **1 a** esp. *hist.* piece of armor held in front of the body for protection when fighting. **b** thing serving to protect. **2** shield-shaped trophy, protective screen on machinery, etc. • *v.tr.* protect or screen. □□ **shield′less** *adj.*

■ *n.* **1 b** protection, guard, safeguard, defense. **2** see SHELL *n.* 1. • *v.* guard, safeguard, keep, defend, shelter.

shi•er *compar.* of SHY¹.

shi•est *superl.* of SHY¹.

shift /shift/ • *v.* **1** *intr.* & *tr.* change or move or cause to change or move from one position to another. **2** *intr.* manage as best one can. **3 a** *tr.* change (gear) in a vehicle. **b** *intr.* change gear. • *n.* **1 a** act or instance of shifting. **b** substitution of one thing for another; rotation. **2 a** relay of workers. **b** time for which they work. **3 a** device, stratagem, or expedient. **b** dodge, trick, or evasion. **4 a** woman's straight unwaisted dress. **b** *archaic* loose-fitting undergarment. **5** (in full **shift key**) key on a keyboard used to switch between lowercase and uppercase, etc. **6** gear lever in a motor vehicle. □□ **shift′a•ble** *adj.* **shift′er** *n.*

■ *v.* **1** switch; edge, budge; relocate, transpose. **2** make do, scrape by or through. • *n.* **1 a** change, movement, switch, transfer. **b** see SUBSTITUTE *n.* **2 a** workforce, crew, staff. **b** stint. **3 a** see STRATAGEM 1. **b** see TRICK *n.* 1, EVASION 2. **4 a** smock, muu-muu, caftan, chemise. **b** *hist.* chemise.

shift•less /shiftlis/ *adj.* lacking resourcefulness; lazy; inefficient. □□ **shift′less•ly** *adv.* **shift′less•ness** *n.*

■ unambitious, indolent, idle, lackadaisical, aimless.

shift•y /shiftee/ *adj. colloq.* (**shift•i•er, shift•i•est**) evasive; deceitful. □□ **shift′i•ly** *adv.* **shift′i•ness** *n.*

■ tricky, artful, shrewd, canny, cunning, foxy, wily.

shill /shil/ *n.* person employed to decoy or entice others into buying, gambling, etc.

shil•le•lagh /shiláylee, -lə/ *n.* = CUDGEL.

shil•ling /shíling/ *n. hist.* former British coin and monetary unit worth one-twentieth of a pound or twelve pence.

shil•ly-shal•ly /shíleeshálee/ *v.intr.* (**-lies, -lied**) be undecided; vacillate.

shim /shim/ • *n.* thin strip of material used in machinery, etc., to make parts fit. • *v.tr.* (**shimmed, shim•ming**) fit or fill up with a shim.

shim•mer /shímər/ • *v.intr.* shine with a tremulous or faint diffused light. • *n.* such a light. □□ **shim′mer•ing•ly** *adv.* **shim′mer•y** *adj.*

■ *v.* gleam, glow, glimmer, glint, glisten, ripple. • *n.* shimmering, shine, gleam, glow, glimmer.

shin /shin/ • *n.* **1** front of the leg below the knee. **2** cut of beef from the lower foreleg. • *v.tr. & [usu. foll. by up, down] intr.* (**shinned, shin•ning**) climb quickly by clinging with the arms and legs.

shin•bone /shínbōn/ = TIBIA.

shin•dig /shíndig/ *n. colloq.* festive, esp. noisy, party.

shine /shīn/ • *v.* (*past* and *past part.* **shone** /shon/ or **shined**) **1** *intr.* emit or reflect light; be bright; glow. **2** *intr.* (of the sun, a star, etc.) be visible. **3** *tr.* cause (a lamp, etc.) to shine. **4** *tr.* (*past* and *past part.* **shined**) polish. **5** *intr.* be brilliant; excel. • *n.* **1** light; brightness, esp. reflected. **2** high polish; luster. □□ **shin'ing•ly** *adv.*

■ *v.* **1** gleam, shimmer, radiate, beam, glare, flare. **4** burnish, rub, buff, brush, brighten. **5** stand out, be outstanding *or* excellent. • *n.* gleam, glow, shimmer, sparkle, radiance.

shin•er /shínər/ *n. colloq.* black eye.

shin•gle /shínggəl/ • *n.* **1** rectangular tile used on roofs, spires, or esp. walls. **2** a shingled hair. **b** act of shingling hair. **3** small signboard, esp. of a doctor, lawyer, etc. • *v.tr.* **1** roof or clad with shingles. **2** cut hair very short.

shin•gles /shínggəlz/ *n.pl.* [usu. treated as *sing.*] acute painful viral inflammation of the nerve ganglia, with a skin eruption often forming a girdle around the middle of the body.

Shin•to /shíntō/ *n.* official religion of Japan, incorporating the worship of ancestors and nature spirits. □□ **Shin'to•ism** *n.* **Shin'to•ist** *n.*

shin•y /shínee/ *adj.* (**shin•i•er, shin•i•est**) **1** having a shine. **2** (of clothing, esp. the seat of pants, etc.) having the nap worn off. □□ **shin'i•ly** *adv.* **shin'i•ness** *n.*

■ **1** gleaming, glowing, shimmering, glossy, shimmery, lustrous, radiant, bright, beaming, glistening, polished.

ship /ship/ • *n.* **1** large seagoing vessel. **2** aircraft. **3** spaceship. • *v.* (**shipped, ship•ping**) **1** *tr.* put, take, or send as in a ship, etc. **2** *tr.* a take in (water) over the side of a ship, boat, etc. **b** take (oars) from the rowlocks and lay them inside a boat. **3** *intr.* embark. □□ **ship'pa•ble** *adj.*

■ *n.* **1** boat. • *v.* **1** deliver, dispatch, haul; ferry, transport. **3** take ship, set sail.

-ship /ship/ *suffix* forming nouns denoting: **1** quality or condition (*hardship*). **2** status, office, or honor (*authorship*). **3** tenure (*chairmanship*). **4** skill (*workmanship*). **5** collective individuals of a group (*membership*).

ship•board /shípbawrd/ *n.* [usu. *attrib.*] used or occurring on board a ship.

ship•build•er /shípbildər/ *n.* person, company, etc., that constructs ships. □□ **ship'build•ing** *n.*

ship•mate /shípmayt/ *n.* fellow member of a ship's crew.

ship•ment /shípmənt/ *n.* **1** amount of goods shipped; consignment. **2** act or instance of shipping goods, etc.

ship•per /shípər/ *n.* person or company that sends or receives goods.

ship•ping /shíping/ *n.* **1** act or instance of shipping goods, etc. **2** ships, esp. the ships of a country, port, etc.

ship•shape /shípshayp/ *adv. & predic.adj.* in good order; trim and neat.

■ spotless, orderly, spick-and-span, tidy.

ship•wreck /shíprek/ • *n.* **1 a** destruction of a ship by a storm, foundering, etc. **b** ship so destroyed. **2** [often foll. by *of*] destruction of hopes, dreams, etc. • *v.* **1** *tr.* inflict shipwreck on (a ship, a person's hopes, etc.). **2** *intr.* suffer shipwreck.

■ *n.* **1 b** wreck, hulk, ruins.

ship•wright /shíprīt/ *n.* **1** shipbuilder. **2** ship's carpenter.

ship•yard /shípyaard/ *n.* place where ships are built, repaired, etc.

shirk /shərk/ • *v.tr.* [also *absol.*] avoid (duty, work, responsibility, fighting, etc.). • *n.* (also **shirk'er**) person who shirks.

■ *v.* evade, shun, dodge, get out of, shrink from. • *n.* see TRUANT *n.*

shirr /shər/ • *n.* two or more rows of gathered threads in a garment. • *v.tr.* **1** gather (material) with parallel threads. **2** bake (eggs) without shells. □□ **shirr'ing** *n.*

shirt /shərt/ *n.* upper-body garment, often having a collar and sleeves.

shirt•tail /shərttayl/ *n.* lower curved part of a shirt below the waist.

shirt•waist /shərtwayst/ *n.* woman's dress with a bodice like a shirt.

shish ke•bab /shish kibób/ *n.* pieces of marinated meat and vegetables grilled and served on skewers.

shiv•er /shívər/ • *v.intr.* **1** tremble with cold, fear, etc. **2** shudder. • *n.* **1** momentary shivering movement. **2** [in *pl.*] attack of shivering (*got the shivers in the dark*). □□ **shiv'er•er** *n.* **shiv'er•ing•ly** *adv.* **shiv'er•y** *adj.*

■ *v.* shake, quake, quiver, quaver. • *n.* **1** shake, tremble, shivering, tremor, flutter. **2** (*shivers*) trembling; (*the shivers*) the shakes.

shiv•er[2] /shívər/ • *n.* [esp. in *pl.*] small piece or splinter. • *v.* break into shivers.

■ *n.* fragment, shard, chip, sliver. • *v.* shatter, fragment, disintegrate, explode.

shoal[1] /shōl/ • *n.* **1** great number of fish swimming together. **2** multitude. • *v.intr.* (of fish) form shoals.

shoal[2] /shōl/ • *n.* **1** area of shallow water. **2** submerged sandbank visible at low water. • *v.intr.* (of water) get shallower. • *adj. archaic* (of water) shallow.

shock[1] /shok/ • *n.* **1** violent collision, impact, tremor, etc. **2** sudden and disturbing effect on the emotions, etc. **3** acute state of prostration following a wound, pain, etc., esp. when much blood is lost. • *v.tr.* **1 a** horrify; outrage. **b** cause shock. **2** affect with an electric or pathological shock. □□ **shock'a•ble** *adj.*

■ *n.* **1** jolt; see also IMPACT *n.* 1. **2** surprise, thunderbolt, bombshell; trauma. • *v.* **1** frighten, scare, petrify, traumatize, appall; disgust, nauseate, repel; stun, numb, paralyze.

shock² /shok/ • *n.* group of usu. twelve sheaves of grain stood up with their heads together in a field. • *v.tr.* arrange (grain) in shocks.

shock³ /shok/ *n.* unkempt or shaggy mass of hair.

shock•er /shókər/ *n. colloq.* **1** shocking, horrifying, etc., person or thing. **2** *hist.* sordid or sensational novel, etc.

shock•ing /shóking/ • *adj.* causing indignation or disgust. • *adv. colloq.* shockingly. □□ **shock′ing•ly** *adv.*
   ■ *adj.* disgusting, revolting, nauseating, sickening, repulsive, abominable, hideous, horrible.

shock•proof /shókpro͞of/ *adj.* resistant to the effects of (esp. physical) shock.

shod *past* and *past part.* of SHOE.

shod•dy /shóde/ • *adj.* (**shod•di•er, shod•di•est**) **1** trashy; shabby; poorly made. **2** counterfeit. • *n.* (*pl.* **–dies**) **1** inferior cloth made partly from the shredded fiber of old woolen cloth. **2** such fiber. □□ **shod′di•ly** *adv.* **shod′di•ness** *n.*
   ■ *adj.* **1** inferior, poor, tawdry.

shoe /sho͞o/ • *n.* **1** outer foot coverings having a sturdy sole and not reaching above the ankle. **2** metal rim nailed to the hoof of a horse, etc.; horseshoe. **3** (also **brake shoe**) part of a brake that presses against a wheel rim or drum. • *v.tr.* (**shoes, shoe•ing**; *past* and *past part.* **shod** /shod/) **1** fit (esp. a horse, etc.) with a shoe or shoes. **2** (as **shod** *adj.*) [in *comb.*] having shoes, etc., of a specified kind (dry-shod, roughshod). □ **shoe tree** shaped block for keeping a shoe in shape when not worn. □□ **shoe′less** *adj.*

shoe•horn /sho͞ohawrn/ *n.* curved piece of horn, metal, etc., for easing one's heel into a shoe.

shoe•lace /sho͞olays/ *n.* cord for lacing up shoes.

shoe•mak•er /sho͞omaykər/ *n.* maker of boots and shoes. □□ **shoe′mak•ing** *n.*

shoe•string /sho͞ostring/ *n.* **1** shoelace. **2** *colloq.* small, esp. inadequate amount of money. **3** [*attrib.*] barely adequate; precarious (*shoestring majority*).

sho•far /shófər, shawfaàr/ *n.* (*pl.* **sho•froth** /shófrōt/) ram's-horn trumpet used by Jews in religious ceremonies.

sho•gun /shógən, –gun/ *n. hist.* any of a succession of Japanese hereditary commanders in chief and virtual rulers before 1868. □□ **sho•gun•ate** /–nət, –nayt/ *n.*

shone *past* and *past part.* of SHINE.

shoo /sho͞o/ • *int.* exclamation used to frighten away birds, children, etc. • *v.* (**shoos, shooed**) **1** *intr.* utter the word "shoo!". **2** *tr.* [usu. foll. by *away*] drive (birds, etc.) away by shooing.

shook /shook/ *past* of SHAKE. • *predic. adj. colloq.* [foll. by *up*] emotionally or physically disturbed; upset.

shoot /sho͞ot/ • *v.* (*past* and *past part.* **shot** /shot/) **1** *tr.* **a** cause (a gun, bow, etc.) to fire. **b** discharge (a bullet, arrow, etc.) from a gun, bow, etc. **c** kill or wound (a person, animal, etc.) with a bullet, arrow, etc. **2** *intr.* discharge a gun, etc., esp. in a specified way (*shoots well*). **3** *tr.* send out, discharge, etc., esp. swiftly (*shot a glance at his neighbor*). **4** *intr.* come or go swiftly or vigorously. **5** *intr.* **a** (of a plant, etc.) put forth buds, etc. **b** (of a bud, etc.) appear. **6** *tr.* film or photograph. **7** *tr. Basketball, etc.* **a** score (a goal). **b** take a shot at (the goal). **8** *intr.* (of a pain) pass with a stabbing sensation. **9** *tr.* [foll. by *up*] *sl.* inject, esp. oneself with (a drug). • *n.* **1** act or instance of shooting. **2** young branch or new growth of a plant. **3** hunting party, etc. • *int. colloq.* **1** demand for a reply, information, etc. **2** *euphem.* exclamation of disgust, anger, etc. □ **shoot-out** *colloq.* decisive gunfight; showdown. □□ **shoot′er** *n.* **shoot′ing** *n. & adj.*
   ■ *v.* **1 b** fire, let fly, launch, propel, project. **c** hurt, harm, injure; gun (down). **3** see EJECT 1. **4** dart, whisk, speed, bolt, run, race. **5** sprout, germinate; grow, spring up; mushroom. • *n.* **1** sprout, stem, bud, offshoot. *int.* **1** *colloq.* spill the beans, spit it out. **2** *damn, colloq.* hell.

shop /shop/ • *n.* **1** place for the retail sale of goods or services; store. **2** place for manufacture or repair; workshop. **3** *colloq.* institution, establishment, place of business, etc. • *v.* (**shopped, shop•ping**) **1** *intr.* go to buy goods. **2** = *window-shop.* □ **shop around** look for the best bargain. □□ **shop′per** *n.*
   ■ *n.* **1** boutique. **2** machine shop; see also FACTORY. **3** see ESTABLISHMENT 2a.

shop•keep•er /shópkeepər/ *n.* owner and manager of a store. □□ **shop′keep•ing** *n.*

shop•lift•er /shópliftər/ *n.* person who steals goods while appearing to shop. □□ **shop′lift** *v.* **shop′lift•ing** *n.*

shop•ping /shóping/ *n.* **1** [often *attrib.*] purchase of goods, etc. **2** goods purchased (*put the shopping on the table*). □ **shopping cen•ter** area or complex of stores, with associated facilities.

shop•worn /shópwawrn/ *adj.* **1** (of an article) soiled or faded by display in a shop. **2** (of a person, idea, etc.) grubby; tarnished; no longer fresh or new.

shore¹ /shawr/ *n.* land that adjoins the sea or a large body of water. □□ **shore′less** *adj.* **shore′ward** *adj. & adv.* **shore′wards** *adv.*

shore² /shawr/ • *v.tr.* [often foll. by *up*] support with or as if with a shore or shores; hold up. • *n.* prop or beam set obliquely against a ship, wall, tree, etc., as a support. □□ **shor′ing** *n.*
   ■ *v.* see SUPPORT¹ *v.* 1, 2, 4, 6. • *n.* see PROP *n.* 1.

shore•line /sháwrlīn/ *n.* line along which a stretch of water, esp. a sea or lake, meets the shore.

shorn *past part.* of SHEAR.

short /shawrt/ • *adj.* **1 a** measuring little; not long from end to end. **b** not long in duration. **2** of small height; not tall. **3 a** [usu. foll. by *of, on*] deficient; scanty. **b** *colloq.* having little money. **c** not far-reaching. **4 a** concise; brief. **b** curt; uncivil. **5** (of the memory) unable to remember distant events. **6** (of pastry) crumbling; flaky. **7** esp.

Stock Exch. (of stocks, etc.) sold or selling when the amount is not in hand, with reliance on getting the deficit in time for delivery. • *adv.* **1** abruptly. **2** rudely; uncivilly. • *n.* **1** short circuit. **2** short movie. • *v.* short-circuit. □ **be caught short** **1** be put at a disadvantage. **2** be unprepared. **for short** as a short name (*Tom for short*). **short circuit** electric circuit through small resistance, esp. instead of the resistance of a normal circuit. **short-circuit** *v.* **1** cause a short circuit (in). **2** shorten or avoid by taking a more direct route, etc. **short cut** **1** route shortening the distance traveled. **2** quick way of accomplishing something. **short for** abbreviation for. **short-list** *v.tr.* put on a shortlist. **short-lived** ephemeral; not longlasting. **short-order** **a** prepared or provided quickly, esp. simple restaurant fare. **b** pertaining to one who provides this (*a short-order cook*). **short story** story with a fully developed theme but shorter than a novella. **short-winded** easily becoming breathless. □□ **short'ish** *adj.* **short'ness** *n.*

■ *adj.* **1 b** quick, limited; short-lived; see also BRIEF *adj.* 1. **2** little, diminutive, elfin; midget, squat. **3 a** (*short of* or *on*) lacking in, needful of, low on. **b** impecunious, straitened, pinched; see also BROKE. **c** close, near. **4 a** compact, abbreviated, abridged; laconic, terse, succinct; direct, straightforward. **b** terse, sharp, blunt, bluff. • *adv.* **1** suddenly, peremptorily, without warning. **2** bluntly, shortly, curtly, brusquely. □ – **short-lived** evanescent, temporary, fleeting. **short-winded** short of or out of breath, winded, breathless, panting.

short•age /sháwrtij/ *n.* deficiency; lack. See synonym study at LACK.

■ deficit, shortfall, dearth, scarcity, want, paucity.

short•bread /sháwrtbred/ *n.* crisp, rich, crumbly type of cookie made with butter, flour, and sugar.

short•cake /sháwrtkayk/ *n.* cake, pastry or biscuit with fruit and whipped cream.

short•change /sháwrtcháynj/ *v.tr.* rob or cheat by giving insufficient money as change.

short•com•ing /sháwrtkumming/ *n.* failure to come up to a standard; defect. See synonym study at FAULT.

■ deficiency, weakness, frailty, drawback, liability.

short•en /sháwrt'n/ *v.* become or make shorter or short; curtail.

■ cut, reduce, diminish, condense; trim.

short•en•ing /sháwrt'ning, sháwrtning/ *n.* fat used for making pastry, bread, etc.

short•fall /sháwrtfawl/ *n.* deficit below what was expected.

short•hand /sháwrt-hand/ *n.* **1** [often *attrib.*] method of rapid writing in abbreviations and symbols, esp. for taking dictation. **2** abbreviated mode of expression.

short•hand•ed /sháwrt-hánded/ *adj.* understaffed.

short•horn /sháwrt-horn/ *n.* **1** animal of a breed of cattle with short horns. **2** this breed.

short•list /sháwrtlist/ *n.* selective list of candidates from which a final choice is made.

short•ly /sháwrtlee/ *adv.* **1** soon. **2** briefly. **3** curtly.

■ **1** presently, before long, in a (little) while. **3** abruptly, peremptorily, brusquely, bluntly, rudely.

shorts /shawrts/ *n.pl.* **1** pants reaching only to the knees or higher. **2** underpants.

short•sight•ed /sháwrtsítid/ *adj.* **1** = NEARSIGHTED. **2** lacking imagination or foresight. □□ **short'sight'ed•ly** *adv.* **short'sight'ed•ness** *n.*

■ **2** unimaginative, unprogressive, improvident, imprudent, injudicious, rash, impolitic, limited.

short•stop /sháwrtstop/ *n.* baseball fielder positioned between second and third base.

short•wave /sháwrtwáyv/ *n.* radio that receives long-distance signals carried by waves shorter than those used for commercial broadcasts.

short•y /sháwrtee/ *n.* (also **short'ie**) (*pl.* –**ies**) *colloq.* person or garment shorter than average.

Sho•sho•ne /shəshón, –shónee/ *n.* (also **Sho•sho'ni**) **1 a** N. American people native to the western US. **b** member of this people. **2** language of this people.

shot[1] /shot/ *n.* **1** firing of a gun, cannon, etc. **2** attempt to hit by shooting or throwing, etc. **3 a** single nonexplosive missile for a cannon, gun, etc. **b** (*pl.* same or **shots**) small lead pellet used in quantity in a single charge or cartridge in a shotgun. **c** (as *pl.*) these collectively. **4 a** photograph. **b** film sequence photographed continuously by one camera. **5 a** stroke or kick in a ball game. **b** *colloq.* an attempt to guess or do something (*let her have a shot at it*). **6** *colloq.* person having a specified skill with a gun, etc. **7** heavy ball thrown by a shot-putter. **8** launch of a space rocket (*a moonshot*). **9** *colloq.* **a** drink of liquor. **b** hypodermic injection. □ **shot put** athletic contest in which a heavy metal ball is thrown a great distance. **shot-putter** athlete who puts the shot. □□ **shot'proof** *adj.*

■ **1** blast. **3** bullet, ball, slug, cannonball, projectile; buckshot. **4 a** print, snapshot, picture. **5 a** see KICK *n.* 1. **b** try, opportunity, chance. **6** marksman, shooter. **9 a** jigger, dram, nip, slug. **b** inoculation, vaccination.

shot[2] /shot/ *past* and *past part.* of SHOOT. • *adj.* **1** (of colored material) woven so as to show different colors at different angles. **2** *colloq.* exhausted; finished.

shot•gun /shótgun/ *n.* smoothbore gun for firing small-shot.

should /shood/ *v.aux.* (*3rd sing.* **should**) *past* of SHALL, used esp.: **1 a** to express a duty, obligation, or likelihood; ought to (*you should be more careful*). **b** (in the 1st person) to express a tentative suggestion (*I should like to say something*). **2** forming an indefinite clause (*if you should see him*).

shoul•der /shóldər/ • *n.* **1 a** part of the body at which the arm, foreleg, or wing is attached. **b** (in full **shoul'der joint**) the end of the upper arm joining with the clavicle and scapula. **c** either of the two projections below the neck from which the arms hang. **2** upper foreleg and shoulder blade of a pig, lamb, etc., when butchered. **3** [often in *pl.*] **a** the upper part of the back and arms. **b** this part of the body regarded as capable of bearing a burden or blame, providing comfort, etc. **4** strip of land next to a paved road. • *v.* **1 a** *tr.* push with the shoulder. **b** *intr.* make one's way by jostling. **2** *tr.* take on (a burden, etc.). □ **shoulder blade** *Anat.* either of the large flat bones of the upper back; the scapula. □□ **shoul'dered** *adj.* [also in *comb.*]

■ *n.* **4** side, edge. • *v.* **1 a** shove, jostle, hustle, thrust, elbow, force. **2** support, carry, bear, assume.

shouldn't /shóod'nt/ *contr.* should not.

shout /showt/ • *v.* **1** *intr.* speak or cry loudly. **2** *tr.* say or express loudly. • *n.* **1** loud cry. □□ **shout'er** *n.*

■ *v.* bellow, bawl, roar (out), call (out), yell, scream. • *n.* **1** yell, scream, bellow, howl, yelp.

shove /shuv/ • *v.* **1** *tr.* push vigorously. **2** *intr.* make one's way by pushing. **3** *tr. colloq.* put somewhere (*shoved it in the drawer*). • *n.* act of shoving. □ **shove off 1** start from the shore in a boat. **2** *sl.* depart; go away (*told him to shove off*).

■ *v.* **1** see PUSH *v.* 1. **2** thrust or elbow or force or jostle one's way; see also PUSH *v.* 6. **3** see STUFF *v.* 2. ■ *n.* push, thrust, nudge.

shov•el /shúvəl/ • *n.* spadelike tool with raised sides for shifting quantities of earth, snow, etc. • *v.tr.* **1** shift or clear (coal, etc.) with or as if with a shovel. **2** *colloq.* move (esp. food) in large quantities or roughly (*shoveled peas into his mouth*). □□ **shov'el•ful** *n.* (*pl.* **–fuls**).

show /shó/ • *v.* (*past part.* **shown** /shōn/ or **showed**) **1** *intr. & tr.* be, allow, or cause to be visible; manifest. **2** *tr.* offer, exhibit, or produce for scrutiny, etc. **3** *tr.* indicate or reveal (one's feelings). **4** *intr.* (of feelings, etc.) be manifest. **5** *tr.* **a** demonstrate. **b** cause (a person) to understand. **6** *tr.* conduct or lead. **7** *intr.* finish third in a race. • *n.* **1** act or instance of showing; state of being shown. **2 a** spectacle, display, exhibition, etc. **b** collection of things, etc., shown for public entertainment or in competition (*flower show*). **3 a** play, etc., esp. a musical. **b** entertainment program on television, etc. **c** any public entertainment or performance. **4** outward appearance or display. □ **show off 1** display to advantage. **2** *colloq.* act pretentiously. **show-off** *n. colloq.* person who shows off. **show up 1** make or be conspicuous or clearly visible. **2** expose (a fraud, impostor, inferiority, etc.). **3** *colloq.* appear; arrive.

■ *v.* **1** appear, become visible, peek through; represent, symbolize, depict. **2** display, present. **3** demonstrate, register; (lay) bare, disclose; grant, bestow. **4** be apparent, show through. **5 a** prove, point out, illustrate, confirm. **b** teach, instruct, inform,

give a lesson in. **6** escort, accompany, usher, guide, direct. • *n.* **2 a** see DISPLAY *n.* 2. **b** display, exhibition, exposition, fair, expo. **3** production, presentation. **4** see SEMBLANCE 1. □ **show off** make an exhibition or a spectacle of, flaunt, advertise, display, parade; pose, swagger, posture, boast, brag. **show-off** braggart, exhibitionist, egotist, boaster. **show up 1** stand out, be noticeable, contrast; reveal, show. **2** reveal; see also *give away* 3. **3** make or put in an appearance, show one's face.

show•case /shókays/ • *n.* **1** glass case used for exhibiting goods, etc. **2** event, etc., for presenting (esp. attractively) to general attention. • *v.tr.* display in or as if in a showcase.

show•down /shódown/ *n.* final test or confrontation; decisive situation.

show•er /shówər/ • *n.* **1** brief fall of esp. rain, hail, sleet, or snow. **2 a** brisk flurry of bullets, dust, etc. **b** similar flurry of gifts, honors, etc. **3 a** cubicle, bath, etc., in which one bathes under a spray of water. **b** apparatus used for this. **c** act of bathing in a shower. **4** party for giving presents to a prospective bride, expectant mother, etc. • *v.* **1** *tr.* **a** discharge (water, missiles, etc.) in a shower. **b** make wet with (or as if with) a shower. **2** *intr.* bathe in a shower. **3** *tr.* lavishly bestow (gifts, etc.). **4** *intr.* descend in a shower. □□ **show'er•y** *adj.*

■ *n.* **1** sprinkle, sprinkling, drizzle, precipitation. **2** deluge, torrent, flood, stream. • *v.* **1** sprinkle, rain, pour, spray. **3** heap. **4** fall, hail, pelt; rain, sprinkle.

show•girl /shógərl/ *n.* actress who sings and dances in musicals, variety shows, etc.

show•ing /shóing/ *n.* **1** act or instance of showing. **2** usu. specified quality of performance.

■ **1** exhibition; see also DEMONSTRATION 3.

show•man /shómən/ *n.* (*pl.* **–men**) **1** proprietor or manager of a circus, etc. **2** person skilled in self-advertisement or publicity. □□ **show'man•ship** *n.*

shown *past part.* of SHOW.

show•piece /shópees/ *n.* **1** item presented for exhibition or display. **2** outstanding specimen.

show•place /shóplays/ *n.* house, etc., that tourists go to see.

show•room /shóroom, –room/ *n.* room used to display goods for sale.

show•stop•per /shóstopər/ *n. colloq.* act or performance receiving prolonged applause.

show•y /shóee/ *adj.* (**show•i•er, show•i•est**) **1** brilliant; gaudy, esp. vulgarly so. **2** striking. □□ **show'i•ly** *adv.* **show'i•ness** *n.*

■ flashy, garish, flamboyant, conspicuous; elaborate, fancy, florid, ornate.

shrank *past* of SHRINK.

shrap•nel /shrápnəl/ *n.* **1** fragments of an exploded artillery shell, bomb, etc. **2** artillery shell designed to scatter metal fragments.

shred /shred/ • *n.* **1** scrap, fragment, or bit. **2** least amount. • *v.tr.* (**shred•ded, shred•ding**) tear or cut into shreds. □□ **shred'der** *n.*

■ *n.* **1** remnant, snippet, piece, tatter. **2**

atom, trace, whit, grain; see also FRAGMENT n.
• v. rip (up), fragment; destroy, demolish.

shrew /shrōō/ n. 1 small, usu. insect-eating, mouselike mammal with a long pointed snout. 2 bad-tempered or scolding woman. □□ **shrew′ish** adj. (in sense 2).

shrewd /shrōōd/ adj. astute; clever and judicious. See synonym study at KEEN. □□ **shrewd′ly** adv. **shrewd′ness** n.
■ smart, cunning, acute, sharp, discerning, wise, sagacious.

shriek /shreek/ • v. 1 intr. a utter a shrill screeching sound. b [foll. by of] provide a clear or blatant indication of. 2 tr. a utter (sounds or words) by shrieking (shrieked his name). b indicate clearly or blatantly. • n. high-pitched piercing cry or scream. □□ **shriek′er** n.
■ screech, squeal, squawk, squall.

shrift /shrift/ n. □ **short shrift** curt or dismissive treatment.

shrike /shrīk/ n. bird of prey with a strong hooked and toothed bill. (Also called **butcher-bird**).

shrill /shril/ • adj. 1 piercing and high pitched in sound. 2 derog. (esp. of a protester) sharp; unrestrained; unreasoning. • v. 1 intr. (of a cry, etc.) sound shrilly. 2 tr. (of a person, etc.) utter or send out (a complaint, etc.) shrilly. □□ **shril′ly** adv. **shrill′ness** n.
■ adj. 1 high, earsplitting, piping, screeching, penetrating.

shrimp /shrimp/ • n. 1 (pl. same or **shrimps**) small (esp. marine) edible crustaceans. 2 colloq. [often derog.] very small slight person. • v.intr. go catching shrimps. □□ **shrimp′er** n.

shrine /shrīn/ • n. 1 a chapel, church, altar, etc., sacred to a saint, holy person, relic, etc. b tomb of a saint, etc. c casket, esp. containing holy relics. 2 place associated with or containing memorabilia of a particular event, etc. • v.tr. poet. enshrine.

shrink /shringk/ • v. (past **shrank** /shrangk/; past part. **shrunk** /shrungk/ or [esp. as adj.] **shrunk•en** /shrúngkən/) 1 tr. & intr. make or become smaller, esp. from moisture, heat, or cold. 2 intr. [usu. foll. by from] a retire; recoil; flinch; cower. b be averse from doing. 3 (as **shrunk•en** adj.) (esp. of a face, person, etc.) having grown smaller, esp. because of age, illness, etc. • n. 1 act or instance of shrinking; shrinkage. 2 sl. psychiatrist (from "headshrinker"). **shrink-wrap** v.tr. (**-wrapped**, **-wrap•ping**) enclose (an article) in film that shrinks tightly on to it. n. plastic film used to shrink-wrap. □□ **shrink′a•ble** adj. **shrink′er** n. **shrink′proof** adj.
■ v. 1 wither, shrivel (up), contract; diminish, dwindle; reduce. 2 a withdraw, draw back, retreat; cringe.

shrink•age /shríngkij/ n. 1 a process or fact of shrinking. b degree or amount of shrinking. 2 allowance made for loss due to wastage, theft, etc.

shrive /shrīv/ v.tr. (past **shrove** /shrōv/; past part. **shriv•en** /shrívən/) Eccl. archaic 1 (of a priest) hear the confession of, assign penance to, and absolve. 2 [refl.] (of a penitent) submit oneself to a priest for confession, etc.

shriv•el /shrívəl/ v. contract or wither into a wrinkled, folded, rolled-up, contorted, or dried-up state.
■ shrink, pucker (up), curl (up); wilt, dry up, desiccate.

shroud /shrowd/ • n. 1 sheetlike garment for wrapping a corpse for burial. 2 anything that conceals. 3 [in pl.] Naut. ropes supporting the mast or topmast. • v.tr. 1 clothe (a body) for burial. 2 cover, conceal, or disguise. □□ **shroud′less** adj.
■ n. 2 veil, cover, shield, cloak, blanket, mask. • v. swathe, wrap; screen, veil, mask; see also ENVELOP.

shrub /shrub/ n. any woody plant smaller than a tree; bush. □□ **shrub′by** adj.

shrub•ber•y /shrúbəree/ n. (pl. **-ies**) 1 area planted with shrubs. 2 shrubs, collectively.

shrug /shrug/ • v. (**shrugged, shrug•ging**) 1 intr. slightly and momentarily raise the shoulders to express indifference, helplessness, contempt, etc. 2 tr. a raise (the shoulders) in this way. b shrug the shoulders to express (indifference, etc.) (shrugged his consent). • n. act or instance of shrugging. □ **shrug off** dismiss as unimportant.

shtick /shtik/ n. sl. theatrical routine, gimmick, etc.

shuck /shuk/ • n. 1 husk or pod. 2 shell of an oyster or clam. 3 [in pl.] colloq. expression of contempt or regret or self-deprecation in response to praise. • v.tr. 1 remove the shucks of; shell. 2 peel off or remove. □□ **shuck′er** n.

shud•der /shúdər/ • v.intr. 1 shiver, esp. convulsively, from fear, cold, repugnance, etc. 2 feel strong repugnance. • n. act or instance of shuddering. □□ **shud′der•ing•ly** adv. **shud′der•y** adj.
■ v. 1 quiver, shake, tremble, convulse. 2 see DREAD v. • n. quiver, paroxysm, spasm, quaver; vibration, rattle.

shuf•fle /shúfəl/ • v. 1 drag (the feet) in walking. 2 tr. rearrange or intermingle (playing cards, papers, etc.). 3 intr. a equivocate; prevaricate. b fidget. • n. 1 shuffling movement. 2 act or instance of shuffling cards. 3 general change of relative positions. 4 piece of equivocation. 5 quick alternation of the position of the feet in dancing. □□ **shuf′fler** n.
■ v. 1 scuff (one's feet), scrape along, shamble; see also HOBBLE v. 1. 2 mix (up), intermix, disarrange, jumble, confuse; shift (about), move up. 3 a bumble, cavil, fence, be evasive. b see FIDGET v. 1. • n. 1 shamble, shambling, scuffing, scraping. 3 rearrangement, reorganization, shake-up. 4 sidestep, evasion.

shuf•fle•board /shúfəlbawrd/ n. game played by pushing disks with a long-handled cue over a marked surface.

shun /shun/ v.tr. (**shunned, shun•ning**) avoid; keep clear of.
■ keep or shy away from, shrink from, give up; disdain.

shunt /shunt/ • v. 1 intr. & tr. redirect or cause (a train) to be redirected, esp. onto a siding. **2** *tr. Electr.* provide (a current) with a shunt. **3** *tr.* **a** postpone or evade. **b** divert (a decision, etc.) on to another person, etc. • *n.* **1** act or instance of shunting. **2** *Electr.* bypass for diverting current. **3** *Surgery* bypass for the circulation of the blood.

shush /shŏŏsh, shush/ • *int.* = HUSH *int.* • *v.* **1** *intr.* call for silence by saying *shush.* **2** *tr.* make or attempt to make silent.

shut /shut/ *v.* (**shut•ting**; *past* and *past part.* **shut**) **1** *tr.* **a** move (a door, window, lid, etc.) to block an aperture. **b** close (a room, window, box, eye, mouth, etc.) by moving a door, etc. **2** *intr.* become or be capable of being closed. **3** *tr.* fold or contract (a book, hand, telescope, etc.). **4** *tr.* [usu. foll. by *in, out*] keep (a person, sound, etc.) in or out of a room, etc. □ **shut down** stop (a factory, nuclear reactor, etc.) from operating. **2** (of a factory, etc.) stop operating. **shut-eye** *colloq.* sleep. **shut-in** invalid confined to home, bed, etc. **shut off 1** stop the flow of (water, gas, etc.). **2** separate from society, etc. **shut out 1** exclude. **2** prevent (an opponent) from scoring. **shut up 1** close all doors and windows. **2** imprison. **3** [esp. in *imper.*] *colloq.* stop talking.
  ■ **1, 2** fasten, secure, bolt, lock (up), seal (up); latch. **3** close. **4** (*shut in*) confine, seclude. □ **shut down** switch *or* turn *or* shut off; close down, cease. **shut-eye** see NAP[1] *n.* **shut off 1** switch *or* turn off; shut down. **2** isolate, seclude, segregate, sequester. **shut out 1** eliminate, bar, debar, lock out; screen. **shut up 1** see SHUT 1, 2 above. **2** confine, shut in; jail, incarcerate.

shut•down /shútdown/ *n.* closure of a factory, etc.

shut•ter /shútər/ • *n.* **1** person or thing that shuts. **2** **a** movable, often louvered, cover for a window. **b** structure of slats on rollers used for the same purpose. **3** device that exposes the film in a camera. • *v.tr.* put up the shutters of.

shut•tle /shút'l/ • *n.* **1** bobbin with two pointed ends used for carrying the weft thread across between the warp threads in weaving. **2** train, bus, etc., going back and forth over a short route continuously. **3** = SHUTTLECOCK. **4** = *space shuttle.* • *v.* **1** move or cause to move back and forth like a shuttle. **2** transport by or travel in a shuttle.

shut•tle•cock /shút'lkok/ *n.* device struck in badminton.

shy /shī/ • *adj.* (**shy•er, shy•est** *or* **shi•er, shi•est**) **1 a** diffident or uneasy in company; timid. **b** (of an animal, bird, etc.) easily startled; timid. **2** avoiding; wary of. **3** [in *comb.*] showing fear of or distaste for (*gun-shy*). • *v.intr.* (**shies, shied**) **1** (esp. of a horse) start suddenly aside in fright. **2** [usu. foll. by *away from, at*] avoid. • *n.* sudden startled movement. □□ **shy'er** *n.* **shy'ly** *adv.* **shy' ness** *n.*
  ■ *adj.* **1** coy, bashful, retiring, withdrawn. **2** cautious, chary, guarded, afraid, fearful.

shy•ster /shístər/ *n. colloq.* unscrupulous lawyer.

Si *symb. Chem.* silicon.

Si•a•mese /sīəmeez/ • *n.* (*pl.* same) **1 a** native of Siam (now Thailand) in SE Asia. **b** language of Siam. **2** (in full **Si'a•mese cat'**) **a** cat of a cream-colored short-haired breed with a brown face and ears and blue eyes. **b** this breed. • *adj.* of or concerning Siam, its people, or language. □ **Siamese twins** twins born joined at any part of the body.

sib•i•lant /síbilənt/ • *adj.* **1** (of a letter or set of letters, as *s, sh*) sounded with a hiss. **2** hissing. • *n.* sibilant letter or sound. □□ **sib'i•lance** *n.*

sib•ling /síbling/ *n.* brother or sister.

sib•yl /síbil/ *n.* pagan prophetess. □□ **sib•yl• line** /síbilīn, –leen/ *adj.*

sic[1] /sik/ *v.tr.* (**sicced, sic'cing**; also **sicked** /sikt/, **sick'ing**) [usu. in *imper.*] urge (a dog) to attack.

sic[2] /sik, seek/ *adv.* [usu. in brackets] used, spelled, etc., as written.

sick /sik/ *adj.* **1** [often in *comb.*] vomiting or tending to vomit (*seasick*). **2** ill; affected by illness. **3 a** esp. mentally perturbed. **b** pining; longing (*lovesick*). **4** [often foll. by *of*] *colloq.* **a** disgusted. **b** angry (*am sick of being teased*). **5** *colloq.* (of humor, etc.) jeering at misfortune, etc.; morbid. □ **sick leave** leave granted because of illness. □□ **sick'ish** *adj.*
  ■ *adj.* **1** nauseated, queasy; seasick, carsick, airsick, sick to one's stomach. **2** unwell, unhealthy, sickly. **3 a** affected, troubled, miserable; mad, insane, deranged. **4** sickened, put out, upset, appalled; annoyed, chagrined, irritated; surfeited; *colloq.* turned off; (*sick of*) (sick and) tired of, bored with, fed up with. **5** peculiar, unconventional, far-out, strange, weird; black.

sick•bay /síkbay/ *n.* **1** part of a ship used as a hospital. **2** any room, etc., for sick people.

sick•bed /síkbed/ *n.* invalid's bed.

sick•en /síkən/ *v.tr.* **1** affect with loathing or disgust. **2** (as **sickening** *adj.*) loathsome; disgusting. □□ **sick'en•ing•ly** *adv.*
  ■ **1** make ill *or* sick, afflict, disgust; put off.

sick•le /síkəl/ *n.* **1** short-handled tool with a semicircular blade, used for cutting grain, lopping, or trimming. **2** anything sickle-shaped, esp. the crescent moon. □ **sickle cell** sickle-shaped blood cell, esp. as found in a type of severe hereditary anemia.

sick•ly /síklee/ *adj.* (**sick•li•er, sick•li•est**) **1 a** of weak health; apt to be ill. **b** faint or pale. **2** causing ill health. **3** sentimental or mawkish. □□ **sick'li•ness** *n.*
  ■ **1 a** see SICK[1] *adj.* 2. **b** languid, ailing, feeble, delicate; see also PALE *adj.* 1.

sick•ness /síknis/ *n.* **1** state of being ill; disease. **2** nausea.

side /sīd/ • *n.* **1 a** each of the surfaces bounding an object. **b** inner or outer surface. **c** such a surface as distinct from the top or bottom, front or back. **2 a** half of a person or animal that is on the right or the left, esp. of the torso. **b** left or right part of a specified part of a thing, etc. **c** [often in *comb.*] a position next to a person or thing (*seaside*). **d** direction. **3** either surface of a thing having two surfaces. **4** any of several aspects of a question, character, etc. **5** each of two sets of opponents in war, politics, games, etc. **6 a** part or region near the edge and remote from the center. **b** [*attrib.*] subordinate, peripheral, or detached part. **7** each of the bounding lines of a plane figure. **8** line of hereditary descent through the father or the mother. • *v.intr.* [usu. foll. by *with*] be on the same side as a disputant, etc. (*sided with his father*). □ **on the side 1** as a sideline. **2** secretly or illicitly. **3** as a side dish. **side arm** pistol or other weapon worn at the belt. **side dish** extra dish subsidiary to the main course. **take sides** support one cause, etc., in a dispute. □□ **side'less** *adj.*

■ *n.* **1 a** face, plane; facet. **b** flank, edge, face. **4** see ASPECT 1a. **5** army; faction, interest, camp; team. **6 a** edge, margin, verge; perimeter, periphery. **b** (*attrib.*) secondary, incidental, tangential, subsidiary • *v.* (*side with*) take sides with, show preference for, be partial to.

side•board /sídbawrd/ *n.* flat-topped cupboard for dishes, table linen, decanters, etc.

side•burns /sídbərnz/ *n.pl. colloq.* hair grown by a man down the sides of his face.

side•car /sídkaar/ *n.* **1** small car for a passenger attached to the side of a motorcycle. **2** cocktail of orange liqueur, lemon juice, and brandy.

side•kick /sídkik/ *n. colloq.* close associate.

side•line /sídlīn/ • *n.* **1** work, etc., done in addition to one's main activity. **2** [usu. in *pl.*] **a** line bounding the side of a football field, tennis court, etc. **b** space next to these where spectators, etc., sit. • *v.tr.* remove (a player) from a team through injury, suspension, etc.

side•long /sídlawng, –lóng/ • *adj.* oblique. • *adv.* obliquely.

■ *adj.* indirect, sideways, lateral, covert, surreptitious, sly. • *adv.* see SIDEWAYS *adv.*

si•de•re•al /sīdeereeəl/ *adj.* of the constellations or fixed stars.

side•sad•dle /sídsad'l/ • *n.* saddle having supports for both feet on the same side of the horse. • *adv.* riding in this position on a horse.

side•show /sídshō/ *n.* minor show or attraction in an exhibition or entertainment.

side•split•ting /sídspliting/ *adj.* causing violent laughter.

side•step /sídstep/ • *n.* step taken sideways • *v.tr.* (**-stepped**, **-step•ping**) **1** avoid by stepping sideways. **2** evade. □□ **side'step•per** *n.*

side•swipe /sídswīp/ • *n.* glancing blow on or from the side. • *v.tr.* hit with or as if with a sideswipe.

side•track /sídtrak/ *v.tr.* **1** shunt. **2 a** postpone, evade, or divert consideration of. **b** divert (a person) from considering, etc.

■ *v.* **1** divert. **2** deflect, distract.

side•walk /sídwawk/ *n.* paved track for pedestrians.

side•wall /sídwawl/ *n.* part of a tire between the tread and the wheel rim.

side•ways /sídwayz/ • *adv.* **1** to or from a side. **2** with one side facing forward. • *adj.* to or from a side. □□ **side'wise** *adv. & adj.*

■ *adv.* obliquely, laterally, edgeways, edgewise, edge on, sidelong, crabwise; indirectly. • *adj.* see SIDELONG *adj.*

sid•ing /síding/ *n.* **1** short track at the side of a railroad line, used for switching trains. **2** material for the outside of a building, e.g., clapboards, shingles, etc.

si•dle /síd'l/ • *v.intr.* walk in a timid, furtive, stealthy, or cringing manner. • *n.* act or instance of sidling.

■ *v.* edge, slink, steal; see also CREEP *v.* 2.

SIDS /sidz/ *abbr.* sudden infant death syndrome; crib death.

siege /seej/ *n.* **1** military action of surrounding and blockading a town, building, etc. **2** period during which a siege lasts. □ **lay siege to** esp. *Mil.* conduct the siege of.

■ **1** blockade, encirclement. □ **lay siege to** besiege, blockade, beleaguer, cordon off, encircle.

si•er•ra /seeérə/ *n.* long jagged mountain chain.

si•es•ta /seeéstə/ *n.* afternoon sleep or rest esp. in hot countries.

sieve /siv/ • *n.* utensil having a perforated or meshed bottom for separating solids or coarse material from liquids or fine particles. • *v.tr.* **1** sift. **2** examine (evidence, etc.) to select or separate. □□ **sieve'like** *adj.*

sift /sift/ *v.tr.* **1** sieve (material) into finer and coarser parts. **2** [usu. foll. by *from*, *out*] separate (finer or coarser parts) from material. **3** examine (evidence, facts, etc.). □□ **sift'er** *n.* [also in *comb.*].

■ **1** strain, riddle, filter. **2** (*sift out*) winnow, weed out, select, choose. **3** sift through, analyze, probe. □□ **sifter** riddle, sieve, colander.

sigh /sī/ • *v.intr.* **1** emit a long, deep, audible breath expressive of sadness, weariness, relief, etc. **2** [foll. by *for*] yearn for (a lost person or thing). **3** (of the wind, etc.) make a sound like sighing. • *n.* act or instance of sighing.

■ *v.* **1** breathe; groan, moan. **2** (*sigh for*) long or pine for; bemoan, lament or mourn for, bewail. **3** sough, moan. • *n.* exhalation; murmur, sound.

sight /sīt/ • *n.* **1 a** faculty of seeing. **b** act or instance of seeing; state of being seen. **2** thing seen. **3** range of vision. **4** [usu. in *pl.*] noteworthy features of a town, etc. **5** a device on a gun or optical instrument for assisting the precise aim or observation. **b** aim or observation so gained. **6** *colloq.* person or thing having a ridiculous, repulsive, or disheveled appearance. • *v.tr.* **1** get sight of, esp. by approaching (*they sighted land*). **2** observe (esp. aircraft, animals, etc.) (*sighted buffalo*). **3** aim (a gun, etc.). • **at** (or **on**) **sight** as soon as seen (*liked him on sight*). **sight-read** (*past* and *past part.* **-read** /-red/) read and perform (music) at sight. □□ **sight'er** *n.*

■ *n.* **1 a** eyesight, vision, visual acuity. **b** glimpse, glance, look; see also VIEW *n.* 3. **2** spectacle, scene, display, show; rarity, marvel; pageant. **3** field of view, ken, perception.

6 mess, disaster, eyesore, monstrosity, fright.
• v. **1, 2** spot, see, catch sight of, mark, view.
sight•ed /sítid/ adj. **1** not blind. **2** [in comb.] having a specified kind of sight (farsighted).
sight•less /sítlis/ adj. blind. □□ **sight′less•ly** adv. **sight′less•ness** n.
sight•ly /sítlee/ adj. attractive to the sight. □□ **sight′li•ness** n.
sight•se•er /sítseeər/ n. person who visits places of interest; tourist. □□ **sight′see** v. **sight′see•ing** n.
■ traveler, globetrotter, visitor.
sig•ma /sígmə/ n. eighteenth letter of the Greek alphabet (Σ, σ, or, when final, ς).
sign /sīn/ • n. **1** thing indicating a quality, state, etc.; thing perceived as indicating a future state or occurrence (violence is a sign of weakness) **b** portent. **2** mark, symbol, etc. **3** gesture or action conveying information, an order, etc. **4** signboard or signpost. **5** any of the twelve divisions of the zodiac. See synonym study at EMBLEM. • v. **1** tr. **a** write (one's name, initials, etc.). **b** sign (a document) as authorization. **2** intr. & tr. communicate by gesture, esp. using sign language. **3** tr. & intr. engage or be engaged by signing a contract, etc. (see also sign on, sign up). **4** tr. mark with a sign (esp. with the sign of the cross in baptism). □ **sign away** convey (one's right, property, etc.) by signing a deed, etc. **sign for** acknowledge receipt of by signing. **sign language** system of communication by hand gestures, used esp. by the hearing impaired. **sign of the cross** Christian sign made in blessing or prayer, by tracing a cross with the hands. **sign off** **1** end work, broadcasting, a letter, etc. **2** acknowledge by signature. **sign on** **1** agree to a contract, employment, etc. **2** begin work, broadcasting, etc. **3** employ (a person). **sign up** **1** engage or employ (a person). **2** enlist in the armed forces. **3 a** commit (another person or oneself) by signing, etc. **b** enroll. □□ **sign′a•ble** adj. **sign′er** n.
■ n. **1** token, symbol, indication; notice; trace, evidence; omen, augury. **2** device, emblem, trademark, logo(type), colophon; monogram. **3** movement, motion, signal, cue; nod, wave. **4** advertisement, billboard, placard; shingle. • v. **1** inscribe, mark; autograph, endorse. **2** see SIGNAL v. 1, 2a. □ **sign away** forgo, relinquish, give up, abandon (claim to); **sign over**, transfer. **sign off 1** close down, end (off), terminate. **sign on 1** sign up, enroll, enlist, register, volunteer, join (up), contract. **3** sign up, enroll, hire. **sign up 1** enroll, hire. **2, 3b** see sign on 1 above.

SYNONYM STUDY: sign

AUGURY, INDICATION, MANIFESTATION, OMEN, SIGNAL, SYMPTOM, TOKEN. What's the difference between a **sign** and a **signal**? The former is a general term for anything that gives evidence of an event, a mood, a quality of character, a mental or physical state, or a trace of something (a sign of approaching rain; a sign of good breeding; a sign that someone has

entered the house). While a sign may be involuntary, or even unconscious, a **signal** is always voluntary and is usually deliberate. A ship that shows signs of distress may or may not be in trouble; but one that sends a distress signal is definitely in need of help. **Indication**, like sign, is a comprehensive term for anything that serves to indicate or point out (he gave no indication that he was lying). A **manifestation** is an outward or perceptible indication of something (the latter was a manifestation of his guilt), and a **symptom** is an indication of a diseased condition (a symptom of pneumonia). Something that proves the actual existence of something that has no physical existence is called a **token** (she gave him a locket as a token of her love). **Omen** and **augury** both pertain to foretelling future events, with augury being the general term for predicting the future and omen being a definite sign foretelling good or evil (they regarded the stormy weather as a bad omen).

---

sig•nal /sígnəl/ • n. **1 a** usu. prearranged sign conveying information, guidance, etc. **b** message made up of such signs (signals made with flags). **2** immediate cause of action, etc. **3** Electr. **a** electrical impulse or impulses or radio waves transmitted as a signal. **b** sequence of these. See synonym study at SIGN. • v. **1** intr. make signals. **2** tr. **a** [often foll. by to + infin.] make signals to; direct. **b** transmit by signal; announce. □□ **sig′nal•er** or **sig′nal•ler** n.
■ n. **1** see SIGN n. 1, 3. **2** incitement, stimulus, spur. • v. **1, 2a** motion, indicate, gesticulate, whistle, wink, blink, nod, semaphore. **2 b** see COMMUNICATE 1a.
sig•nal•man /sígnəlmən/ n. (pl. **-men**) operator of signals, as in the army or on a railroad.
sig•na•to•ry /sígnətawree/ • n. (pl. **-ries**) party or esp. a nation that has signed an agreement or esp. a treaty. • adj. having signed such an agreement, etc.
sig•na•ture /sígnəchər/ n. **1 a** person's name, initials, or mark used in signing. **b** act of signing a document, etc. **2** Mus. **a** group of sharps or flats indicating the key. **b** notation showing tempo. **3** Printing section of a book made from one folded sheet.
sign•board /sínbawrd/ n. board displaying a name, symbol, etc.
sig•net /sígnit/ n. small seal, as on a ring.
sig•nif•i•cant /signífikənt/ adj. **1** having a meaning; indicative. **2** noteworthy; important; consequential. □ **significant other** spouse or lover. □□ **sig•nif′i•cance** n. **sig•nif′i•cant•ly** adv.
■ **1** meaningful, informative; eloquent. **2** weighty, momentous, critical, considerable, substantial. □□ **significance** weight, consequence, relevance, noteworthiness; meaning; gist, connotation. **significantly** see MATERIALLY.
sig•ni•fy /signifí/ v. (**-fies**, **-fied**) **1** tr. be a sign or indication of. **2** tr. mean. **3** tr. make known. **4** intr. be of importance; matter. □□ **sig•ni•fi•ca′tion** n. **sig′ni•fi•er** n.
■ **1, 2** indicate, symbolize, express, denote, say; imply, connote, intimate. **3** sign, signal,

communicate. **4** count, be significant, carry weight.

si•gnor /seenyáwr/ *n.* (*pl.* **si•gno•ri** /–nyó-ree/) **1** title or form of address used of or to an Italian-speaking man, corresponding to Mr. or sir. **2** Italian man.

si•gno•ra /seenyáwrə/ *n.* **1** title or form of address used of or to an Italian-speaking married woman, corresponding to Mrs. or madam. **2** married Italian woman.

si•gno•ri•na /séenyəreénə/ *n.* **1** title or form of address used of or to an Italian-speaking unmarried woman. **2** Italian unmarried woman.

sign•post /sínpōst/ *n.* **1** post with a sign indicating direction. **2** means of guidance; indication.

si•lage /sílij/ *n.* green fodder stored in a silo.

si•lence /síləns/ • *n.* **1** absence of sound. **2** abstinence from speech or noise. **3** avoidance of mentioning a thing, betraying a secret, etc. • *v.tr.* make silent, esp. by coercion or superior argument.

  ■ *n.* **1** quiet, quietness, stillness, soundlessnes, hush, quietude, tranquillity, peace, peacefulness, serenity. **2, 3** speechlessness, muteness; reticence, taciturnity, reserve, secretiveness. • *v.* quiet, mute, hush; mollify, propitiate, pacify; repress, restrain, subdue.

si•lenc•er /sílənsər/ *n.* device for reducing the noise emitted by a gun, etc.

si•lent /sílənt/ *adj.* **1** not speaking; not uttering or making or accompanied by any sound. **2** (of an agreement) unspoken; unrecorded. □ **silent partner** non-working financial partner. □□ **si'lent•ly** *adv.*

  ■ **1** unspeaking, mute, speechless; quiet, still, soundless, tranquil; calm, serene, placid. **2** unexpressed, unrecorded, tacit, understood, implicit. □□ **silently** quietly, soundlessly, noiselessly, stealthily; wordlessly, speechlessly, mutely.

sil•hou•ette /sílōó-ét/ • *n.* **1** representation of a person or thing showing the outline only, usu. in solid black on white or cut from paper. **2** dark shadow or outline against a lighter background. • *v.tr.* represent or [usu. in *passive*] show in silhouette.

sil•i•ca /sílikə/ *n.* silicon dioxide, occurring as quartz, etc. □ **silica gel** hydrated silica in a hard granular form used as a desiccant.

sil•i•cate /sílikayt, –kət/ *n.* compound of a metal with silicon and oxygen.

sil•i•con /sílikən, –kon/ *n.* *Chem.* nonmetallic element occurring widely in silica and silicates. ¶Symb.: **Si**.

sil•i•cone /sílikōn/ *n.* any organic compound of silicon.

silk /silk/ *n.* **1** fine, strong, soft lustrous fiber produced by silkworms. **2** thread or cloth from this. □ **silk-screen printing** process in which ink is pressed through a silk stencil bearing a design to the surface below. □□ **silk'like** *adj.*

silk•worm /sílkwərm/ *n.* caterpillar that spins its cocoon of silk.

silk•y /sílkee/ *adj.* (**silk•i•er, silk•i•est**) **1** like silk in smoothness, softness, fineness, or luster. **2** suave; insinuating. □□ **silk'i•ly** *adv.* **silk'i•ness** *n.*

  ■ **1** silken, silklike, delicate, fine, sleek, soft, smooth.

sill /sil/ *n.* slab of stone, wood, or metal at the foot of a window or doorway.

sil•ly /sílee/ • *adj.* (**sil•li•er, sil•li•est**) **1** lacking sense; foolish; imprudent; unwise. **2** - weak-minded. • *n.* (*pl.* **–lies**) *colloq.* foolish person. □□ **sil'li•ness** *n.*

  ■ *adj.* **1** senseless, nonsensical, absurd, ridiculous, ludicrous, laughable, idiotic, foolish, foolhardy, stupid. • *n.* fool, nincompoop, dunce, clown, jackass.

si•lo /sílō/ • *n.* (*pl.* **–los**) **1** pit or airtight structure in which green crops are stored for fodder. **2** pit or tower for the storage of grain, cement, etc. **3** underground storage chamber for a guided missile. • *v.tr.* (**–oes, –oed**) make silage of.

silt /silt/ • *n.* sediment deposited by water in a channel, harbor, etc. • *v.* choke or be choked with silt. □□ **silt'y** *adj.*

  ■ *n.* deposit, alluvium, ooze, sludge, slime. • *v.* silt up *or* over; clog, obstruct.

sil•ver /sílvər/ • *n.* *Chem.* **1** grayish-white, lustrous, precious metallic element. ¶Symb.: **Ag**. **2** color of silver. **3** silver coins. **4** household cutlery. • *adj.* **1** made wholly of or chiefly of silver. **2** colored like silver. • *v.tr.* coat or plate with silver. □ **silver jubilee** 25th anniversary. **silver lining** consolation or hopeful feature in misfortune. **silver medal** medal of silver, usu. awarded as second prize. **silver plate** vessels, spoons, etc., plated with silver. **silver screen** [usu. prec. by *the*] motion pictures collectively.

  ■ *n.* **2** grayish, white, whitish-gray, silver-gray, gray. **4** silverware, sterling; hollowware; flatware. • *adj.* **2** silvery, shining, polished, lustrous; silver-gray, whitish-gray.

sil•ver•fish /sílvərfish/ *n.* (*pl.* same or **–fishes**) silvery wingless insect.

sil•ver•smith /sílvərsmith/ *n.* worker in silver; manufacturer of silver articles. □□ **sil'ver•smith•ing** *n.*

sil•ver•ware /sílvərwair/ *n.* **1** articles of or coated with silver. **2** tableware of any metal.

sim•i•an /símeeən/ • *adj.* **1** of or concerning the anthropoid apes. **2** like an ape or monkey. • *n.* ape or monkey.

sim•i•lar /símilər/ *adj.* **1** like; alike. **2** [often foll. by *to*] having a resemblance. **3** of the same kind, nature, or amount. □□ **sim•i•lar•i•ty** /–láritee/ *n.* (*pl.* **–ties**). **sim'i•lar•ly** *adv.* See synonym study at LIKENESS.

  ■ **1, 3** almost identical, comparable, equivalent, akin, kindred, related. **2** (*similar to*) resembling, like, corresponding to, comparable with.

sim•i•le /símilee/ *n.* comparison of one thing with another of a different kind, as an illustration or ornament (e.g., *as brave as a lion*).

si•mil•i•tude /símilitōōd, –tyōōd/ *n.* likeness, guise, or outward appearance. See synonym study at LIKENESS.

sim•mer /símər/ • *v.* **1** *intr. & tr.* be or keep bubbling or boiling gently. **2** *intr.* be in a state of suppressed anger or excitement. • *n.*

simmering condition. □ **simmer down** become calm or less agitated.

■ v. **1** stew, cook, boil, bubble. **2** chafe, seethe, stew, steam, smolder, fume, rage, burn. □ **simmer down** cool down, cool off, become quiet, control oneself.

si•mo•ny /sím∂nee, sím–/ n. buying or selling of ecclesiastical privileges, e.g., pardons or benefices.

sim•per /símp∂r/ • v. **1**, intr. smile in a silly or affected way. **2** tr. express by or with simpering. • n. such a smile. □□ **sim′per•ing•ly** adv.

sim•ple /símp∂l/ adj. **1** easily understood or done. **2** not complicated or elaborate; without luxury or sophistication. **3** not compound. **4** absolute; unqualified; straightforward. **5** foolish or ignorant; gullible; feeble-minded.

■ **1** uncomplicated, plain, uninvolved, comprehensible, clear, lucid, esp. Computing user-friendly. **2** uncomplicated; plain, unadorned, undecorated, basic, fundamental, elemental, modest. **4** see PURE 1. **5** naive, green, credulous, slow, slow-witted.

sim•ple•mind•ed /símp∂lmíndid/ adj. **1** natural; unsophisticated. **2** feeble-minded. □□ **sim′ple•mind′ed•ly** adv. **sim′ple•mind′ed•ness** n.

sim•ple•ton /símp∂lt∂n/ n. fool.

sim•plic•i•ty /simplísitee/ n. fact or condition of being simple.

■ understandability, comprehensibility, lucidity; plainness, cleanness; stupidity, foolishness; sincerity, openness, artlessness, candor, ingenuousness, naïveté; directness, rusticity.

sim•pli•fy /símplifī/ v.tr. (**–fies, –fied**) make simple or simpler. □□ **sim•pli•fi•ca′tion** n.

■ clarify, clear up, make easy, untangle, streamline.

sim•plis•tic /símplístik/ adj. **1** excessively or affectedly simple. **2** oversimplified so as to conceal or distort difficulties. □□ **sim•plis′ti•cal•ly** adv.

sim•ply /símplee/ adv. **1** in a simple manner. **2** absolutely; without doubt. **3** merely.

■ **1** distinctly, unambiguously, obviously, unmistakably; naively, artlessly, guilelessly, openly, innocently. **2** totally, completely, altogether, entirely. **3** purely, only, just.

sim•u•late /símyəlayt/ v.tr. **1 a** pretend to have or feel (an attribute or feeling). **b** pretend to be. **2** imitate or counterfeit. **3** (as **simulated** adj.) made to resemble the real thing. □□ **sim•u•la′tion** /–láyshən/ n. **sim′u•la•tor** n.

si•mul•ta•ne•ous /síməltáyneeəs, sím–/ adj. occurring or operating at the same time. □□ **si•mul•ta′ne•ous•ly** adv.

■ coincident, coinciding, concurrent, contemporaneous, synchronous; contemporary.

sin¹ /sin/ • n. **1 a** breaking of divine or moral law, esp. by a conscious act. **b** such an act. **2** offense against good taste or propriety, etc. • v.intr. (**sinned, sin•ning**) **1** commit a sin. **2** [foll. by against] offend. □□ **sin′ful** adj. **sin′ful•ly** adv. **sin′ful•ness** n. **sin′less**

adj. **sin′less•ly** adv. **sin′less•ness** n. **sin′ner** n.

■ n. **1** wickedness, sinfulness, vice, corruption, ungodliness, unrighteousness, badness, evil; transgression, offense. **2** see SCANDAL 1. • v. **1** transgress, offend, fall (from grace), lapse, go astray. **2** err. □□ **sinful** corrupt, evil, wicked, profane, immoral.

SYNONYM STUDY: sin

CRIME, FAULT, INDISCRETION, OFFENSE, TRANSGRESSION, VICE. If you've ever driven through a red light or chewed with your mouth open, you've committed an **offense**, which is a broad term covering any violation of the law or of standards of propriety and taste. A **sin**, on the other hand, is an act that specifically violates a religious, ethical, or moral standard (to marry someone of another faith was considered a sin). **Transgression** is a weightier and more serious word for sin, suggesting any violation of an agreed-upon set of rules (their behavior was clearly a transgression of the terms set forth in the treaty). A **crime** is any act forbidden by law and punishable upon conviction (a crime for which he was sentenced to death). A **vice** has less to do with violating the law and more to do with habits and practices that debase a person's character (alcohol was her only vice). **Fault** and **indiscretion** are gentler words, although they may be used as euphemisms for sin or crime. Fault appears to excuse bad conduct by suggesting that perfection is impossible (a fault in one's character), while indiscretion refers to an unwise or improper action (speaking to the media was an indiscretion for which she was chastised). In recent years, however, indiscretion has become a euphemism for such sins as adultery, as if to excuse such behavior by attributing it to a momentary lapse of judgment (his indiscretions were no secret).

sin² /sin/ abbr. sine.

since /sins/ • prep. throughout or during the period after (must have happened since yesterday). • conj. **1** during or in the time after (has not spoken since the dog died). **2** because; inasmuch as. • adv. **1** from that time or event until now. **2** ago.

sin•cere /sinseér/ adj. (**sin•cer•er, sin•cer•est**) **1** free from pretense or deceit. **2** genuine; honest; frank. □□ **sin•cere′ly** adv. **sin•cer•i•ty** /–séritee/ n.

■ truthful, true, genuine, bona fide, unfeigned, open. □□ **sincerely** truly, honestly, seriously, earnestly, genuinely. **sincerity** honesty, truthfulness, straightforwardness, openness.

sine /sīn/ n. Math. ratio of the side opposite a given angle (in a right triangle) to the hypotenuse.

si•ne•cure /síniky σ̄σ̄r, sín–/ n. position that requires little or no work but usu. yields profit or honor.

si•ne qua non /sínay kwaa nón/ n. indispensable condition or qualification.

sin•ew /sínyσ̄σ̄/ n. **1** tough fibrous tissue uniting muscle to bone; tendon. **2** [in pl.] muscles; bodily strength; wiriness. □□ **sin′ew•less** adj. **sin′ew•y** adj.

■ **1** ligament. **2** (*sinews*) force, power, energy, brawn, vigor. □□ **sinewy** strong, powerful, muscular, mighty, stout, wiry; strapping, brawny, burly.

sing /sing/ • *v.* (*past* **sang** /sang/; *past part.* **sung** /sung/) **1** *intr.* utter musical sounds, esp. words with a set tune. **2** *tr.* utter or produce by singing. **3** *intr.* (of the wind, a kettle, etc.) make humming, buzzing, or whistling sounds. **4** *intr. sl.* turn informer. • *n.* act or spell of singing. □□ **sing′a•ble** *adj.* **sing′er** *n.*

■ *v.* **1, 2** chant, intone, carol, serenade, vocalize, croon. **3** peep, tootle; drone, whir, murmur. **4** tell, tattle, name names. □□ **singer** vocalist, songster, crooner, chanteuse, caroler, chorister.

singe /sinj/ • *v.* (**singe•ing**) burn superficially or lightly. See synonym study at BURN. • *n.* superficial burn.

■ *v.* char, blacken, sear, scorch.

sin•gle /singgəl/ • *adj.* **1** one only. **2** united or undivided. **3 a** designed or suitable for one person (*single room*). **b** used or done by one person, etc. **4** one by itself; not one of several. **5** separately. **6** not married. • *n.* **1** single thing, or item in a series. **2** recording with one item on each side. **3** *Baseball* hit that allows the batter to reach first base safely. **4** [usu. *in pl.*] game, esp. tennis, with one player on each side. **5** unmarried person. • *v.* **1** *tr.* [foll. by *out*] choose as an example or as distinguishable or to serve some purpose. **2** *intr. Baseball* hit a single. □ **single-breasted** (of a coat, etc.) having only one set of buttons and buttonholes, not overlapping. **single file** line of people or things arranged one behind another. **single-handed** *adv.* **1** without the help of another. **2** with one hand. *adj.* **1** done, etc., single-handed. **2** for one hand. **single-handedly** in a single-handed way. **single-minded** having or intent on only one purpose. **single parent** person bringing up a child or children without a partner. □□ **sin′gle•ness** *n.* **sin′gly** *adv.*

■ *adj.* **1, 4** sole, lone, unique, solitary; singular, individual, distinct. **5** distinct, individual, solitary. **6** unmarried, unwed, unattached, free. • *v.* **1** (*single out*) select, separate, target, earmark. □ **single-handed 1** (*adv.*) by oneself, alone, independently. **1** (*adj.*) solo, lone, unaided, unassisted. **single-handedly** see *single-handed* (*adv.*) above. **single-minded** dedicated, devoted, resolute, steadfast, persevering, firm, determined, dogged, unswerving. □□ **singleness** bachelorhood, spinsterhood, celibacy; see also UNITY 1. **singly** one at a time, separately, individually, one by one.

sin•gle•ton /singgəltən/ *n.* **1** *Cards* one card only of a suit, esp. as dealt to a player. **2** single person or thing.

sing•song /singsawng, –song/ • *adj.* uttered with a monotonous rhythm or cadence. • *n.* singsong manner. • *v.* (*past* and *past part.* **sing′songed**) speak or recite in a singsong manner.

sin•gu•lar /singyələr/ • *adj.* **1** unique; much beyond the average; extraordinary. **2** eccen-

tric or strange. **3** *Gram.* (of a word or form) denoting a single person or thing. • *n. Gram.* **1** singular word or form. **2** singular number. □□ **sin•gu•lar•i•ty** /–láritee/ *n.* (*pl.* **–ties**) **sin′gu•lar•ly** *adv.*

■ *adj.* **1** outstanding, prominent, eminent, notable. **2** unusual, different, atypical. □□ **singularity** individuality, distinctiveness, uniqueness, eccentricity, quirk.

Sin•ha•lese /sínhəleéz, sínə–/ (*also* **Sin•gha•lese** /sínggə–/) • *n.* (*pl.* same) **1** member of a people originally from N. India and now forming the majority of the population of Sri Lanka. **2** Indic language spoken by this people. • *adj.* of or relating to this people or language.

sin•is•ter /sínistər/ *adj.* **1** suggestive of evil; looking malignant or villainous. **2** wicked or criminal (*a sinister motive*). **3** ominous.

■ **1, 3** dark, gloomy, black; alarming, frightening; forbidding, threatening, menacing. **2** evil, bad, corrupt, base, malevolent, malignant.

sink /singk/ • *v.intr.* (*past* **sank** /sangk/ or **sunk** /sungk/; *past part.* **sunk** or **sunk•en**) **1** fall or come slowly downward. **2** disappear below the horizon. **3 a** go or penetrate below the surface esp. of a liquid. **b** (of a ship) go to the bottom of the sea, etc. **4** settle down comfortably (*sank into a chair*). **5 a** gradually lose strength or value or quality, etc.; decline. **b** (of the voice) descend in pitch or volume. **c** (of a sick person) approach death. • *n.* **1** basin with a water supply and outflow pipe. **2** place where foul liquid collects. **3** place of vice or corruption. □ **sink in 1** (*also sink into*) penetrate or make its way in. **2** become gradually comprehended. **sinking fund** money set aside for the gradual repayment of a debt. □□ **sink′a•ble** *adj.* **sink′age** *n.*

■ *v.* **1** descend, drop, fall; sag, droop; slump; settle. **2** set, go down, drop; vanish. **3** become submerged, go down, go under, dive; see also FOUNDER v. 1. **5 a, c** weaken, worsen, degenerate; die, expire; languish. • *n.* **1** washbasin, washbowl, lavabo; *Ch.* font, stoup, piscina. **2** cesspool, cesspit, hellhole, den of iniquity. □ **sink in 1** (*sink into*) seep in, soak in, permeate; see also PENETRATE 1b. **2** be understood, penetrate, register.

sink•er /singkər/ *n.* **1** weight used to sink a fishing line or sounding line. **2** *Baseball* pitch that curves sharply downward.

Sino- /síno/ *comb. form* Chinese; Chinese and (*Sino-American*).

sin•u•ous /sínyōōəs/ *adj.* with many curves; tortuous; undulating. □□ **sin′u•ous•ly** *adv.* **sin′u•ous•ness** *n.*

si•nus /sínəs/ *n.* cavity of bone or tissue, esp. in the skull connecting with the nostrils.

si•nus•i•tis /sínəsítis/ *n.* inflammation of a nasal sinus.

-sion /shən, zhən/ *suffix* forming nouns (see -ION) from Latin participial stems in -s- (*mansion, mission, persuasion*).

Sioux /sōō/ *n.* (*pl.* same) **1 a** group of native N. American peoples. (Also called **Dakota**).

b member of these peoples. **2** language of this group. □□ **Siou•an** /sốōən/ *adj. & n.*

sip /sip/ • *v.* (**sipped**, **sip•ping**) drink in small amounts or by spoonfuls. • *n.* **1** small mouthful of liquid. **2** act of taking this. □□ **sip′per** *n.*

■ *v.* taste, sample, sup. • *n.* taste, sample, drop, bit, spoonful, thimbleful, nip, dram; swallow.

si•phon /sīfən/ (also **sy′phon**) • *n.* **1** tube for conveying liquid from a container to a lower level by atmospheric pressure. **2** (in full **si′phon bot′tle**) aerated-water bottle from which liquid is forced out through a tube by the pressure of gas. • *v.* **1** conduct or flow through a siphon. **2** divert or set aside (funds, etc.). □□ **si′phon•age** *n.*

sir /sər/ *n.* **1** polite form of address or reference to a man. **2** (**Sir**) titular prefix to the forename of a knight or baronet.

sire /sīr/ • *n.* **1** male parent of an animal, esp. a stallion. **2** *archaic* respectful form of address, now esp. to a king. **3** *archaic poet.* father or male ancestor. • *v.tr.* (esp. of a stallion) beget.

si•ren /sīrən/ *n.* **1** device for making a loud prolonged signal or warning sound. **2** *Gk. mythol.* woman or winged creature whose singing lured unwary sailors onto rocks. **3** dangerously fascinating woman; temptress.

■ **1** whistle, horn, foghorn; alarm, alert. **3** seductress, enchantress, charmer, sorceress, femme fatale.

sir•loin /sórloyn/ *n.* choicer part of a loin of beef.

si•roc•co /sirókō/ *n.* (*pl.* **–cos**) hot Saharan wind that blows over S. Europe.

sis /sis/ *n. colloq.* sister.

si•sal /sīsəl/ *n.* **1** fiber made from a Mexican agave. **2** this plant.

sis•sy /sisee/ *colloq.* • *n.* (*pl.* **–sies**) effeminate or cowardly person. • *adj.* (**sis•si•er**, **sis•si•est**) effeminate; cowardly. □□ **sis′si•fied** *adj.* **sis′sy•ish** *adj.*

■ *n.* milksop, namby-pamby, weakling, coward, baby.

sis•ter /sistər/ *n.* **1** woman or girl in relation to sons and other daughters of her parents. **2 a** (often as a form of address) close female friend or associate. **b** female fellow member of a labor union, class, etc. **3** nun. **4** [*attrib.*] of the same type or design or origin, etc. □ **sister-in-law** (*pl.* **sisters-in-law**) **1** sister of one's spouse. **2** wife of one's brother. **3** wife of one's brother-in-law. □□ **sis′ter•hood** *n.* **sis′ter•less** *adj.* **sis′ter•ly** *adj.* **sis′ter•li•ness** *n.*

Sis•y•phe•an /sisifeeən/ *adj.* (of toil) endless and fruitless like that of Sisyphus in Greek mythology (whose task in Hades was to push uphill a stone that at once rolled down again).

sit /sit/ *v.* (**sit•ting**; *past* and *past part.* **sat** /sat/) **1** *intr.* rest the buttocks on the ground or a raised seat, etc., with the torso upright. **2** *tr.* cause to sit; place in a sitting position. **3** *intr.* **a** (of a bird) perch or remain on its nest to hatch its eggs. **b** (of an animal) rest with the hind legs bent and the body close to the ground. **4** *intr.* (of a committee, etc.) be in session. **5** *intr.* pose (for a portrait). **6** *intr.* act as a babysitter. □ **sit down 1** sit after standing. **2** cause to sit. **sit-down** *adj.* (of a meal) eaten sitting at a table. **sit-down strike** strike in which workers refuse to leave their place of work. **sit in 1** occupy a place as a protest. **2** [foll. by *for*] take the place of. **3** [foll. by *on*] be present as a guest or observer at (a meeting, etc.). **sit-in** *n.* protest involving sitting in. **sit out 1** take no part in (a dance, etc.). **2** stay till the end of (esp. an ordeal). **sit tight** *colloq.* remain firmly in one's place. **sit up 1** rise from a lying to a sitting position. **2** sit firmly upright. **3** go to bed later than the usual time. **sit-up** *n.* physical exercise in which a person sits up without raising the legs from the ground. □□ **sit′ter** *n.*

■ **1** be *or* get seated, settle, sit down, rest, perch. **2** seat, sit down, install, put. **3 a** nest, roost; brood, incubate. **4** assemble, meet, convene; gather. **5** model. □ **sit in 2** substitute, fill in, double. **3** (*sit in on*) observe, watch, attend; join in. **sit-in** see DEMONSTRATION 2. **sit out 2** wait out, last through, live through. **sit tight** wait, hang back, be patient, delay.

si•tar /sitár, sitaar/ *n.* long-necked E. Indian lute with movable frets. □□ **si•tar•ist** /sitaárist/ *n.*

sit•com /sitkom/ *n. colloq.* situation comedy.

site /sīt/ • *n.* place; location. • *v.tr.* locate or place.

■ *n.* plot, ground, spot, setting, locale, neighborhood. • *v.* position, put, situate, install.

sit•ting /sīting/ • *n.* **1** continuous period of being engaged in an activity (*finished the book in one sitting*). **2** session. **3** session in which a meal is served (*dinner will be served in two sittings*). • *adj.* **1** having sat down. **2** (of an animal or bird) not running or flying. **3** (of a hen) engaged in hatching. □ **sitting duck** (or **target**) *colloq.* vulnerable person or thing. **sitting room 1** living room. **2** space enough to accommodate seated persons.

■ *n.* **2** see SESSION 1, 2. • *adj.* **1** sedentary, seated. □ **sitting room 1** see PARLOR.

sit•u•ate /síchōō-ayt/ *v.tr.* **1** put in a certain position or circumstances. **2** establish or indicate the place of; put in a context.

■ **1** place, locate, set, site, spot, put, install.

sit•u•a•tion /síchōō-áyshən/ *n.* **1** place and its surroundings. **2** circumstances; position; state of affairs. **3** employee's job. □ **situation comedy** television comedy in which the humor derives from the situations the characters are placed in. □□ **sit•u•a′tion•al** *adj.*

■ **1** position, location, spot, site, locale, setting. **2** condition, case, status (quo); plight, predicament. **3** position, place, employment.

six /siks/ *n.* **1** one more than five, or four less than ten. **2** symbol for this (6, vi, VI). □ **at sixes and sevens** in confusion or disagreement. **six-gun** = *six-shooter*. **six-pack** package of six cans or bottles, as of beer, soft drink, etc. **six-shooter** revolver with six chambers.

six•teen /síksteén/ n. **1** one more than fifteen, or six more than ten. **2** symbol for this (16, xvi, XVI). □□ **six'teenth** adj. & n.

sixth /siksth/ • n. **1** next after fifth. **2** each of six equal parts of a thing. • adj. that is the sixth. □ **sixth sense** supposed faculty giving intuitive or extrasensory knowledge.

six•ty /síkstee/ n. (pl. **–ties**) **1** six times ten. **2** symbol for this (60, lx, LX). **3** [in pl.] numbers from 60 to 69, esp. the years of a century or of a person's life. □□ **six'ti•eth** adj. & n. **six'ty•fold** adj. & adv.

siz•a•ble /sízəbəl/ adj. (also **size'a•ble**) large or fairly large. □□ **siz'a•bly** adv.

size[1] /siz/ n. **1** relative dimensions; magnitude. **2** each of the classes, usu. numbered, into which similar things are divided according to size. • v.tr. sort or group in sizes or according to size. □ **size up 1** estimate the size of. **2** colloq. form a judgment of. □□ **sized** adj. [also in comb.]. **siz'er** n.

■ n. **1** largeness, bulk, extent, scope, range; breadth, width, length, height, depth; amount; hugeness, vastness. • v. see SORT v. □ **size up 1** see ESTIMATE v. 1, 2. **2** assess, judge, evaluate, measure.

size[2] /siz/ • n. gelatinous solution used in glazing paper, stiffening textiles, etc. • v.tr. glaze, stiffen, etc.

siz•zle /sízəl/ • v.intr. **1** sputter or hiss, esp. in frying. **2** colloq. be in a state of great heat or excitement, etc. • n. **1** sizzling sound. **2** colloq. state of great heat or excitement. □□ **siz'zler** n. **siz'zling** adj. & adv.

SJ abbr. Society of Jesus (Jesuit).

skate[1] /skayt/ • n. **1** metal blade, usu. attached to a boot, for gliding on ice. **2** (in full **roller skate**) metal frame with small wheels, fitted to shoes for riding on a hard surface. • v. **1** intr. move on skates. **2** tr. perform a (specified figure) on skates. □□ **skat'er** n.

skate[2] /skayt/ n. (pl. same or **skates**) large, flat, raylike marine fish used as food.

skate•board /skáytbawrd/ • n. short narrow board on roller-skate wheels for riding on while standing. • v.intr. ride on a skateboard. □□ **skate'boarder** n.

ske•dad•dle /skidád'l/ colloq. • v.intr. run away; depart quickly; flee. • n. hurried departure or flight.

skeet /skeet/ n. shooting sport in which a clay target is thrown from a trap to simulate the flight of a bird.

skein /skayn/ n. **1** loosely-coiled bundle of yarn or thread. **2** flock of wild geese, etc., in flight.

skel•e•ton /skélit'n/ n. **1 a** hard internal or external framework of bones, cartilage, woody fiber, etc., supporting or containing the body of an animal or plant. **b** dried bones of a human being or other animal fastened together in the same relative positions as in life. **2** supporting framework or structure of a thing. □ **skeleton key** key designed to fit many locks by having the interior of the bit hollowed. □□ **skel'e•tal** adj. **skel'e•tal•ly** adv. **skel'e•ton•ize** v.tr.

skep•tic /sképtik/ n. person inclined to doubt all accepted opinions; cynic. □□ **skep'ti•cal** adj. **skep'ti•cal•ly** adv. **skep•ti•cism** /–tisizəm/ n.

■ doubter, questioner, scoffer. □□ **skeptical** doubting, dubious, doubtful, questioning, critical. **skepticism** doubt, dubiousness, doubtfulness, disbelief, incredulity.

sketch /skech/ • n. **1** a rough or unfinished drawing or painting. **2** rough draft or general outline. **3** very short play, usu. humorous and limited to one scene. • v. **1** tr. make or give a sketch of. **2** intr. draw sketches. **3** tr. [often foll. by in, out] indicate briefly or in outline.

sketch•y /skéchee/ adj. (**sketch•i•er, sketch•i•est**) **1** giving only a slight or rough outline, like a sketch. **2** colloq. unsubstantial or imperfect, esp. through haste. □□ **sketch'i•ly** adv. **sketch'i•ness** n.

■ cursory, superficial, incomplete, patchy, perfunctory. □□ **sketchily** skimpily, vaguely, imperfectly, crudely, hastily, hurriedly.

skew /skyōō/ • adj. oblique; slanting. • n. slant. • v. **1** tr. make skew. **2** tr. distort. **3** intr. move obliquely.

skew•er /skyōōər/ • n. long pin designed for holding meat compactly together while cooking. • v.tr. fasten together or pierce with or as with a skewer.

■ n. see SPIKE[1] n. 1b. • v. see PIERCE 1.

ski /skee/ • n. (pl. **skis** or **ski**) **1** each of a pair of long narrow pieces of wood, etc., for traveling over snow. **2** = water ski. • v. (**skis, skied** /skeed/; **ski•ing**) **1** intr. travel on skis. **2** tr. ski at (a place). □ **ski lift** device for carrying skiers up a slope, usu. on seats hung from an overhead cable. □□ **ski'a•ble** adj. **ski'er** n.

skid /skid/ • v. (**skid•ded, skid•ding**) **1** intr. (of a vehicle, a wheel, or a driver) slide on slippery ground, esp. sideways or obliquely. **2** tr. cause (a vehicle, etc.) to skid. • n. **1** act or instance of skidding. **2** strong base for supporting heavy objects during moving. **3** braking device. **4** runner beneath an aircraft for use when landing. □ **on the skids** colloq. about to be discarded or defeated. **put the skids under** colloq. hasten the downfall or failure of. **skid row** colloq. part of a town frequented by vagrants, alcoholics, etc.

skiff /skif/ n. light rowboat or scull.

skill /skil/ n. expertness; practiced ability; facility in an action; dexterity or tact. □□ **skilled** adj. **skill'ful** adj. **skill'ful•ly** adv. **skill'ful•ness** n

■ talent, aptitude, expertise, mastery; accomplishment, forte, strength. □□ **skillful** accomplished, adept, adroit, dexterous, expert.

skil•let /skílit/ n. frying pan.

skim /skim/ • v. (**skimmed, skim•ming**) **1** tr. take a floating layer from the surface of (a liquid). **2** tr. **a** keep touching lightly or nearly touching (a surface) in passing over. **b** deal with or treat (a subject) superficially. **3** intr. go or glide lightly. **4 a** tr. read superficially; look over cursorily. **b** intr. read or look over cursorily. • *n.* act or instance of skimming. □ **skim** (or **skimmed**) **milk** milk from which the cream has been removed. □□ **skim'mer** *n.*

■ *v.* **1** cream (off), separate, remove. **3** soar, skate, slide, sail. **4** skim through, scan, thumb *or* leaf through, glance at.

skimp /skimp/ • *v.tr.* be stingy. • *adj.* scanty.

skimp•y /skímpee/ *adj.* (**skimp•i•er**, **skimp•i•est**) meager; not ample or sufficient. □□ **skimp'i•ly** *adv.* **skimp'i•ness** *n.*

skin /skin/ • *n.* **1** flexible continuous covering of a human or other animal body. **2** skin of a flayed animal with or without the hair, etc. **3** outer layer or covering, esp. of a plant, fruit, or sausage. • *v.tr.* (**skinned**, **skin•ning**) **1** remove the skin from. **2** *sl.* fleece or swindle. □ **skin-deep** superficial; not deep or lasting. **skin diver** person who swims underwater without a diving suit, usu. with scuba, flippers, etc. □□ **skin'less** *adj.* **skin'like** *adj.* **skinned** *adj.* [also in *comb.*]

■ *n.* **1** epidermis, dermis. **2** hide, pelt, fleece. **3** coat, casing, integument, crust, husk, peel, rind, shell. • *v.* **1** flay, strip; peel, hull, husk, shell; abrade, scrape. **2** see FLEECE *v.* 1. □ **skin-deep** shallow, surface, slight, trivial.

skin•flint /skínflint/ *n.* miserly person.

skin•head /skínhed/ *n.* youth with close-cropped hair, esp. one of an aggressive gang.

skin•ny /skínee/ *adj.* (**skin•ni•er**, **skin•ni•est**) thin or emaciated. See synonym study at THIN. □ **skinny-dipping** *colloq.* swimming in the nude. □□ **skin'ni•ness** *n.*

■ underweight, gaunt, bony, spare, half-starved.

skin•tight /skíntít/ *adj.* (of a garment) very close-fitting.

skip /skip/ • *v.* (**skipped**, **skip•ping**) **1** *intr.* **a** move along lightly, esp. with alternate hops. **b** jump lightly from the ground, esp. so as to clear a jump rope. **c** jump about; gambol. **2** *intr.* move quickly from one point, subject, etc., to another. **3** *tr.* omit in dealing with a series or in reading (*skip every tenth row*). **4** *tr. colloq.* not participate in. **5** *tr. colloq.* leave hurriedly. • *n.* **1** skipping movement or action. **2** *Computing* action of passing over part of a sequence of data or instructions.

■ *v.* **1** leap, caper, frisk, prance, spring, bound. **2** see FLIT 1. **3** leave out, pass by, overlook, pass over, avoid. **4** see AVOID 1. • *n.* **1** prance, jump, bound, dance, hop, romp.

skip•per /skípər/ • *n.* **1** sea captain, esp. the master of a small trading or fishing vessel. **2** captain of an aircraft. • *v.tr.* act as captain of.

■ *n.* commander; leader, chief, *colloq.* boss. • *v.* see LEAD¹ *v.* 6, 7a.

skir•mish /skə́rmish/ • *n.* minor battle. • *v.intr.* engage in a skirmish. □□ **skir'mish•er** *n.*

■ *n.* fight, encounter, fray, brush, clash, engagement. • *v.* fight, clash, struggle, battle, tussle.

skirt /skərt/ • *n.* **1** woman's outer garment

hanging from the waist. **2** part of a coat, etc., that hangs below the waist. • *v.tr.* **1** go along or around or past the edge of. **2** avoid. □□ **skirt'ed** *adj.* [also in *comb.*]. **skirt'less** *adj.*

skit /skit/ *n.* light, usu. short, piece of satire or burlesque.

skit•tish /skítish/ *adj.* **1** lively; playful. **2** (of a horse, etc.) nervous; inclined to shy. □□ **skit'tish•ly** *adv.* **skit'tish•ness** *n.*

skiv•vy /skívee/ *n.* (*pl.* **–vies**) *sl.* [in *pl.*] men's underwear of T-shirt and shorts.

skul•dug•ger•y /skuldúgəree/ *n.* (also **skull•dug'ger•y**) trickery; unscrupulous behavior.

skulk /skulk/ *v.intr.* move stealthily, lurk, or keep oneself concealed. □□ **skulk'er** *n.*

skull /skul/ *n.* **1** bony case of the brain of a vertebrate. **2** the head as the seat of intelligence. □□ **skulled** *adj.* [also in *comb.*].

skull•cap /skúlkap/ *n.* small, close-fitting, peakless cap.

skunk /skungk/ • *n.* **1** black cat-sized mammal with white stripes on the back that emits a powerful stench as a defense. **2** *colloq.* thoroughly contemptible person. • *v.tr. sl.* defeat soundly.

sky /ski/ *n.* (*pl.* **skies**) [in *sing.* or *pl.*] atmosphere and outer space seen from the earth. □ **sky-high** *adv. & adj.* very high.

■ *n.* heaven(s), vault of heaven, (wild) blue (yonder), ether.

sky•box /skíboks/ *n.* elevated enclosure in a sports stadium containing plush seating, food services, and other amenities.

sky•cap /skíkap/ *n.* airport porter.

sky•div•ing /skídiving/ *n.* sport of performing acrobatic maneuvers under free fall with a parachute. □□ **sky'dive** *v.intr.* **sky'div'er** *n.*

sky•jack /skíjak/ *sl.* • *v.tr.* hijack (an aircraft). • *n.* act of skyjacking. □□ **sky'jack•er** *n.*

sky•light /skílit/ *n.* window in a roof or ceiling.

sky•line /skílin/ *n.* outline of buildings, etc., defined against the sky.

sky•rock•et /skírokkit/ • *n.* fireworks rocket. • *v.intr.* (esp. of prices, etc.) rise very rapidly.

sky•scrap•er /skískraypər/ *n.* very tall building.

sky•ward /skíwərd/ • *adv.* (also **sky•wards** /–wərdz/) toward the sky. • *adj.* moving skyward.

sky•writ•ing /skíriting/ *n.* writing traced in the sky by an airplane's smoke trails.

slab /slab/ • *n.* flat, broad, fairly thick piece of solid material. • *v.tr.* (**slabbed**, **slab•bing**) remove slabs from (a log or tree) to prepare it for sawing into planks.

■ *n.* slice, wedge, hunk, chunk, block, brick.

slack /slak/ • *adj.* **1** (of rope, etc.) not taut. **2** inactive or sluggish. **3** negligent or remiss. **4** (of tide, etc.) neither ebbing nor flowing. • *n.* **1** slack part of a rope. **2** slack period. **3** [in *pl.*] informal trousers. • *v.* **1** *tr. & intr.* slacken. **2** *tr.* loosen (rope, etc.). □□ **slack'ly** *adv.* **slack'ness** *n.*

■ *adj.* **1** loose, limp. **2** indolent, lazy, idle, slothful. **3** careless, lax, neglectful, inattentive. • *n.* **2** lull, pause, inactivity, cutback, falloff. • *v.* **1** relax, let up (on); delay, reduce speed; loose, release. □□ **slackness** looseness, play, give, leeway; see also NEGLECT *n*. 1.

slack·en /slákən/ *v.* make or become slack.

slack·er /slákər/ *n.* shirker; indolent person.
■ loafer, idler, skulker, gold brick.

slag /slag/ *n.* refuse left after smelting. □□ **slag·gy** *adj.* (**slag·gi·er, slag·gi·est**).

slain *past part.* of SLAY.

slake /slayk/ *v.tr.* **1** satisfy (thirst, desire, etc.). **2** disintegrate (quicklime) by combination with water.
■ **1** quench, gratify, satiate, allay, ease.

sla·lom /slaáləm/ *n.* ski race down a zigzag obstacle course.

slam[1] /slam/ • *v.* (**slammed, slam·ming**) **1** *tr. & intr.* shut forcefully and loudly. **2** *intr.* move violently. **3** *tr. sl.* criticize severely. • *n.* sound or action of slamming.
■ *v.* **1** fling closed, bang; go bang. **3** attack, vilify, pillory, disparage. • *n.* see IMPACT *n.* 1.

slam[2] /slam/ *n. Cards* winning of every trick in a game. □ **grand slam 1** *Bridge* winning of 13 tricks. **2** winning of all of a group of championships or matches in a sport. **small** (or **little**) **slam** *Bridge* winning of 12 tricks.

slan·der /slándər/ • *n.* **1** malicious, false, and injurious statement spoken about a person. **2** uttering of such statements. • *v.tr.* utter slander about. See synonym study at MALIGN. □□ **slan·der·er** *n.* **slan·der·ous** *adj.* **slan·der·ous·ly** *adv.*
■ *n.* defamation (of character), calumny, obloquy; slur, smear. • *v.* defame, calumniate, disparage, malign. □□ **slanderous** defamatory, calumnious, injurious, scandalous, malicious.

slang /slang/ *n.* words, phrases, and uses that are regarded as very informal or taboo or are peculiar to a specified profession, class, etc. (*racing slang*). See synonym study at DIALECT. □□ **slang·i·ly** *adv.* **slang·i·ness** *n.* **slang·y** *adj.* (**slang·i·er, slang·i·est**).

slant /slant/ • *v.* **1** *intr.* slope; lie or go at an angle. **2** *tr.* cause to do this. **3** *tr.* (often as **slanted** *adj.*) present (information), esp. in a biased or unfair way. • *n.* **1** oblique position. **2** point of view, esp. a biased one. • *adj.* sloping, oblique.
■ *v.* **1, 2** tilt, angle, incline, pitch, cant, bend, lean. **3** bend, distort, deviate, twist. • *n.* incline, tilt, ramp, gradient. **2** angle, standpoint; bias, prejudice.

slap /slap/ • *v.* (**slapped, slap·ping**) **1** *tr. & intr.* strike with the palm or a flat object, so as to make a similar noise. **2** *tr.* lay forcefully (*slapped the money on the table*). **3** *tr.* put hastily or carelessly. • *n.* blow with the palm or a flat object. **2** rebuke; insult.
■ *v.* **1** smack, cuff; spank; clout; flap, whip, beat; see also HIT *v.* 1a. **3** fling, toss, hurl, sling. • *n.* **1** smack, cuff, whack.

slap·dash /slápdash/ • *adj.* hasty and careless. See synonym study at SUPERFICIAL. • *adv.* in a slapdash manner.

slap·hap·py /sláp-hápee/ *adj. colloq.* **1** cheerfully casual or flippant. **2** punch-drunk.

slap·stick /slápstik/ *n.* **1** boisterous knockabout comedy. **2** flexible divided lath used by a clown.

slash /slash/ • *v.* **1** *intr.* make a sweeping cut or cuts with a knife, etc. **2** *tr.* make such a cut or cuts at. **3** *tr.* reduce (prices, etc.) drastically. • *n.* **1 a** slashing cut or stroke. **b** wound or slit made by this. **2** oblique stroke; solidus. □□ **slash·er** *n.*
■ *v.* **2** gash, hack, score, slit, slice; wound; scar. **3** cut, decrease, drop, mark down. • *n.* **1** gash, incision, slit; wound.

slat /slat/ *n.* thin, narrow piece of wood, etc.

slate /slayt/ • *n.* **1** fine-grained, esp. bluishgray, rock easily split into flat smooth plates. **2** piece of this used as roofing material or for writing on. **3** color of slate. **4** list of nominees for office, etc. • *v.tr.* **1** cover with slates esp. as roofing. **2** nominate for office, etc. • *adj.* made of slate. □□ **slat·y** *adj.*

slath·er /sláthər/ *v.tr. colloq.* spread thickly.

slat·tern /slátərn/ *n.* slovenly woman.

slaugh·ter /sláwtər/ • *n.* **1** killing of animals for food. **2** killing of many people or animals at once or continuously; carnage; massacre.
• *v.tr.* **1** kill (people) in a ruthless manner or on a great scale. **2** kill for food; butcher. See synonym study at KILL. □□ **slaugh·ter·er** *n.*
■ *n.* **1** butchery. **2** bloodshed, bloodbath, murder, extermination, genocide. • *v.* **1** butcher, murder, execute, exterminate, massacre.

slaugh·ter·house /sláwtərhows/ *n.* **1** place for the slaughter of animals as food. **2** place of carnage.
■ **1** abattoir.

Slav /slaav/ • *n.* member of a group of peoples in Central and Eastern Europe speaking Slavic languages. • *adj.* **1** of or relating to the Slavs. **2** Slavic. □□ **Slav·ism** *n.*

slave /slayv/ • *n.* **1** person who is the legal property of and has to serve another. **2** drudge; hard worker. **3** helpless victim of some dominating influence (*slave to duty*). • *v. intr.* work very hard. □ **slave driver 1** overseer of slaves. **2** person who works others hard. **slave trade** *hist.* dealing in slaves.
■ *n.* **1** lackey, bondsman, *hist.* serf. **2** workhorse, hack, laborer. • *v.* **1** labor, toil, grub, drudge.

slav·er[1] /sláyvər/ *n. hist.* ship or person engaged in the slave trade.

slav·er[2] /slávər/ • *n.* **1** saliva running from the mouth. **2 a** fulsome or servile flattery. **b** drivel; nonsense. • *v.intr.* drool; dribble.
■ *n.* **1** drool, dribble, spit, spittle. **2 a** see FLATTERY. **b** rubbish, twaddle. • *v.* drivel, spit; salivate, slobber.

slav·er·y /sláyvəree, sláyvree/ *n.* **1** condition of a slave. **2** drudgery. **3** custom of having slaves.
■ **1** enslavement, bondage, servitude; subjugation, captivity. **2** toil, grind, strain.

Slav·ic /sláavik/ • *adj.* **1** of or relating to the group of Indo-European languages including Russian, Polish, and Czech. **2** of or relating to the Slavs. • *n.* Slavic language group.

slav·ish /sláyvish/ *adj.* **1** like slaves. **2** without originality. □□ **slav·ish·ly** *adv.* **slav·ish·ness** *n.*

slay /slay/ *v.tr.* (*past* **slew** /slōō/; *past part.* **slain** /slayn/) **1** *literary* or *joc.* kill. **2** *sl.* overwhelm, esp. with laughter. See synonym study at KILL. □□ **slay'er** *n.*

sleaze /sleez/ *colloq. n.* **1** sleaziness. **2** person of low moral standards.

slea•zy /sléezee/ *adj.* (**slea•zi•er, slea•zi•est**) **1** squalid; tawdry. **2** slatternly. **3** (of textiles, etc.) flimsy. □□ **slea'zi•ly** *adv.* **slea'zi•ness** *n.*

■ **1** disreputable, low-grade, filthy, shabby, mangy, seedy, sordid, base. **2** slovenly, shabby, dirty. **3** unsubstantial, thin, slight.

sled /sled/ • *n.* **1** vehicle on runners for use on snow. **2** toboggan. • *v.intr.* (**sled•ded, sled•ding**) ride on a sled.

sledge /slej/ • *n.* large, heavy sled. • *v.* travel or convey by sledge.

sledge•ham•mer /sléjhamər/ *n.* heavy, long-handled hammer used to break stone, etc.

sleek /sleek/ • *adj.* **1** (of hair, fur, skin, etc.) smooth and glossy. **2** looking well-fed and comfortable. • *v.tr.* make sleek, esp. by stroking or pressing down. □□ **sleek'ly** *adv.* **sleek'ness** *n.*

■ *adj.* **1** velvety, lustrous, shiny, silky. **2** contented, complacent, thriving.

sleep /sleep/ • *n.* **1** naturally recurring condition of suspended consciousness, with the eyes closed and the muscles relaxed. **2** state like sleep, such as rest, quiet, etc. • *v.* (*past* and *past part.* **slept** /slept/) **1** *intr.* **a** be in a state of sleep. **b** fall asleep. **2** *tr.* provide sleeping accommodation for. **3** *intr.* have sexual intercourse (with). □ **put to sleep 1** anesthetize. **2** kill (an animal) mercifully. **sleeping bag** padded bag to sleep in esp. when camping, etc. **sleeping car** railroad car with berths; Pullman. **sleeping sickness** tropical disease causing extreme lethargy. □□ **sleep'less** *adj.* **sleep'less•ly** *adv.* **sleep'less•ness** *n.*

■ *v.* **1** doze, (take a) nap, rest, repose, drowse. □ **put to sleep 2** see *put down* 6 (PUT[1]). □□ **sleepless** restless, wakeful; disturbed; insomniac.

sleep•er /sléepar/ *n.* **1** person or animal that sleeps. **2** railroad tie or similar supporting beam. **3 a** sleeping car. **b** berth in this.

sleep•walk /sléepwawk/ *v.intr.* walk or perform other actions while asleep. □□ **sleep' walk•er** *n.* **sleep'walk•ing** *n.*

sleep•y /sléepee/ *adj.* (**sleep•i•er, sleep•i•est**) **1** drowsy; ready for sleep. **2** quiet; inactive. □□ **sleep'i•ly** *adv.* **sleep'i•ness** *n.*

■ **1** somnolent, tired, nodding; weary, exhausted. **2** boring, dull, soporific; gentle, relaxed.

sleet /sleet/ • *n.* snow and rain falling together. • *v.intr.* [prec. by *it* as subject] sleet falls (*it is sleeting*). □□ **sleet'y** *adj.*

sleeve /sleev/ *n.* **1** part of a garment that covers an arm. **2** cover of a phonograph record. **3** tube enclosing a rod or smaller tube. □ **up one's sleeve** concealed but in reserve. □□ **sleeved** *adj.* [also in *comb.*]. **sleeve'less** *adj.*

sleigh /slay/ • *n.* = SLED. • *v.intr.* travel on a sleigh.

sleight /slīt/ *n.* □ **sleight of hand 1** dexterity, esp. in conjuring or fencing. **2** display of dexterity.

slen•der /sléndər/ *adj.* (**slen•der•er, slen• der•est**) **1 a** of small girth or breadth. **b** gracefully thin. **2** relatively small or scanty; inadequate. See synonym study at THIN. □□ **slen'der•ly** *adv.* **slen'der•ness** *n.*

■ **1** slim, lean, willowy, sylphlike, lithe; attenuated, tenuous. **2** slim, slight, little; narrow, remote; meager, poor; limited.

slept *past* and *past part.* of SLEEP.

sleuth /slōōth/ *colloq. n.* detective.

■ (private) investigator, *colloq.* private eye.

slew[1] /slōō/ (also **slue**) • *v.* turn or swing forcibly to a new position. • *n.* such a change of position.

slew[2] *past* of SLAY.

slew[3] /slōō/ *n. colloq.* large number or quantity.

slice /slīs/ • *n.* **1** thin piece or wedge cut off or out. **2** share; part. **3** *Golf* & *Tennis* slicing stroke. • *v.* **1** *tr.* cut into slices. **2** *tr.* cut (a piece) off. **3** *intr.* cut (as) with a knife. **4** *tr.* **a** *Golf* strike (the ball) so that it deviates away from the striker. **b** (in other sports) propel (the ball) forward at an angle. □□ **slice'a• ble** *adj.* **slic'er** *n.* [also in *comb.*].

■ *n.* **1** portion, segment, slab, helping; shaving. **2** helping, cut, portion, piece. • *v.* **1–3** divide, *Biol.* section; shear; carve.

slick /slik/ • *adj. colloq.* **1 a** skillful or efficient. **b** superficially or pretentiously smooth and dexterous. **c** glib. **2 a** sleek; smooth. **b** slippery. • *n.* patch of oil, etc., esp. on the sea. • *v.tr. colloq.* **1** make sleek or smart. **2** flatten (one's hair, etc.). □□ **slick' ly** *adv.* **slick'ness** *n.*

■ *adj.* **1 a** smooth, clever, adroit, dexterous. **b** shallow, meretricious, specious, glib. **c** smooth, urbane, suave; disingenuous, artful, wily; sycophantic, unctuous. **2 a** glossy, silky, silken, shiny. **b** glassy, greasy. • *v.* **2** slick down, smooth, plaster down.

slick•er /slíkər/ *n.* **1** *colloq.* [usu. *derog.*] **a** plausible rogue. **b** (in full **city slicker**) smart and sophisticated city dweller. **2** raincoat of smooth material.

■ **1 a** confidence man, cheat, swindler.

slide /slīd/ • *v.* (*past* and *past part.* **slid** /slid/) **1 a** *intr.* move along a smooth surface with continuous contact. **b** *tr.* cause to do this (*slide the drawer into place*). **2** *intr.* move quietly; glide. • *n.* **1 a** act or instance of sliding. **b** decline. **2** inclined plane down which children, goods, etc., slide. **3 a** piece of glass holding an object for a microscope. **b** mounted transparency viewed with a projector. □ **let things slide** be negligent; allow deterioration. **slide rule** ruler with a sliding central strip, graduated logarithmically for making rapid calculations. **sliding scale** scale of fees, taxes, wages, etc., that varies according to some standard. □□ **slid'er** *n.*

■ *v.* **1, 2** slip; coast, skim, skid, slither. • *n.* **1 b** see DECLINE[1] *n.* 1, 2. **2** see CHUTE.

slight /slīt/ • *adj.* **1 a** inconsiderable; of little significance. **b** barely perceptible. **c** inadequate; scanty. **2** slender; frail-looking. • *v.tr.* treat disrespectfully; neglect. See synonym study at NEGLECT. • *n.* failure to show due respect. □□ **slight′ing•ly** *adv.* **slight′ish** *adj.* **slight′ly** *adv.* **slight′ness** *n.*

■ *adj.* **1 a** small, little, minor, negligible, insignificant. **b** trifling, tiny, minute. **c** see SCANTY, SLENDER 2. **2** slim, thin, small, petite, feeble, delicate. • *v.* disregard, ignore, disdain, scorn; insult, offend. • *n.* snub, insult, affront, slur, indignity. □□ **slightly** a little, somewhat, to a certain extent, marginally; moderately, rather.

slim /slim/ • *adj.* (**slim•mer, slim•mest**) **1 a** of long, narrow shape. **b** gracefully thin. **2** slight; insufficient. • *v.* (**slimmed, slim• ming**) **1** *intr.* become slimmer by dieting, exercise, etc. **2** *tr.* make slimmer or slimmer. □□ **slim′ly** *adv.* **slim′mer** *n.* **slim′ming** *n. & adj.* **slim′mish** *adj.* **slim′ness** *n.*

■ *adj.* **1** see SLENDER 1. **2** see SLENDER 2. • *v.* **1** reduce, lose *or* shed weight, diet, slenderize.

slime /slīm/ • *n.* thick slippery or sticky substance. • *v.tr.* cover with slime. □□ **slim′i•ly** *adv.* **slim′i•ness** *n.* **slim′y** *adj.* (**slim•i•er, slim•i•est**).

■ □□ **slimy** oozy, slippery, mucky, viscous; unctuous, obsequious, servile.

sling /sling/ • *n.* **1** strap, etc., to support or raise a hanging weight. **2** bandage looped around the neck to support an injured arm. **3** straplike device for flinging a stone or other missile. • *v.tr.* (*past* and *past part.* **slung** /slung/) **1** *colloq.* throw. **2** suspend with a sling.

■ *n.* **1, 2** band; belt. **3** catapult, slingshot. • *v.* **1** catapult, propel, hurl, shy, toss, cast, pitch. **3** hang, dangle, swing.

sling•shot /slingshot/ *n.* forked stick, etc., with elastic for shooting stones, etc.

slink /slingk/ *v.intr.* (*past* and *past part.* **slunk** /slungk/) move in a stealthy or guilty manner.

■ sneak, creep, steal, prowl, skulk, slip.

slink•y /slingkee/ *adj.* (**slink•i•er, slink•i• est**) **1** stealthy. **2** (of a garment) close-fitting and flowing; sinuous. **3** gracefully slender. □□ **slink′i•ly** *adv.* **slink′i•ness** *n.*

slip¹ /slip/ • *v.* (**slipped, slip•ping**) **1** *intr.* slide unintentionally, esp. for a short distance; lose one's footing or balance. **2** *intr.* go or move with a sliding motion. **3** *intr.* escape by being slippery or hard to hold. **4** *intr.* **a** go unobserved or quietly. **b** [foll. by *by*] (of time) go by rapidly or unnoticed. **5** *intr.* **a** make a careless or casual mistake. **b** fall below standard. **6** *tr.* [foll. by *on, off*] pull (a garment) hastily on or off. **7** *tr.* escape from; give the slip to. • *n.* **1** act or instance of slipping. **2** accidental or slight error. **3 a** petticoat. **b** pillowcase. **4** bay in a dock for mooring a vessel. □ **let slip** utter inadvertently. **slip-on** *adj.* (of shoes or clothes) that can be easily slipped on and off. *n.* slip-on shoe or garment. **slipped disk** disk between vertebrae. **slip up** *colloq.* make a mistake.

■ *v.* **1** skid, glide; stumble, trip; fall, tumble. **4 a** sneak, slink, steal, creep; (*slip in*) enter, get in, sneak in. **b** (*slip by*) pass, elapse,

vanish. **5 a** see *slip up* below. **b** see DETERIORATE. • *n.* **2** blunder, mistake, fault, oversight. □ **let slip** reveal, divulge, blurt out, leak. **slip up** err, blunder, miscalculate.

slip² /slip/ *n.* **1** small piece of paper. **2** cutting taken from a plant for grafting or planting; scion. □ **slip of a** small and slim.

■ **1** note, chit; permit, permission, pass. **2** shoot, set, sprout, runner, offshoot.

slip³ /slip/ *n.* clay in a creamy mixture with water, for decorating earthenware.

slip•cov•er /slipkəvər/ • *n.* **1** removable fabric covering for usu. upholstered furniture. **2** jacket or slipcase for a book. • *v.tr* cover with a slipcover.

slip•knot /slipnot/ *n.* knot that can be undone by a pull.

slip•page /slipij/ *n.* act, amount, or instance of slipping.

slip•per /slipər/ *n.* **1** light, loose, comfortable indoor shoe. **2** light slip-on shoe for dancing, etc.

slip•per•y /slipəree/ *adj.* **1** difficult to hold. **2** (of a surface) causing sliding or slipping by its smoothness or slickness. **3** unreliable; unscrupulous. □□ **slip′per•i•ness** *n.*

■ **1, 2** slick, sleek, slimy, icy, glassy, greasy. **3** evasive, devious, undependable, untrustworthy.

slip•shod /slipshod/ *adj.* **1** careless; unsystematic. **2** slovenly.

■ slapdash, haphazard, messy, untidy, disorganized.

slip•stream /slipstreem/ • *n.* **1** current of air or water driven back by a propeller or jet engine. **2** partial vacuum created in the wake of a moving vehicle, esp. as used by other vehicles in a race to assist in passing. • *v.intr.* (esp. in car racing) follow closely behind another vehicle, traveling in its slipstream.

slip-up /slipəp/ *n.* mistake; blunder.

slit /slit/ • *n.* straight, narrow incision or opening. • *v.tr.* (**slit•ting**; *past* and *past part.* **slit**) **1** make a slit in. **2** cut into strips. □□ **slit′ter** *n.*

■ *n.* split, cut, gash, fissure, groove, slash, rift. • *v.* **1** split, slash, gash, slice.

slith•er /slithər/ • *v.intr.* slide unsteadily. • *n.* instance of slithering. □□ **slith′er•y** *adj.*

■ *v.* worm, snake, slip, slink, glide, skitter, creep, crawl.

sliv•er /slivər/ • *n.* long, thin piece cut or split off; splinter. • *v.* **1** break off as a sliver. **2** break or form into slivers.

■ *n.* fragment, shard, shred, slip, slice.

slob /slob/ *n. colloq.* lazy, untidy person. □□ **slob′bish** *adj.*

■ oaf, boor, lout, churl, yahoo, barbarian.

slob•ber /slobər/ • *v.intr.* **1** slaver. **2** show excessive sentiment. • *n.* saliva running from the mouth; slaver. □□ **slob′ber•y** *adj.*

sloe /slō/ *n.* **1** = BLACKTHORN. **2** its small bluish-black fruit with a sharp sour taste.

slog /slog/ • *v.intr.* (**slogged, slog•ging**) walk or work doggedly. • *n.* hard steady work or walking. □□ **slog′ger** *n.*

■ *v.intr.* see WALK *v.* 1, 2. • *n.* see *drudgery* (DRUDGE), WALK *n.* 2.

slo•gan /slṓgən/ n. **1** short catchy phrase used in advertising, etc. **2** party cry; watchword or motto.
■ catchword, byword, catchphrase; jingle, saying.

sloop /slo͞op/ n. one-masted, fore-and-aft-rigged vessel.

slop /slop/ • v. (**slopped, slop•ping**) **1** intr. spill or flow over the edge of a vessel. **2** tr. allow to do this. • n. **1** liquid spilled or splashed. **2** [in pl.] dirty waste water. **3** [in sing. or pl.] unappetizing, weak, liquid food.
■ v. **1** see SPILL v. 1. ■ n. **2** (slops) see GARBAGE 1a.

slope /slōp/ • n. **1** inclined position, state, or direction. **2** piece of rising or falling ground. **3** difference in level between the two ends or sides of a thing. • v. **1** intr. have or take a slope; slant. **2** tr. cause to slope.
■ n. **1–3** incline, decline, ascent, descent, acclivity, declivity, rise, fall, ramp, dip, sink, drop, angle, slant. • v. **1** incline, decline, ascend, descend, rise, fall, dip, sink, drop (off), angle, cant, pitch. **2** slant, angle, bevel, cant, grade.

slop•py /slópee/ adj. (**slop•pi•er, slop•pi•est**) **1 a** (of the ground) full of puddles. **b** (of food, etc.) watery and disagreeable. **2** unsystematic; careless. **3** weakly emotional; maudlin. □□ **slop′pi•ly** adv. **slop′pi•ness** n.
■ **1 a** wet, slushy, soggy, sopping, sodden. **b** thin, runny, messy, slushy. **2** slovenly, slipshod, shoddy, slapdash. **3** sentimental, gushy, mawkish, mushy.

slosh /slosh/ v. **1** intr. splash or flounder about; move with a splashing sound. **2** tr. colloq. pour (liquid) clumsily.
■ v. **1** see SPLASH v. 3.

sloshed /slosht/ adj. sl. drunk.

slot /slot/ • n. **1** slit in a machine for a coin. **2** allotted place in an arrangement or schedule. • v. (**slot•ted, slot•ting**) **1** tr. & intr. place or be placed into or as if into a slot. **2** tr. provide with slots. □ **slot machine** gambling machine worked by the insertion of a coin in a slot.
■ n. **1** groove, fissure, notch, opening, hollow. **2** opening, position, vacancy, place, niche. • v. **1** assign, schedule, position. **2** groove, fissure, notch, slit.

sloth /slawth, slōth/ n. **1** laziness or indolence. **2** slow-moving nocturnal mammal of S. America that hangs upside down in trees. □□ **sloth′ful** adj. **sloth′ful•ly** adv. **sloth′ful•ness** n.
■ **1** idleness, slothfulness, inertia, apathy. □□ **slothful** idle, lazy, indolent; sluggish, laggard.

slouch /slowch/ • v.intr. stand, move, or sit in a drooping fashion. • n. **1** slouching posture or movement. **2** sl. incompetent or indifferent worker. □□ **slouch′y** adj. (**slouch•i•er, slouch•i•est**).
■ v. sag, stoop, slump; hunch. • n. **1** stoop, sag, droop, slump; hunch. **2** sloven, loafer, sluggard.

slough¹ /slow, slo͞o (for 2)/ n. **1** swamp; miry place. **2** marshy pond, backwater, etc. **3** state of hopeless depression.
■ see SWAMP n.

slough² /sluf/ • n. **1** part that an animal casts or molts, esp. a snake's cast skin. **2** dead tissue that drops off from living flesh, etc. • v. **1** tr. cast off as a slough. **2** intr. [often foll. by off] drop off as a slough.

Slo•vak /slṓvaak, –vak/ • n. **1** member of a Slavic people inhabiting Slovakia in central Europe, formerly part of Czechoslovakia and now an independent republic. **2** West Slavic language of this people. • adj. of or relating to this people or language.

slov•en /slúvən/ n. person who is habitually untidy or careless. □□ **slov′en•ly** adj. & adv. **slov′en•li•ness** n.

slow /slō/ • adj. **1 a** taking a relatively long time to do a thing. **b** not quick; acting or moving or done without speed. **2** gradual. **3** not conducive to speed. **4** (of a clock, etc.) showing a time earlier than is the case. **5** (of a person) not understanding or learning readily. **6** slack or sluggish. **7** Photog. (of a film) needing long exposure. • adv. [often in comb.] slowly (slow-moving traffic). • v. [usu. foll. by down, up] **1** intr. & tr. reduce one's speed or the speed of (a vehicle, etc.). **2** intr. reduce one's pace of life. □ **slow motion** speed of a film in which actions, etc., appear much slower than usual. □□ **slow′ish** adj. **slow′ly** adv. **slow′ness** n.
■ adj. **1** lagging, laggard, dawdling, sluggish, sluggardly; see also LATE adj. 1. **2** progressive, moderate, almost imperceptible. **4** behindhand, unpunctual, behind time. **5** dense, dull, slow-witted, dull-witted, obtuse. **6** inactive, quiet; unproductive. • adv. unhurriedly, cautiously; easy, leisurely; tardily. • v. (slow down or up) **1** slack off, decelerate, go slower, put on the brakes; see also RETARD v. **2** relax, take it easy, ease up, let up. □□ **slowly** see gradually (GRADUAL), SLOW adv. above.

slow•down /slṓdown/ n. deliberate slowing down of productivity.

SLR abbr. Photog. single-lens reflex.

sludge /sluj/ n. **1** thick, greasy mud or sediment. **2** sewage. □□ **sludg′y** adj.
■ **1** mire, ooze, slime, dregs, silt, residue.

slue var. of SLEW¹.

slug¹ /slug/ n. **1** small shell-less mollusk destructive to plants. **2 a** bullet. **b** missile for an airgun. **3** shot of liquor. **4** counterfeit coin.
■ **2** see SHOT¹ 3. **3** see DRINK n. 2b.

slug² /slug/ • v.tr. (**slugged, slug•ging**) strike with a hard blow. • n. hard blow. □□ **slug′ger** n.
■ v. see PUNCH¹ v. 1. ■ n. see PUNCH¹ n. 1. □□ **slugger** see PUGILIST.

slug•gard /slúgərd/ n. lazy, sluggish person. □□ **slug′gard•ly** adj. **slug′gard•li•ness** n.

slug•gish /slúgish/ adj. slow-moving; indolent. □□ **slug′gish•ly** adv. **slug′gish•ness** n.
■ see TORPID 1. □□ **sluggishness** sloth, laziness, idleness.

sluice /slo͞os/ • n. **1** (also **sluice gate, sluice valve**) sliding gate, etc., for controlling the flow of water, etc. **2** water so regulated.

3 artificial channel with a sluice gate, esp. one for washing ore. **4** act or instance of rinsing. • *v.tr.* **1** provide or wash with a sluice or sluices. **2** rinse, pour, or throw water freely upon.
■ *n.* **1** lock. **3** see CHANNEL *n.* 5a.

slum /slum/ • *n.* **1** overcrowded and squalid back street, district, etc., usu. in a city. **2** house or building unfit for human habitation. • *v.intr.* (**slummed, slum•ming**) **1** live in slumlike conditions. **2** visit slums, as out of curiosity. □□ **slum′my** *adj.* (**slum•mi•er, slum•mi•est**) **slum′mi•ness** *n.*
■ *n.* **1** ghetto, warren, shanty town. **2** see HOLE *n.* 3a. □□ **slummy** see SHABBY 1, 2.

slum•ber /slúmbər/ *poet. rhet.* *v. & n.* sleep. □□ **slum′ber•er** *n.* **slum′ber•ous** *adj.*

slump /slump/ • *n.* sudden fall in prices and trade. • *v.intr.* **1** undergo a slump; fail. **2** sit or fall heavily or limply. **3** lean or subside.
■ *n.* dip, trough, depreciation, decline, downturn, recession; nosedive, tailspin. • *v.* **1** decline, slip, recede, fall (off), plunge. **2** sink, flop, drop, collapse. **3** sink; see also SLOUCH *v.*

slung *past* and *past part.* of SLING.

slunk *past* and *past part.* of SLINK.

slur /slər/ • *v.* (**slurred, slur•ring**) **1** *tr. & intr.* pronounce indistinctly so that the sounds run into one another. **2** *tr. Mus.* **a** perform (notes) legato. **b** mark (notes) with a slur. **3** *tr.* put a slur on (a person or a person's character). **4** *tr.* [usu. foll. by *over*] pass over (a fact, fault, etc.) lightly. • *n.* **1** imputation of wrongdoing. **2** act or instance of slurring. **3** *Mus.* curved line joining notes to be slurred.
■ *v.* **1** mumble, garble. **3** see SLANDER *v.* **4** (*slur over*) gloss over, disregard, overlook. • *n.* **1** smear, insult, calumny, aspersion, affront, stigma.

slurp /slərp/ • *v.tr.* eat or drink noisily. • *n.* sound of this.

slur•ry /slúree/ *n.* (*pl.* **-ries**) thin, semiliquid mud, cement, etc.

slush /slush/ *n.* **1** thawing, muddy snow. **2** silly sentiment. □ **slush fund** reserve fund, esp. for political bribery. □□ **slush′y** *adj.* (**slush•i•er, slush•i•est**) **slush′i•ness** *n.*

slut /slut/ *n. derog.* **1** slovenly woman. **2** prostitute. □□ **slut′tish** *adj.* **slut′tish•ness** *n.*

sly /slī/ *adj.* (**sli•er, sli•est** or **sly•er, sly•est**) **1** cunning; crafty; wily. **2 a** (of a person) practicing secrecy or stealth. **b** (of an action, etc.) done, etc., in secret. **3** mischievous; knowing; insinuating. □ **on the sly** secretly; covertly. □□ **sly′ly** *adv.* (also **sli•ly**). **sly′ness** *n.*
■ **1** artful, clever, guileful, underhand(ed), scheming. **2** see STEALTHY. **3** impish, elfish, roguish. □ **on the sly** quietly, surreptitiously, privately, stealthily. □□ **slyly** see *on the sly* (SLY) above. **slyness** see STEALTH.

smack¹ /smak/ • *n.* **1** sharp slap or blow. **2** hard hit in baseball, etc. **3** loud kiss. **4** loud, sharp sound. • *v.* **1** *tr.* slap. **2** *tr.* part (one's lips) noisily in eager anticipation of food. **3** *tr. & intr.* move, hit, etc., with a

smack. • *adv. colloq.* **1** with a smack. **2** suddenly; directly; violently. **3** exactly.
■ *n.* **1** see SLAP *n.* **2** see HIT *n.* 1a. **3** see KISS *n.* • *v.* **1** see SLAP *v.* 1. **3** see HIT *v.* 1a. • *adv.* **2, 3** see SLAP *adv.*

smack² /smak/ • *v.intr.* **1** have a flavor of; taste of. **2** suggest the presence or effects of. • *n.* **1** flavor. **2** barely discernible quality.
■ *v.* **1** savor. **2** see SUGGEST 2. • *n.* **1** see TASTE *n.* 1a. **2** see TOUCH *n.* 3.

smack³ /smak/ *n.* single-masted sailboat.

smack⁴ /smak/ *n. sl.* heroin.

smack•er /smákər/ *n. sl.* **1** loud kiss. **2** resounding blow. **3** (usu. *pl.*) *sl.* dollar bill.

small /smawl/ • *adj.* **1** not large or big. **2** slender; thin. **3** not great in importance, amount, number, strength, or power. **4** petty; mean. **5** young. • *n.* slenderest part of something (esp. *small of the back*). • *adv.* into small pieces. □ **feel** (or **look**) **small** be humiliated. **small arms** portable firearms. **small fry** *colloq.* **1** young child or children. **2** insignificant things or people. **small print** inconspicuous and usu. unfavorable limitations, etc., in a contract. **small talk** light social conversation. **small-time** *colloq.* unimportant or petty. □□ **small′ish** *adj.* **small′ness** *n.*
■ *adj.* **1** little, tiny, short, diminutive; compact; wee. **2** see THIN *adj.* 4. **3** slight, secondary, insignificant, trivial, inconsequential. **4** skimpy, niggardly, stingy; paltry, measly. **5** immature, under age, undeveloped. □ **feel** (or **look**) **small** feel embarrassed *or* ashamed *or* foolish. **small fry 1** see YOUNG *n.* **small print** see CONDITION *n.* 1, CATCH *n.* 3b. **small talk** see CHAT *n.* 1. **small-time** small-scale, piddling, minor, insignificant.

SYNONYM STUDY: small

DIMINUTIVE, LITTLE, MINIATURE, MINUTE, PETITE, TINY. Why do we call a house **small** and a woman **petite**? *Small* and *little* are used interchangeably to describe people or things of reduced dimensions, but *small* is preferred when describing something concrete that is of less than the usual size, quantity, value, or importance (*a small matter to discuss; a small room; a small price to pay*), while *little* more often refers to absolute concepts (*through little fault of his own; an issue of little importance*) or to a more drastic reduction in scale (*a little shopping cart just like the one her mother used*). **Diminutive** and *petite* intensify the meaning of *small*, particularly with reference to women's figures that are very trim and compact (*with her diminutive figure, she had to shop in stores that specialized in petite sizes*). **Tiny** is used to describe what is extremely *small*, often to the point where it can be seen only by looking closely (*a tiny flaw in the material, a tiny insect*), while **minute** not only describes what is seen with difficulty but may also refer to a very small amount of something (*minute traces of gunpowder on his glove*). **Miniature** applies specifically to a copy, a model, or a representation of something on a very *small* scale (*a child's mobile consisting of miniature farm animals*).

small-mind•ed /smáwlmíndid/ *adj.* petty; narrow in outlook. □□ **small'-mind'ed•ly** *adv.* **small'-mind'ed•ness** *n.*

small•pox /smáwlpoks/ *n. hist.* acute contagious viral disease, with fever and pustules, usu. leaving permanent scars.

smart /smaart/ • *adj.* **1** clever; ingenious; quickwitted. **2** well-groomed; neat. **3** in good repair. **4** stylish; fashionable. **5** quick; brisk. **6** painfully severe. • *v.intr.* **1** feel or give pain. **2** (of an insult, grievance, etc.) rankle. **3** [foll. by *for*] suffer the consequences of. • *n.* sharp pain. • *adv.* smartly; in a smart manner. □ **smart aleck** *colloq.* person displaying ostentatious or smug cleverness. **smart-ass** *sl.* = SMART ALECK. **smart bomb** bomb that can be guided directly to its target by use of radio waves, television, or lasers. □□ **smart'ing•ly** *adv.* **smart'ly** *adv.* **smart'ness** *n.*

■ *adj.* **1** intelligent, bright, brilliant, sharp, acute, astute. **2** trim, dapper, spruce, soigné(e), elegant, chic. **3** spick and span, bright, gleaming. **4** see STYLISH 1, PROMINENT 3. **5** vigorous, animated, active; quick, swift, alert, jaunty. **6** stiff, smarting, stinging. • *v.* **1** sting, hurt, pinch, ache. • *n.* injury, harm, pang. □□ **smartness** see INGENUITY, PANACHE.

smart•en /smáart'n/ *v.* make or become smart.

smash /smash/ • *v.* **1** *tr. & intr.* **a** break into pieces; shatter. **b** bring or come to sudden destruction, defeat, or disaster. **2** *tr.* move with great force and impact. **3** *tr.* (as **smashed** *adj.*) *sl.* intoxicated. • *n.* **1** act or instance of smashing; violent fall, collision, or disaster. **2** sound of this. **3** (in full **smash hit**) very successful play, song, performer, etc.

■ *v.* **1a** see SHATTER 1. **1b** see DESTROY 1, 2. **2** see BUMP *v.* 1, 2. **3** (**smashed**) see DRUNK *adj.* 1. • *n.* **1** see COLLISION 1. **3** see HIT *n.* 3.

smash•ing /smáshing/ *adj. colloq.* superlative; excellent; wonderful; beautiful. □□ **smash' ing•ly** *adv.*

smash•up /smáshəp/ *n. colloq.* violent collision.

smear /smeer/ • *v.tr.* **1** daub or mark with a greasy or sticky substance. **2** smudge. **3** defame; slander. • *n.* **1** act or instance of smearing. **2** *Med.* **a** material smeared on a microscopic slide, etc., for examination. **b** specimen taken from this. □□ **smear'er** *n.* **smear'y** *adj.* (**smear•i•er, smear•i•est**).

■ *v.* **1** spread, cover, coat; dirty, smudge, stain. **2** blot, blur. **3** blacken, besmirch, discredit, denigrate, tarnish. • *n.* **1** smudge, daub, stain; slander, libel, vilification, defamation, calumny.

smell /smel/ • *n.* **1** faculty of perceiving odors. **2** quality perceived by this. **3** unpleasant odor. **4** act of inhaling to ascertain

smell. • *v.* (*past* and *past part.* **smelled** or **smelt** /smelt/) **1** *tr.* perceive or examine by smell. **2** *intr.* emit odor. **3** *tr.* perceive; detect. **4** *intr.* have or use a sense of smell. □ **smelling salts** ammonium carbonate mixed with scent to be sniffed as a restorative in faintness, etc. □□ **smell'a•ble** *adj.* **smell' er** *n.* **smell'-less** *adj.*

■ *n.* **2** odor, scent, aroma, perfume, fragrance, bouquet. **3** stink, stench, fetidness. • *v.* **1** scent, sniff, nose (out), get wind of. **3** see DETECT.

SYNONYM STUDY: smell

AROMA, BOUQUET, FRAGRANCE, ODOR, PERFUME, SCENT, STENCH, STINK. Everyone appreciates the **fragrance** of fresh-cut flowers, but the **stench** from the paper mill across town is usually unwelcome. Both have a distinctive **smell**, which is the most general of these words for what is perceived through the nose, but there is a big difference between a pleasant *smell* and a foul one. An **odor** may be either pleasant or unpleasant, but it suggests a *smell* that is more clearly recognizable and can usually be traced to a single source (*the pungent odor of onions*). An **aroma** is a pleasing and distinctive *odor* that is usually penetrating or pervasive (*the aroma of fresh-ground coffee*), while **bouquet** refers to the delicate *aroma* of a fine wine (*After swirling the wine around in her glass, she sniffed the bouquet*). A **scent** is usually delicate and pleasing, with an emphasis on the source rather than on an olfactory impression (*the scent of balsam associated with Christmas*). Fragrance and **perfume** are both associated with flowers, but *fragrance* is more delicate; a *perfume* may be so rich and strong that it is repulsive or overpowering (*The air was so dense with the perfume of lilacs that I had to go indoors*). Stench and stink are reserved for *smells* that are foul, strong, and pervasive, although *stink* implies a sharper sensation, while *stench* refers to a more sickening one (*the stink of sweaty gym clothes, the stench of a rotting animal*).

---

smell•y /smélee/ *adj.* (**smell•i•er, smell•i•est**) having a strong or unpleasant smell. □□ **smell'i•ness** *n.*

■ malodorous, evil-smelling, foul-smelling, fetid, putrid, reeky, stinking, rank, offensive.

smelt¹ /smelt/ *v.tr.* **1** separate metal from (ore) by melting. **2** extract or refine (metal) in this way. □□ **smelt'er** *n.*

smelt² *past* and *past part.* of SMELL.

smelt³ /smelt/ *n.* (*pl.* same or **smelts**) small edible green and silver fish.

smid•gen /smíjən/ *n.* (also **smid'gin**) *colloq.* small bit.

smile /smīl/ • *v.* **1** *intr.* relax the features into a pleased or kind or gently skeptical expression, with the lips parted and the corners of the mouth turned up. **2** *tr.* express by smiling (*smiled their consent*). **3** *intr.* [foll. by *on, upon*] encourage. • *n.* **1** act or instance of smiling. **2** smiling expression or aspect. □□ **smile'less** *adj.* **smil'er** *n.* **smil'ing•ly** *adv.*

■ *v.* **1** grin, beam; smirk, simper. **3** (*smile*

on or *upon*) see FAVOR *v.* 2. • *n.* grin; smirk, simper.

smirch /smərch/ • *v.tr.* mark, soil, or discredit. • *n.* spot or stain.
■ *v.* see MUDDY *v.*, STAIN *v.* 2. • *n.* see STAIN *n.* 2.

smirk /smərk/ • *n.* affected, conceited, or silly smile. • *v.intr.* make such a smile. □□ **smirk′er** *n.* **smirk′ing•ly** *adv.* **smirk′** *adj.* **smirk′i•ly** *adv.*
■ *n.* leer, sneer, grin, grimace, simper, simpering smile. • *v.* sneer, grin, grimace, leer, simper.

smite /smīt/ *v.tr.* (*past* **smote** /smōt/; *past part.* **smit•ten** /smit′n/) *archaic* or *literary* **1** hit. **2** chastise; defeat. **3** [in *passive*] **a** have a sudden strong effect on. **b** infatuate; fascinate. □□ **smit′er** *n.*
■ **1** see HIT *v.* 1a. **3** (*smitten*) **a** affected, afflicted, troubled, distressed. **b** captivated, fascinated, enthralled, struck, bewitched, enchanted.

smith /smith/ • *n.* **1** [esp. in *comb.*] worker in metal (*goldsmith*). **2** blacksmith. • *v.tr.* make or treat by forging.

smith•er•eens /smithəreenz/ *n.pl.* small fragments (*smash into smithereens*).

smith•y /smithee/ *n.* (*pl.* **-ies**) blacksmith's workshop; forge.

smit•ten *past part.* of SMITE.

smock /smok/ • *n.* loose shirtlike garment for protecting the clothing. • *v.tr.* adorn with smocking.

smock•ing /smoking/ *n.* ornamental effect on cloth made by gathering the material tightly and embroidering in a decorative pattern.

smog /smog, smawg/ *n.* fog intensified by smoke. □□ **smog′gy** *adj.* (**smog•gi•er, smog•gi•est**)
■ see FOG *n.* 1. □□ **smoggy** see THICK *adj.* 6.

smoke /smōk/ • *n.* **1** visible vapor from a burning substance. **2** act of smoking tobacco. **3** *colloq.* cigarette or cigar. • *v.* **1** *intr.* emit smoke or visible vapor. **2 a** *intr.* inhale and exhale the smoke of a cigarette, etc. **b** *intr.* do this habitually. **3** *tr.* preserve by the action of smoke. □ **smoke out** drive out by means of smoke. **smoke screen 1** cloud of smoke diffused to conceal (esp. military) operations. **2** ruse for disguising one's activities. □□ **smok′a•ble** *adj.* (also **smoke′a•ble**). **smoke′less** *adj.* **smok′er** *n.* **smok′i•ly** *adv.* **smok′i•ness** *n.* **smok′y** *adj.* (**smok•i•er, smok•i•est**)
■ *n.* **1** see FUME *n.* • *v.* **1** see FUME *v.* 1. **2** see PUFF *n.* 2. **3** see PRESERVE *v.* 3. □ **smoke screen 2** see COVER *n.* 3a.

smoke•stack /smōkstak/ *n.* chimney.

smol•der /smōldər/ • *v.intr.* **1** burn slowly without a flame. **2** (of emotions, etc.) exist in a suppressed state. **3** (of a person) show silent anger, hatred, etc. • *n.* smoldering fire.
■ *v.* burn, smoke. **2, 3** burn, seethe, simmer, chafe, rage, fume, stew, fester; see red.

smooch /smōōch/ *colloq.* • *v.intr.* kiss. • *n.* kiss. □□ **smooch′er** *n.* **smooch′y** *adj.* (**smooch•i•er, smooch•i•est**).

smooth /smōōth/ • *adj.* **1** having an even and regular surface. **2** not wrinkled, pitted,

---

scored, or hairy. **3** (of a journey, etc.) untroubled by difficulties. **4** suave; conciliatory. **5** (of movement, etc.) not suddenly varying; not jerky. • *v.* **1** *tr. & intr.* make or become smooth. **2 a** *tr.* reduce or get rid of (differences, faults, difficulties, etc.). **b** *intr.* (of difficulties, etc.) become less obtrusive. • *n.* **1** smoothing touch or stroke. **2** easy part of life (*take the rough with the smooth*). • *adv.* smoothly. □ **smooth-tongued** insincerely flattering. □□ **smooth′a•ble** *adj.* **smooth′er** *n.* **smooth′ish** *adj.* **smooth′ly** *adv.* **smooth′ness** *n.*
■ *adj.* **1** flush, flat, level, plane; unbroken. **2** unwrinkled, uniform, slick, sleek; silky, velvety, satiny; hairless, bare, naked, cleanshaven. **3** unobstructed, easy, effortless, uninterrupted. **4** slippery, unctuous, glib, urbane; scheming, crafty, shrewd. **5** see GRACEFUL. • *v.* **1** flatten, even, level, iron, press. **2 a** assuage, allay, calm, minimize. □ **smooth-tongued** see SMOOTH *adj.* 4 above. □□ **smoothly** see EASILY 1. **smoothness** see *fluency* (FLUENT), SAVOIR FAIRE.

smooth•ie /smōōthee/ *n. colloq.* person who is smooth (see SMOOTH *adj.* 4).

smor•gas•bord /smáwrgəsbawrd/ *n.* buffet offering a variety of hot and cold meats, salads, hors d'oeuvres, etc.

smote *past* of SMITE.

smoth•er /smuthər/ *v.tr.* **1** suffocate; stifle. **2** overwhelm with (kisses, attentions, etc.). **3** cover entirely in or with. **4** extinguish (a fire) by covering it.
■ **1** choke, asphyxiate. **2, 3** overcome, blanket, inundate; envelop, wrap. **4** put out, snuff out, quench.

smudge /smuj/ • *n.* **1** blurred or smeared spot, stain or mark; blot. **2** stain or blot on a person's character, etc. • *v.* **1** *tr.* make a smudge on. **2** *intr.* become smeared or blurred. **3** *tr.* smear or blur the lines of (writing, drawing, etc.). □□ **smudge′less** *adj.* **smudg′i•ly** *adv.* **smudg′i•ness** *n.* **smudg′y** *adj.* (**smudg•i•er, smudg•i•est**).
■ *n.* **1** see BLOT *n.* 1. **2** see STAIN *n.* 2. • *v.* see SMEAR *v.* 1, 2.

smug /smug/ *adj.* (**smug•ger, smug•gest**) self-satisfied; complacent. □□ **smug′ly** *adv.* **smug′ness** *n.*
■ holier-than-thou, self-important, conceited. □□ **smugness** see PRIDE *n.* 2.

smug•gle /smugəl/ *v.tr.* **1** import or export (goods) illegally, esp. without payment of customs duties. **2** convey secretly. **3** [foll. by *away*] put into concealment; hide. □□ **smug′gler** *n.* **smug′gling** *n.*

smut /smut/ *n.* **1** small flake of soot, etc. **2** spot or smudge made by this. **3** obscene or lascivious talk, pictures, or stories. **4** fungal disease of cereals. □□ **smut′ty** *adj.* (**smut•ti•er, smut•ti•est**) (esp. in sense 3 of *n.*). **smut′ti•ly** *adv.* **smut′ti•ness** *n.*
■ **3** see DIRT² 3. **4** see MOLD. □□ **smutty** see OBSCENE 1.

Sn *symb. Chem.* tin.

snack /snak/ • *n.* **1** light, casual, or hurried meal. **2** small amount of food eaten between meals. • *v.intr.* eat a snack. □ **snack bar** place where snacks are sold.

■ *n.* bite, nibble, morsel, tidbit, refreshment(s). • *v.* nibble, pick, *sl.* nosh.

snaf•fle /snáfəl/ • *n.* (in full **snaf´fle bit**) bridle bit without a curb. • *v.tr.* put a snaffle on.

snag /snag/ • *n.* **1** unexpected obstacle or drawback. **2** jagged or projecting point. **3** tear in material, etc. • *v.tr.* (**snagged, snag´ging**) catch or tear on a snag. □□ **snagged** *adj.* **snag´gy** *adj.*

■ *n.* **1** hitch, catch, problem, (stumbling) block, bottleneck, complication. • *v.* rip.

snail /snayl/ *n.* slow-moving mollusk with a spiral shell. □□ **snail´like** *adj.*

■ □□ **snaillike** see SLOW *adj.* 1.

snake /snayk/ • *n.* **1 a** long, limbless reptile. **b** limbless lizard or amphibian. **2** (also **snake in the grass**) treacherous person or secret enemy. **3** plumber's snakelike device for clearing obstructed pipes. • *v.intr.* move or twist like a snake. □ **snake charmer** person appearing to make snakes move by music, etc. □□ **snake´like** *adj.*

■ *n.* **1** viper, cobra, boa, python, *usu. literary* serpent. **2** traitor, turncoat, Judas, quisling, betrayer, double-crosser. • *v.* slither, glide, wriggle; wind, curve, bend, meander. □□ **snakelike** see SERPENTINE *adj.* 2.

snak•y /snáykee/ *adj.* **1** of or like a snake. **2** winding; sinuous. **3** showing coldness, ingratitude, treachery, or guile. □□ **snak´i•ly** *adv.* **snak´i•ness** *n.*

snap /snap/ • *v.* (**snapped, snap•ping**) **1** *intr. & tr.* break suddenly or with a snap. **2** *intr. & tr.* emit or cause to emit a sudden sharp crack. **3 a** *intr.* [often foll. by *at*] speak irritably or spitefully (to a person). **b** *tr.* say irritably or spitefully. **4** *intr.* [often foll. by *at*] (esp. of a dog, etc.) make a sudden audible bite. **5** *tr. & intr.* move quickly. **6** *tr.* take a snapshot of. **7** *tr.* *Football* put (the ball) into play on the ground by a quick backward movement. • *n.* **1** act or sound of snapping. **2** [often in *comb.*] crisp cookie (*gingersnap*). **3** snapshot. **4** (in full **cold snap**) sudden brief spell of cold weather. **5** vigor or liveliness; zest. **6** *sl.* easy task (*it was a snap*). **7** fastener for clothing, etc., that closes with a snapping sound. **8** *Football* beginning of a play, when the ball is passed quickly back. • *adv.* with the sound of a snap. • *adj.* made or done on the spur of the moment. □□ **snap´pa•ble** *adj.* **snap´per** *n.* **snap´ping•ly** *adv.* **snap´pish** *adj.*

■ *v.* **1** separate, crack; split, fracture. **2** click; pop; crack. **3** (*snap at*) **a** attack, lunge at, lash out at, snarl at, growl at. **4** (*snap at*) nip, gnash at, snatch at. **5** jump, leap; see also SPRING *v.* 1. **6** shoot, photograph, catch. • *n.* **1** crack, crackle, pop, click. **3** photograph, photo, picture. **5** energy, animation, vitality. **6** *colloq.* cinch, pushover. • *adj.* abrupt, sudden, precipitate, hurried, hasty.

snap•drag•on /snápdragən/ *n.* plant with a bag-shaped flower like a dragon's mouth.

snap•py /snápee/ *adj.* (**snap•pi•er, snap•pi-**

est) *colloq.* **1** brisk; full of zest. **2** neat and elegant. **3** irritable; ill-tempered. □ **make it snappy** be quick. □□ **snap´pi•ly** *adv.* **snap´pi•ness** *n.*

■ **1** quick, sharp, smart, crisp, rapid, speedy, lively. **2** fashionable, chic, sharp, smart, stylish.

snap•shot /snápshot/ *n.* casual photograph.

snare /snair/ • *n.* **1** trap for catching birds or animals. **2** trick or temptation. **3** [in *sing.* or *pl.*] *Mus.* twisted strings of gut, hide, or wire stretched across the lower head of a snare drum. **4** (in full **snare drum**) small, double-headed drum fitted with snares. • *v.tr.* **1** catch (a bird, etc.) in a snare. **2** ensnare; lure or trap (a person). □□ **snar´er** *n.* [also in *comb.*]

■ *n.* **2** see TEMPTATION 2. • *v.* trap, entrap, seize, capture, ensnare; net, bag, hook; lure, decoy.

snarl¹ /snaarl/ • *v.intr.* **1** (of a dog) growl with bared teeth. **2** (of a person) speak cynically or angrily. • *n.* act or sound of snarling. □□ **snarl´er** *n.* **snarl´ing•ly** *adv.* **snarl´y** *adj.* (**snarl•i•er, snarl•i•est**).

■ *v.* **1** snap. • *n.* growl.

snarl² /snaarl/ • *v.* **1** *tr.* twist; entangle; hamper the movement of (traffic, etc.). **2** *intr.* become entangled, congested, or confused. • *n.* knot or tangle.

■ *v.* **1** tangle, complicate, confuse; impede, obstruct; scramble, muddle. **2** tangle, knot, twist, ravel, jam, kink. • *n.* entanglement, snag, jungle, maze, labyrinth.

snatch /snach/ • *v.tr.* **1** seize quickly, eagerly, or unexpectedly. **2** steal (a wallet, handbag, etc.) by grabbing. **3** *sl.* kidnap. **4** [foll. by *at*] **a** try to seize. **b** take (an offer, etc.) eagerly. • *n.* **1** act of snatching. **2** fragment. **3** short spell of activity, etc. □□ **snatch´er** *n.* (esp. in sense 3 of *n.*).

■ *v.* **1** grasp, clasp, clutch, pluck, capture, snap up. **2** see PILFER. **4 b** see JUMP at. • *n.* **1** grab, clutch, grasp. **2** scrap, bit, snippet; specimen, sample.

snaz•zy /snázee/ *adj.* (**snaz•zi•er, snaz•zi•est**) *sl.* smart or attractive, esp. in an ostentatious way. □□ **snaz´zi•ly** *adv.* **snaz´zi•ness** *n.*

■ see STYLISH 1.

sneak /sneek/ • *v.* **1** *intr. & tr.* go or convey furtively; slink. **2** *tr. sl.* steal unobserved; make off with. **3** *intr.* (as **sneaking** *adj.*) **a** furtive; undisclosed. **b** troubling. • *n.* mean-spirited, underhanded person. • *adj.* acting or done without warning; secret. □□ **sneak´i•ly** *adv.* **sneak´ing•ly** *adv.* **sneak´i•ness** *n.* **sneak´y** *adj.* (**sneak•i•er, sneak•i•est**).

■ *v.* **1** lurk, steal, creep, skulk, cower, prowl; smuggle. **2** see STEAL *v.* 1. **3** (**sneaking**) **a** innate, intuitive, inherent, private, secret. **b** persistent, lingering, lurking, worrying. □□ **sneaky** underhand(ed), devious, furtive, sly, slippery, stealthy.

sneak•er /sneekər/ *n.* rubber-soled shoe for sport or casual wear.

sneer /sneer/ • *n.* derisive smile or remark. • *v.* **1** *intr.* smile derisively. **2** *tr.* say sneeringly. **3** *intr.* [often foll. by *at*] comment on derisively, esp. covertly or ironically. □□ **sneer′er** n. **sneer′ing•ly** adv.

■ n. jeer, scoff, boo, hiss, hoot, gibe, taunt. • v. 1 smirk, curl one's lip. 3 (sneer at) scorn, disdain, despise, sniff at, scoff at, jeer at, laugh at, deride, mock, ridicule.

sneeze /sneez/ • n. 1 sudden involuntary expulsion of air from the nose and mouth. 2 sound of this. • v. intr. make a sneeze. □□ **sneez′er** n. **sneez′y** adj.

snick•er /snikər/ n. & v. intr. = SNIGGER v. □□ **snick′er•ing•ly** adv.

snide /snīd/ adj. sneering; slyly derogatory. □□ **snide′ly** adv. **snide′ness** n.

sniff /snif/ • v. 1 intr. draw up air audibly through the nose. 2 tr. [often foll. by up] draw in (a scent, drug, liquid, or air) through the nose. 3 tr. draw in the scent of (food, flowers, etc.) through the nose. • n. 1 act or sound of sniffing. 2 amount sniffed up. □ **sniff at** try the smell of; show interest in. 2 show contempt for. **sniff out** detect. □□ **sniff′er** n. **sniff′ing•ly** adv.

■ v. 1 snivel, snuffle, snuff. 2 snuff, breathe in, inhale. 3 smell, scent; nose (out). • n. 1 snuffle, snuffle. 2 whiff, breath, odor, scent. □ **sniff at** 2 see SNEER v. 3. **sniff out** see DETECT v.

snif•fle /snifəl/ • v. intr. sniff slightly or repeatedly. • n. 1 act of sniffling. 2 [in sing. or pl.] cold in the head causing a running nose and sniffling. □□ **snif′fler** n. **sniff′ly** adj.

■ v. snivel, snuffle. • n. 1 sniff, snuffle.

snif•ter /sniftər/ n. 1 balloon glass for brandy. 2 sl. small drink of alcohol.

snig•ger /snigər/ esp. Brit. • n. half-suppressed secretive laugh. • v. intr. utter such a laugh. □□ **snig′ger•er** n. **snig′ger•ing•ly** adv.

■ snicker, chuckle, giggle, titter.

snip /snip/ • v. tr. (**snipped**, **snipping**) cut with scissors, esp. in small, quick strokes. • n. 1 act of snipping. 2 piece snipped off. 3 sl. something easily achieved. 4 [in pl.] hand shears for metal cutting (tin snips). □□ **snip′ping** n.

■ v. nip, clip, crop, lop, prune, dock, trim. • n. 1 cut, slit, gash. 2 bit, scrap, shred, snippet. 3 see BREEZE n. 2. 4 (snips) scissors.

snipe /snīp/ • n. (pl. same or snipes) wading bird with a long, straight bill. • v. 1 intr. fire shots from hiding, usu. at long range. 2 tr. kill by sniping. 3 intr. [foll. by at] make a sly critical attack. □□ **snip′er** n.

■ v. 1 shoot. 3 (snipe at) attack, criticize, deride, find fault with, carp at, pick apart. □□ **sniper** see SHOT[1] 6.

snip•pet /snipit/ n. 1 small piece cut off. 2 [usu. in pl.; often foll. by of] scrap or fragment (of information).

■ 1, 2 see FRAGMENT n.

snip•py /snipee/ adj. (**snip•pi•er**, **snip•pi•est**) (also **snip′pet•y**) colloq. faultfinding and snappish. □□ **snippily** adv. **snippiness** n.

snit /snit/ n. rage; sulk.

snitch /snich/ sl. • v. 1 tr. steal. 2 intr. inform on a person. • n. informer.

sniv•el /snivəl/ • v. intr. 1 weep with sniffling. 2 run at the nose. 3 show weak or tearful sentiment. • n. 1 running mucus. 2 hypo-

791   sneeze ~ snow

critical talk; cant. □□ **sniv′el•er** n. **sniv′el•ing** adj. **sniv′el•ing•ly** adv.

■ v. 1, 2 snuffle, sniff; blubber, whimper; cry. □□ **sniveling** see TEARFUL 1, groveling (GROVEL).

snob /snob/ n. 1 person who despises those considered socially, intellectually, etc., inferior. 2 person who behaves with servility to social superiors. □□ **snob′ber•y** n. (pl. **–ies**). **snob′bish** adj. **snob′bish•ly** adv. **snob′bish•ness** n. **snob′by** adj. (**snob•bi•er**, **snob•bi•est**).

■ □□ **snobbery, snobbishness** pretentiousness, haughtiness, superciliousness, condescension, arrogance; vanity, egotism. **snobbish** condescending, superior, patronizing, arrogant, haughty, disdainful, supercilious, contemptuous.

snood /snood/ n. ornamental hairnet usu. worn at the back of the head.

snoop /snoop/ colloq. • v. intr. pry. • n. 1 act of snooping. 2 person who snoops; detective. □□ **snoop′er** n. **snoop′y** adj.

■ v. spy, interfere, meddle, intrude. • n. 2 busybody, meddler, spy, intruder; private detective or investigator. □□ **snoopy** see NOSY.

snoot /snoot/ n. sl. the nose.

snooze /snooz/ colloq. • n. short sleep, esp. in the daytime. • v. intr. take a snooze. □□ **snooz′er** n. **snooz′y** adj. (**snooz•i•er**, **snooz•i•est**).

snore /snawr/ • n. snorting or grunting sound in breathing during sleep. • v. intr. make this sound. □□ **snor′er** n.

snor•kel /snawrkəl/ • n. 1 breathing tube for an underwater swimmer. 2 device for supplying air to a submerged submarine. • v. intr. use a snorkel. □□ **snor′kel•er** n.

snort /snawrt/ • n. 1 explosive sound made by the sudden forcing of breath through the nose. 2 colloq. small drink of liquor. 3 sl. inhaled dose of a (usu. illegal) powdered drug. • v. 1 intr. make a snort. 2 tr. sl. inhale (esp. cocaine or heroin). 3 tr. express (defiance, etc.) by snorting.

■ n. 1 see GASP n. 2 see DRINK n. 2b. • v. 2 see SNIFF v. 2.

snot /snot/ n. sl. 1 nasal mucus. 2 term of contempt.

snot•ty /snotee/ adj. (**snot•ti•er**, **snot•ti•est**) sl. 1 running or foul with nasal mucus. 2 colloq. contemptible. 3 colloq. supercilious; conceited. □□ **snot′ti•ly** adv. **snot′ti•ness** n.

■ 3 see CONCEITED. □□ **snottiness** see snobbery (SNOB).

snout /snowt/ n. 1 projecting nose and mouth of an animal. 2 derog. person's nose. □□ **snout′ed** adj. [also in comb.]. **snout′like** adj. **snout′y** adj.

■ 1 muzzle, trunk, proboscis; see also MOUTH n. 1. 2 sl. snoot, beak.

snow /snō/ • n. 1 frozen atmospheric vapor falling to earth in light white flakes. 2 fall or layer of this. 3 sl. cocaine. • v. 1 intr. [prec. by it as subject] fall as snow (it is snowing). 2 tr. sl. deceive or charm with plausible words. □ **be snowed under** be overwhelmed, esp. with work. □□ **snow′less** adj. **snow′like** adj.

■ n. **1, 2** see PRECIPITATION 3a.

snow•ball /snṓbawl/ • n. **1** snow pressed together into a ball, esp. for throwing in play. **2** anything that increases rapidly like a snowball rolled on snow. • v. **1** intr. & tr. throw or pelt with snowballs. **2** intr. increase rapidly.

■ v. **2** see INCREASE v. 1.

snow•blow•er /snṓblōər/ n. machine that clears snow by blowing it to the side of the road, etc.

snow•board /snṓbawrd/ n. board similar to a wide ski, ridden over snow in an upright or surfing position. □□ **snow′board•er** n.

snow•bound /snṓbownd/ adj. prevented by snow from going out or traveling.

snow•drift /snṓdrift/ n. bank of snow heaped up by the action of the wind.

snow•drop /snṓdrop/ n. bulbous plant with white drooping flowers in the early spring.

snow•fall /snṓfawl/ n. **1** fall of snow. **2** Meteorol. amount of snow that falls on one occasion.

snow•flake /snṓflayk/ n. each of the flakes of ice crystals in which snow falls.

snow•man /snṓman/ n. (pl. **–men**) figure resembling a human, made of compressed snow.

snow•mo•bile /snṓməbeel, –mō–/ n. motor vehicle, esp. with runners or revolving treads, for traveling over snow.

snow•plow /snṓplow/ n. device, or a vehicle equipped with one, for clearing roads of thick snow.

snow•shoe /snṓshōō/ n. racket-shaped attachment to a boot for walking on snow without sinking in. □□ **snow•sho′er** n.

snow•storm /snṓstawrm/ n. heavy fall of snow, esp. with a high wind.

snow•y /snṓee/ adj. (**snow•i•er, snow•i•est**) **1** of or like snow. **2** with much snow. □□ **snow′il•y** adv.

snub /snub/ • v.tr. (**snubbed, snub•bing**) rebuff or humiliate. • n. act of snubbing; rebuff. • adj. short and blunt in shape. □□ **snub′ber** n.

snuff[1] /snuf/ • n. charred part of a candlewick. • v.tr. trim the snuff from (a candle). □ **snuff out 1** extinguish by snuffing. **2** kill; put an end to.

snuff[2] /snuf/ n. powdered tobacco or medicine taken by sniffing. □ **up to snuff** colloq. up to standard.

snuff•box /snúfboks/ n. small box for holding snuff.

snug /snug/ adj. (**snug•ger, snug•gest**) **1** cozy; comfortable; sheltered. **2** close-fitting. □□ **snug′ly** adv. **snug′ness** n.

■ **1** intimate, relaxing, restful, warm, secure, friendly, easy, homely, casual. **2** see TIGHT adj. 1, 2.

snug•gle /snúgəl/ v. [usu. foll. by down, up, together] settle or draw into a warm comfortable position.

■ cuddle, nestle, nuzzle.

so[1] /sō/ • adv. **1** to such an extent. **2** [foll. by that or as + clause] to the degree or in the manner implied (so expensive that few can afford it). **3** (adding emphasis) to that extent; in that or a similar manner (I want to leave and so does she). **4** very (I am so glad). **5** (with verb of saying or thinking, etc.) as previously mentioned or described (I think so). • conj. **1** with the result that (there was none left, so we had to go without). **2** in order that (came home early so that I could see you). **3** and then; as the next step. □ **and so on** (or **forth**) **1** and others of the same kind. **2** and in other similar ways. **so as to** in order to. **so-called** commonly designated or known as, often incorrectly. **so long!** colloq. good-bye. **so-so** adj. [usu. predic.] indifferent; not very good. adv. indifferently. **so what?** colloq. why should that be considered significant?.

so[2] var. of SOL.

soak /sōk/ • v. **1** tr. & intr. make or become thoroughly wet through saturation with or in liquid. **2** tr. [foll. by in, up] **a** absorb (liquid). **b** acquire (knowledge, etc.) copiously. **3** intr. (of liquid) make its way or penetrate by saturation. **4** tr. colloq. overcharge. • n. soaking. □□ **soak′age** n. **soak′er** n. **soak′ing** n. & adj.

■ v. **1** drench, wet; immerse, submerge, sop; macerate; marinate. **2 a** take in or up, sponge up, sop up. **b** absorb, take in, assimilate, learn. **3** see IMPREGNATE v. 1, 2. **4** see STING v. 4. □□ **soaking** (n.) drenching, wetting, saturating. (adj.) wet, sopping, drenched.

so-and-so /sṓəndsō/ n. (pl. **so-and-sos**) **1** particular person or thing not needing to be specified (told me to do so-and-so). **2** colloq. person disliked or regarded with disfavor.

soap /sōp/ • n. **1** cleansing agent yielding lather when rubbed in water. **2** colloq. = soap opera. • v.tr. apply soap to. □ **soap opera** broadcast melodrama, usu. serialized in many episodes. □□ **soap′i•ly** adv. **soap′i•ness** n. **soap′less** adj. **soap′like** adj. **soap′y** adj. (**soap•i•er, soap•i•est**).

soap•box /sṓpboks/ n. makeshift stand for a public speaker.

soap•stone /sṓpstōn/ n. talc in the form of stone.

soar /sawr/ v.intr. **1** fly or rise high. **2** reach a high level. **3** fly without using power. □□ **soar′er** n. **soar′ing•ly** adv.

■ **1** ascend. **2** rise, increase, escalate, climb, mount, spiral upward, rocket. **3** hover, float, hang, glide.

sob /sob/ • v. (**sobbed, sob•bing**) **1** intr. draw breath in convulsive gasps usu. with weeping. **2** tr. utter with sobs. • n. convulsive drawing of breath, esp. in weeping. □ **sob sister** journalist who writes or edits sentimental stories. □□ **sob′ber** n. **sob′bing•ly** adv.

■ v. cry, shed tears, weep, blubber, snivel, whimper.

so•ber /sṓbər/ • adj. (**so•ber•er, so•ber•est**) **1** not affected by alcohol. **2** not given to excessive drinking of alcohol. **3** moderate; tranquil; sedate; serious. **4** (of a color, etc.)

quiet and inconspicuous. • *v.* [often foll. by *down, up*] make or become sober. □□ **so′ber•ing•ly** *adv.* **so′ber•ly** *adv.*

■ *adj.* **1** clear-headed, lucid, rational, sensible, in control. **2** temperate, abstemious; teetotal. **3** solemn, earnest, dispassionate, unruffled, steady. **4** sedate, somber, plain. • *v.* detoxify, recover, dry out.

so•bri•e•ty /səbrī-itee/ *n.* state of being sober.
■ abstemiousness, temperance, teetotalism; seriousness, solemnity, staidness, gravity, temperateness.

so•bri•quet /sóbrikay, –ket/ *n.* (also **sou•bri•quet** /soo–/) **1** nickname. **2** assumed name.

Soc. *abbr.* **1** Socialist. **2** Society.

soc•cer /sókər/ *n.* game played by two teams of eleven players with a round ball that cannot be touched with the hands during play except by the goalkeepers.

so•cia•ble /sóshəbəl/ *adj.* liking the society of other people; gregarious; friendly. □□ **so•cia•bil′i•ty** *n.* **so′cia•ble•ness** *n.* **so′cia•bly** *adv.*
■ social, outgoing, extrovert(ed), companionable.

so•cial /sóshəl/ • *adj.* **1** of or relating to society or its organization. **2** concerned with the mutual relations of human beings or of classes of human beings. **3** living in organized communities. **4** needing companionship; gregarious. • *n.* social gathering, esp. one organized by a club, congregation, etc. □ **social disease** venereal disease. **social science** study of human society and social relationships. **social scientist** student of or expert in the social sciences. **social security** (usu. **Social Security**) federal program of assistance to the elderly, disabled, etc. **social services** services provided by the government, esp. education, health, and housing. **social work** work of benefit to those in need of help or welfare, esp. done by specially trained personnel. **social worker** person trained to do social work. □□ **so′cial•ly** *adv.*
■ *adj.* **1, 2** communal, community, common, collective, group, public. **4** see SOCIABLE. • *n.* see DANCE *n.*, RECEPTION 3. □ **social climber** see PARVENU *n.*

so•cial•ism /sóshəlizəm/ *n.* **1** political and economic theory of social organization advocating state ownership and control of the means of production, distribution, and exchange. **2** policy or practice based on this theory. □□ **so′cial•ist** *n. & adj.* **so•cial•is′tic** *adj.*

so•cial•ite /sóshəlīt/ *n.* person prominent in fashionable society.

so•cial•ize /sóshəlīz/ *v.* **1** *intr.* act in a sociable manner. **2** *tr.* make social. **3** *tr.* organize on socialistic principles. □□ **so•cial•i•za′tion** *n.*
■ **1** mix, get together, fraternize; associate, hobnob.

so•ci•e•ty /səsī̄ətee/ *n.* (*pl.* **–ties**) **1** sum of human conditions and activity regarded as a whole functioning interdependently. **2** social community. **3 a** social mode of life. **b** customs and organization of an ordered community. **4** socially advantaged or prominent members of a community. **5** companionship; company. **6** association; club. □ **Society of Friends** see QUAKER. **Society of Jesus** see JESUIT. □□ **so•ci′e•tal** *adj.* (esp. in sense 1). **so•ci′e•tal•ly** *adv.*
■ **2, 3** culture, civilization, way of life, world; system. **4** high society, upper classes, elite, gentry. **5** camaraderie, friendship, fellowship. **6** organization, circle, league, academy, group.

so•ci•ol•o•gy /sóseeóləjee, sóshee–/ *n.* the study of society and social problems. □□ **so•ci•o•log•i•cal** /–əlójikəl/ *adj.* **so•ci•o•log′i•cal•ly** *adv.* **so•ci•ol′o•gist** *n.*

so•ci•o•path /sóseeopáth, sóshee–/ *n. Psychol.* person who is an antisocial psychopath. □□ **so•ci•o•path′ic** *adj.*

sock¹ /sok/ *n.* (*pl.* **socks** or *colloq.* **sox** /soks/) short knitted covering for the foot, usu. not reaching the knee.

sock² /sok/ *colloq.* • *v.tr.* hit forcefully. • *n.* hard blow.

sock•et /sókit/ *n.* hollow for something to fit into.

So•crat•ic /səkrátik, sō–/ *adj.* of or relating to the Greek philosopher Socrates (d. 399 BC) or his philosophy, esp. the method associated with him of seeking the truth by a series of questions and answers.

sod /sod/ *n.* **1** turf or a piece of turf. **2** surface of the ground.

so•da /sódə/ *n.* **1** sodium bicarbonate. **2 a** (also **so′da pop**) sweet effervescent soft drink. **b** (in full **soda water**) preparation of effervescent water used in mixed drinks, etc. **c** soda water, ice cream, and flavoring combined as a sweet drink. □ **soda fountain** counter for preparing and serving sodas, sundaes, and ice cream.

sod•den /sódən/ *adj.* saturated with liquid; soaked through; soggy. □□ **sod′den•ly** *adv.*

so•di•um /sódeeəm/ *n. Chem.* soft silver white reactive metallic element. ¶Symb.: **Na**. □ **sodium bicarbonate** white soluble powder used in the manufacture of fire extinguishers and effervescent drinks. **sodium chloride** common salt. **sodium hydroxide** deliquescent compound that is strongly alkaline and used in the manufacture of soap and paper.

sod•om•y /sódəmee/ *n.* sexual intercourse involving anal or oral copulation. □□ **sod′om•ite** *n.* **sod′om•ize** *v.tr.*

so•fa /sófə/ *n.* long upholstered seat with a back and arms. □ **sofa bed** sofa that can be converted into a bed.

sof•fit /sófit/ *n.* underside of an architrave, arch, etc.

soft /sawft, soft/ • *adj.* **1** lacking hardness or firmness; yielding to pressure; easily cut. **2** (of cloth, etc.) smooth; not rough or coarse. **3** (of air, etc.) mellow; mild. **4** (of water) free from mineral salts. **5** (of a light or color, etc.) not brilliant or glaring. **6** gentle and pleasing. **7** (of an outline, etc.) not sharply defined. **8** gentle; conciliatory; complimentary; amorous. **9** compassionate; sympathetic. **10** *colloq.* (of a job, etc.) easy.

11 (of drugs) mild; not likely to cause addiction. **12** *Stock Exch.* (of currency, prices, etc.) likely to fall in value. • *adv.* softly (*play soft*). □ **soft-boiled** (of an egg) lightly boiled with the yolk soft or liquid. **soft drink** nonalcoholic usu. effervescent drink. **soft palate** rear part of the palate. **soft pedal** pedal on a piano that makes the tone softer. **soft-pedal** *v.* refrain from emphasizing; be restrained (about). **soft sell** restrained, low key or subtly persuasive salesmanship. **soft soap** *colloq.* persuasive flattery. **soft-soap** *v.tr. colloq.* persuade (a person) with flattery. **soft-spoken** speaking with a gentle voice. **soft touch** *colloq.* gullible person, esp. over money. □□ **soft′ish** *adj.* **soft′ly** *adv.* **soft′ness** *n.*

■ *adj.* **1** cushiony, plushy, spongy, flabby, squeezable, compressible. **2** downy, silken, satiny; furry. **3** gentle, balmy, pleasant. **5** pastel, pale, faint, delicate. **6** subdued, muted, low, quiet, melodious. **7** fuzzy, woolly, blurred, indistinct, diffuse(d). **8** goodtempered, mild, soothing, pacific. **9** tenderhearted, understanding, caring, humane, benign. **10** comfortable, undemanding, *colloq.* cushy. **11** harmless, nonaddictive. □ **soft drink** pop, soda.

soft•ball /sáwftbawl, sóft–/ *n.* **1** ball like a baseball but larger and pitched underhand. **2** form of baseball using this.

soft•cov•er /sáwftcəvər/ • *adj.* (of a book) bound in flexible covers. ■ *n.* softcover book.

soft•en /sáwfən, sófən/ *v.* make or become soft or softer. □□ **soft′en•er** *n.*

■ muffle, deaden, damp, soft-pedal, lower, still, quiet, tone down.

soft•heart•ed /sáwft-haártid, sóft–/ *adj.* tender; compassionate; easily moved. □□ **soft′heart′ed•ness** *n.*

■ tenderhearted, warmhearted, sentimental, charitable, sympathetic.

soft•ware /sáwftwair, sóft–/ *n.* programs for a computer.

soft•y /sáwftee, sóftee/ *n.* (also **soft′ie**) (*pl.* **soft′ies**) *colloq.* weak or silly or softhearted person.

sog•gy /sógee/ *adj.* (**sog•gi•er, sog•gi•est**) sodden; saturated; dank. □□ **sog′gi•ly** *adv.* **sog′gi•ness** *n.*

soil[1] /soyl/ *n.* **1** upper layer of earth in which plants grow. **2** ground belonging to a nation; territory (*on British soil*). □□ **soil′less** *adj.*

■ **1** earth, loam, dirt, ground, turf; clay, marl. **2** land.

soil[2] /soyl/ • *v.tr.* **1** make dirty; smear or stain with dirt. **2** tarnish; defile; bring discredit to. • *n.* **1** dirty mark. **2** filth; refuse.

■ *v.* **1** dirty, begrime, muddy, spot. **2** pollute, contaminate, sully; foul; blot. • *n.* **2** dirt, muck, mire, mud; excrement, waste (matter), sewage.

soi•rée /swaaráy/ *n.* evening party.

so•journ /sójərn/ • *n.* temporary stay. • *v.intr.* stay temporarily. □□ **so′journ•er** *n.*

■ *n.* stop, stopover, visit, rest, holiday, vacation. • *v.* stop (over), visit, rest, holiday, vacation.

sol /sōl/ *n.* (also **so** /sō/) *Mus.* fifth note of a major scale.

sol•ace /sóləs/ • *n.* comfort. • *v.tr.* give solace to.

■ *n.* consolation, condolence, relief; reassurance, cheer. • *v.* comfort, console, condole, support, help, succor; soothe, allay, alleviate; cheer (up), hearten.

so•lar /sōlər/ *adj.* of, relating to, or reckoned by the sun (*solar time*). □ **solar battery** (or **cell**) device converting solar radiation into electricity. **solar plexus** complex of radiating nerves at the pit of the stomach. **solar system** the sun and the celestial bodies whose motion it governs.

so•lar•i•um /səláireeəm/ *n.* (*pl.* **so•lar•i•ums** or **so•lar•i•a** /–reeə/) room with sun lamps or extensive areas of glass for sunbathing.

sold *past* and *past part.* of SELL.

sol•der /sódər/ • *n.* **1** fusible alloy used to join less fusible metals or wires, etc. **2** cementing or joining agency. • *v.tr.* join with solder. □□ **sol′der•er** *n.*

sol•dier /sóljər/ • *n.* **1** person serving in or having served in an army. **2** (in full **com′mon sol′dier**) enlisted person in an army. • *v.intr.* serve as a soldier (*was off soldiering*). □ **soldier of fortune** mercenary; adventurer. **soldier on** *colloq.* persevere doggedly. □□ **sol′dier•ly** *adj.*

■ *n.* serviceman, servicewoman, regular (soldier), GI, recruit, draftee, conscript. □ **soldier on** continue, persist, struggle on.

sole[1] /sōl/ • *n.* **1** undersurface of the foot. **2** part of a shoe, sock, etc., under the foot (esp. excluding the heel). • *v.tr.* provide (a shoe, etc.) with a sole. □□ **–soled** *adj.* [in *comb.*].

sole[2] /sōl/ *n.* flatfish used as food.

sole[3] /sōl/ *adj.* [*attrib.*] one and only; single; exclusive. □□ **sole′ly** *adv.*

■ lone, singular, unique; particular, individual.

sol•e•cism /sólisizəm/ *n.* mistake of grammar or idiom. □□ **sol′e•cist** *n.* **sol′e•cis′tic** *adj.*

■ error, slip, violation, misusage, blunder, gaffe.

sol•emn /sóləm/ *adj.* **1** serious and dignified. **2** formal. **3** mysteriously impressive. **4** serious or cheerless in manner; grave; sober. □□ **sol′emn•ly** *adv.* **sol′emn•ness** *n.*

■ **1** ceremonial, ritual, formal, stately. **2** ceremonial, sacramental, ritualistic, official. **3** imposing, awe-inspiring, awesome. **4** reserved, earnest, sedate; morose, mirthless, gloomy, somber, grim; glum, saturnine.

so•lem•ni•ty /səlémnitee/ *n.* (*pl.* **–ties**) **1** being solemn. **2** rite or celebration; piece of ceremony.

■ **1** solemnness, gravity, seriousness, soberness, reserve.

sol•em•nize /sóləmnīz/ *v.tr.* **1** duly perform (a ceremony, esp. of marriage). **2** celebrate (a festival, etc.). **3** make solemn. □□ **sol•em•ni•za′tion** *n.*

so•le•noid /sólənoyd, sól–/ *n.* cylindrical coil of wire acting as a magnet when charged.

so•lic•it /səlísit/ *v.* **1** *tr. & [foll. by for]* *intr.* ask repeatedly or earnestly for or seek or invite (business, etc.). **2** *tr.* accost as a prostitute.

See synonym study at BEG. ▢▢ **so•lic•i•ta'tion** *n.*

■ **1** entreat, beseech, implore, petition (for), importune, appeal for or to, crave. **3** approach, entice, lure, *colloq.* proposition, *sl.* hustle.

so•lic•i•tor /səlísitər/ *n.* **1** person who solicits. **2** canvasser. **3** chief law officer of a city, county, etc.

so•lic•i•tous /səlísitəs/ *adj.* **1** showing interest or concern. **2** eager; anxious. ▢▢ **so•lic'i•tous•ly** *adv.*

■ **1** caring, considerate, thoughtful, tender, attentive. **2** earnest, keen, avid.

so•lic•i•tude /səlísitōōd, -tyōōd/ *n.* being solicitous.

■ concern, consideration, regard, disquiet, uneasiness, anxiety, apprehension.

sol•id /sólid/ • *adj.* (**sol•id•er, sol•id•est**) **1** firm and stable in shape; not liquid or fluid (*solid food*). **2** of a single material throughout, not hollow or containing cavities (*solid sphere*). **3** of the same substance throughout (*solid silver*). **4** of strong material or construction or build; not flimsy or slender, etc. **5** three dimensional. **6** sound; reliable. **7** uninterrupted; continuous. **8** unanimous; undivided. • *n.* **1** solid substance or body. **2** [in *pl.*] solid food. □ **solid-state** *adj.* using semiconductors instead of vacuum tubes. ▢▢ **sol'id•ly** *adv.*

■ *adj.* **1** hard, compact, rigid. **2** see DENSE[1] 1. **3** consistent, homogeneous, uniform, unalloyed. **4** stable, sturdy, strong, substantial. **5** cubic. **6** cogent, concrete, weighty, sensible, rational, sober, authoritative. **7** undivided, unbroken, unrelieved. ▢▢ **solidly** see *firmly* (FIRM), SURELY 3.

sol•i•dar•i•ty /sólidáritee/ *n.* unity or agreement of feeling or action, esp. among individuals with a common interest.

■ unanimity, accord, concord, concordance, harmony, concurrence.

so•lid•i•fy /səlídifī/ *v.* (**-fies, -fied**) make or become solid. ▢▢ **so•lid•i•fi•ca'tion** *n.* **so•lid'i•fi•er** *n.*

■ harden, freeze, set, firm up; compact, compress; gel, jell.

so•lid•i•ty /səlíditee/ *n.* state of being solid; firmness.

sol•i•dus /sólidəs/ *n.* (*pl.* **sol•i•di** /-dī/) virgule (/).

so•lil•o•quy /səlíləkwee/ *n.* (*pl.* **-quies**) **1** act of talking when alone or regardless of any hearers, esp. in drama. **2** part of a play involving this. ▢▢ **so•lil'o•quist** *n.* **so•lil'o•quize** *v.intr.*

sol•i•taire /sólitáir/ *n.* **1** diamond or other gem set by itself. **2** any of several card games for one player.

sol•i•tar•y /sóliteree/ *adj.* **1** living alone; not gregarious. **2** secluded or unfrequented. **3** single or sole (*solitary instance*). ▢▢ **sol•i•tar'i•ly** *adv.*

■ **1** alone, single; unattended, solo, companionless, unsocial, secluded. **2** remote, distant, out-of-the-way. **3** lone, individual, isolated; unique.

sol•i•tude /sólitōōd, -tyōōd/ *n.* **1** state of being solitary. **2** lonely place.

■ **1** aloneness, isolation, seclusion; loneliness, remoteness. **2** emptiness, wilderness; desert island.

so•lo /sólō/ • *n.* **1** (*pl.* **-los** or **so•li** /-lee/) vocal or instrumental piece or passage, or dance, performed by one person with or without accompaniment. **2** (*pl.* **-los**) **a** unaccompanied flight by a pilot in an aircraft. **b** anything done by one person unaccompanied. • *v.intr.* (**-loes, -loed**) perform a solo. • *adv.* unaccompanied; alone. ▢▢ **so'lo•ist** *n.*

■ *adv.* solus, on one's own, single-handed(ly).

sol•stice /sólstis, sól-, sáwl-/ *n.* time or date, about June 21 (*summer solstice*) and December 22 (*winter solstice*), at which the sun's path is farthest from the equator. ▢▢ **sol•sti'tial** /-stíshəl/ *adj.*

sol•u•ble /sólyəbəl/ *adj.* **1** that can be dissolved, esp. in water. **2** that can be solved. ▢▢ **sol•u•bil'i•ty** *n.*

so•lute /sólyōot, sólōot/ *n.* dissolved substance.

so•lu•tion /səlōoshən/ *n.* **1** act or a means of solving a problem or difficulty. **2 a** conversion of a solid or gas into a liquid by mixture with a liquid. **b** mixture produced by this.

■ **1** solving, working or figuring out, unraveling, explication, decipherment, elucidation, clarification. **2 a** dissolving, mixing, blending.

solve /solv/ *v.tr.* answer or effectively deal with (a problem or difficulty). ▢▢ **solv'a•ble** *adj.* **solv'er** *n.*

■ work or figure out, unravel, disentangle, untangle, sort out, clarify, clear up, make plain or clear, interpret.

sol•vent /sólvənt/ • *adj.* **1** able to dissolve or form a solution with something. **2** having enough money to meet one's liabilities. • *n.* solvent liquid, etc. ▢▢ **sol'ven•cy** *n.* (in sense 2).

■ *adj.* **2** (financially) sound, solid, reliable; debt-free.

So•ma•li /sōmáalee, sə-/ • *n.* **1** (*pl.* same or **So•ma'lis**) member of a Hamitic Muslim people of Somalia in NE Africa. **2** the Cushitic language of this people. • *adj.* of or relating to this people or language. ▢▢ **So•ma'li•an** *adj.*

so•mat•ic /sōmátik, sə-/ *adj.* of or relating to the body, esp. as distinct from the mind. ▢▢ **so•mat'i•cal•ly** *adv.*

som•ber /sómbər/ *adj.* dark; gloomy; dismal. ▢▢ **som'ber•ly** *adv.* **som'ber•ness** *n.*

■ shadowy, murky, leaden; morose, lugubrious, funereal; foreboding, bleak, depressing.

som•bre•ro /sombráirō/ *n.* (*pl.* **-ros**) broad-brimmed felt or straw hat worn esp. in Mexico and the southwest US.

some /sum/ • *adj.* **1** unspecified amount or number of (*some apples*). **2** that is unknown or unnamed (*some day*). **3** denoting an approximate number (*some twenty minutes*). **4** considerable (*went to some trouble*). **5** at least a small amount of (*have some consideration*). • *pron.* some number or amount (*I* *have some already*). • *adv. colloq.* to some extent (*do it some more*).

-some[1] /səm/ *suffix* forming adjectives meaning: **1** productive of (*fearsome*). **2** characterized by being (*lithesome*).

-some[2] /səm/ *suffix* forming nouns from numerals, meaning 'a group of (so many)' (*foursome*).

-some[3] /sōm/ *comb. form* denoting a portion of a body, esp. of a cell (*chromosome, ribosome*).

some•bod•y /súmbodee, –budee, –bədee/ • *pron.* some person. • *n.* (*pl.* **–ies**) person of importance.

some•day /súmday/ *adv.* at some time in the future.

some•how /súmhow/ *adv.* for some unstated reason or way.
  ■ (in) one way or another, no matter how, by hook or by crook.

some•one /súmwun/ *n. & pron.* = SOMEBODY.

some•place /súmplays/ *adv. colloq.* = SOMEWHERE.

som•er•sault /súmərsawlt/ (also **sum′mer•sault**) • *n.* leap or roll in which a person turns head over heels and lands on the feet. • *v.intr.* perform a somersault.

some•thing /súmthing/ *n. & pron.* **1** some unspecified or unknown thing (*something has happened*). **2** unexpressed quantity, quality, or extent (*something of a fool*). **3** *colloq.* notable person or thing. □ **something else 1** something different. **2** *colloq.* something exceptional.

some•time /súmtīm/ • *adv.* **1** at some unspecified time. **2** formerly. • *attrib.adj.* former (*sometime mayor*).
  ■ *adv.* **1** someday, one day, on a future occasion. **2** see FORMERLY. • *adj.* erstwhile, past, one-time.

some•times /súmtīmz/ *adv.* at some times; occasionally.
  ■ on occasion, (every) now and then, on and off, from time to time.

some•what /súmhwut, –hwot, –hwət, –wut, –wot, –wət/ *adv.* to some extent.
  ■ rather, quite, relatively, moderately.

some•where /súmhwair, –wair/ • *adv.* in or to some place. • *pron.* some unspecified place.

som•nam•bu•lism /somnámbyəlizəm/ *n.* sleepwalking. □□ **som•nam′bu•list** *n.*

som•no•lent /sómnələnt/ *adj.* **1** sleepy; drowsy. **2** inducing drowsiness. **3** *Med.* in a state between sleeping and waking. □□ **som′no•lence** *n.* **som′no•lent•ly** *adv.*

son /sun/ *n.* **1** boy or man in relation to his parents. **2** male descendant. □ **son-in-law** (*pl.* **sons-in-law**) husband of one's daughter. □□ **son′less** *adj.* **son′ship** *n.*

so•nar /sónaar/ *n.* **1** system for the underwater detection of objects by reflected sound. **2** apparatus for this.

so•na•ta /sənáatə/ *n.* composition for one or two instruments, usu. in several movements.

song /sawng, song/ *n.* **1** words set to music or meant to be sung. **2** singing or vocal music. **3** musical cry of some birds. □ **for a**

---

song *colloq.* very cheaply. **song and dance** *colloq.* fuss or commotion. □□ **song′less** *adj.*
  ■ **1** tune, air, melody; lay, ballad, madrigal, serenade, chantey, jingle; hymn, carol, anthem.

song•bird /sáwngbərd, sóng–/ *n.* bird with a musical call.

son•ic /sónik/ *adj.* of or relating to or using sound or sound waves. □ **sonic barrier** = *sound barrier* (see SOUND[1]). **sonic boom** loud explosive noise made when an aircraft surpasses the speed of sound.

son•net /sónit/ *n.* poem of 14 lines using any of a number of rhyme schemes and usu. having ten syllables per line.

son•ny /súnee/ *n. colloq.* familiar form of address to a young boy.

son•o•gram /sónəgram/ *n. Med.* image produced by ultrasound waves, used for diagnostic purposes.

so•no•rous /sónərəs, sənáwrəs/ *adj.* **1** having a loud, full, or deep sound; resonant. **2** (of a speech, style, etc.) imposing; grand. □□ **so•nor•i•ty** /sənáwritee/ *n.* **so•no•rous•ly** *adv.* **so′no•rous•ness** *n.*

soon /sōōn/ *adv.* **1** in a short time. **2** quickly; before long. **3** readily or willingly (*would as soon stay behind*). □ **sooner or later** at some future time; eventually. □□ **soon′ish** *adv.*
  ■ **1** before long, presently, in the near future, any minute (now). **2** early, fast; swiftly, speedily. **3** gladly, happily. □ **sooner or later** some time, one day, in time, in due course.

soot /sōōt/ *n.* black powdery deposit from smoke.

soothe /sōōth/ *v.tr.* **1** calm (a person or feelings). **2** soften or mitigate (pain). □□ **sooth′er** *n.* **sooth′ing** *adj.* **sooth′ing•ly** *adv.*
  ■ **1** see CALM *v.* **2** see MITIGATE. □□ **soothing** relaxing, restful, serene, peaceful; mollifying, comforting.

sooth•say•er /sṓthsayər/ *n.* diviner or seer.

soot•y /sōōtee/ *adj.* (**soot•i•er, soot•i•est**) **1** covered with or full of soot. **2** like soot; black. □□ **soot′i•ly** *adv.* **soot′i•ness** *n.*

SOP *abbr.* (also **S.O.P.**) standard operating procedure.

sop /sop/ • *n.* **1** piece of bread, etc., dipped in gravy, etc. **2** thing given or done to pacify or bribe. • *v.* (**sopped, sop•ping**) **1** *intr.* be drenched. **2** *tr.* [foll. by *up*] absorb (liquid) in a towel, etc. **3** *tr.* wet thoroughly; soak.

soph. /sof/ *abbr.* sophomore.

soph•ism /sófizəm/ *n.* false argument, esp. one intended to deceive.

soph•ist /sófist/ *n.* one who reasons with clever but fallacious arguments. □□ **so•phis′tic** *adj.* **so•phis′ti•cal** *adj.*
  ■ □□ **sophistic, sophistical** specious, fallacious, deceptive, deceitful, misleading.

so•phis•ti•cate • *v.tr.* /səfístikayt/ **1** make educated, cultured, or refined. **2** make highly developed or complex. • *n.* /səfístikət/ sophisticated person. □□ **so•phis•ti•ca•tion** /–káyshən/ *n.*
  ■ □□ **sophistication** worldliness, urbanity, culture, refinement, cosmopolitanism, pol-

ish, elegance, poise, suavity; intricacy, subtlety, refinement.

so•phis•ti•cat•ed /səfistikaytid/ *adj.* **1** (of a person) educated and refined; worldly-wise. **2** (of a thing, idea, etc.) highly developed and complex. See synonym study at URBANE.
■ **1** cultured, experienced, worldly, cosmopolitan. **2** advanced, complicated, intricate.

soph•ist•ry /sófistree/ *n.* (*pl.* **–ries**) **1** use of sophisms. **2** a sophism.

soph•o•more /sófəmawr, sófmawr/ *n.* second year college or high school student. □□ **soph•o•mor•ic** *adj.*

sop•o•rif•ic /sópərífik/ • *adj.* inducing sleep. • *n.* soporific drug or influence. □□ **sop•o•rif•er•ous** /–rífərəs/ *adj.* **sop•o•rif•i•cal•ly** *adv.*

sop•py /sópee/ *adj.* (**sop•pi•er**, **sop•pi•est**) **1** *colloq.* **a** silly or foolish in a feeble or self-indulgent way. **b** mawkishly sentimental. **2** soaked with water.

so•pran•o /səpránō, –prā‑/ *n.* (*pl.* **–os** or **so•pran•i** /–nee/) **1 a** highest pitched singing voice. **b** female or boy singer with this voice. **c** a part written for it. **2 a** instrument of a high or the highest pitch in its family. **b** its player.

sor•bet /sawrbáy, sáwrbit/ *n.* sweetened frozen confection, usu. with fruit flavoring.

sor•cer•er /sáwrsərər/ *n.* (*fem.* **sor•cer•ess** /–ris/) magician; wizard. □□ **sor•cer•y** *n.* (*pl.* **–ies**)
■ magus, necromancer, enchanter, witch doctor; (*sorceress*) witch, enchantress. □□ **sorcery** witchcraft, enchantment, sortilege, necromancy, wizardry.

sor•did /sáwrdid/ *adj.* **1** dirty or squalid. **2** ignoble, mean, or mercenary. □□ **sor•did•ly** *adv.* **sor•did•ness** *n.*
■ **1** foul, filthy, unclean, unsanitary, offensive; wretched, miserable, poor. **2** base, vile, corrupt, low, debased.

sore /sawr/ • *adj.* **1** (of a part of the body) painful. **2** (of a person) suffering pain. **3** angry or vexed. **4** grievous or severe (*in sore need*). • *n.* sore place on the body. □ **sore point** subject causing distress or annoyance. □□ **sore•ness** *n.*
■ *adj.* **1** sensitive, tender, raw; irritated, inflamed, chafed. **3** angered, aggrieved, annoyed, irritated. **4** dire, serious, acute, extreme; painful, troublesome, distressing. • *n.* swelling, rawness, infection, inflammation, bruise.

sore•ly /sáwrlee/ *adv.* extremely; badly (*am sorely tempted*).

sor•ghum /sáwrgəm/ *n.* tropical cereal grass.

so•ror•i•ty /səráwritee, –rór‑/ *n.* (*pl.* **–ties**) female students' society in a university or college, usu. for social purposes.

sor•rel /sáwrəl, sór‑/ • *adj.* of a light reddish-brown color. • *n.* **1** this color. **2** sorrel animal, esp. a horse.

sor•row /sáwrō, sór‑/ • *n.* **1** mental distress caused by loss or disappointment, etc. **2** cause of sorrow. • *v.intr.* **1** feel sorrow. **2** mourn. □□ **sor•row•er** *n.* **sor•row•ing** *adj.*
■ *n.* **1** sadness, heartbreak, grief, unhappiness. **2** affliction, trouble, trial, tribulation,

misfortune. • *v.* grieve, lament, weep, moan, wail; (*sorrow for or over*) regret, bemoan.

sor•row•ful /sáwrōfŏŏl, sór‑/ *adj.* **1** feeling or showing sorrow. **2** distressing; lamentable. □□ **sor•row•ful•ly** *adv.* **sor•row•ful•ness** *n.*
■ **1** sad, unhappy, regretful, depressed, dejected, crestfallen, gloomy. **2** doleful, unfortunate, bitter.

sor•ry /sáwree, sór‑/ *adj.* (**sor•ri•er**, **sor•ri•est**) **1** [*predic.*] pained or regretful or penitent. **2** [*predic.*; foll. by *for*] feeling pity or sympathy for. **3** wretched; in a poor state. □□ **sor•ri•ly** *adv.*
■ **1** remorseful, contrite, conscience-stricken, penitential; see also SORROWFUL 1. **2** (*feel sorry for*) see PITY *v.* **3** abject, miserable, pitiful, pathetic.

sort /sawrt/ • *n.* **1** group of things, etc., with common attributes; class or kind. **2** [foll. by *of*] roughly of the kind specified (*is some sort of doctor*). • *v.tr.* arrange systematically or according to type, class, etc. □ **of a sort** (or **of sorts**) *colloq.* not fully deserving the name (*a holiday of sorts*). **out of sorts** slightly unwell. **sort of** *colloq.* as it were; to some extent. □□ **sort•a•ble** *adj.* **sort•er** *n.* **sort•ing** *n.*
■ *n.* **1** variety, type, classification, category; manner; species, genus, family, race. **2** kind, type. • *v.* assort, classify, file, order, rank; combine, merge, organize; describe, characterize. □ **out of sorts** not oneself, ailing, indisposed, (slightly) ill.

sor•tie /sáwrtee, sawrtée/ *n.* **1** sally, esp. from a besieged garrison. **2** operational flight by a single military aircraft.

SOS /ésō‑és/ *n.* (*pl.* **SOSs**) international code signal of extreme distress, used esp. by ships at sea.

sot /sot/ *n.* habitual drunkard.

sot•to vo•ce /sótō vóchee, sáwt‑tō váwche/ *adv.* in an undertone or aside.

sou•bri•quet var. of SOBRIQUET.

souf•flé /soofláy/ *n.* light dish usu. made with flavored egg yolks added to stiffly beaten egg whites and baked.

sought *past* and *past part.* of SEEK.

soul /sōl/ *n.* **1** spiritual or immaterial part of a human being, often regarded as immortal. **2** moral or emotional or intellectual nature of a person or animal. **3** personification or pattern of something (*the very soul of discretion*). **4** an individual (*not a soul in sight*). **5** animating or essential part. **6** African-American culture, music, ethnic pride, etc. □ **soul mate** person ideally suited to another. **soul music** a kind of music incorporating elements of rhythm and blues and gospel music, popularized by African Americans.
■ **1, 2** (vital) spirit or force, being, essence, psyche. **3** incarnation, embodiment, epitome, model. **4** person, man, woman, mortal, (human) being.

soul•ful /sólfŏŏl/ *adj.* having or expressing or evoking deep feeling. □□ **soul•ful•ly** *adv.* **soul•ful•ness** *n.*
■ sincere, deep, profound, heartfelt, moving, ardent.

soul•less /sṓl-lis/ *adj.* **1** lacking sensitivity or noble qualities. **2** having no soul. □□ **soul′less•ly** *adv.* **soul′less•ness** *n.*

sound[1] /sownd/ • *n.* **1** sensation caused in the ear by the vibration of air or other medium. **2** vibrations causing this sensation. **3** what is or may be heard. **4** idea or impression conveyed by words (*don't like the sound of that*). • *v.* **1** *intr. & tr.* emit or cause to emit sound. **2** *tr.* utter or pronounce (*sound a note of alarm*). **3** *intr.* convey an impression when heard (*you sound worried*). □ **sound barrier** high resistance of air to objects moving at speeds near that of sound. **sound bite** short extract from a recorded interview, chosen for its pungency or appropriateness. **sound effect** sound other than speech or music made artificially for use in a play, movie, etc. □□ **sound′less** *adj.* **sound′less•ly** *adv.* **sound′less•ness** *n.*

■ *n.* **1** tone, noise, din, cacophony, report. **4** ring, tone, quality, effect, aspect, look, feel. • *v.* **1** resound, reverberate, echo, resonate; see also BLARE[2] *v.*, RING *v.* 1. **2** articulate, enunciate; voice, vocalize. **3** seem, appear.

sound[2] /sownd/ • *adj.* **1** healthy; not diseased, injured, or rotten. **2** (of an opinion or policy, etc.) correct; orthodox; well-founded; judicious; legally valid. **3** financially secure. **4** restful; undisturbed. • *adv.* soundly (*sound asleep*). □□ **sound′ly** *adv.* **sound′ness** *n.*

■ *adj.* **1** robust, vigorous, blooming; undiseased, uninjured; undamaged, whole, intact; firm, solid, substantial. **2** good, reliable, useful; sane, balanced, normal, rational. **3** safe, good, solid; profitable. **4** unbroken, uninterrupted, untroubled.

sound[3] /sownd/ *v.tr.* **1** test the depth or quality of the bottom of (the sea or a river, etc.). **2** [often foll. by *out*] inquire (esp. cautiously or discreetly) into the opinions or feelings of (a person). □□ **sound′er** *n.*

■ **1** plumb, probe, fathom. **2** plumb, probe, test, check (into), question, poll, canvass, investigate.

sound[4] /sownd/ *n.* **1** narrow passage of water connecting two seas or a sea with a lake, etc. **2** arm of the sea.

■ **1** strait(s), inlet, fiord, firth, cove.

sound•ing /sównding/ *n.* **1** measurement of the depth of water. **2** [in *pl.*] waters close to shore. □ **sounding board 1** canopy over a pulpit, etc., to direct sound toward the congregation. **2** person, etc., used as a trial audience.

sound•proof /sówndprōōf/ • *adj.* impervious to sound. • *v.tr.* make soundproof.

sound•track /sówndtrak/ *n.* the sound element of a movie, television broadcast, etc.

soup /sōōp/ • *n.* liquid dish made by boiling meat, fish, or vegetables, etc., in stock or water. • *v.tr.* [usu. foll. by *up*] *colloq.* **1** increase the power and efficiency of (an engine). **2** enliven. □ **in the soup** *colloq.* in difficulties.

soup•çon /sōōpsáwn, sóōpsón/ *n.* small quantity; dash.

soup•y /sóōpee/ *adj.* (**soup•i•er, soup•i•est**)

1 of or resembling soup. **2** *colloq.* sentimental. □□ **soup′i•ly** *adv.* **soup′i•ness** *n.*

sour /sowr/ • *adj.* **1** acid in taste or smell. **2** (of food, esp. milk or bread) bad because of fermentation. **3** (of a person, temper, etc.) harsh; morose; bitter. **4** (of a thing) unpleasant; distasteful. • *v.* make or become sour (*soured the cream*). □ **sour grapes** resentful disparagement of something one cannot personally acquire. □□ **sour′ish** *adj.* **sour′ly** *adv.* **sour′ness** *n.*

■ *adj.* **1** acidic, tart, vinegary, lemony, sharp. **2** turned, curdled, rancid, spoiled. **3** acrimonious, embittered, unpleasant, bad-tempered, crusty, curmudgeonly. **4** disagreeable, bad, nasty, bitter. • *v.* turn, go bad, ferment; embitter, disenchant.

source /sawrs/ *n.* **1** place, person, or thing from which something issues or originates. **2** person or document, etc., providing evidence (*reliable sources of information*). See synonym study at ORIGIN.

■ **1** (fountain)head, wellhead, origin; provenance, inception, start; originator, initiator. **2** authority, documentation; informant, horse's mouth.

sour•puss /sówrpŏŏs/ *n. colloq.* ill-tempered person.

souse /sows/ • *v.* **1** *tr.* put (pickles, fish, etc.) in brine. **2** *tr. & intr.* plunge into liquid. **3** *tr.* [usu. foll. by *in*] soak (a thing) in liquid. • *n.* **1 a** pickling brine made with salt. **b** pickled food. **2** a dip, plunge, or drenching in water.

south /sowth/ • *n.* **1** point of the horizon 90° clockwise from east. **2** compass point corresponding to this. **3** direction in which this lies. **4** (usu. **the South**) **a** part of the world or a country or a town lying to the south. **b** southern states of the US, especially those that were part of the Confederacy. • *adj.* **1** toward, at, near, or facing the south. **2** coming from the south (*south wind*). • *adv.* **1** toward, at, or near the south. **2** [foll. by *of*] further south than. □ **South African** *adj.* of or relating to the republic of South Africa. *n.* **1** native or inhabitant of South Africa. **2** person of South African descent. **South American** *adj.* of or relating to South America. *n.* native or inhabitant of South America.

southeast *n.* **1** point midway between south and east. **2** direction in which this lies. *adj.* of, toward, or coming from the southeast. *adv.* of, toward, or coming from the southeast. **southeasterly** *adj. & adv.* = *southeast.* **southeastern** lying on the southeast side.

south pole see POLE[2]. **South Sea** southern Pacific Ocean. **southwest** *n.* **1** point midway between south and west. **2** direction in which this lies. *adj.* of, toward, or coming from the southwest. *adv.* toward, at, or near the southwest. **southwesterly** *adj. & adv.* = *southwest.* **southwestern** lying on the southwest side.

south•east•er /sówtheester, sou-eéstər/ *n.* southeast wind.

south•er•ly /sútherlee/ • *adj. & adv.* **1** in a southern position or direction. **2** (of a wind) blowing from the south. • *n.* (*pl.* **−lies**) southerly wind.

south•ern /sútherrn/ *adj.* esp. *Geog.* of, toward, or in the south. □ **southern hemisphere** the half of the earth below the equator. □□ **south′ern•er** n. **south′ern•most** adj.

south•paw /sówthpaw/ *colloq.* • n. left-handed person, esp. as a pitcher in baseball. • adj. left-handed.

south•ward /sówthwərd/ • adj. & adv. (also **south′wards**) toward the south. • n. southward direction or region.

south•west•er /sówthwéstər, sow-wéstər/ n. southwest wind.

sou•ve•nir /sóovəneér/ n. [often foll. by *of*] memento of an occasion, place, etc.

sou′west•er /sow-wéstər/ n. **1** = SOUTHWESTER. **2** waterproof hat with a broad flap covering the neck.

sov•er•eign /sóvrin/ • n. **1** supreme ruler, esp. a monarch. **2** *Brit. hist.* gold coin nominally worth £1. • adj. **1** supreme. **2** possessing independent national authority (*a sovereign state*). □□ **sov′er•eign•ty** n. (pl. **-ties**). See synonym study at JURISDICTION.
■ adj. **1** paramount, highest, principal, foremost, dominant. **2** see INDEPENDENT adj. 1b. □□ **sovereignty** suzerainty, hegemony, dominion, rule; kingship, queenship.

so•vi•et /sóveeət, sóv-/ • n. (in the former USSR) **1** elected local, district, or national council. **2** (**Soviet**) citizen of the USSR. **3** revolutionary council of workers, peasants, etc., before 1917. • adj. (usu. **Soviet**) of or concerning the former Soviet Union.

sow¹ /sō/ *v.tr.* (past **sowed** /sod/; past part. **sown** /sōn/ or **sowed**) **1** [also *absol.*] a scatter or put (seed) on or in the earth. b [often foll. by *with*] plant (a field, etc.) with seed. **2** initiate; arouse. □□ **sow′er** n. **sow′ing** n.
■ **1** plant, strew, spread; seed.

sow² /sow/ n. female adult pig, esp. after farrowing.

sox *colloq.* pl. of SOCK¹.

soy /soy/ n. (also **soy•a** /sóyə/) **1** (also **soy sauce**) sauce from pickled soya beans. **2** (in full **soy bean**) = *soya bean*.

soy•a /sóyə/ n. (in full **soy′a bean**) **1** a leguminous plant, cultivated for the edible oil and flour it yields, and used as a replacement for animal protein in certain foods. b seed of this. **2** (also **soya sauce**) = SOY 1.

spa /spaa/ n. place or resort with facility offering use of exercise equipment, steam baths, etc.

space /spays/ • n. **1 a** continuous unlimited area or expanse which may or may not contain objects, etc. b interval between points or objects. **c** empty area; room. **2** = *outer space*. **3** place, seat, berth, etc., made available (*no space on the bus*). **4** interval of time. • v.tr. set or arrange at intervals. □ **space age** era when space travel has become possible. **space shuttle** a spacecraft for repeated use. **space station** artificial satellite used as a base for operations in space. **space-time** (or **space-time continuum**) fusion of the concepts of space and time, esp. as a four-dimensional continuum. □□ **spac′er** n.
■ n. **1 a** extent, compass, tract. b interspace, interstice, gap, opening, lacuna, hiatus. **c** place, capacity, leeway, margin.

4 lapse, period, time, hiatus, lacuna. • v. organize, array, align, lay out.

space•craft /spáyskraft/ n. vehicle for traveling in space.

space•man /spáysman/ n. (pl. **-men**; fem. **space•wom•an**, pl. **-wom•en**) astronaut.

space•ship /spáys-ship/ n. spacecraft.

space•suit /spáys-soot, -syoot/ n. garment designed to allow an astronaut to survive in space.

space•y /spáysee/ adj. (also **spac′y**) (**spac•i•er**, **spac•i•est**) sl. **1** seemingly out of touch with reality; disoriented. **2** being in a confused or dazed state because of the influence of mind-altering drugs.

spa•cial var. of SPATIAL.

spa•cious /spáyshəs/ adj. having ample space; covering a large area; roomy. □□ **spa′cious•ly** adv. **spa′cious•ness** n.
■ vast, large, extensive, enormous, wide, broad.

spade¹ /spayd/ • n. tool used for digging or cutting the ground, etc., with a sharp-edged metal blade and a long handle. • v.tr. dig over (ground) with a spade. □ **call a spade a spade** speak plainly or bluntly. □□ **spade′ful** n. (pl. **-fuls**).

spade² /spayd/ n. **1** playing card of a suit denoted by black inverted heart-shaped figures with small stalks. **2** [in pl.] this suit. □ **in spades** sl. to a high degree; with great force.

spade•work /spáydwərk/ n. hard or routine preparatory work.

spa•ghet•ti /spəgéttee/ n. pasta made in long thin strings.

span /span/ • n. **1** full extent from end to end in space or time. **2** each arch or part of a bridge between piers or supports. **3** maximum distance between the tips of the thumb and little finger (approx. 9 inches). • v. (**spanned**, **span•ning**) **1** tr. stretch from side to side of; extend across. **2** bridge (a river, etc.).
■ n. **1** reach, spread, sweep, breadth, width; course, interval, stretch, duration, period, time. • v. cross, stretch over or across, reach over or across, go over or across, straddle.

span•drel /spándril/ n. *Archit.* space between an arch and a cornice or exterior wall.

span•gle /spánggəl/ • n. **1** sequin. **2** a small sparkling object. • v.tr. (esp. as **spangled** adj.) cover with or as with spangles (*spangled costume*). □□ **span•gly** /spánglee/ adj.

Span•iard /spányərd/ n. **1** native or inhabitant of Spain in southern Europe. **2** person of Spanish descent.

span•iel /spányəl/ n. **1** dog of any of various breeds with a long silky coat and drooping ears. **2** any of these breeds.

Span•ish /spánish/ • adj. of or relating to Spain or its people or language. • n. **1** language of Spain and Spanish America. **2** [prec. by *the*; treated as pl.] the people of Spain. □ **Spanish America** those parts of America orig. settled by Spaniards, including Central and South America and part of the West Indies.

spank /spangk/ • v.tr. slap, esp. on the buttocks, with the open hand. • *n.* slap, esp. on the buttocks.

■ *v.* smack, put *or* take over one's knee, thrash, hit, paddle, *colloq.* whack. • *n.* see SLAP *n.*

spank•ing /spángking/ • *adj.* **1** brisk or lively. **2** *colloq.* striking; excellent. • *adv. colloq.* very; exceedingly (*spanking clean*). • *n.* slapping on the buttocks.

■ *adj.* **1** quick, rapid, swift, lively; crisp, bracing, fresh, freshening. **2** see EXCELLENT. • *adv.* see EXCEEDINGLY 1.

spar[1] /spaar/ *n.* stout pole, esp. as a ship's mast, etc.

■ mast, yard, yardarm, boom, gaff.

spar[2] /spaar/ *v.intr.* (**sparred, spar•ring**) **1** make the motions of boxing without landing heavy blows. **2** argue.

■ **1** fight, box, exchange blows; shadowbox. **2** dispute, quarrel, bicker, squabble, wrangle, bandy words.

spare /spair/ • *adj.* **1** extra. **2** lean; thin. **3** scanty; frugal; not copious (*spare diet*). See synonym study at THIN. • *n.* **1** spare part. **2** *Bowling* knocking down of all the pins with the first two balls. • *v.tr.* **1** afford to give or do without (*can spare you a couple*). **2 a** abstain from killing, hurting, wounding, etc. **b** abstain from inflicting or causing; relieve from (*spare my blushes*). **3** be frugal or grudging of. □□ **spare'ly** *adv.* **spare'ness** *n.* **spar'er** *n.*

■ *adj.* **1** surplus, excess, supernumerary; odd, left over; unoccupied, free; in reserve, in addition. **2** skinny, scrawny, cadaverous, gaunt. **3** meager, small, skimpy, economical, mean, sparing; plain, sparse, stark. • *v.* **1** allow, relinquish, give, donate, part with, dispense with. **2 a** pardon, let go, release, let off. **b** save from, rescue from, deliver from; exempt from.

spare•ribs /spáir-ríbz/ *n.* closely trimmed ribs of esp. pork.

spar•ing /spáiring/ *adj.* **1** inclined to save; economical. **2** restrained; limited. See synonym study at ECONOMICAL. □□ **spar'ing•ly** *adv.*

■ **1** thrifty, saving, frugal, spare, careful, prudent. **2** sparse, meager, scant.

spark /spaark/ • *n.* **1** fiery particle thrown off from a fire. **2** particle of a quality, etc. (*not a spark of life*). **3** flash of light between electric conductors, etc. **4** flash of wit, etc. • *v.* **1** *intr.* emit sparks of fire or electricity. **2** *tr.* stir into activity; initiate (a process) suddenly. □ **spark plug** device for firing the explosive mixture in an internal combustion engine. □□ **spark'less** *adj.* **spark'y** *adj.*

■ *n.* **2** scintilla, flicker, glimmer. **3** see FLASH *n.* 1. • *v.* **1** see FLASH *v.* 2. **2** set *or* touch off, ignite, kindle, electrify, animate, trigger, energize; set in motion, bring about, start (up), begin.

spar•kle /spáarkəl/ • *v.intr.* **1** emit or seem to emit sparks; glitter; scintillate. **2** (of wine, etc.) effervesce. • *n.* **1** gleam or spark. **2** vivacity; liveliness. □□ **spark'ly** *adj.*

■ *v.* **1** glisten, glint, gleam, flicker, shine. **2** fizz, bubble. • *n.* **1** glitter, scintillation,

twinkle, dazzle. **2** fire, brightness, wittiness, effervescence, ebullience.

spar•kler /spáarklər/ *n.* **1** handheld sparkling firework. **2** *colloq.* diamond or other gem.

spar•row /spárō/ *n.* small brownish-gray bird.

sparse /spaars/ *adj.* thinly dispersed or scattered; not dense. □□ **sparse'ly** *adv.* **sparse'ness** *n.* **spar'si•ty** *n.*

■ few (and far between), meager, spread out, scarce.

Spar•tan /spáart'n/ • *adj.* **1** of Sparta in ancient Greece. **2** rigorous; frugal; austere. • *n.* citizen of Sparta.

■ *adj.* **2** strict, severe, harsh, stern, rigid, ascetic.

spasm /spázəm/ *n.* **1** sudden involuntary, convulsive muscular contraction. **2** *colloq.* brief spell of an activity.

■ **1** convulsion, throe, fit, twitch, tic, paroxysm, shudder. **2** burst, eruption, spurt.

spas•mod•ic /spazmódik/ *adj.* **1** of, caused by, or subject to, a spasm or spasms. **2** occurring or done by fits and starts (*spasmodic efforts*). □□ **spas•mod'i•cal•ly** *adv.*

■ **2** fitful, irregular, intermittent, random.

spas•tic /spástik/ • *adj.* of or afflicted with spasms. • *n. offens.* person suffering from cerebral palsy. □□ **spas'ti•cal•ly** *adv.* **spas•tic'i•ty** /-tisītee/ *n.*

spat[1] *past* and *past part.* of SPIT[1].

spat[2] /spat/ *n.* **1** [usu. in *pl.*] *hist.* short gaiter covering a shoe. **2** cover for an aircraft wheel.

spat[3] /spat/ *n. colloq.* petty quarrel. See synonym study at QUARREL.

spate /spayt/ *n.* large or excessive amount.

■ flood, inundation, onrush, rush, deluge.

spathe /spayth/ *n. Bot.* large bract or pair of bracts enveloping a spadix or flower cluster.

spa•tial /páyshəl/ *adj.* (also **spa'cial**) of or concerning space. □□ **spa•ti•al•i•ty** /-sheeálitee/ *n.* **spa'tial•ly** *adv.*

spat•ter /spátər/ • *v.* **1** *tr.* **a** splash (a person, etc.). **b** scatter or splash (liquid, mud, etc.). **2** *intr.* (of rain, etc.) fall here and there. • *n.* **1** splash; drop. **2** quick pattering sound.

■ *v.* **1 a** speckle, pepper, bespatter, spray, shower, scatter. **b** bespatter, spray, shower, daub, sprinkle, splatter. **2** see FALL[1] *v.* 1. • *n.* **1** see SPLASH *n.* 2, 3. **2** see PATTER *n.*

spat•u•la /spáchələ/ *n.* broad-bladed flat implement used for spreading, lifting, stirring, mixing (food), etc.

spawn /spawn/ • *v.* **1 a** *tr.* [also *absol.*] (of a fish, frog, mollusk, or crustacean) produce (eggs). **b** be produced as eggs or young. **2** *tr.* produce or generate, esp. in large numbers. • *n.* eggs of fish, frogs, etc. □□ **spawn'er** *n.*

■ *v.* **1a** yield, bear. **2** give rise to, bring about, cause, give birth to, bring forth, breed, beget, create.

spay /spay/ *v.tr.* sterilize (a female animal) by removing the ovaries.

SPCA *abbr.* Society for the Prevention of Cruelty to Animals.

speak /speek/ *v.* (*past* **spoke** /spōk/; *past part.* **spok•en** /spōkən/) **1** *intr.* make articulate verbal utterances. **2** *tr.* utter (words, the truth, etc.). **3** *intr.* **a** [foll. by *to, with*] hold a conversation. **b** [foll. by *of*] mention in writing, etc. **c** [foll. by *for*] articulate the feelings of (another person, etc.) in speech or writing. **4** *intr.* make a speech. **5** *tr.* use or be able to use (a specified language). □ **speak out** speak loudly or freely; give one's opinion. **speak up** = *speak out.* **speak volumes** (of a fact, etc.) be very significant. **speak volumes** (or **well**, etc.) **for 1** be abundant evidence of. **2** place in a favorable light. □□ **speak'a•ble** *adj.*

■ **1** talk, converse, discourse, vocalize. **2** express, talk, say, state; articulate, communicate. **3 a** talk to or with, say something to, chat to or with. **b** allude to, refer to, comment on. **c** act in behalf of, act for, represent. **4** address, lecture on, talk about. **5** talk, communicate in, converse in. □ **speak out** or **speak up** talk (more) loudly or clearly, make oneself heard, raise one's voice.

speak•eas•y /spéekeezee/ *n.* (*pl.* **–ies**) illicit liquor store or drinking club during Prohibition in the US.

speak•er /spéekər/ *n.* **1** person who speaks, esp. in public. **2** person who speaks a specified language (esp. in *comb.*: *French speaker*). **3** (**Speaker**) presiding officer in a legislative assembly, esp. the US House of Representatives. **4** = LOUDSPEAKER.

■ **1** orator, lecturer, speechmaker; spokesperson, spokesman, spokeswoman; rabblerouser.

speak•er•phone /spéekərfon/ *n.* telephone equipped with a microphone and loudspeaker, allowing it to be used without picking up the handset.

spear /speer/ • *n.* **1** weapon with a pointed usu. steel tip and a long shaft. **2** pointed stem of asparagus, etc. • *v.tr.* pierce or strike with or as if with a spear (*speared an olive*).

spear•head /spéerhed/ • *n.* **1** point of a spear. **2** individual or group chosen to lead a thrust or attack. • *v.tr.* act as the spearhead of (an attack, etc.).

■ *n.* **2** vanguard, advance guard, van, forefront, front line. • *v.* **1** launch, initiate, lead (the way in), take the initiative in, pioneer, blaze the trail for.

spear•mint /spéermint/ *n.* common garden mint used in flavoring.

spec[1] /spek/ *n. colloq.* commercial speculation or venture. □ **on spec** in the hope of success; as a gamble.

spec[2] /spek/ *n. colloq.* specification.

spe•cial /spéshəl/ • *adj.* **1 a** particularly good; exceptional. **b** peculiar, specific. **2** for a particular purpose. **3** denoting education for children with particular needs, e.g., the disabled. • *n.* special edition of a newspaper, dish on a menu, etc. □ **special delivery** delivery of mail in advance of the regular delivery. **special edition** extra edition of a newspaper including later news than the ordinary edition. **special effects** movie or television illusions created by props, camera work, etc. □□ **spe'cial•ly** *adv.* **spe'cial•ness** *n.*

■ *adj.* **1 a** uncommon, especial, rare, unusual, out of the ordinary, extraordinary; dis-

tinguished, notable, noteworthy; significant, important, momentous; gala, festive; particular, extra, pointed, concerted, deliberate, determined. **b** particular, different, unorthodox, unconventional. **2** exclusive, express, individual, tailor-made, specialized, specific. • *n.* extra; see also SPECIALTY. □□ **specially** especially, particularly, custom-, expressly, exclusively, specifically.

spe•cial•ist /spéshəlist/ *n.* person who is trained in a particular branch of a profession, esp. medicine. □□ **spe'cial•ism** *n.*

■ consultant; expert; authority, professional, master.

spe•cial•ize /spéshəliz/ *v.* **1** *intr.* **a** be or become a specialist. **b** devote oneself to an area of interest, skill, etc. **2** *tr.* adapt for a particular purpose. □□ **spe•cial•i•za'tion** *n*

spe•cial•ty /spéshəltee/ *n.* (*pl.* **–ties**) special pursuit, product, operation, etc., to which a company or a person gives special attention.

■ expertise, talent, genius, gift, skill, aptitude, trade, craft; sphere, field, area, line, subject, concentration.

spe•cie /spéeshee, –see/ *n.* coin as opposed to paper money.

spe•cies /spéesheez, –seez/ *n.* (*pl.* same) **1** class of things having some characteristics in common. **2** *Biol.* category in the system of classification of living organisms consisting of similar individuals capable of exchanging genes or interbreeding. **3** kind or sort.

■ **2** breed, stock, strain. **3** see SORT *n.* 1.

spe•cif•ic /spisífik/ • *adj.* **1** clearly defined; definite. **2** relating to a particular subject; peculiar (*a style specific to that*). • *n.* specific aspect or factor (*shall we discuss specifics?*). □ **specific gravity** the ratio of the density of a substance to the density of a standard, as water for a liquid and air for a gas. □□ **spe•cif'i•cal•ly** *adv.* **spec•i•fic'i•ty** /spésifisitee/ *n.*

■ *adj.* **1** precise, exact, particular, explicit. **2** unique (to), typical (of), characteristic (of), discrete. see DETAIL *n.* 1.

spec•i•fi•ca•tion /spésifikáyshən/ *n.* **1** act of specifying. **2** [esp. in *pl*] detailed description of the construction, workmanship, materials, etc., of work done or to be done.

■ **1** identification, description, particularization, naming; requirement, qualification. **2** itemization, list, listing, checklist, inventory, list of particulars, detail(s).

spec•i•fy /spésifi/ *v.tr.* (**–fies, –fied**) **1** name or mention expressly or as a condition. **2** include in specifications. □□ **spec'i•fi•er** *n.*

■ particularize, enumerate, itemize, denominate, be specific about, list, indicate, mention, identify, cite.

spec•i•men /spésimən/ *n.* **1** individual or part taken as an example of a class or whole. **2** *Med.* sample of fluid or tissue for testing.

■ **1** sample, instance, exemplar, representative; illustration, case (in point), type, model, pattern.

spe•cious /spéeshəs/ *adj.* plausible but wrong. □□ **spe•ci•os•i•ty** /–sheeósitee/ *n.* **spe'cious•ly** *adv.* **spe'cious•ness** *n.*

■ deceptive, superficial, ostensible, misleading.

speck /spek/ • *n.* **1** small spot or stain. **2** particle. • *v.tr.* (esp. as **specked** *adj.*) mark with specks. □□ **speck′less** *adj.*

■ *n.* **1** see SPOT *n.* 1. **2** spot, dot, fleck; crumb, iota, jot (or tittle), whit, atom. • *v.* (**specked**) see *speckled* (SPECKLE *v.*).

speck•le /spékəl/ • *n.* speck, esp. one of many. • *v.tr.* (esp. as **speckled** *adj.*) mark with speckles or patches.

■ *v.* (**speckled**) spotted, mottled, dotted, flecked; discolored, spattered.

specs /speks/ *n.pl. colloq.* pair of eyeglasses.

spec•ta•cle /spéktəkəl/ *n.* **1** public show, ceremony, etc. **2** anything attracting public attention.

■ **1** display, performance, event, extravaganza, spectacular. **2** sight, exhibition, marvel, wonder.

spec•ta•cles /spéktəkəlz/ *n.pl. old-fashioned* or *joc.* eyeglasses.

spec•tac•u•lar /spektákyələr/ • *adj.* striking; amazing; lavish. • *n.* spectacular show. □□ **spec•tac′u•lar•ly** *adv.*

spec•ta•tor /spéktaytər/ *n.* person who looks on at a show, game, incident, etc.

■ witness, eyewitness, observer, viewer, onlooker.

spec•ter /spéktər/ *n.* **1** ghost. **2** haunting presentiment.

■ **1** phantom, wraith, apparition. **2** shadow, image, vision.

spec•tral /spéktrəl/ *adj.* **1 a** of or relating to specters or ghosts. **b** ghostlike. **2** of a spectrum. □□ **spec′tral•ly** *adv.*

■ **1** phantom, eerie, unearthly, supernatural, weird.

spec•trom•e•ter /spektrómitər/ *n.* instrument used for the measurement of observed spectra. □□ **spec•tro•met•ric** /spéktrəmét-rik/ *adj.* **spec•trom•e•try** /–trómitree/ *n.*

spec•tro•scope /spéktrəsköp/ *n.* instrument for producing and recording spectra for examination. □□ **spec•tro•scop•ic** /–skópik/ *adj.* **spec•tro•scop′i•cal** *adj.* **spec•tros•co•py** /–tróskəpee/ *n.*

spec•trum /spéktrəm/ *n.* (*pl.* **spec•tra** /–trə/) **1** band of colors, as seen in a rainbow, etc. **2** distribution of visible electromagnetic radiation arranged in a progressive series according to wavelength. **3** entire range or a wide range of anything arranged by degree or quality, etc.

spec•u•late /spékyəlayt/ *v.* **1** *intr.* form a theory or conjecture. **2** *tr.* conjecture; consider. **3** *intr.* invest in stocks, etc., in the hope of gain but with the possibility of loss. □□ **spec•u•la•tion** /–láyshən/ *n.* **spec′u•la•tor** *n.*

■ **1, 2** reflect, meditate, cogitate, think, mull (over); ponder, contemplate; weigh, judge. **3** gamble, wager, play the market. □□ **speculation** thinking, rumination, cogitation, contemplation; conjecture, guess, hypothesis; gamble, wager.

spec•u•la•tive /spékyələtiv, –lay–/ *adj.* **1** of speculation. **2** (of a business investment) involving the risk of loss (*a speculative builder*). □□ **spec′u•la•tive•ly** *adv.*

■ **1** intellectual, abstract, notional, theoretical, hypothetical. **2** risky, hazardous, uncertain.

spec•u•lum /spékyələm/ *n.* (*pl.* **spec•u•la** /–lə/ or **spec•u•lums**) **1** *Surgery* instrument for dilating the cavities of the human body for inspection. **2** mirror, usu. of polished metal, esp. in a reflecting telescope.

sped *past* and *past part.* of SPEED.

speech /speech/ *n.* **1** faculty, act, or manner of speaking. **2** formal public address. **3** language of a nation, region, group, etc. □□ **speech′ful** *adj.*

■ **1** communication, talking, articulation; diction, expression, enunciation. **2** lecture, disquisition, sermon; monologue, soliloquy; tirade. **3** dialect, idiolect, jargon, idiom.

speech•less /speechlis/ *adj.* **1** temporarily unable to speak. **2** mute. □□ **speech′less•ly** *adv.* **speech′less•ness** *n.*

■ **1** dumbfounded, dumbstruck, wordless, silent, struck dumb, tongue-tied. **2** dumb, voiceless.

speed /speed/ • *n.* **1** rapidity of movement. **2** rate of progress or motion over a distance in time. **3** arrangement of gears yielding a specific ratio in a bicycle or automobile transmission. **4** *Photog.* **a** sensitivity of film to light. **b** light-gathering power of a lens. **c** duration of an exposure. **5** *sl.* amphetamine drug. • *v.* (*past* and *past part.* **sped** /sped/) **1** *intr.* go fast. **2** (*past* and *past part.* **speed•ed**) *intr.* travel at an illegal or dangerous speed. **3** *tr.* send fast or on its way. □ **speed bump** raised ridge across a roadway to force slow travel. **speed up** move or work at greater speed. □□ **speed′er** *n.*

■ *n.* **1** quickness, swiftness, velocity, hastiness, alacrity; suddenness, precipitousness, abruptness. **2** see PACE *n.* 1. • *v.* **1** hasten, hurry, rush. **speed up** accelerate, hurry up, quicken.

speed•boat /speedbot/ *n.* high-speed motorboat.

speed•om•e•ter /spidómitər/ *n.* instrument on a motor vehicle, etc., indicating its speed to the driver.

speed•way /speedway/ *n.* racetrack used for automobiles, motorcycles, etc.

speed•y /speedee/ *adj.* (**speed•i•er, speed•i•est**) **1** moving quickly; rapid. **2** done without delay; prompt (*we need a speedy answer*). □□ **speed′i•ly** *adv.* **speed′i•ness** *n.*

■ **1** nimble, fast, swift, brisk. **2** immediate, expeditious, quick.

spe•le•ol•o•gy /spéeleeóləjee/ *n.* the study of caves. □□ **spe•le•o•log•i•cal** /–leeəlójikəl/ *adj.* **spe•le•ol′o•gist** *n.*

spell[1] /spel/ *v.tr.* (*past* and *past part.* **spelled** or **spelt**) **1** write or name correctly the letters that form (a word, etc.). **2 a** (of letters) form (a word, etc.). **b** result in; involve (*spell ruin*). □ **spell out 1** make out (words, writing, etc.) letter by letter. **2** explain in detail. □□ **spell′a•ble** *adj.*

■ **2 b** augur, portend, presage, promise. □ **spell out 2** specify, delineate, clarify, elucidate.

spell² /spel/ n. **1** form of words used as a magical charm or incantation. **2** attraction or fascination exercised by a person, activity, quality, etc.
■ **1** incantation, formula, charm, conjuration. **2** lure, allure, appeal.

spell³ /spel/ • n. **1** short or fairly short period (*a cold spell in April*). **2** turn of work (*did a spell of woodwork*). • v.tr. relieve or take the place of (a person) in work, etc.
■ n. **1** interval, time, term, season; snap. **2** stint, run, course, shift. • v. **1** relieve, replace, substitute for, take over for *or* from.

spell-bind /spélbind/ v.tr. (*past and past part.* **spell-bound** /spélbownd/) bind with or as if with a spell; cast a spell on or over. □□ **spell'bind-er** n. **spell'bind-ing-ly** adv.
■ bewitch, charm, mesmerize, hypnotize; captivate, fascinate, enthrall, enchant.

spell-er /spélər/ n. **1** person who spells, esp. in a specified way (*is a poor speller*). **2** book on spelling.

spell-ing /spélling/ n. **1** writing or naming the letters of a word, etc. **2** way a word is spelled. **3** ability to spell. □ **spelling bee** spelling competition.

spe-lunk-er /spilúngkər, speélung–/ n. person who explores caves, esp. as a hobby. □□ **spe'lunk-ing** n.

spend /spend/ v.tr. (*past and past part.* **spent** /spent/) **1** pay out (money). **2 a** use or consume (time or energy) **b** use up; exhaust; wear out. □□ **spend'a-ble** adj. **spend'er** n.
■ **1** disburse, expend, lay out, squander. **2 a** devote, allot, assign, invest, put in, pass, occupy. **b** consume, expend, drain, deplete, tire, fatigue, weary, prostrate, (as **spent** adj.) emptied, gone, finished; drained, prostrate, fatigued, weary.

spend-thrift /spéndthrift/ • n. extravagant person; prodigal. • adj. extravagant; prodigal.
■ n. profligate, wastrel, squanderer. • adj. free-spending, profligate.

sperm /spərm/ n. (*pl.* same or **sperms**) **1** = SPERMATOZOON. **2** male reproductive fluid containing spermatozoa; semen. □ **sperm whale** large whale yielding valuable oil.

sper-ma-to-zo-on /spərmátəzóon, –ən, spórma–/ n. (*pl.* **sper-ma-to-zo-a** /–zóə/) mature motile sex cell in animals. □□ **sper-ma-to-zo'an** adj.

sper-mi-cide /spórmisīd/ n. substance able to kill spermatozoa. □□ **sper-mi-cid'al** adj.

spew /spyoo/ v. **1** tr. & intr. vomit. **2** (often foll. by *out*) **a** tr. expel (contents) rapidly and forcibly. **b** intr. (of contents) be expelled in this way. □□ **spew'er** n.
■ **1** see VOMIT v. **1**. **2** spout, discharge, gush, spurt; vomit (up), eject.

SPF abbr. sun protection factor.

sp. gr. abbr. specific gravity.

sphere /sfeer/ n. **1** solid figure, or its surface, with every point on its surface equidistant from its center. **2** object having this shape; ball or globe. **3** field of action, influence, etc. □□ **spher-i-cal** /–ikəl/, sfér–/ adj. See synonym study at ROUND
■ **1, 2** orb, globule, spherule; bubble; spheroid. **3** area, province, territory, subject, dis-

cipline, range, specialty, forte. □□ **spherical** globular, round, globelike.

spher-oid /sféeroyd/ n. spherelike but not perfectly spherical body. □□ **sphe-roi'dal** adj.

sphinc-ter /sfíngktər/ n. Anat. ring of muscle surrounding and serving to guard or close an opening or tube, esp. the anus.

sphinx /sfingks/ n. **1** (**Sphinx**) Gk. mythol. winged monster of Thebes, having a woman's head and a lion's body. **2** Antiq. **a** any of several ancient Egyptian stone figures having a lion's body and a human or animal head. **b** (**the Sphinx**) the huge stone figure of a sphinx near the Pyramids at Giza. **3** enigmatic or inscrutable person.

sphyg-mo-ma-nom-e-ter /sfigmōmənómitər/ n. instrument for measuring blood pressure.

spice /spīs/ • n. **1** aromatic or pungent vegetable substance used to flavor food. **2** interesting or piquant quality. • v.tr. flavor with spice. □□ **spic'y** adj.
■ n. **1** condiment, relish, seasoning, flavor(ing); herb. **2** zest, spiciness, piquancy, tang, pungency. • v. season. □□ **spicy** zesty, piquant, tangy, hot; pungent; suggestive, risqué; indecent; scandalous, sensational.

spick-and-span /spík ənd spán/ (also **spic'-and-span'**) adj. **1** fresh and new. **2** neat and clean.

spi-der /spídər/ n. **1** arachnid, many species of which spin webs for the capture of insects as food. **2** frying pan, esp. one with legs or feet.

spi-der-y /spídəree/ adj. elongated and thin.

spiel /speel, shpeel/ sl. n. glib speech or story, esp. a salesman's patter. □□ **spiel'er** n

spif-fy /spífee/ adj. (**spif-fi-er**, **spif-fi-est**) sl. stylish; smart. □□ **spif'fi-ly** adv.

spig-ot /spígət/ n. **1** small peg or plug, esp. in a cask. **2** faucet.

spike¹ /spīk/ • n. **1 a** sharp point. **b** pointed piece of metal, esp. the top of an iron railing, etc. **2 a** any of several metal points set into the sole of a running shoe to prevent slipping. **b** (in pl.) pair of running shoes with spikes. **3** large stout nail. • v.tr. **1 a** fasten or provide with spikes. **b** fix on or pierce with spikes. **2** (of a newspaper editor, etc.) reject (a story), esp. by filing it on a spike. **3** colloq. lace (a drink) with alcohol, a drug, etc. **4** make useless; put an end to; thwart (an idea, etc.). □□ **spik'i-ly** adv. **spik'i-ness** n. **spik'y** adj. (**spik-i-er**, **spik-i-est**)
■ n. **1 a** see POINT n. **1**. **b** skewer, spit, stake, prong. • v. **1** impale, transfix, stab, stick, skewer. **2** strengthen, sl. slip a Mickey Finn into; drug, poison. **3** disable, stymie, nullify, disarm.

spike² /spīk/ n. Bot. flower cluster formed of many flower heads attached closely on a long stem. □□ **spike'let** n.

spill¹ /spil/ • v. (*past and past part.* **spilled** or **spilt**) **1** intr. & tr. fall or run or cause (a liquid, powder, etc.) to fall or run out of a vessel, esp. unintentionally. **2 a** tr. & intr. throw (a person, etc.) from a vehicle, saddle, etc.

b *intr.* (esp. of a crowd) tumble out quickly from a place, etc. **3** *tr. sl.* disclose (information, etc.). • *n.* **1** spilling or being spilled. **2** tumble or fall, esp. from a horse, etc. □ **spill the beans** *colloq.* divulge information, etc., esp. unintentionally or indiscreetly. **spill blood** be guilty of bloodshed. □□ **spil′lage** /spílij/ *n.* **spil′ler** *n.*

■ *v.* **1** pour (out *or* over), overflow, slop *or* run *or* brim over; leak, escape; see also UPSET *v.* 1a. **2 a** dislodge, unseat, unhorse; shed, discharge, tip. **b** see STREAM *v.* 1. **3** see DISCLOSE 1. • *n.* **1** spillage, outpouring, flood, leak, leakage. **2** accident, *colloq.* header, *sl.* cropper.

spill•way /spílway/ *n.* passage for surplus water from a dam.

spin /spin/ • *v.* (**spin•ning**; *past* and *past part.* **spun** /spun/) **1** *intr. & tr.* turn or cause to turn or whirl around quickly. **2** *tr.* [also *absol.*] **a** draw out and twist (wool, cotton, etc.) into threads. **b** make (yarn) in this way. **3** *tr.* (of a spider, silkworm, etc.) make (a web, gossamer, a cocoon, etc.) by extruding a fine viscous thread. **4** *tr.* tell or write (a story, essay, article, etc.). **5** *intr.* (of a person's head, etc.) be dizzy through excitement, astonishment, etc. • *n.* **1** spinning motion; whirl. **2** aircraft's diving descent combined with rotation. **3** revolving motion through the air, esp. in a rifle bullet or in a ball. **4** *colloq.* brief drive, esp. in a car. **5** emphasis; interpretation. □ **spin doctor** political operative who attempts to influence press coverage of events. **spin off 1** throw off by centrifugal force in spinning. **2** create or establish as a by-product or derivative endeavor. □□ **spin′ner** *n.*

■ *v.* **1** revolve, rotate, wheel, gyrate, twirl, swirl, twist, reel. **4** invent, concoct, make up, devise, produce, fabricate; weave, relate, retail, recount. **5** suffer vertigo, swim, whirl, reel, be giddy. • *n.* **1, 3** twirl, turn, gyration, reel, pirouette, revolution, rotation. **4** whirl, ride, tour, excursion, outing. □ **spin off 1** separate.

spi•na bi•fi•da /spínə bífidə/ *n.* congenital defect of the spine.

spin•ach /spínich, –nij/ *n.* dark green vegetable with edible leaves.

spi•nal /spín′l/ *adj.* of or relating to the spine. □ **spinal column** spine. **spinal cord** cylindrical structure of the central nervous system enclosed in the spine.

spin•dle /spínd′l/ *n.* **1 a** pin in a spinning wheel used for twisting and winding the thread. **b** small bar with tapered ends used for the same purpose in hand spinning. **2** pin or axis that revolves or on which something revolves. **3** turned piece of wood used as a banister, chair leg, etc.

spin•dly /spíndlee/ *adj.* (**spin•dli•er**, **spin•dli•est**) long or tall and thin; thin and weak. (*spindly trees that lined the driveway*).

spine /spin/ *n.* **1** series of vertebrae extending from the skull to the small of the back; backbone. **2** *Zool. & Bot.* any hard pointed process or structure. **3** sharp ridge or projection. **4** part of a book's jacket or cover that encloses the fastened edges of the pages. □ **spine-chilling** (esp. of a story, etc.) frightening. **spine-tingling** thrilling; pleasurably exciting. □□ **spined** *adj.*

■ **1** backbone, vertebrae, spinal column. **2** thorn, needle, barb, spike, spur, prong, quill, ray, bristle. **3** see CREST *n.* 2, RIDGE.

spine•less /spínlis/ *adj.* **1** having no spine; invertebrate. **2** lacking resolve; weak. □□ **spine′less•ly** *adv.* **spine′less•ness** *n.*

■ **2** feeble, flabby, irresolute, indecisive, ineffectual; cowardly, pusillanimous, timorous, lily-livered, craven.

spin•et /spínit, spinét/ *n. Mus.* small upright piano.

spin•ner•et /spínəret/ *n.* spinning organ in a spider, etc.

spin•ning /spíning/ *n.* **1** the act or an instance of spinning. **2** exercise of fast pedaling on a stationary exercise bicycle. □ **spinning jenny** *hist.* machine for spinning with more than one spindle at a time. **spinning wheel** household machine for spinning yarn or thread with a spindle driven by a wheel attached to a crank or treadle.

spin•ster /spínstər/ *n.* **1** unmarried woman. **2** woman, esp. elderly, thought unlikely to marry. □□ **spin′ster•hood** *n.* **spin′ster•ish** *adj.*

spin•y /spínee/ *adj.* (**spin•i•er**, **spin•i•est**) **1** full of spines; prickly. **2** perplexing; troublesome; thorny. □□ **spin′i•ness** *n.*

spi•ral /spírəl/ • *adj.* coiled in a plane or as if around a cylinder or cone. • *n.* **1** plane or three-dimensional spiral curve. **2** spiral thing. **3** progressive rise or fall. • *v.intr.* **1** move in a spiral course. **2** esp. *Econ.* (of prices, wages, etc.) rise or fall, esp. rapidly. □□ **spi′ral•ly** *adv.*

■ *adj.* helical, screw, corkscrew, cochlear; scrolled, volute(d), whorled. • *n.* **1** helix, coil, corkscrew, screw, scroll; whorl, volute, turn, curl.

spire /spir/ *n.* tapering cone- or pyramid-shaped structure built esp. on a church tower.

■ pinnacle, flèche; column, belfry; steeple.

spi•re•a /spíreeə/ *n.* (also **spi•rae′a**) shrub with clusters of small white or pink flowers.

spir•it /spírit/ • *n.* **1** vital animating essence of a person or animal; soul. **2** ghost. **3** prevailing mental or moral condition or attitude; mood; tendency (*public spirit*). **4** [in *pl.*] strong distilled liquor. **5 a** person's mental or moral nature or qualities, usu. specified (*unbending spirit*). **b** person viewed as possessing these (*is an ardent spirit*). **c** (in full **high spirit**) courage; energy; vivacity. **6** real meaning (*spirit of the law*). • *v.tr.* [usu. foll. by *away, off,* etc.] convey rapidly and secretly or as if by spirits.

■ *n.* **1** breath, life, vitality, vital spirit, consciousness, psyche, self, heart. **2** see SPECTER 1. **3** principle, thought, idea, inspiration, notion, feeling, inclination, impulse; atmosphere; temper, sentiment, cheer, humor; morale, esprit de corps, team spirit. **4** (*spirits*) alcohol, strong drink, *colloq.* booze, firewater, *colloq.* hooch. **5 a** character, temperament, temper, persona, disposition, heart, mind, will, willpower. **b** character, soul. **c** bravery, grit, backbone, valor, pluck, daring, mettle, stoutheartedness, manfulness, manliness; ardor, desire, impetus, drive, urge, eagerness; zest, zeal, zealousness, fire, passion, pungency, piquancy, warmth, animation; vim, spunk, get-up-and-go, (right) stuff, guts. **6** sense, tenor, signification, purport, intent, intention, purpose, aim, implication. • *v.* abduct, make off *or* away with, carry off, transport, take away, kidnap.

spir•it•ed /spíritid/ *adj.* full of spirit; animated, lively, brisk, *or* courageous. □□ **spir'it•ed•ly** *adv.* **spir'it•ed•ness** *n.*
   ■ sprightly, energetic, vigorous; frisky, playful; ardent, impassioned; plucky, mettlesome.

spir•it•less /spíritlis/ *adj.* lacking courage, vigor, *or* vivacity. □□ **spir'it•less•ly** *adv.*

spir•i•tu•al /spírichŏŏəl/ • *adj.* **1** of *or* concerning the spirit as opposed to matter. **2** religious; divine; inspired. • *n.* religious song derived from the musical traditions of African-American people. □□ **spir•i•tu•al•i•ty** /-chŏŏ-álitee/ *n.* **spir'i•tu•al•ly** *adv.* **spir'i•tu•al•ness** *n.*
   ■ *adj.* **1** nonmaterial, incorporeal, psychic(al), mental, psychological, inner. **2** sacred, ecclesiastical(al), churchly, clerical, priestly, devotional, holy.

spir•i•tu•al•ism /spírichŏŏəlizəm/ *n.* belief that the spirits of the dead can communicate with the living, esp. through mediums. □□ **spir'i•tu•al•ist** *n.*

spir•i•tu•ous /spírichŏŏəs/ *adj.* **1** containing much alcohol. **2** distilled, as whiskey, rum, etc.

spi•ro•chete /spírōkeet/ *n.* (also **spi'ro•chaete**) any of various flexible spiral-shaped bacteria.

spit¹ /spit/ • *v.* (**spit•ting**; *past* and *past part.* **spat** /spat/ *or* **spit**) **1** *intr.* **a** eject saliva from the mouth. **b** do this as a sign of hatred *or* contempt (*spat at him*). **2** *tr.* [usu. foll. by *out*] **a** eject (saliva, blood, food, etc.) from the mouth (*spit the meat out*). **b** utter (oaths, threats, etc.) vehemently. **3** *intr.* (of a fire, pen, pan, etc.) send out sparks, ink, hot fat, etc. • *n.* **1** spittle. **2** the act *or* an instance of spitting. □ **spit and polish** military cleaning and polishing. **spitting distance** very short distance. **spitting image** [foll. by *of*] *colloq.* the exact double of (another person *or* thing). □□ **spit'ter** *n.*
   ■ *v.* **1 a** expectorate; dribble, salivate, drool, slaver. **2 a** expectorate, discharge, spew (forth). **3** hiss, sputter, splutter; fizz. • *n.* **1** saliva, drool, sputum, slaver. □ **spitting image** twin, duplicate, clone, image, counterpart, likeness, look-alike.

spit² /spit/ • *n.* **1** rod on which meat is skewered before being roasted on a fire, etc. **2** small point of land projecting into the sea. • *v.tr.* (**spit•ted, spit•ting**) **1** thrust a spit through. **2** pierce *or* transfix with a sword, etc.

spit•ball /spítbawl/ *n.* **1** ball of chewed paper, etc., used as a missile. **2** baseball moistened by the pitcher to affect its flight. □□ **spit'ball•er** *n.*

spite /spit/ • *n.* feeling of ill will; malice. • *v.tr.* thwart; mortify; annoy (*does it to spite me*). □ **in spite of** notwithstanding.
   ■ *n.* spitefulness, maliciousness, malevolence, malignity, venom, spleen, rancor, animosity; grievance, resentment. • *v.* irritate, vex, upset, disconcert, offend, provoke, discomfit, pique, put out. □ **in spite of** despite, regardless of, ignoring, in defiance of.

spite•ful /spítfŏŏl/ *adj.* motivated by spite; malevolent. See synonym study at VINDICTIVE. □□ **spite'ful•ly** *adv.* **spite'ful•ness** *n.*
   ■ malicious, malignant, venomous, vindictive, hateful, invidious, hostile, antagonistic, unfriendly.

spit•fire /spítfir/ *n.* person with a fiery temper.

spit•tle /spít'l/ *n.* saliva.

spit•toon /spitŏn/ *n.* vessel to spit into.

splash /splash/ • *v.* **1** *intr. & tr.* spatter *or* cause (liquid) to spatter in small drops. **2** *tr.* cause (a person) to be spattered with liquid, etc. (*splashed them with mud*). **3** *intr.* **a** (of a person) cause liquid to spatter (*was splashing about in the bath*). **b** move while spattering liquid, etc. **4** *tr.* display (news) prominently. • *n.* **1** act *or* instance of splashing. **2** quantity of liquid splashed. **3** spot *or* patch of dirt, etc., splashed on to a thing. □ **make a splash** attract much attention. □□ **splash'y** *adj.* (**splash•i•er, splash•i•est**).
   ■ *v.* **1** bespatter, spray, shower, scatter, daub, sprinkle, splatter, *colloq.* slosh. **2** spatter, speckle, bespatter, spray, shower, scatter, dabble, daub. **3** splatter, slosh, plash, wade, dabble, paddle. **4** blazon, spread, plaster. • *n.* **2** splatter, spatter, slosh, *colloq.* splosh. **3** spatter, spray, sprinkle, stain, smear, smudge, blotch.

splash•down /splashdown/ *n.* landing of a spacecraft in the sea.

splat¹ /splat/ *n.* flat piece of thin wood in the center of a chair back.

splat² /splat/ *colloq.* • *n.* sharp cracking *or* slapping sound. • *adv.* with a splat. • *v.* (**splat•ted, splat•ting**) fall *or* hit with a splat.

splat•ter /splátər/ *v.* splash, esp. with a continuous noisy action.

splay /splay/ • *v.tr.* spread out. • *adj.* **1** wide and flat. **2** turned outward.

spleen /spleen/ *n.* **1** abdominal organ involved in maintaining the proper condition of blood in most vertebrates. **2** moroseness. □□ **spleen'ful** *adj.*

splen•did /spléndid/ *adj.* **1** magnificent; sumptuous. **2** dignified; impressive. **3** excellent; fine. □□ **splen'did•ly** *adv.*
   ■ **1** resplendent, dazzling, marvelous, spectacular, grand; eminent, prominent, superior, illustrious. **3** extraordinary, exceptional, unbelievable.

splen•dor /spléndər/ *n.* **1** great *or* dazzling brightness. **2** magnificence; grandeur.
   ■ **1** brilliance, shine, luster, light, glitter, dazzle, luminosity. **2** brilliance, display, radiance, resplendence, sumptuousness, stateliness, majesty, panoply, spectacle, show, glory, pomp.

sple•net•ic /splinétik/ *adj.* ill-tempered; peevish. □□ **sple•net'i•cal•ly** *adv.*

splice /splīs/ • *v.tr.* **1** join the ends of (ropes) by interweaving strands. **2** join (pieces of timber, tape, film, etc.) in an overlapping position. **3** (esp. as **spliced** *adj.*) *colloq.* join in marriage. • *n.* joint made by splicing. □□ **splic'er** *n.*

■ *v.* **1** entwine, intertwine, braid, plait, twist, interlace. **2** dovetail, mesh, fit (together), knit, interlock, engage. **3** unite, marry, bind, conjoin. • *n.* union, connection, tie, bond, binding, fastening, linkage.

splint /splint/ • *n.* **1** strip of rigid material used for holding a broken bone, etc., when set. **2** rigid or flexible strip of esp. wood used in basketwork, etc. • *v.tr.* secure (a broken limb, etc.) with a splint or splints.

splin•ter /splíntər/ • *v.* break into fragments. • *n.* small thin sharp-edged piece broken off from wood, glass, etc. □□ **splin'ter•y** *adj.*

■ *v.* shatter, fragment, split, disintegrate, shiver. • *n.* sliver, shiver, fragment, piece; scrap, shard, shred.

split /split/ • *v.* (**split•ting**; *past* and *past part.* **split**) **1** *intr. & tr.* **a** break or cause to break forcibly into parts, esp. with the grain or into halves. **b** divide into parts; esp. equal shares. **2** *tr. & intr.* remove or be removed by breaking, separating, or dividing. **3** *intr. & tr.* **a** separate esp. through discord. **b** quarrel or cease association. **4** *intr. & tr. sl.* leave, esp. suddenly. **5** *intr.* (as **splitting** *adj.*) very painful; acute. • *n.* **1** act or result of splitting. **2** separation into parties; schism. **3** [in *pl.*] athletic feat of leaping in the air or sitting down with the legs at right angles to the body in front and behind, or at the sides with the trunk facing forward. □ **split infinitive** infinitive with an adverb, etc., inserted between *to* and the verb, e.g., *seems to really like it.* **split-level** (of a building) having a room or rooms a fraction of a story higher than other parts. **split pea** dried pea split in half for cooking. **split personality** alteration or dissociation of personality occurring in some mental illnesses, esp. schizophrenia and hysteria. □□ **split'ter** *n.*

■ *v.* **1a** split up or apart, divide, separate, cut or chop apart, cut or chop in two, pull or tear apart, snap apart, bisect, dichotomize, halve; burst, *colloq.* bust. **b** apportion, deal out, dole out, distribute, allot; branch, fork, bifurcate, diverge, separate. **3a** divorce, go separate ways, break up, part company, *colloq.* bust up. **4** see LEAVE¹ *v.* 1b, 3. **5** (**splitting**) severe, bad, *colloq.* awful, thumping. • *n.* **1** crack, cleft, fissure, chink, cranny, slit, slot, crevice; gap, hiatus, lacuna, opening; rift, break, rupture, fracture; slash, gash, tear. see also SEPARATION. **2** division, dichotomy, breach, rupture, partition, disunion, dissociation, discord; break, divorce.

splotch /sploch/ *n. & v.tr. colloq.* **1** daub, blot, or smear. • *v.tr.* make a splotch on. □□ **splotch'y** *adj.*

splurge /splərj/ *colloq.* • *n.* **1** ostentatious display or effort. **2** instance of sudden great

extravagance. • *v.intr.* spend large sums of money.

■ *n.* **1** show, ostentation, splash. **2** indulgence, fling, *colloq.* spree. • *v.* squander or dissipate *or* waste money, burn (up) money.

splut•ter /splútər/ • *v.* **1** *intr.* **a** speak in a hurried, vehement, or choking manner. **b** emit spitting sounds. **2** *tr.* speak rapidly or incoherently. • *n.* rapid, incoherent speech. □□ **splut'ter•er** *n.* **splut'ter•ing•ly** *adv.*

spoil /spoyl/ • *v.* (*past* and *past part.* **spoiled** *or* **spoilt**) **1** *tr.* **a** damage; diminish the value of. **b** reduce a person's enjoyment, etc., of. **2** *tr.* overindulge (esp. a child, pet, etc.). **3** *intr.* (of food) go bad; decay. **4** *tr. literary* plunder or deprive (a person of a thing) by force or stealth. • *n.* **1** [usu. in *pl.*] plunder. **2** esp. *joc.* profit or advantages gained by succeeding to public office, high position, etc. □□ **spoil'age** *n.* **spoil'er** *n.*

■ *v.* **1** ruin, destroy, wreck, blight, queer, mess up, bungle, botch, upset, demolish, sabotage, undermine, harm, vitiate, mar. **2** baby, mollycoddle, coddle, cosset, indulge, pamper. **3** turn, go off, deteriorate, curdle, molder, decompose, perish, become addle(d), rot. • *n.* **1** loot, booty, pillage, prizes, pickings, takings, take. **2** benefits, perquisites, *colloq.* perks.

spoke¹ /spōk/ *n.* each of the bars running from the hub to the rim of a wheel.

spoke² *past* of SPEAK.

spo•ken /spṓkən/ *past part.* of SPEAK. *adj.* [in *comb.*] speaking in a specified way (*well-spoken*). □ **spoken for** claimed.

■ □ **spoken for** reserved, bespoke, set aside, accounted for, chosen, selected, requisitioned.

spokes•man /spṓksmən/ *n.* (*pl.* **–men**; *fem.* **spokes•wom•an**, *pl.* **–wom•en**) person speaking for a group, etc.

spokes•per•son /spṓkspərsən/ *n.* (*pl.* **–per•sons** *or* **–peo•ple**) spokesman or spokeswoman.

spo•li•a•tion /spṓleeáyshən/ *n.* plunder or pillage.

spon•dee /spóndee/ *n. Prosody* metrical foot consisting of two long (or stressed) syllables. □□ **spon•da•ic** /–dáyik/ *adj.*

sponge /spunj/ • *n.* **1** any aquatic animal with pores in its body wall and a rigid internal skeleton. **2 a** skeleton of a sponge, esp. the soft light elastic absorbent kind used in bathing, etc. **b** piece of porous rubber or plastic, etc., used similarly. **3** thing of spongelike absorbency or consistency. **4** (also **sponger**) person who lives off another's means. • *v.* **1** *tr.* wipe, clean, or absorb with or as with a sponge. **2** *intr.* live as a parasite. □ **sponge cake** very light cake with a spongelike consistency. □□ **spong•a•ble** *adj.* **sponge'like** *adj.* **spon'gi•form** *adj.* (esp. in senses 1, 2).

spong•y /spúnjee/ *adj.* (**spong•i•er**, **spong•i•est**) **1** like a sponge. **2** (of metal) finely divided and loosely coherent. □□ **spong'i•ly** *adv.* **spong'i•ness** *n.*

spon•sor /spónsər/ • *n.* **1** person who supports an activity; backer. **2** business organization that promotes a broadcast program in return for advertising time. **3** *Eccles.* godparent at baptism or esp. a person who presents a candidate for confirmation. • *v.tr.* be a sponsor for. □□ **spon•so•ri•al** /sponsáwreeəl/ *adj.* **spon'sor•ship** *n.*

■ *n.* **1** supporter, promoter, patron, Maecenas, benefactor, subsidizer, *sl.* angel. **2** (radio *or* television) advertiser. • *v.* back, support, promote, fund, patronize, subsidize, finance, underwrite.

spon•ta•ne•ous /spontáyneeəs/ *adj.* **1** acting or done or occurring without external cause. **2** instinctive; automatic; natural. □ **spontaneous combustion** ignition of a mineral or vegetable substance from internal heat. □□ **spon•ta•ne•i•ty** /spóntənéeitee, -náyitee/ *n.* **spon•ta'ne•ous•ly** *adv.*

■ **2** unconstrained, unforced, unstudied, unaffected; involuntary, instinctual, unconscious, reflex, mechanical, immediate, offhand, unguarded.

spoof /spoof/ *n. & v. colloq.* **1** parody. **2** hoax.

spook /spook/ ■ *n. colloq.* ghost. • *v. sl.* **1** *tr.* frighten; unnerve; alarm. **2** *intr.* take fright; become alarmed.

spook•y /spookee/ *adj.* (**spook•i•er, spook•i•est**) **1** *colloq.* ghostly; eerie. **2** *sl.* nervous; easily frightened. □□ **spook'i•ly** *adv.* **spook'i•ness** *n.*

spool /spool/ ■ *n.* **1** reel for winding magnetic tape, yarn, etc. **2** revolving cylinder of an angler's reel. • *v.tr.* wind on a spool.

spoon /spoon/ ■ *n.* **1 a** utensil consisting of an oval or round bowl and a handle for conveying food (esp. liquid) to the mouth, for stirring, etc. **b** spoonful. • *v.* **1** *tr.* take (liquid, etc.) with a spoon. **2** *colloq. intr.* behave in an amorous way, esp. foolishly. □□ **spoon'er** *n.* **spoon'ful** *n.* (*pl.* **-fuls**).

spoon•bill /spoonbil/ *n.* large wading bird having a bill with a very broad flat tip.

spoo•ner•ism /spoonərizəm/ *n.* transposition, usu. accidental, of the initial letters, etc., of two or more words, e.g., *you have hissed the mystery lectures* for *you have missed the history lectures.*

spoon•feed /spoonfeed/ *v.tr.* (*past and past part.* **-fed**) **1** feed with a spoon. **2** provide help, information, etc., to (a person) without requiring any effort on the recipient's part.

spo•rad•ic /spərádik, spaw–/ *adj.* occurring only here and there or occasionally; separate; scattered. □□ **spo•rad'i•cal•ly** *adv.*

■ occasional, intermittent, random, casual, odd, irregular, patchy, spotty, uneven, erratic, chance, unexpected; spasmodic(al), fitful, periodic(al).

spore /spawr/ *n.* **1** specialized reproductive cell of many plants and microorganisms. **2** these collectively.

sport /spawrt/ ■ *n.* **1 a** game or competitive activity, esp. an outdoor one involving physical exertion, e.g., baseball, football, racing, hunting. **b** [usu. in *pl.*] such activities collectively (*world of sports*). **2** amusement; diversion; fun. **3** *colloq.* fair or generous person. **4** plaything or laughingstock (*was the sport of Fortune*). • *v.* **1** *intr.* **a** divert oneself; take part in a pastime. **b** frolic; gambol. **2** *tr.*

wear, exhibit, or produce, esp. ostentatiously. □ **in sport** jestingly. **make sport of** make fun of; ridicule. **sports car** low-built fast car. **sports coat** (*or* **jacket**) man's jacket for informal wear. □□ **sport'er** *n.*

■ *n.* **1 a** pastime, recreation. **b** games, recreation, play. **2** recreation, entertainment, play, distraction, relaxation. **3** sportsman, sportswoman. • *v.* **1** amuse oneself; romp, caper, play, frisk, rollick. **2** show off, flaunt, display, parade, flourish. □ **in sport** in jest, jokingly, in fun, teasingly, playfully. **make sport of** tease, deride, make a laughingstock of, make a fool of.

sport•ing /spáwrting/ *adj.* **1** interested in sports (*sporting man*). **2** sportsmanlike; generous (*sporting offer*). **3** concerned about, active in, or involved in sports (*sporting dog*). □ **sporting chance** some possibility of success. □□ **sport'ing•ly** *adv.*

sport•ive /spáwrtiv/ *adj.* playful

■ frisky, gamboling, frolicking, romping.

sports•man /spáwrtsmən/ *n.* (*pl.* **-men**; *fem.* **sports•wom•an**, *pl.* **-wom•en**) **1** person who takes part in sports. **2** person who behaves fairly and generously. □□ **sports'man•like** *adj.* **sports'man•ly** *adj.* **sports'man•ship** *n.*

■ □□ **sportsmanship** fair play, fairness, honesty, honor.

sports•wear /spáwrtswair/ *n.* clothes worn for sports or for casual use.

sport•y /spáwrtee/ *adj.* (**sport•i•er, sport•i•est**) *colloq.* **1** fond of sports. **2** rakish; showy □□ **sport'i•ly** *adv.* **sport'i•ness** *n.*

■ **2** informal, casual; stylish, chic, smart, fashionable, modish, à la mode, up to date, swanky, loud, flashy.

spot /spot/ ■ *n.* **1 a** small roundish part of the surface of a thing distinguished by color, texture, etc. **b** blemish; defect. **2** particular place; definite locality. **3** = SPOTLIGHT. **4** *colloq.* awkward or difficult situation (esp. in *in a* (*tight, etc.*) *spot*). • *v.* (**spot•ted, spot•ting**) **1** *tr.* **a** *colloq.* identify; recognize; catch sight of. **b** watch for and take note of (trains, talent, etc.). **2** *tr. & intr.* mark or become marked with spots. □ **on the spot 1** at the scene of an action or event. **2** *colloq.* in a position such that response or action is required. □□ **spot'ter** *n.*

■ *n.* **1** mark, patch, dot, speck, blot, blotch, speckle, fleck, particle, mote, macula, smudge, stain; eruption, pimple, pustule, blackhead, whitehead; see also STIGMA 1. **2** site, locale, location, position, scene, setting, section, area, neighborhood, quarter. **4** predicament, tricky situation, quandary, mess, trouble, straits, *colloq.* pickle, jam, fix. • *v.* **1** pick out, distinguish, single out, detect, locate, discern, see, sight, glimpse. **2** stain, fleck, speckle, spray, splash, spatter, bespatter, soil, dirty, taint.

spot•less /spótlis/ *adj.* immaculate; absolutely clean or pure. □□ **spot'less•ly** *adv.* **spot'less•ness** *n.*

■ gleaming, shiny, spick-and-span; unsullied, flawless, impeccable.

spot•light /spótlit/ • *n.* **1** beam of light directed on a small area. **2** lamp projecting this. **3** full attention or publicity. • *v.tr.* (*past* and *past part.* **–light•ed** or **–lit**) **1** direct a spotlight on. **2** draw attention to.

■ *n.* **1, 2** arc light, searchlight, spot. **3** focus (of attention), limelight, public eye. • *v.* light (up), illuminate, focus light upon *or* on, shine light upon *or* on; emphasize, highlight, make conspicuous, focus upon *or* on, feature, give prominence to.

spot•ty /spótee/ *adj.* (**spot•ti•er, spot•ti•est**) **1** marked with spots. **2** patchy; irregular. □□ **spot′ti•ly** *adv.* **spot′ti•ness** *n.*

■ **1** spotted, dotted, speckled, freckled, flecked, blotched, blotchy, stained; soiled, dirty; *colloq.* splotchy, splotched; pimply, pimpled, acned. **2** uneven, erratic, sporadic, capricious, fitful; see also IRREGULAR 4.

spouse /spows, spowz/ *n.* husband or wife.

spout /spowt/ • *n.* **1** projecting tube or lip through which a liquid, etc., is poured from a teapot, kettle, pitcher, etc., or issues from a fountain, pump, etc. **2** jet or column of liquid, grain, etc. • *v.* **1** discharge or issue forcibly in a jet. **2** utter (verses, etc.) or speak in a declamatory manner; speechify. □□ **spout′er** *n.* **spout′less** *adj.*

■ *n.* **1** gargoyle, duct, waterspout, drain, outlet, conduit, downspout. **2** see GUSH *n.* 1. • *v.* **1** squirt, spurt, spit, shoot, gush, pour (out *or* forth), disgorge; emit, eject, vomit (up *or* forth); flow, stream, jet. **2** ramble on, rant, rave, carry on, pontificate, declaim.

sprain /sprayn/ • *v.tr.* wrench (an ankle, wrist, etc.) so as to cause pain and swelling. • *n.* such a wrench.

sprang *past* of SPRING.

sprat /sprat/ *n.* small European herringlike fish, much used as food.

sprawl /sprawl/ • *v.* **1 a** *intr.* sit or lie or fall with limbs flung out or in an ungainly way. **b** *tr.* spread (one's limbs) in this way. **2** *intr.* (of handwriting, a plant, a town, etc.) be of irregular or straggling form. • *n.* sprawling movement, position, or mass. □□ **sprawl′ing•ly** *adv.*

■ *v.* **1 a** spread out, stretch out, loll, lounge, slouch, slump, recline, lie about *or* around. **2** spread (out), stretch (out), ramble, meander, wander, straggle.

spray¹ /spray/ • *n.* **1** water or other liquid flying in small drops. **2** device for creating this. • *v.tr.* [also *absol.*] **1** throw (liquid) in the form of spray. **2** sprinkle (an object) with small drops or particles. □ **spray gun** gunlike device for spraying paint, etc. □□ **spray′a•ble** *adj.* **spray′er** *n.*

■ *n.* **1** shower, sprinkling, drizzle, mist, sprinkle, spindrift. **2** atomizer, sprayer, sprinkler, vaporizer, aerosol, spray gun. • *v.* **1** sprinkle, shower, spatter, scatter, disperse, diffuse, spread. **2** shower, spatter, besprinkle; see WATER *v.* 1.

spray² /spray/ *n.* sprig of flowers or leaves.

■ flower *or* floral arrangement, nosegay, posy, bouquet.

spread /spred/ • *v.* (*past* and *past part.*

spread) **1** *tr.* **a** open or extend the surface of. **b** cause to cover a larger surface. **c** display to the eye or the mind. **2** *intr.* have a wide or increasing extent (*spreading trees*). **3** *intr. & tr.* become or make widely known, felt, etc. (*rumors are spreading*). **4** *tr.* lay (a table). • *n.* **1** act or an instance of spreading. **2** extent of spreading. **3** diffusion (*spread of learning*). **4** increased bodily girth (*middle-aged spread*). **5** difference between two rates, prices, scores, etc. **6** *colloq.* elaborate meal. **7** food for spreading on bread, etc. **8** bedspread. **9** printed matter spread across more than one column. **10** ranch or farm with extensive land. □ **spread eagle** in the shape of an eagle with legs and wings extended. **spread-eagle** *v.tr.* (usu. as **spread-eagled** *adj.*) place in a position with limbs extended. □□ **spread′a•ble** *adj.* **spread′er** *n.*

■ *v.* **1 a** unfold, draw out, display, stretch out, lay out, fan out, unroll, unfurl. **b** smear, apply, smooth, put, rub; diffuse, distribute, disperse, disseminate. **c** lay out, unfurl, unfold. **2** grow, develop, increase, broaden, expand, extend, widen. **3** spread about *or* around, broadcast, publicize, bruit about, air, televise, circulate, publish, distribute, disseminate. **4** set, arrange. • *n.* **1** extension, expansion, enlargement, development, increase, proliferation, broadening, growth, widening, mushrooming, dispersion, dispersal. **2** expanse, area, span, sweep, vastness, stretch, reach, breadth, depth, size. **3** see CIRCULATION 2a. **4** range, extent, scope, span. **5** feast, banquet, dinner, barbecue; table; *colloq.* feed. **7** butter, margarine, oleomargarine, jam, jelly, preserve, conserve, paste, pâté. **8** counterpane, coverlet, bedcover, cover, quilt, eiderdown, duvet. **10** landholding, holding, property, place, plantation, farm, homestead.

spread•sheet /sprédsheet/ *n.* computer program allowing manipulation of esp. tabulated numerical data.

spree /spree/ *colloq. n.* **1** lively extravagant outing (*shopping spree*). **2** bout of fun or drinking, etc.

■ **1** trip, jaunt, fling, *colloq.* splurge. **2** frolic, romp, revel, wild party, fling, debauch, orgy; drinking bout, carousal, blowout, *sl.* bender, binge, jag.

sprig /sprig/ *n.* small branch or shoot.

spright•ly /sprítlee/ *adj.* (**spright•li•er, spright•li•est**) vivacious; lively; brisk. □□ **spright′li•ness** *n.*

■ spry, cheerful, gay, animated, sportive, active.

spring /spring/ • *v.* (*past* **sprang** /sprang/ also **sprung** /sprung/; *past part.* **sprung**) **1** *intr.* jump; move rapidly or suddenly (*sprang from his seat*). **2** *intr.* move rapidly as from a constrained position or by the action of a spring. **3** *intr.* originate or arise (*springs from an old family*). **4** *intr.* come into being; appear, esp. suddenly (*a breeze sprang up*). **5** *tr.* produce or develop or make known suddenly or unexpectedly (*loves to spring surprises*). **6** *tr. sl.* contrive the escape or release of. • *n.* **1** jump (*took a spring*). **2** recoil, e.g., of a bow. **3** elasticity. **4** resilient device usu. of bent or coiled metal used esp. to drive clockwork or for cushioning in furniture or vehicles. **5 a** season in which vegetation begins to appear, first season of the year. **b** early stage of life, etc. **6** place where water, oil, etc., wells up from the earth. □ **spring fever** restless or lethargic feeling sometimes associated with spring. □□ **spring′less** *adj.* **spring′like** *adj.*

■ *v.* **1** leap, bound, hop, vault, dart, fly, bounce, start. **3** begin, start, evolve; proceed, stem, issue, descend, derive, come, develop. **4** arise, grow, develop, come up, rise, come into existence, be born, emerge. **5** broach, pop, introduce suddenly *or* unexpectedly, divulge suddenly *or* unexpectedly. ■ *n.* **1** leap, bound, hop, vault, bounce, skip. **3** bounciness, bounce, resiliency, resilience, springiness, buoyancy. **5** springtime, (*attrib.*) vernal. **6** source, fountain, fountainhead, wellspring, well, spa, geyser.

spring•board /spríngbawrd/ *n.* **1** springboard giving impetus in leaping, diving, etc. **2** point of departure.

spring•y /springee/ *adj.* (**spring•i•er**, **spring•i•est**) resilient; bouncy; elastic. □□ **spring′i•ly** *adv.* **spring′i•ness** *n.*

sprin•kle /springkəl/ • *v.tr.* **1** scatter in small drops or particles. **2** subject to sprinkling with liquid, etc. **3** distribute in small amounts. • *n.* **1** light shower. **2** = SPRINKLING. □□ **sprin′kler** *n.*

■ *v.* **1, 3** see SCATTER *v.* 1. ■ *n.* **1** see SHOWER *n.* 1.

sprin•kling /springkling/ *n.* sparse number or amount.

sprint /sprint/ • *v.* **1** *intr.* run a short distance at full speed. **2** *tr.* run (a specified distance) in this way. • *n.* **1** such a run. **2** similar short spell of maximum effort in cycling, swimming, auto racing, etc. □□ **sprint′er** *n.*

sprite /sprit/ *n.* elf, fairy, or goblin.

spritz•er /spritsər/ *n.* mixture of wine and soda water.

sprock•et /sprókit/ *n.* each of several teeth on a wheel engaging with links of a chain.

sprout /sprowt/ • *v.* **1** *tr.* put forth; produce (shoots, hair, etc.). **2** *intr.* begin to grow; put forth shoots. • *n.* shoot of a plant.

■ *v.* **1** grow. **2** bud, germinate, come up, arise, begin.

spruce[1] /sprōōs/ • *adj.* neat in dress and appearance; smart. • *v.* [also *refl.*; usu. foll. by *up*] make or become neat and fashionable.
■ *adj.* dapper, trim, tidy, well turned out. • *v.* tidy (up), neaten (up), primp, preen, clean (up).

spruce[2] /sprōōs/ *n.* **1** conifer with dense foliage. **2** wood of this tree used as timber.

sprung *past. and past part.* of SPRING.

spry /spri/ *adj.* (**spry•er**, **spry•est**) active; lively. □□ **spry′ly** *adv.* **spry′ness** *n.*

■ see LIVELY 1.

spud /spud/ *n. sl.* potato.

spume /spyōōm/ *n. & v.intr.* froth; foam. □□ **spum′y** *adj.* (**spum•i•er**, **spum•i•est**).

spun *past* and *past part.* of SPIN.

spunk /spungk/ *n. colloq.* courage; mettle; spirit.

■ nerve, pluck, gameness, resolve, resolu-

tion, heart, grit, backbone, marrow, *colloq.* guts.

spunk•y /spúngkee/ *adj.* (**spunk•i•er**, **spunk•i•est**) *colloq.* brave; spirited. □□ **spunk′i•ly** *adv.*

spur /spər/ • *n.* **1** device with a small spike or a spiked wheel worn on a rider's heel for urging a horse forward. **2** stimulus or incentive. **3** spur-shaped thing, esp.: **a** projection from a mountain or mountain range. **b** branch road or railway. • *v.tr.* (**spurred, spur•ring**) **1** prick (a horse) with spurs. **2** incite; stimulate. □ **on the spur of the moment** on a momentary impulse; impromptu. □□ **spur′less** *adj.*

■ *n.* **2** goad, prod, impulse, impetus, incitement, instigation, pressure, stimulation. **3** prong, spike, spine, gaff, barb, quill, tine. • *v.* goad, prod, urge, egg on, impel, prompt, press, push, pressure; provoke, induce, encourage, excite. □ **on the spur of the moment** impetuously, impulsively, unthinkingly; unpremeditatedly; rashly, thoughtlessly, recklessly.

spu•ri•ous /spyooreeəs/ *adj.* not genuine; not being what it purports to be. □□ **spu′ri•ous•ly** *adv.* **spu′ri•ous•ness** *n.*

■ false, counterfeit, sham, fake.

SYNONYM STUDY: **spurious**

APOCRYPHAL, ARTIFICIAL, COUNTERFEIT, ERSATZ, SYNTHETIC. These adjectives pertain to what is false or not what it appears to be, although not all have negative connotations. **Artificial** implies man-made, especially in imitation of something natural (*artificial flowers; artificial turf*). A **synthetic** substance or material is one produced by a chemical process and used as a substitute for the natural substance it resembles (*boots made from synthetic rubber*). Something that is **counterfeit** is an imitation of something else—usually something rarer, finer, or more valuable—and is intended to deceive or defraud (*counterfeit bills*). **Spurious** also means false rather than true or genuine, but it carries no strong implication of being an imitation (*spurious letters falsely attributed to Winston Churchill*). **Ersatz** refers to an *artificial* substitute that is usually inferior (*ersatz tea made from birch bark and herbs*). The meaning of **apocryphal**, however, is much more restricted. It applies to accounts of the past whose truth or accuracy cannot be ascertained (*an apocryphal story about George Washington as a boy*).

---

spurn /spərn/ *v.* reject with disdain; treat with contempt. □□ **spurn′er** *n.*

■ disdain, scorn, despise, rebuff, repudiate, refuse, sneer at, snub, cold-shoulder, brush off, turn down.

spurt /spərt/ • *v.* **1 a** *intr.* gush out in a jet or stream. **b** *tr.* cause (liquid, etc.) to do this. **2** *intr.* make a sudden effort. • *n.* **1** sudden gushing out; jet. **2** short sudden effort or increase of pace, esp. in racing.

■ *v.* **1 a** spew, squirt, shoot, spout, stream, spray, jet, erupt, burst, surge. **b** spew, squirt, shoot, spout, stream, spray. • *n.* **1** see GUSH *n.* 1. **2** burst, access, outbreak; advance, acceleration, rise; see also DASH *n.* 1.

sput•nik /spŏŏtnĭk, spŭt–/ *n.* each of a series of Russian artificial satellites launched from 1957.

sput•ter /spŭtər/ • *v.* **1** *intr.* emit spitting sounds. **2** *intr.* speak in a hurried or vehement fashion. **3** *tr.* emit with a spitting sound. **4** *tr.* speak or utter rapidly or incoherently. • *n.* sputtering. □□ **sput′ter•er** *n.*

spu•tum /spyŏŏtəm/ *n.* (*pl.* **spu•ta** /–tə/) **1** saliva; spittle. **2** expectorated matter, usu. a sign of disease.

spy /spī/ • *n.* (*pl.* **spies**) **1** person who secretly collects and reports information on the activities, movements, etc., of an enemy, competitor, etc. **2** person who keeps watch on others, esp. furtively. • *v.* (**spies**, **spied**) **1** *tr.* discern; see. **2** *intr.* act as a spy. □□ **spy′ ing** *n.*

■ *n.* double agent, foreign agent, secret (-service) agent, fifth columnist, CIA man *or* woman *or* agent; informer, informant, stool pigeon, *colloq.* mole, snoop, snooper. • *v.* **1** glimpse, spot, catch sight of, sight, catch a glimpse of, make out. **2** follow, shadow, trail, watch, observe, reconnoiter. □□ **spying** espionage, undercover work, intelligence, surveillance.

spy•glass /spīglas/ *n.* small telescope.

sq. *abbr.* square.

squab /skwob/ *n.* young pigeon or other bird.

squab•ble /skwobəl/ • *n.* petty or noisy quarrel. See synonym study at QUARREL. • *v.intr.* engage in a squabble. □□ **squab′bler** *n.*

squad /skwod/ *n.* **1** small group of people sharing a task, etc.; esp. of soldiers or policemen. **2** *Sports* team. □ **squad car** police car.

■ unit, band, company, crew, force, troop, cohort, corps.

squad•ron /skwodrən/ *n.* unit of aircraft, warships, etc.

squal•id /skwolĭd/ *adj.* **1** filthy. **2** mean or poor. □□ **squa•lid′i•ty** /skwolĭd′ĭtē/ *n.* **squal′id•ly** *adv.* **squal′id•ness** *n.*

squall /skwawl/ • *n.* **1** sudden or violent wind, esp. with rain or snow or sleet. **2** discordant cry; scream (esp. of a baby). • *v.intr.* utter a squall; scream. □□ **squal′ly** *adj.*

squa•lor /skwolər/ *n.* state of being filthy or squalid.

squan•der /skwondər/ *v.tr.* spend (money, time, etc.) wastefully. □□ **squan′der•er** *n.*

square /skwair/ • *n.* **1** equilateral rectangle. **2** open (usu. four-sided) area surrounded by buildings. **3** product of a number multiplied by itself (*81 is the square of 9*). **4** L-shaped or T-shaped instrument for obtaining or testing right angles. **5** *sl.* conventional or old-fashioned person. • *adj.* **1** having the shape of a square. **2** having or in the form of a right angle (*table with square corners*). **3** angular and not round. **4** designating the area of a square whose side is the length of the unit specified (*square mile*). **5** level; parallel. **6** at right angles. **7** equal; settled. **8** fair and honest. **9** *sl.* conventional or old-fashioned.

• *adv.* squarely. • *v.* **1** *tr.* make square. **2** *tr.* multiply (a number) by itself (*3 squared is 9*). **3** *tr. & intr.* reconcile (*the results do not square with your conclusions*). **4** *tr.* settle or pay (a bill, etc.). **5** *tr.* place (one's shoulders, etc.) squarely facing forward. □ **square dance** dance with usu. four couples facing inward from four sides. **square meal** substantial and satisfying meal. **square off** assume the attitude of a boxer. **square root** number that multiplied by itself gives a specified number. □□ **square′ly** *adv.* **square′ness** *n.* **squar′ish** *adj.*

■ *n.* **2** plaza, piazza, place, park, (village) green, marketplace, market (square), quadrangle; parade ground. **5** conservative, conformist, traditionalist, bourgeois, (old) fogy, die-hard; *colloq.* straight, stuffed shirt. • *adj.* **1** equilateral, quadrangular, rectangular, quadrilateral, four-sided, boxy. **2** right-angled. **5** equal, on a par, even; quits, settled, balanced. **7** straight, straightened out, organized, arranged; even, level, drawn, tied. **8** honorable, upright, straightforward, decent, ethical. **9** conservative, unsophisticated, provincial, behind the times, conformist, straitlaced, bourgeois. • *adv.* see FULL[1] *adv.* 2. • *v.* **3** adapt, adjust, change, modify, harmonize, accommodate, arrange, fit; meet, match (with), conform to *or* with, comply with. **4** see SETTLE[1] 8. **5** stiffen, throw back, straighten (up), tense. □□ **squarely** see FULL[1] *adv.* 2.

squash[1] /skwosh/ • *v.* **1** *tr.* crush or squeeze flat or into pulp. **2** *intr.* make one's way by squeezing. **3** *tr.* dismiss (a proposal, etc.). • *n.* game played with rackets and a small ball against the walls of a closed court. □□ **squash′y** *adj.* (**squash•i•er**, **squash•i•est**). **squash′i•ly** *adv.* **squash′i•ness** *n.*

squash[2] /skwosh/ *n.* (*pl.* same or **squash•es**) plant with gourdlike fruit that may be used as a vegetable.

squat /skwot/ • *v.* (**squat•ted**, **squat•ting**) **1** *intr.* sit on one's heels or on the ground, etc., with the knees drawn up. **2 a** *intr.* act as a squatter. **b** *tr.* occupy (a building) as a squatter. • *adj.* (**squat•ter**, **squat•test**) (of a person, etc.) short and thick; dumpy. • *n.* squatting posture.

■ *v.* **1** see CROUCH *v.* • *adj.* see DUMPY. • *n.* crouch, stoop, hunch.

squat•ter /skwotər/ *n.* person who takes unauthorized possession of unoccupied premises.

squaw /skwaw/ *n.* often *offens.* Native American woman or wife.

squawk /skwawk/ • *n.* **1** loud harsh cry, esp. of a bird. **2** complaint. • *v.* utter with or make a squawk. □□ **squawk′er** *n.*

■ *n.* **1** screech, shriek, yell, yowl, whoop, hoot, scream, call, wail, squall, cackle. **2** grumble, whine, protest, objection, *colloq.* gripe, grouse, grouch, *sl.* beef. • *v.* **1** screech, shriek, yell, yowl, whoop, hoot, scream; complain, grumble, whine, protest, object.

squeak /skwēk/ • *n.* **1** short shrill cry or sound. **2** (also **nar′row squeak**) narrow escape. • *v.* **1** *intr.* make a squeak. **2** *tr.* utter (words) shrilly. **3** *intr.* [foll. by *by*, *through*] *colloq.* pass narrowly. □□ **squeak'er** *n.*

squeak'i•ly *adv.* **squeak'i•ness** *n.* **squeak'y** *adj.* (**squeak•i•er, squeak•i•est**).

■ *n.* **1** see PEEP² *n.* 1. **2** see *near miss.* • *v.* **1, 2** see PEEP² *v.*, SING *v.* 3. **3** see SCRAPE *v.* 7b.

squeal /skweel/ • *n.* prolonged shrill sound, esp. a cry of a child or a pig. • *v.* **1** make a squeal. **2** *tr.* utter (words) with a squeal. **3** *intr. sl.* turn informer. □□ **squeal'er** *n.*

squeam•ish /skweémish/ *adj.* **1** easily nauseated or disgusted. **2** fastidious; sensitive. □□ **squeam'ish•ly** *adv.* **squeam'ish•ness** *n.*

■ **1** qualmish, queasy, easily revolted. **2** dainty, delicate, prudish, qualmish, punctilious, fussy, overscrupulous.

squee•gee /skweéjee/ *n.* rubber-edged implement often set on a long handle and used for cleaning windows, etc.

squeeze /skweez/ • *v.tr.* **1 a** exert pressure on. **b** reduce the size of or alter the shape of by squeezing. **2** force (a person or thing) into or through a small or narrow space. **3 a** harass by exactions; bring pressure to bear on. **b** obtain (money, etc.) by extortion, entreaty, etc. **4** press or hold closely as a sign of sympathy, affection, etc. • *n.* **1** squeezing; being squeezed. **2** close embrace. **3** crowd or crowded state; crush. **4** small quantity produced by squeezing (*a squeeze of lemon*). **5** *Econ.* restriction on borrowing, investment, etc., in a financial crisis. □ **put the squeeze on** *colloq.* coerce or pressure (a person). □□ **squeez'a•ble** *adj.* **squeez'er** *n.*

■ *v.* **1** press, compress, compact, constrict, crush, squash, wring. **2** ram, jam, pack, squash, stuff, cram, crowd. **3 a** milk, bleed, screw, *colloq.* lean on, put the screws on, put the squeeze on, twist a person's arm. **b** extract, wrest, exact, extort, screw, wrench. **4** clasp, clench, clutch, grip, clip; embrace, hug. • *n.* **1** pinch, nip, tweak, grip. **2** clasp, hug, clutch, grasp, grip, *colloq.* clinch. **3** jam, squash, press. **5** pressure, restrictions. □ **put the squeeze on** press, bring pressure to bear on, put the screws on, twist a person's arm.

squelch /skwelch/ • *v.* **1** *intr.* **a** make a sucking sound as of treading in thick mud. **b** move with a squelching sound. **2** *tr.* suppress; silence. • *n.* instance of squelching. □□ **squelch'er** *n.* **squelch'y** *adj.*

■ *v.* **2** subdue, put down, quell, quash, defeat, overcome, humiliate, disconcert, shoot down; stamp on, squash, crush, quash, quell, put an end to.

squib /skwib/ *n.* **1** small hissing firework that finally explodes. **2** short satirical composition; lampoon.

squid /skwid/ *n.* ten-armed cephalopod used as bait or food.

squig•gle /skwígəl/ • *n.* short curly line, esp. in handwriting or doodling. • *v.* make such lines. □□ **squig'gly** *adj.*

squint /skwint/ • *v.intr.* **1** have the eyes turned in different directions; have a squint. **2** look obliquely or with half closed eyes. • *n.* **1** = STRABISMUS. **2** stealthy or sidelong glance. □□ **squint'er** *n.* **squint'y** *adj.*

squire /skwīr/ • *n.* **1** country gentleman, esp.

the chief landowner in a country district. **2** *hist.* knight's attendant. • *v.tr.* (of a man) attend upon or escort (a woman).

squirm /skwərm/ • *v.intr.* **1** wriggle; writhe. **2** show or feel embarrassment. • *n.* squirming movement. □□ **squirm'er** *n.* **squirm'y** *adj.* (**squirm•i•er, squirm•i•est**).

■ *v.* **1** twist, flounder, shift, fidget. **2** be (very) embarrassed, agonize, sweat. • *n.* see WRIGGLE *n.*

squir•rel /skwórəl, skwúr-/ • *n.* **1** tree-dwelling rodent with a bushy tail. **2** fur of this animal. • *v.tr.* hoard.

squirt /skwərt/ • *v.* **1** *tr.* eject (liquid or powder) in a jet. **2** *intr.* be discharged in this way. **3** *tr.* splash with liquid or powder ejected by squirting. • *n.* **1 a** jet of water, etc. **b** small quantity produced by squirting. **2** *colloq.* insignificant but presumptuous person. □□ **squirt'er** *n.*

squish /skwish/ • *n.* slight squelching sound. • *v.intr.* move with a squish. □□ **squish'y** *adj.* (**squish•i•er, squish•i•est**).

Sr *symb. Chem.* strontium.

Sr. *abbr.* **1** Senior. **2** Señor. **3** Signor. **4** *Eccl.* Sister.

Sri Lank•an /shree lángkən, sree/ • *n.* **1** native or inhabitant of Sri Lanka (formerly Ceylon), an island in the Indian Ocean. **2** person of Sri Lankan descent. • *adj.* of or relating to Sri Lanka or its people.

SRO *abbr.* standing room only.

SS *abbr.* **1** steamship. **2** *hist.* Nazi special police force.

SSA *abbr.* Social Security Administration.

SSS *abbr.* Selective Service System.

SST *abbr.* supersonic transport.

St. *abbr.* **1** Street. **2** Saint.

stab /stab/ • *v.* (**stabbed, stab•bing**) **1** *tr.* pierce or wound with a knife, etc. **2** *intr.* aim a blow with or as if with such a weapon. **3** *intr.* cause a sensation like being stabbed. • *n.* **1 a** instance of stabbing. **b** blow or thrust with a knife, etc. **2** wound made in this way. **3** sharp pain. **4** *colloq.* attempt; try. □□ **stab'ber** *n.*

■ *v.* **1** stick, puncture, prick, lance, jab, run through, impale, gore, transfix, knife. **2** lunge, poke, thrust. **3** see SMART *v.* • *n.* **1, 2** jab; prick, puncture. **3** pang, twinge, sting, ache, hurt, stitch. **4** guess, conjecture; *colloq.* crack, go, shot.

sta•bil•i•ty /stəbílitee/ *n.* quality or state of being stable.

■ steadiness, solidity, firmness, soundness, sturdiness, strength; steadfastness, constancy, dependability.

sta•bi•lize /stáybilīz/ *v.* make or become stable. □□ **sta•bi•li•za'tion** *n.*

sta•bi•liz•er /stáybilīzər/ *n.* device or substance used to keep something stable, esp. in a ship or aircraft.

sta•ble¹ /stáybəl/ *adj.* (**sta•bler, sta•blest**) **1** firmly fixed or established. **2** (of a person) well-adjusted; sane; reliable; sensible. □□ **sta'ble•ness** *n.* **sta'bly** *adv.*

■ **1** steady, solid, firm, sound, sturdy, strong, durable, well-founded, fast, sure, deep-rooted. **2** (well-)balanced, responsible, reasonable; competent, accountable.

sta•ble² /stáybəl/ • *n.* **1** building for keeping horses. **2** establishment where racehorses are trained. **3** persons, products, etc., having a common origin or affiliation. • *v.tr.* put or keep in a stable. □□ **sta′ble•ful** *n.* (*pl.* **–fuls**).

stac•ca•to /stəkáató/ esp. *Mus. adv. & adj.* with each sound or note sharply detached or separated from the others.

stack /stak/ • *n.* **1** pile or heap, esp. in orderly arrangement. **2** stacked pile of hay, straw, etc. **3** *colloq.* large quantity. **4** = SMOKE-STACK.. **5** (also **stacks**) part of a library where books are compactly stored. • *v.tr.* **1** pile in a stack or stacks. **2 a** arrange (cards) secretly for cheating. **b** manipulate (circumstances, etc.) to one's advantage. □□ **stack′a•ble** *adj.* **stack′er** *n.*

 ■ *n.* **1** mound, mass, accumulation, hill, mountain, store, stock, bank, deposit, supply. **2** haystack, mow, cock, haycock, rick, hayrick. **3** collection, aggregation, accumulation, mass, load, lot, pile. **4** chimney, chimney stack, funnel. • *v.* **1** stack up, heap, accumulate, amass, store, stock, stockpile, hoard.

sta•di•um /stáydeeəm/ *n.* (*pl.* **sta•di•ums** or **sta•di•a** /–deeə/) athletic or sports arena with tiers of seats for spectators.

staff /staf/ • *n.* **1** (*pl.* **staffs** or **staves** /stayvz/) **a** stick or pole for use in walking or climbing or as a weapon. **b** stick or pole as a sign of office or authority. **2 a** body of persons employed in a business, etc. **b** those in authority within an organization, esp. the teachers in a school. **c** *Mil., etc.* body of officers. **3** (also **staves**) (*pl.* **staffs** or **staves**) *Mus.* set of *usu.* five parallel lines on or between which a note is placed to indicate its pitch. • *v.tr.* provide (an institution, etc.) with staff. □□ **staffed** *adj.* [also in *comb.*].

 ■ *n.* **1** standard, baton, rod, pikestaff, pike, stake, cane, stave, club, truncheon, mace, crook, crozier, scepter, wand. **2** personnel, employees, help, workforce, crew, team, organization. • *v.* man, people, crew.

stag /stag/ • *n.* adult male deer. • *adj.* for men only, as a party, etc.

stage /stayj/ • *n.* **1** point or period in a process or development (*is in the larval stage*). **2 a** raised floor or platform, esp. one on which plays, etc., are performed. **b** [prec. by *the*] theatrical profession. **c** scene of action. **3 a** regular stopping place on a route. **b** distance between two stopping places. **4** *Astronaut.* section of a rocket with a separate engine. • *v.tr.* **1** present (a play, etc.) on stage. **2** arrange the occurrence of (*staged a comeback*). □ **stage fright** nervousness on facing an audience.

 ■ *n.* **1** position, situation, grade, level, step, station, place, spot, juncture, division, phase, lap; status, condition. **2 a** dais, podium; rostrum. **b** (*the stage*) show business, the theater, the boards, the footlights; acting; *colloq.* showbiz. **3 b** see SECTION *n.* 2. • *v.* **1** put on,

produce, mount, exhibit. **2** put on, contrive, organize, originate, devise, make up, concoct, fake.

stage•coach /stáyjkōch/ *n. hist.* large enclosed horse-drawn coach running regularly by stages between two places.

stage•craft /stáyjkraft/ *n.* theatrical skill or experience.

stage•hand /stáyjhand/ *n.* person handling scenery, etc., during a performance on stage.

stag•fla•tion /stagfláyshən/ *n. Econ.* state of inflation without a corresponding increase of demand and employment.

stag•ger /stágər/ • *v.* **1 a** *intr.* walk unsteadily; totter. **b** *tr.* cause to totter. **2** *tr.* shock; confuse. **3** *tr.* arrange (events, hours of work, etc.) so that they do not coincide. **4** *tr.* arrange (objects) so that they are not in line. • *n.* **1** tottering movement. **2** [in *pl.*] disease of the brain and spinal cord, esp. in horses and cattle, causing staggering. □□ **stag′ger•er** *n.*

 ■ *v.* **1 a** dodder, reel, lurch, teeter, sway, stumble, falter. **2** surprise, amaze, astound, astonish, overwhelm, overcome, dumbfound, stupefy, stun. **3, 4** alternate, space (out), vary, rearrange.

stag•ger•ing /stágəring/ *adj.* **1** astonishing; bewildering. **2** that staggers. □□ **stag′ger•ing•ly** *adv.*

stag•nant /stágnənt/ *adj.* **1** (of liquid) motionless; having no current. **2** (of life, action, the mind, etc.) showing no activity; dull; sluggish. □□ **stag′nan•cy** *n.* **stag′nant•ly** *adv.*

 ■ **1** standing, still, quiet, sluggish, unmoving, immobile, flat; stale, foul, putrid.

stag•nate /stágnayt/ *v.intr.* be or become stagnant. □□ **stag•na′tion** /–náyshən/ *n.*

 ■ languish, idle, vegetate, deteriorate, degenerate, decline, decay, rust, molder, decompose, spoil, rot.

staid /stayd/ *adj.* of quiet and steady character; sedate. □□ **staid′ly** *adv.* **staid′ness** *n.*

 ■ rigid, stiff, prim, dignified, sober, calm, quiet.

stain /stayn/ • *v.* **1** *tr. & intr.* discolor or be discolored by the action of liquid sinking in. **2** *tr.* damage (a reputation, character, etc.). **3** *tr.* color (wood, glass, etc.) by a process other than painting or covering the surface. **4** *tr.* impregnate (a specimen) for microscopic examination with coloring matter. • *n.* **1** discoloration; spot; mark. **2 a** blot or blemish. **b** damage to a reputation, etc. **3** substance used in staining. □ **stained glass** dyed or colored glass, esp. in a lead framework in a window (also (with hyphen) *attrib.: stained-glass window*). □□ **stain′a•ble** *adj.* **stain′er** *n.*

 ■ *v.* **1** blot, mark, spot, blotch, speckle, dye, tinge. **2** spoil, defile, ruin, smirch, besmirch, taint, tarnish. • *n.* **1** blot, blotch, smirch, speck, *colloq.* splotch. **2** mark, stigma, smirch, smudge. **3** dye, color, coloring, colorant, tint, tinge, pigment.

stain•less steel /stáynlis steel/ *n.* steel alloy not liable to rust or tarnish under ordinary conditions.

stair /stair/ *n.* **1** each of a set of fixed indoor

steps. **2** [usu. in *pl.*] set of esp. indoor steps (*passed him on the stairs*).

■ see STEP *n.* 4a.

stair•case /stáirkays/ *n.* **1** flight of stairs and the supporting structure. **2** part of a building containing a staircase.

stair•way /stáirway/ *n.* flight of stairs; staircase.

stair•well /stáirwel/ *n.* shaft in which a staircase is built.

stake[1] /stayk/ • *n.* **1** stout, sharpened stick or post driven into the ground as a support, boundary mark, etc. **2** *hist.* post to which a person was tied to be burned alive. • *v.tr.* **1** fasten, secure, or support with a stake or stakes. **2** [foll. by *off*, *out*] mark off (an area) with stakes. **3** establish (a claim). □ **stake out** *colloq.* place under surveillance.

■ *n.* **1** spike, picket, paling, pale, pole, pike; palisade, upright, pillar. • *v.* **1** tether, tie (up), picket, lash, leash, hitch. **2** define, delimit, outline, demarcate; fence (in *or* off), enclose.

stake[2] /stayk/ • *n.* **1** sum of money, etc., wagered. **2** interest or concern, esp financial. **3** [in *pl.*] prize money, esp. in a horse race. • *v.tr.* **1** wager. **2** *colloq.* support, esp. financially. □ **at stake** risked; to be won or lost. □□ **stak'er** *n.*

■ *n.* **1** bet, wager, ante, risk, hazard. **2** investment, share, involvement. **3** (*stakes*) see PRIZE[1] *n.* 2. • *v.* **1** bet, gamble, put, risk, venture, chance, hazard. □ **at stake** at hazard, hazarded, at risk, on the table.

stake•out /stáykowt/ *n. colloq.* period of surveillance.

sta•lac•tite /stəláktīt, stálək-/ *n.* deposit of calcium carbonate having the shape of a large icicle hanging from the roof of a cave, cliff overhang, etc.

sta•lag•mite /stəlágmīt, stáləg-/ *n.* deposit of calcium carbonate in the shape of a large inverted icicle rising from the floor of a cave, etc.

stale /stayl/ • *adj.* (**stal•er**, **stal•est**) **1** not fresh; musty; insipid. **2** trite or unoriginal. • *v.* make or become stale. □□ **stale'ness** *n.*

■ *adj.* **1** old, past its prime, dry, dried-out, hardened, limp, flat, sour, rank. **2** old, banal, overused, antiquated, old-fashioned, threadbare, clichéd, hackneyed.

stale•mate /stáylmayt/ • *n.* **1** *Chess* position counting as a draw, in which a player cannot move except into check. **2** deadlock; drawn contest. • *v.tr.* **1** *Chess* bring (a player) to a stalemate. **2** bring to a standstill.

■ *n.* **1** impasse, standstill, (dead *or* full) stop, tie, draw, checkmate, stand-off.

stalk[1] /stawk/ *n.* main stem of a plant; leaf, flower, fruit, etc. □□ **stalked** *adj.* [also in *comb.*]. **stalk'y** *adj.*

■ trunk, cane, main axis, shaft; leafstalk, spike, shoot.

stalk[2] /stawk/ • *v.* **1 a** *tr.* pursue stealthily. **b** *intr.* steal up to game under cover. **2** *intr.* stride; walk in a stately or haughty manner. • *n.* **1** stalking of game. **2** imposing gait. □□ **stalk'er** *n.* [also in *comb.*].

■ *v.* **1 a** follow, dog, haunt, shadow, trail, track (down), hunt (down), prey on.

stall[1] /stawl/ • *n.* **1** trader's stand or booth in

a market, etc. **2** compartment for one animal in a stable, etc. **3** fixed, usu. partly enclosed, seat in the choir or chancel of a church. **4** compartment for one person in a shower, toilet, etc. **5** loss of engine power. • *v.* **1** *intr.* (of a vehicle or its engine) stop or lose power because of an overload on the engine or an inadequate supply of fuel to it. **2** *tr.* cause to stall.

■ *n.* **1** cubicle, kiosk; compartment, alcove, section, space; counter, table. **2** shed, pen, cote, fold, coop, sty, enclosure. • *v.* **1** halt, die, shut down, fail, cease operating, come to a standstill, quit.

stall[2] /stawl/ *v.* **1** *intr.* play for time when being questioned, etc. **2** *tr.* delay; obstruct; block.

■ **1** delay, dawdle, dally, temporize, equivocate, hesitate, prevaricate; vacillate, dither; beat about the bush, drag one's feet. **2** see OBSTRUCT 2.

stal•lion /stályən/ *n.* uncastrated adult male horse.

stal•wart /stáwlwərt/ • *adj.* **1** strongly built; sturdy. **2** courageous; resolute; determined. • *n.* stalwart person, esp. a loyal partisan. □□ **stal'wart•ly** *adv.*

■ *adj.* **1** robust, stout, strong, mighty, powerful, rugged, staunch, hardy, vigorous. **2** brave, daring, intrepid, valiant, heroic, manly; redoubtable, undaunted, firm, unbending, steadfast, staunch. • *n.* supporter, upholder, sustainer, loyalist; hero, heroine.

sta•men /stáymən/ *n.* male fertilizing organ of a flowering plant, including the anther containing pollen.

stam•i•na /stáminə/ *n.* physical or mental endurance.

■ ruggedness, vigor, vigorousness, fortitude, robustness, indefatigability, (staying) power, energy.

stam•mer /stámər/ • *v.* **1** *intr.* speak with halting articulation, esp. with pauses or rapid repetitions of the same syllable. **2** *tr.* utter (words) in this way (*stammered out an excuse*). • *n.* **1** tendency to stammer. **2** instance of stammering. □□ **stam'mer•er** *n.* **stam'mer•ing•ly** *adv.*

■ *v.* **1** stutter, hesitate, stumble, falter. • *n.* stutter.

stamp /stamp/ • *v.* **1 a** *tr.* bring down (one's foot) heavily on the ground, etc. **b** *tr.* crush or flatten in this way. **c** *intr.* walk with heavy steps. **2** *tr.* **a** impress (a pattern, mark, etc.) on a surface. **b** impress (a surface) with a pattern, etc. **3** *tr.* affix a postage or other stamp to. **4** *tr.* assign a specific character to; characterize; mark out (*stamps the story an invention*). • *n.* **1** instrument for stamping. **2** mark or pattern made by this; esp. as an official authorization or certification. **3** small adhesive piece of paper indicating that a price, fee, or tax has been paid, esp. a postage stamp. **4 a** heavy downward blow with the foot. **b** sound of this. **5 a** characteristic mark or impression (*bears the stamp of genius*). **b** character; kind. □ **stamp out 1** produce by cutting out with a die, etc.

2 put an end to; crush; destroy. □□ **stamp′er** *n.*

■ *v.* **1 b** trample, tramp, squash, press, tread on, *colloq.* squish. **c** tramp, stomp, thump; tread *or* step heavily. **2** mark, imprint, print, brand; engrave, emboss, inscribe. **4** brand, label, tag, term, name, style, identify, categorize, classify. ● *n.* **1** die, block, punch, seal, matrix, plate; signet (ring). **2** seal, trademark, brand, logotype, symbol, representation, colophon, imprint, emblem, insignia, label, *colloq.* logo. **5 a** sign, impress, hallmark, earmark, trait(s), feature(s), characteristic(s). **b** sort, make, fashion, type, cast, mold. □ **stamp out 2** eliminate, eradicate, abolish, get rid of, annihilate; quell, subdue, suppress, squelch, repress.

stam•pede /stampēd′/ ● *n.* **1** sudden flight or hurried movement of animals or people. **2** spontaneous response of many persons to a common impulse. ● *v.* **1** *intr.* take part in a stampede. **2** *tr.* cause to do this. □□ **stam•ped′er** *n.*

■ *n.* rout, scattering, panic, rush, dash. ● *v.* **1** rush, run, race, charge, take to one's heels, dash, flee, take flight. **2** panic, frighten, rush, scatter, rout, put to flight.

stance /stans/ *n.* **1** attitude or position of the body, esp. when hitting a ball, etc. **2** standpoint; attitude of mind.

■ **1** posture, stand, carriage, bearing, deportment. **2** viewpoint, point of view, stand; see also POSITION *n.* 5.

stanch /stawnch, stanch, staanch/ *v.tr.* (also **staunch**) **1** restrain the flow of (esp. blood). **2** restrain the flow from (esp. a wound).

stan•chion /stánshən, –chən/ *n.* **1** post or pillar; upright support; vertical strut. **2** upright bar, pair of bars, or frame for confining cattle in a stall.

stand /stand/ ● *v.* (*past* and *past part.* **stood** /stood/) **1** *intr.* have or take or maintain an upright position, esp. on the feet or a base. **2** *intr.* be situated (*here once stood a village*). **3** *intr.* be of a specified height. **4** *intr.* be in a specified condition (*stands accused*). **5** *tr.* place or set in an upright or specified position (*stood it against the wall*). **6** *intr.* **a** move to and remain in a specified position (*stand aside*). **b** take a specified attitude (*stand aloof*). **7** *intr.* remain valid or unaltered. **8** *tr.* endure; tolerate. **9** *tr.* provide at one's own expense (*stood him a drink*). ● *n.* **1** cessation from motion or progress; a stoppage. **2** resistance to attack or compulsion (esp. *make a stand*). **3** rack, set of shelves, etc. **4** small open-fronted structure for a trader outdoors or in a market, etc. **5** standing place for vehicles. **6 a** [usu. in *pl.*] a raised structure to sit or stand on. **b** witness box. **7 a** *Theatr.*, *etc.* each halt made on a tour to give one or more performances. **b** *Sports* each place in which a traveling team plays one or more games (*two-game stand in Boston*). **8** group of growing plants (*stand of trees*). □ **as it stands 1** in its present condition. **2** in the present circumstances. **stand back 1** withdraw; take up a position further from the front. **2** with-

draw psychologically in order to take an objective view. **stand by 1** look on without interfering. **2** uphold; support (a person). **3** adhere to (terms or promises). **4** wait; stand ready for. **stand a chance** see CHANCE². **stand for 1** represent; signify; imply (*"US" stands for "United States"*). **2** [often with *neg.*] *colloq.* endure; tolerate; acquiesce in. **stand one's ground** maintain one's position, not yield. **stand-in** *n.* deputy or substitute. **stand off** move or keep away; keep one's distance. **stand out 1** be prominent or conspicuous or outstanding. **2** [usu. foll. by *against, for*] hold out; persist in opposition or support or endurance. **stand pat** see PAT. **stand to** be likely or certain to (*stands to lose everything*). **stand up 1 a** rise to one's feet. **b** come to or remain in or place in a standing position. **2** (of an argument, etc.) be valid. **3** *colloq.* fail to keep an appointment with. **stand up for 1** support; side with; maintain (a person or cause). **2** serve as best man, maid of honor, or other attendant in a wedding. **stand up to 1** meet or face (an opponent) courageously. **2** be resistant to the harmful effects of (wear, use, etc.). □□ **stand′er** *n.*

■ *v.* **1** stand up, rise, get up; stay, remain (standing). **2** be, be located *or* positioned, exist, lie. **5** stand up, position; upend. **7** continue, remain, prevail, apply. **8** survive, countenance, face, confront. **9** treat to, buy. ● *n.* **1** see STANDSTILL. **2** defense, effort. **3** frame, bracket; hatstand, coatrack; easel; tripod. **4** counter, booth, stall, table. **5** lot. **6 a** platform, dais, stage. **b** witness stand. **7** stop, stay; performance, show. **8** copse, grove, wood, thicket. □ **stand by 2** defend, back, stand up for, stick up for. **3** stick to, support, maintain, persist in. **stand for 1** symbolize, betoken, mean. **2** see STAND *v.* 8 above. **stand-in** double, stunt man; surrogate, replacement. **stand out 1** be noticeable, be noteworthy; protrude, project, stick out. **stand up 1 a** stand, rise, get up, be upstanding. **b** see STAND *v.* 1 above. **3** jilt. **stand up for 1** defend, take the side of, champion. **stand up to 1** confront, face up to, brave, challenge, dispute. **2** resist, defy, withstand, endure, outlast.

stan•dard /stándərd/ ● *n.* **1** object or quality or measure serving as a basis or example or principle by which others are judged. **2** the degree of excellence, etc., required for a particular purpose. **3** distinctive flag. **4** upright support. **5** tune or song of established popularity. ● *adj.* **1** serving or used as a standard. **2** of a normal or prescribed but not exceptional quality or size, etc. **3** having recognized and permanent value; authoritative. **4** (of language) conforming to established educated usage (*Standard English*). □ **standard-bearer 1** soldier who carries a standard. **2** prominent leader in a cause. **standard of living** degree of material comfort available to a person or class or community. **standard time** uniform time for places in approximately the same longitude, established in a country or region by law or custom.

■ *n.* **1** model, pattern, archetype, paradigm, paragon, exemplar; criterion, measure, benchmark, touchstone, yardstick. **2** quality, grade, level, rating. **3** banner, ensign, jack, emblem, pennant. **4** upright, pole, post, stanchion, lamppost, column, pillar, pedestal. • *adj.* **2–4** recognized, prevailing, prevalent, usual, customary, habitual, orthodox, set, established, prescribed, defined, required, regular, familiar, ordinary, traditional, accepted, approved.

stand•ard•ize /stándərdīz/ *v.tr.* cause to conform to a standard. □□ **stand•ard•i•za'tion** *n.*

stand•by /stándbī/ *n.* (*pl.* **stand•bys**) **1** person or thing ready if needed in an emergency, etc. **2** readiness for duty (*on standby*).

stand•ing /stánding/ • *n.* **1** esteem or repute, esp. high; status; position. **2** duration (*long standing*). • *adj.* **1** upright. **2** established; permanent (*standing rule*). **3** (of a jump, start, race, etc.) performed from rest or from a standing position. **4** (of water) stagnant.

■ *n.* **1** eminence, prominence, reputation; rank, station, footing. **2** endurance, longevity. • *adj.* **1** erect, on one's feet, vertical, unseated. **2** set, standard, conventional, customary, usual, normal, regular, fixed. **4** motionless, unmoving, stationary, still.

stand•off•ish /stándáwfish, -óf-/ *adj.* cold or distant in manner. □□ **stand•off'ish•ly** *adv.* **stand•off'ish•ness** *n.*

■ aloof, haughty, unsocial, reserved, cool, frosty, frigid, withdrawn, remote; Olympian, lordly, pompous.

stand•pipe /stándpīp/ *n.* vertical pipe extending from a water supply.

stand•point /stándpoynt/ *n.* point of view.

■ viewpoint, vantage point, position, stance, perspective, angle, aspect; view, outlook, attitude, opinion.

stand•still /stándstil/ *n.* stoppage; inability to proceed.

■ (dead *or* full) stop, halt, stand, deadlock, impasse.

stank *past of* STINK.

stan•za /stánzə/ *n.* basic metrical unit in a poem *or* verse, typically of four *or* more lines.

sta•ple[1] /stáypəl/ • *n.* U-shaped metal bar *or* piece of wire with pointed ends for driving into and holding together papers, etc. • *v.tr.* provide *or* fasten with a staple. □□ **sta'pler** *n.*

sta•ple[2] /stáypəl/ • *n.* **1** principal *or* important article of commerce. **2** chief element *or* main component. **3** fiber of cotton *or* wool, etc., as determining its quality (*cotton of fine staple*). • *adj.* **1** main *or* principal (*staple commodities*). **2** important as a product or an export.

■ *n.* **1, 2** necessity, essential, basic, fundamental. • *adj.* **1** basic, elementary, essential, necessary, fundamental, primary, chief; standard, usual, habitual.

star /staar/ • *n.* **1** celestial body appearing as a luminous point in the night sky. **2** large naturally luminous gaseous body such as the sun is. **3** celestial body regarded as influencing a person's fortunes, etc. **4** thing resem-

---

bling a star in shape or appearance. **5** figure or object with radiating points esp. as a decoration or mark of rank, or to show a category of excellence (*five-star hotel*). **6 a** famous or brilliant person; principal performer. **b** [*attrib.*] outstanding (*star pupil*). • *v.* (**starred, star•ring**) **1** *tr.* (of a movie, etc.) feature as a principal performer. **2** *intr.* (of a performer) be featured in a movie, etc. □ **Star of David** two interlaced equilateral triangles used as a Jewish and Israeli symbol. **Stars and Stripes** national flag of the US. **star-spangled** (esp. of the US national flag) covered or glittering with stars. □□ **star'dom** *n.* **star'less** *adj.* **star' like** *adj.*

■ *n.* **1** body, heavenly body; fixed star, evening star, morning star, falling star, shooting star, comet. **4** asterisk, pentagram. **6 a** celebrity, personage, dignitary, VIP, name, somebody, luminary, lead, principal, diva, prima donna, hero, heroine, idol, superstar. **b** principal, major, leading, important, celebrated, famous, famed, prominent. • *v.* play *or* perform *or* act *or* take the lead *or* leading part *or* leading role.

star•board /staarbərd/ *Naut. & Aeron.* *n.* right-hand side (looking forward) of a ship, boat, or aircraft.

starch /staarch/ • *n.* **1** polysaccharide obtained chiefly from cereals and potatoes. **2** preparation of this for stiffening fabric before ironing. **3** stiffness of manner; formality. • *v.tr.* stiffen (*clothing*) with starch. □□ **starch'er** *n.*

starch•y /staarchee/ *adj.* (**starch•i•er, starch•i•est**) **1** of, like, or containing much starch. □□ **starch'i•ly** *adv.* **starch'i•ness** *n.*

stare /stair/ • *v.intr.* look fixedly with eyes open, esp. as the result of curiosity, surprise, horror, etc. (*stared in amazement*). • *n.* staring gaze. □□ **star'er** *n.*

■ *v.* gaze, gape, goggle, watch, peer, ogle, *colloq.* gawk, rubberneck. • *n.* (fixed *or* blank) look; goggle, glare.

star•fish /staarfish/ *n.* echinoderm with five *or* more radiating arms.

star•gaz•er /staargayzər/ *n.* *colloq.* usu. *derog.* or *joc.* astronomer or astrologer.

stark /staark/ • *adj.* **1** desolate; bare (*stark landscape*). **2** sharply evident; brutally simple (*in stark contrast*). **3** downright; sheer (*stark madness*). • *adv.* completely; wholly (*stark naked*). □□ **stark'ly** *adv.* **stark'ness** *n.*

■ *adj.* **1** harsh, severe, bleak, barren, dreary, gray, cold, cheerless. **2** clear, plain, obvious, patent, manifest; bare, blunt, unadorned, unembellished. **3** complete, utter, absolute, perfect, pure, thorough, thoroughgoing. • *adv.* utterly, unqualifiedly, absolutely, entirely, quite, totally, fully.

star•let /staarlit/ *n.* **1** promising young performer, esp. a woman. **2** little star.

star•light /staarlīt/ *n.* light of the stars.

star•ling /staarling/ *n.* small gregarious partly migratory bird with blackish-brown speckled iridescent plumage.

star•lit /staárlit/ *adj.* **1** lighted by stars. **2** with stars visible.

star•ry /staáree/ *adj.* (**star•ri•er, star•ri•est**) **1** covered with stars. **2** like a star. □ **starry-eyed** *colloq.* visionary; enthusiastic but impractical. **star'ri•ness** *n.*

start /staart/ • *v.* **1** *tr. & intr.* begin; commence. **2** *tr.* set in motion or action. **3** *intr.* set oneself in motion or action. **4** *intr.* begin a journey, etc. **5 a** *intr.* (of a machine) begin operating. **b** *tr.* cause to begin operating. **6** *tr.* **a** cause or enable (a person) to make a beginning. **b** cause (a person) to begin (doing something). **7** *intr.* make a sudden movement from surprise, pain, etc. **8** *intr.* spring out, up, etc. • *n.* **1** beginning. **2** place from which a race, etc., begins. **3** sudden movement of surprise, pain, etc.

■ *v.* **1, 2** start off *or* up, get going, get under way, open, activate, trigger (off), get *or* start the ball rolling, *colloq.* get off the ground, kick off. **3, 4** start off *or* up *or* out, go, leave, depart, get going, move (off *or* out *or* on), make a move, get under way. **5 b** start up, turn on, switch on, crank up, activate, set in motion. **7** jump, flinch, blench, quail, shy, recoil, wince, shrink, draw back. **8** see SPRING *v.* 1. • *n.* **1** opening, outset, onset, inception, initiation, rise, genesis, creation, emergence, origin, dawn, threshold, brink; *colloq.* kickoff. **2** starting line *or* gate *or* post *or* point. **3** see JUMP *n.* 2, TURN *n.* 10.

start•er /staártər/ *n.* **1** person or thing that starts. **2** esp. automatic device for starting the engine of a motor vehicle, etc. **3** person giving the signal for the start of a race.

star•tle /staárt'l/ *v.tr.* shock; surprise.

■ frighten, alarm, scare, disturb, unsettle, upset.

star•tling /staártling/ *adj.* **1** surprising. **2** alarming (*startling news*). □□ **star'tling•ly** *adv.*

■ amazing, astounding, astonishing, awesome, staggering, disturbing, unsettling, upsetting, terrifying.

starve /staarv/ *v.* **1** *intr.* die of hunger; suffer from malnourishment. **2** *tr.* cause to die of hunger or suffer from lack of food. **3** *intr. colloq.* (esp. as **starved** *or* **starving** *adj.*) feel very hungry. **4** *intr.* feel a strong need or craving for. **5** *tr.* deprive of. **6** *tr.* compel by starving. □□ **star•va'tion** *n.*

■ **3** (**starved** *or* **starving**) (extremely) hungry, famished, ravenous. **4** (*starve for*) yearn for, hanker for, hunger for, pine for, long for; (*be starving for*) be dying for, be hungry for, be burning for. **5** (*be starved for, of*) be in need *or* want of, be lacking, be bereft of. □□ **starvation** hunger, deprivation, undernourishment, malnutrition, malnourishment.

stash /stash/ *colloq.* • *v.tr.* **1** conceal; put in a safe or hidden place. **2** hoard. • *n.* **1** hiding place. **2** thing hidden.

stat. *abbr.* **1** at once. **2** statistics. **3** statute.

state /stayt/ • *n.* **1** existing condition or position of a person or thing. **2** *colloq.* **a** excited, anxious, or agitated mental condition. **b** un-

tidy condition. **3 a** political community under one government. **b** this as part of a federal republic. **c** (**the States**) US. **4** (also **State**) civil government. • *v.tr.* **1** express in speech or writing. **2** specify. **3** *Mus.* introduce (a theme, etc.). □ **in state** with all due ceremony. **state of the art 1** the current stage of development of a practical or technological subject. **2** (usu. **state-of-the-art**) [*attrib.*] using the latest techniques or equipment (*state-of-the-art weaponry*). □□ **stat'a•ble** *adj.* **stat'ed•ly** *adv.* **state'hood** *n.*

■ *n.* **1** circumstance(s), situation, state of affairs, status; shape, structure, form, constitution; trim, order, repair. **2 a** see STEW *n.* 2. **b** see SHAMBLES. **3 a** nation, country, land, commonwealth, body politic. **4** administration. • *v.* **1** assert, asseverate, declare, affirm, report, articulate, formulate, enunciate, voice; say, testify, hold, have it that. **2** fix, define, delineate, designate, determine, set.

state•hood /stáyt-hood/ *n.* condition or status of being a state, esp. a state of the United States.

state•less /stáytlis/ *adj.* **1** (of a person) having no nationality or citizenship. **2** without a state. □□ **state'less•ness** *n.*

state•ly /stáytlee/ *adj.* (**state•li•er, state•li•est**) dignified; imposing; grand. □□ **state'li•ness** *n.*

■ august, solemn, distinguished, impressive, striking, awesome, lofty, elevated, noble, majestic, regal.

state•ment /stáytmənt/ *n.* **1** stating or being stated; expression in words. **2** thing stated. **3** formal account of facts. **4** record of transactions in a bank account, etc. **5** formal notification of an amount due.

■ **1–3** assertion, allegation, declaration, affirmation, asseveration, averment, announcement, annunciation; communiqué, proposition. **5** account, bill, invoice.

state•room /stáytroom, –room/ *n.* private compartment in a passenger ship or train.

states•man /stáytsmən/ *n.* (*pl.* **–men;** *fem.* **states•wom•an,** *pl.* **–wom•en**) distinguished and capable politician or diplomat. □□ **states'man•like** *adj.* **states'man•ship** *n.*

stat•ic /státik/ • *adj.* **1** stationary; not acting or changing; passive. **2** *Physics* concerned with bodies at rest or forces in equilibrium (opp. DYNAMIC). • *n.* electrical disturbances in the atmosphere or the interference with telecommunications caused by this. □ **static electricity** electricity not flowing as a current as that produced by friction. □□ **stat'i•cal•ly** *adv.*

■ *adj.* **1** immovable, immobile, unmoving, motionless, fixed, stagnant, inert, still, unchanging, constant, steady. • *n.* noise, atmospherics.

sta•tion /stáyshən/ • *n.* **1 a** regular stopping place on a railroad, bus, route, etc. **b** building at this. **2** place or building, etc., where a person or thing stands or is placed. **3** establishment involved in radio or television broadcasting. **4** military or naval base. **5** position in life; rank or status. • *v.tr.* **1** assign a station to. **2** put in position. □ **station**

wagon car with passenger seating and storage or extra seating area in the rear, accessible by a rear door.

■ *n.* **1** railroad station, train station; stop, stage; terminus, terminal; bus station, coach station, depot. **2** position, spot, point, post, site. **3** broadcaster, transmitter; channel. **4** see BASE[1] *n.* 3. **5** place, caste, standing, class, level. ● *v.* **1** appoint, post, install, garrison, billet, quarter. **2** position, place, spot, post, site, situate, locate, install, set, stand.

sta•tion•ar•y /stáyshəneree/ *adj.* **1** remaining in one place. **2** not meant to be moved. **3** not changing.

sta•tion•er /stáyshənər/ *n.* person who sells stationery.

sta•tion•er•y /stáyshəneree/ *n.* **1** writing materials such as pens, paper, etc. **2** writing paper, esp. with matching envelopes.

sta•tis•tic /stətístik/ *n.* statistical fact or item.

sta•tis•tics /stətístiks/ *n.pl.* **1** [usu. treated as *sing.*] science of collecting and analyzing numerical data. **2** any systematic collection or presentation of such facts. □□ **sta•tis'ti•cal** *adj.* **sta•tis'ti•cal•ly** *adv.* **stat•is•ti•cian** /státistíshən/ *n.*

stat•u•ar•y /stáchŏoeree/ ● *adj.* of or for statues (*statuary art*). ● *n.* (*pl.* **–ies**) statues collectively.

stat•ue /stáchŏo/ *n.* sculptured figure of a person or animal, esp. life-size or larger.

■ sculpture, figurine, statuette, carving, casting, model, bronze; bust, colossus, figurehead.

stat•u•esque /stáchŏo-ésk/ *adj.* like, or having the dignity or beauty of, a statue. □□ **stat•u•esque'ness** *n.*

■ imposing, impressive, majestic, regal.

stat•u•ette /stáchŏo-ét/ *n.* small statue.

stat•ure /stáchər/ *n.* **1** height of a (esp. human) body. **2** degree of eminence, social standing, or advancement (*recruit someone of his stature*). □□ **stat'ured** *adj.* [also in *comb.*].

sta•tus /stáytəs, státtós/ *n.* **1** rank; social position; relative importance (*not sure of their status in the hierarchy*). **2** prestige. **3** state of affairs. □ **status symbol** possession, etc., taken to indicate a person's high status.

■ **1** see STANDING *n.* 1. **2** eminence, prominence, preeminence, standing, stature, importance, significance, repute, reputation. **3** see SITUATION 2.

sta•tus quo /stáytəs kwó, státtós/ *n.* existing state of affairs.

stat•ute /stáchŏot/ *n.* **1** written law passed by a legislative body. **2** rule of a corporation, founder, etc., intended to be permanent.

stat•u•to•ry /stáchətawree/ *adj.* required, permitted, or enacted by statute. □□ **stat•u•to'ri•ly** *adv.*

staunch[1] /stawnch, staanch/ *adj.* **1** trustworthy; loyal. **2** (of a ship, joint, etc.) strong, watertight, airtight, etc. See synonym study at RESOLUTE. □□ **staunch'ly** *adv.* **staunch' ness** *n.*

■ **1** steadfast, firm, dependable, reliable. **2** solid, sturdy, sound, well-built.

staunch[2] var. of STANCH.

stave /stayv/ ● *n.* **1** each of the curved pieces of wood forming the sides of a cask, barrel,

etc. **2** = STAFF *n.* 3. **3** stanza; verse. ● *v.tr.* (*past* and *past part.* **stove** /stōv/ or **staved**) **1** break a hole in. **2** crush or knock out of shape. □ **stave in** crush by forcing inward. **stave off** avert or defer (danger, etc.).

stay[1] /stay/ ● *v.* **1** *intr.* continue to be in the same place or condition; not depart or change. **2** *intr.* have temporary residence. **3** *archaic* or *literary* **a** *tr.* stop or check. **b** *intr.* [esp. in *imper.*] pause. **4** *tr.* postpone (judgment, decision, execution, etc.). ● *n.* **1 a** act or an instance of staying. **b** duration of this (*just a ten-minute stay*). **2** suspension or postponement of a sentence, judgment, etc. (*stay of execution*). **3** prop or support. □ **staying power** endurance; stamina. **stay put** *colloq.* remain where it is placed or where one is. **stay up** not go to bed (until late). □□ **stay'er** *n.*

■ *v.* **1** remain, stop, wait, linger, loiter; stand, freeze; keep. **2** remain, stop, sojourn, visit; lodge, reside. **3 a** arrest, thwart, prevent, put an end to, halt, interrupt, discontinue, block; stanch, stem, curb, retard. **4** delay, put off, defer, prorogue; see also POSTPONE. ● *n.* **1** stopover, sojourn, visit, stop, stopoff, layover. **2** delay, deferment, deferral, reprieve; moratorium. **3** see SUPPORT *n.* 2.

stay[2] /stay/ *n.* **1** *Naut.* rope or guy supporting a mast, spar, flagstaff, etc. **2** supporting cable on an aircraft, etc.

STD *abbr.* sexually transmitted disease

std. *abbr.* standard.

stead /sted/ *n.* □ **in a person's** (or **thing's**) **stead** as a substitute; instead of him or her or it. **stand a person in good stead** be advantageous or serviceable to him or her.

stead•fast /stédfast/ *adj.* constant; firm; unwavering. □□ **stead'fast•ly** *adv.* **stead'fast• ness** *n.*

■ resolute, determined, persevering, resolved, single-minded, steady, unflinching, unswerving, indefatigable, dependable, immovable, faithful, true, loyal.

stead•y /stédee/ ● *adj.* (**stead•i•er, stead•i•est**) **1** firmly fixed or supported unwavering. **2** uniform and regular. **3 a** constant in mind or conduct. **b** persistent. **4** (of a person) serious and dependable. **5** regular; established (*steady girlfriend*). ● *v.* (**–ies, –ied**) make or become steady (*steady the boat*). ● *adv.* steadily (*hold it steady*). ● *n.* (*pl.* **–ies**) *colloq.* regular boyfriend or girlfriend. □ **go steady** *colloq.* have as a regular boyfriend or girlfriend. **steady state** unvarying condition, esp. in a physical process. □□ **stead'i•er** *n.* **stead'i•ly** *adv.* **stead'i•ness** *n.*

■ *adj.* **1** stable, balanced, poised, settled, firm, fast, secure, solid. **2** even, invariable, unvarying, unfluctuating, unwavering, undeviating, changeless; perpetual, nonstop, around-the-clock, persistent. **3** see STEADFAST. **4** staid, sedate, sober, temperate, moderate, dignified, poised, sensible, down-to-earth. **5** devoted, firm, staunch, faithful, loyal, constant. ● *v.* stabilize, balance, hold fast; brace, secure, support. ● *adv.* firmly, fast, immovably, solidly, securely. • n. sweet-heart, woman, colloq. (regular) fellow or girl, man, guy.

steak /stayk/ n. thick slice of meat (esp. beef) or fish, often cut for grilling, frying, etc.

steal /steel/ • v. (past **stole** /stōl/; past part. **sto•len** /stōlən/) **1** tr. [also absol.] take (another person's property) illegally or without right or permission, esp. in secret. **2** tr. obtain surreptitiously or by surprise (stole a kiss). **3** tr. gain insidiously or artfully. **4** intr. move, esp. silently or stealthily. **5** tr. Baseball run to (a base) while the pitcher is in the act of delivery. • n. colloq. unexpectedly easy task or good bargain. □ **steal the show** outshine other performers, esp. unexpectedly. **steal a person's thunder** use another person's words, ideas, etc., without permission and without giving credit. □□ **steal•er** n. [also in comb.]. **steal•ing** n.

■ v. **1** appropriate, filch, thieve, shoplift, pilfer; embezzle, misappropriate; hijack, usurp; plagiarize, pirate, colloq. lift, swipe. **4** sneak, creep, slip, slink, tiptoe, prowl, lurk. • n. **2** (good) buy, colloq. giveaway. □□ **stealer** see THIEF. **stealing** see THEFT.

stealth /stelth/ • n. secrecy; secret procedure. • adj. Mil. Aeron. designed to avoid detection by radar.

■ stealthiness, furtiveness, clandestinity, clandestineness, surreptitiousness, sneakiness, slyness.

stealth•y /stélthee/ adj. (**stealth•i•er**, **stealth•i•est**) done with stealth; furtive. □□ **stealth'i•ly** adv. **stealth'i•ness** n.

■ secret, sly, clandestine, hugger-mugger, surreptitious, closet, backstairs; secretive, skulking.

steam /steem/ • n. **1** vapor from heated water. **2 a** power obtained from steam. **b** colloq. power or energy generally. • v. **1** tr. **a** cook (food) in steam. **b** treat with steam. **2** intr. give off steam. **3** intr. **a** move under steam power (the ship steamed down the river). **b** [foll. by ahead, away, etc.] colloq. proceed or travel fast or with vigor. **4** tr. & intr. **a** cover or become covered with condensed steam. **b** (as **steamed up** adj.) colloq. angry or excited. □ **steam engine 1** engine which uses steam to generate power. **2** locomotive powered by this. **steam iron** electric iron that emits steam.

■ n. **1** mist, fog, cloud, haze. • v. **4 a** (steam up) see MIST v. **b** (steamed up) see ANGRY 1.

steam•boat /steembōt/ n. boat propelled by a steam engine.

steam•er /steemər/ n. **1** vessel propelled by steam, esp. a ship. **2** vessel for steaming food in.

steam•roll•er /steemrōlər/ • n. **1** heavy slow-moving vehicle with a roller, used to flatten newly laid asphalt, etc. **2** crushing power or force. • v.tr. **1** crush forcibly or indiscriminately. **2** force (a measure, etc.) through a legislature.

steam•ship /steemship/ n. ship propelled by a steam engine.

steam•y /steemee/ adj. (**steam•i•er**, **steam•**

i•est) **1** like or full of steam. **2** colloq. erotic; salacious. □□ **steam'i•ly** adv. **steam'i•ness** n.

■ **1** humid, steaming, damp, moist, muggy, sticky, dank; hazy, cloudy, dim, blurred. **2** passionate, (sexually) exciting, arousing, hot, torrid, sexy.

steed /steed/ n. archaic or poet. horse.

steel /steel/ • n. **1** alloy of iron and carbon with other elements increasing strength and malleability, much used for making tools, weapons, etc. **2** strength; firmness (nerves of steel). **3** [not in pl.] literary sword. • adj. of or like steel. • v.tr. & refl. harden or make resolute. □ **steel wool** abrasive substance consisting of a mass of fine steel shavings. □□ **steel'i•ness** n. **steel'y** adj. (**steel•i•er**, **steel•i•est**).

■ n. **3** sword, dagger, knife, dirk, stiletto, lance. • adj. see steely (STEEL) below. • v. inure, insulate, protect; brace, nerve, stiffen, strengthen; (steel oneself) grit one's teeth, bear up; sl. bite the bullet. □□ **steely** steel; grayish, gray; hard, iron, tough, strong; severe, obdurate, adamant; see also STONY 2.

steel•works /steelwərks/ n.pl. [usu. treated as sing.] place where steel is manufactured. □□ **steel'work•er** n.

steel•yard /steelyaard/ n. balance with a graduated arm along which a weight is moved.

steep[1] /steep/ adj. **1** sloping sharply. **2** (of a rise or fall) rapid. **3** [predic.] colloq. exorbitant; unreasonable (esp. a bit steep). □□ **steep'en** v. **steep'ly** adv. **steep'ness** n.

■ **1** sheer, abrupt, precipitous, scarped, bluff, sharp. **2** sharp, abrupt, sudden. **3** dear, high, excessive, extravagant, extortionate; outrageous.

steep[2] /steep/ v.tr. soak or bathe in liquid. □ **steep in 1** pervade or imbue with. **2** make deeply acquainted with (a subject, etc.).

■ submerge, souse, drench, immerse. □ **steep in** fill with, saturate with, immerse in, soak in; bury in.

stee•ple /steepəl/ n. tall tower, esp. one surmounted by a spire, above the roof of a church. □□ **stee'pled** adj.

stee•ple•chase /steepəlchays/ n. race with ditches, hedges, etc., to jump. □□ **stee'ple•chas•er** n. **stee'ple•chas•ing** n.

stee•ple•jack /steepəljak/ n. person who climbs tall chimneys, steeples, etc., to do repairs, etc.

steer[1] /steer/ v. **1** tr. guide (a vehicle, aircraft, ship, etc.) by a wheel, etc. **2** tr. direct (one's course). **3** intr. direct one's course in a specified direction. **4** tr. guide the movement or trend of. □ **steer clear of** avoid. **steering wheel** wheel by which a vehicle, etc., is steered. □□ **steer'a•ble** adj. **steer'er** n. **steer'ing** n. (esp. in sense 1 of v.).

■ **1** pilot, direct, navigate; manage, control. **3** see HEAD v. 3a. **4** see GUIDE v. 1, 3. □ **steer clear of** dodge, keep away from, shun, circumvent, fight shy of.

steer[2] /steer/ n. castrated male bovine that is raised for beef.

steer•age /steerij/ n. **1** act of steering. **2** part of a ship allotted to passengers traveling at the cheapest rate.

steg•o•sau•rus /stégəsáwrəs/ *n.* plant-eating dinosaur with a double row of large bony plates along the spine.

ste•la /stéelə/ *n.* (*pl.* **ste•lae** /-lee/) *Archaeol.* upright slab or pillar usu. inscribed and sculpted, esp. as a gravestone.

stel•lar /stélər/ *adj.* of a star or stars. □□ **stel′li•form** *adj.*

■ astral, sidereal, star; chief, starring, principal.

stem[1] /stem/ • *n.* **1** main body or stalk of a plant, fruit, flower, leaf, etc. **2** stem-shaped part of an object: **a** slender part of a wine-glass. **b** tube of a tobacco pipe. **c** vertical stroke in a letter or musical note. **3** *Gram.* root or main part of a noun, verb, etc., to which inflections are added. **4** *Naut.* main upright timber or metal piece at the bow of a ship (*from stem to stern*). • *v.intr.* (**stemmed, stem•ming**) spring or originate from. □□ **stem′less** *adj.* **stem′like** *adj.* **stem′med** *adj.* [also in *comb.*].

■ *n.* **1** trunk, cane, stock; shoot, bine, twig. **2** shaft, shank, stalk, support, upright. **4** *Naut.* bow(s), prow, stem post. • *v.* **1** come, arise, develop, derive, issue, flow, generate, emanate, sprout, grow.

stem[2] /stem/ *v.tr.* (**stemmed, stem•ming**) check or stop.

■ halt, stanch, staunch, arrest, curb, control; retard, slow, lessen, diminish, reduce, cut.

stench /stench/ *n.* offensive or foul smell. See synonym study at SMELL.

■ stink, reek, mephitis, fetor, foul odor, effluvium.

sten•cil /sténsil/ • *n.* **1** thin sheet of plastic, metal, card, etc., in which a pattern or lettering is cut, used to produce a corresponding pattern on the surface beneath it by applying ink, paint, etc. **2** pattern so produced. • *v.tr.* (**sten•ciled, sten•cil•ing; sten•cilled, sten•cil•ling**) **1** produce (a pattern) with a stencil. **2** decorate or mark (a surface) in this way.

ste•nog•ra•phy /stənógrəfee/ *n.* shorthand or the art of writing this. □□ **ste•nog′ra•pher** *n.* **sten•o•graph•ic** /sténəgráfik/ *adj.*

■ tachygraphy, phonography, speedwriting. □□ **stenographer** secretary, amanuensis, stenotypist, tachygrapher, phonographer, *colloq.* steno.

sten•to•ri•an /stəntáwreeən/ *adj.* (of a voice) loud and powerful.

step /step/ • *n.* **1 a** complete movement of one leg in walking or running. **b** distance covered by this. **2** unit of movement in dancing. **3** measure taken, esp. one of several. **4** surface of a stair, stepladder, etc.; tread. **5** short distance. **6** footfall. **7** manner of walking, etc. **8** degree in the scale of promotion, advancement, or precedence. **9** stepping (or not stepping) in time with others or music (esp. *in* or *out of step*). • *v.intr.* (**stepped, step•ping**) **1** lift and set down one's foot or alternate feet in walking. **2** come or go in a specified direction by stepping. **3** make progress in a specified way. □ **step aerobics** exercise regimen using a step-climbing motion. **step-by-step** gradu-

ally; cautiously. **step down** resign. **step in 1** enter. **2** intervene to help or hinder. **step on it** *colloq.* accelerate. **step out 1** leave a room, house, etc. **2** be active socially. **stepping-stone 1** raised stone, usu. one of a set in a stream, muddy place, etc., to help in crossing. **2** means of progress. **step up** increase; intensify. □□ **step′like** *adj.* **stepped** *adj.*

■ *n.* **1, 5** pace, footstep, stride. **2** movement, move. **3** action, initiative, activity, procedure, move. **4** (*steps*) stairs, stairway, staircase, stoop; doorstep, ledge, sill. **6** footstep, tread; footprint, trace, spoor, track; imprint. **7** see WALK *n.* **1. 9** (*in step*) in time, in line, in keeping, in harmony, in agreement, harmonious, agreeable, according, concordant; (*out of step*), discordant, inconsistent, nonconforming; offbeat, unconventional. • *v.* **1, 2** tread, move; pace, stride; see also WALK *v.* **1, 2, 3b.** ■ **step-by-step** a step at a time, by stages, by degrees, slowly, steadily. **step down** abdicate, quit, bow out, retire. **step in 1** go in, come in. **2** interfere, intercede, become involved. **step on it** speed up, *colloq.* put one's foot down; hurry (up), make haste, hasten. **step out 1** go outside, go out of doors. **2** go out, socialize. **step up** raise, strengthen, escalate, up, augment, *colloq.* boost.

step- /step/ *comb. form* denoting a relationship like the one specified but resulting from a parent's remarriage.

step•broth•er /stépbruthər/ *n.* son of a stepparent by a union other than with one's father or mother.

step•child /stépchild/ *n.* child of one's husband or wife by a previous marriage.

step•daugh•ter /stépdawtər/ *n.* female stepchild.

step•fa•ther /stépfaathər/ *n.* male stepparent.

step•lad•der /stépladər/ *n.* short ladder with flat steps and a folding support.

step•moth•er /stépmuthər/ *n.* female stepparent.

step•par•ent /stép-pairənt/ *n.* mother's or father's later husband or wife.

steppe /step/ *n.* level grassy unforested plain.

step•sis•ter /stépsistər/ *n.* daughter of a stepparent by a union other than with one's father or mother.

step•son /stépsun/ *n.* male stepchild.

-ster /stər/ *suffix* denoting a person engaged in or associated with a particular activity or thing (*gangster, youngster*).

ste•re•o /stéreeō, stéereeō/ • *n.* (*pl.* **-os**) **1 a** stereophonic record player, tape recorder, etc. **b** stereophonic sound reproduction. • *adj.* **1** = STEREOPHONIC. **2** = stereoscopic (see STEREOSCOPE).

stereo- /stéreeō, stéereeō/ *comb. form* solid; having three dimensions.

ster•e•o•phon•ic /stéreeəfónik, stéereeō-/ *adj.* (of sound reproduction) using two or more channels giving the effect of naturally distributed sound. □□ **ster•e•o•phon′i•cal•ly** *adv.*

ster•e•o•scope /stéreeəskōp, stéereeə-/ *n.*

device for producing a three-dimensional effect by viewing together two slightly different photographs of the same object. □□ **ster·e·o·scop·ic** /-skópik/ *adj.* **ster·e·o·scop′i·cal·ly** *adv.* **ster·e·os·co·py** /-reeóskəpee/ *n.*

ster·e·o·type /stéreeətīp, steéree-/ • *n.* **1 a** a person or thing that conforms to a widely accepted type. **b** such a type, idea, or attitude. **2** printing plate cast from a mold of composed type. • *v.tr.* **1** (esp. as **stereotyped** *adj.*) standardize; cause to conform to a type. **2 a** print from a stereotype. **b** make a stereotype of. □□ **ster·e·o·typ′ic** /-típik/ *adj.* **ster·e·o·typ′i·cal** *adj.* **ster·e·o·typ′i·cal·ly** *adv.*

ster·ile /stérəl, -īl/ *adj.* **1** not able to produce seeds or fruit or (of an animal) young; barren. **2** unfruitful; unproductive (*sterile discussions*). **3** free from living microorganisms, etc. See synonym study at SANITARY. □□ **ster′ile·ly** *adv.* **ste·ril·i·ty** /stərílitee/ *n.*

■ **1** fruitless, unfruitful, childless, arid, infertile. **2** barren, unproductive, fruitless, unprofitable, ineffectual. **3** pure, aseptic, uninfected, unpolluted, uncontaminated, disinfected, sanitary.

ster·il·ize /stérilīz/ *v.tr.* **1** make sterile. **2** deprive of the power of reproduction. □□ **ster·i·li·za′tion** *n.* **ster′i·liz·er** *n.*

■ **1** purify, disinfect, clean, fumigate, depurate. **2** castrate, emasculate, hysterectomize, vasectomize; geld, spay, desex, neuter, caponize, fix, cut, alter.

ster·ling /stárling/ • *adj.* **1** of or in British money (*pound sterling*). **2** (of a person or qualities, etc.) of solid worth; genuine; reliable. • *n.* **1** = *sterling silver*. **2** British money (*paid in sterling*). □ **sterling silver** silver of 92$\frac{1}{2}$% purity.

■ *adj.* **2** excellent, superior, superb, superlative, first-class, exceptional.

stern¹ /stərn/ *adj.* severe; grim; strict; authoritarian (*stern treatment*). See synonym study at SEVERE. □□ **stern′ly** *adv.* **stern′ness** *n.*

■ serious, frowning, forbidding; austere, Spartan, stringent, demanding, critical, rigid, inflexible, harsh.

stern² /stərn/ *n.* **1** rear part of a ship or boat. **2** any rear part. □□ **sterned** *adj.* [also in *comb.*]. **stern′most** *adj.* **stern′ward** *adj.* & *adv.* **stern′wards** *adv.*

ster·num /stárnəm/ *n.* (*pl.* **ster·nums** or **ster·na** /-nə/) breastbone.

ster·oid /steéroyd, stér-/ *n. Biochem.* any of a group of organic compounds including many hormones, alkaloids, and vitamins. □□ **ste·roid·al** /-róyd′l/ *adj.*

ster·ol /steérawl, -ol, stér-/ *n. Chem.* any of a group of naturally occurring steroid alcohols.

ster·to·rous /stártərəs/ *adj.* (of breathing, etc.) labored and noisy.

stet /stet/ *v.intr.* (**stet·ted, stet·ting**) (usu. as an instruction written on printed text, etc.) ignore or cancel the correction or alteration; let the original form stand.

steth·o·scope /stéthəskōp/ *n.* instrument used in listening to the action of the heart, lungs, etc.

Stet·son /stétsən/ *n. propr.* felt hat with a very wide brim and a high crown.

ste·ve·dore /steévədawr/ *n.* person employed in loading and unloading ships.

stew /stoo, styoo/ • *v.* **1** *tr.* & *intr.* cook by long simmering. **2** *intr. colloq.* fret or be anxious. • *n.* **1** dish of stewed meat, etc. **2** *colloq.* agitated or angry state (*be in a stew*).

■ *v.* **1** casserole, braise, boil, simmer, jug. **2** agonize, dither, chafe, burn, smolder, simmer, seethe. • *n.* **1** casserole, fricassee, cassoulet, ragout, hotpot. **2** state of excitement *or* alarm *or* anxiety, bother, lather, *colloq.* sweat, tizzy.

stew·ard /stóoərd, styóo-/ • *n.* **1** passengers' attendant on a ship or aircraft or train. **2** person responsible for supplies of food, etc., for a college or club, etc. **3** property manager. • *v.tr.* act as a steward of. □□ **stew′ard·ship** *n.*

stew·ard·ess /stóoərdis, styóo-/ *n.* female steward, esp. on a ship or aircraft.

stick¹ /stik/ *n.* **1 a** short slender branch or length of wood. **b** this trimmed for use as a support or weapon. **2** implement used to propel the ball in hockey or polo, etc. **3** gear lever. **4** slender piece, often of a group or set, e.g., celery, dynamite, deodorant, etc. □□ **stick′like** *adj.*

■ **1 a** twig, stalk, switch. **b** stake, pole, pike, rod, mace, wand, staff, cane; club, cudgel, truncheon.

stick² /stik/ *v.* (*past* and *past part.* **stuck** /stuk/) **1** *tr.* [foll. by *in, into, through*] insert or thrust (a thing or its point) (*stuck a finger in my eye*). **2** *tr.* stab. **3** *tr.* & *intr.* [foll. by *in, into, on*, etc.] fix or be fixed on a pointed end or thing. **4** *tr.* & *intr.* fix or become or remain fixed by or as by adhesive, etc. (*stick a label on it*). **5** *intr.* endure; make a continued impression (*the name stuck*). **6** *intr.* not open, release, etc.; jam. **7** *colloq.* **a** *tr.* put in a specified position or place. **b** *intr.* remain in a place (*stuck indoors*). □ **be stuck with** *colloq.* be unable to get rid of. **stick around** *colloq.* linger; remain. **stick by** (or **with**) stay loyal or close to. **stick-in-the-mud** *colloq.* unprogressive or old-fashioned person. **stick it out** *colloq.* put up with or persevere with a burden, etc., to the end. **stick one's neck out** expose oneself to censure, etc., by acting or speaking boldly. **stick out** protrude or cause to protrude. **stick to 1** remain close to or fixed on or to. **2** keep to (a subject, etc.) (*stick to the point*). **stick up 1** be or make erect or protruding upward. **2** fasten to an upright surface. **3** *colloq.* rob or threaten with a gun. **stick-up** *n. colloq.* armed robbery. **stick up for** support or defend.

■ **1** put, poke, push, prod, dig, jab. **2** pierce, transfix, pin, spike, impale. **3** attach, fasten, affix, nail, pin, tack. **4** affix, attach, fasten, glue, cement, paste; bond, melt, fuse; cohere, adhere. **5** linger, remain (fixed), continue, stay. **6** become lodged *or* embedded, be jammed, be wedged, be trapped; catch, wedge, lodge. **7 a** drop, place, deposit, plop, plunk, *colloq.* shove. **b** stay, linger. □ **be stuck with** be burdened *or* encumbered *or* saddled *or* charged with, be weighed down with. **stick around** wait, stay, stand by, hang around *or* about, *colloq.* hang on. **stick by** (*or* **with**) stick to, support, be loyal *or* faithful to, stand by. **stick-in-the-mud** (old) fogy, conservative, anachronism, dodo, *colloq.* fossil. **stick it out** persist, stand fast, bear it, be resolute, hold one's ground. **stick out** jut (out), extend, project, poke (out); bulge, obtrude, stand out. **stick to 2** see KEEP *v.* 2. **stick up 1** stand up *or* out, poke out *or* up, protrude, jut, extend, project, obtrude. **2** put up, post, affix, display. **3** mug, hold up, *sl.* heist. **stick up for** stand by, stand up for, champion, speak for.

stick•ball /stíkbawl/ *n.* form of baseball played with a stick or broom handle and a rubber ball.

stick•er /stíkər/ *n.* adhesive label *or* notice, etc. □ **sticker shock** *colloq.* surprise reaction at a higher-than-expected retail price.

stick•ler /stíklər/ *n.* [foll. by *for*] person who insists on something (*stickler for accuracy*).

stick•y /stíkee/ *adj.* (**stick•i•er, stick•i•est**) **1** tending *or* intended to stick or adhere. **2** glutinous; viscous. **3** humid. **4** difficult; awkward. □□ **stick'i•ly** *adv.* **stick'i•ness** *n.*

■ **1** adhesive, gummed, glued; clinging. **2** gluey, gummy, tacky, viscid, *sl.* gooey. **3** clammy, dank, damp, muggy, close, sultry, oppressive. **4** ticklish, tricky, sensitive, delicate, uncomfortable.

stiff /stif/ • *adj.* **1** rigid; not flexible. **2** hard to bend *or* move or turn, etc. **3** needing strength or effort (*stiff climb*). **4** severe or strong (*stiff penalty*). **5** formal, constrained. **6** (of a muscle, person, etc.) aching when used, owing to previous exertion, injury, etc. **7** (of an alcoholic drink) strong. **8** [predic.] *colloq.* to an extreme degree (*bored stiff*). • *n. sl.* **1** corpse. **2** foolish or useless person. □ **stiff-necked** obstinate or haughty. **stiff upper lip** determination; fortitude. □□ **stiff'ish** *adj.* **stiff'ly** *adv.* **stiff'ness** *n.*

■ *adj.* **1, 2** firm, inelastic, unbending, inflexible, hard, unbendable; semisolid, semifluid, viscous, heavy. **3** difficult, hard, steep, uphill, laborious, arduous, onerous, tiring, fatiguing. **4** steady, powerful, fresh, brisk, gusty; harsh, punitive, hurtful, punishing, abusive, torturous, distressing; vigorous, energetic, staunch, dogged, tenacious, resolute. **5** cool, haughty, rigid, wooden, stuffy, aloof, tense, intense, unrelaxed, starchy, forced, pompous, pedantic, turgid. **7** potent, powerful, overpowering, alcoholic. • *n.* **1** body, *Med.* cadaver.

stiff•en /stífən/ *v.* make or become stiff. □□ **stiff'en•er** *n.* **stiff'en•ing** *n.*

■ thicken, coagulate, clot, congeal; brace, reinforce.

sti•fle /stífəl/ *v.* **1** *tr.* suppress. **2** *intr. & tr.* experience or cause to experience constraint of breathing (*stifling heat*). **3** *tr.* kill by suffocating. □□ **sti•fler** /stíflər/ *n.* **sti'fling•ly** *adv.*

■ **1** smother, choke back, withhold, repress. **2, 3** suffocate, smother, throttle, asphyxiate.

stig•ma /stígmə/ *n.* (*pl.* **stig•mas** or esp. in

sense 3 **stig•ma•ta** /-mətə, -máatə/) **1** mark or sign of disgrace or discredit. **2** part of a pistil that receives the pollen in pollination. **3** [in *pl.*] *Eccl.* (in Christian belief) marks corresponding to those left on Christ's body by the Crucifixion, said to have appeared on the bodies of St. Francis of Assisi and others.

■ **1** brand, (bad) mark, blot, smirch, stain, spot, taint.

stig•ma•tize /stígmətīz/ *v.tr.* [often foll. by *as*] describe as unworthy or disgraceful. □□ **stig•ma•ti•za'tion** *n.*

■ brand, disparage, depreciate, discredit, denounce.

stile /stīl/ *n.* arrangement of steps allowing people but not animals to climb over a fence or wall.

sti•let•to /stilétō/ *n.* (*pl.* **-tos**) **1** short dagger with a thick blade. **2** (in full **stiletto heel**) **a** long tapering heel of a woman's shoe. **b** shoe with such a heel.

still[1] /stil/ • *adj.* **1** not or hardly moving. **2** with little or no sound; calm and tranquil (*a still evening*). • *n.* **1** deep silence (*still of the night*). **2** static photograph, esp. a single shot from a movie or videotape. • *adv.* **1** without moving (*stand still*). **2** even now or at a particular time (*why are you still here?*). **3** nevertheless. **4** [with *compar.*, etc.] even; yet; increasingly (*still greater efforts*). • *v.* make or become still. □ **still life** (*pl.* **still lifes**) painting or drawing of inanimate objects such as fruit or flowers. □□ **still'ness** *n.*

■ *adj.* **1** quiet, serene, placid, calm, tranquil, motionless, unmoving, immobile. **2** silent, quiet, noiseless, soundless; hushed, restful. • *n.* **1** stillness, hush, quiet, tranquillity, quietness. • *adv.* **1** motionlessly, quietly, silently, stock-still. **2** even then, at this or at that time, till this or that time, to this day, yet. **3** notwithstanding, yet, all the same, even then or so; see also NEVERTHELESS. • *v.* calm, allay, assuage, alleviate, relieve, pacify, tranquilize; silence, lull, quiet, hush.

still[2] /stil/ *n.* apparatus for distilling alcohol, etc.

still•birth /stílbərth/ *n.* birth of a dead child.

still•born /stílbawrn/ *adj.* **1** born dead. **2** abortive.

stilt /stilt/ *n.* **1** either of a pair of poles with supports for the feet for walking with the body elevated. **2** each of a set of piles or posts supporting a building, etc.

stilt•ed /stíltid/ *adj.* (of a literary style, etc.) stiff and unnatural; bombastic. □□ **stilt'ed•ly** *adv.* **stilt'ed•ness** *n.*

■ awkward, ungraceful, graceless, clumsy, wooden; pretentious, formal, pompous, lofty, grandiloquent.

stim•u•lant /stímyələnt/ *n.* stimulating substance or influence.

stim•u•late /stímyəlayt/ *v.tr.* **1** act as a stimulus to. **2** animate; excite; arouse. See synonym study at ENCOURAGE. See synonym study at QUICKEN. □□ **stim'u•lat•ing** *adj.* **stim•u•la'tion** /-láyshən/ *n.* **stim'u•la•tive** *adj.* **stim'u•la•tor** *n.*

■ rouse, waken, awaken, wake up; incite,

inspire, encourage, spur, sting, quicken, inflame, foment, fire, kindle; increase, encourage, prompt, provoke, quicken; see also VITALIZE. □□ **stimulating** exciting, inspirational, inspiring, arousing, rousing, stirring. **stimulation** see THRILL *n.* 1a.

stim•u•lus /stímyələs/ *n.* (*pl.* **stim•u•li** /-lī/) **1** thing that rouses to activity or energy. **2** stimulating or rousing effect.

sting /sting/ • *n.* **1** sharp wounding organ of an insect, snake, nettle, etc. **2 a** act of inflicting a wound with this. **b** the wound itself or the pain caused by it. **3** painful quality or effect. **4** pungency; sharpness; vigor (*sting in the voice*). **5** *sl.* swindle. • *v.* (*past* and *past part.* **stung** /stung/) **1 a** *tr.* wound or pierce with a sting. **b** *intr.* be able to sting. **2** *intr. & tr.* feel or cause to feel a tingling physical or sharp mental pain. **3** *tr.* [foll. by *into*] incite by a strong or painful mental effect (*stung into replying*). **4** *tr. sl.* swindle. □□ **sting′er** *n.* **sting′ing•ly** *adv.* **sting′less** *adj.* **sting′like** *adj.*

■ *n.* **2 b** tingle; see also PRICK *n.* 3. • *v.* **1 a** prick, stab, stick; bite, nip. **2** hurt, ache, smart; wound, pain, injure, distress, nettle, pique. **3** see STIMULATE. **4** cheat, overcharge, fleece, rook, defraud, *colloq.* rip off, take for a ride, diddle.

sting•ray /sting-ray/ *n.* broad flatfish having a long poisonous serrated spine at the base of its tail.

stin•gy /stínjee/ *adj.* (**stin•gi•er, stin•gi•est**) ungenerous; mean. □□ **stin′gi•ly** *adv.* **stin′gi•ness** *n.*

■ see MEAN² 1. □□ **stinginess** see THRIFT.

stink /stingk/ • *v.* (*past* **stank** /stangk/ or **stunk** /stungk/; *past part.* **stunk**) **1** *intr.* emit a strong offensive smell. **2** *tr.* [often foll. by *up*] fill (a place) with a stink. • *n.* **1** strong or offensive smell. **2** *colloq.* fuss. See synonym study at SMELL.

■ *n.* **1** see SMELL *n.* 3. **2** see FUSS *n.* 1, 2.

stink•er /stíngkər/ *n.* **1** person or thing that stinks. **2** *sl.* objectionable person or thing. **3** *sl.* difficult task.

■ **2** villain, scoundrel, *colloq.* rat.

stink•ing /stíngking/ • *adj.* **1** that stinks. **2** *sl.* very objectionable. • *adv. sl.* extremely and usu. objectionably. □□ **stink′ing•ly** *adv.*

■ *adj.* **1** foul-smelling, evil-smelling, fetid. **2** wretched, vile, contemptible.

stint /stint/ • *v.* **1** *tr.* supply (food or aid, etc.) in an ungenerous amount or grudgingly. **2** *intr.* [foll. by *on*] be grudging or mean about. • *n.* **1** limitation of supply or effort (*without stint*). **2** allotted amount of work (*do one's stint*). □□ **stint′er** *n.* **stint′less** *adj.*

■ *v.* **1** skimp, scrimp, withhold; be stingy. • *n.* **1** control, curb, limit. **2** share, quota, assignment.

sti•pend /stípend/ *n.* fixed regular allowance or salary.

■ pay, wage, remuneration; grant, scholarship, subsidy.

stip•ple /stípəl/ • *v.* draw or paint or engrave, etc., with dots instead of lines. • *n.* **1** stippling. **2** effect of stippling. □□ **stip′pler** *n.* **stip′pling** *n.*

stip•u•late /stípyəlayt/ *v.tr.* demand or specify as part of an agreement. □□ **stip•u•la• tion** /-láyshən/ *n.* **stip′u•la•tor** *n.*

■ require, covenant, set forth, prescribe; call for. □□ **stipulation** condition, demand, essential, requirement.

stir¹ /stər/ • *v.* (**stirred, stir•ring**) **1** *tr.* move an implement around and around in (a liquid, etc.) to mix the ingredients or constituents. **2 a** *tr.* cause to move, esp. slightly. **b** *intr.* be or begin to be in motion. **3** *intr.* rise from sleep. **4** *tr.* arouse or inspire or excite (the emotions, a person, etc.). • *n.* **1** act of stirring. **2** commotion or excitement. □ **stir up 1** incite (trouble, etc.). **2** stimulate; excite; arouse. □□ **stir′rer** *n.*

■ *v.* **1** stir up, agitate, mix (up), scramble, amalgamate. **2 a** disturb, ruffle, shake (up). **b** see MOVE *v.* 1, 4. **3** get up, wake up, waken, awaken; start or begin the day, be up and about. **4** rouse, affect, stimulate, energize, galvanize, electrify. • *n.* **1** beat, whisk, whip, mix, blend, shake. **2** bustle, activity, movement, stirring, action, flurry. □ **stir up 1** whip up, provoke, inspire, foment; motivate, move, encourage, spur. **2** energize, galvanize, electrify, animate, quicken; revive, resuscitate.

stir² /stər/ *n. sl.* prison (esp. *in stir*).

stir-fry /stárfrī/ • *v.tr.* (**-fries, -fried**) fry rapidly while stirring and tossing. • *n.* food cooked this way.

stir•ring /stóring/ *adj.* **1** stimulating; exciting; arousing. **2** actively occupied (*lead a stirring life*). □□ **stir′ring•ly** *adv.*

■ **1** moving, telling, emotional, rousing. **2** see BUSY *adj.* 2.

stir•rup /stárəp, stír-/ *n.* each of a pair of devices attached to each side of a horse's saddle, in the form of a loop with a flat base to support the rider's foot.

stitch /stich/ • *n.* **1** (in sewing or knitting or crocheting, etc.) single pass of a needle or the thread or loop, etc., resulting from this. **2** least bit of clothing (*hadn't a stitch on*). **3** acute pain in the side. • *v.tr.* sew; make stitches (in). □ **in stitches** *colloq.* laughing uncontrollably. □□ **stitch′er** *n.* **stitch′er•y** *n.*

St. Johns wort • *n.* herbaceous plant or shrub with yellow five-petaled flowers and paired oval leaves.

stoat /stōt/ *n.* carnivorous mammal of the weasel family, having brown fur in the summer turning mainly white in the winter. (Also called **ermine**).

stock /stok/ • *n.* **1** store of goods, etc., ready for sale or distribution, etc. **2** supply; quantity. **3** equipment or raw material for manufacture or trade, etc. **4** farm animals or equipment. **5 a** capital of a business company. **b** shares in this. **6** one's reputation or popularity. **7** line of ancestry. **8** liquid made by stewing bones, vegetables, fish, etc., as a basis for soup, gravy, sauce, etc. **9** plant into which a graft is inserted. **10** [in *pl.*] *hist.* wooden frame with holes for the feet and occas. the hands and head, in which offenders were locked as a public punishment. **11** base or support or handle for an imple-

ment or machine. **12** butt of a rifle, etc.
• *adj.* **1** kept in stock and so regularly available (*stock sizes*). **2** hackneyed; conventional (*stock answer*). □ **have or keep (goods) in stock. 2** supply. □ **stock car** specially modified production car for use in racing. **stock exchange 1** place where stocks and shares are bought and sold. **2** dealers working there. **stock-in-trade 1** requisites of a trade or profession. **2** ready supply of characteristic phrases, attitudes, etc. **stock market** = *stock exchange*. **stock-still** without moving. **stock up 1** provide with or get stocks or supplies. **2** [foll. by *with, on*] get in or gather a stock of (food, fuel, etc.). □□ **stock′er** *n.* **stock′less** *adj.*

■ *n.* **1, 2** inventory, stockpile, reserve, reservoir, cache; wares, merchandise, goods, commodities. **4** livestock, cattle, beasts; horses, cows, oxen, sheep, goats. **5** funds; property, assets. **6** see REPUTATION 2. **7** pedigree, bloodline, roots, origins, lineage, family. **8** see BROTH. **12** handle. • *adj.* **1** standard, ordinary, regular, routine, staple. **2** routine, stereotyped, banal, clichéd, unoriginal, commonplace, usual, ordinary, stale, staple, ready-made. • *v.* **1** carry, have *or* make available, handle, deal in, market, sell. **2** fill, provide, furnish; see also OUTFIT *v.* □ **stock up 2** accumulate, amass, pile up, stockpile, garner, hoard, store (up), cache, lay in.

stock•ade /stokáyd/ • *n.* **1** line or enclosure of upright stakes. **2** military prison. • *v.tr.* fortify with a stockade.

stock•brok•er /stókbrōkər/ *n.* dealer in shares of stock. □□ **stock′brok•er•age** /-ij/ *n.* **stock′brok•ing** *n.*

stock•hold•er /stók-hōldər/ *n.* owner of stocks or shares. □□ **stock′hold•ing** *n.*

stock•ing /stóking/ *n.* knitted fabric covering for the leg and foot. □□ **stock′inged** *adj.* [also in *comb.*]. **stock′ing•less** *adj.*

stock•pile /stókpīl/ • *n.* accumulated stock of goods, materials, weapons, etc., held in reserve. • *v.tr.* accumulate a stockpile of. □□ **stock′pil•er** *n.*

stock•room /stókrōōm, -rŏŏm/ *n.* room for storing goods.

stock•tak•ing /stóktayking/ *n.* **1** making an inventory of stock. **2** review of one's position and resources.

stock•y /stókee/ *adj.* (**stock•i•er, stock•i•est**) short and strongly built; thickset. □□ **stock′i•ly** *adv.* **stock′i•ness** *n.*
■ sturdy, chunky, dumpy, solid.

stock•yard /stókyaard/ *n.* enclosure with pens, etc., for the sorting or temporary keeping of cattle.

stodg•y /stójee/ *adj.* (**stodg•i•er, stodg•i•est**) dull; uninteresting; old-fashioned. □□ **stodg′i•ly** *adv.* **stodg′i•ness** *n.*
■ stuffy, heavy, ponderous, boring, tedious, humdrum.

Sto•ic /stóik/ • *n.* **1** member of the ancient Greek school of philosophy that taught control of one's feelings and passions. **2 (stoic)** stoical person. • *adj.* **1** of or like the Stoics. **2 (stoic)** = STOICAL.

sto•i•cal /stóikəl/ *adj.* having or showing great self-control in adversity. □□ **sto′i•cal•ly** *adv.*

■ impassive, resigned, cool, unemotional.

Sto•i•cism /stóisizəm/ *n.* **1** philosophy of the Stoics. **2 (stoicism)** stoical attitude.
■ **2 (stoicism)** self-possession, austerity, self-control, fortitude, calmness, calm, coolness, imperturbability.

stoke /stōk/ *v.tr.* feed and tend (a fire or furnace, etc.).

STOL *abbr. Aeron.* short take-off and landing.

stole[1] /stōl/ *n.* **1** woman's long scarf, worn around the shoulders. **2** strip of silk, etc., worn over the shoulders as a vestment by a priest.

stole[2] *past* of STEAL.

sto•len *past part.* of STEAL.

stol•id /stólid/ *adj.* **1** lacking or concealing emotion or animation. **2** not easily excited or moved. □□ **sto•lid•i•ty** /-líditee/ *n.* **stol′id•ly** *adv.* **stol′id•ness** *n.*
■ impassive, exanimate, phlegmatic, unemotional; vegetating, lethargic, apathetic; wooden, slow.

stom•ach /stúmək/ • *n.* **1 a** internal organ in which food is digested. **b** any of several such organs in animals. **2** lower front of the body. **3** appetite or inclination. • *v.tr.* **1** find sufficiently palatable to swallow or keep down. **2** endure (usu. with *neg.: cannot stomach it*). □□ **stom′ach•ful** *n.* (*pl.* **-fuls**).
■ *n.* **2** abdomen, belly, gut, paunch, *colloq.* tummy, insides, guts. **3** tolerance; taste, desire, hunger, thirst, craving; relish; see also LIKING 2. • *v.* **1** digest, eat. **2** abide, tolerate, stand, bear, suffer, take, accept, swallow.

stomp /stomp/ • *v.intr.* tread or stamp heavily. • *n.* lively jazz dance with heavy stamping. □□ **stomp′er** *n.*

stone /stōn/ • *n.* **1 a** solid nonmetallic mineral matter, of which rock is made. **b** small piece of this. **2** precious stone, esp. used in jewelry. **3 a** thing resembling stone in hardness or form, e.g., the hard case of the kernel in some fruits. **b** *Med.* [often in *pl.*] hard mass forming in certain body organs. **4** (*pl.* same) *Brit.* unit of weight equal to 14 lb. (6.35 kg). • *v.tr.* pelt with stones. □ **leave no stone unturned** try all possible means. **Stone Age** prehistoric period when weapons and tools were made of stone. **stone's throw** short distance. □□ **stoned** *adj.* [also in *comb.*]. **stone′less** *adj.* **ston′er** *n.*

stoned /stōnd/ *adj. sl.* under the influence of alcohol or drugs.

stone•ma•son /stónmaysən/ *n.* person who cuts, prepares, and builds with stone. □□ **stone′ma′son•ry** *n.*

stone•wall /stónwawl/ *v.* obstruct (discussion or investigation) or be obstructive with evasive answers or denials, etc. □□ **stone′wall•er** *n.* **stone′wall•ing** *n.*

stone•ware /stónwair/ *n.* ceramic ware that is impermeable and partly vitrified but opaque.

stone•washed /stónwawsht, -wosht/ *adj.* (esp. of denim) washed with abrasives to produce a worn or faded look.

stone•work /stónwərk/ *n.* walls, etc., made of stone; masonry. □□ **stone′work•er** *n.*

stony ~ storm

ston•y /stṓnee/ *adj.* (**ston•i•er, ston•i•est**)
1 full of stones (*stony soil*). **2 a** hard; rigid.
b cold; unfeeling; uncompromising (*stony
stare*). □□ **ston′i•ly** *adv.* **ston′i•ness** *n.*

■ **1** rocky, pebbly, shingly, shingled, gravelly; rough, rugged. **2** obdurate, adamant,
heartless, unsympathetic.

stood *past* and *past part.* of STAND.

stooge /stōōj/ *colloq. n.* **1** butt or foil, esp. for
a comedian; straight man. **2** assistant or
subordinate, esp. for routine or unpleasant
work.

stool /stōōl/ *n.* **1** single seat without a back or
arms. **2** = FOOTSTOOL. **3** [usu. in *pl.*] = FE-
CES. □ **stool pigeon** police informer or
decoy.

stoop[1] /stōōp/ • *v.* **1** *tr.* bend (one's head or
body) forward and downward. **2** *intr.* carry
one's head and shoulders bowed forward.
3 *intr.* [often foll. by *down*] lower the body by
bending forward, sometimes also bending at
the knee. **4** *intr.* condescend. **5** *intr.* descend
or lower oneself to (some conduct) (*has
stooped to crime*). • *n.* stooping posture.

■ *v.* **1** bow, duck, lean, hunch, double up.
3 stoop down, bow, duck (down), lean
(down), crouch (down), squat. **4, 5** deign,
abase or degrade oneself, sink, humble oneself. • *n.* hunch, slouch, crouch.

stoop[2] /stōōp/ *n.* porch or small veranda or
set of steps in front of a house.

stop /stop/ • *v.* (**stopped, stop•ping**) **1** *tr.*
a put an end to (motion, etc.); completely
check the progress or motion or operation
of. **b** effectively hinder or prevent. **c** discontinue (an action or sequence of actions).
2 *intr.* come to an end. **3** *intr.* cease from
motion or speaking or action. **4** *tr.* defeat.
5 *intr.* stay for a short time. **6** *tr.* block or
close up (a hole or leak, etc.). • *n.* **1** stopping; being stopped. **2** place designated for a
bus or train, etc., to stop. **3** device for stopping motion at a particular point. **4 a** (in an
organ) row of pipes of one character.
b knob, etc., operating these. □ **stop at
nothing** be ruthless. □□ **stop′less** *adj.* **stop′
pa•ble** *adj.*

■ *v.* **1 a** immobilize, paralyze, freeze, deactivate, bring to an end, shut down, arrest; see
also ABOLISH. **b** curb, restrain, thwart, frustrate; block, bar, obstruct, intercept, dam,
keep *or* hold back; slow, impede, stem,
stanch. **c** halt, terminate, cease, break off,
cut off, interrupt, suspend. **2** draw to a
close, be over, come to a stop *or* halt *or* close,
expire, cease. **3** halt, pause, pull up, draw
up; come to a stop *or* halt *or* standstill; pull in
or over. **4** see DEFEAT *v.* 2. **5** pause, break,
take a break; sojourn, rest, remain, put up,
lodge. **6** obstruct, jam (up), plug (up), bung
(up), clog (up), choke (up). • *n.* **1** stop off,
stopover, halt, end, finish, cessation; close,
standstill, conclusion; stoppage; see also *interruption* (INTERRUPT). **2** stopping place, station, terminal, stage, terminus, depot.

stop•cock /stópkok/ *n.* externally operated
valve regulating the flow of a liquid or gas
through a pipe, etc.

stop•gap /stópgap/ *n.* [often *attrib.*] temporary substitute.
■ improvisation; (*often attrib.*) makeshift,
temporary; (*attrib.*) impromptu.

stop•o•ver /stópōvər/ *n.* break in one's journey.

stop•page /stópij/ *n.* **1** condition of being
blocked or stopped. **2** stopping or interruption of work in a factory, etc.

stop•per /stópər/ • *n.* plug for closing a bottle, etc. • *v.tr.* close or secure with a stopper.
■ *n.* stopple, cork, bung, peg, spigot, spile. •
v. see PLUG *v.* 1.

stop•watch /stópwoch/ *n.* watch with a
mechanism for recording elapsed time, used
to time races, etc.

stor•age /stáwrij/ *n.* **1 a** storing of goods, etc.
b space available for storing. **2** cost of storing. **3** electronic retention of data in a computer, etc. □ **storage battery** (or **cell**) battery (or cell) for storing electricity.

store /stawr/ • *n.* **1** quantity of something
kept available for use. **2** [in *pl.*] **a** articles for
a particular purpose accumulated for use.
b supply of these or the place where they are
kept. **3** retail outlet or shop. • *v.tr.* **1** put
(furniture, etc.) in storage. **2** accumulate for
future use. **3** stock or provide with something useful. **4** enter or retain (data) for retrieval. □ **in store 1** kept in readiness.
2 coming in the future. **3** [foll. by *for*] destined or intended. **set store by** consider important. □□ **stor′a•ble** *adj.* **stor′er** *n.*

■ *n.* **1** supply, inventory, collection, accumulation, stock, stockpile, reservoir, reserve.
2 (*stores*) **a** see PROVISION *n.* 2. **b** see STORE-
HOUSE. **3** market, retailer, cooperative
(store), supermarket. • *v.* **1** keep, hold, stow
(away), preserve, warehouse. **2** stock, collect, put by, lay away, set aside, pile (up),
stockpile; hoard. **3** supply, fill. □ **set store
by** give credence to, believe (in), have faith *or*
trust in, value.

store•house /stáwrhows/ *n.* place where
things are stored.
■ warehouse, depository, repository, storeroom, bank, store(s), depot; treasury; arsenal, magazine, armory.

store•keep•er /stáwrkeepər/ *n.* store owner
or manager.

store•room /stáwr-rōōm, –rŏŏm/ *n.* storage
room.

sto•ried /stáwreed/ *adj. literary* celebrated in
or associated with stories or legends.

stork /stawrk/ *n.* long-legged large wading
bird with white plumage, black wingtips, and
a long reddish beak.

storm /stawrm/ • *n.* **1** violent disturbance of
the atmosphere with strong winds and rain
etc. with thunder and rain or snow, etc. **2** violent
political, etc., disturbance. **3** [foll. by *of*] outbreak of applause, indignation, hisses, etc.
4 direct assault by troops on a fortified place.
• *v.* **1** *intr.* rage; bluster. **2** *intr.* move violently or angrily (*stormed out*). **3** *tr.* attack or
capture by storm. See synonym study at AT-
TACK. □ **storm petrel** = *stormy petrel.* **storm
trooper 1** *hist.* member of the Nazi political
militia. **2** member of the shock troops. **take
by storm 1** capture by direct assault. **2** rap-

idly captivate. □□ **storm′less** *adj.* **storm′ proof** *adj.*

■ *n.* **1** tempest, disturbance, turbulence; gale, whirlwind, hurricane, tornado, typhoon, cyclone; shower, cloudburst, downpour; dust storm, sandstorm; blizzard; hailstorm. **2** stir, uproar, furor; turbulence, strife, disorder. **3** shower, torrent, flood; outburst, outcry, outpouring. ● *v.* **1** rant, rave, fume, explode. **2** assault, assail, rush, charge.

storm•y /stáwrmee/ *adj.* (**storm•i•er, storm•i•est**) **1** of or affected by storms. **2** full of angry feeling or outbursts; tempestuous (*stormy meeting*). □ **stormy petrel 1** small black and white petrel of the North Atlantic. **2** person causing unrest. □□ **storm′i•ly** *adv.* **storm′i•ness** *n.*

■ **1** foul, nasty, bad, inclement, wild, rough, squally. **2** violent, turbulent, fierce, fiery, frantic, frenetic.

sto•ry¹ /stáwree/ *n.* (*pl.* **–ries**) **1** account of imaginary or past events; narrative, tale, or anecdote. **2** history of a person or institution, etc. **3** (in full **story line**) narrative or plot of a novel or play, etc. **4** facts or experiences that deserve narration. **5** *colloq.* fib or lie.

■ **1** recounting, yarn; account, recital, record, history; legend, myth, fairy tale or story, novel; epic, saga, allegory, parable; article, piece, composition; version, statement, representation, description. **2, 4** biography, curriculum vitae, life (story); tale, yarn, saga. **3** scenario, (plot) outline, thread, summary. **5** excuse, untruth, falsehood, fabrication; tall tale.

sto•ry² /stáwree/ *n.* (*pl.* **–ries**) horizontal division of a building, from floor to ceiling in each. □□ **–sto•ried** [in *comb.*].

■ floor, level, tier.

sto•ry•board /stáwreebawrd/ *n.* displayed sequence of pictures, etc., outlining the plan of a movie, etc.

sto•ry•tell•er /stáwreetelər/ *n.* **1** person who tells stories. **2** *colloq.* liar. □□ **sto′ry•tell•ing** *n. & adj.*

stout /stowt/ ● *adj.* **1** somewhat fat; corpulent; bulky. **2** thick; strong. **3** brave; resolute. ● *n.* strong, dark brown beer. □□ **stout′ish** *adj.* **stout′ly** *adv.* **stout′ness** *n.*

■ *adj.* **1** obese, tubby, overweight, thickset, heavyset, burly; brawny, beefy, husky. **2** fat, solid, sturdy, robust, substantial. **3** valiant, undaunted, dauntless, hardy, courageous, gallant, plucky, valorous, staunch.

stout•heart•ed /stówt-hártəd/ *adj.* courageous. □□ **stout′heart•ed•ly** *adj.*

stove¹ /stōv/ *n.* closed apparatus burning fuel or electricity for heating or cooking.

■ see RANGE *n.* 5.

stove² *past* and *past part.* of STAVE *v.*

stove•pipe /stōvpīp/ *n.* pipe conducting smoke and gases from a stove to a chimney. □ **stovepipe hat** *colloq.* tall silk hat.

stow /stō/ *v.tr.* pack (goods, etc.) tidily and compactly. □ **stow away 1** place (a thing) where it will not cause an obstruction. **2** be a stowaway on a ship, etc.

■ store, load, deposit, put (away), place, tuck away.

stow•a•way /stóəway/ *n.* person who hides on board a ship or aircraft, etc., to get free passage.

stra•bis•mus /strəbízməs/ *n. Med.* cross eyes; squint. □□ **stra•bis′mal** *adj.* **stra•bis′mic** *adj.*

strad•dle /strád′l/ *v.* **1** *tr.* **a** sit or stand across (a thing) with the legs wide apart. **b** be situated across or on both sides of. **2** *intr.* sit or stand in this way. □□ **strad′dler** *n.*

strafe /strayf/ *v.tr.* harass with gunfire.

strag•gle /strágəl/ *v.intr.* **1** lack or lose compactness or tidiness. **2** be or become dispersed or sporadic. **3** trail behind others in a march or race, etc. □□ **strag′gler** *n.* **strag′gly** *adj.* (**strag•gli•er, strag•gli•est**)

■ **1** see SPRAWL *v.* 2. **2** (*b*) spread (out), disperse, scatter, thin out. **3** stray, ramble, rove, prowl, range; see also TRAIL *v.* 2. □□ **straggly** unkempt, untidy, loose.

straight /strayt/ ● *adj.* **1** extending uniformly in the same direction; without a curve or bend, etc. **2** successive; uninterrupted (*three straight wins*). **3** in proper order or place or condition; level (*put things straight*). **4** honest; candid. **5 a** unmodified. **b** (of a drink) undiluted. **6** *colloq.* **a** (of a person, etc.) conventional or respectable. **b** heterosexual. **7** direct; undeviating. ● *n.* **1** straight condition. **2** sequence of five cards in poker. **3** *colloq.* **a** conventional person. **b** heterosexual. ● *adv.* **1** in a straight line; direct; without deviation or hesitation or circumlocution. **2** correctly. □ **straight man** comedian's set-up man or foil. **straight off** *colloq.* without hesitation. **straight up** *colloq.* **1** truthfully; honestly. **2** (of liquor) without ice. □□ **straight′ly** *adv.* **straight′ness** *n.*

■ *adj.* **1** direct, unbending, undeviating, unswerving, unwavering, regular, linear. **2** see SUCCESSIVE. **3** shipshape, orderly, neat, tidy, arranged; even, square, true, right; vertical, upright, perpendicular, plumb; symmetrical. **4** frank, straightforward, direct, downright, forthright, legitimate, (fair and) square, fair, equitable; unequivocal, unambiguous, plain, simple, explicit. **5** neat, unmixed, pure, unadulterated, uncut, unaltered. **6 a** see CONSERVATIVE *adj.* 1, RESPECTABLE 1. **b** *colloq.* hetero. **7** unswerving; see also DIRECT *adj.* 3. ● *n.* **3 a** see SQUARE *n.* 5. **b** *colloq.* hetero. ● *adv.* **1** directly, right, undeviatingly, unswervingly; as the crow flies, in a beeline; unequivocally, unambiguously, forthrightly, straightforwardly, point-blank, candidly, frankly. **2** properly. □ **straight off** immediately, at once, without delay, instantly, posthaste, summarily, directly. **straight up 1** see STRAIGHT *adv.* 1 above. **2** neat, undiluted, pure.

straight•a•way /stráytəway/ *n.* straight part of a course, track, road, etc.

straight•en /stráyt′n/ *v.* **1** make or become straight. **2** [foll. by *up*] stand erect after bending. □□ **straight′en•er** *n.*

■ **1** uncurl, untangle, unsnarl; straighten

up, rearrange; (*straighten out*) clear (up), settle, resolve; reform, organize, reorganize.

straight•for•ward /stráytfáwrwərd/ *adj.*
1 honest or frank. **2** (of a task, etc.) uncomplicated. □□ **straight′for′ward•ly** *adv.*
straight′for′ward•ness *n.*

■ **1** odd, bizarre, weird, curious, uncommon. **2** unknown, exotic, new. **3** uneasy, uncomfortable, awkward.

strain¹ /strayn/ • *v.* **1** *tr. & intr.* stretch tightly; make or become taut or tense. **2** *tr.* exercise (oneself, one's senses, a thing, etc.) intensely or excessively; press to extremes. **3** *intr.* strive intensely. **4** *intr.* (foll. by *at*) tug; pull. **5** *tr.* distort from the true intention or meaning. **6** *tr.* overwhelm or injure by overuse or excessive demands. **7** *tr.* clear (a liquid) of solid matter by passing it through a sieve, etc.; filter. • *n.* **1 a** act or an instance of straining. **b** force exerted in this. **2** injury caused by straining a muscle, etc. **3 a** severe demand on physical strength or resources. **b** exertion needed to meet this. **4** [in *sing.* or *pl.*] snatch or spell of music or poetry. **5** tone or tendency in speech or writing (*more in the same strain*). □□ **strain′a•ble** *adj.*

■ *v.* **1** crane, tense, tauten, tension; see also TIGHTEN. **2** see TAX *v.* 3. **3** try (hard), struggle, labor, toil, push. **4** push, heave, stretch, twist, wrench, struggle. **5** see STRETCH *v.* 6. **6** hurt, harm, impair, damage, pull, tear; stretch, force, tax, burden, overburden. **7** sift, drain, screen, sieve, leach, separate; percolate, seep. • *n.* **1 a** see *exertion* (EXERT). **2** sprain, wrick, damage, harm, wrench, pull. **3 a** tax, burden, stress, pressure. **b** stress, tension, pressure, overexertion, overwork; anxiety, worry. **4** air, melody, tune, phrase, cadence. **5** tenor, drift, inclination, quality, spirit, mood, humor.

strain² /strayn/ *n.* **1** breed or stock of animals, plants, etc. **2** moral tendency as part of a person's character.

■ **1** family, ancestry, roots, extraction, derivation, background, variety. **2** trace, hint, suggestion, suspicion.

strained /straynd/ *adj.* **1** constrained; forced; artificial. **2** (of a relationship) mutually distrustful or tense.

■ **1** labored, false, stiff, self-conscious, unnatural. **2** awkward, uneasy, uncomfortable, difficult, fraught.

strain•er /stráynər/ *n.* device for straining liquids, etc.

strait /strayt/ *n.* **1** [in *sing.* or *pl.*] narrow passage of water connecting two seas or large bodies of water. **2** [usu. in *pl.*] difficulty; distress. □□ **strait′ly** *adv.* **strait′ness** *n.*

■ **1** narrows, channel, sound, neck. **2** trouble, need, predicament.

strait•ened /stráytnd/ *adj.* characterized by poverty.

strait•jack•et /stráytjakit/ *n.* **1** strong garment with long arms for confining a violent person. **2** restrictive measures.

strait•laced /stráytláyst/ *adj.* puritanical.

■ priggish, prim, Victorian, prudish.

strand¹ /strand/ • *v.* **1** *tr. & intr.* run aground. **2** *tr.* (as **stranded** *adj.*) in difficulties, esp. without money or means of transport. • *n. rhet.* or *poet.* shoreline, beach.

strand² /strand/ *n.* **1** each of the threads or wires twisted around each other to make a rope or cable. **2** single thread or strip of fiber **b** constituent filament. **3** lock of hair. **4** element or strain in any composite whole.

strange /straynj/ *adj.* **1** unusual; peculiar; surprising; eccentric; novel. **2** unfamiliar; alien; foreign. **3** not at ease; out of one's element (*felt very strange in such company*). □□ **strange′ly** *adv.* **strange′ness** *n.*

strang•er /stráynjər/ *n.* **1** person new to a particular place or company. **2** person one does not know. **3** person entirely unaccustomed to (a feeling, experience, etc.).

■ **1** foreigner, outlander, outsider, alien, newcomer.

stran•gle /stránggəl/ *v.tr.* **1** squeeze the windpipe or neck of, esp. so' as to kill. **2** hamper or suppress. □□ **stran′gler** *n.*

■ **1** throttle, choke, garrotte. **2** see SUPPRESS.

stran•gle•hold /stránggəlhōld/ *n.* **1** illegal throttling hold in wrestling. **2** deadly grip. **3** complete and exclusive control.

stran•gu•late /stránggyəlayt/ *v.tr. Surgery* prevent circulation through (a vein, intestine, etc.) by compression.

stran•gu•la•tion /stránggyəláyshən/ *n.* **1** act of strangling or the state of being strangled. **2** the act of strangulating.

strap /strap/ • *n.* **1** strip of leather, etc., often with a buckle or other fastening for holding things together, etc. **2** thing like this for keeping a garment in place. • *v.tr.* (**strapped, strap•ping**) secure or bind with a strap.

strap•ping /stráping/ *adj.* (esp. of a person) large and sturdy.

stra•ta *pl.* of STRATUM.

strat•a•gem /strátəjəm/ *n.* **1** cunning plan or scheme, esp. for deceiving an enemy. **2** trickery.

■ **1** trick, artifice, device, dodge, subterfuge, lure, wile, ruse, deceit, deception, plot. **2** see TRICKERY.

stra•te•gic /strəteéjik/ *adj.* **1** of or serving the ends of strategy; useful or important with regard to strategy. **2** (of materials) essential in fighting a war. **3** (of bombing or weapons) done or for use as a longer-term military objective. □□ **stra•te′gi•cal** *adj.* **stra•te′gi•cal•ly** *adv.* **stra•te′gics** *n.pl.* [usu. treated as *sing.*].

■ **1** calculated, planned, deliberate, politic, tactical, wise.

strat•e•gy /strátijee/ *n.* (*pl.* **–gies**) **1** art of war or military deployment. **2** plan of action or policy in business or politics, etc. (*economic strategy*). □□ **strat′e•gist** *n.*

■ generalship, military science; tactic(s), design, procedure, approach, maneuver, scheme.

strat•i•fy /strátifi/ *v.tr.* (**–fies, –fied**) **1** (esp. as **stratified** *adj.*) arrange in strata. **2** construct in layers, social grades, etc. □□ **strat•i•fi•ca′tion** *n.*

strat•o•sphere /strátəsfeer/ *n.* layer of atmospheric air above the troposphere extending to about 30 miles above the earth's surface. □□ **strat·o·spher'ic** adj.

stra·tum /stráytəm, strát–/ n. (pl. **stra·ta** /–tə/ or **stratums**) **1** esp. Geol. or Archaeol. layer or set of layers of any deposited substance. **2** atmospheric layer. **3** social class. □□ **stra'tal** adj.

■ **1, 2** level, stratification; lamina, sheet, thickness; plane. **3** level, caste, rank, echelon, station, status.

straw /straw/ n. **1** dry cut stalks of grain for use as fodder or as material for packing, etc. **2** single stalk or piece of straw. **3** thin tube for sucking a drink from a glass, etc. **4** pale yellow color. □ **straw vote** (or **poll**) unofficial ballot as a test of opinion.

straw·ber·ry /stráwberee/ n. (pl. **–ries**) **1** plant with white flowers, trifoliate leaves, and runners. **2** pulpy red edible fruit of this, having a seed-studded surface.

stray /stray/ • v.intr. **1 a** wander from the right place or from one's companions, etc.; go astray. **b** digress. **2** deviate morally. • n. person or thing that has strayed, esp. a domestic animal. • adj. **1** strayed or lost. **2** isolated; found or occurring occasionally (hit by a stray bullet). □□ **stray'er** n.

■ v. **1** roam, rove, range, straggle, drift; deviate, diverge, ramble. **2** see SIN¹ v. **n.** straggler, vagrant, dogie. • adj. **1** vagrant, roving, roaming, wandering, homeless. **2** separate(d), lone, odd, single; random, casual, chance, accidental, haphazard, singular.

streak /streek/ • n. **1** long thin usu. irregular line or band, esp. of color. **2** strain or element in a person's character. **3** spell or series (winning streak). • v. **1** tr. mark with streaks. **2** intr. move very rapidly. **3** intr. colloq. run naked in a public place. □□ **streak'er** n. **streak'ing** n.

■ n. **1** stripe, strip, stroke, bar, mark, smear; vein, layer, seam, stratum. **2** see VEIN 5. **3** period, stretch, run, spate. • v. **1** stripe, line, bar, smear, daub. **2** race, run, rush, dash, sprint, dart, hurtle, fly, flit, speed, zip.

streak·y /streekee/ adj. (**streak·i·er**, **streak·i·est**) full of streaks. □□ **streak'i·ly** adv. **streak'i·ness** n.

stream /streem/ • n. **1** flowing body of water, esp. a small river. **2** flow of a fluid, a mass of people, questions, etc. **3** current; direction (against the stream). • v.intr. **1** flow or move as a stream. **2** run with liquid.

■ n. **1** brook, rivulet, tributary, branch. **2** current, outpouring, effluence, rush, spurt; swarm, tide, spate. **3** course, tide, mainstream; see also TREND n. • v. **1** run, course, glide; pour, issue, gush; teem, swarm; file, proceed, march.

stream·er /streemər/ n. **1** long narrow flag. **2** long narrow strip of ribbon or paper.

■ **1** pennant, banner, pennon, banderole, gonfalon.

stream·line /streemlīn/ v.tr. **1** give (a vehicle, etc.) the form which presents the least resistance to motion. **2** make simple or more efficient or better organized. **3** (as **streamlined** adj.) **a** aerodynamic. **b** having a sim-

---

827 **stratum ~ stress**

plified and more efficient structure or organization.

■ **3** (**streamlined**) **a** curved, curvilinear; smooth, flowing, sleek. **b** modernized, labor-saving, (well-)organized, efficient, automated, well-run.

street /street/ n. **1 a** public road in a city, town, or village. **b** this with the houses or other buildings on each side. **2** persons who live or work on a particular street. □ **on the streets 1** living by prostitution. **2** homeless.

■ **1** thoroughfare, way, main road, roadway, avenue, concourse, boulevard, lane, drive, terrace.

street·car /streetkaar/ n. commuter vehicle that operates on rails in city streets.

street·walk·er /streetwawkər/ n. prostitute seeking customers on the street. □□ **street' walk·ing** n. & adj.

street·wise /streetwīz/ n. familiar with the ways of modern urban life.

strength /strengkth, strength, strenth/ n. **1** being strong; degree or manner of this. **2 a** person or thing affording strength. **b** positive attribute. **3** number of persons present or available. **4** full complement. □ **in strength** with the force of large numbers. **on the strength of** on the basis of.

■ **1** power, might, force, mightiness, robustness, toughness; durability, reliability, resistance, solidity, stamina; fortitude, backbone, tenacity, tenaciousness, willpower, perseverance, persistence; concentration, intensity, potency; efficacy, persuasiveness. **2 a** see PILLAR 2. **b** talent, ability, aptitude, endowment, gift.

strength·en /stréngkthən, strén–/ v. make or become stronger. □□ **strength'en·er** n.

■ reinforce, renew, bolster, fortify; confirm, consolidate, back up; step up, increase, intensify; encourage, hearten, invigorate, rejuvenate, nourish, steel.

stren·u·ous /strényōōəs/ adj. **1** requiring or using great effort. **2** energetic. □□ **stren'u·ous·ly** adv. **stren'u·ous·ness** n.

■ **1** demanding, taxing, tough, arduous, laborious. **2** active, vigorous, enthusiastic, zealous, earnest, dynamic, intense, indefatigable, tireless.

strep·to·coc·cus /stréptəkókəs/ n. (pl. **strep·to·coc·ci** /–kóksī, –kókī/) bacterium of a type often causing infectious diseases. □□ **strep·to·coc'cal** adj.

strep·to·my·cin /stréptəmísin/ n. antibiotic effective against many disease-producing bacteria.

stress /stres/ • n. **1** pressure; tension. **2** physical or mental strain or distress. **3 a** emphasis. **b** accentuation; emphasis laid on a syllable or word. • v.tr. **1** emphasize. **2** subject to stress. □ **stressed out** lethargic owing to long-term stress. □□ **stress'less** adj.

■ n. **1** see PRESSURE n. 1a, b, TENSION n. 1. **2** burden, anxiety, worry, pain, grief. **3 a** importance, weight, force. **b** force, forcefulness, accent. • v. **1** accent, accentuate, lay stress or emphasis on, underscore, dwell on, insist on, focus on, spotlight. **2** strain, upset, disturb, burden, worry, distress.

stress•ful /strésfŏŏl/ *adj.* causing stress; mentally tiring. □□ **stress′ful•ly** *adv.* **stress′ful•ness** *n.*

stretch /strech/ • *v.* **1** *tr. & intr.* draw or be drawn or admit of being drawn out into greater length or size. **2** *tr. & intr.* make or become taut. **3** *tr. & intr.* place or lie at full length or spread out. **4** *tr.* [also *absol.*] **a** extend (an arm, leg, etc.). **b** [often *refl.*] thrust out one's limbs and tighten one's muscles after being relaxed. **5** *intr.* have a specified length or extension; extend. **6** *tr.* strain; exaggerate (*stretch the truth*). • *n.* **1** continuous extent or expanse or period. **2** stretching or being stretched. **3** [*attrib.*] elastic (*stretch fabric*). **4** *colloq.* period of imprisonment; military service, etc. **5** straight side of a racetrack. □ **at a stretch** in one continuous period. **stretch a point** agree to something not normally allowed. □□ **stretch′a•ble** *adj.* **stretch•a•bil′i•ty** *n.* **stretch′y** *adj.* **stretch′i•ness** *n.*

■ *v.* **1** distend, lengthen, elongate, widen, broaden, swell. **3** see SPREAD *v.* 1a. **5** reach, continue; span; spread. **6** overtax, overextend, overburden, tax; warp, distort, bend, break; overstate. • *n.* **1** reach, span, distance, length, spread; see also PERIOD *n.* 1. **3** (*attrib.*) see ELASTIC *adj.* 1, 2. **4** stint, spell, term; *colloq.* time; tour (of duty).

stretch•er /stréchər/ *n.* framework of two poles with canvas, etc., between, for carrying a person in a lying position.

strew /strōō/ *v.tr.* (*past part.* **strewn** or **strewed**) **1** scatter or spread about over a surface. **2** [usu. foll. by *with*] spread (a surface) with scattered things. □□ **strew′er** *n.*

■ bestrew, sprinkle, litter; disperse, toss, distribute.

stri•ate /stríət/ *adj.* (also **stri•at•ed** /stríáytid/) *Anat., Zool., Bot.,* and *Geol.* marked with parallel lines, ridges, etc. □□ **stri•a•tion** /stríáyshən/ *n.*

strick•en /stríkən/ *adj.* affected or overcome with illness or misfortune, etc. (*stricken with measles*).

■ **1** broken, crushed, demoralized; (*stricken by* or *with*) struck (down) by, laid low by or with, afflicted with.

strict /strikt/ *adj.* **1** precisely limited or defined; undeviating. **2** requiring complete compliance or exact performance (*gave strict orders*). See synonym study at SEVERE. □□ **strict′ly** *adv.* **strict′ness** *n.*

■ **1** rigorous, narrow, close, confining, constricting, constrictive, rigid, precise, accurate. **2** rigid, set, unalterable, invariable, hard-and-fast, tight.

stric•ture /stríkchər/ *n.* **1** [usu. in *pl.*] critical or censorious remark. **2** restriction.

stride /strīd/ • *v.* (*past* **strode** /strōd/; *past part.* **strid•den** /stríd′n/) **1** *intr. & tr.* walk with long firm steps. **2** *tr.* cross with one step. **3** *tr.* bestride; straddle. • *n.* **1 a** single long step. **b** length of this. **2** person's gait as determined by the length of stride. **3** [usu.

in *pl.*] progress (*great strides*). **4** settled rate of progress (*get into one's stride*). □ **take in one's stride** manage without difficulty. □□ **strid′er** *n.*

stri•dent /stríd′nt/ *adj.* loud and harsh. See synonym study at VOCIFEROUS. □□ **stri′den•cy** *n.* **stri′dent•ly** *adv.*

■ shrill, raucous, clamorous, noisy, grating, stridulant, scraping, scratching, scratchy, screeching, grinding.

strife /strīf/ *n.* conflict; struggle.

■ discord, disharmony, disagreement, difference, rivalry, competition, contention, dispute, animosity, friction, hard feelings, bad feeling(s).

strike /strīk/ • *v.* (*past* **struck** /struk/; *past part.* **struck** or *archaic* **strick•en** /stríkən/) **1 a** *tr.* subject to an impact. **b** *tr.* deliver (a blow) or inflict a blow on; hit. **2** *tr.* come or bring sharply into contact with (*ship struck a rock*). **3** *tr.* propel or divert with a blow (*struck the ball into the pond*). **4** *intr.* [foll. by *at*] try to hit. **5** *tr.* ignite (a match) or produce (sparks, etc.) by rubbing. **6** *tr.* make (a coin) by stamping. **7** *tr.* produce (a musical note) by striking. **8 a** *tr.* [also *absol.*] (of a clock) indicate (the time) with a chime, etc. **b** *intr.* (of time) be indicated in this way. **9** *tr.* **a** attack or affect suddenly. **b** (of a disease) afflict. **10** *tr.* cause to become suddenly (*struck dumb*). **11** *tr.* reach or achieve (*strike a balance*). **12** *tr.* agree on (a bargain). **13** *tr.* assume (an attitude) suddenly and dramatically. **14** *tr.* **a** discover or find. **b** find (oil, etc.) by drilling. **15** occur to or appear to (*strikes me as silly*). **16 a** *intr.* (of employees) engage in a strike. **b** *tr.* act in this way against (an employer). **17 a** *tr.* lower or take down (a flag, tent, stage set, etc.). **b** *intr.* signify surrender by striking a flag. • *n.* **1** act or instance of striking. **2** organized refusal by employees to work until some grievance is remedied. **3** sudden find or success (*lucky strike*). **4** an attack, esp. from the air. **5** *Baseball* pitched ball counted against a batter, either for failure to hit it fair or because it passes through the strike zone. □ **on strike** taking part in an industrial, etc., strike. **strike home** **1** deal an effective blow. **2** have an intended effect (*my words struck home*). **strike out** **1** hit out. **2** act vigorously. **3** delete (an item or name, etc.). **4** *Baseball* **a** dismiss (a batter) by means of three strikes. **b** be dismissed in this way. **c** *sl.* fail. **strike up** **1** start (an acquaintance, conversation, etc.) off-handedly or casually. **2** [also *absol.*] begin playing (a tune), etc.). □□ **strik′a•ble** *adj.* **strik′er** *n.*

■ *v.* **1** knock, smack, thump, trounce. **2** hit, collide with, land on or in or against, run into. **3** see HIT *v.* 8a. **4** see SWIPE *v.* 1. **5** light. **6** impress, print, punch, mint. **8 a** see CHIME *v.* 1. **9 a** seize, beset, overcome, assail; penetrate, hit; see also CONSUME 3. **b** affect, attack. **11** arrive at, attain; see also REALIZE 4. **12** make, reach; agree or settle (on), ratify. **13** adopt, put on, display, affect. **14** encounter, come or happen upon. **15** come to, dawn on, register with. **16 a** walk out (of the job), go on strike, stop or quit working. **17 a** remove, take apart, dismantle; pull *or* haul down. • *n.* **1** see HIT *n.* 1a. **2** walkout, sit-down (strike), sit-in, stoppage. **3** see WIND-FALL. **4** see ASSAULT *n.* 1.

strike·break·er /stríkbraykər/ *n.* person working or employed in place of strikers. □□ **strike′break** *v.intr.*

strik·ing /stríking/ *adj.* impressive; attracting attention. See synonym study at NOTICEABLE. □□ **strik′ing·ly** *adv.*

■ remarkable, astounding, astonishing, amazing, awe-inspiring, awesome, imposing, great; conspicuous, noticeable, prominent, salient; *colloq.* smashing.

string /string/ • *n.* **1** twine or narrow cord. **2** piece of this. **3** length of catgut or wire, etc., on a musical instrument, producing a note by vibration. **4 a** [in *pl.*] stringed instruments in an orchestra, etc. **b** [*attrib.*] relating to or consisting of stringed instruments (*string quartet*). **5** [in *pl.*] condition; complication (*offer has no strings*). • *v.tr.* (*past and past part.* **strung** /strung/) **1** supply with a string or strings. **2** thread (beads, etc.) on a string. **3** arrange in or as a string. □ **string along** *colloq.* **1** deceive. **2** keep company (with). **string out** extend; prolong (esp. unduly). **string up** **1** hang up on strings, etc. **2** kill by hanging. □□ **string′less** *adj.* **string′like** *adj.*

■ *n.* **1** line, thread, fiber, rope, cable, strand, filament. **2** tie, lace, cord, line; leash, lead, leader. **5** (*strings*) stipulations, provisos, qualifications, requirements, prerequisites, terms. • *n.* **3** line up, align, array, connect, link, join, chain together. □ **string along 1** fool, bluff, dupe, cheat. **2** (*string along with*) accompany, go *or* tag along with, associate with, hang around with. **string out** stretch; drag out, protract, spin out. **string up 1** festoon, loop, drape, suspend, sling, array. **2** hang, lynch.

stringed /stringd/ *adj.* (of musical instruments) having strings (also in *comb.*: *twelve-stringed guitar*).

strin·gent /strínjənt/ *adj.* (of rules, etc.) strict; precise. □□ **strin′gen·cy** *n.* **strin′gent·ly** *adv.*

string·er /stríngər/ *n.* **1** longitudinal structural member in a framework, esp. of a ship or aircraft. **2** *colloq.* newspaper correspondent not on the regular staff.

string·y /stríngee/ *adj.* (**string·i·er**, **string·i·est**) (of food, etc.) fibrous; like string. □□ **string′i·ly** *adv.* **string′i·ness** *n.*

■ chewy, sinewy, gristly; stringlike, ropy, threadlike.

strip[1] /strip/ • *v.* (**stripped**, **strip·ping**) **1** *v.* remove the clothes or covering from. **2** *intr.* undress oneself. **3** *tr.* deprive (a person) of property or titles. **4** *tr.* leave bare. **5** *tr.* remove the accessory fittings of or take apart (a machine, etc.). **6** *tr.* tear the thread from (a screw). **7** *tr.* tear the teeth from (a gearwheel). • *n.* act of stripping, esp. of undressing in striptease. □ **strip mine** mine worked by removing the material that overlies the ore, etc. **strip search** *n.* search of a person involving the removal of all clothes. *v.tr.* search in this way.

■ *v.* **1** disrobe, undress; peel, skin, bare, uncover, expose; fleece, shear, pluck; defoliate. **2** get undressed, unclothe (oneself); get naked, strip down to nothing, peel off one's clothes; (do a) striptease. **3** see DEPRIVE 1. **4** clear; gut, clean out, clear out, empty. **5** dismantle.

strip[2] /strip/ *n.* long narrow piece (*strip of land*).

■ band, ribbon, fillet, belt, swathe, stripe, slat, lath.

stripe /strip/ *n.* **1** long narrow band or strip differing in color or texture from the surface on either side of it (*black with a red stripe*). **2** *Mil.* chevron, etc., denoting military rank. **3** category of character, opinion, etc. (*man of that stripe*).

■ **1** bar, striation, streak, vein, thread, line. **3** style, kind, sort, class, type, complexion, character, nature.

striped /stript/ *adj.* marked with stripes (also in *comb.*: *red-striped*).

■ stripy, streaked, lined, banded, *Anat. & Zool.* striated.

strip·ling /strípling/ *n.* youth not yet fully grown.

strip·per /strípər/ *n.* **1** person or thing that strips something. **2** striptease performer.

strip·tease /strípteez/ *n.* entertainment in which the performer slowly and erotically undresses. □□ **strip·teas′er** *n.*

strive /striv/ *v.intr.* (*past* **strove** /strov/; *past part.* **striv·en** /strívən/) **1** try hard. **2** struggle or contend. □□ **striv′er** *n.*

■ **1** endeavor, strain, struggle, make an *or* every effort, take pains, attempt, work; exert oneself, work at, give (it) one's all, go all out. **2** compete, fight, battle.

strobe /strob/ *n. colloq.* stroboscope.

stro·bo·scope /strobəskōp/ *n.* **1** *Physics* instrument for determining speeds of rotation, etc., by shining a bright light at intervals so that a rotating object appears stationary. **2** lamp made to flash intermittently. □□ **stro·bo·scop·ic** /-skópik/ *adj.*

strode *past of* STRIDE.

stroke /strok/ • *n.* **1** act of striking; blow or hit. **2** sudden disabling attack caused esp. by thrombosis. **3 a** action or movement esp. as one of a series. **b** slightest such action (*stroke of work*). **4** whole of the motion (of a wing, oar, etc.) until the starting position is regained. **5** mode of moving the arms and legs in swimming. **6** specially successful or skillful effort (*a stroke of diplomacy*). **7** mark made by the movement in one direction of a pen or pencil or paintbrush. **8** sound made by a striking clock. **9** act or a spell of stroking. • *v.tr.* **1** caress lightly. **2** act as the stroke of (a boat or crew). **3** *colloq.* flatter; seek to influence by flattery.

■ *n.* **1** rap, tap, thump, knock, lash, smack, slam. **2** seizure, fit, apoplexy, apoplectic fit, spasm. **3 a** motion, go, move, feat, achievement. **b** bit, jot (or tittle), scrap, iota, touch, stitch. **6** achievement; feat, act, action, work. **7** flourish, movement, gesture; mark, dash, sweep. **8** pat, touch, caress, rub, massage. • v. 1 pet, pat, fondle; massage, rub, soothe.

stroll /strōl/ • v.intr. saunter or walk in a leisurely way. • n. short leisurely walk (go for a stroll).

■ v. amble, ramble, wander, promenade, meander. • n. amble, ramble, saunter, wander, constitutional.

stroll•er /strōlər/ n. 1 person who strolls. 2 folding chair on wheels, for pushing a child in.

strong /strawng, strong/ • adj. (**strong•er** /stráwnggər, stróng–/; **strong•est** /stráwnggist, stróng–/) 1 having the power of resistance; not easily damaged, overcome, or disturbed. 2 healthy. 3 capable of exerting great force or of doing much; muscular; powerful. 4 forceful or powerful in effect (strong wind). 5 decided or firmly held (strong views). 6 (of an argument, etc.) convincing or striking. 7 intense; concentrated. 8 formidable (strong candidate). 9 (of a group) having a specified number (200 strong). 10 Gram. forming inflections by change of vowel within the stem (e.g., swim, swam). • adv. strongly. □ **come on strong** act aggressively. **strong-arm** using force (strong-arm tactics). □□ **strong′ly** adv.

■ adj. 1 solid, sturdy, substantial, stout, tough, sound, well-built, reinforced, heavy-duty, durable. 2 see HEALTHY 1. 3 mighty, brawny, strapping, robust, sturdy, stalwart, burly, stout, sinewy. 4 vigorous, heavy; urgent, strongly worded, emphatic, assertive; effective, efficacious, effectual. 5 firm, definite, unshakable, unwavering; deep-felt, deep-seated, deep-rooted, basic, intense, fervent. 6 well-supported, irrefutable, well-substantiated, cogent, forceful, powerful, potent, substantial, weighty, solid. 7 dazzling, glaring, bright, garish; powerful, compelling; pungent, potent; fortified, stiff, alcoholic. 8 likely; competent, talented, able, experienced; forthright, positive, willful. 9 numerically, in number, in strength. □ **strong-arm** threatening, menacing, bullying, high-pressure, thuggish, violent.

strong•box /stráwngboks, stróng–/ n. strongly made small chest for valuables.

strong•hold /stráwnghōld, stróng–/ n. 1 fortified place. 2 secure refuge. 3 center of support for a cause, etc.

■ 1 fortress, bulwark, bastion, fastness, fortification, fort, castle. 2 see REFUGE 1. 3 bastion, fortress, bulwark.

strong•room /stráwngrōōm, –rŏŏm, stróng–/ n. room designed to protect valuables against fire and theft.

stron•ti•um /strónteeəm/ n. Chem. soft silver white metallic element occurring naturally in various minerals. ¶Symb.: **Sr**. □ **strontium 90** radioactive isotope of strontium.

strop /strop/ • n. device, esp. a strip of leather, for sharpening razors. • v.tr. (**stropped, strop•ping**) sharpen on or with a strop.

strove past of STRIVE.

struck past and past part. of STRIKE.

struc•ture /strúkchər/ • n. 1 a constructed unit, esp. a building. b way in which a building, etc., is constructed. 2 framework. • v.tr. give structure or shape to; organize; frame. □□ **struc′tur•al** adj. **struc′tured** adj. [also in comb.]. **struc′ture•less** adj.

■ n. 1 a edifice, house, construction. b construction, fabric, framework, design. 2 form, shape, configuration, construction, organization; system, setup, mechanism, nature, character. • v. construct, build, design, form, shape, arrange, systematize.

stru•del /strōōd′l/ n. confection of thin pastry rolled up around a filling and baked (apple strudel).

strug•gle /strúgəl/ • v.intr. 1 make forceful or violent efforts to get free of restraint or constriction. 2 try hard under difficulties. 3 [foll. by with, against] contend; fight. 4 make one's way with difficulty (struggled to my feet). 5 (esp. as **struggling** adj.) have difficulty in gaining recognition or a living. • n. 1 act or spell of struggling. 2 hard or confused contest. 3 determined effort under difficulties. □□ **strug′gler** n.

■ v. 1, 2 strive, strain, exert oneself, labor, toil; wriggle, squirm, writhe, twist, worm. 3 wrestle, battle, war, grapple; tussle, scuffle. 4 see FLOUNDER¹ v., SCRAMBLE v. 1. • n. 1, 3 exertion, strain, endeavor; toil, work, labor; trial, colloq. grind. 2 contention, competition, battle, fight, combat, tussle.

strum /strum/ • v.tr. (**strummed, strum•ming**) 1 play on (a stringed or keyboard instrument), esp. carelessly or unskillfully. 2 play (a tune, etc.) in this way. • n. sound made by strumming. □□ **strum′mer** n.

strung past and past part. of STRING.

strut /strut/ • n. 1 bar forming part of a framework and designed to resist compression. 2 strutting gait. • v.intr. (**strut•ted, strut•ting**) walk with a pompous or affected stiff erect gait. □□ **strut′ter** n. **strut′ting•ly** adv.

■ n. 1 see BRACE n. 1b. 2 prance, swagger. • v. swagger, parade, promenade, prance.

strych•nine /stríknīn, –nin, –neen/ n. vegetable alkaloid, bitter and highly poisonous, formerly used as a stimulant and (in small amounts) a medication. □□ **strych′nic** adj.

stub /stub/ • n. 1 shortened remnant of a pencil, cigarette, etc., after use. 2 part of a check, receipt, etc., retained as a record. 3 stump. • v.tr. (**stubbed, stub•bing**) 1 strike (one's toe) against something. 2 extinguish (a cigarette) by pressure.

■ n. 1, 3 butt (end), end, tail (end). 2 tally, ticket. • v. 1 bump, knock, hit. 2 (stub out) put out.

stub•ble /stúbəl/ n. 1 cut stalks of cereal plants left sticking up after the harvest. 2 a cropped hair or cropped beard. b short growth of unshaven hair. □□ **stub′bled** adj. **stub′bly** adj.

stub•born /stúbərn/ adj. obstinate; inflexible. □□ **stub′born•ly** adv. **stub′born•ness** n.

■ unyielding, obdurate, intransigent, intractable, uncompromising, mulish, pigheaded, adamant, dogged.

SYNONYM STUDY: **stubborn**

DOGGED, INTRACTABLE, OBDURATE, OBSTINATE, PERTINACIOUS, PERVERSE. If you're the kind of person who takes a stand and then refuses to back down, your friends might say you have a **stubborn** disposition, a word that implies an innate resistance to any attempt to change one's purpose, course, or opinion. People who are *stubborn* by nature exhibit this kind of behavior in most situations, but they might be **obstinate** in a particular instance (*a stubborn child, he was obstinate in his refusal to eat vegetables*). *Obstinate* implies sticking persistently, especially in the face of persuasion or attack, to an opinion, purpose, or course of action. While *obstinate* is usually a negative term, **dogged** can be either positive or negative, implying both tenacious, often sullen, persistence (*dogged pursuit of a college degree, even though he knew he would end up in the family business*) and great determination (*dogged loyalty to a cause*). **Obdurate** usually connotes a *stubborn* resistance marked by harshness and lack of feeling (*to be obdurate in ignoring their pleas*), while **intractable** means *stubborn* in a headstrong sense and difficult for others to control or manage (*intractable pain*). No matter how *stubborn* you are, you probably don't want to be called **pertinacious**, which implies persistence to the point of being annoying or unreasonable (*a pertinacious panhandler*).

stub•by /stúbee/ *adj.* (**stub•bi•er, stub•bi•est**) short and thick. □□ **stub'bi•ly** *adv.* **stub'bi•ness** *n.*

stuc•co /stúkō/ • *n.* (*pl.* **-coes** or **-cos**) plaster or cement for coating walls. • *v.tr.* (**-coes, -coed**) coat with stucco.

stuck *past* and *past part.* of STICK².

stuck-up /stúk úp/ *adj.* conceited.

stud¹ /stud/ • *n.* **1** large-headed nail, boss, or knob, esp. for ornament. **2** double button for a collar, shirt front, etc. • *v.tr.* (**stud•ded, stud•ding**) **1** set with or as with studs. **2** (as **studded** *adj.*) [foll. by *with*] thickly set or strewn.

stud² /stud/ *n.* **1** (in full **stud horse**) stallion. **2** *colloq.* young man (esp. one noted for sexual prowess). **3** (in full **stud poker**) form of poker in which some cards are dealt face up. □ **at stud** (of a male horse) hired out for breeding.

stu•dent /stōōd'nt, styōōd-/ *n.* person who is studying, esp. at school, college, etc.

■ pupil, learner, undergraduate, postgraduate, schoolboy, schoolgirl, schoolchild, trainee, apprentice.

stu•di•o /stōōdeeō, styōō-/ *n.* (*pl.* **-os**) **1** workroom of a painter or photographer, etc. **2** place where movies, recordings, or broadcast programs are made. □ **studio couch** couch that can be converted into a bed.

stu•di•ous /stōōdeeəs, styōō-/ *adj.* **1** assiduous in study. **2** painstaking. □□ **stu'di•ous•ly** *adv.* **stu'di•ous•ness** *n.*

■ **1** scholarly, bookish, academic. **2** assiduous, sedulous, diligent, industrious, attentive, careful, thorough, deliberate.

stud•y /stúdee/ • *n.* (*pl.* **-ies**) **1** acquisition of knowledge, esp. from books. **2** [in *pl.*] pursuit of academic knowledge. **3** room used for reading, writing, etc. **4** piece of work, esp. a drawing, done for practice or as an experiment (*a study of a head*). **5** thing worth observing closely (*your face was a study*). **6** thing that has been or deserves to be investigated. • *v.* (**-ies, -ied**) **1** *tr.* make a study of; investigate or examine (a subject) (*study law*). **2** *intr.* apply oneself to study. **3** *tr.* scrutinize or earnestly contemplate (*studied their faces*). **4** *tr.* learn (one's role, etc.). **5** *tr.* (as **studied** *adj.*) deliberate; affected.

■ *n.* **1, 2** learning, lessons, schooling, education, training, instruction, bookwork, work, reading, contemplation, investigation. **3** library, reading room, study hall, haunt, studio, retreat, den, workroom, office. **4** see PORTRAIT 1, 2. **6** project, program; analysis, review, examination, survey, inquiry, investigation, research, exploration. • *v.* **1, 3** look into *or* over *or* at, go into *or* over, scan, examine, analyze, inspect; learn (about), read; consider, reflect on, think over *or* about. **2** burn the midnight oil, cram, *colloq.* bone up. **4** memorize, practice, rehearse, go over, run through, *colloq.* bone up on. **5** (**studied**) premeditated, calculated, measured, planned, contrived, feigned, forced, labored.

stuff /stuf/ • *n.* **1** material; fabric. **2** unspecified content, things, etc. **3** particular knowledge *or* activity (*know one's stuff*). • *v.* **1** *tr.* pack (a receptacle) tightly. **2** *tr.* [foll. by *in, into*] force or cram (a thing). **3** *tr.* fill out the skin of (a preserved animal or bird, etc.) to restore the original shape. **4** *tr.* fill (poultry, vegetables, etc.) with a mixture, esp. before cooking. **5 a** *tr. & refl.* fill (a person or oneself) with food. **b** *tr. & intr.* eat greedily. **6** *tr.* [usu. in *passive*] block up (a person's nose, etc.) □ **stuffed shirt** *colloq.* pompous person. □□ **stuff'er** *n.* [also in *comb.*].

■ *n.* **1** substance, matter, ingredients, constituents, essence, essentials. **2** matter, substance, material; articles, objects, creations; goods, gear, equipment, materials, trappings, lumber, junk. • *v.* **1, 3** line, pad. **2** jam, ram, crowd, compress, pack, press, squeeze. **5 a** overfeed, satiate, glut, surfeit; (*stuff oneself*) overeat, gorge, overindulge. **b** see DEVOUR 1. **6** (*stuff up*) clog (up), congest, bung up; choke, plug (up), obstruct, stop up.

stuff•ing /stúfing/ *n.* **1** padding used to stuff cushions, etc. **2** mixture used to stuff food, esp. before cooking.

stuff•y /stúfee/ *adj.* (**stuff•i•er, stuff•i•est**) **1** (of a room, etc.) lacking fresh air. **2** (of a person's nose, etc.) stuffed up. **3** dull and conventional. □□ **stuff'i•ly** *adv.* **stuff'i•ness** *n.*

■ **1** close, airless, unventilated, oppressive, stifling. **2** blocked up, congested, clogged up. **3** dreary, uninteresting; pompous, pedantic, narrow-minded, self-important, self-centered, stodgy.

stul•ti•fy /stúltifī/ *v.tr.* (**-fies, -fied**) make

ineffective, useless, or futile, esp. as a result of tedious routine (*stultifying boredom*). □□ **stul•ti•fi•ca'tion** *n.* **stul'ti•fi•er** *n.*

stum•ble /stŭmbəl/ • *v.intr.* **1** involuntarily lurch forward or have a partial fall. **2** walk with repeated stumbles. **3** make a mistake or repeated mistakes in speaking, etc. **4** [foll. by *on, upon, across*] find by chance (*stumbled on an abandoned well*). • *n.* act of stumbling. □ **stumbling block** obstacle. □□ **stum'bler** *n.* **stum'bling•ly** *adv.*

■ *v.* **1** slip, trip, stagger, flounder, totter, tumble. **2** see HOBBLE *v.* 1. **3** pause, hesitate, stammer, stutter, blunder. **4** chance *or* come *or* happen (up)on, hit *or* light (up)on, come *or* run across, discover, encounter, *colloq.* bump into. • *n.* see TRIP *n.* 2. □ **stumbling block** impediment, bar, block, obstruction, hurdle, hindrance, balk, barrier, difficulty, snag.

stump /stŭmp/ • *n.* **1** projecting remnant of a cut or fallen tree. **2** similar remnant cut off or worn down. • *v.tr.* **1** (of a question, etc.) be too hard for; puzzle. **2** [also *absol.*] travel through (a state, etc.) making political speeches. □□ **stump•y** *adj.* (**stump•i•er, stump•i•est**).

■ *n.* **1, 2** stub, butt, end. • *v.* **1** be beyond, mystify, confuse, perplex, bewilder, foil, baffle, confound. **2** campaign, electioneer, canvass, barnstorm.

stun /stŭn/ *v.tr.* (**stunned, stun•ning**) **1** knock senseless; stupefy. **2** bewilder or shock. **3** (of a sound) deafen temporarily.

■ **1** daze, numb, benumb, knock out; paralyze. **2** astonish, daze, paralyze, stagger, stupefy, transfix.

stung *past* and *past part.* of STING.

stunk *past* and *past part.* of STINK.

stun•ning /stŭning/ *adj. colloq.* extremely impressive or attractive. □□ **stun'ning•ly** *adv.*

■ beautiful, dazzling, brilliant, spectacular, ravishing, sensational, extraordinary, prodigious, remarkable, marvelous, stupendous, wonderful, superb, grand.

stunt[1] /stŭnt/ *v.tr.* **1** retard the growth or development of. **2** dwarf; cramp. □□ **stunt'ed•ness** *n.*

■ **1** impede, hamper, hinder, inhibit, slow (down). **2** limit, delimit, restrict, check, curb, stop, arrest.

stunt[2] /stŭnt/ *n.* **1** something unusual done to attract attention. **2** trick or daring maneuver.

■ feat, act, deed, tour de force, exploit.

stu•pe•fy /stōōpĭfī, styōō–/ *v.tr.* (**–fies, –fied**) **1** make stupid or insensible. **2** stun with astonishment. □□ **stu•pe•fa'cient** /–fāyshənt/ *adj. & n.* **stu•pe•fac'tion** /–fákshən/ *n.* **stu'pe•fy•ing** *adj.* **stu'pe•fy•ing•ly** *adv.*

stu•pen•dous /stōōpéndəs, styōō–/ *adj.* amazing or prodigious, esp. in terms of size or degree. □□ **stu•pen'dous•ly** *adv.* **stu•pen'dous•ness** *n.*

stu•pid /stōōpĭd, styōō–/ (**stu•pid•er, stu•pid•est**) *adj.* **1** unintelligent; slow-witted; foolish. **2** typical of stupid persons. **3** unin-

teresting or boring. □□ **stu•pid•i•ty** /–pídi-tee/ *n.* (*pl.* **–ties**) **stu'pid•ly** *adv.*

■ **1** fatuous, obtuse, dull, simple; feeble-minded, dull-witted. **2** foolish, silly, asinine, harebrained, insane. **3** insipid, dull, tedious, humdrum. □□ **stupidity** fatuousness, obtuseness, dullness, *colloq.* halfwittedness, insanity, madness.

stu•por /stōōpər, styōō–/ *n.* dazed, torpid, or helplessly amazed state. □□ **stu'por•ous** *adj.*

■ insensibility, stupefaction, torpor, torpidity, lethargy; inertness, coma, trance, daze, unconsciousness.

stur•dy /stôrdee/ *adj.* (**stur•di•er, stur•di•est**) **1** robust; strongly built. **2** vigorous (*sturdy resistance*). □□ **stur'di•ly** *adv.* **stur'di•ness** *n.*

■ **1** strong, solid, stout, rugged, tough; sound, durable; strapping, muscular, powerful. **2** stalwart, staunch, steadfast, resolute, firm, determined.

stur•geon /stôrjən/ *n.* large sharklike fish used as food and a source of caviar and isinglass.

stut•ter /stútər/ • *v.intr.* stammer, esp. by involuntarily repeating the first consonants of words. • *n.* act or habit of stuttering. □□ **stut'ter•er** *n.* **stut'ter•ing•ly** *adv.*

■ *v.* see STAMMER *v.* • *n.* see STAMMER *n.*

sty[1] /stī/ *n.* (*pl.* **sties**) **1** pen or enclosure for pigs. **2** *colloq.* filthy room or dwelling.

sty[2] /stī/ *n.* (also **stye**) (*pl.* **sties** or **styes**) inflamed swelling on the edge of an eyelid.

style /stīl/ • *n.* **1** kind or sort, esp. in regard to appearance and form (*elegant style of house*). **2** manner of writing or speaking or performing. **3** distinctive manner of a person or school or period. **4 a** superior quality or manner (*do it in style*). **b** fashion in dress, etc. • *v.tr.* **1** design or make, etc., in a particular (esp. fashionable) style. **2** designate in a specified way.

■ *n.* **1** type, variety, category, genre, manner, mode, make, design. **2, 3** quality, character, approach, treatment, vein; tenor, tone, wording, phraseology; phrasing; fashion, trend, vogue, mode. **4 a** chic, stylishness, taste, smartness, flair, dash, élan; luxury, high style, comfort. • *v.* **1** fashion, arrange, set, do, cut, tailor, shape, form. **2** characterize, denominate, call, name, term, label, tag.

styl•ish /stīlish/ *adj.* **1** fashionable; elegant. **2** having a superior quality, manner, etc. □□ **styl'ish•ly** *adv.* **styl'ish•ness** *n.*

■ **1** chic, smart, à la mode, modish, in style *or* fashion *or* vogue, neat, dapper; chichi, in, *colloq.* with it, classy.

styl•ist /stīlist/ *n.* **1 a** designer of fashionable styles, etc. **b** hairdresser. **2** stylish writer or performer.

styl•is•tic /stīlístik/ *adj.* of or concerning esp. literary style. □□ **styl•is'ti•cal•ly** *adv.*

styl•ize /stīlīz/ *v.tr.* (esp. as **stylized** *adj.*) paint, draw, etc., in a conventional nonrealistic style. □□ **styl•i•za'tion** *n.*

sty•lus /stīləs/ *n.* (*pl.* **–li** /–lī/ or **–luses**) **1** needle following a groove in a phonograph record and transmitting the recorded sound for reproduction. **2** pointed writing tool.

sty•mie /stímee/ (also **sty′my**) • *n.* (*pl.* **–mies**) *Golf* situation where an opponent's ball lies between the player and the hole. • *v.tr.* (**sty•mies, sty•mied, sty•my•ing** or **sty•mie•ing**) obstruct; thwart.

styp•tic /stíptik/ • *adj.* (of a drug, etc.) that checks bleeding. • *n.* styptic drug or substance.

sty•rene /stíreen/ *n. Chem.* liquid hydrocarbon easily polymerized and used in making plastics, etc.

Sty•ro•foam /stírəfōm/ *n. propr.* brand of expanded rigid lightweight polystyrene plastic.

sua•sion /swáyzhən/ *n. formal* persuasion as opposed to force (*moral suasion*). □□ **sua′sive** /swáysiv/ *adj.*

suave /swaav/ *adj.* smooth; polite; sophisticated. See synonym study at URBANE. □□ **suave′ly** *adv.* **suave′ness** *n.* **suav•i•ty** /-vitee/ *n.* (*pl.* **–ties**)

▪ debonair, urbane, cosmopolitan, worldly, gracious, nonchalant, civilized.

sub /sub/ *colloq.* • *n.* **1** submarine. **2** subscription. **3** substitute. • *v.intr.* (**subbed, sub•bing**) [usu. foll. by *for*] act as a substitute for a person.

sub- /sub, səb/ *prefix* **1** at or to or from a lower position (*subordinate, submerge, subtract*). **2** secondary or inferior position (*subclass, subtotal*). **3** nearly; more or less (*subarctic*).

sub•base•ment *n.*	**sub•form** *n.*
sub•branch *n.*	**sub•ge′nus** *n.*
sub•cat′e•go•ry *n.*	**sub•group′** *n.*
sub•cat•e•go•rize *v.*	**sub•king′dom** *n.*
sub•cat•e•go•ri•za′tion *n.*	**sub•or′der** *n.*
sub′class *n.*	**sub•phy′lum** *n.*
sub′clause *n.*	**sub•sec′tion** *n.*
sub•cra′ni•al *adj.*	**sub•spe′cies** *n.*
sub•fam′i•ly *n.*	**sub•ze′ro** *adj.*

sub•a•tom•ic /súbətómik/ *adj.* occurring in or smaller than an atom.

sub•com•mit•tee /súbkəmitee/ *n.* committee formed from another committee for a specialized task.

sub•com•pact /səbkómpakt/ *n. & adj.* car that is smaller than a compact.

sub•con•scious /súbkónshəs/ • *adj.* of or concerning the part of the mind which is not fully conscious but influences actions, etc. • *n.* this part of the mind. □□ **sub•con′scious•ly** *adv.* **sub•con′scious•ness** *n.*

▪ *adj.* subliminal, unconscious, suppressed, preconscious, hidden, latent, repressed, inner, innermost, underlying. • *n.* unconscious, inner self, psyche, id; heart.

sub•con•ti•nent /súbkóntinənt/ *n.* extensive landmass, smaller than a continent. □□ **sub•con•ti•nen•tal** /-nént′l/ *adj.*

sub•con•tract • *v.tr.* /súbkəntrákt/ employ a firm, etc., to do (work) as part of a larger project. • *n.* /súbkóntrakt/ secondary contract. □□ **sub•con•trac•tor** /-kóntraktər/ *n.*

sub•cul•ture /súbkulchər/ *n.* distinct cultural group within a larger culture. □□ **sub•cul•tur•al** /-kúlchərəl/ *adj.*

sub•cu•ta•ne•ous /súbkyōōtáyneeəs/ *adj.* under the skin. □□ **sub•cu•ta′ne•ous•ly** *adv.*

sub•di•vide /súbdivíd/ *v.* divide again after a

first division. □□ **sub•di•vi•sion** /súbdivízhən/ *n.*

sub•due /səbdōō, -dyōō/ *v.tr.* (**sub•dues, sub•dued, sub•du•ing**) **1** conquer, subjugate, or tame. **2** (as **subdued** *adj.*) softened; lacking in intensity; toned down (*subdued light*).

▪ **1** put down, beat down, quell, repress, suppress, quash, crush, control, curb. **2** (**subdued**) quiet, mellow(ed), moderate(d), tempered, hushed; low-key, unenthusiastic, restrained, peaceful; chastened, sober, sobered.

sub•head /súbhed/ *n.* (also **sub′head•ing**) subordinate heading or title in a chapter, article, etc.

sub•hu•man /súbhyōōmən/ *adj.* (of behavior, intelligence, etc.) less than human.

subj. *abbr.* **1** subject. **2** subjective. **3** subjunctive.

sub•ject • *n.* /súbjikt/ **1** matter, theme, etc., to be discussed, described, represented, dealt with, etc. **2** field of study. **3** *Gram.* noun or its equivalent about which a sentence is predicated and with which the verb agrees. **4** any person living under a government. **5** person or animal undergoing treatment, examination, or experimentation. • *adj.* /súbjikt/ **1** owing obedience to a government, colonizing power, force, etc. **2** [foll. by *to*] liable, exposed, or prone to (*subject to infection*). **3** under the power or authority of. • *adv.* /súbjikt/ [foll. by *to*] conditionally upon (*subject to your consent, I propose to try again*). • *v.tr.* /səbjékt/ [foll. by *to*] make liable; expose; treat (*subjected us to hours of waiting*). □□ **sub•jec•tion** /səbjékshən/ *n.* **sub•ject•less** /súbjiktlis/ *adj.*

▪ *n.* **1** topic; issue, thesis, gist, substance, business, affair, concern, point. **2** course (of study), area, discipline, department, branch of knowledge. **4** citizen, national; taxpayer, voter. **5** participant, case, patient, guinea pig, testee. • *adj.* **1** dependent, subjugated, enslaved, captive; (*subject to*) answerable to, accountable to, amenable to, responsible to, bound by, obedient to. **2** open to, vulnerable to, susceptible to, disposed to. **3** dependent (up)on, contingent (up)on. • *v.* lay open to, submit to, put through, impose on, cause to undergo. □□ **subjection** subordination, domination, conquest, subjugation, enslavement, servitude.

sub•jec•tive /səbjéktiv/ *adj.* **1** (of art, literature, written history, a person's views, etc.) personal; not impartial or literal. **2** esp. *Philos.* of the individual consciousness or perception; imaginary, partial, or distorted. □□ **sub•jec′tive•ly** *adv.* **sub•jec•tive•ness** *n.* **sub•jec•tiv′i•ty** *n.*

▪ individual, idiosyncratic; prejudiced, biased; self-centered, egoistic, egocentric, selfish, self-serving.

sub•join /súbjóyn/ *v.tr.* add or append (an illustration, anecdote, etc.) at the end.

sub•ju•gate /súbjəgayt/ *v.tr.* bring into subjection; subdue; vanquish. □□ **sub•ju•ga•tion** /-gáyshən/ *n.* **sub′ju•ga•tor** *n.*

■ dominate, subordinate, enslave, enthrall, crush, humble, subject, oppress, suppress, put down.

sub•junc•tive /səbjúngktiv/ *Gram.* • *adj.* (of a mood) denoting what is imagined or wished or possible (e.g., *if I were you, be that as it may*). • *n.* **1** the subjunctive mood. **2** a verb in this mood.

sub•lease • *n.* /súblees/ lease of a property by a tenant to a subtenant. • *v.tr.* /súbleés/ lease to a subtenant.

sub•let • *n.* /súblet/ = SUBLEASE *n.* • *v.tr.* /súblét/ (**–let•ting**; *past and past part.* **–let**) = SUBLEASE *v.*

sub•li•mate /súblimayt/ *v.* **1** *tr. & intr.* divert (the energy of a primitive impulse, esp. sexual) into a culturally more acceptable activity. **2** *tr. & intr. Chem.* convert (a substance) from the solid state directly to its vapor by heat, and usu. allow it to solidify again. **3** *tr.* refine; purify; idealize. □□ **sub•li•ma•tion** /–máyshən/ *n.*

■ **1** transmute, alter, transform; channel, redirect. **3** sublime, rarefy; elevate.

sub•lime /səblím/ • *adj.* **sub•lim•er**, **sub•lim•est**) **1** of the most exalted, grand, or noble kind; awe-inspiring (*sublime genius*). **2** arrogantly unruffled; extreme (*sublime ignorance*). • *v. Chem.* = SUBLIMATE *v.* 2. □□ **sub•lime•ly** *adv.* **sub•lim•i•ty** /–límitee/ *n.*

■ *adj.* **1** lofty, high, supreme, elevated; honorable, ennobled, eminent, glorified; great, magnificent, majestic; awesome, overwhelming, inspiring. **2** lofty, supreme, utmost.

sub•li•mi•nal /səblíminəl/ *adj. Psychol.* (of a stimulus, etc.) below the threshold of sensation or consciousness. □□ **sub•lim'in•al•ly** *adv.*

■ subconscious, unconscious, vague, indefinable.

sub•ma•chine gun /súbməsheén/ *n.* handheld lightweight machine gun.

sub•ma•rine /súbməreén/ • *n.* vessel, esp. an armed warship, capable of operating under water. • *adj.* existing, occurring, done, or used under the surface of the sea (*submarine cable*). □ **submarine sandwich** sandwich made with a long bread roll. □□ **sub•mar•i•ner** /–mareéner, səbmárinər/ *n.*

■ □ **submarine sandwich** hero, hoagy *or* hoagie, sub, grinder, torpedo, poor boy.

sub•merge /səbmérj/ *v.tr.* place, go, or dive under water. □□ **sub•mer'gence** *n.* **sub•mer•sion** /–mórzhən, –shən/ *n.*

■ flood, immerse, swamp; plunge, submerse, drench; plunge, descend, sink.

sub•mers•i•ble /səbmórsibəl/ • *n.* submarine operating under water for short periods. • *adj.* capable of submerging.

sub•mis•sion /səbmíshən/ *n.* **1 a** submitting or being submitted. **b** anything that is submitted. **2** submissiveness.

■ **1 a** concession, acquiescence, capitulation, surrender, yielding, giving in. **b** offering, tender, proposal, proposition, suggestion, contribution, entry. **2** obedience, compliance, deference, resignation; humility, meekness, docility, passivity.

sub•mis•sive /səbmísiv/ *adj.* humble; obedient. □□ **sub•mis'sive•ly** *adv.* **sub•mis'sive•ness** *n.*

■ deferential, biddable, compliant, yielding, acquiescent, tractable; obsequious, abject, subservient, servile.

sub•mit /səbmít/ *v.* (**sub•mit•ted, sub•mit•ting**) **1** [usu. foll. by *to*] *intr.* cease resistance; give way; yield. **2** *tr.* present for consideration. **3** *tr.* subject (a person or thing) to an operation, process, treatment, etc. □□ **sub•mit'ter** *n.*

■ **1** surrender, capitulate, give in *or* up; bow *or* bend, succumb; agree, concede, consent; (*submit to*) respect, accept, comply with, resign oneself to. **2** offer, proffer, tender, put in, advance, put forward; hand *or* give in. **3** see SUBJECT *v.*

sub•nor•mal /súbnáwrməl/ *adj.* (esp. as regards intelligence) below or less than normal. □□ **sub•nor•mal•i•ty** /–málitee/ *n.*

sub•or•di•nate • *adj.* /səbáwrd'nət/ of inferior importance or rank; secondary; subservient. • *n.* /səbáwrd'nət/ person working under another. • *v.tr.* /səbáwrd'nayt/ [usu. foll. by *to*] make or treat as subordinate. □ **subordinate clause** clause modifying or dependent on a main clause. □□ **sub•or'di•nate•ly** *adv.* **sub•or•di•na•tion** /–náyshən/ *n.*

■ *adj.* minor; inferior, lower, lesser, second; (*subordinate to*) next to, below, beneath, under. • *n.* assistant, aide, junior, staff member; staffer; inferior, servant, slave. • *v.* see REDUCE 6, SUBJUGATE.

sub•orn /səbáwrn/ *v.tr.* induce by bribery, etc., to commit perjury, etc. □□ **sub•or•na'tion** *n.* **sub•orn'er** *n.*

sub•plot /súbplot/ *n.* subordinate plot in a play, etc.

sub•poe•na /səpeénə/ • *n.* writ ordering a person to appear in court. • *v.tr.* (*past* and *past part.* **sub•poe•naed**) serve a subpoena on.

sub ro•sa /sub rózə/ *adj. & adv.* in secrecy or confidence.

sub•scribe /səbskríb/ *v.* **1** *tr. & intr.* contribute (a specified sum) or make or promise a contribution to a fund, project, charity, etc., esp. regularly. **2** *intr.* express one's agreement with an opinion, resolution, etc. (*cannot subscribe to that*). **3** *tr. & intr.* arrange to receive a periodical, cable television service, etc., regularly. □□ **sub•scrib'er** *n.*

■ **1** (*subscribe to*) support, give to, donate to, pledge to. **2** endorse, support, underwrite, advocate, back (up), approve of, agree with *or* to.

sub•script /súbskript/ • *adj.* written or printed below the line. • *n.* subscript number or symbol.

sub•scrip•tion /səbskrípshən/ *n.* **1** subscribing. **2** agreement to take and pay for usu. a specified number of issues of a newspaper, magazine, etc.

■ **1** obligation, pledge, promise, commitment.

sub•se•quent /súbsikwənt/ *adj.* [usu. foll. by *to*] following a specified event, etc., in time, esp. as a consequence. □□ **sub'se•quent•ly** *adv.*

■ succeeding, following, ensuing, next, future, later; (*subsequent to*) after, following, succeeding, in the wake or aftermath of. □□ **subsequently** later (on), afterwards, afterward.

sub·ser·vi·ent /səbsérveeənt/ *adj.* 1 servile. 2 subordinate. □□ **sub·ser'vi·ence** *n.* **sub·ser'vi·ent·ly** *adv.*

sub·set /súbset/ *n.* 1 secondary part of a set. 2 *Math.* a set, all the elements of which are contained in another set.

sub·side /səbsíd/ *v.intr.* 1 become tranquil; abate (*excitement subsided*). 2 (of water, etc.) sink. □□ **sub·sid·ence** /-síd'ns, súbsid'ns/ *n.*
■ 1 quiet (down), calm (down), moderate, let up, decrease, diminish. 2 drop (down), go down, recede, descend, decline; settle; cave in, collapse.

sub·sid·i·ar·y /səbsídee–airee/ • *adj.* 1 supplementary; auxiliary. 2 (of a company) controlled by another. • *n.* (*pl.* **-ies**) subsidiary thing, person, or company.
■ *adj.* ancillary, additional, supplemental, complementary, adjuvant. • *n.* accessory, auxiliary, extra, assistant, subordinate; adjunct, supplement.

sub·si·dize /súbsidīz/ *v.tr.* 1 pay a subsidy to. 2 reduce the cost of by subsidy. □□ **sub·si·di·za'tion** *n.* **sub'si·diz·er** *n.*
■ 1 fund, finance, support, aid, sponsor, maintain.

sub·si·dy /súbsidee/ *n.* (*pl.* **-dies**) grant of money, esp. by the government.
■ funding, sponsorship, assistance, aid, contribution, support, endowment.

sub·sist /səbsíst/ *v.intr.* 1 keep oneself alive; be kept alive. 2 remain in being; exist. □□ **sub·sist'ent** *adj.*

sub·sis·tence /səbsístəns/ *n.* 1 state or an instance of subsisting. 2 a means of supporting life; livelihood. b minimal level of existence or the income providing this.
■ 1 existence, living, survival, being.

sub·soil /súbsoyl/ *n.* soil immediately under the surface soil.

sub·son·ic /súbsónik/ *adj.* relating to speeds less than that of sound. □□ **sub·son'i·cal·ly** *adv.*

subst. *abbr.* 1 substantive. 2 substitute.

sub·stance /súbstəns/ *n.* 1 particular kind of material having uniform properties. 2 reality; solidity. 3 content or essence as opposed to form, etc. 4 wealth and possessions.
■ 1 matter, stuff, fabric, composition, makeup. 2 corporeality, actuality, concreteness. 3 theme, subject, gist, thrust; meaning, import, significance; quintessence, pith, heart, core. 4 means, property, riches, resources, affluence, assets.

sub·stand·ard /súbstándərd/ *adj.* of less than the required or normal quality or size; inferior.

sub·stan·tial /səbstánshəl/ *adj.* 1 a of real importance, value, or validity. b large. 2 solid; stout (*substantial house*). 3 commercially successful; wealthy. 4 essential; true in large part. 5 having substance; real. □□ **sub·stan'tial·ly** *adv.*
■ 1 a material, considerable, significant, great, worthwhile, well-founded, sound,

weighty, solid. b ample, goodly, respectable, abundant, generous, big. 2 strong, well-built, durable, sound, sturdy; big, large, massive. 3 well-to-do, rich, affluent, prosperous. 4 basic, fundamental; virtual; see also ESSENTIAL *adj.* 2. 5 see MATERIAL *adj.* 1. □□ **substantially** essentially, at bottom, fundamentally, basically, in essence, intrinsically; in substance; largely, to a large extent, in large measure, materially, practically.

sub·stan·ti·ate /səbstánsheeayt/ *v.tr.* prove the truth of (a charge, claim, etc.). □□ **sub·stan·ti·a·tion** /-áyshən/ *n.*
■ confirm, affirm, attest, corroborate, support, sustain, back up, bear out, authenticate, show (clearly).

sub·stan·tive /súbstəntiv/ • *adj.* (also /səbstántiv/) having separate and independent existence. • *n. Gram.* = NOUN. □□ **sub·stan·ti·val** /-tívəl/ *adj.* **sub·stan'tive·ly** *adv.* esp. *Gram.*

sub·sti·tute /súbstitōot, –tyōot/ • *n.* [also *attrib.*] person or thing acting or serving in place of another. • *v.* act or cause to act as a substitute. □□ **sub·sti·tut'a·ble** *adj.* **sub·sti·tu·tion** /-tōoshən, –tyōo–/ *n.* **sub'sti·tu·tive** *adj.*
■ *n.* substitution, replacement, alternative, relief, supply, representative, proxy, deputy, delegate. • *v.* take the place of, stand in for, step in for, fill in for; double for; supersede, displace, supplant. □□ **substitution** see SUBSTITUTE *n.* above, CHANGE *n.* 4.

sub·strate /súbstrayt/ *n.* 1 = SUBSTRATUM. 2 surface to be painted, printed, etc., on.

sub·stra·tum /súbstraytəm, –strát–/ *n.* (*pl.* **sub·stra·ta** /–tə/ or **substratums**) underlying layer or substance.

sub·struc·ture /súbstrúkchər/ *n.* underlying or supporting structure. □□ **sub·struc'tur·al** *adj.*

sub·sume /səbsōom, –syōom/ *v.tr.* include (an instance, idea, category, etc.) in a rule, class, category, etc. □□ **sub·sum'a·ble** *adj.*

sub·ter·fuge /súbtərfyōoj/ *n.* 1 evasive or conspiratorial lying or deceit. 2 statement, etc., used for such a purpose.
■ 1 artifice, trick, device, stratagem, maneuver, scheme, evasion, deception, dodge, feint, shift, excuse.

sub·ter·ra·ne·an /súbtəráyneeən/ *adj.* underground; concealed.

sub·text /súbtekst/ *n.* underlying theme.

sub·ti·tle /súbtīt'l/ • *n.* 1 secondary or additional title of a book, etc. 2 caption at the bottom of a movie, etc., esp. translating dialogue. • *v.tr.* provide with a subtitle or subtitles.

sub·tle /sút'l/ *adj.* (**sub·tler**, **sub·tlest**) 1 evasive or mysterious; hard to grasp (*subtle charm*). 2 (of scent, color, etc.) faint; delicate (*subtle perfume*). 3 a perceptive (*subtle senses*). b ingenious (*subtle device*). □□ **sub'tle·ness** *n.* **sub'tle·ty** *n.* **sub'tly** *adv.*
■ 1 abstruse, arcane, recondite, remote, deep, profound; refined, fine, nice. 2 fine, refined, exquisite, nice; elusive. 3 a see ACUTE *adj.* 1a. b see SOPHISTICATED 2.

□□ **subtlety** treachery, guile, insidiousness, casuistry, cunning, artfulness, craftiness; refinement, nicety, delicacy, exquisiteness, intricacy.

sub·to·tal /súbtōt'l/ *n.* total of one part of a group of figures to be added.

sub·tract /səbtrákt/ *v.tr.* [often foll. by *from*] deduct (a part, quantity, or number) from another. □□ **sub·tract'er** *n.* **sub·trac·tion** /-trákshən/ *n.* **sub·trac'tive** *adj.*

■ take away *or* off; (*subtract from*) take from.

sub·trop·ics /súbtrópiks/ *n.pl.* regions adjacent to or bordering on the tropics. □□ **sub·trop'i·cal** *adj.*

sub·urb /súbərb/ *n.* outlying district of a city. □□ **sub·ur·ban** /səbŕbən/ *adj.*

sub·ur·bi·a /səbŕbeeə/ *n.* often *derog.* suburbs, their inhabitants, and their way of life.

sub·ver·sive /səbvŕsiv/ • *adj.* seeking to subvert (esp. a government). • *n.* subversive person. □□ **sub·ver·sion** /-vŕzhən, -shən/ *n.* **sub·ver'sive·ly** *adv.* **sub·ver'sive·ness** *n.*

■ *adj.* seditious, treasonous, treacherous, traitorous, mutinous, revolutionary, insurrectionary; undermining, destabilizing. • *n.* traitor, insurgent, subverter, saboteur, fifth columnist, collaborator, collaborationist; dissident, defector. □□ **subversion** overthrow, ruin, destruction, undermining; see also MUTINY *n.*

sub·vert /səbvŕt/ *v.tr.* esp. *Polit.* overturn, overthrow, or upset (religion, government, morality, etc.). □□ **sub·vert'er** *n.*

■ ruin, destroy, undermine, destabilize, topple.

sub·way /súbway/ *n.* underground, usu. electrically powered commuter railroad.

■ underground, metro.

suc- /suk, sək/ *prefix* assim. form of SUB- before *c*.

suc·ceed /səkseéd/ *v.* **1** *intr.* have success; be successful. **2 a** *tr.* follow in order. **b** *intr.* come next. **3** *intr.* come by an inheritance, office, title, or property (*succeeded to the throne*). **4** *tr.* take over an office, property, inheritance, etc., from (*succeeded his father*).

■ **1** make good, thrive, prosper, flourish, progress, advance, win; be effective, work, bear fruit. **2** come (next) after, be subsequent to. **3** (*succeed to*) see INHERIT 1. **4** be successor to, follow, be next to, replace.

suc·cess /səksés/ *n.* **1** accomplishment of an aim; favorable outcome. **2** attainment of wealth, fame, or position. **3** thing or person that turns out well.

■ **1** good *or* happy result *or* outcome, good fortune, achievement, triumph. **3** star, superstar, success story, celebrity.

suc·cess·ful /səksésfool/ *adj.* having success; prosperous. □□ **suc·cess'ful·ly** *adv.* **suc·cess'ful·ness** *n.*

■ victorious, triumphant, first, winning; famous, well-known, famed, celebrated, renowned, eminent; prominent, preeminent, popular, leading; effective, lucrative, booming, profitable; wealthy, rich.

suc·ces·sion /səkséshən/ *n.* **1 a** process of following in order; succeeding. **b** series or sequence. **2 a** succeeding to a throne, office, inheritance, etc. **b** those having such a right. □ **in succession** one after another. □□ **suc·ces'sion·al** *adj.*

■ **1** progression, order, course, flow, run, chain, train, string, line. **2 a** birthright, privilege. **b** lineage, descent, dynasty, ancestry, descendants, bloodline. □ **in succession** one behind the other, at intervals, successively, consecutively, in a row, running.

suc·ces·sive /səksésiv/ *adj.* following one after another; continuing; consecutive. □□ **suc·ces'sive·ly** *adv.* **suc·ces'sive·ness** *n.*

■ uninterrupted, continuous, unbroken, straight, succeeding.

suc·ces·sor /səksésər/ *n.* [often foll. by *to*] person or thing that succeeds another.

suc·cinct /səksíngkt/ *adj.* briefly expressed; terse; concise. See synonym study at TERSE. □□ **suc·cinct'ly** *adv.* **suc·cinct'ness** *n.*

■ compact, brief, pithy, terse, short, compressed.

suc·cor /súkər/ • *n.* aid; assistance, esp. in time of need. • *v.tr.* give succor to.

suc·cu·lent /súkyələnt/ • *adj.* **1** juicy; palatable. **2** *Bot.* (of a plant, its leaves, or stems) thick and fleshy. • *n. Bot.* succulent plant. □□ **suc'cu·lence** *n.* **suc'cu·lent·ly** *adv.*

■ *adj.* **1** rich, luscious, mouthwatering, toothsome, tasty.

suc·cumb /səkúm/ *v.intr.* **1** surrender; be overcome. **2** die.

■ **1** yield, give in, give up, give way, accede, submit.

such /such/ • *adj.* **1** of the kind or degree indicated (*such people, people such as these*). **2** so great; in such high degree (*not such a fool as to believe them*). **3** of a more than normal kind or degree (*such crude language*). • *pron.* such a person; such a thing. □ **as such** as being what has been indicated or named (*there is no theater as such*). **such as** for example.

such·like /súchlīk/ *colloq.* • *adj.* of such a kind. • *n.* things, people, etc., of such a kind.

suck /suk/ • *v.* **1** *tr.* draw (a fluid) into the mouth by suction. **2** *tr.* [also *absol.*] draw fluid from (a thing) in this way. **3** *tr.* roll the tongue around (a candy, etc.). **4** *tr.* engulf, smother, or drown in a sucking movement. **5** *intr. sl.* be or seem very unpleasant, contemptible, or unfair. • *n.* act or instance of sucking. □ **suck in 1** absorb. **2** involve (a person) in an activity, etc., esp. against his or her will. **suck up 1** *colloq.* behave obsequiously. **2** absorb.

suck·er /súkər/ *n.* **1** *sl.* **a** a gullible person. **b** [foll. by *for*] person especially susceptible to. **2 a** rubber cup, etc., that adheres to a surface by suction. **b** similar organ of an organism. **3** *Bot.* shoot springing from a root, stem, or axil.

■ **1** dupe, pigeon, victim, butt, fool, greenhorn, easy *or* fair game.

suck·le /súkəl/ *v.* **1** *tr.* **a** feed (young) from the breast or udder. **b** nourish (*suckled his talent*). **2** *intr.* feed by sucking the breast, etc. □□ **suck'ler** *n.*

suck·ling /súkling/ *n.* unweaned child or animal.

su•crose /sóokrōs/ n. Chem. sugar from sugar cane, sugar beet, etc.

suc•tion /súkshən/ n. **1** act or instance of sucking. **2 a** production of a partial vacuum by the removal of air, etc., in order to force in liquid, etc., or procure adhesion. **b** force produced by this process (*suction keeps the lid on*).

sud•den /súd'n/ adj. occurring or done unexpectedly or without warning; abrupt; hurried; hasty (*sudden storm*). □ **all of a sudden** suddenly. **sudden death** colloq. decision in a tied game, etc., dependent on one move, card, toss of a coin, etc. **sudden infant death syndrome** Med. death of a seemingly healthy infant from an unknown cause; crib death. □□ **sud′den•ly** adv. **sud′den•ness** n.

■ unexpected, unannounced, unanticipated; surprising, startling; precipitate, quick, immediate, rapid; impetuous, rash, impulsive, snap. □□ **suddenly** in a flash, in a moment, in a split second, all at once, instantly; quickly, abruptly, swiftly, speedily, rapidly; hastily, hurriedly, feverishly.

suds /sudz/ n.pl. froth of soap and water. □□ **suds′y** adj.

sue /soo/ v. (**sues, sued, su•ing**) **1** tr. [also absol.] Law institute legal proceedings against (a person). **2** intr. Law make application to a court of law for redress. **3** intr. make entreaty to a person for a favor. □□ **su•er** n.

■ **1** proceed or move or act (against), take (legal) action (against), bring suit (against), prefer charges (against), prosecute; summon(s), charge, accuse. **3** petition, beg, plead (with), entreat, pray, request, solicit.

suede /swayd/ n. [often attrib.] **1** leather with the flesh side rubbed to a nap. **2** cloth resembling suede.

su•et /soo-it/ n. hard white fat from the kidneys or loins of cattle, etc., used in cooking, etc. □□ **su•et•y** adj.

suf- /suf, səf/ prefix assim. form of SUB- before f.

suf•fer /súfər/ v. **1** intr. undergo pain, grief, damage, etc. **2** tr. undergo, experience, or be subjected to (pain, loss, grief, defeat, change, etc.) (*suffered banishment*). **3** tr. tolerate (*does not suffer fools gladly*). **4** tr. archaic allow (*let suffer•a•ble* adj. **suf′fer•er** n. **suf′fer•ing** n.

■ **1** agonize, smart, hurt, writhe, sweat, ache, decline, deteriorate, diminish. **2** endure, feel, bear, live or go through, withstand. **3** take, abide, put up with, bear, stand. □□ **suffering** pain, agony, anguish, distress, misery, grief, sorrow.

suf•fer•ance /súfərəns, súfrəns/ n. tacit consent.

suf•fice /səfís/ v. **1** intr. be enough or adequate. **2** tr. satisfy.

■ **1** serve, do, be sufficient, answer, colloq. do the trick. **2** sate, satiate, do, serve, meet the needs of.

suf•fi•cien•cy /səfíshənsee/ n. (pl. **-cies**) adequate amount.

suf•fi•cient /səfíshənt/ adj. sufficing; adequate; enough (*is sufficient for a family*). □□ **suf•fi′cient•ly** adv.

suf•fix /súfiks/ n. verbal element added at the end of a word to form a derivative (e.g., *-ation, -fy, -ing, -itis*).

suf•fo•cate /súfəkayt/ v. **1** tr. choke or kill by stopping breathing, esp. by pressure, fumes, etc. **2** tr. produce a choking or breathlessness in. **3** intr. be or feel suffocated. □□ **suf′fo•cat•ing** adj. **suf′fo•cat•ing•ly** adv. **suf•fo•ca•tion** /-káyshən/ n.

suf•fra•gan /súfrəgən/ n. bishop appointed to help a diocesan bishop.

suf•frage /súfrij/ n. right to vote in political elections. □□ **suf′fra•gist** n.

suf•fra•gette /súfrəjét/ n. hist. woman seeking the right to vote through organized protest.

suf•fuse /səfyóoz/ v.tr. (of color, moisture, etc.) overspread throughout. □□ **suf•fu•sion** /-fyóozhən/ n.

■ imbue, spread through or over, permeate, pervade, flood, flush, charge, penetrate, saturate, mantle.

Su•fi /sóofee/ n. (pl. **Su•fis**) Muslim ascetic and mystic. □□ **Su′fic** adj. **Su′fism** n.

sug- /sug, səg/ prefix assim. form of SUB- before g.

sug•ar /shoogər/ • n. **1** sweet crystalline substance obtained from various plants, esp. the sugar cane and sugar beet, used in cooking, etc.; sucrose. **2** Chem. soluble usu. sweet-tasting crystalline carbohydrate, e.g., glucose. • v.tr. sweeten or coat with sugar. □ **sugar beet** beet from which sugar is extracted. **sugar cane** Bot. tropical grass from which sugar is made. **sugar-coated 1** (of food) enclosed in sugar. **2** made superficially attractive. **sugar daddy** sl. older man who lavishes gifts on a younger partner. □□ **sug′ar•less** adj.

sug•ar•y /shoogəree/ adj. **1** containing or resembling sugar. **2** excessively sweet or esp. sentimental. □□ **sug′ar•i•ness** n.

sug•gest /səgjést, səjést/ v.tr. **1** propose (a theory, plan, or hypothesis). **2 a** evoke, etc. (*this poem suggests peace*). **b** hint at. □□ **sug•gest′er** n.

■ **1** advance, propound, recommend, endorse, commend, urge, advise. **2** call to mind, bring up, imply, insinuate, intimate, indicate, communicate.

sug•gest•i•ble /səgjéstəbəl, səjés-/ adj. **1** capable of being suggested. **2** easily swayed.

■ **2** impressionable, susceptible, receptive, impressible, susceptive, open (to suggestion), moldable.

sug•ges•tion /səgjéschən, səjés-/ n. **1** suggesting or being suggested. **2** theory, plan, etc., suggested (*made a helpful suggestion*). **3** slight trace; hint.

■ **1** counseling, prompting, urging, inducement. **2** proposal, proposition, recommendation, advice, counsel. **3** indication, whisper, soupçon, touch, tinge.

sug•ges•tive /səgjéstiv, səjés-/ adj. **1** conveying a suggestion; evocative. **2** (esp. of a remark, joke, etc.) indecent; improper; racy. □□ **sug•ges′tive•ly** adv. **sug•ges′tive•ness** n.

■ **1** reminiscent, redolent, indicative; pregnant, significant, meaningful. **2** provocative, risqué, ribald, bawdy, earthy, lusty, rude, indelicate, unseemly.

su•i•cid•al /soõisīd'l/ *adj.* **1** inclined to commit suicide. **2** of suicide. **3** self-destructive; rash. □□ **su•i•cid'al•ly** *adv.*

su•i•cide /soõisīd/ *n.* **1 a** intentional killing of oneself. **b** person who commits suicide. **2** self-destructive action or course (*political suicide*).

su•i ge•ne•ris /soõ-ī jénəris, soõ-ee, soõ-ee gén-/ *adj.* of its own kind; unique.

suit /soõt/ • *n.* **1** set of dress clothes of matching material, usu. of a jacket and trousers, or a jacket and a skirt; [esp. in *comb.*] set of clothes for a special occasion, etc. (*playsuit*). **2** any of the four sets (spades, hearts, diamonds, clubs) in a pack of cards. **3** lawsuit. **4** courting a woman (*paid suit to her*). • *v.tr.* **1** go well with (a person's figure, features, etc.). **2** [also *absol.*] meet the demands or requirements of; satisfy. **3** make fitting; accommodate. □ **suit oneself** do as one chooses.

■ *n.* **1** costume, outfit; uniform, habit; garb, clothing. **3** action, case, proceeding, trial; litigation. **4** courtship, wooing; court, attentions, addresses. • *v.* become, befit, look good on, be appropriate or suitable for. **2** please, fill or meet or answer a person's needs, gratify, be suitable (to or for); conform (to), agree with, fit in (with). **3** adapt, fit, adjust, tailor, gear.

suit•a•ble /soõtəbəl/ *adj.* [usu. foll. by *to, for*] well fitted for the purpose; appropriate. □□ **suit•a•bil'i•ty** *n.* **suit'a•ble•ness** *n.* **suit'a•bly** *adv.*

■ apt, apposite, fit, fitting, befitting, becoming, right, proper, correct; timely, opportune.

suit•case /soõtkays/ *n.* usu. oblong case with a handle for carrying clothes, etc. □□ **suit' case•ful** *n.* (*pl.* **–fuls**)

■ bag, trunk, overnight bag, traveling bag, valise.

suite /sweet/ *n.* **1** set of things belonging together, esp.: **a** set of rooms in a hotel, etc. **b** furniture intended for the same room. **2** *Mus.* set of instrumental compositions to be played as a unit. **3** set of people in attendance; retinue.

■ **1** series, collection, number; arrangement. **3** following, entourage, train, cortège, attendants.

suit•or /soõtər/ *n.* **1** man seeking to marry a specified woman; wooer. **2** plaintiff or petitioner in a lawsuit.

■ **1** admirer, beau; boyfriend, lover, inamorato, escort.

sul•fa /súlfə/ *n.* any anti-bacterial sulfonamide drug.

sul•fate /súlfayt/ *n.* salt or ester of sulfuric acid.

sul•fide /súlfīd/ *n. Chem.* binary compound of sulfur.

sul•fite /súlfīt/ *n. Chem.* salt or ester of sulfurous acid.

sul•fon•a•mide /sulfónəmīd/ *n.* any of a class of antibiotic drugs containing sulfur.

sul•fur /súlfər/ *n. Chem.* pale yellow non-metallic element burning with a blue flame and a suffocating smell. ¶Symb.: **S**. □ **sulfur dioxide** colorless pungent gas formed by burning sulfur in air and used as a food preservative. □□ **sul•fur•ous** /–fərəs, –fyoõr–/ *adj.* **sul'fur•y** *adj.*

sul•fu•ric ac•id /sulfyoõrik/ *adj.* dense, oily, colorless, highly corrosive acid.

sulk /sulk/ • *v.intr.* be sulky. • *n.* period of sullen, esp. resentful, silence. □□ **sulk'er** *n.*

■ *v.* mope, brood, pout, lower, be sullen or moody.

sulk•y /súlkee/ *adj.* (**sulk•i•er, sulk•i•est**) sullen, morose, or silent, esp. from resentment. □□ **sulk'i•ly** *adv.* **sulk'i•ness** *n.*

sul•len /súlən/ *adj.* **1** morose; resentful; sulky. **2** dismal; melancholy (*sullen sky*). See synonym study at GLUM. □□ **sul'len•ly** *adv.* **sul'len•ness** *n.*

■ **1** sulking, brooding, pouting, moody. **2** see LEADEN 4.

sul•ly /súlee/ *v.tr.* (**–lies, –lied**) disgrace; tarnish.

■ besmirch, stain, smirch, blemish, mar, defile, soil.

sul•tan /súlt'n/ *n.* Muslim sovereign. □□ **sul•tan•ate** /–nayt/ *n.*

sul•ta•na /sultánə, –taänə/ *n.* **1** seedless raisin. **2** mother, wife, concubine, or daughter of a sultan.

sul•try /súltree/ *adj.* (**sul•tri•er, sul•tri•est**) **1** (of the atmosphere or the weather) hot or oppressive; close. **2** (of a person, etc.) passionate; sensual. □□ **sul'tri•ly** *adv.* **sul'tri•ness** *n.*

■ **1** humid, sticky, stuffy, stifling, muggy, steamy. **2** lusty, lustful, erotic, seductive, voluptuous.

sum /sum/ • *n.* **1** total resulting from addition. **2** particular amount of money. **3** arithmetical problem. • *v.tr.* (**summed, summing**) find the sum of. □ **sum up 1** (esp. of a judge) recapitulate or review the evidence in a case, etc. **2** form or express an idea of the character of (a person, situation, etc.). **3** collect into or express as a total or whole.

■ *n.* **1** aggregate, grand total, sum total, whole; result, tally, score. **2** figure, quantity. **3** question. • *v.* see ADD 2. □ **sum up 1** summarize, encapsulate, synopsize, digest, abridge, condense. **2** estimate, evaluate, assess, size up, measure (up), take the measure of. **3** reckon, add up, calculate, total.

su•mac /soõmak, shoõ–/ *n.* (also **su'mach**) **1** shrub having reddish cone-shaped fruits used as a spice in cooking. **2** dried and ground leaves of this used in tanning and dyeing.

sum•ma•rize /súmərīz/ *v.tr.* make or be a summary of; sum up. □□ **sum•ma•ri•za'tion** *n.* **sum'ma•riz•er** *n.*

sum•ma•ry /súməree/ • *n.* (*pl.* **–ries**) brief account. • *adj.* dispensing with needless details or formalities; brief. □□ **sum•mar•i•ly** /səmáirilee/ *adv.*

■ *n.* summarization, recapitulation, encapsulation, compendium, synopsis, abstract, digest, abridgment. • *adj.* **1** abrupt, sudden, short, quick, laconic, perfunctory. □□ **sum-**

marily immediately, at once, straightaway, directly; suddenly, without warning.

sum•ma•tion /səmáyshən/ n. **1** finding of a total or sum; an addition. **2** summing-up.
□□ **sum•ma′tion•al** adj.

sum•mer /súmər/ • n. warmest season of the year. • v.intr. pass the summer. □ **summer solstice** see SOLSTICE. □□ **sum′mer•less** adj. **sum′mer•y** adj.

sum•mer•time /súmərtīm/ n. season or period of summer.

sum•mit /súmit/ n. **1** highest point; apex. **2** highest degree. **3** (in full **sum•mit meet•ing, talks,** etc.) discussion between heads of government. □□ **sum′mit•less** adj.
  ■ **1, 2** peak, top, acme, pinnacle, zenith, crown, height; culmination, apogee, climax.

sum•mon /súmən/ v.tr. **1** call upon to appear, esp. at a court of law. **2** call upon (*summoned her to assist*). **3** call together. □ **sum•mon up** gather (courage, spirits, resources, etc.). □□ **sum′mon•er** n.
  ■ **1, 2** subpoena; send for, command, order. **3** assemble, convene, send for, invite, muster, rally. □ **summon up** call or draw (up)on, draw up, mobilize, muster (up), work up, whip up, invoke.

sum•mons /súmənz/ n. (pl. **sum•mons•es**) authoritative or urgent call to attend on some occasion or do something.

su•mo /sóōmō/ n. (pl. **-mos**) style of Japanese wrestling practiced by very heavy competitors.

sump /sump/ n. pit, well, hole, etc., to collect liquid.

sump•tu•ous /súmpchōōəs/ adj. rich; lavish; costly. □□ **sump′tu•ous•ly** adv. **sump′tu•ous•ness** n.
  ■ expensive, extravagant, exorbitant, dear; luxurious, deluxe, opulent, palatial, royal, majestic.

Sun. abbr. Sunday.

sun /sun/ • n. **1** star around which the earth orbits and from which it receives light and warmth. **2** any similar star. • v. (**sunned, sun•ning**) refl. bask in the sun. □ **sun lamp** lamp giving ultraviolet rays for an artificial suntan, therapy, etc. □□ **sun′less** adj. **sun′proof** adj.

sun•bathe /súnbayth/ v.intr. bask in the sun, esp. to tan the body. □□ **sun′bath•er** n.

sun•beam /súnbeem/ n. ray of sunlight.

sun•burn /súnbərn/ • n. reddening and inflammation of the skin caused by overexposure to the sun. • v.intr. **1** suffer from sunburn. **2** (as **sunburned** or **sunburnt** adj.) suffering from sunburn; brown or tanned.

sun•dae /súnday, -dee/ n. dish of ice cream with fruit, nuts, syrup, etc.

Sun•day /súnday, -dee/ n. first day of the week, the Christian sabbath and day of worship.

sun•der /súndər/ v. archaic or literary separate; sever.

sun•dial /súndīəl/ n. instrument showing the time by the shadow of a pointer cast by the sun onto a graduated disk.

sun•down /súndown/ n. sunset.

sun•dry /súndree/ • adj. various; several. • n.

(pl. **-dries**) [in pl.] items or oddments not mentioned individually.
  ■ adj. varied, miscellaneous, assorted, different, mixed. • n. **1** (**sundries**) miscellanea, oddments, et ceteras.

sun•fish /súnfish/ n. almost spherical fish, esp. a large ocean variety.

sun•flow•er /súnflōwər/ n. very tall plant with large, showy, golden-rayed flowers.

sung past part. of SING.

sun•glass•es /súnglasiz/ n. glasses tinted to protect the eyes from sunlight or glare.

sunk past and past part. of SINK.

sunk•en /súngkən/ adj. **1** at a lower level; submerged. **2** (of the eyes, cheeks, etc.) hollow; depressed.
  ■ buried, underground, in-ground, below ground, settled; undersea, underwater. **2** haggard, drawn.

sun•light /súnlīt/ n. light from the sun.

sun•lit /súnlit/ adj. illuminated by sunlight.

Sun•ni /sóōnee/ • n. (pl. same or **Sun•nis**) adherent of one of the two main branches of Islam. • adj. (also **Sun′nite**) of or relating to Sunnis.

sun•ny /súnee/ adj. (**sun•ni•er, sun•ni•est**) **1** bright with or warmed by sunlight. **2** cheery and bright in temperament. □□ **sun′ni•ly** adv. **sun′ni•ness** n.
  ■ **1** sunlit, sunshiny, brilliant, radiant, fair, fine. **2** cheery, happy, joyous, joyful, light-hearted, warm, friendly.

sun•rise /súnrīz/ n. **1** sun's rising. **2** time of this.

sun•roof /súnrōōf/ n. section of an automobile roof that can be slid open.

sun•set /súnset/ • n. **1** sun's setting. **2** time of this. • adj. pertaining to a law or government program subject to review for its continuation.

sun•shine /súnshīn/ n. **1 a** light of the sun. **b** area lit by the sun. **2** good weather. **3** cheerfulness.

sun•spot /súnspot/ n. one of the dark patches, lasting for varying periods, observed on the sun's surface.

sun•stroke /súnstrōk/ n. acute prostration or collapse from the excessive heat of the sun.

sun•tan /súntan/ • n. brownish coloring of skin caused by exposure to the sun. • v.intr. (**-tanned, -tan•ning**) color the skin with a suntan.

sun•up /súnup/ n. sunrise.

sup /sup/ v.intr. (**supped, sup•ping**) archaic eat supper.

sup- /sup, səp/ prefix assim. form of SUB- before p.

su•per /sóōpər/ • adj. colloq. [also as int.] exceptional; splendid. • n. colloq. superintendent.

super- /sóōpər/ comb. form forming nouns, adjectives, and verbs, meaning: **1** above, beyond, or over in place or time or conceptually (*superstructure, supernormal*). **2** to a great or extreme degree (*superabundant*). **3** extra good or large of its kind (*supertanker*). **4** of a higher kind (*superclass*).

su•per•a•bun•dant /sóōpərəbúndənt/ adj.

abounding beyond what is normal or right. □□ **su•per•a•bun′dance** *n.* **su•per•a•bun′dant•ly** *adv.*

su•per•an•nu•ate /sōō͞pərányōōayt/ *v.tr.* **1** retire (a person) with a pension. **2** dismiss or discard as too old for use, work, etc. **3** (as **superannuated** *adj.*) too old for work or use; obsolete. □□ **su•per•an•nu•a′tion** *n.*

su•perb /sōōpórb/ *adj.* **1** splendid; grand (*superb courage*). **2** *colloq.* excellent; fine. □□ **su•perb′ly** *adv.* **su•perb′ness** *n.*

■ wonderful, marvelous, excellent, superior, gorgeous, glorious, majestic, magnificent, outstanding, exquisite, fine, unequaled, sensational, noteworthy, great, impressive, admirable, peerless, matchless.

su•per•charge /sōōpərchaarj/ *v.tr.* **1** charge (the atmosphere, etc.) with energy, emotion, etc. **2** use a supercharger on (an internal combustion engine).

su•per•charg•er /sōōpərchaarjər/ *n.* device supplying air or fuel under pressure to an internal combustion engine for added power.

su•per•cil•i•ous /sōōpərsileeəs/ *adj.* contemptuous; haughty. □□ **su•per•cil′i•ous•ly** *adv.* **su•per•cil′i•ous•ness** *n.*

■ superior, snobbish, disdainful, arrogant, condescending, patronizing, overbearing, scornful, lordly.

su•per•con•duc•tiv•i•ty /sōōpərkónduktívi-tee/ *n. Physics* property of zero electrical resistance in some substances at very low absolute temperatures. □□ **su•per•con•duct′ing** /–kəndúkting/ *adj.* **su•per•con•duc′tive** *adj.*

su•per•con•duc•tor /sōōpərkəndúktər/ *n. Physics* substance having superconductivity.

su•per•e•go /sōōpəreegō, –égō/ *n.* (*pl.* **–gos**) *Psychol.* part of the mind that acts as a conscience.

su•per•er•o•ga•tion /sōōpərérəgáyshən/ *n.* doing more than duty requires. □□ **su•per•e•rog′a•to•ry** /–irógətawree/ *adj.*

su•per•fi•cial /sōōpərfíshəl/ *adj.* **1** of or on the surface; lacking depth (*superficial wounds*). **2** swift or cursory. **3** apparent but not real (*superficial resemblance*). **4** (esp. of a person) shallow. □□ **su•per•fi•ci•al•i•ty** /–sheeálitee/ *n.* (*pl.* **–ties**). **su•per•fi′cial•ly** *adv.*

■ **1** surface, external, exterior, shallow, skindeep. **2** slapdash, quick, hurried, hasty, perfunctory. **3** surface, slight, external, skindeep, outward, insignificant; cosmetic. **4** trivial, frivolous, empty-headed, hollow.

SYNONYM STUDY: **superficial**

CURSORY, HASTY, SLAPDASH, SHALLOW. No one wants to be accused of being **superficial** or **shallow**, two adjectives that literally indicate a lack of depth (*a superficial wound, a shallow grave*). *Superficial* suggests too much concern with the surface or obvious aspects of something, and it is considered a derogatory term because it connotes a personality that is not genuine or sincere. *Shallow* is even more derogatory because it implies not only a refusal to explore something deeply but an inability to feel, sympathize, or understand. It

is unlikely that a *shallow* person, in other words, will ever have more than *superficial* relationships with his or her peers. **Cursory**, which may or may not be a derogatory term, suggests a lack of thoroughness or attention to details rather than a concentration on *superficial* aspects (*a cursory glance at the newspaper*), while **hasty** emphasizes a refusal or inability to spend the necessary time on something (*a hasty review of the facts*). If you are **slapdash** in your approach, it means that you are both careless and *hasty* (*a slapdash job of cleaning up*).

---

su•per•flu•i•ty /sōōpərflóoitee/ *n.* (*pl.* **–ties**) **1** state of being superfluous. **2** superfluous amount or thing.

■ **1** excess, superabundance, overabundance, surplus, surfeit, glut, superfluousness, profusion, plethora. **2** excess, surplus, leftovers, overflow.

su•per•flu•ous /sōōpórflōōəs/ *adj.* more than enough; redundant; needless. □□ **su•per′flu•ous•ly** *adv.* **su•per′flu•ous•ness** *n.*

■ excessive, excess, superabundant, overabundant, supererogatory, surplus, dispensable, gratuitous.

superhighway /sōōpərhíway/ *n.* multilane, limited-access divided highway for fast travel.

su•per•hu•man /sōōpərhyóōmən/ *adj.* **1** beyond normal human capability. **2** above what is human. □□ **su•per•hu′man•ly** *adv.*

■ **1** heroic, Herculean, godlike, legendary, valiant, courageous, brave, daring. **2** see DIVINE *adj.* 2a.

su•per•im•pose /sōōpərimpóz/ *v.tr.* lay (a thing) on something else. □□ **su•per•im•po′si•tion** /–pəzíshən/ *n.*

su•per•in•tend /sōōpərinténd/ *v.* supervise; direct. □□ **su•per•in•tend′ence** *n.* **su•per•in•tend′en•cy** *n.*

su•per•in•tend•ent /sōōpərinténdənt/ *n.* **1** person who superintends; director. **2** caretaker of a building.

■ **1** supervisor, foreman, overseer, manager, administrator, chief, head; governor, controller, conductor; *colloq.* boss, super.

su•pe•ri•or /sōōpéereeər/ • *adj.* **1** in a higher position; of higher rank. **2 a** above the average in quality, etc. (*made of superior leather*). **b** supercilious; haughty. **3** better or greater in some respect. **4** *Printing* (of figures or letters) placed above the line. • *n.* **1** person superior to another in rank, character, etc. (*is her superior in courage*). **2** (*fem.* also **superioress** /–ris/) *Eccl.* head of a monastery or other religious institution (*Mother Superior*).

■ *adj.* **1** higher, upper, loftier, higher-ranking, higher-level, senior; greater. **2 a** high-class, elevated, first-rate, distinguished, exceptional, excellent, better, preferred, choice, select. **b** see SUPERCILIOUS. • *n.* **1** better, senior, elder; see also *supervisor* (SUPERVISE).

su•pe•ri•or•i•ty /sōōpéeree-áwritee, –ór–/ *n.* state of being superior.

■ ascendancy, preeminence, supremacy, leadership, lead, dominance; excellence, greatness, peerlessness, matchlessness, inimitability, superlativeness.

su•per•la•tive /sōōpórlətiv/ • *adj.* **1** of the

highest quality or degree (*superlative wisdom*). **2** *Gram.* (of an adjective or adverb) expressing the highest degree of a quality (e.g., *bravest, most fiercely*). • *n.* **1** *Gram.* superlative expression or form of an adjective or adverb. **2** exaggerated or excessive statement, comment, expression, etc. □□ **su•per′la•tive•ly** *adv.* **su•per′la•tive•ness** *n.*

■ *adj.* **1** unsurpassed, paramount, supreme, consummate, superior, best, choicest, finest, matchless, peerless, unequaled, unrivaled, unbeatable, singular, unique.

su•per•man /s○○pərman/ *n.* (*pl.* **-men**) *colloq.* man of exceptional strength or ability.

su•per•mar•ket /s○○pərmaarkit/ *n.* large self-service store selling foods, household goods, etc.

su•per•nat•u•ral /s○○pərnáchərəl/ • *adj.* attributed to or thought to reveal some force above the laws of nature; magical; mystical. • *n.* [prec. by *the*] supernatural, occult, or magical forces, effects, etc. □□ **su•per•nat′u•ral•ism** *n.* **su•per•nat′u•ral•ist** *n.* **su•per•nat′u•ral•ly** *adv.*

■ *adj.* preternatural, unusual, extraordinary, exceptional, unnatural, miraculous; metaphysical, hyperphysical, superphysical, extramundane, divine, occult, paranormal, psychic.

su•per•no•va /s○○pərnóvə/ *n.* (*pl.* **-no•vae** /-vee/ or **-no•vas**) *Astron.* star that suddenly increases very greatly in brightness because of an explosion ejecting most of its mass.

su•per•nu•mer•ar•y /s○○pərn○○mərereе, -nyо̄ō-/ • *adj.* in excess of the normal number; extra. • *n.* (*pl.* **-ies**) **1** extra or unwanted person or thing. **2** actor without a speaking part; extra.

su•per•pow•er /s○○pərpowr/ *n.* extremely powerful nation.

su•per•script /s○○pərskript/ • *adj.* written or printed above the line. • *n.* superscript number or symbol.

su•per•sede /s○○pərseed/ *v.tr.* **1 a** adopt or appoint another person or thing in place of. **b** set aside; cease to employ. **2** (of a person or thing) take the place of. See synonym study at REPLACE. □□ **su•per•sed′ence** *n.*

■ **1** replace, put in place of, change. **2** replace, succeed, displace, supplant, oust, take over from.

su•per•son•ic /s○○pərsónik/ *adj.* designating or having a speed greater than that of sound. □□ **su•per•son′i•cal•ly** *adv.*

su•per•star /s○○pərstaar/ *n.* extremely famous or renowned actor, movie star, athlete, etc. □□ **su′per•star•dom** *n.*

su•per•sti•tion /s○○pərstíshən/ *n.* **1** credulity regarding the supernatural. **2** irrational fear of the unknown. **3** practice, opinion, or religion based on these tendencies. □□ **su•per•sti′tious** *adj.* **su•per•sti′tious•ly** *adv.*

su•per•struc•ture /s○○pərstrukchər/ *n.* **1** part of a building above its foundations. **2** structure built on top of something else. □□ **su•per•struc′tur•al** *adj.*

su•per•vene /s○○pərveen/ *v.intr.* occur as an interruption in or a change from some state. □□ **su•per•ven′ient** *adj.* **su•per•ven′tion** /-vénshən/ *n.*

su•per•vise /s○○pərviz/ *v.tr.* superintend; oversee. □□ **su•per•vi•sion** /-vízhən/ *n.* **su′per•vi•sor** *n.* **su•per•vi′so•ry** *adj.*

■ overlook, watch (over), manage, run, control, govern. □□ **supervisor** overseer, foreman, manager, controller, superintendent, superior, director; *colloq.* boss, super. **supervisory** managerial, administrative, executive.

su•pine /s○○pín/ *adj.* **1** lying face upward. **2** inert; indolent. □□ **su•pine′ly** *adv.* **su•pine′ness** *n.*

■ **1** flat (on one's back); lying (down), recumbent. **2** lazy, lethargic, idle, listless, indifferent, apathetic, unconcerned, uninterested, torpid.

sup•per /súpər/ *n.* light evening meal. □□ **sup′per•less** *adj.*

sup•plant /səplánt/ *v.tr.* dispossess and take the place of, esp. by underhand means. See synonym study at REPLACE. □□ **sup•plant′er** *n.*

■ replace, displace, oust, turn out, eject, remove, expel, dismiss, unseat, supersede, substitute for.

sup•ple /súpəl/ *adj.* (**sup•pler, sup•plest**) **1** flexible; pliant; easily bent. **2** compliant; avoiding overt resistance; artfully or servilely submissive. See synonym study at FLEXIBLE. □□ **sup′ple•ness** *n.*

■ **1** bendable, elastic, resilient, pliable; willowy, lithe, limber. **2** tractable, yielding, accommodating, obliging, complaisant, acquiescent.

sup•ple•ment • *n.* /súplimənt/ **1** thing or part added to improve or provide further information. **2** separate section of a newspaper or periodical. • *v.tr.* also /súplimént/ provide a supplement for. □□ **sup•ple•men•tal** /-mént′l/ *adj.* **sup•ple•men′tal•ly** *adv.* **sup•ple•men•ta•tion** /-məntáyshən/ *n.*

■ *n.* **1** addition, extension, appendage; addendum, addition, appendix, codicil. **2** insert, appendix, extra; (color) magazine. • *v.* add to, extend, augment.

sup•ple•men•ta•ry /súpliméntərее/ *adj.* forming or serving as a supplement; additional.

■ added, annexed, adjunct, new; supplemental, supportive, contributory, ancillary; extraneous, adventitious, supervenient, extra.

sup•pli•ant /súpleeənt/ • *adj.* supplicating. • *n.* supplicating person. □□ **sup•pli′ant•ly** *adv.*

sup•pli•cate /súplikayt/ *v.* **1** *tr.* petition humbly to (a person) or for (a thing). **2** *intr.* make a petition. □□ **sup′pli•cant** *adj. & n.* **sup•pli•ca•tion** /-áyshən/ *n.*

■ □□ **supplicant** (*adj.*) supplicatory, suppliant, imploring, solicitous. (*n.*) applicant, suppliant, petitioner, suitor; *Law* pleader, appellant, plaintiff. **supplication** entreaty, petition, prayer, appeal, pleading, plea.

sup•ply /səplí/ • *v.tr.* (**-plies, -plied**) **1** provide or furnish (a thing needed). **2** provide (a person, etc., with a thing needed). **3** meet or make up for (a deficiency or need, etc.).

• *n. (pl.* **–plies**) **1** providing what is needed. **2** stock, store, amount, etc. **3** [in *pl.*] provisions; equipment. □□ **sup•pli′er** *n.*

■ *v.* **1, 2** give, endow, donate, present, purvey, deliver; stock, accommodate, afford, equip; victual. **3** satisfy, replenish, fill. • *n.* **1** provision, purveyance, distribution, delivery. **2** inventory, quantity, reservoir, reserve, cache. **3** see KIT[1] **1**, PROVISION *n.* **2**.

sup•port /səpáwrt/ • *v.tr.* **1** carry all or part of the weight of. **2** keep from falling or sinking or failing. **3** provide for (a family, etc.). **4** give strength to; encourage. **5** bear out; substantiate. **6** give help or countenance to; further. **7** speak in favor of. • *n.* **1** supporting or being supported. **2** person or thing that supports. □□ **sup•port′a•ble** *adj.* **sup port′er** *n.*

■ *v.* **1, 2** bear, take, hold up, sustain; brace, prop (up); strengthen, shore up, reinforce, fortify, buttress. **3** maintain, keep, pay for, fund, finance. **4, 6** back (up), stand by, stick by, help, assist, aid, bolster; champion, promote, forward, second, advance, advocate. **5** verify, corroborate, authenticate, vouch for, endorse, confirm, affirm. **7** argue in favor of, recommend, advocate, favor. • *n.* **1** help, backing, backup, reinforcement, encouragement, assistance, aid; contribution, allegiance, patronage, sponsorship. **2** brace, prop, stay, frame, foundation, underpinning, substructure, shoring, staging, truss, beam; sustenance, (living) expenses, keep, maintenance. □□ **supportable** tolerable, bearable, endurable, acceptable, sufferable; defensible, confirmable, verifiable, demonstrable, enthusiast, champion, promoter, fan, aficionado, devotee, admirer, backer, follower, support, advocate.

sup•port•ive /səpáwrtiv/ *adj.* providing support or encouragement. □□ **sup•port′ive•ly** *adv.* **sup•port′ive•ness** *n.*

■ helpful, sustaining, supporting, encouraging, sympathetic, understanding, reassuring.

sup•pose /səpóz/ *v.tr.* **1** assume, be inclined to think. **2** take as a possibility or hypothesis. **3** require as a condition (*design in creation supposes a creator*). **4** [in *passive*] **a** be expected or required (*was supposed to write to you*). **b** [with *neg.*] not have to; not be allowed to. □□ **sup•pos′a•ble** *adj.*

■ **1** presume, presuppose, surmise, take; believe, think; take it. **2** hypothesize, theorize, postulate, posit, assume. **3** presuppose, assume; see also INVOLVE **2**. **4 a** be obliged, be meant, be intended.

sup•pos•ed•ly /səpózidlee/ *adv.* as is generally supposed.

■ allegedly, reputedly, theoretically, hypothetically.

sup•po•si•tion /súpəzíshən/ *n.* **1** fact or idea, etc., supposed. **2** act or an instance of supposing. □□ **sup•po•si′tion•al** *adj.*

■ assumption, presumption, surmise, inference; belief, thought, fancy, idea, guess; postulation.

sup•pos•i•to•ry /səpózitawree/ *n. (pl.* **–ries**)

medical preparation that is inserted in the rectum or vagina.

sup•press /səprés/ *v.tr.* **1** put an end to, esp. forcibly. **2** prevent from being done, seen, heard, or known. □□ **sup•pres•sion** /-préshən/ *n.* **sup•pres′sor** *n.*

■ **1** end, discontinue, cut off, cease, stop, terminate, halt, prohibit, preclude, prevent, repress, put down, quell, crush, squelch, quash. **2** keep down, control, keep under control, swallow, stifle, repress, cover up, censor, conceal, hide. □□ **suppression** end, discontinuation, cutoff, cessation, stop, termination, halt, check, extinction; control, restraint.

sup•pu•rate /súpyərayt/ *v.intr.* **1** form pus. **2** fester. □□ **sup•pu•ra•tion** /-ráyshən/ *n.* **sup•pu•ra•tive** /-rətiv/ *adj.*

supra- /sóōprə/ *prefix* **1** above. **2** beyond; transcending.

su•pra•na•tion•al /sóōprənáshənəl/ *adj.* transcending national limits.

su•prem•a•cy /sooprémasee/ *n. (pl.* **–cies**) being supreme.

■ transcendency, preeminence, supremeness, superiority, ascendancy, predominance, excellence.

su•preme /soopréém/ *adj.* **1** highest in authority or rank. **2** greatest; most important. **3** (of a penalty or sacrifice, etc.) involving death. □ **Supreme Court** highest judicial court in a nation, etc. □□ **su•preme′ly** *adv.* **su•preme′ness** *n.*

■ **1** loftiest, topmost, greatest, first, foremost, principal, unsurpassed, top, uppermost. **2** best, first, outstanding, preeminent, unexcelled, leading; superlative, matchless, peerless, incomparable. **3** greatest, maximum, extreme, uttermost, utmost, ultimate. □□ **supremely** very, extremely, exceedingly, completely; see also *preeminently* (PREEMINENT). **supremeness** see SUPREMACY.

Supt. *abbr.* Superintendent.

sur-[1] /sər/ *prefix* = SUPER- (*surcharge, surrealism*).

sur-[2] /sər/ *prefix* assim. form of SUB- before *r.*

sur•charge • *n.* /sórchaarj/ additional charge or payment. • *v.tr.* /sórchaarj, –chaárj/ exact a surcharge from.

surd /sərd/ • *adj. Math.*(of a number) irrational. • *n. Math.*surd number, esp. the root of an integer.

sure /shoōr/ • *adj.* **1** having or seeming to have adequate reason for a belief or assertion. **2** convinced. **3** confident. **4** reliable or unfailing (*there is one sure way to find out*). **5** certain. **6** undoubtedly true or truthful. • *adv. colloq.* certainly. □ **make sure** make or become certain; ensure. **sure-fire** *colloq.* certain to succeed. **sure-footed** never stumbling or making a mistake. **to be sure 1** it is undeniable or admitted. **2** it must be admitted. □□ **sure′ness** *n.*

■ *adj.* **1, 2** certain, assured, persuaded, positive, definite; unwavering, unswerving, unflinching, steadfast. **3** satisfied, certain. **4** accurate, dependable, tried-and-true, unerring; established, firm, solid, stable; certain, inevitable, indubitable. **5** see CERTAIN *adj.* **2**. **6** see CERTAIN *adj.* **1b**. • *adv.* see SURELY **1**.

sure•ly /shŏŏrlee/ *adv.* **1** with certainty. **2** as an appeal to likelihood or reason. **3** with safety; securely.

■ **1** certainly, to be sure, positively, absolutely, definitely, undoubtedly, indubitably, unquestionably. **3** firmly, solidly, confidently, unfalteringly, steadily.

sure•ty /shŏŏritee/ *n.* (*pl.* **–ties**) **1** person who takes responsibility for another's debt, obligation, etc. **2** certainty.

surf /sərf/ • *n.* **1** swell of the sea breaking on the shore or reefs. **2** foam produced by this. • *v. intr.* ride the surf, with or as with a surfboard. □□ **surf′er** *n.*

sur•face /sŏrfis/ • *n.* **1 a** outside of a material body. **b** area of this. **2** any of the limits terminating a solid. **3** upper boundary of a liquid or of the ground, etc. **4** outward or superficial aspect of anything. **5** *Geom.* set of points that has length and breadth but no thickness. • *v.* **1** *tr.* give the required surface to (a road, paper, etc.). **2** *intr. & tr.* rise or bring to the surface. **3** *intr.* become visible or known. □□ **sur•faced** *adj.* [usu. in *comb.*].

sur′fac•er *n.*

■ *n.* **1** exterior, covering, top, skin, integument, façade, face, boundary. **2** side, face; boundary, *Geom.* superficies. **3** top; surface film. **4** exterior, outside, top, skin, façade, face; (*on the surface*) superficially, at first glance. **5** plane, *Geom.* superficies. • *v.* **1** coat, finish, top; pave, concrete, tar. **2, 3** appear, show up, come up, pop up, crop up, emerge.

surf•board /sŏrfbawrd/ *n.* long narrow board used in surfing.

sur•feit /sŏrfit/ • *n.* **1** excess, esp. in eating or drinking. **2** feeling of satiety or disgust resulting from this. • *v.* **1** *tr.* overfeed. **2** *intr.* overeat. **3** *intr. & tr.* [foll. by *with*] be or cause to be wearied through excess.

■ *n.* **1** over-abundance, superabundance, plethora, glut, surplus, overdose, satiety. **2** nausea, sickness, disgust. • *v.* **1** gorge, satiate, sate, stuff. **2** sate, satiate, cloy, glut, pall.

surg. *abbr.* **1** surgeon. **2** surgery. **3** surgical.

surge /sərj/ • *n.* **1** sudden rush. **2** swell of the waves at sea. **3** heavy forward or upward motion. **4** rapid increase in price, activity, etc. **5** sudden marked increase in voltage. • *v. intr.* **1** (of the sea, etc.) swell. **2** move suddenly and powerfully forward. **3** increase suddenly.

■ *n.* **1** see OUTBURST. **2** surf, upsurge, eddy, rush, gush; see also WAVE *n.* 1, 2. **4** see SWELL *n.* 1. • *v.* **1** billow, bulge, heave, roll, undulate, well forth *or* up, rise and fall, ebb and flow. **2** rush, gush, flood, stream, flow.

sur•geon /sŏrjən/ *n.* medical practitioner qualified to practice surgery.

sur•ger•y /sŏrjəree/ *n.* (*pl.* **–ies**) medical treatment of injuries or disorders by incision, manipulation or alteration of organs, etc., with the hands or with instruments.

sur•gi•cal /sŏrjikəl/ *adj.* **1** of or used by surgeons or in surgery. **2** extremely precise. □□ **sur′gi•cal•ly** *adv.*

sur•ly /sŏrlee/ *adj.* (**sur•li•er, sur•li•est**) bad-tempered and unfriendly; churlish. See synonym study at BRUSQUE. □□ **sur′li•ness** *n.*

■ unpleasant, rude, crusty, cantankerous,

curmudgeonly, crabby, crabbed, choleric, splenetic, dyspeptic, bilious, temperamental, cross, crotchety, sullen.

sur•mise /sərmíz/ • *n.* conjecture. • *v.* **1** *tr.* infer doubtfully. **2** *tr.* suspect the existence of. **3** *intr.* make a guess.

■ *n.* guess, speculation, notion, hypothesis, theory, supposition, assumption, presumption. • *v.* **1** imagine, guess, conjecture, speculate, suppose, hypothesize, theorize, assume, presume, conclude, gather. **3** guess, conjecture, speculate.

sur•mount /sərmównt/ *v. tr.* **1** overcome or get over (a difficulty or obstacle). **2** cap or crown. □□ **sur•mount′a•ble** *adj.*

sur•name /sŏrnaym/ *n.* family or last name.

sur•pass /sərpás/ *v. tr.* outdo; be greater or better than. **2** (as **surpassing** *adj.*) preeminent. □□ **sur•pass′ing•ly** *adv.*

■ **1** exceed, excel, go *or* pass beyond, beat, worst, better, outstrip, outdistance, outperform, outclass. **2** (**surpassing**) excessive, extraordinary, great, enormous, incomparable, unrivaled, unparalleled. □□ **surpassingly** exceedingly, extraordinarily, incomparably.

sur•plice /sŏrplis/ *n.* loose white linen vestment worn over a cassock by clergy and choristers. □□ **sur′pliced** *adj.*

sur•plus /sŏrpləs, –plus/ • *n.* **1** amount left over. **2** excess of revenue over expenditure. • *adj.* exceeding what is needed or used.

■ *n.* **1** overage, excess, superfluity, surfeit, overabundance; remainder, residue, balance. • *adj.* leftover, extra, spare, overabundant, superfluous.

sur•prise /sərpríz/ • *n.* **1** unexpected or astonishing event or circumstance. **2** emotion caused by this. **3** catching or being caught unawares. • *v. tr.* **1** turn out contrary to the expectations of (*your answer surprised me*). **2** [usu. in *passive*] shock; scandalize (*I am surprised at you*). **3** capture or attack by surprise. **4** come upon (a person) unawares. □□ **sur•pris•ed•ly** /–prízidlee/ *adv.* **sur•pris′ing** *adj.* **sur•pris′ing•ly** *adv.*

■ *n.* **1** blow, jolt, bombshell, *colloq.* shocker, eye-opener. **2** shock, astonishment, amazement, stupefaction, wonder. • *v.* **1** shock, astound, astonish, amaze, take by surprise, disconcert, nonplus, dumbfound. **2** appall, dismay, horrify, outrage. **3, 4** ambush, ambuscade, pounce on, swoop on, startle; catch off guard, discover, detect, catch out.

sur•re•al /səréəl/ *adj.* **1** having the qualities of surrealism. **2** strange; bizarre. □□ **sur•re′al•ly** *adv.*

sur•re•al•ism /səréəlizəm/ *n.* 20th-c. movement in art and literature aiming at expressing the subconscious mind, e.g., by the irrational juxtaposition of images. □□ **sur′re•al•ist** *n. & adj.* **sur•re•al•is′tic** *adj.* **sur•re•al•is′ti•cal•ly** *adv.*

sur•ren•der /səréndər/ • *v.* **1** *tr.* hand over; relinquish. **2** *intr.* submit, esp. to an enemy. **3** *intr. & refl.* [foll. by *to*] give oneself over to a habit, emotion, influence, etc. **4** *tr.* abandon (hope, etc.). See synonym study at

RELINQUISH. • *n.* act or an instance of surrendering.

■ *v.* **1** give up, yield, let go (of), deliver (up), forgo, forsake, turn over, turn in. **2** give (oneself) up, yield, quit, cry quits, capitulate, succumb, give way, acquiesce, comply, give in. **4** give up. • *n.* submission, capitulation, yielding, renunciation, transferral, transfer, transference, handover.

sur•rep•ti•tious /sə́rəptíshəs/ *adj.* done by stealth; clandestine. □□ **sur•rep•ti′tious•ly** *adv.*

■ furtive, secret, stealthy, devious, covert.

sur•ro•gate /sə́rəgət, –gayt, súr–/ *n.* **1** substitute. **2** judge in charge of probate, inheritance, and guardianship. □ **surrogate mother** woman who bears a child on behalf of another woman, usu. from her own egg fertilized by the other woman's partner. □□ **sur′ro•ga•cy** *n.*

sur•round /sərównd/ *v.tr.* come or be all around; encircle; enclose. See synonym study at CIRCUMSCRIBE. □□ **sur•round′ing** *adj.*

■ encompass, envelop, hem in, hedge in, fence in, box in, ring; cover, coat, encase; beset, besiege. □□ **surrounding** nearby, neighboring, local, adjoining, neighborhood, adjacent, bordering, abutting.

sur•round•ings /sərówndingz/ *n.pl.* things in the neighborhood of, or conditions affecting, a person or thing.

sur•tax /sə́rtaks/ *n.* additional tax.

sur•veil•lance /sərváyləns/ *n.* close observation, esp. of a suspected person.

■ watch, scrutiny, reconnaissance.

sur•vey • *v.tr.* /sərváy/ **1** take or present a general view of. **2** examine the condition of (a building, etc.). **3** determine the boundaries, extent, ownership, etc., of (a district, etc.). • *n.* /sə́rvay/ **1** general view or consideration. **2 a** act of surveying opinions, etc. **b** result or findings of this, esp. in a written report. **3** inspection or investigation. **4** map or plan made by surveying.

■ *v.* **1, 2** view, look at, contemplate, scan, observe; consider, review; appraise, evaluate, inspect. **3** measure, size up, take the measure of; plot, map (out); explore, reconnoiter. • *n.* **1, 3** observation, sight, contemplation; examination, appraisal, evaluation, assessment; canvass, poll, census.

sur•vey•or /sərváyər/ *n.* person who surveys land and buildings, esp. professionally.

sur•viv•al /sərvívəl/ *n.* **1** surviving. **2** relic.

sur•vive /sərvív/ *v.* **1** *intr.* continue to live or exist; be still alive or existent. **2** *tr.* live or exist longer than. **3** *tr.* remain alive in spite of (a danger, accident, etc.). □□ **sur•vi′vor** *n.*

■ **1** last, live (on), carry on, persist, subsist, pull through. **2** outlast, outlive. **3** see WEATHER *v.*

sus- /sus, səs/ *prefix* assim. form of SUB- before *c*, *p*, *t*.

sus•cep•ti•bil•i•ty /səséptibílitee/ *n.* (*pl.* **–ties**) **1** state of being susceptible. **2** [in *pl.*] person's sensitive feelings.

sus•cep•ti•ble /səséptibəl/ *adj.* **1** impressionable; sensitive. **2** [*predic.*] **a** [foll. by *to*]

liable or vulnerable. **b** [foll. by *of*] allowing; admitting (*facts not susceptible of proof*). □□ **sus•cep′ti•bly** *adv.*

■ **1** influenceable, vulnerable, reachable, accessible, credulous; susceptive; emotional. **2 a** open, prone, subject, disposed, predisposed. **b** permitting.

su•shi /sŏŏshee/ *n.* Japanese dish of balls of cold rice flavored and garnished, esp. with raw fish or shellfish.

sus•pect • *v.tr.* /səspékt/ **1** have an impression of the existence or presence of. **2** believe tentatively, without clear ground. **3** be inclined to think. **4** mentally accuse. **5** doubt the genuineness or truth of. • *n.* /súspekt/ person under suspicion. • *adj.* /súspekt/ subject to or deserving suspicion.

■ *v.* **3** feel, think, believe, sense, fancy, imagine, theorize, guess. **4, 5** disbelieve, mistrust, distrust, have suspicions about or of, be suspicious of. • *adj.* suspicious, questionable, doubtful, dubious, unreliable, untrustworthy, shady.

sus•pend /səspénd/ *v.tr.* **1** hang up. **2** keep inoperative or undecided for a time; defer. **3** bar temporarily from a school, function, office, privilege, etc. **4** (as **suspended** *adj.*) (of particles or a body in a fluid) sustained somewhere between top and bottom. See synonym study at POSTPONE. □ **suspended animation** temporary deathlike condition. □□ **sus•pens•i•ble** /səspénsibəl/ *adj.*

■ **1** attach, fasten, dangle, swing, sling. **2** hold up or off (on), withhold, put off, shelve, postpone, delay, interrupt, table. **3** exclude, eliminate, reject, expel, eject, evict; blackball; see also *lay off* 1 (LAY¹).

sus•pend•ers /səspéndərz/ *n.* [*pl.*] straps worn across the shoulders and supporting trousers, a skirt, etc.

sus•pense /səspéns/ *n.* state of anxious uncertainty or expectation. □□ **sus•pense′ful** *adj.*

■ anxiety, tension, apprehension, nervousness, agitation; indefiniteness, insecurity.

sus•pen•sion /səspénshən/ *n.* **1** suspending or being suspended. **2** means by which a vehicle is supported on its axles. **3** substance consisting of particles suspended in a medium. □ **suspension bridge** bridge with a roadway suspended from cables supported by structures at each end.

■ **1** intermission, moratorium, deferral, deferment, holdup, delay; debarment, exclusion; disbarment.

sus•pi•cion /səspíshən/ *n.* **1** feeling or thought of a person who suspects. **2** suspecting or being suspected. **3** slight trace of.

■ **1** hunch, guess, presentiment; qualm, doubt, misgiving; dubiousness, mistrust, distrust, skepticism, wariness. **3** inkling, suggestion, hint, vestige, flavor, soupçon, taste, dash, glimmer, tinge.

sus•pi•cious /səspíshəs/ *adj.* **1** prone to or feeling suspicion. **2** prompting suspicion (*suspicious lack of surprise*). □□ **sus•pi′cious•ly** *adv.*

■ **1** mistrustful, distrustful, doubtful, in doubt, skeptical, suspecting, disbelieving, unbelieving. **2** doubtful, in doubt, dubious, questionable, debatable, suspect, suspected, under suspicion.

sus•tain /səstáyn/ v.tr. **1** support, bear the weight of, esp. for a long period. **2** encourage; support. **3** (of food) give nourishment to. **4** endure; stand; bear up against. **5** undergo or suffer (defeat or injury, etc.). **6** (of a court, etc.) uphold or decide in favor of (an objection, etc.). **7** corroborate. **8** maintain. □□ **sus•tain'a•ble** adj. **sus•tain'er** n. **sus•tain'ment** n.

■ **1** carry, take, hold. **2** carry, bear, bolster, buoy (up), reinforce, strengthen, shore up. **3** nourish, feed, support, keep (alive), maintain. **4, 5** withstand, put up with, experience, tolerate, weather, brave. **6** recognize, allow, admit, approve, ratify, sanction. **7** see SUBSTANTIATE. **8** uphold, support, keep up, continue, keep going, keep alive, prolong, persist in.

sus•te•nance /sústinəns/ n. **1 a** nourishment; food. **b** process of nourishing. **2** means of support; livelihood.

■ **1 a** nutriment, daily bread, rations, victuals, provisions, groceries, edibles. **2** maintenance, upkeep, keep, (means of) subsistence, daily bread, living.

su•ture /sōōchər/ n. **1** Surgery joining of the edges of a wound or incision by stitching. **2** thread or wire used for this. □□ **su'tured** adj.

svelte /svelt/ adj. slender; graceful. See synonym study at THIN.

SW abbr. **1** southwest. **2** southwestern.

swab /swob/ • n. **1** mop. **2 a** absorbent pad used in surgery. **b** specimen of a secretion taken with a swab for examination. • v.tr. (**swabbed, swab•bing**) **1** clean with a swab. **2** [foll. by up] absorb (moisture) with a swab.

■ n. see WIPE n. 1.

swad•dle /swód'l/ v.tr. swathe (esp. an infant) tightly.

swag /swag/ n. ornamental display of flowers, drapery, etc., hanging decoratively in a curve.

swag•ger /swágər/ • v.intr. walk or behave arrogantly. • n. swaggering gait or manner. □ **swagger stick** short cane carried by a military officer. □□ **swag'ger•er** n. **swag'ger•ing•ly** adv.

■ v. strut, prance, parade; boast, brag, crow; see also lord it over. • n. strut, prance, caper; braggadocio, arrogance, bravado, bluster, boastfulness.

Swa•hi•li /swaahéelee/ n. (pl. same) **1** member of a Bantu people of Zanzibar and adjacent coasts. **2** their language, widely spoken in E. Africa.

swain /swayn/ n. **1** archaic country youth. **2** poet. young male lover or suitor.

swal•low¹ /swólō/ • v. **1** tr. cause or allow (food, etc.) to pass down the throat. **2** intr. perform the muscular movement of the esophagus required to do this. **3** tr. accept meekly or credulously. **4** tr. repress (swallow one's pride). **5** tr. engulf or absorb. • n. **1** act of swallowing. **2** amount swallowed in one action. □□ **swal'low•er** n.

■ v. **1** eat, consume, devour, ingest; guzzle,

gobble, bolt; drink, imbibe, gulp. **3** see also TOLERATE. **4** keep back or down, choke back or down, suppress, hold in, control, stifle. **5** swamp, envelop, enfold, consume, assimilate. • n. drink, gulp, guzzle, sip, sup, colloq. swig; bite, nibble, morsel, mouthful.

swal•low² /swólō/ n. migratory swift-flying insect-eating bird with a forked tail and long pointed wings.

swam past of SWIM.

swa•mi /swaamee/ n. (pl. **swa•mis**) Hindu male religious teacher.

swamp /swaamp/ • n. piece of waterlogged ground. • v. **1 a** tr. overwhelm, flood, or soak with water. **b** intr. become swamped. **2** tr. overwhelm with an excess or large amount of something. □□ **swamp'y** adj. (**swamp•i•er, swamp•i•est**).

■ n. bog, fen, marsh, quagmire, mire, slough; marshland, wetlands; moor. • v. inundate, submerge, immerse, deluge; soak, drench, engulf, swallow up; overcome, overload, overtax, overburden.

swan /swon/ n. large, usu. white, water bird having a long flexible neck and webbed feet. □ **swan song** person's last work or act before death or retirement, etc. □□ **swan'like** adj. & adv.

swank /swangk/ colloq. • n. ostentation; swagger. • adj. = SWANKY.

swank•y /swángkee/ adj. (**swank•i•er, swank•i•est**) ostentatiously stylish or showy. □□ **swank'i•ly** adv. **swank'i•ness** n.

■ fashionable, chic, chichi, fancy, luxurious.

swap /swop/ (also **swop**) • v. (**swapped, swap•ping**) exchange or barter (one thing for another). • n. **1** act of swapping. **2** thing swapped. □□ **swap'per** n.

swarm /swawrm/ • n. **1** cluster of bees leaving the hive with the queen to establish a new colony. **2** large cluster of insects, birds, or people. **3** [in pl.; foll. by of] great numbers. • v.intr. **1** move in or form a swarm. **2** (of a place) be overrun, crowded, or infested.

■ n. **1, 2** throng, horde, army, host, multitude, hive, herd, mob, mass. • v. **1** throng, mass, crowd, congregate, cluster; flood, stream, flow, pour, surge. **2** crawl, abound, throng, teem, burst, bristle.

swarth•y /swáwrthee/ adj. (**swarth•i•er, swarth•i•est**) dark; dark-complexioned. □□ **swarth'i•ness** n.

■ dusky, brown, tanned, weather-beaten.

swash /swosh/ v.intr. (of water, etc.) wash about; make the sound of washing or rising and falling.

swash•buck•ler /swóshbuklər/ n. swaggering adventurer, esp. in a novel, movie, etc. □□ **swash'buck•ling** adj. & n.

■ □□ **swashbuckling** (adj.) adventurous, daring, daredevil, swaggering, roisterous, bold, dashing, flamboyant.

swas•ti•ka /swóstikə/ n. **1** ancient symbol formed by an equal-armed cross with each arm continued at a right angle. **2** this with clockwise continuations as the symbol of Nazi Germany.

swat /swot/ • v.tr. (**swat•ted, swat•ting**)

1 crush (a fly, etc.) with a sharp blow. **2** hit hard and abruptly. • *n.* swatting blow.

swatch /swoch/ *n.* sample, esp. of cloth or fabric.

swath /swoth, swawth/ *n.* **1** ridge of cut grass or grain, etc. **2** space left clear by a mower, etc. **3** broad strip.
■ path, belt, strip, ribbon.

swathe /swoth, swayth/ • *v.tr.* bind or enclose in bandages or garments, etc. • *n.* bandage or wrapping.

sway /sway/ • *v.* **1** *intr. & tr.* lean or cause to lean unsteadily in different directions alternately. **2** *intr.* oscillate irregularly; waver. **3** *tr.* **a** control the motion or direction of. **b** have influence or rule over. • *n.* **1** rule, influence, or government (*hold sway*). **2** swaying motion or position. See synonym study at JURISDICTION.
■ *v.* **1** bend, roll, rock, swing (to and fro *or* back and forth *or* from side to side *or* backward and forward), wave, fluctuate. **2** see OSCILLATE. **3 a** move, incline, divert, veer, tilt, lean. **b** influence, persuade, impress, win over, bring around; move, incline, affect. • *n.* **1** control, power, command, authority, jurisdiction, dominion; grip, clutches, grasp. **2** sweep, wave, swing, (period of) oscillation, libration.

swear /swair/ *v.* (*past* **swore** /swor/; *past part.* **sworn** /sworn/) **1** *tr.* **a** [often foll. by *to* + infin. or *that* + clause] state or promise solemnly or on oath. **b** take (an oath). **2** *tr. colloq.* insist (*swore he had not seen it*). **3** *tr.* cause to take an oath. **4** *intr.* use profane or indecent language. **5** *intr.* **a** appeal to as a witness in taking an oath (*swear by Almighty God*). **b** *colloq.* have or express great confidence in. **6** *intr.* admit the certainty of (*could not swear to it*). □ **swear off** *colloq.* promise to abstain from (drink, etc.). □□ **swear′er** *n.*
■ **1a, 2** declare, assert, solemnly affirm, testify, promise, take an oath. **4** curse, blaspheme, imprecate, use profanity, *colloq.* cuss. **5 b** trust (in), believe in, rely on, count on. **6** see PROVE 1. □ **swear off** forswear, renounce, abjure, go off, forgo, shun.

sweat /swet/ • *n.* **1** moisture exuded through the pores of the skin, esp. from heat or nervousness. **2** state or period of sweating. **3** *colloq.* drudgery; effort. • *v.* (*past* and *past part.* **sweat** or **sweat•ed**) **1** *intr.* exude sweat. **2** *intr.* be terrified, suffering, etc. **3** *intr.* (of a wall, etc.) exhibit surface moisture. **4** *intr.* drudge; toil. **5** *tr.* emit (blood, gum, etc.) like sweat. **6** *tr.* cause to drudge or toil. □ **no sweat** *colloq.* there is no need to worry. **sweat blood** *colloq.* **1** work strenuously. **2** be extremely anxious. **sweat it out** *colloq.* endure a difficult experience to the end.
■ *n.* **1, 2** perspiration, lather, *Med.* diaphoresis. **3** (hard) work, labor, exertion, laboriousness, toil, *colloq.* grind. • *v.* **1** perspire, glow. **2** worry, be anxious, agonize, anguish, fret, fuss, torture *or* torment oneself, lose sleep. **4** slave (away), labor, grind, slog, work like a Trojan. **5** ooze, exude, squeeze out, transude. □ **no sweat** don't

worry, everything is taken care of, all is well, that presents no difficulty, *colloq.* not to worry.

sweat•band /swétband/ *n.* band of absorbent material inside a hat or around a wrist, etc., to soak up sweat.

sweat•er /swétər/ *n.* knitted garment for the upper body, usu. worn over a shirt, etc.

sweat•pants /swétpants/ *n.pl.* loose pants of absorbent cotton material worn for exercise, etc.

sweat•shirt /swétshərt/ *n.* pullover shirt of absorbent material.

sweat•y /swétee/ *adj.* (**sweat•i•er, sweat•i•est**) **1** sweating; covered with sweat. **2** causing sweat. □□ **sweat′i•ly** *adv.* **sweat′i•ness** *n.*

Swede /sweed/ *n.* **1** native or national of Sweden. **2** person of Swedish descent.

Swed•ish /sweédish/ • *adj.* of or relating to Sweden or its people or language. • *n.* language of Sweden.

sweep /sweep/ • *v.* (*past* and *past part.* **swept** /swept/) **1** *tr.* clean or clear with or as with a broom. **2** *intr.* clean a room, etc., in this way. **3** *tr.* collect or remove (dirt, etc.) by sweeping. **4** *tr.* **a** push with or as with a broom. **b** dismiss abruptly. **5** *tr.* carry or drive along with force. **6** *tr.* remove or clear forcefully. **7** *tr.* traverse swiftly or lightly. **8** *intr.* **a** glide swiftly; speed along. **b** go majestically. **9** *tr.* win every game, etc., in (a series). • *n.* **1** act or motion of sweeping. **2** range or scope. See synonym study at RANGE. □ **make a clean sweep of** completely abolish or expel. □□ **sweep′er** *n.*
■ *v.* **1** brush, dust, tidy up. **4 b** see REJECT *v.* 1, 3. **6** wash away; expel, eliminate, get rid of, dispose of. **8 a** sail; swoop, skim, dash, charge, fly. **b** sail, glide, flounce, march, parade. • *n.* **1** see WHISK *n.* 1. **2** extent, compass, reach, stretch, swing.

sweep•ing /sweéping/ • *adj.* **1** wide in range or effect (*sweeping changes*). **2** taking no account of particular cases or exceptions (*sweeping statement*). • *n.* [in *pl.*] dirt, etc., collected by sweeping. □□ **sweep′ing•ly** *adv.*
■ *adj.* **1** comprehensive, (all-)inclusive, general, extensive, universal, broad, widespread, across-the-board, wholesale, complete, total. **2** broad, generalized, unspecific, nonspecific, imprecise, inexact.

sweep•stake /sweépstayk/ *n.* **1** form of gambling in which all competitors' stakes are paid to the winners. **2** race with betting of this kind. **3** prize or prizes won in a sweepstake.

sweet /sweet/ • *adj.* **1** tasting of sugar. **2** fragrant. **3** melodious or harmonious. **4** highly gratifying or attractive. **5** amiable; pleasant; charming. **6** [foll. by *on*] *colloq.* fond of; in love with. • *n.* **1** something sweet. **2** sweetness. **3** [usu. *pl.*] candy. □ **sweet pea** any dwarf or climbing plant with fragrant flowers. **sweet pepper** see PEPPER. **sweet potato 1** tropical climbing plant with sweet tuberous roots used for food. **2** root of this. **sweet talk** *colloq.* flattery; blandishment. **sweet-talk** *v.tr. colloq.* flatter in order to persuade.

sweet tooth liking for sweet-tasting foods. □□ **sweet′ly** adv.

■ adj. **1** sugary, honeylike, honeyed, sweetened; luscious, saccharine, cloying. **2** perfumed, scented, aromatic, ambrosial, sweet-smelling. **3** sweet-sounding, euphonious, dulcet, musical, tuneful, euphonic, mellifluous. **4** satisfying, pleasant, nice; dear, beloved, precious, prized. **5** gentle, agreeable, genial, warm, friendly; nice; considerate, attentive, solicitous, thoughtful; attractive, appealing, endearing, winning. **6** taken with, keen on, devoted to, enamored of, infatuated with, colloq. wild or crazy about, nuts about.

sweet·bread /sweétbred/ n. pancreas or thymus of an animal, esp. as food.

sweet·bri·er /sweétbriər/ n. wild rose of Europe and central Asia with small fragrant pink flowers.

sweet·en /sweét'n/ v. **1** make or become sweet or sweeter. **2** make agreeable or less painful. □ **sweeten the pill** see PILL. □□ **sweet′en·ing** n.

■ **1** sugar, sugarcoat. **2** dress up, make more attractive, sugarcoat, embellish; mitigate, alleviate, assuage.

sweet·en·er /sweét'nər/ n. **1** substance used to sweeten food or drink. **2** colloq. bribe or inducement.

sweet·heart /sweét-haart/ n. **1** lover or darling. **2** term of endearment (esp. as a form of address).

■ **1** girlfriend, boyfriend, friend, admirer, dear, love, beloved, inamorato, inamorata, ladylove. **2** see DEAR n.

sweet·meat /sweétmeet/ n. **1** candy. **2** small fancy cake.

sweet·ness /sweétnis/ n. being sweet; fragrance.

swell /swel/ • v. (past part. **swol·len** /swólən/ or **swelled**) **1** intr. & tr. grow or cause to grow bigger or louder or more intense. **2** intr. & tr. rise or raise up. **3** intr. bulge. **4** intr. (of the heart, etc.) feel full of joy, pride, relief, etc. **5** intr. [foll. by with] be hardly able to restrain (pride, etc.). • n. **1** act or state of swelling. **2** heaving of the sea with waves that do not break. **3** crescendo. **4** colloq. stylish person. • adj. colloq. fine; splendid; excellent.

■ v. **1** increase, enlarge, expand, blow up or out, dilate; mushroom, snowball, multiply; raise, augment, step up, build up. **3** bloat, billow, belly, balloon, fatten, puff up or out. **5** be filled with, be full of, be bursting with, brim with, overflow with. • n. **1** enlargement, broadening, increase, extension, spread. **2** surge, waves, rollers, billows. **4** fop, dandy, coxcomb, colloq. clotheshorse. • adj. marvelous, thrilling, spectacular, first-rate, colloq. great.

swell·ing /sweling/ n. abnormal protuberance.

swel·ter /sweltər/ • v.intr. (usu. as **sweltering** adj.) be uncomfortably hot. • n. sweltering atmosphere or condition. □□ **swel′ter·ing·ly** adv.

■ v. (**sweltering**) hot, torrid, steamy, sultry, stifling, sticky, suffocating, roasting, blistering, burning.

swept past and past part. of SWEEP.

swerve /swarv/ • v. change or cause to change direction, esp. abruptly. • n. swerving movement. □□ **swerv′er** n.

■ v. veer, career, swing, diverge, deviate, dodge, skew.

swift /swift/ • adj. **1** quick; rapid. **2** prompt. • n. swift-flying insect-eating bird with long wings. □□ **swift′ly** adv. **swift′ness** n.

■ adj. fast, speedy, hasty; lively, nimble; brisk, sudden, abrupt; meteoric; prompt, expeditious. □□ **swiftly** fast, quick(ly), speedily, rapidly, expeditiously; briskly, hurriedly, hastily, posthaste, suddenly, abruptly.

swig /swig/ colloq. • v. (**swigged**, **swig·ging**) drink in large swallows. • n. swallow of drink, esp. a large amount. □□ **swig′ger** n.

swill /swil/ • v. drink greedily. • n. **1** mainly liquid refuse as pig food. **2** inferior liquor. □□ **swill′er** n.

■ v. guzzle, swallow, toss off, polish off, colloq. swig. • n. **1** hogwash, pigswill, refuse, pigwash, slop(s).

swim /swim/ • v. (**swim·ming**; past **swam** /swam/; past part. **swum** /swum/) **1** intr. propel the body through water with limbs, fins, or tail. **2** tr. a traverse (a stretch of water or its distance) by swimming. **b** use (a swimming stroke). **3** intr. have a dizzy effect or sensation. **4** intr. [foll. by in, with] be flooded. • n. spell or act of swimming. □□ **swim′ma·ble** adj. **swim′mer** n.

swim·ming·ly /swiminglee/ adv. with easy progress.

■ smoothly, easily, effortlessly, well, successfully.

swim·suit /swimsoot/ n. garment worn for swimming.

swin·dle /swind'l/ • v.tr. cheat (a person) of money, possessions, etc. • n. act of swindling. □□ **swin′dler** n.

■ v. defraud, deceive, double-cross, hoodwink, take in, flimflam, fleece, rook, dupe, fool, mulct, gull. • n. fraud, confidence trick, deception, racket, colloq. fiddle, rip-off, sl. con, gyp, scam. □□ **swindler** cheat, confidence man, hoaxer, charlatan, scoundrel, sharper, racketeer, fraud, colloq. sharp, shark.

swine /swin/ n. (pl. same) **1** pig. **2** colloq. (pl. **swine** or **swines**) contemptible person. □□ **swin′ish** adj. (esp. in sense 2). **swin′ish·ly** adv.

swing /swing/ • v. (past and past part. **swung** /swung/) **1 a** intr. & tr. move or cause to move with a to-and-fro or curving motion; sway. **b** hang so as to be free to sway. **c** oscillate or cause to oscillate. **2** intr. & tr. revolve or cause to revolve. **3** intr. move by gripping something and leaping, etc. **4** intr. go with a swinging gait (swung out of the room). **5** intr. [foll. by around] move around to the opposite direction. **6** intr. change from one opinion or mood to another. **7** intr. [foll. by at] attempt to hit. **8 a** intr. play music with a swing rhythm. **b** tr. play (a tune) with swing. **9** colloq. (of a party, etc.) be lively, successful, etc. **10** tr. have a decisive influence on (esp. voting, etc.). **11** tr. colloq.

deal with or achieve; manage. **12** *intr. colloq.*
a enjoy oneself. **b** be promiscuous. • *n.*
1 act, motion, or extent of swinging.
2 swinging or smooth gait or rhythm or action. **3** seat slung by ropes, etc., for swinging on or in. **4 a** rhythmic jazz or dance music.
b the rhythmic feeling of this. □□ **swing′er** *n.* (esp. in sense 12 of *v.*).

■ *v.* **1a, c** move *or* go back and forth, come and go, rock, flourish, flap, fluctuate. **1 b** dangle, sling, suspend; be suspended. **5** see WHEEL *v.* 2. **6** see OSCILLATE. **7** swipe, lash out. **10** see SWAY *v.* 3b. **11** see ACCOMPLISH, WANGLE *v.* ■ *n.* **1** sway, toing and froing, fluctuation, flap, oscillation; sweep, scope, range.

swipe /swīp/ *colloq.* • *v.* **1** *tr. &* [often foll. by *at*] *intr.* hit hard and recklessly. **2** *tr.* steal. • *n.* reckless hard hit or attempted hit. □□ **swip′er** *n.*

■ *v.* **1** strike, *sl.* belt, wallop; (*swipe at*) lash out at, swing at. **2** filch, pilfer, snatch; *colloq.* lift, snaffle. • *n.* swing, strike, stroke, clip.

swirl /swərl/ • *v.* move or flow or carry along with a whirling motion. • *n.* **1** swirling motion. **2** twist or curl, esp. as part of a pattern or design. □□ **swirl′y** *adj.*

■ *v.* whirl, spin, eddy, churn; twist, curl, roll, furl. • *n.* whirl, roll, twirl, spiral; see also EDDY *n.*

swish /swish/ • *v.* **1** *tr.* swing (a scythe or stick, etc.) audibly through the air, grass, etc. **2** *intr.* move with or make a swishing sound. • *n.* swishing action or sound.

■ *v.* **2** hiss, whisk, rustle, whoosh, swoosh, whisper. • *n.* hiss, hissing sound, whoosh, swoosh, rustle, whistle.

Swiss /swis/ • *adj.* of Switzerland in Western Europe or its people. • *n.* (*pl.* same) **1** native or inhabitant of Switzerland. **2** person of Swiss descent. □ **Swiss cheese** hard cheese with large holes that form during ripening.

switch /swich/ • *n.* **1** device for making and breaking the connection in an electric circuit. **2 a** transfer, changeover, or deviation. **b** exchange. **3** slender flexible shoot cut from a tree. **4** light tapering rod. **5** device at the junction of railroad tracks for transferring a train from one track to another. • *v.* **1** *tr.* turn (an electrical device) on or off. **2** *intr.* change or transfer position, subject, etc. **3** *tr.* change or transfer. **4** *tr.* exchange. **5** *tr.* beat or flick with a switch. □□ **switch′er** *n.*

■ *n.* **1** circuit breaker. **2 a** change, alteration, shift, reversal, deflection. **b** trade, swap; see also EXCHANGE *n.* 1. **3, 4** twitch, lash, whip, birch (rod), scourge. • *v.* **2** deviate, shift, seesaw. **3** shift, turn, rechannel, redirect, direct. **4** change, shift, swap, reverse, replace, substitute. **5** lash, whip, birch, strike, thrash.

switch•back /swíchbak/ *n.* [often *attrib.*] railroad or road with alternate sharp ascents and descents.

switch•board /swíchbawrd/ *n.* apparatus for varying connections between electric circuits, esp. in telephony.

swiv•el /swívəl/ • *n.* coupling between two parts enabling one to revolve without turning the other. • *v.* turn on or as on a swivel.

■ *n.* pivot, elbow joint, gimbals, ball-and-socket joint. • *v.* pivot, rotate, spin, revolve, wheel, turn, gyrate.

swiz•zle stick /swízəl/ *n.* rod used for stirring drinks.

swol•len *past part.* of SWELL.

swoon /swōon/ *literary* • *v.intr.* faint. • *n.* occurrence of fainting.

swoop /swōop/ • *v.intr.* **1** descend rapidly like a bird of prey. **2** make a sudden attack. • *n.* swooping or snatching movement or action.

■ *v.* **1** dive, sweep down, pounce, stoop. **2** see RAID *v.* 1. • *n.* descent, dive, sweep, pounce.

swop var. of SWAP.

sword /sawrd/ *n.* weapon usu. of metal with a long blade and hilt with a handguard. □□ **sword′like** *adj.*

sword•fish /sáwrdfish/ *n.* large marine fish with an extended swordlike upper jaw.

swords•man /sáwrdzmən/ *n.* (*pl.* **-men**) person of (usu. specified) skill with a sword. □□ **swords′man•ship** *n.*

swore *past* of SWEAR.

sworn /swawrn/ **1** *past part.* of SWEAR. **2** *adj.* bound by or as by an oath (*sworn enemies*).

swum *past part.* of SWIM.

swung *past* and *past part.* of SWING.

syb•a•rite /síbərīt/ *n.* person who is self-indulgent or devoted to sensuous luxury.

syc•a•more /síkəmawr/ *n.* **1** plane tree of N. America or its wood. **2** (in full **syc′a•more ma′ple**) large Eurasian maple or its wood.

syc•o•phant /síkəfant, síkə–/ *n.* flatterer; toady. □□ **syc′o•phan•cy** *n.* **syc•o•phan•tic** /–fántik/ *adj.* **syc•o•phan′ti•cal•ly** *adv.*

syl•lab•ic /silábik/ *adj.* of, relating to, or based on syllables. □□ **syl•lab′i•cal•ly** *adv.*

syl•lab•i•ca•tion /silábikáyshən/ *n.* (also **syl•lab•i•fi•ca′tion**) division into or articulation by syllables. □□ **syl•lab′i•fy** *v.tr.* (**–fies, –fied**)

syl•la•ble /síləbəl/ *n.* **1** unit of pronunciation forming the whole or a part of a word and usu. having one vowel sound. **2** character or characters representing a syllable. □□ **syl′la•bled** *adj.* [also in *comb.*].

syl•la•bus /síləbəs/ *n.* (*pl.* **syl•la•bus•es** or **syl•la•bi** /–bī/) program or outline of a course of study, teaching, etc.

syl•lo•gism /síləjizəm/ *n.* reasoning in which a conclusion is drawn from two given or assumed propositions. □□ **syl•lo•gis′tic** *adj.* **syl•lo•gis′ti•cal•ly** *adv.*

sylph /silf/ *n.* **1** elemental spirit of the air. **2** slender graceful woman or girl. □□ **sylph′like** *adj.*

syl•van /sílvən/ *adj.* (also **sil•van**) **1 a** of the woods. **b** having woods; wooded. **2** rural.

sym. *abbr.* **1** symbol. **2** symphony.

sym– /sim/ *prefix* assim. form of SYN– before *b, m, p.*

sym•bi•o•sis /símbee-ōsis, –bī–/ *n.* (*pl.* **sym•bi•o•ses** /–seez/) **1** close coexistence and interaction of two different organisms, usu. to the advantage of both. **2** mutually advantageous association. □□ **sym•bi•ot•ic** /-bīótik/ *adj.* **sym•bi•ot′i•cal•ly** *adv.*

sym•bol /símbəl/ *n.* **1** thing conventionally regarded as typifying, representing, or recalling something. **2** representative mark, sign, logo, etc. See synonym study at EMBLEM. □□ **sym•bol•ic** /-bólik/ *adj.* **sym•bol′i•cal•ly** *adv.* **sym•bol•o•gy** /-bólɔjee/ *n.*
■ representation, figure, metaphor, allegory, token; insignia, badge, logotype, hallmark, stamp, trademark, shibboleth, watchword, code word; banner, flag. □□ **symbolic** symbolical, figurative, allegoric(al), metaphoric(al); emblematic, typical, representative.

sym•bol•ism /símbəlizəm/ *n.* **1 a** use of symbols to represent ideas. **b** symbols collectively. **2** artistic and poetic movement or style using symbols and indirect suggestion to express ideas, emotions, etc. □□ **sym′bol•ist** *n.* **sym•bol•is′tic** *adj.*

sym•bol•ize /símbəlīz/ *v.tr.* **1** be a symbol of. **2** represent by means of symbols. □□ **sym′bol•i•za′tion** *n.*
■ **1** represent, stand for, denote, connote, suggest, express, imply, signify, mean, indicate, typify.

sym•me•try /símitree/ *n.* (*pl.* **-tries**) **1** correct or beautiful proportion of parts; balance; harmony. **2** repetition of exactly similar parts facing each other or a center. □□ **sym•met•ric** /simétrik/ *adj.* **sym•met′ri•cal** *adj.* **sym•met′ri•cal•ly** *adv.*
■ evenness, order, orderliness, regularity, uniformity, congruity, congruousness. □□ **symmetric, symmetrical** (well)balanced, proportionate, proportional, well-proportioned, orderly, congruous; equal, mirror image, mirrorlike.

sym•pa•thet•ic /símpəthétik/ *adj.* **1** of, showing, or expressing sympathy. **2** pleasant; likable. **3** inclined to favor. □□ **sym•pa•thet′i•cal•ly** *adv.*
■ **1** compassionate, commiserative, understanding, supportive, caring, concerned, interested, solicitous, warmhearted, kindhearted; comforting, consoling. **2** appealing, congenial, agreeable, attractive, simpatico. **3** (*sympathetic to*) well-disposed to, favorably disposed to, supportive of, approving of, agreeable to. □□ **sympathetically** compassionately, kindly, benignantly, considerately, supportively, empathetically; see also *favorably* (FAVORABLE).

sym•pa•thize /símpəthīz/ *v.intr.* [often foll. by *with*] **1** feel or express sympathy. **2** agree. □□ **sym′pa•thiz•er** *n.*
■ **1** (*sympathize with*) suffer *or* grieve *or* mourn with, feel (sorry) for, have pity for, condole with; empathize with, harmonize with, get along with, relate to, identify with. **2** (*sympathize with*) go along with, favor, support, understand, appreciate. □□ **sympathizer** condoner, approver, conspirator, co-conspirator, collaborator, accomplice, accessory, supporter, ally; see also PATRON 1.

sym•pa•thy /símpəthee/ *n.* (*pl.* **-thies**) **1 a** state of being simultaneously affected with the same feeling as another. **b** capacity for this. **2** [in *sing.* or *pl.*] compassion or

commiseration; condolences. **3** [in *sing.* or *pl.*] agreement in opinion or desire.
■ **2** pity, concern, feeling, tenderness, empathy, understanding. **3** harmony, compatibility, rapport, concord, accord; fellow feeling, congeniality, communion.

sym•pho•ny /símfənee/ *n.* (*pl.* **-nies**) **1** elaborate composition usu. for full orchestra, and in several movements. **2** interlude for orchestra alone in a large-scale vocal work. **3** = *symphony orchestra*. □ **symphony orchestra** large orchestra suitable for playing symphonies, etc. □□ **sym•phon•ic** /-fónik/ *adj.* **sym•phon•i•cal•ly** /-fóniklee/ *adv.*

sym•po•si•um /simpōzeeəm/ *n.* (*pl.* **sym•po•si•ums** or **sym•po•si•a** /-zeeə/) **1** conference or meeting to discuss a particular subject. **2** collection of essays or papers for this purpose.

symp•tom /símptəm/ *n.* **1** *Med.* physical or mental sign of disease. **2** sign of the existence of something. See synonym study at SIGN.
■ manifestation, evidence, mark, token, indication, indicator, cue, clue, (warning) sign, characteristic.

symp•tom•at•ic /símptəmátik/ *adj.* serving as a symptom. □□ **symp•to•mat′i•cal•ly** *adv.*
■ indicative, representative, suggestive, characteristic.

syn. *abbr.* **1** synonym. **2** synonymous. **3** synonymy.

syn /sin/ *prefix* connoting 'with; together;' or 'at the same time' (in words of Greek origin).

syn•a•gogue /sínəgog/ *n.* **1** house of worship where a Jewish assembly or congregation meets for religious observance and instruction. **2** assembly itself. □□ **syn•a•gog′al** /-gógəl/ *adj.* **syn•a•gog•i•cal** /-gójikəl/ *adj.*

syn•apse /sínaps, sináps/ *n.* *Anat.* junction of two nerve cells.

sync /singk/ (also **synch**) *colloq.* ● *n.* synchronization. ● *v.* synchronize. □ **in** (or **out of**) **sync** harmonizing or agreeing well (or badly).
■ □ **out of sync** see WRONG *adj.* 4.

syn•chron•ic /singkrónik/ *adj.* describing a subject as it exists at one point in time. □□ **syn•chron′i•cal•ly** *adv.*
■ see CONTEMPORARY *adj.* 1.

syn•chro•nize /síngkrənīz/ *v.* **1** *intr.* be simultaneous. **2** *tr.* cause to occur at the same time. **3** *tr.* make the sound and picture of (a movie, etc.), coincide. **4 a** *tr.* cause (clocks, etc.) to show a standard or uniform time. **b** *intr.* (of clocks, etc.) be synchronized. □□ **syn•chro•ni•za′tion** *n.* **syn′chro•niz•er** *n.*
■ **1** see COINCIDE 1. **2, 4a** see COORDINATE *v.* 1.

syn•chro•nous /síngkrənəs/ *adj.* existing or occurring at the same time. □□ **syn′chro•nous•ly** *adv.*
■ see SIMULTANEOUS.

syn•cline /síngklīn/ *n.* rock bed forming a trough. □□ **syn•cli′nal** *adj.*

syn•co•pate /síngkəpayt/ *v.tr.* **1** *Mus.* displace the beats or accents in (a passage) so that strong beats become weak and vice versa. **2** shorten (a word) by dropping interior sounds or letters, as *symbology* for *symbolology*. □□ **syn•co•pa•tion** /–páyshən/ *n.* **syn'co•pa•tor** *n.*

synd. *abbr.* **1** syndicate. **2** syndicated.

syn•di•cate • *n.* /síndikət/ **1** combination of individuals or businesses to promote a common interest. **2** agency supplying features, columns, etc. to newspapers, etc. • *v.tr.* /síndikayt/ **1** form into a syndicate. **2** publish (material) through a syndicate. □□ **syn•di•ca•tion** /–káyshən/ *n.*

■ *n.* **1** trust, monopoly, pool, bloc, cartel, association, alliance, consortium, cooperative, collective, federation, confederation, coalition, league, union. **2** Cosa Nostra, Mafia. • *v.* **1** ally, amalgamate, consolidate, combine.

syn•drome /síndrōm/ *n.* **1** group of concurrent symptoms of a disease. **2** characteristic combination of opinions, emotions, behavior, etc. □□ **syn•drom•ic** /–drómik/ *adj.*

syn•ec•do•che /sinékdəkee/ *n.* figure of speech in which a part is made to represent the whole or vice versa (e.g., *new faces at the meeting*). □□ **syn•ec•doch•ic** /–dókik/ *adj.*

syn•er•gism /sínərjizəm/ *n.* (also **syn•er•gy** /sínərjee/) combined effect of drugs, organs, etc., that exceeds the sum of their individual effects. □□ **syn•er•get•ic** /–jétik/ *adj.* **syn•er'gic** *adj.* **syn'er•gist** *n.* **syn•er•gis'tic** *adj.* **syn•er•gis'ti•cal•ly** *adv.*

syn•od /sínəd/ *n.* **1** church council of delegated clergy and sometimes laity. **2** governing body in certain Christian churches.

syn•o•nym /sínənim/ *n.* word or phrase that means the same as another (e.g., *shut* and *close*). □□ **syn•o•nym'ic** *adj.* **syn•o•nym'i•ty** *n.*

syn•on•y•mous /sinóniməs/ *adj.* **1** having the same meaning. **2** (of a name, idea, etc.) suggestive of or associated with another. □□ **syn•on'y•mous•ly** *adv.* **syn•on'y•mous•ness** *n.*

■ **1** (*synonymous with*) equal to, equivalent to; the same as. **2** (*synonymous with*) suggestive of, corresponding to or with.

syn•op•sis /sinópsis/ *n.* (*pl.* **syn•op•ses** /–seez/) summary; outline; brief general survey. □□ **syn•op'size** *v.tr.*

■ abstract, précis, résumé; run-through, review. □□ **synopsize** see *sum up* 1.

syn•o•vi•a /sinóveeə, sī–/ *n.* *Physiol.* viscous fluid lubricating joints and tendon sheaths. □□ **syn•o'vi•al** *adj.*

syn•tax /síntaks/ *n.* **1** grammatical arrangement of words. **2** rules for or analysis of this. □□ **syn•tac•tic** /–táktik/ *adj.* **syn•tac'ti•cal•ly** *adv.*

syn•the•sis /sínthisis/ *n.* (*pl.* **syn•the•ses**

/–seez/) **1** combining of elements into a whole. **2** *Chem.* artificial production of compounds from their constituents.

■ **1** combination, amalgamation, integration, fusion, mix; merging; blend, compound, composite, mixture. **2** manufacture.

syn•the•size /sínthisīz/ *v.tr.* **1** make a synthesis of. **2** combine into a coherent whole.

■ see COMBINE *v.* 3.

syn•the•siz•er /sínthisīzər/ *n.* electronic console or keyboard, producing a variety of instrumental sounds.

syn•thet•ic /sinthétik/ • *adj.* **1** made by chemical synthesis, esp. to imitate a natural product. **2** affected; insincere. See synonym study at SPURIOUS. • *n.* synthetic substance. □□ **syn•thet'i•cal•ly** *adv.*

■ *adj.* **1** artificial, man-made, manufactured; fake, false, counterfeit, sham, bogus, imitation, pseudo, plastic, *colloq.* phony. **2** see ARTIFICIAL 3.

syph•i•lis /sífilis/ *n.* contagious venereal disease. □□ **syph•i•lit•ic** /–lítik/ *adj.*

Syr•i•an /séereeən/ • *n.* native or inhabitant of Syria; person of Syrian descent. • *adj.* of or relating to Syria.

sy•ringe /sirínj/ • *n.* device for sucking in and ejecting liquid in a fine stream. • *v.tr.* sluice or spray with a syringe.

syr•up /sírəp, sór–/ *n.* **1** sweet sauce of sugar dissolved in water. **2** any thick, esp. sweet liquid. **3** excessive sweetness of style or manner. □□ **syr'up•y** *adj.*

■ □□ **syrupy** see SWEET *adj.* 1.

sys•tem /sístəm/ *n.* **1 a** complex whole; set of connected things or parts. **b** organized arrangement; network. **2 a** set of organs in the body with a common structure or function (*digestive system*). **b** human or animal body as a whole. **3** method; scheme of procedure or classification. **4** orderliness. **5** [prec. by *the*] prevailing political or social order. □ **get a thing out of one's system** *colloq.* be rid of a preoccupation or anxiety.

■ **1** group; structure, setup; see also FRAME *n.* 5. **3** approach, modus operandi, way, technique, plan, process, practice, routine; logic, principles, rules, categorization. **4** see ORDER *n.* 1. **5** regime, government, bureaucracy, status quo, Establishment, powers that be.

sys•tem•at•ic /sístəmátik/ *adj.* **1** methodical; according to a system. **2** regular; deliberate. □□ **sys•tem•at'i•cal•ly** *adv.*

■ **1** organized, planned, businesslike, well-organized, orderly, routine. **2** habitual, persistent.

sys•tem•a•tize /sístəmətīz/ *v.tr.* **1** make systematic. **2** devise a system for. □□ **sys•tem•a•ti•za'tion** *n.* **sys'tem•a•tiz•er** *n.*

sys•tem•ic /sistémik/ *adj.* of or concerning the whole body. □□ **sys•tem'i•cal•ly** *adv.*

sys•to•le /sístəlee/ *n.* normal rhythmic contraction of the heart. □□ **sys•tol•ic** /sistólik/ *adj.*

Tt

T¹ /tee/ *n.* (also **t**) (*pl.* **Ts** or **T's; t's**) **1** twentieth letter of the alphabet. **2** T-shaped thing (esp. *attrib.*: *T-joint*). □ **to a T** exactly; to perfection.

T² *abbr.* **1** tera-. **2** tesla. **3** tablespoon. **4** temperature.

T³ *symb. Chem.* tritium.

t. *abbr.* **1** ton(s). **2** teaspoon. **3** temperature.

Ta *symb. Chem.* tantalum.

tab¹ /tab/ • *n.* **1** small flap or strip attached for grasping, fastening, or hanging up, or for identification. **2** *colloq.* bill; check (*picked up the tab*). • *v.tr.* (**tabbed, tab•bing**) provide with a tab or tabs. □ **keep tabs on** *colloq.* have under observation.
■ *n.* **1** tag, loop, ticket, sticker, label, flag, strap, handle. **2** charge, account. • *v.* see TAG¹ *v.* 1.

tab² /tab/ *n.* device on a computer keyboard or typewriter for advancing to a sequence of set positions.

Ta•bas•co /təbáskō/ *n. propr.* pungent hot pepper sauce.

tab•by /tábee/ *n.* (*pl.* **–bies**) **1** gray, orange, or brownish cat with dark stripes. **2** any domestic cat, esp. female.

tab•er•na•cle /tábərnakəl/ *n.* **1** *hist.* tent used as a sanctuary by the Israelites during the Exodus. **2** *Eccl.* niche or receptacle esp. for the Eucharistic elements. **3** large place of worship.

ta•bla /táablə, túb–/ *n. Ind. Mus.* pair of small drums played with the hands.

ta•ble /táybəl/ • *n.* **1** flat surface with one or more legs, used for eating, working at, etc. **2 a** food provided in a household (*keeps a good table*). **b** group seated for dinner, etc. **3** set of facts or figures in columns, etc. (*a table of contents*). • *v.tr.* postpone consideration of (a matter). □ **table tennis** indoor game played with paddles and a ball bounced on a table divided by a net. **turn the tables** reverse circumstances to one's advantage. **under the table** *colloq.* **1** drunk. **2** (esp. of a payment) covertly; secretly. □□ **ta'ble•ful** *n.* (*pl.* **–fuls**). **ta'bling** *n.*
■ *n.* **2 a** victuals, edibles, fare, provisions. **3** listing, register, record, chart, index. • *v.* shelve, defer, suspend, put off, *colloq.* put on ice. □ **table tennis** Ping-Pong.

tab•leau /tabló, táblō/ *n.* (*pl.* **tab•leaux** /–lōz/) **1** picturesque presentation. **2** silent and motionless group of people arranged to represent a scene.
■ **1** sight, spectacle, picture, image, representation, view. **2** composition, arrangement, grouping.

ta•ble•cloth /táybəlklawth, –kloth/ *n.* cloth spread over the top of a table, esp. for meals.

ta•ble•land /táybəl-land/ *n.* plateau.

ta•ble•spoon /táybəlspoon/ *n.* **1** large spoon for serving food. **2** unit of measure equal to

15 ml. or ½ fl. oz. □□ **ta'ble•spoon•ful** *n.* (*pl.* **–fuls**).

tab•let /táblit/ *n.* **1** solid dose of a medicine, etc. **2** flat slab of stone or wood, usu. inscribed. **3** writing pad.
■ **1** pill, capsule, lozenge. **2** plaque, plate, panel; gravestone, headstone, tombstone. **3** notepad, (spiral(-bound)) notebook, scratch pad.

tab•loid /tábloyd/ *n.* small-sized, usu. sensationalized newspaper.

ta•boo /təbóō, ta–/ • *n.* **1** ritual isolation of a person or thing apart as sacred or accursed. **2** prohibition imposed by social custom. • *adj.* avoided or prohibited, esp. by social custom (*taboo words*). • *v.tr.* (**ta•boos, ta•booed**) **1** put under taboo. **2** exclude or prohibit by authority or social influence.
■ *n.* anathema, excommunication, curse; consecration, sanctification. **2** proscription, ban, restriction; see also BOYCOTT *n.* • *adj.* forbidden, off limits, out of bounds; censored, unacceptable, dirty, explicit; outlawed, illegal, illicit, unlawful. • *v.* forbid, interdict, proscribe, ban.

tab•u•lar /tábyələr/ *adj.* of or arranged in tables or lists.

tab•u•late /tábyəlayt/ *v.tr.* arrange (figures or facts) in tabular form. □□ **tab•u•la'tion** /–láyshən/ *n.* **tab'u•la•tor** *n.*
■ organize, order, group, list, classify, categorize; record, note. □□ **tabulation** see TABLE *n.* 3.

ta•chom•e•ter /takómitər, ta–/ *n.* instrument measuring velocity or rate of rotation of a shaft, esp. of a vehicle.

tac•it /tásit/ *adj.* understood or implied without being stated (*tacit consent*). □□ **tac'it•ly** *adv.*
■ unspoken, silent, unexpressed, implicit.

tac•i•turn /tásitərn/ *adj.* saying little; uncommunicative. □□ **tac•i•tur'ni•ty** *n.* **tac'i•turn•ly** *adv.*
■ silent, reticent, reserved, tight-lipped, closemouthed, quiet, secretive. □□ **taciturnity** see SILENCE *n.* 2, 3.

tack¹ /tak/ • *n.* **1** small sharp broad-headed nail. **2** = THUMBTACK. **3** long stitch for fastening fabrics, etc., lightly or temporarily together. **4** direction or temporary change of direction in sailing to take advantage of a side wind, etc. **5** course of action or policy. • *v.* **1** *tr.* fasten with tacks. **2** *tr.* stitch lightly together. **3** *tr.* [foll. by *to, on*] annex (a thing). **4** *intr.* **a** change a ship's course by turning its head to the wind. **b** make a series of tacks. **5** *intr.* change one's conduct or policy, etc. □□ **tack'er** *n.*
■ *n.* **2** pin. **4** bearing, heading. **5** approach, procedure, method, technique. • *v.* **1** attach, secure, staple, screw, bolt, rivet. **2** baste, sew, bind. **3** (*tack on*) add (on), append. **4** zigzag; veer off *or* away.

tack[2] /tak/ *n.* saddle, bridle, etc., of a horse.
■ harness, tackle, gear, kit, outfit, rigging.

tack•le /tákəl/ • *n.* **1** equipment for a task or sport (*fishing tackle*). **2** mechanism, esp. of ropes, pulley blocks, etc., for lifting weights, etc. **3** act of tackling in football, etc. **4** *Football* **a** either of two linemen. • *v.tr.* **1** try to deal with (a problem or difficulty). **2** grapple with (an opponent). **3** enter into discussion with. **4** *Football* stop (a player with the ball). **5** secure by means of tackle. □ **tackle block** pulley over which a rope runs. □□ **tack′ler** *n.* **tack′ling** *n.*
■ *n.* **1** gear, rig, things, rigging, kit, outfit, tools, implements, apparatus. **2** block (and tackle), hoist. • *v.* **1** come to grips with, take on, face up to, confront, address. **2, 4** attack; intercept, block.

tack•y[1] /tákee/ *adj.* (**tack•i•er, tack•i•est**) (of glue, paint, etc.) still slightly sticky after application. □□ **tack′i•ness** *n.*
■ gummy, viscous, *sl.* gooey.

tack•y[2] /tákee/ *adj.* (**tack•i•er, tack•i•est**) *colloq.* **1** showing poor taste or style. **2** shoddy; seedy. □□ **tack′i•ly** *adv.* **tack′i•ness** *n.*
■ **1** tawdry, cheap, gaudy, chintzy, tasteless, vulgar. **2** shabby, sleazy.

ta•co /taakō/ *n.* (*pl.* **-cos**) tortilla filled with meat, cheese, lettuce, tomatoes, etc.

tact /takt/ *n.* adroitness in dealing with others, esp. in delicate situations; intuitive social grace. □□ **tact′ful** *adj.* **tact′ful•ly** *adv.* **tact′ful•ness** *n.*
■ discretion, diplomacy, sensitivity, savoir faire, finesse, dexterity, skill, acumen, perception. □□ **tactful** discreet, judicious, prudent, understanding, considerate, thoughtful, polite, courteous. **tactfulness** see TACT.

tac•tic /táktik/ *n.* tactical maneuver. □□ **tac′ti•cal** *adj.* **tac′ti•cal•ly** *adv.*
■ move, plan, strategy, stratagem, line, tack, device, ruse, plot, scheme, design, *colloq.* ploy. □□ **tactical** artful, clever, cunning, shrewd, adroit, strategic, calculated.

tac•tics /táktiks/ *n.pl.* **1** [also treated as *sing.*] disposition of armed forces, esp. in war. **2** procedure to achieve an end. □□ **tac•ti•cian** /taktíshən/ *n.*
■ **1** military science. **2** strategy, campaign, approach, game plan; scheme(s), stratagem(s). □□ **tactician** strategist, mastermind.

tac•tile /táktəl, -tīl/ *adj.* **1** of the sense of touch. **2** perceived by touch. **3** tangible. □□ **tac•til•i•ty** /-tílitee/ *n.*

tact•less /táktlis/ *adj.* having or showing no tact. □□ **tact′less•ly** *adv.* **tact′less•ness** *n.*
■ coarse, boorish, uncivilized, unsophisticated, rough, rude, uncouth, discourteous, crude, impertinent, disrespectful, uncivil, impolite, insensitive, awkward, bungling, clumsy, inept, thoughtless, unthinking, inconsiderate, indiscreet, unwise.

tad /tad/ *n. colloq.* small amount (often used adverbially: *a tad salty*).

tad•pole /tádpōl/ *n.* larva of an amphibian, esp. a frog or toad.

tae kwon do /tí kwón dố/ *n.* martial art similar to karate.

taf•fe•ta /táfitə/ *n.* fine lustrous silk or silklike fabric.

taf•fy /táfee/ *n.* (*pl.* **-fies**) chewy boiled sugar or molasses candy.

tag[1] /tag/ • *n.* **1** label, esp. attached to an object. **2** metal or plastic point at the end of a lace, etc. **3** epithet; nickname. **4** loose or ragged end of anything. • *v.tr.* (**tagged, tag•ging**) **1** provide with a tag or tags. **2** join; attach. □ **tag along** go along or accompany passively.
■ *n.* **1** name *or* price tag, marker, tab, ticket, sticker, stub. **3** name, designation, title, *colloq.* handle. • *v.* **1** label, mark, ticket, identify, earmark; call, dub, christen, baptize. **2** (*tag on*) add on. □ **tag along** (*tag along with*) attend, escort; trail (along) after.

tag[2] /tag/ • *n.* children's chasing game. • *v.tr.* (**tagged, tag•ging**) touch in or as in a game of tag.

Ta•ga•log /təgaaləg, -lawg/ • *n.* **1** member of the principal people of the Philippine Islands. **2** language of this people. • *adj.* of or relating to this people or language.

Ta•hi•tian /təheeshən/ • *n.* **1** native or inhabitant of Tahiti. **2** language of Tahiti. • *adj.* of or relating to Tahiti or its people or language.

t'ai chi ch'uan /tí chee chwaán/ *n.* (also **t'ai chi**) Chinese martial art and system of calisthenics consisting of sequences of very slow controlled movements.

tail[1] /tayl/ • *n.* **1** hindmost part of an animal, esp. extending beyond the rest of the body. **2 a** thing like a tail, esp. a rear extension. **b** rear of a procession, etc. **3** rear part of an airplane, rocket, or vehicle. **4** luminous trail following a comet. **5** part of a shirt or coat below the waist at the back. **6** [in *pl.*] *colloq.* **a** tailcoat. **b** evening dress including this. **7** [in *pl.*] reverse of a coin. **8** *colloq.* person following another. **9** buttocks. • *v.tr. & [foll. by after*] *intr. colloq.* shadow or follow closely. □ **tail wind** wind blowing in the direction of travel of a vehicle or aircraft, etc. **with one's tail between one's legs** in a state of dejection or humiliation. □□ **tailed** *adj.* [also in *comb.*]. **tail′less** *adj.*
■ *n.* **1** appendage, brush (*of a fox*), scut (*of a hare, rabbit,* or *deer*), dock. **2 b** see REAR[1] *n.* 1. **9** seat, rump, posterior, *colloq.* backside, bottom, behind, rear (end). • *v.* dog, pursue, trail, stalk, track.

tail•back /táylbak/ *n.* Football offensive player positioned behind the quarterback.

tail•coat /táylkōt/ *n.* man's formal coat with a long divided flap at the back.

tail•gate /táylgayt/ • *n.* hinged or removable flap or door at the rear of a motor vehicle. • *v. colloq.* **1** *intr.* drive too closely behind another vehicle. **2** *tr.* follow (a vehicle) too closely. □□ **tail′gat•er** *n.*

tail•light /táyl-līt/ *n.* rear light of a vehicle.

tai•lor /táylər/ • *n.* maker or fitter of clothes. • *v.tr.* **1** make (clothes) as a tailor. **2** make or adapt for a special purpose. □ **tailor-made** *adj.* **1** made to order by a tailor. **2** made or suited for a particular purpose (*a job tailor-made for me*). □□ **tai′lor•ing** *n.*

■ *n.* couturier, costumer, seamstress, dress-maker. • *v.* **2** fit, suit, adjust, alter, accommodate, fashion. □ **tailor-made** *adj.* **1** - custom-made. **2** ideal, perfect, customized, (just) right.

tai•lored /táylərd/ *adj.* (of clothing) well or closely fitted.

tail•pipe /táylpīp/ *n.* rear exhaust pipe.

tail•spin /táylspin/ • *n.* **1** spin by an aircraft with the tail spiraling. **2** chaos or panic; rapid decline. • *v.intr.* (**-spin•ning**; *past* and *past part.* **-spun**) perform a tailspin.

taint /taynt/ • *n.* spot or trace of decay, infection, corruption, etc. • *v.* **1** *tr.* affect with a taint. **2** *tr.* [foll. by *with*] affect slightly. **3** *intr.* become tainted. See synonym study at POLLUTE.

■ *n.* stain, blot, blemish, stigma, flaw, scar, defect; discredit, dishonor. • *v.* **1** sully, tarnish, smear, damage, contaminate, pollute, adulterate, dirty, soil, spoil, defile, ruin, destroy, poison. **2** see TINT *v.*

take /tayk/ • *v.* (**took** /tŏŏk/; **tak•en** /táykən/) **1** *tr.* lay hold of; get into one's hands. **2** *tr.* acquire; capture; earn; win. **3** *tr.* get by purchase, hire, or formal agreement. **4** *tr.* (in a recipe) use. **5** *tr.* occupy (*take a chair*). **6** *tr.* make use of (*take precautions*). **7** *tr.* consume as food or medicine. **8** *intr.* be effective (*inoculation did not take*). **9** *tr.* **a** require or use up (*these things take time*). **b** hold (*takes three quarts*). **10** *tr.* carry; convey (*bus will take you*). **11** *tr.* **a** remove; steal. **b** annihilate (*took her own life*). **c** [often foll. by *for*] *sl.* swindle. **12** *tr.* **a** experience (*take pleasure*). **b** exert (*take courage*). **13** *tr.* find out and note (*took my temperature*). **14** *tr.* understand (*I take your point*). **15** *tr.* treat or regard in a specified way (*took it badly*). **16** *tr.* [foll. by *for* or *to be*] regard as being (*do you take me for an idiot?*). **17** *tr.* **a** accept (*take the offer*). **b** submit to (*take a joke*). **18** *tr.* choose; assume (*took responsibility*). **19** *tr.* derive (*takes its name from the inventor*). **20** *tr.* [foll. by *from*] subtract (*take 3 from 9*). **21** *tr.* make; undertake; perform (*take notes, take an oath*). **22** *tr.* teach; be taught or examined in (a subject). **23** *tr.* make (a photograph). **24** *tr.* use as an instance (*take Napoleon*). **25** *tr. Gram.* have or require as part of a construction (*this verb takes an object*). **26** *tr.* [in passive; foll. by *by, with*] be attracted or charmed by. • *n.* **1** amount taken or caught in one session or attempt, etc. **2** film sequence photographed continuously at one time. **3** money received by a business, esp. at a theater for seats. □ **have what it takes** *colloq.* have the necessary qualities, etc., for success. **on the take** *sl.* accepting bribes. **take after** resemble (a parent, etc.). **take away 1** remove or carry elsewhere. **2** subtract. **take back 1** retract (a statement). **2** convey (a person or thing) to his or her or its original position. **3** carry in thought to a past time. **take a bath** *sl.* lose money. **take the cake** *colloq.* be the most remarkable. **take down 1** write down (spoken words). **2** remove by separating into pieces. **3** humiliate. **take five** (or **ten**) take a break, esp. from work. **take from** diminish; weaken; detract from. **take heart** be encouraged.

take the heat endure criticism, punishment, etc. **take home** earn. **take-home pay** pay received after taxes, etc. **take in 1** accept as a boarder, etc. **2** make (a garment, etc.) smaller. **3** cheat. **4** include. **5** *colloq.* visit (a place) on the way to another (*shall we take in the White House?*). **7** arrest. **take it 1** assume (*I take it that you have finished*). **2** see TAKE *v.* 15. **take it from me** (or **take my word for it**) I can assure you. **take it or leave it** [esp. in *imper.*] accept it or not. **take it out on** relieve one's frustration by attacking or treating harshly. **take off 1** deduct. **2** depart, esp. hastily. **3** become airborne. **4** (of a scheme, enterprise, etc.) become successful. **5** have (a period) away from work. **take on 1** undertake (work, etc.). **2** engage (an employee). **3** be willing or ready to meet (an adversary, etc.). **4** acquire (a new meaning, etc.). **take out 1** remove; extract. **2** escort; date. **3** buy (food) for eating elsewhere. **4** *sl.* murder or destroy. **take-out** *adj.* (of food) bought cooked for eating elsewhere. □ *n.* this food. **take over 1** succeed to the management or ownership of. **2** take control. **take that!** an exclamation accompanying a blow, etc. **take one's time** not hurry. **take to 1** begin or fall into the habit of (*took to drink*). **2** form a liking for. **3** make for (*took to the hills*). **take up 1** become interested or engaged in (a pursuit, etc.). **2** occupy (time or space). **3** begin (residence, etc.). **4** accept (an offer, etc.). **5** shorten (a garment). **6** absorb (*sponges take up water*). **7** pursue (a matter, etc.) further. **take a person up on** accept (a person's offer, etc.). **take up with** begin to associate with. □□ **tak•a•ble** *adj.* (also **take'a•ble**). **tak'er** *n.*

• *v.* **1** grip, seize, grasp, clasp, hold, grab, snatch, clutch, lay hands on, *sl.* nab. **2** obtain, procure, gain (possession of), catch, abduct; secure. **3** reserve, book, engage; rent, lease; board. **4** employ, adopt, put into effect, apply; resort to, turn to. **7** swallow, eat, ingest, gulp down, drink, inhale. **8** take effect, take hold, work, *colloq.* do the trick. **9 a** demand, need, necessitate, call for; consume. **b** contain, accommodate, have room for, accept, fit in. **10** conduct, escort, lead; bear, transport, run, bring, deliver, ferry, haul. **11 a** appropriate, pilfer, filch, palm, pocket, walk *or* make off with; embezzle; *colloq.* lift, swipe, rip off, pinch. **b** end, terminate, wipe out. **c** cheat, defraud, *sl.* bilk, con. **12 a** entertain, feel. **14** gather, interpret, perceive, deduce, conclude, infer, assume, suppose, imagine. **15** bear, accept, receive. **16** believe, think, judge, hold; (*take for*) consider (as), view as. **17 a** take up, jump at. **b** withstand, stand, endure, weather, tolerate, abide, brave, go through, undergo, suffer, put up with, stomach. **18** pick, select, opt for; undertake. **19** adopt; draw, receive, inherit. **20** deduct. **22** take up, study, learn; read, tackle. **23** see PHOTOGRAPH *v.* **26** (*be taken*) be captivated, be enchanted, be infatuated. • *n.* **3** revenue, takings, yield, return, receipts, proceeds, gain, profit(s); gate (money). □ **take after** look like, be the spitting image of, favor. **take away 1** see CONFISCATE, REMOVE v. 2. **2** see SUBTRACT. **take back 1** withdraw, recant, disavow, repudiate, rescind. **2** see RETURN v. 2. **take down 1** make a note of, record, document, transcribe, chronicle. **2** see *knock down* 4. **3** debase, deflate, lower, diminish, belittle, depreciate, humble, shame, degrade, disgrace. **take from** see DETRACT. **take home** see EARN 1. **take-home pay** see PAY n. **take in 1** accommodate, receive, lodge, house, put up. **3** deceive, fool, trick, dupe, mislead, hoax, hoodwink, swindle, *sl.* con. **4** embrace, comprise, cover, encompass, contain, incorporate. **5** see VISIT v. 1. **take it 1** see SUPPOSE 1. **take off 1** see DEDUCT. **2** leave, go (away), flee; *colloq.* skedaddle, scram, *sl.* beat it, split, hit the road. **3** fly (off), take wing, lift off, blast off. **take on 1** assume, accept, tackle. **2** hire, employ, enroll, enlist, sign up, retain, appoint, recruit. **3** challenge, face, contend with, fight. **take out 1** see EXTRACT v. 1. **2** invite out; court, woo. **4** see MURDER v. 1. **take over 1** seize, assume control *or* possession *or* command of, usurp. **take one's time** dawdle, dilly-dally, delay, linger, loiter. **take to 2** find pleasant *or* pleasing, feel affection for. **3** leave for, depart for, run for, head for, flee to. **take up 1** embark on, start, begin; support, sponsor, advocate. **2** cover, use (up), consume. **4** agree to, accede to. **7** deal with, treat, consider, discuss, bring up, raise. **take up with** see FRATERNIZE.

take•off /táykawf/ *n.* **1** act of becoming airborne. **2** *colloq.* act of mimicking.
■ **1** launch, lift-off, blast-off; flight. **2** satire, lampoon, parody, *colloq.* spoof, send-up.

take•o•ver /táykōvər/ *n.* assumption of control (esp. of a business).

tak•ing /táyking/ *adj.* attractive; captivating.
■ alluring, engaging, winning, winsome, charming, entrancing, enchanting, bewitching, fetching, fascinating, delightful, irresistible, compelling, intriguing.

talc /talk/ • *n.* **1** talcum powder. **2** magnesium silicate used as a lubricant, etc. • *v.tr.* (**talcked, talck•ing**) treat (a surface) with talc.

tal•cum /tálkəm/ *n.* (in full **tal′cum pow′der**) powdered talc for toilet and cosmetic use, usu. perfumed.

tale /tayl/ *n.* **1** narrative or story, esp. fictitious. **2** gossip. **3** lie; falsehood.
■ **1** report, account, record, chronicle, history, saga, narration, anecdote, myth, legend, romance, fable; fabrication, fairy tale, *colloq.* yarn, tall tale. **2** rumor, slander, allegation, libel, *colloq.* scuttlebutt.

tal•ent /tálənt/ *n.* **1** special aptitude or faculty. **2** high mental ability. **3** person or persons of talent. **4** ancient weight and unit of currency, esp. Greek. □ **talent scout** person looking for talented performers, esp. in sports and entertainment. □□ **tal′ent•ed** *adj.* **tal′ent•less** *adj.*
■ **1** flair, capacity, knack, expertise, forte,

strength; endowment. **3** see VIRTUOSO 1.
□□ **talented** gifted, accomplished, skilled, skillful, expert, adept, clever, proficient.

tal•is•man /tálizmən/ *n.* (*pl.* **tal•is•mans**) ring, stone, etc., supposed to have magic powers, esp. of bringing good luck. □□ **tal•is•man•ic** /-mánik/ *adj.*
■ amulet, charm, fetish, mascot; wishbone, rabbit's foot.

talk /tawk/ • *v.* **1** *intr.* converse or communicate by spoken words. **2** *intr.* [foll. by *about*] [in *imper.*] *colloq.* as an emphatic statement (*talk about expense!*). **3** *tr.* express; utter; discuss (*talking nonsense*). **4** *tr.* use (a language) in speech (*talking Spanish*). **5** *intr.* reveal secrets. **6** *intr.* gossip (*people will talk*). **7** *intr.* have influence (*money talks*). • *n.* **1** conversation; talking. **2** particular mode of speech (*baby talk*). **3** address or lecture. **4** a rumor or gossip (*talk of a merger*). **b** its theme (*the talk of the town*). **c** empty words (*mere talk*). **5** [often in *pl.*] discussions; negotiations. □ **now you're talking** *colloq.* I like what you say, suggest, etc. **talk back** reply defiantly. **talk big** *colloq.* boast. **talk down** denigrate; belittle. **talk down to** patronize or condescend to. **talk of 1** discuss; mention. **2** express some intention of (*talked of moving*). **talk over** discuss at length. **talk shop** talk about one's occupation, etc. **talk show** television or radio program featuring guest interviews. **talk through one's hat** *colloq.* **1** exaggerate. **2** bluff. **3** talk wildly or nonsensically. **talk to** reprove or scold (a person). **talk up** discuss (a subject) in order to arouse interest in it. □□ **talk′er** *n.*
■ *v.* **1** speak, lecture; confer, consult, chat; prattle, babble, rattle on; *sl.* rap, chew the fat. **3** see DISCUSS, SPEAK 3. **5** confess, tell, *colloq.* come clean, spill the beans, rat, *sl.* squeal, sing. **6** see GOSSIP v. • *n.* **1** conference, discussion, dialogue; *colloq.* confab, chitchat, *sl.* rap session. **2** dialect, language, jargon, *colloq.* lingo. **3** oration, presentation, speech, report, dissertation; sermon; tirade, *sl.* spiel. **4 a** hearsay, news, report. **b** subject *or* topic of conversation, *colloq.* info, *sl.* dope. **4 c** claptrap, prattle, rubbish, balderdash, *colloq.* malarkey, *sl.* bull. **5** see *negotiation* (NEGOTIATE). □ **talk big** brag, crow, bluster, exaggerate, *colloq.* show off. **talk down** disparage, diminish, criticize, *colloq.* knock, put down. **talk of 1** see DISCUSS, MENTION v. 1, 2. **talk over** see DISCUSS. **talk to** see SPEAK 4. **talk up** promote, support, sponsor, advertise, publicize, push, *colloq.* plug, *sl.* hype. □□ **talker** speaker, lecturer, orator, speechmaker, demagogue; show-off.

talk•a•tive /táwkətiv/ *adj.* fond of or given to talking.
■ garrulous, loquacious, verbose, longwinded, wordy, chatty, *colloq.* gabby.

talk•ie /táwkee/ *n.* (esp. *hist.*) movie with a soundtrack.

tall /tawl/ • *adj.* **1** of more than average height. **2** of a specified height (*about six feet tall*). **3** *colloq.* extravagant or excessive (*tall story*). • *adv.* as if tall; proudly (*sit tall*). □ **tall order** exorbitant or unreasonable demand. □□ **tall′ish** *adj.*

■ *adj.* **1** lanky, rangy, long-legged; big, giant; high, towering, lofty. **3** far-fetched, improbable, unbelievable, incredible, preposterous, outrageous.

tall•boy /táwlboy/ *n.* tall chest of drawers.

tal•low /tálō/ *n.* hard (esp. animal) fat melted down to make candles, soap, etc. □□ **tal′low•ish** *adj.* **tal′low•y** *adj.*

tal•ly /tálee/ • *n.* (*pl.* **–lies**) **1** reckoning of a debt or score. **2** total score or amount. **3** mark registering the number of objects delivered or received. **4** ticket or label for identification. • *v.* (**–lies, –lied**) [often foll. by *with*] **1** *intr.* agree; correspond. **2** *tr.* record or reckon by tally. □□ **tal′li•er** *n.*

■ *n.* **1** count, account, register, addition, tabulation, listing. **2** sum. **4** mark, marker, tag. • *v.* **1** coincide, fit, match (up), concur, *colloq.* jibe. **2** enumerate, itemize, calculate, compute.

tal•ly•ho /táleehō/ • *int.* huntsman's cry on sighting a fox. • *n.* (*pl.* **–hos**) utterance of this. • *v.* (**–hoes, –hoed**) **1** *intr.* utter a cry of "tallyho." **2** *tr.* indicate (a fox) or urge (hounds) with this cry.

Tal•mud /taalmŏŏd, –məd, tál–/ *n.* body of Jewish civil and ceremonial law and tradition. □□ **Tal•mud•ic** /–mŏŏdik, myŏŏ–/ *adj.* **Tal•mud′i•cal** *adj.* **Tal′mud•ist** *n.*

tal•on /tálən/ *n.* claw, esp. of a bird of prey. □□ **tal′oned** *adj.*

ta•lus /táyləs, tál–/ *n.* (*pl.* **ta•li** –lī/) *Anat.* ankle bone supporting the tibia.

tam /tam/ *n.* /tam/ = TAM-O'-SHANTER.

ta•ma•le /təmaalee/ *n.* Mexican food of seasoned meat and corn flour steamed or baked in corn husks.

tam•a•rind /támarind/ *n.* **1** tropical evergreen tree. **2** its edible fruit.

tam•bou•rine /támbəréen/ *n.* percussion instrument consisting of a hoop with pairs of jingling disks around the hoop. □□ **tam•bou•rin′ist** *n.*

tame /taym/ • *adj.* **1** (of an animal) domesticated; not wild or shy. **2** insipid; dull. **3** (of a person) amenable and submissive. • *v. tr.* **1** make tame; domesticate. **2** subdue; curb. □□ **tam′a•ble** *adj.* **tame′ly** *adv.* **tame′ness** *n.* **tam′er** *n.* [also in *comb.*]

■ *adj.* **1** docile, obedient, housebroken; mild, gentle, unafraid. **2** boring, tedious, tiresome, bland, lifeless, flat, vapid, uninspired, uninspiring, run-of-the-mill, ordinary. **3** tractable, compliant, meek, passive; unassertive, ineffectual. • *v.* **1** break, train, master, subdue. **2** calm, control, mollify, humble, pacify, soften, tone down.

Tam•il /támil, túm–, taá–/ • *n.* **1** member of a people of South India and Sri Lanka. **2** language of this people. • *adj.* of this people or their language. □□ **Tam•il′ian** *adj.*

tam-o′-shanter /táməshántər/ *n.* round woolen or cloth beret of Scottish origin.

tamp /tamp/ *v. tr.* ram down tightly by a series of taps. □□ **tam′per** *n.* **tamp′ing** *n.*

tam•per /támpər/ *v. intr.* [foll. by *with*] **1** meddle with or make unauthorized changes in. **2** exert a secret or corrupt influence upon; bribe. □□ **tam′per•er** *n.* **tam′per•proof** *adj.*

■ **1** interfere, tinker, mess *or* fiddle *or* fool (about *or* around), monkey (around).

tam•pon /támpon/ *n.* plug of soft material used to absorb fluid, esp. blood.

tan¹ /tan/ • *n.* **1** brown skin color from exposure to ultraviolet light. **2** yellowish-brown color. • *adj.* yellowish-brown. • *v.* (**tanned, tan•ning**) **1** *tr. & intr.* make or become brown by exposure to ultraviolet light. **2** *tr.* convert (raw hide) into leather. **3** *tr. sl.* beat; whip. □□ **tan′na•ble** *adj.* **tan′ning** *n.* **tan′nish** *adj.*

■ *v.* **1** see SUN *v.* **3** see BEAT *v.* 1. □□ **tanning** see *thrashing* (THRASH).

tan² /tan/ *abbr.* tangent.

tan•a•ger /tánəjər/ *n.* small American bird, the male usu. having brightly colored plumage.

tan•dem /tándəm/ *n.* set of two with one following the other. □ **in tandem** one behind another.

tan•door•i /tandŏŏree/ *n.* spicy Indian food cooked over charcoal in a clay oven.

tang /tang/ *n.* **1** strong taste or smell. **2** characteristic quality. **3** projection on a blade fitting into a handle.

■ **1** pungency, piquancy, bite, zest, sharpness. **2** flavor, feel, essence. **3** tab, tongue, shank.

tan•ge•lo /tánjəlō/ *n.* (*pl.* **–los**) hybrid of tangerine and grapefruit.

tan•gent /tánjənt/ *n.* **1** straight line, curve, or surface that meets a curve but does not intersect it. **2** ratio of the sides opposite and adjacent to an angle in a right triangle. □ **on a tangent** diverging from a previous course of action or thought, etc. □□ **tan′gen•cy** *n.*

tan•gen•tial /tanjénshəl/ *adj.* **1** of or along a tangent. **2** divergent. **3** peripheral. □□ **tan•gen′tial•ly** *adv.*

■ **3** beside the point, irrelevant, unrelated.

tan•ger•ine /tánjəréen/ *n.* **1** small sweet orange-colored citrus fruit with a thin skin. **2** deep orange-yellow color.

tan•gi•ble /tánjəbəl/ *adj.* **1** perceptible by touch. **2** definite; clearly intelligible; not elusive (*tangible proof*). □□ **tan•gi•bil′i•ty** *n.* **tan′gi•ble•ness** *n.* **tan′gi•bly** *adv.*

■ **1** touchable, tactile. **2** material, real, physical, solid, concrete, evident, actual, perceptible.

tible odor of garlic). **Sensible** means that which can clearly be perceived through the senses or which makes a strong impression on the mind through the medium of sensations. In contrast to *perceptible*, something that is *sensible* is more obvious or immediately recognized (*a sensible shift in the tenor of the conversation*). **Corporeal** means *tangible* or material, in contrast to things that are immaterial or spiritual (*corporeal goods*). Something that is **appreciable** is large enough to be measured, weighed, valued, estimated, or considered significant. An *appreciable* change in temperature, for example, can be determined by looking at a thermometer; a *palpable* change in temperature may be slight, but still great enough to be felt; and a *perceptible* change in temperature might be so slight that it almost—but not quite—escapes notice.

tan•gle /tánggəl/ • *v.* **1 a** *tr.* intertwine (threads, hairs, etc.) in a confused mass; entangle. **b** *intr.* become tangled. **2** *intr.* [foll. by *with*] *colloq.* become involved (esp. in conflict) with. • *n.* **1** confused mass of intertwined threads, etc. **2** confused or complicated state.
 ■ *v.* **1** knot, entwine, jumble; snarl, twist, snag. **2** contend, lock horns, cross swords, disagree. • *n.* **1** jam, mess, web. **2** muddle, jumble, mix-up.

tan•go /tánggō/ • *n.* (*pl.* **–gos**) **1** slow S. American ballroom dance. **2** music for this.
 • *v.intr.* (**–goes, –goed**) dance the tango.

tan•gram /tánggram/ *n.* Chinese puzzle square cut into seven pieces to be combined into various figures.

tang•y /tángee/ *adj.* (**tang•i•er, tang•i•est**) having a strong usu. spicy tang. □□ **tang′i•ness** *n.*

tank /tangk/ • *n.* **1** large container usu. for liquid or gas. **2** heavy armored fighting vehicle moving on a tracked carriage. **3** *colloq.* prison cell or holding cell. • *v.* **1** *tr.* fill the tank of (a vehicle, etc.) with fuel. **2** *intr.* & *colloq. tr.* [in *passive*] become drunk. □ **tank top** sleeveless, close-fitting, collarless upper garment. □□ **tank′ful** *n.* (*pl.* **–fuls**).

tan•kard /tángkərd/ *n.* tall mug with a handle and sometimes a hinged lid, esp. for beer.

tank•er /tángkər/ *n.* ship, aircraft, or truck for carrying liquids or gases in bulk.

tan•ki•ni /tangkeénee/ • *n.* bathing suit consisting of a tank top and bikini bottom.

tan•ner /tánər/ *n.* person who tans hides.

tan•ner•y /tánəree/ *n.* (*pl.* **–ies**) place where hides are tanned.

tan•nic /tánik/ *adj.* astringent; tasting of tannin. □ **tannic acid** organic compound of a yellowish color used as a mordant and astringent.

tan•sy /tánzee/ *n.* (*pl.* **–sies**) plant with yellow button-like flowers and aromatic leaves.

tan•ta•lize /tántəlīz/ *v.tr.* torment or tease by the sight or promise of what is unobtainable. □□ **tan•ta•li•za′tion** *n.* **tan′ta•liz•er** *n.* **tan′ta•liz•ing•ly** *adv.*

 ■ taunt, provoke, torture, tempt, lead on, frustrate.

tan•ta•lum /tántələm/ *n. Chem.* rare hard white metallic element. ¶Symb.: **Ta**. □□ **tan•tal•ic** /–tálik/ *adj.*

tan•ta•mount /tántəmownt/ *predic. adj.* equivalent (to). See synonym study at SAME.
 ■ (*tantamount to*) amounting to, as good as, like.

tan•tra /tántrə, tún–/ *n.* any of a class of Hindu or Buddhist mystical and magical writings.

tan•trum /tántrəm/ *n.* outburst of bad temper or petulance.
 ■ fit, explosion, storm, rage, fury, *colloq.* blowup.

Tao•ism /tówizəm, dów–/ *n.* Chinese philosophy advocating humility and religious piety. □□ **Tao′ist** *n.* **Tao•is′tic** *adj.*

tap¹ /tap/ • *n.* **1** = FAUCET. **2** wiretapping. • *v.tr.* (**tapped, tap•ping**) **1 a** provide (a cask) with a tap. **b** let out (liquid) by means of, or as if by means of, a tap. **2** draw sap from (a tree) by cutting into it. **3** obtain information or supplies from. **4** install a secret listening device. □ **on tap** *colloq.* ready for immediate use. **tap root** tapering root growing vertically downward. **tap water** water from a piped supply. □□ **tap′pa•ble** *adj.*
 ■ *n.* **1** see FAUCET. **2** bugging; bug. • *v.* **1 b** drain, draw (off), siphon off. **2** sap, milk. **3** mine, draw on *or* upon, exploit. **4** eavesdrop on, wiretap, *sl.* bug. □ **on tap** available, on *or* at hand.

tap² /tap/ • *v.* (**tapped, tap•ping**) **1** *intr.* [foll. by *at, on*] strike a gentle but audible blow. **2** *tr.* strike lightly (*tapped me on the shoulder*). **3** *intr.* = tap-dance. • *n.* **1 a** light blow; rap. **b** sound of this. **2 a** = *tap dance n.* **b** metal attachment on a tap dancer's shoe. **3** [in *pl.*, usu. treated as *sing.*] military bugle call. □ **tap dance** *n.* rhythmic dance performed wearing shoes with metal taps. **tap-dance** *v.intr.* perform a tap dance. □□ **tap′danc•er** *n.* **tap′ danc•ing** *n.* **tap′per** *n.*
 ■ *v.* **1, 2** rap, knock, pat, hit, peck; drum, beat.

tape /tayp/ • *n.* **1** narrow strip of woven material for tying up, fastening, etc. **2 a** this across the finishing line of a race. **b** similar strip for marking off an area. **3** (in full **ad•he′sive tape**) strip of adhesive plastic, etc., for fastening, masking, etc. **4 a** = *magnetic tape*. **b** tape recording. **5** = *tape measure*. • *v.tr.* **1** tie up, join, seal, mark off, etc., with tape. **2** record on magnetic tape. □ **tape deck** device for playing and recording magnetic tape. **tape measure** strip of tape or flexible material marked for measuring lengths. **tape-record** record (sounds) on magnetic tape. **tape recorder** apparatus for recording and replaying sounds on magnetic tape. **tape recording** recording on magnetic tape. □□ **tape′a•ble** *adj.*
 ■ *n.* **1** band, strap, belt, ribbon. **4** reel, spool, cassette, video, videotape. • *v.* **1** bind; fix, stick.

ta•per /táypər/ • *n.* **1** wick coated with wax, etc., for lighting fires, candles, etc. **2** slender candle. • *v.* **1** diminish or reduce in thickness toward one end. **2** make or become gradually less.

■ *n.* **1** see LIGHT¹ *n.* 2. • *v.* **1** narrow (down), thin, attenuate. **2** wind down, fade, lessen, peter out, wane, subside, let up, slacken, die away *or* down *or* off *or* out, decline, slow (down *or* up), weaken, drop (off).

tap•es•try /tápistree/ *n.* (*pl.* **–tries**) thick fabric in which colored weft threads are woven to form pictures or designs.

tape•worm /táypwərm/ *n.* parasitic intestinal flatworm with a segmented body.

tap•i•o•ca /tápeeókə/ *n.* starchy substance in hard white grains, obtained from cassava and used for puddings, etc.

ta•pir /táypər, təpeér/ *n.* nocturnal hoofed mammal of Central and S. America and Malaysia, with a short flexible snout.

tap•pet /tápit/ *n.* lever or projecting part in machinery giving intermittent motion.

tap•room /táproom, -room/ *n.* barroom.

tar¹ /taar/ • *n.* **1** dark, thick, flammable liquid distilled from wood, coal, etc., used as a preservative of wood and iron, in making roads, etc. **2** similar substance formed in the combustion of tobacco, etc. • *v.tr.* (**tarred, tarring**) cover with tar. □ **tar and feather** smear with tar and then cover with feathers as a punishment. **tarred with the same brush** having the same faults.

tar² /taar/ *n. colloq.* sailor.

tar•an•tel•la /tárəntélə/ *n.* **1** whirling S. Italian dance. **2** music for this.

ta•ran•tu•la /tərántʃələ/ *n.* **1** large, hairy tropical spider. **2** large black S. European spider.

tar•dy /taárdee/ *adj.* (**tar•di•er, tar•di•est**) **1** slow to act, come, or happen. **2** delaying; delayed. □□ **tar′di•ly** *adv.* **tar′di•ness** *n.*

■ **1** belated, reluctant, lethargic, languid. **2** late, behind schedule, overdue. □□ **tardily** see SLOW *adv.*

tare¹ /tair/ *n.* **1** vetch, esp. as a weed or fodder. **2** [in *pl.*] *Bibl.* injurious grain weed (Matt. 13:24-30).

tare² /tair/ *n.* **1** allowance made for the weight of the packing or wrapping around goods. **2** weight of a vehicle without its fuel or load.

tar•get /taárgit/ • *n.* **1** mark fired or aimed at, esp. an object marked with concentric circles. **2** person or thing aimed or fired at. **3** [also *attrib.*] objective (*target date*). **4** butt for criticism, abuse, etc. • *v.tr.* **1** identify or single out (a person or thing) as an object of attention or attack. **2** aim or direct (*target our efforts*). □□ **tar′get•a•ble** *adj.*

■ *n.* **1, 3** goal, aim, end. **2, 4** quarry, prey, victim. • *v.* **1** see DIRECT *v.* 4.

tar•iff /tárif/ *n.* **1** table of fixed charges. **2** duty on a particular class of goods.

■ **1** price list. **2** tax, assessment, excise, levy, impost, toll.

Tar•mac /taármak/ • *n. propr.* **1** = TARMAC-ADAM. **2** surface made of this, e.g., a runway. • *v.tr.* (**tarmac**) (**tar•macked, tar•mack•ing**) apply tarmacadam to.

tar•mac•ad•am /taárməkádəm/ *n.* material of stone or slag bound with tar, used in paving roads, etc.

tarn /taarn/ *n.* small mountain lake.

tar•na•tion /taarnáyshən/ *int.* esp. *dial. sl.* damn; blast.

tar•nish /taárnish/ • *v.* **1** *tr.* lessen or destroy the luster of (metal, etc.). **2** *tr.* sully. **3** *intr.* (of metal, etc.) lose luster. • *n.* **1** loss of luster, esp. as a film on a metal's surface. **2** blemish; stain. □□ **tar′nish•a•ble** *adj.*

■ *v.* **1, 3** dull, blacken, discolor. **2** disgrace, taint, blot, soil, defame, mar, damage, harm, hurt, dishonor. • *n.* **2** see DISCREDIT *n.* 1.

ta•ro /taáro, tárō/ *n.* (*pl.* **–ros**) tropical plant with edible tuberous roots.

ta•rot /tárō, tərō/ *n.* **1** [in *sing.* or *pl.*] pack of mainly picture cards used in fortune-telling. **2** any card from a fortune-telling pack.

tar•pau•lin /taarpáwlin, taárpə-/ (also *colloq.* **tarp**) *n.* **1** heavy-duty waterproof cloth, esp. of canvas or plastic. **2** sheet or covering of this.

tar•pon /taárpon/ *n.* **1** large silvery tropical Atlantic fish. **2** similar Pacific fish.

tar•ra•gon /tárəgon/ *n.* bushy herb with leaves used as a flavoring.

tar•ry /táree/ *v.intr.* (**–ries, –ried**) linger; stay; wait. □□ **tar′ri•er** *n.*

■ loiter, procrastinate, dawdle, remain, bide one's time.

tar•sus /taársəs/ *n.* (*pl.* **tar•si** /-sī, -see/) bones of the ankle and upper foot. □□ **tar′sal** *adj.*

tart¹ /taart/ *n.* small pie containing jam, etc. □□ **tart′let** *n.*

■ pastry, turnover.

tart² /taart/ *n. sl.* prostitute; promiscuous woman. □□ **tart′y** *adj.* (**tart′i•er, tart′i•est**).

tart³ /taart/ *adj.* **1** sharp or acid in taste. **2** (of a remark, etc.) cutting, bitter. □□ **tart′ly** *adv.* **tart′ness** *n.*

■ **1** lemony; tangy, astringent, acerbic, acrid, bitter, pungent, piquant. **2** biting, caustic, harsh, stinging, sharp, barbed, nasty.

tar•tan /taárt'n/ *n.* **1** plaid pattern, esp. denoting a Scottish Highland clan. **2** woolen fabric woven in this pattern.

Tar•tar /taártər/ (also **Ta•tar** /taátər/ except in sense 3 of *n.*) • *n.* **1 a** member of a group of Central Asian peoples including Mongols and Turks. **b** Turkic language of these peoples. **2** (**tartar**) violent-tempered or intractable person. • *adj.* **1** of Tartars. **2** of Central Asia east of the Caspian Sea. □ **tartar sauce** sauce of mayonnaise and chopped pickles, etc. □□ **Tar•tar•i•an** /-táireeən/ *adj.*

tar•tar /taártər/ *n.* **1** hard deposit that forms on the teeth. **2** deposit that forms a hard crust in wine.

task /task/ • *n.* piece of work to be done. • *v.tr.* make great demands on (a person's powers, etc.). □ **take to task** rebuke; scold. **task force 1** *Mil.* armed force organized for a special operation. **2** unit specially organized for a task.

■ *n.* duty, assignment, business, job, mission, chore. • *v.* see TAX¹ *v.* 3. □ **take to task** reprimand, censure, reproach, reprove, criticize, lecture, *colloq.* tell off. **task force 1** see FLEET.

task•mas•ter /táskmastər/ *n.* (*fem.* **task•mis•tress** /–mistris/) person who makes others work hard.

Tas•ma•ni•an /tazmáyneeən/ • *n.* **1** native of Tasmania. **2** person of Tasmanian descent. • *adj.* of or relating to Tasmania. □ **Tasmanian devil** nocturnal, badgerlike carnivorous marsupial of Tasmania.

tas•sel /tásəl/ *n.* **1** decorative tuft of loosely hanging threads or cords. **2** tassellike flowerhead of some plants, esp. corn. □□ **tas′seled** *adj.*

taste /tayst/ • *n.* **1 a** sensation caused in the mouth by contact of the taste buds with a substance. **b** faculty of perceiving. **2** small sample of food or drink. **3** slight experience (*taste of success*). **4** liking or predilection (*expensive tastes*). **5** aesthetic discernment in art, conduct, etc. • *v.* **1** *tr.* sample the flavor of (food, etc.). **2** *tr.* [also *absol.*] perceive the flavor of (*cannot taste with a cold*). **3** *tr.* [esp. with *neg.*] eat or drink a small portion of (*had not tasted food for days*). **4** *tr.* experience (*never tasted failure*). **5** *intr.* have a specified flavor (*tastes of onions*). □ **taste bud** cells or nerve ending on the surface of the tongue by which things are tasted. □□ **taste′a•ble** *adj.* **tast′er** *n.*

 ■ *n.* **1 a** flavor, smack, tang. **2** morsel, bite, nibble, tidbit; sip, nip, swallow, drop; dash, pinch. **4** palate, desire, inclination, penchant, fancy, preference, fondness. **5** discrimination, judgment, style, grace, polish. • *v.* **1** savor, try, test. **3** nibble. **4** have knowledge of, encounter.

taste•ful /táystfool/ *adj.* having, or done in, good taste. □□ **taste′ful•ly** *adv.* **taste′ful•ness** *n.*

 ■ refined, polite, polished, fitting, discriminating, elegant, stylish, graceful, charming. □□ **tastefulness** see GRACE *n.* 2.

taste•less /táystlis/ *adj.* **1** lacking flavor. **2** having, or done in, bad taste. □□ **taste′less•ly** *adv.* **taste′less•ness** *n.*

 ■ **1** insipid, bland, dull, flat. **2** garish, gaudy, cheap, flashy; improper, indelicate, unseemly, uncouth, gauche, distasteful, coarse, crude, vulgar, base, low, tacky.

tast•y /táystee/ *adj.* (**tast•i•er, tast•i•est**) (of food) pleasing in flavor; appetizing. □□ **tast′i•ly** *adv.* **tast′i•ness** *n.*

 ■ delicious, flavorful, savory, scrumptious. □□ **tastiness** see FLAVOR *n.* 1.

tat[1] /tat/ *v.* (**tat•ted, tat•ting**) **1** *intr.* do tatting. **2** *tr.* make by tatting.

tat[2] see TIT[2].

Ta•tar var. of TARTAR.

tat•er /táytər/ *n. sl.* = POTATO.

tat•ter /tátər/ *n.* [usu. in *pl.*] rag; irregularly torn cloth or paper, etc. □ **in tatters** *colloq.* (of a negotiation, etc.) ruined; demolished. □□ **tat′tered** *adj.*

 ■ (*tatters*) scraps, shreds, bits, pieces. □□ **tattered** ragged, torn, frayed, threadbare, shabby.

tat•ting /táting/ *n.* **1** kind of knotted lace used as trim, etc. **2** process of making this.

tat•tle /tát'l/ *v.* **1** *intr.* chatter; gossip. **2** *tr.* reveal (secrets).

 ■ *v.* **1** prattle, babble, jabber; blab, tell, *sl.* squeal. **2** see BLURT.

tat•tle•tale /tát'ltayl/ *n.* one who tells tales or informs.

 ■ *sl.* fink, rat, squealer, stool pigeon, stoolie.

tat•too[1] /tatōō/ *n.* **1** evening drum or bugle signal recalling soldiers to quarters. **2** rhythmic tapping or drumming.

tat•too[2] /tatōō/ • *v.tr.* **1** mark (skin) indelibly by puncturing it and inserting pigment. **2** make (a design) in this way. • *n.* such a design. □□ **tat•too′er** *n.* **tat•too′ist** *n.*

tau /tow, taw/ *n.* nineteenth letter of the Greek alphabet (Τ, τ).

taught *past* and *past part.* of TEACH.

taunt /tawnt/ • *n.* insult; provocation. • *v.tr.* insult; reproach (a person) contemptuously. □□ **taunt′er** *n.* **taunt′ing•ly** *adv.*

 ■ *n.* jeer, gibe, slap (in the face), *colloq.* dig. • *v.* tease, mock, torment, annoy, poke fun at, deride, heckle, sneer at, scoff at, ridicule, *colloq.* kid, rib.

taupe /tōp/ *adj. & n.* dark, brownish gray.

Tau•rus /táwrəs/ *n.* **1** constellation and second sign of the zodiac (the Bull). **2** person born under this sign. □□ **Tau′re•an** *adj. & n.*

taut /tawt/ *adj.* **1** (of a rope, muscles, etc.) tight; not slack. **2** (of nerves) tense. **3** (of a ship, etc.) in good condition. □□ **taut′en** *v.* **taut′ly** *adv.* **taut′ness** *n.*

 ■ **1** stretched, rigid, stiff. **2** strained. **3** neat, tidy, shipshape. □□ **tauten** see TENSE[1] *v.* **tautness** see TENSION 1, 2.

tau•tol•o•gy /tawtóləjee/ *n.* (*pl.* **–gies**) saying of the same thing twice in different words, esp. as a fault of style (e.g., *arrived one after the other in succession*). □□ **tau•to•log•ic** /–t′lójik/ *adj.* **tau•to•log′i•cal** *adj.* **tau•to•log′i•cal•ly** *adv.* **tau•tol′o•gist** *n.* **tau•tol′o•gize** *v.intr.* **tau•tol•o•gous** /–ləgəs/ *adj.*

 ■ repetition, redundancy, duplication.

tav•ern /távərn/ *n.* inn or bar.

taw•dry /táwdree/ *adj.* (**taw•dri•er, taw•dri•est**) **1** showy but worthless. **2** gaudy; vulgar. □□ **taw′dri•ly** *adv.* **taw′dri•ness** *n.*

 ■ cheap, flashy, garish, tasteless, *colloq.* tacky.

taw•ny /táwnee/ *adj.* (**taw•ni•er, taw•ni•est**) orangish or yellowish brown. □□ **taw′ni•ness** *n.*

tax /taks/ • *n.* **1** government revenue compulsorily levied on individuals, property, or businesses. **2** strain; heavy demand; burdensome obligation. • *v.tr.* **1** impose a tax on. **2** deduct tax from (income, etc.). **3** make heavy demands on (a person's powers or resources, etc.). □□ **tax′a•ble** *adj.* **tax′er** *n.*

 ■ *n.* **1** levy, impost, duty, tariff, toll, excise, customs, dues. **2** onus, weight, load, encumbrance, imposition, pressure. • *v.* **1** charge. **3** try, task; overwork, stretch, exhaust, drain; encumber, weigh down, saddle.

tax•a *pl.* of TAXON.

tax•a•tion /taksáyshən/ *n.* imposition or payment of tax.

tax•i /táksee/ • *n.* (*pl.* **taxis**) (in full **tax′i•cab**) automobile licensed for hire and usu.

fitted with a meter. • *v.* (**tax•is, tax•ied, tax•i•ing** or **tax•y•ing**) **1 a** *intr.* (of an aircraft or pilot) move along the ground before takeoff or after landing. **b** *tr.* cause (an aircraft) to taxi. **2** *intr. & tr.* go or convey in a taxi.

▪ *n.* cab, hack. • *v.* **2** drive, chauffeur; take a cab.

tax•i•der•my /táksidərmee/ *n.* art of preparing, stuffing, and mounting the skins of animals. □□ **tax′i•der•mist** *n.*

tax•i•me•ter /tákseemeetər/ *n.* device fitted to a taxi, recording distance traveled and fare payable.

tax•on /tákson/ *n.* (*pl.* **tax•a** /táksə/) any taxonomic group.

tax•on•o•my /taksónəmee/ *n.* classification of living and extinct organisms. □□ **tax•o•nom′ic** /–sənómik/ *adj.* **tax•o•nom′i•cal** *adj.* **tax•o•nom′i•cal•ly** *adv.* **tax•on′o•mist** *n.*

tax•pay•er /tákspayər/ *n.* person who pays taxes.

TB *abbr.* **1** tubercle bacillus. **2** tuberculosis.

Tb *symb. Chem.* terbium.

T-bone /teébōn/ *n.* T-shaped bone, esp. in steak from the thin end of a loin.

tbs. *abbr.* (also **tbsp.**) tablespoon.

Tc *symb. Chem.* technetium.

TD *abbr.* **1** touchdown. **2** Treasury Department.

Te *symb. Chem.* tellurium.

te var. of TI.

tea /tee/ *n.* **1 a** (in full **tea plant**) evergreen shrub or small tree of Asia. **b** its dried leaves. **2** drink made by infusing tea leaves in boiling water. **3** infusion of herbal or other leaves. **4** afternoon party, reception, or light meal at which tea is served. □ **tea and sympathy** *colloq.* hospitable behavior toward a troubled person. **tea bag** small porous bag of tea leaves for infusion. **tea ball** ball of perforated metal to hold tea leaves for infusion. **tea rose** hybrid rose shrub with a tea-like scent.

teach /teech/ *v.tr.* (*past* and *past part.* **taught** /tawt/) **1 a** give systematic information to (a person) or about (a subject or skill). **b** [*absol.*] practice this professionally. **c** enable (a person) to learn by instruction and training (*taught me how to dance*). **2** advocate as a moral, etc., principle (*taught me tolerance*). **3** [foll. by *to* + infin.] impress upon by example or punishment (*will teach you not to laugh*). □□ **teach′a•ble** *adj.*

▪ **1** show; drill, educate, school, guide, tutor, coach, enlighten, edify. **2** instill (in); imbue (with).

teach•er /teéchər/ *n.* person who teaches, esp. in a school.

▪ schoolteacher, educator, instructor, professor, tutor, coach, trainer, mentor, guru, counselor; rabbi.

teach•ing /teéching/ *n.* **1** profession of a teacher. **2** [often in *pl.*] what is taught; doctrine.

▪ **1** see EDUCATION 1. **2** see DOCTRINE.

tea•cup /teékup/ *n.* **1** cup from which tea, etc., is drunk. **2** amount held by this. □□ **tea′cup•ful** *n.* (*pl.* **–fuls**).

teak /teek/ *n.* **1** large deciduous tree of India and SE Asia. **2** its hard durable wood.

teal /teel/ *n.* (*pl.* same) **1** small freshwater duck. **2** dark, greenish blue color.

team /teem/ • *n.* **1** set of players forming one side in a game, debate, etc. **2** two or more persons working together. **3** set of draft animals. • *v.* join in a team or in common action.

▪ *n.* **1** club, squad. **2** pair, group, partnership, band, gang, alliance, body, corps, crew. **3** yoke, tandem. • *v.* unite, ally, collaborate; conspire; coordinate.

team•mate /teémmayt/ *n.* member of the same team.

team•ster /teémstər/ *n.* driver of a truck or a team of animals.

team•work /teémwərk/ *n.* combined action; cooperation.

tea•pot /teépot/ *n.* pot with a handle, spout, and lid, for brewing and pouring tea.

tear[1] /tair/ • *v.* (*past* **tore** /tor/; *past part.* **torn** /torn/) **1** *tr.* pull apart or to pieces with some force. **2** *tr.* make a hole or rent in by tearing. **3** *tr. & intr.* pull violently (*tore off the cover*). **4** *tr.* violently disrupt or divide (*torn by conflicting emotions*). **5** *intr. colloq.* go hurriedly. **6** *intr.* undergo tearing (*the curtain tore down the middle*). • *n.* **1** hole or split caused by tearing. **2** torn part of cloth, etc. **3** *sl.* spree; drinking bout. □ **be torn between** have difficulty in choosing between. **tear apart 1** search (a place) exhaustively. **2** criticize forcefully. **3** distress deeply. **tear into 1** attack verbally; reprimand. **2** start (an activity) vigorously. **tear oneself away** leave reluctantly. **tear one's hair out** behave with extreme desperation or anger. □□ **tear′a•ble** *adj.* **tear′er** *n.*

▪ *v.* **1** rip, rupture, shred, mutilate, claw. **2** gash, pierce. **3** snatch, seize, wrench. **4** split, rend. **5** dash, fly, race, rush, shoot, speed, bolt, dart, zoom, zip. • *n.* **1** rip, fissure, rift. **3** see BENDER[2]. □ **tear apart 1** see SCOUR. **tear one's hair out** see FRET[1] 1.

tear[2] /teer/ *n.* **1** drop of clear salty liquid secreted by glands in the eye. **2** tearlike thing; drop. **6 in tears** crying; shedding tears. **tear gas** gas that disables by causing severe irritation to the eyes. □□ **tear′like** *adj.*

tear•ful /teérfŏol/ *adj.* **1** crying or inclined to cry. **2** sad (*tearful event*). □□ **tear′ful•ly** *adv.* **tear′ful•ness** *n.*

▪ **1** weeping, in tears, sobbing, whimpering, *colloq.* weepy. **2** see SAD 2, SENTIMENTAL.

tear•jerk•er /teérjərkər/ *n. colloq.* sentimental story, film, etc.

tea•room /teéroŏm, –rŏŏm/ *n.* small restaurant or café where tea, etc., is served.

tease /teez/ • *v.tr.* [also *absol.*] **1 a** make fun of playfully, unkindly, or annoyingly. **b** tempt or allure, esp. sexually. **2** pick (wool, hair, etc.) into separate fibers. **3** dress (cloth) esp. with teasels. • *n.* **1** *colloq.* person fond of teasing. **2** instance of teasing. □□ **teas′er** *n.* **teas′ing•ly** *adv.*

▪ *v.* **1 a** bait, taunt, torment, harass, bedevil, bother, pester, irritate, goad, badger, provoke, vex, pick on, mock, *sl.* rag, razz, bug. **b** see FLIRT *v.* 1. • *n.* **1** see NUISANCE, FLIRT *n.*

tea•sel /téezəl/ (also **tea'zel, tea'zle**) • *n.* **1** plant with large prickly heads that are dried and used to raise the nap on woven cloth. **2** device used as a substitute for teasels. • *v.tr.* dress (cloth) with teasels. □□ **tea'sel•er** *n.*

tea•spoon /téespōōn/ *n.* **1** spoon for stirring tea, etc. **2** amount held by this, approx. ¹/₆ fl. oz. □□ **tea'spoon•ful** *n.* (*pl.* **–fuls**)

teat /teet/ *n.* mammary nipple, esp. of an animal.

tech /tek/ *n. colloq.* **1** technician. **2** technical college.

tech•ne•tium /teknéeshəm, –sheeəm/ *n. Chem.* artificially produced radioactive metallic element. ¶Symb.: **Tc**.

tech•ni•cal /téknikəl/ *adj.* **1** of the mechanical arts and applied sciences (*technical college*). **2** of a particular subject, etc., or its techniques. **3** (of a book, discourse, etc.) using technical language. **4** due to mechanical failure. **5** strictly or legally interpreted. □ **technical knockout** ruling by the referee that a boxer has lost on the grounds of a contestant's inability to continue, the opponent being declared the winner. □□ **tech'ni•cal•ly** *adv.*
■ **1** industrial, polytechnic, technological. **2, 3** complex, detailed, specialized.

tech•ni•cal•i•ty /téknikálitee/ *n.* (*pl.* **–ties**) **1** being technical. **2** technical expression. **3** technical point or detail.
■ **3** see DETAIL *n.* 1, *triviality* (TRIVIAL).

tech•ni•cian /tekníshən/ *n.* person skilled in artistic, scientific, mechanical, etc., technique.

Tech•ni•col•or /téknikulər/ *n. propr.* process of color cinematography.

tech•nique /teknéek/ *n.* **1** mechanical skill; applicable method. **2** manner of artistic execution in music, painting, etc.
■ **1** craftsmanship, artistry, craft, knack, talent, gift, expertise; approach, mode, style, procedure.

tech•noc•ra•cy /teknókrəsee/ *n.* (*pl.* **–cies**) rule or control by technical experts. □□ **tech'no•crat** *n.* **tech•no•crat'ic** *adj.*

tech•nol•o•gy /teknóləjee/ *n.* (*pl.* **–gies**) **1** study or use of the mechanical arts and applied sciences. **2** these subjects collectively. □□ **tech•no•log'i•cal** *adj.* **tech•no•log'i•cal•ly** *adv.* **tech•nol'o•gist** *n.*

tec•ton•ic /tektónik/ *adj.* **1** *Geol.* relating to deformation of the earth's crust or to structural changes caused by this. **2** of building or construction. □□ **tec•ton'i•cal•ly** *adv.*

tec•ton•ics /tektóniks/ *n.pl.* [usu. treated as *sing.*] study of the earth's large-scale structural features.

ted•dy /tédee/ *n.* (*pl.* **–dies**) (in full **ted'dy bear**) stuffed toy bear.

te•di•ous /téedeeəs/ *adj.* tiresomely long; wearisome. □□ **te'di•ous•ly** *adv.* **te'di•ous•ness** *n.*
■ prolonged, endless, unending, monoto-

nous, unchanging, wearying, tiring, exhausting, fatiguing, boring, dull, flat, uninteresting, banal, unexciting, repetitious, mechanical.

te•di•um /téedeeəm/ *n.* state of being tedious; boredom.
■ monotony, ennui, dreariness, routine.

tee /tee/ • *n. Golf* **1** cleared space from which a golf ball is struck at the beginning of play for each hole. **2** small wood or plastic support for a golf ball. • *v.tr.* (**tees, teed**) *Golf* place (a ball) on a tee. □ **tee off** **1** *Golf* play a ball from a tee. **2** *colloq.* start; begin.

tee-hee /teehée/ (also **te-hee'**) • *n.* **1** titter. **2** restrained or contemptuous laugh. • *v.intr.* (**tee-hees, tee-heed**) titter or laugh in this way.

teem /teem/ *v.intr.* **1** be abundant. **2** be full of or swarming (*teeming with ideas*).
■ **1** proliferate, be prolific. **2** abound, crawl, overflow, brim.

teen /teen/ • *adj.* = TEENAGE. • *n.* = TEENAGER.

-teen /teen/ *suffix* forming numerals from 13 to 19.

teen•age /téenayj/ *adj.* of or characteristic of teenagers. □□ **teen'aged** *adj.*

teen•ag•er /téenayjər/ *n.* person from 13 to 19 years of age.
■ teen, adolescent, youth, juvenile, minor.

teens /teenz/ *n.pl.* years of age from 13 to 19.

teen•sy /téensee/ *adj.* (**teen•si•er, teen•si•est**) *colloq.* = TEENY. □ **teensy-weensy** = *teeny-tweeny.*

tee•ny /téenee/ *adj.* (**tee•ni•er, tee•ni•est**) *colloq.* tiny. □ **teeny-weeny** very tiny.
■ see TINY.

tee•ny•bop•per /téeneebopər/ *n. colloq.* young teenager, usu. a girl, who follows the latest fashions.

tee•pee var. of TEPEE.

tee•shirt var. of T-SHIRT.

tee•ter /téetər/ *v.intr.* totter; move unsteadily.
■ wobble, rock, sway, waver, tremble, stagger.

teeth *pl.* of TOOTH.

teethe /teeth/ *v.intr.* grow or cut teeth, esp. baby teeth. □□ **teeth'ing** *n.*

tee•to•tal /téetôt'l/ *adj.* of or advocating total abstinence from alcohol. □□ **tee•to'tal•er** *n.* (also **tee•to'tal•ler**). **tee•to'tal•ism** *n.*
■ see SOBER *adj.* 2. □□ **teetotalism** see TEMPERANCE 2.

Tef•lon /téflon/ *n. propr.* nonstick coating for kitchen utensils, etc.

tel. *abbr.* **1** telephone. **2** telegraph.

tele- /télee/ *comb. form* **1** at or to a distance (*telekinesis*). **2** television (*telecast*). **3** by telephone (*teleconference*).

tel•e•cast /télikast/ • *n.* television broadcast. • *v.tr.* transmit by television. □□ **tel'e•cast•er** *n.*
■ *n.* see BROADCAST *n.* • *v.* see BROADCAST *v.* 1a.

tel•e•com•mu•ni•ca•tion /télikəmyōōkhnikáyshən/ *n.* **1** communication over a distance by cable, telegraph, telephone lines, etc. **2** [usu. in *pl.*] technology using these means.

tel•e•com•mute /télikəmyōōt/ *v.intr.* (**tel•e•**

com·mut·ed, tel·e·com·mut·ing) work, esp. at home, communicating electronically with one's employer, etc., by computer, fax, and telephone.

tel·e·con·fer·ence /télikónfərəns, –frəns/ n. conference with participants linked by telecommunication devices. □□ **tel′e·con·fer·enc·ing** n.

tel·e·gram /téligram/ n. message sent by telegraph.
■ cable, cablegram, telex, colloq. wire.

tel·e·graph /téligraf/ • n. 1 system or device for transmitting messages or signals over a distance esp. by making and breaking an electrical connection. 2 [attrib.] used in this system (telegraph pole). • v.tr. 1 send a message to by telegraph. 2 send by telegraph. 3 give advance indication of. □□ **te·leg·ra·pher** /tilégrəfər, téligrafər/ n. **tel·e·graph′ic** adj. **tel·e·graph′i·cal·ly** adv. **te·leg·ra·phy** /təlégrəfee/ n.
■ v. 1, 2 see TRANSMIT 1a.

tel·e·ki·ne·sis /télikineésis, –kī/ n. supposed paranormal force moving objects at a distance. □□ **tel·e·ki·net·ic** /–nétik/ adj.

tel·e·mar·ket·ing /télimaárkiting/ n. marketing by unsolicited telephone calls. □□ **tel′e·mar·ket·er** n.

te·lep·a·thy /təlépəthee/ n. supposed paranormal communication of thoughts. □□ **tel·e·path·ic** /tilipáthik/ adj. **tel·e·path′i·cal·ly** adv. **te·lep′a·thist** n.
■ □□ telepathic clairvoyant, magical; see also PSYCHIC adj. 1.

tel·e·phone /télifōn/ • n. 1 apparatus for transmitting and receiving sound (esp. speech) over a distance by using optical or electrical signals. 2 system of communication using a network of telephones. • v. 1 tr. speak to or send (a message) by telephone. 2 intr. make a telephone call. □ **telephone booth** public booth, etc., with a telephone. □□ **tel·e·phon·ic** /–fónik/ adj. **tel·e·phon′i·cal·ly** adv.
■ n. 1 handset, colloq. phone, horn. • v. dial, colloq. phone, give a person a ring or call or buzz.

te·leph·o·ny /təléfənee/ n. use or system of telephones.

tel·e·pho·to /télifōtō/ n. (pl. –tos) (in full **tel′e·pho′to lens**) lens used in telephotography.

tel·e·pho·tog·ra·phy /télifətógrəfee/ n. photographing of distant objects with a system of magnifying lenses. □□ **tel·e·pho′to·graph·ic** /–fōtəgráfik/ adj.

Tel·e·Promp·Ter /télipromptər/ n. propr. device used in television and filmmaking to display a speaker's script.

tel·e·scope /téliskōp/ • n. 1 optical instrument using lenses or mirrors to magnify distant objects. 2 = radio telescope. • v. 1 tr. press or drive (sections of a tube, etc.) together so that one slides into another. 2 intr. be capable of closing in this way. 3 tr. compress in space or time. □□ **tel·e·scop·ic** /téliskópik/ adj. **tel·e·scop′i·cal·ly** adv.
■ n. 1 spyglass, glass; refracting telescope, reflecting telescope. • v. 1 squash, crush. 3 shorten, compact, abbreviate, contract, condense.

tel·e·thon /télithon/ n. exceptionally long television program, esp. to raise money for a charity.

Tel·e·type /télitīp/ n. propr. telegraphic apparatus for direct exchange of printed messages.

tel·e·vise /télivīz/ v.tr. transmit by television.

tel·e·vi·sion /télivízhən/ n. 1 system for reproducing on a screen visual images transmitted (usu. with sound) by radio waves. 2 (in full **tel′e·vi·sion set**) device with a screen for receiving these signals. 3 television broadcasting.
■ 2, 3 TV, small screen, colloq. tube, sl. boob tube.

tel·ex /téleks/ (also **Telex**) • n. system of telegraphy for printed messages using a public telecommunications network. • v.tr. communicate by telex.

tell /tel/ v. (past and past part. **told** /tōld/) 1 tr. relate in speech or writing. 2 tr. make known; express in words (tell me what you want). 3 tr. reveal or signify to (a person) (your face tells me everything). 4 intr. a divulge information, etc.; reveal a secret. b [foll. by on] colloq. inform against. 5 tr. instruct; order (tell them to wait) 6 tr. assure (it's true, I tell you). 7 tr. decide; predict; distinguish (cannot tell what might happen). 8 intr. produce a noticeable effect or influence. □ **tell apart** distinguish between. **tell off** colloq. reprimand; scold. **tell tales** report a discreditable fact about another. **there is no telling** it is impossible to know. □□ **tell′a·ble** adj.
■ 1 narrate, recount, recite, report, chronicle. 2 say, mention, utter, state, declare, proclaim, announce, publish, broadcast, communicate, impart, refer to, inform, notify, describe, depict, explain; disclose, release, bring to light, admit. 3 express, show, convey, indicate. 4 a colloq. let the cat out of the bag, spill the beans. b (tell on) betray, colloq. blow the whistle on, rat on. 5 command, require, charge, direct. 6 swear to, promise. 7 ascertain, determine, perceive, understand, know; prophesy, forecast, foretell, foresee; confirm, know for sure or certain; discern, identify, recognize, differentiate. 8 register; carry weight. □ **tell apart** see DISTINGUISH 1. **tell off** berate, rebuke, colloq. tear into, bawl out, chew out. **tell tales** tattle, gossip, blab.

tell·er /télər/ n. 1 person employed to receive and pay out money in a bank, etc. 2 person who tells esp. stories (teller of tales).

tell·ing /téling/ adj. 1 having a marked effect; striking. 2 significant. □□ **tell′ing·ly** adv.
■ effective, strong, compelling, considerable.

tell·tale /téltayl/ n. 1 person who reveals secrets about another. 2 [attrib.] that reveals or betrays (telltale smile). 3 device for automatic indicating, monitoring, or registering of a process, etc.
■ 2 (attrib.) see MEANINGFUL.

tel·lu·ri·um /teloóreeəm/ n. Chem. rare lustrous silver-white element used in semiconductors. ¶Symb.: **Te**. □□ **tel•lu•ride** /télyə-rīd/ *n.* **tel•lu•rite** /télyərīt/ *n.* **tel'lu•rous** *adj.* **tel•lu'ric** *adj.*

te•mer•i•ty /tımérıtee/ *n.* **1** rashness. **2** audacity; impudence.

■ **2** see EFFRONTERY.

SYNONYM STUDY: temerity

AUDACITY, EFFRONTERY, FOOLHARDINESS, GALL, IMPETUOSITY, RASHNESS. The line that divides boldness from foolishness or stupidity is often a fine one. Someone who rushes boldly into a situation without thinking about the consequences might be accused of **rashness**, while **temerity** implies exposing oneself needlessly to danger while failing to estimate one's chances of success. *Rashness*, which applies primarily to bodily acts, may be considered a positive trait; but *temerity*, which usually applies to mental or social acts, is always negative (*she had the temerity to criticize her teacher in front of the class*). **Audacity** describes a different kind of boldness, one that disregards moral standards or social conventions (*he had the audacity to ask her if she would mind paying for the trip*). Someone who behaves with **foolhardiness** is reckless or downright foolish (*climbing the mountain after dark was foolhardiness and everyone knew it*), while **impetuosity** describes an eager impulsiveness or behavior that is sudden, *rash*, and sometimes violent (*his impetuosity had landed him in trouble before*). **Gall** and **effrontery** are always derogatory terms. *Effrontery* is a more formal word for the flagrant disregard of the rules of propriety, courtesy, etc. (*she had the effrontery to call the president by his first name*), while *gall* is more colloquial and suggests outright insolence (*he was the only one who had the gall to tell the boss off*).

temp /temp/ *colloq.* • *n.* temporary employee. • *v. intr.* work as a temp.

temp. /temp/ *abbr.* **1** temperature. **2** temporary.

tem•per /témpər/ • *n.* **1** mood; mental disposition. **2** irritation; anger (*fit of temper*). **3** tendency to have fits of anger. **4** composure; calmness (*lose one's temper*). **5** hardness or elasticity of metal. • *v. tr.* **1** bring (metal or clay) to a proper hardness or consistency. **2** moderate (*temper justice with mercy*). See synonym study at ALLEVIATE. □□ **tem'per•a•ble** *adj.* **tem'pered** *adj.*

■ *n.* **1** temperament, character, personality, nature, makeup, constitution; humor, state *or* frame of mind. **2** passion, rage; tantrum, fury. **3** irritability, volatility, surliness, churlishness. **4** self-control, self-possession, coolness, *sl.* cool. • *v.* **1** anneal, toughen, strengthen, harden. **2** modify, assuage, mollify, soften, cushion, tone down, allay, soothe, mitigate, relax, slacken, lighten, appease. □□ **tempered** see *subdued* (SUBDUE 2).

tem•per•a /témpərə/ *n.* method of painting using an emulsion, e.g., of pigment with egg, esp. on canvas.

tem•per•a•ment /témprəmənt/ *n.* person's or animal's nature and character.

■ see DISPOSITION 1.

tem•per•a•men•tal /témprəmént'l/ *adj.* **1** of temperament. **2** moody; unreliable. □□ **tem•per•a•men'tal•ly** *adv.*

■ erratic, sensitive, touchy, volatile, testy, short-tempered, excitable; inconsistent, undependable, unpredictable.

tem•per•ance /témpərəns, témprəns/ *n.* **1** moderation, esp. in eating and drinking. **2** abstinence from alcohol. See synonym study at ABSTINENCE.

■ **1** (self-)restraint, (self-)control. **2** teetotalism, sobriety; prohibition.

tem•per•ate /témpərət, témprət/ *adj.* **1** avoiding excess. **2** moderate. **3** (of a region or climate) mild. □□ **tem'per•ate•ly** *adv.* **tem'per•ate•ness** *n.*

■ **1, 2** reasonable, (self-)restrained, disciplined, controlled, composed, stable, sober; chaste, celibate; coolheaded, calm, unperturbed, self-possessed, quiet. **3** see MILD 3. □□ **temperately** see EASY *adv.* **temperateness** see SOBRIETY.

tem•per•a•ture /témprichər/ *n.* **1** measured or perceived degree of heat or cold of a body, thing, region, etc. **2** body temperature above normal (*have a temperature*).

tem•pest /témpist/ *n.* **1** violent storm. **2** violent agitation. □□ **tem•pes•tu•ous** /-péschōōəs/ *adj.* **tem•pes'tu•ous•ly** *adv.* **tem•pes'tu•ous•ness** *n.*

■ **1** hurricane, typhoon, tornado, cyclone, squall, thunderstorm, gale. **2** commotion, disturbance, upheaval, disruption, furor, tumult, riot, chaos, uproar. □□ **tempestuous** stormy, wild, uncontrollable, turbulent, frenzied, frenetic, passionate. **tempestuousness** see FURY 2.

tem•plate /témplit, -playt/ *n.* piece of thin board or metal plate used as a pattern in cutting, drilling, etc.

■ mold, guide, model, die.

tem•ple[1] /témpəl/ *n.* building for the worship of a god or gods.

■ place *or* house of worship, holy place, house of God, church, synagogue, mosque, pagoda, cathedral, sanctuary, chapel, tabernacle, shrine.

tem•ple[2] /témpəl/ *n.* flat part of either side of the head between the forehead and the ear.

tem•po /témpō/ *n.* (*pl.* **-pos** or **tem•pi** /-pee/) **1** speed at which music is or should be played. **2** rate of motion or activity.

■ **1** cadence, rhythm, beat, time, pulse. **2** pace.

tem•po•ral /témpərəl, témprəl/ *adj.* **1** worldly as opposed to spiritual; secular. **2** of time. **3** of the temples of the head (*temporal artery*). □□ **tem'po•ral•ly** *adv.*

■ **1** earthly, terrestrial, mundane; lay, laic(al); material, civil, mortal.

tem•po•rar•y /témpəréree/ • *adj.* lasting or meant to last only for a limited time. • *n.* (*pl.* **-ies**) person employed temporarily. □□ **tem•po•rar•i•ly** /-pəráirilee/ *adv.*

■ *adj.* makeshift, standby, provisional; *pro tempore*, transient, brief, short-lived. • *n.* stand-in, *colloq.* temp. □□ **temporarily** for the time being, in the interim, (in *or* for the) meantime, for now; *colloq.* pro tem.

EPHEMERAL, EVANESCENT, FLEETING, TRANSIENT, TRANSITORY. Things that don't last long are called **temporary**, which emphasizes a measurable but limited duration (*a temporary appointment as chief of staff*). Something that is **fleeting** passes almost instantaneously and cannot be caught or held (*a fleeting thought; a fleeting glimpse*). **Transient** also applies to that which lasts or stays but a short time (*transient house guests*), while **transitory** refers to something that is destined to pass away or come to an end (*the transitory pleasure of eating*). *Evanescent* and *ephemeral* describe what is even more short-lived. *Ephemeral* literally means lasting for only a single day, but is often used to describe anything that is slight and perishable (*his fame was ephemeral*). *Evanescent* is a more lyrical word for whatever vanishes almost as soon as it appears. In other words, a job might be *temporary*, an emotion *fleeting*, a visitor *transient*, a woman's beauty *transitory*, and glory *ephemeral*, but the flash of a bird's wing across the sky would have to be called *evanescent*.

tem•po•rize /témpəriz/ *v.intr.* **1** avoid committing oneself so as to gain time. **2** comply temporarily; adopt a time-serving policy. □□ **tem•po•ri•za′tion** *n.* **tem′po•riz•er** *n.*
  ■ **1** see PROCRASTINATE.

tempt /tempt/ *v.tr.* **1** entice or incite (a person) to do a wrong or forbidden thing. **2** allure; attract. **3** risk provoking (fate, etc.). □□ **tempt′a•ble** *adj.* **tempt′er**, **tempt′ress** *n.*
  ■ **1** lead, induce, persuade, prompt, coax, cajole, *?* lure, draw (in), invite, seduce, captivate. **3** dare, (put to the) test. □□ **tempter, temptress** charmer, seducer; (*temptress*) seductress, siren, femme fatale; see also DEVIL *n.* 1, 2.

temp•ta•tion /temptáyshən/ *n.* **1** tempting; being tempted; incitement esp. to wrongdoing. **2** attractive thing or course of action.
  ■ **1** enticement, seduction, persuasion. **2** invitation, draw, lure, inducement, bait, *sl.* come-on.

tempt•ing /témpting/ *adj.* attractive; inviting. □□ **tempt′ing•ly** *adv.*
  ■ seductive, enticing, alluring, captivating, tantalizing, appealing, irresistible; (*of food*) appetizing, mouthwatering, delicious, delectable.

tem•pu•ra /tempóorə/ *n.* Japanese dish of fish, shellfish, or vegetables, dipped in batter and deep-fried.

ten /ten/ *n.* **1** one more than nine. **2** symbol for this (10, x, X). **3** ten-dollar bill.

ten•a•ble /ténəbəl/ *adj.* maintainable or defensible against attack or objection (*tenable position*). □□ **ten•a•bil′i•ty** *n.* **ten′a•ble•ness** *n.*
  ■ supportable, justifiable, plausible, reasonable, credible, possible.

te•na•cious /tináyshəs/ *adj.* **1** keeping a firm hold. **2** (of memory) retentive. **3** persistent;

resolute. □□ **te•na′cious•ly** *adv.* **te•na′cious•ness** *n.* **te•nac•i•ty** /tinásitee/ *n.*
  ■ **1** (*tenacious of*) clinging, grasping, retaining. **3** unfaltering, determined, diligent, staunch, steadfast, unwavering, stubborn, adamant, immovable, inflexible, unyielding. □□ **tenaciousness, tenacity** persistence, stamina; toughness, resilience; viscosity.

ten•an•cy /ténənsee/ *n.* (*pl.* **–cies**) **1** status of a tenant; possession as a tenant. **2** duration of this.
  ■ occupancy, occupation, holding, tenure, residency.

ten•ant /ténənt/ *n.* **1** person who rents land or property from a landlord. **2** occupant of a place.
  ■ **1** lessee, renter, leaseholder. **2** resident, inhabitant.

tend¹ /tend/ *v.intr.* **1** be apt or inclined (*to*). **2** be moving; hold a course (*tends to the same conclusion*).
  ■ **1** be prone, be likely, have a tendency. **2** lean, gravitate; (*tend to*) favor.

tend² /tend/ *v.* **1** *tr.* take care of; look after. **2** *intr.* (foll. by *to*) give attention to.
  ■ **1** watch over, mind, minister to, protect. **2** (*tend to*) attend to, see to, deal with, handle.

ten•den•cy /téndənsee/ *n.* (*pl.* **–cies**) leaning; inclination.
  ■ bent, disposition, propensity, proclivity, penchant, partiality, affinity, bias.

ten•den•tious /tendénshəs/ *adj. derog.* (of writing, etc.) calculated to promote a particular cause or viewpoint; having an underlying purpose. □□ **ten•den′tious•ly** *adv.* **ten•den′tious•ness** *n.*
  ■ □□ **tendentiousness** see BIAS *n.* 1.

ten•der¹ /téndər/ *adj.* (**tend•er•er**, **tend•er•est**) **1** easily cut or chewed; not tough. **2** susceptible to pain or grief (*tender heart*). **3** sensitive; delicate; fragile. **4** loving; affectionate. **5** requiring tact or careful handling (*tender subject*). **6** (of age) immature (*of tender years*). □ **tender-hearted** easily moved by pity, etc. **tender mercies** *iron.* attention or treatment which is not in the best interests of its recipient. □□ **ten′der•ly** *adv.* **ten′der•ness** *n.*
  ■ **1** chewable, soft. **2** see SENSITIVE 2. **3** sore, raw, painful; frail, feeble; gentle, light. **4** fond, kindhearted, mild, compassionate, considerate, humane, sympathetic, thoughtful, warm, caring, merciful; touching, emotional, moving, stirring, heartfelt. **5** touchy, ticklish, difficult, tricky. **6** young, youthful, inexperienced, impressionable, vulnerable, green, raw, callow. □ **tender-hearted** see SYMPATHETIC *adj.* 1. □□ **tenderly** see *warmly* (WARM). **tenderness** see FEELING *n.* 3.

tend•er² /téndər/ • *v.* **1** *tr.* offer; present (one's services, payment, resignation, etc.). **2** *intr.* make a tender for the supply of a thing or the execution of work. • *n.* offer, esp. in writing, to execute work or supply goods at a fixed price.
  ■ *v.* **1** proffer, propose, put forward, extend, hold out, submit, advance, put up,

hand in, give. **2** bid, put in a bid, quote. • *n.* bid, proposal, *colloq.* quote.

tend•er[3] /téndər/ *n.* **1** person who looks after people or things. **2** vessel attending a larger one. **3** car coupled to a steam locomotive to carry fuel, water, etc.
  ■ **2** dinghy, skiff, launch.

ten•der•ize /téndərīz/ *v.tr.* make tender, esp. make (meat) tender by beating, etc. □□ **ten′der•iz•er** *n.*

ten•der•loin /téndərloyn/ *n.* tender cut of beef or pork loin.

ten•don /téndən/ *n.* cord of strong tissue attaching a muscle to a bone, etc.

ten•dril /téndril/ *n.* slender leafless shoots by which some climbing plants cling.

ten•e•ment /ténimənt/ *n.* overcrowded or run-down apartment house.

ten•et /ténit/ *n.* doctrine; dogma; principle.
  ■ belief, credo, creed, precept, position, axiom.

ten•fold /ténfōld/ *adj. & adv.* **1** ten times as much or as many. **2** consisting of ten parts.

Tenn. *abbr.* Tennessee.

ten•nis /ténis/ *n.* game in which two or four players strike a ball with rackets over a net stretched across a court. □ **tennis elbow** inflammation of the elbow caused by overuse.

ten•on /ténən/ *n.* projecting piece of wood made for insertion into a cavity (esp. a mortise) in another piece.

ten•or /ténər/ *n.* **1 a** male singing voice between baritone and alto or countertenor. **b** singer with this voice. **2** general purport or drift. **3** prevailing course, esp. of a person's life or habits.
  ■ **2** tone, spirit, essence, character, gist, theme, implication. **3** direction, inclination, trend.

ten•pins /ténpinz/ *n.* [usu. treated as *sing.*] □ bowling game using ten pins.

tense[1] /tens/ • *adj.* **1** stretched tight; strained. **2** causing tenseness (*tense moment*). • *v.* make or become tense. □□ **tense′ly** *adv.* **tense′ness** *n.* **ten′si•ty** *n.*
  ■ *adj.* taut, stiff, rigid; intense, nervous, anxious, on edge, keyed up, worked up, upset, worried, edgy, *colloq.* wound up. **2** worrisome, distressing, stressful, nerve-racking. • *v.* tense up; tighten. □□ **tensely** see *tightly* (TIGHT). **tenseness** see TENSION *n.* 1, 2, STRESS *n.* 2.

tense[2] /tens/ *n. Gram.* form taken by a verb to indicate the time (also the continuance or completeness) of the action, etc. (*present tense, imperfect tense*).

ten•sile /ténsəl, –sīl/ *adj.* **1** of tension. **2** capable of being stretched. □□ **ten•sil•i•ty** /tensílitee/ *n.*
  ■ **2** see FLEXIBLE 1.

ten•sion /ténshən/ *n.* **1** stretching; being stretched; tenseness. **2** mental strain or excitement. **3** strained (political, social, etc.) state or relationship. **4** stress produced by forces pulling apart. **5** electromagnetic force (*high tension, low tension*).

  ■ *n.* **1** tightness, tautness, pull, pressure. **2** nervousness, anxiety, suspense, distress; see also *excitement* (EXCITE).

ten•sor /ténsər/ *n.* muscle that tightens or stretches a part.

tent /tent/ *n.* **1** portable shelter or dwelling of canvas, cloth, etc., supported by poles and ground pegs. **2** tentlike enclosure.

ten•ta•cle /téntəkəl/ *n.* long, slender, flexible appendage of an (esp. invertebrate) animal, used for feeling, grasping, or moving. □□ **ten′ta•cled** *adj.* [also in *comb.*].
  ■ feeler, antenna.

ten•ta•tive /téntətiv/ *adj.* **1** experimental. **2** hesitant; not definite (*tentative suggestion*). □□ **ten′ta•tive•ly** *adv.* **ten′ta•tive•ness** *n.*
  ■ *adj.* **1** speculative, trial, provisional. **2** unsure, uncertain, indecisive, indefinite. □□ **tentatively** see GINGERLY *adv.*

ten•ter•hook /téntərhŏŏk/ *n.* hook to which cloth is fastened for stretching. □ **on tenterhooks** in a state of anxiety or uncertainty.
  ■ □ **on tenterhooks** see TENSE[1] *adj.* 1.

tenth /tenth/ • *n.* **1** next after ninth. **2** each of ten equal parts of a thing. • *adj.* that is the tenth. □□ **tenth′ly** *adv.*

ten•u•ous /tényŏŏəs/ *adj.* **1** slight; insubstantial. **2** (of a distinction, etc.) oversubtle. **3** thin; slender; small. **4** rarefied. □□ **ten′u•ous•ly** *adv.* **ten′u•ous•ness** *n.*
  ■ **1** flimsy, weak, feeble, frail, meager. **2** hairsplitting, quibbling, *colloq.* nit-picking. **3** fine, delicate, gossamer, diaphanous, fragile. **4** see *rarefied* (RAREFY 1).

ten•ure /tényər/ *n.* **1** right or title under which (esp. real) property is held. **2** period of this. **3** guaranteed permanent employment, esp. as a teacher or professor. □□ **ten′ured** *adj.*
  ■ **1, 2** possession, holding, ownership. **3** (job) security.

te•pee /téepee/ *n.* (also **tee′pee**) conical tent orig. used by Native Americans.

tep•id /tépid/ *adj.* **1** slightly warm. **2** unenthusiastic. □□ **te•pid′i•ty** *n.* **tep′id•ly** *adv.* **tep′id•ness** *n.*
  ■ **1** lukewarm, warmish. **2** cool, indifferent, uninterested, nonchalant, blasé.

te•qui•la /tekeélə/ *n.* Mexican liquor made from an agave.

tera- /térə/ *comb. form* denoting a factor of 10^{12}.

ter•bi•um /tórbeeəm/ *n. Chem.* silvery metallic element of the lanthanide series. ¶Symb.: **Tb**.

ter•cen•te•nar•y /tórsenténəree, tərséntineree/ • *n.* (*pl.* **–ies**) **1** three-hundredth anniversary. **2** celebration of this. • *adj.* of this anniversary.

ter•cen•ten•ni•al /tórsentenéeəl/ • *adj.* **1** occurring every three hundred years. **2** lasting three hundred years. • *n.* tercentenary.

ter•i•ya•ki /tereeyókee/ *n.* usu. grilled dish of meat, poultry, or fish that has been marinated in soy sauce.

term /tərm/ • *n.* **1** word for a definite concept, esp. specialized. **2** [in *pl.*] language used; mode of expression (*in no uncertain terms*). **3** [in *pl.*] relationship (*on familiar terms*). **4** [in *pl.*] **a** stipulations (*cannot accept* *your terms*). **b** charge; price (*his terms are $20 a lesson*). **5** limited, usu. specified, period (*term of five years*). **6** *Math.* each of the two in a ratio, series, or expression. **7** completion of a normal length of pregnancy. • *v.tr.* call; assign a term to (*the music termed classical*). □ **bring to terms** cause to accept conditions. **come to terms with 1** reconcile oneself to (a difficulty, etc.). **2** conclude an agreement with. **in terms of 1** in the language peculiar to. **2** by way of. **on terms** on terms of friendship or equality.

■ *n.* **1** name, title, designation, label; expression, phrase. **3** (*terms*) standing, position, footing. **4** (*terms*) **a** conditions, provisions, provisos; qualifications, basis. **b** payment, schedule, rates. **5** time, interval, duration, spell, stint, course; stretch. • *v.* name, label, designate, dub; nickname. □ **come to terms with 1** accept, adjust to, cope with, face up to. **2** come to *or* reach an understanding with. **in terms of 2** as, as regards, concerning, regarding, with regard to, in the matter of.

ter•ma•gant /tə́rməgənt/ • *n.* overbearing woman; virago. • *adj.* violent; turbulent; shrewish.

■ *n.* **1** see SHREW.

ter•mi•na•ble /tə́rminəbəl/ *adj.* that may be terminated.

ter•mi•nal /tə́rminəl/ • *adj.* **1 a** (of a disease) fatal. **b** (of a patient) dying. **c** *colloq.* ruinous; very great (*terminal laziness*). **2** of or forming a limit or terminus. • *n.* **1** terminating thing; extremity. **2** terminus for planes, trains, or long-distance buses. **3** point of connection for closing an electric circuit. **4** apparatus for transmission of messages between a user and a computer, communications system, etc. □ **terminal velocity** velocity of a falling body such that the resistance of the air, etc., prevents further increase of speed under gravity. □□ **ter•mi•nal•ly** *adv.*

■ *adj.* **1 a** deadly, mortal, lethal, incurable. **2** closing, concluding, terminating, ending, final, ultimate, extreme. • *n.* **1** see TIP¹ n. 1. **2** station, end of the line, depot. **3** wire, connector, coupler, coupling, conductor. **4** keyboard, monitor, workstation, visual display unit, PC, CRT, screen. □□ **terminally** see *severely* (SEVERE).

ter•mi•nate /tə́rminayt/ *v.* **1** *tr. & intr.* bring or come to an end. **2** *intr.* (foll. by *in*) (of a word) end in (a specified letter, syllable, etc.). □□ **ter•mi•na′tion** *n.* **ter′mi•na•tor** *n.*

■ **1** stop, finish, cease; put an end to, discontinue; expire, sign off; abort. □□ **termination** end, cancellation, expiration, close, conclusion, completion.

ter•mi•nol•o•gy /tə́rminóləjee/ *n.* (*pl.* **–gies**) **1** system of specialized terms. **2** science of the proper use of terms. □□ **ter•mi•nol′o•gist** *n.*

■ **1** nomenclature, vocabulary, language, wording, phraseology, jargon, *colloq.* lingo, *often derog.*

ter•mi•nus /tə́rminəs/ *n.* (*pl.* **ter•mi•ni** /–nī/ or **ter•mi•nus•es**) end of a bus route, pipeline, etc.; end point.

■ see TERMINAL *n.* 2, DESTINATION.

ter•mite /tə́rmīt/ *n.* antlike social insect destructive to wood.

tern /tərn/ *n.* marine bird like a gull but usu. smaller and with a long forked tail.

terp•si•cho•re•an /tə́rpsikəreéən, –káwreeən/ *adj.* of dancing.

terr. *abbr.* **1** terrace. **2** territory.

ter•race /térəs/ • *n.* **1** flat area formed on a slope and used for cultivation. **2** patio. • *v.tr.* form into or provide with a terrace or terraces.

ter•ra-cot•ta /térəkótə/ *n.* **1** unglazed, usu. brownish red earthenware. **2** its color.

ter•ra fir•ma /térə fə́rmə/ *n.* dry land; firm ground.

ter•rain /təráyn/ *n.* tract of land as regarded by the physical geographer or the military tactician.

■ topography, landscape, ground, country, territory, zone.

ter•ra•pin /térəpin/ *n.* N. American edible freshwater turtle.

ter•rar•i•um /təráireeəm/ *n.* (*pl.* **ter•rar•i•ums** or **ter•ra•ri•a** /–reeə/) usu. glass enclosure for plants or small land animals.

ter•res•tri•al /tərréstreeəl/ • *adj.* **1** of or on the earth; earthly. **2** of or on dry land. • *n.* inhabitant of the earth.

■ *adj.* worldly; earthbound, global. • *n.* earthling, mortal, human.

ter•ri•ble /téribəl/ *adj.* **1** *colloq.* very great or bad (*terrible bore*). **2** *colloq.* very incompetent (*terrible at tennis*). **3** causing terror; awful; dreadful. **4** (*predic.*) *colloq.* full of remorse; sorry (*I felt terrible*). □□ **ter′ri•ble•ness** *n.*

■ **1** serious, grave, severe, acute, distressing, unbearable, intolerable, unpleasant, disagreeable, miserable, wretched, unfortunate. **2** see INCOMPETENT *adj.* 2. **3** gruesome, grisly, grotesque, brutal, savage, horrible, horrendous, terrifying, harrowing, horrid, horrifying, ghastly, frightening, frightful, fearsome, awesome, monstrous, wicked, grievous, appalling, shocking, alarming, foul, disgusting, revolting, nauseating, offensive, abominable, loathsome, hideous, evil, vile, rotten. **4** remorseful, regretful, contrite, ashamed, guilty.

ter•ri•bly /tériblee/ *adv.* **1** *colloq.* very; extremely (*terribly nice*). **2** in a terrible manner.

■ **1** exceedingly, thoroughly, decidedly, really, unbelievably, incredibly. **2** dreadfully, fearfully, awfully; see also BADLY 1.

ter•ri•er /téreeər/ *n.* small dog of various breeds originally used to ferret out game.

ter•rif•ic /tərifik/ *adj.* **1** *colloq.* **a** huge; intense. **b** excellent (*did a terrific job*). **2** causing terror. □□ **ter•rif′i•cal•ly** *adv.*

■ **1 a** see HUGE 1, INTENSE 1, 3. **b** wonderful, marvelous, splendid, breathtaking, extraordinary, outstanding, magnificent, exceptional, sensational, superb, great, fantastic, fabulous, incredible, super. **2** see TERRIBLE 3.

ter•ri•fy /térifī/ *v.tr.* (**–fies, –fied**) fill with

terror. □□ ter'ri•fi•er *n.* ter'ri•fy•ing *adj.* ter'ri•fy•ing•ly *adv.*

■ alarm, frighten, scare, terrorize, shock, horrify.

ter•ri•to•ri•al /tértáwreeəl/ *adj.* **1** of territory or a district. **2** tending to defend one's territory. □□ ter•ri•to'ri•al•ly *adv.*

ter•ri•to•ry /téritawree/ *n.* (*pl.* –ries) **1** extent of land under a ruler, nation, city, etc. **2** (**Territory**) division of a country, esp. one not yet having full rights. **3** sphere of action or thought; province. **4** designated business or sales area. **5** human's or animal's defended space or area.

■ **1** area, region, district, neighborhood, zone, country. **3** haunt, stamping ground, *sl.* turf. **5** domain.

ter•ror /térər/ *n.* **1** extreme fear. **2 a** terrifying person or thing. **b** (also **holy terror**) *colloq.* formidable person; troublesome person or thing. **3** use of organized intimidation. □ **reign of terror** period of remorseless repression, esp. during the French Revolution 1793–94. **terror-stricken** (or **-struck**) affected with terror.

■ **1** fright, dread, horror, anxiety, dismay. **2** demon, brute, monster, fiend, devil. **3** terrorism. □ **terror-stricken** (or **-struck**) see *panic-stricken* (PANIC).

ter•ror•ist /térərist/ *n.* [also *attrib.*] person who uses violent methods of coercing a government or community. □□ ter'ror•ism *n.* ter•ror•is'tic *adj.*

■ subversive, radical, insurgent, revolutionary, anarchist, nihilist; bomber, arsonist; hijacker; thug.

ter•ror•ize /térəriz/ *v.tr.* **1** fill with terror. **2** use terrorism against. □□ ter•ror•i•za'tion *n.* ter'ror•iz•er *n.*

■ **1** see INTIMIDATE.

ter•ry /téree/ • *n.* (*pl.* –ries) pile fabric with the loops uncut, used esp. for towels. • *adj.* of this fabric.

terse /ters/ *adj.* (ters•er, ters•est) **1** (of language) brief; concise. **2** curt; abrupt. □□ terse'ly *adv.* terse'ness *n.*

■ **1** short, compact, pithy, succinct, short and sweet, to the point; condensed, abbreviated, abridged. **2** brusque, blunt, gruff, petulant, rude. □□ terseness see ECONOMY 3.

SYNONYM STUDY: terse

CONCISE, LACONIC, PITHY, SENTENTIOUS, SUCCINCT. If you don't like to mince words, you'll make every effort to be **concise** in both your writing and speaking, which means to remove all superfluous details (*a concise summary of everything that happened*). **Succinct** is very close in meaning to *concise*, although it emphasizes compression and compactness in addition to brevity (*succinct instructions for what to do in an emergency*). If you're **laconic**, you are brief to the point of being curt, brusque, or even uncommunicative (*his laconic reply left many questions unanswered*). **Terse** can also mean clipped or abrupt (*a terse command*), but it usually connotes something that is both *concise* and pol-

ished (*a terse style of writing that was much admired*). A **pithy** statement is not only *succinct* but full of substance and meaning (*a pithy argument that no one could counter*). **Sententious** comes from a Latin word meaning opinion. Although it describes a condensed and *pithy* style or approach, it also connotes a pompous or moralizing attitude or tone (*the speaker was so sententious that half the audience slipped out before he was finished*).

---

ter•ti•ar•y /tórshee-eree, –shəri/ • *adj.* **1** third in order or rank, etc. **2** (**Tertiary**) *Geol.* of the first period in the Cenozoic era. • *n.* (**Tertiary**) *Geol.* Tertiary period.

tes•la /téslə/ *n.* unit of magnetic flux density.

tes•sel•lat•ed /tésəlaytid/ *adj.* **1** of or resembling mosaic. **2** *Bot.* & *Zool.* regularly checkered. □□ tes•sel•la'tion *n.*

test /test/ • *n.* **1** critical examination or trial of a person's or thing's qualities. **2** means of so examining. **3** oral or written examination. • *v.tr.* **1** cause to undergo a test. **2** try severely. **3** *Chem.* examine by means of a reagent. □ **test pattern** still television picture designed for use in judging the quality and position of the image. **test pilot** pilot who tests the performance of aircraft. **test tube** thin glass tube closed at one end used for chemical tests, etc. **test-tube baby** *colloq.* baby conceived by *in vitro* fertilization. □□ test'a•ble *adj.* test•a•bil'i•ty *n.* test'er *n.*

■ *n.* **1** experiment, evaluation, checkup, investigation, inspection, appraisal, assessment, study, analysis. **2** see PROOF *n.* 2. **3** exam. • *v.* **1** try (out), question, prove, put to the test, probe; screen, audition, sample. **2** see TAX *v.* 3. **3** assay, analyze.

Test. *abbr.* Testament.

tes•ta•ment /téstəmənt/ *n.* **1** will (esp. *last will and testament*). **2** evidence; proof (*testament to his loyalty*). **3** *Bibl.* a covenant; dispensation. **b** (**Testament**) division of the Christian Bible (see *Old Testament, New Testament*). □□ tes•ta•men'ta•ry *adj.*

■ **1** last wishes. **2** see MONUMENT 3, PROOF *n.* 1.

tes•tate /téstayt/ • *adj.* having left a valid will at death. • *n.* testate person. □□ tes•ta•cy /–təsee/ *n.* (*pl.* –cies).

tes•ta•tor /téstaytər, téstaytər/ *n.* (*fem.* tes•ta•trix /téstáytriks/) (esp. deceased) person who has made a will.

tes•tes *pl.* of TESTIS.

tes•ti•cle /téstikəl/ *n.* male organ that produces spermatozoa, etc., esp. one of a pair in the scrotum of a man and most mammals. □□ tes•tic•u•lar /–stikyələr/ *adj.*

tes•ti•fy /téstifi/ *v.* (–fies, –fied) **1** *intr.* (of a person or thing) bear witness (*testified to the facts*). **2** *intr.* give evidence. **3** *tr.* affirm; declare (*testified that she had lied*). □□ tes'ti•fi•er *n.*

■ **1** attest. **2** give testimony. **3** state, assert, swear, say, avow, proclaim. □□ **testifier** see WITNESS *n.* 2.

tes•ti•mo•ni•al /téstimóneeəl/ *n.* **1** statement of character, conduct, or qualifications. **2** gift presented to a person (esp. in public) as a mark of esteem, gratitude, etc.

■ **1** endorsement, certification, commendation, (letter of) recommendation. **2** see TRIBUTE 1.

tes•ti•mo•ny /téstimōnee/ *n.* (*pl.* **–nies**) **1** witness's statement under oath. **2** declaration or statement of fact. **3** evidence (*produce testimony*).

■ **1, 2** affirmation, avowal, deposition, affidavit; confirmation, verification, authentication. **3** see DEMONSTRATION 4.

tes•tis /téstis/ *n.* (*pl.* **tes•tes** /–teez/) *Anat. & Zool.* testicle.

tes•tos•ter•one /testóstərōn/ *n.* sex hormone formed in the testicles.

tes•ty /téstee/ *adj.* (**tes•ti•er, tes•ti•est**) irritable; touchy. □□ **tes'ti•ly** *adv.* **tes'ti•ness** *n.*

■ short-tempered, cross, grumpy, crabby, contentious, disagreeable, ill-tempered, edgy, cantankerous, cranky, *colloq.* grouchy. □□ **testily** see SHORTLY 3.

tet•a•nus /tét'nəs/ *n.* bacterial disease causing painful spasm of the voluntary muscles.

tête-à-tête /táytaatáyt, tétaatét/ • *n.* private conversation between two persons. See synonym study at CONVERSATION. • *adv.* together in private (*dined tête-à-tête*).

■ *n.* chat, dialogue, heart-to-heart, interview, *colloq.* confab. • *adv.* intimately, privately, face to face, confidentially, secretly, à deux.

teth•er /téthər/ • *n.* rope, etc., confining an animal. • *v.tr.* tie (an animal) with a tether. □ **at the end of one's tether** having reached the limit of one's patience, resources, abilities, etc.

■ *n.* lead, leash, cord, restraint, halter, tie, chain. • *v.* restrain, fetter, secure, fasten. □ **at the end of one's tether** see DESPERATE 1.

tetra- /tétrə/ *comb. form* (also **tetr-** before a vowel) four.

tet•ra•cy•cline /tétrəsikleen, –klin/ *n.* antibiotic with a molecule of four rings.

Tet•ra•gram•ma•ton /tétrəgráməton/ *n.* Hebrew name of God written in four letters, articulated as *Yahweh*, etc.

tet•ra•he•dron /tétrəhéedrən/ *n.* (*pl.* **tet•ra•he•dra** /–drə/ or **tet•ra•he•drons**) four-sided solid; triangular pyramid. □□ **tet•ra•he'dral** *adj.*

te•tral•o•gy /tetrálɔjee, –tról–/ *n.* (*pl.* **–gies**) group of four related literary or operatic works.

te•tram•e•ter /tetrámitər/ *n. Prosody* verse of four measures.

tet•ra•pod /tétrəpod/ *n. Zool.* animal with four feet. □□ **tet•ra•pod•ous** /titrápədəs/ *adj.*

te•trarch /tétraark/ *n.* **1** *Rom.Hist.* **a** governor of a fourth part of a country or province. **b** subordinate ruler. **2** one of four joint rulers. □□ **te'trarch•ate** *n.* **te•trar'chi•cal** *adj.* **te•trar'chy** *n.* (*pl.* **–chies**)

Teu•ton /tōōt'n, tyōō-/ *n.* member of a Teutonic nation, esp. a German.

Teu•ton•ic /tōōtónik, tyōō-/ *adj.* **1** of the Germanic peoples or languages. **2** German.

Tex. *abbr.* Texas.

Tex•an /téksən/ • *n.* native or inhabitant of Texas. • *adj.* of or relating to Texas.

Tex-Mex /téksméks/ *adj.* combining cultural

elements from Texas and Mexico, as in cooking, music, etc.

text /tekst/ *n.* **1** main body of a book as distinct from notes, etc. **2** original words of an author or document. **3** passage from Scripture, esp. as the subject of a sermon. **4** subject; theme. **5** textbook.

■ **1** wording, content, (subject) matter; printed matter, contents. **2** script, transcript. **3** extract, abstract, section, quotation, part, paragraph, verse, line; lesson. **4** topic, motif, issue, focus.

text•book /tékstbŏŏk/ • *n.* book for use in studying, esp. a standard account of a subject. • *attrib.adj.* **1** exemplary; accurate. **2** instructively typical. □□ **text'book•ish** *adj.*

■ *n.* schoolbook, reader, manual, handbook, primer.

tex•tile /tékstil/ • *n.* **1** any woven material. **2** any cloth. • *adj.* **1** of weaving or cloth (*textile industry*). **2** woven (*textile fabrics*).

tex•tu•al /tékschōōəl/ *adj.* of, in, or concerning a text. □□ **tex'tu•al•ly** *adv.*

tex•ture /tékschər/ • *n.* **1** feel or appearance of a surface or substance. **2** arrangement of threads, etc., in textile fabric. **3** quality or style of music, writing, etc., resulting from composition. • *v.tr.* (usu. as **textured** *adj.*) provide with a texture. □□ **tex'tur•al** *adj.* **tex'tur•al•ly** *adv.*

■ *n.* **1, 2** finish, nap, character, grain, weave. **3** nature, structure, fabric.

TGIF • *abbr.* thank god (or goodness) it's Friday.

Th *symb. Chem.* thorium.

Th. *abbr.* Thursday.

-th /th/ *suffix* (also **-eth** /ith/) forming ordinal and fractional numbers from four onward (*fourth, thirtieth*).

Thai /ti/ • *n.* (*pl.* same or **Thais**) **1 a** native or inhabitant of Thailand in SE Asia. **b** person of Thai descent. **2** language of Thailand. • *adj.* of or relating to Thailand or its people or language.

thal•a•mus /thálɔməs/ *n.* (*pl.* **thal•a•mi** /–mī/) *Anat.* either of two masses of gray matter in the forebrain, serving as relay stations for sensory tracts. □□ **tha•lam•ic** /thəlámik, thálɔmik/ *adj.*

tha•lid•o•mide /thəlídəmīd/ *n.* sedative drug found to cause fetal malformation when taken early in pregnancy.

thal•li•um /tháleeəm/ *n. Chem.* rare soft white metallic element. ¶ Symb.: **Tl.** □□ **thal'lic** *adj.* **thal'lous** *adj.*

than /than, thən/ *conj.* **1** introducing a comparison (*you are older than he*). **2** introducing an element of difference (*anyone other than me*).

thane /thayn/ *n. hist.* former English or Scottish noble rank.

thank /thangk/ • *v.tr.* **1** express gratitude to. **2** hold responsible (*you can thank yourself for that*). • *n.* [in *pl.*] **1** gratitude. **2** expression of gratitude (*give thanks*). **3** thank you. □ **thank goodness** (or **God** or **heavens**, etc.) **1** *colloq.* an expression of relief or pleasure. **2** an expression of pious gratitude.

thanks to as the (good or bad) result of (*thanks to my foresight*). **thank you** polite formula expressing gratitude.

■ *v.* 2 blame, credit. • *n.* (*thanks*) 1 appreciation, gratefulness, acknowledgment, recognition. 2 thanksgiving. □ **thanks to** owing to, because of, as a consequence of, through, by virtue of, on account of, *disp.* due to.

thank•ful /thángkfool/ *adj.* 1 grateful; pleased. 2 (of words or acts) expressive of thanks. □□ **thank′ful•ness** *n.*

■ 1 appreciative, indebted, glad, beholden. □□ **thankfulness** see GRATITUDE.

thank•ful•ly /thángkfoolee/ *adv.* 1 in a thankful manner. 2 *disp.* fortunately (*thankfully, nobody was hurt*).

thank•less /thángklis/ *adj.* 1 not expressing or feeling gratitude. 2 (of a task, etc.) giving no pleasure. □□ **thank′less•ly** *adv.* **thank′less•ness** *n.*

■ 1 ungrateful, unappreciative. 2 unappreciated, unrecognized, unrewarded, fruitless, vain, futile.

thanks•giv•ing /thángksgiving/ *n.* 1 expression of gratitude, esp. as a prayer. 2 (**Thanksgiving** or **Thanksgiving Day**) national holiday for giving thanks, the fourth Thursday in November in the US.

■ 1 see GRATITUDE.

that /that/ • *demons.pron.* (*pl.* **those** /thōz/) 1 person or thing indicated, named, or understood (*who is that in the yard?*). 2 (contrasted with *this*) the further or less immediate or obvious, etc., of two (*this is much heavier than that*). 3 action, behavior, or circumstances just observed or mentioned (*don't do that again*). 4 (esp. in relative constructions) the one, the person, etc., specified in some way (*those who have cars*). 5 (*pl.* **that**) used instead of *which* or *whom* to introduce a defining clause (*there is nothing here that matters*). • *demons.adj.* (*pl.* **those** /thōz/) 1 designating the person or thing indicated, named, understood, etc. (cf. sense 1 of *pron.*) (*look at that dog*). 2 contrasted with *this* (cf. sense 2 of *pron.*) (*this is heavier than that one*). • *adv.* 1 to such a degree; so (*have done that much*). 2 *colloq.* very (*not that good*). 3 at which, on which, etc. (*the day that I first met her*). • *conj.* introducing a subordinate clause indicating: 1 statement or hypothesis (*they say that he is better*). 2 purpose (*we live that we may eat*). 3 result (*am so sleepy that I cannot think*). □ **all that** very (*not all that good*). **and all that** and so forth. **that is** (or **that is to say**) formula introducing or following an explanation of a preceding word or words. **that's** *colloq.* you are (*that's a good boy*). **that's that** formula concluding a narrative or discussion or indicating completion of a task. **that will do** no more is needed or desirable.

■ □ **that is (to say)** see NAMELY[1], LIKE *adj.* 1.

thatch /thach/ • *n.* roofing material of straw, reeds, palm leaves, or similar material. • *v.tr.* [also *absol.*] cover with thatch. □□ **thatch′er** *n.*

thaw /thaw/ • *v.* 1 *intr.* (of a frozen thing) pass into a liquid or unfrozen state. 2 *intr.* become warm enough to melt ice, etc. 3 *intr.* become genial. 4 *tr.* cause to thaw. 5 *tr.* make cordial. • *n.* 1 thawing. 2 warmth of weather that thaws.

■ *v.* 1, 4 defrost. 3, 5 soften, become (more) friendly, relax, yield, relent, let oneself go.

the /before a vowel thee, before a consonant thə, when stressed thee/ • *adj.* [called the definite article] 1 denoting one or more persons or things already mentioned, under discussion, implied, or familiar (*gave the man a wave*). 2 describing as unique (*the president*). 3 a [foll. by defining adj.] which is, who are, etc. (*the embarrassed Mr. Smith*). b [foll. by adj. used *absol.*] denoting a class described (*from the sublime to the ridiculous*). 4 best known (with *the* stressed: *no relation to the Hemingway*). 5 indicating a following defining clause or phrase (*the best I can do*). 6 speaking generically (*plays the harp well*). • *adv.* [preceding comparatives in expressions of proportional variation] in or by that (or such a) degree (*the more the merrier*).

theat. *abbr.* 1 theater. 2 theatrical.

the•a•ter /theéətər/ *n.* (esp. *Brit.* **the′a•tre**) 1 a building or outdoor area for dramatic performances. b (in full **mov′ie the•ater**) building for showing movies. 2 writing and production of plays. 3 room or hall for lectures, etc., with seats in tiers. 4 scene or field of action (*theater of war*). □ **theater-goer** frequenter of theaters. **theater-in-the-round** performance on a stage surrounded by spectators.

■ 1 a playhouse, (opera) house, (music) hall, auditorium, amphitheater, colosseum, hippodrome. 2 drama, stagecraft, acting, performing; the stage, show business, *colloq.* showbiz. 4 area, arena, sphere of action, setting, site.

the•at•ric /theeátrik/ • *adj.* = THEATRICAL. • *n.* [in *pl.*] theatrical actions.

the•at•ri•cal /theeátrikəl/ • *adj.* 1 of or for the theater; of acting or actors. 2 calculated for effect; showy. • *n.* [in *pl.*] dramatic performances (*amateur theatricals*). □□ **the•at′ri•cal•ism** *n.* **the•at•ri•cal•i•ty** /-kálitee/ *n.* **the•at′ri•cal•ly** *adv.*

■ *adj.* 1 stage, thespian; repertory. 2 overdone, melodramatic, exaggerated, overacted, affected, artificial, *colloq.* phony. • *n.* □□ **theatricalism, theatricality** see DRAMA 4.

thee /thee/ *pron. objective case of* THOU[1].

theft /theft/ *n.* act of stealing.

■ robbery, larceny, pilfering, filching, shoplifting, thievery, thieving, embezzlement, misappropriation, fraud, *colloq.* lifting, swiping, rip-off, *sl.* heist.

their /thair/ *poss.pron.* [attrib.] of or belonging to them.

theirs /thairz/ *poss.pron.* the one or ones belonging to or associated with them (*theirs are over here*). □ **of theirs** of or belonging to them (*friend of theirs*).

the•ism /theéizəm/ *n.* belief in gods or a god. □□ **the′ist** *n.* **the•is′tic** *adj.*

them /them, thəm/ • *pron.* 1 *objective case of*

THEY (*I saw them*). **2** *colloq.* they (*it's them again*). • *adj. sl.* or *dial.* those (*them bones*).

theme /theem/ *n.* **1** subject, topic, or recurrent focus. **2** *Mus.* prominent melody in a composition. **3** school exercise, esp. an essay, on a given subject. □ **theme park** amusement park organized around a unifying idea. **theme song 1** recurrent melody in a musical. **2** signature tune. □□ **the•mat•ic** /–mátik/ *adj.* **the•mat'i•cal•ly** *adv.*

■ **1** idea, notion, concept, gist, essence, issue. **2** see MOTIF. **3** paper, composition, article, story, piece, thesis, dissertation.

them•selves /themsélvz, –thəm–/ *pron.* **1 a** *emphat. form* of THEY or THEM. **b** *refl. form* of THEM. **2** in their normal state of body or mind (*are quite themselves again*).

■ **2** see NORMAL *adj.* 2.

then /then/ • *adv.* **1** at that time. **2 a** next; after that. **b** and also. **3 a** in that case (*then you should have said so*). **b** (implying grudging or impatient concession) if you must have it so. **c** used parenthetically to resume a narrative, etc. (*finally, then, he knocked on the door*). • *adj.* such at the time in question (*the then senator*). • *n.* that time (*until then*). □ **then and there** immediately and on the spot.

■ *adv.* **2 b** see FURTHER *adv.* **3 a** see THUS 2. □ **then and there** see *immediately* (IMMEDIATE).

thence /thens/ *adv.* **1** from that place. **2** for that reason.

thence•forth /thénsfáwrth/ *adv.* from that time onward.

thence•for•ward /thénsfáwrward/ *adv. formal* thenceforth.

theo– /thee-o/ *comb. form* God or gods.

the•o•cen•tric /thee-əséntrik/ *adj.* having God or a god as its center.

the•oc•ra•cy /thee-ókrəsee/ *n.* (*pl.* **–cies**) form of government by God or a god directly or through a priestly order, etc. □□ **the•o•crat** /thee-əkrat/ *n.* **the•o•crat•ic** *adj.* **the•o•crat'i•cal•ly** *adv.*

the•od•o•lite /thee-ódəlīt/ *n.* surveying instrument for measuring angles with a rotating telescope. □□ **the•od•o•lit•ic** /–lítik/ *adj.*

theol. *abbr.* **1** theological. **2** theology.

the•o•lo•gian /thee-əlójən/ *n.* person trained in theology.

the•ol•o•gy /thee-óləjee/ *n.* (*pl.* **–gies**) study or system of theistic (esp. Christian) religion. □□ **the•o•log•i•cal** /thee-əlójikəl/ *adj.* **the•o•log'i•cal•ly** *adv.* **the•ol'o•gist** *n.*

the•o•rem /thee-ərəm, theerəm/ *n.* esp. *Math.* **1** general proposition not self-evident but proved by reasoning. **2** rule in algebra, etc., esp. one expressed by symbols or formulae.

■ **1** hypothesis, assumption, conjecture, statement, deduction, thesis, postulate. **2** principle.

the•o•ret•ic /thee-ərétik/ *adj.* = THEORETICAL.

the•o•ret•i•cal /thee-ərétikəl/ *adj.* **1** concerned with knowledge but not with its practical application. **2** based on theory rather than experience. □□ **the•o•ret'i•cal•ly** *adv.*

■ **1** impractical, pure, ideal, abstract, academic. **2** hypothetical, conjectural, specula-

tive, unproven. □□ **theoretically** see *ideally* (IDEAL).

the•o•rist /thee-ərist, theerist/ *n.* holder or inventor of a theory or theories.

■ speculator, hypothesizer, philosopher.

the•o•rize /thee-ərīz, theerīz/ *v.intr.* evolve or indulge in theories. □□ **the•o•riz•er** *n.*

■ hypothesize, conjecture, speculate, surmise, guess.

the•o•ry /thee-əree, theeree/ *n.* (*pl.* **–ries**) **1** supposition or system of ideas explaining something, esp. one based on general principles. **2** speculative (esp. fanciful) view. **3** sphere of abstract knowledge (*works well in theory, but not in practice?*). **4** exposition of the principles of a science, etc. **5** *Math.* collection of propositions.

■ **1** see DOCTRINE 2. **2** see VIEW *n.* 4, FEELING 4a. **4** see LAW 6.

the•os•o•phy /thee-ósəfee/ *n.* (*pl.* **–phies**) any of various philosophies professing to achieve knowledge of God by spiritual ecstasy, direct intuition, or special individual relations, esp. a modern movement following Hindu and Buddhist teachings and seeking universal brotherhood. □□ **the•o•soph•i•cal** /–sóf–/ *adj.* **the•o•soph'i•cal•ly** *adv.* **the•os'o•phist** *n.*

ther•a•peu•tic /thérəpyóotik/ *adj.* **1** of, for, or contributing to the cure of disease. **2** healing; soothing. □□ **ther•a•peu'ti•cal•ly** *adv.*

■ **1** curative, remedial, restorative, corrective, medicinal. **2** healthy, beneficial, salubrious.

ther•a•peu•tics /thérəpyóotiks/ *n.pl.* [usu. treated as *sing.*] branch of medicine concerned with cures and remedies.

ther•a•py /thérəpee/ *n.* (*pl.* **–pies**) nonsurgical treatment of physical or mental disorders. □□ **ther'a•pist** *n.*

■ healing, cure; treatment, remedy; analysis, counseling. ■ **therapist** practitioner; psychologist, analyst, psychiatrist, psychoanalyst, counselor, adviser, *sl.* shrink.

there /thair/ • *adv.* **1** in, at, or to that place or position (*lived there for years*). **2** at that point (*in speech, performance, writing, etc.*). **3** in that respect (*I agree with you there*). **4** used for emphasis in calling attention (*you there!*). **5** used to indicate the fact or existence of something (*there is a house on the corner*). • *n.* that place (*lives near there*). • *int.* **1** expressing confirmation, triumph, dismay, etc. (*there! what did I tell you?*). **2** used to soothe a child, etc. (*there, there, now*). □ **so there** *colloq.* that is my final decision (*whether you like it or not*). **there you are** (or **go**) *colloq.* **1** this is what you wanted, etc. **2** expressing confirmation, triumph, resignation, etc.

there•abouts /tháirəbowts/ *adv.* (also **there'a•bout**) **1** near that place. **2** near that number, quantity, etc.

there•af•ter /tháiráftər/ *adv.* after that.

there•by /tháirbí/ *adv.* by that means; as a result of that.

there•fore /tháirfawr/ *adv.* for that reason; consequently.

■ so, as a result, hence, ergo, accordingly, then, that being so *or* the case.

there•in /tháirín/ *adv.* **1** in that place, etc. **2** in that respect.

there•of /tháirúv, –óv/ *adv.* of that or it.

there•to /tháirtóō/ *adv.* **1** to that or it. **2** in addition; to boot.

there•up•on /tháirəpón, –páwn/ *adv.* **1** in consequence of that. **2** soon or immediately after that.

ther•mal /thə́rməl/ • *adj.* **1** of, for, or producing heat. **2** promoting the retention of heat (*thermal underwear*). • *n.* rising current of heated air. □ **British thermal unit** amount of heat needed to raise 1 lb. of water at maximum density through one degree Fahrenheit, equivalent to 1.055×10^3 joules. □□ **ther′mal•ly** *adv.*

thermo- /thə́rmō/ *comb. form* denoting heat.

ther•mo•dy•nam•ics /thə́rmōdīnámiks/ *n.pl.* [usu. treated as *sing.*] science of the relations between heat and other forms of energy. □□ **ther•mo•dy•nam′ic** *adj.* **ther•mo•dy•nam′i•cal•ly** *adv.*

ther•mom•e•ter /thərmómitər/ *n.* instrument for measuring temperature, esp. a graduated glass tube containing mercury or alcohol.

ther•mo•nu•cle•ar /thə́rmōnōōkleeər, –nyōō–/ *adj.* **1** relating to nuclear reactions that occur only at very high temperatures. **2** (of weapons) using thermonuclear reactions.

ther•mo•plas•tic /thə́rmōplástik/ • *adj.* (of a substance) that becomes plastic on heating and hardens on cooling. • *n.* thermoplastic substance.

ther•mos /thə́rməs/ *n.* (in full **ther′mos bot′tle** or **flask**) *propr.* bottle, etc., with a double wall enclosing a vacuum, used to keep liquids hot or cold.

ther•mo•stat /thə́rməstat/ *n.* device that automatically regulates or responds to temperature. □□ **ther•mo•stat′ic** *adj.* **ther•mo•stat′i•cal•ly** *adv.*

the•sau•rus /thisáwrəs/ *n.* (*pl.* **the•sau•ri** /–rī/ or **the•sau•rus•es**) book that categorizes or lists synonyms and related concepts.

these *pl.* of THIS.

the•sis /théesis/ *n.* (*pl.* **the•ses** /–seez/) **1** proposition to be maintained or proved. **2** dissertation, esp. by a candidate for a degree.

■ **1** argument, theory, contention, belief, idea, premise, assumption, view, assertion, precept, opinion, notion, theorem, axiom, postulate, hypothesis. **2** treatise, tract, monograph, paper, essay, discourse.

thes•pi•an /théspeeən/ • *adj.* of drama. • *n.* actor or actress.

■ *adj.* dramatic, theatric(al). • *n.* performer, trouper, player; star; *sl.* ham.

the•ta /tháytə, thée–/ *n.* eighth letter of the Greek alphabet (Θ, ϑ).

they /thay/ *pron.* (*obj.* **them**; *poss.* **their, theirs**) **1** *pl.* of HE, SHE, IT. **2** people in general (*they say we are wrong*). **3** those in authority (*they have raised the fees*).

they'd /thayd/ *contr.* **1** they had. **2** they would.

they'll /thayl/ *contr.* **1** they will. **2** they shall.

they're /thair/ *contr.* they are.

they've /thayv/ *contr.* they have.

thi•a•mine /thíəmin, –meen/ *n.* (also **thi′a•min**) vitamin of the B complex, found in unrefined cereals, beans, and liver, a deficiency of which causes beriberi. (Also called **vitamin B₁**).

thick /thik/ • *adj.* **1 a** of great or specified extent between opposite surfaces (*thick wall*). **b** of large diameter. **2** (of a line, etc.) broad; not fine. **3** arranged closely; crowded together; dense. **4** densely covered or filled (*air thick with snow*). **5 a** firm in consistency; containing much solid matter. **b** made of thick material. **6** muddy; cloudy; impenetrable by sight (*thick darkness*). **7** *colloq.* stupid; dull. **8 a** (of a voice) indistinct. **b** (of an accent) pronounced; exaggerated. **9** *colloq.* intimate or very friendly (esp. *thick as thieves*). • *n.* thick part of anything. • *adv.* thickly (*snow was falling thick*). □ **in the thick of 1** at the busiest part of. **2** heavily occupied with. **thick-skinned** not sensitive to reproach or criticism. **through thick and thin** in spite of all difficulties. □□ **thick′ish** *adj.* **thick′ly** *adv.*

■ *adj.* **1** ample, substantial, chunky, stout. **2** fat, wide. **3** compact, condensed, compressed, packed; abundant, plentiful; lush. **4** deep, chock-full, teeming, swarming, alive, brimming. **5 a** viscous, concentrated, jelled; stiff. **b** heavy, bulky. **6** soupy, murky, misty, foggy, smoggy, smoky, opaque, obscure, hazy. **7** thickheaded, slow-witted, obtuse; dim-witted. **8 a** guttural, hoarse, throaty, raspy, rough, husky, grating, gravelly. **b** marked, obvious, noticeable. **9** close, inseparable, *colloq.* chummy. • *n.* core, heart, center, middle, focus, midst. □ **in the thick of 1** see AMID. **thick-skinned** callous, numb(ed), steeled, hardened, tough, unfeeling, impervious.

thick•en /thíkən/ *v.* **1** *tr. & intr.* make or become thick or thicker. **2** *intr.* become more complicated (*the plot thickens*). □□ **thick′en•er** *n.*

■ **1** coagulate, clot, congeal, gel, set, solidify, stiffen, harden, firm up, cake, *colloq.* jell.

thick•et /thíkit/ *n.* tangle of shrubs or trees.

■ copse, brake, grove, coppice, covert, wood, brush.

thick•head•ed /thík-hedid/ *n. adj. colloq.* stupid. □□ **thick′head•ed•ness** *n.*

■ see STUPID *adj.* 1, 3.

thick•ness /thíknis/ *n.* **1** being thick. **2** extent to which a thing is thick. **3** layer of material (*three thicknesses of cardboard*).

■ **1** see BODY¹ *n.* 7, *stupidity* (STUPID). **2** see BREADTH 1. **3** see PLY 1.

thick•set /thíksét/ *adj.* **1** heavily or solidly built. **2** set or growing close together.

■ **1** see STOCKY. **2** see THICK *adj.* 3.

thief /theef/ *n.* (*pl.* **thieves** /theevz/) person who steals, esp. secretly.

■ robber, burglar, shoplifter; embezzler; pickpocket, purse snatcher, bandit, outlaw; pirate; cheat, swindler, *sl.* con man, con artist.

thieve /theev/ *v.* **1** *intr.* be a thief. **2** *tr.* steal (a thing). □□ **thiev′ish** adj. **thiev′ish•ly** adv. **thiev′ish•ness** n.

thiev•er•y /ˈθēvəree/ n. act or practice of stealing.

■ see THEFT.

thieves pl. of THIEF.

thigh /thī/ n. part of the leg between the hip and the knee.

thim•ble /ˈθimbəl/ n. metal or plastic cap worn to protect the finger and push the needle in sewing. □□ **thim′ble•ful** (pl. **–fuls**) n.

thin /thin/ • adj. (**thin•ner**, **thin•nest**) **1** having opposite surfaces close together; of small thickness. **2** (of a line, etc.) narrow or fine. **3** made of thin material. **4** lean; not plump. **5** not dense or copious (thin hair). **6** of slight consistency. **7** weak; lacking an important ingredient (thin blood, thin voice). **8** (of an excuse, etc.) flimsy or transparent. • adv. thinly (cut the bread very thin). • v. (**thinned**, **thin•ning**) **1** tr. & intr. make or become thin or thinner. **2** tr. & intr. make or become less dense or crowded or numerous. **3** tr. remove some of a crop to improve the growth of the rest. □ **thin air** state of invisibility or nonexistence (vanished into thin air). **thin on top** balding. **thin-skinned** sensitive to reproach or criticism. □□ **thin′ly** adv. **thin′ness** n. **thin′nish** adj.

■ adj. **2** threadlike. **3** airy, filmy, diaphanous, gossamer, sheer, light, delicate, chiffon, silky, silken, translucent, see-through. **4** slim, slender, skinny, wispy, willowy, scrawny. **5** sparse, scant, slight, skimpy, meager, paltry. **6** watery, runny, dilute(d). **8** feeble, tenuous, poor, lame. • v. **1** trim, prune, sharpen, taper. **2** thin out, decrease, reduce, diminish. □ **thin-skinned** see SENSITIVE adj. **2**.

SYNONYM STUDY: thin

GAUNT, LEAN, SKINNY, SLENDER, SPARE, SVELTE. You can't be too rich or too **thin**, but you can be too **skinny**. *Thin* describes someone whose weight is naturally low in proportion to his or her height, although it may also imply that the person is underweight (she looked pale and thin after her operation). *Skinny* is a more blunt and derogatory term for someone who is too *thin*, and it often implies underdevelopment (a skinny little boy; a tall, skinny fashion model). Most women would rather be called **slender**, which combines thinness with gracefulness and good proportions (the slender legs of a Queen Anne table), or better yet, **svelte**, a complimentary term that implies a slim, elegant figure (after six months of dieting, she looked so svelte I hardly recognized her). **Lean** and **spare** are used to describe people who are naturally *thin*, although *spare* suggests a more muscular leanness (a tall, spare man who looked like Abraham Lincoln). **Gaunt**, on the other hand, means so *thin* that the angularity of the bones can be seen beneath the skin (looking gaunt after her latest bout with cancer).

thine /thīn/ poss.pron. archaic or dial. **1** [predic. or absol.] of or belonging to thee. **2** [attrib. before a vowel] = THY.

thing /thing/ n. **1** entity, action, etc.,

that is or may be thought about or perceived. **2** inanimate material object. **3** unspecified item (a few things to buy). **4** act, idea, or utterance (silly thing to do). **5** event (unfortunate thing to happen). **6** colloq. **a** one's special interest (not my thing). **b** obsession, fear, or prejudice (have a thing about spiders). **7** colloq. fashion (latest thing in footwear). **8** [in pl.] personal belongings or clothing (where are my things?). **9** [in pl.] affairs in general (not in the nature of things). **10** [in pl.] circumstances; conditions (things look good). □ **do things to** colloq. affect remarkably. **make a thing of** colloq. cause a fuss about. **one** (or **just one**) **of those things** colloq. something unavoidable or to be accepted.

■ **2, 3** device, gadget, article, commodity, mechanism, contrivance, apparatus, instrument, utensil; whatnot, doodad, colloq. thingamajig, thingamabob, sl. gizmo. **4** deed, activity, proceeding; chore, task, job, responsibility; statement; subject, detail, feature, aspect, element, factor, point, particular. **5** happening, circumstance, occurrence, incident. **6** concern, fancy, love, passion, mania, fetish; see also BAG n. **6 b** fixation; phobia, loathing, dislike, aversion, sl. hangup; bias. **7** fad, trend, mode, rage. **8** (things) luggage, baggage, possessions, paraphernalia, effects, goods, stuff, junk, colloq. gear. **9** (things) matters, business, concerns. **10** (things) prospects; life.

thing•a•ma•bob /ˈθingəməbob/ n. (also **thing•a•ma•jig** /ˈθingəməjig/) colloq. person or thing whose name one has forgotten or does not know, etc.

■ see THING 2, 3.

think /thingk/ v. (past and past part. **thought** /thawt/) **1** tr. [foll. by that + clause] be of the opinion **2** tr. [foll. by that + clause or to + infin.] judge or consider (is thought to be a fraud). **3** intr. exercise the mind (let me think). **4** tr. [foll. by of or about] consider, imagine. **5** tr. have a half-formed intention (I think I'll stay). **6** tr. [foll. by to + infin.] remember (did not think to lock the door). □ **think again** revise one's plans or opinions. **think out loud** (or **aloud**) utter one's thoughts as soon as they occur. **think back to** recall (a past event or time). **think better of** change one's mind after reconsideration. **think for oneself** have an independent mind or attitude. **think little** (or **nothing**) **of** consider to be insignificant or unremarkable. **think much** (or **highly**) **of** have a high opinion of. **think out** consider carefully. **think over** reflect upon in order to reach a decision. **think tank** body of experts providing advice and ideas on specific national or commercial problems. **think through** reflect fully upon (a problem, etc.). **think twice** use careful consideration, avoid hasty action, etc. **think up** colloq. devise. □□ **think′er** n.

■ v. **1** see BELIEVE **2**. **2** reckon, regard as, characterize as, view as, assume, deem. **3** contemplate, cogitate, ruminate, reflect, meditate, ponder, deliberate, reason, concentrate, use one's head. **4** weigh, mull over, have in mind, propose. **5** expect, dream, fancy, fantasize, suppose. □ **think back to** remember, recollect, call *or* bring to mind. **think little** (or **nothing**) **of** see UNDERESTIMATE *v.* **think much** (or **highly**) **of** see RESPECT *v.* 1. **think through** see PUZZLE *v.* 2. **think twice** see SCRUPLE *v.*; (*think twice about*) see SCRUPLE *v.* **think up** think of, concoct, contrive, come up with, invent, conceive (of), dream up, create, make up, improvise, mastermind. □□ **thinker** sage, wise man, philosopher, scholar, intellectual.

think•ing /thíngkíng/ • *adj.* using thought or rational judgment. • *n.* opinion or judgment. □ **put on one's thinking cap** *colloq.* meditate on a problem.
■ *adj.* sensible, intelligent, reasoning, reasonable; contemplative, reflective, philosophical, thoughtful. • *n.* belief, thought, point of view, viewpoint, assessment, evaluation, theory, reasoning, conclusion, idea, philosophy, outlook.

thin•ner /thínǝr/ *n.* volatile liquid used to dilute paint, etc.

third /thǝrd/ • *n.* **1** next after second. **2** each of three equal parts of a thing. • *adj.* that is the third. □ **third-class** *adj.* lower quality; inferior. **third degree** long and severe questioning, esp. by police to obtain information or a confession. **third-degree** *Med.* denoting burns of the most severe kind, affecting lower layers of tissue. **third person** *Gram.* see PERSON. **third-rate** inferior; very poor in quality. **Third World** [usu. prec. by *the*] developing countries of Asia, Africa, and Latin America. □□ **third'ly** *adv.*

thirst /thǝrst/ • *n.* **1** need to drink liquid; feeling of discomfort caused by this. **2** strong desire; craving (*thirst for power*). • *v.intr.* **1** feel thirst. **2** have a strong desire. □□ **thirst'y** *adj.* **thirst'i•ly** *adv.* **thirst'i•ness** *n.*
■ *n.* **1** thirstiness, dryness. **2** appetite, hunger, lust, passion, *colloq.* yen. • *v.* **2** (*thirst for* or *after*) crave, want, long for, yearn for, wish for. □□ **thirsty** parched, dry, dehydrated, arid; desirous, avid, eager, ravenous, voracious, burning, greedy, itching.

thir•teen /thǝrtéen/ • *n.* **1** one more than twelve, or three more than ten. **2** symbol for this (13, xiii, XIII). • *adj.* that amount to thirteen. □□ **thir'teenth** *adj. & n.*

thir•ty /thǝrtee/ *n.* (*pl.* **-ties**) **1** product of three and ten. **2** symbol for this (30, xxx, XXX). **3** [in *pl.*] numbers from 30 to 39, esp. the years of a century or of a person's life. □ **thirty-first, -second,** etc., ordinal numbers between thirtieth and fortieth. **thirty-one, -two,** etc., cardinal numbers between thirty and forty. □□ **thir'ti•eth** *adj. & n.*

this /this/ • *demons.pron.* (*pl.* **these** /theez/) **1** person or thing close at hand or indicated or already known or understood (*this is my cousin*). **2** (contrasted with *that*) person or thing nearer to hand or more immediately in mind. • *demons.adj.* (*pl.* **these** /theez/) **1** des-

ignating the person or thing close at hand, etc. (cf. senses 1, 2 of *pron.*). **2** (of time): the present or current (*am busy all this week*). **3** *colloq.* (in narrative) designating a person or thing previously unspecified (*then up came this policeman*). • *adv.* to this degree or extent (*knew him when he was this high*). □ **this and that** *colloq.* various unspecified things.

this•tle /thísǝl/ *n.* prickly plant, usu. with globular heads of purple flowers.

thith•er /thíthǝr, thí-/ *adv. archaic* to or toward that place.

tho' var. of THOUGH.

thong /thong/ *n.* narrow strip of hide or leather.

tho•rax /tháwraks, thôr-/ *n.* (*pl.* **tho•rax•es** or **tho•ra•ces** /tháwrǝseez/) *Anat. & Zool.* part of the trunk between the neck and the abdomen. □□ **tho•rac•ic** /thawrásik/ *adj.*

tho•ri•um /tháwreeǝm, thôr-/ *n. Chem.* radioactive metallic element. ¶Symb.: **Th.**

thorn /thawrn/ *n.* **1** sharp-pointed projection on a plant. **2** thorn-bearing shrub or tree. □ **thorn in one's side** (or **flesh**) constant annoyance.
■ **1** barb, spine, brier, burr, bramble. □ **thorn in one's side** (or **flesh**) bother, nuisance, vexation, pest, affliction, irritant, bane, *colloq.* headache, pain in the neck.

thorn•y /tháwrnee/ *adj.* (**thorn•i•er, thorn•i•est**) **1** having many thorns. **2** (of a subject) hard to handle without offense; problematic. □□ **thorn'i•ly** *adv.* **thorn'i•ness** *n.*
■ **1** prickly, barbed, spiny. **2** difficult, hard, tough, ticklish, delicate, complex, complicated, involved, tricky, troublesome, *colloq.* sticky.

thor•ough /thúrō/ *adj.* **1** complete and unqualified; not superficial. **2** acting or done with great care and completeness. **3** absolute (*thorough nuisance*). □□ **thor'ough•ly** *adv.* **thor'ough•ness** *n.*
■ **1** extensive, exhaustive, detailed, indepth, comprehensive, full, all-inclusive, all-embracing, profound. **2** painstaking, meticulous, careful, scrupulous, particular, conscientious, methodical, intensive. **3** thoroughgoing, downright, perfect, total, real, unmitigated, out-and-out, sheer, utter. □□ **thoroughly** throughout, from top to bottom, from stem to stern, backward and forward, in every nook and cranny; wholly, fully, definitely, quite.

thor•ough•bred /thúrōbred, thôrǝ-, thúr-/ • *adj.* of pure breeding. • *n.* thoroughbred animal, esp. a horse.

thor•ough•fare /thúrōfair, thôrǝ-, thúr-/ *n.* road or path open at both ends, esp. for traffic.
■ see ROAD 1, PATH 1, PASSAGEWAY.

thor•ough•go•ing /thúrōgóing, thôrǝ-, thúr-/ *adj.* complete; uncompromising; not superficial.
■ see EXHAUSTIVE, *out-and-out* 1.

those pl. of THAT.

thou¹ /thow/ *pron. archaic* or *dial.* (*obj.* **thee** /thee/; *poss.* **thy** or **thine**; *pl.* **ye** or **you**) second person singular pronoun.

thou² /thow/ *n.* (*pl.* same or **thous**) *colloq.* thousand.

though /thō/ • *conj.* **1** in spite of being; despite the fact that. **2** [introducing a possibility] even if (*ask him, though he may refuse*). **3** and yet; nevertheless. • *adv. colloq.* however; all the same (*I wish you had told me, though*).

■ *conj.* **1** although, granted, allowing *or* admitting that. **2** supposing, even though. • *adv.* nonetheless, nevertheless, yet, still, even so, be that as it may, notwithstanding, *colloq.* still and all.

thought¹ /thawt/ *n.* **1** process or power of thinking; the faculty of reason. **2** way of thinking associated with a particular time, people, etc. (*medieval European thought*). **3** reflection; consideration; regard. **4** idea or piece of reasoning produced by thinking. **5** [usu. in *pl.*] what one is thinking; one's opinion. See synonym study at IDEA.

■ **1** intellect, intelligence, rationality. **2** see THINKING *n.* **3** meditation, contemplation, cogitation, musing, pondering, rumination, introspection; concentration, deliberation; thoughtfulness, care, concern, compassion, kindness, attention. **4** notion, observation, conclusion, conjecture, conception, brainstorm. **5** see OPINION 1, 3.

thought² *past* and *past part.* of THINK.

thought·ful /tháwtfool/ *adj.* **1** engaged in or given to meditation. **2** (of a book, writer, remark, etc.) giving signs of serious thought. **3** considerate. □□ **thought′ful·ly** *adv.* **thought′ful·ness** *n.*

■ **1** contemplative, pensive, reflective, pondering. **2** see THINKING *adj.* **3** kind, compassionate, caring, tender, sympathetic, concerned, helpful, prudent, cautious, mindful, careful. □□ **thoughtfully** see KINDLY 1. **thoughtfulness** see CONSIDERATION 2.

thought·less /tháwtlis/ *adj.* **1** careless of consequences *or* of others' feelings. **2** due to lack of thought. □□ **thought′less·ly** *adv.* **thought′less·ness** *n.*

■ **1** unthinking, inconsiderate, rude, impolite, insensitive, tactless, undiplomatic, uncaring, unfeeling; remiss, absentminded, forgetful, inattentive. **2** rash, imprudent, negligent, neglectful, reckless; foolish, stupid, silly. □□ **thoughtlessly** see *blindly* (BLIND). **thoughtlessness** see *imprudence* (IMPRUDENT).

thou·sand /thówzənd/ • *n.* (*pl.* **thou·sands** or (in sense 1) **thou·sand**) [in *sing.* prec. by *a* or *one*] **1** product of a hundred and ten. **2** symbol for this (1,000; m; M). **3** [in *sing.* or *pl.*] *colloq.* large number. • *adj.* that amount to a thousand. □□ **thou′sand·fold** *adj. & adv.* **thou′sandth** *adj. & n.*

■ *n.* **3** (*thousands*) see SCORE *n.* 3.

thrall /thrawl/ *n. literary* **1** slave. **2** bondage; slavery (*in thrall*). □□ **thrall′dom** *n.* (also **thral′dom**)

thrash /thrash/ • *v.* **1** *tr.* beat or whip severely. **2** *tr.* defeat thoroughly in a contest. **3** *intr.* (of a paddle wheel, branch, etc.) act like a flail; deliver repeated blows. **4** *intr.* [foll. by *about, around*] move or fling the limbs about violently or in panic. **5** *tr.* = THRESH 1. • *n.* act of thrashing. □ **thrash out** discuss to a conclusion. □□ **thrash′ing** *n.*

■ *v.* **1** see BEAT *v.* 1. **2** see DEFEAT *v.* 1. **4** (*thrash about* or *around*) see FLAP *v.* 1. • *n.* see *thrashing* (THRASH) below. □ **thrash out** see DEBATE *v.*, RESOLVE *v.* 1. □□ **thrashing** beating, drubbing, whipping, flogging, caning, lashing, pounding; punishment, chastisement, discipline, *sl.* tanning.

thrash·er /thráshər/ *n.* long-tailed N. American thrushlike birds.

thread /thred/ • *n.* **1 a** spun cotton, silk, glass, etc.; yarn. **b** length of this. **2** thin cord of twisted yarns used esp. in sewing and weaving. **3** continuous aspect of a thing (*the thread of life*). **4** spiral ridge of a screw. **5** [in *pl.*] *sl.* clothes. • *v. tr.* **1** pass a thread through (a needle). **2** put (beads) on a thread. **3** insert (a strip of film, tape, etc.) into equipment. **4** make (one's way) carefully through a crowded place, etc. □ **hang by a thread** be in a precarious state, position, etc. □□ **thread′er** *n.* **thread′like** *adj.*

■ *n.* **1** fiber, filament, strand. **2** string, line, twine. **3** theme, plot, storyline, drift, direction. **5** (*threads*) see CLOTHES. • *v.* **2** string, lace. **4** (*thread one's way*) file, weave, wind (one's way).

thread·bare /thrédbair/ *adj.* **1** (of cloth) with the nap worn and the thread visible. **2** (of a person) wearing such clothes. **3 a** hackneyed. **b** feeble (*threadbare excuse*).

■ **1** frayed, ragged, moth-eaten, tattered, shabby. **2** scruffy, seedy, slovenly. **3 a** trite, stale, tired, timeworn, banal, dull, tedious, tiresome, *colloq.* old hat. **b** see THIN *adj.* 8.

throat /thrōt/ *n.* **1** declaration of an intention to punish or hurt. **2** imminence of something undesirable (*threat of war*). **3** person or thing as a likely cause of harm, etc.

■ **1** intimidation, warning. **2** omen, presage, portent, foreboding, forewarning. **3** menace, danger, hazard, peril.

threat·en /thrét'n/ *v. tr.* **1 a** make a threat or threats against. **b** constitute a threat to. **2** be a sign of (something undesirable). **3** [also *absol.*] present imminent danger of (*clouds were threatening rain*). □□ **threat′en·er** *n.* **threat′en·ing** *adj.* **threat′en·ing·ly** *adv.*

■ **1 a** intimidate, terrorize, bully, warn, caution. **b** imperil, put at risk, endanger, jeopardize. **3** portend, forebode. □ **threatening** menacing; ominous, sinister, looming, impending.

three /three/ • *n.* **1 a** one more than two, or seven less than ten. **b** symbol for this (3, iii, III). • *adj.* that amount to three. □ **three-dimensional** having or appearing to have length, breadth, and depth. **three-ring circus** 1 circus with three rings for simultaneous performances. 2 extravagant display. **the three Rs** reading, writing (*joc.* 'riting), and arithmetic (*joc.* 'rithmetic).

three·fold /thréefōld/ *adj. & adv.* **1** three times as much or as many. **2** consisting of three parts.

three·score /thréeskáwr/ *n. archaic* sixty.

three·some /thréesəm/ *n.* group of three persons.

thren·o·dy /thrénədee/ *n.* (also **thre·node**

/thrénōd/) (*pl.* **–dies** or **thre•nodes**) song of lamentation or mourning.

thresh /thresh/ *v.* **1** *tr.* beat out or separate grain from (wheat, etc.). **2** *intr.* = THRASH *v.* 4. **3** *tr.* [foll. by *over*] analyze (a problem, etc.) in search of a solution. □ **thresh out** = *thrash out.* □□ **thresh′er** *n.*

thresh•old /thréshōld, thrésh-hōld/ *n.* **1** strip of wood or stone forming the bottom of a doorway. **2** point of entry or beginning (*threshold of a new century*). **3** limit (*pain threshold*).

■ **1** sill, doorsill, doorstep; entrance. **2** brink, verge, edge, beginning, inception, outset, start, dawn.

threw *past of* THROW.

thrice /thrīs/ *adv. archaic* or *literary* **1** three times. **2** [esp. in *comb.*] highly (*thrice-blessed*).

thrift /thrift/ *n.* frugality. □ **thrift shop** store selling secondhand items.

■ economy, care, prudence.

thrift•y /thríftee/ *adj.* (**thrift•i•er**, **thrift•i•est**) economical; frugal. See synonym study at ECONOMICAL. □□ **thrift′i•ly** *adv.* **thrift′i•ness** *n.*

■ careful, prudent, sparing, scrimping, skimping; closefisted, tightfisted, niggardly, stingy, miserly, penny-pinching, cheap. □□ **thriftiness** see THRIFT.

thrill /thril/ • *n.* **1 a** wave or nervous tremor of emotion or sensation (*thrill of joy*). **b** thrilling experience. **2** throb; pulsation. • *v.* **1** *intr. & tr.* feel or cause to feel a thrill. **2** *intr.* quiver or throb with or as with emotion. □ **thrills and spills** excitement of potentially dangerous activities. □□ **thrill′ing** *adj.* **thrill′ing•ly** *adv.*

■ *n.* **1a** excitement, shiver, tingle, tremble, flutter, *colloq.* kick, *sl.* buzz. **2** quiver, shudder, vibration. • *v.* **1** (*tr.*) stimulate, electrify, titillate, impassion, arouse. □□ **thrilling** stirring, moving, rousing, gripping, wild, sensational, riveting, spine-tingling.

thrill•er /thrílər/ *n.* exciting or sensational story or play, etc., esp. one involving crime or espionage.

thrive /thrīv/ *v.intr.* (*past* **throve** /thrōv/ or **thrived**; *past part.* **thriv•en** /thrívən/ or **thrived**) **1** prosper; flourish. **2** grow rich. **3** grow vigorously.

■ **1** succeed, boom, advance, do well. **3** bloom, blossom, develop, ripen.

throat /thrōt/ *n.* **1 a** windpipe or gullet. **b** front part of the neck. **2** narrow passage, entrance, or exit. □ **cut one's own throat** bring about one's own downfall. **ram down a person's throat** force (a thing) on a person's attention. □□ **–throat′ed** *adj.* [in *comb.*].

throat•y /thrōtee/ *adj.* (**throat•i•er**, **throat•i•est**) (of a voice) hoarsely resonant. □□ **throat′i•ly** *adv.* **throat′i•ness** *n.*

■ see GRUFF 1a, THICK *adj.* 8a.

throb /throb/ • *v.intr.* (**throbbed**, **throb•bing**) **1** pulsate, esp. with more than the usual force or rapidity. **2** vibrate with a persistent rhythm or with emotion. • *n.* **1** throbbing. **2** (esp. violent) pulsation.

■ *v.* see PULSATE, ACHE *v.* 1, VIBRATE 1–3. • *n.* see PULSE *n.* 5, THRILL *n.* 2.

throe /thrō/ *n.* [usu. in *pl.*] **1** violent pang, esp. of childbirth or death. **2** anguish. □ **in the throes of** struggling with the task of.

■ **1** pain, spasm; fit, seizure, convulsion. **2** (*throes*) struggle, turmoil, tumult; see also AGONY 2.

throm•bo•sis /thrombōsis/ *n.* (*pl.* **throm•bo•ses** /–seez/) coagulation of the blood in a blood vessel or organ. □□ **throm•bot•ic** /–bótik/ *adj.*

throne /thrōn/ *n.* **1** chair of state for a sovereign, bishop, etc. **2** sovereign power (*came to the throne*).

throng /thrawng, throng/ • *n.* crowd, esp. of people. • *v.* **1** *intr.* come in great numbers. **2** *tr.* flock into or crowd around; fill with or as with a crowd.

■ *n.* horde, host, assembly, gathering, mass, multitude, rabble, herd, mob, pack. • *v.* **1** swarm; gather, congregate. **2** pack (into), cram (into), jam *or* pour into.

throt•tle /thrótl/ • *n.* **1** valve controlling flow of fuel, steam, etc., in an engine. **2** lever or pedal operating this. • *v.tr.* **1** choke; strangle. **2** prevent the utterance, etc., of. **3** control (an engine or steam, etc.) with a throttle.

■ *v.* **1** see CHOKE *v.* 1. **2** see GAG *v.* 2.

through /thrōō/ (also **thru**) • *prep.* **1 a** from end to end or from side to side of. **b** going in one side or end and out the other. **2** between or among. **3** from beginning to end of (*read through the letter*). **4** because of (*lost it through carelessness*). **5** up to and including (*Monday through Friday*). • *adv.* through a thing; from side to side, end to end, or beginning to end. • *attrib.adj.* (of traffic) going through a place to its destination. □ **be through** *colloq.* **1** have finished. **2** cease to have dealings. **3** have no further prospects (*is through as a politician*). **through and through** thoroughly; completely.

■ *prep.* **1** over, across. **3** during, throughout. **4** on account of, owing to, as a result of, by virtue of, via, by means of, by way of, due to. • *adv.* by, past; entirely, totally, wholly, utterly, fully. □ **be through 2** (*be through with*) have washed one's hands of. **3** *sl.* washed up. **through and through** see THROUGH *adv.* above.

through•out /thrōō-ówt/ • *prep.* right through; from end to end of. • *adv.* in every part or respect.

■ *prep.* during; all over. • *adv.* through and through, everywhere, entirely, completely.

through•put /thrōōpŏŏt/ *n.* amount of material put through a process, esp. in manufacturing or computing.

through•way /thrōō-way/ *n.* (also **thru′way**) thoroughfare, esp. a highway.

■ see ROAD 1.

throve *past of* THRIVE.

throw /thrō/ • *v.tr.* (*past* **threw** /thrōō/; *past part.* **thrown** /thrōn/) **1** propel with force through the air. **2** force violently into a specified position or state. **3** compel suddenly to be in a specified condition (*thrown out of work*). **4** turn or move (part of the body) quickly or suddenly (*threw an arm out*).

5 project or cast (light, a shadow, etc.). **6 a** bring to the ground in wrestling. **b** (of a horse) unseat (its rider). **7** *colloq.* disconcert (*the question threw me*). **8 a** cast (dice). **b** obtain (a specified number) by throwing dice. **9** extend or provide (*threw a bridge across the river*). **10** operate (a switch or lever). **11** have (a fit or tantrum, etc.). **12** give (a party). **13** *colloq.* lose (a contest or race, etc.) intentionally. • *n.* **1** act of throwing or being thrown. **2** distance a thing is or may be thrown. **3** light cover for furniture, etc. **4** [prec. by *a*] *sl.* each; per item (*sold at $10 a throw*). □ **throw away 1** discard as useless or unwanted. **2** waste or fail to make use of (an opportunity, etc.). **throw down the gauntlet** (or **glove**) issue a challenge. **throw good money after bad** incur further loss in a hopeless attempt to recoup a previous loss. **throw one's hand in 1** abandon one's chances in a card game, esp. poker. **2** give up; withdraw from a contest. **throw in 1** interpose (a word or remark). **2** include at no extra cost. **throw in the towel** admit defeat. **throw off 1** discard **2** write or utter in an offhand manner. **3** confuse or distract (a person) from the matter in hand. **4** emit. **throw oneself at** seek blatantly as a spouse or sexual partner. **throw oneself into** engage vigorously in. **throw out 1** put out forcibly or suddenly. **2** discard as unwanted. **throw over** desert or abandon. **throw stones** cast aspersions. **throw together 1** assemble hastily. **2** bring into casual contact. **throw up 1** *colloq.* vomit. **2** erect hastily. **throw one's weight around** (or **about**) *colloq.* act with unpleasant self-assertiveness. □□ **throw·a·ble** *adj.* **throw'er** *n.* [also in *comb.*].

■ *v.* **1, 2** toss, hurl, fling, pitch, bowl, send, launch, lob, *colloq.* chuck, heave, sling. **5** shed. **6 b** dislodge, buck off. **7** dismay, confound, confuse, baffle, unnerve, unsettle, *colloq.* rattle, faze. • *n.* **1** delivery. **3** see SPREAD[1] *n.* 8. □ **throw away 1** cast off, dispose of, get rid of, scrap, junk, dump, *sl.* ditch. **2** squander, lose, *sl.* blow. **throw in the towel** see SURRENDER *v.* 2. **throw off 1** shake off, reject, renounce, repudiate. **3** divert, see also THROW *v.* 7 above. **throw out 1** expel, eject, evict, turn or toss or kick or boot out, *sl.* bounce. **2** see *throw away* 1 above. **throw over** jilt, leave, forsake, walk out on, *colloq.* drop. **throw together 1** see *throw up* 2 below. **2** see LUMP *v.* 1. **throw up 1** spit up, spew (up), be sick; regurgitate, *sl.* puke, barf. **2** slap or knock together.

throw·a·way /thróöway/ • *adj.* **1** meant to be thrown away after (one) use. **2** (of lines, etc.) deliberately underemphasized. • *n.* thing to be thrown away after (one) use.

■ **1** see DISPOSABLE *adj.* 1.

throw·back /thróbak/ *n.* **1** reversion to ancestral character. **2** instance of this.

thru var. of THROUGH.

thrum /thrum/ • *v.* (**thrummed, thrumming**) **1** *tr.* play (a stringed instrument) monotonously or unskillfully. **2** *intr.* drum idly. • *n.* **1** such playing. **2** resulting sound.

■ *v.* **1** strum, pluck, pick, *usu. derog.* twang.

2 see PULSATE[1]. • *n.* **1** strumming. **2** see PATTER *n.*

thrush[1] /thrush/ *n.* any of various songbirds.

thrush[2] /thrush/ *n.* fungal disease, esp. one marked by whitish vesicles in the mouth and throat.

thrust /thrust/ • *v.* (*past* and *past part.* **thrust**) **1** *tr.* push with a sudden impulse or with force. **2** *tr.* [foll. by *on, upon*] impose (a thing) forcibly. **3** *intr.* stab; lunge suddenly. • *n.* **1** sudden or forcible push or lunge. **2** propulsive force developed by a jet or rocket engine. **3** military offensive. **4** stress between the parts of an arch, etc. **5** chief theme or gist of remarks, etc.

■ *v.* **1** shove, drive, ram, propel. **2** press, urge, foist, intrude. **3** jab, poke, pierce. • *n.* **2** propulsion, power, energy, impetus, drive. **5** see IMPORT *n.* 3.

thru·way var. of THROUGHWAY.

thud /thud/ • *n.* low dull sound as of a blow on a nonresonant surface. • *v.intr.* (**thudded, thud·ding**) make or fall with a thud. □□ **thud'ding·ly** *adv.*

■ clunk, thump, bump.

thug /thug/ *n.* vicious ruffian. □□ **thug'ger·y** *n.* **thug'gish** *adj.* **thug'gish·ly** *adv.* **thug'gish·ness** *n.*

■ hooligan, gangster, hoodlum, tough, *sl.* mobster, goon, hood.

thu·li·um /thoöleeəm, thyoö-/ *n. Chem.* soft metallic element of the lanthanide series. ¶Symb.: **Tm**

thumb /thum/ • *n.* **1** short thick finger on the human hand, set apart from the other four, **2** part of a glove, etc., for a thumb. • *v.* **1** wear or soil (pages, etc.) with a thumb (*well-thumbed book*). **2** turn over pages with or as with a thumb. **3** *tr.* request or obtain (a lift) by signaling with a raised thumb. □ **all thumbs** clumsy with one's hands. **thumb one's nose 1** put one's thumb up to one's nose with fingers extended up, a gesture of contempt. **2** display contempt or disdain. **thumbs-down** indication of rejection or failure. **thumbs-up** indication of satisfaction or approval. **under a person's thumb** completely dominated by a person. □□ **thumbed** *adj.* [also in *comb.*].

■ *v.* **2** leaf, flip, riffle, skim, browse. **3** *colloq.* hitch. □ **all thumbs** awkward, maladroit. **thumb one's nose** scoff at, deride, jeer at, mock. **thumbs-down** see VETO *n.* **thumbs-up** see APPROVAL. **under a person's thumb** wrapped around a person's little finger, in the palm of a person's hand.

thumb·nail /thúmnayl/ *n.* **1** nail of a thumb. **2** [*attrib.*] concise (*thumbnail sketch*).

■ **2** (*attrib.*) rough, cursory, sketchy; brief, short, quick; compact, succinct.

thumb·print /thúmprint/ *n.* impression of a thumb, esp. as used for identification.

thumb·screw /thúmskroö/ *n.* **1** instrument of torture for crushing the thumbs. **2** screw with a flattened head for turning with the thumb and forefinger.

thumb·tack /thúmtak/ *n.* tack with a flat head, pressed in with the thumb.

thump /thump/ • v. **1** tr. beat or strike heavily, esp. with the fist. **2** intr. throb strongly. **3** intr. [foll. by at, on, etc.] deliver blows (thumped on the door). **4** intr. tread heavily. • n. **1** heavy blow. **2** sound of this. □□ **thump′er** n.

■ v. **1** see BEAT v. 1. **2** see PULSATE. **3** see KNOCK v. 1. ■ n. see KNOCK n.

thun•der /thúndər/ • n. **1** loud noise heard after a lightning flash and due to the expansion of rapidly heated air. **2** resounding, loud, deep noise. • v. **1** intr. produce sounds of thunder (it is thundering). **2** intr. make a noise like thunder. **3** tr. utter (approval, disapproval, etc.) loudly. **4** intr. [foll. by against, etc.] make violent threats, etc., against. □ **steal a person's thunder** spoil the effect of another's idea, action, etc., by expressing or doing it first. □□ **thun′der•er** n.

■ n. **1**, **2** rumble, rumbling, reverberation, boom, roar, peal. • v. **2** roll, resound; crash, crack. **3** shout, yell, scream, bellow. **4** (thunder against or at) threaten, intimidate; swear at.

thun•der•bolt /thúndərbōlt/ • n. **1** flash of lightning with a simultaneous crash of thunder. **2** unexpected occurrence or item of news.

■ **2** see SHOCK¹ n. 2.

thun•der•clap /thúndərklap/ n. crash of thunder.

thun•der•cloud /thúndərklowd/ n. cumulus cloud charged with electricity and producing thunder and lightning.

thun•der•head /thúndərhed/ n. rounded cumulus cloud projecting upward and heralding a thunderstorm.

thun•der•ous /thúndərəs/ adj. **1** like thunder. **2** very loud. □□ **thun′der•ous•ly** adv. **thun′der•ous•ness** n.

■ roaring, booming, noisy, ear-splitting, deafening.

thun•der•show•er /thándərshowər/ n. brief rain shower accompanied by thunder and sometimes lightning.

thun•der•storm /thúndərstawrm/ n. storm with thunder and lightning and usu. heavy rain or hail.

thun•der•struck /thúndərstruk/ adj. amazed; surprised.

■ dumbfounded, astonished, astounded, speechless, stunned, shocked, dazed, colloq. flabbergasted.

Thur. abbr. Thursday.

Thurs. abbr. Thursday.

Thurs•day /thárzday, -dee/ n. fifth day of the week, following Wednesday.

thus /thus/ adv. **1 a** in this way. **b** as indicated. **2 a** accordingly. **b** as a result or inference. **3** to this extent; so.

■ **1** as follows, colloq. like so. **2** therefore, ergo, consequently, as a result, hence, that being so.

thwart /thwawrt/ • v.tr. frustrate or foil (a person or purpose, etc.). • n. rower's seat.

■ v. impede, check, stymie, baffle, stop, hinder, obstruct, block, oppose. • n. brace; bench.

SYNONYM STUDY: **thwart**

BAFFLE, BALK, FOIL, FRUSTRATE, INHIBIT. These verbs refer to the various ways in which we can outwit or overcome opposing forces. **Thwart** suggests using cleverness rather than force to bring about the defeat of an enemy or to block progress toward an objective (to thwart a rebellion; to have one's goals thwarted by lack of education). **Balk** also emphasizes setting up barriers (a sudden reversal that balked their hopes for a speedy resolution), but it is used more often as an intransitive verb meaning to stop at an obstacle and refuse to proceed (he balked at appearing in front of the angry crowd). To **baffle** is to cause defeat by bewildering or confusing (the police were baffled by the lack of evidence), while **foil** means to throw off course so as to discourage further effort (her plan to arrive early was foiled by heavy traffic). **Frustrate** implies rendering all attempts or efforts useless, so that nothing ever comes of them (frustrated by the increasingly bad weather, they decided to work indoors), while **inhibit** suggests forcing something into inaction (to inhibit wage increases by raising corporate taxes). Both frustrate and inhibit are used in a psychological context to suggest barriers that impede normal development or prevent the realization of natural desires (he was both frustrated by her refusal to acknowledge his presence and inhibited by his own shyness).

thy /thī/ poss.pron. [attrib.] (also **thine** /thīn/ before a vowel) of or belonging to thee.

thyme /tīm/ n. any of several aromatic herbs used for flavoring.

thy•mi pl. of THYMUS.

thy•mus /thíməs/ n. (pl. **-mus•es** or **-mi** /-mī/) Anat. lymphoid organ situated in the neck of vertebrates.

thy•roid /thíroyd/ n. (in full **thy′roid gland**) **1** large ductless gland in the neck of vertebrates, secreting a hormone that regulates growth and development. **2** extract prepared from the thyroid gland of animals and used in treating goiter, etc.

thy•self /thīsélf/ pron. archaic emphat. & refl. form of THOU¹, THEE.

Ti symb. Chem. titanium.

ti /tee/ n. (also **te**) seventh note of a major scale.

ti•ar•a /teeárə, –áirə, –áirə/ n. **1** jeweled ornamental band worn on the front of a woman's hair. **2** three-crowned diadem worn by a pope.

Ti•bet•an /tibét′n/ • n. **1 a** native of Tibet. **b** person of Tibetan descent. **2** language of Tibet. • adj. of or relating to Tibet or its language.

tib•i•a /tibeeə/ n. (pl. **tib•i•ae** /–bee-ee/) Anat. inner of two bones extending from the knee to the ankle. □□ **tib′i•al** adj.

tic /tik/ n. **1** habitual spasmodic contraction of the muscles, esp. of the face. **2** behavioral quirk.

tick¹ /tik/ • n. slight recurring click, esp. that of a watch or clock. • v. **1** intr. **a** (of a clock, etc.) make ticks. **b** [foll. by away] (of time, etc.) pass. **2** intr. (of a mechanism) function

(*see how it ticks*). □ **tick off** *sl.* annoy; anger.
tick-tack-toe (also **tic-tac-toe**) game of marking Xs or Os in a nine-square grid. **what makes a person tick** *colloq.* person's motivation.

■ *v.* **1b** (*tick away*) see GO[1] *v.* 9. **2** see WORK *v.* 4. □ **tick off** see ANNOY 1.

tick[2] /tik/ *n.* parasitic arachnid on the skin of warm-blooded vertebrates.

tick[3] /tik/ *n.* **1** cover of a mattress or pillow. **2** = TICKING.

tick•er /tíkər/ *n. colloq.* **1** heart. **2** machine that receives and prints telegraphed messages onto paper tape. □ **ticker tape 1** paper strip from a ticker. **2** this or similar material thrown from windows, etc., to greet a celebrity.

tick•et /tíkit/ • *n.* **1** written or printed piece of paper or card entitling the holder to admittance, travel by public transport, etc. **2** notification of a traffic offense, etc. **3** label giving price, etc. **4** list of a political party's candidates. **5** [prec. by *the*] *colloq.* what is correct or needed. • *v.tr.* attach or serve a ticket to. □□ **tick'et•ed** *adj.*

■ *n.* **3** see TAG[1] *n.* 1. • *v.* see TAG[1] *v.* 1.

tick•ing /tíking/ *n.* stout, usu. striped material used to cover mattresses, etc.

tick•le /tíkəl/ • *v.* **1 a** *tr.* apply light touches or strokes to (a person, etc.) so as to produce laughter and spasmodic movement. **b** *intr.* feel this sensation (*my foot tickles*). **2** *tr.* excite agreeably; amuse. • *n.* **1** act of tickling. **2** tickling sensation. □ **tickled pink** (or **to death**) *colloq.* extremely amused or pleased. □□ **tick'ler** *n.* **tick'ly** *adj.*

■ *v.* **1 a** titillate. **2** delight, please, gratify, thrill. • *n.* **2** see ITCH *n.* 1. □ **tickled pink** (or **to death**) see GLAD *adj.* 1.

tick•lish /tíklish/ *adj.* **1** sensitive to tickling. **2** (of a matter or person) requiring careful handling. □□ **tick'lish•ly** *adv.* **tick'lish•ness** *n.*

■ **2** uncertain, unstable, touch and go; delicate, precarious, risky, thorny, awkward, difficult, tricky, sensitive, touchy. □□ **ticklishness** see DELICACY 3.

tid•al /tíd'l/ *adj.* relating to, like, or affected by tides. □ **tidal wave 1** = TSUNAMI. **2** widespread manifestation of feeling, etc. □□ **tid'al•ly** *adv.*

■ □ **tidal wave 2** see FLOOD *n.* 2b.

tid•bit /tídbit/ *n.* **1** small morsel. **2** choice item of news, etc.

■ **1** delicacy, treat, goody.

tid•dly-winks /tídleewingks/ *n.* game played by flicking counters into a cup, etc.

tide /tíd/ *n.* **1 a** periodic rise and fall of the sea due to the attraction of the moon and sun. **b** water as affected by this. **2** time or season (usu. in *comb.*: *Yuletide*). **3** marked trend of opinion, fortune, or events. □ **tide over** enable (a person) to deal with a difficult period, etc.

■ *n.* **3** see TREND *n.*

tide•ta•ble /tídtaybəl/ *n.* table indicating the times of high and low tides at a place.

tide•wa•ter /tídwawtər, –wotər/ *n.* **1** water brought by or affected by tides. **2** [*attrib.*] affected by tides (*tidewater region*).

ti•dings /tídingz/ *n.* [as *sing.* or *pl.*] news; information.

ti•dy /tídee/ • *adj.* (**ti•di•er, ti•di•est**) **1** neat; orderly. **2** *colloq.* considerable (*tidy sum*). • *v.tr.* (**–dies, –died**) [also *absol.*] put in good order; make tidy. □□ **ti'di•ly** *adv.* **ti'di•ness** *n.*

■ *adj.* **1** trim, shipshape, spick-and-span, clean; organized. **2** respectable, sizable, significant, substantial, appreciable, handsome, ample. • *v.* straighten (out *or* up), fix (up); spruce up; see also GROOM *v.* 1. □□ **tidiness** see ORDER *n.* 1.

tie /tí/ • *v.* (**ty•ing**) **1** *tr.* **a** attach or fasten with string, cord, etc. **b** link conceptually. **2** *tr.* **a** form (a string, ribbon, shoelace, necktie, etc.) into a knot or bow. **b** form (a knot or bow) in this way. **3** *tr.* restrict (a person) as to conditions, place, etc (*tied to his job*). **4** *intr.* achieve the same score or place as another competitor. • *n.* **1** cord, line, etc., used for fastening. **2** strip of material worn around the collar and tied in a knot at the front. **3** bond (*family ties*). **4** draw, dead heat, or equality of score among competitors. **5** beam laid horizontally as a support for railroad rails. □ **fit to be tied** *colloq.* very angry. **tie down** = TIE *v.* 3 above. **tie-dye** method of producing irregular dyed patterns by tying string, etc., to the fabric. **tie in** [foll. by *with*] bring into or have a close association or agreement. **tie-in** *n.* connection or association. **tie the knot** *colloq.* get married. **tie up 1** bind securely with cord, etc. **2** invest or reserve (capital, etc.) so that it is not immediately available for use. **3** secure (a boat, animal, etc.). **4** complete (an undertaking, etc.). **5** [usu. in *passive*] fully occupy (a person).

■ *v.* **1 a** make fast, lash, truss (up), tether. **b** connect, associate, join, affiliate, ally, team (up). **3** confine, restrain; limit, curb. **4** (*tie with*) equal, match, be neck and neck with. • *n.* **1** lace, rope, thong, band, leash. **2** cravat, bow tie, necktie. **3** relationship, affiliation, involvement, entanglement. **4** deadlock, stalemate. □ **fit to be tied** see ANGRY 1. **tie in** coordinate; correspond, coincide. **tie-in** relationship, link. **tie up 1, 3** see TIE *v.* 1a above. **2** commit, sink, obligate. **4** clinch, wrap up, nail down. **5** engage, (keep) busy, engross.

tie•pin /típin/ *n.* ornamental pin for holding a tie in place.

tier /teer/ *n.* vertical or sloped row, rank, or unit of structure. □□ **tiered** *adj.* [also in *comb.*].

■ line, level, stratum, story. □□ **tiered** see SERRIED.

tiff /tif/ *n.* slight or petty quarrel.

■ *n.* disagreement, dispute, argument, squabble, *colloq.* spat.

ti•ger /tígər/ *n.* **1** large Asian feline with a yellowish brown coat with black stripes. **2** domestic cat with similar striping. **3** fierce, energetic, or formidable person. □ **tiger-eye** (or **tiger's-eye**) lustrous, yellowish brown, striped gem. **tiger lily** tall garden lily with dark-spotted orange flowers.

tight /tīt/ • *adj.* **1** closely held, drawn, fastened, etc. **2** too closely fitting. **3** impermeable; impervious, esp. [in *comb.*] to a specified thing (*watertight*). **4** tense; stretched. **5** *colloq.* drunk. **6** *colloq.* stingy. **7** (of money or materials) not easily obtainable. **8 a** (of precautions, etc.) stringent. **b** presenting difficulties (*tight situation*). **9** *colloq.* friendly; close. • *adv.* tightly (*hold tight!*). □ **tight-fisted** stingy. **tight-lipped** secretive; taciturn. □□ **tight′ly** *adv.* **tight′ness** *n.*

■ *adj.* **1** secure, firm, fast, fixed, snug. **2** constricting, (too) small. **3** sealed, leakproof, impenetrable, airtight, waterproof. **4** taut. **5** tipsy, intoxicated, *colloq.* high, woozy. **6** niggardly, mean, miserly, penny-pinching. **7** scarce, rare; dear, expensive. **8 a** strict, restrictive, severe, tough, rigorous, stern, harsh, inflexible. **b** trying, dangerous, risky, hazardous, touchy, tricky, precarious, *colloq.* sticky. □ **tight-lipped** closemouthed, silent, quiet, reticent, reserved, *colloq.* mum. □□ **tightly** closely, tensely; densely; firmly, fast. **tightness** see TENSION *n.* 1.

tight•en /tīt′n/ *v.* make or become tighter.
■ strengthen; stiffen; fasten, fix, secure.

tight•rope /tītrōp/ *n.* rope stretched tightly high above the ground, on which acrobats perform.

tights /tīts/ *n.pl.* thin but not sheer close-fitting wool or nylon, etc., garment covering the legs and lower body.

tight•wad /tītwod/ *n. colloq.* person who is miserly or stingy.

ti•gress /tīgris/ *n.* **1** female tiger. **2** fierce or passionate woman.

tike var. of TYKE.

til•de /tíldə/ *n.* mark (˜), put over a letter, e.g., over a Spanish *n* when pronounced *ny* (as in *señor*).

tile /tīl/ • *n.* **1** thin slab of concrete, baked clay, etc., used for roofing, paving, etc. **2** similar slab of glazed pottery, cork, linoleum, etc., for covering a floor, wall, etc. **3** thin flat piece used in a game (esp. mahjongg). • *v.tr.* cover with tiles. □□ **til′er** *n.*

til•ing /tīling/ *n.* **1** process of fixing tiles. **2** area of tiles.

till¹ /til/ • *prep.* **1** up to or as late as (*wait till six o'clock*). **2** up to the time of (*waited till the end*). • *conj.* **1** up to the time when (*wait till I return*). **2** so long that (*laughed till I cried*).

till² /til/ *n.* drawer for money in a store, bank, etc.
■ cash register.

till³ /til/ *v.tr.* cultivate (land). □□ **till′a•ble** *adj.* **till′er** *n.*
■ plow, farm, work, dig, hoe, harrow.

till•age /tilij/ *n.* **1** preparation of land for bearing crops. **2** tilled land.

till•er /tilər/ *n.* horizontal bar fitted to the head of a boat's rudder to turn it in steering.

tilt /tilt/ • *v.* **1 a** *intr. & tr.* assume or cause to assume a sloping position; heel over. **b** lean or cause to lean toward one side of an opinion, action, etc. **2** *intr.* [foll. by *at*] strike, thrust, or run at with a weapon. **3** *intr.* [foll.

by *with*] engage in a contest. • *n.* **1** tilting. **2** sloping position. **3** inclination or bias. **4** (of medieval knights, etc.) charging with a lance against an opponent or at a mark. □ **full** (or **at full**) **tilt 1** at full speed. **2** with full force. □□ **tilt′er** *n.*

■ *v.* **1 a** slant, incline, tip, pitch, list. **2** (*tilt at*) lunge at, attack. **3** (*tilt with*) compete with, contend with, cross swords with. • *n.* **2** inclination. **4** tournament, match, contest; dispute. □ **full** (or **at full**) **tilt 2** see *at full blast* (BLAST).

tim•ber /timbər/ *n.* **1** standing trees suitable for lumber. **2** [esp. as *int.*] warning cry that a tree is about to fall. **3** piece of wood or beam, esp. as the rib of a vessel. □ **timber wolf** large N. American gray wolf. □□ **tim′ber•ing** *n.*
■ **1** see WOOD 2. **3** board, plank, lumber.

tim•ber•line /timbərlīn/ *n.* line or level above which no trees grow.

tim•bre /támbər, táNbrə/ *n.* distinctive character of a musical sound or voice apart from its pitch and intensity.
■ tone (color *or* quality), tonality, color, resonance.

Tim•buk•tu /tímbuktoo/ *n. colloq.* any distant or remote place.

time /tīm/ • *n.* **1** indefinite continued progress of existence, events, etc., in past, present, and future, regarded as a whole. **2** progress of this as affecting persons or things (*stood the test of time*). **3** portion of time; period (*prehistoric times*). **4** allotted or available portion of time (*no time to visit*). **5** point of time, esp. in hours and minutes (*the time is 7:30*). **6** [prec. by *a*] indefinite period (*waited for a time*). **7** particular reckoning of time (*in record time, eight o'clock Eastern time*). **8** occasion (*last time*). **9** opportune occasion or moment (*shall we set a time?*). **10** [in *pl.*] expressing multiplication (*five times six is thirty*). **11** [in *sing.* or *pl.*] **a** the conditions of life or of a period (*hard times*). **b** [prec. by *the*] the present age, or that being considered. **12** *colloq.* prison sentence (*is doing time*). **13** period of apprenticeship or military service. **14** date or expected date of childbirth or death. **15** any of several rhythmic patterns of music. • *v.tr.* **1** choose the time for. **2** do at a chosen or correct time. **3** arrange the time of arrival of. **4** ascertain the time taken by. **5** regulate the duration or interval of. □ **against time** with utmost speed. **ahead of time** earlier than expected. **ahead of one's time** having ideas too advanced to be accepted by one's contemporaries. **all the time 1** throughout. **2** constantly. **at one time 1** in a known but unspecified past period. **2** simultaneously. **at the same time 1** simultaneously. **2** nevertheless. **for the time being** until some other arrangement is made. **have no time for 1** be unable or unwilling to spend time on. **2** dislike. **have the time 1** be able to spend the time needed. **2** know from a watch, etc., what time it is. **in no** (or **less than no**) **time 1** very soon. **2** very quickly. **in time 1** punctual. **2** eventually. **3** in accordance with a given rhythm or tempo.

know the time of day be well informed. lose no time act immediately. on (also in) one's own time outside working hours. pass the time of day *colloq.* exchange a greeting or casual remarks. time after time repeatedly; on many occasions. time and (or time and time) again on many occasions. time and a half rate of payment for work at one and a half times the normal rate. time bomb bomb designed to explode at a preset time. time capsule box, etc., containing objects typical of the present time, buried for discovery in the future. time clock clock with a device for recording workers' hours of work. time exposure exposure of photographic film for longer than the maximum normal shutter setting. time-honored esteemed by tradition or through custom. time immemorial longer time than anyone can remember or trace. time off time for rest or recreation, etc. time of one's life occasion of exceptional enjoyment. time out brief intermission in a game, etc. time-share share in a property under a time-sharing arrangement. time-sharing use of a vacation home at agreed different times by several joint owners. time warp imaginary distortion of space in relation to time. time was there was a time (*time was when I could do that*). time zone range of longitudes where a common standard time is used.

■ *n.* 3 age, epoch, era, lifetime. 4, 6 interval, stretch, spell, span, phase, season, term, session, duration. 5, 9 point, instant, juncture, date. 8 opportunity, chance. 11 circumstances, conditions, culture. 15 tempo, beat, meter, measure. ● *v.* 2, 3 schedule, program, organize, adjust, fix. 4 *colloq.* clock. □ ahead of time prematurely, beforehand. all the time 2 always, ever, continuously. at one time 1 previously, formerly. 2 all together, in unison. at the same time 1 see *at one time* 2 (TIME) above. 2 all the same, yet, even so, but, however, be that as it may, just the same. for the time being for now, for the present, meanwhile, temporarily. in no (or less than no) time 1 at once, immediately, before you know it, right away. 2 swiftly, rapidly, in an instant. in time 1 in timely fashion, in the nick of time. 2 soon, one of these days, sometime, someday, one day. time and (or time and time) again repeatedly, (over and over) again, frequently, often. time-honored established, traditional, conventional, age-old; respected. time off see BREAK *n.* 2. time was see FORMERLY.

time•keep•er /tímkeepər/ *n.* 1 person who records time, esp. of workers or in a game. 2 watch or clock as regards accuracy. □□ **time′keep•ing** *n.*

time•less /tímlis/ *adj.* not affected by the passage of time; eternal. □□ **time′less•ly** *adv.* **time′less•ness** *n.*

■ everlasting, immortal, undying, endless, unending, perpetual. □□ **timelessness** see ETERNITY 1, 3.

time•ly /tímlee/ *adj.* (**time•li•er**, **time•li•est**) opportune; coming at the right time. □□ **time′li•ness** *n.*

■ well-timed, propitious, favorable, auspicious.

SYNONYM STUDY: timely

OPPORTUNE, PROPITIOUS, SEASONABLE. Some people seem to have a knack for doing or saying the right thing at the right time. A timely act or remark is one that comes at a moment when it is of genuine value or service (*a timely interruption*), while an opportune one comes in the nick of time, as if by accident, and exactly meets the needs of the occasion (*the taxi pulled up at an opportune moment, saving her the embarrassment of a prolonged farewell*). Seasonable applies to whatever is suited to the season of the year or fits in perfectly with the needs of the moment or the character of the occasion (*seasonable weather; a seasonable menu for a cold winter day*). Propitious means presenting favorable conditions. While a warm day in December might not be *seasonable*, in other words, it might very well be *propitious* for the sailor setting off on a round-the-world cruise.

time•piece /tímpees/ *n.* clock or watch.

tim•er /tímər/ *n.* 1 person or device that measures or records time taken. 2 automatic mechanism for activating a device, etc., at a preset time.

time•ta•ble /tímtaybəl/ *n.* list of times on a schedule, esp. arrivals and departures of buses, trains, etc.

tim•id /tímid/ *adj.* easily frightened; apprehensive; shy. □□ **ti•mid′i•ty** *n.* **tim′id•ly** *adv.* **tim′id•ness** *n.*

■ shy, retiring, bashful, fearful, fainthearted, mousy, scared, nervous, cowardly, chicken-hearted, *colloq.* yellow. □□ **timidity, timidness** see COWARDICE. **timidly** see *fearfully* (FEARFUL).

tim•ing /tíming/ *n.* 1 way an action or process is timed. 2 regulation of the opening and closing of valves in an internal combustion engine.

tim•o•rous /tímərəs/ *adj.* timid; fearful. □□ **tim′or•ous•ly** *adv.* **tim′or•ous•ness** *n.*

■ see TIMID, AFRAID. □□ **timorously** see *fearfully* (FEARFUL), GINGERLY *adv.* **timorousness** see COWARDICE, HUMILITY.

tim•pa•ni /tímpanee/ *n.pl.* (also **tym′pa•ni**) kettledrums. □□ **tim′pa•nist** *n.*

tin /tin/ • *n.* 1 *Chem.* silvery white metallic element used esp. in alloys and to form tin plate. ¶Symb.: **Sn** 2 = *tin plate*. • *v.tr.* (**tinned, tin•ning**) cover or coat with tin. □ **tin can** tin-plated container, esp. an empty one. **tin foil** foil made of tin, aluminum, or tin alloy, used for wrapping food. **Tin Pan Alley** the world of composers and publishers of popular music. **tin plate** sheet iron or sheet steel coated with tin. **tin-plate** *v.tr.* coat with tin.

tinc•ture /tíngkchər/ • *n.* 1 slight flavor or trace. 2 tinge (of a color). 3 medicinal solution (of a drug) in alcohol (*tincture of quinine*). • *v.tr.* 1 color slightly; tinge, flavor. 2 (often foll. by *with*) affect slightly (with a quality).

■ *n.* **1, 2** see TINT *n.* 1, 2.

tin•der /tíndər/ *n.* dry substance that readily catches fire from a spark.

tin•der•box /tíndərboks/ *n.* **1** *hist.* box containing tinder, flint, and steel, for kindling fires. **2** potentially explosive or violent person, place, situation, etc.

tine /tīn/ *n.* prong, tooth, or point of a fork, comb, antler, etc. □□ **tined** *adj.* [also in *comb.*].

tinge /tinj/ • *v.tr.* (**tinge•ing** or **ting•ing**) **1** color slightly. **2** affect slightly. • *n.* **1** tendency toward or trace of some color. **2** slight admixture of a feeling or quality.

■ *v.* **1** see COLOR *v.* 1. ■ **1** see TINT *n.* 1. **2** see SHADE *n.* 5.

tin•gle /tínggəl/ • *v.* *intr.* feel or cause to feel a slight prickling, stinging, or throbbing sensation. • *n.* tingling sensation. □□ **tin′gly** *adj.*

■ *v.* see PRICKLE *v.* ■ *n.* see PRICKLE *n.* 3.

tin•ker /tíngkər/ • *n.* itinerant mender of kettles, pans, etc. • *v.* *intr.* [foll. by *at, with*] work or repair in an amateurish or desultory way. □□ **tin′ker•er** *n.*

■ *v.* trifle, dabble, toy, fiddle (around), monkey (around).

tin•kle /tíngkəl/ • *v.* **1** *intr. & tr.* make or cause to make a succession of short light ringing sound. **2** *intr.* *colloq.* urinate. • *n.* tinkling sound.

■ *v.* **1** see RING² *v.* 1. **2** see URINATE². • *n.* see RING *n.* 1.

tin•ni•tus /tínītəs, tíni–/ *n.* *Med.* ringing in the ears.

tin•ny /tínee/ *adj.* (**tin•ni•er, tin•ni•est**) **1** of or like tin. **2** flimsy; insubstantial. **3** (of sound) thin and metallic. □□ **tin′ni•ly** *adv.* **tin′ni•ness** *n.*

■ *adj.* **2** shabby, shoddy, inferior, cheap. **3** harsh, twangy.

tin•sel /tínsəl/ *n.* **1** glittering metallic strips, threads, etc., used as decoration. **2** superficial brilliance or splendor. □□ **tin′seled** *adj.*

tint /tint/ • *n.* **1** light or delicate variety of a color. **2** tendency toward or admixture of a different color (*red with a blue tint*). **3** hair dye. • *v.tr.* apply a tint to; color. □□ **tint′er** *n.*

■ *n.* **1** hue, cast, shade, tone. **2** tincture, tinge, touch, hint, trace, dash, suggestion. **3** rinse, coloring.

tin•tin•nab•u•la•tion /tíntinábyəláyshən/ *n.* ringing or tinkling of bells.

ti•ny /tínee/ *adj.* (**ti•ni•er, ti•ni•est**) very small or slight. See synonym study at SMALL. □□ **ti′ni•ness** *n.*

■ microscopic, infinitesimal, minute, minuscule, little, miniature, micro–, mini–, petite, elfin; trifling, paltry, puny, *colloq.* pintsize, wee, teeny, teensy-weensy, itsy-bitsy.

-tion /shən/ *suffix* forming nouns of action, condition, etc. (see -ION, -ATION, -ITION, -UTION).

tip¹ /tip/ • *n.* **1** extremity or end, esp. of a small or tapering thing. **2** small piece or part attached to the end of a thing. • *v.tr.* (**tipped, tip•ping**) provide with a tip. □ **on the tip of one's tongue** about to be said,

esp. after difficulty in recalling to mind. **tip of the iceberg** small evident part of something much larger.

■ *n.* **1** peak, apex, summit, top, pinnacle, head, point, finial. **2** cap, nib. • *v.* top, cap, crown.

tip² /tip/ • *v.* (**tipped, tip•ping**) **1** *intr.* lean or slant. **2** *tr.* cause to do this. • *n.* slight push or tilt. □ **tip the balance** make the critical difference.

■ *v.* **1** incline, list, tilt; upend; discharge, spill, pour out. • *n.* see LIST² *n.*

tip³ /tip/ • *v.* (**tipped, tip•ping**) **1** *tr.* make a small present of money to, esp. for a service given. **2** *tr.* strike or touch lightly. • *n.* **1** small gift of money, esp. for a service given. **2** piece of private or special information, esp. regarding betting or investment. **3** small or casual piece of advice. □ **tip off** give a hint or warning. **tip-off** helpful information or warning. **tip-off** hint or warning, etc. □□ **tip′per** *n.*

■ *v.* **1** reward, remunerate. • *n.* **1** gratuity, *colloq.* little something. **2** clue, hint, prediction. **3** suggestion, recommendation, *colloq.* pointer. □ **tip off** advise, caution, alert, forewarn, notify. **tip-off** see TIP³ *n.* 2 above.

tip•ple /típəl/ *v.intr.* drink intoxicating liquor habitually. □□ **tip′pler** *n.*

tip•sy /típsee/ *adj.* (**tip•si•er, tip•si•est**) slightly intoxicated. □□ **tip′si•ly** *adv.* **tip′si•ness** *n.*

■ see TIGHT *adj.* 5.

tip•toe /típtó/ • *n.* tips of the toes. • *v.intr.* (**tip•toes, tip•toed, tip•toe•ing**) walk on tiptoe, or very stealthily. • *adv.* (also **on tiptoe**) with the heels off the ground.

tip-top /típtóp/ *colloq.* • *adj. & adv.* highest in excellence. • *n.* highest point of excellence.

■ *adj.* see EXCELLENT.

ti•rade /tírayd, tiráyd/ *n.* long vehement denunciation or declamation.

■ harangue, diatribe, outburst, onslaught, rant.

tire¹ /tīr/ *v.* **1** *tr. & intr.* make or grow weary. **2** *tr.* bore. **3** *tr.* [in *passive*; foll. by *of*] have had enough of (*tired of arguing*).

■ **1** tire out, fatigue, exhaust, wear out, drain, sap, enervate, debilitate, weaken. **2** exasperate, irritate, annoy, bother. **3** (*be tired of*) be fed up (to here) with, *colloq.* be sick (and tired) of.

tire² /tīr/ *n.* rubber covering, usu. inflatable, that fits around a wheel rim.

tired /tīrd/ *adj.* **1** weary; ready for sleep. **2** hackneyed. □□ **tired′ly** *adv.* **tired′ness** *n.*

■ **1** exhausted, worn out, fatigued, sleepy, drowsy, spent, drained, all in, *colloq.* bushed, pooped, beat, tuckered out, *sl.* wiped out. **2** overworked, overused, stereotypic(al), unimaginative, trite, stale, unoriginal, commonplace. □□ **tiredness** see FATIGUE *n.* 1.

SYNONYM STUDY: tired
EXHAUSTED, FATIGUED, TUCKERED, WEARY. **Tired** is what you are after you've cleaned the house, spent two hours reading a dull report, or trained for a marathon; it means that you are drained of your strength and energy, without any indication of degree. **Weary**, on

the other hand, is how you feel after you've had to interrupt your dinner five or six times to answer the phone. It implies not only a depletion of energy but also the vexation that accompanies having to put up with something that is, or has become, disagreeable. **Exhausted** means that you are totally drained of strength and energy, a condition that may even be irreversible (*exhausted by battling a terminal disease*). **Fatigued** is a more precise word than either *tired* or *weary*; it implies a loss of energy through strain, illness, or overwork to the point where rest or sleep is essential (*fatigued after working a 24-hour shift*). **Tuckered** comes close in meaning to *fatigued* or *exhausted*, but often carries the suggestion of loss of breath (*tuckered out after running up six flights of stairs*).

tire•less /tírlis/ *adj.* having inexhaustible energy. □□ **tire′less•ly** *adv.* **tire′less•ness** *n.*
■ energetic, vital, vigorous, dynamic, spirited, lively, industrious, untiring, persistent, tenacious, diligent. □□ **tirelessly** see NONSTOP *adv.* **tirelessness** see *perseverance* (PERSEVERE).

tire•some /tírsəm/ *adj.* wearisome; tedious. □□ **tire′some•ly** *adv.* **tire′some•ness** *n.*
■ boring, dull, monotonous, tiring, bland. □□ **tiresomeness** see TEDIUM.

'tis /tiz/ *archaic* it is.

tis•sue /tíshoo/ *n.* **1** any coherent mass of specialized cells of which animals or plants are made. **2** = *tissue paper.* **3** disposable piece of thin, soft, absorbent paper for wiping, drying, etc. **4** fine, gauzy fabric. □ **tissue paper** thin, soft paper for wrapping, etc.

tit[1] /tit/ *n.* any of various small birds.

tit[2] /tit/ *n.* □ **tit for tat** /tat/ blow for blow; retaliation.

Ti•tan /tít'n/ *n.* (often **titan**) person of very great strength, intellect, or importance.

ti•tan•ic /títánik/ *adj.* gigantic; colossal. □□ **ti•tan′i•cal•ly** *adv.*
■ see GIGANTIC.

ti•ta•ni•um /títáyneeəm, tee–/ *n. Chem.* gray metallic element. ¶Symb.: **Ti**.

tithe /tīth/ • *n.* one tenth of the annual product of land or labor, formerly taken as a church tax. • *v. intr.* pay tithes. □□ **tith′ing** *n.*

tit•il•late /tít'layt/ *v.tr.* **1** excite pleasantly. **2** tickle. □□ **tit′il•lat•ing•ly** *adv.* **tit•il•la•tion** /–láyshən/ *n.*
■ **1** see EXCITE 1. □□ **titillation** see THRILL *n.* 1a.

ti•tle /tít'l/ • *n.* **1** name of a book, work of art, etc. **2** heading of a chapter, document, etc. **3** book, etc., regarded in terms of its title (*published 20 new titles*). **4** caption or credit in a movie, broadcast, etc. **5** nomenclature indicating a person's status (e.g., *professor, queen*) or used as a form of address (e.g., *Mr.*). **6** championship. **7** *Law* a right to ownership of property with or without possession. **b** (foll. by *to*) just or recognized claim. • *v.tr.* give a title to. □ **title role** part in a play, etc., that gives its name (e.g., *Othello*).
■ *n.* **2** inscription, headline, subtitle. **5** des-

---

881   **tireless ~ toast**

ignation, epithet, form of address; office, rank. **6** crown. **7 a** interest, privilege, entitlement, possession, tenure. **b** right. • *v.* call, designate, label, term, christen, baptize, nickname, dub. □ **title role** see PROTAGONIST.

ti•tled /tít'ld/ *adj.* having a title of nobility or rank.

tit•mouse /títmows/ *n.* (*pl.* **tit•mice** /–mīs/) any of various small birds.

tit•ter /títər/ • *v.intr.* laugh furtively; giggle. • *n.* furtive laugh.
■ *v. & n.* chuckle, snicker, chortle, giggle, snigger.

tit•tle /tít'l/ *n.* **1** small stroke or dot. **2** particle.

tit•u•lar /tíchələr/ *adj.* **1** of or relating to a title. **2** in name or title only (*titular ruler*). □□ **tit′u•lar•ly** *adv.*
■ *adj.* **2** nominal, so-called, token, theoretical.

tiz•zy /tízee/ *n.* (*pl.* **–zies**) *colloq.* state of nervous agitation (*in a tizzy*).
■ see STEW *n.* 2, FLAP *n.* 3.

TKO *abbr. Boxing* technical knockout.

Tl *symb. Chem.* thallium.

TLC *abbr. colloq.* tender loving care.

Tlin•git /tlíngkət, gət, klíng–/ *n.* **1 a N.** American people native to southern Alaska. **b** member of this people. **2** language of this people.

TM *abbr.* transcendental meditation.

Tm *symb. Chem.* thulium.

TN *abbr.* Tennessee (in official postal use).

TNT *abbr.* trinitrotoluene, a high explosive.

to /too; tə (when unstressed)/ • *prep.* **1** introducing a noun expressing: **a** what is reached, approached, or touched (*fell to the ground*). **b** what is aimed at (*throw it to me*). **c** as far as (*went on to the end*). **d** what is followed (*made to order*). **e** what is considered or affected (*am used to that*). **f** what is caused or produced (*turn to stone*). **g** what is compared (*won by three to two*). **h** what is increased (*add it to mine*). **i** what is involved or composed as specified (*there is nothing to it*). **2** introducing the infinitive: **a** as a verbal noun (*to get there*). **b** expressing purpose, consequence, or cause (*we eat to live*). **c** as a substitute for *to* + infinitive (*wanted to come but was unable to*). • *adv.* **1** in the normal or required position or condition (*come to, heave to*). **2** (of a door) in a nearly closed position. □ **to and fro** backward and forward.

toad /tōd/ *n.* **1** froglike amphibian breeding in water but living chiefly on land. **2** repulsive or detestable person. □□ **toad′ish** *adj.*

toad•stool /tṓdstool/ *n.* poisonous mushrooms.

toad•y /tṓdee/ • *n.* (*pl.* **–ies**) sycophant. • *v.tr. & (foll. by to) intr.* (**–ies, –ied**) behave servilely to; fawn upon. □□ **toad′y•ish** *adj.* **toad′y•ism** *n.*
■ *n.* see FLUNKY 2. • *v.* see TRUCKLE *v.* □□ **toadyish** see OBSEQUIOUS, SERVILE. **toadyism** see *servility* (SERVILE).

toast /tōst/ • *n.* **1** sliced bread browned on both sides by radiant heat. **2 a** person or thing in whose honor a company is request-ed to drink. **b** call to such a drink or an in-stance of it. • *v.* **1** *tr.* cook or brown by radi-ant heat. **2** *intr.* (of bread, etc.) become brown· in this way. **3** *tr.* warm (one's feet, oneself, etc.) at a fire, etc. **4** *tr.* drink to the health or in honor of (a person or thing).

■ *n.* **2 a** heroine, hero, favorite. **b** health, pledge. • *v.* **1** grill. **4** pay tribute to, salute, raise one's glass to.

toast•er /tóstər/ *n.* electrical device for mak-ing toast.

toast•mas•ter /tóstmastər/ *n.* (*fem.* **toast• mis•tress** /–mistris/) person who announces toasts at a public occasion.

to•bac•co /təbákó/ *n.* (*pl.* **–cos**) **1** plant with narcotic leaves used for smoking, chewing, or snuff. **2** its leaves, esp. as prepared for smoking.

to•bog•gan /təbógən/ • *n.* narrow, runner-less sled curled up at the front, for use on snow. • *v.intr.* ride on a toboggan. □□ **to• bog′gan•er** *n.* **to•bog′gan•ing** *n.* **to•bog′ gan•ist** *n.*

to•coph•er•ol /tōkófərawl, –rol/ *n.* any of sev-eral closely related vitamins, found in wheat germ oil, egg yolk, and leafy vegetables. (Also called **vitamin E**).

to•day /tədáy/ • *adv.* .**1** on this present day. **2** nowadays. • *n.* **1** this present day. **2** mod-ern times.

tod•dle /tód′l/ • *v.intr.* walk with short un-steady steps. • *n.* toddling walk.

■ *v.* see WADDLE *v.*

tod•dler /tódlər/ *n.* child who is just begin-ning to walk.

tod•dy /tódee/ *n.* (*pl.* **–dies**) drink of liquor with hot water, sugar, etc.

to-do /tədóō/ *n.* commotion or fuss.

■ see FUSS *n.* 1, 2.

toe /tō/ • *n.* **1** any of the five digits of the foot. **2** part of footwear that covers the toes. • *v.* (**toes, toed, toe•ing**) **1** *tr.* touch (a starting line, etc.) with the toes. **2** *intr.* [foll. by *in*, *out*] converge (or diverge) slightly at the front. □ **on one's toes** alert. **toe the line** conform, esp. unwillingly or under pressure. □□ **toed** *adj.* [also in *comb.*]. **toe′ less** *adj.*

toe•nail /tónayl/ *n.* nail at the tip of each toe.

tof•fee /táwfee, tóf–/ *n.* firm or hard candy made by boiling sugar, butter, etc.

to•fu /tófōō/ *n.* curd made from mashed soy beans.

tog /tog/ *n. colloq.* [usu. in *pl.*] item of cloth-ing.

■ *n.* (*togs*) see CLOTHES.

to•ga /tógə/ *n. hist.* ancient Roman citizen's loose flowing outer garment. □□ **to′gaed** *adj.*

to•geth•er /təgéthər/ • *adv.* **1** in company or conjunction (*walking together*). **2** simultane-ously (*both shouted together*). **3** one with an-other (*were talking together*). **4** so as to unite (*tied them together*). **5** into company or com-panionship. • *adj. colloq.* well organized or controlled. □ **together with** as well as.

■ *adv.* **2** see *at once* 2 (ONCE), *at one time* 2

(TIME). • *adj.* see POISED 1. □ **together with** see PLUS *prep.*

to•geth•er•ness /təgéthərnis/ *n.* **1** being to-gether. **2** feeling of comfort from being to-gether.

tog•gle /tógəl/ *n.* **1** pin or other crosspiece put through the eye of a rope, a link of a chain, etc., to keep it in place. **2** *Computing* switch action that is operated the same way but with opposite effect on successive occa-sions. □ **toggle switch** electric switch with a lever to be moved usu. up and down.

toil /toyl/ • *v.intr.* **1** work laboriously or in-cessantly. **2** make slow painful progress. • *n.* prolonged or intensive labor; drudgery. See synonym study at LABOR. □□ **toil′er** *n.*

■ *v.* **1** see LABOR *v.* 1, 2. **2** see LABOR *v.* 5. • *n.* see LABOR *n.* 1.

toi•let /tóylit/ *n.* **1 a** fixture, as in a bathroom, etc., for defecating and urinating. **b** lavatory. **2** process of washing oneself, dressing, etc. □ **toilet paper** (or **tissue**) paper for clean-ing oneself after excreting. **toilet water** di-luted perfume.

■ **1** rest room, washroom, outhouse, privy, men's room, ladies' room, powder room, uri-nal; *Mil.* latrine, *Naut.* head; sl. john, can. **2** grooming, toilette. □ **toilet water** see PER-FUME *n.* 2.

toi•let•ry /tóylitree/ *n.* (*pl.* **–ries**) [usu. in *pl.*] any of various articles or cosmetics used in washing, dressing, etc.

toi•lette /twaalét/ *n.* = TOILET 2.

toil•some /tóylsəm/ *adj.* involving toil; labo-rious.

■ arduous, strenuous, backbreaking, ex-hausting, tiring.

to•ken /tókən/ *n.* **1** thing serving as a symbol, reminder, or mark (*token of affection*). **2** any-thing used to represent something else, esp. a metal disk, etc., used instead of money. **3** [*attrib.*] **a** nominal or perfunctory (*token effort*). **b** chosen by tokenism to represent a particular group (*token woman on the commit-tee*). See synonym study at EMBLEM. See syn-onym study at SIGN. □ **by the same token 1** similarly. **2** moreover.

■ **1** sign, marker, badge, emblem; souvenir, memento, keepsake. **2** voucher; coin, counter. **3** (*attrib.*) **a** superficial, surface, minimal, slight. **b** symbolic, representative.

to•ken•ism /tókənizəm/ *n.* **1** esp. *Polit.* grant-ing of minimum concessions, esp. to appease radical demands, etc. **2** making only a token effort.

told *past* and *past part.* of TELL.

tol•er•a•ble /tólərəbəl/ *adj.* **1** endurable. **2** fairly good. □□ **tol′er•a•bly** *adv.*

■ **1** bearable, permissible, acceptable. **2** or-dinary, average, so-so, run-of-the-mill, pass-able, *colloq.* OK, okay, not (too) bad, pretty good.

tol•er•ance /tólərəns/ *n.* **1** willingness or ability to tolerate; forbearance. **2** capacity to tolerate. **3** allowable variation in any meas-urable property.

■ **1** open-mindedness, broad-mindedness, lenience, patience. **3** play, clearance, allow-ance.

tol•er•ant /tólərənt/ *adj.* **1** disposed to toler-

ate. **2** [foll. by *of*] enduring or patient.
□□ **tol′er•ant•ly** *adv.*

■ **1** open-minded, forgiving, unprejudiced, broad-minded, lenient; fair, considerate.

tol•er•ate /tólərayt/ *v.tr.* **1** allow the existence or occurrence of without interference. **2** endure (suffering, etc.). **3** be able to take (a drug, radiation, etc.) without harm. □□ **tol•er•a•tion** /–áyshən/ *n.* **tol′er•a•tor** *n.*

■ **1** permit, accept, condone, put up with. **2, 3** bear, stand, sustain, weather.

toll[1] /tōl/ *n.* **1** charge to use a bridge, road, etc. **2** cost or damage caused by a disaster, etc. **3** charge for a long distance telephone call. □ **take its toll** be accompanied by loss, injury, etc.

■ **1** fee, tariff; excise, duty, levy, tax. **2** loss.

toll[2] /tōl/ • *v.* **1 a** *intr.* (of a bell) sound with slow, uniform strokes. **b** *tr.* ring (a bell) in this way. **2** *tr.* strike (the hour). • *n.* **1** tolling. **2** stroke of a bell.

■ peal, chime, knell.

toll•booth /tólbōōth/ *n.* booth on toll road, bridge, etc., from which tolls are collected.

Tol•tec /tóltek, tól / *n.* **1 a** N. American people that flourished in Mexico before the Aztecs. **b** member of this people. **2** language of this people.

tom /tom/ *n.* male animal, esp. a cat (in full **tom′cat**) or a turkey.

tom•a•hawk /tóməhawk/ *n.* Native American war ax.

to•ma•to /təmáytō, –máa–/ *n.* (*pl.* **-toes**) glossy red or yellow, pulpy edible fruit. **2** plant bearing this. □□ **to•ma′to•ey** *adj.*

tomb /tōōm/ *n.* **1** burial vault. **2** grave.

■ sepulcher, crypt, catacomb, final resting place.

tom•boy /tómboy/ *n.* girl who behaves in a traditionally boyish way. □□ **tom′boy•ish** *adj.* **tom′boy•ish•ness** *n.*

tomb•stone /tōōmstōn/ *n.* stone over a grave, usu. with an epitaph.

■ gravestone, headstone, tablet, marker, monument.

tome /tōm/ *n.* large heavy book or volume.

■ see BOOK *n.* 1.

tom•fool•er•y /tómfōōləree/ *n.* (*pl.* **-ies**) foolish behavior.

tom•my gun /tómee/ *n.* type of submachine gun.

tom•my•rot /tómeerot/ *n. sl.* nonsense.

to•mog•ra•phy /təmógrəfee/ *n.* method of radiography displaying details in a selected plane within the body.

to•mor•row /təmáwrō, –mór– / • *adv.* **1** on the day after today. **2** at some future time. • *n.* **1** the day after today. **2** the near future.

■ *n.* **2** days *or* time to come.

tom-tom /tómtom/ *n.* **1** early drum beaten with the hands. **2** tall drum used in jazz bands, etc.

ton /tun/ *n.* **1** (in full **short ton**) unit of weight equal to 2,000 lb. (907.19 kg). **2** (in full **long ton**) unit of weight equal to 2,240 lb. (1016.05 kg). **3** = *metric ton.* **4** (in full **dis•place′ment ton**) unit of measurement of a ship's weight or volume. **5** [usu. in *pl.*] *colloq.* large number or amount (*tons of money*). □ **weigh a ton** *colloq.* be very heavy.

■ **5** see HEAP *n.* 2, MANY *n.*

ton•al /tónəl/ *adj.* **1** of or relating to tone or tonality. **2** (of a fugue, etc.) having repetitions of the subject at different pitches in the same key. □□ **ton′al•ly** *adv.*

to•nal•i•ty /tōnálitee/ *n.* (*pl.* **-ties**) **1** *Mus.* **a** relationship between the tones of a musical scale. **b** observance of a single tonic key as the basis of a composition. **2** color scheme of a picture.

tone /tōn/ • *n.* **1** musical or vocal sound, esp. with reference to its pitch, quality, and strength. **2** [often in *pl.*] expressive vocal manner or quality. **3** manner of expression in writing or speaking. **4** *Mus.* musical sound, esp. of a definite pitch and character. **5 a** general coloration or contrast in a picture. **b** tint or shade of a color. **6** prevailing attitude or sentiment. **7** proper firmness of bodily organs. • *v.tr.* **1** give the desired tone to. **2** modify the tone of. □ **tone arm** movable arm supporting the pickup of a record player. **tone-deaf** unable to perceive differences of musical pitch accurately. **tone down** make or become softer in tone. **tone up** make or become stronger in tone. □□ **tone′less** *adj.* **tone′less•ly** *adv.*

■ *n.* **1** note. **2** stress, emphasis, accent, intonation, inflection, pitch, tonality, timbre, fullness. **3** style, approach. **5** tinge, hue, cast. **6** feeling, air, atmosphere, mood, aspect, character, tenor, drift, temper, vein, spirit. □ **tone down** modify, moderate, quiet, lower, subdue. **tone up** firm (up), (re)vitalize; see also INTENSIFY. □□ **toneless** muffled, dull, flat, low; see also TONELESS *adj* 2, 4.

ton•er /tónər/ *n.* black or colored powder used in photocopiers, etc., to make letters, images, etc. on paper.

tongs /tawngz, tongz/ *n.pl.* (also **pair of tongs** *sing.*) instrument with two arms for grasping and holding.

tongue /tung/ • *n.* **1** fleshy muscular organ in the mouth used in tasting, licking, and swallowing, and (in humans) for speech. **2** tongue of an ox, etc., as food. **3** faculty of or tendency in speech (*a sharp tongue*). **4** particular language (*the German tongue*). **5** thing like a tongue in shape or position, esp.: **a** a long low promontory. **b** a strip of leather, etc., under the laces in a shoe. **c** a projecting strip on a board, etc., fitting into the groove of another. • *v.* (**tongues, tongued, tongu•ing**) **1** *tr.* produce staccato, etc., effects with (a flute, etc.) by means of tonguing. **2** *intr.* use the tongue in this way. □ **gift of tongues** power of speaking in unknown languages, as one of the gifts of the Holy Spirit (Acts 2). **tongue-and-groove** applied to boards in which a tongue along one edge fits into a groove along the edge of the next. **tongue-in-cheek** *adj.* ironic; slyly humorous. *adv.* insincerely or ironically. **tongue-lashing** severe scolding. **tongue-tied** too shy, embarrassed, or surprised to speak. **tongue twister** sequence of words difficult to pronounce quickly and correctly.

with one's **tongue hanging out** eagerly or expectantly. □□ **tongued** adj. [also in comb.].
tongue′less adj.
■ n. 4 speech; dialect, idiom, talk, vernacular. □ **tongue-in-cheek** adj. see PLAYFUL 2.

tongue-lashing berating, rebuke, reprimand, chastisement, colloq. talking-to.
tongue-tied speechless, at a loss for words, struck dumb, dumbfounded.

ton•ic /tónik/ • n. 1 invigorating medicine. 2 anything serving to invigorate. 3 = *tonic water*. 4 *Mus.* keynote. • adj. invigorating. □ **tonic water** carbonated water containing quinine. □□ **ton′i•cal•ly** adv.
■ n. 1, 2 stimulant, pick-me-up, refresher, colloq. bracer. • adj. restorative, fortifying, bracing, refreshing.

to•night /tənít/ • adv. on the present or approaching evening or night. • n. the evening or night of the present day.

ton•nage /túnij/ n. 1 ship's internal cubic capacity or freight-carrying capacity. 2 charge per ton on freight or cargo.

tonne /tun/ n. = metric ton.

ton•sil /tónsəl/ n. either of two small organs, one on each side of the root of the tongue.

ton•sil•lec•to•my /tónsiléktəmee/ n. (pl. –mies) surgical removal of the tonsils.

ton•sil•li•tis /tónsilítis/ n. inflammation of the tonsils.

ton•so•ri•al /tonsáwreeəl/ adj. usu. joc. of or relating to a barber or hairdressing.

ton•sure /tónshər/ • n. 1 shaving of the crown of the head or the entire head, esp. of a person entering a monastic order. 2 bare patch made in this way. • v.tr. give a tonsure to.

too /too/ adv. 1 to a greater extent than is desirable, permissible, etc. (*too large*). 2 colloq. extremely (*too kind*). 3 in addition (*are they coming, too?*). 4 moreover (*consider, too, the time of year*). □ **none too** barely or not at all (*feeling none too good*).
■ 1 see OVERLY. 2 see VERY adv. 3 see in addition (ADDITION). 4 see MOREOVER.

took past of TAKE.

tool /tool/ • n. 1 implement used to carry out mechanical functions manually or by machine. 2 thing used in an occupation or pursuit (*tools of one's trade*). 3 person used as a mere instrument by another. • v.tr. 1 dress (stone) with a chisel. 2 impress a design on (leather). 3 [foll. by *along, around*, etc.] sl. drive or ride, esp. in a casual or leisurely manner. □□ **tool′er** n.
■ n. 1 utensil, instrument, device, apparatus, appliance, contrivance, mechanism, gadget. 2 (*tools*) kit, gear, tackle, paraphernalia; technique, method, medium. 3 puppet, pawn, dupe, colloq. stooge, sl. sucker. • v. 1 work, carve, cut. 2 embellish, decorate.

SYNONYM STUDY: tool
APPARATUS, APPLIANCE, IMPLEMENT, INSTRUMENT, UTENSIL. A wrench is a **tool**, meaning that it is a device held in and manipulated by the hand and used by a mechanic, plumber, carpenter, or other laborer to work, shape,

move, or transform material (*he couldn't fix the drawer without the right tools*). An **implement** is a broader term referring to any tool or mechanical device used for a particular purpose (*agricultural implements*). A washing machine is an **appliance**, which refers to a mechanical or power-driven device, especially for household use (*The newly married couple went shopping for appliances*). A **utensil** is also for domestic use (*eating utensils*), while an **instrument** is used for scientific or artistic purposes (*musical instrument, surgical instrument*). **Apparatus** refers to a collection of distinct *instruments, tools*, or other devices that are used in connection with one another for a certain purpose (*the gym was open, but the exercise apparatus had not been set up*).

tool•mak•er /toolmaykər/ n. person who makes precision tools. □□ **tool′mak•ing** n.

toot /toot/ • n. 1 short sharp sound as made by a horn. 2 sl. drinking session; binge. • v. 1 tr. sound (a horn, etc.) with a short sharp sound. 2 intr. give out such a sound. □□ **toot′er** n.

tooth /tooth/ n. (pl. **teeth** /teeth/) 1 each of a set of hard, bony, enamel-coated structures in the jaws of most vertebrates, used for biting and chewing. 2 toothlike part or projection, e.g., the cog of a gearwheel, point of a saw or comb, etc. 3 [in pl.] force; effectiveness (*penalties give the contract teeth*). □ **armed to the teeth** completely and elaborately armed. **fight tooth and nail** fight very fiercely. **get** (or **sink**) **one's teeth into** devote oneself seriously to. **in the teeth of** 1 in spite of (opposition or difficulty, etc.). 2 contrary to (instructions, etc.). 3 directly against (the wind, etc.). □□ **toothed** adj. [also in comb.]. **tooth′less** adj. **tooth′like** adj.
■ □ **in the teeth of** 1 see DESPITE prep.

tooth•ache /toothayk/ n. pain in a tooth or teeth.

tooth•brush /toothbrush/ n. brush for cleaning the teeth.

tooth•paste /toothpayst/ n. paste for cleaning the teeth.

tooth•pick /toothpik/ n. small sharp instrument for removing food lodged between the teeth.

tooth•some /toothsəm/ adj. 1 delicious. 2 attractive. □□ **tooth′some•ly** adv. **tooth′some•ness** n.
■ see DELICIOUS.

tooth•y /toothee/ adj. (**tooth•i•er, tooth•i•est**) having large, numerous, or prominent teeth.

too•tle /tootl/ v.intr. 1 toot gently or repeatedly. 2 colloq. move casually or aimlessly. □□ **too′tler** n.

top[1] /top/ • n. 1 highest point or part. 2 highest rank or place. 3 upper part or surface. 4 garment for the upper part of the body. 5 lid of a jar, saucepan, etc. 6 utmost degree; height (*at the top of his voice*). 7 [in pl.] colloq. person or thing of the best quality (*tops at swimming*). • adj. 1 highest in position (*top shelf*). 2 highest in degree or importance (top speed). • v.tr. (topped, top•ping) 1 provide with a top, cap, etc. 2 be higher or better than; surpass (topped the list). □ on top in a superior position; above. on top of 1 fully in command of. 2 in close proximity to. 3 in addition to. on top of the world *colloq.* exuberant. top banana 1 *Theatr. sl.* comedian who tops the bill of a show. 2 *sl.* head of an organization, etc. top brass esp. *Mil. colloq.* highest ranking officers, etc. top dog *colloq.* victor or master. top drawer *colloq.* high social position or origin. top-drawer *colloq.* of high social standing; of the highest level or quality. top-notch *colloq.* first rate. top off 1 put an end or the finishing touch to (a thing). 2 fill up, esp. a container already partly full. top secret of the highest secrecy. □□ top′most adj.

■ n. 1 summit, apex, peak, acme, crest, pinnacle, tip. 5 stopper, cork, cover, cap. 7 (tops) see high-class. • adj. 1 uppermost, topmost. 2 greatest, maximum; best, foremost, leading, preeminent, first, first-rate, premier, finest; excellent, superior, superb, supreme, unequaled. • v. 1 cover, crown; garnish. 2 exceed, outdo, excel, beat. □ on top overhead, on high. on top of the world ecstatic, delighted, elated, overjoyed; *colloq.* on cloud nine. top banana 2 see HEAD¹ n. 4. top dog see MASTER n. 1, VICTOR. top-drawer see high-class. top-notch see first-rate adj. top off 1 see COMPLEMENT v. 1. □□ topmost see TOP adj. above, UPPERMOST adj. 1.

top² /top/ n. twirling toy that spins on a point.

to•paz /tópaz/ n. transparent or translucent mineral, usu. yellow, used as a gem.

top•coat /tópkōt/ n. 1 overcoat. 2 outer coat of paint, etc.

top-heav•y /tóphévee/ adj. 1 disproportionately heavy at the top. 2 (of an organization, etc.) having a disproportionately large number of people in administrative positions. □□ top′-heav•i•ness n.

to•pi•ar•y /tópee əree/ • adj. of or formed by clipping shrubs, trees, etc., into ornamental shapes. • n. (pl. -ies) topiary art.

top•ic /tópik/ n. subject of a discourse, conversation, argument, etc.

■ matter, issue, question, point, thesis, theme.

top•i•cal /tópikəl/ adj. 1 dealing with the news, current affairs, etc. 2 (of medicine, etc.) applied to or affecting a part of the body. □□ top•i•cal•i•ty / kálitee/ n. top′i•cal•ly adv.

■ 1 contemporary, up-to-date, timely. 2 localized.

top•knot /tópnot/ n. knot, tuft, crest, or bow worn or growing on the head.

top•less /tóplis/ adj. 1 without a top. 2 a (of clothes) having no upper part. b (of a person) barebreasted. c (of a place) where women go or work topless. □□ top′less•ness n.

top•mast /tópmast/ n. *Naut.* mast next above the lower mast.

to•pog•ra•phy /təpógrəfee/ n. 1 detailed description, mapping, etc., of the features of a town, district, etc. 2 such features. □□ to•pog′ra•pher n. top•o•graph•ic /tópəgráfik/

adj. top•o•graph•i•cal adj. top•o•graph•i•cal•ly adv.

top•ping /tóping/ n. thing that tops another thing, as on cake, ice cream, pizza, etc.

top•ple /tópəl/ v. [usu. foll. by over, down] 1 fall or cause to fall as if top-heavy. 2 overthrow.

■ 1 drop, collapse, keel over, tumble down; upset, upend, knock down or over, fell, capsize. 2 bring or throw down, overcome, overturn, unseat, oust.

top•sail /tópsayl, -səl/ n. square sail next above the lowest; fore-and-aft sail on a gaff.

top•side /tópsīd/ n. side of a ship above the waterline.

top•soil /tópsoyl/ n. top layer of soil.

top•spin /tópspin/ n. spinning motion imparted to a ball in tennis, etc., by hitting it forward and upward.

top•sy-tur•vy /tópseetúrvee/ adv. & adj. 1 upside down. 2 in utter confusion.

■ adj. 1 head over heels, backward, vice versa. 2 chaotic, disorderly, mixed-up, *colloq.* every which way.

toque /tōk/ n. woman's small brimless hat.

tor /tor/ n. hill or rocky peak.

torch /tawrch/ • n. 1 thing lit for illumination. 2 source of heat, illumination, or enlightenment (torch of freedom). • v.tr. *sl.* set alight with or as with a torch. □ carry a torch for suffer from unrequited love for. torch song popular song of unrequited love.

■ n. 1 flambeau, lamp, light

tore *past* of TEAR¹.

tor•e•a•dor /táwreeədor/ n. bullfighter, esp. on horseback.

to•ri•i /táwree-ee/ n. (pl. same) gateway of a Shinto shrine, with two uprights and two crosspieces.

tor•ment • n. /táwrment/ 1 severe physical or mental suffering. 2 cause of this. • v.tr. /tawrmént/ 1 subject to torment. 2 tease or worry excessively. □□ tor•men′tor n.

■ n. 1 agony, wretchedness, anguish, distress, misery, pain, torture, hell. 2 vexation, harassment, ordeal, persecution, nuisance, bane, irritation, bother, affliction, curse, plague, scourge. • v. 1 torture, abuse, mistreat, distress. 2 trouble, annoy, badger, pester, nag, victimize, bully; taunt, *colloq.* needle, *sl.* rag. □□ tormentor see *oppressor* (OPPRESS).

torn *past part.* of TEAR¹.

tor•na•do /tawrnáydō/ n. (pl. -does) violent, usu. localized storm with whirling winds in a funnel-shaped cloud.

tor•pe•do /tawrpeedō/ • n. (pl. -does) cigar-shaped, self-propelled, underwater explosive missile. • v.tr. (-does, -doed) 1 destroy or attack with a torpedo. 2 destroy (a policy, institution, plan, etc.).

tor•pid /táwrpid/ adj. 1 sluggish; inactive; dull; apathetic. 2 (of a hibernating animal) dormant. □□ tor•pid′i•ty n. tor′pid•ly adv. tor′pid•ness n.

■ 1 slow-moving, lethargic, passive, inert, languid, lifeless, listless, indifferent. 2 see DORMANT 1. □□ torpidity, torpidness see TORPOR.

tor•por /táwrpər/ *n.* torpidity. □□ **tor•por•if•ic** /-pərífik/ *adj.*

■ sluggishness, lethargy, apathy, indolence, passivity, drowsiness, sleepiness, inactivity, inertia, languor, laziness, listlessness, indifference.

torque /tawrk/ *n. Mech.* moment of a system of forces tending to cause rotation.

tor•rent /táwrənt, tór-/ *n.* **1** a rushing stream of liquid. **2** [usu. in *pl.*] great downpour of rain. **3** violent or copious flow. □□ **tor•ren•tial** /tərénshəl/ *adj.* **tor•ren'tial•ly** *adv.*

■ **1, 3** flood, deluge, effusion, gushing, outburst, outpouring, inundation. **2** see DOWNPOUR. □□ **torrential** streaming, copious, profuse, teeming, relentless; fierce, ferocious.

tor•rid /táwrid, tór-/ *adj.* **1 a** (of the weather) very hot and dry. **b** (of land, etc.) parched by such weather. **2** passionate; intense. □ **torrid zone** the part of the earth between the Tropics of Cancer and Capricorn. □□ **tor'rid•ly** *adv.* **tor'rid•ness** *n.*

■ **1 a** fiery, sultry, stifling, sweltering; broiling; tropical. **b** scorched, arid. **2** fervent, ardent, impassioned, lustful, amorous. □□ **torridness** see HEAT *n.* 1.

tor•sion /táwrshən/ *n.* twisting, esp. of one end of a body while the other is held fixed.

tor•so /táwrsō/ *n.* (*pl.* **–sos** or **tor•si**) **1** trunk of the human body. **2** statue of this.

tort /tawrt/ *n. Law* breach of duty (other than under contract) leading to liability for damages.

torte /tawrt/ *n.* elaborate sweet cake.

tor•til•la /tawrtéeyə/ *n.* thin, flat, orig. Mexican corn or wheat bread eaten with or without a filling.

tor•toise /táwrtəs/ *n.* turtle, esp. a land turtle. □□ **tor'toise•like** *adj. & adv.*

tor•toise•shell /táwrtəs-shel/ • *n.* yellowish brown, mottled or clouded outer shell of some turtles, used for jewelry, etc. • *adj.* having the coloring or appearance of tortoiseshell.

tor•tu•ous /táwrchŏŏəs/ *adj.* **1** full of twists and turns. **2** devious; circuitous. □□ **tor•tu•os•i•ty** /-ósitee/ *n.* (*pl.* **–ties**) **tor'tu•ous•ly** *adv.* **tor'tu•ous•ness** *n.*

■ **1** winding, serpentine, meandering, curvy. **2** roundabout, indirect, complicated, convoluted, warped, crooked, tricky, misleading, deceptive. □□ **tortuosity** see MEANDER *n.*

tor•ture /táwrchər/ • *n.* **1** infliction of severe bodily pain, esp. as a punishment or a means of persuasion. **2** severe physical or mental suffering. • *v.tr.* subject to torture. □□ **tor'tur•er** *n.* **tor'tur•ous** *adj.* **tor'tur•ous•ly** *adv.*

■ *n.* **1** see *persecution* (PERSECUTE). **2** see TORMENT *n.* 1. • *v.* see PERSECUTE, TORMENT *v.*

To•ry /táwree/ • *n.* (*pl.* **–ries**) **1** esp. *Brit. colloq.* a supporter or member of the Conservative party. **2** *Hist.* member of the British party that gave rise to the Conservative party (opp. WHIG). **3** colonist loyal to the English during the American Revolution. • *adj.* col-

loq. of or characteristic of Conservatives or the Conservative party. □□ **To'ry•ism** *n.*

toss /taws, tos/ • *v.* **1** *tr.* throw up (a ball, etc.). **2** *tr. & intr.* roll about, throw, or be thrown, restlessly or from side to side. **3** *tr.* throw (a thing) lightly or carelessly. **4** *tr.* **a** throw (a coin) into the air to decide a choice, etc., by the side on which it lands. **b** [also *absol.*] settle a question or dispute with (a person) in this way (*tossed him for the armchair*). **5** *tr.* prepare (salads, etc.) by mixing or shaking. • *n.* **1** act of tossing (a coin, etc.). **2** fall, esp. from a horse. □ **toss-up** *n.* **1** doubtful matter; even chance (*it's a toss-up whether he wins*). **2** tossing of a coin. □□ **toss'er** *n.*

■ *v.* **1** cast, lob, pitch, fling, hurl, heave, launch, send, let fly, propel, catapult, sling. **2** lurch, bob; agitate, jiggle; wriggle, squirm, thrash. **4 a** flip.

tot /tot/ *n.* small child.

to•tal /tót'l/ • *adj.* **1** complete; comprising the whole. **2** absolute (*in total ignorance*). • *n.* total number or amount. • *v.* (**to•taled, to•tal•ing; to•talled, to•tal•ing**) **1** *tr.* **a** amount in number to (*they totaled 131*). **b** find the total of (things, a set of numbers, etc.). **2** *intr.* [foll. by *to, up to*] amount to. **3** *tr. sl.* demolish. □□ **to'tal•ly** *adv.*

■ *adj.* **1** entire, full, gross. **2** unmitigated, utter, out-and-out, thorough, perfect, outright, downright. • *n.* sum (total), aggregate. • *v.* **1 b** add (up), reckon, compute. **2** (*total up to*) add up to, come to, make. **3** see TRASH *v.* 1.

to•tal•i•tar•i•an /tótàlitáireeən/ • *adj.* of a dictatorial government requiring complete subservience. • *n.* person advocating such a system. □□ **to•tal•i•tar'i•an•ism** *n.*

■ *adj.* absolute, autocratic, oppressive, despotic, tyrannical. • *n.* absolutist, authoritarian, fascist, Nazi.

to•tal•i•ty /tótálitee/ *n.* complete amount.

■ total, whole, entirety, beginning and end.

tote /tōt/ *v.tr. colloq.* carry; convey. □ **tote bag** open-topped bag for shopping, etc. □□ **tot'er** *n.* [also in *comb.*]

■ see CARRY *v.* 1, 2.

to•tem /tótəm/ *n.* **1** natural object or animal adopted by Native American people as an emblem of a clan or individual. **2** image of this. □ **totem pole** pole on which totems are carved or hung. □□ **to•tem•ic** /-témik/ *adj.* **to'tem•ism** *n.*

tot•ter /tótər/ • *v.intr.* **1** stand or walk unsteadily or feebly. **2 a** shake as if about to collapse. **b** (of a system of government, etc.) be about to fall. • *n.* unsteady or shaky movement. □□ **tot'ter•er** *n.* **tot'ter•y** *adj.*

■ *v.* dodder, falter, stagger; tremble, teeter, sway, rock, reel, wobble, quiver, quake.

tou•can /tóŏkan/ *n.* tropical American fruiteating bird with an immense beak and brightly colored plumage.

touch /tuch/ • *v.* **1** *tr.* come into or be in physical contact with (another thing). **2** *tr.* bring the hand, etc., into contact with. **3 a** *intr.* (of two things, etc.) be in or come into contact. **b** *tr.* bring (two things) into contact (*they touched hands*). **4** *tr.* rouse tender or painful feelings in (*touched by his appeal*). **5** *tr.* strike lightly. **6** *tr.* [usu. with *neg.*] **a** disturb or harm (*don't touch my things*). **b** have any dealings with (*won't touch that subject*). **c** consume; make use of (*dare not touch alcohol, need not touch your savings*). **7** *tr.* concern. **8** *tr.* [usu. with *neg.*] approach in excellence, etc. (*can't touch him for style*). **9** *tr.* (as **touched** *adj.*) slightly mad. • *n.* **1** act of touching. **2 a** faculty of perception through physical contact, esp. with the fingers. **b** qualities of an object, etc., as perceived in this way (*soft touch of silk*). **3** small amount; slight trace. **4 a** manner of playing keys or strings. **b** response of the keys or strings. **c** distinguishing style of workmanship, writing, etc. **5** *sl.* act of asking for and getting money, etc., from a person. □ **easy touch** *sl.* person who readily parts with money. **finishing touch** (or **touch'es**) final details completing and enhancing a piece of work, etc. **in touch** [often foll. by *with*] **1** in communication. **2** up to date, esp. regarding news, etc. **3** aware. **lose touch 1** cease to be informed. **2** cease to be in contact. **lose one's touch** not show one's customary skill. **out of touch 1** not in correspondence. **2** not up to date. **3** lacking in awareness (*out of touch with his son's beliefs*). **soft touch** = *easy touch* (above). **touch and go** risky. **touch base (with)** make contact with. **touch down** (of an aircraft or spacecraft) make contact with the ground in landing. **touch football** football with touching in place of tackling. **touch-me-not** any of various plants with ripe seed capsules bursting open when touched. **touch off 1** explode by touching with a match, etc. **2** initiate (a process) suddenly. **touch on** (or **upon**) **1** refer to or mention casually. **2** verge on (*touches on impudence*). **touch-tone** of or relating to a tone dialing telephone system. **touch-type** type without looking at the keys. **touch typing** this skill. **touch-typist** person who touch-types. **touch up** give finishing touches to or retouch. □□ **touch·a·ble** *adj.* **touch'er** *n.*

■ *v.* **1** border, adjoin. **2** feel, handle; see also FONDLE. **3 a** meet. **4** affect, impress, disturb, move, stir, excite. **5** brush, graze, tap. **6 a** meddle with, tamper with; come near, approach. **b** have to do with, handle. **c** drink, eat, taste; employ, get. **7** see CONCERN *v.* 1a. **8** rival, match, equal, compare with, come up to, be on a par with, be in the same league as or with, reach, hold a candle to, measure up to or against, *colloq.* stack up to. **9** (**touched**) see MAD *adj.* 1. • *n.* **1** pat, tap, dab, blow, hit, stroke, brush, caress. **2 a** feeling. **b** feel, texture. **3** dash, hint, suggestion, pinch, tinge, taste, suspicion, smattering, smack, drop, scent, smell. **4 a, c** approach, technique, execution, method; see also INSTINCT *n.* 2. **b** responsiveness. □ **in touch 2** see INFORMED 1. **3** (*in touch with*) see SENSIBLE 4. **touch and go** see PRECARIOUS. **touch down** alight, come to earth. **touch off 1** detonate, ignite, light. **2** instigate, set in motion, set off, trigger, provoke, foment, cause, give rise to. **touch on** (or

upon) **1** pertain to, relate to, have a bearing on, regard, allude to. **2** border on, resemble. **touch up** edit, polish; beautify, enhance, renovate, restore, spruce up. □□ **touchable** tangible, tactile, palpable.

touch•down /túchdown/ *n.* **1** act of landing by an aircraft. **2** *Football* act or instance of scoring by crossing the goal line.

■ **1** see LANDING 1a.

tou•ché /tooshay/ *int.* **1** acknowledgment of a hit by a fencing opponent. **2** acknowledgment of a justified accusation, witticism, or point made in reply to one's own.

touch•ing /túching/ *adj.* moving; pathetic. □□ **touch'ing•ly** *adv.*

■ stirring, emotional, tender, heartwarming, poignant, heartrending, heartbreaking, sad, pitiful, distressing, distressful.

touch•stone /túchstōn/ *n.* **1** dark schist or jasper used for testing alloys by marking it with them. **2** criterion.

■ **2** standard, yardstick, benchmark, test, norm.

touch•y /túchee/ *adj.* (**touch·i·er, touch·i·est**) **1** apt to take offense; overly sensitive. **2** not to be touched without danger; ticklish; risky; awkward. □□ **touch'i·ly** *adv.* **touch'i·ness** *n.*

■ **1** high-strung, thin-skinned, testy, irritable, edgy, short-tempered, cross, *colloq.* grouchy, cranky. **2** touch and go, precarious, hazardous, chancy, unsure, uncertain, *sl.* hairy; see also AWKWARD 3. □□ **touchiness** see SENSITIVITY (SENSITIVE).

tough /tuf/ • *adj.* **1** hard to break, cut, tear, or chew. **2** able to endure hardship; hardy. **3** unyielding; difficult. **4** *colloq.* **a** acting sternly. **b** (of circumstances, luck, etc.) severe; hard. **5** *colloq.* criminal or violent (*tough guys*). • *n.* tough person, esp. a hoodlum. □ **tough it out** *colloq.* endure or withstand difficult conditions. □□ **tough'en** *v.* **tough'en•er** *n.* **tough'ly** *adv.* **tough'ness** *n.*

■ *adj.* **1** firm, durable, heavy-duty, strong, rugged, sturdy, sound, indestructible, unbreakable, resilient; stiff, inflexible. **2** stalwart, brawny, powerful, virile, intrepid, vigorous, robust, strapping. **3** demanding, exacting; arduous, taxing, strenuous, puzzling, tricky; stubborn, obstinate, adamant. **4 a** harsh, strict, unbending, unfeeling, callous, cold, *colloq.* hard-nosed. **b** see SEVERE² 1. • *n.* hooligan, rowdy, thug, ruffian, *sl.* hood. □ **tough it out** see *stick it out* (STICK). □□ **toughen** see STRENGTHEN. **toughness** see STRENGTH 1.

tou•pee /toopáy/ *n.* hairpiece to cover a bald spot.

tour /toor/ • *n.* **1** pleasure journey from place to place. **2** term of military or diplomatic duty. **3** series of performances, games, etc., at different places. • *v.* **1** *intr.* make a tour (*toured through Italy*). **2** *tr.* make a tour of (a country, etc.). □ **on tour** (esp. of a team, theater company, etc.) touring.

■ *n.* **1** trip, excursion, outing, expedition, trek, jaunt, junket. **2** spell, shift, stint, assignment, turn, stretch. • *v.* **1** travel, sightsee, cruise. **2** visit, see, explore, *colloq.* take in, do.

tour de force /tŏŏr də fôrs/ *n.* feat of strength or skill.

tour•ism /tŏŏrizəm/ *n.* tourist booking and travel.

■ tourist *or* leisure industry.

tour•ist /tŏŏrist/ *n.* person traveling for pleasure (often *attrib.: tourist accommodations*).

■ traveler, voyager, visitor, sightseer, vacationer.

tour•ma•line /tŏŏrməlin, –leen/ *n.* mineral of various colors used in electrical and optical instruments and as a gemstone.

tour•na•ment /tŏŏrnəmənt, tôr–/ *n.* **1** large contest of many rounds. **2** *hist.* pageant with jousting.

■ **1** competition, championship, match, event, meet. **2** tilt.

tour•ney /tŏŏrnee, tôr–/ *n.* tournament.

tour•ni•quet /tərnikit, tŏŏr–/ *n.* device for stopping arterial blood flow.

tou•sle /tŏwzəl/ *v.tr.* make (esp. the hair) untidy; rumple.

■ dishevel, disarrange, mess (up), *colloq.* muss (up).

tout /towt/ • *v.* **1** *tr. & intr.* solicit patronage persistently. **2** *intr.* **a** spy out the movements and condition of racehorses in training. **b** offer racing tips for profit. • *n.* person who touts. □□ **tout'er** *n.*

■ *v.* **1** hawk, peddle, sell, promote, talk up, push, *colloq.* plug. • *n.* barker, tipster.

tow /tō/ • *v.tr.* pull along by a rope, etc. • *n.* towing; being towed. □ **have in tow 1** be towing. **2** be accompanied by and often in charge of (a person).

■ drag, draw, haul, lug, tug, trawl.

to•ward /tawrd, təwawrd, twawrd/ (also **to•wards** /tawrdz, təwawrdz, twawrdz/) *prep.* **1** in the direction of (*set out toward town*). **2** as regards; in relation to (*attitude toward death*). **3** as a contribution to; for (*toward your expenses*). **4** near (*toward the end of our journey*).

■ **1** to; for, on the way *or* road to. **2** concerning, about, regarding, with respect to. **3** supporting, promoting, assisting. **4** close to, approaching, shortly before.

tow•el /tŏwəl/ • *n.* piece of absorbent cloth or paper used for drying after washing. • *v.* **1** *tr.* [often *refl.*] wipe or dry with a towel. **2** *intr.* wipe or dry oneself with a towel. □□ **tow'el•ing** *n.*

tow•er /tŏwər/ • *n.* **1** tall structure, often part of a church, castle, etc. **2** fortress, etc., with a tower. **3** tall structure housing machinery, etc. (*cooling tower, control tower*). • *v.intr.* **1** reach or be high or above; be superior. **2** (as **towering** *adj.*) **a** high; lofty (*towering intellect*). **b** violent (*towering rage*).

■ *n.* **1** bell tower, minaret, obelisk; belfry, turret, steeple. **2** citadel, stronghold. • *v.* **1** loom, soar, rise, ascend, rear; (*tower above*) see OVERSHADOW 1. **2** (*towering*) **a** sky-high; great, impressive, imposing, huge, gigantic, mighty; unequaled, unrivaled, unparalleled, unsurpassed. **b** excessive, in-

tense, overwhelming, extreme, colossal, enormous.

tow•head /tōhed/ *n.* person with very light blond hair. □□ **tow'head•ed** *adj.*

town /town/ *n.* **1 a** defined area between a village and a city in size. **b** densely populated area, esp. as opposed to the country. **2** central business area in a neighborhood (*going into town*). □ **go to town** *colloq.* act with energy or enthusiasm. **on the town** *colloq.* enjoying the entertainments of a town; celebrating. **town hall** building for the administration of local government. **town house 1** town residence, esp. of a person with a house in the country. **2** house in a development.

■ **1** community; municipality, township. **2** downtown.

town•ie /townee/ *n. colloq.* person living in a town, esp. as opposed to a student, etc.

towns•folk /townzfōk/ *n.* inhabitants of a town.

town•ship /township/ *n.* division of a county in some states, having limited corporate powers.

towns•peo•ple /townzpeepəl/ *n.pl.* inhabitants of a town.

tox•e•mi•a /tokseemeeə/ *n.* blood poisoning.

tox•ic /tóksik/ *adj.* **1** of poison. **2** poisonous. □□ **tox•ic'i•ty** /–sisitee/ *n.*

■ **2** see *poisonous* (POISON). □□ **toxicity** see *virulence* (VIRULENT).

tox•i•col•o•gy /tóksikóləjee/ *n.* scientific study of poisons. □□ **tox•i•co•log•i•cal** /–kəlójikəl/ *adj.* **tox•i•col'o•gist** *n.*

tox•in /tóksin/ *n.* poison produced by a living organism.

■ see POISON *n.* 1.

toy /toy/ • *n.* **1** plaything. **2** thing regarded as providing amusement. **3** [usu. *attrib.*] diminutive breed of dog, etc. • *v.intr.* [usu. foll. by *with*] **1** trifle; amuse oneself; flirt. **2** move a thing idly.

■ *n.* trifle, trinket. **3** [*attrib.*] miniature, tiny, small, dwarf. • *v.* **1** dally, play, *colloq.* dillydally. **2** (*toy with*) fool with, fiddle with, tinker with, finger.

tp. *abbr.* **1** (also **t.p.**) title page. **2** township. **3** troop.

tpk. *abbr.* turnpike.

trace[1] /trays/ • *v.tr.* **1 a** observe, or find vestiges or signs of by investigation. **b** follow or mark the track or position of. **c** follow to its origins (*can trace my family to the 12th century*). **2** copy (a drawing, etc.) by drawing over its lines on superimposed translucent paper. **3** mark out, often laboriously (*traced out a plan*). **4** pursue one's way along (a path, etc.). • *n.* **1 a** indication of something having existed; vestige. **b** very small quantity. **2** track; footprint. □ **trace element 1** chemical element occurring in minute amounts. **2** chemical element required only in minute amounts by living organisms for normal growth. □□ **trace'a•ble** *adj.* **trace•a•bil'i•ty** *n.*

■ *v.* **1 a, c** discover, ascertain, detect, determine, search for, hunt down. **b** dog, pursue, stalk, track (down), locate, shadow, trail, *colloq.* tail. **2** reproduce. **3** delineate, outline, describe, map, chart, sketch. • n. 1 a hint, intimation, sign, token, suggestion, relic, remains, remnant, record, evidence, clue. b bit, spot, speck, grain, jot, drop, dash, touch, fragment, shred, taste, iota. 2 spoor.

SYNONYM STUDY: trace

REMNANT, TRACK, TRAIL, VESTIGE. You can follow the **track** of a deer in the snow, the **trace** of a sleigh, or the **trail** of someone who has just cut down a Christmas tree and is dragging it back to the car. A *track* is a line or a series of marks left by the passage of something or someone; it often refers specifically to a line of footprints or a path worn into the ground or grass by the feet (*to follow the track of a grizzly bear*). **Trace** usually refers to a line or a rut made by someone or something that has been present or passed by; it may also refer to a mark serving as evidence that something has happened or been there (*traces of mud throughout the house*). **Trail** may refer to the *track* created by the passage of animals or people, or to the mark or marks left by something being dragged along a surface (*they followed the trail of the injured dog*). **Vestige** and **remnant** come closer in meaning to *trace*, as they refer to what remains after something has passed away. A *vestige* is always slight when compared to what it recalls (*the last vestiges of a great civilization*), while a *remnant* is a fragment or scrap of something (*all that remained of the historic tapestry after the fire were a few scorched remnants*).

trace² /trays/ n. each of two straps, chains, or ropes by which a horse draws a vehicle.

trac•er /tráysər/ n. 1 person or thing that traces. 2 bullet, etc., that is visible in flight because of flames, etc., emitted. 3 radioactive isotope that can be followed through the body by the radiation it produces

trac•er•y /tráysəree/ n. (pl. **-ies**) 1 ornamental stone openwork, esp. in the upper part of a Gothic window. 2 fine decorative pattern.

tra•che•a /tráykeeə/ n. (pl. **tra•che•ae** /-kee-ee/ or **tra•che•as**) windpipe. □□ **tra'che•al** adj.

tra•che•ot•o•my /traykeeótəmee/ n. (pl. **-mies**) incision in the trachea to relieve an obstruction.

trac•ing /tráysing/ n. 1 copy of a drawing, etc., made by tracing. 2 act of tracing. □ **tracing paper** translucent paper for tracing.

track /trak/ • n. 1 mark or marks left by a person, animal, or thing in passing. 2 rough path, esp. one beaten by use. 3 continuous line of railroad rails. 4 a racecourse. b prepared course for runners, etc. c various sports performed on a track, as running or hurdles. 5 section of a record, compact disc, etc., containing one song, etc. 6 line of travel or motion. 7 line of reasoning or thought. See synonym study at TRACE. • v.tr. 1 follow the track of. 2 trace (a course, development, etc.). 3 make a track with (dirt, etc.) from the feet. □ **in one's tracks** colloq. where one stands (*stopped him in his tracks*). **keep** (or **lose**) **track of** follow (or fail to follow) the

course of. **make tracks** colloq. go or run away. **off the track** away from the subject. **on the wrong side of the tracks** colloq. in an inferior or dubious part of town. **on the wrong** (or **right**) **track** following the wrong (or right) line of inquiry. **track down** reach or capture by tracking. **track record** person's past performance.

■ n. 1 spoor, footprint(s), print(s), trace(s), scent, wake. 2 trail, route, footpath, course, road. 4 racetrack. 6 see COURSE¹ n. 2. 7 see LINE n. 14. • v. 1 dog, pursue, stalk, shadow, hunt down, chase, *colloq.* tail. 2 see *keep track of* (TRACK) below. □ **keep track of** keep an eye on, monitor, supervise, oversee, watch, keep a record of or on. **lose track of** misplace, mislay, lose sight of, forget. **track down** find, discover, seek out, ferret out, hunt down, apprehend, sniff out, run down. **track record** see RECORD n. 5.

tract¹ /trakt/ n. 1 region or area of indefinite, esp. large, extent. 2 *Anat.* bodily organ or system (*respiratory tract*).

■ 1 stretch, territory, expanse, zone, sector, quarter, district; plot, parcel, lot.

tract² /trakt/ n. pamphlet, esp. political or religious.

■ treatise, article, paper; booklet, brochure, leaflet.

trac•ta•ble /tráktəbəl/ adj. easily handled; manageable. □□ **trac•ta•bil'i•ty** n.

■ docile, tame, compliant, submissive, obedient, yielding; workable, adaptable, malleable, pliable, pliant, flexible. □□ **tractability** see *flexibility* (FLEXIBLE).

trac•tion /trákshən/ n. 1 act of drawing or pulling a thing over a surface. 2 therapeutic pulling on a limb, muscle, etc. 3 gripping power on a surface.

■ 2 see TENSION n. 1. 3 drag, friction, adhesion.

trac•tor /tráktər/ n. vehicle used for hauling machinery, heavy loads, etc. □ **tractor-trailer** truck consisting of a tractor or cab unit attached to a trailer.

trade /trayd/ • n. 1 a buying and selling. b this between nations, etc. c business conducted for profit (esp. as distinct from a profession). d business of a specified nature or time (*tourist trade*). 2 skilled professional craft. 3 transaction, esp. a swap. 4 [usu. in pl.] = trade wind. • v. 1 intr. engage in trade; buy and sell. 2 a. a exchange in commerce; barter (goods). b exchange (insults, blows, etc.). 3 intr. have a transaction with a person for a thing. □ **trade deficit** extent by which a country's imports exceed its exports. **trade in** exchange (esp. a used car, etc.) in part payment for another. **trade-in** n. thing exchanged in this way. **trade off** exchange, esp. as a compromise. **trade-off** n. such an exchange. **trade on** take advantage of (a person's reputation, etc.). **trade secret** 1 secret device or technique used esp. in a trade. 2 joc. any secret. **trade wind** wind blowing continually toward the equator and deflected westward. □□ **trad'a•ble**, **trade'a•ble** adj.

■ n. 1 a, b commerce, traffic. d clientele,

patrons, following. **2** calling, occupation, pursuit, employment, line (of work), job, vocation, career, profession. **3** exchange, profession. deal. • *v.* **1** transact *or* do business. □ **trade in** see REDEEM 3.

trade•mark /tráydmaark/ *n.* **1** device, word, or words, secured by law or custom as representing a company, product, etc. **2** distinctive characteristic, etc.

■ **1** see BRAND *n.* lb. **2** see HALLMARK *n.* 2.

trad•er /tráydər/ *n.* person, ship, etc., engaged in trade.

■ dealer, merchant, broker, distributor, vendor, buyer, purchaser, retailer, wholesaler.

trades•man /tráydzmən/ *n.* (*pl.* **–men**; *fem.* **trades•wom•an**, *pl.* **–wom•en**) person engaged in trading or a trade.

■ craftsman, journeyman, handicraftsman.

trad•ing /tráyding/ *n.* act of engaging in trade. □ **trading post** store, etc., in a remote or unsettled region.

tra•di•tion /trədíshən/ *n.* **1 a** custom, opinion, or belief handed down to posterity. **b** this process of handing down. **2** valued convention or observance. **3** artistic, literary, etc., principles based on experience and practice. □□ **tra•di•tion•al** *adj.* **tra•di•tion•al•ly** *adv.*

■ **1, 2** practice, habit, ritual, rite, unwritten law, institution, form, lore, folklore. □□ **traditional** customary, usual, routine, habitual, standard, stock, time-honored, classical, established, well-known, conventional, orthodox, historic, old, ancestral.

tra•di•tion•al•ism /trədíshənəlizəm/ *n.* respect for tradition, esp. in religion. □□ **tra•di•tion•al•ist** *n.*

■ □□ **traditionalist** SEE REACTIONARY *n.*

tra•duce /trədoos, -dyoos/ *v.tr.* speak ill of; misrepresent. □□ **tra•duce′ment** *n.* **tra•duc′er** *n.*

traf•fic /tráfik/ • *n.* **1** [often *attrib.*] vehicles moving on a public highway, in the air, or at sea. **2** trade, esp. illegal. **3** comings and goings. **4** dealings between people, etc. **5 a** transmitted messages. **b** volume of these. • *v.* (**traf•ficked, traf•fick•ing**) **1** *intr.* [usu. foll. by *in*] deal in something, esp. illegally. **2** *tr.* deal in; barter. □ **traffic circle** road junction at which traffic moves in one direction around a central island. **traffic jam** traffic at a standstill. **traffic light** *or* **traf′fic sig•nal**) signal with colored lights to control road traffic. □□ **traf′fick•er** *n.*

■ *n.* **3** movement, conveyance, shipping, transportation. **4** see DEALINGS. • *v.* (*traffic in*) see DEAL *v.* 2. □ **traffic circle** rotary. **traffic jam** gridlock, congestion, backup.

tra•ge•di•an /trəjeedeeən/ *n.* **1** writer of tragedies. **2** actor in tragedy.

trag•e•dy /trájidee/ *n.* (*pl.* **–dies**) **1** serious accident, crime, disaster, etc.; great misfortune. **2 a** play dealing with tragic events and with an unhappy ending, esp. concerning the downfall of the protagonist. **b** tragic plays as a genre.

■ **1** catastrophe, calamity, adversity, blow.

trag•ic /trájik/ *adj.* **1** sad; calamitous; greatly distressing. **2** of tragedy. □□ **trag′i•cal•ly** *adv.*

■ **1** depressing, lamentable, unhappy, mournful, grievous, dismal, pitiful, appalling, wretched, dreadful, awful, terrible, horrible, deplorable, miserable, heartrending, disturbing, upsetting, shocking, unfortunate, ill-fated, catastrophic, disastrous.

trag•i•com•e•dy /trájikómidee/ *n.* (*pl.* **–dies**) play or situation having a mixture of comedy and tragedy. □□ **trag•i•com′ic** *adj.*

trail /trayl/ • *n.* **1** track left by a moving thing, person, etc. **2** beaten path or track, esp. through a wild region. **3** part dragging behind a thing or person (*trail of smoke*). See synonym study at TRACE. • *v.* **1** *tr. & intr.* draw or be drawn along behind, esp. on the ground. **2** *intr.* walk wearily (behind); lag. **3** *tr.* follow the trail of; pursue. **4** *intr.* be losing in a contest. **5** *intr.* [usu. foll. by *off*] peter out. **6** *intr.* **a** (of a plant, etc.) grow or hang over a wall, along the ground, etc. **b** (of a garment, etc.) hang loosely.

■ *n.* **1** spoor, scent, smell, trace, footsteps, footprints, path, wake. **2** footpath, route, course. • *v.* **1** tow, drag (along), haul, pull, trawl; stream, sweep, dangle. **2** dawdle, loiter, linger, follow, straggle, bring up the rear. **3** dog, shadow, stalk, track, chase, hunt, *colloq.* tail. **4** be down. **5** (*trail off* or *away*) diminish, disappear, dwindle, subside, taper off, weaken, grow faint or dim.

trail•blaz•er /tráylblayzər/ *n.* **1** person who marks a new track through wild country. **2** pioneer. □□ **trail′blaz•ing** *n.*

trail•er /tráylər/ *n.* **1** scenes from a movie, etc., used to advertise it in advance. **2** vehicle towed by another. **3** mobile home. □ **trailer park** place where trailers are parked as dwellings.

train /trayn/ • *v.* **1 a** *tr.* teach (a person, animal, oneself, etc.) a specified skill, esp. by practice. **b** *intr.* undergo this process. **2** *tr. & intr.* bring or come into a state of physical fitness by exercise, diet, etc. **3** *tr.* cause (a plant) to grow in a required shape. **4** (usu. as **trained** *adj.*) make (the mind, eye, etc.) discerning through practice. **5** *tr.* point or aim (a gun, camera, etc.). • *n.* **1** series of railroad cars drawn by an engine. **2** thing dragged along behind or forming the back part of a dress, robe, etc. **3** succession or series of people, things, events, etc. □ **train of thought** sequence or direction in one's thinking process. □□ **train•ee** /-neé/ *n.* **train′ing** *n.*

■ *v.* **1 a** discipline, tutor, coach, drill, instruct, prepare, educate, edify, rear, raise. **2** work out. **4** (**trained**) see EXPERIENCED 2. **5** see AIM *v.* 2. • *n.* **1** *colloq.* choo-choo. **3** line, procession, chain, caravan, parade, column, file, row; retinue, entourage, following, attendants. □□ **trainee** see NOVICE. **training** workout; practice, rehearsal; see also EDUCATION 1.

train•er /tráynər/ *n.* **1** person who prepares horses, athletes, etc., for competition. **2** aircraft or simulator used to train pilots.

■ **1** see TEACHER.

traipse /trayps/ *v.intr. colloq.* tramp or trudge wearily.

trait /trayt/ *n.* distinguishing feature or characteristic.

■ attribute, quality, peculiarity, idiosyncrasy, hallmark.

trai·tor /tráytər/ *n.* (*fem.* **trai·tress** /-tris/) person who is treacherous or disloyal, esp. to his or her country. □□ **trai'tor·ous** *adj.* **trai'tor·ous·ly** *adv.*

■ turncoat, Judas, double-crosser, snake (in the grass), double-dealer, *colloq.* two-timer. □□ **traitorous** seditious, subversive, insurgent, deceitful, untrue, unfaithful. **traitorously** behind a person's back.

tra·jec·to·ry /trəjéktəree/ *n.* (*pl.* **-ries**) path of an object moving under given forces.

■ flight path, course, track.

tram·mel /tráməl/ • *n.* **1** [usu. in *pl.*] impediment; hindrance. **2** triple dragnet for fish. • *v.tr.* confine; hamper.

■ *n.* **1** (*trammels*) shackle(s), restriction(s), restraint(s), deterrent(s), constraint(s), hitch(es), snag(s), (stumbling) block(s), obstacle(s). • *v.* impede, hinder, handicap, curb, deter, block, obstruct.

tramp /tramp/ • *v.* **1** *intr.* **a** walk heavily and firmly. **b** go on foot, esp. a distance. **2** *tr.* cross on foot, esp. wearily or reluctantly. **3** *tr.* tread on; trample; stamp on. • *n.* **1** itinerant vagrant or beggar. **2** sound of a person, or esp. people, walking, marching, etc., or of horses' hooves. **3** long walk. **4** *sl. derog.* promiscuous woman. **5** (also **tramp steam·er**) merchant ship that takes on any cargo available.

■ *v.* **1 a** plod, stomp, clump, clomp, trudge, lumber. **b** march, hike, trudge, plow. **2** see TRAVERSE *v.*, WALK *v.* 1, 2, 3b. **3** see TRAMPLE *v.* 1. • *n.* **1** derelict, vagabond, drifter, hobo, bum. **2** step, footstep. **4** see SLUT.

tram·ple /trámpəl/ *v.tr.* **1** tread underfoot. **2** crush in this way.

■ *v.* **1** stamp (on), stomp (on), step on. **2** press, squash, flatten; stamp out, extinguish, put out, destroy, rout, defeat.

tram·po·line /trámpəleen/ • *n.* strong fabric sheet connected by springs to a horizontal frame, used for gymnastic jumping. • *v.intr.* use a trampoline. □□ **tram·po·lin'ist** *n.*

trance /trans/ *n.* **1 a** sleeplike state without response to stimuli. **b** hypnotic or cataleptic state. **2** state of rapture; ecstasy.

■ *n.* **1** daze, stupor; reverie. **2** exaltation; see also ECSTASY.

tran·quil /trángkwil/ *adj.* calm; serene; unruffled. See synonym study at CALM. □□ **tran· quil'li·ty** *n.* **tran'quil·ly** *adv.*

■ placid, quiet, peaceful, still, smooth, relaxed, restful; sedate, steady, cool, composed. □□ **tranquillity** see CALM *n.* 1. **tranquilly** see EASY *adv.*

tran·quil·ize /trángkwilīz/ *v.tr.* make tranquil, esp. by a drug, etc.

■ calm, soothe, pacify, still, quiet, relax, lull, sedate.

tran·quil·iz·er /trángkwilīzər/ *n.* drug used to diminish anxiety.

■ barbiturate, opiate, sedative.

trans- /trans, tranz/ *prefix* **1** across; beyond

(*transcontinental*). **2** on or to the other side of (*transatlantic*). **3** into another state or place (*transform*).

trans. *abbr.* **1** transaction. **2** transfer. **3** transitive. **4** (also **transl.**) translated; translation; translator. **5** transmission. **6** transportation.

trans·act /tranzákt, –sákt/ *v.tr.* perform or carry through (business). □□ **trans·ac'tor** *n.*

■ do, carry on *or* out, conduct, administer, discharge, perform, enact, conclude, complete, finish.

trans·ac·tion /tranzákshən, –sák-/ *n.* **1 a** business agreement; deal. **b** management of business, etc. **2** [in *pl.*] published reports of the proceedings of a learned society.

■ **1** negotiation, matter, affair, arrangement. **2** (*transactions*) record(s), acts, minutes, annals, report(s).

trans·at·lan·tic /tránzətlántik, trans-/ *adj.* **1** beyond the Atlantic Ocean. **2** crossing the Atlantic (*a transatlantic flight*).

tran·scend /transénd/ *v.tr.* **1** be beyond the range or grasp of (human experience, reason, belief, etc.). **2** excel; outdo; surpass. □□ **tran·scend'ence** *n.* **tran·scend'en·cy** *n.* **tran·scend'ent** *adj.* **tran·scend'ent·ly** *adv.*

■ **1** lie outside, exceed. **2** outdistance, outdo, overshadow, top, rise above, outshine, eclipse, beat. □□ **transcendence, transcendency** see *predominance* (PREDOMINANT) **transcendent** peerless, incomparable, unequaled, unrivaled, unparalleled, unique, superior, supreme, preeminent, sublime, superb, magnificent, marvelous.

tran·scen·den·tal /tránsendént'l/ *adj.* **1** = *transcendent* (TRANSCEND). **2 a** not based on experience; a priori. **b** innate in the mind. **3** visionary, abstract. □ **transcendental meditation** method of detaching oneself from anxiety, etc., by meditation. □□ **tran· scen·den'tal·ism** *n.* **tran·scen·den'tal·ist** *n.* **tran·scen·den'tal·ly** *adv.*

■ see OCCULT *adj.*

trans·con·ti·nen·tal /tránzkontinént'l/ *adj.* (of a railroad, etc.) extending across a continent.

tran·scribe /transkríb/ *v.tr.* **1** make a copy of, esp. in writing. **2** transliterate. **3** write out (shorthand, notes, etc.). **4** arrange (music) for a different instrument, etc. □□ **tran· scrib'er** *n.* **tran·scrip'tion** /-skripshən/ *n.*

■ **1** reproduce, replicate, duplicate, record. **2, 3** translate, render, interpret. □□ **transcriber** see SCRIBE *n.* 1. **transcription** see TRANSCRIPT.

tran·script /tránskript/ *n.* written or recorded copy.

■ record, transliteration; carbon copy, duplicate, photocopy, facsimile, fax, reproduction.

trans·duc·er /tranzdoosar, –dyoo-, trans-/ *n.* device for converting a nonelectrical signal into an electrical one, e.g., pressure into voltage.

tran·sect /transékt/ *v.tr.* cut across or transversely. □□ **tran·sec·tion** /-sékshən/ *n.*

tran•sept /tránsept/ n. either arm of a cross-shaped church at right angles to the nave (north transept, south transept).

trans•fer • v. /transfár/ (**trans•ferred, trans•fer•ring**) 1 tr. [often foll. by to] a convey, remove, or hand over. b make over the possession of (property, rights, etc.) to a person. 2 tr. & intr. change or move to another group, club, department, etc. 3 intr. change from one station, route, etc., to another on a journey. 4 tr. convey (a drawing, etc.) from one surface to another. • n. /tránsfar/ 1 transferring or being transferred. 2 design, etc., conveyed or to be conveyed from one surface to another. 3 a conveyance of property, a right, etc. b document effecting this. 4 ticket for transferring during travel. □□ **trans•fer′a•ble** adj.

■ v. 1 a move, transport, carry, take, deliver, bring, transmit, cart, haul, shift, turn over, give, pass (on or along or over). b see make over 1. 2 see TRANSPLANT v. 1, MOVE v. 1, 2. 3 switch. • n. 1 conveyance, transmission, delivery, transferral.

trans•fer•ence /transfárans, tránsfar–/ n. 1 transferring; being transferred. 2 Psychol. redirection of childhood emotions to a new object, esp. to a psychoanalyst.

trans•fig•ure /transfigyar/ v.tr. change in form or appearance, esp. so as to elevate or idealize. □□ **trans•fig•u•ra′tion** n.

■ see TRANSFORM v.

trans•fix /transfiks/ v.tr. 1 pierce with a sharp implement or weapon. 2 paralyze with horror or astonishment.

■ 1 pin, fix, impale, skewer, nail, spear, spike, stick, stab. 2 enrapture, hypnotize, mesmerize, rivet, fascinate, bewitch, enchant, engross, stun, colloq. stop a person in his or her tracks.

trans•form /transfáwrm/ v. 1 tr. make a thorough or dramatic change in the form, appearance, character, etc., of. 2 intr. [often foll. by into, to] undergo such a change. □□ **trans•for•ma′tion** n.

■ modify, transfigure, alter, transmute, turn into, convert, mutate. □□ **transformation** metamorphosis, conversion, permutation, revolution.

trans•form•er /transfáwrmar/ n. apparatus for reducing or increasing the voltage of an electrical current.

trans•fuse /transfyóoz/ v.tr. 1 permeate. 2 a transfer (blood) from one person or animal to another. b inject (liquid) into a blood vessel to replace lost fluid. □□ **trans•fu•sion** /-fyóozhan/ n.

■ 1 infuse, imbue; instill, transmit.

trans•gress /transgrés/ v.tr. [also absol.] go beyond the bounds or limits set by (a commandment, law, etc.); violate. □□ **trans•gres•sion** /-gréshan/ n. **trans•gres′sor** n. See synonym study at SIN

■ sin, err, fall from grace, misbehave, go wrong or astray; break or overstep or disobey the law. □□ **transgression** offense, error, disobedience, misdeed, misdemeanor,

crime, wrongdoing, infraction. **transgressor** sinner, criminal, felon, culprit, lawbreaker, reprobate, villain.

tran•sient /tránzhant, –shant, –zeeant/ • adj. of short duration; passing. See synonym study at TEMPORARY. • n. temporary visitor, worker, etc. □□ **tran′sience** n.

■ adj. transitory, temporary, brief, fleeting, ephemeral, short-lived, short-term. • n. see MIGRANT n.

tran•sis•tor /tranzístar/ n. 1 semiconductor device with three connections, capable of amplification in addition to rectification. 2 (in full **tran•sis′tor ra′dio**) portable radio with transistors.

■ 2 see RADIO n.

tran•sit /tránzit, –sit/ n. 1 going, conveying, or being conveyed, esp. over a distance. 2 passage; route. 3 apparent passage of a celestial body across the meridian of a place or across the sun or a planet. □ **in transit** while going or being conveyed. □ in transit while going or being conveyed.

■ n. 1 moving, movement, travel, traveling, motion, passing, progress, progression, transition; transport, transportation, conveyance, transfer, transference.

tran•si•tion /tranzíshan, –síshan/ n. passing or change from one place, state, condition, style, etc., to another.

■ alteration, metamorphosis, changeover, transformation, transmutation, mutation, development, evolution, conversion, modification; progress, progression, passage. □□ **transitional** see INTERMEDIATE adj.

tran•si•tive /tránzitiv, –si–/ adj. Gram. (of a verb or sense of a verb) that takes a direct object (whether expressed or implied), e.g., saw in saw the donkey, saw that she was ill.

tran•si•to•ry /tránzitawree/ adj. not permanent; transient. See synonym study at TEMPORARY. □□ **tran′si•to•ri•ly** adv. **tran′si•to•ri•ness** n.

■ see BRIEF adj. 1, TRANSIENT adj.

trans•late /tránzláyt, tráns–/ v. 1 tr. [also absol.] express the sense of (a word, text, etc.) in another language. 2 intr. be translatable (does not translate well). 3 tr. express (an idea, book, etc.) in another, esp. simpler, form. 4 tr. interpret (translated his silence as dissent). □□ **trans•lat′a•ble** adj. **trans•la•tion** /-láyshan/ n. **trans′la•tor** n.

■ 1 convert (into), rewrite (in), transcribe (into); decipher. 3 explain, rephrase, reword, elucidate, spell out. 4 construe, take, understand, read; infer as. □□ **translation** rewording; rendering, rendition, version, decipherment, decoding.

trans•lit•er•ate /tranzlítarayt, tráns–/ v.tr. represent (a word, etc.) in the closest corresponding characters of a different language. □□ **trans•lit•er•a•tion** /-ráyshan/ n.

■ see TRANSCRIBE 2, 3. □□ **transliteration** see TRANSCRIPT.

trans•lu•cent /tranzlóosant, tráns–/ adj. allowing light to pass through; semitransparent. □□ **trans•lu′cence** n. **trans•lu′cen•cy** n. **trans•lu′cent•ly** adv.

■ see CLEAR¹ adj. 3, see-through (SEE).

trans•mi•grate /tranzmígrayt, tráns–/ v.intr. 1 (of the soul) pass into a different body at death. 2 migrate. □□ **trans•mi•gra•tion** /-gráyshən/ *n.*

trans•mis•sion /tranzmíshən, trans–/ *n.*
1 transmitting; being transmitted. 2 broadcast program. 3 mechanism by which power is transmitted from an engine to the axle in a vehicle.
■ 1 transfer, transference, transferral, conveyance, carriage, movement, transportation, transport, forwarding, shipping, shipment, transmittal, dispatch; dissemination, communication. 2 telecast, show.

trans•mit /tranzmít, trans–/ *v.tr.* (**trans•mitted**, **trans•mit•ting**) 1 a pass or hand on; transfer. b communicate. 2 allow to pass through; conduct. 3 broadcast (a radio or television program). □□ **trans•mis•si•ble** /-mísəbəl/ *adj.* **trans•mit•ta•ble** *adj.* **transmit•tal** *n.*
■ 1 a send, convey, relay, deliver, forward, dispatch, post, ship, radio, telegraph, fax, telex, mail, *colloq.* phone, wire. b see COMMUNICATE 1a. 2 direct, channel. 3 see BROADCAST *v.* 1a. □□ **transmissible** see CATCHING. **transmittal** see TRANSMISSION 1.

trans•mit•ter /tránzmítər, trans–/ *n.* 1 person or thing that transmits. 2 equipment used to transmit radio or other electronic signals.

trans•mog•ri•fy /tranzmógrifī, trans–/ *v.tr.* (**-fies, -fied**) *joc.* transform, esp. in a magical or surprising manner. □□ **trans•mog•ri•fi•ca•tion** *n.*

trans•mute /tranzmyóot, trans–/ *v.tr.* 1 change the form, nature, or substance of. 2 *Alchemy hist.* subject (base metals) to transmutation. □□ **trans•mut•a•ble** *adj.* **trans•mut•a•bil•i•ty** *n.* **trans•mu•ta•tion** *n.*

trans•o•ce•an•ic /tránzósheeánik, tráns–/ *adj.* 1 beyond the ocean. 2 crossing the ocean (*transoceanic flight*).

tran•som /tránsəm/ *n.* 1 horizontal bar of wood or stone across a window or the top of a door. 2 (in full **transom window**) window above a door or larger window.

trans•par•en•cy /tranzpáirənsee, –páiransee, trans–/ *n.* (*pl.* **-cies**) 1 being transparent. 2 photograph, picture, inscription, etc., made visible by a light behind it.

trans•par•ent /tranzpáirənt, –páirənt, trans–/ *adj.* 1 allowing light to pass through; clear and usu. colorless. 2 a (of a disguise, pretext, etc.) easily seen through. b (of a motive, quality, etc.) evident; obvious. 3 easily understood, frank, open. □□ **trans•par•ent•ly** *adv.*
■ 1 crystal clear, diaphanous, see-through, sheer. 2 plain, apparent, patent, manifest, unmistakable, as plain as day. 3 candid, direct, unequivocal, *colloq.* on the level.

tran•spire /t}transpír/ *v.* 1 *intr.* [usu. prec. by it as subject] turn out; prove to be the case (*it transpired he knew nothing about it*). 2 *intr.* occur; happen. 3 *tr. & intr.* emit (vapor, sweat, etc.), or be emitted, through the skin, lungs, or leaves. See synonym study at HAPPEN. □□ **tran•spi•ra•tion** *n.*
■ 1 come to light, emerge. 2 take place, come about, come to pass, materialize, arise.

---

trans•plant • *v.tr.* /tranzplánt, trans–/ 1 plant in or move to another place. 2 *Surgery* transfer (living tissue or an organ) to another part of the body or to another body. • *n.* /tránzplant, tráns–/ 1 *Surgery* a transplanting of an organ or tissue. b such an organ, etc. 2 thing, esp. a plant, transplanted. □□ **trans•plan•ta•tion** *n.*
■ *v.* 1 displace, relocate, shift, uproot, resettle. 2 graft. • *n.* 1 implantation, implant.

tran•spon•der /tranzpóndər, trans–/ *n.* device for receiving a radio signal and automatically transmitting a different signal.

trans•port • *v.tr.* /tranzpáwrt, trans–/ 1 take or carry to another place. 2 (as **transported** *adj.*) affected with strong emotion. • *n.* /tránzpawrt, tráns–/ 1 system or vehicle for conveyance. 2 ship, aircraft, etc., used to carry soldiers, stores, etc. 3 [esp. in *pl.*] vehement emotion (*transports of joy*). See synonym study at RAPTURE. □□ **trans•port•a•ble** *adj.* **trans•port•er** *n.*
■ *v.* 1 move, transfer, ferry, deliver, bring, ship, haul, cart, transmit, send, forward. 2 (**transported**) carried away, captivated, delighted, fascinated; overjoyed, ecstatic, elated. • *n.* 1 transportation, shipment, carriage. 2 rapture, ecstasy.

trans•por•ta•tion /tránzpərtáyshən, tráns–/ *n.* 1 conveying; being conveyed. 2 a system of conveying. b means of this.
■ See TRANSIT *n.* 1.

trans•pose /tranzpóz, trans–/ *v.tr.* 1 a cause (two or more things) to change places. b change the position of (a thing) in a series. 2 change the order or position of (words of a word) in a sentence. 3 *Mus.* write or play in a different key. □□ **trans•pos•er** *n.* **trans•po•si•tion** *n.*
■ 1, 2 exchange, interchange, rearrange, reverse, switch, swap, trade, commute, transfer.

trans•sex•u•al /tránséksh<oo>əl/ • *adj.* having the physical characteristics of one sex but psychological identification with the other. • *n.* 1 transsexual person. 2 person whose sex has been changed by surgery. □□ **trans•sex•u•al•ism** *n.*

tran•ship /tranz-híp, trans–/ *v.tr.* (**-shipped, -ship•ping**) transfer from one ship or form of transport to another. □□ **tran•ship′ment** *n.*

tran•sub•stan•ti•a•tion /tránsəbstánsheeáyshən/ *n. Theol. & RC Ch.* conversion of the Eucharistic elements wholly into the body and blood of Christ.

trans•verse /tránzvórs, tráns–/ *adj.* crosswise. □□ **trans•verse′ly** *adv.*

trans•ves•tite /tranzvéstīt, trans–/ *n.* person who derives pleasure from wearing clothes of the opposite sex. □□ **trans•ves′tism** *n.*

trap /trap/ • *n.* 1 device, often baited, for catching animals. 2 trick betraying a person into speech or an act. 3 arrangement to catch an unsuspecting person. 4 device for hurling an object such as a clay pigeon into the air to be shot at. 5 curve in a downpipe, etc., that fills with liquid and forms a seal against the upward passage of gases. **6** *Golf* bunker. **7** two-wheeled carriage. **8** = TRAPDOOR. **9** *sl.* mouth (esp. *shut one's trap*). **10** [esp. in *pl.*]. *colloq.* percussion instrument, esp. in a jazz band. • *v.tr.* (**trapped, trapping**) **1** catch (an animal) in a trap. **2** catch (a person) by means of a trick, etc. **3** stop and retain in or as in a trap.

■ *n.* **1** snare, pitfall. **2** subterfuge, wile, ruse, stratagem, deception, *colloq.* ploy. **3** ambush, booby trap, setup. **9** *sl.* yap. • *v.* **1** ensnare, capture, net, corner. **2** deceive, fool, dupe, inveigle. **3** imprison, confine, hold, keep, pin down.

trap•door /tráps•dáwr/ *n.* hinged door in a horizontal surface.

tra•peze /trapéez/ *n.* crossbar suspended by ropes used as a swing for acrobatics, etc.

tra•pe•zi•um /trapéezeeam/ *n.* (*pl.* **tra•pe•zi•a** /-zeea/ or **tra•pe•zi•ums**) quadrilateral with no two sides parallel.

trap•e•zoid /trápizoyd/ *n.* quadrilateral with only one pair of sides parallel. □□ **trap•e•zoi′dal** *adj.*

trap•per /trápər/ *n.* person who traps wild animals, esp. to obtain furs.

trap•pings /trápingz/ *n.pl.* **1** ornamental accessories. **2** harness of a horse, esp. when ornamental.

■ **1** accoutrements, paraphernalia, gear, embellishment(s), trimmings.

Trap•pist /trápist/ *n.* monk of an order vowed to silence.

trash /trash/ • *n.* **1** worthless material; rubbish. **2** worthless person or persons. • *v.tr. colloq.* wreck; vandalize; discard.

■ *n.* **1** junk, odds and ends; litter, garbage, waste, refuse, debris, rubble, scrap. **2** see RABBLE 2. • *v.* destroy, ruin, deface, *sl.* total; see also DISCARD *v.*

trash•y /tráshee/ *adj.* (**trash•i•er, trash•i•est**) worthless; poorly made. □□ **trash′i•ness** *n.*

■ see WORTHLESS.

trau•ma /tráwmə, tráw–/ *n.* (*pl.* **trau•ma•ta** /-mətə/ or **trau•mas**) **1** physical injury. **2** physical shock following this. **3** profound emotional shock. □□ **trau′ma•tize** *v.tr.* **trau•ma•ti•za′tion** *n.*

■ **1** see WOUND[1] *n.* 1. **2** see SHOCK[1] *n.* **□□ traumatize** see WOUND[1] *v.*, SHOCK[1] *v.* 1.

trau•mat•ic /trəmátik, trow–, traw–/ *adj.* **1** of or causing trauma. **2** *colloq.* distressing (*traumatic experience*). □□ **trau•mat′i•cal•ly** *adv.*

■ shocking, upsetting, disturbing, painful, agonizing, harmful, hurtful, injurious, damaging, harrowing.

trav. *abbr.* **1** travel. **2** traveler.

tra•vail /trəváyl, trávayl/ *n.* **1** painful or laborious effort. **2** pangs of childbirth. See synonym study at LABOR.

■ *n.* **1** see LABOR *n.* 1. **2** see LABOR *n.* 3.

trav•el /trávəl/ • *v.* **1** *intr.* go from one place to another; make a journey, esp. of some length or abroad. **2** *tr.* **a** journey along or through (a country). **b** cover (a distance) in traveling. **3** *intr.* move or proceed as specified (*light travels faster than sound*). **4** *intr. colloq.* move quickly. **5** *intr.* (of a machine or part) move or operate in a specified way. • *n.* **1 a** traveling, esp. in foreign countries. **b** [often in *pl.*] time or occurrence of this (*returned from their travels*). **2** range, rate, or mode of motion of a part in machinery. □□ **trav′el•er** *n.* **trav′el•ing** *adj.*

■ *v.* **1** move, proceed, roam, rove, tour, take a trip, commute. **2** see TRAVERSE *v.* 1. **3** advance, progress. • *n.* **1 a** tourism. **b** expedition(s), excursion(s), voyage(s), trek(s), pilgrimage(s). □□ **traveler** *n.* tourist, vacationer, sightseer, globe-trotter, rover, wayfarer. **traveling** itinerant, wandering, nomadic, migratory, restless.

trav•eled /trávəld/ *adj.* experienced in traveling (also in *comb.*: *much traveled*).

trav•e•logue /trávəlog/ *n.* (also **trav′e•log**) movie or illustrated lecture about travel.

tra•verse /trávərs, trəvárs/ • *v.tr.* travel or lie across (*traversed the country*). • *n.* **1** traversing. **2** thing that crosses another. □□ **tra•vers′al** *n.* **tra•vers′er** *n.*

■ *v.* crisscross, pass over or through; walk, wander, range; bridge, span, intersect. • *n.* **1** see TRANSIT *n.* 1. □□ **traversal** see PASSAGE 1.

trav•es•ty /trávistee/ • *n.* (*pl.* **–ties**) grotesque misrepresentation or imitation (*travesty of justice*). See synonym study at CARICATURE. • *v.tr.* (**–ties, –tied**) make or be a travesty of.

■ *n.* see PARODY *n.* 2, MOCKERY 1, 2. • *v.* see MOCK *v.* 2.

trawl /trawl/ • *v.* **1** *intr.* fish with a trawl or seine. **2** *tr.* catch by trawling. • *n.* **1** act of trawling. **2** (in full **trawl net**) large widemouthed fishing net dragged by a boat along the sea bottom.

trawl•er /tráwlər/ *n.* boat used for trawling.

tray /tray/ *n.* **1** flat board, usu. with a raised rim, for carrying dishes, etc. **2** shallow lidless box for small articles, papers, etc.

treach•er•ous /tréchərəs/ *adj.* **1** guilty of or involving treachery. **2** (of the weather, ice, the memory, etc.) unreliable; hazardous. □□ **treach′er•ous•ly** *adv.* **treach′er•ous•ness** *n.*

■ **1** see *perfidious* (PERFIDY), *traitorous* (TRAITOR). **2** see DANGEROUS.

treach•er•y /tréchəree/ *n.* (*pl.* **–ies**) violation of faith or trust; betrayal.

■ see *betrayal* (BETRAY).

trea•cle /tréekəl/ *n.* **1** esp. *Brit.* molasses. **2** cloying sentiment. □□ **trea′cly** *adj.*

tread /tred/ • *v.* (**trod** /trod/; **trod•den** /tród′n/ or **trod**) **1** *intr.* set down one's foot; walk; step. **2** *tr.* walk upon. **3** *tr.* perform (steps, etc.) by walking. • *n.* **1** manner or sound of walking. **2** top surface of a step or stair. **3** surface pattern on a tire. **4** shoe part that rests on the ground. □ **tread the boards** be an actor; appear on the stage. **tread water** maintain an upright position in the water by moving the feet and hands.

■ *v.* **1, 3** see WALK *v.* 1, 2, 3b. **2** see TRAMPLE *v.* 1. • *n.* **1** footstep, footfall.

trea•dle /trédəl/ *n.* lever worked by the foot and imparting motion to a machine.

tread•mill /trédmil/ n. **1** device for producing motion by the weight of persons or animals stepping on the inner surface of a revolving upright wheel. **2** monotonous routine work.

■ **2** see RUT¹ 2, LABOR n. 1.

trea•son /tréezən/ n. betrayal of one's nation. □□ **trea'son•a•ble** adj. **trea'son•ous** adj.

■ see PERFIDY. □□ **treasonable** see traitorous (TRAITOR).

treas•ure /trézhər/ • n. **1 a** precious metals or gems. **b** hoard of these. **c** accumulated wealth. **2** thing valued for its rarity, workmanship, associations, etc. **3** colloq. much loved or highly valued person. • v.tr. value highly. • **treasure trove** discovered treasure of unknown ownership.

■ n. **1** wealth, riches, fortune, cache. **3** pride (and joy), delight, darling, apple of one's eye, pearl. • v. hold dear, cherish, appreciate.

treas•ur•er /trézhərər/ n. person in charge of the funds of an organization, etc.

treas•ur•y /trézhəree/ n. (pl. -ies) **1** place or building where treasure is stored. **2** funds or revenue of a nation, institution, or society. **3** (Treasury) **a** department managing the public revenue of a country. **b** offices and officers of this.

■ **1** storehouse, repository, mine, hoard, cache; bank, coffers. **2** purse, resources, finances, money(s). **3** exchequer.

treat /treet/ • v. **1** tr. act or behave toward or deal with in a certain way. **2** tr. apply a process to (treat with acid) **3** tr. apply medical care or attention to. **4** tr. present or deal with (a subject) in literature or art. **5** tr. pay for food, drink, entertainment, etc. **6** intr. negotiate terms (with a person). **7** intr. discuss. • n. **1** delightful event or circumstance. **2** meal, entertainment, etc., paid for by another. □□ **treat'a•ble** adj. **treat'er** n. **treat'ing** n.

■ v. **1** handle, manage; use; consider, regard, look upon, view. **2** prepare, make, produce, **3** nurse, doctor, attend, care for, look after, tend, medicate. **4** touch on or upon, study, examine, explore, investigate, scrutinize, analyze, go into, probe, criticize, review. **5** take out, entertain, play host to; wine and dine; sl. spring for. **7** (treat of) see SPEAK 5. • n. **1** see LUXURY, JOY n. 2. **2** favor, gift, present, bonus, premium, colloq. freebie.

trea•tise /tréetis/ n. written work dealing formally and systematically with a subject.

■ see PAPER n. 6.

treat•ment /tréetmənt/ n. **1** process or manner of behaving toward or dealing with a person or thing. **2** medical care or attention. **3** manner of treating a subject in literature or art.

■ **1** behavior, conduct, action, handling; usage, use. **2** therapy, healing, remedy, cure, medication.

trea•ty /tréetee/ n. (pl. -ties) formal agreement between nations.

■ pact, alliance, covenant, contract, compact, accord, colloq. deal.

tre•ble /trébəl/ • adj. threefold; triple. • n. Mus. = SOPRANO. • v. make or become three

times as much or many; increase threefold. □ **treble clef** Mus. clef placing G above middle C on the second lowest line of the staff.

tree /tree/ • n. **1** branched perennial plant with a woody, self-supporting main stem or trunk. **2** piece or frame of wood, etc., for various purposes (shoe tree). **3** = family tree. • v.tr. **1** force to take refuge in a tree. **2** put into a difficult position. □ **tree line** = TIMBERLINE. **up a tree** cornered; nonplussed. □□ **tree'less** adj.

trek /trek/ • v.intr. (**trekked, trek•king**) travel or make one's way arduously. • n. **1** journey or walk made by trekking. **2** organized migration of a body of persons. □□ **trek'ker** n.

trel•lis /trélis/ n. lattice of light wooden or metal bars, esp. as a support for climbing plants.

trem•a•tode /trémətōd, trée-/ n. type of parasitic flatworm.

trem•ble /trémbəl/ • v.intr. **1** shake involuntarily from weakness, etc. **2** be in a state of extreme apprehension. **3** quiver. • n. trembling; quiver. □□ **trem'bly** adj.

■ v. quake, shiver, shudder, quaver; vibrate, rock, dodder. • n. tremor; vibration.

tre•men•dous /triméndəs/ adj. **1** awe inspiring; overpowering. **2** colloq. remarkable; considerable; excellent. □□ **tre•men'dous•ly** adv.

■ **2** see EXCELLENT, GREAT adj. 1a.

trem•o•lo /tréməlō/ n. Mus. tremulous effect in music.

trem•or /trémər/ n. **1** shaking; quivering. **2** thrill. **3** slight earthquake.

■ n. **1** see QUIVER¹ n. **2** see THRILL n. 1. **3** quake.

trem•u•lous /trémyələs/ adj. trembling. □□ **trem•u•lous•ly** adv. **trem•u•lous•ness** n.

■ atremble, quivering, shaking, quaking, shivering, shuddering, quavering, shaky, colloq. trembly; timid, fearful, nervous, jumpy, colloq. jittery.

trench /trench/ n. **1** long, narrow, usu. deep ditch. **2** Mil. this dug by troops as a shelter from enemy fire. □ **trench coat** loose belted raincoat.

■ n. **1** see FURROW n.

tren•chant /trénchənt/ adj. (of style or language, etc.) incisive; terse; vigorous. □□ **tren'chan•cy** n. **tren'chant•ly** adv.

■ cutting, keen, acute, sharp, pointed, poignant, penetrating, biting, bitter, acerbic, caustic.

tren•cher•man /trénchərmən/ n. (pl. -men) person who eats well, or in a specified manner.

trend /trend/ n. general direction and tendency (esp. of events, fashion, or opinion).

■ n. leaning, bias, bent, drift, course, inclination; style, vogue, mode, look, rage, craze, fad, colloq. thing.

trend•set•ter /tréndsetər/ n. person who leads the way in fashion, etc. □□ **trend'set•ting** adj.

trend•y /tréndee/ adj. colloq. (**trend•i•er,**

trend•i•est) often *derog.* fashionable.
□□ **trend′i•ly** *adv.* **trend′i•ness** *n.*
■ stylish, modern, latest, up-to-the-minute, in vogue, in, all the rage, *colloq.* with it.
□□ **trendiness** see *popularity* (POPULAR).

trep•i•da•tion /trépidáyshən/ *n.* fear; anxiety.
■ see ALARM *n.* 3.

tres•pass /tréspəs, –pas/ • *v.intr.* **1** make an unlawful or unauthorized intrusion (esp. on land or property). **2** encroach (*trespass on your hospitality*). • *n. Law* act of trespassing. □□ **tres′pass•er** *n.*
■ *v.* see ENCROACH. □□ **trespasser** see IN-TRUDER.

tress /tres/ *n.* **1** long lock of human hair. **2** [in *pl.*] head of hair.
■ *n.* **1** see LOCK² 1. **2** (*tresses*) *colloq.* mane.

tres•tle /trésəl/ *n.* **1** supporting structure for a table, etc., usu. consisting of a bar with two divergent pairs of legs. **2** open braced framework to support a bridge, etc.

trey /tray/ *n.* the three on dice or cards.

tri- /trī/ *comb. form* three or three times.

tri•ad /trī́ad/ *n.* group of three (esp. notes in a chord).

tri•age /tree-aázh, trée-aazh/ *n.* assignment of priorities for treatment of wounds, illnesses, etc.

tri•al /trī́əl/ *n.* **1** judicial examination and determination of issues between parties by a judge with or without a jury. **2** tryout; test. **3** affliction (*trials of old age*). □ **on trial 1** being tried in a court of law. **2** to be proved or tested. **trial and error** repeated (usu. unsystematic) attempts continued until successful. **trial run** preliminary operational test.
■ **1** hearing, inquiry, inquisition, litigation, judicial proceeding, lawsuit, contest. **2** experiment, *colloq.* dry run; attempt, endeavor, effort. **3** trouble, hardship, adversity, suffering, misery, distress, misfortune, ordeal; bother, annoyance, hassle.

tri•an•gle /trī́anggəl/ *n.* **1** plane figure with three sides and angles. **2** three things not in a straight line, with imaginary lines joining them. **3** implement of this shape. **4** triangular steel musical instrument struck with a small steel rod. **5** situation, esp. an emotional relationship, involving three people. □□ **tri•an′gu•lar** *adj.*

tri•an•gu•late /trīánggyəlayt/ *v.tr.* measure and map (an area) by dividing it into triangles. □□ **tri•an•gu•la•tion** /–láyshən/ *n.*

Tri•as•sic /trīásik/ *Geol.* • *adj.* of the earliest period of the Mesozoic era. • *n.* this period.

tri•ath•lon /trīáthlən, –lon/ *n.* three-event competition, usu. comprising running, swimming, and bicycling. □□ **tri•ath′lete** /–leét/ *n.*

trib. *abbr.* **1** tribunal. **2** tribune. **3** tributary.

tribe /trīb/ *n.* **1** group of (esp. primitive) families or communities, usu. linked by cultural ties and having a recognized leader. **2** any similar natural or political division. □□ **trib′al** *adj.* **trib′al•ism** *n.*
■ race, nation, breed, people, clan, dynasty, house.

tribes•man /trī́bzmən/ *n.* (*pl.* **–men**) member of a tribe.

trib•u•la•tion /tríbyəláyshən/ *n.* great affliction.
■ see *affliction* (AFFLICT).

tri•bu•nal /trībyōōnəl, tri–/ *n.* **1** board appointed to adjudicate in some matter. **2** court of justice. **3** seat or bench for a judge or judges.
■ **1** see BOARD *n.* 3. **2** bar.

trib•une /trī́byōōn, tribyṓōn/ *n.* **1** popular leader. **2** official in ancient Rome chosen by the people to protect their interests.

trib•u•tar•y /tríbyəteree/ • *n.* (*pl.* **–ies**) **1** river or stream flowing into a larger river or lake. **2** *hist.* person or nation paying or subject to tribute. • *adj.* **1** (of a river, etc.) that is a tributary. **2** *hist.* **a** paying tribute. **b** serving as tribute.
■ *n.* **1** branch, offshoot, feeder, brook, creek, rivulet, run, rill, runnel.

trib•ute /tríbyōōt/ *n.* **1** thing said, done, or given as a mark of respect or affection. **2** *hist.* periodic payment by one nation or ruler to another.
■ **1** honor, homage, recognition, celebration, esteem, testimonial, compliment, acclaim, praise, accolade, eulogy. **2** tax, impost, duty, tariff, surcharge, contribution, offering, gift; ransom.

trice /trīs/ *n.* □ **in a trice** in a moment; instantly.

tri•ceps /trī́seps/ *adj.* muscle (esp. in the upper arm) with three points of attachment at one end.

tri•cer•a•tops /trīsérətops/ *n.* dinosaur with three sharp horns on the forehead and a wavy neck crest.

trich•i•no•sis /tríkinósis/ *n.* disease caused by hairlike worms, ingested in undercooked meat.

trick /trik/ • *n.* **1** action or scheme to fool, outwit, or deceive. **2** illusion (*trick of the light*). **3** special technique; knack. **4** feat of skill or dexterity. **5** practical joke. **6 a** cards played in one round of a card game. **b** point gained in this. **7** [*attrib.*] done to deceive or mystify (*trick photography, trick question*). • *v.tr.* **1** deceive by a trick; outwit. **2** swindle (*tricked out of their savings*). □ **do the trick** *colloq.* achieve the required result. **how's tricks?** *colloq.* how are you?
■ *n.* **1** ruse, deceit, fraud, subterfuge, sham, *sl.* con. **2** deception. **3** art, skill, secret, gift. **4** accomplishment, deed; stunt, *archaic* sleight of hand. **5** prank, hoax, gag. • *v.* fool, hoodwink, dupe, cheat, defraud, take in, *colloq.* bamboozle, take for a ride, *sl.* bilk. □ **do the trick** work, suffice, solve the problem, fill or fit the bill.

trick•er•y /tríkəree/ *n.* (*pl.* **–ies**) deception; use of tricks.
■ chicanery, deceit, guile, craftiness, duplicity, fraud, *colloq.* monkey business.

trick•le /tríkəl/ • *v.* **1** *intr. & tr.* flow or cause to flow in drops or a small stream. **2** *intr.* come or go slowly or gradually (*information trickles out*). • *n.* trickling flow.
■ *v.* **1** drip, drop, dribble, drizzle; ooze, seep, leak. • *n.* seepage, spill.

trick•ster /tríkstər/ n. deceiver; rogue.
■ see ROGUE n. 1.

trick•y /trikee/ adj. (**trick•i•er, trick•i•est**)
1 requiring care and adroitness. 2 crafty; deceitful. □□ **trick'i•ly** adv. **trick'i•ness** n.
■ 1 ticklish, risky, hazardous, sensitive, delicate, touch-and-go, thorny, difficult, awkward, complex, complicated, intricate, knotty, uncertain, colloq. iffy, sticky. 2 shady, deceptive, shrewd, cunning, dishonest, devious, sly, slippery, colloq. shifty. □□ **trickiness**
SEE ARTIFICE 2.

tri•col•or /tríkulər/ • n. flag of three colors, esp. the French national flag of blue, white, and red. • adj. (also **tri'col•ored**) having three colors.

tri•corn /tríkawrn/ • adj. (of a hat) having a brim turned up on three sides. • n. tricorn hat.

tri•cot /treekō/ n. knitted fabric.

tri•cy•cle /trísikəl/ n. three-wheeled pedal-driven vehicle.

tri•dent /tríd'nt/ n. three-pronged spear.

tried past and past part. of TRY.

tri•en•ni•al /trī-éneeəl/ adj. lasting or recurring every three years. □□ **tri•en'ni•al•ly** adv.

tri•fect•a /trīféktə/ n. form of betting in which the first three places in a race must be predicted in the correct order.

tri•fle /trífəl/ • n. 1 thing of slight value or importance. 2 a small amount, esp. of money. b [prec. by a] somewhat (a trifle annoyed). • v. intr. 1 talk or act frivolously. 2 [foll. by with] treat or deal with frivolously.
■ n. 1 knickknack, trinket, bauble, plaything, triviality, doodad. 2 b little, bit, drop, iota, dash, dab, pinch, colloq. smidgen, tad. • v. 2 flirt, toy, play.

tri•fling /trífling/ adj. 1 unimportant; petty. 2 frivolous.
■ 1 trivial, insignificant, puny, minor, paltry, slight, inconsequential, superficial, incidental, negligible, colloq. piddling. 2 see IDLE adj. 5, 6.

tri•fo•cal /trīfōkəl/ • adj. having three focuses, esp. of a lens with different focal lengths. • n. [in pl.] trifocal eyeglasses.

tri•fo•ri•um /trīfáwreeəm/ n. (pl. **tri•fo•ri•a** /-reeə/) upper gallery or arcade in a church.

trig /trig/ n. colloq. trigonometry.

trig•ger /trígər/ • n. 1 movable device for releasing a spring or catch and so setting off a mechanism (esp. that of a gun). 2 event, occurrence, etc., that sets off a chain reaction. • n.tr. set (an action or process) in motion; precipitate. □ **trigger-happy** apt to shoot without or with slight provocation. □□ **trig'gered** adj.
■ v. see INITIATE v. 1.

trig•o•nom•e•try /trígənómitree/ n. branch of mathematics dealing with the relations of the sides and angles of triangles and with the relevant functions of angles. □□ **trig•o•no•met•ric** /-nəmétrik/, **trig•o•no•met'ri•cal** adj.

tri•lat•er•al /trīlátərəl/ adj. 1 of, on, or with three sides. 2 involving three parties, countries, etc.

trill /tril/ • n. 1 quavering sound, esp. a rapid

---

alternation of sung or played notes. 2 bird's warbling. 3 pronunciation of r with a vibration of the tongue. • v. 1 intr. produce a trill. 2 tr. warble (a song) or pronounce (r, etc.) with a trill.
■ n. 2 see CHIRP n. • v. see CHIRP v.

tril•lion /trílyən/ n. (pl. same or **tril•lions**) a million million (1,000,000,000,000 or 10^{12}). □□ **tril'lionth** adj. & n.

tri•lo•bite /trílɔbīt/ n. kind of three-lobed fossil marine arthropod.

tril•o•gy /trílɔjee/ n. (pl. **–gies**) group of three related literary or operatic works.

trim /trim/ • v.tr. (**trimmed, trim•ming**)
1 make neat or of the required size or form, esp. by cutting. 2 cut off (unwanted parts). 3 ornament; decorate. 4 adjust the balance of (a ship or aircraft) by arranging its cargo, etc. 5 arrange (sails) to suit the wind. • n. 1 state of readiness or fitness (in perfect trim). 2 ornament; decorative material. 3 cutting of a person's hair. • adj. 1 neat, slim, or tidy. 2 in good order; well arranged or equipped. □□ **trim'ly** adv. **trim'ness** n.
■ v. 1 shorten, abbreviate, mow, shape, tidy. 2 snip (off), prune, pare, lop (off), crop, clip, shave, shear. 3 embellish, dress up, adorn, deck out. • n. 1 condition, repair, shape. 2 trimming, edging, piping, rickrack, embroidery, frill, fringe. • adj. 1 well-kept, smart, dapper, shipshape, sl. spiffy; slender, clean-cut, streamlined, compact. 2 in fine fettle, fit (as a fiddle); in apple-pie order.

tri•ma•ran /trímaran/ n. vessel like a catamaran, with three hulls side by side.

tri•mes•ter /trimestar/ n. period of three months, esp. of human gestation or as a college or university term.

trim•e•ter /trímitər/ n. Prosody verse of three measures.

trim•ming /tríming/ n. 1 ornamentation or decoration. 2 [in pl.] colloq. usual accompaniments, esp. of the main course of a meal. 3 [in pl.] pieces cut off in trimming.
■ 1 see ORNAMENT n. 1. 2 (trimmings) see TRAPPINGS.

tri•ni•tro•tol•u•ene /trínitrōtólyōoeen/ n. (also **tri•ni•tro•tol•u•ol** /-tólyōo-awl, –ōl/) = TNT.

trin•i•ty /trínitee/ n. (pl. **–ties**) 1 state of being three. 2 group of three. 3 (**Trinity** or **HolyTrinity**) Theol. the three persons of the Christian Godhead (Father, Son, and Holy Spirit).

trin•ket /tríngkit/ n. trifling ornament, esp. a piece of jewelry. □□ **trin'ket•ry** n.
■ see BAUBLE.

tri•o /tree-ō/ n. (pl. **–os**) 1 group of three. 2 Mus. a composition for three performers. b group of three performers.
■ 1 threesome, trilogy, triad, triple, triplet.

trip /trip/ • v. (**tripped, trip•ping**) 1 intr. a move with quick light steps. b (of a rhythm, etc.) run lightly. 2 tr. & intr. a stumble or cause to stumble, esp. by catching the feet. b [foll. by up] make or cause to make a slip or blunder. 3 tr. release (part of a machine) suddenly by knocking aside a catch, etc. **4** *intr. colloq.* have a hallucinatory experience caused by a drug. • *n.* **1** journey or excursion, esp. for pleasure. **2 a** stumble; blunder. **b** tripping or being tripped up. **3** nimble step. **4** *colloq.* hallucinatory experience caused by a drug. See synonym study at JOURNEY. □ **trip the light fantastic** *joc.* dance. **trip wire** wire stretched close to the ground, operating an alarm, etc., when disturbed.

■ *v.* **1** dance, caper, skip, frolic, hop, spring, scamper, cavort. **2 a** slip, misstep, fall (down), tumble, topple. **b** (*trip up*) err; trick, throw off. **3** detonate, set off, trigger, activate. **4** *colloq.* freak out, turn on. • *n.* **1** tour, outing, expedition, voyage, trek, pilgrimage, jaunt, junket, drive. **2** false step; faux pas, error, mistake, oversight; *colloq.* slip-up.

tri•par•tite /trípaartīt/ *adj.* **1** consisting of three parts. **2** shared by or involving three parties.

tripe /trīp/ *n.* **1** first or second stomach of a ruminant, esp. an ox, as food. **2** *colloq.* nonsense; rubbish.

tri•ple /trípəl/ • *adj.* **1** consisting of three usu. equal parts or things; threefold. **2** involving three parties. **3** three times as much or many. • *n.* **1** threefold number or amount. **2** set of three. **3** *Baseball* hit on which the batter reaches third base. • *v.* **1** multiply by three. **2** hit a triple. □ **triple crown** winning of all three of a group of important events in horse racing, etc. **triple jump** athletic contest comprising a hop, step, and jump.

■ *n.* **2** see TRIO.

trip•let /tríplit/ *n.* **1** each of three children or animals born at one birth. **2** set of three things, esp. of equal notes played in the time of two.

trip•li•cate • *adj.* /tríplikət/ **1** existing in three examples or copies. **2** having three corresponding parts. **3** tripled. • *n.* /tríplikət/ each of a set of three copies or corresponding parts. • *v.tr.* /tríplikayt/ **1** make in three copies. **2** multiply by three. □□ **trip•li•ca•tion** /-káyshən/ *n.*

tri•pod /trípod/ *n.* three-legged stand for a camera, etc.

trip•tych /tríptik/ *n.* picture or relief carving on three usu. hinged panels.

tri•sect /trīsékt/ *v.tr.* divide into three (usu. equal) parts. □□ **tri•sec•tion** /-sékshən/ *n.* **tri•sec′tor** *n.*

tris•mus /trízməs/ *n. Med.* variety of tetanus with spasm of the jaw muscles causing the mouth to remain tightly closed; lockjaw.

trite /trīt/ *adj.* (of a phrase, opinion, etc.) hackneyed; worn out by constant repetition. □□ **trite′ly** *adv.* **trite′ness** *n.*

■ see BANAL.

tri•ti•um /tríteeəm/ *n. Chem.* radioactive isotope of hydrogen with a mass about three times that of ordinary hydrogen. ¶ Symb.: **T**.

tri•umph /tríəmf, -umf/ • *n.* **1 a** state of victory or success. **b** great success or achievement. **2** supreme example (*a triumph of engineering*). • *v.intr.* **1** gain a victory; be successful. **2** [often foll. by *over*] exult.

■ *n.* **1 b** conquest, achievement, accomplishment, attainment, coup, smash (hit), winner, *colloq.* knockout, hit. • *v.* **1** win, carry the day, dominate, prevail; (*triumph over*) defeat, beat, rout, best, conquer, overcome. **2** see EXULT.

tri•um•phal /trīúmfəl/ *adj.* of or used in or celebrating a triumph.

■ celebratory, rapturous, jubilant, joyful, exultant.

tri•um•phant /trīúmfənt/ *adj.* **1** victorious; successful. **2** exultant. □□ **tri•um′phant•ly** *adv.*

■ **1** conquering, winning. **2** see *exultant* (EXULT).

tri•um•vi•rate /trīúmvirət/ *n.* ruling group of three persons.

tri•va•lent /trīváylənt/ *adj. Chem.* having a valence of three. □□ **tri•va′lence** *n.* **tri•va′len•cy** *n.*

triv•et /trívit/ *n.* tripod or bracket for a hot pot, kettle, or dish to stand on.

triv•i•a /tríveeə/ *n.pl.* trifles or trivialities.

triv•i•al /tríveeəl/ *adj.* of small value or importance; trifling. □□ **triv•i•al•i•ty** /-veeálitee/ *n.* (*pl.* **-ties**) **triv′i•al•ly** *adv.*

■ see TRIFLING 1, BANAL. □□ **triviality** insignificance, inconsequence, pettiness; trifle, technicality.

triv•i•al•ize /tríveeəlīz/ *v.tr.* make trivial or apparently trivial; minimize. □□ **triv•i•al•i•za′tion** *n.*

■ belittle, denigrate, lessen, depreciate, underestimate, make light of, laugh off, underplay, dismiss, slight, scoff at, scorn, run down, decry, play down, pooh-pooh, *colloq.* put down.

tro•che /trókee/ *n.* small medicated tablet or lozenge.

tro•chee /trókee/ *n. Prosody* foot consisting of one long followed by one short syllable.

trod *past* and *past part.* of TREAD.

trod•den *past part.* of TREAD.

trog•lo•dyte /tróglədīt/ *n.* cave dweller, esp. of prehistoric times. □□ **trog•lo•dyt•ic** /-dítik/ *adj.*

troi•ka /tróykə/ *n.* **1 a** Russian vehicle with a team of three horses abreast. **b** this team. **2** group of three people, esp. as an administrative council.

Tro•jan /trójən/ • *adj.* of ancient Troy in Asia Minor. • *n.* native or inhabitant of Troy. □ **Trojan Horse 1** hollow wooden horse used by the Greeks to enter Troy. **2** person or device secreted, intended to bring about ruin.

troll[1] /trōl/ *n.* (in Scandinavian folklore) fabled being, esp. a giant or dwarf dwelling in a cave.

troll[2] /trōl/ *v.* fish by drawing bait along in the water.

trol•ley /trólee/ *n.* **1** (in full **trol′ley wheel**) wheel attached to a pole, etc., used to carry current from an overhead electric wire to drive a vehicle. **2** = *trolley car.* □ **off one's trolley** *sl.* crazy. **trolley car** electric streetcar using a trolley wheel.

■ □ **off one's trolley** see CRAZY 1.

trol•lop /tróləp/ *n.* **1** disreputable woman. **2** prostitute.

trom•bone /tromb*ō*n/ *n.* brass wind instrument with a sliding tube. □□ **trom•bon′ist** *n.*

trompe-l'œil /trɒ**N**plŏyə, trámpláy, –loi/ *n.* still life painting, etc., designed to give an illusion of reality.

-tron /tron/ *suffix Physics* forming nouns denoting: **1** elementary particle (*positron*). **2** particle accelerator.

troop /troop/ • *n.* **1** assembled company; assemblage of people or animals. **2** [in *pl.*] soldiers; armed forces. **3** cavalry unit under a captain. **4** unit of Girl Scouts, Boy Scouts, etc. • *v.intr.* come together or move in large numbers.

■ *n.* **1** see FLOCK[2] *n.* 2. **2** (*troops*) see SERVICE *n.* 8. • *v.* see FILE *v.*

troop•er /troopər/ *n.* **1** soldier in a cavalry or armored unit. **2** mounted or state police officer.

trop. *abbr.* **1** tropic. **2** tropical.

tro•phy /trofee/ *n.* (*pl.* **–phies**) **1** cup, statuette, etc., awarded as a prize in a contest. **2** memento or souvenir taken in hunting, war, etc.

■ **1** laurel(s), medal. **2** token, remembrance, keepsake; booty, spoils.

trop•ic /trópik/ *n.* **1** parallel of latitude 23°27′ north (**tropic of Cancer**) or south (**tropic of Capricorn**) of the Equator. **2** (**the Tropics**) warm-weather region between the tropics of Cancer and Capricorn. □□ **trop′i•cal** *adj.*

tro•po•sphere /trópəsfeer, trō–/ *n.* lowest layer of atmosphere air extending upward from the earth's surface. □□ **tro•po•spher′ic** *adj.*

trot /trot/ • *v.* (**trot•ted, trot•ting**) **1** *intr.* run at a moderate pace. **2** *intr.* (of a horse) proceed at a steady pace faster than a walk, lifting each diagonal pair of legs alternately. • *n.* **1** action or exercise of trotting. **2** (**the trots**) *sl.* diarrhea.

■ *v.* **1** jog; hurry, scamper, *colloq.* scoot, skedaddle.

troth /trawth, trŏth/ *n. archaic* **1** faith; loyalty. **2** truth. □ **pledge** (or **plight**) **one's troth** pledge one's word esp. in marriage or betrothal.

trou•ba•dour /troobədawr/ *n.* **1** French medieval lyric poet singing of courtly love. **2** singer or poet.

■ see MINSTREL.

trou•ble /trúbəl/ • *n.* **1** difficulty or distress; vexation; affliction. **2 a** inconvenience; unpleasant exertion; bother. **b** cause of this. **3** perceived failing (*that's the trouble with you*). **4** dysfunction (*engine trouble*). **5** strife; disturbance. • *v.* **1** *tr.* cause distress or anxiety to; disturb. **2** *tr.* afflict; cause pain, etc., to. **3** *tr. & intr.* [often *refl.*] subject or be subjected to inconvenience or unpleasant exertion (*sorry to trouble you*).

■ *n.* **1** worry, concern, grief, suffering, adversity, misfortune, hardship, anxiety, torment, anguish. **2 a** effort, pains, care. **b** annoyance, irritation, nuisance, burden, pest. **3** shortcoming, problem. **4** defect, malfunction, disability, disease, ailment, illness, sickness, disorder, complaint. **5** unrest, discord,

turmoil, rebellion, revolt, uprising, fighting. • *v.* **1, 2** upset, alarm, agitate, perturb, oppress; annoy, irritate, irk, vex, plague, pester, harass, provoke, *colloq.* hassle, *sl.* bug. **3** impose on, put out; take pains.

trou•ble•mak•er /trúbəlmaykər/ *n.* person who habitually causes trouble. □□ **trou′ble•mak•ing** *n.*

■ rabble-rouser, malcontent, instigator, ringleader, meddler, agitator, busybody; see also DELINQUENT *n.*

trou•ble•shoot•er /trúbəlshōōtər/ *n.* **1** mediator in a dispute. **2** person who corrects faults in machinery, etc. □□ **trou′ble•shoot•ing** *n.*

trou•ble•some /trúbəlsəm/ *adj.* causing trouble; vexing.

■ difficult, awkward, inconvenient, onerous, trying, tough; uncooperative, unruly, unmanageable; worrisome, annoying, irksome, irritating, distressing, *colloq.* pesky.

trough /trawf, trof/ *n.* **1** long, narrow, open receptacle for water, animal feed, etc. **2** channel or hollow like this. **3** elongated region of low barometric pressure.

■ **2** see CHANNEL 5a.

trounce /trowns/ *v.tr.* **1** defeat heavily. **2** beat; thrash. □□ **trounc′ing** *n.*

■ **1** see DEFEAT *v.* 1. **2** see BEAT *v.* 1, PUNISH 1. □□ **trouncing** see DEFEAT *n.*, *thrashing* (THRASH), PUNISHMENT 1, 2.

troupe /troop/ *n.* company of actors or acrobats, etc.

■ see COMPANY *n.* 4.

troup•er /troopər/ *n.* **1** member of a theatrical troupe. **2** staunch, reliable person, esp. during difficult times.

trou•sers /trówzərz/ *n.pl.* **1** = PANTS. **2** (**trouser**) [*attrib.*] designating part of this (*trouser leg*).

trous•seau /troosō, troosō/ *n.* (*pl.* **trous•seaus** or **trous•seaux** /-sōz/) bride's collection of clothes, linens, etc.

trout /trowt/ *n.* (*pl.* same or **trouts**) food fish related to salmon.

trove /trov/ *n.* = treasure trove.

trow•el /trówəl/ *n.* **1** small flat-bladed tool used to spread mortar, etc. **2** scoop for lifting plants or earth.

troy /troy/ *n.* (in full **troy weight**) system of weights used for precious metals and gems.

tru•ant /trooənt/ • *n.* **1** child who stays away from school without permission. **2** person missing from work, etc. • *adj.* shirking; idle; wandering. □□ **tru′an•cy** *n.*

■ *n.* malingerer, runaway, absentee, dodger, loafer, *colloq.* goldbrick. • *adj.* delinquent.

truce /troos/ *n.* temporary agreement to cease hostilities.

■ armistice, cease-fire, moratorium, respite, letup.

truck¹ /truk/ • *n.* **1** vehicle for carrying loads. **2** handcart. • *v.* **1** convey on or in a truck. **2** *intr.* drive a truck. □□ **truck′er** *n.*

truck² /truk/ *n.* dealings. □ **have no truck with** avoid dealing with.

■ business, transaction, trade, barter, communication, connection.

truck•le /trúkəl/ • n. (in full **truck'le bed**) = trundle bed. • v.intr. [foll. by to] submit obsequiously. □□ **truck'ler** n.

■ v. kowtow, toady, fawn, bow, scrape, genuflect, submit, yield, cower, cringe, grovel, crawl, lick a person's boots, colloq. suck up; (truckle to) butter up. □□ **truckler** see flatterer (FLATTER).

tru•cu•lent /trúkyələnt/ adj. **1** aggressively defiant. **2** fierce; savage. □□ **truc'u•lence** n. **truc'u•lent•ly** adv.

■ surly, sullen, bad-tempered, ill-tempered, unpleasant, nasty, rude, harsh, belligerent, hostile, contentious, violent.

trudge /truj/ • v. **1** intr. go on foot, esp. laboriously. **2** tr. traverse (a distance) in this way. • n. trudging walk.

■ v. see TRAMP v. 1.

true /tróo/ • adj. **1** in accordance with fact or reality. **2** genuine; authentic. **3** loyal; faithful. **4** accurately conforming (to a standard or expectation, etc.) (true to form). **5** correctly positioned or balanced; upright; level. **6** exact; accurate (true aim). • adv. accurately. • v.tr. (**trues, trued, true•ing** or **tru•ing**) bring (a tool, wheel, frame, etc.) into the position required. □ **come true** actually happen. **true-blue** adj. extremely loyal or orthodox.

■ adj. **1** accurate, truthful, literal, actual, factual; realistic, valid. **2** bona fide, legitimate, rightful, legal, proper, real, veritable. **3** staunch, devoted, steadfast, trustworthy, dependable, sincere, reliable. **5** square, parallel; see also LEVEL¹ adj. 1. **6** proper, unerring, correct, precise, right. □ **come true** occur, take place, become a reality. **true-blue** (adj.) see STAUNCH 1, CONSERVATIVE adj. 1a.

truf•fle /trúfəl/ n. **1** edible, rich-flavored underground fungus. **2** candy made of chocolate covered with cocoa, etc.

tru•ism /tróoizəm/ n. obviously true or hackneyed statement.

■ platitude, bromide, axiom, cliché, maxim, saw.

tru•ly /tróolee/ adv. **1** sincerely; genuinely. **2** really; indeed. **3** faithfully; loyally. **4** accurately.

■ **1** actually, honestly, in fact. **2** definitely, beyond (the shadow of) a doubt, unquestionably, absolutely, positively. **3** devotedly, steadfastly. **4** correctly, literally.

trump /trump/ • n. **1** playing card of a suit ranking above the others. **2** this suit. • v. **1** a tr. defeat (a card or its player) with a trump. **b** intr. play a trump card when another suit has been led. **2** tr. colloq. gain a surprising advantage over. □ **trump card** **1** card belonging to a trump suit. **2** colloq. surprise move to gain an advantage. **trump up** fabricate or invent (an accusation, etc.).

■ v. **2** see DISCOMFIT 2, OUTDO. □ **trump up** see FABRICATE 2.

trum•per•y /trúmpəree/ n. (pl. **-ies**) **1** worthless finery. **2** worthless article; junk.

trum•pet /trúmpit/ • n. **1** brass instrument with a flared bell and a bright penetrating tone. **2** trumpet-shaped thing (ear trumpet).

3 sound of or like a trumpet. • v. **1** intr. a blow a trumpet. **b** (of an enraged elephant, etc.) make a trumpetlike cry. **2** tr. proclaim loudly (a person's or thing's merit). □□ **trum'pet•er** n.

■ v. **2** see PROCLAIM 1.

trun•cate /trúngkayt/ v.tr. cut the top or the end from; shorten. □□ **trun•ca•tion** /-káyshən/ n.

trun•cheon /trúnchən/ n. short club carried esp. by a police officer.

trun•dle /trúnd'l/ v. roll or move heavily or noisily, esp. on or as on wheels. □ **trundle bed** wheeled bed stored under a larger bed.

trunk /trungk/ n. **1** main stem of a tree. **2** body apart from the limbs and head. **3** main part of any structure. **4** large box with a hinged lid for luggage, storage, etc. **5** usu. rear storage compartment of an automobile. **6** elephant's elongated prehensile nose. **7** [in pl.] men's shorts worn for swimming, etc. □ **trunk line** main line of a railroad, etc.

■ **1** bole. **2** torso. **4** chest, locker, case. **6** snout, proboscis. **7** (trunks) bathing suit.

truss /trus/ • n. **1** framework supporting a roof, bridge, etc. **2** surgical appliance worn to support a hernia. • v.tr. **1** tie up (a fowl) for cooking. **2** support (roof, bridge, etc.) with a truss or trusses.

trust /trust/ • n. **1** firm belief in the reliability, truth, or strength, etc., of a person or thing. **2** confident expectation. **3** responsibility (in a position of trust). **4** commercial credit. **5** Law **a** arrangement whereby a person or group manages property on another's behalf. **b** property so held. **6** body of trustees. **7** association of companies for reducing competition, etc. • v. **1** tr. place trust in; believe in. **2** tr. [foll. by with] allow to have or use (a thing) (trust them with my books). **3** tr. have faith, confidence, hope that a thing will take place. **4** intr. [foll. by in] place reliance in (we trust in you). **5** intr. [foll. by to] place (esp. undue) reliance on (trust to luck). □ **in trust** Law held on the basis of trust (see sense 5 of n.).

■ n. confidence, reliance, faith, conviction, certainty, assurance. **3** see RESPONSIBILITY 2, OBLIGATION 2. **5 a** custody, care, keeping, charge, guardianship, protection, safe keeping, trusteeship. **7** monopoly, cartel; corporation, conglomerate, syndicate. • v. **1** rely on or upon, confide in, depend or bank or count on or upon. **2** (trust with) entrust with, empower to. **3** see HOPE v. 1, 2. **4** (trust in) see TRUST v. 1 above. **5** (trust to) see TRUST v. 1 above.

trus•tee /trustée/ n. **1** Law person managing property in trust. **2** member of an administrative board. □□ **trust•ee'ship** n.

trust•ful /trústfŏŏl/ adj. full of trust or confidence. □□ **trust'ful•ly** adv. **trust'ful•ness** n.

trust•ing /trústing/ adj. having trust; trustful. See synonym study at GULLIBLE. □□ **trust'ing•ly** adv.

■ confident, unsuspecting; naive, innocent, gullible.

trust•wor•thy /trústwurthee/ adj. deserving of trust; reliable. □□ **trust'wor•thi•ness** n.

**dependable; responsible, steadfast, loyal, faithful, (tried and) true, honorable, honest, ethical.

trust•y /trústee/ *adj.* (**trust•i•er, trust•i•est**) archaic or joc. trustworthy (*a trusty steed*).

truth /trŏŏth/ *n.* (*pl.* **truths** /trŏŏthz, trŏŏths/) **1** quality or a state of being true. **2** what is true.

■ **1** veracity, truthfulness, verity, correctness, accuracy, authenticity, fact. **2** reality; truism, rule, law, principle, gospel.

truth•ful /trŏŏthfŏŏl/ *adj.* **1** speaking the truth. **2** (of a story, etc.) true. □□ **truth′ful•ly** *adv.* **truth′ful•ness** *n.*

■ **1** honest, reliable, faithful, trustworthy, straightforward, candid, frank, sincere. **2** accurate, factual, correct, true to life, unvarnished, unadulterated. □□ **truthfully** see TRULY 1.

try /trī/ • *v.* (**tries, tried**) **1** *intr.* make an effort with a view to success. **2** *tr.* make an effort to achieve (*tried my best*). **3** *tr.* test by use or experiment. **4** *tr.* tax (*tries my patience*). **5** *tr.* examine the effectiveness of for a purpose (*try cold water*). **6** *tr.* ascertain the state of fastening of (a door, window, etc.). **7** *tr.* **a** investigate and decide (a case or issue) judicially. **b** subject (a person) to trial (*tried for murder*). **8** *intr.* aim; strive (*try for a gold medal*). • *n.* (*pl.* **tries**) effort to accomplish something. □ **tried and true** proved reliable by experience. **try on for size** try out or test for suitability. **try one's hand** see how skillful one is, esp. at the first attempt.

■ *v.* **1, 2** attempt, endeavor, aim, undertake, venture, strive, struggle, tackle, have a go (at), *colloq.* have a stab (at), take a shot or crack (at). **3** prove, evaluate, examine, inspect, investigate, sample, appraise, assay, look over, analyze, scrutinize, assess, judge, check out. **4** strain. **7** hear, sit on, adjudicate, judge, adjudge. • *n.* undertaking, go. □ **tried and true** (or **tested**) see SAFE *adj.* 3.

try•ing /trī-ing/ *adj.* annoying; hard to endure.

■ irritating, frustrating, irksome, infuriating, maddening, bothersome, tiresome, vexing, troublesome, worrisome, distressing, disquieting, upsetting, dispiriting, taxing, demanding, tough, stressful, difficult, tiring.

tryst /trist/ *n.* meeting, esp. a secret one of lovers.

tsar var. of CZAR.

tsa•ri•na var. of *czarina* (CZAR).

tset•se /tsétsee, tét-, tseétsee, tee–/ *n.* African fly that feeds on blood and transmits sleeping sickness.

TSH *abbr.* thyroid-stimulating hormone.

T-shirt /téeshərt/ *n.* (also **tee shirt**) short-sleeved, collarless casual top having the form of a T when spread out.

tsp. *abbr.* (*pl.* **tsps.**) teaspoon; teaspoonful.

T square /tée skwair/ *n.* T-shaped instrument for drawing or testing right angles.

tsu•na•mi /tsŏŏnáamee/ *n.* (*pl.* **tsu•na•mis**) long, high sea wave caused by underwater earthquakes, etc.

Tswa•na /tswáanə, swáa–/ *n.* (also **Set•swa•na** /setswáanə/) Bantu language used in

Botswana and neighboring areas of South Africa.

tub /tub/ *n.* **1** open, flat-bottomed, usu. round container for various purposes. **2** tub-shaped carton. **3** *colloq.* clumsy, slow boat.

tu•ba /tŏŏbə, tyŏŏ–/ *n.* (*pl.* **tu•bas**) low-pitched brass wind instrument.

tub•by /túbee/ *adj.* (**tub•bi•er, tub•bi•est**) short and fat. □□ **tub′bi•ness** *n.*

■ see FAT *adj.* 1. □□ **tubbiness** see *fatness* (FAT).

tube /tŏŏb, tyŏŏb/ *n.* **1** long, hollow cylinder. **2** pliable cylinder sealed at one end for holding a semiliquid substance (*tube of toothpaste*). **3** hollow, cylindrical organ in the body. **4** [prec. by *the*] *colloq.* television. **5** = *inner tube*. □□ **tube′like** *adj.*

■ **1** see PIPE *n.* 1. **4** (*the tube*) see TELEVISION 2, 3.

tu•ber /tŏŏbər, tyŏŏ–/ *n.* thick, rounded part of a stem or rhizome, usu. found underground, e.g., a potato. □□ **tu′ber•ous** *adj.*

tu•ber•cle /tŏŏbərkəl, tyŏŏ–/ *n.* small, rounded swelling on the body or in an organ, esp. as characteristic of tuberculosis. □□ **tu•ber′cu•lar** *adj.* **tu•ber′cu•lous** *adj.*

tu•ber•cu•lo•sis /tŏŏbárkyəlṓsis, tyŏŏ–/ *n.* infectious disease characterized by tubercles, esp. in the lungs.

tub•ing /tŏŏbing, tyŏŏ–/ *n.* **1** length of tube. **2** quantity of tubes.

tu•bu•lar /tŏŏbyələr, tyŏŏ–/ *adj.* **1** tube-shaped. **2** having or consisting of tubes.

tu•bule /tŏŏbyŏŏl, tyŏŏ–/ *n.* small tube in a plant or animal body.

tuck /tuk/ • *v.* **1** draw, fold, or turn the outer or end parts of (cloth or clothes, etc.) close together so as to be held; thrust in the edge of (a thing). **2** draw together into a small space (*tucked its head under its wing*). **3** stow (*tucked in a corner*). **4** make a stitched fold in (material, a garment, etc.). • *n.* flattened, usu. stitched fold in material, etc.

tuck•er /túkər/ *v.tr.* [esp. in *passive*; often foll. by *out*] *colloq.* tire; exhaust. □□ **tuck•ered** *adj.* See synonym study at TIRED

-tude /tŏŏd, tyŏŏd/ *suffix* forming abstract nouns (*altitude*).

Tu•dor /tŏŏdər, tyŏŏ–/ *adj.* **1** of the royal family of England 1485–1603 or this period. **2** of the architectural style of this period.

Tues. *abbr.* (also **Tue.**) Tuesday.

Tues•day /tŏŏzday, -dee, tyŏŏz/ *n.* third day of the week, following Monday.

tuft /tuft/ *n.* bunch or collection of threads, grass, feathers, hair, etc., held or growing together at the base. □□ **tuft′ed** *adj.* **tuft′y** *adj.*

■ see WISP.

tug /tug/ • *v.* (**tugged, tug•ging**) **1** *tr. & intr.* pull hard or violently; jerk. **2** *tr.* tow (a ship, etc.) with a tugboat. • *n.* **1** hard, violent, or jerky pull. **2** sudden strong emotion. **3** = TUGBOAT. □ **tug-of-war 1** trial of strength between two sides pulling against each other on a rope. **2** decisive or severe contest.

■ *v.* **1** draw, drag, haul; *colloq.* yank. **2** pull. • *n.* **2** wrench, pang.

tug•boat /túgbōt/ *n.* small, powerful boat for towing or pushing ships, barges, etc.

tu•i•tion /tŏō-íshən, tyŏō–/ *n.* 1 teaching. 2 fee for this.

■ 1 education, training, schooling, instruction.

tu•lip /tŏōlip, tyŏō–/ *n.* 1 bulbous spring-flowering plant with showy cup-shaped flowers. 2 its flower.

tulle /tŏōl/ *n.* soft fine silk, etc., net for veils and dresses.

tum•ble /túmbəl/ • *v.* 1 *tr. & intr.* fall or cause to fall suddenly, clumsily, or headlong. 2 *intr.* fall rapidly in amount, etc. (*prices tumbled*). 3 *intr.* roll or toss to and fro. 4 *intr.* move or rush in a headlong or blundering manner. 5 *intr.* perform acrobatic feats, esp. somersaults. • *n.* 1 sudden or headlong fall. 2 somersault or other acrobatic feat.

■ *v.* 1 pitch, turn end over end, go head over heels, flop, collapse, topple, stumble. 2 drop, nosedive, plummet, take a dive. 3 see ROLL *v.* 1. • *n.* 1 slip, spill, *colloq.* header.

tum•ble•down /túmbəldown/ *adj.* falling or fallen into ruin.

■ ramshackle, dilapidated, decrepit, rickety, shaky, falling apart *or* to pieces, disintegrating, tottering, broken-down, crumbling, derelict, gone to rack and ruin.

tum•bler /túmblər/ *n.* 1 drinking glass. 2 acrobat. 3 pivoted piece in a lock that holds the bolt until lifted by a key or a combination.

■ 1 see GLASS *n.* 2.

tum•ble•weed /túmbəlweed/ *n.* plant whose globular bush breaks off in late summer and is tumbled about by the wind.

tum•brel /túmbrəl/ *n.* (also **tum•bril** /–ril/) *hist.* open cart in which condemned persons were taken to the guillotine during the French Revolution.

tu•mes•cent /tŏōmésənt, tyŏō–/ *adj.* swelling. □□ **tu•mes′cence** *n.*

tu•mid /tŏōmid, tyŏō–/ *adj.* 1 swollen; inflated. 2 (of a style, etc.) inflated; bombastic. □□ **tu•mid′i•ty** *n.* **tu′mid•ly** *adv.*

tum•my /túmee/ *n.* (*pl.* **–mies**) *colloq.* stomach.

■ see STOMACH *n.* 2.

tu•mor /tŏōmər, tyŏō–/ *n.* swelling, esp. from an abnormal growth of tissue. □□ **tu′mor•ous** *adj.*

■ melanoma, sarcoma, carcinoma, growth, lump.

tu•mult /tŏōmult, tyŏō–/ *n.* 1 uproar or din, esp. of a disorderly crowd. 2 angry demonstration; riot. 3 emotional agitation.

■ 1, 2 commotion, disturbance, disorder, disquiet, insurrection, unrest, bedlam, chaos, brouhaha, fracas, hubbub, stir, pandemonium, hullabaloo, turmoil, ruckus. 3 confusion, upset.

tu•mul•tu•ous /tŏōmúlchŏōəs, tyŏō–/ *adj.* noisily vehement; uproarious; agitated. □□ **tu•mul′tu•ous•ly** *adv.*

■ clamorous, boisterous, disorderly, turbulent, violent, chaotic, frenzied, furious, excited, hectic, riotous, rowdy, unruly, wild, frantic, stormy.

tun /tun/ *n.* large beer or wine cask.

tu•na /tŏōnə, tyŏō–/ *n.* (*pl.* same or **tu•nas**) 1 large edible marine fish. 2 (in full **tu′na fish**) its flesh as food.

tun•dra /túndrə/ *n.* vast, level, treeless Arctic region usu. with underlying permafrost.

tune /tŏōn, tyŏōn/ • *n.* melody. • *v.* 1 *tr.* put (a musical instrument) in tune. 2 **a** *tr.* adjust (a radio, etc.) to the frequency of a signal. **b** *intr.* [foll. by *in*] adjust a radio receiver to the required signal (*tuned in to the news*). 3 *tr.* adjust (an engine, etc.) to run smoothly and efficiently. □ **in tune** 1 having the correct pitch. 2 harmonizing (with one's associates, surroundings, etc.). **to the tune of** *colloq.* to the considerable amount of. **tuned in** 1 (of a radio, etc.) adjusted to a particular frequency, station, etc. 2 *colloq.* up to date; aware of what is going on. □□ **tun′a•ble** *adj.* (also **tune′a•ble**)

■ *n.* air, song, strain, motif, theme. • *v.* 1 adjust, modulate, temper. 3 calibrate, regulate, adapt, attune, align, set, fine-tune. □ **in tune**, see STEP *n.* 9.

tune•ful /tŏōnfŏŏl, tyŏō–/ *adj.* melodious; musical. □□ **tune′ful•ly** *adv.* **tune′ful•ness** *n.*

■ melodic, euphonious, mellifluous, harmonic, catchy, mellow, smooth, rich, rhythmic, *colloq.* easy on the ear(s). □□ **tunefulness** see MELODY.

tune•less /tŏōnlis, tyŏō–/ *adj.* 1 unmelodious; unmusical. 2 out of tune. □□ **tune′less•ly** *adv.* **tune′less•ness** *n.*

tun•er /tŏōnər, tyŏō–/ *n.* 1 person who tunes musical instruments, esp. pianos. 2 device for tuning a radio receiver.

tung•sten /túngstən/ *n. Chem.* dense metallic element with a very high melting point. ¶Symb.: **W**.

tu•nic /tŏōnik, tyŏō–/ *n.* 1 blouselike garment extending to the hips, sometimes belted. 2 loose, often sleeveless garment, esp. as worn in ancient Greece and Rome.

tun•ing /tŏōning, tyŏō–/ *n.* process of putting a musical instrument in tune. □ **tuning fork** two-pronged steel fork that gives a particular note when struck.

tun•nel /túnəl/ • *n.* 1 underground passage dug through a hill or under a road, river, etc., esp. for a railroad or road. 2 underground passage dug by an animal. • *v.* 1 *intr.* make a tunnel through. 2 *tr.* make (one's way) by tunneling. □ **tunnel vision** 1 vision that is normal only in a small central area. 2 *colloq.* inability to grasp a situation's wider implications. □□ **tun′nel•er** *n.*

■ *n.* 1 shaft, subway, underpass. 2 burrow, hole. • *v.* 1 excavate, penetrate, mine, bore, drill.

tu•pe•lo /tŏōpilō, tyŏō–/ *n.* (*pl.* **–los**) 1 any of various Asian and N. American deciduous trees with colorful foliage and growing in swamps. 2 its wood.

Tu•pi /tŏōpee/ • *n.* (*pl.* same or **Tu•pis**) 1 member of a Native American people native to the Amazon valley. 2 their language. • *adj.* of this people or language.

tur•ban /túrbən/ *n.* 1 man's headdress of fabric wound around a cap or the head, worn esp. by Muslims and Sikhs. **2** woman's headdress resembling this. ▫ **tur'baned** *adj.*

tur•bid /tɔ́rbid/ *adj.* **1** muddy; thick; not clear. **2** (of a style, etc.) confused; disordered. ▫ **tur•bid'i•ty** *n.*

■ **1** see OPAQUE *adj.* 1, 2. **2** see INCOHERENT 2, DISORDERLY 1.

tur•bine /tɔ́rbin, –bīn/ *n.* rotary motor driven by a flow of water, steam, gas, wind, etc.

turbo- /tɔ́rbō/ *comb. form* turbine.

tur•bo•charg•er /tɔ́rbōchaarjər/ *n.* supercharger driven by a turbine powered by the engine's exhaust gases.

tur•bo•jet /tɔ́rbōjet/ *n.* **1** jet engine in which the jet also operates a turbine-driven air compressor. **2** aircraft powered by this.

tur•bo•prop /tɔ́rbōprop/ *n.* **1** jet engine in which a turbine is used as in a turbojet and also to drive a propeller. **2** aircraft powered by this.

tur•bot /tɔ́rbət/ *n.* any of various flatfishes prized as food.

tur•bu•lent /tɔ́rbyələnt/ *adj.* **1** disturbed; in commotion. **2** (of air, water, etc.) varying irregularly. **3** tumultuous; riotous. ▫ **tur'bu•lence** *n.* **tur'bu•lent•ly** *adv.*

■ **1, 3** see DISORDERLY 2, TUMULTUOUS.

tu•reen /tooréén, tyoo–/ *n.* deep covered dish for soup, etc.

turf /tɔrf/ • *n.* **1 a** layer of grass, etc., with earth and its roots. **b** piece of this. **2** slab of peat. **3** [prec. by *the*] **a** horse racing generally. **b** general term for racetracks. **4** *sl.* person's territory or sphere of influence. • *v.tr.* cover (ground) with turf.

■ *n.* **1** sod, lawn, green. **4** area, neighborhood, backyard, stamping ground, home ground, haunt; domain.

tur•gid /tɔ́rjid/ *adj.* **1** swollen; inflated. **2** (of language) pompous; bombastic. ▫ **tur•gid'i•ty** *n.*

■ **1** see *swollen* (SWELL *v.* 5). **2** see POMPOUS. ▫ **turgidity** see RANT *n.*

Turk /tɔrk/ *n.* **1 a** native or inhabitant of Turkey. **b** person of Turkish descent. **2** member of a Central Asian people from whom the Ottomans derived.

tur•key /tɔ́rkee/ *n.* **1** large bird orig. of N. America, wild or bred for food. **2** its flesh as food. **3** *sl.* theatrical failure; flop. ▫ **talk turkey** *colloq.* talk frankly; get down to business.

Turk•ish /tɔ́rkish/ • *adj.* of Turkey, the Turks, or their language. • *n.* this language. ▫ **Turkish bath** hot-air or steam bath followed by washing, massage, etc. **Turkish towel** thick towel made of cotton terry cloth.

tur•mer•ic /tɔ́rmərik/ *n.* **1** E. Indian plant of the ginger family. **2** its powdered rhizome used for yellow dye or as a spice, esp. in curry powder.

tur•moil /tɔ́rmoyl/ *n.* **1** confusion; agitation. **2** din and bustle.

■ **1** see CONFUSION. **2** see *excitement* (EXCITE).

turn /tɔrn/ • *v.* **1** *tr. & intr.* move around a point or axis; give or receive a rotary motion. **2** *tr. & intr.* change in position; invert; reverse. **3 a** *tr.* give a new direction to. **b** *intr.*

---

903   turbid ~ turn

take a new direction. **4** *tr.* aim in a certain way (*turned the hose on them*). **5** *tr. & intr.* [foll. by *into*] change in nature, form, or condition (*turned into a dragon*). **6** *intr.* [foll. by *to*] **a** set about (*turned to doing the ironing*). **b** have recourse to (*turned to me for help*). **c** go on to consider next (*we'll now turn to your report*). **7** *tr. & intr.* become or cause to become (*turned sour*). **8 a** *tr. & intr.* [foll. by *against*] make or become hostile to (*turned them against us*). **b** *intr.* [foll. by *on, upon*] become hostile to; attack (*suddenly turned on them*). **9** *intr.* change color. **10** *intr.* (of milk, etc.) become sour. **11** *intr.* (of the stomach) be nauseated. **12** *tr.* move to the other side of; go around (*turned the corner*). **13** *tr.* pass the age of (*he has turned 40*). **14** *tr.* **a** perform (a somersault, etc.) with rotary motion. **b** twist (an ankle) out of position; sprain. **15** *tr.* make (a profit). **16** *tr.* shape (an object) on a lathe. **17** *tr.* give an (esp. elegant) form to (*turn a compliment*). **18** *tr. & intr.* (of the tide) change or cause to change direction. • *n.* **1** turning; rotary motion. **2** change of direction or tendency (*sudden turn to the left*). **3** point at which a turning or change occurs. **4** change of direction of the tide. **5** tendency or disposition (*mechanical turn of mind*). **6** opportunity or obligation, etc., that comes successively (*my turn to read*). **7** short walk or ride (*take a turn around the block*). **8** short performance. **9** service of a specified kind (*did me a good turn*). **10** momentary nervous shock (*gave me quite a turn*). ▫ **at every turn** continually; at each new stage, etc. **by turns** in rotation; alternately. **in turn** in succession. **out of turn 1** when it is not one's turn. **2** inappropriately (*speak out of turn*). **take turns** act alternately. **to a turn** (esp. cooked) perfectly.

turn back 1 begin or cause to retrace one's steps. **2** fold back. **turn the corner** pass the critical point in an illness, difficulty, etc. **turn down 1** reject (a proposal, application, etc.). **2** reduce the volume or strength of (sound, heat, etc.) by turning a knob, etc. **3** fold down. **turn in 1** hand in; deliver. **2** achieve or register (a performance, score, etc.). **3** *colloq.* go to bed. **4** fold or incline inward. **turn off 1 a** stop the flow or operation of (water, electricity, etc.) by tap, switch, etc. **b** operate (a tap, switch, etc.) to achieve this. **2 a** enter a side road. **b** (of a side road) lead off from another road. **3** *colloq.* cause to lose interest. **turn on 1 a** start the flow or operation of (water, electricity, etc.) by a tap, switch, etc. **b** operate (a tap, switch, etc.) to achieve this. **2** *colloq.* stimulate the interest of, esp. sexually. **3** *tr. & intr. colloq.* intoxicate or become intoxicated with drugs. **turn-on** *n. colloq.* person or thing that causes (esp. sexual) arousal. **turn one's stomach** make one nauseous or disgusted. **turn out 1** expel. **2** extinguish (an electric light, etc.). **3** produce (goods, etc.). **4** *colloq.* assemble; attend a meeting, etc. **5** prove to be the case; result (*how things turn out*). **turn over 1** reverse the position of (*turn over the page*).

2 upset; fall or cause to fall over. **3 a** cause (an engine) to run. **b** (of an engine) start running. **4** consider thoroughly. **5** [foll. by *to*] transfer or delegate. **6** do business to the amount of. **turn over a new leaf** improve one's conduct or performance. **turn the other cheek** respond meekly to insult or abuse. **turn signal** flashing light on an automobile that indicates that the vehicle is about to turn or change lanes. **turn tail** run away. **turn the tide** reverse the trend of events. **turn up 1** increase the volume or strength of (sound, heat, etc.) by turning a knob, etc. **2** discover; reveal. **3** be found, esp. by chance. **4** arrive. **5** shorten (a garment). **turn up one's nose** (or **turn one's nose up**) react with disdain.

■ *v.* **1** rotate, revolve, spin, roll, reel, circle, gyrate, pirouette, whirl, wheel, pivot, orbit, swivel, spiral, twirl. **2** turn upside down, turn inside out. **3 b** veer, swing, swerve, corner, deviate, divert, shift, switch; twist, wind, snake, curve, bend, arc, coil, loop, meander, zigzag. **4** direct, point. **5** alter, adapt, remodel, modify, remake, refashion, reshape, reform, transform; (*turn into*) become. **6** (*turn to*) **a** see *set about* (SET[1]). **b** appeal to, apply to, resort to. **c** proceed to, refer to, pick *or* take up. **7** grow; make. **8 a** (*turn against*) defy, rise (up) against. **b** (*turn on*) assail, set upon, tear into. **10** go bad, spoil, curdle. **14 b** wrench. **17** make up, fashion, formulate, construct, cast, create, coin, concoct, express. • *n.* **1** revolution, rotation, cycle. **2** trend, drift; deviation, detour. **3** crossroads, junction, watershed. **4** inclination, bent, bias, leaning. **6** chance, say, round, shift, stint, tour (of duty), *colloq.* crack, shot, go. **7** stroll; drive, *colloq.* spin. **8** see ACT[1] *n.* 3a. **9** deed, act; (*bad turn*) disservice, harm, injury, wrong; (*good turn*) favor, good deed, (act of) kindness, courtesy. **10** fright, surprise, start, scare. □ **at every turn** everywhere, constantly, always, all the time. **by turns** reciprocally, successively. **in turn** sequentially, one after the other. **out of turn 1** out of sequence, out of order. **2** indiscreetly, improperly, tactlessly. **take turns** vary, rotate, exchange. **turn back 1** return; reverse, retrace, repel, rebuff, drive *or* beat back. **turn down 1** refuse, rebuff, spurn, decline, forgo, pass up, deny. **2** mute. **turn in 1** hand over, submit, offer, proffer, tender, surrender, yield; inform on, betray, *colloq.* rat on, tell on, *sl.* squeal on, finger. **3** retire, call it a day, *colloq.* hit the sack *or* hay. **turn off 1** deactivate; disconnect. **2** deviate, diverge, branch off. **3** disillusion, disenchant, alienate, repel, repulse, bore, offend, put off, displease, sicken, nauseate, disgust. **turn on 1** energize, activate, set in motion. **2** excite, thrill, arouse, titillate, work up, impassion. **turn out 1** eject, evict, throw out, kick out, oust, remove, dismiss, ax, *colloq.* sack, *sl.* fire. **2** see EXTINGUISH 1. **3** make, form, shape, construct, build, assemble, manufacture, put out. **4** come, arrive, appear, meet, *colloq.* show (up), surface. **5** develop, evolve, hap-

pen, occur, arise, emerge; end up. **turn over 1** invert, turn upside down. **2** overturn, knock *or* flip over; capsize. **3 b** kick over. **4** ponder (over), contemplate, reflect on. **6** sell. **turn over a new leaf** see REFORM *v.* 1. **turn tail** flee, bolt, take to one's heels, take off, *colloq.* scram, *sl.* beat it. **turn up 1** amplify, intensify, raise. **2** uncover, find, unearth, come across, hit upon, dig up, expose, disclose, bring to light. **3** see *come to light* (LIGHT). **4** come up, arise, happen, present itself, crop up, pop up; surface, appear, put in an appearance, show one's face, *colloq.* show (up).

turn•a•bout /tɚnəbowt/ *n.* **1** act of turning about. **2** abrupt change of policy, etc.
■ reversal, U-turn, about-face.

turn•a•round /tɚnərownd/ *n.* **1** = TURNABOUT. **2** space needed for a vehicle to turn around.

turn•buck•le /tɚnbukəl/ *n.* device for tightly connecting parts of a metal rod or wire.

turn•coat /tɚnkōt/ *n.* person who changes sides in a conflict, dispute, etc.
■ renegade, traitor, betrayer, deserter, fifth columnist, double agent, defector, snake in the grass.

turn•ing /tɚning/ *n.* □ **turning point** point at which a decisive change occurs.

tur•nip /tɚnip/ *n.* **1** plant with a large white globular root. **2** its root as a vegetable.
□□ **tur'nip•y** *adj.*

turn•key /tɚnkee/ • *n.* jailer. • *adj.* (of a process, etc.) fully ready for operation.

turn•off /tɚnof/ *n.* **1** turning off a main road. **2** *colloq.* something that repels or causes a loss of interest.

turn•out /tɚnowt/ *n.* **1** number of people attending a meeting, etc. **2** quantity of goods produced in a given time. **3** set or display of equipment, clothes, etc.
■ **1** assemblage, attendance, audience, crowd, gate, gathering. **2** output, production. **3** gear, outfit, apparatus, rig, apparel.

turn•o•ver /tɚnōvər/ *n.* **1** act of turning over. **2** amount of money taken in a business. **3** rate at which people enter and leave employment, etc. **4** small pastry made by folding crust over a filling. **5** rate at which goods are sold and replaced.
■ **2** (gross) revenue, volume. **4** see TART[1].

turn•pike /tɚnpīk/ *n.* highway on which a toll is usu. charged.

turn•stile /tɚnstīl/ *n.* gate with revolving arms, allowing people through singly.

turn•ta•ble /tɚntaybəl/ *n.* circular revolving plate on which records are played.

tur•pen•tine /tɚpəntīn/ *n.* resin secreted by several trees and used in various commercial preparations.

tur•pi•tude /tɚpitōōd, -tyōōd/ *n.* depravity; wickedness.
■ see EVIL *n.* 2.

tur•quoise /tɚkwoyz, -koyz/ • *n.* **1** semiprecious stone, usu. opaque and greenish blue or blue. **2** greenish blue color. • *adj.* of this color.

tur•ret /tɚrit, tur-/ *n.* **1** small tower, esp. decorating a building. **2** low, flat, usu. revolving armored tower for a gun and gunners in a ship, aircraft, fort, or tank. **3** rotating holder for tools in a lathe, etc. □□ **tur′ret•ed** adj.

tur•tle /tə́rt′l/ n. **1** terrestrial or aquatic reptile encased in a shell of bony plates, and having flippers or webbed toes. **2** flesh of the turtle, esp. used for soup. □ **turn turtle** capsize.

■ □ **turn turtle** overturn, upset, upend.

tur•tle•dove /tə́rt′lduv/ n. wild dove noted for its soft cooing and affection for its mate.

tur•tle•neck /tə́rt′lnek/ n. **1** high, close-fitting, turned over collar on a garment. **2** such a garment.

Tus•ca•ro•ra /təskərɔ́rə, -ráwr-/ n. **1 a** N. American people native to N. Carolina and later to New York. **b** member of this people. **2** language of this people.

tusk /tusk/ n. long, pointed tooth, esp. protruding from a closed mouth, as in the elephant, walrus, etc. □□ **tusked** adj. [also in comb.].

tus•sle /túsəl/ • n. scuffle. • v.intr. engage in a tussle.

■ n. see STRUGGLE n. 2.

tus•sock /túsək/ n. clump of grass, etc. □□ **tus′sock•y** adj.

tu•te•lage /tóōt′lij, tyóō-/ n. **1** guardianship. **2** being under this. **3** instruction.

tu•te•lar•y /tóōt′lairee, tyóō-/ adj. **1** serving as guardian. **2** giving protection.

tu•tor /tóōtər, tyóō-/ • n. private teacher. • v. **1** tr. act as a tutor to. **2** intr. work as a tutor. □□ **tu′tor•ship** n.

■ n. instructor, educator, coach, mentor, guru. • v. **1** train, enlighten, advise, direct. **2** teach.

tu•to•ri•al /tóōtáwreeal, tyóō-/ • adj. of a tutor or tuition. • n. period of individual instruction.

tut•ti /tóōtee/ Mus. • adv. with all voices or instruments together. • n. such a passage.

tut•ti-frut•ti /tóōteefróōtee/ n. ice cream flavored with mixed fruits.

tu•tu /tóōtōō/ n. ballet dancer's short skirt of stiffened frills.

tux /tuks/ n. colloq. = TUXEDO.

tux•e•do /tukseédō/ n. (pl. -dos or -does) **1** man's short black formal jacket. **2** suit of clothes including this.

TV abbr. television.

TVA abbr. Tennessee Valley Authority.

twad•dle /twód′l/ n. silly writing or talk.

twain /twayn/ adj. & n. archaic two.

twang /twang/ • n. **1** sound made by the plucked string of a musical instrument or bow. **2** nasal quality of a voice. • v. emit or cause to emit this sound. □□ **twang′y** adj.

'twas /twuz, twoz/ archaic it was.

tweak /tweek/ • v.tr. pinch and twist sharply. • n. instance of tweaking.

■ nip, twitch, squeeze, jerk, grip, pull.

tweed /tweed/ n. **1** rough-surfaced woolen cloth, usu. of mixed colors. **2** [in pl.] clothes made of tweed.

tweet /tweet/ • n. chirp of a small bird. • v.intr. make a chirping noise.

■ n. see CHIRP n. • v. see CHIRP v.

tweet•er /tweétər/ n. loudspeaker for high frequencies.

tweeze /tweez/ v.tr. pluck out with tweezers.

tweez•ers /tweézərz/ n.pl. small pair of pincers for picking up small objects, plucking out hairs, etc.

twelfth /twelfth/ • n. **1** next after eleventh. **2** each of twelve equal parts of a thing. • adj. that is the twelfth.

twelve /twelv/ n. **1** one more than eleven. **2** symbol for this (12, xii, XII).

twelve•fold /twélvfōld/ adj. & adv. **1** twelve times as much or as many. **2** consisting of twelve parts.

twen•ty /twéntee/ n. (pl. -ties) **1** product of two and ten. **2** symbol for this (20, xx, XX). **3** [in pl.] numbers from 20 to 29, esp. the years of a century or of a person's life. □ **twenty-twenty** (or **20/20**) **1** vision of normal acuity. **2** colloq. denoting clear perception or hindsight. □□ **twen′ti•eth** adj. & n.

■ **1** score.

24/7 • adv. colloq. occurring, applying, or available twenty-four hours a day, seven days a week (don't worry, we're on the job 24/7).

'twere /twər/ archaic it were.

twerp /twərp/ n. (also **twirp**) sl. stupid or objectionable person.

■ see FOOL n. 1.

twice /twis/ adv. **1** two times; on two occasions. **2** in double degree or quantity (twice as good).

twid•dle /twid′l/ • v. **1** tr. & intr. twirl, adjust, or play randomly or idly. **2** intr. move twirlingly. • n. act of twiddling □ **twiddle one's thumbs 1** make one's thumbs rotate around each other. **2** have nothing to do. □□ **twid′dler** n. **twid′dly** adj.

■ v. **1** fiddle (with), toy with, fool with, mess with, monkey with. □ **twiddle one's thumbs 2** while away (the) time, waste time.

twig /twig/ n. small branch or shoot of a tree or shrub. □□ **twig′gy** adj.

■ sprig, stem, stick. □□ **twiggy** see THIN adj. 4.

twi•light /twílit/ n. **1** light from the sky when the sun is below the horizon, esp. in the evening. **2** period of this. **3** faint light. **4** period of decline or destruction.

■ **1, 2** dusk, sunset, sundown. **2** nightfall. **4** decay, weakening, declination, diminution.

twi•lit /twílit/ adj. dimly illuminated by or as by twilight.

twill /twil/ n. fabric so woven as to have a surface of diagonal parallel ridges. □□ **twilled** adj.

'twill /twil/ archaic it will.

twin /twin/ • n. **1** each of a closely related or associated pair, esp. of children or animals born at one birth. **2** exact counterpart of a person or thing. **3** (**the Twins**) zodiacal sign or constellation Gemini. • adj. forming, or being one of, such a pair (twin brothers). • v. (**twinned, twin•ning**) **1** tr. & intr. **a** join intimately together. **b** [foll. by with] pair. **2** intr. bear twins. □ **twin bed** each of a pair of single beds. □□ **twin′ning** n.

■ n. **2** double, clone, duplicate, look-alike, colloq. spitting image, sl. (dead) ringer. • adj.

identical, corresponding. • v. **1** match, yoke, link, couple, combine, connect, associate.

twine /twīn/ • n. **1** strong string of twisted strands of fiber. **2** coil; twist. • v. **1** intr. coil; wind. **2** intr. & refl. (of a plant) grow in this way. □□ **twin′er** n.

■ n. **1** cord, thread; rope, cable, yarn. • v. entwine, braid, twist, weave.

twinge /twinj/ n. sharp momentary local pain or pang.

■ stab, cramp, spasm, pinch, stitch.

twin•kle /twingkəl/ • v.intr. **1** (of a star, light, etc.) shine with rapidly intermittent gleams. **2** (of the eyes) sparkle. **3** (of the feet) move lightly and rapidly. • n. **1** sparkle or gleam of the eyes. **2** slight flash of light; glimmer. **3** short, rapid movement. □□ **twin′kler** n. **twin′kling** n.

■ v. **1, 2** scintillate, shimmer, flicker, glisten, glint. • n. **1, 2** twinkling. □□ **twinkling** instant, wink of an eye.

twirl /twərl/ • v. spin, swing, or twist quickly and lightly around. • n. **1** twirling motion. **2** flourish made with a pen. □□ **twirl′er** n. **twirl′y** adj.

■ v. whirl, rotate, turn, gyrate, pivot, wind (about or around). • n. **1** revolution, pirouette. **2** whorl, spiral.

twirp var. of TWERP.

twist /twist/ • v. **1 a** tr. change the form of by rotating one end and not the other, or the two ends in opposite directions. **b** intr. undergo such a change. **c** tr. wrench or pull out of shape with a twisting action (*twisted my ankle*). **2** tr. wind (strands, etc.) around each other. **3 a** tr. give a spiral form to. **b** intr. take a spiral form. **4** tr. (foll. by *off*) break off by twisting. **5** tr. misrepresent the meaning of (words). **6 a** intr. take a winding course. **b** tr. make (one's way) in a winding manner. **7** intr. dance the twist. • n. **1** act of twisting. **2** twisted state. **3** thing formed by twisting. **4** point at which a thing twists or bends. **5** unexpected turn in a story, etc. **6** curled peel of lemon, etc., to flavor a drink. **7** [prec. by *the*] dance with a twisting movement, popular in the 1960s. □ **twist a person's arm** colloq. apply coercion, esp. by moral pressure. □□ **twist′y** adj. (**twist•i•er, twist•i•est**).

■ v. **1 a, b** contort, screw up, buckle, warp; crumple. **c** turn, sprain. **2** plait, braid, weave, entwine, intertwine, splice, interlace, tangle, entangle. **3** see WIND² v. 4. **4** see WRENCH v. 1a. **5** distort, pervert, alter, change, color, falsify, misquote; misinterpret, misunderstand, misconstrue. **6 a** snake, meander, zigzag. **b** wriggle, worm, squirm, writhe, wiggle. • n. **1** rotation, turn, roll, twirl, spin. **2** see TANGLE n. 1. **4** coil, spiral, corkscrew, helix, convolution, skew, curve, angle, bend, bow, kink, loop, curl. □ **twist a person's arm** coerce or bully or pressure a person, colloq. put the squeeze on.

twist•er /twistər/ n. colloq. tornado, waterspout, etc.

■ cyclone, typhoon, hurricane, whirlwind.

twit¹ /twit/ n. sl. silly or foolish person.

■ nincompoop, ass, idiot, simpleton, colloq. nitwit, halfwit, moron, lamebrain, sl. jerk.

twit² /twit/ v.tr. (**twit•ted, twit•ting**) reproach or taunt, usu. good-humoredly.

■ tease, cajole, jeer (at), make fun of, rag, mock; berate, deride, scorn, censure, revile, upbraid, colloq. kid.

twitch /twich/ • v. **1** intr. (of features, muscles, etc.) move or contract spasmodically. **2** tr. pull sharply at. • n. **1** sudden involuntary contraction or movement. **2** sudden pull or jerk.

■ v. **1** see JERK¹ v. 1. **2** see JERK¹ v. 2. • n. see JERK¹ n. 1, 2.

twit•ter /twitər/ • v. **1** intr. (of or like a bird) emit a succession of light tremulous sounds. **2** tr. utter or express in this way. • n. **1** act of twittering. **2** colloq. tremulously excited state. □□ **twit′ter•y** adj.

■ v. peep, cheep, tweet, chirp, warble, trill; chatter, prattle, titter, snicker. • n. **2** flutter, whirl, agitation, colloq. dither, tizzy.

two /too/ • n. **1** one more than one. **2** symbol for this (2, ii, II). • adj. that amount to two. □ **in two** in or into two pieces. **put two and two together** infer from known facts. **that makes two of us** colloq. that is true of me also. **two-bit** colloq. cheap; petty. **two-dimensional 1** having or appearing to have length and breadth but no depth. **2** lacking depth or substance; superficial. **two-faced 1** having two faces. **2** insincere; deceitful. **two-ply** of two strands, webs, or thicknesses. **two-step** dance in march or polka time. **two-time** colloq. **1** be unfaithful to (a lover). **2** swindle. **two-timer** colloq. one who two-times. **two-tone** having two colors or sounds. **two-way 1** involving two ways or participants. **2** (of a radio) capable of transmitting and receiving signals.

■ adj. a couple or pair. □ **put two and two together** see REASON v. 1. **two-bit** see CHEAP adj. 3. **two-dimensional 2** see SUPERFICIAL 1, 3. **two-faced 2** double-dealing, duplicitous, treacherous, dishonest, untrustworthy, scheming, crafty. **two-time** see DECEIVE 1, 2. **two-timer** see TRAITOR.

two•fold /toofōld/ adj. & adv. **1** twice as much or as many. **2** consisting of two parts.

■ adj. **1** double. **2** dual.

two•some /toosəm/ n. two persons together.

■ couple, pair, duo.

'twould /twood/ archaic it would.

twp. abbr. township.

TX abbr. Texas (in official postal use).

-ty¹ /tee/ suffix forming nouns denoting quality or condition (*cruelty, plenty*).

-ty² /tee/ suffix denoting tens (*twenty, thirty, ninety*).

ty•coon /tīkoon/ n. business magnate.

■ baron, financier, (multi)millionaire, billionaire, colloq. wheeler-dealer, mogul, big shot.

ty•ing pres. part. of TIE.

tyke /tīk/ n. (also **tike**) small child.

tym•pa•ni var. of TIMPANI.

tym•pa•num /timpənəm/ n. (pl. **tym•pa•nums** or **tym•pa•na** /-nə/) **1** middle ear. **2** eardrum. □□ **tym•pan′ic** adj.

type /tīp/ • n. **1** class; kind; sort. **2** person,

thing, or event exemplifying a group or class.
3 [in *comb.*] made of, resembling, or functioning as (*ceramic-type material*). **4** *colloq.* person, esp. of a specified character (*quiet type, not my type*). **5** object, conception, or work serving as a model for subsequent artists. **6** *Printing* **a** piece of metal, etc., with a raised letter or character on its upper surface for printing. **b** kind or size of such pieces (*printed in large type*). See synonym study at EMBLEM. • *v.* **1** *tr. & intr.* write with a typewriter or keyboard. **2** *tr.* esp. *Biol. & Med.* assign to a type; classify. **3** *tr.* = TYPECAST.

■ *n.* **1** category, classification, genre, run, order, variety, breed, race, species, strain, genus; brand, make, line, version. **2** prototype, paradigm, archetype, epitome, embodiment, model, specimen, illustration, example, symbol, pattern, personification, standard. **6** *Printing* typeface, font, lettering.

type·cast /típkast/ *v.tr.* (*past* and *past part.* **–cast**) assign (an actor or actress) repeatedly to the same type of role.

type·face /típfays/ *n. Printing* **1** set of type or characters in one design. **2** inked surface of type.

type·script /típskript/ *n.* typewritten document.

type·set·ter /típsetər/ *n. Printing* **1** person who composes type. **2** composing machine. □□ **type'set·ting** *n.*

type·writ·er /típrītər/ *n.* machine with keys for producing printlike characters on paper inserted around a roller.

type·writ·ten /típrīt'n/ *adj.* produced with a typewriter.

ty·phoid /tífoyd/ *n.* (in full **ty'phoid fe'ver**) infectious bacterial fever attacking the intestines.

ty·phoon /tīfoon/ *n.* violent hurricane in E. Asia.
■ see HURRICANE 1.

ty·phus /tífəs/ *n.* infectious fever with a purple rash, headaches, and usu. delirium. □□ **ty'phous** *adj.*

typ·i·cal /típikəl/ *adj.* **1** serving as a characteristic example; representative. **2** characteristic; to be expected. See synonym study at NORMAL. □□ **typ·i·cal·i·ty** /-kálitee/ *n.* **typ'i·cal·ly** *adv.*

■ conventional, normal, standard, ordinary, average, regular, run-of-the-mill, orthodox, classic; in character, in keeping, usual, customary, common; see also *symbolic* (SYMBOL). □□ **typically** see *ordinarily* (ORDINARY).

typ·i·fy /típifī/ *v.tr.* (**–fies, –fied**) **1** be typical of. **2** represent by or as a type or symbol. □□ **typ·i·fi·ca'tion** *n.* **typ'i·fi·er** *n.*
■ **1** exemplify, epitomize, personify, characterize, embody. **2** symbolize, stand for, suggest. □□ **typification** see SOUL 3, TYPE *n.* 2.

typ·ist /típist/ *n.* person who types.

ty·po /típō/ *n.* (*pl.* **–pos**) *colloq.* typographical error
■ see MISPRINT *n.*

ty·pog·ra·phy /típógrəfee/ *n.* **1** printing as an art. **2** style and appearance of printed matter. □□ **ty·pog'ra·pher** *n.* **ty·po·graph'i·cal** *adj.* **ty·po·graph'i·cal·ly** *adv.*

ty·ran·ni·cal /tiránikəl/ *adj.* despotic. □□ **ty·ran'ni·cal·ly** *adv.*
■ oppressive, dictatorial, autocratic, authoritarian, imperious, unjust, harsh, heavy-handed. □□ **tyrannically** see *severely* (SEVERE), *arbitrarily* (ARBITRARY).

ty·ran·nize /tírənīz/ *v.tr. & [foll. by over] intr.* treat despotically or cruelly.
■ bully, subjugate, dominate, intimidate, browbeat, oppress, persecute, subdue, suppress.

ty·ran·no·sau·rus /tírənəsáwrəs/ *n.* (also **ty·ran'no·saur**) carnivorous dinosaur with short front legs and a long well-developed tail.

tyr·an·ny /tírənee/ *n.* (*pl.* **–nies**) **1** cruel and arbitrary use of authority. **2** rule by a tyrant. □□ **tyr'an·nous** *adj.* **tyr'an·nous·ly** *adv.*
■ autocracy, authoritarianism, despotism, dictatorship, oppression, suppression, subjugation; fascism. □□ **tyrannous** see TYRANNICAL.

ty·rant /tírənt/ *n.* **1** oppressive or cruel ruler. **2** person exercising power arbitrarily or cruelly.
■ dictator, despot, autocrat, martinet, Hitler, bully, oppressor, authoritarian, slave driver.

ty·ro /tírō/ *n.* (*pl.* **–ros**) beginner; novice.

Uu

U¹ /yoo/ *n.* (also **u**) (*pl.* **Us** or **U's; u's**) **1** twenty-first letter of the alphabet. **2** U-shaped object or curve.

U² *abbr.* (also **U.**) university.

U³ *symb. Chem.* uranium.

-ubility /yoobílitee/ *suffix* forming nouns from, or corresponding to, adjectives in *–uble* (*solubility, volubility*).

u·biq·ui·tous /yoobíkwitəs/ *adj.* **1** present everywhere or in several places simultaneously.

2 often encountered. □□ **u·biq'ui·tous·ly** *adv.* **u·biq'ui·tous·ness** *n.* **u·biq'ui·ty** *n.*
■ see PERVASIVE. □□ **ubiquitously** see EVERYWHERE. **ubiquitousness, ubiquity** see *prevalence* (PREVALENT).

-uble /yəbəl/ *suffix* forming adjectives meaning 'that may or must be' (see –ABLE) (*soluble, voluble*).

-ubly /yəblee/ *suffix* forming adverbs corresponding to adjectives in *–uble*.

U-boat /yōōbōt/ *n. hist.* German submarine.

ud•der /údər/ *n.* baglike mammary gland of cattle, sheep, etc., with several teats.

UFO /yōō-ef-ō̄, yōōfṓ/ *n.* (also **ufo**) (*pl.* **UFOs** or **ufos**) unidentified flying object.

u•fol•o•gy /yōōfóləjee/ *n.* the study of UFOs. □□ **u•fol´o•gist** *n.*

ugh /əkh, ug, ukh/ *int.* expressing disgust or horror.

ug•ly /úglee/ *adj.* (**ug•li•er, ug•li•est**) **1** unpleasing or repulsive to see or hear. **2** unpleasantly suggestive (*ugly rumors are about*). **3** threatening; dangerous (*the sky has an ugly look*). **4** morally repulsive (*ugly vices*). □□ **ug´li•ly** *adv.* **ug´li•ness** *n.*

■ **1** unattractive, unlovely, unshapely, unsightly, hideous, grotesque, offensive, horrible, horrid. **3** hostile, nasty; forbidding, sinister, ominous, menacing, perilous, hazardous. **4** objectionable, offensive, nasty, loathsome, repellent, repugnant, revolting, sickening, disgusting, obnoxious, rotten, corrupt, filthy, vile, heinous, sordid, evil, foul, perverted, immoral, depraved, degenerate.

UHF *abbr.* ultrahigh frequency.

UK *abbr.* United Kingdom.

Ukrai•ni•an /yōōkráyneeən/ • *n.* **1** native of Ukraine. **2** language of Ukraine. • *adj.* of or relating to Ukraine or its people or language.

u•ku•le•le /yōōkəláylee/ *n.* small, four-stringed Hawaiian (orig. Portuguese) guitar.

-ular /yələr/ *suffix* forming adjectives, sometimes corresp. to nouns in *-ule* (*pustular*) but often without diminutive force (*angular, granular*). □□ **-ularity** /-láritee/ *suffix* forming nouns

ul•cer /úlsər/ *n.* **1** open sore on or in the body, often forming pus. **2 a** moral blemish. **b** corroding or corrupting influence, etc. □□ **ul•cered** *adj.* **ul´cer•ous** *adj.*

■ **1** lesion, abscess, canker, chancre, boil, eruption, carbuncle, inflammation, *Med.* furuncle. **2** cancer, canker, blight, scourge, pestilence, plague.

ul•cer•ate /úlsərayt/ *v.* form into or affect with an ulcer. □□ **ul´cer•a•ble** *adj.* **ul•cer•a•tion** /-ráyshən/ *n.* **ul´cer•a•tive** *adj.*

-ule /əl, yōōl/ *suffix* forming diminutive nouns (*capsule, globule*).

-ulent /yələnt/ *suffix* forming adjectives meaning 'abounding in; full of' (*fraudulent*). □□ **-ulence** *suffix* forming nouns

ul•na /úlnə/ *n.* (*pl.* **ul•nae** /-nee/) the thinner and longer of the two forearm bones (cf. RADIUS 3). □□ **ul´nar** *adj.*

-ulous /yələs/ *suffix* forming adjectives (*fabulous, populous*).

ul•ster /úlstər/ *n.* long, loose overcoat of rough cloth.

ult. *abbr.* **1** ultimo. **2** ultimate.

ul•te•ri•or /ultéereeər/ *adj.* existing in the background; hidden; secret (esp. *ulterior motive*). □□ **ul•te´ri•or•ly** *adv.*

■ concealed, covert, unrevealed, undisclosed, unexpressed, underlying, surreptitious, underhand(ed).

ul•ti•mate /últimət/ • *adj.* **1** last or last possible; final. **2** fundamental; primary (*ultimate*

truths). **3** maximum (*ultimate tensile strength*). • *n.* **1** best achievable or imaginable. **2** final or fundamental fact or principle. □□ **ul´ti•mate•ly** *adj.* **ul´ti•mate•ness** *n.*

■ *adj.* **2** elemental, basic, underlying, root, essential, unanalyzable, final. **3** final, greatest, supreme, utmost, paramount. □□ **ultimately** finally, eventually, in the end, when all is said and done, in the long run.

ul•ti•ma•tum /últimáytəm/ *n.* (*pl.* **ul•ti•ma•tums** or **ul•ti•ma•ta** /-tə/) final demand or statement of terms in negotiations.

■ condition(s), stipulation(s), requirement(s).

ul•ti•mo /últimō/ *adj. Commerce* of last month (*the 28th ultimo*).

ul•tra /últrə/ *adj.* favoring extreme views or measures, esp. in religion or politics.

■ die-hard, rabid, fundamentalist, extremist, prejudiced, opinionated, bigoted, *colloq.* hard-nosed.

ultra- /últrə/ *comb. form* **1** beyond; on the other side of. **2** extreme(ly), excessive(ly) (*ultraconservative, ultramodern*).

ul•tra•high /últrəhī/ *adj.* **1** (of a frequency) in the range 300 to 3,000 megahertz. **2** extremely high (*ultrahigh prices*).

ul•tra•ma•rine /últrəməreén/ • *n.* brilliant blue pigment or color. • *adj.* **1** of this color. **2** *archaic* situated beyond the sea.

ul•tra•mon•tane /últrəmontáyn/ *adj.* situated on the other side of the mountains (esp. the Alps) from the point of view of the speaker.

ul•tra•son•ic /últrəsónik/ *adj.* of or involving sound waves with a frequency above the upper limit of human hearing. □□ **ul•tra•son´i•cal•ly** *adv.*

ul•tra•sound /últrəsownd/ *n.* ultrasonic waves, esp. as used in medicine.

ul•tra•vi•o•let /últrəvī´ələt/ *adj. Physics* **1** having a wavelength (just) beyond the violet end of the visible spectrum. **2** of or using such radiation.

ul•u•late /úlyəlayt, yōōl-/ *v.intr.* howl; wail; make a hooting cry. □□ **ul´u•lant** *adj.* **ul•u•la•tion** /-láyshən/ *n.*

um /um, əm/ *int.* expressing hesitation or a pause in speech.

um•bel /úmbəl/ *n. Bot.* flower cluster in which stalks nearly equal in length spring from a common center and form a flat or curved surface, as in parsley. □□ **um´bel•lar** *adj.* **um•bel•lif•er•ous** /-ifərəs/ *adj.*

um•ber /úmbər/ • *n.* natural pigment or color like ocher but darker and browner. • *adj.* **1** of this color. **2** dark; dusky.

um•bil•i•cal /umbílikəl/ *adj.* of, situated near, or affecting the navel. □ **umbilical cord** flexible, cordlike structure attaching a fetus to the placenta.

um•bil•i•cus /umbílikəs/ *n.* (*pl.* **um•bil•i•ci** /-bílisī/ or **um•bil•i•cus•es**) *Anat.* navel.

um•bra /úmbrə/ *n.* (*pl.* **um•bras** or **um•brae** /-bree/) *Astron.* **1** total shadow usu. cast on the earth by the moon during a solar eclipse. **2** dark central part of a sunspot. □□ **um´bral** *adj.*

um•brage /úmbrij/ *n.* offense; sense of slight or injury.

um•brel•la /umbrélə/ *n.* **1** light, portable device for protection against rain, strong sun, etc., consisting of a usu. circular canopy of cloth mounted by means of a collapsible metal frame on a central stick. **2** protection or patronage. **3** coordinating or unifying agency (*umbrella organization*). □□ **um•brel•laed** /-ləd/ *adj.* **um•brel′la•like** *adj.*

■ **1** parasol, sunshade. **2** cover, coverage, aegis, shield, screen.

u•mi•ak /ṓōmeeak/ *n.* Inuit skin-and-wood open boat propelled with paddles.

um•laut /ṓōmlowt/ *n.* **1** mark ([¨]) used over a vowel, esp. in Germanic languages, to indicate a vowel change. **2** such a vowel change.

ump /ump/ *n. colloq.* umpire.

um•pire /úmpīr/ • *n.* person chosen to enforce the rules and settle disputes esp. in various sports. • *v.* act as umpire.

■ *n.* referee, arbiter, judge, adjudicator, arbitrator; official; *colloq.* ref. • *v.* officiate; referee, arbitrate, judge, moderate, adjudicate.

ump•teen /úmpteen/ *sl.* • *adj.* indefinitely many; a lot of. • *pron.* indefinitely many. □□ **ump•teenth′** *adj.*

■ *adj.* a lot of, many, innumerable, countless, numerous.

UN *abbr.* United Nations.

un-¹ /un/ *prefix* **1** added to adjectives and participles and their derivative nouns and adverbs, meaning: **a** not: denoting the absence of a quality or state (*unusable*, *unhappiness*). **b** reverse of, usu. with an implication of approval or disapproval (*unselfish*, *unscientific*). **2** (less often) added to nouns, meaning 'a lack of' (*unrest*, *untruth*).

un-² /un/ *prefix* added to verbs and (less often) nouns, forming verbs denoting: **1** reversal or cancellation of an action or state (*undress*, *unsettle*). **2** deprivation or separation (*un-*

mask). **3** release from (*unburden*). **4** causing to be no longer (*unman*).

'un /ən/ *pron. colloq.* one (*that's a good 'un*).

un•a•bat•ed /únəbáytid/ *adj.* not abated; undiminished. □□ **un•a•bat′ed•ly** *adv.*

un•a•bridged /únəbríjd/ *adj.* (of a text, etc.) complete; not abridged.

■ uncut, whole, full-length, entire; unexpurgated; extensive, thorough, comprehensive, full, exhaustive, all-encompassing, (all-)inclusive.

un•ac•a•dem•ic /únakədémik/ *adj.* **1** not academic (esp. not scholarly or theoretical). **2** (of a person) not suited to academic study.

un•ac•com•pa•nied /únəkúmpəneed/ *adj.* **1** not accompanied. **2** *Mus.* without accompaniment.

■ **1** alone, solo, lone, on one's own, by oneself, *archaic* sole. **2** solo, *Mus.* a cappella.

un•ac•com•plished /únəkómplisht/ *adj.* **1** not accomplished; uncompleted. **2** lacking accomplishments.

un•ac•count•a•ble /únəkówntəbəl/ *adj.* **1** unable to be explained. **2** unpredictable or strange in behavior. **3** not responsible. □□ **un•ac•count•a•bil′i•ty** *n.* **un•ac•count′a•ble•ness** *n.* **un•ac•count′a•bly** *adv.*

■ **1, 2** unexplained, inexplicable, unexplainable, mysterious, strange, puzzling, baffling, mystifying, peculiar, odd, bizarre.

un•ac•count•ed /únəkówntid/ *adj.* of which no account is given.

un•ac•cus•tomed /únəkústəmd/ *adj.* **1** (usu. foll. by *to*) not accustomed. **2** not customary; unusual (*unaccustomed silence*). □□ **un•ac•cus′tomed•ly** *adv.*

■ **1** (*unaccustomed to*) unused to, inexperi-

un•a•bashed′ *adj.*	un•as•sist′ed *adj.*
un•ab′lc *adj.*	un•at•tain′a•ble *adj.*
un•ac•cept′a•ble *adv.*	un•at•trac′tive *adj.*
un•ac•cept′a•bly *adv.*	un•at•trac′tive•ly *adv.*
un•ar•chive′a•ble *adj.*	un•au′thor•ized *adj.*
un•ac•knowl′edged *adj.*	un•a•vail′a•ble *adj.*
un•ac•quaint′ed *adj.*	un•a•vail•a•bil′i•ty *n.*
un•ad•ver′tised *adj.*	un•a•void′a•ble *adj.*
un•af•fil′i•at•ed *adj.*	un•a•void′a•bly *adv.*
un•a•fraid′ *adj.*	un•bear′a•ble *adj.*
un•aid′ed *adj.*	un•bear′a•bly *adv.*
un•al′ter•a•ble *adj.*	un•beat′a•ble *adj.*
un•al′ter•a•bly *adv.*	un•bi′ased *adj.*
un•al′tered *adj.*	un•bleached′ *adj.*
un•am•big′u•i•ty *n.*	un•blem′ished *adj.*
un•am•big′u•ous *adj.*	un•bound′ *adj.*
un•am•big′u•ous•ly *adv.*	un•break′a•ble *adj.*
un•am•bi′tious *adj.*	un•buck′le *v.*
un•an•nounced′ *adj.*	un•but′ton *v.*
un•an′swered *adj.*	un•ceas′ing *adj.*
un•an•tic′i•pat•ed *adj.*	un•ceas′ing•ly *adv.*
un•ap•peal′ing *adj.*	un•cen′sored *adj.*
un•ap•peal′ing•ly *adv.*	un•chal′lenged *adj.*
un•ap•pe′tiz•ing *adj.*	un•change′a•ble *adj.*
un•ap•pre′ci•at•ed *adj.*	un•changed′ *adj.*
un•ap•pre′cia•tive *adj.*	un•chang′ing *adj.*
un•ap•proved′ *adj.*	un•chap′er•oned *adj.*
un•ar′gu•a•ble *adj.*	un•char•ac•ter•is′tic *adj.*
un•asked′ *adj.*	un•char•ac•ter•is′ti•cal•ly *adv.*
un•as•sail′a•ble *adj.*	

un•checked′ *adj.*	un•cooked′ *adj.*
un•civ′i•lized *adj.*	un•co•op′er•a•tive *adj.*
un•claimed′ *adj.*	un•cor•rob′o•rat•ed *adj.*
un•claimed′ *adj.*	un•crit′i•cal *adj.*
un•clas′si•fied *adj.*	un•cross′ *v.*
un•clean′ *adj.*	un•cul′ti•vat•ed *adj.*
un•clean′ *n.*	un•nurud′ *adj.*
un•cloud′ed *adj.*	un•dam′aged *adj.*
un•clut′tered *adj.*	un•dat′ed *adj.*
un•combed′ *adj.*	un•daunt′ed *adj.*
un•com•plain′ing *adj.*	un•de•clared′ *adj.*
un•com•plain′ing•ly *adv.*	un•de•feat′ed *adj.*
un•com•plet′ed *adj.*	un•de•fend′ed *adj.*
un•com•pli′cat•ed *adj.*	un•de•fined′ *adj.*
un•com•pli•men′ta•ry *adj.*	un•de•mand′ing *adj.*
un•com•pre•hend′ing *adj.*	un•de•mo•crat′ic *adj.*
un•con•cealed′ *adj.*	un•de•pend′a•ble *adj.*
un•con•fined′ *adj.*	un•de•served′ *adj.*
un•con•firmed′ *adj.*	un•de•serv′ed•ly *adv.*
un•con′quer•a•ble *adj.*	un•de•serv′ing *adj.*
un•con′quered *adj.*	un•de•tect′a•ble *adj.*
un•con•strained′ *adj.*	un•de•tect′a•bly *adv.*
un•con•tam′i•nat•ed *adj.*	un•de•tect′ed *adj.*
un•con•test′ed *adj.*	un•de•ter′mined *adj.*
un•con•trol′la•ble *adj.*	un•de•terred′ *adj.*
un•con•trol′la•bly *adv.*	un•de•vel′oped *adj.*
un•con•trolled′ *adj.*	un•di•gest′ed *adj.*
un•con•vinced′ *adj.*	un•dig′ni•fied *adj.*
un•con•vinc′ing *adj.*	un•di•lut′ed *adj.*
un•con•vinc′ing•ly *adv.*	un•di•min′ished *adj.*

enced in *or* at, unfamiliar with, uninitiated in. **2** unfamiliar, rare, unwonted, curious, peculiar, atypical, untypical.

un·a·dorned /únədáwrnd/ *adj.* not adorned; plain.

■ simple, unembellished, undecorated, unornamented, stark, bare, austere.

un·a·dul·ter·at·ed /únədúltəraytid/ *adj.* **1** not adulterated; pure; concentrated. **2** sheer; complete; utter.

■ **1** see PURE[1] 1. **2** see SHEER *adj.* 1.

un·ad·vis·a·ble /únədvízəbəl/ *adj.* **1** not open to advice. **2** (of a thing) inadvisable.

un·ad·vised /únədvízd/ *adj.* **1** indiscreet; rash. **2** not having had advice. □□ **un·ad·vis′ed·ly** /–zidlee/ *adv.* **un·ad·vis′ed·ness** *n.*

■ **1** see *ill-advised* 2.

un·af·fect·ed /únəféktid/ *adj.* **1** [usu. foll. by *by*] not affected. **2** free from affectation; genuine; sincere. □□ **un·af·fect′ed·ly** *adv.* **un·af·fect′ed·ness** *n.*

■ **1** (*unaffected by*) impervious to, immune to, untouched by, unmoved by, unresponsive to, unswayed by, aloof from. **2** real, natural, simple, unpretentious, unassuming, ingenuous, unstudied, honest, guileless, artless, unfeigned. □□ **unaffectedly** see NATURALLY 1. **unaffectedness** see *sincerity* (SINCERE).

un·a·lien·a·ble /únáyleeənəbəl/ *adj. Law* = INALIENABLE.

un·a·ligned /únəlínd/ *adj.* **1** = NONALIGNED. **2** not physically aligned.

un·a·live /únəlív/ *adj.* **1** lacking in vitality. **2** [foll. by *to*] not fully susceptible or awake to.

un·al·loyed /únəlóyd, únál–/ *adj.* **1** not alloyed; pure. **2** complete; utter (*unalloyed joy*).

■ see PURE 1.

un-A·mer·i·can /únəmérikən/ *adj.* **1** not in accordance with American characteristics, etc. **2** contrary to the interests of the US. □□ **un-A·mer′i·can·ism** *n.*

u·nan·i·mous /yŏŏnánimɔs/ *adj.* **1** all in agreement (*the committee was unanimous*). **2** (of an opinion, vote, etc.) held or given by general consent (*the unanimous choice*). □□ **u′na·nim′i·ty** /–nənímitee/ *n.* **u·nan′i·mous·ly** *adv.*

■ □□ **unanimity** see ACCORD *n.* 1.

un·an·swer·a·ble /únánsərəbəl/ *adj.* **1** unable to be refuted. **2** unable to be answered (*an unanswerable question*). □□ **un·an′swer·a·bly** *adv.*

un·ap·proach·a·ble /únəprÓchəbəl/ *adj.* **1** not approachable; remote; inaccessible. **2** (of a person) unfriendly. □□ **un·ap·proach·a·bil′i·ty** *n.* **un·ap·proach·a′bly** *adv.*

■ **2** distant, remote, aloof, reserved, standoffish, austere, withdrawn, unsociable, antisocial, forbidding, chilly, cool, cold, frigid.

un·ap·pro·pri·at·ed /únəprÓpreeaytid/ *adj.* **1** not allocated or assigned. **2** not taken into possession by anyone.

un·apt /únápt/ *adj.* **1** [usu. foll. by *for*] not suitable. **2** [usu. foll. by *to* + infin.] not apt. □□ **un·apt′ly** *adv.* **un·apt′ness** *n.*

■ **2** see EXTRANEOUS 2.

un·armed /únaármd/ *adj.* not armed; without weapons.

■ unprotected, defenseless, weaponless.

un·ar·tic·u·lat·ed /únaartíkyəlaytid/ *adj.* not articulated or distinct.

un·dip·lo·mat′ic *adj.*	**un·ex·plain′a·ble** *adj.*
un·dis′ci·plined *adj.*	**un·ex·plain′a·bly** *adv.*
un·dis·closed′ *adj.*	**un·ex·plained′** *adj.*
un·dis·cov′ered *adj.*	**un·ex·plored′** *adj.*
un·dis·guised′ *adj.*	**un·ex·posed′** *adj.*
un·dis·mayed′ *adj.*	**un·ex·pressed′** *adj.*
un·dis·put′ed *adj.*	**un·fad′ing** *adj.*
un·dis·tin′guished *adj.*	**un·fal′ter·ing** *adj.*
un·dis·turbed′ *adj.*	**un·fa·mil′iar** *adj.*
un·di·vid′ed *adj.*	**un·fa·mil·i·ar′i·ty** *n.*
un·dressed′ *adj.*	**un·fash′ion·a·ble** *adj.*
un·drink′a·ble *adj.*	**un·fash′ion·a·bly** *adv.*
un·eat′en *adj.*	**un·fas′tened** *adj.*
un·ec·o·nom′ic *adj.*	**un·fath′om·a·ble** *adj.*
un·ec·o·nom′i·cal *adj.*	**un·fa′vor·a·ble** *adj.*
un·ec·o·nom′i·cal·ly *adv.*	**un·fa′vor·a·bly** *adv.*
un·ed′it·ed *adj.*	**un·fit′** *adj.*
un·ed′u·cat·ed *adj.*	**un·flat′ter·ing** *adj.*
un·em·phat′ic *adj.*	**un·flat′ter·ing·ly** *adv.*
un·en·cum′bered *adj.*	**un·flinch′ing** *adj.*
un·end′ing *adj.*	**un·flinch′ing·ly** *adv.*
un·en·dur′a·ble *adj.*	**un·fore·see′a·ble** *adj.*
un·en·dur′a·bly *adv.*	**un·fore·seen′** *adj.*
un·en·light′ened *adj.*	**un·for·giv′a·ble** *adj.*
un·en·thu·si·as′tic *adj.*	**un·for·giv′a·bly** *adv.*
un·en·thu·si·as′ti·cal·ly *adv.*	**un·for·giv′en** *adj.*
	un·for·giv′ing *adj.*
un·en′vi·a·ble *adj.*	**un·for·got′ten** *adj.*
un·e·vent′ful *adj.*	**un·ful·filled′** *adj.*
un·e·vent′ful·ly *adv.*	**un·fur′nished** *adj.*

un·gen′tle·man·ly *adj.*	**un·in·formed′** *adj.*
un·grace′ful *adj.*	**un·in·hab′it·a·ble** *adj.*
un·grace′ful·ly *adv.*	**un·in·hab′it·ed** *adj.*
un·gram·mat′i·cal *adj.*	**un·in·hib′it·ed** *adj.*
un·gram·mat′i·cal·ly *adv.*	**un·in′jured** *adj.*
un·grate′ful *adj.*	**un·in·sured′** *adj.*
un·grate′ful·ly *adv.*	**un·in·tel′li·gi·ble** *adj.*
un·grudg′ing *adj.*	**un·in·tend′ed** *adj.*
un·grudg′ing·ly *adv.*	**un·in·ten′tion·al** *adj.*
un·ham′pered *adj.*	**un·in·ten′tion·al·ly** *adv.*
un·harmed′ *adj.*	**un·in·ter·rupt′ed** *adj.*
un·help′ful *adj.*	**un·just′** *adj.*
un·help′ful·ly *adv.*	**un·just′ly** *adv.*
un·hes′i·tat·ing *adj.*	**un·jus·ti·fi′a·ble** *adj.*
un·hes·i·tat′ing·ly *adv.*	**un·jus·ti·fi′a·bly** *adv.*
un·hin′dered *adj.*	**un·jus′ti·fied** *adj.*
un·hook′ *v.*	**un·la′beled** *adj.*
un·hoped′-for *adj.*	**un·lace′** *v.*
un·hur′ried *adj.*	**un·li′censed** *adj.*
un·hurt′ *adj.*	**un·lined′** *adj.*
un·i·den′ti·fi·a·ble *adj.*	**un·list′ed** *adj.*
un·i·den′ti·fied *adj.*	**un·lit′** *adj.*
un·i·ma′gi·na·ble *adj.*	**un·made′** *adj.*
un·im·paired′ *adj.*	**un·man′age·a·ble** *adj.*
un·im·ped′ed *adj.*	**un·man′age·a·bly** *adv.*
un·im·por′tant *adj.*	**un·man′ly** *adj.*
un·im·pressed′ *adj.*	**un·marked′** *adj.*
un·im·pres′sive *adj.*	**un·mar′ried** *adj.*
un·im·proved′ *adj.*	**un·matched′** *adj.*
un·in·cor′po·rat·ed *adj.*	**un·mer′it·ed** *adj.*

un•ar•tis•tic /únaartístik/ *adj.* not artistic, esp. not concerned with art. □□ **un•ar•tis′ti•cal•ly** *adv.*

un•a•shamed /únəsháymd/ *adj.* 1 feeling no guilt; shameless. 2 blatant; bold. □□ **un•a•sham′ed•ly** *adv.* **un•a•sham′ed•ness** *n.*
■ 1 see SHAMELESS. 2 see BLATANT 1.

un•as•sum•ing /únəsōoming/ *adj.* not pretentious or arrogant; modest. □□ **un•as•sum′ing•ly** *adv.*
■ see MODEST 1, 2.

un•at•tached /únətácht/ *adj.* 1 not attached, esp. to a particular body, organization, etc. 2 not engaged or married.
■ 1 separate, unconnected, detached, independent, unaffiliated, self-governing, self-regulating, autonomous, self-reliant, self-sustaining, self-sustained. 2 single, unmarried, uncommitted, not spoken for.

un•at•tend•ed /únəténdid/ *adj.* 1 not attended. 2 (of a person, vehicle, etc.) not accompanied; alone; uncared for.
■ 2 see UNACCOMPANIED 1.

un•at•trib•ut•a•ble /únətríbyətəbəl/ *adj.* (esp. of information) that cannot or may not be attributed to a source, etc. □□ **un•at•trib′ut•a•bly** *adv.*

un•a•vail•ing /únəváyling/ *adj.* not availing; achieving nothing; ineffectual. □□ **un•a•vail′ing•ly** *adv.*

un•a•ware /únəwáir/ • *adj.* 1 not aware; ignorant (*unaware of her presence*). 2 (of a person) insensitive; unperceptive. • *adv.* = UNAWARES. □□ **un•a•ware′ness** *n.*
■ *adj.* 1 oblivious, unknowing, unsuspecting, unwitting, unconscious, uninformed, unenlightened. 2 see THOUGHTLESS 1. □□ **unawareness** see IGNORANCE.

un•a•wares /únəwáirz/ *adv.* 1 unexpectedly

(*met them unawares*). 2 inadvertently (*dropped it unawares*).
■ 1 abruptly, by surprise, suddenly, off (one's) guard. 2 unconsciously, unintentionally, unknowingly, unwittingly.

un•bal•ance /únbáləns/ *v.tr.* 1 upset the physical or mental balance of (*unbalanced by the blow, the shock unbalanced him*). 2 (as **unbalanced** *adj.*) **a** not balanced. **b** (of a mind or a person) unstable or deranged.
■ 2 (**unbalanced**) **a** uneven, unsymmetric(al), lopsided, wobbly, unsteady; one-sided, biased. **b** mad, certifiable, crazy, insane, eccentric, disturbed, of unsound mind, *sl.* daffy, nuts, bananas, out of one's head.

un•bear•a•ble /únbáirəbəl/ *adj.* not bearable. □□ **un•bear′a•bly** *adv.*
■ intolerable, unendurable, insufferable, oppressive, overwhelming, ruling too much.

un•be•com•ing /únbikúming/ *adj.* 1 not flattering a person. 2 not fitting; unsuitable. □□ **un•be•com′ing•ly** *adv.*
■ 1 unsuitable. 2 unbefitting; indecorous, improper, offensive, tasteless; inappropriate, out of place.

un•be•known /únbinón/ *adj.* (also **un•be•knownst** /-nōnst/) without the knowledge of (*was there all day unbeknown to us*).

un•be•lief /únbiléef/ *n.* lack of belief, esp. in religious matters. □□ **un•be•liev′er** /-léevər/ *n.* **un•be•liev′ing** *adj.*
■ see *skepticism* (SKEPTIC). □□ **unbelieving** incredulous, doubting, mistrusting, suspicious; faithless.

un•be•liev•a•ble /únbileevəbəl/ *adj.* not believable; incredible. □□ **un•be•liev′a•bly** *adv.*

■ preposterous, inconceivable, unimaginable, improbable, unthinkable; amazing, extraordinary, fantastic, *colloq.* mind-boggling, *sl.* mind-blowing. □□ **unbelievably** see TERRIBLY 1.

un•bend /únbénd/ *v.* (*past* and *past part.* **unbent**) **1** *tr. & intr.* straighten. **2** *intr.* relax from strain or severity; become affable.

un•bend•ing /únbénding/ *adj.* **1** inflexible. **2** firm; austere (*unbending rectitude*).
■ **1** see INFLEXIBLE 1. **2** see INFLEXIBLE 2.

un•blink•ing /únblingking/ *adj.* **1** not blinking. **2** steadfast; not hesitating. **3** stolid; cool. □□ **un•blink´ing•ly** *adv.*
■ **1, 3** see STEADY *adj.* 4. **2** see STEADFAST.

un•bolt /únbólt/ *v.tr.* release (a door, etc.) by drawing back the bolt.

un•born /únbáwrn/ *adj.* **1** not yet born (*an unborn child*). **2** never to be brought into being (*unborn hopes*).

un•bos•om /únbŏŏzəm/ *v.tr.* **1** disclose (thoughts, etc.). **2** [*refl.*] unburden (oneself) of one's thoughts, etc.

un•bound•ed /únbówndid/ *adj.* infinite (*unbounded optimism*).
■ see *limitless* (LIMIT).

un•bri•dle /únbrídˊl/ *v.tr.* **1** remove a bridle from (a horse). **2** remove constraints from (one's tongue, a person, etc.). **3** (as **unbridled** *adj.*) unconstrained (*unbridled insolence*).

un•bro•ken /únbrókən/ *adj.* **1** not broken. **2** not tamed (*unbroken horse*). **3** not interrupted (*unbroken sleep*). **4** not surpassed (*unbroken record*).
■ **1** see INTACT 1. **3** see CONTINUOUS.

un•bur•den /únbúrdˊn/ *v.tr.* **1** relieve of a burden. **2** [*esp. refl.*] relieve (oneself, one's conscience, etc.) by confession, etc.
■ **1** (*unburden of*) see RELIEVE 4.

un•called /únkáwld/ *adj.* not summoned or invited. □ **uncalled-for** (of an opinion, action, etc.) impertinent or unnecessary (*an uncalled-for remark*).

un•can•ny /únkánee/ *adj.* (**un•can•ni•er**, **un•can•ni•est**) seemingly supernatural; mysterious. □□ **un•can´ni•ly** *adv.*
■ see EERIE.

un•cared-for /únkáirdfawr/ *adj.* disregarded; neglected.

un•car•ing /únkáiring/ *adj.* lacking compassion for others.

un•cer•e•mo•ni•ous /únserimṓneeəs/ *adj.* **1** informal. **2** abrupt; discourteous. □□ **un•cer•e•mo´ni•ous•ly** *adv.*
■ **1** see INFORMAL. **2** see CURT.

un•cer•tain /únsárt'n/ *adj.* **1** not certainly knowing or known (*the result is uncertain*). **2** unreliable (*his aim is uncertain*). **3** changeable; erratic (*uncertain weather*). □ **in no uncertain terms** clearly and forcefully. □□ **un•cer´tain•ly** *adv.* **un•cer´tain•ty** *n.*
■ **1** unsure, undecided, unclear, hesitant; indeterminate, unpredictable, unforeseeable, unresolved, unsettled, speculative, debatable, doubtful, questionable. **2** unpredictable, haphazard, random. **3** variable, inconstant, irregular, fickle, wavering, unreliable; unsystematic.

un•char•i•ta•ble /únchárritəbəl/ *adj.* censorious; severe in judgment. □□ **un•char´i•ta•bly** *adv.*
■ see UNKIND.

un•chart•ed /únchaártid/ *adj.* not mapped or surveyed.
■ unknown, unexplored, strange, virgin, trackless.

un•chris•tian /únkríschən/ *adj.* **1** contrary to Christian principles, esp. uncaring or selfish. **2** not Christian.

un•ci•al /únsheeəl, únshəl/ • *adj.* of or written in rounded, unjoined letters found in manuscripts of the 4th–8th c., from which modern capitals are derived. • *n.* **1** uncial letter. **2** uncial style or manuscript.

un•civ•il /únsívil/ *adj.* ill-mannered; impolite. See synonym study at RUDE. □□ **un•civ´il•ly** *adv.*

un•cle /úngkəl/ *n.* **1 a** brother of one's father or mother. **b** aunt's husband. **2** *colloq.* name given by children to a male family friend. □ **Uncle Sam** *colloq.* federal government personified (*will fight for Uncle Sam*). **Uncle Tom** *derog.* black person considered to be servile, cringing, etc. (from the hero of H. B. Stowe's *Uncle Tom's Cabin*, 1852).

un•clean /únkléen/ *adj.* **1** not clean. **2** religiously impure. **3** *Bibl.* (of a spirit) wicked.
■ **1** see DIRTY *adj.* 1. **2** profane, adulterated, not kosher.

un•clear /únkléer/ *adj.* **1** not clear or easy to understand; obscure. **2** (of a person) doubtful; uncertain (*I'm unclear as to what you mean*). □□ **un•clear´ly** *adv.*

un•cloud•ed /únklówdid/ *adj.* **1** not clouded; clear; bright. **2** untroubled (*unclouded serenity*).

un•coil /únkóyl/ *v.* unwind.

un•com•fort•a•ble /únkúmftəbəl, –kúmfərtə–/ *adj.* **1** not comfortable. **2** uneasy; disquieting (*uncomfortable silence*). □□ **un•com´fort•a•bly** *adv.*
■ **1** see *cramped* (CRAMP 4b), OPPRESSIVE 2. **2** see AWKWARD 3, 4.

un•com•mit•ted /únkəmítid/ *adj.* **1** not committed. **2** unattached to any specific political cause or group.
■ see NEUTRAL *adj.* 1, NONALIGNED.

un•com•mon /únkómən/ *adj.* **1** unusual; remarkable. **2** remarkably great, etc. (*uncommon fear of spiders*). □□ **un•com´mon•ly** *adv.* **un•com•mon•ness** /–mən-nis/ *n.*
■ **1** see UNUSUAL. **2** see EXTREME *adj.* 1. □□ **uncommonly** see ESPECIALLY. **uncommonness** see RARITY 1, *singularity* (SINGULAR).

un•com•mu•ni•ca•tive /únkəmyṓŏnikətiv/ *adj.* not wanting to communicate; taciturn.
■ see TACITURN.

un•com•pro•mis•ing /únkómprəmizing/ *adj.* unwilling to compromise; stubborn; unyielding. □□ **un•com´pro•mis•ing•ly** *adv.*
■ see RESOLUTE. □□ **uncompromisingly** see DOWNRIGHT *adv.*

un•con•cern /únkənsórn/ *n.* indifference; apathy. □□ **un•con•cerned´** *adj.* **un•con•cern´ed•ly** /–nidlee/ *adv.*
■ see *indifference* (INDIFFERENT). □□ **unconcerned** see INDIFFERENT 1.

un•con•di•tion•al /únkəndíshənəl/ *adj.* not subject to conditions; complete (*unconditional surrender*). □□ **un•con•di′tion•al•ly** *adv.*

■ see UNQUALIFIED[1] 3, FULL *adj.* 5.

un•con•di•tioned /únkəndíshənd/ *adj.* **1** not subject to conditions or to an antecedent condition. **2** (of behavior, etc.) not .determined by conditioning; natural.

un•con•nec•ted /únkənéktid/ *adj.* **1** not physically joined. **2** not connected or associated. **3** (of speech, etc.) disconnected; not joined in order or sequence (*unconnected ideas*).

■ **1** see LOOSE *adj.* 2. **2** see EXTRANEOUS 2. **3** see DISCONNECTED 2.

un•con•scion•a•ble /únkónshənəbəl/ *adj.* **1 a** having no conscience. **b** contrary to conscience. **2** excessive (*an unconscionable length of time*). □□ **un•con′scion′a•bly** *adv.*

■ **1** unscrupulous, amoral, unprincipled. **2** egregious, extreme, unwarranted, unreasonable, outrageous.

un•con•scious /únkónshəs/ • *adj.* not conscious (*unconscious of any change; fell unconscious on the floor*). • *n.* that part of the mind that is inaccessible to the conscious mind but that affects behavior, emotions, etc. □□ **un•con′scious•ly** *adv.* **un•con′scious•ness** *n.*

■ *adj.* insensible, knocked out, stunned, comatose, *colloq.* out (cold); heedless, insensitive, unmindful, involuntary, mechanical; unaware, oblivious. • *n.* see SUBCONSCIOUS *n.* □□ **unconsciously** see UNAWARES 2. **unconsciousness** see FAINT *n.*, STUPOR.

un•con•sti•tu•tion•al /únkonstitốoshənəl, -tyốo-/ *adj.* not in accordance with the political constitution or with procedural rules. □□ **un•con•sti′tu′tion•al•ly** *adv.*

un•con•ven•tion•al /únkənvénshənəl/ *adj.* unusual; unorthodox. □□ **un•con•ven′tion•al′i•ty** /-nálitee/ *n.* **un•con•ven′tion•al•ly** *adv.*

un•co•or•di•nat•ed /únko áwrd′naytid/ *adj.* **1** not coordinated. **2** (of a person's movements, etc.) clumsy.

■ **1** see INDISCRIMINATE 2. **2** see CLUMSY 1.

un•cork /únkáwrk/ *v.tr.* **1** draw the cork from (a bottle). **2** allow (feelings, etc.) to be vented.

un•count•ed /únkówntid/ *adj.* **1** not counted. **2** very many; innumerable.

un•cou•ple /únkúpəl/ *v.tr.* **1** release from couplings. **2** unfasten.

un•couth /únkốoth/ *adj.* (of a person, manners, appearance, etc.) lacking in ease and polish; uncultured; rough (*uncouth voices, behavior was uncouth*). See synonym study at RUDE.

■ see ROUGH *adj.* 3.

un•cov•er /únkúvər/ *v.* **1** *tr.* **a** remove a cover or covering from. **b** make known; disclose. **2** *intr.* remove one's hat, cap, etc. **3** *tr.* (as **uncovered** *adj.*) **a** not covered by a roof, clothing, etc. **b** not wearing a hat.

■ **1 a** see BARE *v.* **b** see BARE *v.*, DISCOVER 1. **3 a** (**uncovered**) see BALD *adj.* 1.

unc•tion /úngkshən/ *n.* **1 a** anointing with oil, etc., as a religious rite. **b** oil, etc., so used. **2 a** soothing words or thought. **b** excessive or insincere flattery. **3 a** anointing for medical purposes. **b** ointment so used.

unc•tu•ous /úngkchốoəs/ *adj.* **1** (of behavior, speech, etc.) unpleasantly flattering; oily. **2** (esp. of minerals) having a greasy or soapy feel; oily. □□ **unc′tu•ous•ly** *adv.*

un•cut /únkút/ *adj.* **1** not cut. **2** (of a book, film, etc.) complete; uncensored. **3** (of a stone, esp. a diamond) not shaped by cutting.

■ **1** see INTACT 1. **2** see ENTIRE.

un•de•cid•ed /úndisídid/ *adj.* **1** not settled or certain. **2** hesitating; irresolute.

■ **1** see UNRESOLVED 2. **2** see IRRESOLUTE 1.

un•de•mon•stra•tive /úndimónstrətiv/ *adj.* not expressing feelings, etc., outwardly; reserved.

un•de•ni•a•ble /úndiníəbəl/ *adj.* **1** unable to be disputed; certain. **2** excellent (*of undeniable character*). □□ **un•de•ni′a•bly** *adv.*

■ **1** see CERTAIN *adj.* 1b. □□ **undeniably** see undoubtedly (UNDOUBTED).

un•der /úndər/ • *prep.* **1 a** in or to a position lower than; below; beneath (*fell under the table*). **b** on the inside of (a surface, etc.) (*vest under his jacket*). **2 a** inferior to; less than (*a captain is under a major, is under 18*). **b** at or for a lower cost than (*under $20*). **3 a** subject to; controlled by (*lives under oppression, the country prospered under him*). **b** undergoing (*a house under repair*). **c** classified or subsumed in (*that book goes under biology*). **4** at the foot of or sheltered by (*hid under the wall, under the cliff*). **5** powered by (*sail, steam, etc.*). • *adv.* **1** in or to a lower position or condition (*kept him under*). **2** *colloq.* in a state of unconsciousness (*put her under for the operation*). • *adj.* lower (*the under jaw*). □ **under the sun** anywhere in the world. **under way** in motion, in progress. □□ **un′der•most** *adj.*

■ *prep.* **1 a** underneath. **b** within, covered by, beneath. **2 a** second to, subservient to, below, subordinate to, answerable to. **b** less than. **3 a** liable to, at the beck and call of, at the mercy of, directed or supervised or bound by; under the protection or care of. **c** included in or under, comprised in or under. **4** under the lee of. • *adv.* **1** below, beneath, down, out of sight; underwater. • *adj.* inferior. □ **under way** proceeding, on the move, advancing, going, started, in the pipeline, operating, functioning, *colloq.* in the works.

under- /úndər/ *prefix* in senses of UNDER: **1** below; beneath (*underground*). **2** lower in status; subordinate (*undersecretary*). **3** insufficiently; incompletely (*undercook, underdeveloped*).

un•der•a•chieve /úndərəcheév/ *v.intr.* do less well than might be expected (esp. scholastically). □□ **un•der•a•chiev′er** *n.*

un•der•act /úndərákt/ *v.* **1** *tr.* act (a part, etc.) with insufficient force. **2** *intr.* act a part in this way.

un•der•age /úndəráyj/ *adj.* not old enough, esp. not yet of adult status.

un•der•arm /úndəráarm/ • *adj. & adv.*

1 *Sports* with the arm below shoulder level.
2 under the arm. 3 in the armpit. • *n.*
armpit.

un•der•bel•ly /úndərbélee/ *n. (pl.* **–lies**) underside of an animal, vehicle, etc., esp. as an area vulnerable to attack.

un•der•bid /úndərbíd/ *v.tr.* (**–bid•ding**; *past* and *past part.* **–bid**) 1 make a lower bid than. 2 [also *absol.*] *Bridge*, etc., bid less on (one's hand) than warranted. □□ **un'der•bid'der** *n.*

un•der•brush /úndərbrúsh/ *n.* undergrowth in a forest.

un•der•car•riage /úndərkárij/ *n.* 1 wheeled, retractable structure beneath an aircraft used for landing, etc. 2 supporting frame of a vehicle.

un•der•charge /úndərcháarj/ *v.tr.* 1 charge too little for (a thing) or to (a person). 2 give too little charge to (a gun, battery, etc.).

un•der•class /úndərklás/ *n.* subordinate social class.

un•der•clothes /úndərklóz, –klóthz/ *n.pl.* clothes worn under others, esp. next to the skin.

■ underwear, lingerie, *colloq.* underthings, *joc.* unmentionables.

un•der•coat /úndərkót/ • *n.* 1 layer of paint under a topcoat. 2 animal's under layer of hair or down. • *v.tr.* seal the underpart of a car against rust, etc., with an undercoat. □□ **un'der•coat•ing** *n.*

un•der•cov•er /úndərkúvər/ *adj.* [usu. *attrib.*] 1 surreptitious. 2 spying, esp. by infiltration (*undercover agent*).

■ secret, private, clandestine, covert, stealthy.

un•der•cur•rent /úndərkə́rənt, –kúr–/ *n.* 1 current below the surface. 2 underlying, often contrary, feeling, activity, or influence (*undercurrent of protest*).

■ 1 undertow, riptide. 2 undertone, trend, tendency, suggestion, trace, implication, sense; vibrations, *colloq.* vibes.

un•der•cut /úndərkút/ *v.tr.* (**–cut•ting**; *past* and *past part.* **–cut**) 1 sell or work at a lower price than. 2 cut away the part below or under (a thing). 3 render unstable or less firm; undermine.

■ 1 undercharge, sell cheaply *or* at a loss. 2 undermine, excavate, hollow out. 3 weaken, sabotage, impair, disable.

un•der•de•vel•oped /úndərdivéləpt/ *adj.* 1 not fully developed; immature. 2 (of a country, etc.) below its potential economic level. □□ **un'der•de•vel'op•ment** *n.*

un•der•dog /úndərdawg, –dog/ *n.* 1 oppressed person. 2 person whose loss in a contest, etc., is expected.

■ loser, scapegoat, victim; *sl.* fall guy.

un•der•done /úndərdún/ *adj.* (of food) not sufficiently cooked.

un•der•em•ployed /úndərimplóyd/ *adj.* having employment inadequate to one's abilities, education. etc. □□ **un•der•em•ploy'ment** *n.*

un•der•es•ti•mate • *v.tr.* /úndəréstimayt/ form too low an estimate of. • *n.* /úndərés-

timət/ estimate that is too low. □□ **un•der•es•ti•mation** /–máyshən/ *n.*

■ *v.* undervalue, underrate, misjudge, trivialize, not do justice to, fail to appreciate.

un•der•ex•pose /úndəriksp*óz/ *v.tr. Photog.* expose (film) for too short a time. □□ **un•der•ex•po•sure** /–pózhər/ *n.*

un•der•foot /úndərfóöt/ *adv.* 1 under one's feet. 2 in the way.

un•der•gar•ment /úndərgaarmənt/ *n.* piece of underwear.

un•der•go /úndərgó/ *v.tr.* (*3rd sing. present* **–goes**; *past* **–went**; *past part.* **–gone**) be subjected to; suffer; endure.

■ bear, experience, live *or* go through, weather, withstand.

un•der•grad•u•ate /úndərgrájōōət/ *n.* student at a college or university who has not yet taken a degree.

un•der•ground • *adv.* /úndərgrównd/ 1 beneath the ground. 2 in or into secrecy or hiding. • *adj.* /úndərgrownd/ 1 situated underground. 2 secret; subversive. 3 unconventional; experimental (*underground press*). • *n.* /úndərgrownd/ 1 secret subversive group or activity. 2 *Brit.* subway system.

■ *adv.* 1 see BENEATH *adv.* • *adj.* 1 subterranean, buried, covered. 2 clandestine, hidden, undercover. 3 alternative, radical, nonconformist. • *n.* 1 resistance, partisans, freedom fighters, guerrillas, revolutionaries; fifth column, saboteurs. 2 metro, *colloq.* tube.

un•der•growth /úndərgróth/ *n.* dense growth of shrubs, etc., esp. under large trees.

un•der•hand • *adj.* /úndərhánd/ 1 secret; deceptive; crafty. 2 *Sports* underarm. • *adv.* /úndərhánd/ in an underhand manner.

■ *adj.* 1 see FURTIVE 1, 2, DISHONEST.

un•der•lie /úndərlí/ *v.tr.* (**–ly•ing**; *past* **–lay**; *past part.* **–lain**) 1 [also *absol.*] lie under (a stratum, etc.). 2 [also *absol.*] (esp. as **underlying** *adj.*) be the basis of (a doctrine, law, conduct, etc.). 3 exist beneath the superficial aspect of.

■ 2 (**underlying**) see BASIC *adj.* 2.

un•der•line /úndərlín/ *v.tr.* 1 draw a line under. 2 emphasize; stress.

■ 1 underscore. 2 see EMPHASIZE.

un•der•ling /úndərling/ *n.* usu. *derog.* subordinate.

un•der•ly•ing *pres. part.* of UNDERLIE.

un•der•mine /úndərmín/ *v.tr.* 1 injure, weaken, or wear out secretly or insidiously. 2 wear away the base of (*rivers undermine their banks*). 3 make an excavation under.

■ 1 drain, disable, debilitate, threaten, sabotage, damage. 2 wash away, erode. 3 undercut, mine *or* dig *or* burrow under, hollow out.

un•der•neath /úndərnééth/ • *prep.* 1 at or to a lower place than, below. 2 on the inside of; within. • *adv.* 1 at or to a lower place. 2 inside. • *n.* lower surface or part. • *adj.* lower.

■ *adv.* 1 see BELOW *adv.* 2a.

un•der•pants /úndərpánts/ *n.pl.* undergarment covering the lower part of the torso.

un•der•pass /úndərpás/ *n.* road, etc., passing under a railroad, another road, etc.

un•der•pay /úndərpáy/ *v.tr.* (*past* and *past*

part. –paid) pay too little to (a person) or for (a thing). □□ un•der•pay′ment n.

un•der•pin /úndərpín/ v.tr. (–pinned, –pin•ning) 1 support from below with masonry, etc. 2 support; strengthen.

■ 2 see SUSTAIN 2.

un•der•play /úndərpláy/ v. 1 tr. play down the importance of. 2 intr. & tr. Theatr. underact.

un•der•pop•u•lat•ed /úndərpópyəláytid/ adj. having an insufficient or very small population.

■ see deprived (DEPRIVE 2).

un•der•priv•i•leged /úndərprivilijd, –privlijd/ adj. not enjoying the normal standard of living or rights in a society.

un•der•rate /úndərayt/ v.tr. have too low an opinion of.

un•der•score /úndərskáwr/ v.tr. = UNDERLINE v.

un•der•sea /úndərseé/ adj. below the sea or its surface.

un•der•sec•re•tar•y /úndərsékrətaree/ n. (pl. –ies) subordinate official, esp. a junior minister or senior civil servant.

un•der•sell /úndərsél/ v.tr. (past and past part. –sold) sell at a lower price than (another seller).

■ see UNDERCUT v. 1.

un•der•shirt /úndərshórt/ n. undergarment worn under a shirt.

un•der•shoot /úndərshoot/ v.tr. (past and past part. –shot) 1 land short of (a runway, etc.). 2 shoot short of or below.

un•der•shorts /úndərshawrts/ n. short un•derpants; trunks.

un•der•shot /úndərshót/ adj. (of a water wheel) turned by water flowing under it.

un•der•side /úndərsíd/ n. lower or under side or surface.

un•der•signed /úndərsínd/ adj. whose signature is appended (we, the undersigned, wish to state . . .).

un•der•skirt /úndərskərt/ n. skirt worn under another; petticoat.

un•der•staffed /úndərstáft/ adj. having too few staff.

■ short-staffed, undermanned, short-handed.

un•der•stand /úndərstánd/ v. (past and past part. –stood /–stood/) 1 tr. perceive the meaning of (words, a person, a language, etc.) (understood you perfectly, cannot understand French). 2 tr. perceive the significance or explanation or cause of (do not understand why he came). 3 tr. sympathize with; know how to deal with (understand your difficulty, cannot understand him at all). 4 tr. a infer esp. from information received; take as implied; take for granted (I understand that it begins at noon). b [absol.] believe or assume from knowledge or inference (he is coming tomorrow, I understand). 5 tr. supply (a word) mentally (the verb may be either expressed or understood). □□ un•der•stand′a•ble adj. un•der•stand′a•bly adv.

■ 1 grasp, comprehend, see, make sense of, follow, appreciate, interpret, know, apprehend, fathom, colloq. get, catch on to, get a handle on, sl. dig. 3 empathize with, show

915   underpin ~ undertow

compassion for; accept, tolerate. 4 hear, gather, be told or informed or advised, have found out or learned, interpret, assume, conclude. □□ understandable see INTELLIGIBLE.

un•der•stand•ing /úndərstánding/ • n. 1 a ability to understand or think; intelligence. b power of apprehension; power of abstract thought. 2 individual's perception of a situation, etc. 3 agreement, esp. informally (had an understanding with the rival company). 4 sympathy or tolerance. • adj. 1 having understanding or insight or good judgment. 2 sympathetic. □□ un•der•stand′ing•ly adv.

■ n. 1 intellect, mind, brain, sense, reason, wisdom, insight, sl. savvy; comprehension, awareness, knowledge; conception, mastery. 2 reading, interpretation, judgment. 3 contract, arrangement, accord, treaty, alliance, settlement. 4 empathy, rapport, feeling, compassion, sensitivity. • adj. 1 see JUDICIOUS. 2 see SYMPATHETIC adj. 1.

un•der•state /úndərstáyt/ v.tr. (often as understated adj.) 1 express in greatly restrained terms. 2 represent as being less than it actually is. □□ un•der•state′ment n.

■ understated 1 subtle, low-key, simple, basic, unadorned.

un•der•stood past and past part. of UNDERSTAND.

un•der•stud•y /úndərstúdee/ esp. Theatr. n. (pl. –ies) person ready to act at short notice in the absence of another. • v.tr. (–ies, –ied) 1 study (a role, etc.) as an understudy. 2 act as an understudy to (a person).

■ n. second, substitute, stand-in, colloq. sub. • v. 2 substitute for, back up, double for, replace.

un•der•take /úndərtáyk/ v.tr. (past –took; past part. –tak•en) 1 bind oneself to perform; make oneself responsible for; engage in; enter upon (work, an enterprise, a responsibility). 2 accept an obligation; promise. 3 guarantee; affirm.

■ 1 assume, take on, accept, begin, tackle, try. 2 agree, consent, contract, pledge. 3 see SWEAR v. 1a, 2.

un•der•tak•er /úndərtaykər/ n. person whose business is to make arrangements for funerals.

■ funeral director, mortician.

un•der•tak•ing /úndərtáyking/ n. 1 work, etc., undertaken; enterprise (a serious undertaking). 2 pledge or promise.

■ 1 affair, business, project, effort. 2 commitment, assurance, contract, agreement, vow, guarantee.

un•der•things /úndərthingz/ n.pl. colloq. underclothes.

un•der•tone /úndərtōn/ n. 1 subdued tone of sound or color. 2 underlying quality. 3 undercurrent of feeling.

■ 1 see MURMUR n. 1, TINT n. 2. 2, 3 see UNDERCURRENT 2.

un•der•tow /úndərtō/ n. current below the surface of the sea moving in the opposite direction to the surface current.

un•der•val•ue /úndərvályōō/ *v.tr.* (**-val•ues,** **-val•ued, -val•u•ing**) **1** value insufficiently. **2** underestimate. □□ **un•der•val•u•a'tion** *n.*

■ **2** see UNDERESTIMATE *v.*

un•der•wa•ter /úndərwáwtər, -wótər/ • *adj.* situated or done under water. • *adv.* in and covered by water.

■ *adj.* submarine; see also SUNKEN 1. • *adv.* undersea, submerged, flooded.

un•der•wear /úndərwáir/ *n.* underclothes.

un•der•weight /úndərwáyt/ *adj.* weighing less than is normal or desirable.

■ see LIGHT² *adj.* 2.

un•der•whelm /úndərhwélm, -wélm/ *v.tr. joc.* fail to impress.

un•der•world /úndərwórld/ *n.* **1** those who live by organized crime and immorality. **2** mythical abode of the dead under the earth.

■ **1** syndicate, Mafia, Cosa Nostra, criminals, *colloq.* mob, gangland. **2** nether regions *or* world, lower regions *or* world, Hades, hell.

un•der•write /úndər-rít/ *v.* (*past* **-wrote;** *past part.* **-writ•ten**) **1 a** *tr.* sign and accept liability under (an insurance policy, etc.). **b** *tr.* accept (liability) in this way. **c** *intr.* practice (marine) insurance. **2** *tr.* undertake to finance or support. **3** *tr.* engage to buy all the unsold stock in (a company, etc.). □□ **un'der•writ•er** *n.*

■ **1 a, b** subscribe to, endorse, sign, approve, validate, *colloq.* OK, okay. **2** back (up), invest in, subsidize, guarantee.

un•de•signed /úndizínd/ *adj.* unintentional.

un•de•sir•a•ble /úndizírəbəl/ • *adj.* objectionable; unpleasant. • *n.* undesirable person. □□ **un•de•sir•a•bil'i•ty** *n.*

■ *adj.* unwanted, offensive, unwelcome, disliked, repugnant. • *n.* pariah, outcast, exile, reject, leper.

un•did *past* of UNDO.

un•dies /úndeez/ *n.pl. colloq.* (esp. women's) underclothes.

un•dif•fer•en•ti•at•ed /úndifərénsheeaytid/ *adj.* not differentiated; amorphous.

un•do /úndōō/ *v.tr.* (*3rd sing. present* **-does;** *past* **-did;** *past part.* **-done**) **1** unfasten or untie (a coat, button, package, etc.). **2** annul; cancel (*cannot undo the past*). **3** ruin the prospects, reputation, or morals of.

■ **1** loosen, open, unzip, unbutton, unbuckle; unlock, unbolt, unlatch; unwrap, uncover; unravel; disconnect, release, unscrew, unplug. **2** rescind, void, reverse, invalidate. **3** see RUIN *v.* 1.

un•doc•u•ment•ed /úndókyəmentid/ *adj.* **1** not having the appropriate document. **2** not supported by written evidence.

■ **2** unrecorded.

un•do•ing /úndōōing/ *n.* **1** ruin or cause of ruin. **2** reversing what has been done. **3** opening or unfastening.

■ **1** destruction, defeat, downfall, overthrow, fall, collapse, humiliation, shame, disgrace; curse, misfortune, *poet.* bane.

un•done /úndún/ *adj.* **1** not done; incomplete (*left the job undone*). **2** not fastened (*left the buttons undone*). **3** ruined.

■ **1** unfinished, omitted, neglected, missed, forgotten. **2** open, loose, untied, detached. **3** lost, wrecked, destroyed, defeated.

un•doubt•ed /úndówtid/ *adj.* certain; not questioned. □□ **un•doubt'ed•ly** *adv.*

■ see CERTAIN *adj.* 1b. □□ **undoubtedly** without (a) doubt, unquestionably, beyond (a *or* the shadow of a) doubt, definitely, unmistakably, clearly, of course.

un•dreamed /úndreémd, úndrémt/ *adj.* (also **un•dreamt** /úndrémt/) not dreamed or thought of or imagined.

un•dress /úndrés/ • *v.* **1** *intr.* take off one's clothes. **2** *tr.* take the clothes off (a person). • *n.* **1** ordinary dress as opposed to full dress or uniform. **2** casual or informal dress.

un•due /úndōō, -dyōō/ *adj.* excessive; disproportionate. □□ **un•du'ly** *adv.*

■ see *excessive* (EXCESS).

un•du•late • *v.* /únjəlayt, -dyə-, -də-/ have or cause to have a wavy motion or look. • *adj.* /únjələt, -dyə-, -də-/ wavy (*leaves with undulate margins*). □□ **un•du•la•tion** /-láyshən/ *n.*

■ *v.* see WAVE *v.* 2.

un•dy•ing /úndí-ing/ *adj.* **1** immortal. **2** never-ending (*undying love*). □□ **un•dy'ing•ly** *adv.*

■ see IMMORTAL *adj.* 1a. □□ **undyingly** see ALWAYS 1.

un•earned /únórnd/ *adj.* not earned. □ **unearned income** income from investments, etc., as opposed to salary, etc.

un•earth /únórth/ *v.tr.* discover by searching, digging, or rummaging.

■ exhume; excavate, dredge up, mine.

un•earth•ly /únórthlee/ *adj.* **1** supernatural; mysterious. **2** *colloq.* absurdly early or inconvenient (*unearthly hour*). □□ **un•earth'li•ness** *n.*

■ **1** unnatural, psychic(al); weird, bizarre, macabre, *colloq.* spooky, creepy. **2** strange, unusual, out of the ordinary, outrageous; ridiculous, unreasonable, *colloq.* ungodly, *sl.* god-awful.

un•ease /úneéz/ *n.* lack of ease; discomfort; distress.

un•eas•y /úneézee/ *adj.* (**un•eas'i•er, un•eas'i•est**) **1** nervous; anxious. **2** disturbing (*had an uneasy suspicion*). □□ **un•eas'i•ly** *adv.* **un•eas'i•ness** *n.*

■ **1** see ANXIOUS 1, RESTLESS 2. **2** see *disturbing* (DISTURB).

un•e•mo•tio•nal /únimóshənəl/ *adj.* not emotional; lacking emotion.

■ see COLD *adj.* 4, COOL *adj.* 2.

un•em•ploy•a•ble /únimplóyəbəl/ *adj.* unfit for paid employment. □□ **un•em•ploy•a•bil'i•ty** *n.*

un•em•ployed /únimplóyd/ *adj.* **1** out of work. **2** not in use. □□ **un•em•ploy'ment** *n.*

■ **1** jobless, laid off, unoccupied, between assignments, at leisure. **2** unused, inactive.

un•e•qual /úneékwəl/ *adj.* **1** not equal. **2** of varying quality. **3** unfair (*an unequal bargain*). □□ **un•e'qual•ly** *adv.*

un•e•qualed /úneékwəld/ *adj.* superior to all others.

■ see *peerless* (PEER²).

un•e•quiv•o•cal /únikwívəkəl/ *adj.* not ambiguous; plain; unmistakable. □□ **un•e• quiv'o•cal•ly** *adv.*

■ see PLAIN² *adj.* 1, 2, CATEGORICAL. □□ **unequivocally** see *expressly* (EXPRESS).

un•err•ing /únéring/ *adj.* not erring; true; certain. □□ **un•err'ing•ly** *adv.* **un•err'ing•ness** *n.*

■ see CERTAIN *adj.* 3, TRUE *adj.* 6. □□ **unerringly** see EXACTLY 1.

UNESCO /yōōnéskō/ *abbr.* United Nations Educational, Scientific, and Cultural Organization.

un•eth•i•cal /únéthikəl/ *adj.* not ethical, esp. unscrupulous in business or professional conduct. □□ **un•eth'i•cal•ly** *adv.*

un•e•ven /únéevən/ *adj.* 1 not level or smooth. 2 not uniform. 3 (of a contest) unequal. □□ **un•e'ven•ly** *adv.* **un•e'ven•ness** *n.*

■ 1, 2 see IRREGULAR *adj.* 1, 2. 3 see DISPROPORTIONATE. □□ **unevenness** see *irregularity* (IRREGULAR), DISPROPORTION.

un•ex•am•pled /únigzámpəld/ *adj.* without precedent.

un•ex•cep•tion•a•ble /úniksépshənəbəl/ *adj.* entirely satisfactory. □□ **un•excep'tion•a• bly** *adv.*

■ see FAULTLESS.

un•ex•cep•tion•al /úniksépshənəl/ *adj.* not out of the ordinary; usual; normal. □□ **un• ex•cep'tion•al•ly** *adv.*

un•ex•pect•ed /únikspéktid/ *adj.* not expected; surprising. □□ **un•ex•pect'ed•ly** *adv.* **un•ex•pect'ed•ness** *n.*

■ □□ **unexpectedly** see *suddenly* (SUDDEN).

un•ex•pur•gat•ed /únékspərgaytid/ *adj.* (esp. of a text) complete.

un•fail•ing /únfáyling/ *adj.* 1 not failing. 2 not running short. 3 constant. 4 reliable. □□ **un•fail'ing•ly** *adv.*

■ 1 see CERTAIN *adj.* 3. 2 see INEXHAUSTIBLE 1. 3 see CONSTANT *adj.* 3. 4 see RELIABLE. □□ **unfailingly** see *consistently* (CONSISTENT).

un•fair /únfáir/ *adj.* 1 not equitable or honest (*obtained by unfair means*). 2 not impartial or according to the rules. □□ **un•fair'ly** *adv.* **un•fair'ness** *n.*

■ 1 see DISHONEST. 2 see IRREGULAR *adj.* 3, *prejudiced* (PREJUDICE). □□ **unfairly** see ILL *adv.* 1. **unfairness** see INJUSTICE 1.

un•faith•ful /únfáythfool/ *adj.* 1 not faithful, esp. adulterous. 2 not loyal. 3 treacherous. □□ **un•faith'ful•ly** *adv.* **un•faith'ful•ness** *n.*

■ see UNTRUE 2. □□ **unfaithfulness** see INFIDELITY 1, PERFIDY.

un•fas•ten /únfásən/ *v.* 1 *tr. & intr.* make or become loose. 2 *tr.* open the fastening(s) of. 3 *tr.* detach.

■ see LOOSEN, UNDO 1.

un•feel•ing /únféeling/ *adj.* unsympathetic; harsh. □□ **un•feel'ing•ly** *adv.*

un•feigned /únfáynd/ *adj.* genuine; sincere.

■ see SINCERE.

un•fin•ished /únfínisht/ *adj.* not finished; incomplete.

■ see INCOMPLETE.

un•fit•ting /únfíting/ *adj.* not suitable; unbecoming. □□ **un•fit'ting•ly** *adv.*

un•fix /únfiks/ *v. tr.* 1 release or loosen. 2 detach.

un•flag•ging /únfláging/ *adj.* tireless; persistent. □□ **un•flag'ging•ly** *adv.*

un•flap•pa•ble /únfláppəbəl/ *adj. colloq.* imperturbable; calm. □□ **un•flap•pa•bil'i•ty** *n.* **un•flap'pa•bly** *adv.*

■ see COOL *adj.* 2.

un•fold /únfóld/ *v.* 1 *tr.* open the fold(s) of; spread out. 2 *tr.* reveal (thoughts, etc.). 3 *intr.* become opened out. 4 *intr.* develop.

■ 1, 3 unfurl, stretch out, extend, straighten out. 2 see BARE *v.* 4 evolve, take place, be divulged.

un•forced /únfáwrst/ *adj.* 1 easy; natural. 2 not compelled or constrained.

■ 1 see SPONTANEOUS 2. 2 see OPTIONAL.

un•for•get•ta•ble /únfərgétəbəl/ *adj.* that cannot be forgotten; memorable; wonderful (*an unforgettable experience*). □□ **un•for•get' ta•bly** *adv.*

■ see MEMORABLE.

un•formed /únfáwrmd/ *adj.* 1 not formed. 2 shapeless. 3 not developed

un•for•tu•nate /únfáwrchənət/ • *adj.* 1 having bad fortune; unlucky. 2 unhappy. 3 regrettable. 4 disastrous. • *n.* unfortunate person. □□ **un•for'tu•nate•ly** *adv.*

■ *adj.* 1 hapless; cursed, poor, doomed, ill-fated, *colloq.* jinxed. 2 miserable, wretched, dismal. 3 deplorable, lamentable, disturbing. 4 catastrophic, grievous, terrible, dire; inauspicious. • *n.* see WRETCH 1. □□ **unfortunately** sadly.

un•found•ed /únfówndid/ *adj.* having no foundation (*unfounded hopes, unfounded rumor*).

■ baseless, unwarranted, unjustified, unsupported.

un•friend•ly /únfréndlee/ *adj.* (**un•friend'li• er**, **un•friend'li•est**) not friendly. □□ **un• friend'li•ness** *n.*

un•fun•ny /únfúnee/ *adj.* (**un•fun•ni•er**, **un• fun•ni•est**) not amusing (though meant to be). □□ **un•fun'ni•ly** *adv.*

un•furl /únfárl/ *v.* 1 *tr.* spread out (a sail, etc.). 2 *intr.* become spread out.

■ 1 see SPREAD *v.* 1a.

un•gain•ly /úngáynlee/ *adj.* awkward; clumsy □□ **un•gain'li•ness** *n.*

■ see AWKWARD 2.

un•god•ly /úngódlee/ *adj.* 1 impious; wicked. 2 *colloq.* outrageous (*ungodly hour*). □□ **un•god'li•ness** *n.*

■ 1 sinful, blasphemous, heretical, atheist(ic), irreverent; depraved, corrupt, immoral, evil. 2 awful, indecent, monstrous, *colloq.* unearthly, beastly, *sl.* god-awful. □□ **ungodliness** see SIN¹ *n.* 1.

un•gov•ern•a•ble /úngúvərnəbəl/ *adj.* uncontrollable; violent. □□ **un•gov•ern•a•bil'i•ty** *n.* **un•gov'ern•a•bly** *adv.*

■ unruly, intractable, unmanageable, rebellious, wild.

un•gra•cious /úngráyshəs/ *adj.* not kindly or courteous; unkind. □□ **un•gra'cious•ly** *adv.* **un•gra'cious•ness** *n.*

■ overbearing, rude, uncivil, impolite,

ill-bred, ill-mannered, gruff, abrupt, inconsiderate.

un•guard•ed /úngaárdid/ *adj.* **1** incautious; thoughtless (*unguarded remark*). **2** not guarded. □□ **un•guard′ed•ly** *adv.* **un•guard′ed•ness** *n.*

■ **1** indiscreet, careless, imprudent; inattentive, inadvertent. **2** defenseless, unprotected, open, vulnerable.

un•guent /únggwənt/ *n.* soft substance used as ointment or for lubrication.

■ see OINTMENT.

un•gu•late /úngyələt, –layt/ • *adj.* hoofed. • *n.* hoofed mammal.

un•hal•lowed /únhálōd/ *adj.* **1** not consecrated. **2** not sacred; unholy; wicked.

un•hand /únhánd/ *v.tr. rhet.* or *joc.* **1** take one's hands off (a person). **2** release from one's grasp.

un•hap•py /únhápee/ *adj.* (**un•hap•pi•er**, **un•hap•pi•est**) **1** miserable. **2** unsuccessful; unfortunate. **3** disastrous. □□ **un•hap′pi•ly** *adv.* **un•hap′pi•ness** *n.*

■ **1** sad, depressed, blue, dejected, melancholy, gloomy, downhearted, sorrowful, crestfallen, glum, tearful, *colloq.* down. **2** unlucky, cursed, frustrated, disappointed, *colloq.* jinxed. **3** see UNFORTUNATE *adj.* 2. □□ **unhappily** sadly. **unhappiness** see MISERY 1.

un•health•y /únhélthee/ *adj.* (**un•health•i•er**, **un•health•i•est**) **1** not in good health. **2 a** (of a place, etc.) harmful to health. **b** unwholesome. **c** *sl.* dangerous to life. □□ **un•health′i•ly** *adv.* **un•health′i•ness** *n.*

■ **1** ailing, unwell, ill, frail, unsound, in poor condition. **2 a, b** sickly, noxious, detrimental. **c** risky, perilous.

un•heard /únhérd/ *adj.* **1** not heard. **2** (usu. **unheard-of**) unprecedented; unknown.

■ **2** (**unheard-of**) unfamiliar, obscure, unidentified; unbelievable, inconceivable, unusual; shocking, offensive, outrageous.

un•hinge /únhínj/ *v.tr.* **1** take (a door, etc.) off its hinges. **2** (esp. as **unhinged** *adj.*) unsettle or disorder (a person's mind, etc.), make (a person) crazy.

■ **1** see UNDO 1. **2** (**unhinged**) see CRAZY 1.

un•hitch /únhích/ *v.tr.* **1** release from a hitched state. **2** unhook; unfasten.

■ see DISCONNECT, UNDO 1.

un•ho•ly /únhṓlee/ *adj.* (**un•ho′li•er**, **un•hol′i•est**) **1** impious; wicked. **2** *colloq.* dreadful; outrageous (*made an unholy ordeal out of nothing*). □□ **un•ho′li•ness** *n.*

■ **1** see IMPIOUS. **2** see DREADFUL *adj.* 1.

uni- /yṓóni/ *comb. form* one; having or consisting of one.

u•ni•cam•er•al /yṓónikámərəl/ *adj.* with a single legislative chamber.

UNICEF /yṓónisef/ *abbr.* United Nations Children's Fund. (orig. International Children's Emergency) Fund.

u•ni•cel•lu•lar /yṓónisélyələr/ *adj.* (of an organism, organ, tissue, etc.) consisting of a single cell.

u•ni•corn /yṓónikawrn/ *n.* mythical animal with a horse's body and a single straight horn.

u•ni•cy•cle /yṓónisīkəl/ *n.* single-wheeled cycle, esp. as used by acrobats. □□ **u′ni•cy•clist** *n.*

u•ni•form /yṓónifawrm/ • *adj.* **1** not changing in form or character; unvarying (*present a uniform appearance, of uniform size*). **2** conforming to the same standard, rules, or pattern. • *n.* distinctive clothing worn by members of the same body, e.g., by soldiers, police, and schoolchildren. □□ **u′ni•formed** *adj.* **u•ni•for′mi•ty** *n.* **u′ni•form•ly** *adv.*

■ *adj.* **1, 2** homogeneous, consistent, constant; regimented, standard; ordered, equal, identical; even, unbroken, regular. • *n.* livery, habit, costume, outfit. □□ **uniformity** regularity, similarity, consistency, agreement; harmony; dullness, monotony, lack of variety. **uniformly** see ALIKE *adv.*

u•ni•fy /yṓónifī/ *v.tr.* [also *absol.*] (**–fies, –fied**) reduce to unity or uniformity. □□ **u•ni•fi•ca′tion** *n.* **u′ni•fi•er** *n.*

■ consolidate, combine, bring together, join, merge, incorporate, integrate. □□ **unification** see UNION 1.

u•ni•lat•er•al /yṓónilátərəl/ *adj.* **1** performed by or affecting only one person or party (*unilateral disarmament*). **2** one-sided. □□ **u•ni•lat′er•al•ly** *adv.*

un•i•mag•i•na•tive /únimájinətiv/ *adj.* lacking imagination; stolid; dull. □□ **un•i•mag′i•na•tive•ly** *adv.*

■ see PROSAIC.

un•im•peach•a•ble /únimpéechəbəl/ *adj.* beyond reproach or question. □□ **un•im•peach′a•bly** *adv.*

■ see IRREPROACHABLE.

un•i•ni•ti•at•ed /úninísheeaytid/ *adj.* not initiated; not admitted or instructed.

un•in•spired /úninspírd/ *adj.* **1** not inspired. **2** (of oratory, etc.) commonplace.

■ **2** see PROSAIC.

un•in•ter•est•ed /úníntrəstid, –təristid, –tərəs–/ *adj.* **1** not interested. **2** unconcerned; indifferent. □□ **un•in′ter•est•ed•ly** *adv.*

■ see INDIFFERENT 1.

un•in•vit•ing /úninvíting/ *adj.* unattractive; repellent. □□ **un•in•vit′ing•ly** *adv.*

■ repulsive, offensive, unappealing, unpleasant, disagreeable, sickening.

un•ion /yṓónyən/ *n.* **1** uniting; being united. **2 a** whole resulting from the combination of parts or members. **b** political unit formed in this way, esp. (**Union**) the US (esp. as distinct from the Confederacy during the Civil War), the UK, or South Africa. **3** = *labor union.* **4** marriage. **5** concord; agreement (*lived together in perfect union*). **6** *Math.* totality of the members of two or more sets. □ **Union Jack** national flag of the United Kingdom formed by the union of the crosses of St. George, St. Andrew, and St. Patrick.

■ **1** unification, combination, junction, association, coalition, bond, marriage, confederation, synthesis, blend, mixture. **2** alliance, society, club, team, syndicate, coalition, party, federation, consortium, cartel. **4** matrimony, wedlock, partnership. **5** accord, harmony, coherence, compatibility, unanimity.

un•ion•ize /yŏŏnyəníz/ v. bring or come under labor-union organization or rules. □□ **un•ion•i•za'tion** n.

u•nique /yŏŏneék/ adj. 1 of which there is only one; unequaled; having no like, equal, or parallel (*this vase is considered unique*). 2 *disp.* unusual; remarkable (*the most unique man I ever met*). □□ **u•nique'ly** adv. **u•nique'ness** n.

■ 1 single, (one and) only, solitary, individual, distinctive; unrivaled, incomparable, second to none. 2 see EXCEPTIONAL. □□ **uniqueness** see *singularity* (SINGULAR).

u•ni•sex /yŏŏniseks/ adj. (of clothing, hairstyles, etc.) designed to be suitable for both sexes.

u•ni•son /yŏŏnisən/ n. 1 *Mus.* coincidence in pitch of sounds or notes. 2 agreement; concord (*acted in perfect unison*).

■ 2 see UNITY 2; (*in unison*) in harmony, together, as one, harmonious; (*in unison with*) corresponding exactly to *or* with, in (perfect) accord with.

u•nit /yŏŏnit/ n. 1 a individual thing, person, or group regarded as single and complete. b each of the (smallest) separate individuals or groups into which a complex whole may be analyzed (*the family as the unit of society*). 2 quantity as a standard in terms of which other quantities may be expressed (*unit of heat, mass per unit volume*). 3 device with a specified function forming part of a complex mechanism. 4 group of buildings, wards, etc., as in a hospital. 5 the number 'one'. □ **unit cost** cost of producing one item. **unit price** price charged for each unit of goods supplied.

■ 1, 3 element, component, entity, part, item, constituent, piece, portion, segment, member, section, module.

un•i•tard /yŏŏnətaard/ n. one-piece leotard that covers the legs as well as the torso.

U•ni•tar•i•an /yŏŏnitáireeən/ • n. 1 person who believes that God is not a Trinity but one being. 2 member of a religious body maintaining this and advocating freedom from formal dogma *or* doctrine. • adj. of *or* relating to the Unitarians. □□ **U•ni•tar'i•an•ism** n.

u•ni•tar•y /yŏŏniteree/ adj. 1 of a unit or units. 2 marked by unity or uniformity.

u•nite /yŏŏnít/ v. 1 join together; combine. 2 join in marriage. 3 form or cause to form a physical *or* chemical whole (*oil will not unite with water*).

■ 1, 3 bond, fuse *or* stick *or* bind *or* fasten *or* fix *or* fit (together); integrate, incorporate, blend, mix, consolidate. 2 marry, link, connect, *colloq.* get hitched.

u•ni•ty /yŏŏnitee/ n. (pl. **–ties**) 1 oneness; being one, single, or individual; being formed of parts that constitute a whole (*disturbs the unity of the idea, national unity*). 2 harmony or concord between persons, etc. 3 thing forming a complex whole (*a person regarded as a unity*). 4 *Math.* the number 'one,' the factor that leaves unchanged the quantity on which it operates.

■ 1 singularity, integrity, identity, similarity; cohesion, union. 2 consistency, unanimity,

uniformity, consensus, accord, solidarity, compatibility, sympathy, like-mindedness.

Univ. *abbr.* University.

u•ni•va•lent /yŏŏniváylənt/ adj. *Chem.* having a valence of one.

u•ni•valve /yŏŏnivalv/ *Zool.* • adj. having one valve. • n. univalve mollusk.

u•ni•ver•sal /yŏŏnivórsəl/ • adj. of, belonging to, or done, etc., by all; applicable to all cases (*met with universal approval*). • n. 1 *Logic* universal proposition. 2 *Philos.* a term or concept of general application. b nature or essence signified by a general term. □ **universal joint** (or **coupling**) joint or coupling that can transmit rotary power by a shaft at any angle. **Universal Product Code** bar code on products that can be read by an electronic scanner, usu. providing price and product identification. □□ **u•ni•ver•sal•i•ty** /–sálitee/ n. **u•ni•ver'sal•ize** v. tr. **u•ni•ver'sal•ly** adv.

■ adj. 1 prevailing, general, global, widespread; infinite, limitless, all-inclusive, wide-ranging. □□ **universality** see *prevalence* (PREVALENT). **universally** in every case *or* instance, without exception, always, extensively, widely, everywhere.

SYNONYM STUDY: universal

CATHOLIC, COMMON, COSMIC, ECUMENICAL, GENERAL, GENERIC. Something that is **universal** applies to every case or individual in a class or category (*a universal practice among aboriginal tribesmen; a universal truth*). **General**, on the other hand, is less precise; it implies applicability to all or most of a group or class, whether the members of that group are clearly defined or only casually associated (*a drug that has come into general use among women but has not yet won the universal acceptance of doctors*). **Generic** is often used in place of *general* when referring to every member of a genus or clearly-defined scientific category (*a generic characteristic of insects*); with reference to language, it means referring to both men and women (*a generic pronoun*). **Common** implies participation or sharing by all members of a class (*a common interest in French culture*) or frequently occurring (*a common complaint*). **Catholic** implies a wide-ranging or inclusive attitude (*known for his catholic tastes in music*), while **ecumenical** means pertaining to the whole Christian church or promoting unity among religious groups or divisions (*an ecumenical marriage ceremony*).

---

u•ni•verse /yŏŏnivərs/ n. 1 a all existing things; the cosmos. b sphere of existence, influence, activity, etc. 2 all humankind. 3 *Statistics & Logic* all the objects under consideration.

■ 1 a creation; world. b world, province, domain, circle, territory, microcosm. 2 humanity, people, society.

u•ni•ver•si•ty /yŏŏnivórsitee/ n. (pl. **–ties**) educational institution designed for instruction, examination, or both, of students in many branches of advanced learning, conferring degrees in various faculties, and often embodying colleges and similar institutions.

un•kempt /únkémpt/ *adj.* **1** untidy; of neglected appearance. **2** disheveled. □□ **un•kempt′ly** *adv.* **un•kempt′ness** *n.*

■ **1** ungroomed, messy, bedraggled, rumpled, slovenly, *colloq.* scruffy, mussed (up). **2** uncombed, tousled, disordered, messed-up, *colloq.* scruffy.

un•kind /únkínd/ *adj.* **1** not kind. **2** harsh; cruel. **3** unpleasant. □□ **un•kind′ly** *adv.* **un•kind′ness** *n.*

■ inconsiderate, thoughtless, unfeeling, unsympathetic, unchristian, hard-hearted, rigid, callous, tough, inflexible, stern, malicious, inhuman, brutal, *colloq.* beastly. □□ **unkindness** see DISSERVICE.

un•know•a•ble /únnốəbəl/ • *adj.* that cannot be known. • *n.* **1** unknowable thing. **2** **(the Unknowable)** the postulated absolute or ultimate reality.

un•know•ing /únnốing/ *adj.* not knowing; ignorant; unconscious. □□ **un•know′ing•ly** *adv.*

■ see UNAWARE *adj.* 1. □□ **unknowingly** see UNAWARES 2.

un•known /únnốn/ • *adj.* not known; unfamiliar (*his purpose was unknown to me*). • *n.* **1** unknown thing or person. **2** unknown quantity (*equation in two unknowns*). □ **Unknown Soldier** unidentified soldier killed in war, given burial with special honors in a national memorial.

■ *adj.* unrecognized, strange, anonymous, incognito, unspecified; obscure, unheard-of, undistinguished; unexplored, mysterious, uncharted, dark. • *n.* **1** see NOBODY *n.*

un•law•ful /únláwfŏŏl/ *adj.* illegal; not permissible. □□ **un•law′ful•ly** *adv.* **un•law′ful•ness** *n.*

■ illicit, against the law, illegitimate, criminal; outlawed, banned, prohibited; unauthorized, *colloq.* crooked.

un•lead•ed /únlédid/ *adj.* **1** (of gasoline, etc.) without added lead. **2** not covered, weighted, or framed with lead.

un•learn /únlŕn/ *v.tr.* (*past* and *past part.* **un•learn•ed** or **un•learnt**) **1** discard from one's memory. **2** rid oneself of (a habit, false information, etc.).

un•learn•ed /únlŕrnid/ *adj.* not well educated; untaught; ignorant.

un•leash /únléesh/ *v.tr.* release from a leash or restraint.

■ see RELEASE *v.* 1, LOOSE *v.* 3.

un•leav•ened /únlévənd/ *adj.* made without yeast or other raising agent.

un•less /únlés, ən–/ *conj.* if not; except when (*shall go unless I hear from you, always walked unless I had a bicycle*).

un•let•tered /únlétərd/ *adj.* **1** illiterate. **2** not well educated.

un•like /únlík/ • *adj.* **1** not like; different from (*is unlike both his parents*). **2** uncharacteristic of (*such behavior is unlike him*). **3** dissimilar; different. • *prep.* differently from (*acts quite unlike anyone else*).

■ *adj.* **1** dissimilar to, distinct from, opposite from *or* to, separate from, far from. **2** atypical of. **3** unalike, distinct, opposite, contrasting, incompatible, ill-matched, unequal. • *prep.* in contrast with *or* to, as opposed to.

un•like•ly /únlíklee/ *adj.* (**un•like•li•er**, **un•like•li•est**) **1** improbable (*unlikely tale*). **2** not expected (*he's unlikely to be available*). **3** unpromising (*unlikely candidate*). □□ **un•like′li•hood** *n.* **un•like′li•ness** *n.*

■ **1** doubtful, dubious, remote, unthinkable, unimaginable. **3** unpropitious, inauspicious.

un•lim•it•ed /únlímitid/ *adj.* without limit; unrestricted; very great in number or quantity (*unlimited possibilities, unlimited expanse of sea*). □□ **un•lim′it•ed•ness** *n.*

■ unrestrained, unqualified, indefinite, far-reaching; boundless, vast, immense, innumerable, never-ending, infinite, extensive.

un•load /únlốd/ *v.tr.* **1** [also *absol.*] remove a load from (a vehicle, etc.). **2** remove the charge from (a firearm, etc.). **3** *colloq.* get rid of. **4** [often foll. by *on*] *colloq.* **a** divulge (information). **b** [also *absol.*] give vent to (feelings). □□ **un•load′er** *n.*

■ **1** empty, dump, unpack; unburden. **3** see DUMP[1] *v.* **4** **a** see DISCLOSE 1. **b** see FREE *v.* 2, VENT *v.* 2.

un•lock /únlók/ *v.tr.* **1 a** release the lock of (a door, box, etc.). **b** release or disclose by unlocking. **2** release thoughts, feelings, etc., from (one's mind, etc.).

■ **1 a** see OPEN *v.* 1, 2, UNDO 1. **1b, 2** see RELEASE *v.* 1.

un•looked-for /únlŏŏktfawr/ *adj.* unexpected; unforeseen.

un•loose /únlŏŏs/ *v.tr.* (also **un•loos′en**) loose; set free.

un•luck•y /únlúkee/ *adj.* (**un•luck′i•er**, **un•luck′i•est**) **1** not fortunate or successful. **2** wretched. **3** bringing bad luck. **4** ill-judged. □□ **un•luck′i•ly** *adv.* **un•luck′i•ness** *n.*

■ **1** see UNFORTUNATE *adj.* 1. **2** see TRAGIC. **4** see *ill-advised* 2. □□ **unluckily** sadly.

un•make /únmáyk/ *v.tr.* (*past* and *past part.* **un•made**) undo the making of; destroy; depose; annul.

un•man /únmán/ *v.tr.* (**un•manned**, **un•man′ning**) deprive of supposed manly qualities (e.g., self-control, courage); cause to weep, etc.; discourage.

un•mask /únmásk/ *v.* **1** *tr.* **a** remove the mask from. **b** expose the true character of. **2** *intr.* remove one's mask. □□ **un•mask′er** *n.*

■ **1 b** see EXPOSE 5.

un•men•tion•a•ble /únménshənəbəl/ • *adj.* that cannot be (properly) be mentioned. • *n.* **1** [in *pl.*] *joc.* undergarments. **2** person or thing not to be mentioned. □□ **un•men′tion•a•bly** *adv.*

■ *adj.* unspeakable, unprintable, taboo, scandalous, forbidden; disgraceful, rude, shameful, shocking, obscene. • *n.* **1** (*unmentionables*) underclothes, underwear, lingerie, *colloq.* undies.

un•mer•ci•ful /únmŕrsifŏŏl/ *adj.* merciless. □□ **un•mer′ci•ful•ly** *adv.*

■ pitiless, unsparing, unkind, relentless, heartless, unfeeling, inhuman, harsh, savage, barbarous. □□ **unmercifully** see *roughly* (ROUGH).

un•mis•tak•a•ble /únmistáykəbəl/ *adj.* that cannot be mistaken or doubted; clear. □□ **un•mis•tak′a•bly** *adv.*

■ see CLEAR² *adj.* 6, OBVIOUS. □□ **unmistakably** see *obviously* (OBVIOUS), *expressly* (EXPRESS), *undoubtedly* (UNDOUBTED).

un•mit•i•gat•ed /únmítigaytid/ *adj.* **1** not mitigated or modified. **2** absolute; unqualified (*an unmitigated disaster*). See synonym study at SEVERE. □□ **un•mit′i•gat•ed•ly** *adv.*

■ **1** undiluted, untempered, unabated, oppressive, relentless. **2** out-and-out, thorough, downright, sheer, complete, total, perfect, utter. □□ **unmitigatedly** see DOWNRIGHT *adv.*

un•mor•al /únmáwrəl, –mór–/ *adj.* not concerned with morality (cf. IMMORAL). □□ **un•mor′al•i•ty** /–rálitee/ *n.* **un•mor′al•ly** *adv.*

un•moved /únmóovd/ *adj.* **1** not moved. **2** not changed in one's purpose. **3** not affected by emotion. □□ **un•mov′a•ble** *adj.* (also **un•move′a•ble**).

■ **2** see RELENTLESS 1. **3** cool, aloof, calm, unsympathetic, apathetic, dispassionate, indifferent, stony, hard-hearted. □□ **unmovable** see IMMOVABLE *adj.*

un•nat•u•ral /ún-náchərəl/ *adj.* **1** contrary to nature; not normal. **2** a lacking natural feelings **b** extremely cruel or wicked. **3** artificial. **4** affected. □□ **un•nat′u•ral•ly** *adv.*

■ **1** outlandish, weird, peculiar, strange, supernatural, grotesque, bizarre, extraordinary; unexpected, uncharacteristic. **2** abnormal, perverse, monstrous, improper; deviant, depraved; unfeeling, callous, inhuman, *colloq.* kinky, *sl.* bent. **3** see ARTIFICIAL 1, 2. **4** labored, forced, stilted, insincere, contrived, self-conscious, theatrical, *colloq* phony.

un•nec•es•sar•y /ún-nésəseree/ *adj.* **1** not necessary. **2** more than is necessary (*with unnecessary care*). □□ **un•nec•es•sar′i•ly** *adv.*

■ **1** unneeded, dispensable, disposable, expendable, unwanted, nonessential. **2** surplus, superfluous, redundant, extra. □□ **unnecessarily** unduly.

un•nerve /ún-nə́rv/ *v.tr.* deprive of strength or resolution. □□ **un•nerv′ing•ly** *adv.*

■ upset, agitate, fluster, unsettle, intimidate, stun, shatter, *colloq.* shake (up), rattle, faze, throw.

un•num•bered /ún-númbərd/ *adj.* **1** not marked with a number. **2** not counted. **3** countless.

■ **3** see UMPTEEN *adj.*

un•ob•tru•sive /únəbtró͞osiv/ *adj.* not making oneself or itself noticed. □□ **un•ob•tru′sive•ly** *adv.* **un•ob•tru′sive•ness** *n.*

■ inconspicuous, low-key, modest, unpretentious, quiet, nonassertive, subdued, discreet. □□ **unobtrusively** see *quietly* (QUIET).

un•or•gan•ized /únáwrgənīzd/ *adj.* **1** not organized (cf. DISORGANIZE). **2** not represented by a labor union.

un•pack /únpák/ *v.tr.* **1** [also *absol.*] open

and remove the contents of (a package, luggage, etc.). **2** take (a thing) out from a package, etc. □□ **un•pack′er** *n.*

un•pal•at•a•ble /únpálətəbəl/ *adj.* **1** not pleasant to taste; inedible. **2** (of an idea, suggestion, etc.) disagreeable; distasteful. □□ **un•pal•at•a•bil′i•ty** *n.*

■ unsavory, unattractive, repugnant, nasty, offensive, objectionable.

un•par•al•leled /únpárəleld/ *adj.* having no parallel or equal.

■ incomparable, unrivaled, unmatched, superior, special, singular, rare, unique, exceptional.

un•pleas•ant /únplézənt/ *adj.* not pleasant; disagreeable. □□ **un•pleas′ant•ly** *adv.* **un•pleas′ant•ness** *n.*

■ see NASTY 1, 3. □□ **unpleasantly** see AWFULLY 1. **unpleasantness** see TROUBLE *n.* 1.

un•plug /únplúg/ *v.tr.* (**un•plugged**, **un•plug•ging**) **1** disconnect (an electrical device) by removing its plug from the socket. **2** unstop.

un•plumbed /únplúmd/ *adj.* **1** not plumbed. **2** not fully explored or understood. □□ **un•plumb′a•ble** *adj.*

un•pop•u•lar /únpópyələr/ *adj.* not popular; not liked by the public or by people in general. □□ **un•pop•u•lar′i•ty** /–láritee/ *n.* **un•pop′u•lar•ly** *adv.*

■ out of favor, avoided, snubbed, ignored, rejected, outcast, despised, unloved, friendless.

un•prac•ticed /únpráktist/ *adj.* **1** not experienced or skilled. **2** not put into practice.

■ **1** see INEXPERIENCED (INEXPERIENCE).

un•prec•e•dent•ed /únprésidentid/ *adj.* **1** having no precedent; unparalleled. **2** novel. □□ **un•prec′e•dent•ed•ly** *adv.*

■ **1** see EXTRAORDINARY 1, 2. **2** see ORIGINAL *adj.* 2.

un•pre•pos•sess•ing /únpreepəzésing/ *adj.* unattractive.

un•pre•ten•tious /únpriténshəs/ *adj.* not making a great display; simple; modest. □□ **un•pre•ten′tious•ly** *adv.* **un•pre•ten′tious•ness** *n.*

■ see MODEST 1, 2, 4.

un•prin•ci•pled /únprínsipəld/ *adj.* lacking or not based on good moral principles.

■ see UNSCRUPULOUS.

un•print•a•ble /únpríntəbəl/ *adj.* that cannot be printed, esp. because too indecent or libelous or blasphemous. □□ **un•print′a•bly** *adv.*

un•pro•fes•sion•al /únprəféshənəl/ *adj.* **1** contrary to professional standards of behavior, etc. **2** not belonging to a profession; amateur. □□ **un•pro•fes′sion•al•ly** *adv.*

■ **1** unbecoming, improper, unethical, negligent; incompetent, second-rate, inefficient, low-quality. **2** lay, unspecialized, inexperienced, untrained, unskilled. □□ **unprofessionally** see POORLY *adv.*

un•prompt•ed /únprómptid/ *adj.* spontaneous.

■ see VOLUNTARY *adj.* 1.

un•qual•i•fied /únkwólifīd/ *adj.* **1** not competent (*unqualified to give an answer*). **2** not legally or officially qualified (*unqualified practitioner*). **3** complete (*unqualified success*).

■ **1** ineligible, unfit, unable. **2** untrained, unprepared, amateur. **3** unrestricted, unconditional, categorical, outright, pure (and simple), true, perfect, absolute.

un•ques•tion•a•ble /únkwéschənəbəl/ *adj.* that cannot be disputed or doubted. □□ **un•ques'tion•a•bly** *adv.*

■ undeniable, certain, positive, irrefutable, obvious, clear, definite, unmistakable, conclusive. □□ **unquestionably** see *undoubtedly* (UNDOUBTED).

un•ques•tioned /únkwéschənd/ *adj.* **1** not disputed or doubted; definite; certain. **2** not interrogated.

un•ques•tion•ing /únkwéschəning/ *adj.* **1** asking no questions. **2** done, etc., without asking questions. □□ **un•ques'tion•ing•ly** *adv.*

■ **2** see IMPLICIT 2. □□ **unquestioningly** see *willingly* (WILLING), *implicitly* (IMPLICIT).

un•qui•et /únkwíət/ *adj.* **1** restless; agitated. **2** perturbed; anxious. □□ **un•qui'et•ly** *adv.* **un•qui'et•ness** *n.*

un•quote /únkwót/ *v.tr.* [as *int.*] (in reading aloud, etc.) indicate the presence of closing quotation marks (cf. QUOTE *v.* 3).

un•rav•el /únrávəl/ *v.* **1** *tr.* cause to be no longer raveled, tangled, or intertwined. **2** *tr.* probe and solve (a mystery, etc.). **3** *tr.* undo (a fabric, esp. a knitted one). **4** *intr.* become disentangled or unknitted.

■ **1** unsnarl, sort out. **2** see SOLVE. **3** see UNDO 1.

un•read /únréd/ *adj.* **1** (of a book, etc.) not read. **2** (of a person) not well-read.

un•read•a•ble /únréedəbəl/ *adj.* **1** too dull or too difficult to be worth reading. **2** illegible. □□ **un•read•a•bil'i•ty** *n.* **un•read'a•bly** *adv.*

■ **2** see ILLEGIBLE.

un•real /únréel/ *adj.* **1** not real. **2** imaginary; illusory. **3** *sl.* incredible. □□ **un•re•al'i•ty** /–reélitee/ *n.* **un•re'al•ly** *adv.*

■ **1** artificial, synthetic, mock, false, counterfeit, make-believe. **2** theoretical, hypothetical, mythical, fabulous, fanciful, dreamlike, nonexistent. **3** see INCREDIBLE.

un•rea•son /únréezən/ *n.* lack of reasonable thought or action.

un•rea•son•a•ble /únréezənəbəl/ *adj.* **1** going beyond the limits of what is reasonable or equitable (*unreasonable demands*). **2** not guided by or listening to reason. See synonym study at ABSURD. □□ **un•rea'son•a•ble•ness** *n.* **un•rea'son•a•bly** *adv.*

■ **1** excessive, outrageous, exorbitant, extravagant, unjust, unwarranted, improper, unjustified; inappropriate, unrealistic. **2** irrational, illogical, absurd, foolish, mindless, mad, moronic, stupid, ridiculous, unperceptive, short-sighted. □□ **unreasonableness** see *absurdity* (ABSURD), FOLLY 1. **unreasonably** unduly.

un•re•gen•er•ate /únrijénərət/ *adj.* not re-

generate; obstinately wrong or bad. □□ **un•re•gen'er•a•cy** *n.* **un•re•gen'er•ate•ly** *adv.*

un•re•lent•ing /únrilénting/ *adj.* **1** not relenting or yielding. **2** unmerciful. □□ **un•re•lent'ing•ly** *adv.*

■ see RELENTLESS 1.

un•re•li•a•ble /únrilíəbəl/ *adj.* not reliable; erratic. □□ **un•re•li•a•bil'i•ty** *n.* **un•re•li'a•bly** *adv.*

■ untrustworthy, undependable, irresponsible, uncertain, fickle, inconsistent, temperamental, treacherous, flimsy, risky, *sl.* dicey, iffy. □□ **unreliability** see *inconstancy* (INCONSTANT[2]). **unreliably** see *by fits and starts* (FIT).

un•re•lieved /únrileévd/ *adj.* **1** lacking the relief given by contrast or variation. **2** not aided or assisted.

■ **1** see UNMITIGATED 1.

un•re•mit•ting /únrimíting/ *adj.* never relaxing or slackening; incessant. □□ **un•re•mit'ting•ly** *adv.* **un•re•mit'ting•ness** *n.*

■ see RELENTLESS 2.

un•re•quit•ed /únrikwítid/ *adj.* (of love, etc.) not returned. □□ **un•re•quit'ed•ly** *adv.*

un•re•served /únrizə́rvd/ *adj.* **1** not reserved (*unreserved seats*). **2** without reservations; absolute (*unreserved confidence*). □□ **un•re•serv'ed•ly** *adv.*

■ **1** see FREE *adj.* 7. **2** see WHOLEHEARTED. □□ **unreservedly** see ABSOLUTELY 1.

un•re•solved /únrizólvd/ *adj.* **1 a** uncertain how to act; irresolute. **b** undecided. **2** (of questions, etc.) undetermined; undecided; unsolved.

■ **1** unsure, ambivalent, wavering, hesitant. **2** unsettled, open, up in the air, moot, pending, debatable, questionable, unanswered.

un•rest /únrést/ *n.* restlessness; disturbance; agitation.

■ uneasiness, distress, anxiety, anguish, concern, turmoil, rioting, trouble, strife.

un•right•eous /únríchəs/ *adj.* not righteous; unjust; wicked; dishonest. □□ **un•right'eous•ly** *adv.* **un•right'eous•ness** *n.*

un•ri•valed /únrívəld/ *adj.* having no equal; peerless.

■ see *peerless* (PEER[2]).

un•roll /únról/ *v.* **1** open out from a rolled-up state. **2** display or be displayed in this form.

un•ruf•fled /únrúfəld/ *adj.* **1** not agitated or disturbed; calm. **2** not physically ruffled.

■ **1** see CALM *adj.* 2.

un•rul•y /únróolee/ *adj.* (**un•rul•i•er**, **un•rul•i•est**) not easily controlled or disciplined; disorderly. □□ **un•rul'i•ness** *n.*

■ unmanageable, ungovernable, uncontrollable, lawless, insubordinate, rebellious, headstrong, stubborn, uncooperative, wild, violent, stormy, *colloq.* rambunctious.

un•sad•dle /únsád'l/ *v.tr.* **1** remove the saddle from (a horse, etc.). **2** dislodge from a saddle.

un•sat•u•rat•ed /únsáchəraytid/ *adj.* **1** *Chem.* (of a compound, esp. a fat or oil) having double or triple bonds in its molecule and therefore capable of further reaction. **2** not saturated. □□ **un•sat•u•ra•tion** /–ráyshən/ *n.*

un•sa•vor•y /únsáyvəree/ *adj.* **1** disagreeable; disgusting. **2** morally offensive. □□ **un•sa′vor•i•ness** *n.*

■ unappetizing, inedible; distasteful, objectionable, unpleasant, repugnant, nasty, sickening, noxious.

un•scathed /únskáythd/ *adj.* without suffering any injury.

■ unhurt, undamaged, safe and sound, intact, whole, as new, *colloq.* like new.

un•schooled /únskóoold/ *adj.* **1** uneducated; untaught. **2** untrained; undisciplined.

■ **2** see *inexperienced* (INEXPERIENCE).

un•sci•en•tif•ic /únsīəntifík/ *adj.* not in accordance with scientific principles. □□ **un•sci•en•tif′i•cal•ly** *adv.*

un•scram•ble /únskrámbəl/ *v.tr.* restore from a scrambled state, esp. interpret (a scrambled transmission, etc.). □□ **un•scramb′ler** *n.*

■ see DECIPHER 1.

un•screw /únskróō/ *v.* **1** *tr. & intr.* unfasten or be unfastened by removing a screw or screws or by twisting like a screw. **2** *tr.* loosen (a screw).

un•script•ed /únskríptid/ *adj.* (of a speech, etc.) delivered without a prepared script.

■ see EXTEMPORANEOUS.

un•scru•pu•lous /únskróōpyələs/ *adj.* having no scruples; unprincipled. □□ **un•scru′pu•lous•ly** *adv.* **un•scru′pu•lous•ness** *n.*

■ unconscionable, amoral, unethical, immoral, dishonorable, corrupt, dishonest, *colloq.* shifty, crooked.

un•seal /únséel/ *v.tr.* break the seal of; open (a letter, receptacle, etc.).

un•sea•son•a•ble /únséezənəbəl/ *adj.* **1** not appropriate to the season. **2** untimely; inopportune. □□ **un•sea′son•a•bly** *adv.*

■ **2** unsuitable, inappropriate, ill-timed, inexpedient.

un•seat /únséet/ *v.tr.* **1** remove from a seat, esp. in an election. **2** dislodge from a seat, esp. on horseback.

■ **1** see TOPPLE 2.

un•seem•ly /únséemlee/ *adj.* (**un•seem•li•er, un•seem•li•est**) **1** indecent. **2** unbecoming. □□ **un•seem′li•ness** *n.*

■ **1** improper, indelicate, in poor or bad taste, risqué, naughty, obscene, off-color. **2** unrefined, undignified, disreputable, inappropriate. □□ **unseemliness** see IMPROPRIETY 1.

un•seen /únséen/ *adj.* **1** not seen. **2** invisible.

■ **1** see BACKGROUND 2. **2** see INVISIBLE 1, 2.

un•self•ish /únsélfish/ *adj.* mindful of others' interests. □□ **un•self′ish•ly** *adv.* **un•self′ish•ness** *n.*

■ unsparing, giving, bighearted, magnanimous, considerate, thoughtful, selfless, self-sacrificing. □□ **unselfishness** see ALTRUISM.

un•set•tle /únsét′l/ *v.* **1** disturb the settled state or arrangement of; discompose. **2** *tr.* derange. **3** *intr.* become unsettled. □□ **un•set′tling** *adj.*

■ **1** upset, agitate, perturb, fluster, dismay, *colloq.* shake (up), rattle; see also DISORDER *v.* **2** see UPSET *v.* 3. □□ **unsettling** unnerving, upsetting, disturbing, disconcerting.

un•set•tled /únsét′ld/ *adj.* **1** not (yet) settled.

2 liable or open to change or further discussion. **3** (of a bill, etc.) unpaid.

■ **1** unfixed, unstable, changing, variable, unpredictable, uncertain; disoriented, confused; bewildered, turbulent, agitated, *colloq.* rattled, riled. **2** see UNRESOLVED 2.

un•shak•a•ble /únsháykəbəl/ *adj.* (also **un•shake′able**) firm; obstinate. □□ **un•shak•a•bil′i•ty** *n.* **un•shak′a•bly** *adv.*

■ see FIRM[1] *adj.* 2a, b.

un•shrink•ing /únshríngking/ *adj.* unhesitating; fearless. □□ **un•shrink′ing•ly** *adv.*

un•sight•ly /únsítlee/ *adj.* unpleasant to look at; ugly. □□ **un•sight′li•ness** *n.*

■ hideous, awful-looking, horrible, grotesque, offensive, unattractive.

un•skilled /únskild/ *adj.* lacking or not needing special skill or training.

■ see MENIAL *adj.*, AMATEUR *adj.*, *inexperienced* (INEXPERIENCE).

un•so•lic•it•ed /únsəlísitid/ *adj.* not asked for; given or done voluntarily.

■ unlooked-for, gratuitous, free, voluntary, uninvited, unbidden.

un•so•phis•ti•cat•ed /únsəfístikaytid/ *adj.* **1** artless; simple; natural; ingenuous. **2** not adulterated or artificial. See synonym study at GULLIBLE. □□ **un•so•phis′ti•cat•ed•ly** *adv.*

■ **1** naive, inexperienced, callow, childlike, unworldly, innocent, unaffected, guileless. **2** simple, crude, undeveloped, primitive, uncomplicated.

un•sought /únsáwt/ *adj.* **1** not searched out or sought for. **2** unasked; without being requested.

■ **1** see GRATUITOUS 2.

un•sound /únsównd/ *adj.* **1** unhealthy; diseased. **2** rotten; weak. **3 a** ill-founded; fallacious. **b** unorthodox; heretical. □□ **un•sound′ly** *adv.* **un•sound′ness** *n.*

■ **1** ill, afflicted, delicate, injured. **2** frail, flimsy, shaky, unstable, wobbly, decrepit, defective. **3 a** illogical, faulty, flawed, invalid, groundless, unfounded, erroneous, defective.

un•spar•ing /únspáiring/ *adj.* **1** lavish; profuse. **2** merciless. □□ **un•spar′ing•ly** *adv.*

■ **1** see LAVISH *adj.* 1, 2. **2** see MERCILESS.

un•speak•a•ble /únspéekəbəl/ *adj.* **1** that cannot be expressed in words. **2** indescribably bad or objectionable. □□ **un•speak′a•ble•ness** *n.* **un•speak′a•bly** *adv.*

■ see INEXPRESSIBLE, OUTRAGEOUS 3. □□ **unspeakably** see BADLY 1.

un•sta•ble /únstáybəl/ *adj.* (**un•sta•bler, un•sta•blest**) **1** not stable. **2** changeable. **3** showing a tendency to sudden mental or emotional changes. □□ **un•sta′ble•ness** *n.* **un•sta′bly** *adv.*

■ **1** see SHAKY. **2, 3** variable, unsteady, inconsistent, capricious, fickle, unpredictable, unreliable, erratic, volatile, moody, indecisive, irresolute, unsettled, unbalanced, twisted.

un•stead•y /únstédee/ *adj.* (**un•stead•i•er, un•stead•i•est**) **1** not steady or firm. **2** changeable; fluctuating. **3** not uniform or regular. □□ un•stead'i•ly adv. un•stead'i•ness n.

■ 1 see SHAKY, *doddering* (DODDER), FAINT *adj.* 2. 2 see VARIABLE *adj.* 2. □□ **unsteadiness** see *fluctuation* (FLUCTUATE), *inconstancy* (INCONSTANT).

un•stint•ing /únstínting/ *adj.* ungrudging; lavish. □□ **un•stint'ing•ly** *adv.*

■ see GENEROUS 1, WHOLEHEARTED.

un•stop /únstóp/ *v.tr.* (**un•stopped, un•stop•ping**) 1 free from obstruction. 2 remove the stopper from.

un•stressed /únstrést/ *adj.* 1 (of a word, syllable, etc.) not pronounced with stress. 2 not subjected to stress.

un•string /únstríng/ *v.tr.* (*past* and *past part.* **un•strung**) 1 remove or relax the string(s) of (a bow, harp, etc.). 2 remove from a string. 3 (esp. as **unstrung** *adj.*) unnerve.

un•struc•tured /únstrúkchərd/ *adj.* 1 not structured. 2 informal.

■ 1 see INCOHERENT 2. 2 see INFORMAL.

un•stud•ied /únstúdeed/ *adj.* easy; natural; spontaneous.

un•sub•stan•tial /únsəbstánshəl/ *adj.* having little or no solidity, reality, or factual basis. □□ **un•sub•stan•tial•i•ty** /–sheeálitee/ *n.* **un•sub•stan'tial•ly** *adv.*

un•suit•ed /únsóotid/ *adj.* 1 [usu. foll. by *for*] not fit for a purpose. 2 [usu. foll. by *to*] not adapted.

■ see UNQUALIFIED 1, INCOMPATIBLE 1, 3.

un•sung /únsúng/ *adj.* 1 not celebrated; unknown. 2 not sung.

■ 1 unrecognized, unglorified, unnoticed, disregarded, unheard-of, anonymous, obscure, insignificant, inconspicuous.

un•swerv•ing /únswórving/ *adj.* 1 steady; constant. 2 not turning aside. □□ **un•swerv'ing•ly** *adv.*

■ 1 see CONSTANT *adj.* 3. □□ **unswervingly** see *consistently* (CONSISTENT).

un•tan•gle /úntánggəl/ *v.tr.* disentangle.

■ see STRAIGHTEN, EXTRICATE.

un•tapped /úntápt/ *adj.* not (yet) tapped or used.

un•taught /úntáwt/ *adj.* 1 not instructed by teaching; ignorant. 2 not acquired by teaching; natural; spontaneous.

■ 2 see INBORN, NATURAL *adj.* 4.

un•ten•a•ble /únténəbəl/ *adj.* not tenable; that cannot be defended. □□ **un•ten•a•bil'i•ty** *n.* **un•ten'a•bly** *adv.*

■ unsupportable, indefensible, unjustified, baseless, unfounded, flawed, weak, illogical, unreasonable, unsound, invalid.

un•think•a•ble /únthíngkəbəl/ *adj.* 1 that cannot be imagined or grasped by the mind. 2 *colloq.* highly unlikely or undesirable. □□ **un•think'a•bly** *adv.*

■ 1 inconceivable, unbelievable, incomprehensible, extraordinary, *colloq.* mind-boggling, *sl.* mind-blowing. 2 unacceptable, unattractive, absurd, illogical, out of the question, ridiculous.

un•think•ing /únthíngking/ *adj.* 1 thoughtless. 2 unintentional; inadvertent. □□ **un•think'ing•ly** *adv.*

■ 1 inconsiderate, impolite, tactless, rude, undiplomatic, discourteous, uncivil, indiscreet, negligent, careless, mindless, unreasonable, illogical, foolish, rash, impetuous, stupid, silly, shortsighted, *colloq.* crazy, moronic. 2 see INADVERTENT 1. □□ **unthinkingly** see *blindly* (BLIND).

un•ti•dy /úntídee/ *adj.* (**un•ti•di•er, un•ti•di•est**) not neat or orderly. □□ **un•ti'di•ly** *adv.* **un•ti'di•ness** *n.*

■ messy, disheveled, unkempt, slovenly, bedraggled, rumpled, sloppy, *colloq.* scruffy; littered, cluttered, chaotic, disorganized, topsy-turvy, messed-up. □□ **untidiness** see DISORDER *n.* 1.

un•tie /úntí/ *v.tr.* (*pres. part.* **un•ty•ing**) 1 undo (a knot, the cords of a package, etc.). 2 release from bonds or attachment.

■ 1 see UNDO 1. 2 see RELEASE *v.* 1.

un•til /əntíl, un–/ *prep. & conj.* till; before; up to the time that. ¶Used esp. when beginning a sentence and in formal style, e.g., *until you told me, I had no idea; he resided there until his decease.*

un•time•ly /úntímlee/ *adj.* 1 inopportune. 2 (of death) premature. □□ **un•time'li•ness** *n.*

■ 2 see PREMATURE 1.

un•to /úntoō, úntə/ *prep. archaic =* TO *prep.* (in all uses except as the sign of the infinitive); (*do unto others, faithful unto death, take unto oneself*).

un•told /úntóld/ *adj.* † not told. 2 not (able to be) counted or measured (*untold misery*).

■ 1 unpublished, unrevealed, unreported, private, hidden, secret. 2 innumerable, incalculable, inestimable; unlimited; inexpressible, unimaginable, inconceivable, unthinkable, unspeakable.

un•touch•a•ble /úntúchəbəl/ • *adj.* that may not or cannot be touched. • *n.* member of a hereditary Hindu group held to defile members of higher castes on contact. □□ **un•touch•a•bil'i•ty** *n.* **un•touch'a•ble•ness** *n.*

un•touched /úntúcht/ *adj.* 1 not touched. 2 not affected physically. 3 not affected by emotion.

■ 2 see UNUSED 1b, UNSCATHED. 3 see UNMOVED 3.

un•to•ward /úntáwrd, –təwáwrd/ *adj.* 1 inconvenient; unlucky. 2 awkward. 3 unseemly. □□ **un•to•ward'ly** *adv.* **un•toward' ness** *n.*

■ 1 adverse, unfavorable, discouraging, bad, unfortunate. 3 unbecoming, inappropriate, unsuitable, impolite, rude, indelicate, unwarranted, undiplomatic, tactless; ill-conceived, silly, foolish, stupid, ill-timed.

un•tram•meled /úntráməld/ *adj.* unhampered.

un•tried /úntríd/ *adj.* 1 not tried or tested. 2 inexperienced.

■ 1 unproved, unproven, new. 2 see RAW *adj.* 3.

un•trou•bled /úntrúbəld/ *adj.* not troubled; calm; tranquil.

■ see TRANQUIL.

un•true /úntroō/ *adj.* 1 not true; contrary to what is the fact. 2 [often foll. by *to*] not faithful or loyal. **3** deviating from an accepted standard. □□ **un•tru'ly** *adv.*

■ **1** wrong, false, inaccurate, misleading, mistaken, distorted. **2** disloyal, fickle, undependable, untrustworthy, false, dishonest, insincere, two-faced, devious, deceitful, treacherous. **3** inexact, imprecise, imperfect.

un•truth /úntrŏŏth/ *n.* (*pl.* **un•truths** /–trŏŏthz, –trŏŏths/) **1** state of being untrue; falsehood. **2** false statement (*told me an untruth*). □□ **un•truth'ful** *adj.* **un•truth'ful•ly** *adv.* **un•truth'ful•ness** *n.*

■ **2** see LIE² *n.* □□ **untruthful** FALSE *adj.* 1, 2b, DECEITFUL.

un•tu•tored /úntŏŏtərd, –tyŏŏ–/ *adj.* uneducated; untaught.

un•twist /úntwíst/ *v.* open from a twisted or spiraled state.

un•used *adj.* **1** /únyŏŏzd/ **a** not in use. **b** never having been used. **2** /únyŏŏst/ [foll. by *to*] not accustomed.

■ **1 a** abandoned, neglected, idle, vacant, empty, free. **b** (brand-)new, untouched, original, fresh, firsthand; leftover, remaining, surplus. **2** (*unused to*) unfamiliar with, inexperienced in or at.

un•u•su•al /únyŏŏzhŏŏəl/ *adj.* **1** not usual. **2** exceptional; remarkable. □□ **un•u'su•al•ly** *adv.*

■ **1** uncommon, rare, unexpected, surprising, unconventional. **2** atypical, different, singular, abnormal, irregular, extraordinary, odd, curious, bizarre, eccentric, *colloq.* wayout, *disp.* unique, *sl.* off-the-wall. □□ **unusually** see ESPECIALLY.

un•ut•ter•a•ble /únútərəbəl/ *adj.* inexpressible; beyond description (*unutterable torment*). □□ **un•ut'ter•a•bly** *adv.*

■ see INEXPRESSIBLE.

un•var•nished /únváarnisht/ *adj.* **1** not varnished. **2** plain and straightforward (*the unvarnished truth*).

■ **2** simple, pure, unembellished, direct, honest, naked, stark, sincere, frank, candid, outspoken.

un•veil /únváyl/ *v.* **1** *tr.* remove a veil from. **2** *tr.* remove a covering from (a statue, plaque, etc.) as part of the ceremony of the first public display. **3** *tr.* disclose; reveal; make publicly known. **4** *intr.* remove one's veil.

■ **1–3** expose, uncover; divulge, bring to light.

un•voiced /únvóyst/ *adj.* **1** not spoken. **2** *Phonet.* not voiced.

■ **1** see TACIT, *sneaking* (SNEAK *v.* 3a).

un•war•rant•ed /únwáwrəntid, –wór / *adj.* **1** unauthorized. **2** unjustified.

■ **2** uncalled-for, indefensible, unfair, unworthy, improper, inexcusable, undeserved, excessive.

un•wary /únwáiree/ *adj.* **1** not cautious. **2** [often foll. by *of*] not aware of possible danger, etc. □□ **un•war'i•ly** *adv.* **un•war'i•ness** *n.*

■ **1** heedless, careless, hasty, unsuspecting, foolhardy, unthinking, unwise. **2** see UNAWARE *adj.* 1.

un•washed /únwósht, –wáwsht/ *adj.* not washed or clean. □ **the great unwashed** *colloq.* the masses; the common people.

925 **untruth ~ unwrap**

■ dirty; filthy, grimy, soiled. □ **the great unwashed** the rabble, the hoi polloi, people (at large *or* in general), the population, the man in the street, the working class(es), most people, the (silent) majority, Middle America.

un•wea•ry•ing /únweéreeing/ *adj.* **1** persistent. **2** not causing or producing weariness. □□ **un•wea'ry•ing•ly** *adv.*

un•well /únwél/ *adj.* not in good health; (somewhat) ill.

un•whole•some /únhólsəm/ *adj.* **1** not promoting, or detrimental to, physical or moral health. **2** unhealthy-looking. □□ **un•whole'some•ly** *adv.* **un•whole'some•ness** *n.*

■ **1** unhealthy, deleterious, unhygienic, insanitary, harmful, toxic, injurious, destructive; corrupt, immoral, sinful; demoralizing, degrading, corrupting. **2** ill, ailing, sickly, pale.

un•wield•y /únweéldee/ *adj.* (**un•wield•i•er, un•wield•i•est**) cumbersome, or hard to manage, owing to size, shape, etc. □□ **un•wield'i•ness** *n.*

■ awkward, bulky, burdensome, ungainly, inconvenient. □□ **unwieldiness** see INCONVENIENCE *n.* 1.

un•will•ing /únwíling/ *adj.* not willing or inclined; reluctant. □□ **un•will'ing•ly** *adv.* **un•will'ing•ness** *n.*

■ see RELUCTANT. □□ **unwillingly** see *under* protest (PROTEST).

un•wind /únwínd/ *v.* (*past and past part.* **un•wound** /–wównd/) **1 a** *tr.* draw out (a thing that has been wound). **b** *intr.* become drawn out after being wound. **2** *intr.* & *tr. colloq.* relax.

■ **2** see RELAX 1.

un•wise /únwíz/ *adj.* foolish; imprudent. □□ **un•wise'ly** *adv.*

■ see IMPRUDENT.

un•wit•ting /únwíting/ *adj.* **1** unaware (*unwitting offender*). **2** unintentional. □□ **un•wit'ting•ly** *adv.* **un•wit'ting•ness** *n.*

■ **1** see UNAWARE *adj.* 1. **2** see INADVERTENT 1. □□ **unwittingly** see UNAWARES 2.

un•wont•ed /únwáwntid, –wón–, –wún–/ *adj.* not customary or usual. □□ **un•wont'ed•ly** *adv.* **un•wont'ed•ness** *n.*

■ infrequent, uncommon, unfamiliar, rare, abnormal, peculiar, strange, unconventional, unorthodox.

un•world•ly /únwárldlee/ *adj.* **1** spiritual. **2** naive. □□ **un•world'li•ness** *n.*

■ **1** see SPIRITUAL *adj.*

un•wor•thy /únwúrthee/ *adj.* (**un•wor•thi•er, un•wor•thi•est**) **1** [often foll. by *of*] not worthy or befitting the character of a person, etc. **2** discreditable; unseemly. **3** contemptible; base. □□ **un•wor'thi•ly** *adv.* **un•wor'thi•ness** *n.*

■ **1** unmerited, inferior, menial, mediocre, unqualified, ineligible; (*unworthy of*) inappropriate to, unfit for, beneath. **2** dishonorable, improper, undignified, shameful. **3** see CONTEMPTIBLE.

un•wrap /únráp/ *v.* (**un•wrapped, un•wrap•**

ping) **1** *tr.* remove the wrapping from. **2** *tr.* open or unfold. **3** *intr.* become unwrapped.
■ undo, open.

un•writ•ten /únrít'n/ *adj.* **1** not written. **2** (of a law, etc.) resting originally on custom or judicial decision, not on statute.
■ **1** see VERBAL *adj.* 2.

un•yield•ing /únyéelding/ *adj.* **1** not yielding to pressure, etc. **2** firm; obstinate. □□ **un•yield'ing•ly** *adv.* **un•yield'ing•ness** *n.*
■ **1** see FIRM¹ *adj.* 1. **2** see FIRM¹ *adj.* 2, OBSTINATE.

up /up/ • *adv.* **1** at, in, or toward a higher place or position (*jumped up in the air, what are they doing up there?*). **2** to or in a place regarded as higher, esp. northward (*up in New England*). **3** *colloq.* ahead, etc., as indicated (*went up front*). **4 a** to or in an erect position or condition (*stood it up*). **b** to or in a prepared or required position (*wound up the watch*). **c** in or into a condition of efficiency, activity, or progress (*stirred up trouble, the house is up for sale*). **5** in a stronger or winning position or condition (*our team was three goals up*). **6** (of a computer, machine, etc.) running and available for use. **7** to the place or time in question or where the speaker, etc., is (*a child came up to me, has been fine up till now*). **8** at or to a higher price or value (*our costs are up*). **9 a** completely or effectually (*burn up, eat up, use up*). **b** more loudly or clearly (*speak up*). **10** completed; past (*time is up*). **11** into a compact, accumulated, or secure state (*pack up, save up, tie up*). **12 a** awake. **b** out of bed (*are you up yet?*). **13** (of the sun, etc.) having risen. **14** happening, esp. unusually or unexpectedly (*something is up*). **15** [usu. foll. by *on*] informed about. **16** *Baseball* at bat (*he struck out his last time up*). • *prep.* **1** upward along, through, or into (*climbed up the ladder*). **2** from the bottom to the top of. **3** along (*walked up the road*). **4 a** at or in a higher part of (*is situated up the street*). **b** toward the source of (a river). • *adj.* [often in *comb.*] directed upward (*upstroke*). • *n.* spell of good fortune. • *v.* (**upped, up•ping**) **1** *intr. colloq.* start up; begin abruptly to say or do something (*upped and hit him*). **2** *tr.* increase or raise, esp. abruptly (*upped all their prices*). □ **on the up and up** *colloq.* honest(ly); on the level. **up against 1** close to. **2** *colloq.* confronted with (*up against a problem*). **up and about** (or **doing**) having risen from bed; active. **up-and-coming** *colloq.* making good progress and likely to succeed. **up and down 1** in every direction. **2** *colloq.* in varying health or spirits. **up for** available for or being considered for (office, etc.). **up-front** *adv.* (usu. **up front**) **1** at the front; in front. **2** (of payments) in advance. *adj.* **1** honest; open; frank. **2** (of payments) made in advance. **3** at the front or most prominent. **ups and downs** mixed fortune. **up to 1** until (*up to the present*). **2** less than or equal to (*adds up to $10*). **3** incumbent on (*it is up to you to say*). **4** capable of or fit for (*am not up to a long walk*). **5** occupied or busy with (*what have you been up to?*).

■ *adv.* **15** see INFORMED. □ **on the up and up** see SINCERE, ABOVEBOARD. **up and down 1** see ABOUT *adv.* 3.

up- /up/ *prefix* in senses of UP, added: **1** as an adverb to verbs and verbal derivations, = 'upward' (*update*). **2** as a preposition to nouns forming adverbs and adjectives (*up-country, uphill*). **3** as an adjective to nouns (*upland, upstroke*).

up•beat /úpbeet/ • *n.* unaccented beat in music. • *adj. colloq.* optimistic or cheerful.
■ *adj.* positive, favorable, encouraging, heartening.

up•braid /upbráyd/ *v.tr.* chide or reproach (a person). See synonym study at SCOLD. □□ **up•braid'ing** *n.*
■ scold, rebuke, reprimand, berate, castigate, haul a person over the coals, *colloq.* tell off, dress down, jump on, bawl out. □□ **upbraiding** see REPRIMAND *n.*

up•bring•ing /úpbringing/ *n.* care and education of a child.
■ raising, parenting, nurture, instruction, cultivation, breeding.

UPC *abbr.* = *Universal Product Code* (UNIVERSAL).

up•chuck /úpchuk/ *v. sl.* vomit.

up•com•ing /úpkúming/ *adj.* forthcoming; about to happen.
■ see FORTHCOMING 1.

up•date • *v.tr.* /úpdáyt/ bring up to date. • *n.* /úpdayt/ **1** updating. **2** updated information, etc. □□ **up•dat'er** *n.*
■ *v.* see MODERNIZE, REVISE *v.* 1.

up•end /úpénd/ *v.* set or rise up on end.

up•grade • *v.tr.* /úpgráyd/ **1** raise in rank, etc. **2** improve (equipment, etc.). • *n.* /úpgrayd/ **1** upgrading. **2** improvement. **3** upward slope. □□ **up'grad•er** *n.*
■ *v.* **1** see PROMOTE 1. **2** see IMPROVE 1a. • *n.* **1** see *promotion* (PROMOTE).

up•heav•al /uphéeval/ *n.* violent or sudden change or disruption.
■ upset, unrest, commotion, revolution, cataclysm, turbulence, disturbance, disorder, confusion, chaos, uproar, furor.

up•hill /úphíl/ • *adv.* up a hill, slope, etc. • *adj.* **1** sloping up; ascending. **2** arduous; difficult (*an uphill task*).
■ *adj.* **2** see LABORIOUS 1.

up•hold /úphóld/ *v.tr.* (*past* and *past part.* **up•held'** /–held/) **1** confirm. **2** support (a person, practice, etc.). □□ **up•hold'er** *n.*
■ **1** see CONFIRM 1, 2. **2** maintain, sustain, defend, protect, back, champion, stick up for. □□ **upholder** see PROPONENT *n.*

up•hol•ster /uphólstar, apól–/ *v.tr.* provide (furniture) with upholstery. □□ **up•hol'ster•er** *n.*

up•hol•ster•y /uphólstaree, apól–/ *n.* **1** covering, padding, springs, etc., for furniture. **2** upholsterer's work.

up•keep /úpkeep/ *n.* **1** maintenance in good condition. **2** cost or means of this.
■ **1** repair, preservation, conservation, operation. **2** (operating) costs, (running) expenses, outlay, expenditure, overhead.

up•land /úpland/ • *n.* the higher or inland parts of a country. • *adj.* of or relating to these parts.

up•lift • *v.tr.* /úplíft/ 1 raise; lift up. 2 elevate morally or spiritually. • *n.* /úplíft/ *colloq.* morally or spiritually elevating influence. □□ **up•lift'er** *n.* **up•lift'ing** *adj.* (esp. in sense 2 of *v.*).

■ *v.* 1 see RAISE *v.* 1. 2 see INSPIRE 1, 2. □□ **uplifting** see *exhilarating* (EXHILARATE).

up•mar•ket /úpmaárkit/ *adj. & adv.* = UP-SCALE.

up•on /əpón, əpáwn/ *prep.* = ON. ¶*Upon* is sometimes more formal, and is preferred in *once upon a time* and *upon my word*, and in uses such as *row upon row of seats* and *Christmas is almost upon us.*

up•per[1] /úpər/ • *adj.* 1 higher in place; situated above (*upper lip*). 2 higher in rank or dignity, etc. (*upper class*). • *n.* part of a boot or shoe above the sole. □ **on one's uppers** *colloq.* extremely short of money. **upper class** highest class of society. **upper crust** *colloq.* high society. **upper hand** dominance or control. **upper house** the higher house in a legislature, e.g., the U.S. Senate.

■ *adj.* 1 loftier, topmost, superior. 2 see SUPERIOR *adj.* 1. □ **on one's uppers** poor, destitute, penniless, needy, down and out, *colloq.* strapped (for cash), flat broke, *sl.* stone-broke; see also BROKE. **upper class, upper crust** élite, aristocracy, nobles, the blue-blooded. **upper hand** advantage, authority, power, supcriority, edge.

up•per[2] /úpər/ *n. sl.* stimulant drug, esp. an amphetamine.

up•per•case /úpərkáys/ • *adj.* (of letters) capital. • *n.* capital letters. • *v.tr.* set or print in uppercase.

up•per•cut /úpərkut/ • *n.* upward blow delivered with the arm bent. • *v.tr.* hit with an uppercut.

up•per•most /úpərmōst/ • *adj.* (also **up•most** /úpmōst/) 1 highest. 2 predominant. • *adv.* at or to the uppermost position.

■ *adj.* 1 topmost, loftiest, supreme. 2 foremost, first, most important *or* influential, principal, paramount, preeminent.

up•pi•ty /úpitee/ *adj. colloq.* arrogant; snobbish.

■ see *snobbish* (SNOB).

up•right /úprīt/ • *adj.* 1 erect; vertical (*an upright posture*). 2 (of a piano) with vertical strings. 3 honorable or honest. • *adv.* vertically. • *n.* 1 post or rod fixed upright, esp. as a structural support. 2 upright piano. □□ **up'right•ly** *adv.* **up'right•ness** *n.*

■ *adj.* 1 perpendicular, on end, straight up and down. 3 moral, principled, ethical, virtuous, righteous, *colloq.* straight. • *adv.* perpendicularly, straight up (and down). • *n.* 1 pole, column, pillar, vertical. □□ **uprightly** see UPRIGHT *adv.* above, HONESTLY 1. **uprightness** see RECTITUDE.

up•ris•ing /úprīzing/ *n.* rebellion or revolt.

■ mutiny, revolution, insurrection, coup d'état.

SYNONYM STUDY: uprising

INSURGENCY, INSURRECTION, MUTINY, PUTSCH, REBELLION, REVOLUTION. There are a number of ways to defy the established order or overthrow a government. You can stage an **uprising,** which is a broad term referring to a small and usually unsuccessful act of popular resistance (*uprisings among angry workers all over the country*). An *uprising* is often the first sign of a general or widespread **rebellion,** which is an act of armed resistance against a government or authority; this term is usually applied after the fact to describe an act of resistance that has failed (*a rebellion against the landowners*). If it is successful, however, a *rebellion* may become a **revolution,** which often implies a war or an outbreak of violence (*the American Revolution*). Although a *revolution* usually involves the overthrow of a government or political system by the people, it can also be used to describe any drastic change in ideas, economic institutions, or moral values (*the sexual revolution*). An **insurrection** is an organized effort to seize power, especially political power, while an **insurgency** is usually aided by foreign powers. If you're on a ship, you can stage a **mutiny,** which is an *insurrection* against military or naval authority. But if you're relying on speed and surprise to catch the authorities off guard, you'll want to stage a **putsch,** which is a small, popular *uprising* or planned attempt to seize power.

up•roar /úprawr/ *n.* tumult; violent disturbance.

■ clamor, hubbub, commotion, pandemonium, turmoil, outburst, chaos, fracas, brawl; *colloq.* row, rumpus, *sl.* hoopla.

up•roar•i•ous /upráwreeəs/ *adj.* 1 very noisy. 2 provoking loud laughter. □□ **up•roar'i•ous•ly** *adv.*

■ 1 clamorous, deafening, frenzied, rowdy, wild. 2 hilarious, sidesplitting, *colloq.* hysterical.

up•root /úpróot, róot/ *v.tr.* 1 pull (a plant, etc.) up from the ground. 2 displace. 3 eradicate; destroy. □□ **up•root'er** *n.*

■ 1 root out, dig out *or* up, tear out. 2 transfer; exile, banish. 3 extirpate, weed out; demolish, ruin, eliminate, exterminate.

up•scale /úpskáyl/ *adj. & adv.* toward or relating to the more affluent or upper sector of society or the market.

up•set • *v.* /úpsét/ (**up'set•ting**; *past* and *past part.* **up'set**) 1 a *tr. & intr.* overturn or be overturned. b *tr.* overcome; defeat. 2 *tr.* disturb the composure or digestion of. 3 *tr.* disrupt. • *n.* /úpsét/ 1 condition of upsetting or being upset (*a stomach upset*). 2 surprising result in a game, etc. • *adj.* /úpsét/ disturbed (*upset stomach*). □□ **up•set'ter** *n.* **up•set'ting•ly** *adv.*

■ *v.* 1 a capsize, topple, upend, knock over. b overthrow, beat, conquer, win out over. 2 agitate, distress, unsettle, frighten, annoy, irritate, *colloq.* rattle, *joc.* discombobulate. 3 disturb, derange, disorganize, confuse; defeat, ruin, spoil, interfere with, destroy, *colloq.* gum up, *sl.* screw up. • *n.* 1 disorder, ailment; see also DISTURBANCE 1, 3. 2 unexpected event; defeat, rout; triumph, victory.

• adj. (of digestion) sick, queasy; (of a person) perturbed, disquieted, worried, distracted, apprehensive, nervous, frightened; angry, irate, furious, mad, colloq. fit to be tied, freaked out.

up•shot /úpshot/ n. outcome or conclusion.
■ result, ending, effect, fallout, wake, repercussion, feedback, resolution, sl. payoff.

up•side down /úpsīd dówn/ • adv. **1** with the upper part where the lower part should be; inverted. **2** in or into total disorder.
• adj. (also **up'side-down'**) attrib. inverted.
■ see TOPSY-TURVY.

up•si•lon /úpsilon, yōōp–/ n. twentieth letter of the Greek alphabet (Υ, υ).

up•stage /úpstáyj/ • adj. & adv. nearer the back of a stage. • v.tr. divert attention from (a person) to oneself; outshine.

up•stairs /úpstáirz/ • adv. to or on an upper floor. • adj. (also **up'stair**) situated upstairs. • n. upper floor.

up•stand•ing /úpstánding/ adj. **1** standing up. **2** honest.
■ **1** see UPRIGHT adj. 1. **2** see UPRIGHT adj. 3.

up•start /úpstaart/ • n. newly successful, esp. arrogant, person. • adj. of or characteristic of an upstart.
■ n. parvenu(e), nouveau riche, status seeker, whippersnapper. • adj. parvenu(e), social-climbing, status-seeking.

up•state /úpstáyt/ • n. part of a state remote from its large cities, esp. the northern part.
• adj. of or relating to this part. • adv. in or to this part. □□ **up'stat'er** n.

up•stream /úpstreém/ • adv. against the flow of a stream, etc. • adj. moving upstream.
■ see REVIVAL 1, 3, RISE n. 3.

up•surge /úpsərj/ n. upward surge; rise (esp. in feelings, etc.).
■ see REVIVAL 1, 3, improvement (IMPROVE).

up•swing /úpswing/ n. upward movement or trend.

up•take /úptayk/ n. **1** colloq. understanding; comprehension (esp.quick or slow on the uptake). **2** taking up.
■ **1** apprehension, grasp, perception, insight, sensitivity.

up•thrust /úpthrust/ n. **1** upward thrust. **2** Geol. = UPHEAVAL.

up•tight /úptīt/ adj. colloq. **1** nervously tense or angry. **2** rigidly conventional.

up•town /úptówn/ • adj. **1** of or in the residential part of a town or city. **2** of affluent or sophisticated people. • adv. in or into this part. • n. this part. □□ **up'town'er** n.

up•turn • n. /úptərn/ upward trend; improvement. • v.tr. /úptúrn/ turn up or upside down.
■ n. see REVIVAL 1, improvement (IMPROVE).

up•ward /úpwərd/ • adv. (also **up'wards**) toward what is higher, superior, larger in amount, or more important. • adj. moving, extending, pointing, or leading upward. □ **upward of** more than (found upward of forty specimens).

up•ward•ly /úpwərdlee/ adv. in an upward direction. □ **upwardly mobile** able or aspiring to advance socially or professionally.

up•wind /úpwind/ adj. & adv. against the direction of the wind.

u•ra•ni•um /yōōráyneeəm/ n. Chem. radioactive, gray, dense metallic element, capable of nuclear fission and used as a source of nuclear energy. ¶Symb.: U. □□ **u•ran'ic** /–ránik/ adj.

U•ra•nus /yōōrənəs, yōōráynəs/ n. seventh planet from the sun.

ur•ban /árbən/ adj. of, living in, or situated in a town or city (an urban population) (opp. RURAL).

ur•bane /ərbáyn/ adj. courteous; suave; elegant and refined in manner. □□ **ur•bane'ly** adv. **ur•ban'i•ty** /ərbánitee/ n.
■ see COURTEOUS, ELEGANT 1, 2.

SYNONYM STUDY: urbane
COSMOPOLITAN, GENTEEL, SOPHISTICATED, SUAVE. In his long career as a film star, Cary Grant was known for playing **urbane**, **sophisticated** roles. Urbane in this context suggests the social poise and polished manner of someone who is well-traveled and well-bred, while sophisticated means worldlywise as opposed to naive (a sophisticated young girl who had spent her childhood in Paris and London). **Cosmopolitan** describes someone who is at home anywhere in the world and is free from provincial attitudes (a cosmopolitan man who could charm women of all ages and nationalities), while **suave** suggests the gracious social behavior of urbane combined with a certain glibness or superficial politeness (she was taken in by his expensive clothes and suave manner). At one time **genteel** meant well-bred or refined, but nowadays it has connotations of self-consciousness or pretentiousness (too genteel to drink wine from a juice glass).

ur•ban•ize /árbənīz/ v.tr. **1** make urban. **2** destroy the rural quality of (a district). □□ **ur•ban•i•za'tion** n.

ur•chin /árchin/ n. mischievous child, esp. young and raggedly dressed.
■ see RAGAMUFFIN.

Ur•du /ŏŏrdōō, ór–/ n. language related to Hindi but with many Persian words, used in Pakistan and India.

-ure /ər/ suffix forming: **1** nouns of action or process (seizure). **2** nouns of result (scripture). **3** collective nouns (nature).

u•re•a /yōōreéə/ n. Biochem. soluble, nitrogenous compound contained esp. in urine. □□ **u•re'al** adj.

u•re•ter /yōōreétər/ n. duct by which urine passes from the kidney to the bladder.

u•re•thane /yōōríthayn/ n. Chem. crystalline amide, ethyl carbamate, used in plastics and paints.

u•re•thra /yōōreéthrə/ n. (pl. **u•re'thras** or **u•re'thrae** /–ree/) duct by which urine is discharged from the bladder.

urge /ərj/ • v.tr. **1** drive forcibly; impel (urged the horses forward). **2** encourage or entreat earnestly or persistently (urged them to go). **3** advocate (an action or argument, etc.) emphatically (to a person). • n. **1** urging impulse or tendency. **2** strong desire.
■ v. **1** press, push, hurry, hasten, prod.

2 press, prod, egg on, prompt, induce, incite, demand, ask, beg, implore, persuade. **3** advise, argue. • *n.* **1** pressure, compulsion, drive. **2** longing, yearning, craving, wish, *colloq.* yen.

ur•gent /ə́rjənt/ *adj.* **1** requiring immediate action or attention. **2** persistent in demand. See synonym study at CRUCIAL. □□ **ur′gen•cy** *n.* **ur′gent•ly** *adv.*

■ **1** imperative, compelling, vital, life-and-death, desperate, emergency. **2** begging, solicitous, earnest, tenacious, forceful. □□ **urgency** imperativeness, pressure, stress, necessity, exigency, emergency. **urgently** see HARD *adv.* 1.

u•ric /yŏŏrik/ *adj.* of or relating to urine.

u•ri•nal /yŏŏrinəl/ *n.* place or receptacle for urination by men.

u•ri•nal•y•sis /yŏŏrinálisis/ *n.* (*pl.* **u•ri•nal′y•ses** /-seez/) chemical analysis of urine, esp. for diagnostic purposes.

u•ri•nate /yŏŏrinayt/ *v.intr.* discharge urine. □□ **u•ri•na•tion** /-náyshən/ *n.*

■ pass *or* make water, void, relieve oneself; *colloq.* (have a) pee, tinkle, *colloq.* take a pee, *euphem.* go to the men's *or* ladies' room, excuse (oneself), go to the bathroom, go to the powder room. □□ **urination** passing water, voiding, excretion.

u•rine /yŏŏrin/ *n.* pale-yellow fluid secreted as waste from the blood by the kidneys, stored in the bladder, and discharged through the urethra. □□ **u′ri•na•ry** *adj.*

urn /ərn/ *n.* **1** vase with a foot and usu. a rounded body, esp. for storing the ashes of the dead. **2** large vessel with a tap, in which tea or coffee, etc., is made or kept hot. □□ **urn′ful** *n.* (*pl.* **-fuls**).

u•ro•gen•i•tal /yŏŏrəjénit′l/ *adj.* of or relating to urinary and genital products or organs.

u•rol•o•gy /yŏŏróləjee/ *n.* scientific study of the urinary system. □□ **u•ro•log′ic** /-rəlójik/ *adj.* **u•rol′o•gist** *n.*

ur•sine /ə́rsin/ *adj.* of or like a bear.

US or **U.S.** *abbr.* United States (of America).

us /us, əs/ *pron.* **1** objective case of WE (*they saw us*). **2** *colloq.* = WE (*it's us again*). **3** *colloq.* = ME (*give us a kiss*).

USA *abbr.* **1** United States of America. **2** United States Army.

us•a•ble /yŏŏzəbəl/ *adj.* (also **use′a•ble**) that can be used. □□ **us•a•bil′i•ty** *n.* **us′a•ble•ness** *n.*

■ see SERVICEABLE 1, 2, USEFUL.

USAF *abbr.* United States Air Force.

us•age /yŏŏsij/ *n.* **1** use; treatment (*damaged by rough usage*). **2** habitual or customary practice, esp. as creating a right, obligation, or standard.

■ **1** management, handling. **2** use (and wont), routine, tradition.

USB port • *n.* computer port accepting different peripheral devices (from universal serial bus).

U.S.C. *abbr. Law* United States Code.

USCG *abbr.* United States Coast Guard.

use • *v.tr.* /yŏŏz/ **1 a** cause to act or serve for a purpose; bring into service (*rarely uses the car*). **b** consume or take (alcohol, a drug, etc.), esp. habitually. **2** treat (a person) in a specified manner (*they used him shamefully*). **3** exploit for one's own ends (*they are just using you, used his position*). **4** [in past /yŏŏst/; foll. by *to* + infin.] did or had in the past (but no longer) as a customary practice or state (*I used to be an archaeologist, it did not use to rain so often*). **5** (as used *adj.*) secondhand. **6** (as **used** /yŏŏst/ *predic. adj.*) [foll. by *to*] familiar by habit; accustomed (*not used to hard work*). • *n.* /yŏŏs/ **1** using or being used (*put it to good use, worn and polished with use*). **2** right or power of using (*lost the use of my right arm*). **3 a** ability to be used (*a flashlight would be of use*). **b** purpose for which a thing can be used (*it's no use talking*). **4** custom or usage (*long use has reconciled me to it*). □ **have no use for 1** be unable to find a use for. **2** dislike or be impatient with. **use up** consume completely; use the whole of. □□ **us′er** *n.*

■ *v.* **1 a** employ, put into practice, operate, utilize, exercise, apply, avail oneself of. **b** eat, drink, smoke, ingest, inject, *sl.* do, shoot (up). **2** handle, act *or* behave toward. **3** take advantage of, manipulate, abuse; capitalize on. **5** (used) cast-off, old, worn, hand-me-down. **6** (used to) acclimated to, adapted to, hardened to *or* against, tolerant of; acquainted with. • *n.* **1** application, employment, utilization; handling; consumption. **2** usefulness, utility, function, service(s). **3 a** utility, service. **b** advantage, benefit; point, object; demand, need, urgency. **4** see USAGE. □ **have no use for 2** detest, despise, scorn, reject. **use up** exhaust, expend, run out of; waste, squander, fritter away, *sl.* blow.

use•ful /yŏŏsfŏŏl/ *adj.* **1 a** of use; serviceable. **b** producing or able to produce good results (*gave me some useful hints*). **2** *colloq.* highly creditable or efficient (*a useful performance*). □□ **use′ful•ly** *adv.* **use′ful•ness** *n.*

■ **1** utilitarian, functional, practical, beneficial, advantageous, valuable, helpful, effective, worthwhile. □□ **usefulness** utility, purpose, practicality, benefit, value, effectiveness, worth.

use•less /yŏŏslis/ *adj.* **1** serving no purpose; unavailing (*protest is useless*). **2** *colloq.* feeble or ineffectual (*a useless gadget*). □□ **use′less•ly** *adv.* **use′less•ness** *n.*

■ **1** ineffective, impractical, pointless, futile, unproductive, worthless. **2** inefficient, incompetent, unproductive, no-good, inept, *sl.* out to lunch; see also DUD *adj.* 1. □□ **uselessness** see *incompetence* (INCOMPETENT), VANITY 2.

us•er-friend•ly /yŏŏzər-fréndlee/ *adj.* esp. *Computing* (of a machine or system) designed to be easy to use.

■ simple, practicable, accommodating, understandable, accessible.

ush•er /úshər/ • *n.* person who shows people to their seats in a theater, church, etc. • *v.tr.* **1** act as usher to. **2** announce or show in, etc. (*ushered us into the room*).

USIA *abbr.* United States Information Agency.

USMC *abbr.* United States Marine Corps.

USN *abbr.* United States Navy.

USO *abbr.* United Service Organizations.

USPS *abbr.* United States Postal Service.

USS *abbr.* United States Ship.

USSR *abbr. hist.* Union of Soviet Socialist Republics.

usu. *abbr.* **1** usual. **2** usually.

u•su•al /yōōzhōōəl/ *adj.* **1** customary; habitual (*the usual formalities, it is usual to tip them, forgot my keys as usual*). **2** [prec. by *the, my,* etc.] *colloq.* person's usual drink, etc. See synonym study at NORMAL. □□ **u′su•al•ly** *adv.*
   ■ **1** same, familiar, common, established, traditional, time-honored, old, standard, regular, routine, typical, run-of-the-mill, hackneyed, trite, predictable, unexceptional, unremarkable. □□ **usually** as a rule, generally (speaking), most of the time, for the most part, on the whole, normally, chiefly, by and large, *colloq.* as per usual.

u•surp /yōōzə́rp, –sə́rp/ *v.* **1** *tr.* seize or assume (a throne or power, etc.) wrongfully. **2** *intr.* [foll. by *on, upon*] encroach. □□ **u•sur•pa′tion** *n.* **u•surp′er** *n.*
   ■ **1** see APPROPRIATE *v.* 1.

u•su•ry /yōōzhəree/ *n.* **1** lending of money at an exorbitant or illegal rate of interest. **2** interest at this rate. □□ **u′su•rer** *n.* **u•su•ri•ous** /–zhóoreeəs/ *adj.*

UT *abbr.* Utah (in official postal use).

Ute /yōōt/ *n.* (*pl.* same or **Utes**) **1 a** N. American people native to the Colorado, New Mexico, Utah, and Arizona area. **b** member of this people. **2** language of this people.

u•ten•sil /yōōténsəl/ *n.* implement or vessel, esp. for domestic use (*cooking utensils*). See synonym study at TOOL.

u•ter•us /yōōtərəs/ *n.* (*pl.* **u•ter•i** /–rī/) the womb. □□ **u•ter•ine** /–in, –in/ *adj.*

u•til•i•tar•i•an /yōōtilitáireeən/ *adj.* **1** designed to be useful rather than attractive; severely practical. **2** of utilitarianism.
   ■ **1** see PRACTICAL *adj.* 2.

u•til•i•tar•i•an•ism /yōōtilitáireeənizəm/ *n.* doctrine that actions are right if they are useful or benefit a majority.

u•til•i•ty /yōōtílitee/ *n.* (*pl.* **–ties**) **1** being useful or profitable. **2** useful thing. **3** = *public utility.* □ **utility room** room equipped with appliances for washing, ironing, and other domestic work.
   ■ **1** see *usefulness* (USEFUL).

u•ti•lize /yōōt′līz/ *v.tr.* make practical use of; use effectively. □□ **u′ti•liz•a•ble** *adj.* **u•ti•li•za′tion** *n.* **u•ti•liz•er** *n.*
   ■ see USE *v.* 1a. □□ **utilization** see USE *n.* 1, 2.

-ution /ṓōshən/ *suffix* forming nouns, = -ATION (*solution*).

ut•most /útmōst/ • *adj.* furthest, extreme, or greatest (*showed the utmost reluctance*). • *n.* utmost point or degree, etc.
   ■ *adj.* see MAXIMUM *adj.* • *n.* see MAXIMUM *n.*

U•to•pi•a /yōōtṓpeeə/ *n.* imagined perfect place or state of things. □□ **U•to′pi•an** *adj. & n.*
   ■ paradise, (seventh) heaven, Shangri-la, perfection.

ut•ter¹ /útər/ *attrib.adj.* complete; total; absolute (*utter misery, saw the utter absurdity of it*). □□ **ut′ter•ly** *adv.*
   ■ see COMPLETE *adj.* 3, TOTAL *adj.* 2. □□ **utterly** perfectly, thoroughly, entirely, unreservedly, (with) no holds barred; extremely.

ut•ter² /útər/ *v.tr.* **1** emit audibly. **2** express in words. □□ **ut′ter•a•ble** *adj.* **ut′ter•er** *n.*
   ■ see VOICE *v.*

ut•ter•ance /útərəns/ *n.* **1** act of uttering. **2** thing spoken. **3 a** power of speaking. **b** manner of speaking.
   ■ **1** see EXPRESSION 1. **2** see STATEMENT 1–3, OBSERVATION 3.

ut•ter•most /útərmōst/ *adj.* furthest; extreme.
   ■ see MAXIMUM *adj.*

U-turn /yōōtərn/ *n.* **1** turning of a vehicle so as to face in the opposite direction. **2** reversal of policy.

UV *abbr.* ultraviolet.

u•vu•la /yōōvyələ/ *n.* (*pl.* **u•vu•las** or **u•vu•lae** /–lee/) fleshy extension of the soft palate hanging above the throat. □□ **u′vu•lar** *adj.*

ux•o•ri•al /uksáwreeəl, ugzáwr–/ *adj.* of or relating to a wife.

ux•o•ri•ous /uksáwreeəs, ugzáwr–/ *adj.* greatly or excessively fond of one's wife. □□ **ux•o′ri•ous•ly** *adv.* **ux•o′ri•ous•ness** *n.*

Uz•bek /ŏozbek–, úz–/ *n.* (also **Uz•beg** /–beg/) **1** member of a Turkic people living mainly in Uzbekistan, a country of south central Asia. **2** language of this people.

Vv

V¹ /vee/ *n.* (also **v**) (*pl.* **Vs** or **V's; v's**) **1** twenty-second letter of the alphabet. **2** V-shaped thing. **3** (as a Roman numeral) five.

V² *abbr.* (also **V.**) volt(s).

V³ *symb. Chem.* vanadium.

v. *abbr.* **1** verse. **2** verso. **3** versus. **4** very. **5** *vide.*

VA *abbr.* **1** Veterans Administration. **2** Virginia (in official postal use).

Va. *abbr.* Virginia.

va•can•cy /váykənsee/ *n.* (*pl.* **–cies**) **1** being vacant or empty. **2** unoccupied position or job (*there are three vacancies for computer specialists*). **3** available room in a hotel, etc.
 ■ **1** blankness; void, gap, deficiency, opening, space, vacuum. **2** (job) opening, slot, post, situation; (*vacancies*) help wanted.

va•cant /váykənt/ *adj.* **1** not filled nor occupied; empty. **2** not mentally active; showing no interest. □□ **va′cant•ly** *adv.*
 ■ **1** free, unused, void, uninhabited, abandoned. **2** blank, expressionless, deadpan, inane. □□ **vacantly** vaguely, absently.

va•cate /váykayt, vaykáyt/ *v.tr.* **1** leave vacant or cease to occupy (a room, etc.). **2** give up (a post, etc.).
 ■ **1** leave, depart (from), evacuate; desert, abandon. **2** relinquish, resign, abdicate.

va•ca•tion /vaykáyshən, və–/ • *n.* time of rest, recreation, etc., esp. spent away from home. • *v.intr.* take a vacation, esp. away from home for pleasure and recreation. □□ **va•ca′tion•er** *n.*
 ■ *n.* break, time off, leave (of absence), recess.

vac•ci•nate /váksinayt/ *v.tr.* inoculate to immunize against a disease. □□ **vac•ci•na′tion** *n.*

vac•cine /vákséen/ *n.* antigenic preparation used to stimulate the production of antibodies and procure immunity from disease.

vac•il•late /vásiluyt/ *v.intr.* **1** fluctuate; be irresolute. **2** move from side to side. □□ **vac•il•la′tion** /–láyshən/ *n.* **vac′il•la•tor** *n.*
 ■ see OSCILLATE. □□ **vacillation** see *fluctuation* (FLUCTUATE).

va•cu•i•ty /vakyōotee, və–/ *n.* **1** state of being vacuous. **2** something, such as a comment, that is senseless or inane. **3** empty space.

vac•u•ole /vákyōo-ōl/ *n. Biol.* tiny space in the cytoplasm of a cell containing air, fluid, etc. □□ **vac•u•o•lar** /vakyōo-ōlər, vákyooələr/ *adj.* **vac•u•o•la′tion** *n.*

vac•u•ous /vákyōoəs/ *adj.* **1** lacking expression. **2** unintelligent. **3** empty. □□ **va•cu•i•ty** /vakyōo-itee/ *n.* **vac′u•ous•ly** *adv.*
 ■ **1** see BLANK *adj.* 3a. **2** see INANE 1.

vac•u•um /vákyōoəm, –yōom, –yəm/ • *n.* (*pl.* **vac•u•ums** or **vac•u•a** /–yōoə/) **1** space entirely devoid of matter. **2** space from which the air has been completely or partly removed by a pump, etc. **3** absence of the normal or previous content, activities, etc. **4** (*pl.* **vac•u•ums**) *colloq.* vacuum cleaner. • *v. colloq.* **1** *tr.* clean with a vacuum cleaner. **2** *intr.* use a vacuum cleaner. □ **vacuum cleaner** apparatus for removing dust, etc., by suction. **vacuum-packed** sealed after partial removal of air. **vacuum tube** *Electronics* tube with a near-vacuum that regulates electric current.
 ■ *n.* **3** see VOID *n.*

vag•a•bond /vágəbond/ • *n.* **1** wanderer, esp. an idle one. **2** *colloq.* rascal. • *adj.* wandering. □□ **vag′a•bond•age** *n.*
 ■ *n.* **1** gypsy, drifter, hobo, rolling stone, derelict, *colloq.* panhandler, *sl.* bum. **2** see RASCAL. • *adj.* vagrant, transient, homeless.

va•ga•ry /váygəree/ *n.* (*pl.* **–ries**) caprice; eccentric idea or act (*the vagaries of Fortune*).
 ■ see QUIRK 1.

va•gi•na /vəjínə/ *n.* (*pl.* **va•gi•nas** or **va•gi•nae** /–nee/) canal between the uterus and vulva in female mammals. □□ **va•gi•nal** /vájin'l/ *adj.* **vag•i•ni•tis** /vájinítis/ *n.*

va•grant /váygrənt/ • *n.* **1** person without a home or work. **2** wanderer or vagabond. • *adj.* wandering or roving (*a vagrant musician*). □□ **va•gran•cy** /–grənsee/ *n.* **va′grant•ly** *adv.*
 ■ *n.* see TRAMP *n.* 1.

vague /vayg/ *adj.* **1** uncertain or ill-defined (*gave a vague answer*). **2** (of a person or mind) imprecise; inexact in thought, expression, or understanding. □□ **vague′ly** *adv.* **vague′ness** *n.*
 ■ **1** indefinite, indistinct, inexact, unclear, confused, vague, ambiguous; indefinable, unexplained; hazy, fuzzy, obscure, blurred, shadowy, foggy, barely discernible. **2** wishy-washy, indecisive, irresolute, uncertain; vacant, blank; see also ABSENTMINDED. □□ **vaguely** ambiguously, imprecisely, unclearly, nebulously; remotely, indefinitely, dimly, absentmindedly, distractedly. **vagueness** see *imprecision* (IMPRECISE).

vain /vayn/ *adj.* **1** excessively proud or conceited, esp. about one's own attributes. **2** empty; trivial (*vain boasts*). **3** useless; futile. □ **in vain** without success (*it was in vain that we protested*). □□ **vain′ly** *adv.* **vain′ness** *n.*
 ■ **1** arrogant, puffed up, egotistical, *colloq.* bigheaded, stuck-up. **2** see EMPTY *adj.* 3a. **3** worthless, pointless, unsuccessful, ineffective; abortive. □ **in vain** futilely, unsuccessfully, fruitlessly. □□ **vainness** see VANITY.

vain•glo•ry /vaynglǻwree/ *n. literary* boastfulness; extreme vanity. See synonym study at PRIDE. □□ **vain•glo′ri•ous** *adj.* **vain•glo′ri•ous•ly** *adv.*

val•ance /váləns, váyl–/ *n.* short curtain around the frame or canopy of a bed, above a window, or under a shelf. □□ **val′anced** *adj.*

vale /vayl/ n. archaic or poet. (except in place-names) valley (Vale of the White Horse).
■ see VALLEY.

val•e•dic•tion /válidíkshən/ n. 1 bidding farewell. 2 words used in this.

val•e•dic•to•ri•an /válidiktáwreeən/ n. person who gives a valedictory, esp. the highest-ranking member of a graduating class.

val•e•dic•to•ry /válidiktəree/ • adj. serving as a farewell. • n. (pl. **–ries**) farewell address.
■ n. see PARTING 1.

va•lence /váyləns/ n. Chem. combining power of an atom measured by the number of hydrogen atoms it can displace or combine with.

val•en•tine /váləntīn/ n. 1 card or gift sent as a mark of love or affection on St. Valentine's Day (Feb. 14). 2 sweetheart chosen on this day.

va•let /valáy, válit, –lay/ • n. 1 gentleman's personal attendant. 2 hotel, etc., employee with similar duties. 3 standing rack for holding one's suit, coat, etc. • v. 1 intr. work as a valet. 2 tr. act as a valet to.
■ n. 1 see MAN n. 4b.

val•e•tu•di•nar•i•an /válitŏŏd'náireeən, –tyŏŏd–/ • n. person of poor health or unduly anxious about health. • adj. of poor health. □□ **val•e•tu•di•nar'i•an•ism** n.

Val•hal•la /valhálə, vaalhaalə/ n. (in Norse mythology) palace in which the souls of slain heroes feasted for eternity.

val•iant /váylyənt/ adj. brave; courageous. □□ **val'iant•ly** adv.
■ see BRAVE adj. 1.

val•id /válid/ adj. 1 (of a reason, objection, etc.) sound or defensible. 2 a legally acceptable (valid passport). b not having reached its expiration date. □□ **va•lid'i•ty** n. **val'id•ly** adv.
■ 1 see LEGITIMATE adj. 3. 2 a see LEGITIMATE adj. 1, 2. b see in force (FORCE). □□ **validity** legitimacy, truth, authenticity; see also FORCE n. 4.

val•i•date /válidayt/ v.tr. make valid; ratify. □□ **val•i•da'tion** /–dáyshən/ n.
■ see RATIFY. □□ **validation** see SANCTION n. 2.

val•ise /vəlées/ n. small suitcase; traveling bag.

Val•i•um /váleeəm/ n. propr. drug (diazepam) used as a tranquilizer.

Val•kyr•ie /valkéeree, válkiree/ n. (in Norse mythology) maidens who selected heroes destined to be slain in battle and escorted them to Valhalla.

val•ley /válee/ n. (pl. **–leys**) low area between hills and usu. with a stream flowing through it.
■ glen, dale, dell, hollow, basin, gorge, ravine, gulch, canyon.

val•or /válər/ n. courage, esp. in battle. □□ **val'or•ous** adj.
■ see COURAGE.

val•u•able /vályŏŏəbəl, vályə–/ • adj. of great value, price, or worth. • n. [usu. in pl.] valuable thing. □□ **val'u•a•bly** adv.
■ adj. see advantageous (ADVANTAGE), PRECIOUS adj. 1.

val•u•a•tion /vályŏŏ-áyshən/ n. 1 estimation (esp. by a professional) of a thing's worth. 2 worth estimated. □□ **val'u•ate** v.tr.

val•ue /vályŏŏ/ • n. 1 worth, desirability, or utility (the value of regular exercise). 2 worth as estimated. 3 amount of money or goods for which a thing can be exchanged in the open market. 4 ability of a thing to serve a purpose or cause an effect (news value, nuisance value). 5 [in pl.] one's principles or standards; one's judgment of what is valuable or important in life. 6 Mus. duration of a note. 7 Math. amount denoted by an algebraic term. • v.tr. (**val'ues, val•ued, val•u•ing**) 1 estimate the value of (esp. professionally) (valued the property at $200,000). 2 have a high or specified opinion of (a valued friend). □ **value-added tax** tax on the amount by which the value of an article has been increased at each stage of its production. **value judgment** subjective estimate of quality, etc. □□ **val'ue•less** adj.
■ n. 1 see usefulness (USEFUL). 3 see PRICE n. 1. 5 (values) see PHILOSOPHY 2. • v. 1 see ESTIMATE v. 2. 2 see APPRECIATE 1a, b.

valve /valv/ n. 1 device controlling the flow of fluid through a pipe, etc. 2 Anat. & Zool. part of an organ, etc., allowing a flow of blood, etc., in one direction only. 3 device to vary the effective length of the tube in a brass musical instrument. 4 each of the two shells of an oyster, mussel, etc. □□ **val'vate** /–vayt/ adj. **valved** adj. [also in comb.]. **valve'less** adj. **val'vu•lar** adj.

va•moose /vamŏŏs, və–/ v.intr. [esp. as int.] sl. depart hurriedly.

vamp¹ /vamp/ • n. 1 upper front part of a boot or shoe. 2 improvised musical accompaniment. • v. 1 tr. & intr. improvise a musical accompaniment (to). 2 tr. improvise (a musical accompaniment).

vamp² /vamp/ colloq. • n. woman who uses sexual attraction to exploit men. • v. intr. act as a vamp.

vam•pire /vámpīr/ n. 1 supposedly reanimated corpse that sucks the blood of sleeping persons. 2 colloq. person who preys ruthlessly on others. 3 (in full **vam'pire bat**) tropical (esp. South American) bloodsucking bat.

van¹ /van/ n. 1 covered vehicle for conveying goods, etc., esp. a large truck or trailer (moving van). 2 smaller such vehicle, similar to a panel truck and used esp. for carrying passengers, etc.

van² /van/ n. 1 = VANGUARD. 2 forefront (in the van of progress).
■ 2 see FRONT n. 6; (be in the van of) see SPEARHEAD v.

va•na•di•um /vənáydeeəm/ n. Chem. hard, gray, metallic element used for strengthening some steels. ¶ Symb.: **V**.

van•dal /vánd'l/ n. person who willfully or maliciously damages property. □□ **van'dal•ism** n. **van'dal•ize** v.
■ hooligan, ruffian, tough, hoodlum, sl. punk, lug, hood. □□ **vandalize** see DAMAGE v. 1, MUTILATE 2.

Van•dyke beard /vandík/ n. neat, pointed beard.

vane /vayn/ *n.* **1** (in full **weather vane**) revolving pointer on a barn roof or other high place to show the direction of the wind (cf. WEATHERCOCK). **2** blade of a propeller, windmill, etc. □□ **vaned** *adj.* **vane′less** *adj.*

van•guard /vángaard/ *n.* **1** foremost part of an advancing army, etc. **2** leaders of a movement, etc.
■ see SPEARHEAD *n.*

va•nil•la /vənílə/ *n.* **1 a** tropical climbing orchid with fragrant flowers. **b** (in full **va•nil′la bean**) fruit of these. **2** substance obtained from the vanilla bean or synthesized and used to flavor ice cream, chocolate, etc.

van•ish /vánish/ *v.intr.* **1** disappear. **2** cease to exist. □ **vanishing point** point at which receding parallel lines viewed in perspective appear to meet.
■ **1** see DISAPPEAR 1. **2** see DISAPPEAR 2.

van•i•ty /vánitee/ *n.* (*pl.* **–ties**) **1** conceit about one's appearance or attainments. **2** futility or unsubstantiality (*the vanity of human achievement*). **3** ostentatious display. **4** dressing table. See synonym study at PRIDE. □ **vanity bag** (or **case**) bag or case for carrying a small mirror, makeup, etc.
■ **1** egotism, arrogance, cockiness, self-importance, pride, self-worship, *Psychol.* narcissism. **2** emptiness, worthlessness, unreality, pointlessness, folly, foolishness. **3** see OSTENTATION.

van•quish /vángkwish/ *v.tr.* literary conquer or overcome. □□ **van′quish•a•ble** *adj.* **van′quish•er** *n.*
■ see OVERCOME 1.

van•tage /vántij/ *n.* (also **van′tage point**) place affording a good view or prospect.
■ see PERCH[1] *n.* 2.

vap•id /vápid/ *adj.* insipid; lacking interest; flat; dull. □□ **va•pid′i•ty** *n.,* **vap′id•ly** *adv.* **vap′id•ness** *n.*
■ bland, watered down, wishy-washy, dreary, tedious, trite, wearisome, *colloq.* blah. □□ **vapidity** see TEDIUM.

va•por /váypər/ *n.* **1** moisture or another substance diffused or suspended in air, e.g., mist or smoke. **2** *Physics* gaseous form of a substance (cf. GAS). □ **vapor trail** trail of condensed water from an aircraft or rocket at high altitude, seen as a white streak against the sky. □□ **va′por•ous** *adj.* **va′por•ous•ly** *adv.* **va′por•y** *adj.*
■ **1** fog, haze, steam, cloud, smog, fumes.

va•por•ize /váypəriz/ *v.* convert or be converted into vapor. □□ **va′por•iz•a•ble** *adj.* (also **va′por•a•ble**). **va•por•i•za′tion** *n.* **va′por•i•zer** *v.*
■ see EVAPORATE[1] 1, 2. □□ **vaporization** evaporation. **vaporizer** see SPRAY *n.* 2.

va•ri•a•ble /váireeabəl/ • *adj.* **1** changeable; adaptable. **2** apt to vary; not constant (*variable fortunes*). **3** *Math.* (of a quantity) indeterminate; able to assume different numerical values. • *n.* variable thing or quantity. □□ **var•i•a•bil′i•ty** *n.* **var′i•a•bly** *adv.*
■ *adj.* **1** adjustable. **2** changeable, fluid, fickle, unsteady, unreliable, inconsistent. □□ **variability** see *inconstancy* (INCONSTANT).

var•i•ance /váireeəns/ *n.* **1** difference of opinion; dispute; lack of harmony (*a theory at variance with all known facts*). **2** discrepancy. **3** officially allowed exception to regulations, zoning laws, etc.
■ **1** disagreement, controversy, argument; (*at variance*) conflicting, clashing, at odds. **2** difference, disparity, inconsistency.

var•i•ant /váireeənt/ • *adj.* **1** differing in form or details from the main one (*variant spelling*). **2** having different forms. • *n.* variant form, spelling, type, etc.
■ *adj.* **1** alternative, deviant. **2** separate, distinct. • *n.* alternative, modification.

var•i•a•tion /váireeáyshən/ *n.* **1** varying. **2** departure from a former or normal condition, action, or amount, or from a standard or type (*prices are subject to variation*). **3** extent of this. **4** thing that varies. **5** *Mus.* theme in a changed or elaborated form. □□ **var•i•a′tion•al** *adj.*
■ **1** change, alteration, modification, difference. **2, 3** variety, choice; diversity, inconsistency, change of pace, deviation (from the norm). **4** see VARIANT *n.*

var•i•col•ored /váirikúlərd, vári–/ *adj.* of various colors.

var•i•cose /várikōs/ *adj.* permanently and abnormally dilated (*varicose veins*). □□ **var•i•cos•i•ty** /–kósitee/ *n.*

var•ied /váireed/ *adj.* showing variety. □□ **var′ied•ly** *adv.*
■ diverse, miscellaneous; assorted; see also VARIOUS 1.

var•ie•gat•ed /váirigaytid, váireea–, vár–/ *adj.* **1** with irregular patches of different colors. **2** *Bot.* (of plants) having leaves of two or more colors. □□ **var•i•e•ga′tion** /–gayshən/ *n.*
■ multicolored, many-colored, harlequin, polychromatic.

va•ri•e•tal /vərfət′l/ *adj.* (of wine) made from a single designated variety of grape. □□ **va•ri′e•tal•ly** *adv.*

va•ri•e•ty /vərfitee/ *n.* (*pl.* **–ties**) **1** diversity; absence of uniformity (*not enough variety in our lives*). **2** quantity or collection of different things (*for a variety of reasons*). **3** different form of a thing, quality, etc. **4** *Biol.* subspecies.
■ **1** difference, heterogeneity, contrast, many-sidedness. **2** diversity, range, assortment, medley, mixture, combination. **3** see VERSION 3.

var•i•ous /váireeəs/ *adj.* **1** different; diverse. **2** more than one; several. □□ **var′i•ous•ly** *adv.*
■ **1** distinct, individual, varied. **2** different, a number of, diverse, numerous, miscellaneous.

var•let /vaárlit/ *n.* **1** archaic or joc. rascal. **2** hist. knight's attendant. □□ **var′let•ry** *n.*

var•mint /vaármint/ *n.* dial. objectionable person or animal.

var•nish /vaárnish/ • *n.* **1** resinous solution used to give a hard shiny transparent coating. **2** external appearance or display without an underlying reality. • *v.tr.* **1** apply varnish to. **2** gloss over (a fact). □□ **var′nish•er** *n.*

var•si•ty /vaársitee/ *n.* (*pl.* **–ties**) principal

team representing a high school, college, etc., in a sport.

var•y /váiree/ v. (**-ies, -ied**) **1** tr. make different; modify; diversify. **2** intr. **a** undergo change; become or be different. **b** be of different kinds (his mood varies).
■ **1** change, reshape, adjust, reorganize. **2 a** deviate, diverge, shift. **b** change, switch, alternate, fluctuate.

vas•cu•lar /váskyələr/ adj. of or containing vessels for conveying blood or sap, etc. (vascular tissue). □□ **vas'cu•lar•ly** adv.

vas def•er•ens /vas défərenz/ n. (pl. **va•sa def•er•en•ti•a** /váysə défərénsheeə/) Anat. sperm duct from the testicle to the urethra.

vase /vays, vayz, vaaz/ n. vessel used as an ornament or container, esp. for flowers. □□ **vase'ful** n. (pl. **-fuls**).

va•sec•to•my /vəséktəmee/ n. (pl. **-mies**) surgical removal of part of each vas deferens for sterilization.

Vas•e•line /vásileen/ n. propr. type of petroleum jelly used as an ointment, lubricant, etc.

vas•o•mo•tor /váyzōmótər/ adj. causing constriction or dilatation of blood vessels.

vas•sal /vásəl/ n. **1** hist. feudal land tenant. **2** humble dependent. □□ **vas'sal•age** n.

vast /vast/ adj. immense; huge. □□ **vast'ly** adv. **vast'ness** n.
■ infinite, unlimited, indeterminate, extensive; enormous, tremendous, great, substantial, massive, voluminous, considerable, monumental, colloq. jumbo, sl. humongous. □□ **vastly** immensely, enormously, (almost) entirely, extremely, profoundly, very (much). **vastness** see SIZE[1] n.

VAT /vat, vee-ay-tée/ abbr. value-added tax.

vat /vat/ n. large tank or other vessel, esp. for holding liquids. □□ **vat'ful** n. (pl. **-fuls**).

Vat•i•can /vátikən/ n. seat of the Roman Catholic Church in Rome, Italy.

vaude•ville /váwdvil, váwdə-/ n. stage show of dances, songs, comedy acts, etc. □□ **vaude•vil•li•an** /-vílyən/ adj. & n.

vault /vawlt/ • n. **1** arched roof. **2** vaultlike covering (the vault of heaven). **3** underground chamber: **a** as a place of storage. **b** as a place of interment. **4** act of vaulting. • v. **1** intr. leap, esp. using the hands or a pole. **2** tr. spring over (a gate, etc.) in this way. **3** tr. (esp. as **vaulted**) make in the form of a vault. □□ **vault'er** n.
■ v. **1, 2** see LEAP v. **1, 2**.

vault•ing /váwlting/ n. **1** arched work in a vaulted roof or ceiling. **2** gymnastic exercise in which participants vault over obstacles. □ **vaulting horse** padded rectangular apparatus to be vaulted over by gymnasts.

vaunt /vawnt/ literary • v. **1** intr. boast; brag. **2** tr. boast of. • n. boast. □□ **vaunt'er** n. **vaunt'ing•ly** adv.

VCR abbr. videocassette recorder.

VD abbr. venereal disease.

VDT abbr. video display terminal.

've abbr. (chiefly after pronouns) = HAVE (I've, they've).

veal /veel/ n. calf's flesh as food.

vec•tor /véktər/ n. Math. & Physics **1** quantity having direction as well as magnitude (radius vector). **2** carrier of disease. □□ **vec•to•ri•al** /-táwreeəl/ adj.

Ve•da /váydə, vée-/ n. [in sing. or pl.] most ancient Hindu scriptures. □□ **Ve'dic** adj.

vee•jay /véejay/ n. video jockey.

veer /veer/ • v.intr. **1** change direction. **2** change in course, opinion, conduct, emotions, etc. • n. change of direction.
■ v. **1** see DEVIATE v.

veg /vej/ v. = VEGETATE 1.

veg•an /véjən, véegən/ • n. person who does not eat or use animal products. • adj. using or containing no animal products.

veg•e•ta•ble /véjtəbəl, véjitəbəl/ • n. **1** Bot. herbaceous plant used for food, e.g., a cabbage, potato, turnip, bean, etc. **2** colloq. **a** person who is incapable of normal intellectual activity, esp. through brain injury, etc. **b** dull or inactive person. • adj. **1** of, derived from, relating to, or comprising plant life. **2** of or relating to vegetables as food.

veg•e•tar•i•an /véjitáireeən/ • n. person who abstains from eating meat or fish. • adj. excluding animal food, esp. meat (vegetarian diet). □□ **veg•e'tar'i•an•ism** n.

veg•e•tate /véjitayt/ v.intr. **1 a** live an uneventful or monotonous life. **b** spend time lazily or passively. **2** grow as plants do. □□ **veg'e•ta•tive** adj.
■ **1** see STAGNATE n.

veg•e•ta•tion /véjitáyshən/ n. plants collectively; plant life. □□ **veg•e•ta'tion•al** adj.

veg•gie /véjee/ n. colloq. **1** vegetable. **2** vegetarian.

ve•he•ment /véeəmənt/ adj. showing or caused by strong feeling; forceful; ardent. □□ **ve'he•mence** n. **ve'he•ment•ly** adv.
■ see IMPASSIONED. □□ **vehemence** see FERVOR. **vehemently** see warmly (WARM).

ve•hi•cle /véeikəl/ n. **1** conveyance for transporting people, goods, etc., esp. on land. **2** medium for thought, feeling, or action (the stage is the best vehicle for their talents). **3** liquid, etc., as a medium for suspending pigments, drugs, etc. □□ **ve•hic•u•lar** /veehíkyələr/ adj.
■ **2** means, channel, mechanism, conduit, instrument.

veil /vayl/ • n. **1** piece of usu. transparent fabric attached to a woman's hat, etc. **2** part of a nun's headdress. **3** thing that conceals (under the veil of friendship, a veil of mist). • v.tr. **1** cover with a veil. **2** (esp. as **veiled** adj.) partly conceal (veiled threats). □ **take the veil** become a nun. □□ **veil'less** adj.
■ n. **1** covering. **3** covering, screen, camouflage, cloak, shroud; pretext. • v. disguise, shield, obscure; (veiled) hidden, masked, obscure, subtle.

vein /vayn/ n. **1 a** any of the tubes by which blood is conveyed to the heart (cf. ARTERY). **b** (in general use) any blood vessel. **2** rib of an insect's wing or of a leaf. **3** streak of a different color in wood, marble, cheese, etc. **4** fissure in rock filled with ore. **5** distinctive character or tendency; mood (spoke in a sarcastic vein). □□ **vein'less** n. **vein'like** adj. **vein'y** adj. (**vein•i•er, vein•i•est**).

■ **3** seam, stripe, thread. **4** seam, lode, deposit, pocket. **5** inclination; spirit, tone, attitude, disposition; way, manner, style.

Vel•cro /vélkrō/ *n. propr.* fastener for clothes, etc., consisting of two strips of nylon fabric, one looped and one burred, which adhere when pressed together. □□ **Vel′croed** *adj.*

veld /velt, felt/ *n.* (also **veldt**) *S.Afr.* open country; grassland.

vel•lum /véləm/ *n.* **1 a** fine parchment orig. calfskin. **b** manuscript on this. **2** smooth writing paper imitating vellum.

ve•loc•i•ty /vilósitee/ *n.* (pl. **–ties**) speed, esp. of an inanimate object in a given direction.
■ swiftness, pace, rate of speed, miles per hour, m.p.h., kilometers per hour, km/hr.

ve•lo•drome /vélədrōm/ *n.* arena or building with a track for cycling.

ve•lour /vəlŏŏr/ *n.* (also **ve•lours′**) plushlike woven fabric.

vel•um /véeləm/ *n.* (pl. **ve•la** /–lə/) *Biol. & Anat.* membrane, membranous covering, or flap.

vel•vet /vélvit/ • *n.* **1** woven fabric of silk, cotton, etc., with a thick short pile. **2** furry skin on a deer's growing antler. • *adj.* of, like, or soft as velvet. □□ **vel′vet•ed** *adj.* **vel′vet•y** *adj.*
■ □□ **velvety** see SOFT *adj.* 2.

vel•ve•teen /vélviteen/ *n.* cotton fabric with a pile like velvet.

ve•nal /véenəl/ *adj.* able to be bribed or corrupted. □□ **ve•nal′i•ty** /–nálitee/ *n.* **ve′nal•ly** *adv.*
■ buyable, avaricious, greedy, *sl.* bent; mercenary, unprincipled, *colloq.* crooked. □□ **venality** see VICE[1] 1, 2.

vend /vend/ *v.tr.* offer (small wares) for sale. □ **vending machine** machine that dispenses small articles for sale when a coin or token is inserted. □□ **ven′dor** *n.*

ven•det•ta /vendétə/ *n.* **1** blood feud. **2** prolonged bitter quarrel.
■ **2** dispute, contest, rivalry; hostility, bitterness, hatred.

ve•neer /vineer/ • *n.* **1** thin covering of fine wood, etc. **2** deceptive outward appearance of a good quality, etc. • *v.tr.* **1** apply a veneer to (wood, furniture, etc.). **2** disguise (an unattractive character, etc.) with a more attractive manner, etc.
■ *n.* **1** overlay, surface, finish, skin. **2** gloss, façade, pretense, mask, surface. • *v.* **1** see FACE *v.* 4.

ven•er•a•ble /vénərəbəl/ *adj.* entitled to respect on account of character, age, associations, etc. □□ **ven•er•a•bil′i•ty** *n.* **ven′er•a•ble•ness** *n.* **ven′er•a•bly** *adv.*
■ honorable, estimable, esteemed, revered, worshiped; old.

ven•er•ate /vénərayt/ *v.tr.* regard with deep respect. □□ **ven•er•a•tion** /–ráyshən/ *n.* **ven′er•a•tor** *n.*
■ honor, esteem, revere, worship. □□ **veneration** reverence, devotion, admiration.

ve•ne•re•al /vineereeəl/ *adj.* of sexual desire or intercourse. □ **venereal disease** any of various diseases contracted by sexual intercourse with an infected person. □□ **ve•ne′re•al•ly** *adv.*

935

■ see SEXUAL, EROTIC.

ve•ne•tian blind /vineeshən/ *n.* window blind of adjustable horizontal slats to control the light.

ven•geance /vénjəns/ *n.* punishment inflicted for wrong to oneself or to a person, etc., whose cause one supports. □ **with a vengeance** in a higher degree than was expected or desired; in the fullest sense.
■ revenge, retaliation, retribution. □ **with a vengeance** violently, ferociously, vehemently; to the utmost *or* fullest *or* limit, enthusiastically.

venge•ful /vénjfŏŏl/ *adj.* vindictive; seeking vengeance. See synonym study at VINDICTIVE. □□ **venge′ful•ly** *adv.* **venge′ful•ness** *n.*
■ see VINDICTIVE 1. □□ **vengefulness** see RANCOR.

ve•ni•al /véeneeəl/ *adj.* (of a sin or fault) pardonable; not mortal. □□ **ve•ni•al•i•ty** /–neeálitee/ *n.* **ve′ni•al•ly** *adv.*
■ forgivable, tolerated, minor, insignificant, unimportant.

ven•i•son /vénisən, –zən/ *n.* deer's flesh as food.

Venn di•a•gram /ven/ *n.* diagram of usu. circular areas representing mathematical sets, the areas intersecting where they have elements in common.

ven•om /vénəm/ *n.* **1** poisonous fluid of snakes, scorpions, etc., usu. transmitted by a bite or sting. **2** malignity. □□ **ven′om•ous** *adj.* **ven′om•ous•ly** *adv.* See synonym study at VINDICTIVE.
■ **1** toxin. **2** malice, ill will, animosity, hatred, hostility, antagonism, spite, bitterness, virulence, *sl.* gall.

ve•nous /véenəs/ *adj.* of, full of, or contained in veins. □□ **ve•nos•i•ty** /vinósitee/ *n.* **ve′nous•ly** *adv.*

vent[1] /vent/ • *n.* **1** opening allowing the passage of air, etc. **2** outlet; free expression (*gave vent to their indignation*). • *v.* **1** *tr.* **a** make a vent in. **b** provide (a machine) with a vent. **2** *tr.* give free expression to (*vented my anger on the cat*). **3** *tr. & intr.* discharge. □ **vent one's spleen on** scold or illtreat without cause. □□ **vent′less** *adj.*
■ *n.* **1** slit, slot, hole, aperture, orifice, outlet, duct, pipe. **2** free play *or* passage. • *v.* **2** verbalize, articulate, declare, voice, let loose, **3** release, emit, send out, *colloq.* unload.

vent[2] /vent/ *n.* slit in a garment, esp. in the lower edge of the back of a coat.

ven•ti•late /véntlayt/ *v.tr.* **1** cause air to circulate freely in (a room, etc.). **2** air (a question, grievance, etc.). **3** *Med.* **a** oxygenate (the blood). **b** admit or force air into (the lungs). □□ **ven•ti•la•tion** /–láyshən/ *n.*

ven•ti•la•tor /véntilaytər/ *n.* **1** appliance or aperture for ventilating a room, etc. **2** *Med.* = RESPIRATOR 2.

ven•tral /véntrəl/ *adj. Anat. & Zool.* of or on the abdomen (cf. DORSAL). □□ **ven′tral•ly** *adv.*

ven•tri•cle /véntrikəl/ *n. Anat.* hollow part of an organ, esp. in the brain or heart. □□ **ven•tric•u•lar** /–trikyələr/ *adj.*

ven•tril•o•quism /ventrílǝkwizǝm/ n. skill of speaking without moving the lips, esp. as entertainment. □□ **ven•tril'o•quist** v.intr. **ven•tril'o•quize** v.intr.

ven•ture /vénchǝr/ • n. **1** risky undertaking. **2** commercial speculation. • v. **1** intr. dare; not be afraid (did not venture to stop them). **2** intr. dare to go (out), esp. outdoors. **3** tr. dare to put forward (an opinion, suggestion, etc.). **4 a** tr. expose to risk; stake (a bet, etc.). **b** intr. take risks. **5** intr. dare to engage in, etc. (ventured on a longer journey).
■ n. chance, hazardous undertaking, enterprise, speculation, gamble. • v. **1** make bold, presume, take the liberty, try. **3** risk, hazard, offer, advance. **4 a** jeopardize, endanger; wager, chance.

ven•ture•some /vénchǝrsǝm/ adj. **1** disposed to take risks. **2** risky. □□ **ven'ture•some•ly** adv. **ven'ture•some•ness** n.
■ **1** daring, bold, courageous, audacious, daredevil, fearless. **2** rash, reckless, hazardous.

ven•ue /vényoo/ n. **1** place for a sports event, meeting, concert, etc. **2** Law hist. place where a jury must be gathered and a cause tried (orig. the neighborhood of the crime, etc.).
■ **1** see LOCALE.

Ve•nus /véenǝs/ n. **1** planet second from the sun in the solar system. **2** poet. **a** (pl. Ve'nus•es) beautiful woman. **b** sexual love; amorous influences or desires. □□ **Ve•nu•si•an** /vinóoshǝn, –sheeǝn, –zeeǝn, –nyoo–/ adj. & n.

ve•ra•cious /vǝráyshǝs/ adj. **1** speaking the truth. **2** (of a statement, etc.) true. □□ **ve•ra'cious•ly** adv. **ve•rac'i•ty** n.
■ **1** see TRUTHFUL 1. **2** see TRUTHFUL 2. □□ **veracity** see TRUTH 1.

ve•ran•da /vǝrándǝ/ n. = PORCH[2].

verb /vǝrb/ n. Gram. word used to indicate an action, state, or occurrence (e.g., hear, become, happen).

ver•bal /vórbǝl/ • adj. **1** of words (made a verbal distinction). **2** oral; not written (gave a verbal statement). **3** Gram. of or in the nature of a verb (verbal inflections). **4** talkative. • n. Gram. **1** = verbal noun. **2** word(s) functioning as a verb. □ **verbal noun** Gram.noun derived from a verb (e.g., smoking in smoking is forbidden: see -ING[1]). □□ **ver'bal•ly** adv.
■ adj. **1** lexical; attrib. word, vocabulary. **2** spoken, vocal, articulated, word-of-mouth.

ver•bal•ize /vórbǝliz/ v. **1** tr. express in words. **2** intr. be verbose. □□ **ver•bal•i•za'tion** n. **ver'bal•iz•er** n.
■ **1** see EXPRESS[1] 1, 2. □□ **verbalization** see EXPRESSION 1.

ver•ba•tim /vǝrbáytim/ adv. & adj. in exactly the same words; word for word (copied it verbatim).
■ adv. literally, precisely, accurately, faithfully, to the letter, strictly. • adj. literal, precise, accurate, faithful, strict.

ver•be•na /vǝrbéenǝ/ n. plant bearing clusters of fragrant flowers.

ver•bi•age /vórbeeij/ n. needless accumulation of words.
■ verbosity; see hot air.

ver•bose /vǝrbós/ adj. using more words than are needed. □□ **ver•bose'ly** adv. **ver•bos•i•ty** /–bósitee/ n.
■ see WORDY. □□ **verbosity** see RHETORIC 2.

ver•dant /vórd'nt/ adj. **1** green, esp. bright and fresh-colored. **2** (of a person) unsophisticated. □□ **ver•dan•cy** /–d'nsee/ n. **ver'dant•ly** adv.
■ **1** see LUSH[1] 1. **2** raw, green.

ver•dict /vórdikt/ n. **1** decision on an issue of fact in a civil or criminal cause or an inquest. **2** decision; judgment.
■ see DECISION 2, 3.

ver•di•gris /vórdigrees, –gris, –gree/ n. green substance that forms on copper and its alloys.

ver•dure /vórjǝr/ n. **1** green vegetation. **2** the greenness of this. □□ **ver'dured** adj.

verge[1] /vǝrj/ n. **1** edge or border. **2** extreme limit beyond which something happens (on the verge of tears). See synonym study at BORDER.
■ **1** boundary, margin, brink. **2** (on the verge of) about to, ready to, close to, on the brink of; preparing to.

verge[2] /vǝrj/ v.intr. **1** incline downward or in a specified direction (the now verging sun, verge to a close). **2** [foll. by on] border on; approach closely (verging on the ridiculous).
■ **1** lean, tend, stretch, turn; draw, move. **2** (verge on) come close to or near (to).

ver•i•fy /vérifi/ v.tr. (–fies, –fied) establish the truth or correctness of by examination (must verify the statement, verified my figures). □□ **ver•i•fi'a•ble** adj. **ver•i•fi'a•bly** adv. **ver•i•fi•ca'tion** n. **ver'i•fi•er** n.
■ affirm, confirm, check out, testify to, vouch for, support, substantiate, demonstrate, authenticate, certify, guarantee. □□ **verifiable** see DEMONSTRABLE.

ver•i•ly /vérilee/ adv. archaic really; truly.

ver•i•si•mil•i•tude /vérisimílitood, –tyood/ n. appearance of being true or real.

ver•i•ta•ble /véritǝbǝl/ adj. real; rightly so called (a veritable feast). See synonym study at GENUINE. □□ **ver'i•ta•bly** adv.
■ true, genuine, proper, actual.

ver•i•ty /véritee/ n. (pl. –ties) **1** true statement, esp. one of fundamental import. **2** truth.

ver•mi•cel•li /vórmichélee/ n. pasta made in long slender threads.

ver•mi•cide /vórmisīd/ n. substance that kills worms.

ver•mic•u•lite /vǝrmíkyǝlīt/ n. hydrous silicate mineral used as an insulation material and as a medium for plant growth.

ver•mi•form /vérmifawrm/ adj. wormshaped. □ **vermiform appendix** see APPENDIX 1.

ver•mil•ion /vǝrmílyǝn/ • n. **1** cinnabar. **2 a** brilliant red pigment made by grinding this or artificially. **b** color of this. • adj. of this color.

ver•min /vórmin/ n. [usu. treated as pl.] **1** mammals, insects, and birds injurious to game, crops, etc. **2** vile persons. □□ **ver'min•ous** adj.

ver•mouth /vərmo͞oth/ *n.* wine flavored with aromatic herbs.

ver•nac•u•lar /vərnákyələr/ • *n.* **1** language or dialect of a particular country. **2** language of a particular clan or group. **3** plain, everyday speech. See synonym study at DIALECT. • *adj.* (of language) native; not foreign or formal. □□ **ver•nac'u•lar•ism** *n.* **ver•nac'u•lar•ly** *adv.*

■ *n.* **1** tongue. **2** jargon, idiom, speech, *colloq.* lingo. • *adj.* local, regional, indigenous; pópular, colloquial, familiar, everyday; plain, simple.

ver•nal /vórnəl/ *adj.* of, in, or appropriate to spring (*vernal breezes*). □ **vernal equinox** see EQUINOX. □□ **ver'nal•ly** *adv.*

ver•ni•er /vórneeər/ *n.* small, movable graduated scale for reading fractional parts on a fixed scale of a barometer, etc.

ver•sa•tile /vórsət'l, –tīl/ *adj.* **1** turning easily or readily from one subject or occupation to another; capable of dealing with many subjects (*a versatile mind*). **2** (of a device, etc.) having many uses. □□ **ver•sa•til'i•ty** /-tílhtee/ *n.*

■ **1** adaptable, resourceful, all-around, multifaceted, handy. **2** all-purpose, handy, flexible. □□ **versatility** adaptability, flexibility, adjustability.

verse /vərs/ • *n.* **1 a** poetry. **b** particular type of this (*English verse*). **2** stanza of a poem or song. **3** each of the short numbered divisions of the Bible or other scripture. • *v tr.* [usu. *refl.*; foll. by *in*] instruct; make knowledgeable.
■ *n.* **1** versification; see also POEM.

versed /vərst/ *predic.adj.* [foll. by *in*] experienced or skilled in; knowledgeable about.

■ (*versed in*) well read in, (well-)informed about, (well-)trained in, (well-) educated in, literate in, competent in, accomplished in, expert in *or* at, familiar with

ver•si•fy /vórsifī/ *v.* (**-fies, -fied**) **1** *tr.* turn into or express in verse. **2** *intr.* compose verses. □□ **ver•si•fi•ca'tion** *n.* **ver'si•fi•er** *n.*

ver•sion /vórzhən, –shən/ *n.* **1** account of a matter from a particular point of view (*told them my version of the incident*). **2** book, etc., in a particular edition or translation (*Authorized Version*). **3** form or variant of a thing as performed, adapted, etc. □□ **ver'sion•al** *adj.*

■ **1** story, report, description, rendition, interpretation, understanding, side. **2** adaptation, interpretation. **3** variation, style, adaptation, rendition, interpretation.

ver•so /vórsō/ *n.* (*pl.* **-sos**) **1 a** left-hand page of an open book. **b** back of a printed leaf (opp. RECTO). **2** reverse of a coin.

ver•sus /vórsəs, –səz/ *prep.* against. ¶Abbr.: **v., vs.**

ver•te•bra /vórtibrə/ *n.* (*pl.* **ver•te•brae** /-bray, -hree/) each segment of the backbone. □□ **ver'te•bral** *adj.*

ver•te•brate /vórtibrət, -brayt/ • *n.* animal having a spinal column, including mammals, birds, reptiles, amphibians, and fishes. • *adj.* of or relating to the vertebrates.

ver•tex /vórteks/ *n.* (*pl.* **ver•ti•ces** /-tiseez/ or **ver•tex•es**) **1** highest point; top or apex.

2 *Geom.* **a** each angular point of a polygon, etc. **b** meeting point of lines that form an angle.

■ **1** tip, extremity, zenith, apogee, peak, acme, summit.

ver•ti•cal /vórtikəl/ • *adj.* **1** at right angles to a horizontal plane; perpendicular. **2** in a direction from top to bottom. **3** of or at the vertex or highest point. • *n.* vertical line or plane. □□ **ver•ti•cal•i•ty** /-kálitee/ *n.* **ver'ti•cal•ly** *adv.*

■ *adj.* **1, 2** see PERPENDICULAR *adj.* □□ **vertically** see UPRIGHT *adv.*

ver•tig•i•nous /vərtíjinəs/ *adj.* of or causing vertigo. □□ **ver•tig'i•nous•ly** *adv.*

ver•ti•go /vórtigō/ *n.* condition with a sensation of whirling and a tendency to lose balance; dizziness; giddiness.

■ light-headedness, instability, unsteadiness; *colloq.* wooziness.

verve /vərv/ *n.* enthusiasm; vigor.

■ spirit, vitality, life, liveliness, animation, sparkle, energy, exuberance, zeal, gusto, *colloq.* pep, zing, *sl.* pizzazz, oomph.

ver•y /vérée/ • *adv.* **1** in a high degree (*did it very easily, had a very bad cough*). **2** in the fullest sense [foll. by *own* or superl. *adj.* *at the very latest, my very own room*]. • *adj.* **1** [usu. prec. by *the, this, his*, etc.] actual; truly such (emphasizing identity, significance, or extreme degree: *the very thing we need, those were his very words*). **2** mere; sheer (*the very idea of it was horrible*). □ **not very 1** in a low degree. **2** far from being.

■ *adv.* **1** extremely, really, to a great extent, deeply, acutely, perfectly, thoroughly, unusually, especially, absolutely, completely, *colloq.* damn(ed), terribly, awfully, *sl.* plumb. • *adj.* **1** exact, precise; selfsame, particular; real. **2** least, bare, barest; utter, pure, simple.

ves•i•cle /vésikəl/ *n.* **1** *Anat., Zool.,* & *Bot.* small bladder, bubble, or hollow structure. **2** *Med.* blister. □□ **ve•sic•u•lar** /-síkyələr/ *adj.* **ve•sic•u•late** /-síkyəlayt/ *adj.* **ve•sic•u•la•tion** /-láyshən/ *n.*

ves•pers /véspərz/ *n.* evening prayer service.

ves•sel /vésəl/ *n.* **1** hollow receptacle esp. for liquid, e.g., a cask, cup, pot, bottle, or dish. **2** ship or boat, esp. a large one. **3 a** *Anat.* duct or canal, etc., holding or conveying blood or other fluid, esp. = *blood vessel.* **b** *Bot.* woody duct carrying or containing sap, etc.

■ **1** container, utensil, repository. **2** craft, ark. **3** tube; vein.

vest /vest/ • *n.* waist-length close-fitting, sleeveless garment, often worn under a suit jacket, etc. • *v.* **1** *tr.* [esp. in *passive*; foll. by *with*] bestow (powers, authority, etc.) on (a person). **2** *intr.* [foll. by *in*] (of property, a right, etc.) come into the possession of (a person). □ **vested interest 1** *Law* interest (usu. in land or money held in trust) recognized as belonging to a person. **2** personal interest in a state of affairs, usu. with an expectation of gain. **vest-pocket** small enough to fit into a pocket.

ves•tal /vést'l/ *adj.* chaste; pure. ■ **vestal**

virgin *Rom. Antiq.* virgin consecrated to the goddess Vesta, vowed to chastity, and charged with maintaining the sacred fire burning on the goddess's altar.

■ see PURE 2, 3.

ves•ti•bule /véstibyŏŏl/ *n.* hall or lobby next to the outer door of a building.

■ see HALL 1.

ves•tige /véstij/ *n.* **1** trace or sign (*vestiges of an earlier civilization, found no vestige of their presence*). **2** slight amount; particle (*without a vestige of clothing*). **3** atrophied part or organ of an animal or plant. See synonym study at TRACE. □□ **ves•tig•i•al** /-tijeeəl, -jəl/ *adj.*

■ **1** suggestion, hint, evidence, mark; scrap, fragment, remains. **2** trace, suggestion, suspicion, touch; iota, speck, scrap, shred, bit, fragment. □□ **vestigial** imperfect, undeveloped, incomplete.

vest•ment /véstmənt/ *n.* official robes, esp. those worn by clergy, choristers, etc., during divine service.

ves•try /véstree/ *n.* (*pl.* **–tries**) **1** chasuble; church room or building for keeping vestments in. **2** *hist.* a meeting of parishioners for parochial business. **b** parishioners meeting this way. □□ **ves'tral** *adj.*

vet[1] /vet/ • *n. colloq.* veterinarian. • *v.tr.* (**vet'ted, vet•ting**) make a critical examination of (a scheme, work, candidate, etc.).

■ *v.* review, investigate, scrutinize, inspect; authenticate; check out, *colloq.* size up.

vet[2] /vet/ *n. colloq.* veteran.

vetch /vech/ *n.* plant of the pea family largely used for silage or fodder.

vet•er•an /vétərən, vétrən/ *n.* **1** person with long experience in esp. military service or an occupation (*war veteran, veteran marksman*). **2** ex-serviceman; ex-servicewoman. □ **Veteran's Day** US holiday on November 11 honoring all veterans.

■ **1** old hand, past master, trouper, *colloq.* warhorse, old-timer. **2** returned soldier, *colloq.* vet.

vet•er•i•nar•i•an /vétərináreeən, vétrə–/ *n.* doctor who practices veterinary medicine or surgery.

vet•er•i•nar•y /vétərineree, vétrə–/ *adj.* of or for diseases and injuries of animals, or their treatment.

ve•to /véetō/ • *n.* (*pl.* **–toes**) **1 a** right to reject a bill, resolution, etc. **b** such a rejection. **2** prohibition (*put one's veto on a proposal*). • *v.tr.* (**–toes, –toed**) **1** exercise a veto against (a measure, etc.). **2** forbid authoritatively. □□ **ve'to•er** *n.*

■ *n.* denial, stoppage, block, prevention, interdiction, taboo. • *v.* stop, ban, turn down, say no to, disallow, rule out, prevent, prohibit, *colloq.* kill, *sl.* nix.

vex /veks/ *v.tr.* **1** anger by a petty annoyance; irritate. **2** *archaic* grieve; afflict. □□ **vex'er** *n.* **vex'ing** *adj.* **vex'ing•ly** *adv.*

■ **1** see ANGER *v.* □□ **vexing** see IRKSOME.

vex•a•tion /veksáyshən/ *n.* **1** vexing; being vexed. **2** annoying or distressing thing. □□ **vex•a•tious** /-áyshəs/ *adj.*

■ **1** see ANGER *n.* **2** see PEST 1, WORRY *n.* 1. □□ **vexatious** see IRKSOME.

vexed /vekst/ *adj.* **1** irritated; angered. **2** (of a problem, issue, etc.) difficult and much discussed; problematic. □□ **vex'ed•ly** *adv.*

VF *abbr.* (also **V.F.**) **1** video frequency. **2** visual field.

VHF *abbr.* very high frequency.

VI *abbr.* Virgin Islands.

vi•a /véeə, víə/ *prep.* by way of; through.

■ by means of; see also THROUGH *prep.* 4.

vi•a•ble /víəbəl/ *adj.* **1** (of a plan, etc.) feasible; practicable esp. from an economic standpoint. **2** (of a fetus or newborn child) capable of maintaining life. □□ **vi•a•bil'i•ty** *n.* **vi'a•bly** *adv.*

■ **1** sustainable, reasonable, applicable, workable, possible, achievable.

vi•a•duct /víədukt/ *n.* **1** long bridge esp. a series of arches, carrying a road or railroad across a valley, etc. **2** such a road or railroad.

vi•al /víəl/ *n.* small vessel esp. for medicines. □□ **vi'al•ful** *n.* (*pl.* **–fuls**).

vi•and /víənd/ *n. formal* **1** article of food. **2** [in *pl.*] provisions; victuals.

vibes /vībz/ *n.pl. colloq.* **1** = VIBRATION 2. **2** = VIBRAPHONE.

■ **1** sensations, resonance(s), rapport, empathy, sympathy.

vi•brant /víbrənt/ *adj.* **1** vibrating. **2** (of a person or thing) thrilling; quivering (*vibrant with emotion*). **3** (of sound) resonant. **4** (of color) vivid. □□ **vi•bran•cy** /–rənsee/ *n.* **vi' brant•ly** *adv.*

■ **2** see ANIMATED 1. **4** see RICH 6.

vi•bra•phone /víbrəfōn/ *n.* percussion instrument of tuned metal bars with motor-driven resonators and metal tubes giving a vibrato effect. □□ **vi'bra•phon•ist** *n.*

vi•brate /víbrayt/ *v.* **1** *intr. & tr.* move or cause to move continuously and rapidly to and fro; oscillate. **2** *intr.* (of a sound) throb; continue to be heard. **3** *intr.* [foll. by *with*] quiver; thrill (*vibrating with passion*). **4** *intr.* (of a pendulum) swing to and fro. □□ **vi'bra•tor** *n.* **vi•bra•to•ry** /–brətawree/ *adj.*

■ **1, 3** shiver, fluctuate, shake, tremble, throb, pulsate. **2** pulse, reverberate, resonate. **4** oscillate.

vi•bra•tion /víbráyshən/ *n.* **1** vibrating; oscillation. **2** [in *pl.*; also **vibes**] characteristic atmosphere or feeling in a place, regarded as communicable to people present in it. □□ **vi• bra'tion•al** *adj.*

vi•bra•to /vibraátō/ *n. Mus.* rapid slight variation in pitch in singing or playing an instrument, producing a tremulous effect (cf. TREMOLO).

vi•bur•num /víbórnəm, vee–/ *n. Bot.* any of various shrubs usu. with white flowers, of the honeysuckle family.

vic•ar /víkər/ *n.* **1** (in the Church of England) parish priest receiving a stipend rather than tithes (cf. RECTOR). **2** *RC Ch.* deputy of a bishop.

vic•ar•age /víkərij/ *n.* residence of a vicar.

vi•car•i•ous /víkáireeəs/ *adj.* **1** experienced in the imagination through another person (*vicarious pleasure*). **2** acting or done for another (*vicarious suffering*). **3** deputed; delegated (*vicarious authority*). □□ vi•car'i•ous•ly *adv.* vi•car'i•ous•ness *n.*

■ **1** indirect, secondhand. **2** substitute(d), surrogate. **3** commissioned, assigned.

vice[1] /vīs/ *n.* **1 a** evil or immoral conduct. **b** particular form of this, esp. prostitution, drugs, etc. **2** defect of character or behavior (*drunkenness was not among his vices*). See synonym study at SIN. □ **vice squad** police department enforcing laws against prostitution, drug abuse, etc. □□ vice'less *adj.*

■ **1** corruption, depravity, villainy, wrongdoing, sin, transgression. **2** fault, shortcoming, weakness, foible.

vice[2] /vīsee, -sə/ *prep.* in the place of; in succession to.

vice- /vīs/ *comb. form* forming nouns meaning: **1** as a substitute or deputy for (*vice chancellor*). **2** next in rank to (*vice admiral*).

vice pres•i•dent /vīs-prézidənt, –dent/ *n.* official ranking below and deputizing for a president. □□ vice' pres'i•den•cy *n.* (*pl.* –cies). vice' pres•i•den'tial /–dénshəl/ *adj.*

vice•roy /vísroy/ *n.* sovereign's deputy ruler in a colony, province, etc.

vice ver•sa /vísə vársə, vīs/ *adv.* with the order of the terms changed; the other way around (*from left to right or vice versa*).

■ conversely, to or on the contrary, the reverse.

vi•chys•soise /vísheeswáhz, vée–/ *n.* creamy soup of leeks and potatoes, usu. served chilled.

vi•cin•i•ty /visínitee/ *n.* (*pl.* –ties) **1** surrounding district. **2** [foll. by *to*] nearness or closeness of place or relationship.

■ **1** area, neighborhood, locale, territory, region, proximity.

vi•cious /víshəs/ *adj.* **1** bad-tempered, spiteful. **2** violent. **3** of the nature of or addicted to vice. **4** (of language or reasoning, etc.) faulty or unsound. □ vicious circle self-perpetuating, harmful sequence of cause and effect. □□ vi'cious•ly *adv.* vi'cious•ness *n.*

■ **1** savage, ferocious, brutal; malicious, nasty, bitter, vindictive, *sl.* rotten, bitchy. **2** see SAVAGE *adj.* **1**. **3** immoral, depraved, wicked, shameful, sinful. □□ viciousness see BARBARITY 1.

vi•cis•si•tude /visísitood, –tyood/ *n.* change of circumstances, esp. variation of fortune.

■ alteration, variety, shift, contrast, fluctuation, unpredictability, uncertainty; (*vicissitudes*) ups and downs.

vic•tim /víktim/ *n.* **1** person injured or killed as a result of an event or circumstance. **2** person or thing injured or destroyed in pursuit of an object or in gratification of a passion, etc. **3** prey; dupe (*fell victim to a con man*).

■ **1, 2** sufferer, casualty, fatality, martyr. **3** quarry, target; fool, butt, fair game, *colloq.* chump, *sl.* sucker, patsy.

vic•tim•ize /víktimīz/ *v.tr.* make (a person, etc.) a victim. □□ vic•tim•i•za'tion *n.* vic'tim•i•zer *n.*

■ prey on, pick on, take advantage of, oppress; cheat, outwit, *colloq.* outsmart, suck in, *sl.* bilk. □□ victimization see *persecution* (PERSECUTE).

vic•tor /víktər/ *n.* winner in battle or in a contest.

■ champion, conqueror, prizewinner, *colloq.* top dog.

Vic•to•ri•an /viktáwreeən/ • *adj.* **1** of the time of Queen Victoria. **2** prudish; morally strict. • *n.* person of this time. □□ Vic•to'ri•an•ism *n.*

vic•to•ri•ous /viktáwreeəs/ *adj.* **1** conquering; triumphant. **2** marked by victory (*victorious day*). □□ vic•to'ri•ous•ly *adv.*

■ **1** successful, champion, prevailing, winning.

vic•to•ry /víktəree/ *n.* (*pl.* –ries) defeat of an enemy or an opponent.

■ triumph, superiority, success, mastery, winning; conquest.

vict•ual /vít'l/ *n.* [usu. in *pl.*] food, provisions, esp. as prepared for use. □□ vict'ual•less *adj.*

■ (*victuals*) see FOOD 1.

vi•cu•ña /vikoonə, –nyə, –kyoo–, vi–/ *n.* (also vi•cu'na) **1** S. American mammal, related to the llama, with fine silky wool. **2** its wool or an imitation.

vi•de•li•cet /videliset, vī–/ *adv.* = VIZ.

vid•e•o /videeō/ • *adj.* **1** relating to the recording, reproducing, or broadcasting of visual images, and usu. sound, on magnetic tape. **2** relating to the broadcasting of television pictures. • *n.* (*pl.* –os) **1** such recording, reproducing, or broadcasting. **2** *colloq.* = videocassette recorder. **3** a movie, etc., on videotape. • *v.tr.* (–oes, –oed) make a video recording of. □ video display terminal Computing monitor. video game game played by electronically manipulating images produced by a computer program on a television screen. video jockey person who introduces music videos, as on television.

■ *n.* **3** see TAPE *n.* 4, FILM *n.* 3. • *v.* see FILM *v.* 1.

vid•e•o•cas•sette /videeōkaset, –kəsét/ *n.* cassette of videotape. □ videocassette recorder apparatus for recording and playing videotapes.

vid•e•o•tape /videeōtayp/ • *n.* magnetic tape for recording moving pictures and sound. • *v.tr.* record on this. □ videotape recorder = videocassette recorder.

■ *n.* see TAPE *n.* 4. • *v.* see FILM *v.* 1.

vie /vī/ *v.intr.* (vy•ing) [often foll. by *with*] compete; strive for superiority (*vied with each other for recognition*).

■ contend, struggle.

Vi•en•nese /veeəneez/ • *adj.* of, relating to, or associated with Vienna in Austria. • *n.* (*pl.* same) native or citizen of Vienna.

Vi•et•nam•ese /vee-étnəmeez/ • *adj.* of or relating to Vietnam in SE Asia. • *n.* (*pl.* same) **1** native or national of Vietnam. **2** language of Vietnam.

view /vyoo/ • *n.* **1** range of vision (*came into view*). **2** what is seen from a particular point; scene or prospect (*room with a view*). **3** inspection by the eye or mind. **4 a** opinion (*holds strong views on morality*). **b** manner of considering a thing (*took a long-term view of*) it). • *v.* **1** *tr.* look at; survey visually; inspect (*we are going to view the house*). **2** *tr.* examine; survey mentally (*different ways of viewing a subject*). **3** *tr.* consider (*does not view the matter in the same light*). **4** *intr.* watch. **5** *tr.* see. □ **have in view 1** have as one's object. **2** bear (a circumstance) in mind. **in view of** considering. **with a view to** with the hope or intention of. □□ **view'a•ble** *adj.*

■ *n.* **1** sight. **2** outlook, aspect, perspective, vista, panorama, spectacle; landscape. **3** survey, observation, contemplation. **4** angle, approach, position, judgment, belief, attitude, impression. • *v.* **1** see, watch, observe, scrutinize, contemplate, regard, witness. **2** see SURVEY *v.* 1, 2. **3** regard, think of, hold, estimate, assess. □ **in view of** in light of, having regard to, because of, on account of. **with a view to** with the aim *or* objective *or* expectation *or* dream of. □□ **viewable** see PUBLIC *adj.* 3, OPEN *adj.* 8, 9.

view•er /vyōŏər/ *n.* **1** person who views. **2** device for looking at film transparencies, etc.

view•er•ship /vyōŏərship/ *n.* viewing audience, especially of a television program.

view•find•er /vyōŏfīndər/ *n.* device on a camera showing the area covered by the lens in taking a photograph.

view•point /vyōŏpoynt/ *n.* point of view.
■ standpoint, attitude, position, perspective.

vig•il /vijil/ *n.* **1** keeping awake during the night, etc., esp. to keep watch or pray (*keep vigil*). **2** *Eccl.* eve of a festival or holy day.
■ **1** wake, see also WATCH *n.* 2.

vig•i•lance /vijilans/ *n.* watchfulness; caution. □□ **vig'i•lant** *adj.*
■ alertness, observance, circumspection, care. □□ **vigilant** watchful, alert, sharp, guarded, awake, wary, on the lookout, eagle-eyed, on one's toes.

SYNONYM STUDY: vigilant

CAREFUL, CAUTIOUS, CIRCUMSPECT, WARY, WATCHFUL, ALERT. All of these adjectives connote being on the lookout for danger or opportunity. **Watchful** is the most general term, meaning closely observant (*a watchful young man who noticed everything*). If you're **vigilant**, you are *watchful* for a purpose (*to be vigilant in the presence of one's enemies*), and **wary** suggests being on the lookout for treachery or trickery (*wary of his neighbor's motives in offering to move the fence*). If you're **alert**, you are quick to apprehend a danger, an opportunity, or an emergency (*she was much more alert after a good night's sleep*), and if you're **careful**, you may be able to avoid danger or error altogether. **Cautious** and **circumspect** also emphasize the avoidance of danger or unpleasant situations. To be *circumspect* is to be *watchful* in all directions and with regard to all possible consequences; to be *cautious* is to guard against contingencies (*a cautious approach*).

---

vig•i•lan•te /vijilántee/ *n.* member of a self-appointed group maintaining order.

vi•gnette /vinyét/ *n.* **1** short description or character sketch. **2** illustration or design, esp. on a book's title page without a definite border. **3** photograph showing only the head and shoulders with the background shaded off. **4** brief scene in a movie, etc. □□ **vi•gnet'tist** *n.*
■ **1** see PROFILE *n.* 2.

vig•or /vígər/ *n.* **1** physical strength or energy. **2** healthy growth. **3 a** mental strength. **b** forcefulness. □□ **vig'or•ous** *adj.* **vig'or•ous•ly** *adv.*
■ **1** vitality, resilience, power, potency, endurance, spirit, exuberance, brio, zest, *colloq.* spunk, pep, get-up-and-go, *sl.* pizzazz, oomph. **2** see HEALTH 1. □□ **vigorous** energetic, active, dynamic, forceful, strong, hardy, vital, fit, *colloq.* peppy, full of get-up-and-go, zippy, snappy. **vigorously** energetically, actively, vivaciously, briskly, robustly, strenuously, *colloq.* like mad, like crazy.

Vi•king /víking/ • *n.* of the Scandinavian seafaring pirates and traders who raided and settled in parts of NW Europe in the 8th–11th c. • *adj.* of the Vikings or their time.

vile /vīl/ *adj.* **1** disgusting. **2** morally base; depraved. **3** *colloq.* abominably bad (*vile weather*). See synonym study at DEPRAVED. □□ **vile'ly** *adv.* **vile'ness** *n.*
■ **1** nasty, sickening, offensive, objectionable, revolting. **2** contemptible, degenerate, bad, immoral, sinful, despicable, heinous, corrupt, miserable, shameful. **3** atrocious, foul, unpleasant, miserable, *colloq.* lousy, *sl.* rotten. □□ **vileness** see EVIL *n.* 2.

vil•i•fy /vílifī/ *v.tr.* (**-fies, -fied**) defame; speak evil of. See synonym study at MALIGN. □□ **vil•i•fi•ca'tion** *n.* **vil'i•fi•er** *n.*
■ deprecate, disparage, discredit, defile, smear, tarnish, malign, run down, badmouth, *sl.* knock. □□ **vilification** see SLANDER *n.*

vil•la /víla/ *n.* country house, esp. a luxurious one.

vil•lage /vílij/ *n.* **1 a** group of houses and associated buildings, larger than a hamlet and smaller than a town, esp. in a rural area. **b** inhabitants of a village regarded as a community. **2** small municipality with limited corporate powers. □□ **vil'lag•er** *n.*

vil•lain /vílən/ *n.* **1** person guilty or capable of great wickedness. **2** (in a play, etc.) character whose evil actions or motives are important in the plot. □□ **vil'lain•ous** *adj.* **vil'lain•y** *n.*
■ wretch, evildoer, criminal, malefactor, scoundrel, cur, snake in the grass, *colloq.* crook, baddie. □□ **villainous** treacherous, unscrupulous, corrupt, criminal; contemptible, depraved, atrocious, immoral, wicked, *colloq.* crooked.

vil•lein /vílin, –ayn, viláyn/ *n. hist.* feudal tenant entirely subject to a lord or attached to a manor. □□ **vil'lein•age** /vílinij/ *n.*

vil•lus /víləs/ *n.* (*pl.* **vil•li** /–lī/) **1** *Anat.* each of the short, fingerlike processes on some membranes, esp. on the mucous membrane of the small intestine. **2** *Bot.* [in *pl.*] long, soft hairs covering fruit, flowers, etc. □□ **vil•lous** /–əs/ *adj.*

vim /vim/ *n. colloq.* vigor.
■ see VIGOR 1.

vin·ai·grette /vínigrét/ *n.* salad dressing of oil, vinegar, and seasoning.

vin·di·cate /víndikayt/ *v.tr.* **1** clear of blame or suspicion. **2** establish the existence, merits, or justice of (one's courage, conduct, assertion, etc.). **3** justify. □□ **vin·di·ca·tion** /-káyshən/ *n.* **vin·di·ca·tive** /vindíkativ, vindíkaytiv/ *adj.* **vin·di·ca·tor** *n.*
■ **1** exonerate, absolve, acquit, excuse. **2** uphold, prove, defend. **3** defend, bear out, back up. □□ **vindication** see DEFENSE *n.*

vin·dic·tive /vindíktiv/ *adj.* **1** tending to seek revenge. **2** spiteful. See synonym study at ABSOLVE. □□ **vin·dic·tive·ly** *adv.* **vin·dic· tive·ness** *n.*
■ **1** avenging, retaliatory, punitive. **2** unforgiving, malicious, resentful. □□ **vindictiveness** see REVENGE *n.*, RANCOR.

SYNONYM STUDY: vindictive

RANCOROUS, SPITEFUL, VENGEFUL, VENOMOUS. Someone who is motivated by a desire to get even might be described as **vindictive**, a word that suggests harboring grudges for imagined wrongs (*a vindictive person who had alienated friends and neighbors alike*). **Spiteful** is a stronger term, implying a bitter or vicious vindictiveness (*a spiteful child who broke the toy she had been forced to share*). **Vengeful** implies a strong urge to actually seek vengeance (*vengeful after losing her husband in hit-and-run accident*). Someone who is **rancorous** suffers from a deep-seated and lasting bitterness, although it does not imply a desire to hurt or to be *vindictive* (*his rancorous nature made him difficult to befriend*). **Venomous** takes its meaning from "venom" referring to someone or something of a spiteful, malignant nature and suggesting a poisonous sting (*a critic's venomous attack on an author's first novel*).

vine /vin/ *n.* **1** climbing or trailing woody-stemmed plant, esp. one bearing grapes. **2** stem of this. □□ **vin'y** *adj.*

vin·e·gar /vínigər/ *n.* sour liquid obtained from wine, cider, etc., by fermentation and used as a condiment or for pickling. □□ **vin' e·gar·ish** *adj.* **vin'e·gar·y** *adj.*

vine·yard /vínyərd/ *n.* plantation of grapevines, esp. for wine-making.

vi·no /véenō/ *n. sl.* wine, esp. a red Italian wine.

vin·tage /víntij/ • *n.* **1 a** season's produce of grapes. **b** wine from this. **2** wine of high quality from a particular year and district. **3 a** year, etc., when a thing was made, etc. **b** thing made, etc., in a particular year, etc. • *adj.* **1** of high quality, esp. from the past or characteristic of the best period of a person's work. **2** of a past season
■ *n.* **1** year, crop, harvest. **3** period, generation, origin. • *adj.* **1** choice, superior, select, classic; aged, mature(d). **2** antiquated, old-fashioned, *colloq.* over the hill.

vint·ner /víntnər/ *n.* wine merchant.

vi·nyl /vínəl/ *n.* plastic made by polymerization.

vi·ol /víəl/ *n.* medieval stringed musical in-

strument, played with a bow and held vertically on the knees or between the legs.

vi·o·la /vee-ólə/ *n.* **1 a** instrument larger than the violin and of lower pitch. **b** viola player. **2** viol.

vi·o·late /víəlayt/ *v.tr.* **1** disregard; fail to comply with (an oath, treaty, law, etc.). **2** treat (a sanctuary, etc.) profanely or with disrespect. **3** disturb (a person's privacy, etc.). **4** rape. □□ **vi·o·la·ble** *adj.* **vi·o·la· tion** /-láyshən/ *n.* **vi·o·la·tor** *n.*
■ **1** break, breach, disobey, ignore. **2** dishonor, desecrate, profane. **3** invade, abuse, trespass on. **4** ravage, molest, assault (sexually), outrage. □□ **violation** infringement, breach, disobedience; sacrilege, desecration, dishonor; rape, attack, outrage, assault.

vi·o·lence /víələns/ *n.* **1** being violent. **2** violent conduct or treatment. **3** *Law* **a** unlawful exercise of physical force. **b** intimidation by the exhibition of this.
■ **1** (brute *or* physical) force, power, severity, vehemence, ferocity; destructiveness, brutality, cruelty, passion. **2** see OUTRAGE *n.* 1.

vi·o·lent /víələnt/ *adj.* **1** involving or using great physical force (*violent person, violent storm*). **2 a** intense; vehement; passionate; furious (*violent contrast, violent dislike*). **b** vivid (*violent colors*). **3** resulting from or caused by violence. □□ **vi'o·lent·ly** *adv.*
■ **1** wild, brutal, barbarous, savage, fierce, vicious, uncontrollable, raging, raving, *colloq.* fit to be tied; destructive, catastrophic, cataclysmic, devastating. **2 a** severe, extreme, harsh, virulent, energetic, forceful, impassioned, tempestuous. **b** see VIVID 1. □□ **violently** see MADLY 2a, *fiercely* (FIERCE).

vi·o·let /víələt/ • *n.* **1** plant, esp. the sweet violet, with usu. purple, blue, or white flowers. **2** bluish-purple color seen at the end of the spectrum opposite red. • *adj.* of this color.

vi·o·lin /víəlín/ *n.* musical instrument with four strings of treble pitch played with a bow. **2** violin player. □□ **vi·o·lin'ist** *n.*
■ fiddle.

vi·o·lon·cel·lo /véeələnchélō, ví-/ *n.* (pl. **-los**) *formal* = CELLO. □□ **vi·o·lon·cel'list** *n.*

VIP *abbr.* very important person.

vi·per /vípər/ *n.* **1** small venomous snake, esp. the common viper (see ADDER). **2** treacherous person. □□ **vi'per·ous** *adj.*

vi·ra·go /viráagō, -ráygō/ *n.* (pl. **-gos**) fierce or abusive woman.

vi·ral /vírəl/ *adj.* of or caused by a virus. □□ **vi'ral·ly** *adv.*

vir·e·o /víreeō/ *n.* (pl. **-os**) small American songbird.

vir·gin /vérjin/ • *n.* **1** person who has never had sexual intercourse. **2** (**the Virgin**) Christ's mother, the Blessed Virgin Mary. **3** (**the Virgin**) zodiacal sign or constellation Virgo. • *adj.* **1** that is a virgin. **2** of or befitting a virgin (*virgin modesty*). **3** not yet used, penetrated, or tried (*virgin soil*). **4** undefiled; spotless. □□ **vir'gin·al** *adj.* **vir·gin'i·ty** *n.*
■ *adj.* **1, 2** see PURE 2, 3. **3** see UNUSED 1b, UNCHARTED.

Vir•gin•ia creep•er /vərjínyə/ *n.* ornamental N. American vine.

Vir•gin•ia reel /vərjínyə/ *n.* country dance done by partners in two facing rows.

Vir•go /vérgō/ *n.* (*pl.* **-gos**) **1** constellation and sixth sign of the zodiac (the Virgin). **2** person born under this sign.

vir•gule /vérgyōol/ *n.* **1** slanting line used to mark division of words or lines. **2** = SOLIDUS.

vir•ile /vírəl, -íl/ *adj.* **1** of a man; having masculine vigor or strength. **2** of or having procreative power. **3** of a man as distinct from a woman or child. See synonym study at MALE. □□ **vi•ril•i•ty** /virílitee/ *n.*

■ **1** see MANLY 1. □□ **virility** see MACHISMO.

vi•rol•o•gy /vīróləjee/ *n.* the scientific study of viruses. □□ **vi•ro•log•i•cal** /–rəlójikəl/ *adj.* **vi•ro•log•i•cal•ly** *adv.* **vi•rol´o•gist** *n.*

vir•tu•al /vérchōoəl/ *adj.* that is such for practical purposes though not in name or according to strict definition (*is the virtual manager of the business*). □ **virtual reality** generation by computer software of an image or environment that appears real to the senses. □□ **vir•tu•al•i•ty** /–álitee/ *n.* **vir´tu•al•ly** *adv.*

■ effective; practical, understood, accepted. □□ **virtually** essentially, effectively, practically, almost, to all intents and purposes, for all practical purposes.

vir•tue /vérchōo/ *n.* **1** moral excellence; goodness. **2** particular form of this (*patience is a virtue*). **3** chastity. **4** good quality (*has the virtue of being adjustable*). **5** efficacy; inherent power (*no virtue in such drugs*). See synonym study at GOODNESS. □ **by** (or **in**) **virtue of** on the strength or ground of (*got the job by virtue of his experience*). □□ **vir´tue•less** *adj.*

■ **1** high-mindedness, honor, righteousness, integrity, decency, nobility, character, respectability. **3** virginity, innocence, purity. **4** credit, merit, advantage, asset. □ **by** (or **in**) **virtue of** owing to, thanks to, by reason of, because of, on account of.

vir•tu•o•so /vérchōo-ōsō, -zō/ *n.* (*pl.* **vir•tu•o•si** /–see, –zee/ or **-sos**) **1** person highly skilled in the technique of a fine art, esp. music. **2** [*attrib.*] displaying the skills of a virtuoso. □□ **vir•tu•os•i•ty** /–ósitee/ *n.*

■ **1** master, maestro, expert, genius, prodigy, old hand, *colloq.* maven, whiz kid. **2** masterful, brilliant, excellent, superb, extraordinary. □□ **virtuosity** (technical) skill, technique, ability, expertise, *sl.* razzle-dazzle.

vir•tu•ous /vó rchōoəs/ *adj.* **1** possessing or showing moral rectitude. **2** chaste. See synonym study at MORAL. □□ **vir´tu•ous•ly** *adv.* **vir´tu•ous•ness** *n.*

■ **1** honorable, ethical, upstanding, high-principled, righteous, incorruptible, just, fair, scrupulous. **2** innocent, virginal, pure; decent, proper. □□ **virtuousness** see HONOR *n.* 2, 3.

vir•u•lent /víryələnt, vírə–/ *adj.* **1** strongly poisonous. **2** (of a disease) violent or malignant. **3** bitterly hostile (*virulent animosity*). □□ **vir´u•lence** *n.* **vir´u•lent•ly** *adv.*

■ **1, 2** lethal, life-threatening, deadly, fatal, toxic, dangerous, detrimental. **3** vicious, venomous, spiteful, acrimonious, caustic. □□ **virulence** toxicity, deadliness, destructiveness; acrimony, poison, malevolence, malice, spite, hostility.

vi•rus /vírəs/ *n.* **1** microscopic organism often causing diseases. **2** *Computing* = *computer virus*.

vi•sa /véezə/ *n.* endorsement on a passport, etc., esp. allowing the holder to enter or leave a country.

vis•age /vízij/ *n. literary* face. □□ **vis´aged** *adj.* [also in *comb.*].

■ see FACE *n.* 1.

vis-à-vis /véezaavée/ • *prep.* **1** in relation to. **2** opposite to. • *adv.* facing one another.

■ *prep.* **1** re, with reference to, regarding, with regard to. **2** see OPPOSITE *prep.*

vis•cer•a /vísərə/ *n.pl.* interior organs of the body (e.g., brain, heart, liver), esp. in the abdomen (e.g., the intestines).

vis•cer•al /vísərəl/ *adj.* **1** of the viscera. **2** feelings rather than reasoning. □□ **vis´cer•al•ly** *adv.*

vis•cid /vísid/ *adj.* glutinous; sticky. □□ **vis•cid´i•ty** *n.*

■ see STICKY *adj.* 2.

vis•cose /vískōs/ *n.* cellulose in a highly viscous state, used for making rayon.

vis•count /víkownt/ *n.* British nobleman ranking between an earl and a baron.

vis•count•ess /víkowntəs/ *n.* **1** viscount's wife or widow. **2** woman holding the rank of viscount in her own right.

vis•cous /vískəs/ *adj.* **1** glutinous; sticky. **2** semifluid. **3** *Physics* not flowing freely. □□ **vis´cous•ly** *adv.* **vis•cos´i•ty** /vískósitee/ *n.*

■ **1** see STICKY *adj.* 2. **2** see THICK *adj.* 5a.

vise /vīs/ *n.* instrument, esp. attached to a workbench, with two movable jaws holding an object so as to leave the hands free to work on it. □□ **vise´like** *adj.*

Vish•nu /víshnōo/ *n.* Hindu god regarded by his worshipers as the supreme deity and savior, by others as the second member of a triad with Brahma and Siva. □□ **Vish´nu•ism** *n.*

vis•i•bil•i•ty /vízibílitee/ *n.* **1** being visible. **2** range or possibility of vision as determined by the light and atmosphere (*visibility was 50 yards*).

vis•i•ble /vízibəl/ *adj.* **1** that can be seen by the eye. **2** that can be perceived or ascertained (*has no visible means of support, spoke with visible impatience*). □□ **vis´i•ble•ness** *n.* **vis´i•bly** *adv.*

■ **1** perceptible, detectable, noticeable, obvious; visual. **2** obvious, conspicuous, evident. □□ **visibly** see *outwardly* (OUTWARD).

vi•sion /vízhən/ *n.* **1** act or faculty of seeing (*impaired his vision*). **2 a** thing or person seen in a dream or trance. **b** supernatural or prophetic apparition. **3** thing or idea perceived vividly in the imagination (*romantic visions of youth*). **4** imaginative insight. **5** statesmanlike foresight; sagacity in planning. **6** person, etc., of unusual beauty. □□ **vi´sion•less** *adj.*

■ **1** perception, sight. **2** phantom, delusion, mirage, ghost. **3** perspective, perception, dream, plan, notion. **4, 5** farsightedness, perception. **6** sight for sore eyes, (welcome) sight, picture.

vi•sion•ar•y /vízhəneree/ • *adj.* **1** given to seeing visions; indulging in fanciful theories. **2** of a vision or the imagination. **3** not practicable. • *n.* (*pl.* **–ies**) visionary person.

■ *adj.* **1** dreamy, idealistic, unrealistic; see also IMAGINATIVE. **2** dreamlike, unreal; see also IMAGINARY. **3** unrealistic, Utopian. • *n.* dreamer, idealist, romantic, Don Quixote, Utopian.

vis•it /vízit/ • *v.* **1** *tr.* [also *absol.*] go or come to see (a person, place, etc.) as an act of friendship or ceremony, on business or for a purpose, or from interest. **2** *tr.* reside temporarily with (a person) or at (a place). **3** *intr.* be a visitor. **4** *tr.* (of a disease, calamity, etc.) come upon; attack. • *n.* **1 a** act of visiting; call on a person or at a place. **b** temporary stay with a person or at a place. **2** [foll. by *to*] occasion of going to a doctor, dentist, etc. **3** formal or official call. **4** chat. □□ **vis′i•tor** *n.*

■ *v.* **1** call (on), look in on, stop by, pop in, *colloq.* drop by or in (on). **2** see STAY[1] *v.* 2. **4** afflict, seize, scourge, descend upon. • *n.* **1** call, stop, stopover. **3** visitation. □□ **visitor** caller, guest, company.

vis•i•tant /vízit'nt/ *n.* visitor, esp. a supernatural one.

vis•i•ta•tion /vízitáyshən/ *n.* **1** official visit of inspection. **2** divine punishment. **3** legally permitted visits, as to one's children after a divorce.

■ **1** tour. **2** affliction, ordeal, trial, plague, pestilence.

vi•sor /vízər/ *n.* **1 a** movable part of a helmet covering the face. **b** projecting front part of a cap. **2** shield (fixed or movable) to protect the eyes from unwanted light, esp. at the top of a vehicle windshield. □□ **vi′sored** *adj.* **vi′sor•less** *adj.*

VISTA /vístə/ *abbr.* Volunteers in Service to America.

vis•ta /vístə/ *n.* **1** long, narrow view as between rows of trees. **2** mental view of a series of events. □□ **vis′taed** *adj.*

■ see VIEW *n.* 2.

vis•u•al /vízhōoəl/ • *adj.* of or used in seeing. • *n.* [usu. in *pl.*] visual image or display; picture. □□ **vis′u•al•ly** *adv.*

■ *n.* see PICTURE *n.* 1.

vis•u•al•ize /vízhōoəlīz/ *v.tr.* imagine visually. □□ **vis•u•al•i•za′tion** *n.*

■ see PICTURE *v.* 2.

vi•tal /vít'l/ • *adj.* **1** of or essential to organic life. **2** essential. **3** full of life or activity. **4** fatal to life or to success, etc. • *n.* [in *pl.*] the body's vital organs, e.g., the heart and brain. □ **vital signs** pulse rate, rate of respiration, and body temperature considered as signs of life. **vital statistics** number of births, marriages, deaths, etc. □□ **vi′tal•ly** *adv.*

■ *adj.* **1** living, animate; life-giving, invigorating. **2** imperative, necessary, required, fundamental, life-and-death. **3** lively, vivacious,

943   **visionary ~ vivid**

spirited. **4** grave, serious. • *n.* (*vitals*) see GUT *n.* 1, 2. □□ **vitally** essentially, indispensably.

vi•tal•i•ty /vītálitee/ *n.* **1** liveliness; animation. **2** (of an institution, language, etc.) ability to endure and to perform its functions.

■ **1** energy, vigor, intensity, exuberance, go, zip, *colloq.* zing, pep, vim, *sl.* pizzazz, oomph. **2** stamina, hardiness, robustness.

vi•tal•ize /vít'līz/ *v.tr.* **1** endow with life. **2** infuse with vigor. See synonym study at QUICKEN. □□ **vi•tal•i•za′tion** *n.*

■ stimulate, activate, revive, fortify, perk up, *colloq.* pep up.

vi•ta•min /vítəmin/ *n.* any of various organic compounds essential for many living organisms to maintain normal health and development.

vi•ti•ate /víshee ayt/ *v.tr.* **1** impair; corrupt; debase. **2** make invalid or ineffectual. □□ **vi•ti•a′tion** /–shee áyshən/ *n.* **vi′ti•a•tor** *n.*

■ **1** spoil, ruin, harm, contaminate, weaken, diminish, undermine. **2** destroy, delete, cancel. □□ **vitiation** see *impairment* (IMPAIR).

vit•i•cul•ture /vítikulchər/ *n.* cultivation of grapevines; study of this. □□ **vit•i•cul′tur•al** *adj.* **vit•i•cul′tur•ist** *n.*

vit•re•ous /vítreeəs/ *adj.* of or like glass. □ **vitreous humor** (or **body**) *Anat.* transparent jellylike tissue filling the eyeball. □□ **vit′re•ous•ness** *n.*

vit•ri•fy /vítrifī/ *v.* (**–fies, –fied**) convert or be converted into glass or a glasslike substance, esp. by heat. □□ **vit•ri•fac•tion** /–fákshən/ *n.* **vit′ri•fi•a•ble** *adj.* **vit•ri•fi•ca′tion** *n.*

vit•ri•ol /vítreeōl, –əl/ *n.* **1** sulfuric acid or a sulfate, orig. one of glassy appearance. **2** caustic or hostile speech, criticism, or feeling. □□ **vit•ri•ol•ic** /–ólik/ *adj.*

■ **2** see GALL[1] 2, 3. □□ **vitriolic** see SCATHE.

vi•tu•per•ate /vītoopərayt, –tyoo–, vi–/ *v.tr.* revile; abuse. See synonym study at SCOLD. □□ **vi•tu•per•a•tion** /–ráyshən/ *n.* **vi•tu•per•a•tive** /–rətiv, –ráytiv/ *adj.*

■ berate, reproach, vilify, denounce, *sl.* knock. □□ **vituperation** see ABUSE *n.* 2. **vituperative** abusive, derogatory, belittling, contemptuous, insulting.

vi•va /véevə/ • *int.* long live. • *n.* cry of this as a salute, etc.

vi•va•ce /vivaáchay/ *adv. Mus.* in a lively brisk manner.

vi•va•cious /viváyshəs/ *adj.* lively; sprightly; animated. □□ **vi•va′cious•ly** *adv.* **vi•va′cious•ness** *n.* **vi•vac•i•ty** /vivásitee/ *n.*

■ energetic, effervescent, cheerful, *colloq.* peppy, zippy, chipper, *poet.* blithe. □□ **vivaciousness, vivacity** see VITALITY 1.

viv•id /vívid/ *adj.* **1** (of color) strong; intense (*vivid green*). **2** (of a mental faculty, impression, or description) clear; lively; graphic (*vivid imagination, vivid recollection of the scene*). □□ **viv′id•ly** *adv.* **viv′id•ness** *n.*

■ **1** brilliant, bright, dazzling, rich, bold. **2** detailed, sharp, realistic; fruitful, creative, active.

viv•i•fy /vívifī/ *v.tr.* (**–fies, –fied**) enliven; animate; make lively or living. □□ **viv•i•fi•ca′ tion** *n.*

vi•vip•a•rous /vīvípərəs, vi–/ *adj.* Zool. bringing forth live young. □□ **vi•vip′a•rous•ly** *adv.*

viv•i•sec•tion /vívisékshən/ *n.* surgery on living animals for purposes of scientific research. □□ **viv′i•sect** *v.* **viv•i•sec′tion•al** *adj.* **viv•i•sec′tion•ist** *n.* **viv•i•sec•tor** /–sektər/ *n.*

vix•en /víksən/ *n.* **1** female fox. **2** spiteful woman. □□ **vix′en•ish** *adj.* **vix′en•ly** *adj.*

■ **2** see SHREW.

viz. /viz/ *adv.* (usu. introducing a gloss or explanation) namely; that is to say; in other words. Abbr. of (**videlicet**).

■ see NAMELY.

vi•zier /vizéər, víziər/ *n. hist.* high official in the Ottoman Empire. □□ **vi•zier•i•al** /vizéereeəl/ *adj.* **vi•zier′ship** *n.*

VJ *abbr.* video jockey.

V.M.D. *abbr.* doctor of veterinary medicine.

voc. *abbr.* **1** vocational. **2** vocative.

vocab. *abbr.* vocabulary.

vo•cab•u•lar•y /vōkábyəleree/ *n.* (*pl.* **–ies**) **1** words used by a particular language, individual, book, branch of science, etc., or by a particular author. **2** list of these, arranged alphabetically with definitions or translations.

■ **1** see TERMINOLOGY.

vo•cal /vókəl/ • *adj.* **1** of or uttered by the voice (*vocal communication*). **2** outspoken (*was very vocal about her rights*). **3** (of music) written for or produced by the voice. • *n.* [in *sing.* or *pl.*] sung part of a musical composition. □ **vocal cords** folds of the lining membrane of the larynx near the opening of the glottis, with edges vibrating in the air stream to produce the voice. □□ **vo•cal′i•ty** /vəkálitee/ *n.* **vo′cal•ly** *adv.*

■ *adj.* **1** see ORAL *adj.*

vo•cal•ist /vókəlist/ *n.* singer, esp. of jazz or popular songs.

■ soloist; diva, prima donna, chanteuse; cantor, crooner.

vo•cal•ize /vókəlīz/ *v.* **1** *tr.* form (a sound), utter (a word), or sing. **2** *intr.* utter a vocal sound. □□ **vo•cal•i•za′tion** *n.* **vo′cal•iz•er** *n.*

■ **1, 2** see ENUNCIATE 1.

vo•ca•tion /vōkáyshən/ *n.* **1** strong feeling of fitness for a particular career (in religious contexts, a divine call). **2 a** person's employment. **b** trade or profession. □□ **vo•ca′tion•al** *adj.*

■ **1** calling. **2** mission, business, occupation, career, job, line (of work).

voc•a•tive /vókətiv/ *Gram.* • *n.* case of nouns used in addressing a person or thing. • *adj.* of or in this case.

vo•cif•er•ate /vōsífərayt/ *v.* **1** *tr.* utter (words, etc.) noisily. **2** *intr.* shout; bawl. □□ **vo•cif•er•a′tion** /–rávshən/ *n.*

vo•cif•er•ous /vōsífərəs/ *adj.* **1** noisy; clamorous. **2** insistent. □□ **vo•cif′er•ous•ly** *adv.* **vo•cif′er•ous•ness** *n.*

■ **1** see OBSTREPEROUS. **2** see INSISTENT 2.

□□ **vociferously** see *warmly* (WARM).

---

vod•ka /vódkə/ *n.* alcoholic spirit distilled from rye, etc.

vogue /vōg/ *n.* **1** prevailing fashion. **2** popularity (*has had a great vogue*). □ **in vogue** in fashion. □□ **vogu′ish** *adj.*

■ **1** mode, style, trend, rage. **2** favor, preference, acceptance. □ **in vogue** see FASHIONABLE.

voice /voys/ • *n.* **1 a** sound formed in the larynx and uttered by the mouth, esp. by a person. **b** ability to produce this (*has lost her voice*). **2 a** spoken or written words (esp. *give voice*). **b** opinion so expressed. **c** right to express an opinion (*I have no voice in the matter*). **d** medium for expression. **3** *Gram.* set of verbal forms showing the relation of the subject to the action (*active voice, passive voice*). **4** *Mus.* **a** vocal part in a composition. **b** vocal ability, esp. in singing. • *v.tr.* **1** express (*the letter voices our opinion*). **2** (esp. as **voiced** *adj.*) *Phonet.* utter with vibration of the vocal cords (e.g., b, d, g, v, z). □ **voice box** larynx. **voice mail** automatic telephone answering system that records messages from callers. **voice-over** narration in a movie, etc., not accompanied by a picture of the speaker. **with one voice** unanimously. □□ **–voiced** *adj.*

■ *n.* **2 a** speech, utterance, expression. **c** vote, participation, decision. **d** spokesperson, representative, agent; organ, vehicle, publication. • *v.* **1** utter, articulate, enunciate, present, communicate, state. □ **voice-over** see *narration* (NARRATE).

void /voyd/ • *adj.* **1 a** empty; vacant. **b** [foll. by *of*] lacking; free from (*a style void of affectation*). **2** esp. *Law* invalid; not binding (*null and void*). **3** useless; ineffectual. • *n.* empty space; vacuum (*cannot fill the void made by death*). • *v.tr.* **1** render invalid. **2** [also *absol.*] excrete. □□ **void′a•ble** *adj.*

■ *adj.* **1 a** unused, clear; deserted. **b** (*void of*) without; destitute of. **2** inoperative, unenforceable. **3** futile, ineffective, vain, pointless. • *n.* emptiness, nothingness; hole, space, opening, gap. • v. **1** nullify, annul, cancel. **2** evacuate, expel, drain; urinate, defecate.

voile /voyl, vwaal/ n. thin, semitransparent dress material of cotton, wool, or silk.

vol. abbr. volume.

vol•a•tile /vólət'l, –til/ adj. **1** evaporating rapidly (*volatile salts*). **2** changeable; fickle. **3** apt to break out into violence. □□ **vol•a•til•i•ty** /–tílitee/ n.

■ adj. **1** vaporizing, evaporative. **2** flighty, inconstant, erratic, restless. **3** explosive, hair-trigger, charged, eruptive, tense. □□ **volatility** see *inconstancy* (INCONSTANT).

vol•can•ic /volkánik/ adj. of, like, or produced by a volcano. □□ **vol'can'i•cal•ly** adv.

vol•ca•no /volkáynō/ n. (pl. **–noes** or **–nos**) mountain from which lava, cinders, steam, gases, etc., escape through openings in the earth's crust.

vole /vōl/ n. small plant-eating rodent.

vo•li•tion /vəlíshən/ n. **1** exercise of the will. **2** power of willing. □□ **vo•li'tion•al** adj. **vo•li'tion•al•ly** adv. **vol•i•tive** /vólitiv/ adj.

■ **1** choice, option, discretion, preference. □□ **volitional** see VOLUNTARY adj. 1.

vol•ley /vólee/ • n. (pl. **–leys**) **1 a** simultaneous discharge of a number of weapons. **b** bullets, etc., discharged in a volley. **2** torrent of oaths, etc. **3** *Tennis* return of a ball in play before it touches the ground. **4** *Soccer* kicking of a ball in play before it touches the ground. • v. (**–leys, –leyed**) **1** tr. [also absol.] *Tennis & Soccer* return or send (a ball) by a volley. **2** n. & absol. discharge (bullets, abuse, etc.) in a volley. **3** intr. (of bullets, etc.) fly in a volley. □□ **vol'ley•er** n.

■ n. **1** salvo, bombardment, barrage. **2** outpouring, flood, burst, storm, outbreak. • v. **3** see HAIL[1] v. 2.

vol•ley•ball /vóleebawl/ n. game for two teams of six hitting a large ball by hand over a net.

volt /vōlt/ n. unit of electromotive force, the difference of potential that would carry one ampere of current against one ohm resistance. ¶Abbr.: **V**.

volt•age /vōltij/ n. electromotive force expressed in volts.

vol•ta•ic /voltáyik/ adj. archaic of electricity from a primary battery; galvanic (*voltaic battery*).

volt•me•ter /vōltmeetər/ n. instrument for measuring an electric charge.

volt•me•ter /vōltmeetər/ n. instrument for measuring electric potential in volts.

vol•u•ble /vólyəbəl/ adj. speaking or spoken at length. □□ **vol•u•bil'i•ty** n. **vol'u•ble•ness** n. **vol'u•bly** adv.

■ **1** talkative, glib, fluent, loquacious, garrulous, chatty

vol•ume /vólyŏŏm/ n. **1** single book forming part or the whole of a work. **2 a** solid content; bulk. **b** space occupied by a gas or liquid. **3** quantity or power of sound. □□ **vol'umed** adj. [also in comb.].

■ **1** book, tome. **2 a** mass, content. **b** capacity, size, dimensions, measure. **3** loudness.

vo•lu•mi•nous /vəlŏŏminəs/ adj. **1** large in volume; bulky. **2** (of drapery, etc.) loose and

---

945   **voile ~ votary**

ample. **3** (of a writer) producing many books. □□ **vo•lu'mi•nous•ly** adv. **vo•lu'mi•nous•ness** n.

■ **1** extensive, great, spacious, capacious. **2** billowing, full. **3** copious, prolific.

vol•un•ta•rism /vóləntərizəm/ n. principle of relying on voluntary action rather than compulsion.

vol•un•tar•y /vólənteree/ • adj. **1** done, acting, or able to act of one's own free will; not compulsory. **2** unpaid. **3** supported by voluntary contributions. **4** brought about, produced, etc., by voluntary action. **5** controlled by the will. • n. (pl. **–ies**) **1** organ solo played before or after a church service. □□ **vol•un•tar'i•ly** adv.

■ adj. **1** free, elective, willing, spontaneous, unsolicited. □□ **voluntarily** freely, willingly, without prompting; by choice.

vol•un•teer /vólənteer/ • n. **1** person who voluntarily undertakes a task or enters military service. • v. **1** tr. undertake or offer voluntarily. **2** intr. make a voluntary offer of one's services; be a volunteer.

■ v. see OFFER v. 3, ENROL 1.

vo•lup•tu•ar•y /vəlúpchōoeree/ n. (pl. **–ies**) person given up to luxury and sensual pleasure.

vo•lup•tu•ous /vəlúpchŏŏəs/ adj. **1** of, tending to, occupied with, or derived from, sensuous or sensual pleasure. **2** full of sexual promise, esp. through shapeliness or fullness. □□ **vo•lup'tu•ous•ly** adv. **vo•lup'tu•ous•ness** n.

■ **1** sensualistic, luxurious, sybaritic(al). **2** seductive, erotic, sexy, attractive, desirable, beautiful, tempting.

vo•lute /vəlōōt/ n. *Archit.* spiral-shaped ornamental scroll. □□ **vo•lut'ed** adj.

vom•it /vómit/ • v.tr. **1** eject (matter) from the stomach through the mouth. **2** (of a volcano, etc.) eject violently; belch (forth). • n. matter vomited from the stomach. □□ **vom'iter** n.

■ v. **1** spew, bring up; regurgitate, gag, retch, heave. **2** spew out or up, spit up.

voo•doo /vōōdōō/ • n. **1** religious witchcraft, esp. as practiced in the W. Indies. **2** object used in voodoo practice. • v.tr. affect by voodoo; bewitch. □□ **voo'doo•ism** n. **voo'doo•ist** n.

vo•ra•cious /vawráyshəs, və–/ adj. **1** greedy in eating; ravenous. **2** very eager. □□ **vo•ra'cious•ly** adv. **vo•ra'cious•ness** n. **vo•rac•i•ty** /vərásitee/ n.

■ **1** insatiable, gluttonous, ravening, rapacious, piggish. **2** thirsty, hungry, desirous, avid, fervent.

vor•tex /váwrteks/ n. (pl. **vor•ti•ces** /–tiseez/ or **vor•tex•es**) **1** whirlpool or whirlwind or any whirling motion or mass. **3** thing viewed as swallowing up or engulfing. □□ **vor•ti•cal** /–tikəl/ adj. **vor'ti•cal•ly** adv. **vor•tic•i•ty** /vortísitee/ n. **vor•ti•cose** /–tikōs/ adj.

vo•ta•ry /vōtəree/ n. (pl. **–ries**; fem. **vo•ta•ress**) **1** person vowed to religious service. **2** devoted follower, adherent, or advocate of a person, system, occupation, etc. □□ **vo'ta‑rist** *n.*

vote /vōt/ • *n.* **1** formal expression of choice or opinion by a ballot, show of hands, etc. **2** right to vote. **3** opinion expressed by a majority of votes. **4** votes given by or for a particular group. • *v.* **1** *intr.* give a vote. **2** *tr.* enact or resolve by vote. □ **vote with one's feet** *colloq.* indicate an opinion by one's presence or absence. □□ **vot'a‑ble** *adj.* **vote'less** *adj.* **vot'er** *n.*

■ *n.* **1** election, poll, referendum, plebiscite. **2** suffrage, franchise, voice, say. **3** preference, selection, choice. **4** voter(s), elector(s). • *v.* **1** cast one's vote, ballot; (*vote for*) choose, elect; (*vote against*) come out against, veto, reject. **2** decide, pass.

vo‑tive /vōtiv/ *adj.* offered or consecrated in fulfillment of a vow.

vouch /vowch/ *v.intr.* [foll. by *for*] answer for; be surety for.

■ (*vouch for*) support, guarantee, endorse, sponsor.

vouch‑er /vówchər/ *n.* **1** document exchangeable for goods or services. **2** receipt.

■ token, coupon; see also CHECK *n.* 5.

vouch‑safe /vówchsáyf/ *v.tr. formal* condescend to grant.

■ offer, give (up), yield, accord, supply, grant, impart.

vow /vow/ • *n. Relig.* solemn promise, esp. in the form of an oath to God. • *v.tr.* promise solemnly.

■ *n.* oath, pledge, agreement; (solemn) word (of honor). • *v.* **1** swear, pledge, assure.

vow‑el /vówəl/ *n.* **1** speech sound made with vibration of the vocal cords but without audible friction. **2** letter representing this, as *a, e, i, o, u.* □□ **vow'eled** *adj.* [also in *comb.*]. **vow'el‑less** *adj.*

vox po‑pu‑li /vóks pópyəlee, –lī/ *n.* public opinion.

voy‑age /vó yij/ • *n.* journey, esp. a long one by sea or in space. See synonym study at JOURNEY. • *v.intr.* make a voyage. □□ **voy'ag‑er** *n.*

■ *n.* see JOURNEY *n.* • *v.* see JOURNEY *v.* □□ **voyager** see *traveler* (TRAVEL).

vo‑ya‑geur /vwáayaazhőr/ *n. hist.* French Canadian explorer or trader in colonial N. America.

voy‑eur /vwaayőr/ *n.* person who obtains sexual gratification from observing others' sexual actions or organs. □□ **vo‑yeur'ism** *n.* **voy‑eur‑is'tic** *adj.* **voy‑eur‑is'ti‑cal‑ly** *adj.*

VP *abbr.* VICE PRESIDENT.

VS *abbr.* veterinary surgeon.

vs. *abbr.* **1** versus. **2** verse.

VT *abbr.* Vermont (in official postal use).

Vt. *abbr.* Vermont.

VTOL /véetol/ *abbr.* vertical takeoff and landing.

vul‑can‑ize /vúlkənīz/ *v.tr.* treat (rubber, etc.) with sulfur at a high temperature to increase its strength. □□ **vul‑can‑i‑za'tion** *n.* **vul'can‑iz‑er** *n.*

vul‑gar /vúlgər/ *adj.* **1 a** of or characteristic of the common people. **b** coarse in manners; low. **2** common; prevalent. □□ **vul‑gar‑i‑ty** /–gárity/ *n.* **vul'gar‑ly** *adv.*

■ **1 a** plebeian, uncultured, uncultivated. **b** indelicate, boorish, uncouth; indecent, rude. **2** popular, vernacular, ordinary, everyday. □□ **vulgarity** coarseness, crudeness, indelicacy; impropriety, ribaldry, lewdness.

vul‑gar‑i‑an /vulgáireeən/ *n.* vulgar (esp. rich) person.

vul‑gar‑ism /vúlgərizəm/ *n.* word or expression in coarse or uneducated use.

vul‑gar‑ize /vúlgərīz/ *v.tr.* **1** make vulgar. **2** popularize. □□ **vul‑gar‑i‑za'tion** *n.*

Vul‑gate /vúlgayt, –gət/ *n.* 4th-Century Latin version of the Bible.

vul‑ner‑a‑ble /vúlnərəbəl/ *adj.* **1** easily wounded or harmed. **2** [foll. by *to*] exposed to damage by a weapon, criticism, etc. □□ **vul‑ner‑a‑bil'i‑ty** *n.* **vul'ner‑a‑ble‑ness** *n.* **vul'ner‑a‑bly** *adv.*

■ **1** exposed, defenseless, weak, sensitive, unprotected. **2** (*vulnerable to*) see SUSCEPTIBLE 2a. □□ **vulnerability, vulnerableness** see FRAILTY 1, 2.

vul‑pine /vúlpīn/ *adj.* **1** of or like a fox. **2** crafty; cunning.

vul‑ture /vúlchər/ *n.* **1** large carrion-eating bird of prey. **2** rapacious person. □□ **vul‑tur‑ine** /–rīn/ *adj.* **vul'tur‑ous** *adj.*

vul‑va /vúlvə/ *n.* (*pl.* **vul‑vas**) *Anat.* external female genitals.

vy‑ing *pres. part.* of VIE.

Ww

W[1] /dúbəlyōō/ *n.* (also **w**) (*pl.* **Ws** or **W's**; **w's**) twenty-third letter of the alphabet.

W[2] *abbr.* (also **W.**) **1** watt(s). **2** West; Western. **3** women's (size). **4** Welsh.

W[3] *symb. Chem.* tungsten.

w. *abbr.* **1** warden. **2** wide(s). **3** with. **4** wife. **5** watt(s).

WA *abbr.* **1** Washington (state) (in official postal use). **2** Western Australia.

Wac /wak/ *n.* member of the US Army's Women's Army Corps.

wack‑o /wákō/ (also **whack'o**) sl. • *adj.* crazy. • *n.* (*pl.* **–os** or **–oes**) crazy person.

wack‑y /wákee/ (also **whack'y**) sl. • *adj.* (**wack‑i‑er, wack‑i‑est**) crazy. • *n.* (*pl.* **–ies**) crazy person. □□ **wack'i‑ly** *adv.* **wack'i‑ness** *n.*

wad /wod/ • *n.* **1** lump of soft material.

2 disk of felt, etc., keeping powder or shot in place in a gun. **3** number of bills of currency or documents placed together. **4** [in *sing.* or *pl.*] large quantity, esp. of money. • *v.tr.* (**wad•ded, wad•ding**) **1** stop up or keep in place with a wad. **2** press (cotton, etc.) into a wad or wadding.
■ *n.* **1** pad, mass, clod, ball, plug, chunk. **3** roll, bundle, pocketful, bankroll.

wad•ding /wóding/ *n.* soft, pliable material of cotton, etc., used for stuffing, etc., or to pack fragile articles.
■ padding, filling, stuffing.

wad•dle /wód'l/ • *v.intr.* walk with short steps and a swaying motion. • *n.* waddling gait. □□ **wad'dler** *n.*
■ *v.* toddle, shuffle, wobble, totter, pad, duckwalk.

wade /wayd/ *v.intr.* **1** walk through water, mud, etc., esp. with difficulty. **2** make one's way with difficulty. **3** [foll. by *through*] read (a book, etc.) in spite of its dullness, etc. **4** [foll. by *into*] *colloq.* attack vigorously. □□ **wad'a•ble** *adj.* (also **wade'a•ble**).
■ **1** paddle, splash, plod, trudge. **2** trek, trudge, plow. **3** (*wade through*) plow through, work one's way through. **4** (*wade into*) approach, get to work on.

wad•er /wáydər/ *n.* **1** long-legged wading bird. **2** [in *pl.*] high waterproof boots, or a waterproof garment for the legs and body, worn in fishing, etc.

wa•di /wáadee/ *n.* (also **wa'dy**) (*pl.* **wa•dis** or **wa•dies**) rocky watercourse in N. Africa, etc., dry except in the rainy season

wa•fer /wáyfər/ *n.* **1** very thin, light, crisp sweet cake, cookie, or biscuit. **2** thin disk of unleavened bread used in the Eucharist. □ **wafer-thin** very thin. □□ **wa'fer•y** *adj.*

waf•fle[1] /wófəl/ *colloq.* • *n.* verbose but aimless, misleading, or ignorant talk or writing. • *v.intr.* indulge in waffle. □□ **waf'fler** *n.* **waf'fly** *adj.*
■ *n.* talk, palaver, verbiage, prattle, twaddle. • *v.* carry on, prate, equivocate, hedge.

waf•fle[2] /wófəl/ *n.* small, crisp batter cake with an indented lattice pattern. □ **waffle iron** utensil, usu. of two shallow metal pans hinged together, for cooking waffles.

waft /woft, waft/ • *v.* convey or travel easily as through air or over water. • *n.* **1** whiff or scent. **2** transient sensation of peace, joy, etc.
■ *v.* drift, float, blow, whiff. • *n.* **1** breath, suggestion, puff, hint.

wag[1] /wag/ • *v.* (**wagged, wag•ging**) shake or wave rapidly to and fro. • *n.* wagging motion.
■ *v.* oscillate, fluctuate, sway, undulate, flutter. • *n.* flap, flip, flicker, shake, vibration, quiver.

wag[2] /wag/ *n.* facetious person; joker.
■ comedian, wit, punster, pundit, jester, comic.

wage /wayj/ • *n.* **1** [in *sing.* or *pl.*] fixed regular payment to an employee, esp. to a manual or unskilled worker. **2** return; recompense. • *v.tr.* carry on (a war, etc.).
■ *n.* **1** pay, compensation, earnings, income. **2** requital, reward. • *v.* pursue, conduct, engage in.

wa•ger /wáyjər/ *n. & v.* = BET.

wag•gish /wágish/ *adj.* playful; facetious. □□ **wag'gish•ly** *adv.* **wag'gish•ness** *n.*

wag•gle /wágəl/ *v. colloq.* wag[1].

wag•gly /wáglee/ *adj.* unsteady.

wag•on /wágən/ *n.* **1** four-wheeled vehicle for heavy loads. **2** = *station wagon.* □ **on the wagon** *sl.* teetotal.

waif /wayf/ *n.* **1** homeless and helpless person, esp. an abandoned child. **2** ownerless object or animal. □□ **waif'ish** *adj.*

wail /wayl/ • *n.* prolonged and plaintive loud, high-pitched cry of pain, grief, etc. • *v.intr.* **1** utter a wail. **2** lament or complain persistently or bitterly. □□ **wail'er** *n.* **wail'ing•ly** *adv.*

wain /wayn/ *n. archaic* wagon.

wain•scot /wáynskət, –skot, –skŏt/ • *n.* wooden paneling on the lower part of an interior wall. • *v.tr.* panel with wainscot.

wain•scot•ing /wáynskōting, –skot–, –skə–/ *n.* **1** wainscot. **2** material for this.

wain•wright /wáynrīt/ *n.* wagon builder or repairer.

waist /wayst/ *n.* **1 a** part of the human body below the ribs and above the hips. **b** circumference of this. **2** similar narrow part in the middle of a violin, hourglass, etc. **3 a** part of a garment encircling or covering the waist. **b** blouse or bodice. □□ **waist'ed** *adj.* [also in comb.] **waist'less** *adj.*

waist•band /wáystband/ *n.* strip of cloth forming the waist of a garment.

waist•line /wáystlīn/ *n.* outline or size of a person's body at the waist.

wait /wayt/ • *v.* **1** *intr.* **a** defer action or departure for a specified time or until some event occurs. **b** be expectant or on the watch. **2** *tr.* await. **3** *tr.* defer (an activity). **4** *intr.* **a** (in full **wait at** or **on tables**) serve food, drinks, etc. **b** act as an attendant to. • *n.* period of waiting. □ **wait and see** await the progress of events. **wait up** [often foll. by *for*] not go to bed until a person arrives or an event happens.
■ *v.* **1 a** linger, hold on, stay, stop, remain. **b** see *watch but* 1. **2** wait for. **3** delay, postpone, shelve. • *n.* **1** delay, pause, interval, stoppage, break, hiatus, lacuna.

wait•er /wáytər/ *n.* person who serves at table in a hotel or restaurant, etc.
■ server, *garçon*, steward, attendant.

wait•ing /wáyting/ *n.* in senses of WAIT *v.* □ **waiting game** abstention from early action in a contest, etc., so as to act more effectively later.

wait•per•son /wáytpərsən/ *n.* waiter or waitress.

wait•ress /wáytris/ *n.* woman who serves at table in a hotel or restaurant, etc.

waive /wayv/ *v.tr.* refrain from insisting on or using (a right, claim, opportunity, legitimate plea, rule, etc.). See synonym study at RELINQUISH.
■ give up, relinquish, renounce, resign, forsake; overlook.

waiv•er /wáyvər/ *n. Law* act or an instance of waiving.

■ renunciation, relinquishment, cession, resignation, surrender, abandonment, deferral, remission.

wake[1] /wayk/ • v. (past **woke** /wōk/ or **waked**; past part. **wok•en** /wōkən/ or **waked**) **1** cease or cause to cease to sleep. **2** become or cause to become alert, attentive, or active. **3** intr. (archaic except as **waking** adj. & n.) be awake. **4** tr. evoke (an echo). • n. watch beside a corpse before burial. □□ **wak′er** n.

■ v. **1** awaken, awake, rouse, waken; stir, get up, rise, come to. **2** awake, waken, animate, stimulate, enliven, galvanize. • n. vigil.

wake[2] /wayk/ n. **1** track left on the water's surface by a moving ship. **2** turbulent air left behind a moving aircraft, etc. □ **in the wake of** following; as a result of.

■ **1** trail, path, backwash, wash, bow wave. **2** turbulence, track, trail, path. □ **in the wake of** behind, after, subsequent to; on account of, because of.

wake•ful /wáykfŏŏl/ adj. **1** unable to sleep. **2** (of a night, etc.) passed with little or no sleep. **3** vigilant. □□ **wake′ful•ly** adv. **wake′ful•ness** n.

■ **1** awake, sleepless, restless, restive, insomniac. **2** sleepless, disturbed, restless. **3** watchful, (on the) alert, on the qui vive, sharp, attentive.

wak•en /wáykən/ v. make or become awake.

wale /wayl/ • n. **1** = WEAL[1]. **2** ridge on corduroy. • v.tr. mark with wales; thrash; whip.

walk /wawk/ • v. **1** intr. **a** (of a person or other biped) progress by lifting and setting down each foot in turn, never having both feet off the ground at once. **b** progress with similar movements (walked on his hands). **c** (of a quadruped) go with the slowest gait. **2** intr. travel or go on foot. **3** tr. **a** tread the floor or surface of. **b** traverse or cover (a specified distance) on foot. **4** tr. cause to walk with one. **5** Baseball **a** intr. reach first base on balls. **b** tr. allow to do this. • n. **1 a** act of walking; the ordinary human gait. **b** slowest gait of an animal. **c** person's manner of walking. **2 a** distance walked. **b** excursion on foot. **3** place, track, or route intended or suitable for walking. **4** Baseball four pitched balls advancing a batter to base. □ **walk all over** colloq. **1** defeat easily. **2** take advantage of. **walk away** (or **off**) **with** colloq. **1** steal. **2** win easily. **walk of life** occupation, profession, or calling. **walk on air** see AIR. **walk out 1** depart suddenly or angrily. **2** cease work, esp. to go on strike. **walk out on** desert; abandon.

■ v. **1, 2, 3 b** advance, proceed, move, stride, tramp, stroll, amble. **3 a** patrol, trace out, stalk, cover. **4** take, accompany, escort; conduct, lead. • n. **1** step, pace, stride. **2 b** constitutional, stroll; hike. **3** path, lane, walkway, trail, footpath. □ **walk all over 1** see ROUT[1] v. **walk away** (or **off**) **with 1** see STEAL[1] v. **1. 2** see WIN v. 2. **walk of life** see SPHERE n. **3. walk out** leave, storm out; walk off the job. **walk out on** see DESERT v. 2.

walk•er /wáwkər/ n. **1** one who walks.

2 a wheeled or footed framework in which a baby can learn to walk. **b** tubular metal frame with rubberized ferrules, used by disabled or elderly people to help them walk.

walk•ie-talk•ie /wáwkeetáwkee/ n. two-way radio carried on the person, esp. by police officers, etc.

Walk•man /wáwkmən/ n. (pl. **–mans**) propr. type of small portable stereo equipment with headphones.

walk•out /wáwkowt/ n. sudden angry departure, esp. as a protest or strike.

walk•way /wáwkway/ n. passage or path (esp. raised) for walking.

wall /wawl/ • n. vertical structure of usu. brick or stone, esp. enclosing, protecting, or dividing a space or supporting a roof. • v.tr. (esp. as **walled** adj.) surround, block off, or protect with a wall. □ **go to the wall** be defeated or ruined. **off the wall** sl. unorthodox; unconventional. **up the wall** colloq. crazy or furious. **wall-to-wall 1** (of a carpet) fitted to cover a whole room, etc. **2** colloq. ubiquitous. □□ **wall′ing** n. **wall′-less** adj.

■ n. barricade, fortification, bulwark, breastwork, parapet, embankment, rampart, palisade, stockade. □ **go to the wall** fail, collapse, lose everything. **off the wall** see OFF-BEAT adj. **up the wall** insane, mad, frantic, out of one's mind.

wal•la•by /wólləbee/ n. (pl. **–bies**) small kangaroo.

wall•board /wáwlbawrd/ n. type of wall covering made from wood pulp, plaster, etc.

wal•let /wólit/ n. usu. pocket-size case for holding paper money, etc.

■ purse, billfold.

wall•eye /wáwlī/ n. **1 a** eye with a streaked or opaque white iris. **b** eye squinting outward. **2** (also **wall′eyed pike**) American perch with large prominent eyes. □□ **wall′eyed** adj.

wall•flow•er /wáwlflowr/ n. colloq. woman sitting out at a dance for lack of partners.

Wal•loon /wolōōn/ • n. **1** member of a French-speaking people inhabiting S. and E. Belgium and neighboring France. **2** French dialect spoken by this people. • adj. of or concerning the Walloons or their language.

wal•lop /wóləp/ sl. • v.tr. thrash; beat. • n. heavy blow. □□ **wal′lop•er** n. **wal′lop•ing** n.

wal•low /wólō/ • v.intr. **1** (esp. of an animal) roll about in mud, etc. **2** (usu. foll. by in) indulge in unrestrained pleasure, misery, etc. • n. **1** act or instance of wallowing. **2** place used for wallowing. □□ **wal′low•er** n.

■ v. **1** writhe, tumble, splash, plash. **2** (wallow in) luxuriate in, bask in, revel in, glory in.

wall•pa•per /wáwlpaypər/ • n. decorative paper for pasting on to interior walls. • v.tr. [often absol.] decorate with wallpaper.

Wall Street /wáwl/ n. U.S. financial world and investment market.

wal•nut /wáwlnut/ n. **1** tree with aromatic leaves and drooping catkins. **2** edible nut of this tree. **3** its timber.

wal•rus /wáwlrəs, wól–/ n. large, amphibious, long-tusked arctic mammal related to the seal and sea lion.

waltz /wawlts, wawls/ • n. **1** ballroom dance

in triple time performed by couples. **2** music for this. • *v.* **1** *intr.* dance a waltz. **2** *intr.* [often foll. by *in, out, around*, etc.] *colloq.* move lightly, casually, etc. □ **waltz′er** *n.*

wam•pum /wómpəm/ *n.* beads made from shells and strung together for use as money, decoration, etc., by N. American Indians.

wan /won/ *adj.* pale; exhausted; weak; worn. See synonym study at PALE. □□ **wan′ly** *adv.* **wan′ness** *n.*

■ white, sickly, pallid, livid, pasty, peaked, ashen.

wand /wond/ *n.* **1** stick used by a magician for effect. **2** staff symbolizing some officials' authority. **3** handheld electronic device which can be passed over a bar code to read the data this represents.

■ baton, staff, rod.

wan•der /wóndər/ *v.* **1** *intr.* go from place to place aimlessly. **2** *intr.* **a** wind about; diverge; meander. **b** stray from a path, etc. **3** *intr.* talk or think incoherently. □ **wan′derer** *n.* **wan′dering** *n.* [esp. in *pl.*].

■ **1** walk, roam, rove, range, stray, ramble, stroll. **2 a** snake, zigzag. **3** digress, turn, stray, drift, depart, go off on a tangent.

wan•der•lust /wóndərlust/ *n.* eagerness for traveling or wandering.

wane /wayn/ • *v.intr.* **1** (of the moon) decrease in apparent size after the full moon (cf. WAX²). **2** decrease in power, vigor, etc. • *n.* process of waning. □ **on the wane** declining.

■ *v.* diminish, lessen, dwindle, shrink, decline, die out, abate. • *n.* **1** decrease, diminution, lessening, dwindling, decline. □ **on the wane** on the decrease *or* ebb, diminishing, decreasing.

wan•gle /wánggəl/ *colloq.* • *v.tr.* obtain (a favor, etc.) by scheming, etc. • *n.* act or instance of wangling. □□ **wan′gler** *n.*

■ *v.* scheme, plot, work out, contrive, maneuver.

wan•na•be /wónabee/ *n. sl.* I avid fan who tries to emulate the person he or she admires ▪ anyone who would like to be someone or something else.

want /wont, wawnt/ • *v.* **1** *tr.* **a** desire; wish for possession of; need. **b** need or desire (a person, esp. sexually). **2** *intr.* lack. **3** *tr.* be without or fall short of. **4** *tr.* (as **wanted** *adj.*) (of a suspected criminal, etc.) sought by the police. • *n.* **1 a** lack, deficiency. **b** poverty; need. **2** craving. See synonym study at LACK. □ **want ad** classified newspaper advertisement, esp. for something sought. □□ **want′er** *n.*

■ *v.* **1 a** crave, long for, fancy, covet. **2, 3** need, miss, require, call for, demand, be deficient in. • *n.* **1 a** need, shortage, dearth, scarcity; absence. **b** indigence, destitution, privation. **2** appetite, hunger, thirst, longing, yearning.

want•ing /wónting, wáwn–/ • *adj.* **1** lacking, not equal to requirements. **2** absent; not supplied.

■ **1** deficient, inadequate, not up to par, insufficient, unsatisfactory, second-rate. **2** missing, lacking, short (of).

wan•ton /wóntən/ • *adj.* **1** licentious; lewd.

2 capricious; arbitrary. **3** luxuriant; unrestrained. • *n. literary* immoral or licentious person, esp. a woman. □□ **wan′ton•ly** *adv.* **wan′ton•ness** *n.*

■ *adj.* **1** immoral, dissolute, profligate, dissipated, depraved, promiscuous. **2** random, indiscriminate, unjustified, unprovoked, purposeless. **3** lavish, extravagant, luxurious; abandoned, undisciplined, ungoverned. • *n.* loose woman, prostitute, voluptuary, trollop, Jezebel.

wa•pi•ti /wópitee/ *n.* N. American deer; elk.

war /wawr/ • *n.* **1 a** armed hostilities, esp. between nations; conflict. **b** specific period or instance of this. **2** (as **the war**) most recent major war. **3 a** hostility or contention between people, groups, etc. **b** sustained campaign against crime, disease, poverty, etc. • *v.intr.* (**warred, war•ring**) make war. □ **at war** engaged in a war. **go to war** declare or begin a war. □□ **war′ring** *adj.*

■ *n.* **1** warfare, combat, fighting, clash. **3 b** drive, crusade, battle, fight. • *v.* do battle, fight, struggle, take up arms. □ **at war** fighting, battling; antagonistic. □□ **warring** rival; antagonistic.

war•ble /wáwrbəl/ • *v.* **1** *intr. & tr.* sing in a gentle, trilling manner. **2** *tr.* speak or utter in a warbling manner. • *n.* warbled song or utterance.

war•bler /wáwrblər/ *n.* person, bird, etc., that warbles.

ward /wawrd/ • *n.* **1** division of a hospital, prison, etc. **2** administrative division of a city or town, esp. an electoral district. **3 a** minor under the care of a guardian or a court. **b** (in full **ward of the court**) minor or mentally deficient person placed under the protection of a court. **4** [in *pl.*] corresponding notches and projections in a key and a lock. **5** *archaic* guardian's control. • *v.tr. archaic* guard; protect. □ **ward heeler** party worker in elections, etc. **ward off 1** parry (a blow). **2** avert (danger, etc.).

■ *n.* **1** district, precinct, section, zone, quarter. **3** dependent, charge, protégé(e). □ **ward off** fend off, repel, avoid, block, thwart.

-ward /wərd/ *suffix* (also **–wards**) added to nouns of place or destination and to adverbs of direction and forming: **1** adverbs meaning 'toward the place, etc.' (*moving backward*). **2** adjectives meaning 'turned or tending toward' (*downward look*). **3** (less commonly) nouns meaning 'the region toward or about' (*look to the eastward*).

war•den /wáwrd'n/ *n.* **1** chief administrator of a prison. **2** supervising official (*game warden*).

ward•er /wáwrdər/ *n.* guard; caretaker.

ward•robe /wáwrdrōb/ *n.* **1** large cupboard for storing clothes. **2** person's entire stock of clothes. **3** costume department or costumes of a theater, a movie company, etc.

■ **1** closet. **2** (collection *or* stock of) clothing *or* clothes *or formal* attire *or* apparel.

ward•room /wáwrdroom, –room/ *n.* mess in a warship for commissioned officers.

ware /wair/ n. [often in comb.] **1** things of the same kind made usu. for sale (chinaware, hardware). **2** [usu. in pl.] articles for sale. **3** ceramics, etc., of a specified material, factory, or kind (Wedgwood ware, delftware).
■ **2** (wares) merchandise, goods, commodities, supplies.

ware•house /wáirhows/ ● n. building in which goods are stored. ● v.tr. (also /–howz/) store, esp. temporarily, in a repository.
■ n. storehouse, storeroom, depository.

war•fare /wáwrfair/ n. campaigning or engaging in war.

war•head /wáwrhed/ n. explosive head of a missile, torpedo, or similar weapon.

war•horse /wáwrhawrs/ n. colloq. veteran soldier, politician, etc.

war•like /wáwrlīk/ adj. **1** hostile. **2** soldierly.
■ **1** combative, militant, belligerent; hawkish, warmongering. **2** see MARTIAL 2.

war•lock /wáwrlok/ n. archaic sorcerer or wizard.

war•lord /wáwrlawrd/ n. military commander, esp. in a warlike nation.

warm /wawrm/ ● adj. **1** of or at a fairly high temperature. **2** (clothes, etc.) affording warmth. **3 a** sympathetic; friendly. **b** enthusiastic. **4** colloq. **a** close to the object, etc., sought. **b** near to guessing. **5** Hunting (of a scent) fresh and strong. ● v. **1** tr. **a** make warm. **b** make cheerful. **2** intr. **a** warm oneself. **b** [often foll. by to] become animated or sympathetic. □ **warm-blooded** having blood that maintains a warm temperature. **warmed-up** (or **-over**) **1** (of food, etc.) reheated. **2** secondhand. **warm front** advancing mass of warm air. **warm up 1** prepare for a contest, performance, etc., by practicing. **2** (of a room, etc.) become warmer. **3** (of a person) become enthusiastic, etc. **4** (of an engine, etc.) reach a temperature for efficient working. **5** reheat (food). **warm-up** n. period of preparatory exercise for a contest or performance. □□ **warm'er** n. [also in comb.] **warm'ish** adj. **warm'ly** adv. **warm'ness** n. **warmth** n.
■ adj. **1** heated, tepid, lukewarm, warmish, cozy. **3 a** amiable, cordial, affable, pleasant, genial. **b** ardent, hearty, wholehearted. ● v. **1 a** heat (up). **b** stir, move, please, delight, gladden. **2 b** (warm to) become less hostile to, become enthusiastic or supportive of. □ **warm-blooded** homeothermic, homeothermal. **warm up 1** see EXERCISE v. 3. **5** heat up, warm over. **warm-up** see EXERCISE n. 3. □□ **warmish** tepid, lukewarm. **warmly** cordially, amiably, amicably; affectionately, tenderly, fondly; well, kindly; vigorously, intensely, fiercely; heatedly, vehemently, vociferously. **warmth** heat, warmness, hotness, torridity; cordiality, heartiness, friendliness; ardor, effusiveness, enthusiasm, irritation, indignation, annoyance.

warm•heart•ed /wáwrmháartid/ adj. kind; friendly. □□ **warm'heart'ed•ly** adv. **warm'heart'ed•ness** n.

war•mon•ger /wáwrmunggər, –mong–/ n.

person who seeks to bring about or promote war. □□ **war'mon•ger•ing** n. & adj.

warn /wawrn/ v.tr. **1 a** inform of danger, etc. **b** advise; inform. **2** admonish. □□ **warn'er** n.
■ caution, notify, apprise, alert.

warn•ing /wáwrning/ n. anything that serves to warn. □ **warning track** (or **path**) Baseball dirt strip that borders the outfield just inside the fence. □□ **warn'ing•ly** adv.
■ caution, admonition, advice, counsel, caveat; lesson, example; omen, sign, signal, indication, hint.

warp /wawrp/ ● v. **1** make or become twisted out of shape. **2** make or become perverted or strange. ● n. **1 a** state of being warped, esp. of lumber. **b** perversion, bitterness, etc., of the mind or character. **2** lengthwise threads in a loom. □□ **warp'age** n. (esp. in sense 1 of v.).
■ v. **1** contort, distort, deform. **2** corrupt, twist. ● n. **1** twist, contortion, distortion, bias, deformity.

war•path /wáwrpath/ n. **1** warlike expedition of N. American Indians. **2** colloq. hostile course or attitude (is on the warpath again).

war•rant /wáwrənt, wór–/ ● n. **1** authorization; justification. **2** written authorization allowing police to search premises, arrest a suspect, etc. ● v.tr. **1** justify. **2** guarantee or attest to. □ **warrant officer** officer ranking between commissioned officers and NCOs. □□ **war'rant•er** n. **war'ran•tor** n.
■ n. **1** sanction, reason, approval, validation. **2** writ, order, authority. ● v. **1** authorize, sanction, explain, approve. **2** promise, assure, ensure, answer for.

war•ran•ty /wáwrəntee, wór–/ n. (pl. **–ties**) guarantee of the ownership or quality of a thing sold, etc., often accepting responsibility for defects or repairs.
■ assurance, promise, commitment.

war•ren /wáwrən, wór–/ n. **1** network of interconnecting rabbit burrows. **2** densely populated or labyrinthine building or district.

war•ri•or /wáwreeər, wór–/ n. person experienced or distinguished in fighting.

war•ship /wáwrship/ n. armored ship used in war.

wart /wawrt/ n. **1** small, hard, round growth on the skin. **2** protuberance on the surface of a plant, etc. □□ **wart'y** adj.

wart•hog /wáwrt-hog/ n. African wild pig.

war•y /wáiree/ adj. (war•i•er, war•i•est) **1** on one's guard; circumspect. **2** cautious. See synonym study at VIGILANT. □□ **war'i•ly** adv. **war'i•ness** n.
■ careful, guarded, prudent, apprehensive.

was 1st & 3rd sing. past of BE.

Wash. abbr. Washington.

wash /wosh, wawsh/ ● v. **1** tr. cleanse with liquid, esp. water. **2** tr. remove (a stain) in this way. **3** intr. wash oneself. **4** intr. wash clothes, etc. **5** intr. [foll. by off, out] (of a stain, etc.) be removed by washing. **6** tr. poet. moisten; water. **7** tr. (of a river, etc.) touch (a coast, etc.). **8** tr. (of moving liquid) carry along in a specified direction (a wave washed him overboard). **9** intr. sweep, move, or splash. **10** *tr.* sift (ore) by the action of water. **11** *tr.* **a** brush a thin coat of watery paint or ink over. **b** coat (inferior metal) with gold, etc. • *n.* **1** act or instance of washing. **2** clothes for washing or just washed. **3** visible or audible motion of agitated water or air, esp. due to the passage of a ship or aircraft. **4** liquid to spread over a surface to cleanse, heal, or color. **5** thin coating of watercolor, wall paint, or metal. □ **come out in the wash** *colloq.* be resolved in the course of time. **wash-and-wear** *adj.* (of a fabric or garment) not requiring ironing. **wash down 1** wash completely. **2** [usu. foll. by *with*] accompany or follow (food) with a drink. **washed out 1** faded. **2** pale. **3** *colloq.* limp; enfeebled. **washed up** *sl.* defeated, having failed. **wash one's hands of** renounce responsibility for. **wash-out** *n.* **1** *colloq.* fiasco; complete failure. **2** breach in a road, railroad track, etc., caused by flooding. □□ **wash•a•bil'i•ty** *n.* **wash'a•ble** *adj.*

■ *v.* **1**, **3** wash up, clean (up), bathe, shower, scrub (up). **2** scrub off, soak out; wear away, remove, delete, erase. **8** move, deposit, sweep. **9** spatter, splatter, dash, run, lap, ripple. **10** purify, filter. **11** overlay, film, paint, glaze; plate. • *n.* **1** scrub, scour, shampoo, bath, shower, sponge, sponge bath; laundering. **2** washing, laundry. **3** wave, wake; flow, swell, ebb and flow. **4** lotion, rinse, salve, emulsion; mouthwash; eyewash. **5** film, overlay, glaze; plating. □ **wash down 1** see WASH *v.* 1, 3 above. **washed out 1** bleached. **2** wan, pallid; blanched, bleached. **3** exhausted, spent, tired out. **washed up** finished, through. **wash one's hands of** keep away from, disown, repudiate. **wash-out 1** disaster, debacle, (total) loss.

wash•board /wóshbawrd, wáwsh–/ *n.* ribbed board of wood or sheet of corrugated zinc on which clothes are scrubbed.

wash•cloth /wóshklòth, wáwsh–/ *n.* cloth for washing the face or body.

■ facecloth.

wash•er /wóshər, wáwsh–/ *n.* **1** person or machine that washes. **2** flat ring of rubber, metal, leather, etc., inserted at a joint to tighten and prevent leakage. **3** similar ring placed under the head of a screw, etc., to disperse its pressure.

wash•er•wom•an /wóshərwŏŏmən, wáwsh–/ *n.* (*pl.* **-wom•en**) (also **wash'wom•an**) woman whose occupation is washing clothes; laundress.

wash•ing /wóshing, wáwsh–/ *n.* quantity of clothes for washing or just washed. □ **washing machine** machine for washing clothes and linen, etc.

■ laundry.

wash•room /wóshrŏŏm, –rŏŏm, wáwsh–/ *n.* bathroom.

wash•stand /wóshstànd, wáwsh–/ *n.* piece of furniture to hold a washbowl, pitcher, soap, etc.

was•n't /wúzənt, wóz/ *contr.* was not.

WASP /wosp/ *n.* (also **Wasp**) usu. *derog.* white Anglo-Saxon Protestant. □□ **Wasp'y** *adj.*

wasp /wosp/ *n.* stinging insect with black and yellow stripes and a very thin waist. □□ **wasp'like** *adj.*

wasp•ish /wóspish/ *adj.* irritable; petulant; sharp in retort. □□ **wasp'ish•ly** *adv.* **wasp'ish•ness** *n.*

■ irascible, bad-tempered, testy, grouchy.

was•sail /wósəl, wósayl, wosáyl/ *archaic* • *n.* **1** festive occasion. **2** spiced ale or cider with which toasts were formerly drunk. • *v.intr.* make merry; celebrate with drinking. □□ **was'sail•er** *n.*

wast•age /wáystij/ *n.* **1** amount wasted. **2** loss by use, wear, or leakage. **3** *Commerce* loss of employees other than by layoffs.

waste /wayst/ • *v.* **1** *tr.* use to no purpose or extravagantly. **2** *tr.* fail to use. **3** *tr. & intr.* wear gradually away; make or become weak. **4** *tr.* **a** devastate. **b** *sl.* murder; kill. **5** *intr.* be expended without useful effect. See synonym study at RAVAGE. • *adj.* **1** superfluous. **2** not inhabited or cultivated. • *n.* **1** act or instance of wasting. **2** waste material or food. **3** waste region. □ **go** (or **run**) **to waste** be wasted. **lay waste** ravage; devastate. □□ **waste'less** *adj.*

■ *v.* **1** squander, misuse, throw away, fritter away. **3** enervate, enfeeble, emaciate, debilitate; diminish, deteriorate, atrophy, wither. **4 a** see DEVASTATE 1. **b** assassinate; see also KILL *v.* 1. • *adj.* **1** extra, leftover, unused; worthless, useless, unproductive. **2** barren, empty, unpopulated. • *n.* **1** extravagance, prodigality, wastefulness, squandering; misuse, misapplication, abuse, neglect. **2** refuse, garbage, dregs, debris. **3** wasteland, desert, wilderness, barrens. □ **lay waste** destroy, demolish, ruin, wreck, pillage, sack.

waste•bas•ket /wáystbaskit/ *n.* receptacle for wastepaper.

waste•ful /wáystfŏŏl/ *adj.* **1** extravagant. **2** causing or showing waste. □□ **waste'ful•ly** *adj.* **waste'ful•ness** *n.*

■ spendthrift, profligate, prodigal, lavish, improvident.

waste•land /wáystland/ *n.* **1** unproductive or useless area of land. **2** place or time considered spiritually or intellectually barren.

■ **1** rough ground, scrub, badlands, bomb site; see also WILD *n.*

waste•pa•per /wáystpaypər/ *n.* spoiled, valueless, or discarded paper. □ **wastepaper basket** = WASTEBASKET.

wast•rel /wáystrəl/ *n.* good-for-nothing person.

■ spendthrift, profligate; idler, loafer, shirker.

watch /woch/ • *v.* **1** *tr.* keep the eyes fixed on. **2** *tr.* **a** keep under observation. **b** monitor carefully. **3** *intr.* [often foll. by *for*] be in an alert state; be vigilant. **4** *intr.* [foll. by *over*] look after; take care of. • *n.* **1** small portable timepiece for carrying on one's person. **2** state of alert or constant observation or attention. **3** *Naut.* **a** four-hour period of duty. **b** ship's crew on watch. **4** guard; security officer. □ **watch it** (or **oneself**) *colloq.* be careful. **watch out 1** [often foll. by *for*] be on one's guard. **2** as a warning of immediate danger. ▫▫ **watch'a•ble** *adj.* **watch'er** *n.* [also in *comb.*].

■ *v.* **1** observe, regard, look at; ogle. **2 a, 4** tend, mind, keep an eye on, watch over; chaperon; babysit. **2 b** observe, note, notice, pay attention to. **3** (*watch for*) watch out for, look for, guard against, keep an eye open for. • *n.* **1** pocket watch, wristwatch; chronometer. **2** vigil, surveillance. **4** sentry, sentinel, lookout, (night) watchman, caretaker. ▫ **watch out 1** look out.

watch•band /wóchband/ *n.* strap or bracelet for fastening a watch on the wrist.

watch•dog /wóchdawg, dog/ • *n.* **1** dog kept to guard property, etc. **2** person or body monitoring others' rights, etc. • *v.tr.* (**-dogged, –dog•ging**) maintain surveillance over.

■ *n.* **1** guard dog. **2** see MONITOR *n.* 1.

watch•ful /wóchfool/ *adj.* **1** on the watch. **2** showing vigilance. See synonym study at VIGILANT. ▫▫ **watch'ful•ly** *adv.* **watch'ful•ness** *n.*

watch•man /wóchmən/ *n.* (*pl.* **–men**) person employed to look after an empty building, etc., at night.

■ (security) guard, sentinel, sentry, lookout.

watch•tow•er /wóchtower/ *n.* tower from which observation can be kept.

watch•word /wóchwərd/ *n.* phrase summarizing a guiding principle.

■ see SLOGAN.

wa•ter /wáwtər, wót–/ • *n.* **1** colorless, transparent, odorless, tasteless liquid compound of oxygen and hydrogen. ¶Chem. formula: H_2O. **2** liquid consisting chiefly of this and found in seas, lakes, rivers, and rain. **3** expanse of water. **4** [in *pl.*] part of a sea or river. **5** (often as **the waters**) mineral water at a spa, etc. **6** state of a tide. • *v.* **1** *tr.* sprinkle or soak with water. **2** *tr.* supply (a plant or animal) with water. **3** *intr.* (of the mouth or eyes) secrete water. **4** *tr.* (as **watered** *adj.*) (of silk, etc.) having irregular wavy glossy markings. **5** *intr.* take in a supply of water. ▫ **make one's mouth water** cause one's saliva to flow; stimulate one's appetite or anticipation. **water bed** mattress filled with water. **water buffalo** common domestic E. Indian buffalo. **water chestnut** nutlike tuber from a sedge used esp. in Chinese cooking. **water lily** aquatic plant with broad flat floating leaves and flowers. **water main** main pipe in a water-supply system. **water moccasin** venomous snake of the southern US; cottonmouth. **water pipe 1** pipe for conveying water. **2** hookah. **water polo** ball game played by swimmers. **water rat** aquatic rodent. **water-repellent** not easily penetrated by water. **water ski** each of a pair of skis for skimming the surface of the water when towed by a motorboat. **water table** level below which the ground is saturated with water. **water tower** tower with an elevated tank to store and distribute water. **water wings** inflated floats fixed on the arms of a person learning to swim. ▫▫ **wa'ter•er** *n.*

wa'ter•less *adj.*

■ *n.* **1, 2** *joc.* Adam's ale; distilled water, tap water, drinking water; brine, salt water; heavy water, deuterium oxide. • *v.* **1** inundate, flood, drench, moisten, dampen. **3** run, stream.

wa•ter•col•or /wáwtərkúlər, wótər–/ *n* **1** pigment diluted with water. **2** picture painted with this. ▫▫ **wa'ter•col•or•ist** *n.*

■ **2** aquarelle.

wa•ter•course /wáwtərkawrs, wótər–/ *n.* **1** brook, stream, or artificial water channel. **2** bed along which this flows.

wa•ter•cress /wáwtərkres, wótər–/ *n.* pungent edible plant growing in running water.

wa•ter•fall /wáwtərfawl, wótər–/ *n.* stream or river flowing over a precipice or down a steep hillside.

■ cascade, cataract, fall(s).

wa•ter•fowl /wáwtərfowl, wótər–/ *n.* [usu. collect. as *pl.*] birds frequenting water, esp. swimming game birds.

wa•ter•front /wáwtərfrunt, wótər–/ *n.* part of a town or city adjoining a river, lake, harbor, etc.

wa•ter•line /wáwtərlīn, wótər–/ *n.* line along which the surface of water touches a ship's side.

wa•ter•logged /wáwtərlawgd, –logd, wótər–/ *adj.* saturated or filled with water.

Wa•ter•loo /wáwtərloo, wótər–/ *n.* decisive defeat or contest.

wa•ter•man /wáwtərmən, wótər–/ *n.* (*pl.* **–men**) person who earns a living on the water, esp. a fisherman, etc.

wa•ter•mark /wáwtərmaark, wótər–/ • *n.* faint identifying design in some paper. • *v.tr.* mark with this.

wa•ter•mel•on /wáwtərmelən, wótər–/ *n.* large, smooth, green melon with sweet, juicy red pulp.

wa•ter•pow•er /wáwtərpowr, wótər–/ *n.* mechanical force derived from the weight or motion of water.

wa•ter•proof /wáwtərprōōf, wótər–/ • *adj.* impervious to water. • *v.tr.* make waterproof.

■ *adj.* watertight, sealed.

wa•ter•shed /wáwtərshed, wótər–/ *n.* **1** line of separation between waters flowing to different rivers, basins, or seas. **2** turning point in affairs.

wa•ter•spout /wáwtərspowt, wótər–/ *n.* gyrating column of water and spray formed by a whirlwind between sea and cloud.

wa•ter•tight /wáwtərtīt, wótər–/ *adj.* ⊥ closely fastened or fitted to prevent the passage of water. **2** (of an argument, etc.) unassailable.

■ **1** sealed, waterproof. **2** impregnable, solid, airtight, flawless, faultless, incontrovertible.

wa•ter•way /wáwtərway, wótər–/ *n.* navigable channel.

wa•ter•works /wáwtərwərks, wótər–/ *n.* **1** establishment for managing a water supply. **2** *colloq.* shedding of tears.

wa•ter•y /wáwtəree, wótər–/ *adj.* **1** containing too much water. **2** too thin in consistency. **3** of or consisting of water. **4** (of the eyes) suffused or running with water. **5** (of conversation, style, etc.) vapid; uninteresting. □□ **wa'ter•i•ness** *n.*

■ **1** wet, swampy, boggy, marshy, soggy, moist, damp, humid. **2** weak, dilute(d), watered down. **3** weeping, teary, tearful. **5** insipid, jejune, flat, dull.

WATS /wots/ *abbr.* Wide-Area Telecommunications Service.

watt /wot/ *n.* the SI unit of electrical power, equivalent to one joule per second. ¶Symb.: **W**.

watt•age /wótij/ *n.* amount of electrical power expressed in watts.

wat•tle[1] /wót'l/ • *n.* interlaced rods and split rods used for fences, etc. • *v.tr.* make of wattle.

wat•tle[2] /wót'l/ • *n.* loose fleshy appendage on the head or throat of a turkey or other birds. □□ **wat'tled** *adj.*

wave /wayv/ • *v.* **1 a** *intr.* [often foll. by *to*] move a hand, etc., to and fro in greeting or as a signal. **b** *tr.* move (a hand, etc.) in this way. **2 a** *intr.* show a sinuous or sweeping motion as of a flag, tree, or a wheat field in the wind. **b** *tr.* impart a waving motion to. **3** *tr.* tell or direct (a person) by waving. **4** *tr.* express (a greeting, etc.) by waving. **5** *tr.* give an undulating form to (hair, etc.). **6** *intr.* (of hair, etc.) be wavy. • *n.* **1** ridge of water between two depressions. **2** such a ridge curling into an arched form and breaking on the shore. **3** fluctuating motion, etc. **4** gesture of waving. **5** undulating form, as in the hair. **6** *Physics* **a** disturbance of the particles of a fluid medium for the propagation or direction of motion, heat, light, sound, etc. **b** single curve in the course of this motion. □ **make waves** *colloq.* cause trouble. □□ **wave'less** *adj.* **wave'like** *adj. & adv.*

■ *v.* **1 a** sign, gesture, gesticulate. **2** undulate, billow, flap, flutter; wag. **3** signal, sign, indicate; gesture, gesticulate. • *n.* **1, 2** swell, undulation, roller, whitecap; ripple, wavelet, breaker, comber. **4** signal, sign, gesticulation.

wave•form /wáyvfawrm/ *n. Physics* curve showing the shape of a wave at a given time.

wave•length /wáyvlengkth, -length, -lenth/ *n.* **1** distance between successive crests of a wave. ¶Symb.: λ. **2** *colloq.* particular mode or range of thinking.

wave•let /wáyvlit/ *n.* small wave on water.

wa•ver /wáyvər/ *v.intr.* **1** be or become unsteady. **2** be irresolute. **3** (of a light) flicker. □□ **wa'ver•er** *n.* **wa'ver•ing•ly** *adv.*

wav•y /wáyvee/ *adj.* (**wav•i•er, wav•i•est**) having waves or alternate contrary curves. □□ **wav'i•ly** *adv.* **wav'i•ness** *n.*

wax[1] /waks/ • *n.* **1** sticky, plastic, yellowish substance secreted by bees as the material of honeycomb cells; beeswax. **2** this used for candles, modeling, etc. **3** any similar substance, e.g., earwax. • *v.tr.* cover or treat with wax. □ **wax bean** yellow-podded snap bean. **wax paper** (also **waxed paper**) paper waterproofed with a layer of wax. □□ **wax'er** *n.* **wax'i•ly** *adv.* **wax'i•ness** *n.* **wax'y** *adj.* (**wax•i•er, wax•i•est**).

wax[2] /waks/ *v.intr.* **1** (of the moon between new and full) increasing in apparent size.

---

2 become larger or stronger. **3** pass into a specified state or mood. □ **wax and wane** undergo alternate increases and decreases.

■ **2** see GROW 1. **3** see BECOME 1.

wax•en /wáksən/ *adj.* of, consisting of, or like wax.

wax•wing /wákswing/ *n.* any of various birds with small tips like red sealing wax to some wing feathers.

wax•work /wákswərk/ *n.* **1** object, esp. a lifelike dummy, modeled in wax. **2** [in *pl.*] exhibition of wax dummies.

way /way/ • *n.* **1** road, track, path, etc. **2** course or route for reaching a place. **3** place of passage into a building, through a door, etc. **4 a** method or plan for attaining an object. **b** the ability to obtain one's object. **5 a** person's desired or chosen course of action. **b** custom or manner of behaving. **6** normal course of events. **7** traveling distance. **8** unimpeded opportunity of advance. **9** impetus; progress. **10** specified direction. **11** [in *pl.*] parts into which a thing is divided. **12** specified condition. **13** respect (*useful in some ways*). **14 a** [in *pl.*] structure of lumber, etc., down which a new ship is launched. **b** parallel rails, etc., as a track for the movement of a machine. • *adv. colloq.* far. □ **by the way** incidentally. **by way of 1** by means of. **2** as a form of. **3** passing through. **give way 1 a** make concessions. **b** yield. **2** (of a structure, etc.) collapse. **go out of one's way** make a special effort. **lead the way** act as guide or leader. **way-out** *colloq.* **1** unusual; eccentric. **2** excellent. **ways and means** methods of achieving something, esp. of raising government revenue.

■ *n.* **1, 2** street, avenue. **4 a** manner, means, system, strategy. **b** knack, skill, ability. **5 b** habit, approach, style; idiosyncrasy, peculiarity, eccentricity. **7** haul. **8** clearance, pathway, opening, space. **9** passage, advance, headway. **12** situation, state. **13** aspect, particular, detail. □ **by the way** by the by, parenthetically, in passing. **by way of 1** via, through. **2** (functioning) as, as a substitute for. **give way 1** surrender, retreat, concede, defer. **2** give, cave in, fall (down). **go out of one's way** see *make a point of* (POINT). **lead the way** see GUIDE *v.* 1, 3. **way-out 1** bizarre, mad, weird, offbeat, outrageous. **2** see SPLENDID 3.

-way /way/ *suffix* = -WAYS.

way•far•er /wáyfairər/ *n.* traveler, esp. on foot. □□ **way'far•ing** *n.*

way•lay /wáylay/ *v.tr.* (*past* and *past part.* **way•laid**) **1** lie in wait for. **2** stop to rob or interview. □□ **way'lay•er** *n.*

■ **1** ambush, await, bushwhack. **2** hold up, detain, intercept, attack.

-ways /wayz/ *suffix* forming adjectives and adverbs of direction or manner (*sideways*).

way•side /wáysīd/ *n.* side of a road.

way•ward /wáywərd/ *adj.* childishly self-willed or perverse. □□ **way'ward•ly** *adv.* **way'ward•ness** *n.*

■ see CAPRICIOUS, PERVERSE 2.

we /wee/ *pron.* (*obj.* **us**; *poss.* **our, ours**) **1** *pl.*

of 1[2] used by and with reference to more than one person. **2** used for or by a royal person, an editor, etc., when speaking.

weak /week/ *adj.* **1** deficient in strength, power, vigor, or number. **2** easily led. **3** unconvincing. **4** (of a syllable, etc.) unstressed. **5** *Gram.* (of a verb) forming inflections by the addition of a suffix to the stem. □ **weak-kneed** *colloq.* lacking resolution. **weak-minded 1** mentally deficient. **2** lacking in resolution. **weak moment** time when one is unusually compliant or temptable. □□ **weak′ish** *adj.*

■ **1** feeble, frail, fragile, flimsy, breakable, shaky, infirm; powerless, helpless, defenseless; (*of visible or audible things*) faint, subdued, indistinct; (*of visible things*) dim, poor, dull, pale, faded, vague, hazy; (*of audible things*) low, soft, hushed, muffled. **2** unassertive, retiring, namby-pamby, spineless, irresolute, impotent, powerless, ineffectual. **3** feeble, lame, half-baked, unpersuasive. □□ **weak-kneed** see WEAK 3 above. **weak-minded 1** dim-witted, feebleminded, simple. **2** see WEAK 3 above.

SYNONYM STUDY: **weak**

DEBILITATED, DECREPIT, FEEBLE, FRAIL, INFIRM. Someone who is *weak* lacks physical, mental, or moral strength (*a weak heart; a weak excuse; too weak to resist temptation*). But there's nothing to suggest what the cause of this lack of strength might be. Someone who is *frail,* on the other hand, is *weak* because he or she has a slight build or delicate constitution (*a small, frail man*). Calling someone *feeble* implies that his or her weakness is pitiable (*too feeble to get out of bed*); when applied to things, *feeble* means faint or inadequate (*a feeble light*). *Infirm* suggests a loss of strength or soundness, as from aging or illness (*poverty and illness had made him infirm*). *Debilitated* and *decrepit* also suggest that strength once present has been lost. But while someone who is young may be *debilitated* by disease, *decrepit* specifically refers to a loss of strength due to advanced age or long use (*a decrepit old woman who seldom left her house; a decrepit building that would soon be torn down*).

---

weak•en /weekən/ *v.* **1** *tr. & intr.* make or become weak or weaker. **2** *intr.* relent; give way; succumb to temptation, etc. □□ **weak′en•er** *n.*

■ **1** debilitate, enfeeble, enervate, emasculate, mitigate; fade, dwindle, decline. **2** give in, acquiesce, yield; soften, bend, ease up, let up, relax; succumb (to temptation).

weak•ling /weekling/ *n.* feeble person or animal.

■ runt, milksop, baby, mollycoddle, lightweight.

weak•ly /weeklee/ • *adv.* in a weak manner. • *adj.* (**weak•li•er, weak•li•est**) sickly; not robust. □□ **weak′li•ness** *n.*

■ *adj.* see PUNY 1, 2, UNHEALTHY 1.

weak•ness /weeknis/ *n.* **1** being weak. **2** weak point. **3** self-indulgent liking.

■ **1** feebleness, frailty, fragility, flimsiness, debility. **2** foible, failing, fault, shortcoming. **3** soft spot, fondness, affection, preference, bent.

weal[1] /weel/ • *n.* ridge raised on the flesh by a stroke of a rod or whip. • *v.tr.* mark with a weal.

weal[2] /weel/ *n. literary* welfare; prosperity; good fortune.

wealth /welth/ *n.* **1** riches. **2** state of being rich. **3** abundance.

■ **1** affluence, money, opulence, prosperity. **2** affluence, prosperity, opulence. **3** profusion, bounty, copiousness, fullness.

wealth•y /welthee/ *adj.* (**wealth•i•er, wealth•i•est**) having an abundance, esp. of money. □□ **wealth′i•ly** *adv.* **wealth′i•ness** *n.*

■ rich, affluent, well off, prosperous, well-to-do, opulent.

SYNONYM STUDY: **wealthy**

AFFLUENT, FLUSH, OPULENT, PROSPEROUS, WELL-TO-DO. If you have more money, possessions, or property than is necessary to satisfy normal needs, you are **rich.** If you're *rich* and are also an established and prominent member of the community whose lifestyle is in keeping with your income, you are **wealthy** (*a wealthy family whose influence on public opinion could not be ignored*). **Affluent** comes from the Latin word meaning to flow, and it connotes a generous income (*an affluent neighborhood*), while **opulent** suggests lavish spending or an ostentatious display of wealth (*an opulent mansion with every imaginable luxury*). One may come from an *affluent* family, in other words, and not have a particularly *opulent* lifestyle. If you're **prosperous**, you are thriving or flourishing (*a prosperous merchant; a prosperous business*). While *prosperous* suggests an economic situation that is on the rise, **flush** means having plenty of money on hand at a particular time (*she was feeling flush after receiving her first paycheck*). **Well-to-do** implies a comfortable income, enough to support easy living but not necessarily enough to be considered rich (*they were known as a well-to-do family with a strong commitment to educating their children*).

---

wean /ween/ *v.tr.* **1** accustom (an infant or other young mammal) to food other than (esp. its mother's) milk. **2** disengage (from a habit, etc.).

weap•on /wepən/ *n.* **1** thing designed or used or usable for inflicting bodily harm. **2** means for trying to gain the advantage in a conflict. □□ **weap′oned** *adj.* [also in *comb.*]. **weap′on•less** *adj.*

■ **2** see DEVICE 2. □□ **weaponless** unarmed, unprotected, defenseless.

wea•pon•ize /wepəniz/ *v. tr.* make suitable for use as a weapon (*anthrax is easily weaponized*). □□ **wea•pon•i•za′tion** *n.*

weap•on•ry /wepənree/ *n.* weapons collectively.

wear /wair/ • *v.* (*past* **wore** /wawr/; *past part.* **worn** /wawrn/) **1** *tr.* have on one's person as clothing or an ornament, etc. **2** *tr.* be dressed habitually in. **3** *tr.* exhibit or present (a facial expression, etc.). **4 a** *tr.* injure the surface of, or partly obliterate or alter, by rubbing, stress, or use. **b** *intr.* undergo such injury or change. **5** *tr. & intr.* [foll. by *off, away*] rub or be rubbed off. **6** *tr. & intr.* exhaust. **7** *tr.* [foll. by *down*] overcome by persistence. **8** *intr.* endure continued use or life. • *n.* **1** wearing or being worn. **2** [often in *comb.*] things worn; clothing (*sportswear*). **3** (in full **wear and tear**) damage sustained from continuous use. □ **wear off** lose effectiveness or intensity. **wear out** use or be used until no longer usable. □□ **wear'a•ble** *adj.* **wear•a•bil•i•ty** /wáirabilitee/ *n.* **wear'er** *n.* **wear'ing** *adj.* **wear'ing•ly** *adv.*

• *v.* **1, 2** be in, sport. **3** display, show, exhibit. **4 wear down** *or* **away**, damage, impair, harm, fray. **6** tire, fatigue, debilitate, weary. **7** (*wear down*) see GRIND *v.* 3. **8** last, survive, hold up, bear up, stand up. • *n.* **1** use, utilization. **2** garb, clothes, dress, apparel. **3** attrition, deterioration, damage. □ **wear off** see SUBSIDE 1. □ **wearing** tiring, exhausting, wearying, enervating; irksome, tedious, vexing.

wea•ri•some /wéereesəm/ *adj.* tedious; tiring by monotony or length. □□ **wea'ri•some•ly** *adv.* **wea'ri•some•ness** *n.*

■ see TEDIOUS.

wea•ry /wéeree/ • *adj.* (**wea•ri•er, wea•ri•est**) **1** very tired. **2** impatient of. **3** tiring or tedious. See synonym study at TIRED. • *v.* (**-ries, -ried**) make or grow weary. □□ **wea'ri•less** *adj.* **wea'ri•ly** *adv.* **wea'ri•ness** *n.* **wea'ry•ing•ly** *adv.*

■ *adj.* **1** fatigued, exhausted, worn out, drained. **2** bored, jaded, blasé, fed up. **3** boring, irksome, irritating, vexing, annoying. • *v.* exhaust, enervate, fatigue, tire, debilitate. □□ **weariness** see LETHARGY 2.

wea•sel /wéezəl/ • *n.* small, flesh-eating mammal related to the stoat and ferret. • *v.* **1** equivocate or quibble. **2** [foll. by *on, out*] default on an obligation. □□ **wea'sel•ly** *adj.*

weath•er /wéthər/ • *n.* state of the atmosphere at a place and time as regards heat, cloudiness, dryness, sunshine, wind, and rain, etc. • *v.* **1** expose to or affect by atmospheric changes. **2 a** *tr.* discolor or partly disintegrate (rock or stones) by exposure to air. **b** *intr.* be discolored or worn in this way. **3** *tr.* come safely through (a storm, difficult period, etc.). **4** *tr.* (of a ship or its crew) get to the windward of (a cape, etc.). □ **under the weather** *colloq.* indisposed or out of sorts; drunk. **weather-beaten** affected by exposure to the weather **weather strip** (or **stripping**) piece of material used to proof a door or window against rain or wind **weather-strip** install a weather strip. **weather vane** see VANE.

■ *n.* **1** (meteorological) condition(s), climate, the elements. • *v.* **3** stand, survive, bear up against, endure, withstand. □ **under the weather** ailing, ill, sickly, unwell; see also DRUNK *adj.* 1. **weather-beaten** dry, craggy, rugged; tanned, brown, bronzed; sunburnt.

weath•er•cock /wéthərkok/ *n.* weather vane in the form of a cock.

weath•er•man /wéthərman/ *n.* (*pl.* **-men**)

meteorologist, esp. one who broadcasts a weather forecast.

weath•er•proof /wéthərproof/ • *adj.* resistant to the effects of bad weather, esp. rain. • *v.tr.* make weatherproof. □□ **weath'er•proofed** *adj.*

weave[1] /weev/ • *v.* (*past* **wove** /wōv/; *past part.* **wo•ven** /wóvən/ *or* **wove**) **1** *tr.* form (fabric) by interlacing long threads in two directions. **2** *intr.* **a** make fabric in this way. **b** work at a loom. **3** *tr.* make (a basket or wreath, etc.) by interlacing rushes or flowers, etc. **4** *tr.* make (facts, etc.) into a story or connected whole. • *n.* style of weaving. □□ **weav'er** *n.*

■ *v.* **1** braid, plait, entwine, intertwine, interweave. **4** blend, combine, fuse, merge, construct, make, contrive.

weave[2] /weev/ *v.intr.* move repeatedly from side to side.

■ zigzag, crisscross, make one's way, wind, dodge, bob and weave, shift, *literary or archaic* wend one's way.

web /web/ *n.* **1 a** woven fabric. **b** amount woven in one piece. **2** connected series (*web of lies*). **3** cobweb, gossamer, or similar product of a spinning creature. **4** membrane between the toes of a swimming animal or bird. **5** large roll of paper used in printing. □ **web-footed** having the toes connected by webs. □□ **webbed** *adj.*

■ **2** net, network, mesh, tangle. **3** spider's web; snare, trap.

web•bing /wébing/ *n.* strong, narrow, closely woven fabric used for belts, etc.

we•ber /wébər, váybər/ *n.* the SI unit of magnetic flux. ¶Abbr.: **Wb**

web•zine /wébzeen/ • *n.* magazine published on the Internet.

Wed. *abbr.* Wednesday.

wed /wed/ *v.* (**wed•ding**; *past* and *past part.* **wed•ded** or **wed**) **1** usu. *formal* or *literary* **a** *tr. & intr.* marry. **b** *tr.* join in marriage **2** *tr.* unite. **3** *tr.* (as **wedded** *adj.*) of or in marriage. **4** *tr.* (as **wedded** *adj.*) [foll. by *to*] obstinately attached.

■ **1** get married, become husband and wife; lead down the aisle. **2** combine, ally, marry, blend, merge. **3** (**wedded**) see *matrimonial* (MATRIMONY). **4** (**wedded to**) intimately attached or connected to, enamored of, devoted to.

we'd /weed/ *contr.* **1** we had. **2** we should; we would.

wed•ding /wéding/ *n.* marriage ceremony.

■ wedding ceremony; nuptials.

wedge /wej/ • *n.* **1** piece of wood or metal, etc., tapering to a sharp edge, driven between two objects or parts to secure or separate them. **2** anything resembling a wedge. • *v.tr.* **1** secure or fasten by means of a wedge. **2** force open or apart with a wedge. **3** pack or thrust (a thing or oneself) tightly in or into. □ **wedge'like** *adj.* **wedge'wise** *adv.*

■ *n.* **1** block, chock, cleat; separator, division, partition, split. **2** see SLAB *n.* • *v.* **3** ram, jam, stuff, cram.

wed•lock /wédlok/ *n.* married state.

■ marriage, matrimony.

Wednes•day /wénzday, –dee/ n. fourth day of the week, following Tuesday.

wee /wee/ adj. (**we•er** /wéeər/; **we•est** /wéeist/) little; tiny.

■ small, diminutive, minuscule, microscopic; unimportant, insignificant.

weed /weed/ • n. **1** plant growing where it is not wanted. **2** sl. **a** marijuana. **b** tobacco. • v. **1** tr. **a** clear (an area) of weeds. **b** remove unwanted plants from. **2** tr. [foll. by out] sort out (inferior or unwanted parts, etc.) for removal. □□ **weed′er** n. **weed′less** adj.

■ v. **2** (weed out) exclude, eliminate, remove, root out; screen, sift, clarify, refine, purge.

weeds /weedz/ n.pl. (in full **widow's weeds**) deep mourning worn by a widow.

weed•y /wéedee/ adj. (**weed•i•er**, **weed•i•est**) **1** having many weeds. **2** of or like a weed. □□ **weed′i•ness** n.

week /week/ n. **1** period of seven days reckoned usu. from and to midnight on Saturday–Sunday. **2** period of seven days reckoned from any point (stay for a week). **3** six days between Sundays. **4 a** Monday to Friday. **b** normal amount of work done in this period.

week•day /wéekday/ n. day other than Sunday or other than at a weekend [often attrib.: (a weekday afternoon)].

week•end /wéekénd/ • n. **1** Saturday and Sunday. **2** this period extended slightly esp. for a vacation, etc. • v.intr. spend a weekend.

week•ly /wéeklee/ • adj. done, produced, or occurring once a week. • adv. once a week. • n. (pl. **–lies**) weekly newspaper or periodical.

weep /weep/ v. (past and past part. **wept** /wept/) **1** intr. shed tears. **2** tr. & [foll. by for] intr. bewail; lament over. **3 a** intr. be covered with or send forth drops. **b** intr. & tr. exude liquid. **4** intr. (as **weeping** adj.) (of a tree) having drooping branches. □□ **weep′er** n. **weep′ing•ly** adv. **weep′y** adj. (**weep•i•er**, **weep•i•est**).

■ v. **1**, **2** cry, bawl, blubber, sob, wail, keen, lament, mourn. **3** ooze, seep, drip.

wee•vil /wéevil/ n. destructive beetle feeding esp. on grain, cotton, etc. □□ **wee′vil•y** adj.

weft /weft/ n. threads woven across a warp to make fabric.

weigh /way/ v. **1** tr. find the weight of. **2** tr. balance in the hands to guess or as if to guess the weight of. **3** compare. **4** tr. be equal to (a specified weight). **5** intr. exert an influence. **6** intr. [often foll. by on] be heavy or burdensome (on). □**weigh anchor** see ANCHOR. **weigh down 1** bring or keep down. **2** be oppressive. □□ **weigh′a•ble** adj. **weigh′er** n.

■ **3** judge, estimate, assess; see also COMPARE v. **2**. **4** weigh in at or out at. **5** matter, count, carry weight, be of value. **6** (weigh on) lie heavy on, burden, depress, prey on, preoccupy. □ **weigh down 1** see WEIGHT v. **2** burden, load, overload, encumber, tax.

weight /wayt/ • n. **1** Physics force experienced by a body as a result of the earth's gravitation. **2** heaviness of a body. **3** quantitative expression of a body's weight. **4** body of a known weight for use in weighing. **5** heavy body, esp. used in a mechanism, etc. **6** load or burden. **7 a** influence; importance. **b** preponderance. • v.tr. **1 a** attach a weight to. **b** hold down with a weight. **2** impede or burden.

■ n. **2**, **3** mass, tonnage, heft. **6** millstone, onus, pressure. **7 a** authority, power, substance. **b** mass, bulk. • v. **1** load, charge, ballast, weigh down.

weight•less /wáytlis/ adj. not apparently acted on by gravity. □□ **weight′less•ly** adv. **weight′less•ness** n.

weight•lift•ing /wáytlifting/ n. sport or exercise of lifting heavy weights. □□ **weight′lift•er** n.

weight•y /wáytee/ adj. (**weight•i•er**, **weight•i•est**) **1** heavy. **2** momentous. **3** (of utterances, etc.) deserving careful consideration. **4** influential; authoritative. See synonym study at HEAVY. □□ **weight′i•ly** adv. **weight′i•ness** n.

■ **1** ponderous; massive, huge, bulky, substantial. **2** important, consequential, significant. **3**, **4** convincing, persuasive, impressive, powerful; forceful. □□ **weightiness** see GRAVITY **3a**.

weir /weer/ n. **1** dam built across a river to raise the level of water upstream or regulate its flow. **2** enclosure of stakes, etc., set in a stream as a trap for fish.

weird /weerd/ adj. **1** uncanny; supernatural. **2** colloq. queer; incomprehensible. □□ **weird′ly** adv. **weird′ness** n.

■ strange, odd, peculiar, bizarre, curious.

weird•o /wéerdō/ n. (pl. **–os**) colloq. odd or eccentric person.

■ madman, madwoman, lunatic, psychotic, crank, colloq. crazy, oddball, queer fish, freak.

welch var. of WELSH.

wel•come /wélkəm/ • n. act of greeting or receiving gladly; kind or glad reception. • int. expressing such a greeting. • v.tr. receive with a welcome. • adj. **1** received with pleasure. **2 a** allowed or invited. **b** iron. gladly given (an unwelcome task, thing, etc.) (here's my work and you are welcome to it). □□ **wel′come•ly** adv. **wel′come•ness** n. **wel′com•er** n. **wel′com•ing•ly** adv.

■ n. reception, salutation, glad hand. • v. greet, hail, meet, offer hospitality to. • adj. **1** accepted, well-received, desirable, appreciated. **2 a** freely permitted, entitled, suffered; (be welcome) may.

weld /weld/ • v.tr. **1 a** hammer or press (heated pieces of metal) into one piece. **b** join by fusion with an electric arc, etc. **c** form by welding into some article. **2** unite; join. • n. welded joint. □□ **weld′a•ble** adj. **weld•a•bil′i•ty** n. **weld′er** n.

■ v. **1** fuse, attach, connect, link; bond. **2** combine, merge, fuse, connect. • n. seam, juncture, union.

wel•fare /wélfair/ n. **1** well-being; happiness; health and prosperity. **2** financial support given by a government to the unemployed, disadvantaged, etc.

■ **1** benefit, good, advantage, (good) fortune. **2** see CHARITY 1.

wel•kin /wélkin/ n. poet. sky; the upper air.

well[1] /wel/ • adv. (**better**, **best**) **1** in a satisfactory way. **2** in the right way. **3** with some distinction. **4** in a kind way. **5 a** thoroughly; carefully. **b** intimately; closely. **6** with approval; favorably. **7** probably; reasonably. **8** to a considerable extent. • adj. (**better**, **best**) **1** in good health. **2 a** satisfactory. **b** advisable. • int. expressing surprise, resignation, insistence, etc. □ **as well as** in addition to. **leave** (or **let**) **well enough alone** avoid needless change or disturbance. **well-advised** prudent. **well-appointed** having all the necessary equipment. **well-balanced** sane; sensible. **well-being** state of being well, healthy, contented, etc. **well-bred** having or showing good breeding or manners. **well-disposed** [often foll. by toward] having a good disposition or friendly feeling (for). **well-done 1** (of meat, etc.) thoroughly cooked. **2** (of a task, etc.) performed well [also as int.]. **well-founded** based on good evidence. **well-groomed** with carefully tended hair, clothes, etc. **well-grounded 1** = well-founded. **2** having good knowledge of the groundwork of a subject. **well-heeled** colloq. wealthy. **well-informed** having much knowledge or information about a subject. **well-intentioned** having or showing good intentions. **well-known 1** known to many. **2** known thoroughly. **well-meaning** (or **-meant**) well-intentioned. **well-off 1** wealthy. **2** in a fortunate situation. **well-preserved** see PRESERVE. **well-read** knowledgeable through much reading. **well-rounded 1** complete and symmetrical. **2** having or showing a fully developed personality, ability, etc. **well-spoken** articulate or refined in speech. **well-to-do** prosperous. See synonym study at WEALTHY. **well-worn 1** much worn by use. **2** (of a phrase, etc.) trite.

• adv. **1** satisfactorily, sufficiently, adequately. **2** appropriately, correctly, accurately. **3** skillfully, expertly, proficiently. **4** kindly, graciously, thoughtfully. **5 a** extensively, exhaustively, intensively. **b** familiarly, personally; thoroughly, profoundly. **6** graciously, kindly, highly, glowingly. **7** likely, in all probability, doubtless(ly). **8** considerably, (very) much; far and away, definitely. • adj. **1** healthy, fit, robust, vigorous, hearty. **2 a** pleasing, agreeable, good. **b** see ADVISABLE[2]. □ **well-advised** wise, sensible, intelligent, smart. **well-balanced** rational, reasonable, levelheaded, sound. **well-being** see WELFARE. **well-bred** polite, decorous, mannerly, refined, courteous, cultivated, gracious, courtly. **well-done 1** completely cooked. **2** properly done, first-class, first-rate. **well-groomed** neat, dapper, fastidious, tidy. **well-heeled** see WEALTHY. **well-informed** knowledgeable, learned, well-read, literate, educated. **well-intentioned** see KIND. **well-known 1** famous, noted, celebrated, renowned, illustrious. **2** familiar, (well-)established, acknowledged, proverbial. **well-meaning** see KIND[2]. **well-off**

1 comfortable, rich, affluent, prosperous. **2** lucky, blessed.

well[2] /wel/ • n. **1** shaft sunk into the ground to obtain water, oil, etc. **2** enclosed space like a well shaft. **3** source. **4** = INKWELL. **5** archaic water spring or fountain. • v.intr. spring as from a fountain.

■ n. **1** bore, borehole; gusher. **3** spring, wellspring, fountain, supply. **4, 5** wellspring, fountain, wellhead. • v. flow, surge, rise; gush, spurt.

we'll /weel, wil/ contr. we shall; we will.

well•born /wélbáwrn/ adj. of a good or esteemed family.

well•head /wélhed/ n. source, esp. of a spring or stream.

well•ness /wélnis/ n. healthful condition through proper diet, exercise, and preventive medicine.

well•nigh /wélní/ adv. archaic or rhet. almost.

Welsh /welsh/ • adj. of or relating to Wales or its people or language. • n. **1** Celtic language of Wales. **2** [prec. by the; treated as pl.] the people of Wales. □ **Welsh rabbit** (or **rarebit** by folk etymology) dish of melted cheese, etc., on toast. □□ **Welsh′man** n. (pl. **-men**). **Welsh′wom•an** n. (pl. **-wom•en**).

welsh /welsh/ v.intr. (also **welch** /welch/) evade an obligation, debt, promise, etc. □□ **welsh′er** n.

■ □□ **welsher** nonpayer, cheat, swindler, sl. deadbeat.

welt /welt/ n. **1** leather rim sewn around the edge of a shoe upper for the sole to be attached to. **2** = WEAL[1]. **3** trimming.

■ **2** bruise, contusion, bump, lump, ridge, scar, weal. **3** bead, ridge, seam, edge, wale, stripe, binding.

wel•ter /wéltər/ • v.intr. roll; wallow. • n. **1** state of general confusion. **2** disorderly mixture or contrast of beliefs, policies, etc. • v. **1** roll (about), flounder. • n. **2** mass, mess, jumble, tangle, confusion, mishmash.

wel•ter•weight /wéltərwayt/ n. **1** weight class in certain sports intermediate between lightweight and middleweight. **2** athlete of this weight.

wen /wen/ n. benign tumor on the skin, esp. of the scalp.

wench /wench/ n. **1** joc. girl or young woman. **2** archaic prostitute. □□ **wench′er** n.

wend /wend/ v. literary or archaic go. □ **wend one's way** make one's way.

went past of GO[1].

wept past of WEEP.

were 2nd sing. past, pl. past, and past subj. of BE.

we're /weer/ contr. we are.

weren't /wərnt, wərónt/ contr. were not.

were•wolf /wéerwoolf, wáir-/ n. (also **werwolf** /wór-/) (pl. **-wolves**) mythical being who at times changes from a person to a wolf.

west /west/ • n. **1 a** point of the horizon where the sun sets at the equinoxes. **b** compass point corresponding to this. **c** direction in which this lies. **2** (usu. **the West**) a European civilization. **b** the nations of western Europe and N. America. **c** western part of a country, etc., esp. the American West. • *adj.* **1** toward, at, near, or facing west. **2** from the west. • *adv.* **1** toward, at, or near the west. **2** [foll. by *of*] further west than. □ **West Indies** islands of Central America, including Cuba and the Bahamas.

west•er•ly /wéstərlee/ • *adj. & adv.* **1** in a western position or direction. **2** (of a wind) blowing from the west. • *n.* (*pl.* **-lies**) wind blowing from the west.

west•ern /wéstərn/ • *adj.* **1** of or in the west. **2** lying or directed toward the west. **3** (**Western**) of or relating to the West (see WEST *n.* 2). • *n.* movie or novel about cowboys in western N. America. □ **western hemisphere** the half of the earth containing the Americas. □□ **west'ern•most** *adj.*

west•ern•er /wéstərnər/ *n.* native or inhabitant of the West.

west•ern•ize /wéstərnīz/ *v.tr.* (also **Wes'ternize**) influence with or convert to the ideas and customs, etc., of the West. □□ **west•ern•i•za'tion** *n.*

west•ward /wéstwərd/ • *adj. & adv.* (also **west'wards**) toward the west. • *n.* westward direction or region.

wet /wet/ • *adj.* (**wet•ter, wet•test**) **1** soaked, covered, or dampened with water or other liquid. **2** rainy. **3** not yet dried. **4** *sl.* allowing sales of liquor. • *v.tr.* (**wet•ting;** *past* and *past part.* **wet** or **wet•ted**) **1** make wet. **2** urinate in or on. • *n.* **1** liquid that wets something. **2** rainy weather. □ **wet behind the ears** immature; inexperienced. **wet nurse** woman employed to suckle another's child. **wet-nurse 1** act as a wet nurse to. **2** *colloq.* treat as if helpless. **wet suit** close-fitting rubber garment worn by skin divers, etc., to keep warm. □□ **wet'ly** *adv.* **wet'ness** *n.* **wet'ta•ble** *adj.* **wet'ting** *n.* **wet'tish** *adj.*

■ *adj.* **1** moist, moistened, damp, soaked, sopping, dripping, saturated. **2** raining, teeming, pouring, drizzling, showery. **3** tacky, sticky. • *v.* **1** dampen, moisten, saturate, drench. • *n.* **1** moisture, water, dampness, humidity. **2** rain, wetness, drizzle. □ **wet behind the ears** see *inexperienced* (INEXPERIENCE). **wet nurse 1** see NURSE *n.* 2. □□ **wetness** see PERSPIRATION, WET *n.* 1 above.

wet•back /wétbak/ *n. offens.* illegal immigrant from Mexico to the US.

wet•lands /wétləndz/ *n.pl.* swamps and other damp areas of land.

we've /weev/ *contr.* we have.

whack /hwak, wak/ *colloq.* • *v.tr.* strike or beat forcefully. • *n.* sharp or resounding blow. □ **have a whack at** *sl.* attempt. **out of whack** *sl.* out of order; malfunctioning. □□ **whack'er** *n.* **whack'ing** *n.*

■ *v.* see BEAT² *v.* 1. • *n.* see BLOW 1. □ **out of whack** see *out of order* 1 (ORDER).

whale¹ /hwayl, wayl/ *n.* (*pl.* same or **whales**) large marine mammal having a streamlined body and horizontal tail, and breathing through a blowhole on the head. □ **a whale**

of a *colloq.* exceedingly good or fine, etc. **whale oil** oil from the blubber of whales.

whale² /hwayl, wayl/ *v.tr. colloq.* beat; thrash.

whale•bone /hwáylbōn, wáyl-/ *n.* elastic horny substance growing in thin parallel plates in the upper jaw of some whales.

whal•er /hwáylər, wáyl-/ *n.* **1** whaling ship. **2** seaman engaged in whaling.

wham /hwam, wam/ *colloq.* • *int.* expressing the sound of a forcible impact. • *n.* such a sound. • *v.* (**whammed, wham•ming**) **1** *intr.* make such a sound or impact. **2** *tr.* strike forcibly.

wham•my /hwámee, wám-/ *n.* (*pl.* **-mies**) *colloq.* evil or unlucky influence.

wharf /hwawrf, wawrf/ • *n.* (*pl.* **wharves** /hwawrvz/ or **wharfs**) level quayside area to which a ship may be moored to load and unload. • *v.tr.* moor (a ship) at a wharf.

what /hwot, wot, hwut, wut/ • *interrog.adj.* **1** asking for a choice from an indefinite number or for a statement of amount, number, or kind. **2** *colloq.* = WHICH. • *adj.* [usu. in exclam.] how great or remarkable (*what luck!*). • *rel.adj.* whatever (*will give you what help I can*). • *pron.* (corresp. to the functions of the *adj.*) **1** what thing or things? **2** (asking for a remark to be repeated) = what did you say?. **3** how much (*what you must have suffered!*). **4** [as *rel.pron.*] that or those which (*what followed was worse*). • *adv.* to what extent (*what does it matter?*). □ **what about** what is the news or position or your opinion of.

what•ev•er /hwotévər, wot–, hwut, wut–/ *adj. & pron.* **1** = WHAT (in relative uses) with the emphasis on indefiniteness. **2** though anything (*we are safe whatever happens*). **3** [with *neg.* or *interrog.*] at all; of any kind (*there is no doubt whatever*).

what•not /hwótnot, wót–, hwút–, wút–/ *n.* **1** indefinite or trivial thing. **2** stand with shelves for small objects.

what•so•ev•er /hwótsō-évər, wót–, hwút–, wút–/ *adj. & pron.* = WHATEVER.

wheat /hweet, weet/ *n.* **1** cereal plant bearing dense four-sided seed spikes. **2** its grain, used in making flour, etc. □ **wheat germ** embryo of the wheat grain, extracted as a source of vitamins. □□ **wheat'en** *adj.*

whee•dle /hweédəl, weédəl/ *v.tr.* coax, influence, or get by flattery or endearments; entice. □□ **whee'dler** *n.* **whee'dling** *adj.* **whee'dling•ly** *adv.*

■ **1** cajole, inveigle, charm, beguile, persuade.

wheel /hweel, weel/ • *n.* **1** circular frame or disk that revolves on an axle. **2** wheellike thing. **3** motion as of a wheel. **4** [in *pl.*] *sl.* car. • *v.* **1 a** turn on an axis or pivot. **b** swing around in line with one end as a pivot. **2 a** *intr.* change direction or face another way. **b** *tr.* cause to do this. **3** *tr.* push or pull (a wheeled thing). □ **at the wheel 1** driving a vehicle. **2** directing a ship. **3** in control of affairs. **wheeler-dealer** *colloq.* person who wheels and deals. □□ **wheeled** *adj.* [also in *comb.*]. **wheel'less** *adj.*

■ *n.* **1** ring, circle, hoop, annulus. **3** see REVOLUTION 3, 4. **4** (*wheels*) see CAR 1. • *v.* **1** see REVOLVE 1, 2. **2** spin, veer, swivel, pivot.

□ **at the wheel 3** in charge, in command; (*be at the wheel*) have the whip hand.

wheel•bar•row /hwééelbarŏ, wéél–/ *n.* small cart with one wheel and two shafts for carrying garden loads, etc.

wheel•base /hwééelbays, wéél–/ *n.* distance between the front and rear axles of a vehicle.

wheel•chair /hwééelchair, wéél–/ *n.* chair on wheels for an invalid or disabled person.

wheel•house /hwééelhows, weel–/ *n.* = PILOT-HOUSE.

wheel•ie /hwééelee, wéé–/ *n. sl.* stunt of riding a bicycle or motorcycle with the front wheel off the ground.

wheel•wright /hwééelrīt, wéél–/ *n.* person who makes or repairs, esp. wooden, wheels.

wheeze /hweez, weez/ • *v.* **1** *intr.* breathe with an audible whistling sound. **2** *tr.* utter in this way. • *n.* sound of wheezing. □□ **wheez'i•ly** *adv.* **wheez'i•ness** *n.* **wheez'ing•ly** *adv.* **wheez'y** *adj.* (**wheez•i•er, wheez•i•est**).

whelk /hwelk, welk/ *n.* edible marine mollusk having a spiral shell.

whelm /hwelm, welm/ *v.tr. poet.* **1** engulf. **2** overwhelm.

whelp /hwelp, welp/ • *n.* **1** young dog; puppy. **2** *archaic* cub. **3** ill-mannered child or youth. • *v.tr.* give birth to (a whelp or whelps).

■ *n.* **1** pup. **3** brat, imp.

when /hwen, wen/ • *adv.* **1** at what time?. **2** on what occasion?. **3** (time) at or on which (*there are times when I could cry*). • *conj.* **1** at the or any time that; as soon as (*come when you like*). **2** although. **3** after which; and then; but just then (*was nearly asleep when the bell rang*). • *pron.* what time? (*till when can you stay?*). • *n.* time; occasion (*have finally decided on the where and when*).

whence /hwens, wens/ *formal* • *adv.* from what place? • *conj.* **1** to the place from which. **2** (often prec. by *place*, etc.) from which (*source whence these errors arise*). **3** and thence (*whence it follows that*).

when•ev•er /hwenévər, wen–/ *conj. & adv.* **1** at whatever time; on whatever occasion. **2** every time that.

when•so•ev•er /hwénsō-évər, wén–/ *conj. & adv. formal* = WHENEVER.

where /hwair, wair/ • *adv.* **1** in or to what place or position? (*where is the milk?*). **2** in what respect? (*where does the argument lead?*). **3** in what book, etc.?; from whom? (*where did you read that?*). **4** in or to which (*places where they meet*). • *conj.* wherever (*go where you like*). • *pron.* what place?. • *n.* place; scene of something (see WHEN *n.*).

where•a•bouts • *adv.* /hwáirəbówts, wáir–/ approximately where? (*whereabouts are they?*). • *n.* /hwáirəbowts, wáir–/ [as *sing.* or *pl.*] person's or thing's location.

■ *adv.* in or at or to what place. • *n.* position, place, site, situation, address, locale.

where•as /hwairáz, wair–/ *conj.* **1** in contrast or comparison with the fact that. **2** (esp. in legal preambles) taking into consideration the fact that.

where•by /hwairbī́, wair–/ *conj.* by what or which means.

where•fore /hwáirfawr, wáir–/ • *adv. archaic* **1** for what reason?. **2** for which reason. • *n.* reason.

where•in /hwairín, wair–/ *formal conj.* in what or which place or respect.

where•of /hwairúv, –óv, wair–/ *formal conj.* of what or which (*the means whereof*).

where•up•on /hwáirəpŏn, –páwn, wáir–/ *conj.* immediately after which.

wher•ev•er /hwairévər, wair–/ • *adv.* in or to whatever place. • *conj.* in every place that.

where•with•al /hwáirwith̄awl, –with–, wáir–/ *n. colloq.* money, etc., needed for a purpose (*has not the wherewithal to do it*).

wher•ry /hwérée, wérée/ *n.* (*pl.* **–ries**) light rowboat usu. for carrying passengers.

whet /hwet, wet/ *v.tr.* (**whet•ted, whet•ting**) **1** sharpen (a tool). **2** stimulate (the appetite or a desire, etc.). □□ **whet'ter** *n.* [also in *comb.*].

■ **1** hone, grind, file, strop. **2** pique, sharpen, awaken, arouse.

wheth•er /hwéth̄ər, wéth̄–/ *conj.* introducing the first or both of alternative possibilities (*I do not know whether they have arrived or not*).

whet•stone /hwétstōn, wét–/ *n.* abrasive stone used with water to sharpen tools.

whew /hwyōō/ *int.* expressing surprise, consternation, or relief.

whey /hway, way/ *n.* watery liquid left when milk forms curds.

which /hwich, wich/ • *adj.* **1** asking for choice from a definite set of alternatives (*which John do you mean?*). **2** being the one just referred to (*ten years, during which time they admitted nothing*). • *pron.* **1** which person or persons. **2** which thing or things. **3** used in place of *that* after *in* or *that* (*the house in which I was born*).

which•ev•er /hwichévər, wich –/ *adj. & pron.* **1** any which (*whichever one you like*). **2** no matter which (*whichever one wins, they both get a prize*).

whiff /hwif, wif/ • *n.* **1** puff or breath of air, smoke, etc. **2** odor. • *v.* **1** *tr. & intr.* blow or puff lightly. **2** *intr.* smell (esp. unpleasant). **3** *tr.* get a slight smell of. **4** *intr. Baseball* strike out by swinging and missing on the third strike. **5** *tr. Baseball* strike out a batter in this way.

■ *n.* **1** see BREATH 2a. **2** see SMELL *n.* 2.

Whig /hwig, wig/ *n. hist.* **1** *Polit.* member of a British reformist party before the 19th c. **2 a** American colonist supporting the American Revolution. **b** member of an American political party in the 19th c. □□ **Whig'ger•y** *n.* **Whig'gish** *adj.* **Whig'gism** *n.*

while /hwīl, wīl/ • *n.* period of time (*waited a while*). • *conj.* **1** during the time that. **2** although (*while I want to believe it, I cannot*). • *v.tr.* [foll. by *away*] pass (time, etc.) in a leisurely or interesting manner. • *adv.* [prec. by *time*, etc.] during which (*the summer while I was abroad*). □ **worth one's while** worth the time or effort spent.

■ *n.* **1** see TIME¹ *n.* 4, 6. • *conj.* **2** see THOUGH *conj.* 1. • *v.* (*while away*) see PASS *v.* 12.

whim /hwim, wim/ *n.* sudden fancy; caprice.

■ see FANCY n. 2.

whim•per /hwímpǝr, wím–/ • v. 1 intr. make feeble, querulous, or frightened sounds. 2 tr. utter whimperingly. • n. whimpering sound.
□□ **whim′per•er** n. **whim′per•ing•ly** adv.
■ v. see CRY v. 2a, WEEP v. 1, 2. • n. see GROAN n.

whim•si•cal /hwímzikǝl, wím–/ adj. 1 capricious. 2 fantastic. 3 odd or quaint; fanciful; humorous. □□ **whim•si•cal•i•ty** /–kálitee/ n.
whim′si•cal•ly adv. **whim′si•cal•ness** n.
■ 1 erratic, eccentric, wavering, flighty. 2, 3 fey, curious, unusual, singular, funny, offbeat.

whim•sy /hwímzee, wím–/ n. (also **whim′sey**) (pl. **–sies** or **–seys**) WHIM.
■ see FANCY n. 2.

whine /hwín, wín/ • n. 1 complaining, longdrawn wail of a dog. 2 similar shrill, prolonged sound. 3 querulous tone or complaint. • v. 1 intr. emit or utter a whine. 2 intr. complain in a querulous tone. 3 tr. utter in a whining tone. □□ **whin′er** n.
whin′ing•ly adv. **whin′y** adj. (**whin•i•er**, **whin•i•est**)
■ n. 1, 2 see HOWL n. 1. 3 see GRIPE n. 2. • v. 1 see HOWL v. 1, 2. see MOAN v.

whin•ny /hwínee, wín–/ • n. (pl. **–nies**) gentle or joyful neigh. • v.intr. (**–nies**, **–nied**) give a whinny.

whip /hwíp, wíp/ • n. 1 lash attached to a stick for urging on animals or punishing, etc. 2 legislative member of a political party appointed to control discipline, tactics, etc. • v. (**whipped, whip′ping**) 1 tr. beat or urge on with a whip. 2 tr. beat (cream or eggs, etc.) into a froth. 3 tr. & intr. take or move suddenly, unexpectedly, or rapidly. 4 tr. sl. **a** excel. **b** defeat. 5 tr. bind with spirally wound twine. 6 tr. sew with overcast stitches. □ **whip hand** 1 hand that holds the whip (in riding, etc.). 2 [usu. prec. by the] advantage or control in any situation. **whip up** 1 excite or stir up (feeling, etc.). 2 prepare (a meal, etc.) hurriedly. □□ **whip′less** adj. **whip′like** adj. **whip′per** n. **whip′ping** n.
■ n. 1 scourge, rawhide, quirt, horsewhip, bullwhip, cane, birch, switch, (riding) crop, hist. cat-o'-nine-tails. • v. 1 thrash, lash, flog, horsewhip, scourge; castigate, chastise, punish, discipline. 2 whisk, fluff up. 3 whisk, pull, jerk, snatch. 4 a see EXCEL 1. **b** trounce, beat, conquer, overwhelm, rout. 5 fasten, tie, Naut. seize. 6 overcast. □ **whip hand** 2 see predominance (PREDOMINANT). **whip up** 1 agitate, arouse, work up, kindle. 2 improvise, throw together.

whip•cord /hwípkawrd, wíp–/ n. 1 tightly twisted cord. 2 close-woven worsted fabric.

whip•lash /hwíplash, wíp–/ n. 1 flexible end of a whip. 2 (in full **whiplash injury**) injury to the neck caused by a jerk of the head, esp. as in a motor vehicle accident.

whip•per•snap•per /hwípǝrsnapǝr, wíp–/ n. 1 small child. 2 insignificant but presumptuous (esp. young) person.

whip•pet /hwípit, wíp–/ n. crossbred dog of the greyhound type used for racing.

whip•ping /hwíping, wíp–/ n. □ **whipping boy** scapegoat.
■ □ **whipping boy** see SCAPEGOAT n.

whip•poor•will /hwípǝrwil, wíp–/ n. nocturnal N. American bird, named for its call.

whir /hwǝr, wǝr/ (also **whirr**) • n. continuous rapid buzzing or softly clicking sound. • v.intr. (**whirred, whir′ring**) make this sound.
■ v. see HUM v. 1.

whirl /hwǝrl, wǝrl/ • v. 1 tr. & intr. swing around and around; revolve rapidly. 2 tr. & intr. send or travel swiftly in an orbit or a curve. 3 intr. **a** (of the brain, etc.) seem to spin around. **b** (of thoughts, etc.) be confused. • n. 1 whirling movement. 2 state of intense activity. 3 state of confusion. □ **give it a whirl** try; attempt. □□ **whirl′er** n. **whirl′ing•ly** adv.
■ v. 1 see REVOLVE 1, 2. 3 see SWIRL v. • n. 1 swirl, twist, spiral; see also EDDY n., SPIN n. 1, 3. 2 see FLURRY n. 3. 3 see MUDDLE n.

whirl•i•gig /hwǝrligig, wǝrl–/ n. spinning or whirling toy.

whirl•pool /hwǝrlpōōl, wǝrl–/ n. powerful circular eddy in the sea, etc., often causing suction to its center.
■ maelstrom, vortex, whirl, swirl.

whirl•wind /hwǝrlwind, wǝrl–/ n. 1 mass or column of air whirling rapidly in a funnel shape over land or water. 2 confused tumultuous process. 3 [attrib.] very rapid (a whirlwind romance).
■ 1 vortex, cyclone, typhoon, hurricane, tornado. 2 confusion, tumult, turmoil, pandemonium. 3 [attrib.] speedy, quick, swift, sudden, precipitous.

whisk /hwisk, wisk/ • v. 1 tr. **a** brush with a sweeping movement. **b** take with a sudden motion. 2 tr. whip (cream, eggs, etc.). 3 tr. & intr. convey or go (esp. out of sight) lightly or quickly. • n. 1 whisking action or motion. 2 utensil for whisking eggs or cream, etc. 3 (in full **whisk broom**) small shorthandled broom.
■ v. 1 sweep. 2 beat, fluff up, stir. 3 speed, rush, carry; dart, flit. • n. 1 sweep, wave, brush, flick. 2 beater, whip.

whisk•er /hwískǝr, wis–/ n. 1 [usu. in pl.] hair growing on a man's face, esp. on the cheeks. 2 each of the bristles on the face of a cat, etc. 3 colloq. very small distance. □□ **whisk′ered** adj. **whisk′er•y** adj.

whis•key /hwískee, wis–/ n. (also **whis′ky**) (pl. **–keys** or **–kies**) alcoholic liquor distilled esp. from grain, such as corn or malted barley.
■ Scotch, rye, bourbon, colloq. booze, firewater, hooch.

whis•per /hwíspǝr, wis–/ • v. 1 **a** intr. speak very softly without vibration of the vocal cords. **b** tr. & intr. talk or say in a barely audible tone. 2 intr. speak privately or conspiratorially. 3 intr. rustle or murmur. • n. 1 whispering speech or sound. 2 thing whispered. □□ **whis′per•er** n. **whis′per•ing** n.
■ v. 1 breathe, murmur, mutter, mumble. 2 gossip, bruit about, noise abroad, murmur, insinuate. 3 swish, sibilate, swoosh, hiss. • n.

1 murmur, undertone, hushed tone(s); swoosh; see also RUSTLE *n.*

whist /hwist, wist/ *n.* card game usu. for four players.

whis•tle /hwisəl, wis-/ • *n.* **1** clear shrill sound made by forcing breath through a small hole between nearly closed lips. **2** similar sound made by a bird, the wind, a missile, etc. **3** instrument used to produce such a sound. • *v.* **1** *intr.* emit a whistle. **2 a** *intr.* give a signal or express surprise or derision by whistling. **b** *tr.* summon or give a signal to (a dog, etc.) by whistling. **3** *tr.* produce (a tune) by whistling. □ **whistle-stop 1** small, unimportant town on a railroad line. **2** politician's brief pause for a campaign speech on tour.

whis•tle-blow•er /hwisəlblōər, wi-/ *n. colloq.* one who publicizes wrongdoing in a workplace or organization.

whit /hwit, wit/ *n.* particle; least possible amount.
■ see PARTICLE 2.

white /hwit, wit/ • *adj.* **1** resembling a surface reflecting sunlight without absorbing any of the visible rays; of the color of milk or fresh snow. **2** approaching such a color; pale esp. in the face. **3 a** having light-colored skin. **b** of or relating to white people. **4** lacking or having lost color. • *n.* **1** white color or pigment. **2** innocent. **3** visible part of the eyeball around the iris. **4** member of a light-skinned race. □ **white cell** (or **blood cell** or **corpuscle**) leukocyte. **white-collar** (of a worker) clerical; professional. **white elephant** useless possession. **white flag** symbol of surrender. **white goods 1** domestic linen. **2** large domestic electrical appliances. **white heat 1** the temperature at which metal emits white light. **2** state of intense passion or activity. **White House** official residence of the US president and offices of the executive branch of government in Washington D.C. **white lie** harmless or trivial untruth. **white light** colorless light, e.g. ordinary daylight. **white meat** poultry, veal, rabbit, and pork. **white noise** noise containing many frequencies with equal intensities. **white-out** dense blizzard allowing no visibility. **white sale** sale of household linen. **white tie** man's white bow tie as part of full evening dress. **white water** rapids; foamy stretch of water. □□ **white'ly** *adv.* **white'ness** *n.* **whit'ish** *adj.*
■ *adj.* **1** snow-white, snowy, chalk-white; silver, hoary. **2** pallid, pasty, wan, ashen, bloodless. **3** Caucasian, fair-skinned, pale-complexioned. □ **white-collar** see CLERICAL² 2. **white elephant** see LUMBER *n.* 2. **white lie** see FIB *n.* □□ **whitish** see WHITE *adj.* 2 above.

white•cap /hwitkap, wit-/ *n.* white-crested wave.

white•head /hwit-hed, wit-/ *n. colloq.* white or white-topped skin pustule.
■ see PIMPLE.

whit•en /hwiton, wit-/ *v.* make or become white. □□ **whit'en•er** *n.* **whit'en•ing** *n.*

white•wall /hwitwawl, wit-/ *n.* tire having a white band encircling the outer sidewall.

---

white•wash /hwitwosh, –wawsh, wit-/ • *n.* **1** solution of lime or whiting for whitening walls, etc. **2** means employed to conceal mistakes or faults. • *v.tr.* **1** cover with whitewash. **2** attempt by concealment to clear the reputation of. □□ **white'wash•er** *n.*
■ *v.* **2** gloss over, cover up, sugar-coat, hide, camouflage.

whith•er /hwithər, with-/ *archaic* • *adv.* to what place, position, or state?. • *conj.* to which place; to whatever place.
■ *adv.* **1** see WHEREABOUTS *adv.*

whit•ing¹ /hwiting, wi-/ *n.* small, white-fleshed fish used as food.

whit•ing² /hwiting, wi-/ *n.* ground chalk used in whitewashing, etc.

Whit•sun•day /hwitsúnday, wit-/ seventh Sunday after Easter, commemorating Pentecost (Acts 2).

whit•tle /hwitəl, witəl/ *v.* **1** *tr. & [foll. by at]* *intr.* carve or pare (wood, etc.) with a knife. **2** *tr.* reduce by repeated subtractions.
■ **1** shave, trim, cut, shape. **2** pare, shave, cut, trim.

whiz /hwiz, wiz/ (also **whizz**) *colloq.* • *n.* (*pl.* **whiz•zes**) **1** sound made by an object moving through the air at great speed. **2** (also **wiz** /wiz/) *colloq.* genius; expert. • *v.intr.* (**whizzed**, **whiz•zing**) move with or make a whiz. □ **whiz kid** *colloq.* brilliant or highly successful young person.
■ *n.* **1** whoosh, swish, whistle. **2** see EXPERT *n.* ● *v.* see FLASH *v.* 3b. □ **whiz kid** see VIRTUOSO 1.

WHO *abbr.* World Health Organization.

who /hoo/ *pron.* (*obj.* **whom** /hoom/ or *colloq.* **who**; *poss.* **whose** /hooz/) **1 a** what or which person or persons? (*who called?*). **b** what sort of person or persons? (*who am I to object?*). **2** (a person) that (*anyone who wishes can come*).

whoa /wō/ *int.* command to stop or slow a horse, etc.

who'd /hood/ *contr.* **1** who had. **2** who would.

who•dun•it /hoodúnit/ *n.* (also **who•dun'nit**) *colloq.* story or play about the detection of a crime, etc., esp. murder.
■ see MYSTERY 3.

who•ev•er /hoo-évər/ *pron.* (*obj.* **whom•ev•er** /hoom-/ or *colloq.* **who•ev•er**; *poss.* **whos•ev•er** /hōz-/) **1** the or any person or persons who. **2** though anyone. **3** *colloq.* (as an intensive) who.

whole /hōl/ • *adj.* **1** uninjured; unbroken; intact; undiminished. **2** not less than; all there is of. **3** with no part removed. • *n.* **1** thing complete in itself. **2** all there is of a thing. **3** all members, etc., of. □ **as a whole** as a unity; not as separate parts. **on the whole** taking everything relevant into account. **whole number** number without fractions; integer. **whole wheat** made of wheat with none of the bran or germ removed. □□ **whole'ness** *n.*
■ *adj.* **1** entire, complete, full, total, uncut; in one piece, unharmed. **2** complete, entire, full, total. • *n.* **1** ensemble, aggregate, com-

posite; everything. **2** entirety, (sum) total, totality, lot. □ **as a whole** see *at large* (LARGE *n.* 2). **on the whole** largely, mostly, usually, for the most part. □□ **wholeness** see EN-TIRETY 1.

whole•heart•ed /hṓlhäartid/ *adj.* **1** completely devoted. **2** done with all possible effort or sincerity. □□ **whole′heart′ed•ly** *adv.* **whole′heart′ed•ness** *n.*

■ dedicated, committed, earnest, sincere, real; (*only of an action, etc.*) unqualified, unmitigated, unreserved. □□ **wholeheartedly** see *sincerely* (SINCERE). **wholeheartedness** see DEDICATION 1.

whole•sale /hṓlsayl/ • *n.* selling of things in large quantities to be retailed by others. • *adj. & adv.* **1** by wholesale. **2** on a large scale. • *v.tr.* sell wholesale. □□ **whole′sal•er** *n.*

■ *adj.* **2** see SWEEPING *adj.* 1.

whole•some /hṓlsəm/ *adj.* **1** promoting or indicating physical, mental, or moral health. **2** prudent. □□ **whole′some•ly** *adv.* **whole′some•ness** *n.*

■ **1** healthful, healthy, nutritious, nourishing. **2** see SOUND[2] *adj.* 3.

whol•ly /hṓlee/ *adv.* **1** entirely; without limitation. **2** purely; exclusively.

■ **1** altogether, absolutely, quite, totally, thoroughly, completely. **2** only, solely, categorically, unequivocally.

whom *objective case* of WHO.

whom•ev•er *objective case* of WHOEVER.

whom•so•ev•er *objective case* of WHOSOEVER.

whoop /hōōp, hwōōp, wōōp/ • *n.* **1** loud cry of or as of excitement, etc. **2** long, rasping, indrawn breath in whooping cough. • *v.intr.* utter a whoop. □□ **whooping cough** infectious bacterial disease, esp. of children, with a series of short, violent coughs followed by a whoop.

■ *n.* **1** shout, shriek, yell, roar, bellow, hoot; cheer, hurrah. • *v.* shout, shriek, yell, screech, squeal, yelp, yowl.

whop•per /hwópər, wóp–/ *n. sl.* **1** something big of its kind. **2** great lie.

whop•ping /hwóping, wóp–/ *adj. sl.* huge (*whopping lie*).

■ great, enormous, colossal, gigantic, immense; outrageous, extravagant, terrible.

whore /hawr/ • *n.* prostitute. • *v.intr.* seek or chase after whores. □□ **whor′er** *n.*

■ *n.* see PROSTITUTE *n.*

whorl /hwawrl, wawrl, hwərl, wərl/ *n.* **1** ring of leaves, etc., around a stem. **2** one turn of a spiral. **3** complete circle in a fingerprint. □□ **whorled** *adj.*

whose /hōōz/ • *pron.* of or belonging to which person (*whose is this book?*). • *adj.* of whom or which (*whose book is this?*).

who•so•ev•er /hōōsō-évər/ *pron.* (*obj.* **whom•so•ev•er** /hōōm–/; *poss.* **whose•so•ev•er** /hōōz–/) *archaic* = WHOEVER.

why /hwī, wī/ • *adv.* **1 a** for what reason or purpose (*why did you do it?*). **b** on what grounds (*why do you say that?*). **2** for which (*reasons why I did it*). • *int.* expressing: **1** surprised discovery or recognition (*why, it's

you!). **2** impatience (*why, of course I do!*). **3** reflection (*why, yes, I think so*). **4** objection (*why, what is wrong with it?*). • *n.* (*pl.* **whys**) reason or explanation (esp. *whys and wherefores*).

WI *abbr.* **1** Wisconsin (in official postal use). **2** West Indies. **3** West Indian.

Wich•i•ta /wíchitaw/ *n.* **1 a** N. American people native to Kansas. **b** member of this people. **2** language of this people.

wick /wik/ • *n.* **1** strip or thread of fibrous or spongy material feeding a flame with fuel in a candle, lamp, etc. **2** *Surgery* gauze strip inserted in a wound to drain it. • *v.tr.* draw (moisture) away by capillary action.

wick•ed /wíkid/ *adj.* (**wick•ed•er**, **wick•ed•est**) **1** sinful; iniquitous. **2** spiteful. **3** playfully malicious. **4** *colloq.* very bad. **5** *sl.* excellent. □□ **wick′ed•ly** *adv.* **wick′ed•ness** *n.*

■ **1** evil, bad, immoral, amoral, unprincipled; depraved, dissolute, degenerate. **2** vicious, beastly, savage, cruel. **3** naughty, mischievous, impish. **4** foul, offensive, pernicious, baleful, disgusting. **5** expert, ingenious, superior, superb, superlative. □□ **wickedly** see BADLY 1. **wickedness** see EVIL *n.* 2.

wick•er /wíkər/ *n.* braided twigs, etc., as material for chairs, baskets, mats, etc.

wick•er•work /wíkərwərk/ *n.* **1** wicker. **2** things made of wicker.

wick•et /wíkit/ *n.* **1** small door or gate, esp. beside or in a larger one. **2** aperture in a door or wall, usu. closed with a sliding panel. **3** croquet hoop.

wide /wīd/ • *adj.* **1 a** having sides far apart; broad, not narrow. **b** considerable; more than is needed (*wide margin*). **2** in width (*foot wide*). **3** extending far. **4** not restricted; loose. **5** open to the full extent. **6 a** not within a reasonable distance of. **b** at a considerable distance from. **7** [in *comb.*] extending over the whole of (*nationwide*). • *adv.* **1** widely. **2** to the full extent. **3** far from the target, etc. □□ **wide awake 1** fully awake. **2** *colloq.* wary; knowing. **wide-eyed** surprised or naive. □□ **wide′ness** *n.* **wid′ish** *adj.*

■ *adj.* **1 a** spacious, roomy, ample, extensive, expansive. **b** substantial, sizable, major. **3** broad, extensive, comprehensive. **4** full, ample, generous; see also LOOSE *adj.* 3. • *adv.* **1** far apart, stretched out. **2** all the way, as much as possible, fully. **3** astray, afield, wide of the mark. □ **wide awake 1** see AWAKE *adj.* 1a. **2** see ALERT *adj.* 1. **wide-eyed** see GULLIBLE. □□ **wideness** see WIDTH 1.

wide•ly /wídlee/ *adv.* **1** to a wide extent; far apart. **2** extensively. **3** by many people. **4** considerably; to a large degree.

■ **3** extensively, thoroughly, universally, popularly. **4** to a large or great extent, extremely, substantially.

wid•en /wíd′n/ *v.* make or become wider. □□ **wid′en•er** *n.*

■ distend, dilate, open out, spread, stretch, enlarge.

wide•spread /wídspréd/ *adj.* widely distributed.

■ see EXTENSIVE 2.

wid•geon /wíjən/ *n.* (also **wi′geon**) species of wild duck.

wid•get /wíjit/ *n. colloq.* any gadget or device.

wid•ow /wídō/ • *n.* **1** woman who has lost her husband by death and has not married again. **2** woman whose husband is often away on or preoccupied with a specified activity (*golf widow*). • *v.tr.* **1** make into a widow or widower. **2** (as **widowed** *adj.*) bereft by the death of a spouse. □□ **wid′ow•hood** *n.*

wid•ow•er /wídōər/ *n.* man who has lost his wife by death and has not married again.

width /width, witth, with/ *n.* **1** measurement from side to side. **2** large extent. **3** strip of material of full width. □□ **width′ways** *adv.* **width′wise** *adv.*

■ **1** breadth, wideness, compass, broadness, span; diameter, caliber, bore; measure. **2** reach, scope, range, breadth.

wield /weeld/ *v.tr.* **1** hold and use. **2** exert or command. □□ **wield′er** *n.*

■ **1** flourish, swing, brandish. **2** exercise, employ, use, utilize.

wie•ner /wéenər/ *n.* = FRANKFURTER.

wife /wīf/ *n.* (*pl.* **wives** /wīvz/) married woman, esp. in relation to her husband. □□ **wife′hood** *n.* **wife′less** *adj.* **wife′like** *adj.* **wife′ly** *adj.* **wife′li•ness** *n.*

■ mate, helpmate, spouse, bride, partner.

wig /wig/ *n.* artificial head of hair. □□ **wigged** *adj.* [also in *comb.*]. **wig′less** *adj.*

wig•eon var. of WIDGEON.

wig•gle /wígəl/ *colloq.* • *v.* move or cause to move quickly from side to side, etc. • *n.* act of wiggling. □□ **wig′gler** *n.*

■ *v.* see WAG[1] *v.* □□ **wiggler** see WAG[1] *n.*

wig•wag /wígwag/ *v.intr.* (**wig•wagged, wig•wag•ging**) *colloq.* **1** move lightly to and fro. **2** wave flags in this way in signaling.

wig•wam /wígwom/ *n.* Native American hut or tent.

wild /wīld/ • *adj.* **1** in its original natural state; not domesticated nor cultivated. **2** not civilized; barbarous. **3** unrestrained; disorderly. **4** tempestuous. **5** intensely eager **b** [foll. by *about*] *colloq.* enthusiastically devoted to. **6** haphazard; ill-aimed. • *adv.* in a wild manner. • *n.* wild tract. □□ **wild card 1** playing card having a rank chosen by the player holding it. **2** *Computing* character that will match any character or sequence of characters. **wild-goose chase** foolish or hopeless quest. **wild rice** N. American aquatic grass with edible grains. **Wild West** western US before the establishment of law and order. □□ **wild′ish** *adj.* **wild′ly** *adv.* **wild′ness** *n.*

■ *adj.* **1** undomesticated, untamed, unbroken, savage. **2** savage, uncivilized, primitive. **3** uncontrolled, unrestricted, free; uncontrollable, unmanageable. **4** turbulent, violent; see also STORMY 1, 2. **5** excited, vehement, passionate, maniac(al), frenzied. **6** random, absurd, crazy, irrational. • *n.* waste, wasteland, wilderness; vastness, emptiness. □□ **wildly** see MADLY 2. **wildness** see NATURE 4.

wild•cat /wíldkat/ • *n.* **1** hot-tempered or violent person. **2** any of various smallish undomesticated cats, as the lynx, bobcat, etc.

963   widgeon ~ willow

3 exploratory oil well. • *adj.* **1** reckless; financially unsound. **2** (of a strike) sudden and unofficial.

■ *adj.* **1** see RECKLESS.

wil•de•beest /wíldəbeest, víl–/ *n.* = GNU.

wil•der•ness /wíldərnis/ *n.* desert; uncultivated and uninhabited region.

■ see DESERT[2] *n.*

wild•fire /wíldfīr/ *n. hist.* **1** rapidly spreading fire. **2** combustible liquid, esp. Greek fire, formerly used in warfare. **3** = WILL-O′-THE-WISP.

wild•fowl /wíldfowl/ *n.* (*pl.* same) game bird.

wild•life /wíldlīf/ *n.* wild animals collectively.

wile /wīl/ • *n.* (usu. in *pl.*) stratagem; trick or cunning procedure. • *v.tr.* lure or entice.

■ *n.* ruse, artifice, subterfuge, dodge, trap, scheme. • *v.* see ENTICE.

will[1] /wil/ *v.aux. & tr.* (3rd sing. present **will**; past **would** /wŏŏd/) **1** (in the 2nd and 3rd persons, and often in the 1st: see SHALL expressing the future tense in statements, commands, or questions (*you will regret this*) **2** (in the 1st person) expressing intention (*I will return soon*). **3** expressing desire, consent, or inclination (*will you have a sandwich?*). **4** expressing ability or capacity (*jar will hold a quart*). **5** expressing habitual or inevitable tendency (*accidents will happen*). **6** expressing probability or expectation (*that will be my wife*).

will[2] /wil/ • *n.* **1** faculty by which a person decides what to do. **2** self-control; willpower. **3** strong desire or intention. **4** power of effecting one's intentions or dominating others. **5** directions (usu. written) in legal form for the disposition of one's property after death. • *v.tr.* **1** intend; desire. **2** exercise willpower. **3** bequeath by the terms of a will. □ **at will** whenever one pleases. □□ **willed** *adj.* [also in *comb.*] **will′less** *adj.*

■ *n.* **2** resolve, commitment, resolution, determination. **3** wish, longing, liking, inclination. **4** drive, purposefulness. **5** (last will and) testament. • *v.* **1** want, wish, choose. **3** leave, hand down or on.

will•ful /wílfŏŏl/ *adj.* **1** intentional; deliberate. **2** obstinate; headstrong. □□ **will′ful•ly** *adv.* **will′ful•ness** *n.*

■ **1** voluntary, conscious, intended, purposeful, premeditated. **2** stubborn, pigheaded, mulish, inflexible. □□ **willfully** see *deliberately* (DELIBERATE). **willfulness** see *obstinacy* (OBSTINATE).

wil•lies /wíleez/ *n.pl. colloq.* nervous discomfort.

will•ing /wíling/ *adj.* **1** ready to consent or undertake. **2** given or done, etc., by a willing person. □□ **will′ing•ly** *adv.* **will′ing•ness** *n.*

■ **1** agreeable, acquiescent, compliant, amenable. □□ **willingly** readily, happily, contentedly, gladly, cheerfully, amenably, agreeably, freely.

will-o′-the-wisp /wíləthəwisp/ *n.* **1** phosphorescent light seen on marshy ground. **2** elusive person. **3** delusive hope or plan.

wil•low /wílō/ *n.* tree, usu. near water, yielding wood and pliant branches for furniture, baskets, etc.

wil•low•y /wilō-ee/ *adj.* lithe and slender.

■ lissome, supple, limber; graceful, slim, thin.

will•pow•er /wilpowr/ *n.* control exercised by deliberate purpose over impulse; self-control.

wil•ly-nil•ly /wileenilee/ • *adv.* whether one likes it or not. • *adj.* existing or occurring willy-nilly.

■ *adv.* inevitably, necessarily, of necessity, one way or the other. • *adj.* necessary, unavoidable, inevitable, involuntary.

wilt /wilt/ • *v.* **1** *intr.* wither; droop. **2** *intr.* lose one's energy. **3** *tr.* cause to wilt. • *n.* plant disease causing wilting.

■ *v.* **1** sag, shrink, shrivel (up *or* away). **2** droop, bow, weaken, sink, wane, wither, tire.

wil•y /wīlee/ *adj.* (**wil•i•er, wil•i•est**) full of wiles; crafty; cunning. □□ **wil'i•ness** *n.*

■ shrewd, sly, artful, guileful, clever, foxy, sharp, canny.

wimp /wimp/ *n. colloq.* feeble or ineffectual person. □□ **wimp'ish** *adj.* **wimp'ish•ly** *adv.* **wimp'ish•ness** *n.* **wimp'y** *adj.*

wim•ple /wimpəl/ • *n.* headdress also covering the neck and the sides of the face, worn by some nuns. • *v.* arrange or fall in folds.

win /win/ • *v.* (**win•ning;** *past* and *past part.* **won** /wun/) **1** *tr.* acquire or secure as a result of a fight, contest, bet, effort, etc. **2** *tr.* be victorious in. **3** *intr.* be the victor. • *n.* victory in a game, etc. □□ **win'na•ble** *adj.*

■ *v.* **1** gain, attain, get, obtain, secure. **2** finish first in, achieve first place in, triumph in. **3** carry the day, conquer, overcome, triumph.

wince /wins/ • *n.* start or involuntary shrinking movement showing pain or distress. • *v.intr.* give a wince. □□ **winc'er** *n.* **winc'ing•ly** *adv.*

■ *v.* see CRINGE *v.*

SYNONYM STUDY: wince

COWER, CRINGE, FLINCH, RECOIL. The same individual might **wince** when receiving a flu shot, **flinch** from a difficult task, and **cower** in fear at the approach of a tornado. All of these verbs mean to draw back in alarm, disgust, faintheartedness, or servility, but there are subtle differences among them. To *wince* is to make a slight recoiling movement, often an involuntary contraction of the facial features, in response to pain or discomfort (*to wince when a singer misses a high note*), while *flinch* may imply a similar drawing-back motion or, more abstractly, a reluctance or avoidance (*to tackle the job without flinching*). *Cower* and *cringe* both refer to stooped postures, although *cower* is usually associated with fearful trembling (*he cowered in the doorway*) while *cringe* is usually linked to servile, cowardly, or fawning behavior (*to cringe before her father's authority*). More than any of the other verbs here, **recoil** suggests a physical movement away from something (*to recoil at the sight of a poisonous snake*), although that movement may also be psychological (*to recoil at the very thought of a family reunion*).

winch /winch/ • *n.* **1** crank of a wheel or axle. **2** windlass. • *v.tr.* lift with a winch. □□ **winch'er** *n.*

wind¹ /wind/ • *n.* **1** air in more or less rapid natural motion. **2 a** breath. **b** power of breathing. **3** mere empty words. **4** gas generated in the bowels, etc. **5** wind instruments of an orchestra collectively. **6** scent carried by the wind, indicating the presence or proximity of an animal, etc. • *v.tr.* **1** exhaust the wind of by exertion or a blow. **2** renew the wind of by rest (*stopped to wind the horses*). **3** detect the presence of by a scent. □ **get wind of 1** smell out. **2** begin to suspect. **in the wind** happening or about to happen. **wind instrument** musical instrument in which sound is produced by a current of air, esp. the breath. **wind sock** canvas cylinder or cone on a mast to show the direction of the wind at an airfield, etc. **wind tunnel** tunnellike device to produce an air stream past models of aircraft, etc., for the study of wind effects on them. □□ **wind'less** *adj.*

■ *n.* **1** breeze, *literary* zephyr; puff, gust, blast, squall. **2** air, puff. **3** puffery, bombast, rodomontade, rhetoric, bluster. **4** flatulence, windiness, flatus. **6** whiff, smell, trace. □ **get wind of 1** see SMELL *v.* 1. **2** hear of, learn of, come to know, pick up, become aware of. **in the wind** around, about, rumored, in the air, detectable, discernible. **wind sock** wind sleeve. □□ **windless** see CALM *adj.* 1.

wind² /wīnd/ • *v.* (*past* and *past part.* **wound** /wownd/) **1** *intr.* go in a circular, spiral, curved, or crooked course. **2** *tr.* make (one's way) by such a course. **3** *tr.* wrap closely; surround with or as with a coil. **4 a** *tr.* coil. **b** *intr.* coil into a ball. **5** *tr.* wind up (a clock, etc.). • *n.* bend or turn in a course.

■ *v.* **1** turn, bend, twist, circle, snake, worm, meander. **3** fold, enfold, encircle, envelop. **4** reel, roll, spiral. **5** crank (up), wind up. ■ *n.* see TURN *n.* 2.

wind•bag /windbag/ *n. colloq.* person who talks a lot but says little of any value.

wind•break /windbrayk/ *n.* row of trees or a fence or wall, etc., serving to break the force of the winds.

wind•break•er /windbraykər/ *n.* wind-resistant outer jacket.

wind•burn /windbərn/ *n.* inflammation of the skin caused by exposure to the wind.

wind•chill /windchil/ *n.* cooling effect of wind blowing on a surface.

wind•fall /windfawl/ *n.* **1** fruit blown to the ground by the wind. **2** unexpected good fortune.

■ **2** bonanza, godsend, stroke of (good) fortune, jackpot.

wind•jam•mer /windjamər/ *n.* merchant sailing ship.

wind•lass /windləs/ • *n.* machine with a horizontal axle for hauling or hoisting. • *v.tr.* hoist or haul with a windlass.

wind•mill /wíndmil/ n. mill worked by the action of the wind on its sails.

win•dow /wíndō/ n. **1 a** opening in a wall, etc., usu. with glass in fixed, sliding, or hinged frames, to admit light or air, etc., and allow the occupants to see out. **b** glass filling this opening. **2** gap. **3** windowlike opening. **4** Comp. on-screen display selected to show a particular category or part of the data. □ **window box** box placed on an outside windowsill for growing flowers. **window dressing 1** display in a store window, etc. **2** adroit presentation of facts, etc., to give a deceptively favorable impression. **window-shop (–shopped, –shop•ping)** look at goods displayed in store windows, usu. without buying anything. **window-shopper** person who window-shops. □□ **win′dowed** adj. [also in comb.]. **win′dow•less** adj.

win•dow•pane /wíndōpayn/ n. pane of glass in a window.

win•dow•sill /wíndōsil/ n. sill below a window.

wind•pipe /wíndpīp/ n. air passage from the throat to the lungs; trachea.

wind•shield /wíndsheeld/ n. shield of glass at the front of a motor vehicle. □ **windshield wiper** rubber blade on an arm, moving in an arc, to keep a windshield clear of rain, etc.

wind•surf•ing /wíndsərfing/ n. sport of riding on water on a sailboard. □□ **wind′surf** v.intr. **wind′surf•er** n.

wind•up /wíndup/ n. **1** conclusion; finish. **2** Baseball motions made by a pitcher, esp. arm swinging, in preparation for releasing a pitch.

wind•ward /wíndwərd/ adj. & adv. on the side from which the wind is blowing opp. LEEWARD. • n. windward direction.

wind•y /wíndee/ adj. (**wind•i•er, wind•i•est**) **1** stormy with wind. **2** exposed to the wind; windswept. **3** colloq. wordy; verbose. □□ **wind′i•ly** adv. **wind′i•ness** n.

■ **1** blustery, blowing, gusting, gusty, wild, squally, stormy. **2** unprotected, bleak. **3** talkative, long-winded, garrulous, prolix, glib, bombastic.

wine /wīn/ • n. **1** fermented grape juice as an alcoholic drink. **2** fermented drink resembling this made from other fruits, etc. **3** dark-red color of red wine. • v. **1** intr. drink wine. **2** tr. entertain with wine. □□ **wine′less** adj. **win′y** adj. (**win•i•er, win•i•est**).

win•er•y /wínəree/ n. (pl. **–ies**) establishment where wine is made.

wing /wing/ • n. **1** each of the limbs or organs by which a bird, bat, or insect is able to fly. **2** winglike structure forming a supporting part of an aircraft. **3** part of a building, etc., extended in a certain direction. **4** section of a political party in terms of the extremity of its views. **5** flank of a battle array. **6 a** air force unit of several squadrons or groups. **b** [in pl.] pilot's badge in the air force, etc. • v. **1** intr. & tr. travel or traverse on wings or in an aircraft. **2** tr. wound in a wing or an arm. **3** tr. equip with wings. **4** tr. enable to fly; send in flight. □ **on the wing** flying or in flight. **take under one's wing** treat as a protégé. **take wing** fly away; soar. **wing nut** nut with projections for the fin-

gers. □□ **winged** adj. [also in comb.]. **wing′less** adj. **wing′let** n. **wing′like** adj.

■ n. **4** faction, group, fringe movement, lobby. • v. **1** see FLY[1] v. **1**. **2** see WOUND[1] v. □ **take under one's wing** see PROVIDE[1] 2b. **take wing** see FLY v. **1**.

wingspan /wíngspan/ n. measurement across the wings from tip to tip.

wink /wingk/ • v. **1 a** tr. close and open (one eye or both eyes) quickly. **b** intr. close and open an eye. **2** intr. [often foll. by at] wink one eye as a signal of friendship or greeting or to convey a message to a person. **3** intr. (of a light, etc.) twinkle; shine or flash intermittently. • n. **1** act or instance of winking. **2** colloq. short sleep. □ **wink at** purposely avoid seeing. **2** connive at (a wrongdoing, etc.). □□ **wink′er** n.

■ v. **3** see TWINKLE v. **wink at** see OVERLOOK v. **1**.

win•ner /wínər/ n. person, racehorse, etc., that wins.

■ victor, champion, titleholder, conqueror.

win•ning /wíning/ • adj. **1** having or bringing victory or an advantage. **2** attractive; persuasive. • n. [in pl.] money won. □□ **win′ning•ly** adv. **win′ning•ness** n.

■ adj. **1** triumphant, conquering, victorious, successful. **2** engaging, appealing, alluring, captivating, endearing. • n. (winnings) see PRIZE[1] n. **2**.

win•now /wínō/ v.tr. **1** blow (grain) free of chaff, etc. **2** get rid of (chaff, etc.) from grain. **3** sift; separate; examine. □□ **win′now•er** n. (in senses 1, 2).

wi•no /wínō/ n. (pl. **–nos**) sl. alcoholic.

win•some /wínsəm/ adj. attractive; engaging. □□ **win′some•ly** adv. **win′some•ness** n.

■ see WINNING adj. **2**.

win•ter /wíntər/ • n. **1** coldest season of the year, in the northern hemisphere from December to February and in the southern hemisphere from June to August. **2** Astron. period from the winter solstice to the vernal equinox. **3** bleak or lifeless period or region, etc. (esp. of a person's age: a man of fifty winters). • adj. characteristic of or suitable for winter. • v.intr. pass the winter. □ **winter solstice** see SOLSTICE. □□ **win′ter•er** n. **win′ter•less** adj.

win•ter•green /wíntərgreen/ n. evergreen plant with red berries, source of all aromatic flavoring oil.

win•ter•ize /wíntərīz/ v.tr. adapt for operation or use in cold weather. □□ **win•ter•i•za′tion** n.

win•ter•time /wíntərtīm/ n. season of winter.

win•try /wíntree/ adj. (also **win•ter•y** /–təree/) (**win•tri•er, win•tri•est**) **1** characteristic of winter. **2** (of a smile, greeting, etc.) lacking warmth or enthusiasm. □□ **win′tri•ly** adv. **win′tri•ness** n.

■ **1** icy, snowy, freezing, frozen, frosty, cold, frigid. **2** cold, chilling; forbidding, bleak, dismal, cheerless.

wipe /wīp/ • v.tr. **1** clean or dry by rubbing. **2** rub (a cloth) over a surface. **3 a** spread or remove by wiping. **b** remove or eliminate completely. • n. **1** act of wiping. **2** piece of material for wiping. □ **wipe out 1** destroy; annihilate. **2** sl. murder. **wiped out** adj. sl. tired out; exhausted. □□ **wipe'a•ble** adj. **wip'er** n.

■ v. **1** wipe off or out or up, usu. formal cleanse; dust (off), polish. **3** smear; clear, get rid of. • n. **1** rub, brush, sweep, polish. □ **wipe out 1** massacre, kill (off), eradicate, exterminate. **2** kill (off), dispose of.

wire /wīr/ • n. **1 a** metal drawn out into a thread or thin flexible rod. **b** piece of this. **c** [attrib.] made of wire. **2** telegram or cablegram. • v.tr. **1** provide, attach, fasten, strengthen, etc., with wire. **2** Electr. install electrical circuits in. **3** colloq. telegraph. □ **wire service** business that gathers news and distributes it to subscribers, usu. newspapers. □□ **wir'er** n.

■ n. **2** see TELEGRAM. • v. **3** cablegram.

wire•haired /wīrhaird/ adj. (esp. of a dog) having stiff or wiry hair.

wire•less /wīrlis/ adj. operating without wires, esp. by electromagnetic waves.

wire•tap /wīrtap/ v. (–tapped, –tap•ping) **1** intr. connect a listening device to (a telephone or telegraph line, etc.) to listen to a call or transmission. **2** tr. obtain (information, etc.) by wiretapping. □□ **wire'tap•per** n. **wire'tap•ping** n.

wir•ing /wīring/ n. system or installation of wires providing electrical circuits.

wir•y /wīree/ adj. (**wir•i•er, wir•i•est**) **1** tough and flexible as wire. **2** (of a person) thin and sinewy. □□ **wir'i•ly** adv. **wir'i•ness** n.

■ **2** muscular, lean, lank, spare; untiring, tireless.

Wis. abbr. Wisconsin.

wis•dom /wizdəm/ n. **1** state of being wise. **2** experience and knowledge together with the power of applying them. **3** sagacity; prudence; common sense. **4** wise sayings, thoughts, etc. See synonym study at KNOWLEDGE. □ **wisdom tooth** each of four hindmost molars not usu. cut before 20 years of age.

■ **2, 3** sageness, judgment, discernment, reason, judiciousness, insight. **4** knowledge, learning, erudition, lore.

wise¹ /wīz/ • adj. **1** having, showing, or dictated by wisdom. **2** prudent; sensible. **3** having knowledge. **4** suggestive of wisdom. **5** colloq. **a** crafty. **b** having (usu. confidential) information (about). • v. [foll. by up] colloq. **1** become aware of. **2** inform (a person about). □ **wise guy** colloq. know-it-all. □□ **wise'ly** adv.

■ adj. **1** sage, sagacious, judicious, reasonable, intelligent, astute. **2** well-advised, advisable, judicious, sagacious. **3** knowledgeable, learned, enlightened, informed, erudite; well-read; well-versed, well-informed, lettered, scholarly. **4** knowing, shrewd, perceptive, understanding. **5 a** see FOXY 1, ALERT adj. 1. **b** aware, knowledgeable, informed. • v. **1** get wise. **2** put wise. □ **wise guy** wiseacre; smart aleck.

wise² /wīz/ n. archaic way, manner, or degree (in solemn wise). □ **in no wise** not at all.

-wise /wīz/ suffix forming adjectives and adverbs of manner (crosswise, lengthwise) or respect (moneywise) (cf. -WAYS).

wise•a•cre /wīzaykər/ n. person who affects a wise manner; wise guy.

wise•crack /wīzkrak/ colloq. • n. smart pithy remark. • v.intr. make a wisecrack. □□ **wise' crack•er** n.

■ n. joke, quip, rejoinder, witticism, pun, barb, jest, gibe. • v. joke, quip, pun, gibe.

wish /wish/ • v. **1** intr. [often foll. by for] have or express a desire or aspiration for. **2** tr. have as a desire or aspiration. **3** tr. want or demand. **4** tr. express one's hopes for. • n. **1 a** desire, request, or aspiration. **b** expression of this. **2** thing desired. □□ **wish'er** n. (in sense 4 of v.); [also in comb.].

■ v. **1** yearn, long, hope, aspire; (wish for) desire, want, crave. **3** require, request, order. • n. **1** whim, want, need, craving.

wish•bone /wishbōn/ n. forked bone between the neck and breast of a fowl.

wish•ful /wishfŏŏl/ adj. desiring. □□ **wish' ful•ly** adv. **wish'ful•ness** n.

■ see DESIROUS 2.

wish•y-wash•y /wisheewôshee, -wáwshee/ adj. **1** feeble, insipid, or indecisive in quality or character. **2** weak; watery.

■ **1** neither here nor there, undecided, indecisive, irresolute, insipid. **2** watered down, thin, vapid, flat, bland, tasteless.

wisp /wisp/ n. **1** small, bundle or twist of straw, etc. **2** small, separate quantity of smoke, hair, etc. **3** small, thin person, etc. □□ **wisp'y** adj. (**wisp•i•er, wisp•i•est**). **wisp'i•ly** adv. **wisp'i•ness** n.

■ **2** streak, shred, scrap, strand, thread, snippet, tuft. □ **wispy** thin, flimsy, insubstantial, gossamer.

wis•te•ri•a /wisteéreeə/ n. (also **wis•tar•i•a** /–stáiriə/) climbing plant with hanging racemes of blue, purple, or white flowers.

wist•ful /wistfŏŏl/ adj. yearningly or mournfully expectant. □□ **wist'ful•ly** adv. **wist' ful•ness** n.

■ melancholy, sad, morose, sorrowful; contemplative, pensive, detached, meditative.

wit¹ /wit/ n. **1** [in sing. or pl.] intelligence; quick understanding. **2 a** quick; unexpected, and humorous combining or contrasting of ideas or expressions. **b** power of giving intellectual pleasure by this. **3** person possessing such a power. □ **at one's wit's** (or **wits'**) **end** utterly at a loss or in despair. □□ **wit'ted** adj. (in sense 1); [also in comb.].

■ **1** brains, mind, (common) sense, cleverness. **2** humor, drollery, levity, repartee, raillery, facetiousness, waggishness, badinage, banter. **3** comedian, comedienne, humorist, comic, wag, joker, parodist, satirist. □ **at one's wit's** (or **wits'**) **end** see FRANTIC 2.

SYNONYM STUDY: wit

HUMOR, IRONY, REPARTEE, SARCASM, SATIRE. If you're good at perceiving analogies between things that are dissimilar and at expressing them in quick, sharp, spontaneous observations or remarks, you have wit. **Humor,** on the other hand, is the ability to perceive and express what is comical, ridiculous, or ludicrous in a situation or character, and to do so in a way that makes others see or feel the same thing. It suggests more sympathy, more tolerance, and more kindliness than *wit* (*to have a sense of humor in the midst of trying circumstances*). **Irony** is the *humor* that is implicit in the contradiction between what is meant and what is expressed, or in the discrepancy between appearance and reality. An example would be to say, in the midst of a hurricane, "What a perfect day for a wedding!" Although **sarcasm** may take the form of *irony,* it is less subtle and is often used harshly or bitterly to wound or ridicule someone. Unlike *irony,* however, *sarcasm* depends on tone of voice for its effect ("*A fine friend you turned out to be!*" *he said, with obvious sarcasm*). **Satire** usually implies the use of *sarcasm* or *irony* for the purpose of ridicule or criticism, often directed at institutions or political figures (*to write a satire exposing government corruption*). If you are good at making quick, witty replies, you will be known for your **repartee,** which is the art of responding pointedly and skillfully, with *wit* or *humor,* in a conversational exchange (*no one could compete with her witty repartee*).

wit² /wit/ v. (*1st & 3rd sing. present* **wot** /wot/; *past* and *past part.* **wist**) *archaic* know. □ **to wit** namely.

witch /wich/ n. **1** sorceress, esp. a woman supposed to have dealings with the devil or evil spirits. **2** hag. **3** fascinating girl or woman. □ **witch doctor** tribal magician of primitive people. **witch hazel 1** American shrub with bark yielding an astringent lotion. **2** this lotion. **witch-hunt** campaign directed against a particular group of those holding unpopular or unorthodox views, esp. communists. □□ **witch'ing** adj. **witch' like** adj.

■ **1** enchantress, sibyl, pythoness. **2** fury, crone, gorgon, ogress. □ **witch doctor** see SORCERER.

witch•craft /wichkraft/ n. use of magic; sorcery.

witch•er•y /wicharee/ n. **1** WITCHCRAFT. **2** power exercised by beauty or eloquence or the like.

with /with, with/ prep. expressing: **1** instrument or means used (*cut with a knife*). **2** association or company (*lives with his mother*). **3** cause (*shiver with fear*). **4** possession (*vase with handles*). **5** circumstances (*sleep with the window open*). **6** manner (*behaved with dignity*). **7** reference or regard (*how are things with you?*). □ **with-it** adj. colloq. in step with the times, fashion, etc. **with that** thereupon.

■ **2** BESIDE 1. □ **with-it** see MODERN adj.

with•al /witháwl, with-/ archaic adv. moreover; as well; at the same time.

with•draw /withdráw, with-/ v. (*past* **with•drew** /-dróo/; *past part.* **with•drawn** /-dráwn/) **1** tr. pull or take aside or back. **2** tr. discontinue; cancel; retract. **3** tr. remove; take away. **4** tr. take (money) out of an

account. **5** intr. retire or go away; move away or back. **6** intr. (as **withdrawn** adj.) abnormally shy and unsociable. □□ **with•draw'er** n.

■ **1** draw back, retract. **2** recall, take back, rescind, recant. **3** extract, pull out; recall. **4** remove, take or get (out). **5** retreat, repair, leave, depart, secede. **6** (**withdrawn**) reserved, detached, distant, remote, standoffish, aloof.

with•draw•al /withdráwəl, with-/ n. **1** act or instance of withdrawing or being withdrawn. **2** process of ceasing to take addictive drugs.

■ **1** extraction, removal; see also RETREAT n. 1a, 2, cancellation (CANCEL).

withe /with, with, with/ n. tough, flexible shoot, esp. of willow, used for binding, basketwork, etc.

with•er /withar/ v. **1** tr. & intr. make or become dry and shriveled. **2** tr. & intr. deprive of or lose vigor, vitality, freshness, or importance. **3** tr. a blight with scorn, etc. **b** (as **withering** adj.) scornful (*withering look*). □□ **with'er•ing•ly** adv.

■ **1** see SHRIVEL. **2** see WASTE v. 3.

with•ers /witharz/ n.pl. ridge between a horse's shoulder blades.

with•hold /with-hóld, with-/ v.tr. (*past* and *past part.* **-held** /-héld/) **1** hold back; restrain. **2** refuse to give, grant, or allow. **3** deduct, esp. from a paycheck. □□ **with•hold'er** n.

■ **1** keep back, deduct, retain, reserve; control, repress, suppress. **2** deny, deprive (of), disallow

with•in /within, with-/ adv. archaic or literary **1** inside, internally. **2** indoors. **3** in spirit (*make me pure within*). • prep. **1** inside; enclosed or contained by. **2 a** not beyond or exceeding. **b** not transgressing **3** not further off than. • n. inside part of a building, etc

■ adv. see INSIDE adv. 1.

with•out /withówt, with-/ • prep. **1** not having, feeling, or showing. **2** with freedom from. **3** in the absence of. **4** with neglect or avoidance of. **5** archaic outside. • adv. archaic or literary **1** outside. **2** out of doors. • n. outside part of a building, etc. • conj. dial. unless (*the dog won't eat without you give him some meat*).

■ prep. **1** see EMPTY adj. 1. **2** see FREE adj. 4. • adv. see OUTSIDE adv.

with•stand /withstánd, with-/ v. (*past* and *past part.* **-stood** /-stóod/) **1** tr. oppose; hold out against. **2** intr. make opposition; offer resistance. □□ **with•stand'er** n.

■ **1** resist, stand (up to), face, defy, confront, endure.

wit•less /witlis/ adj. **1** foolish; stupid. **2** crazy. □□ **wit'less•ly** adv. **wit'less•ness** n.

■ see FOOLISH.

wit•ness /witnis/ • n. **1** EYEWITNESS. **2 a** person giving sworn testimony. **b** person attesting another's signature to a document. **3** testimony; confirming evidence; confirmation. • v. **1** tr. be a witness of (an event, etc.). **2** tr. be witness to the authenticity of. **3** tr. & intr.

give or serve as evidence or an indication of. □ **bear witness to** (or **of**) attest the truth of.
■ *n.* **2** *Law* deponent, testifier, corroborating witness. **3** see TESTIMONY 1, 2. • *v.* **1** see, observe, watch, mark, note, notice. **2** countersign, sign, certify, endorse, substantiate, validate. **3** see *bear witness to* below. □ **bear witness to** (or **of**) testify (to), witness (to), verify, confirm, corroborate.

wit•ti•cism /wítisizəm/ *n.* witty remark.
■ pun, quip, play on words, paronomasia, bon mot, mot.

wit•ty /wítee/ *adj.* (**wit•ti•er, wit•ti•est**) showing verbal wit. □□ **wit′ti•ly** *adv.* **wit′ti•ness** *n.*
■ ingenious, subtle, clever, quick-witted, sharp-witted, humorous, sarcastic, sardonic, piquant, epigrammatic.

wives *pl.* of WIFE.

wiz•ard /wízərd/ *n.* **1** sorcerer; magician. **2** person of remarkable powers; genius. □□ **wiz′ard•ly** *adj.* **wiz′ard•ry** *n.*
■ **1** see MAGICIAN. **2** see VIRTUOSO 1. □□ **wizardry** see MAGIC *n.* 1, 2.

wiz•ened /wízənd/ *adj.* (also **wiz′en**) shriveled-looking.
■ wrinkled, shrunken, withered, gnarled.

wob•ble /wóbəl/ • *v.* **1 a** *intr.* sway or vibrate unsteadily from side to side. **b** *tr.* cause to do this. **2** *intr.* stand or go unsteadily; stagger. **3** *intr.* waver; vacillate. **4** *intr.* (of the voice or sound) quaver; pulsate. • *n.* **1** wobbling movement. **2** instance of vacillation or pulsation. □□ **wob′bler** *n.* **wob′bli•ness** *n.* **wob′bly** *adj.* (**wob•bli•er, wob•bli•est**).
■ *v.* **1** see SHAKE[1] *v.* 1, 2. **2** see STAGGER *v.* 1a. **4** see QUIVER *v.* • *n.* see SHAKE *n.* 1. □□ **wobbly** see SHAKY.

woe /wō/ *n. archaic* or *literary* **1** affliction; bitter grief. **2** [in *pl.*] calamities; troubles.
■ **1** trouble, hardship, adversity, misery, anguish. **2** (*woes*) trials, tribulations, adversities, misfortunes.

woe•be•gone /wóbigon, –gawn/ *adj.* dismal-looking.
■ troubled, miserable, anguished, wretched, desolate.

woe•ful /wófool/ *adj.* **1** sorrowful. **2** causing sorrow or affliction. **3** wretched. □□ **woe′ful•ly** *adv.* **woe′ful•ness** *n.*
■ **1** see SORROWFUL 1. **2** see PATHETIC 1. **3** see AWFUL 1a, b. □□ **woefully** see *painfully* (PAIN).

wok /wok/ *n.* bowl-shaped metal pan used in esp. Chinese cooking.

woke *past* of WAKE[1].

wok•en *past part.* of WAKE[1].

wolf /woolf/ • *n.* (*pl.* **wolves** /woolvz/) **1** wild, flesh-eating mammal related to the dog, and hunting in packs. **2** *sl.* man given to seducing women. • *v.tr.* [often foll. by *down*] devour (food) greedily. □ **cry wolf** raise repeated false alarms (so that a genuine one is disregarded). □□ **wolf′ish** *adj.* **wolf′ish•ly** *adv.* **wolf′like** *adj.* & *adv.*
■ *v.* see DEVOUR 1.

wolf•hound /woolfhownd/ *n.* borzoi or other dog of a kind used orig. to hunt wolves.

wolf•ram /woolfrəm/ *n.* TUNGSTEN.

wol•ver•ine /woolvəreen/ *n.* voracious carnivorous mammal of the weasel family.

wom•an /woomən/ *n.* (*pl.* **wom•en** /wimin/) **1** adult human female. **2** the female sex. **3** [prec. by *the*] emotions or characteristics traditionally associated with women (*brought out the woman in him*). **4** [*comb. form*] woman of a specified nationality, profession, skill, etc. (*Englishwoman, horsewoman, congresswoman*). □ **women's lib** *colloq.* = *women's liberation.* **women's liberation** liberation of women from inequalities and subservient status in relation to men, and elimination of attitudes causing these. □□ **wom′an•less** *adj.* **wom′an•like** *adj.*
■ **1** lady, miss. **2** womankind, womenkind, womenfolk. □□ **womanlike** see FEMININE *adj.* 1.

wom•an•hood /woomənhood/ *n.* **1** female maturity. **2** womanly instinct. **3** womankind.

wom•an•ish /woomənish/ *adj.*, usu. *derog.* (of a man) effeminate; unmanly. □□ **wom′an•ish•ly** *adv.* **wom′an•ish•ness** *n.*
■ see EFFEMINATE.

wom•an•ize /wooməniz/ *v.* **1** *intr.* chase after women; philander. **2** *tr.* make womanish. □□ **wom′an•iz•er** *n.*
■ **1** see PHILANDER. □□ **womanizer** see *philanderer* (PHILANDER).

wom•an•kind /woomənkind/ *n.* (also **wom•en•kind** /wimin–/) women in general.

wom•an•ly /woomənlee/ *adj.* having or showing qualities traditionally associated with women; not masculine nor girlish. □□ **wom′an•li•ness** *n.*
■ see FEMININE *adj.* 1.

womb /woom/ *n.* organ of conception and gestation in a woman and other female mammals; uterus. □□ **womb′like** *adj.*

wom•bat /wómbat/ *n.* burrowing, plant-eating Australian marsupial resembling a small bear, with short legs.

wom•en *pl.* of WOMAN.

wom•en•folk /wiminfok/ *n.* **1** women in general. **2** the women in a family.

wom•en•kind var. of WOMANKIND.

won *past* and *past part.* of WIN.

won•der /wúndər/ • *n.* **1** emotion excited by what is unexpected, unfamiliar, or inexplicable. **2** strange or remarkable person or thing; specimen, event, etc. **3** [*attrib.*] having marvelous or amazing properties, etc. (*wonder drug*). • *v.* **1** *intr.* be filled with wonder. **2** *tr.* be surprised to find. **3** *tr.* desire or be curious to know. □□ **won′der•er** *n.*
■ *n.* **1** awe, astonishment, admiration, amazement. **2** prodigy, phenomenon, spectacle, rarity. • *v.* **1** marvel, goggle, gawk, gape, stare, be awed. **3** ponder, meditate, think, theorize, conjecture, puzzle.

won•der•ful /wúndərfool/ *adj.* very remarkable or admirable. □□ **won′der•ful•ly** *adv.* **won′der•ful•ness** *n.*
■ see TERRIFIC 1b. □□ **wonderfully** see *beautifully* (BEAUTIFUL).

won•der•land /wúndərland/ *n.* **1** enchanted place. **2** land of surprises or marvels.

won•der•ment /wúndərmənt/ *n.* surprise; awe.

won•drous /wŭndrəs/ *poet.* • *adj.* wonderful. • *adv. archaic* or *literary* wonderfully (*wondrous kind*). □□ **won'drous•ly** *adv.* **won'drous•ness** *n.*

wont /wŏnt/ • *predic.adj.* *archaic* or *literary* accustomed (*as we were wont to say*). • *n. formal* or *joc.* what is customary; one's habit (*as is my wont*).
■ *n.* see CUSTOM 1a.

won't /wōnt/ *contr.* will not.

wont•ed /wŏntid, wáwn–, wún–/ *attrib.adj.* habitual; accustomed; usual.

woo /wōō/ *v.tr.* (**woos, wooed**) **1** court; seek the love of. **2** try to win. **3** seek the favor or support of. □□ **woo'a•ble** *adj.* **woo'er** *n.*
■ **1** see COURT *v.* 1. **2** chase, follow, pursue, seek. **3** make advances to, ingratiate oneself with, curry favor with.

wood /wŏŏd/ *n.* **1 a** hard fibrous material that forms the main substance of the trunk or branches of a tree or shrub. **b** this cut for lumber, fuel, etc. **2** [*in sing.* or *pl.*] growing trees densely occupying a tract of land. **3** wooden-headed golf club. □ **out of the woods** (or **wood**) out of danger or difficulty. **wood alcohol** methanol. **wood pulp** wood fiber reduced to pulp as raw material for paper. □□ **wood'ed** *adj.* **wood'less** *adj.*
■ **2** (*wood* or *woods*) woodland, forest, copse, brake, grove, covert, thicket, brush; timber, trees. □□ **wooded** sylvan, forested.

wood•bine /wŏŏdbīn/ *n.* **1** wild honeysuckle. **2** Virginia creeper.

wood•chuck /wŏŏdchuk/ *n.* reddish-brown and gray N. American marmot.

wood•cock /wŏŏdkok/ *n.* (*pl.* same) game bird related to the snipe.

wood•craft /wŏŏdkraft/ *n.* **1** skill in woodwork. **2** knowledge of woodland, esp. in camping, scouting, etc.

wood•cut /wŏŏdkut/ *n.* **1** relief cut on a block of wood. **2** print made from this.

wood•cut•ter /wŏŏdkutər/ *n.* person who cuts wood.

wood•en /wŏŏd'n/ *adj.* **1** made of or like wood. **2 a** stiff, clumsy. **b** expressionless. □□ **wood'en•ly** *adv.* **wood'en•ness** *n.*
■ **1** wood, woody, ligneous. **2 a** rigid, inflexible, stilted, unnatural, awkward, ungainly. **b** vacant, empty, impassive, deadpan, poker-faced.

wood•land /wŏŏdlənd/ *n.* wooded country, woods [often *attrib.: woodland scenery*]. □□ **wood'land•er** *n.*

wood•peck•er /wŏŏdpekər/ *n.* bird that taps tree trunks with its beak in search of insects.

wood•pile /wŏŏdpīl/ *n.* pile of wood, esp. for fuel.

wood•shed /wŏŏdshed/ *n.* shed where wood for fuel is stored.

woods•man /wŏŏdzmən/ *n.* (*pl.* **–men**) person who lives in or is familiar with woodland.

wood•sy /wŏŏdzee/ *adj.* like or characteristic of woods.

wood•wind /wŏŏdwind/ *n.* [often *attrib.*] **1** [*collect.*] wind instruments that were orig. made mostly of wood, e.g., flute and clarinet. **2** [usu. *in pl.*] individual instrument of this kind or its player (*the woodwinds are out of tune*).

wood•work /wŏŏdwərk/ *n.* **1** making of things in wood. **2** things made of wood, esp. paneling, moldings, etc. □□ **wood'work•er** *n.* **wood'work•ing** *n.*

wood•y /wŏŏdee/ *adj.* (**wood•i•er, wood•i•est**) **1** wooded; abounding in woods. **2** like or of wood (*woody tissue*). □□ **wood'i•ness** *n.*

woof[1] /wŏŏf/ • *n.* gruff bark of a dog. • *v.intr.* give a woof.

woof[2] /wŏŏf, wŏŏf/ *n.* = WEFT.

woof•er /wŏŏfər/ *n.* loudspeaker designed to reproduce low frequencies (cf. TWEETER).

wool /wŏŏl/ *n.* **1** fine, soft, wavy hair from the fleece of sheep, goats, etc. **2 a** yarn produced from this hair. **b** cloth or clothing made from it. **3** woollike substances (*steel wool*). □□ **wool'like** *adj.*

wool•en /wŏŏlən/ (also **wool'len**) • *adj.* made of wool. • *n.* [in *pl.*] woolen garments.

wool•ly /wŏŏlee/ (also **wool'y**) *adj.* (**wool•li•er, wool•li•est**) **1** bearing or naturally covered with wool or woollike hair. **2** resembling or suggesting wool (*woolly clouds*). **3** vague or confused. □□ **wool'li•ness** *n.*
■ **1** fleecy, woolen, wool-bearing, downy, fuzzy, furry, fluffy, shaggy. **2** fleecy, fluffy. **3** hazy, fuzzy, unclear, obscure(d), foggy, indistinct.

woo•zy /wŏŏzee/ *adj.* (**woo•zi•er, woo•zi•est**) *colloq.* **1** dizzy or unsteady. **2** slightly drunk. □□ **woo'zi•ly** *adv.* **woo'zi•ness** *n.*
■ **1** see DIZZY *adj.* 1a. **2** see TIGHT *adj.* 5.

word /wərd/ • *n.* **1** sound or combination of sounds forming a meaningful element of speech, writing, or printing. **2** speech, esp. as distinct from action. **3** one's promise or assurance. **4** [in *sing.* or *pl.*] remark or conversation. **5** [in *pl.*] text of a song or an actor's part. **6** [in *pl.*] angry talk. **7** news; intelligence; message. **8** command. • *v.tr.* put into words; select words to express. □ **in other words** expressing the same thing differently. **in so many words** explicitly or bluntly. **in a** (or **one**) **word** briefly. **the Word** (or **Word of God**) the Bible. **word of honor** promise or assurance. **word of mouth** speech (only). **word-of-mouth** verbal; unwritten. **word processor** computer software program for electronically storing text entered from a keyboard, incorporating corrections, and providing a printout. □□ **word'age** *n.* **word'less** *adj.* **word'less•ly** *adv.* **word'less•ness** *n.*
■ *n.* **1** name, term, designation, locution, expression, phrase. **3** pledge, vow, oath, (solemn) word of honor. **4** utterance, expression, declaration, statement; chat, discussion, dialogue. **5** (*words*) lyrics, book, libretto, script, lines. **6** (*words*) quarrel, dispute, argument. **7** information, facts, data, report. **8** order, decree, signal, direction, instruction, password, motto. • *v.* say, couch, express, phrase, utter, state. □ **in a** (or **one**) **word** succinctly, in brief, concisely, in short. **word-of-mouth** see VERBAL *adj.* 2. □□ **wordless** see MUTE *adj.* 1, 2. **wordlessly** see *silently* (SILENT).

word•ing /wórding/ *n.* **1** form of words used. **2** way in which something is expressed.

■ language, phrasing, expression, terminology.

word•play /wórdplay/ *n.* witty use of words, esp. punning.

word•y /wórdee/ *adj.* (**word•i•er**, **word•i•est**) using or expressed in too many words; verbose. □□ **word′i•ly** *adv.* **word′i•ness** *n.*

■ prolix, rambling, long-winded, ponderous; repetitious; garrulous. □□ **wordiness** see RHETORIC 2.

wore *past* of WEAR.

work /wərk/ • *n.* **1** application of mental or physical effort to a purpose; use of energy. **2 a** task to be undertaken. **b** materials for this. **3** thing done or made by work; result of an action. **4** employment or occupation. **5 a** literary or musical composition. **b** [in *pl.*] all such by an author or composer, etc. **6** [in *pl.*] operative part of a clock or machine. **7** [in *pl.*] *colloq.* all that is available; everything needed. **8** [in *pl.*] operations of building or repair. **9** [in *pl.*; often treated as *sing.*] factory. **10** [usu. in *pl.*] *Theol.* meritorious act. See synonym study at LABOR. • *v.* (*past* and *past part.* **worked** or [esp. as *adj.*] **wrought**) **1** *intr.* do work; be engaged in bodily or mental activity. **2** *intr.* a be employed in certain work. **b** [foll. by *with*] be the coworker of (a person). **3** *intr.* [foll. by *in*] be a craftsman (in a material). **4** *intr.* operate or function, esp. effectively. **5** *tr.* carry on, manage, or control. **6** *tr.* a cause to toil (*works the staff very hard*). **b** cultivate (land). **7** *tr.* bring about; produce as a result. **8** *tr.* knead; bring to a desired shape or consistency. **9** *tr.* do, or make by, needlework, etc. **10** *tr. & intr.* (cause to) make (one's way) gradually or with difficulty. **11** *intr.* gradually become (loose, etc.) by constant movement. **12** *tr.* artificially excite (*worked themselves into a rage*). **13** *tr.* a purchase with one's labor instead of money. **b** obtain by labor the money for. **14** *intr.* [foll. by *on*, *upon*] have influence. **15** *intr.* ferment. □ **at work** in action. **work off** get rid of by work or activity. **work out 1** solve or calculate. **2** have a result. **3** provide for the details of. **4** engage in physical exercise or training. **work over 1** examine thoroughly. **2** *colloq.* treat with violence. **work sheet 1** paper for recording work done or in progress. **2** paper listing questions or activities for students, etc., to work through. **work up 1** develop or advance gradually. **2** elaborate or excite by degrees. □□ **work′less** *adj.*

■ *n.* **1** labor, toil, effort, drudgery, exertion, industry. **2** function, duty, assignment, job. **3** feat, achievement, creation, accomplishment. **4** business, vocation, calling, profession, trade. **5** opus, oeuvre, production; creation. **6** (*works*) mechanism, machinery, action. **7** (*the works*) the lot, *sl.* the whole (kit and) caboodle. **9** (*works*) plant, workshop, shop, mill. • *v.* **1** labor, toil, exert oneself. **2 a** have a job, earn a living. **4** run, go, perform; be effective, suc-

ceed. **5** manipulate, maneuver, handle, operate. **6 a** operate, use, employ, put to (good *or* effective) use; drive, exploit. **b** till, plow, farm. **7** effect, accomplish, carry out, make, achieve. **8** hammer, mold, form. **10** wade, plod, plow; maneuver, guide. **14** (*work on*) importune, press, pressure; persuade. **15** see FERMENT² *v.* 1. □ **work out 1** see SOLVE. **2** go, develop, turn out, evolve; succeed, prosper. **3** formulate, work up, contrive, draw up, detail, plan. **4** do callisthenics, do aerobics, jog, lift weights, train. **work over 2** see POUND 1. **work up 1** prepare, (make *or* get) ready, put together; ascend, move up *or* ahead. **2** agitate, inflame, arouse, foment.

work•a•ble /wórkəbəl/ *adj.* **1** that can be worked or will work. **2** that is practicable; feasible. □□ **work•a•bil′i•ty** *n.* **work′a•ble•ness** *n.* **work′a•bly** *adv.*

■ **1** see OPERABLE. **2** see FEASIBLE 1.

work•a•day /wórkəday/ *adj.* ordinary; everyday; practical.

■ see ORDINARY *adj.*

work•a•hol•ic /wórkəhólik/ *n. colloq.* person addicted to working.

work•bench /wórkbench/ *n.* bench for doing mechanical or practical work, esp. carpentry.

work•day /wórkday/ *n.* day on which work is usually done.

work•er /wórkər/ *n.* **1** person who works, esp. a manual or industrial employee. **2** neuter bee or ant.

■ **1** laborer, hand, operator, employee; artisan, craftsman, tradesman, mechanic; journeyman, white-collar worker, blue-collar worker, proletarian, breadwinner, wage earner.

work•force /wórkfawrs/ *n.* **1** workers engaged or available in an industry, etc. **2** number of such workers.

■ see STAFF *n.* 2.

work•horse /wórk-hawrs/ *n.* horse, person, or machine that performs hard work.

■ see SLAVE *n.* 2.

work•ing /wórking/ • *adj.* **1** engaged in work. **2** functioning or able to function. • *n.* activity of work. □ **working class** class of people who are employed for wages, esp. in manual or industrial work. **working-class** *adj.* of the working class.

■ *adj.* **1** see BUSY *adj.* 1. **2** see FUNCTIONAL 1, ACTIVE *adj.* 2, 3. □ **working-class** (*adj.*) see PLEBEIAN *adj.* 1.

work•load /wórklōd/ *n.* amount of work to be done.

work•man /wórkmən/ *n.* (*pl.* **–men**) person employed to do manual labor.

■ see WORKER.

work•man•like /wórkmənlīk/ *adj.* characteristic of a good workman; showing practiced skill.

work•man•ship /wórkmənship/ *n.* degree of skill in doing a task or of finish in the product made.

■ **1** craftsmanship, artistry, technique, skillfulness, mastery.

work•out /wórkowt/ *n.* session of physical exercise or training.

■ see EXERCISE *n.* 3.

work•place /wórkplays/ *n.* place at which a person works.

work•shop /wórkshop/ *n.* **1** room or building in which goods are manufactured. **2** meeting for concerted discussion or activity.

work•sta•tion /wórkstayshən/ *n.* **1** location of a stage in a manufacturing process. **2** computer terminal or the desk, etc., where this is located.

world /wərld/ *n.* **1 a** the earth, or a planetary body like it. **b** its countries and their inhabitants. **c** all people; the earth as known or in some particular respect. **2** the universe or all that exists; everything. **3** secular interests and affairs. **4** human affairs; active life. **5** a specified class, time, domain, or sphere of activity (*world of baseball*). **6** vast amount. □ **world-class** of a quality or standard regarded as high throughout the world. **World Series** the championship for U.S. major-league baseball teams. **world-weary** weary of the world and life in it. **World Wide Web** global computer network for exchange of text, hypertext, graphics, audio, etc. ¶Abbr.: **WWW**

■ **1 a** planet, sphere, globe. **c** humanity, mankind, the human race, world at large. **2** cosmos, existence, creation, life. **4** things, circumstances, events. **5** period, age, era; area, community.

world•ly /wórldlee/ *adj.* (**world•li•er, world•li•est**) **1** temporal or earthly. **2** sophisticated. □ **worldly-wise** having worldly wisdom. □□ **world′li•ness** *n.*

■ **1** mundane, terrestrial, physical, carnal; lay, civic, secular, profane. **2** urbane, suave, cosmopolitan.

world•wide /wórldwíd/ • *adj.* affecting, occurring in, or known in all parts of the world • *adv.* throughout the world.
■ *adj.* see GLOBAL 1

worm /wərm/ • *n.* **1** any of various types of creeping or burrowing invertebrate animals with long, slender bodies and no limbs. **2** long, slender larva of an insect. **3** [in *pl.*] intestinal or other internal parasites. **4** insignificant or contemptible person. **5** spiral part of a screw. • *v.* **1** *intr. & tr.* [often *refl.*] move with a crawling motion. **2** *intr.* (*tr. refl.*) insinuate oneself into a person's favor, confidence, etc. **3** *tr.* [foll. by *out*] obtain by cunning persistence. **4** *tr.* rid of intestinal worms. □ **worm gear** arrangement of a toothed wheel worked by a revolving spiral. □□ **worm′er** *n.* **worm′i•ness** *n.* **worm′like** *adj.* **worm′y** *adj.*

■ *n.* **4** see WRETCH 2. • *v.* **1** see SLITHER *v.* **2** (*worm oneself*) see INSINUATE 2. **3** (*worm out*) see EXTRACT *v.* 2.

worm•wood /wórmwood/ *n.* **1** woody plant with a bitter aromatic taste. **2** bitter mortification or a source of this.

worn /wawrn/ *past part.* of WEAR. • *adj.* **1** damaged by use or wear. **2** looking tired and exhausted. **3** (in full **well-worn**) (of a joke, etc.) stale; often heard.

■ *adj.* **1** shabby, threadbare, tattered, dilapidated. **2** worn out, fatigued, spent.

wor•ri•some /wóreesəm, wúr-/ *adj.* causing

or apt to cause worry or distress. □□ **wor′ri•some•ly** *adv.*
■ see TROUBLESOME.

wor•ry /wóree, wúr-/ • *v.* (**-ries, -ried**) **1** *intr.* give way to anxiety. **2** *tr.* harass; be a trouble or anxiety to. **3** *tr.* (of a dog, etc.) shake or pull about with the teeth. **4** (as **worried** *adj.*) **a** uneasy; troubled in the mind. **b** suggesting worry (*worried look*). • *n.* (*pl.* **-ries**) **1** thing that causes anxiety. **2** disturbed state of mind; anxiety. □□ **wor′ried•ly** *adv.* **wor′ri•er** *n.* **wor′ry•ing•ly** *adv.*

■ *v.* **1** be anxious, be fearful, be apprehensive, be concerned. **2** annoy, irk, pester, nettle, irritate. **4** (**worried**) fearful, apprehensive, anxious. • *n.* **1** concern, care; problem, burden, trouble. **2** anguish, uneasiness, unease, nervousness.

wor•ry•wart /wóreewawrt, wúr-/ *n. colloq.* person who habitually worries unduly.

worse /wərs/ • *adj.* (compar. of BAD). **1** more bad. **2** [*predic.*] in or into worse health or a worse condition. • *adv.* (compar. of BADLY) more badly or more ill. • *n.* **1** worse thing or things. **2** worse condition (*change for the worse*). □ **none the worse** [often foll. by *for*] not adversely affected (by). **worse off** in a worse (esp. financial) position.

wors•en /wórsən/ *v.* make or become worse.
■ exacerbate, aggravate; weaken, deteriorate, degenerate.

wor•ship /wórship/ • *n.* **1 a** homage or reverence paid to a deity. **b** acts, rites, or ceremonies of worship. **2** adoration or devotion (*worship of wealth*). • *v.* (**wor•shiped, wor•ship•ing; wor•shipped, wor•ship•ping**) **1** *tr.* adore as divine; honor with religious rites. **2** *tr.* idolize. **3** *intr.* attend public worship. □□ **wor′ship•er** *n.* (or **wor′ship•per**).

■ *n.* veneration, glorification. • *v.* **1, 2** venerate, revere, reverence, extol, honor, hallow.

worst /wərst/ • *adj.* (superl. of BAD) most bad. • *adv.* (superl. of BADLY) most badly. • *n.* worst part, event, circumstance, or possibility. • *v. tr.* get the better of; defeat. □ **at worst** (or **the worst**) in the worst possible case. **if worst comes to worst** if the worst happens.

wor•sted /woostid, wór-/ *n.* **1** fine smooth yarn spun from combed long, stapled wool. **2** fabric made from this.

wort /wərt, wawrt/ *n.* infusion of malt which after fermentation becomes beer.

worth /wərth/ • *predic.adj.* **1** of a value equivalent to. **2** such as to justify or repay; deserving. **3** possessing or having property amounting to. • *n.* **1** what a person or thing is worth; the (usu. specified) merit of. **2** equivalent of money in a commodity. □ **for what it is worth** without a guarantee of its truth or value.

■ *n.* **1** quality, merit, advantage, benefit, good.

worth•less /wórthlis/ *adj.* without value or merit. □□ **worth′less•ly** *adv.* **worth′less•ness** *n.*

■ unimportant, insignificant; pointless; silly, inane.

worth•while /wórth–hwíl, wíl/ *adj.* worth the time or effort spent; of value or importance. □□ **worth′while•ness** *n.*

■ profitable, justifiable, productive, gainful, rewarding; useful, valuable, invaluable, important.

wor•thy /wórthee/ • *adj.* (**wor•thi•er, wor•thi•est**) **1** estimable; deserving respect. **2** entitled to. **3** deserving. • *n.* (*pl.* **–thies**) worthy person. □□ **wor′thi•ly** *adv.* **wor′thi•ness** *n.*

◙ *adj.* **1** worthwhile, meritorious, praise-worthy, good. **3** meriting, qualified, fit. • *n.* dignitary, personage, notable.

-worthy /wərthee/ *comb. form* forming adjectives meaning: **1** deserving of. **2** suitable for.

would /wood, when unstressed wəd/ *v.aux.* (*3rd sing.* **would**) *past* of WILL[1], used esp.: **1 a** in reported speech (*he said he would be home by evening*). **b** to express the conditional mood (*they would have been killed if they had gone*). **2** to express habitual action (*would wait every evening*). **3** to express a question or polite request (*would you come in, please?*). **4** to express consent (*they would not help*). □ **would-be** *often derog.* desiring or aspiring to be.

■ □ **would-be** professed; see also SELF-STYLED.

would•n't /wood′nt/ *contr.* would not.

wound[1] /woond/ • *n.* **1** injury done to living tissue by a cut or blow, etc. **2** injury to a person's reputation or a pain inflicted on a person's feelings. • *v.tr.* inflict a wound on. □□ **wound′ing•ly** *adv.* **wound′less** *adj.*

■ *n.* **1** damage, hurt, trauma; puncture, cut, gash. **2** slight, damage, insult. • *v.* harm, injure, hurt, traumatize; slight, distress, damage, mortify, insult.

wound[2] *past* and *past part.* of WIND[2].

wove *past* of WEAVE[1].

wo•ven *past part.* of WEAVE[1].

wow /wow/ • *int.* expressing astonishment or admiration. • *n. sl.* sensational success. • *v.tr. sl.* impress or excite greatly.

w.p.m. *abbr.* words per minute.

wrack /rak/ *n.* = RACK[2].

wraith /rayth/ *n.* ghost. □□ **wraith′like** *adj.*

■ see GHOST *n.* 1. □□ **wraithlike** see GHOSTLY.

wran•gle /ránggəl/ • *n.* noisy argument, altercation, or dispute. See synonym study at QUARREL. • *v.* **1** *intr.* engage in a wrangle. **2** *tr.* herd (cattle).

■ *n.* see ARGUMENT 1. • *v.* **1** see ARGUE 1.

wran•gler /rángglər/ *n.* cowboy.

wrap /rap/ • *v.tr.* (**wrapped, wrap•ping**) **1** envelop in folded or soft encircling material. **2** arrange or draw (a pliant covering) around. • *n.* **1** shawl, scarf, etc. **2** material used for wrapping. □ **under wraps** in secrecy. **wrapped up in** engrossed or absorbed in. **wrap up** finish off.

■ *v.* **1** swathe, swaddle, bind, cover, surround. **2** twine, wind, entwine, coil. • *n.*

1 stole, poncho, serape. **2** packaging, covering. □ **under wraps** see SECRET *adj.* 1. **wrapped up in** immersed in, submerged in, involved in, devoted to. **wrap up** complete, conclude, finish, end, bring to a close, terminate, finalize, wind up, settle, tidy up.

wrap•a•round /rápərownd/ • *adj.* **1** (esp. of clothing) designed to wrap around. **2** curving or extending around at the edges. • *n.* anything that wraps around.

wrap•per /rápər/ *n.* **1** that which wraps; cover. **2** loose enveloping robe or gown.

■ **1** envelope, package, packing, wrapping, covering. **2** housecoat, dressing gown, bathrobe, kimono, negligee, peignoir.

wrap•ping /ráping/ *n.* [esp. in *pl.*] material used to wrap. □ **wrapping paper** strong or decorative paper for wrapping packages.

wrasse /ras/ *n.* any of several species of bright-colored marine fish with thick lips and strong teeth.

wrath /rath, roth, rawth/ *n. literary* extreme anger. □□ **wrath′ful** *adj.* **wrath′ful•ly** *adv.* **wrath′ful•ness** *n.*

■ see ANGER *n.*

wreak /reek/ *v.tr.* **1** express (vengeance or one's anger, etc.). **2** cause (damage, etc.). □□ **wreak′er** *n.*

■ **1** inflict, exercise, exert, carry out, unleash, vent.

wreath /reeth/ *n.* (*pl.* **wreaths** /reethz, reeths/) **1** flowers or leaves fastened in a ring. **2** curl or ring of smoke or cloud.

■ **1** see GARLAND *n.* 1.

wreathe /reeth/ *v.* **1** *tr.* encircle as, with, or like a wreath. **2** *intr.* (of smoke, etc.) move in the shape of wreaths. **3** *tr.* form into a wreath.

■ **1** see CIRCLE *v.* 2, TWINE *v.*

wreck /rek/ • *n.* **1** destruction or disablement, esp. of a ship or automobile. **2** ship or automobile, etc., that has suffered a wreck. **3** greatly damaged thing. **4** *colloq.* dilapidated car. • *v.* **1** *tr.* cause the wreck of. **2** *tr.* completely ruin (hopes, chances, etc.). **3** *intr.* suffer a wreck. **4** *tr.* (as **wrecked** *adj.*) involved in a shipwreck.

■ *n.* **1** loss, sinking, devastation, foundering, grounding; demolition, razing; crash. **2** hulk, shipwreck, ruins. **3** mess, disaster, ruin(s); wrack. **4** jalopy. • *v.* **1** sink, scuttle, run aground, founder, capsize; destroy, ruin. **2** destroy, shatter, dash, spoil.

wreck•age /rékij/ *n.* **1** wrecked material. **2** remnants of a wreck. **3** action of wrecking.

■ **1, 2** debris, fragments, pieces, remains, flotsam, rubble, ruin(s), wrack. **3** see WRECK *n.* 1.

wreck•er /rékər/ *n.* **1** person or thing that wrecks or destroys. **2** esp. *hist.* person on the shore who tries to bring about a shipwreck in order to plunder or profit by the wreckage. **3** person who removes wrecks or breaks them up for spares and scrap. **4** vehicle used to remove disabled cars, etc.

wren /ren/ *n.* small, usu. brown, songbird having an erect tail.

wrench /rench/ • *n.* **1** violent twist or oblique pull or tearing off. **2** tool for gripping and turning nuts, etc. **3** painful uprooting or

parting. • *v. tr.* **1 a** twist or pull violently around or sideways. **b** injure (a limb, etc.) by undue straining; sprain. **2** pull off with a wrench. **3** distort (facts) to suit a theory, etc.
■ *n.* **1** jerk, tug, rip. **2** monkey wrench. • *v.* **1 a** jerk, force, tear. **b** strain, rack. **3** twist, pervert, slant, warp.

wrest /rest/ *v. tr.* **1** wrench away from a person's grasp. **2** obtain by effort or with difficulty.
■ *v.* **1** see WRENCH *v.* 1, 3, SNATCH *v.* 1. **2** see EXTRACT *v.* 2.

wres•tle /résəl/ • *n.* **1** contest in which two opponents grapple and try to throw each other to the ground, esp. as an athletic sport. **2** hard struggle. • *v.* **1** *intr.* take part in a wrestle. **2** *tr.* fight (a person) in a wrestle. **3** *intr.* struggle; contend. □□ **wres′tler** *n.* **wres′tling** *n.*
■ *n.* **1** see STRUGGLE *n.* 2. **2** fight, battle, tussle, effort; see also LABOR *n.* 1. • *v.* **1**, **3** battle, fight, tussle, grapple.

wretch /rech/ *n.* **1** unfortunate or pitiable person. **2** reprehensible or contemptible person.
■ **1** miserable creature, down-and-out. **2** scoundrel, blackguard, worm, villain, cur, rogue.

wretch•ed /réchid/ *adj.* (**wretch•ed•er, wretch•ed•est**) **1** unhappy or miserable. **2** of bad quality or no merit; contemptible. **3** unsatisfactory; displeasing. □□ **wretch′ed•ly** *adv.* **wretch′ed•ness** *n.*
■ **1** sad, woebegone, woeful, dismal, downhearted, heartbroken, brokenhearted, dejected. **2** worthless, inferior, shabby; vile, shameful, despicable. **3** miserable, atrocious, deplorable; see also BAD *adj.* 1, REPULSIVE.

wrig•gle /rígəl/ • *v.* **1** *intr.* twist or turn with short, writhing movements. **2** *intr.* make wriggling motions. **3** *tr. & intr.* move or go in this way. **4** *intr.* practice evasion. • *n.* act of wriggling. □□ **wrig′gler** *n.* **wrig′gly** *adj.* (**wrig•gli•er, wrig•gli•est**).
■ *v.* **1**–**3** squirm, snake, worm, slither; wobble, shake, tremble. • *n.* writhing, squirming, slithering, twisting.

wright /rīt/ *n.* [usu. in *comb.*] maker or builder (*playwright, wheelwright*).

wring /ring/ • *v. tr.* (*past* and *past part.* **wrung** /rung/) **1 a** squeeze tightly. **b** squeeze and twist, esp. to remove liquid. **2** distress or torture. **3** extract by squeezing. **4** obtain by pressure or importunity; extort. • *n.* act of wringing; squeeze.
■ *n.* **4** see EXTORT.

wring•er /ríngər/ *n.* **1** device for wringing water from washed clothes, etc. **2** difficult ordeal (*that exam put me through the wringer*).

wrin•kle /ríngkəl/ • *n.* **1** slight crease in the skin such as is produced by age. **2** similar mark in another flexible surface. • *v.* **1** *tr.* make wrinkles in. **2** *intr.* form wrinkles; become marked with wrinkles. □□ **wrin′kly** *adj.* (**wrin•kli•er, wrin•kli•est**).
■ *n.* **1** crow's-foot, fold, line, furrow. **2** crease, fold, crinkle, corrugation, pucker. • *v.* **1** crease, fold, line, crinkle. **2** crease, pucker, rumple, crumple.

wrist /rist/ *n.* **1** joint connecting the hand with the forearm. **2** part of a garment covering the wrist.

wrist•watch /rístwoch/ *n.* small watch worn on the wrist.

writ /rit/ *n.* legal document commanding or forbidding action.
■ warrant.

write /rīt/ *v.* (*past* **wrote** /rōt/; *past part.* **written** /rít′n/) **1** *intr.* mark paper or some other surface by means of a pen, pencil, etc., with symbols, letters, or words. **2** *tr.* form or mark (such symbols, etc.). **3** *tr.* fill or complete (a form, check, etc.). **4** *tr.* put (data) into a computer store. **5** *tr.* compose. **6** *intr.* [foll. by *to*] write and send a letter (to a recipient). □ **write-in** *n.* candidate whose name is written on a ballot by a voter. **write off 1** cancel the record of (a bad debt, etc.); acknowledge the loss of. **2** dismiss as insignificant. **write-off** *n.* thing written off. **write out** write in full or in finished form. **write up** write a full account of. **write-up** *n. colloq.* written or published account; review.
■ **2** inscribe, pen, pencil. **3** pen, dash off; inscribe, make out, draw up. **4** input, load. **5** create, make up, compile. **6** (*write to*) correspond with, communicate with. □ **write off 1** delete, forgive, annul. **write-up** see REPORT *n.* 2.

writ•er /rítər/ *n.* person who writes, esp. as a profession; author.
■ wordsmith, hack, journalist, reporter, correspondent, ghost writer.

writhe /rīth/ • *v.* **1** *intr.* twist or roll oneself about in or as if in acute pain. **2** *intr.* suffer severe mental discomfort or embarrassment. **3** *tr.* twist (one's body, etc.) about. • *n.* act of writhing.
■ *v.* **1**, **3** wriggle, worm, squirm, wiggle, flounder, fidget, shift. **2** see SQUIRM *v.* 2, SWEAT *v.* 2.

writ•ing /ríting/ *n.* **1** group or sequence of letters or symbols. **2** = HANDWRITING. **3** [usu. in *pl.*] author's works.
■ **1** notation, characters, hieroglyphs, runes. **2** composition(s), publication(s); prose, poetry, nonfiction, fiction; book, article, piece, critique, review, editorial.

writ•ten *past part.* of WRITE.

wrong /rawng, rong/ • *adj.* **1** mistaken; not true; in error. **2** unsuitable; less or least desirable. **3** contrary to law or morality. **4** amiss; out of order. • *adv.* in a wrong manner or direction; with an incorrect result. • *n.* **1** what is morally wrong. **2** injustice. • *v. tr.* **1** treat unjustly; do wrong to. **2** mistakenly attribute bad motives to; discredit. □ **in the wrong** responsible for a quarrel, mistake, or offense. **wrong side out** inside out. □□ **wrong′ly** *adv.*
■ *adj.* **1** erroneous, incorrect, inaccurate. **2** incorrect, improper, inappropriate; ill-considered, wrongheaded, imprudent. **3** improper, unjust, unfair, unethical, immoral, iniquitous. **4** not working, faulty, abnormal, awry, defective. • *adv.* awry, imperfectly, incorrectly. • *n.* **1** see SIN¹ *n.* 1. **2** see GRIEV-

ANCE. • *v.* **1** abuse, mistreat, injure, misuse. **2** malign, vilify, slander, libel. □ **in the wrong** see *at fault* (FAULT). **wrong side out** see *inside out.* □□ **wrongly** see ILL *adv.* 1.

wrong•do•er /ráwngdōōər, róng–/ *n.* person who behaves immorally or illegally. □□ **wrong′do•ing** *n.*

■ see *transgressor* (TRANSGRESS). □□ **wrongdoing** see *transgression* (TRANSGRESS).

wrong•ful /ráwngfool, róng–/ *adj.* **1** characterized by unfairness or injustice. **2** contrary to law. □□ **wrong′ful•ly** *adv.* **wrong′ful•ness** *n.*

■ **1** see GRIEVOUS¹ 2, 3. **2** see ILLEGAL 2. □□ **wrongfully** see ILL *adv.* 1. **wrongfulness** see SIN *n.* 1.

wrong•head•ed /ráwnghédid, róng–/ *adj.* perverse and obstinate. □□ **wrong′head•ed•ly** *adv.* **wrong′head•ed•ness** *n.*

■ see PERVERSE 2,3.

wrote *past* of WRITE.

wrought /rawt/ *archaic past* and *past part.* of

WORK. *adj.* (of metals) beaten out or shaped by hammering. □ **wrought iron** tough malleable form of iron.

wrung *past* and *past part.* of WRING.

wry /rī/ *adj.* (**wry•er, wry•est; wri•er, wri•est**) **1** distorted. **2** contorted in disgust, disappointment, or mockery. **3** (of humor) dry and mocking. □□ **wry′ly** *adv.* **wry′ness** *n.*

■ **1** contorted, twisted, lopsided, crooked. **2** distorted, twisted. **3** droll, witty, sardonic.

wt. *abbr.* weight.

wuss /woos/ *n. colloq.* person seen as a coward or weakling. □□ **wuss′y** *adj.*

WV *abbr.* West Virginia (in official postal use).

W.Va. *abbr.* West Virginia.

WW *abbr.* World War (I, II).

WWW *abbr.* World Wide Web.

WY *abbr.* Wyoming (in official postal use).

Wyo. *abbr.* Wyoming.

WYSIWYG /wízeewig/ *adj.* (also **wysiwyg**) *Computing* denoting the representation of text onscreen in a form exactly corresponding to its appearance on a printout (acronym of *what you see is what you get*).

X¹ /eks/ *n.* (also **x**) (*pl.* **Xs** or **X's; x's**) twenty-fourth letter of the alphabet.

X² **1** *Rom. num.* ten. **2** extra. **3** extraordinary. **4** cross-shaped symbol esp. used to indicate position (*X marks the spot*) or incorrectness or to symbolize a kiss or a vote, or as the signature of a person who cannot write. **5** (in full **X-rated**) (of a movie) classified as suitable for adults only.

x *symb.* **1** excess. **2** *Math.* unknown quantity or variable. **3** *Math.* horizontal-axis coordinate.

-x /z/ *suffix* forming the plural of many nouns ending in –*u* taken from French (*beaux, tableaux*).

X chro•mo•some /éks krṓməsōm/ *n.* sex chromosome of which the number in female cells is twice that in male cells.

Xe *symb. Chem.* xenon.

xe•non /zénon, zeé–/ *n. Chem.* heavy, colorless, odorless inert gaseous element. ¶Symb.: **Xe.**

xe•no•pho•bi•a /zénəfṓbeeə, zeénə–/ *n.* deep dislike of foreigners. □□ **xe•no•phobe** /zénəfōb, zeénə–/ *n.* **xe•no•pho′bic** *adj.*

■ see *intolerance* (INTOLERANT). □□ **xeno-phobic** see INHOSPITABLE 1.

xe•rog•ra•phy /zeerógrəfee/ *n.* dry copying

process in which black or colored powder adheres to electrically charged parts of a surface. □□ **xe•ro•graph•ic** /–rəgráfik/ *adj.* **xe•ro•graph′i•cal•ly** *adv.*

Xe•rox /zeéroks/ • *n. propr.* **1** machine for copying by xerography. **2** copy thus made. • *v.tr.* (**xerox**) reproduce by this process.

■ *n.* **2** see DUPLICATE *n.* • *v.* see DUPLICATE *v.*

xi /zī, sī, ksee/ *n.* fourteenth letter of the Greek alphabet (Ξ, ξ).

-xion /kshən/ *suffix* forming nouns (see -ION from Latin participial stems ending in -*x* (*fluxion*).

X•mas /krísməs, éksməs/ *n.* colloq. = CHRISTMAS.

X ray /éksray/ (also **x-ray**) • *n.* **1** [in *pl.*] electromagnetic radiation of short wavelength, able to pass through opaque bodies. **2** photograph made by X rays. • *v.tr.* photograph, examine, or treat with X rays. • *adj.* by, like, or of X rays.

xy•lem /zílem/ *n. Bot.* woody tissue.

xy•lo•phone /zíləfōn/ *n.* musical instrument of graduated wooden or metal bars struck with small wooden hammers. □□ **xy•lo•phon•ic** /–fónik/ *adj.* **xy•lo•phon•ist** /–fōn–/ *n.*

Yy

Y[1] /wī/ *n.* (also **y**) (*pl.* **Ys** or **Y's**; **y's**) twenty-fifth letter of the alphabet.

Y[2] *abbr.* (also **Y.**) **1** yen. **2** = YMCA, YWCA.

Y[3] *symb. Chem.* yttrium.

y *symb. Math.* **1** vertical-axis coordinate. **2** unknown quantity or variable.

y. *abbr.* **1** yard(s). **2** year(s).

-y[1] /ee/ *suffix* forming adjectives: **1** from nouns and adjectives, meaning: full of; having the quality of (*messy*). **2** from verbs, meaning 'inclined to,' 'apt to' (*runny*).

-y[2] /ee/ *suffix* (also **-ey, -ie**) forming diminutives, pet names, etc. (*nightie, Mickey*).

-y[3] /ee/ *suffix* forming nouns denoting: state, condition, or quality (*modesty*).

yacht /yot/ • *n.* **1** sailing vessel for racing, for cruising, etc., esp. for pleasure. • *v.intr.* race or cruise in a yacht. □□ **yacht'ing** *n.*
  ■ *n.* **1** SEE BOAT *n.* 2. • *v.* SEE CRUISE *v.*

yachts•man /yótsmən/ *n.* (*pl.* **-men**; *fem.* **yachts•wom•an,** *pl.* **-wom•en**) person who sails yachts.

ya•hoo /yaáhōō/ *n.* coarse, bestial person.

Yah•weh /yaáway, -we/ *n.* (also **Yah•veh** /-vay, -ve/) = JEHOVAH.

yak /yak/ *n.* long-haired, humped Tibetan ox.

yam /yam/ *n.* **1 a** tropical or subtropical climbing plant. **b** edible starchy tuber of this. **2** sweet potato.

yam•mer /yámər/ *colloq.* or *dial.* • *n.* **1** lament, wail, or grumble. **2** voluble talk. • *v.intr.* **1** utter a yammer. **2** talk volubly. □□ **yam'mer•er** *n.*
  ■ *v.* **1** SEE MOAN *v.* 2. **2** SEE YAP *v.* 2.

yang /yang/ *n.* (in Chinese philosophy) active male principle of the universe (cf. YIN).

Yank /yangk/ *n. colloq.* American.

yank /yangk/ *colloq.* • *v.tr.* pull with a jerk.
  ■ □ bulldozen hard pull.
  ■ *v. & n.* jerk, jolt, tug, wrench, snatch, hitch.

Yan•kee /yángkee/ • *n. colloq.* **1** inhabitant of the U.S. **2** inhabitant of New England or one of the other northern states. **3** *hist.* Union soldier in the American Civil War. • *adj.* characteristic of the Yankees.

yap /yap/ • *v.intr.* **(yapped, yap•ping) 1** bark shrilly. **2** *colloq.* talk noisily, foolishly, or complainingly. • *n.* **1** sound of yapping. **2** *sl.* mouth. □□ **yap'per** *n.*
  ■ *v.* **1** yelp. **2** gabble, babble, blather, chatter, prattle. • *n.* **1** bark, yelp. **2** *sl.* trap.

yard[1] /yaard/ *n.* **1** unit of linear measure equal to 3 feet (0.9144 meter). **2** this length of material. **3** square or cubic yard, esp. (in building) of sand, etc. **4** spar slung across a mast for a sail to hang from.

yard[2] /yaard/ *n.* **1** piece of ground, esp. attached to a building or used for a particular purpose. **2** lawn and garden area of a house.

yard•age /yaárdij/ *n.* number of yards of material, etc.
  ■ see MEASUREMENT 2.

yard•arm /yaárdaarm/ *n.* outer extremity of a ship's yard.

yard•stick /yaárdstik/ *n.* **1** standard used for comparison. **2** measuring rod a yard long, usu. divided into inches, etc.
  ■ **1** measure, benchmark, criterion, norm.

yar•mul•ke /yaárməlkə, yaáməl–/ *n.* (also **yar'mul•ka**) skullcap worn by Jewish men.

yarn /yaarn/ • *n.* **1** spun thread, esp. for knitting, weaving, etc. **2** *colloq.* long or rambling story or discourse. • *v.intr. colloq.* tell yarns.
  ■ *n.* **1** fiber, strand. **2** tale, account, anecdote; tall tale, fable, fabrication, fiction.

yaw /yaw/ • *v.intr.* (of a ship or aircraft, etc.) fail to hold a straight course; go unsteadily. • *n.* yawing of a ship, etc., from its course.
  ■ *v.* see TOSS *v.* 2.

yawl /yawl/ *n.* two-masted sailing vessel with aftermast set astern of the rudder.

yawn /yawn/ • *v.* **1** *intr.* (as a reflex) open the mouth wide and inhale, esp. when sleepy or bored. **2** *intr.* gape; be wide open. **3** *tr.* utter or say with a yawn. • *n.* act of yawning. □□ **yawn'er** *n.* **yawn'ing•ly** *adv.*

yaws /yawz/ *n.pl.* [usu. treated as *sing.*] contagious tropical skin disease with large red swellings.

Yb *symb. Chem.* ytterbium.

Y chro•mo•some /wī-króməsōm/ *n.* sex chromosome occurring only in male cells (cf. X CHROMOSOME).

yd. *abbr.* (*pl.* **yds.**) yard (measure).

ye[1] /yee/ *pron. archaic pl.* of THOU[1].

ye[2] /yee/ *adj. pseudo-archaic* = THE (*ye olde tea shoppe*).

yea /yay/ *formal* • *adv.* **1** yes. **2** indeed. • *n.* "yes" vote or voter.

yeah /yea/ *adv. colloq.* yes.

year /yeer/ *n.* **1** (also **astronomical year, equinoctial year, natural year, solar year, tropical year**) time occupied by the earth in one revolution around the sun, 365 days, 5 hours, 48 minutes, and 46 seconds in length. **2** (also **calendar year, civil year**) period of 365 days (**common year**) or 366 days see leap year from Jan. 1 to Dec. 31. **3 a** period of the same length as this starting at any point (*four years ago*). **b** such a period in terms of a particular activity, etc., occupying its duration (*school year*). **4** [in *pl.*] age or time of life. **5** [usu. in *pl.*] *colloq.* very long time.
  ■ **5** (*years*) see AGE *n.* 2a.

year•book /yeerbŏŏk/ *n.* annual publication dealing with events or aspects of the (usu. preceding) year.
  ■ annual, annal, almanac.

year•ling /yeerling/ • *n.* **1** animal between one and two years old. **2** racehorse in the calendar year after the year of foaling. • *adj.* year old (*yearling heifer*).

year•ly /yeerlee/ • *adj.* **1** done, produced, or occurring once a year. **2** of or lasting a year. • *adv.* once a year; from year to year.

■ *adj.* **1** annual, once-a-year. • *adv.* annually, per year, per annum; perennially, year in (and) year out.

yearn /yərn/ *v.intr.* **1** have a strong emotional longing. **2** be filled with compassion or tenderness. □□ **yearn'er** *n.* **yearn'ing** *n. & adj.* **yearn'ing•ly** *adv.*

■ **1** long, pine, ache, hanker, itch, hunger, thirst, crave. □□ **yearning** *n.* see LONGING *n.* • *adj.* see DESIROUS 2.

yeast /yeest/ *n.* grayish-yellow fungous substance obtained esp. from fermenting malt liquors and used as a fermenting agent, to raise bread, etc. □□ **yeast'less** *adj.* **yeast' like** *adj.*

yeast•y /yeéstee/ *adj.* (**yeast•i•er, yeast•i• est**) **1** frothy or tasting like yeast. **2** in a ferment. **3** light and superficial. □□ **yeast'i•ly** *adv.* **yeast'i•ness** *n.*

yell /yel/ • *n.* **1** loud sharp cry of pain, anger, etc. **2** shout. • *v.* utter with or make a yell.

■ *n.* scream, cry, bellow, bawl, howl, screech, roar.

yel•low /yélō/ • *adj.* **1** of the color between green and orange in the spectrum, as of lemons, egg yolks, or gold. **2** having a yellow skin or complexion. **3** *colloq.* cowardly. **4** (of newspapers, etc.) unscrupulously sensational. • *n.* yellow color or pigment. • *v.* make or become yellow. □ **yellow fever** tropical virus disease with fever and jaundice. **yellow jacket** any of various wasps or hornets with yellow and black bands. **Yellow Pages** (or **yellow pages**) telephone directory of classified business listings, on yellow paper. □□ **yel'low•ish** *adj.* **yel'low•ly** *adv.* **yel'low•ness** *n.* **yel'low•y** *adj.*

■ *adj.* **3** see COWARDLY *adj.* □□ **yellowish** see GOLDEN 2.

yelp /yelp/ • *n.* sharp, shrill cry of or as of a dog in pain or excitement. • *v.intr.* utter a yelp. □□ **yelp'er** *n.*

■ *n.* see HOWL *n.* 1. • *v.* see HOWL *v.* 1.

yen[1] /yen/ *n.* (*pl.* same) chief monetary unit of Japan.

yen[2] /yen/ *colloq. n.* longing or yearning.

■ see LONGING *n.*

yeo•man /yṓmən/ *n.* (*pl.* **–men**) **1** esp. *hist.* man holding and cultivating a small landed estate. **2** in the US Navy, petty officer performing clerical duties on board ship. □□ **yeo'man** (or **yeo'man's**) **service** efficient or useful help in need.

yeo•man•ry /yṓmənree/ *n.* (*pl.* **–ries**) body or class of yeomen.

yep /yep/ *adv. & n.* (also **yup** /yup/) *colloq.* = YES.

yes /yes/ • *adv.* **1** indicating affirmation, consent, assent, etc. **2** (in answer to a summons or address) an acknowledgment of one's presence. • *n.* utterance of the word *yes.* □ **yes?** **1** indeed?. **2** what do you want?. **yes-man** (*pl.* **–men**) *colloq.* weakly acquiescent person.

■ *adv.* **1** *archaic* yea, *archaic or dial.* aye. **2** here, present. □ **yes-man** toady, sycophant, timeserver, hanger-on.

yes•ter•day /yéstərday/ • *adv.* **1** on the day

before today. **2** in the recent past. • *n.* **1** day before today. **2** the recent past.

■ *n.* **2** see PAST *n.* 1.

yes•ter•year /yéstəryeer/ *n. literary* **1** last year. **2** the recent past.

■ **2** see PAST *n.* 1.

yet /yet/ • *adv.* **1** as late as; until; now or then. **2** [with *neg.* or *interrog.*] so soon as; by; now or then. **3** again; in addition. **4** still (*I will do it yet*). **5** even (*a yet more difficult task*). **6** nevertheless. • *conj.* but nevertheless.

■ *adv.* **1** still, even now, up to this time. **2** as yet, up to now, so far. **4** in the future, later, eventually. **6** still, notwithstanding, anyhow. • *conj.* still, but.

yew /yōō/ *n.* **1** dark-leaved evergreen coniferous tree with red berrylike cones. **2** its wood.

yield /yeeld/ • *v.* **1** *tr.* produce or return as a fruit, profit, or result. **2** *tr.* give up; surrender. **3** *intr.* submit; defer to. **4** *intr.* [foll. by *to*] give right of way to (other traffic, etc). See synonym study at RELINQUISH. • *n.* amount yielded or produced. □□ **yield'er** *n.*

■ *v.* **1** bear, supply, bring forth; earn, return, net. **2** give, abandon, relinquish, concede. **3** surrender, give up (the fight *or* struggle), give in, knuckle under. • *n.* crop, harvest, production; return, output, revenue, gain.

yield•ing /yeélding/ *adj.* **1** compliant; submissive. **2** (of a substance) able to bend; not stiff nor rigid. □□ **yield'ing•ly** *adv.*

■ **1** accommodating, docile, amenable, tractable. **2** pliant, flexible, pliable.

yin /yin/ *n.* (in Chinese philosophy) passive female principle of the universe (cf. YANG).

yip /yip/ • *v.intr.* (**yipped, yip•ping**) = YELP *v.* • *n.* = YELP *n.*

yip•pee /yippeé/ *int.* expressing delight or excitement.

YMCA *abbr.* Young Men's Christian Association.

YMHA *abbr.* Young Men's Hebrew Association.

yo•del /yṓd'l/ • *v.* sing with melodious inarticulate sounds and frequent changes between falsetto and the normal voice. • *n.* yodeling cry. □□ **yo'del•er** *n.*

yo•ga /yṓgə/ *n.* Hindu system of philosophic meditation and exercise. □□ **yo•gic** /yṓgik/ *adj.*

yo•gi /yṓgee/ *n.* teacher of yoga. □□ **yo'gism** *n.*

yo•gurt /yṓgərt/ *n.* (also **yo'ghurt**) semisolid sourish food prepared from milk fermented by added bacteria.

yoke /yōk/ • *n.* **1** wooden crosspiece fastened over the necks of two oxen, etc., and attached to the plow or wagon to be drawn. **2** (*pl.* same or **yokes**) pair (of oxen, etc.). **3** object like a yoke in form or function, e.g., wooden shoulder-piece for carrying a pair of pails, etc. **4** dominion or servitude. **5** bond of union, esp. that of marriage. • *v.* **1** *tr.* put a yoke on. **2** *tr.* couple or unite (a pair). **3** *tr.* [foll. by *to*] link (one thing) to (another).

■ *n.* **2** see TEAM *n.* 2. **4** see SLAVERY 1. **5** tie, link. • *v.* **2** see COUPLE *v.* 1.

yo•kel /yṓkəl/ *n.* country bumpkin.

yolk /yōk/ *n.* yellow internal part of an egg. ▫▫ **yolked** *adj.* [also in *comb.*]. **yolk′less** *adj.* **yolk′y** *adj.*

Yom Kip•pur /yawm kípər, keepŏŏr, yōm, yom/ *n.* most solemn holy day of the Jewish year; Day of Atonement.

yon /yon/ *literary & dial.* • *adj. & adv.* yonder. • *pron.* yonder person or thing.

yon•der /yóndər/ • *adv.* over there; at some distance in that direction. • *adj.* situated yonder.

yoo-hoo /yŏŏhŏŏ/ *int.* used to attract a person's attention.

yore /yawr/ *n.* literary long ago. ▫ **of yore** formerly.

you /yŏŏ/ *pron.* (*obj.* **you**; *poss.* **your, yours**) **1** person or persons addressed. **2** [as *int.* with a noun] in an exclamatory statement (*you fools!*). **3** (in general statements) one; a person; people.

you'd /yŏŏd/ *contr.* **1** you had. **2** you would.

you'll /yŏŏl, yŏŏl/ *contr.* you will; you shall.

young /yung/ • *adj.* (**young•er** /yúnggər/; **young•est** /yúnggist/) **1** not far advanced in life, development, or existence; not yet old. **2** immature; inexperienced. **3** of or characteristic of youth. • *n.* offspring. ▫▫ **young′ish** *adj.* **young′ling** *n.*

■ *adj.* **1** youthful, teenage(d), adolescent, prepubescent, minor; new, developing, undeveloped. **2** callow, green, uninitiated. **3** childish, boyish, girlish, puerile, sophomoric. • *n.* babies, little ones, progeny, litter, brood; children.

young•ster /yúngstər/ *n.* child or young person.

■ see YOUTH 3.

your /yŏŏr, yawr/ *poss.pron.* of or belonging to you.

you're /yŏŏr, yawr/ *contr.* you are.

yours /yŏŏrz, yawrz/ *poss.pron.* **1** the one or ones belonging to you. **2** [introducing a formula ending a letter (*yours truly*).

your•self /yŏŏrsélf, yawr–/ *pron.* (*pl.* **your•selves** /–sélvz/) **1 a** *emphat. form* of YOU. **b** *refl. form* of YOU. **2** in your normal state of body or mind (*are quite yourself again*).

youth /yŏŏth/ *n.* (*pl.* **youths** /yŏŏthz/) **1** being young; period between childhood and adult age. **2** vigor, enthusiasm, inexperience, or other characteristic of this period. **3** young person. **4** [*pl.*] young people collectively.

■ **1** prepubescence, pubescence, adolescence, teens, salad days; minority, immaturity. **3** child, youngster, teenager, teen, minor, juvenile, adolescent. **4** children, youngsters, adolescents.

youth•ful /yŏŏthfŏŏl/ *adj.* young or having the characteristics of youth. ▫▫ **youth′ful•ly** *adv.* **youth′ful•ness** *n.*

■ see YOUNG *adj.* 1

SYNONYM STUDY: youthful

ADOLESCENT, CALLOW, IMMATURE, JUVENILE, PUERILE. Everyone wants to look **youthful**, an adjective that means possessing, or appearing to possess, the qualities associated with youth (*a youthful enthusiasm for the job*). But no one wants to be called **immature**, which usually pertains to behavior and atti-

977   **yolk ~ yummy**

tudes rather than to physical appearance and means childish or emotionally undeveloped (*still immature despite the fact that he was almost thirty*). **Juvenile** suggests immaturity of mind or body and is applied especially to things that are designed for boys and girls in their early teens (*juvenile books*), while **adolescent** applies to the period between puberty and maturity and suggests the physical awkwardness and emotional instability associated with the teenage years (*an adolescent response to criticism*). Young men in particular are often described as **callow**, which means immature in terms of experience (*a callow youth who had never lived away from his family*). Of all these words, **puerile** is probably the most insulting, because it is so often used to describe adults who display the *immature* behavior of a child (*a puerile piece of writing; a puerile revolt against his aging parents*).

you've /yŏŏv, yŏŏv/ *contr.* you have.

yowl /yowl/ • *n.* loud, wailing cry. • *v.intr.* utter a yowl.

■ *n.* see HOWL *n.* 1. • *v.* see HOWL *v.* 1.

yo-yo /yóyō/ • *n.* (*pl.* **yo-yos**) **1** *propr.* toy consisting of a pair of disks that can be made to fall and rise on a string. **2** thing that repeatedly falls and rises. • *v.intr.* (**yo-yoes, yo-yoed, yo-yoing**) **1** play with a yo-yo. **2** move up and down; fluctuate.

■ *v.* see FLUCTUATE.

yr. *abbr.* (*pl.* **yrs.**) **1** year(s). **2** yours. **3** younger.

yt•ter•bi•um /itárbeəm/ *n.* Chem. silvery metallic element of the lanthanide series. ¶Symb.: **Yb**.

yt•tri•um /ítreeəm/ *n. Chem.* grayish metallic element resembling the lanthanides. ¶Symb.: **Y**.

Y2K • *adj. colloq.* abbreviation for the year 2000, esp. in reference to expected computer problems at the start of the year.

yu•an /yŏŏ-ààn, yŏŏ-/ *n.* (*pl.* same) chief monetary unit of China.

yuc•ca /yúkə/ *n.* N. American white-flowered liliaceous plant with swordlike leaves.

yuck /yuk/ *int. sl.* expression of strong distaste or disgust.

yuck•y /yúkee/ *adj.* (**–i•er, –i•est**) *sl.* **1** messy, repellent. **2** sickly; sentimental.

■ **1** disgusting, repugnant, unappetizing, revolting. **2** see SENTIMENTAL.

Yu•go•slav /yŏŏgəslaav/ (also **Jugoslav**) *hist.* • *n.* **1** native or national of the former republic of Yugoslavia. **2** person of Yugoslav descent. • *adj.* of or relating to Yugoslavia or its people. ▫▫ **Yu•go•sla′vi•an** *adj. & n.*

yule /yŏŏl/ *n.* (in full **yule′tide**) archaic Christmas festival.

Yu•ma /yŏŏmə/ *n.* **1 a** N. American people native to Arizona. **b** member of this people. **2** language of this people.

yum•my /yúmee/ *adj.* (**yum•mi•er, yum•mi•est**) *colloq.* tasty; delicious.

■ mouthwatering, luscious, appetizing, savory.

yup var. of YEP.

yup•pie /yúpee/ (also **yup′py**) (pl. **–pies**) colloq. usu. derog. • n. young, ambitious professional person working in a city. • adj. characteristic of a yuppie or yuppies. (from young urban professional.).

YWCA abbr. Young Women's Christian Association.

YWHA abbr. Young Women's Hebrew Association.

Z /zee/ n. (also **z**) (pl. **Zs** or **Z's**; **z's**) twenty-sixth letter of the alphabet.

z symb. **1** Math. unknown quantity or variable. **2** Math. coordinate of the third-dimensional axis. **3** Chem. (usu. **Z**) atomic number.

zag /zag/ • n. sharp change of direction in a zigzag course. • v.intr. (**zagged, zag•ging**) move in one of the two directions in a zigzag course.

za•ny /záynee/ • adj. (**za•ni•er, za•ni•est**) comically idiotic; crazily ridiculous. • n. buffoon or jester. □□ **za′ni•ly** adv. **za′ni•ness** n.
  ■ adj. clownish, wild, frolicsome, playful, slapstick. • n. clown, comic, fool, joker, wag, comedian.

zap /zap/ sl. • v. (**zapped, zap•ping**) **1** tr. **a** kill or destroy. **b** hit forcibly. **c** send an electric current, radiation, etc., through (someone or something). **2** intr. move quickly. **3** tr. Computing erase or change (an item in a program). **4** tr. heat or cook (food) by microwave. **5** tr. change (television channels) by remote control. • n. strong emotional effect. • intr. expressing the sound or impact of a bullet, ray gun, etc., or any sudden event.
  ■ v. **1 a** slaughter, annihilate, murder, assassinate, liquidate. **b** see HIT[1] v. 1a. **2** see RUSH v. 1.

zap•per /zápər/ n. colloq. hand-held remote-control device for changing television channels, adjusting volume, etc.

Zar•a•thus•tri•an var. of ZOROASTRIAN.

zeal /zeel/ n. **1** earnestness or fervor. **2** hearty and persistent endeavor. □□ **zeal•ous** /zéləs/ adj. **zeal′ous•ly** adv. **zeal′ous•ness** n.. See synonym study at EAGER
  ■ **1** see ENTHUSIASM 1. **2** diligence, persistence, sedulousness, tirelessness, indefatigability, perseverance. □□ **zealous** see enthusiastic (ENTHUSIASM).

zeal•ot /zélət/ n. extreme partisan; fanatic. □□ **zeal′ot•ry** n.
  ■ **1** extremist, radical, bigot, crank, militant. □□ **zealotry** fanaticism, extremism, radicalism; fervor, obsession.

SYNONYM STUDY: zealot

BIGOT, ENTHUSIAST, EXTREMIST, FANATIC. An **enthusiast** displays an intense and eager interest in something (a sky-diving enthusiast). A **fanatic** is not only intense and eager but possibly irrational in his or her enthusiasm; fanatic suggests extreme devotion and a willingness to go to any length to maintain or carry out one's beliefs (a fly-fishing fanatic who hired a helicopter to reach his favorite stream). A **zealot** exhibits not only extreme devotion but vehement activity in support of a cause or goal (a feminist zealot who spent most of her time campaigning for women's rights). An **extremist** is a supporter of extreme doctrines or practices, particularly in a political context (a Muslim extremist who hated the Americans). But it is the **bigot** who causes the most trouble, exhibiting obstinate and often blind devotion to his or her beliefs and opinions. In contrast to fanatic and zealot, the term bigot implies intolerance and contempt for those who do not agree (a bigot who could not accept his daughter's decision to marry outside her religion).

---

ze•bra /zeebrə/ n. (pl. same or **zebras**) black and white striped African quadruped related to the ass and horse. □□ **ze•brine** /-brīn/ adj.

ze•bu /zéebōō/ n. humped ox of India, E. Asia, and Africa.

zed /zed/ n. Brit. the letter Z.

Zen /zen/ n. form of Mahayana Buddhism emphasizing the value of meditation and intuition. □□ **Zen′ist** n. (also **Zennist**).

ze•nith /zéenith/ n. **1** part of the sky directly above an observer opp. NADIR. **2** any peak or highest point.
  ■ **2** summit, acme, apex, apogee, top.

zeph•yr /zéfər/ n. literary mild gentle breeze.
  ■ see BREEZE n. 1.

zep•pe•lin /zépəlin/ n. hist. German large dirigible airship of the early 20th c., orig. for military use.

ze•ro /zéerō/ • n. (pl. **–ros**) **1 a** the figure 0; naught. **b** no quantity or number; nil. **2** point on the scale from which a positive or negative quantity is reckoned. **3** no; not any. **4** lowest or earliest point. • v.tr. (**–roes, –roed**) **1** adjust (an instrument, etc.) to zero point. **2** set the sights of (a gun) for firing. □ **zero in on 1** take aim at. **2** focus one's attention on. **zero-sum** (of a political situation, etc.) system in which gains and losses are equal.
  ■ n. **1** null, nothing, cipher, goose egg. □ **zero in on 2** pinpoint, fix on.

zest /zest/ n. **1** piquancy; stimulating flavor or quality. **2 a** keen enjoyment or interest. **b** relish. **c** gusto. **3** a scraping of orange or lemon peel as flavoring. □□ **zest′ful** adj. **zest′ful•ly** adv. **zest′i•ness** n. **zest′y** adj. (**zest•i•er, zest•i•est**).
  ■ **1** spice, tang, pungency, edge, bite. **2** eagerness, zestfulness, exuberance. **3** rind. □□ **zestful** see energetic (ENERGY), spicy (SPICE).

ze•ta /záytə, zeé–/ *n.* sixth letter of the Greek alphabet (Ζ, ζ).

zig•gu•rat /zígərat/ *n.* rectangular stepped pyramidal tower in ancient Mesopotamia, surmounted by a temple.

zig•zag /zígzag/ • *n.* **1** line or course having abrupt alternate right and left turns. **2** [often in *pl.*] each of these turns. • *adj.* having the form of a zigzag. • *adv.* with a zigzag course. • *v.intr.* (**zig•zagged, zig•zag•ging**) move in a zigzag course. □□ **zig•zag′ged•ly** *adv.*

■ *n.* see TWIST² n. 4. • *adj.* see TORTUOUS 1. • *v.* see WIND v. 1.

zilch /zilch/ *n. sl.* nothing.

zil•lion /zílyən/ *n. colloq.* indefinite large number. □□ **zil′lionth** *adj. & n.*

zinc /zingk/ *n. Chem.* white metallic element used as a component of brass, in galvanizing, in electric batteries, and in printing plates. ¶Symb.: **Zn**. □□ **zinced** *or* **zincked** *adj.*

zing /zing/ *colloq.* • *n.* vigor; energy. • *v.intr.* move swiftly or with a shrill sound. □□ **zing′er** *n.* **zing′y** *adj.* (**zing•i•er, zing•i•est**).

■ *n.* see VIGOR 1.

zin•ni•a /zíneeə/ *n.* composite plant with showy rayed flowers of various colors.

Zi•on /zíən/ *n.* (also **Sion** /síən/) **1** hill of Jerusalem on which the city of David was built. **2** the Jewish people or religion. **3** (in Christian thought) the kingdom of God in heaven.

Zi•on•ism /zíənizəm/ *n.* movement (orig.) for the re-establishment and (now) the development of a Jewish nation in what is now Israel. □□ **Zi′on•ist** *n.*

zip /zip/ • *n.* **1** light fast sound, as of a bullet passing through air. **2** energy; vigor. • *v.* (**zipped, zip•ping**) **1** *tr. & intr.* [often foll. by *up*] fasten with a zipper. **2** *intr.* move with zip or at high speed.

■ *n.* **2** see ENERGY 1. • *v.* **2** see STREAK v. 2.

zip code /zip/ *n.* (also **ZIP code**) assigned numeric postal code to speed the sorting and delivering mail.

zip•per /zípər/ • *n.* fastening device of two flexible strips with interlocking projections closed or opened by pulling a slide along them. • *v.tr.* [often foll. by *up*] fasten with a zipper. □□ **zip′pered** *adj.*

zip•py /zípee/ *adj.* (**zip•pi•er, zip•pi•est**) *colloq.* **1** bright; fresh; lively. **2** fast; speedy. □□ **zip′pi•ly** *adv.* **zip′pi•ness** *n.*

■ **1** see *energetic* (ENERGY). **2** quick.

zir•con /zərkon/ *n.* zirconium silicate of which some translucent varieties are cut into gems.

zir•co•ni•um /zərkóneeəm/ *n. Chem.* gray metallic element. ¶Symb.: **Zr**.

zit /zit/ *n. sl.* pimple.

zith•er /zíthər/ *n.* musical instrument consisting of a flat wooden sound box with numerous strings stretched across it, placed horizontally and played with the fingers and a plectrum. □□ **zith′er•ist** *n.*

Zn *symb. Chem.* zinc.

zo•di•ac /zṓdeeak/ *n.* **1** imaginary belt of the heavens including all apparent positions of the sun, moon, and planets divided into twelve equal parts (**signs of the zodiac**) named for constellations: Aries, Taurus,

Gemini, Cancer, Leo, Virgo, Libra, Scorpio, Sagittarius, Capricorn(us), Aquarius, Pisces. **2** diagram of these signs. □□ **zo•di•a•cal** /–díəkəl/ *adj.*

zom•bie /zómbee/ *n.* **1** *colloq.* dull or apathetic person. **2** corpse said to be revived by witchcraft.

zone /zōn/ • *n.* **1** area having particular features, properties, purpose, or use (*danger zone*). **2** well-defined region of more or less beltlike form. **3** (in full **time zone**) range of longitudes where a common standard time is used. **4** *Geog.* latitudinal division of the earth see FRIGID, TEMPERATE, TORRID. • *v.tr.* **1** encircle as or with a zone. **2** assign as or to a particular area. □□ **zon′al** *adj.* **zon′ing** *n.* (in sense 2 of *v.*).

■ *n.* **1, 2** quarter, district, sector, section, sphere, belt.

zonked /zongkt/ *adj. sl.* [often foll. by *out*] exhausted; intoxicated.

zoo /zoo/ *n.* park with a collection of animals for exhibition or study.

■ menagerie, (safari *or* wildlife) park.

zool. *abbr.* **1** zoological. **2** zoology.

zo•ol•o•gy /zō-óləjee/ *n.* **1** the scientific study of animals. □□ **zo•o•log•i•cal** /–lój–/ *adj.* **zo•ol′o•gist** *n.*

zoom /zoom/ • *v.* **1** *intr.* move quickly, esp. with a buzzing sound. **2 a** *intr.* cause an airplane to climb at high speed and a steep angle. **b** *tr.* cause (an airplane) to do this. **3 a** *intr.* (of a camera) close up rapidly from a long shot to a close-up. **b** *tr.* cause (a lens or camera) to do this. • *n.* **1** airplane's steep climb. **2** zooming camera shot. □ **zoom lens** lens allowing a camera to zoom by varying the focal length.

zo•o•phyte /zṓəfit/ *n.* plantlike animal, esp. a coral, sea anemone, or sponge. □□ **zo•o•phyt•ic** /–fitik/ *adj.*

Zo•ro•as•tri•an /záwrō-ástreeən/ (also **Zar•a•thus•tri•an** /zárəthoóstreeən/) • *adj.* of or relating to Zoroaster (or Zarathustra) of Persia, or the dualistic religious system taught by him in the 6th *c.* BC. • *n.* follower of Zoroaster. □□ **Zo•ro•as′tri•an•ism** *n.*

Zr *symb. Chem.* zirconium.

zuc•chi•ni /zookeénee/ *n.* (*pl.* same or **zuc•chi•nis**) green variety of smooth-skinned summer squash.

Zu•lu /zoóloo/ • *n.* **1** member of a black South African people orig. inhabiting Zululand and Natal. **2** language of this people. • *adj.* of or relating to this people or language.

Zu•ni /zoónee/ *n.* (also **Zu•ñi** /zoónyee/) **1 a** N. American people native to New Mexico. **b** member of this people. **2** language of this people.

zwie•back /zwíbak, –baak, zweé–, swí–, sweé–/ *n.* a kind of rusk or sweet cake toasted in slices.

zy•gote /zígōt, zíg–/ *n. Biol.* cell formed by the union of two gametes. □□ **zy•got′ic** /–gótik/ *adj.* **zy•got′i•cal•ly** *adv.*

zy•mur•gy /zímərjee/ *n.* the branch of applied chemistry dealing with the use of fermentation in brewing, etc.

Special Reference Sections

Standard Weights and Measures
with Metric Equivalents

Linear Measure

1 inch	= 2.54 centimeters
1 foot = 12 inches	= 0.3048 meter
1 yard = 3 feet	= 0.9144 meter
= 36 inches	
1 (statute) mile = 1,760 yards	= 1.609 kilometers
= 5,280 feet	

Square Measure

1 sq. inch	= 6.45 sq. centimeters
1 sq. foot = 144 sq. inches	= 9.29 sq. decimeters
1 sq. yard = 9 sq. feet	= 0.836 sq. meter
1 acre = 4,840 sq. yards	= 0.405 hectare
1 sq. mile = 640 acres	= 259 hectares

Cubic Measure

1 cu. inch	= 16.4 cu. centimeters
1 cu. foot = 1,728 cu. inches	= 0.0283 cu. meter
1 cu. yard = 27 cu. feet	= 0.765 cu. meter

Capacity Measure

DRY MEASURE

1 pint = 33.60 cu. inches	= 0.550 liter
1 quart = 2 pints	= 1.101 liters
1 peck = 8 quarts	= 8.81 liters
1 bushel = 4 pecks	= 35.3 liters

LIQUID MEASURE

1 fluid ounce	= 29.573 milliliters
1 gill = 4 fluid ounces	= 118.294 milliliters
1 pint = 16 fluid ounces	= 0.473 liter
	= 28.88 cu. inches
1 quart = 2 pints	= 0.946 liter
1 gallon = 4 quarts	= 3.785 liters

Avoirdupois Weight

1 grain	= 0.065 gram
1 dram	= 1.772 grams
1 ounce = 16 drams	= 28.35 grams
1 pound = 16 ounces	= 0.4536 kilograms
= 7,000 grains	= (0.45359237 exactly)
1 stone (British) = 14 pounds	= 6.35 kilograms
1 ton	= 2,000 pounds
1 hundredweight (US)	= 100 pounds
20 hundredweight (US)	= 2,000 pounds

Metric Weights and Measures
with Standard Equivalents

Linear Measure
1 millimeter (mm)	= 0.039 inch
1 centimeter (cm) = 10 millimeters	= 0.394 inch
1 decimeter (dm) = 10 centimeters	= 3.94 inches
1 meter (m) = 10 decimeters	= 1.094 yards
1 decameter = 10 meters	= 10.94 yards
1 hectometer = 100 meters	= 109.4 yards
1 kilometer (km) = 1,000 meters	= 0.6214 mile

Square Measure
1 sq. centimeter	= 0.155 sq. inch
1 sq. meter = 10,000 sq. centimeters	= 1.196 sq. yards
1 are = 100 sq. meters	= 119.6 sq. yards
1 hectare = 100 ares	= 2.471 acres
1 sq. kilometer = 100 hectares	= 0.386 sq. mile

Cubic Measure
1 cu. centimeter	= 0.061 cu. inch
1 cu. meter = 1,000,000 cu. centimeters	= 1.308 cu. yards

Capacity Measure
1 milliliter (ml)	= 0.034 fluid ounce
1 centiliter (cl) = 10 milliliters	= 0.34 fluid ounce
1 deciliter (dl) = 10 centiliters	= 3.38 fluid ounces
1 liter (l) = 10 deciliters	= 1.06 quarts
1 decaliter = 10 liters	= 2.64 gallons
1 hectoliter = 100 liters	= 2.75 bushels

Weight
1 milligram (mg)	= 0.015 grain
1 centigram = 10 milligrams	= 0.154 grain
1 decigram (dg) = 10 centigrams	= 1.543 grains
1 gram (g) = 10 decigrams	= 15.43 grains
1 decagram = 10 grams	= 5.64 drams
1 hectogram = 100 grams	= 3.527 ounces
1 kilogram (kg) = 1,000 grams	= 2.205 pounds
1 ton (metric ton) = 1,000 kilograms	= 0.984 (long) ton

Chemical Elements

Element	Symbol	Atomic Number	Element	Symbol	Atomic Number
actinium	Ac	89	lithium	Li	3
aluminum	Al	13	lutetium	Lu	71
americium	Am	95	magnesium	Mg	12
antimony	Sb	51	manganese	Mn	25
argon	Ar	18	meitnerium*	Mt	109
arsenic	As	33	mendelevium	Md	101
astatine	At	85	mercury	Hg	80
barium	Ba	56	molybdenum	Mo	42
berkelium	Bk	97	neodymium	Nd	60
beryllium	Be	4	neon	Ne	10
bismuth	Bi	83	neptunium	Np	93
bohrium*	Ns	107	nickel	Ni	28
boron	B	5	niobium	Nb	41
bromine	Br	35	nitrogen	N	7
cadmium	Cd	48	nobelium	No	102
calcium	Ca	20	osmium	Os	76
californium	Cf	98	oxygen	O	8
carbon	C	6	palladium	Pd	46
cerium	Ce	58	phosphorus	P	15
cesium	Cs	55	platinum	Pt	78
chlorine	Cl	17	plutonium	Pu	94
chromium	Cr	24	polonium	Po	84
cobalt	Co	27	potassium	K	19
copper	Cu	29	praseodymium	Pr	59
curium	Cm	96	promethium	Pm	61
dubnium*	Db	105	protactinium	Pa	91
dysprosium	Dy	66	radium	Ra	88
einsteinium	Es	99	radon	Rn	86
erbium	Er	68	rhenium	Re	75
europium	Eu	63	rhodium	Rh	45
fermium	Fm	100	rubidium	Rb	37
fluorine	F	9	ruthenium	Ru	44
francium	Fr	87	rutherfordium*	Rf	104
gadolinium	Gd	64	samarium	Sm	62
gallium	Ga	31	scandium	Sc	21
germanium	Ge	32	seaborgium*	Sg	106
gold	Au	79	selenium	Se	34
hafnium	Hf	72	silicon	Si	14
hassium*	Hs	108	silver	Ag	47
helium	He	2	sodium	Na	11
holmium	Ho	67	strontium	Sr	38
hydrogen	H	1	sulfur	S	16
indium	In	49	tantalum	Ta	73
iodine	I	53	technetium	Tc	43
iridium	Ir	77	tellurium	Te	52
iron	Fe	26	terbium	Tb	65
krypton	Kr	36	thallium	Tl	81
lanthanum	La	57	thorium	Th	90
lawrencium	Lr	103	thulium	Tm	69
lead	Pb	82	tin	Sn	50

Element	Symbol	Atomic Number	Element	Symbol	Atomic Number
titanium	Ti	22	ytterbium	Yb	70
tungsten (wolfram)	W	74	yttrium	Y	39
uranium	U	92	zinc	Zn	30
vanadium	V	23	zirconium	Zr	40
xenon	Xe	54			

* Names formed systematically based on atomic numbers are preferred by the International Union of Pure and Applied Chemistry (IUPAC) for numbers from 104 onward. These names are formed from the numerical roots *nil* (= 0), *un* (= 1), *bi* (= 2), etc. (e.g., *unnilquadium* = 104, *unnilpentium* = 105, *unnilhexium* = 106, *unnilseptium* = 107, *unniloctium* = 108, *unnilnovium* = 109, etc.).

Signs and Symbols

General

&	and	×	by, as in *an 8' × 12' room*
&c.	et cetera (and so forth)	w/	with
©	copyright(ed)	w/o	without
®	registered; of a trademark or service mark	§	section (of a text)
†	death; died	"	ditto marks; repeat the word or sign located in the line above
℞	take (Latin *recipe*); used on prescriptions	☠	poison
#	1. number (before a figure) 2. pound(s) (after a figure) 3. space (in printing) 4. pound sign (on a telephone number pad)	☢	radioactive; radiation

Science and Mathematics

♂	male	≅	congruent to (in geometry)
♀	female	:	is to; the ratio of
+	1. plus 2. positive (number or charge)	!	factorial of
		Σ	sum
−	1. minus 2. negative (number or charge)	π	pi; the ratio of the circumference of a circle to its diameter (3.14159265+)
		∞	infinity
±	plus or minus	∴	therefore
× or • or ⋆	multiplied by	∵	since
÷	divided by	∥	parallel to
=	equal to	⊥	perpendicular to
≠	not equal to	√	radical sign; root
>	greater than	°	degree
<	less than	'	1. minute(s) of arc 2. foot, feet
≥	greater than or equal to	"	1. second(s) of arc 2. inch(es)
≤	less than or equal to		
≡	identical with	∅	empty set
≈	approximately equal to		

Commerce and Finance

$	dollar(s)	@	at the rate of
¢	cent(s)	%	percent
£	pound(s) sterling (UK)	€	Euro
p	(new) pence (UK)		
¥	yen (Japan)		

Signs of the Zodiac

Spring
♈ Aries, the Ram
♉ Taurus, the Bull
♊ Gemini, the Twins

Summer
♋ Cancer, the Crab
♌ Leo, the Lion
♍ Virgo, the Virgin

Autumn
♎ Libra, the Balance
♏ Scorpio, the Scorpion
♐ Sagittarius, the Archer

Winter
♑ Capricorn, the Goat
♒ Aquarius, the Water Bearer
♓ Pisces, the Fishes

Diacritical Marks
(to distinguish sounds or values of letters)

´ acute (as in the French word *née*)
` grave (as in the French word *père*)
~ tilde (as in the Spanish word *piñata*)
^ circumflex (as in the word *rôle*)
¯ macron (as used in pronunciation: *āge*, *īce*)
˘ breve (as used in pronunciation: *tăp*, *rĭp*)
¨ dieresis (as in the word *naïve*)
¸ cedilla (as in the word *façade*)

States of the United States of America

State	Traditional & Postal Abbreviations	Capital
Alabama	Ala.; AL	Montgomery
Alaska	Alas.; AK	Juneau
Arizona	Ariz.; AZ	Phoenix
Arkansas	Ark.; AR	Little Rock
California	Calif.; CA	Sacramento
Colorado	Col.; CO	Denver
Connecticut	Conn.; CT	Hartford
Delaware	Del.; DE	Dover
Florida	Fla.; FL	Tallahassee
Georgia	Ga.; GA	Atlanta
Hawaii	Haw.; HI	Honolulu
Idaho	Id.; ID	Boise
Illinois	Ill.; IL	Springfield
Indiana	Ind.; IN	Indianapolis
Iowa	Ia.; IA	Des Moines
Kansas	Kan.; KS	Topeka
Kentucky	Ky.; KY	Frankfort
Louisiana	La.; LA	Baton Rouge
Maine	Me.; ME	Augusta
Maryland	Md.; MD	Annapolis
Massachusetts	Mass.; MA	Boston
Michigan	Mich.; MI	Lansing
Minnesota	Minn.; MN	St. Paul
Mississippi	Miss.; MS	Jackson
Missouri	Mo.; MO	Jefferson City
Montana	Mont.; MT	Helena
Nebraska	Nebr.; NE	Lincoln
Nevada	Nev.; NV	Carson City
New Hampshire	N.H.; NH	Concord
New Jersey	N.J.; NJ	Trenton
New Mexico	N. Mex.; NM	Santa Fe
New York	N.Y.; NY	Albany
North Carolina	N.C.; NC	Raleigh
North Dakota	N. Dak.; ND	Bismarck
Ohio	O.; OH	Columbus
Oklahoma	Okla.; OK	Oklahoma City
Oregon	Ore.; OR	Salem
Pennsylvania	Pa.; PA	Harrisburg
Rhode Island	R.I.; RI	Providence
South Carolina	S.C.; SC	Columbia
South Dakota	S. Dak.; SD	Pierre
Tennessee	Tenn.; TN	Nashville
Texas	Tex.; TX	Austin
Utah	Ut.; UT	Salt Lake City
Vermont	Vt.; VT	Montpelier
Virginia	Va.; VA	Richmond
Washington	Wash.; WA	Olympia
West Virginia	W. Va.; WV	Charleston
Wisconsin	Wis.; WI	Madison
Wyoming	Wyo.; WY	Cheyenne

Presidents of the United States of America

Name and life dates	Party (term in office)
1. George Washington 1732–99	Federalist (1789–97)
2. John Adams 1735–1826	Federalist (1797–1801)
3. Thomas Jefferson 1743–1826	Democratic-Republican (1801–09)
4. James Madison 1751–1836	Democratic-Republican (1809–17)
5. James Monroe 1758–1831	Democratic-Republican (1817–25)
6. John Quincy Adams 1767–1848	Democratic-Republican (1825–29)
7 Andrew Jackson 1767–1845	Democrat (1829–37)
8. Martin Van Buren 1782–1862	Democrat (1837–41)
9. William H. Harrison 1773–1841	Whig (1841)
10. John Tyler 1790–1862	Whig, then Democrat (1841–45)
11. James K. Polk 1795–1849	Democrat (1845–49)
12. Zachary Taylor 1784–1850	Whig (1849–50)
13. Millard Fillmore 1800–74	Whig (1850–53)
14. Franklin Pierce 1804–69	Democrat (1853–57)
15. James Buchanan 1791–1868	Democrat (1857–61)
16. Abraham Lincoln 1809–65	Republican (1861–65)
17. Andrew Johnson 1808–75	Democrat (1865–69)
18. Ulysses S. Grant 1822–85	Republican (1869–77)
19. Rutherford B. Hayes 1822–93	Republican (1877–81)
20. James A. Garfield 1831–81	Republican (1881)
21. Chester A. Arthur 1830–86	Republican (1881–85)
22. Grover Cleveland 1837–1908	Democrat (1885–89)
23. Benjamin Harrison 1833–1901	Republican (1889–93)
24. Grover Cleveland (see above)	Democrat (1893–97)
25. William McKinley 1843–1901	Republican (1897–1901)
26. Theodore Roosevelt 1858–1919	Republican (1901–09)
27. William H. Taft 1857–1930	Republican (1909–13)
28. Woodrow Wilson 1856–1924	Democrat (1913–21)
29. Warren G. Harding 1865–1923	Republican (1921–23)
30. Calvin Coolidge 1872–1933	Republican (1923–29)
31. Herbert Hoover 1874–1964	Republican (1929–33)
32. Franklin D. Roosevelt 1882–1945	Democrat (1933–45)
33. Harry S Truman 1884–1972	Democrat (1945–53)
34. Dwight D. Eisenhower 1890–1969	Republican (1953–61)
35. John F. Kennedy 1917–63	Democrat (1961–63)
36. Lyndon B. Johnson 1908–73	Democrat (1963–69)
37. Richard M. Nixon 1913–94	Republican (1969–74)
38. Gerald R. Ford 1913–	Republican (1974–77)
39. James Earl Carter 1924–	Democrat (1977–81)
40. Ronald W. Reagan 1911–	Republican (1981–89)
41. George H.W. Bush 1924–	Republican (1989–93)
42. William J. Clinton 1946–	Democrat (1993–2001)
43. George W. Bush 1946–	Republican (2001–)

Countries of the World

Country	Capital	Continent/Area	Nationality
Afghanistan	Kabul	Asia	Afghan
Albania	Tirana (Tiranë)	Europe	Albanian
Algeria	Algiers	Africa	Algerian
Andorra	Andorra la Vella	Europe	Andorran
Angola	Luanda	Africa	Angolan
Antigua and Barbuda	Saint John's	North America	Antiguan, Barbudan
Argentina	Buenos Aires	South America	Argentinian
Armenia	Yerevan	Europe	Armenian
Australia	Canberra	Australia	Australian
Austria	Vienna	Europe	Austrian
Azerbaijan	Baku	Europe	Azerbaijani
Bahamas, The	Nassau	North America	Bahamian
Bahrain	Manama	Asia	Bahraini
Bangladesh	Dhaka	Asia	Bangladeshi
Barbados	Bridgetown	North America	Barbadian
Belarus	Minsk	Europe	Belorussian, Belarrussian, *or* Belarusian
Belgium	Brussels	Europe	Belgian
Belize	Belmopan	North America	Belizean
Benin	Porto Novo	Africa	Beninese
Bhutan	Thimphu	Asia	Bhutanese
Bolivia	La Paz; Sucre	South America	Bolivian
Bosnia and Herzegovina	Sarajevo	Europe	Bosnian, Herzegovinian
Botswana	Gaborone	Africa	Motswana, *sing.*, Batswana, *pl.*
Brazil	Brasilia	South America	Brazilian
Brunei	Bandar Seri Begawan	Asia	Bruneian
Bulgaria	Sofia	Europe	Bulgarian
Burkina Faso	Ouagadougou	Africa	Burkinese
Burma (*see* Myanmar)	Rangoon	Asia	Burmese
Burundi	Bujumbura	Africa	Burundian, *n.*; Burundi, *adj.*
Cambodia	Phnom Penh	Asia	Cambodian
Cameroon	Yaoundé	Africa	Cameroonian
Canada	Ottawa	North America	Canadian
Cape Verde	Praia	Africa	Cape Verdean
Central African Republic	Bangui	Africa	Central African
Chad	N'Djamena	Africa	Chadian
Chile	Santiago	South America	Chilean
China	Beijing	Asia	Chinese
Colombia	Bogotá	South America	Colombian
Comoros	Moroni	Africa	Comoran
Congo, Democratic Republic of the (*formerly* Zaire)	Kinshasa	Africa	Congolese

Country	Capital	Continent/Area	Nationality
Congo, Republic of the	Brazzaville	Africa	Congolese, *n.*; Congolese *or* Congo, *adj.*
Costa Rica	San José	North America	Costa Rican
Country	Capital	Continent/Area	Nationality
Côte d'Ivoire	Yamoussoukro	Africa	Ivorian
Croatia	Zagreb	Europe	Croat, *n.*; Croatian, *adj.*
Cuba	Havana	North America	Cuban
Cyprus	Nicosia	Europe	Cypriot
Czech Republic	Prague	Europe	Czech
Denmark	Copenhagen	Europe	Dane, *n.*; Danish, *adj.*
Djibouti	Djibouti	Africa	Djiboutian
Dominica	Roseau	North America	Dominican
Dominican Republic	Santo Domingo	North America	Dominican
East Timor	Dili	Asia	East Timoran
Ecuador	Quito	South America	Ecuadorean
Egypt	Cairo	Africa	Egyptian
El Salvador	San Salvador	North America	Salvadoran
Equatorial Guinea	Malabo	Africa	Equatorial Guinean *or* Equatoguinean
Eritrea	Asmara	Africa	Eritrean
Estonia	Tallinn	Europe	Estonian
Ethiopia	Addis Ababa	Africa	Ethiopian
Fiji	Suva	Oceania	Fijian
Finland	Helsinki	Europe	Finn, *n.*; Finnish, *adj.*
France	Paris	Europe	French
Gabon	Libreville	Africa	Gabonese
Gambia, The	Banjul	Africa	Gambian
Georgia	Tbilisi	Europe	Georgian
Germany	Berlin	Europe	German
Ghana	Accra	Africa	Ghanaian
Greece	Athens	Europe	Greek
Grenada	Saint George's	North America	Grenadian
Guatemala	Guatemala City	North America	Guatemalan
Guinea	Conakry	Africa	Guinean
Guinea-Bissau	Bissau	Africa	Guinea-Bissauan
Guyana	Georgetown	South America	Guyanese
Haiti	Port-au-Prince	North America	Haitian
Holy See	Vatican City	Europe	
Honduras	Tegucigalpa	North America	Honduran
Hungary	Budapest	Europe	Hungarian
Iceland	Reykjavik	Europe	Icelander, *n.*; Icelandic, *adj.*
India	New Delhi	Asia	Indian
Indonesia	Djakarta	Asia	Indonesian
Iran	Tehran	Asia	Iranian
Iraq	Baghdad	Asia	Iraqi
Ireland, Republic of	Dublin	Europe	Irish
Israel	Jerusalem	Asia	Israeli
Italy	Rome	Europe	Italian
Ivory Coast (*See* Côte d'Ivoire)			
Jamaica	Kingston	North America	Jamaican
Japan	Tokyo	Asia	Japanese
Jordan	Amman	Asia	Jordanian

Country	Capital	Continent/Area	Nationality
Kazakhstan	Astana	Asia	Kazakhstani
Kenya	Nairobi	Africa	Kenyan
Kiribati	Bairiki (on Tarawa)	Oceania	I-Kiribati
Country	Capital	Continent/Area	Nationality
Korea, North (see North Korea)			
Korea, South (see South Korea)			
Kuwait	Kuwait City	Asia	Kuwaiti
Kyrgyzstan	Bishkek	Asia	Kyrgyz
Laos	Vientiane	Asia	Lao or Laotian
Latvia	Riga	Europe	Latvian
Lebanon	Beirut	Asia	Lebanese
Lesotho	Maseru	Africa	Mosotho, sing.; Basotho, pl.; Basotho, adj.
Liberia	Monrovia	Africa	Liberian
Libya	Tripoli	Africa	Libyan
Liechtenstein	Vaduz	Europe	Liechtensteiner, n.; Liechtenstein, adj.
Lithuania	Vilnius	Europe	Lithuanian
Luxembourg	Luxembourg	Europe	Luxembourger, n.; Luxembourg, adj.
Macedonia	Skopje	Europe	Macedonian
Madagascar	Antananarivo	Africa	Malagasy
Malawi	Lilongwe	Africa	Malawian
Malaysia	Kuala Lumpur	Asia	Malaysian
Maldives	Male	Asia	Maldivian
Mali	Bamako	Africa	Malian
Malta	Valletta	Europe	Maltese
Marshall Islands	Majuro	Oceania	Marshallese
Mauritania	Nouakchott	Africa	Mauritanian
Mauritius	Port Louis	Africa	Mauritian
Mexico	Mexico City	North America	Mexican
Micronesia	Palikir	Oceania	Micronesian
Moldova	Chişinău	Europe	Moldovan
Monaco	Monaco	Europe	Monacan or Monegasque
Mongolia	Ulaanbaatar	Asia	Mongolian
Montenegro	Podgorica	Europe	Montenegran
Morocco	Rabat	Africa	Moroccan
Mozambique	Maputo	Africa	Mozambican
Myanmar (Burma)	Yangoon	Asia	Burmese
Namibia	Windhoek	Africa	Namibian
Nauru	Yaren District	Oceania	Nauruan
Nepal	Kathmandu	Asia	Nepalese
Netherlands	Amsterdam; The Hague	Europe	Dutchman or Dutchwoman, n.; Dutch, adj.
New Zealand	Wellington	Oceania	New Zealander, n.; New Zealand, adj.
Nicaragua	Managua	North America	Nicaraguan
Niger	Niamey	Africa	Nigerien
Nigeria	Abuja	Africa	Nigerian
North Korea	P'yongyang	Asia	North Korean
Norway	Oslo	Europe	Norwegian
Oman	Muscat	Asia	Omani

Country	Capital	Continent/Area	Nationality
Pakistan	Islamabad	Asia	Pakistani
Palau	Melekeok	Oceania	Palauan
Panama	Panama City	North America	Panamanian
Country	Capital	Continent/Area	Nationality
Papua New Guinea	Port Moresby	Oceania	Papua New Guinean
Paraguay	Asunción	South America	Paraguayan
Peru	Lima	South America	Peruvian
Philippines	Manila	Asia	Filipino, *n.*; Philippine, *adj.*
Poland	Warsaw	Europe	Pole, *n.*; Polish, *adj.*
Portugal	Lisbon	Europe	Portuguese
Qatar	Doha	Asia	Quatari
Romania	Bucharest	Europe	Romanian
Russia	Moscow	Europe & Asia	Russian
Rwanda	Kigali	Africa	Rwandan, Rwandese
Saint Kitts and Nevis	Basseterre	North America	Kittsian; Nevisian
Saint Lucia	Castries	North America	St. Lucian
Saint Vincent and the Grenadines	Kingstown	North America	St. Vincentian or Vincentian
Samoa (*formerly* Western Samoa)	Apia	Oceania	Samoan
San Marino	San Marino	Europe	Sammarinese
São Tomé and Príncipe	São Tomé	Africa	Sao Tomean
Saudi Arabia	Riyadh	Asia	Saudi *or* Saudi Arabian
Scotland	Edinburgh	Europe	Scot, *n.*; Scots *or* Scottish, *adj.*
Senegal	Dakar	Africa	Senegalese
Serbia	Belgrade	Europe	Serb, *n.*; Serbian, *adj.*
Seychelles	Victoria	Indian Ocean	Seychellois, *n.*; Seychelles, *adj.*
Sierra Leone	Freetown	Africa	Sierra Leonean
Singapore	Singapore	Asia	Singaporean, *n.*; Singapore, *adj.*
Slovakia	Bratislava	Europe	Slovak
Slovenia	Ljubljana	Europe	Slovene, *n.*; Slovenian, *adj.*
Solomon Islands	Honiara	Oceania	Solomon Islander
Somalia	Mogadishu	Africa	Somali
South Africa	Pretoria; Cape Town; Bloemfontein	Africa	South African
South Korea	Seoul	Asia	South Korean
Spain	Madrid	Europe	Spanish
Sri Lanka	Colombo	Asia	Sri Lankan
Sudan	Khartoum	Africa	Sudanese
Suriname	Paramaribo	South America	Surinamer, *n.*; Surinamese, *adj.*
Swaziland	Mbabane	Africa	Swazi
Sweden	Stockholm	Europe	Swede, *n.*; Swedish, *adj.*
Switzerland	Bern	Europe	Swiss
Syria	Damascus	Asia	Syrian

Country	Capital	Continent/Area	Nationality
Taiwan	Taipei	Asia	Taiwanese
Tajikistan	Dushanbe	Asia	Tajik
Tanzania	Dar es Salaam	Africa	Tanzanian
Thailand	Bangkok	Asia	Thai
Togo	Lomé	Africa	Togolese
Tonga	Nuku'alofa	Oceania	Tongan
Country	Capital	Continent/Area	Nationality
Trinidad and Tobago	Port-of-Spain	South America	Trinidadian; Tobagonian
Tunisia	Tunis	Africa	Tunisian
Turkey	Ankara	Asia & Europe	Turk, *n.*; Turkish, *adj.*
Turkmenistan	Ashgabat	Asia	Turkmen
Tuvalu	Funafuti	Oceania	Tuvaluan
Uganda	Kampala	Africa	Ugandan
Ukraine	Kiev	Europe	Ukrainian
United Arab Emirates	Abu Dhabi	Africa	Emirian
United Kingdom	London	Europe	Briton, *n.*; British, *collective pl. & adj.*
United States of America	Washington, DC	North America	American
Uruguay	Montevideo	South America	Uruguayan
Uzbekistan	Tashkent	Asia	Uzbek
Vanuatu	Vila	Oceania	Ni-Vanuatu
Venezuela	Caracas	South America	Venezuelan
Vietnam	Hanoi	Asia	Vietnamese
Western Samoa (*see* Samoa)			
Yemen	Sana'a	Asia	Yemeni
Zaire (*see* Congo)			
Zambia	Lusaka	Africa	Zambian
Zimbabwe	Harare	Africa	Zimbabwean

Punctuation Guide

Punctuation is an essential element of good writing because it make author's meaning clear to the reader. Although precise punctuation s may vary somewhat among published sources, there are a number of func mental principles worthy of consideration. Discussed below are the punctu ation marks used in English:

> comma
> semicolon
> colon
> period
> question mark
> exclamation point
> apostrophe
> quotation marks
> parentheses
> dash
> hyphen

Comma

The comma is the most frequently used mark of punctuation in the English language. It signals to the reader a pause, which generally clarifies the author's meaning, and establishes a sensible order to the elements of written language. Among the most typical functions of the comma are the following:

1. It can separate the clauses of a compound sentence when there are two independent clauses joined by a conjunction, especially when the clauses are not very short:

   It never occurred to me to look in the attic, and I'm sure it didn't occur to Rachel either.

   The Nelsons wanted to see the Grand Canyon at sunrise, but they overslept that morning.

2. It can separate the clauses of a compound sentence when there is a series of independent clauses, the last two of which are joined by a conjunction:

   The bus ride to the campsite was very uncomfortable, the cabins were not ready for us when we got there, the cook had forgotten to start dinner, and the rain was torrential.

3. It is used to precede or set off, and therefore indicate, a nonrestrictive dependent clause (a clause that could be omitted without changing the meaning of the main clause):

   I read her autobiography, which was published last July.

   They showed up at midnight, after most of the guests had gone home.

   The coffee, which is freshly brewed, is in the kitchen.

...low an introductory phrase:

...g enjoyed the movie so much, he agreed to see it again.

...rn and raised in Paris, she had never lost her French accent.

In the beginning, they had very little money to invest.

. It can set off words used in direct address:

Listen, people, you have no choice in the matter.

Yes, Mrs. Greene, I will be happy to feed your cat.

6. The comma can separate two or more coordinate adjectives (adjectives that could otherwise be joined with *and*) that modify one noun:

The cruise turned out to be the most entertaining, fun, and relaxing vacation I've ever had.

My Appaloosa was a tall, lean, sleek horse.

Note that cumulative adjectives (those not able to be joined with *and*) are not separated by a comma:

She wore bright yellow rubber boots.

7. Use a comma to separate three or more items in a series or list:

Charlie, Melissa, Stan, and Mark will be this year's soloists in the spring concert.

We need furniture, toys, clothes, books, tools, housewares, and other useful merchandise for the benefit auction.

Note that the comma between the last two items in a series is sometimes omitted in less precise style:

The most popular foods served in the cafeteria are pizza, hamburgers and nachos.

8. Use a comma to separate and set off the elements in an address or other geographical designation:

My new house is at 1657 Nighthawk Circle, South Kingsbury, Michigan.

We arrived in Pamplona, Spain, on Thursday.

9. Use a comma to set off direct quotations (note the placement or absence of commas with other punctuation):

"Kim forgot her gloves," he said, "but we have a pair she can borrow."

There was a long silence before Jack blurted out, "This must be the world's ugliest painting."

"What are you talking about?" she asked in a puzzled manner.

"Happy New Year!" everyone shouted.

10. A comma is used to set off titles after a person's name:

Katherine Bentley, M.D.

Steven Wells, Esq., is the addressee.

Semicolon

The semicolon has two basic functions:

1. It can separate two main clauses, particularly when these clauses are of equal importance:

The crowds gathered outside the museum hours before the doors were opened; this was one exhibit no one wanted to miss.

She always complained when her relatives stayed for the weekend; even so, she usually was a little sad when they left.

2. It can be used as a comma is used to separate such elements as clauses or items in a series or list, particularly when one or more of the elements already includes a comma:

The path took us through the deep, dark woods; across a small meadow; into a cold, wet cave; and up a hillside overlooking the lake.

Listed for sale in the ad were two bicycles; a battery-powered, leaf-mulching lawn mower; and a maple bookcase.

Colon

The colon has five basic functions:

1. It can introduce something, especially a list of items:

In the basket were three pieces of mail: a postcard, a catalog, and a wedding invitation.

Students should have the following items: backpack, loose leaf notebook, pens and pencils, pencil sharpener, and ruler.

2. It can separate two clauses in a sentence when the second clause is being used to explain or illustrate the first clause:

We finally understood why she would never go sailing with us: she had a deep fear of the water.

Most of the dogs in our neighborhood are quite large: two of them are St. Bernards.

3. It can introduce a statement or a quotation:

His parents say the most important rule is this: Always tell the truth.

We repeated the final words of his poem: "And such is the plight of fools like me."

can be used to follow the greeting in a formal or business letter:

Dear Ms. Daniels:

Dear Sir or Madam:

5. In the U.S., use a colon to separate minutes from hours, and seconds from minutes, in showing time of day and measured length of time:

   Please be at the restaurant before 6:45.

   Her best running time so far has been 00:12:35.

Period

The period has two basic functions:

1. It is used to mark the end of a sentence:

   It was reported that there is a shortage of nurses at the hospital. Several of the patients have expressed concern about this problem.

2. It is often used at the end of an abbreviation:

   On Fri., Sept. 12, Dr. Brophy noted that the patient's weight was 168 lbs. and that his height was 6 ft. 2 in. (Note that another period is not added to the end of the sentence when the last word is an abbreviation.)

Question Mark and Exclamation Point

The only sentences that do not end in a period are those that end in either a question mark or an exclamation point.

Question marks are used to mark the end of a sentence that asks a direct question (generally, a question that expects an answer):

Is there any reason for us to bring more than a few dollars?

Who is your science teacher?

Exclamation points are used to mark the end of a sentence that expresses a strong feeling, typically surprise, joy, or anger:

I want you to leave and never come back!

What a beautiful view this is!

Apostrophe

The apostrophe has two basic functions:

1. It is used to show where a letter or letters are missing in a contraction:

   The directions are cont'd [continued] on the next page.

   We've [we have] decided that if she can't [cannot] go, then we aren't [are not] going either.

2. It can be used to show possession:

   a. The possessive of a singular noun or an irregular plural noun is created by adding an apostrophe and an s:

   the pilot's uniform

   Mrs. Mendoza's house

   a tomato's bright red color

   the oxen's yoke

   b. The possessive of a regular plural noun is created by adding just an apostrophe:

   the pilots' uniforms [referring to more than one pilot]

   the Mendozas' house [referring to the Mendoza family]

   the tomatoes' bright red color [referring to more than one tomato]

Quotation Marks

Quotation marks have two basic functions:

1. Quotation marks are used to set off direct quotations (an exact rendering of someone's spoken or written words):

   "I think the new library is wonderful," she remarked to David

   We were somewhat lost, so we asked, "Are we anywhere near the art gallery?"

   In his letter he had written, "The nights here are quiet and starry. It seems like a hundred years since I've been wakened by the noise of city traffic and squabbling neighbors."

   Note that indirect quotes (which often are preceded by that, if, or whether) are not set off by quotation marks:

   He told me that he went to school in Boston.

   We asked if we could still get tickets to the game.

2. Quotation marks can be used to set off words or phrases that have specific technical usage, or to set off meanings of words, or to indicate words that are being used in a special way in a sentence:

   The part of the flower that bears the pollen is the "stamen."

   When I said "plain," I meant "flat land," not "ordinary."

   Oddly enough, in the theater, the statement "break a leg" is meant as an expression of good luck.

   What you call "hoagies," we call "grinders" or "submarine sandwiches."

   He will never be a responsible adult until he outgrows his "Peter Pan" behavior.

Note that sometimes single quotation marks (the 'stamen.'), rather than double quotation marks as above (the "stamen."), may be used to set off words or phrases. What is most important is to be consistent in such usage.

Parentheses

Parentheses are used, in pairs, to enclose information that gives extra detail or explanation to the regular text. Parentheses are used in two basic ways:

1. They can separate a word or words in a sentence from the rest of the sentence:

   On our way to school, we walk past the Turner Farm (the oldest dairy farm in town) and watch the cows being fed.

   The stores were filled with holiday shoppers (even more so than last year). (Note that the period goes outside the parentheses, because the words in the parentheses are only part of the sentence.)

2. They can form a separate complete sentence:

   Please bring a dessert to the dinner party. (It can be something very simple.) I look forward to seeing you there. (Note that the period goes inside the parentheses, because the words in the parentheses are a complete and independent sentence.)

Dash

A dash is used most commonly to replace the usage of parentheses within sentences. If the information being set off is in the middle of the sentence, a pair of dashes is used; if it is at the end of the sentence, just one dash is used:

   On our way to school, we walk past the Turner Farm—the oldest dairy farm in town—and watch the cows being fed.

   The stores were filled with holiday shoppers—even more so than last year.

Hyphen

A hyphen has three basic functions:

1. It can join two or more words to make a compound, especially when so doing makes the meaning more clear to the reader:

   We met to discuss long-range planning.

   There were six four-month-old piglets at the fair.

   That old stove was quite a coal-burner.

2. It can replace the word "to" when a span or range of data is given. This kind of hyphen is sometimes also called a dash:

John Adams was president of the United States 1797–1801.

Today we will look for proper nouns in the L–N section of the dictionary.

The ideal weight for that breed of dog would be 75–85 pounds. .

3. It can indicate a word break at the end of a line. The break must always be between syllables:

   It is important for any writer to know that there are numerous punctuation principles that are considered standard and proper, but there is also flexibility regarding acceptable punctuation. Having learned the basic "rules" of good punctuation, the writer will be able to adopt a specific and consistent style of punctuation that best suits the material he or she is writing.

Proofreading Marks

℘	delete	⁶⁶ ⁹⁹	quotation marks
℘	delete and close up	{ }	parentheses
℘#	delete and leave space	[ ]	square brackets
∧	insert	=	hyphen
#	space	⅟M	em-dash
⊙	period	⅟N	en-dash
⌃	comma	¶	new paragraph
⌃;	semicolon	dictionary	break line or word
⌃ or ⊙	colon	∨	set as superscript
⌄	apostrophe	∧	set as subscript

dictionary	transpose
(tr)	transpose (note in margin)
(3)	spell out
(SP)	spell out (note in margin)
dictionary	capitalize
(cap)	set as capitals (note in margin)
Dictionary	make lower case
(lc)	set in lower case (note in margin)
dictionary	make boldface
(bf)	set in boldface (note in margin)
dictionary	make italic
(ital)	set in italic (note in margin)
dictionary	small caps
(sc)	set in small caps (note in margin)
(lf)	lightface (note in margin)
(rom)	set in roman (note in margin)

International Time Zones

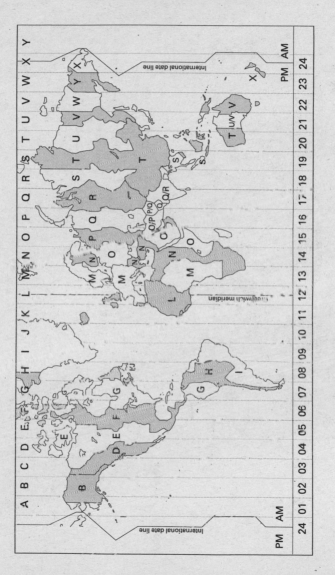

United States Time Zones

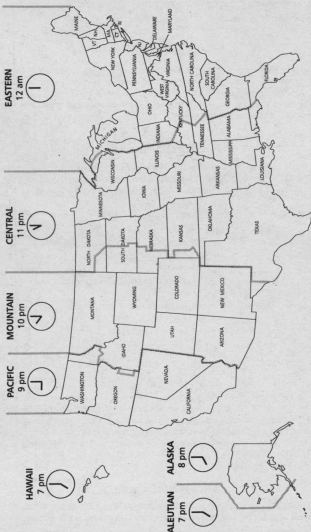

Dictionary Games

There are several fun games that you can play with just a dictionary and a group of friends. A few are listed here.

What's Next?

One player chooses a word from the dictionary and everyone takes turns guessing what the next main entry in the dictionary is. If you want to keep score, give one point for each main entry that comes between the given word and the word a player guesses. The lowest number of points wins, and the winner chooses the next word to play.

Fractured Phrases

Take turns flipping through the dictionary to find pairs of guidewords (the words at the top of each page) that make funny phrases. Then, challenge the other players to make up a sentence using (or explaining) the phrase.

Examples

Fractured phrase	Sentence
electronic ~ elite	"The electronic elite – the people who IM me."
flout ~ flunky	"Don't flout the flunky or you'll never see the big boss!"
impolite ~ impregnate	"It's definitely impolite to impregnate on the first date."
pickle ~ pied-à-terre	"No one is allowed to eat a pickle in his pied-à-terre."
southpaw ~ spank	"Only southpaws really know how to spank."
wrongdoer ~ xylophone	"Every wrongdoer wants a xylophone."

Word Chains

Look up any word in the dictionary, and choose one word in the definition to look up in turn. Then, look up a word in that second word's definition to look up. Keep going until you hit the original word. There are two ways to score: one is to make the shortest chain the winner, and the other is to make the longest chain the winner. (Looking up a, an, the is not allowed in the longest chain version.)

Thesaurus Sleuth

One player chooses a synonym block from this dictionary and reads off the synonyms aloud. The first person to guess the entry word is the winner.